PRENTICE HALL
LITERATURE

TEACHER'S EDITION • THE BRITISH TRADITION, VOLUME 1

COMMON CORE EDITION ©

ISBN-13: 978-0-13-319630-6
ISBN-10:   0-13-319630-5
6 7 8 9 10 V092 15 14 13

ALWAYS LEARNING

PEARSON

Preparing Students for College and Career

Literature opens minds. It should also open doors to a student's future. *Prentice Hall Literature Common Core Edition* is a comprehensive literacy program that teaches the new standards and helps students become better readers, better writers, and better thinkers so they're better prepared for college, careers, and beyond. You can be confident that what you are teaching meets the Common Core framework.

Common Core in *Prentice Hall Literature*

- Leveled support and scaffolding for understanding increasingly complex texts
- Informational texts across content areas
- Emphasis on writing argumentative, informative/explanatory, and narrative texts
- Critical thinking and higher-order thinking skills presented in instruction
- Traditional and performance-based assessments
- Best-in-class digital resources
- Teacher training to implement the new standards

Builds Better Readers

Prentice Hall Literature provides a scaffolded approach to rigorous instruction, enabling students to build a solid literary foundation that is necessary for success in college and careers.

Exposure to rich literature selections with increasing text complexity across genres builds students' literary and cultural knowledge, so they become comfortable reading different text structures and understand the elements that appear in the selections.

Leveled Selection Pairs in the Student Edition let you choose the right text without skipping essential skills.

Text Complexity Rubrics guide you in choosing the selection that's appropriate for your students' abilities.

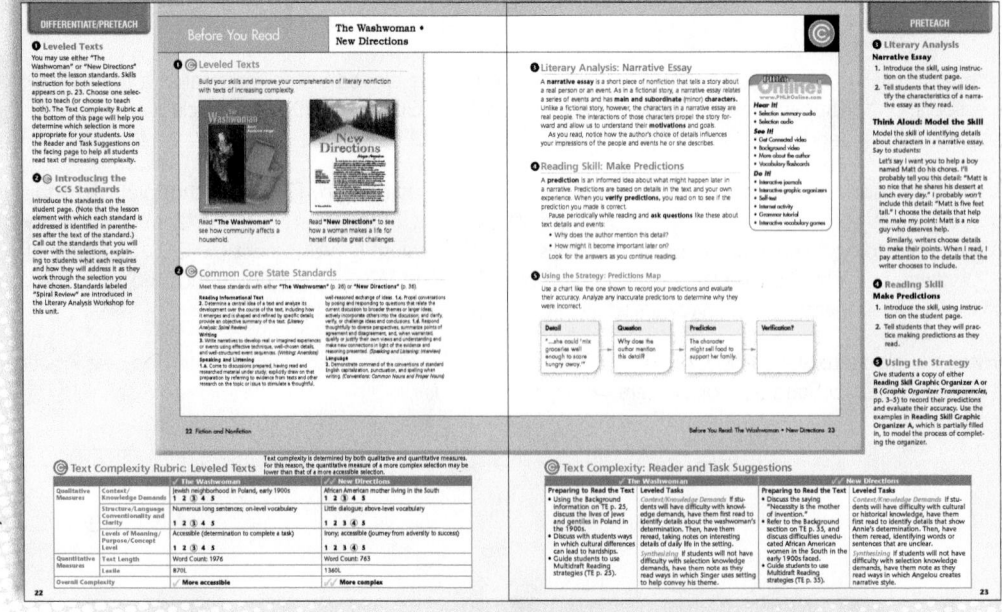

Reader and Task Suggestions offer support to ensure all readers meet achievable challenges.

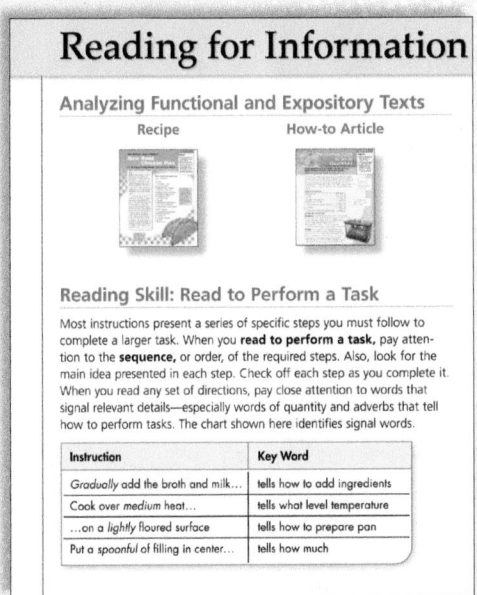

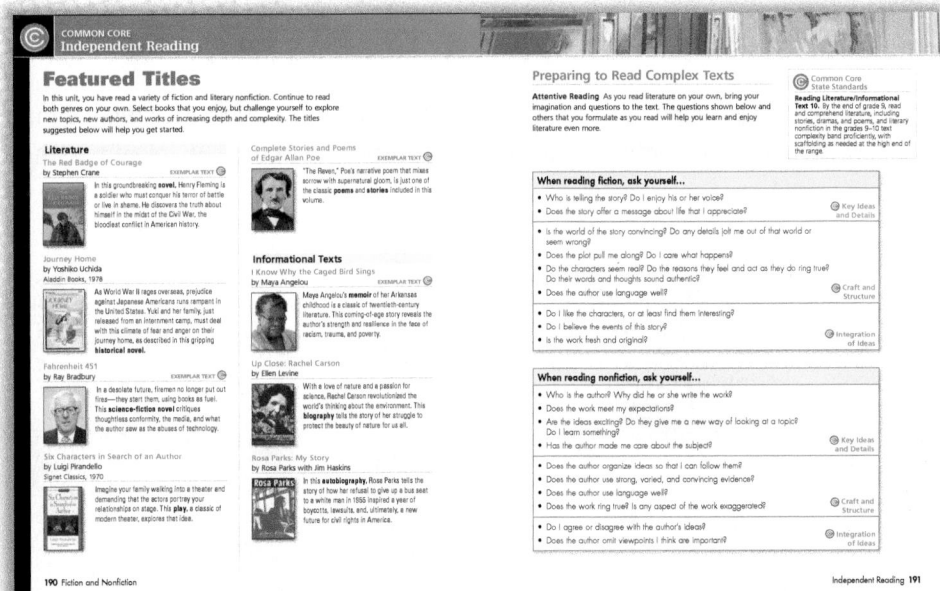

Informational texts provide context for learning and allow for the application of knowledge across science, social studies, and math.

Wide and deep independent readings of increasing complexity challenge learners. Support for reading complex texts is aligned to the Common Core.

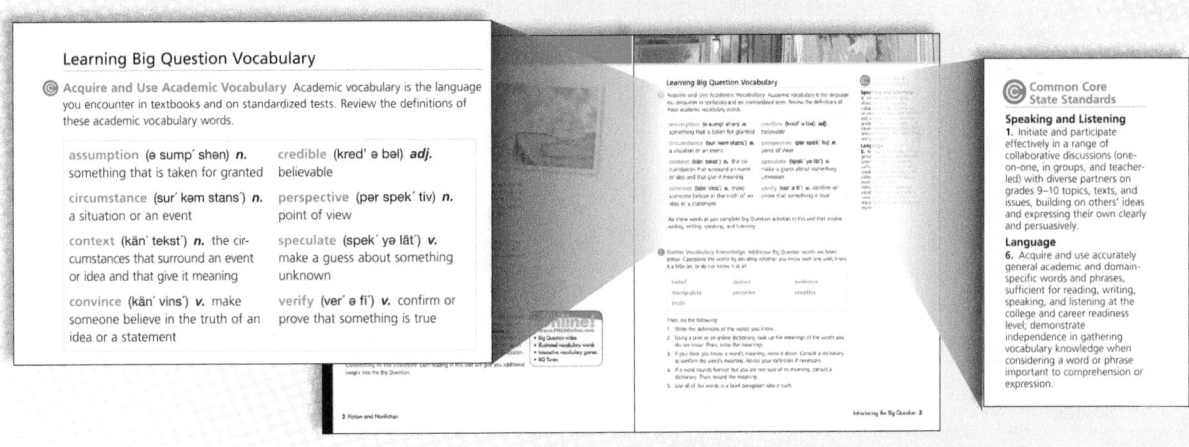

Extensive practice with general and domain-specific vocabulary builds vocabulary knowledge and prepares students for success.

Digital Resources Target Practice with Customized Instruction

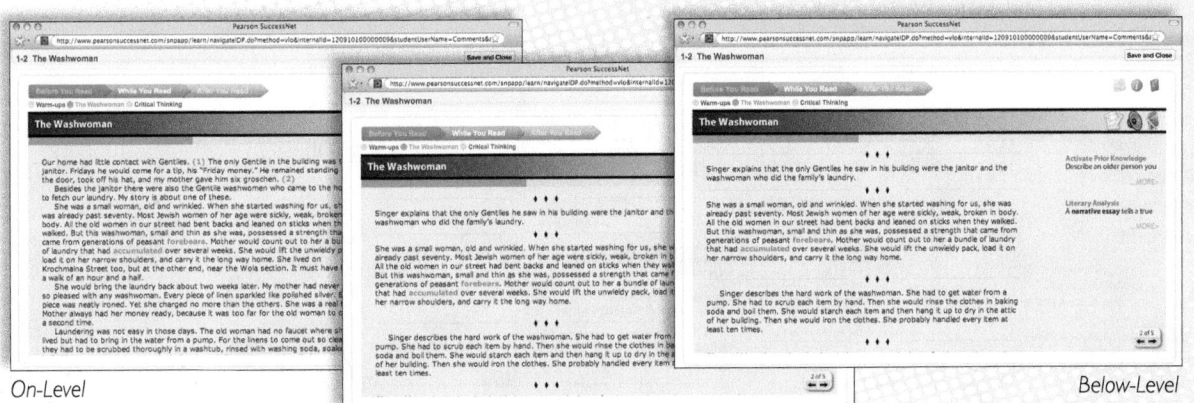

Online instruction instantly responds to students' needs with precise practice and scaffolding. PHLitOnline automatically assigns learner levels based on Diagnostic Test results.

On-Level

English Learner

Below-Level

Better Writers, Better Thinkers

Writing, speaking, and listening are integrated throughout *Prentice Hall Literature* with rigorous, robust skill instruction that takes students to the next level of mastery.

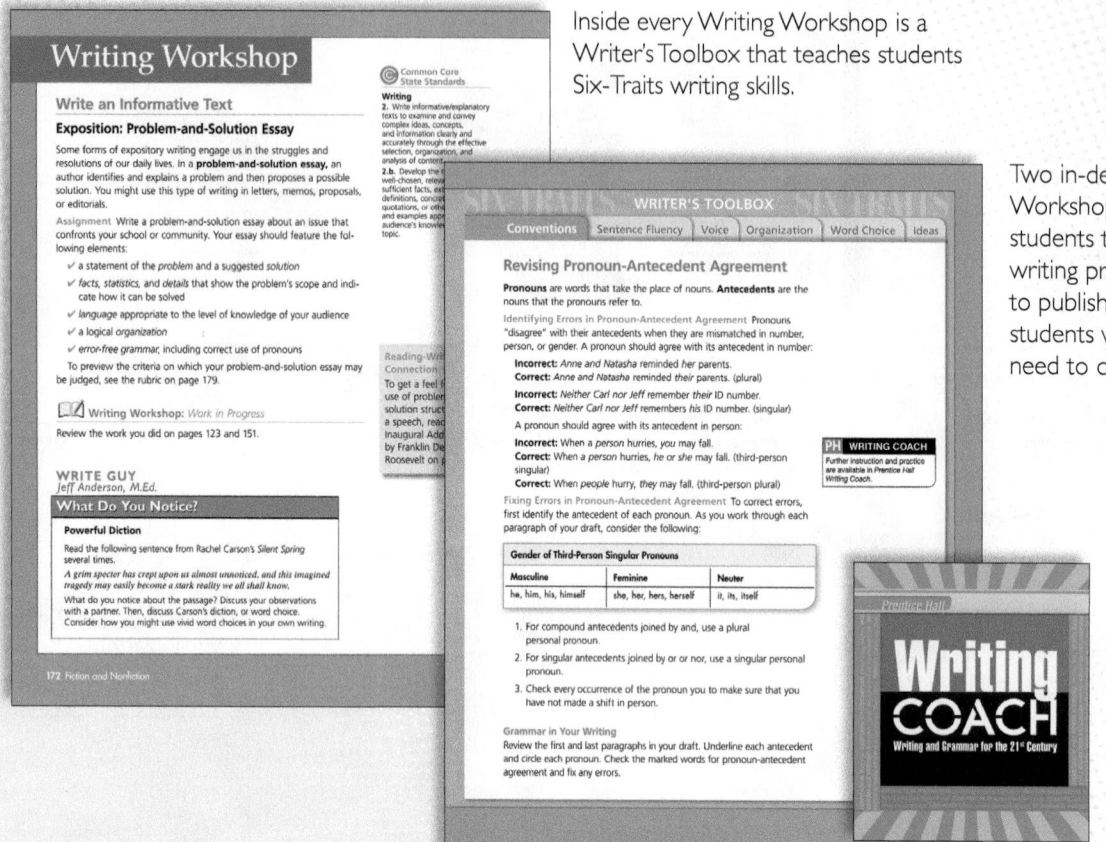

Inside every Writing Workshop is a Writer's Toolbox that teaches students Six-Traits writing skills.

Two in-depth Writing Workshops per unit take students through the complete writing process—from drafting to publishing—equipping students with the tools they need to develop as writers.

Help students become great writers by using guided writing skill instruction from *Writing Coach*.

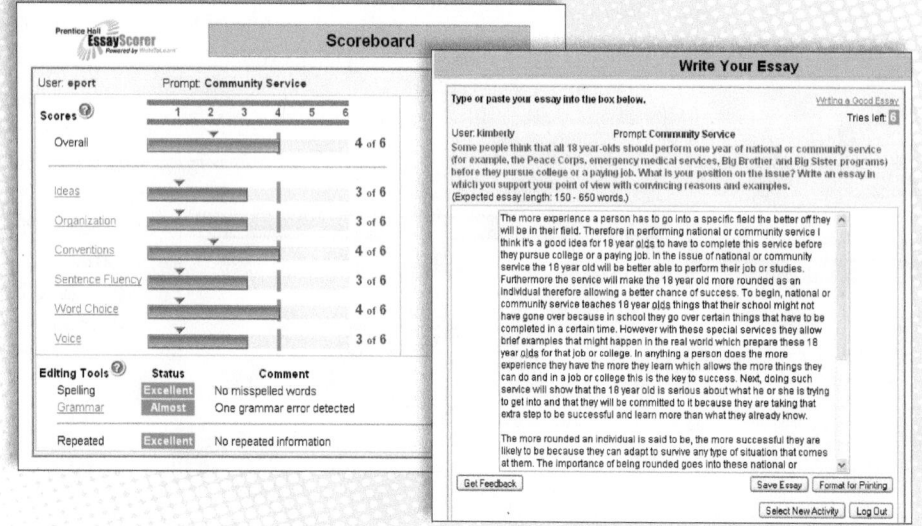

EssayScorer saves you hundreds of hours grading papers by providing students instant feedback on their writing.

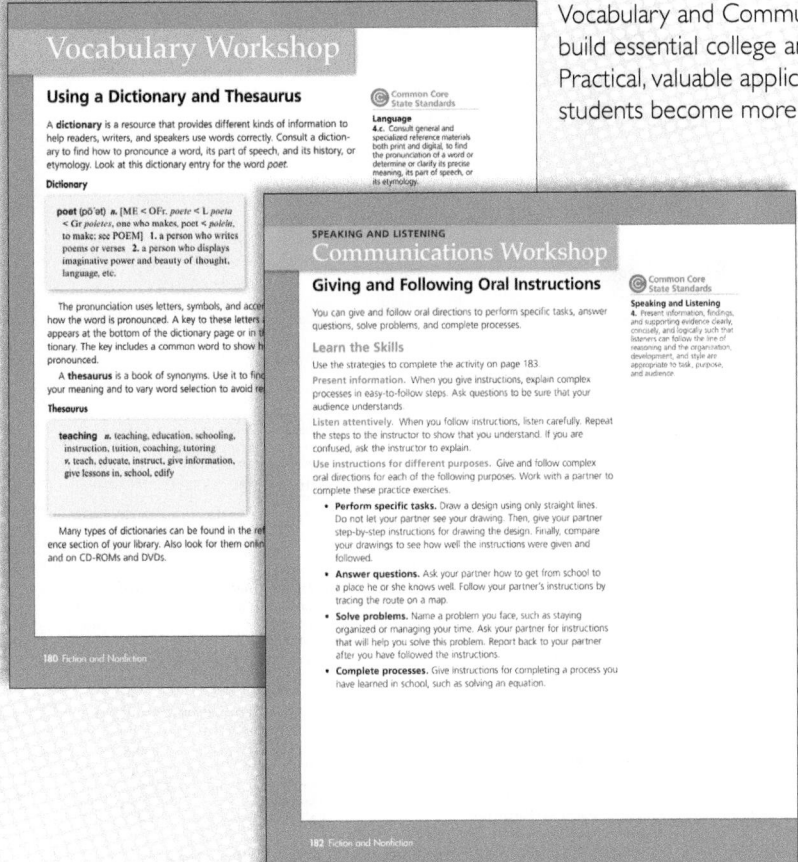

Vocabulary and Communications Workshops build essential college and career-ready skills. Practical, valuable applications are used to help students become more fluent in these skills.

Speaking and Listening are emphasized to help students develop the career-ready skills they need for life and work.

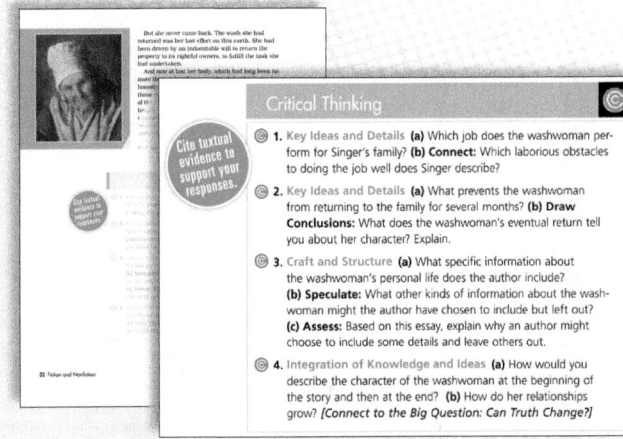

Critical Thinking questions build learning skills by helping students apply their reading.

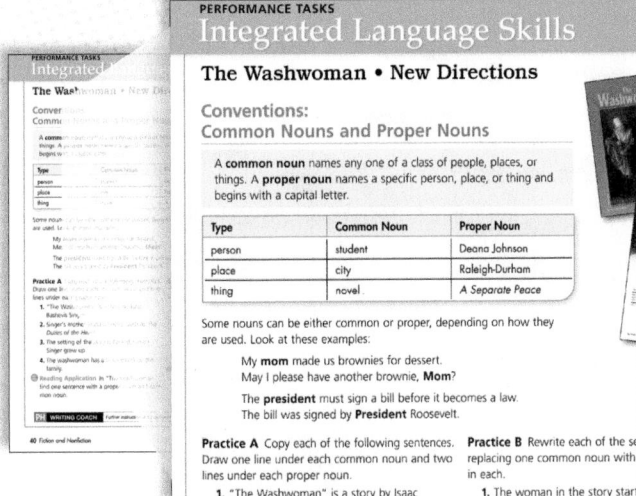

Integrated Language Skills offers full coverage of grammar, writing, speaking and listening, and research.

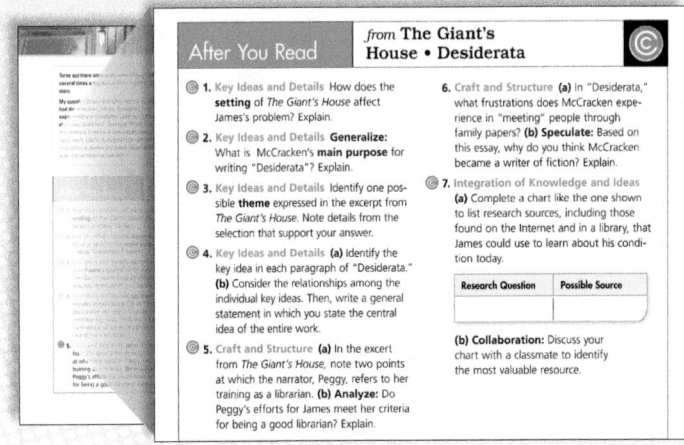

Every selection is followed by critical thinking questions aligned to the organizational structure of the Common Core Reading Domain.

Ensure Mastery

The new standards require new assessments. *Prentice Hall Literature* provides traditional assessments along with new performance-based assessments as called for by the Common Core. Students are given opportunities to apply critical thinking to demonstrate mastery of the standards.

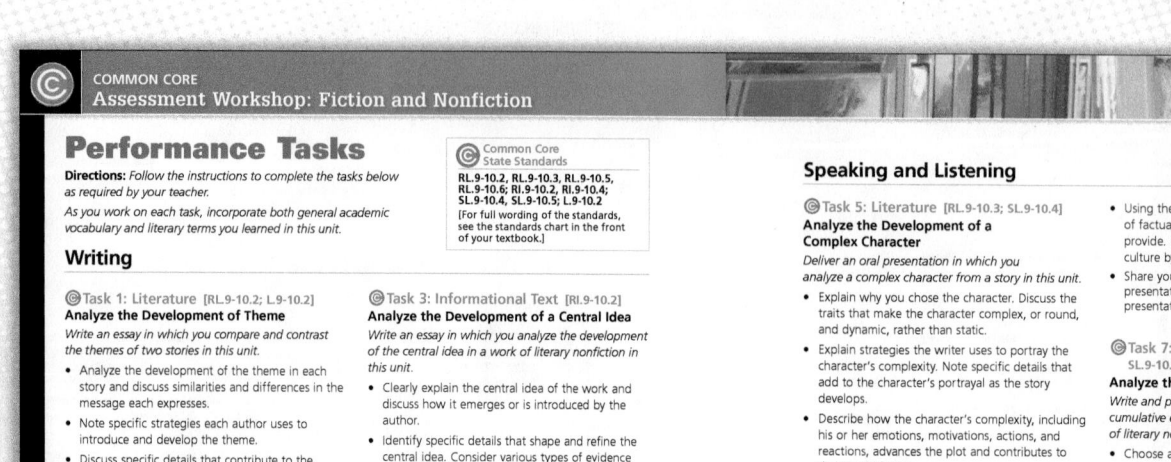

COMMON CORE
Assessment Workshop: Fiction and Nonfiction

Performance Tasks

Directions: *Follow the instructions to complete the tasks below as required by your teacher.*

As you work on each task, incorporate both general academic vocabulary and literary terms you learned in this unit.

Common Core State Standards
RL.9-10.2, RL.9-10.3, RL.9-10.5, RL.9-10.6; RI.9-10.2, RI.9-10.4; SL.9-10.4, SL.9-10.5; L.9-10.2
[For full wording of the standards, see the standards chart in the front of your textbook.]

Writing

Task 1: Literature [RL.9-10.2; L.9-10.2]
Analyze the Development of Theme
Write an essay in which you compare and contrast the themes of two stories in this unit.

• Analyze the development of the theme in each story and discuss similarities and differences in the message each expresses.
• Note specific strategies each author uses to introduce and develop the theme.
• Discuss specific details that contribute to the development of each theme. Explain what each detail adds.
• To ensure that readers understand your analysis, include an objective summary of each story.
• Capitalize proper nouns, including characters' and authors' names, correctly.

Task 2: Literature [RL.9-10.5]
Analyze the Effects of Structure in a Story
Write an essay in which you explain how the structure of a story in this unit leads to a specific emotional effect, such as tension or suspense.

• Identify the story's main conflict and summarize the narrative.
• Describe specific structural choices the writer makes. For example, discuss how much exposition the author provides and how he or she introduces the conflict. Also describe any use of plot devices, such as foreshadowing.
• Finally, explain how the story affects you as a reader and how the author's choices regarding structure contribute to that effect.
• Cite textual evidence to support your assertions.

Task 3: Informational Text [RI.9-10.2]
Analyze the Development of a Central Idea
Write an essay in which you analyze the development of the central idea in a work of literary nonfiction in this unit.

• Clearly explain the central idea of the work and discuss how it emerges or is introduced by the author.
• Identify specific details that shape and refine the central idea. Consider various types of evidence and explain what each adds to the development of the central idea.
• To ensure that readers understand your analysis, include an objective summary of the work.

Task 4: Informational Text [RI.9-10.6]
Analyze an Author's Purpose and Use of Rhetoric
Write an essay in which you determine an author's purpose and point of view and analyze his or her uses of rhetoric in a work of nonfiction in this unit.

• Explain the topic of the work and determine both the author's general and specific purposes for writing.
• Analyze the author's perspective or point of view on the topic. For example, explain whether the author has a positive or negative perspective or expresses a particular attitude toward the topic.
• Note specific examples of the author's uses of rhetoric. For example, identify examples of parallel structure or repetition. Then, explain how those uses of rhetoric work to advance the author's purpose and point of view.

Speaking and Listening

Task 5: Literature [RL.9-10.3; SL.9-10.4]
Analyze the Development of a Complex Character
Deliver an oral presentation in which you analyze a complex character from a story in this unit.

• Explain why you chose the character. Discuss the traits that make the character complex, or round, and dynamic, rather than static.
• Explain strategies the writer uses to portray the character's complexity. Note specific details that add to the character's portrayal as the story develops.
• Describe how the character's complexity, including his or her emotions, motivations, actions, and reactions, advances the plot and contributes to the story's theme.
• Present your analysis and evidence logically so that listeners can follow your line of reasoning. Make sure your overall approach, including both content and style, is appropriate for a classroom presentation on an academic topic.

Task 6: Literature [RL.9-10.6; SL.9-10.5]
Analyze a Cultural Perspective
Present a visual essay in which you analyze a cultural perspective reflected in a story in this unit.

• A visual essay combines images and text to explain an idea. The visual part of your essay may take the form of a slideshow, poster, or other format.
• Choose a story from this unit that reflects a cultural perspective from outside the United States. Explain how that cultural perspective is reflected in the setting and events as well as in characters' thoughts, emotions, actions, and reactions.

• Using the story as an example, discuss the kinds of factual information a work of fiction can provide. Explain what you learned about another culture by reading this story.
• Share your work with the class in an informal presentation. After you have delivered your presentation, answer questions from classmates.

Task 7: Informational Text [RL.9-10.4; SL.9-10.5]
Analyze the Effect of Word Choice on Tone
Write and present an essay in which you analyze the cumulative effect of word choice on tone in a work of literary nonfiction in this unit.

• Choose a work of literary nonfiction from this unit that offers a clear and distinct tone. Explain your choice.
• Identify specific word choices that contribute to the creation of that tone.
• Illustrate your analysis by creating a graphic organizer or chart that captures your ideas visually.
• Present your essay, including charts or graphic organizers, to the class. Use technology to display graphics, or distribute them as handouts.

Can truth change?
At the beginning of Unit 1, you participated in a discussion about the Big Question. Now that you have completed the unit, write a response to the question. Discuss how your initial ideas have either changed or been reinforced. Cite specific examples from the literature in this unit, from other subject areas, and from your own life to support your ideas. Use Big Question vocabulary words (see page 3) in your response.

188 Fiction and Nonfiction

Assessment Workshop **189**

Performance Tasks in the unit Assessment Workshops call for the application of higher-level thinking skills.

Students are assessed across the key Common Core domains of reading, writing, speaking and listening, and language.

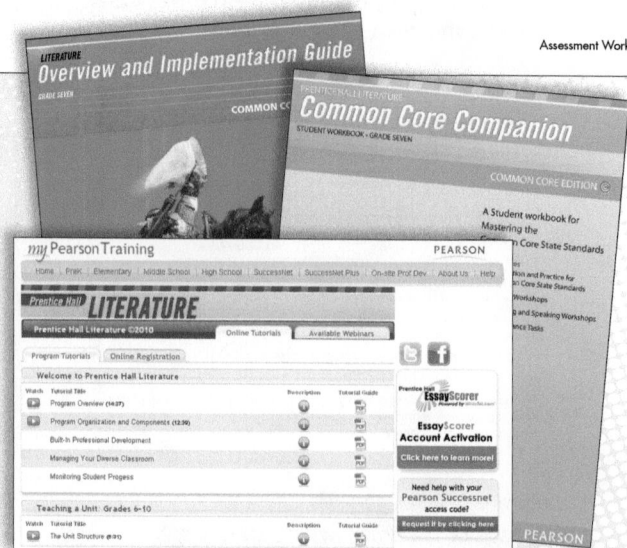

Prentice Hall Literature offers additional resources to ensure a successful implementation.

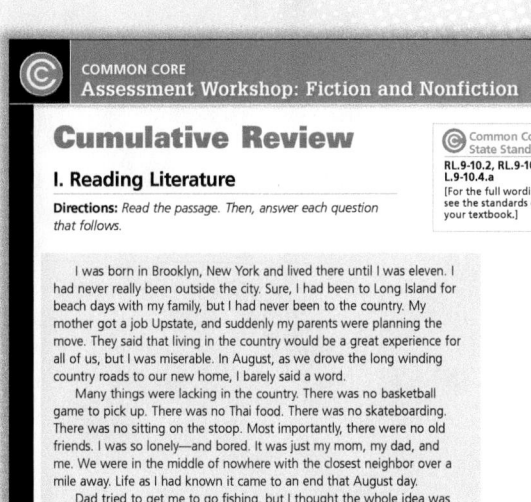

Cumulative Review

I. Reading Literature

Common Core
State Standards

RL.9-10.2, RL.9-10.3, RL.9-10.5;
L.9-10.4.a
[For the full wording of the standards, see the standards chart in the front of your textbook.]

Directions: *Read the passage. Then, answer each question that follows.*

I was born in Brooklyn, New York and lived there until I was eleven. I had never really been outside the city. Sure, I had been to Long Island for beach days with my family, but I had never been to the country. My mother got a job Upstate, and suddenly my parents were planning the move. They said that living in the country would be a great experience for all of us, but I was miserable. In August, as we drove the long winding country roads to our new home, I barely said a word.

Many things were lacking in the country. There was no basketball game to pick up. There was no Thai food. There was no skateboarding. There was no sitting on the stoop. Most importantly, there were no old friends. I was so lonely—and bored. It was just my mom, my dad, and me. We were in the middle of nowhere with the closest neighbor over a mile away. Life as I had known it came to an end that August day.

Dad tried to get me to go fishing, but I thought the whole idea was disgusting. Mom tried to get me to walk in the woods, but I didn't like all the bugs, and the brambles scratched my legs. I wanted to go back to Brooklyn in the worst way. All of that would soon change.

I was petrified when I walked into my homeroom. Everyone there knew everyone else, and I did not know anyone. I was set apart from all the other boys by my pale skin and long hair. I sat in the back, and no one said anything to me. The teacher came in and introduced herself.

"Class, we have two new students with us this year." My ears perked up at the word *two*, and I scanned the room for another outsider.

"First, I want to introduce Dave from Brooklyn." The teacher pointed to me. My face flushed as I said "Hi."

"Next, meet Alexis from Washington, D.C."

"Call me Al," she said to the class, looking as lost as I felt.

I had been staring at the back of her head. Her hair was as short as mine was long. I knew immediately that this was not only the year of the Big Move, but it was also the year of the New Best Friend.

1. From which **point of view** is this story told?

   A. first person
   B. second person
   C. third-person limited
   D. third-person omniscient

2. Which element from the passage helped you determine the **point of view**?

   A. The narrator directly addresses his audience, the reader.
   B. The narrator refers to himself as *I* and *me*.
   C. The narrator knows only one person's thoughts.
   D. The narrator has insight into all the people's thoughts.

3. Which word best describes the **author's voice**?

   A. formal
   B. casual
   C. friendly
   D. sarcastic

4. Which of the following sentences is an example of **foreshadowing**?

   A. All of that would soon change.
   B. I had never really been outside of the city.
   C. I wanted to go back to Brooklyn in the worst way.
   D. The teacher pointed to me.

5. Which event occurs during the **rising action** of the narrative?

   A. Dave is born in Brooklyn.
   B. Dave makes a new friend.
   C. Dave's mom gets a job Upstate.
   D. Dave meets Alexis.

6. Which event is the turning point, or **climax**, of the narrative?

   A. Dave moves in August.
   B. Dave wants to move back to Brooklyn.
   C. Dave refuses to go fishing.
   D. Dave hears the teacher say "two."

7. **Vocabulary** Which word is closest in meaning to the underlined word *petrified*?

   A. angry
   B. terrified
   C. annoyed
   D. disturbed

8. How is the conflict in the story resolved?

   A. Dave makes a new friend in the city.
   B. Dave wants to return to Brooklyn.
   C. Dave's mom does not like her job.
   D. Dave goes fishing with his dad.

9. In what way does the choice of narrator affect the description of the country in paragraph 2?

   A. Life in the country seems frightening.
   B. The country appears to offer lots of fun activities.
   C. Moving to the country sounds like a good idea.
   D. The country seems to lack a lot of things that life in the city has to offer.

⏱ Timed Writing

10. In a well-developed essay, **identify** the conflict in this story. **Explain** how the author of the text establishes the conflict. Cite evidence from the text to support your analysis. [20 minutes]

GO ON

Traditional Cumulative Review prepares students for high-stakes testing.

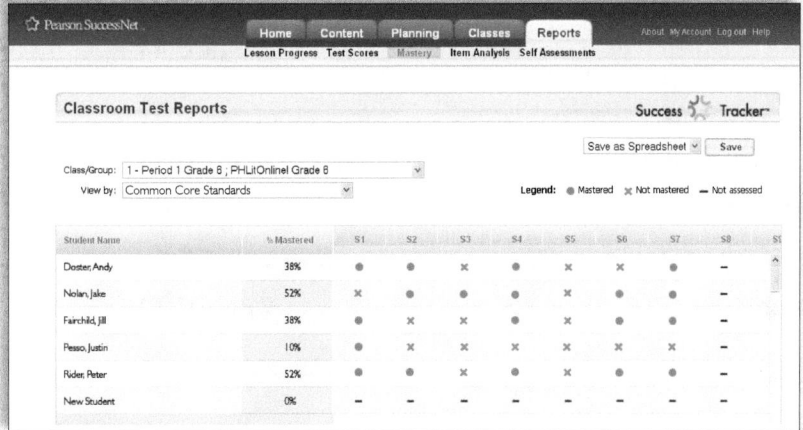

SuccessTracker® includes reporting tools to make progress monitoring easier.

Research Bibliography

▶ **Reading and Concept-Driven Instruction**

Alexander, Patricia A., and Tamara Jetton. "Learning from Text: A Multidimensional and Developmental Perspective." *Handbook of Reading Research*, vol. 3. Ed. M. L. Kamil, P. B. Mosenthal, P. D. Pearson, and R. Barr, 285–310. Mahwah, NJ: Lawrence Erlbaum Associates, 2000.

Blau, Sheridan. *The Literature Workshop: Teaching Texts and Their Readers*. Portsmouth: Heinemann Press, 2003.

Buehl, Doug, Judith L. Irvin, and Ronald M. Klemp. *Reading and the High School Student: Strategies to Enhance Literacy*. Boston: Allyn and Bacon, 2007.

Buehl, Doug, Judith L. Irvin, and Barbara J. Radcliffe. *Strategies to Enhance Literacy and Learning in Middle School Content Area Classrooms*. Boston: Allyn and Bacon, 2007.

Daniels, Harvey. *Literature Circles: Voice and Choice in Book Clubs and Reading Groups*. Portland: Stenhouse Publishers, 2002.

———*Mini-Lessons for Literature Circles*. Portsmouth: Heinemann Press, 2005.

Gallagher, Kelly. *Reading Reasons: Motivational Mini-Lessons for the Middle and High School*. Portland: Stenhouse Publishers, 2003.

Guthrie, John T. and Allan Wigfield. "Engagement and Motivation in Reading." *Handbook of Reading Research*, vol. 3, eds. M. L. Kamil, P. B. Mosenthal, P. D. Pearson, and R. Barr, 403–422. Mahwah: Lawrence Erlbaum Associates, 2000.

Harvey, Stephanie, and Anne Goudvis. "Determining Importance in Text: The Nonfiction Connection." *Strategies That Work: Teaching Comprehension to Enhance Understanding*. Portland: Stenhouse Publishers, 2000.

Langer, Judith. "Beating the Odds: Teaching Middle and High School Students to Read and Write Well," 1999. Center on English Learning and Achievement. May 2003.<http://cela.albany.edu/eie2/main.html>

National Reading Panel. *Teaching Children to Read: An Evidence-Based Assessment of the Scientific Research on Reading and Its Implications for Reading Instruction*. NIH Publication 00–4769. Bethesda: U.S. Department of Health and Human Services, 2000.

Pressley, Michael. "What Should Comprehension Instruction Be the Instruction Of?" *Handbook of Reading Research*, vol. 3, eds. M. L. Kamil, P. B. Mosenthal, P. D. Pearson, and R. Barr, 545–562. Mahwah: Lawrence Erlbaum Associates, 2000.

Scieszka, Jon. *Guys Write for Guys Read*. New York: Penguin Group, 2005.

Wiggins, Grant P., and Jay McTighe. *Understanding by Design*. Alexandria: Association for Supervision and Curriculum Development, 2006.

▶ **Vocabulary, Writing, and Grammar**

Anderson, Jeff. *Mechanically Inclined: Building Grammar, Usage, and Style into Writer's Workshop*. Portland: Stenhouse Publishers, 2005.

Baumann, J. F., and E. J. Kame'enui. *Vocabulary Instruction: From Research to Practice*. New York: Guilford Press, 2004.

Blachowicz, Camille, and Peter Fisher. *Teaching Vocabulary in All Classrooms*, Second Edition. Upper Saddle River: Merrill, 2002.

Feber, Jane. *Creative Book Reports: Fun Projects With Rubrics for Fiction and Nonfiction*. Gainesville: Maupin House Publishing, Inc., 2004.

———*Active Word Play*. Gainesville: Maupin House Publishing, Inc., 2008.

Kinsella, Kate. "Strategies to Teach Academic Vocabulary." *Strategies to Promote Academic Literacy for Second Language Learners Within the English Language Arts Classroom*. 2005.

Kinsella, Kate and Kevin Feldman. *Narrowing the Language Gap: The Case for Explicit Vocabulary Instruction*. New York: Scholastic, 2005.

Marzano, Robert J. "The Developing Vision of Vocabulary Instruction." In Baumann and Kame'enui, *Vocabulary Instruction: From Research to Practice*. New York: Guilford Press, 2004.

▶ **Differentiated Instruction for Universal Access**

Allington, Richard L. *What Really Matters for Struggling Readers: Designing Research Based Programs*. New York: Longman, 2001.

Download the
research report at
pearsonschool.com/phlit

Armbruster, Bonnie, and Thomas H. Anderson. "On Selecting 'Considerate' Content Area Textbooks." *Remedial and Special Education*, 9.1 (1988): 47–52.

Balderrama, María V., and Lynne T. Díaz-Rico. *Teacher Performance Expectations for Educating English Learners*. Boston: Allyn and Bacon, 2006.

Ball, Arnetha F. and Ted Lardner. *African American Literacies Unleashed: Vernacular English and the Composition Classroom*. Carbondale: Southern Illinois University Press, 2005.

Carnie, Douglas, Jerry Silbert, and Edward J. Kame'enui. *Direct Instruction Reading*. 3rd ed. Upper Saddle River: Prentice Hall, 1997.

Deshler, Donald D., Keith B. Lenz, and Brenda R. Kissam. *Teaching Content to All: Evidence-Based Inclusive Practices in Middle and Secondary Schools*. Boston: Allyn and Bacon, 2004.

Francis, David, Mabel Rivera, Nonie Lesaux, Michael Kieffer, and Hector Rivera. *Practical Guidelines for the Education of English Language Learners*. Portsmouth: RMC Research Corporation, Center on Instruction, 2006.

Vaughn, Sharon, Candace S. Bos, and Jeanne Shay Schumm. *Teaching Exceptional, Diverse, and At-Risk Students in the General Education Classroom*. Boston: Allyn and Bacon, 2002.

Pearson Prentice Hall Literature:
A Rich Tradition of Learning Success

▶ The Research Process

Since 1988, *Pearson Prentice Hall Literature* has been at the forefront of language arts instruction, providing teachers and their students with quality instruction and assessment tools to ensure success. Each successive edition builds on the strong heritage of the program. Our research comprised these three design stages:

1. EXPLORATORY NEEDS ASSESSMENT

In conjunction with Pearson Prentice Hall authors, we conducted research proven to explore educational reading methodologies. This research was incorporated into our instructional strategy and pedagogy to create a more effective literature program. This stage included:

- reading research
- review of state standards
- teacher interviews

2. FORMATIVE RESEARCH, DEVELOPMENT, AND FIELD-TESTING

During this phase of the research, we developed and field-tested prototype material with students and teachers. Results informed revisions to the final design and pedagogy. Formative research included:

- field-testing of prototypes in classroom pilots
- classroom observations
- teacher reviews
- supervisor reviews
- educator advisory panels

3. SUMMATIVE RESEARCH AND VALIDATION RESEARCH

Finally, we have conducted and will continue to conduct longer-term research under actual classroom conditions. Research at this phase includes:

- pilot-testing
- prepublication learner verification research
- postpublication validation studies, including validation of test questions
- evaluation of results on standardized tests

Harvey Daniels
Voice and Choice

Excerpts from "Using Leveled Selections" and "Leveled Reading Selections, A Key to Differentiation" by Harvey Daniels

" With leveled texts, all students can understand their selection—and no one is left behind."

Harvey Daniels is known for his passionate work on literacy and student-led book clubs. He is the author of *Literature Circles: Voice and Choice in Book Clubs and Reading Groups* and *Mini-lessons for Literature Circles,* he has been a classroom teacher, writing project director, author, and university professor.

Read the full text of Harvey Daniels's articles at PHLitOnline.

We have all watched it unfold.

You select a wonderful book or article for your class to read. You hand it out to the students and what happens? The text is way too hard for some kids, far too easy for others, and "boring" to still others. Not a good feeling.

Using Leveled Readings.
Happily, research on differentiated instruction shows us a better way: leveled selections. **Prentice Hall Literature** offers two levels of text. All students can understand and enjoy their selection and still learn same required skills—and no one is left behind.

Why are leveled selections so important?

- If we expect kids to grow as readers, they must spend part of each day reading *text they can read.* As the Common Core State Standards put it: "Students need opportunities to stretch their reading abilities but also to experience the satisfaction and pleasure of easy, fluent reading, both of which the Standards allow for."
- A *choice* of texts means that more students will have the background knowledge to understand and enjoy the chosen selection.
- All students need to read increasingly challenging text as the school year unfolds, but every student does not need to read the same texts. As the Common Core standards explain: "Teachers who have had success using particular texts that are easier than those required for a given grade band should feel free to continue to use them, so long as the general movement during a given school year is toward texts of higher levels of complexity."

These are the reasons **Prentice Hall Literature** offers two leveled selections for almost every lesson—one more accessible and one more challenging. Every student can be challenged at his or her own level, from lesson to lesson, throughout the school year.

" When we make accommodations like leveled selections, we often find that such accommodations make learning work better for everyone."

Grant Wiggins
Better Big Questions

Excerpts from "Teaching Literature by Design: Introducing the Big Questions" by Grant Wiggins

" . . . our methods have to foster that questioning and meaning-making."

Grant Wiggins is the co-author of *Understanding By Design,** published by ASCD. He is also the president of Authentic Education in Hopewell, New Jersey. He consults with schools, districts, and state education departments on a variety of reform issues. His work has been supported by the Pew Charitable Trusts, the Geraldine R. Dodge Foundation, and the National Science Foundation.

Read the full text of Grant Wiggins's article at PHLitOnline.

*The Association for Supervision of Curriculum Development (ASCD), publisher of the "Understanding by Design Handbook" co-authored by Grant Wiggins and registered owner of the trademark "Understanding by Design," has not authorized, approved, or sponsored this work and is in no way affiliated with Pearson or its products.

A Big Question is different from many of the questions teachers typically ask students in class.

A Big Question is more of a *why?* or a *so what?* question rather than a *what?* or a *where?* question. We are not looking for an answer, really; we are inviting inquiry and reflection. The Big Questions awaken curiosity and thus provide a purpose for reading.

What Makes a Question "Big"?

"Big" connotes "substantial"—occupying a considerable amount of space and time. A question is "big" or "weighty" if it has significant depth and breadth—occupying a good deal of our psychic space, such as our thoughts and feelings. Another aspect of "bigness" is the time it consumes. Vital issues and inquiries remain alive over days, months, and years, unlike simple or superficial queries. Important questions recur over and through time, as we rethink and reflect on our present and past experiences. **Prentice Hall Literature** provides Big Questions that meet the criteria in ways that others do not.

- The questions cannot be answered with a list or a single answer.
- The questions are designed to allow answers to change to accommodate new information or experience.
- The questions are designed to encourage answers that change over time.

Why Ask Big Questions?
The teacher has a different intent when asking a "big" as opposed to an "academic" question. If we want students to end up asking Big Questions on their own, then our courses have to be designed "backward" from that goal. If we want students to learn from their reading, our methods have to foster that questioning and meaning-making.

" Important questions occur over and through time."

Kelly Gallagher
Multidraft Reading

Excerpts from "The Value of Second Draft Reading" and "Powerful, Purposeful Reading" by Kelly Gallagher

" In our classrooms, we are the 'tour guides.'"

Kelly Gallagher is a full-time English teacher at Magnolia High School in Anaheim, California, where he has taught for twenty-two years. He is the author of several books:

- *Reading Reasons: Motivational Mini-Lessons for the Middle and High School*
- *Deeper Reading: Comprehending Challenging Texts*
- *Teaching Adolescent Writers*
- *Readicide*

Read the full text of Kelly Gallagher's article at PHLitOnline.

Where do adolescents get the idea that they can read complex text one time and get it? More importantly, how can we help our students to understand that much of our deepest thinking comes when we reread? How can we teach our students to recognize the value of second-draft reading?

The Importance of Rereading
The principal strategy that good readers employ when confronted by difficult text is to reread it. If the text is particularly difficult, you might have students read the text first with the sole purpose of monitoring where they were confused. Use the blue dots in the student edition of **Prentice Hall Literature** to help students "chunk" the text into passages with logical pause points to stop, reread, and clarify.

Multi-Lens Reading
Students often read difficult text better when they have been provided a purpose for their reading. In our classrooms, we are the "tour guides." We create student tours by first determining the purpose for each reading. Providing students with a specific purpose gives them a more focused, meaningful reading experience.

Prentice Hall Literature provides the tools for multiple reading purposes.

When students read with a purpose in mind, their anxiety is lowered, their comprehension deepens, and they are given the confidence to approach works they might have otherwise shunned.

" Providing students with a specific purpose gives them a more focused, meaningful reading experience."

Elfrieda H. Hiebert
What Is Text Complexity?

> ". . . greater focus on text complexity will help . . . prepare students for the increasing demands of required reading in college and the workplace."

Dr. Elfrieda "Freddy" H. Hiebert is the President and CEO of TextProject, Inc. Her model of accessible texts for beginning and struggling readers—TExT—has been used to develop several reading programs. Most recently, Dr. Hiebert served on the Common Core State Standards development team focused on text complexity. Dr. Hiebert has published more than 130 research articles, chapters in edited volumes, and books. In particular, Hiebert's interests lie in how fluency, vocabulary, and knowledge can be fostered through appropriate texts.

The Common Core State Standards cite research that shows that the difficulty of texts used in elementary and secondary classrooms in the United States has decreased over the past 50 years, while the difficulty of college texts has not. As a result, students entering post-secondary education are not prepared for the level of text complexity required to be successful.

To address this issue, the Standards have identified text complexity grade bands (K–1, 2–3, 4–5, 6–8, 9–10, 11–12), in which students read increasingly complex texts within a defined spectrum. Ultimately, greater focus on text complexity will help close the gap that exists between secondary and post-secondary education and prepare students for the increasing demands of required reading in college and the workplace.

The Common Core State Standards identify a three-part model for measuring a text's complexity. This model, as detailed below, includes quantitative and qualitative measures as well as variables of individual readers.

Quantitative Dimensions
Quantitative dimensions are aspects of text complexity that can be measured with traditional readability formulas, such as the Lexile measure. These formulas measure such aspects of a text as word length and frequency, total number of words, average sentence length, and text cohesion.

Qualitative Dimensions
Qualitative dimensions consist of "those aspects of text complexity best measured or only measurable by an attentive human reader." Qualitative measures include categories such as a student's familiarity with a text's structure, levels of meaning, language clarity and conventionality, and knowledge demands, or what the reader needs to know to access the text.

Reader and Task Considerations
Reader and task considerations include an evaluation of student variables, such as the reader's motivation, background knowledge, experience, and cognitive abilities. Evaluating text complexity is best done by the classroom teacher, who brings to bear professional judgments concerning subject matter and individual students.

> ". . . students read increasingly complex texts . . ."

Text Complexity: Building Capacity for All Students

To better gauge a text's difficulty, Dr. Elfrieda Hiebert has created a Text Complexity Multi-Index. In this model, four comprehensive measures and considerations are taken into account to determine a text's appropriateness for a student or group of students.

The four parts of Dr. Hiebert's model expand upon the Common Core State Standards' three-part model for measuring text complexity. A critical component of both models is that qualitative measures and reader-task considerations are balanced with quantitative measures to achieve an overall text complexity recommendation. By measuring text complexity, both quantitative and qualitative, teachers can challenge students to read more complex texts as they move toward college and career readiness.

In Dr. Hiebert's Multi-Index, quantitative measures consist of Overall Text Difficulty and Specifics of Text Difficulty. Qualitative Measures include Themes and Knowledge Demands. Reader and Task in the Common Core aligns with Purpose and Task in Dr. Hiebert's index. These four parts of Dr. Hiebert's Text Complexity Multi-Index are explained below.

Text Complexity Multi-Index

❶ Themes and Knowledge Demands

- The reader's familiarity with the theme of a text and the concept presented must be considered as part of the assessment of text complexity.

- Knowledge demands are based on the background knowledge students need to bring to a given text. Teachers can assess background knowledge through informal classroom discussions.

❷ Specifics of Text Difficulty

- Readability scores are based on quantitative variables, such as average sentence length and overall word frequency.

- Sentence length is determined by averaging the number of words in each sentence in a selection. Formulaically speaking, shorter sentences should mean easier reading. However, teachers must consider conceptual and thematic complexity of a selection to accurately assess a text's difficulty.

- Word frequency refers to how often the same words appear in a text. A low score indicates that the text most likely has words that students may not have encountered. This is especially true when dealing with informational texts that may address unfamiliar content and concepts.

❸ Overall Quantitative Text Difficulty

- Overall quantitative text difficulty can be determined by a readability formula. Frequently used readability formulas include Lexile, Dale-Chall, and Spache.

❹ Purpose and Task

- Purpose and task refer to the why and what of reading—questions such as "Why am I reading this text?" and "What tasks are involved before, during, and after reading to build knowledge?"

- To address purpose and task, teachers use professional judgment to assess reader and task compatibility.

The Text Complexity Rubric in *Prentice Hall Literature*

The following is a sample from the Grade 11, Unit 1 book. The leveled texts "Speech in the Virginia Convention" and "Speech in the Convention" are featured in Unit 1 of this grade level. The leveling of these selections relies on many factors as depicted in the measures outlined here.

Analyze the Qualitative and Quantitative measures to determine the complexity of these texts.

© Text Complexity Rubric

		Speech in the Virginia Convention	Speech in the Convention
①	**Qualitative Measures**		
	Context/ Knowledge Demands	Historical knowledge demands (speech) 1 2 ③ 4 5	Historical knowledge demands (speech) 1 2 ③ 4 5
	Structure/Language Conventionality and Clarity	Eighteenth-century vocabulary; complicated sentence structure 1 2 3 ④ 5	Eighteenth-century vocabulary; complicated sentence structure 1 2 3 ④ 5
	Levels of Meaning/ Purpose/Concept Level	Challenging concept (argues against negotiation in favor of armed rebellion) 1 2 3 ④ 5	Challenging concept (complex reasoning; urges acceptance of Constitution) 1 2 3 ④ 5
②	**Quantitative Measures**		
	Lexile/Text Length	980L / 1,212 words	1490L / 656 words
③	**Overall Complexity**	**More complex**	**More complex**

① Themes and Knowledge Demands

Context/Knowledge Demands: The accessibility of texts is dependent in part on the range of students' experiences and their background knowledge.

Structure/Language Conventionality and Clarity: Conventional and unconventional structures as well as domain-specific language and vocabulary all affect the ability of students to access text.

Levels of Meaning/Purpose/Concept Level: An author's use of either single or multiple levels of meaning impacts the accessibility of a text's concepts.

② Specifics of Text Difficulty

Pearson has provided two quantitative measures of text complexity—text length and Lexile score. Use these measures in tandem with qualitative measures to make informed choices.

③ Overall Quantitative Text Difficulty

Based on the criteria cited above for Themes and Knowledge Demands and Specifics of Text Difficulty, texts can be deemed either more accessible or more complex.

© Text Complexity: Reader and Task Suggestions

Speech in the Virginia Convention		Speech in the Convention	
Preparing to Read the Text	**Leveled Tasks**	**Preparing to Read the Text**	**Leveled Tasks**
• Using the Background information on TE p. 99, discuss Henry as a firebrand in the years before the American Revolution. • Ask students what kind of language they might use to persuade an uncertain audience. • Guide students to use Multidraft Reading strategies (TE p. 99).	*Structure/Language* If students will have difficulty with structure, have them skim the selection, looking for the persuasive questions that Henry asks. As students reread, have them find an answer for each question. *Analyzing* If students will not have difficulty with structure, have them give an example of parallel language. Discuss how the parallelism reinforces Henry's persuasive appeal.	• Using the information on TE pp. 104–105, discuss Franklin's role after the American Revolution. • Ask students how they would prepare if they knew their speech might be historic. • Guide students to use Multidraft Reading strategies to deepen their comprehension (TE p. 99).	*Structure/Language* If students will have difficulty with syntax, guide them in paraphrasing a few sentences. Encourage students to continue paraphrasing as they reread, focusing on what Franklin suggests about the serious nature of this moment in history. *Evaluating* If students will not have difficulty with syntax, ask them if they think that the speech would have been more persuasive (or more historic) had Franklin not voiced his initial doubts.

④ Purpose and Task

Specific pre-reading suggestions are given in "Preparing to Read the Text." These are followed by "Leveled Tasks" that will help you guide students' comprehension as they analyze, synthesize, or evaluate the concept development of selections. Teachers may adapt the leveled tasks, as needed, to suit the needs of their students.

Jim Cummins
Second Language Learning

Excerpts from "The Challenge of Learning Academic English" by Jim Cummins

" Students who gain a sense of control over language will want to use it for powerful purposes."

Jim Cummins's research focuses on literacy development in multilingual school contexts as well as English Language Learners' academic trajectories. He has been a recipient of the International Reading Association's Albert J. Harris award, and has published in *Educational Researcher, International Education Journal, NABE Journal, and TESOL Quarterly.*

Read the full text of Jim Cummins's article at PHLitOnline.

Learning difficulties faced by struggling readers can derive from a variety of sources. This is true regardless of whether their home language is English or a language other than English. Intervention should address the specific difficulties they are experiencing.

Scaffold Instruction We can promote literacy engagement among ELL students and struggling readers by using "scaffolds" or supports to make the input more comprehensible (e.g., through graphic organizers, demonstrations, etc.). It is also important to scaffold students' use of language.

Build Background Effective instruction for ELL students and struggling readers will also activate students' prior knowledge and build background knowledge as needed. Learning can be defined as the integration of new knowledge or skills with the knowledge or skills we already possess. Therefore, it is crucial to activate ELL students' preexisting knowledge so that they can relate new information to what they already know.

Validate Culture Identity affirmation is also crucial for literacy engagement. Students who feel their culture and identity validated in the classroom are much more likely to engage with literacy than those who perceive their culture and identity ignored or devalued.

Literacy engagement among ELL students and struggling readers also requires that teachers across the curriculum explain how language works and stimulate students' curiosity about language. Students who gain a sense of control over language will want to use it for powerful purposes.

" Students who feel their culture and identity validated in the classroom are much more likely to engage with literacy. . . ."

Sharroky Hollie
Culturally Responsive Instruction

Excerpts from "Expanding Academic Home Language" and "Navigating Cultural Discourse Styles" by Sharroky Hollie

Students entering the classroom bring with them a variety of experiences, traditions, interpretive frameworks, and learning styles. Culturally responsive instruction begins when a teacher acknowledges this variety as a positive resource for education. By capitalizing on the student's own resources, a teacher ensures success.

What is Culturally Responsive Instruction?
To make academic progress, a student must build on one success to another. How do we ensure that we are teaching to and through students' personal and cultural strengths and prior accomplishments?

- Build bridges from what students already know or have experienced to new knowledge and skills.
- Create a cooperative learning environment rich in affirmations of students' heritages.
- Build not just on individual strengths, but on the new strength that emerges when individuals join together in a community that respects their diversity.

Building on Strength
A key premise for culturally responsive pedagogy is that education proceeds from students' strengths and not students' weaknesses. **Prentice Hall Literature** consistently supports culturally responsive instruction with each selection in the anthology. Integrated throughout each lesson plan are the strategies for using what students bring with them into the classroom to enrich learning and foster success.

> " By capitalizing on the student's own resources, a teacher ensures success."

Sharroky Hollie is the Executive Director of the Center for Culturally Responsive Teaching and Learning. He is an assistant professor at California State University and a visiting professor at Webster University in St. Louis. His work focuses on African American education and on second language methodology. In addition to his university teaching, Dr. Hollie also teaches professional development courses, and he is the co-founding director of the Culture and Language Academy of Success, an independent charter school in Los Angeles.

Read the complete texts of Sharroky Hollie's articles on PHLitOnline.

> " . . . education proceeds from students' strengths and not students' weaknesses."

William G. Brozo
Response to Intervention

"   Within RTI, the frontline of prevention is Tier 1, or the general education classroom, where every student regardless of ability is to receive high-quality instruction. What's revolutionary about these new standards is that they situate literacy and language development squarely within the content areas....Common core proponents assert that prevailing literacy curriculum needs to shift from a focus on developing reading skills and building fluency with simple narratives toward reading and writing to gain knowledge and express new understandings with informational text."

William G. Brozo, "The Role of Content Literacy in an Effective RTI Program,"
The Reading Teacher, (64)2, pp. 147–150

Donald J. Leu
21st-Century Solutions

"   The good news about the Common Core State Standards is that we are going to increasingly support higher-level thinking, reasoning, and comprehension. Locating, evaluating, integrating, and communicating information – all these skills are essential to students' success in the future. We need to help students think in deeper, more complex ways as they read a wider variety of texts, both print and digital."

Karen K. Wixson
The Goal: College and Career Readiness

"   The ELA Common Core State Standards are meant to be read as an integrated English Language Arts program beginning with College and Career Readiness Anchor Standards. It is absolutely essential that teachers and administrators look first at the anchor standards, next the appendices, and lastly at the grade-level standards."

Expanded essays by these authors are available at PHLitOnline.com.

Master Teacher Board

Master Teacher Board **v**

Student Edition Pages

Contributing Authors

The contributing authors guided the direction and philosophy of Pearson Prentice Hall Literature. Working with the development team, they helped to build the pedagogical integrity of the program and to ensure its relevance for today's teachers and students.

Grant Wiggins, Ed.D., is the President of Authentic Education in Hopewell, New Jersey. He earned his Ed.D. from Harvard University and his B.A. from St. John's College in Annapolis. Grant consults with schools, districts, and state education departments on a variety of reform matters; organizes conferences and workshops; and develops print materials and Web resources on curricular change. He is the coauthor, with Jay McTighe, of Understanding by Design and The Understanding by Design Handbook, the award-winning and highly successful materials on curriculum published by ASCD. His work has been supported by the Pew Charitable Trusts, the Geraldine R. Dodge Foundation, and the National Science Foundation. *The Association for Supervision of Curriculum Development (ASCD), publisher of the "Understanding by Design Handbook" co-authored by Grant Wiggins and registered owner of the trademark "Understanding by Design", has not authorized, approved, or sponsored this work and is in no way affiliated with Pearson or its products.*

Jeff Anderson has worked with

struggling writers and readers for almost 20 years. Anderson's specialty is the integration of grammar and editing instruction into the processes of reading and writing. He has published two books, *Mechanically Inclined: Building Grammar, Usage, and Style into Writer's Workshop* and *Everyday Editing: Inviting Students to Develop Skill and Craft in Writer's Workshop,* as well as a DVD, *The Craft of Grammar.* Anderson's work has appeared in *English Journal.* Anderson won the NCTE Paul and Kate Farmer Award for his *English Journal* article on teaching grammar in context.

Arnetha F. Ball, Ph.D., is a

Professor at Stanford University. Her areas of expertise include language and literacy studies of diverse student populations, research on writing instruction, and teacher preparation for working with diverse populations. She is the author of *African American Literacies Unleashed* with Dr. Ted Lardner, and *Multicultural Strategies for Education and Social Change.*

Sheridan Blau is Professor of

Education and English at the University of California, Santa Barbara, where he directs the South Coast Writing Project and the Literature Institute for Teachers. He has served in senior advisory roles for such groups as the National Board for Professional Teaching Standards, the College Board, and the American Board for Teacher Education. Blau served for twenty years on the National Writing Project Advisory Board and Task Force, and is a former president of NCTE. Blau is the author of *The Literature Workshop: Teaching Texts and Their Readers,* which was named by the Conference on English Education as the 2004 Richard Meade Award winner for outstanding research in English education.

William G. Brozo, Ph.D., is

a Professor of Literacy at George Mason University in Fairfax, Virginia. He has taught reading and language arts in junior and senior high school and is the author of numerous texts on literacy development. Dr. Brozo'z work focuses on building capacity among teacher leaders, enriching the literate culture of schools, enhancing the literate lives of boys, and making teaching more responsive to the needs of all students. His recent publications include *Bright Beginnings for Boys: Engaging Young Boys in Active Literacy* and the *Adolescent Literacy Inventory.*

Doug Buehl is a teacher, author, and

national literacy consultant. He is the author of *Classroom Strategies for Interactive Learning* and coauthor of *Reading and the High School Student: Strategies to Enhance Literacy;* and *Strategies to Enhance Literacy and Learning in Middle School Content Area Classrooms.*

Jim Cummins, Ph.D, is a profes-

sor in the Modern Language Centre at the University of Toronto. He is the author of numerous publications, including *Negotiating Identities: Education for Empowerment in a Diverse Society.* Cummins coined the acronyms BICS and CAPT to help differentiate the type of language ability students need for success.

Harvey Daniels, Ph.D., has been

a classroom teacher, writing project director, author, and university professor. "Smokey" serves as an international consultant to schools, districts, and educational agencies. He is known for his work on student-led book clubs, as recounted in *Literature Circles: Voice and Choice in Book Clubs & Reading Groups* and *Mini Lessons for Literature Circles.* Recent works include *Subjects Matter: Every Teacher's Guide to Content-Area Reading* and *Content Area Writing: Every Teacher's Guide.*

Student Edition Pages

Jane Feber taught language arts in Jacksonville, Florida, for 36 years. Her innovative approach to instruction has earned her several awards, including the NMSA Distinguished Educator Award, the NCTE Edwin A. Hoey Award, the Gladys Prior Award for Teaching Excellence, and the Florida Council of Teachers of English Teacher of the Year Award. She is a National Board Certified Teacher, past president of the Florida Council of Teachers of English, and the author of *Creative Book Reports* and *Active Word Play*.

Danling Fu, Ph.D., is Professor of Language and Culture in the College of Education at the University of Florida. She researches and provides inservice to public schools nationally, focusing on literacy instruction for new immigrant students. Fu's books include *My Trouble is My English* and *An Island of English* addressing English language learners in the secondary schools. She has authored chapters in the *Handbook of Adolescent Literacy Research* and in *Adolescent Literacy: Turning Promise to Practice*.

Kelly Gallagher is a full-time English teacher at Magnolia High School in Anaheim, California. He is the former co-director of the South Basin Writing Project at California State University, Long Beach. Gallagher wrote *Reading Reasons: Motivational Mini-Lessons for the Middle and High School, Deeper Reading: Comprehending Challenging Texts 4-12,* and *Teaching Adolescent Writers*. Gallagher won the Secondary Award of Classroom Excellence from the California Association of Teachers of English—the state's top English teacher honor.

Sharroky Hollie, Ph.D., is an assistant professor at California State University, Dominguez Hills, and an urban literacy visiting professor at Webster University, St. Louis. Hollie's work focuses on professional development, African American education, and second language methodology. He is a contributing author in two texts on culturally and linguistically responsive teaching. He is the Executive Director of the Center for Culturally Responsive Teaching and Learning and the co-founding director of the Culture and Language Academy of Success, an independent charter school in Los Angeles.

Dr. Donald J. Leu, Ph.D., teaches at the University of Connecticut and holds a joint appointment in Curriculum and Instruction and in Educational Psychology. He directs the New Literacies Research Lab and is a member of the Board of Directors of the International Reading Association. Leu studies the skills required to read, write, and learn with Internet technologies. His research has been funded by groups including the U.S. Department of Education, the National Science Foundation, and the Bill & Melinda Gates Foundation.

Jon Scieszka founded GUYS READ, a nonprofit literacy initiative for boys, to call attention to the problem of getting boys connected with reading. In 2008, he was named the first U.S. National Ambassador for Young People's Literature by the Library of Congress. Scieszka taught from first grade to eighth grade for ten years in New York City, drawing inspiration from his students to write *The True Story of the 3 Little Pigs!, The Stinky Cheese Man,* the *Time Warp Trio* series of chapter books, and the *Trucktown* series of books for beginning readers.

Sharon Vaughn, Ph.D., teaches at the University of Texas at Austin. She is the previous Editor-in-Chief of the *Journal of Learning Disabilities* and the co-editor of *Learning Disabilities Research and Practice.* She is the recipient of the American Education Research Association SIG Award for Outstanding Researcher. Vaughn's work focuses on effective practices for enhancing reading outcomes for students with reading difficulties. She is the author of more than 100 articles, and numerous books designed to improve research-based practices in the classroom.

Karen K. Wixson is Dean of the School of Education at the University of North Carolina, Greensboro. She has published widely in the areas of literacy curriculum, instruction, and assessment. Wixson has been an advisor to the National Research Council and helped develop the National Assessment of Educational Progress (NAEP) reading tests. She is a past member of the IRA Board of Directors and co-chair of the IRA Commission on RTI. Recently, Wixson served on the English Language Arts Work Team that was part of the Common Core State Standards Initiative.

COMMON CORE
Contents in Brief

The selections in this book are presented through the lens of three Essential Questions:

What is the relationship between literature and place?

How does literature shape or reflect society?

What is the relationship of the writer to tradition?

viii Contents in brief

Student Edition Pages

From Legend to History
The Old English and Medieval Periods (A.D. 449 to 1485)

ⓒ Multiple Perspectives on the Era

Six units explore literature from consecutive periods in British history. Program pacing allows for 3-, 6-, or 9-week intervals.

Each unit develops literary and reading skills, teaching them to mastery.

x Contents

★ INFORMATIONAL TEXT HIGHLIGHTED

Student Edition Pages

Extended Studies provide in-depth exploration of important authors, genres, or themes in history.

Skills workshops provide practice with key language arts skills.

Contents **xi**

Celebrating Humanity
The English Renaissance Period (1485 to 1625)

Ⓒ Multiple Perspectives on the Era

Each unit includes an introduction to the historical context and literature of the period.

Grant Wiggins worked with the Pearson development team to identif the Essential Questions that drive the instruction in this program.

PART ONE: **LOVERS AND THEIR LINES**

Comparing Literary Works: Sonnet Sequences

Comparing Literary Works: Universal Themes

Student Edition Pages

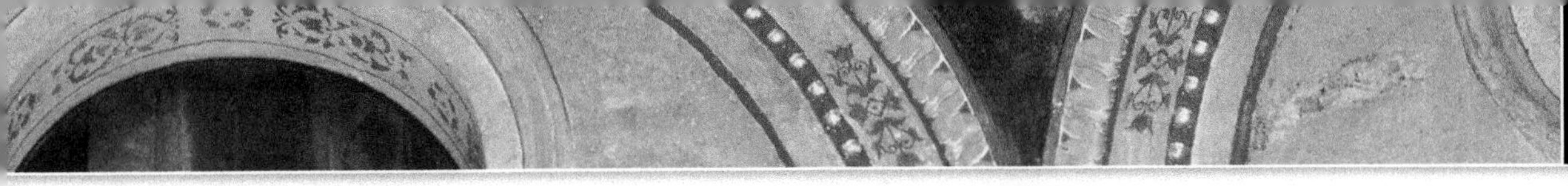

World Literature Connections focus on authors, themes, and genres across world cultures.

Vocabulary, Writing, and Grammar activities link to selection content.

Contents **xiii**

CC 29

Featured unit authors present professional models of writing strategies.

A robust mix of literary and informational texts provides a wide range of reading.

Student Edition Pages

A Turbulent Time
The Seventeenth and Eighteenth Centuries (1625 to 1798)

> Snapshot of the Period features present historical information graphically.

> Literary History features present information about prominent authors, genres, and themes within the historical context of each period.

Contents **xv**

PART THREE: **THE TIES THAT BIND**

Primary Sources documents enhance students' research skills and understanding of literature.

Student Edition Pages

PART TWO: **LYRIC POETRY**

Reading for Information features in each unit present nonfiction forms such as manuals, newspaper articles, Web sites, and other real-life readings.

Assessment Workshops prepare students for questions and formats they will encounter on the SAT and ACT tests.

xx Contents

Student Edition Pages

Progress and Decline
The Victorian Period (1833 to 1901)

Essential Questions drive instruction, shaping selection groupings around critical issues.

Contents **xxi**

Exemplar texts appear throughout the program.

PART THREE: **THE EMPIRE AND ITS DISCONTENTS**

Comparing Literary Works: Mood

THEMES ACROSS CULTURES: Author's Insights

Contemporary Connection: Connecting Victorian Themes

ⓒ **Research Project**: Primary Sources

Student Edition Pages

PART FOUR: **GLOOM AND GLORY**

> Performance Tasks, modeled on those in the Common Core framework, enable students to go beyond multiple-choice assessments.

www.PHLitOnline.com

> Interactive resources provide personalized instruction and activities online.

> All program resources are available online for classroom presentation or individual study.

Contents **xxiii**

A Time of Rapid Change

The Modern and Postmodern Periods (1901 to Present)

Award-winning authors provide scholarly articles that comment on the historical period and related authors and genres.

Comparing Literary Works features support the study of literary and stylistic elements across selections.

xxiv Contents

Student Edition Pages

Contents **xxv**

PART FOUR: **THE POSTMODERN AND BEYOND**

Comparing Literary Works: Meter and Free Verse

Comparing Literary Works: Elegies

Student Edition Pages

Independent Reading suggestions offer opportunities for students to read complex texts independently.

PHLit Online!
www.PHLitOnline.com

Interactive resources provide personalized instruction and activities online.

Contents **xxvii**

Literature

Student Edition Pages

▶ Poetry

xxx Contents

Student Edition Pages

Informational Text—Literary Nonfiction

Student Edition Pages

▶ **Historical and Literary Background**

▶ **The British Tradition—Reading in the Humanities**

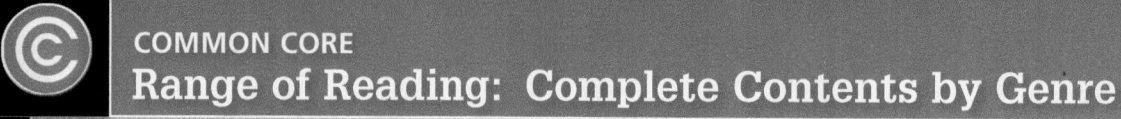
Informational Text—Literary Nonfiction

▶ Literature in Context—Reading in the Content Areas

▶ World Literature Connections

Comparing Across World Literature

World Literature Connection

▶ Literary History

▶ Writing Workshops

▶ Communications Workshops

▶ Vocabulary Workshops

SAT PREP ACT Test-Taking Practice

Contents **xxxv**

Introductory Unit

Building Academic Vocabulary

Academic vocabulary is the language used in school, on standardized tests, and—often—in the business world. Academic terms are more formal and specific than the informal vocabulary most people use among friends and family members. Success in school and later in work requires a clear understanding of different types of academic language. The Common Core State Standards require that you acquire and use grade-appropriate academic words and phrases.

Technical Domain-Specific Academic Vocabulary The literary concepts you will learn throughout this book are one type of academic language. These words are specific to the content area—the subject or discipline—of literature. Other disciplines, such as social studies, the sciences, mathematics, and the arts, have their own academic vocabularies. Some content-area words cross disciplines, or have different meanings when applied to different areas of study.

Technical words are an even more specialized type of domain-specific academic vocabulary. These are words and phrases, such as the following, that identify a precise element in the content area and usually do not appear in other disciplines:

> *Science:* pipette; genome
> *Music:* clef; libretto

Critical Reading and Thinking Terms Many academic terms define modes of thinking, discussing, or writing about ideas. In this book, these words appear in the Critical Reading questions at the ends of the selections. Such academic terms also appear in instructions and writing prompts.

A Note on Etymology
Etymology is the branch of linguistics that deals with word origins and the development of languages. Etymologists trace the history of a word in its own language, and then to even earlier sources in other, more ancient languages. Knowledge of a word's etymology will contribute to your understanding of its meaning and help you determine the meaning of other words that share its history. Etymological information for content-area words appears in the charts on the following pages.

Common Core State Standards

Language 6. Acquire and use accurately general academic and domain-specific words and phrases, sufficient for reading, writing, speaking, and listening at the college and career readiness level; demonstrate independence in gathering vocabulary knowledge when considering a word or phrase important to comprehension or expression.

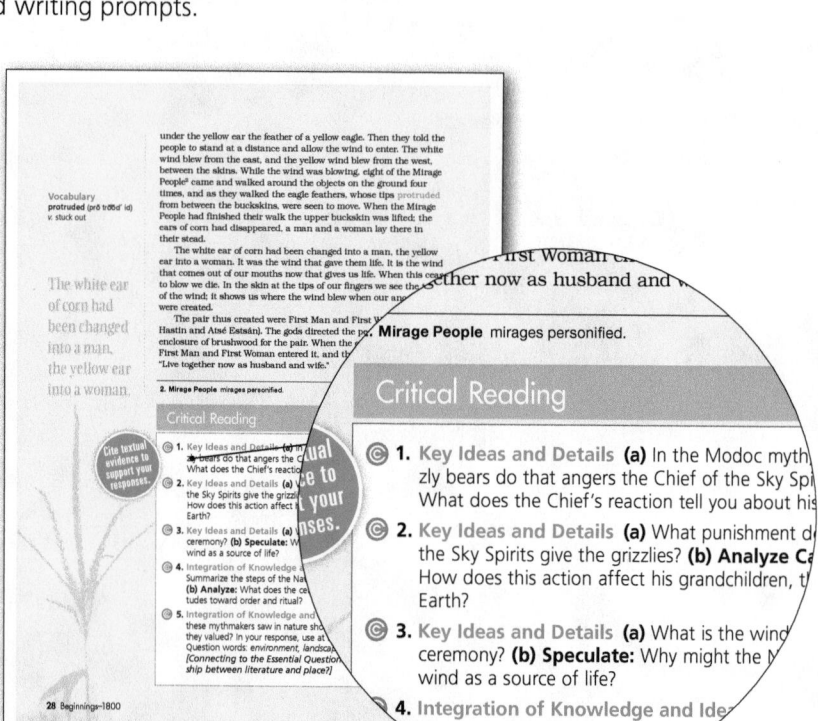

xlviii Building Academic Vocabulary

Technical Domain-Specific Academic Vocabulary

Knowledge of technical content-area academic words, and the roots and affixes that compose them, will help you in all your school courses. As you review the charts below, recognize words that apply to content areas other than those specified here.

Technical Domain-Specific Academic Vocabulary: Science

Term	Meaning	Root/Affix
Accelerate	v. increase speed	Latin root -celer- = swift Words with the same root: accelerator n.; celerity n.
Catalyst	n. something that acts to bring about a result	Latin root -cata- = down; away Words with the same root: cataclysm n.; catapult n.
Chlorophyll	n. green pigment found in plant cells	Greek root -chloro- = green Words with the same root: chlorine n.; chlorosis n.
Chromosome	n. strand of proteins that carries the genes of a living creature	Greek prefix chromo- = color; pigment Words with the same prefix: chromatic adj.; chromate n.
Cytoplasm	n. colorless substance of a cell; outside the nucleus	Greek suffix -plasm = molded; formed Words with the same suffix: bioplasm n.; protoplasm n.
Entropy	n. lack of order which increases over time in a system	Greek root -tropos- = turning; deviation Words with the same root: tropical adj.; trophy n.; heliotrope n.
Enzyme	n. chemical substance produced by living cells that causes changes in other chemicals	Greek suffix -zyme = leavening (an agent that causes fermentation) Words with the same suffix: vitazyme n.; microzyme n.
Mitosis	n. method of cell division	Greek suffix -osis = action; process Words with the same suffix: prognosis n.; psychosis n.
Thermometer	n. instrument for measuring temperature	Greek root -therme- = hot Words with the same root: thermonuclear adj.; thermostat n.
Viscous	adj. having a thick and sticky fluid consistency	Latin prefix visco- = sticky Words with the same prefix: viscometer n.; viscosity n.

> **Ordinary Language:**
> Ice cubes placed in water will begin to break down.
>
> **Academic Language:**
> Ice cubes placed in water will begin the process of entropy.

Exploring Academic Vocabulary: Science

The word *thermometer* combines the Greek roots -*therme*-, which means "heat," and -*metr*-, which means "measure." Using this knowledge, determine the meaning of the following words derived from the same roots:

dynameter   **odometer**   **hypothermia**   **thermography**

Then, use a dictionary to confirm the definitions you proposed. If a general dictionary is not sufficient, consult a specialized science dictionary to find the information you need. Explain how the meaning of each word relates to those of its Greek origins.

COMMON CORE
Workshop

Technical Domain-Specific Academic Vocabulary: Mathematics

Term	Meaning	Root/Affix
Correlate	*v.* show mutual relationship between items	Latin prefix *cor-* = together; with Words with the same prefix: correspond *v.*; corrosion *n.*
Exponent	*n.* symbol placed above and to the right of a number or letter to show how many times that quantity is to be multiplied by itself	Latin suffix *-ponent* = to put; place; set Words with the same suffix: component *n.*; proponent *n.*
Inflection	*n.* change of a curve or arc from convex to concave or the reverse	Latin root *-flectere-* = to bend Words with the same root: reflection *n.*; deflect *v.*
Logarithm	*n.* power to which a base must be raised to produce a given number	Greek prefix *logos-* = word; speech; reason Words with the same prefix: logic *n.*; logotype *n.*
Statistics	*n.* numerical facts or data	Latin root *-stat-* = condition; position; state Words with the same root: statistical *adj.*; static *adj.*
Permutation	*n.* one of the ways in which a set of things can be arranged or ordered	Latin root *-mutare-* = change Words with the same root: mutable *adj.*; mutation *n.*
Estimate	*v.* calculate approximately	Middle French root *-estimer-* = value; appraise Words with the same root: estimation *n.*; esteem *v.*
Graphic	*adj.* relating to the use of diagrams, graphs, curves	Greek root *-graph-* = writing; drawing Words with the same root: telegraph *n.*; biography *n.*; autograph *n.*
Configure	*v.* construct; arrange	Latin root *-figura-* = shape; form; figure Words with the same root: disfigure *v.*; effigy *n.*

Ordinary Language:
We arranged the numerical information in different charts.

Academic Language:
We incorporated statistical data into charts.

Exploring Academic Vocabulary: Mathematics

The word *correlate* is built on the Latin prefix *cor-* (also *com-* or *con-*), which means "with" or "together." Using this knowledge, determine the meaning of the following words derived from the same prefix:

correspond   concert   compress   congruent

Then, use an online or print dictionary to confirm the definitions you proposed. Explain how the meaning of each word relates to that of its Latin ancestor.

I Building Academic Vocabulary

Student Edition Pages

Technical Domain-Specific Academic Vocabulary: Social Studies

Term	Meaning	Root/Affix
Corporation	*n.* organization of many people authorized to act as a single person	Latin root *-corpus-* = body Words with the same root: corporeal *adj.*; incorporate *v.*
Demography	*n.* study of human populations	Greek prefix *demos-* = people Words with the same prefix: demographic *n.*; democracy *n.*
Economy	*n.* system by which a country's money and goods are used and produced	Greek suffix *-nomy* = law; received knowledge Words with the same suffix: agronomy *n.*; taxonomy *n.*
Invest	*v.* give money to a company in order to receive a profit	Latin root *-vestire-* = dress; clothe Words with the same root: vestment *n.*; investigation *n.*
Admiral	*n.* high-ranking naval officer	Arabic root *-amir-* = leader Words with the same root: emirate *n.*; admiralship *n.*
Curfew	*n.* law requiring a population to stay indoors at a stated hour	Old French root *-covrir-* = to cover Words with the same root: covert *adj.*; coverlet *n.*
Lieutenant	*n.* someone who substitutes for another person of greater authority	Old French root *-lieu-* = place Word with the same root: milieu *n.*
Absolutism	*n.* system of government in which a ruler has unlimited power	Latin prefix *ab-* = away; from Word with the same prefix: absolve *v.*
Civic	*adj.* of a city, citizens, or citizenship	Latin root *-civ-* = citizen Words with the same root: civilian *n.*; civilization *n.*

> **Ordinary Language:**
> The government urges citizens to put money into local businesses.
>
> **Academic Language:**
> The government urges citizens to invest in local businesses.

Exploring Academic Vocabulary: Social Studies

The word *economy* is built on the Greek suffix *-nomy*, which means "law; body of received knowledge." Using this knowledge, determine the meaning of the following words derived from the same suffix:

taxonomy   **autonomy**   **astronomy**   **gastronomy**

Then, use an online or print dictionary to confirm the definitions you proposed. Explain how the meaning of each word relates to that of its Greek ancestor.

Building Academic Vocabulary **li**

Technical Domain-Specific Academic Vocabulary: Technology

Term	Meaning	Root/Affix
Gigabyte	*n.* unit of storage capacity in a computer system equal to 1,073,741,824 bytes	Greek prefix *giga-* = giant Words with the same prefix: gigahertz *n.*; gigantic *adj.*
Macro	*n.* single computer instruction that represents a sequence of operations	Greek prefix *macro-* = long, tall, deep, large Words with the same prefix: macrobiotic *adj.*; macrocosm *n.*
Pixel	*n.* smallest unit of an image on a television or computer screen	Old French suffix *–el* = small one Words with the same suffix: satchel *n.*; model *n.*
Processor	*n.* central part of a computer that does the calculations needed to deal with the information it is given	from Latin root *-cedere-* = to go Words with the same root: proceed *v.*; recede *v.*
Simulation	*n.* situation that produces conditions that are not real but appear real	Latin root *-sim-* = like derived through Indo-European base *sem-/som-* = same; as one Words with the same root: ensemble *v.*; simultaneous *adj.*
Streaming	*n.* method of transmitting data so that it can be delivered and received in a steady stream	German root *-strom-* = current; river Words with the same root: mainstream *n.*; streamline *v.*
Transmitter	*n.* equipment that sends out radio or television signals	Latin prefix *trans-* = across Words with the same prefix: transportation *n.*; transcontinental *adj.*
Debug	*v.* find and correct defects	Latin prefix *de-* = down; from Words with the same prefix: defuse *v.*; defrost *v.*
Export	*v.* in computers, to save data in a format usable by another program	Latin root *-portare-* = to carry Words with the same root: import *v.*; airport *n.*
Binary	*adj.* made up of two parts or things; twofold	Latin root *-bin-* = together; double Words with the same root: binocular *n.*; binomial *n.*

Ordinary Language: I asked the technician to clean up my computer.

Academic Language: I asked the technician to debug my operating system.

Exploring Academic Vocabulary: Technology

The word *simulation* comes from the Latin root *-sim-,* which means "like." This Latin root derives from the Indo-European base *sem-/som-,* which means "same; as one." Using your knowledge of these origins, determine the meaning of the following words derived from the same roots:

resemble　　**facsimile**　　**verisimilitude**　　**semblance**

Then, use a dictionary to confirm the definitions you proposed. Explain how the meaning of each word relates to that of its Indo-European base.

lii Building Academic Vocabulary

Student Edition Pages

Technical Domain-Specific Academic Vocabulary: The Arts

Term	Meaning	Root/Affix
Allegro	*adv.* faster than allegretto but not so fast as presto	Latin root -*alacer-/-alacris-* = lively; brisk Words with the same root: allegretto *adj.*; *adv.*; alacrity *n.*
Alignment	*n.* arrangement in a straight line	Old French root -*lignier-* = to line Words with the same root: align *v.*; realign *v.*
Craftmanship	*n.* skill used in making handmade objects	Middle English suffix -*schipe*; derived through Anglian suffix -*scip* = state; condition; quality Words with the same suffix: friendship *n.*; dictatorship *n.*
Decrescendo	*n.* gradual decrease in volume	Old French *creissant*; derived through Latin root -*crescere-* = come forth; spring up; grow; thrive Words with the same root: crescent *n.*; increase *v.*
Baritone	*n.* male singing voice lower than a tenor and higher than a bass	Latin root -*tonus-* = sound; tone Words with the same root: monotone *n.*; intonation *n.*
Medium	*n.* material or technique used in art	Latin root -*medius-* = middle Words with the same root: media *n.*; mediate *v.*; median *adj.*
Musicality	*n.* sensitivity to, knowledge of, or talent for music	Latin suffix -*ity* = quality; state; or degree Words with the same suffix: normality *n.*; publicity *n.*
Technique	*n.* method or procedure in rendering an artistic work	Indo-European prefix *tek-* = shape; make Words with the same prefix: technical *adj.*; technician *n.*
Tempo	*n.* speed at which a composition is performed	Latin root -*tempus-* = time Words with the same root: temporal *adj.*; temporary *adj.*

Ordinary Language: The dancers moved in a perfectly straight line.

Academic Language: The dancers moved in perfect alignment on stage.

Exploring Academic Vocabulary: The Arts

The word *craftsmanship* is built on the Anglian suffix *–scip*, which means "state, condition, quality." Using this knowledge, determine the meaning of the following words derived from the same suffix:

musicianship   **readership**   **friendship**   **partnership**

Then, use an online or print dictionary to confirm the definitions you proposed. Explain how the meaning of each word relates to that of its Anglian ancestor.

Vocabulary Across Content Areas

You might recognize words that apply to content areas other than those specified in the charts on the previous pages. For example, notice how the word *accelerator* relates to two different content areas:

> **Science: accelerator** *n.* nerve or muscle that speeds up a body function

> **Automotive Technology: accelerator** *n.* device, such as the foot throttle of an automobile, for increasing the speed of a machine

While the objects referred to in each definition are different, both of their functions relate to the Latin root *–celer–,* meaning "swift." As you read texts for school, recognize similarities in roots or affixes among words in different content areas. This will help you better understand specific terms and make meaningful connections among topics.

Academic Vocabulary: Critical Thinking Terms

Throughout this book, you will encounter academic vocabulary related to the process of critical thinking. Unlike content-area vocabulary, these words apply equally in all school studies. Being familiar with these academic vocabulary words will be useful as you approach high-stakes standardized tests such as the SAT and ACT. Academic vocabulary will also aid you as you encounter business materials in the workplace.

Term (verb form)	Meaning	Root/Affix
Advocate	Speak or write in support of	Latin root *-voc-* = speak; call Related words: advocate *n.*; advocacy *n.*
Anticipate	Prepare for or signal something	Latin prefix *ante-* = before Related words: anticipatory *adj.*; anticipation *n.*
Arrange	Put into order or sequence	Old French root *-rang-* = rank Related words: arrangement *n.*
Assess	Determine importance; size; or value	Latin root *-sed-/-sess-* = sit Related words: assessment *n.*
Categorize	Place in related groups	Greek prefix *kata-/cata-* = down; against Related words: category *n.*; categorical *adj.*
Compare	Examine in order to discover similarities	Latin root *-par-* = equal Related words: comparison *n.*; comparable *adj.*
Conclude	Determination reached through logical reasoning	Latin root *-clud-* = shut Related words: conclusion *n.*; conclusive *adj.*
Contrast	Examine in order to discover differences	Latin prefix *con-/com-* = with; together Related words: contrastable *adj.*
Debate	Discuss opposing reasons; argue	French root *-batre-* = to beat Related words: debatable *adj.*

Term (verb form)	Meaning	Root/Affix
Deduce	Infer from a general principle	Latin root -duc- = to lead Related words: deduction n.; deductive adj.
Defend	Maintain or support in the face of argument	Latin root -fend- = to strike; push Related words: defense n.; defendant n.
Describe	Represent in words	Latin root -scrib- = to write Related words: description n.; descriptive adj.
Design	Create; fashion or construct according to plan	Latin root -sign- = to mark Related words: design n.; designer n.
Devise	Form in the mind by new combinations of ideas; invent	Latin root -vid- = to separate Related words: devisable adj.
Differentiate	Recognize a difference	Latin suffix -ate = act Related words: different adj.; differentiation n.
Evaluate	Determine significance, worth, or condition through careful study	Old French root -val- = worth; value Related words: evaluation n.; evaluative adj.
Format	Arrange according to a design or plan	Latin root -form- = form, shape Related words: format n.; formation n.
Generalize	Draw a larger principle from details	Latin root -genus- = stock; kind Related words: generalization n.
Hypothesize	Develop a theory about	Greek prefix hypo- = under, beneath Related words: hypothesis n.; hypothetically adv.
Illustrate	Give examples that support an idea	Latin root -lus- = brighten; illuminate Related words: illustration n.; illustrative adj.
Interpret	Explain the meaning of	Latin root -inter- = between Related words: interpretation n.; interpreter n.
Investigate	Make a systematic examination	French root -vestige- = mark; trace; sign Related words: investigation n.; investigative adj.
Paraphrase	Express in one's own words what another person has said or written	Greek prefix para- = beside Related words: paraphraser n.
Predict	Foretell on the basis of observation, experience, or reason	Latin root -dic- = speak, tell, say Related words: prediction n.; predictable adj.
Refute	Prove an argument or statement false or wrong	Latin root -fut- = beat Related words: refutable adj.; refutably adv.
Sort	Put in place according to kind, class, or nature	Old French root -sortir- = allot; assort Related words: sorter n.
Speculate	Use evidence to guess what might happen	Latin root -spec- = look at; view Related words: speculation n.; speculative adj.
Structure	Create a general plot or outline	Latin root -struct- = to build; assemble Related words: structure n.; structural adj.
Validate	Prove to be factual or effective	Latin root -val- = be strong Related words: valid adj.; validity n.

Ordinary Language:
She explained the meaning of the story's symbols.

Academic Language:
She interpreted the meaning of the story's symbols.

Writing an Objective Summary

The ability to write objective summaries is important in college course work and in many careers, such as journalism, business, law, various medical fields, social work, and research. Writing an effective objective summary involves recording the key ideas of a text as well as demonstrating your understanding of the text.

**Common Core
State Standards**

Reading Informational Text
2. Determine two or more central ideas of a text and analyze their development over the course of the text, including how they interact and build on one another to provide a complex analysis; provide an objective summary of the text.
Reading Literature
2. Determine two or more themes or central ideas of a text and analyze their development over the course of the text, including how they interact and build on one another to produce a complex account; provide an objective summary of the text.

Characteristics of an Objective Summary

An effective objective summary is a concise, overview of a text. Following are important elements of an objective summary:

- It is **focused,** relaying the main theme or central idea of a text. It includes specific, relevant details that support that theme or central idea and leaves out unnecessary supporting details.

- It is **brief,** although the writer must be careful to balance brevity and thoroughness and not misrepresent the text by eliminating important parts.

- It is **accurate.** It captures the essence of the longer text it is describing.

- It is **objective.** The writer should refrain from inserting his or her own opinions, judgments, reactions, or personal reflections into the summary.

Remember that an objective summary is *not* a collection of sentences or paragraphs copied from the original source. It is *not* a long retelling of every event, detail, or point in the original text. Finally, a good summary does *not* include evaluative comments, such as the reader's overall opinion of or reaction to the text.

Checklist for Writing an Objective Summary

Before writing an objective summary, be sure you are well acquainted with the text.

- **Understand the entire passage.** You must clearly understand the text's meaning, including any advanced or technical terminology. In your summary, refer to details from the beginning, middle, and end of the text.

- **Prioritize ideas and details.** Determine the main or central ideas of a text and identify the key supporting details. Make sure you recognize which details are less important so that you do not include them in your objective summary.

- **Identify the author's audience and purpose.** Knowing what the author intended to accomplish in the text as well as what audience it was designed to reach will help you summarize accurately.

lvi Introductory Unit

Student Edition Pages

INFORMATIONAL TEXT

Model Objective Summary

Note the key elements of an effective objective summary, called out in the sidenotes. Then, write an objective summary of a text you have recently read. Review your summary, and delete any unnecessary details, opinions, or evaluations.

Summary of "The Story of an Hour"

"The Story of an Hour" by ~~the under-appreciated~~ Kate Chopin is a short story about a woman who is told her husband is dead. Set in the late nineteenth century, the story takes place in the home of Mrs. Louise Mallard.

Because of Mrs. Mallard's heart condition, her sister Josephine tells her the news gently. Richards, a family friend, had been in the newspaper office when a telegram was received that told of a railroad disaster, and Brently Mallard was listed as dead. Mrs. Mallard immediately takes in the news and begins to weep, heading to her room alone.

She sits in an armchair and looks out the window. She notices signs of life everywhere, which contrast with her loss. ~~It is so very sad.~~

Then a thought begins to come to her as she looks at the blue patches in the sky. She breathes heavily as she struggles with the full comprehension of the thought that is trying to possess her, but she gives in. She whispers the word: "Free." She repeats the word over and over. Her eyes brighten, her heart beats quickly, and her body relaxes.

She decides that she will cry at the dead body of the man who loved her, but she welcomes the years beyond that. She looks forward to living independently. The thought of freedom is exhilarating.

Josephine begs her to open the door, but Louise refuses.

She imagines the days ahead and prays that her life will be long, remembering that the day before she had dreaded the thought of a long life. She finally lets her sister in ~~and holds her tight around her waist~~. Together they go downstairs to meet Richards.

Brently Mallard, alive and unharmed, then walks through the front door. He was unaware of the accident at the railroad and surprised at the cry of his wife.

The doctors said her weak heart could not stand such joy; they called it the "joy that kills."

A one-sentence synopsis highlighting the theme or central idea of the story can be an effective start to a summary. Relating the setting of the text gives the summary context.

Opinions should not be included in an objective summary.

These sentences are too detailed and too interpretative to be included in an objective summary. More appropriate would be a simpler statement, such as, "Suddenly a thought came to her."

Eliminate unnecessary details.

The writer includes the last phrase in the story because the irony is a key element of the story.

Writing an Objective Summary **lvii**

Comprehending Complex Texts

As you prepare for higher education and the workplace, you will be required to read increasingly complex texts. A complex text features one or more of the following qualities:

- challenging vocabulary
- long, complex sentences
- figurative language
- multiple levels of meaning
- unfamiliar settings and situations

The selections in this textbook provide you with a range of readings in many genres. Some of these texts will be quite accessible, while others will be, and should be, more challenging. In order to comprehend and interpret complex texts, practice the reading strategies described here.

Strategy 1: Multidraft Reading

Good readers develop the habit of rereading texts in order to comprehend them completely. Similar to listening to a song over and over in order to better understand the lyrics and relive the emotional experience, returning to a text enables readers to more fully enjoy and comprehend it. To fully understand a text, try this multidraft reading strategy:

1st Reading
The first time you read a text, read to gain its basic meaning. If you are reading a narrative text, look for the basics of the plot, character, and setting. If the text is nonfiction, look for central ideas. If you are reading poetry, read first to get a sense of speaker, topic, and mood.

2nd Reading
During your second reading of a text, look for deeper meaning by applying your literary analysis skills. Focus on the artistry or effectiveness of the writing. Look for text structures. Think about why the author chose those organizational patterns. Examine the author's use of language and its effect. For example, consider the effect of rhyme, figurative language, or words with distinct connotations.

3rd Reading
In this reading, search for multiple levels of meaning, considering historical and cultural context. Now is the time to compare and contrast the text with others of its kind you have read. Consider it in the context of its genre, and make connections between texts. You may also make connections between the text and your own experiences. After your third reading, you should be able to evaluate the text's overall effectiveness and its central idea or theme.

lviii Introductory Unit

Student Edition Pages

Common Core
State Standards

Reading Literature
4. Determine the meaning of words and phrases as they are used in the text, including figurative and connotative meanings; analyze the impact of specific word choices on meaning and tone, including words with multiple meanings or language that is particularly fresh, engaging, or beautiful.

Reading Informational Text
4. Determine the meaning of words and phrases as they are used in a text, including figurative, connotative, and technical meanings; analyze how an author uses and refines the meaning of a key term or terms over the course of a text (e.g., how Madison defines *faction* in *Federalist* No. 10).

9. Analyze seventeenth-, eighteenth- and nineteenth-century foundational U.S. documents of historical and literary significance (including the Declaration of Independence, the Preamble to the Constitution, the Bill of Rights, and Lincoln's Second Inaugural Address) for their themes, purposes, and rhetorical features.

Independent Practice

As you read this poem by John Keats, practice the multidraft reading strategy by completing a chart like the one below.

On the Grasshopper and Cricket
by John Keats

The poetry of earth is never dead:

When all the birds are faint with the hot sun,

And hide in cooling trees, a voice will run

From hedge to hedge about the new-mown mead;

That is the Grasshopper's—he takes the lead

In summer luxury—he has never done

With his delights; for when tired out with fun

He rests at ease beneath some pleasant weed.

The poetry of earth is ceasing never:

On a lone winter evening, when the frost

Has wrought a silence, from the stove there shrills

The Cricket's song, in warmth increasing ever,

And seems to one in drowsiness half lost,

The Grasshopper's among some grassy hills.

Multidraft Reading Chart

	My Understanding
1st Reading Look for key ideas and details that reveal basic meaning.	
2nd Reading Read for deeper meanings. Look for ways in which the author used text structures and language to create effects.	
3rd Reading Integrate knowledge and ideas. Consider cultural and historical context and genre. Connect the text to your own experience.	

Comprehending Complex Texts **lix**

Strategy 2: Close Read the Text

Complex texts require close reading and a careful analysis of the writer's choice of words, phrases, and sentences. An awareness of literary and rhetorical techniques and elements, such as parallelism, symbolism, analogy, and text structure, contributes to a deep understanding of a complex text. However, a starting point for close reading is comprehension, which is the foundation for interpretation and analysis. Use the following tips to comprehend the text:

Tips for Close Reading

1. **Break down long sentences into parts.** Look for the subject of the sentence and its verb. Then identify which parts of the sentence modify, or give more information about, its subject.

2. **Reread passages.** When reading complex texts, be sure to reread passages to confirm that you understand their meaning. Look for rhetorical devices and persuasive techniques.

3. **Look for context clues,** such as

   a. Restatement of an idea. For example, in this sentence, *small* restates the adjective *diminutive*.

   She received only a **diminutive** sum, but she was able to make the <u>small</u> amount last the rest of the month.

   b. Definition of sophisticated words. In this sentence, the word *depravity* defines the verb *turpitude*.

   The **turpitude**, or <u>depravity</u>, of the young character in the film stunned the audience to silence.

   c. Examples of concepts and topics. In the following sentence, the underlined text provides examples of words that suggest the meaning of the adjective *melancholy*.

   The **melancholy** territory of gothic literature includes <u>gloomy</u> settings, <u>eerie</u> occurrences, and <u>emotionally troubled</u> characters.

   d. Contrasts of ideas and topics.

   Their **banter** evolved into a <u>serious conversation.</u>

4. **Identify pronoun antecedents.** If long sentences contain pronouns, reread the text to make sure you know to what the pronouns refer. The pronoun *it* in the following sentence refers to the infinitive phrase *to protest injustices,* not to the government.

   The government should assume that **it** is not harmful <u>to protest injustices.</u> (The government should assume that to protest injustices is not harmful.)

5. **Look for conjunctions,** such as *and, or, however, accordingly,* and *yet,* to help you understand relationships between ideas.

6. **Paraphrase,** or restate in your own words, passages of difficult text in order to check your understanding. Remember that a paraphrase is essentially a word-for-word restatement of an original text; it is not a summary.

lx Introductory Unit

Student Edition Pages

INFORMATIONAL TEXT

Close-Read Model

As you read this document, take note of the sidenotes that model ways to unlock meaning in the text.

from "Defending Nonviolent Resistance"
by Mohandas K. Gandhi

Affection cannot be manufactured or regulated by law. If one has an affection for a person or system, one should be free to give the fullest expression to his disaffection, so long as he does not contemplate, promote, or incite to violence. But the section under which Mr. Banker [a colleague in nonviolence] and I are charged is one under which mere promotion of disaffection is as crime. I have studied some of the cases tried under it, and I know that some of the most loved of India's patriots have been convicted under it. I consider it a privilege, therefore, to be charged under that section. I have endeavored to give in their briefest outline the reasons for my disaffection. I have no personal ill will against any single administrator, much less can I have any disaffection toward the king's person. But I hold it to be a virtue to be disaffected toward a government which in its totality has done more harm to India than any previous system. India is less manly under the British rule than she ever was before. Holding such a belief, I consider it to be a sin to have affection for the system. And it has been a precious privilege for me to be able to write what I have in the various articles, tendered in evidence against me.

In fact, I believe that I have rendered a service to India and England by showing in non-cooperation the way out of the unnatural state in which both are living. In my humble opinion, non-cooperation with evil is as much a duty as is cooperation with good. But in the past, non-cooperation has been deliberately expressed in violence to the evildoer. I am endeavoring to show to my countrymen that violent non-cooperation only multiplies evil and that as evil can only be sustained by violence, withdrawal of support of evil requires complete abstention from violence. Nonviolence implies voluntary submission to the penalty for non-cooperation with evil. I am here, therefore, to invite and submit cheerfully to the highest penalty that be inflicted upon me for what in law is a deliberate crime and what appears to me to be the highest duty of a citizen. The only course open to you, the judge, is either to resign your post, and thus dissociate yourself from evil if you feel that the law you are called upon to administer is an evil and that in reality I am innocent, or to inflict on me the severest penalty if you believe that the system and the law you are assisting to administer are good for the people of this country and that my activity is therefore injurious to the public weal.

Note rhetorical devices, such as Gandhi's use of antithesis—connecting contrasting ideas—here.

The conjunction *But* indicates a contrasting idea: Gandhi has no ill will toward a single person, but he does have disaffection toward the totality of the government.

Look for antecedents. The antecedent of the word *it* comes after the pronoun: *to be disaffected toward a government...*

Search for context clues. The words in blue are context clues that help you figure out the meaning of the word that appears in yellow.

Break down this long sentence into parts. The text highlighted in yellow conveys the basic meaning of the sentence. The text highlighted in blue provides additional information.

Comprehending Complex Texts **lxi**

Strategy 3: Ask Questions

Be an attentive reader by asking questions as you read. Throughout this program, we have provided questions for you following each selection. Those questions are sorted into three basic categories that build in sophistication and lead you to a deeper understanding of the texts. Here is an example from this textbook:

Some questions are about **Key Ideas and Details** in the text. You will need to locate and cite explicit information in the text or draw inferences from what you have read.

Some questions are about **Craft and Structure** in the text. To answer these questions, you will need to analyze how the author developed and structured the text. You will also look for ways in which the author artfully used language and how those word choices impacted the meaning and tone of the work.

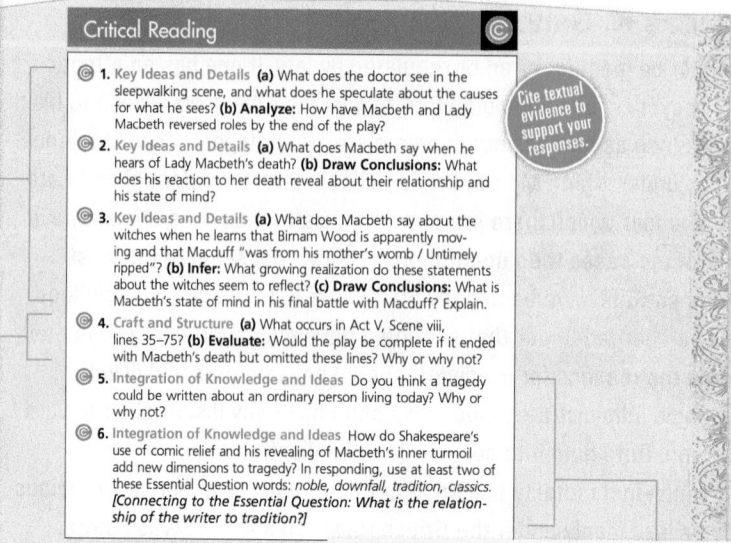

Critical Reading

1. **Key Ideas and Details** (a) What does the doctor see in the sleepwalking scene, and what does he speculate about the causes for what he sees? (b) **Analyze:** How have Macbeth and Lady Macbeth reversed roles by the end of the play?

2. **Key Ideas and Details** (a) What does Macbeth say when he hears of Lady Macbeth's death? (b) **Draw Conclusions:** What does his reaction to her death reveal about their relationship and his state of mind?

3. **Key Ideas and Details** (a) What does Macbeth say about the witches when he learns that Birnam Wood is apparently moving and that Macduff "was from his mother's womb / Untimely ripped"? (b) **Infer:** What growing realization do these statements about the witches seem to reflect? (c) **Draw Conclusions:** What is Macbeth's state of mind in his final battle with Macduff? Explain.

4. **Craft and Structure** (a) What occurs in Act V, Scene viii, lines 35–75? (b) **Evaluate:** Would the play be complete if it ended with Macbeth's death but omitted these lines? Why or why not?

5. **Integration of Knowledge and Ideas** Do you think a tragedy could be written about an ordinary person living today? Why or why not?

6. **Integration of Knowledge and Ideas** How do Shakespeare's use of comic relief and his revealing of Macbeth's inner turmoil add new dimensions to tragedy? In responding, use at least two of these Essential Question words: *noble, downfall, tradition, classics. [Connecting to the Essential Question: What is the relationship of the writer to tradition?]*

Cite textual evidence to support your responses.

Some questions are about the **Integration of Knowledge and Ideas** in the text. These questions ask you to evaluate a text in many different ways, such as comparing texts, analyzing arguments in the text, and using many other methods of thinking critically about a text's ideas.

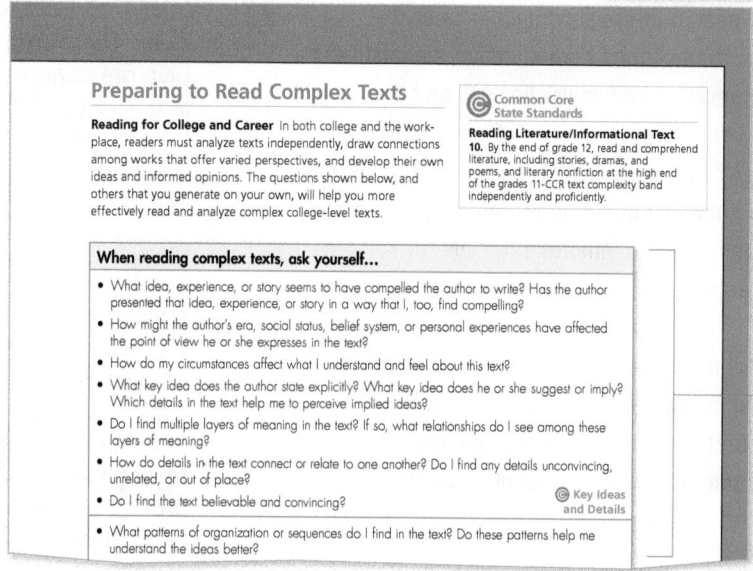

Preparing to Read Complex Texts

Reading for College and Career In both college and the workplace, readers must analyze texts independently, draw connections among works that offer varied perspectives, and develop their own ideas and informed opinions. The questions shown below, and others that you generate on your own, will help you more effectively read and analyze complex college-level texts.

Common Core State Standards

Reading Literature/Informational Text
10. By the end of grade 12, read and comprehend literature, including stories, dramas, and poems, and literary nonfiction at the high end of the grades 11–CCR text complexity band independently and proficiently.

When reading complex texts, ask yourself...

- What idea, experience, or story seems to have compelled the author to write? Has the author presented that idea, experience, or story in a way that I, too, find compelling?
- How might the author's era, social status, belief system, or personal experiences have affected the point of view he or she expresses in the text?
- How do my circumstances affect what I understand and feel about this text?
- What key idea does the author state explicitly? What key idea does he or she suggest or imply? Which details in the text help me to perceive implied ideas?
- Do I find multiple layers of meaning in the text? If so, what relationships do I see among these layers of meaning?
- How do details in the text connect or relate to one another? Do I find any details unconvincing, unrelated, or out of place?
- Do I find the text believable and convincing?

Key Ideas and Details

- What patterns of organization or sequences do I find in the text? Do these patterns help me understand the ideas better?

As you read independently, ask similar types of questions to ensure that you fully enjoy and comprehend any text you choose to read. We have provided sets of questions for you on the Independent Reading pages at the end of each unit.

 INFORMATIONAL TEXT

Model

In this example of a complex text, the call-out boxes show questions
that an attentive reader might ask while reading.

Sample questions:

The Preamble of the United States Constitution

We the people of the United States, in order to form a more perfect union, establish
justice, insure domestic tranquility, provide for the common defense, promote the
general welfare, and secure the blessings of liberty to ourselves and our posterity,
do ordain and establish this Constitution for the United States of America.

**Key Ideas and
Details** What is the
purpose of the
Preamble? What is the
purpose of the
Constitution?

INFORMATIONAL TEXT

Independent Practice

The Bill of Rights

Amendment I Congress shall make no law respecting an establishment of
religion, or prohibiting the free exercise thereof; or abridging the freedom of
speech, or of the press, or the right of the people peaceably to assemble, and
to petition the Government.

Amendment II A well regulated Militia, being necessary to the security of a
free State, the right of the people to keep and bear Arms, shall not be infringed.

Amendment III No Soldier shall, in time of peace be quartered in any house,
without the consent of the Owner, nor in time of war, but in a manner to be
prescribed by law.

Amendment IV The right of the people to be secure in their persons, houses,
papers, and effects, against unreasonable searches and seizures, shall not be
violated, and no Warrants shall issue, but upon probable cause, supported by
Oath or affirmation, and particularly describing the place to be searched, and
the persons or things to be seized.

Amendment V No person shall be held to answer for a capital, or otherwise
infamous crime, unless on a presentment or indictment of a Grand Jury . . . nor
shall any person be subject for the same offence to be twice put in jeopardy of
life or limb, nor shall be compelled in any criminal case to be a witness against
himself . . . nor shall private property be taken for public use, without just
compensation.

Amendment VI In all criminal prosecutions, the accused shall enjoy the right to
a speedy and public trial, by an impartial jury of the State and district wherein
the crime shall have been committed . . . to be confronted with the witnesses
against him . . . and to have the assistance of counsel for his defense.

Amendment VII In Suits at common law, where the value in controversy shall
exceed twenty dollars, the right of trial by jury shall be preserved . . .

Amendment VIII Excessive bail shall not be required, nor excessive fines
imposed, nor cruel and unusual punishments inflicted. . . .

Craft and Structure
What is the effect of
parallel structure here?
How does this pattern
help me follow the
ideas and argument?
What attitude does the
author project?

**Integration of
Knowledge and
Ideas** What other U.S.
documents have themes
similar to those found
in the Preamble and
the Bill of Rights?

Comprehending Complex Texts **lxiii**

Analyzing Arguments

The ability to evaluate an argument, as well as to make one, is critical for success in college and in the workplace.

What Is an Argument?

Chances are you have used the word *argument* to refer to a disagreement between people. A second definition of *argument* is to present one side of a controversial or debatable issue. Through this type of argument, the writer logically supports a particular belief, conclusion, or point of view. A good argument is supported with reasoning and evidence.

Purposes of Argument

There are three main purposes for writing a formal argument:

- to change the reader's mind about an issue
- to convince the reader to accept what is written
- to motivate the reader to take action, based on what is written

---

Elements of Argument

Claim (assertion)—what the writer is trying to prove
Example: The penny should be abolished.

Grounds (evidence)—the support used to convince the reader
Example: There is no profit derived from manufacturing pennies; they actually cost consumers money.

Justification (reasons)—the link between the grounds and the claim; why the grounds are credible
Example: As a unit of currency, pennies are widely viewed as being obsolete.

Evaluating Claims

When reading or listening to an argument, critically assess the claims that are made. Analyze the argument to identify claims that are based on fact or that can be proved true. Also evaluate evidence that supports the claims. If there is little or no reasoning or evidence provided to support the claims, the argument may not be sound or valid.

**Common Core
State Standards**

Language
6. Acquire and use accurately general academic and domain-specific words and phrases, sufficient for reading, writing, speaking, and listening at the college and career readiness level; demonstrate independence in gathering vocabulary knowledge when considering a word or phrase important to comprehension or expression.

Reading Informational Text
6. Determine an author's point of view or purpose in a text in which the rhetoric is particularly effective, analyzing how style and content contribute to the power, persuasiveness, or beauty of the text.

Student Edition Pages

INFORMATIONAL TEXT

Model Argument

from Philadelphia, and Its Solitary Prison
by Charles Dickens

In the outskirts, stands a great prison, called the Eastern Penitentiary: conducted on a plan peculiar to the state of Pennsylvania. The system here is rigid, strict, and hopeless solitary confinement. I believe it, in its effects, to be cruel and wrong.

In its intention, I am well convinced that it is kind, humane, and meant for reformation; but I am persuaded that those who devised this system of Prison Discipline, and those benevolent gentlemen who carry it into execution, do not know what it is that they are doing. I believe that very few men are capable of estimating the immense amount of torture and agony which this dreadful punishment, prolonged for years, inflicts upon the sufferers; and in guessing at it myself, and in reasoning from what I have seen written upon their faces, and what to my certain knowledge they feel within, I am only the more convinced that there is a depth of terrible endurance in it which none but the sufferers themselves can fathom, and which no man has a right to inflict upon his fellow-creature.

I hold this slow and daily tampering with the mysteries of the brain, to be immeasurably worse than any torture of the body: and because its ghastly signs and tokens are not so palpable to the eye and sense of touch as scars upon the flesh; because its wounds are not upon the surface. . . I hesitated once, debating with myself, whether, if I had the power of saying 'Yes' or 'No,' I would allow it to be tried in certain cases, where the terms of imprisonment were short; but now, I solemnly declare, that with no rewards or honours could I walk a happy man beneath the open sky by day, or lie me down upon my bed at night, with the consciousness that one human creature, for any length of time, no matter what, lay suffering this unknown punishment in his silent cell, and I the cause, or I consenting to it in the least degree.

It seems to me that the objection that nothing wholesome or good has ever had its growth in such unnatural solitude, and that even a dog or any of the more intelligent among beasts, would pine, and mope, and rust away, beneath its influence, would be in itself a sufficient argument against this system. But when we recollect, in addition, how very cruel and severe it is, and that a solitary life is always liable to peculiar and distinct objections of a most deplorable nature, which have arisen here, and call to mind, moreover, that the choice is not between this system, and a bad or ill-considered one, but between it and another which has worked well, and is, in its whole design and practice, excellent; there is surely more than sufficient reason for abandoning a mode of punishment attended by so little hope or promise, and fraught, beyond dispute, with such a host of evils.

The introduction sets the stage for the argument that follows, narrowing the focus from the prison to the system of solitary confinement.

Claim: Solitary confinement is cruel and wrong.

Dickens addresses the counterclaim, stating that the intentions of the system were good, and he assumes that the gentlemen do not know how cruel they are being.

Evidence provided includes that people underestimate the unfathomable suffering from the punishment; the punishment is torture. Dickens draws this conclusion based on what he has seen.

Justification: Basic human rights prohibit cruel, inhumane, or unusual punishment.

Dickens reasons that this punishment is worse than physical torture because no one can see the wounds; he also offers the testimony that he would not assent to this punishment in any case.

The last paragraph summarizes the arguments, and the final sentence restates the claim and asks for action: abandon this mode of punishment.

Analyzing Arguments **lxv**

The Art of Argument: Rhetorical Devices and Persuasive Techniques

Rhetorical Devices

Rhetoric is the art of using language in order to make a point or to persuade listeners. Rhetorical devices such as the ones listed below are accepted elements of argument. Their use does not invalidate or weaken an argument. Rather, the use of rhetorical devices is regarded as a key part of an effective argument.

Rhetorical Devices	Examples
Repetition The repeated use of words, phrases, or sentences	Stop the violence! We want to avoid violence! Stop the violence!
Parallelism The repeated use of similar grammatical structures	The strength of the army, the reach of the navy, and the speed of the air force are considered the source of national pride in the military.
Rhetorical Question Calls attention to the issue by implying an obvious answer	Shouldn't civilized nations avoid cruel punishments, even for the most heinous crimes?
Sound Devices The use of alliteration, assonance, rhyme, or rhythm	The sound of the crowd protesting outside the gate drifted to the inmate's ear and lifted his spirits.
Simile and Metaphor Compares two seemingly unlike things or asserts that one thing *is* another	The words in the book became a salve for her wounded soul.

Persuasive Techniques

Persuasive techniques are often found in advertisements and in other forms of informal persuasion. Although techniques like the ones below are sometimes found in formal arguments, they should be avoided in formal arguments.

Persuasive Techniques	Examples
Bandwagon Approach/Anti-Bandwagon Approach Appeals to a person's desire to belong; encourages or celebrates individuality	Don't be the only one without one! Be the first to own our brand.
Emotional Appeal Evokes people's fear, anger, or desire	Our choices today will ensure the health and prosperity of our children! Of our children's children!
Endorsement/Testimony Employs a well-known person to promote a product or idea	These famous authors, actors, politicians, and CEOs are alumnae of our university!
Loaded Language The use of words that are charged with emotion	It is a crisis of unfathomable proportions.
"Plain Folks" Appeal Shows a connection to everyday, ordinary people	I enjoy a good ol' burger and fries, just like everyone else.
Hyperbole Exaggerates to make a point	I'd give my right arm to end the abuse and neglect of animals.

lxvi Introductory Unit

Student Edition Pages

 EXEMPLAR TEXT

Model Speech

The excerpted speech below includes examples of rhetorical devices and persuasive techniques.

Speech on Conciliation with America, by Edmund Burke

. . . The proposition is peace. Not peace through the medium of war; not peace to be hunted through the labyrinth of intricate and endless negotiations; not peace to arise out of universal discord, fomented from principle, in all parts of the empire; not peace to depend on the juridical determination of perplexing questions, or the precise marking the shadowy boundaries of a complex government. It is simple peace, sought in its natural course and in its ordinary haunts.

> The repetition of the word *peace* emphasizes its importance, while the paragraph provides a growing, defining context for the term.

Let the colonies always keep the idea of their civil rights associated with your government—they will cling and grapple to you, and no force under heaven will be of power to tear them from their allegiance. But let it be once understood that your government may be one thing and their privileges another, that these two things may exist without any mutual relation - the cement is gone, the cohesion is loosened, and everything hastens to decay and dissolution. As long as you have the wisdom to keep the sovereign authority of this country as the sanctuary of liberty, the sacred temple consecrated to our common faith, wherever the chosen race and sons of England worship freedom, they will turn their faces towards you . . . Slavery they can have anywhere. It is a weed that grows in every soil . . . But until you become lost to all feeling of your true interest and your natural dignity, freedom they can have from none but you. This is the commodity of price, of which you have the monopoly . . . Deny them this participation of freedom, and you break that sole bond which originally made, and must still preserve, the unity of the empire . . . It is the spirit of the English constitution which, infused through the mighty mass, pervades, feeds, unites, invigorates, vivifies, every part of the empire, even down to the minutest member.

> This metaphor compares slavery to a weed. Burke uses the metaphor to explain why slavery does not create allegiance to a government.

> The alliteration, besides adding to the rhythm of the speech, reinforces the relationship between parts and the whole.

Is it not the same virtue which does every thing for us here in England? Do you imagine, then, that it is the Land-Tax Act which raises your revenue? that it is the annual vote in the Committee of Supply, which gives you your army? or that it is the Mutiny Bill which inspires it with bravery and discipline? No! surely, no! It is the love of the people; it is their attachment to their government, from the sense of the deep stake they have in such a glorious institution, which gives you your army and your navy, and infuses into both that liberal obedience without which your army would be a base rabble and your navy nothing but rotten timber . . .

> This rhetorical question applies the previous conclusions about the empire to England.

> The parallelism in these rhetorical questions builds momentum and leads to the emphatic answer: No!

We ought to elevate our minds to the greatness of that trust to which the order of Providence has called us. By adverting to the dignity of this high calling, our ancestors have turned a savage wilderness into a glorious empire, and have made the most extensive and the only honorable conquests, not by destroying, but by promoting the wealth, the number, the happiness of the human race. Let us get an American revenue as we have got an American empire. English privileges have made it all that it is; English privileges alone will make it all it can be.

> The strongly rhythmic parallelism in the final sentence provides a memorable conclusion.

The Art of Argument **lxvii**

Analyzing Legal Meanings and Reasoning

Reading historical and legal texts requires careful analysis of both the vocabulary and the logical flow of ideas that support a conclusion.

Understanding Legal Meanings

The language of historical and legal documents is formal, precise, and technical. Many words in these texts have specific meanings that you need to understand in order to follow the flow of ideas. For example, the second amendment to the U.S. Constitution states that "A well regulated militia being necessary to the security of a free State, the right of the People to keep and bear arms shall not be infringed." To understand this amendment, it is important to know that in this context *militia* means "armed forces," *bear* means "carry," and *infringed* means "denied." To understand legal meanings:

- Use your knowledge of word roots to help you understand unfamiliar words. Many legal terms use familiar Greek or Latin roots, prefixes, or suffixes.

- Do not assume that you know a word's legal meaning: use a dictionary to check the meanings of key words to be certain that you are applying the correct meaning.

- Paraphrase the text to aid comprehension. Replace difficult words with synonyms to make sure you follow the logic of the argument.

Delineating Legal Reasoning

Works of public advocacy, such as court decisions, political proclamations, proposed laws or constitutional amendments, use careful reasoning to support conclusions. These strategies can help you understand the legal reasoning in an argument:

- State the **purpose** of the document in your own words to help you focus on the writer's primary goal.

- Look for the line of reasoning that supports the **arguments** presented. To be valid and persuasive, key arguments should be backed up by clearly stated logical analysis. Be aware of persuasive techniques, such as citing facts and statistics, referring to expert testimonials, and using emotional language with strong connotations.

- Identify the **premises,** or evidence, upon which a decision rests. In legal texts, premises often include **precedents,** which are earlier examples that must be followed or specifically overturned. Legal reasoning is usually based on the decisions of earlier trials. Be sure you understand precedents in order to identify how the court arrived at the current decision.

lxviii Introductory Unit

Student Edition Pages

INFORMATIONAL TEXT

Model Court Decision

Note the strategies used to evaluate legal meanings and reasoning in this Supreme Court decision from 1954 regarding the legality of segregated, "separate, but equal" schools for black and white students.

from *Brown v. Board of Education of Topeka,* Opinion of the Supreme Court by Chief Justice Earl Warren

We come then to the question presented: Does segregation of children in public schools solely on the basis of race, even though the physical facilities and other "tangible" factors may be equal, deprive the children of the minority group of equal educational opportunities? We believe that it does.

In *Sweatt v. Painter,* in finding that a segregated law school for Negroes could not provide them equal educational opportunities, this Court relied in large part on "those qualities which are incapable of objective measurement but which make for greatness in a law school." In *McLaurin v. Oklahoma State Regents,* the Court, in requiring that a Negro admitted to a white graduate school be treated like all other students, again resorted to intangible considerations: ". . . his ability to study, to engage in discussions and exchange views with other students, and, in general, to learn his profession." Such considerations apply with added force to children in grade and high schools. To separate them from others of similar age and qualifications solely because of their race generates a feeling of inferiority as to their status in the community that may affect their hearts and minds in a way unlikely ever to be undone. The effect of this separation on their educational opportunities was well stated by a finding in the Kansas case by a court which nevertheless felt compelled to rule against the Negro plaintiffs: Segregation of white and colored children in public schools has a detrimental effect upon the colored children. The impact is greater when it has the sanction of the law, for the policy of separating the races is usually interpreted as denoting the inferiority of the negro group. A sense of inferiority affects the motivation of a child to learn. Segregation with the sanction of law, therefore, has a tendency to [retard] the educational and mental development of negro children and to deprive them of some of the benefits they would receive in a racially integrated school system. Whatever may have been the extent of psychological knowledge at the time of *Plessy v. Ferguson,* this finding is amply supported by modern authority. Any language in *Plessy v. Ferguson* contrary to this finding is rejected.

We conclude that, in the field of public education, the doctrine of "separate but equal" has no place. Separate educational facilities are inherently unequal.

> The word *tangible* comes from the Latin root meaning "to touch." In this decision, the court contrasts tangible, measurable features with intangible features that are difficult to measure.

> The court cites two precedents: earlier cases relating to unequal education opportunities for black students.

> Here's one way you might break down the ideas in this sentence when you paraphrase: Segregating black students just because of their race makes them feel as if they are less valued by our society. This separation can have a permanent negative influence on their character.

> The conclusion makes the **purpose** of the decision clear: to overturn the precedent established by *Plessy v. Ferguson.* The **argument** describes the reasons why the Court no longer considers the reasoning in that earlier case to be valid.

Writing About Legal Meanings

Write a detailed analysis of the phrase "segregation with the sanction of law" in the *Brown v. Board of Education of Topeka* decision. Explain the definitions of the terms as they are used in this context and explain how this phrase relates to the courts decision to outlaw "separate but equal" education.

Analyzing Legal Meanings and Reasoning   **lxix**

Composing an Argument

Choosing a Topic

You should choose a topic that matters to people—and to you. The topic should be debatable or controversial to some degree.

Confirm that you can make an arguable claim. Ask yourself:

1. What am I trying to prove? What ideas do I need to get across?
2. Are there people who would disagree with my claim? What counterclaims would they make?
3. Do I have evidence to support my claim? Is my evidence sufficient and relevant?

If you are able to state what you want to prove and answered "yes" to questions 2 and 3, you have an arguable claim.

Introducing the Claim and Establishing Its Significance

Before you begin writing, determine how much your audience already knows about your chosen topic. Then, provide only as much background information as necessary to introduce your claim. If there are issues surrounding your topic, you will need to clarify them for your audience and narrow the focus to your specific claim. Remember that you are not writing a summary of the topic—you are crafting an argument. Once you have provided context for your argument, you should clearly state your claim, or thesis.

Developing Your Claim With Reasoning and Evidence

Now that you have made your claim, you must support it with evidence, or grounds, and reasons for your claim. A good argument should have at least three solid pieces of evidence to support the claim. Evidence can range from personal experience to researched data or expert opinion. Knowing your audience's knowledge level, concerns, values, and possible biases can help you decide what kind of evidence will have the strongest impact. Make sure your evidence is up to date and comes from a credible source. Always credit your sources.

You should also address opposing counterclaims within the body of your argument. Consider points you have made or evidence you have provided that a person might challenge. Decide how best to refute these counterclaims. One technique for defusing an opponent's claims is to agree with selected parts of them.

Writing a Concluding Statement or Section

Restate your claim in the conclusion of your argument, and summarize your main points. The goal of a concluding section is to provide a sense of closure and completeness to an argument. Make your concluding statement strong enough to be memorable and to leave the reader thinking.

 Common Core State Standards

Writing

1.a. Introduce precise, knowledgeable claim(s), establish the significance of the claim(s), distinguish the claim(s) from alternate or opposing claims, and create an organization that logically sequences claim(s), counterclaims, reasons, and evidence.

1.b. Develop claim(s) and counterclaims fairly and thoroughly, supplying the most relevant evidence for each while pointing out the strengths and limitations of both in a manner that anticipates the audience's knowledge level, concerns, values, and possible biases.

1.e. Provide a concluding statement or section that follows from and supports the argument presented.

Student Edition Pages

Practice

Exploring both sides of an issue can be a good way to start planning an argument. Complete a chart like the one below to help you plan your own argument.

Topic:

Issue: _____

_____

Claim:	Counterclaim:
Grounds (Evidence): 1. _____ 2. _____ 3. _____	Grounds (Evidence): 1. _____ 2. _____ 3. _____
Justification: 1. _____ 2. _____ 3. _____	Justification: 1. _____ 2. _____ 3. _____

When you have completed the chart and developed your own, precise claim, consider the following questions:

1. Who is your audience? What type of evidence can you use to best convince those who do not agree with your claim?

2. Is your evidence strong and difficult to dispute? If not, how can you strengthen it or find better evidence?

3. How will you refute the counterclaim? Are there any parts of the counterclaim you agree with?

Correlation to Prentice Hall Literature © 2012

The following correlation shows points at which focused, sustained instruction is provided in the Student Edition. The standards are spiraled and revisited throughout the program, and the Teacher's Edition provides further opportunity to address standards.

Key
SE/TE: Student Edition/Teacher's Edition
CCC: Common Core Companion

		Grade 12 Reading Standards for Literature	Prentice Hall Literature © 2012, Grade 12
Key Ideas and Details	RL.1	Cite strong and thorough textual evidence to support analysis of what the text says explicitly as well as inferences drawn from the text, including determining where the text leaves matters uncertain.	**SE/TE:** 95, 296, 588, 866, 936, 958, 1011, 1154, 1170, 1340 **CCC:** 2, 3, 9
	RL.2	Determine two or more themes or central ideas of a text and analyze their development over the course of the text, including how they interact and build on one another to produce a complex account; provide an objective summary of the text.	**SE/TE:** xlvii, 168, 264, 504, 552, 664, 746, 936, 1040, 1388 **CCC:** 15, 16, 22
	RL.3	Analyze the impact of the author's choices regarding how to develop and relate elements of a story or drama (e.g., where a story is set, how the action is ordered, how the characters are introduced and developed).	**SE/TE:** 38, 95, 137, 321, 360, 378, 400, 541, 588, 976, 997, 1028, 1191, 1209, 1244, 1296, 1358, 1378, 1418, 1434 **CCC:** 28, 29, 35
Craft and Structure	RL.4	Determine the meaning of words and phrases as they are used in the text, including figurative and connotative meanings; analyze the impact of specific word choices on meaning and tone, including words with multiple meanings or language that is particularly fresh, engaging, or beautiful. (Include Shakespeare as well as other authors.)	**SE/TE:** 296, 480, 494, 558, 779, 852, 936, 1138, 1272, 1366 **CCC:** 41, 42, 48
	RL.5	Analyze how an author's choices concerning how to structure specific parts of a text (e.g., the choice of where to begin or end a story, the choice to provide a comedic or tragic resolution) contribute to its overall structure and meaning as well as its aesthetic impact.	**SE/TE:** 18, 123, 252, 272, 342, 521, 797, 818, 880, 936, 1072, 1086, 1218, 1400, 1410 **CCC:** 54, 55
	RL.6	Analyze a case in which grasping point of view requires distinguishing what is directly stated in a text from what is really meant (e.g., satire, sarcasm, irony, or understatement).	**SE/TE:** 604, 628, 1308 **CCC:** 61, 62
Integration of Knowledge and Ideas	RL.7	Analyze multiple interpretations of a story, drama, or poem (e.g., recorded or live production of a play or recorded novel or poetry), evaluating how each version interprets the source text. (Include at least one play by Shakespeare and one play by an American dramatist.)	**SE/TE:** 313, 702 **CCC:** 68, 69
	RL.8	(Not applicable to literature)	
	RL.9	Demonstrate knowledge of eighteenth-, nineteenth-, and early-twentieth-century foundational works of American literature, including how two or more texts from the same period treat similar themes or topics.	**SE/TE:** In addition to the study of the texts included on the pages listed here, this book provides numerous opportunities for students to analyze foundational works of British literature across genres. 644, 662, 850, 1242 **CCC:** 75, 76
Range of Reading and Level of Text Complexity	RL.10	By the end of Grade 12, read and comprehend literature, including stories, dramas, and poems, in the grades 11–CCR text complexity band proficiently, with scaffolding as needed at the high end of the range.	**SE/TE:** xlvii, 233, 421, 461, 713, 1119, 1487 **CCC:** 82, 83

Grade 12 Reading Standards for Informational Texts		Prentice Hall Literature © 2012, Grade 12
Key Ideas and Details	**RI.1** Cite strong and thorough textual evidence to support analysis of what the text says explicitly as well as inferences drawn from the text, including determining where the text leaves matters uncertain.	**SE/TE:** 568, 680, 932, 1062 **CCC:** 90, 91, 97
	RI.2 Determine two or more central ideas of a text and analyze their development over the course of the text, including how they interact and build on one another to provide a complex analysis; provide an objective summary of the text.	**SE/TE:** xlvii, 282, 932, 1284, 1444 **CCC:** 103, 104, 110
	RI.3 Analyze a complex set of ideas or sequence of events and explain how specific individuals, ideas, or events interact and develop over the course of the text.	**SE/TE:** 568, 646, 932, 1062, 1316 **CCC:** 116, 117
Craft and Structure	**RI.4** Determine the meaning of words and phrases as they are used in a text, including figurative, connotative, and technical meanings; analyze how an author uses and refines the meaning of a key term or terms over the course of a text (e.g., how Madison defines *faction* in *Federalist No. 10*).	**SE/TE:** xlvii, 646, 896, 932, 1444 **CCC:** 123, 124, 130
	RI.5 Analyze and evaluate the effectiveness of the structure an author uses in his or her exposition or argument, including whether the structure makes points clear, convincing, and engaging.	**SE/TE:** 82, 598, 810, 1022, 1454, 1462 **CCC:** 136, 137
	RI.6 Determine an author's point of view or purpose in a text in which the rhetoric is particularly effective, analyzing how style and content contribute to the power, persuasiveness, or beauty of the text.	**SE/TE:** xlvii, 436, 896, 910, 932, 1284 **CCC:** 143, 144, 150
Integration of Knowledge and Ideas	**RI.7** Integrate and evaluate multiple sources of information presented in different media or formats (e.g., visually, quantitatively) as well as in words in order to address a question or solve a problem.	**SE/TE:** 16, 70, 198, 250, 441, 478, 730, 956, 1136 **CCC:** 156, 157
	RI.8 Delineate and evaluate the reasoning in seminal U.S. texts, including the application of constitutional principles and use of legal reasoning (e.g., in U.S. Supreme Court majority opinions and dissents) and the premises, purposes, and arguments in works of public advocacy (e.g., *The Federalist,* presidential addresses).	**SE/TE:** 908 **CCC:** 163, 164
	RI.9 Analyze seventeenth-, eighteenth-, and nineteenth-century foundational U.S. documents of historical and literary significance (including The Declaration of Independence, the Preamble to the Constitution, the Bill of Rights, and Lincoln's Second Inaugural Address) for their themes, purposes, and rhetorical features.	**SE/TE:** In addition to the study of the texts included on the pages listed here, this book provides numerous opportunities for students to analyze foundational British documents of historical and literary significance. xlvii, 644, 662 **CCC:** 170, 171
Range of Reading and Level of Text Complexity	**RI.10** By the end of Grade 12, read and comprehend literary nonfiction in the grades 11–CCR text complexity band proficiently, with scaffolding as needed at the high end of the range.	**SE/TE:** 233, 461, 713, 1119, 1487 **CCC:** 177, 178

Grade 12 Writing Standards		Prentice Hall Literature © 2012, Grade 12
Text Types and Purposes		
W.1	Write arguments to support claims in an analysis of substantive topics or texts, using valid reasoning and relevant and sufficient evidence.	**SE/TE:** 32, 65, 89, 166, 358, 442, 514, 603, 987, 1021, 1050, 1094, 1149, 1278 **CCC:** 185, 186, 187, 188, 189, 190, 191, 192, 193, 194, 195
W.1.a	Introduce precise, knowledgeable claim(s), establish the significance of the claim(s), distinguish the claim(s) from alternate or opposing claims, and create an organization that logically sequences claim(s), counterclaims, reasons, and evidence.	**SE/TE:** xlvii, 135, 358, 444, 501, 538, 685, 794, 1050, 1430 **CCC:** 185, 186, 187, 188, 189, 190, 191, 192, 193, 194, 195
W.1.b	Develop claim(s) and counterclaims fairly and thoroughly, supplying the most relevant evidence for each while pointing out the strengths and limitations of both in a manner that anticipates the audience's knowledge level, concerns, values, and possible biases.	**SE/TE:** xlvii, 444, 538, 1430 **CCC:** 185, 186, 187, 188, 189, 190, 191, 192, 193, 194, 195
W.1.c	Use words, phrases, and clauses as well as varied syntax to link the major sections of the text, create cohesion, and clarify the relationships between claim(s) and reasons, between reasons and evidence, and between claim(s) and counterclaims.	**CCC:** 185, 186, 187, 188, 189, 190, 191, 192, 193, 194, 195
W.1.d	Establish and maintain a formal style and objective tone while attending to the norms and conventions of the discipline in which they are writing.	**SE/TE:** 65, 987, 1094 **CCC:** 185, 186, 187, 188, 189, 190, 191, 192, 193, 194, 195
W.1.e	Provide a concluding statement or section that follows from and supports the argument presented.	**SE/TE:** xlvii, 444, 538, 794 **CCC:** 185, 186, 187, 188, 189, 190, 191, 192, 193, 194, 195
W.2	Write informative/explanatory texts to examine and convey complex ideas, concepts, and information clearly and accurately through the effective selection, organization, and analysis of content.	**SE/TE:** 75, 261, 435, 551, 676, 809, 974, 1027, 1038, 1096, 1167, 1215, 1242, 1315, 1337, 1376, 1453, 1459, 1467 **CCC:** 196, 197, 198, 199, 201, 202, 203, 204, 205, 206, 207
W.2.a	Introduce a topic; organize complex ideas, concepts, and information so that each new element builds on that which precedes it to create a unified whole; include formatting (e.g., headings), graphics (e.g., figures, tables), and multimedia when useful to aiding comprehension.	**SE/TE:** 626, 920, 936, 1415 **CCC:** 196, 197, 198, 199, 200, 201, 202, 203, 204, 205, 206, 207
W.2.b	Develop the topic thoroughly by selecting the most significant and relevant facts, extended definitions, concrete details, quotations, or other information and examples appropriate to the audience's knowledge of the topic.	**SE/TE:** 279, 397, 441, 557, 850, 920, 936, 1083, 1242 **CCC:** 196, 197, 198, 199, 200, 201, 202, 203, 204, 205, 206, 207
W.2.c	Use appropriate and varied transitions and syntax to link the major sections of the text, create cohesion, and clarify the relationships among complex ideas and concepts.	**SE/TE:** 75, 270, 922, 1098 **CCC:** 196, 197, 198, 199, 200, 201, 202, 203, 204, 205, 206, 207
W.2.d	Use precise language, domain-specific vocabulary, and techniques such as metaphor, simile, and analogy to manage the complexity of the topic.	**SE/TE:** 850, 1337 **CCC:** 196, 197, 198, 199, 200, 201, 202, 203, 204, 205, 206, 207
W.2.e	Establish and maintain a formal style and objective tone while attending to the norms and conventions of the discipline in which they are writing.	**SE/TE:** 1098 **CCC:** 196, 197, 198, 199, 200, 201, 202, 203, 204, 205, 206, 207

Ⓒ Grade 12 Writing Standards			Prentice Hall Literature © 2012, Grade 12
	W.2.f	Provide a concluding statement or section that follows from and supports the information or explanation presented (e.g., articulating implications or the significance of the topic).	**SE/TE:** 397, 1098 **CCC:** 196, 197, 198, 199, 200, 201, 202, 203, 204, 205, 206, 207
	W.3	Write narratives to develop real or imagined experiences or events using effective technique, well-chosen details, and well-structured event sequences.	**SE/TE:** 196, 214, 305, 340, 376, 596, 1269, 1356, 1387, 1468 **CCC:** 208, 209, 210, 211, 212, 213, 214, 215, 216, 217, 218
	W.3.a	Engage and orient the reader by setting out a problem, situation, or observation and its significance, establishing one or multiple point(s) of view, and introducing a narrator and/or characters; create a smooth progression of experiences or events.	**SE/TE:** 376, 491, 694, 1468 **CCC:** 208, 209, 210, 211, 212, 213, 214, 215, 216, 217, 218
	W.3.b	Use narrative techniques, such as dialogue, pacing, description, reflection, and multiple plot lines, to develop experiences, events, and/or characters.	**SE/TE:** 216, 566, 1468 **CCC:** 208, 209, 210, 211, 212, 213, 214, 215, 216, 217, 218
	W.3.c	Use a variety of techniques to sequence events so that they build on one another to create a coherent whole and build toward a particular tone and outcome (e.g., a sense of mystery, suspense, growth, or resolution).	**SE/TE:** 218, 696, 864, 1306 **CCC:** 208, 209, 210, 211, 212, 213, 214, 215, 216, 217, 218
	W.3.d	Use precise words and phrases, telling details, and sensory language to convey a vivid picture of the experiences, events, setting, and/or characters.	**SE/TE:** 196, 214, 305, 340, 376, 696, 864, 1306, 1356, 1470 **CCC:** 208, 209, 210, 211, 212, 213, 214, 215, 216, 217, 218
	W.3.e	Provide a conclusion that follows from and reflects on what is experienced, observed, or resolved over the course of the narrative.	**SE/TE:** 216, 1409 **CCC:** 208, 209, 210, 211, 212, 213, 214, 215, 216, 217, 218
Production and Distribution of Writing	W.4	Produce clear and coherent writing in which the development, organization, and style are appropriate to task, purpose, and audience.	**SE/TE:** 261, 644, 698, 936, 1098, 1167, 1399, 1443 **CCC:** 219, 220
	W.5	Develop and strengthen writing as needed by planning, revising, editing, rewriting, or trying a new approach, focusing on addressing what is most significant for a specific purpose and audience.	**SE/TE:** 120, 214, 218, 221, 376, 397, 442, 449, 491, 698, 701, 924, 927, 1083, 1100, 1107, 1149, 1185, 1218, 1242, 1269, 1472, 1475 **CCC:** 226, 227
	W.6	Use technology, including the Internet, to produce, publish, and update individual or shared writing products in response to ongoing feedback, including new arguments or information.	**SE/TE:** 221, 701, 920, 927 **CCC:** 233, 234
Research to Build and Present Knowledge	W.7	Conduct short as well as more sustained research projects to answer a question (including a self-generated question) or solve a problem; narrow or broaden the inquiry when appropriate; synthesize multiple sources on the subject, demonstrating understanding of the subject under investigation.	**SE/TE:** 212, 580, 878, 908, 920, 1069, 1096, 1294, 1365 **CCC:** 240, 241, 244
	W.8	Gather relevant information from multiple authoritative print and digital sources, using advanced searches effectively; assess the strengths and limitations of each source in terms of the task, purpose, and audience; integrate information into the text selectively to maintain the flow of ideas, avoiding plagiarism and overreliance on any one source and following a standard format for citation.	**SE/TE:** 212, 580, 878, 1069, 1096, 1102, 1294 **CCC:** 247, 248, 249, 251, 253, 254, 255, 256, 257, 258, 259, 260

COMMON CORE
Common Core State Standards Correlation

Ⓒ Grade 12 Writing Standards			Prentice Hall Literature © 2012, Grade 12
Research to Build and Present Knowledge	W.9	Draw evidence from literary or informational texts to support analysis, reflection, and research.	**SE/TE:** 908 **CCC:** 261, 262, 265, 266
	W.9.a	Apply *grades 11–12 Reading standards* to literature (e.g., "Demonstrate knowledge of eighteenth-, nineteenth- and early-twentieth-century foundational works of American literature, including how two or more texts from the same period treat similar themes or topics").	**SE/TE:** 794, 850, 893, 956, 1242 **CCC:** 261, 262, 265, 266
	W.9.b	Apply *grades 11–12 Reading standards* to literary nonfiction (e.g., "Delineate and evaluate the reasoning in seminal U.S. texts, including the application of constitutional principles and use of legal reasoning [e.g., in U.S. Supreme Court Case majority opinions and dissents] and the premises, purposes, and arguments in works of public advocacy [e.g., *The Federalist,* presidential addresses]").	**SE/TE:** 662 **CCC:** 261, 262, 265, 266
Range of Writing	W.10	Write routinely over extended time frames (time for research, reflection, and revision) and shorter time frames (a single sitting or a day or two) for a range of tasks, purposes, and audiences.	**SE/TE:** 166, 435, 551, 809, 1215 **CCC:** 269, 270, 271, 272, 273, 274, 275, 276

Ⓒ Grade 12 Speaking and Listening Standards			Prentice Hall Literature © 2012, Grade 12
Comprehension and Collaboration	SL.1	Initiate and participate effectively in a range of collaborative discussions (one-on-one, in groups, and teacher-led) with diverse partners on *grades 11–12 topics, texts, and issues,* building on others' ideas and expressing their own clearly and persuasively.	**SE/TE:** 16, 478, 730 **CCC:** 278, 279, 280, 281, 282, 283, 284, 285
	SL.1.a	Come to discussions prepared, having read and researched material under study; explicitly draw on that preparation by referring to evidence from texts and other research on the topic or issue to stimulate a thoughtful, well-reasoned exchange of ideas.	**SE/TE:** 478, 936, 1154, 1433 **CCC:** 278, 279, 280, 281, 282, 283, 284, 285
	SL.1.b	Work with peers to promote civil, democratic discussions and decision-making, set clear goals and deadlines, and establish individual roles as needed.	**SE/TE:** 1154, 1433 **CCC:** 278, 279, 280, 281, 282, 283, 284, 285
	SL.1.c	Propel conversations by posing and responding to questions that probe reasoning and evidence; ensure a hearing for a full range of positions on a topic or issue; clarify, verify, or challenge ideas and conclusions; and promote divergent and creative perspectives.	**SE/TE:** 730, 1433 **CCC:** 278, 279, 280, 281, 282, 283, 284, 285
	SL.1.d	Respond thoughtfully to diverse perspectives; synthesize comments, claims, and evidence made on all sides of an issue; resolve contradictions when possible; and determine what additional information or research is required to deepen the investigation or complete the task.	**SE/TE:** 450, 936, 1433 **CCC:** 278, 279, 280, 281, 282, 283, 284, 285
	SL.2	Integrate multiple sources of information presented in diverse formats and media (e.g., visually, quantitatively, orally) in order to make informed decisions and solve problems, evaluating the credibility and accuracy of each source and noting any discrepancies among the data.	**SE/TE:** 1108, 1476 **CCC:** 286, 287
	SL.3	Evaluate a speaker's point of view, reasoning, and use of evidence and rhetoric, assessing the stance, premises, links among ideas, word choice, points of emphasis, and tone used.	**SE/TE:** 222, 928 **CCC:** 290, 291, 294

Grade 12 Speaking and Listening Standards			Prentice Hall Literature © 2012, Grade 12
Presentation of Knowledge and Ideas	SL.4	Present information, findings, and supporting evidence, conveying a clear and distinct perspective, such that listeners can follow the line of reasoning, alternative or opposing perspectives are addressed, and the organization, development, substance, and style are appropriate to purpose, audience, and a range of formal and informal tasks.	**SE/TE:** 250, 450, 936, 1136 **CCC:** 297, 298, 301
	SL.5	Make strategic use of digital media (e.g., textual, graphical, audio, visual, and interactive elements) in presentations to enhance understanding of findings, reasoning, and evidence and to add interest.	**SE/TE:** 250, 956 **CCC:** 304, 305
	SL.6	Adapt speech to a variety of contexts and tasks, demonstrating a command of formal English when indicated or appropriate.	**SE/TE:** 702, 936, 1136 **CCC:** 306, 307, 310

Grade 12 Language Standards			Prentice Hall Literature © 2012, Grade 12
Conventions of Standard English	L.1	Demonstrate command of the conventions of standard English grammar and usage when writing or speaking.	**SE/TE:** 491, 501, 794, 932 **CCC:** 314, 315, 316, 317
	L.1.a	Apply the understanding that usage is a matter of convention, can change over time, and is sometimes contested.	**SE/TE:** 16, 305, 378, 919 **CCC:** 314, 315
	L.1.b	Resolve issues of complex or contested usage, consulting references (e.g., *Merriam-Webster's Dictionary of English Usage, Garner's Modern American Usage*) as needed.	**SE/TE:** 449, 491 **CCC:** 316, 317
	L.2	Demonstrate command of the conventions of standard English capitalization, punctuation, and spelling when writing.	**SE/TE:** 927, 932, 1107, 1472 **CCC:** 318, 319, 320, 321
	L.2.a	Observe hyphenation conventions.	**SE/TE:** 221 **CCC:** 318, 319
	L.2.b	Spell correctly.	**SE/TE:** 221, 449, 701, 1206, 1475 **CCC:** 320, 321
Knowledge of Language	L.3	Apply knowledge of language to understand how language functions in different contexts, to make effective choices for meaning or style, and to comprehend more fully when reading or listening.	**SE/TE:** 151, 927, 932, 1094, 1185 **CCC:** 322, 323
	L.3.a	Vary syntax for effect, consulting references (e.g., Tufte's *Artful Sentences*) for guidance as needed; apply an understanding of syntax to the study of complex texts when reading.	**SE/TE:** 65, 272, 936, 1167 **CCC:** 322, 323
Vocabulary Acquisition and Use	L.4	Determine or clarify the meaning of unknown and multiple-meaning words and phrases based on *grades 11–12 reading and content,* choosing flexibly from a range of strategies.	**SE/TE:** 151, 501, 704 **CCC:** 324, 325, 326, 327, 328, 329, 330, 331
	L.4.a	Use context (e.g., the overall meaning of a sentence, paragraph, or text; a word's position or function in a sentence) as a clue to the meaning of a word or phrase.	**SE/TE:** 120, 156, 196, 224, 270, 340, 376, 452, 596, 644, 704, 864, 908, 930, 932, 974, 1110, 1269, 1306, 1337, 1430, 1478 **CCC:** 324, 325
	L.4.b	Identify and correctly use patterns of word changes that indicate different meanings or parts of speech (e.g., *conceive, conception, conceivable*).	**SE/TE:** 598, 792, 987, 1356 **CCC:** 326, 327

Grade 12 Language Standards		Prentice Hall Literature © 2012, Grade 12
Vocabulary Acquisition and Use	**L.4.c** Consult general and specialized reference materials (e.g., dictionaries, glossaries, thesauruses), both print and digital, to find the pronunciation of a word or determine or clarify its precise meaning, its part of speech, its etymology, or its standard usage.	**SE/TE:** 156, 224, 416, 536, 662, 704, 797, 930, 936, 1006, 1209, 1478 **CCC:** 328, 329
	L.4.d Verify the preliminary determination of the meaning of a word or phrase (e.g., by checking the inferred meaning in context or in a dictionary).	**SE/TE:** 75, 224, 397, 441, 810, 878, 936, 1006, 1022, 1149, 1204, 1459 **CCC:** 330, 331
	L.5 Demonstrate understanding of figurative language, word relationships, and nuances in word meanings.	**SE/TE:** 32, 65, 89, 279, 340, 452, 491, 626, 878, 893, 1083, 1110, 1167, 1278 **CCC:** 332, 333, 334, 335
	L.5.a Interpret figures of speech (e.g., hyperbole, paradox) in context and analyze their role in the text.	**SE/TE:** 794, 852, 936 **CCC:** 332, 333
	L.5.b Analyze nuances in the meaning of words with similar denotations.	**SE/TE:** 744, 792, 936, 1242 **CCC:** 334, 335
	L.6 Acquire and use accurately general academic and domain-specific words and phrases, sufficient for reading, writing, speaking, and listening at the college and career readiness level; demonstrate independence in gathering vocabulary knowledge when considering a word or phrase important to comprehension or expression.	**SE/TE:** xlvii, 135, 156, 212, 290, 421, 452, 536, 541, 580, 936, 1011, 1069, 1294 **CCC:** 336, 337

The following skills are particularly likely to require continued attention in higher grades as they are applied to increasingly sophisticated writing and speaking.

Grade 12 Language Progressive Skills		Prentice Hall Literature © 2012, Grade 12
Conventions of Standard English	L.9–10.1.a	Use parallel structure.	1207
	L.6.1.c	Recognize and correct inappropriate shifts in pronoun number and person.	795
	L.7.1.c	Place phrases and clauses within a sentence, recognizing and correcting misplaced and dangling modifiers.	539
	L.5.1.d	Recognize and correct inappropriate shifts in verb tenses.	216, 218
	L.6.1.d	Recognize and correct vague pronouns (i.e., ones with unclear or ambiguous antecedents).	795
	L.8.1.d	Recognize and correct inappropriate shifts in verb voice and mood.*	1085
	L.6.1.e	Recognize variations from standard English in their own and others' writing and speaking, and identify and use strategies to improve expression in conventional language.	936
	L.3.1.f	Ensure subject-verb and pronoun-antecedent agreement.	767, 795
	L.4.1.f	Produce complete sentences, recognizing and correcting inappropriate fragments and run-ons.	1151
	L.4.1.g	Correctly use frequently confused words (e.g., to/too/two; there/their).	449
	L.6.2.a	Use punctuation (commas, parentheses, dashes) to set off nonrestrictive/parenthetical elements.	221, 419
Knowledge of Language	L.3.3.a	Choose words and phrases for effect.	446, 663, 1472
	L.7.3.a	Choose language that expresses ideas precisely and concisely, recognizing and eliminating wordiness and redundancy.	446, 663
	L.4.3.b	Choose punctuation for effect.	1475
	L.6.3.b	Maintain consistency in style and tone.	696

Unit	Scholarship and Commentary	Focus on Literary Forms	Literary History	Contemporary Connection
1. From Legend to History: The Old English and Medieval Periods (A.D. 449–1485)	Burton Raffel, "England's Green, Fertile Land" pp. 14–15; Burton Raffel Introduces *Beowulf* pp. 36–37; Seamus Heaney Discusses *Beowulf* pp. 68–69	Defining Epics pp. 34–35	Chaucer's Guided Tour of Medieval Life and Literature pp. 90–91	*Beowulf*: From Ancient Epic to Graphic Novel pp. 76–80
2. Celebrating Humanity: The English Renaissance Period (1485–1625)	Frank Kermode, "Life in Elizabethan and Jacobean England" pp. 248–249; Frank Kermode Introduces *Macbeth* pp. 314–315	Defining Drama pp. 308–309	The Elizabethan Theater, Shakespeare on Film, pp. 310–313	Connecting Elizabeth I, Past and Present pp. 292–295
3. A Turbulent Time: The Seventeenth and Eighteenth Centuries (1625–1798)	Richard Rodriguez Talks About the Time Period pp. 476–477; Richard Rodriguez Introduces *Days of Obligation* pp. 689–693	Defining the Essay pp. 678–679	Making "Darkness Visible": Milton's Epic Ambition pp. 516–517	London: Past and Present pp. 582–587
4. Rebels and Dreamers: The Romantic Period (1798–1832)	Elizabeth McCracken Talks About the Time Period pp. 728–729; Elizabeth McCracken Introduces *Frankenstein* pp. 756–759	Defining Lyric Poetry pp. 774–775	The Muse's Children: Lyric Poets in the World p. 796	Frankenstein: Past and Present pp. 768–772
5. Progress and Decline: The Victorian Period (1833–1901)	James Berry, "Growing up in Colonial Jamaica" pp. 954–955; James Berry, "From Lucy: Englan' Lady," "Time Removed," and "Freedom" pp. 1052–1059	Defining the Novel pp. 990–991	The Curious Workshop of Charles Dickens: Making Myths pp. 992–993	Connecting Victorian Themes pp. 1060–1061
6. A Time of Rapid Change: The Modern and Postmodern Periods (1901–Present)	Anita Desai, "The English Language Takes Root in India" pp. 1134–1135; Anita Desai Introduces "A Devoted Son" pp. 1416–1417	Defining the Contemporary Short Story pp. 1216–1217	T. S. Eliot's World p. 1152–1153; How "The Hollow Men" Was Written pp. 1160–1162; Contemporary British Fiction 1432–1433; New British Nonfiction 1460–1461	Connecting War Writings Past and Present pp. 1280–1283

PHLit Online!
www.PHLitOnline.com

• Essential Question Video • Vocabulary Central	**PHLitOnline** *See It!* Video Bring real writers into your classroom	**PHLitOnline** Interactive Online Test Practice	

Ⓒ Common Core State Standards appear in red throughout the Skills Navigator.

Informational Materials	Writing Workshop	Communications Workshop	Vocabulary Workshop	Test–Taking Practice
Reading for Information pp. 70–75; Primary Sources pp. 198–213	Narration: Autobiographical Narrative pp. 214–221	Evaluate Persuasive Speech pp. 222–223	Using Dictionaries and Other Resources p. 224	Reading Test: Natural Science Passage pp. 226–229 Performance Tasks pp. 230–231 SAT PREP ACT
Primary Sources pp. 282–291; Reading for Information pp. 436–441	Persuasion: Persuasive Essay pp. 442–449	Deliver a Persuasive Speech pp. 450–451	Words from Mythology p. 452	Critical Reading: Paired Passages pp. 454–457 Performance Tasks pp. 458–459 SAT PREP ACT
Primary Sources pp. 568–581; Reading for Information pp. 598–603	Narration: Reflective Essay pp. 694–700	Oral Interpretation of a Literary Work pp. 702–703	Etymology: Political Science/History Terms p. 704	Reading Test: Humanities Passage pp. 706–709 Performance Tasks pp. 710–711 SAT PREP ACT
Reading for Information pp. 810–817; Primary Sources pp. 896–909	Research: Multimedia Presentation pp. 920–927	Analyze a Non-Print Political Advertisement pp. 928–929	Etymology of Science, Medical, and Mathematical Terms p. 930	Critical Reading: Long Reading Passage pp. 932–935 Performance Tasks pp. 936–937 SAT PREP ACT
Reading for Information pp. 1022–1027; Primary Sources pp. 1062–1070	Research: Historical Investigation pp. 1096–1107	Analyze and Evaluate Entertainment Media pp. 1108–1109	Idioms p. 1110	Reading Test: Prose Fiction pp. 1112–1115 Performance Tasks pp. 1116–1117 SAT PREP ACT
Primary Sources pp. 1284–1295; Reading for Information pp. 1454–1459	Narration: Short Story pp. 1468–1475	Compare Media Coverage of Same Event pp. 1476–1477	Cognates and Borrowed Words p. 1478	Critical Reading: Short Reading Passage pp. 1480–1483 Performance Tasks pp. 1484–1485 SAT PREP ACT

PHLitOnline **Essay Scorer:** score essays in seconds	**PHLitOnline** Vocabulary Central: • Games • Audio • Flash cards • Images		

Unit 1: From Legend to History

	Selection	Reading Strategy	Literary Analysis
PART 1	"The Seafarer," (A), translated by Burton Raffel, SE, p. 21; "The Wanderer," (MA), translated by Charles W. Kennedy, SE, p. 27; "The Wife's Lament," (MC), translated by Ann Stanford, SE, p. 30	Understand the Historical Context, SE, p. 18	Anglo-Saxon Lyrics, SE, p. 18 RL.5
PART 2	From *Beowulf* (A), translated by Burton Raffel, SE, p. 36	Determine the Main Idea or Essential Message, SE, p. 38	Epic and Legendary Hero, SE, p. 38 RL.3
PART 2	Online Encyclopedia Article; Wikipedia Article, SE, p. 70	Evaluate Its Validity and Reliability, SE, p. 70 RI.7	Online Encyclopedia Article, SE, p. 70
PART 3	from *A History of the English Church and People* (MC), Bede, translated by Leo Sherley–Price, SE, p. 84	Analyze the Clarity of Meaning, SE, p. 82 RI.5	Historical Writing, SE, p. 82
PART 3	from *The Canterbury Tales:* "The Prologue" (A), Geoffrey Chaucer, translated by Nevill Coghill, SE, p. 96 ©	Questioning, SE, p. 95	Characterization and Social Commentary, SE, p. 95 RL.1, RL.3 Spiral Review, p. 105
PART 3	from *The Canterbury Tales:* "The Pardoner's Tale" (A), Geoffrey Chaucer, translated by Nevill Coghill, SE, p. 124 ©	Reread, SE, p. 123	Allegories and Archetypal Narrative Elements, SE, p. 123 RL.5
PART 3	from *The Canterbury Tales:* "The Wife of Bath's Tale" (A), Geoffrey Chaucer, translated by Nevill Coghill, SE, p. 138 ©	Checking Context Clues, SE, p. 137	Frame Story and Setting, SE, p. 137 RL.3
PART 3	from the *Decameron* by Giovanni Boccaccio, translated by G. H. McWilliam, SE, p. 158	Comparing Frame Stories Across Cultures, SE, p. 156 RL.10	
PART 4	from *Sir Gawain and the Green Knight* (A), translated by Marie Borroff, SE, p. 171; from *Morte d'Arthur,* (A), by Sir Thomas Malory, SE, p. 185	Determine the Main Idea, or Essential Message, SE, p. 168 RL.2	Medieval Romances and Legends, SE, p. 168
PART 4	Letters of Margaret Paston (A), Margaret Paston, SE, p. 201; "Twa Corbies" (MA), SE, p. 205; "Lord Randall" (MA), SE, p. 206; "Get Up and Bar the Door" (MA), SE, p. 207; "Barbara Allan" (MA), SE, p. 209	Analyzing, Evaluating, and Applying Information from Text Features, p. 198 RI.7	Letters and Ballads, SE, p. 198

Key: *UR:* Unit Resources   **A:** Average   **MA:** More Accessible   **MC:** More Challenging   © Indicates an Exemplar Text

Vocabulary	Grammar/Writing	Assessment
Vocabulary, SE, p. 18: admonish, sentinel, fervent, rancor, compassionate, rapture; **Categorize Vocabulary, SE,** p. 32 L.5.a	**Writing: Editorial, SE,** p. 32 W.1	**Critical Reading, SE,** pp. 25, 29, 31; **Selection Tests A and B,** *UR1,* pp. 25–30
Vocabulary, SE, p. 38: reparation, solace, purge, writhing, massive, loathsome; **Word Analysis: Latin Word Root** *-sol-,* **SE,** p. 66; **Vocabulary: Analogies, SE,** p. 66 L.3.a, L.5	**Coordinating Conjunctions, SE,** p. 67; **Writing and Speaking Conventions,** p. 67; **Writing: Job Application, SE,** p. 66 W.1, W.1.d	**Critical Reading, SE,** pp. 37, 64, 69; **Selection Tests A and B,** *UR1,* pp. 46–51
Cross-Curricular Vocabulary, SE, p. 70: manuscripts, didactic, fragmentary, forefront, siege L.4.d	**Timed Writing: Explanatory, SE,** p. 75 W.2, W.2.c	**Critical Reading, SE,** p. 80
Vocabulary, SE, p 82: promontories, cultivated, innumerable, migrated; **Categorize Vocabulary, SE,** p. 89 L.5	**Writing: Business Memo, SE,** p. 89 W.1	**Critical Reading, SE,** p. 88; **Selection Tests A and B,** *UR1,* pp. 64–69
Vocabulary, SE, p. 95: solicitous, garnished, absolution, commission, sanguine, prevarication; **Word Analysis: Latin Suffix** *-tion,* **SE,** p. 121; **Context Clues, SE,** p. 121 L.4.a	**Writing: Pilgrimage Blog, SE,** p. 121 W.5	**Critical Reading, SE,** p. 119; **Selection Tests A and B,** *UR1,* pp. 90–95
Vocabulary, SE, p. 123: pallor, hoary, tarry, apothecary, deftly, sauntered; **Word Analysis: Greek Prefix** *apo-,* **SE,** p. 136; **Relate New to Familiar Words, SE,** p. 136 L.6	**Writing: Persuasive Sermon on Greed, SE,** p. 136 W.1.a	**Critical Reading, SE,** p. 134; **Selection Tests A and B,** *UR1,* pp. 108–113
Vocabulary, SE, p. 137: implored, relates, contemptuous, bequeath, prowess, esteemed, rebuke; **Word Analysis: Multiple-Meaning Words in Context, SE,** p. 152; **Vocabulary: Logical or Illogical?, SE,** p. 152; **Using Resources to Build Vocabulary, SE,** p. 152 L.3, L.4	**Correlative Conjunctions, SE,** p. 154; **Combining: Correlative Conjunctions, SE,** p. 154; **Writing and Speaking Conventions, SE,** p. 154; **Writing: Essay, SE,** p. 153 W.1.a, W.1.e	**Critical Reading, SE,** p. 150; **Selection Tests A and B,** *UR1,* pp. 127–132
Vocabulary, SE, p. 156: courtly, frugally, deference, affably, impertinence, despondent L.4.a, L.4.c	**Timed Writing, SE,** p. 166 W.1, W.10	**Critical Reading, SE,** p. 165; **Selection Tests A and B,** *UR1,* pp. 136–137
Vocabulary, SE, p. 168: adjure, adroitly, largesse, entreated, peril, interred; **Word Analysis: The Word Root** *-droit-,* **SE,** p. 197; **Vocabulary: True or False? SE,** p. 197 L.4.a	**Writing: Interior Monologue, SE,** p. 197 W.3, W.3.d	**Critical Reading, SE,** pp. 183, 195; **Selection Tests A and B,** *UR1,* pp. 150–155
Vocabulary, SE, p. 199: aldermen, succor, certify, remnant, ransacked, asunder, assault, bar, measure, melody L.6	**Research Report, SE,** p. 213 W.7, W.8	**Critical Reading, SE,** pp. 204, 206, 208, 210; **Selection Tests A and B,** *UR1,* pp. 158–159

All selections are supported in the *Reader's Notebooks.*

Unit 2: Celebrating Humanity

	Selection	Reading Strategy	Literary Analysis
PART 1	from *Spenser's Sonnets* (MC, MC, MC), Edmund Spenser, SE, p. 254; from *Sidney's Sonnets* (MA, MA), Sir Philip Sidney, SE, p. 259	Determine the Main Idea or Essential Message, SE, p. 252	Sonnet and Sonnet Sequence, SE, p. 252 RL.5
	"The Passionate Shepherd to His Love" (A), Christopher Marlowe, SE, p. 266; "The Nymph's Reply to the Shepherd" (MC), Sir Walter Raleigh, SE, p. 268	Analyze Similar Themes, SE, p. 264 RL.2	Pastoral, SE, p. 264
	Sonnet 29 (MC), William Shakespeare, SE, p. 275; Sonnet 106 (MC), William Shakespeare, SE, p. 275; Sonnet 116 (A), William Shakespeare, SE, p. 276; Sonnet 130 (A), William Shakespeare, SE, p. 278	Analyze Text Structures, SE, p. 272 RL.5 Spiral Review, p. 278	Shakespearean Sonnet, SE, p. 272
PART 2	"Speech Before Her Troops," Queen Elizabeth I, SE, p. 285; "Examination of Don Luis de Córdoba," SE, p. 288	Summarizing, SE, p. 282 RI.2	Speech and Eyewitness Account, SE, p. 282
	from *The King James Bible* (A), SE, p. 296	Determine the Main Idea, SE, p. 296 RL.1	Psalms, Sermons, Parables, SE, p. 296 RL.4
PART 3	*The Tragedy of Macbeth,* Act I (MC), William Shakespeare, SE, p. 322	Analyzing Information from Text Features, SE, p. 321	Elizabethan Drama, Tragedies, and Soliloquy, SE, p. 321 RL.3
	The Tragedy of Macbeth, Act II (MC), William Shakespeare, SE, p. 342	Analyzing Clarity of Meaning, SE, pp. 342, 358	Blank Verse, SE, p. 342 RL.5 Spiral Review, p. 345, 351
	The Tragedy of Macbeth, Act III (MC), William Shakespeare, SE, p. 361	Identify Cause-and-Effect Relationships, SE, p. 360	Conflict, Climax, and Dramatic Irony, SE, p. 360 RL.3
	The Tragedy of Macbeth, Act IV (MC), William Shakespeare, SE, p. 378	Analyze Text Structures, SE, p. 378	Imagery, SE, p. 378 RL.3
	The Tragedy of Macbeth, Act V (MC), William Shakespeare, SE, p. 401	Relate the Work to the Major Themes and Issues of Its Period, SE, p. 400	Shakespearean Tragedy, SE, p. 400 RL.3
	from *Oedipus the King,* Sophocles, Translated by David Grene, SE, p. 423; from *Faust,* Wolfgang von Goethe, Translated by Louis MacNeice, SE, p. 430	Comparing Tragedy Past and Present, SE, p. 421 RL.10	

Key: *UR: Unit Resources*   **A:** Average   **MA:** More Accessible   **MC:** More Challenging   Ⓒ Indicates an Exemplar Text

Vocabulary	Grammar/Writing	Assessment
Vocabulary, SE, p. 252: design, assay, devise, wan, languished, balm; **Word Analysis: Patterns of Word Changes, SE**, p. 262; **Vocabulary: Context Clues, SE**, p. 262 L.4.a, L.4.b	**Subordinating Conjunctions, SE**, p. 263; **Writing: Manual for a Sonnet, SE**, p. 262 W.2, W.4	**Critical Reading, SE**, pp. 256, 260; **Selection Tests A and B**, *UR2*, pp. 20–25
Vocabulary, SE, p. 264: melodious, madrigals, reckoning, gall, wither; **Word Analysis: Word Origins *gall*, SE**, p. 271; **Vocabulary: Context Clues, SE**, p. 271 L.4.a	**Writing: Compare-and-Contrast Essay, SE**, p. 271 W.2.c	**Critical Reading, SE**, p. 269; **Selection Tests A and B**, *UR2*, pp. 38–43
Vocabulary, SE, p. 272: scope, sullen, chronicle, prefiguring, impediments, alters; **Word Analysis: Greek Root *-chron-*, SE**, p. 280; **Vocabulary: Analogies, SE**, p. 280 L.5	**Writing: Analysis of a Sonnet's Imagery, SE**, p. 280 W.2.b	**Critical Reading, SE**, pp. 276, 278; **Selection Tests A and B**, *UR2*, pp. 57–61
Vocabulary, SE, p. 283: treachery, tyrants, realms, stead, obedience, concord, valor, galleons L.6	**Research Task, SE**, p. 291 W.7, W.8	**Critical Reading, SE**, pp. 287, 289; **Selection Tests A and B**, *UR2*, pp. 64–65
Vocabulary, SE, p. 296: righteousness, stature, prodigal, entreated, transgressed; **Word Analysis: Latin Root *-stat-*, SE**, p. 306; **Vocabulary: Synonyms, SE**, p. 306 L.1.a	**Writing: Parable, SE**, p. 306 W.3, W.3.d	**Critical Reading, SE**, pp. 300, 301, 304; **Selection Tests A and B**, *UR2*, pp. 78–83
Vocabulary, SE, p. 321: valor, treasons, imperial, surmise, sovereign; **Word Analysis: Denotations and Connotations of Political Words, SE**, p. 341; **Vocabulary: Context Clues, SE**, p. 341 L.4.a, L.5	**Writing: Speaker Introduction, SE**, p. 341 W.3, W.3.d	**Critical Reading, SE**, pp. 315, 339; **Selection Tests A and B**, *UR2*, pp. 100–105
Vocabulary, SE, p. 342: augment, palpable, stealthy, multitudinous, equivocate, predominance; **Word Analysis: Latin Word Root *-voc-*, SE**, p. 359; **Vocabulary: Antonyms, SE**, p. 359	**Writing: Interpretation of Comic Relief, SE**, p. 359 W.1, W.1.a	**Critical Reading, SE**, p. 355; **Selection Tests A and B**, *UR2*, pp. 118–123
Vocabulary, SE, p. 360: indissoluble, dauntless, predominant, infirmity, malevolence; **Word Analysis: Latin Prefix *mal-*, SE**, p. 377; **Vocabulary: Context Clues, SE**, p. 377 L.4.a	**Writing: Soliloquy, SE**, p. 377 W.3, W.3.d, W.5	**Critical Reading, SE**, p. 375; **Selection Tests A and B**, *UR2*, pp. 142–147
Vocabulary, SE, p. 378: pernicious, judicious, sundry, intemperance, avarice, credulous; **Word Analysis: Latin Root *-cred-*, SE**, p. 398; **Vocabulary: Analogies, SE**, p. 398 L.4.d	**Writing: Analysis of Archetypal Images, SE**, p. 398 W.2.b, W.2.f, W.5	**Critical Reading, SE**, p. 396; **Selection Tests A and B**, *UR2*, pp. 160–165
Vocabulary, SE, p. 400: perturbation, recoil, antidote, pristine, clamorous, harbingers, vulnerable; **Word Analysis: Latin Root *-turb-*, SE**, p. 417; **Descriptive Adjectives: Words Relating to Tragedy, SE**, p. 417; **Vocabulary: Sentence Completion, SE**, p. 417 L.1, L.4.c	**Conventions and Style: Adjective and Adverb Clauses, SE**, p. 419; **Writing: Response to Literature, SE**, p. 418 W.1.a, W.5	**Critical Reading, SE**, p. 415; **Selection Tests A and B**, *UR2*, pp. 179–184
Vocabulary, SE, p. 421: reverence, rites, infamy, tenacity, insatiableness L.6	**Timed Writing: Explanatory Essay, SE**, p. 435 W.2, W.10	**Critical Reading, SE**, pp. 428, 434; **Selection Tests A and B**, *UR2*, pp. 188–189

All selections are supported in the *Reader's Notebooks*.

Unit 3: A Turbulent Time

	Selection	Reading Strategy	Literary Analysis
PART 1	Works of John Donne (MC), John Donne, SE, p. 482 ©	Analyze the Author's Perspective and How It Affects the Meaning, SE, p. 480 RL.4	Metaphysical Poetry, Conceits, and Paradoxes, SE, p. 480
	"On My First Son" (A), Ben Jonson, SE, p. 496; "Still to Be Neat" (A), Ben Jonson, SE, p. 498; "Song: To Celia" (A), Ben Jonson, SE, p. 500	Comparing and Contrasting Elements, SE, p. 494 RL.4	Lyric, SE, p. 494
	"To His Coy Mistress" (MC), Andrew Marvell, SE, p. 506; "To the Virgins, to Make Much of Time" (MC), Robert Herrick, SE, p. 510; "Song" (A), Sir John Suckling, SE, p. 513	Analyze and Evaluate Similar Themes, SE, p. 504	*Carpe Diem* Theme, SE, p. 504 RL.2 Spiral Review, p. 507
PART 2	Poetry of John Milton (MC), SE, p. 522	Using a Graphic Organizer, SE, p. 521	The Italian Sonnet and Epic, SE, p. 521 RL.5 Spiral Review, p. 532
	from *Inferno*, Dante Alighieri, SE, p. 543	Comparing Epics Around the World, SE, p. 541 RL.3	
	from *The Pilgrim's Progress* (A), John Bunyan, SE, p. 554	Analyzing the Text Structure, SE, p. 552	Allegory, SE, p. 552 RL.2
	from *Eve's Apology in Defense of Women* (A), Amelia Lanier, SE, p. 560; "To Lucasta, on Going to the Wars" (MA), Richard Lovelace, SE, p. 563; "To Althea, from Prison" (A), Richard Lovelace, SE, p. 564	Relate [a Work] to the Major Themes and Issues of Its Historical Period, SE, p. 558	Tradition and Reform, SE, p. 558 RL.4
	from *The Diary* (A), Samuel Pepys, SE, p. 571	Verify and Clarify Facts, SE, p. 568 RI.1, RI.3	Diary and Policy Statement, SE, p. 568
PART 3	from *A Journal of the Plague Year* (A), Daniel Defoe, SE, p. 590	Asking Questions, SE, p. 588	Point of View, SE, p. 588 RL.3
	from *Gulliver's Travels* (A), Jonathan Swift, SE, p. 606; "A Modest Proposal" (A), Jonathan Swift, SE, 617	Analyzing and Evaluating Information from Text Features, SE, p. 604	Satire, SE, p. 604 RL.6 Spiral Review, p. 608

Key: *UR: Unit Resources*   **A:** Average   **MA:** More Accessible   **MC:** More Challenging   © Indicates an Exemplar Text

Vocabulary	Grammar/Writing	Assessment
Vocabulary, SE, p. 480: profanation, laity, trepidation, contention, piety, covetousness; **Word Analysis: Latin Prefix con-, SE**, p. 492; **Vocabulary: Analogies, SE**, p. 492 L.1, L.1.b, L.5	**Comparative and Superlative Adjectives and Adverbs, SE**, p. 493; **Writing and Speaking Conventions, SE**, p. 493; **Writing: Plan for a Biographical Narrative, SE**, p. 492 W.3, W.5	**Critical Reading, SE**, pp. 483, 485, 487, 490; **Selection Tests A and B, *UR3*,** pp. 20–25
Vocabulary, SE, p. 494: fate, lament, presumed, sound, divine, wreath; **Multiple-Meaning Words, SE**, p. 502; **Vocabulary: Synonyms, SE**, p. 502 L.1, L.4	**Participles, Gerunds, and Infinitives, SE**, p. 503; **Writing and Speaking Conventions, SE**, p. 503; **Response to Literature, SE**, p. 502 W.1	**Critical Reading, SE**, pp. 497, 498, 500; **Selection Tests A and B, *UR3*,** pp. 39–44
Vocabulary, SE, p. 504: coyness, amorous, languish, prime, wan, prevail; **Vocabulary: Context, SE**, p. 514	**Public Service Announcement, SE**, p. 514 W.1	**Critical Reading, SE**, pp. 508, 510, 513; **Selection Tests A and B, *UR3*,** pp. 57–62
Vocabulary, SE, p. 521: semblance, illumine, transgress, guile, obdurate, tempestuous, transcendent, ignominy; **Word Analysis: Latin Root -lum-, SE**, p. 537; **Vocabulary: Synonyms, SE**, p. 537; **Using Resources to Build Vocabulary, SE**, p. 537 L.4.c, L.6	**Misplaced and Dangling Modifiers, SE**, p. 539; **Writing and Speaking Conventions, SE**, p. 539; **Writing: Response to Literature, SE**, p. 538 W.2.b, W.2.f	**Critical Reading, SE**, pp. 522, 523, 534, 550; **Selection Tests A and B, *UR3*,** pp. 78–83
Vocabulary, SE, p. 541: cowered, awe, writhes, shrill, nimble; **Vocabulary: Synonyms, SE**, p. 551 L.6	**Timed Writing: Comparison-and-Contrast Essay, SE**, p. 551 W.2, W.10	**Critical Reading, SE**, p. 550; **Selection Tests A and B, *UR3*,** pp. 87–88
Vocabulary, SE, p. 552: heedless, wallowed, burden, endeavored, dominions, substantial	**Casting Memo, SE**, p. 557 W.2.b	**Critical Reading, SE**, p. 555; **Selection Tests A and B, *UR3*,** pp. 101–106
Vocabulary, SE, p. 558: breach, discretion, reprove, inconstancy	**Dramatic Scene, SE**, p. 566 W.3.b	**Critical Reading, SE**, pp. 561, 565; **Selection Tests A and B, *UR3*,** pp. 101–106
Vocabulary, SE, p. 569: apprehensions, abated, lamentable, combustible, malicious, accounts, pernicious, magistrate, eminent, notorious, deliberation L.6	**Research Task, SE**, p. 581	**Critical Reading, SE**, pp. 577, 579; **Selection Tests A and B, *UR3*,** pp. 109–110
Vocabulary, SE, p. 588: lamentations, distemper, delirious, resolution, importuning, prodigious; **Word Analysis: Latin Prefix dis-, SE**, p. 597; **Vocabulary: Context Clues, SE**, p. 597 L.4	**Writing: Reflective Essay, SE**, p. 597 W.3	**Critical Reading, SE**, p. 595; **Selection Tests A and B, *UR3*,** pp. 138–143
Vocabulary, SE, p. 604: conjecture, schism, expedient, sustenance, commodity, censure L.5	**Writing: Plan for a Multimedia Presentation, SE**, p. 627 W.2.a	**Critical Reading, SE**, pp. 616, 625; **Selection Tests A and B, *UR3*,** pp. 162–167

All selections are supported in the *Reader's Notebooks*.

Unit 3: A Turbulent Time *(continued)*

	Selection	Reading Strategy	Literary Analysis
PART 3 (continued)	from *An Essay on Man* (MC), Alexander Pope, SE, p. 628; from *The Rape of the Lock* (MC), Alexander Pope, SE, p. 632	Analyze How an Author's Purpose Affects the Meaning of a Work, SE, p. 628 RL.6, RL.9; RI.9 Spiral Review, p. 642	Parody and Epic Similes, SE, p. 628
	from *A Dictionary of the English Language* (MA), Samuel Johnson, SE, p. 648; from *The Life of Samuel Johnson* (A), James Boswell, SE, p. 655	Analyzing the Author's Purpose, SE, p. 646 RI.3, RI.4, RI.9	Dictionary and Biography, SE, p. 646
	"Elegy Written in a Country Churchyard" (MC), Thomas Gray, SE, p. 666; "A Nocturnal Reverie" (MC), Anne Finch, Countess of Winchilsea, SE, p. 673	Determine the Essential Message, SE, p. 664	Pre-Romantic Poetry, SE, p. 664 RL.2
PART 4	*The Aims of The Spectator* (A), Joseph Addison, SE, p. 682; from *Days of Obligation:* from "In Athens Once" (A), Richard Rodriguez, SE, p. 689	Analyze the Author's Implicit Philosophical Assumptions, SE, p. 680; Explicit Assumptions, SE, p. 680 RL.1	Essay and Historical Period, SE, p. 680

Unit 4: Rebels and Dreamers

	Selection	Reading Strategy	Literary Analysis
	"To a Mouse" (MC), Robert Burns, SE, p. 734; "To a Louse" (MC), Robert Burns, SE, p. 737; "Woo'd and Married and A'" (A), Joanna Baillie, SE, p. 741	Analyze Information from Text Features, SE, p. 732	Dialect, SE, p. 732 RL.4 Spiral Review, p. 735
PART 1	"The Lamb" (MA), William Blake, SE, p. 748; "The Tyger" (MA), William Blake, SE, p. 749; "The Chimney Sweeper" (MA), William Blake, SE, p. 751; "Infant Sorrow" (MA), William Blake, SE, p. 752	Applying Critical Perspectives, SE, p. 746	Archetypes and Social Commentary, SE, p. 746 RL.2
	Introduction to *Frankenstein* (MC), Mary Shelley, SE, p. 760	Make Predictions, SE, p. 758	Gothic Literature and the Romantic Movement, SE, p. 758 RI.3
PART 2	"Lines Composed a Few Miles Above Tintern Abbey" (MC), William Wordsworth, SE, p. 780; from "The Prelude" (MC), William Wordsworth, SE, p. 786; "The World Is Too Much With Us" (A), William Wordsworth, SE, p. 790; "London, 1802" (A), William Wordsworth, SE, p. 791	Evaluating the Influence of the Historical Period, SE, p. 779	Romanticism and Lyric, SE, p. 779 RL.4 Spiral Review, p. 784

Key: *UR: Unit Resources*   **A:** Average   **MA:** More Accessible   **MC:** More Challenging   © Indicates an Exemplar Text

Vocabulary	Grammar/Writing	Assessment
Vocabulary, SE, p. 628: stoic, disabused, obliquely, plebeian, destitute, assignations; **Word Analysis: Words from Political Science, SE**, p. 645; **Vocabulary: Synonyms, SE**, p. 645 L.4.a	**Writing: Essay, SE**, p. 645	**Critical Reading, SE**, pp. 631, 643; **Selection Tests A and B**, *UR3*, pp. 180–185
Vocabulary, SE, p. 646: caprices, adulterations, risible, abasement, credulity, malignity; **Word Analysis: Latin Root** *-dict-*, **SE**, p. 663; **Vocabulary: Cognates, SE**, p. 663 L.4.c	**Writing: Essay, SE**, p. 663 W.9.b	**Critical Reading, SE**, pp. 653, 661; **Selection Tests A and B**, *UR3*, pp. 198–203
Vocabulary, SE, p. 664: penury, circumscribed, ingenuous, nocturnal, temperate, venerable; **Vocabulary Acquisition and Use, SE**, p. 676	**Directions for Reciting a Poem, SE**, p. 676 W.2	**Critical Reading, SE**, pp. 671, 675; **Selection Tests A and B**, *UR3*, pp. 216–221
Vocabulary, SE, p. 680: transient, assiduous, affluence, contentious, trifles, embellishments	**Writing: Letter to the Editor, SE**, p. 685 W.1.a	**Critical Reading, SE**, pp. 684, 688, 693; **Selection Tests A and B**, *UR3*, pp. 236–241

Vocabulary	Grammar/Writing	Assessment
Vocabulary, SE, p. 732: dominion, impudence, winsome, discretion, inconstantly; **Word Analysis: Anglo-Saxon Suffix** *-some*, **SE**, p. 745; **Vocabulary: Synonyms, SE**, p. 745 L.5.b	**Writing: Editorial Speech on the Use of Dialect, SE**, p. 745 W.1.b	**Critical Reading, SE**, pp. 736, 739, 743; **Selection Tests A and B**, *UR4*, pp. 19–24
Vocabulary, SE, p. 746: vales, immortal, symmetry, aspire, sinews, sulk; **Word Analysis: Latin Root** *-spir-*, **SE**, p. 754 L.3.a, L.4.a	**Writing: Explanatory Essay, SE**, p. 754; **Using Introductory Phrases and Clauses, SE**, p. 755; **Writing and Speaking Conventions, SE**, p. 755 W.2.a	**Critical Reading, SE**, p. 752; **Selection Tests A and B**, *UR4*, pp. 38–43
Vocabulary, SE, p. 758: appendage, ungenial, acceded, platitude, phantasm, incitement; **Word Analysis: Relate New Words to Familiar Vocabulary, SE**, p. 766; **Vocabulary: Synonyms, SE**, p. 766 L.4.d	**Writing: Autobiography of a Monster, SE**, p. 766; **Subject-Verb Agreement Problems, SE**, p. 767; **Writing and Speaking Conventions, SE**, p. 767 W.3, W.3.b	**Thinking About the Commentary, SE**, p. 757; **Critical Reading, SE**, pp. 764, 772; **Selection Tests A and B**, *UR4*, pp. 59–64
Vocabulary, SE, p. 779: recompense, roused, presumption, anatomize, sordid, stagnant; **Word Analysis: Forms of** *anatomize*, **SE**, p. 793; **Vocabulary: Synonyms, SE**, p. 793 L.4.b, L.5.a, L.5.b	**Assessing an Analysis of Wordsworth, SE**, p. 794; **Pronoun-Antecedent Agreement Problems, SE**, p. 795; **Writing and Speaking Conventions, SE**, p. 795 W.1.a, W.1.e, W.9.a	**Critical Reading, SE**, pp. 785, 788, 791; **Selection Tests A and B**, *UR4*, pp. 79–84

All selections are supported in the *Reader's Notebooks*.

Unit 4: Rebels and Dreamers *(continued)*

	Selection	Reading Strategy	Literary Analysis
PART 2 *(continued)*	"I Have Visited Again," Alexander Pushkin, translated by D. M. Thomas, p. 799; "Invitation to the Voyage," Charles Baudelaire, translated by Richard Wilbur, p. 802; from *The Book of Songs*, "Thick Grow the Rush Leaves," p. 805; "Jade Flower Palace," Tu Fu, translated by Kenneth Rexroth, p. 806; Tanka by Priest Jakuren, and Ki Tsurayuki, translated by Geoffrey Bownas, p. 807; Tanka by Ono Komachi, translated by Geoffrey Bownas, p. 808		**Comparing Lyric Poetry from Around the World, SE**, p. 797 RL.5
	"The Rime of the Ancient Mariner" (A), Samuel Taylor Coleridge, SE, p. 820; "Kubla Khan" (MA), Samuel Taylor Coleridge, SE, p. 846	**Comparing and Contrasting Sound Devices, SE**, p. 818	**Narrative Poetry and Poetic Sound Devices, SE**, p. 818 Spiral Review, p. 832
	"She Walks in Beauty" (MA), George Gordon, Lord Byron, SE, p. 854; from "Childe Harold's Pilgrimage: Apostrophe to the Ocean" (A), George Gordon, Lord Byron, SE, p. 856; from *Don Juan* (MA), George Gordon, Lord Byron, SE, p. 860	**Question, SE**, p. 852	**Figurative Language, SE**, p. 852 RL.4
	"Ozymandias" (A), Percy Bysshe Shelley, SE, p. 868; "Ode to the West Wind" (MC), Percy Bysshe Shelley, SE, p. 870; "To a Skylark" (MA), Percy Bysshe Shelley, SE, p. 873 ©	**Comparing and Contrasting Elements, SE**, p. 866	**Imagery and Romantic Philosophy, SE**, p. 866 RL.1 Spiral Review, p. 874
	Poetry of John Keats, SE, pp. 883–892 Pablo Neruda's Odes, SE, p. 888 "Ode on a Grecian Urn," SE, p. 890 ©	**Determine the Main Idea, SE**, p. 880; **Paraphrase, SE**, p. 893	**Ode, SE**, p. 880 RL.5
PART 3	"Speech in Favor of Reform," Lord John Russell, SE, p. 899; "Speech Against Reform," Sir Robert Peel, SE, p. 902; "On the Passing of the Reform Bill," Thomas Babington Macaulay, SE, p. 904	**Analyzing Rhetorical Devices, SE**, p. 896 RI.6	**Debate and Letter, SE**, p. 896
	"On Making an Agreeable Marriage" (A), Jane Austen, SE, p. 912; from *A Vindication of the Rights of Woman,* (A) Mary Wollstonecraft, SE, p. 916	**Analyze the Author's Purpose, SE**, p. 910	**Social Commentary and Persuasive Techniques, SE**, p. 910 RI.6

Key: *UR:* Unit Resources   **A:** Average   **MA:** More Accessible   **MC:** More Challenging   © Indicates an Exemplar Text

Vocabulary	Grammar/Writing	Assessment
Vocabulary, SE, p. 797: ancestral, morose, proffering, scurry, pathos, imperceptibly	**Timed Writing: Explanatory Essay, SE**, p. 809 W.2, W.10	**Critical Reading, SE**, pp. 801, 803, 808; **Selection Tests A and B**, *UR4*, pp. 88–89
Vocabulary, SE, p. 818: averred, sojourn, expiated, reverence, sinuous, tumult; **Word Analysis: Latin Root: *-journ-*, SE**, p. 851; **Vocabulary: Antonyms, SE**, p. 851	**Writing Lesson: Comparing Poetic Symbols, SE**, p. 851 W.2.b, W.2.d, W.9.a	**Critical Reading, SE**, pp. 845, 849; **Selection Tests A and B**, *UR4*, pp. 108–113
Vocabulary, SE, p. 852: arbiter, torrid, retort, credulous, copious, avarice; **Word Analysis: Latin Suffix *-ous*, SE**, p. 865; **Vocabulary: Context, SE**, p. 865 L.4.a	**Writing: Interior Monologue of a Modern Byronic Hero, SE**, p. 865 W.3.c, W.3.d	**Critical Reading, SE**, pp. 855, 859, 863; **Selection Tests A and B**, *UR4*, pp. 128–131
Vocabulary, SE, p. 866: verge, sepulcher, impulse, blithe, profuse, satiety; **Word Analysis: Latin Root *-puls-*, SE**, p. 879; **Vocabulary: Analogies, SE**, p. 879 L.4.d, L.5.a	**Writing: Develop a Research Plan for a Report, SE**, p. 879 W.7, W.8	**Critical Reading, SE**, pp. 869, 872, 876; **Selection Tests A and B**, *UR4*, pp. 144–149
Vocabulary, SE, p. 880: ken, surmise, gleaned, teeming, vintage, requiem; **Word Analysis: Multiple Meanings, SE**, p. 894; **Vocabulary: Sentence Completion, SE**, p. 894 L.5	**Writing: Essay**, p. 894 W.9.a	**Critical Reading, SE**, pp. 885, 889, 892; **Selection Tests A and B**, *UR4*, pp. 162–167
Vocabulary, SE, p. 897: measure, grievances, electors, constituency, extravagant, reverence, inauspicious, orthodox L.4.a	**Research Task, SE**, p. 909 W.7, W.9	**Critical Reading, SE**, p. 907; **Selection Tests A and B**, *UR4*, pp. 185–186
Vocabulary, SE, p. 910: amiable, vindication, fastidious, specious, fortitude, gravity; **Vocabulary: Synonyms and Antonyms, SE**, p. 919 L.1.a	**Writing: E-mail Exchange on Marriage, SE**, p. 919	**Critical Reading, SE**, pp. 915, 918; **Selection Tests A and B**, *UR4*, pp. 199–204

All selections are supported in the *Reader's Notebooks*.

Unit 5: Progress and Decline

Selection	Reading Strategy	Literary Analysis
PART 1 — from *In Memoriam, A.H.H.* (A), Alfred, Lord Tennyson, SE, p. 960; "The Lady of Shalott" (A), Alfred, Lord Tennyson, SE, p. 963; "Tears, Idle Tears" (A), Alfred, Lord Tennyson, SE, p. 969; "Ulysses" (MA), Alfred, Lord Tennyson, SE, p. 970	Analyzing an Author's Philosophical Assumptions and Beliefs, SE, p. 958 RL.1	The Speaker in Poetry, SE, p. 958
"My Last Duchess" (A), Robert Browning, SE, p. 979; "Life in a Love" (A), Robert Browning, SE, p. 981; "Porphyria's Lover," Robert Browning, SE, p. 982; "Sonnet 43" (MA), Elizabeth Barrett Browning, SE, p. 986	Compare and Contrast Speakers in Multiple Poems, SE, p. 976	The Dramatic Monologue, SE, p. 976 RL.3
PART 2 — from *Hard Times* (A), Charles Dickens, SE, p. 998	Analyzing an Author's Purpose, SE, p. 997 RL.3 Spiral Review, p. 1001	Ethical and Social Influences, SE, p. 997
"An Upheaval," Anton Chekhov, SE, p. 1013		Comparing Social Criticism in Fiction, SE, p. 1011 RL.1 Spiral Review, p. 1018
Public Documents, Web Site Home Page, Brochure, SE, p. 1022	Predict the Content and Purpose, SE, p. 1022 RI.5	Web Site Home Page, SE, p. 1022
from *Jane Eyre* (MA), Charlotte Brontë, SE, p. 1030 ©	Analyze the Author's Assumptions, SE, p. 1028	Philosophical Assumptions, SE, p. 1028 RL.3 Spiral Review, p. 1032
PART 3 — "Dover Beach" (A), Matthew Arnold, SE, p. 1042; "Recessional"(A), Rudyard Kipling, SE, p. 1045; "The Widow at Windsor" (MC), Rudyard Kipling, SE, p. 1048	Connecting Poems to the Historical Period, SE, p. 1040	Mood and Theme, SE, p. 1040 RL.2
"From Lucy: Englan' Lady," James Berry, SE, p. 1055; "Freedom," James Berry, SE, p. 1057; "Time Removed," James Berry, SE, p. 1058	Analyze the Techniques of Media Messages, SE, p. 1062; Note-Taking Guide, SE, p. 1063 RI.1, RI.3	Newspaper Article and Advertisement, SE, p. 1062; Comparing Primary Sources, SE, p. 1069
PART 4 — "Remembrance" (A), Emily Brontë, SE, p. 1075; "The Darkling Thrush" (MA), Thomas Hardy, SE, p. 1078; "Ah, Are You Digging on My Grave?" (MA), Thomas Hardy, SE, p. 1081	Analyze the Pattern of Stanzas, SE, p. 1072 RL.5	Stanzas, Stanza Structure, and Irony, SE, p. 1072
"God's Grandeur" (A), Gerard Manley Hopkins, SE, p. 1088; "Spring and Fall: To a Young Child" (A), Gerard Manley Hopkins, SE, p. 1090; "To an Athlete Dying Young" (MA) A. E. Housman, SE, p. 1092; "When I Was One-and-Twenty" (MA), A. E. Housman, SE, p. 1093	Analyzing the Author's Beliefs, SE, p. 1086	Rhythm and Feet, SE, p. 1086 RL.5

Key: *UR: Unit Resources*   **A:** Average   **MA:** More Accessible   **MC:** More Challenging   © Indicates an Exemplar Text

Vocabulary	Grammar/Writing	Assessment
Vocabulary, SE, p. 958: chrysalis, diffusive, prosper, waning, prudence, furrows; **Word Analysis: Literal and Figurative Meanings, SE**, p. 975; **Vocabulary: Context, SE**, p. 975 L.4.a	**Writing: Biographical Essay, SE**, p. 975 W.2	**Critical Reading, SE**, pp. 962, 968, 973; **Selection Tests A and B**, *UR5*, pp. 19–24
Vocabulary, SE, p. 976: countenance, officious, munificence, dowry, eludes, sullen; **Word Analysis: Latin Suffix -ence, SE**, p. 988; **Analogies, SE**, p. 988 L.3	**Writing: Writing a Detective's Report on the Duke, SE**, p. 988 W.1, W.1.d	**Critical Reading, SE**, pp. 981, 984, 986; **Selection Tests A and B**, *UR5*, pp. 37–42
Vocabulary, SE, p. 997: monotonous, obstinate, deficient, adversary, indignant, approbation, etymology, syntax; **Word Analysis: Greek Prefix mono-, SE**, p. 1007; **Vocabulary: Antonyms, SE**, p. 1007; **Using Resources to Build Vocabulary, SE**, p. 1007 L.4.c, L.4.d	**Writing: Historical Investigation: Annotated Bibliography, SE**, p. 1008; **Shifts in Verb Tense, SE**, p. 1009; **Writing and Speaking Conventions, SE**, p. 1009 W.2, W.8	**Critical Reading, SE**, p. 1004; **Selection Tests A and B**, *UR5*, pp. 57–62
Vocabulary, SE, p. 1011: turmoil, rummaging, kindred, palpitation, ingratiating	**Timed Writing: Compare-and-Contrast Essay, SE**, p. 1021 W.1	**Critical Reading, SE**, p. 1020; **Selection Tests A and B**, *UR5*, pp. 66–67
Cross-Curricular Vocabulary, SE, p. 1022: manuscripts, agricultural, tenant	**Timed Writing: Persuasive Essay, SE**, p. 1027	**Test Practice: Reading, SE**, 1027
Vocabulary, SE, p. 1028: obscure, comprised, sundry, tumult, truculent	**School Conduct Report, SE**, p. 1038 W.2	**Critical Reading, SE**, p. 1037; **Selection Tests A and B**, *UR5*, pp. 80–85
Vocabulary, SE, p. 1040: tranquil, cadence, turbid, dominion, contrite, awe; **Word Analysis: Word-Phrase Relationships, SE**, p. 1051; **Vocabulary: Antonyms, SE**, p. 1051	**Writing: Essay About the Victorian Age, SE**, p. 1051 W.1, W.1.a	**Critical Reading, SE**, pp. 1043, 1047, 1049; **Selection Tests A and B**, *UR5*, pp. 100–105
Vocabulary, SE, p. 1063: depredation, Macadam, fracture, pulp, gout, bilious, privations L.6	**Research Task, SE**, p. 1070 W.7, W.8	**Critical Reading, SE**, pp. 1038, 1066, 1068
Vocabulary, SE, p. 1072: obscure, languish, rapturous, gaunt, terrestrial, prodding; **Latin Root -terr(a)-, SE**, p. 1084; **Vocabulary: Analogies, SE**, p. 1084 L.5	**Writing: Comparative Analysis, SE**, p. 1084; **Active, Not Passive, Voice, SE**, p. 1085; **Writing and Speaking Conventions, SE**, p. 1085 W.2.b, W.5	**Critical Reading, SE**, pp. 1076, 1080, 1082; **Selection Tests A and B**, *UR5*, pp. 123–128
Vocabulary, SE, p. 1086: grandeur, smudge, brink, blight, lintel, rue; **Word Analysis: Coined Words, SE**, p. 1095; **Vocabulary: Analogies, SE**, p. 1095 L.3	**Writing: Letter of Recommendation, SE**, p. 1095 W.1, W.1.d	**Critical Reading, SE**, pp. 1090, 1093; **Selection Tests A and B**, *UR5*, pp. 141–146

All selections are supported in the *Reader's Notebooks*.

Unit 6: A Time of Rapid Change

	Selection	Reading Strategy	Literary Analysis
PART 1	Poetry of William Butler Yeats (MA, MA, MA, A, MC), William Butler Yeats, SE, p. 1140	Analyze Yeats's Philosophical Assumptions, SE, p. 1138 RL.4	Philosophical System and Symbol, SE, p. 1138
	"Preludes" (A), T. S. Eliot, SE, p. 1156; "Journey of the Magi" (MA), T. S. Eliot, SE, p. 1158; "The Hollow Men" (MC), T. S. Eliot, SE, p. 1163	Relate Eliot's Literary Works to the Historical Period, SE, p. 1154 RL.1	Modernism, SE, p. 1154
	"In Memory of W. B. Yeats" (A), W. H. Auden, SE, p.1172; "Musée des Beaux Arts" (A), W. H. Auden, SE, p. 1177; "Carrick Revisited" (MC), Louis MacNeice, SE, p. 1180; "Not Palaces" (MC), Stephen Spender, SE, p. 1183	Comparing and Contrasting Elements, SE, p. 1170	Allegory and Pastoral, SE, p. 1170 RL.1
PART 2	"The Lady in the Looking Glass: A Reflection," Virginia Woolf, SE, p. 1192; from *Mrs. Dalloway*, Virginia Woolf, SE, p. 1198; "Shakespeare's Sister," Virginia Woolf, SE, p. 1202	Repair Your Comprehension by Asking Questions, SE, p. 1191	Points of View, SE, p. 1191 RL.3
	from "Pedro Páramo," Juan Rulfo, SE, p. 1211; from "The Nine Guardians," Rosario Castellanos, SE, p. 1213		Stream-of-Consciousness Narration, SE, p. 1209 RL.3
	"The Lagoon," Joseph Conrad, SE, p. 1220; "Araby," James Joyce, SE, p. 1236	Identifying Cause-and-Effect Relationships, SE, p. 1218 W.2, W.10 Spiral Review, p. 1226, 1239	Plot Devices and Theme, SE, p. 1218 RL.5
	"The Rocking-Horse Winner," D. H. Lawrence, SE, p. 1246; "A Shocking Accident," Graham Greene, SE, p. 1263	Make Predictions, SE, p. 1244	Theme and Symbol, SE, p. 1244 RL.3
PART 3	"The Soldier" (MA), Rupert Brooke, SE, p. 1274; "Wirers" (MA), Siegfried Sassoon, SE, p. 1276; "Anthem for Doomed Youth," Wilfred Owen, SE, p. 1277	Infer the Essential Message, SE, p. 1272	Tone and Theme, SE, p. 1272 RL.4
	"Wartime Speech" (MC), Sir Winston Churchill, SE, p. 1287; "Evacuation Scheme," SE, p. 1291; Photographs of the London Blitz, SE, p. 1292	Determine the Essential Message, SE, p. 1284	Speech and Government Memorandum, SE, p. 1284
	"The Demon Lover" (A), Elizabeth Bowen, SE, p. 1298	Relate a Literary Work to a Primary Source Document, SE, p. 1296	Ghost Story, Flashback, and Ambiguity, SE, p. 1296 RL.3
	World War II Poets, SE, p. 1310	Author's Purpose, SE, p. 1308	Theme and Irony, SE, p. 1308 RL.6

Key: *UR: Unit Resources*   **A:** Average   **MA:** More Accessible   **MC:** More Challenging   © Indicates an Exemplar Text

Vocabulary	Grammar/Writing	Assessment
Vocabulary, SE, p. 1138: clamorous, conquest, anarchy, conviction, paltry, artifice; **Word Analysis: Greek Root** *-archy-*, **SE**, p. 1150; **Vocabulary: Synonyms, SE**, p. 1150 L.4.d	**Writing Lesson: Response to Literature, SE**, p. 1150; **Grammar in Your Writing, SE**, p. 1151; **Grammar and Style Lesson: Sentence Fragments and Run-ons, SE**, p. 1151; *WG*, Ch. 20, Section 4 W.1, W.5	**Critical Reading, SE**, pp. 1141, 1143, 1146, 1148; **Selection Tests A and B**, *UR6*, pp. 20–25
Vocabulary, SE, p. 1154: galled, refractory, dispensation, supplication, tumid; **Word Analysis: Latin Root** *-fract-*, **SE**, p. 1168; **Vocabulary: Analogies, SE**, p. 1168 L.3.a, L.5	**Writing Lesson: Multi-Genre Response, SE**, p. 1168; **Grammar in Your Writing, SE**, p. 1169; **Grammar and Style Lesson: Transitional Expressions, SE**, p. 1169; *WG*, Ch. 17, Section 4 W.2, W.4	**Critical Reading, SE**, pp. 1157, 1159, 1166; **Selection Tests A and B**, *UR6*, pp. 39–44
Vocabulary, SE, p. 1170: sequestered, topographical, affinities, prenatal, intrigues; **Word Analysis: Greek Root** *-top-*, **SE**, p. 1186; **Vocabulary: Synonyms** L.3	**Writing Lesson: Poem About an Artwork, SE**, p. 1186 W.5	**Critical Reading, SE**, pp. 1175, 1178, 1181, 1184; **Selection Tests A and B**, *UR6*, pp. 57–62
Vocabulary, SE, p. 1191: suffused, transient, upbraidings, evanescence, reticent, vivacious, irrevocable, escapade; **Word Analysis: Latin Root** *-trans-*, **SE**, p. 1205; **Vocabulary: Sentence Completions, SE**, p. 1205; **Precise Words for Movement, SE**, p. 1205 L.4.d	**Writing Lesson: Essay Comparing Narrative Styles, SE**, p. 1206; **Grammar and Style Lesson: Parallel Structure, SE**, p. 1207; *WG*, Ch. 20, Section 6; **Grammar in Your Writing, SE**, p. 1207	**Critical Reading, SE**, pp. 1197, 1200, 1203; **Selection Tests A and B**, *UR6*, pp. 77–82
Vocabulary, SE, p. 1209: palpitations, tendrils, diligent, sated, furtively; **Vocabulary: Analogies, SE**, p. 1215	**Writing to Compare Literary Works: Essay, SE**, p. 1215 W.2, W.10	**Critical Reading, SE**, pp. 1212, 1214; **Selection Tests A and B**, *UR6*, pp. 86–87
Vocabulary, SE, p. 1218: invincible, propitiate, conflagration, imperturbable, garrulous, derided; **Word Analysis: Latin Root** *-vinc-*, **SE**, p. 1243; **Vocabulary: Synonyms, SE**, p. 1243 L.5	**Writing Lesson: Response to Literature, SE**, p. 1243 W.1.a, W.5	**Critical Reading, SE**, pp. 1234, 1241; **Selection Tests A and B**, *UR6*, pp. 100–105
Vocabulary, SE, p. 1244: discreet, obstinately, uncanny, apprehension, embarked, intrinsically; **Word Analysis: Anglo-Saxon Prefix** *un-*, **SE**, p. 1270; **Vocabulary: Context Clues, SE**, p. 1270 L.4.a	**Writing Lesson: Script for a Scene, SE**, p. 1270 W.3, W.5	**Critical Reading, SE**, pp. 1261, 1268; **Selection Tests A and B**, *UR6*, pp. 118–123
Vocabulary, SE, p. 1272: stealthy, ghastly, desolate, mockeries, pallor; **Word Analysis: Anglo-Saxon Roots** *-ghast-* **and** *-ghost-*, **SE**, p. 1279; **Vocabulary: Synonyms, SE**, p. 1279 L.5	**Writing Lesson: Response to Criticism, SE**, p. 1279 W.1	**Critical Reading, SE**, pp. 1275, 1277; **Selection Tests A and B**, *UR6*, pp. 145–150
Vocabulary, SE, p. 1285: intimidated, endurance, formidable, invincible, retaliate, humanitarian, allocation; **Vocabulary: Antonyms, SE**, p. 1294 L.6	**Research Task, Topic: Great Speeches, SE**, p. 1295 W.7, W.8	**Test Practice: Reading, SE**, p. 1295; **Selection Tests A and B**, *UR6*, pp. 171–172
Vocabulary, SE, p. 1296: spectral, dislocation, arboreal, circumscribed, aperture; **Word Analysis: Cognates, SE**, p. 1307; **Vocabulary: Context Clues, SE**, p. 1307 L.4.a	**Writing Lesson: Sequel, SE**, p. 1307 W.3.c, W.3.d	**Critical Reading, SE**, p. 1305; **Selection Tests A and B**, *UR6*, pp. 185–190
Vocabulary, SE, p. 1308: combatants, sprawling, abide, eloquent; **Vocabulary: Analogies, SE**, p. 1315	**Writing: Memorandum, SE**, p. 1315 W.2	**Critical Reading, SE**, pp. 1311, 1312, 1314; **Selection Tests A and B**, *UR6*, pp. 203–208

All selections are supported in the *Reader's Notebooks*.

Unit 6: A Time of Rapid Change (continued)

	Selection	Reading Strategy	Literary Analysis
PART 3 (continued)	"Shooting an Elephant" (A), George Orwell, SE, p. 1318; "No Witchcraft for Sale" (MA), Doris Lessing, SE, p. 1327	Analyze and Evaluate the Similar Themes, SE, p. 1316	Cultural Conflict and Irony, SE, p. 1316 RI.3 Spiral Review, p. 1334
	"The Train from Rhodesia" (MA), Nadine Gordimer, SE, p. 1342; "B. Wordsworth" (A), V. S. Naipaul, SE, p. 1349	Apply Your Background Knowledge of a Historical Period, SE, p. 1340 RL.1	Historical Period, SE, p. 1340 Spiral Review, p. 1350
	from "Midsummer, XXII" (MC), Derek Walcott, SE, p. 1360; from "Omeris" from *Chapter XXVIII* (MC), Derek Walcott, SE, p. 1363	Repair Comprehension by Understanding Allusions, SE, p. 1358 RL.5	Political Critique and Allusions, SE, p. 1358
	"Follower" (MA), Seamus Heaney, SE, p. 1368; "Two Lorries" (A), Seamus Heaney, SE, p. 1370; "Outside History" (A), Eavan Boland, SE, p. 1374	Summarize, SE, p. 1366	Diction and Style, SE, p. 1366 RL.4
PART 4	"Come and Go" (A), Samuel Beckett, SE, p. 1380; "That's All" (A), Harold Pinter, SE, p. 1384	Compare and Contrast Literary Elements, SE, p. 1378 RL.3	Theater of the Absurd, SE, p. 1378
	"Do Not Go Gentle into That Good Night" (A), Dylan Thomas, SE, p. 1390; "Fern Hill" (A), Dylan Thomas, SE, p. 1392; "The Horses" (A), Ted Hughes, SE, p. 1396	Evaluate the Poet's Expression of the Theme, SE, p. 1388 RL.2	Style, SE, p. 1388
	"An Arundel Tomb" (MC), Philip Larkin, SE, p. 1402; "The Explosion" (A), Philip Larkin, SE, p. 1404; "On the Patio" (A), Peter Redgrove, SE, p. 1407; "Not Waving but Drowning" (MA), Stevie Smith, SE, p. 1408	Read It in Sentences, SE, p. 1400	Meter, Free Verse, and Dramatic Structure, SE, p. 1400 RL.5
	"Prayer" (A), Carol Ann Duffy, SE, p. 1412; "In the Kitchen" (A), Penelope Shuttle, SE, p. 1414	Recite the Poem Aloud, SE, p. 1410	Form, SE, p. 1410 RL.5
	"A Devoted Son" (A), Anita Desai, SE, p. 1419	Identify the Causes of the Characters' Actions, SE, p. 1418	Generational Conflicts and Characters, SE, p. 1418 RL.3
	"Next Term, We'll Mash You" (MA), Penelope Lively, SE, p. 1436	Evaluate Social Influences of the Period, SE, p. 1434	Characterization and Theme, SE, p. 1434 RL.3
	"We'll Never Conquer Space" (A), Arthur C. Clarke, SE, p. 1446	Applying an Expository Critique, SE, p. 1444	Argumentative Essay and Analogy, SE, p. 1444 RI.2, RI.4
	"Extra-Terrestrial Relays: Can Rocket Stations Give World-wide Radio Coverage?" Arthur C. Clarke, SE, p. 1455	Analyzing Cause-and-Effect Relationships, SE, p. 1454 RI.5	Technical Article and Press Release, SE, p. 1454
	from *Songbook*: "I'm Like a Bird," Nick Hornby, SE, p. 1464	Outlining Arguments and Strategies, SE, p. 1462 RI.5	Personal Essay, SE, p. 1462

Key: *UR: Unit Resources*   **A:** Average   **MA:** More Accessible   **MC:** More Challenging   © Indicates an Exemplar Text

Vocabulary	Grammar/Writing	Assessment
Vocabulary, SE, p. 1316: imperialism, despotic, dominion, reverently, incredulously, skeptical; **Word Analysis: Etymology of Political Science and History Terms, SE,** p. 1338; **Vocabulary: Contextual Meaning, SE,** p. 1338 L.4.a	**Writing Lesson: Problem-and-Solution Essay, SE,** p. 1338; **Grammar in Your Writing, SE,** p. 1339; **Grammar and Style Lesson: Variety in Sentence Beginnings, SE,** p. 1339; **WG,** Ch. 20, Section 3 W.2, W.2.d	**Critical Reading, SE,** pp. 1326, 1336; **Selection Tests A and B, UR6,** pp. 222–227
Vocabulary, SE, p. 1340: impressionistic, segmented, atrophy, patronize, distill, keenly; **Word Analysis: Patterns of Word Changes, SE,** p. 1357; **Vocabulary: Analogies, SE,** p. 1357 L.4.b	**Writing: Biographical Sketch of a Remarkable Person, SE,** p. 1357 W.3, W.3.d	**Critical Reading, SE,** pp. 1347, 1355; **Selection Tests A and B, UR6,** pp. 240–245
Vocabulary, SE, p. 1358: antic, rancor, eclipse, inducted; **Vocabulary: Synonyms, SE,** p. 1365	**Writing: Multimedia Presentation, SE,** p. 1365 W.2	**Critical Reading, SE,** pp. 1361, 1364; **Selection Tests A and B, UR6,** pp. 250–263
Vocabulary, SE, p. 1366: furrow, nuisance, inklings, mortal, ordeal; **Vocabulary: Context, SE,** p. 1376 L.4.b	**Writing: Directions, SE,** p. 1376	**Critical Reading, SE,** pp. 1369, 1372, 1375; **Selection Tests A and B, UR6,** pp. 276–281
Vocabulary, SE, p. 1378: undeterminable, clasped, appalled, resume; **Vocabulary: Context, SE,** p. 1387	**Writing: Scene, SE,** p. 1387 W.3	**Critical Reading, SE,** pp. 1382, 1386; **Selection Tests A and B, UR6,** pp. 294–299
Vocabulary, SE, p. 1388: grieved, spellbound, tortuous, dregs; **Vocabulary: Context, SE,** p. 1399	**Writing: Parody, SE,** p. 1399 W.4	**Critical Reading, SE,** pp. 1390, 1394, 1398; **Selection Tests A and B, UR6,** pp. 318–323
Vocabulary, SE, p. 1400: effigy, supine, fidelity, larking; **Vocabulary: Antonyms, SE,** p. 1409	**Writing: Reflective Essay, SE,** p. 1409 W.3.e	**Critical Reading, SE,** pp. 1405, 1407, 1408; **Selection Tests A and B, UR6,** pp. 336–341
Vocabulary, SE, p. 1410: utters, scales, lustrous, steadfastly; **Vocabulary: True or False? SE,** p. 1415	**Writing: Radio Introduction, SE,** p. 1415 W.2.a	**Critical Reading, SE,** pp. 1413, 1414; **Selection Tests A and B, UR6,** pp. 354–359
Vocabulary, SE, p. 1418: exemplary, filial, encomiums, complaisant, fathom; **Word Analysis: Latin Root -fil-, SE,** p. 1431; **Vocabulary: Context Clues, SE,** p. 1431 L.4.a	**Writing: Response to Literature, SE,** p. 1431 W.1.a, W.1.b	**Thinking About the Commentary, SE,** p. 1417; **Critical Reading, SE,** p. 1429
Vocabulary, SE, p. 1434: subdued, dappled, assessing, homespun, condescension, haggard; **Vocabulary: Analogies, SE,** p. 1443	**Writing: Magazine Advertisement, SE,** p. 1443 W.4	**Critical Reading, SE,** p. 1442; **Selection Tests A and B, UR6,** pp. 392–397
Vocabulary, SE, p. 1444: ludicrous, irrevocable, instantaneous, enigma, inevitable; **Vocabulary: Antonyms, SE,** p. 1453	**Writing: Expository Essay, SE,** p. 1453 W.2	**Critical Reading, SE,** p. 1451; **Selection Tests A and B, UR6,** pp. 410–415
Cross-Curricular Vocabulary, SE, p. 1454: atmosphere, orbit, velocity, satellite	**Timed Writing: Expository Essay, SE,** p. 1459 W.2, W.4.d	**Test Practice: Reading, SE,** p. 1459
Vocabulary, SE, p. 1462: inane, incessant, cynically, languor, anemic, disposable; **Vocabulary: Context, SE,** p. 1467	**Writing: Explanatory Notes, SE,** p. 1467	**Critical Reading, SE,** p. 1466; **Selection Tests A and B, UR6,** pp. 428–433

All selections are supported in the *Reader's Notebooks.*

1 Where Do I Start?

Right here! These pages will guide you through the program's unique organization and describe the many resources that will enrich your teaching.

2 How Do I Introduce the Essential Questions?

The literature in this book is presented through the lens of three key Essential Questions. Use the **Introduction to the Essential Questions** to give students a framework for understanding the overarching ideas that will guide their reading.

3 How Do I Introduce the Unit?

Each unit in this book presents the literature of a specific time period. Use the unit **Introduction** to examine multiple perspectives on an era and to develop students' understanding and appreciation for literature in its broader context.

> The **Snapshot of the Period** at the beginning of every unit presents key information graphically.

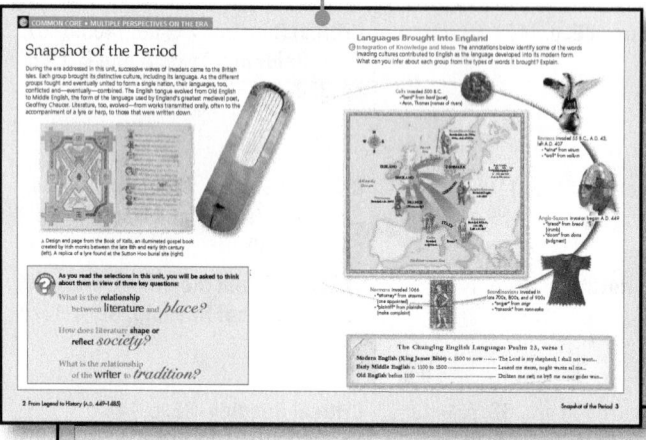

> **Recent Scholarship** features provide students with college-level analyses of the time period and related topics or themes.

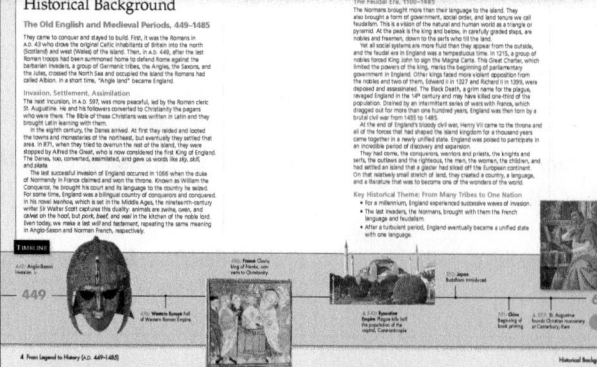

> A **Historical Background** provides students with a deeper understanding of the historical context.

> The **Integrate and Evaluate Information** pages provide both critical-thinking and extension activities.

4 What Should I Use to Plan and Prepare?

Start your planning with the **Time and Resource Manager** that precedes every selection or grouping of texts. This guide provides

- a detailed lesson plan.
- a list of the standards covered in the lesson.
- suggestions for incorporating program resources into your instruction.

For an at-a-glance look at selection resources, see the **Visual Guide to Featured Selection Resources** that precedes each selection or grouping.

Lesson Pacing Guide
Suggested pacing information

Meeting Common Core State Standards
Standard-coverage information

Resources
Suggested resources for differentiated instruction

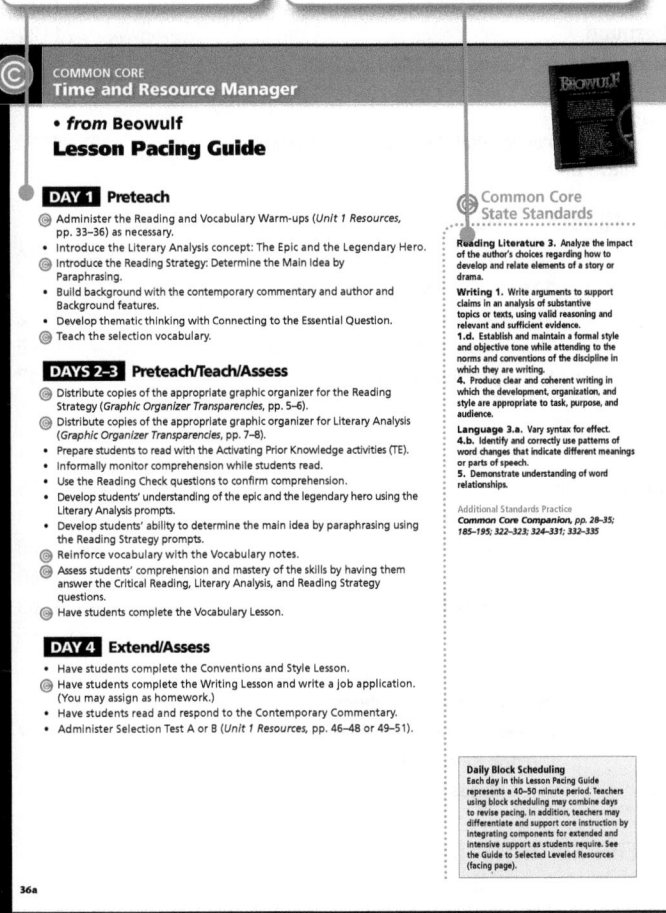

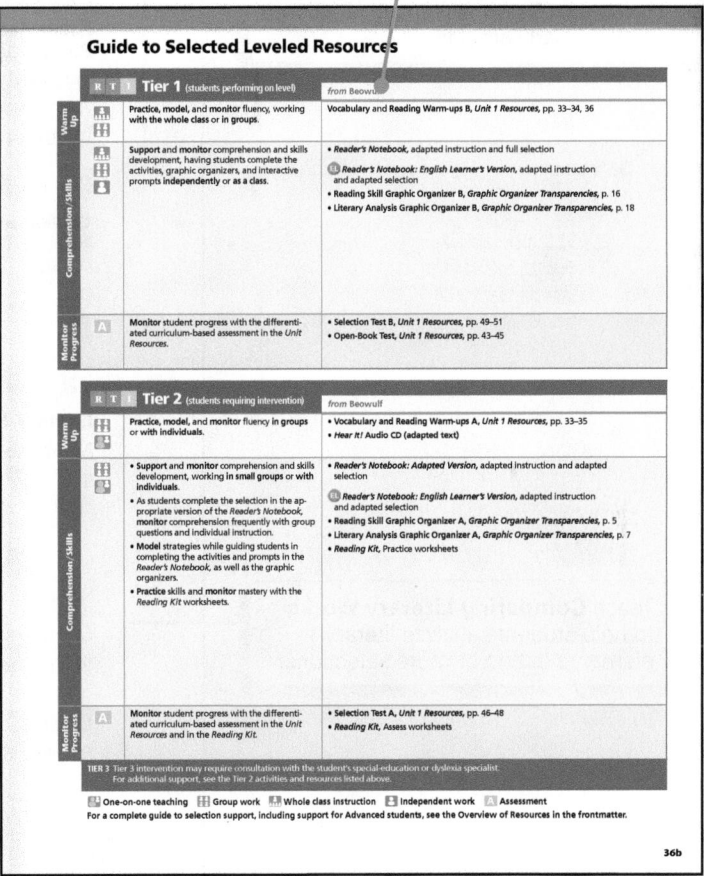

5 How Does the Program Help Me with Pacing?

The program is organized into three-week instructional blocks, with each block focusing on core skills and standards. This consistent organization ensures thorough skills coverage presented in manageable chunks. A benchmark test is provided at the middle and end of each unit, allowing you to administer assessment at three-, six-, or nine-week intervals. This systematic, logical organization with built-in progress monitoring allows you to make sound instructional choices for your class without skipping or missing any skills or standards.

6 How Do I Use Each Feature in a Unit?

COMMON CORE
Unit 6 ▪ Table of Contents

A Time of Rapid Change

The Modern and Postmodern Periods (1901 to Present)

A Introduce students to the literary period through analysis of graphics, historical essays, essential questions, and scholarly articles.

B Teach **Comparing Literary Works** to help students analyze literary elements in two or more selections.

xxiv Contents

UNIT **6**

PART THREE: **CONFLICTS AT HOME AND ABROAD**

C **Extended Studies** expand students' knowledge of literature and culture.

D **Research projects** provide students with the tools they need to be successful in college and in their careers.

Contents **xxv**

7 How Do I Teach a Selection?

Prentice Hall Literature addresses the challenges of today's mixed-ability classrooms through its unique combination of differentiated instruction, online activities, and skills support. When planning lessons for a diverse group of students, look for the **Text Complexity** rubric provided in the Teacher's Edition at the beginning of each selection or grouping. The Text Complexity rubrics provide a snapshot of each text's relative complexity. The Reader and Task suggestions on the following page provide suggestions for ensuring students' comprehension and success. The instruction for each selection or grouping follows a consistent pattern. This approach allows you and your students to appreciate significant works of literature while developing essential literary analysis and critical reading skills.

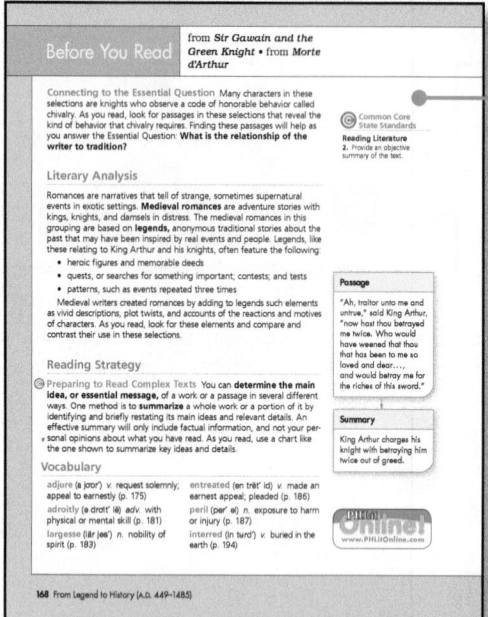

Use the **Before You Read** pages to present a full author biography and instruction on literary analysis, reading strategy, and vocabulary.

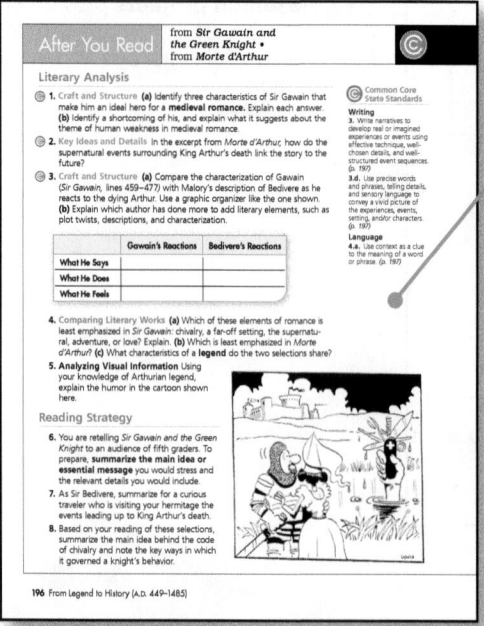

After completing the selection, use the **Critical Reading** and **After You Read** questions and the **Integrated Language Skills** pages to build skills and assess students' understanding.

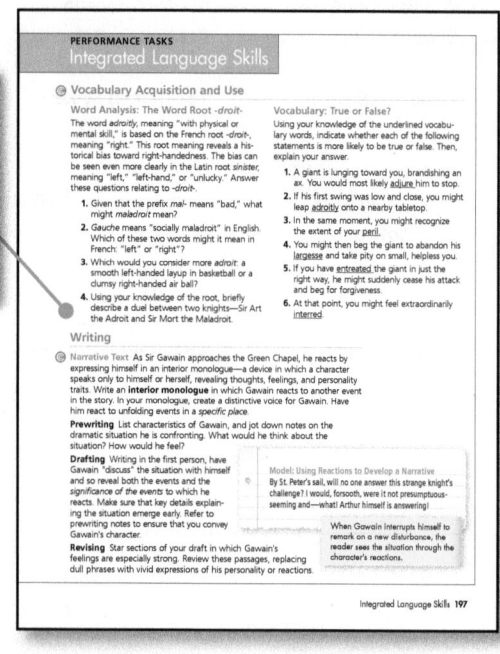

8 How Do I Differentiate Instruction?

Prentice Hall Literature provides unprecedented opportunities for differentiated instruction:

- **Teacher's Edition:** Use the strategies and techniques geared toward different reading levels and learning styles.
- **Reader's Notebooks:** Customize instruction with reading support for struggling readers and English learners.
- **Leveled Vocabulary and Reading Warm-ups:** For each selection, build background, fluency, and vocabulary.
- **Graphic Organizers:** Give struggling readers additional support with completed versions of all organizers in the Student Edition.

Differentiated Instruction for Universal Access

EL Pronunciation for English Learners

Some students may have difficulty pronouncing the /u/ or short *u* sound in the word *love*, which appears repeatedly in Sonnet 31. Many may substitute /oo/, as in the word *pool*.

If students have trouble with the short *u*, provide practice with pairs of words such as *boom/bum, coop/cup, gloom/glum, mood/mud, roost/rust, school/skull, spoon/spun*. Write and read each pair aloud, emphasizing differences in the vowels, and have students repeat. Model

using *love* and the words with the short *u* sound in sentences.

Pair English learners with fluent students to practice pronouncing the pairs and using the words in sentences. Have fluent English speakers correct English learners as needed.

Finally, play a game of telephone, using sentences in which a mispronunciation changes the meaning, such as, "I am looking for my cup."

PHLitOnline provides a customized learning experience for students. Learner levels are assigned to students based on Diagnostic Test results. All selections and support provided are based on that level, creating a truly personalized learning experience!

9 How Do I Monitor Student Progress?

Prentice Hall Literature makes progress monitoring easy with frequent opportunities to evaluate student progress and to reteach material. For more information on the program's assessments, see the Assessment Roadmap in PHLitOnline under Resources & Downloads.

Use the electronic test generator to customize assessment.

- The **Beginning-of-Year Benchmark Test** assesses students' skills and deficiencies at the onset of the year. Test results allow you to tailor your instruction to individual classes or students.

- Use the **Diagnostic Tests** at the beginning of the school year to determine readiness. You will find frequent **reading checks** and suggestions in the Teacher's Edition for monitoring student progress during reading. If taken online, learner levels are assigned automatically based on test results.

- After reading selections, use the **Open Book Tests** and leveled **Selection Tests** to assess comprehension and mastery of the literary, reading, and vocabulary skills.

- As you teach the unit, use the **Assessment Workshop** pages in standardized SAT and ACT test formats to give students practice in applying core skills and in writing for assessment under test-taking conditions. The Performance Task pages provide project-based activities for standards assessment.

- Use the **Benchmark Tests** to monitor progress at regular, frequent intervals. For your convenience, both mid-unit and end-of-unit tests are provided. If taken online, remediation for skills missed is assigned automatically!

- **Mid-Year** and **End-of-Year Summative Tests** provide a measure of student achievement over a longer period of time.

10 When Do I Teach Writing?

This program incorporates opportunities in every unit for both process writing and writing for assessment.

Process Writing: In each unit, a **Writing Workshop** with step-by-step instruction guides students to develop their ideas into full-length compositions, addressing these key stages in the writing process:

- Prewriting
- Drafting
- Revising
- Editing and Proofreading
- Publishing and Presenting

Timed Writing: To address the call for writing in the Common Core State Standards, the program provides numerous opportunities for students to practice writing for assessment. Each **Reading for Information** and **Comparing Literary Works** feature concludes with an annotated timed writing prompt that includes a step-by-step planner to help students complete the assignment. In addition, each Assessment Workshop includes a Timed Writing component.

The **Research Tasks** and **Communications Workshops** in each unit offer additional opportunities for students to engage in ambitious writing, research, and communications projects.

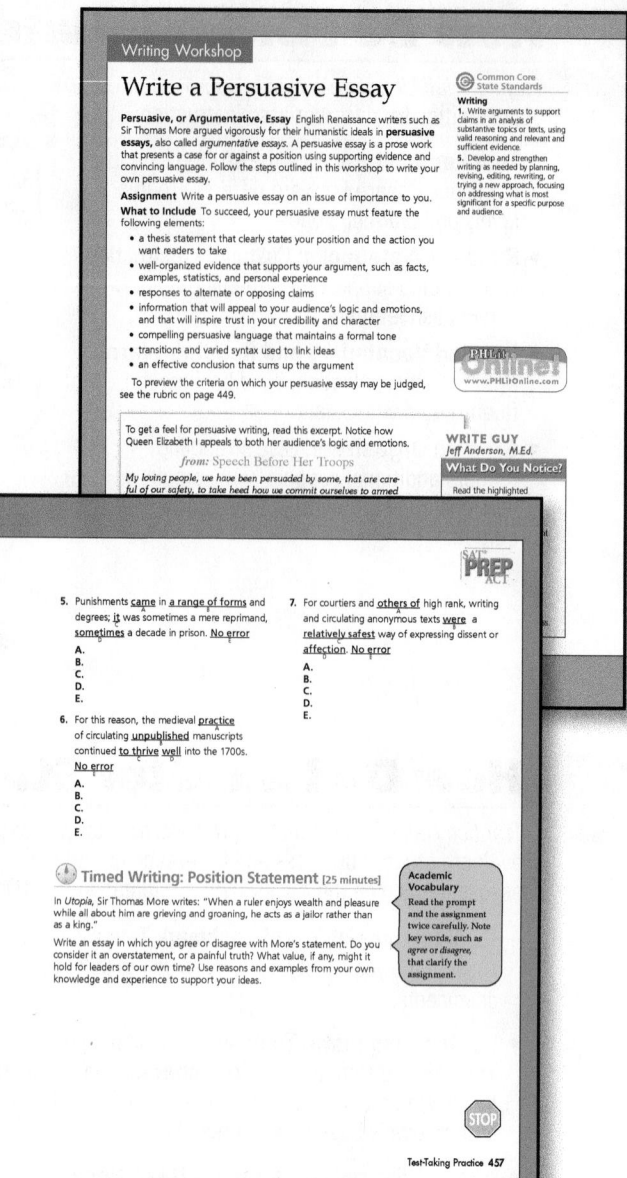

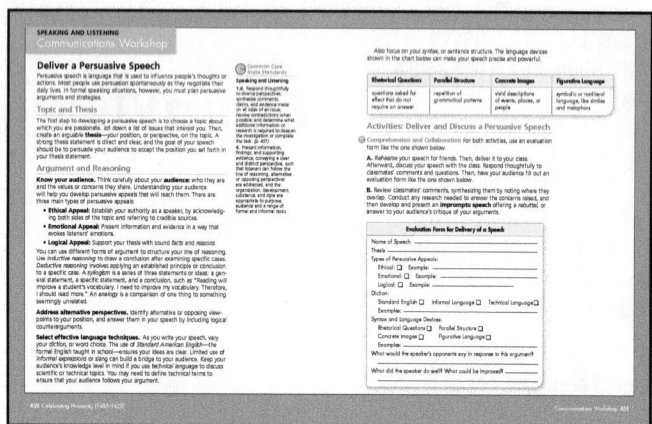

Score student essays in seconds.

Finally, to facilitate your teaching of writing, the **Prentice Hall EssayScorer** provides instant scoring and feedback, plus tips for revision. You save time, and your students become better writers!

11 How Can I Use Technology in My Classroom?

PHLitOnline allows you to teach the entire program without using the print products. It contains all of the components of the program in one central location: all of the print and activity-based materials, PLUS integrated videos, animations, interactive practice activities, songs, and audio. You will navigate through the program by using the Table of Contents, exactly as you would in the textbook.

You can choose to use PHLitOnline only, or you may choose to use it in conjunction with the print program. Supporting resources such as videos, audio, online assessments, lesson planning, and reporting are just what you need to teach literature to your 21st-Century students!

> All tests are scored automatically in PHLitOnline!

Enriched Online Student Edition
- Full narration of selections
- interactive graphic organizers
- linked Get Connected and Background videos
- all worksheets and other student resources

Professional Development
- the Professional Development Guidebook online
- additional professional development essays by program authors

Planning, Assigning, and Monitoring
- software for online assignment of work to students, individually or to the whole class
- a system for tracking and grading student work

12 How Can the Online Resource Help Me in the Classroom?

PHLitOnline Teacher Center has digital and print tools you can use to reach your students, manage your teaching resources, and meet the Common Core State Standards. You can

- provide personal diagnosis, instruction, and remediation to all students.
- tailor instruction for the right level of support for each student's specific needs.
- create customized assignments.
- view Common Core State Standards from within lessons.
- plan with easy-to-use tools.
- access all print resources online.

PHLitOnline Student Center allows students to access the complete printed program while at their computers in the classroom or at home. In addition to all print and activity-based materials, PHLitOnline Student Center offers videos, animations, interactive practice activities, "sticky" notes, songs, and audio features.

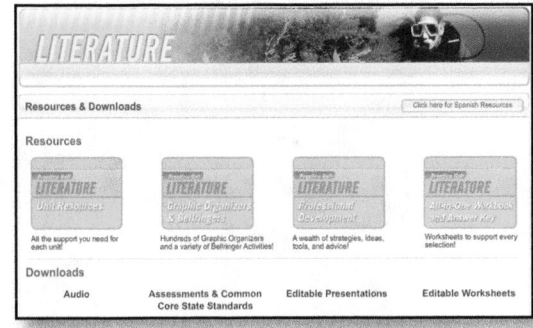

13 How Can PHLitOnline Help Me Personalize Instruction?

PHLitOnline provides personalized differentiated support with **Diagnostic** and **Benchmark** tests. The digital product can assess, diagnose, and auto-assign reading materials and practice at each student's level. Students are assigned a learner level—On-Level, Below-Level, or English Learner. Selections, audio, graphic organizers, and other support served up to students is based on this level. And since you know your students better than anyone, you have the flexibility to change the learner level as needed!

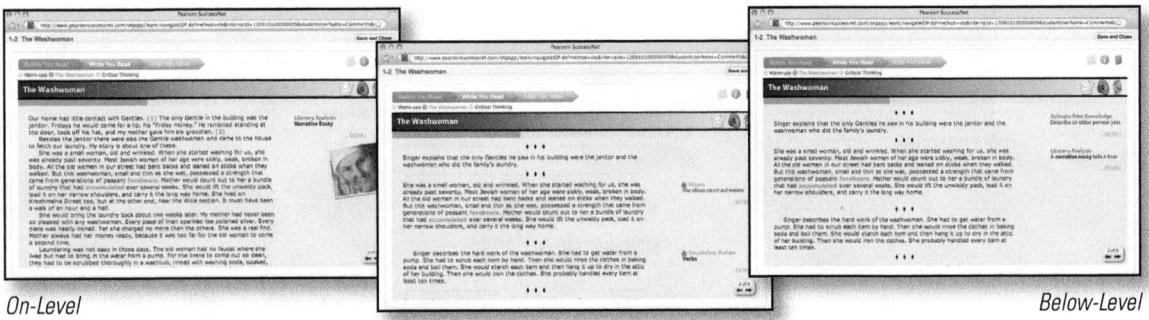

On-Level

English Learner

Below-Level

Full-size versions of these Media Literacy Handbook pages can be found in the Student Edition.

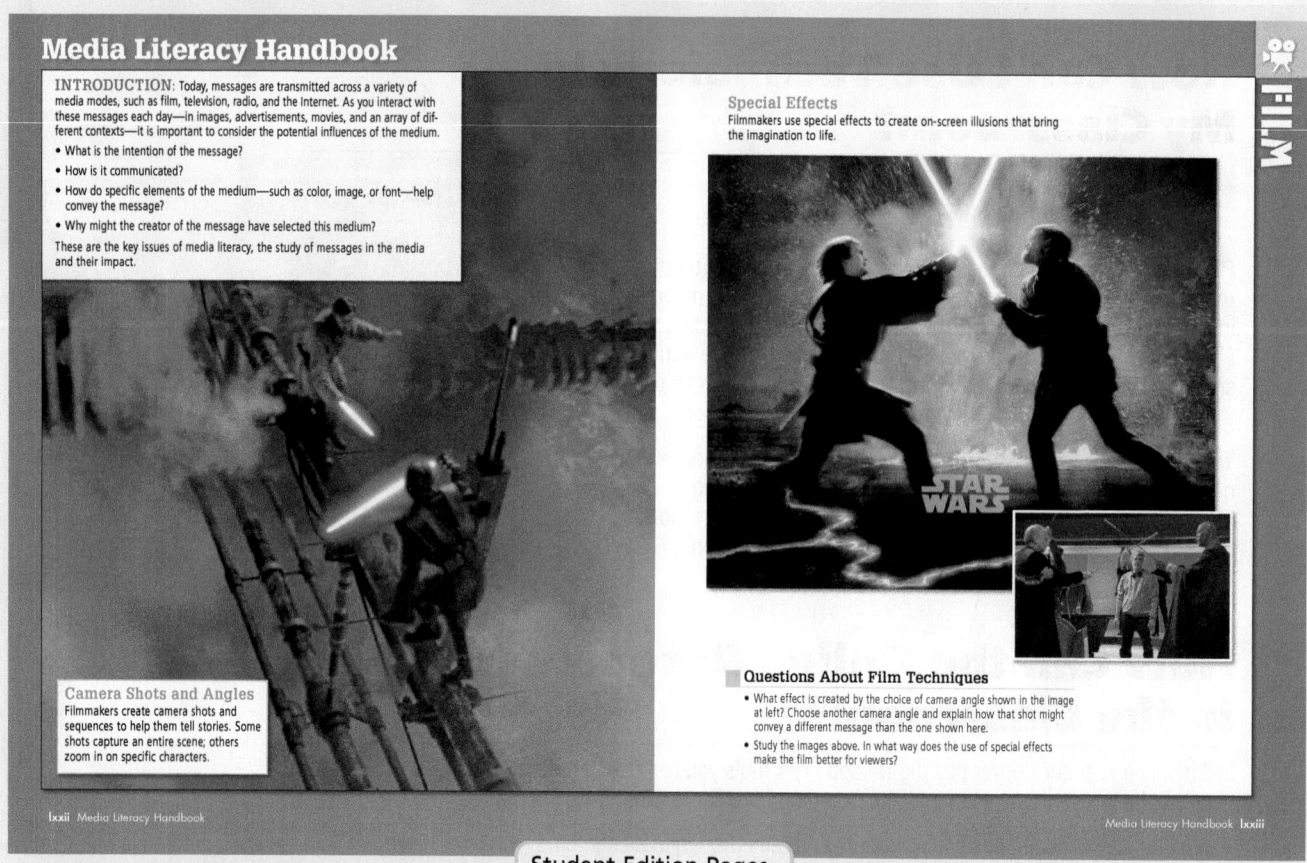

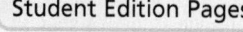
Student Edition Pages

Media Literacy Handbook

FILM

INTRODUCTION: Today, messages are transmitted across a variety of media modes, such as film, television, radio, and the Internet. As you interact with these messages each day—in images, advertisements, movies, and an array of different contexts—it is important to consider the potential influences of the medium.

• What is the intention of the message?
• How is it communicated?
• How do specific elements of the medium—such as color, image, or font—help convey the message?
• Why might the creator of the message have selected this medium?

These are the key issues of media literacy, the study of messages in the media and their impact.

Camera Shots and Angles
Filmmakers create camera shots and sequences to help them tell stories. Some shots capture an entire scene; others zoom in on specific characters.

Special Effects
Filmmakers use special effects to create on-screen illusions that bring the imagination to life.

Questions About Film Techniques

• What effect is created by the choice of camera angle shown in the image at left? Choose another camera angle and explain how that shot might convey a different message than the one shown here.

• Study the images above. In what way does the use of special effects make the film better for viewers?

lxxii Media Literacy Handbook

Media Literacy Handbook lxxiii

Student Edition Pages

Media Literacy Handbook

GRAPHICS/PHOTOS

Special Techniques
Most images you see today have been manipulated or changed in some way. Even a small change—such as an added graphic element or a difference in shading—can alter the mood of an image.

Focus and Framing
A sharp focus captures all details in a photographic image. A softer focus lessens the amount of detail that can be seen. The framing of elements within a photograph directs the eye toward a portion of the image.

Lighting and Shadow
Lighting techniques are used in photography to enhance mood and direct the viewer's focus.

FROM LUCY: ENGLAN' LADY
James Berry

Questions About Graphics and Photos

• What would be the effect if the image at left used a sharp focus instead of a combination of a sharp and soft focus?

• In what way does the use of color and light create mood in the photo at left?

• What special techniques were applied to the original photograph shown above right? What effect does the use of special techniques create?

lxxiv Media Literacy Handbook

Media Literacy Handbook lxxv

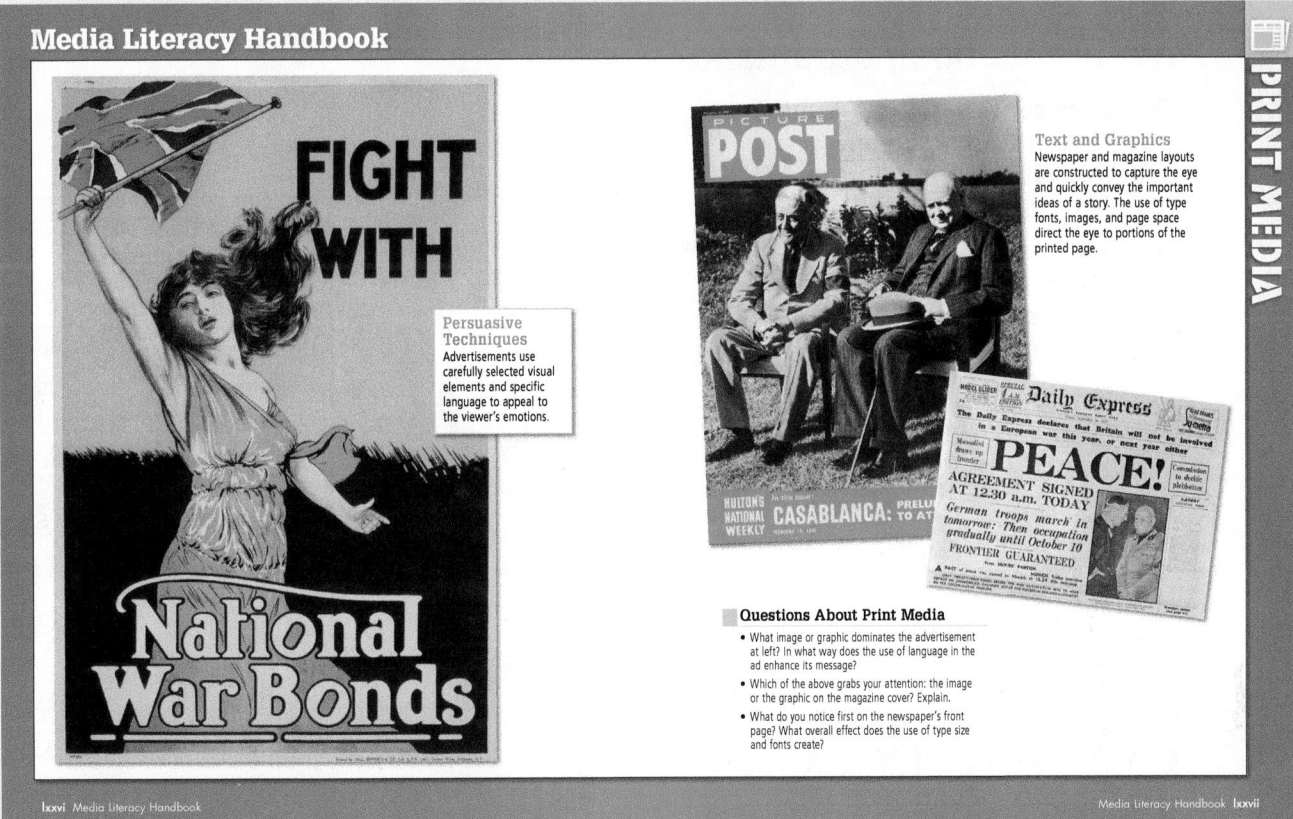

Persuasive Techniques
Advertisements use carefully selected visual elements and specific language to appeal to the viewer's emotions.

Text and Graphics
Newspaper and magazine layouts are constructed to capture the eye and quickly convey the important ideas of a story. The use of type fonts, images, and page space direct the eye to portions of the printed page.

Questions About Print Media

- What image or graphic dominates the advertisement at left? In what way does the use of language in the ad enhance its message?

- Which of the above grabs your attention: the image or the graphic on the magazine cover? Explain.

- What do you notice first on the newspaper's front page? What overall effect does the use of type size and fonts create?

Student Edition Pages

How is this book organized?

- There are six chronological units, starting with Anglo Saxon beginnings and extending to the present.
- Each unit has an introduction that offers multiple perspectives on the history, culture, and literature of the time period.

A **"Snapshot"** shows you key people, places, and innovations. ▶

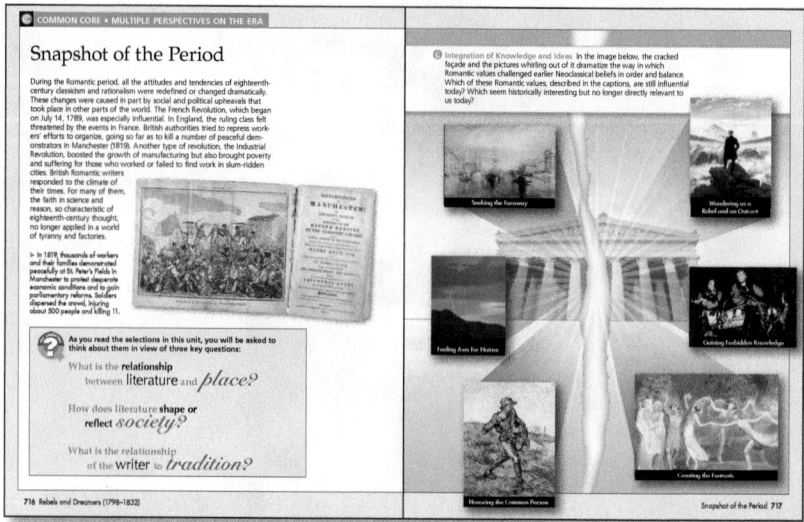

Historical Background summarizes key events of the era. ▼

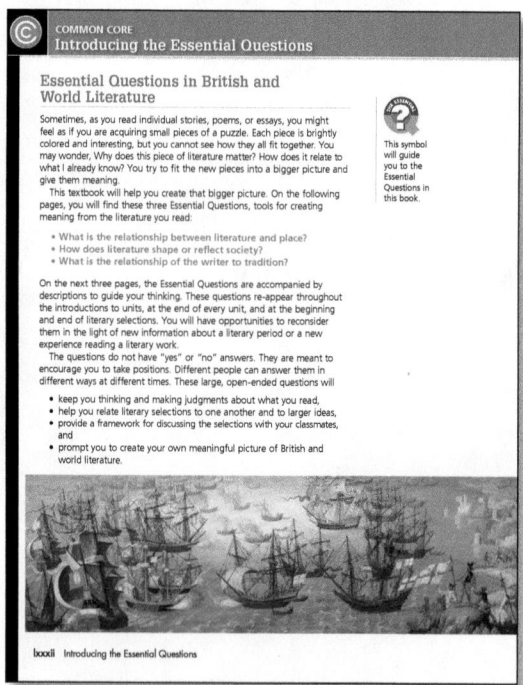

▲ **Essential Questions** help you think about universal themes.

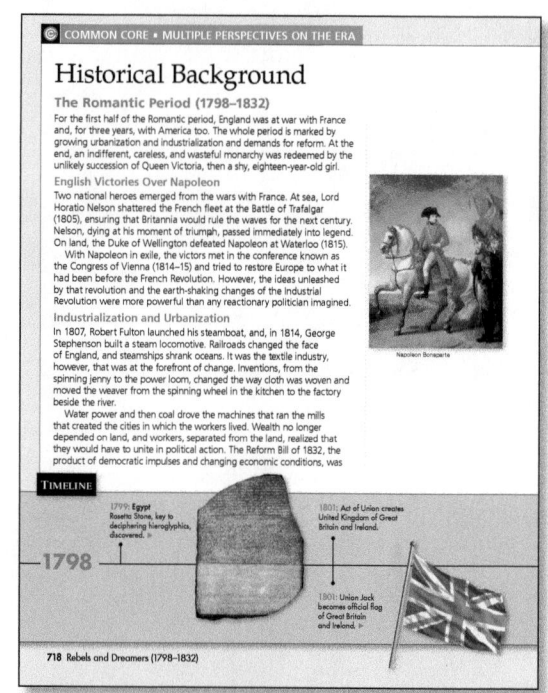

Student Edition Pages

How are the literary selections organized?

- **Each unit contains literary selections from the time period.**
- **Each selection has features to help you better understand the literature.**

Before You Read teaches you important skills and vocabulary. ▶

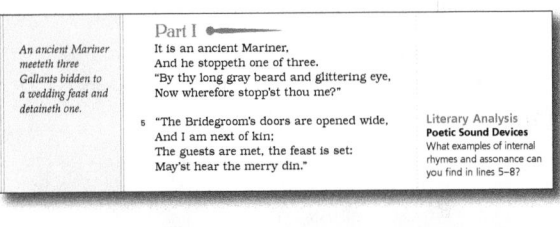

▲ **Author Biography** tells you about the author's life.

◀ **While You Read questions** help you apply the skills as you read.

After You Read helps you practice the skills you have learned. ▶

Skills Practice

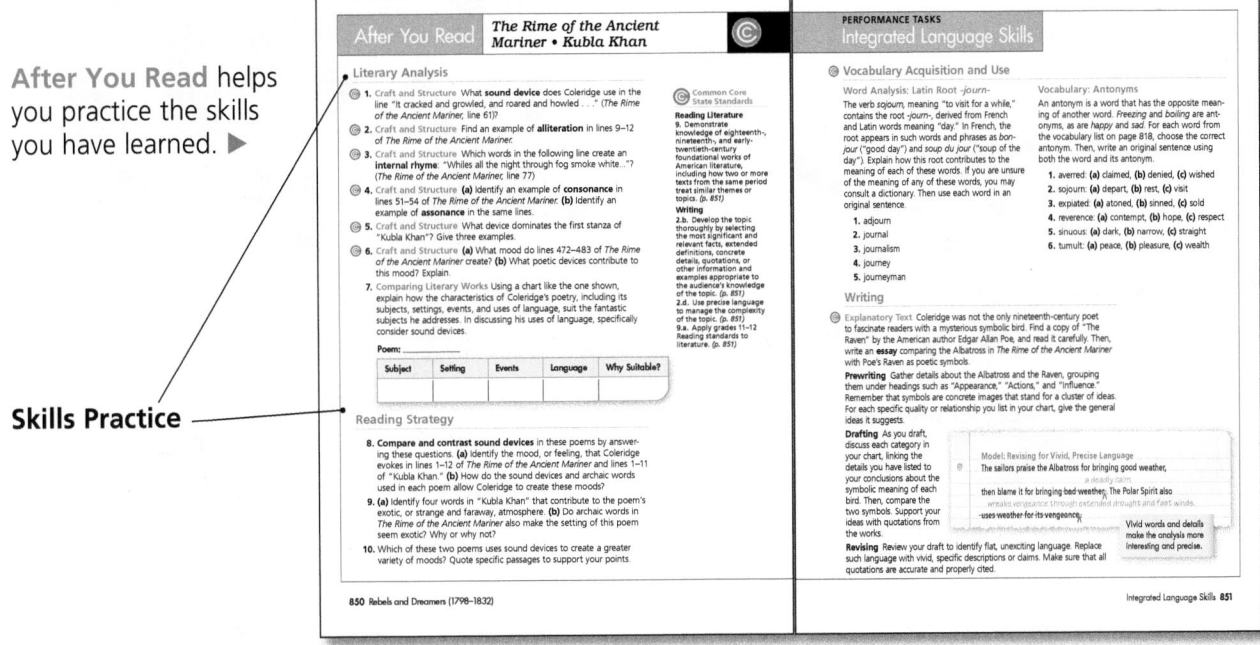

Special Features Bring British and World Literature to Life and Show Why They Matter Today

Extended Study brings you closer to an author's world or allows you to explore a literary movement or genre in great depth. ▶

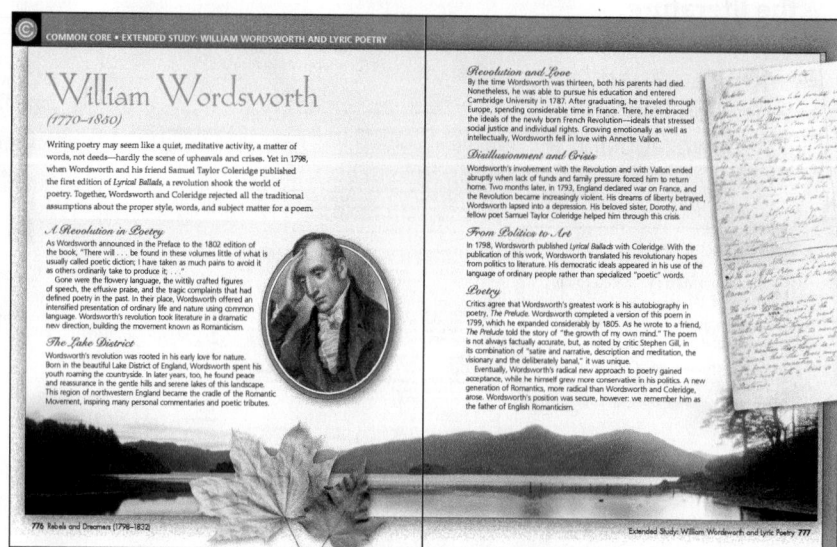

Themes Across Centuries, Genres, or Cultures features essays by today's writers on the topic of the classics. ▼

▲ **Illustrations** help you visualize literary history.

Student Edition Pages

Contemporary Connections links the classics to today. ▶

◀ **Primary Sources** features real documents that made history, and supports in-depth research projects.

◀ **Reading for Information** feature nonfiction texts you will encounter in daily life.

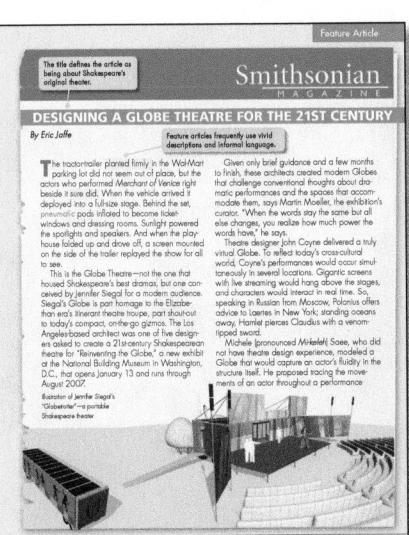

Comparing Literature Past and Present shows the continuity of ideas, themes, and styles. ▶

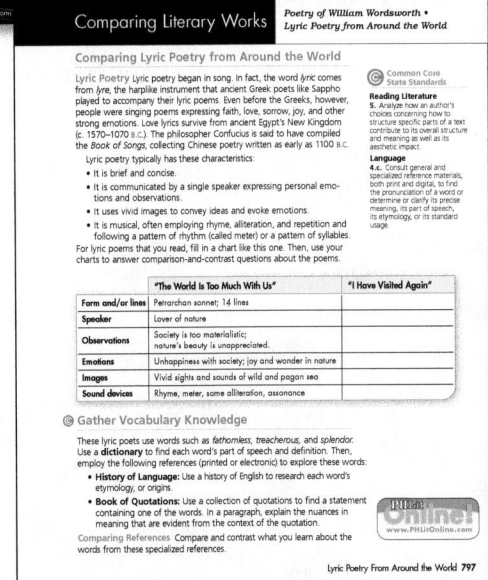

How to Use This Book **lxxxi**

Essential Questions in British and World Literature

This symbol will guide you to the Essential Questions in this book.

Sometimes, as you read individual stories, poems, or essays, you might feel as if you are acquiring small pieces of a puzzle. Each piece is brightly colored and interesting, but you cannot see how they all fit together. You may wonder, Why does this piece of literature matter? How does it relate to what I already know? You try to fit the new pieces into a bigger picture and give them meaning.

This textbook will help you create that bigger picture. On the following pages, you will find these three Essential Questions, tools for creating meaning from the literature you read:

- **What is the relationship between literature and place?**
- **How does literature shape or reflect society?**
- **What is the relationship of the writer to tradition?**

On the next three pages, the Essential Questions are accompanied by descriptions to guide your thinking. These questions re-appear throughout the introductions to units, at the end of every unit, and at the beginning and end of literary selections. You will have opportunities to reconsider them in the light of new information about a literary period or a new experience reading a literary work.

The questions do not have "yes" or "no" answers. They are meant to encourage you to take positions. Different people can answer them in different ways at different times. These large, open-ended questions will

- keep you thinking and making judgments about what you read,
- help you relate literary selections to one another and to larger ideas,
- provide a framework for discussing the selections with your classmates, and
- prompt you to create your own meaningful picture of British and world literature.

lxxxii Introducing the Essential Questions

Student Edition Pages

What is the **relationship** between literature and *place?*

From the beginning, England's geography captured the imagination of its writers. Over a thousand years ago, a monk named Bede began a section of his history, "Britain, formerly known as Albion, is an island in the ocean . . ." As you read the selections in this book, think about how England's island existence and dependence on the sea influenced its literature.

The imagination can shape the perception of a place, and writers play a major part in that imagining. How have different generations of England's writers re-imagined their country? How have they shaped remembered or even unreal places, such as a perfect pastoral community that exists only on the pages of a book?

As you read, watch how writers invest places with reality and invent places with imagination. Stay attuned to the variety of responses to the Essential Question: What is the relationship between literature and place?

Thematic Vocabulary

To help as you explore this Essential Question, use words like these:

boundary	**colonize**	**conquest**
destruction	**empire**	**geography**
immigrant	**isolation**	**mobility**
nature		

"This blessed plot, this earth, this realm, this England."

—William Shakespeare, *Richard II*

Introducing the Essential Questions **lxxxiii**

How does literature
shape or reflect *society?*

We know why we need farmers, carpenters, and doctors, but why do we need writers? Also, how do writers interact with the culture to produce literature that entertains, informs, persuades, challenges, and moves readers?

The writers who create British literature are a vital part of British society. They help to produce its culture, and they are the products of that culture. They are the entertainers who amuse, the critics who confront, and the teachers who share wisdom. Every day, writers celebrate Britain, define it, defy it, and tell its story. As you read this textbook and keep asking this Essential Question, you will become aware of the many relationships between Britain and its writers.

Thematic Vocabulary
To help as you explore this Essential Question, use words like these:

capitalism	dissatisfaction	ideal	independence
industry	loyalty	modernization	
order	revolution	values	

"No man is an island, entire of itself; every man is a piece of the continent, a part of the main."
—John Donne, *Meditation 17*

Student Edition Pages

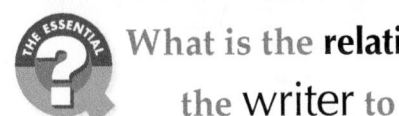

What is the **relationship** of the **writer** to *tradition?*

The past is not past. It is a living part of the present, and tradition is its embodiment. Literary tradition is the record of how men and women imaginatively responded to their times, what they believed was important and beautiful. It is the record of how they chose to express that beauty, the forms and styles and words and images they used. Tradition is the biography of literature.

Every British writer is, in some way, a product of the British literary tradition and a participant in it. As you keep asking this Essential Question throughout this book, you will be getting to the core of what gives British literature its unique character.

Thematic Vocabulary
To help as you explore this Essential Question, use words like these:

authentic	**conventional**	**interpretation**
monarchy	**philosophy**	**piety**
propriety	**reform**	**struggle**
transformation		

"*Let me imagine . . . what would have happened had Shakespeare had a wonderfully gifted sister, called Judith, let us say.*"

—Virginia Woolf, *A Room of One's Own*

LITERARY MAP OF THE BRITISH ISLES

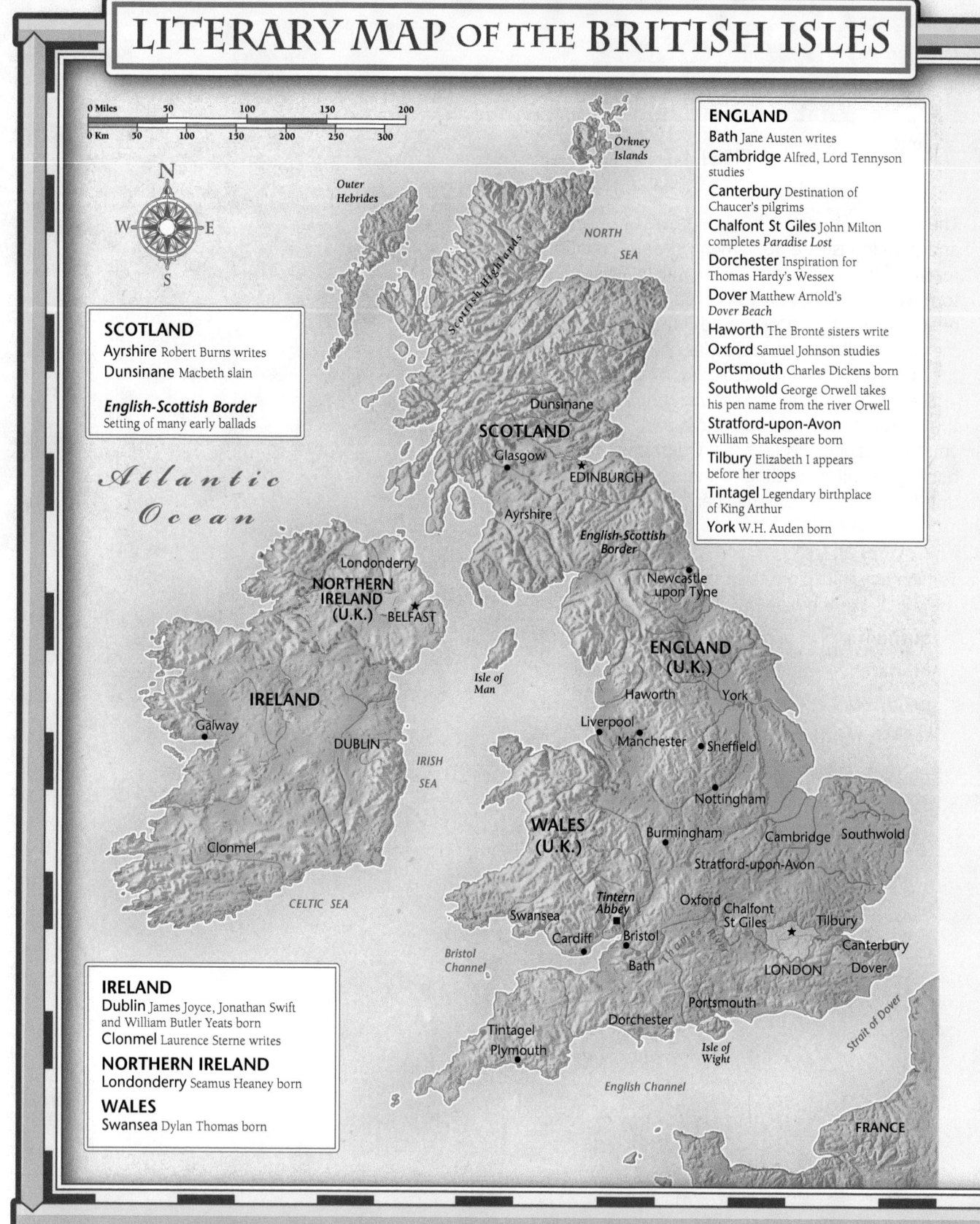

0 Miles 50 100 150 200
0 Km 50 100 150 200 250 300

N
W E
S

Orkney Islands

Outer Hebrides

NORTH SEA

Scottish Highlands

SCOTLAND
Ayrshire Robert Burns writes
Dunsinane Macbeth slain

English-Scottish Border
Setting of many early ballads

Dunsinane

SCOTLAND

Glasgow

★ EDINBURGH

Ayrshire

English-Scottish Border

Atlantic Ocean

Londonderry

NORTHERN IRELAND (U.K.) ★ BELFAST

Newcastle upon Tyne

IRELAND

Galway

DUBLIN

IRISH SEA

Isle of Man

ENGLAND (U.K.)

Haworth York

Liverpool
Manchester Sheffield

Nottingham

Clonmel

CELTIC SEA

WALES (U.K.)

Burmingham

Cambridge Southwold

Stratford-upon-Avon

Tintern Abbey Oxford Chalfont St Giles Tilbury

Swansea

Cardiff Bristol *Thames River* LONDON Canterbury

Bath Dover

Bristol Channel

Dorchester

Portsmouth

Tintagel

Plymouth

Isle of Wight

English Channel

Strait of Dover

FRANCE

IRELAND
Dublin James Joyce, Jonathan Swift and William Butler Yeats born
Clonmel Laurence Sterne writes

NORTHERN IRELAND
Londonderry Seamus Heaney born

WALES
Swansea Dylan Thomas born

ENGLAND
Bath Jane Austen writes
Cambridge Alfred, Lord Tennyson studies
Canterbury Destination of Chaucer's pilgrims
Chalfont St Giles John Milton completes *Paradise Lost*
Dorchester Inspiration for Thomas Hardy's Wessex
Dover Matthew Arnold's *Dover Beach*
Haworth The Brontë sisters write
Oxford Samuel Johnson studies
Portsmouth Charles Dickens born
Southwold George Orwell takes his pen name from the river Orwell
Stratford-upon-Avon William Shakespeare born
Tilbury Elizabeth I appears before her troops
Tintagel Legendary birthplace of King Arthur
York W.H. Auden born

lxxxvi Literary Map of the British Isles

Student Edition Pages

LITERARY MAP OF LONDON

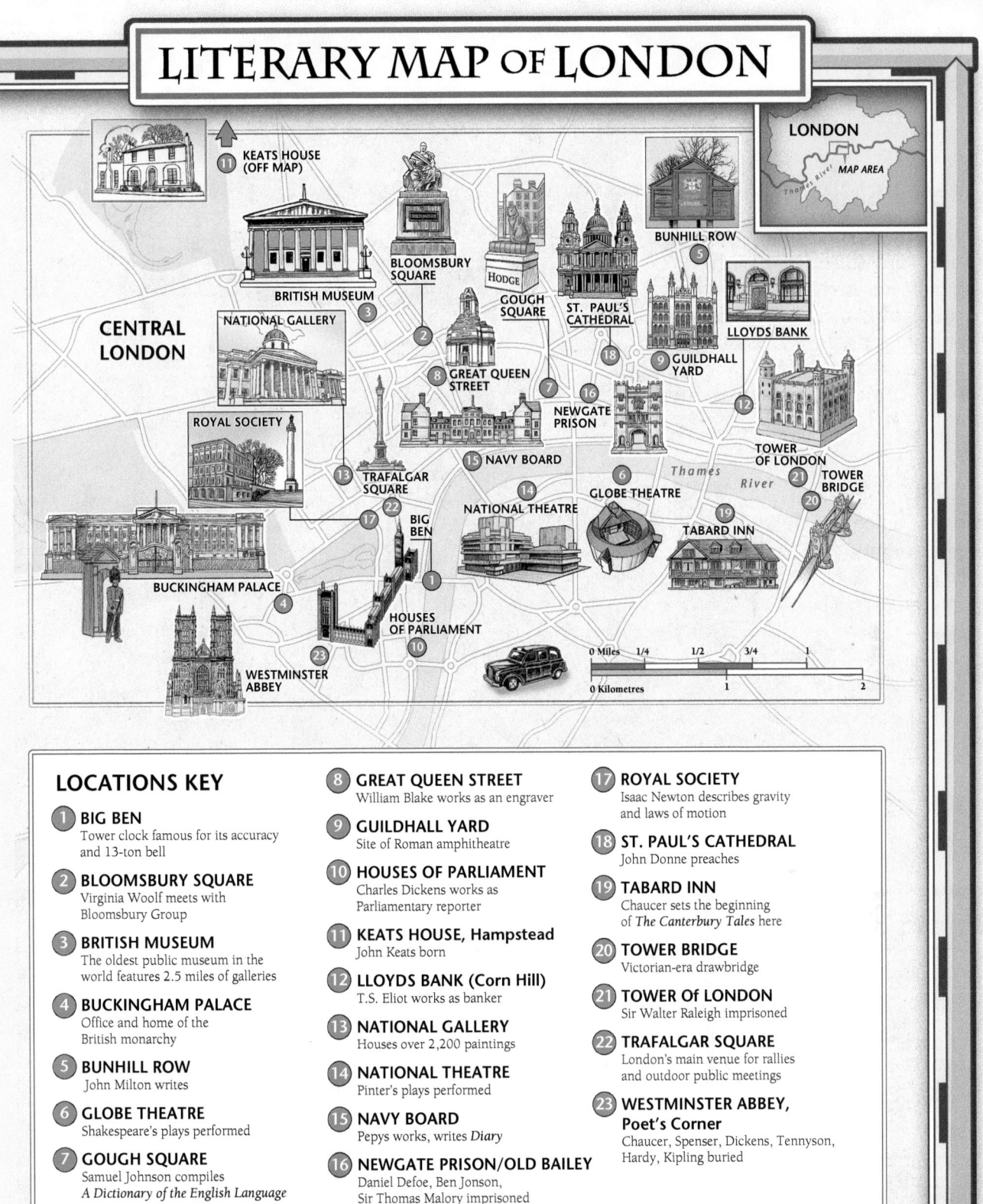

LONDON
MAP AREA

KEATS HOUSE (OFF MAP) 11

BLOOMSBURY SQUARE

BRITISH MUSEUM

CENTRAL LONDON

NATIONAL GALLERY

HODGE

GOUGH SQUARE

ST. PAUL'S CATHEDRAL

BUNHILL ROW 5

ROYAL SOCIETY

LLOYDS BANK

GUILDHALL YARD

GREAT QUEEN STREET 8

NEWGATE PRISON

TOWER OF LONDON

TRAFALGAR SQUARE 13

NAVY BOARD 15

Thames River

TOWER BRIDGE 21 20

BUCKINGHAM PALACE

BIG BEN 17 22

NATIONAL THEATRE 14

GLOBE THEATRE 6

TABARD INN 19

HOUSES OF PARLIAMENT 1

WESTMINSTER ABBEY 23

10

0 Miles   1/4   1/2   3/4   1

0 Kilometres   1   2

LOCATIONS KEY

1 BIG BEN
Tower clock famous for its accuracy and 13-ton bell

2 BLOOMSBURY SQUARE
Virginia Woolf meets with Bloomsbury Group

3 BRITISH MUSEUM
The oldest public museum in the world features 2.5 miles of galleries

4 BUCKINGHAM PALACE
Office and home of the British monarchy

5 BUNHILL ROW
John Milton writes

6 GLOBE THEATRE
Shakespeare's plays performed

7 GOUGH SQUARE
Samuel Johnson compiles *A Dictionary of the English Language*

8 GREAT QUEEN STREET
William Blake works as an engraver

9 GUILDHALL YARD
Site of Roman amphitheatre

10 HOUSES OF PARLIAMENT
Charles Dickens works as Parliamentary reporter

11 KEATS HOUSE, Hampstead
John Keats born

12 LLOYDS BANK (Corn Hill)
T.S. Eliot works as banker

13 NATIONAL GALLERY
Houses over 2,200 paintings

14 NATIONAL THEATRE
Pinter's plays performed

15 NAVY BOARD
Pepys works, writes *Diary*

16 NEWGATE PRISON/OLD BAILEY
Daniel Defoe, Ben Jonson, Sir Thomas Malory imprisoned

17 ROYAL SOCIETY
Isaac Newton describes gravity and laws of motion

18 ST. PAUL'S CATHEDRAL
John Donne preaches

19 TABARD INN
Chaucer sets the beginning of *The Canterbury Tales* here

20 TOWER BRIDGE
Victorian-era drawbridge

21 TOWER Of LONDON
Sir Walter Raleigh imprisoned

22 TRAFALGAR SQUARE
London's main venue for rallies and outdoor public meetings

23 WESTMINSTER ABBEY, Poet's Corner
Chaucer, Spenser, Dickens, Tennyson, Hardy, Kipling buried

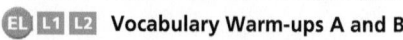
Selection and Skills Support

Every selection is fully supported with worksheets in *Unit Resources*, differentiated for various groups of learners. The Visual Guide to Selected Resources preceding each leveled selection pair gives a sample of the worksheets available. The full complement is presented on these pages.

RESOURCES FOR:

- **L1** Special-Needs Students
- **L2** Below-Level Students (Tier 2)
- **L3** On-Level (Tier 1)
- **L4** Advanced Students (Tier 1)
- **EL** English Learners
- **All** All Students

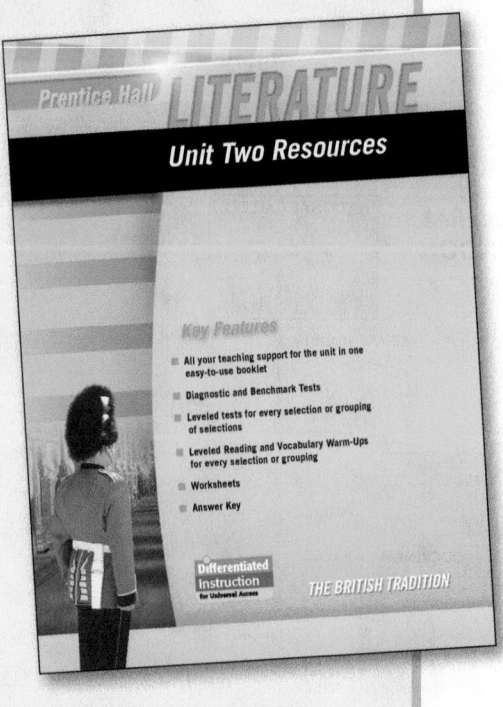

Prentice Hall **LITERATURE**

Unit Two Resources

Key Features

- All your teaching support for the unit in one easy-to-use booklet
- Diagnostic and Benchmark Tests
- Leveled tests for every selection or grouping of selections
- Leveled Reading and Vocabulary Warm-Ups for every selection or grouping
- Worksheets
- Answer Key

Differentiated Instruction for Universal Access

THE BRITISH TRADITION

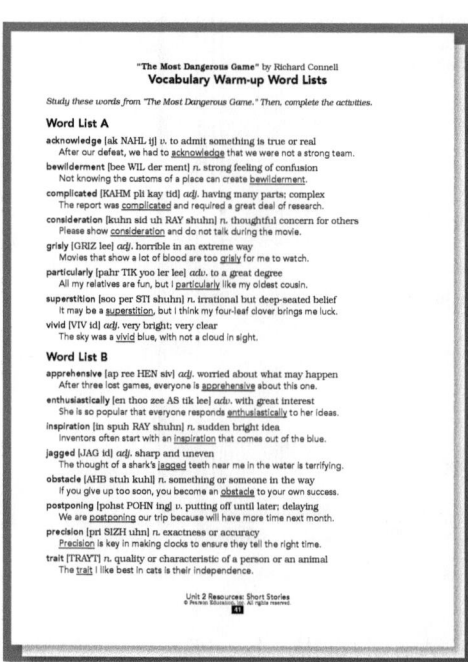

EL **L1** **L2** **Vocabulary Warm-ups A and B**

vocabulary and reading practice for lower-level students and English learners

---

All **Writing About the Big Question**

thematic vocabulary and thought-provoking activities centered around the unit Big Question

---

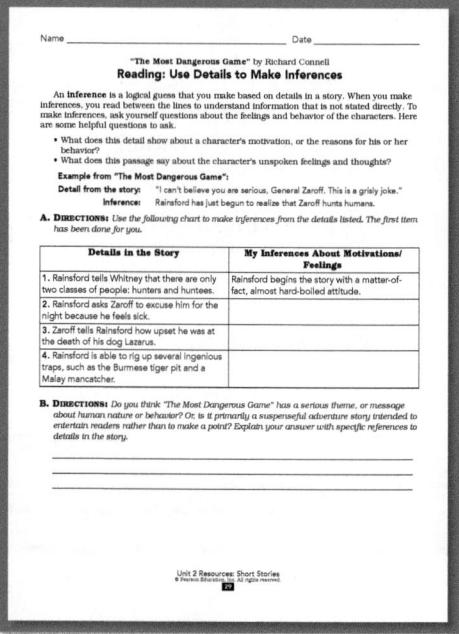

All **Reading**

a full page of support for the Reading Skill taught with the selection

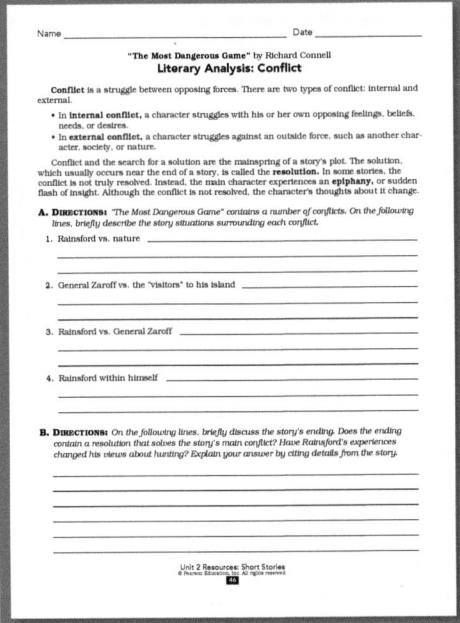

All **Literary Analysis**

a full page of support for the Literary Analysis concept taught with the selection

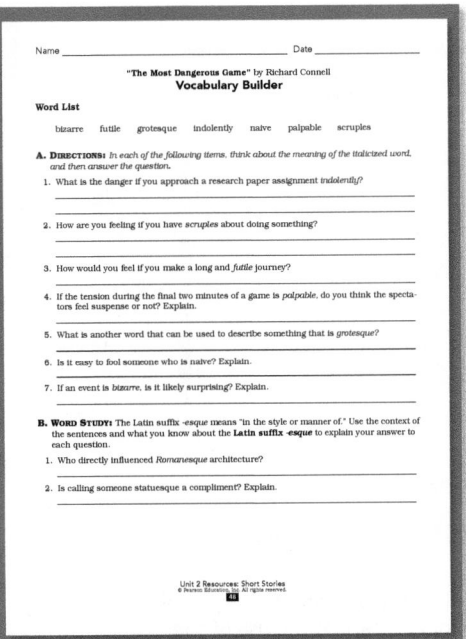

All **Vocabulary Builder**

selection vocabulary and Word Study skill practice

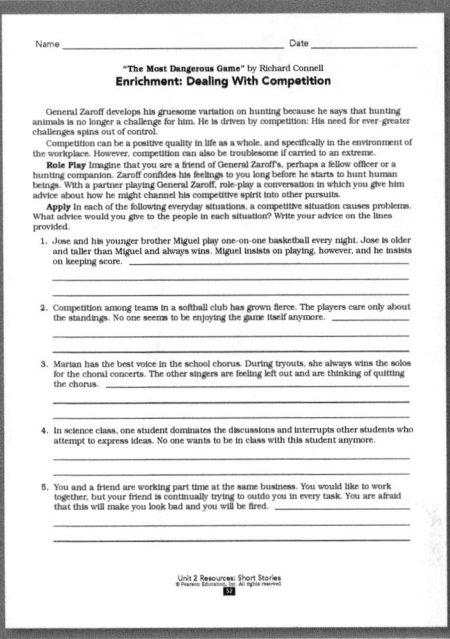

L4 **Enrichment**

a selection-related challenge for advanced learners

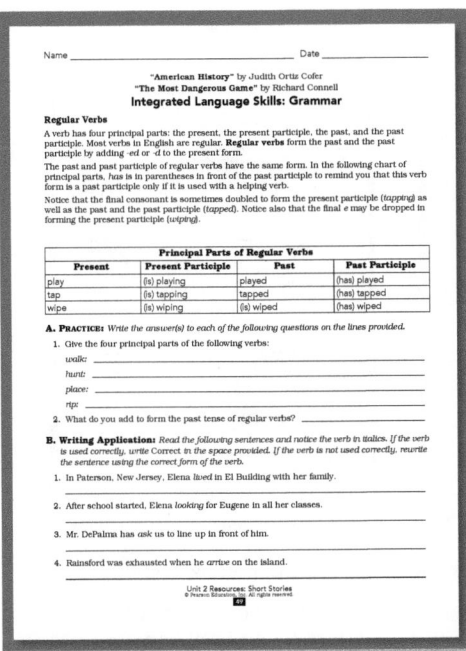

L3 **L4** **Grammar**

more practice with the grammar skill taught with the selection

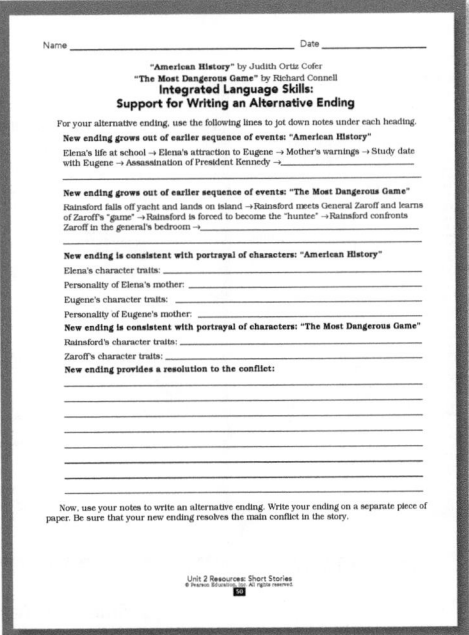

L3 **L4** **Writing**

support for the Writing activity accompanying the selection

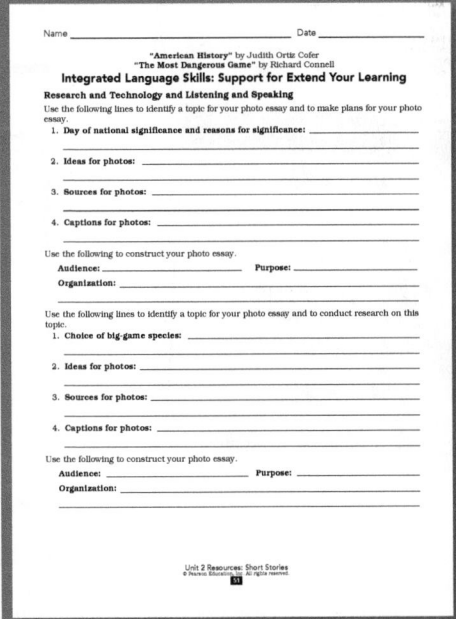

L3 **L4** **Extend Your Learning**

customized support for the Listening and Speaking or Research and Technology activity related to the selection

Selection Support

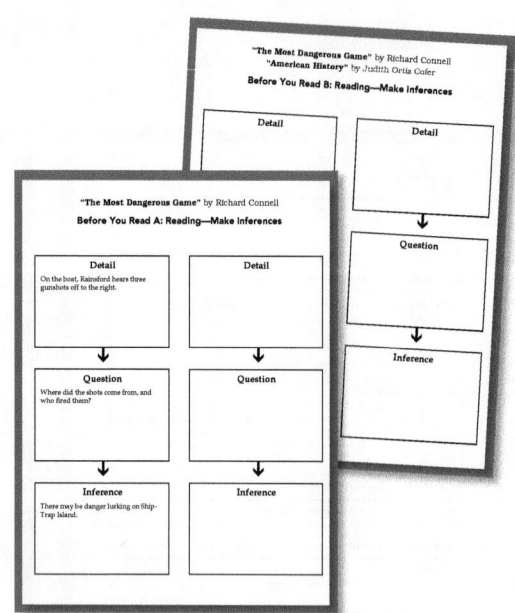

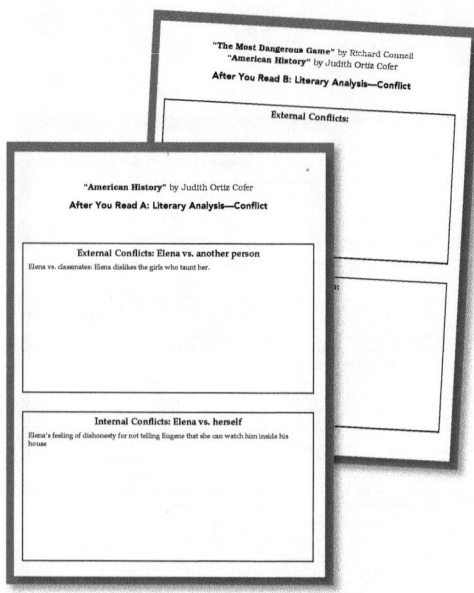

EL L1 L2 Reading Graphic Organizer A

a partially filled-in graphic organizer to model or scaffold the use of the organizer

L3 Reading Graphic Organizer B

the blank version of the organizer

EL L1 L2 Literary Analysis Graphic Organizer A

a partially filled-in graphic organizer to model or scaffold the use of the organizer

L3 Literary Analysis Organizer B

the blank version of the organizer

Assessment

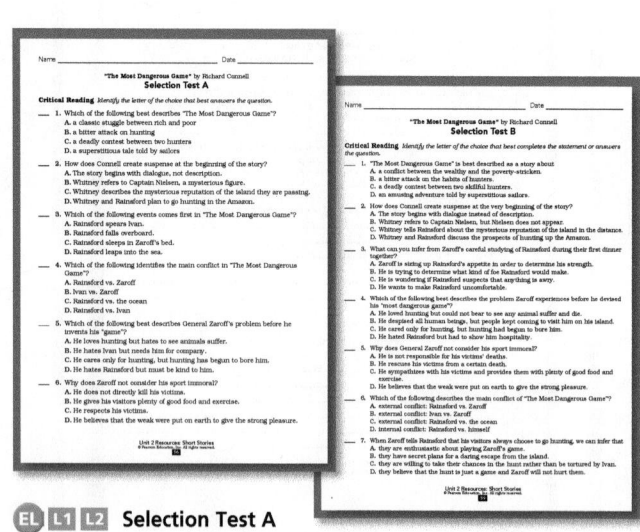

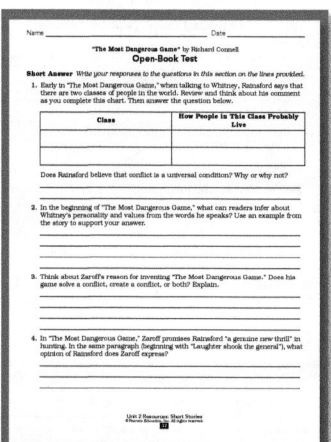

EL L1 L2 Selection Test A

selection test with complete skills coverage, adapted for lower-level students and English learners

EL L3 L4 Selection Test B

selection test with complete skills coverage, including multiple choice and essay items

L3 L4 Open-Book Test

an alternative assessment format for on-level and advanced students

All teacher resources
are available online at
www.PHLitOnline.com

Common Core Companion

The Common Core Companion student workbook provides instruction and practice for all Common Core State Standards. Here is a closer look at this workbook.

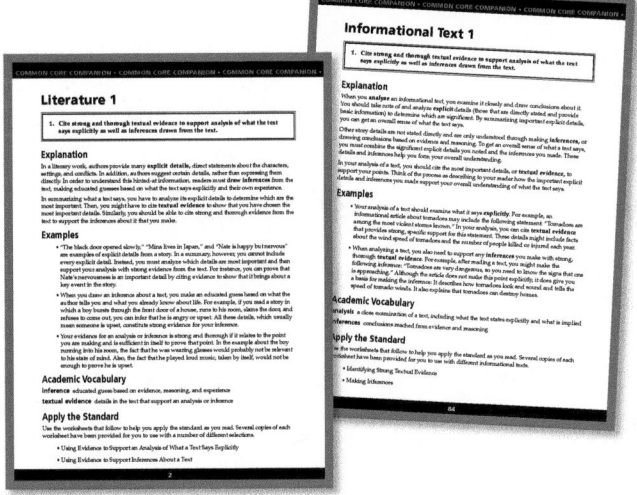

All **Literature and Informational Text**

Direct instruction and practice for each Common Core State Standard. Standards requiring writing or presentation outcomes are supported through process workshops.

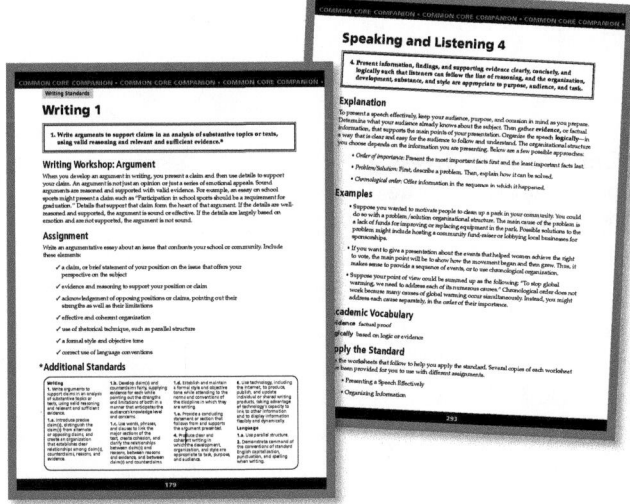

All **Writing and Speaking and Listening**

Full writing process workshops are supported with direct instruction and worksheets. Writing process standards are integrated with Speaking and Listening activities.

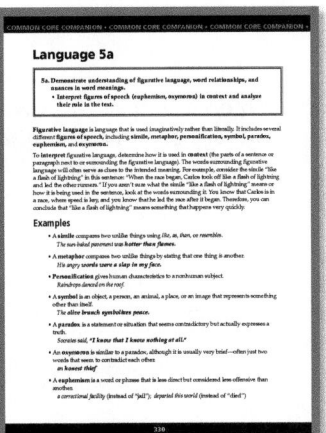

All **Language**

Explicit instruction supports each Language standard. Practice worksheets and graphic organizers provide additional opportunities for mastery.

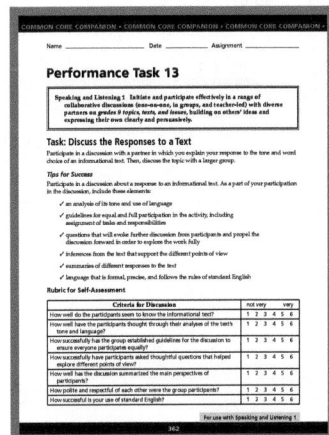

All **Performance Tasks**

Assessment opportunities are provided for each reading standard, along with tips for success and rubrics.

Each unit in this Teacher's Edition begins with a professional development essay by a program author. For more professional development essays, visit www.PHLitOnline.com.

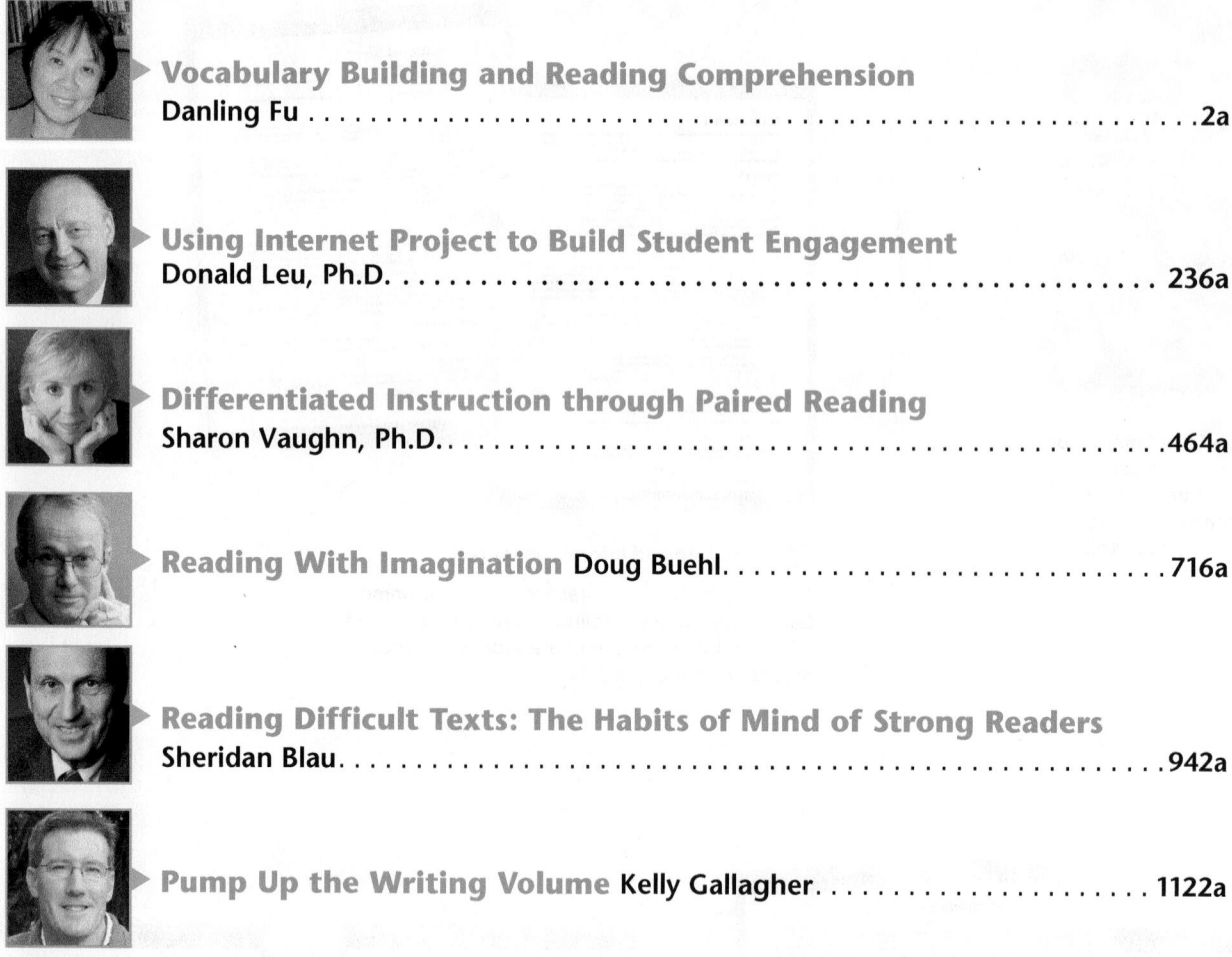

Log on as a teacher at www.PHLitOnline.com to access a library of all Professional Development articles by the Contributing Authors of *Pearson Prentice Hall Literature.*

PRENTICE HALL

LITERATURE

GRADE 12

COMMON CORE EDITION

Upper Saddle River, New Jersey

Boston, Massachusetts

Chandler, Arizona

Glenview, Illinois

WAYS LEARNING

PEARSON

Student Edition Pages

Cover: (Bkgd) ©Ted Mead/Getty Images, (L) ©James Forte/Getty Images, (B) ©Tom Merton/OJO Images/Getty Images, (TL, BC) ©Blaine Harrington III/CORBIS, (CR) ©Uli Wiesmeier/zefa/CORBIS

PEARSON

ISBN-13: 978-0-13-319558-3
ISBN-10:   0-13-319558-9
2 3 4 5 6 7 8 9 10 VO92 15 14 13 12 11

Student Edition Pages

PRENTICE HALL
LITERATURE
TEACHER'S EDITION • *THE BRITISH TRADITION, VOLUME 1*

COMMON CORE EDITION ©

PEARSON

Common Core
State Standards

• Reading Literature 1, 2, 3, 4, 5, 10
• Writing 1, 2, 3, 4, 5, 6, 7, 8
• Language 1, 2, 3, 4, 5, 6

From Legend to History
The Old English and Medieval Periods

"... borne/In the lap
of their shining ship, lined/
With gleaming armor,
going safely/In that oak-hard boat
to where their hearts took them."

—from *Beowulf*

www.PHLitOnline.com

Teaching From Technology

Enriched Online Student Edition
• full narration of selections
• interactive graphic organizers
• linked **Get Connected** and **Background** videos
• all work sheets and other student resources

Professional Development
• the *Professional Development Guidebook* online
• additional professional-development essays by program authors

Planning, Assigning, and Monitoring
• software for online assignment of work to students, individually or to the whole class
• a system for tracking and grading student work

Unit 1

PHLit Online!
www.PHLitOnline.com

Hear It!
- Selection summary audio
- Selection audio

See It!
- Author videos
- Essential Question video
- Get Connected videos
- Background videos
- More about the authors
- Illustrated vocabulary words
- Vocabulary flashcards

Do It!
- Interactive journals
- Interactive graphic organizers
- Grammar tutorials
- Interactive vocabulary games
- Test practice

1

Introduce Unit 1

1. Direct students' attention to the title of the Unit, including the time period covered. Have a volunteer read the quotation. **Ask:** What does the quotation suggest about the period?
   Possible response: Students might offer that the quotation implies they will be reading about epic adventures involving the sea and armored men.

2. Discuss the artwork, *The Viking Sea Raiders*, by Albert Goodwin (1845–1932).
   Ask: What is taking place in this painting?
   Possible response: Students might suggest that Vikings are sailing on a rough sea. Perhaps they are in the middle of a storm, on their way to or from a battle.

3. Have students speculate about the literature of the period, given the quotation and the art.
   Possible response: Students might offer that the literature of this period will involve tales of adventure, battles, and mythology. Certainly, themes of bravery, survival, and courage will be integral.

Unit Resources

Unit 1 Resources includes these pages:

Benchmark Tests assess and monitor student progress.

Vocabulary and Reading Warm-ups provide additional vocabulary support, based on Lexile rankings, for each selection. "A" **Warm-ups** are for students reading two grades below level. "B" **Warm-ups** are for students reading one grade below level.

Selection Support
- **Reading Skill**
- **Literary Analysis**
- **Vocabulary Builder**
- **Support for Writing**
- **Enrichment**

Unit Features

Unit Author
Burton Raffel helps introduce the period in the Unit Introduction, provides Recent Scholarship on literature in the Unit, and offers insight in the Writing Workshop.

Extended Studies
Students explore in depth the works of Geoffrey Chaucer, presented with links to contemporary culture, a Critical Commentary, and a Comparing Literary Works feature.

Comparing Literary Works
Students compare master works in the British tradition with works of world literature.

Primary Sources
Students engage the documents that recorded history as it was made.

Informational Texts
Students learn to use and evaluate various types of informational text.

Themes Across Centuries
Students discover links between canonical literature and the contemporary world.

PHLit Online!
All worksheets and other student resources are also available online at www.PHLitOnline.com.

CLASSROOM STRATEGIES

Vocabulary Building and Reading Comprehension **Danling Fu**

> "Marzano et al (2001) state that "Direct teaching of vocabulary might be one of the most underused activities in K-12 education."

One of the most glaring differences between successful and less successful students, across the grade levels, can be readily seen in their vocabulary knowledge and lexical skills (Biemiller, 2003). Successful comprehension is, in some significant part, dependent on the reader's knowledge of word meanings in a given text. Baker, Simmons, & Kame'enui (1998) state that "there is evidence that the relationship [between reading comprehension and vocabulary knowledge] is largely reciprocal." The good news for teachers from research in vocabulary development is that vocabulary instruction does improve reading comprehension (Stahl and Nagy, 2005). However, not all approaches to teach word meaning will improve comprehension.

Effective Vocabulary Instruction

Effective vocabulary instruction must involve the learner's active engagement in constructing understanding, not simply passively re-presenting information from a text or lecture. For example, teachers should use language, images, examples and other representational forms that are familiar to their students—not simply focus on the definition provided in the glossary or dictionary. The research on effective vocabulary teaching (Stahl & Nagy, 2005) summarizes three critical notions:

1. **Integration**—connecting new vocabulary to prior knowledge;
2. **Meaningful Use**—multiple opportunities to use new words in reading, writing and discussion;
3. **Explicit Instruction on Word-study**

Integration

Rationale: Beck and colleagues (2002) define effective vocabulary instruction as beginning with explanations, NOT definitions. Effective explanations are characterized by language the students already know, examples culled from students background knowledge/world view and images, metaphors, etc. familiar to students.

How to apply it: Connecting new vocabulary to students' prior knowledge can be accomplished in multiple ways: new words connected to the student's familiar background (e.g. loquacious-talk too much); new concepts related to the words the students already know ("culture" in biology); using the metaphors or images and language familiar to students to explain the new words with new concepts (multilingualism=belief in equality of various languages). For instance, to link new words to the students' background, the teacher can contrast the meanings of *admonish* and *rebuke* by comparing the examples of a policeman giving a warning to a driver not wearing a seatbelt and giving a ticket to a driver for speeding.

Meaningful Use

Rationale: Students need multiple exposures to new vocabulary words they encounter as they read. Academic vocabulary at high school level is mostly content specific, which students rarely use such words outside the classrooms. Teachers need to provide students with meaningful contexts in which to encounter and use the words and new concepts associated with them.

How to apply it: Vocabulary learning activities should be meaningfully linked with reading instruction before, during, and after reading.

Before reading: The teacher should select the important new words associated with the key concepts of the text the students will read, and use concept-mapping strategies to explain the meaning of the words before assigning students to preview the parts of the text.

During reading: the teacher should frequently and purposefully use the new words in instruction, so that students can encounter the new words and new concepts in meaningful contexts. In class, students should be given opportunities to use the new words in small-group reading discussions. The discussions should extend from retelling to making text-to-text and text-to-self and -world connections.

After reading: Students should review the parts of the text taught and further discuss in writing the new concepts with the new words, including the connections they have made orally in class with their peers. Through multiple language encounters (listening, speaking, reading, and writing before, during, and after reading), students will deepen their understanding of word meanings as well as of the text they read.

Explicit Instruction on Word-study

Rationale: Marzano et al (2001) state that "Direct teaching of vocabulary might be one of the most underused activities in K-12 education." In addition to the activities listed so far, teachers should also provide 20-30 minutes of explicit instruction in word study. These lessons should focus on teaching word parts (word origins, and derivational meanings), word associations and connotative meanings, and facilitating students' application of word knowledge across contexts.

How to apply it: Linguists estimate that well over 50% of polysyllabic words found in English are of Latin or Greek derivation and a large number of academic vocabulary words share this feature. A study on word origins or etymology can help students build basic knowledge of word structure and help them connect new words to those already known. For instance, draw their attention to the root *"spect=look/see"* and associate it with in*spect,* *spect*acle, pro*spect,* su*spect,* *spect*ator. Explicitly teach high-utility affixes and prefixes, such as the prefix "multi=many": multiple, multifaceted, multilingual, multicultural and the affix "less=without": useless, faceless, childless, senseless, etc. Focused word study on Greek and Latin roots can be of significant assistance to secondary students.

Modeled Strategy

See p. 48 for a point-of-use note modeling these strategies.

Teacher Resources

- *Professional Development Guidebook*
- *Classroom Strategies and Teaching Routines cards*

PHLit Online!

Log on as a teacher at **www.PHLitOnline.com** to access a library of all Professional Development articles by the Contributing Authors of Prentice Hall *Literature*.

Danling Fu

Danling Fu, Ph.D, Professor of Literacy, Language and Culture, College of Education in the University of Florida, teaches courses for both undergraduate and graduate students on teaching methods, composition theory/research, and writing/reading in the content areas.

Supporting Research

Baker, S.K., Simmons, D. C., & Kame'enui, E. J. (1998). Vocabulary acquisition: Instructional and curricular basics and implications. In D.C. Simmons & E. J. Kame'enui (Eds.), *What reading research tells us about children with diverse learning needs* (pp. 219–238). Mahwah, New Jersey: Lawrence Erlbaum Associates.

Beck, I.L., Mckeown, M.G. & Kucan, L. (2002). *Bring words to life: Robust vocabulary instruction*, Guilford Press, New York.

Biemiller, A. (2003). Vocabulary: Needed if more children are to read well. *Reading Psychology*, 24(3), 323–335.

Marzano, R. J., Pickering, D.J. & Pollock, J. E. (2001). Classroom instruction that works: Research based strategies for increasing student achievement. ASCD, Alexandria, VA.

Stahl S. & Nagy, W. E. (2005). *Teaching word Meaning*. New York: Routledge, Taylor & Francis Group.

Reading the Unit Introduction

From Legend to History

Explain to students that this unit covers literature in England from the Anglo-Saxon invasion in 449 to the Middle Ages in the 1400s. The Unit Introduction includes these components:

• a **Snapshot** offering a quick glimpse at the period

• a **Historical Background** section discussing major events

• a **Timeline** that covers the period from 449 to 1485 over a span of eight pages

• a **Unit Essay** examining the literature of the period through the lens of three Essential Questions

• **Following-Through** activities

• a **Recent Scholarship** essay

? Introducing the Essential Questions

1. Introduce each of the Essential Questions on the student page.

2. Show the **Essential Question Video** on the *See It!* DVD. Help students relate the Essential Questions to the unit and their own experiences by asking the following:
   Place and Literature How would you describe the geography of the place where you live? How does the place where you live affect your daily life?
   Literature and Society Choose a television program, book, or movie that you think best reflects current life in your community. How does the program or book reflect life today?
   Writer and Tradition Make a list of stories or traditions that have been passed down in your family from generation to generation. Have these traditions been passed down exactly the same way to each generation? Have they been modified in any way?

3. Explain to students that the ideas they have considered in answering these questions also apply to Britain's early history. Have them begin reading the Unit Introduction, and tell them to look as they read for ideas related to their answers.

Snapshot of the Period

During the era addressed in this unit, successive waves of invaders came to the British Isles. Each group brought its distinctive culture, including its language. As the different groups fought and eventually united to form a single nation, their languages, too, conflicted and—eventually—combined. The English tongue evolved from Old English to Middle English, the form of the language used by England's greatest medieval poet, Geoffrey Chaucer. Literature, too, evolved—from works transmitted orally, often to the accompaniment of a lyre or harp, to those that were written down.

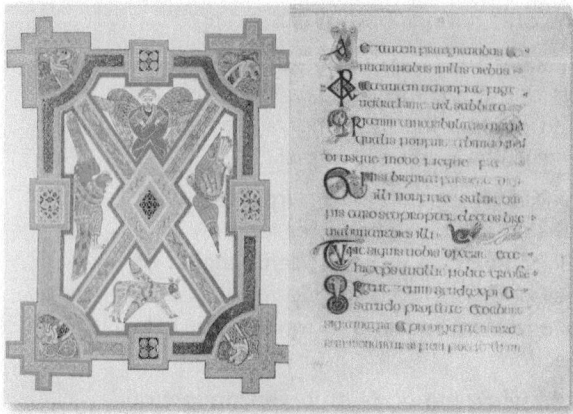

▲ Design and page from the Book of Kells, an illuminated gospel book created by Irish monks between the late 8th and early 9th century (left). A replica of a lyre found at the Sutton Hoo burial site (right).

 As you read the selections in this unit, you will be asked to think about them in view of three key questions:

What is the **relationship** between literature and *place?*

How does literature **shape or reflect** *society?*

What is the relationship of the **writer** to *tradition?*

Teaching Resources

The following resources can be used to support, enrich, or extend the instruction.

Unit 1 Resources
Names and Terms to Know, p. 8
Essential Question, pp. 9–11
Follow-Through, p. 12

▦ *Common Core Companion,*
pp. 9–14, 33–38

▦ *Professional Development Guidebook*
Cross-Curricular Enrichment,
pp. 234, 235, 237

See It! DVD
Essential Question Video: Unit 1
Susan Power Segment 1

PHLit Online! All resources are available at **www.PHLITOnline.com.**

Languages Brought Into England

Ⓒ **Integration of Knowledge and Ideas** The annotations below identify some of the words invading cultures contributed to English as the language developed into its modern form. What can you infer about each group from the types of words it brought? Explain.

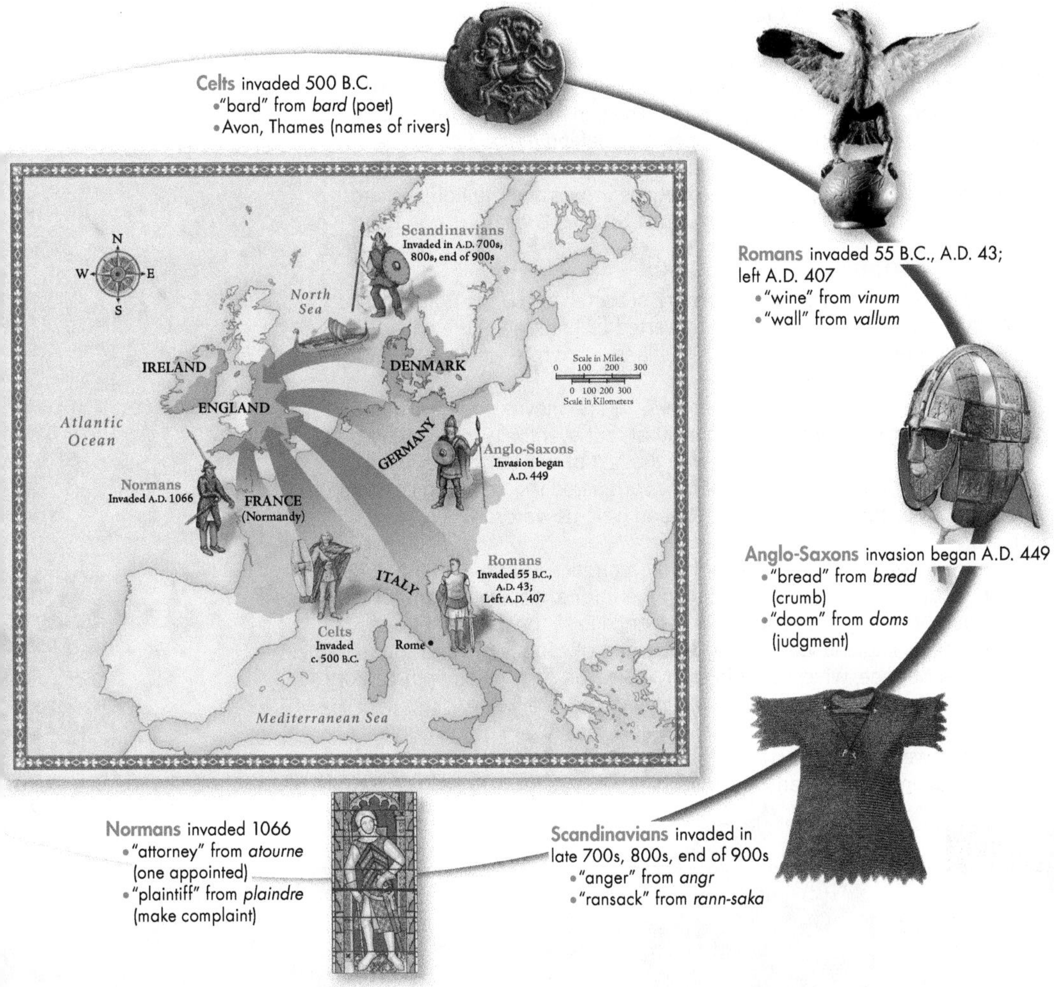

Celts invaded 500 B.C.
- "bard" from *bard* (poet)
- Avon, Thames (names of rivers)

Scandinavians
Invaded in A.D. 700s, 800s, end of 900s

Romans invaded 55 B.C., A.D. 43;
left A.D. 407
- "wine" from *vinum*
- "wall" from *vallum*

Anglo-Saxons
Invasion began
A.D. 449

Normans
Invaded A.D. 1066

Romans
Invaded 55 B.C.,
A.D. 43;
Left A.D. 407

Celts
Invaded
c. 500 B.C.

Anglo-Saxons invasion began A.D. 449
- "bread" from *bread* (crumb)
- "doom" from *doms* (judgment)

Normans invaded 1066
- "attorney" from *atourne* (one appointed)
- "plaintiff" from *plaindre* (make complaint)

Scandinavians invaded in late 700s, 800s, end of 900s
- "anger" from *angr*
- "ransack" from *rann-saka*

The Changing English Language: Psalm 23, verse 1

Modern English (King James Bible) c. 1500 to now ········ The Lord is my shepherd; I shall not want...

Early Middle English c. 1100 to 1500 ··························· Lauerd me steres, noght wante sal me...

Old English before 1100 ······································· Drihten me ræt; ne byð me nanes godes wan...

Snapshot of the Period **3**

3

Teaching the Historical Background

The Historical Background section discusses the most significant events of this period: the invasions first by Romans, then the invasions and settlement in A.D. 449 by Germanic tribes—the Angles, the Saxons, and the Jutes; the incursion by Christian followers of St. Augustine in 597; the invasion and settlement by the Danes in the 700s; and the last invasion of England in 1066 by the Normans of France.

1. Point out that the story of this period includes the effects these groups had on the development of England as a nation in terms of the nation's government, economy, and social order.

2. Have students read the Background. Then **ask** them to list the contributions the following groups made to England and its development as a nation: St. Augustine and his followers, the Danes, and the Normans. **Possible response:** St. Augustine's followers brought Christianity and Latin; the Danes influenced the language; and the Normans brought their language, a form of government, and a pyramid social order in a system known as feudalism.

Critical Viewing

Analyze

1. Call students' attention to the illustration of the helmet.

2. **Ask** students what information about the Anglo-Saxon culture they can deduce from the helmet. **Possible response:** The helmet indicates that the Anglo-Saxon culture was likely warlike. The people were able to work with metal.

Teaching the Timeline

1. Tell students that the Timeline for the period from 449 to 1485 appears on pages 4–13 of this Unit Introduction. Each portion of the Timeline identifies and illustrates some of the major events in Britain and in the world for that period.

2. Have students survey the entire Timeline before they read the rest of the Unit Introduction.

3. Encourage students to identify additional events from the period and share them.

4

Historical Background

The Old English and Medieval Periods, 449–1485

They came to conquer and stayed to build. First, it was the Romans in A.D. 43 who drove the original Celtic inhabitants of Britain into the north (Scotland) and west (Wales) of the island. Then, in A.D. 449, after the last Roman troops had been summoned home to defend Rome against the barbarian invaders, a group of Germanic tribes, the Angles, the Saxons, and the Jutes, crossed the North Sea and occupied the island the Romans had called Albion. In a short time, "Angle land" became England.

Invasion, Settlement, Assimilation

The next incursion, in A.D. 597, was more peaceful, led by the Roman cleric St. Augustine. He and his followers converted to Christianity the pagans who were there. The Bible of these Christians was written in Latin and they brought Latin learning with them.

In the eighth century, the Danes arrived. At first they raided and looted the towns and monasteries of the northeast, but eventually they settled that area. In 871, when they tried to overrun the rest of the island, they were stopped by Alfred the Great, who is now considered the first King of England. The Danes, too, converted, assimilated, and gave us words like *sky, skill,* and *skate.*

The last successful invasion of England occurred in 1066 when the duke of Normandy in France claimed and won the throne. Known as William the Conqueror, he brought his court and its language to the country he seized. For some time, England was a bilingual country of conquerors and conquered. In his novel *Ivanhoe,* which is set in the Middle Ages, the nineteenth-century writer Sir Walter Scott captures this duality: animals are *swine, oxen,* and *calves* on the hoof, but *pork, beef,* and *veal* in the kitchen of the noble lord. Even today, we make a last *will* and *testament,* repeating the same meaning in Anglo-Saxon and Norman French, respectively.

TIMELINE

449: Anglo-Saxon Invasion. ▶

449

476: **Western Europe** Fall of Western Roman Empire.

496: **France** Clovis, king of Franks, converts to Christianity.

4 From Legend to History (A.D. 449–1485)

The Feudal Era, 1100–1485

The Normans brought more than their language to the island. They also brought a form of government, social order, and land tenure we call feudalism. This is a vision of the natural and human world as a triangle or pyramid. At the peak is the king and below, in carefully graded steps, are nobles and freemen, down to the serfs who till the land.

Yet all social systems are more fluid than they appear from the outside, and the feudal era in England was a tempestuous time. In 1215, a group of nobles forced King John to sign the Magna Carta. This Great Charter, which limited the powers of the king, marks the beginning of parliamentary government in England. Other kings faced more violent opposition from the nobles and two of them, Edward II in 1327 and Richard II in 1399, were deposed and assassinated. The Black Death, a grim name for the plague, ravaged England in the 14th century and may have killed one-third of the population. Drained by an intermittent series of wars with France, which dragged out for more than one hundred years, England was then torn by a brutal civil war from 1455 to 1485.

At the end of England's bloody civil war, Henry VII came to the throne and all of the forces that had shaped the island kingdom for a thousand years came together in a newly unified state. England was poised to participate in an incredible period of discovery and expansion.

They had come, the conquerors, warriors and priests, the knights and serfs, the outlaws and the righteous, the men, the women, the children, and had settled an island that a glacier had sliced off the European continent. On that relatively small stretch of land, they created a country, a language, and a literature that was to become one of the wonders of the world.

Key Historical Theme: From Many Tribes to One Nation
- For a millennium, England experienced successive waves of invasion.
- The last invaders, the Normans, brought with them the French language and feudalism.
- After a turbulent period, England eventually became a unified state with one language.

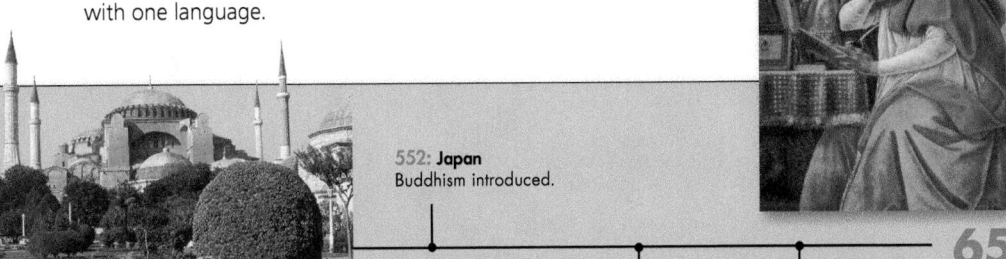

552: Japan Buddhism introduced.

▲ 542: **Byzantine Empire** Plague kills half the population of the capital, Constantinople.

591: **China** Beginning of book printing.

▲ 597: St. Augustine founds Christian monastery at Canterbury, Kent.

656

Historical Background **5**

Connecting to the Literature

1. Point out that, in this unit, students will encounter works from several different periods of English history. These works include "The Seafarer" and "The Wanderer," on page 20. These Anglo-Saxon poems offer first-person accounts of the loneliness and alienation that sea-roving and warfare could prompt. The epic poem *Beowulf,* on page 40, is the story of the Anglo-Saxon hero Beowulf.

2. Explain that Bede's *A History of the English Church and People,* on page 84, describes events of the early Middle Ages. Geoffrey *Chaucer's Canterbury Tales* appears on page 123. This collection of stories offers a snapshot of medieval life in England.

3. Indicate that the excerpt from the medieval poem *Sir Gawain and the Green Knight,* on page 170, illustrates the chivalry and integrity in King Arthur's court. *Morte d'Arthur,* on page 185, was the first prose version about the legendary King Arthur's court.

Key Historical Theme

1. Explain to students that this section of the Historical Background calls out three major historical themes from the whole period.

2. **Ask** students to write a newspaper headline to help them remember each theme.
Sample answer: Possible headlines include When Will These Invasions End?; Normans Make Their Mark; One Nation, One Language.

History Background

Although they descended from the Vikings, the Normans had adopted many French ways over the years. They had become devout Christians. They had accustomed themselves to speaking a dialect of the French language. They had also organized themselves according to the French political and economic system of the times—feudalism.

5

Teaching the Essential Questions

As students read From Legend to History, they will examine its information through the lens of three Essential Questions. Each Essential Question is broken down into "stepping-stone" questions. Work through each stepping-stone question with the class. Then have students pose answers to the Essential Question as it applies to the period.

What is the relationship between literature and place?

1. Before they read this section of the essay, tell students that the work of many early English writers focused on place—the sea they had to cross to arrive in the land that would become England, and the place itself before it became an island nation.

2. Have students read this section of the essay. Then, pose the first stepping-stone question. **Ask:** *How did English writers respond to their island geography?*
Possible response: The English writers responded to their island geography by focusing on the sea. They spoke of the loneliness that men faced on long sea voyages. They also spoke of the sea as a waterway and a means of traveling to a new place for settlement.

(cont. on page 9)

Essential Questions Across Time

The Old English and Medieval Periods (A.D. 449–1485)

 What is the **relationship** between literature and *place?*

In 1399, just before he was deposed and killed, King Richard II returned to England from Ireland. In Shakespeare's version of the scene, the King kneels, touches the sacred soil of England, and says: "Dear earth, I do salute thee with my hand . . . So weeping, smiling, greet I thee, my earth, . . ." This is almost a thousand years after the invading Angles, Saxons, and Jutes set foot on the island's soil, but they neither knelt nor wept. Shakespeare's tragic king, whose feeling for the soil of England is so powerful, shows how the people had shaped a country that had, in turn, shaped them.

How did English writers respond to their island geography?

The Placeless Sea The creation of a sense of place is an important theme in the literature of those who came from elsewhere to dwell on the island. In a way, however, this work of creation begins with an awareness of what is the opposite of place. For islanders, that means the sea, both a protective barrier and an untamable threat. As a watery wilderness, the sea is a kind of placeless place, a vast nowhere that can separate one from home.

"The Seafarer" and "The Wanderer" Two Anglo-Saxon poems chilled by images of the sea, "The Seafarer" and "The Wanderer," are spoken by men on sea voyages. They tell of exile and separation from a remembered home. The bleakness of these poems of lonely struggle is, however, tempered by a different frame of values. Resigned and even bitter as they must have been in their original forms, these poems have come down

TIMELINE

732: France Charles Martel defeats Moors. ▼

656

712: Spain Seville conquered by Moors.

▲ c. 750: Surviving version of *Beowulf* composed.

Enrichment: Understanding Language

Listening to Old and Middle English

Have students listen to the readings in Old English (from *Beowulf*) and in Middle English (from the Prologue to *The Canterbury Tales*) on the **Listening to Literature Audio CDs.**

Before playing the reading from *Beowulf*, have students read lines 530–542 of the poem. Knowing the basic meaning of the passage may help them identify words. Have students listen to the Middle English. After they hear the recording, **ask** them how much they understood, and have them use dictionaries to identify words with Anglo-Saxon and French roots.
Possible responses: An Anglo-Saxon word is *droghte* (drought); a word with a French root is *vertu* (virtue).
Activity: Looking at Words Have students use the **Investigating Language** worksheet, *Professional Development Guidebook*, page 234, to help them record other words with an Old English or Middle English origin. Ask them to analyze what these words might indicate about the people who spoke these languages.

to us in copies made by monks. These monks were aware that Christianity itself begins with a story of exile: Adam and Eve banished from the Garden of Eden. In the Christian tradition, all exile is a model of the exile of humankind from its rightful place in Heaven. In editing "The Seafarer," monks therefore framed the sea-tossed speaker's lament for his life with the overarching Christian theme of exile from Eden, from Heaven, and from God.

The "Sea-Road" The sea also figures in the first epic poem of British literature, *Beowulf*, which contains a distant echo of the journey of the Angles, Saxons, and Jutes to England. In this poem, the hero Beowulf and his men travel by ship to the land of the Danes to face the monster Grendel. The "sea-road," as it is called in the poem, is not merely a threatening watery waste. It is a "road" to fame and honor—and a natural place for these seafaring warriors.

The Mead Hall The destination for Beowulf and his men is not a nation in our modern sense. It is a kingdom, whose capital and command center is Herot, a mead hall. This gathering place—a large building with a single room—probably smelled like a locker room, but it provided warmth, light, food, drink, song, and fellowship for a lord and his warriors. When the monster Grendel comes from the bleak and mysterious darkness to menace Herot, he is striking at the very center of human society, the hearth around which people gather. That is why Beowulf must meet him there and drive him back into the swamp, the dark place from which he comes.

The BRITISH TRADITION

THE CHANGING ENGLISH LANGUAGE
by Richard Lederer

The Beginnings of English

The rise of English as a planetary language is an unparalleled success story that began, long ago, in the middle of the fifth century A.D. Several large tribes of sea rovers—the Angles, Saxons, and Jutes—invaded the islands then known as Britannia. They brought with them a Low Germanic tongue that, in its new setting, became Anglo-Saxon, or Old English. The language came to be called *Englisc*, after *Englaland*, "land of the Angles."

Old English differs so much from modern English that it is harder for us to learn than German is. Still, we can recognize a number of Anglo-Saxon words: *bedd, can-del, eorth,* and *waeter.* Anglo-Saxon words such as these concern the unchanging basics of life. They survived later social upheavals nearly unchanged.

A dramatic evolution in the language came after yet another conquest of England, this one by the Norman French. These Normans (shortened from *Northmen*) had originally been Vikings, but they now spoke French and had taken to French customs. In 1066, under William, Duke of Normandy, the Normans invaded England. One result was that Old Englisc was flooded by the French spoken by the Normans. Examples of French influence include the words *sir, madam, courtesy, honor,* and *royal*. From this infusion of French words emerged a tongue that today we call Middle English.

793: Vikings attack Lindisfarne. ▼

▲ **800: Peru**
Incas build city of Machu Picchu.

861: North Atlantic
Vikings discover Iceland.

863

The British Tradition

The Changing English Language

1. Have students read the sidebar feature about the beginnings of the English language.

2. Tell students that in addition to the Angles, Saxons, Jutes, and Normans, the Danes also brought a Germanic language to England. The Celts, who contributed to the English language, were a group who did not arrive from the European continent, but rather came from Ireland.

3. **Ask** students what kinds of events caused important changes in early English.
   Possible answer: Conquest and invasion contributed to the development of early English.

4. Review the examples of English words with Norman roots. **Ask** students what areas of life they think the English words adapted from the Normans mostly concern.
   Possible answer: Normans dominated the upper strata of society. They influenced the vocabulary of courtly behavior and etiquette.

Critical Viewing

Analyze

1. Direct students to the Timeline illustration on page 7 of the Viking ship. Point out that recent replicas of this kind of ship have actually crossed the Atlantic.

2. **Ask** students how the ship is similar to or different from modern ships.
   Possible response: Modern ships retain the streamlined hull, but not the elaborate decorations. Modern ships are made of steel, are powered by engines, and have rudders in the stern. The Viking ship is made of wood, is powered by sail and oar, and has its rudder at the side.

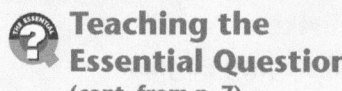
3. **Ask** the second stepping-stone question: *How did literature make a nation of an island?*
Possible response: In writing *A History of the English Church and People,* Bede indicates that England is becoming a nation. His writing indicates that what happened in England is as important as its location or its geography. Chaucer's stories show England as a place in which people move and one in which people share common stories.

Applying the Essential Question

1. Summarize the class discussion of the two stepping-stone questions on pages 6–8.
2. Then **ask** students this question: What would writers today focus on when writing about the United States as a place?
Possible response: Writers might focus on the United States as being a land of diversity, both in terms of physical features as well as population.

Background

Literature

To make literature and other documents more accessible, King Alfred the Great oversaw translations of Bede's *History* and other works from Latin into Anglo-Saxon, the everyday language of the people. In this way he fostered the growth of the English language and its literature. He also began to keep records of English history in *The Anglo-Saxon Chronicle,* one of our principal sources of information on early English life.

How did literature make a nation of an island?

A Place of Shared Stories In the 8th century, Bede, a learned monk, wrote *A History of the English Church and People,* marking an important stage in England's developing sense of itself as an island-nation. With his knowledge of Latin and history, Bede was not interested in merely telling the story of a single clan's mead hall. Instead, he wrote the history of an entire nation—"Britain, formerly known as Albion."

Through Bede's informative prose, the reader can sense how "the island in the ocean" he describes, with its abundant resources, is on its way to becoming the earth to which Shakespeare's Richard II will kneel. Most importantly, Bede is aware that his island is becoming a nation, a place that is as much a product of its history as of its geography; a country is a geographical area with shared stories.

A Nation Created by Imagination Chaucer's *Canterbury Tales,* England's greatest medieval poem, is all about "shared stories" and a sense of England as a nation of different social types. These various characters are on a pilgrimage to the town of Canterbury. There, in 1170, Thomas à Becket, the Archbishop of Canterbury, was murdered in the cathedral on the orders of his former friend King Henry II, to whom he would not yield in matters of church policy. Becket was canonized, or declared a saint, and the cathedral became a shrine. That is why the pilgrims are traveling there, and they will seal their fellowship by telling one another stories along the way.

For Chaucer and his pilgrims, Canterbury is a somewhat distant goal, a symbol of the ultimate sacred place to which people journey on their life's pilgrimage—Heaven. Such was the ideal. Chaucer's pilgrims, however, have a wide range of motives, desires, and needs, many of which are far from noble. A later great poet and critic, John Dryden, was moved to say of Chaucer: "He has taken into the compass of his *Canterbury Tales* the various manners and humors…of the whole English nation…Not a single character has escap'd him."

In the process of inventing English poetry as we know it, Chaucer presents his pilgrims on the road. England is a place in motion, a nation created by the imagination, by the stories people tell one another. It is these shared stories, with all their humble realities, that transform the British Isles to—in the words of Shakespeare's Richard II—"Dear earth."

ESSENTIAL QUESTION VOCABULARY

These Essential Question words will help you think and write about literature and place:

exile (ek´ sīl´) *n.* long time living away from one's country or community, usually involuntary; banishment

geography (jē ăg´ rə fē) *n.* physical features of a region, area, or place

pilgrimage (pil´ grə mij) *n.* long journey to a holy or important place

TIMELINE

863

871: Alfred the Great becomes King of Wessex. ▶

c. 900: **Western Europe** Feudalism develops.

▲ c. 975: Saxon monks copy Old English poems into The Exeter Book.

8 From Legend to History (A.D. 449–1485)

Vocabulary Development

Essential Question Vocabulary
Students will use Essential Question Vocabulary (introduced on pp. 8, 10, and 12) when they discuss and write about the literature in the Unit. Have students practice by completing sentence starters such as these:

1. The characters in *The Canterbury Tales* are making a **pilgrimage** to Canterbury to honor _____.
2. Chaucer's tales reflect the **turbulent** fourteenth century in that they _____.

How does literature **shape or** reflect *society?*

In the ten centuries between the Germanic invasions and the dawn of the modern world, England changed from a place of warrior bands and invading tribes to a country ruled by a king, nobles, and bishops. Indeed, England was increasingly run and organized by merchants and landowners and their representatives in an evolving Parliament. The literature written during this period reflects these changes.

How did writers capture a vanishing world of tribes and clans?

The Hero's Code The world of the Anglo-Saxon epic poem *Beowulf* is that of the tribe and its leader. To become a leader a young warrior must prove himself in battle. So Beowulf crosses the sea to aid his kinsman Hrothgar, who cannot protect his people from the monster Grendel. After his victories over Grendel and Grendel's mother, Beowulf becomes the leader of his own tribe.

Vanishing World, Enduring Values The *Beowulf* poet tells a rousing story, but he also allows his listener to see and feel the world of the hero in both its glory and decline. At the end of the poem, Beowulf, with only the faithful young warrior Wiglaf at his side, battles a dragon and dies for his people. The audience knows that the poet is lamenting not only the death of a hero, but the passing of a hero's way of life.

The BRITISH TRADITION

CLOSE-UP ON HISTORY

Guilds and the Status of Women

By 1000, merchants, traders, and artisans or crafts workers formed a new middle class, ranked between nobles and peasants. This class gained power in medieval towns, with merchants and artisans forming associations called guilds.

The craft guilds of artisans represented workers in one occupation, such as weavers, bakers, or goldsmiths. Guild members made rules to protect the quality of their goods, regulate hours, and set prices. No one except guild members could work in any trade, and becoming a guild member took many years of labor.

Guilds offered opportunities to women, who worked in dozens of crafts and dominated some trades. Young girls became apprentices in trades such as ribbon-making and papermaking. Also, a woman often engaged in the same trade as her father or husband and might inherit his workshop if he died. Chaucer's Wife of Bath, a weaver, represents this type of new middle-class woman.

982: **Greenland** Eric the Red establishes first Viking Colony. ▼

991: English defeated by Danes at Battle of Maldon.

c. 1020: **America** Viking Leif Ericson explores Canadian coast.

1040: Macbeth kills Duncan I.

▲1066: Normans defeat Saxons at Hastings; William the Conqueror becomes king of England.

1070

Essential Questions Across Time **9**

Critical Viewing

Infer

1. Draw students' attention to the Timeline illustration on page 8, which shows a Saxon monk copying poems.

2. **Ask** students: What can you infer about the values of the monks who produced this work?
   Possible response: They valued learning and invested large amounts of time and resources to preserve knowledge.

Teaching the Essential Question

How does literature shape or reflect society?

1. Before they read this section, explain to students that the literature created during this period reflects the changes that occurred in England, such as those in government and society.

2. Have students read this section of the essay. Then **ask** the first stepping-stone question: *How did writers capture a vanishing world of tribes and clans?*
   Possible answer: In *Beowulf,* the writer describes the hero Beowulf who wants to become the leader of his tribe. To do so, he has to prove himself in battle. So Beowulf helps Hrothgar, a fellow tribesman, fight Grendel, a monster. His victory made him a leader of his tribe. In the end, Beowulf fights and dies for his people. At the end of the poem, the writer makes it known that the hero's way of life is coming to an end.

The British Tradition

Guilds and the Status of Women

1. **Ask** students why some workers in the United States join unions, and list students' responses on the board.

2. Have students read the sidebar feature about guilds in the Middle Ages.

3. Then **ask** students what effect they think the craft guilds had on the quality of goods produced by their members.
   Possible response: Because members needed to spend many years working before becoming guild members, and because guilds passed rules to protect the quality of their goods, the goods produced were of the highest quality.

4. **Ask** students whether they think the guilds were ahead of their time in their treatment of women.
   Possible response: The guilds provided women with opportunities and rights that were not available to them in most areas of life during the Middle Ages.

9

3. **Ask** the second stepping-stone
question on this student page:
*How did Chaucer reflect social
trends without preaching?*
Possible response: In his
poems, Chaucer does not preach
about the social ills. Instead, he
presents his characters, the society in which they live, their situations, and their feelings to the
readers. He leaves the analysis of
these characters to the reader.

Applying the Essential Question

1. Summarize the class discussion of
the two stepping-stone questions
on pages 9–10.

2. Then **ask** students on what kind
of social trends authors today
might focus.
Possible answer: Authors
might focus on trends such as the
widespread use of technology for
communication or the changes in
family structure.

How did Chaucer reflect social trends without preaching?

A Poet and His World At the other end of the period, Chaucer provides
the most complete example of the poet's interaction with his world.

Chaucer's lifetime, the late fourteenth century, was a turbulent period
in English history. The country suffered the devastations of the Black
Death and Chaucer vividly describes that plague in "The Pardoner's Tale."
In the preaching of dissident theologian John Wycliffe, the country also
experienced a foreshadowing of the Protestant Reformation, the Protestant
separation from the Catholic Church that would occur in the early sixteenth
century. Wycliffe's criticisms of the church reflected a growing discontent
with the showy wealth of some religious institutions. In the Prologue to
The Canterbury Tales, we meet a number of characters who represent
various religious orders. Their sometimes questionable behavior suggests
the controversy that would lead to the Reformation.

Showing, Not Sermonizing Chaucer, however, does not rant, rave, or
preach about corruption among religious orders or other social ills. Instead,
he shows us characters like the Monk, who spends more time hunting and
feasting than praying and fasting.

Political Turbulence In 1381, England was shaken by The Peasant's
Revolt, in which farmers and laborers demanded a greater share in the
wealth and governance of the country. King Richard II put the rebellion
down, only to lose power himself eighteen years later. London, originally
a Roman settlement on the banks of the Thames River, had by this time
grown into a great city and a center for international trade.

Rising Middle Class Part of this tumult and change involved the
replacement of feudal roles, such as knight and serf, with a newly
empowered urban middle class. Chaucer himself was a member of this
newly-rising group, as is one of his most memorable characters, the Wife
of Bath.

The Writer and Society Writers often address social issues, but not as
sociologists. Writers are interested in the human stories, the individual tale
rather than the mass phenomenon. Readers are often left to figure out
who or what is to blame or praise. The turbulent history of the later Middle
Ages is contained in Chaucer's pilgrimage—between the lines.

ESSENTIAL QUESTION VOCABULARY

These Essential Question
words will help you think
and write about literature
and society:

sociologist (sō′ sē äl′
ə jist) *n.* scientist who
studies societies and the
behavior of people in
groups

turbulent (tur′ byə lənt)
adj. full of commotion or
wild disorder

feudal (fyōod′ 'l) *adj.*
relating to a system in
which overlords granted
land to lesser lords, or
vassals, in return for
military service and in
which poor farmers
worked the land for
vassals

TIMELINE

1070

1073: Canterbury
becomes England's
religious center.

▲ 1096: **Europe and
Middle East** First Crusade
begins.

c. 1100:
France *Song of
Roland* written.

▲ c. 1130: Oxford
becomes a center for
learning.

Think Aloud

Vocabulary: Using Context

Direct students' attention to the word *tumult*
in paragraph 5 on this page. Use the following
"think aloud" to model the skill of using context to infer the meaning of the word. Say to
students:

> I may not know the meaning of the word
> *tumult.* When I read the sentence, however,
> I realize that the writer is using *tumult* to

describe the rebellion and changes occurring in England at this time. In the preceding paragraph, we learn that King Richard II
put down a rebellion by farmers and laborers. So I think *tumult* refers to the disorder
and chaos that English society faced during
Chaucer's time.

What is the relationship of the writer to *tradition?*

You may first have encountered King Arthur and the Knights of the Round Table in a book, a movie, a comic strip, or even a multi-player game. Their stories have been told, reverently and irreverently, for over a thousand years. These tales, in other words, are traditional; they have been handed down. The word *tradition* comes from the Latin *traditio,* meaning "to hand over, to transmit." Tradition in literature, however, does not simply refer to what a writer receives from the past. It also refers to what a writer does with the inheritance.

How do writers change what they have inherited?

Bequest from the Past The King Arthur stories are a kind of bequest from the past. Different authors accepted this literary inheritance but decided to use it in different ways. For example, the poet who wrote *Sir Gawain and the Green Knight* has his knight-hero submit to a series of tests that teach him something about himself. The tests come from earlier folk tales and romances, or adventure stories about knights, and the poet weaves them into a seamless whole.

Sir Thomas Malory, writing in the fifteenth century at the end of the age of chivalry, uses Arthurian legend in a different way. In his book *Morte d'Arthur* ("Death of Arthur"), Malory gathers many legends of Arthur and his companions to write an elegy, or farewell, to the era of knights.

Changing in the Telling The much earlier Anglo-Saxon epic *Beowulf* also ends on a note of farewell, with the dying hero deserted by all but one faithful follower. It is easy to imagine how this story grew in the retelling. Perhaps in the earliest recitals, the hero sails across the sea to rescue his kinsmen and kill the monster. Then, as new audiences clamor for more, the storyteller adds more exploits. Now, Beowulf must also pursue and kill the monster's mother. Still later, in an episode added by another teller, Beowulf is mortally injured by a dragon. Finally, the monk or monks who copy the tale alter it further, adding Christian elements from their own tradition.

1170: Thomas à Becket, Archbishop of Canterbury, murdered.▼

1214: Mongol leader Genghis Khan captures Peking.

▲ 1215: King John forced to sign Magna Carta.

1270

1258: First commoners allowed in Parliament.

Essential Questions Across Time **11**

Enrichment: Investigating a Literary Figure

Geoffrey Chaucer

Geoffrey Chaucer is often referred to as the father of English literature. He was also one of the first writers who wrote in the vernacular English instead of Latin. His most well-known work is *The Canterbury Tales;* however, he also wrote other short stories and poems.

Activity: Research Have students use the **Analyzing a Literary Figure** worksheet, *Professional Development Guidebook,* page 235, to help them record information about Geoffrey Chaucer's life and literary contributions.

Teaching the Essential Question

What is the relationship of the writer to tradition?

1. Before they read this section, explain to students that English writers during this period often built their stories on ones that had been handed down to them.

2. Have students read this section of the essay. Then **ask** the first stepping-stone question: *How do writers change what they have inherited?*

   Possible answer: The poet who wrote *Sir Gawain and the Green Knight* used the King Arthur stories, but in a different way than they were first presented. He wrote about a knight who undergoes a series of tests, which are based on earlier folk tales that the poet then adapts in his poem. Sir Thomas Malory also used the King Arthur stories, but wrote about the end of the era of knighthood.

(cont. on page 12)

Critical Viewing

Analyze

1. Call students' attention to the image in the Timeline of the signing of the Magna Carta. In 1215, King John signed the document, which limited the power of the king and made it clear that everyone, even the king, was subject to the law.

2. **Ask:** From the illustration, what can you tell about King John's feelings about signing the Magna Carta?

   Answer: The illustration indicates that the king was forced to sign the document. His expression shows that he was not happy to do so.

3. Have students read this section of the essay. Then **ask** the second stepping-stone question: *How did Chaucer respond to and create literary traditions?*
   Possible answer: Chaucer knew the work of Italian author Boccaccio, which included a collection of stories. Chaucer used this format in his *Canterbury Tales*.

Applying the Essential Question

1. Summarize the discussion of the two stepping-stone questions on pages 11 and 12.

2. Then **ask** students to think of traditions or stories that have been passed down to them from their parents, grandparents, or other family members. **Ask** them to write their own version of the tradition or story, using the original one as the basis. Have students share their "inherited" stories with the class.
   Possible answer: Students' stories will vary, but they should indicate the original story and then explain how they adapted it as their own.

How did Chaucer respond to and create literary traditions?

Using the Old Geoffrey Chaucer is the supreme literary artist of the English Middle Ages because he is both indebted to traditions and committed to creating them. Consider the idea of his major poem, *The Canterbury Tales*: a varied group of people are thrown together and agree to tell stories to pass the time. In 1353, the Italian author Boccaccio had used the same format in his collection of stories, the *Decameron*, in which a group of aristocrats flee to a castle to avoid the plague and agree to tell one another a hundred tales. Chaucer knew Italian literature and the work of Boccaccio. The idea of a group of stories held together by a frame story is his inheritance.

Making It New Chaucer, however, altered what he inherited. His pilgrims reflect almost all levels of society, from the Knight to the Miller. They are not fleeing from the plague; they are on a religious pilgrimage. Chaucer's approach allows him to explore interesting differences between noble and base motives. For example, the Wife of Bath may be on a pilgrimage not so much to worship at a saint's tomb as to meet her next husband. Chaucer uses each tale to reveal something about the teller.

Inventing The Rhythm of English Poetry Chaucer not only reinvented the frame story; he also reinvented a French verse form to create the iambic pentameter line that would dominate English poetry for hundreds of years. Chaucer knew the ten-syllable lines and rhyming couplets used in French poetry. With the instinct that comes only with real genius, he adapted that form to English. In his rhyming couplets, Chaucer used a line of ten syllables with five alternating accents, the form known as iambic pentameter. This new form, when rediscovered by poets in the sixteenth century, became one of the most enduring traditions in English literature.

Traditions Stretching Backward and Forward The beginnings of literature are lost in the mists of prehistory, when some forms of telling stories came into being. Successive generations used those forms to relate the history of the tribe for each new generation. When these stories came to be written down, traditional forms were established. The wonder of literature in this period is that we can see traditions stretching backward into archeological time and stretching forward to tomorrow.

ESSENTIAL QUESTION VOCABULARY

These Essential Question words will help you think and write about the writer and tradition:

traditional (trə dish´ə nəl) *adj.* relating to or based on old customs, beliefs, and ways of doing things

inheritance (in her´i təns) *n.* goods, ideas, literary creations, or skills received from the past

legend (lej´ənd) *n.* story handed down for generations and believed to be based on actual events

TIMELINE

1270

1275: China Marco Polo visits court of Kubla Khan. ▶

1277: England conquers Wales.

1291: Europe and Middle East End of Crusades.

1325: Mexico Aztecs establish Mexico city and create a dating system with a solar year of 365 days. ▼

12 From Legend to History (A.D. 449–1485)

The BRITISH TRADITION

King Arthur: Legendary Hero, Broadway Star!

In medieval Europe, tales circulated of a legendary king named Arthur. He and his knights represented the ideals of chivalry—rules governing the behavior of knights. Since then, Arthur's story has surfaced in many literary and dramatic works. Most recently, it has been brought to life in *Spamalot*, a musical comedy that pokes fun at the legend, as follows:

- King Arthur's kingdom is a Las Vegas resort, not the town of Camelot.
- The knights of the Round Table are a motley crew who have to be talked into performing heroic deeds.
- Arthur's knights underwent trials and ordeals to prove their courage and virtue. *Spamalot*'s crew, however, must prove themselves by producing a Broadway musical.

Despite its silliness, *Spamalot*'s success proves the ongoing fascination with the legend. Tales of romance and courage never go out of style.

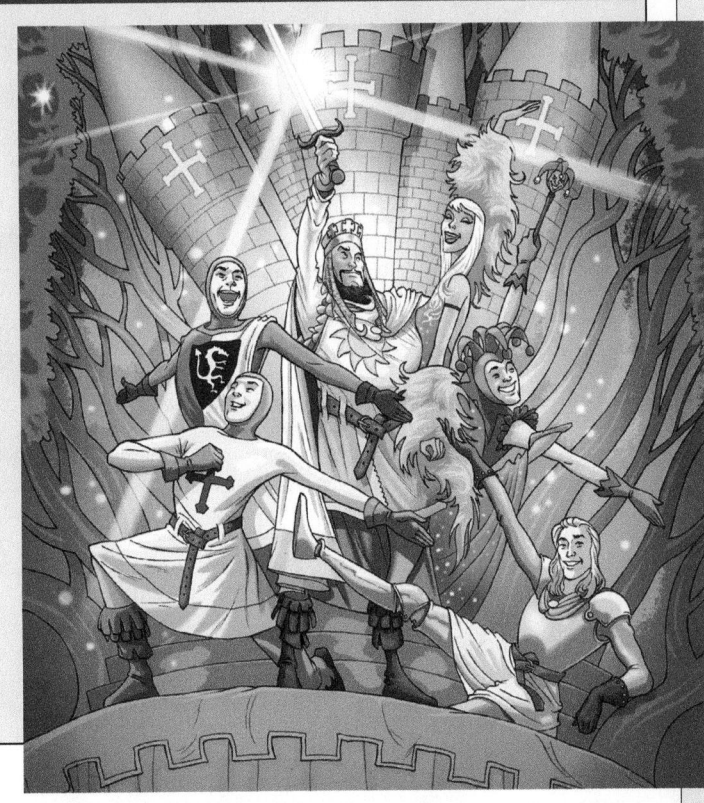

1337: Beginning of the Hundred Years' War with France.

1348: Black Death begins sweeping through England.

1381: Bible first translated into English.

1429: France Joan of Arc leads French in breaking siege of Orléans.

1453: Germany First Gutenberg Bible printed.▼

1455–1485: The Wars of the Roses.

1485

The British Tradition

Contemporary Connection

1. Have students read the sidebar feature about the musical comedy *Spamalot*.

2. Tell students that *Spamalot* is based on the movie *Monty Python and the Holy Grail,* a comedy that spoofs stories of King Arthur and his knights. Explain that *Monty Python* refers to a group of British comedy actors, famous for their comedy show *Monty Python's Flying Circus*.

3. **Ask** students how *Spamalot* illustrates the essential question regarding writer and tradition. **Possible answer:** Like Sir Thomas Malory's *Morte d' Arthur, Spamalot* builds on the stories of King Arthur. Unlike Malory's work, *Spamalot* pokes fun at the legend.

Critical Viewing

Analyze

1. Call students' attention to the image of the printing of the Gutenberg Bible. Tell students that Johannes Gutenberg invented a printing process using moveable type.

2. **Ask:** What does the image show? How do you think this invention affected access to literary works by people in the Middle Ages? **Possible answer:** The illustration shows Gutenberg examining a page printed on his printing press. This invention led to literary works being printed on a larger scale, making them accessible to more people.

Recent Scholarship
Burton Raffel

1. Burton Raffel introduces the unit and provides insights into Britain's early settlers. His introduction to *Beowulf* appears later in the unit on page 36.

2. Have students read the Meet the Author feature about Burton Raffel. Tell students that Raffel has taught at universities in the United States, Israel, and Canada. He practiced law on Wall Street, and besides writing numerous translations, he has written poetry and critical studies.

3. Use the *See It!* DVD to introduce Burton Raffel. Show Segment 1 to provide insights into his career. You can also view the video from this page in the **Enriched Online Student Edition** at **www. PHLitOnline.com.**

4. After students have watched the segment, discuss the role of a translator.

Recent Scholarship

England's Green, Fertile Land

Burton Raffel

We tell jokes about the rainy English climate. A warm ocean current brings that moisture, and makes England the green, fertile land it still is. When the last ice age ended, some three thousand years ago, all across Europe easy hunting ended with it, and people without rich pasturage and easy farming went hungry. The English Channel was not as broad as it is today, and wave after wave of immigrants came pouring across.

Daily Life

Life for England's earliest settlers was in many ways much like that still lived in England, as recently as the early nineteenth century. Cities were, for the most part, a thing of the future, though London was even then beginning to become a rich, bustling port. People lived on and by the land, which was worked by both men and women. Sheep were kept for their wool, pigs for their meat, chickens for their eggs. Most people raised a large percentage of the food they ate. There were no shops where one could buy such necessities as clothing (woven and sewn by hand), though artisans like blacksmiths made tools and other metallic items. Most of the land was owned by nobles, both hereditary and newly created aristocrats, having been made counts and earls as kingly rewards. There were many kingdoms on the island now called England and a good deal of quarreling between and among them.

Kings, Lords, Knights, and Peasants

Society was hierarchical—that is, very little moved upward from the peasant level, and virtually everything proceeded downward from the nobility. No one imagined questioning the necessity for these largely fixed relationships. Without leadership, no community would function, and no stability would have been possible. These were matters as much taken for granted as, today, automobiles and television sets. Most of what we would call "work" was performed by those at the lower levels of society. We have no direct testimony from them, but from drawings and paintings, and surviving documents written by clergy or the minority of

About the Author

Burton Raffel (b. 1928) is a noted scholar and poet. You might also call him a time traveler. His work as a translator of world literature has taken him back in time to Anglo-Saxon England, with his versions of *Beowulf* and "The Seafarer," and to Renaissance France, with his version of Rabelais's *Gargantua and Pantagruel*—to name just two of his many translations. When he is not breaking the time barrier, Raffel serves as a professor of English at the University of Louisiana.

aristocrats who could read and write, there is a sense of relatively prosperous busyness. England was a rich habitat, as its inhabitants well knew. What overseas trading there was usually involved costly goods that only a few could afford. There was a good deal of local trading, most of which was conducted on the barter principle. Aristocrats dressed elaborately and expensively; most others dressed very plainly, both men and women wearing loose-fitting garments very like what we today call "smocks."

People not only worked, but they played. There was a good deal of group dancing: the songs we call "carols" in fact began as dance music. There were harvest and other agricultural festivals, and there were more solemn religious festivals. For both the secular and the holy festivities, there were other entertainments, from storytelling to dramatic presentations.

From Many Kingdoms to One Nation

By the ninth century, some unification of the country's many kingdoms had occurred. Alfred the Great was the most notable English ruler, though still not entirely in control. Immigrants and Anglo-Saxon "natives" pulled and tugged at one another, and continued to fight over the prosperous green land. It was William of Brittany (in France) who finally created as much unity as England was to know for almost another five hundred years. In 1066, at the Battle of Hastings, William the Conqueror defeated an Anglo-Saxon opponent and became the increasingly powerful king of England. The kind of feudal structure he enforced was based on a close accounting of wealth, as reported, at William's direction, by the famous Domesday Book. William's England, now a Norman French "colony," was officially a French-speaking land: indeed, English law courts employed French until the sixteenth century.

But toward the end of the Anglo-Saxon period, we do not know exactly when, someone, somewhere, produced a poetic narrative, probably meant as a guide to proper kingship. This famous book is known as *Beowulf*.

© Collaboration: Speaking and Listening

Burton Raffel refers to the conflict between "Anglo-Saxon 'natives'" and Viking or Danish "immigrants." Suppose you were a council of Viking leaders planning to invade England. Hold a **small group discussion** about the map of Anglo-Saxon Kingdoms below, answering these questions as you make your military plans:

- Which region or regions might aid you in your fight? Why?
- Which regions might oppose your invasion most strongly? Why?
- Would it be easier to sail your war ships down the Ouse River or the Thames? Explain.

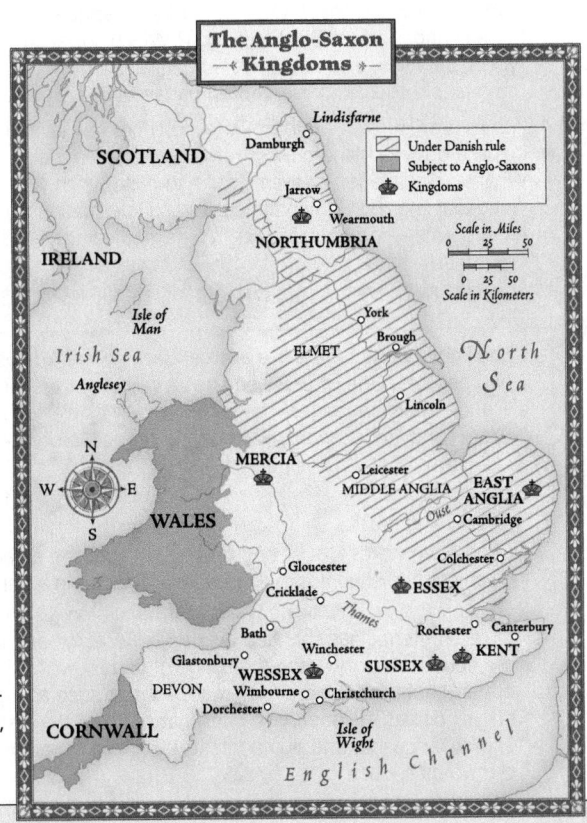

The Anglo-Saxon Kingdoms

Recent Scholarship **15**

Collaboration: Speaking and Listening

1. Review the assignment with students.

2. Organize students into small groups. Instruct each group to discuss answers to the questions for developing their military plans. Remind them to study the map on the page and to locate the area from which the Vikings would be invading (Scandinavia) on a map of Europe.

3. After students discuss the answers to the questions and develop a military plan, ask each group to appoint a representative. Invite student representatives to present the group's military plan to the class. Hold a class discussion to choose the plan the students believe would be most effective for the Viking invasion of England.

4. To help conduct the discussion, use the **Discussion Guide** in the *Professional Development Guidebook*, page 77.

ASSESS

Common Core State Standards

- **Reading Informational Text 7**
- **Language 1.a**
- **Speaking and Listening 1**

Integrate and Evaluate Information

1. Review the chart assignment with the class. Then, ask students to use the Activity I chart in the **Follow-Through** worksheet (p. 12 in *Unit 1 Resources*) to complete this activity.

   Possible response: *Literature and Society: Key Concept*—recapture ideas of leaders and tribes, *Key Author*—Beowulf (author unknown); *Writer and Tradition: Key Concept*—celebrate knights and romance, *Key Author*—Chaucer

2. **Possible response:** The map on p. 3 adds to the understanding of how different languages were brought to England by invaders. The image on p. 11, which shows King John sitting while the nobles stand, adds to the understanding of the nobles' power to force the king to sign the Magna Carta.

3. **Possible response:** England's various social types include royalty, aristocrats, and the middle class. During the medieval period, the social structure of feudalism included kings, nobles and freemen, and serfs. An urban middle class developed with merchants, traders, and artisans, or crafts workers, who formed guilds. Over time, feudalism declined; the middle class replaced the feudal knights and serfs. The monarchy survived but was weakened, and parliamentary government—representing merchants and landowners—was established.

4. **Possible response:** Students might mention stories, films, and video games about Robin Hood or King Arthur and the Knights of the Round Table that bring to mind images of royalty, castles, feasts in huge halls, knights, sword fights, and shooting contests with bow and arrow. Some might also mention the powerful role of the church in medieval society.

Speaking and Listening

1. Review the assignment with the class. Point out that students are to create a list of words for one of the categories and discuss the words' current meanings and etymologies. Students will explain how and why the usage of certain words has changed over time.

2. Then, have students complete Activity II in the **Follow-Through** worksheet (p. 12 in *Unit 1 Resources*).

3. After students have completed their lists, ask each group to choose a representative to participate in the panel discussion and present the group's findings to the class.

 COMMON CORE ▪ MULTIPLE PERSPECTIVES ON THE ERA

Integrate and Evaluate Information

1. Use a chart like the one shown to determine the key ideas expressed in the Essential Question essays on pages 6–12. Fill in two ideas related to each Essential Question and note the authors most closely associated with each concept. One example has been done for you.

Essential Question	Key Concept	Key Author
Literature and Place	Exile to a foreign land	"Seafarer" (author unknown)
Literature and Society		
Writer and Tradition		

2. How do the visual sources in this section—artifacts, paintings, photographs, and illustrations—add to your understanding of the ideas expressed in words? Cite specific examples.

3. On page 8, medieval England is described as "a nation of different social types." Using information from the multiple sources presented in this section, explain how this is so. What social structures produced these "types"? How did these social structures change over time, and how did these changes affect the population? Which social structures—and social types—survived, and which were replaced by others? Cite evidence from the multiple sources presented on pages 4–15 in your answer.

4. **Address a Question** Burton Raffel describes medieval England as a prosperous and bustling island pulsing with commerce, recreation, and, often, war. What stories, images, or events come to mind when you hear the phrase "medieval England"? Integrate details and information from this textbook and other sources—including movies, novels, and games—to support your ideas.

Speaking and Listening: Panel Discussion

The English language is like a large machine that draws its power from two engines. One of these engines is built from the Anglo-Saxon and Scandinavian languages. The other, equally powerful, is fueled by Latin, Greek, and French words. Working in groups, pick one of the following categories:

- Domestic Life
- Law and Politics
- Science and Medicine
- Recreation and Athletics

Choose ten words that belong to your category and determine their current meanings and *etymologies*. Present your findings in a **panel discussion.**

Solve a Research Problem: In your discussion, explain how usage of certain terms has changed over time. Research and describe any moments in history when the usage of certain words caused conflicts or was contested. Consult reference sources such as dictionaries and encyclopedias, secondary sources that describe the history of the English language, and primary texts—such as literary works—in which the words appear.

16 From Legend to History (A.D. 449–1485)

Common Core State Standards

Reading Informational Text

7. Integrate and evaluate multiple sources of information presented in different media or formats as well as in words in order to address a question or solve a problem.

Language

1.a. Apply the understanding that usage is a matter of convention, can change over time, and is sometimes contested.

Speaking and Listening

1. Initiate and participate effectively in a range of collaborative discussions with diverse partners on *grades 11–12 topics, texts, and issues,* building on others' ideas and expressing their own clearly and persuasively.

ESSENTIAL QUESTION VOCABULARY

Use these words in your responses:

Literature and Place
exile
geography
pilgrimage

Literature and Society
sociologist
turbulent
feudal

Writer and Tradition
traditional
inheritance
legend

Earthly Exile, Heavenly Home

PART 1

17

Text Complexity: At a Glance

This chart gives a general text complexity rating for the selections in this part of the unit to help guide instruction. For additional text complexity support, see the Test Complexity Rubric at point of use.

The Seafarer	**More Complex**
The Wanderer	**More Complex**
The Wife's Lament	**More Accessible**

Selection Planning Guide

The selections in this section explore the theme of exile in Anglo-Saxon poetry. "The Seafarer" tells the tale of a sailor whose passion for the sea causes him to undertake dangerous, lonely voyages. The plight of a warrior who must find a new place in the world after his lord dies is described in "The Wanderer." In "The Wife's Lament," a woman whose husband has sent her away describes her misfortune.

Humanities

Viking Ship, 19th Century by Sir Edward Burne-Jones (1833–1898)

Burne-Jones was born in Birmingham, England. A student of Dante Rossetti, he became interested in the revival of traditional stained glass art. In addition to his glassworks, Burne-Jones also painted; designed ceramic tiles, jewelry, and tapestries; and illustrated books. *Viking Ship, 19th Century* exemplifies his narrative style, which was strongly influenced by the Italian Renaissance and by medieval legend.

Use these questions for discussion:

1. Why do you think there was a revival of interest in telling traditional stories through the medium of art glass?
   Possible response: Because of the way the rich jeweled colors of stained glass interact with light, the craftsman can use effects of light and color to create moods and atmosphere. This makes the architectural element well suited to telling dramatic stories.

2. What details of this Viking ship help explain why these people were often depicted as barbaric raiders?
   Possible response: The Viking ship's billowing sail makes it look very swift. It could carry many fierce warriors. The ship also has a dragon on its prow, which suggests pagan influences.

Monitoring Progress

Before students read the Anglo-Saxon poetry selections, refer to the results for the **Diagnostic Test** (*Unit 1 Resources* p. 1). Use this test to guide your choice of selections to teach as well as the depth of preparation you will provide, based on students' readiness for reading and vocabulary skills.

The Seafarer • The Wanderer • The Wife's Lament
Lesson Pacing Guide

DAY 1   Preteach

- © Administer the Reading and Vocabulary Warm-ups (*Unit 1 Resources*, pp. 13–16) as necessary.
- Introduce the Literary Analysis concept: Anglo-Saxon Lyrics and the Elegy.
- © Introduce the Reading Strategy: Understand Historical Context.
- Build background with the author and Background features.
- Develop thematic thinking with Connecting to the Essential Question.
- © Teach the selection vocabulary.

DAY 2   Preteach/Teach/Extend

- © Distribute copies of the appropriate graphic organizer for the Reading Strategy (*Graphic Organizer Transparencies*, pp. 1–2).
- © Distribute copies of the appropriate graphic organizer for Literary Analysis (*Graphic Organizer Transparencies*, pp. 3–4).
- Prepare students to read with the Activating Prior Knowledge activities (TE).
- Informally monitor comprehension while students read.
- Use the Reading Check questions to confirm comprehension.
- Develop students' understanding of Anglo-Saxon lyrics and elegies using the Literary Analysis prompts.
- Develop students' ability to understand historical context using the Reading Strategy prompts.
- © Reinforce vocabulary with the Vocabulary notes.
- © Assess students' comprehension and mastery of the skills by having them answer the Critical Reading, Literary Analysis, and Reading Strategy questions.

DAY 3   Assess

- Have students complete the Vocabulary activity.
- © Have students complete the Writing activity and write an editorial. (You may assign as homework.)
- © Administer Selection Test A or B (*Unit 1 Resources,* pp. 25–27 or 28–30).

© Common Core State Standards

Reading Literature 4. Determine the meaning of words and phrases as they are used in the text, including figurative meanings.
5. Analyze how an author's choices concerning how to structure specific parts of a text contribute to its overall structure and meaning as well as its aesthetic impact.

Writing 1. Write arguments to support claims in an analysis of substantive topics or texts, using valid reasoning and relevant and sufficient evidence.

Language 5. Demonstrate understanding of word relationships and nuances in word meanings.

Additional Standards Practice
Common Core Companion, pp. 41–48; 54–55; 185–195; 332–335

Daily Block Scheduling
Each day in this Lesson Pacing Guide represents a 40–50 minute period. Teachers using block scheduling may combine days to revise pacing. In addition, teachers may differentiate and support core instruction by integrating components for extended and intensive support as students require. See the Guide to Selected Leveled Resources (facing page).

Guide to Selected Leveled Resources

R T I Tier 1 (students performing on level)

The Seafarer • The Wanderer • The Wife's Lament

Warm Up	**Practice, model,** and **monitor** fluency, working **with the whole class** or **in groups**.	**Vocabulary and Reading Warm-ups B,** *Unit 1 Resources,* pp. 13–14, 16
Comprehension/Skills	**Support** and **monitor** comprehension and skills development, having students complete the activities, graphic organizers, and interactive prompts **independently** or **as a class**.	• *Reader's Notebook,* adapted instruction and full selection EL *Reader's Notebook: English Learner's Version,* adapted instruction and adapted selection • **Reading Skill Graphic Organizer B,** *Graphic Organizer Transparencies,* p. 2 • **Literary Analysis Graphic Organizer B,** *Graphic Organizer Transparencies,* p. 4
Monitor Progress	**Monitor** student progress with the differentiated curriculum-based assessment in the *Unit Resources.*	• **Selection Test B,** *Unit 1 Resources,* pp. 28–30 • **Open-Book Test,** *Unit 1 Resources,* pp. 22–24

R T I Tier 2 (students requiring intervention)

The Seafarer • The Wanderer • The Wife's Lament

Warm Up	**Practice, model,** and **monitor** fluency **in groups** or **with individuals**.	• **Vocabulary and Reading Warm-ups A,** *Unit 1 Resources,* pp. 13–15 • *Hear It!* Audio CD (adapted text)
Comprehension/Skills	• **Support** and **monitor** comprehension and skills development, working **in small groups** or **with individuals**. • As students complete the selection in the appropriate version of the *Reader's Notebook,* **monitor** comprehension frequently with group questions and individual instruction. • **Model** strategies while guiding students in completing the activities and prompts in the *Reader's Notebook,* as well as the graphic organizers. • **Practice** skills and **monitor** mastery with the *Reading Kit* worksheets.	• *Reader's Notebook: Adapted Version,* adapted instruction and adapted selection EL *Reader's Notebook: English Learner's Version,* adapted instruction and adapted selection • **Reading Skill Graphic Organizer A,** *Graphic Organizer Transparencies,* p. 1 • **Literary Analysis Graphic Organizer A,** *Graphic Organizer Transparencies,* p. 3 • *Reading Kit,* Practice worksheets
Monitor Progress	**Monitor** student progress with the differentiated curriculum-based assessment in the *Unit Resources* and in the *Reading Kit.*	• **Selection Test A,** *Unit 1 Resources,* pp. 25–27 • *Reading Kit,* Assess worksheets

TIER 3 Tier 3 intervention may require consultation with the student's special-education or dyslexia specialist. For additional support, see the Tier 2 activities and resources listed above.

One-on-one teaching   Group work   Whole class instruction   Independent work   A Assessment

For a complete guide to selection support, including support for Advanced students, see the Overview of Resources in the frontmatter.

18b

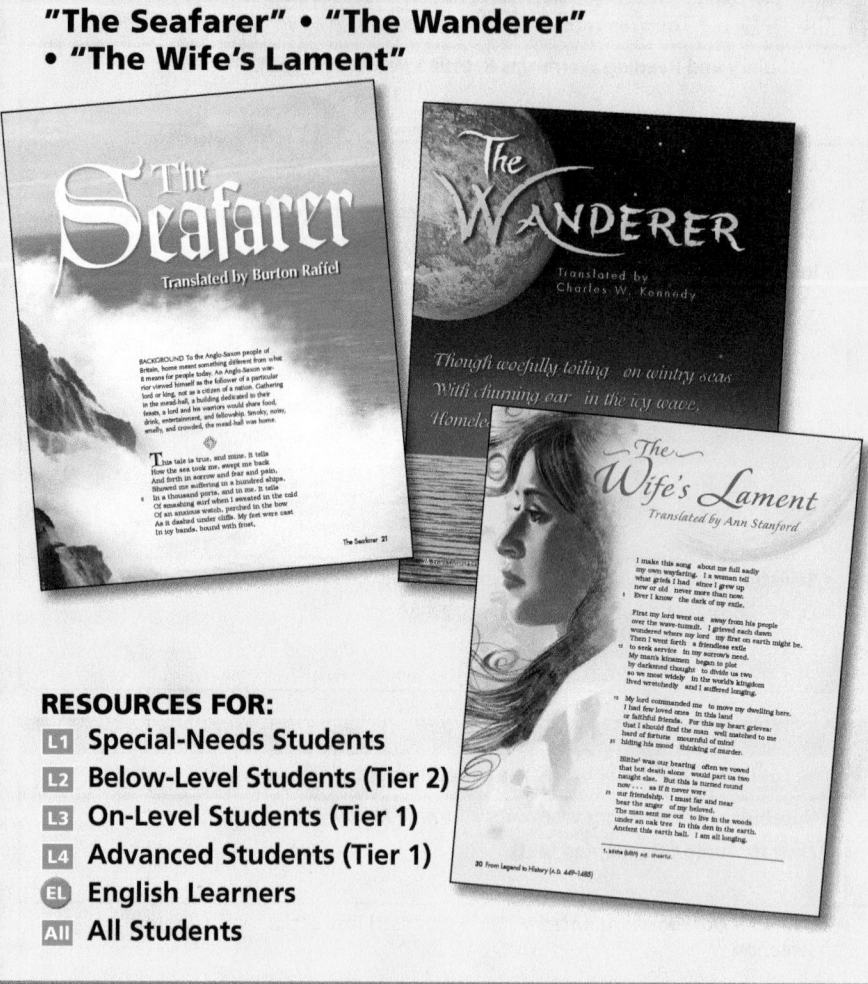

"The Seafarer" • "The Wanderer"
• "The Wife's Lament"

RESOURCES FOR:
- L1 Special-Needs Students
- L2 Below-Level Students (Tier 2)
- L3 On-Level Students (Tier 1)
- L4 Advanced Students (Tier 1)
- EL English Learners
- All All Students

Vocabulary/Fluency/Prior Knowledge

"The Seafarer," translated by Burton Raffel. "The Wanderer," translated by Charles W. Kennedy. "The Wife's Lament," translated by Ann Stanford

Vocabulary Warm-up Word Lists

Study these words from the selections. Then, complete the activities.

Word List A

perched [PURCHT] *v.* seated on a high or insecure resting place
The falcon's nest was perched on the edge of the cliff.

whirled [WHURLD] *v.* moved rapidly in a circular manner
The couple whirled around the dance floor as they waltzed.

terns [TURNZ] *n.* any birds of the seagull family
Hundreds of terns flew over the garbage dump.

unfurl [un FUHRL] *v.* to unfold or unroll
The cabin boy learned to unfurl the sails on the ship.

scorch [SKAWRCH] *v.* to shrivel or parch with heat
The sun can scorch fresh paint, causing it to blister.

billowing [BIL oh ing] *adj.* rising and rolling in large waves
The smoke was billowing from the chimney.

smitten [SMITN] *v.* fascinated with someone or something; in love
The young man was smitten with love when he read the girl's poetry.

strive [STRYV] *v.* try very hard
Always strive to do your best.

Word List B

wretched [RECH id] *adj.* deeply distressed
The wretched child could not stop crying.

desolation [DES oh LAY shun] *n.* lonely grief
The survivors of the plane crash were overcome with desolation.

tarnished [TAHR nishd] *adj.* having lost its shine, beauty, or reputation
Since the brass lamp was tarnished, the price was reduced.

decrees [dee KREEZ] *n.* authoritative orders having the force of law
When our team won, the mayor issued decrees renaming streets in the team's honor.

brood [BROOD] *v.* think about something constantly out of worry or anger
Until he failed the test, the student had no reason to brood about his grades.

fleeting [FLEET ing] *adj.* passing quickly
The star was surrounded by bodyguards, so the crowd only got a fleeting glimpse of him.

mournful [MAWRN full] *adj.* suggesting sadness
Whether played at parades or funerals, the bagpipes have a mournful sound.

naught [NAWT] *n.* nothing
When the rain washed away the seeds, the farmer's work was for naught.

Unit 1 Resources: From Legend to History
© Pearson Education, Inc. All rights reserved.

Unit 1 Resources

EL L1 L2 **Vocabulary Warm-ups A and B,** pp. 13–14

Also available for these selections:
EL L1 L2 **Reading Warm-ups A and B,** pp. 15–16
All **Vocabulary Builder,** p. 19

Reader's Notebooks

Pre- and postreading pages for these selections appear in an interactive format in the *Reader's Notebooks*. Each *Notebook* is differentiated for a different group of learners. The selections in the Adapted and English Learner's versions are abridged.

- L2 L3 *Reader's Notebook*
- L1 *Reader's Notebook: Adapted Version*
- EL *Reader's Notebook: English Learner's Version*
- EL *Reader's Notebook: Spanish Version*

© *Common Core Companion*

Additional instruction and practice for each Common Core State Standard

Selection Support

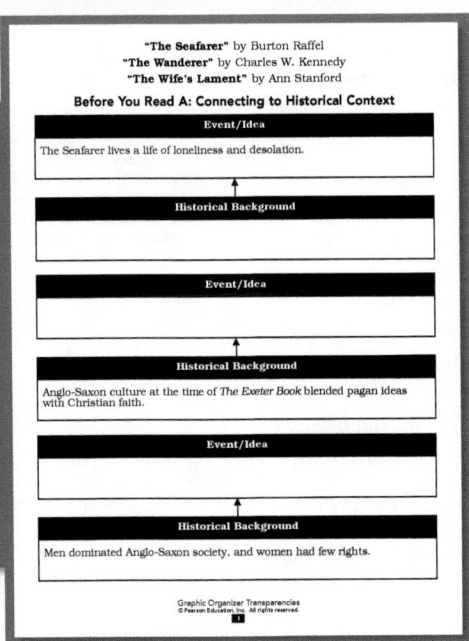

Graphic Organizer Transparencies

"The Seafarer" by Burton Raffel
"The Wanderer" by Charles W. Kennedy
"The Wife's Lament" by Ann Stanford

Before You Read A: Connecting to Historical Context

| Event/Idea |
| The Seafarer lives a life of loneliness and desolation. |

| Historical Background |
| |

| Event/Idea |
| |

| Historical Background |
| Anglo-Saxon culture at the time of *The Exeter Book* blended pagan ideas with Christian faith. |

| Event/Idea |
| |

| Historical Background |
| Men dominated Anglo-Saxon society, and women had few rights. |

EL L3 Reading: Graphic Organizer A (partially filled in), p. 1

Also available for these selections:

EL L1 L2 Reading: Graphic Organizer B, p. 2

EL L1 L2 Literary Analysis: Graphic Organizer A (partially filled in), p. 3

EL L3 Literary Analysis: Graphic Organizer B, p. 4

Skills Development/Extension

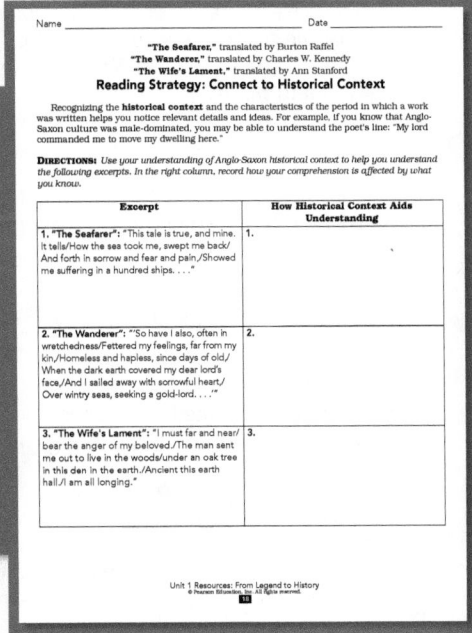

Unit 1 Resources

Name _____ Date _____

"The Seafarer," translated by Burton Raffel
"The Wanderer," translated by Charles W. Kennedy
"The Wife's Lament," translated by Ann Stanford

Reading Strategy: Connect to Historical Context

Recognizing the **historical context** and the characteristics of the period in which a work was written helps you notice relevant details and ideas. For example, if you know that Anglo-Saxon culture was male-dominated, you may be able to understand the poet's line: "My lord commanded me to move my dwelling here."

DIRECTIONS: *Use your understanding of Anglo-Saxon historical context to help you understand the following excerpts. In the right column, record how your comprehension is affected by what you know.*

Excerpt	How Historical Context Aids Understanding
1. "The Seafarer": "This tale is true, and mine. It tells/How the sea took me, swept me back/And forth in sorrow and fear and pain,/Showed me suffering in a hundred ships. . . ."	1.
2. "The Wanderer": "So have I also, often in wretchedness/Fettered my feelings, far from my kin,/Homeless and hapless, since days of old,/When the dark earth covered my dear lord's face,/And I sailed away with sorrowful heart,/Over wintry seas, seeking a gold-lord. . . ."	2.
3. "The Wife's Lament": "I must far and near/bear the anger of my beloved./The man sent me out to live in the woods/under an oak tree in this den in the earth./Ancient this earth hall./I am all longing."	3.

All Reading, p. 18

Also available for these selections:

All Literary Analysis, p. 17

EL L3 L4 Support for Writing, p. 20

L4 Enrichment, p. 21

Assessment

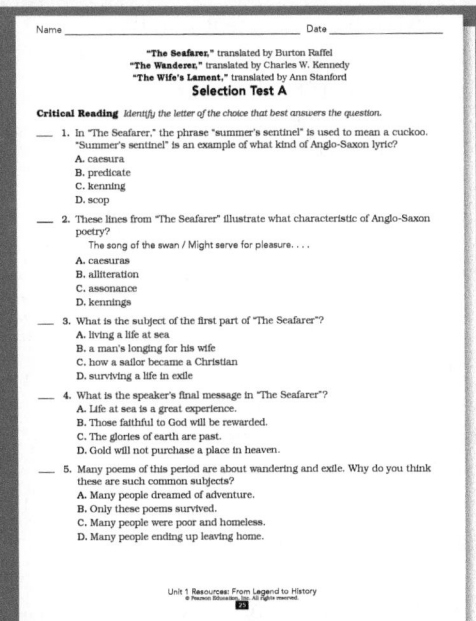

Name _____ Date _____

"The Seafarer," translated by Burton Raffel
"The Wanderer," translated by Charles W. Kennedy
"The Wife's Lament," translated by Ann Stanford

Selection Test A

Critical Reading *Identify the letter of the choice that best answers the question.*

___ 1. In "The Seafarer," the phrase "summer's sentinel" is used to mean a cuckoo. "Summer's sentinel" is an example of what kind of Anglo-Saxon lyric?
A. caesura
B. predicate
C. kenning
D. scop

___ 2. These lines from "The Seafarer" illustrate what characteristic of Anglo-Saxon poetry?
The song of the swan / Might serve for pleasure. . . .
A. caesuras
B. alliteration
C. assonance
D. kennings

___ 3. What is the subject of the first part of "The Seafarer"?
A. living a life at sea
B. a man's longing for his wife
C. how a sailor became a Christian
D. surviving a life in exile

___ 4. What is the speaker's final message in "The Seafarer"?
A. Life at sea is a great experience.
B. Those faithful to God will be rewarded.
C. The glories of earth are past.
D. Gold will not purchase a place in heaven.

___ 5. Many poems of this period are about wandering and exile. Why do you think these are such common subjects?
A. Many people dreamed of adventure.
B. Only these poems survived.
C. Many people were poor and homeless.
D. Many people ending up leaving home.

EL L1 L2 Selection Test A, pp. 25–27

Also available for these selections:

EL L3 L4 Selection Test B, pp. 28–30

L3 L4 Open-Book Test, pp. 22–24

PHLit Online!
www.PHLitOnline.com

Online Resources: All print materials are also available online.

- complete narrated selection text
- a thematically related video with writing prompt
- an interactive graphic organizer
- highlighting feature
- access to all student print resources, adapted to individual student needs
- Spanish and English summaries
- adapted selection translations in Spanish

Background Video

Also available:

Get Connected! (thematic video with writing prompt)
All videos are available in Spanish.

Vocabulary Central (tools, activities, and songs for studying vocabulary)

Also available:

Writer's Journal (with graphics feature)

Before You Read

The Seafarer •
The Wanderer •
The Wife's Lament

❶ Connecting to the Essential Question

1. Review the assignment with the class.

2. Ask students to discuss experiences of homesickness. Then, have them complete the assignment

3. As students read, have them look for specific words revealing the speakers' feelings about their lost homes.

❷ Literary Analysis

Introduce the skill using the instruction on the student page.

Think Aloud: Model the Skill

Model the skill of recognizing Anglo-Saxon lyrics and elegies. Say to students:

When I read a poem, I look for defining characteristics of its period. In "The Wanderer," I see large spaces in the middle of lines. I know that Anglo-Saxon poems use such spaces, called caesuras, to indicate pauses. Now I can search this poem and others for further characteristics of Anglo-Saxon lyrics.

❸ Reading Strategy

1. Introduce the strategy.

2. Give students a copy of **Reading Strategy Graphic Organizer B,** page 2 in *Graphic Organizer Transparencies,* to fill out as they read.

❹ Vocabulary

1. Pronounce each word, giving its definition, and have students say it aloud.

2. For more guidance, see the *Classroom Strategies and Teaching Routines* card for introducing vocabulary.

---

❶ **Connecting to the Essential Question** These poems are about people in exile—those forced from and longing for home. As you read, note what the speakers say about their lost homes. This will help you answer the Essential Question: **What is the relationship between literature and place?**

❷ Literary Analysis

A lyric poem expresses the thoughts and feelings of a single speaker. **Anglo-Saxon lyrics,** composed for easy memorization and recitation, contain the following structural elements:

- Lines with **regular rhythms,** usually with four strong beats
- **Caesuras,** pauses for breath in the middle of lines
- **Kennings,** two-word poetic renamings, like "whales' home" for the sea
- **Assonance,** repeated vowel sounds in unrhymed, stressed syllables
- **Alliteration,** repeated initial consonant sounds in stressed syllables

Comparing Literary Works Shaped by these devices, each lyric in this grouping is an **elegy**—a poem mourning the loss of someone or something. Compare and contrast the types of loss experienced by the speakers in these poems. Also, analyze and compare the ways in which the writers used poetic devices to *convey a mood* of sadness.

❸ Reading Strategy

Ⓒ **Preparing to Read Complex Texts** It is helpful to **understand the historical context** of a literary work, the time in which it was created. Anglo-Saxon England, for example, was a collection of warring kingdoms, not a single nation. In this uncertain situation, people gave loyalty to a lord in return for his protection. Also, men dominated society, and women relied on men for protection. As you read, use a diagram like the one shown to find connections between the characters and settings in these poems and the historical issues of the era.

❹ Vocabulary

admonish (ad män′ ish) *v.* advise; caution (p. 23)

sentinel (sen′ ti nəl) *n.* person or animal that guards (p. 23)

fervent (fur′ vənt) *adj.* having great warmth of feeling (p. 23)

rancor (raŋ′ kər) *n.* ill will; continuing and bitter hate (p. 23)

compassionate (kəm pash′ ən it) *adj.* sympathizing; pitying (p. 27)

rapture (rap′ chər) *n.* joy; great pleasure (p. 28)

Ⓒ **Common Core State Standards**

Reading Literature
5. Analyze how an author's choices concerning how to structure specific parts of a text contribute to its overall structure and meaning as well as its aesthetic impact.

Event/Idea

The speaker is exiled when his lord dies.

Historical Background

Anglo-Saxon warriors depended on the protection of a powerful lord.

18 From Legend to History (A.D. 449–1485)

Vocabulary Development

Vocabulary Knowledge Rating
Create a **Vocabulary Knowledge Rating Chart** *(Professional Development Guidebook,* p. 33*)* for the vocabulary words on the student page. Give each student a copy of the chart with the words on it. Read the words aloud, and have students mark their rating of each in the Before Reading column. When students have completed reading and discussing the group of selections, have them take out their **Vocabulary Knowledge Rating Charts** for the selections. Read the words aloud and have students rate their knowledge again in the After Reading column. Clarify any words that are still problematic. Then, have students complete the Vocabulary practice at the end of the selections.

Vocabulary Central, featuring tools, and activities for studying vocabulary, is available online at **www.PHLitOnline.com.**

⑤ *from* The Exeter Book

"The Seafarer" • "The Wanderer" • "The Wife's Lament"

Imagine what life would be like if there were no television sets and if movies played in theaters only on important occasions. People would gather beforehand, chatting excitedly. The next day, everyone would discuss the film, quoting dialogue and reenacting scenes.

Telling the Story This scenario captures the nature of entertainment during Britain's Anglo-Saxon period, from the fifth to the eleventh century. Few people of the time were able to read, and movies lay centuries in the future. Instead, people turned to traveling storytellers, known as *scops*, who created an oral tradition by memorizing, adapting, and passing along stories and songs. Through the years, many of these works were lost. Others, however, were eventually written down.

An Early Anthology *The Exeter Book* is a collection of manuscripts that includes pieces of this tradition. The book was probably compiled by monks during the reign of Alfred the Great, A.D. 871–899. Without *The Exeter Book*, many stories that came out of the oral tradition would have been lost to us forever. "The Seafarer," "The Wanderer," and "The Wife's Lament" were all discovered in this collection.

Guests Who Came to Stay Those who recited and listened to the tales recorded in *The Exeter Book*—the Anglo-Saxons—were not native to Britain. In the 400s, Roman soldiers stationed in Britain had abandoned the island to defend Rome. The native inhabitants were soon threatened by Picts from Scotland and Scots from Ireland. One British king invited warlike Germanic tribes from Europe to help him defend Britain. These "guests" proved to be the most dangerous invaders of them all. By the 500s, Angles, Saxons, and other Germanic peoples had settled Britain themselves, driving out most of the Britons. By the end of the 600s, these new inhabitants of the island thought of themselves as part of an English nation, and in A.D. 827, King Egbert named Britannia *Englaland*, "land of the Angles."

A Growing Culture The Angles and Saxons brought with them a warrior culture, a seafaring tradition, and pagan beliefs, including a grim, fatalistic view of the world. They were followed by missionaries sent by Rome. Eventually, these missionaries converted Britain to Christianity. Anglo-Saxon culture at the time of *The Exeter Book* was a blend, mixing pagan ideas of fate with Christian faith in heaven, the boasts of proud warriors with lessons about humility. Preserved by scops and monks, this culture gave Britain its first literature.

▲ Anglo-Saxon artifact from the 7th century A.D.: the great gold buckle from the Sutton Hoo ship burial

The Seafarer • The Wanderer • The Wife's Lament **19**

Daily Bellringer

For each class during which you will teach these selections, have students complete one of the five activities for the appropriate week in the *Daily Bellringer Activities* booklet.

Multidraft Reading

To assist struggling readers and to enhance reading for all, assign the text in chunks, as warranted by length, and apply multidraft reading protocols. For each reading, have students set the purpose indicated:

- **First reading**—identifying key ideas and details and answering any Reading Checks.
- **Second reading**—analyzing craft and structure and responding to the side-column prompts.
- **Third reading**—integrating knowledge and ideas, connecting to other texts and the world, and answering the end-of-selection questions.

For more guidance, refer to the *Classroom Strategies and Teaching Routines* card on multidraft reading.

⑤ Background
More About the Authors

No one knows the names of the authors of these poems, but we do know much about the era in which they were collected. Alfred the Great, King of Wessex from 871–899, was a brilliant soldier and wise ruler, but his greatest legacy was his passion for learning and literacy, which he actively promoted. He directed all young freemen to learn to read English. He learned Latin and translated many works into English. The poems in this grouping, collected during this era, are found in *The Exeter Book*, the largest collection of Old English poetry in existence and one of only four collections from the period to survive to present day. Exeter, in the southwest of England, was an important city during the Middle Ages. Around 975, this collection of poems was copied, and the manuscript was given by Bishop Leofric to Exeter Cathedral, where the book remains to this day.

❶ About the Selection

The lonely seafarer of this poem drifts in icy waters, far from human companionship. Yet, though the seafarer is "drowning in desolation" at sea, he returns to it again and again. Life itself, he realizes, no matter where it is spent, is exile: The only home is heaven.

❷ Activating Prior Knowledge

Have students share what they know about the hardships people face when leaving family and friends to relocate to an unfamiliar area, and discuss how those hardships might have been different at the time when these selections were written. Have students write a list predicting what difficulties and feelings the poets might record.

Concept Connector ➡

Tell students they will return to their responses after reading the selection.

20 From Legend to History (A.D. 449–1485)

© Text Complexity Rubric

	The Seafarer	The Wanderer	The Wife's Lament
Qualitative Measures			
Context/ Knowledge Demands	Anglo-Saxon oral tradition 1 2 ③ 4 5	Anglo-Saxon oral tradition 1 2 ③ 4 5	Anglo-Saxon oral tradition 1 2 ③ 4 5
Structure/Language Conventionality and Clarity	Long sentences; vocabulary 1 2 ③ 4 5	Archaic language; vocabulary 1 2 ③ 4 5	Poetic diction and syntax 1 2 ③ 4 5
Levels of Meaning/ Purpose/Concept Level	Challenging (abstract truths) 1 2 3 ④ 5	Challenging (accepting one's fate) 1 2 3 ④ 5	Accessible (personal feelings) 1 2 ③ 4 5
Quantitative Measures			
Lexile/Text Length	NP / 912 words	NP / 735 words	NP / 357 words
Overall Complexity	**More complex**	**More complex**	**More accessible**

The Seafarer

Translated by Burton Raffel

❶
❷

BACKGROUND To the Anglo-Saxon people of Britain, home meant something different from what it means for people today. An Anglo-Saxon warrior viewed himself as the follower of a particular lord or king, not as a citizen of a nation. Gathering in the mead-hall, a building dedicated to their feasts, a lord and his warriors would share food, drink, entertainment, and fellowship. Smoky, noisy, smelly, and crowded, the mead-hall was home.

This tale is true, and mine. It tells
How the sea took me, swept me back
And forth in sorrow and fear and pain,
Showed me suffering in a hundred ships,
5   In a thousand ports, and in me. It tells
Of smashing surf when I sweated in the cold
Of an anxious watch, perched in the bow
As it dashed under cliffs. My feet were cast
In icy bands, bound with frost,

❸

❹

The Seafarer **21**

21

The Literature of Exile

Poet Marina Tsvetaeva (1892–1941) and novelist Vladimir Nabokov (1899–1977), among others, left their homeland after the Russian Revolution. For many, the alternative to exile was silence. Boris Pasternak (1890–1960) was eventually forced to stop publishing his own original writing. Awarded the Nobel Prize in 1958, Pasternak was pressured by his government to refuse it.

For some Russian writers, then, exile made literature possible—they were free to write only if they left their homeland. Exile may be a condition for literature in another, deeper sense as well—from the singing laments of "The Seafarer" to the word play of Nabokov's novels, literature is the work of those who place their faith in words after home has been lost.

Connect to the Literature After students have read The Literature of Exile note, **ask** students: Do you think that the exile of the speaker in "The Seafarer" can touch readers in the twenty-first century? Why or why not?

Possible response: The speaker in "The Seafarer can touch readers in the twenty-first century because even today, people are exiled from their homelands. This similarity connects the speaker to readers today.

6 **Engaging the Essential Question**

1. Point out to students that in "The Seafarer," the poet's experience of the sea is juxtaposed against and colored by his experiences of other places in the world. The poet acknowledges that both pleasures and sorrow accompany life either on the sea or on land.

2. **Ask** students: What lines or words reveal the poet's memories of and feelings toward life away from the sea?
   Possible responses: In lines 48–49, the poet remembers sights on land as being beautiful. In lines 27–30, he shows feelings of disconnectedness from worldly life in the city. In lines 82–88, he laments the loss of earth's king-doms' former glory.

5 **World LITERATURE CONNECTION**

The Literature of Exile

"The Seafarer" is about exile, a long stay away from home that is often enforced but sometimes self-imposed. The theme of exile has run through world literature since ancient times. Over the centuries, many writers suffered exile, an experience that colored their work. Some fled for safety. Others were banished for political reasons.

In A.D. 8, for example, the Roman ruler Augustus Caesar sent the poet Ovid into the provinces for writing *The Art of Love*, which was deemed immoral. Ovid remained there until his death, writing *Sorrows*, among other works.

Italian poet Dante Alighieri was sentenced to exile by his political enemies in 1302. Banished from his beloved native city of Florence, he wrote the *Divine Comedy*, an epic that describes a journey through Hell, Purgatory, and Heaven. In the fol-lowing passage from that work, he evokes the suffering of the outcast: "You shall leave everything you love most:/this is the arrow that the bow of exile/shoots first."

Just as Ovid and Dante went into exile, so did many twentieth-century writers. For example, after the Russian Revolution, poet Marina Tsvetaeva left Moscow, following her husband to Europe, where she wrote poetry filled with longing for her lost home.

Connect to the Literature

Do you think that the exile of the speaker in "The Seafarer" can touch readers in the twenty-first century? Why or why not?

---

10 With frozen chains, and hardship groaned
    Around my heart. Hunger tore
    At my sea-weary soul. No man sheltered
    On the quiet fairness of earth can feel
    How wretched I was, drifting through winter
15 On an ice-cold sea, whirled in sorrow,
    Alone in a world blown clear of love,
    Hung with icicles. The hailstorms flew.
    The only sound was the roaring sea,
    The freezing waves. The song of the swan
20 Might serve for pleasure, the cry of the sea-fowl,
    The death-noise of birds instead of laughter,
    The mewing of gulls instead of mead.[1]
    Storms beat on the rocky cliffs and were echoed
    By icy-feathered terns and the eagle's screams;
25 No kinsman could offer comfort there,
    To a soul left drowning in desolation.
        And who could believe, knowing but
    The passion of cities, swelled proud with wine
    And no taste of misfortune, how often, how wearily,
30 I put myself back on the paths of the sea.
    Night would blacken; it would snow from the north;
    Frost bound the earth and hail would fall,
    The coldest seeds. And how my heart
    Would begin to beat, knowing once more
35 The salt waves tossing and the towering sea!
    The time for journeys would come and my soul
    Called me eagerly out, sent me over
    The horizon, seeking foreigners' homes.
        But there isn't a man on earth so proud,
40 So born to greatness, so bold with his youth,
    Grown so brave, or so graced by God,
    That he feels no fear as the sails unfurl,
    Wondering what Fate has willed and will do.
    No harps ring in his heart, no rewards,
45 No passion for women, no worldly pleasures,
    Nothing, only the ocean's heave;
    But longing wraps itself around him.
    Orchards blossom, the towns bloom,
    Fields grow lovely as the world springs fresh,

---

1. mead liquor made from fermented honey and water.

---

22 From Legend to History (A.D. 449–1485)

Enrichment: Investigating Religion and Myth

Fate

Different cultures have different opinions about the role of fate or higher powers in people's lives.

The Greeks believed that human life was subject to the whims of the gods, whereas Chaldean Egyptians believed that planetary position had a direct influence on people's lives. The Catholic church maintains that people have free will, while Hinduism promotes the belief that present life is determined by actions in past lives.

Activity: Poem Rewrite Have groups of stu-dents choose a religion or culture and con-duct research on the beliefs concerning fate. Suggest that they record information in the **Enrichment: Investigating Religion and Myth** worksheet, *Professional Development Guidebook,* page 240.

50   And all these *admonish* that willing mind
     Leaping to journeys, always set
     In thoughts traveling on a quickening tide.
     So summer's *sentinel*, the cuckoo, sings
     In his murmuring voice, and our hearts mourn
55   As he urges. Who could understand,
     In ignorant ease, what we others suffer
     As the paths of exile stretch endlessly on?
          And yet my heart wanders away,
     My soul roams with the sea, the whales'
60   Home, wandering to the widest corners

❼   Of the world, returning ravenous with desire,
     Flying solitary, screaming, exciting me
     To the open ocean, breaking oaths
     On the curve of a wave.
                              Thus the joys of God
65   Are *fervent* with life, where life itself
     Fades quickly into the earth. The wealth

❽   Of the world neither reaches to Heaven nor remains.
     No man has ever faced the dawn
     Certain which of Fate's three threats
70   Would fall: illness, or age, or an enemy's
     Sword, snatching the life from his soul.
     The praise the living pour on the dead
     Flowers from reputation: plant
     An earthly life of profit reaped
75   Even from hatred and *rancor*, of bravery
     Flung in the devil's face, and death
     Can only bring you earthly praise
     And a song to celebrate a place
     With the angels, life eternally blessed
80   In the hosts of Heaven.
                              The days are gone
     When the kingdoms of earth flourished in glory;
     Now there are no rulers, no emperors,
     No givers of gold, as once there were,
     When wonderful things were worked among them

❾   85   And they lived in lordly magnificence.
     Those powers have vanished, those pleasures are dead.
     The weakest survives and the world continues,
     Kept spinning by toil. All glory is tarnished.

Vocabulary

admonish (ad män′ ish) *v.*
advise; caution

sentinel (sen′ ti nel), *n.*
person or animal that guards

fervent (fur′ vent) *adj.*
having great warmth of
feeling

rancor (raŋ′ kər) *n.* ill will;
continuing and bitter hate

Literary Analysis

Anglo-Saxon Lyrics
How does the alliteration of
words beginning with *w, r,*
and *s* affect the sound and
meaning of lines 59–62?

Literary Analysis

**Anglo-Saxon Lyrics
and the Elegy**
What does the speaker
mourn in lines 81–90?

❿  Reading
        Check

What are the "three threats"
mentioned by the speaker?

The Seafarer **23**

Differentiated
Instruction   for Universal Access

EL Pronunciation for English Learners
English learners may struggle with pronunciation of some words on this page. The words
mourn, pour, corners, sword, and *lordly* all contain
the /ô/ sound.

Write the word *mourn* on the board. Model the
pronunciation of the word for the students. Have
students repeat the word. Then write the words
pour, corners, sword, and *lordly* on the board,

one at a time. Model each word's pronunciation.
Have the students repeat each word. Ask for volunteers in pronunciation.

Explain that even though these words are
spelled differently, with different combinations of
-our, -or, -wor, that the /ô/ sound is pronounced
the same.

23

⑪ ▲ **Critical Viewing**
In what ways does the mood of this painting match the mood of the speaker's reflections on "The world's honor"?
[Connect]

⑨ ▲ The world's honor ages and shrinks,
90 Bent like the men who mold it. Their faces
Blanch as time advances, their beards
Wither and they mourn the memory of friends.
The sons of princes, sown in the dust.
The soul stripped of its flesh knows nothing
95 Of sweetness or sour, feels no pain,
Bends neither its hand nor its brain. A brother
Opens his palms and pours down gold
On his kinsman's grave, strewing his coffin
With treasures intended for Heaven, but nothing
100 Golden shakes the wrath of God
For a soul overflowing with sin, and nothing
Hidden on earth rises to Heaven.
    We all fear God. He turns the earth,
He set it swinging firmly in space,
105 Gave life to the world and light to the sky.
Death leaps at the fools who forget their God.
He who lives humbly has angels from Heaven

24 From Legend to History (A.D. 449–1485)

Think Aloud

Literary Analysis: Anglo-Saxon Lyrics
To model the process of looking for ways in which alliteration and assonance are used to enhance meaning, use the following "think aloud." Say to students:

I may be asked to look for connections between a literary device, such as alliteration, and the meaning of a work. For example, line 92 contains alliteration with a repeated *m* sound: "*mourn* the *memory*." To see how this contributes to meaning, I need to think about what meanings can be associated with the *m* sound. The sound is soft and smooth, so it may be associated with fondness or sad feelings. This supports the meaning of the text, which speaks of loss and death.

To carry him courage and strength and belief.
A man must conquer pride, not kill it,
110 Be firm with his fellows, chaste for himself,
Treat all the world as the world deserves,
With love or with hate but never with harm,
Though an enemy seek to scorch him in hell,
Or set the flames of a funeral pyre
115 Under his lord. Fate is stronger
And God mightier than any man's mind.
Our thoughts should turn to where our home is,
Consider the ways of coming there,
Then strive for sure permission for us
120 To rise to that eternal joy,
That life born in the love of God
And the hope of Heaven. Praise the Holy
Grace of Him who honored us,
Eternal, unchanging creator of earth. Amen.

A man must conquer pride, not kill it.

Critical Reading

1. Key Ideas and Details (a) Identify three images related to weather in the first stanza. **(b) Interpret:** What does each convey about the speaker's experiences at sea?

2. Key Ideas and Details (a) What causes the speaker's heart to "begin to beat"? **(b) Generalize:** How can someone dislike something as much as the seafarer dislikes life at sea and yet be drawn to it?

3. Key Ideas and Details (a) What is the seafarer's response to "harps," "rewards," "passion," and the other pleasures of life on the land (lines 44–47)? **(b) Interpret:** Judging from his response to these things, explain whether he is more attached to life on land than he is to life at sea.

4. Key Ideas and Details (a) Interpret: What does the speaker mean when he says in lines 58–61, "And yet my heart wanders away, / My soul roams with the sea, . . . / . . . / . . . returning ravenous with desire, . . ."? **(b) Draw Conclusions:** Is the speaker fully at home on land, on the sea, or in neither place? Explain.

5. Integration of Knowledge and Ideas (a) Interpret: According to the last section of the poem, where is our home? **(b) Synthesize:** Explain the connection between the poem's concluding message and its depiction of the seafarer's wandering existence.

6. Integration of Knowledge and Ideas Can people find a way of life in which they are fully happy, or, like the seafarer, will they always have longings for another place? Explain.

Cite textual evidence to support your responses.

The Seafarer 25

Differentiated Instruction *for Universal Access*

Culturally Responsive Instruction

Culture Connection Students may lack the background knowledge necessary to fully comprehend these selections. Build background knowledge about Anglo-Saxon society. In England during the Middle Ages, there was no national government; instead, people gave their allegiance to a local lord. Lords offered land and protection in return for various services. Some men served as warriors, protecting the lord's property and taking over more land. Others farmed the land, providing food for the lord and all of his followers. If the lord died, this entire mini-society could disintegrate. In contrast, in the United States, if a political leader dies or is unable to continue in his or her position, a new leader usually transitions into the role without much interruption to everyday life for most citizens.

⓬ About the Selection

The wanderer in this poem has experienced the complete collapse of his entire world: His lord has died. With the loss of his lord, he has no more purpose, no more friends, no more hopes of enjoying treasures, no one to feast with, and no one's knee upon which to lay his hand and promise loyalty. He is alone, cast out, left to wander in search of a new lord.

⓭ 🔑 Engaging the Essential Question

1. Discuss with students the types of places that have a hold on their memory or imagination. Lead them to see that the memories of a place may be more poignant if the place is far off or belongs to their past. Point out that the poet of "The Wanderer" writes of not only the physical aspects of the place he has lost but also the relationships and experiences he associates with it.

2. **Ask** students: What people and experiences does the poet remember?
Possible responses: He remembers the hall-men and his lord; he remembers dealing in treasure, feasting, and kneeling before his lord.

3. Next, **ask** students: What physical descriptions does the poet give of his past home?
Possible response: In lines 69–70 and 80, the poet describes impressive structures that are now going to ruin.

4. **Ask** students: How do both aspects of the poet's remembrance affect the way readers perceive the place he remembers?
Possible responses: The details about people and experiences help readers share the poet's nostalgia for the place; the details about the decaying buildings help readers share the poet's sadness over the fading past of the place he remembers.

5. Tell students that as they continue to read, they should pay attention to their feelings about the places described in each poem and notice what the poet has done to create those feelings.

⓬ # The Wanderer

Translated by
Charles W. Kennedy

⓭ *Though woefully toiling   on wintry seas*
With churning oar   in the icy wave,
Homeless and helpless   he fled from fate.

26 From Legend to History (A.D. 449–1485)

Think Aloud

Vocabulary: Using Context

Direct students' attention to the word *winsomeness* in line 30 of "The Wanderer." Use the following "think aloud" to model the skill of using context to infer the meaning of the word. Say to students:

I may not know the exact meaning of the word *winsomeness*. However, I see that the poet writes that Earth's winsomeness is dead. So winsomeness is a quality that Earth used to have but no longer has in the poet's eyes. When I read lines 28–34, I see that the poet remembers better days full of things he enjoyed: time with his companions; the dealing of treasure, and times of celebration and feasting with his lord. Now all of these things are gone. Since Earth's winsomeness is also gone according to the poet, I think these things must have been part of Earth's winsomeness for him. So *winsomeness* may refer to the quality of being enjoyable or delightful, which Earth no longer has.

Oft to the wanderer,   weary of exile,
Cometh God's pity,   compassionate love,
Though woefully toiling   on wintry seas
With churning oar   in the icy wave,
5 Homeless and helpless   he fled from fate.
Thus saith the wanderer   mindful of misery,
Grievous disasters,   and death of kin:
   "Oft when the day broke,   oft at the dawning,
Lonely and wretched   I wailed my woe.
10 No man is living,   no comrade left,
To whom I dare fully   unlock my heart.
I have learned truly   the mark of a man
Is keeping his counsel   and locking his lips,
Let him think what he will!   For, woe of heart
15 Withstandeth not fate: a failing spirit
Earneth no help.   Men eager for honor
Bury their sorrow   deep in the breast.
   "So have I also,   often in wretchedness
Fettered[1] my feelings,   far from my kin,
20 Homeless and hapless,[2]   since days of old,
When the dark earth covered   my dear lord's face,
And I sailed away   with sorrowful heart,
Over wintry seas,   seeking a gold-lord,
If far or near   lived one to befriend me
25 With gift in the mead-hall   and comfort for grief.
   "Who bears it, knows   what a bitter companion,
Shoulder to shoulder,   sorrow can be,
When friends are no more.   His fortune is exile,
Not gifts of fine gold;   a heart that is frozen,
30 Earth's winsomeness dead.   And he dreams of the hall-men,
The dealing of treasure,   the days of his youth,
When his lord bade welcome   to wassail[3] and feast.
But gone is that gladness,   and never again
Shall come the loved counsel   of comrade and king.
35   "Even in slumber   his sorrow assaileth,
And, dreaming he claspeth   his dear lord again,
Head on knee, hand on knee,   loyally laying,
Pledging his liege[4]   as in days long past.
Then from his slumber   he starts lonely-hearted,
40 Beholding gray stretches   of tossing sea.
Sea-birds bathing,   with wings outspread,

---

1. **Fettered** (fet´ ərd) chained; restrained.
2. **hapless** (hap´ lis) unlucky.
3. **wassail** (wäs´ əl) a toast in drinking a person's health, or a celebration at which such toasts are made.
4. **liege** (lēj) lord; sovereign.

The Wanderer **27**

Vocabulary
compassionate (kəm pash´ ən it) *adj.* sympathizing; pitying

15 Reading Check
What is the wanderer's situation?

14 Critical Thinking
Infer
1. Remind students that a kenning is a metaphorical phrase used in place of a concrete noun.
2. Call on a volunteer to read lines 20–25 aloud. Have students identify the kenning.
3. Then, **ask:** How does the kenning "gold-lord" help you infer the wanderer's goal?
   Answer: The kenning suggests that the wanderer's livelihood is intimately connected with his having a lord, or one who will provide him with gold, or money.

15 Reading Check
Answer: The wanderer is bereft because his lord has died, and he is left lonely and without means to support himself or hope of enjoying himself in his lord's company.

Differentiated Instruction   for Universal Access

Support for Special-Needs Students
The unusual line breaks may make this poem difficult to read. Summarize a section or stanza for students. Then have students rewrite it as normal sentences, without line breaks, using punctuation as a guideline. You may do this as a group. Then have students break the sentences into phrases, discussing the meaning of each phrase.

Strategy for Less Proficient Readers
To help students use historical context to make sense of the poem, show them **Reading Skill Graphic Organizer A** (*Graphic Organizer Transparencies* p. 1). The partially completed graphic organizer will serve as a model showing students how to take general historical information and apply it to the specific circumstances of the poem.

Understand Historical Context

1. Have a volunteer read lines 55–65 aloud.

2. Then have students review what they know about Anglo-Saxon values and community life. You may also point students back to the introductory material at the beginning of the selections.

3. Next, **ask** students the Reading Strategy question.
Possible response: The wanderer expresses a contentment with fate and an appreciation for wisdom that comes through experience, which are in keeping with Anglo-Saxon values of accepting one's destiny and proving oneself in acts of courage and bravery.

▶ **Monitor Progress:** To assess students' understanding of the historical context strategy, discuss what they would look for when researching the historical context of a piece of literature.

▶ **Reteach:** If students focus mainly on historical events, remind them that historical context concerns more than events. It also concerns a culture's beliefs and ideas—what is called "worldview."

17 Literary Analysis

Anglo-Saxon Lyrics

1. Remind students that a caesura is a pause. Then, **ask** them the Literary Analysis question.
Answer: Caesuras are indicated by a space mid-line.

2. Divide students into two groups and have them perform a choral reading of the bracketed passage. Have the first group of students read the part of each line before the caesura and the second group of students read the part after the caesura, in "call and response" style.

3. **Ask** students what their reading shows them about the use of the caesura.
Possible response: The repeated pauses add a strong rhythmic element to the poem. The caesura adds to the meaning by calling out the way ideas can echo or oppose each other in a single line.

Vocabulary
rapture (rap chər) *n.* joy; great pleasure

Reading Strategy
Understand Historical Context How does your knowledge of Anglo-Saxon life help you appreciate the mood of these lines?

17 Literary Analysis
Anglo-Saxon Lyrics
How are caesuras indicated on the page?

While hailstorms darken,   and driving snow.
Bitterer then   is the bane of his wretchedness,
The longing for loved one: his grief is renewed.
45   The forms of his kinsmen   take shape in the silence:
In rapture he greets them;   in gladness he scans
Old comrades remembered.   But they melt into air
With no word of greeting   to gladden his heart.
Then again surges   his sorrow upon him;
50   And grimly he spurs   his weary soul
Once more to the toil   of the tossing sea.
      "No wonder therefore,   in all the world,
If a shadow darkens   upon my spirit
When I reflect   on the fates of men—
55   How one by one   proud warriors vanish
From the halls that knew them,   and day by day
All this earth ages   and droops unto death.
No man may know wisdom   till many a winter

16
Has been his portion.   A wise man is patient,
60   Not swift to anger,   nor hasty of speech,
Neither too weak,   nor too reckless, in war,
Neither fearful nor fain,[5]   nor too wishful of wealth,
Nor too eager in vow—   ere he know the event.
A brave man must bide[6]   when he speaketh his boast
65   Until he know surely   the goal of his spirit.
      "A wise man will ponder   how dread is that doom
When all this world's wealth   shall be scattered and waste
As now, over all,   through the regions of earth,
Walls stand rime-covered[7]   and swept by the winds.
70   The battlements crumble,   the wine-halls decay;
Joyless and silent   the heroes are sleeping
Where the proud host fell   by the wall they defended.
Some battle launched   on their long, last journey;
One a bird bore   o'er the billowing sea:
75   One the gray wolf slew;   one a grieving earl
Sadly gave   to the grave's embrace.
The Warden of men   hath wasted this world
Till the sound of music   and revel is stilled,
And these giant-built structures   stand empty of life.
80   "He who shall muse   on these moldering ruins,
And deeply ponder   this darkling life,
Must brood on old legends   of battle and bloodshed,
And heavy the mood   that troubles his heart:
'Where now is the warrior?   Where is the war horse?

---

5. fain (fān) archaic word meaning "eager." In this context it means "too eager."
6. bide (bīd) wait.
7. rime (rīm)-**covered** covered with frost.

Enrichment: Analyzing Forms and Genres

The Homily

Point out to students that the passage in lines 58–65 interrupts an intensely concrete and dramatic scene with a homily, a passage that gives general advice pertaining to morals and conduct.

Some critics have argued that the homiletic passages in "The Wanderer" must be later additions to a poem that is otherwise remarkably terse, lyrical, and dramatic.

Other critics assert that the homilies are perfectly in character, showing the wanderer's belief in justice at those moments when he is most overcome with grief.

Activity: Debate Have students conduct research on the characteristics, history, and use of the homily literary form. Have them use the results of their research to stage a mini-debate on whether lines 58–65 are out of place within the poem.

85   Bestowal of treasure,   and sharing of feast?
     Alas! the bright ale-cup,   the byrny-clad[8] warrior,
     The prince in his splendor—   those days are long sped
     In the night of the past,   as if they never had been!'
18 And now remains only,   for warriors' memorial,
90   A wall wondrous high   with serpent shapes carved.
     Storms of ash-spears   have smitten the earls,
     Carnage of weapon,   and conquering fate.
         "Storms now batter   these ramparts of stone;
     Blowing snow   and the blast of winter
95   Enfold the earth;   night-shadows fall
     Darkly lowering,   from the north driving
     Raging hail   in wrath upon men.
     Wretchedness fills   the realm of earth,
     And fate's decrees   transform the world.
100 Here wealth is fleeting,   friends are fleeting,
     Man is fleeting,   maid is fleeting;
     All the foundation of earth   shall fail!"
         Thus spake the sage   in solitude pondering.
     Good man is he   who guardeth his faith.
105 He must never too quickly   unburden his breast
     Of its sorrow, but eagerly   strive for redress;
     And happy the man who seeketh for mercy
     From his heavenly Father,   our fortress and strength.

---

8. byrny (bər′ nē)**-clad** dressed in a coat of chain-mail armor.

Critical Reading

Cite textual evidence to support your responses.

1. **Key Ideas and Details** **(a)** Who are the speakers in the poem? **(b) Analyze:** What is the relationship between the two? **(c) Analyze:** What effect does the use of two speakers have on the reader's picture of the wanderer?

2. **Key Ideas and Details** **(a)** Why does the wanderer go into exile? **(b) Analyze:** What images does the poet use to convey his isolation and despair?

3. **Key Ideas and Details** **(a)** What are "the fates of men" on which the wanderer reflects? **(b) Connect:** Why might the wanderer's own experiences have led him to such brooding thoughts?

4. **Integration of Knowledge and Ideas** According to the poem, how might reflection on "the fates of men" lead to wisdom?

5. **Integration of Knowledge and Ideas** Do you think dwelling on the sorrowful, painful side of life can give a person wisdom and a valuable perspective on life, or do you think it can be harmful? Explain.

The Wanderer **29**

The speaker of this poem has been sent into exile by her husband. Although she still longs for him, she is bitter and angry about the friendless, lonely, joyless fate she must endure.

20 Critical Thinking

Speculate

1. Have students read lines 6–20 to themselves.

2. **Ask** students to speculate about what type of plot the husband's kinsmen may have used to separate the couple. Have them support their answers with details from the text.

   Possible responses: The kinsmen created financial or political difficulties for the husband (line 19) or invented a story that made the husband angry at his wife (line 20).

The Wife's Lament

Translated by Ann Stanford

I make this song   about me full sadly
my own wayfaring.   I a woman tell
what griefs I had   since I grew up
new or old   never more than now.
5   Ever I know   the dark of my exile.

First my lord went out   away from his people
over the wave-tumult.   I grieved each dawn
wondered where my lord   my first on earth might be.
Then I went forth   a friendless exile
10   to seek service   in my sorrow's need.
My man's kinsmen   began to plot
by darkened thought   to divide us two
so we most widely   in the world's kingdom
lived wretchedly   and I suffered longing.

15   My lord commanded me   to move my dwelling here.
I had few loved ones   in this land
or faithful friends.   For this my heart grieves:
that I should find the man   well matched to me
hard of fortune   mournful of mind
20   hiding his mood   thinking of murder.

Blithe[1] was our bearing   often we vowed
that but death alone   would part us two
naught else.   But this is turned round
now . . .   as if it never were
25   our friendship.   I must far and near
bear the anger   of my beloved.
The man sent me out   to live in the woods
under an oak tree   in this den in the earth.
Ancient this earth hall.   I am all longing.

---

1. **blithe** (blīth) *adj.* cheerful.

Concept Connector

Reading Skill Graphic Organizer
Ask students to review the graphic organizers in which they have made connections between the selections and their historical context. Then, have students share their organizers and compare the connections they made.

Activating Prior Knowledge
Have students return to their responses given to the Activating Prior Knowledge activity. Ask them to compare their lists to the hardships actually described by the poets.

Connecting to the Essential Question
Have students compare their responses to the prompt, which they completed before reading the selections, with their thoughts afterward. Have them work individually or in groups, writing or discussing their thoughts, to formulate their new responses. Then, lead a class discussion, probing for insights regarding the experience of exile that the students gained from the selections and discussing how these insights either support or alter students' initial thoughts. Encourage students to cite specific textual details to support their responses.

21 Literary Analysis
Anglo-Saxon Lyrics and the Elegy
What does the wife mourn in this elegy?

30 The valleys are dark   the hills high
the yard overgrown   bitter with briars
a joyless dwelling.   Full oft the lack of my lord
seizes me cruelly here.   Friends there are on earth
living beloved   lying in bed
35 while I at dawn   am walking alone
under the oak tree   through these earth halls.
There I may sit   the summerlong day
there I can weep   over my exile
my many hardships.   Hence I may not rest
40 from this care of heart   which belongs to me ever
nor all this longing   that has caught me in this life.

May that young man   be sad-minded always
hard his heart's thought   while he must wear
a blithe bearing   with care in the breast
45 a crowd of sorrows.   May on himself depend
all his world's joy.   Be he outlawed far
in a strange folk-land—   that my beloved sits
under a rocky cliff   rimed with frost
a lord dreary in spirit   drenched with water
50 in a ruined hall.   My lord endures
much care of mind.   He remembers too often
a happier dwelling.   Woe be to them
that for a loved one   must wait in longing.

Critical Reading

Cite textual evidence to support your responses.

© **1. Key Ideas and Details (a)** Why did the wife have to leave her home? **(b) Interpret:** What do lines 25–26 suggest about her reaction to this event?

© **2. Craft and Structure (a) Generalize:** How might a listener feel about his or her griefs after hearing the wife's lament? **(b) Draw Conclusions:** Explain why the poem presents the wife as an image of pure longing, rather than as a person who will one day move on.

© **3. Integration of Knowledge and Ideas** Is the wife justified in her anger and sorrow? Explain.

© **4. Integration of Knowledge and Ideas** How does the Anglo-Saxon sense of home compare with ours? In responding, use at least two of these Essential Question words: *exile, community, refuge, sanctuary*. *[Connecting to the Essential Question: What is the relationship between literature and place?]*

The Wife's Lament **31**

Assessment Practice

Sequential Order (For more practice, see *All-in-One Workbook.***)**

Some tests require students to identify the order in which events have occurred. Use this sample test item:

Blithe was our bearing often we vowed/that but death alone would part us two/naught else. But this is turned round/now . . . as if it never were/our friendship. I must far and near/bear the anger of my beloved. /The man sent me out to live in the woods/under an oak tree in this den in the earth.

Which of the following happens last according to the speaker in "The Wife's Lament"?

A The beloved sent the speaker into the woods.

B The two vowed that only death would part them.

C The speaker must bear the beloved's anger.

D The man sent the speaker into the woods.

Have students use verb tenses and signal words such as *now* to help them determine that C is the correct answer.

Answers

1. **Possible responses:**
   Regular rhythms: "The Wanderer"— "A wise man is patient,/ Not swift to anger, nor hasty of speech" (ll. 59–60).
   Caesuras: Caesuras can be found throughout "The Wanderer" and "The Wife's Lament."
   Kennings: "The Wife's Lament"— "wave-tumult," meaning "the ocean."
   Assonance: "The Wife's Lament"—*I, find; fortune, mournful; mind, hiding.*
   Alliteration: "The Wanderer"—*muse, moldering; brood, battle, bloodshed.*

2. (a) Each reflects on something lost or absent. (b) **Possible response:** "The Wanderer" is moving because the speaker's whole world is gone. The poet's use of alliteration calls forth emotion.

3. The wanderer's situation would be impossible to understand without knowing that the sense of purpose and identity of a warrior depended on the warrior's tie to his lord.

4. Knowing the husband had the right to banish his wife and that she had little recourse aids comprehension.

Vocabulary Acquisition and Use

1. synonyms and antonyms
2. synonyms
3. synonyms and antonyms
4. synonyms
5. synonyms
6. synonyms and antonyms

Writing

1. Go over the assignment with students. Help students find a topic by having them chart important places and activities in their lives. For each place or activity, have them list associated people or things that are now absent. Emphasize that the loss of this person or thing should be something that is regretted.

2. Suggest that they allot five minutes for prewriting, ten minutes for drafting, and ten minutes for revising and editing.

3. Have students complete the assignment.

32

After You Read

The Seafarer • The Wanderer • The Wife's Lament

Literary Analysis

1. Craft and Structure Use a graphic organizer like the one shown to find and analyze examples of the following poetic and structural devices in these poems: **regular rhythms, caesuras, kennings, assonance,** and **alliteration.**

Poem	Literary Devices

2. Integration of Knowledge and Ideas (a) What makes each of these poems an **elegy**? **(b)** Which poem do you find most moving? In supporting your response, show how poetic devices help call forth your emotions.

Reading Strategy

3. Why is **understanding the historical context,** relating to a warrior's relationship to his lord, important to appreciating the *setting* and the speaker's *character* in "The Wanderer"?

4. How does understanding the role of women in Anglo-Saxon society help you understand the speaker's plight in "The Wife's Lament"?

PERFORMANCE TASKS
Integrated Language Skills

Vocabulary Acquisition and Use

Categorize Vocabulary Using your knowledge of the vocabulary words, decide whether each item contains synonyms only (words similar in meaning) or synonyms and antonyms (words differing in meaning). Explain your choice.

1. admonish, calm, warn
2. fervent, ardent, impassioned
3. compassionate, malicious, kind
4. rancor, bitterness, spite
5. sentinel, guard, watchman
6. rapture, rest, ecstasy

Writing

Argument Write an **editorial** that is an elegy for someone or something that has gone from your neighborhood or school. In your editorial, persuade members of the community that the loss should be regretted. Use persuasive techniques like the following: a *testimonial* to the value of what was lost, from someone your audience will respect; an *emotional appeal* that associates what was lost with things or people that your audience values; *word choice* or language that your readers will find moving.

32 From Legend to History (A.D. 449–1485)

Common Core State Standards

Writing
1. Write arguments to support claims in an analysis of substantive topics or texts, using valid reasoning and relevant and sufficient evidence.

Language
5. Demonstrate understanding of word relationships and nuances in word meanings.

Assessment Resources

Unit 1 Resources

L1 L2 EL Selection Test A, pp. 25–27.
Administer Test A to less advanced readers.

L3 L4 EL Selection Test B, pp. 28–30.
Administer Test B to on-level and more advanced students.

L3 L4 Open-Book Test, pp. 22–24.
As an alternative, give the Open-Book Test.

All Customizable Test Bank

All Self-tests
Students may prepare for the **Selection Test** by taking the **Self-test** online.

PHLit Online! All assessment resources are available at www.PHLitOnline.com.

Focus on Literary Forms
The Epic

PART 2

33

Selection Planning Guide

The selection in this section provides insight into the nature of the epic hero and the conventions of the epic. The selection consists of excerpts from *Beowulf,* the most famous epic in the British tradition. It includes the battles with Grendel, Grendel's mother, and concludes with his last battle against a fire-breathing dragon.

Humanities

The Grandsons of Gostosmysl: Rurik, Truvori, and Sineus, 1986 by Ilya Glazunov.

Glazunov (1930–) is a contemporary Russian artist from Saint Petersburg. His paintings generally have historic or religious themes. This painting documents the Viking penetration of Eastern Europe. The Vikings gradually merged with the Slavs, adopting Slavic culture. This migration paralleled the voyages of the Norsemen into the British Isles.

Use these questions for discussion:

1. Why would a Russian artist be interested in memorializing images of these ancient Russian traders and warriors?
   Possible response: The helmeted brothers and their long ships are strong and heroic figures. This was probably a crucial episode in the development of the Russian nation, and emphasizes the interconnections between Russian history and the modern world.

2. What details in Glazunov's painting suggest that he views the brothers as brave and heroic?
   Possible response: Their gaze is bold and steady. The wearing of armor and helmets suggests they are ready for battle. The number of long ships in the background on the river suggests they come in force for raids or to establish new settlements.

Monitoring Progress

Before students read from *Beowulf* refer to the results for the **Diagnostic Test** (*Unit 1 Resources,* **p. 1**). Use this test to guide your choice of selections to teach as well as the depth of preparation you will provide, based on students' readiness for reading and vocabulary skills.

© Text Complexity: At a Glance

This chart gives a general text complexity rating for the selections in this part of the unit to help guide instruction. For additional text complexity support, see the Test Complexity Rubric at point of use.

from Beowulf	**More Accessible**

❶ Defining Epics

Have students review the opening paragraph. Explain that a courageous hero is central to the epic. Point out that because many epic heroes are semi-divine, their feats are often superhuman. **Ask:** In what way does the comic book character Superman fulfill the role of epic hero?

Sample response: Superman is noble and possesses superhuman strength. He reflects the values of his culture: His calling is to fight for "the American way."

❷ Types of Epics

Point out that the two types of epics are related; the style and conventions of literary epics come from the older folk epics. **Ask:** In the modern world, movies have adopted the epic form as a means of popular entertainment. What are some examples of movies that portray epics?

Sample response: Examples include the *Star Wars* and *Lord of the Rings* series.

❸ Epic Conventions

Explain that the Muses of Greek mythology presided over the arts and sciences. **Ask:** Why might the poet have considered it necessary to invoke a muse?

Sample response: The poet might have wished to impress his audience with the importance of his task and to demonstrate that no human could recite such a significant poem without divine assistance.

❹ Close Read: Characteristics of the Epic

Review the chart with students. Point out the highlighted text in the model on page 35. Explain that in each case, the color of the highlighting matches the color of the category in the chart. Details that illustrate a given category are highlighted in the color of that category.

THE EPIC IMPARTS SOLEMNITY TO HISTORY. . . .

— VICTOR HUGO

❶ Defining Epics

One of the earliest forms of literature, an **epic** is a long narrative poem written in an elevated style. An epic relates the adventures of a hero in pursuit of goals of national importance. The hero's adventures, which often include a quest, reflect the values of his culture and are usually prominent in the traditions of his people.

❷ Types of Epics In ancient times, stories about heroes were passed down orally. These stories were eventually arranged into larger works called **folk epics** and written down long after they were first composed. Examples include *Beowulf* (Anglo-Saxon), the *Mahabharata* (Indian), and *The Epic of Gilgamesh* (Sumerian). **Literary epics** were composed by individual authors who drew on the conventions of folk epics. Examples include the *Aeneid* by Virgil and *Paradise Lost* by John Milton.

❸ Epic Conventions Most epics share certain literary or formal characteristics called **epic conventions.**

• **Invoking a Muse** At the beginning of an epic, the poet states the subject or purpose of the poem, and then invokes, or calls upon, a muse (a spirit thought to inspire an artist) or supernatural force for help in telling the story. For example, Homer begins the *Iliad,* "Rage— Goddess, sing the rage of Peleus' son Achilles . . ."

• ***In Medias Res*** The plot begins ***in medias res*** (Latin for "in the middle of things")—the action is already underway. Homer's *Iliad,* for example, begins during the tenth year of the Trojan War.

• **Elevated Style** See the chart below for a definition and example of the epic convention of elevated style.

❹ Close Read: Characteristics of the Epic
These elements and conventions of an epic appear in the Model text at right.

Epic Hero on a Quest: The epic hero is the central character in an epic. Often of noble or semi-divine birth, he sets out on a quest, a dangerous journey that tests his spirit. Example: *In* Beowulf, *a noble young warrior goes on a quest to rescue a kingdom from a monster.*	**Supernatural Forces:** Supernatural forces include deities, some of whom may watch over the hero, and monsters. Example: *In the ancient Greek epic the* Iliad, *the goddess Athena helps the hero Achilles.*
Valorous Deeds: Valorous deeds are acts that reveal the epic hero's extraordinary qualities and reflect the values cherished by his culture. Example: Beowulf *shows superhuman strength in fighting the monster Grendel with his bare hands.*	**Elevated Style:** An epic contains lofty diction, or word choice, that heightens the importance of the events retold. It may contain catalogs, or lists, of battles, weapons, and royal gifts. Example: "'Hail, Hrothgar! / Higlac is my cousin and my king; the days / Of my youth have been filled with glory. . . .'" Beowulf, *(lines 236–238)*

34 From Legend to History (A.D. 449–1485)

Differentiated Instruction   for Universal Access

ⓔⓛ Strategy for English Learners

Explain to students that an epic poem such as *Beowulf* will likely contain many unfamiliar words and word uses. They should be prepared to look up new vocabulary, reread, and ask questions to make sure they fully understand what they read. Reassure students that, despite the intimidating language, these epics are good stories, and students should focus on main events and characters and not become bogged down in less important details.

Strategies for Less Proficient Readers

Students may be more familiar with films such as *Star Wars,* or books by authors such as Tolkien or J. K. Rowling, than they are with classic epic tales. List elements of the epic and epic conventions on the board. Then, encourage students to suggest films or books that include these elements. Students may work in pairs to identify epic elements and epic conventions in one or more modern works.

Model

About the Text Gilgamesh, the hero of *The Epic of Gilgamesh,* is a Sumerian king who seeks eternal life. He and Urshanabi, a ferryman, have journeyed to meet Utnapishtim, whom the gods saved from a great flood and to whom they have granted immortality. As the excerpt begins, Gilgamesh and Urshanabi prepare to return home.

from *The Epic of Gilgamesh* (translated by N. K. Sandars)

Then Gilgamesh and Urshanabi launched the boat onto the water and boarded it, and they made ready to sail away; but the wife of Utnapishtim the Faraway said to him, "Gilgamesh came here wearied out, he is worn out; what will you give him to carry him back to his own country?" So Utnapishtim spoke, and Gilgamesh took a pole and brought the boat in to the bank. "Gilgamesh, you came here a man wearied out, you have worn yourself out; what shall I give you to carry you back to your own country? Gilgamesh, I shall reveal a secret thing, it is a mystery of the gods that I am telling you. There is a plant that grows under the water, it has a prickle like a thorn, like a rose; it will wound your hands, but if you succeed in taking it, then your hands will hold that which restores his lost youth to a man."

When Gilgamesh heard this he opened the sluices so that a sweet-water current might carry him out to the deepest channel; he tied heavy stones to his feet and they dragged him down to the water-bed. There he saw the plant growing; although it pricked him he took it in his hands; then he cut the heavy stones from his feet, and the sea carried him and threw him onto the shore. Gilgamesh said to Urshanabi the ferryman, "Come here, and see this marvelous plant. By its virtue a man may win back all his former strength. I will take it to Uruk of the strong walls; there I will give it to the old men to eat. Its name shall be 'The Old Men Are Young Again'; and at last I shall eat it myself and have back all my lost youth." So Gilgamesh returned by the gate through which he had come, Gilgamesh and Urshanabi went together. They traveled their twenty leagues and then they broke their fast; after thirty leagues they stopped for the night.

Gilgamesh saw a well of cool water and he went down and bathed; but deep in the pool there was lying a serpent, and the serpent sensed the sweetness of the flower. It rose out of the water and snatched it away, and immediately it sloughed its skin and returned to the well. Then Gilgamesh sat down and wept, the tears ran down his face, and he took the hand of Urshanabi: "O Urshanabi, was it for this that I toiled with my hands, is it for this I have wrung out my heart's blood? For myself I have gained nothing; not I, but the beast of the earth has joy of it now. Already the stream has carried it twenty leagues back to the channels where I found it. I found a sign and now I have lost it. Let us leave the boat on the bank and go."

After twenty leagues they broke their fast, after thirty leagues they stopped for the night; in three days they had walked as much as a journey of a month and fifteen days. When the journey was accomplished they arrived at Uruk, the strong-walled city. Gilgamesh spoke to him, to Urshanabi the ferryman, "Urshanabi, climb up onto the wall of Uruk, inspect its foundation terrace, and examine well the brickwork; see if it is not of burnt bricks; and did not the seven wise men lay these foundations? One third of the whole is city, one third is garden, and one third is field, with the precinct of the goddess Ishtar. These parts and the precinct are all Uruk."

This too was the work of Gilgamesh, the king, who knew the countries of the world. He was wise, he saw mysteries and knew secret things, he brought us a tale of the days before the flood. He went a long journey, was weary, worn out with labor, and returning engraved on a stone the whole story.

⑤ Supernatural Forces
Utnapishtim is a favorite of the gods, who have granted him immortality. He reveals "a mystery of the gods" that has the supernatural power to restore youth.

⑥ Valorous Deeds
Gilgamesh dives deep underwater to find the magic plant. He wounds his hands to pluck and secure it. These deeds are valorous, demonstrating courage and perseverance. They are also of great consequence—should Gilgamesh succeed, he will help his people conquer death.

⑦ Epic Hero Through his actions, Gilgamesh, like other epic heroes, seeks to better his people. His actions also help to define his culture's concerns and values—the tellers of this epic saw humanity as striving to overcome time and aging.

⑧ Elevated Style Note the formal tone and elevated diction of Gilgamesh's lament. The parallel phrases "toiled with my hands" and "wrung out my heart's blood" heighten the intensity.

Extended Study: The Epic **35**

⑤ Supernatural Forces

Remind students that Gilgamesh's quest has a supernatural goal: to discover the secret of eternal life. In this scene, Utnapishtim reveals the mystery to him. **Ask:** What does Gilgamesh's failure to keep the magic water plant suggest about humanity and the gods?

Sample response: Human beings are meant to die. The gods protect their immortality.

⑥ Valorous Deeds

Read aloud the bracketed passage. Point out that Gilgamesh is well equipped for valorous deeds. **Ask:** What do these references to Gilgamesh's journey suggest about him?

Sample response: Gilgamesh possesses superhuman strength and endurance.

⑦ Epic Hero

Have students read the blue-highlighted passage. **Ask:** How can we infer from this passage that Gilgamesh is not a god?

Sample response: The fact that he desires to recover his lost youth indicates that—despite his great strength—he is mortal.

⑧ Elevated Style

Invite a volunteer to read the bracketed passage dramatically. **Ask:** What is the effect of a lofty lament such as this one?

Sample response: This elevated style of speaking serves to emphasize the importance of the event: Gilgamesh's failure to capture the secret to immortality.

Extend the Lesson

Evaluating Heroes

An epic hero is courageous, valiant, virtuous, and larger-than-life, sometimes even godlike. Not only are epic heroes more than human, they are also more than individuals. Epic heroes embody the values and ideals of a nation or culture. For example, the hero Beowulf is a mighty warrior with supernatural powers, but he is more than a superhero. He represents the strength, love, and loyalty to which Anglo-Saxon England aspired.

Divide students into small groups and have each group choose a different hero from film, fiction, or real life. Have them identify the heroic qualities of their hero, and then discuss how these qualities reflect cultural attitudes and values. Invite groups to share their thoughts with the class.

• *from* Beowulf
Lesson Pacing Guide

DAY 1 Preteach

- Ⓒ Administer the Reading and Vocabulary Warm-ups (*Unit 1 Resources,* pp. 33–36) as necessary.
- • Introduce the Literary Analysis concept: The Epic and the Legendary Hero.
- Ⓒ Introduce the Reading Strategy: Determine the Main Idea by Paraphrasing.
- • Build background with the contemporary commentary and author and Background features.
- • Develop thematic thinking with Connecting to the Essential Question.
- Ⓒ Teach the selection vocabulary.

DAYS 2–3 Preteach/Teach/Assess

- Ⓒ Distribute copies of the appropriate graphic organizer for the Reading Strategy (*Graphic Organizer Transparencies,* pp. 5–6).
- Ⓒ Distribute copies of the appropriate graphic organizer for Literary Analysis (*Graphic Organizer Transparencies,* pp. 7–8).
- • Prepare students to read with the Activating Prior Knowledge activities (TE).
- • Informally monitor comprehension while students read.
- • Use the Reading Check questions to confirm comprehension.
- • Develop students' understanding of the epic and the legendary hero using the Literary Analysis prompts.
- • Develop students' ability to determine the main idea by paraphrasing using the Reading Strategy prompts.
- Ⓒ Reinforce vocabulary with the Vocabulary notes.
- Ⓒ Assess students' comprehension and mastery of the skills by having them answer the Critical Reading, Literary Analysis, and Reading Strategy questions.
- Ⓒ Have students complete the Vocabulary Lesson.

DAY 4 Extend/Assess

- • Have students complete the Conventions and Style Lesson.
- Ⓒ Have students complete the Writing Lesson and write a job application. (You may assign as homework.)
- • Have students read and respond to the Contemporary Commentary.
- • Administer Selection Test A or B (*Unit 1 Resources,* pp. 46–48 or 49–51).

Ⓒ **Common Core
State Standards**

Reading Literature 3. Analyze the impact of the author's choices regarding how to develop and relate elements of a story or drama.

Writing 1. Write arguments to support claims in an analysis of substantive topics or texts, using valid reasoning and relevant and sufficient evidence.
1.d. Establish and maintain a formal style and objective tone while attending to the norms and conventions of the discipline in which they are writing.
4. Produce clear and coherent writing in which the development, organization, and style are appropriate to task, purpose, and audience.

Language 3.a. Vary syntax for effect.
4.b. Identify and correctly use patterns of word changes that indicate different meanings or parts of speech.
5. Demonstrate understanding of word relationships.

Additional Standards Practice
Common Core Companion, pp. 28–35; 185–195; 322–323; 324–331; 332–335

Daily Block Scheduling
Each day in this Lesson Pacing Guide represents a 40–50 minute period. Teachers using block scheduling may combine days to revise pacing. In addition, teachers may differentiate and support core instruction by integrating components for extended and intensive support as students require. See the Guide to Selected Leveled Resources (facing page).

Guide to Selected Leveled Resources

R T I Tier 1 (students performing on level)

from Beowulf

Warm Up	**Practice, model,** and **monitor** fluency, working **with the whole class** or **in groups**.	**Vocabulary** and **Reading Warm-ups B,** *Unit 1 Resources,* pp. 33–34, 36
Comprehension/Skills	**Support** and **monitor** comprehension and skills development, having students complete the activities, graphic organizers, and interactive prompts **independently** or **as a class**.	• *Reader's Notebook,* adapted instruction and full selection **EL** *Reader's Notebook: English Learner's Version,* adapted instruction and adapted selection • **Reading Skill Graphic Organizer B,** *Graphic Organizer Transparencies,* p. 16 • **Literary Analysis Graphic Organizer B,** *Graphic Organizer Transparencies,* p. 18
Monitor Progress	**Monitor** student progress with the differentiated curriculum-based assessment in the *Unit Resources.*	• **Selection Test B,** *Unit 1 Resources,* pp. 49–51 • **Open-Book Test,** *Unit 1 Resources,* pp. 43–45

R T I Tier 2 (students requiring intervention)

from Beowulf

Warm Up	**Practice, model,** and **monitor** fluency **in groups** or **with individuals**.	• **Vocabulary and Reading Warm-ups A,** *Unit 1 Resources,* pp. 33–35 • *Hear It!* **Audio CD (adapted text)**
Comprehension/Skills	• **Support** and **monitor** comprehension and skills development, working **in small groups** or **with individuals**. • As students complete the selection in the appropriate version of the *Reader's Notebook,* **monitor** comprehension frequently with group questions and individual instruction. • **Model** strategies while guiding students in completing the activities and prompts in the *Reader's Notebook,* as well as the graphic organizers. • **Practice** skills and **monitor** mastery with the *Reading Kit* worksheets.	• *Reader's Notebook: Adapted Version,* adapted instruction and adapted selection **EL** *Reader's Notebook: English Learner's Version,* adapted instruction and adapted selection • **Reading Skill Graphic Organizer A,** *Graphic Organizer Transparencies,* p. 5 • **Literary Analysis Graphic Organizer A,** *Graphic Organizer Transparencies,* p. 7 • *Reading Kit,* Practice worksheets
Monitor Progress	**Monitor** student progress with the differentiated curriculum-based assessment in the *Unit Resources* and in the *Reading Kit.*	• **Selection Test A,** *Unit 1 Resources,* pp. 46–48 • *Reading Kit,* Assess worksheets

TIER 3 Tier 3 intervention may require consultation with the student's special-education or dyslexia specialist. For additional support, see the Tier 2 activities and resources listed above.

 One-on-one teaching   Group work   Whole class instruction   Independent work   A Assessment

For a complete guide to selection support, including support for Advanced students, see the Overview of Resources in the frontmatter.

• *from* Beowulf

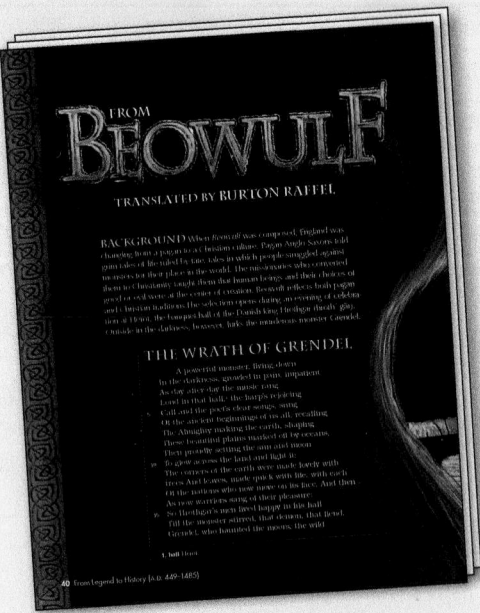

RESOURCES FOR:

- **L1** Special-Needs Students
- **L2** Below-Level Students (Tier 2)
- **L3** On-Level Students (Tier 1)
- **L4** Advanced Students (Tier 1)
- **EL** English Learners
- **All** All Students

Vocabulary/Fluency/Prior Knowledge

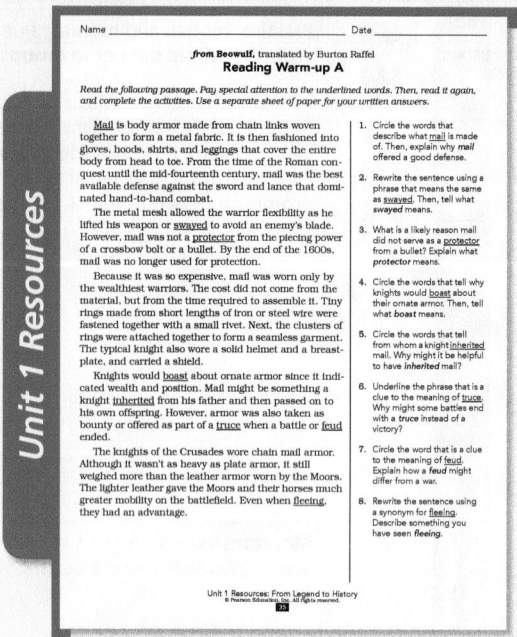

EL L1 L2 Reading Warm-ups A and B, pp. 35–36

Also available for these selections:

EL L1 L2 Vocabulary Warm-ups A and B, pp. 33–34

All Vocabulary Builder, p. 39

Reader's Notebooks

Pre- and postreading pages for this selection, as well as the excerpt from *Beowulf* appear in an interactive format in the *Reader's Notebooks*. Each *Notebook* is differentiated for a different group of learners.

The selections in the Adapted and English Learner's versions are abridged.

L2 L3 Reader's Notebook
L1 Reader's Notebook: Adapted Version
EL Reader's Notebook: English Learner's Version
EL Reader's Notebook: Spanish Version

© Common Core Companion

Additional instruction and practice for each Common Core State Standard

Selection Support

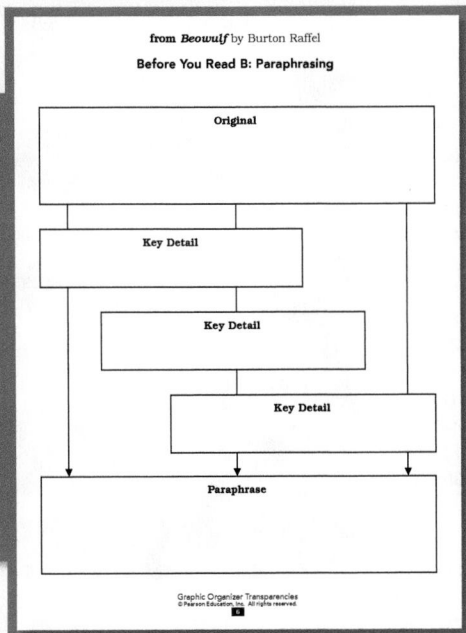

EL **L3** **Reading: Graphic Organizer B,** p. 6

Also available for these selections:

EL **L1** **L2** **Reading: Graphic Organizer A** (partially filled in), p. 5

EL **L1** **L2** **Literary Analysis: Graphic Organizer A** (partially filled in), p. 7

EL **L3** **Literary Analysis: Graphic Organizer B,** p. 8

Skills Development/Extension

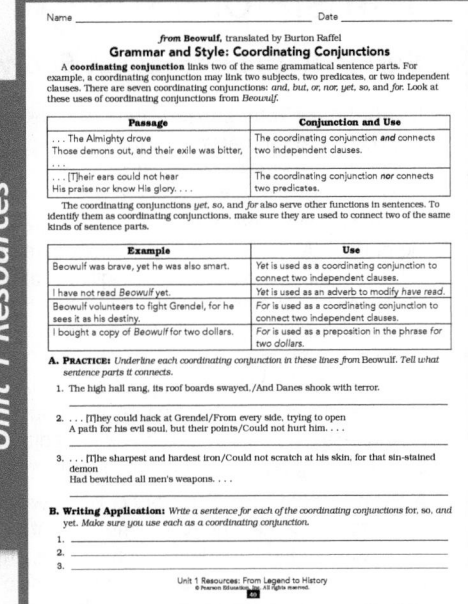

EL **L3** **L4** **Grammar and Style,** p. 40

Also available for these selections:

All **Literary Analysis,** p. 37
All **Reading,** p. 38
EL **L3** **L4** **Support for Writing,** p. 41
L4 **Enrichment,** p. 42

Assessment

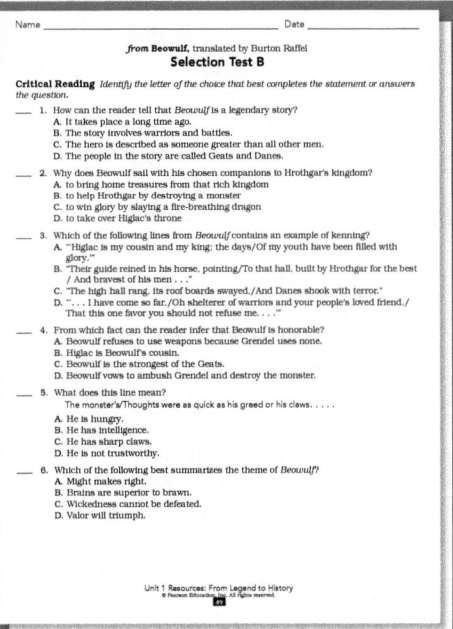

EL **L1** **L2** **Selection Test B,** pp. 49–51

Also available for these selections:

L3 **L4** **Open-Book Test,** pp. 43–45
EL **L3** **L4** **Selection Test A,** pp. 46–48

PHLit Online!
www.PHLitOnline.com

Online Resources: All print materials are also available online.

- complete narrated selection text
- a thematically related video with writing prompt
- an interactive graphic organizer
- highlighting feature
- access to all student print resources, adapted to individual student needs
- Spanish and English summaries
- adapted selection translations in Spanish

Get Connected! (thematic video with writing prompt)

Also available:

Background Video
All videos are available in Spanish.

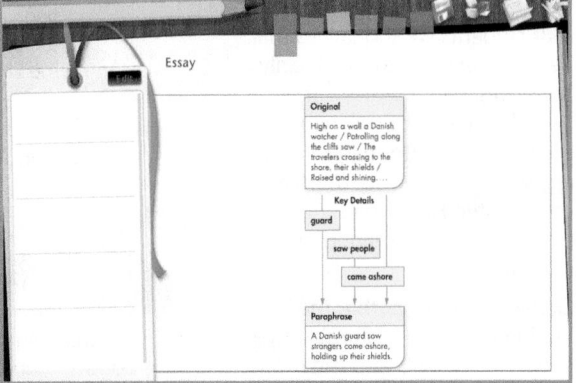

Writer's Journal (with graphics feature)

Also available:

Vocabulary Central (tools and activities for studying vocabulary)

Graphic Organizer Transparencies

Unit 1 Resources

Themes Across Centuries

Burton Raffel

1. Tell students that Burton Raffel is well known as a scholar and translator. He has taught literature and classics at universities around the world, from the United States to Canada to Israel. In addition to translating *Beowulf*, he has translated French, Spanish, Greek, and Russian literature.

2. Show students Segment 2 on Burton Raffel on the *See It!* DVD for insight into Raffel's perspective on *Beowulf*. After students have watched the segment, encourage them to discuss the qualities that make the epic difficult for contemporary readers, as well as the qualities that are still appealing.

3. **Ask** students if, based on the DVD segment, they think they would enjoy reading *Beowulf*. Press students to explain their answers with references to the DVD segment. **Possible responses:** Students may say they will enjoy *Beowulf* because, in addition to being an important early work of English literature, it is an exciting adventure story.

A Legendary Tale, Larger than Life

1. Have volunteers read aloud Raffel's commentary on pages 36–37. Point out that Raffel's first task is to introduce the epic and offer a preview of its plot.

2. **Ask** students what qualities make Beowulf such an extraordinarily heroic figure. **Possible responses:** He has great courage and magical powers, such as the ability to breathe underwater. His name suggests that he is superhuman, part bear and part wolf.

3. Explain to students that the first section of *Beowulf*—the struggle between the hero and the monster Grendel—is suspenseful and exciting. Point out such dramatic events as the arrival of Grendel, Beowulf's journey to Hrothgar's court, and the battle between hero and monster. Use Raffel's summary to build students' anticipation for reading the epic.

Themes Across Centuries: Translator's Insights

Burton Raffel Introduces *Beowulf*

A Legendary Tale, Larger Than Life *Beowulf* is a sweeping, action-packed narrative. Written in highly dramatic language, its characters are almost all kings, princes, and their heroic followers. The plot is energized by a pair of powerful man-eating monsters and, at the end, a greedy, fire-spouting dragon. All three are killed by the poem's principal character, Beowulf, who possesses magical qualities of his own. He can swim for days on end; he can breathe for extended periods underwater; his very name tells us in three ways that he is no mere human. He is Beo, or "bear." He is also Wulf, or "wolf." And most important of all, his name does not begin exactly as his father's name, Edgetho: for everyone in Anglo-Saxon England, this break in tradition would have been a dead giveaway of Beowulf's extraordinary character.

A Grand Beginning The story crackles with wonderfully calculated suspense. The hero himself is not introduced at the start. Man-eating Grendel takes the stage, emerging out of the kind of darkness and terror in which Anglo-Saxon life was steeped. Beowulf comes to help the besieged King Hrothgar. (His exciting travel over the deep waves was the first part of the poem I read, over fifty years ago.) The poem carefully explains his heroic, profoundly social motives. Offering himself as a potential sacrifice to Grendel, he fights with and tears an arm off the monster, who flees back into darkness.

Everyone is overjoyed, there is much celebrating—until Grendel's mother enters the scene, hungry (literally) for revenge. Beowulf promptly accepts the challenge, diving far down into the water, finding the lady demon, and in the end killing her in a very close fight. Loaded with praise and gifts, he returns to his own king, to whose throne he succeeds.

The Passage of Time Fifty years later, the old Beowulf's land is terrorized by a fire-breathing dragon. Unlike a good king, and like some of the bad kings in the poem, the dragon fiercely guards and never shares its treasures. Beowulf does not hesitate. But he is old and not as strong as he was. Significantly, he must have help, and is so badly burned that, after the dragon is dead, Beowulf too dies. His people give him a royal burial and a monument, and sing the praises due to a fearless ruler who so totally embodied the virtues of a warrior king.

36 From Legend to History (A.D. 449–1485)

About the Author

Burton Raffel, the translator of the version of *Beowulf* that follows, has won the Frances Steloff Prize and the Translation Prize for the French-American Foundation. He is the author of numerous poems, screenplays, and novels.

Teaching Resources

The following resources can be used to enrich or extend the instruction for Contemporary Commentary.

Unit 1 Resources
From the Translator's desk: Burton Raffel Introduces Beowulf, p. 31
Listening and Viewing, p. 32

See It! DVD
Burton Raffel, Segment 2

All resources are available at **www.PHLitOnline.com**.

◄ Critical Viewing
Which of the dragon's characteristics might a storyteller share with an audience? [Connect]

The Spirit of *Beowulf* *Beowulf* is not a pagan poem. There are no pagan gods, no idols, no wanton human sacrifices. Anglo-Saxon England had long since been Christianized when *Beowulf* was composed, but the epic is primarily concerned with social, not religious, issues. Still, if not overtly Christian, *Beowulf*'s close identification with ancient Hebraic ways of life marks it as very much an Old Testament poem. "Almighty God," clearly and repeatedly evoked, operates ethically and holds humans to high moral standards. The creation story of Genesis is beautifully paraphrased. Hell is cited as the home of evil; the Abel and Cain tale is mentioned explicitly. And just as evil is punished, good prevails. The message is that men must learn to behave responsibly, and to love and be faithful to one another, exactly as *Beowulf* has shown that they can.

Critical Reading

1. **Key Ideas and Details (a)** What was the first part of *Beowulf* that Burton Raffel read? **(b) Speculate:** Based on Raffel's introduction, what aspects of the poem do you think led to his lifelong interest in *Beowulf*?

2. **Key Ideas and Details (a)** What specific details of the poem allow Raffel to say so definitely that *Beowulf* is not a pagan poem? **(b) Analyze:** What might the religious dimension of *Beowulf* tell us about the culture that produced it?

As You Read *Beowulf* . . .

3. **Integration of Knowledge and Ideas** Be ready to compare and contrast your reaction to the poem with Raffel's.

4. **Integration of Knowledge and Ideas** Think about how Raffel's passion for the poem is revealed in his translation.

Extended Study: The Epic **37**

Differentiated Instruction   for Universal Access

Culturally Responsive Instruction

Culture Connection When one people conquers another, cultures tend to mesh in interesting ways. When the Spanish Conquistadors came to the New World, for example, they sought to spread the Catholic faith among the native peoples, resulting in a hybrid belief system that mixed Catholic and traditional native beliefs.

This principle also occurs with language. When the Anglo-Saxon invasion occurred, two languages clashed—German and the old Celtic language. The result was Old English, the language in which *Beowulf* was originally recorded. Students should be aware that the text in this book is one of many translations of the epic poem, and that the translations may vary greatly in style. It may be a fruitful exercise to bring in short sections of different translations so that students can compare and contrast them and discuss which translations they prefer and for what reasons.

Critical Viewing

Possible responses: A storyteller might share details such as the dragon's yellow eyes, fierce expression, large wings, fiery breath, and sharp claws, fangs, and horns.

ASSESS
Answers

As students answer the questions below, remind them to support their answers with evidence from the text.

1. (a) The first part Raffel read was the description of Beowulf's journey over deep waves to King Hrothgar's court. (b) **Possible response:** Raffel seems to be interested in *Beowulf* because it deals with social issues, establishing moral standards and telling readers that they must be responsible and faithful toward one another. He is also drawn to the poem's excitement and suspense.

2. (a) *Beowulf* includes references to the Judeo-Christian God, the creation story of Genesis, Hell, and the story of Abel and Cain. (b) **Possible response:** The poem was produced by a Christian culture that had moved away from the old gods. It was also a culture concerned with moral and ethical standards of behavior.

3. Students are not likely to embrace *Beowulf* as wholeheartedly as Raffel does. They do not have his academic background, so they will not be familiar with the culture the poem reflects. However, the action and excitement to which Raffel responds so strongly should be gripping for students as well.

4. Students may point to the flow of Raffel's translation and its dramatic building of tension and suspense. They are likely to find that Raffel's translation captures the excitement he first found in *Beowulf*.

Before You Read from *Beowulf*

❶ Connecting to the Essential Question

1. Review the assignment with the class.

2. Discuss movies and books featuring heroes who defeat evil beings or forces.

3. As students read, have them consider ideas of evil.

❷ Literary Analysis

Introduce the skill, using the instruction on the student page.

Think Aloud: Model the Skill

Say to students:

From the beginning, *Beowulf* exhibits the characteristics of an epic. Lines 15–16 read "Hrothgar's men lived happy in his hall/Till the monster stirred. . ." In these lines I notice that a usual way of life is described—the men living happily in the hall. The word *Till* shows that this happy way of life is about to be interrupted—the monster is a threat to that way of life.

❸ Reading Strategy

1. Introduce the strategy, using the instruction on the student page.

2. Give students a copy of **Reading Strategy Graphic Organizer B,** page 6 in *Graphic Organizer Transparencies,* to fill out as they read.

❹ Vocabulary

1. Pronounce each word, giving its definition, and have students say it aloud.

2. For more guidance, see the *Classroom Strategies and Teaching Routines* card for introducing vocabulary.

---

❶ **Connecting to the Essential Question** In *Beowulf*, a brave hero battles swamp-dwelling monsters that threaten a kingdom. As you read, notice descriptions of the monsters in *Beowulf*, and consider what the details suggest about Anglo-Saxon ideas about evil. Doing so will help as you explore the Essential Question: **How does literature shape or reflect society?**

❷ ## Literary Analysis

An **epic** is a long narrative poem, sometimes developed orally, that celebrates heroic deeds and legendary events. Epics, like Homer's *Iliad* from ancient Greece, are among the earliest forms of literature. As such, they reveal the values of the peoples who created them. For example, in *Beowulf*, the action in the mead hall reveals the social and economic relationship between an Anglo-Saxon lord and his followers. This is where the lord provides food, shelter, and fellowship in return for loyalty. It is the center of civilization and all that threatens it is evil. Common features of epics include the following:

- a story told in a serious manner, with elevated language
- a hero battling forces that threaten the world's order

Most epics celebrate the exploits of a **legendary, or epic, hero,** a larger-than-life character. Beowulf's boastful self-confidence, his feats of strength, and his victories in battle make him a classic epic hero. Because he upholds the values of his culture—loyalty, bravery, honor—he can teach modern readers a great deal about the Anglo-Saxon view of the world.

❸ ## Reading Strategy

Ⓒ **Preparing to Read Complex Texts** To **determine the main idea or essential message** of a passage, you can *paraphrase* it—identify the key details and restate them in your own words. This strategy will help you understand the long, involved sentences in this translation of *Beowulf*. Use a graphic organizer like the one shown to help you paraphrase such sentences.

❹ ## Vocabulary

reparation (rep´ ə rā´ shən) *n.* compensation for a wrong (p. 43)

solace (säl´ is) *n.* comfort; relief (p. 44)

purge (purj) *v.* purify; cleanse (p. 48)

writhing (rīth´ iŋ) *adj.* making twisting or turning motions (p. 50)

massive (mas´ iv) *adj.* big and solid; bulky (p. 54)

loathsome (lōth´ səm) *adj.* disgusting (p. 55)

Ⓒ **Common Core State Standards**

Reading Literature
3. Analyze the impact of the author's choices regarding how to develop and relate elements of a story or drama.

Original

High on a wall a Danish watcher / Patrolling along the cliffs saw / The travelers crossing to the shore, their shields / Raised and shining. . . .

Key Details:
guard; saw people; come ashore

Paraphrase

A Danish guard saw strangers come ashore, holding up their shields.

PHLit Online!
www.PHLitOnline.com

38 From Legend to History (A.D. 449–1485)

Vocabulary Development

Vocabulary Knowledge Rating

Create a **Vocabulary Knowledge Rating Chart** (*Professional Development Guidebook,* pp. 32–33) for the vocabulary words on the student page. Give each student a copy of the chart with the words on it. Read the words aloud, and have students mark their rating of each in the Before Reading column. Urge students to attend to these words as they read and discuss the selection.

In order to gauge how much instruction you need to provide, tally how many students are confident in their knowledge of each word. As students read, point out the words and their context.

PHLit Online! **Vocabulary Central,** featuring tools and activities for studying vocabulary, is available online at www.PHLitOnline.com.

⑤ ABOUT *BEOWULF*

During Britain's Anglo-Saxon period, from the fifth to the eleventh century, few people were able to read and movies lay centuries in the future. Although the action takes place in sixth-century Scandinavia, *Beowulf* was originally told in Old English, the language spoken by the Anglo-Saxons of England during the years 500 to 1100.

Beowulf, a Geat from a region that is today southern Sweden, sets sail to aid the Danish King Hrothgar in his fight against the monster Grendel. A terrifying swampland creature whose eyes burn "with gruesome light," Grendel has been terrorizing Hrothgar's great banquet hall, Herot, for twelve years. The battle between Beowulf, a young warrior of great strength and courage, and Grendel, his bloodthirsty foe, is the first of three mortal battles that are fought in this long poem.

Forging an Epic The tales in *Beowulf* originate from a time when stories and poems were passed along by word of mouth. In Anglo-Saxon England, traveling minstrels, called *scops*, captivated audiences with long narrative poems. These poems changed and grew as they were passed from one scop to another. *Beowulf* was told and retold in this fashion throughout England for hundreds of years. In the eleventh c entury, the epic was finally written down.

Beowulf grew out of other, earlier traditions. The monsters and dragons of the tale, the brave warriors steadfastly loyal to their heroic chief, the descent into the eerie regions below the earth— these were familiar elements of Scandinavian or Celtic folk tales. Even a detail as specific as Beowulf's seizure of Grendel's arm can be traced to earlier tales.

A Guide to Life By forging these various traditions into one unified tale and by adding the later influence of Christianity, the Anglo-Saxon scops created a central reference point for their culture. Listening to *Beowulf,* an Anglo-Saxon could learn of bravery and loyalty to one's fellows, of the monsters that spite and hatred could breed, and of the heroism needed to conquer such monsters.

Beowulf and Popular Culture
- Nobel Prize–winner Seamus Heaney's translation of *Beowulf* won the Whitbread Book of the Year Award for Poetry in 1999. (See pages 68–69 for Heaney's comments on his translation.)
- Roger Avary and Neil Gaiman adapted *Beowulf* as a computer animated movie (2007), with voice-overs performed by such stars as Angelina Jolie, Anthony Hopkins, and John Malkovich.
- A *Beowulf* comic-book series was issued in connection with the *Beowulf* movie.

An ancient helmet worn by Anglo-Saxons. ▼

from Beowulf **39**

PHLit Online!
www.PHLitOnline.com

Teaching From Technology

Preparing to Read
Go to **www.PHLitOnline.com** in class or in a lab and display the **Get Connected!** slide show for this grouping. Have the class brainstorm responses to the slide show writing prompt, entering ideas in the interactive journal. Then, have students complete their written responses individually, in a lab or as homework.

To build background, display the features.

Using the Interactive Text
Go to **www.PHLitOnline.com** and display the Enriched Online Student Edition. As the class reads the selection or listens to the narration, record answers to side-column prompts using the graphic organizers accessible on the interactive page. Alternatively, have students use the online edition individually, answering the prompts as they read.

 Daily Bellringer

For each class during which you will teach these selections, have students complete one of the five activities for the appropriate week in the *Daily Bellringer Activities* booklet.

Multidraft Reading

To assist struggling readers and to enhance reading for all, assign the text in chunks as warranted by length and apply multidraft reading protocols. For each reading, have students set the purpose indicated:

- **First reading**—identifying key ideas and details and answering any Reading Checks.
- **Second reading**—analyzing craft and structure and responding to the side-column prompts.
- **Third reading**—integrating knowledge and ideas, connecting to other texts and the world, and answering the end-of-selection questions.

For more guidance, refer to the *Classroom Strategies and Teaching Routines* card on multidraft reading.

⑤ More About the Author

Anglo-Saxons were the descendants of three different Germanic peoples— the Angles, Saxons, and Jutes. These groups migrated to England from Northern Germany in the fifth century. The author of *Beowulf* is unknown, but it seems likely that he was from one of the Anglian settlements. Recent discoveries in this region include burial sites with grave goods that are similar to those in the poem and that are closely linked to Beowulf's homeland, Sweden. While there is no evidence that Beowulf himself ever existed, there are people and events in the poem that are true. For example, Higlac really was king of the Geats. He died in battle sometime in the 520s—which is one reason we know that *Beowulf* was composed after that decade, because the poem mentions Higlac's death. Hrothgar, too, is among many historical characters in the work.

❶ About the Selection

Familiarity with the epic formula of *Beowulf* is a prerequisite for reading major works by Milton and Tennyson, as well as lighthearted mock epics by Chaucer and Pope. However, because of the stirring language and compelling action, *Beowulf* stands on its own merits, drawing readers into the adventures of another time and place.

❷ Activating Prior Knowledge

Have students share stories with which they are familiar in which a hero slays a dragon or other mythical beast. Discuss similarities among these stories, such as obstacles the heroes must overcome on the way to victory and characteristics the heroes share. Have students write a short paragraph predicting how these elements might appear in *Beowulf*.

Concept Connector ➡

Tell students they will return to their responses after reading the selections.

❸ Critical Thinking

Compare and Contrast

Ask students to contrast the description of Herot with the dwelling of the monster Grendel found in the first four lines of the poem.

Possible response: Herot is filled with music and rejoicing, while the monster lives down in the darkness and growls with pain.

FROM

❶ ❷ BEOWULF

TRANSLATED BY BURTON RAFFEL

BACKGROUND When *Beowulf* was composed, England was changing from a pagan to a Christian culture. Pagan Anglo-Saxons told grim tales of life ruled by fate, tales in which people struggled against monsters for their place in the world. The missionaries who converted them to Christianity taught them that human beings and their choices of good or evil were at the center of creation. Beowulf reflects both pagan and Christian traditions. The selection opens during an evening of celebration at Herot, the banquet hall of the Danish king Hrothgar (hroth´ gär). Outside in the darkness, however, lurks the murderous monster Grendel.

THE WRATH OF GRENDEL

A powerful monster, living down
In the darkness, growled in pain, impatient
As day after day the music rang
Loud in that hall,[1] the harp's rejoicing
5   Call and the poet's clear songs, sung
Of the ancient beginnings of us all, recalling
The Almighty making the earth, shaping
These beautiful plains marked off by oceans,
Then proudly setting the sun and moon
10 To glow across the land and light it;
The corners of the earth were made lovely with trees
And leaves, made quick with life, with each
Of the nations who now move on its face. And then
As now warriors sang of their pleasure:
15 So Hrothgar's men lived happy in his hall
Till the monster stirred, that demon, that fiend,
Grendel, who haunted the moors, the wild

---
1. hall Herot.

40 From Legend to History (A.D. 449–1485)

Ⓔ Text Complexity Rubric

from Beowulf

Qualitative Measures	
Context/Knowledge Demands	Anglo-Saxon epic; historical knowledge demands 1 2 ③ 4 5
Structure/Language Conventionality and Clarity	Long, complex sentences 1 2 ③ 4 5
Levels of Meaning/ Purpose/Concept Level	Accessible (heroic figure and deeds) 1 ② 3 4 5
Quantitative Measures	
Lexile	NP	Text Length	6,804 words
Overall Complexity	**More accessible**		

Reader and Task Suggestions

Preparing to Read the Text
- Using the information on SE p. 39, discuss key ideas and attitudes likely to be found in an Anglo-Saxon epic.
- Review strategies for untangling long sentences and for paraphrasing key ideas.
- Guide students to use Multidraft Reading strategies (TE p. 39).

Leveled Tasks

Structure/Language If students will have difficulty with the long sentences, assign the selection's eight sections to different groups to paraphrase key ideas. Then, have them reread the text to focus on key ideas.

Synthesizing If students will not have difficulty with the long sentences, have them synthesize key ideas about Beowulf's deeds and role in his society.

from Beowulf **41**

1. **Ask** students: Before we even know this creature's name, what information do we have about it?
   Possible responses: It is a monster; it lives in the darkness underground; it is subjected to pain and is impatient.

2. **Ask** students: What judgments might we make about this creature's relationship to society? What textual details contribute to these judgments?
   Possible responses: The creature is separate from society since it lives in darkness underground, which generally does not characterize most human societies. Also, the word *monster* is pejorative, indicating a judgment the society has placed on this outside creature.

3. Remind students to look as they read for details about the monsters, which are clues to discovering what evil meant in the Anglo-Saxon mind.

Differentiated Instruction   for Universal Access

Support for Special-Needs Students
Have students complete the **Before You Read** and the **Making Connections** pages for this selection in the *Reader's Notebook: Adapted Version.* These pages provide abbreviated skills instruction, a selection summary, the Before You Read graphic organizer, and a **Note-taking Guide.**

Support for Less Proficient Readers
Have students complete the **Before You Read** and the **Making Connections** pages for this selection in the *Reader's Notebook.* These pages provide abbreviated skills instruction, a selection summary, the Before You Read graphic organizer, and a **Note-taking Guide.**

EL Support for English Learners
Have students complete the **Before You Read** and the **Making Connections** pages for this selection in the *Reader's Notebook: English Learner's Version.* These pages provide additional vocabulary, vocabulary skills, and vocabulary practice, along with a **Getting Ready to Read** activity.

PHLit Online!

This selection is available in interactive format in the **Enriched Online Student Edition,** at **www.PHLitOnline.com,** which includes a thematically related video with writing prompt and an interactive graphic organizer.

Define

1. Have a student volunteer read aloud lines 23–29.

2. **Ask** students to use these lines, especially lines 28 and 29, to write a definition for the word *evil* as the poet might have defined it. **Possible response:** *Evil*, according to the poet, might be defined as "anything that opposes God's will."

6 Reading Strategy

Determine the Main Idea by Paraphrasing

1. Remind students of the paraphrasing technique that can be used to help determine the main idea or ideas in a passage. Encourage students to use this technique as they read lines 34–40 silently.

2. **Ask** students to paraphrase the events that take place in these lines. **Possible responses:** The monster thinks, moves, and kills quickly. His victims are asleep, peaceful, and unaware of their danger. Grendel kills them as they sleep and carries their bodies off. Killing makes Grendel happy.

3. Tell students that they can condense these paraphrased ideas further to express the main idea or ideas of the passage. Then, **ask** students the Reading Strategy question: What are the main ideas in the sentences in lines 34–40? **Possible response:** The monster sneaks up on and violently kills his sleeping victims.

Marshes, and made his home in a hell
Not hell but earth. He was spawned in that slime,
20 Conceived by a pair of those monsters born
Of Cain,[2] murderous creatures banished
By God, punished forever for the crime
Of Abel's death. The Almighty drove
Those demons out, and their exile was bitter,
25 Shut away from men; they split
5 Into a thousand forms of evil—spirits
And fiends, goblins, monsters, giants,
A brood forever opposing the Lord's
Will, and again and again defeated.
30   Then, when darkness had dropped, Grendel
Went up to Herot, wondering what the warriors
Would do in that hall when their drinking was done.
He found them sprawled in sleep, suspecting
Nothing, their dreams undisturbed. The monster's
35 Thoughts were as quick as his greed or his claws:
He slipped through the door and there in the silence
6 Snatched up thirty men, smashed them
Unknowing in their beds and ran out with their bodies,
The blood dripping behind him, back
40 To his lair, delighted with his night's slaughter.
    At daybreak, with the sun's first light, they saw
How well he had worked, and in that gray morning
Broke their long feast with tears and laments
For the dead. Hrothgar, their lord, sat joyless

Reading Strategy
Determine the Main Idea by Paraphrasing What are the main ideas in the sentences in lines 34–40?

---

2. **Cain** oldest son of Adam and Eve, who murdered his brother, Abel.

42 From Legend to History (A.D. 449–1485)

Think Aloud

Reading Strategy: Determine the Main Idea by Paraphrasing
Model the mental processes involved in answering the Reading Strategy question on this page. Say to students:

    To figure out the main ideas in these lines, the first thing I'll do is paraphrase the passage. Lines 34 and 35 say, "The monster's/ Thoughts were as quick as his greed or his claws." In my own words, these lines are saying that the monster's mind was moving quickly, just as his claws would during a fight. In my own words, the next three lines say that the monster sneaks into the silent hall, grabs thirty sleeping men who never saw him coming, then kills them and takes their bodies. Now that I understand what has happened, I know what is important and what is not as important. The main idea in these lines is that the monster killed thirty men in their sleep. The part about the monster thinking quickly adds detail, but it is not the important event of the passage.

45 In Herot, a mighty prince mourning
    The fate of his lost friends and companions,
    Knowing by its tracks that some demon had torn
    His followers apart. He wept, fearing
    The beginning might not be the end. And that night
50 Grendel came again, so set
    On murder that no crime could ever be enough,
    No savage assault quench his lust
    For evil. Then each warrior tried
    To escape him, searched for rest in different
55 Beds, as far from Herot as they could find,
    Seeing how Grendel hunted when they slept.
    Distance was safety; the only survivors
    Were those who fled him. Hate had triumphed.
        So Grendel ruled, fought with the righteous,
60 One against many, and won; so Herot
    Stood empty, and stayed deserted for years,
    Twelve winters of grief for Hrothgar, king
    Of the Danes, sorrow heaped at his door
    By hell-forged hands. His misery leaped
65 The seas, was told and sung in all
    Men's ears: how Grendel's hatred began,
    How the monster relished his savage war
    On the Danes, keeping the bloody feud
    Alive, seeking no peace, offering
70 No truce, accepting no settlement, no price
    In gold or land, and paying the living
    For one crime only with another. No one
    Waited for reparation from his plundering claws:
    That shadow of death hunted in the darkness,
75 Stalked Hrothgar's warriors, old
    And young, lying in waiting, hidden
    In mist, invisibly following them from the edge
    Of the marsh, always there, unseen.
        So mankind's enemy continued his crimes,
80 Killing as often as he could, coming
    Alone, bloodthirsty and horrible. Though he lived
    In Herot, when the night hid him, he never
    Dared to touch King Hrothgar's glorious
    Throne, protected by God—God,
85 Whose love Grendel could not know. But Hrothgar's
    Heart was bent. The best and most noble
    Of his council debated remedies, sat
    In secret sessions, talking of terror
    And wondering what the bravest of warriors could do.
90 And sometimes they sacrificed to the old stone gods,
    Made heathen vows, hoping for Hell's

❼ Burton Raffel
Translator's Insight
A normal feud involves two sides: it takes two to tangle. Literary lore suggests that monsters are interested in fights they know they will win.

Vocabulary
reparation (rep´ ə rā´ shən) *n.* compensation for a wrong

Reading Check
Why do the Danes flee Herot at night?

from Beowulf **43**

❼ Burton Raffel
Translator's Insight
1. Read aloud Raffel's insight about literary lore. **Ask** students what this information reveals about Grendel.
    Possible response: Students may suggest that Grendel only fights the weak. He does not possess any worthy heroic qualities.
2. **Ask** students to brainstorm other real-life or fictional examples of monster or bully figures who display cowardice or want guaranteed wins.
    Possible responses: Students may mention bullies who only pick fights with weaker children or cite fictional characters, such as the Wizard of Oz, who seek to intimidate others with a false image of strength.

❽ Critical Thinking
Analyze
1. Have a volunteer read aloud lines 79–85.
2. Then, **ask** students how the poem establishes that the coming battle is not just a battle between a hero and a monster, but a battle between good and evil.
    Answer: Hrothgar's throne is untouched because it is protected by God, who is unknown to Grendel.

❾ Reading Check
Answer: The Danes flee Herot at night because Grendel hunts at night, while they sleep.

The Latin Word Root -sol-

1. Call students' attention to the word *solace* and its definition. Tell students that the Latin word root *-sol-* is derived from the word *solari*, which means "to console or comfort, to soothe."

2. Point out that, as with other roots, meaning is built with prefixes and suffixes. For example, *disconsolate* would describe someone who lacks (*dis-*) that which gives solace. Write *inconsolable* on the board, circling the root *-sol-*, and **ask** students what they think *inconsolable* would mean.
   Answer: Not able to be comforted.

3. Explain to students that the root *-sol-* may have other meanings as well. For example, in the words *solitary* and *solo*, *-sol-* means "alone."

⑪ **Literary Analysis**

The Epic

1. Remind students that an epic hero embodies the values and ideals of the culture that produces him.

2. Have students take turns reading lines 109–122 aloud.

3. **Ask** students what qualities they think were valued by Anglo-Saxons, based on the descriptions of Beowulf in lines 109–122.
   Answer: Anglo-Saxons valued strength, leadership, willingness to help others, and bravery.

Support, the Devil's guidance in driving
Their affliction off. That was their way,
And the heathen's only hope, Hell
95 Always in their hearts, knowing neither God
Nor His passing as He walks through our world, the Lord
Of Heaven and earth; their ears could not hear
His praise nor know His glory. Let them
Beware, those who are thrust into danger,
100 Clutched at by trouble, yet can carry no solace
In their hearts, cannot hope to be better! Hail
To those who will rise to God, drop off
Their dead bodies and seek our Father's peace!

⑩ **Vocabulary**
solace (säl´ is) *n.* comfort; relief

THE COMING OF BEOWULF

So the living sorrow of Healfdane's son[3]
105 Simmered, bitter and fresh, and no wisdom
Or strength could break it: that agony hung
On king and people alike, harsh
And unending, violent and cruel, and evil.
In his far-off home Beowulf, Higlac's[4]
110 Follower and the strongest of the Geats—greater
And stronger than anyone anywhere in this world—
Heard how Grendel filled nights with horror
And quickly commanded a boat fitted out,
Proclaiming that he'd go to that famous king,
⑪ 115 Would sail across the sea to Hrothgar,
Now when help was needed. None
Of the wise ones regretted his going, much
As he was loved by the Geats: the omens were good,
And they urged the adventure on. So Beowulf
120 Chose the mightiest men he could find,
The bravest and best of the Geats, fourteen
In all, and led them down to their boat;
He knew the sea, would point the prow
Straight to that distant Danish shore.
⑫↓125   Then they sailed, set their ship

---

3. **Healfdane's** (hä´ alf den´ nez) **son** Hrothgar.
4. **Higlac's** (hig´ laks) Higlac was the king of the Geats (gä´ ats) and Beowulf's feudal lord and uncle.

44 From Legend to History (A.D. 449–1485)

Enrichment: Investigating Technology

Nautical Technology

The Geats were excellent sailors whom "the wind hurried … over the waves" and "through the sea like a bird." Acquiring such sailing skill is not a simple matter; it requires an understanding of the forces of wind and water and the capabilities of the ship. The design and features of the ship would have been crucial factors to the success of a nautical journey in this time, as they are today. The Anglo-Saxons developed techniques and technologies to construct sound ships.

Activity: Research Anglo-Saxon Ships Have groups conduct research on the features of Anglo-Saxon ships and the purposes of each feature. Suggest that they record information in the **Enrichment: Investigating Technology** worksheet, *Professional Development Guidebook*, page 242. Have students share their results and discuss whether they believe the illustration on page 45 to be an accurate representation of an Anglo-Saxon ship, and why.

Out on the waves, under the cliffs.
Ready for what came they wound through the currents,
The seas beating at the sand, and were borne
In the lap of their shining ship, lined
130 With gleaming armor, going safely
In that oak-hard boat to where their hearts took them.
The wind hurried them over the waves,
The ship foamed through the sea like a bird
Until, in the time they had known it would take,
135 Standing in the round-curled prow they could see
Sparkling hills, high and green
Jutting up over the shore, and rejoicing
In those rock-steep cliffs they quietly ended
Their voyage. Jumping to the ground, the Geats
140 Pushed their boat to the sand and tied it
In place, mail⁵ shirts and armor rattling
As they swiftly moored their ship. And then
They gave thanks to God for their easy crossing.
        High on a wall a Danish watcher
145 Patrolling along the cliffs saw
The travelers crossing to the shore, their shields
Raised and shining; he came riding down,
Hrothgar's lieutenant, spurring his horse,
Needing to know why they'd landed, these men
150 In armor. Shaking his heavy spear
In their faces he spoke:
                "Whose soldiers are you,
You who've been carried in your deep-keeled ship
Across the sea-road to this country of mine?
Listen! I've stood on these cliffs longer
155 Than you know, keeping our coast free
Of pirates, raiders sneaking ashore
From their ships, seeking our lives and our gold.
None have ever come more openly—
And yet you've offered no password, no sign
160 From my prince, no permission from my people
        for your landing

---

5. **mail** flexible body armor made of metal.

Reading Strategy
Determine the Main Idea by Paraphrasing
Paraphrase lines 125–131. Remember that your paraphrase need not follow the word order of the original.

❸ ☑ Reading Check
Why does Beowulf sail to Denmark?

❷ Reading Strategy
Determine the Main Idea by Paraphrasing
1. Point out the suggestion following the Reading Strategy prompt, and encourage students to keep this in mind as they read silently and paraphrase lines 125–131. Have students jot down their paraphrases on paper.
2. Then, **ask** volunteers to answer the Reading Strategy prompt by sharing their paraphrases. **Possible responses:** The Geats loaded their armor into a strong boat. They felt ready for whatever might happen. Following their hearts, they set sail, traveling safely past cliffs and through ocean currents.

❸ Reading Check
Answer: Beowulf sails to Denmark to help Hrothgar defend his people against the monster Grendel.

Differentiated Instruction for Universal Access

Support for Special-Needs Students
If students are having difficulty following the action of the story, have them read it first in the **Reader's Notebooks**. There is a summary of the story, a story map that outlines the action, and an adapted version of several sections of *Beowulf*, including "The Coming of Beowulf." Once students understand what is happening, encourage them to keep the story map nearby, so that they can keep track of where they are in the tale.

Support for Less Proficient Readers
Students may benefit from reading "The Coming of Beowulf" in the **Reader's Notebooks**. After they read the summary of the story and review the story map, students will find the full text of this section of the tale accompanied by a variety of questions and comments, designed to aid comprehension, that parallel the text.

1. Have students look at lines 173–179 and identify the details of Beowulf's response to the watchman's challenge.

2. Then, **ask** the Literary Analysis question: What does Beowulf's way of identifying himself suggest about the values of a warrior culture?
   Answer: They valued military prowess, leadership, longevity, wisdom, and having a respected father.

⓯ **Engaging the Essential Question**

1. Remind students that Beowulf was shaped in part by Christian ideas about the nature of good and evil. Tell them that biblical language describes the devil as prowling for unsuspecting prey and working undetected while people sleep.

2. **Ask** students: What details are given about Grendel in lines 185–190?
   Possible responses: Grendel is strange and vicious; no one has seen him since he hunts at night.

3. **Ask** students: Do you find it more likely that descriptions such as the one given here of Grendel shaped people's ideas about the nature of evil or that societal notions of evil were reflected in the way evil characters were described in literature? Why?
   Possible response: The latter, since Grendel's description so closely mirrors Christian language about the devil.

4. Tell students to continue looking for descriptions of evil characters as they read.

Literary Analysis ⓮
The Epic and the Legendary Hero
What does Beowulf's way of identifying himself suggest about the values of a warrior culture?

⓯

Here. Nor have I ever seen,
Out of all the men on earth, one greater
Than has come with you; no commoner carries
Such weapons, unless his appearance, and his beauty,
165 Are both lies. You! Tell me your name,
And your father's; no spies go further onto Danish
Soil than you've come already. Strangers,
From wherever it was you sailed, tell it,
And tell it quickly, the quicker the better,
170 I say, for us all. Speak, say
Exactly who you are, and from where, and why."
　　　Their leader answered him, Beowulf unlocking
Words from deep in his breast:
　　　　　　　"We are Geats,
Men who follow Higlac. My father
175 Was a famous soldier, known far and wide
As a leader of men. His name was Edgetho.
His life lasted many winters;
Wise men all over the earth surely
Remember him still. And we have come seeking
180 Your prince, Healfdane's son, protector
Of this people, only in friendship: instruct us,
Watchman, help us with your words! Our errand
Is a great one, our business with the glorious king
Of the Danes no secret; there's nothing dark
185 Or hidden in our coming. You know (if we've heard
The truth, and been told honestly) that your country
Is cursed with some strange, vicious creature
That hunts only at night and that no one
Has seen. It's said, watchman, that he has slaughtered
190 Your people, brought terror to the darkness. Perhaps
Hrothgar can hunt, here in my heart,
For some way to drive this devil out—
If anything will ever end the evils
Afflicting your wise and famous lord.
195 Here he can cool his burning sorrow.
Or else he may see his suffering go on
Forever, for as long as Herot towers
High on your hills."
　　　　　　　The mounted officer
Answered him bluntly, the brave watchman:
200 "A soldier should know the difference between words
And deeds, and keep that knowledge clear
In his brain. I believe your words, I trust in
Your friendship. Go forward, weapons and armor
And all, on into Denmark. I'll guide you
205 Myself—and my men will guard your ship,

Think Aloud

Vocabulary: Using Context
Direct students' attention to the word *gables* (line 219). Use the following "think aloud" to model the skill of using context to infer the meaning of the word. Say to students:

　I may not know the meaning of this word. However, line 220 tells me that the gables are "of Herot." I know that Herot is a building, so *gables* might be something on or near a building. The rest of lines 220 and 221 says that the gables are "covered with hammered gold/And glowing in the sun."

This lets me know that the gables are probably meant to be decorative, since they are covered in gold. Line 222 refers to the "glittering roofs" of Herot. If the gables are covered with hammered gold, they would probably glitter in the sun. This makes me want to guess that the gold-covered gables might be the same thing as the glittering roofs, so *gables* might be another word for *roofs*. *Gables* could also simply refer to part of a building's roof. I could look up the word in a dictionary to check my guess.

Keep it safe here on our shores,
Your fresh-tarred boat, watch it well,
Until that curving prow carries
Across the sea to Geatland a chosen
210 Warrior who bravely does battle with the creature
Haunting our people, who survives that horror
Unhurt, and goes home bearing our love."
        Then they moved on. Their boat lay moored,
Tied tight to its anchor. Glittering at the top
215 Of their golden helmets wild boar heads gleamed,
Shining decorations, swinging as they marched,
Erect like guards, like sentinels, as though ready
To fight. They marched, Beowulf and his men
And their guide, until they could see the gables
220 Of Herot, covered with hammered gold
And glowing in the sun—that most famous of
    all dwellings,
Towering majestic, its glittering roofs
Visible far across the land.
Their guide reined in his horse, pointing
225 To that hall, built by Hrothgar for the best
And bravest of his men; the path was plain,
They could see their way. . . .

*Beowulf and his men arrive at Herot and are called to see
the King.*

                Beowulf arose, with his men
230 Around him, ordering a few to remain
With their weapons, leading the others quickly
Along under Herot's steep roof into Hrothgar's
Presence. Standing on that prince's own hearth,
Helmeted, the silvery metal of his mail shirt
235 Gleaming with a smith's high art, he greeted
The Danes' great lord:
                "Hail, Hrothgar!
Higlac is my cousin[6] and my king; the days
Of my youth have been filled with glory. Now Grendel's
Name has echoed in our land: sailors
240 Have brought us stories of Herot, the best
Of all mead-halls,[7] deserted and useless when the moon
Hangs in skies the sun had lit,
Light and life fleeing together.
My people have said, the wisest, most knowing
245 And best of them, that my duty was to go to the Danes'
Great king. They have seen my strength for themselves,

---

6. **cousin** here, used as a general term for relative.
7. **mead-halls** To reward his thanes, the king in heroic literature would build a hall
   where mead (a drink made from fermented honey) was served.

16 ▼ Critical Viewing
What can you infer about
ancient Scandinavian society
based on the artifacts
displayed on pages 46–47?
[Infer]

18 ☑ Reading Check
Where does the watchman
bring Beowulf?

from Beowulf **47**

16 **Critical Viewing**
Possible responses: The ancient
Scandinavian people valued beauty
and ornate decoration even in
utilitarian objects. The society was
advanced and wealthy enough to
support artisans.

17 **Critical Thinking**
Speculate
1. Read aloud lines 229–233.
2. **Ask** students: Why do you think
   Beowulf ordered some of his men
   to remain outside Herot with
   their weapons?
   Possible response: Even
   though Beowulf and his men had
   been welcomed by the guard,
   they were still in a foreign land,
   and Beowulf did not want to risk
   being tricked or attacked.

18 **Reading Check**
Answer: The watchman brings
Beowulf and his men to Herot so that
they can speak to Hrothgar.

**Differentiated
Instruction** for Universal Access

Enrichment for Gifted/Talented Students
Have students work in small groups to recreate a
scene from *Beowulf* for the stage. Some students
may wish to do a dramatic reading; others may
wish to use the *Hear It!* **Audio CDs** as narration
for their performance. Alternatively, students
may choose to write their own script for a scene
from *Beowulf*. You may have different groups
enact the same scene in order to see and discuss
how different interpretations lead to differences
in performance, or you may have different
groups choose different scenes in order to cover
more of the selection as a class.

Strategy for Advanced Readers
Have students write character analyses for
Grendel and Hrothgar based on what they have
read. Encourage students to use a strategy such
as creating a chart in which they analyze and
compare the characters' physical descriptions,
home environments, actions, motives, and character traits. **Ask** students to address how the
poet aligns these characters with good and evil
based on their behavior and other descriptions
of them in the poem.

The Epic and the Legendary Hero

1. Have students read lines 248–264 silently.

2. Then, **ask** students the Literary Analysis question: How do Beowulf's boasts of past deeds and his announcement of his plan establish him as a hero?
Possible responses: Beowulf relates the type of larger-than-life accomplishments one would expect from a legendary hero, including the defeat of giants, and also establishes that he is famous for his deeds (his people have seen him in battle, and that is why they sent him). Also, his confidence in his ability to defeat Grendel is typical of a legendary hero.

▶ **Monitor Progress: Ask** students to list characteristics that would typify a legendary hero.
Possible responses: A legendary hero would be famous, brave, and have superior strength and skills.

▶ **Reteach:** If students give only a vague description of a legendary hero, remind them that legendary heroes are larger than life, exude self-confidence, and likely have a track record of battle victories and feats of strength to back up their confidence and reputation.

⓴ **Reading Strategy**

Determine the Main Idea by Paraphrasing

1. Have a student volunteer read aloud lines 264–279.

2. Then, have students complete the Reading Strategy prompt:
Paraphrase Beowulf's plans in lines 264–279. Students may need some time to complete this task.
Possible response: Beowulf plans to wait for Grendel in the hall, where he will fight the monster with his bare hands. He realizes that he may be killed and eaten.

3. **Ask** students what Beowulf gives as his reason for fighting barehanded.
Answer: He is afraid that it would be less honorable to use a sword and hide behind a shield. Besides, the battle is in God's hands.

48

Literary Analysis
The Epic and the Legendary Hero ⓳
How do Beowulf's boasts of great deeds and his announcement of his plan establish him as a hero?

Vocabulary
purge (purj) *v.* purify; cleanse

Reading Strategy
Determine the Main Idea by Paraphrasing
Paraphrase Beowulf's plans in lines 264–279.

Have watched me rise from the darkness of war,
Dripping with my enemies' blood. I drove
Five great giants into chains, chased
250 All of that race from the earth. I swam
In the blackness of night, hunting monsters
Out of the ocean, and killing them one
By one; death was my errand and the fate
They had earned. Now Grendel and I are called
255 Together, and I've come. Grant me, then,
Lord and protector of this noble place,
A single request! I have come so far,
O shelterer of warriors and your people's loved friend,
That this one favor you should not refuse me—
260 That I, alone and with the help of my men,
May purge all evil from this hall. I have heard,
Too, that the monster's scorn of men
Is so great that he needs no weapons and fears none.
Nor will I. My lord Higlac
265 Might think less of me if I let my sword
Go where my feet were afraid to, if I hid
Behind some broad linden[8] shield: my hands
Alone shall fight for me, struggle for life
Against the monster. God must decide
270 Who will be given to death's cold grip.
Grendel's plan, I think, will be
What it has been before, to invade this hall
And gorge his belly with our bodies. If he can,
If he can. And I think, if my time will have come,
275 There'll be nothing to mourn over, no corpse to prepare
For its grave: Grendel will carry our bloody
Flesh to the moors, crunch on our bones
And smear torn scraps of our skin on the walls
Of his den. No, I expect no Danes
280 Will fret about sewing our shrouds, if he wins.
And if death does take me, send the hammered
Mail of my armor to Higlac, return
The inheritance I had from Hrethel, and he
From Wayland.[9] Fate will unwind as it must!"

That night Beowulf and his men stay inside Herot. While his men sleep, Beowulf lies awake, eager to meet with Grendel.

---

8. **linden** very sturdy type of wood.
9. **Wayland** from Germanic folklore, an invisible blacksmith.

48 From Legend to History (A.D. 449–1485)

THE BATTLE WITH GRENDEL

285　　Out from the marsh, from the foot of misty
　　Hills and bogs, bearing God's hatred,
　　Grendel came, hoping to kill
　　Anyone he could trap on this trip to high Herot.
　　He moved quickly through the cloudy night,
290　Up from his swampland, sliding silently
　　Toward that gold-shining hall. He had visited Hrothgar's
　　Home before, knew the way—
　　But never, before nor after that night,
　　Found Herot defended so firmly, his reception
295　So harsh. He journeyed, forever joyless,
　　Straight to the door, then snapped it open,
　　Tore its iron fasteners with a touch
　　And rushed angrily over the threshold.
　　He strode quickly across the inlaid
300　Floor, snarling and fierce: his eyes
　　Gleamed in the darkness, burned with a gruesome
　　Light. Then he stopped, seeing the hall
　　Crowded with sleeping warriors, stuffed
　　With rows of young soldiers resting together.
305　And his heart laughed, he relished the sight,
　　Intended to tear the life from those bodies
　　By morning; the monster's mind was hot
　　With the thought of food and the feasting his belly
　　Would soon know. But fate, that night, intended
310　Grendel to gnaw the broken bones
　　Of his last human supper. Human
　　Eyes were watching his evil steps,
　　Waiting to see his swift hard claws.
　　Grendel snatched at the first Geat
315　He came to, ripped him apart, cut
　　His body to bits with powerful jaws,
　　Drank the blood from his veins and bolted
　　Him down, hands and feet; death
　　And Grendel's great teeth came together,
320　Snapping life shut. Then he stepped to another
　　Still body, clutched at Beowulf with his claws,
　　Grasped at a strong-hearted wakeful sleeper
　　—And was instantly seized himself, claws
　　Bent back as Beowulf leaned up on one arm.
325　　That shepherd of evil, guardian of crime,
　　Knew at once that nowhere on earth
　　Had he met a man whose hands were harder;
　　His mind was flooded with fear—but nothing
　　Could take his talons and himself from that tight

21 ▼ Critical Viewing
Why do you think early Scandinavians adorned their ships with figures like the one below? **[Speculate]**

23 ✓ Reading Check
What happens when Grendel grabs Beowulf?

from Beowulf **49**

---

21 Critical Viewing

Possible responses: Early Scandinavians probably wanted to present an image of strength and fearlessness; the sharp teeth on this figurehead make it appear strong and fierce. They also may have been superstitious, believing that such images would ward off evil.

22 Critical Thinking

Analyze

1. Have student volunteers read aloud lines 285–288 and lines 305–309.

2. **Ask** students: What are Grendel's goals as he approaches and enters Herot?
   Answer: He hopes to kill and eat the soldiers he finds there.

3. Then, **ask** students: What is Grendel's motivation to have and work towards these goals? Encourage students to support their responses with details from the text.
   Possible responses: He derives enjoyment from killing and death (line 305); he is hungry or gluttonous (lines 308 and 309).

23 Reading Check

Answer: When Grendel grabs Beowulf, Beowulf grips onto and bends back Grendel's claws, gaining the upper hand.

Differentiated Instruction　　for Universal Access

EL **Pronunciation for English Learners**
Native speakers of some languages have difficulty producing the nasal *n* sound that appears on page 49 at the end of words such as *bearing* (line 286), *hoping* (line 287), and *young* (line 304). Students may "drop the *g*," resulting in pronunciations such as bearin' and yun.

To give students practice with this sound, model the pronunciation of several words from page 49 that contain it. Have students repeat each word after you. Then, to isolate the sound, write the following word pairs on the board: *ton* and *tongue*, *thin* and *thing*, *run* and *rung*.

Practice pronouncing each pair with students.

Point out to students that the nasal *n* sound often appears when verbs take on their *-ing* form. Give some examples, and have students generate other examples. Tell students to be on the lookout for verbs in this form throughout Beowulf, and encourage them to remember this pronunciation lesson whenever they see an *-ing* verb.

Translator's Insight

1. Direct students' attention to the translator's insight note. Point out that Beowulf forces Grendel to finally fight a fair fight. **Ask** students which details from the text show that Grendel is facing more difficulty than he has in the past.
Possible responses: Line 332 states that "this was a different Herot" from the one Grendel had once terrorized; lines 335–336 say that Beowulf fastens Grendel's claws in his fists; and line 339 tells us that Grendel wants to escape.

2. **Ask** students to predict who will win the battle.
Possible response: Students may suggest that Beowulf will win because good always conquers evil, or because they know Beowulf is the hero of the poem.

25 Literary Analysis

The Epic

1. Have students read the description of the battle between Beowulf and Grendel in lines 342–410. You may have students take turns reading or have students read to themselves. Encourage students to record their impressions of the battle as they read.

2. Then, **ask** students the Literary Analysis question: Which details from the description of the battle between Beowulf and Grendel add realism? Which details add epic grandness?
Possible responses: The descriptions of Grendel's screams, shrieks, and tears, combined with those of Beowulf's secure hold on the monster, add realism. Epic grandness is suggested by the description of how Grendel has bewitched the weapons of Beowulf's men, as well as the descriptions of Beowulf as the "mighty protector of men," and of Grendel as "afflictor of men, tormentor of their days."

3. Have students consider Grendel's recognition that he is feuding with God. **Ask** students how this belief might affect him.
Possible responses: It might increase his fear. In the poem, the realization that his real enemy is not just a mortal man also increases his hatred.

Translator's Insight
Like bullies, monsters immediately think of running, as soon as they find themselves in what might be a fair fight.

Vocabulary
writhing (rīth´ in) *adj.* making twisting or turning motions

Literary Analysis
The Epic
Which details from this description of the battle between Beowulf and Grendel add realism? Which details add epic grandness?

330 Hard grip. Grendel's one thought was to run
From Beowulf, flee back to his marsh and hide there:
This was a different Herot than the hall he had emptied.
But Higlac's follower remembered his final
Boast and, standing erect, stopped
335 The monster's flight, fastened those claws
In his fists till they cracked, clutched Grendel
Closer. The infamous killer fought
For his freedom, wanting no flesh but retreat,
Desiring nothing but escape; his claws
340 Had been caught, he was trapped. That trip to Herot
Was a miserable journey for the writhing monster!
      The high hall rang, its roof boards swayed,
And Danes shook with terror. Down
The aisles the battle swept, angry
345 And wild. Herot trembled, wonderfully
Built to withstand the blows, the struggling
Great bodies beating at its beautiful walls;
Shaped and fastened with iron, inside
And out, artfully worked, the building
350 Stood firm. Its benches rattled, fell
To the floor, gold-covered boards grating
As Grendel and Beowulf battled across them.
Hrothgar's wise men had fashioned Herot
To stand forever; only fire,
355 They had planned, could shatter what such skill had put
Together, swallow in hot flames such splendor
Of ivory and iron and wood. Suddenly
The sounds changed, the Danes started
In new terror, cowering in their beds as the terrible
360 Screams of the Almighty's enemy sang
In the darkness, the horrible shrieks of pain
And defeat, the tears torn out of Grendel's
Taut throat, hell's captive caught in the arms
Of him who of all the men on earth
365 Was the strongest.
                    That mighty protector of men
Meant to hold the monster till its life
Leaped out, knowing the fiend was no use
To anyone in Denmark. All of Beowulf's
Band had jumped from their beds, ancestral
370 Swords raised and ready, determined
To protect their prince if they could. Their courage
Was great but all wasted: they could hack at Grendel
From every side, trying to open
A path for his evil soul, but their points
375 Could not hurt him, the sharpest and hardest iron

Think Aloud

Literary Analysis: The Epic
Use the following Think Aloud to model answering the Literary Analysis question. Say to students:

To determine which details on this page are realistic, I imagine what would happen if this battle took place in real life. I know that when two people or creatures fight, it is a very physical ordeal; the participants must grab and hold on to each other to gain the upper hand. Details such as "fastened those claws/In his fists till they cracked" add realism because they help me picture the scene.

Also, participants in a fight often let out screams of pain; for that reason, auditory details such as "the horrible shrieks of pain/And defeat" also lend realism to the description in the epic. On the other hand, when I look for language that adds epic grandness, I want to be looking for non-literal phrases that might exaggerate reality or give grand labels to a character. For example, calling Grendel "the Almighty's enemy" elevates the tone of the text, making it sound more epic.

Could not scratch at his skin, for that sin-stained demon
Had bewitched all men's weapons, laid spells
That blunted every mortal man's blade.
And yet his time had come, his days
380 Were over, his death near; down
To hell he would go, swept groaning and helpless
To the waiting hands of still worse fiends.
Now he discovered—once the afflictor
Of men, tormentor of their days—what it meant
385 To feud with Almighty God: Grendel
Saw that his strength was deserting him, his claws
Bound fast, Higlac's brave follower tearing at
His hands. The monster's hatred rose higher,
But his power had gone. He twisted in pain,
390 And the bleeding sinews deep in his shoulder
Snapped, muscle and bone split
And broke. The battle was over, Beowulf
Had been granted new glory: Grendel escaped,
But wounded as he was could flee to his den,
395 His miserable hole at the bottom of the marsh,
Only to die, to wait for the end
Of all his days. And after that bloody
Combat the Danes laughed with delight.
He who had come to them from across the sea,
400 Bold and strong-minded, had driven affliction
Off, purged Herot clean. He was happy,
Now, with that night's fierce work; the Danes
Had been served as he'd boasted he'd serve them; Beowulf,
A prince of the Geats, had killed Grendel,
405 Ended the grief, the sorrow, the suffering
Forced on Hrothgar's helpless people
By a bloodthirsty fiend. No Dane doubted
The victory, for the proof, hanging high
From the rafters where Beowulf had hung it, was the monster's
410 Arm, claw and shoulder and all.

The Danes celebrate Beowulf's victory. That night, though, Grendel's
mother kills Hrothgar's closest friend and carries off her child's
claw. The next day the horrified king tells Beowulf about the two
monsters and their underwater lair.

THE MONSTERS' LAIR

"I've heard that my people, peasants working
In the fields, have seen a pair of such fiends
Wandering in the moors and marshes, giant
Monsters living in those desert lands.
415 And they've said to my wise men that, as well as they could see,

Reading Strategy
Determine the Main Idea
by Paraphrasing
Paraphrase the sentence
in lines 392–397.

Reading
Check
How does Beowulf's battle
with Grendel end?

from Beowulf 51

26 Reading Strategy
Determine the Main Idea by Paraphrasing

1. Have a student volunteer read aloud lines 392–397 while the other students follow along.

2. Then, have students complete the Reading Strategy prompt: **Paraphrase** the sentence in lines 392–397.
Possible responses: The battle between Grendel and Beowulf ended. Beowulf is more famous than before. Grendel escaped, wounded, and fled to his den at the bottom of the marsh, where he would wait to die.

3. Discuss with students what difference, if any, they see between the concepts of victory and glory. Then, **ask** students which they believe was Beowulf's goal during this episode.
Possible response: Students may say that a victory is a one-time occurrence, while glory is long-lasting. Beowulf wanted victory in this battle, but glory seemed even more important to him, and he has gained this with Grendel's defeat.

27 Reading Check
Answer: Beowulf's battle with Grendel ends when he snaps off Grendel's arm, and the monster flees to his lair to die.

Differentiated
Instruction   for Universal Access
Culturally Responsive Instruction
Culture Connection Point out to students that Beowulf hangs Grendel's arm high in the rafters of Herot as a sort of battle trophy. **Ask** students what purpose they think this serves and whether they can think of examples of similar practices today. (Students may mention hunters or fishers who display their kills on a wall.) Explain that, beginning in ancient times and even continuing into modern times, many cultures have practiced forms of taking human battle trophies. Some Native American tribes practiced scalping when warring with other tribes; enemy scalps were displayed upon returning home as evidence of victory. In many other cultures, a fallen enemy would be beheaded, and the head would be displayed as a trophy. This occurs, for example, in the biblical account of David and the giant Goliath, who was beheaded after his defeat.

Determine the Main Idea by Paraphrasing

1. Have students read lines 420–431 to themselves. As they read, have them write paraphrases that include important ideas written in their own words.

2. After students have completed their paraphrases, have several volunteers read theirs to the class. **Ask** students which elements are key ideas and which may be interesting but unnecessary to understanding the main idea. **Possible responses:** The idea that no one knows whether there are other monsters like Grendel is a key idea. Details such as mist steaming like black clouds are not crucial to the meaning of the passage.

3. Then, **ask** students the Reading Strategy question: What do these lines tell you about Grendel's background?
   Possible response: The lines reveal that Grendel's background is dark and mysterious.

29 **World Literature Connection**

Battling Demons in the *Ramayana*

Rama, the hero of the *Ramayana,* is more than a character in a poem. He is a popular deity worshiped in the Hindu religion. According to Hindu tradition, Rama is an incarnation of the god Vishnu. Rama's main purpose is to demonstrate the righteous path for all living creatures on Earth. Even today, he serves as a model of good conduct, just as Beowulf may have for the Anglo-Saxons.

Connect to the Literature

After students have read Battling Demons in the Ramayana note, **ask** students: What do you think makes the battle with Grendel feel so compelling, despite the brevity of the conflict?
Possible response: Even though the battle between Beowulf and Grendel is brief, the lead-up to the battle makes it compelling. As Beowulf travels across the sea to help Hrothgar and Grendel approaches Herot "hoping to kill," the battle is set up as a showdown of good and evil. Like Rama, Beowulf is the champion of his culture's values, and so the stakes are high.

52

Reading Strategy
Determine the Main Idea by Paraphrasing
Paraphrase lines 420–431. What do these lines tell you about Grendel's background?

World LITERATURE CONNECTION

Battling Demons in the *Ramayana*

Beowulf's fight with Grendel touches on a universal theme. Tales of heroes who battle monsters or demons are common in world literature. One of the most famous battles occurs in the *Ramayana*, the Hindu epic poem that is as well known in India and other areas of Asia as Bible stories are here. The *Ramayana* is part of a living oral tradition; even today, traveling storytellers recite the tales to large audiences. The hero of this epic is the virtuous prince Rama, husband to beautiful Sita. Rama's enemy is the demon king Ravana, who has ten heads and twenty arms, and lives with his warriors in the land of Lanka. After Ravana kidnaps Sita, Rama must wage battle against the demon king to rescue his wife. While Beowulf's battle with Grendel can be told in a few minutes, Rama's attack on Ravana requires many hours over a series of nights to recite. Both poems feature heroes who ultimately triumph over creatures of supernatural strength and size.

Connect to the Literature

What do you think makes the battle with Grendel feel so compelling, despite the brevity of the description?

One of the devils was a female creature.
The other, they say, walked through the wilderness
Like a man—but mightier than any man.
They were frightened, and they fled, hoping to find help
420 In Herot. They named the huge one Grendel:
If he had a father no one knew him,
28 Or whether there'd been others before these two,
Hidden evil before hidden evil.
They live in secret places, windy
425 Cliffs, wolf-dens where water pours
From the rocks, then runs underground, where mist
Steams like black clouds, and the groves of trees
Growing out over their lake are all covered
With frozen spray, and wind down snakelike
430 Roots that reach as far as the water
And help keep it dark. At night that lake
29 Burns like a torch. No one knows its bottom,
No wisdom reaches such depths. A deer,
Hunted through the woods by packs of hounds,
435 A stag with great horns, though driven through the forest
From faraway places, prefers to die
On those shores, refuses to save its life
In that water. It isn't far, nor is it
A pleasant spot! When the wind stirs
440 And storms, waves splash toward the sky,
As dark as the air, as black as the rain
That the heavens weep. Our only help,
Again, lies with you. Grendel's mother
Is hidden in her terrible home, in a place
445 You've not seen. Seek it, if you dare! Save us,
Once more, and again twisted gold,
Heaped-up ancient treasure, will reward you
For the battle you win!"

Beowulf resolves to kill Grendel's monstrous mother. He travels to the lake in which she lives.

THE BATTLE WITH GRENDEL'S MOTHER

Then Edgetho's brave son[10] spoke:

"Remember,
450 Hrothgar, O knowing king, now
When my danger is near, the warm words we uttered,
And if your enemy should end my life

---

10. Edgetho's brave son Beowulf. Elsewhere he is identified by such phrases as "the Geats' proud prince" and "the Geats' brave prince."

Enrichment: Building Context

Pagan and Christian Influences

The popularity of pagan and almost-pagan legends like *Beowulf* was a source of concern and irritation to early Christian leaders. The scholar and monk Alcuin wrote a famous letter home in 797. In it, he criticized the English bishop for allowing Christian priests, while dining, to listen to poetry about the pagan king Ingeld—one of the characters in *Beowulf*. Alcuin argued that the poem was inappropriate for the priests, who needed to be learning the Scripture they would be teaching. Eventually, Christian influences began to filter into the pagan stories. Two centuries later, it was the clergy who recorded *Beowulf*, saving the legend.

Activity: Research Context Have groups work together to research who the early audiences of *Beowulf* would have been and how the text would have been received by various audiences. Suggest that they record information in the **Enrichment: Building Context** worksheet, *Professional Development Guidebook*, page 222.

Then be, O generous prince, forever
The father and protector of all whom I leave
455 Behind me, here in your hands, my beloved
Comrades left with no leader, their leader
Dead. And the precious gifts you gave me,
My friend, send them to Higlac. May he see
In their golden brightness, the Geats' great lord
460 Gazing at your treasure, that here in Denmark
I found a noble protector, a giver
Of rings whose rewards I won and briefly
Relished. And you, Unferth,[11] let
My famous old sword stay in your hands:
465 I shall shape glory with Hrunting, or death
Will hurry me from this earth!"
                            As his words ended
He leaped into the lake, would not wait for anyone's
Answer; the heaving water covered him
Over. For hours he sank through the waves;
470 At last he saw the mud of the bottom.
And all at once the greedy she-wolf
Who'd ruled those waters for half a hundred
Years discovered him, saw that a creature
From above had come to explore the bottom
475 Of her wet world. She welcomed him in her claws,
Clutched at him savagely but could not harm him,
Tried to work her fingers through the tight
Ring-woven mail on his breast, but tore
And scratched in vain. Then she carried him, armor
480 And sword and all, to her home; he struggled
To free his weapon, and failed. The fight
Brought other monsters swimming to see
Her catch, a host of sea beasts who beat at
His mail shirt, stabbing with tusks and teeth
485 As they followed along. Then he realized, suddenly,
That she'd brought him into someone's battle-hall,
And there the water's heat could not hurt him.
Nor anything in the lake attack him through
The building's high-arching roof. A brilliant
490 Light burned all around him, the lake
Itself like a fiery flame.
                            Then he saw
The mighty water witch and swung his sword,
His ring-marked blade, straight at her head;
The iron sang its fierce song,
495 Sang Beowulf's strength. But her guest

11. Unferth Danish warrior who had questioned Beowulf's bravery before the battle with Grendel.

Reading Strategy
Determine the Main Idea by Paraphrasing
Paraphrase lines 467–481.

Burton Raffel
Translator's Insight
True warriors are totally dedicated and fight for fame (honor), not for tangible rewards.

Reading Check
What requests does Beowulf make before he dives into the lake?

from Beowulf 53

53

Anglo-Saxon Metalwork

Metallurgy was fairly advanced in the era in which the poem *Beowulf* was composed and transcribed into English. The Anglo-Saxons used metal tools and weapons and wore jewelry forged from metal ores, and they decorated their simplest implements with metal ornamentation. Many of the artifacts in this unit display the superior skills of metallurgists of this period.

Connect to the Literature

After students have read the *Literature in Context* note in their texts, discuss with them the various reasons why swords were highly valued in Anglo-Saxon culture. Then, **ask** students: Besides its ornate hilt, what else makes Hrunting a valuable property? Encourage students to use details from the text to support their answers.

Possible response: Hrunting is valuable because it is "blessed with … magic" (line 532) and does not fail Beowulf in his efforts.

34 Engaging the Essential Question

1. Discuss with students mental images that they have of Grendel and Grendel's mother. For example, do students picture them as walking on two legs or four? Do they have skin, fur, or scales? What do their faces look like?

2. **Ask** students to find words and phrases on page 92 that give physical descriptions of Grendel's mother.
   Possible responses: *Clutching claws* (line 514) and *squatting* (line 518) may help students picture her body and stature; *wildly tearing* (line 515) provides an image of her physical motion.

3. Then, **ask** students: What do these images suggest about the way Anglo-Saxons conceived of evil?
   Possible response: They seem to have associated evil with wild, animalistic tendencies.

4. Remind students that, as they read, they should continue to examine the ways in which the monsters are described.

Science Connection

Anglo-Saxon Metalwork
The sword that Beowulf discovers is said to have been magically forged by giants—a story reflecting the scarcity and value of swords in Anglo-Saxon times. To form a sword, highly skilled smiths had to heat ore to the melting point of iron (2,800° F), cool it, and then add carbon. The result was a hard, durable metal. A smith's work did not stop at a strong, sharp edge but included the ornamentation of the sword hilt. Handsomely adorned, a sword was at once a deadly weapon and a work of art. Both usable iron and the skills needed to work it were scarce, and a sword's noble owner treasured it, treating it as an individual. Some swords—like Beowulf's Hrunting—were given names.

Connect to the Literature

Besides its ornate hilt, what else makes Hrunting a valuable property? **34**

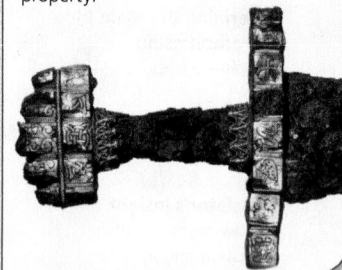

Vocabulary
massive (mas´ iv) *adj.*
big and solid; bulky

Discovered that no sword could slice her evil
Skin, that Hrunting could not hurt her, was useless
Now when he needed it. They wrestled, she ripped
And tore and clawed at him, bit holes in his helmet,
500 And that too failed him; for the first time in years
Of being worn to war it would earn no glory;
It was the last time anyone would wear it. But Beowulf
Longed only for fame, leaped back
Into battle. He tossed his sword aside,
505 Angry; the steel-edged blade lay where
He'd dropped it. If weapons were useless he'd use
His hands, the strength in his fingers. So fame
Comes to the men who mean to win it
And care about nothing else! He raised
510 His arms and seized her by the shoulder; anger
Doubled his strength, he threw her to the floor.
She fell, Grendel's fierce mother, and the Geats'
Proud prince was ready to leap on her. But she rose
At once and repaid him with her clutching claws,
515 Wildly tearing at him. He was weary, that best
And strongest of soldiers; his feet stumbled
And in an instant she had him down, held helpless.
Squatting with her weight on his stomach, she drew
A dagger, brown with dried blood, and prepared
520 To avenge her only son. But he was stretched
On his back, and her stabbing blade was blunted
By the woven mail shirt he wore on his chest.
The hammered links held; the point
Could not touch him. He'd have traveled to the bottom of the earth,
525 Edgetho's son, and died there, if that shining
Woven metal had not helped—and Holy
God, who sent him victory, gave judgment
For truth and right, Ruler of the Heavens,
Once Beowulf was back on his feet and fighting.
530   Then he saw, hanging on the wall, a heavy
Sword, hammered by giants, strong
And blessed with their magic, the best of all weapons
But so massive that no ordinary man could lift
Its carved and decorated length. He drew it
535 From its scabbard, broke the chain on its hilt,
And then, savage, now, angry
And desperate, lifted it high over his head
And struck with all the strength he had left,
Caught her in the neck and cut it through,
540 Broke bones and all. Her body fell
To the floor, lifeless, the sword was wet

Enrichment: Investigating Science

Iron and Steel Manufacture

The process of turning iron ore into usable iron and steel has advanced significantly from the Iron Age to today. Technological advances make it possible to heat the iron ore to high temperatures and expose it to gases that oxidize some of the ore's carbon content. Various methods have been invented to make this process more efficient and to increase the quality of the iron and steel produced.

Activity: Investigate Iron Production Methods Have pairs or individual students research advances that allows natural iron ore to become iron and steel. Also, have them research one method that has been used for this process in the past. Have students create a diagram of this process. Suggest that they record information in the **Enrichment: Investigating Science** worksheet, *Professional Development Guidebook*, page 241. As a class, discuss what method would have been used to create the iron used to make swords at the time *Beowulf* was written.

With her blood, and Beowulf rejoiced at the sight.
    The brilliant light shone, suddenly,
As though burning in that hall, and as bright as Heaven's
545 Own candle, lit in the sky. He looked
At her home, then following along the wall
Went walking, his hands tight on the sword,
His heart still angry. He was hunting another
Dead monster, and took his weapon with him
550 For final revenge against Grendel's vicious
Attacks, his nighttime raids, over
And over, coming to Herot when Hrothgar's
Men slept, killing them in their beds,
Eating some on the spot, fifteen
555 Or more, and running to his loathsome moor
With another such sickening meal waiting
In his pouch. But Beowulf repaid him for those visits,
Found him lying dead in his corner,
Armless, exactly as that fierce fighter
560 Had sent him out from Herot, then struck off
His head with a single swift blow. The body
jerked for the last time, then lay still.
    The wise old warriors who surrounded Hrothgar,
Like him staring into the monsters' lake,
565 Saw the waves surging and blood
Spurting through. They spoke about Beowulf,
All the graybeards, whispered together
And said that hope was gone, that the hero
Had lost fame and his life at once, and would never
570 Return to the living, come back as triumphant
As he had left; almost all agreed that Grendel's
Mighty mother, the she-wolf, had killed him.
The sun slid over past noon, went further
Down. The Danes gave up, left
575 The lake and went home, Hrothgar with them.
The Geats stayed, sat sadly, watching,
Imagining they saw their lord but not believing
They would ever see him again.
                —Then the sword
Melted, blood-soaked, dripping down
580 Like water, disappearing like ice when the world's
Eternal Lord loosens invisible
Fetters and unwinds icicles and frost
As only He can, He who rules
Time and seasons, He who is truly
585 God. The monsters' hall was full of
Rich treasures, but all that Beowulf took
Was Grendel's head and the hilt of the giants'

35 ▲ Critical Viewing
How would this helmet affect the appearance of the person wearing it? **[Infer]**

Vocabulary
loathsome (lōth′ səm)
adj. disgusting

37 Reading Check
Why do the Danes think Beowulf has been slain?

from Beowulf **55**

35 Critical Viewing
Possible response: The helmet would cause the person wearing it to appear menacing and tough. The narrow eye slits appear angry, and since the helmet is made of hard, durable materials, it gives the impression that the wearer is also strong and durable. In addition, the helmet would cover the face of the wearer, de-emphasizing that person's humanity in favor of a warlike appearance.

36 Critical Thinking
Infer

1. Have a volunteer read aloud lines 585–588.
2. **Ask** students: What can we infer about Beowulf's values based on his decision to take home Grendel's head but leave the rich treasures behind?
   Possible response: Beowulf values personal victories in battle far more than he values material possessions and riches.

37 Reading Check
Answer: The Danes believe Beowulf is dead because they see strong waves and blood coming up from the monster's lake.

Differentiated Instruction for Universal Access

Strategy for Special-Needs Students
Explain to students what has happened over these two pages. Write an outline on the board: attacks Grendel's mother, Grendel's mother tries to stab him but his armor protects him, finds magical sword, kills Grendel's mother, kills Grendel, the Danes believe Beowulf is dead while the Geats don't want to believe it, Beowulf swims back to the surface. Then have students, working as a group, find the details in the poem that describe the items in the outline. Finally, have them write what happened in their own words.

EL Strategy for English Learners
The exercise at left might help English learners, too, but they will also need assistance with the vocabulary on these pages. After students understand the general meaning of the passages, have them create a list of unfamiliar words. Then, have them work in groups that include at least one more-fluent student to discover word meanings. Discuss these difficult words with students. Have students then reread the sentences that contain these words, so they understand them in context.

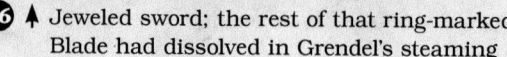

Determine the Main Idea by Paraphrasing

Have students follow the Reading Strategy prompt: In your own words, **paraphrase** the events described in lines 596–611.

Possible response: Beowulf swam back to land. The Geats rejoiced that he was alive. They left and walked away from the lake carrying Grendel's skull so they could show it to the Danes in Herot.

39 Critical Thinking

Criticize

1. Explain to students that *hubris* refers to an overly inflated sense of pride, which often leads literary characters to ruin. Then, read aloud lines 623–628.

2. **Ask** students whether they believe Beowulf exhibits signs of hubris in this passage, and why or why not.
   Possible responses: Students may see signs of hubris in the word *boast* and in Beowulf's claim never to have known fear, his decision to continue seeking fame, and his belief that the dragon has reason to fear him, a mere human. Other students may counter that Beowulf, as an epic hero and based on his former victories, has legitimate claims to pride.

---

36 Jeweled sword; the rest of that ring-marked
    Blade had dissolved in Grendel's steaming
590 Blood, boiling even after his death.
    And then the battle's only survivor
    Swam up and away from those silent corpses;
    The water was calm and clean, the whole
    Huge lake peaceful once the demons who'd lived in it
595 Were dead.
            Then that noble protector of all seamen
    Swam to land, rejoicing in the heavy
    Burdens he was bringing with him. He
    And all his glorious band of Geats

Determine Main Idea by Paraphrasing In your own words, paraphrase the events described in lines 596–611.

    Thanked God that their leader had come back unharmed;
600 They left the lake together. The Geats
    Carried Beowulf's helmet, and his mail shirt.
    Behind them the water slowly thickened
    As the monsters' blood came seeping up.
    They walked quickly, happily, across
605 Roads all of them remembered, left
    The lake and the cliffs alongside it, brave men
    Staggering under the weight of Grendel's skull,
    Too heavy for fewer than four of them to handle—
    Two on each side of the spear jammed through it—
610 Yet proud of their ugly load and determined
    That the Danes, seated in Herot, should see it.
    Soon, fourteen Geats arrived
    At the hall, bold and warlike, and with Beowulf,
    Their lord and leader, they walked on the mead-hall
615 Green. Then the Geats' brave prince entered
    Herot, covered with glory for the daring
    Battles he had fought; he sought Hrothgar
    To salute him and show Grendel's head.
    He carried that terrible trophy by the hair,
620 Brought it straight to where the Danes sat,
    Drinking, the queen among them. It was a weird
    And wonderful sight, and the warriors stared.

After being honored by Hrothgar, Beowulf and his fellow Geats return home, where he eventually becomes King. Beowulf rules Geatland for fifty years. When a dragon menaces his kingdom, Beowulf, now an old man, determines to slay the beast. Before going into battle, he tells his men about the royal house and his exploits in its service.

39

THE LAST BATTLE

    And Beowulf uttered his final boast:
    "I've never known fear, as a youth I fought
625 In endless battles. I am old, now,
    But I will fight again, seek fame still,

Think Aloud

Literary Analysis: The Epic

Students may have difficulty extracting information about Anglo-Saxon values from the text, as they are asked to do in the Literary Analysis question on page 57. To model this literary analysis skill, say to students:

To look for the values that may be behind a text, I need to examine what characteristics the text seems to portray in a positive light. Because Beowulf is the hero of the epic, I can expect that he will be portrayed positively. I also know that as a legendary hero, he upholds the values of his culture. For example, in lines 636–639, Beowulf states that he will stand firm and not run away when the dragon approaches him. His words in these lines show that he is brave and does what he sets out to do. Therefore bravery and integrity are probably characteristics that are highly valued in Anglo-Saxon culture.

If the dragon hiding in his tower dares
To face me."
        Then he said farewell to his followers,
Each in his turn, for the last time:

630   "I'd use no sword, no weapon, if this beast
Could be killed without it, crushed to death
Like Grendel, gripped in my hands and torn
Limb from limb. But his breath will be burning
Hot, poison will pour from his tongue.

635 I feel no shame, with shield and sword
And armor, against this monster: when he comes to me
I mean to stand, not run from his shooting
Flames, stand till fate decides
Which of us wins. My heart is firm,

640 My hands calm: I need no hot
Words. Wait for me close by, my friends.
We shall see, soon, who will survive
This bloody battle, stand when the fighting
Is done. No one else could do

645 What I mean to, here, no man but me
Could hope to defeat this monster. No one
Could try. And this dragon's treasure, his gold
And everything hidden in that tower, will be mine
Or war will sweep me to a bitter death!"

650   Then Beowulf rose, still brave, still strong,
And with his shield at his side, and a mail shirt on his breast,
Strode calmly, confidently, toward the tower, under
The rocky cliffs: no coward could have walked there!
And then he who'd endured dozens of desperate

655 Battles, who'd stand boldly while swords and shields
Clashed, the best of kings, saw
Huge stone arches and felt the heat
Of the dragon's breath, flooding down
Through the hidden entrance, too hot for anyone

660 To stand, a streaming current of fire
And smoke that blocked all passage. And the Geats'
Lord and leader, angry, lowered
His sword and roared out a battle cry,
A call so loud and clear that it reached through

665 The hoary rock, hung in the dragon's
Ear. The beast rose, angry,
Knowing a man had come—and then nothing
But war could have followed. Its breath came first.
A steaming cloud pouring from the stone,

670 Then the earth itself shook. Beowulf
Swung his shield into place, held it
In front of him, facing the entrance. The dragon

㊵ Literary Analysis
The Epic
What does Beowulf's speech in lines 630–649 suggest to you about Anglo-Saxon values?

㊸

☑ Reading Check **㊶**
How does Beowulf plan to fight the dragon?

from Beowulf **57**

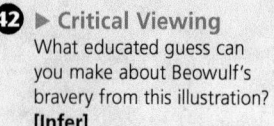

42 Critical Viewing

Possible response: Students might infer that Beowulf has superhuman courage, because although he is very small compared to the monster and is surrounded by huge flames and smoke, he continues to fight to fend off the monster.

43 Reading Strategy

Determine Main Idea by Paraphrasing

1. Give students time to read over lines 650–714 to themselves.

2. Then, have students complete the Reading Strategy prompt: In your own words, **paraphrase** the events of Beowulf's battle with the dragon. Students may need several minutes to complete this task.
   Possible response: Beowulf walks out confidently to meet the dragon and stands firm as the dragon approaches and shoots out flames. Eventually Beowulf's shield begins to melt. Beowulf attacks the dragon with his sword, but the sword does not go deep enough. Beowulf realizes that he may die. The dragon comes toward him, and none of his fellow soldiers come to his aid.

▶ **Monitor Progress:** Challenge students to see who can write the shortest paraphrase that still contains all of the main ideas from the passage.

▶ **Reteach:** If students oversimplify, remind them that a passage may have more than one important idea. Explain that their goal should be to include any key information that may affect someone's understanding of the passage.

44 Literary Analysis

The Epic

1. Have a student volunteer read aloud lines 720–739.

2. Then, **ask** students the Literary Analysis question: What do these lines reveal about the values of warrior culture?
   Possible responses: Good swords and armor were valuable and highly valued, making them a gift of honor. Weapons and armor were among the most important items a son inherited from his father. The pedigree of a warrior's sword and armor was important.

58

---

42 ▶ Critical Viewing
What educated guess can you make about Beowulf's bravery from this illustration? **[Infer]**

43

Reading Strategy
Determine Main Idea by Paraphrasing
In your own words, paraphrase the events of Beowulf's battle with the dragon.

44 Literary Analysis
The Epic
What do these lines reveal about the values of warrior culture?

Coiled and uncoiled, its heart urging it
Into battle. Beowulf's ancient sword
675 Was waiting, unsheathed, his sharp and gleaming
Blade. The beast came closer; both of them
Were ready, each set on slaughter. The Geats'
Great prince stood firm, unmoving, prepared
Behind his high shield, waiting in his shining
680 Armor. The monster came quickly toward him,
Pouring out fire and smoke, hurrying
To its fate. Flames beat at the iron
Shield, and for a time it held, protected
Beowulf as he'd planned; then it began to melt,
685 And for the first time in his life that famous prince
Fought with fate against him, with glory
Denied him. He knew it, but he raised his sword
And struck at the dragon's scaly hide.
The ancient blade broke, bit into
690 The monster's skin, drew blood, but cracked
And failed him before it went deep enough, helped him
Less than he needed. The dragon leaped
With pain, thrashed and beat at him, spouting
Murderous flames, spreading them everywhere.
695 And the Geats' ring-giver did not boast of glorious
Victories in other wars: his weapon
Had failed him, deserted him, now when he needed it
Most, that excellent sword. Edgetho's
Famous son stared at death,
700 Unwilling to leave this world, to exchange it
For a dwelling in some distant place—a journey
Into darkness that all men must make, as death
Ends their few brief hours on earth.
    Quickly, the dragon came at him, encouraged
705 As Beowulf fell back; its breath flared,
And he suffered, wrapped around in swirling
Flames—a king, before, but now
A beaten warrior. None of his comrades
Came to him, helped him, his brave and noble
710 Followers; they ran for their lives, fled
Deep in a wood. And only one of them
Remained, stood there, miserable, remembering,
As a good man must, what kinship should mean.

    His name was Wiglaf, he was Wexstan's son
715 And a good soldier; his family had been Swedish,
Once. Watching Beowulf, he could see
How his king was suffering, burning. Remembering
Everything his lord and cousin had given him,

58 From Legend to History (A.D. 449–1485)

Enrichment: Analyzing Forms and Genres

Epics

Because epics have been used the world over to preserve values and traditions, they are a rich resource for exploring world cultures.

Activity: Examine Epics Have interested students gather information on these epics and share their findings with the class:

Finland: *Kalevala*
France: *Chanson de Roland*
India: *Ramayana* and *Mahabharata*
Italy: *Orlando Furioso*
Japan: *Heike Monogatari*

Norway: *Volsunga Saga*
Ancient Greece: the *Odyssey*, the *Iliad*
Spain: *Poema del Cid*

Suggest that students record information in the **Enrichment: Analyzing Forms and Genres** worksheet, *Professional Development Guidebook*, page 227, as they listen to their classmates' presentations. Discuss similarities and differences between *Beowulf* and the other epics.

from Beowulf 59

45 **Critical Thinking**

Analyze

1. Explain that lines 645–692 represent a turning point.

2. **Ask** students how this battle is different from the others that Beowulf has fought.
Answer: Fate is against the hero for the first time, and Beowulf knows he is going to lose.

46 **Critical Thinking**

Connect

1. Remind students of Burton Raffel's comments about villains throughout the selection, particularly his insight that villains are usually only interested in fights they know they can win.

2. **Ask** students to look for phrases on page 58 that support this insight.
Possible response: The statement that the dragon was "encouraged/As Beowulf fell back" supports this idea.

3. Then, **ask** students: What other characters in *Beowulf* have exhibited similar tendencies?
Possible response: Grendel showed this tendency when he wanted to run away after realizing Beowulf had the power to beat him.

Differentiated Instruction for Universal Access

Culturally Responsive Instruction

Culture Connection Point out to students that Wiglaf is the only solider who remains to support Beowulf. Draw their attention to the phrase "what kinship should mean" in line 713, and explain that in the Anglo-Saxon warrior culture, a soldier's allegiance to his leader was thought to be one of his primary virtues. A lack of loyalty in difficult circumstances would have been looked down upon. **Ask** students to consider ways in which the idea that allegiance to one's leader is of high value is a universal theme; have them brainstorm ways in which this theme appears in different cultures. Encourage them to think about and discuss ways in which various ethnic and national cultures value loyalty to a family leader, a military or political leader, or the leader of one's group of friends.

㊼ Critical Thinking

Make a Judgment

1. Read aloud lines 743–744.

2. **Ask** students whether they agree with the epic poet's judgment that Wiglaf's words about his comrades were deserved, and why or why not.
   Possible responses: Students may agree that the men deserved Wiglaf's words because they should have defended Beowulf and not run away.

3. Encourage students to imagine themselves in the position of Beowulf's men, seeing their brave and strong leader being over-powered by a fierce dragon. **Ask** whether this thought leads any students to reconsider their previous position.
   Possible responses: Some students may say that they probably also would have fled in the face of the danger presented by the dragon; this may prompt some to change their minds. Others, however, still may believe that the right thing to do would have been to defend Beowulf.

㊽ Literary Analysis

The Epic and the Legendary Hero

1. Have students read lines 745–760 to themselves.

2. Then, **ask** students the Literary Analysis question: According to Wiglaf, what is Beowulf's relationship with his followers like?
   Possible response: Beowulf and his followers are bound together by his generous gifts and their oaths. Their bond is one of life and death and trust, since the followers swear to give their lives for Beowulf, while Beowulf relies on his followers to aid him in battle.

3. **Ask** students why, as it says in line 744, Wiglaf feels that this speech is what these men deserve.
   Answer: Beowulf always did what he said, but they have not. They have failed to help a kind and brave leader, betraying not only Beowulf but the whole value system of the warrior culture.

Armor and gold and the great estates
720   Wexstan's family enjoyed, Wiglaf's
    Mind was made up; he raised his yellow
    Shield and drew his sword—an ancient
    Weapon that had once belonged to Onela's
    Nephew, and that Wexstan had won, killing
725   The prince when he fled from Sweden, sought safety
    With Herdred, and found death.[12] And Wiglaf's father
    Had carried the dead man's armor, and his sword,
    To Onela, and the king had said nothing, only
    Given him armor and sword and all,
730   Everything his rebel nephew had owned
    And lost when he left this life. And Wexstan
    Had kept those shining gifts, held them
    For years, waiting for his son to use them,
    Wear them as honorably and well as once
735   His father had done; then Wexstan died
    And Wiglaf was his heir, inherited treasures
    And weapons and land. He'd never worn
    That armor, fought with that sword, until Beowulf
    Called him to his side, led him into war.
740   But his soul did not melt, his sword was strong;
    The dragon discovered his courage, and his weapon,
    When the rush of battle brought them together.
       And Wiglaf, his heart heavy, uttered
    The kind of words his comrades deserved:

Literary Analysis
The Epic and the Legendary Hero
According to Wiglaf, what is Beowulf's relationship with his followers?

745   "I remember how we sat in the mead-hall, drinking
    And boasting of how brave we'd be when Beowulf
    Needed us, he who gave us these swords
    And armor: all of us swore to repay him,
    When the time came, kindness for kindness
750   —With our lives, if he needed them. He allowed us to
       join him,
    Chose us from all his great army, thinking
    Our boasting words had some weight, believing
    Our promises, trusting our swords. He took us
    For soldiers, for men. He meant to kill
755   This monster himself, our mighty king,
    Fight this battle alone and unaided,
    As in the days when his strength and daring dazzled
    Men's eyes. But those days are over and gone
    And now our lord must lean on younger
760   Arms. And we must go to him, while angry
    Flames burn at his flesh, help
    Our glorious king! By almighty God,

---

12. Onela's / Nephew . . . found death When Onela seized the throne of Sweden, his two nephews sought shelter with the king of Geatland, Herdred. Wiglaf's father, Wexstan, killed the older nephew for Onela.

Enrichment: Investigating a Key Person in History

Death of a Heroic Figure

Explain that heroes are usually described in terms of life's peak moments. For example, young Beowulf's early triumphs are dramatized. His death fighting the dragon is also featured in the epic. However, nothing of his fifty-year reign as king is shown in the poem.

Activity: Examine a Historical Hero Have students research events in the life of a heroic historical figure who died as a result of pursuing a cause, such as Joan of Arc, Martin Luther King, Jr., or Abraham Lincoln.

Suggest that students record information in the **Enrichment: Investigating a Key Person in History** worksheet, *Professional Development Guidebook*, page 233. After students finish, have volunteers share their results, and discuss the types of life events that often make it into history books. **Ask** students what similarities and differences they see between the way heroes' lives are described in epics and the way real-life heroes' lives are recorded for historical purposes. Discuss reasons for these similarities and differences.

I'd rather burn myself than see
Flames swirling around my lord.
765 And who are we to carry home
Our shields before we've slain his enemy
And ours, to run back to our homes with Beowulf
So hard-pressed here? I swear that nothing
He ever did deserved an end
770 Like this, dying miserably and alone,
Butchered by this savage beast: we swore
That these swords and armor were each for us all!"
     Then he ran to his king, crying encouragement
As he dove through the dragon's deadly fumes.

49 *Wiglaf and Beowulf kill the dragon, but the old king is mortally wounded. As he dies, Beowulf asks Wiglaf to bring him the treasure that the dragon was guarding.*

THE SPOILS

775   Then Wexstan's son went in, as quickly
As he could, did as the dying Beowulf
Asked, entered the inner darkness
Of the tower, went with his mail shirt and his sword.
Flushed with victory he groped his way,
780 A brave young warrior, and suddenly saw
Piles of gleaming gold, precious
Gems, scattered on the floor, cups
And bracelets, rusty old helmets, beautifully
Made but rotting with no hands to rub
785 And polish them. They lay where the dragon left them;
It had flown in the darkness, once, before fighting
Its final battle. (So gold can easily
Triumph, defeat the strongest of men,
No matter how deep it is hidden!) And he saw,
790 Hanging high above, a golden
Banner, woven by the best of weavers
And beautiful. And over everything he saw
A strange light, shining everywhere,
On walls and floor and treasure. Nothing
795 Moved, no other monsters appeared;
He took what he wanted, all the treasures
That pleased his eye, heavy plates
And golden cups and the glorious banner,
Loaded his arms with all they could hold.
800 Beowulf's dagger, his iron blade,
Had finished the fire-spitting terror
That once protected tower and treasures
Alike; the gray-bearded lord of the Geats

50 **Reading Strategy**
Determine the Main Idea by Paraphrasing What is the main idea in the sentence in lines 779–785?

51  Reading Check

Why does Wiglaf decide to come to Beowulf's aid?

from Beowulf **61**

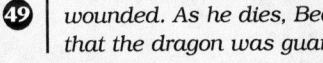
49 **Critical Thinking**
Modify

1. Have a student read aloud the italicized summary section on this page.
2. **Ask** students: How would the outcome of the story have changed if Wiglaf had not stayed behind to fight with Beowulf?
Possible response: The dragon would have killed Beowulf and remained a danger to the other people in the community.

50 **Reading Strategy**

Determine the Main Idea by Paraphrasing

1. Read aloud or have a student volunteer read aloud lines 779–785.
2. Walk through the passage as a class, having volunteers **paraphrase** short sections as you go.
Possible responses: Wiglaf, a brave soldier, was excited by his victory. He searched his way through the dark tower and then saw beautiful treasure scattered all over the floor. The treasure looked as if it had been neglected.
3. Then, **ask** students the Reading Strategy question: What is the main idea in the sentence in lines 779–785?
Possible response: Wiglaf finds the treasure but sees that it has deteriorated due to neglect.
4. Tell students that in almost all legends of dragons, the dragons had hoards of valuable treasure. Dragons were proverbial for greed and acquisitiveness. **Ask** students how this thought influences their interpretation of this passage.
Possible response: The poem implies the message that these treasures were made to be cared for and well used, not to be hoarded for the sake of amassing wealth.

51 **Reading Check**

Answer: Wiglaf comes to Beowulf's aid because Beowulf has been kind and generous to him and the other men: as a result, Wiglaf and the other men had pledged their lives and loyalty to Beowulf.

The Epic

1. Remind students that when Beowulf first landed in Denmark, he identified himself in terms of his father being remembered still (lines 174–179).

2. Read aloud or have a student read aloud lines 823–830.

3. Then, **ask** students: In Beowulf's death scene, what is shown about the importance of the remembrance of individuals after death?
   Answer: Being remembered was important to the individual; a father's glory could aid his son, and undying fame was a way of overcoming death. Beowulf's desire to have a tower reminding people of his life illustrates this principle.

4. **Ask** students to compare the commemoration of an epic hero to the ways in which the dead are remembered today.
   Possible response: Today the dead are often commemorated with a headstone or memorial to remind friends and family of the person's life. Beowulf's commemoration is similar in purpose but much more grand and is intended for a larger audience.

53 **Critical Thinking**

Interpret

1. Have a student volunteer read aloud lines 831–838.

2. **Ask** students: What "family" is Beowulf referring to when he calls Wiglaf "the last of all our far-flung family"?
   Possible responses: Beowulf may be referring to the fact that he and Wiglaf are from the same nation; however, it seems more likely that he is implying that he and Wiglaf are the last of the true warriors. Since the other men in their group left in the face of trouble, they proved not to belong to this group. This leaves Wiglaf to carry on the legacy of the true and noble warrior in Beowulf's absence.

62 From Legend to History (A.D. 449–1485)

Had ended those flying, burning raids
805 Forever.
　　　　　Then Wiglaf went back, anxious
To return while Beowulf was alive, to bring him
Treasure they'd won together. He ran,
Hoping his wounded king, weak
And dying, had not left the world too soon.
810 Then he brought their treasure to Beowulf, and found
His famous king bloody, gasping
For breath. But Wiglaf sprinkled water
Over his lord, until the words
Deep in his breast broke through and were heard.
815 Beholding the treasure he spoke, haltingly:
　　　"For this, this gold, these jewels, I thank
Our Father in Heaven, Ruler of the Earth—
For all of this, that His grace has given me,
Allowed me to bring to my people while breath
820 Still came to my lips. I sold my life
For this treasure, and I sold it well. Take
What I leave, Wiglaf, lead my people,
Help them; my time is gone. Have
The brave Geats build me a tomb,
825 When the funeral flames have burned me, and build it
Here, at the water's edge, high
On this spit of land, so sailors can see
This tower, and remember my name, and call it
Beowulf's tower, and boats in the darkness
830 And mist, crossing the sea, will know it."
　　　　Then that brave king gave the golden
Necklace from around his throat to Wiglaf,
Gave him his gold-covered helmet, and his rings,
And his mail shirt, and ordered him to use them well:
835 　　"You're the last of all our far-flung family.
Fate has swept our race away,
Taken warriors in their strength and led them
To the death that was waiting. And now I follow them."
　　　The old man's mouth was silent, spoke
840 No more, had said as much as it could;
He would sleep in the fire, soon. His soul
Left his flesh, flew to glory.

Wiglaf denounces the warriors who deserted Beowulf. The Geats burn their king's body on a funeral pyre and bitterly lament his death.

Vocabulary Development

Vocabulary Knowledge Rating
When students have completed reading and discussing the selection, have them take out their **Vocabulary Knowledge Rating** charts for the story. Read the words aloud and have students rate their knowledge of words again in the After Reading column. Clarify any words that are still problematic. Have students write their own definitions and example or sentence in the appropriate column. Then, have students complete the Vocabulary Lesson at the end of the selection. Encourage students to use the words in further discussion and written work about the selection. Remind them that they will be accountable for these words on the **Selection Test,** *Unit 1 Resources,* page 46–48 or 49–51.

Vocabulary Central, featuring tools and activities for studying vocabulary, is available online at **www.PHLitOnline.com.**

54 Critical Viewing

Possible response: The mood of the painting is solemn and sad, yet also peaceful. The men's serious faces and formal dress add to the somber quality of the painting, as do the dark colors and overcast sky. However, the background is misty, with light in the distance, which adds a sense of peace and hope despite the mournful scene.

55 Reading Check

Answer: Beowulf's last request is for Wiglaf to lead his people and build a tower in Beowulf's name.

THE FAREWELL

     Then the Geats built the tower, as Beowulf
     Had asked, strong and tall, so sailors
845 Could find it from far and wide; working
     For ten long days they made his monument,
     Sealed his ashes in walls as straight
     And high as wise and willing hands
     Could raise them. And the riches he and Wiglaf
850 Had won from the dragon, rings, necklaces,
     Ancient, hammered armor—all
     The treasures they'd taken were left there, too,
     Silver and jewels buried in the sandy

54 ▲ Critical Viewing
How would you describe the mood of this painting? Does it accurately reflect the conclusion of *Beowulf*? Explain. **[Connect]**

55 **Reading Check**
What is Beowulf's last request?

from Beowulf **63**

Burton Raffel

Translator's Insight

Ask students what Christian figure would be described as Beowulf in lines 867–869.

Possible response: Students may suggest Jesus Christ, who is often referred to as a mild prince in the New Testament.

ASSESS

Answers

Before students respond, you may wish to have them write a brief objective summary of the selection. As they answer the questions below, remind them to support their answers with evidence from the text.

1. (a) Grendel is annoyed by the happiness and singing of the warriors. (b) **Possible response:** The universal conflict behind the attack is the battle between good and evil.

2. (a) He travels to Herot to rid the Danes of Grendel. (b) It shows that he is brave, cares about others, and hates evil and suffering. (c) Grendel hates others and loves evil and suffering. Beowulf is the ideal of goodness; Grendel is the personification of an evil.

3. By conquering Grendel, Beowulf has not only ended the life of the menace that has plagued the Danes, but he has eradicated the presence of an evil from the world.

4. Beowulf embodied the values of the age in which he lived. His culture valued a man who was strong, brave, wise, aware of duty, and God-fearing.

5. **Possible response:** Beowulf's deeds make him a good role model because he helped the Danes and vanquished evil.

6. **Possible responses:** *Beowulf* reveals that Anglo-Saxons' definitions of evil and good were based on both moral and social standards. The evil characters in the poem are portrayed as completely *malignant;* there is no *liminal* characterization. Their actions are portrayed as morally wrong and antisocial. On the other hand, good characters such as Beowulf and Wiglaf live within the moral and social *boundaries.*

Ground, back in the earth, again
855 And forever hidden and useless to men.
And then twelve of the bravest Geats
Rode their horses around the tower,
Telling their sorrow, telling stories
Of their dead king and his greatness, his glory,
860 Praising him for heroic deeds, for a life
As noble as his name. So should all men
Raise up words for their lords, warm
With love, when their shield and protector leaves
His body behind, sends his soul
865 On high. And so Beowulf's followers
Rode, mourning their beloved leader,
Crying that no better king had ever
Lived, no prince so mild, no man
So open to his people, so deserving of praise.

 Burton Raffel

Translator's Insight

"Mild," in line 868, is not a description of Beowulf as we have seen him. But it is a description often used in the New Testament, more evidence that *Beowulf* is not a pagan poem.

Critical Reading

 Cite textual evidence to support your responses.

1. **Key Ideas and Details (a)** What annoys Grendel and leads to his attacks? **(b) Interpret:** What universal conflict lies behind his war with the Danes?

2. **Key Ideas and Details (a)** Why does Beowulf travel to Herot? **(b) Infer:** What do his motives for the trip tell you about his character? **(c) Analyze:** How does the contrast between Grendel and Beowulf turn their conflict into a fight between good and evil?

3. **Integration of Knowledge and Ideas** Beowulf's defeat of Grendel might be described as the defeat of the "dark side" of the warrior's life. Explain.

4. **Integration of Knowledge and Ideas** Explain how the poem, by keeping Beowulf's memory alive, keeps a culture's values alive.

5. **Integration of Knowledge and Ideas** Do you think Beowulf's deeds make him a good role model? Explain.

6. **Integration of Knowledge and Ideas** What does *Beowulf* reveal about the way in which Anglo-Saxons defined evil and good? In responding, use at least two of these Essential Question words: *liminal, boundary, malignant. [Connecting to the Essential Question: How does literature shape or reflect society?]*

64 From Legend to History (A.D. 449–1485)

Concept Connector

Reading Skill Graphic Organizer
Ask students to review the graphic organizers in which they have paraphrased passages from the selection in order to determine main ideas. Then, have students share their organizers and compare the main ideas they identified.

Activating Prior Knowledge
Have students return to the prediction paragraphs they wrote in the Activating Prior Knowledge activity. **Ask** them to explain which of their predictions were correct, and which events surprised them or unfolded in a way that was different from what they expected.

Writing About the Essential Question
Have students compare their responses given to the prompt before they completed reading the selection with their thoughts afterwards. Have them work individually or in groups, writing or discussing their thoughts, to formulate new responses. Then lead a class discussion, probing for what students have observed in the selection that confirms or invalidates their initial thoughts. Encourage students to cite specific textual details to support their responses.

64

After You Read   from *Beowulf*

Literary Analysis

1. **Key Ideas and Details** **Epics** often center on a battle between good and evil. Find evidence in lines 173–198 to indicate that Beowulf is battling for the good.

2. **Integration of Knowledge and Ideas** An epic reflects the values of the culture that produced it. Use a chart like the one shown to identify three features of *Beowulf* that probably pleased its original audience. For each, draw a conclusion about Anglo-Saxon tastes and values.

Feature	Why Pleasing	Values Reflected
boastful speeches	makes hero seem superhuman	

3. **Key Ideas and Details** **(a)** What details show the importance of Christian beliefs in the epic? **(b)** What details reveal the importance of pagan warrior values, such as a belief in fate, a taste for boasting, a pride in loyalty, and a desire for fame?

4. **Integration of Knowledge and Ideas** Frustrated pride may lead to spite, just as loyalty may lead to vengeance, and eagerness for glory may turn into greed. Explain how each creature Beowulf battles represents an extreme and dangerous form of warrior values and behavior.

5. **Key Ideas and Details** **(a)** List two characteristics that make Beowulf a **legendary, or epic, hero**. **(b)** Find a passage that shows his more human side. Explain your choice. **(c)** Identify each main character and the traits that make him a hero.

6. **Integration of Knowledge and Ideas** **(a)** Is Beowulf a believable character, or is he "too heroic"? Explain your answer. **(b)** How does his believability affect your sympathy for him?

7. **Integration of Knowledge and Ideas** Compare the way the epic commemorates Beowulf with the way our culture celebrates its heroes.

Reading Strategy

8. **Determine the main idea** of lines 843–861 from *Beowulf* by *paraphrasing* them.

9. **(a)** Explain which details you did not understand before paraphrasing. **(b)** Compare your paraphrase to the original, citing poetic effects that were lost in your paraphrase.

10. If someone asked you to state the essential message of this epic, which passage would you choose to paraphrase for that person? Why?

Common Core State Standards

Writing
1. Write arguments to support claims in an analysis of substantive topics or texts, using valid reasoning and relevant and sufficient evidence. *(p. 66)*

1.d. Establish and maintain a formal style and objective tone while attending to the norms and conventions of the discipline in which they are writing. *(p. 66)*

Language
3.a. Vary syntax for effect. *(p. 67)*
5. Demonstrate understanding of word relationships. *(p. 66)*

from Beowulf 65

Answers

1. Beowulf says he comes in friendship, and then relates that he wants to drive the evil monster out.

2. The poem has a great hero, there is a lot of action, and good triumphs over evil. The Anglo-Saxon audience probably admired the hero because he reflected virtues they valued, action was a part of life, and they liked to think that good would always triumph. Another sample answer can be found on **Literary Analysis Graphic Organizer A**, page 7 in *Graphic Organizer Transparencies*.

3. (a) The creation story, the labeling of Grendel as the enemy of God, and Beowulf's attributing his gifts to God all reflect Christian beliefs. (b) Beowulf boasts of his skill; he often mentions fate; he speaks of people remembering him.

4. Grendel derived pride from his ability to kill. Grendel's mother fought for revenge and loyalty. The dragon delighted in battle and wanted to protect its treasure.

5. (a) Beowulf is strong and of noble birth. (b) When fighting the dragon, Beowulf "stared at death, unwilling to leave this world." (c) Hrothgar is a nobleman and is a good king. Wiglaf is loyal and an excellent warrior.

6. (a) His accomplishments are not believable, but then neither are his opponents. However, his heroic attitude is believable. (b) His desire to do the right thing and to help others makes him very sympathetic.

7. Contemporary heroes are often given grand burials and monuments like the ones in *Beowulf*.

8. The Geats built the tower Beowulf had requested. They put his ashes inside and buried the dragon's treasure nearby. Geats circled the monument, telling stories about Beowulf.

9. (a) Answers will vary. Discuss how paraphrasing helped students understand the story. (b) Discuss poetic effects that students did not include in their paraphrases.

10. **Possible response:** Bravery and integrity make a person great and worthy of respect.

Assessment Practice

Sequential Order (For more practice, see *All-in-One Workbook*.)

Some tests require students to identify sequential order. Use this sample test item:

The monster's/Thoughts were as quick as his greed or his claws:/He slipped through the door and there in the silence/Snatched up thirty men, smashed them/ Unknowing in their beds and ran out with their bodies,/ The blood dripping behind him, back/To his lair, delighted with his night's slaughter.

Of the four actions described, which did Grendel perform third?

A He happily went back to his lair.
B He came up with an idea quickly.
C He smashed thirty men in their beds.
D He slipped through the door.

The correct answer is **C**. Choices **A, B,** and **D** are all activities that Grendel performs, but they are not the third activity Grendel performs.

Vocabulary Acquisition and Use

Word Analysis

1. **Possible response:** Grendel is inconsolable at first because he cannot stand the men's rejoicing, and later because he has been defeated by Beowulf; *inconsolable* means "not able to be comforted."

2. The warriors might have felt jealous of Beowulf's abilities; *disconsolate* means "dissatisfied" or "disgruntled."

3. Beowulf rid the people of Grendel; *solace* means "peace and comfort."

4. One might remind the warriors of Beowulf's great acts and encourage them to honor his memory with their own; *console* means "to comfort."

Vocabulary

1. loathsome
2. solace
3. massive
4. purge
5. reparation
6. writhing

Writing

1. To guide students in writing this argument, give them the **Support for Writing** page (*Unit 1 Resources,* p. 41).

2. Remind students that they should organize their letter with a general introductory paragraph followed by one or more body paragraphs in which they describe specific skills and experiences in detail.

3. If students have difficulty striking a balance between formality and a personable tone, you might wish to have students practice describing aloud to a partner the qualities and experiences they want to convey before writing them down.

4. Use the **Rubrics for Business Letter,** *Professional Development Guidebook,* pages 291–292, to evaluate students' work.

 COMMON CORE ▪ EXTENDED STUDY: THE EPIC

PERFORMANCE TASKS

Integrated Language Skills

Vocabulary Acquisition and Use

Word Analysis: Latin Word Root -sol-

The root *-sol-* comes from the Latin word *solari,* meaning "to relieve, to comfort." The root appears in the word *solace,* which means "an easing of grief, loneliness, or discomfort." With *-sol-* in mind, answer the following questions. Then, provide a definition of each italicized word.

1. Which character is *inconsolable*?
2. Why might Hrothgar's warriors have felt *disconsolate* after hearing Beowulf's boasts?
3. In what way did Beowulf provide *solace* for Hrothgar's people?
4. How might you *console* the mourning warriors after King Beowulf's death?

Vocabulary: Analogies

An analogy compares two relationships to show their basic similarity. For each item below, analyze the relationship between the first and second words. Then, complete the analogy using a word from the vocabulary list on page 38. Use each word only once, and explain your choice.

1. honest : untruthful :: delightful : _____
2. agreement : discord :: distress : _____
3. elevated : soaring :: huge : _____
4. flee : escape :: rid : _____
5. gift : donation :: reimbursement : _____
6. soothing : disturbing :: unmoving : _____

Writing

Argument Assuming the role of Beowulf, write a **job application** to Hrothgar, explaining why you are best suited to take on Grendel. Strike the same tone you would use in a real-life job letter. Keep in mind both your *purpose* and your *audience*, and choose words and ideas that are appropriate to both.

Prewriting First, review the text and create a list of Beowulf's best and most noble qualities, as well as his prior experience. Then, review your list, eliminating anything unrelated to the task of battling Grendel.

Model: Brainstorming Relevant Ideas
Beowulf's Qualities and Experiences
~~expert sailor~~
~~listens to his advisors~~
survived many wars
bound giants in chains
killed monsters of the ocean

> Beowulf's sailing and listening skills would not be needed in a battle with Grendel.

Drafting In the first paragraph of your letter, state your purpose and give an overview of your main qualifications for the job. In the body of your letter, describe your qualifications and prior experiences in detail. Remember to maintain a formal yet personable tone.

Revising As you read over your draft, revise any words or phrases that sound too casual, inappropriate, or irrelevant.

66 From Legend to History (A.D. 449–1485)

Assessment Resources

Unit 1 Resources

L1 L2 EL **Selection Test A,** pp. 46–48. Administer Test A to less advanced readers.

L3 L4 EL **Selection Test B,** pp. 49–51. Administer Test B to on-level and more advanced students.

L3 L4 **Open-Book Test,** pp. 43–45. As an alternative, give the Open-Book Test.

All **Customizable Test Bank**

All **Self-tests**
Students may prepare for the **Selection Test** by taking the **Self-test** online.

PHLit Online! All assessment resources are available at www.PHLitOnline.com.

Conventions and Style: Coordinating Conjunctions

For a smoother writing style, you can combine short, choppy sentences. One way to combine sentences is by using coordinating conjunctions to join sentence elements. A **coordinating conjunction** connects words or groups of words that have equal importance in the sentence.

Combining Sentences With Coordinating Conjunctions

Choppy	Better
Peace could not be bought with money. Peace could not be bought with land.	Peace could not be bought with money *or land.*
The monster hid in the mist. He terrorized the king's warriors.	The monster hid in the mist *and* terrorized the king's warriors.
The men stayed away from the banquet hall. They feared Grendel.	The men stayed away from the banquet hall, *for they feared Grendel.*

Keep in mind that different coordinating conjunctions show different relationships: *And* shows addition or similarity. *But* and *yet* indicate contrast. *Or* and *nor* indicate a choice. *For* and *so* show a result.

Punctuation Tip: When a coordinating conjunction joins two words, phrases, or subordinate clauses, no comma is needed. When a coordinating conjunction joins three or more elements, insert a comma before each element. When a coordinating conjunction joins two independent clauses, use a comma before the conjunction.

Practice In items 1–4, identify the coordinating conjunction and the words it joins. In items 5–8, use a coordinating conjunction to combine the two sentences.

1. Were pagan or Christian ideas more popular when *Beowulf* was written?
2. The king's council held meetings but could not devise a way to stop the attacks.
3. The people were terrified, but there was one man who could help them.
4. They landed the ship and were greeted by a soldier patrolling the cliffs.
5. He did not take his shield with him to fight Grendel. He did not take his sword either.
6. The monster struggled. He could not escape Beowulf's grip.
7. Her son had been killed. The mother sought revenge.
8. Epics reflect the dominant cultural values of the time. They reflect the dominant religious values too.

© **Writing and Speaking Conventions**

A. Writing For each pair listed, construct a sentence in which you link the two words or word groups using a coordinating conjunction. Tell what relationship is indicated by the conjunction.

1. good—evil
2. outfitted a boat—sailed to a distant land
3. he killed the monster—the people were grateful

   Example: good—evil
   Sentence: Is the king good or evil?
   Relationship: choice

B. Speaking Tell your friends the story of Beowulf's battle with Grendel. Use at least three different coordinating conjunctions.

PH WRITING COACH
Further instruction and practice are available in *Prentice Hall Writing Coach*.

Integrated Language Skills **67**

Extend the Lesson

Sentence Modeling

Choose one or both of the following sentences from the selection:

   His name was Wiglaf, he was Wexstan's son/And a good soldier.
   The monsters' hall was full of/Rich treasures, but all that Beowulf took/Was Grendel's head and the hilt of the giants'/Jeweled sword.

Ask students what they notice about the sentences. Elicit from them that both sentences contain at least one coordinating conjunction. Discuss the relationships indicated by both conjunctions. (In the first sentence, *and* indicates addition; in the second sentence, *but* indicates contrast and *and* indicates addition.) Have students imitate the sentences by writing similar sentences on topics of their own choosing, matching the grammatical features and the relationships indicated by the coordinating conjunctions. Have student volunteers share their sentences with the class.

Conventions and Style

1. Introduce and discuss the skill, using the instruction on the student page.
2. Have students complete the activities

Think Aloud: Model the Skill

Say to students:

   When I want to get an idea across, there is always more than one way to say it. For example, my first draft might say, "He went to the store. He needed to buy milk." I could also say, "He needed to buy milk, so he went to the store." This way explains the reason that he went to the store.

PH WRITING COACH Grade 12

Students will find instruction on and practice with coordinating conjunctions in Chapter 13, section 4.

Practice

1. *Or* joins *pagan* and *Christian.*
2. *But* joins *held meetings* and *could not devise.*
3. *But* joins the two independent clauses.
4. *And* joins *landed the ship* and *were greeted.*

Sample responses for items 5–8:

5. He did not take his shield or his sword with him to fight Grendel.
6. The monster struggled, but he could not escape Beowulf's grip.
7. Her son had been killed, so the mother sought revenge.
8. Epics reflect the dominant cultural and religious values of the time.

Writing and Speaking Conventions

A. Sample responses:

1. **Sentence:** *Beowulf* examines the forces of good and evil. **Relationship:** addition.
2. **Sentence:** He outfitted a boat and sailed to a distant land. **Relationship:** addition.
3. **Sentence:** He killed the monster, so the people were grateful. **Relationship:** result.

B. Answers will vary. Encourage students to vary their use of coordinating conjunctions.

TEACH

Themes Across Centuries

Seamus Heaney

Tell students that Seamus Heaney is much more than just a translator. He is among the world's most renowned poets. He began writing poetry in the 1960s while he was teaching in Ireland. Early on, his work was marked by the heavy rhythms of Anglo-Saxon English—a linguistic interest that is reflected in Heaney's translation of *Beowulf*. In 1995, Heaney was awarded the Nobel Prize for Literature.

Giving Shape to Poetry

1. After students read Heaney's commentary, point out that his focus is on *Beowulf's* language and the linguistic tradition that produced it, rather than the epic's plot and themes.

2. Call students' attention to Heaney's literal translation of the Old English word for poet, *scop*. **Ask** students to explain the question Heaney raises about this term, and the answer he offers. **Possible response:** The question Heaney poses is whether *Beowulf* was composed orally or in its written form. Heaney's answer is that both the oral and written traditions were likely involved.

3. Explain to students that studies have been done to prove that listening to certain types of music while studying aids the memory. Discuss with students how this idea can be related to Heaney's description of the scop.

The Original Beowulf

Call students' attention to the Old English lines from *Beowulf*. Review Heaney's commentary on the Old English lines with the class. Guide them to recognize the evidence of alliteration in the original text.

Critical Viewing

Possible response: Historians may preserve these documents to keep a record of our literary past and to help us learn about the skills and trades involved in creating ancient documents, as well as to help others learn to study and appreciate the documents.

68

COMMON CORE ▪ EXTENDED STUDY: THE EPIC

Themes Across Centuries: Translator's Insights

Seamus Heaney Discusses Beowulf

Giving Shape to Poetry A poet in Old English was called a *scop*, pronounced "shop" and meaning "a shaper." But did he do his shaping with a pen on parchment or with sound-patterns in the ear? Was he a scribe or was he a singer? Was *Beowulf* the result of mouth and ear work, or pen and paperwork?

The answer has to be that it was both. We have evidence that the *scop* chanted his poems to the accompaniment of a harp, so the notes he struck with his voice and his instrument were designed to fasten his words into the ear and the memory. But the intricacy of the patterning suggests that over time his live performance developed into a written score, so the heard melody has come down to us as a manuscript, a word which basically means handwritten marks.

The Original Beowulf In the original, for example, three lines of one passage of *Beowulf* look like this:

> Him ðā gegiredan Gēata lēode
> ād on eorðan unwāclīcne,
> helmum behongen, hilde-bordum.

Look again and you can see words and traces of words that we still use. "Him," obviously, in line 1; "helmets" and "hung" and "boards" in line 3; and once you realize that the strange letter ð is the symbol that Anglo-Saxon scribes used for the "th," you can see "earth" in line 2. But the words were meant to be heard rather than seen, and if you keep looking you can find alliteration that the first audience listened for in every line.

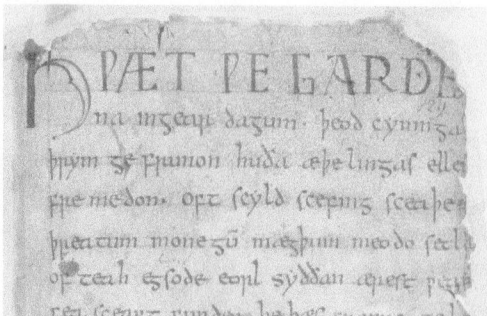

68 From Legend to History (A.D. 449–1485)

About the Author

Seamus Heaney's poetry focuses on the cities and farms of his homeland in Northern Ireland and the political and religious strife that he has witnessed. Among his translations are *Beowulf* (2000) and Sophocles' drama *Antigone* (2004).

◀ **Critical Viewing**
Why do historians preserve documents like this page from *Beowulf*? **[Speculate]**

Teaching Resources

The following resources can be used to enrich or extend the instruction for the Contemporary Commentary.

Unit 1 Resources

Listening and Viewing, p. 32

See It! DVD

Seamus Heaney, Segment 2

The Music of Storytelling Translating an old poem means keeping time, in both the musical and historical sense; it means staying faithful to the original, but not to the point of sounding out of tune. I wanted my version to be a score for performance and tried, therefore, to tune my voice not only to the movement of the Anglo-Saxon lines but to the other voices that had been familiar to me in Northern Ireland. I wrote for my first local accent, imagining the poetry being spoken by old neighbors who always gave their storytelling a natural pace and stress. When I tried out a line, the test would be: do these words sound sure and true if I pretend to be one of those big-voiced elders?

Take, for example, the third line: it tolls like a bell that has been rung four times, and when I translated it I wanted to keep the heavy downbeat of the original alliterating words, so it came out as "hung with helmets, heavy war-shields." I was after a similar effect in later lines such as "funeral fires; fumes of woodsmoke" and "and wailed aloud for their lord's decease."

Still, there is epic pride in the lines as well as elegy, so I wanted them to sound not only mournful but elevated. Ideally, the translator of *Beowulf* will construct something in words that is the equivalent of the burial mound constructed by the Geats, something to make us feel both their hero's greatness and their grief at his loss.

▲ **Critical Viewing**
In what ways does the burial mound pictured here convey both greatness and serenity?
[Interpret]

Critical Reading

© 1. **Craft and Structure (a)** According to Heaney's essay, was the original Old English scop a writer or a musician? **(b) Speculate:** In what ways do you think details in this translation of *Beowulf* were influenced by the manner in which the tale was originally told?

© 2. **Craft and Structure (a)** On what voices does Heaney model his translation? **(b) Infer:** Why might it have helped Heaney to have specific voices in mind as he translated?

As You Think About *Beowulf* . . .

© 3. **Integration of Knowledge and Ideas** Many translators have produced versions of *Beowulf*. In what ways might translators' decisions affect your experience with the epic?

Extended Study: The Epic **69**

The Music of Storytelling

1. Have students compare the third line of the Old English text on page 106 to Heaney's translation. **Ask** them what elements of the original rhythm they can see in the translation.
Possible response: The translation shares the heavy stresses of the original, replicating the four beats of the Old English version.

2. Call students' attention to Heaney's comments on keeping *Beowulf's* Old English rhythm in his translation. Be sure students understand that maintaining the rhythm was a primary concern for the poet and translator. **Ask** students if, based on the examples here, they think Heaney achieved this goal.
Possible response: Most students will agree that he has achieved his goal.

Critical Viewing
Possible response: The sheer size of the burial mound conveys greatness, while its smooth, even curve and the lushness of the grass make it appear serene.

ASSESS

Answers

Remind students to support their answers with evidence from the text.

1. (a) Heaney believes the scop was both writer and musician. (b) **Possible response:** The rhythms of the translation seem to have grown from oral recitations with musical accompaniment. The drama and excitement of the poem may have also grown from its storytelling roots.

2. (a) Heaney models his translation on the voices of Northern Ireland. (b) **Possible response:** Heaney used the voices he had in mind to structure the rhythms of his translation. Keeping specific voices in mind gave the translation a consistency it might have otherwise lacked.

3. **Possible response:** Students are likely to observe that the translators create rhythms that can either enhance or impede their enjoyment of *Beowulf*. Students may also note that the choices translators make can change the plot's focus, its pacing, and even the words of the poem and their connotations.

69

Common Core
State Standards

- Reading Informational Text 7
- Writing 2, 2.c
- Language 4.d

About the Texts

1. Introduce the form using the instruction about an *encyclopedia article* on the student page.

2. Tell students that they will identify the features and elements of each form as they read the selections.

Reading Strategy

1. Introduce the skill using the instruction and chart on the student page.

2. Tell students that they will evaluate each online article's accuracy as an information source as they read the selections.

Think Aloud: Model the Skill

Say to students:

Whenever I am reading an online information source, I evaluate its accuracy. Even before I begin to read, I skim the article for an author's name or a sponsoring organization. Then I look for any references to resources used by the author. I can use these and other texts to verify or clarify statements made in the article.

Content-Area Vocabulary

1. Have students say each word aloud.

2. Next, use each word in a sentence that defines it.

For more guidance, consult the *Classroom Strategies and Teaching Routines* card on introducing vocabulary.

Reading for Information

Analyzing Functional and Expository Texts

Online Encyclopedia Article • Wikipedia Article

About the Texts

An **online encyclopedia article** is a research source, presented as a Web page on the Internet, that provides information on a given topic. Usually, pages addressing specific topics can be accessed through a search engine within the larger encyclopedia site. Most online encyclopedia articles are written by an expert and feature credible information on the topic of the article, clear identification of the author or sponsor of the Web site, and a list of resources or bibliography consulted by the author. Some sites also provide links to other reliable online resources.

A **Wikipedia article** is an online reference that, unlike a traditional encyclopedia article, can be edited and updated by readers. Wikipedia does not charge an access fee and therefore relies on contributions from amateur writers. This practice has caused some experts to question its accuracy.

Reading Strategy

As you read a digital reference, **evaluate its validity and reliability** as a research tool.

- *Consider the source.* Identify the site's sponsor. Determine whether it promotes a particular agenda, such as to sell products, that could result in biased information.

- *Verify and clarify facts.* Confirm information by consulting other reputable sources in various media or formats. For example, compare the presentation of a topic online, in a book, and in a documentary film. Evaluate the accuracy of one source by measuring it against the others.

As you read, use a chart like this one to evaluate a source's validity:

Digital Resource _____			
Author _____			
Facts to Be Verified	**Sources**	**Discrepancies**	**Result**
1. _____	_____	_____	_____
2. _____	_____	_____	_____
3. _____	_____	_____	_____

Common Core
State Standards

Reading Informational Text
7. Integrate and evaluate multiple sources of information presented in different media or formats as well as in words in order to address a question or solve a problem.

Content-Area Vocabulary

These words appear in the selections that follow. They may also appear in other content-area texts:

manuscripts (man´ yo͞o skripts´) *n.* books or documents written by hand before printing was invented

didactic (dī dak´ tik) *adj.* descriptive of a work that is intended to teach people a moral lesson

fragmentary (frag´ mən ter´ ē) *adj.* consisting of broken pieces; disconnected

forefront (fôr´ frunt´) *n.* the position of most activity or importance

siege (sēj) *n.* the surrounding of a place by an opposing force

---

Teaching Resources

Reading Support

L2 L3 *Reader's Notebook*

L1 *Reader's Notebook: Adapted Version*

EL *Reader's Notebook: English Learner's Version*

ENCYCLOPEDIA BRITANNICA online

Jump to: navigation, search

Old English poetry

Home | Blog | Board | Newsletters | International | Store

English Literature — The Major Manuscripts

The Old English period > Poetry > The major manuscripts

Most Old English poetry is preserved in four manuscripts of the late 10th and early 11th centuries. The Beowulf manuscript (British Library) contains *Beowulf*, *Judith*, and three prose tracts; the <u>Exeter Book</u> (Exeter Cathedral) is a miscellaneous gathering of lyrics, riddles, didactic poems, and religious narratives; the <u>Junius Manuscript</u> (Bodleian Library, Oxford)—also called the <u>Caedmon Manuscript</u>, even though its contents are no longer attributed to Caedmon—contains biblical paraphrases; and the <u>Vercelli Book</u> (found in the cathedral library in Vercelli, Italy) contains saints' lives, several short religious poems, and prose homilies. In addition to the poems in these books are historical poems in the <u>Anglo-Saxon Chronicle</u>; poetic renderings of Psalms 51–150; the 31 Metres included in <u>King</u> <u>Alfred the Great</u>'s translation of <u>Boethius</u>'s *De consolatione philosophiae (Consolation of Philosophy)*; magical, didactic, elegiac, and heroic poems; and others, miscellaneously interspersed with prose, jotted in margins, and even worked in stone or metal.

Underlined words in blue are hyperlinks or connections to other sources.

Related Topics

<u>Poetry</u>
   from the English literature *article*
The Norman Conquest worked no immediate transformation on either the language or the literature of the English. Older poetry continued to be copied during the last half of the 11th century; two poems . . .

<u>Development as a poet</u>
   from the Pound, Ezra *article*
Unsettled by the slaughter of World War I and the spirit of hopelessness he felt was pervading England after its conclusion, Pound decided to move to Paris, publishing before he left two of his most . . .

<u>lament</u>
a nonnarrative poem expressing deep grief or sorrow over a personal loss. The form developed as part of the oral tradition along with heroic poetry and exists in most languages. Examples include . . .

<u>Chadwick, H. Munro</u>
English philologist and historian, professor of Anglo-Saxon at the University of Cambridge (1912–41), who helped develop an integral approach to Old English studies.

About Online Encyclopedia Articles

1. Point out to students that the first selection is an encyclopedia article.

2. Refer students to the bulleted list of features of an encyclopedia article on the Preteach page.

3. **Ask** students to identify the features of this online information source.
   Answer: The site has a navigation bar that links to different parts of the site and to its sponsor. It also has links to outside educational and Web resources.

Verify and Clarify

1. Refer students to the bulleted questions about accuracy on the Preteach page.

2. Point out that they will be evaluating the accuracy of an online information source.

3. Have students apply the questions to the encyclopedia article shown here to begin to verify and clarify information.

4. Suggest that students use a chart like the one shown on the Preteach page to organize their findings.

Differentiated Instruction   for Universal Access

Support for Less Proficient Readers

Have students work with partners to analyze how they approach a Web page. Students should write the steps they take in order. For example, the first thing they may do is look at the navigation bar at the top of the page. Once students complete their lists, have them consider additional steps that would help them evaluate the source's accuracy. For example, students might ask, "Do the author's opinions and beliefs come through in this article?" Have pairs share their lists with the class.

EL Strategies for English Learners

Encourage students to practice the techniques in this lesson using an online source written in their home languages. Take a moment to identify the English vocabulary for features, such as *link, button, URL,* and *Web page.* Then have students identify the features of an online article they have found that uses their home language.

71

1. Remind students to look through the article for information to verify or clarify.

2. **Ask** students whether they would trust the information provided by this article, and to explain why.
   Answer: Students should understand that the people who provided the information are experts on the topic.

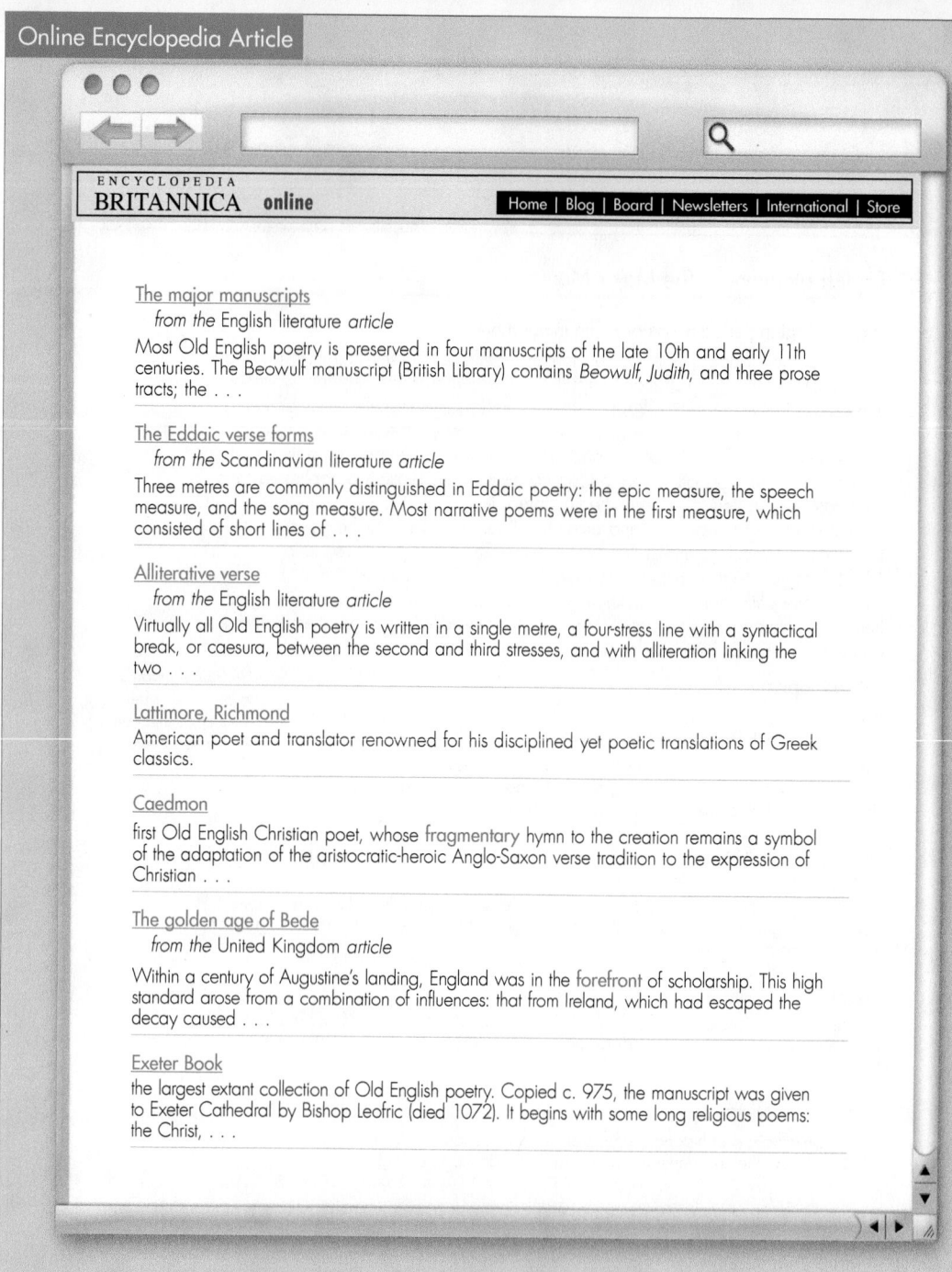

Online Encyclopedia Article

ENCYCLOPEDIA
BRITANNICA online

Home | Blog | Board | Newsletters | International | Store

The major manuscripts
from the English literature *article*

Most Old English poetry is preserved in four manuscripts of the late 10th and early 11th centuries. The Beowulf manuscript (British Library) contains *Beowulf, Judith,* and three prose tracts; the . . .

The Eddaic verse forms
from the Scandinavian literature *article*

Three metres are commonly distinguished in Eddaic poetry: the epic measure, the speech measure, and the song measure. Most narrative poems were in the first measure, which consisted of short lines of . . .

Alliterative verse
from the English literature *article*

Virtually all Old English poetry is written in a single metre, a four-stress line with a syntactical break, or caesura, between the second and third stresses, and with alliteration linking the two . . .

Lattimore, Richmond

American poet and translator renowned for his disciplined yet poetic translations of Greek classics.

Caedmon

first Old English Christian poet, whose fragmentary hymn to the creation remains a symbol of the adaptation of the aristocratic-heroic Anglo-Saxon verse tradition to the expression of Christian . . .

The golden age of Bede
from the United Kingdom *article*

Within a century of Augustine's landing, England was in the forefront of scholarship. This high standard arose from a combination of influences: that from Ireland, which had escaped the decay caused . . .

Exeter Book

the largest extant collection of Old English poetry. Copied c. 975, the manuscript was given to Exeter Cathedral by Bishop Leofric (died 1072). It begins with some long religious poems: the Christ, . . .

72 From Legend to History (A.D. 449–1485)

Vocabulary Development

Content-Area Vocabulary: Language Arts

Review the definitions of the cross-curricular vocabulary with students: *manuscript, didactic, fragmertay,* and *forefront*. Then, examine each word in its context in the article.

When you have finished with the four listed words, ask students to identify other words in the article that relate to the cross-curricular vocabulary. Have students look up their definitions in a dictionary and then use them in sentences about the topic of the encyclopedia article.

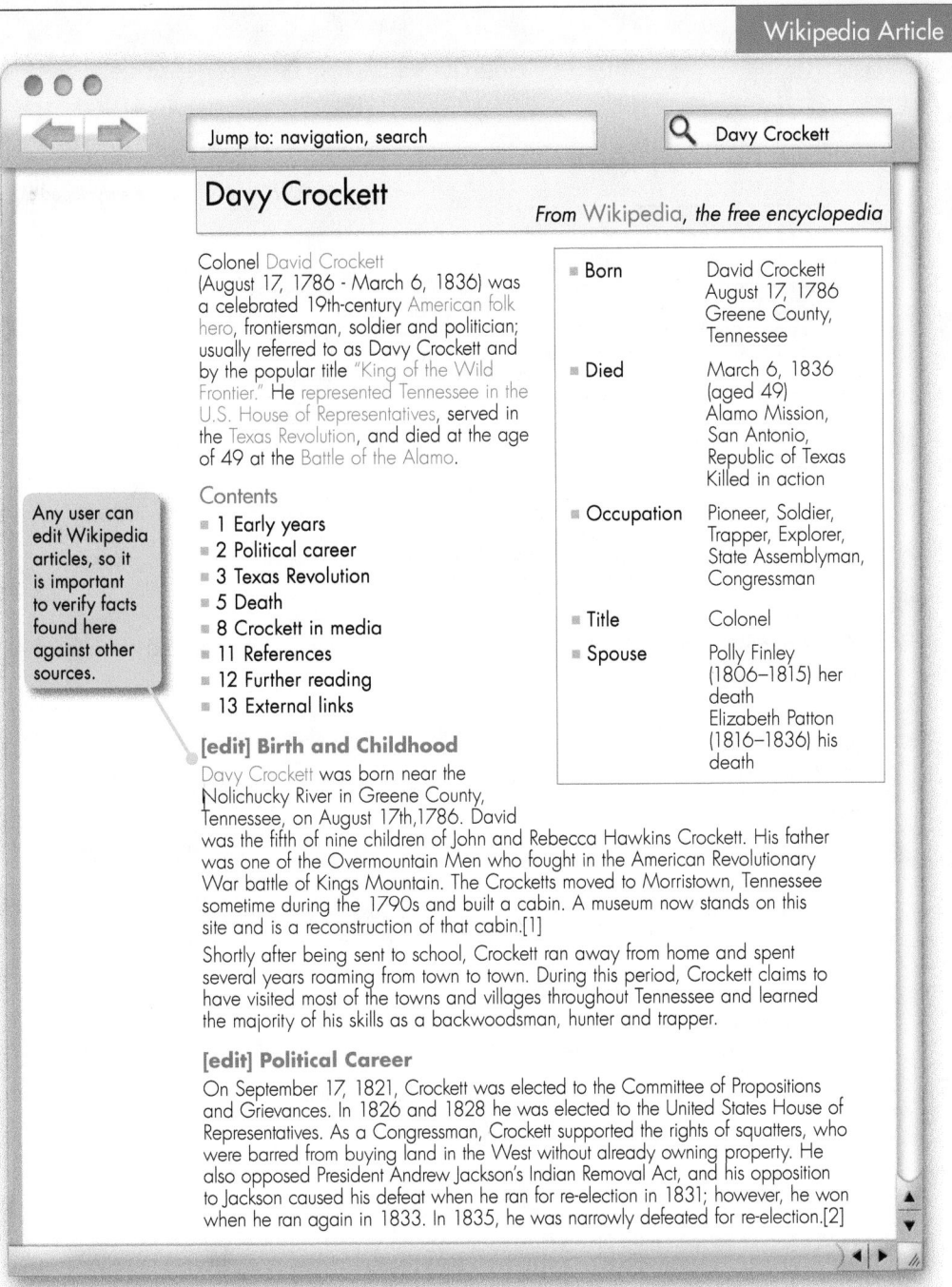

Jump to: navigation, search

Q Davy Crockett

Davy Crockett

From Wikipedia, *the free encyclopedia*

Colonel David Crockett (August 17, 1786 - March 6, 1836) was a celebrated 19th-century American folk hero, frontiersman, soldier and politician; usually referred to as Davy Crockett and by the popular title "King of the Wild Frontier." He represented Tennessee in the U.S. House of Representatives, served in the Texas Revolution, and died at the age of 49 at the Battle of the Alamo.

Born	David Crockett August 17, 1786 Greene County, Tennessee
Died	March 6, 1836 (aged 49) Alamo Mission, San Antonio, Republic of Texas Killed in action
Occupation	Pioneer, Soldier, Trapper, Explorer, State Assemblyman, Congressman
Title	Colonel
Spouse	Polly Finley (1806–1815) her death Elizabeth Patton (1816–1836) his death

Contents

- 1 Early years
- 2 Political career
- 3 Texas Revolution
- 5 Death
- 8 Crockett in media
- 11 References
- 12 Further reading
- 13 External links

> Any user can edit Wikipedia articles, so it is important to verify facts found here against other sources.

[edit] Birth and Childhood

Davy Crockett was born near the Nolichucky River in Greene County, Tennessee, on August 17th,1786. David was the fifth of nine children of John and Rebecca Hawkins Crockett. His father was one of the Overmountain Men who fought in the American Revolutionary War battle of Kings Mountain. The Crocketts moved to Morristown, Tennessee sometime during the 1790s and built a cabin. A museum now stands on this site and is a reconstruction of that cabin.[1]

Shortly after being sent to school, Crockett ran away from home and spent several years roaming from town to town. During this period, Crockett claims to have visited most of the towns and villages throughout Tennessee and learned the majority of his skills as a backwoodsman, hunter and trapper.

[edit] Political Career

On September 17, 1821, Crockett was elected to the Committee of Propositions and Grievances. In 1826 and 1828 he was elected to the United States House of Representatives. As a Congressman, Crockett supported the rights of squatters, who were barred from buying land in the West without already owning property. He also opposed President Andrew Jackson's Indian Removal Act, and his opposition to Jackson caused his defeat when he ran for re-election in 1831; however, he won when he ran again in 1833. In 1835, he was narrowly defeated for re-election.[2]

Informational Text: Wikipedia Article **73**

About Wikipedia Articles

1. Introduce the form, using the instruction about a Wikipedia encyclopedia article on the Preteach page.

2. Remind students that a Wikipedia encyclopedia article differs from a traditional encyclopedia article because it can be edited by anyone. **Ask:** How might Wikipedia's policy of making content editable by anyone strengthen the content? How might it weaken the content?
Possible response: Letting a variety of people edit the content could help to ensure that biases would be edited out or balanced and that content could be updated as soon as new information is available. It could also enable vandals to intentionally include incorrect information and enable inexperienced editors to introduce mistakes unknowingly. However, the system may also be helpful in finding incorrect information as other editors may soon correct glaring errors.

Verify and Clarify

1. Tell students that they will evaluate the article's accuracy as an information source as they read.

2. Remind students to use a chart like the one on the Preteach page to record their findings as they verify and clarify.

Differentiated Instruction   for Universal Access

Support for Special-Needs Students
Have students work with partners to identify the online source's topic and the summary of its contents. Have students make a list of references they might use to verify or clarify information found in this article.

Support for Less Proficient Readers
Have individual students look for a Wikipedia site on a hero who is more familiar to them than Davy Crockett. As they read the article, students should evaluate its accuracy. Students should suggest texts they know of that the author could use to support statements he or she makes and to clarify other information in the article.

Verify and Clarify

1. Remind students to look for information to verify or clarify as they read. Point out that the boxed text near the center of the article is Wikipedia's clue to readers that a portion of the article may not be verifiable.

2. **Ask** students whether they would trust the information provided by this article, and to explain why.
   Answer: Students may acknowledge that Wikipedia is edited by amateurs but that much of the information in this article can be verified.

3. **Ask** students to name situations in which they might use Wikipedia and situations in which they might prefer to use a traditional encyclopedia.
   Possible response: Students may respond that they would use Wikipedia as a starting point before researching a topic they are curious about. However, they might use a traditional encyclopedia as a source for a paper for school.

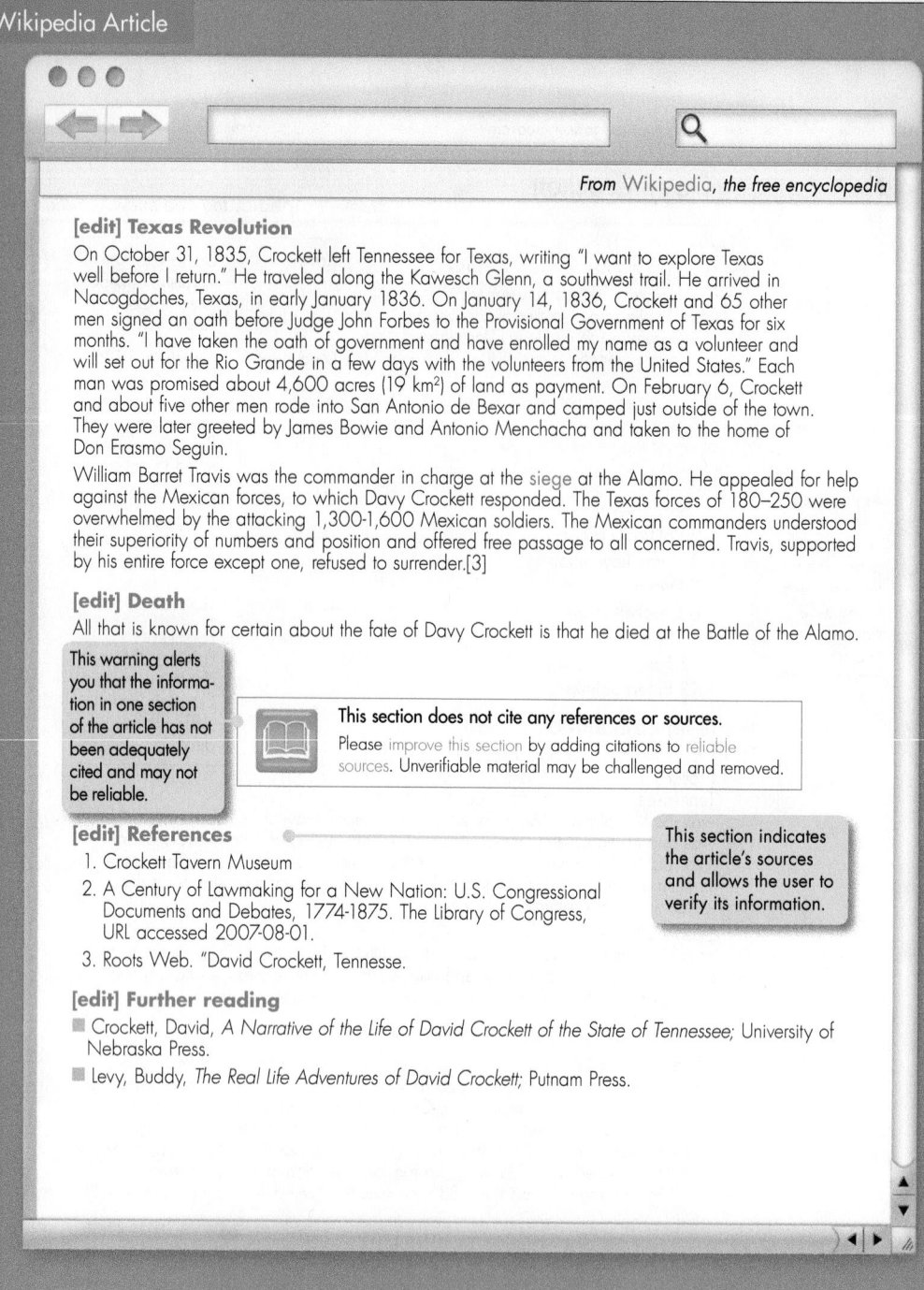

Wikipedia Article

From Wikipedia, *the free encyclopedia*

[edit] Texas Revolution

On October 31, 1835, Crockett left Tennessee for Texas, writing "I want to explore Texas well before I return." He traveled along the Kawesch Glenn, a southwest trail. He arrived in Nacogdoches, Texas, in early January 1836. On January 14, 1836, Crockett and 65 other men signed an oath before Judge John Forbes to the Provisional Government of Texas for six months. "I have taken the oath of government and have enrolled my name as a volunteer and will set out for the Rio Grande in a few days with the volunteers from the United States." Each man was promised about 4,600 acres (19 km²) of land as payment. On February 6, Crockett and about five other men rode into San Antonio de Bexar and camped just outside of the town. They were later greeted by James Bowie and Antonio Menchacha and taken to the home of Don Erasmo Seguin.

William Barret Travis was the commander in charge at the siege at the Alamo. He appealed for help against the Mexican forces, to which Davy Crockett responded. The Texas forces of 180–250 were overwhelmed by the attacking 1,300-1,600 Mexican soldiers. The Mexican commanders understood their superiority of numbers and position and offered free passage to all concerned. Travis, supported by his entire force except one, refused to surrender.[3]

[edit] Death

All that is known for certain about the fate of Davy Crockett is that he died at the Battle of the Alamo.

> This warning alerts you that the information in one section of the article has not been adequately cited and may not be reliable.

This section does not cite any references or sources.
Please improve this section by adding citations to reliable sources. Unverifiable material may be challenged and removed.

[edit] References

> This section indicates the article's sources and allows the user to verify its information.

1. Crockett Tavern Museum
2. A Century of Lawmaking for a New Nation: U.S. Congressional Documents and Debates, 1774-1875. The Library of Congress, URL accessed 2007-08-01.
3. Roots Web. "David Crockett, Tennesse.

[edit] Further reading

- Crockett, David, *A Narrative of the Life of David Crockett of the State of Tennessee*; University of Nebraska Press.
- Levy, Buddy, *The Real Life Adventures of David Crockett*; Putnam Press.

74 From Legend to History (A.D. 449–1485)

Vocabulary Development

Content-Area Vocabulary

Review the definition of the following cross-curricular vocabulary word with students: *siege*. Then, examine the word in its context in the second article.

When you have finished with the listed word, ask students to identify other words in the article that relate to the cross-curricular vocabulary.

Have students look up their definitions in a dictionary and then use them in sentences about the topic of the encyclopedia article.

After You Read

Online Encyclopedia Article •
Wikipedia Article

Critical Reading

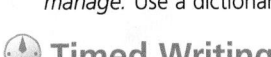 **1. Key Ideas and Details (a)** Identify three distinct features of the Britannica page. Consider both content and components provided for navigation. **(b)** Which feature would be most helpful to you in evaluating the site's reliability and credibility? Explain your choice.

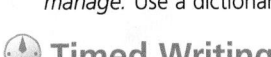 **2. Key Ideas and Details** What other sources might you use to evaluate the validity and reliability of the Britannica article? Explain your choices.

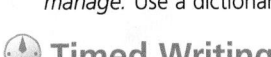 **3. Key Ideas and Details (a)** What is the main difference between Wikipedia and other encyclopedias? **(b)** Which feature or features of the Wikipedia page could you use to evaluate the site's validity and reliability? Explain your choices.

4. Content-Area Vocabulary (a) Explain how the Latin words *manus,* ("hand") and *scribere* ("to write") contribute to the meaning of the word *manuscript.* **(b)** Determine the meaning of these other words derived from the Latin word *manus: manacle, manicure, manipulate, manual,* and *manage.* Use a dictionary to verify the meanings you determined.

◈ Timed Writing

Explanatory Text [40 minutes}

Format

In an **analytical essay,** you break a topic into its elements and examine each one. Write at least one paragraph about each element, and include smooth transitions between ideas.

Write an **analytical essay** in which you **evaluate** the validity and reliability of various digital reference tools. Consider the pages shown here, as well as other sources you may have consulted in the past. Discuss the credibility of the various sites, as well as the information and features each offers. Also, explain how you can use other sources in various media to further verify the credibility of an online reference. End with a discussion of why it is important to verify the reliability of information presented online and elsewhere.

Academic Vocabulary

When you **evaluate** a text, you state your own judgment about it. Be sure to support your judgment with specific details from the texts.

5-Minute Planner

Complete these steps before you begin to write:

1. Read the prompt carefully. List key words.

2. Write a thesis that clearly responds to the prompt.

3. Scan the texts shown here and jot down other details that relate to the prompt.

4. Briefly sketch an outline for your essay. **TIP** In a Timed Writing situation an outline can be a simple numbered list.

5. Reread the prompt, and begin drafting.

© Common Core State Standards

Writing

2. Write informative/explanatory texts to examine and convey complex ideas, concepts, and information clearly and accurately through the effective selection, organization, and analysis of content.

2.c. Use appropriate and varied transitions to clarify the relationships among complex ideas and concepts.

Language

4.d. Verify the preliminary determination of the meaning of a word or phrase.

Reading for Information: Online Encyclopedia Article • Wikipedia Article **75**

Extend the Lesson

Connecting to the Students' World

To give students further practice with online information sources and to help them apply the material to their own world, divide the class into small groups. Provide each group with a Wikipedia article on a topic relevant to your community and have students evaluate its accuracy. To do so, they should verify or clarify facts and statements made by the author. Students should work together to write a brief report of their findings. Ask them to provide source materials to support their evaluation of the assigned article.

75

Contemporary Connection

Hinds's graphic novel consists of three books. The first chronicles Beowulf's defeat of Grendel; the second depicts his battle with Grendel's mother; and the third records Beowulf's final battle with the dragon. Each book was drawn using a different artistic technique. Sample pages from each book may be found through an Internet search. You may wish to show students these samples as an introduction to the scope of Hinds's work and to help them contextualize the segment from Book Three included in this text.

Beowulf: From Ancient Epic to Graphic Novel

1. Students are likely to have heard of the 2007 film version of *Beowulf,* but they may not know of the various other modern interpretations of the ancient tale. For example, John Gardner's novella *Grendel* retells the story of Beowulf's battle with Grendel from the monster's point of view.

2. While Hinds's graphic novel is probably closer to the original tale than Gardner's novella, both are modern artists' reinterpretations of Beowulf's story. **Ask** students what may be gained or lost when an ancient tale is retold or reexamined.
   Possible response: Hearing the story told in a different way may enrich our understanding of the story or introduce themes that are not usually considered in connection with the story; however, a retelling may also distort the original intention of the story, and some may feel that it corrupts the purity of the ancient version.

Gareth Hinds

1. Review the information on Gareth Hinds with students.

2. **Ask:** What advice would Hinds likely give to someone interested in a career in the arts?
   Possible response: Get good training, become well-rounded, and look for opportunities to tell meaningful stories.

CONTEMPORARY CONNECTION

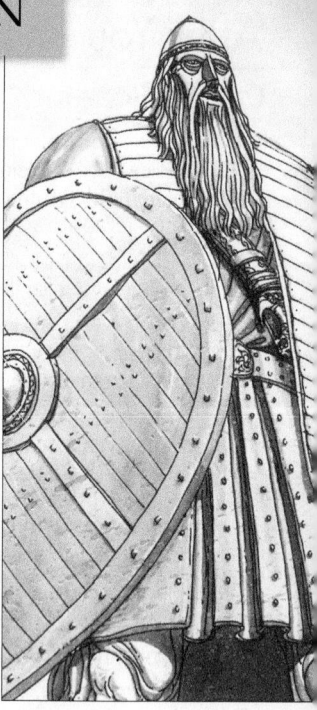

Beowulf: From Ancient Epic to Graphic Novel

It was the superhero in *Beowulf,* the sword-wielding slayer of monsters, that drew comics creator Gareth Hinds to the eighth-century epic. It was the warrior's heroism and realistic fighting style, however, that led the artist in Hinds to render the story as a graphic novel. Above all, as Hinds told one interviewer, *Beowulf* is "an incredibly cool story."

It is so cool and powerful that this tale of a warrior-chieftain has found its way into movies (the latest one directed by Robert Zemeckis, with writer Neil Gaiman sharing a screenwriting credit), TV, and opera. In Hinds's chosen medium, the dragon looks remarkably similar to the one in the movie *Alien* and Beowulf has the fit body of a comic-book superhero.

For his graphic novel, Hinds employed three different art styles: pen and ink, with computer coloring using Adobe Photoshop; paint on wooden panels; and black wash over black ink. All pre-press work was done on his own computer. Thus, while Beowulf's narrative may be timeless, Hinds's techniques are as up-to-the-minute as Hollywood's transformations of paper comic books into movie blockbusters.

Gareth Hinds
artist of *Beowulf*

Gareth Hinds was always drawing when he was child. "I was basically born into it," he says. "But I had a lot of really good training and encouragement along the way. And I'm a very strong believer in the power of good art instruction." So it was only natural that he would study art in school, earning two Bachelors of Fine Art, from Rochester Institute of Technology and Parsons School of Design. He used a grant to self-publish his first graphic novel, *Bearskin*, a Grimm's fairy tale, in 1997. The next year he self-published *Beowulf*. His version of Shakespeare's *King Lear* came out in 2007. Hinds advises aspiring artists to "become well-rounded." Also, the key to artistic success, he insists, is to "tell a story that is meaningful to ordinary people."

76 From Legend to History (A.D. 449–1485)

Enrichment: Analyzing Forms and Genres

Graphic Novels

While graphic novels have long been respected as literature in some parts of the world, they are just beginning to win critical respect in the United States. This may be partly because U.S. comics have traditionally been geared toward children and young adults, while in other countries graphic novels are produced for many different readerships in terms of age and interests. In recent years, the United States has seen growing interest in graphic novels.

They are coming to be seen as an acceptable literary form for adults.
Activity: Review a Graphic Novel Have students find and read a modern graphic novel. Then have students present synopses and reviews of the novels to the class. Suggest that students record information in the **Enrichment: Analyzing Forms and Genres** worksheet, *Professional Development Guidebook,* page 227.

from *Beowulf* **77**

1. Discuss with students their knowledge of the graphic novel genre. While graphic novels have existed in various forms for over a century, they have only recently begun to enjoy critical respect in the United States. Prominent examples include Art Spiegelman's *Maus,* Neil Gaiman's *Sandman* series, and Marjane Satrapi's *Persepolis,* which was adapted into the Oscar-nominated 2007 film. Ask students to list other examples with which they are familiar, and to describe the style of art and amount of text used.

2. Tell students that reading a graphic novel requires a different information-gathering process than reading a text-only version of the story. **Ask** students how the reading process might differ. **Possible response:** Instead of taking words and using them to form a mental picture of what is happening, readers must examine the details in each picture and combine those details with the words provided to piece together the progression of the story.

3. **Ask** students whether they think information can be conveyed more effectively and accurately through pictures or through words. Encourage them to consider advantages and disadvantages of each method. **Possible response:** Students may feel that information may be conveyed more quickly through pictures, but that some ideas are difficult to convey without words, so some information may be lost if mostly pictures are used.

Beowulf: From Ancient Epic to Graphic Novel

1. Point out that the words on this page are all spoken by Beowulf to his troops—there is no narration. As a result, all of the context is provided through the art. **Ask** students what contextual information, such as setting, mood, and circumstances, they can gather from the pictures. Encourage them to support their responses with details from the pictures.

   Possible responses: The occasion is a solemn one, since the men's faces look serious, and they are all gathered around to listen to Beowulf. The men's armor and weapons show that they are warriors ready for battle. Also, the setting seems quiet and barren; all that can be seen is a few treetops and the blank white sky. The blue and black tones add to the solemn mood. The angle from which the upper right-hand picture is drawn makes it evident that Beowulf is highly respected. It places the reader at a position of looking up at Beowulf and makes Beowulf appear large and majestic.

2. **Ask** students what the focal point of the bottom cell is, and how this artistic choice propels the story forward.

   Possible response: The focal point is Beowulf's sword. The effect of this choice is that it makes the viewer acutely aware that Beowulf is headed into battle. The visual emphasis being placed on his sword alone shows that the story is about Beowulf's individual fight, and not that of his army.

As in the old time with Grendel, I would not use sword or other weapon against this Worm. But I know not how, without these, I could fell such an enemy. Thus will I go prepared, but not one foot's space will I yield to him.

Now stand by this barrow and watch, my young comrades, which of us better from the battle-rush shall bear his wounds. To war with the Worm is not for you, nor any man but me alone. One of these two things must be: either I will carry away his treasure or death at last will find me. . . .

78 From Legend to History (A.D. 449–1485)

from Beowulf **79**

1. Ask students to describe what is happening on this page, and what will happen next. Encourage them to think back to what they read about Beowulf's encounter with the dragon.
   Possible response: Beowulf is walking toward the dragon's lair while his army watches. The dragon is said to guard a great treasure, which is probably hidden somewhere down the long passage pictured in the bottom cell on this page. Students should remember that during his encounter with the dragon, Beowulf feels for the first time that he might fail and be killed. Although one of his soldiers comes to his aid, Beowulf eventually dies from his injuries.

2. **Ask** students what artistic techniques Hinds uses to single out Beowulf and depict him as an epic hero.
   Possible response: In the top cell, Beowulf and his shadow draw the eye because they are the darkest point of the picture. His armor and sword make him appear strong and majestic, even next to the towering, solid cliffs. In the lower cell, Beowulf draws the eye because he is portrayed as white and appears to be glowing against the dark backdrop of the cliffs. The glowing appearance is in keeping with the epic conception of Beowulf as having superhuman qualities.

Differentiated
Instruction   for Universal Access

Support for Special-Needs Students
While a pictorial presentation of Beowulf may be more accessible for special-needs students, it may also be difficult for these students to form connections between the various pictures to construct a coherent understanding of the story. To help them string together the ideas, walk students through each cell.

Enrichment for Less Proficient Readers
To make sure that students understand what is happening on each page, have students summarize the events that are taking place. Then encourage students to imagine what other scenes or alternate views Hinds might have included.

EL Support for English Learners
The graphic novel format presents a unique opportunity for English learners to practice narrating a story. Have students write in their own words the story of what is taking place on these pages. Encourage them to include details from the pictures.

Before students respond, you may wish to have them write a brief objective summary of the selection. As they answer the questions below, remind them to support their answers with evidence from the text.

1. **Possible response:** Students may feel that the emotional tone of the graphic novel is similar to what they imagined when reading *Beowulf,* such as the mood portrayed as the soldiers listen to Beowulf's farewell speech, but specifics such as the appearance of the dragon's lair may be different.

2. (a) Hinds shows the soldiers looking at Beowulf in anticipation, which allows us to join them in anticipation. He also builds suspense through setting, such as the mysterious appearance of the long passageway where Beowulf meets the dragon. (b) The words contribute to the suspense because they present the possibilities that await: "either I will carry away his treasure or death at last will find me."

3. (a) Hinds uses close-ups to portray emotion, such as the soldiers' solemn faces and Beowulf's fear when he meets the dragon. He uses middle-distance views to show events, such as the soldiers watching Beowulf approach the dragon's lair. He uses long-distance perspectives to give a sense of the epic scope of the events, such as the bottom cell of page 79, where he shows the towering cliffs and how small the soldiers appear atop them. (b) Students may feel that Hinds effectively combines the perspectives because it allows him to show both the epic proportion of the events through long-perspective views and the epic proportion of the emotions experienced by the characters in close-ups.

4. (a) Storytelling with pictures and words requires readers to gather information from both sources and combine it to piece together the story. (b) **Possible response:** Pictures can convey events and emotions quickly, but some ideas are easier to express in words than in pictures.

Critical Reading

1. **Respond:** In this section from his graphic novel, Hinds depicts the lead-up to the battle with the dragon. Does the way in which Hinds portrays characters and scenes agree with how you pictured them? Why or why not?

2. **(a) Analyze:** In what visual ways does Hinds build suspense for the battle with the dragon? **(b) Analyze:** How do the words in the text boxes work with the images to create suspense?

3. **(a) Classify:** Where does Hinds use close-ups, middle-distance views, and long-distance perspectives in telling the story?
(b) Evaluate: Do you think he effectively combines these different perspectives? Explain.

Use these questions to hold a class discussion of *Beowulf*:

4. **(a)** How does storytelling with pictures and words differ from storytelling with words alone? **(b)** What are the advantages and disadvantages of each method? Explain.

5. Do you find it surprising that a very new form, the graphic novel, draws its subject matter from a very old form, an ancient epic? Why or why not?

80 From Legend to History (A.D. 449–1485)

5. **Possible response:** Students may feel that it is not very surprising that the ancient story has been retold in a new form, because the story contains timeless themes of adventure and heroism.

A National Spirit

PART 3

81

Text Complexity: At a Glance

This chart gives a general text complexity rating for the selections in this part of the unit to help guide instruction. For additional text complexity support, see the Test Complexity Rubric at point of use.

from A History of the English Church and People	**More Complex**
from The Canterbury Tales: The Prologue	**More Accessible**
from The Pardoner's Tale	**More Accessible**
The Wife of Bath's Tale	**More Accessible**

Selection Planning Guide

The selections in this section reveal the development of an English national identity. The excerpts from the medieval history, *A History of the English Church and People* describes events of the early Middle Ages. The excerpts from *The Canterbury Tales* reveal much about the structure of fourteenth-century society and also show the development of a national language.

Humanities

King Richard I and his Barons, Anonymous

Richard I was king of England and ruler of the Angevin Empire from July 6, 1189 until his death. He was known as Richard the Lionheart, or *Coeur de Lion,* even before his accession, because of his reputation as a great military leader. At only age 16, Richard had his own command, putting down rebellions against his father, Henry II. He spent most of his reign outside of England, fighting in the Crusades. In his absence, the country was ruled by his brother John, who succeeded him.

Ask students the following: Why might the use of English (rather than Latin) for important documents enhance national identity?
Possible response: It would imply that England was developing an established language and culture distinct from Roman models.

Monitoring Progress

Before students read the selections in Part 3, refer to the results for the **Diagnostic Test (***Unit 1 Resources,* **p.1).** Use this test to guide your choice of selections to teach as well as the depth of preteaching preparation you will provide, based on students' readiness for the reading and vocabulary skills.

Benchmark

After students have completed the excerpt from *A History of the English Church and People,* administer **Benchmark Test 1.** If the Benchmark Test reveals that some of the students need further work, use the **Interpretation Guide** to determine the appropriate reteaching page in the **Reading Kit** and on the **Success Tracker.**

• *from* A History of the English Church and People

Lesson Pacing Guide

DAY 1 Preteach

- Ⓒ Administer the Reading and Vocabulary Warm-ups (*Unit 1 Resources*, pp. 52–55) as necessary.
- Introduce the Literary Analysis concept: Historical Writing.
- Ⓒ Introduce the Reading Strategy: Analyze the Clarity of Meaning
- Build background with the author and Background features.
- Develop thematic thinking with Connecting to the Essential Question.
- Ⓒ Teach the selection vocabulary.

DAYS 2 Preteach/Teach/Extend

- Ⓒ Distribute copies of the appropriate graphic organizer for the Reading Strategy (*Graphic Organizer Transparencies*, pp. 9–10).
- Ⓒ Distribute copies of the appropriate graphic organizer for Literary Analysis (*Graphic Organizer Transparencies*, pp. 11–12).
- Prepare students to read with the Activating Prior Knowledge activities (TE).
- Informally monitor comprehension while students read.
- Use the Reading Check questions to confirm comprehension.
- Develop students' understanding of historical writing using the Literary Analysis prompts.
- Develop students' ability to analyze the clarity of meaning using the Reading Strategy Prompts.
- Ⓒ Reinforce vocabulary with the Vocabulary notes.
- Ⓒ Assess students' comprehension and mastery of the skills by having them answer the Critical Reading, Literary Analysis, and Reading Strategy questions.

DAY 3 Assess

- Have students complete the Vocabulary activities.
- Ⓒ Have students complete the Writing activity and write a business memo. (You may assign as homework.)
- Ⓒ Administer Selection Test A or B (*Unit 1 Resources*, pp. 64–66 or 67–69).

Ⓒ Common Core State Standards

Reading Literature 1. Cite strong and thorough textual evidence to support analysis of what the text says explicitly as well as inferences drawn from the text. **3.** Analyze the impact of the author's choices regarding how to develop and relate elements of a story or drama.

Informational Text 5. Analyze and evaluate the effectiveness of the structure an author uses in his or her exposition, including whether the structure makes points clear, convincing, and engaging.

Writing 1. Write arguments to support claims in an analysis of substantive topics or texts, using valid reasoning and relevant and sufficient evidence. **5.** Demonstrate understanding of word relationships.

Additional Standards Practice
***Common Core Companion**, pp. 2–9; 28–35; 136–137; 185–195; 226–227*

Daily Block Scheduling
Each day in this Lesson Pacing Guide represents a 40–50 minute period. Teachers using block scheduling may combine days to revise pacing. In addition, teachers may differentiate and support core instruction by integrating components for extended and intensive support as students require. See the Guide to Selected Leveled Resources (facing page).

Guide to Selected Leveled Resources

R T I Tier 1 (students performing on level)

from A History of the English Church and People

Warm Up	**Practice, model,** and **monitor** fluency, working **with the whole class** or **in groups.**	Vocabulary and Reading Warm-ups B, *Unit 1 Resources,* pp. 52–53, 55
Comprehension/Skills	**Support** and **monitor** comprehension and skills development, having students complete the activities, graphic organizers, and interactive prompts **independently** or **as a class.**	• *Reader's Notebook,* adapted instruction and full selection **EL** *Reader's Notebook: English Learner's Version,* adapted instruction and adapted selection • **Reading Skill Graphic Organizer B,** *Graphic Organizer Transparencies,* p. 10 • **Literary Analysis Graphic Organizer B,** *Graphic Organizer Transparencies,* p. 12
Monitor Progress	**Monitor** student progress with the differentiated curriculum-based assessment in the *Unit Resources.*	• **Selection Test B,** *Unit 1 Resources,* pp. 67–69 • **Open-Book Test,** *Unit 1 Resources,* pp. 61–63
Assess/ Screen	**Assess** student progress using Benchmark Test.	• **Benchmark Test 1,** *Unit 1 Resources,* pp. 70–75

R T I Tier 2 (students requiring intervention)

from A History of the English Church and People

Warm Up	**Practice, model,** and **monitor** fluency **in groups** or **with individuals.**	• **Vocabulary and Reading Warm-ups A,** *Unit 1 Resources,* pp. 52–54 • *Hear It!* Audio CD (adapted text)
Comprehension/Skills	• **Support** and **monitor** comprehension and skills development, working **in small groups** or **with individuals.** • As students complete the selection in the appropriate version of the *Reader's Notebook,* **monitor** comprehension frequently with group questions and individual instruction. • **Model** strategies while guiding students in completing the activities and prompts in the *Reader's Notebook,* as well as the graphic organizers. • **Practice** skills and **monitor** mastery with the *Reading Kit* worksheets.	• *Reader's Notebook: Adapted Version,* adapted instruction and adapted selection **EL** *Reader's Notebook: English Learner's Version,* adapted instruction and adapted selection • **Reading Skill Graphic Organizer A,** *Graphic Organizer Transparencies,* p. 9 • **Literary Analysis Graphic Organizer A,** *Graphic Organizer Transparencies,* p. 11 • *Reading Kit,* Practice worksheets
Monitor Progress	**Monitor** student progress with the differentiated curriculum-based assessment in the *Unit Resources* and in the *Reading Kit.*	• **Selection Test A,** *Unit 1 Resources,* pp. 64–66 • *Reading Kit,* Assess worksheets
Assess/ Screen	**Assess** student progress using the Benchmark Test.	*Benchmark Test 1, Unit 1 Resources,* pp. 70–75

TIER 3 Tier 3 intervention may require consultation with the student's special-education or dyslexia specialist. For additional support, see the Tier 2 activities and resources listed above.

One-on-one teaching   Group work   Whole class instruction   Independent work   A Assessment

For a complete guide to selection support, including support for Advanced students, see the Overview of Resources in the frontmatter.

• *from* A History of the English Church and People

Unit 1 Resources

Vocabulary/Fluency/Prior Knowledge

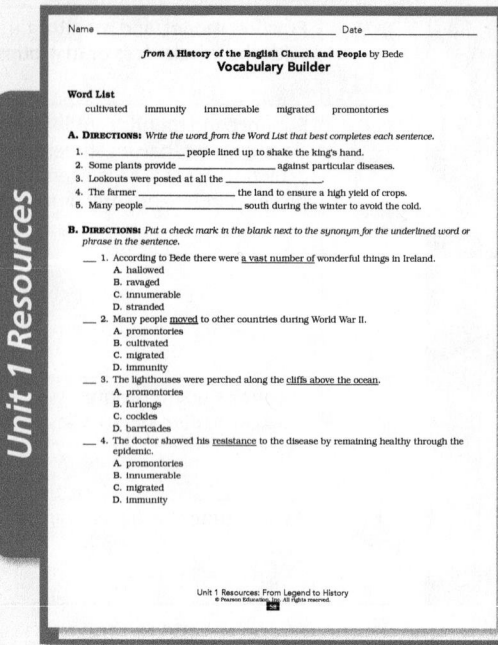

All Vocabulary Builder, p. 58

Also available for these selections:

EL L1 L2 Vocabulary Warm-ups A and B, pp. 52–53

EL L1 L2 Reading Warm-ups A and B, pp. 54–55

RESOURCES FOR:

L1 Special-Needs Students

L2 Below-Level Students (Tier 2)

L3 On-Level Students (Tier 1)

L4 Advanced Students (Tier 1)

EL English Learners

All All Students

Reader's Notebooks

Pre- and postreading pages for this selection appear in an interactive format in the *Reader's Notebooks*. Each *Notebook* is differentiated for a different group of learners.

The selections in the Adapted and English Learner's versions are abridged.

L2 L3 *Reader's Notebook*

L1 *Reader's Notebook: Adapted Version*

EL *Reader's Notebook: English Learner's Version*

EL *Reader's Notebook: Spanish Version*

© *Common Core Companion*

Additional instruction and practice for each Common Core State Standard

Selection Support

from A History of the English Church and People
by Bede

After You Read A: Historical Writing

Clarify Claim	Evidence	Verify Evidence
Britain has copper, iron, lead, silver, and black jet (coal).		
Ireland has a superior climate; it is mild and healthy.	Bede uses the fact that snow rarely lies longer than three days in Ireland (suggesting that the situation is different in Britain).	
	As soon as snakes breathe the lovely air in Ireland, they die.	
Britain has good pasture land for cattle and draft animals.		
Deer and goats are widely hunted in Ireland.		
		Not true: Today's atlas says that Britain is 300 miles across at its widest point; Ireland is 171 miles from east to west.

Graphic Organizer Transparencies

EL L1 L2 Literary Analysis: Graphic Organizer A (partially filled in), p. 11

Also available for these selections:

EL L1 L2 Reading: Graphic Organizer A (partially filled in), p. 9

EL L3 Reading: Graphic Organizer B, p. 10

EL L3 Literary Analysis: Graphic Organizer B, p. 11

Skills Development/Extension

Unit 1 Resources

Name _____ Date _____

from A History of the English Church and People by Bede
Enrichment: Career as a Historian

A. DIRECTIONS: When historical works such as Bede's *A History of the English Church and People* were being written, historians had few reference materials at their disposal. For the most part, authors were dependent on ancient manuscripts in monastic libraries; annual records of such events as planting, births, and deaths; and of course, the oral tradition. By comparison, today's historian has a vast number of references from which to gather information. Using the general categories in the chart below, name as many different kinds of resource materials as you can think of.

Print Materials	Film/Video	Audio Recordings	Other

B. DIRECTIONS: You can certainly think of many advantages to having such a large number of reference materials available for use. But there can also be drawbacks to the situation. Think about what problems a modern historian might encounter as a result of easy access to large amounts of information—problems that Bede or others of his time would not have faced. What are some problems you have encountered in your own research?

_____
_____
_____
_____
_____
_____
_____

L4 Enrichment, p. 60

Also available for these selections:

All Reading, p. 57

All Literary Analysis, p. 56

EL L3 L4 Support for Writing Lesson, p. 59

Assessment

Name _____ Date _____

from A History of the English Church and People by Bede
Open-Book Test

Short Answer *Write your response to the questions in this section on the lines provided.*

1. What was Bede's main reason for writing *A History of the English Church and People*? How do you know?
_____

2. In *A History of the English Church and People*, Bede is not completely accurate. What keeps him from being accurate?
_____

3. Cite two examples from the end of the passage that reflect Bede's idealized view of Ireland.
_____

4. Consider the time in which Bede wrote *A History of the English Church and People*. Which source would probably have provided Bede with the most reliable information that Britain had "twenty-eight noble cities"? Explain.
_____

5. In *A History of the English Church and People*, Bede writes that "all are united in their study of God's truth." What can the reader infer about Bede's attitude toward the English Church from this statement?
_____

6. In the chart below, write four facts and four opinions from *A History of the English Church and People*.

Facts	Opinions

L3 L4 Open-Book Test, pp. 61–63

Also available for these selections:

EL L3 L4 Selection Test A, pp. 64–66

EL L1 L2 Selection Test B, pp. 67–69

PHLit Online!
www.PHLitOnline.com

Online Resources: All print materials are also available online.

- complete narrated selection text
- a thematically related video with writing prompt
- an interactive graphic organizer
- highlighting feature
- access to all student print resources, adapted to individual student needs
- Spanish and English summaries
- adapted selection translations in Spanish

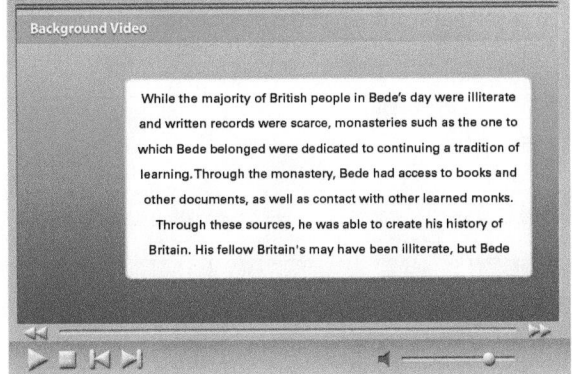

Background Video

While the majority of British people in Bede's day were illiterate and written records were scarce, monasteries such as the one to which Bede belonged were dedicated to continuing a tradition of learning. Through the monastery, Bede had access to books and other documents, as well as contact with other learned monks. Through these sources, he was able to create his history of Britain. His fellow Britain's may have been illiterate, but Bede

Background Video

Also available:

Get Connected! (thematic video with writing prompt)
All videos are available in Spanish.

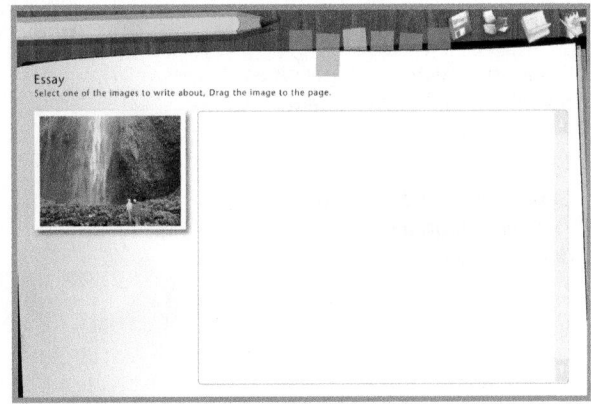

Essay
Select one of the images to write about. Drag the image to the page.

Writer's Journal (with graphics feature)

Also available:

Vocabulary Central (tools and activities for studying vocabulary)

❶  **Connecting to the Essential Question**

1. Review the assignment with the class.

2. Prepare students to write by reminding them that a sense of *place* is not just a geographical term. It can be a state of mind or a sense of values.

3. As students read, have them look not only for facts about early Anglo-Saxon history, but also for the feel of life in the time period.

❷ Literary Analysis

Introduce the skill, using the instruction on the student page.

Think Aloud: Model the Skill

Say to students:

To decide if a statement is fact, superstition, or personal belief, I ask myself, "Can this be proven?" If so, then it is a fact. If not, then it is either a superstition or personal belief. For example, if I read that England is 2,000 miles long, I know that this can be proven. I can go to a map to see how long England really is.

❸ Reading Strategy

1. Introduce the strategy.

2. Give students a copy of **Reading Strategy Graphic Organizer B,** page 10 in *Graphic Organizer Transparencies,* to fill out as they read.

❹ Vocabulary

1. Pronounce each word, giving its definition, and have students say it aloud.

2. For more guidance, see the *Classroom Strategies and Teaching Routines* card for introducing vocabulary.

Before You Read

from *A History of the English Church and People*

❶ Connecting to the Essential Question In this selection, a monk living many years ago describes the distant British Isles for European readers. As you read, notice details that suggest Bede is describing a place that is far away from the known world. Finding such details will help you think about the Essential Question: **What is the relationship between literature and place?**

❷ Literary Analysis

Historical writing tells the story of past events using reliable evidence, such as eyewitness reports and documents. Bede, however, lived at a time when even educated people were more superstitious and less informed. Also, as occurs in any era, his biases and beliefs affected his accounts. In Bede's historical writing, therefore, you will find the following:

- Statements of fact: "Britain, formerly known as Albion, is an island"
- Superstitions: belief that snakes die from breathing Ireland's air
- Personal beliefs: "All are united in their study of God's truth"

Look for examples of each of these elements as you read.

❸ Reading Strategy

Ⓒ Preparing to Read Complex Texts Bede's purpose is to introduce readers to a new place, Britain. Naturally, he tries to do this as clearly as possible. **Analyze the clarity of meaning** he achieves by focusing on these elements of his writing:

- *Patterns of organization,* such as the order in which he discusses Britain and Ireland, and his way of combining facts, examples, description, and narration, or the telling of a story
- *Hierarchical structures,* such as the relative importance he gives to different aspects of Britain
- *Repetition of main ideas,* such as Britain's positive qualities
- *Word choice;* for example, the use of factual language
- *Clear syntax,* or easy-to-understand sentence structure

As you read, use a chart like the one shown to analyze the clarity of Bede's discussion.

❹ Vocabulary

promontories (präm′ ən tôr′ ēz) *n.* peaks of high land sticking out into a body of water (p. 85)

cultivated (kul′ tə vāt′ əd) *v.* grown (p. 85)

innumerable (i nõõ′ mer ə bəl) *adj.* too many to count (p. 85)

migrated (mī′ grāt′ əd) *v.* moved from one region or country to another (p. 86)

Ⓒ Common Core State Standards

Reading Informational Text

5. Analyze and evaluate the effectiveness of the structure an author uses in his or her exposition, including whether the structure makes points clear, convincing, and engaging.

Clarity of Meaning	
Element and Example	Contribution to Clarity

www.PHLitOnline.com

Vocabulary Development

Vocabulary Knowledge Rating

Create a **Vocabulary Knowledge Rating Chart** (*Professional Development Guidebook,* p. 33) for the vocabulary words on the student page. Give each student a copy of the chart with the words on it. Read the words aloud, and have students mark their rating of each in the Before Reading column. When students have completed reading and discussing the selection, have them take out their **Vocabulary Knowledge Rating Charts** for the story. Read the words aloud and have students rate their knowledge again in the After Reading column. Clarify any words that are still problematic. Then, have students complete the Vocabulary practice at the end of the selection.

 **Vocabulary Central,** featuring tools and activities for studying vocabulary, is available online at **www.PHLitOnline.com.**

⑤ BEDE (673–735)

Author of *A History of the English Church and People*

It was as if the lights had gone out. In the fifth century, the Roman Empire abandoned Britain. Rome was the center of the most advanced civilization in the West. As part of the Roman Empire, Britain had been connected with a larger world of trade and culture. Roman missionaries taught reading and writing as they preached Christianity. Roman soldiers patrolled Britain's borders. Once Rome withdrew, however, Britain was isolated, threatened by invasion from without and by strife from within.

Keeping Learning Alive Monasteries, particularly in Ireland, kept knowledge alive during these dark times. Monks studied Latin, the language of the Roman Empire. They laboriously copied books. The more scholarly monks wrote new works.

Much of what we know about England before A.D. 700 is based on the work of one such monk, Bede. A contemporary of the unknown author of *Beowulf*, Bede was the most learned scholar of his day. Although he wrote forty books on various subjects, his reputation would be secure on the basis of one—*A History of the English Church and People*, for which Bede is called the father of English history.

A Daily Reminder Bede was born in Wearmouth (now Sunderland) in northeastern England. At age seven, he entered the nearby monastic school of Jarrow. A diligent student, he stayed on as a priest and scholar. Although Bede lived his whole life at Jarrow, he wrote in Latin, so his work was accessible to scholars throughout the West. His pupils carried his writings to Europe. His work, famous in his own lifetime for its scholarship, has become a part of daily life—Bede helped originate the dating of events from the birth of Christ, a cornerstone of the Western calendar.

A Scholarly Work In the *History*, Bede describes the conquest of Britain by the Anglo-Saxon tribes after the departure of the Romans. His main concern, however, was the expansion of Christianity in England. Bede gathered information from many kinds of documents, interviewed knowledgeable monks, and, in general, proceeded very much like a modern historian.

In the century after his death, Bede's history was translated from Latin into English for King Alfred. In the same century, Bede was honored with the title "the Venerable [respected] Bede."

▲ Detail of a manuscript by the 8th century English Benedictine monk and scholar, the Venerable Bede.

from A History of the English Church and People **83**

Daily Bellringer

For each class during which you will teach this selection, have students complete one of the five activities for the appropriate week in the *Daily Bellringer Activities* booklet.

Multidraft Reading

To assist struggling readers and to enhance reading for all, assign the text in chunks, as warranted by length, and apply multidraft reading protocols. For each reading, have students set the purpose indicated:

- **First reading**—identifying key ideas and details and answering any Reading Checks.
- **Second reading**—analyzing craft and structure and responding to the side-column prompts.
- **Third reading**—integrating knowledge and ideas, connecting to other texts and the world, and answering the end-of-selection questions.

For more guidance, refer to the *Classroom Strategies and Teaching Routines* card on multidraft reading.

⑤ Background
More About the Author

In addition to histories and biographies, Bede wrote treatises on spelling, hymns, figures of speech, poetry, theology, and reckoning time. A diligent scholar, he anxiously assessed the accuracy of his sources and recorded only what he regarded as trustworthy evidence. His work remains an indispensable source for many of the facts and much of the feel of early Anglo-Saxon history. Bede's knowledge, insights, and scholarly enthusiasm were perpetuated at a school founded by Bede's pupil, Archbishop Egbert of York, and were carried to the continent by one of the school's students, Alcuin, who became master of Charlemagne's palace school.

PHLit Online!
www.PHLitOnline.com

Teaching From Technology

Preparing to Read
Go to www.PHLitOnline.com in class or in a lab and display the **Get Connected!** slide show for this selection. Have the class brainstorm responses to the slide show writing prompt, entering ideas in the interactive journal. Then, have students complete their written responses individually, in a lab or as homework.

To build background, display the More About the Author feature.

Using the Interactive Text
Go to www.PHLitOnline.com and display the **Enriched Online Student Edition.** As the class reads the selection or listens to the narration, record answers to side-column prompts using the graphic organizers accessible on the interactive page. Alternatively, have students use the online edition individually, answering the prompts as they read.

① About the Selection

Bede's work, which traced English history from the time of the Roman Invasion (54 B.C.) until A.D. 731, was written in Latin but later translated into English so it could be read by a wider audience.

② Activating Prior Knowledge

Ask students what movies or TV shows they have seen that involved time travel. If time travel really did exist, where would they like to go and during which time period? What they would like to discover about these places, people, or times?

Concept Connector ➤

Tell students they will return to their responses after reading the selection.

③ Background

History

Explain to students that monasteries are places where monks live. Have a volunteer tell the class what a monk is. If no one can, explain that a monk is a man who does not marry, but chooses to join a group of men with whom he studies, prays, and works for his whole life. **Ask** volunteers to name some religions that have monks.
Possible responses: Catholicism, Buddhism, Eastern Orthodoxy, and Christianity. Explain that Bede was a Catholic monk.

from

① A HISTORY OF
② THE ENGLISH
③ CHURCH AND PEOPLE

Translated by Leo Sherley-Price

BACKGROUND Although the majority of British people in Bede's day were illiterate and written records were scarce, monasteries such as the one to which Bede belonged were dedicated to continuing a tradition of learning. Through the monastery, Bede had access to books and other documents, as well as contact with other learned monks. Using these sources, he was able to generate his history of Britain. His fellow Britons may have been illiterate, but Bede had in mind a larger world of readers for his work—the Church to which he belonged and the Roman civilization in which it participated. Bede wrote his account of Britain for such readers, starting at the beginning with the basics.

THE SITUATION OF BRITAIN AND IRELAND: THEIR EARLIEST INHABITANTS

④ Britain, formerly known as Albion, is an island in the ocean, facing between north and west, and lying at a considerable distance from the coasts of Germany, Gaul, and Spain, which together form the greater part of Europe. ⑤

84 From Legend to History (A.D. 449–1485)

© Text Complexity Rubric

from A History of the English Church and People	
Qualitative Measures	
Context/Knowledge Demands	Medieval history; historical knowledge demands 1 2 3 ④ 5
Structure/Language Conventionality and Clarity	Explanatory, factual details 1 2 ③ 4 5
Levels of Meaning/Purpose/Concept Level	Challenging (history and geography) 1 2 3 ④ 5
Quantitative Measures	

Lexile	1280L	Text Length	1,085 words
Overall Complexity	**More complex**		

Reader and Task Suggestions

Preparing to Read the Text
- Using the biographical information on SE and TE p. 83, discuss the kind of information Bede is likely to supply in his history.
- Discuss with students the role that geography can play in the history of a city or nation.
- Guide students to use Multidraft Reading strategies (TE p. 83).

Leveled Tasks

Knowledge Demands If students will have difficulty with the history and geography in the selection, refer them to the map on page 87 to locate England, Scotland, and Ireland. Then have students read the selection, focusing on its factual details.

Analyzing If students will not have difficulty with the history and geography in the selection, have them explain how Britain's location affected people in Bede's day.

It extends 800 miles northwards, and is 200 in breadth, except where a number of promontories stretch farther, the coastline round which extends to 3,675 miles. To the south lies Belgic Gaul,[1] from the nearest shore of which travelers can see the city known as Rutubi Portus, which the English have corrupted to Reptacestir.[2] The distance from there across the sea to Gessoriacum,[3] the nearest coast of the Morini, is 50 miles or, as some write it, 450 furlongs.[4] On the opposite side of Britain, which lies open to the boundless ocean, lie the isles of the Orcades.[5] Britain is rich in grain and timber; it has good pasturage for cattle and draft animals,[6] and vines are cultivated in various localities. There are many land and sea birds of various species, and it is well known for its plentiful springs and rivers abounding in fish. There are salmon and eel fisheries, while seals, dolphins, and sometimes whales are caught. There are also many varieties of shellfish, such as mussels, in which are often found excellent pearls of several colors: red, purple, violet, and green, but mainly white. Cockles[7] are abundant, and a beautiful scarlet dye is extracted from them which remains unfaded by sunshine or rain; indeed, the older the cloth, the more beautiful its color. The country has both salt and hot springs, and the waters flowing from them provide hot baths, in which the people bathe separately according to age and sex. As Saint Basil says: "Water receives its heat when it flows across certain metals, and becomes hot, and even scalding." The land has rich veins of many metals, including copper, iron, lead, and silver. There is also much black jet[8] of fine quality, which sparkles in firelight. When burned, it drives away snakes, and, like amber, when it is warmed by friction, it clings to whatever is applied to it. In old times, the country had twenty-eight noble cities, and innumerable castles, all of which were guarded by walls, towers, and barred gates.

Since Britain lies far north toward the pole, the nights are short in summer, and at midnight it is hard to tell whether the evening twilight still lingers or whether dawn is approaching; for in these northern latitudes the sun does not remain long below the horizon at night. Consequently both summer days and winter nights are long, and when the sun withdraws

---

1. **Belgic Gaul** France.
2. **Reptacestir** Richborough, part of the city of Sandwich.
3. **Gessoriacum** Boulogne, France.
4. **furlongs** units for measuring distance; a furlong is equal to one eighth of a mile.
5. **Orcades** Orkney Isles.
6. **draft animals** animals used for pulling loads.
7. **Cockles** edible shellfish with two heart-shaped shells.
8. **jet** *n.* type of coal.

Vocabulary

promontories
(präm´ ən tôr´ ēz) *n.* peaks of high land sticking out into the water

cultivated
(kul´ tə vāt´ əd) *v.* grown

innumerable
(i noo´ mər ə bəl) *adj.* too many to count

Reading Strategy
Analyze Clarity of Meaning If Britain is unknown to many of his readers, why does it make sense for Bede to begin with a geographical description?

Literary Analysis
Historical Writing Find two facts in this paragraph. Then, identify one claim for which you might need more evidence.

Reading Check
According to Saint Basil, how does water from the hot springs receive its heat?

from A History of the English Church and People **85**

④ Reading Strategy
Analyze Clarity of Meaning
Ask: the Reading Strategy question.
Possible response: It makes sense for Bede to begin with a geographical description because it helps his international readers gain a sense for where Britain is in relation to other countries they may know better.

⑤ Literary Analysis
Historical Writing
1. Remind students that writing from any era will include information that might later be disproved. However, things that are later disproved tell us about the era. For example, the statement that burning jet drives away snakes indicates snakes were a problem.
2. Point out to students that Bede quotes his source when he is not sure of the evidence, as when he attributes the theory of heated water to Saint Basil.
3. **Ask:** students the Literary Analysis question.
   Possible responses: Facts include: Cockles are abundant, a scarlet dye is obtained from cockles, the country has salt and hot springs, the land has metals, jet and amber carry a static charge. The claims about how water is heated and that burning jet drives away snakes need more evidence.

⑥ Reading Check
Answer: According to Saint Basil, water runs over certain metals and becomes hot.

Analyze Clarity of Meaning

1. List the facts and stories of this paragraph on the board in a two-column chart.

2. Then **ask** the Reading Strategy question: In this paragraph, how does Bede weave together facts and narratives, or stories?
Possible response: Bede states a fact about one of the tribes of Britain. Then he tells some stories about the tribe. Then he states a fact about another tribe of Britain and tells some stories about this tribe's members.

⓼ **Critical Thinking**

Analyze

1. Remind students that Bede was (as were most literate people in his day) a priest.

2. Have a student read the first two sentences of the paragraph on this page that begins with "At the present time…"

3. **Ask** students how Bede's religious background is revealed in these two sentences.
Answer: Bede refers to divine law and the study of God's truth.

⓽ 🅠 **Engaging the Essential Question**

1. Point out to students that, like other writers, Bede tries to give his readers a sense of the place of Britain. This is, in fact, his main purpose for writing. Therefore, examples of Bede giving the reader a sense of place are numerous.

2. **Ask** students: What details on this page show that Bede is trying to give his reader a sense of Britain?
Possible answer: He describes the landscape and rivers. He tells about the specific animals of Britain. He describes the cities and buildings.

Reading Strategy
Analyze Clarity of Meaning In this paragraph, how does Bede weave together facts and narratives, or stories?

⓼

⓻

⓽

Vocabulary
migrated (mī´ grāt´ əd) *v.* moved from one region or country to another

southwards, the winter nights last eighteen hours. In Armenia,[9] Macedonia,[10] and Italy, and other countries of that latitude, the longest day lasts only fifteen hours and the shortest nine.

At the present time there are in Britain, in harmony with the five books of the divine law, five languages and four nations—English, British, Scots, and Picts. Each of these have their own language, but all are united in their study of God's truth by the fifth, Latin, which has become a common medium through the study of the scriptures. The original inhabitants of the island were the Britons, from whom it takes its name, and who, according to tradition, crossed into Britain from Armorica,[11] and occupied the southern parts. When they had spread northwards and possessed the greater part of the islands, it is said that some Picts from Scythia[12] put to sea in a few long ships and were driven by storms around the coasts of Britain, arriving at length on the north coast of Ireland. Here they found the nation of the Scots, from whom they asked permission to settle, but their request was refused. Ireland is the largest island after Britain, and lies to the west. It is shorter than Britain to the north, but extends far beyond it to the south towards the northern coasts of Spain, although a wide sea separates them. These Pictish seafarers, as I have said, asked for a grant of land to make a settlement. The Scots replied that there was not room for them both, but said: "We can give you good advice. There is another island not far to the east, which we often see in the distance on clear days. Go and settle there if you wish; should you meet resistance, we will come to your help." So the Picts crossed into Britain, and began to settle in the north of the island, since the Britons were in possession of the south. Having no women with them, these Picts asked wives of the Scots, who consented on condition that, when any dispute arose, they should choose a king from the female royal line rather than the male. This custom continues among the Picts to this day. As time went on, Britain received a third nation, that of the Scots, who migrated from Ireland under their chieftain Reuda, and by a combination of force and treaty, obtained from the Picts the settlements that they still hold. From the name of this chieftain, they are still known as Dalreudians, for in their tongue *dal* means a division.

⓾ Ireland is broader than Britain, and its mild and healthy climate is superior. Snow rarely lies longer than three days, so that

9. **Armenia** region between the Black and the Caspian seas, now divided between the nations of Armenia and Turkey.
10. **Macedonia** region in the eastern Mediterranean, divided among Greece, Yugoslavia, and Bulgaria.
11. **Armorica** Brittany, France.
12. **Scythia** ancient region in southeastern Europe.

Think Aloud

Vocabulary: Using Context
Direct students' attention to the word *medium* on this page. Use the following "think aloud" to model the skill of using context to infer the meaning of the word. Say to students:

I may not know the meaning of the word *medium*. When I read the sentence, I understand that the writer uses the word *medium* when referring to the Latin language. The writer also uses the words *united* and *common* in the same sentence. I know Latin is a language that used to be spoken, especially among educated people of the Roman Empire. The writer is describing how Latin unites the four nations of the English, British, Scots, and Picts. I can infer that a *medium* must be a way in which people communicate with each other. The writer argues that Latin is a language these four nations have in common, and that it unites them. I think the writer is trying to show how Latin used in Biblical scriptures unites different groups of people in Britain.

ATLAS PAGE
THE BRITISH ISLES

An atlas is a book of maps and other information on a country's physical landscape, political makeup, and economic resources. Modern atlases benefit from satellite technology and computer-generated maps. You can use this atlas page to verify and clarify — check the accuracy and clarity of — facts that Bede provides about Britain's geography and resources.

CONNECT TO THE LITERATURE

Use this modern atlas entry for Ireland and the United Kingdom to check the accuracy and clarity of three of Bede's statements of fact about the British Isles.

> At its widest the United Kingdom is 300 miles (500 km) across. From the northern tip of Scotland to the southern coast of England, it is about 600 miles (1,000 km). No part is more than 75 miles (120 km) from the sea.
>
> The greatest distance from north to south in Ireland is 302 miles (486 km), and from east to west it is 171 miles (275 km).

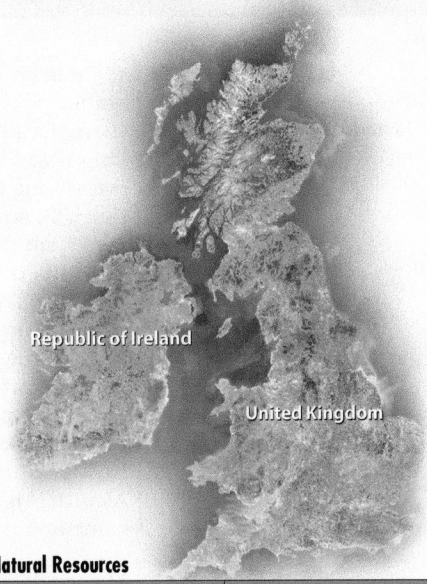

Republic of Ireland

United Kingdom

Natural Resources

United Kingdom	Republic of Ireland
coal, petroleum, natural gas, iron ore, lead, zinc, gold, tin, limestone, salt, clay, chalk, gypsum, potash, silica sand, slate, arable land	natural gas, peat, copper, lead, zinc, silver, barite, gypsum, limestone, dolomite

Animal Life

United Kingdom	Republic of Ireland
Red Deer, badgers, otters, foxes, stoats, weasels, rodents hedgehogs, moles, shrews, rabbits, newts, frogs, toads, lizards, snakes	Red Deer, badgers, otters, foxes, stoats, rodents, hedgehogs, shrews, rabbits, newts, frogs

Climate: Republic of Ireland

Month	Average Max Temp F°	Average Min Temp F°	Daily Hours of Sunshine	Days of Rainfall
March	50	37.4	3	11
June	64.4	48.2	6	12
September	62.6	48.2	4	15
December	46.4	35.6	2	18

Climate: United Kingdom

Month	Max Temp F°	Min Temp F°	Hours of Sunshine	Days of Rainfall
March	47.3	35.42	4	13
June	62.4	47.1	7	11
September	61	47.3	5	13
December	44.4	34.7	1	15

Sunlight: In Britain, daily sunshine hours range from between one and two in midwinter to between five and seven in midsummer.

Land Area

United Kingdom	Republic of Ireland
total: 94,526 sq mi	total: 27,135 sq mi
land: 93,278 sq mi	land: 26,599 sq mi
water: 1,247 sq mi	water: 537 sq mi
coastline: 7,723 mi	coastline: 900 mi

United Kingdom	Republic of Ireland
mostly rugged hills and low mountains; level to rolling plains in east and southeast	mostly level to rolling interior plain surrounded by rugged hills and low mountains; sea cliffs on west coast

from A History of the English Church and People **87**

Literature in Context
Connect to the Literature

1. **Ask** students to review Bede's description of the United Kingdom. Then, have them review the current information about the U.K. excerpted from an atlas.

2. **Ask** students how examining a historic description of climatic, geographic, and economic data is useful in creating a context for events that occurred at that time.
   Possible answer: Migration and conflict over land often concern natural resources. Awareness of topography and climate affects where people might settle. Understanding what people knew about their climate, geography, and resources might explain why they made certain decisions.

3. **Ask** students to compare the natural resources described by Bede to those listed in the modern atlas.
   Answer: Both Bede and the atlas list coal, iron, lead, and land that could be cultivated. In general, Bede lists more renewable resources (e.g. fish, shellfish for dye, timber, hot springs) while the atlas listed many nonrenewable resources. Some of the nonrenewable resources, like natural gas, would not have been used in the seventh century.

4. **Ask** students what they notice about Bede's summary of the animal life in Great Britain in comparison to what is listed by the modern atlas. What might account for this disparity?
   Possible response: Bede lists mainly fish and birds, while the modern atlas more comprehensively lists mammals, reptiles, and amphibians. Bede concentrates on animals that can be used by humans.

Differentiated Instruction for Universal Access

Strategy for Less Proficient Readers
To help students through the detail-packed text, encourage them to break the text into chunks or paragraphs and read one at a time. After reading each paragraph, have them ask themselves: Does this tell about a place or about people?

EL Support for English Learners
The long sentences and unfamiliar names may give students difficulty. To aid comprehension, give them a brief preview of each section before they read it. Additionally, posting a map of Britain that reflects place-names of this period may help students identify places that are mentioned.

Enrichment for Advanced Learners
Ask students to note the types of details that are not included in this selection, such as details about food, transportation, or entertainment. Have students consider what these omissions suggest about the writer's interests or priorities. Students may research these omitted elements.

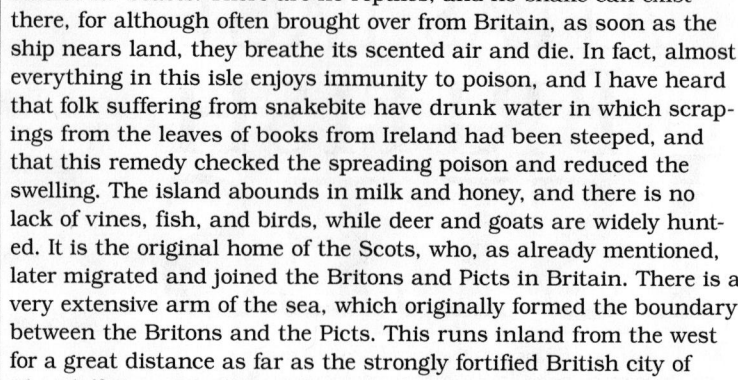

Ask students to reread the paragraph to find one example of a superstition.

Possible response: As soon as a snake breathes air in Ireland, it dies; water steeped with scrapings from leaves of Irish books is a remedy for poisonous snakebites.

ASSESS

Answers

Before students respond, you may wish to have them write a brief objective summary of the selection. As they answer the questions below, remind them to support their answers with evidence from the text.

1. (a) He says the scarlet dye is extracted from cockles and used in cloth. (b) Possible response: This information suggests that the society is highly evolved, and possibly wealthy.

2. (a) Latin unites Britain because it is the common language of the educated in all four nations. (b) The most important factor is the "study of God's truth": that is, the shared religion of Christianity.

3. **Possible response:** Readers would likely have many questions, based on the author's worldview and biases. Students' questions should utilize details from the selection.

4.  **Possible response:** Because Britain is in relative *isolation* from other countries, Bede had to describe its *geography* in terms of *proximity* to other countries with which his foreign readers might be more familiar, such as France or Belgic Gaul.

Literary Analysis
Historical Writing
Find one example of a superstition in this paragraph.

❿

there is no need to store hay in summer for winter use or to build stables for beasts. There are no reptiles, and no snake can exist there, for although often brought over from Britain, as soon as the ship nears land, they breathe its scented air and die. In fact, almost everything in this isle enjoys immunity to poison, and I have heard that folk suffering from snakebite have drunk water in which scrapings from the leaves of books from Ireland had been steeped, and that this remedy checked the spreading poison and reduced the swelling. The island abounds in milk and honey, and there is no lack of vines, fish, and birds, while deer and goats are widely hunted. It is the original home of the Scots, who, as already mentioned, later migrated and joined the Britons and Picts in Britain. There is a very extensive arm of the sea, which originally formed the boundary between the Britons and the Picts. This runs inland from the west for a great distance as far as the strongly fortified British city of Alcuith.[13] It was to the northern shores of this firth[14] that the Scots came and established their new homeland.

---

13. Alcuith Dumbarton, Scotland.
14. firth narrow arm of the sea.

Critical Reading

Cite textual evidence to support your responses.

1. **Key Ideas and Details (a)** What background does Bede give about British scarlet dye? **(b) Infer:** What does this information suggest about the lifestyle or economy of the country?

2. **Key Ideas and Details (a) Interpret:** In what way does Latin unite England? **(b) Interpret:** According to Bede, what factor is most important in uniting people and giving them a common identity?

3. **Integration of Knowledge and Ideas Evaluate:** Does Bede do a good job answering readers' questions about England? Explain, giving three examples of possible questions.

4. **Integration of Knowledge and Ideas** In what ways does Britain's remote location influence Bede's description of it? In responding, use at least two of these Essential Question words: *geography, proximity, isolation. [Connecting to the Essential Question: What is the relationship between literature and place?]*

Concept Connector

Reading Strategy Graphic Organizer
Ask students to review the charts of the elements and examples of clear writing. Then, have students share their charts and compare the elements and examples they identified.

Activating Prior Knowledge
Have students return to their responses to the Activating Prior Knowledge activity about time travel. Ask them to explain whether their thoughts have changed about where they would like to time travel and, if so, how.

Connecting to the Essential Question
Have students compare their responses to the prompt they completed before reading the selection with their thoughts afterwards. Have them work individually or in groups, writing or discussing their thoughts, to formulate their new responses. Then, lead a class discussion, probing for what students have learned that confirms or invalidates their initial thoughts. Encourage students to cite specific textual details to support their responses.

Literary Analysis

1. Integration of Knowledge and Ideas Evaluate Bede's **historical writing** in terms of the evidence he supplies. On a chart like this one, *clarify* several claims Bede makes about Britain or Ireland. For each claim, list his supporting evidence, *verify* it against evidence from a modern atlas page (p. 87), and indicate whether you feel he gives enough support for the claim.

Claim/Clarify	Evidence	Evaluation/Verify

2. Integration of Knowledge and Ideas How do Bede's attitudes and beliefs color the information he provides? Support your answer with examples from the selection.

3. Integration of Knowledge and Ideas **(a)** In Bede's account, contrast factors that are dividing England with those that are uniting it. **(b)** Which factors seem stronger? Why?

Reading Strategy

4. Analyze the clarity of meaning in Bede's writing, taking into account the contributions of elements such as *patterns of organization, hierarchic structures, repetition of main ideas, word choice,* and *syntax.*

5. It is the year 3000, and a writer wants Earthlings to appreciate the value of a new colony on Mars. How could Bede's use of word choice, repetition, and patterns of organization serve as a model for this writer?

PERFORMANCE TASKS
Integrated Language Skills

Vocabulary Acquisition and Use

Categorize Vocabulary Using the list of vocabulary words on page 82, analyze the relationship between the words in each item. Are they synonyms (words with similar meanings) or a combination of synonyms and antonyms (words with opposite meanings)? Use a dictionary if necessary.

1. promontories, capes, headlands
2. grew, destroyed, cultivated
3. innumerable, few, scarce
4. migrated, traveled, journeyed

Writing

Argument Review Bede's *History* as if you were an eighth-century European reader looking for business opportunities. Then, write a **business memo** convincing people to invest in an enterprise in Britain or Ireland. Explain your plan clearly and persuasively, citing passages from the selection to support your points. Use a heading that specifies To, From, Subject, and Date.

from A History of the English Church and People **89**

Common Core State Standards

Writing
1. Write arguments to support claims in an analysis of substantive topics or texts, using valid reasoning and relevant and sufficient evidence.

Language
5. Demonstrate understanding of word relationships.

Answers

1. **Possible response:** Claim: Ireland's climate is superior to Britain's. Evidence: Snow doesn't last, hay doesn't need to be stored for winter, and there are no reptiles. Evaluation: Bede attributes Ireland's lack of reptiles to the fragrant air, which seems like a legend.

2. **Possible response:** He shows his Christian beliefs when he says that all the tribes of Britain are "united in their study of God's truth."

3. (a) **Possible response:** Factors dividing Britain are its different populations and languages. The factors uniting Britain include its Christian faith and its use of Latin. (b) The uniting factors seem stronger because Bede doesn't tell of wars or fights between the clans.

4. **Possible response:** He shows a fairly strong clarity of meaning. He uses patterns of organization to describe Britain and then Ireland. Bede also uses hierarchic structures, especially when describing Britain's geography. He repeats main ideas such as the clans and their languages. He uses strong, definite words.

5. Bede's word choice could serve as a model [strong and definite words to describe geographical landmarks]. The writer could follow Bede's model repetition of important people and places and could use Bede's patterns of organization to describe Earth and the new colony.

Vocabulary Acquisition and Use

1. synonyms
2. synonyms, antonyms
3. antonyms, synonyms
4. synonyms

Writing

1. Review the assignment.
2. Show a sample argument. Ask volunteers to identify the heading and the specifics.
3. Have students complete the assignment. Suggest that they allot five minutes for prewriting, ten minutes for drafting, and ten minutes for revising and editing.
4. Evaluate students' arguments using the **Rubrics for Business Letter,** *Professional Development Guidebook,* pages 291–292.

Assessment Resources

Unit 1 Resources

L1 L2 EL Selection Test A, pp. 64–66. Administer Test A to less advanced readers.

L3 L4 EL Selection Test B, pp. 67–69. Administer Test B to on-level and more advanced students.

L3 L4 Open-Book Test, pp. 61–63. As an alternative, give the Open-Book Test.

All Customizable Test Bank

All Self-tests
Students may prepare for the **Selection Test** by taking the **Self-test** online.

PHLit Online! All assessment resources are available at **www.PHLitOnline.com.**

89

Chaucer's Guided Tour of Medieval Life and Literature

1. Discuss with students their knowledge of medieval life. What have they read or seen in movies or on television about knights? What other people lived at the same time as knights? How did medieval people travel from one place to another?

2. After students have discussed what they already know about medieval life, have them read the article about medieval life and literature.

Background

Thomas à Becket, Archbishop of Canterbury

The pilgrims in *The Canterbury Tales* are on their way to the shrine of Thomas à Becket at the cathedral in Canterbury. Becket was appointed by Henry II as Archbishop of Canterbury and became famous for his struggle to keep the English church free from royal control.

In the 1160s, a series of conflicts ensued between Becket and Henry II over Henry's attempt to control the church. After fleeing to France in 1164, Becket returned to England in 1170 and quickly revived his struggle with Henry. In earshot of his knights, Henry questioned if there was anyone who might get rid of Becket. Four knights interpreted Henry's words as a request and went off to Canterbury, where they killed Becket while he was at evening prayers.

Pope Alexander III made Becket a saint in 1173, and Becket's tomb at Canterbury soon became a popular place for pilgrims. Later, however, King Henry VIII destroyed the shrine that had been dedicated to Becket at Canterbury.

Literary History: Chaucer's World

The Canterbury Tales . . . is actually a story about stories.

Chaucer's Guided Tour of Medieval Life and Literature

Rich people, poor people, stock brokers, artists, farmers, street vendors . . . with all of the different lifestyles in our culture, you may wonder what single event could gather together people from all parts of society. Geoffrey Chaucer found in his own society an orderly, even joyous event that gathered people from diverse backgrounds and occupations—a pilgrimage, or journey to a sacred spot. It is such a pilgrimage that gathers together the diverse characters in his masterpiece, *The Canterbury Tales.*

The Journey Begins Like modern travelers, medieval pilgrims must have been eager to while away their time traveling. Chaucer uses this fact to set his story in motion. *The Canterbury Tales* begins with a Prologue, in which the Narrator, presumably Chaucer himself, meets twenty-nine other pilgrims at the Tabard Inn, located in a suburb of London. As the pilgrims prepare for their journey, the host of the Inn, Harry Bailey, sets a challenge. To make the journey more entertaining, he suggests that each pilgrim tell two stories on the way to Canterbury and two stories on the return trip. The person who tells the best tale will be treated to a feast hosted by the other pilgrims. The pilgrims accept the challenge, and Bailey himself decides to join them and judge the competition.

Each of the following sections of the work consists of one of the pilgrim's tales. Brief transitions, as one storyteller finishes and another begins, link the stories. In this way, the work is actually a story about stories, twenty-four different tales set within the overarching tale of the pilgrimage.

Snapshots of an Era In the Prologue, Chaucer sketches a brief but vivid portrait of each pilgrim, creating a lively sense of medieval life. In itself, the Prologue is a great literary achievement. As critic Vincent Hopper notes,

> The description of the various pilgrims turn in rapid sequence from an article of clothing to a point of character and back again with no apparent organization or desire for it. Yet so effective is this artful artlessness that each pilgrim stands out sharply as a type of medieval personality and also as a highly individualized character. . . .

90 From Legend to History (A.D. 449–1485)

Tales of Tales

Stories that include other stories, such as *The Thousand and One Nights,* were told before Chaucer.

Chaucer's great originality, though, is shown both in the innovations he made in the tales his pilgrims tell and in the presence of each pilgrim as a character. As Chaucer scholar F. N. Robinson points out, the personality of each pilgrim is present throughout, whether in the kind of tales each chooses to tell or in the quarrels and jokes of the pilgrims between the tales.

Activity: Compare and Contrast Have students read the beginning of another famous tale within a tale, such as *The Thousand and One Nights.* Suggest that they record information in the **Enrichment: Analyzing Forms and Genres** worksheet, *Professional Development Guidebook,* page 227. Have them use the results of their research to write a short essay comparing the tale with "The Prologue" to *The Canterbury Tales.*

Chaucer begins his survey of medieval society with the courtly world, which centered on the nobility. Medieval nobles such as Chaucer's Knight held land granted them by a lord or king, for whom they fought in times of war. In the middle ranks of medieval society were learned professionals, such as Chaucer's Doctor, and wealthy businessmen. The lower orders included craftsmen, storekeepers, and minor administrators, such as the Reeve and the Manciple. The various ranks of the Church, a cornerstone of medieval society, are represented by characters from the Prioress to the Summoner.

However, as Chaucer writes about character ranks and types, he presents them as real people, individuals who defy categorizing. For example, though all outward appearances suggest that the Merchant is wealthy, he is, in fact, deeply in debt—a secret he keeps from some of his fellow travelers. Such breaks in stereotype provide readers with an even greater insight into the daily lives of medieval people.

A Literary Tour The popular genres in Chaucer's day included romances (tales of chivalry), *fabliaux* (short, bawdy, humorous stories), the stories of saints' lives, sermons, and allegories (narratives in which characters represent abstractions such as Pride or Honor). Each pilgrim chooses to tell a type of tale consistent with his or her character, and each of the major forms of medieval literature is represented. Chaucer wrote much of the *Tales* using his own form, the heroic couplet, a pair of rhyming lines with five stressed syllables each. For this important innovation, along with his other achievements, he is known as the father of English poetry.

The Endless Road Traveling with Chaucer's pilgrims, a reader may feel that the world is a big place but that, somehow, all of its pieces fit together. *The Canterbury Tales* reminds us that every journey from here to there is filled with stories, waiting to be told.

Speaking and Listening: Discussion

© **Comprehension and Collaboration** Imagine you are taking a long bus or plane trip with a group of modern-day travelers. With a group, discuss the types of people traveling with you. Come up with your own cast of characters for a modern-day version of *The Canterbury Tales*. Use these questions to guide your **discussion:**

- What different kinds of people make up our society today? Identify six types and build a character that matches each.
- In what ways might many of these individuals break the stereotype they outwardly appear to fit?
- What kind of tale might each character tell?

Choose a point person to share your ideas with the class.

Literary History **91**

Background
The Three Estates

Social stratification in medieval Europe consisted primarily of three social classes, or "estates." The first estate comprised the clergy, the second comprised nobility, and the third workers and peasants. However, this traditional division began to break down during the late Middle Ages as a new middle class began to form, consisting of trained urban workers and merchants.

In *The Canterbury Tales,* Chaucer is highly conscious of the social divisions known as the "estates." The Prologue to *The Canterbury Tales* is an example of "estates satire," a genre that satirizes the abuses that occurred within the three traditional Estates—in particular, the clergy

Speaking and Listening: Discussion
Modern Day Travelers

1. Read "Modern Day Travelers" with students. Develop a set of guiding questions as a class so that all students are working from a common basis. Additional starter questions include the following: How do people in our society vary in social, cultural, and economic status? How do people vary in age? What characteristics would not be typical for people of different ages and social, cultural, or economic status?

2. After establishing the guiding questions, divide the class into groups. Encourage students to brainstorm the six stereotypes together and to then build the characters individually. Once students have developed their characters, they can describe the tales their character might tell together.

3. Allow class time for groups to develop their characters and describe their tales. Then have each group's chosen point person share their characters and tales with the class.

• *from* The Canterbury Tales: The Prologue
Lesson Pacing Guide

DAY 1 Preteach

- © Administer the Reading and Vocabulary Warm-ups (*Unit 1 Resources*, pp. 76–79) as necessary.
- • Introduce the Literary Analysis concept: Characterization and Social Commentary.
- © Introduce the Reading Strategy: Questioning.
- • Build background with the Author in Depth and Background features.
- • Develop thematic thinking with Connecting to the Essential Question.
- © Teach the selection vocabulary.

DAYS 2–3 Preteach/Teach/Assess

- © Distribute copies of the appropriate graphic organizer for Reading Strategy (*Graphic Organizer Transparencies*, pp. 13–14).
- • Distribute copies of the appropriate graphic organizer for Literary Analysis (*Graphic Organizer Transparencies*, pp. 15–16).
- • Prepare students to read with the Activating Prior Knowledge activities (TE).
- • Informally monitor comprehension while students read.
- • Use the Reading Check questions to confirm comprehension.
- • Develop students' understanding of characterization and social commentary using the Literary Analysis prompts.
- • Develop students' ability to question using the Reading Strategy prompts.
- © Reinforce vocabulary with the Vocabulary notes.
- © Assess students' comprehension and mastery of the skills by having them answer the Critical Reading, Literary Analysis, and Reading Strategy questions.
- • Have students complete the Vocabulary Lesson.

DAY 4 Extend/Assess

- © Have students complete the Writing Lesson and write a Canterbury blog. (You may assign as homework.)
- © Have students read and respond to the Critical Commentary.
- • Administer Selection Test A or B (*Unit 1 Resources*, pp. 90–92 or 93–95).

© Common Core State Standards

Reading Literature 1. Cite strong and thorough textual evidence to support analysis of what the text says explicitly as well as inferences drawn from the text, including determining where the text leaves matters uncertain.
3. Analyze the impact of the author's choices regarding how to develop and relate elements of a story or drama.

Writing 5. Develop and strengthen writing as needed by planning, revising, editing, rewriting, or trying a new approach, focusing on addressing what is most significant for a specific purpose and audience.

Language 4.a. Use context as a clue to the meaning of a word or phrase.

Additional Standards Practice
Common Core Companion, pp. 2–9; 28–35; 226–227; 324–331

Daily Block Scheduling
Each day in this Lesson Pacing Guide represents a 40–50 minute period. Teachers using block scheduling may combine days to revise pacing. In addition, teachers may differentiate and support core instruction by integrating components for extended and intensive support as students require. See the Guide to Selected Leveled Resources (facing page).

Guide to Selected Leveled Resources

R T I **Tier 1** (students performing on level)

from The Canterbury Tales: The Prologue

Warm Up

Practice, **model**, and **monitor** fluency, working **with the whole class** or **in groups**.

Vocabulary and **Reading Warm-ups B,** *Unit 1 Resources,* pp. 76–77, 79

Comprehension/Skills

Support and **monitor** comprehension and skills development, having students complete the activities, graphic organizers, and interactive prompts **independently** or **as a class**.

- *Reader's Notebook,* adapted instruction and full selection
- EL *Reader's Notebook: English Learner's Version,* adapted instruction and adapted selection
- **Reading Skill Graphic Organizer B,** *Graphic Organizer Transparencies,* p. 14
- **Literary Analysis Graphic Organizer B,** *Graphic Organizer Transparencies,* p. 16

Monitor Progress

A **Monitor** student progress with the differentiated curriculum-based assessment in the *Unit Resources.*

- **Selection Test B,** *Unit 1 Resources,* pp. 93–95
- **Open-Book Test,** *Unit 1 Resources,* pp. 87–89

R T I **Tier 2** (students requiring intervention)

from The Canterbury Tales: The Prologue

Warm Up

Practice, **model,** and **monitor** fluency **in groups** or **with individuals**.

- **Vocabulary and Reading Warm-ups A,** *Unit 1 Resources,* pp. 76–78
- *Hear It!* Audio CD (adapted text)

Comprehension/Skills

- **Support** and **monitor** comprehension and skills development, working **in small groups** or **with individuals**.
- As students complete the selection in the appropriate version of the *Reader's Notebook,* **monitor** comprehension frequently with group questions and individual instruction.
- **Model** strategies while guiding students in completing the activities and prompts in the *Reader's Notebook,* as well as the graphic organizers.
- **Practice** skills and **monitor** mastery with the *Reading Kit* worksheets.

- *Reader's Notebook: Adapted Version,* adapted instruction and adapted selection
- EL *Reader's Notebook: English Learner's Version,* adapted instruction and adapted selection
- **Reading Skill Graphic Organizer A,** *Graphic Organizer Transparencies,* p. 13
- **Literary Analysis Graphic Organizer A,** *Graphic Organizer Transparencies,* p. 15
- *Reading Kit,* Practice worksheets

Monitor Progress

A **Monitor** student progress with the differentiated curriculum-based assessment in the *Unit Resources* and in the *Reading Kit.*

- **Selection Test A,** *Unit 1 Resources,* pp. 90–92
- *Reading Kit,* Assess worksheets

TIER 3 Tier 3 intervention may require consultation with the student's special-education or dyslexia specialist. For additional support, see the Tier 2 activities and resources listed above.

🔲 One-on-one teaching 🔲 Group work 🔲 Whole class instruction 🔲 Independent work 🅰 Assessment

For a complete guide to selection support, including support for Advanced students, see the Overview of Resources in the frontmatter.

• *from* The Canterbury Tales: The Prologue

RESOURCES FOR:
- **L1** Special-Needs Students
- **L2** Below-Level Students (Tier 2)
- **L3** On-Level Students (Tier 1)
- **L4** Advanced Students (Tier 1)
- **EL** English Learners
- **All** All Students

Vocabulary/Fluency/Prior Knowledge

The Prologue *from* The Canterbury Tales by Geoffrey Chaucer
Vocabulary Warm-up Word Lists

Study these words from the selection. Then, complete the activities.

Word List A

adversity [ad VER si tee] *n.* great hardship; misfortune
Forest fires, droughts, and mudslides can cause adversity for people.

courteous [KUR tee us] *adj.* considerate of others; polite
It is important for a receptionist to be courteous to visitors.

devout [di VOWT] *adj.* extremely religious; pious
The devout woman could be seen going to church every day.

dispense [di SPENS] *v.* administer; distribute in portions
It was the head nurse's responsibility to dispense the medicine.

distinguished [di STING gwisht] *adj.* marked by excellence; well-known
All the world leaders respected the distinguished diplomat.

pilgrimages [PIL gruhm ij iz] *n.* journeys to shrines or sacred places
The man has made pilgrimages to Mecca and other religious cities.

prudent [PROOD uhnt] *adj.* using good judgment; acting wisely
The prudent shopper spends less than he or she earns.

repented [ree PENT id] *v.* felt remorse or regret; resolved to reform
The thief repented and returned the stolen items.

Word List B

agility [uh JIL i tee] *n.* ability to move with ease and speed
The player's agility allowed her to return the ball after a difficult serve.

dainty [DAYN tee] *adj.* tiny and delicately beautiful
The dainty teapot, made of fine china, held only one cup of tea.

diligent [DIL uh juhnt] *adj.* marked by effort and care
The diligent employee was valued for her careful, dependable work.

dispatch [di SPACH] *v.* send to a destination or on specific business
The need to dispatch a messenger showed that the matter was urgent.

frugal [FROO guhl] *adj.* thrifty; economical; inexpensive
Her frugal lunch consisted of a peanut butter sandwich and an apple.

prompt [PRAHMPT] *adj.* acting or arriving on time or without delay
If you are prompt and arrive on time, we won't have to wait for you.

sundry [SUHN dree] *adj.* miscellaneous; various
The boy's pockets contained string, rocks, and sundry other items.

unanimously [yoo NAN uh muhs lee] *adv.* with everyone agreeing
The candidate was elected unanimously; not one person voted against her.

Unit 1 Resources: From Legend to History
© Pearson Education, Inc. All Rights reserved.
76

EL L1 L2 Vocabulary Warm-ups A and B, pp. 76–77

Also available for these selections:
EL L1 L2 Reading Warm-ups A and B, pp. 78–79
All Vocabulary Builder, p. 84

Reader's Notebooks
Pre- and postreading pages for this selection, as well as the excerpt from *The Canterbury Tales* appear in an interactive format in the *Reader's Notebooks*. Each *Notebook* is differentiated for a different group of learners.
The selections in the Adapted and English Learner's versions are abridged.

- **L2 L3** *Reader's Notebook*
- **L1** *Reader's Notebook: Adapted Version*
- **EL** *Reader's Notebook: English Learner's Version*
- **EL** *Reader's Notebook: Spanish Version*

© *Common Core Companion*
Additional instruction and practice for each Common Core State Standard

Selection Support

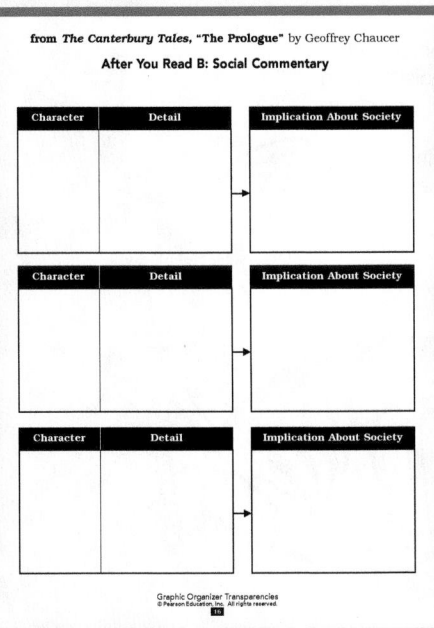

from *The Canterbury Tales*, "The Prologue" by Geoffrey Chaucer

After You Read B: Social Commentary

Graphic Organizer Transparencies

EL **L3** **Literary Analysis: Graphic Organizer B,** p. 16

Also available for these selections:

EL **L1** **L2** **Reading: Graphic Organizer A** (partially filled in), p. 13

EL **L3** **Reading: Graphic Organizer B,** p. 14

EL **L1** **L2** **Literary Analysis: Graphic Organizer A** (partially filled in), p. 15

Skills Development/Extension

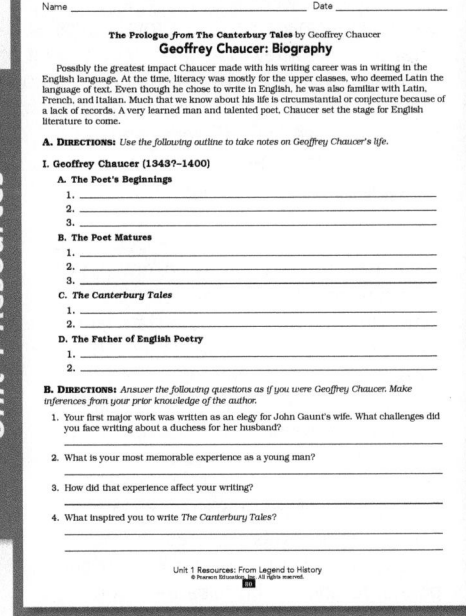

Unit 1 Resources

All **Biography,** p. 80

Also available for these selections:

All **Literary Analysis,** p. 81

All **Literary Analysis,** p. 82

All **Reading,** p. 83

EL **L3** **L4** **Support for Writing,** p. 85

L4 **Enrichment,** p. 86

Assessment

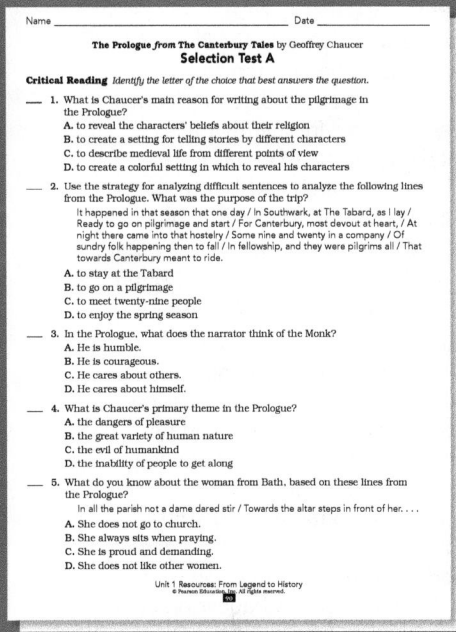

EL **L1** **L2** **Selection Test A,** pp. 90–92

Also available for these selections:

L3 **L4** **Open-Book Test,** pp. 87–89

EL **L3** **L4** **Selection Test B,** pp. 93–95

PHLit Online!
www.PHLitOnline.com

Online Resources: All print materials are also available online.

- complete narrated selection text
- a thematically related video with writing prompt
- an interactive graphic organizer
- highlighting feature
- access to all student print resources, adapted to individual student needs
- Spanish and English summaries
- adapted selection translations in Spanish

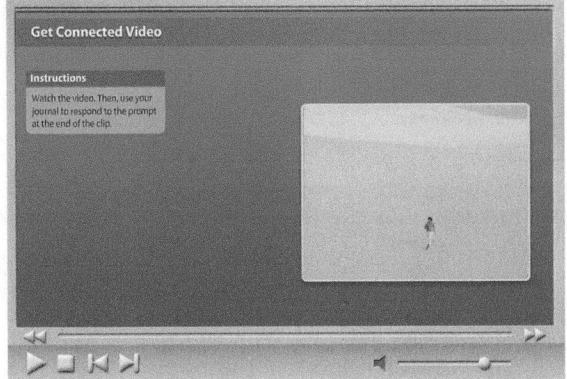

Get Connected! (thematic video with writing prompt)

Also available:

Background Video
All videos are available in Spanish.

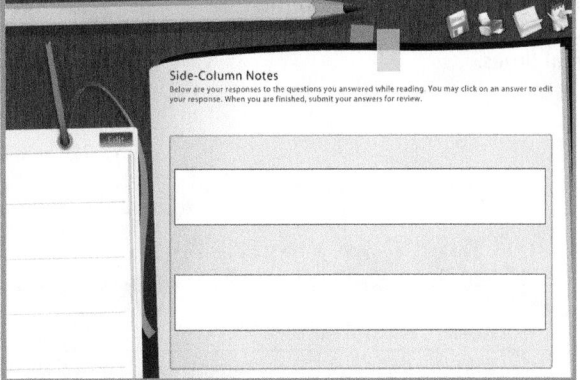

Writer's Journal (with graphics feature)

Also available:

Vocabulary Central (tools and activities for studying vocabulary)

❶ Background

Overview: The Author's Work

Chaucer's first poem, *The Book of the Duchess*, was written to console a friend whose wife died of plague. Later, Chaucer frequently traveled to Italy. There he read Italian poets, including Petrarch and Dante. Chaucer continued to write, beginning with *Hous of Fame*. In this poem, he develops his ironic voice, casting himself as a dimwitted narrator.

After *Hous of Fame*, Chaucer wrote *The Parlement of Foules* and *Troilus and Criseyde*, which many consider to be his greatest work. Then he wrote *The Legend of Good Women*, which, like *The Canterbury Tales*, is a story that contains other stories. Scholars do not regard *The Legend of Good Women* as a very good work, but the piece gave Chaucer practice with the form he was to use for *The Canterbury* Tales, his last work.

The Writer in His Time

Today Chaucer is remembered as a writer and a poet, but writing was not his day job. Chaucer was a civil servant who worked for three kings: Edward II, Richard II, and Henry IV. As an officer of the court, he frequently traveled abroad. He was often in Flanders, France, and Italy.

In 1389, Chaucer became clerk of the king's works. He was in charge of repair and maintenance of buildings such as the Tower of London and Westminster Palace. But in this position, he was robbed and beaten several times.

❶ ❷ Geoffrey Chaucer (1343?–1400)

Son of a merchant, page in a royal house, soldier, diplomat, and royal clerk, Geoffrey Chaucer saw quite a bit of the medieval world. His varied experiences helped prepare him to write *The Canterbury Tales*. This masterpiece provides the best contemporary picture we have of fourteenth-century England. Gathering characters from different walks of life, Chaucer takes the reader on a journey through medieval society.

The Poet's Beginning The exact date of Geoffrey Chaucer's birth is unknown, but official records furnish many details of his active life. Born into a middle-class family, Chaucer was sent in his early teens to work as page to the wife of Lionel of Antwerp, a son of the reigning monarch, Edward III. Through this position, middle-class Chaucer was introduced to the aristocratic society of England. In 1359, while serving in the English Army in France, Chaucer was captured and held prisoner. King Edward paid a £16 (sixteen-pound) ransom for his release—a sum that was eight times what a simple laborer might make in a year. In 1366, Chaucer married Philippa Pan, a lady-in-waiting to the queen. Their eldest child, Thomas, continued his father's rise in the world, marrying a noblewoman and acquiring great wealth.

The Poet Matures Chaucer began writing in his twenties, practicing his skills as a poet as he rose through the ranks of medieval society. His early poems were based on the works of European poets. These were followed by various translations of French poetry. His first major work, *The Book of the Duchess*, was probably completed in early 1369, almost one year after the death of Blanche of Lancaster, for whose grieving husband, John of Gaunt, he wrote the poem. As Chaucer grew older, he developed a mature style of his own and displayed a deep insight into human character.

ⓒ Text Complexity Rubric

The Prologue *from* The Canterbury Tales

Qualitative Measures	
Context/Knowledge Demands	Social commentary; historical knowledge demands 1 2 ③ 4 5
Structure/Language Conventionality and Clarity	Complex sentences; above-level vocabulary 1 2 3 ④ 5
Levels of Meaning/Purpose/Concept Level	Accessible (human nature) 1 2 ③ 4 5

Quantitative Measures			
Lexile	NP	**Text Length**	6,775 words
Overall Complexity	**More accessible**		

Reader and Task Suggestions

Preparing to Read the Text

- Using the Background on TE p. 90, discuss the reasons that people would make a pilgrimage to Canterbury.
- Have students work together on a chart they might use to list the characters in Chaucer's Prologue by rank or social importance.
- Guide students to use Multidraft Reading strategies to deepen their comprehension (TE p. 93).

Leveled Tasks

Knowledge Demands If students will have difficulty with the historical context, have them skim the Prologue, charting each character they encounter. Then, have students read the Prologue, using their character list to guide them.

Evaluating If students will not have difficulty with the historical context, have them evaluate Chaucer's use of clothing as a form of indirect characterization.

The Canterbury Tales Chaucer wrote *The Canterbury Tales* in his later years. No one knows for certain what prompted him to begin this work. Chaucer's inspiration may have come from his own participation in the pilgrimage to Canterbury. A pilgrimage is a long journey to a shrine or holy site, undertaken by people who wish to express their devotion. The Canterbury Cathedral was the focus of devotion because St. Thomas à Becket was murdered there in 1170. Chaucer certainly had the opportunity to observe many pilgrims starting their journeys—a window of his London home overlooked the pilgrim road that led to Canterbury.

In this masterwork, each character tells a tale on the way to Canterbury. Just as the tellers of *The Canterbury Tales* come from the length and breadth of medieval society, the tales encompass medieval literature—from romance to comedy, from rhyme to prose, from crude humor to religious mysteries. Only 24 of the projected 120 tales were finished, but they stand together as a complete work.

The Father of English Poetry In his own lifetime, Geoffrey Chaucer was considered the greatest English poet. Recognized as a shrewd storyteller, he was also praised by a contemporary as the first to "rain the gold dewdrops of speech and eloquence" into English literature. Throughout history, new generations of poets writing in English have studied his work for both inspiration and insight.

Chaucer lies buried in Westminster Abbey. In recognition of his unique position in England's literary tradition, Westminster's honorary burial area for distinguished writers, the Poets' Corner, was established around his tomb. The words in Middle English at the right are from Chaucer's poem *Troilus and Criseyde*. They are not on his tomb, but they serve to measure both his distance from us and his closeness to us.

Ye knowe eek, that in forme of speche is chaunge

Withinne a thousand yeer, and wordes tho

That hadden prys, now wonder nyce and straunge

Us thinketh hem; and yet they spake hem so,

And spedde as wel in love as men now do . . .

Geoffrey Chaucer **93**

Daily Bellringer

For each class during which you will teach this selection, have students complete one of the five activities for the appropriate week in the *Daily Bellringer Activities* booklet.

Multidraft Reading

To assist struggling readers and to enhance reading for all, assign the text in chunks, as warranted by length, and apply multidraft reading protocols. For each reading, have students set the purpose indicated:

- **First reading**—identifying key ideas and details and answering any Reading Checks.
- **Second reading**—analyzing craft and structure and responding to the side-column prompts.
- **Third reading**—integrating knowledge and ideas, connecting to other texts and the world, and answering the end-of-selection questions.

For more guidance, refer to the *Classroom Strategies and Teaching Routines* card, **Multidraft Reading**.

❷ Background

More About the Author

The name Chaucer is derived from the French word *chaussier*, meaning a maker of footwear. The family had, in fact, made its fortune from leather, as well as from wine. Chaucer spoke French, Latin, and Italian, in addition to Middle English. Chaucer was no mere clerk—he was sufficiently important within the government to attain a guaranteed income for life.

Chaucer was appointed a justice of the peace for Kent in 1385, and in 1386 he became a knight for the shire of Kent, to attend Parliament. He was a courtier, diplomat, civil servant, and trusted aide to three kings.

Differentiated Instruction for Universal Access

Enrichment for Gifted/Talented Students

As students read Chaucer's Prologue, page 96, have them take notes on the social status and ethical qualities of each character. Then, have students draw a scene of the pilgrims en route, drawing on Chaucer's descriptions and conveying a sense of the event and the times.

Alternatively, you may want to have each student choose a character to portray in person. Pick a day to have students come to class in costume, dressed as a character from *The Canterbury Tales*.

PHLit Online!

For more about Geoffrey Chaucer's additional background, and a **Get Connected!** video, go online at **www.PHLitOnline.com**.

❶ Chaucer's Sharp Eye
for Dress

1. Have student volunteers describe how they prefer to dress. **Ask** how the clothes they wear reflect their station in life. Then brainstorm occasions when they dress differently than they do at school (e.g., for athletic events, formal parties).

2. Point out that many people in the Middle Ages, especially travelers, did not have a wide variety of clothing from which to choose. Tell students that clothing differed quite a bit by social station. Wealthier people wore clothing (long tunics for men and flowing gowns for women) that was not designed for labor, to make it obvious that they did not have to work.

3. Point out that people in the Middle Ages wore more layers than people today. Women wore petticoats under their skirts, and they also wore long tunics. Men wore tunics and trousers. People needed these additional layers during the Middle Ages because neither cloaks nor houses were as warm as they are today, and people spent more time outdoors.

4. Tell students that members of Holy Orders, such as priests, monks, and nuns, wore habits that showed the Order to which they belonged. One order of Franciscan nuns had to petition the Pope for permission to wear wool socks.

❶ CHAUCER'S SHARP EYE FOR DRESS

Do you dress to impress? Or for success?

Medieval Dress Codes In the 14th century, rules dictating style depended on whether you were rich, middle-class, or poor. No one below the rank of knight could wear fur, for example; merchants could wear the same clothes as knights only if they were five times wealthier, and women were forbidden from wearing silk head coverings.

In the Prologue to *The Canterbury Tales*, Chaucer relies on the details of the pilgrims' clothing and a general knowledge of the do's and don'ts of fashion laws to reveal their personalities, positions on the social ladder, and attempts at modesty or deception.

Modest Dress The Knight's coarse tunic "stained and dark" could have fooled fashion watchers into believing he was without rank. Yet knights were members of the nobility and were allowed to adorn themselves with fur and gold.

Pleasure Loving A Franklin, a member in good standing of the top tier of 14th century hierarchy, was a pleasure-loving fellow. This landowner carried "a little purse of silk…" that Chaucer aptly describes as "white as morning milk."

The Wife of Bath's "flowing mantle" hid her "large hips," her handkerchiefs were finely woven, her stockings "were of the finest scarlet red" and her shoes "soft and new." Her clothing revealed her as a member of the middle class.

Clothing That Suits the Profession A Doctor in the group was adorned alarmingly in "blood-red garments…lined with taffeta," almost as if he were advertising his profession. Yet Chaucer wrote that the Doctor watched every cent and was "rather close as to expenses."

Bottom line: No matter what you wear or when you live, your clothes say a lot about who you are, where you fit, and what you aspire to be.

Knight   **Franklin**   **Wife of Bath**   **Doctor**

94 From Legend to History (A.D. 449–1485)

Vocabulary Development

Vocabulary Knowledge Rating

Create a **Vocabulary Knowledge Rating Chart** (*Professional Development Guidebook*, p. 32-33) for this selection, using the selection vocabulary from the next page. Give students a copy of the chart. Read the words aloud, and have students mark their rating in the Before Reading column. Urge them to be alert to these words as they read and discuss the selection.

Tally how many students think they know a word to gauge how much instruction to provide. As students read and discuss the selection, point out the words and their context.

PHLit **Online!** **Vocabulary Central**, featuring student tools for recording and studying vocabulary, is available online at **www.PHLitOnline.com.**

Before You Read

from *The Canterbury Tales: The Prologue*

❷ Connecting to the Essential Question In the Prologue to *The Canterbury Tales*, Chaucer describes different medieval social types. Briefly describe some social types at your school. In describing social types, you probably described their clothes. As you read, note what Chaucer's descriptions of clothes reveal about his characters. Doing so will help you explore the Essential Question: **How does literature shape or reflect society?**

❸ Literary Analysis

As you read the Prologue, look for these forms of **characterization**—techniques of revealing character:

- **Direct characterization** presents direct statements about a character, like Chaucer's statement that the Knight "followed chivalry. . . ."
- **Indirect characterization** uses actions, thoughts, dialogue, and description to reveal a character's personality. By saying the Knight Is "not gaily dressed," Chaucer suggests that he is not vain.

Each character in the selection represents a different segment of society in Chaucer's time. By using characterization to reveal the virtues and faults of each, Chaucer provides **social commentary,** writing that offers insight into society, its values, and its customs. As you read, determine what Chaucer's characters suggest about his views of English society and of life.

❹ Reading Strategy

Ⓒ Preparing to Read Complex Texts When you do not understand a long, involved sentence you are reading, repair your comprehension by **questioning.** For example, you may have trouble understanding the eighteen-line sentence at the start of Chaucer's Prologue. To analyze the sentence, ask the questions *When?, Who?, Where?, What?, Why?,* and *How?* to identify essential information. Use a chart like the one shown to finish analyzing Chaucer's first sentence.

❺ Vocabulary

solicitous (sə lis′ ə təs) *adj.* showing care or concern (p. 101)

garnished (gär′ nisht) *adj.* decorated; trimmed (p. 102)

absolution (ab′ sə lōō′ shən) *n.* act of freeing someone of a sin or criminal charge (p. 103)

commission (kə mish′ ən) *n.* authorization; act of giving authority to an individual (p. 105)

sanguine (saṅ′ gwin) *adj.* confident; cheerful (p. 106)

prevarication (pri var′ i kā′ shən) *n.* evasion of truth (p. 115)

Common Core State Standards

Reading Literature

1. Cite strong and thorough textual evidence to support analysis of what the text says explicitly as well as inferences drawn from the text, including determining where the text leaves matters uncertain.

3. Analyze the impact of the author's choices regarding how to develop and relate elements of a story or drama.

Analyze Difficult Sentences	
When?	in April
Who?	people; palmers
Where?	
What?	
Why?	
How?	

PHLit Online! www.PHLitOnline.com

from The Canterbury Tales: The Prologue 95

---

❷ Connecting to the Essential Question

1. Review the assignment with the class.

2. Have students brainstorm about the different adult social types that they see in their community. Then, have them complete the assignment.

3. As students read, have them look for clues to the social status of each character.

❸ Literary Analysis

Introduce the skill, using the instruction on the student page.

Think Aloud: Model the Skill

Say to students:

I want to look at Chaucer's characterization of the Friar. I read lines 212 to 279. Chaucer writes as though he is praising the Friar. But I see that the Friar prefers the company of rich people, he likes pretty women, and he wears expensive clothes. I consider what Chaucer's opinion of the Friar's faith was.

❹ Reading Strategy

1. Introduce the strategy using the instruction on the student page.

2. Give students a copy of **Reading Strategy Graphic Organizer B**, page 14 in *Graphic Organizer Transparencies,* to fill out as they read.

❺ Vocabulary

1. Pronounce each word, giving its definition, and have students say it aloud.

2. For more guidance, see the *Classroom Strategies and Teaching Routines* card for vocabulary instruction.

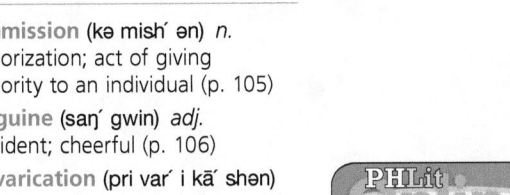
PHLit Online! www.PHLitOnline.com

Teaching From Technology

Preparing to Read

Go to www.PHLitOnline.com and display the **Get Connected!** slide show for this selection. Have the class brainstorm for responses to the writing prompt, entering ideas in the interactive journal. Then have students complete their responses individually. You may also have students complete the assignment as homework.

To build background, display the **Background** video and **More About the Author** features.

Using the Interactive Student Edition

Go to www.PHLitOnline.com and display the **Enriched Online Student Edition.** As the class reads the selection or listens to the narration, record answers to side-column prompts using the graphic organizers accessible on the interactive page. Alternatively, have students use the online edition individually, answering the prompts as they read.

❶ About the Selection

Chaucer's collection of fourteenth-century heroes and rogues offers a rare snapshot of medieval life and values. Moreover, it provides enduring evidence that human nature changes very little. In Chaucer's characters, we see something of ourselves and the people around us.

❷ Activating Prior Knowledge

Have students preview the illustrations accompanying this selection prior to reading it. Encourage them to share their impressions of the characters based on the illustrations.

EXEMPLAR TEXT ©

from the

Canterbury Tales
The Prologue

Geoffrey Chaucer
translated by Nevill Coghill

❶
❷

96 From Legend to History (A.D. 449–1485)

3   **4**   Lines 1–18 of the Prologue in Chaucer's original Middle English are followed by the entire Prologue in a modern translation.

Whan that Aprill with his shoures soote
The droghte of March hath perced to the roote,
And bathed every veyne in swich licour
Of which vertu engendred is the flour;
5   Whan Zephirus eek with his sweete breeth
Inspired hath in every holt and heeth
The tendre croppes, and the yonge sonne
Hath in the Ram his halve cours yronne,
And smale foweles maken melodye,
10   That slepen al the nyght with open ye
(So priketh hem nature in hir corages);
Thanne longen folk to goon on pilgrimages,
And palmeres for to seken straunge strondes,
To ferne halwes, kowthe in sondry londes;
15   And specially from every shires ende
Of Engelond to Caunterbury they wende,
The hooly blisful martir for to seke,
That hem hath holpen whan that they were seeke.

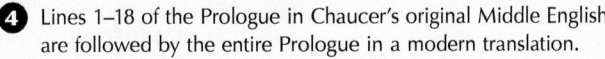

W̲hen in April the sweet showers fall
And pierce the drought of March to the root, and all
The veins are bathed in liquor of such power
As brings about the engendering of the flower,
5   When also Zephyrus[1] with his sweet breath
Exhales an air in every grove and heath
Upon tender shoots, and the young sun
His half-course in the sign of the Ram[2] has run,
And the small fowl are making melody
10   That sleep away the night with open eye
(So nature pricks them and their heart engages)
Then people long to go on pilgrimages
And palmers[3] long to seek the stranger strands[4]
Of far-off saints, hallowed in sundry lands,
15   And specially, from every shire's end
In England, down to Canterbury they wend
To seek the holy blissful martyr,[5] quick
To give his help to them when they were sick.

---

1. **Zephyrus** (zefʹ ə rəs) the west wind.
2. **Ram** Aries, the first sign of the zodiac. The pilgrimage began on April 11, 1387.
3. **palmers** pilgrims who wore two crossed palm leaves to show that they had visited the Holy Land.
4. **strands** shores.
5. **martyr** St. Thomas à Becket, the Archbishop of Canterbury, who was murdered in Canterbury Cathedral in 1170.

from The Canterbury Tales: The Prologue   **97**

❺ Reading Strategy

Questioning

1. Remind students that by asking questions such as when, who, what, how, where, and why when reading a passage, they can analyze its meaning and identify the essential information it conveys.

2. Point out that in these lines, *who* refers to the Knight, and *when* means from the time the Knight first began to ride.

3. Then, **ask** students the Reading Strategy question: According to lines 43–46, what values does the Knight follow?
   Answer: The knight follows the values of chivalry, truth, honor, generousness, and courtesy.

❻ Literary Analysis

Characterization

1. **Ask** students why they think Chaucer started with the Knight.
   Possible response: He possessed the highest social standing among the pilgrims.

2. Explain to students that, when Chaucer describes the Knight as the epitome of chivalry, he is talking about an ideal from the past. By the 1380s, when Chaucer began *The Canterbury Tales,* feudalism and chivalry had nearly disappeared from England.

3. **Ask** students the Literary Analysis question: What do lines 54–65 indirectly suggest about the Knight's character?
   Answer: He is brave, loves action and adventure, really believes in the ideals of chivalry—and must be an excellent fighter to have survived so many battles.

4. **Ask** students which lines use direct characterization, and what details are added about the Knight's character.
   Answer: Lines 70–74 describe his character directly, stating that he is wise, modest, and true.

Reading Strategy ❺

Questioning

According to lines 43–46, what values does the Knight follow?

Literary Analysis ❻

Characterization

What do lines 54–65 indirectly suggest about the Knight's character?

It happened in that season that one day
20 In Southwark,[6] at The Tabard,[7] as I lay
Ready to go on pilgrimage and start
For Canterbury, most devout at heart,
At night there came into that hostelry
Some nine and twenty in a company
25 Of sundry folk happening then to fall
In fellowship, and they were pilgrims all
That towards Canterbury meant to ride.
The rooms and stables of the inn were wide;
They made us easy, all was of the best.
30 And shortly, when the sun had gone to rest,
By speaking to them all upon the trip
I soon was one of them in fellowship
And promised to rise early and take the way
To Canterbury, as you heard me say.
35   But nonetheless, while I have time and space,
Before my story takes a further pace,
It seems a reasonable thing to say
What their condition was, the full array
Of each of them, as it appeared to me
40 According to profession and degree,
And what apparel they were riding in;
And at a Knight I therefore will begin.
There was a *Knight*, a most distinguished man,
Who from the day on which he first began
45 To ride abroad had followed chivalry,
Truth, honor, generousness and courtesy.
He had done nobly in his sovereign's war
And ridden into battle, no man more,
As well in Christian as heathen places,
50 And ever honored for his noble graces.
    When we took Alexandria,[8] he was there.
He often sat at table in the chair
Of honor, above all nations, when in Prussia.
In Lithuania he had ridden, and Russia,
55 No Christian man so often, of his rank.
When, in Granada, Algeciras sank
Under assault, he had been there, and in
North Africa, raiding Benamarin;
In Anatolia he had been as well
60 And fought when Ayas and Attalia fell,

---

6. **Southwark** (suth′ erk) suburb of London at the time.
7. **The Tabard** (ta′ berd) an inn.
8. **Alexandria** site of one of the campaigns fought by Christians against groups who posed a threat to Europe during the fourteenth century. The place names that follow refer to other battle sites in these campaigns, or crusades.

98 From Legend to History (A.D. 449–1485)

Enrichment: Understanding Culture

The Knight

The Knight is said to have done nobly in "his sovereign's war." Scholars suggest that this is a reference to the campaigns of the Hundred Years' War between England and France. However, based on the other references, the Knight must have served some forty years in northeastern Europe, the western Mediterranean, the Turkish empire of the eastern Mediterranean, and North Africa.

Activity: Analyzing Culture

Have students trace the travels of the Knight and report on the culture and customs of the people occupying those regions today.

Suggest that they record information on the **Enrichment: Investigating Culture** worksheet, *Professional Development Guidebook,* page 223.

For all along the Mediterranean coast
He had embarked with many a noble host.
In fifteen mortal battles he had been
And jousted for our faith at Tramissene
65 Thrice in the lists, and always killed his man.
This same distinguished knight had led the van[9]
Once with the Bey of Balat,[10] doing work
For him against another heathen Turk;
He was of sovereign value in all eyes.
70 And though so much distinguished, he was wise
And in his bearing modest as a maid.
He never yet a boorish thing had said
In all his life to any, come what might;
He was a true, a perfect gentle-knight.
75 Speaking of his equipment, he possessed
Fine horses, but he was not gaily dressed.
He wore a fustian[11] tunic stained and dark
With smudges where his armor had left mark;
❼ Just home from service, he had joined our ranks
80 To do his pilgrimage and render thanks.
    He had his son with him, a fine young *Squire*,
A lover and cadet, a lad of fire
With locks as curly as if they had been pressed.
He was some twenty years of age, I guessed.
85 In stature he was of a moderate length,
With wonderful agility and strength.
❽ He'd seen some service with the cavalry
In Flanders and Artois and Picardy[12]
And had done valiantly in little space
90 Of time, in hope to win his lady's grace.
He was embroidered like a meadow bright
And full of freshest flowers, red and white.
Singing he was, or fluting all the day;
He was as fresh as is the month of May.
95 Short was his gown, the sleeves were long and wide;
He knew the way to sit a horse and ride.
He could make songs and poems and recite,
Knew how to joust and dance, to draw and write.
He loved so hotly that till dawn grew pale
100 He slept as little as a nightingale.
Courteous he was, lowly and serviceable,
And carved to serve his father at the table.

---

9. **van** the part of the army that goes before the rest (short for *vanguard*).
10. **Bey of Balat** pagan leader.
11. **fustian** (fus´ chən) *n.* coarse cloth of cotton and linen.
12. **Flanders . . . Picardy** regions in Belgium and France.

Reading Strategy
Questioning What motivates the Squire in lines 85–90?

❾ Reading Check

What are some of the military accomplishments of the Knight?

from The Canterbury Tales: The Prologue **99**

❼ **Literary Analysis**
Characterization

1. Remind students that the details that help characterize someone in this work (as well as in others) are not always obvious—and not always part of the individual's description.

2. Point out that the comment in lines 78–80 shows that the Knight has just returned from another battle.

3. **Ask** students what additional information we gain about the Knight in the first few lines of the description of the Squire.
   Answer: We learn that the Knight has a son, the Squire, and we learn that the Knight is no youngster, if his son is already twenty.

❽ **Reading Strategy**
Questioning

1. Remind students that asking questions can help them to understand a character.

2. Point out that becoming a squire involves work and risk.

3. **Ask** students the Reading Strategy question: What motivates the Squire in lines 85–90?
   Answer: The Squire is hoping to impress a lady.

❾ **Reading Check**

Answer: The Knight has served in Alexandria, Prussia, Lithuania, Russia, Granada, North Africa, Anatolia, Tramissene, and Turkey.

Differentiated
Instruction for Universal Access

Strategy for
Less Proficient Readers
To help students keep track of details, write the titles of the various characters being described on the board or on an overhead transparency. Then, as students read one description at a time, have them suggest character traits and descriptive elements, and list these beneath the appropriate title.

EL **Background for**
English Learners
Use illustrations in the text to point out items described. For characters not illustrated, you may wish to bring in more pictures. In addition, students may benefit from seeing images of horses, a medieval town, and even of Canterbury Cathedral. Also, review footnotes with students to make certain they understand the words in the definitions. For example, defining *Prioress* in terms of an abbey helps only if students know what an abbey is.

⑩ Humanities

The Yeoman, 1946,
by Arthur Szyk

In this miniature, painted in 1946 for *The Canterbury Tales,* the artist shows a fully equipped medieval yeoman. He appears ready for any occurrence in the forest, from the appearance of game to an attack by a highwayman. He is portrayed as a sturdy fellow with a serious expression. In painting these miniatures, Arthur Szyk, with patience and meticulous care, imitates monkish manuscript painters. Through this painstaking effect, he succeeds in capturing the charm and medieval flavor of that art.
Use these questions for discussion:

1. How does Szyk's depiction of the Yeoman compare with your image of him?
   Possible responses: Some students may say that the art matches their image of the Yeoman. For many students, the Yeoman will match their images of Robin Hood.

2. What details of this illustration would you like to change?
   Possible response: Students may suggest ways to make the illustration match Chaucer's description more closely, such as changing the Yeoman's jacket to green, or putting a brace on his arm.

⑪ Critical Viewing

Possible response: The Yeoman's arrows are slung over his shoulder, rather than hanging at his belt as in Chaucer's description. The artist has also chosen to omit the arm brace, the medal of St. Christopher, and the hunting horn. Some students may dispute whether the coat and hood are green, as only the lining appears to be green.

The Yeoman, Arthur Szyk for The Canterbury Tales

⑩

▲ **Critical Viewing ⑪**
Compare this portrait with Chaucer's description of the Yeoman. What details did the artist choose to change or omit? **[Compare and Contrast]**

100 From Legend to History (A.D. 449–1485)

There was a *Yeoman*[13] with him at his side,
No other servant; so he chose to ride.
105 This Yeoman wore a coat and hood of green,
And peacock-feathered arrows, bright and keen
And neatly sheathed, hung at his belt the while
—For he could dress his gear in yeoman style,
His arrows never drooped their feathers low—
110 And in his hand he bore a mighty bow.
His head was like a nut, his face was brown.
He knew the whole of woodcraft up and down.
A saucy brace[14] was on his arm to ward
It from the bow-string, and a shield and sword
115 Hung at one side, and at the other slipped
A jaunty dirk,[15] spear-sharp and well-equipped.
A medal of St. Christopher[16] he wore
Of shining silver on his breast, and bore
A hunting-horn, well slung and burnished clean,
120 That dangled from a baldric[17] of bright green.
He was a proper forester I guess.
      There also was a *Nun,* a Prioress.[18]
Her way of smiling very simple and coy.
Her greatest oath was only "By St. Loy!"[19]
125 And she was known as Madam Eglantyne.
And well she sang a service,[20] with a fine
Intoning through her nose, as was most seemly,
And she spoke daintily in French, extremely,
After the school of Stratford-atte-Bowe;[21]
130 French in the Paris style she did not know.
At meat her manners were well taught withal;
No morsel from her lips did she let fall,
Nor dipped her fingers in the sauce too deep;
But she could carry a morsel up and keep
135 The smallest drop from falling on her breast.
For courtliness she had a special zest,
And she would wipe her upper lip so clean
That not a trace of grease was to be seen
Upon the cup when she had drunk; to eat,

---

13. **Yeoman** (yō′ mən) *n.* attendant.
14. **brace** bracelet.
15. **dirk** *n.* dagger.
16. **St. Christopher** patron saint of travelers.
17. **baldric** *n.* belt worn over one shoulder and across the chest to support a sword.
18. **Prioress** *n.* in an abbey, the nun ranking just below the abbess.
19. **St. Loy** St. Eligius, patron saint of goldsmiths and courtiers.
20. **service** daily prayer.
21. **Stratford-atte-Bowe** nunnery near London.

---

140 She reached a hand sedately for the meat.
    She certainly was very entertaining,
    Pleasant and friendly in her ways, and straining
    To counterfeit a courtly kind of grace,
    A stately bearing fitting to her place,
145 And to seem dignified in all her dealings.
    As for her sympathies and tender feelings,
    She was so charitably *solicitous*
    She used to weep if she but saw a mouse
    Caught in a trap, if it were dead or bleeding.
150 And she had little dogs she would be feeding
    With roasted flesh, or milk, or fine white bread.
    And bitterly she wept if one were dead
    Or someone took a stick and made it smart;
    She was all sentiment and tender heart.
155 Her veil was gathered in a seemly way,
    Her nose was elegant, her eyes glass-gray;
    Her mouth was very small, but soft and red,
    Her forehead, certainly, was fair of spread,
    Almost a span[22] across the brows, I own;
160 She was indeed by no means undergrown.
    Her cloak, I noticed, had a graceful charm.
    She wore a coral trinket on her arm,
    A set of beads, the gaudies[23] tricked in green,
    Whence hung a golden brooch of brightest sheen
165 On which there first was graven a crowned *A*,
    And lower, *Amor vincit omnia*.[24]
        Another *Nun*, the chaplain at her cell,
    Was riding with her, and *three Priests* as well.
        A *Monk* there was, one of the finest sort
170 Who rode the country; hunting was his sport.
    A manly man, to be an Abbot able;
    Many a dainty horse he had in stable.
    His bridle, when he rode, a man might hear
    Jingling in a whistling wind as clear,
175 Aye, and as loud as does the chapel bell
    Where my lord Monk was Prior of the cell.
    The Rule of good St. Benet or St. Maur[25]
    As old and strict he tended to ignore;
    He let go by the things of yesterday

---

22. **span** nine inches.
23. **gaudies** large green beads that marked certain prayers on a set of prayer beads.
24. **Amor vincit omnia** (ä´ môr´ vin´ chit ôm´ nē ä´) "love conquers all" (Latin).
25. **St. Benet or St. Maur** St. Benedict, author of monastic rules, and St. Maurice, one of his followers. Benet and Maur are French versions of Benedict and Maurice.

Vocabulary
solicitous (sə lis´ ə təs) *adj.*
showing care or concern

Literary Analysis
Characterization
What can you infer about the Prioress based on this detailed description of her jewelry?

Reading Check
How does the Nun show her "sympathies and tender feelings"?

from The Canterbury Tales: The Prologue **101**

---

⑫ Literary Analysis
Characterization

1. Review with students how indirect and direct characterization reveal something about a character (p. 95 of text).

2. Then, **ask** students the Literary Analysis question: What can you infer about the Prioress based on this detailed description of her jewelry?
   Possible response: Most students will realize that the jewelry indicates wealth. Students may also suggest that it indicates a degree of worldliness.

3. Point out the reference to Eglantyne in line 125, and explain that Eglantyne is a type of wild rose whose long, thorny stems readily entangle passersby. Eglantyne was also the name of several "clinging-vine" heroines in medieval romances.

4. **Ask** students what Chaucer is saying about the Prioress by calling her Madam Eglantyne.
   Possible response: He is saying that she is clinging, helpless, and perhaps a bit too dainty.

5. Have students identify other elements of the description that show that the Prioress was excessively dainty, in Chaucer's view.
   Possible response: Comments about her wiping "her upper lip so clean," and about being reduced to tears by seeing a mouse in a trap suggest that Chaucer thinks her daintiness is extreme.

⑬ Reading Check
Answer: She weeps if anything happens to a mouse or to her dogs, and she tenderly feeds her dogs scraps of food from the table.

101

⑭ Humanities

The Monk, 1946, by Arthur Szyk

In this miniature, Szyk shows the massive and richly robed monk described in the Prologue. His wealth is apparent from his fine fur-trimmed robes, gold brooch, elaborate sword, and tooled wallet. Szyk painted the worldly cleric with humor and wit, emphasizing the incongruity between wealth and the man's humble vocation.

Use these questions for discussion:

1. How does Szyk's representation of the Monk compare with Chaucer's description?
   Answer: The miniature closely matches Chaucer's description.

2. Does this depiction look realistic or exaggerated?
   Possible response: Students may say the depiction is stylized but contains some realistic details in the Monk's facial features.

⑮ Critical Viewing

Possible response: Students may point to the Monk's size and weight as evidence that he eats well. His fur-trimmed clothing and fine purse indicate a degree of wealth. The spurs and sword suggest he rides and possibly hunts or engages in sport.

⑯ Literary Analysis

Characterization and Social Commentary

Monitor Progress

To monitor students' comprehension of the Literary Element, **ask** students to give examples of direct and indirect characterization from the characters they have already read about.

Reteach

Remind them that social commentary provides insights into society, its values, and its customs. By helping us understand the era of a work, social commentary helps us understand the motives and lives of the individuals who lived in that society. Review the Literary Analysis information on page 95.

The Monk, Arthur Szyk for *The Canterbury Tales*

▲ Critical Viewing ⑮
What can you infer from this picture about the Monk's style of living? List three details supporting your conclusion. **[Infer]**

Vocabulary
garnished (gär′ nisht) *adj.* decorated; trimmed

180 And took the modern world's more spacious way.
He did not rate that text at a plucked hen
Which says that hunters are not holy men
And that a monk uncloistered is a mere
Fish out of water, flapping on the pier,
185 That is to say a monk out of his cloister.
That was a text he held not worth an oyster;
And I agreed and said his views were sound;
Was he to study till his head went round
Poring over books in cloisters? Must he toil
190 As Austin[26] bade and till the very soil?
Was he to leave the world upon the shelf?
Let Austin have his labor to himself.
　　This Monk was therefore a good man to horse;
Greyhounds he had, as swift as birds, to course.
195 Hunting a hare or riding at a fence
Was all his fun, he spared for no expense.
I saw his sleeves were garnished at the hand
With fine gray fur, the finest in the land,
And on his hood, to fasten it at his chin
200 He had a wrought-gold cunningly fashioned pin;
Into a lover's knot it seemed to pass.
His head was bald and shone like looking-glass;
So did his face, as if it had been greased.
He was a fat and personable priest;
205 His prominent eyeballs never seemed to settle.
They glittered like the flames beneath a kettle;
Supple his boots, his horse in fine condition.
He was a prelate fit for exhibition,
He was not pale like a tormented soul.
210 He liked a fat swan best, and roasted whole.
His palfrey[27] was as brown as is a berry.
　　There was a *Friar*, a wanton[28] one and merry
A Limiter,[29] a very festive fellow.
In all Four Orders[30] there was none so mellow,
215 So glib with gallant phrase and well-turned speech.
He'd fixed up many a marriage, giving each
Of his young women what he could afford her.
He was a noble pillar to his Order.
Highly beloved and intimate was he

---

26. Austin English version of St. Augustine, who criticized lazy monks.
27. palfrey *n.* saddle horse.
28. wanton *adj.* jolly.
29. Limiter friar who is given begging rights for a certain limited area.
30. Four Orders There were four orders of friars who supported themselves by begging: Dominicans, Franciscans, Carmelites, and Augustinians.

Enrichment: Investigating Career Connections

The Clergy

In the Middle Ages, some entered the clergy because they felt called to a life of devotion. However, this was not always the case. Because inheritance laws gave all land and titles to firstborn sons, other sons had to make their own fortunes. Generally, second sons became knights, while third sons went into the church. It was common for members of the clergy to be wealthy, because they came from noble families. It was also common for them to have only as much interest in religion as was necessary to get ahead. This situation resulted in many abuses

Activity: Investigate Careers Have students research the job of a clergyperson today. Suggest that they record information in the **Enrichment: Investigating Career Connections** worksheet, *Professional Development Guidebook,* page 221. Have them use the results of their research to compare the role of the clergy in the Middle Ages with the role of the clergy today.

220   With County folk[31] within his boundary,
     And city dames of honor and possessions;
     For he was qualified to hear confessions,
     Or so he said, with more than priestly scope;
     He had a special license from the Pope.
225   Sweetly he heard his penitents at shrift[32]
     With pleasant absolution, for a gift.
     He was an easy man in penance-giving
     Where he could hope to make a decent living;
     It's a sure sign whenever gifts are given
230   To a poor Order that a man's well shriven,[33]
     And should he give enough he knew in verity
     The penitent repented in sincerity.
     For many a fellow is so hard of heart
     He cannot weep, for all his inward smart.
235   Therefore instead of weeping and of prayer
     One should give silver for a poor Friar's care.
     He kept his tippet[34] stuffed with pins for curls,
     And pocket-knives, to give to pretty girls.
     And certainly his voice was gay and sturdy,
240   For he sang well and played the hurdy-gurdy.[35]
     At sing-songs he was champion of the hour.
     His neck was whiter than a lily-flower
     But strong enough to butt a bruiser down.
     He knew the taverns well in every town
245   And every innkeeper and barmaid too
     Better than lepers, beggars and that crew,
     For in so eminent a man as he
     It was not fitting with the dignity
     Of his position, dealing with a scum
250   Of wretched lepers; nothing good can come
     Of dealings with the slum-and-gutter dwellers,
     But only with the rich and victual-sellers.
     But anywhere a profit might accrue
     Courteous he was and lowly of service too.
255   Natural gifts like his were hard to match.
     He was the finest beggar of his batch,
     And, for his begging-district, payed a rent;
     His brethren did no poaching where he went.
     For though a widow mightn't have a shoe,
260   So pleasant was his holy how-d'ye-do
     He got his farthing from her just the same

---

31. **County folk** The phrase refers to rich landowners.
32. **shrift** *n.* confession.
33. **well shriven** *adj.* absolved of his sins.
34. **tippet** *n.* hood.
35. **hurdy-gurdy** stringed instrument played by cranking a wheel.

from The Canterbury Tales: The Prologue   **103**

---

17 Vocabulary
absolution (ab′ sə lōō′ shən)
n. act of freeing someone of a sin or of a criminal charge

Literary Analysis
Characterization
In lines 244–254, is Chaucer using direct characterization or indirect characterization? Explain.

19 Reading Check
How does the Friar earn his living?

---

17 Vocabulary
Latin Suffix *-tion*

1. Call students' attention to the word *absolution* and its definition. Explain that the suffix *-tion* is derived from Latin and means "the act or process of."

2. Have students **suggest** other words and phrases that contain this Latin suffix, and list them on the board.
Possible responses: solution, illustration, assignation, motivation, illumination.

3. Have students look up any unfamiliar words in a dictionary.

18 Literary Analysis
Characterization

1. Review with students the differences between indirect and direct characterization.

2. Then, **ask** students the Literary Analysis question: In lines 244–254, is Chaucer using direct characterization or indirect characterization? Explain.
Answer: Chaucer is using an indirect method of characterization: He describes who the Friar knew and where he spent his time.

19 Reading Check
Answer: The Friar earns his living by skillful begging.

Humanities

The Student, 1946,
by Arthur Szyk

In the miniature Szyk cleverly shows the Oxford Cleric's preference for intellectual attainment over worldly matters. His drab tunic and patched knees contrast with his intent expression as he reads his book. He absently gestures with his left hand as if in conversation with himself, unaware of the picture he presents to others. Although not as decorative as the other, more richly dressed characters illustrated by Szyk, the student is detailed with care and skill.

Use these questions for discussion:

1. Do you think Szyk's miniature captures the personality of the Oxford Cleric as Chaucer has portrayed him?
   Possible responses: Students will probably say that the miniature captures the Oxford Cleric's "unworldly," studious personality.

2. Does Szyk's student remind you of any young scholar you have ever seen?
   Answer: Students may be reminded of classmates or acquaintances whom they characterize as bookworms or nerds.

㉑ Critical Viewing

Possible responses: Students may conclude that the student likes to read and lives rather frugally. These characteristics are suggested by the following details: He is reading; his hose are patched at the knees; and he lacks the more luxurious purses, swords, and adornment seen in the pictures of the other pilgrims.

The Student, Arthur Szyk for *The Canterbury Tales*

㉑ ▼ Critical Viewing
What can you infer from this picture about the Oxford Cleric's style of living?
[Infer]

Before he left, and so his income came
To more than he laid out. And how he romped,
Just like a puppy! He was ever prompt
265 To arbitrate disputes on settling days
(For a small fee) in many helpful ways,
Not then appearing as your cloistered scholar
With threadbare habit hardly worth a dollar,
But much more like a Doctor or a Pope.
270 Of double-worsted was the semi-cope[36]
Upon his shoulders, and the swelling fold
About him, like a bell about its mold
When it is casting, rounded out his dress.
He lisped a little out of wantonness
275 To make his English sweet upon his tongue.
When he had played his harp, or having sung,
His eyes would twinkle in his head as bright
As any star upon a frosty night.
This worthy's name was Hubert, it appeared.
280   There was a *Merchant* with a forking beard
And motley dress, high on his horse he sat,
Upon his head a Flemish[37] beaver hat
And on his feet daintily buckled boots.
He told of his opinions and pursuits
285 In solemn tones, and how he never lost.
The sea should be kept free at any cost
(He thought) upon the Harwich-Holland range,[38]
He was expert at currency exchange.
This estimable Merchant so had set
290 His wits to work, none knew he was in debt,
He was so stately in negotiation,
Loan, bargain and commercial obligation.
He was an excellent fellow all the same;
To tell the truth I do not know his name.
295   An *Oxford Cleric*, still a student though,
One who had taken logic long ago,
Was there; his horse was thinner than a rake,
And he was not too fat, I undertake,
But had a hollow look, a sober stare;

---

36. semi-cope cape.
37. Flemish from Flanders.
38. Harwich-Holland range the North Sea between England and Holland.

Enrichment: Investigating Geography

Chaucer's Travels

Considering Chaucer's characters have traveled it is interesting to trace the advances and reversals of the author himself. In *The History of English Literature,* Peter Quennell reports the following:

Between 1370 and 1386, Chaucer undertook a variety of important diplomatic missions. Thus he made an official journey to Italy toward the end of 1372, when he visited Genoa, Pisa, and Florence, and remained for over ten months; in 1377 he was dispatched to Flanders and France; in 1378 he was returned to France and, soon afterward, set forth on another errand to Italy.

Activity: Investigate Geography Have students research Chaucer's travels. Suggest that they record information in the **Enrichment: Investigate Geography** worksheet, *Professional Development Guidebook,* page 228. Have them make a map of Chaucer's journeys.

300 The thread upon his overcoat was bare.
He had found no preferment in the church
And he was too unworldly to make search
For secular employment. By his bed
He preferred having twenty books in red
305 And black, of Aristotle's[39] philosophy,
To having fine clothes, fiddle or psaltery.[40]

22 Though a philosopher, as I have told,
He had not found the stone for making gold.[41]
Whatever money from his friends he took
310 He spent on learning or another book
And prayed for them most earnestly, returning
Thanks to them thus for paying for his learning.
His only care was study, and indeed
He never spoke a word more than was need,
315 Formal at that, respectful in the extreme,
Short, to the point, and lofty in his theme.
The thought of moral virtue filled his speech
And he would gladly learn, and gladly teach.

     A *Sergeant at the Law* who paid his calls,
320 Wary and wise, for clients at St. Paul's[42]
There also was, of noted excellence.
Discreet he was, a man to reverence,
Or so he seemed, his sayings were so wise.
He often had been Justice of Assize
325 By letters patent, and in full commission.
His fame and learning and his high position
Had won him many a robe and many a fee.
There was no such conveyancer[43] as he;
All was fee-simple[44] to his strong digestion,
330 Not one conveyance could be called in question.
Nowhere there was so busy a man as he;
But was less busy than he seemed to be.
He knew of every judgment, case and crime
Recorded, ever since King William's time.
335 He could dictate defenses or draft deeds;
No one could pinch a comma from his screeds,[45]

---

39. Aristotle's (ar´ is tät´ əlz) referring to the Greek philosopher (384–322 B.C.).
40. psaltery (sôl´ tər ē) ancient stringed instrument.
41. stone : . . gold At the time, alchemists believed that a "philosopher's stone" existed that could turn base metals into gold.
42. St. Paul's London cathedral near the center of legal activities in the city. Lawyers often met near there to discuss cases.
43. conveyancer one who draws up documents for transferring ownership of property.
44. fee-simple unrestricted ownership.
45. screeds long, boring speeches or pieces of writing.

105

Reading Strategy

Questioning

1. Tell students to check the foot-notes regularly and to think about what the information provided adds to the descriptions.

2. Remind students that, as with most poetry, a line end does not mean the end of a sentence. Encourage students to be guided by punctuation, rather than by line breaks, as they read.

3. **Ask** students the Reading Strategy question: What question do lines 346–348 answer about the main idea in line 345?
Possible response: The lines answer the question *why*, revealing why the Franklin lived for pleasure.

25 Literary Analysis

Characterization

1. Tell students that the word *frank-lin* comes from a Middle English word, *frankelein*, which means free man.

2. Explain that, in Chaucer's day, the social position of franklin was a relatively new one. The middle class was just emerging. During most of the Middle Ages, a free landowner who was not part of the nobility simply did not exist.

3. **Ask** students the Literary Analysis question: What are the Franklin's interests?
Possible response: He loves food and drink. He loves to enter-tain and has a reputation for hospitality. He is also involved in community affairs.

4. You may wish to **discuss** with students why someone like the Franklin, might have the interests the Franklin has.
Possible response: It seems natural that people who had been locked out of both govern-ment and the possibility of wealth and landownership would eagerly exercise these options once they were free to do so.

Vocabulary
sanguine (saṇ´ gwin) *adj.*
confident; cheerful

Reading Strategy
Questioning What question do lines 346–348 answer about the main idea in line 345?

Literary Analysis
Characterization
What are the Franklin's interests?

And he knew every statute off by rote.
He wore a homely parti-colored coat
Girt with a silken belt of pin-stripe stuff;
340   Of his appearance I have said enough.
         There was a *Franklin*[46] with him, it appeared;
White as a daisy-petal was his beard.
A sanguine man, high-colored and benign,
He loved a morning sop[47] of cake in wine.
345   He lived for pleasure and had always done,
For he was Epicurus[48] very son,
In whose opinion sensual delight
Was the one true felicity in sight.
As noted as St. Julian[49] was for bounty
350   He made his household free to all the County.
His bread, his ale were the finest of the fine
And no one had a better stock of wine.
His house was never short of bake-meat pies,
Of fish and flesh, and these in such supplies
355   It positively snowed with meat and drink
And all the dainties that a man could think.
According to the seasons of the year
Changes of dish were ordered to appear.
He kept fat partridges in coops, beyond,
360   Many a bream and pike were in his pond.
Woe to the cook whose sauces had no sting
Or who was unprepared in anything!
And in his hall a table stood arrayed
And ready all day long, with places laid.
365   As Justice at the Sessions[50] none stood higher;
He often had been Member for the Shire.[51]
A dagger and a little purse of silk
Hung at his girdle, white as morning milk.
As Sheriff he checked audit, every entry.
370   He was a model among landed gentry.
         A *Haberdasher*, a *Dyer*, a *Carpenter*,
A *Weaver* and a *Carpet-maker* were
Among our ranks, all in the livery
Of one impressive guild-fraternity.[52]

---

46. *Franklin* wealthy landowner.
47. **sop** piece.
48. **Epicurus'** (ep´ i kyoor´ əs) referring to a Greek philosopher (341–270 B.C.) who believed that happiness is the most important goal in life.
49. **St. Julian** patron saint of hospitality.
50. **Sessions** court sessions.
51. **Member . . . Shire** Parliamentary representative for the county.
52.
     guild-fraternity In the Middle Ages, associations of men practicing the same craft or trade, called guilds, set standards for workmanship and protected their members by controlling competition.

106 From Legend to History (A.D. 449–1485)

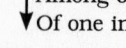
Think Aloud

Vocabulary: Using Context
Direct students' attention to the word *felicity* in line 348. Use the following "think aloud" to model the skill of using context to infer the meaning of the word. Say to students:

I may not know the meaning of the word *felicity*. When I read the sentence, however, I realize that the writer is using *felicity* when he describes how Epicurus felt about life— "that sensual delight was the one true felic-ity in sight"—and he describes the Franklin as Epicurus' son. If I go back to the begin-ning of the sentence, it says that "He lived for pleasure and had always done." I infer that the Franklin lives for pleasure because it makes him happy. So I can infer that *felicity* means happiness.

They were so trim and fresh their gear would pass
For new. Their knives were not tricked out with brass
But wrought with purest silver, which avouches
A like display on girdles and on pouches.
Each seemed a worthy burgess,[53] fit to grace
A guild-hall with a seat upon the dais.
Their wisdom would have justified a plan
To make each one of them an alderman;
They had the capital and revenue,
Besides their wives declared it was their due.
And if they did not think so, then they ought;
To be called "*Madam*" is a glorious thought,
And so is going to church and being seen
Having your mantle carried like a queen.
        They had a *Cook* with them who stood alone
For boiling chicken with a marrow-bone,
Sharp flavoring-powder and a spice for savor.
He could distinguish London ale by flavor,
And he could roast and seethe and broil and fry,
Make good thick soup and bake a tasty pie.
But what a pity—so it seemed to me,
That he should have an ulcer on his knee.
As for blancmange,[54] he made it with the best.
        There was a *Skipper* hailing from far west;
He came from Dartmouth, so I understood.
He rode a farmer's horse as best he could,
In a woolen gown that reached his knee.
A dagger on a lanyard[55] falling free
Hung from his neck under his arm and down.
The summer heat had tanned his color brown,
And certainly he was an excellent fellow.
Many a draught of vintage, red and yellow,
He'd drawn at Bordeaux, while the trader snored.
The nicer rules of conscience he ignored.
If, when he fought, the enemy vessel sank,
He sent his prisoners home; they walked the plank.
As for his skill in reckoning his tides,
Currents and many another risk besides,
Moons, harbors, pilots, he had such dispatch
That none from Hull to Carthage was his match.
Hardy he was, prudent in undertaking;
His beard in many a tempest had its shaking,
And he knew all the havens as they were
From Gottland to the Cape of Finisterre,

Line numbers:
375, 380, 385, 390, 395, 400, 405, 410, 415

26 Literary Analysis

27 Literary Analysis

---

53. **burgess** member of a legislative body.
54. **blancmange** (blə mänzh´) at the time, the name of a creamy chicken dish.
55. **lanyard** loose rope around the neck.

from The Canterbury Tales: The Prologue **107**

Literary Analysis
Characterization and
Social Commentary
What point is Chaucer
making about the
relationship between these
men and their wives?

Literary Analysis
Characterization
What picture of the
Skipper is created by the
mixture of details about his
heartlessness with details
about his competence?

28 Reading Check
What are two characteristics
of the Skipper?

26 **Literary Analysis**

Characterization and Social Commentary

1. Point out that this group of successful, skilled workers would be part of the new, middle class, perhaps even achieving, the status of upper class.

2. **Ask** students the first Literary Analysis question: What point is Chaucer making about the relationship between these men and their wives?
Possible response: It seems that their wives are eager social climbers who urge their husbands to run for office. The fact that the men are stylishly dressed shows that they either agree with their wives or are motivated by their wives' wishes.

27 **Literary Analysis**

Characterization

1. **Ask** students what they can infer from line 400.
Answer: The Skipper rides badly, because he lives at sea.

2. Point out that the places named in Chaucer's description were as far as anyone was sailing in those days, and suggest the Skipper's considerable experience.

3. **Ask** students the second Literary Analysis question.
Possible response: He is ruthless with enemies but is very competent. He is able to withstand hardship and is a careful, judicious planner.

4. Point out that the name of his barge, *The Maudelayne,* is the word from which we get *maudlin,* which means "weepy sentimentality" or "tearful and silly due to drunkenness." Discuss with students why Chaucer chose this name.
Possible responses: Irony, because the Skipper seems unsentimental.

28 **Reading Check**

Answer: The Skipper is a skilled navigator but is ruthless in dealing with enemies.

Differentiated
Instruction   **for Universal Access**

EL **Pronunciation for English Learners**
Native speakers of some languages have difficulty producing the nasal *n* sound that appears at the end of words such as *being* (line 387), *having* (line 388), and *boiling* (line 390). Students may "drop the final *g*," resulting in pronunciations such as *bein'* and *havin'*.
    To give students practice with this sound, model the pronunciation of several words that contain it. Have students repeat each word after you. Then, to isolate the sound, write the following word pairs on the board: *ton* and *tongue, thin* and *thing, run* and *rung.* Practice pronouncing each pair with students.

Point out to students that the nasal *n* sound often appears when verbs take on their *-ing* form. Give some examples, and then have students find examples on the page (*flavoring:* line 391; *hailing:* line 398; *falling:* line 402; *reckoning:* line 411; *undertaking:* line 415; *shaking:* line 416).

Questioning

1. Explain that *astronomy* in line 424 really means *astrology* in this context. Astronomy is the scientific study of the universe; astrology is the divination of the supposed influence of the stars on human events.

2. Tell students that people didn't know about germs until the nineteenth century. Point out the footnote about humors, and explain that some of the ways in which humors were "balanced" were through purging or bleeding patients.

3. Explain that an effigy (line 428) was usually a human figure, and **ask** students why they think an effigy might have been used to "treat" a disease.
   Possible responses: Students may be reminded of voodoo, where pins are stuck in a doll to hurt the person the doll represents. This would be the reverse, using the doll to heal the person represented. They may also be aware of the practice of burning enemies in effigy.

4. Students may be interested to know that the line (448) about not reading the Bible very much probably has two applications for this character: the Bible has clear instruction about washing before and after caring for the sick, which would relate to his medical practice, and the Bible also states that "the love of money is the root of all kinds of evil," which would connect to line 454 .

5. To help students learn more about the Doctor's practices, **ask** them the Reading Strategy question.
   Answer: The Doctor watches people's stars (rather than their illnesses) and makes charms and magic images based on "lucky hours," rather than on any diagnosis of disease.

Reading Strategy
Questioning In the sentence in lines 421–428, what is said about *how* the Doctor practices medicine?

27
420 And every creek in Brittany and Spain;
The barge he owned was called *The Maudelayne.*
    A *Doctor* too emerged as we proceeded;
No one alive could talk as well as he did
On points of medicine and of surgery,
29
425 For, being grounded in astronomy,
He watched his patient's favorable star
And, by his Natural Magic, knew what are
The lucky hours and planetary degrees
For making charms and magic effigies.
The cause of every malady you'd got
430 He knew, and whether dry, cold, moist or hot;[56]
He knew their seat, their humor and condition.
He was a perfect practicing physician.
These causes being known for what they were,
He gave the man his medicine then and there.
435 All his apothecaries[57] in a tribe
Were ready with the drugs he would prescribe,
And each made money from the other's guile;
They had been friendly for a goodish while.
He was well-versed in Aesculapius[58] too
440 And what Hippocrates and Rufus knew
And Dioscorides, now dead and gone,
Galen and Rhazes, Hali, Serapion,
Averroes, Avicenna, Constantine,
Scotch Bernard, John of Gaddesden, Gilbertine.[59]
445 In his own diet he observed some measure;
There were no superfluities for pleasure,
Only digestives, nutritives and such.
He did not read the Bible very much.
In blood-red garments, slashed with bluish-gray
450 And lined with taffeta,[60] he rode his way;
Yet he was rather close as to expenses
And kept the gold he won in pestilences.
Gold stimulates the heart, or so we're told.
He therefore had a special love of gold.
455   A worthy *woman* from beside Bath[61] city
Was with us, somewhat deaf, which was a pity.
In making cloth she showed so great a bent

56. **The cause . . . hot** It was believed that the body was composed of four "humors" (cold and dry, hot and moist, hot and dry, cold and moist) and that diseases resulted from a disturbance of one of these "humors."
57. **apothecaries** (ə päth′ə ker′ ēz) persons who prepared medicines.
58. **Aesculapius** (es′ kyoo lā′ pē əs) in Roman mythology, the god of medicine and healing.
59. **Hippocrates . . . Gilbertine** famous physicians and medical authorities.
60. **taffeta** (taf′ i tə) fine silk fabric.
61. **Bath** English resort city.

Enrichment: Investigating Health and Medicine

Plague

Plague is primarily a disease of rats and the fleas that feed upon them. There are three forms of plague in humans: bubonic, pneumonic, and septicemic. Bubonic plague is characterized by swellings (buboes) of the lymph nodes and is transmitted from person to person by fleas. Pneumonic plague is a severe infection of the lungs that can be transmitted directly from one person to another. Because of the way plague is transmitted, the most severe epidemics have occurred in crowded, urban areas where people live close to rats—such as medieval cities.

Activity: Investigate Health and Medicine
Have students research treatments for plague. Suggest that they record information in the **Enrichment: Investigate Health and Medicine** worksheet, *Professional Development Guidebook*, page 229. Have them use their research to write an essay comparing and contrasting the treatment of plague in medieval times with its treatment today.

She bettered those of Ypres and of Ghent.[62]
In all the parish not a dame dared stir
460 Towards the altar steps in front of her,
And if indeed they did, so wrath was she
As to be quite put out of charity.
Her kerchiefs were of finely woven ground;[63]
I dared have sworn they weighed a good ten pound,
465 The ones she wore on Sunday, on her head.
Her hose were of the finest scarlet red
And gartered tight; her shoes were soft and new.
Bold was her face, handsome, and red in hue.
A worthy woman all her life, what's more
470 She'd had five husbands, all at the church door,
Apart from other company in youth;
No need just now to speak of that, forsooth.
And she had thrice been to Jerusalem,
Seen many strange rivers and passed over them;
475 She'd been to Rome and also to Boulogne,
St. James of Compostella and Cologne,[64]
And she was skilled in wandering by the way.
She had gap-teeth, set widely, truth to say.
Easily on an ambling horse she sat
480 Well wimpled[65] up, and on her head a hat
As broad as is a buckler[66] or a shield;
She had a flowing mantle that concealed
Large hips, her heels spurred sharply under that.
In company she liked to laugh and chat
485 And knew the remedies for love's mischances,
An art in which she knew the oldest dances.

    A holy-minded man of good renown
There was, and poor, the *Parson* to a town,
Yet he was rich in holy thought and work.
490 He also was a learned man, a clerk,
Who truly knew Christ's gospel and would preach it
Devoutly to parishioners, and teach it.
Benign and wonderfully diligent,
And patient when adversity was sent
495 (For so he proved in great adversity)
He much disliked extorting tithe[67] or fee,
Nay rather he preferred beyond a doubt
Giving to poor parishioners round about

---

62. Ypres (ē′ prə) **and of Ghent** (gent) Flemish cities known for wool making.
63. ground composite fabric.
64. Jerusalem . . . Rome . . . Boulogne . . . St. James of Compostella . . . Cologne famous pilgrimage sites at the time.
65. wimpled wearing a scarf covering the head, neck, and chin.
66. buckler small round shield.
67. tithe (tīth) one tenth of a person's income, paid as a tax to support the church.

from The Canterbury Tales: The Prologue **109**

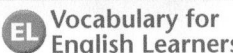

The Wife of Bath, Arthur Szyk for The Canterbury Tales

31 ▼ **Critical Viewing**
What does the Wife of Bath's pose convey about her character?
[Analyze]

30

32 Reading Check
What is the Parson's main characteristic?

30 **Humanities**

***The Wife of Bath,* 1946,** by Arthur Szyk

In this miniature, the artist shows the good Wife of Bath to be an imposing and decorative figure. The provocative posture and bold eyes are in keeping with Chaucer's description of her. The tiny details of dress, such as the gold buttons and the heart pattern on her belt, show the extreme skill of the artist. When discussing this painting with your class, point out similarities between Szyk's portrait of the Wife of Bath and Chaucer's written account of her.

Use these questions for discussion:

1. What impression of the Wife's personality does the painting express? **Possible response:** She is bold, saucy, and outspoken.

2. What does Chaucer's description of her convey that the painting does not? **Possible response:** Students may point out physical details that the artist chose not to include, such as her wimple or gap-teeth. Chaucer's description also includes details that cannot be shown in the portrait, such as her skill at cloth making, and her anger when others do not defer to her.

31 **Critical Viewing**

Possible response: Students may say that the Wife's self-assured, bold stance suggests confidence, independence, and even superiority to others on the journey. Her cane, gold buttons, and fur-trimmed attire imply a degree of wealth.

32 **Reading Check**

Answer: The Parson's main characteristic is that he lives out what he professes to believe.

Differentiated Instruction for Universal Access

Strategy for Less Proficient Readers
Help students break down the sentence in lines 421–428 into individual clauses. Then have them paraphrase the meaning of each clause. Help them discover the meanings of words that may be unfamiliar, such as *effigies* or *planetary degrees.* The first clause might be paraphrased, "It turned out that one member of our group was a doctor." Guide them through the paraphrasing of the rest of this long sentence.

EL **Vocabulary for English Learners**
It is important that students be aware of the words they need to know in order to understand the story, and be guided away from worrying about words that do not affect the meaning of the narrative. For example, they will need to know what *mischances* means in order to know what is being said about the Wife of Bath, but they do not need to translate Compostella and Cologne. Discuss each character, pointing out key words and phrases that describe the individual.

Characterization and Social Commentary

1. Encourage students to list specific things that Chaucer identifies as either actions or traits of the Parson.

2. You may want to discuss in class which of these traits have already been shown to be lacking in other members of the clergy in the group. For example, the Parson gives to the poor, while the Friar was described as taking the farthing from the poor widow (lines 259–263).

3. **Ask** students the Literary Analysis question: How does Chaucer use his characterization of the Parson to comment on the way priests ought to behave?
   Answer: He shows that the Parson not only knows well what he says he believes, he also lives out his beliefs. He leads by example. Most of the virtues he exhibits are in direct contrast to traits of others in the group, from the hypocrisy of the clergy to the vanity and greed of the merchants to the ruthlessness of the Skipper.

4. Because Chaucer says that the Parson is "an example to his sheep," what can we assume that Chaucer feels about how others ought to behave, even if they are not in the clergy? **Answer:** It is evident that Chaucer feels that others should share the traits of integrity, kindness, and generosity exhibited by the Parson.

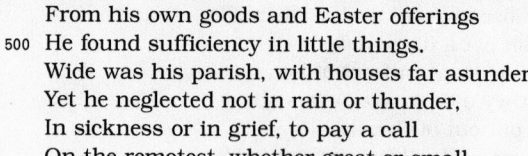

Literary Analysis
Characterization and Social Commentary
How does Chaucer use his characterization of the Parson to comment on the way priests ought to behave?

33

From his own goods and Easter offerings
500 He found sufficiency in little things.
Wide was his parish, with houses far asunder,
Yet he neglected not in rain or thunder,
In sickness or in grief, to pay a call
On the remotest, whether great or small,
505 Upon his feet, and in his hand a stave.
This noble example to his sheep he gave,
First following the word before he taught it,
And it was from the gospel he had caught it.
This little proverb he would add thereto
510 That if gold rust, what then will iron do?
For if a priest be foul in whom we trust
No wonder that a common man should rust;
And shame it is to see—let priests take stock—
A soiled shepherd and a snowy flock.
515 The true example that a priest should give
Is one of cleanness, how the sheep should live.
He did not set his benefice to hire[68]
And leave his sheep encumbered in the mire
Or run to London to earn easy bread
520 By singing masses for the wealthy dead,
Or find some Brotherhood and get enrolled.
He stayed at home and watched over his fold
So that no wolf should make the sheep miscarry.
He was a shepherd and no mercenary.
525 Holy and virtuous he was, but then
Never contemptuous of sinful men,
Never disdainful, never too proud or fine,
But was discreet in teaching and benign.
His business was to show a fair behavior
530 And draw men thus to Heaven and their Savior,
Unless indeed a man were obstinate;
And such, whether of high or low estate,
He put to sharp rebuke to say the least.
I think there never was a better priest.
535 He sought no pomp or glory in his dealings,
No scrupulosity had spiced his feelings.
Christ and His Twelve Apostles and their lore
He taught, but followed it himself before.
       There was a *Plowman* with him there, his brother.
540 Many a load of dung one time or other
He must have carted through the morning dew.
He was an honest worker, good and true,

---

68. **set . . . hire** pay someone else to perform his parish duties.

110 From Legend to History (A.D. 449–1485)

Enrichment: Investigating a Key Person in History

Thomas à Becket

The murder of Thomas à Becket is a well-known event in English history. Thomas was Archbishop of Canterbury and Chancellor of England. Thomas and the King became engaged in a bitter quarrel over the right of the courts to try members of the clergy. On December 29, 1170, the King's knights killed the archbishop in his cathedral at Canterbury. Thomas was canonized in 1173, and the pope took the unusual step of forcing Henry to do public penance. Historians dispute whether Henry gave orders for the assassination.

Activity: Investigating a Key Person in History Have students choose either Thomas à Becket or Henry II to research. Suggest that they record information in the **Enrichment: Investigating a Key Person in History** worksheet, *Professional Development Guidebook*, page 233. Divide the class into two groups and have half research Becket, while half research Henry II. Organize Becket/Henry II pairs, and have each pair present their research to each other.

Living in peace and perfect charity,
And, as the gospel bade him, so did he,
545 Loving God best with all his heart and mind
And then his neighbor as himself, repined
At no misfortune, slacked for no content,
For steadily about his work he went
To thrash his corn, to dig or to manure
550 Or make a ditch; and he would help the poor
For love of Christ and never take a penny
If he could help it, and, as prompt as any,
He paid his tithes in full when they were due
On what he owned, and on his earnings too.
555 He wore a tabard[69] smock and rode a mare.
There was a *Reeve*,[70] also a *Miller*, there,
A College *Manciple*[71] from the Inns of Court,
A papal *Pardoner*[72] and, in close consort,
A Church-Court *Summoner*,[73] riding at a trot,
560 And finally myself—that was the lot.
       The *Miller* was a chap of sixteen stone,[74]
A great stout fellow big in brawn and bone.
He did well out of them, for he could go
And win the ram at any wrestling show.
565 Broad, knotty and short-shouldered, he would boast
He could heave any door off hinge and post,
Or take a run and break it with his head.
His beard, like any sow or fox, was red
And broad as well, as though it were a spade;
570 And, at its very tip, his nose displayed
A wart on which there stood a tuft of hair,
Red as the bristles in an old sow's ear.
His nostrils were as black as they were wide.
He had a sword and buckler at his side,
575 His mighty mouth was like a furnace door.
A wrangler and buffoon, he had a store
Of tavern stories, filthy in the main.
His was a master-hand at stealing grain.
He felt it with his thumb and thus he knew
580 Its quality and took three times his due—
A thumb of gold, by God, to gauge an oat!
He wore a hood of blue and a white coat.
He liked to play his bagpipes up and down
And that was how he brought us out of town.

---

69. **tabard** loose jacket.
70. *Reeve* estate manager.
71. *Manciple* buyer of provisions.
72. *Pardoner* one who dispenses papal pardons.
73. *Summoner* one who serves summonses to church courts.
74. **sixteen stone** 224 pounds. A stone equals 14 pounds.

34

 **35** ▲ **Critical Viewing**
Compare this portrait of the Miller with lines 561–584. What details did the illustrator choose to change or omit? **[Compare and Contrast]**

36 Reading Check
What is the Plowman like?

from The Canterbury Tales: The Prologue **111**

Questioning

Ask the Reading Strategy question: What are the two subjects of the comparison in lines 594–604?

Answer: The two subjects of comparison are the Manciple and his masters.

38 **Literary Analysis**

Characterization

1. Remind students that in medieval times, a reeve was a steward responsible for running the everyday affairs of a feudal manor.

2. Have a volunteer read lines 605–610 aloud.

3. Have another volunteer read lines 615–624.

4. Then **ask** students how the Reeve's physical appearance contrasts with the way others viewed him.
   Possible response: The Reeve was old and thin; his legs were like sticks. He probably was frail-looking. Yet line 624 says he was feared like the plague by those beneath him. This indicates that he knew what he was doing and that people knew they could not get away with trying to trick him.

Reading Strategy
Questioning What are the two subjects of the comparison in lines 594–604?

585 The *Manciple* came from the Inner Temple;
    All caterers might follow his example
    In buying victuals; he was never rash
    Whether he bought on credit or paid cash.
    He used to watch the market most precisely
590 And go in first, and so he did quite nicely.
    Now isn't it a marvel of God's grace
    That an illiterate fellow can outpace
    The wisdom of a heap of learned men?
    His masters—he had more than thirty then—
595 All versed in the abstrusest legal knowledge,
37 Could have produced a dozen from their College
    Fit to be stewards in land and rents and game
    To any Peer in England you could name,
    And show him how to live on what he had
600 Debt-free (unless of course the Peer were mad)
    Or be as frugal as he might desire,
    And they were fit to help about the Shire
    In any legal case there was to try;
    And yet this Manciple could wipe their eye.
605   The *Reeve* was old and choleric and thin;
    His beard was shaven closely to the skin,
    His shorn hair came abruptly to a stop
    Above his ears, and he was docked on top
    Just like a priest in front; his legs were lean,
610 Like sticks they were, no calf was to be seen.
    He kept his bins and garners[75] very trim;
    No auditor could gain a point on him.
38 And he could judge by watching drought and rain
    The yield he might expect from seed and grain.
615 His master's sheep, his animals and hens,
    Pigs, horses, dairies, stores and cattle-pens
    Were wholly trusted to his government.
    And he was under contract to present
    The accounts, right from his master's earliest years.
620 No one had ever caught him in arrears.
    No bailiff, serf or herdsman dared to kick,
    He knew their dodges, knew their every trick;
    Feared like the plague he was, by those beneath.
    He had a lovely dwelling on a heath,
625 Shadowed in green by trees above the sward.[76]
    A better hand at bargains than his lord,
    He had grown rich and had a store of treasure
    Well tucked away, yet out it came to pleasure

---

75. **garners** *n.* buildings for storing grain.
76. **sward** *n.* turf.

Enrichment: Analyzing a Historical Event

Local Historic Site

Point out that the pilgrims set out to visit the site of an important event in their religious and civic history. Perhaps there are places in your area that people come to visit because of a well-known event that occurred there. Tell students that it does not have to be an event that changed history on a large scale. It might be something known primarily to people in the area.

Activity: Analyzing a Historical Event Have interested students conduct research on the historic site. What happened at the site? What were its effects? Why is the site significant? Why do people visit the site? Suggest that they record information on the **Enrichment: Analyzing a Historical Event** worksheet, *Professional Development Guidebook,* page 230.

His lord with subtle loans or gifts of goods,
630 To earn his thanks and even coats and hoods.
When young he'd learnt a useful trade and still
He was a carpenter of first-rate skill.
The stallion-cob he rode at a slow trot
Was dapple-gray and bore the name of Scot.
635 He wore an overcoat of bluish shade
And rather long; he had a rusty blade
Slung at his side. He came, as I heard tell,
From Norfolk, near a place called Baldeswell.
His coat was tucked under his belt and splayed.
640 He rode the hindmost of our cavalcade.
       There was a *Summoner* with us in the place
Who had a fire-red cherubinnish face,[77]
For he had carbuncles.[78] His eyes were narrow,
He was as hot and lecherous as a sparrow.
645 Black, scabby brows he had, and a thin beard.
Children were afraid when he appeared.
No quicksilver, lead ointments, tartar creams,
Boracic, no, nor brimstone,[79] so it seems,
Could make a salve that had the power to bite,
650 Clean up or cure his whelks[80] of knobby white.
Or purge the pimples sitting on his cheeks.
Garlic he loved, and onions too, and leeks,
And drinking strong wine till all was hazy.
Then he would shout and jabber as if crazy,
655 And wouldn't speak a word except in Latin
When he was drunk, such tags as he was pat in;
He only had a few, say two or three,
That he had mugged up out of some decree;
No wonder, for he heard them every day.
660 And, as you know, a man can teach a jay
To call out "Walter" better than the Pope.
But had you tried to test his wits and grope
For more, you'd have found nothing in the bag.
Then "*Questio quid juris*"[81] was his tag.
665 He was a gentle varlet and a kind one,
No better fellow if you went to find one.
He would allow—just for a quart of wine—

---

77. **fire-red . . . face** In the art of the Middle Ages, the faces of cherubs, or angels, were often painted red.
78. **carbuncles** (kär′ buŋ′ kəlz) *n.* pus-filled boils resulting from a bacterial infection under the skin.
79. **quicksilver . . . brimstone** various chemicals and chemical compounds, used as remedies. *Quicksilver* is a name for mercury. *Brimstone* is a name for sulfur.
80. **whelks** *n.* pustules; pimples.
81. **"*Questio quid juris*"** "The question is, What is the point of law?" (Latin).

from The Canterbury Tales: The Prologue 113

➌➒

➍➓ ▲ Critical Viewing
What can you infer from this picture about the Summoner's personality? List three details supporting your conclusion. **[Infer]**

➍➊ ☑ Reading Check

How do serfs and herdsmen view the Reeve?

➌➒ Humanities

The Summoner, 1946,
by Arthur Szyk

Arthur Szyk's finely detailed miniature of the Summoner matches closely with Chaucer's description. Medieval artists painted the faces of cherubs red. However, the red cheeks of the Summoner are more satanic than cherubic. His appearance gives evidence of his many vices.

Use this question for discussion:
  How would you describe the appearance of the Summoner?
  Possible response: Students may say that his appearance is repulsive, disgusting, or gross.

➍➓ Critical Viewing

Answer: Answers may vary. The Summoner is wearing a medallion and head wreath, which suggest he is lavish, he is frowning and seems sullen; and, like most of the pilgrims, he is carrying weapons.

➍➊ Reading Check

Answer: Serfs and herdsmen fear the Reeve as if he was the Plague.

Differentiated Instruction for Universal Access

EL Pronunciation for English Learners
English Learners may have difficulty recognizing and pronouncing the short *i* in words such as *thin, still, it, quicksilver,* and *brimstone*. For these students, begin with the one-syllable word *still*. Write this word on the board, along with *steel*. Pronounce each word as you point to it, having students echo you. Then say each word and have students write down which one you said. When students have mastered this exercise, introduce the words *quicksilver* and *brimstone*, writing them on the board and having students pronounce them after you.

42 Humanities

The Pardoner, 1946,
by Arthur Szyk

The Pardoner's stringy yellow hair and wallet bulging with relics are straight out of Chaucer. The sanctimonious expression and gesture of forgiveness are from the imagination of Arthur Szyk. The miniature is finely detailed and painted in subtle, glowing colors. In discussing Szyk's miniatures with your students, you may wish to mention that the costumes portrayed are close in style to those actually worn in England in Chaucer's time.

Use these questions for discussion:

1. Does the Pardoner look trustworthy?
   Possible responses: Some students may say he looks sneaky. Others may say that he looks like a respectable, highly religious person, which is why he is able to fool country parsons and their congregations.

2. What is the effect of the cross he carries and the crosses on his wallet and satchel?
   Possible responses: Students may say that these enhance the Pardoner's illusion of holiness. Others may say that the number of religious symbols is suspiciously overdone.

43 Critical Viewing

Possible responses: Students may say that the picture matches Chaucer's description quite well. The Pardoner has stringy blond hair, lacks a beard, and has a relic or pilgrim's medal attached to his cap.

42

▲ **Critical Viewing 43**
How well does this picture of the Pardoner match Chaucer's description of him in lines 695–710? **[Assess]**

Any good lad to keep a concubine
A twelvemonth and dispense it altogether!
670 Yet he could pluck a finch to leave no feather:
And if he found some rascal with a maid
He would instruct him not to be afraid
In such a case of the Archdeacon's curse
(Unless the rascal's soul were in his purse)
675 For in his purse the punishment should be.
"Purse is the good Archdeacon's Hell," said he.
But well I know he lied in what he said;
A curse should put a guilty man in dread,
For curses kill, as shriving brings, salvation.
680 We should beware of excommunication.
Thus, as he pleased, the man could bring duress
On any young fellow in the diocese.
He knew their secrets, they did what he said.
He wore a garland set upon his head
685 Large as the holly-bush upon a stake
Outside an ale-house, and he had a cake,
A round one, which it was his joke to wield
As if it were intended for a shield.
       He and a gentle *Pardoner* rode together,
690 A bird from Charing Cross of the same feather,
Just back from visiting the Court of Rome.
He loudly sang *"Come hither, love, come home!"*
The Summoner sang deep seconds to this song,
No trumpet ever sounded half so strong.
695 This Pardoner had hair as yellow as wax,
Hanging down smoothly like a hank of flax.
In driblets fell his locks behind his head
Down to his shoulder which they overspread;
Thinly they fell, like rat-tails, one by one.
700 He wore no hood upon his head, for fun;
The hood inside his wallet had been stowed,
He aimed at riding in the latest mode;
But for a little cap his head was bare
And he had bulging eyeballs, like a hare.
705 He'd sewed a holy relic on his cap;
His wallet lay before him on his lap,
Brimful of pardons come from Rome all hot.
He had the same small voice a goat has got.
His chin no beard had harbored, nor would harbor,
710 Smoother than ever chin was left by barber.
I judge he was a gelding, or a mare.

114 From Legend to History (A.D. 449–1485)

Think Aloud

Vocabulary: Using Context
Direct students' attention to the word *gelding* in line 711. Use the following "think aloud" to model the skill of using context to infer the meaning of the word. Say to students:

> I may not know the meaning of the word *gelding.* When I read the sentence, however, I realize that Chaucer is using *gelding* to describe the Pardoner. In the same sentence, the writer follows that word with "or a mare." I know that a mare is a female horse. If I go back and reread the previous three lines, I see that the Pardoner is described as having a small voice, like a goat. Chaucer goes on to say that his chin was smooth, never having had a beard. When Chaucer compares the Pardoner to a gelding or a mare, I think that he must be trying to say that the Pardoner, although he is a man, seems very feminine. So I infer that a *gelding* is a horse that is male, but doesn't act like one.

114

As to his trade, from Berwick down to Ware
There was no pardoner of equal grace,
For in his trunk he had a pillowcase
715 Which he asserted was Our Lady's veil.
He said he had a gobbet[82] of the sail
Saint Peter had the time when he made bold
To walk the waves, till Jesu Christ took hold.
He had a cross of metal set with stones
720 And, in a glass, a rubble of pigs' bones.
And with these relics, any time he found
Some poor up-country parson to astound,
On one short day, in money down, he drew
More than the parson in a month or two,
725 And by his flatteries and prevarication
Made monkeys of the priest and congregation.
But still to do him justice first and last
In church he was a noble ecclesiast.
How well he read a lesson or told a story!
730 But best of all he sang an Offertory,[83]
For well he knew that when that song was sung
He'd have to preach and tune his honey-tongue
And (well he could) win silver from the crowd.
That's why he sang so merrily and loud.
735   Now I have told you shortly, in a clause,
The rank, the array, the number and the cause
Of our assembly in this company
In Southwark, at that high-class hostelry
Known as *The Tabard*, close beside *The Bell*.
740 And now the time has come for me to tell
How we behaved that evening; I'll begin
After we had alighted at the inn,
Then I'll report our journey, stage by stage,
All the remainder of our pilgrimage.
745 But first I beg of you, in courtesy,
Not to condemn me as unmannerly
If I speak plainly and with no concealings
And give account of all their words and dealings,
Using their very phrases as they fell.
750 For certainly, as you all know so well,
He who repeats a tale after a man

---

82. **gobbet** piece.
83. **Offertory** song that accompanies the collection of the offering at a church service.

from The Canterbury Tales: The Prologue **115**

44 **Literary Analysis**
Characterization
What facts in lines 719–726 indirectly characterize the Pardoner?

Vocabulary
prevarication (pri var′ i kā′ shən) *n.* evasion of truth

45 **Reading Strategy**
Questioning Why does Chaucer apologize in the sentence starting with line 745?

46  **Reading Check**
What two things does Chaucer promise to tell the reader?

44 **Literary Analysis**
Characterization

1. Remind students that indirect characterization uses details to suggest a character's personality, whereas direct characterization specifically describes a character's personality.
2. Then, **ask** students the Literary Analysis question: What facts in lines 719–726 indirectly characterize the Pardoner?
   Answer: The facts of the Pardoner's tricking "poor up-country" folks and making "monkeys of the priest and congregation" indirectly characterize him as a dishonest person.

45 **Reading Strategy**
Questioning

1. Remind students to ask questions of the passage to help them break down difficult sentences.
2. Then, **ask** students the Reading Strategy question: Why does Chaucer apologize in the sentence starting with line 745?
   Answer: He apologizes because he is going to report matters frankly, without euphemisms.

46 **Reading Check**
Answer: Chaucer promises to report the journey, stage by stage, and to give an account of all their words and dealings, concealing nothing.

Differentiated Instruction for Universal Access

EL **Pronunciation for English Learners**
English learners may have difficulty perceiving and pronouncing the initial *w* sound in words such as *walk, waves, well, win, when*, and *with*. Write these words on the board and pro

nounce each word as you point to it, having students echo you. Repeat until students are properly pronouncing the initial *w* sound.

115

The Literature of Social Observation

Students should think about works they have read that involve extensive social observation. Explain that not all works of social observation are critical of society, but many of them are. Students may want to look at the cartoons in local newspapers, many of which are well known for their social commentary and observation. Have them consider in what ways Chaucer's social commentary was a springboard for the types of social observation in contemporary publications.

Connect to the Literature

Encourage students to reread the description of the Wife of Bath before answering the question.
Possible responses: She traveled alone. She knew how to dance, make cloth, and observe the religious conventions of her time. She was a good conversationalist.

---

47 *The* BRITISH TRADITION

The Literature of Social Observation

Chaucer was just one author in a long tradition of British writers who detailed ironic observations of social types. Four centuries later, for instance, eighteenth-century writers such as Joseph Addison held up a mirror to middle-class society, describing the typical characters of the day and their follies.

The tradition of social commentary bloomed with the invention of the novel, a form built around keen observations of character and society. Yet the novel emphasized the individual in a way that earlier literature often did not. The characters of nineteenth-century novelist Charles Dickens, for instance, take on their social roles with extravagant, individual style. In a sense, though, Dickens was only following Chaucer. In pilgrims such as the Wife of Bath, the Skipper, and the Host, you can already detect a spark of vital individuality, deeper than any social role.

Connect to the Literature

Identify three ways in which the Wife of Bath both fits and defies the stereotype of a woman of her time.

Is bound to say, as nearly as he can,
Each single word, if he remembers it,
However rudely spoken or unfit,
755   Or else the tale he tells will be untrue,
The things invented and the phrases new.
He may not flinch although it were his brother,
If he says one word he must say the other.
And Christ Himself spoke broad[84] in Holy Writ,
760   And as you know there's nothing there unfit,
And Plato[85] says, for those with power to read,
"The word should be as cousin to the deed."
Further I beg you to forgive it me
If I neglect the order and degree
765   And what is due to rank in what I've planned.
I'm short of wit as you will understand.
      Our *Host* gave us great welcome; everyone
Was given a place and supper was begun.
He served the finest victuals you could think,
770   The wine was strong and we were glad to drink.
A very striking man our Host withal,
And fit to be a marshal in a hall.
His eyes were bright, his girth a little wide;
There is no finer burgess in Cheapside.[86]
775   Bold in his speech, yet wise and full of tact,
There was no manly attribute he lacked,
What's more he was a merry-hearted man.
After our meal he jokingly began
To talk of sport, and, among other things
780   After we'd settled up our reckonings,
He said as follows: "Truly, gentlemen,
You're very welcome and I can't think when
—Upon my word I'm telling you no lie—
I've seen a gathering here that looked so spry,
785   No, not this year, as in this tavern now.
I'd think you up some fun if I knew how.
And, as it happens, a thought has just occurred
And it will cost you nothing, on my word.
You're off to Canterbury—well, God speed!
790   Blessed St. Thomas answer to your need!
And I don't doubt, before the journey's done

---

84. broad bluntly.
85. Plato Greek philosopher (427?–347? B.C.).
86. Cheapside district in London.

Enrichment: Investigating Language

Different Words, Same Meaning

An idiom is a phrase where the words together have a meaning that is different from the dictionary definitions of the individual words. In line 762, Chaucer quotes Plato, saying "The word should be as cousin to the deed." In today's vernacular, we might say, "Don't talk the talk if you can't walk the walk." Both sayings mean the same thing: "Don't just talk about doing something, do it!" Similar idioms include "Talk is cheap," "Actions speak louder than words," and "Practice what you preach."
Activity: Investigating Language Have interested students research other idioms that are used in the English language and their meanings. Suggest that they record information in the **Enrichment: Investigating Language** worksheet, *Professional Development Guidebook*, page 234.

You mean to while the time in tales and fun.
Indeed, there's little pleasure for your bones
Riding along and all as dumb as stones.
795 So let me then propose for your enjoyment,
Just as I said, a suitable employment.
And if my notion suits and you agree
And promise to submit yourselves to me
Playing your parts exactly as I say
800 Tomorrow as you ride along the way,
Then by my father's soul (and he is dead)
If you don't like it you can have my head!
Hold up your hands, and not another word."
        Well, our consent of course was not deferred,
805 It seemed not worth a serious debate;
We all agreed to it at any rate
And bade him issue what commands he would.
"My lords," he said, "now listen for your good,
And please don't treat my notion with disdain.
810 This is the point. I'll make it short and plain.
Each one of you shall help to make things slip
By telling two stories on the outward trip
To Canterbury, that's what I intend,
And, on the homeward way to journey's end
815 Another two, tales from the days of old;
And then the man whose story is best told,
That is to say who gives the fullest measure
Of good morality and general pleasure,
He shall be given a supper, paid by all,
820 Here in this tavern, in this very hall,
When we come back again from Canterbury.
And in the hope to keep you bright and merry
I'll go along with you myself and ride
All at my own expense and serve as guide.
825 I'll be the judge, and those who won't obey
Shall pay for what we spend upon the way.
Now if you all agree to what you've heard
Tell me at once without another word,
And I will make arrangements early for it."
830   Of course we all agreed, in fact we swore it
Delightedly, and made entreaty too
That he should act as he proposed to do,

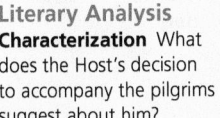

Literary Analysis
Characterization What does the Host's decision to accompany the pilgrims suggest about him?

from The Canterbury Tales: The Prologue **117**

117

Become our Governor in short, and be
Judge of our tales and general referee,

835 And set the supper at a certain price.
We promised to be ruled by his advice
Come high, come low; unanimously thus
We set him up in judgment over us.
More wine was fetched, the business being done;

840 We drank it off and up went everyone
To bed without a moment of delay.
    Early next morning at the spring of day
Up rose our Host and roused us like a cock,
Gathering us together in a flock,

845 And off we rode at slightly faster pace
Than walking to St. Thomas' watering-place;[87]
And there our Host drew up, began to ease
His horse, and said, "Now, listen if you please,

---

87. St. Thomas' watering-place a brook two miles from the inn.

▶ **Critical Viewing 50**
What can you infer about the personalities of these monks from this illustration? **[Infer]**

My lords! Remember what you promised me.
850 If evensong and matins will agree[88]
Let's see who shall be first to tell a tale.
And as I hope to drink good wine and ale
I'll be your judge. The rebel who disobeys,
However much the journey costs, he pays.
855 Now draw for cut[89] and then we can depart;
The man who draws the shortest cut shall start."

---

88. **If evensong . . . agree** "if what you said last night holds true this morning."
89. **draw for cut** draw lots, as when pulling straws from a bunch; the person who pulls the short straw is "it."

Critical Reading

1. **Key Ideas and Details (a)** List three characteristics of the Nun. **(b) Deduce:** What details does Chaucer include in his description of the Nun to make gentle fun of her? Explain.

2. **Key Ideas and Details (a)** Identify two of the main characteristics of the Friar and the Parson. **(b) Compare and Contrast:** What are some of the ways in which the Friar and the Parson differ?

3. **Key Ideas and Details** Judging from the descriptions of the Friar and the Parson, what does Chaucer think can cause a religious person to fail in his or her duty?

4. **Key Ideas and Details** How does Chaucer's attitude toward the Monk differ, if at all, from his attitude toward the Friar? Explain.

5. **Integration of Knowledge and Ideas (a) Apply:** What modern character types match the characters in the Prologue? **(b) Apply:** What types would Chaucer not have anticipated? Explain.

6. **Integration of Knowledge and Ideas (a) Analyze:** From what segments of medieval society do the pilgrims come? **(b) Draw Conclusions:** What does their participation in a common pilgrimage suggest about the times?

7. **Integration of Knowledge and Ideas** Judging from his pilgrims, do you think Chaucer believes people are basically good, basically evil, or often a mix of the two? Give examples to support your answer.

8. **Integration of Knowledge and Ideas** Do you think Chaucer's view of people is justified? Explain.

9. **Integration of Knowledge and Ideas** Explain what a description of clothing reveals about a character and about medieval society. Use two of these Essential Question words: *echelon, distinct, approbation, condemn.* [Connecting to the Essential Question: How does literature shape or reflect society?]

 Cite textual evidence to support your responses.

from The Canterbury Tales: The Prologue **119**

Differentiated Instruction for Universal Access

Support for Less Proficient Readers
To help reinforce what they have learned, have students work through the interactive review of this selection with the *See It!* DVD. Encourage students to note any concepts that are unclear or any questions that they miss, and then review with them where the answers are found in the selection.

EL Vocabulary for English Learners
Review with students the vocabulary list from page 95. Then have them go through the lesson to find the words in context, and have them read aloud the sentence or phrase in which the word appears. Discuss how the definition of the word contributes to understanding the sentence.

Enrichment for Advanced Readers
Encourage students to pick a topic suggested by this selection (for example, medieval medicine, the rise of the middle class, or life at sea) and do further research. Have them write a brief report relating something they discover that sheds additional light on the lives and times of Chaucer's characters.

119

Answers

1. The Doctor cares more about gold than about his patients (direct); he and his apothecaries worked together selling drugs at inflated prices (indirect).

2. **Possible responses:** (a) The Plowman is "an honest worker, good and true"—direct statement. The Reeve is "old and choleric and thin"—use of physical description. The Nun "used to weep if she but saw a mouse/ caught in a trap"—use of action. (b) In the case of the Reeve, the description suggests that he is shrewd and tough. The Nun's action shows she is sentimental.

3. **Possible responses:** (a) Chaucer's description of the Nun's poor French. (b) Chaucer's tone undermines the Nun's efforts at seeming refined.

4. **Possible response:** Students may say that the description of the Miller is vivid because it incorporates physical description.

5. **Possible response:** (a) Pardoner: wallet bulging with pardons. Implication: corruption was rampant in the giving of pardons. (b) Knight: truth, honor, courtesy. Implication: society promoted virtuous behavior.

   For other sample answers, see *Graphic Organizer Transparencies*, **Literary Analysis Graphic Organizer A**, page 15, and the **Additional Answers** section.

6. In medieval society, people may have been defined by their profession or their social role.

7. **Possible responses:** (a) an airplane pilot, a mechanic, a computer programmer (b) a pilot would wear a uniform and speak in technical terms; a mechanic might wear a stained uniform and speak colloquial English; a computer programmer might wear jeans and a shirt and speak using computer terms.

8. Who: A Knight; what: he rode to battle; how much: more than anyone else; how well: very well.

9. Who: The Parson; what: an exemplary figure; why: to draw people to God; how: if a man was difficult, he rebuked him no matter what his social status.

10. Responses will vary but should identify the major questioning points of the sentence selected.

120

After You Read
from *The Canterbury Tales: The Prologue*

Literary Analysis

Ⓒ 1. **Key Ideas and Details** Give three details that Chaucer uses to **characterize** the Doctor. For each, note whether the characterization is **direct** or **indirect**.

Ⓒ 2. **Key Ideas and Details** **(a)** Find one example of each of the following kinds of details in Chaucer's characterizations: direct statement, physical description, character's action. **(b)** Explain how your examples of physical description and action indirectly characterize that pilgrim.

Ⓒ 3. **Craft and Structure** **(a)** Identify an example in which Chaucer uses mild sarcasm in describing a character. **(b)** Explain how his *tone*, or attitude, changes the meaning of the description.

Ⓒ 4. **Craft and Structure** Choose the character sketch you find most effective. Explain the method Chaucer uses to make the sketch so vivid.

Ⓒ 5. **Integration of Knowledge and Ideas** Use a chart like the one shown to reflect on the **social commentary** in the Prologue. **(a)** What social comment does Chaucer make in his sketch of the Pardoner? **(b)** What does the sketch of the Knight suggest were some of the virtues promoted by medieval society?

Character	Detail	Implication About Society

Ⓒ 6. **Integration of Knowledge and Ideas** Most of Chaucer's characters are named after a profession. What does this emphasis on the characters' social roles suggest about medieval society?

Ⓒ 7. **Integration of Knowledge and Ideas** **(a)** If Chaucer were writing today, what three kinds of pilgrims might he consider adding to the group? Explain your choices. **(b)** Describe how each of your twenty-first-century pilgrims would dress and speak.

Reading Strategy

8. Suppose you were having trouble understanding the sentence in lines 47–50. Practice **repairing your comprehension** of the sentence by **questioning**. What essential information do you discover by asking *When?, Who?, Where?, What?, Why?,* and *How?*

9. Use the same questioning technique to analyze the sentence in lines 529–533.

10. Find and analyze another sentence from the Prologue, especially one that continues through many lines. Remember that asking basic questions will help you unlock its meaning.

Common Core State Standards

Writing
5. Develop and strengthen writing as needed by planning, revising, editing, rewriting, or trying a new approach, focusing on addressing what is most significant for a specific purpose and audience. *(p. 121)*

Language
4.a. Use context as a clue to the meaning of a word or phrase. *(p. 121)*

Assessment Practice

Signal Words **(For more practice, see *All-in-One Workbook*.)**

Many tests require students to identify sequence of events. Have students note the signal words that clue the order of events.

"...on homeward way to journey's end
Another two, tales from the days of old;
And then the man whose story is best told
...shall be given a supper, paid by all...
when we come back again from Canterbury."

What does the Host say will happen at the end of the pilgrims' journey?

A Each pilgrim will tell two stories.

B The pilgrims will treat the person who told the best story to supper.

C The person who does not obey rules will pay for all the journey's expenses.

D The host will treat the pilgrim who told the best story to supper.

Responses *A, C,* and *D* are inaccurate. The word *end* signals a later time. The correct answer is *B*.

Integrated Language Skills

Vocabulary Acquisition and Use

Word Analysis: Latin Suffix -tion

The suffix *-tion* means "the act or process of" or "the result of the act or process of." For example, *prevaricate* means "to distort the truth"; *prevarication* means "the act of distorting the truth." Likewise, *absolve* means "to free someone of a sin"; *absolution* refers to the act of freeing someone from a sin, and also to the state of freedom that results from being absolved. With a small group, write a short paragraph about some of Chaucer's pilgrims. Include at least four of the following words in your paragraph:

1. flirtation
2. decoration
3. narration
4. devotion
5. negotiation
6. digestion

Then, choose two of the words used in your paragraph. For each, write a sentence explaining how the suffix *-tion* helps contribute to the meaning of the word.

Writing

Narrative Text A blog is a Web site where entries on a particular subject are written and posted in reverse chronological order on a single homepage. Show your understanding of the Prologue by starting a **pilgrimage blog.** Write an introduction as the Host. Then, add postings from several pilgrims in which they express their thoughts, hopes, and fears about the journey.

Prewriting First, decide on a pilgrimage-related topic—the more controversial, the better. Review Chaucer's description of each character and jot down several opinions each might hold about this topic.

Drafting As you draft your postings, use language that strongly expresses each pilgrim's personality.

Revising As you revise, check to make sure you have written each posting in character and that you have stayed on topic. Revise language that slips out of character, and delete details that are irrelevant.

Vocabulary: Context Clues

The context of a word is the other words, phrases, and sentences that come before and after the word and that may provide clues to its meaning. For each underlined word that appears below, explain how clues in the paragraph help you infer the word's contextual meaning.

A motley group of pilgrims gathered for a journey. The first was a stout, <u>sanguine</u> cook who greeted each newcomer with a jolly "Hallo!" The second was a noblewoman whose gowns were <u>garnished</u> with emeralds and pearls. The third, a young clerk, was traveling on <u>commission</u> from his employer; he made his errand sound so lofty and important that the other pilgrims suspected him of <u>prevarication</u>. The fourth, a widow, believed the clerk was telling the truth and behaved in a kind, <u>solicitous</u> manner toward him. The fifth said he was naught but a sinner, and that he sought naught but <u>absolution</u> for his crimes.

Model: Revising for a Consistent Voice

The Franklin says:

I find the idea of rationing our provisions to be

~~interesting, but a bit extreme~~

~~not only impractical, but downright insulting!~~ It is my custom to carry an abundant supply of cake and beverage, and to indulge at will—and also to share what I have with fellow-travelers.

> The Franklin is a cheerful character, so the angry language doesn't fit. The revision strikes a polite and cordial tone.

Integrated Language Skills **121**

Assessment Resources

Unit 1 Resources

L1 L2 EL Selection Test A, pp. 90–92. Administer Test A to less advanced students

L3 L4 EL Selection Test B, pp. 93–95. Administer Test B to on-level and more advanced students.

L3 L4 Open-Book Test, pp. 87–89. As an alternative, administer the Open-Book Test.

All Customizable Test Bank

All Self-tests
Students may prepare for the **Selection Test** by taking the **Self-test** online.

PHLit Online! All assessment resources are available at **www.PHLitOnline.com.**

Vocabulary Acquisition and Use

Word Analysis
Sample sentences:

The word *decoration* means the act of decorating. The word *devotion* means a feeling of being devoted to something.

Vocabulary
Sample Answers:

sanguine: The cook seems confident and cheerful in each greeting to a newcomer. *Sanguine* means confident and optimistic.

garnished: One would only put jewels on a gown to decorate it. *Garnished* must mean "to decorate."

commission: The clerk is traveling on an errand for his employer. *Commission* must mean that he has been given some authority.

prevarication: The other pilgrims suspect the clerk's truthfulness. *Prevarication* must mean lying.

solicitous: The widow felt concerned. *Solicitous* must mean concerned.

absolution: One would want forgiveness for one's crimes so that must be what *absolution* means.

Writing

You may use this Writing Lesson as timed-writing practice, or you may allow students to develop the narrative text as a writing assignment over several days.

1. Point out to students that most blogs have entries and comments.

2. Work with students to draw up guidelines for their blogs:

   • **Focus** The writer should clearly present a controversial topic.

   • **Organization** The writer should introduce the topic, presenting several points in logical order. Then, the writer should write comments from several pilgrims.

   • **Elaboration** The writer should give details that show the personality of each pilgrim.

   • **Style** The writer should use an informal writing style.

• *from* The Pardoner's Tale
Lesson Pacing Guide

DAY 1 Preteach

© Administer the Reading and Vocabulary Warm-ups (*Unit 1 Resources,* pp. 96–99) as necessary.

• Have students read and respond to the Critical Commentary.

© Introduce the Literary Analysis concept: Allegory and Archetypal Elements.

• Introduce the Reading strategy: Rereading.

• Build Background with the author and Background features.

© Develop thematic thinking with Connecting to the Essential Question.

© Teach the selection vocabulary.

DAYS 2–3 Preteach/Teach /Assess

© Distribute copies of the appropriate graphic organizer for the Reading Strategy (*Graphic Organizer Transparencies,* pp. 17–18).

• Distribute copies of the appropriate graphic organizer for Literary Analysis (*Graphic Organizer Transparencies,* pp. 19–20).

• Prepare students to read with the Activating Prior Knowledge activities (TE).

• Informally monitor comprehension while students read.

• Use the Reading Check questions to confirm comprehension.

• Develop students' understanding of allegory and archetypal elements using the Literary Analysis prompts

© Develop students' ability to repair comprehension by rereading using the Reading Strategy prompts.

© Reinforce vocabulary with the Vocabulary notes.

© Assess students' comprehension and mastery of the skills by having them answer the Critical Reading, Literary Analysis, and Reading Strategy questions.

• Have students complete the Vocabulary Lesson.

DAY 4 Extend/Assess

© Have students complete the Writing Lesson and write a persuasive sermon on greed. (You may assign as homework.)

• Administer Selection Test A or B (*Unit 1 Resources,* pp. 108–110 or 111–113).

© **Common Core**
State Standards

Reading Literature 5. Analyze how an author's choices concerning how to structure specific parts of a text contribute to its overall structure as well as its aesthetic impact.

Writing 1.a. Introduce precise, knowledgeable claim(s), establish the significance of the claim(s), distinguish the claim(s) from alternate or opposing claims, and create an organization that logically sequences claim(s), counter-claims, reasons, and evidence.

Language 6. Acquire and use accurately general academic and domain-specific words and phrases, sufficient for reading, writing, speaking, and listening at the college and career readiness level; demonstrate independence in gathering vocabulary knowledge when considering a word or phrase important to comprehension or expression.

Additional Standards Practice
Common Core Companion, *pp. 54–55; 185–195; 336–337*

Daily Block Scheduling
Each day in this Lesson Pacing Guide represents a 40–50 minute period. Teachers using block scheduling may combine days to revise pacing. In addition, teachers may differentiate and support core instruction by integrating components for extended and intensive support as students require. See the Guide to Selected Leveled Resources (facing page).

Guide to Selected Leveled Resources

R T I Tier 1 (students performing on level)

from The Pardoner's Tale

Warm Up	Practice, **model**, and **monitor** fluency, working **with the whole class** or **in groups**.	Vocabulary and **Reading Warm-ups B**, *Unit 1 Resources*, pp. 96–97, 99
Comprehension/Skills	**Support** and **monitor** comprehension and skills development, having students complete the activities, graphic organizers, and interactive prompts **independently** or **as a class**.	• *Reader's Notebook*, adapted instruction and full selection **EL** *Reader's Notebook: English Learner's Version*, adapted instruction and adapted selection • **Reading Skill Graphic Organizer B**, *Graphic Organizer Transparencies*, p. 18 • **Literary Analysis Graphic Organizer B**, *Graphic Organizer Transparencies*, p. 20
Monitor Progress	**Monitor** student progress with the differentiated curriculum-based assessment in the *Unit Resources*.	• **Selection Test B,** *Unit 1 Resources*, pp. 111–113 • **Open-Book Test,** *Unit 1 Resources*, pp. 105–107

R T I Tier 2 (students requiring intervention)

from The Pardoner's Tale

Warm Up	Practice, **model,** and **monitor** fluency **in groups** or **with individuals**.	• **Vocabulary and Reading Warm-ups A,** *Unit 1 Resources*, pp. 96–98 • *Hear It!* Audio CD (adapted text)
Comprehension/Skills	• **Support** and **monitor** comprehension and skills development, working **in small groups** or **with individuals**. • As students complete the selection in the appropriate version of the *Reader's Notebook*, **monitor** comprehension frequently with group questions and individual instruction. • **Model** strategies while guiding students in completing the activities and prompts in the *Reader's Notebook*, as well as the graphic organizers. • **Practice** skills and **monitor** mastery with the *Reading Kit* worksheets.	• *Reader's Notebook: Adapted Version,* adapted instruction and adapted selection **EL** *Reader's Notebook: English Learner's Version,* adapted instruction and adapted selection • **Reading Skill Graphic Organizer A,** *Graphic Organizer Transparencies*, p. 17 • **Literary Analysis Graphic Organizer A,** *Graphic Organizer Transparencies*, p. 19 • *Reading Kit,* Practice worksheets
Monitor Progress	**Monitor** student progress with the differentiated curriculum-based assessment in the *Unit Resources* and in the *Reading Kit*.	• **Selection Test A,** *Unit 1 Resources*, pp. 108–110 • *Reading Kit,* Assess worksheets

TIER 3 Tier 3 intervention may require consultation with the student's special-education or dyslexia specialist. For additional support, see the Tier 2 activities and resources listed above.

One-on-one teaching   Group work   Whole class instruction   Independent work   Assessment

For a complete guide to selection support, including support for Advanced students, see the Overview of Resources in the frontmatter.

• *from* The Pardoner's Tale

RESOURCES FOR:

- **L1** Special-Needs Students
- **L2** Below-Level Students (Tier 2)
- **L3** On-Level Students (Tier 1)
- **L4** Advanced Students (Tier 1)
- **EL** English Learners
- **All** All Students

Vocabulary/Fluency/Prior Knowledge

Unit 1 Resources

EL L1 L2 Reading Warm-ups A and B, pp. 98–99

Also available for these selections:

EL L1 L2 Vocabulary Warm-ups A and B, pp. 96–97

All Vocabulary Builder, p. 102

Reader's Notebooks

Pre- and postreading pages for this selection appear in an interactive format in the *Reader's Notebooks*. Each *Notebook* is differentiated for a different group of learners.
The selections in the Adapted and English Learner's versions are abridged.

- **L2 L3** *Reader's Notebook*
- **L1** *Reader's Notebook: Adapted Version*
- **EL** *Reader's Notebook: English Learner's Version*
- **EL** *Reader's Notebook: Spanish Version*

© *Common Core Companion*

Additional instruction and practice for each Common Core State Standard

Selection Support

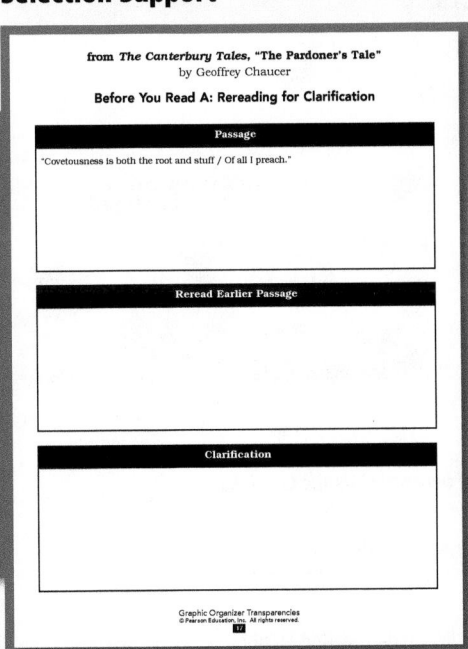

from *The Canterbury Tales*, "The Pardoner's Tale"
by Geoffrey Chaucer

Before You Read A: Rereading for Clarification

Passage
"Covetousness is both the root and stuff / Of all I preach."

Reread Earlier Passage

Clarification

Graphic Organizer Transparencies

EL L3 **Reading: Graphic Organizer A**
(partially filled in), p. 17

Also available for these selections:

EL L1 L2 **Reading: Graphic Organizer B,**
p. 18

EL L1 L2 **Literary Analysis: Graphic Organizer
A** (partially filled in), p. 19

EL L3 **Literary Analysis: Graphic Organizer B,**
p. 20

Skills Development/Extension

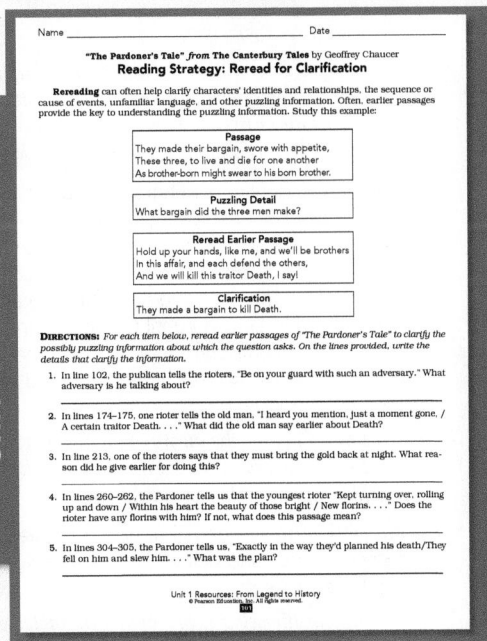

Name _____ Date _____

"The Pardoner's Tale" *from The Canterbury Tales* by Geoffrey Chaucer
Reading Strategy: Reread for Clarification

Rereading can often help clarify characters' identities and relationships, the sequence or cause of events, unfamiliar language, and other puzzling information. Often, earlier passages provide the key to understanding the puzzling information. Study this example:

Passage
They made their bargain, swore with appetite, / These three, to live and die for one another / As brother-born might swear to his born brother.

Puzzling Detail
What bargain did the three men make?

Reread Earlier Passage
Hold up your hands, like me, and we'll be brothers / In this affair, and each defend the others, / And we will kill this traitor Death, I say!

Clarification
They made a bargain to kill Death.

DIRECTIONS: *For each item below, reread earlier passages of "The Pardoner's Tale" to clarify the possibly puzzling information about which the question asks. On the lines provided, write the details that clarify the information.*

1. In line 102, the publican tells the rioters, "Be on your guard with such an adversary." What adversary is he talking about?

2. In lines 174–175, one rioter tells the old man, "I heard you mention, just a moment gone, / A certain traitor Death. . . ." What did the old man say earlier about Death?

3. In line 213, one of the rioters says that they must bring the gold back at night. What reason did he give earlier for doing this?

4. In lines 260–262, the Pardoner tells us that the youngest rioter "Kept turning over, rolling up and down / Within his heart the beauty of those bright / New florins. . . ." Does the rioter have any florins with him? If not, what does this passage mean?

5. In lines 304–305, the Pardoner tells us, "Exactly in the way they'd planned his death/They fell on him and slew him. . . ." What was the plan?

All **Reading,** p. 101

Also available for these selections:

All **Literary Analysis,** p. 100

EL L3 L4 **Support for Writing,** p. 103

L4 **Enrichment,** p. 104

Assessment

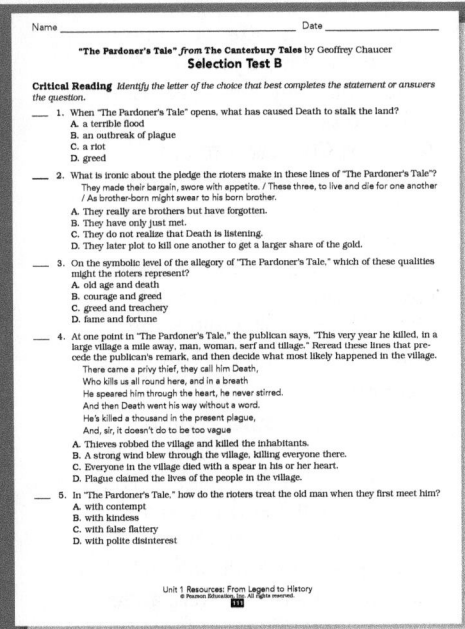

Name _____ Date _____

"The Pardoner's Tale" *from The Canterbury Tales* by Geoffrey Chaucer
Selection Test B

Critical Reading *Identify the letter of the choice that best completes the statement or answers the question.*

_____ 1. When "The Pardoner's Tale" opens, what has caused Death to stalk the land?
A. a terrible flood
B. an outbreak of plague
C. a riot
D. greed

_____ 2. What is ironic about the pledge the rioters make in these lines of "The Pardoner's Tale"?
They made their bargain, swore with appetite. / These three, to live and die for one another / As brother-born might swear to his born brother.
A. They really are brothers but have forgotten.
B. They have only just met.
C. They do not realize that Death is listening.
D. They later plot to kill one another to get a larger share of the gold.

_____ 3. On the symbolic level of the allegory of "The Pardoner's Tale," which of these qualities might the rioters represent?
A. old age and death
B. courage and greed
C. greed and treachery
D. fame and fortune

_____ 4. At one point in "The Pardoner's Tale," the publican says, "This very year he killed, in a large village a mile away, man, woman, serf and tillage." Reread these lines that precede the publican's remark, and then decide what most likely happened in the village.
There came a privy thief, they call him Death,
Who kills us all round here, and in a breath
He speared him through the heart, he never stirred.
And then Death went his way without a word.
He's killed a thousand in the present plague,
And, sir, it doesn't do to be too vague.
A. Thieves robbed the village and killed the inhabitants.
B. A strong wind blew through the village, killing everyone there.
C. Everyone in the village died with a spear in his or her heart.
D. Plague claimed the lives of the people in the village.

_____ 5. In "The Pardoner's Tale," how do the rioters treat the old man when they first meet him?
A. with contempt
B. with kindness
C. with false flattery
D. with polite disinterest

EL L1 L2 **Selection Test B,** pp. 111–113

Also available for these selections:

L3 L4 **Open-Book Test,** pp. 105–107

EL L3 L4 **Selection Test A,** pp. 108–110

PHLit Online!
www.PHLitOnline.com

Online Resources: All print materials are also available online.

- complete narrated selection text
- a thematically related video with writing prompt
- an interactive graphic organizer
- highlighting feature
- access to all student print resources, adapted to individual student needs
- Spanish and English summaries
- adapted selection translations in Spanish

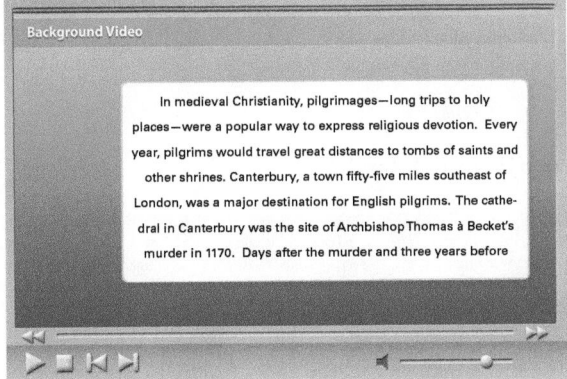

Background Video

In medieval Christianity, pilgrimages—long trips to holy places—were a popular way to express religious devotion. Every year, pilgrims would travel great distances to tombs of saints and other shrines. Canterbury, a town fifty-five miles southeast of London, was a major destination for English pilgrims. The cathedral in Canterbury was the site of Archbishop Thomas à Becket's murder in 1170. Days after the murder and three years before

Background Video

Also available:

Get Connected! (thematic video with writing prompt)
All videos are available in Spanish.

Vocabulary Central

Vocabulary Central (tools and activities for studying vocabulary)

Also available:

Writer's Journal (with graphics feature)

Critical Commentary

1. Direct students' attention to the artwork on this page. **Ask** students what they think its artist is trying to say.

   Answer: Chaucer is to British poetry as George Washington is to the United States. He is considered the "father of English poetry," just as George Washington (who is normally pictured on a dollar bill) is the "Father" of the United States.

2. Point out to students that they have read other English poetry, predating Chaucer: "The Seafarer," "The Wanderer," "The Wife's Lament," and selections from *Beowulf*. **Ask** students if they agree with Addison's statement that the Muses were asleep in Britain until Chaucer came along.

3. **Ask** students whether they would like to meet Chaucer. **Ask** students what they think Chaucer would be like. Remind students to support their answers with text evidence.

4. Have students write their own assessment of Chaucer. They can use the words of Addison, Dryden, Hazlitt, and Chesterton as models, but they should express their own feelings about Chaucer, explaining whether they believe he was important, and why.

Key Ideas and Details

Possible response: Chaucer's *Canterbury Tales* are the length of a novel, and they tell a complete story. *The Canterbury Tales* could be regarded as a novel in verse.

Critical Commentary

Geoffrey Chaucer: Father of English Literature

> *Long had our dull Fore-Fathers slept Supine,*
> *Nor felt the Raptures of the Tuneful Nine;*
> *Till Chaucer first, a merry Bard, arose;*
> *And many a Story told in Rhyme and Prose.*

This stanza, penned by English author Joseph Addison in 1694, expresses the general view of Chaucer expressed by most English writers who followed him. The "Tuneful Nine," or Muses—that is, the nine goddesses said to inspire the arts—were asleep in England until Chaucer came along. Addison's contemporary John Dryden, the great pioneer of English literary criticism, called Chaucer "the father of English poetry":

▲ This imaginary British pound note depicts Chaucer as the Father of English Literature.

> *From Chaucer the purity of the English tongue began. . . . As he is the father of English poetry, so I hold him in the same degree of veneration as the Grecians held Homer or the Romans Virgil.*

Romantic Age author William Hazlitt hailed Chaucer as "the first to tune his native tongue" and named him as a person from the past whom he would most like to meet:

> *He was himself a noble, manly character, standing before his age and striving to advance it; a pleasant humorist withal, who . . . would make as hearty a companion as mine host of the Tabard.*

The attitude toward Chaucer is summed up by twentieth-century author G. K. Chesterton:

> *. . . Shakespeare and Milton were the greatest sons of their country; but Chaucer was the Father of his Country, rather in the style of George Washington. And apart from that, he made something that has altered all Europe more than the Newspaper: the Novel. He was a novelist when there were no novels.*

ⓒ **Key Ideas and Details** In what ways does the Prologue show Chaucer being (in Chesterton's words) "a novelist when there were no novels"? Explain.

Enrichment: Analyzing a Literary Figure

Fathers of Literature

Geoffrey Chaucer is not the only literary figure to be regarded as the father of literature in his homeland. Mark Twain is often called the father of American literature. Chinua Achebe, who wrote *Things Fall Apart* in 1958, is regarded as the father of modern African literature. Harishchandra, who founded the first Hindi literary magazine, is called the father of modern Hindi literature. J.R.R. Tolkien, who wrote *The Hobbit* and *The Lord of the Rings* trilogy, is regarded as the father of fantasy literature.

Activity: Biography Have students choose a "father" or "mother" of literature and research that person's life. Suggest that they record information in the **Enrichment: Investigating a Literary Figure** worksheet, *Professional Development Guidebook*, page 235. Have them use the results of their research to write an essay describing the influence of their research subject on literature.

Before You Read

from *The Pardoner's Tale*

❶ Connecting to the Essential Question In this tale told by Chaucer's Pardoner, greed is an important motivation. Consider what you have observed about the power of greed. As you read, look for examples of greed in this tale, and notice its effects on the characters and action. Considering the influence of this motive will help you explore the Essential Question: **How does literature shape or reflect society?**

❷ Literary Analysis

Allegories are narratives that have both literal and deeper, symbolic meanings. "The Pardoner's Tale" is a kind of allegory called an *exemplum,* Latin for "example." The tale is an exemplum against the sin of greed, and the Pardoner uses the tale to illustrate the point of one of his sermons, "Love of money is the root of all evil."

To teach its lesson effectively, an allegory must be easily understood and remembered by the listeners. For this reason, an allegory may use certain basic storytelling patterns, or **archetypal narrative elements,** found in folk literature around the world. These elements include the following:

- Characters, events, and other things that come in threes
- A test of the characters' morality
- A mysterious guide who helps point the way
- A just ending that rewards good or punishes evil

Because it is structured to contain such elements, the basic story in this tale survived retellings as it traveled from ancient India to Europe. As you read, note the archetypal elements that make the allegory and its moral clear and memorable.

❸ Reading Strategy

© **Preparing to Read Complex Texts** If you cannot fully understand a passage at first, **reread** it and the surrounding passages. Rereading can help you clarify characters' identities, the sequence or causes of events, and puzzling language. As you read "The Pardoner's Tale," use a diagram like the one shown to clarify difficult passages.

❹ Vocabulary

pallor (pal´ ər) *n.* unnatural lack of color; paleness (p. 129)

hoary (hôr´ ē) *adj.* white or gray with age (p. 129)

tarry (tar´ ē) *v.* to delay or linger (p. 132)

apothecary (ə päth´ ə ker´ ē) *n.* pharmacist; druggist (p. 132)

deftly (deft´ lē) *adv.* skillfully; with ease and quickness (p. 132)

sauntered (sôn´ tərd) *v.* walked at an unhurried pace (p. 132)

© **Common Core State Standards**

Reading Literature
5. Analyze how an author's choices concerning how to structure specific parts of a text contribute to its overall structure and meaning.

Passage

"He gathered lots and hid them in his hand...."

Reread Earlier Passage

"'We draw for lots and see the way it goes; / The one who draws the longest, lucky man, ...'"

Clarification

"Drawing lots" must be like drawing straws: The one who draws the longest is "it."

PHLit Online!
www.PHLitOnline.com

from The Pardoner's Tale **123**

© **Common Core State Standards**

- **Reading Literature 5**
- **Writing 1.a; 6**

❶ 🅠 Connecting to the Essential Question

1. Review the assignment with the class.

2. Explain to students that greed can refer to a desire for anything, but most often it refers to a desire for money. Ask students to discuss the lengths people will go to for money. Then have students complete the assignment.

3. As students read, have them look for examples of greed and its effects.

❷ Literary Analysis

Introduce the skill, using the instruction on the student page.

Think Aloud: Model the Skill

Say to students:

I realize that I'm familiar with archetypal elements even though I may not use the term "archetypal elements" often. People get three wishes in fairy tales. In *Macbeth* there are three witches. Events and characters that come in threes are archetypal elements.

❸ Reading Strategy

1. Introduce the strategy using the instruction on the student page.

2. Give students a copy of **Reading Strategy Graphic Organizer B,** page 18 in *Graphic Organizer Transparencies,* to fill out as they read.

❹ Vocabulary

1. Say and define each word. Have students pronounce each word.

2. For more guidance, see the *Classroom Strategies and Teaching Routines* card for introducing vocabulary.

PHLit Online!
www.PHLitOnline.com

Teaching From Technology

Preparing to Read
Go to www.PHLitOnline.com and display the *Get Connected!* slideshow for this selection. Have the class brainstorm for responses to the writing prompt, entering ideas in the interactive journal. Then, have students complete their written responses as homework.

Using the Interactive Student Edition
Go to www.PHLitOnline.com and display the **Enriched Online Student Edition.** As the class reads the selection or listens to the narration, record answers to side-column prompts using the graphic organizers accessible on the interactive page. Alternatively, have students use the online edition individually, answering the prompts as they read.

❶ About the Selection

The Pardoner's unscrupulous ways are set in relief against his tale—an exemplum derived from multiple sources that demonstrates the evils that come from loving money. One of the elements some readers overlook in this tale is the validity of the moral when it comes from one as corrupt as the Pardoner. Encourage students to make a judgment about the Pardoner's reliability as a narrator, and have them determine the relevance of his tale when they have finished reading.

❷ Activating Prior Knowledge

Explain that this tale takes place during a plague. The pestilence, we know now, was not one disease but two occurring simultaneously: bubonic plague and the far more contagious, and usually fatal, pneumonic plague. Have students suggest ways that a highly contagious, fatal disease might affect relationships within a community.

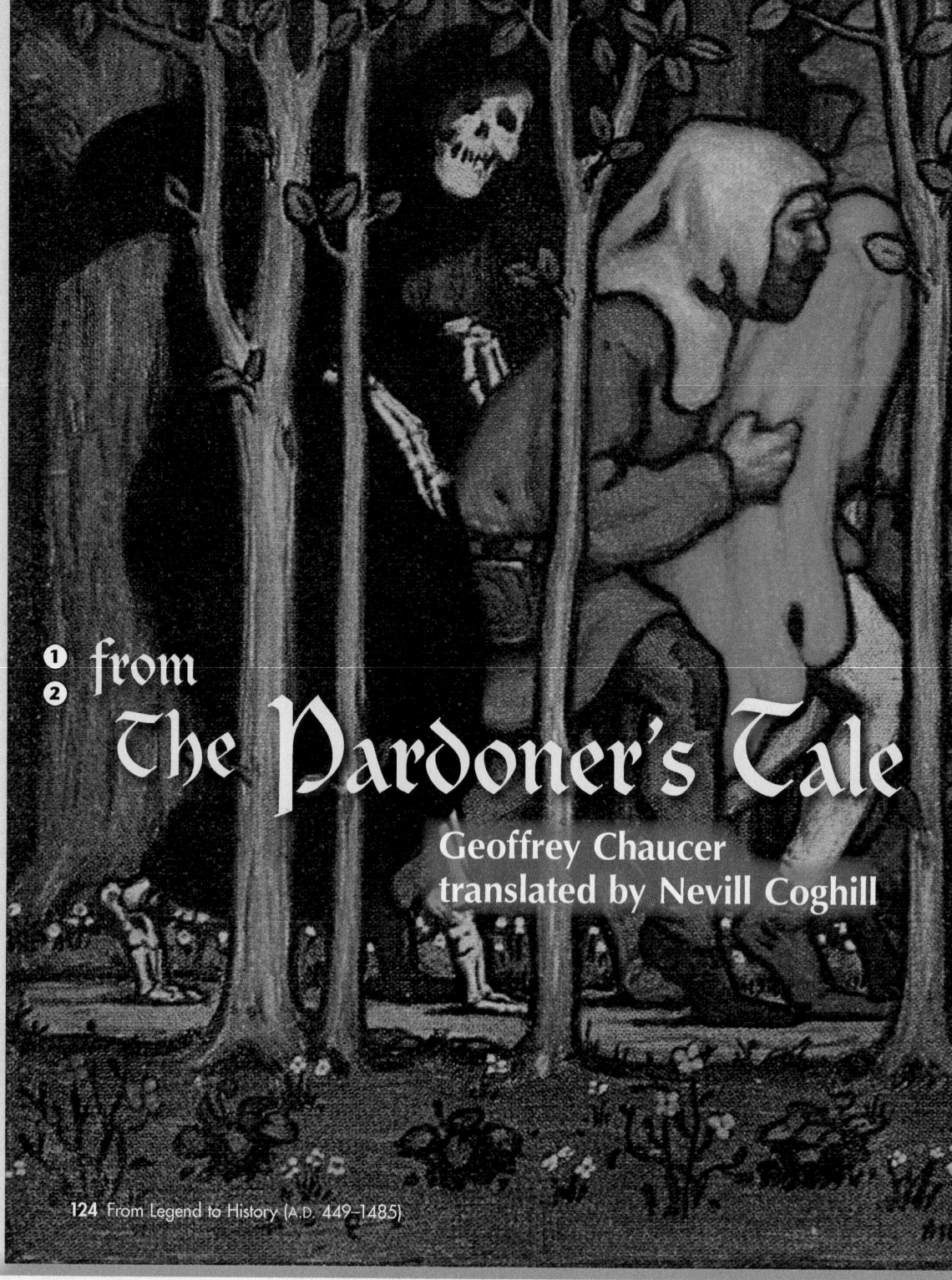

❶❷ from
The Pardoner's Tale

Geoffrey Chaucer
translated by Nevill Coghill

124 From Legend to History (A.D. 449–1485)

Text Complexity Rubric

from The Pardoner's Tale		
Qualitative Measures		
Context/Knowledge Demands	Social criticism; historical knowledge demands	
	1 2 ③ 4 5	
Structure/Language Conventionality and Clarity	Period vocabulary with footnotes	
	1 2 ③ 4 5	
Levels of Meaning/ Purpose/Concept Level	Accessible (greed)	
	1 ② 3 4 5	
Quantitative Measures		
Lexile	NP	Text Length	2,835 words
Overall Complexity	**More accessible**	

Reader and Task Suggestions

Preparing to Read the Text
- Using the information on TE p. 126, discuss social corruption and reform in Chaucer's age.
- Discuss with students the idea of literature as an effective form of social criticism.
- Guide students to use Multidraft Reading strategies to deepen their comprehension (TE p. 93).

Leveled Tasks
Knowledge Demands If students will have difficulty with the social commentary, remind them that the Pardoner is described as greedy. Have students read his tale, focusing on what it shows about greed.

Synthesizing If students will not have difficulty with the social commentary, ask why the Pardoner might tell a tale with the moral he states on p. 125.

The Pardoner's Prologue

"My lords," he said, "in churches where I preach
I cultivate a haughty kind of speech
And ring it out as roundly as a bell;
I've got it all by heart, the tale I tell.
5 I have a text, it always is the same
And always has been, since I learnt the game,
Old as the hills and fresher than the grass,
Radix malorum est cupiditas."[1]

———————

*The Pardoner explains how he introduces
himself to a congregation, showing official documents
and offering relics as cures for various problems.
Next, he explains how he preaches.*

———————

"Then, priestlike in my pulpit, with a frown,
10 I stand, and when the yokels[2] have sat down,
I preach, as you have heard me say before,
And tell a hundred lying mockeries[3] more.
I take great pains, and stretching out my neck
To east and west I crane about and peck
15 Just like a pigeon sitting on a barn.
My hands and tongue together spin the yarn
And all my antics[4] are a joy to see.
The curse of avarice and cupidity[5]
Is all my sermon, for it frees the pelf.[6]
20 Out come the pence, and specially for myself,
For my exclusive purpose is to win

---

1. *Radix malorum est cupiditas* Latin for "Greed is the root of all evil."
2. **yokels** (yō′ kəlz) *n.* unsophisticated people living in a rural area.
3. **mockeries** (mäk′ ər ēz) *n.* stories that are untrue.
4. **antics** (an′ tikz) *n.* playful, silly, or ludicrous acts.
5. **avarice** (av′ ə ris) **and cupidity** (kyōō pid′ ə tē) *n.* desire to gain wealth; greed (synonyms).
6. **pelf** (pelf) *n.* ill-gotten gains of money or wealth.

from The Pardoner's Tale **125**

---

③ **Humanities**

The three Rogues search in the woods for Death, 1904, by Walter Appleton Clark (1876–1906), an American illustrator and artist, was part of a book of color plates made to illustrate the Canterbury Tales. Clark was an illustrator for many magazines, including *Harper's* and *The Saturday Evening Post,* but he considered the color-plate book his most important work. It was the only color-plate book he would illustrate, as he died two years after its publication, at the age of 30, from typhoid fever.

Use the following question for discussion:

• What indications are there about whether or not the three Rogues will be successful in finding Death?
Answer: Death appears to be stalking them from behind. So they may be successful in finding Death, but not the way they had planned.

④ **Critical Thinking**

Analyze

1. Direct students' attention to line 6, where the Pardoner refers to preaching as a "game."

2. As students read, challenge them to find details that explain the Pardoner's strategy in his "game."
Answer: He uses a "haughty kind of speech," stands in the pulpit "with a frown," tells "lying mockeries," and engages in theatrical gestures and other "antics."

Differentiated Instruction   for Universal Access

Support for Special-Needs Students
Have students complete the **Before You Read** and the **Making Connections** pages for this selection in the *Reader's Notebook: Adapted Version.* These pages provide an abbreviated skills instruction, a selection summary, the Before You Read graphic organizer, and a **Note-taking Guide.**

Support for Less Proficient Readers
Have students complete the **Before You Read** and the **Making Connections** pages for this selection in the *Reader's Notebook.* These pages provide an abbreviated skills instruction, a selection summary, the Before You Read graphic organizer, and a **Note-taking Guide.**

EL Support for English Learners
Have students complete the **Before You Read** and the **Making Connections** pages for this selection in the *Reader's Notebook: English Learner's Version.* These pages provide additional vocabulary, vocabulary skills, and vocabulary practice, along with a **Getting Ready to Read** activity.

PHLit Online!

This selection is available in interactive format in the **Enriched Online Student Edition** at www. PHLitOnline.com, which includes a thematically related video with writing prompt and an interactive graphic organizer.

Rereading

1. Explain to students that *Radix malorum est cupiditas* means "Greed is the root of all evil."

2. **Ask** students the Reading Strategy question: Reread lines 41–44 to determine the "principal intent" of the Pardoner's sermons.
   Answer: His intent is to make money.

❻ 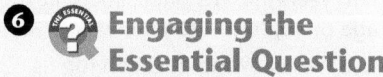 **Engaging the Essential Question**

1. Point out to students that some synonyms for *greed* are *avarice*, *covetousness*, and *cupidity*.

2. **Ask** students: What example of greed can be found in "The Pardoner's Prologue"?
   Answer: The Pardoner only preaches sermons because he wants to be wealthy, not because he cares about people.

3. **Ask** students: What aspects of medieval society make it easy for the Pardoner to exploit people?
   Answer: Religious leaders had a lot of authority, and the people he preached to may have been too uneducated and naive to understand his true nature.

And not at all to castigate[7] their sin.
Once dead what matter how their souls may fare?
They can go blackberrying, for all I care!
25   "Believe me, many a sermon or devotive
Exordium[8] issues from an evil motive.
Some to give pleasure by their flattery
And gain promotion through hypocrisy,
Some out of vanity, some out of hate;
30 Or when I dare not otherwise debate
I'll put my discourse into such a shape,
My tongue will be a dagger; no escape
For him from slandering falsehood shall there be,
If he has hurt my brethren[9] or me.
35 For though I never mention him by name
The congregation guesses all the same
From certain hints that everybody knows,
And so I take revenge upon our foes
And spit my venom forth, while I profess
40 Holy and true—or seeming holiness.
   "But let me briefly make my purpose plain;
I preach for nothing but for greed of gain
And use the same old text, as bold as brass,
Radix malorum est cupiditas.
45 And thus I preach against the very vice
I make my living out of—avarice.
And yet however guilty of that sin
Myself with others I have power to win
Them from it, I can bring them to repent;
50 But that is not my principal intent.
Covetousness[10] is both the root and stuff
Of all I preach. That ought to be enough.
   "Well, then I give examples thick and fast
From bygone times, old stories from the past.
55 A yokel mind loves stories from of old,
Being the kind it can repeat and hold.
What! Do you think, as long as I can preach
And get their silver for the things I teach,
That I will live in poverty, from choice?
60 That's not the counsel of my inner voice!
No! Let me preach and beg from kirk[11] to kirk

Reading Strategy
Rereading Reread lines 41–44 to determine the "principal intent" of the Pardoner's sermons.

❺

❻

---

7. **castigate** (kas´ ti gāt´) *v.* to punish severely.
8. **Exordium** (eg zôr´ dē əm) *n.* the opening part of an oration.
9. **brethren** (breth´ rən) *n.* brothers.
10. **Covetousness** (kuv´ ət əs nis) *n.* greed, especially for what belongs to others.
11. **kirk** *n.* church.

Enrichment: Analyzing a Historical Event

Religious Corruption and Reform

Chaucer's characterization of the Pardoner as a rapacious figure out for personal gain is a satire of the religious state of affairs in his era. Before the Reformation in the sixteenth century, religious abuses were fairly common.

Relic-dealers profited at the expense of the faithful, and sinecures—cushy jobs funded by the coffers of the church—were available to people connected with religious corruption. The Reformation, led by Martin Luther, John Calvin, Ulrich Zwingli, and John Knox,

originated as a protest against these religious abuses. These reformers broke away from the Roman Catholic Church to found various denominations of Protestantism.

Activity: Analyzing a Historical Event Have interested students conduct research on the Reformation. Suggest that they record information on the **Enrichment: Analyzing a Historical Event** worksheet, *Professional Development Guidebook,* page 230.

And never do an honest job of work,
No, nor make baskets, like St. Paul, to gain
A livelihood. I do not preach in vain.
65 There's no apostle I would counterfeit;
I mean to have money, wool and cheese and wheat
Though it were given me by the poorest lad
 Or poorest village widow, though she had
A string of starving children, all agape.
70 No, let me drink the liquor of the grape
And keep a jolly wench in every town!
     "But listen, gentlemen; to bring things down
To a conclusion, would you like a tale?
Now as I've drunk a draught of corn-ripe ale,
75 By God it stands to reason I can strike
On some good story that you all will like.
For though I am a wholly vicious man
Don't think I can't tell moral tales. I can!
Here's one I often preach when out for winning;
80 Now please be quiet. Here is the beginning."

The Pardoner's Tale

   It's of three rioters I have to tell
Who, long before the morning service bell,[12]
Were sitting in a tavern for a drink.
And as they sat, they heard the hand-bell clink
85 Before a coffin going to the grave;
One of them called the little tavern-knave[13]
And said "Go and find out at once—look spry!—
Whose corpse is in that coffin passing by;
And see you get the name correctly too."
90 "Sir," said the boy, "no need, I promise you;
Two hours before you came here I was told.
He was a friend of yours in days of old,
And suddenly, last night, the man was slain,
Upon his bench, face up, dead drunk again.

---

12. **long before . . . bell** long before 9:00 A.M.
13. **tavern-knave** serving boy.

from The Pardoner's Tale **127**

Allegory and Archetypal Elements

1. Have students read the bracketed passage.

2. Then, **ask** them the Literary Analysis question: What details of the publican's comments build the danger of the situation?
Answer: The publican's comments—that Death has killed an entire household in a village only a mile away—builds the danger of the situation.

⑪ Reading Strategy

Rereading

1. Read line 122 aloud to students.

2. Have students use the **Reading Strategy Graphic Organizer** to help them clarify the meaning of line 122.

3. Then, **ask** students the Reading Strategy question: What lines explain the "bargain" the rioters are said to have made in line 122?
Answer: Students should recognize the bargain is their plan to kill Death together, in line 119.

Literary Analysis
Allegory and Archetypal Elements What details of the publican's comments add to the sense of danger?

Reading Strategy
Rereading What lines explain the "bargain" the rioters are said to have made in line 122?

95 There came a privy[14] thief, they call him Death,
    Who kills us all round here, and in a breath
    He speared him through the heart, he never stirred.
    And then Death went his way without a word.
    He's killed a thousand in the present plague,[15]
100 And, sir, it doesn't do to be too vague
    If you should meet him; you had best be wary.
    Be on your guard with such an adversary,
    Be primed to meet him everywhere you go,
    That's what my mother said. It's all I know."
105   The publican[16] joined in with, "By St. Mary,
    What the child says is right; you'd best be wary.
⑩ This very year he killed, in a large village
    A mile away, man, woman, serf at tillage,[17]
    Page in the household, children—all there were.
110 Yes, I imagine that he lives round there.
    It's well to be prepared in these alarms,
    He might do you dishonor." "Huh, God's arms!"
    The rioter said, "Is he so fierce to meet?
    I'll search for him, by Jesus, street by street.
115 God's blessed bones! I'll register a vow!
    Here, chaps! The three of us together now,
    Hold up your hands, like me, and we'll be brothers
    In this affair, and each defend the others,
    And we will kill this traitor Death, I say!
120 Away with him as he has made away
    With all our friends. God's dignity! Tonight!"
⑪   They made their bargain, swore with appetite,
    These three, to live and die for one another
    As brother-born might swear to his born brother.
125 And up they started in their drunken rage
    And made towards this village which the page
    And publican had spoken of before.
    Many and grisly were the oaths they swore,
    Tearing Christ's blessed body to a shred;[18]
130 "If we can only catch him, Death is dead!"
        When they had gone not fully half a mile,
    Just as they were about to cross a stile,
    They came upon a very poor old man
    Who humbly greeted them and thus began,
135 "God look to you, my lords, and give you quiet!"

---

14. privy secretive.
15. plague the Black Death, which killed over a third of the population of Europe from 1347–1351. The plague reached England in 1348.
16. publican innkeeper.
17. tillage plowing.
18. Tearing . . . shred their oaths included such expressions as "God's arms" and "God's blessed bones."

128 From Legend to History (A.D. 449–1485)

Enrichment: Analyzing Forms and Genres

Morality Plays

Allegorical dramas of the late Middle Ages were known as morality plays. Many of them were presented as popular pageants, and they always included abstract personifications, such as Charity, Mercy, Truth, Pity, and Church, rather than figures from history or other individuals. Morality plays are dramatic presentations of sermons. The most famous morality play is *Everyman*, written around 1500. When Everyman receives a summons from Death, he tries in vain to convince his friends Fellowship, Kindred, Worldly Goods, and Beauty to journey with him. Only Good Deeds remains faithful.

Activity: Analyzing Forms and Genres Have interested students conduct further investigation into morality plays. Have them use the **Enrichment: Analyzing Forms and Genres** worksheet on page 227 of the *Professional Development Guidebook* to organize the information. Ask students to summarize their findings for the class.

To which the proudest of these men of riot
Gave back the answer, "What, old fool? Give place!
Why are you all wrapped up except your face?
Why live so long? Isn't it time to die?"

140   The old, old fellow looked him in the eye
And said, "Because I never yet have found,
Though I have walked to India, searching round
Village and city on my pilgrimage,
One who would change his youth to have my age.

145 And so my age is mine and must be still
Upon me, for such time as God may will.
    "Not even Death, alas, will take my life;
So, like a wretched prisoner at strife
Within himself, I walk alone and wait

150 About the earth, which is my mother's gate,
Knock-knocking with my staff from night to noon
And crying, 'Mother, open to me soon!
Look at me, mother, won't you let me in?
See how I wither, flesh and blood and skin!

155 Alas! When will these bones be laid to rest?
Mother, I would exchange—for that were best—
The wardrobe in my chamber, standing there
So long, for yours! Aye, for a shirt of hair[19]
To wrap me in!' She has refused her grace,

160 Whence comes the pallor of my withered face.
    "But it dishonored you when you began
To speak so roughly, sir, to an old man,
Unless he had injured you in word or deed.
It says in holy writ, as you may read,

165 'Thou shalt rise up before the hoary head
And honor it.' And therefore be it said
'Do no more harm to an old man than you,
Being now young, would have another do
When you are old'—if you should live till then.

170 And so may God be with you, gentlemen,
For I must go whither I have to go.'
    "By God," the gambler said, "you shan't do so,
You don't get off so easy, by St. John!
I heard you mention, just a moment gone,

175 A certain traitor Death who singles out
And kills the fine young fellows hereabout.
And you're his spy, by God! You wait a bit.
Say where he is or you shall pay for it,
By God and by the Holy Sacrament!

180 I say you've joined together by consent

---

19. shirt of hair here, a shroud.

⑬ ▲ Critical Viewing
What moral might a medieval illustration like this one have served to teach? **[Hypothesize]**

Vocabulary
pallor (pal′ ər) *n.* unnatural lack of color; paleness

hoary (hôr′ ē) *adj.* white or gray with age

Reading Check
⑭ What do the three rioters swear to do?

from The Pardoner's Tale **129**

⑫ Humanities

La Danse Macabre This French illustration from an illuminated manuscript dates to the 1400s. *La Danse Macabre,* also called the Dance of Death, was a common medieval allegory that represented the all-conquering power of death. The concept originated in the late thirteenth or early fourteenth century and became one of the most common images during the Middle Ages, as the Black Death in the mid-fourteenth century and the Hundred Years' War (1337–1453) devastated Europe. Generally, there is a procession in the image, with people arranged in order of rank, from popes and kings down through children, clerks, and hermits. In the image shown here (which is part of the illustration—the other part is on page 131), a wealthy young man is approached by Death. Another illustration from the manuscript appears on page 133.

Use the following questions for discussion:

1. Why would this allegory include images of people from all levels of society?
   Possible response: It illustrates that death does not respect titles or wealth, but comes to everyone.

2. Why might people surrounded by death include it in their art?
   Possible responses: To remind the evil or vain that death is inevitable. They considered it such a common, inescapable part of life that it seemed natural to include it in their art.

⑬ Critical Viewing

Possible response: Students may say that the medieval illustration may have served to teach that death could come to anyone, even the young, strong, and rich.

⑭ Reading Check

Answer: The three rioters swear to kill Death.

Allegory and Archetypal Elements

▶ **Monitor Progress**

1. **Read** aloud the bracketed passage to students.

2. **Ask** students the Literary Analysis question: What archetypal role does the old man play?
   Answer: The old man is the mysterious guide who helps point the way.

▶ **Reteach:** If students are having difficulty, remind them that an exemplum is a story that teaches a moral lesson. These stories often use basic storytelling patterns, called archetypal elements. Review the archetypal elements listed on page 123.

16 Reading Strategy

Rereading

1. **Read** line 212 aloud to students.

2. **Ask:** What "property" is the rioter talking about?
   Answer: He means the gold. Since they found it, they think it is theirs.

3. **Ask** students the Reading Strategy question: Reread lines 206–211 to clarify the remark in line 212.
   Answer: When people saw this gold, they would assume the men were robbers and would punish them.

Literary Analysis
Allegory and Archetypal Elements What archetypal role does the old man play? **15**

Reading Strategy
Rereading Reread lines 206–211 to clarify the remark in line 212. **16**

To kill us younger folk, you thieving swine!"
    "Well, sirs," he said, "if it be your design
To find out Death, turn up this crooked way
Towards that grove, I left him there today
185 Under a tree, and there you'll find him waiting.
He isn't one to hide for all your prating.[20]
You see that oak? He won't be far to find.
And God protect you that redeemed mankind,
Aye, and amend you!" Thus that ancient man.
190   At once the three young rioters began
To run, and reached the tree, and there they found
A pile of golden florins[21] on the ground,
New-coined, eight bushels of them as they thought.
No longer was it Death those fellows sought,
195 For they were all so thrilled to see the sight,
The florins were so beautiful and bright,
That down they sat beside the precious pile.
The wickedest spoke first after a while.
"Brothers," he said, "you listen to what I say.
200 I'm pretty sharp although I joke away.
It's clear that Fortune has bestowed this treasure
To let us live in jollity and pleasure.
Light come, light go! We'll spend it as we ought.
God's precious dignity! Who would have thought
205 This morning was to be our lucky day?
        "If one could only get the gold away,
Back to my house, or else to yours, perhaps
For as you know, the gold is ours, chaps—
We'd all be at the top of fortune, hey?
210 But certainly it can't be done by day.
People would call us robbers—a strong gang,
So our own property would make us hang.
No, we must bring this treasure back by night
Some prudent way, and keep it out of sight.
215 And so as a solution I propose
We draw for lots and see the way it goes;
The one who draws the longest, lucky man,
Shall run to town as quickly as he can
To fetch us bread and wine—but keep things dark—
220 While two remain in hiding here to mark
Our heap of treasure. If there's no delay,
When night comes down we'll carry it away,
All three of us, wherever we have planned."
        He gathered lots and hid them in his hand
225 Bidding them draw for where the luck should fall.

---

20. prating chatter.
21. florins coins.

Think Aloud

Vocabulary: Using Context

Direct students' attention to the word *prudent* in line 214. Use the following "think aloud" to model the skill of using context to infer the meaning of the word. Say to students:

I am unsure of the meaning of the word *prudent* in line 214. When I reread lines 206–214, I understand that the rioter is talking about how to get the gold back to his house without being seen. He is worried that if people see them, they will think the gold is stolen. So traveling in daylight is too dangerous. Traveling in the dark is safer. *Prudent* must have something to do with being safe. I also notice that *prudent* describes the way they plan to move the gold. They are making a careful plan to make sure nothing goes wrong, so maybe a *prudent* way is a careful, safe, or well-planned way.

It fell upon the youngest of them all,
And off he ran at once towards the town.
    As soon as he had gone, the first sat down
And thus began a parley²² with the other:
230 "You know that you can trust me as a brother;
Now let me tell you where your profit lies;
You know our friend has gone to get supplies
And here's a lot of gold that is to be
Divided equally amongst us three.
235 Nevertheless, if I could shape things thus
So that we shared it out—the two of us—
Wouldn't you take it as a friendly act?"
    "But how?" the other said. "He knows the fact
that all the gold was left with me and you;
240 What can we tell him? What are we to do?"
    "Is it a bargain," said the first, "or no?
For I can tell you in a word or so
What's to be done to bring the thing about."
"Trust me," the other said, "you needn't doubt
245 My word. I won't betray you, I'll be true."
    "Well," said his friend, "you see that we are two,
And two are twice as powerful as one.
Now look; when he comes back, get up in fun
To have a wrestle; then, as you attack,
250 I'll up and put my dagger through his back
While you and he are struggling, as in game;
Then draw your dagger too and do the same.
Then all this money will be ours to spend,
Divided equally of course, dear friend.
255 Then we can gratify our lusts and fill
The day with dicing at our own sweet will."
Thus these two miscreants²³ agreed to slay
The third and youngest, as you heard me say.
    The youngest, as he ran towards the town,
260 Kept turning over, rolling up and down
Within his heart the beauty of those bright
New florins, saying, "Lord, to think I might
Have all that treasure to myself alone!
Could there be anyone beneath the throne
265 Of God so happy as I then should be?"
    And so the Fiend,²⁴ our common enemy,
Was given power to put it in his thought
That there was always poison to be bought,

---

22. **parley** discussion.
23. **miscreants** villains.
24. **Fiend** Satan.

18 ▲ **Critical Viewing**
Compare this illustration to the one on page 129. What point might the artist make by depicting contrasting individuals being taken by death? **[Compare and Contrast]**

19 ☑ Reading Check
What does the old man say the rioters will find under the tree? What do they find there?

from The Pardoner's Tale **131**

㉔ Engaging the Essential Question

1. Point out to students that Chaucer makes it clear that the young man plans to kill the other two rioters without regret ("was utterly content," line 273) and without hesitation ("no thought to tarry," line 275).

2. **Ask** students: What effect has greed had on the youngest rioter?
Answer: He is willing to kill the other two without hesitation.

3. Remind students that this story takes place during a time when people died frequently as a result of plague. **Ask** students: What effect do you think this has on the rioter?
Possible Answer: Students may think that because death was common, it did not trouble him to take a life.

㉑ Vocabulary Builder

Greek Prefix *apo-*

1. Call students' attention to *apothecary,* a word that means "pharmacist," or "druggist." Explain to students that *apothecary* contains the Greek prefix *apo-,* which means "away; off; separate." An apothecary is someone who "puts away" prescriptions (that is, he stores them).

2. Have students suggest other words that contain this Greek prefix, and list them on the chalkboard.
Possible responses: apostrophe, apology, apostle, apostasy

3. Have students look up any unfamiliar words in dictionaries.

Vocabulary

tarry (tar′ ē) *v.* to delay or linger

apothecary (ə päth′ ə ker′ ē) *n.* pharmacist; druggist

㉔

Vocabulary

deftly (deft′ lē) *adv.* skillfully; with ease and quickness

sauntered (sôn′ tərd) *v.* walked at an unhurried pace

And that with poison he could kill his friends.
270 To men in such a state the Devil sends
Thoughts of this kind, and has a full permission
To lure them on to sorrow and perdition;[25]
For this young man was utterly content
To kill them both and never to repent.
275   And on he ran, he had no thought to tarry,
㉑ | Came to the town, found an apothecary
And said, "Sell me some poison if you will,
I have a lot of rats I want to kill
And there's a polecat too about my yard
280 That takes my chickens and it hits me hard;
But I'll get even, as is only right,
With vermin that destroy a man by night."
    The chemist answered, "I've a preparation
Which you shall have, and by my soul's salvation
285 If any living creature eat or drink
A mouthful, ere he has the time to think,
Though he took less than makes a grain of wheat,
You'll see him fall down dying at your feet;
Yes, die he must and in so short a while
290 You'd hardly have the time to walk a mile,
The poison is so strong, you understand."
    This cursed fellow grabbed into his hand
The box of poison and away he ran
Into a neighboring street, and found a man
295 Who lent him three large bottles, He withdrew
And deftly poured the poison into two.
He kept the third one clean, as well he might,
For his own drink, meaning to work all night
Stacking the gold and carrying it away.
300 And when this rioter, this devil's clay,
Had filled his bottles up with wine, all three,
Back to rejoin his comrades sauntered he.
    Why make a sermon of it? Why waste breath?
Exactly in the way they'd planned his death
305 They fell on him and slew him, two to one.
Then said the first of them when this was done,
"Now for a drink. Sit down and let's be merry,
For later on there'll be the corpse to bury."
And, as it happened, reaching for a sup,
310 He took a bottle full of poison up
And drank and his companion, nothing loth,
Drank from it also, and they perished both.

---

25. perdition damnation.

Enrichment: Investigating Daily Life

The Apothecary

Though apothecaries in Chaucer's time were essentially the pharmacists of their era, their roles were actually considerably greater. Unlike pharmacists, they could prescribe cures themselves, and they could care for humans and animals alike. Also, because there were no prepackaged medicines, they had to be able to formulate everything themselves.

Because apothecaries could compound poisons for dealing with pests, they became a source not only of lethal draughts, but also of plot twists. In Shakespeare's *Romeo and Juliet,* for example, Romeo goes to an apothecary to buy the poison with which he will end his life.

Activity: Investigating Daily Life Have interested students conduct research on the treatment of illness during the Middle Ages. Have them record and analyze their findings by completing the **Enrichment: Investigating Daily Life** worksheet on page 224 of the *Professional Development Guidebook.*

(22)

(23) ◄ **Critical Viewing**
What does this illustration say about the relationship between material wealth and death? **[Interpret]**

There is, in Avicenna's long relation[26]
Concerning poison and its operation,
315 Trust me, no ghastlier section to transcend
What these two wretches suffered at their end.
Thus these two murderers received their due,
So did the treacherous young poisoner too.

O cursed sin! O blackguardly excess!
320 O treacherous homicide! O wickedness!
O gluttony that lusted on and diced!
O blasphemy that took the name of Christ
With habit-hardened oaths that pride began!
Alas, how comes it that a mortal man,
325 That thou, to thy Creator, Him that wrought thee,

---

26. Avicenna's long relation book on medicines written by Avicenna (980–1037), an Arab physician, which contains a chapter on poisons.

Literary Analysis
Allegory In addition to avarice, or greed, against what sins does the exemplum preach in lines 319–323?

(25) **Reading Check**
What explanation does the rioter give to the Apothecary for buying the poison?

Differentiated Instruction   for Universal Access

EL **Pronunciation for English Learners**

English learners may have difficulty recognizing and pronouncing the short *i* in words such as *did, sin, wickedness,* and *within.* For these students, begin with the one-syllable words *did* and *sin.* Write these words on the board, along with *seen* and *deed.* Pronounce each word as you point to it, having students echo you.

Then say each word, and have students write down which one you said. When students have mastered this exercise, introduce the words *within* and *wickedness,* writing them on the board and having students pronounce them after you.

---

(22) **Humanities**

La Danse Macabre

This is another image from the fifteenth-century *La Danse Macabre* featured on pages 129 and 131. Here, the artist shows death coming for a rich moneylender, a man who took advantage of others by loaning them money for very high fees.

In addition to being common in paintings, the allegorical theme of the Dance of Death was also represented in drama, poetry, music, and dance. Death is viewed as the great equalizer—both inevitable and impartial. The paintings often adorned churches and were meant to remind people that repentance and loving God would be wise before death—represented then as now by a skeleton—came to escort them to their final destination.

Use the following question for discussion:

Why do you think the moneylender looks pleased and seems to be ignoring Death?
Possible response: He may be thinking about how much money he will gain when the borrower pays back the loan and may not have noticed that Death has come to take him.

(23) **Critical Viewing**

Possible response: Students may say that death comes to the rich as well as the poor, and that a person's wealth cannot keep death away.

(24) **Literary Analysis**

Allegory

1. Have students read the bracketed passage to themselves.
2. Then, **ask** them the Literary Analysis question: In addition to avarice, or greed, against what sins does the exemplum preach in the final lines?
   Answer: The exemplum rails against homicide, gluttony, blasphemy, and pride.

(25) **Reading Check**

Answer: He says he needs to kill rats, as well as a polecat that takes his chickens.

Before students respond, you may wish to have them write a brief objective summary of the selection. As they answer the questions below, remind them to support their answers with evidence from the text.

1. (a) The rioters are drinking. A coffin passing by captures their attention. (b) They are trouble-makers—they are drinking before nine in the morning, and are generally dissolute.

2. **Possible responses:** Some may say that the point of the story is true, even though the Pardoner uses it for the wrong reasons. Some may say that the impact is dulled by the Pardoner's hypocrisy.

3. (a) **Possible response:** It seems that the constant reminder of death makes people either very good, or at least careful, because they are aware of death, or very bad, as they try to forget about or think to cheat death. (b) **Possible response:** Some students may respond that stories such as this one remind people to fear death, which may encourage people to behave in a way that is consistant with a society's accepted morals. Other students may respond that stories such as this one may result in people living selfish lives because life seems brief and meaningless in the face of a constant threat of death.

4. **Possible responses:** The desire for gain purely for the love of gain is destructive. The desire for gain at the expense of others or through questionable actions is destructive. The desire for legitimate and reasonable gain, through diligent work, is not.

5. **Possible Answer:** "The Pardoner's Tale" is a good example of how literature reflects society. During the Middle Ages, some representatives of the church used their authority to live lives of leisure and <u>excess</u> without <u>reproach</u>. The Pardoner's <u>role</u> in society allows him to violate the very <u>principles</u> he preaches.

That paid His precious blood for thee and bought thee,
Art so unnatural and false within?
　　　　Dearly beloved, God forgive your sin
And keep you from the vice of avarice!
330　My holy pardon frees you all of this,
Provided that you make the right approaches,
That is with sterling rings, or silver brooches.
Bow down your heads under this holy bull!²⁷
Come on, you women, offer up your wool!
335　I'll write your name into my ledger; so!
Into the bliss of Heaven you shall go.
For I'll absolve you by my holy power,
You that make offering, clean as at the hour
When you were born. . . . That, sirs, is how I preach.
340　And Jesu Christ, soul's healer, aye, the leech
Of every soul, grant pardon and relieve you
Of sin, for that is best I won't deceive you.

---

27. holy bull an official proclamation by the Catholic Church.

Critical Reading

Cite textual evidence to support your responses.

1. **Key Ideas and Details (a)** When the story opens, what are the rioters doing, and what captures their attention? **(b) Generalize:** What sort of people are they? Explain how you know.

2. **Integration of Knowledge and Ideas** The Pardoner is quite open about the manipulative use to which he puts the tale. Do the Pardoner's reasons for telling the story detract from its moral truth? Explain.

3. **Integration of Knowledge and Ideas** The tale refers to the time of the plague. **(a)** What does the tale suggest about the effects of such a disaster on society? Support your answer. **(b) Apply:** Can stories such as this one encourage people to behave well even in times of crisis? Explain.

4. **Integration of Knowledge and Ideas** Do you think the desire for gain is ultimately destructive, as the Pardoner's tale suggests, or can it lead to positive consequences? Explain.

5. **Integration of Knowledge and Ideas** What can you learn about life in the Middle Ages from "The Pardoner's Tale"? Use at least two of these Essential Question words in your response: *role, principles, reproach, excess. [Connecting to the Essential Question: How does literature shape or reflect society?]*

Think Aloud

Reading Strategy
Remind students that on page 40 they learned to use paraphrasing to help clarify the main idea of a passage. Direct students' attention to lines 335–339. Use the following "think aloud" to model paraphrasing the text. Say to students:

Let's say I don't quite understand what the Pardoner is getting at in these lines. In line 335 he seems to be saying that he has a ledger, and that if he writes a person's name in the ledger they will go to Heaven. A ledger is a book that businesses use to keep track of money. He might be implying that getting into Heaven is like a business transaction. In lines 337–339, the Pardoner says he will absolve the people who make an offering. I think *absolve* means the same thing as *pardon.* So he will pardon people who make an offering, that is, who give him payment. I might paraphrase these lines this way: *If you give me payment, I'll pardon you so you can go to Heaven.*

After You Read | from *The Pardoner's Tale*

Literary Analysis

© 1. Key Ideas and Details (a) Explain why "The Pardoner's Tale" is an **allegory,** and cite a passage to support your point. **(b)** Then, explain how the allegory of "The Pardoner's Tale" proves that greed is the root of all evil.

© 2. Integration of Knowledge and Ideas Identify two ways in which "The Pardoner's Tale" differs from modern short stories.

© 3. Craft and Structure (a) Why is it ironic, or surprising, that the Pardoner tells this story? **(b)** What point might Chaucer be making about moral tales by assigning this one to a rogue?

© 4. Craft and Structure (a) What role does the old man perform in the story? **(b)** What might he symbolize? **(c)** Explain the way in which the old man's presence in the tale benefits the Pardoner and motivates his listeners to adopt a more wholesome existence.

© 5. Integration of Knowledge and Ideas (a) On a chart like the one shown, explain how the tale illustrates the **archetypal elements** listed.

Patterns of Three	Test of Characters	Mysterious Guide	Just Ending

(b) Then, work with a partner to add to your response. Share your combined answers with the class.

© 6. Key Ideas and Details What other familiar elements does the story include?

© 7. Integration of Knowledge and Ideas Why do you think many tales feature things that come in threes?

© 8. Integration of Knowledge and Ideas Do you think that archetypal elements are more likely to be found in tales told orally or in written stories? Explain.

Reading Strategy

9. Find a passage that you had trouble understanding when you first read it. Improve your comprehension by **rereading** the lines leading up to the passage. Then, explain what the passage means. If you have already clarified the passage in this way, explain how you did so.

10. In line 112, the publican tells the rioters, "He might do you dishonor." Reread the previous lines. Then, use the information they provide to explain the publican's meaning.

11. In line 319, the Pardoner speaks of "blackguardly excess" as well as homicide. Reread earlier lines to clarify what he means.

from The Pardoner's Tale **135**

© Common Core State Standards

Writing

1.a. Introduce precise, knowledgeable claim(s), establish the significance of the claim(s), distinguish the claim(s) from alternate or opposing claims, and create an organization that logically sequences claim(s), counterclaims, reasons, and evidence. *(p. 136)*

Language

6. Acquire and use accurately general academic and domain-specific words and phrases, sufficient for reading, writing, speaking, and listening at the college and career readiness level; demonstrate independence in gathering vocabulary knowledge when considering a word or phrase important to comprehension or expression. *(p. 136)*

Answers

1. **(a)** An allegory has both a literal and a symbolic meaning. The Pardoner says that his stories are examples he uses to preach in lines 78–79. **(b)** The exemplum shows that when the rioters become obsessed with gold, they are willing to do anything to get it.

2. **Possible responses:** Students may point to the personification of Death, the methods used for killing, or the sermonlike ending that turns from the point of the story to evil in general.

3. **(a)** It is ironic that the Pardoner tells this story because he is open about his own greed. **(b) Possible response:** Chaucer may be making the point that moral tales are easier to tell than to heed.

4. **Possible responses: (a)** The old man sets the action in motion. **(b)** He symbolizes death as a blessing. Few would want eternal life without eternal youth. **(c)** The old man's presence shows that no one knows when death might come, so forsaking greed and seeking pardon for sins is a wise idea.

5. **(a) and (b)** Patterns of Three: three rioters; Test of Characters: pledge to find and vanquish Death; Mysterious Guide: old man who directs them to Death; Just Ending: murderers are poisoned and poisoner is murdered.

6. **Possible response:** The story includes a mysterious threat to the population and a community of people who treat each other with more or less respect.

7. **Possible response:** Three is rich with mythical associations; it allows for triangular conflict.

8. **Possible response:** Archetypal elements are more common in tales told orally because patterns help storytellers remember information and familiar elements help listeners understand.

9. Answers will vary.

10. The publican means Death might kill them, too.

11. The excesses of the rioters could include their drinking, their greed, their willingness to kill for money, or all of these.

Assessment Practice

Identifying Events

Many tests require students to identify the sequence of events. Use the following as practice:

One of [the rioters] called the little
tavern-knave
And said "Go and find out at once—look
spry!—
Whose corpse is in that coffin passing
by; . . .
"Sir," said the boy, "no need,

I promise you;
Two hours before you came here I was told."
Which event happens first?

   A The rioter called the boy.
   B The boy went to check the coffin.
   C The boy learned who had died.
   D The coffin passed the tavern.

Choice **B** didn't happen. Choices **A** and **D** were happening at the same time. The boy heard "two hours before you came," so the correct answer is **C**.

Vocabulary Acquisition and Use

Word Analysis

Sample Answers

1. apology: words that explain <u>away</u> your offense
2. apogee: the farthest point <u>away</u> from the center
3. apostle: a person who is sent <u>off</u> on a special mission

Vocabulary

Answers

1. sauntered
2. pallor
3. hoary
4. deftly
5. tarry
6. apothecary

Writing

You may use this Writing Lesson as timed-writing practice, or you may allow students to develop the argumentative text as a writing assignment over several days.

Work with students to draw up guidelines, based on the assignment, for their sermons:

1. **Focus and Organization** The writer should clearly state his or her position, and follow with details that support this position.
2. **Elaboration** The writer should use several strategies to support his or her main point, such as examples, arguments, and emotional appeals.
3. **Style** To appeal to a contemporary audience, the content of the sermon must be relevant to today's society.

PERFORMANCE TASKS
Integrated Language Skills

Vocabulary Acquisition and Use

Word Analysis: Greek Prefix *apo-*

The word apothecary, meaning "druggist," combines the Greek prefix *apo-*, meaning "away; off; separate," with a form of a Greek word for "put." An apothecary is one who "puts away," or stores, prescriptions. This prefix can often be found in *scientific terms* and in other words, too.

Write an alternate definition for each numbered word that contains the word *away, off,* or *separate.* An example appears first.

apoapsis *n.* farthest point from gravitational center in the orbit of any satellite

alternate definition: <u>away</u> or separated from gravitational center in a satellite's orbit

1. **apology** *n.* words of regret for an offense
2. **apogee** *n.* the highest or farthest point
3. **apostle** *n.* a person sent on a special mission

Vocabulary: Relate New to Familiar Words

Associating a new word with an already familiar word can help you remember the meaning of the new word. For each of the following items, replace the italicized familiar word with one of the words from the vocabulary list.

1. Death *strolled* down the moonlit lane.
2. His long, craggy face shone with an eerie *paleness*.
3. His long *whitened* beard fluttered in the silent breeze.
4. When a black cat crossed his path, Death stepped *easily* over its scrawny back.
5. Suddenly, Death picked up his pace. "This is no time to *dally*," he thought.
6. "I feel like death, and the *pharmacist* is closing shop in five minutes!"

Writing

Argumentative Text In the final lines of his tale, the Pardoner preaches passionately on the subject of greed (among other sins). Write a **sermon**—a persuasive talk about some aspect of morality—on greed. Your sermon should be directed toward a contemporary audience.

Prewriting First, brainstorm for a list of modern-day examples of greed. Then jot down a few answers to this question: What ill effects do these forms of greed cause for an individual or for society at large?

Drafting Begin your sermon with a strong *claim* or a vivid image. Then, spend the remainder of your sermon developing this claim or image. Support your central idea with examples, arguments, emotional appeals, and word choice suited to a contemporary audience.

Revising As you read your draft, imagine that you disagree with each key point you encounter. Then revise to acknowledge and refute that opposing argument.

> **Model: Revising to Refute Opponents**
>
> ~~may be convenient for a large family, but it is nevertheless~~
> Owning a large, gas-guzzling vehicle is irresponsible. It consumes twice the fuel of smaller cars and puts twice as much pollution into the atmosphere. It therefore gives *you*, the owner, a double ownership in the problem of global warming...
>
> The writer revises to anticipate what the opposition might say.

136 From Legend to History (449–1485)

Assessment Resources

Unit 1 Resources

L1 L2 EL **Selection Test A,** pp. 127–129. Administer Test A to less advanced readers.

L3 L4 EL **Selection Test B,** pp. 130–132. Administer Test B to on-level and more advanced students.

L3 L4 **Open-Book Test,** pp. 124–126. As an alternative, give the Open-Book Test.

All **Customizable Test Bank**

All **Self-tests**
Students may prepare for the **Selection Test** by taking the **Self-test** online.

Before You Read

The Wife of Bath's Tale

❶ Connecting to the Essential Question In her tale, the feisty Wife of Bath asserts the idea that husbands and wives should be equal in marriage. As you read, identify passages in which the Wife of Bath supports the idea of "selfsame sovereignty," or equality in marriage. This will help you address the Essential Question: **How does literature shape or reflect society?**

❷ Literary Analysis

A **frame story** contains—or frames—another story or group of stories. In *The Canterbury Tales,* the frame story is the characters' pilgrimage to Canterbury Cathedral described in the Prologue. Within the frame story are the tales told by the characters on their journey. Here are some ways in which the frame story develops a work of literature:

- Individual tales reflect the description of the storytellers' personalities and lives that you find in the frame story.
- A tale may itself contain a frame story and an inner tale. "The Wife of Bath's Tale" has such a structure.
- The **setting** of the frame story, the time and place of its action, may not match the settings of individual tales. For example, the events in the Prologue occur around Chaucer's time, but the Wife of Bath sets her frame story much earlier, during the reign of King Arthur.

Analyze these interactions and consider their effects as you read "The Wife of Bath's Tale."

❸ Reading Strategy

Ⓒ Preparing to Read Complex Texts You may encounter unfamiliar words while reading. If so, repair your comprehension by **checking context clues**—words and phrases in the surrounding passage that shed light on the meaning of a word. Common context clues are synonyms, antonyms, and examples that clarify a word's meaning. Use a chart like the one shown to find context clues as you read.

❹ Vocabulary

implored (im plôrd′) *v.* begged earnestly (p. 140)

relates (ri lāts′) *v.* tells (p. 141)

contemptuous (kən temp′ chŏŏ əs) *adj.* scornful (p. 145)

bequeath (bē kwēth′) *v.* hand down as an inheritance (p. 146)

prowess (prou′ is) *n.* heroism; distinction (p. 147)

esteemed (ə stēmd′) *adj.* highly respected; held in high regard (p. 147)

rebuke (ri byŏŏk′) *v.* criticize strongly (p. 149)

Ⓒ Common Core State Standards

Reading Literature
3. Analyze the impact of the author's choices regarding how to develop and relate elements of a story or drama.

Passage

"Hundreds of years ago, in days of yore"

↓

Context Clue

Unfamiliar Word: *yore*
Context Clue: Hundreds of years ago
Relation to Word: Similar in meaning

↓

Conclusion

If days of *yore* took place hundreds of years ago, *yore* must mean time long past.

PHLit Online!
www.PHLitOnline.com

The Wife of Bath's Tale **137**

PRETEACH

❶ Connecting to the Essential Question

1. Review the assignment with the class.

2. **Ask** students how the Wife of Bath would probably feel about not being known by a name that asserts her individuality. Have students complete the assignment.

3. As students read, have them look for passages in which the Wife of Bath supports the idea of equality in marriage.

❷ Literary Analysis

Introduce the skill using the instruction on the student page.

Think Aloud: Model the Skill

Say to students:

I have seen frames in other stories I have read. In *The Thousand and One Nights,* Queen Scheherazade tells the king a different story each night to save her life. The frame is the story in which Scheherazade is in danger of being killed.

❸ Reading Strategy

1. Introduce the strategy using the instruction on the student page.

2. Give students a copy of **Reading Strategy Graphic Organizer B,** page 22 in *Graphic Organizer Transparencies,* to fill out as they read.

❹ Vocabulary

1. Pronounce each word, giving its definition, and have students say it aloud.

2. For more guidance, see the *Classroom Strategies and Teaching Routines* card for introducing vocabulary.

PHLit Online!
www.PHLitOnline.com

Teaching From Technology

Preparing to Read
Go to **www.PHLitOnline.com** and display the *Get Connected!* slide show for this selection. Have the class brainstorm for responses to the writing prompt, entering ideas in the interactive journal. Then have students complete their responses as homework.

To build background, display the Background video and More About the Author features.

Using the Interactive Student Edition
Go to **www.PHLitOnline.com** and display the **Enriched Online Student Edition.** As the class reads the selection or listens to the narration, record answers to side-column prompts using the graphic organizers accessible on the interactive page. Alternatively, have students use the online edition individually, answering the prompts as they read.

• The Wife of Bath's Tale
Lesson Pacing Guide

DAY 1 Preteach

- Ⓒ Administer the Reading and Vocabulary Warm-ups (*Unit 1 Resources*, pp. 114–117) as necessary.
- • Introduce the Literary Analysis concept: Frame.
- Ⓒ Introduce the Reading Strategy: Checking Context Clues.
- • Build Background with the author and Background features.
- • Develop thematic thinking with Connecting to the Essential Question.
- Ⓒ Teach the selection vocabulary.

DAYS 2–3 Preteach/Teach/Assess

- Ⓒ Distribute copies of the appropriate graphic organizer for the Reading Strategy (*Graphic Organizer Transparencies*, pp. 21–22).
- Ⓒ Distribute copies of the appropriate graphic organizer for Literary Analysis (*Graphic Organizer Transparencies*, pp. 23–24).
- • Prepare students to read with the Activating Prior Knowledge activities (TE).
- • Informally monitor comprehension while students read.
- • Use the Reading Check questions to confirm comprehension.
- • Develop students' understanding of frame using the Literary Analysis prompts.
- • Develop students' ability to check context clues using the Reading Strategy prompts.
- Ⓒ Reinforce vocabulary with the Vocabulary notes.
- Ⓒ Assess students' comprehension and mastery of the skills by having them answer the Critical Reading, Literary Analysis, and Reading Strategy questions.
- Ⓒ Have students complete the Vocabulary Lesson.

DAY 4 Extend/Assess

- Ⓒ Have students complete the Conventions and Style Lesson.
- Ⓒ Have students complete the Writing Lesson and write a response to literature. (You may assign as homework.)
- • Administer Selection Test A or B (*Unit 1 Resources*, pp. 127–129 or 130–132).

Ⓒ Common Core State Standards

Reading Literature 3. Analyze the impact of author's choices regarding how to develop and relate elements of a story or drama.

Writing 1.a Create an organization that logically sequences claims, counterclaims, reasons, and evidence.
1.e Provide a concluding statement or section that follows from and supports the argument presented.

Language 3. Apply knowledge of language to understand how language functions in different contexts, to make effective choices for meaning or style, and to comprehend more fully when reading or listening.
4. Determine or clarify the meaning of unknown and multiple-meaning words and phrases based on grades 11–12 reading and content, choosing flexibly from a range of strategies.

Additional Standards Practice
Common Core Companion, pp. 28–35; 185–195; 322–323; 324–331

Daily Block Scheduling
Each day in this Lesson Pacing Guide represents a 40–50 minute period. Teachers using block scheduling may combine days to revise pacing. In addition, teachers may differentiate and support core instruction by integrating components for extended and intensive support as students require. See the Guide to Selected Leveled Resources (facing page).

Guide to Selected Leveled Resources

R T I Tier 1 (students performing on level)

The Wife of Bath's Tale

Warm Up	Practice, model, and monitor fluency, working with the whole class or in groups.	Vocabulary and Reading Warm-ups B, *Unit 1 Resources,* pp. 114–115, 117
Comprehension/Skills	Support and monitor comprehension and skills development, having students complete the activities, graphic organizers, and interactive prompts independently or as a class.	• *Reader's Notebook,* adapted instruction and full selection **EL** *Reader's Notebook: English Learner's Version,* adapted instruction and adapted selection • **Reading Skill Graphic Organizer B,** *Graphic Organizer Transparencies,* p. 22 • **Literary Analysis Graphic Organizer B,** *Graphic Organizer Transparencies,* p. 24
Monitor Progress **A**	Monitor student progress with the differentiated curriculum-based assessment in the *Unit Resources.*	• **Selection Test B,** *Unit 1 Resources,* pp. 130–132 • **Open-Book Test,** *Unit 1 Resources,* pp. 124–126

R T I Tier 2 (students requiring intervention)

The Wife of Bath's Tale

Warm Up	Practice, model, and monitor fluency in groups or with individuals.	• **Vocabulary and Reading Warm-ups A,** *Unit 1 Resources,* pp. 114–116 • *Hear It!* Audio CD (adapted text)
Comprehension/Skills	• Support and monitor comprehension and skills development, working in small groups or with individuals. • As students complete the selection in the appropriate version of the *Reader's Notebook,* monitor comprehension frequently with group questions and individual instruction. • Model strategies while guiding students in completing the activities and prompts in the *Reader's Notebook,* as well as the graphic organizers. • Practice skills and monitor mastery with the *Reading Kit* worksheets.	• *Reader's Notebook: Adapted Version,* adapted instruction and adapted selection **EL** *Reader's Notebook: English Learner's Version,* adapted instruction and adapted selection • **Reading Skill Graphic Organizer A,** *Graphic Organizer Transparencies,* p. 21 • **Literary Analysis Graphic Organizer A,** *Graphic Organizer Transparencies,* p. 23 • *Reading Kit,* Practice worksheets
Monitor Progress **A**	Monitor student progress with the differentiated curriculum-based assessment in the *Unit Resources* and in the *Reading Kit.*	• **Selection Test A,** *Unit 1 Resources,* pp. 127–129 • *Reading Kit,* Assess worksheets,

TIER 3 Tier 3 intervention may require consultation with the student's special-education or dyslexia specialist. For additional support, see the Tier 2 activities and resources listed above.

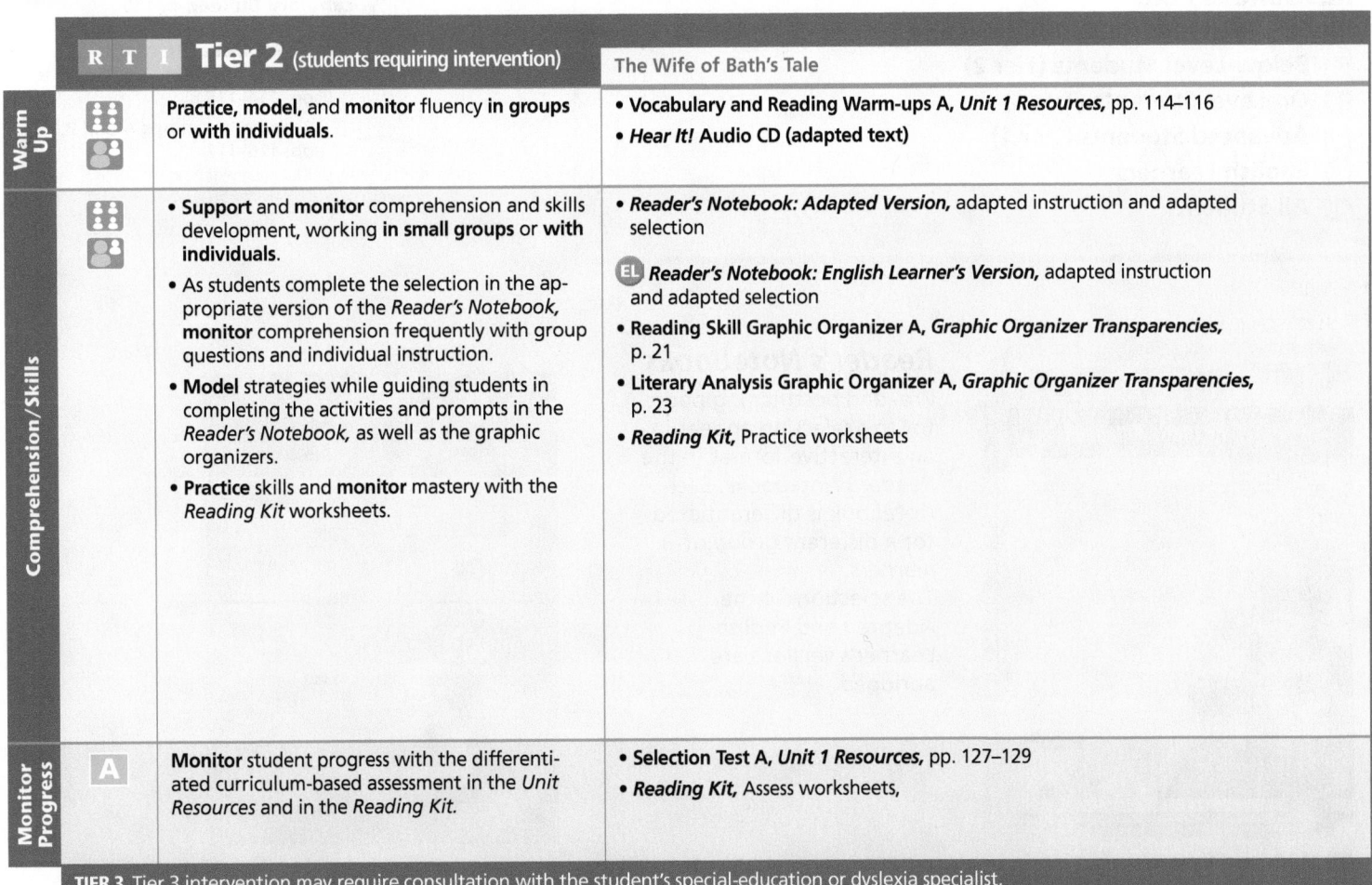 One-on-one teaching   Group work   Whole class instruction   Independent work   **A** Assessment

For a complete guide to selection support, including support for Advanced students, see the Overview of Resources in the frontmatter.

• The Wife of Bath's Tale

RESOURCES FOR:

L1 Special-Needs Students

L2 Below-Level Students (Tier 2)

L3 On-Level Students (Tier 1)

L4 Advanced Students (Tier 1)

EL English Learners

All All Students

Vocabulary/Fluency/Prior Knowledge

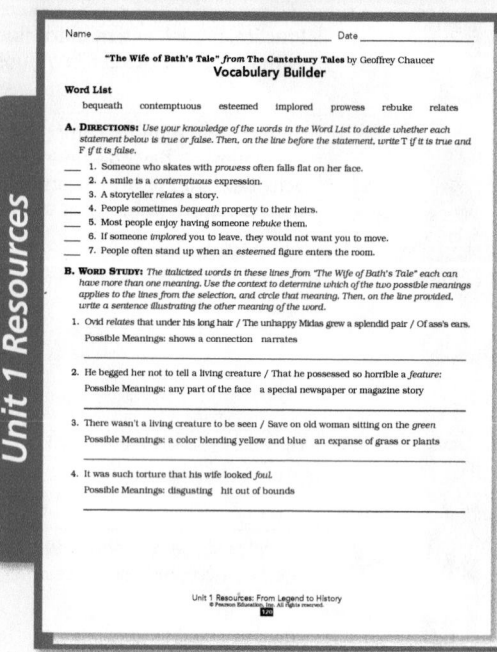

All Vocabulary Builder, p. 120

Also available for these selections:

EL L1 L2 Vocabulary Warm-ups A and B, pp. 114–115

EL L1 L2 Reading Warm-ups A and B, pp. 116–117

L2 L3 *Reader's Notebook*

L1 *Reader's Notebook: Adapted Version*

EL *Reader's Notebook: English Learner's Version*

EL *Reader's Notebook: Spanish Version*

Reader's Notebooks

Pre- and postreading pages for this selection appear in an interactive format in the *Reader's Notebooks*. Each *Notebook* is differentiated for a different group of learners.

The selections in the Adapted and English Learner's versions are abridged.

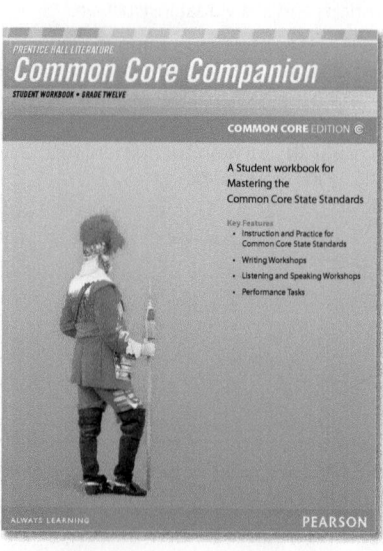

© *Common Core Companion*

Additional instruction and practice for each Common Core State Standard

Selection Support

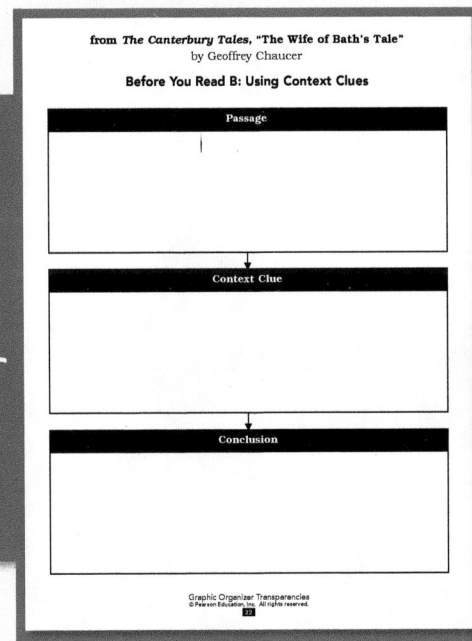

Graphic Organizer Transparencies

from *The Canterbury Tales*, "The Wife of Bath's Tale"
by Geoffrey Chaucer

Before You Read B: Using Context Clues

Passage

Context Clue

Conclusion

EL L3 Reading: Graphic Organizer B, p. 22

Also available for these selections:

EL L1 L2 Reading: Graphic Organizer A
(partially filled in), p. 21

EL L1 L2 Literary Analysis: Graphic Organizer A (partially filled in), p. 23

EL L3 Literary Analysis: Graphic Organizer B, p. 24

Skills Development/Extension

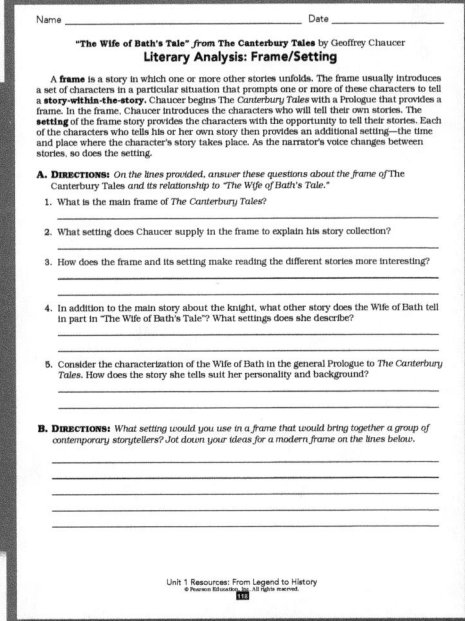

Unit 1 Resources

"The Wife of Bath's Tale" *from* The Canterbury Tales by Geoffrey Chaucer
Literary Analysis: Frame/Setting

A **frame** is a story in which one or more other stories unfolds. The frame usually introduces a set of characters in a particular situation that prompts one or more of these characters to tell a **story-within-the-story**. Chaucer begins The Canterbury Tales with a Prologue that provides a frame. In the frame, Chaucer introduces the characters who will tell their own stories. The **setting** of the frame story provides the characters with the opportunity to tell their stories. Each of the characters who tells his or her own story then provides an additional setting—the time and place where the character's story takes place. As the narrator's voice changes between stories, so does the setting.

A. DIRECTIONS: *On the lines provided, answer these questions about the frame of* The Canterbury Tales *and its relationship to "The Wife of Bath's Tale."*

1. What is the main frame of *The Canterbury Tales*?

2. What setting does Chaucer supply in the frame to explain his story collection?

3. How does the frame and its setting make reading the different stories more interesting?

4. In addition to the main story about the knight, what other story does the Wife of Bath tell in part in "The Wife of Bath's Tale"? What settings does she describe?

5. Consider the characterization of the Wife of Bath in the general Prologue to *The Canterbury Tales*. How does the story she tells suit her personality and background?

B. DIRECTIONS: *What setting would you use in a frame that would bring together a group of contemporary storytellers? Jot down your ideas for a modern frame on the lines below.*

Unit 1 Resources: From Legend to History

All Literary Analysis, p. 118

Also available for these selections:

All Reading, p. 119

EL L3 L4 Support for Writing, p. 121

EL L3 L4 Grammar and Style, p. 122

L4 Enrichment, p. 123

Assessment

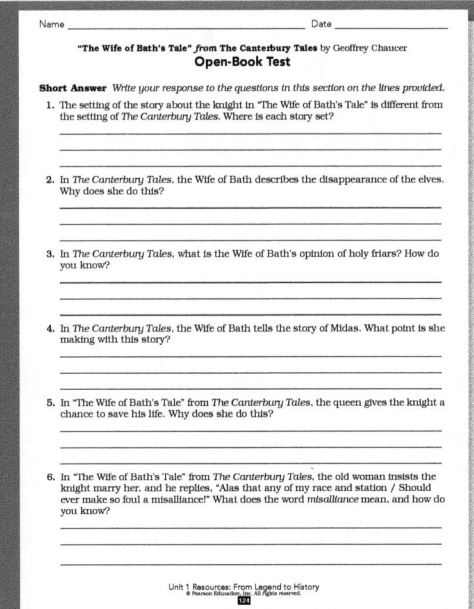

"The Wife of Bath's Tale" *from* The Canterbury Tales by Geoffrey Chaucer
Open-Book Test

Short Answer *Write your response to the questions in this section on the lines provided.*

1. The setting of the story about the knight in "The Wife of Bath's Tale" is different from the setting of *The Canterbury Tales*. Where is each story set?

2. In *The Canterbury Tales*, the Wife of Bath describes the disappearance of the elves. Why does she do this?

3. In *The Canterbury Tales*, what is the Wife of Bath's opinion of holy friars? How do you know?

4. In *The Canterbury Tales*, the Wife of Bath tells the story of Midas. What point is she making with this story?

5. In "The Wife of Bath's Tale" from *The Canterbury Tales*, the queen gives the knight a chance to save his life. Why does she do this?

6. In "The Wife of Bath's Tale" from *The Canterbury Tales*, the old woman insists the knight marry her, and he replies, "Alas that any of my race and station / Should ever make so foul a misalliance!" What does the word *misalliance* mean, and how do you know?

Unit 1 Resources: From Legend to History

L3 L4 Open-Book Test, pp. 124–126

Also available for these selections:

EL L3 L4 Selection Test A, pp. 127–129

EL L1 L2 Selection Test B, pp. 130–132

Online Resources: All print materials are also available online.

- complete narrated selection text
- a thematically related video with writing prompt
- an interactive graphic organizer
- highlighting feature
- access to all student print resources, adapted to individual student needs
- Spanish and English summaries
- adapted selection translations in Spanish
- adapted selection translations in Spanish

Get Connected! (thematic video with writing prompt)

Also available:
Background Video
All videos are available in Spanish.

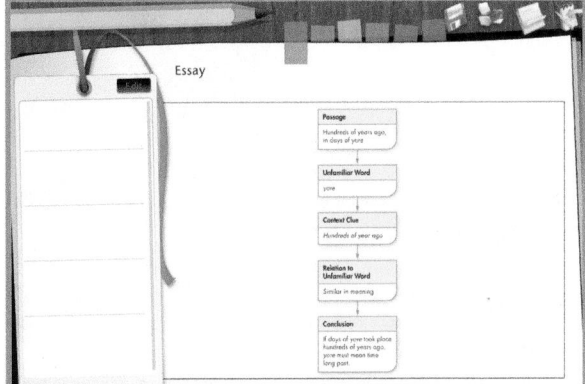

Writer's Journal (with graphics feature)

Also available:
Vocabulary Central (tools and activities for studying vocabulary)

❶❷ THE WIFE of BATH'S TALE

Geoffrey Chaucer
translated by Nevill Coghill

❶ About the Selection

"The Wife of Bath's Tale" addresses what women desire the most. In order to save his life, a knight embarks on a quest to answer the queen's question of what women desire most. On his journey, he meets an old woman who agrees to tell the knight the answer if he does whatever she says. The knight returns to the court and delivers the correct answer. The old woman tells the knight he has to marry her. He agrees, unwillingly. The wife then lectures the knight about all his objections to her as a wife. The tale ends with the knight yielding to his wife and receiving a welcome surprise.

❷ Activating Prior Knowledge

Ask students what the most important quality for a long-lasting relationship is. What does a woman or man want most for herself or himself in a long-term relationship? Encourage students to go beyond the obvious and superficial. Have students list their responses. Tell students that they will find an answer in this story, and that it is most likely one that they have not thought of.

Concept Connector ➡️

Tell students they will return to their responses after reading the selection.

Ⓒ Text Complexity Rubric

The Wife of Bath's Tale

Qualitative Measures	
Context/Knowledge Demands	Medieval romance; historical knowledge demands 1 2 ③ 4 5
Structure/Language Conventionality and Clarity	Archaic syntax and language; poetic diction 1 2 ③ 4 5
Levels of Meaning/ Purpose/Concept Level	Accessible (ideas about women and marriage) 1 ② 3 4 5

Quantitative Measures			
Lexile	NP	**Text Length**	3,318 words
Overall Complexity	**More accessible**		

Reader and Task Suggestions

Preparing to Read the Text
- Using the information about the Wife of Bath in the General Prologue (pp. 108–109), discuss the likely content of her story.
- Review strategies for using context clues to determine the meanings of unfamiliar words.
- Guide students to use Multidraft Reading strategies to deepen their comprehension (TE p. 93).

Leveled Tasks
Structure/Language If students will have difficulty with archaic language, have them read the selection focusing on vocabulary. Tell them to list unfamiliar terms, try using context, and check definitions. Then, have students reread the selection for content.

Evaluating If students will not have difficulty with archaic language, have them consider why such language is well suited to the Wife of Bath's tale.

When good King Arthur ruled in ancient days,
(A king that every Briton loves to praise.)
This was a land brim-full of fairy folk.
The Elf-Queen and her courtiers joined and broke
5   Their elfin dance on many a green mead,
Or so was the opinion once, I read,
Hundreds of years ago, in days of yore.
But no one now sees fairies any more.
For now the saintly charity and prayer
10   Of holy friars seem to have purged the air;
They search the countryside through field and stream
As thick as motes[1] that speckle a sun-beam,
Blessing the halls, the chambers, kitchens, bowers,
Cities and boroughs, castles, courts and towers,
15   Thorpes,[2] barns and stables, outhouses and dairies,
And that's the reason why there are no fairies.
Wherever there was wont to walk an elf
To-day there walks the holy friar himself
As evening falls or when the daylight springs,
20   Saying his matins[3] and his holy things,
Walking his limit round from town to town.
Women can now go safely up and down.
By every bush or under every tree;
There is no other incubus but he,
25   So there is really no one else to hurt you
And he will do no more than take your virtue.
        Now it so happened, I began to say,
Long, long ago in good King Arthur's day,
There was a knight who was a lusty liver.
30   One day as he came riding from the river
He saw a maiden walking all forlorn
Ahead of him, alone as she was born.
And of that maiden, spite of all she said,
By very force he took her maidenhead.
35   This act of violence made such a stir,
So much petitioning of the king for her,
That he condemned the knight to lose his head
By course of law. He was as good as dead
(It seems that then the statutes took that view)

---

1. **motes** dust particles.
2. **Thorpes** villages.
3. **matins** morning prayers.

◄ **Critical Viewing** Which details in this picture of the Wife of Bath suggest she is a self-confident middle-class woman? **[Analyze]**

The Wife of Bath's Tale **139**

Checking Context Clues

1. Point out that the meanings of some words can be determined fairly accurately by using context clues.

2. **Ask** students to summarize lines 50–58.
   Answer: The queen tells the knight that he shall live if he can correctly answer what it is that women desire most. She tells him that if he cannot answer now, he can have a year and a day to find an answer.

3. **Ask** students to respond to the first Reading Strategy prompt: Use the surrounding lines to determine the meaning of the word *concede* in line 54.
   Answer: Beginning in line 53, the Queen tells the knight that if he cannot answer the question now she will give him a period of time in which to find an answer. Students may suggest that *concede* means "allow," "grant," or "give."

4. If possible, have students confirm their meaning in a dictionary or thesaurus.

❺ 🅠 **Engaging the Essential Question**

1. Point out to students that the king originally was going to have the knight killed as punishment for his crime.

2. **Ask** students: Why isn't the knight killed?
   Answer: The queen intervenes, and the knight's fate is left in her hands.

3. **Ask** students: Do you think this is an example of equality in marriage? Why or why not?
   Answer: Students may say that it is an example of equality because the queen gets her way. Others may feel that the use of *implored* suggests that the queen had to ask permission, and *ceaselessly* suggests that he gave in only because the queen was unusually persistent in asking.

Vocabulary
implored (im plôrd′) *v.*
begged earnestly

Reading Strategy
Checking Context Clues
Use the surrounding lines to determine the meaning of the word *concede* in line 54.

But that the queen, and other ladies too,
40   implored the king to exercise his grace
So ceaselessly, he gave the queen the case
And granted her his life, and she could choose
Whether to show him mercy or refuse.
❺   The queen returned him thanks with all her might,
45   And then she sent a summons to the knight
At her convenience, and expressed her will:
"You stand, for such is the position still,
In no way certain of your life," said she,
50   "Yet you shall live if you can answer me:
❹   What is the thing that women most desire?
Beware the axe and say as I require.
          "If you can't answer on the moment, though,
I will concede you this: you are to go
55   A twelvemonth and a day to seek and learn
Sufficient answer, then you shall return.
I shall take gages⁴ from you to extort
Surrender of your body to the court."
          Sad was the knight and sorrowfully sighed,
60   But there! All other choices were denied,
And in the end he chose to go away
And to return after a year and day
Armed with such answer as there might be sent
To him by God. He took his leave and went.

65   He knocked at every house, searched every place,
Yes, anywhere that offered hope of grace.
What could it be that women wanted most?
But all the same he never touched a coast,
Country or town in which there seemed to be
70   Any two people willing to agree.
          Some said that women wanted wealth and treasure,
"Honor," said some, some "Jollity and pleasure,"
Some "Gorgeous clothes" and others "Fun in bed,"
❻   " To be oft widowed and remarried," said
75   Others again, and some that what most mattered
Was that we should be cosseted⁵ and flattered.
That's very near the truth, it seems to me;

---

4. **gages** guarantees.
5. **cosseted** pampered.

140 From Legend to History (A.D. 449–1485)

Enrichment: Investigating Culture

The Changing Meaning of Chivalry

People sometimes say that chivalry is dead—meaning that men no longer hold doors open for women or practice other forms of polite behavior. Originally, however, chivalry had little to do with politeness; it had to do with codes of conduct and ideal qualities such as bravery and honor. Men who were chivalrous were knights who rode horses and fought on behalf of their kings. Knights who practiced chivalry were loyal to God, their temporal master or king, and their love (which was usually platonic). This system of ideals experienced its height in the twelfth and thirteenth centuries.

Activity: Investigating Culture
In the twelfth and thirteenth centuries, the practice of chivalry grew into a culture of its own. Have interested students conduct research on this "culture" of chivalry. Have students record information on the **Enrichment: Investigating Culture** worksheet, *Professional Development Guidebook,* page 223.

A man can win us best with flattery.
To dance attendance on us, make a fuss,
Ensnares us all, the best and worst of us.

     Some say the things we most desire are these:
Freedom to do exactly as we please,
With no one to reprove our faults and lies,
Rather to have one call us good and wise.
Truly there's not a woman in ten score
Who has a fault, and someone rubs the sore,
But she will kick if what he says is true;
You try it out and you will find so too.
However vicious we may be within
We like to be thought wise and void of sin.
Others assert we women find it sweet
When we are thought dependable, discreet
And secret, firm of purpose and controlled,
Never betraying things that we are told.
But that's not worth the handle of a rake;
Women conceal a thing? For Heaven's sake!
Remember Midas?[6] Will you hear the tale?

     Among some other little things, now stale,
Ovid *relates* that under his long hair
The unhappy Midas grew a splendid pair
Of ass's ears; as subtly as he might,
He kept his foul deformity from sight;
Save for his wife, there was not one that knew.
He loved her best, and trusted in her too.
He begged her not to tell a living creature
That he possessed so horrible a feature.
And she—she swore, were all the world to win,
She would not do such villainy and sin
As saddle her husband with so foul a name;
Besides to speak would be to share the shame.
Nevertheless she thought she would have died
Keeping this secret bottled up inside;
It seemed to swell her heart and she, no doubt,
Thought it was on the point of bursting out.

     Fearing to speak of it to woman or man,
Down to a reedy marsh she quickly ran
And reached the sedge. Her heart was all on fire
And, as a bittern[7] bumbles in the mire,

---

6. **Midas** In mythology, King Midas had the magic touch that turned everything to gold. Here, Chaucer makes reference to Ovid's *Metamorphoses*.
7. **bittern** small wading bird.

The Wife of Bath's Tale **141**

Sidebar Notes

Reading Strategy
Checking Context Clues
Which context clues might help you figure out the meaning of *ensnares* in line 80?

Vocabulary
relates (ri lāts´) *v.* tells

Literary Analysis
Frame Story
What clues in lines 97–99 signal the beginning of a tale-within-a-tale?

Reading Check ⑧
What punishment does the queen demand of the knight?

Teacher Margin

⑥ Reading Strategy
Checking Context Clues

1. **Ask** students to summarize the answers the knight finds in lines 71–80.
   Answer: Some women want wealth, and some want honor; some want pleasure; some want nice clothes; and others want fun in bed. Others want to be married and widowed. Most want to be flattered, because men who flatter women often catch them.

2. Have students use the **Reading Strategy Graphic Organizer** to clarify the meaning of *ensnares* in line 80.

3. **Ask** students the Reading Strategy question: Which context clues help you figure out the meaning of *ensnares* in line 80?
   Possible response: Line 78 talks about the best way for a man to "win" a woman. Lines 79–80 further expand on how flattery works on all women. Therefore, *ensnares* must mean "catches or traps."

⑦ Literary Analysis
Frame

1. Remind students that a frame is a story that brackets another story or group of stories. For example, the story of the pilgrimage to Canterbury is the frame for the stories of the individual travelers.

2. Point out that "The Wife of Bath's Tale" is a frame, too. On page 179, the Wife interrupts her own tale to retell the story of King Midas.

3. **Ask** the Literary Analysis question: What clues in lines 97–99 signal the beginning of the tale-within-a-tale?
   Answer: The clues that indicate the beginning of the tale-within-a-tale are the questions "Remember Midas? Will you hear the tale?" (line 97).

⑧ Reading Check

Answer: The queen demands that the knight find the answer to the question "What do women most desire?"

Differentiated Instruction — for Universal Access

EL Support for English Learners

Students may be confused by some of the inverted phrases used in this tale. Have students look at the phrases "Sad was the knight" (line 59) and "…were all the world to win" (line 107). Explain that the phrase "Sad was the knight" can be reordered to make it easier to understand: "The knight was sad." Explain that in line 107 the speaker says that the woman would not betray her husband even if she won all the world.

Enrichment for Advanced Readers

Point out to students that the Wife's tale is a quest story. The knight's quest is to find the answer to a question. Along the way, the knight meets different characters who have wide-ranging answers to his question. Have students name other quest stories they have read or seen in movies or on television. **Ask** students to write a brief essay comparing the knight's quest (its focus, its motivation, its lesson) with another quest. Have students present their ideas to the class.

Imagery

1. Read aloud lines 135–144. **Ask** students to describe what the knight sees as he approaches the wood.
   Answer: He sees a group of women dancing in the wood, but when he gets closer they vanish.

2. **Ask** students: What image from the beginning of "The Wife of Bath's Tale" does this remind you of?
   Answer: The image of the elf-queen and her courtiers dancing on the green.

3. **Ask** students who they think the old woman is.
   Possible Answer: The old woman may be the elf-queen.

❿ **Critical Viewing**

Possible response: The knight's weapons and armor show that he is armed for battle. His well-groomed presentation suggests that he also has a social role in the court.

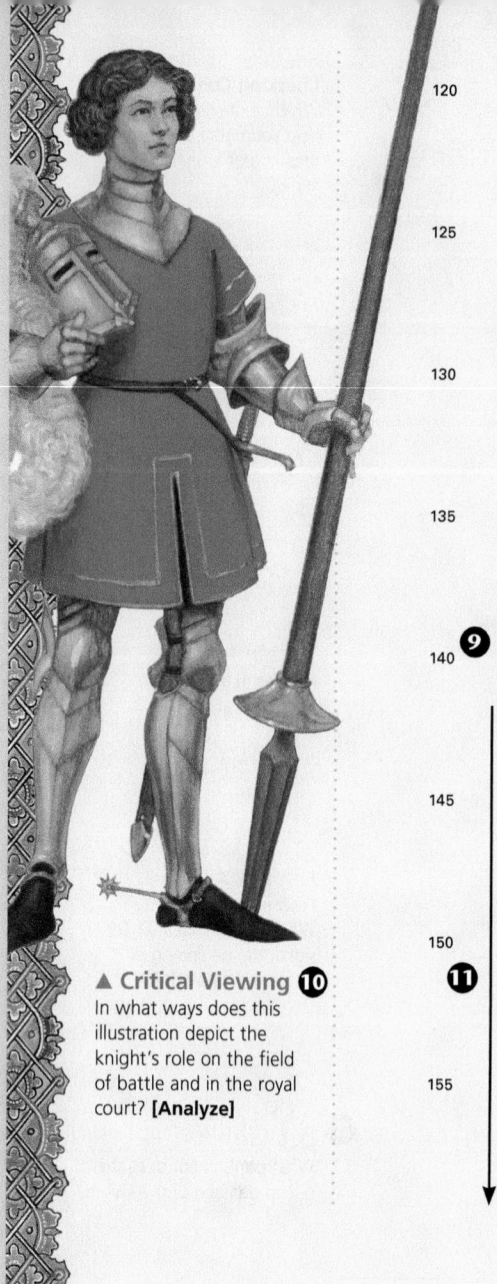

▲ Critical Viewing ❿
In what ways does this illustration depict the knight's role on the field of battle and in the royal court? **[Analyze]**

She whispered to the water, near the ground,
120 "Betray me not, O water, with thy sound!
To thee alone I tell it: it appears
My husband has a pair of ass's ears!
Ah! My heart's well again, the secret's out!
I could no longer keep it, not a doubt."
125 And so you see, although we may hold fast
A little while, it must come out at last,
We can't keep secrets; as for Midas, well,
Read Ovid for his story; he will tell.
      This knight that I am telling you about
130 Perceived at last he never would find out
What it could be that women loved the best.
Faint was the soul within his sorrowful breast
As home he went, he dared no longer stay;
His year was up and now it was the day.
135   As he rode home in a dejected mood
Suddenly, at the margin of a wood,
He saw a dance upon the leafy floor
Of four and twenty ladies, nay, and more.
Eagerly he approached, in hope to learn
140 Some words of wisdom ere he should return;
But lo! Before he came to where they were,
Dancers and dance all vanished into air!
There wasn't a living creature to be seen
Save one old woman crouched upon the green.
145 A fouler-looking creature I suppose
Could scarcely be imagined. She arose
And said, "Sir knight, there's no way on from here.
Tell me what you are looking for, my dear,
For peradventure that were best for you;
150 We old, old women know a thing or two."
      "Dear Mother," said the knight, "alack the day!
I am as good as dead if I can't say
What thing it is that women most desire;
If you could tell me I would pay your hire."
155 "Give me your hand," she said, "and swear to do
Whatever I shall next require of you
—If so to do should lie within your might—
And you shall know the answer before night."
"Upon my honor," he answered, "I agree."

Enrichment: Analyzing Forms and Genres

The Tale of King Midas
The figure of King Midas appears in several ancient Greek myths. The story that the Wife of Bath cites is a lesser known one.
King Midas sprouted the ears of an ass because he had offended the god Apollo. While serving as a judge in a musical contest between Apollo and the satyr Marsyas, Midas judged in favor of the satyr. The angry god took his revenge by changing the king's ears into those of a donkey.

Activity: Analyzing Forms and Genres
Have interested students conduct further investigation into Greek mythology. Have them locate different retellings of Greek myths, including the story of King Midas. Encourage them to use the **Enrichment: Analyzing Forms and Genres** worksheet on page 227 of the *Professional Development Guidebook* to organize the information.

160 ❶❶ ↑ "Then," said the crone, "I dare to guarantee
Your life is safe; I shall make good my claim.
Upon my life the queen will say the same.
Show me the very proudest of them all
In costly coverchief or jewelled caul[8]

165 That dare say no to what I have to teach.
Let us go forward without further speech."
And then she crooned her gospel in his ear
And told him to be glad and not to fear.
    They came to court. This knight, in full array,

170 Stood forth and said, "O Queen, I've kept my day
And kept my word and have my answer ready."
    There sat the noble matrons and the heady
Young girls, and widows too, that have the grace
Of wisdom, all assembled in that place,

175 And there the queen herself was throned to hear
And judge his answer. Then the knight drew near
And silence was commanded through the hall.
    The queen then bade the knight to tell them all
What thing it was that women wanted most.

180 He stood not silent like a beast or post,
But gave his answer with the ringing word
Of a man's voice and the assembly heard:
    "My liege and lady, in general," said he,
"A woman wants the self-same sovereignty

185 ❶❷ Over her husband as over her lover,
And master him; he must not be above her.
That is your greatest wish, whether you kill
Or spare me; please yourself. I wait your will."
    In all the court not one that shook her head

190 Or contradicted what the knight had said;
Maid, wife and widow cried, "He's saved his life!"
    And on the word up started the old wife,
The one the knight saw sitting on the green,
And cried, "Your mercy, sovereign lady queen!

195 Before the court disperses, do me right!
'Twas I who taught this answer to the knight,
For which he swore, and pledged his honor to it,
That the first thing I asked of him he'd do it,
So far as it should lie within his might.

200 Before this court I ask you then, sir knight,

---

8. **coverchief. . .caul** kerchief, and a decorative cap, both worn as headgear by medieval women.

Reading Strategy
Checking Context Clues
What clues in the context hint at the meaning of *crone* in line 160?

Reading Strategy
Checking Context Clues
Which context clues might help you figure out the meaning of *sovereignty* in line 184?

❶❸ Reading Check
How does the setting described in lines 169–177 differ from that described in the Prologue?

The Wife of Bath's Tale **143**

---

❶❶ **Reading Strategy**
Checking Context Clues

1. **Read** aloud the bracketed passage.

2. **Ask** the Reading Strategy question: What clues in context hint at the meaning of *crone* in line 160? **Answer:** Lines 143–146 provide the best description of the old woman. As she is the only woman speaking here, a crone must be a very old woman.

❶❷ **Reading Strategy**
Checking Context Clues

1. **Have** a student volunteer read aloud lines 183–188.

2. **Ask** the Reading Strategy question: What context clues might help you figure out the meaning of *sovereignty* in line 184? **Answer:** The phrases "over her husband," "master him," and "not be above her" all indicate that *sovereignty* means "ruling over" or "having authority over."

❶❸ **Reading Check**

Answer: The setting of these lines is the royal court during the time of King Arthur. The Prologue takes place on the road to Canterbury during the thirteenth century.

Differentiated
Instruction   for Universal Access

Strategy for
Less Proficient Readers
Help students understand that the tale of the Wife of Bath has a moral or lesson. A lesson, like a theme, is often expressed through the characters' words and actions. **Ask** students to consider the lesson that the knight learns. Help students understand that the knight learns women should be treated with respect, something he did not know at the beginning of the story. Have students pay attention to how the knight treats women at different points in the story.

Enrichment for
Gifted/Talented Students
Have students create a comic strip of the knight's quest. **Ask** them to depict his encounters with people and the answers they provide. Students can elaborate on the story by mentioning places the knight travels to or even creating new scenes or scenarios for the knight in his journey. Have students address the knight's attitude toward women. Does he get annoyed on his journey, or does he become more respectful?

from illuminated manuscript *Les Très Riches Heures du Duc de Berry*, 1400s, by the Limbourg Brothers

Pol, Herman, and Jehanequin de Limbourg were artists who lived during the early fifteenth century. These three Flemish brothers worked as a team to produce fine illuminated manuscripts decorated with real gold and silver. Illuminated manuscripts were books with elaborate, colorful illustrations, in which the use of real precious metals made the illustrations, and even some of the text, seem to give off light. This illustration is from the calendar for the month of May in a book commissioned by the French aristocrat.

Use these questions for discussion:

1. **Ask:** How does the artwork idealize the figures?
   Answer: The figures are elongated and curved in graceful, arcing lines.

2. **Ask:** How does this procession of figures on horseback contrast with the procession of pilgrims on the road to Canterbury?
   Answer: These people are all from the same social and economic class, while the pilgrims are a much more diverse group.

144

Enrichment: Analyzing Forms and Genres

Fairy Tales and Folk Tales

"The Wife of Bath's Tale" contains elements of fairy tales. The wife discusses fairies as if they were real. Also, like most fairy tales, hers is set in a time steeped in legend and lore. Finally, her story, like every fairy tale, has a happy ending. The Wife's tale enters the realm of folklore when it presents its lesson. Folk tales contained lessons about proper behavior. The tale is a modern story, blending elements of traditional tales and creating something new.

Activity: Analyzing Forms and Genres
Have interested students do further research on fairy tales and folk tales. Have them organize their information using the **Enrichment: Analyzing Forms and Genres** worksheet on page 227 of the *Professional Development Guidebook*.

To keep your word and take me for your wife:
For well you know that I have saved your life.
If this be false, deny it on your sword!"
    "Alas!" he said, "Old lady, by the Lord
205 I know indeed that such was my behest,
But for God's love think of a new request,
Take all my goods, but leave my body free."
"A curse on us," she said, "if I agree!
I may be foul, I may be poor and old,
210 Yet will not choose to be, for all the gold
That's bedded in the earth or lies above,
Less than your wife, nay, than your very love!"
    "My love?" said he. "By Heaven, my damnation!
Alas that any of my race and station
215 Should ever make so foul a misalliance!"
Yet in the end his pleading and defiance
All went for nothing, he was forced to wed.
He takes his ancient wife and goes to bed.

———

Now peradventure some may well suspect
220 A lack of care in me since I neglect
To tell of the rejoicings and display
Made at the feast upon their wedding-day.
I have but a short answer to let fall;
I say there was no joy or feast at all,
225 Nothing but heaviness of heart and sorrow.
He married her in private on the morrow
And all day long stayed hidden like an owl,
It was such torture that his wife looked foul.
    16 Great was the anguish churning in his head
230 When he and she were piloted to bed;
He wallowed back and forth in desperate style.
His ancient wife lay smiling all the while;
At last she said, "Bless us! Is this, my dear,
How knights and wives get on together here?
235 Are these the laws of good King Arthur's house?
Are knights of his all so contemptuous?
I am your own beloved and your wife,
And I am she, indeed, that saved your life;
And certainly I never did you wrong.

15 ◀ **Critical Viewing**
In what ways does this picture help you visualize the kind of medieval nobles who listened to the knight's answer? **[Connect]**

Reading Strategy
Checking Context Clues
What is the meaning of *anguish* in line 229? Identify the context clues that helped you to determine the meaning.

Vocabulary
contemptuous
(kən temp´ chōō əs) *adj.*
scornful

17 ☑ Reading
Check

In addition to becoming the knight's wife, what more does the old woman demand?

15 **Critical Viewing**
Possible response: The people are dressed in elaborate clothing, ride fine horses, and appear to be engaged in a leisurely garden party complete with musicians. They do not seem to be people for whom hard work is a daily activity.

16 **Reading Strategy**
Checking Context Clues
1. **Ask** students to summarize lines 226–231.
   Possible response: The knight marries the old woman in a private ceremony, and he stays inside all day because he does not want anyone to see how ugly she is. On his wedding night, he is miserable and desperate.
2. **Ask** students the Reading Strategy question: What is the meaning of *anguish* in line 229? Identify the context clues that helped you to determine the meaning.
   Answer: Students should identify the words *torture, churning, wallowing,* and *desperate* as clues to the meaning of *anguish,* which means "deep distress." All the words suggest that the knight is suffering.

17 **Reading Check**
Answer: She wants to become his "very love."

Differentiated
Instruction   for Universal Access

Strategy for
Gifted/Talented Students
Invite students to go on a quest of their own. Have students ask the knight's question to their female family members, friends, and acquaintances, and then make a list of all the answers. Challenge students to tally the answers and write a short essay that analyzes their results. Students should compare the answers from modern women to the answers the knight received in "The Wife of Bath's Tale." **Ask** volunteers to share the results of their research with the class.

Enrichment for
Advanced Readers
Point out that a scene in which someone receives judgment at court is a plot device that even today causes suspense. Have students relate this device to courtroom scenes they have read (a classic example is the courtroom scenes in *To Kill a Mockingbird*) or seen in crime dramas in movies or on television. Have students reread or view a modern courtroom scene and then write a short essay in which they compare it with the scene in which the knight appears before the queen and her court.

Frame Story

Ask students the Literary Analysis question: By the standards set forth in lines 255–262, is the Knight from the Prologue a gentleman? Why or why not?

Possible Answer: Students may suggest that the knight is a gentleman because he is described as being wise as well as modest in both bearing and dress (lines 70–74 of the Prologue).

⓳ Literature in Context

Selfsame Sovereignty

Since the days of the Norman Conquest in the eleventh century, English law held that a woman was the subordinate partner in a marriage. The legal term that described the relationship was *coverture.* The word literally means "cover." In other words, a woman was under the protection, or cover, of her husband. When a woman married, coverture caused a woman to lose her own rights, individuality, and property in the eyes of the law. It relieved a woman of all legal responsibilities. For example, a woman could not be sued and did not have to pay taxes. On the other hand, a woman's property was entirely controlled by her husband, and she had no rights when it came to her income, her property, or her children during marriage or in the event of a divorce.

Coverture was in effect in the United States until 1839, when married women obtained some of their legal rights. Women argued that they needed to control their money and property while their men were away for long periods fighting in wars or pioneering new lands.

Connect to the Literature

Encourage students to review the tale and the Wife's description in the Prologue before answering the question.

Answer: Unlike the women of her day, the Wife of Bath exerted control over the men she had married and confidently told a tale in which a woman triumphed over her husband. She was independent and was traveling to Canterbury as an equal among men.

146

Literary Analysis
Frame Story
By the standards set forth in lines 255–262, is the Knight from the Prologue a gentleman? Why or why not?

Vocabulary
bequeath (bē kwē*th*) *v.* hand down as an inheritance

> 240 Then why, this first of nights, so sad a song?
>   You're carrying on as if you were half-witted
>   Say, for God's love, what sin have I committed?
>   I'll put things right if you will tell me how."
>   "Put right?" he cried. "That never can be now!
> 245 Nothing can ever be put right again!
>   You're old, and so abominably plain,
>   So poor to start with, so low-bred to follow;
>   It's little wonder if I twist and wallow!
>   God, that my heart would burst within my breast!"
> 250   "Is that," said she, "the cause of your unrest?"
>   "Yes, certainly," he said, "and can you wonder?"
>   "I could set right what you suppose a blunder,
>   That's if I cared to, in a day or two,
>   If I were shown more courtesy by you.
> 255 Just now," she said, "you spoke of gentle birth,
>   Such as descends from ancient wealth and worth.
>   If that's the claim you make for gentlemen
> ⓲   Such arrogance is hardly worth a hen.
>   Whoever loves to work for virtuous ends,
> 260 Public and private, and who most intends
>   To do what deeds of gentleness he can,
>   Take him to be the greatest gentleman.
>   Christ wills we take our gentleness from Him,
>   Not from a wealth of ancestry long dim,
> 265 Though they bequeath their whole establishment
>   By which we claim to be of high descent.
>   Our fathers cannot make us a bequest

⓳ LITERATURE IN CONTEXT

Selfsame Sovereignty

The Wife of Bath uses the story of the knight and the old woman to express her own belief in selfsame sovereignty, or equality in marriage between a husband and wife. Whether such an idea meant that women shared ownership of property and family wealth, or whether it meant they had an equal share in decision-making, such a belief was definitely well ahead of the times.

In medieval England, women could inherit property only if there were no male heirs in the family. Usually, property was entailed, or assigned to the male survivors, the women being left under the men's care until marriage or death. Moreover, at marriage a woman was often required to renounce any further claims to her father's property. Often, any property she did bring to the marriage was immediately forfeited to her husband, leaving her with virtually no further claim to it. Only in 1857 did Great Britain's Married Women's Property Acts first allow a woman the right to property in her own name.

Connect to the Literature

The Wife of Bath refuses to play a subordinate role in her society. In what ways does Chaucer's description of the Wife of Bath, as well as her tale, suggest that she was an unusual woman for her time?

Enrichment: Investigating Daily Life

Ranks and Titles in "The Wife of Bath's Tale"

The ranks and titles mentioned in "The Wife of Bath's Tale" are remnants of a feudalistic society. The definitions of some of the ranks and titles that appear in "The Wife of Bath's Tale."

liege: This is a feudal term; it is the lord to whom a knight or peasant owed service.

sovereign: The term for the chief or leader with highest rank—the king or queen; the term still refers to the ruler of England.

duke: In medieval times it referred to a prince who ruled his own independent territory; today, it is the rank of someone who is born royal but is not a prince.

knight: In the Middle Ages, it meant a military servant of the king; today it is an honorary rank.

Activity: Investigating Daily Life

Have interested students investigate the daily life of a peasant in the feudalistic society of medieval England. Have them use the **Enrichment: Investigating Daily Life** worksheet on page 224 of the *Professional Development Guidebook.*

Of all those virtues that became them best
And earned for them the name of gentleman,
270　But bade us follow them as best we can.
　　　"Thus the wise poet of the Florentines,
Dante[9] by name, has written in these lines,
For such is the opinion Dante launches:
'Seldom arises by these slender branches
275　prowess of men, for it is God, no less,
Wills us to claim of Him our gentleness.'
For of our parents nothing can we claim
Save temporal things, and these may hurt and maim.
　　　"But everyone knows this as well as I;
280　For if gentility were implanted by
The natural course of lineage down the line,
Public or private, could it cease to shine
In doing the fair work of gentle deed?
No vice or villainy could then bear seed.
285　　　"Take fire and carry it to the darkest house
Between this kingdom and the Caucasus,[10]
And shut the doors on it and leave it there,
It will burn on, and it will burn as fair
As if ten thousand men were there to see,
290 **20** For fire will keep its nature and degree,
I can assure you, sir, until it dies.
　　　"But gentleness, as you will recognize,
Is not annexed in nature to possessions,
Men fail in living up to their professions;
295　But fire never ceases to be fire.
God knows you'll often find, if you enquire,
Some lording full of villainy and shame.
If you would be esteemed for the mere name
Of having been by birth a gentleman
300　And stemming from some virtuous, noble clan,
And do not live yourself by gentle deed
Or take your fathers' noble code and creed,
You are no gentleman, though duke or earl.
Vice and bad manners are what make a churl.
305　　　"Gentility is only the renown
For bounty that your fathers handed down,
Quite foreign to your person, not your own;
Gentility must come from God alone.
That we are gentle comes to us by grace

---

9. **Dante** Dante Alighieri (dän´ tā al əg yer´ ē) (1265–1321) Italian poet who wrote the *Divine Comedy*.
10. **Caucasus** (kô´ kə səs) mountain range between southeastern Europe and western Asia.

Vocabulary

prowess (prou´ is) *n.*
heroism; distinction
esteemed (ə stēmd´) *adj.*
highly respected

21 Reading Check
According to the old woman, what makes a man a gentleman?

The Wife of Bath's Tale **147**

---

20 Critical Commentary

Analyze

1. Have students read the analogy the woman makes between a burning fire and gentility in lines 285–295.

2. **Ask** them to restate those lines in their own words.
   Possible response: If you take fire and let it burn in the darkest house, it burns whether someone sees it or not. Gentility, or gentleness, is not a result or reflection of one's wealth or birth. It is a quality that, like fire, exists whether you can see it or not.

3. Finally, **ask** students what point the woman is trying to make.
   Possible response: People who possess true gentility are always gentle. The quality of gentility is expressed in one's actions and cannot be inherited or bought.

21 Reading Check

Possible response: The desire to do good deeds and work for virtue's sake, public or private, makes a man a gentleman.

Differentiated Instruction for Universal Access

EL Vocabulary for English Learners
Point out to students that today the word *gentle* usually means "not harsh or rough," but the original meaning of the word is "of high birth." Provide students with the words below, all of which have the same root—*gentil*. Discuss how the words are generally used today and how these uses are different from the words' original meanings.

| gentility | genteel |
| gentle | gentleman/gentlewoman |

Strategy for Advanced Readers
Students should understand that the long exchange between the knight and the old woman on their wedding night provides the lesson of the tale. For every objection raised by the knight, the old woman has a counterargument. Have students work in pairs to summarize the points and objections each character makes and to identify the point at which the knight learns his lesson. Then **ask** students to evaluate the two characters' arguments.

Analyze

1. Have students read aloud lines 323–336. Explain that, in these lines, the woman is setting forth her own definition of "true" poverty and wealth.

2. **Ask** students: Who does the old woman say is truly rich?
Answer: The poor who accept their poverty and do not covet what others have.

3. **Ask** students: Who does she say are truly poor?
Answer: Those who whine and are jealous of what others have.

4. You may want to give students the opportunity to agree or disagree with the old woman. The idea that the poor should accept their poverty may not be one all students accept.

23 **Critical Viewing**

Possible response: Idealistic elements include the grace and beauty of the maiden as well as her slender figure, compared with the stooping, heavier figure of the old woman. The clothing each woman is wearing seems realistic, and the way the maiden averts her eyes may reflect the social conventions of the time.

The crone may be better able to teach the knight a lesson because he won't be distracted by beauty as he would be with the maiden. When talking to the crone, the knight has to focus on something other than outer beauty, which is part of her lesson.

▼ Critical Viewing 23
Compare the illustrations of the crone and maiden. Why is the crone better able to teach the knight a lesson? [Speculate]

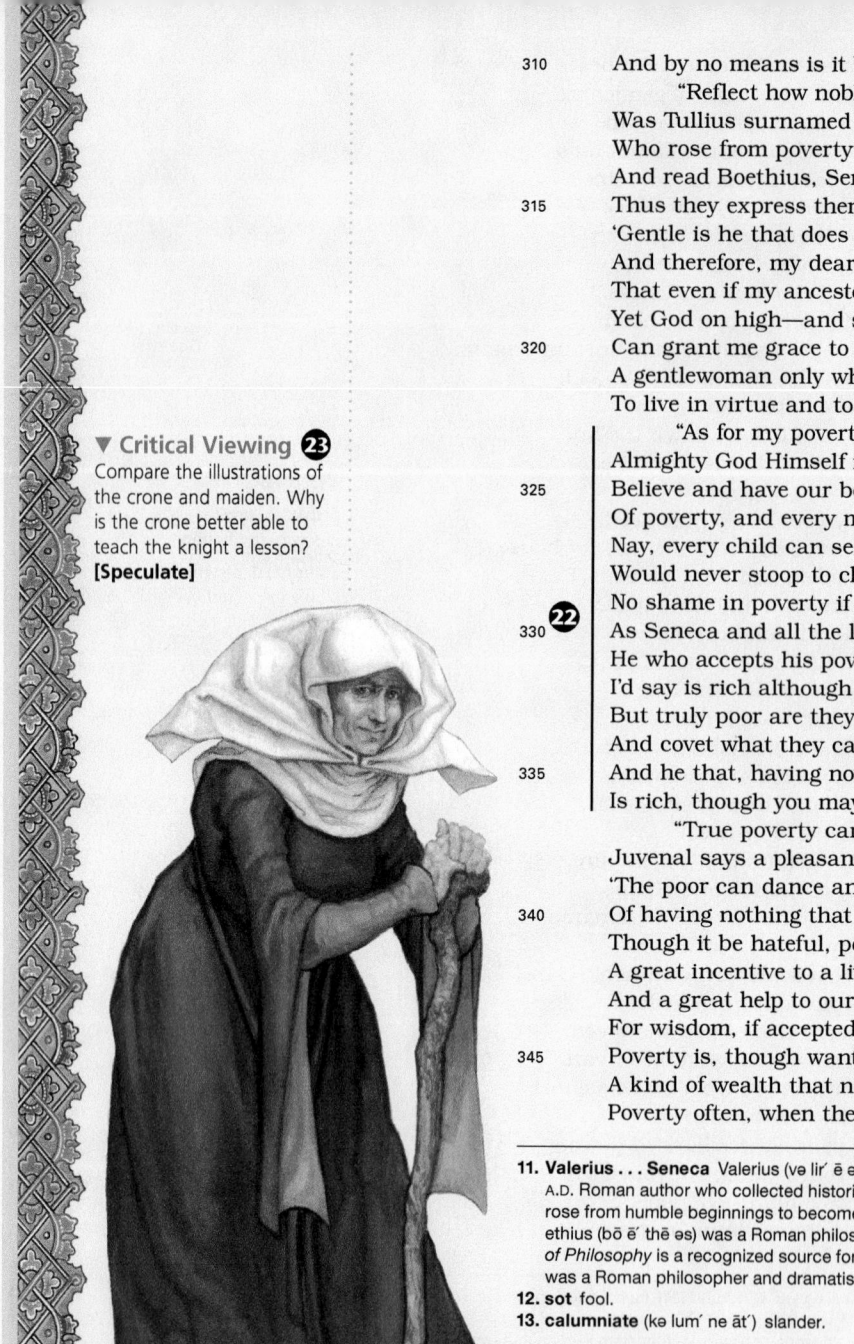

148

310 And by no means is it bequeathed with place.
       "Reflect how noble (says Valerius)[11]
       Was Tullius surnamed Hostilius,
       Who rose from poverty to nobleness.
       And read Boethius, Seneca no less,
315   Thus they express themselves and are agreed:
       'Gentle is he that does a gentle deed.'
       And therefore, my dear husband, I conclude
       That even if my ancestors were rude,
       Yet God on high—and so I hope He will—
320   Can grant me grace to live in virtue still,
       A gentlewoman only when beginning
       To live in virtue and to shrink from sinning.
       "As for my poverty which you reprove,
       Almighty God Himself in whom we move,
325   Believe and have our being, chose a life
       Of poverty, and every man or wife
       Nay, every child can see our Heavenly King
       Would never stoop to choose a shameful thing.
       No shame in poverty if the heart is gay,
330   As Seneca and all the learned say.
       He who accepts his poverty unhurt
       I'd say is rich although he lacked a shirt.
       But truly poor are they who whine and fret
       And covet what they cannot hope to get.
335   And he that, having nothing, covets not,
       Is rich, though you may think he is a sot.[12]
       "True poverty can find a song to sing.
       Juvenal says a pleasant little thing:
       'The poor can dance and sing in the relief
340   Of having nothing that will tempt a thief.'
       Though it be hateful, poverty is good,
       A great incentive to a livelihood,
       And a great help to our capacity
       For wisdom, if accepted patiently.
345   Poverty is, though wanting in estate,
       A kind of wealth that none calumniate.[13]
       Poverty often, when the heart is lowly,

---

11. **Valerius . . . Seneca** Valerius (və lir′ ē əs) Maximus was a first-century A.D. Roman author who collected historical anecdotes. Tullius Hostilius rose from humble beginnings to become a legendary king of Rome. Boethius (bō ē′ thē əs) was a Roman philosopher whose *The Consolation of Philosophy* is a recognized source for Chaucer's writings. Seneca was a Roman philosopher and dramatist.
12. **sot** fool.
13. **calumniate** (kə lum′ ne āt′) slander.

Vocabulary Development

Vocabulary Knowledge Rating

When students have completed reading and discussing the selections, have them take out the **Vocabulary Knowledge Rating** charts they worked on earlier. Read the words aloud and have students rate their knowledge of the words again in the After Reading column. Clarify any words that are still problematic. Have students write their own definitions and example or sentence in the appropriate column. Then have students complete the Vocabulary lesson at the end of this selection. Encourage students to use the words in further discussion and written work about the selections. Remind them that they will be accountable for these words on the *Selection Test, Unit 1 Resources,* pages 127–129 or 130–132.

Brings one to God and teaches what is holy,
Gives knowledge of oneself and even lends
350   A glass by which to see one's truest friends.
And since it's no offence, let me be plain;
Do not rebuke my poverty again.

      "Lastly you taxed me, sir, with being old.
Yet even if you never had been told
355   By ancient books, you gentlemen engage
Yourselves in honor to respect old age.
To call an old man 'father' shows good breeding,
And this could be supported from my reading.
      "You say I'm old and fouler than a fen.
360   You need not fear to be a cuckold, then.
Filth and old age, I'm sure you will agree,
Are powerful wardens upon chastity.
Nevertheless, well knowing your delights,
I shall fulfil your worldly appetites.

365   "You have two choices; which one will you try?
To have me old and ugly till I die,
But still a loyal, true and humble wife
That never will displease you all her life,
Or would you rather I were young and pretty
370   And chance your arm what happens in a city
Where friends will visit you because of me,
Yes, and in other places too, maybe.
Which would you have? The choice is all your own."

      The knight thought long, and with a piteous groan
375   At last he said, with all the care in life,
"My lady and my love, my dearest wife,
I leave the matter to your wise decision.
You make the choice yourself, for the provision
24 Of what may be agreeable and rich
380   In honor to us both, I don't care which;
Whatever pleases you suffices me."

      "And have I won the mastery?" said she,
"Since I'm to choose and rule as I think fit?"
"Certainly, wife," he answered her, "that's it."
385   "Kiss me," she cried. "No quarrels! On my oath
And word of honor, you shall find me both,
That is, both fair and faithful as a wife;
May I go howling mad and take my life
Unless I prove to be as good and true
390   As ever wife was since the world was new!
And if to-morrow when the sun's above
I seem less fair than any lady-love,

Vocabulary
rebuke (ri byoōk´) v.
criticize strongly

25 Reading Check

Identify two benefits that the old woman says can come with poverty.

The Wife of Bath's Tale **149**

---

24 Engaging the Essential Question

1. Have students reread lines 374–384 in which the knight and the old woman set up the terms of their marital relationship.
2. **Ask** students to explain how the relationship between the knight and his wife shows "selfsame sovereignty."
   Possible response: The knight recognizes the wisdom of his wife and agrees to let her make the decision that will affect both of them.

25 Reading Check

Possible response: Benefits include having nothing worth stealing, self-knowledge, and greater spirituality.

Differentiated Instruction for Universal Access

Strategy for Less Proficient Readers
Students may benefit from some guidance as they read the old woman's arguments on pages 148–153. Draw a three-column chart on the board and label the columns Gentility (lines 271–310), Poverty (lines 311–352), and Old Age/Beauty (lines 353–373). Have students work in pairs to identify key ideas and phrases for each topic. After students complete their analysis, discuss the three ideas as a class. Work together to analyze students' findings, and then generate statements that reflect what the old woman says about each idea.

Strategy for Gifted/Talented Students
Students may enjoy turning the ending of the story into an episode of a talk show. Have several students act out the last section of the story, in which the old woman outlines the benefits and drawbacks of having an old and ugly wife or a young and beautiful wife. Have the knight be present on the stage along with a young mystery woman. Students should act out the interaction between the three people. Which woman does the knight choose?

26 Literary Analysis

Frame

Ask students the Literary Analysis question: Which words serve as a clue that the interior story is finished and that the Wife has turned her attention toward her riding companions?

Answer: The traditional words "So they lived ever after" are a clue that the story is finished.

ASSESS

Answers

Before students respond, you may wish to have them write a brief objective summary of the selection. As they answer the questions below, remind them to support their answers with evidence from the text.

1. (a) The king sentences the knight to death. (b) **Possible response:** The king might be a husband who defers to his wife's decisions. (c) They understand equality in marriage.

2. (a) The tale illustrates the Wife's point that women can't keep secrets. (b) Students may respond negatively; it simply shows that the Wife is aware that women have faults.

3. (a) The knight agrees to do what the old woman wants after she tells him the secret to what women desire most. (b) **Possible response:** The queen believes the knight should marry the woman to keep his honor.

4. (a) The old woman offers the knight a choice between an old, ugly, loyal wife and an unfaithful, young, beautiful wife. (b) By letting his wife make the decision, the knight shows he has understood her lesson. (c) **Possible response:** Yes; he worked hard and honored his promise to the old woman. He learned his lesson and received his reward.

5. **Possible Response:** Chaucer is clearly trying to influence society. In medieval times wives did not own property; therefore they had no <u>independence</u>. A woman like the Wife of Bath, who demanded <u>parity</u> in a marriage, was most likely unusual in Chaucer's time.

150

Than any queen or empress east or west,
Do with my life and death as you think best.
395 Cast up the curtain, husband. Look at me!"
    And when indeed the knight had looked to see,
Lo, she was young and lovely, rich in charms.
In ecstasy he caught her in her arms,
His heart went bathing in a bath of blisses
400 And melted in a hundred thousand kisses,
And she responded in the fullest measure
With all that could delight or give him pleasure.
    So they lived ever after to the end
In perfect bliss; and may Christ Jesus send
405 Us husbands meek and young and fresh in bed,
And grace to overbid them when we wed.
And—Jesu hear my prayer!—cut short the lives
Of those who won't be governed by their wives;
And all old, angry niggards of their pence,[14]
410 God send them soon a very pestilence!

Literary Analysis
Frame Story
Which words serve as a clue that the interior story is finished and that the Wife has turned her attention toward her riding companions?

---

14. niggards (nig´ ərdz) **of their pence** misers stingy with their money.

Critical Reading

Cite textual evidence to support your responses.

1. **Key Ideas and Details (a)** What punishment does the king initially order for the knight? **(b) Speculate:** Why might the king willingly allow his wife to effect a different punishment instead? **(c) Apply:** What philosophy about relationships do the king and queen share with the Wife of Bath?

2. **Key Ideas and Details (a)** What character flaw is the tale-within-a-tale of Midas's wife meant to illustrate? **(b) Evaluate:** In your opinion, does this inner story undercut the main point of the Wife's tale? Explain.

3. **Key Ideas and Details (a)** What bargain does the knight make with the old woman? **(b) Analyze:** Why do you think the queen forces the knight to keep his part of the bargain?

4. **Key Ideas and Details (a)** What final choice does the old woman offer the knight? **(b) Infer:** In what way does his response show that he has finally learned his lesson about the nature of women? **(c) Make a Judgment:** Has the knight experienced sufficient punishment and redemption for his crime? Explain.

5. **Integration of Knowledge and Ideas** By discussing selfsame sovereignty, was Chaucer reflecting or trying to influence social trends? In responding, use at least two of these words: *parity, independence, reciprocate.* *[Connecting to the Essential Question: How does literature shape or reflect society?]*

150 From Legend to History (A.D. 449–1485)

Concept Connector

Activating Prior Knowledge
Have students return to their responses to the Activating Prior Knowledge activity in which they explained what they thought men and women want from a long-lasting relationship. **Ask** them to compare their answer to the answer given in "The Wife of Bath's Tale." **Ask** them to explain whether their thoughts on the subject have changed and, if so, how.

Writing About the Essential Question
Have students compare their responses to the prompt before they completed reading "The Wife of Bath's Tale" with their thoughts afterward. Have them work in groups to discuss how "The Wife of Bath's Tale" either supports or opposes their own view. Encourage students who agree with the idea of equality in marriage to examine whether they agree with the Wife of Bath's interpretation of the ideal marriage. Is what she proposes really equality? **Ask** groups to share their ideas with the class.

After You Read | *The Wife of Bath's Tale*

Literary Analysis

🅒 **1. Integration of Knowledge and Ideas** Reread the description of the Wife of Bath in the General Prologue, or the **frame story** for the Wife's tale. **(a)** Compare the characteristics of the Wife to those of the old woman in the Wife's tale. **(b)** Do you think the Wife identifies with the old woman? Why or why not?

🅒 **2. Integration of Knowledge and Ideas** In the frame story, the Host declares he will judge the pilgrims' tales on their "good morality and general pleasure" (Prologue line 818), their ability to teach a moral or lesson, and the entertainment value for the listeners. As the Host, how would you respond to the Wife's tale? **(a)** Use the first two boxes in the chart below to note details from the tale. **(b)** Then, use the details to determine a final judgment.

Good Morality/ Lesson	General Pleasure/ Entertainment Value	→	Final Judgment

🅒 **3. Craft and Structure** In what ways does the **setting** of "The Wife of Bath's Tale" compare or contrast with the setting of the frame story, the pilgrimage to Canterbury?

🅒 **4. Key Ideas and Details (a)** In what ways do the details of the setting in lines 135–144 echo the description of "ancient days" in lines 3–7? **(b)** Describe the way these details hint at, or foreshadow, the happy ending of the tale.

🅒 **5. Integration of Knowledge and Ideas** In what ways is a story like "The Wife of Bath's Tale" an important commentary on the lives of medieval women?

🅒 **6. Integration of Knowledge and Ideas (a)** In today's society, where might you find individuals who would agree with the Wife and the philosophy she illustrates with her story? **(b)** Who might argue against such opinions?

7. Analyzing Visual Information: Does the caricature of Chaucer on this page suggest that he knew and appreciated many people like the characters he invented? Why or why not?

Reading Strategy

8. (a) If you were unfamiliar with the word "dejected," in line 135, how might you repair your comprehension by **checking context clues**? **(b)** Identify three words you might use instead of "dejected" that would retain the meaning of the lines around the word.

9. Define the word "suffices" as it is used in line 381, explaining which context clues enabled you to determine its meaning.

10. Which type of context clue—synonyms, antonyms, examples, or another type of clue—has been most useful to you in figuring out the meaning of new words? Explain.

ⓒ **Common Core State Standards**

Language
3. Apply knowledge of language to understand how language functions in different contexts, to make effective choices for meaning or style, and to comprehend more fully when reading or listening. *(p. 152)*
4. Determine or clarify the meaning of unknown and multiple-meaning words and phrases based on *grades 11–12 reading and content,* choosing flexibly from a range of strategies. *(p. 152)*

The Wife of Bath's Tale **151**

---

9. *Suffices* means "satisfies, is enough, is adequate." Students should understand that the knight's insistence that he does not care and will be pleased by whatever his wife decides is a context clue.

10. Possible response: Examples are the most reliable type of clue, because the context almost always provides some sort of example, while synonyms and antonyms are less frequent.

7. Possible response: In the caricature, Chaucer looks sly and not very trustworthy. It seems to suggest that he shared many of the same vices and acquaintances as his characters.

8. (a) The clues include the knight's perception that he will never find the answer he needs and his decision to return to the Queen. **(b)** Possible synonyms include *brokenhearted, despondent,* and *melancholy.*

Answers

1. (a) Unlike the old woman in the story, the Wife of Bath is well off, well dressed, and well traveled. Like the old woman, the Wife is wise and confident in her abilities. **(b)** The Wife certainly identifies with the old woman who is wise, just, articulate, and persuasive.

2. (a) Good Morality/Lesson: knight receives merciful punishment; he is forced to marry old woman; gentility is defined as gift from God and the exercise of good values; poverty is not shameful; knight rewarded for deferring to wife's judgment. General Pleasure/ Entertainment Value: ridicule of friars; description of the court and the knight's journey; story of King Midas; magical characters; knight's anguish at marrying old woman; twists and turns of plot. **(b)** Final Judgment: The host would probably be entertained by the tale, although he might disagree with the Wife's idea that women should master their husbands.

3. Although the frame story's setting is contemporary with the author, the Wife's story is set centuries before, during the age of King Arthur. The frame story begins in the English town of Southwark; the Wife's tale takes place in the countryside and in the royal court.

4. (a) Both scenes are set in the countryside and contain magical dancing creatures. **(b)** The rural setting and the magical creatures suggest that a happy, fairy-tale ending will follow.

5. Possible response: The fairy-tale nature of the story suggests that women in medieval times had little autonomy or influence over their husbands. Also, the Wife of Bath's comments about women's lack of safety among friars and the knight's rough treatment of the old woman suggest that life for medieval women could be difficult or dangerous.

6. Possible response: (a) Many modern women would probably agree with the Wife of Bath. **(b)** People who do not see men and women as equals might disagree with the Wife of Bath.

151

Vocabulary Acquisition and Use

Multiple-Meaning Words in Context
Sample Answers

1. *B; relate* does not take an object in the sentence.
2. *B;* the word *an* indicates *act* is used as a noun.
3. *A;* because *bluff* describes "her tale," it cannot mean "a high steep bank." It has to mean "lie."

Vocabulary
Sample Answers

1. "Let us give more consideration to the rights of women," the Wife of Bath implored.
2. The story the Pardoner relates is a warning against the destructiveness of greed.
3. When asked why he is unhappy in his marriage, the knight replied in a contemptuous way.
4. The old woman in the tale says that our fathers can bequeath us their wealth, but not their virtue.
5. According to the old wife in the story, the prowess of men should be their gentleness.
6. The Wife's tale suggests that gentlemen should be esteemed only for their gentleness.
7. The old woman in the Wife's tale changes into a young woman because the knight ceases to rebuke her.

Using Resources to Build Vocabulary
Sample Answers

line 281: <u>contrasting</u> for <u>motley</u>; "Motley" suggests carelessness, while "contrasting" suggests a deliberate, elaborate effect.

line 320: <u>cautious</u> for <u>wary</u>; "Wary" has a negative connotation, but "cautious" does not.

line 375: <u>neat</u> and <u>clean</u> for <u>fresh</u> and <u>trim</u>; The connotations are similar.

line 562: <u>fat</u> for <u>stout</u>; "Stout" implies muscular girth, but "fat" implies girth due to overeating.

line 565: <u>wide</u> for <u>broad</u>; "Wide" suggests obesity, but "broad" suggests strength.

152

PERFORMANCE TASKS
Integrated Language Skills

ⓒ Vocabulary Acquisition and Use

Multiple-Meaning Words in Context

Many English words have more than one meaning. For example, *relates* as a verb with an object can mean "tells a story or recounts," or, as a verb without an object, "to have or establish a relation (to)." Often, the meaning of the word changes according to its part of speech, which can be determined by the context. Note these examples:

> *The Wife relates her tale.*
> *He relates to what she is saying.*

In the first sentence, that *relates* takes an object provides a clue to its correct meaning, as does the fact that the object, "tale," is a narrative. In the second sentence, *relates* does not take an object, suggesting that it means "to have or establish a relation (to)."

For each of the following, explain how context helps you know which definition corresponds to the italicized word.

1. The Wife *relates* best to submissive men.
   a. tells   **b.** has a relation to
2. Is her desire for power merely an *act*?
   a. to take action   **b.** performance
3. If so, her *bluff* is as compelling as her tale!
   a. lie   **b.** high, steep bank

Using Resources to Build Vocabulary

Lively Descriptive Adjectives and Their Connotations
In the Prologue, Chaucer uses lively adjectives to help you visualize his characters. For example, in line 299, he refers to the Oxford Cleric's "hollow look" and "sober stare." Following are other examples of lively adjectives:

motley (line 281)	wary (line 320)	trim (line 375)
fresh (line 375)	stout (line 562)	broad (line 565)

Review these words in context. Then, use a *print or digital thesaurus* to find synonyms for each. Rewrite the passage by replacing the word with a synonym. Next, read your new lines, and briefly explain how they differ from Chaucer's originals. Tell how the *connotative meanings,* or associations, of the adjectives make them better or worse for describing the characters, although their *denotative meanings,* or definitions, are similar.

152 From Legend to History (A.D. 449–1485)

Vocabulary: Logical or Illogical?

Review the vocabulary words on page 137. Then, for each item below, revise the sentence so that the underlined vocabulary word is used logically. Be sure not to change the vocabulary word.

Example: When the dark clouds moved in, the water in the puddles <u>glistened</u>.

After the dark clouds moved away, the water in the puddles <u>glistened</u>.

1. Let us give less consideration to the rights of women, the Wife of Bath <u>implored</u>.
2. The story the Wife of Bath <u>relates</u> is a warning against the destructiveness of greed.
3. When asked what women wanted most, the knight replied in a <u>contemptuous</u> way.
4. The old woman in the tale says that our fathers <u>bequeath</u> us their wealth and virtue.
5. According to the old wife in the story, the <u>prowess</u> of men is their fierceness.
6. The Wife's tale suggests that gentlemen should be <u>esteemed</u> only for their rank.
7. The old woman in the Wife's tale changes into a young woman because the knight continues to <u>rebuke</u> her.

Assessment Resources

Unit 1 Resources   **All**
- **L1 L2 EL** **Selection Test A**, pp. 127–129. Administer Test A to less advanced readers.
- **L3 L4 EL** **Selection Test B**, pp. 130–132. Administer Test B to on-level and more advanced students.
- **L3 L4** **Open-Book Test**, pp. 124–126. As an alternative, give the Open-Book Test.

   All
Customizable Test Bank

Self-tests
Students may prepare for the **Selection Test** by taking the **Self-test** online.

PHLit Online!   All assessment resources are available at **www.PHLitOnline.com**.

Writing

 **Argumentative Text** Chaucer's outlandish, rule-breaking pilgrims have long been the subject of critical speculation. Through such characters, did Chaucer hope to reform the flawed institutions they represent—the church, the nobility, the government, and marriage, among others? Or did he intend to censure the pilgrims themselves and others like them?

Perhaps he meant to do neither. In his book *Chaucer and the Energy of Creation,* critic Edward I. Condren writes:

> To view Chaucer as a reformer . . . is to overlook his evident love affair with the world he creates—a world he neither condemns, endorses, burdens with ideology, nor seeks to improve, but a world he shows as a dynamic, human, endlessly fascinating entity unto itself.

Do you agree or disagree with Condren's take on Chaucer? Do you, too, believe that the poet's main intent was to capture life in all its teeming glory, or do you suspect that he had an agenda of reform or censure? Write an **essay** in which you evaluate Condren's view and state your own judgment about Chaucer's purpose, supporting your claims with evidence from the texts.

Prewriting Before formulating an opinion, review the texts with an open mind. Gather details, including *imagery* and *figures of speech*, that describe pilgrims acting unconventionally and evoke your emotions. Is the *tone* of each detail comically affirming or darkly disapproving?

Drafting Use these steps as you compose your essay:

- In your introduction, include a *thesis* statement supporting or refuting Condren's remark. Try to express your thesis in a way that engages the interest of the reader.

- In your essay, *support your thesis* with information and examples from your prewriting notes. Return to the texts for additional support, if necessary.

- Close the essay by restating your thesis and by echoing your strongest evidence.

Revising Your essay may discuss social and religious institutions that some readers may value. Review your draft, placing a star next to passages that might lead to *misunderstandings*. For each star, rephrase the idea so that your meaning is clear and your tone is inoffensive.

 **Common Core State Standards**

Writing
1.a. Create an organization that logically sequences claims, counterclaims, reasons, and evidence.
1.e. Provide a concluding statement or section that follows from and supports the argument presented.

Model: Revising to Eliminate False Generalizations

Chaucer writes of the Monk that "Hunting a hare or riding at a fence / Was all his fun, he spared for no expense."

Here, Chaucer suggests that this monk, for one, lived a life of indulgence rather than poverty.

★ ~~Clearly, Chaucer wanted to point out that most religious people at that time lived lives of indulgence rather than poverty.~~

The generalization "most religious people" makes a false generalization from Chaucer's passage. The writer replaces it with a specific reference to the monk.

Integrated Language Skills **153**

Writing

You may use this Writing lesson as timed-writing practice, or you may allow students to develop the argumentative text as a writing assignment over several days.

- **Focus** The writer should clearly express his or her thesis, supporting or refuting Condren's remark. The thesis should be interesting and engaging.

- **Organization** The writer should support the thesis with information and examples that support the thesis. The examples should be clearly stated and relevant to the thesis.

- **Style** Whenever religious, cultural, or political topics are discussed, writers need to maintain an objective, inoffensive tone. The content of the essay should appeal to a broad audience of various religious and cultural backgrounds.

Teaching Resources

Unit 1 Resources
- L3 L4 **Vocabulary Builder,** p. 120.
- L3 L4 **Support for Writing Lesson,** p. 121.
- L3 L4 **Grammar and Style,** pp. 122.
- L4 **Enrichment,** p. 123.
- All *Common Core Companion,* pp. 28–35; 185–195

All **Enriched Online Student Edition**
Internet Research Activity: available under After You Read for this selection
Interactive Grammar Lesson: available under After You Read for this selection

All *Professional Development Guidebook*
Rubrics for Self-Assessment: pp. 245–304

PHLit Online!
All resources are available at **www.PHLitOnline.com.**

PHLit Online!
Direct students to **www.PHLitOnline.com** to view rubrics, use interactive prewriting and drafting graphic organizers, and get revision suggestions.

Conventions and Style
Practice

1. either, or
2. both, and; not only, but also
3. not only, but also; both, and
4. either, or
5. not only, but also; both, and
6. *Both* the narrator *and* the characters are storytellers.
7. The host of the tavern serves *both* as a travel guide *and* as a judge of the tales.
8. The pardoner is *both* greedy *and* hypocritical.
9. The knight must *either* answer the queen's question correctly *or* surrender himself to the court.
10. *Neither* the old man's words *nor* his actions hurt the rioters.

Writing and Speaking Conventions

A. Sample Responses

1. The stories serve not only as entertainment but also as competition.
2. A knight should be not only honorable but also courteous.
3. You may either read the poem aloud or listen to a recording.

B. Sample Response

I would like to go on a pilgrimage to the Sistine Chapel. I would like to see the ceiling that Michelangelo worked so hard to complete. This pilgrimage would be both religious and artistic. Unfortunately, neither my mother nor my father wants to pay for the trip.

PH WRITING COACH | Grade 12

Students will find instruction on and practice with correlative conjunctions in Chapter 13, section 4

 COMMON CORE ▪ EXTENDED STUDY: GEOFFREY CHAUCER

PERFORMANCE TASKS
Integrated Language Skills

Conventions and Style: Correlative Conjunctions

Too many short sentences can make your writing sound dull or stilted. When two short sentences have related ideas, you might be able to combine them using a **correlative conjunction,** a word pair connecting similar words or groups of words.

Combining: Correlative Conjunctions
The correlative conjunction you should use depends on the relationship between the ideas.

Two Short Sentences

The Carpenter is not described in detail. The Weaver isn't either.

The young man was the knight's Squire. He was also the knight's son.

The Cleric will buy books. The Cleric might take a course instead.

Combined

Neither the Weaver *nor* the Carpenter is described in detail.

The young man was *not only* the knight's Squire *but also* his son.

The Cleric will *either* buy books *or* take a course.

Practice In items 1–5, supply a correlative conjunction to complete the sentence. In items 6–10, use a correlative conjunction to combine the two sentences.

1. Each pilgrim must _____ tell four stories _____ pay for the journey.
2. The parson shows _____ generosity _____ patience in his behavior toward others.
3. The old woman urges the knight to respect _____ poverty _____ old age.
4. The travelers briefly considered _____ to accept _____ reject the Host's proposal.
5. Knights were supposed to be _____ honest _____ generous.
6. The narrator is a storyteller. The characters are storytellers too.
7. The host of the tavern serves as a travel guide. He serves as a judge of the tales.
8. The pardoner is greedy. He is hypocritical.
9. The knight must answer the queen's question correctly. Otherwise, he must surrender himself to the court.
10. The old man had not hurt the rioters by his words. He had not hurt them by his actions.

Punctuation Tip: Do not use a comma to separate items joined by a correlative conjunction, except when they are independent clauses.

© Writing and Speaking Conventions

A. Writing For each pair, write a sentence using a correlative conjunction to link the words or phrases.
1. entertainment—competition
2. honorable—courteous
3. read the poem aloud—listen to a recording

Example: entertainment—competition
Sentence: The stories serve as both an entertainment and a competition.

B. Speaking Describe a pilgrimage you have taken or would like to take. Include at least two sentences with correlative conjunctions.

PH WRITING COACH
Further instruction and practice are available in *Prentice Hall Writing Coach.*

Extend the Lesson

Sentence Modeling
Display for students the following sentences from "The Pardoner's Tale" and "The Wife of Bath's Tale":

"Covetousness is both the root and stuff / Of all I preach." ("The Pardoner's Tale")

On my oath / And word of honor, you shall find me both, / That is, both fair and faithful as a wife; / May I go howling mad and take my life / Unless I prove to be as good and true / As ever wife was since the world was new!" ("The Wife of Bath's Tale")

Ask students what similarity they notice about the sentences. (They use the correlative conjunction pair "both/and.") Then, **ask** what differences they notice. (The sentence from "The Wife of Bath's Tale" is longer and more complex. Also, it repeats the word "both.")

Have students imitate the first sentence by writing a simple sentence using a correlative conjunction. Then have them expand their sentence into a stanza of poetry that uses the same correlative conjunction pair.

GALLERY OF FRAME STORIES

To delay her execution, Scheherazade...

... tells stories that she leaves incomplete until the next night.

The Thousand and One Nights
MEDIEVAL ARABIA

Escaping the plague, residents of Florence, Italy,...

... tell stories to entertain one another.

The Decameron
BY GIOVANNI BOCCACCIO (ITALIAN; 1313–1375)

Pilgrims traveling to Canterbury, England,...

... enter into a storytelling competition.

The Canterbury Tales
BY GEOFFREY CHAUCER (ENGLISH; 1343?–1400)

Marco Polo, visiting Kublai Khan...

... tells him stories about fantastic cities.

Invisible Cities (1972)
BY ITALO CALVINO (ITALIAN; 1923–1985)

Gallery of Frame Stories

1. Tell students that a frame story is a literary technique that uses a main story in part for the purpose of organizing a set of shorter stories.

2. Direct student attention to the picture frame showing *The Thousand and One Nights.* **Ask** a volunteer to identify the story-teller, the premise of the frame story, and some of her familiar stories.
   Answer: Shaherazade tells a series of fairy tales to entertain her husband, the sultan of Arabia. Each night she stops just before the climax, saying the story is "to be continued" the next night. Since the sultan wants to hear the ending, he postpones her execution. Among the familiar stories are the tales of Aladdin, Ali Babba, and Sinbad.

3. Point out to students that they have just read another frame story, and direct their attention to the picture frame showing Chaucer's *Canterbury Tales.* **Ask:** What is the premise of this frame story?
   Answer: A group of pilgrims from all layers of society tell stories to pass the time while they journey to Canterbury.

4. **Ask** students to name some of the tales within this larger frame story.
   Answer: The Knight's Tale, Pardoner's Tale, and the Wife of Bath's Tale

5. Point out the picture frame showing Marco Polo. **Ask:** What does this frame story appear to have in common with the Arabian Nights?
   Answer: The storyteller is telling fantastic tales to entertain a ruler.

6. **Ask:** What other frame stories have you encountered before in literature?
   Possible responses: Bronte's *Wuthering Heights,* Shelley's *Frankenstein,* Carroll's *Alice in Wonderland,* and Goldman's *The Princess Bride.*

7. Explain that the next selection is also a frame story. Direct them to the picture frame for *Decameron.* **Ask** a volunteer to identify the premise of the frame story from the student page.
   Answer: A group of people escaping from the plague tell stories to entertain each other.

155

**Common Core
State Standards**

- **Reading Literature 10**
- **Writing 1, 10**
- **Language 4.a, c; 6**

Comparing Frame Stories Across Cultures

1. Have students read the discussion of frame stories on page 156.

2. **Ask** students if they can think of other examples of frame stories.

3. Point out that sometimes movies use frame stories. For example, the classic children's movie *Rudolph the Red-Nosed Reindeer* uses a frame. The story is told by a snowman who seems to be remembering it. As students mention other frame stories, list them on the board.

4. Have students examine the comparison chart on page 156. Tell students that they can ask questions to help them find the information they will need to complete the chart. Prompt students to think of questions they might ask: When does the story take place? Who is telling the story? Why? What types of stories are included?

Gather Vocabulary Knowledge

Have print and online resources available for students to consult as they explore the etymologies of the words.

Display a key to the symbols and abbreviations used in etymology notation. Preview with students and clarify any symbols or abbreviations they do not understand.

Comparing Literary Works

from *The Canterbury Tales* •
from the *Decameron:
Federigo's Falcon*

Comparing Frame Stories Across Cultures

Frame Stories A frame story is a type of narrative in which the author creates one long story that contains within it another story or group of stories. It has been used as a literary device by writers from diverse time periods and regions. Early frame stories, like those of *The Thousand and One Nights*, wove together tales from a variety of sources. Chaucer did so when he wrote *The Canterbury Tales*, but he also developed stories and characters of his own. Here are some advantages of a frame story:

- ties together stories of all different kinds
- presents fantastic stories in the realistic context of the frame
- captures the natural quality of oral storytelling

As you read the selection from the *Decameron*, use a chart like the one shown to compare it with the selections from *The Canterbury Tales*.

	The Canterbury Tales	*Decameron*
Frame-story setting	England in the 1300s	
Storytellers' backgrounds	people of all ages from different walks of life	
Storytellers' purpose for gathering	to make a pilgrimage to Becket's shrine in Canterbury	
Storytellers' purpose for storytelling	to pass the time and compete for best story	
Types of stories within the frame	stories of many kinds set in many times and places	

Gather Vocabulary Knowledge

In the third paragraph of the excerpt from the *Decameron*, Boccaccio uses the words *pre-eminence, eloquence,* and *sumptuous*. Read the paragraph, and then use the following exercises to further explore the words.

- **Context** Reread the words and try to define them using context—the words immediately surrounding the word you are trying to define. Then, use a print or online **dictionary** to verify your definitions and to find the parts of speech.
- **Etymologies** Use a print or online dictionary or a book of etymologies to determine the etymologies, or origins, of the three words.

After you have familiarized yourself with the words, form a small group with classmates and use the words in a brief paragraph about attending a formal event at a banquet hall or a palace. Then, elect a speaker and share your writing with the rest of the class.

156 From Legend to History (A.D. 449–1485)

**Common Core
State Standards**

Reading Literature
10. By the end of grade 12, read and comprehend literature, including stories, at the high end of the grades 11–CCR text complexity band independently and proficiently.

Language
4.a. Use context as a clue to the meaning of a word or phrase.
4.c. Consult general and specialized reference materials, both print and digital, to find the pronunciation of a word or determine or clarify its precise meaning, its part of speech, or its etymology.
6. Demonstrate independence in gathering vocabulary knowledge when considering a word or phrase important to comprehension or expression.

www.PHLitOnline.com

Teaching Resources

The following resources can be used to enrich, extend, or differentiate the instruction.

All *Unit 1 Resources,* pp. 133–137

All Enriched Online Student Edition

All *Common Core Companion,*
pp. 82–83; 185–195, 269–276; 324–331, 336–337

PHLit Online! All resources are available at
www.PHLitOnline.com.

Giovanni Boccaccio (1313–1375)

Author of the *Decameron: Federigo's Falcon*

When Giovanni Boccaccio (jō vän´ ē bō kä´ chō) was ten years old, his father, an associate of a well-known banking firm, sent the boy away from his native Florence to work at the firm's bank in Naples. Here he remained for many years, attending the court of Robert of Anjou, who ruled Naples at the time.

Enjoying the splendor and sophistication of Robert's court, Boccaccio showed little interest in becoming a businessman or a lawyer, as his father wanted him to do. Instead, he began writing—something he did prolifically for the rest of his life.

A Wider Worldview In 1340, financial problems caused Boccaccio's family to recall him to Florence, where at first he found the middle-class life not to his tastes. However, the change broadened his understanding of all different kinds and classes of people, an experience that would prove useful in his writing. In time, he became more sympathetic to Florence and its citizens, even engaging in local politics and serving as a Florentine ambassador.

Scholarship and Authorship In 1350, Boccaccio met the Italian poet and scholar Francesco Petrarch, with whom he began a lifelong friendship. Petrarch encouraged Boccaccio's writing, including many scholarly works in Latin.

However, while Boccaccio himself was proudest of these works, it is for an Italian work that he is best remembered. That masterpiece is the *Decameron*, a collection of stories that reveal his impressive literary versatility while exploring deeply human universal themes of love, loss, deception, fate, and honor.

"Human it is to have compassion on the unhappy."

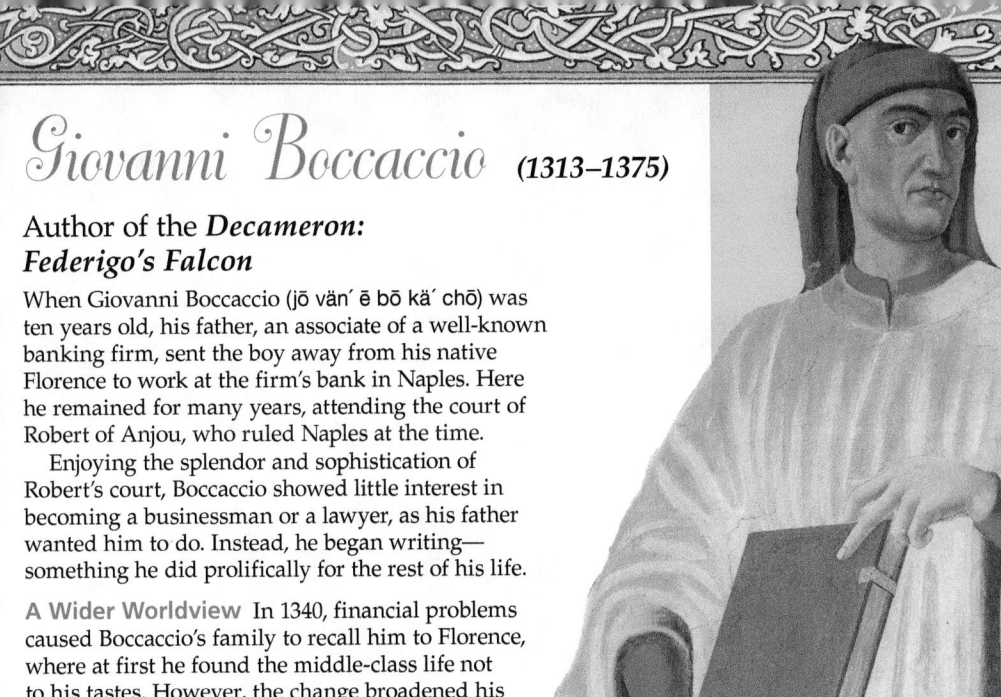

from the Decameron: Federigo's Falcon **157**

❶ About the Selection

Set in medieval Italy, the *Decameron* contrasts the tragedy of the plague with the playful liveliness of a group of aristocrats who try to entertain each other as they wait out the epidemic. The *Decameron* is divided into ten days, but includes 100 stories. Each member of the party has a day in which to serve as king or queen of the others. Each day has a theme: some days are given over to stories of adventure, and others to stories of unrequited love, happy love, or trickery and deceit.

❷ Activating Prior Knowledge

Tell students that this story begins with the tale of a man who loves a woman but is not loved by her in return. **Ask** students what other stories of unrequited love they know. Write the names of stories on the board. Then **ask** students what they think a person should do if his or her love is unrequited. Should a lover ever give up hope of love being returned? How might a lover try to inspire love in the object of his or her affections?

❶
❷ *from the* **Decameron**

Giovanni Boccaccio

translated by G.H. McWilliam

158 From Legend to History (A.D. 449–1485)

Enrichment: Building Context

Medieval Italy

During the 1300s, Italy was not yet a nation-state. Instead, it was composed of several small city-states: Sicily, Naples, Rome (where the Catholic Church was a political as well as religious authority), Florence, Milan, and Venice. Minor city-states included Mantua, Montferrat, Lucca, and Siena. People were loyal to their city-state, not to Italy, and only a few would have ever even heard the word *Italia*. Even dialects of Italian varied greatly from one city-state to another.

Activity: Investigating the City-State Have each student pick a medieval Italian city-state to research. Suggest that they record information in the **Enrichment: Building Context** worksheet, *Professional Development Guidebook*, page 222. Direct students to use the results of their research to develop oral presentations. Then have students make their oral presentations to the class.

③

❸ Humanities

The Decameron, 1916, by John William Waterhouse

This work, entitled *The Decameron,* was painted by John William Waterhouse in 1916. Waterhouse was an English painter, born in Rome in 1849. Throughout his life, Waterhouse returned several times to Italy to learn more about his craft.

Waterhouse is referred to as a Pre-Raphaelite painter. Much of his work involves particularly beautiful, sometimes tragic women, and plein-air (or, outdoor) paintings. Waterhouse painted subjects from mythology and literature, as well as historical figures, and portraits of young women of antiquity and medieval legend.

Here, one imagines the young women, listening enthralled to the stories of the young man speaking.

Use these questions for discussion:

1. **Ask:** What story do you imagine this young man is telling?
   Possible response: Students may offer that he is, in fact, telling "Federigo's Falcon," told on the fifth day in the *Decameron.*

2. **Ask:** What can we guess about the social class of the subjects?
   Possible response: Students may suggest that the young men and women in this painting seem to be from an upper or aristocratic class. They are wearing fine clothing, the young man is holding a musical instrument, they are in an idyllic setting, and they have the time and means to sit and listen to a story.

❹ Background

The Plague

The *Decameron* lasts ten days, but in real life, nobles could not hope to be safe simply by waiting out the plague. Going to the countryside made them a little safer, because the countryside was not hit as hard as the cities, where people lived in tighter spaces. But the countryside was hit as well. Italy's city-states experienced numerous plague epidemics from the 1340s through the early 1400s. Scholars estimate that approximately 25 million Europeans died of bubonic plague. Europe did not reach its pre-plague population again until the early 1500s.

❹ BACKGROUND In 1348, bubonic plague swept Europe, killing more than half the population of Florence, including Boccaccio's parents. The *Decameron* begins with a group of ten young aristocrats—seven women and three men— taking up residence on a country estate where they hope to wait out the plague in Florence. To entertain themselves, each of them tells one story a day for ten days—the name Decameron means "ten days." Each day they elect a "king" or "queen" to preside over the day's storytelling and suggest the theme of the stories. "Federigo's Falcon" is told on the fifth day.

from the Decameron: Federigo's Falcon **159**

Culturally Responsive Instruction

Culture Focus Point out to students that frame stories appear in the literature of many different cultures. Two of the oldest frame stories are the *Mahabharata* (composed around the year AD 400) and the *Ramayana* (composed around 300 BC). Both are epic poems written in Sanskrit. The *Mahabharata* tells the story of the struggle for power between two groups of cousins. But most of the poem is made up of other stories.

The *Ramayana* tells the story of the birth of the prince Rama and his adventures during years of exile in the forest. The *Ramayana* became extremely popular and spread to Cambodia, Indonesia, and Thailand. It is still told in traditional Javanese-Balinese theatre, dance, and shadow plays, and events that occur in it are carved on monuments in Indonesia. **Ask** students to share frame stories from their own cultures.

5 Comparing Frame Stories

1. Point out to students that this story contains a frame within a frame. The queen tells the story, but she claims the story originally came from Coppo di Borghese Domenichi.

2. **Ask** students the Comparing Frame Stories question: Why do you think the "queen" introduces another storyteller, Coppo di Borghese Domenichi?
Sample answer: The queen may be modest and prefers to give credit for her story to someone else, or she may be unsure what the party will think of the story, and she prefers to blame someone else.

3. **Ask** students: In *The Canterbury Tales,* does Chaucer also use the device of a frame within a frame?
Answer: Yes, he appears in the story himself as the storyteller, but he has the pilgrims tell the stories.

6 Critical Thinking

Deduce

1. **Ask** students to name the characters the queen introduces on this page as she prepares to tell her story.
Answer: On this page, the queen mentions Coppo di Borghese Domenichi, Messer Filippo Alberighi, Federigo Alberighi, and Monna Giovanna.

2. **Ask:** What can we deduce as the reason why the queen refers to each character's attributes as she introduces them?
Answer: As the storyteller, the queen introduces each character as a fine, honorable person, in order to give her story interest and credence.

5 Comparing Frame Stories
Why do you think the "queen" introduces another storyteller, Coppo di Borghese Domenichi, in the third paragraph of the story?

Vocabulary
courtly (kôrt′ ly)
adj. elegantly dignified; polite

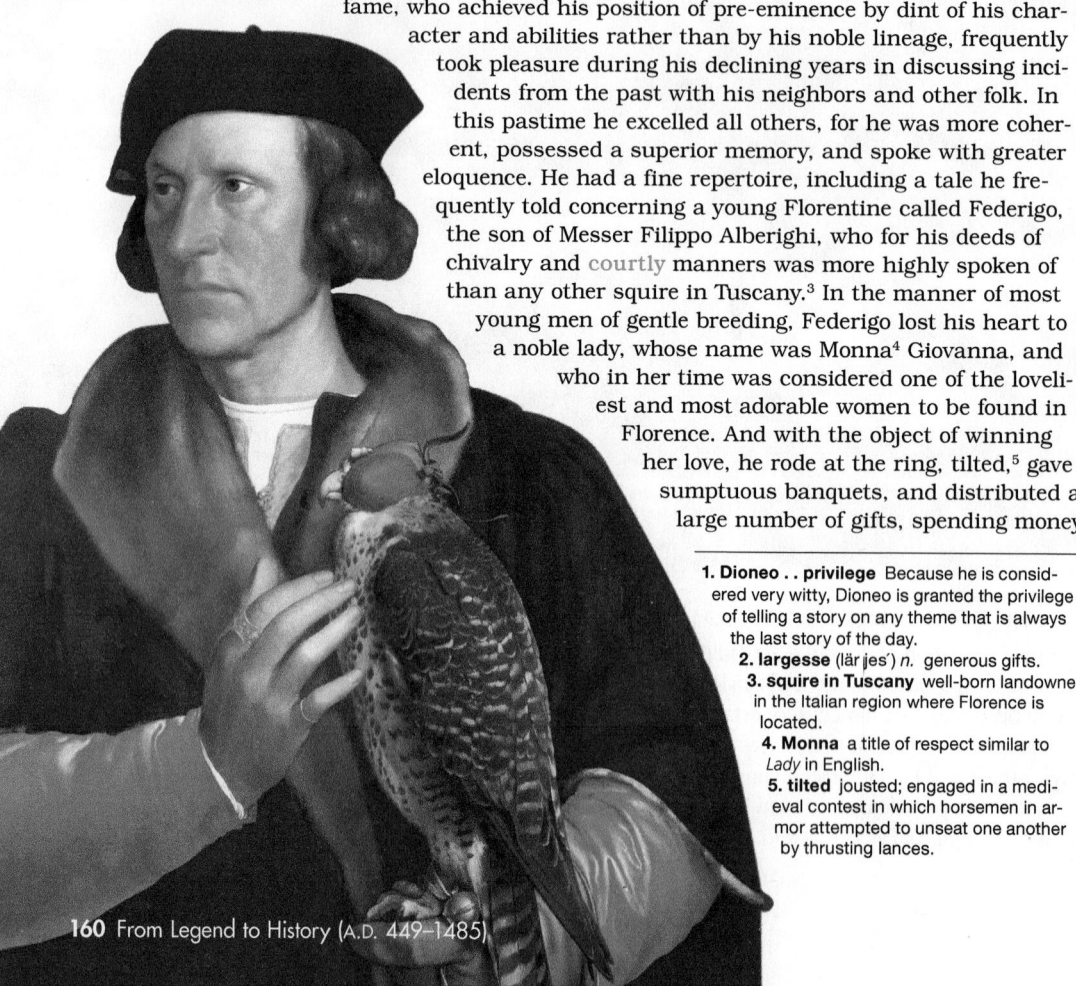

160 From Legend to History (A.D. 449–1485)

Once Filomena had finished, the queen, finding that there was no one left to speak apart from herself (Dioneo being excluded from the reckoning because of his privilege[1]), smiled cheerfully and said:

It is now my own turn to address you, and I shall gladly do so, dearest ladies, with a story similar in some respects to the one we have just heard. This I have chosen, not only to acquaint you with the power of your beauty over men of noble spirit, but so that you may learn to choose for yourselves, whenever necessary, the persons on whom to bestow your largesse,[2] instead of always leaving these matters to be decided for you by Fortune, who, as it happens, nearly always scatters her gifts with more abundance than discretion.

You are to know, then, that Coppo di Borghese Domenichi, who once used to live in our city and possibly lives there still, one of the most highly respected men of our century, a person worthy of eternal fame, who achieved his position of pre-eminence by dint of his character and abilities rather than by his noble lineage, frequently took pleasure during his declining years in discussing incidents from the past with his neighbors and other folk. In this pastime he excelled all others, for he was more coherent, possessed a superior memory, and spoke with greater eloquence. He had a fine repertoire, including a tale he frequently told concerning a young Florentine called Federigo, the son of Messer Filippo Alberighi, who for his deeds of chivalry and courtly manners was more highly spoken of than any other squire in Tuscany.[3] In the manner of most young men of gentle breeding, Federigo lost his heart to a noble lady, whose name was Monna[4] Giovanna, and who in her time was considered one of the loveliest and most adorable women to be found in Florence. And with the object of winning her love, he rode at the ring, tilted,[5] gave sumptuous banquets, and distributed a large number of gifts, spending money

1. **Dioneo . . privilege** Because he is considered very witty, Dioneo is granted the privilege of telling a story on any theme that is always the last story of the day.
2. **largesse** (lär jes′) *n.* generous gifts.
3. **squire in Tuscany** well-born landowner in the Italian region where Florence is located.
4. **Monna** a title of respect similar to *Lady* in English.
5. **tilted** jousted; engaged in a medieval contest in which horsemen in armor attempted to unseat one another by thrusting lances.

Think Aloud

Reading Strategy: Reread for Clarification
To model the skill of rereading for clarification, use the following "think aloud." Say to students:

As I read the queen's introduction, I may be confused. Why does she say that ladies should not allow "these matters to be decided for you by Fortune"? Looking at the sentence about Fortune, I see that Fortune has a capital *F* and is referred to as *her.* So I can infer that Fortune is a personification of an abstract idea. That idea is luck, or chance. Boccaccio says that Fortune "scatters her gifts with more abundance than discretion." What can this mean? I may have to use a dictionary to look up the word *discretion.* When I do, I find that *discretion* means "using good judgment to avoid embarrassing others." So, I can infer that the queen is warning the ladies that if they leave their love lives up to chance, they may end up embarrassed.

without any restraint whatsoever. But since she was no less chaste than she was fair, the lady took no notice, either of the things that were done in her honor, or of the person who did them.

In this way, spending far more than he could afford and deriving no profit in return, Federigo lost his entire fortune (as can easily happen) and reduced himself to poverty, being left with nothing other than a tiny little farm, which produced an income just sufficient for him to live very frugally, and one falcon of the finest breed in the whole world. Since he was as deeply in love as ever, and felt unable to go on living the sort of life in Florence to which he aspired, he moved out to Campi, where his little farm happened to be situated. Having settled in the country, he went hunting as often as possible with his falcon, and, without seeking assistance from anyone, he patiently resigned himself to a life of poverty.

Now one day, while Federigo was living in these straitened circumstances, the husband of Monna Giovanna happened to fall ill, and, realizing that he was about to die, he drew up his will. He was a very rich man, and in his will he left everything to his son, who was just growing up, further stipulating that, if his son should die without legitimate issue, his estate should go to Monna Giovanna, to whom he had always been deeply devoted.

Shortly afterward he died, leaving Monna Giovanna a widow, and every summer, in accordance with Florentine custom, she went away with her son to a country estate of theirs, which was very near Federigo's farm. Consequently this young lad of hers happened to become friendly with Federigo, acquiring a passion for birds and dogs; and, having often seen Federigo's falcon in flight, he became fascinated by it and longed to own it, but since he could see that Federigo was deeply attached to the bird, he never ventured to ask him for it.

And there the matter rested, when, to the consternation of his mother, the boy happened to be taken ill. Being her only child, he was the apple of his mother's eye, and she sat beside his bed the whole day long, never ceasing to comfort him. Every so often she asked him whether there was anything he wanted, imploring him to tell her what it was, because if it was possible to acquire it, she would move heaven and earth to obtain it for him.

After hearing this offer repeated for the umpteenth time, the boy said:

"Mother, if you could arrange for me to have Federigo's falcon, I believe I should soon get better."

On hearing this request, the lady was somewhat taken aback, and began to consider what she could do about it. Knowing that Federigo had been in love with her for a long time, and that she had never deigned to cast so much as a single glance in his direction, she said to herself: "How can I possibly go to him, or even send anyone, to ask him for this falcon, which to judge from all I have heard is the

Vocabulary
frugally (froo′ gə lē)
adv. in a way that is careful with money

❼ ◀ Critical Viewing
In what ways might this portrait be an accurate representation of Federigo?
[Analyze]

❽ ☑ Reading Check
What remains of Federigo's fortune after pursuing Monna Giovanna?

Differentiated Instruction   for Universal Access

Strategy for Special-Needs Students
Students may need assistance with the flow of events in the story. List the main characters on the board. Then discuss who each character is. Then, on the board, list the events of the story so far. **Ask** students what they think might happen next. Have students continue listing events as they read through the story.

Enrichment for Advanced Readers
Have students check out copies of the *Decameron* from the library. Then have students each choose one or two other stories from the *Decameron* to read and analyze. Suggest students offer at least one note of historical context with each story they analyze. Have students present the stories they have read and analyzed.

Enrichment for Gifted/Talented Students
Have students create a mini-play based on the selection. Students can set a modern scene, write new dialogue, and consider alternative endings to the story. Students should work with the same narrative device of the frame story. **Ask** students to perform their play for their classmates.

Falconry

Falconry, or hawking, is an ancient sport. It has been practiced since before the beginning of writing. Archaeologists have found cave paintings depicting falcons and falconers. The sport was not introduced to Europe, however, until the Middle Ages, when merchants, adventurers, and Crusaders began to visit the Middle East. They learned about falconry and brought the sport back to Europe.

Falconers teach their falcons to come to them to be fed. They keep the falcons in a room of their own, in a special house called a mew. When they are hunting, a falcon may bring down prey, such as a rabbit, but often cannot carry it to the falconer, because prey large enough for a falconer to hunt is often too large for a bird to carry.

During the medieval period, falconry flourished throughout Europe. When the shotgun was invented, its popularity waned. However, some people still practice falconry.

❿ Critical Thinking

Speculate

1. Direct students' attention to the paragraph beginning, "'My lady,' replied Federigo…." Have a volunteer read the paragraph.

2. **Ask** students: Given the tone of Federigo's words to Monna Giovanna, what might you speculate will happen when she asks him to give her his falcon?
   Possible response: Students may offer that because he is so in love with her, he will surely give her his falcon.

❾

❿

finest that ever flew, as well as being the only thing that keeps him alive? And how can I be so heartless as to deprive so noble a man of his one remaining pleasure?"

Her mind filled with reflections of this sort, she remained silent, not knowing what answer to make to her son's request, even though she was quite certain that the falcon was hers for the asking.

At length, however, her maternal instincts gained the upper hand, and she resolved, come what may, to satisfy the child by going in person to Federigo to collect the bird, and bring it back to him. And so she replied:

"Bear up, my son, and see whether you can start feeling any better. I give you my word that I shall go and fetch it for you first thing tomorrow morning."

Next morning, taking another lady with her for company,[6] his mother left the house as though intending to go for a walk, made her way to Federigo's little cottage, and asked to see him. For several days, the weather had been unsuitable for hawking, so Federigo was attending to one or two little jobs in his garden, and when he heard, to his utter astonishment, that Monna Giovanna was at the front door and wished to speak to him, he happily rushed there to greet her.

When she saw him coming, she advanced with womanly grace to meet him. Federigo received her with a deep bow, whereupon she said:

"Greetings, Federigo!" Then she continued: "I have come to make amends for the harm you have suffered on my account, by loving me more than you ought to have done. As a token of my esteem, I should like to take breakfast with you this morning, together with my companion here, but you must not put yourself to any trouble."

"My lady," replied Federigo in all humility, "I cannot recall ever having suffered any harm on your account. On the contrary I have gained so much that if ever I attained any kind of excellence, it was entirely because of your own great worth and the love I bore you. Moreover I can assure you that this visit which you have been generous enough to pay me is worth more to me than all the money I ever possessed, though I fear that my hospitality will not amount to very much."

So saying, he led her unassumingly into the house, and thence into his garden, where, since there was no one else he could call upon to chaperon her, he said:

"My lady, as there is nobody else available, this good woman, who is the wife of the farmer here, will keep you company whilst I go and see about setting the table."

Though his poverty was acute, the extent to which he had squandered his wealth had not yet been fully borne home to Federigo; but on this particular morning, finding that he had nothing to set before

---

6. **taking . . . company** It was not considered proper for a young woman of the upper classes to go out by herself.

Think Aloud

Vocabulary: Using Context Clues

To model the skill of using context clues, use the following "think aloud." Say to students:

As I read this page, I may be confused by some of the words, such as *amends, hospitality, acute,* and *squandered*. But even if I do not know these words, I may be able to guess what they mean. For example, Monna Giovanna says to Federigo, "I have come to make amends for the harm you have suffered." I know that *mend* means to fix something, and I wonder if *amend* is a related word. I also know that *make up* is often used to mean "make something better." So I can infer that by *amends*, Monna Giovanna means that she wants to make up to Federigo for ignoring him in the past.

the lady for whose love he had entertained so lavishly in the past, his eyes were well and truly opened to the fact. Distressed beyond all measure, he silently cursed his bad luck and rushed all over the house like one possessed, but could find no trace of either money or valuables. By now the morning was well advanced, he was still determined to entertain the gentlewoman to some sort of meal, and, not wishing to beg assistance from his own farmer (or from anyone else, for that matter), his gaze alighted on his precious falcon, which was sitting on its perch in the little room where it was kept. And having discovered, on picking it up, that it was nice and plump, he decided that since he had nowhere else to turn, it would make a worthy dish for such a lady as this. So without thinking twice about it he wrung the bird's neck and promptly handed it over to his housekeeper to be plucked, dressed, and roasted carefully on a spit. Then he covered the table with spotless linen, of which he still had a certain amount in his possession, and returned in high spirits to the garden, where he announced to his lady that the meal, such as he had been able to prepare, was now ready.

The lady and her companion rose from where they were sitting and made their way to the table. And together with Federigo, who waited on them with the utmost deference, they made a meal of the prize falcon without knowing what they were eating.

On leaving the table they engaged their host in pleasant conversation for a while, and when the lady thought it time to broach the subject she had gone there to discuss, she turned to Federigo and addressed him affably as follows:

"I do not doubt for a moment, Federigo, that you will be astonished at my impertinence when you discover my principal reason for coming here, especially when you recall your former mode of living and my virtue, which you possibly mistook for harshness and cruelty. But if you had ever had any children to make you appreciate the power of parental love, I should think it certain that you would to some extent forgive me.

"However, the fact that you have no children of your own does not exempt me, a mother, from the laws common to all other mothers. And being bound to obey those laws, I am forced, contrary to my own wishes and to all the rules of decorum and propriety, to ask you for something to which I know you are very deeply attached—which is only natural, seeing that it is the only consolation, the only pleasure, the only recreation remaining to you in your present extremity of fortune. The gift I am seeking is your falcon, to which my son has taken so powerful a liking, that if I fail to take it to him I fear he will succumb to the illness from which he is suffering, and consequently I shall lose him. In imploring you to give me this falcon, I appeal, not

Vocabulary

deference (def′ ər əns) *n.* courteous regard or respect

affably (af′ ə blē) *adv.* in a friendly manner

impertinence (im purt′ ə nəns) *n.* rudeness; impudence

Reading Check

Why has Monna Giovanna visited Federigo?

from the Decameron: Federigo's Falcon **163**

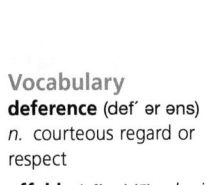

Background
Medieval Manors

Students may wonder why Federigo was able to afford to employ a housekeeper, when he did not have enough money for food. They may also be confused by the statement that Federigo did not wish "to beg assistance from his own farmer." Federigo's farm, although small, was a medieval manor, and it included tenants who lived there and worked the land. The farmer and housekeeper were tenants of Federigo's manor.

The manorial system in place in medieval Europe was a complex social and political arrangement. The lord of the manor, who could be a king, a baron, or a noble, owned the manor. Peasants worked the land in exchange for protection from the lord. Tenants also paid dues, either in currency or services, to live and work on the manor. The lord of the manor was expected to care for his tenants; for example, if a harvest was particularly poor, the lord would be expected to use his own monies to prevent starvation.

The small, economic units of the manorial system declined as a result of three main factors: the centralization of monarchies, the growth of urban centers, and the development of capitalist economies.

Reading Check

Answer: Monna Giovanna hopes that Federigo will give her his falcon, and that having the falcon will help her son to recover from his illness.

Differentiated Instruction   for Universal Access

(EL) Vocabulary for English Learners

Point out to students the two ways in which the word *possess* is used in the first paragraph on this page. Boccaccio writes that Federigo rushes "all over the house like one possessed" and later, that he still had some spotless linen "in his possession." Explain that in English, *possess* has more than one meaning. It can mean "to own something," such as a linen tablecloth and napkins. But it can also mean "to take control of somebody."

Vocabulary for Less Proficient Readers

Direct students' attention to the word *broach* in the third paragraph on this page. Explain that like *possess*, *broach* also has several meanings. It can mean "to come through the surface of water," for instance, or it can mean "to start talking about a difficult topic." Ask students if they have ever had a hard time broaching a difficult topic, or if they can imagine a topic that would be difficult to broach.

⓭ Literary Analysis

Frame

1. Have a volunteer read the second full paragraph on the page, which begins with, "'My lady,' he said..."

2. **Ask** students: What words from Federigo indicate that he is preparing to tell Monna Giovanna a mini-story, or a story within this story?
Answer: The last line of the second full paragraph, "The reason is simple, and I shall explain it in few words."

3. **Ask** students: How does Federigo add to the drama of his explanation of why he cannot give Monna Giovanna the falcon?
Answer: Federigo dumps the feathers, talons, and beak of the falcon on the table in front of her.

⓮ Critical Thinking

Evaluate

1. Have a volunteer read the last paragraph on the page, which begins, "In confirmation of his words...".

2. **Ask** students: What two reactions does Monna Giovanna have when she learns the fate of the falcon?
Answer: First, Monna Giovanna is angry with Federigo; she "reproached him for killing so fine a falcon." Then her reaction moves to "admiration for his magnanimity of spirit."

3. Then, **ask** students: How might the reader evaluate her response?
Possible answer: Students might suggest that Monna Giovanna experiences a change of heart on the spot, and that her realization of the sacrifice Federigo made for her transforms the way she thinks and feels about him.

---

to your love, for you are under no obligation to me on that account, but rather to your noble heart, whereby you have proved yourself superior to all others in the practice of courtesy. Do me this favor, then, so that I may claim that through your generosity I have saved my son's life, thus placing him forever in your debt."

When he heard what it was that she wanted, and realized that he could not oblige her because he had given her the falcon to eat, Federigo burst into tears in her presence before being able to utter a single word in reply. At first the lady thought his tears stemmed more from his grief at having to part with his fine falcon than from any other motive, and was on the point of telling him that she would prefer not to have it. But on second thoughts she said nothing, and waited for Federigo to stop crying and give her his answer, which eventually he did.

⓭ "My lady," he said, "ever since God decreed that you should become the object of my love, I have repeatedly had cause to complain of Fortune's hostility towards me. But all her previous blows were slight by comparison with the one she has dealt me now. Nor shall I ever be able to forgive her, when I reflect that you have come to my poor dwelling, which you never deigned to visit when it was rich, and that you desire from me a trifling favor which she has made it impossible for me to concede. The reason is simple, and I shall explain it in few words.

"When you did me the kindness of telling me that you wished to breakfast with me, I considered it right and proper, having regard to your excellence and merit, to do everything within my power to prepare a more sumptuous dish than those I would offer to my ordinary guests. My thoughts therefore turned to the falcon you have asked me for and, knowing its quality, I reputed it a worthy dish to set before you. So I had it roasted and served to you on the trencher this morning, and I could not have wished for a better way of disposing of it. But now that I discover that you wanted it in a different form, I am so distressed by my inability to grant your request that I shall never forgive myself for as long as I live."

⓮ In confirmation of his words, Federigo caused the feathers, talons and beak to be cast on the table before her. On seeing and hearing all this, the lady reproached him at first for killing so fine a falcon, and serving it up for a woman to eat; but then she became lost in admiration for his magnanimity[7] of spirit, which no amount of poverty had managed to diminish, nor ever would. But now that her hopes of obtaining the falcon had vanished she began to feel seriously concerned for the health of her son, and after thanking Federigo for his hospitality and good intentions, she took her leave of him, looking all despondent, and returned to the child. And to his mother's indescribable sorrow, within the space of a few days, whether through his dis-

Vocabulary
despondent (di spän′ dent) *adj.* hopeless; dejected

---

7. **magnanimity** (mag′ nə nim′ ə tē) *n.* noble generosity.

Think Aloud

Reading Strategy: Reread for Clarification
To model the skill of rereading for clarification, use this "think aloud." Say to students:

Now I am starting to understand the queen's remarks in her introduction to this story on page 198. I remember that she said she had chosen "to acquaint with the power of beauty over men of noble spirit." At first it seemed as though she might have meant that men tend to fall in love with beautiful women. But now I see that she is referring to Federigo's actions. Federigo was so in love with Monna Giovanna that he thought nothing of sacrificing his beloved falcon simply to provide a fancy breakfast for her. I ask myself, I wonder what the queen thinks of this action? I think the queen might think that it shows great generosity and nobility of spirit.

appointment in not being able to have the falcon, or because he was in any case suffering from a mortal illness, the child passed from this life.

After a period of bitter mourning and continued weeping, the lady was repeatedly urged by her brothers to remarry, since not only had she been left a vast fortune but she was still a young woman. And though she would have preferred to remain a widow, they gave her so little peace that in the end, recalling Federigo's high merits and his latest act of generosity, namely to have killed such a fine falcon in her honor, she said to her brothers:

"If only it were pleasing to you, I should willingly remain as I am; but since you are so eager for me to take a husband, you may be certain that I shall never marry any other man except Federigo degli Alberighi."

Her brothers made fun of her, saying:

"Silly girl, don't talk such nonsense! How can you marry a man who hasn't a penny with which to bless himself?"

"My brothers," she replied, "I am well aware of that. But I would sooner have a gentleman without riches, than riches without a gentleman."

Seeing that her mind was made up, and knowing Federigo to be a gentleman of great merit even though he was poor, her brothers fell in with her wishes and handed her over to him, along with her immense fortune. Thenceforth, finding himself married to this great lady with whom he was so deeply in love, and very rich into the bargain, Federigo managed his affairs more prudently, and lived with her in happiness to the end of his days.

 Comparing Frame Stories Which words let you know that the interior story has finished?

Critical Reading

Cite textual evidence to support your responses.

© 1. **Key Ideas and Details** (a) What early efforts does Federigo make to win Monna Giovanna's love? (b) **Summarize:** How does she respond to those efforts? (c) **Analyze:** What does her behavior reveal about her character?

© 2. **Key Ideas and Details** (a) **Connect:** In what ways do Federigo's gestures of hospitality when Monna Giovanna visits reflect his former life as a wealthy gentleman? (b) **Infer:** Why is killing the bird such a sacrifice for him? (c) **Analyze:** What does his sacrifice show about his character?

© 3. **Key Ideas and Details** (a) **Infer:** Why is it difficult for Monna Giovanna to ask Federigo for the falcon? (b) **Analyze:** What does her making the request show about her character?

© 4. **Integration of Knowledge and Ideas** (a) **Evaluate:** Do you think Monna Giovanna makes the right decision in marrying Federigo in the end? (b) **Support:** Cite reasons and story details to support your evaluation.

from the Decameron: Federigo's Falcon **165**

1. **Ask** students whether they consider the ending of the story to be a happy one.
   Possible response: The deaths of the son and the falcon are tragic, but the marriage is a happy one.

2. **Ask** students whether Monna Giovanna and Federigo will be happy in their marriage.
   Possible response: Some students may notice that Monna Giovanna "would have preferred to remain a widow."

3. **Ask** students the Comparing Frame Stories question: Which words let you know that the interior story has finished?
   Answer: The story ends with a "happily ever after" statement: "Federigo...lived with her in happiness to the end of his days."

ASSESS

Answers

Before students respond, you may wish to have them write a brief objective summary of the selection. As they answer the questions below, remind them to support their answers with evidence from the text.

1. (a) Federigo gives banquets and gifts. He also jousts in Monna Giovanna's honor. (b) She paid no attention to Federigo. (c) She is a chaste woman.

2. (a) Federigo always gave his guests the best meals possible. (b) Federigo loves his falcon. (c) He is a very generous person, willing to go to any length for true love.

3. (a) Monna Giovanna realizes that she has always ignored Federigo's attentions, and that she has no right to now ask him for his most precious possession. (b) Monna Giovanna's strong maternal instinct is revealed in her request.

4. (a) **Sample answer:** Yes, she makes the right decision. (b) She now realizes what a generous person he is, and how much he really loves her. The story says that she recalls "Federigo's high merits and his latest act of generosity," and that she regards him as a true gentleman.

Answers

Comparing Frame Stories

1. (a) Ten aristocrats are waiting out the plague on a country estate. They tell stories. (b) Chaucer's pilgrims also tell stories. But Chaucer's pilgrims come from all walks of life; they are not all aristocrats. (c) **Sample answer:** Chaucer's frame story is more effective, because the characters are more varied than Boccaccio's. The variety adds to the interest of the stories.

2. **Sample answer:** Boccaccio's story is more like oral storytelling. Chaucer seems to describe a pilgrim telling a story—it is as if Chaucer has two frames, the story of the pilgrims, and Chaucer's perspective.

3. **Sample answer:** I disagree. Frame stories show the values of the narrator. Chaucer's *Prologue* shows what he thinks of each pilgrim, which reveals his values. "Federigo's Falcon" shows that the queen thinks women need instruction on how their beauty affects men.

Timed Writing

1. Teach the Academic Vocabulary. Discuss the words with students, and their related forms, including *comparison, comparatively, in contrast, insightful,* and *interpretation.* Encourage students to use the words as appropriate as they compare and contrast the selections.

2. Use the prompt to help students identify elements and qualities their interpretation of a literary text should have:

   • A statement about the relationship between the themes of the two works

   • An interpretation of the two themes

   • Specific text references that illustrate how the themes are developed through events and characters

   • An interpretation of how the two themes are similar and different in their message, development, and delivery

   • Detailed and specific text references that illustrate and support the interpretation of similarities and differences

---

After You Read

from *The Canterbury Tales* •
from the *Decameron:*
Federigo's Falcon

Comparing Frame Stories

1. **Integration of Knowledge and Ideas** **(a)** In the **frame story** of Boccaccio's *Decameron*, what is the premise or reason for the storytelling? **(b)** How is that premise like and unlike the premise for the storytelling in Chaucer's work? **(c)** Which premise makes for a more effective frame story? Why?

2. **Integration of Knowledge and Ideas** One advantage of a frame story is that it can capture, in written form, the qualities of oral storytelling. Which author, Boccaccio or Chaucer, better conveys those qualities? Explain.

3. **Integration of Knowledge and Ideas** Consider this statement: Frame stories are not effective for revealing character because the only action people perform is telling stories. Explain why you agree or disagree with this assertion, citing evidence from "Federigo's Falcon" and *The Canterbury Tales* as support.

⏱ Timed Writing

Argumentative Text: Essay

Although Chaucer and Boccaccio both use the device of the frame story, they do not always deal with similar themes in exactly the same way.

Assignment: Write an **interpretation of a literary text** in which you compare and contrast the theme of "Federigo's Falcon" with the theme of "The Wife of Bath's Tale" or "The Pardoner's Tale." **[40 minutes]**
Your essay should explore these types of questions:

   • How does the sequence of events and outcome of each tale offer a clue to its theme?

   • How does the theme of each tale reflect or suggest the personality, background, or motives of the character in the frame story who narrates the tale?

   • What do the themes of the two tales have in common, and how are they different?

   As you write, support your ideas with accurate and detailed references to the texts.

5-Minute Planner

Complete these steps before you begin to write:

1. Read the assignment carefully. Identify key words and phrases.

2. Scan the selections, looking for details related to your assignment.
   TIP As you scan, jot down quotations that you might use in your essay.

3. Write a rough outline for your essay.

4. Reread the prompt and begin drafting.

Common Core State Standards

Writing

1. Write arguments to support claims in an analysis of substantive topics or texts, using valid reasoning and relevant and sufficient evidence.

10. Write routinely over extended time frames and shorter time frames for a range of tasks, purposes, and audiences.

USE ACADEMIC VOCABULARY

As you write, use academic language, including the following words or their related forms:

   compare
   contrast
   insight
   interpret

For more about academic language, see the vocabulary charts in the introduction to this book.

Encourage students to focus on these points when they are planning and revising their essays.
Tell students they will have 40 minutes to plan and write the essay. Call students' attention to the 5-Minute Planner. Encourage students to budget their time to allow 5 minutes for outlining, 5 minutes for identifying some initial supporting text references in the works, and 10 minutes for revision and proofreading.

Assessment Resources

Unit 1 Resources
L1 L2 EL **Selection Test,** pp. 136–137.

 Students may use the Self-test, online at **www. PHLitOnline.com,** to prepare for the Selection Test.

Perils and Adventures

PART 4

167

Text Complexity: At a Glance

This chart gives a general text complexity rating for the selections in this part of the unit to help guide instruction. For additional text complexity support, see the Test Complexity Rubric at point of use.

from Sir Gawain and the Green Knight	**More Accessible**
from Morte de'Arthur	**More Accessible**

Selection Planning Guide

The selections in this section are full of the perils and adventures that characterize medieval legends. In this excerpt from *Sir Gawain and the Green Knight,* the hero faces challenges that test his courage, loyalty, and honesty—virtues all knights of King Arthur's court should possess. King Arthur battles and kills his own son, Mordred, in the excerpt from *Morte d'Arthur.* The letters of Margaret Paston provide an insight into the perils of maintaining an estate. The ballads tell of perils faced by several unfortunate individuals.

Humanities

St. George and the Dragon,
ca. 1620 by Peter Paul Rubens

In his painting of St. George and the dragon, Rubens provides a drama-filled scene. St. George is the patron saint of England. The most famous legend associated with St. George is his slaying of a dragon and rescue of a princess.

Use these questions for discussion:

1. What is the impression created by Rubens's painting of St. George?
   Possible response: He has clearly charged up on a white horse to save the maiden, who looks strangely calm, and kill the dragon; the dragon looks like a fearsome menace with glowing eyes.

2. What details of the painting suggest the heroic stature of St. George?
   Possible response: Details such as the knight's forceful posture, his splendid armor, the white horse's flowing mane and flaring nostrils, and the broken lance contribute to the heroic picture.

Monitoring Progress

Before students read from the medieval legends selections refer to the results for the **Diagnostic Test** (*Unit 1 Resources* **p. 1**). Use this diagnostic portion of the test to guide your choice of selections to teach, as well as the depth of preparation you will provide, based on students' readiness for reading and vocabulary skills.

from Sir Gawain and the Green Knight
• *from* Morte d'Arthur
Lesson Pacing Guide

DAY 1 Preteach

- ©️ Administer the Reading and Vocabulary Warm-ups (*Unit 1 Resources*, pp. 138–141) as necessary.
- • Introduce the Literary Analysis concept: Medieval Romance.
- ©️ Introduce the Reading Strategy: Summarizing.
- • Build background with the author and Background features.
- • Develop thematic thinking with Connecting to the Essential Question.
- ©️ Teach the selection vocabulary.

DAYS 2–3 Preteach/Teach/Assess

- ©️ Distribute copies of the appropriate graphic organizer for the Reading Strategy (*Graphic Organizer Transparencies*, pp. 27–28).
- ©️ Distribute copies of the appropriate graphic organizer for Literary Analysis (*Graphic Organizer Transparencies*, pp. 29–30).
- • Prepare students to read with the Activating Prior Knowledge activities (TE).
- • Informally monitor comprehension while students read.
- • Use the Reading Check questions to confirm comprehension.
- • Develop students' understanding of medieval romance using the Literary Analysis prompts.
- • Develop students' ability to summarize using the Reading Strategy prompts.
- ©️ Reinforce vocabulary with the Vocabulary notes.
- ©️ Assess students' comprehension and mastery of the skills by having them answer the Critical Reading, Literary Analysis, and Reading Strategy questions.
- ©️ Have students complete the Vocabulary Lesson.

DAY 4 Extend/Assess

- ©️ Have students complete the Writing Lesson and write an interior monologue. (You may assign as homework.)
- ©️ Administer Selection Test A or B (*Unit 1 Resources*, pp. 150–152 or 153–155).

©️ ## Common Core
State Standards

Reading Literature 2. Provide an objective summary of the text.

Writing 3. Write narratives to develop real or imagined experiences or events using effective technique, well-chosen details, and well-structured event sequences.
3.d. Use precise words and phrases, telling details, and sensory language to convey a vivid picture of the experiences, events, setting, and/or characters.

Language 4.a. Use context as a clue to the meaning of a word or phrase.

Additional Standards Practice
Common Core Companion, *pp. 15–22; 208–218; 324–331*

Daily Block Scheduling
Each day in this Lesson Pacing Guide represents a 40–50 minute period. Teachers using block scheduling may combine days to revise pacing. In addition, teachers may differentiate and support core instruction by integrating components for extended and intensive support as students require. See the Guide to Selected Leveled Resources (facing page).

Guide to Selected Leveled Resources

R T I Tier 1 (students performing on level)

from Sir Gawain and the Green Knight • *from* Morte d'Arthur

Warm Up	**Practice, model,** and **monitor** fluency, working **with the whole class** or **in groups.**	**Vocabulary** and **Reading Warm-ups B,** *Unit 1 Resources,* pp. 138–139, 141
Comprehension/Skills	**Support** and **monitor** comprehension and skills development, having students complete the activities, graphic organizers, and interactive prompts **independently** or **as a class.**	• *Reader's Notebook,* adapted instruction and full selection **EL** *Reader's Notebook: English Learner's Version,* adapted instruction and adapted selection • **Reading Skill Graphic Organizer B,** *Graphic Organizer Transparencies,* p. 28 • **Literary Analysis Graphic Organizer B,** *Graphic Organizer Transparencies,* p. 30
Monitor Progress	**A** **Monitor** student progress with the differentiated curriculum-based assessment in the *Unit Resources.*	• **Selection Test B,** *Unit 1 Resources,* pp. 153–155 • **Open-Book Test,** *Unit 1 Resources,* pp. 147–149
Assess/ Screen	**A** **Assess** student progress using Benchmark Test. **Preassess** instructional needs using the Vocabulary in Context section of the test.	• **Benchmark Test 2, Unit 1 Resources,** 165–173, including Vocabulary in Context diagnostic items

R T I Tier 2 (students requiring intervention)

from Sir Gawain and the Green Knight • *from* Morte d'Arthur

Warm Up	**Practice, model,** and **monitor** fluency **in groups** or **with individuals.**	• **Vocabulary and Reading Warm-ups A,** *Unit 1 Resources,* pp. 138–140 • *Hear It!* Audio CD (adapted text)
Comprehension/Skills	• **Support** and **monitor** comprehension and skills development, working **in small groups** or **with individuals.** • As students complete the selection in the appropriate version of the *Reader's Notebook,* **monitor** comprehension frequently with group questions and individual instruction. • **Model** strategies while guiding students in completing the activities and prompts in the *Reader's Notebook,* as well as the graphic organizers. • **Practice** skills and **monitor** mastery with the *Reading Kit* worksheets.	• *Reader's Notebook: Adapted Version,* adapted instruction and adapted selection **EL** *Reader's Notebook: English Learner's Version,* adapted instruction and adapted selection • **Reading Skill Graphic Organizer A,** *Graphic Organizer Transparencies,* p. 27 • **Literary Analysis Graphic Organizer A,** *Graphic Organizer Transparencies,* p. 29 • *Reading Kit,* Practice worksheets
Monitor Progress	**A** **Monitor** student progress with the differentiated curriculum-based assessment in the *Unit Resources* and in the *Reading Kit.*	• **Selection Test A,** *Unit 1 Resources,* pp. 150–152 • *Reading Kit,* Assess worksheets
Assess/ Screen	**A** **Assess** student progress using Benchmark Test. **Preassess** instructional needs using the Vocabulary in Context section of the test.	• **Benchmark Test 2, Unit 1 Resources,** 165–173, including Vocabulary in Context diagnostic items

TIER 3 Tier 3 intervention may require consultation with the student's special-education or dyslexia specialist. For additional support, see the Tier 2 activities and resources listed above.

One-on-one teaching　　Group work　　Whole class instruction　　Independent work　　**A** Assessment
For a complete guide to selection support, including support for Advanced students, see the Overview of Resources in the frontmatter.

from *Sir Gawain and the Green Knight*
• from *Morte d'Arthur*

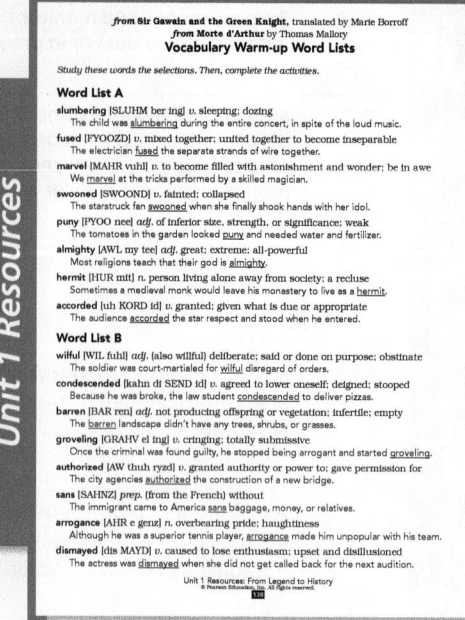

RESOURCES FOR:

- **L1** Special-Needs Students
- **L2** Below-Level Students (Tier 2)
- **L3** On-Level Students (Tier 1)
- **L4** Advanced Students (Tier 1)
- **EL** English Learners
- **All** All Students

Vocabulary/Fluency/Prior Knowledge

from Sir Gawain and the Green Knight, translated by Marie Borroff
from Morte d'Arthur by Thomas Mallory
Vocabulary Warm-up Word Lists

Study these words the selections. Then, complete the activities.

Word List A

slumbering [SLUHM ber ing] *v.* sleeping; dozing
The child was slumbering during the entire concert, in spite of the loud music.

fused [FYOOZD] *v.* mixed together; united together to become inseparable
The electrician fused the separate strands of wire together.

marvel [MAHR vuhl] *v.* to become filled with astonishment and wonder; be in awe
We marvel at the tricks performed by a skilled magician.

swooned [SWOOND] *v.* fainted; collapsed
The starstruck fan swooned when she finally shook hands with her idol.

puny [PYOO nee] *adj.* of inferior size, strength, or significance; weak
The tomatoes in the garden looked puny and needed water and fertilizer.

almighty [AWL my tee] *adj.* great; extreme; all-powerful
Most religions teach that their god is almighty.

hermit [HUR mit] *n.* person living alone away from society; a recluse
Sometimes a medieval monk would leave his monastery to live as a hermit.

accorded [uh KORD id] *v.* granted; given what is due or appropriate
The audience accorded the star respect and stood when he entered.

Word List B

wilful [WIL fuhl] *adj.* (also willful) deliberate; said or done on purpose; obstinate
The soldier was court-martialed for wilful disregard of orders.

condescended [kahn di SEND id] *v.* agreed to lower oneself; deigned; stooped
Because he was broke, the law student condescended to deliver pizzas.

barren [BAR ren] *adj.* not producing offspring or vegetation; infertile; empty
The barren landscape didn't have any trees, shrubs, or grasses.

groveling [GRAHV el ing] *v.* cringing; totally submissive
Once the criminal was found guilty, he stopped being arrogant and started groveling.

authorized [AW thuh ryzd] *v.* granted authority or power to; gave permission for
The city agencies authorized the construction of a new bridge.

sans [SAHNZ] *prep.* (from the French) without
The immigrant came to America sans baggage, money, or relatives.

arrogance [AHR e genz] *n.* overbearing pride; haughtiness
Although he was a superior tennis player, arrogance made him unpopular with his team.

dismayed [dis MAYD] *v.* caused to lose enthusiasm; upset and disillusioned
The actress was dismayed when she did not get called back for the next audition.

Unit 1 Resources: From Legend to History
© Pearson Education, Inc. All rights reserved.

EL **L1** **L2** **Vocabulary Warm-ups A and B,**
pp. 138–139

Also available for these selections:

EL **L1** **L2** **Reading Warm-ups A and B,**
pp. 140–141

All **Vocabulary Builder,** p. 144

Reader's Notebooks

Pre- and postreading pages for both selections, as well as the selection from *Morte d'Arthur*, appear in an interactive format in the *Reader's Notebooks*. Each *Notebook* is differentiated for a different group of learners.
The selections in the Adapted and English Learner's versions are abridged.

- **L2** **L3** *Reader's Notebook*
- **L1** *Reader's Notebook: Adapted Version*
- **EL** *Reader's Notebook: English Learner's Version*
- **EL** *Reader's Notebook: Spanish Version*

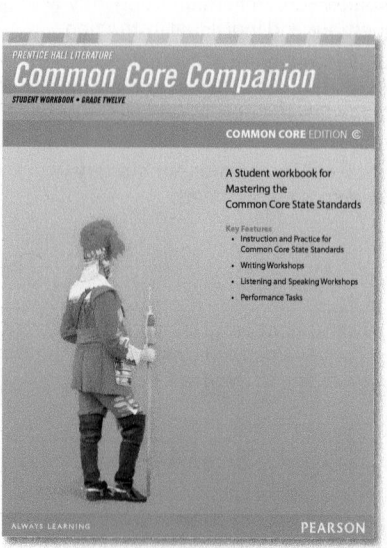

© *Common Core Companion*

Additional instruction and practice for each Common Core State Standard

Selection Support

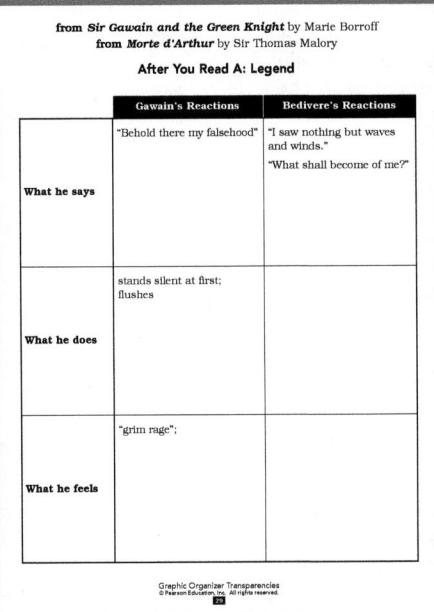

from Sir Gawain and the Green Knight by Marie Borroff
from Morte d'Arthur by Sir Thomas Malory

After You Read A: Legend

	Gawain's Reactions	Bedivere's Reactions
What he says	"Behold there my falsehood"	"I saw nothing but waves and winds." "What shall become of me?"
What he does		stands silent at first; flushes
What he feels	"grim rage";	

**EL L1 L2 Literary Analysis: Graphic
Organizer A** (partially filled in),
p. 29

Also available for these selections:

EL L1 L2 Reading: Graphic Organizer A
(partially filled in), p. 27

EL L3 Reading: Graphic Organizer B, p. 28

EL L3 Literary Analysis: Graphic Organizer B,
p. 30

Skills Development/Extension

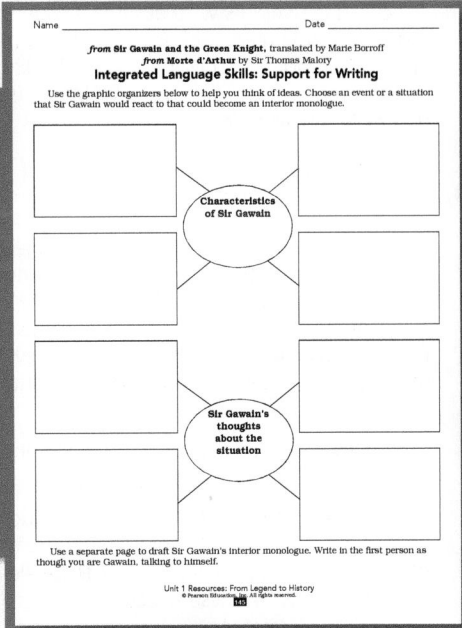

Name _____ Date _____

from Sir Gawain and the Green Knight, translated by Marie Borroff
from Morte d'Arthur by Sir Thomas Malory
Integrated Language Skills: Support for Writing

Use the graphic organizers below to help you think of ideas. Choose an event or a situation that Sir Gawain would react to that could become an interior monologue.

Characteristics of Sir Gawain

Sir Gawain's thoughts about the situation

Use a separate page to draft Sir Gawain's interior monologue. Write in the first person as though you are Gawain, talking to himself.

Unit 1 Resources: From Legend to History

EL L3 L4 Support for Writing, p. 145

Also available for these selections:

All Literary Analysis, p. 142

All Reading, p. 143

L4 Enrichment, p. 146

Assessment

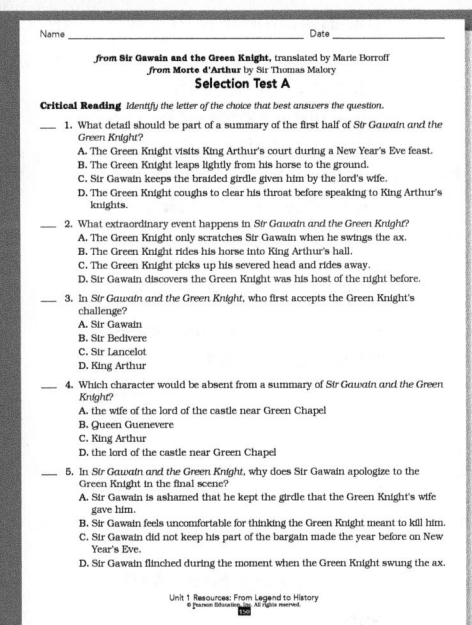

Name _____ Date _____

from Sir Gawain and the Green Knight, translated by Marie Borroff
from Morte d'Arthur by Sir Thomas Malory
Selection Test A

Critical Reading *Identify the letter of the choice that best answers the question.*

____ 1. What detail should be part of a summary of the first half of *Sir Gawain and the Green Knight*?
A. The Green Knight visits King Arthur's court during a New Year's Eve feast.
B. The Green Knight leaps lightly from his horse to the ground.
C. Sir Gawain keeps the braided girdle given him by the lord's wife.
D. The Green Knight coughs to clear his throat before speaking to King Arthur's knights.

____ 2. What extraordinary event happens in *Sir Gawain and the Green Knight*?
A. The Green Knight only scratches Sir Gawain when he swings the ax.
B. The Green Knight rides his horse into King Arthur's hall.
C. The Green Knight picks up his severed head and rides away.
D. Sir Gawain discovers the Green Knight was his host of the night before.

____ 3. In *Sir Gawain and the Green Knight*, who first accepts the Green Knight's challenge?
A. Sir Gawain
B. Sir Bedivere
C. Sir Lancelot
D. King Arthur

____ 4. Which character would be absent from a summary of *Sir Gawain and the Green Knight*?
A. The wife of the lord of the castle near Green Chapel
B. Queen Guenevere
C. King Arthur
D. the lord of the castle near Green Chapel

____ 5. In *Sir Gawain and the Green Knight*, why does Sir Gawain apologize to the Green Knight in the final scene?
A. Sir Gawain is ashamed that he kept the girdle that the Green Knight's wife gave him.
B. Sir Gawain feels uncomfortable for thinking the Green Knight meant to kill him.
C. Sir Gawain did not keep his part of the bargain made the year before on New Year's Eve.
D. Sir Gawain flinched during the moment when the Green Knight swung the ax.

Unit 1 Resources: From Legend to History

EL L1 L2 Selection Test A, pp. 150–152

Also available for these selections:

L3 L4 Open-Book Test, pp. 147–149

EL L3 L4 Selection Test B, pp. 153–155

PHLit Online!
www.PHLitOnline.com

Online Resources: All print materials are also available online.

- complete narrated selection text
- a thematically related video with writing prompt
- an interactive graphic organizer
- highlighting feature
- access to all student print resources, adapted to individual student needs
- Spanish and English summaries
- adapted selection translations in Spanish

Background Video

Also available:

Get Connected! (thematic video with writing prompt)
All videos are available in Spanish.

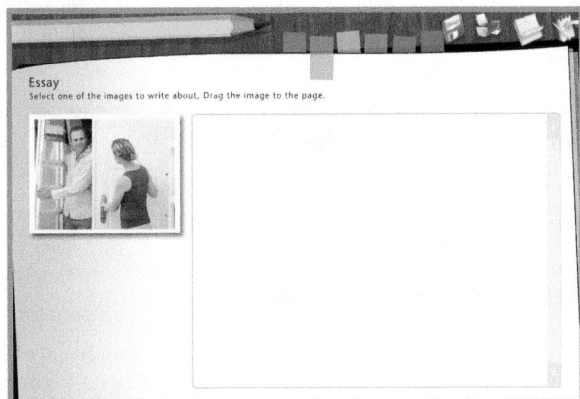

Writer's Journal (with graphics feature)

Also available:

Vocabulary Central (tools and activities for studying vocabulary)

❶ Connecting to the Essential Question

1. Review the assignment with the class.

2. Prepare students to write by defining the phrase *code of behavior*. Tell students that a code of behavior is like a list of beliefs that tell you how to act. **Ask** volunteers to suggest examples of codes of behavior. Then have students complete the assignment.

3. As students read, have them look for passages that reveal the kind of behavior that chivalry requires.

❷ Literary Analysis

Introduce the skill using the instruction on the student page.

Think Aloud: Model the Skill

Say to students:

As I read, I will look for vivid descriptions or passages and for plot twists or sudden changes. Finally, I will look for accounts of the reactions and motivations of the characters. Finding these elements will help me identify a Medieval romance.

❸ Reading Strategy

1. Introduce the strategy using the instruction on the student page.

2. Give students a copy of **Reading Strategy Graphic Organizer B,** p. 28 in *Graphic Organizer Transparencies,* to fill out as they read.

❹ Vocabulary

1. Pronounce each word, giving its definition, and have students say it aloud.

2. For more guidance, see the *Classroom Strategies and Teaching Routines* card for introducing vocabulary.

Before You Read

from *Sir Gawain and the Green Knight* • from *Morte d'Arthur*

❶ **Connecting to the Essential Question** Many characters in these selections are knights who observe a code of honorable behavior called chivalry. As you read, look for passages in these selections that reveal the kind of behavior that chivalry requires. Finding these passages will help as you answer the Essential Question: **What is the relationship of the writer to tradition?**

 **Common Core State Standards**

Reading Literature
2. Provide an objective summary of the text.

❷ ### Literary Analysis

Romances are narratives that tell of strange, sometimes supernatural events in exotic settings. **Medieval romances** are adventure stories with kings, knights, and damsels in distress. The medieval romances in this grouping are based on **legends,** anonymous traditional stories about the past that may have been inspired by real events and people. Legends, like these relating to King Arthur and his knights, often feature the following:

- heroic figures and memorable deeds
- quests, or searches for something important; contests; and tests
- patterns, such as events repeated three times

Medieval writers created romances by adding to legends such elements as vivid descriptions, plot twists, and accounts of the reactions and motives of characters. As you read, look for these elements and compare and contrast their use in these selections.

❸ ### Reading Strategy

© **Preparing to Read Complex Texts** You can **determine the main idea, or essential message,** of a work or a passage in several different ways. One method is to **summarize** a whole work or a portion of it by identifying and briefly restating its main ideas and relevant details. An effective summary will only include factual information, and not your personal opinions about what you have read. As you read, use a chart like the one shown to summarize key ideas and details.

❹ ### Vocabulary

adjure (a joor´) *v.* request solemnly; appeal to earnestly (p. 175)

adroitly (ə droit´ lē) *adv.* with physical or mental skill (p. 181)

largesse (lär jes´) *n.* nobility of spirit (p. 183)

entreated (en trēt´ id) *v.* made an earnest appeal; pleaded (p. 186)

peril (per´ əl) *n.* exposure to harm or injury (p. 187)

interred (in turd´) *v.* buried in the earth (p. 194)

Passage

"Ah, traitor unto me and untrue," said King Arthur, "now hast thou betrayed me twice. Who would have weened that thou that has been to me so loved and dear…, and would betray me for the riches of this sword."

Summary

King Arthur charges his knight with betraying him twice out of greed.

 **PHLit Online!** www.PHLitOnline.com

168 From Legend to History (A.D. 449–1485)

Vocabulary Development

Vocabulary Knowledge Rating
Create a **Vocabulary Knowledge Rating Chart** (*Professional Development Guidebook,* p. 33) for the vocabulary words on the student page. Give each student a copy of the chart with the words on it. Read the words aloud, and have students mark their rating in the Before Reading column. Urge students to attend to these words as they read and discuss the selections.

In order to gauge how much instruction you need to provide, tally how many students are confident in their knowledge of each word. As students read, point out the words and their context.

 **PHLit Online!** **Vocabulary Central,** featuring tools and activities for studying vocabulary, is available online at **www.PHLitOnline.com.**

❺ KNIGHTS OF LEGEND

Medieval Europe depended on a few powerful words—the promise of loyalty a knight gave to his lord. By A.D. 1000, a simple promise had blossomed into a social order called feudalism.

A Society of Promises Feudalism was a system both of government and of land ownership. In exchange for a nobleman's oath of loyalty, a king would give him lands. The nobleman ruled these lands, judging legal cases, imposing taxes, and maintaining an army—powers granted him in exchange for his promise of loyalty to his king.

The Code of Chivalry As an expression of feudal ideals of honor, nobles developed a code of conduct called chivalry. This code demanded that knights be brave warriors and virtuous Christians who would selflessly fight for justice.

King Arthur and His Knights The ideals of chivalry gave rise to legends and songs, such as the tales of King Arthur and his knights of the Round Table. In the eleventh century, as feudalism established itself throughout Europe, stories about Arthur's court became widespread.

Sir Gawain and the Green Knight In *Sir Gawain and the Green Knight,* a medieval poem, the chivalry of Gawain, Arthur's loyal nephew, is tested by three challenges. In meeting them, Gawain proves admirable but not invulnerable. As one critic writes, the hero "gains in human credibility what he loses in ideal perfection."

We know little about the poet of *Sir Gawain,* who is credited with three other poems in alliterative verse. In his work, though, with its combination of humor and fervent ideals, he has helped shape an enduring vision of personal integrity.

from Sir Gawain and the Green Knight • from Morte d'Arthur **169**

Daily Bellringer

For each class during which you will teach these selections, have students complete one of the five activities for the appropriate week in the *Daily Bellringer Activities* booklet.

Multidraft Reading

To assist struggling readers and to enhance reading for all, assign the text in chunks, as warranted by length, and apply multidraft reading protocols. For each reading, have students set the purpose indicated:

- **First reading**—identifying key ideas and details and answering any Reading Checks.
- **Second reading**—analyzing craft and structure and responding to the side-column prompts.
- **Third reading**—integrating knowledge and ideas, connecting to other texts and the world, and answering the end-of-selection questions.

For more guidance, refer to the *Classroom Strategies and Teaching Routines* card on multidraft reading.

❺ Background
More About the Author

Little is known about the author of *Sir Gawain and the Green Knight.* However, the story of the green knight who tests the honesty and bravery of Arthur's knight Gawain still remains one of the most popular of the Arthurian legends. The author's vivid descriptions, lively language, and dramatic picture of life in medieval times have a timeless appeal for students, and the story's skillful use of alliteration and rhyme makes it an excellent introduction to Arthurian legends.

PHLit Online!
www.PHLitOnline.com

Teaching From Technology

Preparing to Read
Go to **www.PHLitOnline.com** and display the *Get Connected!* slideshow for these selections. Have the class brainstorm for responses to the writing prompt, entering ideas in the interactive journal. Then, have students complete their written responses as homework.

To build background, display the Background and More About the Author feature.

Using the Interactive Text
Go to **www.PHLitOnline.com** and display the **Enriched Online Student Edition.** As the class reads the selections or listens to the narration, record answers to side-column prompts using the graphic organizers accessible on the interactive page. Alternatively, have students use the online edition individually, answering the prompts as they read.

TEACH

❶ About the Selection

In *Sir Gawain and the Green Knight*, an enormous green knight bursts into Arthur's hall and challenges King Arthur to strike the first blow in a duel, provided that in a year's time he seek out the Green Knight and allow him to deal the first blow. Gawain takes the challenge on Arthur's behalf and promptly chops off the intruder's head.

❷ Activating Prior Knowledge

Point out that these selections contain many features of popular action-adventure stories: brave heroes, adventure, action, humor, and hints of magic. Have students recall tales from the Arthurian legend and cite instances of these features.

❸ Critical Thinking

Speculate

1. **Ask** students to study the picture and consider the following questions: What materials were used to make the picture? Who or what does it depict? Was this picture made in modern or medieval times? What makes you think this? Write the questions on the board.

2. Have pairs of students discuss the questions. Then have a class discussion about their responses.
Possible answers: The picture is a sketch made from pen or pencil on paper. It depicts a knight on a horse. It may be Gawain or King Arthur. The drawing seems to have been made in modern times because it looks like a contemporary portrayal of a person.

170

Ⓒ Text Complexity Rubric

	from **Sir Gawain and the Green Knight**	*from* **Morte d'Arthur**
Qualitative Measures		
Context/ Knowledge Demands	Arthurian legend; historical and cultural demands 1 2 ③ 4 5	Arthurian legend; historical and cultural demands 1 2 ③ 4 5
Structure/Language Conventionality and Clarity	Period language; archaic syntax 1 2 3 ④ 5	Period language; long sentences 1 2 ③ 4 5
Levels of Meaning/ Purpose/Concept Level	Accessible (courtly love) 1 ② 3 4 5	Accessible (King Arthur and his knights) 1 ② 3 4 5
Quantitative Measures		
Lexile/Text Length	NP / 4,606 words	1270L / 3,165 words
Overall Complexity	**More accessible**	**More accessible**

FROM
❶❷ SIR GAWAIN
AND THE
GREEN KNIGHT

TRANSLATED BY MARIE BORROFF

❹ BACKGROUND The legend of King Arthur may have been based on the life of one or more Celtic warriors who fought the Anglo-Saxon invaders of England in the late fifth and early sixth centuries. The Britons, the island's Celtic inhabitants, told stories celebrating his just rule and championship of the oppressed. The Arthurian stories set an ideal for knights, and ideals are never fully realized in the present. Their true home may be the legendary past, or a future yet to come. The selection begins at the start of a New Year's Eve feast at King Arthur's Court in Camelot. Before anyone has started eating, the festivities are interrupted by an immense green knight who suddenly appears at the hall door. The knight rides a green horse and is armed with a gigantic ax.

❺
This horseman hurtles in, and the hall enters;
Riding to the high dais,[1] recked he no danger;
Not a greeting he gave as the guests he o'erlooked,
Nor wasted his words, but "Where is," he said,
5 "The captain of this crowd? Keenly I wish
To see that sire with sight, and to himself say my say."
     He swaggered all about
     To scan the host so gay;
     He halted, as if in doubt
10   Who in that hall held sway.

---

1. **dais** (dā′ is) *n.* platform.

from Sir Gawain and the Green Knight **171**

❹ Literary Analysis
Medieval Romance

1. Explain to students that the English word *romance* comes from the French *roman,* which is similar in meaning to the English word *novel*—that is, a long work of fiction. It did not, originally, have any connection to love, except in a peripheral way—because pure, unrequited love is an important element of chivalry, and chivalry is the real core of the medieval romance.

2. Review the elements of medieval romance: vivid descriptions, plot twists, heroic figures, memorable deeds, quests and adventure.
   Ask: What examples of medieval romance and chivalry can you think of from movies you have seen?
   Answer: Answers will vary. Ensure students differentiate between the characteristics of medieval romance and romantic love.

❺ Reading Strategy
Summarizing

1. Point out that a summary is a short review of the most important events or main points in a story.

2. Have students practice verbally summarizing familiar songs or the plots of television shows they have recently watched.

3. **Ask** pairs of students to summarize the first stanza. Remind them to tell the main idea and important details.
   Possible response: A knight on a horse rides into a crowded hall, looking for the leader of the group.

4. Have volunteers read and write their summaries on the board.

© Text Complexity: Reader and Task Suggestions

from Sir Gawain and the Green Knight		*from* Morte d'Arthur	
Preparing to Read the Text	**Leveled Tasks**	**Preparing to Read the Text**	**Leveled Tasks**
• Using the information on SE p. 169, discuss the code of chivalry and the feudal ideals that inspired it. • Review strategies for summarizing to determine main ideas and key details. • Guide students to use Multidraft Reading strategies to deepen their comprehension (TE p. 169).	*Structure/Language* If students will have difficulty with the period language, assign student pairs different sections to decipher and summarize. After students share their summaries, have them read the whole selection, focusing on its key ideas. *Analyzing* If students will not have difficulty with the period language, have them discuss what the ideas of conciliation and reconciliation tell us about the medieval world view.	• Using the information on SE and TE p. 184, discuss the legend of King Arthur and its continued popularity. • Remind students that to unravel long sentences, they need to focus on the subjects performing the actions and the actions they perform. • Guide students to use Multidraft Reading strategies (TE p. 169).	*Structure/Language* If students will have difficulty with the long sentences, have them read the selection first with a focus on key characters and the deeds they perform. After they list these characters and their actions, have students reread the selection. *Analyzing* If students will not have difficulty with the long sentences, have them consider the deeds characters perform and the ideals of medieval romance that they convey.

171

❻ Literary Analysis

Medieval Romance

1. **Ask** students what aspect of medieval romance is introduced in lines 11–19.
   Answer: The elements of strange events and fantasy are introduced here.

2. Have students identify other elements of medieval romance that are mentioned on these pages.
   Answer: Elements of medieval romance include a king (King Arthur), knights, ladies, banquet hall, courtesy, bravery, armor, weapons, contest/fight.

3. Remind students that accounts of the reactions and motivations of characters are another element of medieval romance. **Ask** students to explain how the knights in the hall feel when they see the Green Knight.
   Answer: They are stunned into silence. They are all amazed and some are frightened.

❼ Reading Strategy

Summarizing

1. Have students read lines 34–51.

2. **Ask** students to name key words or phrases that reveal the Green Knight's purpose.
   Possible response: The knight mentions an errand (line 35) and that he sought out King Arthur specifically (line 42).

3. Then **ask** students the Reading Strategy question: What are three main points of the Green Knight's speech in lines 34–51?
   Answer: The Green Knight has heard glowing reports of King Arthur and his knights, he comes in peace, and he would enter into a contest with King Arthur.

There were stares on all sides as the stranger spoke,
For much did they marvel what it might mean
That a horseman and a horse should have such a hue,
Grow green as the grass, and greener, it seemed.
❻ 15 Then green fused on gold more glorious by far.
All the onlookers eyed him, and edged nearer,
And awaited in wonder what he would do,
For many sights had they seen, but such a one never,
So that phantom and fairy the folk there deemed it,
20 Therefore chary[2] of answer was many a champion bold,
And stunned at his strong words stone-still they sat
In a swooning silence in the stately hall.
As all were slipped into sleep, so slackened their speech apace.
    Not all, I think, for dread,
25   But some of courteous grace
    Let him who was their head
    Be spokesman in that place.

Then Arthur before the high dais that entrance beholds,
And hailed him, as behooved, for he had no fear.
30 And said "Fellow, in faith you have found fair welcome;
The head of this hostelry Arthur am I;
Leap lightly down, and linger, I pray,
And the tale of your intent you shall tell us after."
"Nay, so help me," said the other, "He that on high sits,
35 To tarry here any time, 'twas not mine errand;
But as the praise of you, prince, is puffed up so high,
And your court and your company are counted the best,
Stoutest under steel-gear on steeds to ride,
Worthiest of their works the wide world over,
40 And peerless to prove in passages of arms,
And courtesy here is carried to its height,
And so at this season I have sought you out.
You may be certain by the branch that I bear in hand
That I pass here in peace, and would part friends,
45 For had I come to this court on combat bent,
I have a hauberk[3] at home, and a helm beside,
A shield and a sharp spear, shining bright,
And other weapons to wield, I ween well, to boot,
But as I willed no war, I wore no metal.
50 But if you be so bold as all men believe,
You will graciously grant the game that I ask by right."

Reading Strategy
Summarizing What are the three main points of the Green Knight's speech in lines 34–51?

---

2. **chary** (cher′ ē) *adj.* not giving freely.
3. **hauberk** (hô′ bərk) *n.* coat of armor.

172 From Legend to History (A.D. 449–1485)

Enrichment: Investigating Culture

New Year's Celebrations

The Green Knight has arrived at a New Year's celebration, at which people are feasting. Although not everyone celebrates the New Year on the same date, cultures throughout the world do celebrate it on some day.

Many New Year's festivities involve traditional foods. Most foods eaten on New Year's are chosen because they are associated with some combination of good luck, wealth, or fertility. The foods are thought to help ensure these in the coming year.

Activity: Research a Cultural Tradition Have pairs or groups of students choose a culture and conduct research on the way they celebrate New Year's. Suggest that they record information in the **Enrichment: Investigating Culture** worksheet, *Professional Development Guidebook,* p. 223. Have them write and then present an oral presentation based on the information they gathered.

Arthur answer gave
And said, "Sir courteous knight,
If contest here you crave,
55   You shall not fail to fight."

"Nay, to fight, in good faith, is far from my thought;
There are about on these benches but beardless children,
Were I here in full arms on a haughty[4] steed,
For measured against mine, their might is puny.
60   And so I call in this court for a Christmas game,
For 'tis Yule, and New Year, and many young bloods about;
If any in this house such hardihood claims,
Be so bold in his blood, his brain so wild,
As stoutly to strike one stroke for another,
65   I shall give him as my gift this gisarme[5] noble,
This ax, that is heavy enough, to handle as he likes,
And I shall bide the first blow, as bare as I sit.
If there be one so wilful my words to assay,
Let him leap hither lightly, lay hold of this weapon;
70   I quitclaim it forever, keep it as his own,
And I shall stand him a stroke, steady on this floor,
So you grant me the guerdon to give him another, sans blame.[6]
        In a twelvemonth[7] and a day
        He shall have of me the same;
75   Now be it seen straightway
        Who dares take up the game."

If he astonished them at first, stiller were then
All that household in hall, the high and the low;
The stranger on his green steed stirred in the saddle,
80   And roisterously his red eyes he rolled all about,
Bent his bristling brows, that were bright green,
Wagged his beard as he watched who would arise.
When the court kept its counsel he coughed aloud,
And cleared his throat coolly, the clearer to speak:
85   "What, is this Arthur's house," said that horseman then,
"Whose fame is so fair in far realms and wide?
Where is now your arrogance and your awesome deeds,
Your valor and your victories and your vaunting words?
Now are the revel and renown of the Round Table
90   Overwhelmed with a word of one man's speech,
For all cower and quake, and no cut felt!"

---

4. **haughty** (hôt′ ē) *adj.* lofty.
5. **gisarme** (gi zärm′) *n.* battle-ax.
6. **I shall . . . blame** "I will stand firm while he strikes me with the ax provided that you reward me with the opportunity to do the same to him without being blamed for it."
7. **twelvemonth** a year.

from Sir Gawain and the Green Knight **173**

Summarizing

1. **Ask** students to summarize lines 95–112.
   Possible response: King Arthur tells the Green Knight that he is wrong about the knights in his court. Then he takes the Green Knight's ax and gets ready to hit him. The Green Knight climbs off his horse and calmly waits.

2. Then **ask:** How does King Arthur feel about the Green Knight's challenge? What is King Arthur's motivation? How does the Green Knight react?
   Possible responses: King Arthur is angered by the Green Knight's words. He is motivated to prove that he and his knights are brave. The Green Knight is calm and undaunted.

13 Critical Viewing

Compare and Contrast

If necessary, suggest students draw a Venn diagram or a chart to compare and contrast the picture with Gawain's self-assessment.

Possible response: The picture shows that Gawain is strong, good-looking, and even smart, but he says that he is weak, feeble of wit, and his body is barren of worth. The picture depicts a Gawain who is the very opposite of the man whom he describes.

▲ **Critical Viewing**
Read Gawain's description of himself in lines 128–130. In what ways does this illustration of Gawain contrast with those lines?
[Compare and Contrast]

With this he laughs so loud that the lord grieved;
The blood for sheer shame shot to his face, and pride.
  With rage his face flushed red,
95   And so did all beside.
  Then the king as bold man bred
  Toward the stranger took a stride.

And said, "Sir, now we see you will say but folly,
Which whoso has sought, it suits that he find.
100 No guest here is aghast of your great words.
Give to me your gisarme, in God's own name,
And the boon you have begged shall straight be granted."
He leaps to him lightly, lays hold of his weapon;
The green fellow on foot fiercely alights.
105 Now has Arthur his ax, and the haft[8] grips,
And sternly stirs it about, on striking bent.
The stranger before him stood there erect,
Higher than any in the house by a head and more;
With stern look as he stood, he stroked his beard,
110 And with undaunted countenance drew down his coat,
No more moved nor dismayed for his mighty dints
Than any bold man on bench had brought him a drink of wine.
    Gawain by Guenevere
    Toward the king doth now incline:
115   "I beseech, before all here,
    That this melee may be mine."

"Would you grant me the grace," said Gawain to the king,
"To be gone from this bench and stand by you there,
If I without discourtesy might quit this board,
120 And if my liege lady[9] misliked it not,
I would come to your counsel before your court noble.
For I find it not fit, as in faith it is known,
When such a boon is begged before all these knights,
Though you be tempted thereto, to take it on yourself
125 While so bold men about upon benches sit,
That no host under heaven is hardier of will,
Nor better brothers-in-arms where battle is joined;
I am the weakest, well I know, and of wit feeblest;
And the loss of my life would be least of any;
130 That I have you for uncle is my only praise;
My body, but for your blood, is barren of worth;
And for that this folly befits not a king,
And 'tis I that have asked it, it ought to be mine,
And if my claim be not comely let all this court judge in sight."

8. **haft** *n.* handle of a weapon or tool.
9. **liege** (lēj) **lady** Guenevere, the wife of the lord, Arthur, to whom Gawain is bound to give service and allegiance.

Enrichment: Analyzing Historical Patterns, Trends, and Periods

Chivalry

Though few could maintain all the virtues of chivalry all the time, the ideal was seriously pursued by knights of the age. The virtues of chivalry included humility, loyalty to God, king, and country, courage, honor, being true to one's word, protection of the weak, respect for women, generosity, fairness to enemies, courtesy, developing one's skills, and determination to fight evil.

Activity: Identify Chivalry Today Have pairs of students complete the chart on chivalry in the

Enrichment: Analyzing Historical Patterns, Trends, and Periods worksheet, *Professional Development Guidebook,* p. 231. Then instead of completing the timeline at the bottom of the worksheet, ask them to consider one part of the chivalric code that still exists today in their culture. Have students list examples of the chivalric code today and then present their ideas to the class.

135 The court assays the claim,
    And in counsel all unite
    To give Gawain the game
    And release the king outright.

Then the king called the knight to come to his side,
140 And he rose up readily, and reached him with speed,
Bows low to his lord, lays hold of the weapon,
And he releases it lightly, and lifts up his hand,
And gives him God's blessing, and graciously prays
That his heart and his hand may be hardy both.
145 "Keep, cousin," said the king, "what you cut with this day,
And if you rule it aright, then readily, I know,
You shall stand the stroke it will strike after."
Gawain goes to the guest with gisarme in hand,
And boldly he bides there, abashed not a whit.
150 Then hails he Sir Gawain, the horseman in green:
"Recount we our contract, ere you come further.
First I ask and adjure you, how you are called
That you tell me true, so that trust it I may."
"In good faith," said the good knight, "Gawain am I
155 Whose buffet befalls you,[10] whate'er betide after,
And at this time twelvemonth take from you another
With what weapon you will, and with no man else alive."
    The other nods assent:
    "Sir Gawain, as I may thrive,
160   I am wondrous well content
    That you this dint[11] shall drive."

"Sir Gawain," said the Green Knight, "By God, I rejoice
That your fist shall fetch this favor I seek,
And you have readily rehearsed, and in right terms,
165 Each clause of my covenant with the king your lord,
Save that you shall assure me, sir, upon oath,
That you shall seek me yourself, wheresoever you deem
My lodgings may lie, and look for such wages[12]
As you have offered me here before all this host."
170 "What is the way there?" said Gawain, "Where do you dwell?
I heard never of your house, by Him that made me,
Nor I know you not, knight, your name nor your court.
But tell me truly thereof, and teach me your name,
And I shall fare forth to find you, so far as I may,
175 And this I say in good certain, and swear upon oath."
"That is enough in New Year, you need say no more,"

---
10. Whose . . . you "whose blow you will receive."
11. dint n. blow.
12. wages n. payment; that is, a strike with the ax.

from Sir Gawain and the Green Knight **175**

Literary Analysis
Medieval Romance
How are Gawain's words in lines 128–134 and the court's decision consistent with the ideals of chivalry?

Vocabulary
adjure (ə joor') *v.* request solemnly; appeal to earnestly

 **Reading Check**
What does Gawain do to the Green Knight?

---

14 Literary Analysis
Medieval Romance
1. **Ask** volunteers to review the code of chivalry. List their responses on the board.
Answer: The virtues of chivalry included humility, loyalty to God, king, and country, courage, honor, being true to one's word, protection of the weak, respect for women, generosity, fairness to enemies, courtesy, developing one's skills, and determination to fight evil.

2. **Ask** students the Literary Analysis question: How are Gawain's words in lines 128–134 and the court's decision consistent with the ideals of chivalry?
Answer: Gawain's words reflect the ideal qualities of humility, loyalty to the king, courage, and courtesy. The court's decision reflects the ideals of loyalty to the king and being true to one's word in that King Arthur must be formally released from his word before he can step down.

15 Reading Strategy
Summarizing
1. Have students read lines 150–155.
2. **Ask** students to summarize the key points.
Possible response: Whatever happens, Gawain must seek out the knight in a year. He can bring any weapon he wants, but he must come alone.

16 Engaging the Essential Question
1. Have students read lines 162–175.
2. **Ask:** How is the Green Knight chivalrous in his reply to Gawain?
Possible answer: The Green Knight is courteous in his reply, but also emphasizes the importance of Gawain's chivalry.

3. What words underscore the importance of a knight's promise?
Possible response: Words such as *covenant, upon oath, oath,* and *swear upon oath* underscore the importance of a knight's word.

17 Reading Check
Answer: Gawain chops off the Green Knight's head.

175

Summarizing

1. Suggest that, to make summarizing easier, students break the longer passage into individual events. Noting where one action or event ends and another begins will make it easier to identify which are the main ones.

2. **Ask** students the Reading Strategy question: How would you summarize the event in lines 188–213?
Answer: The Green Knight bows his head and bares his neck. Gawain picks up the ax and deals a sharp blow, cutting off the Green Knight's head. The head rolls across the floor. To everyone's surprise, the knight reaches out with one arm, grabs the head, and mounts his horse.

3. Have students identify the details in this stanza that are realistic and those that are supernatural.
Answer: Details from the beheading are realistic; what follows is supernatural.
Reteach: If students have difficulty summarizing, help them locate relevant details in the text and ask them to make notes to help with their summaries.

19 **Literary Analysis**

Medieval Romance

1. **Ask** students what is happening in this stanza (line 214 and following).
Answer: The Green Knight is holding his severed head, and the head is talking.

2. Remind students that this poem was intended to be fun. While it upholds the ideas of the era, it also contains a lot of humor.

3. **Ask** students the Literary Analysis question: What two characteristics of a medieval romance are reflected in lines 214–231?
Answer: Sir Gawain's honor is being put to the test. The dramatic language and supernatural actions are also characteristics of medieval romance.

Said the knight in the green to Gawain the noble,
"If I tell you true, when I have taken your knock,
And if you handily have hit, you shall hear straightway
180 Of my house and my home and my own name;
Then follow in my footsteps by faithful accord.
And if I spend no speech, you shall speed the better:
You can feast with your friends, nor further trace my tracks.[13]
      Now hold your grim tool steady
185   And show us how it hacks."
      "Gladly, sir; all ready,"
      Says Gawain; he strokes the ax.

18 **Reading Strategy**
Summarizing How would you summarize the event described in lines 188–213?

The Green Knight upon ground girds him with care:
Bows a bit with his head, and bares his flesh:
190 His long lovely locks he laid over his crown,
Let the naked nape for the need be shown
Gawain grips to his ax and gathers it aloft—
The left foot on the floor before him he set—
Brought it down deftly upon the bare neck,
195 That the shock of the sharp blow shivered the bones
And cut the flesh cleanly and clove it in twain,[14]
That the blade of bright steel bit into the ground.
The head was hewn off and fell to the floor;
Many found it at their feet, as forth it rolled;
200 The blood gushed from the body, bright on the green,
Yet fell not the fellow, nor faltered a whit,
But stoutly he starts forth upon stiff shanks,
And as all stood staring he stretched forth his hand,
Laid hold of his head and heaved it aloft,
205 Then goes to the green steed, grasps the bridle,
Steps into the stirrup, bestrides his mount,
And his head by the hair in his hand holds,
And as steady he sits in the stately saddle
As he had met with no mishap, nor missing were his head.
210   His bulk about he haled,
      That fearsome body that bled;
      There were many in the court that quailed
      Before all his say was said.

19 **Literary Analysis**
Medieval Romance What two characteristics of a medieval romance are reflected in lines 214–231?

For the head in his hand he holds right up;
215 Toward the first on the dais directs he the face,
And it lifted up its lids, and looked with wide eyes,
And said as much with its mouth as now you may hear:
"Sir Gawain, forget not to go as agreed,

---

13. **If I tell you . . . tracks** The Green Knight tells Gawain that he will let him know where he lives after he has taken the blow. If he is unable to speak following the blow, there will be no need for Gawain to know.
14. **clove it in twain** split it in two.

176 From Legend to History (A.D. 449–1485)

Enrichment: Investigating Daily Life

Knights

As populations grew and wealth increased, it was possible for people to specialize. No longer did a family have to defend their own property. They could rely on the local lord and his knights. A knight was, in essence, a professional soldier.

Knighthood originally included only those men who could afford the high cost of a horse and armor. During the eleventh century, most knights were nobles, landowners, or freemen with money. But the boundaries were fluid,

and anyone who managed to get the training and equipment to be a knight could eventually enter that class.

Activity: Research Have students conduct research on medieval knights and modern soldiers. Have students record the knights' information on the **Enrichment: Investigating Daily Life** worksheet, *Professional Development Guidebook*, p. 224. Then students can compare knights with modern soldiers in the chart at the bottom of the page.

And cease not to seek till me, sir, you find,
220 As you promised in the presence of these proud knights.
To the Green Chapel come, I charge you, to take
Such a dint as you have dealt—you have well deserved
That your neck should have a knock on New Year's morn.
The Knight of the Green Chapel I am well-known to many,
225 Wherefore you cannot fail to find me at last;
Therefore come, or be counted a recreant[15] knight."
With a roisterous rush he flings round the reins,
Hurtles out at the hall door, his head in his hand,
That the flint fire flew from the flashing hooves.
230 Which way he went, not one of them knew
Nor whence he was come in the wide world so fair.
　　The king and Gawain gay
　　Make a game of the Green Knight there,
　　Yet all who saw it say
235 　　'Twas a wonder past compare.

Though high-born Arthur at heart had wonder,
He let no sign be seen, but said aloud
To the comely queen, with courteous speech,
"Dear dame, on this day dismay you no whit;
240 Such crafts are becoming at Christmastide,
Laughing at interludes, light songs and mirth,
Amid dancing of damsels with doughty knights.
Nevertheless of my meat now let me partake,
For I have met with a marvel, I may not deny."
245 He glanced at Sir Gawain, and gaily he said,
"Now, sir, hang up your ax, that has hewn enough,"
And over the high dais it was hung on the wall
That men in amazement might on it look,
And tell in true terms the tale of the wonder.
250 Then they turned toward the table, those two together,
The good king and Gawain, and made great feast,
With all dainties double, dishes rare,
With all manner of meat and minstrelsy both,
Such happiness wholly had they that day in hold.
255 　　Now take care, Sir Gawain,
　　That your courage wax not cold
　　When you must turn again
　　To your enterprise foretold.

------

15. **recreant** *adj.* cowardly.

22 ▲ Critical Viewing
Identify two elements in this illustration of Arthur that portray him as a powerful ruler. **[Analyze]**

23 Reading Check
What happens after Gawain chops off the Green Knight's head?

㉔ Background:

Vocabulary: Girdle

1. Explain to students that a *girdle* is a garment that women wear under their dresses to make their waists appear smaller.

2. Next, explain that the green girdle that the lady of the castle gives Gawain is a green scarf. Both meanings of the word *girdle* come from the verb *to gird*.

3. **Ask** students to look up *gird* in the dictionary and relate the definition to both meanings you shared.
Possible answer: *Gird*, which means "to tie around the body," relates to a woman's girdle because it is wrapped around the body, and to a scarf, because it is wrapped around the neck.

㉕ Critical Viewing

Possible response: Gawain might be tempted to stay at the castle because he might feel safe in the castle and insecure in the frightening wilderness.

㉖ Reading Strategy

Summarizing

1. Have two volunteers read aloud lines 262–286. Remind students to pay careful attention to the details about the setting described in this passage.

2. **Ask** students to relate how the setting in this passage adds to the story.
Possible response: The setting mirrors Gawain's mental state and creates suspense.

3. **Ask** students: How would you summarize the description of the setting in lines 262–286?
Answer: The area is wild and rugged. It is not what Gawain expected. Instead of a formal church, he finds a grass mound with entrance holes, much like a cave.

The following November, Sir Gawain sets out to fulfill his promise to the Green Knight. For weeks, he travels alone through the cold, threatening woods of North Wales. Then, after he prays for shelter, he comes upon a wondrous castle on Christmas Eve, where he is greeted warmly by the lord of the castle and his lady. The lord assures Sir Gawain that the Green Chapel is nearby and promises to provide him with a guide to lead him there on New Year's Day. Before the lord and Sir Gawain retire for the night, they agree to exchange whatever they receive during the next three days. Sir Gawain keeps his pledge for the first two days, but he fails to give the lord the magic green girdle that the lady gives him on the third day, because she gives it with the promise that it will protect him from harm. The next day, Gawain sets out for the Green Chapel. His guide urges him not to proceed, but Gawain feels that it would be dishonorable not to fulfill his pledge. He is determined to accept his fate; however, he wears the magic green girdle that the lady has given him.

㉕ ▼ Critical Viewing
Examine this illustration of Gawain's journey through the wilderness. Why might Gawain be tempted to stay in the castle and give up his quest? **[Speculate]**

He puts his heels to his horse, and picks up the path;
260 Goes in beside a grove where the ground is steep,
     Rides down the rough slope right to the valley;
     And then he looked a little about him—the landscape was wild,
     And not a soul to be seen, nor sign of a dwelling,
     But high banks on either hand hemmed it about,
265 With many a ragged rock and rough-hewn crag;
     The skies seemed scored by the scowling peaks.
     Then he halted his horse, and hoved there a space,
     And sought on every side for a sight of the Chapel,
     But no such place appeared, which puzzled him sore,
270 Yet he saw some way off what seemed like a mound,
     A hillock high and broad, hard by the water,
     Where the stream fell in foam down the face of the steep
     And bubbled as if it boiled on its bed below.
     The knight urges his horse, and heads for the knoll;
275 Leaps lightly to earth; loops well the rein
     Of his steed to a stout branch, and stations him there.
     He strides straight to the mound, and strolls all about,
     Much wondering what it was, but no whit the wiser;
     It had a hole at one end, and on either side,
280 And was covered with coarse grass in clumps all without,
     And hollow all within, like some old cave,
     Or a crevice of an old crag—he could not discern aright.
         "Can this be the Chapel Green?
         Alack!" said the man, "Here might
285   The devil himself be seen
         Saying matins[16] at black midnight!"

16. matins *n.* morning prayers.

178 From Legend to History (A.D. 449–1485)

Enrichment: Building Context

Sir Gawain

Sir Gawain and the Green Knight is only one of many tales in which Gawain appears. Gawain was the greatest knight of the Round Table long before Lancelot was introduced into Arthurian legend. The handsome, chivalrous Gawain enjoyed centuries of popularity with an astonishing variety of audiences. His adventures were recited publicly throughout the Middle Ages and Renaissance.

Activity: Building Context Have students conduct research on the time periods in which Sir Gawain's tales were written. Suggest that they record information in the **Enrichment: Building Context** worksheet, *Professional Development Guidebook*, p. 222. Have them use the results of their research to write a one-page description on the impact of these tales.

"Now by heaven," said he, "it is bleak hereabouts;
This prayer house is hideous, half covered with grass!
Well may the grim man mantled in green
290 Hold here his orisons,[17] in hell's own style!
Now I feel it is the Fiend, in my five wits,
That has tempted me to this tryst,[18] to take my life;
This is a Chapel of mischance, may the mischief take it!
As accursed a country church as I came upon ever!"

295 With his helm on his head, his lance in his hand,
He stalks toward the steep wall of that strange house.
Then he heard, on the hill, behind a hard rock,
Beyond the brook, from the bank, a most barbarous din:
Lord! it clattered in the cliff fit to cleave it in two,
300 As one upon a grindstone ground a great scythe!
Lord! it whirred like a mill-wheel whirling about!
Lord! it echoed loud and long, lamentable to hear!
Then "By heaven," said the bold knight, "That business up there
Is arranged for my arrival, or else I am much misled.

305   Let God work! Ah me!
       All hope of help has fled!
       Forfeit my life may be
       But noise I do not dread."

Then he listened no longer, but loudly he called,
310 "Who has power in this place, high parley to hold?
For none greets Sir Gawain, or gives him good day;
If any would a word with him, let him walk forth
And speak now or never, to speed his affairs."
"Abide," said one on the bank above over his head,
315 "And what I promised you once shall straightway be given."
Yet he stayed not his grindstone, nor stinted its noise,
But worked awhile at his whetting before he would rest,
And then he comes around a crag, from a cave in the rocks,
Hurtling out of hiding with a hateful weapon,
320 A Danish ax[19] devised for that day's deed,
With a broad blade and bright, bent in a curve,
Filed to a fine edge—four feet it measured
By the length of the lace that was looped round the haft.
And in form as at first, the fellow all green,
325 His lordly face and his legs, his locks and his beard,
Save that firm upon two feet forward he strides,
Sets a hand on the ax-head, the haft to the earth;
When he came to the cold stream, and cared not to wade,

---

17. **orisons** *n.* prayers.
18. **tryst** (trist) *n.* meeting.
19. **Danish ax** long-bladed ax.

from Sir Gawain and the Green Knight **179**

Literary Analysis
Medieval Romance and Legend In what way does Gawain's speech in lines 287–294 add a dimension to the story that might not have been present in the original legend?

Reading Check
What is the Green Knight doing when Gawain arrives at the Green Chapel?

㉗ Literary Analysis

Medieval Romance and Legend

1. Remind students that knighthood arose only as a result of the growing influence of Christianity, so mentions of heaven and hell are not new concepts to the audience.

2. Suggest that students think about prose tales of adventure stories, and then consider how this speech differs from how they might retell an adventurous scene from a movie.

3. **Ask** students the Literary Analysis question: In what way does Gawain's speech in lines 287–294 add a dimension to the story that might not have been present in the original legend?
   Possible response: There is more imagery and alliteration here than would normally be found in the telling of an adventure tale. The bleakness of the place reflects the bleakness of Gawain's feelings and situation. The alliteration is a tool used throughout this poem to make it memorable and entertaining.

㉘ Reading Check

Answer: The Green Knight is grinding, or sharpening, his ax in preparation for dealing Gawain a blow.

Differentiated Instruction   for Universal Access

Strategy for Less Proficient Readers
Help students identify each of the pronouns in a selected passage. Which refer to Gawain? Which refer to the Green Knight? Helping students to trace the pronouns will help them more clearly understand what each character is doing and saying throughout the poem.

Support for English Learners
Help students break down the complex sentences of lines 309–334. Give each a photocopy of the stanza. Have them underline or highlight the phrases or words that describe the Green Knight, his words, and his actions. Help students learn the meaning of unfamiliar words. Then ask them to summarize the passage.

Enrichment for Advanced Readers
Have students research Gawain and his adventures, including rescues, combat, and the "loathly lady." Encourage them to find other tales and relate common themes. They could also read the full text of the poem from which this selection is excerpted.

㉙ Critical Viewing

Compare and Contrast

Possible response: Some students might mention that the illustration paints a much more attractive image of the Green Knight than what they had imagined.

㉚ Literary Analysis

Medieval Romance

1. **Ask** students which of the virtues of knighthood they feel would apply to the current situation.
   Possible response: Bravery and keeping one's word would apply. Fairness to enemies, honor, and loyalty to king might also be named.

2. Then **ask** students the Literary Analysis question: How do Gawain's actions in lines 359–387 reflect or depart from the ideals of knighthood?
   Answer: The ideals are shown in Gawain's baring his neck for the blow and in his promise not to flinch the second time. He departs from them when he winces.

3. Explain that it is the inclusion of human emotions that made this poem popular. It presented heroes who possessed chivalric virtues, but who still had human qualities. The author gently mocks the tradition of the flawless hero and still upholds the pursuit of the ideal.

㉙ ▲ Critical Viewing
In what ways does this illustration of the Green Knight compare or contrast with your mental image of him? **[Compare and Contrast]**

Literary Analysis
Medieval Romance
How do Gawain's actions in lines 359–387 reflect or depart from the ideals of knighthood?

He vaults over on his ax, and advances amain
330 On a broad bank of snow, overbearing and brisk of mood.
    Little did the knight incline
    When face to face they stood;
    Said the other man, "Friend mine,
    It seems your word holds good!"

335 "God love you, Sir Gawain!" said the Green Knight then,
    "And well met this morning, man, at my place!
    And you have followed me faithfully and found me betimes,
    And on the business between us we both are agreed:
    Twelve months ago today you took what was yours,
340 And you at this New Year must yield me the same.
    And we have met in these mountains, remote from all eyes:
    There is none here to halt us or hinder our sport;
    Unhasp your high helm, and have here your wages;
    Make no more demur[20] than I did myself
345 When you hacked off my head with one hard blow."
    "No, by God," said Sir Gawain, "that granted me life,
    I shall grudge not the guerdon[21] grim though it prove;
    And you may lay on as you like till the last of my part be paid."
        He proffered, with good grace,
350   His bare neck to the blade,
        And feigned a cheerful face:
        He scorned to seem afraid.

    Then the grim man in green gathers his strength,
    Heaves high the heavy ax to hit him the blow.
355 With all the force in his frame he fetches it aloft,
    With a grimace as grim as he would grind him to bits;
    Had the blow he bestowed been as big as he threatened,
    A good knight and gallant had gone to his grave.
    But Gawain at the great ax glanced up aside
360 As down it descended with death-dealing force,
    And his shoulders shrank a little from the sharp iron.
    Abruptly the brawny man breaks off the stroke,
    And then reproved with proud words that prince among knights.
    "You are not Gawain the glorious," the green man said,
365 "That never fell back on field in the face of the foe,
    And now you flee for fear, and have felt no harm:
    Such news of that knight I never heard yet!
    I moved not a muscle when you made to strike,
    Nor caviled[22] at the cut in King Arthur's house;
370 My head fell to my feet, yet steadfast I stood,
    And you, all unharmed, are wholly dismayed—

20. demur (dē mur') protest; delay.
21. guerdon *n.* reward.
22. caviled raised trivial objections

Enrichment: Analyzing an Image

Illuminated Manuscripts

In the Middle Ages, part of the population was highly educated, but many people were only partially literate. Because producing a single book involved a great deal of work, most books were designed to appeal to both of these groups, with both text and illustrations.

Books were laboriously copied by hand. Most medieval manuscripts were created by monks, who beautifully hand lettered each page before turning them over to illuminators. An illuminated manuscript did not simply have a few illustrations. It had highly decorative initial letters and ornate borders in all the margins, and it included little paintings called miniatures.

Activity: Analyzing an Illuminated Manuscript Ask students to locate and research an example of a page from an illuminated manuscript from the medieval period. Then, have them analyze it using the **Enrichment: Analyzing an Image** worksheet, *Professional Development Guidebook*, p. 232.

Wherefore the better man I, by all odds, must be."
    Said Gawain, "Strike once more;
    I shall neither flinch nor flee;
    But if my head falls to the floor
375   There is no mending me!"

"But go on, man, in God's name, and get to the point!
Deliver me my destiny, and do it out of hand,
For I shall stand to the stroke and stir not an inch
380 Till your ax has hit home—on my honor I swear it!"
"Have at thee then!" said the other, and heaves it aloft,
And glares down as grimly as he had gone mad.
He made a mighty feint, but marred not his hide;
Withdrew the ax adroitly before it did damage.
385 Gawain gave no ground, nor glanced up aside,
But stood still as a stone, or else a stout stump
That is held in hard earth by a hundred roots.
Then merrily does he mock him, the man all in green:
"So now you have your nerve again, I needs must strike;
390 Uphold the high knighthood that Arthur bestowed,
And keep your neck-bone clear, if this cut allows!"
Then was Gawain gripped with rage, and grimly he said,
"Why, thrash away, tyrant, I tire of your threats;
You make such a scene, you must frighten yourself."
395 Said the green fellow, "In faith, so fiercely you speak
That I shall finish this affair, nor further grace allow."
    He stands prepared to strike
    And scowls with both lip and brow;
    No marvel if the man mislike
400   Who can hope no rescue now.

He gathered up the grim ax and guided it well:
Let the barb at the blade's end brush the bare throat;
He hammered down hard, yet harmed him no whit
Save a scratch on one side, that severed the skin;
405 The end of the hooked edge entered the flesh,
And a little blood lightly leapt to the earth.
And when the man beheld his own blood bright on the snow,
He sprang a spear's length with feet spread wide,
Seized his high helm, and set it on his head,
410 Shoved before his shoulders the shield at his back,
Bares his trusty blade, and boldly he speaks—
Not since he was a babe born of his mother
Was he once in this world one half so blithe—
"Have done with your hacking—harry me no more!
415 I have borne, as behooved, one blow in this place;
If you make another move I shall meet it midway
And promptly, I promise you, pay back each blow with brand.

from Sir Gawain and the Green Knight **181**

---

31 Vocabulary
adroitly (ə droit′ lē) *adv.*
with physical or mental skill

Reading Strategy
Summarizing
Summarize what happens after the Green Knight's third stroke with the ax.

33  Reading Check
How does Gawain react when the Green Knight first lifts his axe?

181

Medieval Romance

1. Explain to students that lines 441–462 refer to events at the castle where Gawain stayed before his final search for the Green Chapel. The lady of the castle, described as incredibly beautiful, is part of a test that has been set up for Gawain—without Gawain's knowledge. The lord of the castle goes hunting for three days, while Gawain remains in the castle. The lady tests Gawain's chastity and virtue by acting as if she wishes to seduce him. The lord tests Gawain's honor by asking that they exchange whatever they get during the three days. The first two days, Gawain receives a chaste kiss from the lady, and returns this to the lord in exchange for the animal from the hunt. The third day, Gawain gets the green girdle, which he keeps, hoping it will protect him. While he has maintained his virtue and chastity, his honor has been compromised, because he did not give the lord the green girdle.

2. Tell students the result of this test, and of Gawain's failure, is that the Green Knight makes three passes with the ax: two without touching, for the days when Gawain kept his word, and one with a scratch, for Gawain's failure.

3. **Ask** students: What theme of medieval romance is suggested in lines 441–443?
   Answer: The lines suggest the medieval theme of honor.

35 Critical Viewing

Possible response: Gawain might feel guilty and ashamed of himself when he remembers the image of the Green Knight's wife.

35 ▲ **Critical Viewing**
In view of what has happened, how might Gawain feel when he remembers this image of the Green Knight's wife? **[Speculate]**

```
             One stroke acquits me here;
             So did our covenant stand
420          In Arthur's court last year—
             Wherefore, sir, hold your hand!"

     He lowers the long ax and leans on it there,
     Sets his arms on the head, the haft on the earth,
     And beholds the bold knight that bides there afoot,
425  How he faces him fearless, fierce in full arms,
     And plies him with proud words—it pleases him well.
     Then once again gaily to Gawain he calls,
     And in a loud voice and lusty, delivers these words:
     "Bold fellow, on this field your anger forbear!
430  No man has made demands here in manner uncouth,
     Nor done, save as duly determined at court.
     I owed you a hit and you have it; be happy therewith!
     The rest of my rights here I freely resign.
     Had I been a bit busier, a buffet, perhaps,
435  I could have dealt more directly; and done you some harm.
     First I flourished with a feint, in frolicsome mood,
     And left your hide unhurt—and here I did well
     By the fair terms we fixed on the first night;
     And fully and faithfully you followed accord:
440  Gave over all your gains as a good man should.
     A second feint, sir, I assigned for the morning
     You kissed my comely wife—each kiss you restored.
     For both of these there behooved but two feigned blows by right.
             True men pay what they owe;
445          No danger then in sight.
             You failed at the third throw,
             So take my tap, sir knight.

     "For that is my belt about you, that same braided girdle,
     My wife it was that wore it; I know well the tale,
450  And the count of your kisses and your conduct too,
     And the wooing of my wife—it was all my scheme!
     She made trial of a man most faultless by far
     Of all that ever walked over the wide earth;
     As pearls to white peas, more precious and prized,
455  So is Gawain, in good faith, to other gay knights.
     Yet you lacked, sir, a little in loyalty there,
     But the cause was not cunning, nor courtship either,
     But that you loved your own life; the less, then, to blame."
     The other stout knight in a study stood a long while,
460  So gripped with grim rage that his great heart shook.
     All the blood of his body burned in his face
     As he shrank back in shame from the man's sharp speech.
     The first words that fell from the fair knight's lips:
```

34

35

Enrichment: Investigating Religion and Myth

Redemption

The conclusion of this tale reflects a common theme of Arthurian legends—that of reconciliation and redemption. Throughout the tales, one finds King Arthur's knights battling evil kings or bad knights, then showing them kindness, at which point they realize that virtue and civilization are better than evil and barbarity, vow allegiance to Arthur, and usually join the Round Table.

While much of this obviously reflects the influence of the church and the Christian ideals of redemption and forgiveness, it also reflects the emergence of society from barbarity.

Activity: Religions that Shape Society Ask students to choose a religion and analyze how it has shaped or influenced the society from which it came. Students can use the worksheet **Enrichment: Investigating Religion and Myth**, in *Professional Development Guidebook*, p. 240, to guide their research and to record their findings. Have students share their research results with the class.

"Accursed be a cowardly and covetous heart!
465 In you is villainy and vice, and virtue laid low!"
Then he grasps the green girdle and lets go the knot,
Hands it over in haste, and hotly he says:
"Behold there my falsehood, ill hap betide it!
Your cut taught me cowardice, care for my life,
470 And coveting came after, contrary both
To largesse and loyalty belonging to knights.
Now am I faulty and false, that fearful was ever
Of disloyalty and lies, bad luck to them both! and greed.
    I confess, knight, in this place,
475   Most dire is my misdeed;
    Let me gain back your good grace,
    And thereafter I shall take heed."

Then the other laughed aloud, and lightly he said,
"Such harm as I have had, I hold it quite healed.
480 You are so fully confessed, your failings made known,
And bear the plain penance of the point of my blade,
I hold you polished as a pearl, as pure and as bright
As you had lived free of fault since first you were born.
And I give you sir, this girdle that is gold-hemmed
485 And green as my garments, that, Gawain, you may
Be mindful of this meeting when you mingle in throng
With nobles of renown—and known by this token
How it chanced at the Green Chapel, to chivalrous knights.
And you shall in this New Year come yet again
490 And we shall finish out our feast in my fair hall with cheer."

Critical Reading

1. **Key Ideas and Details (a)** How do Arthur's knights first respond to the Green Knight's challenge? **(b) Analyze:** Why does the Green Knight laugh at their response?

2. **Key Ideas and Details (a)** What does Gawain offer to do? **(b) Analyze:** How does he make his offer seem humble, not boastful?

3. **Key Ideas and Details (a) Interpret:** In lines 464–477, how does Sir Gawain react when he considers his own actions? **(b) Draw Conclusions:** What has Sir Gawain learned from his second encounter with the Green Knight?

4. **Integration of Knowledge and Ideas** Using the example of Sir Gawain, explain whether it is more important to achieve goals or to learn from mistakes.

Cite textual evidence to support your responses.

from Sir Gawain and the Green Knight **183**

Vocabulary
largesse (lär jes´) *n.* nobility of spirit

Reading Strategy
Summarizing How would you summarize Sir Gawain's response to the Green Knight in lines 459–477?

36 Reading Strategy
Summarizing

1. **Ask** students the Reading Strategy question: How would you summarize Sir Gawain's response to the Green Knight in lines 459–477? **Answer:** Gawain admits to his failure to live up to his end of the pledge. He is angry with himself and ashamed, and asks forgiveness.

2. Point out that, in the following stanza, the Green Knight gladly grants forgiveness, and invites Gawain to return to his castle to celebrate New Year's.

ASSESS

Answers

Before students respond, you may wish to have them write a brief objective summary of the selection. As they answer the questions below, remind them to support their answers with evidence from the text.

1. (a) The knights are at first silent with astonishment. (b) The Green Knight laughs because the reaction of Arthur's knights does not live up to their reputation.

2. (a) Gawain offers to take Arthur's place in the contest. (b) He makes the offer seem humble by playing down his strength and skills.

3. (a) Gawain is upset at himself for being false, greedy, cowardly, and disloyal to his code. (b) He may have learned that it is always best to keep your word and act honorably, no matter what fears you may have.

4. **Possible response:** It is more important to learn from one's mistakes. The Green Knight tells Gawain to remember the lesson he learned from him always.

Differentiated Instruction for Universal Access

Support for Less Proficient Readers
It may help students if they see a chart of what has happened, and why, in these last stanzas. List on the board the three attempts with the ax, and then next to each attempt, identify the reason for the outcome (two where Gawain kept his promise; one where he did not). Then, have students reread the stanzas that cover this information, one incident at a time.

Enrichment for Advanced Readers
Armor changed considerably during the Middle Ages. Have students research the types of armor worn at different periods, noting why changes were made and when. Students may also wish to research the real games that were common in the era (jousting, as opposed to beheading green giants) and what armor was worn for tournaments.

183

Most speculation about the identity of the author is based on the fact that within the text of *Morte d'Arthur,* there is a note that states that a "Syr Thomas Meleore knyght" finished the work during the reign of Edward IV and that he hoped for deliverance from prison. (He denied all charges of wrongdoing.)

There are records of the era of a Sir Thomas Malory of Warwickshire, who was imprisoned at various times, and a "Thomas Malorie (or Malarie), knight" was excluded from general pardons granted by Edward IV to political prisoners in 1468 and 1470. It is thought that he is probably the author of *Morte d'Arthur.*

This Sir Thomas Malory served in the train of the earl of Warwick at the siege of Calais. He was knighted in 1442. At his death in 1471, he was buried in the Chapel of St. Francis at Grey Friars, near Newgate, the prison where he had spent most of his time after 1460.

38 About the Selection

No one knows for sure whether King Arthur was real, but his name has popped up since the sixth century, and by the ninth century, he was a folk hero. During the fourteenth and fifteenth centuries, there was a revival of interest in Arthurian legends, mainly due to *Sir Gawain and the Green Knight* and to *Morte d'Arthur.* Unlike the former, written in verse, *Morte d'Arthur* was the first English prose version of King Arthur's life. After reading, students will understand why, with its realistic detail and natural dialogue, it has become a classic.

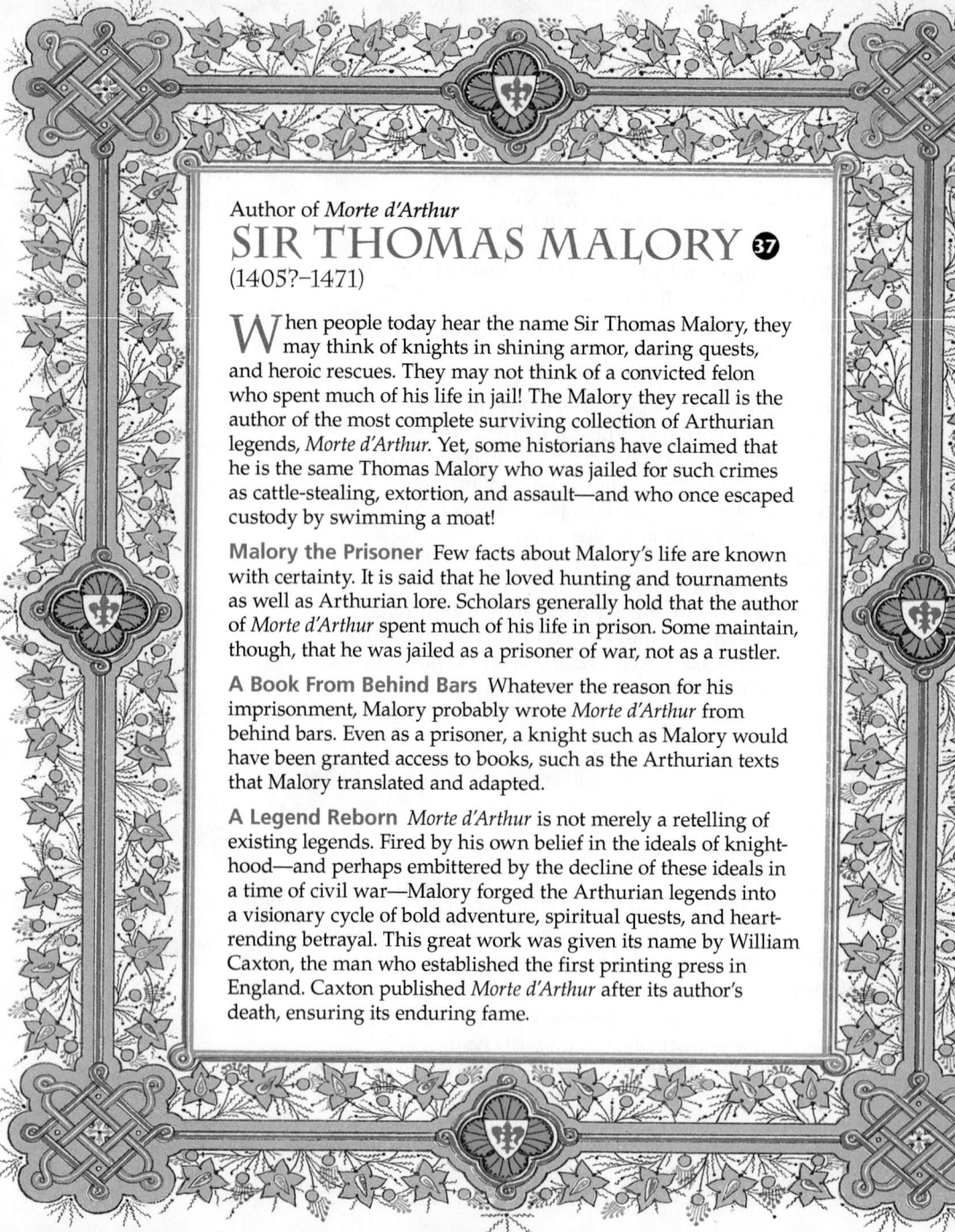

Author of *Morte d'Arthur*

SIR THOMAS MALORY **37**
(1405?–1471)

When people today hear the name Sir Thomas Malory, they may think of knights in shining armor, daring quests, and heroic rescues. They may not think of a convicted felon who spent much of his life in jail! The Malory they recall is the author of the most complete surviving collection of Arthurian legends, *Morte d'Arthur.* Yet, some historians have claimed that he is the same Thomas Malory who was jailed for such crimes as cattle-stealing, extortion, and assault—and who once escaped custody by swimming a moat!

Malory the Prisoner Few facts about Malory's life are known with certainty. It is said that he loved hunting and tournaments as well as Arthurian lore. Scholars generally hold that the author of *Morte d'Arthur* spent much of his life in prison. Some maintain, though, that he was jailed as a prisoner of war, not as a rustler.

A Book From Behind Bars Whatever the reason for his imprisonment, Malory probably wrote *Morte d'Arthur* from behind bars. Even as a prisoner, a knight such as Malory would have been granted access to books, such as the Arthurian texts that Malory translated and adapted.

A Legend Reborn *Morte d'Arthur* is not merely a retelling of existing legends. Fired by his own belief in the ideals of knighthood—and perhaps embittered by the decline of these ideals in a time of civil war—Malory forged the Arthurian legends into a visionary cycle of bold adventure, spiritual quests, and heart-rending betrayal. This great work was given its name by William Caxton, the man who established the first printing press in England. Caxton published *Morte d'Arthur* after its author's death, ensuring its enduring fame.

184 From Legend to History (A.D. 449–1485)

Enrichment: Investigating Religion

The Holy Grail

In Arthurian legend, the Grail was the cup Jesus used at the Last Supper. However, at least some of the mystical properties attributed to the cup were probably inspired by classical or Celtic mythologies, in which one finds many magic drinking horns or life-restoring caldrons.

Robert de Borron's thirteenth-century poem *Roman de l'estoire dou Graal* had a particularly large impact on the image of the Grail in Arthurian legend, because it was one of the texts used by Malory to create *Le Morte d'Arthur.*

Activity: Images of the Holy Grail Ask students to research images and stories about the Holy Grail. They can record their findings on the **Enrichment: Investigating Religion and Myth** worksheet, *Professional Development Guidebook,* p. 240.

FROM MORTE D'ARTHUR

SIR THOMAS MALORY

38

This selection begins after King Arthur has traveled to France at the insistence of his nephew, Gawain, to besiege his former friend and knight, Lancelot, for his involvement with Queen Guenevere. However, the king's attempts to punish Lancelot are halfhearted, and he is soon forced to abandon them altogether when he learns that his illegitimate son, Mordred, has seized control of England. Arthur leads his forces back to England, and Mordred attacks them upon their landing. Gawain is killed in the fighting, but before he dies, he manages to send word to Lancelot that Arthur is in need of his assistance.

39

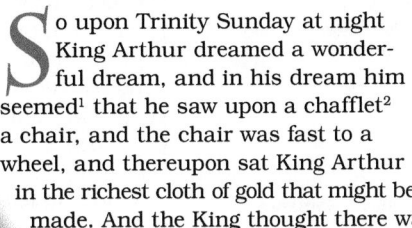

So upon Trinity Sunday at night King Arthur dreamed a wonderful dream, and in his dream him seemed[1] that he saw upon a chafflet[2] a chair, and the chair was fast to a wheel, and thereupon sat King Arthur in the richest cloth of gold that might be made. And the King thought there was under him, far from him, an hideous deep black water, and therein was all manner of serpents, and worms, and wild beasts, foul and horrible. And suddenly the King thought that the wheel turned upside down, and he fell among the serpents, and every beast took him by a limb. And then the King cried as he lay in his bed, "Help, help!"

And then knights, squires, and yeomen awaked the King, and then he was

40 ◀ **Critical Viewing**
Compare and contrast the details in this picture with those in Malory's account of Arthur's dream. **[Compare and Contrast}**

1. **him seemed**

    It seemed to him.
2. **chafflet**

platform. *from* Morte d'Arthur **185**

39 **Critical Thinking**

Speculate

1. **Reteach:** Remind students that medieval romance includes such elements as kings, knights, battles between good and evil, honor, love, and elements of the supernatural.

2. **Ask** students to speculate what elements of medieval romance they might find in the first paragraphs of this selection.
   Possible response: Elements of medieval romance in the first paragraphs might include a king, knights, squires, yeomen, imagery of a battle against evil, and elements of the supernatural, as the dead Sir Gawain appears to Arthur.

40 **Critical Viewing**

Answer: In both the picture and the dream, Arthur is seated at the head of a wheel. However, only in the dream is there a pit with serpents and other beasts below him. Also, in the dream only he falls into the pit. In the picture he remains at the head of the wheel.

Differentiated Instruction   for Universal Access

Culturally Responsive Instruction
Culture Connection Students may lack the background knowledge necessary to fully comprehend the selection. Before students read, review background knowledge about King Arthur. Ask volunteers to tell any stories they know about King Arthur. If no one has shared a story about Arthur's boyhood, tell the legend of the sword: As a young boy, Arthur pulled the dead king's sword out of the stone, proving that he was the true king of England. Merlin, a wise magician, became the young king's advisor. Take this opportunity as well to share the legend of Lancelot and Guinevere: Lancelot was Arthur's best, most loyal knight. He fell in love with Guinevere, Arthur's wife. She, too, fell in love with Lancelot. Their love devastated Arthur.

41 **Reading Strategy**

Summarizing

1. Have students review Arthur's dream, first to identify what kind of dream it is.
   Answer: Arthur is having a nightmare—or possibly a prophetic vision.

2. **Ask** students the Reading Strategy question: What are three key points of Sir Gawain's speech in the dream?
   Answer: Gawain says that God has sent him to tell Arthur that he will be killed if he fights tomorrow, that he should delay the fight for a month, and that Lancelot will slay Mordred in battle if the fight is delayed.

▶ **Monitor Progress:** Gawain opens with a description of the ladies with him. Why is this not a key point of his speech?
   Possible response: It is not part of the message; it is simply in response to Arthur's question.

42 **Literary Analysis**

Medieval Romance

1. Remind students of the Christian influence on the code of chivalry. **Ask** students to name some elements of the dream that reflect this Christian influence.
   Possible responses: Students might mention that the dream takes place on Trinity Sunday, that in the dream Gawain speaks of an afterlife and God's grace, and that Arthur and Gawain extol the name of "Almighty Jesu." Also, students may realize that prophetic dreams appear frequently in the Bible and in Christian tradition.

2. Then **ask** students the Literary Analysis question: What characteristic of medieval romance is illustrated by the dream and Arthur's response to it?
   Answer: The dream suggests that Christian beliefs played a strong role in medieval romance. In addition, both the idea of a prophetic dream and Arthur's immediate willingness to accept the dream as true are characteristic of the supernatural aspects of medieval romance.

186

41

Reading Strategy
Summarizing What are three key points of Sir Gawain's speech in the dream?

Literary Analysis
Medieval Romance
What characteristic of medieval romance is illustrated by the dream and Arthur's response to it?

42

Vocabulary
entreated (en trēt´ id) v. made an earnest appeal; pleaded

---

so amazed that he wist[3] not where he was. And then so he awaked until it was nigh day, and then he fell on slumbering again, not sleeping nor thoroughly waking. So the King seemed[4] verily that there came Sir Gawain unto him with a number of fair ladies with him. So when King Arthur saw him, he said, "Welcome, my sister's son. I weened ye had been dead. And now I see thee on-live, much am I beholden unto Almighty Jesu. Ah, fair nephew and my sister's son, what been these ladies that hither be come with you?"

"Sir," said Sir Gawain, "all these be ladies for whom I have foughten for when I was man living. And all these are those that I did battle for in righteous quarrels, and God hath given them that grace, at their great prayer, because I did battle for them for their right, that they should bring me hither unto you. Thus much hath given me leave God, for to warn you of your death. For and ye fight as tomorn[5] with Sir Mordred, as ye both have assigned, doubt ye not ye must be slain, and the most party of your people on both parties. And for the great grace and goodness that Almighty Jesu hath unto you, and for pity of you and many more other good men there shall be slain, God hath sent me to you of his special grace to give you warning that in no wise ye do battle as tomorn, but that ye take a treaty for a month from today. And proffer you largely[6] you so that tomorn ye put in a delay. For within a month shall come Sir Lancelot with all his noble knights and rescue you worshipfully and slay Sir Mordred and all that ever will hold with him."

Then Sir Gawain and all the ladies vanished. And anon the King called upon his knights, squires, and yeomen, and charged them wightly[7] to fetch his noble lords and wise bishops unto him. And when they were come the King told them of his avision,[8] that Sir Gawain had told him and warned him that, and he fought on the morn, he should be slain. Then the King commanded Sir Lucan the Butler and his brother Sir Bedivere the Bold, with two bishops with them, and charged them in any wise to take a treaty for a month from today with Sir Mordred. "And spare not: proffer him lands and goods as much as ye think reasonable."

So then they departed and came to Sir Mordred where he had a grim host of an hundred thousand, and there they entreated Sir Mordred long time. And at the last Sir Mordred was agreed for to have Cornwall and Kent by King Arthur's days, and after that, all England, after the days of King Arthur.

Then were they condescended[9] that King Arthur and Sir Mordred should meet betwixt both their hosts, and each of them should bring

---

3. **wist** knew.
4. **the King seemed** It seemed to the King.
5. **and . . . tomorn** "if you fight tomorrow."
6. **proffer you largely** make generous offers.
7. **wightly** quickly.
8. **avision** dream.
9. **condescended** agreed.

186 From Legend to History (A.D. 449–1485)

Enrichment: Investigating Career Connections

The Armed Forces

In these selections, knights perform the function that the armed forces perform today. Though the "chivalric code" has obviously changed, much of what we expect of a professional military was, in fact, established during the Middle Ages. Loyalty to country, fairness to enemies, protection of the weak, bravery, and skill with weapons are ideals established then that are valued today.

Today, many young people consider one of the armed forces as a career. Over a million men and women now serve in the U.S. Army, the Air Force, the Navy, the Marine Corps, and the Coast Guard. Each of these services is associated with a four-year academy that provides academic as well as military instruction.

Activity: Career Research Have students conduct research on a branch of the military. Suggest that they record information in the **Enrichment: Investigating Career Connections** worksheet, *Professional Development Guidebook,* p. 221. Have students share their research results with classmates.

fourteen persons. And so they came with this word unto Arthur. Then said he, "I am glad that this is done," and so he went into the field.

And when King Arthur should depart, he warned all his host that, and they see any sword drawn, "Look ye come on fiercely and slay that traitor Sir Mordred, for I in no wise trust him." In like wise Sir Mordred warned his host that "And ye see any manner of sword drawn, look that ye come on fiercely, and so slay all that ever before you standeth, for in no wise I will not trust for this treaty." And in the same wise said Sir Mordred unto his host, "For I know well my father will be avenged upon me."

And so they met as their pointment[10] was and were agreed and accorded thoroughly. And wine was fetched and they drank together. Right so came an adder out of a little heathbush, and it stung a knight in the foot. And so when the knight felt him so stung, he looked down and saw the adder. And anon he drew his sword to slay the adder, and thought none other harm. And when the host on both parties saw that sword drawn, then they blew beams,[11] trumpets, horns, and shouted grimly. And so both hosts dressed them together. And King Arthur took his horse and said, "Alas, this unhappy day!" and so rode to his party, and Sir Mordred in like wise.

And never since was there never seen a more dolefuller battle in no Christian land, for there was but rushing and riding, lunging and striking; and many a grim word was there spoken of either to other, and many a deadly stroke. But ever King Arthur rode throughout the battle[12] of Sir Mordred many times and did full nobly, as a noble king should do, and at all times he fainted never. And Sir Mordred did his devoir[13] that day and put himself in great peril.

And thus they fought all the long day, and never stinted[14] till the noble knights were laid to the cold earth. And ever they fought still till it was near night, and by then was there an hundred thousand laid dead upon the down. Then was King Arthur wood-wroth[15] out of measure when he saw his people so slain from him. And so he looked about him and could see no more of all his host, and good knights left no more on-live, but two knights: the t'one was Sir Lucan the Butler and the other his brother Sir Bedivere. And yet they were full sore wounded.

"Jesu, mercy," said the King, "where are all my noble knights become? Alas that ever I should see this doleful day! For now," said King Arthur, "I am come to mine end. But would to God," said he,

---

10. **pointment** arrangement.
11. **beams** type of trumpet.
12. **battle** battalion.
13. **devoir** (də vwär′) *n.* duty (from the French; obsolete).
14. **stinted** stopped.
15. **wood-wroth** wild with rage.

And when they were come the King told them of his avision, that Sir Gawain had told him and warned him that, and he fought on the morn, he should be slain.

Vocabulary
peril (per′ əl) *n.* exposure to harm or injury

Reading Check

What causes the two armies to start fighting?

from Morte d'Arthur **187**

43 Reading Strategy

Summarizing

1. **Ask** students to reread the first two paragraphs on the page, beginning with "And when King Arthur…" and "And so they met…."

2. Then have pairs of students write summaries of the paragraphs. Read them aloud to the class and discuss whether they are good summaries and why.

Answer: Arthur and his knights went to the field to try to reach a truce with Mordred. Arthur and Mordred both warned their men that if anyone should draw their sword they all should draw swords and begin the fight. During their negotiations, one of Mordred's men was bitten by a snake. He drew his sword to kill the snake. All men drew their swords and the battle began.

44 Literary Analysis

Medieval Romance and Legend

1. Read the paragraph about the battle that begins "And thus they fought…" aloud. Tell students to listen for elements that show that this tale may have been intended for public performance.

2. Have students review the paragraph in the book, looking for elements that identify this as "legendary."

3. **Ask** students the Literary Analysis question: What features of this account seem more typical of a legend than of written forms of storytelling?

Possible response: There is much alliteration ("noble knights," "near night") and poetic phrasing ("all the long day," "ever they fought," "laid dead upon the down"). These traits reflect the oral tradition of such tales. Also, the huge number of casualties and the fact that Arthur and Mordred are still standing at the end are elements that identify this as a legend.

45 Reading Check

Answer: The two armies started fighting because a knight drew his sword to kill a snake. The drawing of the sword was misinterpreted and the battle began.

Differentiated Instruction for Universal Access

Culturally Responsive Instruction

Culture Connection Students may lack the background knowledge or context-building experiences necessary to fully comprehend the significance of the legendary Sir Mordred. Provide the following background knowledge to help students better access this legend.

Mordred has always been associated with Arthurian legend in some way. In Malory's recounting of the legend, young Arthur is seduced by the witch Morgause, unaware that she is his half sister. The child of this union is Mordred.

Merlin predicts that Mordred's birth will lead to the destruction of Camelot. Arthur tries to get rid of the child, but Mordred survives and returns to Camelot as a knight. He cannot hide his hatred for everything in Camelot, and his reputation as a false knight grows.

In some tales, Mordred seduces Arthur's queen, Guinevere, but in Malory's account, though he desires her, she spurns his advances. However, Mordred uses her love for Lancelot to destroy Camelot and Arthur.

46 Humanities

The Battle Between King Arthur and Sir Mordred, 1910, by William Hatherell

This painting, which is early twentieth century, depicts legendary King Arthur (in red) as he drives a spear through Sir Mordred during the Battle of Salisbury Plain (also known as the Battle of Camlaan). Arthur's spear kills Mordred, but not before Mordred lands a fatal retaliatory blow that similarly dispatches Arthur.

Use this question for discussion:

Ask: Why do you think Arthur is depicted in red and Mordred in black?

Possible answer: Red is a color associated with royalty and blood. Both these associations are appropriate to highlight Arthur's true royalty, the bloodiness of the battle, and his blood relation to Mordred. Black is commonly a color associated with evil and darkness. Mordred, as Arthur's enemy, is evil and brings darkness to the otherwise civilized society.

188 From Legend to History (A.D. 449–1485)

Think Aloud

Literary Analysis: Medieval Romance
Ask students to consider how the painting on this page represents characteristics of the medieval romance. To model the process of looking for elements of medieval romance, use the following "think aloud." Say to students:

I may be asked to look for connections between a piece of art and a literary work. First, I review the elements of medieval romance: (say and list the elements on the board) heroic figures, memorable deeds, quests, contests, tests, patterns, supernatural events, exotic set- tings, vivid descriptions, plot twists, reactions and motives of characters. Then I look at each element and see if I find evidence of it in the painting. The subject of the painting demonstrates three elements of medieval romance: heroic figures, memorable deeds, and a contest. King Arthur and Mordred are heroes; their battle is an important memorable deed and it is also a contest. When I look for details like these, I can make connections between art and literature.

"that I wist now where were that traitor Sir Mordred that has caused all this mischief."

Then King Arthur looked about and was ware where stood Sir Mordred leaning upon his sword among a great heap of dead men.

"Now give me my spear," said King Arthur unto Sir Lucan, "for yonder I have espied the traitor that all this woe hath wrought."

49 "Sir, let him be," said Sir Lucan, "for he is unhappy. And if ye pass this unhappy day ye shall be right well revenged upon him. And, good lord, remember ye of your night's dream, and what the spirit of Sir Gawain told you tonight, and yet God of his great goodness hath preserved you hitherto. And for God's sake, my lord, leave off by this, for, blessed be God, ye have won the field: for yet we been here three on-live, and with Sir Mordred is not one on-live. And therefore if ye leave off now, this wicked day of destiny is past."

"Now, tide[16] me death, tide me life," said the King, "now I see him yonder alone, he shall never escape mine hands. For at a better avail shall I never have him."

"God speed you well!" said Sir Bedivere.

Then the King got his spear in both his hands and ran toward Sir Mordred, crying and saying, "Traitor, now is thy deathday come!"

And when Sir Mordred saw King Arthur he ran until him with his sword drawn in his hand, and there King Arthur smote Sir Mordred under the shield, with a thrust of his spear, throughout the body more than a fathom. And when Sir Mordred felt that he had his death's wound, he thrust himself with the might that he had up to the burr[17] of King Arthur's spear, and right so he smote his father King Arthur with his sword holden in both his hands, upon the side of the head, that the sword pierced the helmet and the casing of the brain. And therewith Sir Mordred dashed down stark dead to the earth.

And noble King Arthur fell in a swough[18] to the earth, and there he swooned oftentimes, and Sir Lucan and Sir Bedivere ofttimes heaved him up. And so, weakly betwixt them, they led him to a little chapel not far from the seaside, and when the King was there, him thought him reasonably eased. Then heard they people cry in the field. "Now go thou, Sir Lucan," said the King, "and do me to

---

16. **tide** befall.
17. **burr** hand guard.
18. **swough** forcible movement

 ◄ **Critical Viewing 47**
In this picture of the battle between King Arthur and Sir Mordred, which details contribute to the grim mood? Explain. **[Analyze]**

48

Reading Strategy
Summarizing Summarize the events leading to the death of Mordred and the mortal wounding of King Arthur.

 Reading Check **50**

What does Sir Lucan urge King Arthur to do?

from Morte d'Arthur **189**

---

47 **Critical Viewing**
Analyze
Answer: The sky is cloudy. The earth in both the foreground and the background is murky and dark. The clothing of the characters is blood red and black. Arthur's facial expression is grim. Finally, there are the skulls and bones on the ground.

48 **Reading Strategy**
Summarizing
1. Have students read page 189, making note of the main points.
2. Then **ask** the Reading Strategy question: Summarize the events leading to the death of Mordred and the mortal wounding of King Arthur.
   Answer: Everyone on Mordred's side is dead, and Arthur has only two men left. Sir Lucan tries to dissuade Arthur, but the king realizes he will never have a better opportunity, so he attacks Mordred and gives him a mortal wound. As he dies, Mordred strikes Arthur's head with his sword.

49 **Critical Thinking**
Make a Judgment
1. **Ask** students whether they think the advice offered by Sir Lucan is good and wise.
   Possible response: It is excellent advice. Even if the prophecy were not true, Arthur had won the day and was still alive, and so it would have been wise to quit.
2. Point out that, even today, we refer to the place where a battle takes place as a battlefield. In having held his ground, Arthur "won the field." Note that these terms—*holding one's ground* and *winning the field*—show that warfare is usually about land.
3. **Ask** students what reasons Arthur might have for ignoring Lucan's advice.
   Possible responses: He was too excited from the battle to stop. He wanted to make certain Mordred could never be a threat again. He did not want to live, now that almost all of his knights were dead.

50 **Reading Check**
Answer: Sir Lucan urges King Arthur to stop fighting and leave Mordred, as he had already won the battle.

51 Literary Analysis

Medieval Romance

1. Have students read the paragraph beginning with "So Sir Lucan departed…."

2. **Ask** students: What note of realism does this paragraph strike?
Answer: Criminals have come to strip valuables off the bodies of fallen knights. They are even killing knights so they can take their equipment. There are always those who take advantage of the misfortune of others, so this is realistic.

3. Discuss with students why those who loot and kill in the wake of such disasters—rather than helping the wounded or trying to make things better—have always been viewed as being even worse than enemies.
Possible response: Individuals who are willing to hurt their own people for illegal gain are parasites. They are worse than enemies because you expect your own people to help you.

4. Point out that in the following paragraphs, Sir Lucan's noble actions contrast with the ignoble actions of the robbers. Though seriously wounded, Sir Lucan is willing to help others, although doing so costs him his life.

52 Critical Viewing

Interpret

Possible response: I think the boat is supernatural because it is transparent and the figures onboard seem almost transparent and imbued with light.

52 ▼ Critical Viewing In this picture of Sir Bedivere and the dying Arthur, do you think the boat that Bedivere sees is real or supernatural? Why? **[Interpret]**

wit[19] what betokens that noise in the field."

51 So Sir Lucan departed, for he was grievously wounded in many places. And so as he walked he saw and harkened by the moonlight how that pillagers and robbers were come into the field to pill and to rob many a full noble knight of brooches and bracelets and of many a good ring and many a rich jewel. And who that were not dead all out there they slew them for their harness and their riches. When

19. me to wit "let me know."

190 From Legend to History (A.D. 449–1485)

Enrichment: Investigating Religion and Myth

Magic and Myth

If magic was so evident in everyday life, then it would certainly be operating at a higher level in legend. Hence, Arthurian legend is shot through with magic. The blend of paganism and Christianity is often fairly obvious, but the Roman Empire had controlled England until only shortly before Arthur, so Roman myth also contributes to the tales. For example, Arthur's magical half sister is Morgan Le Fay. *Fay* means "fairy" and is related to the word *fate*, which would have been adopted from Rome's three Fates.

Activity: Debate Have students conduct research on one of the three religious influences to the *Morte d'Arthur*: Christianity, Paganism, and Roman Mythology. Suggest they record their findings in the **Enrichment: Investigating Religion and Myth** worksheet, *Professional Development Guidebook*, p. 240. Then ask students to conduct a mini-debate about which religious tradition influences *Morte d'Arthur* most.

50 Sir Lucan understood this work, he came to the King as soon as he might and told him all what he had heard and seen. "Therefore by my read,"[20] said Sir Lucan, "it is best that we bring you to some town."

"I would it were so," said the King, "but I may not stand, my head works so. Ah, Sir Lancelot," said King Arthur, "this day have I sore missed thee. And alas that ever I was against thee, for now have I my death, whereof Sir Gawain me warned in my dream."

Then Sir Lucan took up the King the t'one party[21] and Sir Bedivere the other party; and in the lifting up the King swooned and in the lifting Sir Lucan fell in a swoon that part of his guts fell out of his body, and therewith the noble knight's heart burst. And when the King awoke he beheld Sir Lucan how he lay foaming at the mouth and part of his guts lay at his feet.

"Alas," said the King, "this is to me a full heavy sight to see this noble duke so die for my sake, for he would have helped me that had more need of help than I. Alas that he would not complain him for his heart was so set to help me. Now Jesu have mercy upon his soul."

Then Sir Bedivere wept for the death of his brother.

"Now leave this mourning and weeping gentle knight," said the King, "for all this will not avail me. For wit thou well, and might I live myself, the death of Sir Lucan would grieve me evermore. But my time passeth on fast," said the King. "Therefore," said King Arthur unto Sir Bedivere, "take thou here Excalibur my good sword and go with it to yonder water's side; and when thou comest there I charge thee throw my sword in that water and come again and tell me what thou sawest there."

"My lord," said Sir Bedivere, "your commandment shall be done, and I shall lightly[22] bring you word again."

So Sir Bedivere departed. And by the way he beheld that noble sword, that the pommel and the haft[23] was all precious stones. And then he said to himself, "If I throw this rich sword in the water, thereof shall never come good, but harm and loss." And then Sir Bedivere hid Excalibur

---

20. **read** advice.
21. **party** side.
22. **lightly** quickly.
23. **pommel . . . haft** hilt and hand guard.

Literary Analysis
53 **Medieval Romance**
What note of realism does this one-sentence paragraph strike?

Reading Check
54 What does Arthur ask Sir Bedivere to do with Excalibur?

from Morte d'Arthur **191**

---

53 **Literary Analysis**
Medieval Romance

1. Tell students that earlier parts of the story tell tales of Excalibur. Actually, Malory relates two different tales of how Arthur got this sword. One is the familiar account of Arthur pulling the sword from the stone that identified Arthur as king. In the other, Merlin takes Arthur to the Lady of the Lake to get the sword, after the original broke in battle.

2. **Ask** students the Literary Analysis question: What note of realism does this one-sentence paragraph strike?
Answer: It is realistic because Bedivere weeps for his brother's death, which is something that happens in real life.

54 **Reading Check**

Answer: King Arthur asks Bedivere to throw Excalibur into the lake.

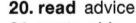

Differentiated
Instruction   for Universal Access

EL **Support for**
English Learners

Have students paraphrase the page in their own words. As they paraphrase, direct students to write down words that are unknown to them. Have students work in pairs to discuss and define the unknown words. Direct pairs of students to share some of their words with other pairs of English learners. Make a list of pairs' common unknown words, and define them as a group.

Enrichment for
Gifted/Talented Students

Ask students to use a Venn diagram to compare and contrast *Morte d'Arthur* with *Sir Gawain and the Green Knight.* Direct students to focus on characters, themes, and literary style. Students can then write a short essay explaining how the pieces are similar and different, citing examples and quotes from both.

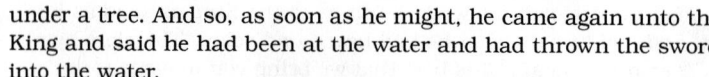

55 **Critical Viewing**

Infer

Possible response: I think the three women are mourning King Arthur and perhaps waiting for God to wake him up so that he can go on to perform more great deeds.

56 **Literary Analysis**

Medieval Romance

1. Explain to students that Arthur had some idea what might happen when the sword was thrown. Earlier in Malory's tale, Arthur and Merlin row to the center of this lake to get the sword from an arm that reaches out of the water.

2. Point out that, as with Gawain in the previous tale, there are three "trials" for Bedivere. Gawain succeeded twice and failed once; Bedivere failed twice and succeeded once. Trials were believed to come in threes, as when the apostle Peter denied knowing Jesus three times the night before the crucifixion.

▶ **Monitor Progress: Ask** students what elements of the chivalric code Bedivere has failed to uphold in the first two trials. **Possible response:** He has not been loyal to the king; he has not been honest or honorable. His greed would be the opposite of the ideal of generosity.

3. **Ask** students the Literary Analysis question: What element does the appearance of the hand add to the tale? **Possible response:** It heightens the sense of mystery and contributes to the sense that this is an awful tragedy. It also adds to the fantasy elements of the story.

4. Tell students that elements of Arthurian legend still appear in modern books and films—sometimes in modern settings. For example, such Arthurian elements as Merlin, Pendragon, the Fisher-King, and Arthur's mysterious end figure in *That Hideous Strength,* the final book of C.S. Lewis's acclaimed space trilogy, set at a modern university. Becoming familiar with the legends can help students understand many other allusions.

192

55 ▶ **Critical Viewing**
What do you think the three women around the dead or dying Arthur are doing? Explain. **[Infer]**

Literary Analysis
Medieval Romance **56**
What element does the appearance of the hand add to the tale?

under a tree. And so, as soon as he might, he came again unto the King and said he had been at the water and had thrown the sword into the water.

"What saw thou there?" said the King.

"Sir," he said, "I saw nothing but waves and winds."

"That is untruly said of thee," said the King. "And therefore go thou lightly again and do my commandment; as thou art to me loved and dear, spare not, but throw it in."

Then Sir Bedivere returned again and took the sword in his hand. And yet him thought sin and shame to throw away that noble sword. And so eft[24] he hid the sword and returned again and told the King that he had been at the water and done his commandment.

"What sawest thou there?" said the King.

"Sir," he said, "I saw nothing but waters wap and waves wan."[25]

"Ah, traitor unto me and untrue," said King Arthur, "now hast thou betrayed me twice. Who would have weened that thou that has been to me so loved and dear, and thou art named a noble knight, and would betray me for the riches of this sword. But now go again lightly, for thy long tarrying putteth me in great jeopardy of my life, for I have taken cold. And but if thou do now as I bid thee, if ever I may see thee I shall slay thee mine own hands, for thou wouldest for my rich sword see me dead."

Then Sir Bedivere departed and went to the sword and lightly took it up, and so he went to the water's side; and there he bound the girdle about the hilts, and threw the sword as far into the water as he might. And there came an arm and an hand above the water and took it and clutched it, and shook it thrice and brandished; and then vanished away the hand with the sword into the water. So Sir Bedivere came again to the King and told him what he saw.

"Alas," said the King, "help me hence, for I dread me I have tarried overlong."

Then Sir Bedivere took the King upon his back and so went with him to that water's side. And when they were at the water's side, even fast[26] by the bank floated a little barge with many fair ladies in it; and among them all was a queen; and all they had black hoods, and all they wept and shrieked when they saw King Arthur.

"Now put me into that barge," said the King; and so he did softly. And there received him three ladies with great mourning, and so they set them down. And in one of their laps King Arthur laid his head, and then the queen said, "Ah, my dear brother, why have ye tarried so long from me? Alas, this wound on your head hath caught overmuch cold." And anon they rowed fromward the land, and Sir Bedivere beheld all those ladies go froward him.

---

24. eft again.
25. waters . . . wan waters lap and waves grow dark.
26. fast close.

Think Aloud

Literary Analysis: Medieval Romance
To model the process of determining what the element of the appearance of the hand adds to the tale, use the following "think aloud." Say to the students:

First I reread the paragraph again to make sure I understand what is happening. Then I review the list of elements of a medieval romance. I remember they include heroic figures, memorable deeds, quests, contests, or tests, patterns, supernatural events, exotic setting, vivid descriptions, plot twists, and the reactions or motivations of characters. I then compare the appearance of the hand to this list of elements. I determine that because Arthur is a heroic figure, the hand appearing makes him seem even more important, and therefore his death more tragic. Clearly, this is a supernatural event that adds to the mystery and fantasy of the legend. Finally, Malory uses vivid descriptions to tell how the hand emerged and brandished the sword.

from Morte d'Arthur **193**

57 Humanities

The Last Sleep of Arthur in Avalon, 1898, by Sir Edward Burne-Jones

This is a detail, or small part, of a very large painting, which measures 9 feet tall and 21 feet wide, by Pre-Raphaelite painter Sir Edward Burne-Jones. He began the painting in 1881 and still had not completed it at the time of his death in 1898. In the rest of the painting, there are five other women watching Arthur sleep; a marble canopy over King Arthur, on which the legend of the Holy Grail is depicted; architectural attributes that range from medieval castles to Eastern-influenced columns; and a garden full of trees and bushes. In this detail, the women seem to be waiting for Arthur to wake up and perform more great deeds.

Use the following question for discussion:

Ask: How does the painting relate to the tale? To which paragraph on page 192 might the painting relate? How is the painting different from the tale? How is it similar to it?

Answer: The painting relates to the tale in that it depicts a portion of it, beginning at the paragraph on page 192 that starts: "Then Sir Bedivere took the King...." The painting is similar to the tale in that it shows the three women, with Arthur's head on one of their laps. The women are mourning, but unlike the tale, the women are not shrieking or crying.

Differentiated Instruction for Universal Access

Support for Special-Needs Students
Help students understand the story's end by explaining what is occurring before they read. Point out which elements are fantasy and which are realistic. Make certain students know who the characters are and that King Arthur is still the focus of the tale, even though many other people appear.

Enrichment for Gifted/Talented Students
Have students illustrate some aspect of the story's end, such as Sir Bedivere throwing the sword, the Lady of the Lake, or the women coming for Arthur. Have them use details from the story, but encourage them to do additional research. Ask students to share their illustrations with the class.

Enrichment for Advanced Readers
Suggest that students read either all of *Morte d'Arthur* or a good synopsis and then find a twentieth-century work that retells the legend. Have them compare the old and new works. Great, fun books might include T.H. White's *The Once and Future King* or Mary Stewart's Merlin trilogy.

58 Literary Analysis

Medieval Romance and Legend

1. Have students identify the specific elements of Bedivere's reaction to the events, and discuss how they fit into the ideals of chivalry.
Possible response: Specific elements include asking Arthur what he will do without a king to follow, weeping at Arthur's departure, swooning at news of Arthur's death, and vowing to stay by the grave and pray. Loyalty to one's king is the foremost element of chivalry here, but Christian piety is also present.

2. Point out that Malory says he got the story from the hermit, who had gotten it from Bedivere. This "eyewitness" device is a common one in fiction, still used today to give the appearance of credibility to a far-fetched tale.

3. **Ask** students the Literary Analysis question: Does the description of Sir Bedivere's reaction sound more like a description you might find in a folk tale or in a modern short story? Explain.
Possible response: The response seems to suit a folk tale. It seems unlikely that a warrior would be portrayed as swooning or weeping in a modern story. Also, such devotion to a king seems more legendary than modern.

59 Reading Strategy

Summarizing

1. Have students review the page.

2. Then **ask** students the Reading Strategy question: What happens to Sir Bedivere after Arthur departs on the barge?
Answer: As soon as the barge disappeared, Sir Bedivere wept and then ran into the forest. He ran through the forest all night. In the morning, he found a hermitage where a monk was just finishing burying a man whom many women brought to him to bury.

58 Literary Analysis
Medieval Romance and Legend Does the description of Sir Bedivere's reaction sound more like a description you might find in a folk tale or in a modern short story? Explain.

Vocabulary
interred (in turd') *v.* buried in the earth

Reading Strategy
Summarizing What happens to Sir Bedivere after Arthur departs on the barge?

Then Sir Bedivere cried and said, "Ah, my lord Arthur, what shall become of me, now ye go from me and leave me here alone among mine enemies?"

"Comfort thyself," said the King, "and do as well as thou mayest, for in me is no trust for to trust in. For I must into the vale of Avilion[27] to heal me of my grievous wound. And if thou hear nevermore of me, pray for my soul."

But ever the queen and ladies wept and shrieked, that it was pity to hear. And as soon as Sir Bedivere had lost sight of the barge he wept and wailed, and so took the forest and went all that night.

And in the morning he was ware, betwixt two bare woods, of a chapel and an hermitage. Then was Sir Bedivere glad, and thither he went, and when he came into the chapel he saw where lay an hermit groveling on all fours, close thereby a tomb was new dug. When the hermit saw Sir Bedivere he knew him well, for he was but little tofore Bishop of Canterbury, that Sir Mordred put to flight.

"Sirs," said Sir Bedivere, "what man is there here interred that you pray so fast for?"

"Fair son," said the hermit. "I wot not verily but by guessing. But this same night, at midnight, here came a number of ladies and 58 brought here a dead corpse and prayed me to inter him. And here 59 they offered an hundred tapers, and gave me a thousand gold coins."

"Alas," said Sir Bedivere, "that was my lord King Arthur, which lieth here buried in this chapel."

Then Sir Bedivere swooned, and when he awoke he prayed the hermit that he might abide with him still, there to live with fasting and prayers:

"For from hence will I never go," said Sir Bedivere, "by my will, but all the days of my life here to pray for my lord Arthur."

"Sir, ye are welcome to me," said the hermit, "for I know you better than ye think that I do: for ye are Sir Bedivere the Bold, and the full noble duke Sir Lucan the Butler was your brother."

Then Sir Bedivere told the hermit all as you have heard tofore, and so he stayed with the hermit that was beforehand Bishop of Canterbury. And there Sir Bedivere put upon him poor clothes, and served the hermit full lowly in fasting and in prayers.

Thus of Arthur I find no more written in books that been authorized, neither more of the very certainty of his death heard I nor read, but thus was he led away in a ship wherein were three queens; that one was King Arthur's sister, Queen Morgan le Fay, the other was the Queen of North Galis, and the third was the Queen of the Waste Lands.

Now more of the death of King Arthur could I never find, but that these ladies brought him to his grave, and such one was interred there which the hermit bare witness that was once Bishop of

---

27. **Avilion** legendary island where Arthur is said to dwell until his return.

Vocabulary Development

Vocabulary Knowledge Rating
When students have completed reading and discussing the group of selections, have them take out their **Vocabulary Knowledge Rating Charts** for the story. Read the words aloud and have students rate their knowledge of words again in the After Reading column. Clarify any words that are still problematic. Have students write their own definitions and example or sentence in the appropriate column. Then, have students complete the Vocabulary Lesson at the end of the selections. Encourage students to use the words in further discussion and written work about the selections. Remind them that they will be accountable for these words on the **Selection Test,** *Unit 1 Resources,* pp. 150–152 or pp.153–155.

Canterbury. But yet the hermit knew not in certain that he was verily the body of King Arthur; for this tale Sir Bedivere, a knight of the Table Round, made it to be written.

Yet some men say in many parts of England that King Arthur is not dead, but carried by the will of our Lord Jesu into another place; and men say that he shall come again, and he shall win the Holy Cross. Yet I will not say that it shall be so, but rather I would say: here in this world he changed his life. And many men say that there is written upon the tomb this:

HIC IACET ARTHURUS, REX QUONDAM, REXQUE FUTURUS[28]

28. HIC . . . FUTURUS

Here lies Arthur, who was once king and king will be again.

Critical Reading

Cite textual evidence to support your responses.

1. **Key Ideas and Details** **(a)** What warning does King Arthur receive in his dream? **(b)** How do circumstances frustrate his attempt to heed this warning? **(c) Interpret:** How does this series of events make the ending of the tale seem fated?

2. **Key Ideas and Details** **(a)** What is the relationship between Mordred and Arthur? **(b) Interpret:** How does the conflict between them emphasize the theme of betrayal in the tale?

3. **Integration of Knowledge and Ideas** **(a) Compare and Contrast:** How does the description of Sir Lucan's death contrast with the speech in which Arthur bemoans his passing? **(b) Draw Conclusions:** What conclusions can you draw from this contrast about the range of medieval taste in literature?

4. **Integration of Knowledge and Ideas** At the tale's end, rightful authority has been betrayed and may yet return, but it is not here now. What idea of leadership and loyalty in the present does this ending suggest?

5. **Integration of Knowledge and Ideas** Do you think leaders are "Arthurs"—those who should receive perfect obedience—or should people sometimes question their leader's decisions? Explain.

6. **Integration of Knowledge and Ideas** Do the authors of these selections accept or question the code of chivalry? In your response, use at least two of these Essential Question words: *traditional, ideal, conform. [Connecting to the Essential Question: What is the relationship of the writer to tradition?]*

from Morte d'Arthur **195**

Concept Connector

Reading Skill Graphic Organizer
Ask students to review the graphic organizers in which they have recorded the main ideas and details of each part of the selections. Then, have students share their organizers and compare the summaries they made.

Activating Prior Knowledge
Have students return to their responses to the Activating Prior Knowledge activity. Ask them to compare and describe the medieval romance elements from the two selections.

Writing About the Essential Question
Have students compare their responses to the prompt made before they completed reading the selections with their thoughts afterward. Have them work individually or in groups, writing or discussing their thoughts, to formulate their new responses. Then, lead a class discussion, probing for insights regarding the code of chivalry that the students gained from the selections and discussing how these insights either support or alter students' initial thoughts. Encourage students to cite specific textual details to support their responses.

Answers

1. **Possible response:** (a) Gawain is humble in his address to the king, brave and honorable in looking for the Green Knight, and chaste in his dealing with the lady of the castle. (b) Gawain fails to keep his word when he keeps the green girdle. The stories recognize human weaknesses, but use them as lessons.

2. Arthur is taken by magic women, many say he lives and will return, and the writing on his tomb says he will be king again, in the future.

3. (a) Gawain's reactions: Gawain confesses to having lied, admits he did not live up to ideals, repents, feels shame. Bedivere's reactions: Bedivere hides the sword, lies at first about throwing it, says he does not know what he will do without Arthur, weeps as Arthur departs, stays at the chapel, feels loss. (b) **Possible response:** The author of *Sir Gawain and the Green Knight* has added more characterization and plot twists. Gawain is more developed than Bedivere, and the identity of the lord and lady of the castle is a surprise.

4. (a) Love is the least emphasized element. Gawain meets the lady of the castle, but there is no romance. (b) A far-off setting is missing. In fact, Arthur comes home for this battle. (c) Both have heroic figures and memorable deeds. Both have contests (beheading, battle) and quests (chapel, Lady of the Lake). Both have events grouped in threes.

5. This cartoon is humorous because instead of brandishing a sword, the hand in the lake is brandishing a Swiss Army knife. This tool would have been useful to a knight, but not more so than a sword, which was his essential tool. It is humorous therefore to see a modern object being offered to a medieval knight, who looks surprised and as if he does not even know what the knife is.

6. For fifth graders, students will likely pick elements such as the challenge, the Green Knight's appearance, and the outcome, with Gawain still alive at the end, to relate.

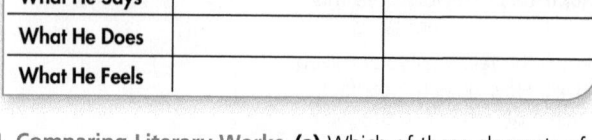

Literary Analysis

1. **Craft and Structure** (a) Identify three characteristics of Sir Gawain that make him an ideal hero for a **medieval romance.** Explain each answer. (b) Identify a shortcoming of his, and explain what it suggests about the theme of human weakness in medieval romance.

2. **Key Ideas and Details** In the excerpt from *Morte d'Arthur,* how do the supernatural events surrounding King Arthur's death link the story to the future?

3. **Craft and Structure** (a) Compare the characterization of Gawain (*Sir Gawain,* lines 459–477) with Malory's description of Bedivere as he reacts to the dying Arthur. Use a graphic organizer like the one shown. (b) Explain which author has done more to add literary elements, such as plot twists, descriptions, and characterization.

	Gawain's Reactions	Bedivere's Reactions
What He Says		
What He Does		
What He Feels		

4. **Comparing Literary Works** (a) Which of these elements of romance is least emphasized in *Sir Gawain:* chivalry, a far-off setting, the supernatural, adventure, or love? Explain. (b) Which is least emphasized in *Morte d'Arthur*? (c) What characteristics of a **legend** do the two selections share?

5. **Analyzing Visual Information** Using your knowledge of Arthurian legend, explain the humor in the cartoon shown here.

Reading Strategy

6. You are retelling *Sir Gawain and the Green Knight* to an audience of fifth graders. To prepare, **summarize the main idea or essential message** you would stress and the relevant details you would include.

7. As Sir Bedivere, summarize for a curious traveler who is visiting your hermitage the events leading up to King Arthur's death.

8. Based on your reading of these selections, summarize the main idea behind the code of chivalry and note the key ways in which it governed a knight's behavior.

Common Core State Standards

Writing
3. Write narratives to develop real or imagined experiences or events using effective technique, well-chosen details, and well-structured event sequences. (p. 197)

3.d. Use precise words and phrases, telling details, and sensory language to convey a vivid picture of the experiences, events, setting, and/or characters. (p. 197)

Language
4.a. Use context as a clue to the meaning of a word or phrase. (p. 197)

---

7. Students' responses should include not only important details from the story but also some effort to show that Bedivere is speaking.

8. The main idea behind the code of chivalry was selflessness. A chivalrous knight could be brave in battle because he put aside his concern for self-preservation; loyal to the king because he cared for the king's affairs more than his own; chaste with women because he thought of their good, not his own desires; holy because he did what God wanted, not what he wanted.

PERFORMANCE TASKS
Integrated Language Skills

Vocabulary Acquisition and Use

Word Analysis: The Word Root -droit-

The word *adroitly*, meaning "with physical or mental skill," is based on the French root *-droit-*, meaning "right." This root meaning reveals a historical bias toward right-handedness. The bias can be seen even more clearly in the Latin root *sinister*, meaning "left," "left-hand," or "unlucky." Answer these questions relating to *-droit-*.

1. Given that the prefix *mal-* means "bad," what might *maladroit* mean?
2. *Gauche* means "socially maladroit" in English. Which of these two words might it mean in French: "left" or "right"?
3. Which would you consider more *adroit*: a smooth left-handed layup in basketball or a clumsy right-handed air ball?
4. Using your knowledge of the root, briefly describe a duel between two knights—Sir Art the Adroit and Sir Mort the Maladroit.

Vocabulary: True or False?

Using your knowledge of the underlined vocabulary words, indicate whether each of the following statements is more likely to be true or false. Then, explain your answer.

1. A giant is lunging toward you, brandishing an ax. You would most likely <u>adjure</u> him to stop.
2. If his first swing was low and close, you might leap <u>adroitly</u> onto a nearby tabletop.
3. In the same moment, you might recognize the extent of your <u>peril.</u>
4. You might then beg the giant to abandon his <u>largesse</u> and take pity on small, helpless you.
5. If you have <u>entreated</u> the giant in just the right way, he might suddenly cease his attack and beg for forgiveness.
6. At that point, you might feel extraordinarily <u>interred.</u>

Writing

Narrative Text As Sir Gawain approaches the Green Chapel, he reacts by expressing himself in an interior monologue—a device in which a character speaks only to himself or herself, revealing thoughts, feelings, and personality traits. Write an **interior monologue** in which Gawain reacts to another event in the story. In your monologue, create a distinctive voice for Gawain. Have him react to unfolding events in a *specific place*.

Prewriting List characteristics of Gawain, and jot down notes on the dramatic situation he is confronting. What would he think about the situation? How would he feel?

Drafting Writing in the first person, have Gawain "discuss" the situation with himself and so reveal both the events and the *significance of the events* to which he reacts. Make sure that key details explaining the situation emerge early. Refer to prewriting notes to ensure that you convey Gawain's character.

Revising Star sections of your draft in which Gawain's feelings are especially strong. Review these passages, replacing dull phrases with vivid expressions of his personality or reactions.

> **Model: Using Reactions to Develop a Narrative**
> By St. Peter's sail, will no one answer this strange knight's challenge? I would, forsooth, were it not presumptuous-seeming and—what! Arthur himself is answering!
>
> When Gawain interrupts himself to remark on a new disturbance, the reader sees the situation through the character's reactions.

Integrated Language Skills **197**

Assessment Resources

Unit 1 Resources
L1 L2 EL Selection Test A, pp. 150–152. Administer Test A to less advanced readers.
L3 L4 EL Selection Test B, pp. 153–155. Administer Test B to on-level and more advanced students.

L3 L4 Open-Book Test, pp. 147–149. As an alternative, administer the Open-Book Test.

All Customizable Test Bank

All Self-tests
Students may prepare for the **Selection Test** by taking the **Self-test** online.

PHLit Online! All assessment resources are available at **www.PHLitOnline.com**.

ASSESS/EXTEND

Answers

Vocabulary Acquisition and Use
1. Introduce the skill using the instruction on the student page.
2. Have students complete the Word Analysis activity and the Vocabulary practice.

Word Analysis
1. *Maladroit* means "unskilled."
2. *Gauche* means "left."
3. A smooth left-handed layup is more <u>adroit</u>.
4. Sir Art the <u>Adroit</u> drew his sword and swung it acrobatically over his head. Sir Mort the <u>Maladroit</u> grunted and fumbled for his sword. Sir Art the <u>Adroit</u> leaped at him with the gracefulness and power of a puma. Sir Mort the <u>Maladroit</u> stumbled back, impaling himself on his own sword.

Vocabulary
1. True. You would want him to stop.
2. True. It makes sense for you to leap agilely out of the way.
3. True. You would recognize how much danger you were in.
4. False. The giant is not showing nobility of spirit by attacking you.
5. True. If you begged the giant he might stop his attack.
6. False. You would not feel buried, but rather grateful.

Writing
1. Discuss with students how to choose a topic.
2. Explain that interior monologue helps readers know what characters are thinking.
3. Point out that a monologue must supply information that the reader does not already have.
4. Have students complete the assignment.
5. To guide students in writing this narrative text, give them the **Support for Writing** page (*Unit 1 Resources*, p.145).
6. Use the **Response to Literature** rubrics, pp. 250–251 in the *Professional Development Guidebook*, to evaluate student work.

197

 **Common Core**
State Standards

- **Reading Informational Text 7**
- **Writing 7, 8**
- **Language 6**

❶ About the Text Forms

1. Introduce the letter and ballad forms using the instruction on the student page.

2. **Ask** students what parallels and what differences exist between e-mail communications today and letters written in the days before e-mail existed.

Possible responses: Students may say that e-mail is used for communicating news and plans, and letters served a similar purpose. However, e-mails can be sent frequently to give up-to-date news, while letters were sent less frequently and contained news of events over a longer period of time.

3. **Ask** students if they think modern culture has any art form similar to the ballad.

Possible response: Students may say that some modern songs tell stories that reflect cultural attitudes.

❷ Reading Strategy

Introduce the strategy using the instruction on the student page.

Model the Strategy:

Say to students:

If a document contains text features, first I decide which ones to look at before I read. If there is an introductory or background note, I should read that first, since that will give context and help me understand the document. If I see footnotes that define words, I know that the document may contain advanced vocabulary or unfamiliar terms.

PH WRITING COACH | Grade 12

Students will find additional information on research writing in Chapter 11.

198

© **COMMON CORE ▪ RESEARCH PROJECT**

Primary Sources

Letters
Letters of Margaret Paston

Ballads
Four Folk Ballads

© **Common Core**
State Standards

Reading Informational Text
7. Integrate and evaluate multiple sources of information presented in different media or formats as well as in words in order to address a question or solve a problem.

❶ About the Text Forms

A **letter** is a written communication to a person or group. In the centuries before telephones and e-mail, letters were a basic means of sharing information over a distance. Carried on foot, by horse, or by ship, letters were written for business and diplomatic reasons as well as personal ones. Today, letters from earlier eras are primary sources of information that shed light on the events, personalities, and daily life of times past.

During the Middle Ages, most people could neither read nor write. One of the ways in which they transmitted information was in story poems set to music, called **ballads.** Telling of sensational events and everyday calamities, **folk ballads** were anonymously composed and passed orally from singer to singer among the common folk. They often use four-line *stanzas,* in which only the second and fourth lines rhyme, and contain *dialogue* and repeated lines or phrases called **refrains.** Today, folk ballads of old are still being sung. As primary sources, they provide valuable glimpses into the lives and attitudes of ordinary people.

As you prepare to read these texts, consider questions you have about English life in the late Middle Ages. Look for answers among the details these primary sources provide.

❷ Reading Strategy

The scholars who prepare primary sources for publication often include text aids to help you understand these sources from a different era. You can improve your comprehension of primary sources by **analyzing, evaluating, and applying information from text features.** Such features may include *introductory and side notes* that give background or *footnotes* that clarify unfamiliar terms or words in *dialect,* the variety of a language spoken by people in a particular region or group.

❸ How does literature **shape or** reflect *society?*

Letters and ballads can both reflect and influence their times. As you read, consider how passages in Margaret Paston's letters show her responding to and trying to influence events. Also consider how ballads hint at certain *assumptions* about love and death and speculate how people in medieval times may have reacted to those assumptions.

---

❸ How does literature shape or reflect society?

Tell students that, as they read, they should make a list of cultural values that they see reflected in Margaret Paston's actions as well as in the stories relayed in the ballads.

Teaching Resources

- ⒶⒾⒾ *Unit 1 Resources,* pp. 156–157
- ⒶⒾⒾ Enriched Online Student Edition
- ⒶⒾⒾ *Common Core Companion,* pp. 156–157; 240–260; 336–337

 All resources are available at
www.PHLitOnline.com

Primary-source documents are a rich source of information for researchers. As you read these documents, use a note-taking guide like the one shown to organize relevant and accurate information.

1 Type of Document (check one)
☐ Newspaper ☐ Letter ☐ Diary ☐ Map ☐ Government Document
☐ Advertisement ☐ Speech ☐ Other (specify): _____

2 Date(s) or Period Composed _____

3 Author (if known) _____
Author's Position (if known) _____

4 Intended Audience _____

5 Purpose and Message
  a Why was this document composed? (check the main purpose)
    ☐ to entertain ☐ to inform ☐ to persuade ☐ to describe ☐ to reflect
  b Which word or words best describe the tone? ☐personal
    ☐ formal ☐ humorous ☐ dramatic ☐ emotional ☐ unsentimental
  c Summarize the message or main events in a sentence or two.
    _____
    _____

  d What does this document show about life in the time and place in which it was composed?
    _____
    _____

> **Reading Strategy**
> **Using Text Features**
> Features such as introductory notes, side notes, and footnotes may clarify details about time and place. As you read, analyze and apply information from text features to better understand the documents.

This guide was adapted from the **U.S. National Archives** document analysis worksheet.

❺ Vocabulary

aldermen (ôl´ dər mən) *n.* chief officers in a shire, or county (p. 202)

succor (suk´ ər) *v.* help; aid; relieve (p. 202)

certify (sʉrt´ ə fī´) *v.* declare a thing true or accurate; verify; attest (p. 202)

remnant (rem´ nənt) *n.* what is left over; remainder (p. 202)

ransacked (ran´ sakt´) *v.* searched through to find goods to rob; looted (p. 203)

asunder (ə sun´ dər) *adv.* into parts or pieces (p. 203)

assault (ə sôlt´) *v.* violently attack (p. 203)

bar (bär) *n.* one of the vertical lines dividing written music into equal sections called measures (p. 205)

measure (mezh´ ər) *n.* a section of written music between two vertical lines called bars (p. 205)

melody (mel´ ə dē) *n.* a sequence of single tones that together create a tune or song (p. 205)

---

❹ Note-Taking Guide

1. Walk the class through the **Note-Taking Guide**, pointing out the different types of information students will be recording.

2. Discuss items 4 and 5 on the **Note-taking Guide** with students in greater detail, asking students to discuss how they might determine this information. For example, discuss what questions students might ask themselves in order to determine the intended audience for a selection, and what criteria students can use to determine why a document was written and what its tone is.

3. Point out that students can use the technique of paraphrasing to help them identify the message or main events of a selection for item 5c in the **Note-Taking Guide**.

❺ Vocabulary

1. Have students preview the selection vocabulary, pronouncing the words and reading their definitions. Have students identify any words with which they are already familiar.

2. Use each word in a sentence with sufficient context to define the word. Then repeat or rephrase your definitional sentence with the vocabulary word missing, prompting the class to "fill in the blank" orally. Here is an example:

To certify a statement is to declare that it is true. If a child told his mother that he needed money for a field trip, the mother might call his teacher to [students say "certify"] her child's claim.

Differentiated Instruction for Universal Access

Support for Special-Needs Students
Have students complete the **Before You Read** and the **Making Connections** pages for these selections in the *Reader's Notebook: Adapted Version.* These pages provide abbreviated skills instruction, a selection summary, the Before You Read graphic organizer, and a **Note-Taking Guide.**

Support for Less Proficient Readers
Have students complete the **Before You Read** and the **Making Connections** pages for these selections in the *Reader's Notebook.* These pages provide abbreviated skills instruction, a selection summary, the Before You Read graphic organizer, and a **Note-Taking Guide.**

EL Support for English Learners
Have students complete the **Before You Read** and the **Making Connections** pages for these selections in the *Reader's Notebook: English Learner's Version.* These pages provide additional vocabulary, vocabulary skills, and vocabulary practice, along with a **Getting Ready to Read** activity.

⑥ Background

The Story Behind the Documents

Margaret Mauteby married John Paston when he was 19 and she was between the ages of 12 and 18. An only child of a well-connected family, she brought valuable land to her marriage. Margaret and John had seven children: five boys and two girls.

The Paston letters were collected by William Worcester, servant of Sir John Fastolf, a friend and neighbor of John Paston. Several of the lawsuits for which the letters were needed as evidence involved Fastolf—including the dispute mentioned on page 200 of this selection.

(Fastolf achieved some degree of immortality when he was transformed by Shakespeare into Sir John Falstaff. However, the real Fastolf, a career soldier who fought with distinction, bore little resemblance to Shakespeare's cowardly clown.)

It is not known how the letters were kept from the fifteenth to the eighteenth century, but they reemerged in 1735. The letters were divided between Oxford's Bodleian Library and the British Museum. The collection, edited and published in six volumes, remains an important source of information about fifteenth-century England.

⑦ Critical Viewing

Possible response: Students may note that the tower and high windows would have allowed manor residents to see enemies approaching at a distance and fight them off with weapons such as arrows. The moat around the manor would also have provided protection and made it difficult for enemies to climb over the walls.

⑥ THE STORY BEHIND THE DOCUMENTS

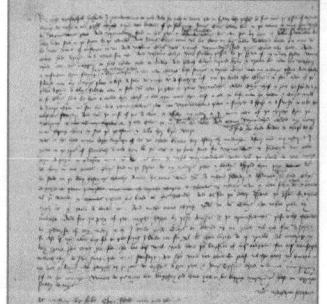

Dating from 1477, this letter from the Paston collection may be the first Valentine message in English. Margery Brews writes to her fiancé, John Paston, "Be my olde Valentine."

Margaret Paston (1423–1484) was born Margaret Mautby in the eastern English county of Norfolk. In about 1442 she married John Paston, a Norfolk lawyer and landowner. The Pastons had only recently acquired their wealth, however, and had to fight hard to keep it. During John's frequent visits to London to work on legal matters, it fell to his wife to run the estates, settle land disputes, and defend Paston manors against hostile raids.

Because they were often separated, Margaret and John exchanged many letters discussing family matters, local politics, and the everyday business of running an estate. Their letters are part of the more than one thousand Paston family documents originally preserved as evidence for lawsuits. Today these documents are a treasure trove of information about life in fifteenth-century England.

In the fifteenth century, when the weak rule of Henry VI plunged England into chaos, many families like the Pastons were able to rise from poverty, taking properties for which their legal claim was not firm. In one instance, the powerful Duke of Suffolk challenged the Pastons' claim to the manor of Hellesdon and bribed the mayor of the city of Norwich (nôr´ ij) to help force the Pastons out. Although Margaret Paston, with a garrison of sixty warriors, repelled the first attacks, the duke eventually seized and looted Hellesdon. In the first two letters presented here, Margaret writes to her husband with news of the duke's success. In the third letter, composed after her husband's death, she writes to her son Sir John Paston about defending another Paston property called Caister.

Unlike Margaret and John Paston, most people in the fifteenth century could not write or read. One way the common folk passed along sensational news and entertaining stories was in brief storytelling poems set to music called folk ballads.

The first English folk ballads probably go back to the twelfth century, but many more date to the Pastons' era of the fifteenth. Anonymously composed and transmitted orally from singer to singer, folk ballads exist in many different versions. The four presented here are versions from the border area between England and Scotland and use words and pronunciations in Scots dialect.

In 1765, Bishop Thomas Percy collected and published folk ballads in a book called *Reliques of Ancient English Poetry*. As other collections followed, people began to appreciate the literary value of folk ballads and the fascinating glimpses they offered of daily life and attitudes among people in times past.

⑦ ▶ **Critical Viewing** The Paston manor homes were often attacked. Judging from this photograph of a manor house, how easy would it have been to defend such a building? Explain. **[Speculate]**

200 From Legend to History (A.D. 449–1485)

Enrichment: Investigating Career Connections

Information Science

Along with advances in technology, the ways in which we are able to search for and consume information are constantly changing. Careers in information and library science range from those who archive and preserve ancient documents to those who develop ways to bring these documents to the computer screens of users all over the world. A degree in information science does not always lead to a school or public library—it can be the gateway to a broad range of career opportunities, from museum archivists to university librarians to computer database developers.

Activity: Research Careers in Information Science Present students with a list of careers in information science, and have individuals or pairs of students choose a career path to research. Suggest that they record information in the **Enrichment: Investigating Career Connections** worksheet, *Professional Development Guidebook*, page 221.

Letters of
MARGARET PASTON

Margaret Paston

❶ Background

History

The Paston letters found their first public audience in 1787 when their owner, John Fenn, edited and published a collection of them under the title *Original letters, Written during the Reigns of Henry VI., Edward IV. and Richard III. by Various Persons of Rank or Consequence.* Although Fenn was by no means a famous figure at this point, the entire first printing of his book was sold within a week of its publication, and a second edition was soon requested. The book was read not only by those with a specific interest in and knowledge of England's history, but by many members of polite society, who enjoyed discussing the anecdotes of real family life in another time. Public interest in the letters was so great that Fenn put them on display in the Library of the Society of Antiquaries. This public display served a second purpose as well—with the book's popularity came questions about the authenticity of the letters.

❷ About the Selection

Letters are a way of sharing life's news, and, in the case of Margaret Paston, the news is dramatic, detailed, and very directly stated. Letters can also go a long way toward revealing the personality of the writer. In the first pair of letters, Paston tells her husband that one of their homes, Hellesdon, has been attacked, seized, and ransacked by the Duke of Suffolk. As she details the events, her outrage is palpable.

The third letter, written almost two years later, warns her son of yet another impending attack. This letter reveals Paston's keen awareness of political turmoil.

By reading these letters, students will receive firsthand information about life in the Middle Ages. They will also come to appreciate and respect Margaret Paston herself. She was a remarkable woman.

❸ Primary Sources

Letters

1. Read aloud or have a student read aloud the first paragraph on page 202.

2. Then **ask** students the Primary Sources question: What does this letter show about the loyalties of others to a newly wealthy family like the Pastons?
Possible response: The letter shows that the nobility show no loyalty to the newly rich. Instead, the Pastons are treated with suspicion and hardness; the nobility punishes anyone who tries to aid the Pastons or their men.

❹ Background

Language

Students may be unfamiliar with the term *Dowager* in the second paragraph on this page. A *dowager* is a widow whose deceased husband has left her with property or a noble title, such as Duchess. The "old Lady" referred to on this page was probably the Duke's mother. Although her husband, the original Duke, was no longer alive, she retained the title of Duchess and maintained a stake in the property of which her son, the new Duke, was the steward.

202

Primary Sources
Letters What does this letter show about the loyalties of others to a newly wealthy family like the Pastons?

Vocabulary
aldermen (ôl´ dər mən) *n.* chief officers in a shire, or county

succor (suk´ ər) *v.* help; aid; relieve

certify (sʉrt´ ə fī´) *v.* declare a thing true or accurate; verify; attest

remnant (rem´ nənt) *n.* what is left over; remainder

❷ *Margaret Paston to John Paston*
17 October 1465
Norwich

. . . The Duke came to Norwich on Tuesday at 10 o'clock with some 500 men. And he sent for the mayor and aldermen with the Sheriffs, desiring them in the King's name that they should make enquiry of the constables of every ward in the City as to what men had gone to help or succor your men at any time during these gatherings and, if they could find any, that they should take and arrest and correct them, and certify to him the names by 8 o'clock on Wednesday. Which the Mayor did and will do anything that he may for him and his men. . . .

I am told that the old Lady [the Dowager Duchess] and the Duke are fiercely set against us on the information of Harleston, the bailiff of Costessey . . . and such other false shrews which would have this matter carried through for their own pleasure. . . . And as for Sir John Heveningham, Sir John Wingfield and other worshipful men, they are but made their doggebolds [lackeys], which I suppose will cause their disworship hereafter. I spoke with Sir John Heveningham and informed him of the truth of the matter and of all our demeaning at Drayton, and he said he would that all things were well, and that he would inform my Lord what I told him, but that Harleston had all the influence with the Duke here, and at this time he was advised by him and Dr. Aleyn.

The lodge and the remnant of your place was beaten down on Tuesday and Wednesday and the Duke rode on Wednesday to Drayton and so forth to Costessey while the lodge at Hellesdon was being beaten down. And this night at midnight Thomas Slyforth . . . and others had a cart and fetched away feather-beds and all our stuff that was left at the parson's and Thomas Waters' house to be kept. . . . I pray you send me word how I shall act—whether you wish that I abide at Caister or come to you at London. . . .

Margaret Paston to John Paston
27 October 1465
Norwich

. . . Please you to know that I was at Hellesdon on Thursday last and saw the place there, and, in good faith, nobody would believe how foul and horrible it appears unless they saw it. There come many people daily to wonder at it, both from Norwich and

---

Enrichment: Investigating Daily Life

Manors and Tenants

The manor system began at the end of the Roman Empire. Farmers and laborers traded their land, freedom, or services for the protection of powerful landowners, who could afford to support a military force. The landowners, who became lords or kings over time, gained the benefit of laborers to work their fields.

The typical manor included a manor house, land for farming and grazing livestock, and the cottages, barns, and gardens of its tenants. These were often gathered into a small village.

There might also be a church and shops.
Activity: Research Manor Life Have pairs or groups of students conduct research on daily life in a fifteenth-century English manor. Suggest that they record information in the **Enrichment: Investigating Daily Life** worksheet, *Professional Development Guidebook,* page 224. Students may use their results to create a map of what they believed the Paston's manor may have looked like, or to draw a scene that may have taken place there.

many other places, and they speak of it with shame. The Duke would have been a £1000 better off if it had not happened, and you have the more good will of the people because it was so foully done. They made your tenants of Hellesdon and Drayton, with others, break down the walls of both the place and the lodge—God knows full much against their wills, but they dare not refuse for fear. I have spoken with your tenants of Hellesdon and Drayton and comforted them as well as I can. The Duke's men ransacked the church and bore away all the goods that were left there, both of ours and of the tenants, and even stood upon the high altar and ransacked the images and took away those that they could find, and put the parson out of the church till they had done, and ransacked every man's house in the town five or six times. . . . As for lead, brass, pewter, iron, doors, gates and other stuff of the house, men from Costessey and Cawston have it, and what they might not carry away they have hewn asunder in the most spiteful manner. . . .

At the reverence of God, if any worshipful and profitable settlement may be made in your matters, do not forsake it, to avoid our trouble and great costs and charges that we may have and that may grow hereafter. . . .

The following letter was sent to Sir John Paston, Margaret's knighted son. Caister, a castle with many manors and estates, had been willed to the Paston family by Sir John Fastolf, for whom John Paston worked as financial advisor. There followed years of legal wrangles during which the Pastons faced numerous challenges to the will. Because her husband had died the year before, Margaret turned to her son Sir John for help defending Caister. Sir John sent his younger brother, also named John, to protect the castle. John failed, however, surrendering the castle after his protector, King Edward IV, was captured during the Wars of the Roses.

Margaret Paston to Sir John Paston
11 July 1467
Norwich

. . . Also this day was brought me word from Caister that Rising of Fritton had heard in divers places in Suffolk that Fastolf of Cowhawe gathers all the strength he may and intends to assault Caister and to enter there if he may, insomuch that it

Vocabulary
ransacked (ranʹsaktʹ)
v. searched through to find goods to rob; looted

asunder (ə sunʹdər) *adv.*
into parts or pieces

assault (ə sôltʹ) *v.* violently attack

Reading Strategy
Text Features What does
❺ this note clarify about the social position of the Pastons and the dangers they faced?

❻ **Reading Check**
What has the Duke done against the Pastons?

Primary Sources: Letters **203**

---

❺ Reading Strategy
Text Features

1. Have a student read aloud the italicized background paragraph on page 203.

2. Then **ask** students the Reading Strategy question: What does this note clarify about the Pastons' social position and the dangers they faced?
Possible response: The note reveals that although the Pastons were respected by nobles such as Sir John Fastolf and King Edward IV, their social position was not high enough to protect them from lawsuits challenging their rights to own certain properties.

3. **Ask** students: Based on this note, what information do you expect to find in the letter that follows, and what tone do you expect it to have?
Possible response: The letter may inform Sir John about the specifics of plots to challenge the Pastons' right to Caister. Its tone will likely be anxious and worried.

4. Then **ask** students: How will these predictions make it easier for you to get meaning out of the letter?
Possible response: Students will not need to spend as much time trying to figure out what people, places, and events the writer is referring to, and can instead focus on the underlying motivations and feelings of Margaret Paston.

❻ Reading Check
Answer: The Duke has destroyed the Pastons' manors at Hellesdon and Drayton, taking the Pastons' property as well as their tenants', and forcing the Pastons' tenants to tear down the walls of manor buildings.

Differentiated
Instruction for Universal Access

Strategy for Special-Needs Students
The number of details and unfamiliar names in these letters may make them hard for some students to follow. List on the board the "good guys," the "bad guys," and the places. This will help students realize that while Harleston is a person, Hellesdon is the manor. Explain to students, one letter at a time, what Margaret Paston is reporting, and then have students read that letter and look for details that relate to the outline you have given.

Enrichment for Gifted/Talented Students
Ask students to imagine that Margaret Paston's letters are the inspiration for a movie. Have them create a brief outline of the events they would want to include in the movie (including details from the Background, if desirable). They should also give a brief description of how they would want to portray Margaret. Students may also wish to find pictures of English manor homes that might work as film locations or of clothing from the period for the costume designer.

203

Before students respond, you may wish to have them write a brief objective summary of the selection. As they answer the questions below, remind them to support their answers with evidence from the text.

1. (a) The Duke made the tenants of Hellesdon help destroy the buildings of the manor. Then he ransacked the place, taking the belongings of both the Pastons and the tenants. (b) She is upset and believes the Duke's actions to be cruel and wrong. She expects the tenants to have similar feelings of loss and dismay, which is shown by the way she attempts to comfort them after the Duke forced them to destroy their homes.

2. (a) Emotion is revealed by word choice: calling associates "lackeys," describing destruction as "foul and horrible" and people's reactions as "wonder" and "shame." She also writes that "I have been afraid" and "I marvel." However, she uses reason consistently, offering details, outlining causes and effects, and asking advice. For example, she uses reason when she observes that the soldiers do not respect her as much as they might respect a man, and she therefore asks her son to send a man or men to take control of the situation. (b) Margaret seems to have honest, straightforward relationships with both her husband and her son. She is very open in her writing, and one gets the feeling she and her husband discussed everything. She is open with her son, too, but he appears to be busy with his own battles.

3. (a) Life in the Middle Ages offered opportunities but was hard and uncertain. (b) **Possible response:** Today, one has legal recourse if someone tries to take one's property by force.

---

is said that he has five score men ready and daily sends spies to know what men guard the place. By whose power or favor or support he will do this I know not, but you know well that I have been afraid there before this time, when I had other comfort than I had now: I cannot guide nor rule soldiers well and they set not by [do not respect] a woman as they should by a man. Therefore I would that you should send home your brothers or else Daubeney to take control and to bring in such men as are necessary for the safeguard of the place. . . . And I have been about my livelode to set a rule therein, as I have written to you, which is not yet all performed after my desire, and I would not go to Caister till I had done. I do not want to spend more days near thereabouts, if I can avoid it; so make sure that you send someone home to keep the place and when I have finished what I have begun I shall arrange to go there if it will do any good—otherwise I had rather not be there. . . .

. . . I marvel greatly that you send me no word how you do, for your enemies begin to grow right bold and that puts your friends in fear and doubt. Therefore arrange that they may have some comfort, so that they be not discouraged, for if we lose our friends, it will be hard in this troublous world to get them again . . .

Critical Reading

Cite textual evidence to support your responses.

© 1. **Key Ideas and Details (a)** What does the duke force the Pastons' tenants to do? **(b) Interpret:** How does Margaret Paston feel about the duke's actions, and how does she expect the tenants to feel?

© 2. **Craft and Structure (a) Analyze:** Cite examples of emotional appeals and logical reasons that Margaret Paston uses in requesting help from her husband and son. **(b) Draw Conclusions:** What sort of relationship does she have with her husband and son?

© 3. **Integration of Knowledge and Ideas (a) Generalize:** What do the letters suggest to you about life in the Middle Ages? **(b) Evaluate:** What do you think is the most important difference, positive or negative, between life then and today? Why?

Enrichment: Investigating Health and Medicine

Medieval Medicine

People in the Middle Ages viewed illness and death differently from most people today—differences in living conditions and medical knowledge in the Middle Ages resulted in illness being much more common. As a result, it was viewed as an expected part of life rather than a rare inconvenience. Common illnesses included tertian malaria, dysentery, jaundice, pleurisy, pneumonia, influenza, and the common cold.

Activity: Research Illnesses in Medieval Times and Today Have pairs or groups of students conduct research on an illness common in fifteenth-century England, looking not only for causes and symptoms but also for historical and modern treatments of the illness. Suggest that they record information in the **Enrichment: Investigating Health and Medicine** worksheet, *Professional Development Guidebook,* page 229. When students are finished, have them present their findings to the class.

⑦ TWA CORBIES

⑧ *BACKGROUND During the Middle Ages, death before the age of thirty-five was the norm. The stark facts of life and death promoted the unsentimental outlook of medieval folk ballads.*

As I was walking all alane,
I heard twa corbies[1] making a mane.[2]
The tane unto the tither did say,
"Whar sall we gang and dine the day?"

5 "In behint yon auld fail dyke,[3]
I wot[4] there lies a new-slain knight;
And naebody kens[5] that he lies there
But his hawk, his hound, and his lady fair.

"His hound is to the hunting gane,
10 His hawk to fetch the wild-fowl hame,
His lady's ta'en anither mate,
So we may mak our dinner sweet.

"Ye'll sit on his white hause-bane,[6]
And I'll pike out his bonny blue e'en;[7]
15 Wi' ae lock o' his gowden hair
We'll theek[8] our nest when it grows bare.

"Mony a one for him maks mane,
But nane sall ken whar he is gane.
O'er his white banes, when they are bare,
20 The wind sall blaw for evermair."

---

1. **twa corbies** two ravens.
2. **mane** moan.
3. **fail dyke** bank of earth.
4. **wot** know.
5. **kens** knows.
6. **hause-bane** neck-bone.
7. **e'en** eyes.
8. **theek** thatch.

---

⑨ LITERATURE IN CONTEXT

Cultural Connection

Folk Ballads
Following are some terms that will help you to understand the musical basis of folk ballads:

bar (bär) *n.* one of the vertical lines dividing written music into equal sections called measures

measure (mezh´ ər) *n.* a section of written music between two vertical lines called bars

melody (mel´ ə dē) *n.* a sequence of single tones that together create a tune or song
A typical ballad tune is made up of sixteen bars of music, with a rhythm that is mostly two beats per measure. The tune lasts as long as each ballad stanza, so the singer repeats it each time he or she begins a new stanza.

Connect to the Literature

Look at the stanzas in these ballads. In what way is the ballad stanza both a unit of meaning and a unit of music?

---

⑦ About the Selections

Death by murder or accident is one of the most common themes of ballads. These two ballads are no exception. In the first, a young knight lies slain, unmourned by his hawk, his hound, or his lady love. The story unfolds through a conversation between two ravens that look at the whole affair in a matter-of-fact, cold-blooded way.

Students may be familiar with a version of "Lord Randall," What they may not have realized, however, is that this is a tale of treachery. The handsome young man, comes home to his mother to die, for he has been poisoned by his "true-love."

⑧ Background
Mortality Rates in the Middle Ages

People in the Middle Ages knew little about germs and diseases; they had few medicines and lacked knowledge about disease prevention. For this reason, mortality rates were much higher than they are today, especially during childhood. People estimate the child mortality rate during the Middle Ages as being between 30 and 50 percent.

⑨ Literature in Context
Cultural Connection

1. Discuss with students the three terms defined on the student page, having musically knowledgeable students contribute their own understandings of these terms.

2. Have musically knowledgeable students flesh out what is explained in the paragraph beginning "A typical ballad tune...." Encourage students to give an example of a well-known song that fits this pattern.

Connect to the Literature

Ask students the Connect to the Literature question: In what way is the ballad stanza both a unit of meaning and a unit of music?
Possible response: The stanzas divide the lyrics into small, easily digestible messages that form the whole story when put together. The stanzas are also units of music since each stanza was probably set to the same tune.

Differentiated Instruction   for Universal Access

Support for Less Proficient Readers
Play the readings of "Twa Corbies" and "Lord Randall" from the *Hear It!* **Audio CD.** asking that students read along with the recordings. Pause after each stanza to discuss what is happening, and have students identify key words or phrases they used to understand the action.

Enrichment for Gifted/ Talented Students
Have students create a ballad on a topic of their choosing. You may wish to challenge them to use dialect in their work, as well. Encourage them to review the characteristics of ballads and to use at least two of them. Have them share their ballads with the class.

Vocabulary for Advanced Readers
Students may wish to do further research into how words of dialect are related to words in standard English. You may wish to direct them to the Robert Burns poems in this volume for more words of dialect. Larger dictionaries, online etymologies, and dictionaries of dialect will be useful resources.

⑩ Reading Strategy

Text Features

1. Point out the first two footnotes and the places where the words appear in the text.

2. Then, **ask** students the Reading Strategy question: What words and pronunciations in Scots dialect are explained in the first two footnotes? Why do you think there are no footnotes for the dialect in lines 1–3?
   Possible response: They explain that "fain" means gladly and "wald" means would; Lines 1–3 do not have unfamiliar words.

⑪ Primary Sources

Folk Ballads

1. Have a student read aloud the fourth stanza of "Lord Randall."

2. Then **ask** students the Primary Sources question: What do the details in the fourth stanza of "Lord Randall" reveal about medieval life among the nobility?
   Possible response: The details reveal that the nobility had time for leisure activities and money for luxuries.

ASSESS

Answers

Remind students to support their answers with evidence from the text.

1. (a) The knight's hawk, hound, and lady know where he lies.
   (b) **Possible response:** Students may guess that the lady's new mate killed the knight.

2. (a) The corbies' tone is matter-of-fact and unsentimental. (b) People accepted it as part of life.

3. (a) **Possible responses:** Students who think he was truly poisoned may note that he has just eaten with his love, and his bloodhounds died. Others may say that he is only playing on the meaning of his mother's words and is not really sick. b) Love can make people vulnerable to great hurt.

206

© COMMON CORE ■ RESEARCH PROJECT

LORD RANDALL

⑩ **Reading Strategy**
Text Features What words and pronunciations in Scots dialect are explained in the first two footnotes? Why do you think there are no footnotes for the dialect in lines 1–3?

Primary Sources
Folk Ballads What do the details in the fourth stanza of "Lord Randall" reveal about medieval life among the nobility?

⑩ O where hae ye been, Lord Randall, my son?
O where hae ye been, my handsome young man?"
"I hae been to the wild wood; mother, make my bed soon,
For I'm weary wi' hunting, and fain[1] wald[2] lie down."

5 "Where gat ye your dinner, Lord Randall, my son?
Where gat ye your dinner, my handsome young man?"
"I dined wi' my true-love; mother, make my bed soon,
For I'm weary wi' hunting, and fain wald lie down."

"What gat ye to your dinner, Lord Randall, my son?
10 What gat ye to your dinner, my handsome young man?"
"I gat eels boil'd in broo;[3] mother, make my bed soon,
For I'm weary wi' hunting, and fain wald lie down."

⑪ "What became of your bloodhounds, Lord Randall, my son?
What became of your bloodhounds, my handsome young man?"
15 "O they swell'd and they died; mother, make my bed soon,
For I'm weary wi' hunting, and fain wald lie down."

"O I fear ye are poison'd, Lord Randall, my son!
O I fear ye are poison'd, my handsome young man!"
"O yes! I am poison'd; mother, make my bed soon,
20 For I'm sick at the heart, and I fain wald lie down."

---

1. fain gladly.
2. wald would.
3. broo broth.

Critical Reading

© **1. Key Ideas and Details (a)** Besides the two corbies, or ravens, who are the only ones that know where the new-slain knight lies? **(b) Infer:** Who or what do you think has caused the knight's death? Why?

© **2. Craft and Structure (a) Infer:** How would you describe the corbies' tone in discussing the knight's death? **(b) Interpret:** What does the tone suggest about the medieval attitude toward death?

© **3. Integration of Knowledge and Ideas (a) Analyze Cause and Effect:** Do you think Lord Randall was poisoned, or do you think he is simply sick at heart? Cite details to support your analysis. **(b) Draw Conclusions:** What view of love does "Lord Randall" express?

Cite textual evidence to support your responses.

206 From Legend to History (A.D. 449–1485)

Enrichment: Analyzing Forms and Genres

Ballads and the Oral Tradition

Ballads are part of the oral tradition. Often, oral literature consists of myths and tales; in particular, it emphasizes creation myths. This is the case in the Native American and African literary traditions.

Ballads, which tell stories without much character development, resemble many early myths in which the emphasis is on plot and especially outcome, rather than on motivation or any other psychological dimension of human action.

Activity: Compare Myths and Ballads Have pairs or groups of students research examples of myths from the Native American and African traditions. Suggest that they record information in the **Enrichment: Analyzing Forms and Genres** worksheet, *Professional Development Guidebook,* page 227. After students are finished, lead a discussion about similarities in purpose and form between the ballads students have read and the myths they researched.

GET UP AND BAR THE DOOR

It fell about the Martinmas time,[1]
    And a gay time it was then,
When our goodwife got puddings to make,
    She's boild them in the pan.

5 The wind sae cauld blew south and north.
    And blew into the floor;
Quoth our goodman to our goodwife,
    "Gae out and bar the door."

"My hand is in my hussyfskap,[2]
10   Goodman, as ye may see;
An it should nae be barrd this hundred year,
    It's no be barrd for me."[3]

They made a paction[4] tween them twa.
    They made it firm and sure.
15 That the first word whaeer shoud speak,
    Shoud rise and bar the door.

Then by there came two gentlemen,
    At twelve o'clock at night,
And they could neither see house nor hall,
20   Nor coal nor candlelight.

"Now whether is this a rich man's house,
    Or whether it is a poor?"
But neer a word wad ane o' them[5] speak,
    For barring of the door.

25 And first they[6] ate the white puddings,
    And then they ate the black:

---

1. **Martinmas time** November 11.
2. **hussyfskap** household duties.
3. **An it should . . . me** "If it has to be barred by me, then it will not be barred in a hundred years."
4. **paction** agreement.
5. **them** the man and his wife.
6. **they** the strangers.

⓭

⓮ ▲ **Primary Source: Art**
What does this painting tell you about domestic life in medieval times? **[Infer]**

⓯ ✓ Reading Check
What is it that neither the husband nor the wife wants to do?

Primary Sources: Ballads **207**

---

16 Reading Strategy

Text Features

1. As a class, read each of the footnotes for this ballad, and discuss the lines in which each word or phrase appears so that students understand the meaning of each line.

2. Then, **ask** students the Reading Strategy question: How do the footnotes for this ballad help explain or clarify what occurs? **Possible response:** The footnotes clarify unclear pronoun references (e.g., footnotes 5 and 6) and explain characters' speech (e.g., footnotes 8, 9, 10, and 11).

ASSESS

Answers

Before students respond, you may wish to have them write a brief objective summary of the selection. As they answer the questions below, remind them to support their answers with evidence from the text.

1. (a) They agree that the first to speak shall get up and bar the door. (b) She is busy, he is lazy, and both are stubborn.

2. (a) The goodman and his wife are probably members of the lower class of tenants, rather than wealthy landowners. The wife does housework, rather than a servant, and there is no water in the house. (b) People of this class were probably very vulnerable to burglary and violence since they had only a door to protect them and not the strong fortifications of a manor house.

3. (a) They must decide which is worse, being burglarized or losing the bet. (b) She wins because the goodman is the first to speak. Neither the goodwife nor the goodman wins, in that their home is burglarized. (c) Stubbornness is often stupid and can be harmful.

Tho muckle[7] thought the goodwife to hersel,
    Yet neer a word she spake.

Then said the one unto the other,
30   "Here, man, take ye my knife;
Do ye tak aff the auld man's beard,
    And I'll kiss the goodwife."

"But there's nae water in the house,
    And what shall we do than?"
35 "What ails ye at the pudding broo,[8]
    That boils into[9] the pan?"

O up then started our goodman,
    An angry man was he:
"Will ye kiss my wife before my een,
40   And scad[10] me wi pudding bree?"[11]

Then up and started our goodwife,
    Gied three skips on the floor:
"Goodman, you've spoken the foremost word;
    Get up and bar the door."

Reading Strategy
Text Features How do the footnotes for this ballad help explain or clarify what occurs?

---

7. **muckle** much.
8. **What . . . broo** "What's the matter with pudding water?"
16 9. **into** in.
10. **scad** scald.
11. **bree** broth.

Cite textual evidence to support your responses.

Critical Reading

© 1. **Key Ideas and Details (a)** What agreement do the goodman and his wife make? **(b) Analyze:** What situation and/or character traits prompt them to make this agreement?

© 2. **Key Ideas and Details (a) Interpret:** To what class of society do the goodman and his wife belong? Cite details to support your answer. **(b) Draw Conclusions:** What does the strangers' treatment of them suggest about the dangers people of this class faced in medieval times?

© 3. **Key Ideas and Details (a) Summarize:** What dilemma does the couple face when the strangers arrive? **(b) Analyze:** In what way does the wife "win"? In what way do neither she nor her husband win? **(c) Interpret:** What point about stubbornness does the ballad make?

208 From Legend to History (A.D. 449–1485)

Enrichment: Investigating Popular Culture

Popularizing Ballads

By the seventeenth century, English presses were beginning to pour out ballad texts printed on broadsides. (Broadsides are large sheets of paper printed on one side only.) However, most of these ballad texts disappeared almost as quickly as most of today's pop songs.

Ballad singers hawked the broadsides around country towns and at places for social entertainments, such as fairs and public houses, so a few of the street ballad texts passed into oral circulation.

Activity: Examine the Modern Music Industry
Have pairs or groups of students research the rise and fall of several recent pop songs to gather information on the typical life span of a song in today's music industry. Suggest that they record information in the **Enrichment: Investigating Popular Culture** worksheet, *Professional Development Guidebook,* page 238. After students are finished, have them share some of their findings.

BARBARA ALLAN

It was in and about the Martinmas time,[1]
    When the green leaves were a-fallin';
That Sir John Graeme in the West Country
    Fell in love with Barbara Allan.

5 He sent his man down through the town
    To the place where she was dwellin':
"O haste and come to my master dear,
    Gin[2] ye be Barbara Allan."

O slowly, slowly rase[3] she up,
10   To the place where he was lyin',
And when she drew the curtain by:
    "Young man, I think you're dyin'."

"O it's I'm sick, and very, very sick,
    And 'tis a' for Barbara Allan."
15 "O the better for me ye sal[4] never be,
    Though your heart's blood were a-spillin'.

"O dinna ye mind,[5] young man," said she,
    "When ye the cups were fillin',
That ye made the healths gae round and round,
20   And slighted Barbara Allan?"

He turned his face unto the wall,
    And death with him was dealin':
"Adieu, adieu, my dear friends all,
    And be kind to Barbara Allan.

---

1. **Martinmas time** November 11.
2. **Gin** if.
3. **rase** rose.
4. **sal** shall.
5. **dinna ye mind** don't you remember.

Primary Sources
Folk Ballads What does the phrase "his man" tell you about the society of the time?

Reading Check
Why does Sir John Graeme send his man to Barbara Allan?

---

⑰ About the Selection
Over time, "Barbara Allan" has had more than a dozen titles and has been spoken in countless local accents. A ballad historian found ninety-two versions in Virginia alone!

In this popular ballad, Barbara Allan uses her last moments with Graeme, on his deathbed, to remind him that he slighted her. Yet, when she returns home, it is only to die tomorrow, because Graeme, her own true love, died today. (Actually, this ballad is still popular, especially among people of Scottish descent. It commonly appears on recordings of Scottish songs.)

⑱ Primary Sources
Folk Ballads

1. Direct students' attention to lines 5 and 6, and read these lines aloud.
2. Then, **ask** students the Primary Sources question: What does the phrase "his man" tell you about the society of the time? **Possible response:** Servants were viewed either as the property of their masters or as inextricably bound to them—not as independent individuals.

⑲ Reading Check
Answer: Sir John sends his man to summon Barbara Allan to come to his bedside because he knows he is dying.

Differentiated Instruction for Universal Access

Strategy for Less Proficient Readers
Have students make a flowchart of the actions presented in the ballad. Each stanza should be summarized in one phrase or short sentence. Help students use context clues and the footnote definitions to understand what is happening. When all the summaries are complete, help students put the actions in chronological order.

Enrichment for Advanced Readers
Have students reread the ballad, looking at the order in which the events are presented. **Ask** students to compare this to the previous ballads. Which are in chronological order and which are not? Is there a difference in how one learns of the actions presented? Discuss the effects of, and possible artistic purposes for, retelling past events out of order. Students may also explore this topic further by examining films that present events out of chronological order and discussing the filmmaker's aim in using this technique.

209

Primary Sources

Folk Ballad

1. Have a student read aloud the last stanza of "Barbara Allan."

2. Then, **ask** students the Primary Sources questions: Who speaks the dialogue in the last stanza? What general purpose does all the dialogue in the ballad serve? **Possible responses:** Barbara Allan speaks the dialogue in the last stanza. The dialogue in the ballad serves to express the internal feelings of the characters, such as Sir John's heartsickness and Barbara Allan's remorse at the end of the poem.

ASSESS

Answers

Before students respond, you may wish to have them write a brief objective summary of the selection. As they answer the questions below, remind them to support their answers with evidence from the text.

1. (a) He is sick because of Barbara Allan. (b) She acts unconcerned because he slighted her in public. (c) She is controlling her feelings for him.

2. At the end of the poem, Barbara Allan reveals that she loves Sir John, so it is possible that his death inspired her emotions.

3. (a) Barbara Allan realizes that she loves Sir John, but now it is too late since he has died; in her remorse she wants to die. (b) The ultimate expression of love is to die for love. (c) Students may appreciate and agree with this romantic sentiment, or they may find it too extreme.

4. (a) Sir John slights Barbara Allan, Sir John realizes his love and sends for Barbara Allan, Barbara Allan refuses him because of the earlier slight, Sir John dies of heartsickness, Barbara Allan realizes her love too late. (b) The common folk may have felt that satisfaction in love was important because unrequited love could have a detrimental effect on one's physical health.

210

---

25 And slowly, slowly rase she up,
  And slowly, slowly left him;
 And sighing said she could not stay,
  Since death of life had reft[6] him.

 She had not gane a mile but twa,[7]
30   When she heard the dead-bell knellin',
 And every jow[8] that the dead-bell ga'ed[9]
  It cried, "Woe to Barbara Allan!"

➍ "O mother, mother, make my bed,
  O make it soft and narrow:
35 Since my love died for me today,
  I'll die for him tomorrow."

Primary Sources
Folk Ballad Who speaks the dialogue in the last stanza? What general purpose does all the dialogue in the ballad serve?

---

6. **reft** deprived.
7. **not . . . twa** gone but two miles.
8. **jow** stroke.
9. **ga'ed** made.

Critical Reading

Cite textual evidence to support your responses.

© 1. **Key Ideas and Details** **(a)** What reason does Sir John give for his ailment? **(b)** What reason does Barbara Allan give for acting unconcerned about his plight? **(c) Interpret:** What is another reason she might put on a show of indifference?

© 2. **Key Ideas and Details** **Interpret:** Do you think Barbara Allan loved Sir John before her visit, or do you think the knowledge that he is dying inspires her love? Explain.

© 3. **Integration of Knowledge and Ideas** **(a) Summarize:** Sum up Barbara Allan's realization and feelings in the final stanza. **(b) Interpret:** What does the ballad suggest is the ultimate expression of love? **(c) Evaluate:** Do you agree with this view? Why or why not?

© 4. **Integration of Knowledge and Ideas** **(a) Analyze:** What chain of causes and effects leads to the outcome of the story in this ballad? **(b) Infer:** What do these events suggest about attitudes toward love among the common folk who listened to ballads? Explain.

Enrichment: Analyzing Music

Medieval Music

Many modern musical artists seek to preserve musical traditions of the past by recording music from various eras, including medieval music. Find recordings by groups that specialize in medieval music, looking especially for songs that feature the instruments described on page 211. Play selections from these songs for the class.

Activity: Analyze Medieval Music As you play the recordings, have students take notes in the **Enrichment: Analyzing Music** worksheet, *Professional Development Guidebook*, page 236. After the recordings are over, have students share their reactions to the music. Then discuss which musical selections students would choose to accompany each ballad, and the reasons for each choice.

The Sound of Medieval Music

Nobody knows for sure when the old English and Scottish folk ballads were first composed, who their authors were, or how they were performed. Based on versions in circulation today, we can guess that the narratives were sung and that the singers probably accompanied themselves on string instruments such as harps or lutes. Musicians playing woodwinds similar to recorders and flutes, as well as percussion instruments like the tabor, may have joined in. A bagpiper might even have contributed an interlude between verses.

Medieval musicians tuned their instruments differently from the way most Western musicians do today, and were probably influenced by Middle Eastern scales. The Islamic rule of the Iberian Peninsula (711–1492) and the Crusades (1095–1291) had introduced Europeans to Arabic vocal and instrumental traditions. During the Middle Ages, North African and Middle Eastern tonalities probably colored much of the music in Europe and the British Isles.

▲ Medieval musicians often combined string instruments with drums, horns, and bagpipes.

CONNECT TO THE LITERATURE

How would music enhance or detract from the stories in these ballads? Explain.

BAGPIPES
In the Middle Ages, bagpipes were played throughout Britain and Scotland as well as India and North Africa. With its loud, plaintive sound, it was the perfect instrument for the outdoors.

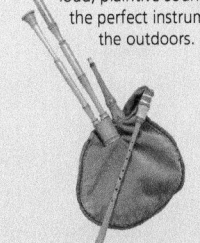

PIPE and TABOR
The pipe and tabor could be played by one person, who beat the tabor with one hand, while playing the pipe with the other. The tabor, a simple drum, is still used in the British Isles.

HARP
The word *harp* comes from Anglo-Saxon and Old German and originally meant, "to pluck." Triangular harps were used in Scotland as far back as the 9ᵗʰ century. Strings were made of twisted animal gut, horsehair, or even silk.

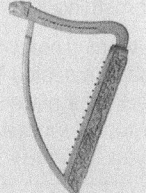

LUTE and PLECTRUM
The European lute was the predecessor to the modern guitar. It was an offspring of the oud, a stringed instrument introduced into Spain by the Arabs, during Islamic rule (711–1492). Like the oud, the early medieval lute was plucked with a pencil-thin tool called a plectrum.

Primary Sources: Ballads **211**

The Sound of Medieval Music

The instruments that medieval musicians used to accompany their ballads were, for the most part, small and easily portable. This was for a reason—musicians traveled from place to place, spreading news and popular ballads around the country. At one point in time, nobles would employ minstrels (the name for court musicians) to entertain them. However, minstrels were gradually replaced by troubadours, or traveling musicians. These musicians performed their songs for both nobles and the common people.

Connect to the Literature

Possible response: It is possible that music might distract some listeners from the lyrics of the ballads. However, it is most likely that music enhanced people's enjoyment and understanding of the stories in the ballads, since the music could shape and enhance the emotional impact of the stories.

Differentiated Instruction   for Universal Access

Culturally Responsive Instruction

Culture Focus Students are likely to feel a disconnect between the concerns of their daily lives and much of the subject matter of the ballads. To help bridge this gap, find modern songs—preferably current songs that students know and enjoy, whether the songs are rap, country, pop, punk, or some other genre—that contain similar themes to those of the ballads in this text. For example, a song about a doomed relationship might be paired with "Barbara Allan," or a song about a lover's betrayal might be paired with "Lord Randall." Display the lyrics for one ballad along with the lyrics for the similarly themed song. Discuss with the class how the lyrics for the ballad might be changed to express the same events and themes in more modern language, and how the lyrics of the modern song might be changed to fit the patterns exhibited in the ballad. Emphasize that people in the Middle Ages experienced similar emotions and situations to many that we experience today, but the different literary conventions of that time resulted in these emotions being expressed in a different form.

Comparing Primary Sources

1. **Possible response:** Paston's letters express indignation and sadness at the violence done to her family's property, while the ballads treat death matter-of-factly. The sadness expressed in the ballads is only in relation to death as a result of lovesickness or when it prevents love from being realized.

2. **Possible response:** Letters: Specific audience, personal letter form, purpose was to convey personal information. Ballads: General audience, song form, purpose was to entertain. Both: Purpose was to communicate news and information.

3. **Possible response:** The letters have more detailed and historically reliable information about people and places. However, the ballads contain reliable information about cultural values and daily life via inference.

Vocabulary Acquisition and Use

New Vocabulary

1. A kind person will succor the poor and needy.

2. An invading army will assault a village.

3. A remnant would be the last piece.

4. A paper can be more easily torn asunder.

Content-Area Vocabulary

1. False, because a measure contains a certain number of beats

2. True, because the melody is the tune of a song.

3. False, because a bar is just a visible divider on a piece of written music.

4. True, because aldermen were officers in power.

5. False, because to certify something is to say it is true.

Etymology Study

In addition to *looted*, two synonyms of *ransacked* are *ravished*, which means "to seize and carry away by force" and *pillaged*, which means "to deprive of money or property through violence."

212

Letters • Ballads

Comparing Primary Sources

Refer to your Note-Taking Guide to complete these questions.

1. How are the perspectives on death and violence expressed in Paston's letters and in the ballads similar and different? Cite specific details to support your analysis.

2. Using a Venn diagram like this one, compare and contrast the letters and ballads with regard to their forms, audiences, and purposes.

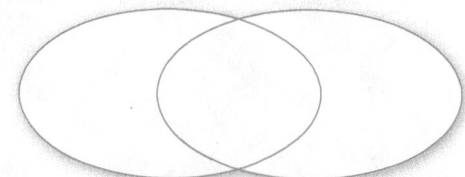

Paston Letters   Ballads

3. **(a)** Cite two questions about life in England during the Middle Ages that these texts can help you answer. Explain. **(b)** Which texts do you find more informative, and in what ways?

Vocabulary Acquisition and Use

New Vocabulary Answer each question. Then, explain how your understanding of the italicized vocabulary word helped you answer.

1. Who will *succor* the poor and needy, a kind person or a cruel one?

2. Who will *assault* a village, an invading army or a tired traveler?

3. Would a *remnant* of a meat loaf be the first piece or the last?

4. Which can more easily be torn *asunder*, a stone or a piece of paper?

Content-Area Vocabulary Use your knowledge of the italicized vocabulary words to decide whether each statement is true or false. Explain your answers.

1. A *measure* generally contains just one note.

2. To teach someone a song, you might hum the *melody*.

3. The *bar* tells you how quickly or slowly to play a piece of music.

4. *Aldermen* generally had influence in their communities.

5. When you *certify* something, you challenge it in court.

Etymology Study The word *ransacked*, from the Old Norse *rann*, meaning "house," and *saka*, meaning "seek," comes from the common medieval practice of attacking a place in search of valuables. A synonym of *ransacked* often used today is *looted*. Use a print or an online thesaurus to find two more synonyms for this word.

Common Core State Standards

Writing
7. Conduct short as well as more sustained research projects to answer a question or solve a problem; narrow or broaden the inquiry when appropriate; synthesize multiple sources on the subject, demonstrating understanding of the subject under investigation.
8. Gather relevant information from multiple authoritative print and digital sources, using advanced searches effectively; assess the strengths and limitations of each source in terms of the task, purpose, and audience; integrate information into the text selectively to maintain the flow of ideas, avoiding plagiarism and overreliance on any one source and following a standard format for citation.

Language
6. Acquire and use accurately general academic and domain-specific words and phrases, sufficient for reading, writing, speaking, and listening at the college and career readiness level; demonstrate independence in gathering vocabulary knowledge when considering a word or phrase important to comprehension or expression.

Enrichment: Investigating Language

The History of English

The original inhabitants of the British Isles spoke Celtic languages, but as various peoples invaded and conquered, the languages spoken on these islands morphed and evolved, incorporating features of Latin, Anglo-Saxon, and Norse languages. The earliest variety of English, called Old English, was first spoken around 400 or 500 AD. The language incorporated other foreign influences, particularly French, and slowly evolved to become Middle English, which was spoken between about 1000 and 1400 AD. A variety of English close to today's modern English has been spoken since around 1500 AD; Shakespeare wrote in modern English.

Activity: Word Study Have individual students or pairs choose an English word that has its origins in another language and research the history of the word's use in English. Suggest that students record information in the **Enrichment: Investigating Language** worksheet, *Professional Development Guidebook*, page 234.

Research Task

Topic: The Manor in Medieval England

Margaret Paston and her husband owned several significant properties, including two manor houses—the Hellesdon Manor and the Manor at Gresham. A manor was more than just a house. Under Feudalism, it was the center—both physical and symbolic—of the related economic system called Manorialism.

Assignment: With a group, write a **research report** on the English manor and the social order it represented. Discuss how key architectural elements reflect economic and legal relationships between the occupants of the manor and the people who lived in the surrounding area. Consider the following items:

- The relationship of the manor house to the surrounding land
- Activities, such as legal proceedings, that took place in a manor home
- The typical layout of the manor home, including the great hall, and the uses of these features
- Changes in manor homes as Feudalism waned in England

Formulate your research plan. In a group, brainstorm to formulate research questions about English manors and Manorialism. Then, discuss and decide on a plan to answer those questions.

Gather sources. Use library and computer searches to locate and explore a full range of relevant sources that answer the research questions. Organize the information into categories that address specific aspects of your topic. For all sources you consult, keep records that include the information you will need to construct thorough citations.

Synthesize information. When you synthesize information, you can decide which ideas and evidence to use and which to discard, arriving at the best response to your research question. A graphic organizer can clarify information and help you to compare and contrast it. For example, by listing specific features of a typical manor, you can better understand the picture of medieval life they convey.

Model: Using a Chart to Synthesize Information

Item	Description	Picture of Culture It Conveys

Organize and present your ideas. Write your report on the English manor and Manorialism. Account for both the physical features of these structures as well as the social, legal, and economic system they represent. Include specific examples, and include graphic elements that will help your readers understand your ideas and evidence. Be sure to cite all sources, both print and electronic, accurately.

RESEARCH TIP

There are many online sites dealing with specific English manor homes. You may want to include graphics from these sites and cite them in your report.

Use a checklist like the one shown to evaluate your work.

Research Checklist

☐ Have I answered the research questions?
☐ Have I organized information to support my central ideas?
☐ Have I accurately and thoroughly cited my sources?
☐ Have I presented my reasons clearly?

Research Task **213**

The Manor in Medieval England

Introduce the Assignment

1. Review the assignment. Point out that the assignment calls for a research report about the connection between the English manor and the legal and economic relationships of Feudalism.

2. Have students formulate their research plans by turning the assignment into a series of questions: What was the relationship of the manor house to the surrounding land? What activities took place in a manor home? What was the typical layout of the manor home? How did manor homes change over time?

Guide Student Research

1. Students should explore a range of relevant print and online sources. Additionally, they should make sure that they are using reliable sources. Online, these will primarily be identified by URLs ending with *.edu* and *.org*.

2. Remind students to distinguish between factual data and complex inferences—interpretations of the significance of the facts.

Think Aloud: Model the Skill

Say to students:

When I am researching information, I do not write down everything I read. I ask myself, "What does this say about my topic?" For example, if I read about the kinds of entertainment enjoyed by the lord and lady of the manor, I consider what that says about the social order and culture of medieval England.

Guide Student Writing

1. Have students use the chart they have completed as they develop their reports.

2. Students might include a diagram in their report to illustrate the manor house and surrounding areas. The diagram can act as an organizing feature for a discussion of the social, legal, and economic aspects of manorialism.

213

Common Core State Standards

• Writing 3, 3.b, c, d, e; 5, 6
• Language 2.a, b

Introducing the Writing Assignment

Review the assignment and the criteria, using the instruction on the student page.

What Do You Notice?

1. Read the excerpt from "Introduction to *Frankenstein*." Discuss the passage with students.

2. Have a student read the highlighted sentence aloud. **Ask** what makes the sentence special. (**Possible responses:** its figurative language; its brevity; its pointed expression)

3. Direct students' attention to the subordinate clause "I had to myself" at the end of this sentence. Then, **ask** how this clause functions in the sentence. (**Answer:** as an adjective) **Ask** what word this clause modifies. (**Answer:** *room*)

4. Have students recall a room they had to themselves. **Ask** what feelings this room gave them. (**Possible responses:** a sense of belonging, privacy, ownership, and attachment) Then, ask what the author suggests about fear by comparing it to her only room to herself. (**Possible responses:** Fear triggered by scary movies and tales gave the author her own private place away from other family members.)

5. Suggest that students occasionally end a sentence in their narratives with a brief adjective clause.

Burton Raffel on Autobiographical Narratives

Show students Segment 3 on Burton Raffel on the *See It!* DVD or via the link in the **Enriched Online Student Edition** at www.PHLitOnline.com. Discuss the "creative room" Raffel finds in translating, and suggest that students can find room for creativity in writing autobiographical narratives.

214

Write a Narrative

Autobiographical Narrative The best stories are often true—they tell about real events in a writer's life. From memories of childhood to funny anecdotes to dramatic encounters, true stories touch and inspire us. Such stories are called **autobiographical narratives.** Follow the steps outlined in this workshop to write your own autobiographical narrative.

Assignment Write an autobiographical narrative about an event in your life that marked a significant change or led to an important insight.

What to Include Your autobiographical narrative should include the following elements:

• Characters, with a focus on one main character—you, the writer
• A setting with specifically located scenes and incidents and with *concrete sensory details* such as sights, sounds, and smells
• A *sequence of events* that forms a plot and whose *significance* is clear
• Conflict between characters or between a character and another force
• Insights that you gained from the experience

To preview the criteria on which your autobiographical narrative may be assessed, see the rubric on page 221.

To get a feel for autobiographical narratives, read this mentor text in which Elizabeth McCracken describes the thrill of scary stories. Notice how she uses the idea of a "room" in both a literal and a figurative way.

from: Introduction to *Frankenstein*

Like most seven-year-olds, I was never really alone except in dreams. Someone was always in a nearby room. I liked the terrifying movies I saw on TV, so many different versions of Frankenstein—Frankenstein, Bride of Frankenstein, Abbott and Costello Meet Frankenstein. I liked fairy tales with dark woodcuts of dense forests that might hide any number of monsters. Fear was the only room I had to myself.

Common Core State Standards

Writing
3. Write narratives to develop real or imagined experiences or events using effective technique, well-chosen details, and well-structured event sequences.
3.d. Use telling details to convey a vivid picture of the experiences, events, setting, and/or characters.
5. Develop and strengthen writing as needed by planning, focusing on addressing what is most significant for a specific purpose and audience.

WRITE GUY
Jeff Anderson, M.Ed.

What Do You Notice?

Read the highlighted sentence several times. Then, with a partner, discuss the qualities that make it special. You might consider the following elements:

• Word choice
• Sentence Length
• Rhythm
• Structure

Share your group's observations with the class.

Teaching Resources

Unit 1 Resources
All Writing Workshop, pp. 160–161
All *Common Core Companion,* pp. 208–218; 226–234; 318–321
All *Professional Development Guidebook*
Rubrics for Self-Assessment: Autobiographical Narrative, pp. 248–249

All *Graphic Organizer Transparencies*
Rubric for Self-Assessment: Autobiographical Narrative, p. 33
Plot Diagram, p. 297
Three-Column Chart, p. 299

All *See It!* DVD
Burton Raffel, Segments 3 and 4

All resources are available at **www.PHLitOnline.com.**

Prewriting and Planning

Choosing Your Topic

To choose an event for your essay, use one of these strategies:

- **Listing** Create a chart with three columns, labeled *People*, *Places*, and *Events*. List memorable parts of your life under each column. Then, look for connections among the items you listed. When you find a connection, circle the items and draw an arrow to link them. Review your connections for narrative ideas.

- **Using Sentence Starters** Complete these sentences to generate ideas:

  - The funniest thing happened when _____.
  - My favorite holiday was _____.
  - My strongest memory from childhood is _____.

Narrowing Your Topic

Find your insight. Make your topic more specific by focusing on one idea you want to convey. Narrow a general topic to focus on one key event that highlights a meaningful insight.

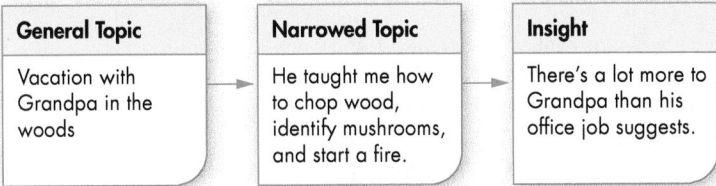

General Topic	Narrowed Topic	Insight
Vacation with Grandpa in the woods	He taught me how to chop wood, identify mushrooms, and start a fire.	There's a lot more to Grandpa than his office job suggests.

Gathering Details

Look for concrete details. List specific details you will include. Consider sensory details that convey the sights, sounds, and smells of the scenes. Look for details about characters' actions, movements, thoughts, words, and gestures. As you collect details, think about where each one will fit best in your narrative. Estimate about how much space and emphasis you will give to specific elements. The plan shown works for many narratives.

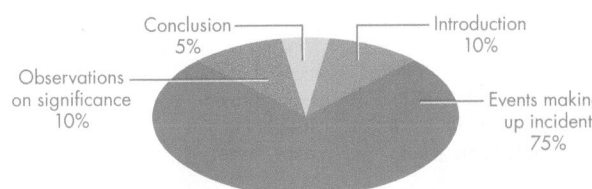

Conclusion 5%
Introduction 10%
Observations on significance 10%
Events making up incident 75%

Applying Understanding by Design Principles

Clarifying Expected Outcomes: Using Rubrics

- Before students begin work on this assignment, have them preview the **Rubric for Self-Assessment**, page 221, to learn what qualities their autobiographical narratives must have. A copy of this rubric appears in the *Professional Development Guidebook*, page 248.

- Review the criteria in the Rubric with the class. Before students use the Rubric to assess their own writing, work with them to rate the Student Model (page 220) using the Rubric.

- If you wish to assess students' autobiographical narratives with either a 4-point or 6-point scoring rubric, see the *Professional Development Guidebook*, pages 248–249.

Prewriting and Planning

1. Introduce the prewriting strategies using the instruction on the student page.

2. Have students apply the strategies to choose and narrow a topic and gather details.

Teaching the Strategies

1. Use the Three-Column Chart (*Graphic Organizer Transparencies*, page 299) to model the Listing strategy. **Ask** volunteers to complete the chart on the board. Distribute the chart.

2. For students using Sentence Starters to generate ideas, suggest examples.

3. Encourage students to create charts as they gather details. Charts can list sensory details or chronology.

Think Aloud: Model Choosing Your Topic

To model the strategy of choosing a topic, use the following "think aloud." Say to students:

Before I write about experience, I like to go through photo albums. Seeing pictures that remind me of my life helps me reconnect with who I was. This gives me ideas.

Six Traits Focus

✔	Ideas		Word Choice
✔	Organization		Sentence Fluency
	Voice		Conventions

PH WRITING COACH | Grade 12

Students will find additional instruction on narrative in Chapter 5.

Prentice Hall **EssayScorer**

A writing prompt for this mode of writing can be found on the *Prentice Hall EssayScorer* at **www.PHLitOnline.com**.

215

Drafting

1. Introduce the drafting strategies, using the instruction on the student page.

2. Have students apply the strategies as they draft their autobiographical narratives.

Teaching the Strategies

1. Explain to students that openings are strong only if they are appropriate for the narrative. For example, if the narrative focuses on a relationship, it might be appropriate to start with a character. If the narrative focuses on an event, it might be more appropriate to start with dialogue.

2. To help students pace their narratives effectively, use the Plot Diagram (*Graphic Organizer Transparencies,* page 297). Recommend that students keep expositions short and begin to build toward their climaxes quickly. Point out that in a test-taking situation, getting bogged down in background details will eat up time. (For more on details, see Burton Raffel's comments on the next page.)

3. Review the models of flat and vivid conflicts with the class. Explain that to be striking, a conflict needs more than vivid language; it should have significance beyond the superficial or obvious. Students should focus their narratives on conflicts that were important to their lives and have had a lasting effect on them.

4. **Ask** students to read their closing paragraphs to the class. Discuss what strategy each closing uses. Do the closings offer epilogues, sum up what the characters learned, or answer questions that would otherwise go unanswered? Do the closings add a finishing touch for readers, or would a different ending work better?

Six Traits Focus

✔	Ideas	✔	Word Choice
✔	Organization		Sentence Fluency
✔	Voice		Conventions

Drafting

Shaping Your Writing

Start out strong. Catch your readers' interest with a strong opening. Consider the options in this chart.

Opening Strategy	Example
Introduce a Character: A description of a character is effective if your narrative centers on a relationship.	Bob doesn't say much, no matter what may be going on, but when you see that gleam in his eye, you know you're in trouble.
Focus on Setting: This approach works well if time and place are critical elements.	The wind whistled through the cracks in the attic window.
Begin with Dialogue: An intriguing line of dialogue can quickly pull readers in.	"I said, did anybody leave this package on the counter?"

Pace your writing. Make sure you do not get bogged down in insignificant details. Establish background information quickly and then set your main incident in motion.

Providing Elaboration

Highlight a striking conflict. Describe the central conflict vividly, showing your readers the reason for the conflict instead of just telling them.

Flat: Grandpa wanted me to chop wood, but I didn't know how.

Vivid: "Henry, do me a favor and chop up a few logs, OK?" I nodded and hurried out to the woodpile so Grandpa wouldn't see the terror on my face. What did I know about chopping wood? The ax taunted me. Just thinking about swinging it made my toes hurt because I knew the ax was way more likely to land on my foot than the log.

End well. Devise an interesting closing. You might put the finishing touch on your story or leave readers hoping for more. Consider ending with an epilogue about what happened after the incident, a summary of your insights, or an unanswered question related to the conflict.

> **Model: Devising a Good Closing**
> I was sweating and my muscles ached, but there was my pile of chopped-up logs. I felt proud, as if this two-foot-high stack of wood was a house I had built with my own hands. The discarded splinters seemed like my own fears, cast away in the act of chopping.

The writer ends on a note of accomplishment, providing an insight into the experience.

Common Core State Standards

Writing
3.b. Use narrative techniques, such as dialogue, pacing, description, reflection, and multiple plot lines, to develop experiences, events, and/or characters.
3.e. Provide a conclusion that follows from and reflects on what is experienced, observed, or resolved over the course of the narrative.

Strategies for Test-Taking

Students may encounter standardized tests that require them to write about personal experiences—in other words, to write autobiographical narratives. Remind students not to waste time agonizing over a topic when faced with such prompts. They should choose topics with an eye toward drafting. Ideal topics for timed writing situations will have striking conflicts that drive the pace, as well as clear climaxes and resolutions. For example, a friend with whom you were once close but from whom you have drifted apart slowly would probably not be an ideal topic. A brief but dramatic experience, such as a sudden loss, would be a more effective topic. Often, the farther back students go in their lives, the clearer the situation will be.

Writers on Writing

Burton Raffel On Shaping a Narrative

Burton Raffel is the author of the introduction to *Beowulf* (p. 36).

This is an excerpt from an autobiographical piece I wrote about thirty years ago. It tries to re-create, in adult language, some of those well-rubbed but rarely verbalized feelings that all small children surely have. Children are not simply the "small adults" that our civilization used to think they were. Nor is childhood merely another, though different, route to the same landing place.

"I realized that I was inventing a reality that wasn't real."

—*Burton Raffel*

from *Out in the Backyard of My Mind*

When I think of myself, as a small child, I remember, first, the sensation of offensive clothing—floppy clothing. Clothing buttoned and snapped and fastened in places I could not reach and affixed for reasons I knew I would not approve of if I could have understood what they were. I remember my shirts strapped to my back, somehow; and I remember ghastly knickers of worn corduroy, hanging baggy at the knees; and floppy coats that had belonged to cousins and uncles unseen, handed down, a little shabbier and floppier each time, until they came to me. I remember the faintly dank smell of cheap wool (mixed with what?), and especially its coarse, hairy feel—and the good, powdery smell and full softness of a big brown automobile lap robe, always and still called "the horse blanket." Skin was no better: if I was ever without clothing, in those days, I do not remember it, nor remember any pleasure from it. And I can remember hiding from my nakedness. Not just the way all little children do, sometimes, but compulsively, fiercely. One summer—I was eight, I think—my mother had a serious operation and I spent two months with a relative. Two summer months, and hot work of it, playing outdoors, but I did not know how to take a bath by myself and I would not let anyone give me a bath; no one unauthorized was to be allowed to see me unclothed.

> These first two sentences are not "laundry lists": their detail is simply what they, and the piece as a whole, are about.

> The details of the third sentence introduce a quiet shift in focus, from myself to the exterior world: walking, first, and then cars.

> The last sentences move the focus of the piece even further into society.

Writing Workshop **217**

Burton Raffel on Shaping a Narrative

Review the passage on the student page with the class, using Burton Raffel's comments to deepen students' understanding of the process of writing an autobiographical narrative.

Teaching from the Professional Model

1. Show students Segment 4 on Burton Raffel on *From the Author's Desk DVD* or from this page in the **Enriched Online Student Edition**. Discuss the relationships that Raffel sees between the classic literature he teaches and translates and the daily experiences of contemporary students and readers.

2. Point out to students that the subject of this excerpt from the autobiographical *Out in the Backyard of My Mind* is not a character, an event, or a setting, but the childhood experience of wearing clothes. Explain that any important aspect of a writer's life and experiences can be a compelling topic for an autobiographical narrative.

3. Call students' attention to Raffel's comments about *Out in the Backyard of My Mind.* Be sure students recognize that the details Raffel uses are central to the narrative. Tell students that they should enrich their own autobiographical narratives with details that are important to their topics.

Differentiated Instruction for Universal Access

Support for Special-Needs Students
Before students read the excerpt, explain that Raffel uses vivid details to express feelings he had as a child. Read the first two sentences with students, making sure they understand that the details deal only with Raffel's feelings. Have them read the next two sentences on their own. Point out that in these sentences, Raffel refers to his relatives, to walking, and to riding in a car. Then have students read the rest of the excerpt. Guide them to see how Raffel's discomfort with clothes extends to a discomfort with the outside world.

Strategy for Less Proficient Readers
Have students reread the excerpt from *Out in the Backyard of My Mind,* writing down every sensory detail they find. Review the list with students, and guide them to recognize the points at which Raffel moves from his own feelings to his actions, and then to his interactions with other people. Suggest that in their own autobiographical narratives, students give details both of their own feelings and the outside world.

Revising

1. Introduce the revising strategies, using the instruction on the student page.

2. Have students apply the strategies as they revise their autobiographical narratives.

Teaching the Strategies

1. Point out that many autobiographical narratives unfold in more than one time and place. Ask students to list the settings—the times and locations—that appear in their narratives.

2. Use the Revising to Clarify Time and Place model to demonstrate the revising strategy for students. Be sure they recognize that shifts in time and place need descriptive words and transitional phrases to be clear.

3. Have students work on the revising strategy in pairs. You may wish to have peers review drafts before students star time and location shifts and underline transitional words and phrases. Then, have students conduct peer reviews for clarity after revising the structures of their narratives.

4. After students revise the structures of their narratives, have them focus on eliminating unnecessary changes in verb tense. Tell students to look for changes in tense where they have made shifts in place and, especially, time. Passages they have revised for clarity may still have unnecessary shifts in tense.

5. Tell students to pay special attention to tenses of such verbs as *to be* (*is/are, was/were*) and *to have* (*has/have, had*).

Six Traits Focus

Ideas		✔	Word Choice
✔	Organization		Sentence Fluency
	Voice		Conventions

Revising

Revising Your Overall Structure

Clarify the time and place. Be sure that you have clearly indicated *shifts in time and place* and have *paced actions* to accommodate these *changes*.

1. Star any place where the time or location changes.

2. Underline in red the words you have used to indicate the change. Have a partner check to make sure that each shift is clear and complete and that the actions do not seem abrupt.

3. Revise by adding transitional phrases or descriptive words. Insert a paragraph break to highlight the impact of a time or place shift.

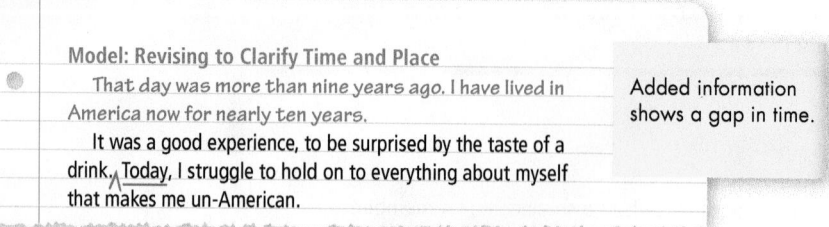

Model: Revising to Clarify Time and Place

That day was more than nine years ago. I have lived in America now for nearly ten years.

It was a good experience, to be surprised by the taste of a drink. Today, I struggle to hold on to everything about myself that makes me un-American.

Added information shows a gap in time.

Peer Review: Share your draft with a classmate. Explain why you made your revision choices, and ask your reader to give you feedback about the time and place shifts you included.

Revising Your Content

Add significance. Consider conveying the significance of events to your audience by adding an ***interior monologue,*** in which a character reacts to events and reveals his or her feelings and thoughts about them.

Revising Your Sentences

Eliminate unnecessary tense changes. Even though you may be moving back and forth in time in your narrative, do not change tenses unnecessarily. Do not shift tenses without a good reason.

Original Sentence:

It was midnight when the vote tally is finally complete.

Corrected Sentence:

It was midnight when the vote tally was finally completed.

Common Core State Standards

Writing

3.c. Use a variety of techniques to sequence events so that they build on one another to create a coherent whole and build toward a particular tone and outcome.

5. Develop and strengthen writing as needed by revising, focusing on addressing what is most significant for a specific purpose and audience.

Strategies for Test-Taking

Students may be expected to revise the compositions they write for standardized tests. However, time constraints of the test-taking situation put strict limits on how much revising students can complete. Suggest to students that the most time-effective revision strategy is planning and, especially, drafting carefully. For example, students should pay close attention to shifts in time or location as they write their initial drafts. They may mark these shifts as they draft, making them easier to review. Rather than rewriting the entire composition, students should make simple changes to clarify setting shifts directly on their drafts. You may wish to have students practice by giving them 15 minutes to plan, write, and revise an opening paragraph for an autobiographical narrative.

Developing Your Style

Vivid Word Choice

Word Choice Choose strong verbs and adjectives that bring the characters, events, setting, and conflict of your autobiographical narrative to life. Avoid words that are weak, dull, or vague.

Weak: I drank the soda and it was delicious.

Strong: I took a sip of the soda and savored its tangy surprises: a tart kick of lime and extra-fizzy bubbles that tickled the inside of my mouth and made me feel as if I were smelling a lime air freshener.

Instead of settling for general, overused verbs and adjectives, take time to find precise, vivid examples.

Find It in Your Reading

Read the selection "Letters of Margaret Paston" on pages 201–204.

1. Find two sentences from Paston's letters in which the author uses strong verbs and two sentences in which the author uses strong adjectives.

2. Choose two words from the selection that you find particularly vivid.

sped — ran — dashed

sauntered — walked — strutted

went — ambled — slithered

Apply It to Your Writing

Review the draft of your autobiographical narrative, focusing on your choice of words. Follow these steps as you read:

- Circle any words that seem dull, weak, or vague. Also circle any uses of jargon or clichés.
- Challenge yourself to replace each circled word with a more vivid alternative, especially one that brings a setting to life with concrete sensory details of sights, sounds, and smells.
- Use a thesaurus or dictionary, and check to be sure that your new words accurately reflect what you want to say about your characters, setting, or conflict.

PH WRITING COACH
Further instruction and practice are available in *Prentice Hall Writing Coach*.

Developing Your Style

1. Introduce the concept of careful word choice to students, using the instruction on the student page.
2. Have students complete the Find It in Your Reading and Apply It to Your Writing activities.

Teaching the Strategies

1. Tell students that their autobiographical narratives will be more compelling if their word choice is as vivid as the characters and events their narratives describe.
2. Read the examples of weak and strong passages with the class. Point to the verb *tickled* and adjectives *tart, tangy,* and *extra-fizzy* as examples of strong, vivid word choices.
3. Explain to students that verbs and adjectives are often the weakest words in any piece of writing. Extensive use of common verbs such as *walked, ran,* and *went,* for example, can make their narratives overly general and dull. Tell students to pay special attention to verbs and adjectives as they revise for style.
4. Have students read the strong sentences they find in "Letters of Margaret Paston," pages 202–204. Write these sentences on the board, underlining the strongest words. Discuss with the class what Paston's vivid word choices add to her letters.
5. Tell students to use the Apply It to Your Writing strategy on their narratives. Point out that on standardized tests, they will have limited time for revising. In test-taking situations, students can look for weak word choices as they edit for grammar, usage, and mechanics.

Six Traits Focus

Ideas		✔ Word Choice
Organization		Sentence Fluency
Voice		Conventions

Strategies for
Improving Word Choice

Give students these suggestions for developing their style by focusing on vivid word choice.

- Prepare a list of strong, vivid words that you might want to include in your autobiographical narrative. Think about your topic, and write down any vivid words that come to mind. Strong verbs and adjectives will be especially useful.
- Look for places in your draft where words—especially verbs and adjectives—are vague, overly general, or repetitive. Mark these words for possible revision, and see whether any words from your list will fit in their places.
- Be careful not to overload your autobiographical narrative with vivid words. Your style should be strong and exciting, but not overblown. Too many vivid words will clutter your narrative, making your plot difficult to follow.

Student Model

Review the Student Model with the class, using the annotations to analyze the writer's incorporation of the elements of an autobiographical narrative.

Teaching the Strategies

1. Explain that the Student Model is an example and that autobiographical narratives may be longer.

2. Point out that Mircea Vlaicu's narrative unfolds at a specific time and place. **Ask** students to identify the setting.
Answer: The setting is a center aisle of a 747 sitting outside a Chicago airport.

3. Be sure students recognize that Mircea uses his description of the many choices of soda available to him to establish his main focus: the conflict of cultures he faces.

4. Discuss with the class how Mircea paces his narrative. Be sure students understand that the details about soda are not insignificant; they are essential to the experience he is describing.

5. Call students' attention to Mircea's use of sensory details and vivid word choices. Help them recognize how his language enriches the narrative.

6. Remind students that a strong closing is an important part of an autobiographical narrative. **Ask** them how Mircea closes his narrative.
Possible response: Mircea connects his experience on the plane with the insight he gained about how things often differ from their appearance.

Connecting to Real-Life Writing

Explain to students that many college applications will ask them to write about a significant event in their lives and how it has shaped them. Ask a volunteer to explain why a college might ask an applicant to write this kind of narrative. Guide students to recognize that these narratives can reveal a great deal about the writer's character and personal strengths. Point out that a challenge or a problem they have faced or a change they have gone through can be an excellent focus for these narratives.

220

Student Model: Mircea Viaicu, Palm Springs, CA

A Toast to the Future

I came to this country on a plane. Just a kid, not even eight years old yet, I sat on the center aisle of a huge 747 in Chicago waiting to fly to Los Angeles. These names—Chicago, Los Angeles—were abstract to me. All I knew was that I was in America, the place where everybody drives a nice car and lives in a great house or apartment and the bad guys always lose. At least, that was what the television back in Romania had shown me.

> Mircea clearly establishes the setting of his story.

I was very thirsty, sitting in that center aisle. I kept asking my mom when they were going to bring us drinks. I don't know how much time went by before the cart came around, but it finally arrived.

That moment was my first real encounter with America. There were so many cans to choose from, so many colors. I had no idea which one to take. I chose the blue one since blue was my favorite color. I opened it up and poured it in my clear plastic cup. The soda was also clear, and I was very disappointed. Out of all those different cans I had to choose club soda, a drink I already knew the taste of. But I was wrong. I took a sip, and to my joyous surprise, it was sweet and refreshing, and the bubbles tickled the inside of my mouth. It tasted nothing like club soda. It was a good experience, to be surprised by the taste of a drink.

> The narrative centers on the conflict of cultures.

> Mircea devotes several sentences to the choice of sodas, using pacing to focus his reader's attention and build interest.

That day was more than nine years ago. I have lived in America now for nearly ten years. I have since passed through feelings of isolation and fears of being different. I have learned to make friends and to lead life as I want to.

> Vivid sensory details draw a reader into Mircea's experience. See Developing Your Style, p. 219.

Today, I struggle to hold on to everything about myself that makes me un-American. I try not to forget the Romanian language, I try to remember that I was not born in America. I think about Romania every day. I will not forget it, ever. A Romanian flag hangs in my bedroom alongside pictures of American rock stars. The thought of my homeland always makes me feel a certain way. I feel a kind of bittersweet feeling, calm, a feeling of happiness. I picture a warm sunny day on which I am walking alone on the little winding street that surrounded our building complex.

When I think of the future, though, I have a simple hope. I hope the future will be like the moment one tastes the first sip of sweet, crisp, bubbly soda, when a second before it looked like just plain old club soda.

> Mircea clearly states the insight he has gained and poetically links it to the narrative.

220 From Legend to History (A.D. 449–1485)

Differentiated Instruction for Universal Access

EL Strategy for English Learners

Students may have had experiences similar to the one Mircea describes in his narrative on this page. Encourage students to focus on their experiences learning a new culture to help them generate a topic for their own autobiographical narrative. For example, they could describe an experience that, while familiar in their original country, differs greatly in the United States—as does Mircea's experience of drinking a soda.

Strategy for Advanced Writers

Encourage students to pay close attention to Mircea's use of sensory details in his narrative. Discuss the way strong, vivid words enhance the sensory images, helping readers to see the soda can and feel the soda in their mouths. Remind students that these details are connected to Mircea's central focus, the positive experience of a new culture. Point out that sensory details and strong word choice can make students' autobiographical narratives as compelling as Mircea's.

Editing and Proofreading

Focus on punctuation. To punctuate direct quotations, place commas or periods inside the final quotation mark and place semicolons or colons outside it. Place a question mark inside the closing quotation mark only if it is part of the quotation.

    Inside: My grandfather asked, "Where do you think you're going?"

    Outside: Will I be able to say "I'm sorry"?

Focus on spelling. When the prefix *ex-* means "out," do not use a hyphen after it: *extract, export, exhaust.* When it means "former," use a hyphen: *ex-president, ex-wife.*

Spiral Review: Conventions Earlier in this unit, you learned about correlative conjunctions (page 154). Check your narrative to be sure you have used those conventions correctly.

Publishing, Presenting, and Reflecting

Consider one of the following ways to share your writing with your classmates.

Maintain a portfolio. Follow your growth as a writer by keeping your autobiographical narrative with other works in a writing portfolio.

Publish a literary magazine. Collect your classmates' narratives for publication in a student magazine, which you might post on the Internet. Have writers provide illustrations and introductions for their works.

Reflect on your writing. Jot down your thoughts on the experience of writing an autobiographical narrative. Begin by answering this question: What did you learn about yourself as a writer by completing this narrative?

Rubric for Self-Assessment

Evaluate your reflective essay using the following criteria and rating scale.

Criteria	Rating Scale
Focus: How well do you describe yourself, the main character, and the other characters in your narrative?	1 2 3 4 5
Organization: How effectively do you organize the sequence of events?	1 2 3 4 5
Support/Elaboration: How well do you use details to describe scenes and events?	1 2 3 4 5
Style: How vivid is your word choice, especially your use of strong verbs and adjectives to bring characters, events, settings, and conflicts to life?	1 2 3 4 5
Conventions: How correct is your grammar, especially your use of punctuation?	1 2 3 4 5

Rating Scale: *not very* 1 2 3 4 5 *very*

Common Core State Standards

Writing

5. Develop and strengthen writing as needed by editing, focusing on addressing what is most significant for a specific purpose and audience.

6. Use technology, including the Internet, to produce, publish, and update individual or shared writing products in response to ongoing feedback, including new arguments or information.

Language

2.a. Observe hyphenation conventions.

2.b. Spell correctly.

PH WRITING COACH

Further instruction and practice are available in *Prentice Hall Writing Coach*.

Editing and Proofreading

1. Introduce the editing and proofreading focuses, using the instruction on the student page.

2. Have students read their autobiographical narratives carefully, marking them for line edits. Make sure they check for errors of the type noted on the student page.

Teaching the Strategies

1. Remind students that in timed writing situations, they will need to edit quickly. To do so, students should focus only on grammar, usage, and mechanics.

2. Explain that quotations often punctuate dialogue in autobiographical narratives. Review the rules for using quotation marks.

Six Traits Focus

Ideas		Word Choice	
Organization	✓	Sentence Fluency	
Voice		Conventions	✓

ASSESS

Publishing, Presenting, and Reflecting

1. Help students reserve time and space for a storytelling festival, possibly bringing in adults from the community.

2. Point out that the audience for a student magazine would include their classmates, teachers, and parents.

3. Before they begin writing in their journals, encourage students to discuss how their ideas have changed and evolved.

Strategies for Using Technology in Writing

Students may find it helpful to use computers as they plan a storytelling festival. They can use word processing programs to create advertisements, flyers, and schedules. Graphics programs can be used to design posters and maps of the event space. Students may want to use the Internet to promote their festival. Supervise students who want to create a Web site for the festival or send promotional e-mails.

Students interested in assembling and publishing a literary magazine will also find a computer to be useful. Most word processing programs offer features that will help students format a magazine. Students may want to illustrate their magazine with appropriate digital photographs. An appropriately supervised Web site might also serve as an excellent way to seek and receive submissions for the magazine.

Types of Prepositions

1. Present the four types of prepositions, using the instruction on the student page.

2. Review the examples of each type of preposition. Guide students to determine additional examples of proposition of fact, proposition of value, proposition of problem, and proposition of policy.

Identify Persuasive Techniques

1. Review with students the various persuasive techniques pertaining to Content and Message and their characteristics.

   • Explain that an ethical appeal gives validity to an argument because of the credibility of the speaker.

   • Have students brainstorm other examples of emotional appeals, such as ads that use pictures of exotic locations to sell vacation packages or pictures of adorable dogs to sell pet products.

   • Discuss how the use of logic gives validity to an argument and "sells" the idea by presenting statistics that support it. Explain that inductive reasoning moves from the specific to the general, while deductive reasoning moves from the general to the specific. Caution students to make sure that the two premises of a syllogism reach a true and logical conclusion.

Evaluate Persuasive Speech

Persuasive speech, also called argument, includes a range of uses, from a presidential address to a lawyer's closing remarks. Persuasion happens whenever one person speaks to convince another to think or act in a certain way.

Types of Propositions

Persuasive speech includes four types of propositions.

Propositions	Example
Fact—asserts that something is	Average annual temperatures have been rising.
Value—claims that something is good or bad or is better or worse than something else	Kenneth Branagh's adaptation of *Hamlet* is the best.
Problem—demonstrates that a problem exists	Our team's name, The Ants, is a problem because...
Policy—argues that something should be done	Our school should start a debate club.

Identify Persuasive Techniques

Persuasive Appeals Different types of persuasive speech rely on varied types of appeals, evidence, and patterns of logic:

   • **Ethos, an ethical appeal,** cites the speaker's authority, as in a famous surgeon endorsing a heart medicine.

   • **Pathos, an emotional appeal,** tugs at the audience's emotions, as in an ad that uses a smiling infant to sell baby food.

   • **Logos, a logical appeal,** applies reasoning and facts to build convincing arguments.

Syllogisms are arguments made up of two premises and a conclusion. Example: "All men are mortal. Socrates is a man. Socrates is mortal."

Inductive reasoning draws a conclusion from examples. Example: "I touched three icicles and they were cold. I think all icicles are cold."

Deductive reasoning applies a general principle to specific cases. Example: "I know ice is frozen, so I know this icicle will be cold."

Analogies are comparisons. A letter of recommendation comparing your writing to a professional's will probably create a good impression.

Common Core
State Standards

**Speaking and Listening
3.** Evaluate a speaker's point of view, reasoning, and use of evidence and rhetoric, assessing the stance, premises, links among ideas, word choice, points of emphasis, and tone used.

Identify Persuasive Techniques (continued)

Uses of Language Effective speakers use various techniques to achieve clarity, force, and aesthetic effect:

- **rhetorical questions:** questions not meant to be answered but used to establish solidarity with an audience
- **parallelism:** repetition of similar ideas in similar grammatical forms
- **figurative language:** nonliteral language, such as similes and metaphors, that add interest and encourage active listening

Negative Techniques Speakers may also resort to *negative persuasive techniques,* including the misuse of logic, in order to sway listeners. Many **logical fallacies,** such as those listed below, may seem plausible at first:

- *ad hominem* **attack:** an attack on a person's character
- **false causality:** the idea that A happened before B, so A caused B
- **red herring:** an irrelevant distraction from more important points
- **overgeneralization:** a conclusion based on too little evidence
- **bandwagon effect:** the idea that you should do something because everyone does it

Activities: Evaluate Persuasive Speech

Comprehension and Collaboration With a classmate, complete the following activities, using the evaluation form shown below to guide your work.

A. Find a persuasive speech in a play or on the Internet. Describe the proposition and evaluate the use of specific persuasive techniques.

B. Identify logical fallacies in three different speeches. Then, discuss why the speakers might have resorted to using fallacies.

Evaluation Form for Persuasive Speech

Name of Speech _____

Media Type _____

Intended Audience _____

Purpose _____

Type of Proposition _____

Appeal to Ethos _____

Appeal to Pathos _____

Appeal to Logos (Include syllogisms or analogies, if possible) _____

Uses of Language _____

Negative Persuasive Techniques _____

In your opinion, does this speaker argue persuasively and ethically? Why or why not? _____

Differentiated Instruction for Universal Access

Strategy for Less Proficient Readers

These students may have difficulty distinguishing among the four kinds of persuasive speeches. Encourage students, when they are listening to a persuasive speech, to consider what the speaker is trying to achieve by persuading the audience. Help students identify the purpose of each type of persuasive speech. A proposition of fact attempts to prove a claim about facts. A proposition of value attempts to apply values to facts. A proposition of problem attempts to create con-

cern to establish that a situation is an important problem. A proposition of policy attempts to support a course of action. By identifying the purpose of a particular speech, less proficient students can determine what kind of speech it is. For example, if the speech addresses the need for crosswalks to enable people to cross a busy street, students might say the speaker is trying to support a course of action and that the speech is a proposition of policy.

Identify Persuasive Techniques (cont.)

2. Review with students persuasive techniques pertaining to Uses of Language and their characteristics.

- Explain that rhetorical questions like *Could it be any easier?* establish a connection between speaker and audience.
- Give an example of parallelism, such as: *Scientists note that average temperatures are rising and greenhouse gas concentrations are increasing.*
- Discuss how similes and metaphors create connections between something new and something known.
- Review the various persuasive techniques pertaining to negative techniques.
- Explain how an *ad hominem* attack might be used in a political campaign.
- Explain that false causality shows a correlation between two seemingly related situations that are not, in fact, connected.
- Tell students that the expression *red herring* originated when it was suggested that someone drag a fish across the trail during a foxhunt to disguise the fox's scent and confuse the dogs.
- Point out that an overgeneralization does not explore specific points that would negate an argument.

Activities: Evaluate Persuasive Speech

1. Present the two activities. Help students find plays that incorporate persuasive speeches. Review negative techniques before students begin Activity B.

2. Have students fill out an evaluation form for both activities.

3. After students complete the Activity on the student page, have them discuss which types of persuasive speech and which persuasive techniques seemed especially effective.

4. To evaluate students' analyses, use the Analyzing Persuasive Techniques rubric, page 295 in the *Professional Development Guidebook.*

223

EXTEND

Common Core
State Standards

• Language 4.a, c, d

Using Dictionaries and Other Resources

1. Teach the skills, using the instruction and samples on the student page.

2. If possible, demonstrate the use of an electronic dictionary on computers in a lab or the classroom.

Think Aloud: Model the Skills

Say to students:

When I look up a word, I always check the etymology, which is the story of where the word comes from. Often, a word's origin grabs my interest and helps me remember the meaning. For example, I learn that *devout* comes from the Latin meaning "to vow." When I think of the fact that *devout* means "very religious," I imagine people saying wedding vows in a church, temple, or mosque. If I hear or read other forms of *devout,* I will think of vows and imagine a religious building, which will help me figure out the meaning of the word. For example, if Sara speaks *devoutly,* I know that she is speaking in a very religious manner (*Devout* means "very religious"; the suffix *–ly* means "in a ____ manner.").

Vocabulary Workshop

Common Core
State Standards

Using Dictionaries and Other Resources

A **dictionary** is a reference tool that contains information about words. Each entry lists the word's correct spelling and pronunciation, grammatical function, meanings, and etymology, or origin. **Print dictionaries** are organized alphabetically. **Electronic dictionaries** offer a search list or require you to enter your word. **Specialized dictionaries** define words and phrases in a particular field, such as medicine, law, art, or literature.

Sample Dictionary Entry

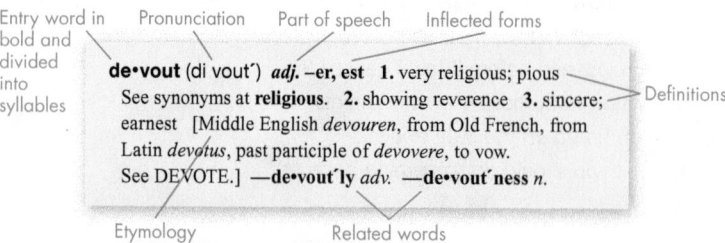

A **thesaurus** is a reference tool providing, for each entry, lists of synonyms and some antonyms. The synonyms share the *denotative,* or literal, meaning of the entry word. However, they do not always share the *connotative* meaning, or associations a word suggests. For example, *precise* and *prim* have similar meanings, but *precise* has a positive connotation while *prim* suggests a self-conscious fussiness. After choosing a synonym, it is a good idea to check its meaning in a dictionary to see how it will fit in your sentence.

Sample Thesaurus Entry

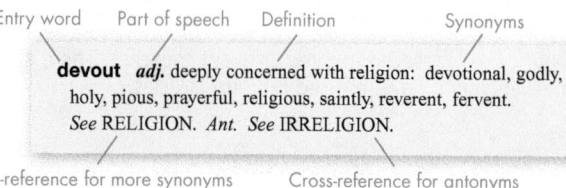

Practice

Directions: Answer each question as directed.

1. Use a dictionary to discover the etymology of *barbarous.* Analyze the word's origin and explain how it relates to the etymology of *brave.*

2. Analyze a thesaurus entry for *brave.* **(a)** Choose two words with positive connotations. Use each in a sentence about Beowulf or another epic hero. **(b)** Then, choose two synonyms with negative connotations. Use each in a sentence that illustrates its meaning.

3. Use a dictionary to trace the etymologies of these words: *shield, destiny, fame, hero, dragon, sword.* Which derive from Old English?

4. Trace the etymologies of these words: *kingdom, nation.*

224 From Legend to History (A.D. 449–1485)

Language

4.a. Use context as a clue to the meaning of a word or phrase.

4.c. Consult general and specialized reference materials, both print and digital, to find the pronunciation of a word or determine or clarify its precise meaning, its part of speech, its etymology, or its standard usage.

4.d. Verify the preliminary determination of the meaning of a word or phrase.

Practice

Answers

1. *Barbarous* is derived from the Greek *barbaros.* The Latin *barbarus* evolved from meaning "non-Greek, strange, foreign, or rude" to include connotations of wildness and savagery. The Italian word *bravo,* meaning "courageous or wild," has its roots in *barbarus. Bravo* is the origin of *brave.*

2. (a) The <u>courageous</u> Beowulf dared to battle Grendel, who had already killed many men. When Hercules's weapons prove useless against the Nemean lion, he is <u>confident</u> enough to battle the lion with his bare hands. (b) It is <u>foolhardy</u> to drive in an ice storm. A <u>defiant</u> swimmer ignored the No Swimming sign, and the lifeguard had to rescue him.

3. *Destiny* and *fame* derive from the Latin words for "send" and "fame," respectively. *Hero* is originally a Greek word meaning "demigod," from an Indo-European root meaning "protect." *Shield, dragon,* and *sword* derive from Old English.

4. *Kingdom:* Middle English, from Old English *cyningdom. Nation:* Old French *nacion,* from Latin *nationem,* "nation, stock, race," literally "that which has been born," from *natus,* "be born."

224

Vocabulary Acquisition and Use: Context Clues

Context clues are words or phrases that help readers clarify the meanings of unfamiliar words in a text. By using context clues, you can determine the word or words that complete a sentence. Sentence Completion questions appear in most standardized tests. In these types of questions, you are given sentences with one or more missing words. Your task is to use the context to choose the correct word or words to complete each sentence logically. Try this strategy: (1) Read the sentence. (2) Read *all* of the answer choices, and mark those that might work. (3) Of the ones you marked, choose the answer that works best.

Practice

This exercise is modeled after the Sentence Completion exercises that appear in the Critical Reading section of the SAT.

Directions: Each of the following sentences is missing one or two words. Choose the word or set of words that best completes each sentence.

Test-Taking Tip
Immediately rule out any answer choices you know are wrong.

1. Violent, ___?___ creatures such as Grendel appear frequently in heroic literature.
   A. fervent
   B. solicitous
   C. genteel
   D. loathsome
   E. compassionate

2. The beast often makes it a habit to ___?___ and consume the people of a nearby community.
   A. assault
   B. purge
   C. cultivate
   D. befriend
   E. purge

3. Before the entire village has been torn ___?___, a noble traveler—often a distant kinsman— will arrive on the scene.
   A. adroitly
   B. aloft
   C. asunder
   D. obliquely
   E. apologetically

4. Next, at his own ___?___, the hero will confront the mighty beast.
   A. predicament
   B. peril
   C. prevarication
   D. pallor
   E. prowess

5. Though he is sometimes wounded, the hero takes ___?___ in his sacrifice.
   A. rancor
   B. prevarication
   C. absolution
   D. solace
   E. reparation

6. The hero proves his ___?___ from death.
   A. solace
   B. immunity
   C. largesse
   D. authority
   E. vulnerability

ASSESS/EXTEND

Answers

Practice

1. Introduce the skill, using the instruction on the student page. Be sure students understand how context clues can reveal the meaning of an unknown word.

2. You may wish to go over the first item with students, applying the "read all of the answer choices" strategy. Read the first item to the class, including all of the answer choices. As you read the list of choices the second time, ask students to raise their hands when they think a choice might work. Point out that *fervent,* which means passionately enthusiastic; *solicitous,* which means an attitude of concern and consideration; *interred,* which means buried; and *compassionate,* which means feelings of sympathy for someone's suffering, clearly do not fit the context of the sentence. Choice D—*loathsome,* something or someone that arouses intense dislike and disgust—is clearly the correct choice.

3. Assign the remaining items in the Practice Test. Allow students six minutes to complete the questions.

Answers:

1. D
2. A
3. C
4. B
5. D
6. B

Strategies for
Test Taking

After students have read each answer choice for a question, they may still be torn between possible choices. To help narrow these down, students can try substituting a synonym for each word choice to see if the sentence still makes sense.

Test-Taking Practice

In this Test-Taking Practice (pp. 226–229), students apply the skills in Unit 1. The Practice is divided into three sections.

1. Before assigning each section, review the relevant Unit skills with students. Discuss the characteristics of each type of test and specific strategies for test questions, using the instruction that precedes each Practice.

2. Set a time limit for the multiple-choice items in each Practice, allowing a little more than one minute per question. Use the designated time allowance set for the Timed Writing section.

3. Administer each section. Have students write the starting time at the top of their papers. When the time for the multiple-choice items has half run out, ask students to write the time next to the answer on which they are working. Have them make similar notes when the time is three-quarters through and again when time is up. Follow a similar procedure for the Timed Writing assignment.

4. Review with students the pacing reflected in their notes.

Reteaching

Have students complete each Practice. Then, use the Reteach charts to determine which skills require reteaching, based on the items students answer incorrectly. Reteach these skills prior to assigning the **Benchmark Test** *Unit 1 Teaching Resources,* pp. 165–170.

Test-Taking Practice

Reading Test: Natural Science Passages

Natural science passages are one type of reading selection found on standardized tests. These passages may relate to biology, chemistry, geology, or other sciences. They may have a social or historical perspective as well. Natural science passages are informational, but they also express the author's point of view either directly or indirectly. Questions following these passages may focus on main idea, text structure, and author's purpose. They will also test your comprehension of key facts and details.

 Common Core State Standards

RI.11-12.1, RI.11-12.2, RI.11-12.3, RI.11-12.4, RI.11-12.5; L.11-12.3, L.11-12.4, L.11-12.6
[For the full wording of the standards, see the standards chart in the front of your textbook.]

Practice

The following exercise is modeled after the ACT Reading Test, Natural Science section. The full reading test has 40 questions.

Directions: Read the following passage, taken from Bede's *A History of the English Church and People.* Then, choose the best answer to each question.

Ireland is broader than Britain, and its mild and healthy climate is superior. Snow rarely lies longer than three days, so that there is no need to store hay in summer for winter use or to build stables for beasts. There are no reptiles, and no snake can exist there, for
5 although often brought over from Britain, as soon as the ship nears land, they breathe its scented air and die. In fact, almost everything in this isle enjoys immunity to poison, and I have heard that folk suffering from snakebite have drunk water in which scrapings from the leaves of books from Ireland had been steeped, and that this
10 remedy checked the spreading poison and reduced the swelling. The island abounds in milk and honey, and there is no lack of vines, fish, and birds, while deer and goats are widely hunted. It is the original home of the Scots, who, as already mentioned, later migrated and joined the Britons and Picts in Britain. There is a very extensive
15 arm of the sea, which originally formed the boundary between the Britons and the Picts. This runs inland from the west for a great distance as far as the strongly fortified British city of Alcuith. It was to the northern shores of this firth that the Scots came and established their new homeland.

Strategy

Scan, then read.

- **First, scan the passage.** Take 20 seconds to skim the text. Look for a main topic and a few key terms.

- **Second, read the passage in full.** Ask yourself: *What information is most important? How does the author present this information?*

226 From Legend to History (A.D. 449–1485)

Strategies for Test Taking

Point out that questions about a reading passage on the ACT may ask about main ideas and details that are expressed explicitly, or about those that are inferred. As you read, underline or bracket important points. This will help you locate information when answering questions, saving you valuable time during the timed test.

1. It can reasonably be inferred that at the time of the writing
   A. the environment in northern Europe was drastically different than it is today.
   B. the geography of northern Europe had recently and dramatically shifted.
   C. many people in Europe were suffering from poor health.
   D. most people in Europe knew little about Ireland.

2. Which of the following statements best paraphrases lines 2–3?
   F. Winter weather is harsh, but summer is easy on both animals and farmers.
   G. Because the snow is quick-melting, it does not interfere with the storage of hay or the building of shelters.
   H. Mild, dry winters eliminate the need for hay storage and animal shelters.
   J. The animals are hearty enough to go without food or shelter during the mild winter months.

3. The author includes the detail about the snakebite remedy (lines 7–10) in order to
   A. entertain his readers with a local legend.
   B. support the idea that Ireland's environment is healthful.
   C. encourage his readers to try the remedy for themselves.
   D. illustrate how uncivilized Ireland is.

4. The author writes that the island "abounds in milk and honey" (line 11).
   This phrase
   F. symbolizes the island's people.
   G. denotes the contents of the island.
   H. identifies an important limitation.
   J. connotes wholesome abundance.

5. In the context of the passage, the main function of lines 12–19 is to
   A. situate the island of Ireland in relation to Britain.
   B. provide background information about the Scots.
   C. indicate that Britain is home to many different peoples.
   D. suggest that Ireland is largely free of inhabitants.

6. Which conclusion can best be drawn about the author of the passage?
   F. He is native to Ireland.
   G. He is objective and credible.
   H. His motives are questionable.
   J. He has a background in medicine.

7. In the context of lines 14–18, it can reasonably be inferred that a *firth* is
   A. the shore of an island.
   B. a unit of measurement.
   C. an arm of the sea.
   D. the outer boundary of a city.

Differentiated Instruction   for Universal Access

Support for Less Proficient Students

Read the passage with students and help them to summarize it. Then, go over the first test item as a class, guiding students to eliminate incorrect answer choices.

EL Support for English Learners

Read the entire passage with the class and help students to summarize it. Make sure that students understand *Britons* and *Picts* in line 14, *fortified* in line 17, and *paraphrases* in Question 2. Allow students to ask clarifying questions about any of the question choices, but be careful not to reveal correct answers. Once students understand the questions, have them complete the test on their own. Allow five minutes for reading the passage and twelve minutes for the questions.

Reading Test
Natural Science Passage

1. Introduce the passage using the instruction on page 226. Be sure students understand the strategy set off in the boxed section.

2. You may wish to review the first test item with students before they take the test. Have students read the passage silently, then, as a class, analyze each choice in the first test item.

   A—There is no substantial difference in the environment of Northern Europe in Bede's day and today. (Eliminate)

   B—Nothing in the passage suggests a recent shift in geography. (Eliminate)

   C—The passage does not address the health of Europeans. (Eliminate)

   D—Correct answer. The details Bede includes imply that he is describing Ireland for people who knew little about it.

3. Assign the Practice exercise. Have students read the passage and answer the questions on their own. Allow fifteen minutes for this process, announcing when they have five minutes and one minute remaining.

Answers
1. D
2. H
3. A
4. J
5. B
6. G
7. C

Question	Pages to Reteach
1	82
2	38
3	168
4	123
5	137
6	38
7	137

Grammar and Writing

Editing in Context

1. Introduce the skill using the instruction on the student page. Be sure students understand the strategy set off in the boxed section.

2. Read the first paragraph of the Practice passage; then, go over the first test item with students, modeling the "try out each answer" strategy.

3. To determine what might be lost from the passage were the author to delete the sentence underlined in paragraph 1, read the passage aloud without the sentence. Students should be able to eliminate Choice A, since the definition of *hoo* is not important to the essay's main concept. Choice C can be eliminated, since the definition does not relay a critical fact or relate to the writer's credibility. If the sentence were eliminated, readers would not know the meaning of *hoo,* which might distract them as they read. This eliminates Choice D. Point out that the word *hoo* is unusual and will likely draw the reader's eye and curiosity, making Choice B the correct choice.

4. Have students complete questions 2–8 on their own. Allow students eight minutes to complete the questions.

Grammar and Writing: Editing in Context

Some tests feature a passage with numbered sentences or parts of sentences, some of which contain errors in grammar, style, and usage. Your task is to choose the best version of the sentence from the choices offered. Some questions may also refer to the passage as a whole or to the numbered paragraphs contained in the passage.

Practice

This exercise is modeled after the ACT English Test.

Directions: For each underlined sentence or portion of a sentence, choose the best alternative. If an item asks a question about the underlined portion, choose the best answer to the question.

[1]

Edith May Pretty had lived on the Sutton Hoo estate near Suffolk, England, for twelve years. <u>The word *hoo* means "spur of a hill."</u> Mrs. Pretty, her
₁
husband, <u>nor</u> her son had never quite been sure what to make of the
₂
nineteen large mounds visible throughout the grounds. Now infested with rabbits, the mounds were rumored to hold ancient mysteries.

[2]

<u>After</u> her husband died, Pretty's curiosity got the best of her. In 1938, she
₃
hired an archaeologist named Basil Brown to open some of the smaller mounds, which held a few interesting treasures, <u>so</u> nothing as wondrous or
₄
mysterious as legend had predicted. Unsatisfied, Pretty instructed Brown to open Mound One, the largest of them all.

[3]

In the spring of 1939, Brown and two helpers began to dig a trench from the east end of the mound. Soon, the men encountered some large iron rivets,
<u>or</u> fasteners, laid out in a <u>long, repetitive pattern,</u> like a subterranean
₅ ₆
ribcage. As more of the pattern emerged, the men realized that they were standing in the remains of the bottom hull of a colossal boat. More than 80 feet long, the ship had served as the burial vessel of an Anglo-Saxon king. Fully equipped for the afterlife, the ship's hold contained forty-one items of solid gold, silverware inscribed in Greek, a silver dish bearing the stamp of the

Strategy

Try out each answer.
Mentally test each answer before you choose one of them. The one that sounds the best is probably correct.

228 From Legend to History (A.D. 449–1485)

Strategies for Test Taking

Point out to students that in editing in context tests such as the one on this page, some test answer choices simply list words or phrases; students are expected to select the best alternative word or phrase for that sentence. Items 2, 4, 5, and 6 are of this type.

Other test items require more careful interpretation. Some items are preceded by statements or questions, or may ask the reader to summarize or analyze part or all of the passage. Items 1, 3, 7, and 8 are of this type. Tell students to

read these questions twice, making sure they understand exactly what change the writer is contemplating before testing out the item's choices.

Since these questions may take more time, students might work through the "simpler" test items first, and then go back to the more detailed test items. Also, if students complete the test with time remaining, they should review their answers to the detailed test items.

Byzantine emperor, and a bronze bowl from the Middle East. In addition to satisfying Edith May Pretty's curiosity, this astounding archaeological discovery greatly expanded contemporary understanding of Anglo-Saxon culture.

1. Upon reviewing paragraph 1, the writer considers deleting the indicated sentence. If the writer were to delete the sentence, the paragraph would primarily lose

   A. an explanation of one of the essay's central concepts.

   B. a colorful detail that draws the reader into the essay.

   C. an impressive fact that establishes the writer's credibility.

   D. nothing; it should be deleted.

2. **F.** NO CHANGE

   G. and

   H. but also

   J. though

3. What is the function of this word?

   A. It is used as a correlative conjunction.

   B. It is used as a coordinating conjunction.

   C. It is used as a subordinating conjunction.

   D. It has no function and should be deleted.

4. **F.** NO CHANGE

   G. than

   H. or

   J. but

5. **A.** NO CHANGE

   B. as though

   C. nor

   D. and

6. **F.** NO CHANGE

   G. repetitive pattern

   H. long pattern

   J. pattern

7. What is the most accurate summary of paragraph 3?

   A. It contains specific information and historical details.

   B. It describes the great Anglo-Saxon archaeological discovery that was made.

   C. It is the conclusion of the story.

   D. It persuades people to study archaeology.

8. *This question refers to the passage as a whole.* What is the main idea of this passage?

   F. Archaeology is a more established science today than it once was.

   G. People should be more curious.

   H. Old rumors may be true.

   J. Old tales, curiosity, and hard work lead to an important discovery.

 Timed Writing: Position Statement [30 minutes]

Burton Raffel, translator of *Beowulf,* has remarked that one of the most satisfying aspects of that poem is "the poet's insight into people." One might also argue that Bede, author of *A History of the English Church and People,* had equally deep insight into people and places.

In your view, which kind of text—a work of fiction like *Beowulf* or a work of nonfiction like Bede's *History*—sheds greater light on an ancient culture and its people? Write an essay developing your view on this issue. Support your position with reasoning and examples based on your reading, studies, or observations.

> **Academic Vocabulary**
>
> An **issue** is a debatable idea. There is no one right or wrong position on an issue. Choose the position for which you can offer the strongest support.

Question	Pages to Reteach
1	—
2	154
3	154
4	154
5	154
6	86
7	168
8	168

Benchmark

Reteach skills as indicated by students' performance, following the Reteach charts on pp. 227 and 229. Then, administer the end-of-unit **Benchmark Test** *(Unit 1 Resources,* pp. 165–170). The Benchmark Test concludes instruction in the Unit skills. Follow the **Interpretation Guide** for the test *(Unit 1 Resources,* p. 174) to assign reteaching pages as necessary in the *Reading Kit.* Use the built-in tracking software online to automatically assign these pages.

Answers

1. B
2. G
3. C
4. J
5. A
6. F
7. B
8. J

Timed Writing

Position Statement

1. Go over the two paragraphs of the timed writing assignment on the student page.

2. Tell students that they can quickly formulate a thesis statement for their position statements by choosing their position.

3. Encourage students to budget adequate time for prewriting and revising/editing. Students should spend about 8 minutes in the prewriting stage, 12 minutes drafting, and 5 minutes revising and editing. Reinforce this by announcing elapsed time at the 8, 12, and 20 minute marks as students respond to the assignment.

4. Use the **Rubric for Writing Assessment,** *Professional Development Guidebook,* pages 258–259 to evaluate students' work.

The Benckmark Tests are available online at www.PHLitOnline.com.

229

Performance Tasks

Assigning Tasks/Reteaching Skills

Use the chart below to choose appropriate Performance Tasks by identifying which tasks assess lessons in the textbook that you have taught. Use the same lessons for reteaching when students' performance indicates a failure to fully master a standard. For additional instruction and practice, assign the *Common Core Companion* pages indicated for each task.

Task	Where Taught/ Pages to Reteach	Common Core Companion Pages
1	35, 90, 94, 95, 98, 106–107, 123, 197	2–14, 196–207
2	70, 82, 198, 212	136–142, 185–195
3	18, 38, 68, 122	54–60, 185–195
4	16, 168, 189, 213	2–14, 297–303
5	36, 95, 98, 101, 123, 137, 156	28–40, 297–303, 306–312
6	18, 28, 156, 205, 222	54–60, 297–303

Assessment Pacing

In assigning the Writing Tasks on this student page, allow a class period for the completion of a task. As an alternative, assign tasks as homework. In assigning the Speaking and Listening Tasks on the facing page, consider having students do any required preparation as a homework assignment. Then, allow a class period for the presentations themselves.

Evaluating Performance Tasks

Use the rubric at the bottom of this Teacher Edition page to evaluate students' mastery of the standards as demonstrated in their Performance Task responses. Review the rubric with students before they begin work so they know the criteria by which their work will be evaluated.

Performance Tasks

Directions: *Follow the instructions to complete the tasks below as required by your teacher. As you work on each task, incorporate both general academic vocabulary and literary terms you learned in this unit.*

Common Core
State Standards

RL.11-12.1; RL.11-12.3, RL.11-12.5;
RI.11-12.5; W.11-12.1.d, W.11-12.1.e,
W.11-12.2; SL.11-12.1, SL.11-12.4,
SL.11-12.6
[For the full wording of the standards, see the standards chart in the front of your textbook.]

Writing

Task 1: Literature [RL.11-12.1; W.11-12.2]
Analyze Character

Write an essay in which you analyze a character from a literary work in this unit.

- Select a character who is central to the work in which he or she appears.
- Describe the character as fully as possible, based on the information provided in the work. Details in the text may provide either direct information or indirect clues about the character.
- Once you have described the character, analyze the character's significance in the work. For example, the character may stand for a type of person or may be archetypal. He or she may have a particular role or motivation.
- Remember to support your inferences with evidence from the text.
- Provide a conclusion that follows from the information you presented and also creates a sense of closure.

Task 2: Informational Text [RI.11-12.5; W.11-12.1.e]
Analyze Text Structure

Write an essay in which you analyze how a text's structure contributes to its meaning in a nonfiction work from this unit.

- Choose a work of nonfiction from this unit in which the author's choices concerning text structure help to clarify and develop central ideas.
- Determine which text structure is being used. Evaluate the way in which the structure helps to introduce and clarify points.

- Include a judgment as to how effective the author's use of text structure is.
- Provide examples from the text to support your ideas.
- Use a variety of sentence lengths in your writing. Combine short, choppy sentences by using coordinating or correlative conjunctions.
- End your essay with a conclusion that follows from your discussion and sums up your main points.

Task 3: Literature [RL.11-12.5; W.11-12.1.d]
Analyze Poetic Structure

Write an essay in which you analyze how an author's choices concerning structure add to the overall meaning of a poem.

- Choose a poem from this unit and briefly describe its overall structure and important structural elements. For example, the length of a poem or a distinct rhythm might be considered structural choices.
- Write a thesis sentence that describes the impact that the structure of the poem has upon its meaning.
- Discuss the relationship between structure and meaning in detail, providing evidence from the text to support your reasoning.
- Establish and maintain a formal style and objective tone in your writing.
- Finish your essay with a strong conclusion that sums up your main points and makes a statement about the relationship between poetic form and meaning.

230 From Legend to History (A.D. 449–1485)

Performance Task Rubric: Standards Mastery	Rating Scale
Critical Thinking: How clearly and consistently does the student pursue the specific mode of reasoning or discourse required by the standard, as specified in the prompt (e.g., comparing and contrasting, analyzing, explaining)?	not very very 1 2 3 4 5
Focus: How well does the student understand and apply the focus concepts of the standard, as specified in the prompt (e.g., development of theme or of complex characters, effects of structure, and so on)?	1 2 3 4 5
Support/Elaboration: How well does the student support points with textual or other evidence? How relevant, sufficient, and varied is the evidence provided?	1 2 3 4 5
Insight: How original, sophisticated, or compelling are the insights the student achieves by applying the standard to the text(s)?	1 2 3 4 5
Expression of Ideas: How well does the student organize and support ideas? How well does the student use language, including word choice and conventions, in the expression of ideas?	1 2 3 4 5

Speaking and Listening

Task 4: Literature [RL.11-12.1; SL.11-12.1]

Make Inferences

Conduct a **small group discussion** exploring inferences that can be made about culture based upon one of the literary works in this unit.

- Choose a work that contains clues about the culture in which it originated.

- Identify details that point to values, beliefs, the historical framework, and the social structure of the culture.

- Explain how these details help you to make connections and draw inferences about the culture.

- Prepare for the discussion. Create a list of questions based on your analysis designed to stimulate discussion.

- As group members contribute, build on their ideas. Pose further questions and point to evidence from the work.

- Respond thoughtfully to diverse perspectives and points of view.

Task 5: Literature [RL.11-12.3; SL.11-12.4, 6]

Analyze Story Elements

Prepare and deliver an **oral presentation** in which you analyze and evaluate the presentation and development of story elements in a literary work from this unit.

- Explain which work you chose and briefly summarize the setting, situation, characters, conflict, and plot.

- Discuss how the author orders events and how he or she introduces and develops characters or new situations.

- Explain how the author's choices about the development of the story elements contribute to the narrative's larger meaning or themes.

- Apply the conventions of Standard English grammar and usage in your speaking.

- As you present, speak clearly and loudly enough to be understood by your audience.

Task 6: Literature [RL.11-12.5; SL.11-12.4]

Analyze Text Structure

Prepare and deliver an **oral presentation** in which you analyze the effect of text structure on the meaning as well as the artistry and beauty of a literary work from this unit.

- Identify a work in which the structure of the text is deeply connected to its meaning and is also aesthetically significant. Caesuras, rhyming quatrains, or frame story structure are all examples of text structures.

- Define the text structure and its impact on the text's meaning.

- Discuss what you perceive to be artful or aesthetically pleasing about this text structure and in what way it engaged you as a reader. Draw a conclusion as to why the author made specific choices regarding structure.

- Present your interpretation and supporting evidence in an organized and clear way, so that your audience can follow your reasoning.

How does literature shape or reflect society?

What is Home? Over the thousand years covered in this unit, England evolved from a collection of clans to a more unified nation. You can trace this evolution in the different ideas of home expressed by various writers.

Assignment Choose three works from this unit that express different perspectives on the significant idea of home. Write a **comparison-and-contrast essay** about these perspectives, showing how the idea of home changed over time.

Performance Tasks **231**

Supporting Speaking and Listening

1. Consider having students work with partners or in groups to complete Performance Tasks involving listening and speaking. For tasks that you assign for individual work, you may still wish to have students rehearse with partners, who can provide constructive feedback.

2. As students rehearse, have them keep in mind these tips:
   - Present findings and evidence clearly and concisely.
   - Observe conventions of standard English grammar and usage.
   - Be relaxed and friendly but maintain a formal tone.
   - Make eye contact with the audience, pronounce words clearly, and vary your pace.
   - When working with a group, respond thoughtfully to others' positions, modifying your own in response to new evidence.

Linking Performance Tasks to Independent Reading

If you wish to cover the standards with students' independent reading, adapt Performance Tasks of your choice to the works they have selected. (Independent reading suggestions appear on the next page.)

 How does literature shape or reflect society?

1. Remind students of the Essential Question, "How does literature shape or reflect society?"

2. Have students complete their responses to the prompt on the student page. Point out that in this unit, they have read a variety of British literature of the Old English and Medieval periods and that they should draw on these selections in their responses. Remind them that they can also draw on their own experiences and what they have learned in other subject areas in formulating their answers.

231

EXTEND

Independent Reading

Titles featured on the Independent Reading pages at the end of each unit represent a range of reading, including stories, dramas, and poetry, as well as literary nonfiction and other types of informational text. Throughout, labels indicate the works that are CCSS Exemplar Texts. Choosing from among these featured titles will help students read works at increasing levels of text complexity in the grades 11–12 text complexity band.

Using Literature Circles

A literature circle is a temporary group in which students independently discuss a book.

Use the guidance in the *Professional Development Guidebook*, pp. 47–49, as well as the teaching notes on the facing page, for additional suggestions for literature circles.

Meeting Unit 1 CCS Standards

Students can use books listed on this page to apply and reinforce their mastery of the CCS Standards covered in this unit.

Introducing Featured Titles

Have students choose a book or books for independent reading. Assist them by previewing the titles, noting their subject matter and level of difficulty. **Note:** Before recommending a work to students, preview it, taking into account the values of your community as well as the maturity of your students.

Featured Titles

In this unit, you have read a variety of British literature of the Old English and Medieval periods. Continue to read works related to this era on your own. Select books that you enjoy, but challenge yourself to explore new topics, new authors, and works offering varied perspectives or approaches. The titles suggested below will help you get started.

LITERATURE

Beowulf: A Verse Translation
Translated by Burton Raffel

 **Epic** This Old English poem tells how Beowulf heroically defeats three fearsome monsters: Grendel, Grendel's mother, and a dragon. Thrill to the ultimate in gore from a time when audiences heard their heroic tales told aloud instead of going to the multiplex to see them.

[An excerpt from Beowulf appears on page 40 of this book. Build knowledge by reading the full text.]

The Canterbury Tales
Geoffrey Chaucer
Translated by Nevil Coghill   EXEMPLAR TEXT ©

 **Poetry** As part of a storytelling contest, each character in this medieval classic tells a tale while on a pilgrimage from London to Canterbury Cathedral. The stories range from bawdy and hilarious to innocent and virtuous, depending on the personality of the storyteller.

[An excerpt from The Canterbury Tales appears on page 96 of this book. Build knowledge by reading the full text.]

Sir Gawain and the Green Knight
Translated by Brian Stone

 **Poetry** In this acclaimed medieval romance, Sir Gawain is the young nephew of King Arthur. The Green Knight tests Gawain's chivalric ideals by posing three challenges.

[An excerpt from Sir Gawain and the Green Knight appears on page 170 of this book. Build knowledge by reading the full text.]

The Once and Future King
T. H. White
Ace, 1987

 **Novel** In this modern classic, White retells a variety of exciting tales about the legendary King Arthur and his Knights of the Round Table. White's humorous, imaginative, and suspenseful retellings will delight today's readers.

INFORMATIONAL TEXTS

Historical Texts

The Ecclesiastical History of the English People
Bede
Translated by Leo Sherley-Price

 **History** Written in A.D. 731 by a Christian monk named Bede, this book describes England from the first-century invasion by the Romans to Anglo-Saxon life in Bede's own day. It is a fascinating account of the ebb and flow of peoples and belief systems in the early centuries of Britain.

[An excerpt from the same work—using the slightly different title A History of the English Church and People—appears on page 84 of this book. Build knowledge by reading the full text.]

The Book of Margery Kempe
Margery Kempe
Translated by B. A. Windeatt

 **Autobiography** Considered the first autobiography in English, this book was dictated to a priest. It narrates the spiritual and everyday struggles of one woman in the fifteenth century as she deals with bankruptcy, the pressures of maintaining a household with fourteen children, and divine revelations that send her on pilgrimages far from home.

Contemporary Scholarship

A Distant Mirror: The Calamitous 14th Century
Barbara W. Tuchman
Ballantine Books, 1978

 **History** Told from the perspective of nobleman Enguerrand de Coucy (1340–1397), this book explores important events in the fourteenth century, including the Black Death, The Hundred Years' War, and the Crusades.

The Story of English
Robert McCrum, Robert MacNeil, and William Cran

 **Linguistics** This book presents a stimulating and comprehensive record of spoken and written English—from its Anglo-Saxon origins to the present day, when English is the dominant language of commerce and culture, with more than one billion English speakers throughout the world.

232 From Legend to History (A.D. 449–1485)

© Text Complexity: Aligning Texts With Readers and Tasks

TEXTS	READERS AND TASKS
• *The Once and Future King* (Lexile: 1080L)	**Below-Level Readers** Allow students to focus on reading for content, and challenge them to interpret multiple perspectives.
• *Beowulf: A Verse Translation* • *The Canterbury Tales* • *Sir Gawain and the Green Knight* • *A Distant Mirror* • *The Story of English*	**Below-Level Readers** Challenge students as they read for content. **On-Level Readers** Allow students to focus on reading for content, and challenge them to interpret multiple perspectives. **Advanced Readers** Allow students to focus on interpreting multiple perspectives.
• *The Ecclesiastical History of the English People* (Lexile: 1430L) • *The Book of Margery Kempe*	**On-Level Readers** Challenge students as they read for content. **Advanced Readers** Allow students to focus on reading for content, and challenge them to interpret multiple perspectives.

Preparing to Read Complex Texts

Reading for College and Career In both college and the workplace, readers must analyze texts independently, draw connections among works that offer varied perspectives, and develop their own ideas and informed opinions. The questions shown below, and others that you generate on your own, will help you more effectively read and analyze complex college-level texts.

 **Common Core State Standards**

Reading Literature/Informational Text

10. By the end of grade 12, read and comprehend literature, including stories, dramas, and poems, and literary nonfiction at the high end of the grades 11-CCR text complexity band independently and proficiently.

When reading complex texts, ask yourself...

- What idea, experience, or story seems to have compelled the author to write? Has the author presented that idea, experience, or story in a way that I, too, find compelling?
- How might the author's era, social status, belief system, or personal experiences have affected the point of view he or she expresses in the text?
- How do my circumstances affect what I understand and feel about this text?
- What key idea does the author state explicitly? What key idea does he or she suggest or imply? Which details in the text help me to perceive implied ideas?
- Do I find multiple layers of meaning in the text? If so, what relationships do I see among these layers of meaning?
- How do details in the text connect or relate to one another? Do I find any details unconvincing, unrelated, or out of place?
- Do I find the text believable and convincing?

Key Ideas and Details

- What patterns of organization or sequences do I find in the text? Do these patterns help me understand the ideas better?
- What do I notice about the author's style, including his or her diction, uses of imagery and figurative language, and syntax?
- Do I like the author's style? Is the author's style memorable?
- What emotional attitude does the author express toward the topic, the story, or the characters? Does this attitude seem appropriate?
- What emotional attitude does the author express toward me, the reader? Does this attitude seem appropriate?
- What do I notice about the author's voice—his or her personality on the page? Do I like this voice? Does it make me want to read on?

Craft and Structure

- Is the work fresh and original?
- Do I agree with the author's ideas entirely, or are there elements I find unconvincing?
- Do I disagree with the author's ideas entirely, or are there elements I can accept as true?
- Based on my knowledge of British literature, history, and culture, does this work reflect the British tradition? Why or why not?

Integration of Ideas

Text Complexity: Reader and Task Support Suggestions

INDEPENDENT READING

Increased Support Suggest that students choose a book that they feel comfortable reading and one that is a bit more challenging.

Pair a more proficient reader with a less proficient reader and have them work together on the more challenging text. Partners can prepare to read the book by reviewing questions on this student page. They can also read difficult passages together, sharing questions and insights. They can use the questions on the student page to guide after-reading discussion.

Increased Challenge Encourage students to integrate knowledge and ideas by combining the Essential Questions and the unit concepts in their approach to two or more featured titles.

For example, students might compare and contrast the ways in which chivalry is presented in *Sir Gawain and the Green Knight* and *The Once and Future King*. Students can focus on how a time period can be treated very differently depending on whether a text was written during that period or well after.

Preparing to Read Complex Texts

1. Tell students they can be attentive readers by bringing their experience and imagination to the texts they read and by actively questioning those texts. Explain that the questions they see on the student page are examples of types of questions to ask about works of fiction and nonfiction.

2. Point out that, like writing, reading is a "multidraft" process, involving several readings of complete works or passages, revising and refining one's understanding each time.

Key Ideas and Details

3. Review and amplify the first bulleted point in the Key Ideas and Details box. **Ask:** What details in the text lead you to conclude that this idea or experience compelled the author to write?

   Possible response: Students may point out that the cited idea is the central idea of the text, or that it is the idea that is treated with the most passion.

Craft and Structure

4. **Ask:** What elements of craft can you point to in the text that establish the author's unique voice?

   Possible response: Students may point to the author's diction, syntax, and rhythm as the elements of craft that establish voice.

Integration of Ideas

5. Focus on the first bulleted point in the Integration of Ideas box. **Ask:** Do the ideas in this work seem original today? Might they have been more original when first published?

   Possible response: The ideas in the work do not seem original today. However, most of the works suggested were written during the Old English or Medieval periods. It is possible that these ideas were very original in their time.

6. Finally, explain to students that they should cite key ideas and details, examples of craft and structure, or instances of the integration of ideas as evidence to support their points during a discussion of fiction, nonfiction, or poetry. After hearing the evidence, the group might reach a consensus or might agree to disagree.

233

Common Core State Standards

- **Reading Literature 1, 2, 3, 4, 5, 7, 10**
- **Reading Informational Text 2, 6, 7**
- **Writing 1, 2, 3, 4, 5, 7, 8, 10**
- **Speaking and Listening 4, 5**
- **Language 1, 3, 4, 5, 6**

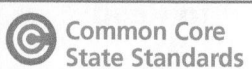

Celebrating Humanity

The English Renaissance Period

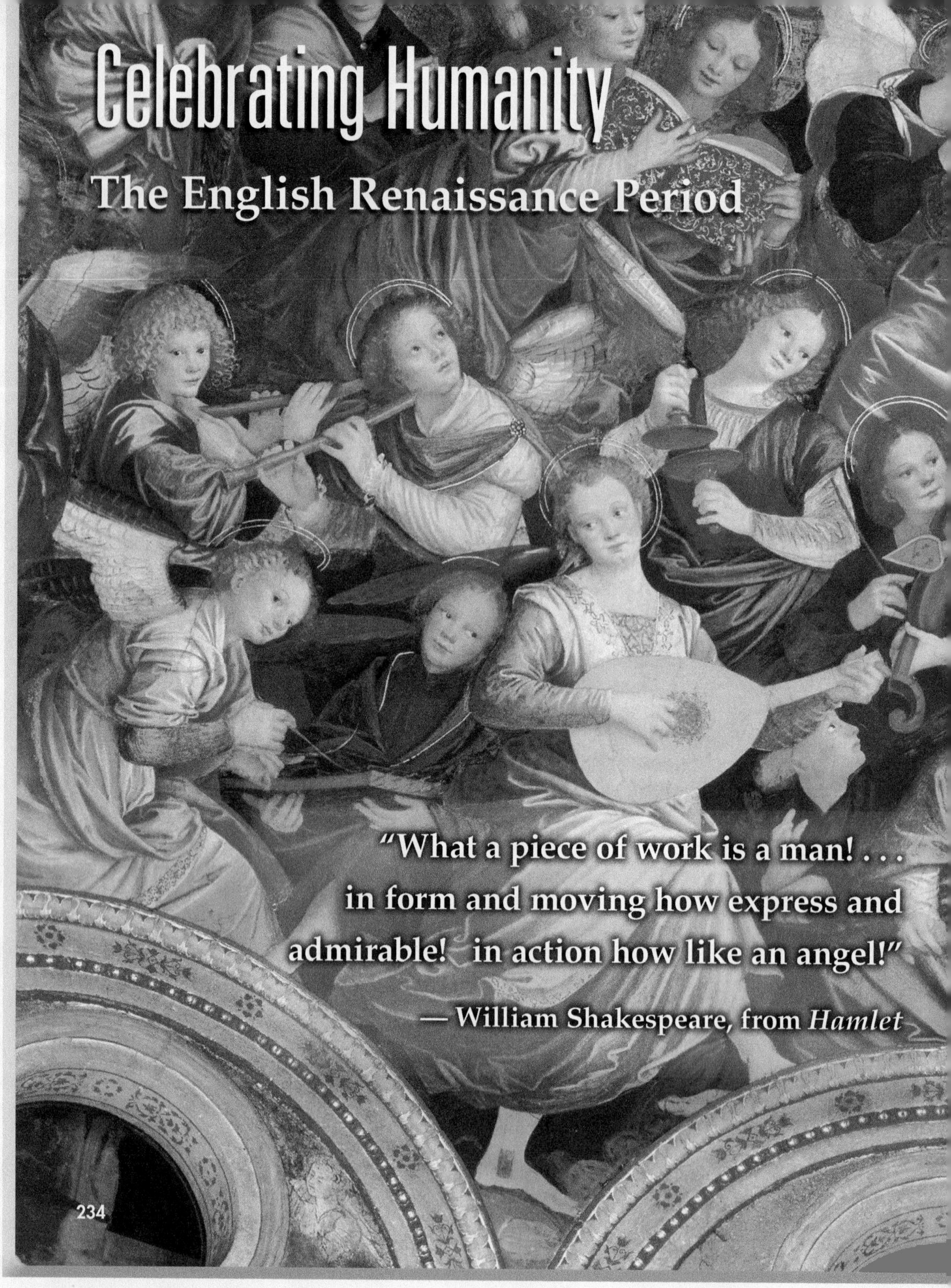

"What a piece of work is a man! . . . in form and moving how express and admirable! in action how like an angel!"

— William Shakespeare, from *Hamlet*

234

PHLit Online!
www.PHLitOnline.com

Teaching From Technology

Enriched Online Student Edition
- full narration of selections
- interactive graphic organizers
- linked **Get Connected** and **Background** videos
- all work sheets and other student resources

Professional Development
- the ***Professional Development Guidebook*** online
- additional professional-development essays by program authors

Planning, Assigning, and Monitoring
- software for online assignment of work to students, individually or to the whole class
- a system for tracking and grading student work

(1485–1625)

Unit
2

PHLit Online!
www.PHLitOnline.com

Hear It!
- Selection summary audio
- Selection audio

See It!
- Author videos
- Essential Question video
- Get Connected videos
- Background videos
- More about the authors
- Illustrated vocabulary words
- Vocabulary flashcards

Do It!
- Interactive journals
- Interactive graphic organizers
- Grammar tutorials
- Interactive vocabulary games
- Test practice

235

Introduce Unit 2

1. Direct students' attention to the title of the Unit, including the time period covered. Have a volunteer read the quotation. **Ask:** What does the quotation suggest about the spirit of the period? **Possible response:** The quotation implies a focus on man, which aligns with the humanist expressions in art and literature during the Renaissance.

2. Discuss the artwork, *Musical Angels*, a fresco painted by Gaudenzio Ferrari (1475–1546). **Ask:** How does this painting reflect the English Renaissance period? **Possible response:** Students might suggest that Renaissance art, like medieval art, still had a strong religious focus.

3. Have students speculate about the literature of the period, given the quotation and the art. **Possible response:** Students might offer that the literature in this period will fuse themes of humanism and religion.

Unit Resources

Unit 2 Resources includes these pages:

Benchmark Tests assess and monitor student progress.

Vocabulary and Reading Warm-ups provide additional vocabulary support, based on Lexile rankings, for each selection. "A" **Warm-ups** are for students reading two grades below level. "B" **Warm-ups** are for students reading one grade below level.

Selection Support
- **Reading Skill**
- **Literary Analysis**
- **Vocabulary Builder**
- **Support for Writing**
- **Enrichment**

PHLit Online!
All worksheets and other student resources are also available online at www.PHLitOnline.com.

Unit Features

Unit Author
Frank Kermode helps introduce the period in the Unit Introduction, provides an Author's Insights on literature in the Unit, and offers insight in the Writing Workshop.

Extended Study
Students explore in depth the works of William Shakespeare, presented with links to contemporary culture, a Critical Commentary, and a Comparing Literary Works feature.

Comparing Literary Works
Students compare master works in the British tradition with works of world literature.

Primary Sources
Students engage the documents that recorded history as it was made.

Informational Texts
Students learn to use and evaluate various types of informational text.

Themes Across Centuries
Students discover links between canonical literature and the contemporary world.

CLASSROOM STRATEGIES

Using Internet Project To Build Student Engagement **Donald Leu**

"What would you think if, each day, your class exchanged responses to a common reading selection with classes around the world?"

Our world is shrinking as the Internet brings us closer together. We are beginning to truly understand the diverse nature of our fragile planet. The diversity that defines us also enriches us.

How can we increase student engagement as we develop a better understanding of our global diversity? What would you think if, each day, your class exchanged responses to a common reading selection with other classes around the world? This is what happens with Internet Project (Leu, 2001; Leu, Leu, & Coiro, 2004), an instructional model that can increase reading engagement, develop new literacies, and inspire our students to appreciate the powerful benefits that diversity provides.

Internet Project

Internet Project is an instructional model where you collaborate online with other classrooms in order to learn and make our world a better place (Harris, 1999). It can take place at a common site where everything is provided, such as at *Journey North* (http://www.learner.org/jnorth/). It can also take place when you organize the learning experience and invite partners to join you, using sites such as *EPals Book Club* (http://www.epals.com/projects/book_club/).

International collaborative learning can be highly engaging and effective. Developing an email or blog exchange project to discuss a common work of literature with other classrooms around the world increases engagement, develops a global understanding of diversity, and increases new, online literacy skills. (International Reading Association, 2002).

Getting Started

Visit some of these project sites to see how Internet Project might be used in your classroom:

- EPals Book Club: http://www.epals.com/projects/book_club/
- Global SchoolNet's Collaboration Center: http://www.globalschoolnet.org/gsncenter/
- Oz Projects: http://www.ozprojects.edna.edu.au/sibling/home
- Global Gateway: http://www.globalgateway.org.uk/Default.aspx?page=7

Look for the location at each site where projects are described. To find additional sites for Internet Project, simply do a search with key words such as: *Internet Project registry.*

Advertising for Partner Classrooms To advertise for partners, write a project description. The description should contain:

- a summary of the project;
- a clear list of learning goals;
- expectations you have for collaborating classrooms;
- a description of how and where responses will be exchanged; and
- a projected timeline for beginning and ending the project.

Post the project description several months in advance at one of the project sites listed on the previous page. When you hear from interested teachers by email, arrange the collaboration details.

Directly Contacting Teachers Another way to gather partner classrooms is to locate and contact teachers directly by email. It is easy to locate potential partner classrooms in specific countries with a search engine. Use keyword strings such as: *English class secondary schools Japan home page.* Then visit school sites, locate the email addresses of English teachers, and email invitations.

Blogging If you wish to move beyond email for projects like this, consider using a blog. Blogs are easy to set up and provide a more flexible forum for individual students to share responses to reading selections. Some are free. If you are interested in developing a blog for a project like this, explore the tools available for you at either Blogspot (https://www.blogger.com) or Typepad (http://www.typepad.com). Both are common starting points for bloggers.

Two Examples of Internet Project

A Daily Message Project Each day, your class composes an email message and sends it to four other classrooms who have joined you. The other classrooms do the same. Each daily message describes what students are reading, their responses to the selections, and important events taking place in their part of the world. Each day, your students will have several messages from around the world to read, discuss, and respond to. It is an exciting way to begin the day's activities. Moreover, it allows your class to compose a message for other participants with new questions and new information. The activity engages students in new forms of literacy as they meet other students around the world.

A Reading Response Project Locate partners around the world who would like to read the same book as your class. Then, each day, exchange responses to chapters as you read and discuss the selection. You will discover that different cultural contexts prompt different types of responses and interpretations of the same work of literature. As a variation, consider reading and responding to a set of poems that are selected in advance.

Teacher Resources
- *Professional Development Guidebook*
- *Classroom Strategies and Teaching Routines cards*

PHLit Online!

Log on as a teacher at **www.PHLitOnline.com** to access a library of all Professional Development articles by the Contributing Authors of Prentice Hall *Literature*.

Donald J. Leu

Donald J. Leu, Ph.D., holds the Neag Endowed Chair in Literacy and Technology at the University of Connecticut and directs the New Literacies Research Lab. He is a member of the Reading Hall of Fame, and a former President of the National Reading Conference.

Supporting Research

Harris, J. (1999). First steps in telecollaboration. *Learning and Leading with Technology,* 27(3), 54–57.

International Reading Association. (2001). *Integrating literacy and technology in the curriculum: A position statement of the International Reading Association.* Newark, DE: Author.

Leu, D. J., Jr. (2001). Internet project: Preparing students for new literacies in a global village. The Reading Teacher, 54, 568–585.

Leu, D. J., Jr., Leu, D. D. & Coiro, J. (2004). *Teaching with the Internet: New literacies for new times (4th ed.).* Norwood, MA: Christopher-Gordon.

Reading the Unit Introduction

Celebrating Humanity

Explain to students that this unit covers literature in England during the English Renaissance from 1485 to 1625. The Unit Introduction includes these components:

–a **Snapshot** offering a quick glimpse at the period

–a **Historical Background** section discussing major events

–a **Timeline** that covers the period from 1485 to 1625, over a span of ten pages

–a **Unit Essay** examining the literature of the period through the lens of three Essential Questions

–**Following-Through** activities

–a **Recent Scholarship** essay

 Introducing the Essential Questions

1. Introduce each of the Essential Questions on the student page.

2. Show the **Essential Question** video on the *See It!* DVD. Help students relate the Essential Questions to the unit and their own experiences by asking the following:
   Literature and Place If you were asked to write a story about a place that is important to you, what would that place be? What would you want to say about it?
   Literature and Society How do novels such as *The Great Gatsby* give you a glimpse of society at a certain period of time? What other novels have you read that offer a glimpse of society at a certain time?
   Writer and Tradition Do you think that keeping traditions is important? Do you think traditions should ever be changed? Why?

3. Explain to students that the ideas they have considered in answering these questions also apply to the Renaissance period in England. Have them begin reading the Unit Introduction, telling them to look as they read for ideas related to their answers.

Snapshot of the Period

Renaissance and Reformation

Two major movements influenced the thought and literature of this period: the Renaissance and the Reformation. The Renaissance, meaning "rebirth," was characterized by innovations in art, science, and exploration, and a rediscovery of long-neglected classical works. Beginning in Italy, it gradually spread northward. Renaissance scholars of northern Europe, like Erasmus, attempted to reform the Catholic Church. The German theologian Martin Luther, however, initiated the movement known as the Reformation (reform-ation), which led to the founding of Protestantism. Luther stressed the Bible, rather than the Pope, as the source of authority and the importance of faith, rather than good works, for salvation.

Of the two major English works of this period, Shakespeare's plays and the King James Bible, the first is a product of the Renaissance and the second a product of the Reformation.

▲ This 16th-century engraving shows the new technology of book printing. The printing press, developed by Gutenberg in the mid-15th century, helped spread the ideas of the Renaissance and the Reformation.

> **As you read the selections in this unit, you will be asked to think about them in view of three key questions:**
>
> What is the **relationship** between literature and *place?*
>
> How does literature **shape or reflect** *society?*
>
> What is the relationship of the **writer** to *tradition?*

236 Celebrating Humanity (1485–1625)

Teaching Resources

The following resources can be used to support, enrich, or extend the instruction.

Unit 2 Resources
Names and Terms to Know Worksheet, p. 2
Essential Question Worksheets, pp. 3–5.
Listening and Viewing, p. 85
Follow Through Activities, p. 6

All *Common Core Companion,* pp. 9–14; 33–38

All *Professional Development Guidebook*
Cross-Curricular Enrichment Worksheets, pp. 230, 234, 241

See It! DVD
Sir Frank Kermode, Segment 4

All resources are available at **www.PHLitOnline.com.**

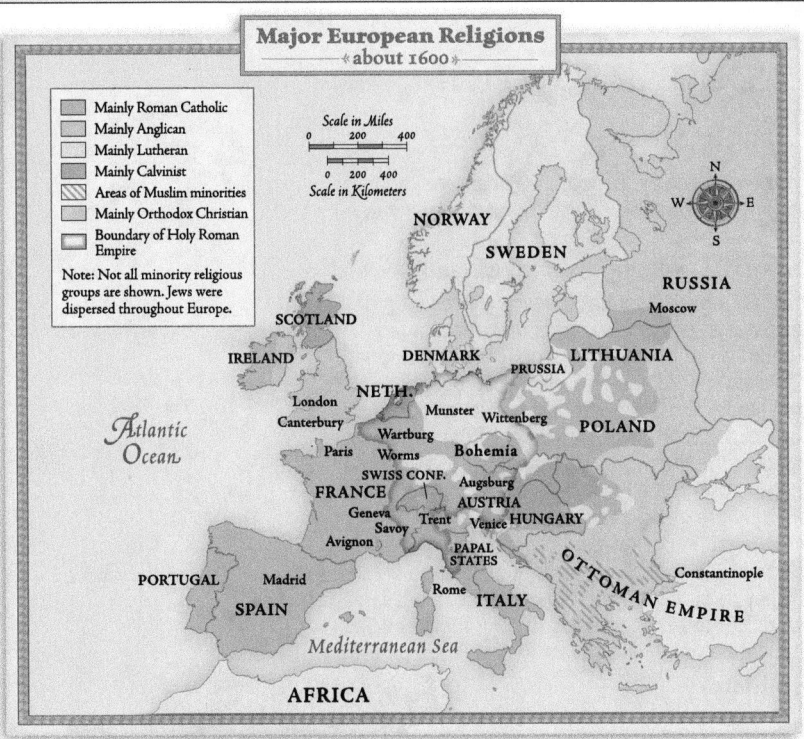

Major European Religions
about 1600

Mainly Roman Catholic
Mainly Anglican
Mainly Lutheran
Mainly Calvinist
Areas of Muslim minorities
Mainly Orthodox Christian
Boundary of Holy Roman Empire

Note: Not all minority religious groups are shown. Jews were dispersed throughout Europe.

Scale in Miles
0   200   400

Scale in Kilometers
0   200   400

A Time of Change in Religion & Science

Ⓒ Integration of Knowledge and Ideas The Reformation led to sharp religious divisions in Europe, shown on the map above. Which territories were controlled by Roman Catholics and which by Protestant denominations—Anglican, Calvinist, or Lutheran? How does this map help explain the war between England and Spain, which broke out in 1588? Review the timeline below. Which Renaissance inventions shown would you consider the most important? Why?

Renaissance Inventions

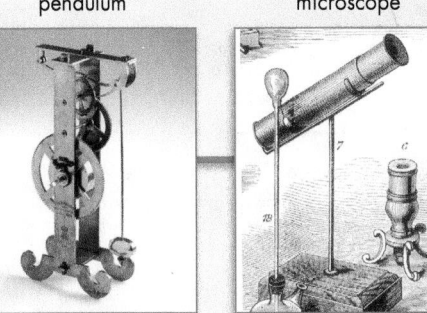
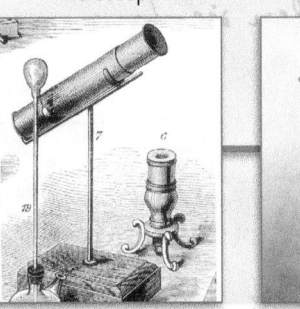
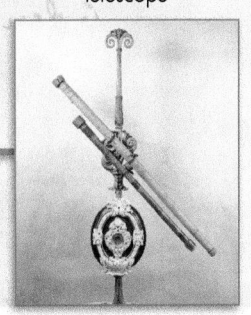

1496
paper mill; wall paper

1581
pendulum

1590
microscope

1608
telescope

Snapshot of the Period **237**

Background

Science

Tell students that Hans Lippershey, a Dutch optician, is credited with making the first telescope in 1608. However, he most likely was not the first to actually make one. Lippershey's telescope was made with two glass lenses mounted in a narrow tube. Galileo used a similar telescope and was the first person to use a telescope to study the sky. He observed the moon's craters, Jupiter's moons, and Saturn's rings.

Critical Viewing

Interpreting Illustrations

Draw students' attention to the map. **Ask** the question on the student page: Which territories were controlled by Roman Catholics and which by Protestant denominations—Anglican, Calvinist, or Lutheran? How does this map help explain the war between England and Spain, which broke out in 1588? Which Renaissance inventions in the timeline would you consider the most important? Why?

Possible response: Spain, Portugal, and Italy were controlled by Roman Catholics; England and part of Ireland were Anglican; Scotland, the Netherlands, Switzerland, and parts of Hungary were Calvinist; Germany, Norway, and Sweden were mostly Lutheran. The war occurred between Roman Catholic Spain and Anglican England. The paper mill is an important invention because it would make books accessible to a greater number of people.

Differentiated Instruction *for Universal Access*

For Less Proficient Readers

Before students read the Unit Introduction, distribute copies of the **Names and Terms to Know** worksheet (*Unit 2 Resources,* page 2). Ask students to preview the worksheet. On the board, list the names and terms on the worksheet. Ask students to predict (or guess) the possible significance of these terms. Record several predictions or guesses next to each term on the board. As students read the Unit Introduction, have them check the accuracy of the predictions on the board. Correct each as necessary. Finally, when students have finished reading the Unit Introduction, erase the board, and have the class complete the worksheet, referring back to the Unit Introduction.

237

Teaching the Historical Background

The Historical Background section discusses the most significant events of this period: Renaissance scholars reviving the learning of ancient Greece and Rome to bring about a rebirth of civilization; the questioning of the authority of the Roman Catholic Church; and an eventual split with the Church.

1. Point out that the story of this period is a story of the effects of these events on the development of the English Renaissance.

2. Have students read the Background. Then **ask** them to explain how the Reformation affected the government of England between 1485 and 1625.
   Possible response: Henry VIII founded the Protestant church when the Catholic Pope wouldn't abide by his wishes. Elizabeth firmly established the nation as Protestant and let England into a golden age of prosperity.

Background

History

During this period, England supported Protestant Dutch rebels against Catholic Spain, the superpower of the day. Spanish ships returning from the New World, loaded with treasure, were attacked by English raiders like Sir Francis Drake. Spain finally sent a fleet of 130 battleships, called the Armada, to invade England in 1588. The smaller, more maneuverable English fleet did well against the ponderous Spanish ships, attacking with cannons and burning ships filled with gunpowder. Many surviving Spanish ships were wrecked by storms when they fled. England was on its way to ending Spanish naval supremacy.

Teaching the Timeline

Tell students that the Timeline for the period from 1485 to 1625 appears on pages 238–247 of this Unit Introduction. Each portion of the Timeline identifies and illustrates some of the major events in England during that period.

Historical Background

The English Renaissance Period (1485–1625)

The two major European movements of this period, the Renaissance and the Reformation, both involved a return to old sources that led to cultural innovations.

Renaissance and Reformation: Going Back to Move Forward

The Renaissance, which means "rebirth," sought to revive the learning of ancient Greece and Rome. It was a secular movement that encouraged voyages of discovery and emphasized human aspiration. During this period, the very dimensions of the world shifted and enlarged, as Europeans discovered new parts of the globe, and Polish scientist Nicolaus Copernicus first proposed that the sun, not the Earth, was the center of the solar system. Renaissance ideas blossomed first in the Italian city states (1350–1550) and slowly spread northward, giving rise to the English Renaissance (1485–1625).

The Reformation, inspired by the ideas of the German theologian Martin Luther (1483–1546), began in part as a reaction against what many perceived as corruption in the Catholic Church. Reformation thinkers wanted to return to what they took to be a more pure idea of Christianity. Once again, an attempt to return to early ideas led to something new, as reformers created a denomination of Christianity known as Protestantism.

The Drama of English History

England became swept up in both of these two wider European movements, sometimes in a dramatic, even bloody, fashion. In the late 1400s, England was beginning to heal after thirty years of civil war. By the early 1500s, the country had plunged into the religious controversies of the Reformation. At the same time, the spirit of the Renaissance breathed new life into the arts.

The story begins in 1485, when Henry Tudor became King Henry VII, ending a civil war and reconciling the two factions in the war, the House of York and the the House of Lancaster. With him began the reign of the Tudors. His son, Henry VIII, inherited a strong, stable country. Henry VIII married his older brother's widow, Catherine of Aragon, and she bore him

TIMELINE

1485 Henry VII becomes the first Tudor king. ▼

1492: Columbus lands in Western Hemisphere.

1497: Africa Vasco da Gama rounds Cape of Good Hope.

1500: *Everyman* first performed.

1503: Italy Leonardo da Vinci paints *Mona Lisa.* ▶

238 Celebrating Humanity (1485–1625)

Enrichment: Investigating Geography

Defeat of the Spanish Armada

The English navy gained supremacy on the sea after defeating the Spanish Armada in 1588. War tactics used by the English contributed to their success.

Activity: History Report Have students use the **Analyzing a Historical Event** worksheet, *Professional Development Guidebook*, page 230, to find out about the events that led to the conflict between England and Spain, the historical figures involved in the conflict, the main events in the conflict, and the effects of the defeat of the Spanish Armada. Then ask students to report their findings to the class.

a daughter, Mary. However, Henry then fell in love with Anne Boleyn, a beautiful lady of the court. He also wanted a male heir, which Catherine had not provided him. He therefore petitioned the Pope for a divorce on the grounds that his marriage to his brother's widow was invalid.

Henry had written a treatise attacking Luther, and the Pope had designated Henry "Defender of the Faith," a title English monarchs retain to this day. However, when the Pope denied his petition to remarry, Henry refused to comply, marrying Anne Boleyn in 1533 and eventually severing all ties with Rome. In 1534, he established the Protestant Church of England with himself at its head. Religious affiliation and allegiance to the king were suddenly united.

The woman who was to become perhaps the greatest of England's monarchs, Elizabeth I, was born to Henry and Anne Boleyn in 1533. Before Elizabeth took the throne in 1558, Catholics and Protestants struggled for control of the country, and Elizabeth's ascent to the throne was marked by turmoil and death. When Elizabeth took power, however, she firmly established England as a Protestant nation and ushered in a golden age of prosperity and peace. The greatest threat to her rule came in 1588, when Catholic Spain assembled an armada, or fleet of warships, to conquer England. Elizabeth rallied her people, and the English fleet, aided by bad weather, shattered the armada. This glorious moment produced a surge of spirit and sense of power that swept the entire nation.

Elizabeth I never married and had no heir. The final days of her reign were clouded with questions of who would succeed her. In 1603, James I became her successor and the first of the ill-starred Stuart line. By the end of his reign, his struggles with Parliament foreshadowed the civil war that would come during the reign of his son, Charles I.

Key Historical Theme: Going Back to Create Something New

- Renaissance scholars turned to classical authors for inspiration, and Reformation thinkers broke with the Catholic Church in their attempt to return Christianity to its original principles.
- Renaissance ideas stimulated literary, artistic, and scientific achievement in England.
- Influenced by the Reformation, England became a Protestant country.

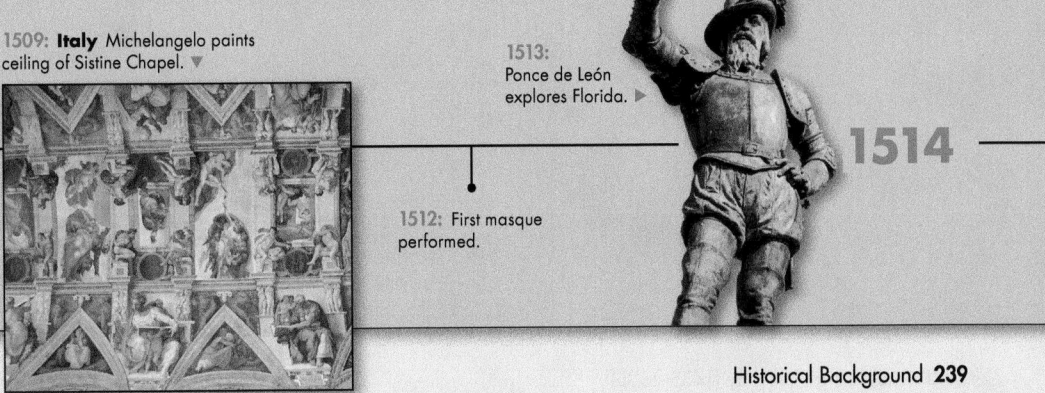

1509: **Italy** Michelangelo paints ceiling of Sistine Chapel. ▼

1513: Ponce de León explores Florida. ▶

1512: First masque performed.

1514

Historical Background 239

239

As students read Celebrating Humanity, they will examine its information through the lens of three Essential Questions. Each Essential Question is broken down into "stepping-stone" questions. Work through each stepping-stone question with the class. Then have students pose answers to the Essential Question as it applies to the period.

What is the relationship between Literature and Place?

1. Before they read this section of the essay, tell students that the theater became an important place to the literature of the English Renaissance. At the same time, England became an important nation on the world's stage.

2. Have students read this section of the essay. Then, pose the first stepping-stone question. **Ask:** What did England come to mean? **Possible response:** England came to mean a source of identity with connections to other parts of the world. After defeating the Spanish, England was recognized as a participant in world events, including the age of Exploration; The literature of England, especially the works of Shakespeare, Sidney, and Spenser, celebrated both a national and individual identity and had an influence on literature.

3. Then **ask** the second intermediary question: What was London's role in this literary explosion? **Possible response:** Theaters, including the Globe Theatre, were located outside London's city limits because actors were regarded as disreputable. However, London grew as writers, actors, patrons, and publishers arrived there.

(continued on p. 241)

Critical Viewing

Drawing Conclusions

1. Direct students to the Timeline illustration on page 240 of northern Africa.

2. **Ask** students what conclusions they can draw about the environment of North Africa from the photograph.

240

Essential Questions Across Time

The English Renaissance Period (1485–1625)

 What is the **relationship** between **literature** and *place?*

What did England come to mean?

"This England" It was in a theater that one of the most enduring descriptions of England was delivered. In Shakespeare's *Richard II*, first performed in 1595, the Duke of Lancaster, John of Gaunt, articulates his vision of what England should be: "This blessed plot, this earth, this realm, this England." His words reflect the exhilaration that followed the defeat of the Spanish Armada in 1588. At the time, Spain was one the world's superpowers, feared for her military might. Spain was also a champion of the Catholic Church, which Henry VIII had rejected. By defeating the Armada, England had established its place as a player in the drama of world history.

The Age of Exploration England also sought a place on the world stage through exploration. Fueled by the Renaissance thirst for knowledge, European navigators ventured far and wide, aided by the invention of the compass and by advances in astronomy. Their explorations culminated in Columbus's arrival in the Americas in 1492. England's participation in the Age of Exploration began in 1497, when the Italian-born explorer John Cabot, sailing for an English company, reached present-day Canada. Cabot laid the basis for future English claims in North America.

Forging a Literature of England Even as England was redefining itself politically as a world power, its poets and dramatists were taking a new hold on the English language, transforming it into an instrument of new literary power. The English poets Edmund Spenser, Sir Philip Sidney, and William Shakespeare pioneered new forms of the sonnet and wrote extended sonnet sequences (see p. 246). Embarking on his own voyage of discovery,

ESSENTIAL QUESTION VOCABULARY

These Essential Question words will help you think and write about literature and place:

exhilaration (eg zil′ə rā′shən) *n.* liveliness; high spirits

pastoral (pas′tər əl) *n.* genre of literature portraying rural life as peaceful and simple

climate (klī′mət) *n.* prevailing or average weather conditions of a place

---

TIMELINE

1514

◄ **1518: Africa** Algiers and Tunisia founded.

1521: Italy Pope Leo X excommunicates Martin Luther.

1532: France Rabelais publishes *Gargantua and Pantagruel*, Book 1.

1532: Peru Pizzaro conquers Incas.

240 Celebrating Humanity (1485–1625)

Vocabulary Development

Essential Question Vocabulary

Students will use Essential Question Vocabulary (introduced on pp. 240, 244, and 246) when they discuss and write about the Essential Questions. Have students practice by completing sentence starters such as these:

Writers responded to London's urban filth with the **pastoral** as a way to _____.

Because England's official religion changed so swiftly and so often, **heretics** of one religion might become the _____.

The new drama, one of the Renaissance's **innovations**, was formed using _____.

Shakespeare explored the heights and depths of the English language in his plays, rediscovering the words of philosophers and kings as well as of rogues and laborers, and adding along the way his own coinages. Through redefinitions of forms and new uses of English, the poets of England created a literature that was truly of England, strong enough to, in turn, influence writers across the world.

What was London's role in this literary explosion?

Theater in London During this period, London, a bustling port city on the river Thames, thrived, becoming a center of world commerce. As the wealth and population of the city grew, theater came to flourish there. Actors were regarded as disreputable by Puritanical city officials. As a result, plays were staged in theaters outside the city limits, on the south bank of the Thames. That is where the famous Globe theater, home for Shakespeare's troupe, opened in 1599. Drama was edging London southward. As the city grew, more writers came, attracted by the presence of the theaters, of patrons, and of publishers.

Londoners' Rural Dreams As poets and writers flocked to smoky London—soft coal was the principal source of heat—they dreamed about the country. Following the models of the classical literature they had studied, they turned to the pastoral as a literary form. (*Pastor* is the Latin word for shepherd.) Greek and Roman literature had depicted shepherds and shepherdesses tending flocks in some innocent garden world. Walking the wet and stinking streets of London, poets imagined a green and carefree world, the world of English poet Christopher Marlowe's "The Passionate Shepherd to His Love."

The BRITISH TRADITION

THE CHANGING ENGLISH LANGUAGE, by Richard Lederer

"A Man of Fire-New Words"

Time has proved the truth of what Shakespeare's contemporary, Ben Jonson, said of him: "He was not of an age but for all time." William Shakespeare's words, as well as his works, were not just of an age, but for all time. He was, quite simply, the greatest word maker who ever lived. Of the 20,138 different words that Shakespeare employs in his plays, sonnets, and other poems, his is the first known use of more than 1,700 of them.

Consider the following list of thirty representative words that, as far as we can tell, Shakespeare was the first to use in writing: aerial, amazement, assassination, auspicious, baseless, bedroom, bump, castigate, countless, courtship, critic, dishearten, dislocate, dwindle, exposure, frugal, generous, gloomy, hurry, impartial, invulnerable, lapse, laughable, lonely, majestic, monumental, perusal, pious, sneak, useless.

The striking compound that Shakespeare fashioned to describe a character in *Love's Labour's Lost* is an important label for the playwright himself: "a man of fire-new words."

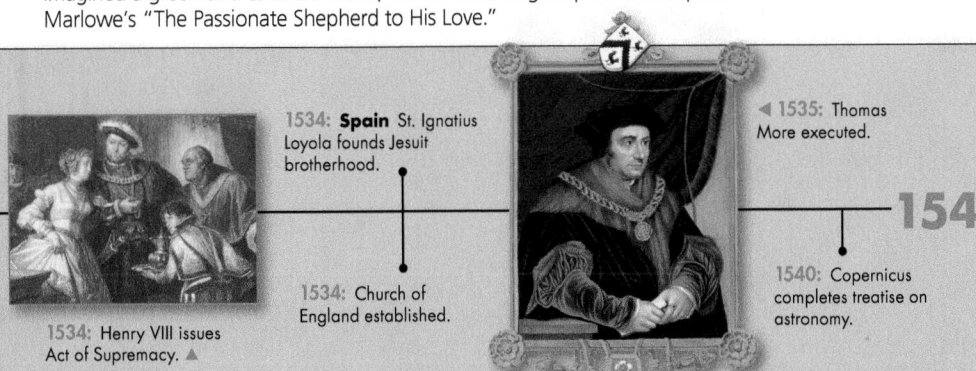

1534: **Spain** St. Ignatius Loyola founds Jesuit brotherhood.

1534: Henry VIII issues Act of Supremacy. ▲

1534: Church of England established.

◀ 1535: Thomas More executed.

1541

1540: Copernicus completes treatise on astronomy.

Critical Viewing

Drawing Conclusions

(cont.)

Possible response: The region appears to have a dry climate; the topography and building structures are different from those of Europe.

Applying the Essential Question

1. Summarize the class discussion of the two stepping-stone questions on page 240.

2. Then, **ask** students how place and literature contribute to ideas of identity today.

   Possible response: Today, people form opinions about other places and cultures based on movies, plays, and books. Although in Elizabethan England, many of these connections were made through drama and poetry, in contemporary times, people watch documentaries as well.

The British Tradition

The Changing English Language

1. Have students read the sidebar feature about the words that William Shakespeare originated in his plays.

2. **Ask** students what other factor, besides his innovativeness, might account for the fact that for many words, Shakespeare's use was their first appearance in print?

   Possible response: The people of Shakespeare's day may have used some of these words in their speech, but considered them unfit—too ordinary or vulgar—to put into writing.

3. **Ask** students to speculate on how the people of Shakespeare's day would have "heard" his style. Ask students to draw evidence from the chart.

   Possible response: Some students may argue that his success proves that his audiences found his style interesting and memorable.

Enrichment: Language

The Language of Technology

Shakespeare flooded our language with new coinages, some invented or derived from other languages. Explain to students that, in our own time, science and technology have become a major source of new words.

Activity: Have students find words in use today that have evolved from science and technology.

Have students use the **Investigating Language** worksheet, *Professional Development Guidebook,* page 234, to help them record the words, cite their origin, and provide their meaning.

How does literature shape or reflect society?

1. Before they read this section, explain to students that during this time period, what to believe was a major question. People questioned religious beliefs, politics, and the nature of Earth and the universe.

2. Have students read this section of the essay. Then **ask** the first stepping-stone question: Why was belief an issue?

   Possible response: England's official religion changed four times within thirty years, and the questions of what was the true church and true worship became a major issue. Religion at times represented a threat to political authority. Sir Thomas More refused to cooperate with Henry VIII and was executed. Many believers chose to be burned rather than convert for Mary. While religion was challenging political authority, scientific discoveries challenged the authority of religion.

Background

The *Book of Common Prayer*

Explain to students that the *Book of Common Prayer*, published in 1549, was a radical departure from the past and would influence English literature in times to come. The new Church of England needed standard texts for prayers and services. The Archbishop of Canterbury, Thomas Cranmer, prepared these texts—in English. The solemn Latin of Catholic Church services had been replaced by the plain, everyday speech of England.

How does literature shape or reflect *society?*

What to believe? That was the question, and it was a question that affected everything, from religion, to politics, to the very nature of the Earth and the universe.

Why was belief an issue?

Changing Beliefs The official religion of England changed four times in less than thirty years. This series of upheavals began in 1534, when King Henry VIII took England out of the Catholic camp and made it a Protestant country.

Political Allegiance and Religious Belief The new link between politics and religion often had tragic consequences. Consider Sir Thomas More, a trusted advisor of King Henry VIII. A man of principle, More would not support Henry's petition for divorce. After he refused to acknowledge Henry as the head of the Church of England, Henry had him executed. More's tragic end announced a new, sometimes fatal struggle between warring religious convictions.

Mary I, daughter of Henry VIII and Catherine, became queen in 1553. She denied the validity of the church her father founded and used the power of the state to return the country to Catholicism. Those she thought the worst heretics she had burned at the stake, but this only fortified the resolve of those who had embraced Protestantism. Her successor, Elizabeth I, re-established the monarch's supremacy in the Church of England, restoring Protestantism as the country's official religion. Elizabeth strove for moderation in religious matters. Even so, she contended with Catholic plots against her throne and eventually had Mary, Queen of Scots—her Catholic cousin and rival—executed.

Other Shifts in Belief Even as Protestantism had shaken the Pope's claim to be at the center of the religious world, developments in science

TIMELINE

1547: Henry VIII dies.

1541

◀ 1549: *The Book of Common Prayer* issued.

1558: Elizabeth I becomes queen.

1563: More than 20,000 Londoners die in plague.

Enrichment: Investigating Science

Renaissance Science

Explain to students that Renaissance science, like much of Renaissance painting, was born of a new thirst for observation. Yet, at the same time, the claims of ancient authorities on people's beliefs were strong. The bold explorers of the time had already shaken one Ptolemaic theory: They had discovered a new continent in the West. In 1540, the Polish astronomer Nicolaus Copernicus dealt Ptolemy another blow—the Earth, he said, went around the sun.

It would take some time before Copernicus's theory gained wide acceptance.

Activity: Research Have students speculate about other links they can see between the exploration of the world and the science of the time, using the **Enrichment: Investigating Science** worksheet from the *Professional Development Guidebook,* page 241, to guide them.

The BRITISH TRADITION

High Fashion in the Elizabethan Age

A more trivial version of the question, What to believe?, is the question, What to wear? For the Elizabethan nobility, however, that second question was almost as urgent as the first. Women and men alike took dress very seriously. Noblewomen looked like dolls on display, tightly laced into dresses that resembled giant bells. Noblemen were arrayed like showy peacocks in close-fitting jackets and wide collars that seemed to serve up their heads on plates of lace. As demonstrated in the accompanying portraits—one of Queen Elizabeth I and one of Nicholas Hilliard—clothing was elaborate and theatrical in an age that loved the drama and also loved to dramatize itself.

Two devices that helped create these theatrical effects were the ruff and the farthingale, both of which came from the Spanish court. Even after the English navy defeated the Spanish Armada in 1588, Spanish fashions held sway among the English nobility. The ruff was a pleated, starched collar worn by both sexes. It varied in size, but as you can see from the portrait of Hilliard, it could expand to the size of a large platter. The farthingale was a linen underskirt stretched over a thick iron wire that supported a skirt or dress and gave it the bell shape that Elizabeth's dress has in the portrait.

and exploration were overturning old pictures of the universe. Explorers confirmed that the Earth is round, not flat. They discovered the Americas, previously unknown to Europeans, and estimates of the size of the Earth doubled. Add to these discoveries the new Copernican theory that the sun, not the Earth, is at the center of the solar system, and the result was the upending of centuries of belief.

◀ 1564: William Shakespeare born.

1567: **South America** 2 million Indians die of typhoid.

1567: **Brazil** Rio de Janeiro founded by Portuguese. ▶

1569

Essential Questions Across Time **243**

The British Tradition

High Fashion in the Elizabethan Age

1. Ask students how they would describe today's fashion style. Then have students read the sidebar feature about fashion in the Elizabethan Age.

2. Then **ask** students to speculate about the types of lives led by the people who could afford the kind of clothes pictured in the feature.
Possible response: People who wore such clothes must have attended occasions at which display counted for a great deal—the clothing was not designed for comfort or ease of movement.

3. Refer students to the devices used in the clothing being described in the feature. Discuss how fashion has changed over the centuries. **Ask** students to name other items that were once the height of fashion.
Possible response: Students may suggest flapper dresses, poodle skirts, and corsets.

Critical Viewing

Draw Conclusions

1. Draw students' attention to the Timeline photograph of Rio de Janeiro on this page.

2. **Ask** students: What information about Rio de Janeiro does the photograph provide?
Possible response: Christianity is a major religion in Rio de Janeiro.

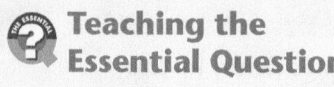

Teaching the Essential Question
(cont.)

4. **Ask** the second stepping-stone question, on this student page: How did writers respond to problems of belief?

Possible response: The King James version of the Bible was an attempt by King James to settle some of the doubts and questions of Christian beliefs. The idea that the Earth was round and not the center of the universe challenged long-held beliefs. Literature reflected these problems of belief. For example, Shakespeare's *Macbeth* is a play about illusion and reality, about what appears to be true and what really is true.

Applying the Essential Question

1. Summarize discussion of the two stepping-stone questions on pages 242–244.

2. Then, **ask** students what scientific beliefs and ideas today are changing or being reexamined.

Possible response: Changing ideas include ideas about how the universe was formed and the impact of the human activities on the planet.

How did writers respond to problems of belief?

One True Bible Protestantism emphasized the authority of scripture, and to answer concerns about existing translations, King James I convened a group of fifty-four scholars to produce a new translation of the Bible. There would be one, authentic, accurate version for the entire realm. The scholars he commissioned to translate the work produced a Bible that remains a standard text and a masterpiece of English writing. (See page 246 for more details.) However, it did not resolve all conflicts. Even as men and women now read the same words, they argued about what those words meant.

The Place of the Individual Just as the Renaissance emphasized the glory of humanity and the value of the individual, Reformation thinkers such as Luther stressed the role of the individual's faith in achieving salvation. At the same time, religious controversy could demand an individual decision about what to believe. The new prominence of the individual is mirrored in the literature of the period. From Astrophel's complaints in Sidney's sonnet sequence *Astrophel and Stella* to the powerful soliloquies in Shakespeare's plays, in which characters lay bare the conflicts that tear at their souls, Elizabethan literature turned a new eye on the inner life.

Deciding What to Believe Columbus, Luther, and Copernicus never came to England, but they shaped the new worlds in which everyone had to learn to live all over again. It was a time of incredible turmoil: intellectual, religious, political, artistic. In the midst of that turmoil, ordinary people struggled to decide what to believe, how to worship, and whom to obey. The glorious literature of the period gave them new terms in which to think, opening the way to modern ideas of the individual.

> **ESSENTIAL QUESTION VOCABULARY**
>
> These Essential Question words will help you think and write about literature and society:
>
> **petition** (pə tish′ən) *n.* solemn request to a person or group in authority
>
> **heretics** (her′ə tiks) *n.* those holding opinions at odds with accepted religious beliefs
>
> **turmoil** (tur′moil′) *n.* commotion; uproar; confusion

TIMELINE

▲ **1579:** Sir Francis Drake lands near site of San Francisco on his voyage around the globe.

— **1569** —

1582: Italy Pope Gregory XIII introduces new calendar. ▼

c. **1582:** Sir Philip Sidney writes *Astrophel and Stella*.

244 Celebrating Humanity (1485–1625)

Think Aloud

Vocabulary: Using Context
Direct students' attention to the word *realm* in the first paragraph on this page. Use the following "think aloud" to model the skill of using context to infer the meaning of the word. Say to students:

> I may not know the meaning of the word *realm*. The preceding sentence discusses the determination of King James to settle questions about the Bible. When I read the second sentence, however, I realize that the writer is using *realm* to describe the area under King James's rule. So I think *realm* refers to the English kingdom.

What is the relationship of the writer to *tradition?*

Renaissance and Reformation are the words that define the period. *Renaissance* means rebirth and refers to the revival of classical learning at this time. Reformation was the re-forming of the church, bringing it back to its earlier, basic forms. Both went back to older traditions to make something new.

What did writers rediscover in the classics?

Humanism The ancient language of Latin had never gone away—its study was still an important part of an education. What was rediscovered in this period was not a language, but the "purer" forms in which the classical writers of ancient Greece and Rome wrote. The classics also offered a view of life different from the Christian vision that had dominated Europe. Ancient Greek and Roman authors offered ethics without reference to heaven and hell and philosophy that was about the natural world, not about the supernatural. They emphasized what it was to be human, so the new way of thinking based on the classics was called Humanism.

How did rediscovery encourage originality?

Translation and Invention The champions of Humanism wanted the classics to reach a wide audience. They therefore undertook a series of translations that made the ancient works more widely available while at the same time enriching the English language. English poet and dramatist George Chapman translated the *Iliad,* the ancient Greek poet Homer's epic poem about the fall of ancient Troy. Sir Thomas North translated the ancient writer Plutarch's brief biographies of famous Greeks and Romans and provided Shakespeare with material for five plays. Perhaps most important, when the English poet Henry Howard, Earl of Surrey, translated the *Aeneid*, the Roman poet Virgil's epic on the founding of Rome, he used unrhymed lines of iambic pentameter. This supple form, "blank verse," was quickly adapted for the stage, and Elizabethan playwright Christopher

1588: English navy defeats Spanish Armada.

1590: Edmund Spenser publishes *The Faerie Queen*, Part I.

◄ 1594: Shakespeare writes *Romeo and Juliet.*

1597

1595: **South America** Sir Walter Raleigh explores Orinoco River.

Essential Questions Across Time **245**

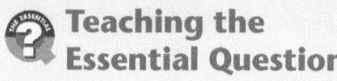

4. **Ask** the third stepping-stone question: In religion, how did writers move forward by going back?

Possible response: Writers consulted Latin, Greek, and Hebrew texts in order to translate the bible into an official English version, the King James Bible. The new version is a masterpiece of English prose.

Applying the Essential Question

1. Summarize discussion of the two stepping-stone questions on pages 245–246.

2. Then **ask** students to give examples of current or recent movies, plays, or novels that are based on older works.

Possible response: The movie *West Side Story* is based on Shakespeare's *Romeo and Juliet*. The movie *O Brother, Where Art Thou?* is based on Homer's *The Odyssey*.

Critical Viewing

1. Draw students' attention to the Timeline illustration on page 246 depicting a sketch of the Globe Theatre.

2. Then **ask:** What does the illustration suggest about the location of the theater? How might this sketch have been used?

Possible response: The illustration shows the theater being close to the city, close to a residential area. The sketch might have been used as an advertisement for the Globe Theatre.

Marlowe's version of blank verse, his "mighty line," inspired Shakespeare to imitate it and then make it his special instrument. The invention of blank verse shows that, as often happened in this period, the return to older sources led to innovations.

A New Form of Drama The drama itself was a mixture of two traditions, one native and one classical. The native tradition began in the medieval church and involved the reenactment of scenes from the Bible. These "plays" moved into the marketplace, adding depictions of the struggles of vice and virtue. Shakespeare probably saw such performances as a boy. Onto this native stock of theatrical representation, the new writers grafted classical models of comedy and tragedy. The result was a new form of English drama.

Borrowing and Reinventing One of the most enduring forms of English poetry, the sonnet, entered the English tradition through translation. In this period, writers from all over Europe borrowed ideas and literary models from Italy, where the Renaissance began. English poets imported a fourteen-line Italian poem called the *sonetto*. Sidney, Spenser, and Shakespeare worked individual variations on the challenging form (see page 241), as would poets of later centuries.

In religion, how did writers move forward by going back?

Remaking the Bible, in English Translation was crucial to the Reformation as well. When James I came to the throne, it was obvious that the Church of England, in existence for sixty-nine years, should have one recognized English Bible. There were English translations, but none was standard. King James appointed a committee of scholars to make a new translation. Not only did they consult the Latin version of St. Jerome, which had been used in Europe for more than a thousand years, but working with Latin, Greek, and Hebrew texts, in a blend of the new learning and the new religious fervor, they produced the required Bible, a masterpiece of English prose.

Once again, writers had gone back to traditional sources and used them to make something new and enduring. Other translations may now be used in church services, but as long as English is spoken, "The Lord is my shepherd" will be remembered.

ESSENTIAL QUESTION VOCABULARY

These Essential Question words will help you think and write about the writer and tradition:

ethics (eth´iks) *n.* study of standards of conduct and moral judgment

theology (thē äl´ə jē) *n.* study of religious doctrines and matters of divinity

innovations (in´ ə vā´shənz) *n.* new methods or devices

TIMELINE

1599: Globe theater opens. ▼

1597

1603: Elizabeth I dies.

1600: East India Company founded.

▲ 1606: Guy Fawkes executed for Gunpowder Plot.

Enrichment: Investigating Religion and Myth

Religion in the United States

Most people in the United States consider themselves to be practitioners of a religion. Almost every religion in the world has some sort of organized institution in the U.S. Approximately 77% of people in the U.S. consider themselves Christian. The most prominent groups of religious non-Christians are Jews, Muslims, Buddhists, Unitarians, and Hindus, which together represent approximately 3% of the population. About 14% of people in the US do not identify with any religion.

Activity: Investigating Religion in the United States Encourage students to do further research on the different types of religions in the United States. Have them focus their research on a single religion and use the **Investigating Religion and Myth** worksheet, *Professional Development Guidebook,* p. 240, to record and analyze their findings.

The BRITISH TRADITION

CONTEMPORARY CONNECTION

William Shakespeare: To Be or Not to Be . . . A Rocker!

Shakespeare's sonnets may seem an unlikely inspiration for contemporary musicians, composers, and singers. In 2007, however, the Royal Shakespeare Company commissioned pop artists to set their favorite sonnet to music. Here are some of the surprising results:

- Irish singer Gavin Friday found his inspiration in Sonnet 40: "Take my loves, love, yea take them all. . . ." One reviewer wrote that Friday's performance was "extraordinary," describing his intonation of the sonnet as "a kind of strangulated speech-song."
- Former 10,000 Maniacs lead singer Natalie Merchant picked melancholy Sonnet 73, with its reflections on advancing age: "To love that well which thou must leave ere long."
- Romanian violinist Alexander Balanescu's choice was Sonnet 43, with its speaker's expression of longing to see his love: "All days are nights to see till I see thee."
- Electronic artist Mira Calix decided on Sonnet 130, a parody of love poetry, which begins, "My mistress's eyes are nothing like the sun." Calix liked "the idea that it appears to be a diss."

For artists and audience alike, the experience proved the timelessness of the sonnets. As Merchant commented in wonder, "How could an Englishman writing at the beginning of the seventeenth century and I have so much in common?"

PERFORMING TONIGHT WILLIAM SHAKESPEARE

1607: North America British colony established at Jamestown.

1618: Germany Kepler proposes laws of planetary motion.

1623: First patent laws passed.

1625

1609: Italy Galileo builds first telescope.

▲ **1620: North America** Pilgrims land at Plymouth Rock.

1625: James I dies.

Essential Questions Across Time **247**

Differentiated Instruction   for Universal Access

Support for Special-Needs Students
These students may benefit from creating their own Graphic Organizer to help master this unit's treatment of three Essential Questions. The organizer should be very simple: It can consist of three boxes, with the Essential Question written at the top of each, and each stepping-stone question listed under the Essential Question. Students might work in groups of three, with each student creating a box for one of the three Essential Questions.

Enrichment for Gifted/Talented Students
Have musical students put together a kind of "sound essay"—a mix of music and sound effects that suggests the times and events referred to in this Unit Introduction. They could focus in on one event or span the entire time covered by the unit; they could use recorded material or compose original music and sound effects. Sounds could include religious music for the Reformation; ocean and boat sounds for the overseas voyages; and love songs for the period's literature, such as the sonnets and Shakespeare's plays.

The British Tradition
Contemporary Connection

1. Before students read the feature, tell them that the artists were part of a two-part project titled *Nothing Like the Sun: The Sonnet Project*. The project is the work of composer Gavin Bryars, who was inspired by Shakespeare's sonnets. The first part of the project includes the commissioned works of the artists mentioned in the feature. The second part of the project involves Bryars's own 40-minute composition inspired by several of Shakespeare's sonnets.

2. Direct students' attention to the end of the feature, to the quote by Natalie Merchant. **Ask** students why they think people today can still connect to Shakespeare's sonnets. **Possible response:** The sonnets can still connect to people today because their themes—love, mortality, beauty—are still relevant to people today.

247

Sir Frank Kermode

1. Frank Kermode introduces the unit and provides insights into life in Elizabethan and Jacobean England.

2. Have students read the Meet the Author feature about Sir Frank Kermode. Tell students that he is a respected academic. His book *Shakespeare's Language* addresses the intellectual demands of reading Shakespeare.

3. Use the *See It!* DVD to introduce Frank Kermode. Show Segment 1 to provide insights into his writing. You can also view the video from this page in the Enriched Online Student Edition at **www.PHLitOnline.com.**

4. After students have watched the segment, discuss the role of a literary critic.

Life in Elizabethan and Jacobean England

Sir Frank Kermode

London expanded greatly during the reign of Queen Elizabeth I, becoming one of the largest and wealthiest European capitals. Essentially a medieval city, its southern boundary was the River Thames, which was also its principal thoroughfare. To the north was the old Roman wall, but the city was spreading beyond it. Upstream was Westminster, the historic seat of the court and the national government. And across the river was Southwark, outside the jurisdiction of the City of London and therefore the favored site for enterprises, including theaters, deplored by the virtually autonomous and puritanical city government.

The population was swollen by country people, escaping the restrictions of rural life and famine, and by immigrants from Europe. The narrow, traffic-crowded streets were lined by shops and workshops, by civic mansions and rich halls of the trade guilds, and by the Inns of Court, haunts of lawyers and young gentlemen continuing their studies after leaving Oxford or Cambridge. The class system was strict—clothes were appropriate to rank, whether gentleman, citizen, craftsman, or laborer.

About the Author

Sir Frank Kermode is a literary critic who has written in-depth analyses of works ranging from the Bible to those of Shakespeare and beyond. He is a former professor of modern English at University College, London, and was knighted by Queen Elizabeth in 1991.

248 Celebrating Humanity (1485–1625)

All video resources are available online at **www.PHLitOnline.com.**

The Challenges of Urban Life

London was not clean or healthy. Sanitation was crude—the Thames was a beautiful sewer. Deadly diseases—plague, malaria, smallpox—ensured a high mortality rate. Cheats, tricksters, and thieves abounded. Men carried weapons—swords or pistols—in the street. Meanwhile, as the fields and woods were built over, access to country air grew more difficult.

Inflation was unchecked but money flowed freely. Among the expensive luxuries of the day were ostentatious clothes and tobacco, a recent import from the New World. London was perpetual bustle, noise, and display. Imagine how a young man from the provinces, like Shakespeare, might react to it. Shakespeare's Stratford, though a sturdy community with its own guilds and its good grammar school, hardly offered adequate preparation for London, a great port and the gateway to the larger world. The splendor of the river and the mansions lining its bank won the keen admiration of foreign visitors, who compared its magnificence to that of Paris and other great European cities.

From Stratford to London

In Shakespeare's day, the journey from Stratford to London took four days on foot, two on a horse.

Shakespeare, new to London, probably took time to settle down. His London was the area around the old St. Paul's cathedral. The theaters were across the river in wicked Southwark. Westminster, site of Whitehall Palace, was a couple of miles to the west. There, in ancient halls, the great affairs of state were decided. There the queen contended with the Pope and her other foreign and domestic enemies. Later, James catered to his favorites and dreamed of establishing absolute monarchy and universal peace. However, their majesties both liked plays, so there was hope for an aspiring playwright. There was the prospect of pleasure and success, though there was also risk. Perhaps that's why Shakespeare left his family in Stratford: to take his place in the London theater—and eventually, literary immortality.

© Speaking and Listening: Collaboration

Sir Frank Kermode refers to London's "perpetual bustle, noise and display." With a few classmates, study the picture showing the display at a feast held across the river from the Tower of London (c. 1570). Then, participate in a **small group discussion** pointing out the features of the scene that might have interested Shakespeare. Look for such items as these:

- a nobleman riding with a hawk on his arm
- children dressed like little adults
- fashionably dressed people strolling
- a servant holding a shield on his back

Speaking and Listening: Collaboration

Small Group Discussion

1. Review the assignment with students.
2. Instruct students to carefully study the picture. Have them find other items that might have interested Shakespeare and list them.
3. Then hold a class discussion and list the additional items students have observed. Have students explain why Shakespeare might have been interested in each of these items and how he might have incorporated them in his work.
4. To help conduct the discussion, use the Discussion Guide in the *Professional Development Guidebook,* page 65.

Common Core
State Standards

- **Reading Informational Text 7**
- **Speaking and Listening 4, 5**

Integrate and Evaluate Information

1. Review the chart assignment with the class. Then, ask students to use the Activity A chart in the **Following Through** worksheet (p. 6 in *Unit 2 Resources*) to complete this activity.
   Possible responses: *Literature and Place: Key Concept*—writer writes about both real and imaginary places, *Key Author*—William Shakespeare; *Literature and Society: Key Concept*—changing beliefs, *Key Author*—King James

2. **Possible responses:** The image of the telescope on p. 237 is representative of the Renaissance, which fostered innovation in science. The image of *The Book of Common Prayer* on p. 242 is representative of the Reformation because of the focus on the Bible as the source of authority.

3. **Possible responses:**
   (a) Translations of Greek and Roman classics made the classics accessible to a wide audience and also led to the development of blank verse, which was used both by Marlowe and Shakespeare.
   (b) The Renaissance shaped a new idea of the value of the individual within the context of Humanism. The Reformation shaped an idea of the individual as one who required faith to achieve salvation.

4. **Possible responses:** Students willing to ignore some discomfort might enjoy visiting such an interesting and exciting destination. In their answers, students should cite details from Kermode's essay and the feature.

Integrate and Evaluate Information

1. Use a chart like the one shown to determine the key ideas expressed in the Essential Question essays on pages 240–246. Fill in two ideas related to each Essential Question and note the authors most closely associated with each concept. One item has been completed for you.

Essential Question	Key Concept	Key Author
Literature and Place		
Literature and Society		
Writer and Tradition	New uses of the sonnet	William Shakespeare

2. Review the visual images in this section. Choose one that, in your view, is representative of the movement known as the Renaissance, and one that is representative of the movement known as the Reformation. Explain your choices.

3. Both the Renaissance and the Reformation sought to recover earlier perspectives: the former by reviving the literature of ancient Greece and Rome, and the latter by returning to Christian scripture (rather than the pope) for religious guidance. (a) Describe one effect of Renaissance ideas on the literature of the time. (b) Explain how the Renaissance and Reformation shaped new ideas of the individual.

4. **Address a Question:** In his essay on pages 248–249, Sir Frank Kermode writes that Renaissance London "was not clean or healthy" but that the splendor and vitality of the city was widely admired. Would you like to have visited London during this period in history? Why or why not? Integrate information from this textbook and other sources, such as an online history of the city, to support your ideas.

Speaking and Listening: "Welcome" Talk

Shakespearean drama had its home in London's Globe theater. Destroyed by Puritans in the mid-1600s, the Globe was rebuilt in 1997. Today, the new Globe serves as a theater, information center and exhibition space.

Play the role of a docent, or tour guide, at the new Globe, and prepare a multimedia **"welcome" talk** for visitors. Your talk should include a brief history of the original Globe theater, as well as a description of the resources at the modern Globe. Make sure to address alternative views of the theater's history and construction. To accompany your talk, prepare a brief slide presentation that includes photographs or diagrams of the theater. Select images that will lend interest or that will help your audience understand your points.

Solve a Research Problem: This assignment requires you to research both the history and present-day existence of the Globe. Begin by formulating a research plan. Review both print and media sources, and consult the ones that you determine will provide reliable information about the Globe. You may also want to contact an actual Globe docent for information about the talks given to visitors.

Common Core
State Standards

Reading Informational Text
7. Integrate and evaluate multiple sources of information presented in different media or formats as well as in words in order to address a question or solve a problem.

Speaking and Listening
4. Present information, findings, and supporting evidence, conveying a clear and distinct perspective, such that listeners can follow the line of reasoning, alternative or opposing perspectives are addressed, and the organization, development, substance, and style are appropriate to purpose, audience, and a range of formal and informal tasks.

5. Make strategic use of digital media in presentations to enhance understanding of findings, reasoning, and evidence and to add interest.

ESSENTIAL QUESTION VOCABULARY

Use these words in your responses:

Literature and Place
exhilaration
pastoral
climate

Literature and Society
petition
heretics
turmoil

Writer and Tradition
ethics
theology
innovations

Speaking and Listening

1. Clarify that students will create a multimedia "welcome" talk for visitors to the new Globe theater.

2. Analyze the activity and identify its key terms: *Globe theater; docent/tour guide; 1600s; resources; "welcome" talk; slide presentation; print and media sources.*

3. Then, have students complete Activity B in the **Following Through** worksheet (p. 6 in *Unit 2 Resources*). Suggest that they create an outline to help structure their talk.

4. Have students deliver their talks to the class and answer questions about the original and modern Globe theaters.

Lovers and Their Lines

PART 1

251

The poems in this section celebrate love—witty love, sincere love, and love for love's sake. Edmund Spenser, in "little love poems," is unique in his choice of romantic subject (his wife). Sir Philip Sidney, unlike Spenser, wrote of his agonized love for a woman who would not or could not return his ardor. Shakespeare's sonnets run the gamut from quiet introspection about the nature of love and marriage to a backhanded celebration of his unlovely love. Christopher Marlowe's idealistic pastoral poem contrasts with Sir Walter Raleigh's tart, commonsense response.

Humanities

Henry Percy, 9th Earl of Northumberland, ca. 1595, by Nicholas Hilliard.

Nicholas Hilliard (1547–1619) was an English goldsmith and miniaturist best known for his portrait miniatures of members of the court of Elizabeth 1 and James 1 of England. He was the author of a work of scholarship on miniature painting, called *The Art of Limning* (c.1600). Henry Percy was called the Wizard Earl for his scientific and alchemical experiments, his passion for cartography, and his large library. He is pictured reclining in a hedged garden.

Use these questions for discussion:

1. What is the young man in this painting doing?

   Possible response: He appears to be lying down in a garden, resting his head on his hand.

2. What details in this painting suggest that Henry Percy was reading poetry?

   Possible response: There is a book on the lawn near his head and his body language appears contemplative as if he is lost in thought.

Text Complexity: At a Glance

This chart gives a general text complexity rating for the selections in this part of the unit to help guide instruction. For additional text complexity support, see the Text Complexity Rubric at point of use.

Sonnet 1 (Spenser)	**More Complex**	The Nymph's Reply to the Shepherd	**More Complex**
Sonnet 35 (Spenser)	**More Complex**	Sonnet 29 (Shakespeare)	**More Complex**
Sonnet 75 (Spenser)	**More Complex**	Sonnet 106 (Shakespeare)	**More Complex**
Sonnet 31 (Sidney)	**More Accessible**	Sonnet 116 (Shakespeare)	**More Accessible**
Sonnet 39 (Sidney)	**More Accessible**	Sonnet 130 (Shakespeare)	**More Accessible**
The Passionate Shepherd to His Love	**More Accessible**		

Monitoring Progress

Before students read the poetry selections, refer to the results for the **Vocabulary in Context** items on **Benchmark Test 2** (*Unit 1 Resources* p. 171). Use this diagnostic portion of the test to guide your choice of selections to teach, as well as the depth of preparation you will provide, based on students' readiness for reading and vocabulary skills.

COMMON CORE
Time and Resource Manager

from Spenser's Sonnets • *from* Sidney's Sonnets
Lesson Pacing Guide

DAY 1 Preteach

-  Administer the Reading and Vocabulary Warm-ups (*Unit 2 Resources,* pp. 7–10) as necessary.
- Introduce the Literary Analysis concept: Sonnet.
- Introduce the Reading Strategy: Essential Message.
- Build Background with the author and Background features.
- Develop thematic thinking with Connecting to the Essential Question.
- Teach the selection vocabulary.

DAYS 2–3 Preteach/Teach/Assess

- Distribute copies of the appropriate graphic organizer for the Reading Strategy (*Graphic Organizer Transparencies,* pp. 34–35).
- Distribute copies of the appropriate graphic organizer for Literary Analysis (*Graphic Organizer Transparencies,* pp. 36–37).
- Prepare students to read with the Activating Prior Knowledge activities (TE).
- Informally monitor comprehension while students read.
- Use the Reading Check questions to confirm comprehension.
- Develop students' understanding of sonnets using the Literary Analysis prompts.
- Develop students' ability to identify the Essential Message using the Reading Strategy prompts.
- Reinforce vocabulary with the Vocabulary notes.
- Assess students' comprehension and mastery of the skills by having them answer the Critical Reading, Literary Analysis, and Reading Strategy questions.
- Have students complete the Vocabulary Lesson.

DAY 4 Extend/Assess

- Have students complete the Conventions and Style Lesson.
- Have students complete the Writing Lesson and write a manual for a sonnet. (You may assign as homework.)
- Administer Selection Test A or B (*Unit 2 Resources,* pp. 20–22 or 23–25).

Common Core State Standards

Reading Literature 5. Analyze how an author's choices concerning how to structure specific parts of a text contribute to its overall structure and meaning as well as its aesthetic impact.

Writing 2. Write informative/explanatory texts to examine and convey complex ideas, concepts, and information clearly and accurately through the effective selection, organization, and analysis of content.
4. Produce clear and coherent writing in which the development, organization, and style are appropriate to task, purpose, and audience.

Language 4.a. Use context as a clue to the meaning of a word or phrase.
4.b. Identify and correctly use patterns of word changes that indicate different meanings or parts of speech.

Additional Standards Practice
Common Core Companion, *pp. 54–55; 196–207; 219–220; 324–341*

Daily Block Scheduling
Each day in this Lesson Pacing Guide represents a 40–50 minute period. Teachers using block scheduling may combine days to revise pacing. In addition, teachers may differentiate and support core instruction by integrating components for extended and intensive support as students require. See the Guide to Selected Leveled Resources (facing page).

Guide to Selected Leveled Resources

R T I Tier 1 (students performing on level)

from Spenser's Sonnets • *from* Sidney's Sonnets

Warm Up

Practice, model, and **monitor** fluency, working **with the whole class** or **in groups.**

Vocabulary and **Reading Warm-ups B,** *Unit 2 Resources,* pp. 7–8, 10

Comprehension/Skills

Support and **monitor** comprehension and skills development, having students complete the activities, graphic organizers, and interactive prompts **independently** or **as a class.**

• *Reader's Notebook,* adapted instruction and summary

EL *Reader's Notebook: English Learner's Version,* adapted instruction and summary

• **Reading Skill Graphic Organizer B,** *Graphic Organizer Transparencies,* p. 35

• **Literary Analysis Graphic Organizer B,** *Graphic Organizer Transparencies,* p. 37

Monitor Progress

A

Monitor student progress with the differentiated curriculum-based assessment in the *Unit Resources.*

• **Selection Test B,** *Unit 2 Resources,* pp. 23–25
• **Open-Book Test,** *Unit 2 Resources,* pp. 17–19

R T I Tier 2 (students requiring intervention)

from Spenser's Sonnets • *from* Sidney's Sonnets

Warm Up

Practice, model, and **monitor** fluency **in groups** or **with individuals.**

• **Vocabulary** and **Reading Warm-ups A,** *Unit 2 Resources,* pp. 7–9
• *Hear It!* Audio CD

Comprehension/Skills

• **Support** and **monitor** comprehension and skills development, working **in small groups** or **with individuals.**

• As students complete the selection in the appropriate version of the *Reader's Notebook,* **monitor** comprehension frequently with group questions and individual instruction.

• **Model** strategies while guiding students in completing the activities and prompts in the *Reader's Notebook,* as well as the graphic organizers.

• **Practice** skills and **monitor** mastery with the *Reading Kit* worksheets.

• *Reader's Notebook: Adapted Version,* adapted instruction and summary

EL *Reader's Notebook: English Learner's Version,* adapted instruction and summary

• **Reading Skill Graphic Organizer A,** *Graphic Organizer Transparencies,* p. 34

• **Literary Analysis Graphic Organizer A,** *Graphic Organizer Transparencies,* p. 36

• *Reading Kit,* Practice worksheets

Monitor Progress

A

Monitor student progress with the differentiated curriculum-based assessment in the *Unit Resources* and in the *Reading Kit.*

• **Selection Test A,** *Unit 2 Resources,* pp. 20–22
• *Reading Kit,* Assess worksheets

TIER 3 Tier 3 intervention may require consultation with the student's special-education or dyslexia specialist. For additional support, see the Tier 2 activities and resources listed above.

One-on-one teaching   Group work   Whole class instruction   Independent work   **A** Assessment

For a complete guide to selection support, including support for Advanced students, see the Overview of Resources in the frontmatter.

from Spenser's Sonnets
• *from* Sidney's Sonnets

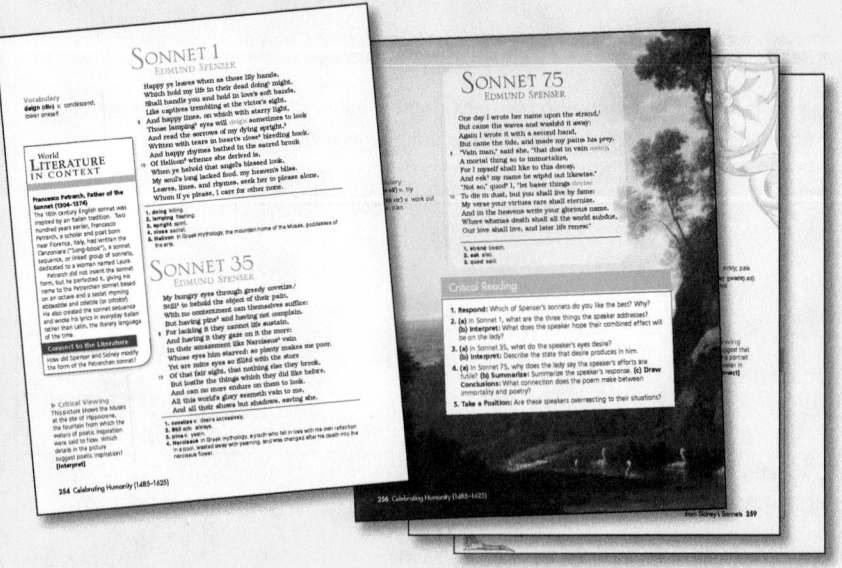

RESOURCES FOR:

- **L1** Special-Needs Students
- **L2** Below-Level Students (Tier 2)
- **L3** On-Level Students (Tier 1)
- **L4** Advanced Students (Tier 1)
- **EL** English Learners
- **All** All Students

Vocabulary/Fluency/Prior Knowledge

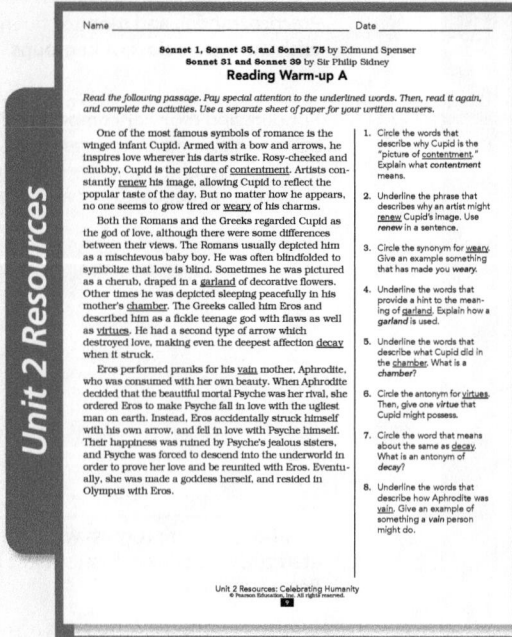

EL L1 L2 Reading Warm-ups A and B, pp. 9–10

Also available for these selections:

EL L1 L2 Vocabulary Warm-ups A and B, pp. 7–8

All Vocabulary Builder, p. 13

Reader's Notebooks

Pre- and postreading pages for these selections appear in an interactive format in the *Reader's Notebooks*. Each *Notebook* is differentiated for a different group of learners. The selections in the Adapted and English Learner's versions are abridged.

- **L2 L3** *Reader's Notebook*
- **L1** *Reader's Notebook: Adapted Version*
- **EL** *Reader's Notebook: English Learner's Version*
- **EL** *Reader's Notebook: Spanish Version*

© *Common Core Companion*

Additional instruction and practice for each Common Core State Standard

Selection Support

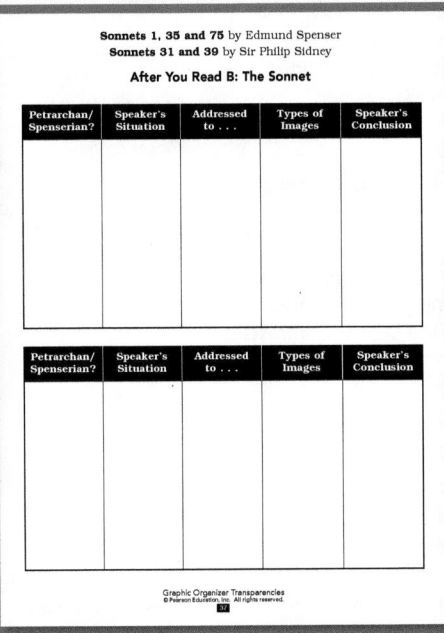

EL **L3** **Literary Analysis: Graphic Organizer B**, p. 37

Also available for these selections:

EL **L1** **L2** **Reading: Graphic Organizer A** (partially filled in), p. 34

EL **L3** **Reading: Graphic Organizer B**, p. 35

EL **L1** **L2** **Literary Analysis: Graphic Organizer A** (partially filled in), p. 36

Skills Development/Extension

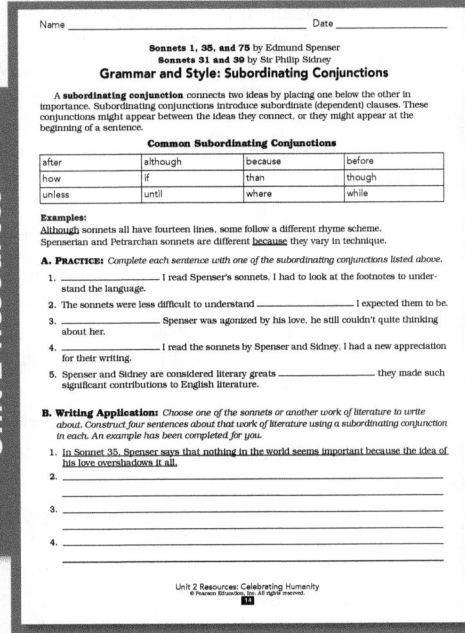

EL **L3** **L4** **Grammar and Style**, p. 14

Also available for these selections:

All **Literary Analysis**, p. 11

All **Reading**, p. 12

EL **L3** **L4** **Support for Writing**, p. 15

L4 **Enrichment**, p. 16

Assessment

EL **L1** **L2** **Selection Test B**, pp. 23–25

Also available for these selections:

L3 **L4** **Open-Book Test**, pp. 17–19

EL **L3** **L4** **Selection Test A**, pp. 20–22

Online Resources: All print materials are also available online.

- complete narrated selection text
- a thematically related video with writing prompt
- an interactive graphic organizer
- highlighting feature
- access to all student print resources, adapted to individual student needs
- Spanish and English summaries
- adapted selection translations in Spanish

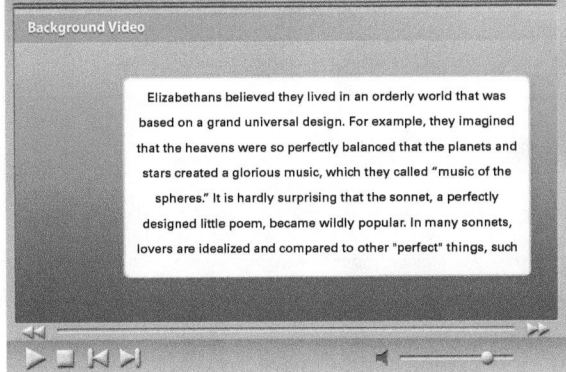

Background Video

Also available:

Get Connected! (thematic video with writing prompt)
All videos are available in Spanish.

Vocabulary Central (tools and activities for studying vocabulary)

Also available:

Writer's Journal (with graphics feature)

❶ 🔍 Connecting to the Essential Question

1. Review the assignment with the class.

2. Prepare students to write by discussing which song lyrics they find moving, and why. Then have them complete the assignment.

❷ Literary Analysis

Introduce the skill using the instruction on the student page.

Think Aloud: Model the Skill

Say to students:

Both Petrarchan and Spenserian sonnets have the same number of lines and the same meter, but they have different rhyme schemes. I can tell a Petrarchan sonnet from a Spenserian sonnet by looking at the sonnet's end rhymes—the rhymes at the end of lines.

❸ Reading Strategy

1. Introduce the skills.

2. Give students a copy of **Reading Strategy Graphic Organizer B,** page 35 in *Graphic Organizer Transparencies,* to fill out as they read.

Think Aloud: Model the Skill

Say to students:

Whenever I put a new idea into my own words, I'm paraphrasing. For example, when someone gives me directions, I might repeat them in my own words. Then, the person can hear what I think he means and he can correct anything that was miscommunicated. When I'm reading by myself, I can check that my paraphrasing makes sense. If it does not make sense, I know that I have probably misunderstood something.

❹ Vocabulary

1. Pronounce each word, giving its definition, and have students say it aloud.

2. For more guidance, see the *Classroom Strategies and Teaching Routines* card for introducing vocabulary.

Before You Read
from *Spenser's Sonnets* • from *Sidney's Sonnets*

❶ **Connecting to the Essential Question** Like modern songwriters, Elizabethan poets used strongly emotional language to express their love. As you read, notice the different poetic forms these poets used to express love. This will help you answer the Essential Question: **What is the relationship of the writer to tradition?**

❷ **Literary Analysis**

A **sonnet** is a fourteen-line lyric poem with a single theme. Each line in a sonnet is usually in iambic pentameter—five groups of two syllables, each with the accent on the second syllable. Sonnet forms include these:

- The **Petrarchan sonnet** is divided into an eight-line octave, rhyming *abbaabba*, followed by a six-line sestet, rhyming *cdecde*. Often, the octave poses a problem that is answered in the sestet. Contrasts between the octave and the sestet allow poets to develop meaning and achieve beautiful effects.
- The **Spenserian sonnet** rhymes *abab bcbc cdcd ee*.

In a **sonnet sequence,** sonnets are linked by theme or person addressed.

Comparing Literary Works Notable writers of the Elizabethan Age, such as Spenser and Sidney, made their mark by writing sonnet sequences. To connect one hundred or more poems without growing dull, they used a basic fictional situation: The speaker in the sequence is deeply in love, but his love is often unfulfilled.

As you read, compare Spenser's and Sidney's uses of this basic situation.

❸ **Reading Strategy**

© **Preparing to Read Complex Texts** To better understand what you read, **determine the main idea or essential message** of literary works or passages. For instance, you can determine the main idea of a passage of poetry by *paraphrasing* it, or restating it in your own words. First read the passage to find a complete thought. Then, separate the essential from the nonessential information, and express the essential information in your own language. Use a chart like the one shown to help you write a paraphrase.

❹ **Vocabulary**

deign (dān) *v.* condescend; lower oneself (p. 254)

assay (a sā´) *v.* try (p. 256)

devise (di vīz´) *v.* work out or create; plan (p. 256)

wan (wän) *adj.* sickly; pale (p. 259)

languished (laŋ´ gwisht) *adj.* weakened; dulled (p. 259)

balm (bäm) *n.* ointment or other thing that heals or soothes (p. 260)

Common Core State Standards

Reading Literature
5. Analyze how an author's choices concerning how to structure specific parts of a text contribute to its overall structure and meaning as well as its aesthetic impact.

Poet's Lines

"One day I wrote her name upon the strand,/ But came the waves and washèd it away:"

↓

Paraphrase

One day the speaker wrote his beloved's name in the sand at the beach, but the waves came and erased his writing.

Vocabulary Development

Vocabulary Knowledge Rating

Create a **Vocabulary Knowledge Rating Chart** (*Professional Development Guidebook,* p. 33) for the vocabulary words on the student page. Give each student a copy of the chart with the words on it. Read the words aloud, and have students mark their rating of each in the Before Reading column. When students have completed reading and discussing the sonnets, have them take out their **Vocabulary Knowledge Rating Charts** for the story. Read the words aloud and have students rate their knowledge again in the After Reading column. Clarify any words that are still problematic. Then have students complete the Vocabulary practice at the end of the selections.

Vocabulary Central, featuring tools and activities for studying vocabulary, is available online at **www.PHLitOnline.com.**

5 EDMUND SPENSER

(1552–1599)

Author of *Spenser's Sonnets*

Born into a working-class family, Edmund Spenser attended the Merchant Taylors' School on a scholarship and managed to work his way through Cambridge University. During his university years, Spenser published his first poems.

Pay for Poetry Unlike many other poets of the day, Spenser depended on the payments he received for his work. When the queen's treasurer balked at paying him, he sent this verse to the queen: "I was promised on a time / To have reason for my rhime. / From that time unto this season / I have received nor rhime, nor reason." Spenser was paid immediately.

The Faerie Queene In 1580, Spenser took a position as secretary to the Lord Deputy of Ireland. On a visit to Ireland in 1589, Sir Walter Raleigh (see p. 265) read and was impressed with one of Spenser's unfinished poems. He persuaded Spenser to take the first three books of this long poem to London for publication. That poem became Spenser's greatest work, *The Faerie Queene*.

Written in an intentionally archaic style, *The Faerie Queene* recounts the adventures of several knights, each representing a virtue. This allegory of good and evil, dedicated to Queen Elizabeth I (who appears as the Faerie Queene in the poem), brought Spenser a small pension.

A Poet's Poet Spenser was an innovative poet. In *The Faerie Queene*, he created a new type of nine-line stanza, which was later named for him. He also created a sonnet form, known as the Spenserian sonnet, containing a unique structure and rhyme scheme. His sonnet sequence *Amoretti* is unique among such works—it is addressed to the poet's own wife, not some inaccessible, idealized beauty.

The noblest mind the best contentment has.

—*Edmund Spenser*

from Spenser's Sonnets **253**

Daily Bellringer

For each class during which you will teach these selections, have students complete one of the five activities for the appropriate week in the *Daily Bellringer Activities* booklet.

Multidraft Reading

To assist struggling readers and to enhance reading for all, assign the text in chunks, as warranted by length, and apply multidraft reading protocols. For each reading, have students set the purpose indicated:

- **First reading**—identifying key ideas and details and answering any Reading Checks.
- **Second reading**—analyzing craft and structure and responding to the side-column prompts.
- **Third reading**—integrating knowledge and ideas, connecting to other texts and the world, and answering the end-of-selection questions.

For more guidance, refer to the *Classroom Strategies and Teaching Routines* card on multidraft reading.

5 Background
More About the Author

Edmund Spenser's knowledge of Latin and Greek classics and Italian, French, and English literature provided a foundation for his highly original work. Many scholars consider Spenser's book *The Shepheardes Calendar*, which was dedicated to Philip Sidney, to be the first work of the English literary Renaissance. Surrounded by conflict (Protestant *v.* Catholic, Irish *v.* English), Spenser saw his poetry as a way to illuminate the human experience, the battle between good and evil, and the importance of virtue.

www.PHLitOnline.com

Teaching From Technology

Preparing to Read
Go to **www.PHLitOnline.com** in class or in a lab and display the *Get Connected!* slide show for these selections. Have the class brainstorm responses to the slide show writing prompt, entering ideas in the interactive journal. Then, have students complete their written responses individually, in a lab or as homework

To build background, display the More About the Author features.

Using the Interactive Text
Go to **www.PHLitOnline.com** and display the **Enriched Online Student Edition.** As the class reads the selection or listens to the narration, record answers to side-column prompts using the graphic organizers accessible on the interactive page. Alternatively, have students use the online edition individually, answering the prompts as they read.

❶ About the Selections

The three sonnets by Edmund Spenser in this section come from a longer work—the sonnet sequence *Amoretti*, Italian for "little love poems." The sonnet sequence is unique in that it is addressed to the poet's wife, Elizabeth Boyle, not to some distant, unattainable, or unrequited love.

In Spenser's sonnets, his love inspires the speaker's poetry (Sonnet 1) and the speaker claims that he suffers because he cannot focus on anything but his beloved (Sonnet 35). However, the poet's triumph will be to immortalize her in verse (Sonnet 75).

❷ Activating Prior Knowledge

These sonnets by Spenser and Sidney recount the conflicting emotions inherent in romantic love. One of the authors writes about being happily in love, the other about the sadness love can bring.

To stimulate interest, have students assume the role of an advice columnist. What advice would they give to:

- someone who has been rejected by the person he or she loves?
- a person who is too shy to announce his or her love?

Have students write a short response to one of the above questions.

Concept Connector ➡

Tell students they will return to their responses after reading the selections.

Vocabulary
deign (dān) *v.* condescend; lower oneself

❸ World LITERATURE IN CONTEXT

Francesco Petrarch, Father of the Sonnet (1304–1374)
The 16th century English sonnet was inspired by an Italian tradition. Two hundred years earlier, Francesco Petrarch, a scholar and poet born near Florence, Italy, had written the *Canzoniere* ("Song-book"), a sonnet sequence, or linked group of sonnets, dedicated to a woman named Laura.

Petrarch did not invent the sonnet form, but he perfected it, giving his name to the Petrarchan sonnet based on an octave and a sestet rhyming *abbaabba* and *cdecde* (or *cdcdcd*). He also created the sonnet sequence and wrote his lyrics in everyday Italian rather than Latin, the literary language of the time.

Connect to the Literature

How did Spenser and Sidney modify the form of the Petrarchan sonnet?

❺ ▶ Critical Viewing

This picture shows the Muses at the site of Hippocrene, the fountain from which the waters of poetic inspiration were said to flow. Which details in the picture suggest poetic inspiration? **[Interpret]**

---

❶❷ SONNET 1
EDMUND SPENSER

Happy ye leaves when as those lily hands,
Which hold my life in their dead doing[1] might,
Shall handle you and hold in love's soft bands,
Like captives trembling at the victor's sight,
5 And happy lines, on which with starry light,
Those lamping[2] eyes will deign sometimes to look
And read the sorrows of my dying spright,[3]
Written with tears in heart's close[4] bleeding book.
And happy rhymes bathed in the sacred brook
10 Of Helicon[5] whence she derived is,
When ye behold that angel's blessed look,
My soul's long lacked food, my heaven's bliss.
Leaves, lines, and rhymes, seek her to please alone,
Whom if ye please, I care for other none.

1. **doing** killing.
2. **lamping** flashing.
3. **spright** spirit.
4. **close** secret.
5. **Helicon** In Greek mythology, the mountain home of the Muses, goddesses of the arts.

SONNET 35
EDMUND SPENSER

My hungry eyes through greedy covetize,[1]
Still[2] to behold the object of their pain,
With no contentment can themselves suffice:
But having pine[3] and having not complain.
5 For lacking it they cannot life sustain,
And having it they gaze on it the more:
In their amazement like Narcissus[4] vain
Whose eyes him starved: so plenty makes me poor.
Yet are mine eyes so fillèd with the store
❹ 10 Of that fair sight, that nothing else they brook,
But loathe the things which they did like before,
And can no more endure on them to look.
All this world's glory seemeth vain to me,
And all their shows but shadows, saving she.

1. **covetize** *v.* desire excessively.
2. **Still** *adv.* always.
3. **pine** *v.* yearn.
4. **Narcissus** in Greek mythology, a youth who fell in love with his own reflection in a pool, wasted away with yearning, and was changed after his death into the narcissus flower.

© Text Complexity Rubric

	Sonnet 1	Sonnet 35	Sonnet 75	Sonnets 31 and 39
Qualitative Measures				
Context/ Knowledge Demands	Elizabethan sonnet 1 2 ③ 4 5	Elizabethan sonnet 1 2 ③ 4 5	Elizabethan sonnet 1 ② 3 4 5	Elizabethan sonnets 1 ② 3 4 5
Structure/Language Conventionality and Clarity	Archaic diction and syntax 1 2 ③ 4 5	Archaic diction and syntax 1 2 ③ 4 5	Archaic diction and syntax 1 2 ③ 4 5	Archaic diction and syntax 1 2 ③ 4 5
Levels of Meaning/ Purpose/Concept Level	Accessible (love) 1 2 ③ 4 5	Moderate (love) 1 2 ③ 4 5	Moderate (love and immortality) 1 2 ③ 4 5	Accessible (love) 1 ② 3 4 5
Quantitative Measures				
Lexile/Text Length	NP / 112 words	NP / 110 words	NP / 115 words	NP / 115; 118 words
Overall Complexity	**More complex**	**More complex**	**More complex**	**More accessible**

Francesco Petrarch, Father of the Sonnet

Petrarch abandoned his legal studies to study classical authors and religion. In bridging these two traditions, he founded Humanism, a movement that encouraged inquiry and that opened the way to a new emphasis on the individual and on the value of human experience.

Connect to the Literature

Ask students the Connect to the Literature question: How did Spenser and Sidney modify the form of the Petrarchan sonnet?

Answer: Spenser and Sidney modified the Petrarchan sonnet by using three quartets each linked by rhyme scheme and a final couplet, rather than an octave and sestet.

❹ Reading Strategy

Determine Main Idea or Essential Message

Ask students to paraphrase the essential information. Have students write their paraphrases in a graphic organizer like the one on page 252 (see *Graphic Organizer Transparencies,* page 35).

Possible response: I like looking at my loved one so much that I don't want to look at any others. I can't stand to look at women I used to think were beautiful.

❺ Critical Viewing

Possible responses: The Muses are all beautiful women, and Spenser's poetic inspiration seems to be the beauty of his loved one. The tablet one of the Muses is holding could also be an inspiration to write.

Ⓒ Text Complexity: Reader and Task Suggestions

Sonnets 1, 35, and 75		Sonnets 116 and 130	
Preparing to Read the Text	**Leveled Tasks**	**Preparing to Read the Text**	**Leveled Tasks**
• Using the About the Selections information on TE p. 254, discuss the distinction between writing a poem for a person you know versus some unreachable person. • Discuss the different purposes of love poems. • Guide students to use Multidraft Reading strategies (TE p. 253).	*Levels of Meanings* If students will have difficulty with the poems' meaning, help them use sonnet structure to focus on the main point of the first four lines, the next four lines, the next four lines, and the last two lines. Then, have them reread each poem. *Analyzing* If students will not have difficulty with the poems' meaning, have them analyze imagery that helps convey ideas about the relationship between love and immortality.	• Using the About the Selections information on TE p. 257, discuss Sidney's use of the names Astrophel and Stella. • Remind students of the strategies for paraphrasing a poem in order to determine its main idea. • Guide students to use Multidraft Reading strategies (TE p. 253).	*Structure/Language* If students will have difficulty with the language or syntax, have them first read each poem to find its complete thoughts. Then, ask them to separate essential from nonessential information. Finally, have them paraphrase the poem. *Analyzing* If students will not have difficulty with the language or syntax, have them analyze and explain the moon imagery in Sonnet 31 or the sleep imagery in Sonnet 39.

Before students respond, you may wish to have them write a brief objective summary of the selection. As they answer the questions below, remind them to support their answers with evidence from the text.

1. (a) The speaker addresses the leaves (pages of a book), lines, and rhymes. (b) The speaker hopes their combined effect will please the lady who beholds them.

2. (a) The speaker's eyes desire to gaze on his love. (b) Constant desire to behold his beloved produces a state of pain and grief in the speaker, because the more he looks, the more he wants to look at nothing else.

3. (a) The lady says the speaker's efforts are futile because she will eventually die and be forgotten. (b) The speaker believes that his lines of poetry will forever capture or immortalize his love. (c) The poem claims that verse has the power to make immortal the relationship between the speaker and his beloved.

4. **Possible responses:** No, the speakers are not overreacting to their situations; they are convinced of the gravity of their feelings for the women they love. Students may also point out that this highly charged style of writing was the tradition of Spenser's times, so was not an overreaction, but a traditional one. Yes, the speakers are overreacting to their situations; they are driven by their emotions and cannot recognize that their feelings are causing them to be irrational.

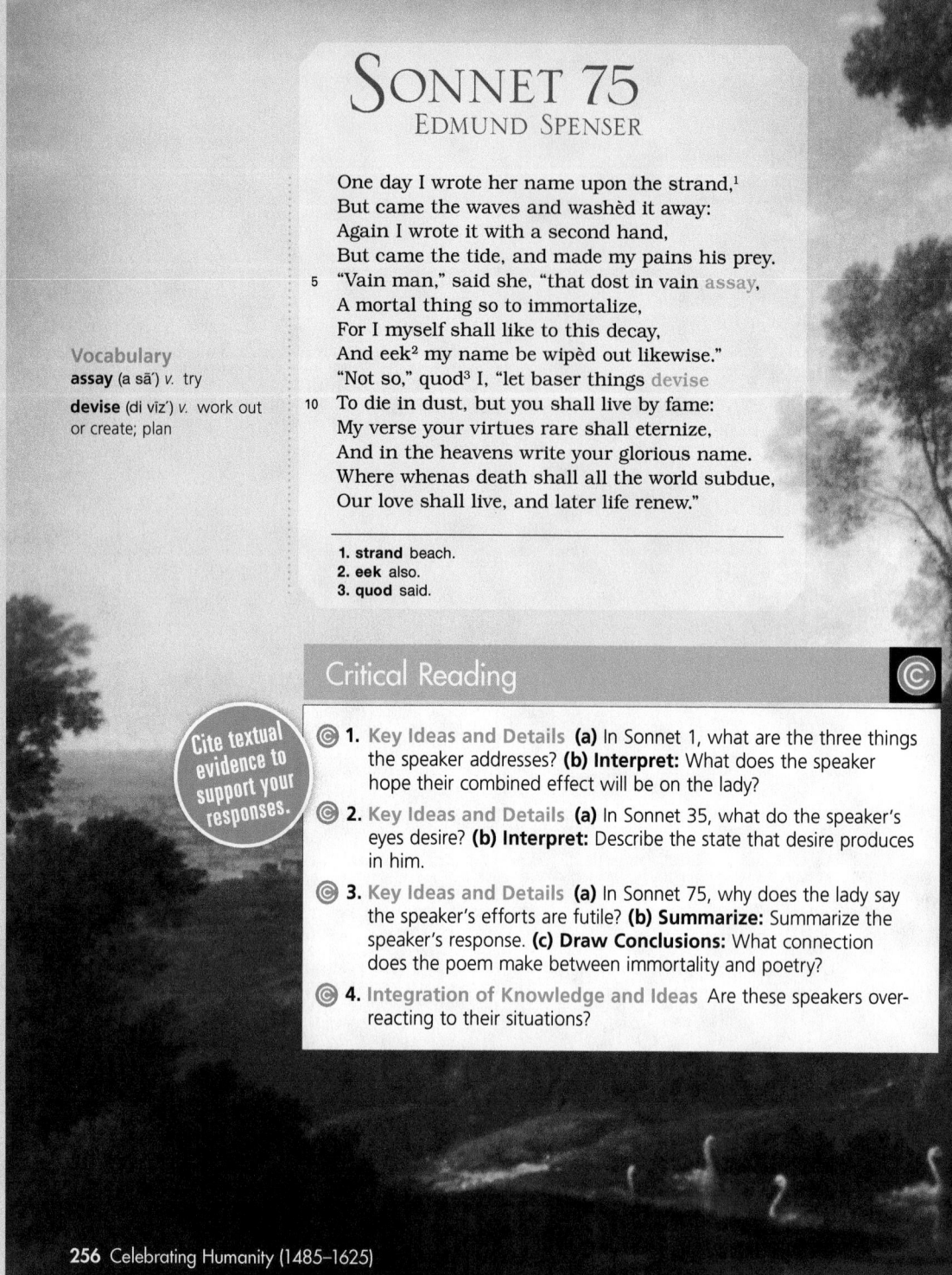

SONNET 75
EDMUND SPENSER

One day I wrote her name upon the strand,[1]
But came the waves and washèd it away:
Again I wrote it with a second hand,
But came the tide, and made my pains his prey.
5 "Vain man," said she, "that dost in vain assay,
A mortal thing so to immortalize,
For I myself shall like to this decay,
And eek[2] my name be wipèd out likewise."
"Not so," quod[3] I, "let baser things devise
10 To die in dust, but you shall live by fame:
My verse your virtues rare shall eternize,
And in the heavens write your glorious name.
Where whenas death shall all the world subdue,
Our love shall live, and later life renew."

Vocabulary
assay (a sā′) *v.* try
devise (di vīz′) *v.* work out or create; plan

1. **strand** beach.
2. **eek** also.
3. **quod** said.

Critical Reading

Cite textual evidence to support your responses.

1. **Key Ideas and Details (a)** In Sonnet 1, what are the three things the speaker addresses? **(b) Interpret:** What does the speaker hope their combined effect will be on the lady?

2. **Key Ideas and Details (a)** In Sonnet 35, what do the speaker's eyes desire? **(b) Interpret:** Describe the state that desire produces in him.

3. **Key Ideas and Details (a)** In Sonnet 75, why does the lady say the speaker's efforts are futile? **(b) Summarize:** Summarize the speaker's response. **(c) Draw Conclusions:** What connection does the poem make between immortality and poetry?

4. **Integration of Knowledge and Ideas** Are these speakers overreacting to their situations?

256 Celebrating Humanity (1485–1625)

Enrichment: Investigating Psychology

Sleeping and Dreaming

Throughout history, sleep and dreams have been a source of mystery and debate. In the late nineteenth century, the psychoanalyst Sigmund Freud proposed that one's dreams revealed important information about that individual. However, psychologists differ strongly on the issue. It has been only recently that sleeping and dreaming have been subjected to controlled, scientific study under laboratory conditions.

Activity: Research on Dreams and Psychologists Have pairs or groups of students conduct research on sleeping and dreaming, how views about them have changed over time, and/or key psychologists who have studied sleep and dreams. Have students record information in the **Enrichment: Investigating Psychology** worksheet, *Professional Development Guidebook,* page 239. Invite them to share and discuss their findings.

Sir Philip Sidney
(1554–1586)

Author of *Sidney's Sonnets*

Sir Philip Sidney was a courtier, scholar, poet, and soldier—a true "Renaissance man." He attended both Oxford and Cambridge, and furthered his knowledge by traveling extensively through Europe. He became a favorite in the court of Queen Elizabeth I.

Groomed for Success Nephew of the earl of Leicester and son of the statesman Sir Henry Sidney, Philip Sidney was certainly well connected. Throughout his life, though, he carried himself with remarkable modesty. His schoolmate and, later, biographer Fulke Greville remarked on his "staidness of mind, [and] lovely and familiar gravity."

A Brave Soldier Around 1580, Sidney fell out of favor with the queen when he wrote a letter urging her not to marry the duke of Anjou. Eventually, he regained status with her and was knighted in 1583. In 1586, during a military engagement against the Spanish Catholics in Holland, Sidney was severely wounded. As he lay on the battle-field, he bravely insisted that the water offered to him be given to another wounded soldier. Twenty-six days later he died, to the great grief of his country.

Pioneering Sonneteer Sidney wrote the first great sonnet sequence in English, *Astrophel and Stella.* Before Sidney, Sir Thomas Wyatt and others had written excellent sonnets, but Sidney's were the first linked by subject matter and theme. Each sonnet addresses an aspect of Astrophel's love for Stella. This sonnet sequence was inspired by Penelope Devereux (Stella), to whom Sir Philip (Astrophel) had been engaged. The engagement was later broken, and Penelope married Lord Rich. Yet, for most readers, Stella's name will forever be linked with Astrophel's.

Either I will find a way, or I will make one.
—Sir Philip Sidney

❻ Background

More About the Author

Sir Philip Sidney was considered the ideal gentleman of his day. He was an excellent horseman, and was among the few Englishmen of his time who were interested in the Americas. His *Defence of Poesie* introduced the critical ideas of Renaissance theorists to England. His travels in Europe made it possible for him to perfect his Latin, French, and Italian, and to gain a knowledge of European politics and ideas.

❼ About the Selections

The sonnet sequence *Astrophel and Stella* includes 108 sonnets, plus 11 songs. Because it is known that *Astrophel and Stella* deals with Sidney's love for Penelope Devereaux, we know that Astrophel represents Sidney and Stella represents Devereaux. In fact, the name *Astrophel,* created from ancient Greek word parts, *astro-* meaning "star" and *-phil,* meaning "lover," is thought to be a pun using Sidney's first name, Philip, as well as a description of Astrophel's role in the sonnets as the one who loves Stella, the star.

The sequence of sonnets reflects the course of Astrophel's love. In Sonnet 31, a frustrated lover sees his own lovesickness mirrored in the pale moon, and in Sonnet 39, he seeks in sleep a release from his suffering.

Differentiated Instruction   for Universal Access

Support for Special-Needs Students

Pick a sonnet and write it on the board. Beside the original sonnet, write a paraphrased version in sentences, rather than in sonnet format. Supply and call attention to substitutes for words students might not understand, and point out to students where you change word order. Discuss the meaning of the paraphrased version, connecting to stories, songs, or real-life experiences of students. Link each sentence to the relevant lines of the whole sonnet so students understand what the poem says.

Enrichment for Gifted/Talented Students

Have students imagine that the moon, which Sidney addresses in Sonnet 31, can actually hear the poet. Have students write a sonnet that gives the moon's reply to the author. Is Sidney wrong about the moon's sadness? What or who might the moon love?

All video resources are available online at www.PHLitOnline.com.

❽ Humanities

Unknown Youth Leaning Against a Tree among Roses, c. 1590, by Nicholas Hilliard (1547-1619)

Hilliard was an accomplished miniaturist and goldsmith who served as court artist to both Elizabeth I and James I. He painted some of the most famous people of his time, including Francis Drake, Walter Raleigh, and Mary Queen of Scots.

Like several other of his miniatures, *Unknown Youth Leaning Against a Tree among Roses* shows his subject in a detailed natural setting and uses even lighting across the entire scene. Hilliard's work was an influence on many other portrait artists of his time. Use this question for discussion:

In this minature, does Hilliard seem concerned with accurately portraying his subject? Explain.

Possible response: Hilliard includes many precise details in this minature, but as a whole, the image does not seem realistic. The man's pose and his perfectly-placed hair and clothing seem to indicate that Hilliard is more interested in portraying a stylized ideal than a realistic image.

❾ Critical Thinking

Infer

1. Review with students the background material they have read and heard, including biographical information about Sir Philip Sidney, and information about the sonnet sequence *Astrophel and Stella*.

2. Tell students that they can combine what they have learned so far from the text with their own personal knowledge, such as that gained from reading Spenser's sonnets, to infer, or predict, what Sonnet 31 will be like.

3. **Ask:** What do you predict will be the mood and subject of Sonnet 31?

    Possible responses: Students will likely predict that the mood will be sad, and they may infer from Sidney's biography that the sonnet will be about love that does not work out.

258 Celebrating Humanity (1485–1625)

Think Aloud

Vocabulary: Using Context

Direct students' attention to the word *deemed* in line 10. Use the following "think aloud" to model the skill of using context to infer the meaning of the words. Say to students:

> I may not know what *deemed* means, but in this question, it seems to be used as a past-tense verb. I know that *but* often means the same thing as "nothing but" or "just the same as." So *deemed* seems to say that *constant love* is the same as *want of wit*. I know that a want of something means a lack of

it, and the footnote says *wit* means "intelligence." So this verb is linking constant love with stupidity. That sounds sort of judgmental or like name-calling. Maybe that is what *deem* means. Let me try paraphrasing the question with that meaning: "Is constant love judged as nothing but stupidity?" Yes, that seems like a good guess. I can confirm it later by looking it up in the dictionary.

⑨ SONNET 31

SIR PHILIP SIDNEY

With how sad steps, O Moon, thou climb'st the skies!
How silently, and with how *wan* a face!
What, may it be that even in heavenly place
That busy archer[1] his sharp arrows tries?
5   Sure, if that long-with-love-acquainted eyes
Can judge of love, thou feel'st a lover's case.
⑩   I read it in thy looks, thy *languished* grace,
To me, that feel the like, thy state descries.[2]
Then even of fellowship, O Moon, tell me
10 Is constant love deemed there but want of wit?[3]
Are beauties there as proud as here they be?
Do they above love to be loved, and yet
Those lovers scorn whom that love doth possess?
Do they call virtue there ungratefulness?

---

1. **busy archer** Cupid, the Roman god of love.
2. **descries** reveals.
3. **wit** intelligence.

Vocabulary

wan (wän) *adj.* sickly; pale

languished (laŋ′ gwisht) *adj.* weakened; dulled

◀ **Critical Viewing**
Which details suggest that the subject of this portrait might be the speaker in Sonnet 31? **[Connect]**

from Sidney's Sonnets **259**

⑩ Engaging the Essential Question

1. Remind students that, although all sonnets have fourteen lines, usually in iambic pentameter, sonneteers varied the rhyme schemes to create different forms. Review the rhyme scheme of the octave and sestet in a Petrarchan sonnet, *abbaabba cdecde,* and of a Spenserian sonnet, *abab bcbc cdcd ee.*

2. **Ask** students to determine the rhyme scheme in lines 1–8.
Answer: *abbaabba.* **Ask** which sonnet form this scheme matches.
Answer: Petrarchan.

3. Next, have students look at the next six lines. Help them to understand that people in Sidney's time would consider *yet* to rhyme with *wit.* **Ask** students to determine the rhyme scheme of lines 9-14.
Answer: *cdcd ee.* **Ask** which sonnet form this scheme matches.
Answer: Spenserian.

4. Point out that Sidney has blended two forms in Sonnet 31. **Ask** students to discuss whether this blend means that he is respecting sonnet traditions or violating them.
Possible response: He respects the basic rules of the form, but uses the flexibility of the rules about rhyme to do something new.

5. **Ask** students to speculate on reasons why Sidney would want to innovate.
Possible responses: In writing more than 100 sonnets, he may have wanted some variety. He might have been unable to say the things about love he wanted to express using the existing rhyme schemes.

⑪ Critical Viewing

Possible responses: The blue shades in the picture suggest the scene is lit by moonlight. He is alone, without a partner. He holds his hand over his heart as though it aches with sadness.

259

Literary Analysis

The Sonnet

1. **Ask** students the Literary Analysis question: How does the rhyme scheme of lines 1–8 make this sonnet different from a typical Spenserian or Petrarchan sonnet? **Answer:** The rhyme scheme Sidney uses is *abab abab*, rather than the Spenserian *abab bcbc* or the Petrarchan *abba abba*.

▶ **Monitor Progress: Ask** students to identify the rhyme scheme of the last six lines. Then have them identify which of the two forms this sonnet is more like. **Answer:** The rhyme scheme is *cdcdee*, so this sonnet is more like a Spenserian sonnet.

▶ **Reteach:** Remind students that Petrarchan sonnets have a rhyme scheme of *abba abba cdecde*, while Spenserian sonnets have a rhyme scheme of *abab bcbc cdcdee*.

ASSESS

Answers

Before students respond, you may wish to have them write a brief objective summary of the selection. As they answer the questions below, remind them to support their answers with evidence from the text.

1. (a) The moon appears sad. (b) The speaker thinks that the moon is lovesick. (c) The speaker reveals his own situation by claiming that the moon looks as pale as he feels, prompting his questions—all of which tell something of his own experience.

2. (a) Sleep assures one of peace; it restores the keen mind; it heals sorrows; it is the poor man's wealth; it allows the prisoner to wander far and wide in his dreams; and it treats all people the same. (b) The speaker promises sleep the reward of seeing Stella's image in the speaker's dreams. (c) The speaker craves sleep because he will dream of Stella.

3. **Possible response:** Students may say that the limitations of the <u>form</u> force the poets to express their feelings in a compact and memorable way, which explains the <u>influence</u> the poems continue to have.

SONNET 39
SIR PHILIP SIDNEY

Vocabulary
balm (bäm) *n.* ointment or other thing that heals and soothes

Literary Analysis
The Sonnet How does the rhyme scheme of lines 1–8 make this sonnet different from a typical Spenserian or Petrarchan sonnet?

⓬

Come sleep! O sleep, the certain knot of peace,
The baiting place[1] of wit, the balm of woe,
The poor man's wealth, the prisoner's release,
The indifferent[2] judge between the high and low;
5   With shield of proof[3] shield me from out the prease[4]
Of those fierce darts Despair at me doth throw:
O make in me those civil wars to cease;
I will good tribute pay, if thou do so.
Take thou of me smooth pillows, sweetest bed,
10   A chamber deaf to noise, and blind to light,
A rose garland, and a weary head:
And if these things, as being thine by right,
Move not thy heavy grace, thou shalt in me,
Livelier than elsewhere, Stella's image see.

---

1. **baiting place** place for refreshment.
2. **indifferent** impartial.
3. **proof** proven strength.
4. **prease** crowd.

Critical Reading

Cite textual evidence to support your responses.

© 1. **Key Ideas and Details** **(a)** In Sonnet 31, how does the moon appear to the speaker? **(b) Infer:** To what does the speaker attribute the moon's mood? **(c) Analyze:** How does the speaker reveal his own situation by addressing the moon?

© 2. **Key Ideas and Details** **(a)** What benefits does the speaker attribute to sleep in lines 1–4 of Sonnet 39? **(b)** What "reward" does he promise sleep in lines 13–14? **(c) Interpret:** Judging from this "reward," why does he crave sleep?

© 3. **Craft and Structure** What, if anything, do the regular rhymes and briefness of the sonnet form add to these poets' expressions of love? Explain. In your response, use at least two of these Essential Question words: *form, imitation, influence, Renaissance*. [Connecting to the Essential Question: What is the relationship of the writer to tradition?]

260 Celebrating Humanity (1485–1625)

Concept Connector

Reading Strategy Graphic Organizer
Ask students to review the graphic organizers in which they have restated the essential information in the selections by paraphrasing. Then have students share their organizers and compare how they paraphrased poets' lines.

Activating Prior Knowledge
Have students return to their responses to the Activating Prior Knowledge activity. Ask them to explain whether their thoughts have changed and, if so, how.

Connecting to the Essential Question
Have students compare their responses to the prompt, given before they completed reading the sonnets, with their thoughts afterward. Have them work individually or in groups, writing or discussing their thoughts, to formulate their new responses. Then lead a class discussion, probing for what students have learned that confirms or invalidates their initial thoughts. Encourage students to cite specific textual details to support their responses.

Literary Analysis

1. Craft and Structure Reread Sidney's Sonnets 31 and 39, and analyze their rhyme schemes. Do these **sonnets** more closely follow the **Spenserian** or the **Petrarchan** form? Explain.

2. Craft and Structure Review Spenser's three sonnets. Then, explain what poets can achieve in a **sonnet sequence** that they cannot in individual poems. Consider such factors as shifting moods and developing characters.

3. Comparing Literary Works Using a chart like the one here, compare and contrast one of Sidney's sonnets with one of Spenser's.

Petrarchan/ Spenserian?	Speaker's Situation	Addressed to...	Types of Images	Speaker's Conclusion

4. Craft and Structure (a) Compare the person or thing addressed in each of the sonnets you entered in the chart. **(b)** Explain how the basic **sonnet sequence** situation justifies or motivates each choice of addressee.

5. Craft and Structure (a) Compare the dominant purpose of each sonnet in the chart—to express hope, to persuade, to complain, and so on. **(b)** Explain how the sonnet sequence situation justifies or motivates each purpose.

6. Integration of Knowledge and Ideas Explain how, in each sonnet, the writer goes beyond the basic sonnet situation to give a general insight into the nature of love or life.

7. Integration of Knowledge and Ideas (a) Renaissance poets compared those they loved to "perfect" things in nature or to timeless figures from mythology. To what "perfect" things do songwriters compare their loves today? **(b)** In what other ways are modern songwriters similar to or different from Renaissance sonneteers?

Reading Strategy

8. Reread the octave of Sidney's Sonnet 39. **(a) Determine the essential message** of lines 1–4 by writing a *paraphrase* of them. **(b)** Then, paraphrase lines 5–8. **(c)** What problem do lines 1-8 set up?

9. (a) Reread and then paraphrase the sestet of Sonnet 39. You may break the sestet into smaller sections for paraphrasing. **(b)** What does the sestet suggest about the reason for the problem in the octave? Explain.

Common Core State Standards

Writing
2. Write informative/ explanatory texts to examine and convey complex ideas, concepts, and information clearly and accurately through the effective selection, organization, and analysis of content. (p. 262)
4. Produce clear and coherent writing in which the development, organization, and style are appropriate to task, purpose, and audience. (p. 262)

Language
4.a. Use context as a clue to the meaning of a word or phrase. (p. 262)
4.b. Identify and correctly use patterns of word changes that indicate different meanings or parts of speech. (p. 262)

Answers

1. Sonnet 31 is half Petrarchan (*abba abba*) and half Spenserian (*cdcd ee*); Sonnet 39 comes closer to Spenserian, but is still a slight variation (*abab abab cdcdee*).

2. In a sonnet sequence, the poet can develop characters, explore a relationship, and show how things unfold.

3. **Possible responses:** Sonnet 35: Spenserian; speaker longs to gaze upon his beloved; addressed to himself or the reader; image is hungry eyes; conclusion is that the world's glory is dark compared to his love. Sonnet 31: Petrarchan/Spenserian blend; speaker is lovesick; addressed to the moon; image is pale moon; conclusion is that love is cruel.

4. (a) Spenser addresses his writing to his reader; Sidney addresses the moon. (b) The basic situation is unrequited love. Spenser's speaker, bewildered by the constant torment of love, speaks to himself or the reader to make sense of his situation. Sidney's despairing speaker finds solace in his loneliness by holding a conversation with the moon.

5. (a) Spenser's sonnets express hope, and then persuade and praise. Sidney complains, and then seeks escape. (b) The sequence is natural in both cases—Spenser progresses from hope to love; Sidney progresses from pain to escape.

6. In the Spenser sonnets, we gain insight into the progression of a successful relationship. Sidney shows the more painful side of love, where the object of desire is unattainable.

7. **Possible responses:** (a) Songwriters today compare their loves to angels or other spiritual figures, dreams, or "perfect" technologies such as satellites or life preservers. (b) Modern songwriters work within formulas and exaggerate their emotions. Few, however, create linked sequences of more than 100 songs.

8. (a) **Possible response:** Please, wonderful sleep, I'll reward you if you help me escape from my despair. (b) The speaker is miserable and wants to find some relief in sleep, but cannot. (c) The speaker wants to sleep to forget Stella, but when he is asleep, he will dream of her.

Answers continued

9. (a) **Possible response:** Sleep, take everything that already belongs to sleep, but if these things do not move you, know that you will see Stella when I dream. (b) Thinking and dreaming about Stella are the reasons for the speaker's despair and sleeplessness.

261

Vocabulary Acquisition and Use

1. Introduce the skill using the instruction on the student page.

2. Have students complete the Word Analysis activity and the vocabulary practice.

Hard Analysis

1. languor
2. languid
3. languished

Vocabulary

1. The word *weakened* provides a clue that *languished* might mean "became weak."

2. The sentence says her skin tone *matched* her hankie, suggesting that *wan* means "pale."

3. The word *soothing* suggests that a *balm* is something that would make her feel better.

4. *Devise* is used as a verb and the sentence says she devised plans, which suggests that *devise* means "made" or "created."

5. The word *haughty*, which suggests pride, is a clue that *deign* might mean "lower herself."

6. *Assay* is used as a verb and the sentence says he would assay an approach, which suggests that *assay* means "try" or "attempt."

Writing

1. To guide students in writing their explanatory texts, give them the **Support for Writing** page (*Unit 2 Resources,* p. 15).

2. Remind students that they should create a how-to guide for someone who knows nothing about sonnets.

3. If students have difficulty understanding the assignment, suggest that they mentally compare the sonnet to a bicycle that must be put together. Like an instruction book for a bike, their manuals should name and explain all the parts of the sonnet.

4. Use the **Rubrics for How-to-Essay,** *Professional Development Guidebook,* pages 254–255, to evaluate students' work.

Vocabulary Acquisition and Use

Word Analysis: Patterns of Word Changes

Words often change form and *meaning* when they serve different *functions*. For example, the verb *languish,* which means "to become weak," has the past participle form *languished.* This form can be used as an adjective ("languished grace") or as a verb ("He languished under the weight of illness"). Other forms of the word are *languid,* an adjective that means "drooping" or "weak," and the noun *languor,* meaning "weakness."

For each sentence below, decide what function or meaning the missing word should have. Then identify the form of *languish* that belongs in the blank, explaining each choice.

1. His _____ was caused by overexertion.
2. The worker's movements were _____ at the end of the day.
3. Everyone _____ in the heat.

Writing

Explanatory Text As a technical writer, you have been contracted to compose a *manual* explaining *procedures* for putting together a Petrarchan sonnet. The manual will be used by the company's newest sonneteers, so it should be clear, accurate, and easy to follow. It should also employ and briefly define the *technical* terms for each element of the sonnet, including *octave, sestet, iambic pentameter,* and *rhyme scheme.*

Prewriting Consider using some or all of the following: a preface, a table of contents, an overview of the product, in-depth descriptions of each part, step-by-step instructions, an FAQ section (Frequently Asked Questions), and a Where to Find Help page.

Drafting As you draft your manual, keep your readers in mind. Define all technical terms and put all concepts into clear, concise language.

Revising Revise with an eye to format. Have you included too much information on a single page? Can your reader glance at a page and understand what the page contains? Add headings, bullets, boldfacing, and other text features as needed.

Model: Anticipating Reader Confusion
II. The Sestet
The second half of the sonnet is made up of a *sestet.*
A **sestet** is a group of six lines with the rhyme scheme *cdecde.*

The writer has anticipated and answered the following questions: *What is a sestet? What is its rhyme scheme?*

Vocabulary: Context Clues

Context clues are words and phrases in a text that help you reason out the meaning of an unfamiliar word. For each underlined word below, explain how clues in the sentence help you identify the word's *contextual meaning.*

1. The young woman <u>languished</u>, weakened by neglect.
2. Her <u>wan</u> complexion matched the washed-out hue of her hankie.
3. Even a glimpse of her beloved would be a soothing <u>balm</u> to her broken heart.
4. Desperate, she began to <u>devise</u> an array of complicated plans.
5. Then, she grew haughty; she would never <u>deign</u> to answer his call.
6. Just let him <u>assay</u> an approach, she muttered.

262 Celebrating Humanity (1485–1625)

Assessment Resources

Unit 2 Resources

L1 L2 EL **Selection Test A,** pp. 20–22. Administer Test A to less advanced readers.

L3 L4 EL **Selection Test B,** pp. 23–25. Administer Test B to on-level and more advanced students.

L3 L4 **Open-Book Test,** pp. 17–19. As an alternative, give the Open-Book Test.

All **Customizable Test Bank**

All **Self-tests**
Students may prepare for the **Selection Test** by taking the **Self-test** online.

All assessment resources are available at www.PHLitOnline.com.

Conventions and Style: Subordinating Conjunctions

For a smoother flow and more variety in your writing, try using subordinating conjunctions to combine sentences. A **subordinating conjunction** joins two complete ideas by making one idea subordinate to, or dependent on, the other.

Common Subordinating Conjunctions

after	as though	if	unless
although	because	now that	until
as if	before	since	when
as soon as	even though	so that	while

When you use **subordination** to combine sentences, you show which idea is more important.

Use Subordination to Combine Sentences

Simple Sentences: Philip Sidney regained the queen's favor. Then he was knighted.
Combined: Philip Sidney was knighted *after* he regained the queen's favor.

Simple Sentences: The speaker describes leaves. He is really talking about a book.
Combined: *Although* the speaker describes leaves, he is really talking about a book

Ⓔ Writing and Speaking Conventions

A. Writing For each pair of ideas, construct a sentence that uses a subordinating conjunction to join the ideas.

1. the poet is happy—he is gazing at his beloved

2. her name was washed away—the tide came in

> **Example:** the moon climbs the skies—it does so with sad steps
> **Sentence:** Although the moon climbs the skies, it does so with sad steps.

Punctuation Tip: Use a comma after a subordinate clause that comes at the beginning of a sentence but not, in most cases, before a subordinate clause that comes at the end of a sentence.

B. Speaking Choose one of the sonnets and summarize it to a classmate. In your summary, correctly use two subordinating conjunctions.

Practice In items 1–5, supply an appropriate subordinating conjunction to complete each sentence. In items 6–10, combine the two sentences using a subordinating conjunction.

1. According to the poet's guess, the moon is sad _____ it has lost in love.

2. Poets often compare lovers to the moon or stars, _____ their beloved is perfect.

3. The poems will keep her memory alive _____ she dies.

4. The moon appears _____ it feels weak or sick.

5. He asks for smooth pillows, a comfortable bed, and a dark and quiet room _____ he can sleep soundly.

6. He has looked at her. He does not want to look at anything else.

7. The writing is finished. The sea washes it away.

8. He will still love her. She does not return his feelings.

9. He wants to please her. He loves her.

10. The poet addresses the moon. He acts as if the moon understands him.

> **PH** WRITING COACH
> Further instruction and practice are available in *Prentice Hall Writing Coach*.

Extend the Lesson

Sentence Modeling

Write and read aloud the following lines:
Where whenas death shall the world subdue, /Our love shall live, and later life renew. (Spenser, Sonnet 75, lines 13–14)
Provide explanation of the lines, as needed. Then **ask** students to identify the subordinating conjunction.
Answer: *where whenas*
Discuss with students the progress of the sentence from the legalistic conjunctions to the proclamation of love's triumph over death to the rhythmically emphasized assertion that it will renew life. Have students imitate each feature discussed in a sentence on a topic of their choice.

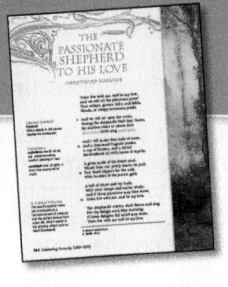

The Passionate Shepherd to His Love
• The Nymph's Reply to the Shepherd
Lesson Pacing Guide

DAY 1 Preteach

- Administer the Reading and Vocabulary Warm-ups (*Unit 2 Resources*, pp. 26–29) as necessary.
- Introduce the Literary Analysis concept: Pastoral Tradition.
- Introduce the Reading Strategy: Analyzing Similar Themes.
- Build background with the author and Background features.
- Develop thematic thinking with Connecting to the Essential Question.
- Teach the selection vocabulary.

DAYS 2–3 Preteach/Teach/Assess

- Distribute copies of the appropriate graphic organizer for the Reading Strategy (*Graphic Organizer Transparencies*, pp. 38–39).
- Distribute copies of the appropriate graphic organizer for Literary Analysis (*Graphic Organizer Transparencies*, pp. 40–41).
- Prepare students to read with the Activating Prior Knowledge activities (TE).
- Informally monitor comprehension while students read.
- Use the Reading Check questions to confirm comprehension.
- Develop students' understanding of pastoral tradition using the Literary Analysis prompts.
- Develop students' ability to analyze similar themes using the Reading Strategy prompts.
- Reinforce vocabulary with the Vocabulary notes.
- Assess students' comprehension and mastery of the skills by having them answer the Critical Reading, Literary Analysis, and Reading Strategy questions.
- Have students complete the Vocabulary Lesson.

DAY 4 Extend/Assess

- Have students complete the Writing Lesson and write compare-and-contrast essay. (You may assign as homework.)
- Administer Selection Test A or B (*Unit 2 Resources*, pp. 38–40 or 41–43).

Common Core State Standards

Reading Literature 2. Determine two or more themes or central ideas of a text and analyze their development over the course of the text, including how they interact and build on one another to produce a complex account.

Writing 2.c. Use appropriate and varied transitions and syntax to link the major sections of the text, create cohesion, and clarify the relationships among complex ideas and concepts.

Language 4.a. Use context as a clue to the meaning of a word or phrase.

Additional Standards Practice
Common Core Companion, *pp. 15–22; 196–207; 324–331*

Daily Block Scheduling
Each day in this Lesson Pacing Guide represents a 40–50 minute period. Teachers using block scheduling may combine days to revise pacing. In addition, teachers may differentiate and support core instruction by integrating components for extended and intensive support as students require. See the Guide to Selected Leveled Resources (facing page).

Guide to Selected Leveled Resources

RTI Tier 1 (students performing on level)

The Passionate Shepherd to His Love • The Nymph's Reply to the Shepherd

Warm Up	**Practice, model,** and **monitor** fluency, working **with the whole class** or **in groups.**	Vocabulary and **Reading Warm-ups B,** *Unit 2 Resources,* pp. 26–27, 29
Comprehension/Skills	**Support** and **monitor** comprehension and skills development, having students complete the activities, graphic organizers, and interactive prompts **independently** or **as a class.**	• *Reader's Notebook,* adapted instruction and summary **EL** *Reader's Notebook: English Learner's Version,* adapted instruction and summary • **Reading Skill Graphic Organizer B,** *Graphic Organizer Transparencies,* p. 39 • **Literary Analysis Graphic Organizer B,** *Graphic Organizer Transparencies,* p. 41
Monitor Progress [A]	**Monitor** student progress with the differentiated curriculum-based assessment in the *Unit Resources.*	• **Selection Test B,** *Unit 2 Resources,* pp. 41–43 • **Open-Book Test,** *Unit 2 Resources,* pp. 35–37

RTI Tier 2 (students requiring intervention)

The Passionate Shepherd to His Love • The Nymph's Reply to the Shepherd

Warm Up	**Practice, model,** and **monitor** fluency **in groups** or **with individuals.**	• **Vocabulary and Reading Warm-ups A,** *Unit 2 Resources,* pp. 26–28 • *Hear It!* Audio CD
Comprehension/Skills	• **Support** and **monitor** comprehension and skills development, working **in small groups** or **with individuals.** • As students complete the selection in the appropriate version of the *Reader's Notebook,* **monitor** comprehension frequently with group questions and individual instruction. • **Model** strategies while guiding students in completing the activities and prompts in the *Reader's Notebook,* as well as the graphic organizers. • **Practice** skills and **monitor** mastery with the *Reading Kit* worksheets.	• *Reader's Notebook: Adapted Version,* adapted instruction and summary **EL** *Reader's Notebook: English Learner's Version,* adapted instruction and summary • **Reading Skill Graphic Organizer A,** *Graphic Organizer Transparencies,* p. 38 • **Literary Analysis Graphic Organizer A,** *Graphic Organizer Transparencies,* p. 40 • *Reading Kit,* Practice worksheets
Monitor Progress [A]	**Monitor** student progress with the differentiated curriculum-based assessment in the *Unit Resources* and in the *Reading Kit.*	• **Selection Test A,** *Unit 2 Resources,* pp. 38–40 • *Reading Kit,* Assess worksheets

TIER 3 Tier 3 intervention may require consultation with the student's special-education or dyslexia specialist. For additional support, see the Tier 2 activities and resources listed above.

🖥 One-on-one teaching   👥 Group work   👫 Whole class instruction   👤 Independent work   [A] Assessment

For a complete guide to selection support, including support for Advanced students, see the Overview of Resources in the frontmatter.

The Passionate Shepherd to His Love
• The Nymph's Reply to the Shepherd

RESOURCES FOR:

L1 Special-Needs Students

L2 Below-Level Students (Tier 2)

L3 On-Level Students (Tier 1)

L4 Advanced Students (Tier 1)

EL English Learners

All All Students

Vocabulary/Fluency/Prior Knowledge

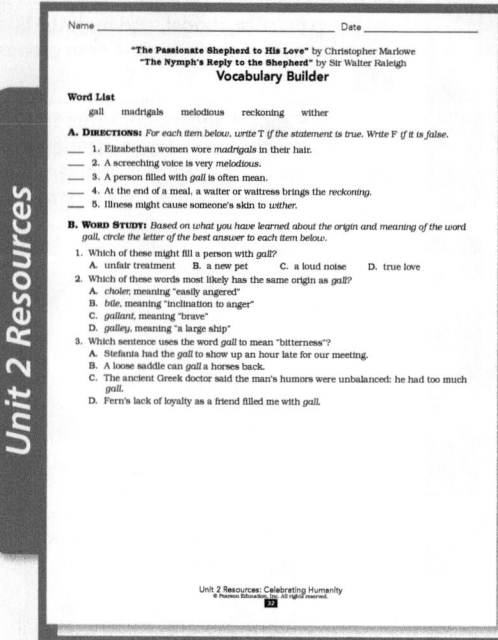

All **Vocabulary Builder,** p. 32

Also available for these selections:

EL **L1** **L2** Vocabulary Warm-ups A and B, pp. 26–27

EL **L1** **L2** Reading Warm-ups A and B, pp. 28–29

Reader's Notebooks

Pre- and postreading pages for these selection appear in an interactive format in the *Reader's Notebooks.* Each *Notebook* is differentiated for a different group of learners. The selections in the Adapted and English Learner's versions are abridged.

L2 **L3** *Reader's Notebook*

L1 *Reader's Notebook: Adapted Version*

EL *Reader's Notebook: English Learner's Version*

EL *Reader's Notebook: Spanish Version*

© *Common Core Companion*

Additional instruction and practice for each Common Core State Standard

Selection Support

Graphic Organizer Transparencies

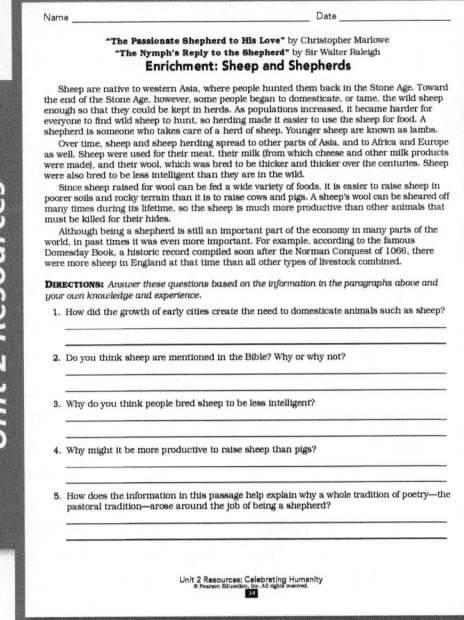

"The Passionate Shepherd to His Love" by Christopher Marlowe
"The Nymph's Reply to the Shepherd" by Sir Walter Raleigh

Before You Read A: Analyzing Similar Themes

"The Passionate Shepherd to His Love"	Both	"The Nymph's Reply to the Shepherd"
Uses the phrase "live with me, and be my love" in first, fifth, and sixth stanzas	Written in iambic pentameter—lines in which most feet are iambs (an unstressed syllable followed by a stressed syllable) and there are five feet in each line.	Uses the phrase "live with thee, and be thy love" in first and sixth stanzas; uses the phrase "come to thee and be thy love" in the fifth stanza

EL **L3** **Reading: Graphic Organizer A**
(partially filled in), p. 38

Also available for these selections:

EL **L1** **L2** **Reading: Graphic Organizer B,**
p. 38

EL **L1** **L2** **Literary Analysis: Graphic**
Organizer A (partially filled in), p. 40

EL **L3** **Literary Analysis: Graphic Organizer B**
p. 41

Skills Development/Extension

Unit 2 Resources

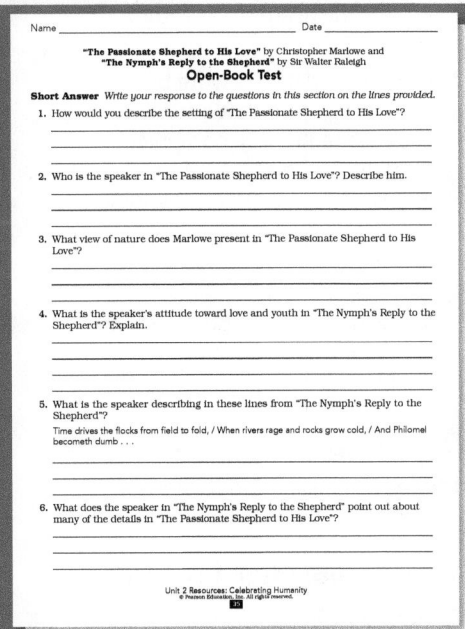

Name _____ Date _____

"The Passionate Shepherd to His Love" by Christopher Marlowe
"The Nymph's Reply to the Shepherd" by Sir Walter Raleigh
Enrichment: Sheep and Shepherds

Sheep are native to western Asia, where people hunted them back in the Stone Age. Toward the end of the Stone Age, however, some people began to domesticate, or tame, the wild sheep enough so that they could be kept in herds. As populations increased, it became harder for everyone to find wild sheep to hunt, so herding made it easier to use the sheep for food. A shepherd is someone who takes care of a herd of sheep. Younger sheep are known as lambs.

Over time, sheep and sheep herding spread to other parts of Asia, and to Africa and Europe as well. Sheep were used for their meat, their milk (from which cheese and other milk products were made), and their wool, which was bred to be thicker and thicker over the centuries. Sheep were also bred to be less intelligent than they are in the wild.

Since sheep raised for wool can be fed a wide variety of foods, it is easier to raise sheep in poorer soils and rocky terrain than it is to raise cows and pigs. A sheep's wool can be sheared off many times during its lifetime, so the sheep is much more productive than other animals that must be killed for their hides.

Although being a shepherd is still an important part of the economy in many parts of the world, in past times it was even more important. For example, according to the famous Domesday Book, a historic record compiled soon after the Norman Conquest of 1066, there were more sheep in England at that time than all other types of livestock combined.

DIRECTIONS: *Answer these questions based on the information in the paragraphs above and your own knowledge and experience.*

1. How did the growth of early cities create the need to domesticate animals such as sheep?

2. Do you think sheep are mentioned in the Bible? Why or why not?

3. Why do you think people bred sheep to be less intelligent?

4. Why might it be more productive to raise sheep than pigs?

5. How does the information in this passage help explain why a whole tradition of poetry—the pastoral tradition—arose around the job of being a shepherd?

L4 **Enrichment: Sheep and Shepherds** p. 34

Also available for these selections:

All **Literary Analysis,** p. 30

All **Reading,** p. 31

EL **L3** **L4** **Support for Writing,** p. 33

Assessment

Name _____ Date _____

"The Passionate Shepherd to His Love" by Christopher Marlowe and
"The Nymph's Reply to the Shepherd" by Sir Walter Raleigh
Open-Book Test

Short Answer *Write your response to the questions in this section on the lines provided.*

1. How would you describe the setting of "The Passionate Shepherd to His Love"?

2. Who is the speaker in "The Passionate Shepherd to His Love"? Describe him.

3. What view of nature does Marlowe present in "The Passionate Shepherd to His Love"?

4. What is the speaker's attitude toward love and youth in "The Nymph's Reply to the Shepherd"? Explain.

5. What is the speaker describing in these lines from "The Nymph's Reply to the Shepherd"?
Time drives the flocks from field to fold, / When rivers rage and rocks grow cold, / And Philomel becometh dumb . . .

6. What does the speaker in "The Nymph's Reply to the Shepherd" point out about many of the details in "The Passionate Shepherd to His Love"?

L3 **L4** **Open-Book Test,** pp. 35–37

Also available for these selections:

EL **L3** **L4** **Selection Test A,** pp. 38–40

EL **L1** **L2** **Selection Test B,** pp. 41–43

Online Resources: All print materials are also available online.

- complete narrated selection text
- a thematically related video with writing prompt
- an interactive graphic organizer
- highlighting feature
- access to all student print resources, adapted to individual student needs
- Spanish and English summaries
- adapted selection translations in Spanish

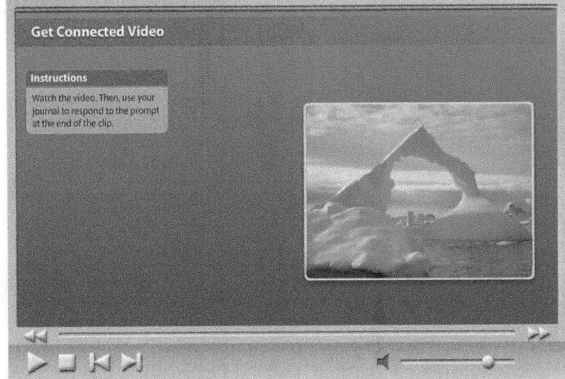

Get Connected! (thematic video with writing prompt)

Also available:

Background Video
All videos are available in Spanish.

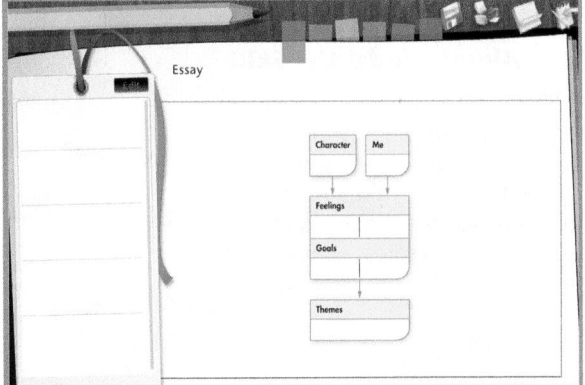

Writer's Journal (with graphics feature)

Also available:

Vocabulary Central (tools and activities for studying vocabulary)

❶ 🔍 Connecting to the Essential Question

1. Review the assignment with the class.

2. Prepare students to write by reminding them that a sense of *place* is not just a geographical term. It can be a state of mind or a sense of values that gives someone a basic orientation in the world.

3. As students read, have them look for examples of the poets' imagination and observation of the world.

❷ Literary Analysis

Introduce the skill using the instruction on the student page.

Think Aloud: Model the Skill

Say to students:

As I read, I am looking for examples of pastoral conventions. I am also looking for how these conventions are ordered and repeated. I want to see if they convey any universal themes about love, youth, nature, and time.

❸ Reading Strategy

1. Introduce the strategy using the instruction on the student page.

2. Give students a copy of **Reading Strategy Graphic Organizer B,** page 39 in *Graphic Organizer Transparencies,* to fill out as they read.

Think Aloud: Model the Skill

Say to students:

To analyze similar themes in poems, I compare and contrast which themes they present, how they organize the themes, and the views they express about the themes.

❹ Vocabulary

1. Pronounce each word, giving its definition, and have students say it aloud.

2. For more guidance, see the *Classroom Strategies and Teaching Routines* card for introducing vocabulary.

264

Before You Read

The Passionate Shepherd to His Love • The Nymph's Reply to the Shepherd

❶ **Connecting to the Essential Question** As you read, notice which poem's setting is shaped more by the imagination and which by observation of the world. Making this distinction will help you answer this Essential Question: **What is the relationship between literature and place?**

❷ **Literary Analysis**

Works in the **pastoral** tradition, in poetry or prose, celebrate the pleasures of country life. This tradition, dating back to ancient Greece, was developed by authors writing for an urban audience. These conventions of the pastoral allowed city dwellers to imagine a country life:

- shepherds addressing or describing a beloved shepherdess
- a natural setting that seems perfect in every respect
- simple pleasures and games, including singing contests

Comparing Literary Works While addressing pastoral conventions differently, Marlowe and Raleigh touch on a number of **universal themes:** the link between love and the delights of youth and nature, and the relationship of love to time—love conquering time or being conquered by it.

Note the variations in these themes as you read. Also, consider this *nuance:* Although Raleigh seems to be writing against the pastoral tradition, is he in some way part of it?

❸ **Reading Strategy**

ⓒ **Preparing to Read Complex Texts** As you read a poem, determine if it contains multiple themes. Then, decide how multiple themes add to the meaning of the poem. For example, do the themes build on or contradict each other?

When reading a pair of related poems, **analyze similar themes** in the two by comparing and contrasting their *patterns of organization* and *repetition.* For example, Marlowe and Raleigh use similar patterns of organization to create contrasting versions of pastoral themes. Use a chart like the one on this page to help you summarize each poem and then compare and contrast themes.

❹ **Vocabulary**

melodious (mə lō′ dē əs) *adj.* sweet-sounding; tuneful; pleasing to hear (p. 266)

madrigals (ma′ dri gəlz) *n.* short love poems set to music (p. 266)

reckoning (rek′ ən iŋ) *n.* accounting (p. 268)

gall (gôl) *n.* bitter feeling; deep spite (p. 268)

wither (wit͟h′ ər) *v.* dry up (p. 268)

Common Core State Standards

Reading Literature
2. Determine two or more themes or central ideas of a text and analyze their development over the course of the text, including how they interact and build on one another to produce a complex account.

Marlowe

Stanza #1
argument Come be my love and enjoy the countryside with me.
key words live, love, pleasures
themes pastoral, love and youth

Raleigh

Stanza #1
response I would be your love if you were telling the truth.
repeated words live, love, pleasures
themes anti-pastoral, untruthful lover

PHLit Online!
www.PHLitOnline.com

Vocabulary Development

Vocabulary Knowledge Rating
Create a **Vocabulary Knowledge Rating Chart** (*Professional Development Guidebook,* p. 33) for the vocabulary words on the student page. Give each student a copy of the chart with the words on it. Read the words aloud, and have students mark their rating of each in the Before Reading column.

Urge students to attend to these words as they read and discuss the selections.

In order to gauge how much instruction you need to provide, tally how many students are confident in their knowledge of each word. As students read, point out the words and their context.

Vocabulary Central, featuring tools and activities for studying vocabulary, is available online at **www.PHLitOnline.com.**

(1564–1593)

⑤ CHRISTOPHER MARLOWE

Author of "The Passionate Shepherd to His Love"

Killed before the age of thirty, Christopher Marlowe nonetheless managed to achieve renown as a brilliant playwright and poet. He spent his college days writing plays and serving as a government agent.

A Pioneer in Drama *Tamburlaine*, Marlowe's first drama, dazzled the public with its dynamic characterization of the tyrant-hero. All of Marlowe's subsequent plays may be seen as variations on a single theme: the larger-than-life hero who "overreaches," seeking to dominate everything around him.

The most famous example is the protagonist in *Doctor Faustus*, who thirsts for supreme knowledge and sells his soul to the devil. Marlowe matched the grandeur of his heroes with the grandeur of language, forging blank verse into a powerfully expressive medium for the first time in English drama.

A Life of Intrigue Marlowe has been described as a scoundrel, a ladies' man, and a hothead. By all accounts, his personal magnetism attracted both friends and enemies. When the court of Queen Elizabeth I wrote a letter implying that Marlowe had performed important government services, rumors flew about that he was a spy.

A Violent Death Marlowe was knifed to death in a tavern brawl in 1593. To this day, scholars question whether his death was really caused by his drunken refusal to pay his bill or whether he was murdered because of his undercover activities on behalf of the government.

(1554?–1618)

SIR WALTER RALEIGH

Author of "The Nymph's Reply to the Shepherd"

Sir Walter Raleigh is famed for having been a courtier, a navigator, a poet, and a historian.

A Charmed Life The half-brother of a famous sailor and an explorer, Raleigh began to satisfy his taste for adventure early in life, when he volunteered as a teenager for army service in France. A favorite of Queen Elizabeth I, he was given estates and prestigious appointments. In 1584, he set up a colony in Virginia.

Disaster When it was discovered that Raleigh had been secretly married to one of the queen's maids of honor, he and his wife were imprisoned in the Tower of London for a time but then released. Following the queen's death in 1603, Raleigh was accused of conspiring against King James I and was imprisoned again in the Tower, where he remained for thirteen years. He was eventually released to seek out gold along the Orinoco River in Venezuela. Despite a royal command not to engage in battle with Spain, Raleigh's fleet entered Spanish territory. In the ensuing fight, Raleigh lost his son and was forced to return to England. There, Raleigh was executed for disobeying the king's orders.

Literary Achievements Raleigh was a friend of some of the leading poets of his age, including Sir Philip Sydney and Edmund Spenser. Like them, he wrote elegant verse, rich in vivid imagery and classical allusions. Among Raleigh's numerous prose works is an ambitious book entitled *The History of the World* (1614), composed while he was in prison.

The Passionate Shepherd to His Love • The Nymph's Reply to the Shepherd **265**

Multidraft Reading

To assist struggling readers and to enhance reading for all, assign the text in chunks, as warranted by length, and apply multidraft reading protocols. For each reading, have students set the purpose indicated:

- **First reading**—identifying key ideas and details and answering any Reading Checks.
- **Second reading**—analyzing craft and structure and responding to the side-column prompts.
- **Third reading**—integrating knowledge and ideas, connecting to other texts and the world, and answering the end-of-selection questions.

For more guidance, refer to the *Classroom Strategies and Teaching Routines* card, **Multidraft Reading**.

⑤ Background

More About the Authors

Christopher Marlowe was born in Canterbury in 1564, the same year as William Shakespeare. He received his bachelor's and master's degrees from Corpus Christi College in Cambridge. School records show that his numerous absences nearly prevented him from earning a degree.

Sir Walter Raleigh, an adventurer and sailor, was affiliated with a poetic group called the "School of Night." This group, which included Christopher Marlowe, gained notoriety for being atheists because of their critical interpretation of Scripture.

PHLit Online! www.PHLitOnline.com

Teaching From Technology

Preparing to Read
Go to **PHLitOnline.com** and display the **Get Connected!** slideshow for this selection. Have the class brainstorm for responses to the writing prompt, entering ideas in the interactive journal. Then, have students complete their written responses as homework.
To build background, display the Background and More About the Author feature.

Using the Interactive Text
Go to **www.PHLitOnline.com** and display the **Enriched Online Student Edition**. As the class reads the selection or listens to the narration, record answers to side-column prompts using the graphic organizers accessible on the interactive page. Alternatively, have students use the online edition individually, answering the prompts as they read.

TEACH

❶ About the Selections

"The Passionate Shepherd to His Love" is perhaps one of the world's best-known examples of pastoral poetry. It has a lyric that celebrates the beauty and pleasures of country life. The poem also makes use of a number of traditional conventions: The speaker is a shepherd addressing a shepherdess with whom he is in love.

In Raleigh's "The Nymph's Reply to the Shepherd," the nymph (shepherdess) replies to the earnest, idealistic shepherd of Marlowe's poem in a skeptical, clear-eyed fashion, turning down his proposal.

❷ Activating Prior Knowledge

These poems by Marlowe and Raleigh are an exchange between a shepherd and his love. To stimulate interest, have students discuss what they would offer in an attempt to win over the person they love.

❸ Literary Analysis

Pastoral

1. Remind students that pastoral poetry uses imagery to create an idealized portrait of nature. Then, read aloud the second stanza of Marlowe's poem.

2. **Ask** students the Literary Analysis question: Which details in this stanza idealize the landscape?
Answer: The shepherds feeding their flocks, the "shallow rivers," and the "melodious" songs of the birds all create an unthreatening, idyllic vision of the landscape.

THE PASSIONATE SHEPHERD TO HIS LOVE ❶ ❷

CHRISTOPHER MARLOWE

Literary Analysis
Pastoral
Which details in this stanza idealize the landscape?

Vocabulary
melodious (mə lō′ dē əs)
adj. sweet-sounding; tuneful; pleasing to hear

madrigals (ma′ dri gəlz) *n.* short love poems set to music

❺ ▶ **Critical Viewing**
The poem's speaker views the countryside as a luxurious source of pleasure and the perfect escape from urban life. Which details in this painting reflect such an ideal? **[Connect]**

Come live with me, and be my love,
And we will all the pleasures prove[1]
That valleys, groves, hills, and fields,
Woods, or steepy mountain yields.

5 And we will sit upon the rocks,
❸ Seeing the shepherds feed their flocks,
By shallow rivers to whose falls
Melodious birds sing madrigals.

And I will make thee beds of roses,
10 And a thousand fragrant posies,
A cap of flowers, and a kirtle[2]
Embroidered all with leaves of myrtle;

A gown made of the finest wool,
Which from our pretty lambs we pull;
15 Fair lined slippers for the cold,
With buckles of the purest gold;

A belt of straw and ivy buds,
With coral clasps and amber studs;
And if these pleasures may thee move,
20 Come live with me, and be my love.

The shepherds' swains shall dance and sing
For thy delight each May morning;
If these delights thy mind may move,
Then live with me and be my love.

1. **prove** experience.
2. **kirtle** skirt.

266 Celebrating Humanity (1485–1625)

© Text Complexity Rubric

	The Passionate Shepherd to His Love	The Nymph's Reply to the Shepherd
Qualitative Measures		
Context/ Knowledge Demands	Elizabethan pastoral verse 1 ② 3 4 5	Elizabethan reply poem (to Marlowe's poem) 1 ② 3 4 5
Structure/Language Conventionality and Clarity	Archaic diction and syntax 1 ② 3 4 5	Archaic diction and syntax 1 ② 3 4 5
Levels of Meaning/ Purpose/Concept Level	Accessible (nature idealized; invitation to love) 1 ② 3 4 5	Challenging (realistic view of nature and of human experience) 1 2 ③ 4 5
Quantitative Measures		
Lexile/Text Length	NP / 157 words	NP / 166 words
Overall Complexity	**More accessible**	**More complex**

266

④ Humanities

Orpheus Leading Eurydice from the Underworld, detail by Jean-Baptiste-Camille Corot

Corot was a French landscape painter who lived from 1796 to 1875. He was born to prosperous parents, but did not have success in his family's merchant business. At age 25 or 26, he went to art school. He painted mostly realistic landscape paintings. Ask this question:

This is a painting of a god named Orpheus rescuing a woman from the underworld. What evidence do you see of a godlike quality? How are the people in the painting different from the shepherd and shepherdess Marlowe describes?

Possible responses: The man is strong, richly dressed, and has a kingly countenance. The people in the painting are not dressed in simple shepherd's wool and straw belts, nor are they wearing flower hats.

⑤ Critical Viewing

Connect

1. Have students study the landscape or details around the people in the painting.

2. Then **ask** the Critical Viewing question: Which details in this painting reflect the ideal of the countryside as a luxurious source of pleasure and the perfect escape from urban life?
   Possible response: The abundant, lush green trees and undergrowth; soft light; flawless depiction; and rich colors make the landscape seem rich, perfect, and ideal.

© Text Complexity: Reader and Task Suggestions

The Passionate Shepherd to His Love		The Nymph's Reply to the Shepherd	
Preparing to Read the Text	**Leveled Tasks**	**Preparing to Read the Text**	**Leveled Tasks**
• Using the biographical information on SE p. 265, discuss why Marlowe chose to idealize simple country life. • Discuss the effect of pleasant details—flowers, music, and so on—in love poetry. • Guide students to use Multidraft Reading strategies (TE p. 265).	*Structure/Language* If students will have difficulty with the poem's details, read it aloud, capturing its tone and mood. Then, have students read it, using context clues to help them understand unfamiliar details. Finally, have students reread it, focusing on the main idea. *Evaluating* If students will not have difficulty with the poem's details, have them evaluate the effectiveness with which its imagery captures tone and mood.	• Using the Background on SE p. 268, discuss why one poet might respond to another's poem. • Have students predict the kind of response Raleigh's nymph is likely to make to the invitation in Marlowe's poem. • Guide students to use Multidraft Reading strategies (TE p. 265).	*Levels of Meaning* If students will have difficulty with the poem's meaning, have them focus first on the structure of its argument: *If A were true, I would do B, but the opposite of A is true, as shown by C, D, etc., so I cannot do B.* Then, have students reread the poem, filling in details. *Evaluating* If students will not have difficulty with the poem's meaning, have them evaluate the effectiveness of Raleigh's reply to Marlowe's poem.

THE NYMPH'S REPLY TO THE SHEPHERD

SIR WALTER RALEIGH

BACKGROUND "The Passionate Shepherd to His Love" and "The Nymph's Reply to the Shepherd" are examples of reply poems. Many poets travel in similar social circles, and their association with each other sometimes motivates them to construct poems in response to one another's work. In addition to Sir Walter Raleigh, for example, John Donne also wrote a reply poem, "The Bait," to Marlowe's "The Passionate Shepherd to His Love." Such linkages can be found in many literary epochs and cultures: for example, twentieth-century Chinese poet Shu Ting composed a poem, titled "Also All," in response to Bei Dao's poem "All."

Reading Strategy

Analyzing Similar Themes

1. **Ask** students to reread the first stanza, noting which words and ideas are repeated and what Raleigh's lines say about Marlowe's.

2. List the student responses in a Reading Strategy chart that you copy onto the board.
   Possible responses: Raleigh repeats *pretty pleasures; move;* and *to live with thee and be thy/ my love.* Raleigh comments on Marlowe's poem by suggesting that the shepherd is not being honest and that love dies quickly.

3. Then **ask** the Reading Strategy question: How do the first four lines of this poem compare with the opening of "The Passionate Shepherd to His Love"?
   Possible response: Raleigh repeats many of the same ideas, but only to criticize or refute them.

Literary Analysis

Pastoral and Common Themes

1. Remind students that the imagery in Marlowe's poem portrays an idealized natural world in which one can live a carefree life. Raleigh's poem shatters this vision.

2. Then **ask:** What contrast does the nymph draw between the idealized world and the real world?
   Answer: Verses: 5 *flocks from field to fold;* 13 *beds of roses;* 17 *belt of straw and ivy buds;* 18 *coral clasps and amber studs*
   Answer: In the real world, the idyllic elements described in Marlowe's poem fade with time.

Reading Strategy

Analyzing Similar Themes

Ask students to consider the context of the pastoral conventions that they recorded in the previous activity. Have them compare and contrast these references to the same ones in Marlowe's poem.
Possible response: Raleigh recalls each of Marlowe's images and describes how they will turn cold, fade, or die. Raleigh describes the realistic version of the pastoral images.

Reading Strategy

Analyzing Similar Themes
How do the first four lines of this poem compare with the opening lines of "The Passionate Shepherd to His Love"?

Vocabulary
reckoning (rek´ ən in) *n.* accounting

gall (gôl) *n.* bitter feeling; deep spite

wither (with´ ər) *v.* dry up

6

If all the world and love were young
And truth in every shepherd's tongue
These pretty pleasures might me move
To live with thee, and be thy love.

5 Time drives the flocks from field to fold,
When rivers rage and rocks grow cold,
And Philomel[1] becometh dumb,
The rest complains of cares to come.

7 10 The flowers do fade, and wanton fields
8 To wayward winter reckoning yields:
A honey tongue, a heart of gall,
Is fancy's spring, but sorrow's fall.

Thy gowns, thy shoes, thy beds of roses,
Thy cap, thy kirtle,[2] and thy posies
15 Soon break, soon wither, soon forgotten,
In folly ripe, in reason rotten.

1. **Philomel** the nightingale.
2. **kirtle** skirt.

Differentiated Instruction for Universal Access

Strategy for Less Proficient Readers
Have students use a Venn diagram to compare these poems. Students should include the following elements in each circle of the diagram: the speaker, the speaker's main point, and the tone. Students should also list in the overlapping portion at least one similarity between the poems.

EL Vocabulary for English Learners
Students may have difficulty with the words *thee* and *thy.* Explain that these words are archaic, or no longer in general use. Then, explain that *thee* means "you" and *thy* means "your." Encourage students to substitute *you* and *your* for the archaic words as they read both poems.

Enrichment for Advanced Readers
Explain to students that a nymph is a figure in Greek mythology. Certain nymphs represented different natural features. Encourage students to research one or more of the following nymphs: Oceanids, Oreads, Limoniads, Limniads, and Napaea. Have students present their findings to the class.

7 Thy belt of straw and ivy buds,
Thy coral clasps and amber studs,
8 All these in me no means can move
20 To come to thee and be thy love.

But could youth last and love still breed,
Has joy no date[3] nor age no need,
Then these delights my mind might move,
To live with thee and be thy love.

---
3. **date** ending.

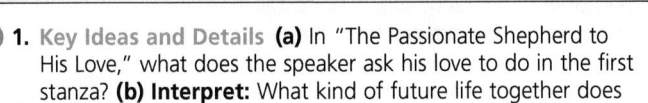

Critical Reading

1. **Key Ideas and Details (a)** In "The Passionate Shepherd to His Love," what does the speaker ask his love to do in the first stanza? **(b) Interpret:** What kind of future life together does the speaker envision?

2. **Key Ideas and Details (a)** What happens to the nightingale in line 7 of "The Nymph's Reply"? **(b) Compare and Contrast:** According to lines 5 through 8, in what ways is the nymph's world different from that of the shepherd? **(c) Analyze:** Which words in this stanza evoke a feeling of ruin or despair? Explain.

3. **Key Ideas and Details (a)** According to lines 21–22 of "The Nymph's Reply," what might persuade the nymph to live with the shepherd? **(b) Speculate:** Do you think these lines would console the shepherd? **(c) Analyze:** How does the nymph present a realistic portrayal of time and change?

4. **Integration of Knowledge and Ideas** If you were the shepherd, what counterargument might you make in response to the "The Nymph's Reply"?

5. **Integration of Knowledge and Ideas** What is the good, if any, of using literature to imagine an ideal setting? In your answer, use at least two of these Essential Question words: *perfection, escape, pastoral, realistic. [Connecting to the Essential Question: What is the relationship between literature and place?]*

Cite textual evidence to support your responses.

The Nymph's Reply to the Shepherd **269**

269

Answers

1. **(a) Sample Answer:** Shepherd's Idealism: melodious birds, beds of roses, fragrant posies, cap of flowers, finest wool, pretty lambs, purest gold, coral clasps; dancing and singing swains; Nymph's Realism: time drives the flocks, rivers rage, rocks grow cold, the rest complains, flowers fade, fields yield to winter **(b)** The shepherd is an optimist who buys into romantic conventions; the nymph recognizes the impermanence of these conventions.

2. The opposing images of "ripe" and "rotten" demonstrate time's toll. The elements of nature that the shepherd sees as eternally flourishing in reality waste away.

3. **(a)** Raleigh presents negative view of pastoral conventions. **(b)** It is a nuance. In being anti-pastoral, it is part of the pastoral tradition, though counter-traditional.

4. **(a)** Marlowe's shepherd shows in his offering of gifts that he believes love to be true and eternal; Raleigh's nymph directly describes love as fleeting and often untrue. **(b)** They are worlds apart in their opinions on nature, love, and time. **(c)** Both poets write in complex sentences with inverted order. However, Raleigh uses more strong verbs.

5. **(a)** The shepard urges the nymph to take advantage of his offers. The nymph rejects him in order to live her own life. **(b)** People of all cultures can have an opinion about it.

6. **Possible answer:** His smug expression and haughty stance suggest Raleigh's cynicism about love proposals. The cartoon may be a play on the saying "the pen is mightier than the sword," as there is a rapier on Raleigh's belt and a quill in his cap, indicating that he put as much value in the written word as in armed exploits.

7. **(a)** Raleigh repeats all of Marlowe's images, but only to describe them as realistic and negative. **(b)** Raleigh recalls Marlowe's images in the same order Marlowe wrote them. This way, he can contrast all of Marlowe's ideals.

8. **(a) Possible answer:** The nymph may have had a lover who did not keep his promises. **(b)** Answers will vary.

270

After You Read

The Passionate Shepherd to His Love • The Nymph's Reply to the Shepherd

Literary Analysis

1. **Key Ideas and Details** Although both Marlowe and Raleigh's poems reflect the **pastoral** tradition, the speakers present opposing views of rural life. **(a)** Use a chart like the one shown to identify details that signal the shepherd's idealized view and the nymph's more realistic view of country life.

Shepherd's Idealism	Nymph's Realism

   (b) Based on their attitudes toward nature, what conclusions can you draw about the personalities of the shepherd and the nymph?

2. **Craft and Structure** In line 16 of "The Nymph's Reply to the Shepherd," in what way does the speaker's word choice reveal a striking balance of opposites to illustrate the theme of the harmful effects of time?

3. **Integration of Knowledge and Ideas (a)** In what ways can Raleigh's poem be considered anti-pastoral? **(b)** Is it a *nuance* or *ambiguity* of Raleigh's poem that it is also part of the pastoral tradition? For instance, could you argue that this shepherd and nymph are engaged in a pastoral singing contest? Explain.

4. **Integration of Knowledge and Ideas** The worth of love is one of the **universal themes** explored in these poems, but the speakers present contrasting views. **(a)** Compare and contrast the views of each speaker on the worth and reliability of love. **(b)** Although these speakers, a shepherd and a nymph, are supposedly part of the same landscape, how are they "worlds apart"? **(c)** Compare their syntax, or sentence structure.

5. **Comparing Literary Works** Renaissance lyric poems often linked the inevitable passage of time with the Latin motto *carpe diem*, meaning "seize the day," or enjoy yourself in the present. **(a)** How does this motto apply to each of these poems? **(b)** How is this theme universal, rather than specific to a particular culture?

6. **Analyzing Visual Information** Does this caricature of Sir Walter Raleigh suggest he might have shared the Nymph's cynical view of love proposals? Explain.

Reading Strategy

7. **(a)** If you **analyze similar themes** in both poems, what similarities and *repetitions* do you find in them? **(b)** How does Raleigh's *pattern of organization* make it easier for him to contrast his views on pastoral, love, and time with those of Marlowe?

8. **(a)** What experiences might have shaped the nymph's attitudes in "The Nymph's Reply"? **(b)** If you were the nymph, what kind of future might you project for the shepherd?

Common Core State Standards

Writing
2.c. Use appropriate and varied transitions and syntax to link the major sections of the text, create cohesion, and clarify the relationships among complex ideas and concepts. *(p. 271)*

Language
4.a. Use context as a clue to the meaning of a word or phrase. *(p. 271)*

270 Celebrating Humanity (1485–1625)

Vocabulary Development

Vocabulary Knowledge Rating

When students have completed reading and discussing the selections, have them take out their **Vocabulary Knowledge Rating Charts** for the poems. Read the words aloud and have students rate their knowledge of words again in the After Reading column. Clarify any words that are still problematic. Have students write their own definitions and example or sentence in the appropriate column. Then have students complete the Vocabulary Lesson at the end of the selections. Encourage students to use the words in further discussion and written work about the selections. Remind them that they will be accountable for these words on the **Selection Test,** *Unit 2 Resources,* pages 38–40 or 41–43.

Vocabulary Acquisition and Use

Word Analysis: *gall*

The *medical etymology* of the word *gall* goes back to the Greek word *chole*, or "bile." Bile is the bitter yellowish fluid secreted by the liver to aid in digestion. In ancient Greek medicine, bile referred to one of two bodily humors, or fluids: black bile, thought to cause melancholy, or yellow bile, thought to cause anger. The other two humors were blood, which made a person cheerful and confident; and phlegm, which made a person calm and detached. In a healthy person, these four fluids were thought to be held in balance. This theory remained the most common view of the human body in Europe until the 1800s.

In each sentence below, replace *gall* with a word of similar meaning.

1. The gall of defeat was difficult to swallow.
2. He could no longer contain his gall and began to yell.

Writing

Informative Text Marlowe's and Raleigh's poems present opposing points of view on the same subject. Write an **essay** in which you develop a *coherent thesis*, or consistent central idea, about the poems' *similarities and differences*. Focus on the viewpoints expressed by the speakers in the poems.

Prewriting Use a chart like the one shown to compare the poems. Then, draw a conclusion about their similarities and differences.

Model: Compare and Contrast Essay	Love	Nature	Time	World
"The Passionate Shepherd"	sees it as life's highest pleasure			
"The Nymph's Reply"	sees it as a mistake			

Using generalizations here will help the writer see major similarities and differences in the speakers' viewpoints.

Drafting Incorporate your conclusion into a clear thesis statement. Then, in the body of your essay, develop this thesis by comparing the viewpoints expressed in the poems. Use transition words and phrases such as *similarly*, *in contrast*, and *by comparison*.

Revising Revise your draft, focusing on redundant ideas. Remove any words or sentences that do not directly relate to or support your thesis.

Vocabulary: Context Clues

Review the vocabulary words on page 264. Then, for each item below, explain how the meaning of the vocabulary word and the *context* in which it is used help you identify each statement as correct or incorrect.

1. The poet adapted her works as *madrigals* and participated in a performance of them.
2. Her strong, *melodious* voice was perfectly suited to the poems' deep emotion.
3. At the end of the stunning performance, she even had the *gall* to sing several encores and take additional bows.
4. According to one *reckoning*, the show drew the largest crowd in the whole history of the opera house.
5. These facts suggest the conclusion that the poet's fame will *wither* within days.

Vocabulary Acquisition and Use

Word Analysis

1. disappointment
2. anger

Vocabulary

1. correct; *Madrigals* are songs and orchestras are used to play songs.
2. correct; *Melodious* means sweet sounding, which would be suiting to a poem's deep emotion.
3. incorrect; *Gall* is a negative word; stunning tells that the performance was positive, not negative.
4. correct; *Reckoning* would show how large a crowd was.
5. incorrect; Facts could show how someone's fame *withers* quickly, but not in just days.

Writing

1. Read and go over the assignment with students.
2. Show a sample Compare and Contrast Essay. Ask volunteers to identify the topic of each paragraph.
3. Have students complete the assignment. Suggest that they allot five minutes for prewriting, ten minutes for drafting, and ten minutes for revising and editing.
4. Evaluate students' informative texts using the **Rubrics for Compare and Contrast Essays**, *Professional Development Guidebook*, pages 260–261.

Assessment Resources

Unit 2 Resources

L1 L2 EL **Selection Test A**, pp. 38–40. Administer Test A to less advanced readers.

L3 L4 EL **Selection Test B**, pp. 41–43. Administer Test B to on-level and more advanced students.

L3 L4 **Open-Book Test**, pp. 35–37. As an alternative, administer the Open-Book Test.

All **Customizable Test Bank**

All **Self-tests**
Students may prepare for the **Selection Test** by taking the **Self-test** online.

PHLit Online! All assessment resources are available at **www.PHLitOnline.com**.

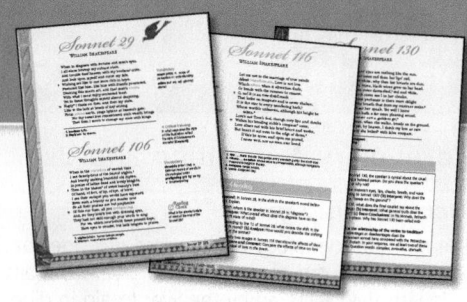
Sonnet 29 • Sonnet 106 • Sonnet 116 • Sonnet 130
Lesson Pacing Guide

DAY 1 Preteach

- © Administer the Reading and Vocabulary Warm-ups (*Unit 2 Resources,* pp. 44–47) as necessary.
- Introduce the Literary Analysis concept: Shakespearean Sonnet.
- © Introduce the Reading Strategy: Analyzing Text Structures.
- Build background with the author and Background features.
- Develop thematic thinking with Connecting to the Essential Question.
- © Teach the selection vocabulary.

DAYS 2–3 Preteach/Teach/Assess

- © Distribute copies of the appropriate graphic organizer for the Reading strategy (*Graphic Organizer Transparencies,* pp. 42–43).
- © Distribute copies of the appropriate graphic organizer for Literary Analysis (*Graphic Organizer Transparencies,* pp. 44–45).
- Prepare students to read with the Activating Prior Knowledge activities (TE).
- Informally monitor comprehension while students read.
- Use the Reading Check questions to confirm comprehension.
- Develop students' understanding of Shakespearean sonnet using the Literary Analysis Prompts.
- Develop students' ability to analyze text structures using the Reading Strategy Prompts.
- © Reinforce vocabulary with the Vocabulary notes.
- © Assess students' comprehension and mastery of the skills by having them answer the Critical Reading, Literary Analysis, and Reading Strategy questions.
- © Have students complete the Vocabulary Lesson.

DAY 4 Extend/Assess

- © Have students complete the Writing Lesson and write an analysis of sonnet's imagery. (You may assign as homework.)
- © Administer Selection Test A or B (*Unit 2 Resources,* pp. 56–58 or 59–61).

Common Core State Standards

Reading Literature 5. Analyze how an author's choices concerning how to structure specific parts of a text contribute to its overall structure and meaning as well as its aesthetic impact.

Writing 2.b. Develop the topic thoroughly by selecting the most significant and relevant facts, extended definitions, concrete details, quotations, or other information and examples appropriate to the audience's knowledge of the topic.

Language 3.a Apply an understanding of syntax to the study of complex texts when reading.
5. Demonstrate understanding of figurative language, word relationships, and nuances in word meanings.

Additional Standards Practice
Common Core Companion, *pp. 54–60; 196–207; 322–323, 332–337*

Daily Block Scheduling
Each day in this Lesson Pacing Guide represents a 40–50 minute period. Teachers using block scheduling may combine days to revise pacing. In addition, teachers may differentiate and support core instruction by integrating components for extended and intensive support as students require. See the Guide to Selected Leveled Resources (facing page).

Guide to Selected Leveled Resources

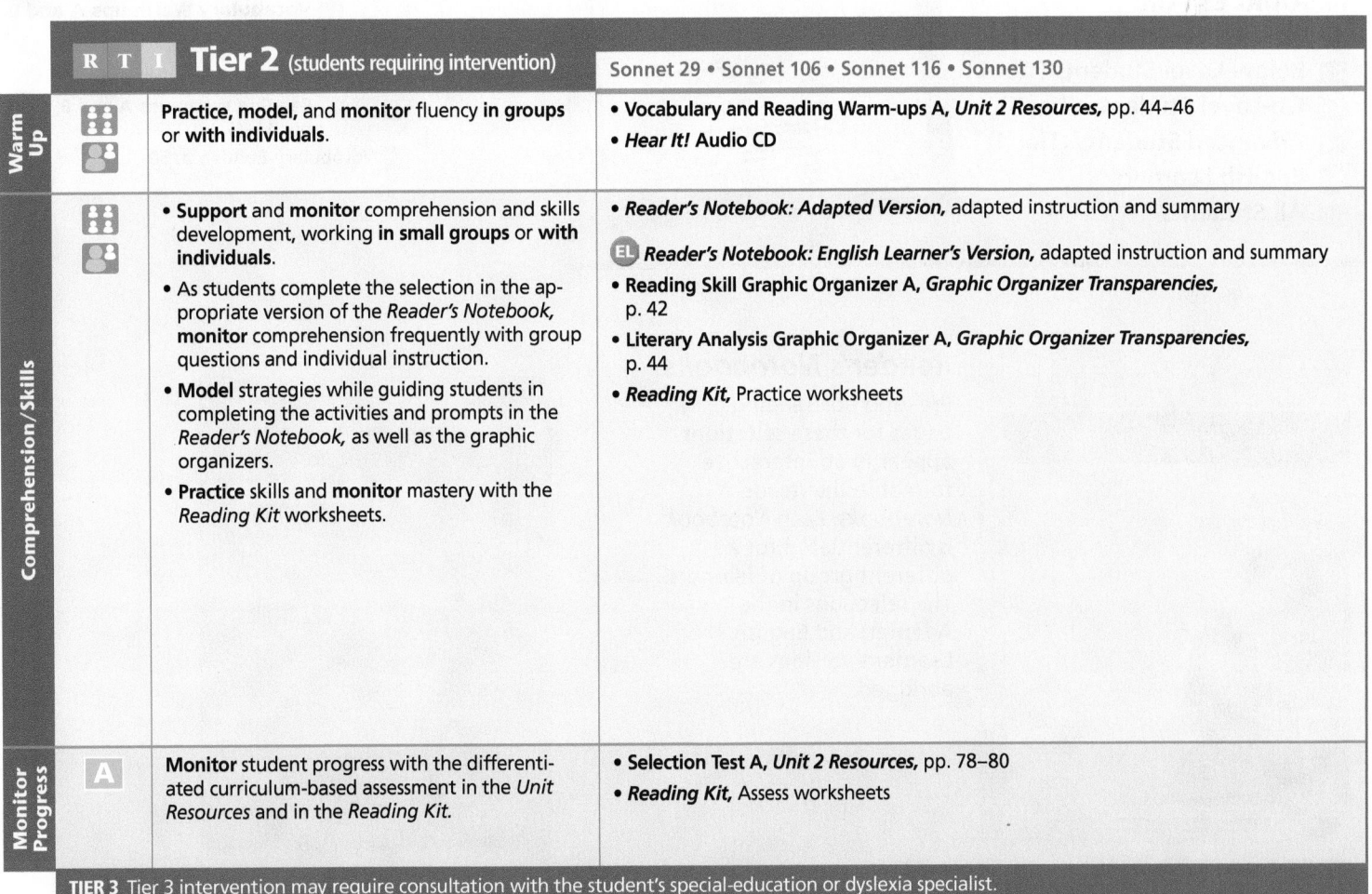

R T I **Tier 1** (students performing on level)

Sonnet 29 • Sonnet 106 • Sonnet 116 • Sonnet 130

Warm Up

Practice, **model**, and **monitor** fluency, working **with the whole class** or **in groups**.

Vocabulary and **Reading Warm-ups B**, *Unit 2 Resources*, pp. 44–45, 47

Comprehension/Skills

Support and **monitor** comprehension and skills development, having students complete the activities, graphic organizers, and interactive prompts **independently** or **as a class**.

- *Reader's Notebook,* adapted instruction and summary
- **EL** *Reader's Notebook: English Learner's Version,* adapted instruction and summary
- **Reading Skill Graphic Organizer B**, *Graphic Organizer Transparencies,* p. 43
- **Literary Analysis Graphic Organizer B**, *Graphic Organizer Transparencies,* p. 45

Monitor Progress

Monitor student progress with the differentiated curriculum-based assessment in the *Unit Resources*.

- **Selection Test B**, *Unit 2 Resources*, pp. 59–61
- **Open-Book Test**, *Unit 2 Resources*, pp. 53–55

R T I **Tier 2** (students requiring intervention)

Sonnet 29 • Sonnet 106 • Sonnet 116 • Sonnet 130

Warm Up

Practice, **model**, and **monitor** fluency **in groups** or **with individuals**.

- **Vocabulary and Reading Warm-ups A**, *Unit 2 Resources*, pp. 44–46
- *Hear It!* Audio CD

Comprehension/Skills

- **Support** and **monitor** comprehension and skills development, working **in small groups** or **with individuals**.
- As students complete the selection in the appropriate version of the *Reader's Notebook,* **monitor** comprehension frequently with group questions and individual instruction.
- **Model** strategies while guiding students in completing the activities and prompts in the *Reader's Notebook,* as well as the graphic organizers.
- **Practice** skills and **monitor** mastery with the *Reading Kit* worksheets.

- *Reader's Notebook: Adapted Version,* adapted instruction and summary
- **EL** *Reader's Notebook: English Learner's Version,* adapted instruction and summary
- **Reading Skill Graphic Organizer A**, *Graphic Organizer Transparencies,* p. 42
- **Literary Analysis Graphic Organizer A**, *Graphic Organizer Transparencies,* p. 44
- *Reading Kit,* Practice worksheets

Monitor Progress

Monitor student progress with the differentiated curriculum-based assessment in the *Unit Resources* and in the *Reading Kit.*

- **Selection Test A**, *Unit 2 Resources*, pp. 78–80
- *Reading Kit,* Assess worksheets

TIER 3 Tier 3 intervention may require consultation with the student's special-education or dyslexia specialist. For additional support, see the Tier 2 activities and resources listed above.

One-on-one teaching　Group work　Whole class instruction　Independent work　A Assessment

For a complete guide to selection support, including support for Advanced students, see the Overview of Resources in the frontmatter.

Sonnet 29 • Sonnet 106 • Sonnet 116 • Sonnet 130

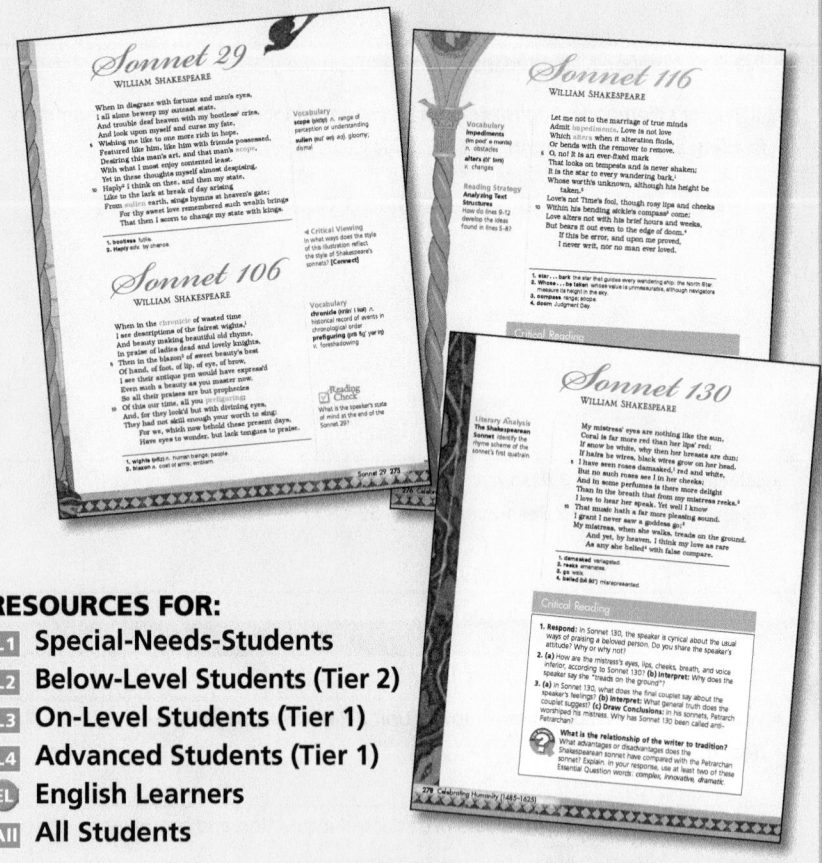

RESOURCES FOR:

- L1 Special-Needs-Students
- L2 Below-Level Students (Tier 2)
- L3 On-Level Students (Tier 1)
- L4 Advanced Students (Tier 1)
- EL English Learners
- All All Students

Vocabulary/Fluency/Prior Knowledge

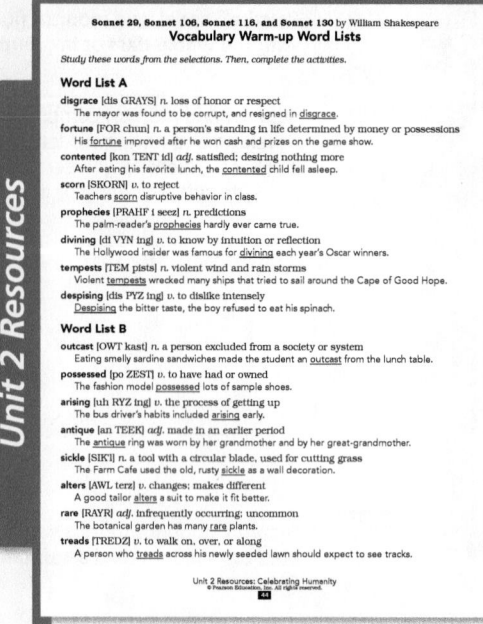

EL L1 L2 **Vocabulary Warm-ups A and B,** pp. 44–45

Also available for these selections:

EL L1 L2 **Reading Warm-ups A and B,** pp. 46–47

All **Vocabulary Builder, p. 50**

Reader's Notebooks

Pre- and postreading pages for these selections appear in an interactive format in the *Reader's Notebooks*. Each *Notebook* is differentiated for a different group of learners. The selections in the Adapted and English Learner's versions are abridged.

- L2 L3 *Reader's Notebook*
- L1 *Reader's Notebook: Adapted Version*
- EL *Reader's Notebook: English Learner's Version*
- EL *Reader's Notebook: Spanish Version*

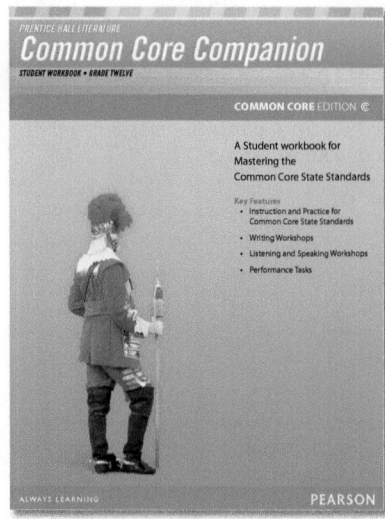

© *Common Core Companion*

Additional instruction and practice for each Common Core State Standard

Selection Support

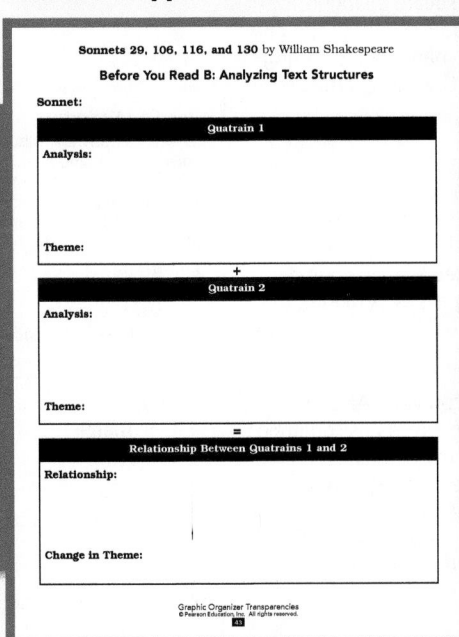

Graphic Organizer Transparencies

EL L3 **Literary Analysis: Graphic Organizer B,** p. 43

Also available for these selections:

EL L1 L2 **Literary Analysis: Graphic Organizer A** (partially filled in), p. 42

EL L1 L2 **Reading: Graphic Organizer A,** (partially filled in) p. 44

EL L3 **Reading: Graphic Organizer B,** p. 45

Skills Development/Extension

Unit 2 Resources

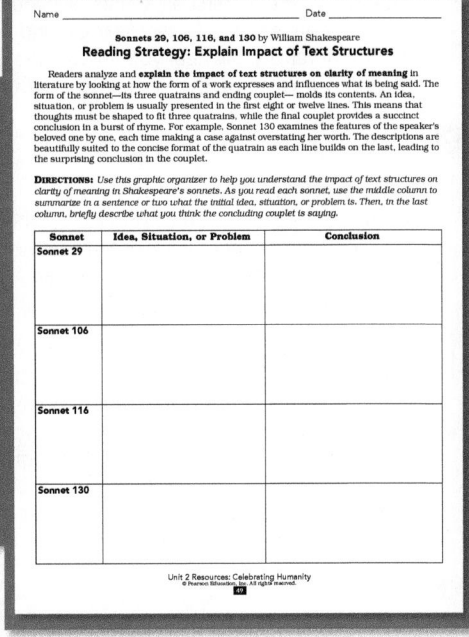

All **Reading,** p. 49

Also available for these selections:

All **Literary Analysis,** p. 48

EL L3 L4 **Support for Writing,** p. 51

L4 **Enrichment,** p. 52

Assessment

EL L1 L2 **Selection Test A,** pp. 56–58

Also available for these selections:

L3 L4 **Open-Book Test,** pp. 53–55

EL L3 L4 **Selection Test B,** pp. 59–61

PHLit Online!
www.PHLitOnline.com

Online Resources: All print materials are also available online.

- complete narrated selection text
- a thematically related video with writing prompt
- an interactive graphic organizer
- highlighting feature
- access to all student print resources, adapted to individual student needs
- Spanish and English summaries
- adapted selection translations in Spanish

Get Connected! (thematic video with writing prompt)

All videos are available in Spanish.

Writer's Journal (with graphics feature)

Also available:

Vocabulary Central (tools and activities for studying vocabulary)

❶ Ⓠ Connecting to the Essential Question

1. Review the assignment with the class.

2. As students read, have them analyze Shakespeare's rhyme scheme and contrast it to Petrarch's.

❷ Literary Analysis

Introduce the skill using the instruction on the student page.

Think Aloud: Model the Skill

Say to students:

When I read Sonnet 29, I can easily identify the rhyme scheme. For example, lines 1 and 3 rhyme, and so do lines 2 and 4. The second and third quatrains follow the same pattern. The ending couplet is one long sentence. The last words in each line rhyme.

❸ Reading Strategy

1. Introduce the strategy.

2. Give students a copy of **Reading Strategy Graphic Organizer B**, page 43 in *Graphic Organizer Transparencies,* to fill out as they read.

Think Aloud: Model the Skill

Say to students:

When I read Sonnet 29, I can understand how Shakespeare's quatrains and couplets follow the description. The first two quatrains explain the speaker's sullen state of mind. In the third quatrain, a new thought distracts him from his depressed state. With the ending couplet, he describes a dramatic shift of mind.

❹ Vocabulary

1. Pronounce each word, giving its definition, and have students say it aloud.

2. For more guidance, see the *Classroom Strategies and Teaching Routines* card for introducing vocabulary.

Before You Read

Sonnet 29 • Sonnet 106 • Sonnet 116 • Sonnet 130

❶ **Connecting to the Essential Question** Shakespeare changed the structure of the Petrarchan sonnet. As you read, identify some of the differences between the Shakespearean and the Petrarchan sonnet. Noting these differences will help you answer the Essential Question: **What is the relationship of the writer to tradition?**

❷ Literary Analysis

A **Shakespearean sonnet** has fourteen lines, with five iambic feet to the line (an iambic foot is an unstressed syllable followed by a stressed one).

Unlike Petrarchan and Spenserian sonnets, a Shakespearean sonnet follows the rhyme scheme *abab cdcd efef gg,* giving it this structure:

• three **quatrains,** or four-line stanzas
• a rhyming **couplet** that dramatically restates or redefines a theme

As you read, notice Shakespeare's quatrains and couplets. Also notice how his sentences often continue past lines and sometimes past quatrains.

Though all Shakespearean sonnets have fourteen rhyming lines, there are no rules about the number or types of sentences. Shakespeare uses this freedom of **syntax,** or sentence structure, to create dazzling dramatic effects. By saving his main idea until the end of one long sentence (lines 13–14), he makes Sonnet 106 build like a lawyer's statement to a jury.

❸ Reading Strategy

ⓒ **Preparing to Read Complex Texts** A sonnet's rhyme scheme, stanzas, and syntax are text structures. You can better understand a sonnet by **analyzing its text structures,** noticing how they contribute to the sonnet's clarity of meaning and aesthetic impact. For example, each quatrain helps develop the main problem or argument, which the couplet then dramatically restates or redefines. Use a chart like the one shown to analyze each sonnet's *pattern of organization*.

❹ Vocabulary

scope (skōp) *n.* range of perception or understanding (p. 275)

sullen (sul´ ən) *adj.* gloomy; dismal (p. 275)

chronicle (krän´ i kəl) *n.* historical record of events in chronological order (p. 275)

prefiguring (prē fig´ yər iŋ) *v.* foreshadowing (p. 275)

impediments (im ped´ ə mənts) *n.* obstacles (p. 276)

alters (ôl´ tərz) *v.* changes (p. 276)

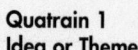

Common Core State Standards

Reading Literature
5. Analyze how an author's choices concerning how to structure specific parts of a text contribute to its overall structure and meaning as well as its aesthetic impact.

Language
3.a. Apply an understanding of syntax to the study of complex texts when reading.

Quatrain 1 Idea or Theme

↓

Quatrain 2 Idea or Theme

↓

Quatrain 3 Idea or Theme

↓

Couplet Idea or Theme

www.PHLitOnline.com

Vocabulary Development

Vocabulary Knowledge Rating

Create a **Vocabulary Knowledge Rating Chart** (*Professional Development Guidebook,* p. 33) for the vocabulary words on the student page. Give each student a copy of the chart with the words on it. Read the words aloud, and have students mark their rating in the Before Reading column. Urge students to attend to these words as they read and discuss the selections.

In order to gauge how much instruction you need to provide, tally how many students are confident in their knowledge of each word. As students read, point out the words and their context.

Vocabulary Central, featuring tools and activities for studying vocabulary, is available online at **www.PHLitOnline.com.**

William Shakespeare (1564–1616)

Author of Sonnet 29 • Sonnet 106 • Sonnet 116 • Sonnet 130

Shakespeare may be the most admired author of all time. If he were living today, he would be a celebrity, and the facts of his life would be widely available in magazine articles, books, and Web pages. Instead, we know few facts about him, and these few had to be painstakingly traced from legal and church records or deduced from references in his work.

Bare-Bones Biography Shakespeare was born in the country town of Stratford-on-Avon and probably attended the town's free grammar school. When he was eighteen, he married twenty-six-year-old Anne Hathaway. They had a daughter, Susanna, and twins, Hamnet and Judith.

Shakespeare acquired a public reputation as an actor and a playwright. In addition, he was part owner of a London theater called the Globe, where many of his plays were performed. (For more about Shakespeare and his work as a dramatist, see pages 316–319.)

The Sonnet In the years 1592–1594, London's theaters were closed because of an outbreak of the plague. This general misfortune may have had at least one benefit: It may have provided the time that Shakespeare needed to write some of his 154 sonnets.

In writing a long sequence of sonnets, Shakespeare was being fashionable. Elizabethan poets enjoyed the sonnet form, writing fourteen-line lyric poems to both real and imaginary lovers.

The great Italian poet Petrarch (1304–1374) pioneered the writing of sonnet sequences. His sequence charts each pang and longing of the speaker's unfulfilled love for an idealized lady. This poetic device led to endless inventiveness—the beloved's beauty invites extravagant comparisons, and she provides a focus for the poet's ingenuity.

Shakespeare's Sequence Like the sonnet sequences of other poets, Shakespeare's 154 sonnets are numbered. Most of them are addressed to a handsome, talented young man, urging him to marry and have children who can carry on his talents. Readers treasure Shakespeare's masterful use of the sonnet to bring the fundamental experiences of life—time, death, love, and friendship—into tight focus.

> "Not marble nor the gilded monuments Of princes shall outlive this pow'rful rhyme . . ."
> —William Shakespeare, from Sonnet 55

Sonnet 29 • Sonnet 106 • Sonnet 116 • Sonnet 130 **273**

Teaching From Technology

Preparing to Read
Go to **www.PHLitOnline.com** in class or in a lab and display the **Get Connected!** slide show for these selections. Have the class brainstorm responses to the slide show writing prompt, entering ideas in the interactive journal. Then have students complete their written responses individually, in a lab or as homework.

To build background, display the More About the Author feature.

Using the Interactive Text
Go to **www.PHLitOnline.com** and display the **Enriched Online Student Edition**. As the class reads the selections or listens to the narration, record answers to side-column prompts using the graphic organizers accessible on the interactive page. Alternatively, have students use the online edition individually, answering the prompts as they read.

Daily Bellringer

For each class during which you will teach these selections, have students complete one of the five activities for the appropriate week in the *Daily Bellringer Activities* booklet.

Multidraft Reading

To assist struggling readers and to enhance reading for all, assign the text in chunks, as warranted by length, and apply multidraft reading protocols. For each reading, have students set the purpose indicated:

- **First reading**—identifying key ideas and details and answering any Reading Checks.
- **Second reading**—analyzing craft and structure and responding to the side-column prompts.
- **Third reading**—integrating knowledge and ideas, connecting to other texts and the world, and answering the end-of-selection questions.

For more guidance, refer to the *Classroom Strategies and Teaching Routines* card on multidraft reading.

5 Background
More About the Author

It is clear that Shakespeare made the most of his education. His astonishingly large vocabulary and broad knowledge of history and literature indicate that he read widely, and did so throughout his life.

There is a gap in the record between the birth of his children and Shakespeare's appearance in London theater records. But in 1592, dramatist Robert Greene declared in a pamphlet that an "upstart crow" had appeared on the scene. The insult brought a swift response from many corners, indicating that Shakespeare had already made many influential friends in London.

His life was not without sadness. His only son, Hamnet, died at age 11. But his daughters survived and married.

Probably the most famous comment made about Shakespeare was written by his contemporary Ben Jonson: "He was not of an age, but for all time!"

TEACH

❶ About the Selections

In Sonnet 29, when things are going badly, the speaker has only to remember a special person's love to feel joyous again.

In Sonnet 106, previous descriptions of handsome men and beautiful women only anticipated the beauty of a special person the poet knows.

In Sonnet 116, Shakespeare praises the constancy of true love.

In Sonnet 130, Shakespeare makes fun of the language that Petrarchan poets used to describe their ideal mistresses.

❷ Activating Prior Knowledge

What is love? How long does it truly last? Engage students with questions like these. Then have them respond to the following statements as true or false.

- A person who has true love is better off than the richest king.
- People no longer express their love as well as they used to.
- True love lasts forever; nothing on earth stops it.
- It is better to be honest about someone's shortcomings than to glorify them.

Allow students to share their responses and discuss reasons for their opinions. Tell them that Shakespeare addresses each of these issues in these sonnets.

Concept Connector ➡

Tell students they will return to their responses after reading the selections.

274 Celebrating Humanity (1485–1625)

ⓒ Text Complexity Rubric

	Sonnet 29	Sonnet 106	Sonnet 116	Sonnet 130
Qualitative Measures				
Context/Knowledge Demands	Elizabethan sonnet 1 2 ③ 4 5	Elizabethan sonnet 1 2 ③ 4 5	Elizabethan sonnet 1 2 ③ 4 5	Elizabethan sonnet 1 ② 3 4 5
Structure/Language Conventionality and Clarity	Archaic diction and syntax 1 2 ③ 4 5	Archaic diction and syntax 1 2 ③ 4 5	Archaic diction and syntax 1 2 ③ 4 5	Archaic diction and syntax 1 2 ③ 4 5
Levels of Meaning/Purpose/Concept Level	Moderate (hope) 1 2 ③ 4 5	Moderate (beauty) 1 2 ③ 4 5	Accessible (love) 1 ② 3 4 5	Accessible (beauty) 1 ② 3 4 5
Quantitative Measures				
Lexile/Text Length	NP / 114 words	NP / 110 words	NP / 109 words	NP / 123 words
Overall Complexity	**More complex**	**More complex**	**More accessible**	**More accessible**

Sonnet 29

WILLIAM SHAKESPEARE

When in disgrace with fortune and men's eyes,
I all alone beweep my outcast state,
And trouble deaf heaven with my bootless¹ cries,
And look upon myself and curse my fate,
5   Wishing me like to one more rich in hope,
Featured like him, like him with friends possessed,
Desiring this man's art, and that man's scope,
With what I most enjoy contented least.
Yet in these thoughts myself almost despising,
10 Haply² I think on thee, and then my state,
Like to the lark at break of day arising
From sullen earth, sings hymns at heaven's gate;
     For thy sweet love remembered such wealth brings
     That then I scorn to change my state with kings.

1. **bootless** futile.
2. **Haply** *adv.* by chance.

Sonnet 106

WILLIAM SHAKESPEARE

When in the chronicle of wasted time
I see descriptions of the fairest wights,¹
And beauty making beautiful old rhyme,
In praise of ladies dead and lovely knights,
5 Then in the blazon² of sweet beauty's best
Of hand, of foot, of lip, of eye, of brow,
I see their antique pen would have express'd
Even such a beauty as you master now.
So all their praises are but prophecies
10 Of this our time, all you prefiguring;
And, for they look'd but with divining eyes,
They had not skill enough your worth to sing:
     For we, which now behold these present days,
     Have eyes to wonder, but lack tongues to praise.

1. **wights** (wīts) *n.* human beings; people.
2. **blazon** *n.* here, catalog of lover's physical attributes.

Vocabulary
scope (skōp) *n.* range of perception or understanding
sullen (sul´ ən) *adj.* gloomy; dismal

◀ **Critical Viewing**
In what ways does the style of this illustration reflect the style of Shakespeare's sonnets? **[Connect]**

Vocabulary
chronicle (krän´ i kəl) *n.* historical record of events in chronological order
prefiguring (prē fig´ yer iŋ) *v.* foreshadowing

☑ **Reading Check**
What is the speaker's state of mind at the end of Sonnet 29?

Sonnet 29 **275**

---

❸ Reading Strategy

Analyzing Text Structure

1. Remind students that Shakespeare uses the structure of the sonnet to help develop its meaning.

2. After students have read Sonnet 29, have them suggest what the speaker is saying in lines 5–7. **Answer:** He envies people who have friends and hope, and he desires the creativity and intelligence that others possess.

3. Ask how the third quatrain relates to the first two. **Answer:** It marks the beginning of a change in direction. The first two quatrains show alienation and envy, but in the third one he thinks of something other than misery.

❹ Critical Viewing

Possible response: The bright colors, stylized poses of the figures, and the elegant composition parallel Shakespeare's use of and musings about conventional imagery and forms.

❺ Vocabulary Builder

Greek Root: -*chron*-

1. Call students' attention to the word *chronicle* in Sonnet 106 and its definition. Tell them that the word *chronicle* contains the root -*chron*- from the Greek word *chronos*, meaning "time."

2. Have students suggest words that contain this root, and list them on the board. **Possible responses:** *chronic, chronology, chronometer*

❻ Reading Check

Answer: The speaker's state of mind at the end of the poem is one of contentment and self-satisfaction.

©️ Text Complexity: Reader and Task Suggestions

Sonnets 29 and 106		Sonnets 116 and 130	
Preparing to Read the Text	**Leveled Tasks**	**Preparing to Read the Text**	**Leveled Tasks**
• Using the information on SE p. 273, note that Shakespeare likely wrote many sonnets while thwarted by the closing of theaters. • Note to students that Shakespeare's sonnets almost always touch upon universal themes. • Guide students to use Multidraft Reading strategies (TE p. 273).	*Levels of Meanings* If students will have difficulty with the sonnets' meanings, have them first read each poem to find its complete thoughts. Then, ask them to separate essential from nonessential information. Finally, have them paraphrase the poem. *Evaluating* If students will not have difficulty with the poems' meanings, have them evaluate the effectiveness of each poem's imagery and diction in conveying the speaker's feelings.	• Using the information on TE p. 257, stress that the speaker in Sonnet 130 uses an odd approach to describe his beloved. • Remind students of the structure of Shakespearean sonnets. • Guide students to use Multidraft Reading strategies (TE p. 253).	*Structure/Language* If students will have difficulty with the poem's structure and meaning, help them use sonnet structure to focus on the main point of the three four-line segments. Then, have students reread each poem. *Analyzing* If students will not have difficulty with the poem's structure and meaning, have them analyze the use of negatives or understatement to express key ideas in each sonnet.

1. Have students reread lines 5–12.

2. Then, **ask** the Reading Strategy question.

   Possible response: In lines 5–8, the writer is stating that true love remains the same. In lines 9–12, he writes that true love lasts forever, even "to the edge of doom."

ASSESS

Answers

Before students respond, you may wish to have them write a brief objective summary of the selection. As they answer the questions below, remind them to support their answers with evidence from the text.

1. (a) He is in disgrace with luck and people's opinions. (b) It makes him curse his fate and hate his life.

2. (a) Thoughts of his beloved cause the shift in mood. (b) The first eight lines are somber and dark in mood, while the final six lines are happy and bright.

3. (a) **Possible response:** The effects of time include the death of "rosy lips and cheeks" within Time's sickle, and the passing of "brief hours and weeks." (b) Time has little or no effect on love; love outlasts time.

Sonnet 116
WILLIAM SHAKESPEARE

Vocabulary
impediments
(im pedʹ ə mənts)
n. obstacles

alters (ôlʹ tərs)
v. changes

Let me not to the marriage of true minds
Admit impediments. Love is not love
Which alters when it alteration finds,
Or bends with the remover to remove.
5   O, no! It is an ever-fixèd mark
That looks on tempests and is never shaken;
It is the star to every wandering bark,[1]
Whose worth's unknown, although his height be taken.[2]
Love's not Time's fool, though rosy lips and cheeks
10   Within his bending sickle's compass[3] come;
Love alters not with his brief hours and weeks,
But bears it out even to the edge of doom.[4]
     If this be error, and upon me proved,
     I never writ, nor no man ever loved.

❼

---

1. **star . . . bark** the star that guides every wandering ship: the North Star.
2. **Whose . . . be taken** whose value is unmeasurable, although navigators measure its height in the sky.
3. **compass** range; scope.
4. **doom** Judgment Day.

Critical Reading

Cite textual evidence to support your responses.

© 1. **Key Ideas and Details (a)** With whom is the speaker in Sonnet 29 in "disgrace"? **(b) Analyze:** What overall effect does this disgrace have on the speaker's state of mind?

© 2. **Key Ideas and Details (a)** According to line 12 of Sonnet 29, what causes the shift in the speaker's mood? **(b) Analyze:** How would you describe the shifting moods in the sonnet?

© 3. **Integration of Knowledge and Ideas (a)** Identify two images in Sonnet 116 that show the effects of time. **(b) Compare and Contrast:** Compare the effects of time on love with the ideal of love in the poem.

Vocabulary Development

Vocabulary Knowledge Rating
When students have completed reading and discussing the selections, have them take out their **Vocabulary Knowledge Rating Charts.** Read the words aloud and have students rate their knowledge of words again in the After Reading column. Clarify any words that are still problematic. Have students write their own definitions and example or sentence in the appropriate column. Then have students complete the Vocabulary Lesson at the end of the selections. Encourage students to use the words in further discussion and written work about the selections. Remind them that they will be accountable for these words on the **Selection Test,** *Unit 2 Resources,* pages 56–58 or 59–61.

The Mystery of the SONNETS

For centuries, readers have puzzled over Shakespeare's sonnet sequence, which tells a story of love and betrayal. The early poems address a beautiful young man, whom the poet urges to get married and have children. The later poems concern a dark-haired woman, who torments the poet with jealousy. Midway through the sequence, a rival poet makes an appearance, further complicating the situation.

Were these characters real people? Or were they simply creations of Shakespeare's dramatic imagination? Literary detectives have proposed various historical figures as the characters in the sonnets. But the only facts we know for sure are that the sonnet sequence was published in 1609 and dedicated to a "Mr. W.H."

CONNECT TO THE LITERATURE

Does knowing the story told by the sonnets make reading individual sonnets more interesting? Why or why not?

Title page from the 1609 edition of *Shake-Speares Sonnets.* ▼

SHAKE-SPEARES

SONNETS.

Neuer before Imprinted.

AT LONDON
By G. Eld for T. T. and are
to be solde by John Wright, dwelling
at Christ Church gate.
1609.

WILLIAM HERBERT

Some think William Herbert, the third Earl of Pembroke and a patron of the arts, was the young man of the sonnets. Shakespeare's "First Folio" was dedicated to him.

GEORGE CHAPMAN

His powerful translation of Homer inspired John Keats. Chapman is thought by many to be the rival poet of Shakespeare's Sonnets.

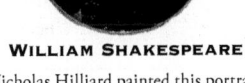

WILLIAM SHAKESPEARE

Nicholas Hilliard painted this portrait, which some believe to be the young Shakespeare, in 1588.

CHRISTOPHER MARLOWE

Poet and dramatist Christopher Marlowe (1564–1593) may have been the rival poet.

EMILIA BASSANO

Some historians think Emilia Bassano, the daughter of a court musician, was Shakespeare's mysterious "Dark Lady."

HENRY WRIOTHESLY

The third Earl of Southampton, Wriothesly became Shakespeare's patron in 1593. Many believe he was the "fair youth" of the sonnets.

Sonnet 116 **277**

The Mystery of the Sonnets

1. Remind students that people seem to enjoy filling the gaps in historical narratives. **Ask** students if they can think of some examples of when a mysterious historical event captured the public imagination and created speculation similar to the hypotheses regarding the subjects of Shakespeare's sonnets.
   Possible responses: Students might suggest theories about King Tutankhamen's murder or about what really happened to Amelia Earhart.

2. Explain to students that many scholars agree that it is unlikely that these poems represent a narrative of Shakespeare's love life. Thematically, sonnets often dealt with love, but this love could easily have been a hypothetical exercise in style.

Connect to the Literature

1. **Ask** students the **Connect to the Literature** question: Does knowing the story told by the sonnets make reading individual sonnets more interesting? Why or why not? **Possible answers:** Students might say yes, arguing that the narrative behind the sonnets contextualizes them and provides possible explanations for the language Shakespeare used. Other students might offer that the sonnets stand on their artistic merit alone and do not need speculation to make them interesting.

2. Point out to students that in Elizabethan England, wealthy nobility often provided artists with sponsorship in exchange for commissioned work. This relationship enhanced the prestige of the noble and advanced the career of the artist. **Ask** students how this relationship might affect the nature of what the artist produced.
   Possible answers: If the artist were dependent upon a sponsor, he might be inclined to dedicate the work to that sponsor. Even if the works were not really about the sponsor, it would behoove the artist to create that impression.

Enrichment for Advanced Readers

Suggest that students read additional works by William Shakespeare. Provide students with copies of Sonnets 18, 30, and 73. You may wish to use *Authors In Depth, The British Tradition*, which contains the following selections:
- from *Antony and Cleopatra*
- from *The Merchant of Venice*
- Sonnets 15, 30, 71, 73, 77, 128
- "Fear No More the Heat o' the Sun"

- "O Mistress Mine, Where Are You Roaming"
  After students have read additional works by Shakespeare, have them form discussion groups in which they compare and contrast what they have read. Suggest criteria for comparison, such as theme, language, sentiment, style, and ideas. To extend that activity, have volunteers present to the class brief oral reports on their favorite works.

Literary Analysis

The Shakespearean Sonnet

1. Review with students the rhyme scheme and iambic meter of Shakespearean sonnets.

2. Then **ask** students the Literary Analysis question: Identify the rhyme scheme of the sonnet's first quatrain.

   Answer: The rhyme scheme of the first quatrain is *abab*.

Spiral Review

Check Context Clues

1. Remind students that they studied context clues earlier.

2. **Ask** the Spiral Review question.

   Possible response: The speaker has honestly stated that his beloved fails to live up to trite notions of beauty. "False compare" suggests that these notions are untrue and irrelevant to his beloved's "rare" qualities.

Remind students to support their answers with evidence from the text.

1. (a) Her lips are not red as coral; her cheeks are not like roses; her breath is not like perfume; her voice is not music. (b) He may mean that she is an earthly being, as opposed to idealized lovers who are compared to angels.

2. (a) He says his love is as delightful as any of those who are praised with false comparisons. (b) That true love is based on reality. (c) It is anti-Petrarchan because it does not idealize the state of love; instead, it shows the speaker's love with all her imperfections.

3. **Possible response:** The structure of the Shakespearean sonnet—four sections rather than the two in Petrarchan sonnet—allows for a more <u>complex</u> development of thought. The three quatrains lead to the ending couplet, which offers a <u>dramatic</u> flourish of surprise or an <u>innovative</u> twist on the overall theme.

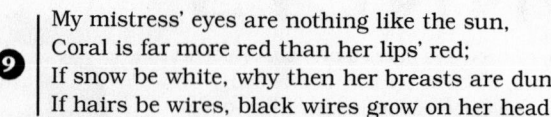

Sonnet 130
WILLIAM SHAKESPEARE

 Literary Analysis

The Shakespearean Sonnet Identify the rhyme scheme of the sonnet's first quatrain.

Spiral Review

Check Context Clues Based on the context of the poem as a whole, what is the meaning of the term "false compare" in the last line?

My mistress' eyes are nothing like the sun,
Coral is far more red than her lips' red;
If snow be white, why then her breasts are dun;
If hairs be wires, black wires grow on her head.
5 I have seen roses damasked,[1] red and white,
But no such roses see I in her cheeks;
And in some perfumes is there more delight
Than in the breath that from my mistress reeks.[2]
I love to hear her speak. Yet well I know
10 That music hath a far more pleasing sound.
I grant I never saw a goddess go;[3]
My mistress, when she walks, treads on the ground.
    And yet, by heaven, I think my love as rare
    As any she belied[4] with false compare.

1. **damasked** variegated.
2. **reeks** emanates.
3. **go** walk.
4. **belied** (bē līd´) misrepresented.

Critical Reading

Cite textual evidence to support your responses.

1. **Key Ideas and Details (a)** How are the mistress's eyes, lips, cheeks, breath, and voice inferior, according to Sonnet 130? **(b) Interpret:** Why does the speaker say she "treads on the ground"?

2. **Integration of Knowledge and Ideas (a)** In Sonnet 130, what does the final couplet say about the speaker's feelings? **(b) Interpret:** What general truth does the couplet suggest? **(c) Draw Conclusions:** In his sonnets, Petrarch worshiped his mistress. Why has Sonnet 130 been called anti-Petrarchan?

3. **Integration of Knowledge and Ideas** What advantages or disadvantages does the Shakespearean sonnet have compared with the Petrarchan sonnet? Explain. In your response, use at least two of these Essential Question words: *complex, innovative, dramatic.* [Connecting to the Essential Question: What is the relationship of the writer to tradition?]

Concept Connector

Reading Skill Graphic Organizer
Ask students to review the graphic organizers in which they have recorded the progress of theme as it relates to structure. Then have students share their organizers and compare their ideas and conclusions.

Activating Prior Knowledge
Have students return to their responses to the Activating Prior Knowledge activity. Ask them to explain whether their thoughts have changed and, if so, how.

Connecting to the Essential Question
Have students compare their responses to the prompt, given before they completed reading the sonnets, with their thoughts afterward. Have them work individually or in groups, writing or discussing their thoughts, to formulate their new responses. Then lead a class discussion, probing for what students have learned that confirms or invalidates their initial thoughts. Encourage students to cite specific textual details to support their responses.

Literary Analysis

© **1. Craft and Structure (a)** Identify the three quatrains and the couplet of the **Shakespearean sonnet** using Sonnet 106 as an example. **(b)** Which rhyming words represent the *a*'s, *b*'s, *c*'s, *d*'s, *e*'s, *f*'s, and *g*'s of the rhyme scheme?

© **2. Craft and Structure** Choose a sonnet and use a chart like the one shown to map out its **syntax.**

Number of Sentences	Number of Lines in Each Sentence	Syntax is Straightforward or Complicated?

© **3. Craft and Structure (a)** Which two of the sonnets use complicated **syntax,** featuring sentences full of phrases and clauses? **(b)** Compare the complicated syntax of these sonnets with the simpler syntax of the other two sonnets. **(c)** In each case, explain how effectively the elaborate or the simple syntax conveys the meaning.

© **4. Key Ideas and Details** Explain how Shakespeare uses references to other poetry in Sonnets 106 and 130. In each case, how do these references support the argument he is making?

© **5. Integration of Knowledge and Ideas** If Shakespeare had adapted one of these sonnets to the Petrarchan form (an eight-line octet followed by a six-line sestet), how might the new form have affected the way he presented his message?

© **6. Integration of Knowledge and Ideas (a)** Which sonnet do you think best expresses modern attitudes? Support your choice with examples. **(b)** Do you think the sonnet is a form suited to today's world? Why or why not?

Reading Strategy

7. (a) Analyze text structures in Shakespeare's sonnets by listing the main idea of each section of Sonnets 106 and 116. **(b)** Does each idea correspond to a quatrain or couplet? Explain.

8. Analyze the effects of the couplet in each of these sonnets. Does it restate what has been said, provide a different perspective on it, or reverse it? Cite evidence from the poems to support your point.

9. In Sonnet 29, line 9 marks a turn in the meaning. By contrast, in Sonnet 116, lines 1–12 express a single thought in different ways. Which pattern of organization do you prefer, a sonnet that swerves in meaning or one that builds to a conclusion? Why?

Sonnet 29 • Sonnet 106 • Sonnet 116 • Sonnet 130 **279**

© **Common Core State Standards**

Writing
2.b. Develop the topic thoroughly by selecting the most significant and relevant facts, extended definitions, concrete details, quotations, or other information and examples appropriate to the audience's knowledge of the topic. *(p. 280)*

Language
5. Demonstrate understanding of word relationships. *(p. 280)*

8. Possible responses: Sonnet 29: shift in thought. Sonnet 106: different perspective. Sonnet 116: reaffirmation of poet's assertion. Sonnet 130: reversal of previous ideas.

9. Possible response: I prefer a sonnet that swerves in meaning, because it is more interesting to follow and gives more insight into the poet's thought patterns.

Answers

1. (a) Quatrains: lines 1–4, 5–8, 9–12; couplet: lines 13–14. (b) time, rhyme = a; wights, knights = b; best, express'd = c; brow, now = d; prophecies, eyes = e; prefiguring, sing = f; days, praise = g.

2. **Possible response:** Sonnet 106. Number of sentences: 2. Lines in each sentence: 8; 6. The syntax of the first sentence is somewhat complicated, because the sentence contains many nested clauses, which makes it difficult to connect its different ideas. The syntax of the second sentence is more straightforward, because it is clearly broken up using the semicolon and colon.

3. (a) Sonnets 29 and 106 use complex syntax. (b) in sonnets 116 and 130, ideas are completed in a few lines. (c) In Sonnets 29 and 106, the complex syntax matches the wandering thoughts. In Sonnets 116 and 130, the precise language matches the speaker's certainty.

4. Shakespeare's references give his poems authority while allowing him to set his words and love apart.

5. **Possible response:** Shakespeare's message might have to be simplified to fit the octet-sestet format. For instance, in Sonnet 29, the division into quatrains plus a couplet supports shifts in theme that a division into only two parts might eliminate.

6. **Possible responses:** (a) Sonnet 130 seems more typical of our times. In today's world, idealized beauty is still in conflict with reality. (b) **Possible responses:** Yes, if it were set to music, it might resemble a modern love song.

7. (a) and (b) **Possible response:** Sonnet 106: Q1–People have praised beauty in the past. Q2–They tried to describe beauty like yours. Q3–Everything they said was a prophecy of your beauty, even if their skills were inadequate. Couplet–We get to look on you in wonder, but words fail us. Sonnet 116: Q1–Love that changes is not love. Q2–Love is constant, unshaken, and a reliable guide. Q3–Love is not changed by time. Couplet–If this is false, then love does not exist.

279

Vocabulary Acquisition and Use

1. Introduce the skill using the instruction on the student page.
2. Have students complete the Word Analysis activity and the Vocabulary practice.

Word Analysis

1. c
2. a
3. b
4. d

Vocabulary

1. prefiguring
2. sullen
3. impediments
4. alters
5. chronicle
6. scope

Writing

1. Review with students their understanding of imagery.
2. Tell students that in preparing their analyses, they should look for passages that include images that express emotions and ideas.
3. Model the Prewriting chart for students to help stimulate their thinking about Shakespeare's use of imagery.
4. Give students the Support for Writing Lesson, page 49 in *Unit 2 Resources,* to guide them in developing their informative texts.
5. Use the **Rubrics for Response to Literature,** pages 250–251 in **Professional Development Guidebook,** to evaluate students' essays.

Ⓒ Vocabulary Acquisition and Use

Word Analysis: Greek Root -chron-

The word *chronicle* contains the Greek root *-chron-,* meaning "time." This root is important in words relating to history. For example, a chronicle is a record of events arranged in their order of occurrence. Keeping in mind the meaning of *-chron-,* match the following words with their definitions.

1. chronology
2. chronicler
3. chronological
4. chronometer

  a. person who records events by date
  b. arranged in order of occurrence
  c. a list of important events by date
  d. a device that measures time

Vocabulary: Analogies

An *analogy* is a comparison of two pairs of words that have the same relationship. For each item, determine the relationship between the first and second words. Then, using a word from the vocabulary list on page 272, fill in the blank to complete the analogy. Explain your choice.

1. Humming : singing :: _____ : occurring
2. Careful : rash :: _____ : cheerful
3. Principles : beliefs :: _____ : obstacles
4. Wavers : decides :: _____ : preserves
5. Desk : drawer :: _____ : entry
6. Speed : reduced :: _____ : limited

Writing

Ⓒ **Argumentative Text** In his sonnets, Shakespeare uses imagery—words that appeal to the senses—to suggest the complexities of love. In an **essay,** analyze the imagery in one of his sonnets. Consider how the images are used both to communicate central ideas and to evoke readers' emotions. Support your ideas and reasoning with relevant quotations and details from the poem.

Prewriting Describe the images in a sonnet of your choice. Next to each image, note the idea that it expresses and its relationship to other images in the poem. Use a chart like the one shown.

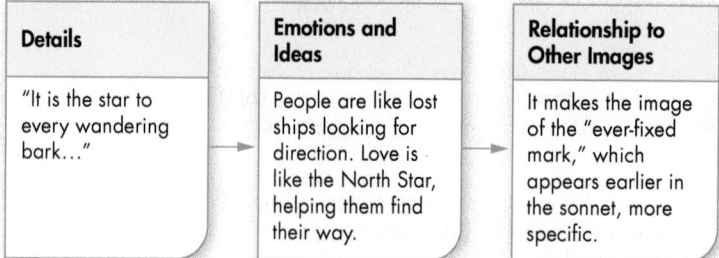

Details	Emotions and Ideas	Relationship to Other Images
"It is the star to every wandering bark..."	People are like lost ships looking for direction. Love is like the North Star, helping them find their way.	It makes the image of the "ever-fixed mark," which appears earlier in the sonnet, more specific.

Drafting Begin with a strong thesis statement. Then, use details to support your ideas. Note relationships of similarity, contrast, or development among images.

Revising Review your analysis. If necessary, refine your thesis to fit the details or add details as support. Then, consider your audience's knowledge of the topic. If you think that any of your points will not be easily understood, add clarifications, such as defining a difficult word or explaining a connection you have made.

Assessment Resources

Unit 2 Resources

L1 L2 EL **Selection Test A,** pp. 56–58. Administer Test A to less advanced readers.

L3 L4 EL **Selection Test B,** pp. 59–61. Administer Test B to on-level and more advanced students.

L3 L4 **Open-Book Test,** pp. 53–55. As an alternative, administer the Open-Book Test.

All **Customizable Test Bank**

All **Self-tests**
Students may prepare for the **Selection Test** by taking the **Self-test** online.

The Influence of the Monarchy

Text Complexity: At a Glance

This chart gives a general text complexity rating for the selections in this part of the unit to help guide instruction. For additional text complexity support, see the Test Complexity Rubric at point of use.	
Psalm 23	**More Complex**
Psalm 137	**More Complex**
from the Sermon on the Mount	**More Accessible**
from the Parable of the Prodigal Son	**More Accessible**

Selection Planning Guide

The selections in this section demonstrate the influence of British monarchs on the literature of the sixteenth and early seventeenth centuries. For example, Elizabeth I's "Speech Before Defeating the Spanish Armada" reveals the public persona of this powerful monarch. A committee appointed by Elizabeth's successor, James I, produced one of the most enduring and influential works of English literature, the King James Bible.

Humanities

Henry VIII, c. 1540, after Hans Holbein the Younger

This portrait is often mistakenly attributed to Holbein. There are few portraits of Henry VIII that can be attributed to Holbein with certainty. Those portraits, however, were impressive enough to influence all other artists who painted the king, so most of Henry VIII's portraits appear Holbein-esque. Consider this portrait—the king faces us directly, one hand clutching a glove and the other resting above a jeweled sword. The rings on his fingers are similar as well; the most obvious difference is the color of his sleeves. This portrait is at the Galleria Nazionale d'Arte Antica in Rome.

Use these questions for discussion:

1. What impression of Henry VIII do you form from this painting?
   Possible response: Students may say that he projects wealth, leadership, power, and dignity.

2. What details in the painting contribute to this overall impression?
   Possible response: Students may cite such details as his pose, straight posture, serious expression, and expensive clothing.

Monitoring Progress

Before students read the selections in Part 2, refer to the results for the **Vocabulary in Context** items on **Benchmark Test 2** (*Unit 1 Resources,* p. 171). Use this diagnostic portion of the test to guide your choice of selections to teach as well as the depth of prereading preparation you will provide, based on students' readiness for the reading and vocabulary skills.

281

Primary Sources

Speech
Speech Before Her Troops

Eyewitness Account
Examination of Don Luis de Córdoba

Common Core State Standards

Reading Informational Text 2. Determine two or more central ideas of a text and analyze their development over the course of the text, including how they interact and build on one another to provide a complex analysis; provide an objective summary of the text.

❶ About the Text Forms

A **speech,** or talk given to an audience, is one of the oldest means of communication, serving purposes like these: to persuade, entertain, or inform. Before recording technology was invented, a speech was always immediate. Those not present had to read, or be read, a written record of the speaker's words. Such transcripts are valuable primary sources.

An **eyewitness account** is an oral or written narrative of events by someone who saw what happened. Even if it has some inaccuracy or bias, an eyewitness account of historical events can still be a valuable primary source, especially when considered along with other accounts of the same events.

❷ Reading Strategy

One of the best ways of remembering the details in a primary source and understanding the relationships between them is by **summarizing,** or briefly restating the writer's central ideas and listing the key facts that support these ideas.

Once you have summarized the central ideas and key supporting details in a text, identify ways in which the central ideas interact. Here is an example:

Central Idea 1: Elizabeth I loves and trusts her people.
Supporting Detail: She has come to address them even though her advisers warn of treachery.
Central Idea 2: She will reward her troops.
Supporting Detail: She knows that they deserve reward.
Interaction of Ideas: Her promise reflects her love.

After reading each of these primary sources, summarize it. Then, use your summary to analyze the development of central ideas and their interaction. Prepare for your summary by using *anecdotal scripting*—note-taking—as you read.

❸ What is the **relationship** between *literature* and *place?*

England was at war, but the troops were still unpaid. What might inspire them to go on? Elizabeth I had an answer. As you read her speech, consider what her leadership and her words suggest about the answer to the Essential Question shown above.

Common Core State Standards

• Reading Informational Text 2
• Writing 7, 8
• Language 6

❶ About the Text Forms

1. Have students suggest types of speeches that are common today, such as campaign speeches and have students identify the main purpose(s) of each type of speech.

2. Encourage students to compare the benefits and drawbacks of both types of primary documents. For example, an eyewitness account may have details and an emotional impact that a more objective account might not include, but it is only one person's point of view.

❷ Reading Strategy

Introduce the strategy using the instruction on the student page.

Think Aloud: Model the Skill

Say to students:

To help organize the facts and ideas in a text, I pause often to summarize, or restate a main idea in my own words. Putting an idea in my own words helps me understand what I am reading.

❸ What is the relationship between literature and place?

After reading the Essential Question note, have students discuss ways that leaders' speeches to their soldiers might be different in different circumstances.

Teaching Resources

All *Unit 2 Resources,* pp. 62–65

All *Common Core Companion,* pp. 103–110; 240–260; 336–337

All Enriched Online Student Edition

All resources are available at **www.PHLitOnline.com.**

Note-Taking Guide

Primary source documents are a rich source of information for researchers. As you read these documents, use a note-taking guide like the one shown to organize relevant and accurate information.

1 Type of Document (check one)
☐ Newspaper ☐ Letter ☐ Diary ☐ Map ☐ Speech ☐ Advertisement
☐ Government Document ☐ Eyewitness Account ☐ Memorandum ☐ Other

2 Date of Document _____

3 Author _____
Author's Position _____

4 Original Audience _____

5 Purpose and Importance
  a What was the original purpose? _____
    Write down two details that support your answer. _____
    _____

  b What are the key ideas or observations in this document? _____
    _____

  c What does this document show about the time and place in which it was
    composed? _____
    _____

> **Reading Strategy**
> **Summarizing Information**
> Sometimes you need to organize the basic information found in a primary source document. One way of doing this is **summarizing,** briefly restating main points and key details. As you read, summarize the key ideas in each document.

This guide was adapted from the **U.S. National Archives** document analysis worksheet.

Vocabulary

treachery (trech´ ər ē) *n.* betrayal of trust or loyalty (p. 285)

tyrants (tī´ rənts) *n.* cruel, oppressive rulers (p. 285)

realms (relmz) *n.* regions under the rule of a king or queen (p. 287)

stead (sted) *n.* position being filled by a replacement (p. 287)

obedience (ō bē´ dē əns; ō bēd´ yəns) *n.* the act of following orders or instructions (p. 287)

concord (kän´ kôrd´) *n.* friendly relations; harmony (p. 287)

valor (val´ ər) *n.* courageous behavior (p. 287)

galleons (gal´ ē ənz) *n.* large sailing ships used for war or trade (p. 289)

---

4 Note-Taking Guide

1. Explain to students that they will need to have separate note-taking guides for each selection, and that some of the items can be completed before they begin reading.

2. Encourage students to set up a note-taking guide for each selection before they read, filling in type and date of document, author information, and original audience before beginning to read the selections.

3. Read aloud the Reading Strategy note on the student page. Point out that item *5b* corresponds to the Reading Strategy.

5 Vocabulary

1. Have students preview the selection vocabulary, pronouncing the words and reading their definitions. Have students identify any words with which they are familiar.

2. Use each word in a sentence with sufficient context to define the word. Then have students take turns using each vocabulary word in their own sentences.

❻ Background

The Story Behind the Documents

Why was the Spanish Armada defeated by the English? The Armada was known to be a formidable force, and it seemed unlikely that England would be able to stand up to its power. One contributing factor was leadership. Philip II had been planning for many years to invade England, but shortly before the 1588 invasion was launched, the commander of the Armada, Santa Cruz, unexpectedly died. The Duke of Medina Sedonia, who took over in place of Santa Cruz, did not have the experience necessary to make the venture a success.

❻ THE STORY BEHIND THE DOCUMENTS

Elizabeth I (1533–1603), who became England's queen in 1558 when she was barely out of her teens, ruled at a time when few thought a woman could succeed as a leader. The young queen, however, using courage and judgment, brought stability and prosperity to her nation. Today she is often named as England's greatest monarch. A dramatic moment in her reign came when King Philip II of Spain sent an Armada, or war fleet, to invade England. Her speech to her troops at this dangerous time reveals her skill as an inspirational leader.

Don Luis de Córdoba was a Spanish aristocrat, the son of a high official in Philip II's court. Sailing with the Armada, he survived the fighting, but his ship was wrecked off the west coast of Ireland. There the English executed most Armada survivors, but the high-born Don Luis was allowed to live. His eyewitness account of his experiences provides a valuable record of a major historical event.

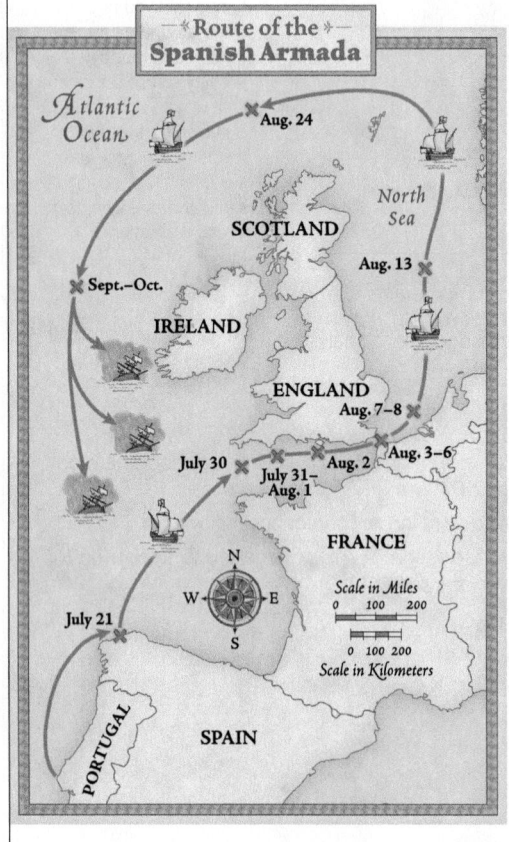

Route of the **Spanish Armada**

The defeat of the Spanish Armada was the climax of what might be described as a religious war, a national feud, and a family dispute rolled into one. It all began with a royal divorce.

In 1533, King Henry VIII of England, a headstrong man, divorced the Spanish princess Catherine of Aragon to marry Anne Boleyn. This caused him to split with the Roman Catholic Church. As a result, England became a Protestant nation. Spain remained a champion of Roman Catholicism. In addition, England and Spain were rivals for colonial possessions in the New World.

Family disputes added fuel to the fires. Mary, daughter of Henry VIII and Catherine of Aragon, became England's queen and wed the future king of Spain, Philip II. Philip and Bloody Mary, as she was called for persecuting Protestants, tried to make England Catholic again. Mary was highly suspicious of her Protestant half-sister and royal rival, Elizabeth. With Protestants rebelling and maybe plotting to bring Elizabeth to the throne, Mary kept Elizabeth in the Tower of London or under house arrest.

When Mary died and Elizabeth became queen, most of England welcomed the change. Roman Catholics at home and abroad, however, schemed to overthrow Elizabeth. Philip II of Spain was at the heart of such conspiracies. In 1588, he sent a large fleet, the Spanish Armada, to conquer England and bring it back into the Catholic fold.

284 Celebrating Humanity (1485–1625)

The Elizabethan Age

It is almost impossible to overstate the brilliance and influence of Queen Elizabeth I. She loved learning and set aside large sums of money for public education. A skilled dancer and poet, she enthusiastically supported the arts. She was friend and patron to some of the most famous individuals in English history, including Sir Francis Drake, Sir Walter Raleigh, and William Shakespeare.

Today, Elizabeth I is regarded as one of the finest English monarchs. Highly intelligent, beloved by her subjects, she governed during a time of artistic achievement, military success, and economic advances.

Activity: Investigating Daily Life Have interested students conduct further investigation into life during the Elizabethan Age. What was daily life like for the subjects of Queen Elizabeth I? Students can use the **Enrichment: Investigating Daily Life** worksheet on page 224 of the *Professional Development Guidebook* to help them record what they learn about the Elizabethan Age.

SPEECH BEFORE HER TROOPS

Queen Elizabeth I

▲ These Dangers Averted medals celebrated the defeat of the Spanish Armada.

BACKGROUND By the 1580s, Philip II was king of Portugal as well as Spain and ruled over vast New World colonies. He also ruled the Spanish Netherlands (today's Netherlands and some adjoining areas), where his repression of Protestants prompted the Dutch to rebel. Philip's Protestant half-sister-in-law, Elizabeth I, queen of England, aided the Dutch rebels and quietly supported attacks on Spanish ships by English sea captains. In 1587, when a plot to replace her with her Catholic cousin Mary, Queen of Scots, ended in failure, Elizabeth had Mary executed. A year later, Philip sent his Armada of warships to collect troops fighting in the Netherlands and invade England.

With Elizabeth's navy fighting the Spanish fleet, her land forces massed in the English port of Tilbury, anticipating an invasion that never came. Nerves frayed and soldiers began to grumble about delays in pay. Then Elizabeth, dramatically dressed in a white gown and silver breast-plate, appeared before the troops and made the following famous speech.

Primary Sources
Speech When Elizabeth delivered this speech, which words in the first two sentences do you think she emphasized? Why?

Vocabulary
treachery (trech′ ər ē) *n.* betrayal of trust or loyalty

tyrants (tī′ rənts) *n.* cruel, oppressive rulers

My loving people, we have been persuaded by some, that are careful of our safety, to take heed how we commit ourselves to armed multitudes,[1] for fear of treachery: but I assure you, I do not desire to live to distrust my faithful and loving people. Let tyrants fear; I have always so behaved myself that, under God, I have placed my chiefest strength and safeguard in the loyal hearts and good will of my subjects. And therefore I am come amongst you at this time, not as for my recreation or sport, but being resolved, in the midst and heat of the battle, to live or die amongst you all; to lay down, for my God, and for my kingdom, and for my people, my honor and my blood, even the dust. I know I have but the body of a weak and

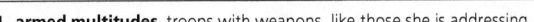

1. armed multitudes troops with weapons, like those she is addressing.

TEACH

❶ Background

History

As the final words of this speech clearly illustrate, the English people believed that God was on their side. When strong winds gave a clear advantage to the English ships during the battle, the English people saw it as an example of divine intervention on their behalf. After it became known that they had indeed defeated the mighty Spanish Armada, the words *God blew and they were scattered* were engraved on a commemorative medal in celebration.

❷ Primary Sources

Speech

1. Have students read the first two sentences to themselves, then ask several volunteers to read them aloud. Have students note what words each student emphasized when reading aloud.

2. **Ask** students the Primary Sources question: When Elizabeth delivered this speech, which words in the first two sentences do you think she emphasized? Why? **Possible Answer:** She may have emphasized *loving, assure, faithful, loving, loyal hearts,* and *good will* to communicate her love and admiration for her subjects, thus appealing to their good natures and inspiring their love and loyalty.

Differentiated Instruction for Universal Access

Background for Special-Needs Students
Explain to students that Elizabeth I was speaking to soldiers. Spain had threatened to invade. Elizabeth is reminding the soldiers of how wonderful England is, and how the country is worth defending, as well as how highly she regards the soldiers and their sense of duty. She also states that she is prepared to die with them, if necessary. Listening to this selection on *Hear It!* Audio CDs may help students better understand what is being said.

Enrichment for Gifted/Talented Students
Have students make a collage in which they illustrate or excerpt parts of Elizabeth I's speech that suggest the theme of monarch as hero. Encourage students to reread the speech independently, noting words, passages, or persuasive elements that allude to Elizabeth I's heroism. Then, have students work in small groups to make an illustration that conveys the way in which the theme is broached in her speech. Students may want to listen to the speech on the *Hear It!* Audio CDs.

PHLit Online!

These selections are available in interactive format in the **Enriched Online Student Edition,** at **www.PHLitOnline.com,** which includes a thematically related video with writing prompt and an interactive graphic organizer.

Portrait of Queen Elizabeth I, Anonymous

Many portraits were painted of Elizabeth I, emphasizing many different aspects. This painting, known as the Armada portrait, stresses her victory over Spain.

Use these questions for discussion:

- What are some of the clues in the painting that the woman portrayed is the queen of an empire?
  Answer: The crown to the right of the queen suggests royalty. Her hand is on the globe of the Earth, suggesting conquest and the idea that the world is under her control. Her jewelry and clothing indicate that she is a person of wealth and importance.

- What evidence is there in the picture that Spain's famed Armada had met its end?
  Answer: The images of ships in the background allude to the naval battle, and the picture at left of the Armada broken and battered on a stormy sea reflects its defeat.

- Monarchs were viewed as the embodiment of their nation. What does Elizabeth's appearance tell you about England during this period?
  Answer: On the basis of Elizabeth's appearance, one might guess that England was formal, wealthy, powerful, and in control.

286 Celebrating Humanity (1485–1625)

Enrichment: Understanding the Monarchy

Rulers

The beliefs people have about their monarchs have varied across time and place. The ancient Egyptian pharaohs, and later some Roman emperors, were considered gods, and their subjects were expected to revere them as such. The Aztec "sun kings" were seen as gods and expected human sacrifice.

The seventeenth-century French king Louis XIV made the famous statement, "I am the State." Today, several countries still have monarchs. Generally, today's rulers are dedicated to help-ing their people and strengthening their countries. Good examples of this trend are found in Thailand and Spain.

Activity: Investigating Culture Have interested students conduct further investigation into the relationship between a ruler and the people. Students should pay special attention to the way rulers are viewed in this culture. They may use the **Enrichment: Investigating Culture** worksheet on page 223 of the *Professional Development Guidebook* to organize their information.

feeble woman; but I have the heart of a king, and of a king of England, too; and think foul scorn that Parma[2] or Spain, or any prince of Europe, should dare to invade the borders of my realms: to which, rather than any dishonor should grow by me, I myself will take up arms; I myself will be your general, judge, and rewarder of every one of your virtues in the field. I know already, by your forwardness, that you have deserved rewards and crowns;[3] and we do assure you, on the word of a prince, they shall be duly paid you. In the mean my lieutenant general shall be in my stead, than whom never prince commanded a more noble and worthy subject; not doubting by your obedience to my general, by your concord in the camp, and by your valor in the field, we shall shortly have a famous victory over the enemies of my God, of my kingdom, and of my people.

---

2. **Parma** Alessandro Farnese (1545–1592), duke of the Italian state of Parma and commander of Philip II's troops fighting rebels in the Spanish Netherlands.
3. **crowns** coins depicting the monarch's head, used to pay the troops.

Vocabulary

realms (relmz) *n.* regions under the rule of a king or queen

stead (sted) *n.* position being filled by a replacement

obedience (ō bē′ dē əns; ō bēd′ yəns) *n.* the act of following orders or instructions

concord (kän′ kôrd′) *n.* friendly relations; harmony

valor (val′ ər) *n.* courageous behavior

Critical Reading

1. **Key Ideas and Details** (a) According to the speech, what have Elizabeth's advisers warned her not to do, and why does she do it anyway? (b) **Interpret:** What effect is the inclusion of this information designed to have on her audience?

2. **Key Ideas and Details** (a) What does Elizabeth tell her audience she already knows, and what does she promise to do? (b) **Analyze Cause and Effect:** How do you think her audience reacted to this information? Why?

3. **Craft and Structure** (a) **Analyze:** Where does Elizabeth exaggerate in her speech? (b) **Evaluate:** Do you think the exaggeration makes her speech more or less persuasive? Explain your answer.

Cite textual evidence to support your responses.

◀ **Critical Viewing** What does this rendering of Elizabeth indicate about the importance of pageantry—ceremony and theatrical presence—in her court? Explain your reasoning. **[Interpret]**

Speech Before Her Troops **287**

Differentiated Instruction for Universal Access

Strategy for Less Proficient Readers
Make sure students understand that Elizabeth is responding to concerns that the soldiers have: the concern that a woman should not lead soldiers, concern that they will not win, and concern that they will not be rewarded. Have students find where Elizabeth reassures her subjects.

EL Strategy for English Learners
Help English learners break up the long, complex sentences in this speech into shorter sentences. For example, the first sentence of the speech can easily be broken up into two sentences by ending at *treachery* and deleting the word *but* in line 3.

Enrichment for Advanced Readers
Queen Elizabeth's speech exemplifies some of the techniques that a persuasive speaker uses, including flattery and rhetorical devices such as repetition and parallel structure. Encourage students to find examples of these techniques in the Queen's speech.

---

4 Primary Sources

Speech

Have a volunteer read aloud the final sentence of the speech and identify the part of the sentence that reveals the Queen's feelings about the Spanish Armada.

Answer: The Queen's feelings are reflected in the phrase "the enemies of my God, of my Kingdom, and of my people."

5 Critical Viewing

Answer: Elizabeth's elaborate dress and jewelry suggest that she was an important symbol of majesty and empire to her subjects, as well as to those who might visit from other countries. Pageantry emphasized the glory and power of both Elizabeth and the country as a whole.

ASSESS

Answers

Before students respond, you may wish to have them write a brief objective summary of the selection. As they answer the questions below, remind them to support their answers with evidence from the text.

1. (a) Elizabeth's advisors have warned her to avoid close, personal contact with her subjects, but Elizabeth trusts her people. (b) This introduction is designed to have her audience feel close to the Queen.

2. (a) Elizabeth says she already knows that her soldiers deserve to be rewarded for their service, and she promises to make sure they get their reward. **Possible Response:** (b) Her audience probably reacted favorably to this news, since they were concerned about payment.

3. (a) She exaggerates by saying that she herself will fight, be their general, and reward them personally. (b) I think they reveal her passion and help communicate her emotions to the audience.

287

History

Although Spain and England had roughly the same number of ships, their strategy in battle was quite different. The Spanish Armada included many large ships used for carrying soldiers. They intended to carry out the invasion by depositing an overwhelming number of troops on land. The English wanted to stop the Armada before it reached its destination, so they developed a naval strategy using artillery and fireships to drive the Spanish ships away.

7 Primary Sources

Eyewitness Account

1. Have students read the first three sentences of Don Luis's testimony. **Ask** them what clues in the text show that Don Luis is giving this account to English interrogators, rather than to his own countrymen.
   Answer: Spanish officials probably would not refer to "the Queen."

2. Then **ask** students the Primary Sources question: How might the circumstances under which Don Luis was questioned affect the accuracy of his information?
   Possible Answer: Because Don Luis is being questioned by his enemies, he may not have felt compelled to give accurate information, and he may have been inclined to make the Spanish seem courageous and unlucky rather than unorganized and unprepared.

Examination of
6 DON LUIS DE CÓRDOBA

BACKGROUND: THE SPANISH ARMADA VS. THE ENGLISH FLEET

	Spain	England
Statistics	about 130 ships: 40 are 1st rate best warships: large, slow, with fewer and lighter guns; gunners not well trained	about same number best warships: small, fast, with more and heavier guns; gunners well trained
Battle Plan	• sail up English Channel • at Flanders, pick up troops for invasion	• attack early • break up Spanish battle formation
Results	• English outmaneuver Spanish but do no real damage • Spanish fleet anchors off Calais (ka lā´), France • English set boats afire and send them toward Spanish fleet • Spanish formation breaks up; English win decisive battle • Bad weather drives Spanish away; they sail northward • Many Spanish ships, including Don Luis de Córdoba's, are wrecked on the west coast of Ireland	

Primary Sources
Eyewitness Account
How might the circumstances under which Don Luis was questioned affect the accuracy of his information?

7

Don Lewes from Cordoba in Andalucia:[1] Captain of the men shipwrecked on the shore of the land of Sir Murrough ne Doe (Galway), says that when the Spanish fleet got near to Plymouth, there were 140 different types of boats including 96 great ships for the battle, and the rest were pataches[2] and small boats for transport. Off the coast of Plymouth, they met about 70 of Queen Elizabeth's ships. The Queen's ships gained the weather gage[3] and shot at them. They kept going towards Calais and returned fire for 2 or 3 hours. During this battle, Don Pedro and his ship were captured, as he was left behind the fleet when a cannon ball broke the main mast. The next day was calm and therefore nothing happened between them, except that a Spanish ship of 700 ton was burned accidentally, but most of the men were rescued. On the 3rd day they fought for 5 or 6 hours without losing any ships. On the 4th day they fought for 4 hours without losing any ships. On the

---

1. **Andalucia** the region of southern Spain where the city of Córdoba is located.
2. **pataches** *n.* small, fast, well-armed Portuguese ships that sailed with the Armada.
3. **gained the weather gage** positioned the ships so that the wind blew into their sails, giving them the advantage of more speed.

Enrichment: Understanding Historical Figures

Sir Francis Drake

One of the leaders of English forces against the Spanish Armada, Francis Drake had a lifelong career on the sea. He was involved in the slave trade in the 1560s and sailed as a merchant through the early 1570s. After this, he spent several years making a nuisance of himself to the Spanish—plundering their ships for cargos of gold bullion and robbing their ports of valuable merchandise.

In addition to his fame as a pirate and his role in the defeat of the Armada, Sir Francis Drake is also well known as a sailor. Perhaps his greatest distinction is being the first Englishman to sail around the entire Earth.

Activity: Investigating a Key Person in History Have interested students conduct further investigation into the life and accomplishments of Sir Francis Drake. Students should use the **Enrichment: Investigating a Key Person in History** worksheet on page 233 of the *Professional Development Guidebook* to gather and organize their information.

5th day they reached Calais where they anchored and chained themselves together and at the same time, 25 more ships came to join the Queen's fleet. During the night, the Spanish saw 6 ships on fire sailing down upon them, which forced them to cut their cables and set sail; at this point a great ship was burned amongst them, and a galleas[4] was shipwrecked on the sands. After this, the English ships entered into a fierce fight with the Spanish, in which 2 of the greatest Spanish Galleons were so beaten, that they were forced to come ashore at Flanders and sent the men to their other ships. That day, if the fire had not stopped them, they were going to put 7000 men on the shore at Calais to go to the prince (Duke) of Parma to find out his plans. He was going to be in charge of them and they had some unopened orders addressed to him, which were lost in the burnt ship. When they were stopped by this fire, they were broken and so fought very hard, and after 3 days moved out of the sight of the (English) coast, so that the Queen's ships left them and returned home, celebrating by firing off a lot of cannons. After this, the Duke of Medina moved his remaining ships together and found that he had lost 6 ships. He ordered his forces to return to Spain. But around Norway, the great storm took them and beat them towards our coast; the Duke had already warned them about the dangers of our coastline.

***

4. **galleas** *n.* a large warship powered by both oars and sails.

Vocabulary
galleons (gal´ ē ənz) *n.* large sailing ships used for war or trade

Reading Strategy
Summarizing Information
Summarize the information that Don Luis supplies about events near Norway.

Critical Reading

@ 1. **Key Ideas and Details** **(a) Summarize:** What happened off the coast of Plymouth? **(b) Infer:** Why do you think Don Luis mentions that the English got the advantage from the wind?

@ 2. **Key Ideas and Details** **(a)** What was the purpose of the "ships of fire," or fireships, that the English sent out? **(b) Infer:** How do you think Don Luis felt as he told what happened near Calais? Why?

@ 3. **Key Ideas and Details** **(a) Analyze Cause and Effect:** What prevented the Duke of Parma from giving and receiving orders? **(b) Draw Conclusions:** What do the details suggest about communications among the Spanish forces?

Cite textual evidence to support your responses.

Examination of Don Luis de Córdoba **289**

❽ Reading Strategy
Organizing Information

1. Point out to students that because Don Luis provides many details in his account, creating a chronological summary of the events he recounts would be helpful for their understanding.

2. **Ask** the Reading Strategy question: Summarize the information that Don Luis supplies about events near Norway.
   Possible response: A great storm pushed the Spanish fleet toward the English coast.

ASSESS
Answers

Before students respond, you may wish to have them write a brief objective summary of the selection. As they answer the questions below, remind them to support their answers with evidence from the text.

1. (a) The Spanish were engaged in battle by many English ships, and Don Pedro and his ship were captured. (b) **Possible Response:** Don Luis wants to provide an excuse for their poor performance in this battle.

2. (a) The fireships forced the Spanish to set sail and hampered their efforts to organize an effective attack against the English. (b) **Possible Response:** He probably felt saddened and disappointed by the way Spanish forces were defeated by the English, because they expected to be successful in their invasion.

3. (a) Fire stopped the Duke from giving and receiving orders. (b) These details suggest that communications were already rather unorganized, and that events made them even more so.

Differentiated Instruction   for Universal Access

Culturally Responsive Instruction
Culture Focus Students may lack the background knowledge or context-building experiences to fully comprehend the selection. Specifically, it may be confusing that two of the people mentioned in the document are called *Don*: Don Pedro and Don Luis. Point out to students that while *Don* is a man's name, often short for *Donald* in English, it is a form of address indicating that the person is of some importance in Spanish-speaking cultures. Have students suggest similar titles from other cultures, including English-speaking cultures.

Comparing Primary Sources

1. (a) Queen Elizabeth's speech was meant to inspire her troops, while the account by Don Luis de Córdoba to his English captors seeks to paint the Spanish forces in the best possible light (b) These contrasts explain why Elizabeth's speech shows her affection and trust in her subjects, while Don Luis's is filled with facts meant to satisfy his captors.

2. (a) The statement, "and think foul scorn that Parma or Spain, or any other prince of Europe, should dare to invade the borders of my realms" reveals that forces were trying to invade England. The statement "he ordered his forces to return to Spain" reveals that the Spanish Armada retreated from the battle after its great losses. (b) Answers will vary.

3. Queen Elizabeth's speech is helpful to historians studying the dynamics of leadership that led to the defeat of the Armada. The account of Don Luis may be helpful to those who need more details about the actual battles.

Vocabulary Acquisition and Use

1. obedience: The child was *obedient* to her parents.

2. treachery: *Treachery* is another way of describing a betrayal.

3. valor: *Valor* is a synonym for bravery.

4. stead: The substitute taught the class in the teacher's *stead*.

Using Content-Area Vocabulary

5. dictators; The *dictators* of the two nations refused to compromise.

6. kingdoms: The *realms* of France and England were in conflict.

7. warships: The *galleons* were damaged in the battle.

Etymology Study

To be in *accord* means to be in agreement, and *cordial* is used to describe the behavior shown by those who agree.

Speech ▪ Eyewitness Account

Comparing Primary Sources

Refer to your Note-Taking Guide to complete these questions.

1. (a) Contrast the authors' purposes and audiences in these documents arising from the same historical event. (b) How do these contrasts explain the differences in tone, or attitude?

2. (a) Use a chart like the one below to identify one statement from each document and what it reveals about this historic battle. (b) From which document do you learn more? Explain.

Author	Statement	What It Reveals
Queen Elizabeth I		
Don Luis de Córdoba		

3. (a) Summarize each source, listing the central ideas along with key supporting details. (b) For each source, analyze the development and interaction of central ideas, explaining whether they reinforce or contrast with each other.

4. Write a paragraph exploring how each primary source, in its own way, would be useful to historians studying the Armada.

Vocabulary Acquisition and Use

Using New Vocabulary Choose the Word Bank word that is most clearly related to the situation in each sentence. Explain your choices.

treachery   stead   obedience   valor

1. A child heeded all the instructions her parents gave her.
2. A spy pretending to be a friend betrayed the king's trust.
3. The soldier showed great courage during the battle.
4. When the teacher fell ill, a substitute filled in for her.

Content-Area Vocabulary Identify the letter of the choice that is a synonym for the boldfaced word. Then, use the word in a sentence.

5. **tyrants:** (a) monarchs (b) trends (c) dictators (d) quarrels
6. **realms:** (a) kingdoms (b) treaties (c) truths (d) valuables
7. **galleons:** (a) ropes (b) amounts (c) kitchens (d) warships

Etymology Study *Concord* comes from the Latin word *concordia*, meaning "agreement," which includes the Latin root *cord*, meaning "heart." People or things in *concord* seem to have the same heart. The words *accord* and *cordial* have the same Latin root.

Using an online or print dictionary, explain how the root's meaning is reflected in each of these words.

Common Core State Standards

Writing

7. Conduct short as well as more sustained research projects to answer a question or solve a problem; narrow or broaden the inquiry when appropriate; synthesize multiple sources on the subject, demonstrating understanding of the subject under investigation. *(p. 291)*

8. Gather relevant information from multiple authoritative print and digital sources, using advanced searches effectively; assess the strengths and limitations of each source in terms of the task, purpose, and audience; integrate information into the text selectively to maintain the flow of ideas, avoiding plagiarism and overreliance on any one source and following a standard format for citation. *(p. 291)*

Language

6. Acquire and use accurately general academic and domain-specific words and phrases, sufficient for reading, writing, speaking, and listening at the college and career readiness level; demonstrate independence in gathering vocabulary knowledge when considering a word or phrase important to comprehension or expression.

Assessment Practice

Many tests require students to recognize propaganda. Use this item to reinforce the concept:

My loving people . . . being resolved, in the midst and heat of the battle, to live or die amongst you all; . . . by your valor in the field, we shall . . . have a famous victory over the enemies of my God, of my kingdom, and of my people.

The passage can be characterized as propaganda because

A it was spoken by a political leader.
B it contains examples of hyperbole.
C it is very dramatic.
D its purpose was to persuade the people to support the speaker's cause.

Choice **D** is correct, because the purpose of propaganda is to persuade people to support a particular cause.

Research Task

Topic: The Defeat of the Spanish Armada

News traveled slowly in 1588. When Queen Elizabeth I delivered her "Speech Before Her Troops" to rally them against the expected Spanish invasion, the Armada had already been defeated. Using effective research, you can find out about the battle faster, and perhaps more fully, than Elizabeth could.

Assignment: Write a **research report** about one of these aspects of the battle with the Spanish Armada:

- historical causes of the conflict
- forces and weapons of each side
- military tactics used by each side
- sequence of the battle's events

During the battle with the Armada, the English attacked the Spanish fleet with fireships.

Formulate a research plan. Brainstorm and consult with others to decide upon a topic. Formulate an open-ended research question to address your topic, such as "In the battle with the Spanish Armada, what were the differences between the English and the Spanish tactics?" Then, formulate a plan for in-depth research on your topic.

Gather sources. Follow your plan, determining, locating, and exploring the full range of relevant sources.

- Gather evidence, distinguishing between reliable and unreliable sources. Avoid overreliance on one source.
- Systematically organize information to support your central idea. Outline your ideas using a conceptual map or timeline.

Model: Using a Timeline to Organize Information

July 20 Armada sets sail for England.	July 27 Armada anchors off Calais.	July 29 English use fireships.

RESEARCH TIP

Be sure to separate factual data and the complex inferences you make based on the data. Also, differentiate among primary, secondary, and other sources.

Use a checklist like the one shown to evaluate your work.

> **Research Checklist**
> ☐ Have I answered the research question?
> ☐ Have I gathered and synthesized information from reliable sources?
> ☐ Have I organized all the information clearly?
> ☐ Have I cited sources accurately, using a style manual?

Synthesize information. Critique your research process at each step, modifying your process or research question as needed. Differentiate between theories and evidence, and determine whether the evidence for a theory is weak or strong. As you draft, maintain a flow by selecting and synthesizing related, relevant ideas from your sources.

Organize and present ideas. Provide an analysis that does not simply restate facts but supports and develops your personal opinions. Give your report sufficient length and depth to address the complexities of the topic. Avoid plagiarism, citing your sources for ideas not your own, following a standard format.

Research Task **291**

The Defeat of the Spanish Armada

Introduce the Assignment

1. Review the research assignment. As you define the scope of students' research reports, be sure to specify your requirements for length, format, and method of source citation.

2. Point out that, based on the expected length of their reports, students will need to focus their research questions. For example, "What tactics did English sailors use against the Armada?" might be too broad for a short research report. A more focused question might assure an appropriate depth of coverage: "What was the most effective tactic used by the English against the Armada?"

Guide Student Research

1. Using the library and the Internet, students should locate and explore a range of relevant sources.

2. Advise students to be open-minded throughout the research process and to be prepared to adjust their ideas when they encounter "inconvenient" facts that do not support their initial thesis.

Think Aloud: Model the Skill

Say to students:

The worst mistake I can make in a research report is to present another writer's interpretations as my own. To avoid this problem, I use different colors or different fonts to record factual information and others' insights.

Guide Student Writing

1. Encourage students writing about historical causes or the sequence of the battle to present their data in chronological order.

2. Students writing about the resources or tactics of each side of the battle should find a comparison-contrast pattern useful.

291

Contemporary Connection

"Disappearing Act" gives students biographical information about Australian actress Cate Blanchett. Blanchett is an award-winning actress who has portrayed Queen Elizabeth I twice in films. You may want to have students read the entire interview. It was published in *The New Yorker* magazine, February 12, 2007.

Connecting Elizabeth I, Past and Present

1. Tell students that Elizabeth I was queen during England's golden age of literature. During her reign, poetry and drama flourished, in part because of her patronage. English writers, including Elizabeth herself, began to write sonnets and blank verse. William Shakespeare, Christopher Marlowe, and Edmund Spenser all lived during Elizabeth's reign.

2. The text invites a comparison between Cate Blanchett and Elizabeth herself. **Ask** students how Blanchett and Elizabeth are similar and different.
Possible response: They both have public personas, and a famous actress in our culture has much of the celebrity of a queen.

John Lahr

1. Review the information on John Lahr with students.
2. **Ask:** Why might Lahr feel that he had interviewed an actress who "disappeared" into her characters? Is this comment a compliment, or a criticism, of Blanchett?
Possible response: Some actresses act so well that it is very hard to see anything of the actress in the character. A good actor can convince an audience that he or she is a different person. Lahr's is a compliment.

Connecting Elizabeth I, Past and Present

Famous actresses have portrayed Elizabeth I over the years, including Sarah Bernhardt and Helen Mirren. It was, however, a young unknown who in 1998 portrayed the transformation of Elizabeth on screen from a fragile, endangered girl to one of the most respected and iconic monarchs in history. In doing so, Australian actress Cate Blanchett also transformed herself into a star.

Blanchett, who even as a child loved to perform, studied Elizabeth I's letters to better understand the monarch. "It was there I could see the mechanics of her brain and her thought processes," she explained, "and the way she was able to play people off against each other, as well as her extraordinary intelligence."

The young actress came to think of Elizabeth herself as a kind of actress, and once said of her: "You know, she was in her element in front of a large crowd. She had the instincts of a performer. . . ."

Cate Blanchett has played royalty more than once. After starring as Elizabeth I in Indian director Shekhar Kapur's *Elizabeth*, which earned her an Academy Award Best Actress nomination, she portrayed the Elf Queen Galadriel in the immensely popular *The Lord of the Rings* trilogy (2001–2003). In 2005, Blanchett won the Oscar for Best Supporting Actress for her role as Hollywood cinema queen Katharine Hepburn in *The Aviator*.

Cate Blanchett's performance in **Elizabeth** *made the Australian actress into a celebrity.*

John Lahr
Drama Critic/Interviewer

John Lahr, who interviewed Cate Blanchett for *The New Yorker* magazine, has show business blood in his veins. His father, Bert Lahr, played *The Wizard of Oz*'s Cowardly Lion.

As a senior drama critic for *The New Yorker*, Lahr is interested in how actors create their public images as well as how they perform on stage and screen. "When you become a public personality and have a public persona, you have created 'you,'" he once said. "The public 'you' is your greatest invention."

In interviewing Blanchett, however, Lahr encountered an actress who seemed to disappear into the characters she portrayed.

Enrichment: Analyzing Film

Two Elizabeths

Cate Blanchett has acted the role of Elizabeth I twice. She was nominated for an Academy Award in 1999 for *Elizabeth* and in 2008 for *Elizabeth: The Golden Age.* Both films had the same director, Shekhar Kapur. Blanchett was also nominated for a Golden Globe Award for Best Actress for both films. Only for the 1998 film, *Elizabeth,* did she win this award.

Activity: Connecting Genres Have students watch *Elizabeth* and *Elizabeth: The Golden Age.* Suggest that students record information in the **Enrichment: Analyzing Film** worksheet, *Professional Development Guidebook,* page 226. Be sure to give them two copies of the worksheet, one for each movie. Have them use the results of their research to write an essay explaining why they think Blanchett won the Golden Globe for *Elizabeth* but not for *Elizabeth: The Golden Age.*

from
DISAPPEARING ACT

Interview with Cate Blanchett
conducted *by John Lahr*

Blanchett grew up in Ivanhoe, a leafy suburb of Melbourne, beside the Yarra River. She was the middle child, between an older brother, Bob, who had a mild case of cerebral palsy, and Genevieve. (Bob works as a computer programmer; Genevieve is studying architecture, after a successful career as a stage designer.)

Of the siblings, Blanchett was, by her own admission, the most adventurous. "I felt very free as a child," she said. Together, she and Genevieve invented characters, which Blanchett would play, for days at a time, around the house. "My sister and I would dress me up in something," she said "I'd pull a face or a stance; she'd give them names and an identity."

When Blanchett was around nine, her enthusiasm for performance took the form of knocking on strangers' doors to see if she could talk her way inside their homes with a tall tale about a lost dog. "It was the adrenaline rush, really," she said. "My friends hid in the bushes. I remember the woman at the door saying, 'I haven't seen a dog. Come in. I'll ask my husband.' I looked at the bushes thinking, Oh, my God, what am I doing? I remember the look in this woman's

from Disappearing Act **293**

1. Direct students' attention to Lahr's comment, that "when you become a public personality and have a public persona, you have created 'you.' The public 'you' is your greatest invention." **Ask** students to give an example from Blanchett's life of a time when her public persona differed from her private persona.
   Answer: When Blanchett knocked on doors and pretended to have lost a dog, she was creating a public persona for herself that differed from her true, private persona.

2. **Ask** students how, in ordinary life, an actor's public and private persona might differ.
   Possible response: An actor's public persona might be connected to the characters he or she has portrayed. Cate Blanchett might be queenly in public, for example. But few people are dignified all the time in private. Some actors work to separate themselves from the public persona they have created.

3. **Ask:** Does everyone have a public persona, or only celebrities?
   Possible response: Everyone has a public persona. There are many things we do in private that we would never do in public. But some people consider their public persona to be who they really are, while others consider their private persona to be far more important. Some are extremely introverted and consider most of the things they enjoy doing to be very private. Other people are extroverted and enjoy being in the public eye.

from "Disappearing Act"

1. As students read, have them note the way that Lahr presents information to his readers. Tell students that Lahr interviewed Blanchett for *The New Yorker,* but he does not present the interview in question-and-answer format. **Ask** students why Lahr might have chosen to write about Blanchett in narrative form.
Possible response: Lahr probably had limited space, and he chose to focus on certain aspects of Blanchett's life. He may have condensed what she said, summarizing some things and including interesting quotations from Blanchett in other places.

2. Review the paragraphs that describe Blanchett's relationship with her father, and her reaction to his death. Then **ask:** Why do you think that Blanchett became so interested in horror movies after her father died?
Possible response: She was very upset, and she needed something that would engage her emotionally, pulling her out of her grief to be, instead, afraid.

3. **Ask** students whether they agree with Blanchett's husband's remark that acting, like watching horror movies, is cheating death.
Possible response: Acting is like cheating death because the character ceases to exist when the actor stops acting. But acting is *unlike* cheating death, because actors do not actually die when they walk offstage. They can bring their characters back to life at any time they choose.

eyes when she started to think, You haven't lost a dog, have you? It suddenly had become a real thing."

Blanchett continued, "My whole childhood was like that. If someone dared me, I'd do it."

"Cate is willing to throw herself into a chaotic state out of which something will arise," the director Shekhar Kapur told me. "The fluidity you get in Cate is also because of the contradictions inside her." Blanchett is both candid and private, gregarious and solitary, self-doubting and daring, witty and melancholy. It was these contradictions that prompted Kapur to cast her as Elizabeth I in *Elizabeth,* one of the films that made Blanchett an international star.

Blanchett's mother, June, was a jazz-loving schoolteacher. Her Texas-born father, Robert, who met June when his Navy ship broke down in Melbourne, had, according to Blanchett, "a very dry sense of humor." He had quit school at fourteen—"I went to the school for bums," he told his daughter. Robert put himself through night school, worked at a television station, returned to Australia to marry June, and got into advertising. Then, when Blanchett was ten, he died. "I was playing the piano," she has recalled. "He walked past the window. I waved goodbye. He was going off to work. He had a heart attack that day. He was only forty."

The fact that she hadn't embraced him before he left haunted Blanchett. "I developed this ritual where I couldn't leave the house until I could actually physically say goodbye to everyone," she said. . . .

After Robert died, Blanchett developed a passion for horror movies. "I loved being terrified," she said. "It used to be a badge of honor if you could sit through *Halloween II.*" Some of the thrill of horror movies lies in the thrill of surviving them, of, in a sense, cheating death. It's a thrill that carries over, as Upton [her husband] pointed out, to acting. "You go onstage and you're alive," he said. "You walk offstage, then the character's gone. You survive the experience. . . ."

294 Celebrating Humanity (1485–1625)

"The fluidity you get in Cate is also because of the contradictions inside her."

Critical Reading

1. **(a)** How would Blanchett perform as a child? **(b) Infer:** Why did Blanchett enjoy this kind of performance?

2. **(a)** According to the interviewer, what is part of the thrill of horror movies? **(b) Interpret:** What connection does Blanchett's husband see between this thrill and the experience of acting? Explain.

3. **(a) Summarize:** Briefly summarize the childhood experiences Blanchett discusses in this interview. **(b) Draw Conclusions:** How might her childhood experiences, actions, and interests have helped her develop skills she needs to act?

Use these questions to focus a class discussion of "Disappearing Act":

4. In what ways are actresses and monarchs—like Cate Blanchett and Elizabeth I—both performers? Explain the reasons for your answer.

5. **(a)** How might creating a public image, as actresses and monarchs do, be a kind of deception? **(b)** How might it be a true expression of an individual's personality?

from Disappearing Act **295**

Answers

Remind students to support their answers with evidence from the tex

1. (a) She would knock on the doors of strangers' homes and try to talk her way inside the home. (b) **Possible response:** She probably found it humorous to trick a stranger.

2. (a) According to the interviewer, part of the thrill of horror movies is surviving them and feeling as though you have cheated death. (b) Blanchett's husband says that acting is like cheating death, because the character "dies" when the actor walks offstage.

3. (a) Blanchett was an adventurous child who enjoyed dressing up and acting. Her father died suddenly of a heart attack and she was deeply affected by the loss. After his death, she became fascinated with horror movies. (b) **Possible response:** Blanchett's experience of trying to trick strangers probably helped her to be more realistic in her acting later in life. Her interest in movies may also have inspired her to consider acting as a career.

4. **Possible response:** Actresses and monarchs both must create a public persona. Monarchs must act as the representatives of their countries, not as private individuals. Actresses are always on display, because reporters and photographers follow them around.

5. (a) **Possible response:** A public image suggests to the public that the image is who one really is. But an actress, or a monarch, may have many interests that she chooses not to share with the public (b) **Possible response:** A public image may be partially true, because it shows interests that the actress really has and actions that she really has taken.

Differentiated Instruction for Universal Access

Support for Less Proficient Readers
Students may need help understanding Shekhar Kapur's comment that Blanchett is fluid "because of the contradictions inside her." Read the following lines from Walt Whitman's *Song of Myself* to students: "Do I contradict myself? / Very well then, I contradict myself./ (I am large, I contain multitudes.)" Ask students if they have ever felt two contradicting opinions at once. Explain that an actor can call upon those kinds of feelings while acting.

Enrichment for Gifted/Talented Students
Challenge students to consider their own private and public personas. Encourage students to write a poem about the differences between their public and private personas. If students would like an extra challenge, have them write a sonnet or write in blank verse. Alternatively, if you have students who are very visual, have them paint a self-portrait that shows the differences between their public and private personas.

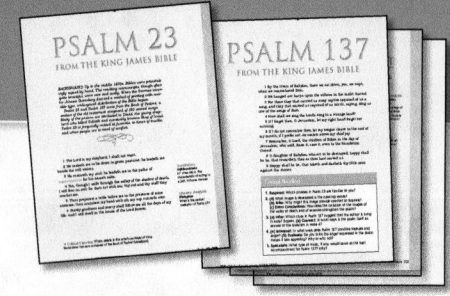

• *from* The King James Bible

Lesson Pacing Guide

DAY 1 Preteach

- Administer the Reading and Vocabulary Warm-ups (*Unit 2 Resources,* pp. 66–69) as necessary.
- Introduce the Literary Analysis concept: Psalm, Sermon, Parable, and Metaphor.
- Introduce the Reading Strategy: Determine the Main Idea.
- Build background with the author and Background features.
- Develop thematic thinking with Connecting to the Essential Question.
- Teach the selection vocabulary.

DAYS 2–3 Preteach/Teach/Assess

- Distribute copies of the appropriate graphic organizer for the Reading Strategy (*Graphic Organizer Transparencies,* pp. 48–49).
- Distribute copies of the appropriate graphic organizer for Literary Analysis (*Graphic Organizer Transparencies,* pp. 50–51).
- Prepare students to read with the Activating Prior Knowledge activities (TE).
- Informally monitor comprehension while students read.
- Use the Reading Check questions to confirm comprehension.
- Develop students' understanding of psalms, sermons, parables, and metaphors using the Literary Analysis prompts.
- Develop students' ability to determine the main idea using the Reading Strategy prompts.
- Reinforce vocabulary with the Vocabulary notes.
- Assess students' comprehension and mastery of the skills by having them answer the Critical Reading, Literary Analysis, and Reading Strategy questions.
- Have students complete the Vocabulary Lesson.

DAY 4 Extend/Assess

- Have students complete the Writing Lesson and write a parable. (You may assign as homework.)
- Administer Selection Test A or B (*Unit 2 Resources,* pp. 78–80 or 81–83).

Common Core State Standards

Reading Literature 1. Cite strong and thorough textual evidence to support analysis of what the text says explicitly as well as inferences drawn from the text, including determining where the text leaves matters uncertain.

4. Determine the meaning of words and phrases as they are used in the text, including figurative meanings.

Writing 3. Write narratives to develop real or imagined experiences or events using effective technique, well-chosen details, and well-structured event sequences.

3.d. Use precise words and phrases, telling details, and sensory language to convey a vivid picture of the experiences, events, setting, and/or characters.

Language 1.a. Apply the understanding that usage is a matter of convention, can change over time, and is sometimes contested.

Additional Standards Practice
Common Core Companion, pp. 2–9; 41–48; 208–218; 314–317

Daily Block Scheduling
Each day in this Lesson Pacing Guide represents a 40–50 minute period. Teachers using block scheduling may combine days to revise pacing. In addition, teachers may differentiate and support core instruction by integrating components for extended and intensive support as students require. See the Guide to Selected Leveled Resources (facing page).

Guide to Selected Leveled Resources

R T I Tier 1 (students performing on level)

from The King James Bible

Warm Up	Practice, model, and monitor fluency, working with the whole class or in groups.	Vocabulary and Reading Warm-ups B, *Unit 2 Resources*, pp. 66–67, 69
Comprehension/Skills	Support and monitor comprehension and skills development, having students complete the activities, graphic organizers, and interactive prompts independently or as a class.	• *Reader's Notebook*, adapted instruction and summary **EL** *Reader's Notebook: English Learner's Version*, adapted instruction and summary • **Reading Skill Graphic Organizer B**, *Graphic Organizer Transparencies*, p. 49 • **Literary Analysis Graphic Organizer B**, *Graphic Organizer Transparencies*, p. 51
Monitor Progress **A**	Monitor student progress with the differentiated curriculum-based assessment in the *Unit Resources*.	• **Selection Test B**, *Unit 2 Resources*, pp. 81–83 • **Open-Book Test**, *Unit 2 Resources*, pp. 75–77

R T I Tier 2 (students requiring intervention)

from The King James Bible

Warm Up	Practice, model, and monitor fluency in groups or with individuals.	• **Vocabulary and Reading Warm-ups A**, *Unit 2 Resources*, pp. 66–68 • *Hear It!* Audio CD
Comprehension/Skills	• **Support** and **monitor** comprehension and skills development, working in small groups or with individuals. • As students complete the selection in the appropriate version of the *Reader's Notebook*, monitor comprehension frequently with group questions and individual instruction. • **Model** strategies while guiding students in completing the activities and prompts in the *Reader's Notebook*, as well as the graphic organizers. • **Practice** skills and **monitor** mastery with the *Reading Kit* worksheets.	• *Reader's Notebook: Adapted Version*, adapted instruction and summary **EL** *Reader's Notebook: English Learner's Version*, adapted instruction and summary • **Reading Skill Graphic Organizer A**, *Graphic Organizer Transparencies*, p. 48 • **Literary Analysis Graphic Organizer A**, *Graphic Organizer Transparencies*, p. 50 • *Reading Kit*, Practice worksheets
Monitor Progress **A**	Monitor student progress with the differentiated curriculum-based assessment in the *Unit Resources* and in the *Reading Kit*.	• **Selection Test A**, *Unit 2 Resources*, pp. 78–80 • *Reading Kit*, Assess worksheets

TIER 3 Tier 3 intervention may require consultation with the student's special-education or dyslexia specialist. For additional support, see the Tier 2 activities and resources listed above.

One-on-one teaching   Group work   Whole class instruction   Independent work   **A** Assessment

For a complete guide to selection support, including support for Advanced students, see the Overview of Resources in the frontmatter.

• *from* The King James Bible

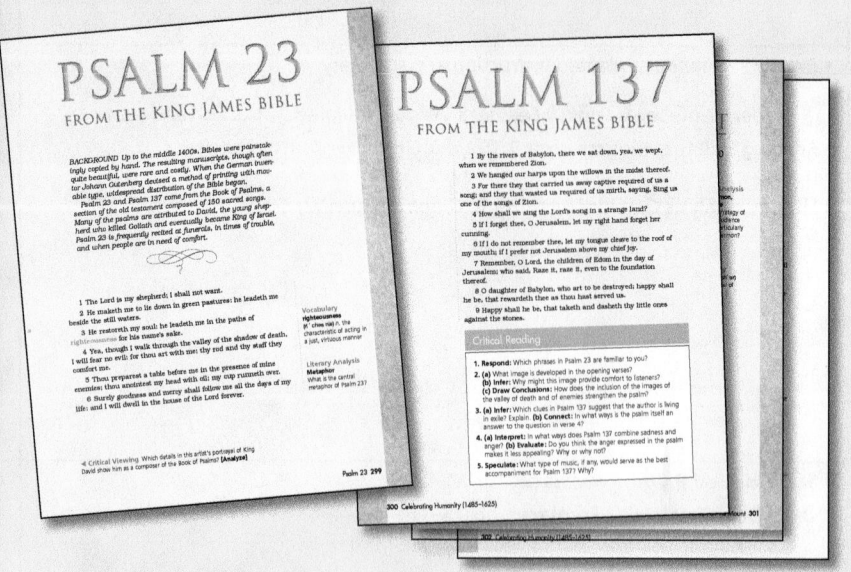

RESOURCES FOR:

L1 Special-Needs Students

L2 Below-Level Students (Tier 2)

L3 On-Level Students (Tier 1)

L4 Advanced Students (Tier 1)

EL English Learners

All All Students

Vocabulary/Fluency/Prior Knowledge

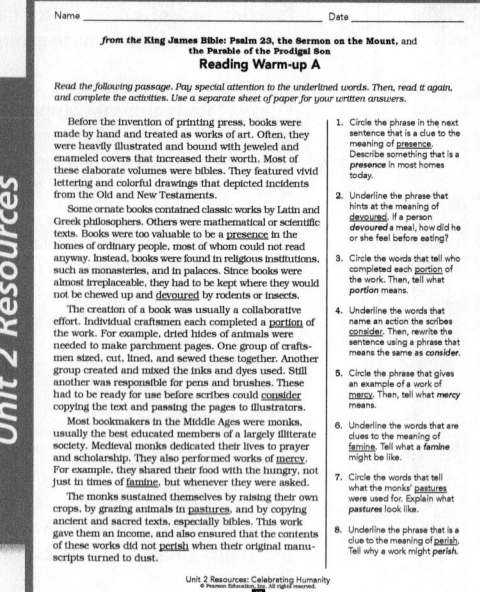

EL L1 L2 **Reading Warm-ups A and B,** pp. 68–69

Also available for these selections:

EL L1 L2 **Vocabulary Warm-ups A and B,** pp. 66–67

All **Vocabulary Builder,** p. 72

Reader's Notebooks

Pre- and postreading pages for this selection appear in an interactive format in the *Reader's Notebooks*. Each *Notebook* is differentiated for a different group of learners.

The selections in the Adapted and English Learner's versions are abridged.

L2 L3 *Reader's Notebook*

L1 *Reader's Notebook: Adapted Version*

EL *Reader's Notebook: English Learner's Version*

EL *Reader's Notebook: Spanish Version*

© *Common Core Companion*

Additional instruction and practice for each Common Core State Standard

Selection Support

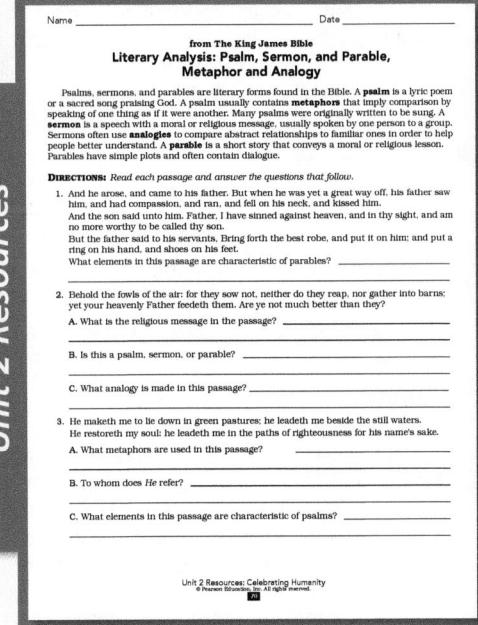

from *The King James Bible*
After You Read A: Psalm, Sermon, and Parable

Images: Familiar / Unfamiliar	Simple / Difficult?	Memorable? Why?
Psalm 23 Familiar: sheep, pastures, "still waters," leading someone on a path, a valley full of shadows, a table set for a meal, living in a house	Simple: comfort, rest, and security; no fear in the shadow of death; eating and drinking	Memorable: easily understood and based on ordinary aspects of rural life
Sermon on the Mount		
Parable of the Prodigal Son		

Graphic Organizer Transparencies

EL L1 L2 **Literary Analysis: Graphic Organizer A,** p. 50

Also available for these selections:

EL L1 L2 **Reading: Graphic Organizer A,** (partially filled in), p. 48

EL L3 **Reading: Graphic Organizer B,** p. 49

EL L3 **Literary Analysis: Graphic Organizer B,** p. 51

Skills Development/Extension

Unit 2 Resources

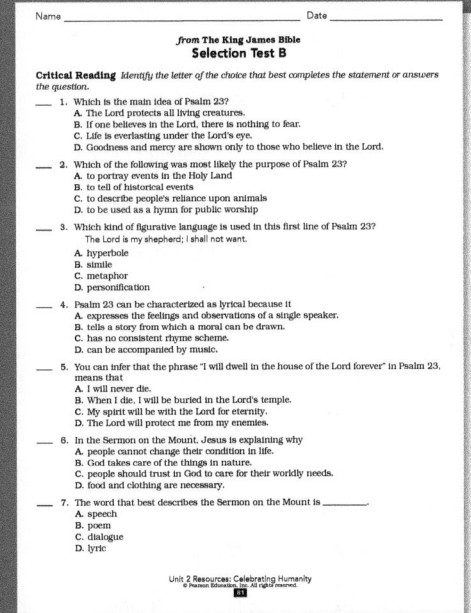

Name _____ Date _____

from The King James Bible
Literary Analysis: Psalm, Sermon, and Parable, Metaphor and Analogy

Psalms, sermons, and parables are literary forms found in the Bible. A **psalm** is a lyric poem or a sacred song praising God. A psalm usually contains **metaphors** that imply comparison by speaking of one thing as if it were another. Many psalms were originally written to be sung. A **sermon** is a speech with a moral or religious message, usually spoken by one person to a group. Sermons often use **analogies** to compare abstract relationships to familiar ones in order to help people better understand. A **parable** is a short story that conveys a moral or religious lesson. Parables have simple plots and often contain dialogue.

DIRECTIONS: *Read each passage and answer the questions that follow.*

1. And he arose, and came to his father. But when he was yet a great way off, his father saw him, and had compassion, and ran, and fell on his neck, and kissed him.
   And the son said unto him, Father, I have sinned against heaven, and in thy sight, and am no more worthy to be called thy son.
   But the father said to his servants, Bring forth the best robe, and put it on him; and put a ring on his hand, and shoes on his feet.
   What elements in this passage are characteristic of parables? _____

2. Behold the fowls of the air: for they sow not, neither do they reap, nor gather into barns; yet your heavenly Father feedeth them. Are ye not much better than they?
   A. What is the religious message in the passage? _____
   B. Is this a psalm, sermon, or parable? _____
   C. What analogy is made in this passage? _____

3. He maketh me to lie down in green pastures: he leadeth me beside the still waters. He restoreth my soul: he leadeth me in the paths of righteousness for his name's sake.
   A. What metaphors are used in this passage? _____
   B. To whom does *He* refer? _____
   C. What elements in this passage are characteristic of psalms? _____

All **Literary Analysis,** p. 70

Also available for these selections:

All **Reading,** p. 71

EL L3 L4 **Support for Writing,** p. 73

L4 **Enrichment,** p. 74

Assessment

Name _____ Date _____

from The King James Bible
Selection Test B

Critical Reading *Identify the letter of the choice that best completes the statement or answers the question.*

___ 1. Which is the main idea of Psalm 23?
   A. The Lord protects all living creatures.
   B. If one believes in the Lord, there is nothing to fear.
   C. Life is everlasting under the Lord's eye.
   D. Goodness and mercy are shown only to those who believe in the Lord.

___ 2. Which of the following was most likely the purpose of Psalm 23?
   A. to portray events in the Holy Land
   B. to tell of historical events
   C. to describe people's reliance upon animals
   D. to be used as a hymn for public worship

___ 3. Which kind of figurative language is used in this first line of Psalm 23?
   The Lord is my shepherd; I shall not want.
   A. hyperbole
   B. simile
   C. metaphor
   D. personification

___ 4. Psalm 23 can be characterized as lyrical because it
   A. expresses the feelings and observations of a single speaker.
   B. tells a story from which a moral can be drawn.
   C. has no consistent rhyme scheme.
   D. can be accompanied by music.

___ 5. You can infer that the phrase "I will dwell in the house of the Lord forever" in Psalm 23, means that
   A. I will never die.
   B. When I die, I will be buried in the Lord's temple.
   C. My spirit will be with the Lord for eternity.
   D. The Lord will protect me from my enemies.

___ 6. In the Sermon on the Mount, Jesus is explaining why
   A. people cannot change their condition in life.
   B. God takes care of the things in nature.
   C. people should trust in God to care for their worldly needs.
   D. food and clothing are necessary.

___ 7. The word that best describes the Sermon on the Mount is _____.
   A. speech
   B. poem
   C. dialogue
   D. lyric

EL L1 L2 **Selection Test B,** pp. 81–83

Also available for these selections:

L3 L4 **Open-Book Test,** pp. 75–77

EL L3 L4 **Selection Test A,** pp. 78–80

PHLit Online!
www.PHLitOnline.com

Online Resources: All print materials are also available online.

- complete narrated selection text
- a thematically related video with writing prompt
- an interactive graphic organizer
- highlighting feature
- access to all student print resources, adapted to individual student needs
- Spanish and English summaries
- adapted selection translations in Spanish

Background Video

Also available:

Get Connected! (thematic video with writing prompt)
All videos are available in Spanish.

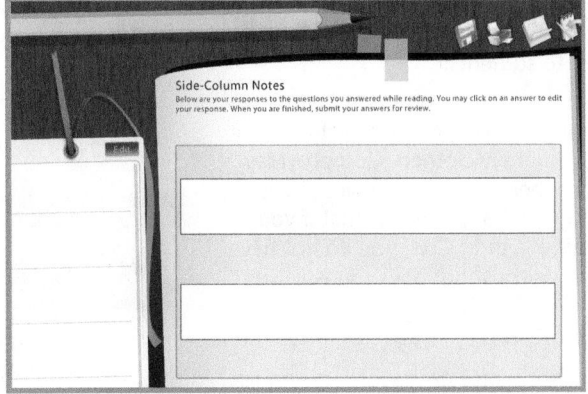

Writer's Journal (with graphics feature)

Also available:

Vocabulary Central (tools and activities for studying vocabulary)

❶ **Connecting to the Essential Question**

1. Review the assignment with the class.

2. Prepare students for the assignment by telling them that many common expressions, such as *the blind leading the blind*, come from the King James Bible. Then have them complete the assignment.

3. As students read, have them listen to the language.

❷ Literary Analysis

Introduce the skill using the instruction on the student page.

Think Aloud: Model the Skill

Say to students:

Some of my favorite songs use metaphors to compare something to something else. This is what psalms do. Sermons are similar to some classes in which the teacher uses analogies, such as comparing the human heart to a pump, to help get a point across. Parables teach a moral lesson, as a fable such as "The Boy Who Cried Wolf" does.

❸ Reading Strategy

1. Introduce the strategy.

2. Give students a copy of **Reading Strategy Graphic Organizer B**, page 49 and 51 in *Graphic Organizer Transparencies*, to fill out as they read.

Think Aloud: Model the Skill

Say to students:

In the Sermon on the Mount, Jesus says lilies do not work, yet they are beautifully clothed. God provides for them. I infer from what he is saying that he means that if you have faith in God, you do not have to worry about how you will live.

❹ Vocabulary

1. Pronounce each word, giving its definition, and have students say it aloud.

2. For more guidance, see the *Classroom Strategies and Teaching Routines* card for introducing vocabulary.

Before You Read | from *The King James Bible*

❶ Connecting to the Essential Question The King James Bible has been for centuries an important book for many Protestants. As you read, identify qualities of language and rhythm that contribute to the appeal and influence of this great prose work. This will help you answer the Essential Question: **How does literature shape or reflect society?**

❷ Literary Analysis

The Bible conveys themes of faith in a few genres, including these:

• **Psalms**—sacred songs or lyric poems in praise of God.

• **Sermons**—speeches offering religious or moral instruction. The Sermon on the Mount contains the basic teachings of Christianity.

• **Parables**—simple stories from which a moral or religious lesson can be drawn. The most famous are in the New Testament.

Comparing Literary Works Psalms, sermons, and parables all convey deep messages about life. Each communicates a message in a manner suited to its form. Psalms are songs. To engage an audience, psalms may feature vivid figurative language including **metaphors**—comparisons of unlike things. To help listeners understand, sermons may feature **analogies**—explanations comparing abstract relationships to familiar ones. Parables are **narratives**—stories illustrating a message.

As you read, compare the methods by which each selection conveys its message and the appeal and effectiveness of each.

❸ Reading Strategy

 Preparing to Read Complex Texts In some portions of the Bible, the *main idea* is implied rather than directly stated. You can **determine the main idea** by *making inferences*—identifying key details in the text and then relating them to other details and to your own experience. When making inferences, consider what the text suggests as well as what it leaves uncertain. Use a chart like the one shown.

❹ Vocabulary

righteousness (rī′ chəs nis) *n.* the characteristic of acting in a just, virtuous manner (p. 299)

stature (stach′ ər) *n.* height; level of achievement (p. 301)

prodigal (präd′ i gəl) *adj.* recklessly wasteful (p. 302)

entreated (en trēt′ id) *v.* begged; pleaded with (p. 304)

transgressed (trans grest′) *v.* overstepped or broke (a law or commandment) (p. 304)

© **Common Core State Standards**

Reading Literature
1. Cite strong and thorough textual evidence to support analysis of what the text says explicitly as well as inferences drawn from the text, including determining where the text leaves matters uncertain.
4. Determine the meaning of words and phrases as they are used in the text, including figurative and connotative meanings.

Text
The Lord is my shepherd.

↓

Textual Evidence	Associations
Verses 1–4: Lord acts as a shepherd.	A shepherd protects and leads.

Inference ↓

Main Idea
The Lord watches over faithful people, protecting them from danger.

Vocabulary Development

Vocabulary Knowledge Rating

Create a **Vocabulary Knowledge Rating Chart** (*Professional Development Guidebook,* p. 33) for the vocabulary words on the student page. Give each student a copy of the chart with the words on it. Read the words aloud, and have students mark their ratings in the Before Reading column. Urge students to attend to these words as they read and discuss the selections.

In order to gauge how much instruction you need to provide, tally how many students are confident in their knowledge of each word. As students read, point out the words and their context.

 **Vocabulary Central,** featuring tools and activities for studying vocabulary, is available online at **www.PHLitOnline.com.**

5 FROM THE KING JAMES BIBLE

The King James Bible (completed 1611)

For centuries, the Bible was the cornerstone of European culture—the ultimate reference for rulers and priests, the ultimate authorization for laws and religious practices, a treasury of images and subjects for art. Yet, the book was inaccessible to the majority of Europeans. During the Reformation, in the 1500s, the need for a closer study of the Bible was widely acknowledged, which led to translations of the work into the vernacular, or common languages. For the first time, this grounding work became widely accessible.

The King James Bible, the authoritative English translation, was created at the command of King James I. In 1604, James commissioned fifty-four scholars and clergymen to compare all known texts of the Bible and prepare the definitive English edition.

Early Bibles The Bible, a collection of books developed over more than 1,200 years, consists of two main parts—the Old Testament, written in Hebrew, and the New Testament, written in Greek. In about A.D. 405, St. Jerome finished translating the Bible into Latin. This translation, the Vulgate, remained the standard Bible of the West for centuries. King James's translators, though, were to review the original sources, as well as translations of the work.

A Systematic Plan The project was carefully organized from the start. The books of the Bible were divided among six groups of scholars in Westminster, Oxford, and Cambridge.

The groups took four years to produce their initial drafts. Then, two scholars from each region spent nine months in London reviewing and revising the draft. After laboring for seven years, the group produced one of the great works of English literature. The King James Bible has been called "the only classic ever created by a committee."

Tyndale's Legacy The King James Bible was not the first English translation of the book. James's translators were greatly influenced by William Tyndale's translation. Tyndale, a Protestant chaplain and tutor in England, fled clerical oppression at home and published his translation of the New Testament in Germany. Before he had completed work on the Old Testament, however, he was arrested for heresy and executed near Brussels, Belgium, in 1536.

As England became more Protestant, Tyndale came to be viewed, not as a heretic, but as a hero. King James's committee closely followed the magnificent diction and rhythms of Tyndale's groundbreaking translation.

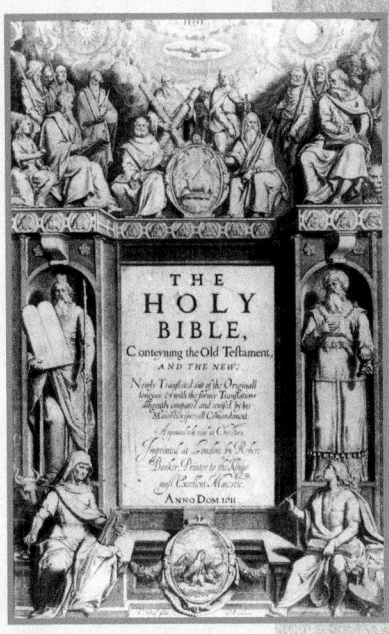

▲ Title page of the 1611 edition of the King James Bible

from The King James Bible **297**

PHLit Online!
www.PHLitOnline.com

Teaching From Technology

Preparing to Read
Go to **www.PHLitOnline.com** in class or in a lab and display the **Get Connected!** slide show for this grouping. Have the class brainstorm responses to the slide show writing prompt, entering ideas in the interactive journal. Then have students complete their written responses individually, in a lab or as homework.

To build background, display the More About the Authors feature.

Using the Interactive Text
Go to **www.PHLitOnline.com** and display the Enriched Online Student Edition. As the class reads the selection or listens to the narration, record answers to side-column prompts using the graphic organizers accessible on the interactive page. Alternatively, have students use the online edition individually, answering the prompts as they read.

PRETEACH

🐦 Daily Bellringer
For each class during which you will teach these selections, have students complete one of the five activities for the appropriate week in the *Daily Bellringer Activities* booklet.

Multidraft Reading
To assist struggling readers and to enhance reading for all, assign the text in chunks, as warranted by length, and apply multidraft reading protocols. For each reading, have students set the purpose indicated:

- **First reading**—identifying key ideas and details and answering any Reading Checks.
- **Second reading**—analyzing craft and structure and responding to the side-column prompts.
- **Third reading**—integrating knowledge and ideas, connecting to other texts and the world, and answering the end-of-selection questions.

For more guidance, refer to the *Classroom Strategies and Teaching Routines* card on multidraft reading.

5 Background
More About the Authors
When translating the Bible, scholars have a greater number of ancient documents from which to work than for any other literature of such age. Its historical record is so accurate that archaeologists in the Middle East have used it to locate lost cities. But more significant is its impact on Western culture. From the Bible we get ideas as diverse as trial by jury, the right of women to inherit property, and fair wages. Much writing in English contains at least some biblical allusion, from Edgar Allan Poe's "The Masque of the Red Death" to Shakespeare's *Measure for Measure*.

❶ About the Selection

Although the Book of Psalms contains 150 sacred poems, Psalm 23 and Psalm 137 are among the best known. Psalm 23 portrays God as a shepherd who cares for his sheep Psalm 137 refers to the period of Jewish history known as the Babylonian Captivity. In 586 B.C. the Babylonian King Nebuchadnezzar invaded Jerusalem and took many Jews captive, deporting them to Mesopotamia (modern-day Iraq). The psalm is a lament for the Jews' lost homeland.

❷ Activating Prior Knowledge

As students read the following psalms, sermon, and parable, encourage students to put themselves in the role of each speaker. Under what circumstances would they say the psalm, give the sermon, or tell the parable? Who would be the audience in each case?

Concept Connector ➞

Tell students they will return to their responses after reading the selection.

❸ Humanities

King David Playing the Harp, by Domenico Zampieri (1581–1641) Zampieri paid particular attention to the expressions of the human face. Art critics have praised his warm and harmonious use of color, his simple style, his superb use of light and shade, and his interesting groups of accessories.

298 Celebrating Humanity (1485–1625)

Text Complexity Rubric

	Psalms 23 and 137	*from the* **Sermon on the Mount**	*from the* **Parable of the Prodigal Son**
Qualitative Measures			
Context/ Knowledge Demands	Sacred songs; historical context 1 2 ③ 4 5	Biblical sermon 1 2 ③ 4 5	Biblical parable 1 ② 3 4 5
Structure/Language Conventionality and Clarity	Archaic diction 1 2 ③ 4 5	Archaic diction; rhetorical questions 1 ② 3 4 5	Archaic diction; oral storytelling 1 ② 3 4 5
Levels of Meaning/ Purpose/Concepts	Accessible (faith, comfort, and sorrow) 1 2 ③ 4 5	Moderate (faith and God's care) 1 2 ③ 4 5	Moderate (redemption) 1 2 ③ 4 5
Quantitative Measures			
Lexile/Text Length	870L / 123, 174 words	890L / 206 words	1350L / 529 words
Overall Complexity	**More complex**	**More accessible**	**More accessible**

❶❷ PSALM 23
FROM THE KING JAMES BIBLE

BACKGROUND Up to the middle 1400s, Bibles were painstakingly copied by hand. The resulting manuscripts, though often quite beautiful, were rare and costly. When the German inventor Johann Gutenberg devised a method of printing with movable type, widespread distribution of the Bible began.

Psalm 23 and Psalm 137 come from the Book of Psalms, a section of the old testament composed of 150 sacred songs. Many of the psalms are attributed to David, the young shepherd who killed Goliath and eventually became King of Israel. Psalm 23 is frequently recited at funerals, in times of trouble, and when people are in need of comfort.

1 The Lord is my shepherd; I shall not want.

2 He maketh me to lie down in green pastures: he leadeth me beside the still waters.

❺ 3 He restoreth my soul: he leadeth me in the paths of righteousness for his name's sake.

❻ 4 Yea, though I walk through the valley of the shadow of death, I will fear no evil: for thou art with me; thy rod and thy staff they comfort me.

5 Thou preparest a table before me in the presence of mine enemies; thou anointest my head with oil; my cup runneth over.

6 Surely goodness and mercy shall follow me all the days of my life: and I will dwell in the house of the Lord forever.

Vocabulary
righteousness
(rī´ chəs nis) *n.* the characteristic of acting in a just, virtuous manner

Literary Analysis
Metaphor
What is the central metaphor of Psalm 23?

❹
◀ **Critical Viewing** Which details in this artist's portrayal of King David show him as a composer of the Book of Psalms? **[Analyze]**

Psalm 23 **299**

❺ Literary Analysis
Metaphor

1. Have a volunteer read the psalm.

2. Then, **ask** students the Literary Analysis question: What is the central metaphor of Psalm 23? **Answer:** It is that of God as a shepherd of sheep.

3. **Ask:** What details support the metaphor of God as shepherd? **Answer:** Students should mention the "green pastures" and "still waters" where sheep graze and get water in verse 2, and the "rod and staff" that are used by shepherds in verse 4.

❻ ⁇ Engaging the Essential Question

1. Point out to students that the King James Bible has endured for four hundred years and is still widely read today.

2. **Ask** students: What qualities of the language and rhythm in this psalm might contribute to the appeal of the King James Bible? **Possible response:** Students may suggest that the metaphor in verse 1 and the beauty of the imagery in verses 2–5 all contribute to the appeal.

3. **Ask:** How has the King James Bible shaped or reflected society? **Possible response:** The King James Bible has contributed phrases that are used by speakers of English around the world. For centuries it has been a central reference point for many English-speaking Christians.

ⓒ Text Complexity: Reader and Task Suggestions

	Psalms 23 and 137	*from the* Sermon on the Mount	*from the* Parable of the Prodigal Son
Preparing to Read the Texts • Using the Background on TE p. 297, discuss why biblical allusions are so common in literature. • Ask students to consider what faith generally brings to the faithful and what it generally requires. • Guide students to use Multidraft Reading strategies (TE p. 297).	**Leveled Tasks** *Structure/Language* If students will have difficulty with the archaic diction, have them rewrite the psalms with modern English verbs and pronouns. Then, have them reread the psalms, focusing on the ideas expressed. *Evaluating* If students will not have difficulty with the archaic diction, have them focus on the emotional content.	**Leveled Tasks** *Levels of Meaning* If students will have difficulty with abstract ideas, have them focus on God's care for fowls and lilies. As they reread, have them consider how that care applies to people. *Synthesizing* If students will not have difficulty with the abstract ideas, have them restate the sermon's view of God's relationship to living things.	**Leveled Tasks** *Levels of Meaning* If students will have difficulty with levels of meaning, have them focus on the parable's characters and events. Then, have students consider whom the father may symbolize and what types of people the sons represent. *Analyzing* If students will not have difficulty with the levels of meaning, have them explore the parable's theme of redemption.

Making Inferences

1. Ask a volunteer to read the brack-eted passage.

2. **Ask:** What does the speaker offer to sacrifice if he forgets his home-land?
Answer: He offers to sacrifice the use of his right hand and the power of speech.

3. Then **ask:** What can you infer about the speaker's attitude toward his homeland in verses 5 and 6?
Answer: You can infer that the speaker loves his homeland, he is homesick, and he is determined to remember his home.

ASSESS

Answers

Before students respond, you may wish to have them write a brief objective summary of the selection. As they answer the questions below, remind them to support their answers with evidence from the text.

1. (a) God cares for the speaker, as a shepherd cares for his sheep. (b) It shows God as provider and protector. (c) It shows that things can look bad, but God is still there.

2. (a) The speaker mentions that he "remembered Zion" and would not forget Jerusalem and that "they carried us away captive." (b) The psalm is the song, which speaks of longing for home and wanting revenge.

3. (a) The psalm speaks of weeping and remembering Zion in verses 1–6. Verses 7–9 express anger at the destruction of Jerusalem and the hope for revenge. (b) Some students may suggest that the anger makes the psalm less appealing since it calls for violent revenge; others may say that the anger is justified, and it does not make the psalm less appealing.

4. Students may suggest that a harp would be the best accompani-ment, since a harp is mentioned in verse 2.

PSALM 137

FROM THE KING JAMES BIBLE

1 By the rivers of Babylon, there we sat down, yea, we wept, when we remembered Zion.

2 We hanged our harps upon the willows in the midst thereof.

3 For there they that carried us away captive required of us a song; and they that wasted us required of us mirth, saying, Sing us one of the songs of Zion.

4 How shall we sing the Lord's song in a strange land?

5 If I forget thee, O Jerusalem, let my right hand forget her cunning.

❼ 6 If I do not remember thee, let my tongue cleave to the roof of my mouth; if I prefer not Jerusalem above my chief joy.

7 Remember, O Lord, the children of Edom in the day of Jerusalem; who said, Raze it, raze it, even to the foundation thereof.

8 O daughter of Babylon, who art to be destroyed; happy shall he be, that rewardeth thee as thou hast served us.

9 Happy shall he be, that taketh and dasheth thy little ones against the stones.

Critical Reading

Cite textual evidence to support your responses.

ⓒ **1. Craft and Structure (a)** What image is developed in the opening verses of Psalm 23? **(b) Infer:** Why might this image provide com-fort to listeners? **(c) Draw Conclusions:** How does the inclusion of the images of the valley of death and of enemies strengthen the psalm?

ⓒ **2. Key Ideas and Details (a) Infer:** Which clues in Psalm 137 sug-gest that the author is living in exile? Explain. **(b) Connect:** In what ways is the psalm itself an answer to the question in verse 4?

ⓒ **3. Key Ideas and Details (a) Interpret:** In what ways does Psalm 137 combine sadness and anger? **(b) Evaluate:** Do you think the anger expressed in the psalm makes it less appealing? Why or why not?

ⓒ **4. Integration of Knowledge and Ideas** What type of music, if any, would serve as the best accompaniment for Psalm 137? Why?

300 Celebrating Humanity (1485–1625)

Think Aloud

Vocabulary: Using Context
Direct students' attention to verse 7 of Psalm 137. Use the following "think aloud" to model the skill of using context to infer the meaning of the word. Say to students:

In verse 7 of Psalm 137, the speaker says, "Remember, O Lord, the children of Edom in the day of Jerusalem; who said, Raze it, raze it, even to the foundation thereof." I may not know the meaning of the word *raze*. When I read the verse, however,

I realize that the speaker is using the word to describe what happens to Jerusalem, "even to the foundation thereof." I know that the inhabitants of Jerusalem were taken captive and taken to Babylon, as described in verses 1–3. I further see in verse 8 that the speaker hopes Babylon will be destroyed "even as thou hast served us." I can infer, therefore, that *raze* must mean "destroy" or "knock down to the foundations."

From the SERMON ON THE MOUNT

FROM THE KING JAMES BIBLE MATTHEW 6: 24-30

24 No man can serve two masters: for either he will hate the one, and love the other; or else he will hold to the one, and despise the other. Ye cannot serve God and mammon.[1]

25 Therefore I say unto you, Take no thought for your life, what ye shall eat, or what ye shall drink; nor yet for your body, what ye shall put on. Is not the life more than meat, and the body than raiment?[2]

26 Behold the fowls of the air: for they sow not, neither do they reap, nor gather into barns; yet your heavenly Father feedeth them. Are ye not much better than they?

27 Which of you by taking thought can add one cubit unto his stature?

28 And why take ye thought for raiment? Consider the lilies of the field, how they grow; they toil not, neither do they spin:

29 And yet I say unto you, That even Solomon[3] in all his glory was not arrayed like one of these.

30 Wherefore, if God so clothe the grass of the field, which to day is, and to morrow is cast into the oven, *shall he* not much more *clothe* you, O ye of little faith?

---

1. **mammon** (mam´ ən) *n.* money, personified as a false god.
2. **raiment** (rā´ mənt) *n.* clothing; wearing apparel.
3. **Solomon** (säl´ ə mən) *n.* tenth-century B.C. king of Israel.

Literary Analysis
Psalm, Sermon, and Parable
Why is the strategy of asking the audience questions particularly suited to a sermon?

10 Vocabulary
stature (stach´ ər) *n.* height; level of achievement

Critical Reading

1. **Key Ideas and Details (a)** What human activities do the fowls and lilies of the sermon avoid? **(b) Analyze:** How does this "omission" affect their lives? **(c) Interpret:** Describe the attitude towards life that Jesus advocates.

2. **Key Ideas and Details** Does Jesus, the speaker of this sermon, mean that his followers should literally "take no thought for life"? Explain.

3. **Integration of Knowledge and Ideas** Explain what a life lived like the lilies might be like.

Cite textual evidence to support your responses.

---

8 About the Selection
Many people consider the Sermon on the Mount to be the most important teaching in the Bible. Jesus spoke these words to the public and to his disciples. The sermon as a whole teaches the virtues and actions that are the essence of Christianity.

9 Literary Analysis
Psalm, Sermon, and Parable

1. Have a volunteer define *sermon*.

2. Read aloud the questions in the bracketed passage.

▶ **Monitor Progress: Ask** the Literary Analysis question: Why is the strategy of asking the audience questions particularly suited to a sermon?
Answer: Asking questions forces the audience to think about the ideas and issues in the sermon and can make the audience feel more involved.

▶ **Reteach:** If students have difficulty understanding the function of the sermon, have them reread the discussion of Literary Analysis on page 296. Point out that a sermon is similar to a class lesson, in which the speaker (or teacher) is trying to impart a lesson. Just as a teacher asks questions, so might someone giving a sermon.

10 Vocabulary Builder
Latin Word Root: -stat-

1. Point out the word *stature* and its definition. Tell students that the Latin root -stat- means "to stand."

2. Have students suggest words that contain this root, and list them on the chalkboard.
Possible responses: *statue; stationary; status*

3. Have students look up any unfamiliar words in the dictionary.

ASSESS
Answers

Before students respond, you may wish to have them write a brief objective summary of the selection. As they answer the questions below, remind them to support their answers with evidence from the text.

1. (a) The fowls "sow not" and the lilies "toil not." (b) This omission does not affect their lives; God

provides for them. (c) Jesus advocates a life in which one trusts God to provide rather than worrying over buying clothes and food.

2. Jesus means that his followers should not worry about their lives, because God will provide for them.

3. **Possible responses:** Some may say that such a life is impossible. Others may point to the lives of people of many faiths who live simple lives.

301

❶❶

❶ About the Selection

Many religions, including Judaism and Zen Buddhism, teach lessons by means of parables. In this parable, a young man demands his inheritance and leaves home. Later, he returns home in disgrace but is welcomed back by his father with open arms. This parable symbolizes God's readiness to forgive those who fall from grace.

❷ World Literature Connection

Parables Around the World

The parables of Jesus have been the model for preachers throughout the Western world for centuries. Christian preachers quickly recognized the parable as an effective teaching tool. From the early days of the church, preachers not only relied on New Testament parables, they began to invent their own to teach simple lessons about how a good Christian should behave. These Christian parables were collected in a variety of handbooks. The parables use a wide variety of subjects to make their point, from simple stories about magicians and prophets to knights, ladies, and emperors—subjects guaranteed to hold the interest of the preachers' congregations.

Connect to the Literature

Have students read the feature, and share the additional background above. Then, **ask** the Connect to the Literature question.

Possible response: This parable takes place in a society where a father was responsible for the honor of the family and protection of the family inheritance. When his son returns home, the father's love and forgiveness are at odds with the attitudes of the society.

❸ Critical Viewing

Possible response: Verses 21 and 22 are best illustrated. These verses describe the moment when the son, weary from his experiences, returns and is embraced by the father. In the image, the tattered clothes of the son and the father's embrace clearly illustrate these verses.

❶ from the Parable of the Prodigal Son

FROM THE KING JAMES BIBLE LUKE 15: 11-32

Vocabulary
prodigal (präd´ i gəl) *adj.*
recklessly wasteful

❷ World LITERATURE CONNECTION

Parables Around the World

The oral traditions of Zen Buddhists, Islamic Sufis and Jewish Hassidim all use parables to teach ideas about morality, philosophy and religion.

A Sufi story tells of a man who is chased by a hungry tiger. Finally the man turns around and cries to the tiger, "Why don't you leave me alone?" "Why don't you stop being so appetizing?" responds the tiger. This parable points out that there is always more than one way to see a situation.

Connect to the Literature

In what way does The Parable of the Prodigal Son challenge long-standing attitudes?

11 And he said, A certain man had two sons:

12 And the younger of them said to his father, Father, give me the portion of goods that falleth to me. And he divided unto them his living.

13 And not many days after the younger son gathered all together, and took his journey into a far country, and there wasted his substance with riotous living.

14 And when he had spent all, there arose a mighty famine in that land; and he began to be in want.

15 And he went and joined himself to a citizen of that country; and he sent him into his fields to feed swine.

16 And he would fain[1] have filled his belly with the husks that the swine did eat: and no man gave unto him.

17 And when he came to himself, he said, How many hired servants of my father's have bread enough and to spare, and I perish with hunger!

18 I will arise and go to my father, and will say unto him, Father, I have sinned against heaven, and before thee,

19 And am no more worthy to be called thy son: make me as one of thy hired servants.

20 And he arose, and came to his father. But when he was yet a great way off, his father saw him, and had compassion, and ran, and fell on his neck, and kissed him.

21 And the son said unto him, Father, I have sinned against heaven, and in thy sight, and am no more worthy to be called thy son.

---

1. fain *adv.* gladly.

❸ ▶ **Critical Viewing** Which verses from the selection are best illustrated by this painting? Explain. **[Interpret]**

Vocabulary Development

Vocabulary Knowledge Rating

When students have completed reading and discussing the selections, have them take out their **Vocabulary Knowledge Rating Charts** for the selections. Read the words aloud and have students rate their knowledge of words again in the After Reading column. Clarify any words that are still problematic. Have students write their own definitions and example or sentence in the appropriate column. Then have students complete the Vocabulary Lesson at the end of the selections. Encourage students to use the words in further discussion and written work about the selections. Remind them that they will be accountable for these words on the **Selection Test,** *Unit 2 Resources,* pages 78–80 or 81–83.

from The Parable of the Prodigal Son **303**

⑭ Humanities

The Return of the Prodigal Son, by Lionello Spada

Italian baroque painter Lionello Spada (1576–1622) studied art in his hometown of Bologna, Italy, at the workshop of the Carraci brothers. He later became a follower of Caravaggio, frequently creating dramatic oil renditions of biblical scenes and the lives of saints and martyrs. Spada's style reflects Caravaggio's paintings, which used dramatic effects of light and shadow and realistic portrayals of ordinary people in the roles of biblical figures. Caravaggio's focus on naturalistic portrayals of religious figures was a radical departure from the idealized beauty depicted in earlier Renaissance treatments of similar themes in religious art.

In Spada's interpretation of the parable, the believably tattered and grubby clothing of the son, the warm colors of the father's clothing, and the contrast between the father's lined visage and the youth's expressive face bring to life the characters of forgiving father and prodigal son.

Use these questions for discussion.

1. Which verse of the parable might have inspired Spada's painting?
   Possible responses: Some students may say that Spada's painting depicts verse 21, in which the son apologizes. Other students may say that it represents verse 24, in which the father rejoices that his son is alive.

2. How does this painting illustrate the theme of this unit—Celebrating Humanity?
   Possible response: Spada's painting dramatizes a scene from the parable in a way that makes clear the human emotions of the participants. The figures in the painting are everyday people, not remote, unapproachable ideals or abstract symbols of sin and forgiveness.

Differentiated Instruction *for Universal Access*

Strategy for Special-Needs Students
Relate to students the basic ideas and actions of the story. Identify the verses in which key events occur, one event at a time, and have students read those verses. Then discuss how the verses relate to the basic story. Lead students through the ideas that the son ruins his life, comes to his senses, returns to his father, and is welcomed back by the father. Remind students that the story is a parable, intended to show God's forgiveness.

Enrichment for Gifted/Talented Students
Suggest that students create a script for performing the tale of the prodigal son. They could do it as a dramatic reading. They could tell the tale from the different points of view (the prodigal, the father, the older brother). Or they could script the story as is, from the son's asking for his inheritance to his return home. Encourage them to rehearse and present to the class whatever they prepare.

Before students respond, you may wish to have them write a brief objective summary of the selection. As they answer the questions below, remind them to support their answers with evidence from the text.

1. **(a)** He is starving. **(b)** The father is happy, excited, and welcoming. The older son complains.

2. **(a)** The older son complains that he has obediently served his father, but he was never given so much as a young goat. **(b)** The father lets the older son know that everything the father has belongs to the older son. The father reminds the older son of the years of grief he has suffered, thinking his younger son was dead, and that the party is about his happiness.

3. **(a)** The son had disappeared and, as far as his father knew, was probably dead. His return was like a return from death. **(b) Possible response:** The lesson might apply today to someone who has made a serious mistake and asks forgiveness of his or her family or, as originally intended, to someone who, in times of trouble, turns to God.

4. **Possible response:** Students may suggest that the solemn tone used in the translation is suited to the content; they may also suggest that the majestic language is so appealing that the translation has been used by generations of readers. Many of the sayings we use today in everyday language are taken directly from the King James Bible.

22 But the father said to his servants, Bring forth the best robe, and put *it* on him; and put a ring on his hand, and shoes on *his* feet:

23 And bring hither the fatted calf, and kill *it*; and let us eat, and be merry:

24 For this my son was dead, and is alive again; he was lost, and is found. And they began to be merry.

25 Now his elder son was in the field: and as he came and drew nigh to the house, he heard music and dancing.

26 And he called one of the servants, and asked what these things meant.

27 And he said unto him, Thy brother is come; and thy father hath killed the fatted calf, because he hath received him safe and sound.

28 And he was angry, and would not go in: therefore came his father out, and entreated him.

29 And he answering said to *his* father, Lo, these many years do I serve thee, neither transgressed I at any time thy commandment: and yet thou never gavest me a kid, that I might make merry with my friends:

30 But as soon as this thy son was come, which hath devoured thy living with harlots, thou hast killed for him the fatted calf.

31 And he said unto him, Son, thou art ever with me, and all that I have is thine.

32 It was meet[2] that we should make merry, and be glad: for this thy brother was dead, and is alive again; and was lost, and is found.

2. **meet** *adj.* fitting.

Vocabulary

entreated (en trēt´ id) *v.* begged; pleaded with

transgressed (trans grest´) *v.* overstepped or broke (a law or commandment)

Critical Reading

Cite textual evidence to support your responses.

1. **Key Ideas and Details (a)** What causes the younger son to return home? **(b) Compare and Contrast:** Contrast the father's and the older son's responses to the younger son's return.

2. **Key Ideas and Details (a)** What specific complaint does the older son make? **(b) Assess:** How effectively does the father address his concerns?

3. **Integration of Knowledge and Ideas (a) Interpret:** Why does the father say that the younger son is "alive again"? **(b) Apply:** In what circumstances might the lesson of the parable apply today?

4. **Integration of Knowledge and Ideas** What made the King James Bible so influential? In your response, use at least two of the following Essential Question words: *majestic, clarity, solemn, preach.* [*Connecting to the Essential Question: How does literature shape or reflect society?*]

Concept Connector

Reading Strategy Graphic Organizer
Ask students to review the graphic organizers, in which they have identified key details and determined the main idea by making inferences. Then have students share their organizers and compare their inferences.

Activating Prior Knowledge
Have students return to their responses to the Activating Prior Knowledge activity. Ask them to explain whether their thoughts have changed and, if so, how.

Connecting to the Essential Question
Have students compare their responses given to the prompt before they completed reading the selections with their thoughts afterward. Have them work individually or in groups, writing or discussing their thoughts, to formulate their new responses. Then, lead a class discussion, probing for what students have learned that confirms or invalidates their initial thoughts. Encourage students to cite specific textual details to support their responses.

Literary Analysis

1. Key Ideas and Details (a) What is the message of the selection from the Sermon on the Mount? **(b)** Why is the form of a **sermon** suited to this lesson?

2. Key Ideas and Details (a) What is the chief moral lesson of the Parable of the Prodigal Son? **(b)** Why is the form of a **parable** suited to this lesson?

3. Craft and Structure (a) Contrast the styles of the **psalm**, the sermon, and the parable. **(b)** How is the style of each selection appropriate to its purpose?

4. Integration of Knowledge and Ideas The **metaphor** of the shepherd in Psalm 23, the **analogy** of the birds in the Sermon on the Mount, and the **narrative** in the Parable of the Prodigal Son are all designed to appeal to their original audience of uneducated, rural folk. Explain, using a chart like the one below.

Images: Familiar / Unfamiliar?	Simple / Difficult?	Memorable? Why?

5. Comparing Literary Works Of the following, which did you find easiest to understand: the metaphor of the shepherd, the analogy of the lilies, or the lesson of the prodigal son? For each, explain what was clear and what was complex.

Reading Strategy

6. For Psalm 23, **determine the main idea** by *making inferences* about the meaning of this quotation: "I will dwell in the house of the Lord forever." Consider, for example, what "the house of the Lord" might mean and why the word *dwelling* may have a connotation stronger than that of the word *living*.

7. What inference can you make from the fact that this excerpt from the Sermon on the Mount closes with "O ye of little faith"?

8. After reading the Parable of the Prodigal Son, what inference can you make about the value the Bible places on forgiveness?

9. Do you think that mercy and forgiveness are more important than, less important than, or equal in importance to justice? Explain, using examples from the parable.

10. Make inferences about the meaning of this quote from the Sermon on the Mount: "Which of you by taking thought can add one cubit unto his stature?"

Common Core State Standards

Writing
3. Write narratives to develop real or imagined experiences or events using effective technique, well-chosen details, and well-structured event sequences. *(p. 306)*
3.d. Use precise words and phrases, telling details, and sensory language to convey a vivid picture of the experiences, events, setting, and/or characters. *(p. 306)*

Language
1.a. Apply the understanding that usage is a matter of convention, can change over time, and is sometimes contested. *(p. 306)*

Assessment Practice

Fact and Opinion (For more practice, see *All-in-One Workbook*.)

Many tests require students to distinguish between fact and opinion. Use the following sample item to show students how certain words can signal a statement of opinion.

Which of the following lines from the Sermon on the Mount is an opinion?

A Behold the fowls of the air: for they sow not . . .

B Consider the lilies of the field . . . they toil not . . .

C That even Solomon . . . was not arrayed like one of these (lilies)

D . . . the grass of the field . . . is cast into the oven . . .

Lead students to recognize that judgments about what is beautiful or wonderful often signal a statement of opinion. Such statements are difficult to prove, and a fact must be provable. The correct answer is **C.**

Answers

1. **(a)** The message is that believers should not focus on money and things, or live in worry; God will take care of them. **(b)** Points about attitudes are being made, and the sermon form suits this type of teaching.

2. **(a)** The chief moral lesson is God's readiness to forgive those who fall from grace and later repent. **(b)** A parable works because people can understand the emotions of the characters.

3. **(a)** The psalm is formal and lyric. The sermon is more structured. The parable has an informal, storylike "feel." **(b)** The lyricism of the psalm is suitable for a song of praise. The precise structure of the sermon presents ideas clearly. The parable presents its message in an appealing way.

4. **Possible responses:** Psalm, familiar: sheep, water, pasture, difficult: no fear in shadow of death; memorable because easy to understand. Sermon, familiar: birds, lilies; difficult: Solomon's glory; memorable because good examples. Parable, familiar: father's love; difficult: jealous brother; memorable because emotions are universal. Another sample answer can be found on the **Literary Analysis Graphic Organizer** A, page 50 in *Graphic Organizer Transparencies*.

5. **Possible response:** Students may find that the rebellious child and the loving father are the easiest to understand, because these are still parts of people's lives.

6. The main idea is that "I will have a place in heaven"; heaven is God's house.

7. "O ye of little faith" suggests that many people listening to the sermon were unable to trust God.

8. Students should infer that the Bible valued forgiveness highly.

9. **Possible responses:** Students may say that mercy and forgiveness are more important, because they are aspects of love. Others may say that they are less important than justice, which is essential to an orderly society. Still others may say that all are equally important, because all three are necessary for a contented society.

10. The meaning is, "Who can add anything to their height simply by thinking about it?"

Vocabulary Acquisition and Use

1. Introduce the skill using the instruction on the student page.

2. Have students complete the Word Analysis activity and the Vocabulary practice.

Word Analysis

1. d
2. b
3. a
4. e
5. c

Vocabulary

1. A person needs the quality of <u>righteousness</u> to be a good judge.

2. I would advise a <u>prodigal</u> friend that she could not repay borrowed money if she wasted it.

3. Some people might wish they had <u>transgressed</u> the laws, because they would have enjoyed the excitement.

4. It makes most people uncomfortable to be <u>entreated</u> for something, so they are less likely to respond favorably.

5. People with <u>stature</u> are admired by others, and some people want to be admired.

Writing

1. To guide students in writing this narrative text, give them the **Support for Writing** page (*Unit 2 Resources*, p. 73).

2. Review with students the definition of a parable as a simple story from which a moral is drawn.

3. Tell students that they should reread the Parable of the Prodigal Son to help them capture the style, tone, and impact. Encourage students to think about ideals and virtues that are important to them. Suggest that they think of incidents in their lives or stories they know that might illustrate these ideals.

4. Use the **Rubrics for Persuasive Essays**, *Professional Development Guidebook*, pages 256–257, to evaluate students' work.

© Vocabulary Acquisition and Use

Word Analysis: Latin Root -stat-

The word *stature*, meaning "height when standing," comes from the Latin root *-stat-*, sometimes spelled *-stit-*, which means "to stand" or "to set up." Over time, the word *stature* has taken on a figurative meaning in addition to its literal one: though it sometimes refers to a person's actual height, it can also refer to a person's prominence or position in society or in some other organization or ranking.

Use the meaning of the root *-stat-* to match the following words with their definitions.

1. statue   a. to set up a procedure
2. stationary   b. standing still
3. institute   c. rank
4. constitution   d. a figure that stands
5. status   e. act of setting up

Vocabulary: Synonyms

Write a complete sentence to answer each question. For each item, use a vocabulary word from page 296 in place of the underlined words.

1. In what jobs or professions would a person need a good deal of <u>fairness</u> and <u>honesty</u>?

2. What might you say to a friend who was being <u>recklessly wasteful</u> with money she had borrowed?

3. Why do you think people often identify with a book or movie character who has <u>broken a law</u>?

4. Why might a person who is <u>begged</u> for something respond less favorably than one who is asked politely?

5. In your view, why is social <u>standing</u> so important to so many people?

Writing

© **Narrative Text** Write a **parable** in the King James style about a modern-day issue or situation that supports a moral in which you believe. Study the style of the Parable of the Prodigal Son, and adapt it to your purposes.

Prewriting Choose a moral to teach, and sketch the plot of a story to illustrate it. Then reread the Parable of the Prodigal Son, taking notes on the style in which it is told.

Drafting Follow your notes as you draft, setting out the events of your story in clear sequence. Emphasize those elements—character traits or events—that will lead the reader to understand your parable. Use sensory details to make the scenes vivid and specific in your reader's mind. Conclude the parable with a moral.

Revising Highlight parts of your work that do not fit the general style you have adopted. Rewrite marked passages for consistency.

> Model: Revising for Consistent Style
> And, lo, the bully descended like a wolf on the playground. "Out of my way, meathead," he said.
> ~~laid about him mightily.~~
> And he started wailing on the nearest person.

The revision maintains the style: formal, simple, biblical-sounding narration contrasting with the character's slang dialogue.

306 Celebrating Humanity (1485–1625)

Assessment Resources

Unit 2 Resources

L1 L2 EL **Selection Test A**, pp. 78–80. Administer Test A to less advanced readers.

L3 L4 EL **Selection Test B**, pp. 81–83. Administer Test B to on-level and more advanced students.

L3 L4 **Open-Book Test**, pp. 75–77. As an alternative, administer the Open-Book Test.

All Customizable Test Bank

All Self-tests
Students may prepare for the **Selection Test** by taking the **Self-test** online.

PHLit Online! All assessment resources are available at **www.PHLitOnline.com.**

Focus on Literary Forms
Drama

Text Complexity: At a Glance

This chart gives a general text complexity rating for the selections in this part of the unit to help guide instruction. For additional text complexity support, see the Test Complexity Rubric at point of use.

Macbeth	More Complex

Selection Planning Guide

William Shakespeare's *The Tragedy of Macbeth* is one of the greatest dramatic tragedies ever staged. *Macbeth* works on many levels: it is a human tragedy wherein the war hero develops a raging lust for power that leads him to commit murder and lose his humanity. It is also an exciting, gruesome tale of fate, war, the supernatural, greed, and retribution.

Humanities

Ellen Terry as Lady Macbeth, 1889, by John Singer Sargent

John Singer Sargent, popular for his portraits of prestigious men and women, painted this portrait of Shakespearean actress Ellen Terry characterizing Lady Macbeth, perhaps her most famous role. Of the painting, Terry said that Sargent was able to communicate all she'd hoped to communicate through her actual performance.

Use this question for discussion: Ask students to describe what is happening in the painting. Then **ask:** Why might Terry have been pleased with Sargent's work? Though it contains no words, how does it accurately depict Lady Macbeth's character?

Possible responses: Students may say that in showing Lady Macbeth crowning herself, the character's power-hungry qualities are very evident. Additionally, the expression on Terry's face is very cold and true to Lady Macbeth's actions that help spur her husband on to murder.

Monitoring Progress

Before students read *Macbeth*, refer to the results for the **Vocabulary in Context** items on **Benchmark Test 2** (*Unit 1 Resources,* p. 171). Use this diagnostic portion of the test to guide your choice of selections to teach as well as the depth of prereading preparation you will provide, based on students' readiness for the reading and vocabulary skills.

Benchmark

After students have completed *The Tragedy of Macbeth, Act II,* administer **Benchmark Test 3** (*Unit 2 Resources* pp. 124–129). If the Benchmark Test reveals that some of the students need further work, use the appropriate reteaching pages in the **Reading Kit.**

❶ Defining Drama

Point out that because a drama, or play, has to hold the interest of a live audience, the usual ingredients of plot are heightened. **Ask:** What does the word "dramatic" mean when we use it to describe human behavior, and why might we have come to use it that way?

Sample response: We use the word "dramatic" to refer to emotional intensity. This meaning derives from the way literary drama intensifies the usual ingredients of plot, heightening conflict, complications, and resolution.

❷ Types of Drama

Review the two types of drama, noting that there can be moments of comedy within a tragic play, and that serious topics may be discussed in a comedy. Invite students to offer examples of dramatic writing in film or television that combine these two genres.

❸ Stage Directions

Point out that stage directions are essential to actors performing in a play, because the directions tell them how to move and deliver their lines. **Ask:** How are stage directions also essential to the reader of a play?

Sample response: Stage directions enable a reader to visualize the action.

❹ Close Read: Elements of Shakespearean Drama

Review the chart with students. Point out the highlighted text in the model on page 309. Explain that in each case, the color of the highlighting matches the color of the category in the chart. Details that illustrate a given category are highlighted in the color of that category.

"DRAMA IS LIFE WITH THE DULL BITS CUT OUT."

— ALFRED HITCHCOCK

❶ Defining Drama

Drama is a form of literature that tells a story through performances by actors.

❷ **Types of Drama** The ancient Greeks developed drama into a sophisticated art form. They created two broad categories of drama: tragedy and comedy.

- **Tragedies** end with the downfall or death of the protagonist, or main character. In ancient Greek and Shakespearean tragedy, the main character is the *tragic hero*—an outstanding person of high rank who falls to his or her ruin.
- **Comedies** feature ordinary protagonists in conflicts that are resolved happily.

Elements of Drama The text of a play consists of dialogue and stage directions.

- **Dialogue** The term **dialogue** refers to the lines characters speak in conversation with each other. Playwrights also use these types of speech: **monologues,** or long speeches delivered by one character to others; **asides,** or private remarks to another character or to the audience that are not heard by other characters onstage; and **soliloquies,** or speeches voicing a character's inner thoughts, not heard by others.

❸ • **Stage Directions** Many playwrights include **stage directions,** or instructions, about the setting, costumes, lighting, scenery, and props, or objects used onstage. Stage directions may also indicate how and when characters should move and with what expression they should deliver their lines.

❹ **Close Read: Elements of Shakespearean Drama** These literary elements appear in the Model text.

Soliloquy: A soliloquy is a long speech expressing private thoughts, not heard by others. Example: *Before murdering King Duncan, Macbeth delivers a soliloquy expressing his fears and doubts, beginning "If it were done when 'tis done . . . " (Macbeth, I, vii, 1).*	**Internal Conflict and Characterization:** An internal conflict is a character's struggle with his or her own conflicting motivations. In his soliloquies, Shakespeare turns a powerful psychological spotlight on characters' internal conflicts. Example: ***"Hamlet.** To be or not to be, that is the question. . . ." (Hamlet, III, i, 62)*
Imagery: The mind's power to make sense of the world is part of Shakespearean drama. Imagery, or word pictures, in the dialogue shows characters' minds and hearts at work. Example: ***"Romeo.** But soft! What light through yonder window breaks? / It is the East, and Juliet is the sun!" (Romeo and Juliet, II, ii, 2–3)*	**Blank Verse:** Shakespeare's noble characters often speak in a type of poetry called blank verse, consisting of unrhymed lines each containing five stressed syllables. Each stressed syllable is preceded by an unstressed syllable in a "da-DUM, da-DUM" rhythm. Example: ***"Antony.** O mighty Caesar! Dost thou lie so low?" (Julius Caesar, III, i, 148)*

308 Celebrating Humanity (1485–1625)

Differentiated Instruction   for Universal Access

Strategies for Less Proficient Readers

Help familiarize students with a drama's appearance on the page. First, have students compare a page of prose text with a page of *Macbeth,* and ask students to describe the differences they see. Then, have them analyze a page of *Macbeth,* identifying the elements that help readers and performers, such as the names of the speakers, the stage directions, and the numbering of acts and scenes.

EL Strategy for English Learners

Remind students that stage directions are not read aloud when performing a play. Have them notice that the stage directions are written in italics and are set apart from the dialogue in brackets. To illustrate, have students listen to Act 1, Scene 3, of *Macbeth* on the *Hear It!* Audio CD as they follow along in the text.

Model

About the Text In Shakespeare's *Hamlet,* Hamlet's uncle Claudius has murdered Hamlet's father, the king of Denmark, and then married Hamlet's mother, taking the throne of Denmark. In this soliloquy, Claudius ponders his crime.

from *The Tragedy of Hamlet,* Act III, Scene iii, Lines 39–75
William Shakespeare

KING CLAUDIUS

5

40   O, my offence is rank, it smells to heaven;
    It hath the primal eldest curse[1] upon't,
    A brother's murder. Pray can I not,
    Though inclination be as sharp as will:
    My stronger guilt defeats my strong intent;
    And, like a man to double business bound,
45   I stand in pause where I shall first begin,
    And both neglect. What if this cursed hand
    Were thicker than itself with brother's blood,
    Is there not rain enough in the sweet heavens
    To wash it white as snow? Whereto serves mercy
50   But to confront the visage of offence?[2]
    And what's in prayer but this two-fold force,
    To be forestalled ere we come to fall,

6
    Or pardon'd being down? Then I'll look up;
    My fault is past. But, O, what form of prayer

7
55   Can serve my turn? 'Forgive me my foul murder'?
    That cannot be; since I am still possess'd
    Of those effects for which I did the murder,
    My crown, mine own ambition and my queen.
    May one be pardon'd and retain the offence?
60   In the corrupted currents of this world
    Offence's gilded hand may shove by justice,
    And oft 'tis seen the wicked prize itself
    Buys out the law: but 'tis not so above;
    There is no shuffling, there the action lies
65   In his true nature; and we ourselves compell'd,
    Even to the teeth and forehead of our faults,
    To give in evidence. What then? What rests?
    Try what repentance can. What can it not?
    Yet what can it when one can not repent?
70   O wretched state! O bosom black as death!
    O limed[3] soul, that, struggling to be free,
    Art more engaged! Help, angels! Make assay!

8
    Bow, stubborn knees; and, heart with strings of steel,
    Be soft as sinews of the newborn babe!
75   All may be well.

1. primal eldest curse the curse of Cain. In the Bible, Cain killed his brother Abel.

2. Whereto serves mercy . . . visage of offence? What is mercy's purpose if not to contest condemnation?

3. limed trapped, as a bird caught in birdlime, a sticky substance used in traps.

5 Soliloquy In this speech, Claudius reveals his thoughts alone onstage, confessing that he has murdered his brother, who was Hamlet's father and the king of Denmark.

6 Blank Verse The rhythm of the blank verse helps carry Claudius's analysis of prayer and forgiveness to its conclusion.

7 Internal Conflict In these lines Claudius elaborates on his internal conflict—the fact that he is "to double business bound." He cannot truly repent of the murder as long as he is still attached to what it has brought him: a crown and a wife.

8 Imagery The contrast between the images of "strings of steel" and "sinews of the newborn babe" reflects Claudius's agonized struggle—he is torn between his stubborn attachment to his crime and his desire to repent.

Extended Study: Shakespearean Drama **309**

---

5 Soliloquy

Remind students that a soliloquy expresses a character's private thoughts. **Ask:** If a soliloquy reveals thoughts not intended for others, why might a playwright have a character speak his or her thoughts aloud?

Sample response: While a soliloquy includes thoughts not intended for other characters on stage, it *is* intended for the audience. The audience gains knowledge that helps them understand the plot and the characters' motivations.

6 Blank Verse

Have students review the definition of *blank verse* on page 308. Point out that while Shakespeare wrote much of his drama in blank verse, not all his lines are perfect examples of the form. Invite a volunteer to read lines 51 to 54 aloud. **Ask:** Which lines are irregular examples of blank verse? Explain.

Answer: Lines 51 and 52 each have too few syllables.

7 Internal Conflict

Invite a volunteer to read the green-highlighted sentence. **Ask:** What internal conflict does Claudius reveal?

Answer: Claudius wants to pray; he can't because he is consumed by guilt for his brother's death and because he still possesses the very things for which he committed the murder.

8 Imagery

Read aloud the bracketed passage. **Ask:** Why does Claudius employ the image of a "newborn babe"?

Sample response: It is wishful thinking. Claudius is a guilty murderer. He wants his heart to become as innocent as a baby's.

Extend the Lesson

Understanding Drama

Because a drama depends on dialogue, playwrights must find creative ways to reveal information that otherwise might go into a character description, a description of the setting, or a flashback. In particular, Shakespeare's plays were written to be performed with minimal sets and few props. Have students read or listen to a recording of *Macbeth* Act 1, Scene 1. Discuss the following questions with students:

- How does the king find out what happened in the battle with Macdonwald?
- How might this information have been presented in a modern film adaptation of the play?

Tell students that, as they read a drama, they should be aware of how details of setting and off-stage action are revealed in the dialogue.

• *Macbeth*, Act 1
Lesson Pacing Guide

DAY 1 Preteach

- Ⓒ Administer the Reading and Vocabulary Warm-ups (*Unit 2 Resources*, pp. 86–89) as necessary.
- Ⓒ Introduce the Literary Analysis concept: Elizabethan Drama.
- • Introduce the Reading Strategy: Analyze Information from Text Features.
- Ⓒ Build background with the Author in Depth and Background features.
- • Develop thematic thinking with Connecting to the Essential Question.
- Ⓒ Teach the selection vocabulary.

DAYS 2–3 Preteach/Teach

- Ⓒ Have students read and respond to the Contemporary Commentary.
- • Distribute copies of the appropriate graphic organizer for the Reading Strategy (*Graphic Organizer Transparencies*, pp. 52–53).
- • Distribute copies of the appropriate graphic organizer for Literary Analysis (*Graphic Organizer Transparencies*, pp. 54–55).
- • Prepare students to read with the Activating Prior Knowledge activities (TE).
- • Informally monitor comprehension while students read.
- • Use the Reading Check questions to confirm comprehension.
- Ⓒ Develop students' understanding of Elizabethan Drama using the Literary Analysis prompts.
- • Develop students' ability to analyze information using text features using the Reading Strategy prompts.
- Ⓒ Reinforce vocabulary with the Vocabulary notes.

DAY 4 Assess

- • Assess students' comprehension and mastery of the skills by having them answer the Critical Reading, Literary Analysis, and Reading Strategy questions.
- Ⓒ Have students complete the Vocabulary Lesson.

DAY 5 Extend/Assess

- Ⓒ Have students complete the Writing Lesson and write a speaker introduction. (You may assign as homework.)
- • Administer Selection Test A or B (*Unit 2 Resources*, pp. 100–102 or 103–105).

Ⓒ Common Core State Standards

Reading Literature 3. Analyze the impact of the author's choices regarding how to develop and relate elements of a story or drama.

Writing 3. Write narratives to develop real or imagined experiences or events using effective technique, well-chosen details, and well-structured event sequences.
3.d. Use precise words and phrases, telling details, and sensory language to convey a vivid picture of the experiences, events, setting, and/or characters.

Language 4.a. Use context as a clue to the meaning of a word or phrase.
5. Demonstrate understanding of nuances in word meanings.

Additional Standards Practice
Common Core Companion, *pp. 28–35; 208–218; 324–335*

Daily Block Scheduling
Each day in this Lesson Pacing Guide represents a 40–50 minute period. Teachers using block scheduling may combine days to revise pacing. In addition, teachers may differentiate and support core instruction by integrating components for extended and intensive support as students require. See the Guide to Selected Leveled Resources (facing page).

Guide to Selected Leveled Resources

R T I	**Tier 1** (students performing on level)	Macbeth, *Act 1*

Warm Up		**Practice, model,** and **monitor** fluency, working with the whole class or in groups.	**Vocabulary** and **Reading Warm-ups B,** *Unit 2 Resources,* pp. 86–87, 89
Comprehension/Skills		**Support** and **monitor** comprehension and skills development, having students complete the activities, graphic organizers, and interactive prompts **independently** or **as a class**.	• *Reader's Notebook,* adapted instruction and summary **EL** *Reader's Notebook: English Learner's Version,* adapted instruction and summary • **Reading Skill Graphic Organizer B,** *Graphic Organizer Transparencies,* p. 53 • **Literary Analysis Graphic Organizer B,** *Graphic Organizer Transparencies,* p. 55
Monitor Progress	**A**	**Monitor** student progress with the differentiated curriculum-based assessment in the *Unit Resources.*	• **Selection Test B,** *Unit 2 Resources,* pp. 103–105 • **Open-Book Test,** *Unit 2 Resources,* pp. 97–99

R T I	**Tier 2** (students requiring intervention)	Macbeth, *Act 1*

Warm Up		**Practice, model,** and **monitor** fluency **in groups** or **with individuals**.	• **Vocabulary and Reading Warm-ups A,** *Unit 2 Resources,* pp. 86–88 • *Hear It!* Audio CD
Comprehension/Skills		• **Support** and **monitor** comprehension and skills development, working **in small groups** or **with individuals**. • As students complete the selection in the appropriate version of the *Reader's Notebook,* **monitor** comprehension frequently with group questions and individual instruction. • **Model** strategies while guiding students in completing the activities and prompts in the *Reader's Notebook,* as well as the graphic organizers. • **Practice** skills and **monitor** mastery with the *Reading Kit* worksheets.	• *Reader's Notebook: Adapted Version,* adapted instruction and summary **EL** *Reader's Notebook: English Learner's Version,* adapted instruction and summary • **Reading Skill Graphic Organizer A,** *Graphic Organizer Transparencies,* p. 52 • **Literary Analysis Graphic Organizer A,** *Graphic Organizer Transparencies,* p. 54 • *Reading Kit,* Practice worksheets
Monitor Progress	**A**	**Monitor** student progress with the differentiated curriculum-based assessment in the *Unit Resources* and in the *Reading Kit.*	• **Selection Test A,** *Unit 2 Resources,* pp. 100–102 • *Reading Kit,* Assess worksheets

TIER 3 Tier 3 intervention may require consultation with the student's special-education or dyslexia specialist. For additional support, see the Tier 2 activities and resources listed above.

One-on-one teaching   Group work   Whole class instruction   Independent work   **A** Assessment

For a complete guide to selection support, including support for Advanced students, see the Overview of Resources in the frontmatter.

• *Macbeth*, Act 1

Vocabulary/Fluency/Prior Knowledge

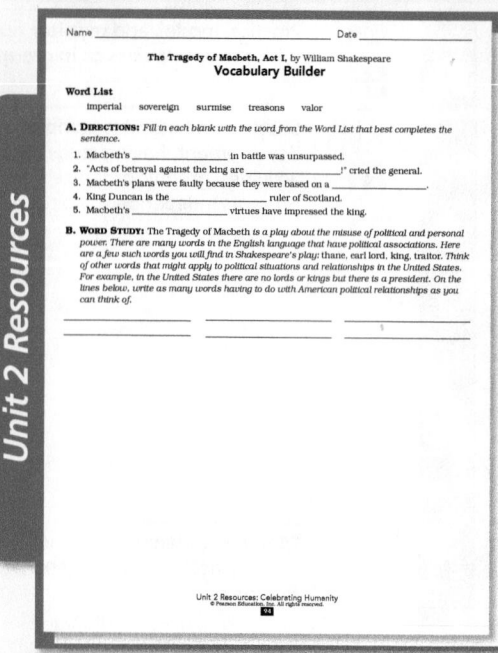

Unit 2 Resources

RESOURCES FOR:

L1	Special-Needs Students
L2	Below-Level Students (Tier 2)
L3	On-Level Students (Tier 1)
L4	Advanced Students (Tier 1)
EL	English Learners
All	All Students

All **Vocabulary Builder,** p. 94

Also available for these selections:

EL L1 L2 **Vocabulary Warm-ups A and B,** pp. 86–87

EL L1 L2 **Reading Warm-ups A and B,** pp. 88–89

Reader's Notebooks

Pre- and postreading pages for this selection appear in an interactive format in the *Reader's Notebooks.* Each *Notebook* is differentiated for a different group of learners.

The selections in the Adapted and English Learner's versions are abridged.

L2 L3 *Reader's Notebook*

L1 *Reader's Notebook: Adapted Version*

EL *Reader's Notebook: English Learner's Version*

EL *Reader's Notebook: Spanish Version*

© *Common Core Companion*

Additional instruction and practice for each Common Core State Standard

Selection Support

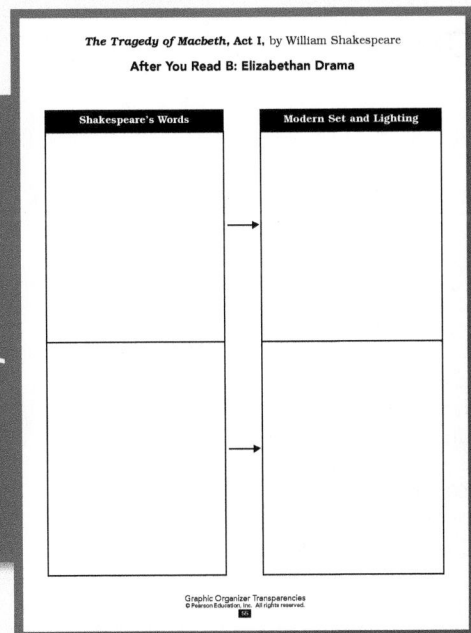

The Tragedy of Macbeth, Act I, by William Shakespeare

After You Read B: Elizabethan Drama

Shakespeare's Words	Modern Set and Lighting

Graphic Organizer Transparencies
© Pearson Education, Inc. All rights reserved.

EL L3 Literary Analysis: Graphic Organizer B, p. 55

Also available for these selections:

EL L3 Reading: Graphic Organizer A (partially filled in), p. 52

EL L3 Reading: Graphic Organizer B, p. 53

EL L1 L2 Literary Analysis: Graphic Organizer A (partially filled in), p. 54

(left margin) Graphic Organizer Transparencies

Skills Development/Extension

Name _____ Date _____

Macbeth
William Shakespeare: Biography

William Shakespeare's influence ranges far and wide from his lifetime even until today. His works have influenced major artists, writers, and all speakers of the English language. Some of the biggest names in modern literature call upon Shakespearean tradition, including James Joyce, T.S. Elliot, and Virginia Woolf. Contemporary authors, such as Jane Smiley in *One Thousand Acres*, call upon Shakespeare (*King Lear* in Smiley's case). His theatrical works have been inspiration for other playwrights and moviemakers. Some movies are direct remakes, sharing the same titles as the plays. Others call upon the famous plots, such as *West Side Story*'s retelling of *Romeo and Juliet*.

A. DIRECTIONS: *Use the following chart to organize your notes on Shakespeare's life and influence.*

William Shakespeare (1564—1616)				
Early Years	**Marriage and Family**	**Acting/Writing Career**	**Literary Works**	**Influence**

Unit 2 Resources: Celebrating Humanity
© Pearson Education, Inc. All rights reserved.
90

All Biography, p. 90

Also available for these selections:

All Literary Analysis, p. 91
All Literary Analysis, p. 92
All Reading: p. 93
EL L3 L4 Support for Writing, p. 95
L4 Enrichment, p. 96

(left margin) Unit 2 Resources

Assessment

Name _____ Date _____

The Tragedy of Macbeth, *Act 1* by William Shakespeare
Open-Book Test

Short Answer *Write your response to the questions in this section on the lines provided.*

1. Act I of *The Tragedy of Macbeth* opens with a scene of witches. What role do the witches play in the act? Explain.

2. Act 1 of *The Tragedy of Macbeth* includes numbered side notes. What aspect of the play do the notes help readers understand?

3. In her soliloquy in Act 1 of *The Tragedy of Macbeth*, Lady Macbeth says "Glamis thou art, and Cawdor, and shalt be / What thou art promised." What does she mean by this?

4. Why do the stage directions in Act 1 of *The Tragedy of Macbeth* make no detailed references to lighting or sets? Explain.

5. Based on the information in Act 1 of *The Tragedy of Macbeth*, what appears to be Macbeth's character flaw? Explain.

6. If you were watching *The Tragedy of Macbeth* at the Globe Theater in Shakespeare's time, how would the illusions of time and space be created?

Unit 2 Resources: Celebrating Humanity
© Pearson Education, Inc. All rights reserved.
97

L3 L4 Open-Book Test, pp. 97–99

Also available for these selections:

EL L3 L4 Selection Test A, pp. 100–102
EL L1 L2 Selection Test B, pp. 103–105

PHLit Online!
www.PHLitOnline.com

Online Resources: All print materials are also available online.

- complete narrated selection text
- a thematically related video with writing prompt
- an interactive graphic organizer
- highlighting feature
- access to all student print resources, adapted to individual student needs
- Spanish and English summaries
- adapted selection translations in Spanish

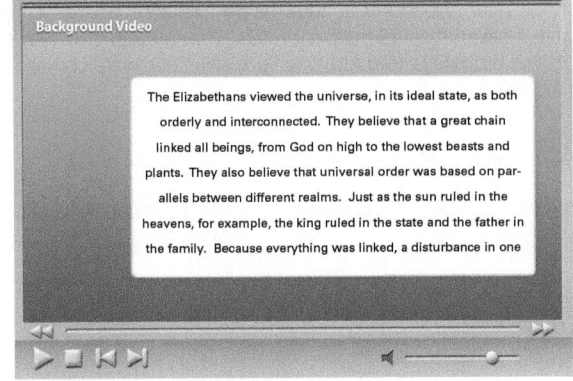

Background Video

The Elizabethans viewed the universe, in its ideal state, as both orderly and interconnected. They believe that a great chain linked all beings, from God on high to the lowest beasts and plants. They also believe that universal order was based on parallels between different realms. Just as the sun ruled in the heavens, for example, the king ruled in the state and the father in the family. Because everything was linked, a disturbance in one

Background Video

Also available:

Get Connected! (thematic video with writing prompt)
All videos are available in Spanish.

Vocabulary Central

Vocabulary Central (tools and activities for studying vocabulary)

Also available:

Writer's Journal (with graphics feature)

Literary History: Shakespeare's Globe

1. Lead a discussion with students about theater and performance spaces they may have visited, including movie theaters, school auditoriums, concert halls, or performance halls for live theater. Guide them to focus on the physical details that affect their experiences as an audience member, such as seating, view of the stage or screen, and sound quality.

2. After students have discussed today's performance spaces, have them read the article about the Elizabethan theater.

Background

Although Shakespeare did not have the advantages of modern theaters to draw on, the theaters of his day must be considered highly sophisticated. The greatest dramas in our language were produced on the sixteenth-century English stage. This fact alone suggests how advanced the theater arts were when Shakespeare was writing his masterpieces.

Most of Shakespeare's plays were performed at the Globe. It was built by Richard and Cuthbert Burbage, sons of James Burbage, who had constructed The Theatre, London's first theater. Richard Burbage was multitalented: He was a leading actor in Shakespeare's acting company!

The foundation of the original Globe was discovered in 1989. The excavation revealed clues about the theater itself as well as the actors and the audience. The tiny part of the foundation that was originally uncovered yielded a great number of hazelnuts shells. Hazelnuts were the Elizabethan equivalent of popcorn.

Literary History: Shakespeare's Globe

"Can this cockpit hold
The vasty fields of France? Or may we cram
Within this wooden O the very casques
That did affright the air at Agincourt?"

—*Shakespeare, from* Henry V

The Elizabethan Theater

English drama came of age during the reign of Elizabeth I, developing into a sophisticated and popular art form. Although playwrights like Shakespeare were mainly responsible for the great theatrical achievements of the time, audiences and theater buildings were equally important.

Before the reign of Elizabeth I, traveling theater companies put on plays wherever they could find an audience, often performing in the open courtyards of inns. Spectators watched from the ground or from balconies or galleries above.

England's First Playhouse

When Shakespeare was twelve years old, an actor named James Burbage built London's first theater, called simply The Theater. Actors—even prominent and well-to-do actors like James Burbage—were frowned upon by the city fathers. Nonetheless, they were wildly popular with the common people and were called on frequently to perform at court. A man like Burbage enjoyed a reputation somewhat like a rock star's today.

The Globe In 1597, the city fathers closed down The Theater. In late 1598, Richard Burbage (James Burbage's son) and his men dismantled it and hauled it in pieces across the Thames to Southwark. It took them six months to rebuild it, and when they did, they renamed it the Globe.

Scholars disagree about what the Globe actually looked like because there are no surviving drawings from the time or detailed descriptions. Shakespeare refers to the building in *Henry V* as "this wooden O." The building had to have been small enough for the actors to be heard, and we know that performances drew as many as 2,500 to 3,000 people. These truly packed houses must have been uncomfortable—especially when you consider that people of the era didn't bathe or change their clothes very often! Most spectators stood throughout the performance. Some of the audience sat in a gallery behind the performers. Though they saw only the actors' backs and probably could not hear very well, they were content to be seen by the rest of the audience.

There were no sets or lighting at the Globe. Plays were performed in sunlight, and a playwright's words alone had to create moods like the one in the eerie first scene of *Macbeth*. Holding an audience spellbound was complicated by the fact that most spectators ate and drank throughout the performance.

The first Globe met its demise in 1613, when a cannon fired as part of a performance of *Henry VIII* ignited the theater's thatched roof. Everyone escaped unharmed, but the Globe burned to the ground. Although the theater was rebuilt, the Puritans had it permanently closed in 1642.

The New Globe

Building a replica of Shakespeare's Globe was the American actor Sam Wanamaker's dream. After long years of fundraising and construction, the theater opened to its first full season on June 8, 1997, with a production of *Henry V.* Like the earlier Globe, this one is made of wood, with a thatched roof and lime plaster covering the walls. The stage and the galleries are covered, but the "bear pit," where the modern-day groundlings stand, is open to the skies.

Perhaps the most striking aspect of seeing Shakespeare's plays performed at the Globe is the immediacy of the action. The performers, as Benedict Nightingale noted in the *London Times,* "are talking to you, asking you questions, involving you in their fears." Is that not what theater is all about?

A performance at the modern Globe

Speaking and Listening: Discussion

Ⓒ **Comprehension and Collaboration** Today, most patrons expect a certain level of comfort and technical sophistication when attending a theatrical event—whether a concert, a Broadway show, or a school assembly.

With a group, discuss your experiences while attending live performances. Use these questions to guide your discussion:

- In what ways do modern shows compare with what you have read about Elizabethan theater?
- Do you think live theater is more popular or less popular today than in Shakespeare's day? Explain.

Choose a point person to share your group's ideas with the class.

Literary History **311**

Background
The New Globe

London's new Globe Theatre is located on the Thames. It retains the characteristics of the original—including its circular shape, open center, and thatched roof. Since few details of the original remain, the builders referred to the building contracts that exist for the rival theaters, the Rose and the Fortune, which were built by the same master carpenter who built the Globe.

The new Globe seats 1,000 people. Because the seats curve around the stage, everyone has a different view of the action. The yard, or pit, has room for 450 groundlings. As in Elizabethan times, the audience tends to join in the proceedings, commenting on the action.

Plays are performed as they would have been in Shakespeare's time, with little or no scenery, people moving around in the yard, and vendors circulating to sell refreshments. The experience contrasts with performances in modern theaters, which usually take place in a darkened, quiet theater with an attentive and respectful audience.

Speaking and Listening: Discussion

1. Read the discussion topic and clarify it as needed. Remind students to review the article for details about the lack of physical comforts available to patrons of the old Globe. Explain that "technical sophistication" refers to lighting, sound, sets, costuming, and special effects.

2. Then organize students into small groups. Suggest that they begin by discussing the differences between modern movies and plays presented in an Elizabethan theater. If any students in the group have attended a live theater performance, encourage them to share their experiences.

3. Suggest that students may wish to research attendance figures for Broadway and off-Broadway plays, or for local live theater performances, before they discuss the second question.

4. Allow class time for groups to share and discuss their ideas with the class.

311

Background

Shakespeare on Film

Moviemakers today are often torn between the desire to appeal to the broadest possible tastes and the desire to make artistic statements. From the 1920s through the 1940s, the Hollywood studio system turned out profitable movies that often met high artistic standards. Under the system, a few competing companies contracted for long-term relations with actors and directors and owned chains of theaters. Though profits were still the bottom line, the studio system nurtured individual talent, supporting the vision of gifted, even idiosyncratic directors and screenwriters such as Ernst Lubitsch, Howard Hawks, and Orson Welles.

Those who ran the studio system were interested in respectability, even an appearance of culture. Early versions of Shakespeare on film reflect this ambition and help explain why a studio would have spent millions on George Cukor's reconstruction of Verona for *Romeo and Juliet* in 1936.

At the end of the studio era, movie making began to split up between the creation of popular movies with little pretension to sophistication and "highbrow" films. With the development of the category of the "art film," attempts to commit Shakespeare to celluloid became painstaking labors of authenticity or artistic innovation. It is only more recently that growing intellectual comfort with popular culture has enabled productions like the 1996 *Romeo and Juliet*.

Literary History: Shakespeare on Film

Adapting Shakespeare

William Shakespeare wrote for the same audience that filmmakers write for today. Recognizing his wide appeal, filmmakers have adapted many of Shakespeare's plays as films. On these two pages, you will see examples of some of the more notable adaptations.

◄ The 1956 science-fiction film *Forbidden Planet* adapted Shakespeare's drama *The Tempest*, transforming the play's mysterious island into a distant planet.

Japanese director Akira Kurosawa's samurai epic *Throne of Blood* (1957) is considered one of the best film adaptations of *Macbeth*. Toshiro Mifune (shown here) plays the character based on Shakespeare's tragic hero. ▶

312 Celebrating Humanity (1485–1625)

Enrichment: Investigating Popular Culture

Film

The first movie camera was invented in Thomas Edison's laboratories in 1888. Early films were short features, generally of exotic scenes, displayed through devices that accommodated one viewer at a time. Later, filmmakers such as Georges Méliès in France began to tell stories on film. His *Voyage to the Moon* (1902), a spoof of Jules Verne's science fiction, was internationally distributed. For decades, silent feature films were an important form of popular entertainment.

Activity: Research Silent Film Have pairs or groups of students conduct research on the history of silent film, as well as its features and examples of the genre. Suggest that they record information in the **Enrichment: Investigating Popular Culture** worksheet, *Professional Development Guidebook*, p. 238. Have students share their results and lead a class discussion about the difficulties that might arise when turning a play into a silent film.

◄ The musical *West Side Story* (1961) updated *Romeo and Juliet* to the mean streets of New York City. The warring families of Shakespeare's drama become rival gangs.

In 1996, Claire Danes (shown here) played Juliet to Leonardo DiCaprio's Romeo in Baz Luhrmann's version of *Romeo and Juliet*. Luhrmann used Shakespeare's dialogue, but set the play in a hip modern suburb. ▶

ⓒ **Common Core State Standards**

Reading Literature
7. Analyze multiple interpretations of a story, drama, or poem, evaluating how each version interprets the source text.

Reading Literature: Group Discussion

ⓒ **Analyzing Multiple Interpretations** After reading Shakespeare's *Macbeth*, view two or more productions of the play. Consider the 1948 film version directed by Orson Welles as well as any current theatrical versions. Then, in small groups, compare the interpretations you viewed. Use these prompts to guide discussion:

• Did the characters in each version match the characters you imagined while reading *Macbeth*? Were the portrayals effective?

• Describe and evaluate the use in each production of techniques specific to the medium—for film, for example, you might discuss the use of camera point of view, including distance shots and close-ups.

• Did the production depart from Shakespeare's text by introducing, updating, or omitting elements? Evaluate each change.

Based on your discussion, evaluate the effectiveness of each production.

Extended Study: Shakespearean Drama **313**

Group Discussion

1. **Ask:** Which films based on a Shakespeare play are you most interested in watching?
   Possible response: Students should support their choices with reference to specific criteria, such as entertainment value, artistry, depth of insight into human nature, or their own preferences among the plays.

2. Have students select a play to read and film version to watch. You may have them choose from the films represented on pages 312-313. In addition, there are hundreds of other modern-day Shakespeare-related films to consider, including *Hamlet* (1948), starring Sir Laurence Olivier; *A Midsummer Night's Dream* (1999), starring Michelle Pfeiffer; and *Ran* (1985), the Japanese adaptation of *King Lear*, directed by Akira Kurosawa.

3. Have students read the play and watch the film version. Note that the viewing time may have to extend over two or more class periods.

4. Provide students with focus questions, such as the following, with which to begin their small-group discussions: What liberties, if any, did the film take with the text, plot, setting, or character? Did the film emphasize elements of characterization, plot, or theme that you found surprising? Did the film provide new insights into the play, or did it provide a faulty understanding of Shakespeare's meaning?

5. Allow students to summarize their small-group discussions and present their ideas to the class as a whole.

TEACH

Themes Across Centuries
Sir Frank Kermode

1. Tell students that Sir Frank Kermode has written and taught extensively about Shakespeare as a professor at Cambridge University and as the author of books such as *Shakespeare's Language*. He finds that the job of a literary critic is to "help make available the great works to non-specialists."

2. Show Segment 2 on Kermode on the *See it! DVD* to provide insight into the work of a literary critic. After students have watched the segment, **ask:** How can reading books about Shakespeare's plays help readers better understand the text? **Answer:** Reading books can help readers see the text's nuances and complexities. It can also show the successes and failures of the text.

Portraying the Tumult of Mind and Conscience

1. Have students read Kermode's comments about the play's revelations of Macbeth's thoughts.

2. Explain to students that Kermode says Macbeth's soliloquy is famous because it provides a "vivid expression to an acute crisis of conscience."
   Ask students why a soliloquy might be a good format for exploring a "crisis of conscience."
   Possible response: A soliloquy provides an opportunity to think out loud. The performance of a soliloquy may appear more spontaneous than an essay or other written format in which a character examines a decision.

Critical Viewing

Possible response: Physical appearance, good nature, and military abilities would be worthy of note in a young king.

Themes Across Centuries: Scholar's Insights

Sir Frank Kermode on *Macbeth*

Macbeth's Dramatic History *Macbeth,* first performed in 1606, is a play about the murder of a good king of Scotland, its cruel consequences for his country, and the final overthrow of the murderous usurper. Shakespeare takes many liberties with history, for King Duncan was not really a saintly character and Macbeth not a particularly evil one. Banquo is presented in a favorable light because he was held to be the ancestor of King James, the Scottish king who inherited Elizabeth's throne in 1603. Shakespeare's company was called The King's Men; as servants of the king, they had good reason to praise his ancestry and his virtues. Considering the period background, the play is remarkable for the allusions it makes to events in the early years of James's reign.

Portraying the Tumult of Mind and Conscience Yet these allusions are matters of secondary interest to the modern reader. *Macbeth* is a work of the author's full maturity. He had already written the tragedies *Hamlet, Othello,* and *King Lear* and had learned how to represent not merely outward actions but the tumults of the mind and conscience.

In the passage shown from Act I, Macbeth is at the moment of decision, the interim between desire and action, debating within himself whether to go ahead with the plot he devised with his wife to murder the king, their guest. He is weighing the benefits that act would bring him against the powerful reasons for not doing it. He knows that time won't stand still when Duncan is dead. The killing will start a train of events calling for further action.

He is willing to risk judgment after death but knows it will happen in this life. In the here and now. And he gives ordinary social, human reasons for not committing the crime: He is Duncan's kinsman and his host. Moreover, for a subject to kill an innocent monarch is an offense so horrible that his imagination foretells the dreadful disturbances and great sorrows that must ensue. And he admits he has no motive except overweening ambition.

About the Author

Literary critic Sir Frank Kermode wrote the award-winning *Shakespeare's Language* in 2000. Other works by Kermode include *The Uses of Error* (1991) and *An Appetite for Poetry* (1989).

▼ **Critical Viewing**
What general traits might be worthy of note in a tribute to a young king, like James I pictured here? **[Speculate]**

Assessment Resources

The following resources can be used to enrich or extend the instruction for the Contemporary Commentary.

Unit 2 Resources
  Frank Kermode, p. 84
  Listening and Viewing, p. 85
See It! DVD
  Frank Kermode, Segment 2

PHLit Online! All assessment resources are available at **www.PHLitOnline.com.**

The Actions of a Common Man The reason why Macbeth's soliloquy is so famous is not that it concerns the early history of Scotland, and the foundation of the Stuart dynasty, but that it gives incomparably vivid expression to an acute crisis of conscience. For a moment, Macbeth is every man or woman, who must, in the course of his or her life, be faced by the need to decide which of two choices is the right one.

The language of this soliloquy is sometimes unusual and full of feverish excitement. But, at first, do not bother too much about the details; just allow yourself to be swept along by the movement of passionate thought.

This soliloquy indicates the extraordinary range and flexibility of the play's language, incomparably greater than English could have provided even fifty or sixty years before. This new fluency owes something to sixteenth-century Bible translations.

Religious and Ethical Thought As this soliloquy also reflects, *Macbeth* is notable for complying with native ethical traditions. Shakespeare is not often explicitly religious, but Macbeth speaks as one aware of the Christian religion—he understands the danger to his soul, yet gives his "eternal jewel" to "the common enemy of man" (3.1.68–69). Behind such remarks there is a great weight of religious and ethical thought.

"He's here in double trust:
First, as I am his kinsman and his subject,
Strong both against the deed; then, as his host,
Who should against his murderer shut the door,
Not bear the knife myself. Besides, this Duncan
Hath borne his faculties so meek, hath been
So clear in his great office, that his virtues
Will plead like angels, trumpet-tongue'd, against
The deep damnation of his taking-off . . .
 I have no spur
To prick the sides of my intent, but only
Vaulting ambition, which o'erleaps itself
And falls on th'other." — *Macbeth*, Act I, Scene vii

Critical Reading

1. **Key Ideas and Details (a)** What English king did Shakespeare intend to honor by writing *Macbeth?* **(b) Speculate:** What benefits might a company of actors and playwrights reap by presenting their king in a favorable light?

2. **Key Ideas and Details (a)** According to Kermode, what reason does Macbeth provide for wanting to kill King Duncan? **(b) Speculate:** If, in the course of the play, Macbeth is punished for killing the king, what message might this send to the audience in Shakespeare's day?

As You Read Macbeth . . .

3. **Integration of Knowledge and Ideas** Note moments in which Banquo and most kings in the play are presented in a positive light as a way to honor James I of England.

4. **Integration of Knowledge and Ideas** Look for evidence that supports Kermode's characterization of Macbeth as "every man or woman . . . faced by the need to decide which of two choices is the right one."

The Actions of a Common Man

1. Have students read Macbeth's soliloquy and Kermode's explanation of its importance.

2. Then **ask:** What does Macbeth's speech reveal about his feelings regarding the murder he is about to perform?
   Answer: Macbeth is conflicted because he knows that murdering Duncan will violate the laws of kinship and hospitality. He recognizes that he is driven by ambition.

Religious and Ethical Thought

Encourage students to look for other instances of references to religious or ethical thoughts as they read *Macbeth*. Discuss how the weight of religious defiance affects Macbeth's conscience and actions.

ASSESS

Answers

Before students respond, you may wish to have them write a brief objective summary of the selection. As they answer the questions below, remind them to support their answers with evidence from the text.

1. (a) Shakespeare intended to honor King James, the Scottish king, by writing *Macbeth*. (b) Actors who presented their king in a favorable light might be invited to perform for the king. Royal performances might receive more publicity and increase their company's attendance.

2. (a) Macbeth is ambitious and wants to kill Duncan so he can advance himself. (b) Macbeth's punishment might send the message not to challenge the king's authority.

❶ Background

Overview: The Author's Work

Like Chaucer before him, Shakespeare was a gifted story-teller—of others' stories. Most of the stories portrayed in his dramas had already been told before. In Shakespeare's hands, however, these stories became instruments of a new knowledge. Rummaging through old histories and legends, Shakespeare found the tools he needed to lay bare the human condition. His success has guaranteed him a central place in Western culture.

His ability to use just the right word or phrase is evident in the many familiar expressions first penned by the Bard of Avon: "Now is the winter of our discontent . . ." (Richard III); ". . . parting is such sweet sorrow . . ." (Romeo and Juliet); ". . . it was Greek to me" (Julius Caesar); "All the world's a stage . . ." (As You Like It).

Although best known as a play-wright, Shakespeare also wrote 154 sonnets and 2 narrative poems, "Venus and Adonis," (1593) and "The Rape of Lucrece" (1594), as well as another long poem, "The Phoenix and the Turtle."

❶ WILLIAM SHAKESPEARE
(1564–1616)

Because of his deep understanding of human nature, his compassion for all types of people, and the power and beauty of his language, William Shakespeare is regarded as the greatest writer in English. Nearly four hundred years after his death, Shakespeare's plays continue to be read widely and produced throughout the world. They have the same powerful impact on today's audiences as they had when they were first staged.

THE PLAYWRIGHT IN HIS OWN TIME

It is a myth that we know absolutely nothing about Shakespeare's life. As critic Irving Ribner attests, "we know more about him than we do about virtually any other of his contemporary dramatists, with the exception of Ben Jonson." Shakespeare was born on April 23, 1564, in Stratford-on-Avon,

"The poet's eye, in a fine frenzy rolling,
Doth glance from heaven to earth, from earth
*   to heaven;*
And, as imagination bodies forth
The forms of things unknown, the poet's pen
Turns them to shapes, and gives to airy nothing
A local habitation and a name."

—William Shakespeare,
from A Midsummer Night's Dream

316 Celebrating Humanity (1485–1625)

ⓒ Text Complexity Rubric

Macbeth		
Qualitative Measures		
Context/Knowledge Demands	Five-act drama; historical knowledge demands 1 2 ③ 4 5	
Structure/Language Conventionality and Clarity	Archaic diction and syntax 1 2 3 ④ 5	
Levels of Meaning/ Purpose/Concept Level	Accessible (ambition) 1 2 ③ 4 5	
Quantitative Measures		
Lexile	NP	
	Text Length	18,031 words
Overall Complexity	**More complex**	

Reader and Task Suggestions

Preparing to Read the Text
- Using the information on SE p. 319, explain that Shakespeare wrote *Macbeth* in part to please King James I, a Scot.
- Remind students that stage directions will help them visualize setting and events.
- Guide students to use Multidraft Reading strategies to deepen their comprehension (TE p. 317).

Leveled Tasks
Structure/Language If students will have difficulty understanding the play's language, have them focus first to sense the flow of action. On second reading they should focus on characters' behavior and motivations.

Synthesizing If students will not have great difficulty with the play's language, have them read each scene several times to get a full appreciation of the dialogue and characterization.

which is northwest of London. (The date is based on a record of his baptism on April 26.) Stratford, with a population of about two thousand in Shakespeare's day, was the market town for a fertile agricultural region.

Shakespeare's father, John, was a successful glove maker and businessman who held a number of positions in the town's government. His mother, whose maiden name was Mary Arden, was the daughter of John's landlord. Their marriage, therefore, boosted the Shakespeare family's holdings. Nevertheless, there is evidence that in the late 1570s, John Shakespeare began to suffer financial reverses.

SHAKESPEARE'S EDUCATION

No written evidence of Shakespeare's boyhood exists—not even a name on a school attendance list. However, given his father's status, it is highly probable that he attended the Stratford Grammar School, where he acquired a knowledge of Latin.

Although Shakespeare did not go on to study at a university, his attendance at the grammar school from ages seven to sixteen would have provided him with a good education. Discipline at such a school was strict, and the school day lasted from 6:00 A.M. in the summer (7:00 in the winter) until 5:00 P.M. From 11:00 to 1:00, students were dismissed to eat lunch with their families. At 3:00, they were allowed to play for a quarter of an hour!

SHAKESPEARE'S MARRIAGE AND FAMILY

Shakespeare's name enters the official records again in November 1582, when he received a license to marry Anne Hathaway. The couple had a

Speaking Shakespeare

You may not realize the extent to which you already "speak" Shakespeare. For example, have you ever used or heard any of these phrases used in *Macbeth*?

He's full of *milk of human kindness* (I, v, 17)
Don't worry about it, *what's done is done!* (II, ii, 12)
That will last until *the crack of doom.* (IV, i, 117)
She finished the jobs in *one fell swoop.* (IV, iii, 219)

Shakespeare invented each of these now common phrases, which were unknown in English before their appearance in *Macbeth*. Look for them as you read and discover if their meanings have changed since Shakespeare's time.

William Shakespeare **317**

Daily Bellringer

For each class during which you will teach the play, have students complete one of the five activities for the appropriate week in the *Daily Bellringer Activities* booklet.

Multidraft Reading

To assist struggling readers and to enhance reading for all, assign the text in chunks, as warranted by length, and apply multidraft reading protocols. For each reading, have students set the purpose indicated:

- **First reading**—identifying key ideas and details and answering any Reading Checks.
- **Second reading**—analyzing craft and structure and responding to the side-column prompts.
- **Third reading**—integrating knowledge and ideas, connecting to other texts and the world, and answering the end-of-selection questions.

For more guidance, refer to the *Classroom Strategies and Teaching Routines* card on multidraft reading.

Differentiated Instruction for Universal Access

Enrichment for Advanced Readers

There is a persistent argument in some circles that Shakespeare did not actually write the plays attributed to him. Those who make this argument overlook the fact that everyone who knew Shakespeare acknowledged him as the author. Ben Jonson, a contemporary and one of Shakespeare's more vocal critics, wrote that Shakespeare was a naturally gifted writer who lacked discipline—but Jonson never questioned his authorship. In an era when gossip was a national pastime, it seems unlikely that Jonson and Shakespeare's many theatrical associates would have kept such a secret quiet.

Activity: A Shakespeare Summary To help students organize their knowledge about Shakespeare, have pairs or groups of students research and record information about his life and works. Suggest that they record information in the **Enrichment: Analyzing a Literary Figure** worksheet, *Professional Development Guidebook,* page 235. Have groups share the events and works they recorded. You may wish to have students create a timeline and chart of Shakespeare's works on the board.

Background

The Writer in His Time

England, with a population of about three million, was largely rural during Shakespeare's time. The English economy was largely based on agricultural products, with wool being the most important. Sharp social and economic divisions separated the wealthy landowning classes from poor farm laborers.

During the reign of Queen Elizabeth I, England underwent significant political, religious, and social change. Henry VIII, Elizabeth's father, had created an unstable religious situation, separating England from the Catholic Church to get a divorce from his wife Catherine. When Elizabeth's half-sister Mary became queen, she returned England to Catholicism and even had Elizabeth imprisoned on suspicion of aiding the Protestant cause. Mary died childless, and Elizabeth became queen. She ratified her father's decision, establishing the Church of England as the official church of England with herself at its head, thereby ensuring the enmity of the Catholic powers of the world, including mighty Spain.

During Shakespeare's time, England felt the constant threat of an invasion by Spain, whose heavily armed galleons ruled the seas. When in 1588, the feared Spanish armada, retreating from a battle with England, shipwrecked in a storm, the English took it as a sign of God's favor.

The messy political intrigues of the day and the anxious question of who will rule, together with a new-found English self-confidence, find echoes in Shakespeare's plays. Questions of legitimate rule and of the nature of social bonds abound there. In the end, his resolution of these questions may lie in a tragic self-knowledge. England blossomed in the Elizabethan Era, and Shakespeare celebrates his land, but his awareness of the ambiguities of power is pervasive and compelling.

daughter, Susanna, in 1583, and twins, Judith and Hamnet, in 1585. Beyond names and years in which his children were born, we know little about his family life. Some writers have made much of the fact that Shakespeare left his wife and children behind when he went to London not long after his twins were born. However, he visited his family in Stratford regularly during his years as a playwright, and they may have lived with him for a time in London.

ACTOR AND PLAYWRIGHT

It is uncertain how Shakespeare became connected with the theater in the late 1580s and early 1590s. By 1594, however, he had become a part owner and the principal playwright of the Lord Chamberlain's Men, one of the most successful theater companies in London.

In 1599, the company built the famous Globe theater on the south bank of the Thames River, in Southwark. This is where most of

The painting below presents a view of London from the south during Shakespeare's lifetime. Londoners from all walks of life used the Thames River for transportation and recreation. Church spires dominated the skyline of the north bank. London Bridge provided a means of crossing the Thames, as well a popular location for shops and homes. In order to avoid city restrictions, many theaters (including the Globe, pictured to the left) were built beyond the city limits, on the south bank of the river.

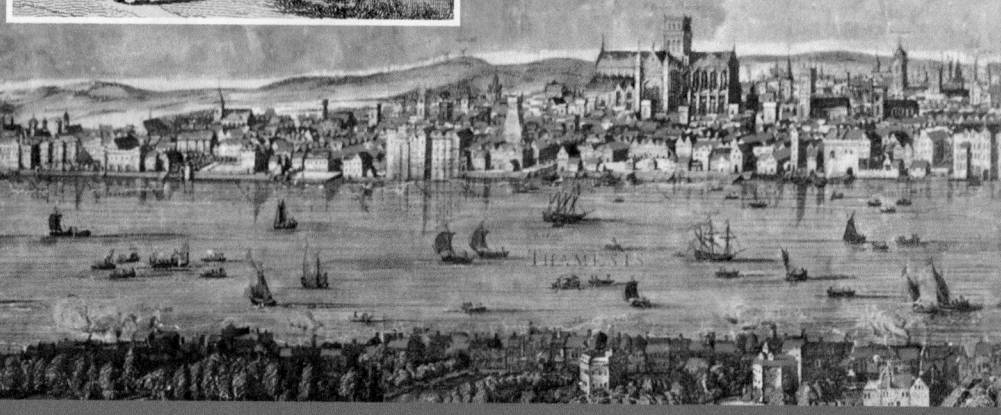

318 Celebrating Humanity (1485–1625)

Shakespeare's plays were performed. When James I became king in 1603, after the death of Elizabeth I, James took control of the Lord Chamberlain's Men and renamed the company the King's Men.

RETIREMENT

In about 1610, Shakespeare retired to Stratford, where he continued to write plays. He was a prosperous middle-class man, who profited from his share in a successful theater company. Six years later, on April 23, 1616, he died and was buried in Holy Trinity Church in Stratford. Because it was a common practice to move bodies after burial to make room for others, Shakespeare wrote the following as his epitaph:

> Blest be the man that spares these stones,
> And curst be he that moves my bones.

HIS LITERARY RECORD

Shakespeare did not think of himself as a man of letters. He wrote his plays to be performed and did not bring out editions of them for the reading public. The first published edition of his work, called the First Folio, was issued in 1623 by two members of his theater company, John Heminges and Henry Condell. It contained thirty-six of the thirty-seven plays now attributed to him.

Shakespeare's varied output includes romantic comedies, like *A Midsummer Night's Dream* and *As You Like It*; history plays, like *Henry IV*, Parts 1 and 2; tragedies, like *Romeo and Juliet, Hamlet, Othello, King Lear,* and *Macbeth*; and later romances, like *The Tempest*. In addition to his plays, he wrote 154 sonnets and three longer poems.

Background
More About the Author

The known facts regarding Shakespeare's life tell us little about him as a person. Born in April 1564 in Stratford-on-Avon, Shakespeare probably attended grammar school there. The principal subject of Elizabethan grammar school was Latin, so Shakespeare no doubt read the works of Cicero, Ovid, and Virgil. Frequent allusions are made to such classics in his works.

Shakespeare showed so much talent early in his career that he elicited the envy of other playwrights. Robert Greene, a contemporary of Shakespeare's, called Shakespeare ". . . an upstart crow, beautified with our feathers, that with his Tiger's heart wrapped in a player's hide, supposes he is as well able to bombast out a blank verse as the best of you: and being an absolute *Johannes fac totum,* is in his own conceit the only Shake-scene in a country."

In 1582, Shakespeare married Anne Hathaway. They had three children. Shakespeare died in Stratford-on-Avon in 1616 and was buried near the altar in the church. His wife died seven years later.

William Shakespeare **319**

Differentiated
Instruction   for Universal Access

Enrichment for Gifted/Talented

The Globe Theater is one of three theaters in London associated with William Shakespeare. The Globe was largely owned by a group of actors and other theater-folk, including Shakespeare.

Have students work in pairs to research the history of the original Globe Theater and its modern reconstruction. Ask pairs to make a diagram or three-dimensional model of the Globe. Have pairs present their material to the class.

For more about Shakespeare, additional background, and a **Get Connected!** video, go online at www.PHLitOnline.com.

The following is Holinshed's version of Macbeth's encounter with the three witches:

Shortly after happened a strange and uncouth wonder, which afterward was the case of much trouble in the realm of Scotland, as ye shall after hear. It fortuned as Macbeth and Banquo journeyed toward Forres, where the king then lay, they went sporting by the way together without other company, save only themselves, passing through the woods and fields, when suddenly in the midst of a laund [lawn, open place] there met them three women in strange and wild apparel, resembling creatures of elder world, whom when they attentively beheld, wondering much at the sight, the first of them spake and said: "All hail, Macbeth, Thane of Glammis!" (for he had lately entered into that dignity and office by the death of his father Sinell). The second of them said: "Hail, Macbeth, Thane of Cawdor!" But the third said: "All hail, Macbeth, that hereafter shall be King of Scotland!"

❶ MACBETH
SHAKESPEARE'S SOURCES

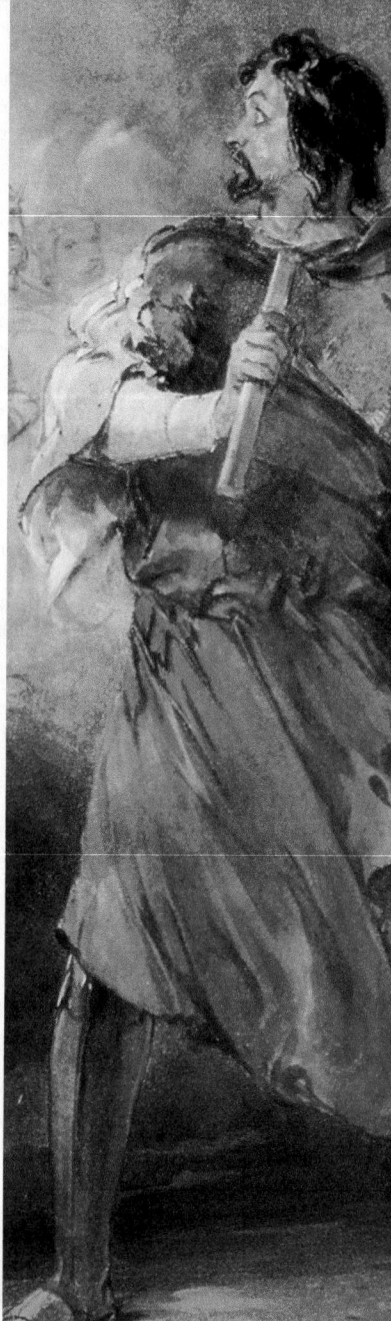

FACT AND LEGEND

By Shakespeare's time, the story of the eleventh-century Scottish king Macbeth was a mixture of fact and legend. Shakespeare and his contemporaries, however, probably regarded the account of Macbeth in Raphael Holinshed's *Chronicles of England, Scotland, and Ireland* as completely factual. The playwright drew on the *Chronicles* as a source for the play, yet, as you will see, he freely adapted the material for his own purposes.

HOLINSHED'S CHRONICLES

Holinshed's account contains a description of a meeting between Macbeth and the witches. His account also tells how Macbeth and his friends, angry at the naming of King Duncan's son Malcolm as Prince of Cumberland, ambush and slay Duncan. However, the historical Macbeth's claim to the throne has some basis. (See page 408 for an explanation of the ancient Scottish custom of choosing kings.) Finally, Holinshed indicates that Banquo is Macbeth's accomplice in the assassination. Lady Macbeth, prominent in Shakespeare's play, does not play a significant role in Holinshed.

SHAKESPEARE'S MACBETH

Shakespeare took what he needed from the *Chronicles* and shaped it into a tragic plot. Seeing the theatrical possibilities of the meeting with the witches, Shakespeare staged such an encounter in Act I, Scene iii. However, he changed Holinshed's account in order to make King Duncan an innocent victim: Shakespeare's Macbeth does not have a legitimate claim to the throne. Further, Shakespeare used another story in the *Chronicles*—one in which a wife urges her husband to kill a friend and guest—as the basis for the character Lady Macbeth. She becomes Macbeth's co-conspirator, replacing Banquo. Shakespeare, of course, had political motives for holding Banquo innocent. Banquo was considered the ancestor of the new king, James I!

Vocabulary Development

Vocabulary Knowledge Rating

Create a **Vocabulary Knowledge Rating Chart** (*Professional Development Guidebook*, p. 33) for the vocabulary words on the student page. Give each student a copy of the chart with the words on it. Read the words aloud, and have students mark their rating of each in the Before Reading column. Urge students to attend to these words as they read and discuss the selection.

In order to gauge how much instruction you need to provide, tally how many students are confident in their knowledge of each word. As students read, point out the words and their context.

PHLit Online! **Vocabulary Central**, featuring tools and activities for studying vocabulary, is available online at www.PHLitOnline.com.

Before You Read   *Macbeth, Act I*

❷ Connecting to the Essential Question In *Macbeth*, a noble person's downfall results from a character flaw. As you read, note that *Macbeth*, unlike classical tragedies, includes comedy in its portrayal of a noble character's downfall. Finding such moments will help you answer the Essential Question: **What is the relationship of the writer to tradition?**

❸ Literary Analysis

During the late 1500s, **Elizabethan drama** blossomed. Using models from ancient Greece and Rome, writers reintroduced **tragedies**—plays in which disaster befalls a character. Dramatists also began writing their plays in carefully crafted unrhymed verse, using rich language and vivid imagery.

Because the Globe, like other Elizabethan theaters, had no lighting, plays were performed in broad daylight. There were also no sets, so the words of the play had to create the illusion of time and place for the audience.

Playwrights made key choices about how to develop and relate character. One device they used was called a **soliloquy,** a long speech usually made by a character who is alone (the Latin *solus* means "alone"). This speech reveals thoughts and feelings to the audience. In Shakespeare's tragedies, the greatest works of Elizabethan drama, tragic characters reveal secret desires or fears through their soliloquies.

As you read the following soliloquies in this act, note the inner struggles each reveals.

- Lady Macbeth's soliloquy, Act I, Scene v, lines 1–30
- Macbeth's soliloquy, Act I, Scene vii, lines 1–28

❹ Reading Strategy

Ⓒ Preparing to Read Complex Texts Like many dramas, Shakespeare's plays were meant to be performed, not read. By **analyzing information from text features** like introductory *background notes*, *stage directions* in brackets, *illustrations*, and *footnotes* on the side of the text, you can picture the action in your mind. You can also better understand the meaning and tone of the characters' words. Use a chart like the one shown to analyze information from text features and clarify the meaning of passages.

❺ Vocabulary

valor (val′ ər) *n.* bravery (p. 324)

treasons (trē′ zənz) *n.* betrayals of one's country (p. 330)

imperial (im pir′ ē əl) *adj.* having supreme authority (p. 330)

surmise (sər mīz′) *n.* imaginings; speculation (p. 331)

sovereign (säv′ rən) *adj.* supreme in power or authority (p. 336)

Common Core State Standards

Reading Literature
3. Analyze the impact of the author's choices regarding how to develop and relate elements of a story or drama.

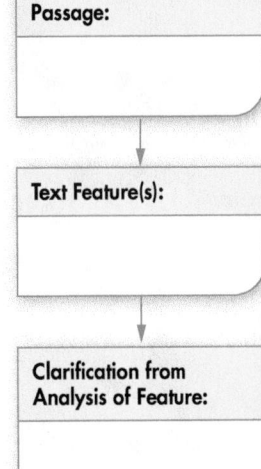

Passage:

Text Feature(s):

Clarification from Analysis of Feature:

Macbeth, Act I **321**

---

❷ Connecting to the Essential Question

1. Review the assignment with the class.

2. Lead students in discussing ways a person's flaws, such as overconfidence, can bring about his or her downfall. Then, have them complete the assignment.

3. As students read, have them look for moments of comedy.

❸ Literary Analysis

1. Introduce the skills using the instruction on the student page.

2. Give students **Literary Analysis Graphic Organizer B**, page 53 in *Graphic Organizer Transparencies,* to use as they read *Macbeth,* Act 1.

Think Aloud: Model the Skill

Say to students:

If I overhear a friend muttering to himself, "That's not fair," I know I am hearing the truth—my friend's thoughts, born of some internal struggle, uttered aloud. When Shakespeare wants to show the conflicting energies driving his heroes, he gives them voice in a soliloquy. These speeches are more complicated than a muttered remark, but they have the same urgency, and the same power to reveal. I can learn much about Macbeth from his soliloquies.

❹ Reading Strategy

Introduce the strategy using the instruction on the student page.

Think Aloud: Model the Skill

Say to students:

When I need help understanding a knotty sentence in Shakespeare, I look for a gloss, or note, that explains the meaning of his words. Other text features, such as background notes, can help me fill in the big picture.

❺ Vocabulary

1. Pronounce each word, giving its definition, and have students say it aloud.

2. For more guidance, see the *Classroom Strategies and Teaching Routines* card for introducing vocabulary.

PHLit Online! www.PHLitOnline.com

Teaching From Technology

Preparing to Read
Go to **PHLitOnline.com** and display the **Get Connected!** slideshow for this selection. Have the class brainstorm for responses to the writing prompt, entering ideas in the interactive journal. Then, have students complete their written responses as homework.
To build background, display the Background and More About the Author feature.

Using the Interactive Text
Go to **www.PHLitOnline.com** and display the **Enriched Online Student Edition.** As the class reads the selection or listens to the narration, record answers to side-column prompts using the graphic organizers accessible on the interactive page. Alternatively, have students use the online edition individually, answering the prompts as they read.

❶ About the Selection

In *The Tragedy of Macbeth,* Act I, the war hero Macbeth returns home and, on the way, encounters three witches who prophesy that he will one day be king of Scotland. Seized by ruthless ambition and spurred on by his wife, Macbeth plans to murder King Duncan, thus setting in motion a series of events that will lead to his eventual downfall.

❷ Activating Prior Knowledge

Write the word *Fate* on the board and ask students to offer definitions. Then have students write a paragraph explaining whether they believe events occur as the result of fate, human choice, or some combination of the two.

Concept Connector ➡

Tell students they will return to their responses after reading the selection.

❸ Background

Reading Shakespeare

Many students will find Shakespeare's language a challenge. He uses words and structures not familiar to the modern ear. Underscore that the richness of the language and insights into human nature make Shakespeare worth the work.

Encourage students to watch one of the recent film versions of Shakespeare's plays to hear how the language sounds in performance. You may also wish to listen in class to the *Hear It!* **Audio CDs.**

Because some words are no longer in common use or have evolved different meanings, encourage students to refer often to the margin notes. Also, Shakespeare plays with standard English word order. When students confront a difficult sentence, they should look for the subject and verb and then determine how other sentence parts fit.

As with poetry, students should read in sentences, rather than in lines. A sentence may extend over a number of lines, so encourage students to be guided by the punctuation.

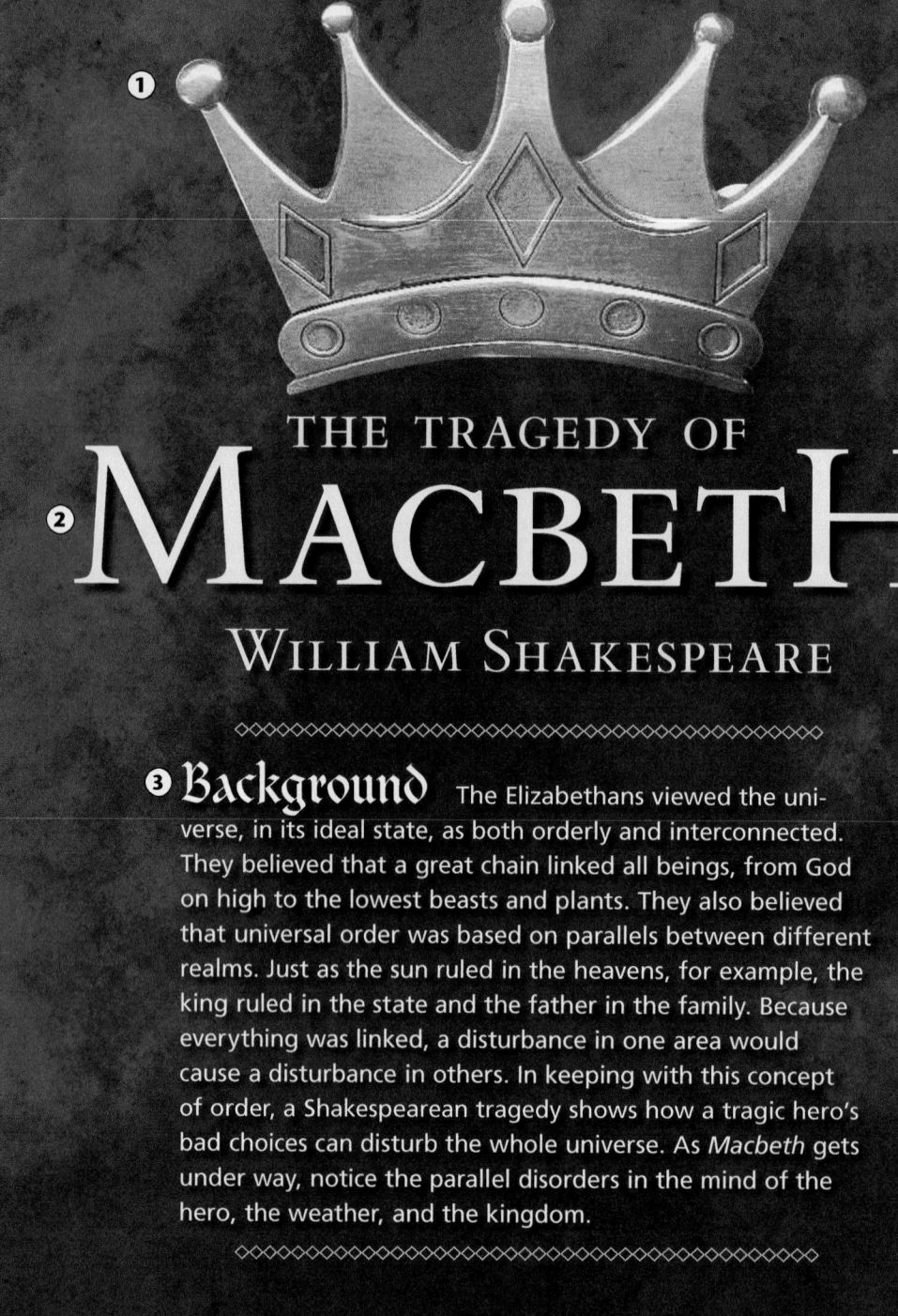

❶

THE TRAGEDY OF
❷ MACBETH
WILLIAM SHAKESPEARE

❸ **Background**   The Elizabethans viewed the universe, in its ideal state, as both orderly and interconnected. They believed that a great chain linked all beings, from God on high to the lowest beasts and plants. They also believed that universal order was based on parallels between different realms. Just as the sun ruled in the heavens, for example, the king ruled in the state and the father in the family. Because everything was linked, a disturbance in one area would cause a disturbance in others. In keeping with this concept of order, a Shakespearean tragedy shows how a tragic hero's bad choices can disturb the whole universe. As *Macbeth* gets under way, notice the parallel disorders in the mind of the hero, the weather, and the kingdom.

322 Celebrating Humanity (1485–1625)

CHARACTERS

DUNCAN, King of Scotland

MALCOLM
DONALBAIN } his sons

MACBETH
BANQUO
MACDUFF
LENNOX } noblemen
ROSS } of Scotland
MENTEITH
ANGUS
CAITHNESS

FLEANCE, son to Banquo

SIWARD, Earl of Northumberland, general of the English forces

YOUNG SIWARD, his son

SEYTON, an officer attending on Macbeth
SON TO MACDUFF
AN ENGLISH DOCTOR
A SCOTTISH DOCTOR
A PORTER
AN OLD MAN
THREE MURDERERS
LADY MACBETH
LADY MACDUFF
A GENTLEWOMAN attending on Lady Macbeth
HECATE
WITCHES
APPARITIONS
LORDS, OFFICERS, SOLDIERS, ATTENDANTS, AND MESSENGERS

Setting: Scotland; England

ACT I

Scene i. An open place.

[*Thunder and lightning. Enter* THREE WITCHES.]

FIRST WITCH. When shall we three meet again?
In thunder, lightning, or in rain?

SECOND WITCH. When the hurlyburly's done,
When the battle's lost and won.

5   **THIRD WITCH.** That will be ere the set of sun.

FIRST WITCH. Where the place?

SECOND WITCH.   Upon the heath.

THIRD WITCH. There to meet with Macbeth.

FIRST WITCH. I come, Graymalkin.[1]

SECOND WITCH. Paddock[2] calls.

THIRD WITCH.   Anon![3]

10   **ALL.** Fair is foul, and foul is fair.
Hover through the fog and filthy air.   [*Exit.*]

Scene ii. A camp near Forres, a town in northeast Scotland.

[*Alarum within.*[1] *Enter* KING DUNCAN, MALCOLM, DONALBAIN, LENNOX, *with* ATTENDANTS, *meeting a bleeding* CAPTAIN.]

Reading Strategy

Analyze Text Features

Who or what are Graymalkin and Paddock in lines 8 and 9? How do you know?

1. **Graymalkin** first witch's helper, a gray cat.

2. **Paddock** second witch's helper, a toad.

3. **Anon** at once.

1. **Alarum within** trumpet call offstage.

6 ☑ **Reading Check**

Where, when, and with whom will the witches next meet?

Macbeth, Act I, Scene i **323**

---

4 Reading Strategy

Analyze Text Features

1. Read aloud lines 7–9 ("There to... Anon!").

2. Then **ask** students the Reading Strategy question: Who or what are Graymalkin and Paddock in lines 8 and 9? How do you know? **Answer:** Graymalkin is the first witch's helper, a gray cat, and Paddock is the second witch's helper, a toad. The margin notes explain this.

3. **Ask** students what other sources they might have consulted to find this information if they had not been given the margin notes. **Possible responses:** Ideas might include illustrated books, videos of the play, or Internet sites or books that are related to Shakespeare, theatre, or the concept of witches during the era.

5 Critical Thinking

Analyze

1. Explain to the class that Shakespeare often uses rhyming couplets to end scenes. Then have students read lines 10–11.

2. **Ask** students why Shakespeare might have chosen to end the first scene with these lines. **Possible response:** The couplet reinforces the mysterious mood of the scene; the use of alliteration and the rhyme make the couplet memorable; it makes it clear that the scene is over.

6 Reading Check

Answer: The witches will meet with Macbeth upon the heath, when the hurlyburly's done and when the battle's lost and won.

Differentiated Instruction for Universal Access

Support for Special-Needs Students

Have students complete the **Before You Read** and the **Making Connections** pages for this selection in the *Reader's Notebook: Adapted Version.* These pages provide an abbreviated skills instruction, a selection summary, the Before You Read graphic organizer, and a **Note-taking Guide.**

Support for Less Proficient Readers

Have students complete the **Before You Read** and the **Making Connections** pages for this selection in the *Reader's Notebook.* These pages provide an abbreviated skills instruction, a selection summary, the Before You Read graphic organizer, and a **Note-taking Guide.**

EL **Support for English Learners**

Have students complete the **Before You Read** and the **Making Connections** pages for this selection in the *Reader's Notebook: English Learner's Version.* These pages provide additional vocabulary, vocabulary skills, and vocabulary practice, along with a **Getting Ready to Read** activity.

PHLit Online!

This selection is available in interactive format in the **Enriched Online Student Edition**, at www.PHLitOnline.com, which includes a thematically related video with writing prompt and an interactive graphic organizer.

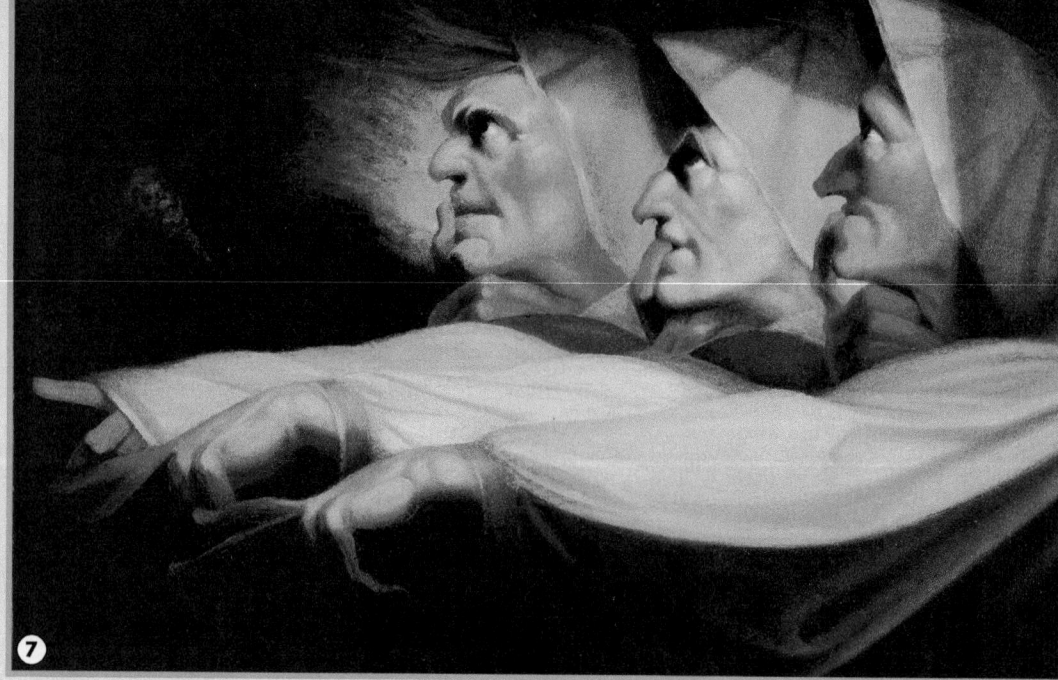

➐ Humanities

The Three Witches, 1783, by Henry Fuseli

Henry Fuseli (1741–1825), a Swiss-born English artist, began as a writer, but with the encouragement of Sir Joshua Reynolds, the head of the Royal Academy of Art, he began to paint. His formal art education consisted of an eight-year residence in Rome, where he studied the art of the Italian master Michelangelo. His style is a combination of romanticism, fantasy, and the grotesque. Throughout his life, Fuseli was influenced by literature, especially the works of William Shakespeare.

The strong composition is enhanced by the rhythm of the three outstretched arms ending in talon-like hands.

Use these questions for discussion:

1. Read Banquo's description of the witches in lines 40–47 of Scene 3. Is Fuseli's painting faithful to this description?
Possible response: The witches appear to be withered, with choppy fingers and skinny lips, as described by Banquo.

2. Does this painting give you a better understanding of the fright felt by the characters upon encountering the witches?
Possible responses: Yes, they certainly seem strange; no, they are merely old women, nothing to be afraid of.

➑ Critical Viewing

Possible response: Fuseli's shrouding of the witches in darkness and his repetition of the same mysterious gesture captures the eerie mood of their presence in Act 1, Scene 1.

➑ ▲ **Critical Viewing** Examine Fuseli's rendering of the witches. Does the mood he creates correspond to the mood in Act I, Scene i? Why or why not? **[Connect]**

2. **sergeant** officer.

3. **broil** battle.

4. **choke their art** prevent each other from swimming.

5. **Western Isles** the Hebrides, off Scotland.

6. **Of kerns and gallowglasses** with lightly armed Irish foot soldiers and heavily armed soldiers.

7. **damned quarrel** accursed cause.

8. **Showed . . . whore** falsely appeared to favor Macdonwald.

9. **minion** favorite.

Vocabulary
valor (val′ ər) *n.* marked courage or bravery

KING. What bloody man is that? He can report,
As seemeth by his plight, of the revolt
The newest state.

MALCOLM.   This is the sergeant[2]
Who like a good and hardy soldier fought
'Gainst my captivity. Hail, brave friend!
Say to the king the knowledge of the broil[3]
As thou didst leave it.

CAPTAIN.   Doubtful it stood,
As two spent swimmers, that do cling together
And choke their art.[4] The merciless Macdonwald—
Worthy to be a rebel for to that
The multiplying villainies of nature
Do swarm upon him—from the Western Isles[5]
Of kerns and gallowglasses[6] is supplied;
And fortune, on his damnéd quarrel[7] smiling,
Showed like a rebel's whore:[8] but all's too weak:
For brave Macbeth—well he deserves that name—
Disdaining fortune, with his brandished steel,
Which smoked with bloody execution,
Like valor's minion[9] carved out his passage

5

10

15

324 Celebrating Humanity (1485–1625)

Enrichment: Analyzing Historical Patterns, Trends, and Periods

Witchcraft in the English Renaissance

Scholars believe that one reason Shakespeare included witches in *Macbeth* is the fact that the king, James I, had openly expressed his belief in witches. Witchcraft was a topic of controversy in seventeenth-century Europe and America. Some regarded the existence of witches to be nothing more than a harmless superstition. Others felt witches to be real and a source of evil that had to be wiped out.

As a result, waves of hysteria over witches swept over the land. Between the fifteenth and eighteenth centuries, thousands of people were convicted of being witches and executed.

Activity: Investigate Witch Executions Have pairs or groups of students conduct research on the reasons for and effects of witch executions in this period, as well as significant examples and other related events. Suggest that they record information in the **Enrichment: Analyzing Historical Patterns, Trends, and Periods** worksheet, *Professional Development Guidebook*, page 231.

20 Till he faced the slave;
Which nev'r shook hands, nor bade farewell to him,
Till he unseamed him from the nave to th' chops,[10]
And fixed his head upon our battlements.

KING. O valiant cousin! Worthy gentleman!

25 CAPTAIN. As whence the sun 'gins his reflection[11]
Shipwracking storms and direful thunders break,
So from that spring whence comfort seemed to come
Discomfort swells. Mark, King of Scotland, mark:
No sooner justice had, with valor armed,
30 Compelled these skipping kerns to trust their heels
But the Norweyan lord,[12] surveying vantage,[13]
With furbished arms and new supplies of men,
Began a fresh assault.

KING.   Dismayed not this
Our captains, Macbeth and Banquo?

CAPTAIN.   Yes;
35 As sparrows eagles, or the hare the lion.
If I say sooth,[14] I must report they were
As cannons overcharged with double cracks;[15]
So they doubly redoubled strokes upon the foe.
Except[16] they meant to bathe in reeking wounds,
40 Or memorize another Golgotha,[17]
I cannot tell—
But I am faint; my gashes cry for help.

KING. So well thy words become thee as thy wounds;
They smack of honor both. Go get him surgeons.

[Exit CAPTAIN, attended.]

[Enter ROSS and ANGUS.]
Who comes here?

45 MALCOLM.   The worthy Thane[18] of Ross.

LENNOX. What a haste looks through his eyes! So should he look
That seems to[19] speak things strange.

ROSS.   God save the king!

KING. Whence cam'st thou, worthy Thane?

ROSS.   From Fife, great King;
Where the Norweyan banners flout the sky
50 And fan our people cold.
Norway[20] himself, with terrible numbers,
Assisted by that most disloyal traitor
The Thane of Cawdor, began a dismal[21] conflict;
Till that Bellona's bridegroom, lapped in proof,[22]

Literary Analysis
Elizabethan Drama
What offstage scene does
the captain describe in this
speech (lines 7–23)?

10. **unseamed . . . chops**
split him open from the
navel to the jaws.

11. **'gins his reflection**
rises.

12. **Norweyan lord** king of
Norway.

13. **surveying vantage**
seeing an opportunity.

14. **sooth** truth.

15. **cracks** explosives.

16. **except** unless.

17. **memorize . . . Golgotha**
(gôl´ gə thə) make the
place as memorable for
slaughter as Golgotha, the
place where Christ was
crucified.

18. **Thane** Scottish title
of nobility.

19. **seems to** seems about to.

20. **Norway** king of Norway.

21. **dismal** threatening.

22. **Bellona's . . . proof**
Macbeth is called the mate
of Bellona, the goddess of
war, clad in tested armor.

Literary Analysis
Elizabethan Drama
How do Lennox's words here
(lines 46–47) supply a clue
for the actor playing Ross?

Reading Check
What role has Macbeth
played in the battle?

Macbeth, Act I, Scene ii **325**

---

9 Literary Analysis
Elizabethan Drama

1. Have a student volunteer read the Captain's speech in lines 7–23.

2. Then **ask** students the first Literary Analysis question: What offstage scene does the Captain describe in this speech? **Answer:** The Captain describes a battle between Macdonwald and Macbeth in which Macbeth was victorious.

3. **Ask** students why Shakespeare might have chosen to have a character relate this scene rather than have it performed. **Possible responses:** The battle would have been difficult to represent on stage; the story of the battle serves mainly to introduce Macbeth's character and reputation, so it was not necessary to show it.

10 Literary Analysis
Elizabethan Drama

1. Explain to students that most of the audience in the Globe would not have been close enough to the stage to see the small details of actors' facial expressions. These nuances were often conveyed through dialogue and through the characters' actions on stage. Then read aloud Lennox's words in lines 46–47.

2. **Ask** students the second Literary Analysis question: How do Lennox's words here supply a clue for the actor playing Ross? **Possible responses:** The comment that haste looks through Ross's eyes and that he looks like he is going to speak strange things would be clues to the actor playing Ross that there is a sense of urgency in his behavior. He should probably look excited, as if he were eager to share what he knows. It might also suggest that he would enter quickly, because he has important news.

11 Reading Check

Answer: Macbeth was the hero of the day, killing Macdonwald in hand-to-hand combat, then helping to defeat the Norwegians.

Differentiated Instruction for Universal Access

Support for Special-Needs Students
To help students understand the role of soliloquies in *Macbeth,* show them **Literary Analysis Graphic Organizer A** (*Graphic Organizer Transparencies*, p. 52). This partially filled in sample will model how to interpret the details of a soliloquy to understand a character. Students can use the completed graphic organizer as a model for making further interpretations.

Enrichment for Gifted/Talented Students
Students may enjoy exploring aspects of early Scottish society. Encourage them to research one of the many colorful, often highly visual symbols associated with Scotland, such as tartans, clan emblems, flags, highland dress, Scottish landscapes, bagpipes, weapons, or military dances (for example, the sword dance). Have them prepare displays, collages, or demonstrations to share with the class what they discover. (If you need resources, many cities have Scottish societies that would assist you or your students with this effort.)

Analyze Information from Text Features

1. Point out the text aids that open Scene 3.

2. Then **ask** students the Reading Strategy question: What information about the setting for Scene 3 do you learn from the italicized stage directions?
   Answer: The stage directions state that the scene takes place on a heath near Forres; thunder sounds, and the three witches enter.

3. Explain that a heath is an open wasteland with heather or low bushes growing on it, but few or no trees. It is similar to what the English call a moor.

4. **Ask** students how standing in an open wasteland enhances the eeriness of the scene.
   Possible response: The characters are exposed and unprotected from the lightning and thunder. Also, it makes the appearance of the witches more surprising.

⓭ Critical Thinking

Draw Conclusions

1. Have students read the first witch's speech in lines 3–10 to themselves.

2. **Ask** students what they think the first witch means by "I'll do, I'll do, and I'll do" in line 10.
   Possible responses: She'll seek to injure the sailor to get revenge on the sailor's wife.

3. **Ask** students what is being established about the witches in Scene 3.
   Possible response: The witches are evil, murderous, and destructive.

---

23. self-comparisons counter movements.

24. lavish insolent.

25. composition terms of peace.

26. St. Colme's Inch island near Edinburgh, Scotland.

27. our bosom interest my heart's trust.

28. present immediate.

Reading Strategy
Analyze Information from Text Features
What information about the setting for Scene iii do you learn from the italicized ⓬ stage directions?

1. Killing swine It was commonly believed that witches killed domestic animals.

2. Aroint thee Be off. ⓭

3. rump-fed ronyon fat-rumped, scabby creature.

4. Aleppo trading center in Syria.

5. sieve It was commonly believed that witches often sailed in sieves.

6. rat . . . tail According to popular belief, witches could assume the form of any animal, but the tail would always be missing.

7. they blow to which the winds blow.

8. card compass.

9. penthouse lid eyelid.

10. forbid cursed.

---

55 Confronted him with self-comparisons,[23]
Point against point, rebellious arm 'gainst arm,
Curbing his lavish[24] spirit: and, to conclude,
The victory fell on us.

KING.   Great happiness!

ROSS.   That now
Sweno, the Norways' king, craves composition;[25]
60 Nor would we deign him burial of his men
Till he disbursed, at Saint Colme's Inch,[26]
Ten thousand dollars to our general use.

KING. No more that Thane of Cawdor shall deceive
Our bosom interest:[27] go pronounce his present[28] death,
65 And with his former title greet Macbeth.

ROSS. I'll see it done.

KING. What he hath lost, noble Macbeth hath won.

                                                [*Exit.*]

Scene iii. A heath near Forres. ⓬

[*Thunder. Enter the* THREE WITCHES.]

FIRST WITCH. Where hast thou been, sister?

SECOND WITCH. Killing swine.[1]

THIRD WITCH. Sister, where thou?

FIRST WITCH. A sailor's wife had chestnuts in her lap,
And mounched, and mounched, and mounched.
5   "Give me," quoth I.
"Aroint thee,[2] witch!" the rump-fed ronyon[3] cries.
Her husband's to Aleppo[4] gone, master o' th' Tiger:
But in a sieve[5] I'll thither sail,
And, like a rat without a tail,[6]
10 I'll do, I'll do, and I'll do.

SECOND WITCH. I'll give thee a wind.

FIRST WITCH. Th' art kind.

THIRD WITCH. And I another.

FIRST WITCH. I myself have all the other;
15 And the very ports they blow,[7]
All the quarters that they know
I' th' shipman's card.[8]
I'll drain him dry as hay:
Sleep shall neither night nor day
20 Hang upon his penthouse lid;[9]
He shall live a man forbid:[10]

Enrichment: Investigating Geography

Scotland

After centuries of bitter hostility, Scotland and England were joined in 1707 to form Great Britain, a single kingdom. However, the Scots have retained a distinct culture that is deeply embedded in their history and the rugged terrain of the countryside. For example, the steep mountains forced Scottish highlanders to live in small groups called clans. Most clans consisted of people with the same surname, such as MacDonald, MacKinnon, and MacLeod. They each developed their own fabric pattern, or tartan, and displayed it on kilts—short skirts that made it easy to climb hills—and other clothing.

Activity: Mapping Scotland Have students create topographical maps of Scotland and Great Britain to gain an understanding of the physical setting of *Macbeth.* Suggest that they record information in the **Enrichment: Investigating Geography** worksheet, *Professional Development Guidebook,* page 228.

Weary sev'nights[11] nine times nine
Shall he dwindle, peak,[12] and pine:
Though his bark cannot be lost,
25   Yet it shall be tempest-tossed.
Look what I have.

SECOND WITCH. Show me, show me.

FIRST WITCH. Here I have a pilot's thumb,
Wracked as homeward he did come.

[*Drum within.*]

30 **THIRD WITCH.** A drum, a drum!
Macbeth doth come.

ALL. The weird[13] sisters, hand in hand,
Posters[14] of the sea and land,
Thus do go about, about:
35   Thrice to thine, and thrice to mine,
And thrice again, to make up nine.
Peace! The charm's wound up.

[*Enter* MACBETH *and* BANQUO.]

MACBETH. So foul and fair a day I have not seen.

BANQUO. How far is 't called to Forres? What are these
40   So withered, and so wild in their attire,
That look not like th' inhabitants o' th' earth,
And yet are on 't? Live you, or are you aught
That man may question? You seem to understand me,
By each at once her choppy[15] finger laying
45   Upon her skinny lips. You should be women,
And yet your beards forbid me to interpret
That you are so.

MACBETH.   Speak, if you can: what are you?

FIRST WITCH. All hail, Macbeth! Hail to thee, Thane of Glamis!

SECOND WITCH. All hail, Macbeth! Hail to thee, Thane of Cawdor!

50 **THIRD WITCH.** All hail, Macbeth, that shalt be King hereafter!

BANQUO. Good sir, why do you start, and seem to fear
Things that do sound so fair? I' th' name of truth,
Are you fantastical,[16] or that indeed
Which outwardly ye show? My noble partner
55   You greet with present grace[17] and great prediction
Of noble having[18] and of royal hope,
That he seems rapt withal:[19] to me you speak not.
If you can look into the seeds of time,
And say which grain will grow and which will not,

---

11. **sev'nights** weeks.
12. **peak** waste away.

13. **weird** destiny-serving.
14. **Posters** swift travelers.

Literary Analysis
Elizabethan Drama
What descriptive details does Banquo use in his speech about the witches (lines 39–47)?

15. **choppy** chapped.

16. **fantastical** imaginary.
17. **grace** honor.
18. **having** possession.
19. **rapt withal** entranced by it.

16 ✓ Reading Check
What has Macbeth earned through his exploits?

Macbeth, Act I, Scene iii **327**

---

14 Literary Analysis
Elizabethan Drama

1. Have a student volunteer read lines 39–47.

2. Then **ask** students the Literary Analysis question: What descriptive details does Banquo use in his speech about the witches? **Answer:** Banquo describes the witches as withered, wild in their dress, not human, ghostly, with dry hands and skinny lips, womanish in appearance, but with beards.

15 Engaging the Essential Question

1. Remind students that witches and witchcraft were subject to differing opinions in Shakespeare's day; King James I was a staunch believer, while others dismissed the idea. Because of this, it is likely that the first audiences for *Macbeth* consisted of people holding both views. Also remind students that the weird sisters in *Macbeth* harkened back to the Fates of Greek mythology.

2. **Ask** students whether they believe Shakespeare's portrayal of the witches was influenced more by views of witches in his culture, or by Greek ideas about the Fates. **Possible response:** Shakespeare may have combined both traditions, making his witches a trio in order to echo the Greek concept of the Fates, while also incorporating popular ideas about witches from his time and culture to satisfy his audience. By exaggerating his culture's ideas about witches and drawing attention to the trio's odd appearance, he could create humor.

16 Reading Check

Answer: Macbeth has earned a new title, Thane of Cawdor, through his exploits.

---

⑰ Humanities

Macbeth and the Witches, by Clarkson Stanfield

Clarkson Stanfield (1793–1867) did not start out as a painter. He was a sailor who passed time on board ship by painting, drawing marine scenes, and making scenery for the sailors' plays. Upon leaving the navy, Stanfield took a job as a scene painter in a London theater. There, he gained an outstanding reputation for his painted scenery. This watercolor, *Macbeth and the Witches,* was done for a production of *Macbeth* at one of the theaters in which Stanfield worked. It was painted between 1813 and 1829. This skillfully executed design serves to explain the popularity Stanfield enjoyed in theater circles.

⑱ Critical Viewing

Answer: The soldier on the right seems taller and appears to be more nobly attired, suggesting that this soldier is Macbeth.

⑲ Literary Analysis

Elizabethan Drama

1. After students have read through line 109, **ask** them what Banquo and Macbeth have learned in this scene.
   Answer: They have learned that the witches predict that Macbeth will become Thane of Cawdor and king, while Banquo will have descendants that become kings.

2. Then **ask** students the Literary Analysis question: How could Elizabethan actors have made this scene with the witches mysterious without help from special lighting effects?
   Possible responses: Actors could make this scene mysterious with actions and voices. The witches could act threatening and other-worldly. Macbeth and Banquo could act shaken, horrified, and disbelieving. They could show shock at the entrance and disappearance of the witches.

⑰

⑱ ▲ **Critical Viewing** Which of the two soldiers on the right do you think is Macbeth? Explain your reasoning. **[Deduce]**

⑲ **Literary Analysis**
Elizabethan Drama
How could Elizabethan actors have made this scene with the witches mysterious without help from special lighting effects?

20. **happy** fortunate.

21. **imperfect** incomplete.

22. **Sinel's** (sī´ nelz) Macbeth's father's.

23. **owe** own.

24. **intelligence** information.

60   Speak then to me, who neither beg nor fear
       Your favors nor your hate.

      FIRST WITCH. Hail!

      SECOND WITCH. Hail!

      THIRD WITCH. Hail!

65 **FIRST WITCH.** Lesser than Macbeth, and greater.

      SECOND WITCH. Not so happy,[20] yet much happier.

      THIRD WITCH. Thou shalt get kings, though thou be none.
        So all hail, Macbeth and Banquo!

      FIRST WITCH. Banquo and Macbeth, all hail!

70 **MACBETH.** Stay, you imperfect[21] speakers, tell me more:
        By Sinel's[22] death I know I am Thane of Glamis;
        But how of Cawdor? The Thane of Cawdor lives,
        A prosperous gentleman; and to be King
        Stands not within the prospect of belief,
75   No more than to be Cawdor. Say from whence
        You owe[23] this strange intelligence?[24] Or why

Enrichment: Analyzing Themes and Symbols

The Fates

In Greek mythology, a person's fate was determined by three women, sometimes called the "weird sisters." They were usually pictured spinning or weaving the fabric of a person's life, which was then arbitrarily cut. In fact, the Middle English word *werde* meant "fate."

In *Macbeth,* three witches appear throughout the play to foretell Macbeth's future—and determine his fate. Shakespeare was not the only author to draw upon this image from Greek mythology: many other authors and filmmakers have created their own versions of the weird sisters.

Activity: The Weird Sisters Then and Now
Have students examine the way the sisters have been represented in at least two different works. These works might be two film versions of *Macbeth* or other films, such as Disney's *Hercules.* Suggest that they record information in the **Enrichment: Analyzing Themes and Symbols** worksheet, *Professional Development Guidebook,* page 243.

Upon this blasted heath you stop our way
With such prophetic greeting? Speak, I charge you.

[WITCHES *vanish*.]

BANQUO. The earth hath bubbles as the water has,
80   And these are of them. Whither are they vanished?

MACBETH. Into the air, and what seemed corporal[25] melted
As breath into the wind. Would they had stayed!

BANQUO. Were such things here as we do speak about?
Or have we eaten on the insane root[26]
85   That takes the reason prisoner?

MACBETH. Your children shall be kings.

BANQUO.   You shall be King.

MACBETH. And Thane of Cawdor too. Went it not so?

BANQUO. To th' selfsame tune and words. Who's here?

[*Enter* ROSS *and* ANGUS.]

ROSS. The King hath happily received, Macbeth,
90   The news of thy success; and when he reads[27]
Thy personal venture in the rebels' fight,
His wonders and his praises do contend
Which should be thine or his.[28] Silenced with that,
In viewing o'er the rest o' th' selfsame day,
95   He finds thee in the stout Norweyan ranks,
Nothing afeard of what thyself didst make,
Strange images of death.[29] As thick as tale
Came post with post,[30] and every one did bear
Thy praises in his kingdom's great defense,
And poured them down before him.

100 **ANGUS.**   We are sent
To give thee, from our royal master, thanks;
Only to herald thee into his sight,
Not pay thee.

ROSS. And for an earnest[31] of a greater honor,
105   He bade me, from him, call thee Thane of Cawdor;
In which addition,[32] hail, most worthy Thane!
For it is thine.

BANQUO. [*Aside*] What, can the devil speak true?

MACBETH. The Thane of Cawdor lives: why do you dress me
In borrowed robes?

ANGUS.   Who was the thane lives yet,
110   But under heavy judgment bears that life
Which he deserves to lose. Whether he was combined[33]

25. **corporal** real.

26. **insane root** henbane or hemlock, believed to cause insanity.

Reading Strategy
Analyze Information from Text Features
What does Banquo mean by the "insane root" (line 84)?

27. **reads** considers.

28. **His wonders . . . his** His admiration contends with his desire to praise you.

29. **Nothing . . . death** killing, but not being afraid of being killed.

30. **As thick . . . post** as fast as could be counted came messenger after messenger.

31. **earnest** pledge.

32. **In which addition** with this new title.

33. **combined** allied.

㉑  Reading Check
What do the witches promise Macbeth and Banquo?

Macbeth, Act I, Scene iii **329**

㉛ Reading Strategy

Analyze Information from Text Features

1. Have students follow along as you read aloud lines 83–84.

2. Then **ask** students the Reading Strategy question: What does Banquo mean by the "insane root"?
   Answer: Banquo means henbane, or hemlock, a plant believed to cause insanity.

▶ **Monitor Progress: Ask** students what clue in the text helped them come to this conclusion. **Answer:** The text annotation in the margin explains what the "insane root" means, and the number 26 after the word root in the text indicates that a margin note is present.

㉑ Reading Check

Answer: The witches promise Macbeth that he will be Thane of Cawdor and king. They promise Banquo that his descendants shall be kings.

Differentiated Instruction   for Universal Access

Enrichment for Advanced Readers
Suggest that students read additional works by Shakespeare. You might provide students with copies of *Sonnets*, *The Merchant of Venice*, or *Julius Caesar*. You may also wish to use **Authors in Depth, The British Tradition**, which contains the following selections:
• from *Antony and Cleopatra*, Act 2, Scene 2
• from *The Merchant of Venice*, Act 2, Scene 7
• Sonnets 15, 30, 71, 73, 77, 128
• "Fear No More the Heat o' the Sun"
• "O Mistress Mine, Where Are You Roaming?"

After students have read these or other works by William Shakespeare, have them form discussion groups in which they compare and contrast the selections they have just read. Suggest criteria for comparison, such as genre, theme, and characters. To extend the activity, have volunteers present to the class brief oral reports on their favorite Shakespeare selections.

Analyze Information from Text Features

1. Have student volunteers read aloud lines 118 (beginning "Do you not…") through 122.

2. Then **ask** students the Reading Strategy question: Using the side notes, how would you rephrase lines 120–121 in modern English? **Possible response:** If that part of the witches' prediction is believed, it might encourage you to hope that you will become king.

23 Critical Thinking

Interpret

1. Explain that, in these speeches, we begin to see the first glimmerings of the evil to come. Direct students' attention to Banquo's comments in lines 123–126, and read them aloud.

2. **Ask** students to explain what Banquo means. **Possible response:** The witches may have told a partial truth to lure Macbeth into evil and ruin.

3. Point out that Macbeth acknowledges Banquo's "two truths"— that the witches' words might be for good or for ill. It is the first time we learn that Macbeth even considers violence as an option.

24 Critical Viewing

Possible responses: The design includes several crosses and fleurs-de-lis (stylized flowers that were sometimes used as symbols of the Christian Trinity).

---

34. line support.

35. vantage assistance.

36. wrack ruin.

Vocabulary
treasons (trē′ zenz) *n.* betrayals of one's country or oath of loyalty

37. behind still to come.

Reading Strategy
Analyze Information from Text Features
Using the side notes, how would you rephrase lines 120–121? **22**

38. home fully.

39. enkindle you unto encourage you to hope for.

40. Cousins often used as **23** a term of courtesy between fellow noblemen.

41. swelling . . . theme stately idea that I will be King.

Vocabulary
imperial (im pir′ ē əl) *adj.* of an empire; having supreme authority

42. suggestion thought of murdering Duncan.

43. seated fixed.

44. Against . . . nature in an unnatural way.

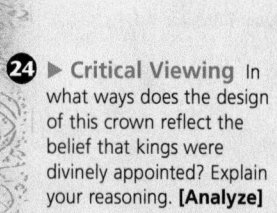

24 ▶ **Critical Viewing** In what ways does the design of this crown reflect the belief that kings were divinely appointed? Explain your reasoning. **[Analyze]**

With those of Norway, or did line[34] the rebel
With hidden help and vantage,[35] or that with both
He labored in his country's wrack,[36] I know not;
115   But treasons capital, confessed and proved,
Have overthrown him.

MACBETH.   [Aside] Glamis, and Thane of Cawdor:
The greatest is behind.[37] [To ROSS and ANGUS]
Thanks for your pains.
[Aside to BANQUO] Do you not hope your children shall be kings,
When those that gave the Thane of Cawdor to me
Promised no less to them?

120 **BANQUO.** [Aside to MACBETH] That, trusted home,[38]
Might yet enkindle you unto[39] the crown,
Besides the Thane of Cawdor. But 'tis strange:
And oftentimes, to win us to our harm,
The instruments of darkness tell us truths,
125   Win us with honest trifles, to betray 's
In deepest consequence.
Cousins,[40] a word, I pray you.

MACBETH.   [Aside] Two truths are told,
As happy prologues to the swelling act
Of the imperial theme.[41]—I thank you, gentlemen.—
130   [Aside] This supernatural soliciting
Cannot be ill, cannot be good. If ill,
Why hath it given me earnest of success,
Commencing in a truth? I am Thane of Cawdor:
If good, why do I yield to that suggestion[42]
135   Whose horrid image doth unfix my hair
And make my seated[43] heart knock at my ribs,
Against the use of nature?[44] Present fears
Are less than horrible imaginings.

Enrichment: Understanding Political Science

A Leader Deposed

In Shakespeare's *Macbeth,* the original Thane of Cawdor is forced from his seat by allegations of treason. This type of overthrow is by no means uncommon today; modern leaders, whether political, religious, or otherwise, may be forced out of office for immoral conduct, treason, crimes against humanity, or simply dissatisfaction among the people. Some deposed leaders, such as Saddam Hussein, have been tried and executed for their crimes, while others, such as former Haitian president Jean-Bertrand Aristide, are able to seek refuge in a different country.

Activity: Profiles of Deposed Leaders Have pairs or groups of students choose a deposed historical leader and research the events that led to that leader being overthrown. Suggest that they record information in the **Enrichment: Understanding Political Science** worksheet, *Professional Development Guidebook,* page 237.

My thought, whose murder yet is but fantastical
140 Shakes so my single[45] state of man that function
     Is smothered in *surmise*, and nothing is
     But what is not.

BANQUO.   Look, how our partner's rapt.

MACBETH. [*Aside*] If chance will have me King, why,
     chance may crown me,
     Without my stir.

BANQUO.   New honors come upon him,
145 Like our strange[46] garments, cleave not to their mold
     But with the aid of use.

MACBETH.   [*Aside*] Come what come may,
     Time and the hour runs through the roughest day.

BANQUO. Worthy Macbeth, we stay upon your leisure.[47]

MACBETH. Give me your favor.[48] My dull brain was wrought
150 With things forgotten. Kind gentlemen, your pains
     Are registered where every day I turn
     The leaf to read them. Let us toward the King.
     [*Aside to* BANQUO] Think upon what hath chanced,
       and at more time,
     The interim having weighed it,[49] let us speak
     Our free hearts[50] each to other.

155 BANQUO.   Very gladly.

MACBETH. Till then, enough. Come, friends.

                                    [*Exit.*]

Scene iv. Forres. The palace.

[*Flourish.*[1] *Enter* KING DUNCAN, LENNOX, MALCOLM, DONALBAIN,
and ATTENDANTS.]

     KING. Is execution done on Cawdor? Are not
        Those in commission[2] yet returned?

     MALCOLM.   My liege,[3]
        They are not yet come back. But I have spoke
        With one that saw him die, who did report
   5   That very frankly he confessed his treasons,
        Implored your Highness' pardon and set forth
        A deep repentance: nothing in his life
        Became him like the leaving it. He died
        As one that had been studied[4] in his death,
  10   To throw away the dearest thing he owed[5]
        As 'twere a careless[6] trifle.

45. **single** unaided, weak.

Reading Strategy
Analyze Information from Text Features
What does the stage direction for line 153 indicate to the actor playing Macbeth?

46. **strange** new.

Vocabulary
surmise (sər miz´) *n.*
imaginings; speculation

47. **stay upon your leisure** await your convenience.

48. **favor** pardon.

49. **The interim . . . it** when we have had time to think about it.

50. **Our free hearts** our minds freely.

1. **Flourish** trumpet fanfare.

2. **in commission** commissioned to oversee the execution.

3. **liege** (lēj) *n.* lord or king.

4. **studied** rehearsed.

5. **owed** owned.

6. **careless** worthless.

Reading Check
27 As Macbeth thinks about what the witches have promised, what "horrid image" frightens him?

Macbeth, Act I, Scene iv **331**

25 Critical Thinking
Interpret

1. Read aloud Macbeth's aside in lines 143–144.

2. Then **ask** students to explain what Macbeth means by these lines.
   Answer: If chance (fate) wants him as king, then chance will make it happen, without his doing anything.

3. **Ask** students whether they believe these lines show that Macbeth has made up his mind not to murder Duncan.
   Possible response: Some students may feel that these lines show that Macbeth has truly decided against this course of action. Others may believe that, instead, Macbeth is trying to talk himself out of feeling guilty by saying he will not be able to help it if he becomes king by some chain of events.

26 Reading Strategy
Analyze Information from Text Features

1. Direct students' attention to the stage direction in line 153 and tell them to think about how it would affect delivery of the line.

2. Then **ask** the Reading Strategy question: What does this stage direction indicate to the actor playing Macbeth?
   Answer: It indicates that the actor playing Macbeth should turn to Banquo or speak only to him.

3. Point out the stage directions in lines 143 and 146. **Ask** how they differ from the one in line 153.
   Answer: They don't specify to whom Macbeth speaks.

4. **Ask** students what they think these stage directions mean—who do they think Macbeth is speaking to in lines 143 and 146?
   Answer: Shakespeare often has characters speak directly to the audience in "asides," to let the audience know what characters are thinking.

27 Reading Check
Answer: Macbeth is frightened by the horrible image of his murdering Duncan to achieve the events the witches foretold.

Differentiated
Instruction for Universal Access

Strategy for Special-Needs Students
Before moving on, review the events on these pages. Macbeth has seen one prophecy come true. **Ask** students which prophecy has been realized (he is now Thane of Cawdor). If necessary, take them back to the place in the text where the witches predicted this (line 49). Emphasize that Macbeth is already having his first thoughts of what might need to happen to make the next prophecy come true—King Duncan would have to die.

EL Strategy for English Learners
Discuss the events that have occurred thus far in the play, so that students do not lose the thread of the story. Then take time to make certain that students understand the definitions given in the side notes. For example, the definition of *treasons* includes the words *betrayals* and *loyalty*, both of which might be new to English learners.

331

Interpret

1. Have a student volunteer read the king's statement in lines 11–14 (through "O worthiest cousin!").

2. Then **ask** students to explain what the king is saying in these lines.
   Answer: You can't determine a person's character by outward appearances. He had trusted Cawdor.

3. **Ask** students why it is significant that he says this just before Macbeth enters.
   Answer: Macbeth appears honorable and loyal, and the king trusts him. But we already know that Macbeth has thoughts of murdering the king.

29 **Critical Viewing**

Answer: The use of blue and white colors conveys an icy, deathlike coldness consistent with the coldblooded murder of the king. The steep walls and surrounding water reflect both the isolation and the power experienced by Macbeth in the play.

30 **Humanities**

This photograph, taken by Anne Van De Vaeken, is of Eilean Donan Castle in Dornie, Scotland. Castles were places of safety from which occupants could defend themselves against attack. The castle in this picture is situated on a small island. The only access is across a narrow bridge.

Use these questions for discussion:

1. What might be the drawbacks and advantages of living in a castle such as this one?
   Possible responses: It is remote and isolated, and it would be easy for enemies to cut off your supplies or escape; food (fish) and water would be abundant, and it would be easy to defend.

2. When the King arrives at Macbeth's castle (Scene 6), he says that the castle has "a pleasant seat" and fragrant air. How does that compare with this image?
   Possible responses: Some may say that the cold isolation suggested in the photo contrasts with the description of Macbeth's castle. Others may say that this castle matches the description: it is well situated, would have great views, and the air would be fresh.

332

---

7. **mind's construction** person's character.

KING.   There's no art
To find the mind's construction[7] in the face:
He was a gentleman on whom I built
An absolute trust.

28

[*Enter* MACBETH, BANQUO, ROSS, *and* ANGUS.]

                                  O worthiest cousin!
15   The sin of my ingratitude even now
     Was heavy on me: thou art so far before,
     That swiftest wing of recompense is slow
     To overtake thee. Would thou hadst less deserved,
     That the proportion both of thanks and payment
20   Might have been mine![8] Only I have left to say,
     More is thy due than more than all can pay.

8. **Would . . . mine** If you had been less worthy, my thanks and payment could have exceeded the rewards you deserve.

9. **pays itself** is its own reward.

MACBETH. The service and the loyalty I owe,
     In doing it, pays itself.[9] Your Highness' part
     Is to receive our duties: and our duties
25   Are to your throne and state children and servants;
     Which do but what they should, by doing every thing
     Safe toward[10] your love and honor.

10. **Safe toward** with sure regard for.

KING.   Welcome hither.
     I have begun to plant thee, and will labor
31
     To make thee full of growing. Noble Banquo,
30   That hast no less deserved, nor must be known

29 ▼ **Critical Viewing** How does this Scottish castle reflect the mood of the play? **[Connect]**

332 Celebrating Humanity (1485–1625)

Enrichment: Analyzing an Image

Photo Composition

Studying the underlying characteristics of a work of art can add to one's appreciation of it. For example, when viewing a photograph, one should study its composition—is the photograph visually balanced from side to side and top to bottom? What elements provide that balance? One should also pay attention to what the eye is drawn to in the picture. What is the main subject? What visual lines are created by various elements in the photograph, and how do these draw the eye and help to provide balance?

Activity: Photo Analysis Have students work individually or in pairs to analyze the photograph on this page using the questions above, as well as other considerations such as color, mood, and symbolism. Suggest that they record information in the **Enrichment: Analyzing an Image** worksheet, *Professional Development Guidebook*, page 232.

No less to have done so, let me enfold thee
And hold thee to my heart.

BANQUO.   There if I grow,
The harvest is your own.

KING.   My plenteous joys,
Wanton[11] in fullness, seek to hide themselves
35 In drops of sorrow. Sons, kinsmen, thanes,
And you whose places are the nearest, know,
We will establish our estate upon
Our eldest, Malcolm,[12] whom we name hereafter
The Prince of Cumberland: which honor must
40 Not unaccompanied invest him only,
But signs of nobleness, like stars, shall shine
On all deservers. From hence to Inverness,[13]
And bind us further to you.

MACBETH. The rest is labor, which is not used for you.[14]
45 I'll be myself the harbinger,[15] and make joyful
The hearing of my wife with your approach;
So, humbly take my leave.

KING.   My worthy Cawdor!

MACBETH. [Aside] The Prince of Cumberland! That is a step
On which I must fall down, or else o'erleap,
50 For in my way it lies. Stars, hide your fires;
Let not light see my black and deep desires:
The eye wink at the hand;[16] yet let that be
Which the eye fears, when it is done, to see.   [Exit.]

KING. True, worthy Banquo; he is full so valiant,
55 And in his commendations I am fed;
It is a banquet to me. Let's after him,
Whose care is gone before to bid us welcome.
It is a peerless kinsman.   [Flourish. Exit.]

Scene v. Inverness. Macbeth's castle.

[Enter MACBETH'S WIFE, alone, with a letter.]

LADY MACBETH. [Reads] "They met me in the day of
success; and I have learned by the perfect'st report
they have more in them than mortal knowledge.
When I burned in desire to question them further,
5 they made themselves air, into which they vanished.
Whiles I stood rapt in the wonder of it, came
missives[1] from the King, who all-hailed me 'Thane
of Cawdor'; by which title, before, these weird sisters
saluted me, and referred me to the coming on
10 of time, with 'Hail, King that shalt be!' This have I

31 Literary Analysis
Elizabethan Drama

1. Have students read lines 28–33. Encourage them to focus on the imagery in the dialogue.

2. Then **ask** students the Literary Analysis question: From what area of human activity do King Duncan and Banquo draw their imagery?
   Answer: King Duncan and Banquo draw on imagery from agriculture or farming.

3. **Ask** students to interpret the meaning of the imagery: what are King Duncan and Banquo saying?
   Possible response: King Duncan expresses a wish to help Macbeth and Banquo grow to reach their full potential, and Banquo replies that if he is able to do so, it will be thanks to King Duncan's support, and "the harvest" will go to Duncan—Banquo will repay Duncan for his investment.

4. **Ask** students why they think Shakespeare chose to use this imagery.
   Possible response: The image reveals King Duncan's role in the success of Macbeth and Banquo; the rich images and language are also characteristic of Elizabethan dramas.

32 Reading Strategy
Analyze Information from Text Features

1. Direct students' attention to line 48, and the stage direction there.

2. Then **ask** students the Reading Strategy question: What do the stage directions with line 48 tell you about how Macbeth is to deliver this speech?
   Answer: Macbeth is to deliver his comment as an aside, speaking to the audience, as if speaking to himself. He should turn away from the king and toward the audience.

33 Reading Check
Answer: Duncan names his son Malcolm as heir to his throne and Prince of Cumberland.

Differentiated Instruction   for Universal Access

Strategy for Less Proficient Readers
Have students compare the way Macbeth addresses the king in lines 22–27 and 44–47 with the thoughts he expresses in his aside to the audience in lines 48–53. You may wish to have students first paraphrase these passages to make sure they understand what Macbeth is saying. Do students think Macbeth is being honest with the king? Make sure students know that, by making his eldest son heir to the throne, the king has put a barrier in Macbeth's way. Discuss what Macbeth wants hidden in line 52—what deed he wants the eye to "wink at."

Strategy for Gifted/Talented Students
Have students pick a speech from Act 1 and prepare it for a dramatic reading. Remind students to look at text aids for clues (are they on a battlefield, is this an aside), but explain that it is primarily from the emotions and ideas expressed that they will gain an understanding of how to deliver the speech. Encourage them to think about how a person would speak and act when coming from a battle or plotting a murder, for example.

333

34 Literary Analysis

Elizabethan Drama and Soliloquy

1. Remind students that a soliloquy is a long speech, usually made by a character who is alone. Soliloquies were important elements of Elizabethan drama.

2. Point out that in the soliloquy running from line 1 through line 30, lines 1–14 show Lady Macbeth reading a letter from her husband about his meeting with the witches and the fulfillment of the first promise.

3. Have a student volunteer read lines 1–14 aloud. Then **ask:** What do lines 11–14 tell us about Macbeth's feelings for his wife? **Answer:** He loves her, sees her as an equal, and knows that she, too, is ambitious.

4. Have another volunteer read aloud lines 15–30. Then **ask** the Literary Analysis question: What does Lady Macbeth's soliloquy in lines 15–30 reveal about her ambitions and plans? **Answer:** Lady Macbeth decides that the witches' prophecy will come true, and that she plans to persuade Macbeth to fulfill his destiny.

5. **Ask** students how, based on lines 18–25, Lady Macbeth thinks Macbeth would approach the situation. **Answer:** She sees Macbeth as not being sufficiently wicked to accomplish his ambitions. She says he would rather do it "holily" (in a holy manner) and would rather not play false and win dishonestly. But she also says that she thinks that he would be willing to accept the results of foul play, even if he did not consider them his first choice.

35 Critical Thinking

Compare and Contrast

1. Have a student read aloud lines 38–53.

2. Then **ask** students how Lady Macbeth's reaction to the situation contrasts with Macbeth's. **Answer:** While Macbeth is reluctant to consider murder, Lady Macbeth embraces the idea immediately and calls on the forces of evil to help her.

---

2. **deliver thee** report to you.

Literary Analysis
Elizabethan Drama and Soliloquy
What does Lady Macbeth's soliloquy in lines 15–30 reveal about her ambitions and plans?

3. **nearest** quickest.

4. **illness** wickedness.

5. **that which . . . undone** What you are afraid of doing you would not wish undone once you have done it.

6. **round** crown.

7. **had . . . him** overtook him.

8. **mortal** deadly.

9. **remorse** compassion.

10. **compunctious . . . nature** natural feelings of pity.

11. **fell** savage.

12. **effect** fulfillment.

13. **milk for gall** kindness in exchange for bitterness.

14. **ministers** agents.

15. **sightless** invisible.

16. **wait on** assist.

---

thought good to deliver thee,[2] my dearest partner of greatness, that thou mightst not lose the dues of rejoicing, by being ignorant of what greatness is promised thee. Lay it to thy heart, and farewell."

15 Glamis thou art, and Cawdor, and shalt be
What thou art promised. Yet do I fear thy nature;
It is too full o' th' milk of human kindness
To catch the nearest[3] way. Thou wouldst be great,
Art not without ambition, but without
20 The illness[4] should attend it. What thou wouldst highly,
That wouldst thou holily; wouldst not play false,
And yet wouldst wrongly win. Thou'dst have, great Glamis,
That which cries "Thus thou must do" if thou have it;
And that which rather thou dost fear to do
25 Than wishest should be undone.[5] Hie thee hither,
That I may pour my spirits in thine ear,
And chastise with the valor of my tongue
All that impedes thee from the golden round[6]
Which fate and metaphysical aid doth seem
To have thee crowned withal.

[*Enter* MESSENGER.]

30   What is your tidings?

MESSENGER. The King comes here tonight.

LADY MACBETH.   Thou'rt mad to say it!
Is not thy master with him, who, were't so,
Would have informed for preparation?

MESSENGER. So please you, it is true. Our thane is coming.
35 One of my fellows had the speed of him,[7]
Who, almost dead for breath, had scarcely more
Than would make up his message.

LADY MACBETH.   Give him tending;
He brings great news.   [*Exit* MESSENGER.]
                    The raven himself is hoarse
That croaks the fatal entrance of Duncan
40 Under my battlements. Come, you spirits
That tend on mortal[8] thoughts, unsex me here,
And fill me, from the crown to the toe, top-full
Of direst cruelty! Make thick my blood,
Stop up th' access and passage to remorse[9]
45 That no compunctious visitings of nature[10]
Shake my fell[11] purpose, nor keep peace between
Th' effect[12] and it! Come to my woman's breasts,
And take my milk for gall,[13] you murd'ring ministers,[14]
Wherever in your sightless[15] substances
50 You wait on[16] nature's mischief! Come, thick night,

Enrichment: Analyzing Forms and Genres

Shakespeare's Tragedies

William Hazlitt (1778–1830), one of the most outspoken critics in the Romantic era, made the following observation about the scope of Shakespeare's work:

Macbeth and *Lear, Othello* and *Hamlet,* are usually reckoned Shakespeare's four principal tragedies. . . . If the force of genius shown in each of these works is astonishing, their variety is not less so. They are like different creations of the same mind, not one of which has the slightest reference to the rest. This distinctness and originality is indeed the necessary consequence of truth and nature. Shakespeare's genius alone appeared to possess the resources of nature. He is "your only tragedy maker."

Activity: Compare Shakespeare's Tragedies
Have students research the characters, themes, and plot of another Shakespearean tragedy and compare it to *Macbeth.* Have them use the **Enrichment: Analyzing Forms and Genres** worksheet, *Professional Development Guidebook,* page 227.

36

37 ◄ Critical Viewing This is an artist's rendering of nineteenth-century actress Ellen Terry playing Lady Macbeth. Judging by the picture, how do you think Terry would have spoken lines 38-54 in Act I, Scene v? [Deduce]

35 | And pall[17] thee in the dunnest[18] smoke of hell,
That my keen knife see not the wound it makes,
Nor heaven peep through the blanket of the dark,
To cry "Hold, hold!"

[*Enter* MACBETH.]

55   Great Glamis! Worthy Cawdor!
Greater than both, by the all-hail hereafter!
Thy letters have transported me beyond
This ignorant[19] present, and I feel now
The future in the instant.[20]

MACBETH.   My dearest love,
Duncan comes here tonight.

LADY MACBETH.   And when goes hence?

MACBETH. Tomorrow, as he purposes.

17. **pall** enshroud.

18. **dunnest** darkest.

19. **ignorant** unknowing.

20. **instant** present.

38 Reading Check
What does Lady Macbeth feel is Macbeth's weakness?

Macbeth, Act I, Scene v **335**

36 Humanities

Ellen Terry as Lady Macbeth, 1889, from a photograph by Hindau and Grove

Ellen Terry was a brilliant actress and one of the most socially prominent people of the time. Her pose is theatrical and impressive. The drapery of the costume is painted in many tones and textures to convey the richness of nobility. The image reveals more of the actress than of the character she represents.

Use this question for discussion:

> What has the costume designer tried to communicate with the outfit made for Ellen Terry?
> **Possible response:** The costume is very dramatic. It reflects a vaguely medieval image, with the flowing sleeves and multiple belts. The richness of the colors and all the gold accentuate nobility and power.

37 Critical Viewing

Possible response: The actress's thoughtful pose and expression suggest that she may have spoken these lines with measured strength and deliberation, but also with the confidence that comes from being sure of one's course of action.

38 Reading Check

Answer: Lady Macbeth feels Macbeth's kindness is his weakness.

Differentiated Instruction for Universal Access

EL **Pronunciation for English Learners**
Students who are native speakers of some languages may have difficulty with the voiced /th/ sound common in Shakespearean language, in words such as *thee, thou* and *thy.* They may replace /th/ with /b/ or /f/. For example, a student might say *bee* or *fee* instead of *thee.* To help students distinguish between these sounds, first point out one /th/ word on these pages and have students repeat it after you several times, emphasizing the initial consonant. Then create three columns of words on the board. In the first column, write *that, thee,* and *though;* in the second, *bat, bee,* and *bow;* in the third, *fat, fee,* and *foe.* Discuss the meanings of any unfamiliar words; then play a game in which one student at a time pronounces one of the words and a second student points to the word on the board.

39 Vocabulary Builder

1. Point out the word *sovereign* in line 70, and its definition in the side margin.

2. Tell students that, like many other words, *sovereign* came into English through the French-speaking Normans. The French word is *souverain*. *Royal* also came from the French. The French word for king is *roi,* kingship is *royauté,* and kingly is *royal.* Ultimately, the English *sovereign* and French *souverain* both relate back to the Latin word *super,* which means "over" (as in "higher than").

3. **Ask** students to brainstorm other words that relate back to the Latin word *super.*
   Possible responses: *supervisor, superlative, superb.*

4. Point out that *sovereign* can be used as a noun or as an adjective. In this case, it is an adjective that modifies *sway.* Explain that *sway* here means "influence" or "control." **Ask** students what Lady Macbeth is saying that their deeds will give them.
   Answer: Their deeds will result in them having sovereign, or authoritative, influence over others.

40 Critical Thinking

Analyze

1. Have a student read aloud Lady Macbeth's speech in lines 14–20.

2. **Ask** students to paraphrase these lines.
   Possible response: Any service we can do for you is nothing compared to what you have done for us by honoring us with your presence.

3. Then **ask** students: Knowing what we know about Lady Macbeth's plans for King Duncan, why would she show such humility and respect for him?
   Possible response: She wants to make sure he is not suspicious; she wants to make sure others will not suspect her; she is playing the role she would be expected to play, even though it does not match her true feelings.

---

21. **beguile the time** deceive the people tonight.
22. **dispatch** management.
23. **look up clear** appear innocent.

39 Vocabulary

sovereign (säv´ rən) *adj.* supreme in power, rank, or authority

24. **To alter . . . fear** to show a disturbed face will arouse suspicion.

1. **Hautboys** oboes announcing the arrival of royalty.
2. **seat** location.
3. **gentle** soothed.
4. **temple-haunting martlet** martin, a bird that usually nests in churches. In Shakespeare's time, *martin* was a slang term for a person who is easily deceived.
5. **approve** show.
6. **mansionry** nests.
7. **jutty** projection.
8. **coign of vantage** advantageous corner.
9. **procreant** (prō´ krē ənt) **cradle** nest where the young are hatched.
10. **haunt** visit.
11. **The love . . . trouble** Though my visit inconveniences you, you should ask God to reward me for coming, because it was my love for you that prompted my visit.
12. **single business** feeble service.
13. **rest your hermits** remain your dependents bound to pray for you. Hermits were often paid to pray for another person's soul.

---

60 **LADY MACBETH.**   O, never
Shall sun that morrow see!
Your face, my Thane, is as a book where men
May read strange matters. To beguile the time,[21]
Look like the time; bear welcome in your eye,
65 Your hand, your tongue: look like th' innocent flower,
But be the serpent under 't. He that's coming
Must be provided for: and you shall put
This night's great business into my dispatch;[22]
Which shall to all our nights and days to come
70 Give solely sovereign sway and masterdom.

MACBETH. We will speak further.

LADY MACBETH.   Only look up clear.[23]
To alter favor ever is to fear.[24]
Leave all the rest to me.   [*Exit.*]

Scene vi. Before Macbeth's castle.

[*Hautboys.*[1] *Torches. Enter* KING DUNCAN, MALCOLM, DONALBAIN, BANQUO, LENNOX, MACDUFF, ROSS, ANGUS, *and* ATTENDANTS.]

KING. This castle hath a pleasant seat;[2] the air
Nimbly and sweetly recommends itself
Unto our gentle[3] senses.

BANQUO.   This guest of summer,
The temple-haunting martlet,[4] does approve[5]
5 By his loved mansionry[6] that the heaven's breath
Smells wooingly here. No jutty,[7] frieze,
Buttress, nor coign of vantage,[8] but this bird
Hath made his pendent bed and procreant cradle.[9]
Where they most breed and haunt,[10] I have observed
The air is delicate.

[*Enter* LADY MACBETH.]

10 **KING.**   See, see, our honored hostess!
The love that follows us sometime is our trouble,
Which still we thank as love. Herein I teach you
How you shall bid God 'ield us for your pains
And thank us for your trouble.[11]

LADY MACBETH.   All our service
15 In every point twice done, and then done double,
Were poor and single business[12] to contend
Against those honors deep and broad wherewith
Your Majesty loads our house: for those of old,
And the late dignities heaped up to them,
We rest your hermits.[13]

336 Celebrating Humanity (1485–1625)

Enrichment: Analyzing a Historical Event

Assassins

Macbeth's soliloquy at the opening of Scene 7 centers around the question of whether he should assassinate Duncan. History is fraught with examples of assassins and attempted assassinations, from the well-known assassinations of Abraham Lincoln and John F. Kennedy to the lesser-known attempted assassinations of Adolf Hitler and Malcolm X.

Activity: Research an Assassination Have pairs or groups of students conduct research on a historical assassination or attempted assas-

sination. Suggest that they record information in the **Enrichment: Analyzing a Historical Event** worksheet, *Professional Development Guidebook,* page 230. When students are finished, have each group record a summary of their research on the board and present it to the class. Then discuss with the class which assassins might have faced similar thoughts to Macbeth's, which were unlikely to have had those thoughts, and why.

336

KING.   Where's the Thane of Cawdor?
20 We coursed[14] him at the heels, and had a purpose
To be his purveyor:[15] but he rides well,
And his great love, sharp as his spur, hath holp[16] him
To his home before us. Fair and noble hostess,
We are your guest tonight.

25 LADY MACBETH.   Your servants ever
Have theirs, themselves, and what is theirs, in compt,[17]
To make their audit at your Highness' pleasure,
Still[18] to return your own.

KING.   Give me your hand.
Conduct me to mine host: we love him highly,
30 And shall continue our graces towards him.
By your leave, hostess.   [Exit.]

Scene vii. Macbeth's castle.

[*Hautboys. Torches. Enter a* SEWER,[1] *and diverse* SERVANTS *with dishes and service over the stage. Then enter* MACBETH.]

MACBETH. If it were done[2] when 'tis done, then 'twere well
It were done quickly. If th' assassination
Could trammel up the consequence, and catch,
With his surcease, success;[3] that but this blow
5 Might be the be-all and the end-all—here,
But here, upon this bank and shoal of time,
We'd jump the life to come.[4] But in these cases
We still have judgment here; that we but teach
Bloody instructions, which, being taught, return
10 To plague th' inventor: this even-handed[5] justice
Commends[6] th' ingredients of our poisoned chalice[7]
To our own lips. He's here in double trust:
First, as I am his kinsman and his subject,
Strong both against the deed; then, as his host,
15 Who should against his murderer shut the door,
Not bear the knife myself. Besides, this Duncan
Hath borne his faculties[8] so meek, hath been
So clear[9] in his great office, that his virtues
Will plead like angels trumpet-tongued against
20 The deep damnation of his taking-off;
And pity, like a naked newborn babe,
Striding the blast, or heaven's cherubin[10] horsed
Upon the sightless couriers[11] of the air,
Shall blow the horrid deed in every eye,
25 That tears shall drown the wind. I have no spur
To prick the sides of my intent, but only
Vaulting ambition, which o'erleaps itself
And falls on th' other—

14. **coursed** chased.

15. **purveyor** advance supply officer.

16. **holp** helped.

17. **compt** trust.

18. **Still** always.

Literary Analysis
Elizabethan Drama
What details does Banquo use in Scene vi, lines 3–10 to paint a word picture of Macbeth's castle?

1. **sewer** chief butler.

2. **done** over and done with.

3. **If . . . success** if the assassination could be done successfully and without consequence.

4. **We'd . . . come** I would risk life in the world to come.

5. **even-handed** impartial.

6. **commends** offers.

7. **chalice** cup.

8. **faculties** powers.

9. **clear** blameless.

10. **cherubin** angels.

11. **sightless couriers** unseen messengers (the wind).

Literary Analysis
Elizabethan Drama and Soliloquy
What doubts does Macbeth reveal in his soliloquy (lines 1–28)?

Reading Check
What deed does Lady Macbeth urge her husband to perform?

Macbeth, Act I, Scene vii **337**

41 Literary Analysis
Elizabethan Drama

1. Have students read to themselves Banquo's speech in lines 3–10. Tell them to focus on the descriptive content of the images in the passage.

2. Then ask students the first Literary Analysis question: What details does Banquo use in Scene vi, lines 3–10 to paint a word picture of Macbeth's castle?
Answer: Banquo notes that martins, birds usually drawn to churches, are plentiful here. Every projection and vantage point has a nest where chicks hatch. He also writes that the air has a lovely smell, which he gives as the reason that all of the birds choose to nest there.

42 Literary Analysis
Elizabethan Drama and Soliloquy

1. Have one or more students read aloud Macbeth's soliloquy, lines 1–28.

2. Then ask students the second Literary Analysis question: What doubts does Macbeth reveal in his soliloquy?
Answer: Macbeth has doubts about the consequences of his deed—his plans may go awry. He also expresses doubts about the deed due both to his obligations as kinsman, subject, and host of Duncan and to Duncan's own virtues.

43 Reading Check
Answer: Lady Macbeth urges her husband to look innocent and leave the murder plot to her.

Differentiated Instruction   for Universal Access

Support for Special-Needs Students
Summarize the events and thoughts on these pages. Then focus on Macbeth's soliloquy, lines 1–28. Go over the speech one sentence at a time, so that students can discuss the ideas in more manageable amounts. You may wish to create overhead transparencies with two columns, the first containing portions of the text, and the second with space to paraphrase the meaning of the passage. Once students understand what is being said, have them discuss what the images reveal about Macbeth.

EL Vocabulary for English Learners
Briefly explain what Macbeth is saying in lines 1–28. With guidance from the teacher or more fluent students, have students go through the speech slowly, stopping to determine meanings for unfamiliar words. Any pictures you can supply to illustrate such images as a bank and shoal (line 6), chalice (line 11), or trumpet-tongued angels (line 19) would aid comprehension. The overhead strategy suggested in the note for Special-Needs Students might also benefit English Learners.

44 Reading Strategy

Analyze Text Features

1. Direct students' attention to line 42.

2. **Ask** students the Reading Strategy question: In line 42, what does Lady Macbeth mean by the "ornament of life"? **Answer:** The "ornament of life" to which Lady Macbeth refers is the crown.

3. Point out that the sentence in which this expression appears is easier to understand in context. In the previous sentence, Lady Macbeth states that Macbeth is afraid to be the same in action as he is in desire. The sentence that follows notes that Macbeth wishes but will not act.

4. Have students paraphrase the sentence that includes "ornament of life." **Possible response:** Do you want to have the crown, and yet continue to be a coward about it?

45 Critical Thinking

Interpret

1. Have students read to themselves Lady Macbeth's speech in lines 47–59.

2. Then **ask** students what arguments Lady Macbeth uses to convince Macbeth to carry out the murder. **Answer:** Lady Macbeth asks Macbeth if his hopes have all died out. She implies that her love is directly linked to his ambitions. She also accuses him of being cowardly.

---

12. **bought** acquired.

Reading Strategy
Analyze Text Features
In line 42, what does Lady Macbeth mean by the "ornament of life"?

13. **ornament of life** the crown.

14. **wait upon** follow.

15. **poor . . . adage** from an old proverb about a cat who wants to eat fish but is afraid of getting its paws wet.

16. **break** reveal.

17. **Did then adhere** was then suitable (for the assassination)

18. **that their** their very.

19. **But** only.

20. **sticking-place** the notch that holds the bowstring of a taut crossbow.

[*Enter* LADY MACBETH.]

How now! What news?

LADY MACBETH. He has almost supped. Why have you left the chamber?

MACBETH. Hath he asked for me?

30 **LADY MACBETH.** Know you not he has?

MACBETH. We will proceed no further in this business:
He hath honored me of late, and I have bought[12]
Golden opinions from all sorts of people,
Which would be worn now in their newest gloss,
Not cast aside so soon.

35 **LADY MACBETH.** Was the hope drunk
Wherein you dressed yourself? Hath it slept since?
And wakes it now, to look so green and pale
At what it did so freely? From this time
Such I account thy love. Art thou afeard

40 To be the same in thine own act and valor
As thou art in desire? Wouldst thou have that
Which thou esteem'st the ornament of life,[13]
And live a coward in thine own esteem,
Letting "I dare not" wait upon[14] "I would,"
Like the poor cat i' th' adage?[15]

45 **MACBETH.** Prithee, peace!
I dare do all that may become a man;
Who dares do more is none.

LADY MACBETH. What beast was 't then
That made you break[16] this enterprise to me?
When you durst do it, then you were a man;

50 And to be more than what you were, you would
Be so much more the man. Nor time nor place
Did then adhere,[17] and yet you would make both.
They have made themselves, and that their[18] fitness now
Does unmake you. I have given suck, and know

55 How tender 'tis to love the babe that milks me:
I would, while it was smiling in my face,
Have plucked my nipple from his boneless gums,
And dashed the brains out, had I so sworn as you
Have done to this.

MACBETH. If we should fail?

LADY MACBETH. We fail?

60 But[19] screw your courage to the sticking-place[20]
And we'll not fail. When Duncan is asleep—
Whereto the rather shall his day's hard journey
Soundly invite him—his two chamberlains

338 Celebrating Humanity (1485–1625)

Vocabulary Development

Vocabulary Knowledge Rating

When students have completed reading and discussing the selection, have them take out their **Vocabulary Knowledge Rating Charts** for the story. Read the words aloud and have students rate their knowledge of words again in the After Reading column. Clarify any words that are still problematic. Have students write their own definitions and example or sentence in the appropriate column. Then, have students complete the Vocabulary Lesson at the end of the selection. Encourage students to use the words in further discussion and written work about the selection. Remind them that they will be accountable for these words on the **Selection Test,** *Unit 2 Resources,* pages 118–120 or 121–123.

Will I with wine and wassail[21] so convince,[22]
65 That memory, the warder of the brain,
Shall be a fume, and the receipt of reason
A limbeck only:[23] when in swinish sleep
Their drenchèd natures lies as in a death,
What cannot you and I perform upon
70 Th' unguarded Duncan, what not put upon
His spongy[24] officers, who shall bear the guilt
Of our great quell?[25]

MACBETH.   Bring forth men-children only;
For thy undaunted mettle[26] should compose
Nothing but males. Will it not be received,
75 When we have marked with blood those sleepy two
Of his own chamber, and used their very daggers,
That they have done 't?

LADY MACBETH.   Who dares receive it other,[27]
As we shall make our griefs and clamor roar
Upon his death?

MACBETH.   I am settled, and bend up
80 Each corporal agent to this terrible feat.
Away, and mock the time[28] with fairest show:
False face must hide what the false heart doth know.   [*Exit.*]

---

21. **wassail** carousing.
22. **convince** overpower.
23. **That . . . only** that memory, the guardian of the brain, will be confused by the fumes of the drink, and the reason become like a still, distilling confused thoughts.
24. **spongy** sodden.
25. **quell** murder.
26. **mettle** spirit.
27. **other** otherwise.
28. **mock the time** mislead the world.

Critical Reading

@ **1. Key Ideas and Details (a)** What statements do the witches and Macbeth make about "foul and fair"? **(b) Interpret:** What meaning (or meanings) does each remark have?

@ **2. Key Ideas and Details (a)** Describe Banquo's and Macbeth's reactions to the witches. **(b) Compare and Contrast:** Compare and contrast their reactions to the witches.

@ **3. Key Ideas and Details (a)** In his soliloquy at the beginning of Scene vii, what arguments against killing Duncan does Macbeth express? **(b) Analyze Cause and Effect:** Which of these arguments seems to influence him the most? Explain.

@ **4. Integration of Knowledge and Ideas (a)** What is Lady Macbeth's opinion of her husband's character? **(b) Analyze:** How does she use her knowledge of his character to convince him to kill Duncan?

Cite textual evidence to support your responses.

Macbeth, Act I, Scene vii **339**

Concept Connector

Reading Strategy Graphic Organizer
Ask students to review the graphic organizers in which they have analyzed information from text features. Then have students share their organizers and compare the features they identified.

Activating Prior Knowledge
Have students return to the paragraphs they wrote in the Activating Prior Knowledge activity. Ask them to explain whether their thoughts have changed and, if so, how.

Writing About the Essential Question
Have students list instances of comedy from *Macbeth,* Act 1, and record these on the board. Ask students why they believe Shakespeare included these moments. Was it because he felt they contributed to the artistic value of his play? Was it because that was the convention of theater in his day? Then have students work individually or in groups, to formulate their responses to the Essential Question. Encourage students to consider to what extent Shakespeare's work was formed by the traditions of his day and to what extent Shakespeare helped to shape the traditions of his day.

Answers

1. (a) In Elizabethan drama, costumes helped identify characters and their positions in society, and borrowing robes would be taking another's part. (b) It shows that Macbeth is uneasy with taking on a title that is not his.

2. If their predictions are to come true, people must die.

3. **Possible response:** Macbeth's meeting with the witches suggests that opportunities for evil can present themselves unbidden; however, it is only with Macbeth's decision to act on their words that the witches effectively bring evil to pass.

4. **Possible response:** Students may mention Julius Caesar, who killed others in his quest for power.

5. 1, i, 10–11: fair is foul, foul is fair, fog and filthy air; modern sets: fog machine; austere stage and backdrop. 1, vi, 3–10: sweet air, birds nesting; modern sets: bright stage, bird sounds, attractive castle as backdrop. Another sample can be found on **Literary Analysis Graphic Organizer B,** page 53 in *Graphic Organizer Transparencies.*

6. (a) Lady Macbeth reveals that she is ready to do whatever it takes, but worries that her husband is too kind. She resolves to talk him into killing the king. (b) Macbeth thinks he should get it over with. However, his concern over consequences and his dislike for injuring a guest make him hesitate.

7. **Possible response:** The soliloquies reveal more, because Macbeth is more open.

8. Their soliloquies add to the sense that they are moving toward disaster, because they are talking themselves into horrible acts.

9. (a) Act 1, Scene 1: The witches enter an open place; there is thunder and lightning. They refer to their helpers, a cat and a toad, and depart. Act 1, Scene 5: lady Macbeth is alone; she reads a letter. A messenger enters. (b) The stage directions were most helpful since they describe the action.

10. (a) *Anon* means "at once." (b) *Thane* was a Scottish title of nobility. (c) *Cousins* was a courtesy used between noblemen.

340

COMMON CORE ▪ EXTENDED STUDY: SHAKESPEAREAN DRAMA

After You Read *Macbeth, Act I*

Literary Analysis

1. Craft and Structure (a) What vivid image, typical of **Elizabethan drama,** does Shakespeare create when Macbeth says to Ross, "why do you dress me / In borrowed robes?" (Act I, Scene iii, lines 108–109)? **(b)** What uneasiness in Macbeth does this word picture reveal?

2. Craft and Structure How does Macbeth's encounter with the witches show that the play will probably be a **tragedy?**

3. Integration of Knowledge and Ideas Does Macbeth's meeting with the witches suggest that evil is something people choose, a force that seeks people out, or some combination of the two? Explain.

4. Integration of Knowledge and Ideas Identify a person in history who is similar to a character in Macbeth. Then, explain your choice.

5. Integration of Knowledge and Ideas Using a chart like this one, analyze the details of setting in the lines shown. Then, indicate how modern sets and lighting might produce such a setting.

Shakespeare's Words	Modern Sets and Lighting
I, i, 10–11	
I, vi, 3–10	

6. Craft and Structure What do each of the following **soliloquies** reveal about their speaker's thoughts and plans: **(a)** Lady Macbeth, Act I, Scene v, lines 1–30 and **(b)** Macbeth, Act I, Scene vii, lines 1–28?

7. Craft and Structure In Act I, which type of speech directed to the audience is more effective in revealing Macbeth's thoughts: asides or a soliloquy? Explain.

8. Integration of Knowledge and Ideas Do Lady Macbeth's and Macbeth's soliloquies add to the sense that the characters are moving toward disaster? Why or why not?

Reading Strategy

9. (a) Analyze information from text features such as stage directions, side notes, and illustrations to describe the action in Act I, Scene i, and the beginning of Act I, Scene v. **(b)** Which text features were most helpful in describing the action? Provide reasons for your choice or choices.

10. Use the side notes to clarify the meaning of the following terms: **(a)** anon, **(b)** Thane, **(c)** cousins.

340 Celebrating Humanity (1485–1625)

Common Core State Standards

Writing
3. Write narratives to develop real or imagined experiences or events using effective technique, well-chosen details, and well-structured event sequences. *(p. 341)*
3.d. Use precise words and phrases, telling details, and sensory language to convey a vivid picture of the experiences, events, setting, and/or characters. *(p. 341)*

Language
4.a. Use context as a clue to the meaning of a word or phrase. *(p. 341)*
5. Demonstrate understanding of nuances in word meanings. *(p. 341)*

Assessment Practice

Fact and Opinion (For more practice, see *All-in-One Workbook*.)

Many tests require students to distinguish between fact and opinion. Have students read Act 1, Scene 2, lines 7–23. Use the following sample item to teach students to extract facts from statements that contain both fact and opinion.

Which of the following statements is a fact from the Captain's report?

A Fortune favored Macdonwald.
B Macbeth killed Macdonwald.
C Macbeth and Banquo fought like lions.
D Macdonwald is a slave.

Help students identify literary devices in the Captain's report, such as personification (choice **A**), simile (choice **C**), and metaphor (choice **D**). Point out that literary devices are usually indications of opinion. The correct answer is **B.**

340

PERFORMANCE TASKS
Integrated Language Skills

© **Vocabulary Acquisition and Use**

Word Analysis: Denotations and Connotations of Political Words

A word's **denotation** is its dictionary meaning—what it means, free of associations it might call to mind. A word's **connotation** is the set of associations and feelings that it stirs up. The denotation of *liege* is "king" or "subject." In addition to these denotative meanings, the word carries connotations of deep allegiance between ruler and subject. Another word with strong connotations is the adjective *sovereign*, suggesting a formal and absolute power, unlike its weaker synonym *dominant*.

For each of these political words, use a thesaurus to find a word with the same denotation but weaker connotations. Then, explain your choice.

1. reign (n.)   3. monarch   5. dominion
2. imperial   4. realm   6. majesty

Writing

© Narrative Text As Macbeth, write a **speech** introducing the visiting Duncan to your household. Include details you would use in a real-life introduction of a speaker.

Prewriting List facts about Duncan, such as his title and accomplishments. Then, list the traits that make him a good king.

Drafting Begin with a flattering anecdote. Then use your prewriting lists to craft an engaging narrative account of his life and accomplishments.

Revising Revise to add subtlety by telling a flattering story about Duncan that may not be widely known to the listeners. Also, place stars next to boring, overused words or phrases. Then, replace them with language that is more vivid and specific. Use words and phrases that would seem flattering to Duncan but also ironically suggest your plan to do away with him.

Model: Revising for Subtlety

These last weeks have been difficult for our liege. We can only
                                    fading
hope that his time among us will provide a ~~tired~~ king with
  long spell of bodily repose   *this realm*
a ~~bit of rest~~, and that he shall leave ~~our home~~ in a state
  heavenly rejuvenation.
of ~~renewal and health.~~

The writer replaces weak, everyday words and phrases with language that is both lofty—befitting a king—and subtly suggestive of treason.

Vocabulary: Context Clues

Each sentence below features an underlined word from the vocabulary list on page 321. If the word's meaning makes sense in the context, identify the sentence as logical. If not, identify the sentence as illogical and revise it to make it logical. Do not change the vocabulary word.

1. Macbeth's fearfulness in battle proved that he was a man of <u>valor</u>.

2. The <u>imperial</u> air with which Macbeth commanded caused others to obey him instantly.

3. Macbeth's assassination plan was aided by his habit of engaging in anxious <u>surmise</u>.

4. The witches had appealed to Macbeth's image of himself as <u>sovereign</u>.

5. Duncan believed in Macbeth and knew he was capable of <u>treason</u>.

Integrated Language Skills **341**

Vocabulary Acquisition and Use

Word Analysis

1. *Rule* is not as majestic.

2. *Royal* does not sound as powerful.

3. *Ruler* does not imply royalty.

4. *Territory* does not sound as inspiring.

5. *Leadership* does not sound as imperial.

6. *Greatness* does not sound as awe-inspiring.

Vocabulary

1. The sentence is logical.

2. The sentence is logical.

3. The sentence is illogical; change *aided to hindered*.

4. The sentence is logical.

5. The sentence is illogical; change *capable to incapable*.

Writing

1. To guide students in writing this narrative text, give them the **Support for Writing** page (*Unit 2 Resources,* page 95).

2. Remind students that even though a speech is spoken, it should still be organized in a logical way. They should organize their speech into an introductory section followed by a series of main points in which they use evidence to demonstrate Duncan's characteristics and actions.

3. If students have difficulty identifying boring or overused words and phrases in their writing, you might wish to have students underline adjectives and other descriptive phrases in their writing. Encourage students to go through these phrases one at a time, brainstorming new ways of saying the same thing. Then have students choose the best of their ideas.

4. Use the **Biographical Essay Rubrics,** *Professional Development Guidebook,* pp. 278–279, to evaluate students' work.

Assessment Resources

Unit 2 Resources

L1 L2 EL **Selection Test A,** pp. 100–102. Administer Test A to less advanced readers.

L3 L4 EL **Selection Test B,** pp. 103–105. Administer Test B to on-level and more advanced students.

L3 L4 **Open-Book Test,** pp. 97–99. As an alternative, administer the Open-Book Test.

All Customizable Test Bank

All Self-tests
Students may prepare for the **Selection Test** by taking the **Self-test** online.

PHLit Online! **PHLitOnline** All assessment resources are available at **www.PHLitOnline.com.**

341

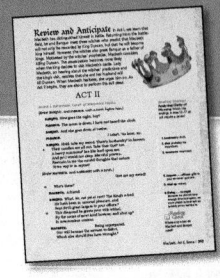

• *Macbeth*, Act II
Lesson Pacing Guide

DAY 1 Preteach

- © Administer the Reading and Vocabulary Warm-ups (*Unit 2 Resources*, pp. 106–109) as necessary.
- © Introduce the Literary Analysis concept: Blank Verse, Prose, and Comic Relief.
- • Introduce the Reading Strategy: Analyzing Clarity of Meaning.
- © Build background with Background features.
- • Develop thematic thinking with Connecting to the Essential Question.
- © Teach the selection vocabulary.

DAYS 2–3 Preteach/Teach/Assess

- • Distribute copies of the appropriate graphic organizer for the Reading Strategy (*Graphic Organizer Transparencies*, pp. 56–57).
- • Distribute copies of the appropriate graphic organizer for Literary Analysis (*Graphic Organizer Transparencies*, pp. 58–59).
- • Prepare students to read with the Activating Prior Knowledge activities (TE).
- • Informally monitor comprehension while students read.
- • Use the Reading Check questions to confirm comprehension.
- © Develop students' understanding of blank verse, prose, and comic relief using the Literary Analysis prompts.
- • Develop students' ability to clarify meaning using the Reading Strategy prompts.
- © Reinforce vocabulary with the Vocabulary notes.
- • Assess students' comprehension and mastery of the skills by having them answer the Critical Reading, Literary Analysis, and Reading Strategy questions.
- © Have students read and respond to the contemporary commentary.
- © Have students complete the Vocabulary Lesson.

DAY 4 Extend/Assess

- © Have students complete the Writing Lesson and write an interpretation of comic relief. (You may assign as homework.)
- • Have students read and respond to the Critical Commentary.
- • Administer Selection Test A or B (*Unit 2 Resources*, pp. 118–120 or 121–123).

© Common Core
State Standards

Reading Literature 5. Analyze how an author's choices concerning how to structure specific parts of a text contribute to its overall structure and meaning as well as its aesthetic impact.

Writing 1. Write arguments to support claims in an analysis of substantive topics or texts, using valid reasoning and relevant and sufficient evidence.
1.a. Introduce precise, knowledgeable claim(s), establish the significance of the claim(s), distinguish the claim(s) from alternate or opposing claims, and create an organization that logically sequences claims, counterclaims, reasons, and evidence.

Additional Standards Practice
Common Core Companion, pp. 54–55; 185–195

Daily Block Scheduling
Each day in this Lesson Pacing Guide represents a 40–50 minute period. Teachers using block scheduling may combine days to revise pacing. In addition, teachers may differentiate and support instruction by integrating components for extended and intensive support as students require. See the Guide to Selected Leveled Resources (facing page).

Guide to Selected Leveled Resources

R T I Tier 1 (students performing on level)

Macbeth, *Act II*

Warm Up		**Practice, model,** and **monitor** fluency, working with the whole class or in groups.	Vocabulary and Reading Warm-ups B, *Unit 2 Resources,* pp. 106–107, 109
Comprehension/Skills		**Support** and **monitor** comprehension and skills development, having students complete the activities, graphic organizers, and interactive prompts **independently** or **as a class.**	• *Reader's Notebook,* adapted instruction and summary EL *Reader's Notebook: English Learner's Version,* adapted instruction and summary • **Reading Skill Graphic Organizer B,** *Graphic Organizer Transparencies,* p. 57 • **Literary Analysis Graphic Organizer B,** *Graphic Organizer Transparencies,* p. 59
Monitor Progress	A	**Monitor** student progress with the differentiated curriculum-based assessment in the *Unit Resources.*	• **Selection Test B,** *Unit 2 Resources,* pp. 121–123 • **Open-Book Test,** *Unit 2 Resources,* pp. 115–117
Assess/ Screen	A	**Assess** student progress using Benchmark Test 2.	• **Benchmark Test 3,** *Unit 2 Resources,* pp. 124–129

R T I Tier 2 (students requiring intervention)

Macbeth, *Act II*

Warm Up		**Practice, model,** and **monitor** fluency **in groups** or **with individuals.**	• **Vocabulary and Reading Warm-ups A,** *Unit 2 Resources,* pp. 106–108 • *Hear It!* Audio CD
Comprehension/Skills		• **Support** and **monitor** comprehension and skills development, working **in small groups** or **with individuals.** • As students complete the selection in the appropriate version of the *Reader's Notebook,* **monitor** comprehension frequently with group questions and individual instruction. • **Model** strategies while guiding students in completing the activities and prompts in the *Reader's Notebook,* as well as the graphic organizers. • **Practice** skills and **monitor** mastery with the *Reading Kit* worksheets.	• *Reader's Notebook: Adapted Version,* adapted instruction and summary EL *Reader's Notebook: English Learner's Version,* adapted instruction and summary • **Reading Skill Graphic Organizer A,** *Graphic Organizer Transparencies,* p. 56 • **Literary Analysis Graphic Organizer A,** *Graphic Organizer Transparencies,* p. 58 • *Reading Kit,* Practice worksheets
Monitor Progress	A	**Monitor** student progress with the differentiated curriculum-based assessment in the *Unit Resources* and in the *Reading Kit.*	• **Selection Test A,** *Unit 2 Resources,* pp. 118–120 • *Reading Kit,* Assess worksheets
Assess/ Screen	A	**Assess** student progress using Benchmark Test 1.	**Benchmark Test 3,** *Unit 2 Resources,* pp. 124–129

TIER 3 Tier 3 intervention may require consultation with the student's special-education or dyslexia specialist. For additional support, see the Tier 2 activities and resources listed above.

One-on-one teaching ▪ Group work ▪ Whole class instruction ▪ Independent work ▪ A Assessment

For a complete guide to selection support, including support for Advanced students, see the Overview of Resources in the frontmatter.

• *Macbeth*, Act II

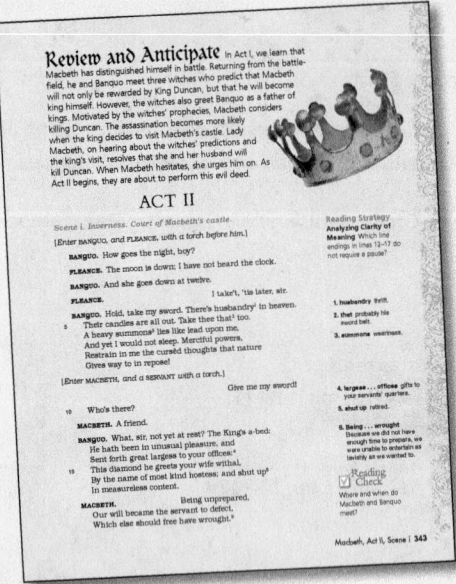

RESOURCES FOR:
- **L1** Special-Needs Students
- **L2** Below-Level Students (Tier 2)
- **L3** On-Level Students (Tier 1)
- **L4** Advanced Students (Tier 1)
- **EL** English Learners
- **All** All Students

Vocabulary/Fluency/Prior Knowledge

EL L1 L2 Vocabulary Warm-ups A and B, pp. 106–107

Also available for these selections:

EL L1 L2 Reading Warm-ups A and B, pp. 108–109

All Vocabulary Builder, p. 112

Reader's Notebooks

Pre- and postreading pages for this selection appear in an interactive format in the *Reader's Notebooks*. Each *Notebook* is differentiated for a different group of learners.
The selections in the Adapted and English Learner's versions are abridged.

- **L2 L3** *Reader's Notebook*
- **L1** *Reader's Notebook: Adapted Version*
- **EL** *Reader's Notebook: English Learner's Version*
- **EL** *Reader's Notebook: Spanish Version*

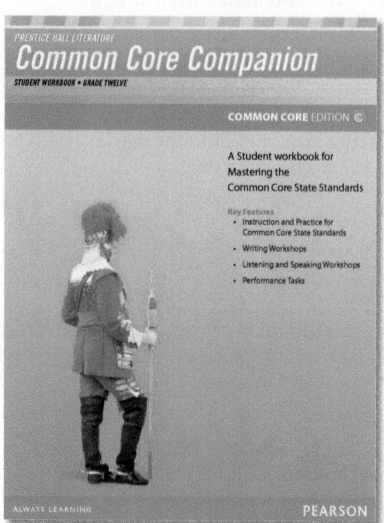

© *Common Core Companion*
Additional instruction and practice for each Common Core State Standard

Selection Support

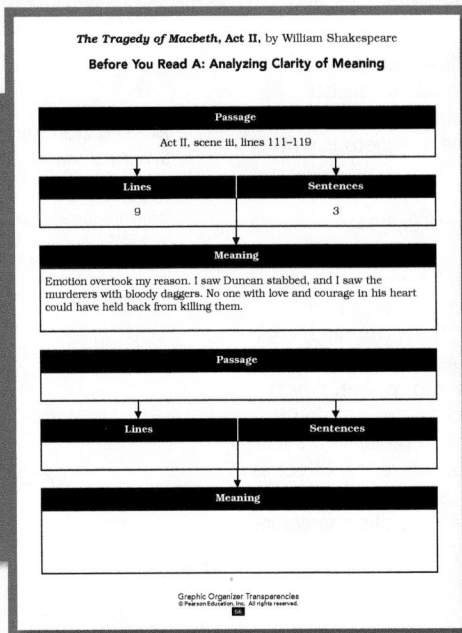

The Tragedy of Macbeth, Act II, by William Shakespeare

Before You Read A: Analyzing Clarity of Meaning

Passage
Act II, scene iii, lines 111–119

Lines	Sentences
9	3

Meaning
Emotion overtook my reason. I saw Duncan stabbed, and I saw the murderers with bloody daggers. No one with love and courage in his heart could have held back from killing them.

Passage

Lines	Sentences

Meaning

Graphic Organizer Transparencies
© Pearson Education, Inc. All rights reserved.

EL L3 Reading Graphic Organizer A (partially filled in), p. 56

Also available for these selections:

EL L1 L2 Reading: Graphic Organizer B, p. 57

EL L1 L2 Literary Analysis: Graphic Organizer A (partially filled in), p. 58

EL L3 Literary Analysis: Graphic Organizer B, p. 59

Skills Development/Extension

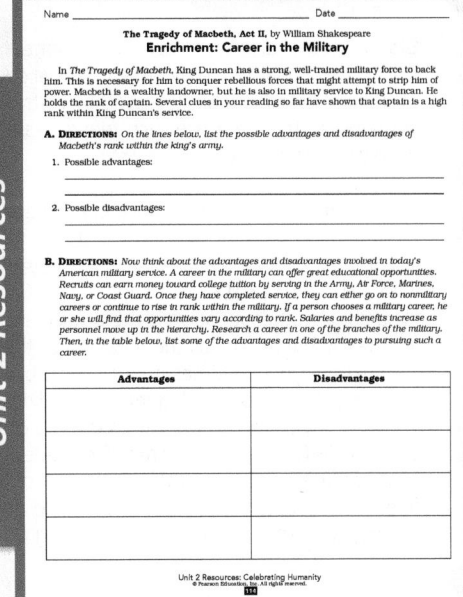

Name _____ Date _____

The Tragedy of Macbeth, Act II, by William Shakespeare
Enrichment: Career in the Military

In *The Tragedy of Macbeth,* King Duncan has a strong, well-trained military force to back him. This is necessary for him to conquer rebellious forces that might attempt to strip him of power. Macbeth is a wealthy landowner, but he is also in military service to King Duncan. He holds the rank of captain. Several clues in your reading so far have shown that captain is a high rank within King Duncan's service.

A. DIRECTIONS: *On the lines below, list the possible advantages and disadvantages of Macbeth's rank within the king's army.*

1. Possible advantages: _____

2. Possible disadvantages: _____

B. DIRECTIONS: *Now think about the advantages and disadvantages involved in today's American military service. A career in the military can offer great educational opportunities. Recruits can earn money toward college tuition by serving in the Army, Air Force, Marines, Navy, or Coast Guard. Once they have completed service, they can either go on to nonmilitary careers or continue to rise in rank within the military. If a person chooses a military career, he or she will find that opportunities vary according to rank. Salaries and benefits increase as personnel move up in the hierarchy. Research a career in one of the branches of the military. Then, in the table below, list some of the advantages and disadvantages to pursuing such a career.*

Advantages	Disadvantages

Unit 2 Resources: Celebrating Humanity
© Pearson Education, Inc. All rights reserved.

L4 Enrichment, p. 114

Also available for these selections:

All Literary Analysis: p. 110

All Reading, p. 111

EL L3 L4 Support for Writing, p. 113

Assessment

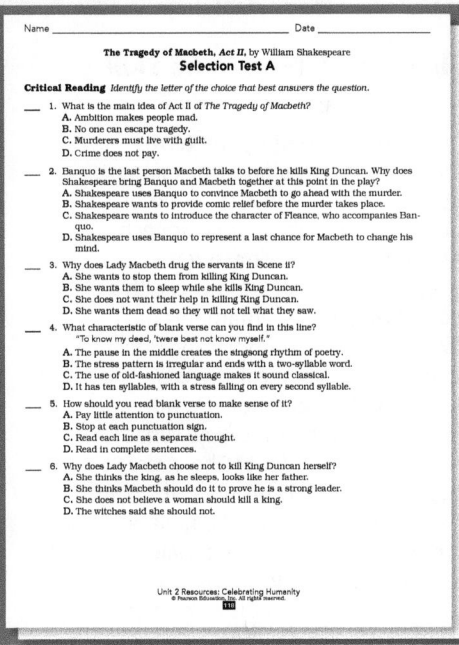

Name _____ Date _____

The Tragedy of Macbeth, Act II, by William Shakespeare
Selection Test A

Critical Reading *Identify the letter of the choice that best answers the question.*

____ 1. What is the main idea of Act II of *The Tragedy of Macbeth?*
A. Ambition makes people mad.
B. No one can escape tragedy.
C. Murderers must live with guilt.
D. Crime does not pay.

____ 2. Banquo is the last person Macbeth talks to before he kills King Duncan. Why does Shakespeare bring Banquo and Macbeth together at this point in the play?
A. Shakespeare uses Banquo to convince Macbeth to go ahead with the murder.
B. Shakespeare wants to provide comic relief before the murder takes place.
C. Shakespeare wants to introduce the character of Fleance, who accompanies Banquo.
D. Shakespeare uses Banquo to represent a last chance for Macbeth to change his mind.

____ 3. Why does Lady Macbeth drug the servants in Scene ii?
A. She wants to stop them from killing King Duncan.
B. She wants them to sleep while she kills King Duncan.
C. She does not want their help in killing King Duncan.
D. She wants them dead so they will not tell what they saw.

____ 4. What characteristic of blank verse can you find in this line?
"To know my deed, 'twere best not know myself."
A. The pause in the middle creates the singsong rhythm of poetry.
B. The stress pattern is irregular and ends with a two-syllable word.
C. The use of old-fashioned language makes it sound classical.
D. It has ten syllables, with a stress falling on every second syllable.

____ 5. How should you read blank verse to make sense of it?
A. Pay little attention to punctuation.
B. Stop at each punctuation sign.
C. Read each line as a separate thought.
D. Read in complete sentences.

____ 6. Why does Lady Macbeth choose not to kill King Duncan herself?
A. She thinks the king, as he sleeps, looks like her father.
B. She thinks Macbeth should do it to prove he is a strong leader.
C. She does not believe a woman should kill a king.
D. The witches said she should not.

Unit 2 Resources: Celebrating Humanity
© Pearson Education, Inc. All rights reserved.

EL L1 L2 Selection Test A, pp. 118–120

Also available for these selections:

L3 L4 Open-Book Test, pp. 115–117

EL L3 L4 Selection Test B, pp. 121–123

Online Resources: All print materials are also available online.

- complete narrated selection text
- a thematically related video with writing prompt
- an interactive graphic organizer
- highlighting feature
- access to all student print resources, adapted to individual student needs
- Spanish and English summaries
- adapted selection translations in Spanish

Get Connected! (thematic video with writing prompt)

Also available:

Background Video
All videos are available in Spanish.

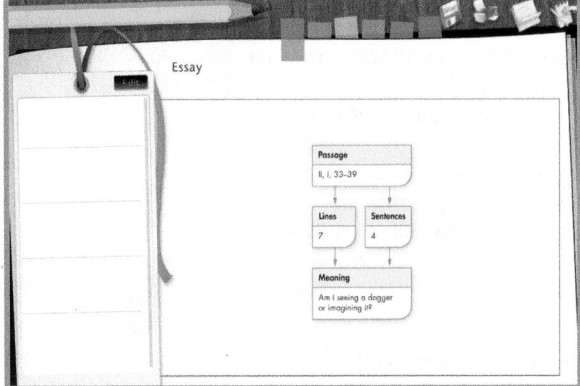

Writer's Journal (with graphics feature)

Also available:

Vocabulary Central (tools and activities for studying vocabulary)

❶ Literary Analysis

Introduce the skill using the instruction on the student page.

Think Aloud: Model the Skill

Say to students:

I may be confused by the terms *iambic pentameter* and *trochaic foot.* But our text says that this kind of poetry sounds like natural speech. An iamb has an unstressed and a stressed syllable. It sounds like this: da DUM. Iambic pentameter has five such units. Examples include: *forgot, escape, agree.* Here is a whole iambic sentence: *Do not forget to feed the cat today.* What about a trochaic foot? The stress should come first this time. It should sound like DUM da. Here are some examples of trochaic feet: *student, essay, homework, gym class, sandwich.* Here is a short trochaic sentence: *Students must do homework.*

❷ Reading Strategy

1. Introduce the skill using the instruction on the student page.

2. Give students a copy of **Reading Strategy Graphic Organizer B,** page 57 in *Graphic Organizer Transparencies,* to fill out as they read.

Think Aloud: Model the Skill

Say to students:

As I read blank verse, I may get mixed up between the ends of the lines and the ends of the sentences. At the beginning of Act 2, the first few lines are also sentences, like *How goes the night, boy?* But then I come to Banquo's third speech, in lines 4 through 9. Here, the ends of lines and ends of sentences do not match. I can make a chart like the one on page 342 to sort it out.

❸ Vocabulary

1. Pronounce each word, giving its definition, and have students say it aloud.

2. For more guidance, see the *Classroom Strategies and Teaching Routines* card for introducing vocabulary.

COMMON CORE ▪ EXTENDED STUDY: SHAKESPEAREAN DRAMA

Before You Read | *Macbeth, Act II*

❶ Literary Analysis

Blank verse—unrhymed iambic pentameter—was invented during the English Renaissance to reflect natural speech. An **iamb** consists of an unstressed syllable followed by a stressed syllable (˘ ´). In iambic pentameter, there are five such feet (units) to the line. *Macbeth* is written mainly in blank verse, as follows:

> Methóught Ĭ héard ă vóice crý, "Sléep ňo móre!" (II,ii,34)

For interest, Shakespeare varies his meter, as when he begins this line with a **trochaic foot** (´ ˘): "List'ning their fear, I could not say 'Amen'" (II, ii, 28). Another variation is the **anapestic foot** (˘ ˘ ´). As you read, listen for the rhythm as well as the meaning of the dialogue.

Shakespeare sometimes interrupts his blank verse with **prose,** which is writing that is not divided into poetic lines and lacks a definite rhythm. In his tragedies, lower-ranking characters often speak in prose to provide **comic relief,** a humorous break from a tense mood. Notice this effect as you read the Porter's speech at the start of Act II, Scene iii. By using different line structures, such as blank verse or prose, for specific characters, Shakespeare adds to the overall meaning of the play.

❷ Reading Strategy

Preparing to Read Complex Texts A key *pattern of organization* in Shakespeare's blank verse is the way in which sentences and blank verse lines interact. By **analyzing** that interaction, you can better understand how Shakespeare achieves **clarity of meaning.** In making your analysis, follow sentences past line endings. For instance, you must follow this sentence past the end of the line to learn what the owl does:

> *"It was the owl that shrieked, the fatal bellman,*
> *Which gives the stern'st good-night. . . ." (II, ii, 3–4).*

Use a chart like this one to distinguish between lines and sentences.

❸ Vocabulary

augment (ôg ment´) *v.* make greater; enlarge (p. 344)

palpable (pal´ pə bəl) *adj.* capable of being touched or felt (p. 344)

stealthy (stel´ thē) *adj.* sly (p. 344)

multitudinous (mul´ tə tōōd´ ′n əs) *adj.* existing in great numbers (p. 344)

equivocate (ē kwiv´ ə kāt´) *v.* to use terms that have two or more meanings to mislead purposely or deceive (p. 348)

predominance (prē däm´ ə nəns) *n.* superiority (p. 354)

---

342 Celebrating Humanity (1485–1625)

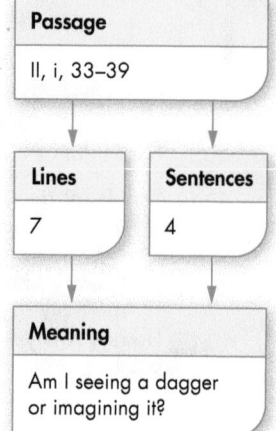

Passage
II, i, 33–39

Lines	Sentences
7	4

Meaning
Am I seeing a dagger or imagining it?

www.PHLitOnline.com

Teaching From Technology

Preparing to Read
Go to **www.PHLitOnline.com** in class or in a lab and display the **Get Connected!** slide show for this act. Have the class brainstorm responses to the slide show writing prompt, entering ideas in the interactive journal. Then have students complete their written responses individually, in a lab or as homework.

To build background, display the Background video and More About the Author slide show.

Using the Interactive Text
Go to **www.PHLitOnline.com** and display the **Enriched Online Student Edition.** As the class reads the selection or listens to the narration, record answers to side-column prompts using the graphic organizers accessible on the interactive page. Alternatively, have students use the online edition individually, answering the prompts as they read.

❶ ❷ Review and Anticipate

In Act I, we learn that Macbeth has distinguished himself in battle. Returning from the battlefield, he and Banquo meet three witches who predict that Macbeth will not only be rewarded by King Duncan, but that he will become king himself. However, the witches also greet Banquo as a father of kings. Motivated by the witches' prophecies, Macbeth considers killing Duncan. The assassination becomes more likely when the king decides to visit Macbeth's castle. Lady Macbeth, on hearing about the witches' predictions and the king's visit, resolves that she and her husband will kill Duncan. When Macbeth hesitates, she urges him on. As Act II begins, they are about to perform this evil deed.

ACT II

Scene i. Inverness. Court of Macbeth's castle.

[*Enter* BANQUO, *and* FLEANCE, *with a torch before him.*]

BANQUO. How goes the night, boy?

FLEANCE. The moon is down; I have not heard the clock.

BANQUO. And she goes down at twelve.

FLEANCE.   I take't, 'tis later, sir.

BANQUO. Hold, take my sword. There's husbandry[1] in heaven.
5   Their candles are all out. Take thee that[2] too.
       A heavy summons[3] lies like lead upon me,
       And yet I would not sleep. Merciful powers,
       Restrain in me the cursèd thoughts that nature
       Gives way to in repose!

[*Enter* MACBETH, *and a* SERVANT *with a torch.*]

                         Give me my sword!

10   Who's there?

MACBETH. A friend.

BANQUO. What, sir, not yet at rest? The King's a-bed:
       He hath been in unusual pleasure, and
       Sent forth great largess to your offices:[4]
15   This diamond he greets your wife withal,
       By the name of most kind hostess; and shut up[5]
       In measureless content.

MACBETH.   Being unprepared,
       Our will became the servant to defect,
       Which else should free have wrought.[6]

---

❸ Reading Strategy

Analyzing Clarity of Meaning Which line endings in lines 12–17 do not require a pause?

1. **husbandry** thrift.

2. **that** probably his sword belt.

3. **summons** weariness.

4. **largess . . . offices** gifts to your servants' quarters.

5. **shut up** retired.

6. **Being . . . wrought** Because we did not have enough time to prepare, we were unable to entertain as lavishly as we wanted to.

❹  Reading Check

Where and when do Macbeth and Banquo meet?

Macbeth, Act II, Scene i **343**

TEACH

❶ About the Selection

In this act, thoughts become deeds. It appears that Macbeth and Lady Macbeth have committed the perfect crime. In fact, it may have been more successful than they had hoped—the attendants are slain and unable to defend themselves, and Duncan's sons flee, casting suspicion upon themselves. However, their plot begins to unravel and hints of tragedy begin to appear. One of the play's major themes—the fatal flaw of excessive ambition—emerges as Macbeth becomes tortured by guilt.

❷ Activating Prior Knowledge

Review the plan Macbeth and Lady Macbeth have made for "the perfect crime." Ask students to write a paragraph detailing what complications Macbeth and Lady Macbeth might anticipate in the execution of their "perfect crime."

Concept Connector ➤

Tell students they will return to their responses after reading the selection.

❸ Reading Strategy

Analyzing Clarity of Meaning

1. Remind students that reading blank verse for meaning often requires following sentences past their line endings.

2. **Ask:** Which line endings in lines 12–17 do not require a pause? **Answer:** Lines 13 and 16 do not require a pause.

❹ Reading Check

Answer: After midnight, in the court of Macbeth's castle, at Inverness.

Differentiated Instruction for Universal Access

Support for Special-Needs Students
Have students complete the **Before You Read** and the **Making Connections** pages for this selection in the *Reader's Notebook: Adapted Version.* These pages provide an abbreviated skills instrucrion, a selection summary, **Before You Read** graphic organizer instrucrion, and a **Note-taking Guide.**

Support for Less Proficient Readers
Have students complete the **Before You Read** and the **Making Connections** pages for this selection in the *Reader's Notebook.* These pages provide an abbreviated skills, a selection summary, the graphic organizer on the **Before You Read** page in the student book, and a **Note-taking Guide.**

EL Support for English Learners
Have students complete the **Before You Read** and the **Making Connections** pages for this selection in the *Reader's Notebook: English Learner's Version.* These pages provide additional vocabulary, vocabulary skills, and vocabulary practice, along with a **Getting Ready to Read** activity.

Analyzing Clarity of Meaning

1. Have students read the exchange between Banquo and Macbeth in lines 19–29.

2. **Ask** how Banquo's words, "All's well," and Macbeth's response, "I think not of them," are similar and different.
   Answer: Both are untrue, but only Macbeth knows that what he is saying is untrue.

3. Point out that Macbeth's next sentence runs almost three lines. He suggests that when he and Banquo have some time, they should talk about the witches.

4. **Ask** students what Macbeth is asking and promising Banquo in lines 25–26.
   Answer: He is asking Banquo to join his cause, and he promises him honor.

5. **Ask** students how Banquo responds.
   Answer: He is not interested in honors that might diminish his own sense of honor. However, if he can have a clear conscience and remain faithful, he would consider promotion.

❻ Critical Thinking

Analyze

1. Have students read Macbeth's soliloquy of lines 33–61.

2. **Ask** what Macbeth sees and what the vision adds to the play.
   Answer: He sees a dagger that keeps moving away from him. The dagger becomes covered with blood. The vision heightens the drama, points to what is to come, and perhaps makes us ask if Macbeth is becoming unhinged.

3. **Ask** students at what point in the passage Macbeth ceases to hallucinate and proceeds with his plan.
   Answer: In line 47, when he says "there's no such thing," the hallucination has ceased—or been dismissed.

4. **Ask:** Of what story element do lines 49–52 remind the audience?
   Answer: These lines tie in with the witchcraft that has perhaps brought Macbeth to this point.

---

7. **cleave . . . 'tis** join my cause when the time comes.

8. **So** provided that.

Vocabulary
augment (ôg ment´) *v.* make greater; enlarge

9. **bosom franchised** heart free (from guilt).

Vocabulary
palpable (pal´ pə bəl) *adj.* capable of being touched or felt

10. **sensible** able to be felt.

11. **marshal'st** leads.

12. **dudgeon** wooden hilt.

13. **gouts** large drops.

14. **informs** takes shape.

15. **abuse** deceive.

16. **Hecate's** (hek´ə tēz) **offerings** offerings to Hecate, the Greek goddess of witchcraft.

Vocabulary
stealthy (stel´ thē) *adj.* sly

17. **Tarquin's** of Tarquin, a Roman tyrant.

---

❺ **BANQUO.**   All's well.
20 I dreamt last night of the three weird sisters:
    To you they have showed some truth.

MACBETH.   I think not of them.
    Yet, when we can entreat an hour to serve,
    We would spend it in some words upon that business,
    If you would grant the time.

BANQUO.   At your kind'st leisure.

25 **MACBETH.** If you shall cleave to my consent, when 'tis,[7]
    It shall make honor for you.

BANQUO.   So[8] I lose none
    In seeking to augment it, but still keep
    My bosom franchised[9] and allegiance clear,
    I shall be counseled.

MACBETH.   Good repose the while!

30 **BANQUO.** Thanks, sir. The like to you!

                                    [*Exit* BANQUO *with* FLEANCE.]

MACBETH. Go bid thy mistress, when my drink is ready,
    She strike upon the bell. Get thee to bed.

                                    [*Exit* SERVANT.]

    Is this a dagger which I see before me,
    The handle toward my hand? Come, let me clutch thee.
35 I have thee not, and yet I see thee still.
    Art thou not, fatal vision, sensible[10]
    To feeling as to sight, or art thou but
    A dagger of the mind, a false creation,
    Proceeding from the heat-oppressèd brain?
40 I see thee yet, in form as palpable
    As this which now I draw.
    Thou marshal'st[11] me the way that I was going;
    And such an instrument I was to use.
    Mine eyes are made the fools o' th' other senses,
45 Or else worth all the rest. I see thee still;
    And on thy blade and dudgeon[12] gouts[13] of blood,
    Which was not so before. There's no such thing.
    It is the bloody business which informs[14]
    Thus to mine eyes. Now o'er the one half-world
50 Nature seems dead, and wicked dreams abuse[15]
    The curtained sleep; witchcraft celebrates
    Pale Hecate's offerings;[16] and withered murder,
    Alarumed by his sentinel, the wolf,
    Whose howl's his watch, thus with his stealthy pace,
55 With Tarquin's[17] ravishing strides, towards his design
    Moves like a ghost. Thou sure and firm-set earth,

344 Celebrating Humanity (1485–1625)

Enrichment: Analyzing Film

Shakespeare Adaptations

Only the Bible has been translated into more languages than Shakespeare's works. In addition Shakespeare's plays have been adapted to other art forms. Japanese film director Akira Kurosawa turned *Macbeth* into a film called *Throne of Blood*. Kurosawa's Macbeth is a samurai lord, and the film is set in medieval Japan. Kurosawa also adapted *King Lear* for his film *Ran*. Leonard Bernstein based *West Side Story* on *Romeo and Juliet*. The sci-fi classic *Forbidden Planet* is based on *The Tempest*.

Activity: Connecting Genres Have students watch a film based on one of Shakespeare's plays. Have them also read the play that the film is based on. Have students write an essay comparing the film to the play Suggest that students record information in the **Enrichment: Analyzing Film** worksheet, found in the *Professional Development Guidebook*, page 226.

Hear not my steps, which way they walk, for fear
Thy very stones prate of my whereabout,
And take the present horror from the time,
6
60 Which now suits with it.[18] Whiles I threat, he lives:
Words to the heat of deeds too cold breath gives.

[*A bell rings.*]

    I go, and it is done: the bell invites me.
Hear it not, Duncan, for it is a knell
That summons thee to heaven, or to hell.   [*Exit.*]

Scene ii. Macbeth's castle

[*Enter* LADY MACBETH.]

LADY MACBETH. That which hath made them drunk hath made
    me bold;
What hath quenched them hath given me fire. Hark! Peace!
It was the owl that shrieked, the fatal bellman,
Which gives the stern'st good-night.[1] He is about it.
5 The doors are open, and the surfeited grooms[2]
7
Do mock their charge with snores. I have drugged their possets,[3]
That death and nature do contend about them,
Whether they live or die.

MACBETH.   [*Within*] Who's there? What, ho?

LADY MACBETH. Alack, I am afraid they have awaked
10 And 'tis not done! Th' attempt and not the deed
Confounds[4] us. Hark! I laid their daggers ready;
He could not miss 'em. Had he not resembled
My father as he slept, I had done 't.

[*Enter* MACBETH.]

                My husband!

MACBETH. I have done the deed. Didst thou not hear a noise?

15 **LADY MACBETH.** I heard the owl scream and the crickets cry.
    Did not you speak?

MACBETH.   When?

LADY MACBETH.   Now.

MACBETH.   As I descended?

8
LADY MACBETH. Ay.

MACBETH. Hark!
    Who lies i' th' second chamber?

LADY MACBETH.   Donalbain.

20 **MACBETH.** This is a sorry[5] sight.

LADY MACBETH. A foolish thought, to say a sorry sight.

Macbeth, Act II, Scene ii **345**

Spiral Review
Soliloquy In what way do lines 31–61 introduce a new sound into poetry, the "sound" of someone thinking aloud on stage?

18. **take . . . it** remove the horrible silence that suits this moment.

1. **bellman . . . good-night** It was customary for a bell to be rung at midnight outside a condemned person's cell on the night before an execution.

2. **surfeited grooms** overfed servants.

3. **possets** warm bedtime drinks.

4. **Confounds** ruins.

Literary Analysis
Blank Verse Notice that the iambic pentameter of line 16 is shared in dialogue between Macbeth and Lady Macbeth. Why might the playwright have chosen this artistry?

5. **sorry** miserable.

Reading Check
What deed have Macbeth and Lady Macbeth performed?

Spiral Review

Soliloquy

  Ask students the Spiral Review question.

  Possible response: Shakespeare uses the soliloquy to give a voice to Macbeth's internal struggle. Although the language retains its poetic rhythm and sound, there is an increased intensity and rawness to the language of a character wrestling with his own emotions and fears.

7 Critical Thinking

Analyze

1. Have students review lines 1–13.

2. **Ask** students what it is that Lady Macbeth has contributed to the murder plot.
  Answer: She has drugged the king's servants and has placed their daggers where they can easily be found.

3. **Ask** students what comments indicate that Lady Macbeth is not as cold as she would like to think.
  Answer: In line 2, she is jumpy, spooked by the owl. In lines 12–13, she admits that she could not have murdered Duncan herself, because he looked like her father while he slept.

8 Literary Analysis

Blank Verse

1. **Ask** students what mood or atmosphere lines 15–20 create.
  Answer: These lines suggest an atmosphere of tension, as if the characters are jumping at the sound of each other's voice.

2. Point out that, though it looks at first as if Shakespeare has abandoned writing in verse, the iambic pentameter is actually continued across these lines of dialogue, starting in line 16.

3. **Ask** students the Literary Analysis question.
  Possible response: The choppy speech contributes to the mood. Also, having Macbeth and Lady Macbeth finishing each other's lines adds to the sense of their complicity in the murder.

9 Reading Check

Answer: They have murdered Duncan.

Differentiated Instruction for Universal Access

Culturally Responsive Instruction

Culture Focus Point out to students the symbols Shakespeare uses to indicate that Duncan is about to die: the bell tolling and the owl shrieking. Tell students that owls are symbols in many cultures. Owls are nocturnal, and they are birds of prey. In some cultures, owls symbolize wisdom. In others, the cry of an owl, or the appearance of an owl, is thought to portend a death. Invite students to share their thoughts about what an owl might symbolize. Then ask students to list other symbols of death or destruction from their own culture or other cultures.

Infer

1. Direct students' attention to lines 25–34.

2. **Ask** students why Macbeth would have listened with such care to what was being said by the two sleepers.
   Answer: He would want to know if they heard him, or if he was about to be discovered.

3. **Ask** students what significance they draw from the fact that Macbeth is unable to respond to the blessing with "Amen."
   Possible responses: Macbeth's inability to engage in prayer suggests that he feels a strong sense of guilt and of divine disapproval of his act. He has descended so far into evil that he can no longer do anything that would be viewed as good or holy.

⑪ **Critical Thinking**

Analyze

1. Have students **analyze** lines 34–38 and list at least three qualities that Macbeth ascribes to sleep. **Possible responses:** Sleep is innocent. Sleep helps untangle the worrisome issues of life. Sleep helps one's body heal from the day's work and one's mind heal from the day's problems. Sleep is nourishing—it builds one up and gives strength.

2. **Ask** students what Macbeth means when he says that he has murdered sleep.
   Possible response: As is stated in line 42, "Macbeth shall sleep no more." Macbeth will be unable to sleep because his mind is troubled.

⑫ **Critical Viewing**

Answer: The sinister shadows reflect the treachery that is hatched in Act 2. The eyes of Macbeth reflect a sense of shock at the horrible nature of the crime. Lady Macbeth's posture and facial expression suggest cold, almost mechanical determination.

---

6. **two** Malcolm and Donalbain, Duncan's sons.

7. **knits . . . sleave** straightens out the tangled threads.

8. **second course** main course; sleep.

9. **unbend** relax.

10. **witness** evidence.

11. **gild** paint.

⑫ ▶ **Critical Viewing** How do these images from a poster advertising a production of *Macbeth* capture the suspense created in Act II? **[Connect]**

MACBETH. There's one did laugh in 's sleep, and one cried "Murder!"
That they did wake each other. I stood and heard them.
But they did say their prayers, and addressed them
Again to sleep.

25 **LADY MACBETH.** There are two[6] lodged together.

MACBETH. One cried "God bless us!" and "Amen" the other,
As they had seen me with these hangman's hands:
List'ning their fear, I could not say "Amen,"
When they did say "God bless us!"

LADY MACBETH. Consider it not so deeply.

⑩ 30 **MACBETH.** But wherefore could not I pronounce "Amen"?
I had most need of blessing, and "Amen"
Stuck in my throat.

LADY MACBETH. These deeds must not be thought
After these ways; so, it will make us mad.

MACBETH. Methought I heard a voice cry "Sleep no more!
35 Macbeth does murder sleep"—the innocent sleep,
Sleep that knits up the raveled sleave[7] of care,
The death of each day's life, sore labor's bath,
Balm of hurt minds, great nature's second course,[8]
Chief nourisher in life's feast—

⑪

LADY MACBETH. What do you mean?

40 **MACBETH.** Still it cried "Sleep no more!" to all the house:
"Glamis hath murdered sleep, and therefore Cawdor
Shall sleep no more: Macbeth shall sleep no more."

LADY MACBETH. Who was it that thus cried? Why, worthy Thane,
You do unbend[9] your noble strength, to think
45 So brainsickly of things. Go get some water,
And wash this filthy witness[10] from your hand.
Why did you bring these daggers from the place?
They must lie there: go carry them, and smear
The sleepy grooms with blood.

MACBETH. I'll go no more.
50 I am afraid to think what I have done;
Look on 't again I dare not.

LADY MACBETH. Infirm of purpose!
Give me the daggers. The sleeping and the dead
Are but as pictures. 'Tis the eye of childhood
That fears a painted devil. If he do bleed,
55 I'll gild[11] the faces of the grooms withal,
For it must seem their guilt.   [*Exit. Knock within.*]

346 Celebrating Humanity (1485–1625)

Enrichment: Investigating Psychology

Guilt

Psychologists have devoted considerable research to the subject of guilt and its effect on an individual who has committed a crime. Shakespeare's *Macbeth* is, to a large degree, also a study of the effects of guilt. In Act 2, the guilt Macbeth feels after he murders Duncan is manifest in several ways: He is unable to answer a blessing with "Amen" and he thinks he hears a voice saying "Sleep no more!" The effects of guilt are manifested even more dramatically in later acts.

Activity: Comparing and Contrasting Have students research the way in which police officers prepare psychological profiles of criminals. Have them use the results of their research to prepare a psychological profile of Macbeth and Lady Macbeth. Suggest that students record information in the **Enrichment: Investigating Psychology** worksheet, *Professional Development Guidebook*, page 239.

Macbeth, Act II, Scene i **347**

Poster for Orson Welles's film of *Macbeth*

Orson Welles, famous for the film *Citizen Kane* and the radio broadcast *War of the Worlds*, adapted Shakespeare's *Macbeth* for the screen and then directed and starred in the production. This 1948 version also featured Jeanette Nolan and Roddy McDowall. The production is notable for its papier-mâché sets and brooding atmosphere.

The shadowy poster for Welles's *Macbeth* emphasizes the darkness of the play's content. Orson Welles's face, made up as Macbeth at various points during the drama, conveys to viewers that the play is about a tortured individual.

Use these questions for discussion:

1. What emotion is portrayed by each of the expressions in Welles's face in this poster?
   Possible responses: Welles's face conjures up images of cold-blooded determination, fear, hate, helplessness, remorse, and resignation.

2. **Ask:** Do you find that the poster captures the essence of *The Tragedy of Macbeth?*
   Possible response: Yes, the various expressions of Macbeth show that it is ultimately a human tragedy; no, the poster focuses too much on Macbeth and not enough on the others.

Differentiated
Instruction   for Universal Access

Strategy for Special-Needs Students
Have students use the *Reader's Notebook: Adapted Version* to help them get involved in the story. The summary and simplified version of the first scene may give them just the start they need to discover the story buried in the language. Then, as students continue reading Act 2 in the Student Edition, summarize each scene so they do not lose the thread of the story. Read important speeches aloud, so that the students can begin to get a feel for the language without getting lost in it.

Enrichment for Gifted/Talented Students
Suggest that students create their own "movie posters" for this play, using color, images, and words to "hook" potential audiences into coming to see *Macbeth*. Encourage them to think about the characters, actions, emotions, and images of the play as they plan their posters. When their posters are done, have students describe what message they were trying to get across, and what elements they chose to highlight. Hang their posters in the classroom.

Blank Verse, Prose, and Comic Relief

1. **Ask** students the Literary Analysis question: How do the shift from verse to prose in Scene 3 and the Porter's remarks affect the mood? **Answer:** The mood shifts from one of great tension to one of lighthearted humor; this scene offers the audience some relief from the tension.

2. Discuss how and why the Porter's reaction to the knocking is different from the reactions of Macbeth and Lady Macbeth in the previous scene.
Possible responses: For the Porter, it is a job; for Macbeth and Lady Macbeth, it is a warning that people approach. Macbeth is appalled, certain that the knocking is related to his guilt; Lady Macbeth views it as a sign to get moving, so they will not get caught; the Porter is annoyed at being awakened.

⓯ **Engaging the Essential Question**

1. Remind students that Shakespeare sometimes interrupts his blank verse with prose. Prose is usually reserved for low-ranking characters. Also, only low-ranking characters were bawdy or vulgar. Their often humorous speeches helped break up the dramatic narrative. This device is called comic relief and is common in Elizabethan drama.

2. **Ask** students to discuss the ways in which Shakespeare employs comedy in Scene 3.
Possible responses: The Porter uses comedic language; the Porter does not want to do his own job. The Porter has had too much to drink and cannot do his job. The juxtaposition of the Porter's behavior with the murder of the king produces a comedic effect.

Vocabulary

multitudinous (mul′ tə tood̄′ 'n əs) *adj.* existing in great numbers

12. **incarnadine** (in kär′ nə dīn) redden.

13. **Your constancy . . . unattended** Your firmness of purpose has left you.

14. **watchers** up late.

Literary Analysis

Blank Verse, Prose, and Comic Relief
How do the shift from verse to prose in Scene iii and the porter's remarks affect the mood?

1. **porter** doorkeeper.

2. **should have old** would have plenty of.

3. **Beelzebub** (bē el′ zə bub′) the chief devil.

4. **a farmer . . . plenty** a farmer who hoarded grain, hoping the prices would come up after a bad harvest.

5. **enow** enough.

Vocabulary

equivocate (ē kwiv′ ə kāt′) *v.* to use terms that have two or more meanings to mislead purposely or deceive

6. **an equivocator . . . scale** a liar who could make two contradictory statements and swear both were true.

7. **stealing . . . hose** stealing some cloth from the hose while making them.

8. **goose** pressing iron.

MACBETH.   Whence is that knocking?
How is 't with me, when every noise appalls me?
What hands are here? Ha! They pluck out mine eyes!
Will all great Neptune's ocean wash this blood
60 Clean from my hand? No; this my hand will rather
The multitudinous seas incarnadine,[12]
Making the green one red.

[*Enter* LADY MACBETH.]

LADY MACBETH. My hands are of your color, but I shame
To wear a heart so white. [*Knock.*] I hear a knocking
65 At the south entry. Retire we to our chamber.
A little water clears us of this deed:
How easy is it then! Your constancy
Hath left you unattended.[13] [*Knock.*] Hark! more knocking.
Get on your nightgown, lest occasion call us
70 And show us to be watchers.[14] Be not lost
So poorly in your thoughts.

MACBETH. To know my deed, 'twere best not know myself. [*Knock.*]
Wake Duncan with thy knocking! I would thou couldst!

[*Exit.*]

⓮

Scene iii. Macbeth's castle.

[*Enter a* PORTER.[1] *Knocking within.*]

PORTER. Here's a knocking indeed! If a man were porter
of hell gate, he should have old[2] turning the key.
[*Knock.*] Knock, knock, knock! Who's there, i' th'
name of Beelzebub?[3] Here's a farmer, that
5 hanged himself on th' expectation of plenty.[4] Come
in time! Have napkins enow[5] about you; here you'll
sweat for 't. [*Knock.*] Knock, knock! Who's there, in
th' other devil's name? Faith, here's an equivocator,
that could swear in both the scales against
⓯ 10 either scale;[6] who committed treason enough for
God's sake, yet could not equivocate to heaven. O,
come in, equivocator. [*Knock.*] Knock, knock, knock!
Who's there? Faith, here's an English tailor come
hither for stealing out of a French hose:[7]
15 come in, tailor. Here you may roast your goose.[8]
[*Knock.*] Knock, knock; never at quiet! What are you?
But this place is too cold for hell. I'll devil-porter it no
further. I had thought to have let in some of all
professions that go the primrose way to th'
20 everlasting bonfire. [*Knock.*] Anon, anon!
[*Opens an entrance.*] I pray you, remember the porter.

Think Aloud

Literary Analysis: Comic Relief
Say to students:

The Porter's speech is another soliloquy. Unlike Macbeth's soliloquy in Scene 1, the Porter's soliloquy is meant to be comic. However, it may be confusing. The Porter keeps pretending to see people: a farmer, an equivocator, a tailor. But those people are not really at the door. Here is a clue: He says, "Who's there, in the name of Beelzebub?" Surely that is not how Macbeth has told the Porter to answer knocking at his gate. The Porter has gotten drunk and is being silly. He is pretending that his master, Macbeth, is the devil himself and that these are the gates of hell. Meanwhile he is ignoring the knocking and invites in his imaginary visitors. Finally, though, he sobers up enough to answer the door. He realizes, "This place is too cold for hell." The Porter does not realize, it, though, but his words are not entirely wrong. The castle has become a hell for Macbeth and his wife, but it is a hell made up of their own thoughts and guilt.

[Enter MACDUFF and LENNOX.]

MACDUFF. Was it so late, friend, ere you went to bed,
That you do lie so late?

25 **PORTER.** Faith, sir, we were carousing till the second
cock:[9] and drink, sir, is a great provoker of three
things.

MACDUFF. What three things does drink especially
provoke?

5

30 **PORTER.** Marry, sir, nose-painting, sleep, and urine.
Lechery, sir, it provokes and unprovokes; it provokes
16 the desire, but it takes away the performance: therefore much drink may be said to be an equivocator
with lechery: it makes him and it mars him; it
35 sets him on and it takes him off; it persuades him
and disheartens him; makes him stand to and not
stand to; in conclusion equivocates him in a sleep,
and giving him the lie, leaves him.

MACDUFF. I believe drink gave thee the lie[10] last night.

40 **PORTER.** That it did, sir, i' the very throat on me: but I
requited him for his lie, and, I think, being too strong
for him, though he took up my legs sometime, yet I
make a shift to cast[11] him.

MACDUFF. Is thy master stirring?

7 [Enter MACBETH.]

Our knocking has awaked him; here he comes.

LENNOX. Good morrow, noble sir.

45 **MACBETH.**   Good morrow, both.

MACDUFF. Is the king stirring, worthy Thane?

MACBETH.   Not yet.

MACDUFF. He did command me to call timely[12] on him:
I have almost slipped the hour.

MACBETH.   I'll bring you to him.

MACDUFF. I know this is a joyful trouble to you;
50 But yet 'tis one.

MACBETH. The labor we delight in physics pain.[13]
This is the door.

MACDUFF.   I'll make so bold to call,
For 'tis my limited service.[14]

[Exit MACDUFF.]

LENNOX. Goes the king hence today?

---

9. **second cock** 3:00 A.M.

10. **gave thee the lie** laid you out.

11. **cast** vomit.

Literary Analysis
Blank Verse and Prose
Why is it appropriate for the dialogue in lines 43–44 to change back from prose to blank verse?

12. **timely** early.

13. **labor . . . pain** labor we enjoy cures discomfort.

14. **limited service** assigned duty.

18 ☑ Reading Check
To what gate does the porter compare the gate of Macbeth's castle?

Macbeth, Act II, Scene iii **349**

---

16 Critical Thinking
Interpret

1. Explain to students that while the Porter's speech does not really further the plot, his slowness does.

2. Point out that the ideas the Porter raises, though apparently off the point, still are tied to the ideas of the play: References to the diabolical reflect the character of Macbeth, and references to drink reflect the condition of the king's servants.

3. Note that the Porter uses two versions of the same word several times. **Ask** students to identify it and determine how it reflects on the play. (Hint: One form is a vocabulary word.)
Answer: *equivocator* (lines 8, 12, 32) and *equivocate* (lines 11, 36). They reflect on what is about to happen—intentional misleading and deception.

17 Literary Analysis
Blank Verse and Prose

1. Direct students' attention to lines 43–44.

2. Then **ask** students the Literary Analysis question: Why is it appropriate for the dialogue in lines 43–44 to change back from prose to blank verse?
Answer: It is appropriate for the dialogue to change back from prose to blank verse because the comic relief provided by the Porter has ended, and serious matters are about to begin. Also, prose is used for low-ranking characters, such as the Porter, so blank verse is appropriate for the high-ranking Macduff and Lennox.

18 Reading Check
Answer: The Porter compares the gate of Macbeth's castle to the gate of hell.

Differentiated
Instruction   for Universal Access

Support for
Less Proficient Readers
Explain that the Porter's speeches are comic interruptions. Other than the delay in opening the door, there is no plot development. "Knock, knock! Who's there" in line 7 adds only humor. Discuss whether the lines are funny, or if the Porter's behavior adds the most humor.

EL **Background for**
English Learners
Explain that low-ranking characters are often vulgar in Shakespeare. Hence, this humorous passage uses images that students may be surprised to see in "serious" literature. Ask them to think of what they know of drunken-ness, as they read lines 29–37. Their knowledge may help them understand the images.

Strategy for
Advanced Readers
Have students discuss the comic impact of the Porter's speech. Ask them to research the use of comic relief in other Shakespearian plays. You may wish to have them share their findings and have them give dramatic presentations of the speeches to the class.

349

Reading Strategy
Analyzing Clarity of Meaning
Read lines 55–62 aloud. How many sentences are there in these lines? ⑲

19 **Reading Strategy**

Analyzing Clarity of Meaning

1. Have students read lines 55–62 aloud.

2. **Ask** students the first Reading Strategy question: How many sentences are there in these lines?
Answer: There are three sentences in lines 55–62.

3. Have students **describe** the night Lennox has experienced.
Answer: The wind was wild and blew down the chimney. There were a lot of ominous sounds. An owl screeched all night. Some reported an earthquake.

20 **Reading Strategy**

Analyzing Clarity of Meaning

1. Have students read lines 75–81.

2. Then **ask** them the second Reading Strategy question: In the latter part of Macduff's speech, lines 75–81, where should you *not* pause at the ends of lines?
Answer: You should *not* pause at the end of line 78.

3. **Ask** what comparison Macduff makes between sleep and death.
Answer: He says that sleep is a counterfeit, or "fake," death.

21 **Literature in Context**

Elizabethan Concepts of Monarchy

The theory of the divine right of kings held that the ruler's authority came from God, not from the people. Under this absolutist philosophy, the ruler was directly accountable only to God. To make their monarch more accountable to the government and the people, the British instituted a constitutional monarchy in 1688, following the Glorious Revolution.

Connect to the Literature Point out the religious imagery Macduff uses in lines 68–69. Share the additional background above. Then **ask** the Connect to the Literature question: How does Macduff's line 68 reflect this concept of monarchy?
Answer: Macduff refers to the king's body as the "Lord's anointed temple" and calls the murder "sacrilegious."

---

15. **combustion** confusion.

16. **obscure bird** bird of darkness, the owl.

17. **Confusion** destruction.

18. **The Lord's anointed temple** the King's body.

Reading Strategy
Analyzing Clarity of Meaning In the latter part of Macduff's speech, lines 75–81, where should you not pause at the ends of lines?

19. **Gorgon** Medusa, a mythological monster whose appearance was so ghastly that those who looked at it turned to stone.

MACBETH. He does: he did appoint so.

55 **LENNOX.** The night has been unruly. Where we lay,
Our chimneys were blown down, and, as they say,
Lamentings heard i' th' air, strange screams of death,
And prophesying with accents terrible
Of dire combustion[15] and confused events
60 New hatched to th' woeful time: the obscure bird[16]
Clamored the livelong night. Some say, the earth
Was feverous and did shake.

MACBETH. 'Twas a rough night.

LENNOX. My young remembrance cannot parallel
A fellow to it.

[*Enter* MACDUFF.]

65 **MACDUFF.** O horror, horror, horror! Tongue nor heart
Cannot conceive nor name thee.

MACBETH AND LENNOX. What's the matter?

MACDUFF. Confusion[17] now hath made his masterpiece.
Most sacrilegious murder hath broke ope
The Lord's anointed temple,[18] and stole thence
The life o' th' building.

70 **MACBETH.** What is 't you say? The life?

LENNOX. Mean you his Majesty?

MACDUFF. Approach the chamber, and destroy your sight
With a new Gorgon:[19] do not bid me speak;
See, and then speak yourselves. Awake, awake!

[*Exit* MACBETH *and* LENNOX.]

75 Ring the alarum bell. Murder and Treason!
Banquo and Donalbain! Malcolm! Awake!
Shake off this downy sleep, death's counterfeit,

21 **LITERATURE IN CONTEXT**

Cultural Connection

Elizabethan Concepts of Monarchy
For the Elizabethans, the monarch was God's representative on Earth. For this reason, the expression "the Lord's anointed" is used to describe the head of state. Killing the ruler, therefore, was not just an act of political assassination; it was also a horrifying desecration of religious values.

Connect to the Literature

How does Macduff's line 68 reflect this concept of monarchy?

350 Celebrating Humanity (1485–1625)

Enrichment: Investigating Career Connections

Forensics

In Shakespeare's time, little was known of blood types, fingerprints, and similar modern evidence-gathering methods. As is seen in Act 2, conclusions about the manner in which a crime was committed and the guilt or innocence of a suspect were made largely on the basis of appearances and unsubstantiated theories.

Today, crime scenes are preserved and investigated in depth. Blood samples and fingerprints are collected. Weapons are scientifically examined, and witnesses, victims, and suspects are questioned.

Activity: Comparing and Contrasting Have students research careers in forensics. Have students use the results of their research to develop a plan for how Duncan's murder could be investigated if it were to happen today. Suggest that students record information in the **Enrichment: Investigating Career Connections** worksheet, *Professional Development Guidebook,* page 221.

And look on death itself! Up, up, and see
80 The great doom's image![20] Malcolm! Banquo!
As from your graves rise up, and walk like sprites,[21]
To countenance[22] this horror. Ring the bell.

[Bell rings. Enter LADY MACBETH.]

LADY MACBETH. What's the business,
That such a hideous trumpet calls to parley[23]
The sleepers of the house? Speak, speak!

MACDUFF.   O gentle lady,
85 'Tis not for you to hear what I can speak:
The repetition, in a woman's ear,
Would murder as it fell.

[Enter BANQUO.]

                         O Banquo, Banquo!
Our royal master's murdered.

LADY MACBETH.   Woe, alas!
What, in our house?

BANQUO.   Too cruel anywhere.
90 Dear Duff, I prithee, contradict thyself,
And say it is not so.

[Enter MACBETH, LENNOX, and ROSS.]

MACBETH. Had I but died an hour before this chance,
I had lived a blessed time; for from this instant
There's nothing serious in mortality:[24]
95 All is but toys.[25] Renown and grace is dead,
The wine of life is drawn, and the mere lees[26]
Is left this vault[27] to brag of.

[Enter MALCOLM and DONALBAIN.]

DONALBAIN. What is amiss?

MACBETH.   You are, and do not know 't.
The spring, the head, the fountain of your blood
100 Is stopped; the very source of it is stopped.

MACDUFF. Your royal father's murdered.

MALCOLM.   O, by whom?

LENNOX. Those of his chamber, as it seemed, had done 't:
Their hands and faces were all badged[28] with blood;
So were their daggers, which unwiped we found
105 Upon their pillows. They stared, and were distracted.
No man's life was to be trusted with them.

MACBETH. O, yet I do repent me of my fury,
That I did kill them.

---

20. great doom's image likeness of Judgment Day.

21. sprites spirits.

22. countenance be in keeping with.

23. parley war conference.

Spiral Review
Metaphor In line 96, what does Macbeth mean by "The wine of life"?

24. serious in mortality worthwhile in mortal life.

25. toys trifles.

26. lees dregs.

27. vault world.

Literary Analysis
Blank Verse Where is there a pause in line 100? How does it reinforce the meaning?

28. badged marked.

Reading Check
According to Lennox, what evidence proves that the guards killed Duncan?

Macbeth, Act II, Scene iii **351**

Spiral Review

Metaphor

Ask students the Spiral Review question.

Sample answer: "The wine of life" is the joy and pleasure of life, drained away by Duncan's death, leaving only a worthless residue ("dregs"). "Wine" and "vault" visually evoke Duncan's bloody chamber.

22 Critical Thinking

Analyze

1. Point out that each of Macbeth's speeches on this page are designed to make him look loyal and loving toward the king.

2. Ask students to paraphrase Macbeth's words in lines 92–97. Possible response: He says that, if he had died without hearing this bad news, he would have had a happy life. From now on, there's nothing worthwhile in his life.

3. Have students compare Macbeth's "act" with that of Lady Macbeth. Does it seem, since the previous night, that the control and passion have shifted from one to the other? Possible response: Lady Macbeth seems to be at a loss now. Suddenly, Macbeth is the one in control, and he springs quite easily into committing the next murder.

23 Literary Analysis

Blank Verse

1. Direct students' attention to line 100.

2. Ask students the Literary Analysis question. Answer: The pause occurs after the phrase "is stopped," at the semicolon. The pause underscores the emotion, as if he is choking back tears.

3. Ask students what Macbeth's words in lines 98–100 mean. Answer: Malcolm and Donalbain are Duncan's sons, so Duncan was the "source" of their blood. They don't know it yet, but their father is dead.

24 Reading Check

Answer: Lennox cites the blood on the guards' hands and faces, as well as their bloody daggers.

Differentiated Instruction for Universal Access

Support for Less Proficient Readers
Work through Scene 3 with students. Have groups of students read dialogue together, slowly, and explain what is happening as they read. Encourage students to write down questions they have about what is happening in Scene 3. If students continue to struggle, have them read Scene 3 in Act 2 of the **Reader's Notebook**.

Enrichment for Gifted/Talented Students
Suggest artistically gifted students create sketches of the main characters in Scene 3. Students should base their sketches on details they find in the dialogue. Students can independently sketch one or more characters, or groups of students can work on character sketches together. Remind students to stay true to the dialogue, and to Shakespeare's characterizations. Have students display their sketches to the class.

351

㉕ Humanities

Lady Macbeth Seizing the Daggers,
1812, by Henri Fuseli

This painting by Henry Fuseli (1741–1825) depicts the scene immediately after the murder of Duncan. It shows the horror Macbeth feels for what he has done and the unshaken control Lady Macbeth has over him. Like most of Fuseli's work, it has a surrealistic, nightmarish quality that reflects the disordered minds of the characters. He created this painting from a sketch he made in 1760 after seeing David Garrick and Mrs. Pritchard in a performance of *Macbeth*. Use these questions for discussion:

1. How does the lack of color contribute to the mood of this scene?
   Answer: The lack of color creates a dream-like scene, as if the characters were ghosts, or from another world. It also makes the blood on the daggers stand out.

2. How does the artist's depiction of these two characters compare with your conception of them?
   Possible responses: Some students will be surprised by the outwardly submissive appearance of Macbeth. Lady Macbeth's aggressive posturing and determined look may be more in keeping with students' mental picture of the character.

㉖ Critical Viewing

Answer: Lady Macbeth's face and body suggest a determined and aggressive personality. She seems to dominate her shrinking, horrified husband.

㉗ Critical Thinking

Interpret

1. Direct students' attention to lines 119–120.

2. **Ask** students if they think Lady Macbeth has actually fainted, or if she is merely pretending to faint to deflect suspicion.
   Possible responses: A case can be made for either position. However, most students will probably think that Lady Macbeth has shown herself to be a treacherous, plotting villain, and her actions are as false as Macbeth's protests of love and loyalty.

㉖ ▲ **Critical Viewing** This painting depicts the moment when Macbeth comes from murdering Duncan (II, ii, 14). However, it also captures the nature of the relationship between Macbeth and Lady Macbeth in the first part of the play. What do their facial expressions and body language suggest about that relationship? **[Interpret]**

MACDUFF.   Wherefore did you so?

MACBETH. Who can be wise, amazed, temp'rate and furious,
110   Loyal and neutral, in a moment? No man.
        The expedition[29] of my violent love
        Outrun the pauser, reason. Here lay Duncan,
        His silver skin laced with his golden blood,
        And his gashed stabs looked like a breach in nature
115   For ruin's wasteful entrance: there, the murderers,
        Steeped in the colors of their trade, their daggers
        Unmannerly breeched with gore.[30] Who could refrain,
        That had a heart to love, and in that heart

29. **expedition** haste.

30. **breeched with gore** covered with blood.

352 Celebrating Humanity (1485–1625)

Think Aloud

Reading Strategy: Analyzing Clarity of Meaning

Direct students' attention to Macbeth's explanation of why he killed the guards (lines 109–119). Use the following "Think Aloud" to model the skill of analyzing clarity of meaning in a passage. Say to students:

I may be confused by Macbeth's answer to Macduff's question. Macbeth has said that he killed the guards in anger; Macduff wants to know why. Macbeth says that his love outran his reason. By *outran*, I suppose he means that his feelings were faster than his logic. I can infer that he killed the guards because he was upset. But he also says that Duncan's skin was silver and his blood was gold. I doubt that this was true. And then he says that the stabs in Duncan looked like a breach against nature. I know Macbeth is trying not to seem guilty. I think he must be trying to show loyalty to the king. Duncan's skin isn't really silver and his blood isn't really gold. But Macbeth is pretending that it is so that he seems more like a loyal follower of the king.

Courage to make 's love known?

LADY MACBETH.   Help me hence, ho!

MACDUFF. Look to the lady.

120 **MALCOLM.** [*Aside to* DONALBAIN] Why do we hold our tongues,
That most may claim this argument for ours?[31]

DONALBAIN. [*Aside to* MALCOLM] What should be spoken here,
Where our fate, hid in an auger-hole,[32]
May rush, and seize us? Let's away:
Our tears are not yet brewed.

125 **MALCOLM.** [*Aside to* DONALBAIN] Nor our strong sorrow
Upon the foot of motion.[33]

BANQUO.   Look to the lady.

                   [LADY MACBETH *is carried out.*]

And when we have our naked frailties hid,[34]
That suffer in exposure, let us meet
130 And question[35] this most bloody piece of work,
To know it further. Fears and scruples[36] shake us.
In the great hand of God I stand, and thence
Against the undivulged pretense[37] I fight
Of treasonous malice.

MACDUFF.   And so do I.

ALL.   So all.

MACBETH. Let's briefly[38] put on manly readiness,
And meet i' th' hall together.

135 **ALL.**   Well contented.

            [*Exit all but* MALCOLM *and* DONALBAIN.]

MALCOLM. What will you do? Let's not consort with them.
To show an unfelt sorrow is an office[39]
Which the false man does easy. I'll to England.

DONALBAIN. To Ireland, I; our separated fortune
140 Shall keep us both the safer. Where we are
There's daggers in men's smiles; the near in blood,
The nearer bloody.[40]

MALCOLM.   This murderous shaft that's shot
Hath not yet lighted,[41] and our safest way
Is to avoid the aim. Therefore to horse;
145 And let us not be dainty of leave-taking,
But shift away. There's warrant[42] in that theft
Which steals itself[43] when there's no mercy left.

            [*Exit.*]

---

31. **That most . . . ours** who are the most concerned with this topic.

32. **auger-hole** tiny hole, an unsuspected place because of its size.

33. **Our tears . . . motion** We have not yet had time for tears nor to turn our sorrow into action.

34. **when . . . hid** when we have put on our clothes.

35. **question** investigate.

36. **scruples** doubts.

37. **undivulged pretense** hidden purpose.

38. **briefly** quickly.

Reading Strategy

Analyzing Clarity of Meaning How do the brief sentences in lines 136–138 reinforce the meaning?

39. **office** function.

40. **the near . . . bloody** The closer we are in blood relationship to Duncan, the greater our chance of being murdered.

41. **lighted** reached its target.

42. **warrant** justification.

43. **that theft . . . itself** stealing away.

③¹ ☑ Reading Check

What do Malcolm and Donalbain decide to do?

Macbeth, Act II, Scene iii **353**

㉘ Critical Thinking

Analyze

1. Duncan's sons are quick to assess their danger. Have students read the exchanges between the brothers (lines 120–126 and 136–147). Then **ask** students what Duncan's sons' biggest concern is.
Answer: They are concerned that whoever is behind the murder will want to murder them too.

2. **Ask** students why they think that Duncan's sons decide to go in different directions.
Answer: They feel that if they are separate, the chances of one of them surviving is greater.

㉙ Critical Thinking

Infer

1. Direct students' attention to lines 127–133.

2. **Ask** students what is significant about Banquo's words.
Answer: Banquo feels that things are not as they appear and warrant further investigation.

3. **Ask** students what two recent events might make Banquo think that someone would have a reason for killing the king.
Answer: Banquo heard the witches promise Macbeth the crown; Malcolm was just named heir to the throne.

㉚ Reading Strategy

Analyzing Clarity of Meaning

1. Have students **explain** what Malcolm is saying in lines 136–138.
Answer: He asks Donalbain what he's going to do. He suggests that they not talk with the others. He states that those who are lying can easily make a show of their sorrow. He says he is heading for England.

2. Then **ask** students the Reading Strategy question: How do the brief sentences in lines 136–138 reinforce the meaning?
Answer: The brief sentences lend a sense of urgency to the conversation.

㉛ Reading Check

Answer: Malcolm and Donalbain decide to flee the scene.

353

Blank Verse

1. Have students read line 23 aloud, listening for the meter.

2. Encourage students to look at metric patterns listed under Meter in the Literary Terms Handbook at the back of their texts.

3. Then **ask** students to answer the Literary Analysis question: What rhythmic variation in the blank verse do you find at the beginning of line 23? **Answer:** The line begins with two stressed syllables creating a spondee: **Those / that /** Mac/ **beth /** hath / **slain.**

33 Critical Thinking

Analyze

1. Point out that, in lines 8–9, Ross notes that it is dark out, when it should be light. **Ask** students what this fact signifies.
   Answer: It is, like the wild night, a sign that the natural order is disrupted by Duncan's murder.

2. Explain to students that the old man's comment that the darkness is unnatural, like the deed that is done, is the first indication that Duncan's sons are suspect. The child's loyalty to a parent was seen as being as much a part of the natural order as a subject's loyalty to the king.

3. Have students look at lines 22–30. **Ask** them what is now believed to have been the plot behind the murder. Why?
   Answer: It is believed that Duncan's sons paid the servants to commit the murder. This is believed because the servants would have nothing to gain from the murder without someone paying them, and Duncan's sons have fled the scene of the crime.

4. Remind students that one of the reasons Macbeth hesitated to kill Duncan is that they were related. What does that explain in this scene?
   Answer: It explains why the crown would come next to Macbeth. A member of the royal family would inherit the throne.

354

Scene iv. Outside Macbeth's castle.

[*Enter* ROSS *with an* OLD MAN.]

1. **sore** grievous.

2. **traveling lamp** the sun.

OLD MAN. Threescore and ten I can remember well:
 Within the volume of which time I have seen
 Hours dreadful and things strange, but this sore[1] night
 Hath trifled former knowings.

ROSS.   Ha, good father,
5 Thou seest the heavens, as troubled with man's act,
 Threatens his bloody stage. By th' clock 'tis day,
 And yet dark night strangles the traveling lamp:[2]
 Is 't night's predominance, or the day's shame,
 That darkness does the face of earth entomb,
 When living light should kiss it?

Vocabulary
predominance (prē däm′ ə nəns) *n.* superiority

10 **OLD MAN.**   'Tis unnatural,
 Even like the deed that's done. On Tuesday last
 A falcon, tow'ring in her pride of place,[3]
 Was by a mousing owl hawked at and killed.

3. **tow'ring . . . place** soaring at its summit.

ROSS. And Duncan's horses—a thing most strange
     and certain—
15 Beauteous and swift, the minions of their race,
 Turned wild in nature, broke their stalls, flung out,
 Contending 'gainst obedience, as they would make
 War with mankind.

4. **eat** ate.

OLD MAN.   'Tis said they eat[4] each other.

ROSS. They did so, to th' amazement of mine eyes,
 That looked upon 't.

[*Enter* MACDUFF.]

32 Literary Analysis
Blank Verse What rhythmic variation in the blank verse do you find at the beginning of line 23?

20   Here comes the good Macduff.
 How goes the world, sir, now?

MACDUFF.   Why, see you not?

ROSS. Is 't known who did this more than bloody deed?

32 | **MACDUFF.** Those that Macbeth hath slain.

ROSS.   Alas, the day!
 What good could they pretend?[5]

5. **pretend** hope for.

6. **suborned** bribed.

33 **MACDUFF.**   They were suborned:[6]
25 Malcolm and Donalbain, the king's two sons,
 Are stol'n away and fled, which puts upon them
 Suspicion of the deed.

ROSS.   'Gainst nature still.
 Thriftless ambition, that will ravin up[7]
 Thine own life's means! Then 'tis most like

7. **ravin up** devour greedily.

354 Celebrating Humanity (1485–1625)

Vocabulary Development

Vocabulary Knowledge Rating
When students have completed reading and discussing both selections, have them take out the **Vocabulary Knowledge Rating Charts** they worked on earlier. Read the words aloud and have students rate their knowledge of the words again in the After Reading column. Clarify any words that are still problematic. Have students write their own definitions and example or sentence in the appropriate column. Then have students complete the Vocabulary lesson at the end of this selection. Encourage students to use the words in further discussion and written work about the selections. Remind them that they will be accountable for these words on the **Selection Test,** *Unit 2 Resources,* pages 118–120 or 121–123.

30 **33** The sovereignty will fall upon Macbeth.

MACDUFF. He is already named, and gone to Scone[8]
  To be invested.

ROSS.   Where is Duncan's body?

MACDUFF. Carried to Colmekill,
  The sacred storehouse of his predecessors
  And guardian of their bones.

35 **ROSS.**   Will you to Scone?

MACDUFF. No, cousin, I'll to Fife.[9]

ROSS.   Well, I will thither.

MACDUFF. Well, may you see things well done there.
    Adieu,
  Lest our old robes sit easier than our new!

ROSS. Farewell, father.

40 **OLD MAN.** God's benison[10] go with you, and with those
  That would make good of bad, and friends of foes!

[*Exit.*]

8. Scone (skoon) where Scottish kings were crowned.

9. Fife where Macduff's castle is located.

10. benison blessing.

Critical Reading

Cite textual evidence to support your responses.

1. **Key Ideas and Details (a)** Describe Macbeth's and Lady Macbeth's reactions to the murder just after it is committed. **(b) Compare and Contrast:** Compare and contrast their reactions to the deed.

2. **Key Ideas and Details (a)** What kind of gate does the porter imagine he is tending? **(b) Interpret:** In what way is the porter's playful fantasy a comment on Macbeth's situation?

3. **Integration of Knowledge and Ideas (a)** What two strange occurrences are reported in this act? **(b) Interpret:** Why would Shakespeare include reports of such occurrences at this point in the play? **(c) Connect:** In what way do these strange occurrences relate to the Elizabethan notion of an orderly and interconnected universe?

4. **Key Ideas and Details (a) Analyze:** What question does Ross ask that indicates he doubts the grooms committed the murder? Explain. **(b) Infer:** Is Ross satisfied by the answer? Explain.

5. **Integration of Knowledge and Ideas** Do you think a political assassination like the one Macbeth commits is ever justifiable? Why or why not?

Macbeth, Act II, Scene iv **355**

Concept Connector

Reading Strategy Graphic Organizer
Ask students to review the graphic organizers in which they have distinguished between lines and sentences. Have students share their graphic organizers.

Activating Prior Knowledge
Have students return to the paragraphs they wrote in the Activating Prior Knowledge activity. Ask students to discuss their paragraphs detailing what complications Macbeth and Lady Macbeth might anticipate in the execution of their "perfect crime."

Writing About the Essential Question
Review the Essential Question on page 321 with students. Have students list instances of comedy from *Macbeth*, Act 2, and record these on the board. Ask students why they believe Shakespeare included these moments. Have students work individually or in groups, writing or discussing their thoughts, to formulate their responses to the Essential Question. Lead a class discussion, encouraging students to cite specific textual details to support their responses.

Before students respond, you may wish to have them write a brief objective summary of the selection. As they answer the questions below, remind them to support their answers with evidence from the text.

1. (a) Macbeth is horrified by his actions and almost incapacitated. Lady Macbeth is practical: wash up, make the servants look guilty, go to bed. (b) Macbeth is immediately swept up in feelings of guilt. Lady Macbeth, on the other hand, seems cool and in charge.

2. (a) The Porter imagines he is tending the gate to hell. (b) The Porter's imaginings are a comment on Macbeth's situation because the murders Macbeth and his wife committed are hellish.

3. (a) Two of the strange things that occur in this act are the sky's remaining dark during the day and Duncan's horses eating each other. (b) Shakespeare reports such occurrences at this point to show that nature is responding to the king's death. (c) The Elizabethan concept that the universe is orderly and interconnected would require that there be consequences to the disruption of order represented by murder—especially the murder of a king.

4. (a) Ross asks what good the groomsmen could have hoped for by killing Duncan. There was no motive, because they had nothing to gain. (b) Ross seems doubtful still, because it would be against nature and foolish to destroy their means of making a living.

5. **Possible response:** Students may feel that political assassinations are sometimes necessary to end the rule of evil dictators. Others may feel that revolutions should be bloodless and that assassinations are never appropriate.

Critical Commentary

1. Have students reread Act 2, Scene 3 (beginning on page 348).

2. Then have students read De Quincey's remarks about the knocking at the gate.

3. **Ask** students how this moment is different from any other moment in the play thus far. Why does this moment have, as De Quincey points out, "a peculiar awfulness and depth of solemnity"?

   Answer: For Macbeth and Lady Macbeth, this is the moment when their crime is about to be discovered. This is the moment when it will be seen whether or not their stories are believed. It is impossible to imagine how others will react to a crime—so the tension of these two characters is high as they wait to find out what the consequences of their action will be.

4. Direct students' attention to the second-to-last paragraph on page 356. **Ask** students: How does Shakespeare create sympathy for Macbeth and Lady Macbeth?

   Possible responses: Shakespeare shows us the humanity of Macbeth and Lady Macbeth. He shows how conflicted Macbeth is about the choice he made to kill Duncan, and has Lady Macbeth admit that she could not commit the murder herself, because Duncan so resembled her father. He also sets up the scene so that Macbeth and Lady Macbeth are present when the crime is discovered, so the audience can see their reactions.

5. Direct students' attention to De Quincey's last paragraph on this page. Then **ask:** How does Shakespeare discriminate between Macbeth and Lady Macbeth? How is the "murderous mind of necessity" similar in both?

   Possible response: Shakespeare makes Macbeth hesitant, and Lady Macbeth determined; in the end, though, they both agree on the crime, and they both feel conflicted and guilty about it.

Critical Commentary

from "On the Knocking at the Gate in *Macbeth*"

Thomas De Quincey

English author Thomas De Quincey published his influential essay on Macbeth *in 1823, more than 200 years after the first performance of the play. In the essay, he does not only express his ideas about the play, but he models the process of criticism: It begins when a reader has a problem with a text that he or she cannot easily solve.*

From my boyish days I had always felt a great perplexity on one point in *Macbeth*. It was this: the knocking at the gate, which succeeds to the murder of Duncan, produced to my feelings an effect for which I never could account. The effect was, that it reflected back upon the murder a peculiar awfulness and a depth of solemnity; yet, however obstinately I endeavored with my understanding to comprehend this, for many years I never could see why it should produce such an effect.

De Quincey's interest in this problem was renewed when he read about a real murder case in which there was "a knocking at the door soon after the work of extermination was complete." This incident caused him to re-examine why the "knocking at the gate" had such a strong "effect" in Macbeth.

. . . at length I solved it to my own satisfaction; and my solution is this. Murder in ordinary cases, where the sympathy is wholly directed to the case of the murdered person, is an incident of coarse and vulgar horror; and for this reason, that it flings the interest exclusively upon the natural but ignoble instinct by which we cleave to life . . .

He goes on to discuss a topic familiar to anyone who enjoys reading thrillers: How can an author help an audience understand the mind of a murderer?

Such an attitude would little suit the purposes of the poet. What then must he do? He must throw the interest on the murderer. Our sympathy must be with him; (of course I mean a sympathy of comprehension, a sympathy by which we enter into his feelings, and are made to understand them,—not a sympathy of pity or approbation.) . . . in the murderer, such a murderer as a poet will condescend to, there must be raging some great storm of passion,—jealousy, ambition, vengeance, hatred,—which will create a hell within him; and into this hell we are to look.

In *Macbeth*, for the sake of gratifying his own enormous and teeming faculty of creation, Shakespeare has introduced two murderers: and, as usual in his hands, they are remarkably discriminated: but, though in Macbeth the strife of mind is greater than in his wife, the tiger spirit not so awake, and his feelings caught chiefly by contagion from her,—yet, as both were finally involved in the guilt of murder, the murderous mind of necessity is finally to be presumed in both. . . .

Enrichment: Analyzing Themes and Symbols

The Knocking at the Gate

Tell students that in literature, those moments when characters are waiting to do something have the potential to be very dull. Good writers, though, find ways to make these moments exciting. They find ways to heighten the tension, so that readers (or the audience) feel they cannot wait to find out what will happen.

Activity: Comparing Symbols Have students compare the knocking at the gate with other moments in *Macbeth* that involve waiting,

such as the moment when Macbeth is waiting to go to Duncan to murder him. Suggest that students record information in the **Enrichment: Analyzing Themes and Symbols** worksheet, *Professional Development Guidebook,* page 243. Have students use the results of their research to write an essay comparing and contrasting the knocking at the gate with other waiting moments in the play.

Here, De Quincey expresses his central idea, that the "knocking at the gate" symbolizes a return to "ordinary life." By contrast, such a return only emphasizes the horror of the murder.

. . . All action in any direction is best expounded, measured, and made apprehensible, by reaction. Now apply this to the case in *Macbeth*. Here, as I have said, the retiring of the human heart and the entrance of the fiendish heart was to be expressed and made sensible. Another world has stepped in; and the murderers are taken out of the region of human things, human purposes, human desires. They are transfigured: Lady Macbeth is "unsexed"; Macbeth has forgot that he was born of woman; both are conformed to the image of devils; and the world of devils is suddenly revealed.

But how shall this be conveyed and made palpable? In order that a new world may step in, this world must for a time disappear. The murderers, and the murder, must be insulated—cut off by an immeasurable gulf from the ordinary tide and succession of human affairs—locked up and sequestered in some deep recess; we must be made sensible that the world of ordinary life is suddenly arrested—laid asleep—tranced—racked into a dread armistice: time must be annihilated; relation to things without abolished; and all must pass self-withdrawn into a deep . . . suspension of earthly passion.

Hence it is, that when the deed is done, when the work of darkness is perfect, then the world of darkness passes away like a pageantry in the clouds: the knocking at the gate is heard; and it makes known audibly that the reaction has commenced: the human has made its reflux upon the fiendish; the pulses of life are beginning to beat again; and the re-establishment of the goings-on of the world in which we live, first makes us profoundly sensible of the awful parenthesis that had suspended them.

ⓒ **Key Ideas and Details** Why did the "knocking at the gate" puzzle De Quincey? What does De Quincey conclude about the scene that puzzled him?

Critical Commentary **357**

Critical Commentary

1. **Ask** students what De Quincey means when he says that Macbeth and Lady Macbeth are "transfigured" and that Lady Macbeth is "unsexed."
   Answer: Macbeth sets aside his doubts to commit the crime. Lady Macbeth acts against the stereotype of womanliness in encouraging this act of violence. Some students may recall that in Act 1, Lady Macbeth calls upon "spirits" to "unsex" her, to "make thick" her blood and to fill her "top-full/Of direst cruelty."

2. **Ask** students: How would the characters be different if it had been Macbeth who was determined to kill the king, and Lady Macbeth who hesitated?
   Possible response: The characters would not have the gender reversal that they currently have. Lady Macbeth would not have been "unsexed." She would be more stereotypically female, and Macbeth would be more stereotypically male.

3. Then **ask:** Why might Shakespeare have chosen to have Macbeth and Lady Macbeth act out the reverse of their gender roles?
   Possible response: It makes the play more compelling to the audience. The audience would have been accustomed to seeing traditional gender roles; the opposite was not something they saw every day.

Key Ideas and Details
Answers

1. He wondered why that moment in the play seemed so awful and solemn.

2. **Possible responses:** De Quincey concludes that the knocking at the gate announces the return of the ordinary world and so throws into relief the hellish world of murder that Macbeth and Lady Macbeth have entered. It helps the audience appreciate their state.

Differentiated Instruction   for Universal Access

Strategy for Special-Needs Students
Give students a photocopy of student pages 356–357. Explain that De Quincey's work is hard to read, but that each paragraph contains one main idea. Have students use highlighters to mark the main idea in each paragraph.

EL Background for English Learners
Preteach the following vocabulary words: *perplexity, obstinately, condescend, discriminate.* These words should help students to comprehend De Quincey's first several paragraphs. Then have students work in groups to find the meanings of the many vocabulary words in the last paragraph.

Enrichment for Gifted/ Talented Students
Have students write a letter to De Quincey, responding to his essay. Students should express their own ideas about the play. They may wish to focus on a different moment in the play, or they may share a different perspective on the knocking at the gate.

357

Answers

1. The first line contains all iambic feet. In the second line, ...-*nocent sleep* is anapestic; all other feet are iambic.

2. (Stressed syllables are bold.)
Will **all** great **Nep**tune's **o**cean **wash** this **blood** / **Clean** from my **hand?** /**No; this** my **hand** will **ra**ther / The multi**tud**inous **seas** in**car**na**dine,** / **Ma**king the **green** one **red.**

3. Line 60 begins with a trochee; the word *multitudinous* breaks out of iambic rhythm and begins with an anapest; line 62 begins with a trochee.

4. (a) The switch from verse to prose is visually obvious—the lines are not broken as they are in verse. Also, there is no consistent meter. (b) Prose is less elegant than verse, just as "low" characters would be less elegant. (c) The speech offers comic relief by contrasting sharply with what has gone on before.

5. **Possible response:** De Quincey is right; the reintroduction of the ordinary creates a contrast that makes the murder seem more dreadful.

6. Macbeth's strong imagination allows him to consider how his killing Duncan would lead to his own advancement. On the other hand, Macbeth's imagination causes him to tremble at the potential consequences of his act.

7. (a) There are two sentences in this passage. (b) One would pause at the end of line 62 because a thought has been completed.

8. **Possible responses:** (a) Reading sentences past the ends of lines was clearer, because the thought continues to the end of the sentence. (b) Earth, don't hear my steps, because you might warn Duncan.

After You Read   *Macbeth, Act II*

Literary Analysis

ⓒ **1. Craft and Structure** To analyze Shakespeare's use of **blank verse**, complete a chart like this one by identifying the rhythm of each of the lines indicated.

Line	Iambic Feet	Trochaic or Anapestic Feet
"It is the bloody business which informs...."		
"'Macbeth does murder sleep' —the innocent sleep,..."		

ⓒ **2. Craft and Structure** Mark stressed and unstressed syllables in Act II, Scene ii, lines 59–62.

ⓒ **3. Craft and Structure** Identify three metrical variations in Act II, Scene ii, lines 59–62.

ⓒ **4. Craft and Structure** **(a)** Contrast the Porter's speech (Act II, Scene iii, lines 1–21) with the two speeches at the end of Act II, Scene ii to show that the Porter's speech is written in **prose** form. **(b)** Why might prose be suitable for a "low" character? **(c)** How does the speech offer **comic relief?**

ⓒ **5. Integration of Knowledge and Ideas** The nineteenth-century English writer Thomas De Quincey argued that the scene with the Porter reinforces the shock of the king's murder by a striking contrast: "The re-establishment of the goings-on of the world in which we live, first makes us profoundly sensible of the awful [episode] that had suspended them." (For a larger excerpt from De Quincey's essay, see pages 356–357.) Do you agree or disagree? Explain.

ⓒ **6. Integration of Knowledge and Ideas** Macbeth has a strong imagination. In what way does this trait both prompt him to commit a crime and make it hard for him to commit it?

Reading Strategy

7. Analyze how Shakespeare achieves **clarity of meaning** by focusing on the interaction between sentences and blank verse lines. **(a)** How many sentences are there in Act II, Scene i, lines 62–64? **(b)** In reading these lines for meaning, would you pause at any of the line ends? Explain.

8. (a) Experiment by using two different ways of reading the sentences in Act II, Scene i, lines 56–61, beginning, "Thou sure . . ." First read them by pausing after each line of blank verse. Then, read them by following sentences past the ends of lines. Which way was clearer? Why? **(b)** In your own words, express the meaning of this passage.

ⓒ **Common Core State Standards**

Writing
1. Write arguments to support claims in an analysis of substantive topics or texts, using valid reasoning and relevant and sufficient evidence. *(p. 359)*

1.a. Introduce precise, knowledgeable claim(s), establish the significance of the claim(s), distinguish the claim(s) from alternate or opposing claims, and create an organization that logically sequences claims, counterclaims, reasons, and evidence. *(p. 359)*

Assessment Practice

Forms of Propaganda (For more practice, see *All-in-One Workbook*.)

Many tests require students to recognize a persuasive speech. Use the following to teach students how to recognize the purpose of a speech.

> Macbeth ....The expedition of my violent love Outrun the pauser, reason. Here lay Duncan, His silver skin laced with his golden blood, ...there, the murderers, Steeped in the colors of their trade, their daggers...

Macbeth speaks these lines in the presence of the other characters *primarily* to—

A explain why he killed the grooms.

B persuade them that the grooms were guilty and that he was loyal to Duncan.

C describe the appearance of the grooms.

D convince them that he lost control and that he killed the grooms out of revenge.

Choices **A, C,** and **D** are true but are not the primary purposes of the speech. The correct answer is **B.**

Integrated Language Skills

Ⓒ Vocabulary Acquisition and Use

Word Analysis: Latin Word Root -voc-

The word *equivocate*, meaning "to speak in two equal voices" or "to mislead," is based on the Latin root -voc-, meaning "voice" or "calling." Words with the root -voc- are useful in interpreting *Macbeth*, whose protagonist is haunted by many voices: the stern voice of his wife; the prophetic voices of witches; the accusing voices of ghosts; and the disturbing voice of his own conscience.

With a small group, write a paragraph that describes Macbeth's central conflict or conflicts. Use at least four of the -voc- words listed below in your description. Use a dictionary if necessary.

vocalize	invocation	vocation
advocate	irrevocable	provoke

Then, choose two of the words in your paragraph and write a sentence explaining how the root -voc- helps create each word's meaning.

Vocabulary: Antonyms

Antonyms are words with opposite meanings. For each sentence, replace the underlined term with an antonym from the vocabulary list on page 342. The antonym should make the sentence logical. Change the form of the vocabulary word if necessary.

1. Macbeth's success in battle gave him a sense of <u>inferiority</u>.
2. He was willing to use <u>straightforward</u> means to become king.
3. Before murdering Duncan, his doubts and fears were <u>few</u>.
4. As Macbeth approached the king's bedchamber, the sense of fear was <u>intangible</u>.
5. The Witches' prophecy served to <u>diminish</u> Macbeth's sense of ambition.
6. He learned the witches always <u>told the truth</u>.

Writing

Ⓒ **Argumentative Text** Reread De Quincey's essay (pages 356–357) on the porter scene. Then, write an **essay** agreeing or disagreeing with his interpretation. Support your ideas with detailed references to the text.

Prewriting Reread Scenes ii and iii of Act II, noting your own feelings and reactions. Then, reread De Quincey's comments. Note how your responses to the scene are like or unlike his.

Drafting Begin by stating your agreement or disagreement in a clear thesis. Then, support your thesis with references to the tone, mood, style, or "sound" of the porter's language. Next, anticipate those who may disagree with your view by providing logical counterarguments.

Revising Review your essay to be sure it is clear and logically organized. Make sure to comment on every quotation you include, and check to see that each claim you make is supported.

> A comparison of the writer's own ideas and de Quincey's reveals that both felt perplexed in response to the Porter's soliloquy.

> **Model: Comparing Responses**
> The first thing I felt when I began reading the Porter's speech was confusion. I was confused not only by his archaic expressions, but also by his exasperated response to something as routine as a knock at the door. Answering the door is, after all, a porter's job.
>
> *De Quincey says he felt "an effect for which [he] could never account."*

Integrated Language Skills **359**

Vocabulary Acquisition and Use

Word Analysis

Possible response: Macbeth is shocked to hear the witches <u>vocalize</u> his ambition to be king. At home, his wife, after an <u>invocation</u> to spirits to make her cruel, <u>advocates</u> murdering the king. Macbeth hesitates to commit such an <u>irrevocable</u> act.

-*Voc-* means voice or calling. Lady Macbeth <u>advocates</u>, or calls for, the murder of Duncan. She <u>invokes</u>, or calls upon, spirits, to make her cruel.

Vocabulary

1. predominance
2. stealthy
3. multitudinous
4. palpable
5. augment
6. equivocated

Writing

You may use this Writing Lesson as timed-writing practice, or you may allow students to develop the response as a writing assignment over several days.

1. Have students reread the excerpt from De Quincey's essay.
2. Have students reread Act 2, Scenes 2 and 3, taking notes on their own reactions.
3. Have students compare their own reactions to the knocking at the gate with De Quincey's.
4. Work with students to draw up guidelines, based on the assignment, for their essays:

- **Focus** The writer should clearly present the similarity or difference between his or her point of view and De Quincey's.
- **Organization** The writer should introduce De Quincey's reaction, and then his or her own, ordering points logically.
- **Elaboration** The writer should give details from De Quincey's essay and from *Macbeth* to support his or her thesis.
- **Style** The audience is not specified, so a formal style is appropriate.

5. Have students draft their argumentative texts.

359

• *Macbeth*, Act III
Lesson Pacing Guide

DAY 1 Preteach

- Administer the Reading and Vocabulary Warm-ups (*Unit 2 Resources,* pp. 130–133) as necessary.
- Introduce the Literary Analysis concepts: Conflict and Irony.
- Introduce the Reading Strategy: Identifying Cause-and-Effect Relationships.
- Build background with Background features.
- Develop thematic thinking with Connecting to the Essential Question.
- Teach the selection vocabulary.

DAYS 2–3 Preteach/Teach/Assess

- Distribute copies of the appropriate graphic organizer for the Reading Strategy (*Graphic Organizer Transparencies,* pp. 60–61).
- Distribute copies of the appropriate graphic organizer for Literary Analysis (*Graphic Organizer Transparencies,* pp. 62–63).
- Prepare students to read with the Activating Prior Knowledge activities (TE).
- Informally monitor comprehension while students read.
- Use the Reading Check questions to confirm comprehension.
- Develop students' understanding of conflict and irony using the Literary Analysis prompts.
- Develop students' ability to identify causes-and-effect relationships using the Reading Strategy prompts.
- Reinforce vocabulary with the Vocabulary notes.
- Assess students' comprehension and mastery of the skills by having them answer the Critical Reading, Literary Analysis, and Reading Strategy questions.
- Have students complete the Vocabulary Lesson.

DAY 4 Extend/Assess

- Have students complete the Writing Lesson and write a soliloquy. (You may assign as homework.)
- Administer Selection Test A or B (*Unit 2 Resources,* pp. 142–144 or 145–147).

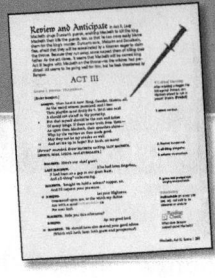

Common Core State Standards

Reading Literature 3. Analyze the impact of the author's choices regarding how to develop and relate elements of a story or drama.

Writing 3. Write narratives to develop real or imagined experiences or events using effective technique, well-chosen details, and well-structured event sequences.
3.a. Engage and orient the reader by setting out a problem, situation, or observation and its significance, establishing one or multiple point(s) of view, and introducing a narrator and/or characters; create a smooth progression of experiences or events.
3.d. Use precise words and phrases, telling details, and sensory language to convey a vivid picture of the experiences, events, setting, and/or characters.
5. Develop and strengthen writing as needed by planning, revising, editing, rewriting, or trying a new approach, focusing on addressing what is most significant for a specific purpose and audience.

Language 1.a. Apply the understanding that usage is a matter of convention, can change over time, and is sometimes contested.
4.a. Use context as a clue to the meaning of a word or phrase.

Additional Standards Practice
Common Core Companion, pp. 28–35; 208–218; 226–227; 324–331

Daily Block Scheduling
Each day in this Lesson Pacing Guide represents a 40–50 minute period. Teachers using block scheduling may combine days to revise pacing. In addition, teachers may differentiate and support core instruction by integrating components for extended and intensive support as students require. See the Guide to Selected Leveled Resources (facing page).

Guide to Selected Leveled Resources

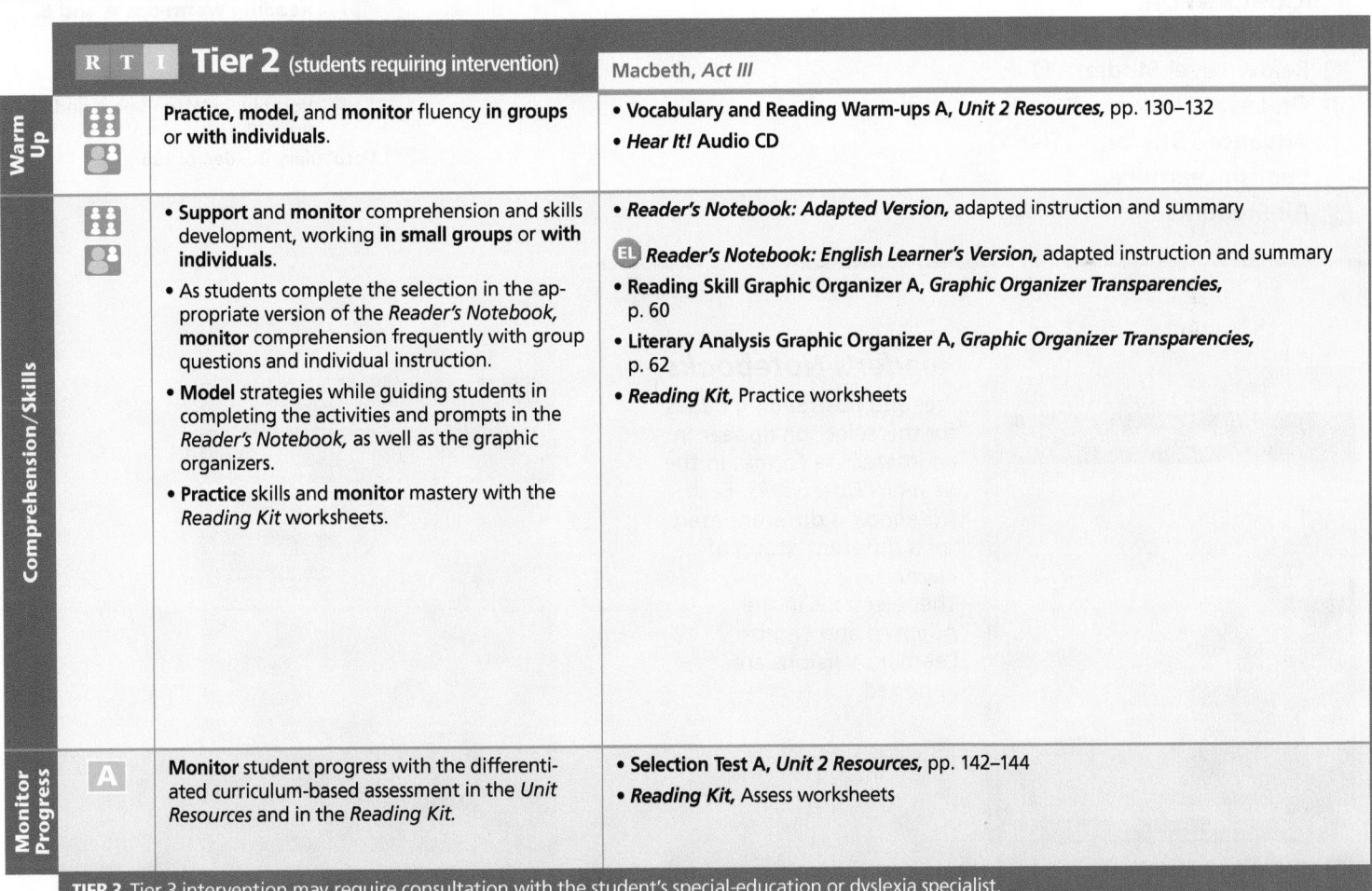

R T I Tier 1 (students performing on level)

Macbeth, *Act III*

Warm Up

Practice, model, and **monitor** fluency, working **with the whole class** or **in groups**.	**Vocabulary** and **Reading Warm-ups B,** *Unit 2 Resources,* pp. 130–131, 133

Comprehension/Skills

Support and **monitor** comprehension and skills development, having students complete the activities, graphic organizers, and interactive prompts **independently** or **as a class**.	• *Reader's Notebook,* adapted instruction and summary **EL** *Reader's Notebook: English Learner's Version,* adapted instruction and summary • **Reading Skill Graphic Organizer B,** *Graphic Organizer Transparencies,* p. 61 • **Literary Analysis Graphic Organizer B,** *Graphic Organizer Transparencies,* p. 63

Monitor Progress

A **Monitor** student progress with the differentiated curriculum-based assessment in the *Unit Resources.*	• **Selection Test B,** *Unit 2 Resources,* pp. 145–147 • **Open-Book Test,** *Unit 2 Resources,* pp. 139–141

R T I Tier 2 (students requiring intervention)

Macbeth, *Act III*

Warm Up

Practice, model, and **monitor** fluency **in groups** or **with individuals**.	• **Vocabulary and Reading Warm-ups A,** *Unit 2 Resources,* pp. 130–132 • *Hear It!* **Audio CD**

Comprehension/Skills

• **Support** and **monitor** comprehension and skills development, working **in small groups** or **with individuals**. • As students complete the selection in the appropriate version of the *Reader's Notebook,* **monitor** comprehension frequently with group questions and individual instruction. • **Model** strategies while guiding students in completing the activities and prompts in the *Reader's Notebook,* as well as the graphic organizers. • **Practice** skills and **monitor** mastery with the *Reading Kit* worksheets.	• *Reader's Notebook: Adapted Version,* adapted instruction and summary **EL** *Reader's Notebook: English Learner's Version,* adapted instruction and summary • **Reading Skill Graphic Organizer A,** *Graphic Organizer Transparencies,* p. 60 • **Literary Analysis Graphic Organizer A,** *Graphic Organizer Transparencies,* p. 62 • *Reading Kit,* Practice worksheets

Monitor Progress

A **Monitor** student progress with the differentiated curriculum-based assessment in the *Unit Resources* and in the *Reading Kit.*	• **Selection Test A,** *Unit 2 Resources,* pp. 142–144 • *Reading Kit,* Assess worksheets

TIER 3 Tier 3 intervention may require consultation with the student's special-education or dyslexia specialist. For additional support, see the Tier 2 activities and resources listed above.

One-on-one teaching Group work Whole class instruction Independent work **A** Assessment

For a complete guide to selection support, including support for Advanced students, see the Overview of Resources in the frontmatter.

• *Macbeth*, Act III

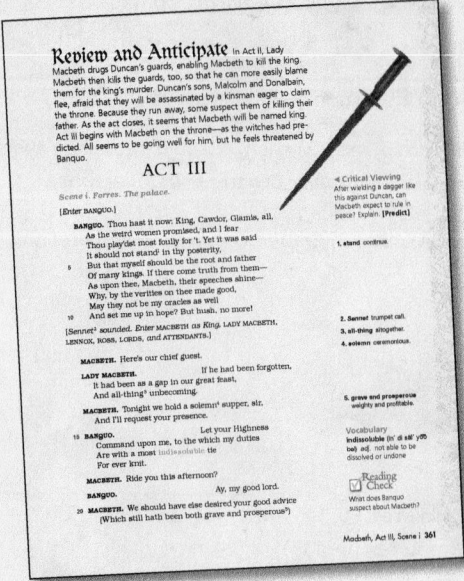

RESOURCES FOR:
- **L1** Special-Needs Students
- **L2** Below-Level Students (Tier 2)
- **L3** On-Level Students (Tier 1)
- **L4** Advanced Students (Tier 1)
- **EL** English Learners
- **All** All Students

Vocabulary/Fluency/Prior Knowledge

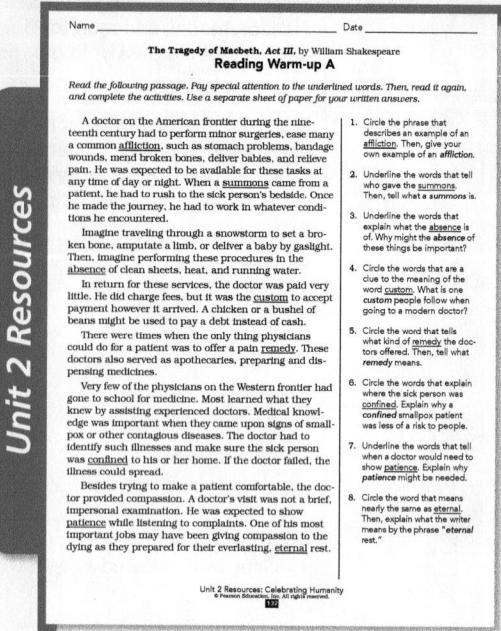

EL **L1** **L2** **Reading Warm-ups A and B,** pp. 132–133

Also available for these selections:

EL **L1** **L2** **Vocabulary Warm-ups A and B,** pp. 130–131

All **Vocabulary Builder,** p. 136

Reader's Notebooks

Pre- and postreading pages for this selection appear in an interactive format in the *Reader's Notebooks*. Each *Notebook* is differentiated for a different group of learners.

The selections in the Adapted and English Learner's versions are abridged.

- **L2** **L3** *Reader's Notebook*
- **L1** *Reader's Notebook: Adapted Version*
- **EL** *Reader's Notebook: English Learner's Version*
- **EL** *Reader's Notebook: Spanish Version*

© *Common Core Companion*

Additional instruction and practice for each Common Core State Standard

Selection Support

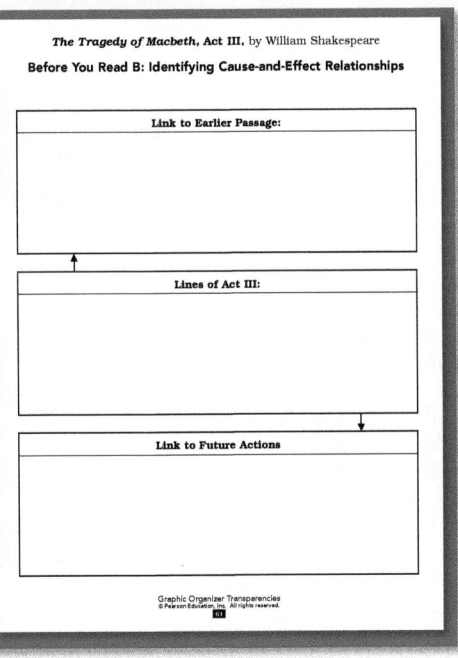

The Tragedy of Macbeth, Act III, by William Shakespeare

Before You Read B: Identifying Cause-and-Effect Relationships

EL **L3** **Reading: Graphic Organizer B,** p. 60

Also available for these selections:

EL **L1** **L2** **Reading: Graphic Organizer A** (partially filled in), p. 61

EL **L1** **L2** **Literary Analysis: Graphic Organizer A** (partially filled in), p. 62

EL **L3** **Literary Analysis: Graphic Organizer B,** p. 63

Skills Development/Extension

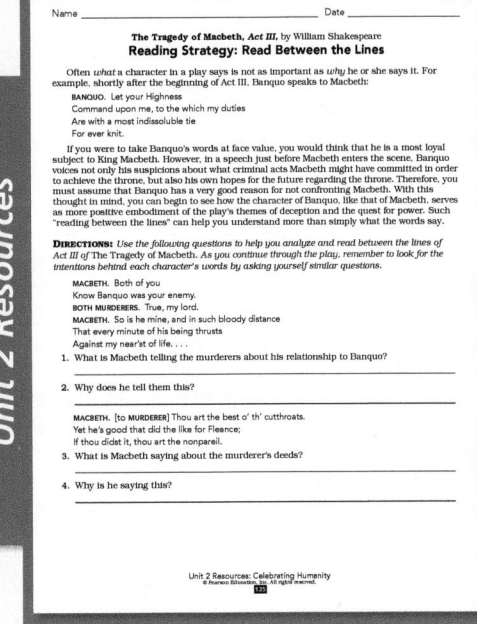

The Tragedy of Macbeth, Act III, by William Shakespeare
Reading Strategy: Read Between the Lines

All **Reading,** p. 135

Also available for these selections:

All **Literary Analysis,** p. 134

EL **L3** **L4** **Support for Writing,** p. 137

L4 **Enrichment,** p. 138

Assessment

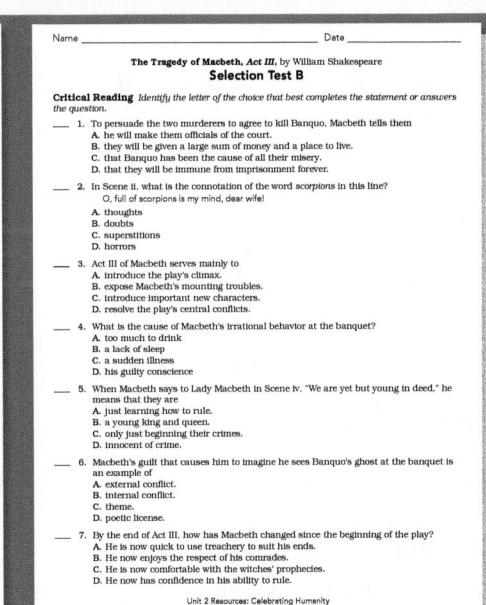

The Tragedy of Macbeth, Act III, by William Shakespeare
Selection Test B

EL **L1** **L2** **Selection Test B,** pp. 145–147

Also available for these selections:

L3 **L4** **Open-Book Test,** pp. 139–141

EL **L3** **L4** **Selection Test A,** pp. 142–144

PHLit Online! www.PHLitOnline.com

Online Resources: All print materials are also available online.

- complete narrated selection text
- a thematically related video with writing prompt
- an interactive graphic organizer
- highlighting feature
- access to all student print resources, adapted to individual student needs
- Spanish and English summaries
- adapted selection translations in Spanish

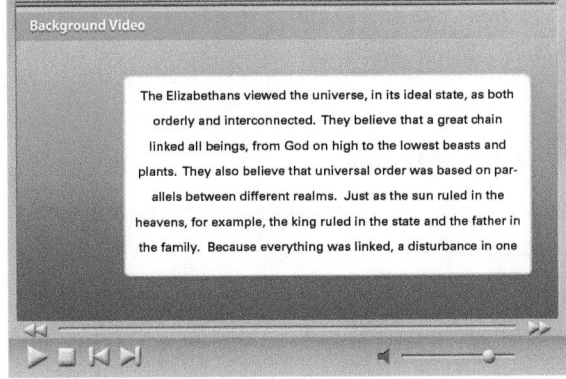

Background Video

Also available:

Get Connected! (thematic video with writing prompt)
All videos are available in Spanish.

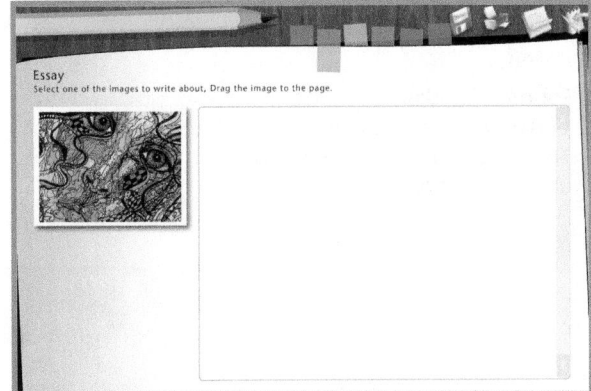

Writer's Journal (with graphics feature)

Also available:

Vocabulary Central (tools and activities for studying vocabulary)

Before You Read *Macbeth,* Act III

❶ Literary Analysis

Introduce the skill using the instruction on the student page.

Think Aloud: Model the Skill

Say to students:

Macbeth is full of internal and external conflict. If I think about Act 2 and remember Macbeth's murder of Duncan and his guards, I recognize that as an *external* conflict. I see the war between his ambition and his guilt as an *internal* conflict. Usually something happens that resolves the story. I understand this point as the *climax.*

❷ Reading Strategy

1. Introduce the strategy using the instruction on the student page.

2. Give students a copy of **Reading Strategy Graphic Organizer B**, page 61 in *Graphic Organizer Transparencies,* to use as they read.

Think Aloud: Model the Skill

Say to students:

I can recognize cause-and-effect in relationships in everyday life. For example, if I forget to set my alarm, I might wake up late. If that happens, I won't be ready to leave on time. As a result, I will probably be late for school.

❸ Vocabulary

1. Pronounce each word, giving its definition, and have students say it aloud.

2. For more guidance, see the *Classroom Strategies and Teaching Routines* card for vocabulary instruction.

❶ Literary Analysis

Conflict—the struggle between two forces—is what creates drama.

- An **external conflict** is a struggle between two characters or groups.
- An **internal conflict** is a struggle within a character.

The action, or series of events, of a play is developed and ordered by an author so that it reaches a **climax**—the point at which the internal and external conflicts are greatest. The impact of the climax on the play as a whole is twofold: The tension is at its highest and the conflicts are resolved.

In Act III of *Macbeth,* notice how the rising action leads the new king to a state dinner and the sight of a guest—a guest who should not be there!

In connection with that dinner, Macbeth makes this critical remark to Banquo in Act III, Scene i, line 27: "Fail not our feast." This invitation is an example of dramatic irony, a device that Shakespeare uses to heighten conflict. **Dramatic irony** occurs when the words or actions of a character take on a meaning for the audience or readers different from the one the character intends.

Observe how Macbeth's remark takes on dramatic irony as events unfold, and becomes a different kind of invitation, answered by a different kind of guest.

❷ Reading Strategy

ⓒ Preparing to Read Complex Texts Connecting different passages in a text will also enable you to **identify cause-and-effect relationships**—to show, for example, how an earlier event or remark (cause) leads to a later one (effect). The Witches' prophecy that Banquo will father kings may be a cause that has many effects in Act III. Use a graphic organizer like the one shown to trace those effects.

❸ Vocabulary

indissoluble (in′ di säl′ yo̅o̅ bəl) *adj.* not able to be undone (p. 361)

dauntless (dônt′ lis) *adj.* fearless; cannot be intimidated (p. 362)

predominant (prē däm′ ə nənt) *adj.* foremost; powerful (p. 363)

infirmity (in fʉr′ mə tē) *n.* physical or mental defect; illness (p. 371)

malevolence (mə lev′ ə ləns) *n.* ill will; spitefulness (p. 375)

Common Core State Standards

Reading Literature
3. Analyze the impact of the author's choices regarding how to develop and relate elements of a story or drama.

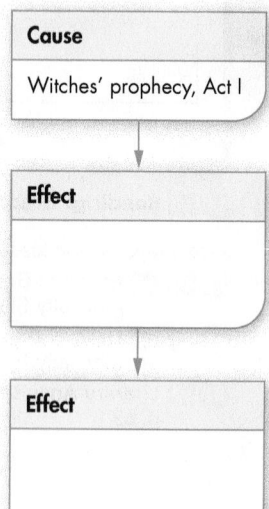

Cause
Witches' prophecy, Act I

Effect

Effect

www.PHLitOnline.com

360 Celebrating Humanity (1485–1625)

Teaching From Technology

www.PHLitOnline.com

Preparing to Read
Go to **www.PHLitOnline.com** and display the **Get Connected!** slide show for this selection. Have the class brainstorm for responses to the writing prompt, entering ideas in the interactive journal. Then have students complete their responses individually. You may also have students complete the assignment as homework.

To build background, display the Background video and More About the Author features.

Using the Interactive Student Edition
Go to **www.PHLitOnline.com** and display the **Enriched Online Student Edition.** As the class reads the selection or listens to the narration, record answers to side-column prompts using the graphic organizers accessible on the interactive page. Alternatively, have students use the online edition individually, answering the prompts as they read.

❶ Review and Anticipate

In Act II, Lady Macbeth drugs Duncan's guards, enabling Macbeth to kill the king. Macbeth then kills the guards, too, so that he can more easily blame them for the king's murder. Duncan's sons, Malcolm and Donalbain, flee, afraid that they will be assassinated by a kinsman eager to claim the throne. Because they run away, some suspect them of killing their father. As the act closes, it seems that Macbeth will be named king. Act III begins with Macbeth on the throne—as the witches had predicted. All seems to be going well for him, but he feels threatened by Banquo.

❷ ACT III

Scene i. Forres. The palace.

[*Enter* BANQUO.]

    BANQUO. Thou hast it now: King, Cawdor, Glamis, all,
        As the weird women promised, and I fear
        Thou play'dst most foully for 't. Yet it was said
        It should not stand[1] in thy posterity,
5   But that myself should be the root and father
        Of many kings. If there come truth from them—
        As upon thee, Macbeth, their speeches shine—
        Why, by the verities on thee made good,
        May they not be my oracles as well
10   And set me up in hope? But hush, no more!

[*Sennet[2] sounded. Enter* MACBETH *as King*, LADY MACBETH, LENNOX, ROSS, LORDS, *and* ATTENDANTS.]

    MACBETH. Here's our chief guest.

    LADY MACBETH.   If he had been forgotten,
        It had been as a gap in our great feast,
        And all-thing[3] unbecoming.

    MACBETH. Tonight we hold a solemn[4] supper, sir,
        And I'll request your presence.

15 **BANQUO.**   Let your Highness
        Command upon me, to the which my duties
        Are with a most indissoluble tie
        For ever knit.

    MACBETH. Ride you this afternoon?

    BANQUO.   Ay, my good lord.

20 **MACBETH.** We should have else desired your good advice
        (Which still hath been both grave and prosperous[5])

---

❸ ◄ Critical Viewing

After wielding a dagger like this against Duncan, can Macbeth expect to rule in peace? Explain. **[Predict]**

1. **stand** continue.

2. **Sennet** trumpet call.

3. **all-thing** altogether.

4. **solemn** ceremonious.

5. **grave and prosperous** weighty and profitable.

Vocabulary

indissoluble (in' di săl' yōō bəl) *adj.* not able to be dissolved or undone

❹ Reading Check

What does Banquo suspect about Macbeth?

Macbeth, Act III, Scene i **361**

361

Interpret

1. Have students look at lines 29–32.

2. Remind students that the term *cousin* in the Elizabethan period meant *kinsman*, not necessarily an actual cousin.

3. **Ask:** Who are the "bloody cousins" referred to by Macbeth. What do we learn about these "cousins"?
   Answer: Duncan's sons are the "bloody cousins" because they are rumored to have plotted their father's murder. We learn that they have reached England and Ireland and are telling "lies"—which, coming from the actual murderer, Macbeth, means they are probably telling the truth.

❻ **Critical Thinking**

Correct

1. **Ask:** What did the witches promise Macbeth and Banquo when they visited them in Act 1?
   Answer: They promised that Macbeth would be king, and that Banquo's heirs will be kings.

2. Have students divide the soliloquy into two parts and describe the topics of each of the two parts.
   Answer: The first part of the soliloquy runs from line 48 to line 57. It reveals that Macbeth fears Banquo. The second part runs from the middle of line 57 through line 72. In this part, Macbeth reveals his resentment of the prophecy that Banquo's descendants, not his own, will sit on the throne in the future.

---

6. **Go not . . . better** unless my horse goes faster than I expect.

7. **invention** lies.

8. **cause . . . jointly** matters of state demanding our joint attention.

9. **While** until.

10. **Sirrah** common address to an inferior.

11. **thus** king.

12. **but** unless.

Vocabulary
dauntless (dônt′ lis) *adj.* fearless; cannot be intimidated

13. **to** added to.

14. **genius is rebuked** guardian spirit is cowed.

15. **chid** scolded.

16. **gripe** grip.

In this day's council; but we'll take tomorrow. Is't far you ride?

BANQUO. As far, my lord, as will fill up the time
  'Twixt this and supper. Go not my horse the better,[6]
  I must become a borrower of the night
  For a dark hour or twain.

MACBETH. Fail not our feast.

BANQUO. My lord, I will not.

MACBETH. We hear our bloody cousins are bestowed
  In England and in Ireland, not confessing
  Their cruel parricide, filling their hearers
  With strange invention.[7] But of that tomorrow,
  When therewithal we shall have cause of state
  Craving us jointly.[8] Hie you to horse. Adieu,
  Till you return at night. Goes Fleance with you?

BANQUO. Ay, my good lord: our time does call upon 's.

MACBETH. I wish your horses swift and sure of foot,
  And so I do commend you to their backs.
  Farewell.   [*Exit* BANQUO.]
  Let every man be master of his time
  Till seven at night. To make society
  The sweeter welcome, we will keep ourself
  Till suppertime alone. While[9] then, God be with you!

          [*Exit* LORDS *and all but* MACBETH *and a* SERVANT.]

  Sirrah,[10] a word with you: attend those men
  Our pleasure?

ATTENDANT. They are, my lord, without the palace gate.

MACBETH. Bring them before us.   [*Exit* SERVANT.]
  To be thus[11] is nothing, but[12] to be safely thus—
  Our fears in Banquo stick deep,
  And in his royalty of nature reigns that
  Which would be feared. 'Tis much he dares;
  And, to[13] that dauntless temper of his mind,
  He hath a wisdom that doth guide his valor
  To act in safety. There is none but he
  Whose being I do fear: and under him
  My genius is rebuked,[14] as it is said
  Mark Antony's was by Caesar. He chid[15] the sisters,
  When first they put the name of King upon me,
  And bade them speak to him; then prophetlike
  They hailed him father to a line of kings.
  Upon my head they placed a fruitless crown
  And put a barren scepter in my gripe,[16]

362 Celebrating Humanity (1485–1625)

Enrichment: Investigating a Key Person in History

Plutarch
Though he was also a mathematician, philosopher, world traveler, politician, educator, and priest of the Delphic oracle, the reputation of the Greek essayist and biographer Plutarch (A.D. 46–c. 119) rested on his writing. Of all his works, the most important is *Parallel Lives*. This collection contains biographies of every important soldier, leader, and orator of ancient Rome and Greece.

Activity: Investigate Plutarch Have pairs or groups of students conduct research on Plutarch. Suggest that they record information in the **Enrichment: Investigating a Key Person in History** worksheet, *Professional Development Guidebook*, page 233. Ask students to include on their worksheet one sentence about how their research on an ancient Greek essayist affects their understanding of Shakespeare's writing.

6

Thence to be wrenched with an unlineal hand,
No son of mine succeeding. If 't be so,
65 For Banquo's issue have I filed[17] my mind;
For them the gracious Duncan have I murdered;
Put rancors in the vessel of my peace
Only for them, and mine eternal jewel[18]
Given to the common enemy of man,[19]
70 To make them kings, the seeds of Banquo kings!
Rather than so, come, fate, into the list,
And champion me to th' utterance![20] Who's there?

[*Enter* SERVANT *and* TWO MURDERERS.]

Now go to the door, and stay there till we call.

[*Exit* SERVANT.]

Was it not yesterday we spoke together?

MURDERERS. It was, so please your Highness.

75 **MACBETH.**   Well then, now
Have you considered of my speeches? Know
That it was he in the times past, which held you
So under fortune,[21] which you thought had been
Our innocent self: this I made good to you
7
80 In our last conference; passed in probation[22] with you,
How you were born in hand,[23] how crossed, the instruments,
Who wrought with them, and all things else that might
To half a soul[24] and to a notion[25] crazed
Say "Thus did Banquo."

FIRST MURDERER.   You made it known to us.

85 **MACBETH.** I did so; and went further, which is now
Our point of second meeting. Do you find
Your patience so predominant in your nature,
That you can let this go? Are you so gospeled,[26]
To pray for this good man and for his issue,
90 Whose heavy hand hath bowed you to the grave
And beggared yours for ever?

8

FIRST MURDERER.   We are men, my liege.

MACBETH. Ay, in the catalogue ye go for[27] men;
As hounds and greyhounds, mongrels, spaniels, curs,
Shoughs, water-rugs[28] and demi-wolves, are clept[29]
95 All by the name of dogs: the valued file[30]
Distinguishes the swift, the slow, the subtle,
The housekeeper, the hunter, every one
According to the gift which bounteous nature
Hath in him closed,[31] whereby he does receive
100 Particular addition,[32] from the bill

---

17. **filed** defiled.
18. **eternal jewel** soul.
19. **common . . . man** the Devil.
20. **champion me to th' utterance** Fight against me to the death.
21. **held . . . fortune** kept you from good fortune.
22. **passed in probation** reviewed the proofs.
23. **born in hand** deceived.
24. **half a soul** halfwit.
25. **notion** mind.
26. **gospeled** ready to forgive.
27. **go for** pass as.
28. **Shoughs** (shuks), **water-rugs** shaggy dogs, long-haired dogs.
29. **clept** called.
30. **valued file** classification by valuable traits.

Vocabulary
predominant (prē däm´ ə nənt) *adj.* foremost; powerful

Reading Strategy
Identifying Cause-and-Effect Relationships
What does the first murderer mean in line 91 when he answers Macbeth, "We are men"?

31. **closed** enclosed.
32. **addition** distinction (to set it apart from other dogs).

9
Reading Check
What has caused Macbeth to hire these murderers?

Macbeth, Act III, Scene i **363**

---

7 Critical Thinking
Infer

1. Direct students' attention to Macbeth's speech in lines 75–84.
2. **Ask** students what they can infer about what Macbeth has told these men.
   Answer: He appears to have told them that whatever miseries they have suffered can be blamed on Banquo.
3. **Ask** students why he might have told them this.
   Answer: He wanted to give them a reason to murder Banquo, to motivate them in a way that would make them feel that they would be solving a problem of their own.

8 Reading Strategy
Identifying Cause-and-Effect Relationships

1. Have students reread Lady Macbeth's views on manhood in Act I, Scene 7, lines 49–54, on page 338.
2. **Ask** students the Reading Strategy question: What does the first murderer mean in line 91 when he answers Macbeth, "We are men"?
   Answer: The murderer means that they, as men, would not let such an outrage go unpunished, which echoes Lady Macbeth's earlier views that it is manly to kill someone who stands in your way.

9 Reading Check
Answer: Macbeth is uncertain in his power. He fears Banquo because Banquo knows about the prophecies and might be suspicious. Also, if Banquo's descendants will be kings, Macbeth's heirs will not sit on the throne. Both things are a threat to Macbeth's power. Thus, he has hired murderers to take care of Banquo.

Differentiated Instruction for Universal Access

Support for Less Proficient Readers
Help students understand the phrase *read between the lines.* Read Banquo's speech as a group. Ask students how much Banquo knows about what Macbeth has done. Also, discuss Banquo's reasons for imagining himself the father of kings. When you finish, analyze one of Macbeth's speeches on page 362 or 363.

(EL) Vocabulary for English Learners
Make certain students understand the definitions given in the side notes. For example, on the facing page, the definition of *dauntless* includes the words *fearless* and *intimidated*, both of which might be new to English learners. Pronounce the words, and make certain students understand them in the story's context.

Strategy for Advanced Readers
Allow students to read Act 3 independently. Have them note lines or speeches that are clues about what is going to happen. Then, have them note where in the play their suspicions are confirmed. Suggest that they also note events that remind them of clues they did not write down, even from other acts.

Conflict

1. **Ask** students the Literary Analysis question: What conflict does Macbeth express in lines 116–126?
   Answer: The external conflicts are between Macbeth and Banquo and between Macbeth and public opinion. An internal conflict, though not directly stated, may be identified as existing between Macbeth and his fear.

   ▶ **Reteach:** If students have difficulty identifying the conflict, review with them their understanding of internal and external conflicts. Reread the definition of conflict on page 360. Explain to students that a conflict can have both internal and external dimensions at the same time.

2. **Ask** students if they believe the reasons Macbeth gives for not killing Banquo himself. What reasons might he really have for not wanting to kill Banquo himself?
   Possible responses: The reasons Macbeth gives are partially true; he would lose friends and allies. However, his having the power is doubtful because none of the things Macbeth has said about Banquo are true. His real reason is that he wants to look innocent of the murder. He may also be concerned about getting injured if he attacks Banquo alone.

⑪ Critical Thinking

Analyze

1. Direct students' attention to lines 134–139.

2. Point out that, in this passage, Macbeth refers to Banquo's son, Fleance, almost as if he were an afterthought. **Ask** students how important Fleance's death is to Macbeth, and why.
   Answer: Fleance's death is very important. The witches said that Banquo would father kings. While Banquo's death is necessary to make Macbeth feel safe, Fleance's death is necessary if Macbeth wants to have his own sons inherit the throne.

3. **Ask** students in which speech Macbeth expressed his reasons for wishing to end Banquo's line.
   Answer: lines 57–72 of this scene.

364

---

33. **file** ranks.

34. **wear . . . life** are sick as long as he lives.

35. **set** risk.

36. **distance** disagreement.

37. **near'st of life** most vital parts.

38. **avouch** justify.

39. **wail his fall** (I must) bewail his death.

Literary Analysis
Conflict What conflict does Macbeth express in lines 116–126?

40. **the perfect . . . on't** exact information of the exact time.

41. **something** some distance.

42. **thought** remembered.

43. **clearness** freedom from suspicion.

44. **rubs** flaws.

45. **Resolve yourselves apart** Make your own decision.

That writes them all alike: and so of men.
Now if you have a station in the file,[33]
Not i' th' worst rank of manhood, say 't,
And I will put that business in your bosoms
105   Whose execution takes your enemy off,
Grapples you to the heart and love of us,
Who wear our health but sickly in his life,[34]
Which in his death were perfect.

SECOND MURDERER.   I am one, my liege,
Whom the vile blows and buffets of the world
110   Hath so incensed that I am reckless what
I do to spite the world.

FIRST MURDERER.   And I another
So weary with disasters, tugged with fortune,
That I would set[35] my life on any chance,
To mend it or be rid on 't.

MACBETH.   Both of you
Know Banquo was your enemy.

115   **BOTH MURDERERS.**   True, my lord.

MACBETH. So is he mine, and in such bloody distance[36]
That every minute of his being thrusts
Against my near'st of life:[37] and though I could
With barefaced power sweep him from my sight
120   And bid my will avouch[38] it, yet I must not,
For certain friends that are both his and mine,
Whose loves I may not drop, but wail his fall[39]
Who I myself struck down: and thence it is
That I to your assistance do make love,
125   Masking the business from the common eye
For sundry weighty reasons.

SECOND MURDERER.   We shall, my lord,
Perform what you command us.

FIRST MURDERER.   Though our lives—

MACBETH. Your spirits shine through you. Within this hour at most
I will advise you where to plant yourselves,
130   Acquaint you with the perfect spy o' th' time,[40]
The moment on 't;[40] for 't must be done tonight,
And something[41] from the palace; always thought[42]
That I require a clearness:[43] and with him—
To leave no rubs[44] nor botches in the work—
135   Fleance his son, that keeps him company,
Whose absence is no less material to me
Than is his father's, must embrace the fate
Of that dark hour. Resolve yourselves apart:[45]

Think Aloud

Reading Strategy: Investigating Cause-and-Effect Relationships

To model the Reading Strategy skill of investigating cause-and-effect relationships, use the following "think aloud." Say to students:

I might be confused about the events in Scene 1. I might wonder how Macbeth is able to hire two murderers. In line 16, Macbeth says to the two murderers, "Both of you / Know Banquo was your enemy." Now I know that the two men Macbeth is trying to convince to do his dirty work already dislike Banquo.

Previously in Scene 1 (in lines 85–110), I learned that Macbeth challenged the manhood of the murderers. In this way, I can see a cause-and-effect relationship come into play. Macbeth needs someone to do a terrible deed; he does not want to kill Banquo himself. Thus, Macbeth stirs up two men he knows are violent, and he is thus able to carry out his plan.

D ↑   I'll come to you anon.

MURDERERS.   We are resolved, my lord.

140 **MACBETH.** I'll call upon you straight.[46] Abide within.
It is concluded: Banquo, thy soul's flight,
If it find heaven, must find it out tonight.   [*Exit.*]

46. straight immediately.

Scene ii. *The palace.*

[*Enter* MACBETH'S LADY *and a* SERVANT.]

LADY MACBETH. Is Banquo gone from court?

SERVANT. Ay, madam, but returns again tonight.

LADY MACBETH. Say to the King, I would attend his leisure
For a few words.

SERVANT.   Madam, I will.   [*Exit.*]

LADY MACBETH.   Nought's had, all's spent,
5   Where our desire is got without content:
'Tis safer to be that which we destroy
Than by destruction dwell in doubtful joy.

[*Enter* MACBETH.]

How now, my lord! Why do you keep alone,
Of sorriest fancies your companions making,
10   Using those thoughts which should indeed have died
With them they think on? Things without all remedy
Should be without regard: what's done is done.

MACBETH. We have scotched[1] the snake, not killed it:
She'll close[2] and be herself, whilst our poor malice
15   Remains in danger of her former tooth.[3]
But let the frame of things disjoint,[4] both the worlds[5] suffer,
Ere we will eat our meal in fear, and sleep
In the affliction of these terrible dreams
That shake us nightly: better be with the dead,
20   Whom we, to gain our peace, have sent to peace,
Than on the torture of the mind to lie
In restless ecstasy.[6] Duncan is in his grave;
After life's fitful fever he sleeps well.
Treason has done his worst: nor steel, nor poison,
25   Malice domestic, foreign levy,[7] nothing,
Can touch him further.

LADY MACBETH.   Come on.
Gentle my lord, sleek o'er your rugged looks;
Be bright and jovial among your guests tonight.

MACBETH. So shall I, love; and so, I pray, be you:

Reading Strategy
Identifying Cause-and-Effect Relationships
What causes Lady Macbeth to say what she does in lines 4–7?

1. scotched wounded.

2. close heal.

3. in . . . tooth in as much danger as before.

4. frame of things disjoint universe collapse.

5. both the worlds heaven and earth.

6. ecstasy frenzy.

7. Malice . . . levy civil and foreign war.

Reading Check
What does Macbeth ask the murderers to do?

Macbeth, Act III, Scene ii **365**

---

12 Reading Strategy
Identifying Cause-and-Effect Relationships

1. **Ask** students the Reading Strategy question: What causes Lady Macbeth to say what she does in lines 4–7? **Answer:** Lady Macbeth is realizing that she and Macbeth have paid a very high price for desires that have left them discontented and worried.

2. Point out that her feelings reflect the uncertainty that Macbeth is feeling—but with a difference: She is beginning to sound doubtful about their actions.

3. **Ask** students why, in their opinion, her four lines are rhymed, when rhyme is normally saved for the end of a scene. **Possible response:** They might reflect a turning point for Lady Macbeth.

4. Explain that, in showing uncertainty, she has now changed places with Macbeth. He was doubtful before Duncan's murder; now she is. We already know more than Lady Macbeth does— that Macbeth has ordered the murder of Banquo and Fleance. We see in the speeches that make up the rest of the scene that Macbeth is now the one in charge and determined to hold to the path of evil.

13 Critical Thinking
Analyze

1. Direct students' attention to lines 13–26.

2. Point out that Shakespeare often makes use of the comparison between sleep and death. It was a relatively common comparison of biblical origin. However, Shakespeare uses it masterfully as a thread in the play. Remind students of the speech in Act 2, Scene 2, when Macbeth says, "Sleep no more! Macbeth does murder sleep."

3. **Ask** students who Macbeth feels is sleeping better than he is, according to this passage. **Answer:** He says that murdered Duncan sleeps better than he does.

14 Reading Check
Answer: Macbeth asks the murderers to kill Banquo and his son.

365

Mrs. Siddons as Lady Macbeth,

by G. H. Harlow

The actress depicted in this painting is Sarah Siddons (1755–1831), one of the greatest English actresses of her time. She came from a family of traveling actors and began acting as a child. She played the part of Lady Macbeth early in her career and performed the role at London's Drury Lane Theater for the first time in 1785, terrifying audiences with her vivid portrayal of the famous character.

Use these questions for discussion:

- **How does Harlow portray Sarah Siddons as Lady Macbeth? Answer:** Harlow portrays Lady Macbeth in a timid posture. She is surrounded by darkness. She looks more fearful and demure than sinister. Her white robe gives her an angelic, or perhaps ghostly, appearance.

- **Ask** students how this portrait of Lady Macbeth compares with the ones on pages 335 and 352. **Possible responses:** Most students will say that this portrait portrays Lady Macbeth as quieter, meeker, and more dainty than the other portraits, in which she is depicted as larger than life, vibrant, and wild.

16 Critical Viewing

Answer: The clasped hands and sad expression suggest the insecurity and unhappiness in lines 4–7 of Scene 2.

17 Literary Analysis

Conflict and Irony

1. Remind students that **dramatic irony** occurs when the words or actions of a character take on a meaning different from the one the character intends.

2. **Ask** students the Literary Analysis question: What is ironic about Macbeth's idea about disguising the couple's real conflict with Banquo? **Answer:** It is ironic that Macbeth is telling Lady Macbeth that they need to disguise their feelings, because he is in the process of having Banquo murdered.

16 ▶ **Critical Viewing** This artist depicted actress Sarah Siddons (1755–1831) playing Lady Macbeth. How does Mrs. Siddons's body language suggest the same inner conflict as do lines 4–7 in Act III, ii? **[Connect]**

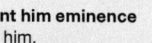

Literary Analysis
Conflict and Irony What is ironic about Macbeth's idea for disguising the couple's real conflict with Banquo (Scene ii, lines 30–35)?

8. **Present him eminence** Honor him.

9. **Unsafe . . . lave** We are unsafe as long as we have to wash.

10. **vizards** (viz´ ərdz) masks

11. **nature's . . . eterne** Nature's lease is not eternal.

12. **jocund** (jäk´ ənd) cheerful; jovial

13. **shard-borne** borne on scaly wings.

30   Let your remembrance apply to Banquo;
    Present him eminence,[8] both with eye and tongue:
    Unsafe the while, that we must lave[9]
    Our honors in these flattering streams
    And make our faces vizards[10] to our hearts,
    Disguising what they are.

35 **LADY MACBETH.**   You must leave this.

  MACBETH. O, full of scorpions is my mind, dear wife!
    Thou know'st that Banquo, and his Fleance, lives.

  LADY MACBETH. But in them nature's copy's not eterne.[11]

  MACBETH. There's comfort yet; they are assailable.
40   Then be thou jocund.[12] Ere the bat hath flown
    His cloistered flight, ere to black Hecate's summons
    The shard-borne[13] beetle with his drowsy hums
    Hath rung night's yawning peal, there shall be done

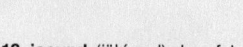

366 Celebrating Humanity (1485–1625)

Think Aloud

Literary Analysis: Dramatic Irony

To model the process of working out the answer to the Literary Analysis question on the student page, use the following "think aloud." Say to students:

I might be confused about dramatic irony. I can remember that one definition of dramatic irony is when the character's words or actions are clear to the audience, but not to the other characters. In Scene 2, lines 29–34, Macbeth is telling Lady Macbeth to honor Banquo, and to disguise feelings of guilt. The audience knows, though, that at the end of Scene 1, Macbeth had already arranged to have Banquo murdered. So I can see that the dramatic irony is the audience knowing Banquo's fate, and Lady Macbeth remaining ignorant about Macbeth's plan.

A deed of dreadful note.

LADY MACBETH.   What 's to be done?

45 **MACBETH.**   Be innocent of the knowledge, dearest chuck,[14]
Till thou applaud the deed. Come, seeling[15] night,
Scarf up[16] the tender eye of pitiful day,
And with thy bloody and invisible hand
Cancel and tear to pieces that great bond[17]
50 Which keeps me pale! Light thickens, and the crow
Makes wing to th' rooky[18] wood.
Good things of day begin to droop and drowse,
Whiles night's black agents to their preys do rouse.
Thou marvel'st at my words: but hold thee still;
55 Things bad begun make strong themselves by ill:
So, prithee, go with me.

                                              [*Exit.*]

Scene iii. Near the palace.

[*Enter* THREE MURDERERS.]

FIRST MURDERER.   But who did bid thee join with us?

THIRD MURDERER.   Macbeth.

SECOND MURDERER.   He needs not our mistrust; since he delivers
Our offices[1] and what we have to do
To the direction just.[2]

FIRST MURDERER.   Then stand with us.
5 The west yet glimmers with some streaks of day.
Now spurs the lated traveler apace
To gain the timely inn, and near approaches
The subject of our watch.

THIRD MURDERER.   Hark! I hear horses.

BANQUO. [*Within*] Give us a light there, ho!

SECOND MURDERER.   Then 'tis he. The rest
10 That are within the note of expectation[3]
Already are i' th' court.

FIRST MURDERER.   His horses go about.[4]

THIRD MURDERER.   Almost a mile: but he does usually—
So all men do—from hence to th' palace gate
Make it their walk.

[*Enter* BANQUO *and* FLEANCE, *with a torch*]

SECOND MURDERER.   A light, a light!

THIRD MURDERER.   'Tis he.

15 **FIRST MURDERER.**   Stand to 't

---

14. **chuck** term of endearment.

15. **seeling** eye-closing. Falconers sometimes sewed a hawk's eyes closed in order to train it.

16. **Scarf up** blindfold.

17. **great bond** between Banquo and fate.

18. **rooky** full of rooks, or crows.

Reading Strategy
Identifying Cause-and-Effect Relationships
To what specific action do you think Macbeth is indirectly referring in lines 45–56?

1. **offices** duties.

2. **direction just** exact detail.

3. **within . . . expectation** on the list of expected guests.

4. **His . . . about** His horses have been taken to the stable.

20   **Reading Check**

What does Macbeth tell Lady Macbeth and what does he hold back from her?

Macbeth, Act III, Scene iii **367**

---

18 **Reading Strategy**

Identifying Cause-and-Effect Relationships

1. Have students read lines 39–56.

2. **Ask** students the Reading Strategy question: To what specific action do you think Macbeth is indirectly referring in lines 45–56?
   Answer: Macbeth is referring to his plot to have Banquo and Fleance killed.

3. **Ask** students why they think Macbeth might have chosen to keep his plans for Banquo's murder from Lady Macbeth.
   Possible responses: He may feel that she would give him away at the banquet that night. He might not trust anyone at this point. He may want to impress her by carrying out this act without urging from her. Maybe he fears that she is losing her "nerve."

19 **Critical Thinking**

Speculate

1. Direct students' attention to the entrance of the three murderers.

2. **Ask** students if they were surprised by the appearance of a third murderer.
   Possible responses: Students may be surprised, but some may say that it is in keeping with Macbeth's actions so far.

3. Then, **ask** students why they think Macbeth sent a third murderer.
   Possible responses: He may not have trusted the first two. He might have thought the others were not strong enough to take on Banquo.

4. Tell students that the identity of the third murderer has been the subject of debate among scholars for centuries. Some suggest that it might be a messenger from the witches or even Macbeth himself in disguise. Whatever Shakespeare had in mind, the third murderer works primarily as a plot device to show Macbeth's growing fear and mistrust.

20 **Reading Check**

Answer: Macbeth tells Lady Macbeth that something will happen to Fleance and Banquo, but he does not reveal that he has plotted with murderers to have them killed.

Differentiated Instruction   **for Universal Access**

Support for Special-Needs Students
To help students stay involved in the story, review the events thus far, briefly for Acts 1 and 2 (witches, murder) and with more detail for Act 3. To help students hear sentence breaks and the meaning contributed by oral interpretation, have them read along with the *Hear It! Audio CDs.*

Support for Less Proficient Readers
To help students gain more experience in using the skills needed for understanding the text, have them complete the **Literary Analysis** and **Reading Strategy** activities, pages 134 and 135 in *Unit 2 Resources.* You may wish to have students work with partners or individually with teacher guidance.

EL **Support for English Learners**
Review the story to this point to make certain students understand what they are reading. Take time to review words or sentence structure that is confusing. Use the *Hear It! Audio CDs* so students can hear words pronounced. Have them read along to connect sounds with printed words.

367

㉑ Literary Analysis

Conflict and Climax

1. **Ask** students to provide a review of the events of Scene 3.
   Answer: A mystery murderer has joined the two hired to kill Banquo. Banquo and his son approach on horseback but dismount and walk the rest of the way to the castle. The three murderers set on them. Fleance escapes and Banquo is killed.

2. Remind students that Banquo is a great warrior, and it is likely that his son, who is probably a teenager, is also skilled in battle. So it is likely that Fleance could escape the fight.

3. **Ask** students why Fleance's escape creates an external conflict for Macbeth.
   Answer: Macbeth had hoped to cheat fate. He had hoped that, though the witches' predictions came true about him, he could keep them from coming true about Banquo and the promised line of kings to come from Banquo.

4. Tell students that many scholars consider the climax of the play to occur with the stage directions "Exit Fleance." **Ask** them why Fleance's escape is important to the drama.
   Answer: The escape is important because it means that Macbeth still has an enemy to reckon with and that the witches' prophecy about Banquo's heirs can still come true. It is the first time that one of Macbeth's plans has gone wrong. It also means someone has lived to tell of an attempted murder, which might lead people to doubt the original story about Duncan's murder—especially because Banquo had probably told Fleance about the prophecies and his concerns.

5. Tell students that, though some scholars feel that Fleance's exit is the climax, others believe the climax is in line 21, when Macbeth learns that Fleance has escaped. You may wish to have students discuss in class which event they feel is more climactic.

368

BANQUO. It will be rain tonight.

FIRST MURDERER.   Let it come down.

[*They set upon* BANQUO.]

BANQUO. O, treachery! Fly, good Fleance, fly, fly, fly!

[*Exit* FLEANCE.]

Thou mayst revenge. O slave! [*Dies.*]

THIRD MURDERER. Who did strike out the light?

FIRST MURDERER.   Was't not the way?[5]

20 **THIRD MURDERER.** There's but one down; the son is fled.

SECOND MURDERER. We have lost best half of our affair.

FIRST MURDERER. Well, let 's away and say how much is done.

[*Exit.*]

Scene iv. The palace.

[*Banquet prepared. Enter* MACBETH, LADY MACBETH, ROSS, LENNOX, LORDS, *and* ATTENDANTS.]

MACBETH. You know your own degrees;[1] sit down:
At first and last, the hearty welcome.

LORDS. Thanks to your Majesty.

MACBETH. Ourself will mingle with society[2]
5   And play the humble host.
Our hostess keeps her state,[3] but in best time
We will require[4] her welcome.

LADY MACBETH. Pronounce it for me, sir, to all our friends,
For my heart speaks they are welcome.

[*Enter* FIRST MURDERER.]

10 **MACBETH.** See, they encounter thee with their hearts' thanks.
Both sides are even: here I'll sit i' th' midst:
Be large in mirth; anon we'll drink a measure[5]
The table round. [*Goes to* MURDERER] There's blood upon thy face.

MURDERER. 'Tis Banquo's then.

15 **MACBETH.** 'Tis better thee without than he within.[6]
Is he dispatched?

MURDERER. My lord, his throat is cut; that I did for him.

MACBETH. Thou art the best o' th' cutthroats.
Yet he's good that did the like for Fleance;
20   If thou didst it, thou art the nonpareil.[7]

5. way thing to do.

1. degrees ranks. At state banquets, guests were seated according to rank.

2. society company.

3. keeps her state remains seated on her throne.

4. require request.

5. measure toast.

6. thee . . . within you outside than he inside.

㉑

7. nonpareil without equal.

368 Celebrating Humanity (1485–1625)

Enrichment: Analyzing Themes and Symbols

Ghosts

When Shakespeare included ghosts in his plays, he knew that many people believed in restless spirits who returned to Earth. Some people in Western culture believe that the ghosts of murdered people appear to seek retribution.

Though the idea of ghosts or restless spirits is fairly universal, different groups have different views. Some groups of Native Americans and Pacific Islanders believe that ghosts return to Earth for both good and evil purposes. In Asia, some people honor the spirits of dead ances-tors, which are believed to bring good fortune to families who show proper respect.

Activity: Ghosts in Literature Direct students to research another author and his or her use of ghosts. Students can then compare that author's use of ghosts with Shakespeare's. Suggest that students use as their research guide the **Enrichment: Analyzing Themes and Symbols** worksheet, *Professional Development Guidebook*, page 243.

MURDERER. Most royal sir, Fleance is 'scaped.

MACBETH. [*Aside*] Then comes my fit again: I had else been perfect,
Whole as the marble, founded as the rock,
As broad and general as the casing[8] air:
25 But now I am cabined, cribbed, confined, bound in
To saucy[9] doubts and fears.—But Banquo's safe?

MURDERER. Ay, my good lord: safe in a ditch he bides,
With twenty trenchèd[10] gashes on his head,
The least a death to nature.[11]

MACBETH. Thanks for that.
30 [*Aside*] There the grown serpent lies; the worm that's fled
Hath nature that in time will venom breed,
No teeth for th' present. Get thee gone. Tomorrow
We'll hear ourselves[12] again. [*Exit* MURDERER.]

LADY MACBETH. My royal lord,
You do not give the cheer.[13] The feast is sold
35 That is not often vouched, while 'tis a-making,
'Tis given with welcome.[14] To feed were best at home;
From thence, the sauce to meat is ceremony;[15]
Meeting were bare without it.

[*Enter the* GHOST *of* BANQUO *and sits in* MACBETH'S *place.*]

MACBETH. Sweet remembrancer!
Now good digestion wait on appetite,
And health on both!

40 **LENNOX.** May't please your Highness sit.

MACBETH. Here had we now our country's honor roofed,[16]
Were the graced person of our Banquo present—

8. as . . . casing as unrestrained as the surrounding.

9. saucy insolent.

10. trenchèd trenchlike.

11. nature natural life.

12. hear ourselves talk it over.

13. give the cheer make the guests feel welcome.

14. The feast . . . welcome The feast at which the host fails to make the guests feel welcome while the food is being prepared is no more than a bought dinner.

15. From . . . ceremony Ceremony adds a pleasant flavor to the food.

16. our . . . roofed the most honorable men in the country under one roof.

Reading Check

What do the murderers fail to do?

LITERATURE IN CONTEXT

Cultural Connection

Stagecraft at the Globe

It took some sophisticated Elizabethan theatrics to manage entrances and exits such as those of Banquo's ghost. (Macbeth reacts to the ghost in this picture.) In the farthest reaches of the Globe Theater's stage was a small area called the rear stage, which was open to the audience but enclosed by a wall at the back and cloth hangings on the sides. A trapdoor in the floor of the rear stage was the means by which Banquo's ghost made an entrance. The trapdoor operated silently, and it was not completely visible to the audience.

Connect to the Literature

What other characters in *Macbeth* might have used a trapdoor for exits or entrances? Explain.

Macbeth, Act III, Scene iv **369**

22 Literary Analysis

Dramatic Irony

1. Explain that this scene contains asides within asides. Macbeth is obviously off to the side talking to the blood-soaked murderers, because no one else sees them (their appearance would certainly have raised questions). Within this side conversation, Macbeth directs asides to the audience.

2. Tell students that the word *worm* in line 30 had a different meaning in Shakespeare's day. Then, it was often used as another word for snake. **Ask** them if lines 30–33 remind them of anything else Macbeth has recently said about snakes.
   Answer: In Scene 2, lines 13–15, Macbeth speaks of danger in general as being a snake and says that killing Duncan has wounded the snake, but not killed it. Killing Banquo and Fleance was a way to remove that danger.

3. **Ask** students to identify the dramatic irony in Macbeth's speech as he converses with his guests.
   Answer: In lines 41–42, Macbeth says that everything would be perfect if Banquo were there. In reality, he has done everything possible to ensure that Banquo will not be there—he has had Banquo murdered.

23 Reading Check

Answer: The murderers fail to kill Fleance.

24 Literature in Context

Cultural Connection

Macbeth is not the only play that needed a trapdoor for a ghost. Another famous apparition was "Great Caesar's ghost" in Shakespeare's *Julius Caesar*. In fact, astonishing entrances were included in most writers' works; special effects have always been popular.

Connect to the Literature

Ask students what other supernatural characters appear in *Macbeth*. Then, ask the Connect to the Literature question: What other characters in *Macbeth* might have used a trapdoor for exits or entrances?
Answer: The three witches might have used a trapdoor to leave quickly—in a way that would appear magic.

Identifying Cause-and-Effect Relationships

1. After students have read Scene 4, **ask** them how it is consistent with the play thus far.
Answer: Macbeth has seen floating daggers, and Duncan's death was accompanied by strange events, so a ghost fits right in.

2. Macbeth is very agitated. Note that in lines 22–26 on page 369, after learning of Fleance's escape, he says "then comes my fit again" and goes on to describe how he is again the prisoner of his fears.

3. **Ask** the Reading Strategy question: How might you connect Macbeth's agitation with his knowledge that Fleance has escaped?
Answer: Macbeth is concerned about the witches' prediction for Fleance as Banquo's son and upset that his murder plot did not succeed and might, therefore, be discovered.

4. **Ask** students what Macbeth's comments in lines 76–84 indicate about his view of murder.
Answer: Macbeth seems to view murder as neither human nor civilized, yet not as particularly evil. His comments indicate that he is more unnerved by seeing ghosts than he is concerned about the immorality of his actions.

26 Literary Analysis

Conflict

1. Remind students that an external conflict is a struggle between two characters or groups, and an internal conflict is a struggle within a character.

2. **Ask** the Literary Analysis question: How does the incident with Banquo's ghost convey Macbeth's inner conflict?
Answer: The ghost appears when Macbeth mentions Banquo, indicating that he may be feeling guilty about Banquo's death, or at least worried and fearful of consequences. Macbeth's shock at the sight of the ghost reveals his agitation—both about the actions he has taken and the course of future events.

370

---

17. Who . . . mischance whom I hope I may reproach for being absent due to discourtesy rather than pity because he has had an accident.

Reading Strategy
Identifying Cause-and-Effect Relationships
How might you connect Macbeth's agitation with his knowledge that Fleance has escaped?

Literary Analysis
Conflict How does the incident with Banquo's ghost convey Macbeth's inner conflict?

18. upon a thought in a moment.

19. passion suffering.

20. flaws gusts of wind; outbursts of emotion.

21. Authorized vouched for.

22. charnel houses vaults containing human bones dug up in making new graves.

23. our . . . kites Because the dead will be devoured by birds of prey, our tombs will be the bellies of those birds.

Who may I rather challenge for unkindness
Than pity for mischance![17]

ROSS.   His absence, sir,
45   Lays blame upon his promise. Please 't your Highness
To grace us with your royal company?

MACBETH. The table's full.

LENNOX. Here is a place reserved, sir.

MACBETH. Where?

LENNOX. Here, my good lord. What is 't that moves your Highness?

MACBETH. Which of you have done this?

50 LORDS.   What, my good lord?

MACBETH. Thou canst not say I did it. Never shake
Thy gory locks at me.

ROSS. Gentlemen, rise, his Highness is not well.

LADY MACBETH. Sit, worthy friends. My lord is often thus,
55   And hath been from his youth. Pray you, keep seat.
The fit is momentary; upon a thought[18]
He will again be well. If much you note him,
You shall offend him and extend his passion.[19]
Feed, and regard him not.—Are you a man?

60 MACBETH. Ay, and a bold one, that dare look on that
Which might appall the devil.

LADY MACBETH.   O proper stuff!
This is the very painting of your fear.
This is the air-drawn dagger which, you said,
Led you to Duncan. O, these flaws[20] and starts,
65   Impostors to true fear, would well become
A woman's story at a winter's fire,
Authorized[21] by her grandam. Shame itself!
Why do you make such faces? When all's done,
You look but on a stool.

MACBETH.   Prithee, see there!
70   Behold! Look! Lo! How say you?
Why, what care I? If thou canst nod, speak too.
If charnel houses[22] and our graves must send
Those that we bury back, our monuments
Shall be the maws of kites.[23]   [Exit GHOST.]

75 LADY MACBETH.   What, quite unmanned in folly?

MACBETH. If I stand here, I saw him.

LADY MACBETH.   Fie, for shame!

Think Aloud

Literary Analysis: Conflict
To model the skill of identifying and analyzing conflict, use the following "think aloud":

In Scene 4, the characters have come together for a banquet. I know by now that Macbeth has had Banquo killed. I also know that he is feeling guilty. Because Macbeth says to Banquo's ghost, in lines 51–52, "Thou canst no say I did it. Never shake / Thy gory locks at me," I know that Macbeth is not settled in any way about having Banquo killed. I think he is worried about getting caught. He is threatened by Banquo's appearance, and does not know if others can see Banquo too. I can identify this as an *internal* conflict. I can also identify an *external* conflict, because Lady Macbeth makes excuses for his behavior in lines 54–59, and she pleads in lines 62–68 for Macbeth to calm down and be a man. Macbeth's internal and external conflicts are threatening to bring them both down.

Scene from Macbeth, Cattermole, The Folger Shakespeare Library, Washington, D.C.

◀ **Critical Viewing** **28**
In what ways does the artist's use of light and shadow suggest the conflict in Act III, Scene iv? **[Interpret]**

MACBETH. Blood hath been shed ere now, i' th' olden time,
Ere humane statute purged the gentle weal;[24]
Ay, and since too, murders have been performed
Too terrible for the ear. The time has been
80 That, when the brains were out, the man would die,
And there an end; but now they rise again,
With twenty mortal murders on their crowns,[25]
And push us from our stools. This is more strange
Than such a murder is.

LADY MACBETH.   My worthy lord,
Your noble friends do lack you.

85 **MACBETH.**   I do forget.
Do not muse at me, my most worthy friends;
I have a strange infirmity, which is nothing
To those that know me. Come, love and health to all!
Then I'll sit down. Give me some wine, fill full.

[*Enter* GHOST.]

90 I drink to th' general joy o' th' whole table,
And to our dear friend Banquo, whom we miss;
Would he were here! To all and him we thirst,[26]
And all to all.

LORDS.   Our duties, and the pledge.

MACBETH. Avaunt![27] and quit my sight! Let the earth hide thee!
95 Thy bones are marrowless, thy blood is cold;

24. Ere . . . weal before humane laws civilized the state and made it gentle.

25. mortal . . . crowns deadly wounds on their heads.

Vocabulary
infirmity (in fur' mə tē) *n.* physical or mental defect; illness

26. thirst drink.

27. Avaunt Be gone!

29
Reading Check
Why is Macbeth startled at the feast?

Macbeth, Act III, Scene iv **371**

27 **Humanities**

Scene from Macbeth,

by George Cattermole

George Cattermole (1800–1868) was born in Norfolk, England. Trained as an architectural draftsman, he often later turned to illustrating historical events, particularly scenes of battles and duels. He is best known for his illustrations and watercolors. Cattermole was good friends with Charles Dickens, whose writings he illustrated. He also created romantic illustrations for works of Lord Byron and Sir Walter Scott. His sense of history drove him to always pay careful attention to such details as the backgrounds and costumes the characters wore.

Use these questions for discussion:

1. **Ask** students: Does Macbeth's body language suggest anything about his state of mind?
   Answer: Though Macbeth is depicted as a large, powerful man, his body language suggests that he is fearful and taken a drawing back.

2. **Ask** what the bright light in the center of the painting might represent.
   Possible response: Some students may say the bright light in the center of the painting represents Macbeth's fear that the truth about the plot will surfacing. It also highlights the line of kings who will descend from Banquo—the good that will survive Macbeth's evil.

28 **Critical Viewing**

Possible response: The artist's use of shadow may symbolize Macbeth's emotional state: He attempts to stay in the light, acting the jovial host, but the shadows, Banquo's ghost, and Macbeth's guilty conscience keep intruding.

29 **Reading Check**

Answer: Macbeth is startled at the feast because he sees the ghost of Banquo.

Differentiated
Instruction   **for Universal Access**

EL **Pronunciation for English Learners:** /r/
Read aloud lines 76–96. Point out that many of these words contain the /r/ sound. Write the following words, which appear in these lines on page 371, on the board: *purged, performed, ear, murders, worthy, dear, thirst, earth.*

Review with students the correct pronunciation of the words listed. Explain that though /r/ is a consonant, it acts more like a vowel; it does not touch anywhere in the mouth.

Practice these words first chorally, and then ask for volunteers to pronounce words. Take time to slowly sound out each /r/ sound.

Then write these words on the board: *brains, rise, crowns, strange.* Point out that these are other words that contain the /r/ sound and that are found on this page. Practice the pronunciation with students.

1. **Ask** the students whether they think Lady Macbeth or any of the guests see Banquo's ghost. Why or why not?

   Possible responses: It seems unlikely that Lady Macbeth sees the ghost, because she is too calm in making excuses, and she is too annoyed with Macbeth's reactions, which she would understand if she saw the ghost. Also, she was not involved in Banquo's murder and does not know about it yet, so it is likely that she would react pretty strongly to the gore-soaked image of a butchered Banquo. However, some students may feel that she must see the ghost, because of her own guilt. They should point out that, in line 117, Ross asks, "What sights, my lord?" So it is clear that the other guests do not see the ghost.

2. **Ask** students the Reading Strategy question: What effects do you think Macbeth's behavior will have on the guests?

   Possible response: They might be confused or worried, thinking that Macbeth is hallucinating, insane, or unwell.

31 **Critical Thinking**

Interpret

1. Direct students' attention to lines 97–99 and 118–121.

2. **Ask** students why they think Lady Macbeth is covering up for Macbeth.

   Answer: Although it seems likely that she is worried only about Duncan's murder, not yet having been told about Banquo, Lady Macbeth knows that her own security rests on Macbeth's crime remaining a secret. She aided in the crime and would therefore be condemned. Even if Macbeth fell and she escaped punishment, she would no longer be queen, and her ambition is also behind Duncan's murder.

---

28. **speculation** sight.
29. **Hyrcan** (her´ ken) from Hyrcania, a province of the ancient Persian and Macedonian empires south of the Caspian Sea.

30. **that** Banquo's shape.
31. **desert** place where neither of us could escape.
32. **inhabit** remain indoors.

33. **admired** amazing.
34. **overcome us** come over us.
35. **disposition. . . owe** my own nature.

30

What effects do you think Macbeth's behavior will have on the guests?

36. **Stand . . . going** Do not wait to depart in order of rank. **31**

37. **Augures and understood relations** omens and the relationship between the omens and what they represent.
38. **maggot-pies and choughs** (chufs) magpies and crows.
39. **man of blood** murderer.
40. **at odds** disputing.

> Thou hast no speculation[28] in those eyes
> Which thou dost glare with.
>
> **LADY MACBETH.** Think of this, good peers, **31**
> But as a thing of custom, 'tis no other.
> Only it spoils the pleasure of the time.
>
> 100 **MACBETH.** What man dare, I dare.
> Approach thou like the rugged Russian bear,
> The armed rhinoceros, or th' Hyrcan[29] tiger;
> Take any shape but that,[30] and my firm nerves
> Shall never tremble. Or be alive again,
> 105 And dare me to the desert[31] with thy sword.
> If trembling I inhabit[32] then, protest me
> The baby of a girl. Hence, horrible shadow!
> Unreal mock'ry, hence! [*Exit* GHOST.]
> Why, so: being gone,
> I am a man again. Pray you, sit still.
>
> **LADY MACBETH.** You have displaced the mirth, broke the
> 110 good meeting,
> With most admired[33] disorder.
>
> **MACBETH.** Can such things be,
> And overcome us[34] like a summer's cloud,
> Without our special wonder? You make me strange
> Even to the disposition that I owe,[35]
> 115 When now I think you can behold such sights,
> And keep the natural ruby of your cheeks,
> When mine is blanched with fear.
>
> **ROSS.** What sights, my lord?
>
> **LADY MACBETH.** I pray you, speak not: He grows worse and worse;
> Question enrages him: at once, good night.
> 120 Stand not upon the order of your going,[36]
> But go at once.
>
> **LENNOX.** Good night; and better health
> Attend his Majesty!
>
> **LADY MACBETH.** A kind good night to all!
>
> [*Exit* LORDS.]
>
> **MACBETH.** It will have blood, they say: blood will have blood.
> Stones have been known to move and trees to speak;
> 125 Augures and understood relations[37] have
> By maggot-pies and choughs[38] and rooks brought forth
> The secret'st man of blood.[39] What is the night?
>
> **LADY MACBETH.** Almost at odds[40] with morning, which is which.
>
> **MACBETH.** How say'st thou, that Macduff denies his person

---

Enrichment: Investigating Religion and Myth

Hecate and Scene 5

Hecate (pronounced *hekaty*) was a goddess in early Greek religion. She was probably derived from an early people in southwest Asia Minor. The name in Greek means "she who works her will." Hecate was the chief goddess of magic and spells. Because of associations between magic and the moon, she was often identified with the moon goddess Diana. However, Hecate was considered the infernal aspect of the moon.

Activity: Investigating Greek Mythology Have students research an aspect of Greek mythology that they have come across thus far in *Macbeth*. Students may focus on Hecate or pick up on Shakespeare's use of the three witches, which resemble the Greek fates. Suggest that students use as their research guide the **Enrichment: Investigating Religion and Myth** worksheet, *Professional Development Guidebook,* page 240. Ask students to present their findings to the class.

At our great bidding?

130 **LADY MACBETH.** Did you send to him, sir?

MACBETH. I hear it by the way, but I will send:
There's not a one of them but in his house
I keep a servant fee'd.[41] I will tomorrow,
And betimes [42] I will, to the weird sisters:

135 More shall they speak, for now I am bent [43] to know
By the worst means the worst. For mine own good
All causes shall give way. I am in blood
Stepped in so far that, should I wade no more,
Returning were as tedious as go o'er.

140 Strange things I have in head that will to hand,
Which must be acted ere they may be scanned.[44]

LADY MACBETH. You lack the season of all natures,[45] sleep.

MACBETH. Come, we'll to sleep. My strange and self-abuse[46]
Is the initiate fear that wants hard use.[47]

145 We are yet but young in deed. *[Exit.]*

Scene v. A witches' haunt.

[Thunder. Enter the THREE WITCHES, *meeting* HECATE.]

FIRST WITCH. Why, how now, Hecate! you look angerly.

HECATE. Have I not reason, beldams[1] as you are,
Saucy and overbold? How did you dare
To trade and traffic with Macbeth
5 In riddles and affairs of death;
And I, the mistress of your charms,
The close contriver [2] of all harms,
Was never called to bear my part,
Or show the glory of our art?
10 And, which is worse, all you have done
Hath been but for a wayward son,
Spiteful and wrathful; who, as others do,
Loves for his own ends, not for you.
But make amends now: get you gone,
15 And at the pit of Acheron[3]
Meet me i' th' morning: thither he
Will come to know his destiny.
Your vessels and your spells provide,
Your charms and everything beside.
20 I am for th' air; this night I'll spend
Unto a dismal and a fatal end:
Great business must be wrought ere noon.
Upon the corner of the moon
There hangs a vap'rous drop profound;

---

41. fee'd paid to spy.

42. betimes quickly.

43. bent determined.

Literary Analysis
Conflict How do lines
136–139 in Scene iv mark a
turning point in Macbeth's
inner conflict?

44. scanned examined.

45. season . . . natures
preservative of all living
creatures.

46. My . . . self-abuse my
strange delusion.

47. initiate . . . use beginner's
fear that will harden with
experience.

1. beldams hags.

2. close contriver secret
inventor.

3. Acheron (ak′ ər än′) hell;
in Greek mythology the river
of Hades.

Why will Macbeth visit
"the weird sisters" again?

Macbeth, Act III, Scene v **373**

---

32 Literary Analysis
Conflict

1. Have students read Macbeth's comments in lines 131–141 and 143–145 carefully.

2. **Ask** them to identify the comment that lets them know that Macbeth already doesn't trust anyone.
   Answer: In lines 132–133, he says he is paying servants in everyone's households to spy for him.

3. **Ask** students the Literary Analysis question: How do lines 136–139 in Scene iv mark a turning point in Macbeth's inner conflict?
   Answer: Macbeth has come to the point at which he feels that he will do anything to protect his position, without his previous doubts. He has reached what he himself views as the point of no return, where he has gone so far that it is as far forward as it is back.

4. **Ask** students what they think these lines, along with the comment in line 145, tell the audience about what events they can expect in the future.
   Answer: The lines indicate that Macbeth will visit the witches, but also that more people will be murdered. "We are yet but young in deed" indicates that the killing has only just begun.

▶ **Monitor Progress:** Remind students that the climax of a play is the point at which the conflict reaches its highest point, and after that the action falls as the conflicts are resolved. **Ask** them how Macbeth's attitude at this point reflects the beginning of the resolution of conflicts.
Possible response: Macbeth's inner conflict appears to have been resolved; he no longer seems to be slowed by any sense of guilt or fear of consequences. The decision to resolve the exter-nal conflict has been made, as Macbeth spies on and plans to kill his enemies.

33 Reading Check

Answer: Macbeth decides to visit "the weird sisters" again to demand that they tell him more about his future, now that he has done so much.

373

Interpret

1. As students read Scene 6, tell them to look for subtle comments that would let the audience know that Lennox and the other lord are not as fond of Macbeth as they might at first seem. In fact, you may wish to tell them to read the scene with the idea in mind that the two hate Macbeth.

2. **Ask** students to identify the word (lines 22–26) that both men use that tells us their true feelings about Macbeth.
   Answer: Both use the word *tyrant*, which implies injustice and a usurped throne.

3. **Ask** how the second lord's description of England's Edward lets us know that this lord feels that Duncan's son is innocent.
   Answer: He calls him pious and holy, which implies that he would be on the side of right and goodness. Therefore, if he has received Duncan's son, the son must be innocent.

4. **Ask** students what coming action and events they can anticipate from the information supplied in lines 24–39.
   Answer: Macbeth will probably try to kill Macduff. Macbeth will soon face an English army, as well as unhappy Scots, in battle.

34 Engaging the Essential Question

1. Explain that the inclusion of Hecate (or Hekate) in *Macbeth* is an allusion to the Greek tradition. In Greek mythology, Hekate, was often portrayed as an evil manifestation.

2. **Ask** students why they think Shakespeare included the allusion to Hecate.
   Possible response: Shakespeare may have included Hecate to amplify the evil within Macbeth's heart, which is representative of the evil that dwells in the hearts of all humankind.

3. Then **ask** what Shakespeare's use of the allusion suggests about his relationship to tradition.
   Possible response:
   Shakespeare's relationship to tradition is a close one. In *Macbeth*, Shakespeare uses the allusion to amplify the evil that lies within the human soul.

---

4. **sleights** devices.

5. **artificial sprites** spirits created by magic.

6. **confusion** ruin.

7. **security** overconfidence.

25
I'll catch it ere it come to ground:
And that distilled by magic sleights[4]
Shall raise such artificial sprites[5]
As by the strength of their illusion
Shall draw him on to his confusion.[6]

34 30
He shall spurn fate, scorn death, and bear
His hopes 'bove wisdom, grace, and fear:
And you all know security[7]
Is mortals' chiefest enemy.

[*Music and a song.*]

Hark! I am called; my little spirit, see,
35 Sits in a foggy cloud and stays for me.   [*Exit.*]

[*Sing within,* "Come away, come away," *etc.*]

FIRST WITCH. Come, let's make haste; she'll soon be
back again.   [*Exit.*]

Scene vi. The palace.

[*Enter* LENNOX *and another* LORD.]

1. **hit** coincided with.

2. **Which . . . farther** from which you can draw your own conclusions.

3. **borne** managed.

4. **cannot . . . thought** can fail to think.

5. **fact** deed.

6. **thralls** slaves.

7. **an 't** if it.

8. **broad** unguarded.

9. **due of birth** birthright; claim to the throne.

LENNOX. My former speeches have but hit[1] your thoughts,
Which can interpret farther.[2] Only I say
Things have been strangely borne.[3] The gracious Duncan
Was pitied of Macbeth: marry, he was dead.
5 And the right-valiant Banquo walked too late;
Whom, you may say, if 't please you, Fleance killed,
For Fleance fled. Men must not walk too late.
Who cannot want the thought,[4] how monstrous
It was for Malcolm and for Donalbain
10 To kill their gracious father? Damnèd fact![5]
How it did grieve Macbeth! Did he not straight,
In pious rage, the two delinquents tear,
That were the slaves of drink and thralls[6] of sleep?
Was not that nobly done? Ay, and wisely too;
15 For 'twould have angered any heart alive
To hear the men deny 't. So that I say
He has borne all things well: and I do think
That, had he Duncan's sons under his key—
As, an 't[7] please heaven, he shall not—they should find
20 What 'twere to kill a father. So should Fleance.
But, peace! for from broad[8] words, and 'cause he failed
His presence at the tyrant's feast, I hear,
Macduff lives in disgrace. Sir, can you tell
Where he bestows himself?

35

LORD.   The son of Duncan,
25 From whom this tyrant holds the due of birth,[9]

Vocabulary Development

Vocabulary Knowledge Rating

When students have completed reading and discussing the selection, have them take out their **Vocabulary Knowledge Rating Charts** for the story. Read the words aloud and have students rate their knowledge of words again in the After Reading column. Clarify any words that are still problematic. Have students write their own definitions and example or sentence in the appropriate column. Then have students complete the Vocabulary Lesson at the end of the selection. Encourage students to use the words in further discussion and written work about the selection. Remind them that they will be accountable for these words on the **Selection Test,** *Unit 2 Resources*, pages 142–144 or 145–147.

Lives in the English court, and is received
Of the most pious Edward[10] with such grace
That the malevolence of fortune nothing
Takes from his high respect.[11] Thither Macduff
30 Is gone to pray the holy King, upon his aid[12]
To wake Northumberland and warlike Siward;[13]
That by the help of these, with Him above
To ratify the work, we may again
Give to our tables meat, sleep to our nights,
35 Free from our feasts and banquets bloody knives,
Do faithful homage and receive free honors:[14]
All which we pine for now. And this report
Hath so exasperate the King that he
Prepares for some attempt of war.

LENNOX.   Sent he to Macduff?

40 **LORD.** He did: and with an absolute "Sir, not I,"
The cloudy[15] messenger turns me his back,
And hums, as who should say "You'll rue the time
That clogs[16] me with this answer."

LENNOX.   And that well might
Advise him to a caution, t' hold what distance
45 His wisdom can provide. Some holy angel
Fly to the court of England and unfold
His message ere he come, that a swift blessing
May soon return to this our suffering country
Under a hand accursed!

LORD.   I'll send my prayers with him.   [*Exit.*]

Vocabulary

malevolence (mə lev′ ə ləns)
n. ill will; spitefulness

10. **Edward** Edward the Confessor, king of England 1042–1066.

11. **with . . . respect** does not diminish the high respect he is given.

12. **upon his aid** to aid Malcolm.

13. **To . . . Siward** to call to arms the commander of the English forces, the Earl of Northumberland, and his son Siward.

14. **free honors** honors given to freemen.

15. **cloudy** disturbed.

16. **clogs** burdens.

Critical Reading

©

© 1. **Key Ideas and Details** **(a)** What does Macbeth think as he anticipates the murder of Banquo? **(b) Compare and Contrast:** Compare and contrast Macbeth's thoughts about Banquo's murder with his thoughts before the murder of Duncan.

© 2. **Key Ideas and Details** **(a)** In the banquet scene, what complaint does Macbeth make about murdered men? **(b) Analyze:** Is there anything humorous or even ridiculous in this complaint? Why or why not? **(c) Connect:** Does Shakespeare use humor for comic relief in this scene, as he does in the earlier scene with the porter? Explain.

© 3. **Integration of Knowledge and Ideas** Has the relationship between Macbeth and Lady Macbeth changed? Explain.

© 4. **Integration of Knowledge and Ideas** What does the murder of Banquo suggest about the effects of evil on evildoers? Explain.

Cite textual evidence to support your responses.

Macbeth, Act III, Scene vi **375**

ASSESS

Answers

Before students respond, you may wish to have them write a brief objective summary of the selection. As they answer the questions below, remind them to support their answers with evidence from the text.

1. (a) Macbeth thinks he will have made himself safe by killing Banquo. He is eager to see it done. (b) **Possible response:** Macbeth's thoughts before killing Duncan were quite different. His fear then was about the act of killing; with regard to Banquo, he fears the victim. He hesitated then, but he does not now.

2. (a) Macbeth complains that murdered men do not stay in their graves; they rise again. (b) **Possible response:** There is a kind of grim humor in the passage. It is a ridiculous response to a blood-covered ghost. (c) **Possible response:** The grim humor here, which emanates from guilt and insanity, is not really comparable to the Porter's scene, which was goofy but innocent. The Porter gets a laugh; Macbeth gets a shudder.

3. The relationship has changed. They are no longer partners. Macbeth is not consulting Lady Macbeth or informing her of his decisions. She is no longer urging him to violence; instead, she would rather have him calm down and stop worrying.

4. **Possible response:** The evildoer becomes calloused and no longer has normal feelings of either guilt or love. The evil is never finished, and it continues to produce evil results.

Concept Connector

Reading Strategy Graphic Organizer
Ask students to review the graphic organizers in which they have traced cause-and-effect relationships throughout Act 3. Then have students share their organizers and compare what they identified.

Activating Prior Knowledge
Have students return to the paragraphs they wrote in the Activating Prior Knowledge activity. Have students follow up with each other: Were their predictions correct?

Writing About the Essential Question
Have students list instances of comedy from *Macbeth*, Act 3, and record these on the board. Then have students work individually or in groups, writing or discussing their thoughts, to formulate their responses to the Essential Question. Encourage students to consider to what extent Shakespeare is able to insert moments of comedy, even among the events in Act 3. Lead a class discussion, encouraging students to cite specific textual details to support their responses.

Answers

1. **(a)** Macbeth is involved in this external conflict because the witches predicted that Banquo would father a line of kings. **(b)** He fails to have Banquo's son killed.

2. **Action:** murder of Banquo; Fleance escapes. **Internal Conflict:** Macbeth struggles with fear, first because Fleance is alive, posing a threat, and then because of the appearance of Banquo's ghost. **Proposed Actions:** Macbeth says he will visit the witches; he also says the killing will escalate.

3. **(a)** The fact that Macbeth argues with the ghost, which represents his conscience, is a sign of the internal conflict. **(b)** Macbeth turns his thoughts to Macduff's absence and to his future plans.

4. **Possible response:** Some may say Duncan's son, Malcolm, because he is the rightful heir.

5. **(a)** Macbeth tells Banquo that he will ask his advice tomorrow, asks him to not miss the feast, and wishes Banquo a safe journey. **(b)** Tension is heightened because the audience does not know what to believe.

6. Macbeth's ironic comment about Banquo's absence creates tension because, even without expecting a ghost, one still expects some-one to confront him and reveal his guilt.

7. **Possible response:** Students may suggest a moving camera, to take in the reactions of the guests to Macbeth's outbursts, com-bined with close-ups of Macbeth, to show his reactions.

8. **(a)** Macbeth wants to find a time when Banquo and his son will be together, in order to have them murdered. **(b)** Banquo must die so that he cannot father more potential kings.

9. **Possible responses:** Macbeth might join the murderers to make sure the deed is done. He might not join them because he must be seen to be innocent of the crime. Students may also point out that it is unlikely he was there since he was surprised to learn of Fleance's escape.

10. **Possible response:** They will form an alliance against Macbeth and bring troops to take back the throne for Duncan's son.

376

After You Read   *Macbeth, Act III*

Literary Analysis

1. **Craft and Structure (a)** Why is Macbeth involved in an **external conflict** with Banquo? **(b)** In what way does Macbeth fail to resolve this conflict?

2. **Craft and Structure** Complete a chart like the one below to show the intensification of **conflict** and the movement toward a climax in Act III.

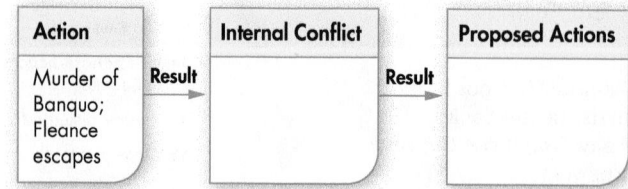

Action	Internal Conflict	Proposed Actions
Murder of Banquo; Fleance escapes	*Result* →	*Result* →

3. **Craft and Structure (a)** How is Macbeth's behavior at the banquet a sign of an **internal conflict? (b)** How does he temporarily resolve this conflict?

4. **Key Ideas and Details** Macbeth is personifying evil. Who do you think will lead the forces of good in a campaign against him? How do you know?

5. **Craft and Structure (a)** Identify three examples of **dramatic irony** in Macbeth's speeches to Banquo in Act III, Scene i, lines 20–38. **(b)** In what way do these examples achieve an aesthetic purpose for Shakespeare by heightening the tension?

6. **Craft and Structure** How does the dramatic irony in Act III, Scene iv, lines 41–44 create an expectation of a tense encounter?

7. **Integration of Knowledge and Ideas** What camera shots would you use to film the banquet scene for a movie version of *Macbeth*? Explain.

Reading Strategy

8. **Identify causes and effects** in the play by explaining how the Witches' prophecy that Banquo will father kings could be viewed as the cause of the following items: **(a)** the question Macbeth asks of Banquo, "'Goes Fleance with you?'" (III, i, 35); **(b)** Macbeth's recruit-ing of the murderers (III, iii)

9. Some critics suggest that the third murderer is Macbeth himself. Argue for or against this interpretation, supporting your points by showing what would cause Macbeth to join the two murderers in person or what would cause him not to join them.

10. In Act III, Scene vi, a lord tells Lennox that Duncan's son is being shel-tered at the English court and that Macduff has gone there to seek his aid. What effects do you think will result from Macduff's visit?

Common Core State Standards

Writing

3. Write narratives to develop real or imagined experiences or events using effective technique, well-chosen details, and well-structured event sequences. *(p. 377)*

3.a. Engage and orient the reader by setting out a problem, situation, or observation and its significance, establishing one or multiple point(s) of view, and introducing a narrator and/or characters; create a smooth progression of experiences or events. *(p. 377)*

3.d. Use precise words and phrases, telling details, and sensory language to convey a vivid picture of the experiences, events, setting, and/or characters. *(p. 377)*

5. Develop and strengthen writing as needed by planning, revising, editing, rewriting, or trying a new approach, focusing on addressing what is most significant for a specific purpose and audience. *(p. 377)*

Language

4.a. Use context as a clue to the meaning of a word or phrase. *(p. 377)*

Assessment Practice

Forms of Propaganda (For more practice, see *All-in-One Workbook*.)

Many tests require students to recognize per-suasive devices. Use this item to show that sometimes rhetorical questions are a persuasive device.

> **Macbeth.** . . . Do you find
> Your patience so predominant in your nature,
> That you can let this go? Are you so gospeled,
> To pray for this good man and for his issue,
> Whose heavy hand hath bowed you to the grave

And beggared yours forever?

Macbeth asks the murderers these questions because he wants them to

   A answer him truthfully.
   B be patient and forgiving.
   C know what Banquo has done to them.
   D agree to kill Banquo.

Macbeth is persuading the murderers to kill Banquo. The correct answer is **D**.

Integrated Language Skills

Vocabulary Acquisition and Use

Word Analysis: Latin Prefix *mal-*

The Latin prefix *mal-* means "bad or badly, poorly, or wrong." *Malevolence*, therefore, means "ill will." The prefix *mal-* can also mean "not," as in *malcontent*. With a group, write a short paragraph describing several qualities that would make a person a poor leader, giving an example of each. Use at least three of the *mal-* words listed below. If any of the words are unfamiliar, refer to a dictionary to clarify their meanings.

maladjusted	malformed
malady	maladministration
malfunction	malicious

Then, for each of the *mal-* words used in your description, tell whether the prefix most nearly means "bad or badly," "poorly," "wrong," or "not."

Writing

Narrative Text Write a **soliloquy** for a lord returning from Macbeth's banquet. At the beginning of the soliloquy, have him clearly establish his point of view (a guest at Macbeth's banquet). Then, have your character relate the events he has seen and explain why they are important.

Prewriting Reread Scene iv. List Macbeth's most striking words and actions, your lord's reactions, and possible sensory details of the scene.

Drafting Using your prewriting list, draft the soliloquy in **blank verse,** unrhymed iambic pentameter. Mimic Shakespeare's style and diction.

Revising Reread your soliloquy to strengthen its figurative language. First, place a star next to descriptive words and phrases that sound too literal. Then, replace each with an imaginative comparison or word picture.

Model: Revising for Figurative Language

                              face as dazed as death
And then the king, with ~~pale and frightened face,~~
rose slowly, staring at—nay, toward—the wall
                    danced
where nothing ~~was~~ except for shadows dark.

The writer replaces the lackluster adjectives with a vivid and eerie comparison. Next, she replaces the flat *to-be* verb with a lively action verb. These changes help the audience "see" what is being described.

Vocabulary: Context Clues

The context of a word—the words, phrases and sentences that surround it—may provide clues to its meaning. In the paragraph below, explain how context clues help you identify the meaning of the underlined vocabulary words:

A <u>predominant</u> nobleman in the court of King Malicia heard rumors of foul play in the neighboring kingdom of Maloria. "Though your reign is <u>indissoluble</u>, my liege," he said to the king, "I am afraid the one next door is a little flimsy." "Does the King of Maloria suffer from physical illness or mental <u>infirmity</u>?" the king queried. "Both, my liege," replied the nobleman. "Though he thinks himself <u>dauntless</u>, he is actually a cowering ninny." "Perfect!" cackled the king. "My unchecked <u>malevolence</u> shall soon make me the evil ruler of not one kingdom, but two!"

Integrated Language Skills **377**

Vocabulary Acquisition and Use

Word Analysis

Possible response: A good leader has to be fair, competent, and get along well with others. *Malicious* people, who would intentionally hurt others, would be poor leaders. Another form of poor leadership is *maladministration* through incompetence. Finally, people who are *maladjusted* cannot understand others' needs and make poor leaders.

1. *malicious* – bad
2. *maladministration* – poor
3. *maladjusted* – poorly

Vocabulary

Possible responses:

1. *predominant* – Because he speaks to the king, he must be influential.
2. *indissoluble* – Since it is contrasted with flimsy, it must be strong.
3. *infirmity* – Since it is paired with *illness,* it is probably similar.
4. *dauntless* – As a contrast to *cowering,* this means *courageous.*
5. *malevolence* – The adjective *evil* is used in the sentence.

Writing

You may use this Writing Lesson as timed-writing practice, or you may allow students to develop the response as a writing assignment over several days.

1. Before they begin, have students discuss how they would react if their host acted like Macbeth.
2. Before they begin their drafts, review **blank verse**.
3. Work with students to develop guidelines for their narrative texts,
   - **Focus** The writer should clearly present the point of the view of the returning lord.
   - **Organization** The writer's character should clearly narrate events leading up to his return.
   - **Elaboration** The writer should include sensory details and figurative language.
   - **Style** The writer should employ blank verse and a formal style.
4. Before they revise, have students discuss the changes made in the model.

Assessment Resources

Unit 2 Resources

L1 L2 EL Selection Test A, pp. 142–144. Administer Test A to less advanced readers.

L3 L4 EL Selection Test B, pp. 145–147. Administer Test B to on-level and more advanced students.

L3 L4 Open-Book Test, Test, pp. 139–141. As an alternative, administer the Open-Book Test.

All Customizable Test Bank

All Self-tests
Students may prepare for the **Selection Test** by taking the **Self-test** online.

PHLit Online! All assessment resources are available at **www.PHLitOnline.com**.

377

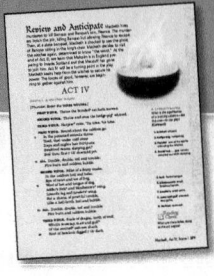

• *Macbeth*, Act IV
Lesson Pacing Guide

DAY 1 Preteach

- Administer the Reading and Vocabulary Warm-ups (*Unit 2 Resources,* pp. 148–151) as necessary.
- Introduce the Literary Analysis concept: Imagery.
- Introduce the Reading Strategy: Analyzing Text Structures.
- Build background with Background features.
- Develop thematic thinking with Connecting to the Essential Question.
- Teach the selection vocabulary.

DAYS 2–3 Preteach/Teach/Assess

- Distribute copies of the appropriate graphic organizer for the Reading Strategy (*Graphic Organizer Transparencies,* pp. 64–65).
- Distribute copies of the appropriate graphic organizer for Literary Analysis (*Graphic Organizer Transparencies*, pp. 66–67).
- Prepare students to read with the Activating Prior Knowledge activities (TE).
- Informally monitor comprehension while students read.
- Use the Reading Check questions to confirm comprehension.
- Develop students' understanding of imagery using the Literary Analysis prompts.
- Develop students' ability to analyze text structures using the Reading Strategy prompts.
- Reinforce vocabulary with the Vocabulary notes.
- Assess students' comprehension and mastery of the skills by having them answer the Critical Reading, Literary Analysis, and Reading Strategy questions.
- Have students complete the Vocabulary Lesson.

DAY 4 Extend/Assess

- Have students complete the Writing Lesson and write an analysis of archetypal images. (You may assign as homework.)
- Have students read and respond to the Critical Commentary.
- Administer Selection Test A or B (*Unit 2 Resources*, pp. 160–162 or 163–165).

Common Core State Standards

Reading Literature 3. Analyze the impact of the author's choices regarding how to develop and relate elements of a story or drama.

Writing 2.b. Develop the topic thoroughly by selecting the most significant and relevant facts, extended definitions, concrete details, quotations, or other information and examples appropriate to the audience's knowledge of the topic.
2.f. Provide a concluding statement or section that follows from and supports the information or explanation presented.
5. Develop and strengthen writing as needed by planning, revising, editing, rewriting, or trying a new approach, focusing on addressing what is most significant for a specific purpose and audience.

Language 1.a. Apply the understanding that usage is a matter of convention, can change over time, and is sometimes contested.
4.d. Verify the preliminary determination of the meaning of a word or phrase.

Additional Standards Practice
Common Core Companion, pp. 28–40; 196–207; 226–227; 324–331

Daily Block Scheduling
Each day in this Lesson Pacing Guide represents a 40–50 minute period. Teachers using block scheduling may combine days to revise pacing. In addition, teachers may differentiate and support core instruction by integrating components for extended and intensive support as students require. See the Guide to Selected Leveled Resources (facing page).

Guide to Selected Leveled Resources

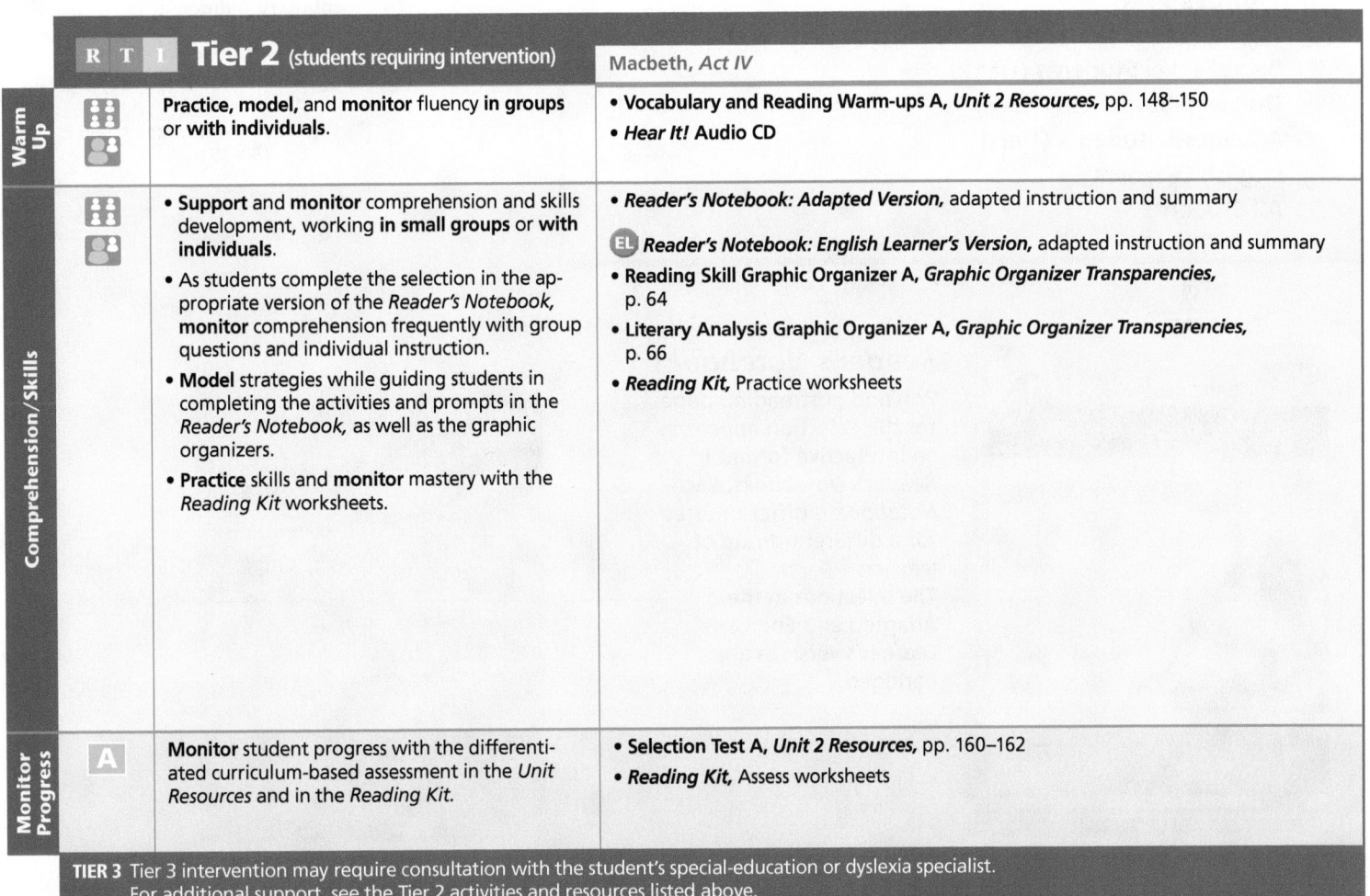

R T I Tier 1 (students performing on level) — Macbeth, *Act IV*

Warm Up

Practice, **model,** and **monitor** fluency, working **with the whole class** or **in groups.**

Vocabulary and **Reading Warm-ups B,** *Unit 2 Resources,* pp. 148–149, 151

Comprehension/Skills

Support and **monitor** comprehension and skills development, having students complete the activities, graphic organizers, and interactive prompts **independently** or **as a class.**

- *Reader's Notebook,* adapted instruction and summary
- **EL** *Reader's Notebook: English Learner's Version,* adapted instruction and summary
- **Reading Skill Graphic Organizer B,** *Graphic Organizer Transparencies,* p. 65
- **Literary Analysis Graphic Organizer B,** *Graphic Organizer Transparencies,* p. 67

Monitor Progress

Monitor student progress with the differentiated curriculum-based assessment in the *Unit Resources.*

- **Selection Test B,** *Unit 2 Resources,* pp. 163–165
- **Open-Book Test,** *Unit 2 Resources,* pp. 157–159

R T I Tier 2 (students requiring intervention) — Macbeth, *Act IV*

Warm Up

Practice, **model,** and **monitor** fluency **in groups** or **with individuals.**

- **Vocabulary** and **Reading Warm-ups A,** *Unit 2 Resources,* pp. 148–150
- *Hear It!* Audio CD

Comprehension/Skills

- **Support** and **monitor** comprehension and skills development, working **in small groups** or **with individuals.**
- As students complete the selection in the appropriate version of the *Reader's Notebook,* **monitor** comprehension frequently with group questions and individual instruction.
- **Model** strategies while guiding students in completing the activities and prompts in the *Reader's Notebook,* as well as the graphic organizers.
- **Practice** skills and **monitor** mastery with the *Reading Kit* worksheets.

- *Reader's Notebook: Adapted Version,* adapted instruction and summary
- **EL** *Reader's Notebook: English Learner's Version,* adapted instruction and summary
- **Reading Skill Graphic Organizer A,** *Graphic Organizer Transparencies,* p. 64
- **Literary Analysis Graphic Organizer A,** *Graphic Organizer Transparencies,* p. 66
- *Reading Kit,* Practice worksheets

Monitor Progress

Monitor student progress with the differentiated curriculum-based assessment in the *Unit Resources* and in the *Reading Kit.*

- **Selection Test A,** *Unit 2 Resources,* pp. 160–162
- *Reading Kit,* Assess worksheets

TIER 3 Tier 3 intervention may require consultation with the student's special-education or dyslexia specialist. For additional support, see the Tier 2 activities and resources listed above.

One-on-one teaching　Group work　Whole class instruction　Independent work　A Assessment

For a complete guide to selection support, including support for Advanced students, see the Overview of Resources in the frontmatter.

• *Macbeth*, Act IV

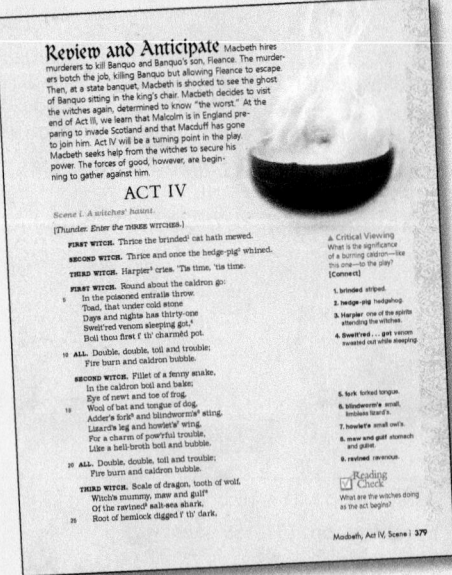

RESOURCES FOR:

L1 Special-Needs Students

L2 Below-Level Students (Tier 2)

L3 On-Level Students (Tier 1)

L4 Advanced Students (Tier 1)

EL English Learners

All All Students

Vocabulary/Fluency/Prior Knowledge

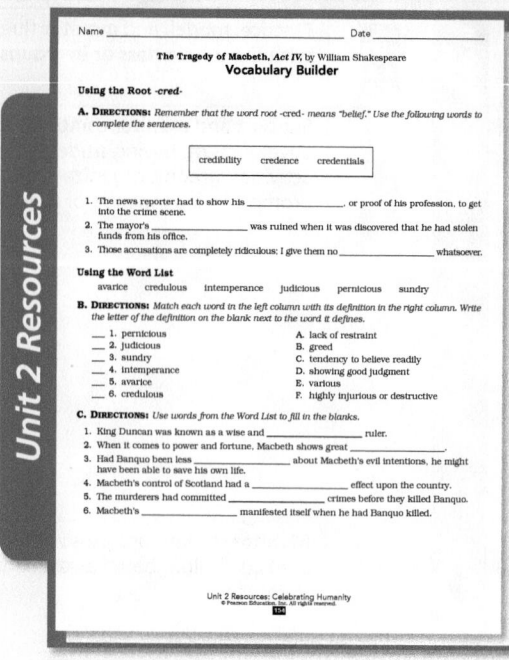

All **Vocabulary Builder,** p. 154

Also available for these selections:

EL L1 L2 **Vocabulary Warm-ups A and B,** pp. 148–149

EL L1 L2 **Reading Warm-ups A and B,** pp. 150–151

L2 L3 *Reader's Notebook*

L1 *Reader's Notebook: Adapted Version*

EL *Reader's Notebook: English Learner's Version*

EL *Reader's Notebook: Spanish Version*

Reader's Notebooks

Pre- and postreading pages for this selection appear in an interactive format in the *Reader's Notebooks*. Each *Notebook* is differentiated for a different group of learners.
The selections in the Adapted and English Learner's versions are abridged.

© *Common Core Companion*

Additional instruction and practice for each Common Core State Standard

Selection Support

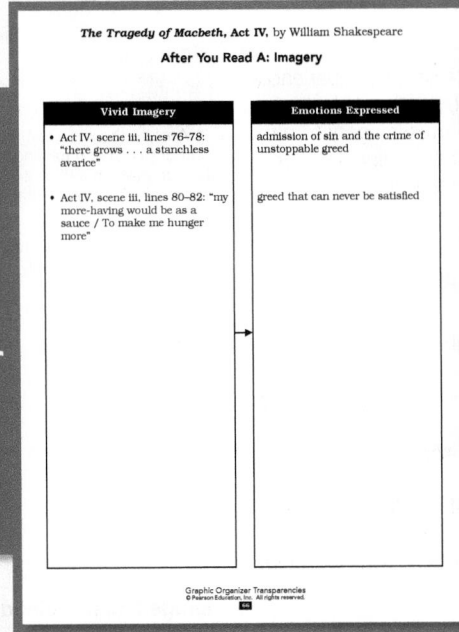

The Tragedy of Macbeth, Act IV, by William Shakespeare

After You Read A: Imagery

Vivid Imagery	Emotions Expressed
• Act IV, scene iii, lines 76–78: "there grows . . . a stanchless avarice"	admission of sin and the crime of unstoppable greed
• Act IV, scene iii, lines 80–82: "my more-having would be as a sauce / To make me hunger more"	greed that can never be satisfied

Graphic Organizer Transparencies
© Pearson Education, Inc. All rights reserved.

EL L1 L2 Literary Analysis: Graphic Organizer A (partially filled in), p. 66

Also available for these selections:

EL L1 L2 Reading: Graphic Organizer A (partially filled in), p. 64

EL L3 Reading: Graphic Organizer B, p. 65

EL L3 Literary Analysis: Graphic Organizer B, p. 67

Skills Development/Extension

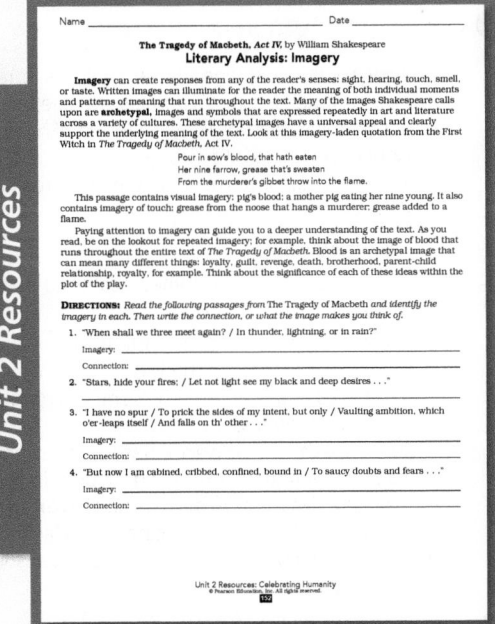

Name _____ Date _____

The Tragedy of Macbeth, Act IV, by William Shakespeare
Literary Analysis: Imagery

Imagery can create responses from any of the reader's senses: sight, hearing, touch, smell, or taste. Written images can illuminate for the reader the meaning of both individual moments and patterns of meaning that run throughout the text. Many of the images Shakespeare calls upon are **archetypal**, images and symbols that are expressed repeatedly in art and literature across a variety of cultures. These archetypal images have a universal appeal and clearly support the underlying meaning of the text. Look at this imagery-laden quotation from the First Witch in *The Tragedy of Macbeth,* Act IV.

> Pour in sow's blood, that hath eaten
> Her nine farrow, grease that's sweaten
> From the murderer's gibbet throw into the flame.

This passage contains visual imagery: pig's blood; a mother pig eating her nine young. It also contains imagery of touch: grease from the noose that hangs a murderer; grease added to a flame.

Paying attention to imagery can guide you to a deeper understanding of the text. As you read, be on the lookout for repeated imagery; for example, think about the image of blood that runs throughout the entire text of *The Tragedy of Macbeth.* Blood is an archetypal image that can mean many different things: loyalty, guilt, revenge, death, brotherhood, parent-child relationship, royalty, for example. Think about the significance of each of these ideas within the plot of the play.

DIRECTIONS: *Read the following passages from The Tragedy of Macbeth and identify the imagery in each. Then write the connection, or what the image makes you think of.*

1. "When shall we three meet again? / In thunder, lightning, or in rain?"

   Imagery: _____

   Connection: _____

2. "Stars, hide your fires: / Let not light see my black and deep desires . . ."

3. "I have no spur / To prick the sides of my intent, but only / Vaulting ambition, which o'er-leaps itself / And falls on th' other . . ."

   Imagery: _____

   Connection: _____

4. "But now I am cabined, cribbed, confined, bound in / To saucy doubts and fears . . ."

   Imagery: _____

   Connection: _____

Unit 2 Resources: Celebrating Humanity
© Pearson Education, Inc. All rights reserved. 152

All Literary Analysis, p. 152

Also available for these selections:

All Reading, p. 153

EL L3 L4 Support for Writing, p. 155

L4 Enrichment, p. 156

Assessment

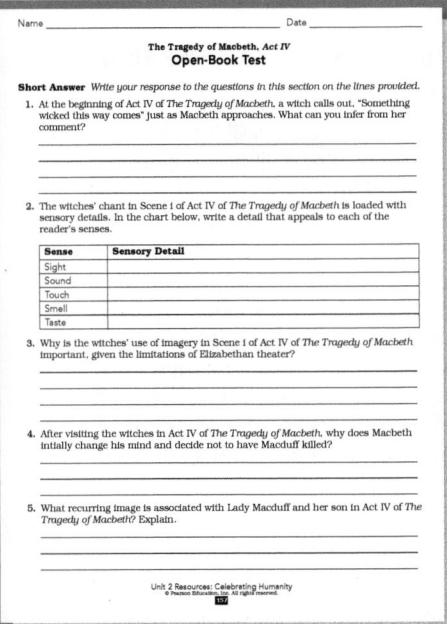

Name _____ Date _____

The Tragedy of Macbeth, Act IV
Open-Book Test

Short Answer *Write your response to the questions in this section on the lines provided.*

1. At the beginning of Act IV of *The Tragedy of Macbeth,* a witch calls out, "Something wicked this way comes" just as Macbeth approaches. What can you infer from her comment?

2. The witches' chant in Scene i of Act IV of *The Tragedy of Macbeth* is loaded with sensory details. In the chart below, write a detail that appeals to each of the reader's senses.

Sense	Sensory Detail
Sight	
Sound	
Touch	
Smell	
Taste	

3. Why is the witches' use of imagery in Scene i of Act IV of *The Tragedy of Macbeth* important, given the limitations of Elizabethan theater?

4. After visiting the witches in Act IV of *The Tragedy of Macbeth,* why does Macbeth initially change his mind and decide not to have Macduff killed?

5. What recurring image is associated with Lady Macduff and her son in Act IV of *The Tragedy of Macbeth?* Explain.

Unit 2 Resources: Celebrating Humanity
© Pearson Education, Inc. All rights reserved. 157

L3 L4 Open-Book Test, pp. 157–159

Also available for these selections:

EL L3 L4 Selection Test A, pp. 160–162

EL L1 L2 Selection Test B, pp. 163–165

PHLit Online!
www.PHLitOnline.com

Online Resources: All print materials are also available online.

• complete narrated selection text
• a thematically related video with writing prompt
• an interactive graphic organizer
• highlighting feature
• access to all student print resources, adapted to individual student needs
• Spanish and English summaries
• adapted selection translations in Spanish

Get Connected! (thematic video with writing prompt)

Also available:

Background Video
All videos are available in Spanish.

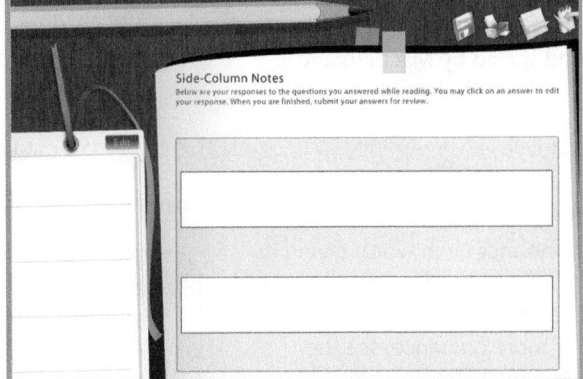

Writer's Journal (with graphics feature)

Also available:

Vocabulary Central (tools and activities for studying vocabulary)

378d

Before You Read   *Macbeth, Act IV*

❶ Literary Analysis

Imagery is the language that writers use to re-create sensory experiences and stir emotions. It is what helps you see, hear, feel, smell, and taste, rather than just read or listen to words. Shakespeare uses imagery to pack sensory experiences and strong emotions into almost every line. Further, he creates these patterns of images that run through the whole play:

- Blood
- Ill-fitting clothes
- Babies and children, sometimes killed by Macbeth and sometimes threatening him

These images reinforce important themes in the play. The last group of images suggests that Macbeth is in some way warring against the future, which babies and children represent. As you read, link patterns of images to the play's central ideas.

Some images are powerful because they are **archetypal**—they relate to ideas and emotions expressed by people in many cultures. In Act IV, for example, **images of banishment from an ideal world**—shrieking, groaning, and bleeding—indicate that Macbeth's Scotland resembles an underworld region where the dead are punished. Look for such archetypal images as you read.

❷ Reading Strategy

Preparing to Read Complex Texts You will better understand and enjoy a literary work if you **analyze its text structures,** or the way it is put together. In *Macbeth,* Shakespeare uses a type of text structure that involves relationships among images and among patterns of images. For example, as indicated above, you will see patterns of images relating to blood and to babies and children.

Use a graphic organizer like the one shown to figure out how a pattern of images reinforces a theme in the play. Then, analyze how the development and relationship of these images adds to the impact and meaning of the play.

❸ Vocabulary

pernicious (pər nish´ əs) *adj.* fatal; deadly (p. 384)

judicious (jōō dish´ əs) *adj.* showing good judgment (p. 385)

sundry (sun´ drē) *adj.* various; miscellaneous (p. 389)

intemperance (in tem´ pər əns) *n.* lack of restraint (p. 390)

avarice (av´ ə ris) *n.* greed (p. 390)

credulous (krej´ ōō ləs) *adj.* tending to believe too readily (p. 391)

Common Core State Standards

Reading Literature
3. Analyze the impact of the author's choices regarding how to develop and relate elements of a story or drama.

Language
1.a. Apply the understanding that usage is a matter of convention, can change over time, and is sometimes contested. (*Literature in Context: Vocabulary Connection, p. 388*)

Image Pattern: Blood

Examples:
• IV, i, 37
•
•
•

↓

Relation to Theme:

---

❶ Literary Analysis

Introduce the skill using the instruction on the student page.

Think Aloud: Model the Skill

Say to students:

As I read this act, I will look for references to blood, ill-fitting clothes, babies/children, or other archetypal images, such as banishment from an ideal world. When I find one of these references, I can pause and consider what the image might mean. Babies and children represent the future. I can ask myself why Shakespeare employs these images. Understanding imagery gives me a deeper connection to this work.

❷ Reading Strategy

1. Introduce the strategy using the instruction on the student page.
2. Give students a copy of **Reading Strategy Graphic Organizer B,** page 61 in *Graphic Organizer Transparencies,* to fill out as they read.

Think Aloud: Model the Skill

Say to students:

After I complete the upper cell of the chart, I am ready to analyze the images. For example, I look at the first reference to blood in Act 4, in Scene 1, line 37: "Cool it with a baboon's blood." I see that this is part of the witches' potion. I think about how this image helps connect the witches to other blood in the play, such as Duncan's blood spilled by Macbeth and Lady Macbeth. I write my associations—"fate" and "murder"—in the lower cell.

❸ Vocabulary

1. Pronounce each word, giving its definition, and have students say it aloud.
2. For more guidance, see the *Classroom Strategies and Teaching Routines* card for introducing vocabulary.

PHLit Online! www.PHLitOnline.com

Teaching From Technology

Preparing to Read
Go to **www.PHLitOnline.com** and display the **Get Connected!** slide show for this selection. Have the class brainstorm for responses to the writing prompt, entering ideas in the interactive journal. Then have students complete their responses individually. You may also have students complete the assignment as homework.

To build background, display the Background video and More About the Author features.

Using the Interactive Student Edition
Go to **www.PHLitOnline.com** and display the **Enriched Online Student Edition.** As the class reads the selection or listens to the narration, record answers to side-column prompts using the graphic organizers accessible on the interactive page. Alternatively, have students use the online edition individually, answering the prompts as they read.

❶ Review and Anticipate Macbeth hires murderers to kill Banquo and Banquo's son, Fleance. The murderers botch the job, killing Banquo but allowing Fleance to escape. Then, at a state banquet, Macbeth is shocked to see the ghost of Banquo sitting in the king's chair. Macbeth decides to visit the witches again, determined to know "the worst." At the end of Act III, we learn that Malcolm is in England preparing to invade Scotland and that Macduff has gone to join him. Act IV will be a turning point in the play. Macbeth seeks help from the witches to secure his power. The forces of good, however, are beginning to gather against him.

❷ ACT IV

Scene i. A witches' haunt.

[*Thunder. Enter the* THREE WITCHES.]

FIRST WITCH. Thrice the brinded[1] cat hath mewed.

SECOND WITCH. Thrice and once the hedge-pig[2] whined.

THIRD WITCH. Harpier[3] cries. 'Tis time, 'tis time.

FIRST WITCH. Round about the caldron go:
5   In the poisoned entrails throw.
   Toad, that under cold stone
   Days and nights has thirty-one
   Swelt'red venom sleeping got,[4]
   Boil thou first i' th' charmèd pot.

10 **ALL.** Double, double, toil and trouble;
   Fire burn and caldron bubble.

❸ **SECOND WITCH.** Fillet of a fenny snake,
   In the caldron boil and bake;
   Eye of newt and toe of frog,
15   Wool of bat and tongue of dog,
   Adder's fork[5] and blindworm's[6] sting,
   Lizard's leg and howlet's[7] wing,
   For a charm of pow'rful trouble,
   Like a hell-broth boil and bubble.

20 **ALL.** Double, double, toil and trouble;
   Fire burn and caldron bubble.

THIRD WITCH. Scale of dragon, tooth of wolf,
   Witch's mummy, maw and gulf[8]
   Of the ravined[9] salt-sea shark,
25   Root of hemlock digged i' th' dark,

❹ ▲ Critical Viewing
What is the significance of a burning caldron—like this one—to the play?
[Connect]

1. **brinded** striped.
2. **hedge-pig** hedgehog.
3. **Harpier** one of the spirits attending the witches.
4. **Swelt'red . . . got** venom sweated out while sleeping.

5. **fork** forked tongue.
6. **blindworm's** small, limbless lizard's.
7. **howlet's** small owl's.
8. **maw and gulf** stomach and gullet.
9. **ravined** ravenous.

❺  **Reading Check**
What are the witches doing as the act begins?

Macbeth, Act IV, Scene i **379**

TEACH

❶ About the Selection
In Act 4, Macbeth's decline is in full swing. He sees apparitions, and Macbeth, grown desperate to secure his throne, interprets the apparitions' words in the most favorable way. Forces begin to gather against Macbeth, and his situation becomes desperate.

❷ Activating Prior Knowledge
Point out that *Macbeth* contains so much blood that it has caused comment. Critic Mark Van Doren claimed, "Never in a play has there been so much of this substance, and never has it been so sickening... We see, feel, and smell it on everything." Have students write a short paragraph about the images of blood they have encountered so far in the play and to speculate about Shakespeare's reasons for making this drama so bloody.

❸ Literary Analysis
Archetypes
1. Tell students that it is often difficult to draw the line between how the culture affected Shakespeare's images and how Shakespeare shaped the culture. This scene, for example, is so familiar that even people who have never read Shakespeare know the chant "double, double, toil and trouble." In this case, Shakespeare has contributed to the culture's image of witches.
2. **Ask** students if they have heard any of this scene before. How many of these images are still associated with witchcraft? **Answer:** Some students will have heard at least part of the speech, and most will be familiar with the cauldron, and magic brew.

❹ Critical Viewing
Possible response: It represents the magic, evil elements of the play, as seen in this passage where the witches prepare their "hell-broth".

❺ Reading Check
Answer: They are making a witches' brew.

379

❻ Humanities

Poster for Macbeth,
by Edmund Dulac

Edmund Dulac (1882–1953) was born in France and settled in England in 1904. He is most widely known as a book illustrator of fairy tales and legends, but he also was a caricaturist and portrait painter. He did a lot of work for the British stage, such as this poster for *Macbeth*. In 1953, he was commissioned to produce a stamp commemorating the coronation of Queen Elizabeth II.

Use these questions for discussion:

1. Why is it ironic that Macbeth should be standing above the witches with his arms crossed?
   Answer: Despite the fact that Macbeth is commanding the three witches, he is actually at their mercy.

2. How does this depiction of the witches compare to the one on page 324?
   Possible responses: Students may say that the picture on page 324 shows three old women who look strange and gnarled, but the picture on this page depicts the witches as more obviously demonic or evil, and even shows one witch as being fairly young.

❼ Critical Viewing

Possible responses: Students may say that the gloomy colors and the ragged appearance of the witches do seem appropriate. They also might say the artist has successfully depicted the witches' brew as a powerful, supernatural force that is capable of bringing forth the apparitions.

380 Celebrating Humanity (1485–1625)

❻

Edmund Dulac

Enrichment: Analyzing Film

Shakespeare, The Entertainer

Remind students that Shakespeare's primary purpose in writing plays was to entertain his audience. Encourage students to think about a scary movie they have seen. Point out that, even though the movie may have depicted something really horrible, it was also entertaining. Point out that this first scene in Act 4 had the same effect on Shakespeare's audiences, many of whom believed in witches and the occult—and that this part of the play still delights audiences today. The witches are evil, and their intent is to deceive Macbeth and pull him into further evil. Tell students to keep in mind the horror-movie aspects of *Macbeth* as they read lines 1–47.

Activity: Compare Films Have pairs of students choose a scene from a scary movie. Suggest that they record information in the **Enrichment: Analyzing Film** worksheet, *Professional Development Guidebook*, page 226. Have them develop an oral presentation comparing the scene from the film with the first scene in *Macbeth's* Act 4.

Liver of blaspheming Jew,
Gall of goat, and slips of yew
Slivered in the moon's eclipse,
Nose of Turk and Tartar's lips,[10]
30 Finger of birth-strangled babe
Ditch-delivered by a drab,
Make the gruel thick and slab:[11]
Add thereto a tiger's chaudron,[12]
For th' ingredience of our caldron.

35 **ALL.** Double, double, toil and trouble;
Fire burn and caldron bubble.

SECOND WITCH. Cool it with a baboon's blood,
Then the charm is firm and good.

[*Enter* HECATE *and the other* THREE WITCHES.]

HECATE. O, well done! I commend your pains;
40 And every one shall share i' th' gains:
And now about the caldron sing,
Like elves and fairies in a ring,
Enchanting all that you put in.

[*Music and a song:* "Black Spirits," *etc. Exit* HECATE *and the
other* THREE WITCHES.]

SECOND WITCH. By the pricking of my thumbs,
45 Something wicked this way comes:
Open, locks,
Whoever knocks!

[*Enter* MACBETH.]

MACBETH. How now, you secret, black, and midnight hags!
What is 't you do?

ALL.   A deed without a name.

50 **MACBETH.** I conjure you, by that which you profess,
Howe'er you come to know it, answer me:
Though you untie the winds and let them fight
Against the churches; though the yesty[13] waves
Confound[14] and swallow navigation up;
55 Though bladed corn be lodged[15] and trees blown down;
Though castles topple on their warders' heads;
Though palaces and pyramids do slope[16]
Their heads to their foundations; though the treasure
Of nature's germens[17] tumble all together,
60 Even till destruction sicken, answer me
To what I ask you.

FIRST WITCH.   Speak.

**10. blaspheming Jew . . .
Tartar's lips** For many in
Shakespeare's audience,
the words *Jew, Turk,* and
Tartar evoked stereotypical
enemies of Christianity.

11. slab sticky.

12. chaudron (shô´ drən)
entrails.

7 ◀ **Critical Viewing**
Has this artist captured the
spirit of the witches as it is
portrayed in IV, i? Explain.
[Evaluate]

8 **Reading Strategy**
Analyzing Text Structures
How does the pattern of
images in Scene i reinforce
the scene's meaning?

13. yesty foamy.

14. Confound destroy.

15. lodged beaten down.

16. slope bend.

17. nature's germens seeds
of all life.

10 **Reading
Check**
What does Macbeth
demand of the witches?

Macbeth, Act IV, Scene i **381**

---

8 **Reading Strategy**
Analyzing Text Structures

1. Tell students that one of the
senses to which this passage
appeals is hearing. Read the
witches' dialogue aloud or play
the Audio CD, so that the music
of the spell weaving can be
heard.

2. **Ask** students the Reading
Strategy question: How does the
pattern of images in Scene 1 reinforce the scene's meaning?
Possible response: The images
are dark and evil, which parallels
the dark and evil deeds to which
Macbeth is surrendering.

3. Point out that, as in Act 3, the
entrance here of Hecate may
have been written and inserted
by someone else.

9 **Literary Analysis**
Imagery

1. In Macbeth's speech, note
the use of the word *conjure.*
It can mean "earnestly ask,"
but Shakespeare likely chose it
because of the strong connection
to magic spells.

2. **Ask** students which images in
lines 50–61 parallel things the
witches have related.
Possible response: The
witches have, particularly in Act
1, described themselves as controlling the winds and sinking
ships ("swallowing navigation").
Mayhem is implied in all they say.
The comments about toppling
castles may refer to the overthrow of governments, of which
Macbeth is a participant.

10 **Reading Check**
Answer: Macbeth demands that the
witches answer whatever he asks.

Differentiated
Instruction for Universal Access

**Strategy for
Less Proficient Readers**
Point out that imagery goes
beyond literature. For example, saying "it's as cold as ice
in here" is imagery—it relates
a sensory experience. Writers
use imagery in a similar way.
Review the list of images in
the play, and encourage students to look for these as they
read.

EL **Support for
English Learners**
Explain that imagery in literature is in some ways similar
to imagery in paintings.
Have students look at the
painting on the facing page
and describe what they see.
Explain that the words they
use to describe a visual image
are, in effect, imagery. They
are translating a visual experience into words.

**Strategy for
Advanced Readers**
Explain that many of
Shakespeare's images are
archetypal, relating to universal ideas and emotions. Have
students record images they
encounter that they feel are
archetypal. Tell them that a
good gauge would be if the
images seem valid today. If
the images survive time, they
are likely archetypal.

PHLit
Online!

This selection is available in
interactive format in the **Enriched
Online Student Edition** at **www.
PHLitOnline.com**, which includes
a thematically related video with
writing prompt and an interactive
graphic organizer.

381

⓫ Literary Analysis

Imagery

⓫ Literary Analysis

Imagery

1. Review with students the patterns of imagery listed on page 378. Tell students that this list does not include all the images in the play, so they can look for others.

2. Explain that an "armed head" would be a head wearing a war helmet. "Armed" refers to armor.

3. **Ask** students the Literary Analysis question: How do the apparitions that Macbeth sees in Scene i, lines 68, 76, and 86 connect with the patterns of imagery in the play? **Possible response:** The first apparition connects with the images of war, which open the play and seem to signal how it will end. The second combines the images of blood—which symbolizes revenge, murder, or guilt—and a child, which represents the future. The third apparition has a child but adds a crown, another recurring image, especially in Macbeth's dreams.

4. **Ask** students if, after reading the third prophecy, they know why the child holds a tree. **Answer:** It probably relates to the prophecy about Birnam Wood.

5. Remind students that an important theme in Macbeth has been things not always being what they seem. In light of this, **ask** students what they predict about the prophecies. **Answer:** At least some of the prophecies are not as positive as Macbeth believes they are.

⓬ Critical Thinking

Analyze

1. Direct students' attention to line 77.

2. Point out that the apparition speaks Macbeth's name three times. Macbeth replies with a comment about three ears. **Ask** students to recall other occurrences of the number three or things occurring in threes. **Possible response:** There are three witches. In Act 1, they hail Macbeth three times. Macbeth heard three prophecies during his first encounter with the witches; during this encounter, he meets three apparitions who will deliver three more prophecies.

382

Literary Analysis
Imagery How do the apparitions that Macbeth sees in Scene i, lines 68, 76, and 86 connect with the patterns of imagery in the play?

18. **farrow** young pigs.
19. **gibbet** (jib´ it) gallows.

20. **office** function.
21. **an Armed Head** symbol of Macduff.

22. **harped** hit upon.

23. **a Bloody Child** symbol of Macduff at birth.

24. **take . . . fate** get a guarantee from fate (by killing Macduff).

25. **a Child . . . hand** symbol of Malcolm.

26. **top of sovereignty** crown.

SECOND WITCH. Demand.

THIRD WITCH. We'll answer.

FIRST WITCH. Say, if th' hadst rather hear it from our mouths, Or from our masters?

MACBETH. Call 'em, let me see 'em.

FIRST WITCH. Pour in sow's blood, that hath eaten
65   Her nine farrow;[18] grease that's sweaten
From the murderer's gibbet[19] throw
Into the flame.

ALL. Come, high or low,
Thyself and office[20] deftly show!

⓫ [*Thunder.* FIRST APPARITION: *an Armed Head.*[21]]

MACBETH. Tell me, thou unknown power—

FIRST WITCH. He knows thy thought:
70   Hear his speech, but say thou nought.

FIRST APPARITION. Macbeth! Macbeth! Macbeth! Beware Macduff! Beware the Thane of Fife. Dismiss me: enough.

[*He descends.*]

MACBETH. Whate'er thou art, for thy good caution thanks: Thou hast harped[22] my fear aright. But one word more—

75 **FIRST WITCH.** He will not be commanded. Here's another, More potent than the first.

⓫ [*Thunder.* SECOND APPARITION: *a Bloody Child.*[23]]

⓬   **SECOND APPARITION.** Macbeth! Macbeth! Macbeth!

MACBETH. Had I three ears, I'd hear thee.

SECOND APPARITION. Be bloody, bold, and resolute! Laugh to scorn
80   The pow'r of man, for none of woman born
Shall harm Macbeth. [*Descends.*]

MACBETH. Then live, Macduff: what need I fear of thee?
But yet I'll make assurance double sure,
And take a bond of fate.[24] Thou shalt not live;
85   That I may tell pale-hearted fear it lies,
And sleep in spite of thunder.

⓫ [*Thunder.* THIRD APPARITION: *a Child Crowned, with a tree in his hand.*[25]]

  What is this,
That rises like the issue of a king,
And wears upon his baby-brow the round
And top of sovereignty?[26]

ALL. Listen, but speak not to 't.

382 Celebrating Humanity (1485–1625)

Enrichment: Investigating Religion and Myth

The Weird Sisters

Scholars have long debated whether Macbeth's tragedy results from the inexorable pressures of fate or from his own free choice of evil. This debate tends to focus on the role of the witches. Shakespearean scholar George Lyman Kittredge argued that these weird sisters were not just run-of-the-mill crones, but arbiters of human destiny who shaped men's lives. Irving Ribner, among other scholars, argued against this position. He felt that Shakespeare was writing from a Christian perspective. While Christians acknowledge the reality of evil, they believe that God gave humans the power to choose evil or good. Macbeth chooses his own course.

Activity: Debate Divide the class in half. Assign one group to argue for Kittredge's thesis and the other to argue for Ribner's. Ask the teams to consider the images and ideas in *Macbeth* and take notes on the **Enrichment: Investigating Religion and Myth** worksheet, *Professional Development Guidebook*, page 240. Then conduct a debate.

90 **THIRD APPARITION.** Be lion-mettled, proud, and take no care
Who chafes, who frets, or where conspirers are:
Macbeth shall never vanquished be until
Great Birnam Wood to high Dunsinane Hill
Shall come against him.   [*Descends.*]

MACBETH.   That will never be.
95 Who can impress²⁷ the forest, bid the tree
Unfix his earth-bound root? Sweet bodements,²⁸ good!
Rebellious dead, rise never, till the Wood
Of Birnam rise, and our high-placed Macbeth
Shall live the lease of nature,²⁹ pay his breath
100 To time and mortal custom.³⁰ Yet my heart
Throbs to know one thing. Tell me, if your art
Can tell so much: shall Banquo's issue ever
Reign in this kingdom?

ALL.   Seek to know no more.

MACBETH. I will be satisfied. Deny me this,
105 And an eternal curse fall on you! Let me know.
Why sinks that caldron? And what noise is this?

[*Hautboys.*]

FIRST WITCH. Show!

SECOND WITCH. Show!

THIRD WITCH. Show!

110 **ALL.** Show his eyes, and grieve his heart;
Come like shadows, so depart!

[*A show of eight* KINGS *and* BANQUO, *last* KING *with a glass*³¹ *in his hand.*]

MACBETH. Thou art too like the spirit of Banquo. Down!
Thy crown does sear mine eyelids. And thy hair,
Thou other gold-bound brow, is like the first.
115 A third is like the former. Filthy hags!
Why do you show me this? A fourth! Start, eyes!
What, will the line stretch out to th' crack of doom?
Another yet! A seventh! I'll see no more.
And yet the eighth appears, who bears a glass
120 Which shows me many more: and some I see
That twofold balls and treble scepters³² carry:
Horrible sight! Now I see 'tis true;
For the blood-boltered³³ Banquo smiles upon me,
And points at them for his.³⁴ What, is this so?

125 **FIRST WITCH.** Ay, sir, all this is so. But why
Stands Macbeth thus amazedly?
Come, sisters, cheer we up his sprites,
And show the best of our delights:

27. **impress** force into service.

28. **bodements** prophecies.

29. **lease of nature** natural lifespan.

30. **mortal custom** natural death.

31. **glass** mirror.

Literary Analysis
Imagery What does Macbeth learn from the images of the eight kings?

32. **twofold . . . scepters** coronation emblems and insignia of the kingdoms of England, Scotland, and Ireland, united in 1603 when James VI of Scotland became James I of England.

33. **blood-boltered** with his hair matted with blood.

34. **his** his descendants.

Reading Check

What do the three apparitions tell Macbeth, and what further vision does he see?

Macbeth, Act IV, Scene i **383**

383

Critical Thinking

16 **Critical Thinking**

Compare and Contrast

1. Have students read lines 144–156.

2. Tell students to think about what Macbeth felt before he murdered Duncan.

3. Then **ask** students to compare Macbeth's attitude toward murdering Macduff and his family with his attitude toward murdering Duncan.
   Possible response: Students should point out that Macbeth has lost all semblance of humanity and is planning the execution of an entire family in cold blood. When he was planning to kill Duncan, he was filled with doubt and guilt.

4. **Ask** students how Macbeth has interpreted the prophecies made by the apparitions, and then have them consider how his interpretation makes the murders he is now planning seem even worse than the others.
   Answer: Macbeth has interpreted the prophecies as meaning he cannot be touched. Therefore, the murders he is currently planning seem much worse because they are completely unnecessary. He gains nothing from them, and they are against people who are not a threat to him.

---

35. antic round grotesque circular dance.

Vocabulary
pernicious (pər nish′ əs) *adj.* fatal; deadly

36. anticipat'st foretold.

37. The flighty . . . it The fleeting plan is never fulfilled unless it is carried out at once.

38. firstlings . . . heart first thoughts, impulses.

39. trace succeed.

I'll charm the air to give a sound,
130 While you perform your antic round,[35]
That this great king may kindly say
Our duties did his welcome pay.

[*Music.* THE WITCHES *dance, and vanish.*]

MACBETH. Where are they? Gone? Let this pernicious hour
Stand aye accursèd in the calendar!
Come in, without there!

[*Enter* LENNOX.]

135 LENNOX.   What's your Grace's will?

MACBETH. Saw you the weird sisters?

LENNOX.   No, my lord.

MACBETH. Came they not by you?

LENNOX.   No indeed, my lord.

MACBETH. Infected be the air whereon they ride,
And damned all those that trust them! I did hear
140 The galloping of horse. Who was 't came by?

LENNOX. 'Tis two or three, my lord, that bring you word
Macduff is fled to England.

MACBETH.   Fled to England?

LENNOX. Ay, my good lord.

MACBETH. [*Aside*] Time, thou anticipat'st[36] my dread exploits.
145 The flighty purpose never is o'ertook
Unless the deed go with it.[37] From this moment
The very firstlings of my heart[38] shall be
The firstlings of my hand. And even now,
To crown my thoughts with acts be it thought and done:
150 The castle of Macduff I will surprise;
Seize upon Fife; give to th' edge o' th' sword
His wife, his babes, and all unfortunate souls
That trace[39] him in his line. No boasting like a fool;
This deed I'll do before this purpose cool:
155 But no more sights!—Where are these gentlemen?
Come, bring me where they are.

[*Exit.*]

Scene ii. Macduff's castle.

[*Enter* MACDUFF'S WIFE, *her* SON, *and* ROSS.]

LADY MACBETH. What had he done, to make him fly the land?

ROSS. You must have patience, madam.

LADY MACDUFF. What had he done, to make him fly the land?

384 Celebrating Humanity (1485–1625)

Enrichment: Building Context

Castles

When Macbeth lived, Scotland and England had long been made up of clans, tribes, and ethnic groups who were frequently at war, either with outside invaders or with each other. Hence, the head of any group usually lived in a castle. Castles were designed for defense. They were built in places that gave them a clear view of approaching enemies or that protected them from that approach, such as on cliffs or islands. They would have heavy doors, thick walls, and numerous places from which weapons could be used. While only the ruler had a castle, all were designed so that everyone from the surrounding villages and farms could be safe inside during times of attack.

Activity: Create a Castle Have students research medieval castles and record their findings on the **Enrichment: Analyzing Historical Patterns** worksheet, *Professional Development Guidebook*, page 231. Then ask them to create a medieval castle in a drawing or sculpture.

LADY MACDUFF. He had none:
His flight was madness. When our actions do not,
Our fears do make us traitors.

ROSS. You know not
5 Whether it was his wisdom or his fear.

LADY MACDUFF. Wisdom! To leave his wife, to leave his babes,
His mansion and his titles,[1] in a place
From whence himself does fly? He loves us not;
He wants the natural touch:[2] for the poor wren,
10 The most diminutive of birds, will fight,
Her young ones in her nest, against the owl.
All is the fear and nothing is the love;
As little is the wisdom, where the flight
So runs against all reason.

ROSS. My dearest coz,[3]
15 I pray you, school[4] yourself. But, for your husband,
He is noble, wise, *judicious*, and best knows
The fits o' th' seasons,[5] I dare not speak much further:
But cruel are the times, when we are traitors
And do not know ourselves;[6] when we hold rumor
20 From what we fear,[7] yet know not what we fear,
But float upon a wild and violent sea
Each way and move. I take my leave of you.
Shall not be long but I'll be here again.
Things at the worst will cease, or else climb upward
25 To what they were before. My pretty cousin,
Blessing upon you!

LADY MACDUFF. Fathered he is, and yet he's fatherless.

ROSS. I am so much a fool, should I stay longer,
It would be my disgrace and your discomfort.[8]
I take my leave at once. [*Exit* ROSS.]

30 **LADY MACDUFF.** Sirrah, your father's dead;
And what will you do now? How will you live?

SON. As birds do, mother.

LADY MACDUFF. What, with worms and flies?

SON. With what I get, I mean; and so do they.

LADY MACDUFF. Poor bird! thou'dst never fear the net nor lime,[9]
35 The pitfall nor the gin.[10]

SON. Why should I, mother? Poor birds they are not set for.
My father is not dead, for all your saying.

LADY MACDUFF. Yes, he is dead: how wilt thou do for a father?

SON. Nay, how will you do for a husband?

Literary Analysis

Imagery What image is suggested by Lady Macduff's use of the words "fly" and "flight" in lines 8 and 13?

1. **titles** possessions.

2. **wants . . . touch** lacks natural affection.

3. **coz** cousin.

4. **school** control.

Vocabulary

judicious (jo͞o dish′ əs) *adj.* showing good judgment

5. **fits o' th' season** disorders of the time.

6. **when . . . ourselves** when we are treated as traitors but do not know of any treason.

7. **when . . . fear** believe rumors based on our fears.

8. **It . . . discomfort:** I would disgrace myself and embarrass you by weeping.

Literary Analysis

Imagery What does the imagery in Scene ii, lines 34–35 suggest about what might happen?

9. **lime** birdlime, a sticky substance smeared on branches to catch birds.

10. **gin** trap.

  Reading Check

Where has Macduff gone, and how will Macbeth revenge himself against Macduff?

Macbeth, Act IV, Scene ii **385**

---

⑰ Literary Analysis

Imagery

1. Tell students to look out for repeated words, ideas, and images throughout this scene. For example, the words *traitor* and *fears* appear frequently, as do *fly* and *flight.*

2. **Ask** the first Literary Analysis question: What image is suggested by Lady Macduff's use of the words *fly* and *flight* in lines 8 and 13?
   Answer: The words *fly* and *flight* suggest images of birds and support the extended metaphor of the Macduffs as birds, used by both Lady Macduff and her son.

3. Further discuss the bird imagery used by Lady Macduff in lines 6–14.
   Ask students how the imagery shows both her nobility and her helplessness.
   Answer: She compares herself to the wren, which she identifies as the smallest of birds. This smallness makes her seem vulnerable. However, she also points out that her love would cause her to fight the owl, a bird of prey, to protect her children.

4. Point out the wordplay in lines 13 and 14: *flight runs.* Remind students to keep an eye out for the ways in which Shakespeare plays with language.

5. You may also want to point out to students that, in the speech that follows, Ross reiterates the idea of fear of traitors. He also, in contrast to Macbeth, shows that he does not have any idea what the future holds.

⑱ Literary Analysis

Imagery

1. Read aloud lines 34–35.

2. Then, have students use the text aids to define *lime* and *gin.*

3. **Ask** the second Literary Analysis question: What does the imagery in Scene II, lines 34–35, suggest about what might happen?
   Answer: These images suggest that Lady Macduff and her son will be trapped by the murderers.

⑲ Reading Check

Answer: Macduff has fled to England, and Macbeth will revenge himself against Macduff by killing his wife and children.

385

Critical Thinking

20 **Critical Thinking**

Analyze

1. Have students read lines 54–55.

2. Explain to students that unlikely characters are often clever in Shakespeare's plays.

3. Then **ask** students why it is significant that Macduff's son makes this observation about liars and swearers, when just eight lines earlier he has to ask what a traitor is.
Possible response: Shakespeare seems to be juxtaposing childlike innocence with a more mature, unadulterated truth. Shakespeare may be implying that children are wiser than the adults around them.

21 **Reading Strategy**

Analyze Text Structures

1. **Ask** students how they think the messenger appears, and what the delivery of his lines would be like.
Possible response: He would probably have been in a hurry, and his lines would probably be delivered in a rushed, somewhat breathless manner.

▶ **Monitor Progress: Ask** students this question: **What do the content of the messenger's speech and the context suggest about his dress, appearance, and manner?**
Answer: He is probably in a hurry, so he may be abrupt. The fact that he observes that he has frightened Lady Macduff (line 68) confirms that he has probably rushed in and just blurted out his warning. He may also be a little disheveled. He says he is "homely;" hence, he is probably dressed in the clothing of a worker or farmer.

▶ **Reteach: Remind students that imagery can appeal to any of the five senses.** Point out, too, that because this is a play and is intended to be visual, there are also often hints about what the people look like or how they behave.

2. You may wish to point out that because the messenger speaks in blank verse, we know that, even if he is simple, he is not a servant or someone who can be ignored.

386

---

11. **sell** betray.

12. **for thee** for a child.

13. **swears and lies** takes an oath and breaks it.

14. **enow** enough.

15. **in . . . perfect** I am fully informed of your honorable rank.

16. **doubt** fear.

17. **homely** simple.

18. **fell** fierce.

---

40   LADY MACDUFF. Why, I can buy me twenty at any market.

SON. Then you'll buy 'em to sell[11] again.

LADY MACDUFF. Thou speak'st with all thy wit, and yet i' faith, With wit enough for thee.[12]

SON. Was my father a traitor, mother?

45   LADY MACDUFF. Ay, that he was.

SON. What is a traitor?

LADY MACDUFF. Why, one that swears and lies.[13]

SON. And be all traitors that do so?

LADY MACDUFF. Every one that does so is a traitor, and must be hanged.

50   SON. And must they all be hanged that swear and lie?

LADY MACDUFF. Every one.

SON. Who must hang them?

LADY MACDUFF. Why, the honest men.

 55   SON. Then the liars and swearers are fools; for there are liars and swearers enow[14] to beat the honest men and hang up them.

LADY MACDUFF. Now, God help thee, poor monkey! But how wilt thou do for a father?

60   SON. If he were dead, you'd weep for him. If you would not, it were a good sign that I should quickly have a new father.

LADY MACDUFF. Poor prattler, how thou talk'st!

[*Enter a* MESSENGER *.*]

MESSENGER. Bless you, fair dame! I am not to you known, Though in your state of honor I am perfect.[15]
65   I doubt[16] some danger does approach you nearly: If you will take a homely[17] man's advice, Be not found here; hence, with your little ones. To fright you thus, methinks I am too savage; To do worse to you were fell[18] cruelty,
70   Which is too nigh your person. Heaven preserve you! I dare abide no longer.   [*Exit* MESSENGER.]

LADY MACDUFF.   Whither should I fly? I have done no harm. But I remember now I am in this earthly world, where to do harm Is often laudable, to do good sometime
75   Accounted dangerous folly. Why then, alas, Do I put up that womanly defense, To say I have done no harm?—What are these faces?

386 Celebrating Humanity (1485–1625)

Enrichment: Analyzing Culture

The Rules of Hospitality

When Macbeth murdered Duncan, he broke two tenets of his society: He killed his king, and he killed a guest under his roof. According to the rules of hospitality in most cultures, guests are to be treated with a deliberate respect and kindness.

In ancient Greek culture, Zeus was the god of hospitality. People treated all guests well, lest they discover that the poor traveler they had treated badly was Zeus in disguise, testing them. Hospitality was also an important part of Middle Eastern culture, and is reflected in ancient Jewish and Christian literature. Even today, in many areas of Latin America, Africa, and Asia, any traveler can expect to receive a warm welcome.

Activity: Interview Have students interview one or more person about their culture's view of hospitality. They can record the information in the **Enrichment: Investigating Culture** worksheet, *Professional Development Guidebook,* page 223. Have students share what they learn.

[*Enter* MURDERERS.]

MURDERER. Where is your husband?

LADY MACDUFF. I hope, in no place so unsanctified
  Where such as thou mayst find him.

80 **MURDERER.**   He's a traitor.

SON. Thou li'st, thou shag-eared[19] villain!

MURDERER.   What, you egg!

       [*Stabbing him.*]

   Young fry[20] of treachery!

SON.   He has killed me, mother:
  Run away, I pray you! [*Dies.*]

       [*Exit* LADY MACDUFF *crying "Murder!" followed by* MURDERERS.]

19. shag-eared hairy-eared.

20. fry offspring

㉒ ☑ Reading Check
Whom do Macbeth's men kill?

㉔ ▼ Critical Viewing
This engraving shows the murderers menacing Macduff's family. In what way does the artist capture the defiance reflected in Act IV, Scene ii, line 81? **[Interpret]**

㉓

Macbeth, Act IV, Scene ii **387**

㉒ Reading Check
Answer: Macbeth's men kill Macduff's son and, though not on stage, Macduff's wife and other children.

㉓ Humanities
Wood Engraving After Sir John Gilbert
This wood engraving was made from a drawing by Sir John Gilbert. He created this drawing of Lady Macduff and the murderers for Mackey's *Shakespeare,* an illustrated book in a series that won Gilbert great acclaim as an illustrator. The ease with which the figures are drawn highlights the superior sketching ability that Gilbert achieved through continual practice. This drawing is balanced in terms of motion and the placement of the characters, yet it contains a deadly tension.

Use these questions for discussion:

1. Judging from this engraving, how did Sir John Gilbert envision the murderers in Act 4, scene 2, of *Macbeth?*
   Answer: Gilbert imagined the murderers as large, brutish men against whom Macduff's family would not have a chance.

2. Does Lady Macduff's protective action seem appropriate given her earlier description of herself as a "wren"?
   Answer: Lady Macduff's protective stance and fierce expression are appropriate. When she described the wren, she described it as small, but willing to fight an attacking predator to protect her children.

㉔ Critical Viewing
Interpret
Answer: As the murderers approach, Lady Macduff's son appears defiant and protective. It matches well with his defiant words, calling the murderers liars and villains.

Imagery

1. **Ask** students the Literary Analysis question: How do the images in Scene III, lines 1–4, help establish a contrast between Malcolm and Macduff?
   Answer: Malcolm is showing a sentimental, emotional side; Macduff is displaying no weakness and remains warrior-like.

2. **Ask** students to what they might attribute the differences between the two men.
   Possible response: Malcolm is young and has just seen his father murdered and his kingdom lost, so he is in an emotional state. Macduff is an experienced soldier.

㉖ **Critical Thinking**

Analyze

1. **Ask** students how Malcolm's comment in line 14 is ironic.
   Answer: Malcolm states Macduff has not yet suffered personal loss at the hands of Macbeth. Neither of them knows that Macduff's entire family has just been murdered at Macbeth's order.

2. Though he is young, Malcolm is not a fool. **Ask** students what Malcolm is saying in lines 15–24.
   Answer: Malcolm is saying that Macduff would have much to gain by turning him over to Macbeth. Even if Macduff is virtuous, he might do it because it was commanded by the king. Also, even angels have fallen.

㉗ **Literature in Context**

Shifting Meanings

1. Direct students' attention to the Literature in Context box.

2. Remind students that language changes over time; however, old and new definitions are usually related. For example, both definitions of *mortal* include the idea of death—and anyone who knows the phrase "mortal combat" would understand Shakespeare's use of *mortal* to mean "deadly."

   Connect to the Literature

   Ask the Connect to the Literature question: What possible meanings might the word recoil have in line 19?

   Answer: The usual meaning of recoil is "to shrink back"; in line 19, it means "to give way."

Literary Analysis
Imagery How do the images in Scene iii, lines 1–4 help establish a contrast between Malcolm and Macduff?

㉕

1. **Bestride . . . birthdom** Protectively stand over our native land.

2. **Like . . . dolor** similar cry of anguish.

3. **deserve . . . me** earn by betraying me to Macbeth.

4. **wisdom** It is wise.

㉖

Scene iii. England. Before the King's palace.

[*Enter* MALCOLM *and* MACDUFF.]

    MALCOLM. Let us seek out some desolate shade, and there
        Weep our sad bosoms empty.

    MACDUFF.   Let us rather
        Hold fast the mortal♦ sword, and like good men
        Bestride our down-fall'n birthdom.[1] Each new morn
5   New widows howl, new orphans cry, new sorrows
        Strike heaven on the face, that it resounds
        As if it felt with Scotland and yelled out
        Like syllable of dolor.[2]

    MALCOLM.   What I believe, I'll wail;
        What know, believe; and what I can redress,
10   As I shall find the time to friend,♦ I will.
        What you have spoke, it may be so perchance.
        This tyrant, whose sole♦ name blisters our tongues,
        Was once thought honest:♦ you have loved him well;
        He hath not touched you yet. I am young; but something
15   You may deserve of him through me;[3] and wisdom[4]
        To offer up a weak, poor, innocent lamb
        T' appease an angry god.

    MACDUFF. I am not treacherous.

㉗ **LITERATURE IN CONTEXT**

Vocabulary Connection

♦ Shifting Meanings
Because language is always changing, some words used by Shakespeare have shifted in meaning.

Mortal (IV, iii, 3) means "deadly," which is somewhat unlike its current meaning, "subject to death or decay."

Friend (IV, iii, 10), which today is a noun, is used as a verb meaning "to be friendly."

Sole (IV, iii, 12), which now means "single" or "one and only," is used as an intensifier meaning "very."

Honest (IV, iii, 13) has the broad sense of "good."

As you read, be alert to shifts in meaning like these, and use the context of a word or phrase as well as the side notes to help you determine Shakespeare's meaning.

Connect to the Literature

What possible meanings might the word *recoil* have in line 19?

Think Aloud

Vocabulary: Relating Modern Meanings with Medieval Meanings
Ask students to read both the modern and the medieval meanings of the words in the Literature in Context box. Then have them discuss with a partner how the modern meanings relate to the medieval meanings. Use the following "think aloud" to model the skill of comparing medieval and modern meaning. Say to students:

When I read the medieval meaning of *friend* I think of the meaning of the modern word *befriend*. I see that *friend,* the medieval verb, and the modern noun *friend* are connected because they have the same meaning, but they are different parts of speech. I can apply this same process to the other words listed. I can understand that meanings of words shift over time.

MALCOLM. But Macbeth is.

A good and virtuous nature may recoil
20 In an imperial charge. But I shall crave your pardon;
That which you are, my thoughts cannot transpose:
Angels are bright still, though the brightest[5] fell!
Though all things foul would wear[6] the brows of grace,
Yet grace must still look so.[7]

MACDUFF. I have lost my hopes.

25 **MALCOLM.** Perchance even there where I did find my doubts.
Why in that rawness[8] left you wife and child,
Those precious motives, those strong knots of love,
Without leave-taking? I pray you,
Let not my jealousies be your dishonors.
30 But mine own safeties.[9] You may be rightly just
Whatever I shall think.

MACDUFF. Bleed, bleed, poor country:

Great tyranny, lay thou thy basis sure,
For goodness dare not check thee: wear thou thy wrongs:
The title is affeered.[10] Fare thee well, lord:
35 I would not be the villain that thou think'st
For the whole space that's in the tyrant's grasp
And the rich East to boot.

MALCOLM. Be not offended:

I speak not as in absolute fear of you.
I think our country sinks beneath the yoke;
40 It weeps, it bleeds, and each new day a gash
Is added to her wounds. I think withal
There would be hands uplifted in my right;[11]
And here from gracious England[12] have I offer
Of goodly thousands: but, for all this,
45 When I shall tread upon the tyrant's head,
Or wear it on my sword, yet my poor country
Shall have more vices than it had before,
More suffer, and more sundry ways than ever,
By him that shall succeed.

MACDUFF. What should he be?

50 **MALCOLM.** It is myself I mean, in whom I know
All the particulars of vice so grafted[13]
That, when they shall be opened,[14] black Macbeth
Will seem as pure as snow, and the poor state
Esteem him as a lamb, being compared
With my confineless harms.[15]

55 **MACDUFF.** Not in the legions
Of horrid hell can come a devil more damned
In evils to top Macbeth.

5. **the brightest** Lucifer.

6. **would wear** desire to wear.

7. **so** like itself.

8. **rawness** unprotected state or condition.

9. **safeties** protections.

10. **affeered** legally confirmed.

Literary Analysis

Imagery Why are the images Malcolm uses to describe Scotland in lines 39–41 more effective than a simple statement that the country is in trouble and getting worse?

11. **in my right** on behalf of my claim.

12. **England** king of England.

Vocabulary

sundry (sun' drē) *adj.*
various; miscellaneous

13. **grafted** implanted.

14. **opened** in bloom.

15. **confineless harms** unbounded evils.

Reading Check

How does Malcolm describe himself to Macduff?

Macbeth, Act IV, Scene iii **389**

30 Critical Thinking

Analyze

1. Point out that, as the dialogue between Malcolm and Macduff progresses, Malcolm stops talking about his worries and his safety and begins talking about how awful he is.

2. **Ask** students if the things Malcolm is saying about himself sound believable.
   Possible response: Students may respond that they do not sound reasonable. First, if he were that bad, he wouldn't tell anyone; he would be secretive, like Macbeth. Second, it is unlikely that he could be that bad and not have anyone notice before now.

3. **Ask** students if they can imagine a reason Malcolm would talk this way about himself.
   Possible responses: Perhaps he is still worried about Macduff and is trying to drive him away. Perhaps he is testing Macduff.

4. Have students consider Macduff's response in lines 84–90. How does he feel about Malcolm's claim of avarice? How does he reply to Malcolm's confession?
   Answer: Macduff considers avarice to be worse than the previously confessed lust. However, Macduff says that Scotland can afford to satisfy Malcolm's greed.

31 Reading Strategy

Analyze Text Structures

1. Discuss with students what Malcolm is saying he will do in line 98.
   Answer: He says that he will destroy the harmony (concord) of life in Scotland.

2. **Ask** students the Reading Strategy question on page 391: How does the image in Act 4, Scene 3, line 98 echo those in Act 1, Scene 5, lines 17 and 47–48?
   Answer: In all three passages, milk represents something good—kindness, concord—and it is shown as the thing that stands between good acts and evil. Hence, Lady Macbeth says Macbeth has too much "milk of human kindness" to kill; she asks to have her milk exchanged for the bitterness of gall. Malcolm threatens to pour this same milk into hell, implying that nothing will then stop him from evil.

390

---

16. **Luxurious** lecherous.
17. **Sudden** violent.

18. **continent impediments** restraints.

Vocabulary
intemperance (in tem´ pər əns) *n.* lack of restraint

19. **nature** man's nature.
20. **Convey** secretly manage.

21. **affection** character.
Vocabulary
avarice (av´ ə ris) *n.* greed
22. **stanchless** never-ending.

23. **summer-seeming** summerlike.
24. **of** that killed.
25. **foisons** (foi´ zənz) plenty.
26. **mere own** own property.
27. **portable** bearable.

28. **division . . . crime** variations of each kind of crime.

29. **confound** destroy.

MALCOLM.   I grant him bloody,
Luxurious,[16] avaricious, false, deceitful,
Sudden,[17] malicious, smacking of every sin
     That has a name: but there's no bottom, none,   60
In my voluptuousness: your wives, your daughters,
Your matrons and your maids, could not fill up
The cistern of my lust, and my desire
All continent impediments[18] would o'erbear,
     That did oppose my will. Better Macbeth   65
Than such an one to reign.

MACDUFF.   Boundless *intemperance*
In nature[19] is a tyranny; it hath been
Th' untimely emptying of the happy throne,
And fall of many kings. But fear not yet
     To take upon you what is yours: you may   70
Convey[20] your pleasures in a spacious plenty,
And yet seem cold, the time you may so hoodwink.
We have willing dames enough. There cannot be
That vulture in you, to devour so many
     As will to greatness dedicate themselves,   75
Finding it so inclined.

MALCOLM.   With this there grows
In my most ill-composed affection[21] such
A stanchless[22] *avarice* that, were I King,
I should cut off the nobles for their lands,
     Desire his jewels and this other's house: 80
And my more-having would be as a sauce
To make me hunger more, that I should forge
Quarrels unjust against the good and loyal,
Destroying them for wealth.

30

MACDUFF.   This avarice
     Sticks deeper, grows with more pernicious root   85
Than summer-seeming[23] lust, and it hath been
The sword of[24] our slain kings. Yet do not fear.
Scotland hath foisons[25] to fill up your will
Of your mere own.[26] All these are portable,[27]
     With other graces weighed.   90

MALCOLM. But I have none: the king-becoming graces,
As justice, verity, temp'rance, stableness,
Bounty, perseverance, mercy, lowliness,
Devotion, patience, courage, fortitude,
     I have no relish of them, but abound   95
In the division of each several crime,[28]
Acting it many ways. Nay, had I pow'r, I should
Pour the sweet milk of concord into hell,

31

Uproar the universal peace, confound[29]

Enrichment: Analyzing Themes and Symbols

The Number Three

The number three appears often in *Macbeth*. Three is significant in an astonishing range of connections.

Celtic art and literature (the Scots were largely Celts) were preoccupied with the number three. One often sees objects repeated three times or with three faces.

The Greeks also used the number three in many ways. There were three fates, three graces, and three furies.

In the Bible, three is important, from the Holy Trinity to the three denials of Peter. Three is often a symbol of things being completed, either in judgment or in redemption.

Activity: Finding the Three Ask students to choose a culture and find the number three symbolized in its religion or myths. They can record their findings on the **Enrichment: Analyzing Themes and Symbols** worksheet, *Professional Development Guidebook,* page 243. Have a class in which you share all the references to the number three that students found.

All unity on earth.

100 **MACDUFF.**   O Scotland, Scotland!

MALCOLM. If such a one be fit to govern, speak:
I am as I have spoken.

MACDUFF.   Fit to govern!
No, not to live. O nation miserable!
With an untitled[30] tyrant bloody-sceptered,
105 When shalt thou see thy wholesome days again,
Since that the truest issue of thy throne[31]
By his own interdiction[32] stands accursed,
And does blaspheme his breed?[33] Thy royal father
Was a most sainted king: the queen that bore thee,
110 Oft'ner upon her knees than on her feet,
Died[34] every day she lived. Fare thee well!
These evils thou repeat'st upon thyself
Hath banished me from Scotland. O my breast,
Thy hope ends here!

MALCOLM.   Macduff, this noble passion,
115 Child of integrity, hath from my soul
Wiped the black scruples, reconciled my thoughts
To thy good truth and honor. Devilish Macbeth
By many of these trains[35] hath sought to win me
Into his power; and modest wisdom[36] plucks me
120 From over-credulous haste: but God above
Deal between thee and me! For even now
I put myself to thy direction, and
Unspeak mine own detraction,[37] here abjure
The taints and blames I laid upon myself,
125 For[38] strangers to my nature. I am yet
Unknown to woman, never was forsworn,
Scarcely have coveted what was mine own,
At no time broke my faith, would not betray
The devil to his fellow, and delight
130 No less in truth than life. My first false speaking
Was this upon myself. What I am truly,
Is thine and my poor country's to command:
Whither indeed, before thy here-approach,
Old Siward, with ten thousand warlike men,
135 Already at a point,[39] was setting forth.
Now we'll together, and the chance of goodness
Be like our warranted quarrel![40] Why are you silent?

MACDUFF. Such welcome and unwelcome things at once
'Tis hard to reconcile.

[*Enter a* DOCTOR.]

140 **MALCOLM.** Well, more anon. Comes the King forth, I pray you?

31 Reading Strategy
Analyzing Text Structures
How does the image in Act IV, Scene iii, line 98 echo those in Act I, Scene v, line 17 and Act I, Scene v, lines 47–48?

30. **untitled** having no right to the throne.

31. **truest . . . throne** child of the true king.

32. **interdiction** exclusion.

33. **blaspheme his breed** slander his ancestry.

34. **Died** prepared for heaven.

35. **trains** enticements.

36. **modest wisdom** prudence.

Vocabulary
credulous (krej´ o͞o ləs) *adj.* tending to believe too readily

37. **detraction** slander.

38. **For** as.

39. **at a point** prepared.

40. **the chance . . . quarrel** May our chance of success equal the justice of our cause.

33 Reading Check
What response by Macduff convinces Malcolm that Macduff is being honest?

Macbeth, Act IV, Scene iii **391**

Literary Analysis
Imagery

1. **Ask** students to notice how many of the recurring themes or ideas of this play are found in lines 102–117.
   Answer: Possibilities include tyrant, blood, child, black, and devilish.

2. Point out that this exchange marks a departure from what has come before. For the first time, a man is exactly what he appears to be. Both Malcolm and Macduff are honest men, who speak without hiding secrets.

3. **Ask** students how Duncan and Macbeth are contrasted in these lines.
   Answer: Duncan was sainted and Macbeth is devilish—so they are total opposites.

4. Point out that, though she isn't mentioned, there is an implied contrast with Lady Macbeth. The saintliness and tender care of Duncan's queen contrast with Lady Macbeth's evil, particularly her comment about her willingness to dash her child's brains out.

5. **Ask** students if Macduff's comment in line 138 reminds them of anything they read earlier in the play.
   Possible response: The line is similar to several lines in which things were opposites, such as Macbeth's comment in Act 1, Scene 3, "So foul and fair a day I have not seen."

33 Reading Check
Answer: Macduff laments that Malcolm is not fit to govern or to live, that he cannot compare to his father Duncan, and he banishes himself from Scotland because he despairs of its ever righting itself with Malcolm in power. This response convinces Malcolm that Macduff is being honest.

Differentiated
Instruction for Universal Access

EL Pronunciation for English Learners

Hard c / Soft c / ch
Explain to students that the letter *c* is pronounced differently depending on the letter that follows it. Say: *When* c *comes before* i *or* e, *it is soft and sounds like an* s, *as in the word* cereal. *When* c *comes before an* h, *it makes the blend* ch *as in the word* church. *When it comes before any other letter, it is hard and sounds like* k *as in the word* car.

On the board, list the words from page 391 that include the letter *c*. Write them in random order. (*Scotland, sceptered, interdiction, since, accursed, Macduff, reconciled, credulous, direction, detraction, scarcely, coveted, child, once, country's command, such, chance, welcome, comes*). Then say each word slowly, clearly, and without distortion. Have students repeat.

Finally, ask pairs of students to organize the words into columns according to their sound: hard *c* (car), soft *c* (cereal), *ch* (church). Pronounce each sound and write them in columns on the board to model for students.

Analyze Text Structures

1. **Ask** students the Reading Strategy question: Connect the images in lines 164–173 with similar images revealing Scotland as a hellish place.

   Possible responses: Students may offer that this description gives an impression of a country in chaos, where death and sorrow are so common no one even comments. The country is so helpless and sad that it is in danger of becoming numb to its own suffering. In the text, sighs, groans, shrieks, the dead man's knell, violent sorrow, graves, and the words *expire, sicken,* and *dying* all contribute to the overall image of Scotland as a hellish place.

2. Explain to students that the "dead man's knell" mentioned in line 170 refers to the old tradition of ringing the church bell when someone in a town died. (Explain that both *knell* and *toll* are other ways of saying *ring*, though both imply the deeper sound of a large bell.) It was a common practice and appears in many works. Among the most famous appearances are in John Donne's "Meditation 17," which begins, "Perchance he for whom this bell tolls may be so ill, as that he knows not it tolls for him," and Ernest Hemingway's novel *For Whom the Bell Tolls.*

---

41. **stay** wait for.
42. **convinces . . . art** defies the efforts of medical science.
43. **presently amend** immediately recover.

44. **evil** scrofula (skräf′ ye le), skin disease called "the king's evil" because it was believed that it could be cured by the king's touch.

45. **mere** utter.
46. **stamp** coin.

47. **gentle** noble.

48. **betimes** quickly.

Reading Strategy

Analyzing Text Structures
Connect the images in lines 164-173 with similar images revealing Scotland as a hellish place.

49. **nothing** no one.

50. **modern ecstasy** ordinary emotion. **34**

51. **The dead . . . who** People can no longer keep track of Macbeth's victims.

52. **nice** exact.

DOCTOR. Ay, sir. There are a crew of wretched souls
　　That stay[41] his cure: their malady convinces
　　The great assay of art;[42] but at his touch,
　　Such sanctity hath heaven given his hand,
　　They presently amend.[43]

145 **MALCOLM.** 　　　　　　　　I thank you, doctor.

　　　　　　　　　　　　　　　　　　[*Exit* DOCTOR.]

MACDUFF. What's the disease he means?

MALCOLM. 　　　　　　　　'Tis called the evil:[44]
　　A most miraculous work in this good King,
　　Which often since my here-remain in England
　　I have seen him do. How he solicits heaven,
150　　Himself best knows: but strangely-visited people,
　　All swoll'n and ulcerous, pitiful to the eye,
　　The mere[45] despair of surgery, he cures,
　　Hanging a golden stamp[46] about their necks,
　　Put on with holy prayers: and 'tis spoken,
155　　To the succeeding royalty he leaves
　　The healing benediction. With this strange virtue
　　He hath a heavenly gift of prophecy,
　　And sundry blessings hang about his throne
　　That speak him full of grace.

[*Enter* ROSS.]

MACDUFF. 　　　　　　　See, who comes here?

160 **MALCOLM.** My countryman; but yet I know him not.

MACDUFF. My ever gentle[47] cousin, welcome hither.

MALCOLM. I know him now: good God, betimes[48] remove
　　The means that makes us strangers!

ROSS. 　　　　　　　　　　　　Sir, amen.

MACDUFF. Stands Scotland where it did?

ROSS. 　　　　　　　　　　　Alas, poor country!
165　　Almost afraid to know itself! It cannot
　　Be called our mother but our grave, where nothing[49]
　　But who knows nothing is once seen to smile;
　　Where sighs and groans, and shrieks that rent the air,
　　Are made, not marked, where violent sorrow seems
170　　A modern ecstasy.[50] The dead man's knell
　　Is there scarce asked for who,[51] and good men's lives
　　Expire before the flowers in their caps,
　　Dying or ere they sicken.

MACDUFF. 　　　　　　　　　O, relation
　　Too nice,[52] and yet too true!

Enrichment: Analyzing Historical Patterns, Trends, and Periods

Facts versus Entertainment

Macbeth was probably performed for King James I during the summer of 1606. Scholars believe that Shakespeare wanted to flatter the king, so he made the characters of Banquo and Fleance more noble than they appeared in Holinshed's account. But flattery was only a small part of Shakespeare's motivation. Shakespeare's audiences knew Holinshed well. These histories were far from accurate, but were widely accepted. However, people didn't expect facts from a play. They expected to be entertained—and no one did that better than Shakespeare.

Activity: Investigate Medieval History Ask students to research Holinshed and Donwald to learn about the medieval people on whom Shakespeare based his play. They can record their findings on the **Enrichment: Analyzing Historical Patterns, Trends, and Periods** worksheet, *Professional Development Guidebook,* page 231.

MALCOLM. What's the newest grief?

175 **ROSS.** That of an hour's age doth hiss the speaker;[53]
    Each minute teems[54] a new one.

MACDUFF. How does my wife?

ROSS. Why, well.

MACDUFF. And all my children?

ROSS. Well too.

MACDUFF. The tyrant has not battered at their peace?

ROSS. No; they were well at peace when I did leave 'em.

180 **MACDUFF.** Be not a niggard of your speech: how goes 't?

ROSS. When I came hither to transport the tidings,
    Which I have heavily borne, there ran a rumor
    Of many worthy fellows that were out;[55]
    Which was to my belief witnessed[56] the rather,
185   For that I saw the tyrant's power[57] afoot.
    Now is the time of help. Your eye in Scotland
35   Would create soldiers, make our women fight,
    To doff[58] their dire distresses.

MALCOLM. Be 't their comfort
    We are coming thither. Gracious England hath
190   Lent us good Siward and ten thousand men;
    An older and a better soldier none
    That Christendom gives out.

ROSS. Would I could answer
    This comfort with the like! But I have words

---

53. That . . . speaker Report of the grief of an hour ago is hissed as stale news.

54. teems gives birth to.

Literary Analysis

Imagery Why do you think Ross uses such an exaggerated image in lines 186–188?

55. out in rebellion.

56. witnessed confirmed.

57. power army.

58. doff put off.

---

36  Reading Check

What report from Scotland does Ross bring?

37 ▼ Critical Viewing
How does this castle compare with your image of Inverness? **[Connect]**

Macbeth, Act IV, Scene iii 393

---

35 **Literary Analysis**

Imagery

1. **Ask** the Literary Analysis question: Why do you think Ross uses such an exaggerated image in lines 186–188?
   Possible responses: Ross uses such an exaggerated image because he wants to convince Malcolm how much his presence would inspire people to fight against Macbeth.

2. **Ask** students what real opinion of Malcolm is reflected in Ross's speech.
   Answer: Ross has a high opinion of Malcolm. He believes people will be inspired by someone who is honorable.

3. Point out that, in the lines preceding this speech, Macduff asks why Ross suddenly has so little to say. (Explain that *niggard* means "stingy.") **Ask** students why Ross might be reluctant to tell Macduff about his family. Also, in what way might saying "they are at peace" be viewed by Ross as kind of a truth?
   Possible responses: Ross is reluctant to speak because no one likes telling someone about a loved one's death. As for what he says about their being "at peace," it is fairly common to say that someone who is dead is at peace, and tombstones often read "Rest in Peace."

36 **Reading Check**

Answer: Ross brings a report from Scotland that the country suffers greatly.

37 **Critical Viewing**

Possible responses: This castle is strongly fortified and looks imposing and regal, as Inverness would. Some students might think that this castle is much more modern than Inverness would be, and much larger. They might also observe that the large number of windows would make it harder to defend, so it does not seem to be the kind of castle one would expect in a warlike era, such as that of the play.

Infer

1. Direct students' attention to lines 199–203.

2. **Ask:** What does Ross mean when he says, "Let not your ears despise my tongue for ever" in line 201?

3. **Answer:** Ross is warning Macduff not to be angry with him, for he has terrible news.

4. **Ask:** What is Ross's terrible news?

5. **Answer:** Ross has news that Macduff's wife, children, and servants have all been slaughtered.

39 **Critical Viewing**

Possible response: The actor portraying Macduff projects power, solemnity, and strength.

394 Celebrating Humanity (1485–1625)

Vocabulary Development

Vocabulary Knowledge Rating

When students have completed reading and discussing the selection, have them take out their **Vocabulary Knowledge Rating Charts** for Act 4. Read the words aloud and have students rate their knowledge of words again in the After Reading column. Clarify any words that are still problematic. Have students write their own definitions and example or sentence in the appropriate column. Then have students complete the Vocabulary Lesson at the end of the selection. Encourage students to use the words in further discussion and written work about the selection. Remind them that they will be accountable for these words on the **Selection Test,** *Unit 2 Resources,* pages 157–159 and 160–162.

That would be howled out in the desert air,
Where hearing should not latch[59] them.

195 **MACDUFF.**   What concern they?
The general cause or is it a fee-grief[60]
Due to some single breast?

ROSS.   No mind that's honest
But in it shares some woe, though the main part
Pertains to you alone.

MACDUFF.   If it be mine,
200 Keep it not from me, quickly let me have it.

ROSS. Let not your ears despise my tongue for ever,
Which shall possess them with the heaviest sound
That ever yet they heard.

MACDUFF.   Humh! I guess at it.

ROSS. Your castle is surprised; your wife and babes
205 Savagely slaughtered. To relate the manner,
Were, on the quarry[61] of these murdered deer,
To add the death of you.

MALCOLM.   Merciful heaven!
What, man! Ne'er pull your hat upon your brows;
Give sorrow words. The grief that does not speak
210 Whispers the o'er-fraught[62] heart and bids it break.

MACDUFF. My children too?

ROSS.   Wife, children, servants, all
That could be found.

MACDUFF.   And I must be from thence!
My wife killed too?

ROSS.   I have said.

MALCOLM.   Be comforted.
Let's make us med'cines of our great revenge,
215 To cure this deadly grief.

MACDUFF. He has no children. All my pretty ones?
Did you say all? O hell-kite![63] All?
What, all my pretty chickens and their dam
At one fell swoop?

MALCOLM. Dispute it[64] like a man.

220 **MACDUFF.**   I shall do so;
But I must also feel it as a man.
I cannot but remember such things were,
That were most precious to me. Did heaven look on,
And would not take their part? Sinful Macduff,

---

59. **latch** catch.

60. **fee-grief** personal grief.

Literary Analysis
Imagery How does the image in line 206 emphasize the ghastly fate of Macduff's family?

61. **quarry** heap of game slain in a hunt.

62. **o'er-fraught** over-burdened.

63. **hell-kite** hellish bird of prey.

64. **Dispute it** Counter your grief.

39 ◀ Critical Viewing
What emotions does this actor playing Macduff project? Explain. **[Interpret]**

---

40 Literary Analysis
Imagery

1. **Ask** students what Ross means by "To relate the manner, were. . . to add the death of you."
   Answer: He means that it was so ghastly that if Macduff heard the whole story, he would die, too.

2. **Ask** students the Literary Analysis question: How does the imagery in line 206 emphasize the ghastly fate of Macduff's family?
   Answer: By comparing them to deer and a heap of game after a hunt, it emphasizes that they were innocent and that they were treated inhumanly.

41 Critical Thinking
Deduce

1. **Ask** students whom Malcolm is addressing in lines 207–210. What is his advice?
   Answer: Malcolm addresses Macduff; he tells him not to hold in his grief.

2. **Ask** students how Macduff's disbelief and then sorrow are reflected in the dialogue that follows.
   Answer: He keeps asking who was killed, as if it is not sinking in; it is too horrible to believe. He then swings from disbelief to sorrow and to fury.

42 Literary Analysis
Imagery

1. Point out that, as the act ends, much of the imagery used thus far appears in the closing speeches.

2. **Ask** students what image used by Lady Macduff to her son in Scene 2 is echoed in lines 217–218.
   Answer: Both use bird imagery.

3. Note that manhood is discussed in line 219 and following. **Ask:** How do these images differ from previous ones?
   Answer: Here, a more traditional image of manhood—loving husband and father, protector, upholder of what is right—contrasts with previous images of manhood as being murderous.

4. Point out that the closing line echoes the recurring theme of light and dark.

Differentiated
Instruction   for Universal Access

Enrichment for Advanced Readers
Give students an opportunity to read a scholarly essay on *Macbeth*. They can research online or at the library. Have students read the essay of their choosing, and then summarize what they read in a short essay of their own. Encourage students to share their findings with each other and with the class.

EL Support for English Learners
For students who might be struggling with the events of *Macbeth* to this point, take some time to review what has happened in the story thus far. Have students work in pairs or small groups and make a flow chart of events. Students can then use these charts for Act 5.

Before students respond, you may wish to have them write a brief objective summary of the selection. As they answer the questions below, remind them to support their answers with evidence from the text.

1. (a) The second apparition says that none of woman born shall harm Macbeth. The third apparition tells Macbeth he will not be vanquished until Birnam Wood comes to Dunsinane. (b) Macbeth accepts the predictions because they appear favorable. Also, the witches' other prophecies came true.

2. (a) Macduff's wife and children are murdered. (b) Macbeth has degenerated into complete, unbridled evil.

3. (a) Malcolm tests Macduff by claiming to be worse than Macbeth. (b) Malcolm is a cautious man, testing Macduff. He is no fool and shows signs of being a great leader. Macduff is an honorable, honest man who is loyal to his country and the vows he has taken.

4. (a) He says that he must feel his grief as a man does. (b) Macduff reacts as a deeply loving man who is staggered by the news of his family's death. (c) Macduff's idea of manhood includes tenderness, love, and honor; earlier definitions do not. However, Macduff and Macbeth both speak of making wrongs right as manly, though Macduff's motives are honorable and Macbeth's are not.

5. (a) **Possible response:** Shakespeare would argue that everyone has free choice. Students should cite evidence from Act IV. (b) **Possible response:** Yes, even though genetics and upbringing play a part in shaping a person's character, it is their own free choice to pursue good or bad ends.

---

65. **Naught** wicked.

225 They were all struck for thee! Naught[65] that I am,
Not for their own demerits but for mine
Fell slaughter on their souls. Heaven rest them now!

MALCOLM. Be this the whetstone of your sword. Let grief
Convert to anger; blunt not the heart, enrage it.

230 **MACDUFF.** O, I could play the woman with mine eyes,
And braggart with my tongue! But, gentle heavens,
Cut short all intermission; front to front[66]

66. **front to front** face to face.

Bring thou this fiend of Scotland and myself;
Within my sword's length set him. If he 'scape,

235 Heaven forgive him too!

MALCOLM. This time goes manly.
Come, go we to the King. Our power is ready;

67. **Our . . . leave** We need only to take our leave.

Our lack is nothing but our leave.[67] Macbeth
Is ripe for shaking, and the pow'rs above

68. **Put . . . instruments** urge us onward as their agents.

Put on their instruments.[68] Receive what cheer you may.

240 The night is long that never finds the day. [*Exit.*]

Critical Reading

Cite textual evidence to support your responses.

1. **Key Ideas and Details (a)** What are the predictions made by the second and third apparitions? **(b) Analyze:** Why does Macbeth readily accept these predictions?

2. **Key Ideas and Details (a)** What happens to Macduff's family? **(b) Infer:** What does the fate of Macduff's family suggest about Macbeth's state of mind?

3. **Key Ideas and Details (a)** How does Malcolm test Macduff? **(b) Analyze:** What does this test reveal about both Malcolm and Macduff? Explain.

4. **Integration of Knowledge and Ideas (a)** How does Macduff respond when asked to take the news about his family "like a man"? **(b) Interpret:** How would you characterize Macduff, based on his reaction to the murder of his wife and son? **(c) Compare and Contrast:** Compare and contrast Macduff's understanding of manhood with definitions of it earlier in the play.

5. **Integration of Knowledge and Ideas (a) Hypothesize:** If Shakespeare were alive today, would he argue that evildoers are primarily influenced by genetics, upbringing, or their own free choice? Base your answer on evidence from Act IV. **(b) Evaluate:** Would you agree with his position? Explain.

396 Celebrating Humanity (1485–1625)

Concept Connector

Reading Strategy Graphic Organizer
Ask students to review the graphic organizers in which they have analyzed text structures. Then have students share their organizers and compare the sensing images they identified, and the patterns of images that help convey the play's meaning.

Activating Prior Knowledge
Have students return to their responses to the Activating Prior Knowledge activity. Ask them to explain whether their thoughts have changed and if so, how.

Writing About the Essential Question
Have students compare their responses to the prompt, given before they completed reading Act 4, with their thoughts afterward. Have them work individually or in groups, writing or discussing their thoughts, to formulate their new responses. Then, lead a class discussion, probing for what students have learned that confirms or invalidates their initial thoughts. Encourage students to cite specific textual details to support their responses.

After You Read   *Macbeth, Act IV*

Literary Analysis

1. Craft and Structure Identify a passage in Act IV that has vivid **imagery.** Using a chart like the one shown, indicate the emotions that the images express.

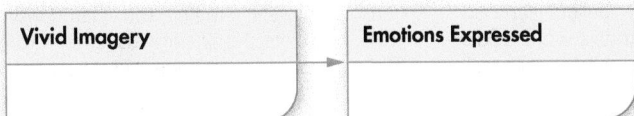

2. Craft and Structure (a) In Act IV, Scene i and Act IV, Scene ii, find images that show children and babies are in danger from Macbeth and also threaten him. **(b)** Why is Macbeth at war with the future, which babies and children represent?

3. Craft and Structure (a) Find two passages in Act IV, Scene iii with images of sickness. **(b)** Explain how these images relate to the conflict between Macbeth and Malcolm.

4. Craft and Structure In Act IV, Scene iii, identify two **archetypal images of banishment from an ideal world,** images that describe Scotland in terms of weeping, bleeding, or both.

5. Integration of Knowledge and Ideas What do the images of

banishment from an ideal world and the references to the Christian underworld indicate about Macbeth's rule over Scotland? Explain.

Reading Strategy

6. Analyze the text structure of *Macbeth* by identifying three patterns of imagery that occur throughout Act IV. Remember that a pattern of imagery is a series of related images—for example, images of blood.

7. Explain how each of the patterns of imagery you identified relates to an important theme—an insight into life or comment on life—in the play.

8. Demonstrate how several patterns of imagery work together to convey the play's meaning.

9. (a) Would *Macbeth* be less rich if Shakespeare had not used imagery to reinforce the themes of his play? Why or why not? **(b)** Is it necessary for the reader to experience the images with his or her senses to make them truly effective? Explain.

10. Some critics have argued that a pattern of imagery is a text structure that appeals to a reader's mind, emotions, and senses. Do you agree or disagree? Why?

 **Common Core State Standards**

Writing
2.b. Develop the topic thoroughly by selecting the most significant and relevant facts, extended definitions, concrete details, quotations, or other information and examples appropriate to the audience's knowledge of the topic. *(p. 398)*
2.f. Provide a concluding statement or section that follows from and supports the information or explanation presented. *(p. 398)*
5. Develop and strengthen writing as needed by planning, revising, editing, rewriting, or trying a new approach, focusing on addressing what is most significant for a specific purpose and audience. *(p. 398)*

Language
4.d. Verify the preliminary determination of the meaning of a word or phrase. *(p. 398)*

Macbeth, Act IV **397**

Answers

1. **Possible response:** Students may choose imagery from Lady Macduff's speech in Scene 2, lines 6–14: "poor wren, / The most diminutive of birds," expresses helplessness and innocence; "the owl" expresses being ravenous and deadly.

2. (a) In Act 4, Scene 1, the second and third apparition—a bloody child and a child crowned—threaten Macbeth. In Act 4, Scene 2, the murder of Macduff's children is an image of children in danger from Macbeth. (b) Macbeth is at war with the future because the future holds the chance of failure, death, and loss of the crown.

3. (a) Scene 3, lines 140–159, and Scene 3, lines 168–174, contain imagery of sickness and disease. (b) Macbeth is the disease, and Malcolm is the cure.

4. In Scene 3, lines 39–41, Malcolm describes Scotland: "It weeps, it bleeds, and each new day a gash is added to her wounds." In Scene 3, lines 168–170, Ross adds that Scotland sighs, groans, and shrieks, and that violence and death are common.

5. These images combined with references to hell, demons, and Lucifer (the fallen angel Malcolm mentions) indicate that Macbeth has chosen evil (the fall) and has turned Scotland into a place of torment.

6. **Possible response:** One pattern of imagery is blood: The witches use baboon blood; a bloody child appears to Macbeth as an apparition; Macbeth also sees bloody Banquo pointing to his descendants on the throne; Macduff describes Scotland as bleeding; Malcolm calls Macbeth bloody. Another pattern of imagery is birds: Lady Macduff uses bird imagery to talk about her husband's leaving—his flight; she uses bird imagery to talk about her son; Macduff uses bird imagery when he talks about his slain family. Another pattern of imagery is children: The witches use a child's finger in their potion; children are two of Macbeth's apparitions.

7. The pattern of blood relates to the theme of murder in *Macbeth*. The pattern of children relates to the theme of future in the

---

Answers continued

play. The pattern of birds relates to hope and despair in the play.

8. In the witches' potion, the apparitions, and the murder of Macduff's children, the patterns of blood and children work together to show the meaning of a bloody future for Scotland and, eventually, Macbeth.

9. **Possible response:** (a) *Macbeth* would be less rich if Shakespeare did not use thematic imagery because imagery is what helps the reader/listener fully imagine the world Shakespeare is creating. (b) Yes, Shakespeare created the images to appeal to the readers'

senses, so readers must do so to fully participate in the play.

10. **Possible response:** Yes, a pattern of imagery does appeal to a reader's mind, emotions, and senses. Because the definition of images is "words that convey sensory impressions," patterns of images must appeal to the senses or they would not be images. Because the reader's mind must be fully engaged to perceive the patterns, the patterns appeal to his or her mind. Finally, most people associate emotions with their sensory experiences. Therefore, powerful imagery would also appeal to readers' emotions.

397

ASSESS/EXTEND

Answers

Vocabulary Acquisition and Use

Word Analysis

1. *Incredible* means "unbelievable."
2. *Incredulous* means "disbelieving."
3. *Credible* means "believable.".
4. *Credulity* means "the tendency to believe something too readily."
5. *Discredit* means "to make unbelievable."
6. *Miscredulity* means "wrong belief."

Vocabulary

1. avarice
2. sundry
3. credulous
4. intemperance
5. judicious
6. pernicious

Writing

Work with students to draw up guidelines, based on the assignment, for their informative texts:

- **Focus** The writer should clearly present the ideal world, why Macbeth falls, and the evil world in which *Macbeth* ends.

- **Organization** The writer should begin the essay describing the ideal world. The body of the essay should explain Macbeth's fall. The conclusion should describe the evil world in which *Macbeth* ends.

- **Elaboration** The writer should give details from the play, explaining how passages might affect reader's emotions.

- **Style** The audience is not specified, so a formal style is appropriate.

PERFORMANCE TASKS
Integrated Language Skills

ⓒ Vocabulary Acquisition and Use

Word Analysis: Latin Word Root -cred-

The Latin root *-cred-* means "belief." For example, to be *credulous* is "to believe something too readily." The word *creed*, meaning "belief," can also be traced back to this root, as can the word *credentials*, meaning "qualifications," or traits that make a person trustworthy or believable.

Working with a partner, use the word parts shown below to build six *-cred-* words. Then, write the meanings of these words.

in-	-ulous
dis-	-ulity
mis-	-ible

When you are done, verify your words and definitions by referring to a dictionary.

Vocabulary: Analogies

An analogy compares two relationships to show their similarity. For each item, determine the relationship between the first and second words. Then, complete the analogy using a word from the vocabulary list on page 378. Use each word only once, and explain your choice.

1. *suspicion : trust ::* _____ *: generosity*
2. *expensive : costly ::* _____ *: assorted*
3. *independent : adult ::* _____ *: child*
4. *formality : ease ::* _____ *: self-control*
5. *offensive : rude ::* _____ *: sensible*
6. *invulnerable : susceptible ::* _____ *: harmless*

Writing

ⓒ Informative Text *Archetypal images of banishment from an ideal world—otherwise known as the archetype of the "fall"—*often appear in works dealing with the loss of innocence or with a character's descent into a state of evil. Write an **essay** analyzing Shakespeare's use of such images in *Macbeth.* Identify the "ideal world" from which one or more characters are expelled, as well as the causes of this banishment. Remember to trace the descent into evil by means of Shakespeare's imagery.

Prewriting Create a flow chart like the one shown to trace a central character's "fall." Identify imagery reflecting the ideal state in which the character exists at first. Then list reasons why this ideal state does not last. (The reasons may be internal character traits, external events, or both.) Finally, describe the evil into which the character has fallen.

Drafting Begin with a statement that summarizes the fall from the ideal state shown in your prewriting chart. Develop your essay by indicating the ways Shakespeare uses imagery to picture this fall. Support your points by making *specific and detailed references* to the text, and note how these passages might affect *readers' or viewers' emotions.*

Revising Revise to add breadth and depth to your essay. Consider adding comparisons or references to other works of literature that use archetypal images of banishment. Alternatively, provide a concluding section about *nuances or complexities* that make Shakespeare's use of these archetypal images more convincing than that of other authors.

Model: Charting a Character's Fall

> Macbeth's "Ideal" State
>
> ↓   ↓   ↓
>
> Macbeth's "Fallen" State

398 Integrated Language Skills

Assessment Resources

Unit 2 Resources

L1 L2 EL Selection Test A, pp. 157–159. Administer Test A to less advanced readers.

L3 L4 EL Selection Test B, pp. 160–162. Administer Test B to on-level and more advanced students.

All Customizable Test Bank

All Self-tests
Students may prepare for the **Selection Test** by taking the **Self-test** online.

PHLit Online! All assessment resources are available at www.PHLitOnline.com.

Critical Commentary

"Macbeth as King"

Ian Johnston

Ian Johnston teaches at Malaspina-University College, Nanaimo, BC, Canada. His analysis of Macbeth's character in the later acts of the play comes from his lecture entitled "Introduction to Macbeth.*"*

. . . It is worth asking ourselves what in Macbeth commands our attention throughout the second half of this play. After all, he is in many respects the least admirable tragic hero of all. In characters like Othello, Romeo, Cleopatra, Lear, Antony, Hamlet . . . we can usually find something to admire. We may not like them (they are not very likable people), but there is something in their characters or their situations on which we can hang some sympathy, even if there is not enough for us to rationalize away their actions. But Macbeth is a mass murderer, who does away with friends, colleagues, woman and children, often for no apparent reason other than his own desires. Why do we keep our attention focused on him?

The answer, I think, has to do with the quality of his mind, his horrible determination to see the entire evil business through. Having, with the murder of Duncan, taken charge of the events which shape his life, he is not now going to relinquish the responsibility for securing his desires. The most remarkable quality of the man in this process is the clear-eyed awareness of what is happening to him personally. He is suffering horribly throughout, but he will not crack or seek any other remedy than what he alone can deliver. If that means damning himself even further, then so be it.

This stance certainly does not make Macbeth likable or (from our perspective) in many respects admirable. But it does confer a heroic quality upon his tragic course of action. He simply will not compromise with the world, and he will pay whatever price that decision exacts from him, even though as his murderous career continues he becomes increasingly aware of what it is costing him.

▲ Macbeth demands to know the future from the Witches.

ⓒ **Key Ideas and Details** According to Johnston, is Macbeth among Shakespeare's more admirable tragic heroes? Explain.

Critical Commentary **399**

Critical Commentary

1. Have students read through Ian Johnston's commentary on Macbeth's character.

2. Point out to students that Johnston frames his commentary by asking and answering a question. **Ask** students to identify the question.
   Answer: He asks, "What in Macbeth commands our attention throughout the second half of this play?"

3. **Ask** students to restate, in their own words, Johnston's answer to this question.
   Answer: Macbeth is a compelling character because of his strength and determination. Once he has set upon his course, nothing will make him waver. Also, he takes personal responsibility for his actions.

4. Draw students' attention to the last sentence of Johnston's commentary. Tell students that, as they read the final act of the play, they should be aware of ways that Macbeth reveals his awareness of the "cost" of his chosen path.

Key Ideas and Details

Possible response: No, Johnston does not hold Macbeth among the most admirable of Shakespearean heroes. In fact, he refers to Macbeth as "the least admirable tragic hero of all" because he does not seem to have qualities with which audiences can sympathize. He seems utterly selfish and coldhearted.

Enrichment: Understanding Theater

Shakespeare's Universal Appeal

All the world is truly Shakespeare's stage. His plays, including **Macbeth**, have been performed continually since they first appeared. Though the plays seem to be about specific places and times, they are actually about universal themes that speak across time and borders.

Because Shakespeare is also about a good story, directors often give his work new looks and new settings, to share their own vision or to reach new audiences. In recent years, movies have been made of *Hamlet, A Midsummer Night's Dream, Much Ado About Nothing, Romeo and Juliet,* and *Henry V.*

Activity: Analyzing Film Have interested students conduct research on film adaptations of Shakespeare's plays. Students may view one or more films and prepare a short presentation for their classmates. Information about each film can be recorded on the **Enrichment: Analyzing Film** worksheet, **Professional Development Guidebook**, page 226.

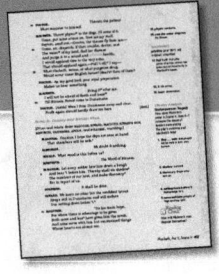

• *Macbeth*, Act V
Lesson Pacing Guide

DAY 1 Preteach

- Administer the Reading and Vocabulary Warm-ups (*Unit 2 Resources,* pp. 166–169) as necessary.
- Introduce the Literary Analysis concept: Shakespearean Tragedy.
- Introduce the Reading Strategy: Relating a Work to the Issues of its Period.
- Build background with Background features.
- Develop thematic thinking with Connecting to the Essential Question.
- Teach the selection vocabulary.

DAYS 2–3 Preteach/Teach/Assess

- Distribute copies of the appropriate graphic organizer for the Reading Strategy (*Graphic Organizer Transparencies,* pp. 68–69).
- Distribute copies of the appropriate graphic organizer for Literary Analysis (*Graphic Organizer Transparencies,* pp. 70–71).
- Prepare students to read with the Activating Prior Knowledge activities (TE).
- Informally monitor comprehension while students read.
- Use the Reading Check questions to confirm comprehension.
- Develop students' understanding of Shakespearean Tragedy using the Literary Analysis prompts.
- Develop students' ability to relate a work to the issues of its period using the Reading Strategy prompts.
- Reinforce vocabulary with the Vocabulary notes.
- Assess students' comprehension and mastery of the skills by having them answer the Critical Reading, Literary Analysis, and Reading Strategy questions.
- Have students complete the Vocabulary Lesson.

DAY 4 Extend/Assess

- Have students complete the Conventions and Style Lesson.
- Have students complete the Writing Lesson and write a response to literature. (You may assign as homework.)
- Administer Selection Test A or B (*Unit 2 Resources,* pp. 179–181 or 182–184).

© Common Core State Standards

Reading Literature 3. Analyze the impact of the author's choices regarding how to develop and relate elements of a story or drama.

Language 4.c. Consult general and specialized reference materials, both print and digital, to find the pronunciation of a word or determine or clarify its precise meaning, its part of speech, its etymology, or its standard usage.

Additional Standards Practice
Common Core Companion, *pp. 28–40; 185–195; 324–331*

Daily Block Scheduling
Each day in this Lesson Pacing Guide represents a 40–50 minute period. Teachers using block scheduling may combine days to revise pacing. In addition, teachers may differentiate and support core instruction by integrating components for extended and intensive support as students require. See the Guide to Selected Leveled Resources (facing page).

Guide to Selected Leveled Resources

R T I Tier 1 (students performing on level) — Macbeth, *Act V*

Warm Up		Practice, **model,** and **monitor** fluency, working **with the whole class** or **in groups.**	**Vocabulary** and **Reading Warm-ups B,** *Unit 2 Resources,* pp. 166–167, 169
Comprehension/Skills		**Support** and **monitor** comprehension and skills development, having students complete the activities, graphic organizers, and interactive prompts **independently** or **as a class.**	• *Reader's Notebook,* adapted instruction and summary **EL** *Reader's Notebook: English Learner's Version,* adapted instruction and summary • **Reading Skill Graphic Organizer B,** *Graphic Organizer Transparencies,* p. 69 • **Literary Analysis Graphic Organizer B,** *Graphic Organizer Transparencies,* p. 71
Monitor Progress	A	**Monitor** student progress with the differentiated curriculum-based assessment in the *Unit Resources.*	• **Selection Test B,** *Unit 2 Resources,* pp. 182–184 • **Open-Book Test,** *Unit 2 Resources,* pp. 176–178
Assess/Screen	A	**Assess** student progress using Benchmark Test 2.	• **Benchmark Test 4,** *Unit 2 Resources,* pp. 195–203

R T I Tier 2 (students requiring intervention) — Macbeth, *Act V*

Warm Up		Practice, **model,** and **monitor** fluency **in groups** or **with individuals.**	• **Vocabulary and Reading Warm-ups A,** *Unit 2 Resources,* pp. 166–168 • *Hear It!* Audio CD
Comprehension/Skills		• **Support** and **monitor** comprehension and skills development, working **in small groups** or **with individuals.** • As students complete the selection in the appropriate version of the *Reader's Notebook,* **monitor** comprehension frequently with group questions and individual instruction. • **Model** strategies while guiding students in completing the activities and prompts in the *Reader's Notebook,* as well as the graphic organizers. • **Practice** skills and **monitor** mastery with the *Reading Kit* worksheets.	• *Reader's Notebook: Adapted Version,* adapted instruction and summary **EL** *Reader's Notebook: English Learner's Version,* adapted instruction and summary • **Reading Skill Graphic Organizer A,** *Graphic Organizer Transparencies,* p. 68 • **Literary Analysis Graphic Organizer A,** *Graphic Organizer Transparencies,* p. 70 • *Reading Kit,* Practice worksheets
Monitor Progress	A	**Monitor** student progress with the differentiated curriculum-based assessment in the *Unit Resources* and in the *Reading Kit.*	• **Selection Test A,** *Unit 2 Resources,* pp. 179–181 • *Reading Kit,* Assess worksheets
Assess/Screen	A	**Assess** student progress using Benchmark Test.	**Benchmark Test 4,** *Unit 2 Resources,* pp. 195–203

TIER 3 Tier 3 intervention may require consultation with the student's special-education or dyslexia specialist. For additional support, see the Tier 2 activities and resources listed above.

 One-on-one teaching   Group work   Whole class instruction   Independent work   A Assessment

For a complete guide to selection support, including support for Advanced students, see the Overview of Resources in the frontmatter.

• *Macbeth*, Act V

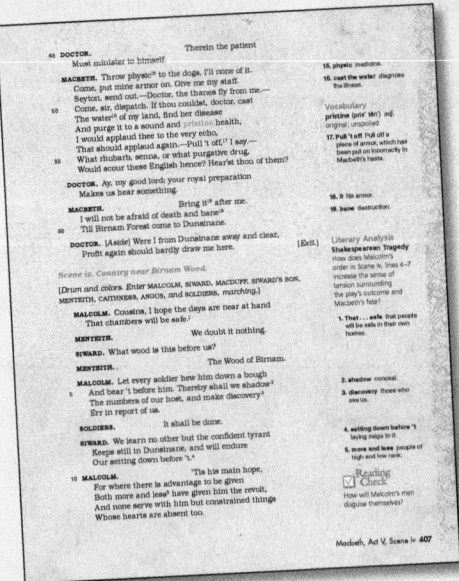

RESOURCES FOR:

- **L1** Special-Needs Students
- **L2** Below-Level Students (Tier 2)
- **L3** On-Level Students (Tier 1)
- **L4** Advanced Students (Tier 1)
- **EL** English Learners
- **All** All Students

Vocabulary/Fluency/Prior Knowledge

EL L1 L2 Vocabulary Warm-ups A and B, pp. 166–167

Also available for these selections:

EL L1 L2 Reading Warm-ups A and B, pp. 168–169

All Vocabulary Builder, p. 172

Reader's Notebooks

Pre- and postreading pages for this selection, as well as *Macbeth*, Act V, Scenes 5–8 appear in an interactive format in the *Reader's Notebooks*. Each *Notebook* is differentiated for a different group of learners. The selections in the Adapted and English Learner's versions are abridged.

- **L2 L3** *Reader's Notebook*
- **L1** *Reader's Notebook: Adapted Version*
- **EL** *Reader's Notebook: English Learner's Version*
- **EL** *Reader's Notebook: Spanish Version*

© Common Core Companion

Additional instruction and practice for each Common Core State Standard

Selection Support

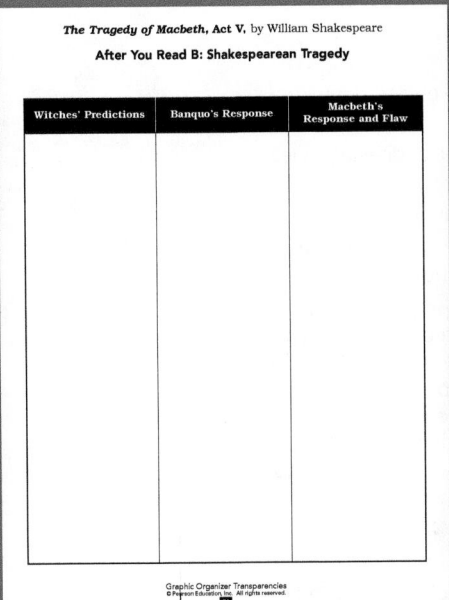

The Tragedy of Macbeth, Act V, by William Shakespeare

After You Read B: Shakespearean Tragedy

Witches' Predictions	Banquo's Response	Macbeth's Response and Flaw

Graphic Organizer Transparencies

Graphic Organizer Transparencies

EL L1 L2 **Literary Analysis: Graphic Organizer A** (partially filled in), p. 70

Also available for these selections:

EL L1 L2 **Reading: Graphic Organizer A** (partially filled in), p. 68

EL L3 **Reading: Graphic Organizer B,** p. 69

EL L3 **Literary Analysis: Graphic Organizer B,** p. 71

Skills Development/Extension

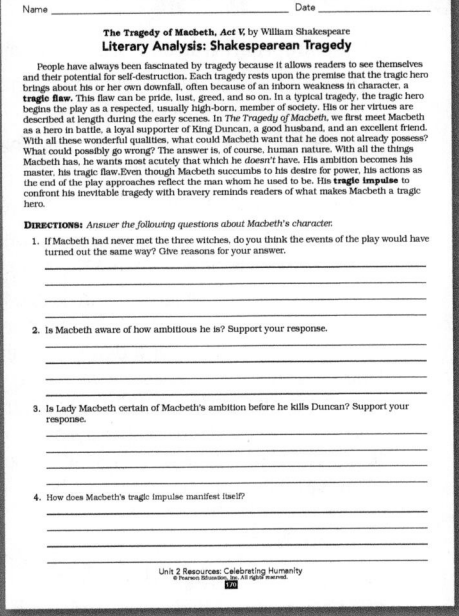

Unit 2 Resources

The Tragedy of Macbeth, Act V, by William Shakespeare
Literary Analysis: Shakespearean Tragedy

All **Literary Analysis,** p. 170

Also available for these selections:

All **Reading,** p. 171

EL L3 L4 **Grammar and Style,** p. 173

EL L3 L4 **Support for Writing,** p. 174

L4 **Enrichment,** p. 175

Assessment

The Tragedy of Macbeth, Act V, by William Shakespeare
Selection Test A

EL L1 L2 **Selection Test A,** pp. 179–181

Also available for these selections:

L3 L4 **Open-Book Test,** pp. 176–178

EL L3 L4 **Selection Test B,** pp. 182–184

PHLit Online! www.PHLitOnline.com

Online Resources: All print materials are also available online.

- complete narrated selection text
- a thematically related video with writing prompt
- an interactive graphic organizer
- highlighting feature
- access to all student print resources, adapted to individual student needs
- Spanish and English summaries
- adapted selection translations in Spanish

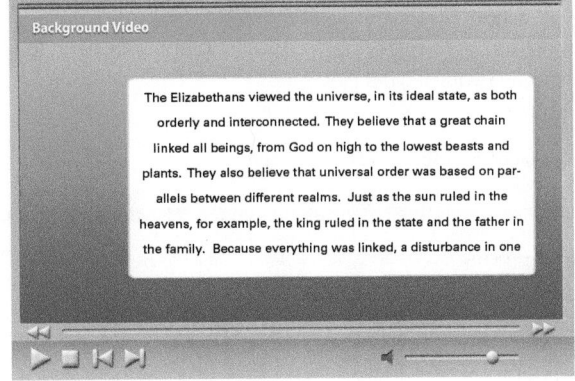

Background Video (thematic video with writing prompt)

Also available:

Get Connected!
All videos are available in Spanish.

Vocabulary Central (tools and activities for studying vocabulary)

Also available:

Writer's Journal (with graphics feature)

Before You Read   *Macbeth, Act V*

❶ Literary Analysis

Introduce the skill using the instruction on the student page.

Think Aloud: Model the Skill

Say to students:

Based on what I have read so far in this play, it is clear that Macbeth's tragic flaw is his ambition. His wife was able to influence him by appealing to his ambition. The information given by the witches also seems to provoke Macbeth to act on his ambition. As for "vivid spectacle," I imagine that on the stage, all the violence could be pretty intense. And the Porter in Act 2 certainly provides some comic relief.

❷ Reading Strategy

1. Introduce the strategy using the instruction on the student page.

2. Give students a copy of **Reading Strategy Graphic Organizer B,** page 65 in *Graphic Organizer Transparencies,* to fill out as they read.

Think Aloud: Model the Skill

Say to students:

Knowing that Elizabethans thought that order in society reflected order in the heavens helps me understand the behavior of Lady Macbeth at the banquet in Act 3. Macbeth is acting crazily and talking to someone no one else can see. Lady Macbeth has to make desperate excuses for her husband, so that no one will worry. If they thought the king was truly mad, they might suspect that he was out of favor with the heavens, or that God did not approve of Macbeth as king.

❸ Vocabulary

1. Pronounce each word, giving its definition, and have students say it aloud.

2. For more guidance, see the *Classroom Strategies and Teaching Routines* card for introducing vocabulary.

❶ Literary Analysis

Shakespearean tragedy usually contains these elements:

- A central character of high rank and personal quality, yet with a **tragic flaw** or weakness
- Causally related events that lead this character to disaster, at least partly through his or her flaw
- An experience of pity, fear, and awe for the audience
- Lively action that creates a vivid spectacle and the use of comic scenes to temper and offset the mood of sadness

As you read, consider how Shakespeare introduces Macbeth as a character (as a war hero) and how the author then develops the character, adding complexity and depth and ultimately revealing a tragic flaw. Note, too, how Shakespeare chooses to include plot events that lead to Macbeth's downfall and that make his tragic flaw evident.

Reading a Shakespearean tragedy is often uplifting despite the disasters that befall the hero. This positive experience results from the **tragic impulse,** which shows the tragic hero acting nobly.

Common Core State Standards

Reading Literature
3. Analyze the impact of the author's choices regarding how to develop and relate elements of a story or drama.

❷ Reading Strategy

Ⓒ Preparing to Read Complex Texts As products of a certain time, great plays reflect the beliefs of their period. To better understand a great play, therefore, you should **relate the work to the major themes and issues of its period.** Following are ways to uncover the philosophical, political, and religious influences that shaped *Macbeth*'s characters and settings:

- Be aware of the importance Elizabethans placed on the king's role in maintaining social order and how they linked order in the heavens with order in society.
- Compare the ideas that characters express with modern ideas.

In using the second method, focus on the ideas expressed by the doctor in Act V, Scene i. Use a chart like the one shown to compare his ideas with those a modern psychiatrist might express.

Comparison of Beliefs

Doctor in *Macbeth*

↓

Modern Psychiatrist

❸ Vocabulary

perturbation (pʉr´ tər bā´ shən) *n.* disturbance (p. 401)

recoil (ri kɔil´) *v.* to draw back in fear, surprise, or disgust (p. 405)

antidote (an´ tə dōt´) *n.* remedy (p. 406)

pristine (pris´ tēn´) *adj.* original; unspoiled (p. 407)

clamorous (klam´ ər əs) *adj.* noisy (p. 410)

harbingers (här´ bin jərz) *n.* forerunners (p. 410)

vulnerable (vul´ nər ə bəl) *adj.* exposed to attack or harm (p. 412)

www.PHLitOnline.com

400 Celebrating Humanity (1485–1625)

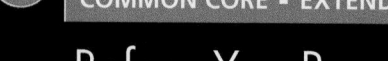
www.PHLitOnline.com

Teaching From Technology

Preparing to Read
Go to www.PHLitOnline.com and display the **Get Connected!** slide show for this selection. Have the class brainstorm for responses to the writing prompt, entering ideas in the interactive journal. Then have students complete their responses individually. You may also have students complete the assignment as homework.

To build background, display the Background video and More About the Author features.

Using the Interactive Student Edition
Go to www.PHLitOnline.com and display the **Enriched Online Student Edition.** As the class reads the selection or listens to the narration, record answers to side-column prompts using the graphic organizers accessible on the interactive page. Alternatively, have students use the online edition individually, answering the prompts as they read.

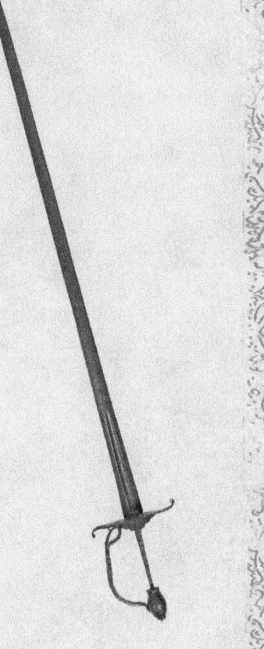

❶❷ Review and Anticipate

In Act IV, Macbeth learns from the witches that he must "Beware Macduff!" but that he need not fear any man "of woman born." He also learns he will never be vanquished until the forest itself marches against him. However, he sees a vision indicating that Banquo will indeed father a long line of kings.

Armed with his new knowledge, Macbeth orders the murder of Macduff's wife and son. Macduff himself is in England to join forces with Malcolm and is overcome when he hears the news. Nevertheless, he and Malcolm will lead an army against Macbeth.

Act V will determine the outcome as Macbeth, grown reckless in evil, battles against Malcolm and his men.

ACT V

Scene i. Dunsinane. In the castle.

[*Enter a* DOCTOR OF PHYSIC *and a* WAITING-GENTLEWOMAN.]

DOCTOR. I have two nights watched with you, but can perceive no truth in your report. When was it she last walked?

5 **GENTLEWOMAN.** Since his Majesty went into the field.[1] I have seen her rise from her bed, throw her nightgown upon her, unlock her closet,[2] take forth paper, fold it, write upon 't, read it, afterwards seal it, and again return to bed; yet all this while in a most fast sleep.

DOCTOR. A great perturbation in nature, to receive at
10 once the benefit of sleep and do the effects of watching![3] In this slumb'ry agitation, besides her walking, and other actual performances, what, at any time, have you heard her say?

15 **GENTLEWOMAN.** That, sir, which I will not report after her.

DOCTOR. You may to me, and 'tis most meet[4] you should.

GENTLEWOMAN. Neither to you nor anyone, having no witness to confirm my speech.

[*Enter* LADY MACBETH, *with a taper.*]

Lo you, here she comes! This is her very guise,[5] and, upon my
20 life, fast asleep! Observe her; stand close.[6]

DOCTOR. How came she by that light?

GENTLEWOMAN. Why, it stood by her. She has light by her continually. 'Tis her command.

25 **DOCTOR.** You see, her eyes are open.

---

❸ ▲ **Critical Viewing**
Who will slay Macbeth with a sword like this one? **[Predict]**

1. **field** battlefield.
2. **closet** chest.

Vocabulary
perturbation (pʉr′ tər bā′ shən) *n.* disturbance

3. **effects of watching** deeds of one awake.
4. **meet** suitable.
5. **guise** custom.
6. **close** hidden.

❹ ☑ Reading Check
Why has the gentlewoman summoned the doctor?

Macbeth, Act V, Scene i **401**

TEACH

❶ About the Selection

This act shows with great poignancy the final effects of Macbeth's actions on himself, his wife, and the kingdom of Scotland. As the act begins, Macbeth has fortified himself behind the stone walls of Dunsinane, armed with the prophecy of the apparitions. Lady Macbeth has suffered a mental and emotional breakdown. As the army of angry Scots who are determined to overthrow Macbeth approaches, Lady Macbeth kills herself. What is left of Macbeth's former glory will not allow him to die without a fight. The final speech by Macbeth is meant to lift the mood of the audience. However, this play's main message is a dark one: Even the noblest and most heroic humans can fall into the depths of depravity and ruin.

❷ Activating Prior Knowledge

Review the last three predictions made by the apparitions in Act 4: Macbeth should beware Macduff; no man born of woman shall ever harm Macbeth; Macbeth will never be vanquished until Birnam Wood comes to Dunsinane. Ask students to write a paragraph with their ideas about how these predictions might or might not come true. Tell them to include a prediction about what will become of Lady Macbeth.

Concept Connector ➡

Tell students they will return to their responses after reading the selection.

❸ Critical Viewing

Answer: Students may predict that Macduff will slay Macbeth with such a sword, because Macbeth has been warned to beware of Macduff.

❹ Reading Check

Answer: The gentlewoman has summoned the doctor because she has seen Lady Macbeth sleepwalking and she wants another witness.

Differentiated Instruction *for Universal Access*

Support for Special-Needs Students
Have students complete the **Before You Read** and the **Making Connections** pages for this selection in the **Reader's Notebook: Adapted Version.** These pages provide an abbreviated skills instruction, a selection summary, the Before You Read graphic organizer, and a **Note-taking Guide.**

Support for Less Proficient Readers
Have students complete the **Before You Read** and the **Making Connections** pages for this selection in the **Reader's Notebook.** These pages provide an abbreviated skills instruction, a selection summary, the Before You Read graphic organizer, and a **Note-taking Guide.**

EL Support for English Learners
Have students complete the **Before You Read** and the **Making Connections** pages for this selection in the **Reader's Notebook: English Learner's Version.** These pages provide additional vocabulary, vocabulary skills, and vocabulary practice, along with a **Getting Ready to Read** activity

401

Lady Macbeth Sleepwalking,
by Henry Fuseli

Henry Fuseli (1741–1825) was considered one of the early Romantics. Like other Romantics, he had an interest in dreams, nightmares, and waking visions. In fact, the first painting to make him famous was titled *The Nightmare.* His interest in the deeply psychological made him a natural for illustrating *Macbeth.* Fuseli loved Shakespeare and illustrated many of his works. Fuseli's pictorial fantasies later influenced the work of William Blake.

This painting captures the nightmarish quality of Lady Macbeth's sleepwalking scene. Painted in 1784, this oil painting on canvas now hangs in the Louvre in Paris.

Use these questions for discussion:

1. How well does this painting capture the feel of the sleepwalking scene? How does your own mental image of the scene compare with the one in the painting?
   Possible responses: Students may say that the painting captures the agitation suffered by Lady Macbeth. Students may say that this painting differs from their own mental image, because Lady Macbeth seems stronger and more vibrant than the character they pictured.

2. In what ways do the colors used in the painting capture the mood of the sleepwalking scene?
   Answer: The bright color of Lady Macbeth's gown and her vivid red hair make her the focal point of the painting. The shadowy dark colors used in the background emphasize that this is a nightmarish scene.

❺

Think Aloud

Literary Analysis: Shakespearean Tragedy
To model the process of working out the answer to the Literary Analysis question on student page 403, use the following "think aloud." Say to students:

If Lady Macbeth is to be a tragic figure in the tradition of Shakespearean tragedy, four things must be true: she must be a person of high rank with a tragic flaw or weakness; events related to this tragic flaw must lead her into disaster; the audience must feel pity, awe, and fear; and there must be elements that offset the sadness, such as "vivid spectacle" and comic scenes. Well, Lady Macbeth is certainly of high rank, and she does have the tragic flaw of overwhelming ambition. This ambition leads her to violence, deceit, and suffering. The audience definitely feels pity for Lady Macbeth during the sleepwalking scene. A sleepwalking woman, trying to wash her hands of imaginary blood while a doctor tries to write down everything she says, might qualify as a "spectacle." It seems to me that Lady Macbeth is shown as a tragic figure in every sense.

GENTLEWOMAN. Ay, but their sense[7] are shut.

DOCTOR. What is it she does now? Look, how she rubs her hands.

GENTLEWOMAN. It is an accustomed action with her, to seem thus washing her hands: I have known her continue in this a quarter of an hour.

LADY MACBETH. Yet here's a spot.

DOCTOR. Hark! She speaks. I will set down what comes from her, to satisfy[8] my remembrance the more strongly.

LADY MACBETH. Out, damned spot! Out, I say! One: two: why, then 'tis time to do 't. Hell is murky. Fie, my lord, fie! A soldier, and afeard? What need we fear who knows it, when none can call our pow'r to accompt?[9] Yet who would have thought the old man to have had so much blood in him?

DOCTOR. Do you mark that?

LADY MACBETH. The Thane of Fife had a wife. Where is she now? What, will these hands ne'er be clean? No more o' that, my lord, no more o' that! You mar all with this starting.

DOCTOR. Go to, go to! You have known what you should not.

GENTLEWOMAN. She has spoke what she should not, I am sure of that. Heaven knows what she has known.

LADY MACBETH. Here's the smell of the blood still. All the perfumes of Arabia will not sweeten this little hand. Oh, oh, oh!

DOCTOR. What a sigh is there! The heart is sorely charged.[10]

GENTLEWOMAN. I would not have such a heart in my bosom for the dignity[11] of the whole body.

DOCTOR. Well, well, well—

GENTLEWOMAN. Pray God it be, sir.

DOCTOR. This disease is beyond my practice. Yet I have known those which have walked in their sleep who have died holily in their beds.

LADY MACBETH. Wash your hands; put on your nightgown; look not so pale! I tell you yet again, Banquo's buried. He cannot come out on 's[12] grave.

DOCTOR. Even so?

LADY MACBETH. To bed, to bed! There's knocking at the gate. Come, come, come, come, give me your hand!

7. sense powers of sight.

8. satisfy support.

9. to accompt into account.

❻ **Literary Analysis**
Shakespearean Tragedy
Does the sleepwalking scene suggest that Lady Macbeth is a tragic heroine? Explain.

10. charged burdened.

11. dignity worth.

❼ ◀ **Critical Viewing**
Identify four details from the sleepwalking scene (V, i) the artist illustrates in this picture. **[Connect]**

12. on 's of his.

❽ **Reading Check**
What does Lady Macbeth do and say as she sleepwalks?

❻ Literary Analysis

Shakespearean Tragedy

1. Review with students the four central aspects of Shakespearean tragedy listed on page 400.
2. Then **ask** the Literary Analysis question: Does the sleepwalking scene suggest that Lady Macbeth is a tragic heroine? Explain.
   Answer: Lady Macbeth is a tragic figure because her flaw, unbridled ambition, has led her to this tragic point, where her conscience has caught up with her and she is suffering for her actions.

❼ Critical Viewing

Possible response: Details of the scene that students might identify include the presence of the female servant (gentlewoman); the presence of the doctor, who appears to be prepared to take notes; Lady Macbeth holding a candle (taper), with her eyes open and looking as if she is suffering "slumb'ry agitation."

❽ Reading Check

Answer: As she sleepwalks, Lady Macbeth rubs her hands, as if to wash them, and speaks of blood, the deaths for which she and Macbeth are responsible, and such elements of previous events as the knocking at the gate.

Differentiated Instruction for Universal Access

Strategy for Less Proficient Readers
Review with students the elements of Shakespearean tragedy that they have already encountered (tragic flaw of ambition, comic scene with porter, lively action with witches and murders). Explain that in Act 5 students will witness more action, but will also see the disaster to which Macbeth's actions have led.

EL Vocabulary for English Learners
Explain that Act 5 reveals the destruction to which Macbeth's actions have led. Review the vocabulary words, but be aware of words in stage directions (for example, *taper* means "candle") and dialogue that may be unfamiliar. For Scene 1, have students study Fuseli's painting for clues to the action.

Strategy for Advanced Readers
Have students discuss how the tragic elements in *Macbeth* are similar to other tragedies with which they are familiar. Ask them to list some common tragic flaws and the problems they created. From what they know of tragedy, ask them to predict what will happen in this act.

Relating a Work to the Issues of Its Period

1. Remind students that the play is set in Scotland in the eleventh century, but that it was written and performed in the seventeenth century.

2. **Ask** students the Reading Strategy question: What can you infer about medicine during this time from the doctor's words in lines 72–80?
   Answer: Students should note that the doctor recognizes that Lady Macbeth's illness stems not from physical suffering, but from emotional suffering. Realizing the depth of her emotional suffering, he admits that while he is unable to help her, perhaps God could. Students should remark that the doctor's willingness to call on divine aid represents a blending of religion and medicine that was characteristic of the time.

❿ Literary Analysis

Shakespearean Tragedy

1. Have students read the speech in lines 12–16 to themselves.

2. Ask them to think about madness, or insanity, and Macbeth's murderous acts.

3. Then **ask** students the Literary Analysis question: Do you agree with those whom Caithness quotes in line 13? Is Macbeth "mad"? Why or why not?
   Possible responses: Students who agree that Macbeth is mad should support their answers by pointing out that the theme of evil runs throughout the play, and that Macbeth has become evil and cannot redeem himself. His lack of restraint or human caring at this point might indicate madness. Those who say he is not mad might state that he is simply a man who has allowed his selfish ambition to rule his judgment, and he is suffering for the actions that resulted from his wrong decisions. They might say that it is a weakness of character, not madness, that drives his actions

---

70   What's done cannot be undone. To bed, to bed, to bed!

[*Exit* LADY MACBETH.]

DOCTOR. Will she go now to bed?

GENTLEWOMAN. Directly.

DOCTOR. Foul whisp'rings are abroad. Unnatural deeds
    Do breed unnatural troubles. Infected minds
    To their deaf pillows will discharge their secrets.
75   More needs she the divine than the physician.
    God, God forgive us all! Look after her;
    Remove from her the means of all annoyance,[13]
    And still keep eyes upon her. So good night.
    My mind she has mated[14] and amazed my sight:
80   I think, but dare not speak.

GENTLEWOMAN.   Good night, good doctor.

[*Exit.*]

Scene ii. The country near Dunsinane.

[*Drum and colors. Enter* MENTEITH, CAITHNESS, ANGUS, LENNOX, SOLDIERS.]

MENTEITH. The English pow'r[1] is near, led on by Malcolm,
    His uncle Siward and the good Macduff.
    Revenges burn in them; for their dear causes
    Would to the bleeding and the grim alarm
    Excite the mortified man.[2]

5   **ANGUS.**   Near Birnam Wood
    Shall we well meet them; that way are they coming.

CAITHNESS. Who knows if Donalbain be with his brother?

LENNOX. For certain, sir, he is not. I have a file[3]
    Of all the gentry: there is Siward's son,
10   And many unrough[4] youths that even now
    Protest[5] their first of manhood.

MENTEITH.   What does the tyrant?

CAITHNESS. Great Dunsinane he strongly fortifies.
    Some say he's mad; others, that lesser hate him,
    Do call it valiant fury: but, for certain,
15   He cannot buckle his distempered cause
    Within the belt of rule.[6]

ANGUS.   Now does he feel
    His secret murders sticking on his hands;
    Now minutely revolts upbraid his faith-breach.[7]
    Those he commands move only in command,
20   Nothing in love. Now does he feel his title

404 Celebrating Humanity (1485–1625)

Reading Strategy
Relating a Work to the Issues of Its Period
What can you infer about medicine during this time from the doctor's words in lines 72–80?

13. **annoyance** injury.

14. **mated** baffled.

1. **pow'r** army.

2. **Would . . . man** would incite a dead man to join the bloody, grim call to arms.

3. **file** list.

4. **unrough** beardless.

5. **Protest** assert.

Literary Analysis
Shakespearean Tragedy
Do you agree with those whom Caithness quotes in Scene ii, line 13? Is Macbeth "mad"? Why or why not?

6. **rule** self-control.

7. **minutely . . . faith-breach** every minute revolts rebuke his disloyalty.

Enrichment: Understanding Neurology

Sleepwalking

Sleepwalking, also known as somnambulism, is a sleep disorder in which people walk around or perform other actions normally associated with being awake while they are actually asleep.

Normal sleep consists of several stages, which occur in cycles throughout the night. Stage 1 sleep is a light sleep. During stage 2 sleep, brainwaves slow down. Stages 3 and 4 are deep sleep. Most sleepwalking occurs during these deep-sleep periods.

Activity: Investigating Health and Medicine
Have interested students conduct further investigation into the causes and treatments of sleepwalking. Students may want to compare the medical opinion of sleepwalking during Shakespeare's time with modern understandings of the disorder. Suggest that students record their analysis in the **Enrichment: Investigating Health and Medicine** worksheet *Professional Development Guidebook*, p. 229.

Hang loose about him, like a giant's robe
Upon a dwarfish thief.

MENTEITH.   Who then shall blame
His pestered[8] senses to recoil and start,
When all that is within him does condemn
Itself for being there?

25 CAITHNESS.   Well, march we on,
To give obedience where 'tis truly owed.
Meet we the med'cine of the sickly weal,[9]
And with him pour we, in our country's purge,
Each drop of us.[10]

LENNOX.   Or so much as it needs
30 To dew the sovereign flower and drown the weeds.[11]
Make we our march towards Birnam.

[*Exit, marching.*]

Scene iii. Dunsinane. In the castle.

[*Enter* MACBETH, DOCTOR, *and* ATTENDANTS.]

MACBETH. Bring me no more reports; let them fly all![1]
Till Birnam Wood remove to Dunsinane
I cannot taint[2] with fear. What's the boy Malcolm?
Was he not born of woman? The spirits that know
5 All mortal consequences[3] have pronounced me thus:
"Fear not, Macbeth; no man that's born of woman
Shall e'er have power upon thee." Then fly, false thanes,
And mingle with the English epicures.[4]
The mind I sway[5] by and the heart I bear
10 Shall never sag with doubt nor shake with fear.

[*Enter* SERVANT.]

The devil damn thee black, thou cream-faced loon.[6]
Where got'st thou that goose look?

SERVANT. There is ten thousand—

MACBETH.   Geese, villain?

SERVANT.   Soldiers, sir.

MACBETH. Go prick thy face and over-red thy fear.
15 Thou lily-livered boy. What soldiers, patch?[7]
Death of thy soul! Those linen[8] cheeks of thine
Are counselors to fear. What soldiers, whey-face?

SERVANT. The English force, so please you.

MACBETH. Take thy face hence.   [*Exit* SERVANT.]

Seyton!—I am sick at heart.

---

8. **pestered** tormented.

Vocabulary
recoil (ri koil´) *v.* to draw back in fear, surprise, or disgust

9. **med'cine . . . weal** Malcolm and his supporters are "the medicine" that will heal "the sickly" commonwealth.

10. **Each . . . us** every last drop of our blood.

11. **dew . . . weeds** water the royal flower (Malcolm) and drown the weeds (Macbeth).

1. **let . . . all** let them all desert me!

2. **taint** become infected.

3. **mortal consequences** future human events.

4. **epicures** gluttons.

5. **sway** move.

6. **loon** fool.

7. **patch** fool.

8. **linen** pale as linen.

12 Reading Check
Why is Macbeth unafraid even though Malcolm's army is marching against him?

Macbeth, Act V, Scene iii **405**

11 **Critical Thinking**
Analyze

1. Point out that this is Macbeth's first appearance since his meeting with the witches in Act 4.

2. **Ask** students what Macbeth's state of mind seems to be in Scene 3, lines 1–10.
Possible response: He seems almost defensive in his overconfidence; "let them fly all"—is like a child's defensive "who needs you anyway?" One can imagine him pacing, raging, repeating out loud the prophecies (except the one about Macduff), as if to reassure himself.

12 **Reading Check**
Answer: Macbeth believes that Malcolm was born of a woman, and the apparitions told him that he need not fear harm from any man born of woman.

Differentiated Instruction for Universal Access

Strategy for Less Proficient Readers
In Scene 2, the stage is being set for the final battle. Help students follow the plot by looking for words that indicate which side the Scottish nobles are on (*good Macduff, give obedience where 'tis truly owed*) and to understand that the battle is coming (mentions of army, blood, and marching).

Enrichment for Gifted/Talented Students
Have students read Act 5, Scene 1, independently. Then, have students work in groups of three to reenact Lady Macbeth's sleepwalking scene. To aid students in interpreting the emotion and delivery of the lines, have them listen to the *Hear It!* Audio CDs.

Enrichment for Advanced Readers
Have students examine the theme of madness as in Lady Macbeth's sleepwalking in Act 5, Scene 1, and Macbeth's condition, as explored in Act 5, Scene 2. Have them address whether or not they think Macbeth and Lady Macbeth are truly mad, and how their actions contributed to bringing about their conditions.

405

Literary Analysis

13 **Literary Analysis**

Shakespearean Tragedy

1. **Ask** students the Literary Analysis question: Do lines 20–28 evoke sympathy for Macbeth? Explain.
Answer: Shakespeare seems to be trying to evoke sympathy for Macbeth at this point. As the possibility of death approaches, Macbeth experiences a moment of truth when the consequences of his actions become clear to him. He knows that life could bring no joy to him now and, in weariness, he makes his peace with the thought of dying.

14 **Reading Strategy**

Relating a Work to the Issues of Its Period

1. Explain to students that medicine, like most sciences, was in its infancy in Shakespeare's time, though it was gaining ground rapidly. Major side effects of the Reformation were a belief in the rational, the invention of the scientific method, and an explosion of experimentation and research.

2. Point out that today, we are rediscovering the close connection between mind and body and the influence of emotions on health.

3. Have students complete the **Reading Strategy Graphic Organizer** as they reread the doctor's words in Scene 3.

4. **Ask** students the Reading Strategy question: Would a modern psychiatrist answer as the doctor does in lines 45–46? Why or why not?
Possible response: Students may respond that, yes, a modern psychiatrist would recognize that Lady Macbeth's distress was caused by mental anguish, not physical illness. Even modern psychoanalysis is largely concerned with leading patients into healing themselves.

---

9. **push** effort.
10. **disseat** unthrone.

11. **the sear** withered state.

Literary Analysis
Shakespearean Tragedy
Do lines 20–28 evoke sympathy for Macbeth? Explain.

12. **moe** more.
13. **skirr** scour.

Reading Strategy
Relating a Work to the Issues of Its Period
Would a modern psychiatrist answer as the doctor does in lines 45–46? Why or why not?

14. **Raze out** erase.

Vocabulary
antidote (an´ tə dōt´)
n. remedy

---

20 When I behold—Seyton, I say!—This push[9]
Will cheer me ever, or disseat[10] me now.
I have lived long enough. My way of life
Is fall'n into the sear,[11] the yellow leaf,
And that which should accompany old age,
25 As honor, love, obedience, troops of friends,
I must not look to have; but, in their stead,
Curses not loud but deep, mouth-honor, breath,
Which the poor heart would fain deny, and dare not.
Seyton!

[*Enter* SEYTON.]

SEYTON. What's your gracious pleasure?

30 MACBETH. What news more?

SEYTON. All is confirmed, my lord, which was reported.

MACBETH. I'll fight, till from my bones my flesh be hacked.
Give me my armor.

SEYTON. 'Tis not needed yet.

MACBETH. I'll put it on.
35 Send out moe[12] horses, skirr[13] the country round.
Hang those that talk of fear. Give me mine armor.
How does your patient, doctor?

DOCTOR. Not so sick, my lord,
As she is troubled with thick-coming fancies
That keep her from her rest.

MACBETH. Cure her of that.
40 Canst thou not minister to a mind diseased,
Pluck from the memory a rooted sorrow,
Raze out[14] the written troubles of the brain,
And with some sweet oblivious antidote
Cleanse the stuffed bosom of that perilous stuff
Which weighs upon the heart?

Enrichment: Understanding Literature

Quotable Shakespeare

Only the Bible has been the source of more titles, quotes, and allusions than Shakespeare.

Titles have been lifted from the text throughout the play, such as Steinbeck's *The Moon is Down* (2, 1), but the famous speech in Act 5, Scene 5, lines 17–28 has been the richest source of titles, from Robert Frost's poem "Out, Out—" to William Faulkner's novel *The Sound and the Fury*. In fact, almost every line of this speech has been used at least once for the title of some work: *Tomorrow and Tomorrow and Tomorrow, This Petty Pace, All Our Yesterdays,* *The Way to Dusty Death, Brief Candle, Walking Shadow, A Poor Player.*

Activity: Analyzing a Literary Figure Have students conduct further research into the author of one of the literary works mentioned above. Students should pay special attention to why the author chose to title his or her work with a Shakespearean quote. Have students record their analysis in the **Enrichment: Investigating a Literary Figure** worksheet, p. 235 *Professional Development Guidebook.*

406

14 45 **DOCTOR.**   Therein the patient
Must minister to himself.

MACBETH. Throw physic[15] to the dogs, I'll none of it.
Come, put mine armor on. Give me my staff.
Seyton, send out.—Doctor, the thanes fly from me.—
50 Come, sir, dispatch. If thou couldst, doctor, cast
15 The water[16] of my land, find her disease
And purge it to a sound and pristine health,
I would applaud thee to the very echo,
That should applaud again.—Pull 't off,[17] I say.—
55 What rhubarb, senna, or what purgative drug,
Would scour these English hence? Hear'st thou of them?

DOCTOR. Ay, my good lord; your royal preparation
Makes us hear something.

MACBETH.   Bring it[18] after me.
I will not be afraid of death and bane[19]
60 Till Birnam Forest come to Dunsinane.

DOCTOR. [*Aside*] Were I from Dunsinane away and clear,
Profit again should hardly draw me here.   [*Exit.*]

Scene iv. Country near Birnam Wood.

[*Drum and colors. Enter* MALCOLM, SIWARD, MACDUFF, SIWARD'S SON,
MENTEITH, CAITHNESS, ANGUS, *and* SOLDIERS, *marching.*]

MALCOLM. Cousins, I hope the days are near at hand
That chambers will be safe.[1]

MENTEITH.   We doubt it nothing.

SIWARD. What wood is this before us?

MENTEITH.   The Wood of Birnam.

MALCOLM. Let every soldier hew him down a bough
16 5 And bear 't before him. Thereby shall we shadow[2]
The numbers of our host, and make discovery[3]
Err in report of us.

SOLDIERS.   It shall be done.

SIWARD. We learn no other but the confident tyrant
Keeps still in Dunsinane, and will endure
Our setting down before 't.[4]

10 **MALCOLM.**   'Tis his main hope,
For where there is advantage to be given
Both more and less[5] have given him the revolt,
And none serve with him but constrained things
Whose hearts are absent too.

---

15. **physic** medicine.

16. **cast the water** diagnose
the illness.

Vocabulary
pristine (pris´ tēn´) *adj.*
original; unspoiled

17. **Pull 't off** Pull off a
piece of armor, which has
been put on incorrectly in
Macbeth's haste.

18. **it** his armor.

19. **bane** destruction.

Literary Analysis
Shakespearean Tragedy
How does Malcolm's
order in Scene iv, lines 4–7
increase the sense of
tension surrounding
the play's outcome and
Macbeth's fate?

1. **That . . . safe** that people
will be safe in their own
homes.

2. **shadow** conceal.

3. **discovery** those who
see us.

4. **setting down before 't**
laying seige to it.

5. **more and less** people of
high and low rank.

17 ☑ Reading
Check
How will Malcolm's men
disguise themselves?

Macbeth, Act V, Scene iv **407**

---

15 **Critical Thinking**
Analyze
1. Point out that Macbeth is talking to more than one person at a
time. In performance, he would
likely be turning, or at least facing, in different directions as he
talks to Seyton, then the doctor,
and then dons his armor.

2. **Ask** students to describe
Macbeth's mental state as he
speaks lines 47–56.
Possible response: Students will
probably say that Macbeth is very
emotional, weighed down by his
wife's illness and the approaching
battle. This mood is shown in his
outbursts and in his impatience.

3. Point out that the idea of the sick
country reemerges in this passage, with Macbeth asking the
doctor how he can cure Scotland
of her illness and purge it of the
English. Explain that rhubarb and
senna were (and still are) commonly used as laxatives.

16 **Literary Analysis**
Shakespearean Tragedy
1. **Ask** students to explain why
Malcolm has suggested the strategy found in lines 4–7.
Answer: Carrying branches
would disguise the number of
soldiers. Malcolm may hope to
approach the castle without
having Macbeth consider
escaping.

2. **Ask** students to recall the prophecy made in Act 4 by the apparition of the child holding a tree.
Answer: The apparition said
that Macbeth should be brave,
because he would not be vanquished until Birnam Wood came
to Dunsinane.

3. **Ask** the Literary Analysis question: How does Malcolm's order
in lines 4–7 increase the tension
surrounding the play's outcome
and Macbeth's fate?
Possible response: The soldiers
carrying boughs would look like
moving trees. Macbeth, seeing
them, would begin to fear that he
was misled by the prophecy.

17 **Reading Check**
Answer: Answer: Malcolm's
men will disguise themselves with
branches of trees from the Wood of
Birnam.

407

Sieges

Macbeth's attitude in Scene 5, lines 1–7, was not bravado—he had reason to believe Dunsinane might withstand attack. Battles were as hard on attackers as on the attacked. It was easier to fight from the castle than to approach unprotected. Poor hygiene, inadequate supplies, and exposure to the elements often seriously diminished the ranks of the besiegers. Also, normally hostile groups that joined together for battle, such as the English and Scottish, sometimes fell to fighting among themselves.

19 Literature in Context

History Connection

Macbeth's claim to the crown was probably stronger than Duncan's. Macbeth was the grandson of Scottish king Kenneth II, and Lady Macbeth (Gruoch) was the granddaughter of Kenneth III.

Duncan's grandfather, Malcolm II, became king after he killed Kenneth III. He wanted to make sure that Duncan became king, so he tried to kill rival claimants. However, Macbeth survived.

Many other references in the play are loosely connected to real people, places, and events. Macbeth vanquished a rebel army near Birnam Wood. Siward, Earl of Northumbria, unsuccessfully attempted to dethrone Macbeth in favor of Malcolm in 1046. Macbeth was eventually killed in battle against Malcolm, who was aided by the English.

Connect to the Literature

1. Remind students that Shakespeare often departed from historical fact to heighten the drama of his plays.

2. Then **ask** the Connect to the Literature question: Use this history of the real Macbeth to predict the end of the play.
   Answer: Students may predict that Macbeth will die in battle.

---

6. **our . . . event** true judgment await the actual outcome.

7. **owe** own.

8. **strokes . . . arbitrate** fighting must decide.

9. **war** army.

MACDUFF.   Let our just censures
15   Attend the true event,[6] and put we on
      Industrious soldiership.

SIWARD.   The time approaches,
      That will with due decision make us know
      What we shall say we have and what we owe.[7]
      Thoughts speculative their unsure hopes relate,
20   But certain issue strokes must arbitrate:[8]
      Towards which advance the war.[9]   [*Exit, marching.*]

Scene v. Dunsinane. Within the castle.

[*Enter* MACBETH, SEYTON, *and* SOLDIERS, *with drum and colors.*]

18

1. **ague** fever.

2. **forced** reinforced.

3. **dareful** boldly.

MACBETH. Hang out our banners on the outward walls.
      The cry is still "They come!" Our castle's strength
      Will laugh a siege to scorn. Here let them lie
      Till famine and the ague[1] eat them up.
5   Were they not forced[2] with those that should be ours,
      We might have met them dareful,[3] beard to beard,
      And beat them backward home.

      [*A cry within of women.*]

                                      What is that noise?

SEYTON. It is the cry of women, my good lord.   [*Exit.*]

4. **fell** scalp.

5. **treatise** story.

MACBETH. I have almost forgot the taste of fears:
10   The time has been, my senses would have cooled
      To hear a night-shriek, and my fell[4] of hair
      Would at a dismal treatise[5] rouse and stir

---

19 LITERATURE IN CONTEXT

History Connection

The Real Macbeth

The real Macbeth, who ruled Scotland from 1040 to 1057, did, in fact, become king by killing King Duncan. However, Macbeth's claim to the throne was legitimate due to the ancient Scottish custom of tanistry.

According to this system, the ablest, oldest male in an extended royal family could declare war on his competitors for the crown. The real Macbeth declared war on King Duncan and killed him fairly in battle. Eventually, Duncan's son Malcolm led a Northumbrian invasion force into Scotland. In 1057, he killed Macbeth.

Connect to the Literature

Use this history of the real Macbeth to predict the end of the play.

THE TRAGEDIE OF MACBETH.

Enrichment: Understanding Elizabethan Theater

Swordplay on the Elizabethan Stage

As soldiers were assembled and battle became imminent, the Elizabethan audience would prepare for an exciting flurry of swordplay. Londoners of Shakespeare's time were connoisseurs of the art of fencing and would have been disappointed to see any half-hearted duel.

Some Elizabethan actors became so skillful at fencing that they won awards for it. Richard Tarleton, for example, a theater star of the 1580s, was made Master of Fence. As the highest degree offered by fencing schools, this designation was akin to today's black belt in karate.

Activity: Investigating Career Connections
Students who are interested in the performing arts may want to investigate one of the behind-the-scenes careers associated with professional theater, such as makeup artist, costume design, set design, or even carpentry. Suggest that students record their analysis in the **Enrichment: Investigating Career Connections** worksheet of the *Professional Development Guidebook,* p. 221.

As life were in 't. I have supped full with horrors.
Direness, familiar to my slaughterous thoughts,
Cannot once start[6] me.

[*Enter* SEYTON.]

15   Wherefore was that cry?

SEYTON. The queen, my lord, is dead.

MACBETH. She should[7] have died hereafter;
      There would have been a time for such a word.[8]
20   Tomorrow, and tomorrow, and tomorrow
      Creeps in this petty pace from day to day,
      To the last syllable of recorded time;
      And all our yesterdays have lighted fools
      The way to dusty death. Out, out, brief candle!
25   Life's but a walking shadow, a poor player
      That struts and frets his hour upon the stage
      And then is heard no more. It is a tale
      Told by an idiot, full of sound and fury
      Signifying nothing.

[*Enter a* MESSENGER.]

      Thou com'st to use thy tongue; thy story quickly!

30 **MESSENGER.** Gracious my lord,
      I should report that which I say I saw,
      But know not how to do 't.

      MACBETH.   Well, say, sir.

      MESSENGER. As I did stand my watch upon the hill,
      I looked toward Birnam, and anon, methought,
      The wood began to move.

35 **MACBETH.**   Liar and slave!

      MESSENGER. Let me endure your wrath, if 't be not so.
      Within this three mile may you see it coming;
      I say a moving grove.

      MACBETH.   If thou speak'st false,
      Upon the next tree shalt thou hang alive,
40   Till famine cling[9] thee. If thy speech be sooth,[10]
      I care not if thou dost for me as much.
      I pull in resolution, and begin
      To doubt th' equivocation of the fiend
      That lies like truth: "Fear not, till Birnam Wood
45   Do come to Dunsinane!" And now a wood
      Comes toward Dunsinane. Arm, arm, and out!
      If this which he avouches[11] does appear,
      There is nor flying hence nor tarrying here.

6. **start** startle.

7. **should** inevitably would.

8. **word** message.

Literary Analysis
Shakespearean Tragedy and the Tragic Impulse
This speech in lines 17–28 is a powerful expression of life's futility. Is Macbeth's story really "a tale/Told by an idiot, full of sound and fury/Signifying nothing"? Why or why not?

Literary Analysis
Shakespearean Tragedy
In lines 42–50, how does Macbeth's allusion to the witches' prophecies disclose a growing awareness of his own doom?

9. **cling** wither.

10. **sooth** truth.

11. **avouches** asserts.

22 ✓ Reading Check

To what two things does Macbeth compare life when he hears Lady Macbeth is dead?

Macbeth, Act V, Scene v **409**

---

20 Literary Analysis
Shakespearean Tragedy and the Tragic Impulse

1. **Ask** students to explain the "tragic impulse" as it was described on page 400. **Answer:** The tragic impulse shows a tragic hero confronting his or her limits in a noble way.

2. Then **ask** students the first Literary Analysis question: Is Macbeth's story really "a tale/ Told by an idiot, full of sound and fury/Signifying nothing"? Why or why not?
   Possible responses: Students who agree may note that Macbeth said in Scene 3 that he lacked most things worth having, and now he has lost his wife. His life has come to nothing. Those who disagree may say that Macbeth's life gains meaning by serving as a warning to others.

▶ **Reteach:** If students have difficulty answering, **ask** them how the speech in lines 17–28 shows Macbeth's "tragic impulse." **Possible response:** Students may think that Macbeth is nobly confronting the limit of his own mortality and powerlessness.

21 Literary Analysis
Shakespearean Tragedy

1. Tell students that *equivocation* in line 43 refers to the ambiguous language of the prophecy.

2. Then **ask** them the second Literary Analysis question: In lines 42–50, how does Macbeth's allusion to the witches' prophecies disclose a growing awareness of his own doom?
   Answer: Macbeth realizes that the promise of the third apparition has misled him. Now Birnam Wood is moving, which means Macbeth might be vulnerable.

22 Reading Check

Answer: Macbeth compares life to an actor and a senseless story.

Differentiated Instruction   for Universal Access

Enrichment for Gifted/Talented Students
Have students choose a favorite medium in which to interpret all or part of Scenes 4–8 from Act 5 of *Macbeth*. They may choose collage, painting, dramatic reading, mime, interpretive dance, puppets, song, theatrical presentation, videotape, or another medium in which to demonstrate the ideas, events, or emotions of these highly charged scenes. Have students share their interpretations with the class.

Enrichment for Advanced Readers
While inferring beliefs of the period is an excellent reading strategy, studying a period's beliefs can often add depth and richness to reading. Have students pick some aspect of life in Shakespeare's time to research and then show how it appears in Shakespeare's play. Aspects might include exploding interest in everything from medicine to classical literature, the impact of the Reformation and new Bible translations, relations between England and Scotland, the reign of James I, sports, entertainment, or ideas of honor.

㉓ Critical Viewing

Possible response: It appears that this is Macbeth and Macduff. The men look as if they are arguing, but are reluctant to fight. The fight between Macbeth and Young Siward is more fighting than talking.

㉔ Critical Thinking

Analyze

1. Have students think back to the Critical Commentary by Ian Johnston. Remind them that one of the reasons Johnston says Macbeth is a compelling character is his awareness of what is happening within his own mind, and his determination to see his actions through to the end.

2. **Ask** students how Macbeth's words in lines 49–52 show this awareness and determination. **Possible response:** Macbeth has just realized that the witches' words may have more than one interpretation. In these lines, he shows signs of weariness and regret for the choices that have set him on this path. Yet, even as he realizes his danger, he determines that if he is to die, at least he will die in battle.

㉓ ▶ Critical Viewing
Do you think this picture portrays the fight between Macbeth and Young Siward (V, vii, 10–11) or that between Macbeth and Macduff (V, viii, 34–35)? Explain. **[Make a Judgment]**

㉔
50
> I 'gin to be aweary of the sun,
> And wish th' estate o' th' world were now undone.
> Ring the alarum bell! Blow wind, come wrack!
> At least we'll die with harness[12] on our back.　　　　　*[Exit.]*

12. **harness** armor.

Scene vi. Dunsinane. Before the castle.

[Drum and colors. Enter MALCOLM, SIWARD, MACDUFF, *and their army, with boughs.]*

MALCOLM. Now near enough. Your leavy[1] screens throw down,
　　And show like those you are. You, worthy uncle,
　　Shall, with my cousin, your right noble son,
　　Lead our first battle.[2] Worthy Macduff and we
5　Shall take upon 's what else remains to do,
　　According to our order.[3]

1. **leavy** leafy.

2. **battle** battalion.

3. **order** plan.

SIWARD.　　　　　　　　　　　Fare you well.
　　Do we find the tyrant's power[4] tonight,
　　Let us be beaten, if we cannot fight.

4. **power** forces.

MACDUFF. Make all our trumpets speak; give them all breath.
10　Those clamorous harbingers of blood and death.

　　　　　　　　　　　　　　　　　[Exit. Alarums continued.]

Vocabulary
clamorous (klam′ ər əs) *adj.* noisy

harbingers (här′ bin jərz) *n.* forerunners

410 Celebrating Humanity (1485–1625)

Enrichment: Understanding Social Context

Bearbaiting

In Scene 7, lines 1–2, Macbeth compares himself to a bear tied to a stake. This metaphor refers to bearbaiting, a form of entertainment popular from the twelfth to the nineteenth century. Bullbaiting was also popular. In these "sports," a bear or bull was chained to a stake by the neck or a leg. The animal was then attacked by specially trained dogs. In fact, the breed of dog we call the bulldog was developed especially for bullbaiting.

　The metaphor shows that Macbeth, for all his bravery, realizes he has little chance of surviving.

Activity: Investigating Popular Culture The entertainment value of bearbaiting may seem strange or barbaric to students. Encourage interested students to investigate Elizabethan society by looking at its entertainment and compare it with modern forms such as professional sports. Suggest that they record the analysis in the **Enrichment: Investigating Popular Culture** worksheet *Professional Development Guidebook,* p. 238.

Scene vii. Another part of the field.

[*Enter* MACBETH.]

MACBETH. They have tied me to a stake; I cannot fly,
But bearlike I must fight the course.[1] What's he
That was not born of woman? Such a one
Am I to fear, or none.

[*Enter* YOUNG SIWARD.]

YOUNG SIWARD. What is thy name?

5 **MACBETH.**   Thou'lt be afraid to hear it.

YOUNG SIWARD. No; though thou call'st thyself a hotter name
Than any is in hell.

MACBETH.   My name's Macbeth.

YOUNG SIWARD. The devil himself could not pronounce a title
More hateful to mine ear.

MACBETH.   No, nor more fearful.

10 **YOUNG SIWARD.** Thou liest, abhorrèd tyrant; with my sword
I'll prove the lie thou speak'st.

          [*Fight, and* YOUNG SIWARD *slain.*]

MACBETH.   Thou wast born of woman.
But swords I smile at, weapons laugh to scorn,
Brandished by man that's of a woman born.   [*Exit.*]

[*Alarums. Enter* MACDUFF.]

MACDUFF. That way the noise is. Tyrant, show thy face!
15 If thou be'st slain and with no stroke of mine,
My wife and children's ghosts will haunt me still.
I cannot strike at wretched kerns, whose arms
Are hired to bear their staves.[2] Either thou, Macbeth,
Or else my sword, with an unbattered edge,
20 I sheathe again undeeded.[3] There thou shouldst be;
By this great clatter, one of greatest note
Seems bruited.[4] Let me find him, Fortune!
And more I beg not.   [*Exit. Alarums.*]

[*Enter* MALCOLM *and* SIWARD.]

SIWARD. This way, my lord. The castle's gently rend'red:[5]
25 The tyrant's people on both sides do fight;
The noble thanes do bravely in the war;
The day almost itself professes yours,
And little is to do.

MALCOLM.   We have met with foes
That strike beside us.[6]

1. **bearlike . . . course** like a bear chained to a stake being attacked by dogs, I must fight until the end.

Literary Analysis
Shakespearean Tragedy
In Scene vii, does Macbeth show signs of bravery or is he just overconfident because of what the witches said? Explain.

2. **staves** spears.

3. **undeeded** unused.

4. **bruited** reported.

5. **gently rend'red** easily surrendered.

6. **strike . . . us** deliberately miss us.

27 ☑ Reading Check
What is the outcome of the hand-to-hand combat between Macbeth and Young Siward?

Macbeth, Act V, Scene vii **411**

25 Literary Analysis
Shakespearean Tragedy
1. Remind students that the prophecy of the second apparition was that no man born of woman can harm Macbeth.

2. Then **ask** the Literary Analysis question: In Scene 7, does Macbeth show signs of bravery or is he just overconfident because of what the witches said?
Possible responses: Students who say Macbeth is showing bravery should note the fact that Shakespeare has left him some of the admirable traits he had in the beginning in order to evoke pity in the audience. Students who say he is simply overconfident should explain that he is overcompensating for the fact that he already knows the truth: he was misled by the prophecies, and there is really no hope left for him.

3. Explain that *kerns,* mentioned in line 17, were hired Irish foot soldiers. The fact that Macbeth's troops are hired underscores the fact that Macbeth is alone.

26 Critical Thinking
Make a Judgment
1. **Ask** if students find it surprising that Macbeth so easily defeats Young Siward. Why or why not?
Possible responses: Students may cite the battles at the beginning of the play as proof of Macbeth's skill as a fighter and proof that he was brave even before he heard from the witches. They may say that now, with almost nothing left to lose, he would be a deadly opponent.

2. **Ask** students why Macbeth still seems to be clinging to the last remaining hope of the witches' promises (lines 11–13).
Possible responses: It may be all he has left to hold onto. He may see his victory over Young Siward as a confirmation of it. He may not really believe it, but may just say it out of habit. It may simply be a plot device, to prepare us for a surprise at the end.

27 Reading Check
Answer: Macbeth kills Young Siward.

Differentiated Instruction *for Universal Access*

Support for Less Proficient Readers
The action of the final battle may prove confusing for students. To clarify the sequence of events, have them make an outline of what happens in Act 5. Students may want to use a three-column chart to list each scene, what happens in that scene, and what characters are present.

Enrichment for Gifted/Talented Students
Point out to students that, on stage, the final battle sequence of the play would be loud, chaotic, and full of action. Set on the field of battle, with alarums (the call to arms of trumpets), clanging swords, and yelling. Have students work in groups to provide the class with a dramatic reading of these scenes, complete with sound effects.

Interpret

1. Point out that when Macduff first heard of his family's death, he called Macbeth a hell-kite (hellish bird of prey), and now, in line 3, he calls him a hell-hound (hounds were used for hunting). Both reflect the evil and bloody image created for Macbeth in this play.

2. **Ask** students why they believe Macbeth has been avoiding Macduff.
   Possible responses: Some may say that it is because of the warning of the first apparition: "Beware Macduff." Others may note that Macbeth says it is because he feels he has shed too much Macduff blood already.

3. **Ask** students whether Macbeth's comments about being "too much charged with blood" show sorrow or fear.
   Possible responses: Some may cite Macbeth's new awareness of the shortness of life and sorrow over the death of his own wife as reasons he would be sad. Others may say that he worries about Macduff's vengeful rage.

4. **Ask** students to explain the significance of Macduff's comments in lines 13–16.
   Answer: Macbeth's last hope is destroyed by this revelation. Because Macduff's mother died, he was delivered by the equivalent of a caesarean section. Hence, faith in an apparition's promise has again misled Macbeth.

---

1. **play . . . sword** die like Brutus or Cassius, who killed themselves with their own swords in the moment of defeat.

2. **Whiles . . . lives** so long as I see living men.

3. **terms . . . out** words can describe you.

4. **intrenchant** incapable of being cut.

5. **impress** make a dent in.

28

Vocabulary
vulnerable (vul′ nər ə bəl) *adj.* exposed to attack or harm

6. **angel** fallen angel; fiend.

7. **his . . . ripped** Macduff's mother died before giving birth to him.

8. **better . . . man** courage.

9. **palter** juggle.

10. **gaze o' th' time** spectacle of the age.

11. **monsters** freaks.

12. **Painted . . . pole** pictured on a banner stuck on a pole by a showman's booth.

SIWARD.   Enter, sir, the castle.

                           [*Exit. Alarum.*]

Scene viii. Another part of the field.

[*Enter* MACBETH.]

MACBETH. Why should I play the Roman fool, and die
On mine own sword?[1] Whiles I see lives,[2] the gashes
Do better upon them.

[*Enter* MACDUFF.]

MACDUFF.   Turn, hell-hound, turn!

MACBETH. Of all men else I have avoided thee.
5   But get thee back! My soul is too much charged
With blood of thine already.

MACDUFF.   I have no words:
My voice is in my sword, thou bloodier villain
Than terms can give thee out![3]

[*Fight. Alarum.*]

MACBETH.   Thou losest labor:
As easy mayst thou the intrenchant[4] air
10   With thy keen sword impress[5] as make me bleed:
Let fall thy blade on vulnerable crests;
I bear a charmèd life, which must not yield
To one of woman born.

MACDUFF.   Despair thy charm,
And let the angel[6] whom thou still hast served
15   Tell thee, Macduff was from his mother's womb
Untimely ripped.[7]

MACBETH. Accursèd be that tongue that tells me so,
For it hath cowed my better part of man![8]
And be these juggling fiends no more believed,
20   That palter[9] with us in a double sense;
That keep the word of promise to our ear,
And break it to our hope. I'll not fight with thee.

MACDUFF. Then yield thee, coward,
And live to be the show and gaze o' th' time:[10]
25   We'll have thee, as our rarer monsters[11] are,
Painted upon a pole,[12] and underwrit,
"Here may you see the tyrant."

MACBETH.   I will not yield,
To kiss the ground before young Malcolm's feet,
And to be baited with the rabble's curse.
30   Though Birnam Wood be come to Dunsinane,

412 Celebrating Humanity (1485–1625)

Enrichment: Understanding Political Context

Malcolm's Reign

As the play closes, Duncan's son Malcolm takes the throne of Scotland. In reality, Malcolm Canmore did become king in 1057, seventeen years after Duncan's death. He reigned as Malcolm III for thirty-five years.

Malcolm had been protected during exile by Edward the Confessor and was later able to return the favor to England. After England was defeated in the Battle of Hastings in 1066 by William of Normandy, the grandchildren of Edmund Ironside, half-brother to Edward

the Confessor, fled in exile to Scotland to be protected by Malcolm. Queen Elizabeth II is descended from this line.

Activity: Investigating a Key Person in History Many of the political figures mentioned above may be unfamiliar to students. Encourage students to conduct further research into the life of one of these people. Suggest they record the analysis in **Enrichment: Investigating a Key Person in History** worksheet *Professional Development Guidebook*, p. 233.

And thou opposed, being of no woman born,
Yet I will try the last. Before my body
I throw my warlike shield. Lay on, Macduff;
And damned be him that first cries "Hold, enough!"

[*Exit, fighting. Alarums.*]

[*Re-enter fighting, and* MACBETH *slain. Exit* MACDUFF, *with* MACBETH.
Retreat and flourish.[13] *Enter, with drum and colors,*
MALCOLM, SIWARD, ROSS, THANES, *and* SOLDIERS.]

35 **MALCOLM.** I would the friends we miss were safe arrived.

SIWARD. Some must go off;[14] and yet, by these I see,
So great a day as this is cheaply bought.

MALCOLM. Macduff is missing, and your noble son.

ROSS. Your son, my lord, has paid a soldier's debt:
40 He only lived but till he was a man;
The which no sooner had his prowess confirmed
In the unshrinking station[15] where he fought,
But like a man he died.

SIWARD.   Then he is dead?

ROSS. Ay, and brought off the field. Your cause of sorrow
45 Must not be measured by his worth, for then
It hath no end.

SIWARD.   Had he his hurts before?

ROSS. Ay, on the front.

SIWARD.   Why then, God's soldier be he!
Had I as many sons as I have hairs,
I would not wish them to a fairer death:
And so his knell is knolled.

50 **MALCOLM.**   He's worth more sorrow,
And that I'll spend for him.

SIWARD.   He's worth no more:
They say he parted well and paid his score:
And so God be with him! Here comes newer comfort.

[*Enter* MACDUFF, *with* MACBETH'S *head.*]

MACDUFF. Hail, King! for so thou art: behold, where stands
55 Th' usurper's cursèd head. The time is free.[16]
I see thee compassed with thy kingdom's pearl,[17]
That speak my salutation in their minds,
Whose voices I desire aloud with mine:
Hail, King of Scotland!

ALL.   Hail, King of Scotland!

[*Flourish.*]

---

13. *Retreat and flourish* trumpet call to withdraw and fanfare.

14. go off die.

15. unshrinking station place where he stood firmly.

Reading Strategy
Relating a Work to the Issues of Its Period
What does Siward's reaction to the death of his son reveal about the values of patriotism and honor at this time (lines 47–53)?

16. The . . . free Our country is liberated.

17. compassed . . . pearl surrounded by the noblest people in the kingdom.

30 Reading Check
Who finally slays Macbeth?

Macbeth, Act V, Scene viii **413**

---

29 **Reading Strategy**
Relating a Work to the Issues of Its Period

1. Have students review lines 39–53.
2. **Ask** students to answer the Reading Strategy question: What does Siward's reaction to the death of his son reveal about the values of patriotism and honor at this time?
   Answer: To die fighting for a good cause was one of the highest honors that a young man could attain.
3. Remind students that manhood has been a theme throughout the play. **Ask** them to consider how the view of manhood here compares with some of the other images of manliness in the play, and how they relate to the idea of manhood in this period.
   Possible responses: Lady Macbeth urges Macbeth to action by saying that a real man just takes what he wants. Macbeth encourages Banquo's murderers by telling them that to kill to redress hardship is manly. Because both of these characters are "bad guys," we know that these images do not reflect the period's understanding of manhood. Then, at the death of his family, there is a discussion of Macduff's showing sorrow like a man, and then avenging their deaths. Here, the idea of tenderness, love, and honor are associated with being a man. Because Macduff is a "good guy," this would be more likely to reflect the period's beliefs.
4. Point out that, at the beginning of the play (Act 1, Scene 4, lines 3–8), the traitorous Cawdor was commended for dying well. Before being executed, he confessed his treasons and repented of his actions.
   Ask students how this compares with Macbeth's end.
   Answer: Macbeth would not surrender, refused to serve Malcolm (lines 27–28), and went out cursing. Hence, Macbeth's death would not receive commendation, because it was without honor.

30 **Reading Check**
Answer: Macduff slays Macbeth.

Differentiated Instruction for Universal Access

Strategy for Less Proficient Readers
Explain to students that Shakespeare often includes characters that contrast in obvious ways with his main characters. In Act 5 of *Macbeth,* there is a clear distinction between the virtuous Macduff and the villainous Macbeth. Even Young Siward is introduced to show us how far Macbeth has fallen from his noble beginnings. Have students choose a character from the play and write a short paragraph comparing and contrasting this character with Macbeth.

Strategy for Advanced Learners
Explain to students that the relationship of father to son is one of the driving forces behind the plot of *Macbeth.* Invite students to identify the father/son pairs in *Macbeth,* then discuss how the plot is affected by these relationships. How would the play be different if Macbeth had an heir, if Duncan or Banquo did not, if Macbeth had not killed Macduff's son, or if Fleance had not escaped?

413

Whole-Class Activity

1. Ask students to describe the scenes from Macbeth in the poster.
   Possible response: The first scene shows Macbeth's encounter with the witches; the middle scene shows Macbeth and Lady Macbeth after the murder of Duncan; the bottom left shows Macbeth seeng the ghost of Banquo at the banquet; the bottom right shows a sword fight between Macbeth and Young Siward or between MacDuff and Macbeth; the central image is the actor Thomas Keene as Macbeth.

2. Ask students whether the images from the poster capture the dramatic action of the play and would motivate them to see Thomas Keene perform Macbeth.
   Possible response: Yes, the images capture the atmosphere and action of Macbeth and would motivate people to attend the performance.

Small-Group Activity

1. Divide students into small groups. Tell students to discuss the images shown in the poster. Have them relate the scenes shown to their reading and write descriptive captions for each scene.

2. Ask one group to summarize the group's ideas.

3. Record students' ideas on the board.

Individual Activity

1. As a class briefly discuss the poster images.

2. Ask students to illustrate a scene not shown in the poster that they found especially compelling. Have them include a relevant quotation and description of the action.

3. Allow students to proofread and revise their posters in class or as homework.

4. Post the student-made posters around the classroom and invite students to discuss their work.

414 Celebrating Humanity (1485–1625)

Vocabulary Development

Vocabulary Knowledge Rating
When students have completed reading and discussing the selections, have them take out the **Vocabulary Knowledge Rating Charts** they worked on earlier. Read the words aloud and have students rate their knowledge of the words again in the After Reading column. Clarify any words that are still problematic. Have students write their own definitions and example or sentence in the appropriate column. Then, have students complete the Vocabulary lesson at the end of this selection. Encourage students to use the words in further discussion and written work about the selections. Remind them that they will be accountable for these words on the **Selection Test**, *Unit 2 Resources,* pages 179–181 or 182–184.

MALCOLM. We shall not spend a large expense of time
60 Before we reckon with your several loves,[18]
   And make us even with you.[19] My thanes and kinsmen,
   Henceforth be earls, the first that ever Scotland
   In such an honor named. What's more to do,
65 Which would be planted newly with the time[20]—
   As calling home our exiled friends abroad
   That fled the snares of watchful tyranny,
   Producing forth the cruel ministers
   Of this dead butcher and his fiendlike queen,
70 Who, as 'tis thought, by self and violent hands
   Took off her life—this, and what needful else
   That calls upon us, by the grace of Grace
   We will perform in measure, time, and place:[21]
   So thanks to all at once and to each one,
75 Whom we invite to see us crowned at Scone.

[Flourish. Exit all.]

18. **reckon . . . loves** reward each of you for your devotion.

19. **make . . . you** pay what we owe you.

20. **What's . . . time** what remains to be done at the beginning of this new age.

21. **in measure . . . place** fittingly at the appropriate time and place.

32 ◀ **Critical Viewing**
Based on the scenes shown in the poster, summarize the play. **[Summarize]**

Critical Reading

1. **Key Ideas and Details (a)** What does the doctor see in the sleepwalking scene, and what does he speculate about the causes for what he sees? **(b) Analyze:** How have Macbeth and Lady Macbeth reversed roles by the end of the play?

2. **Key Ideas and Details (a)** What does Macbeth say when he hears of Lady Macbeth's death? **(b) Draw Conclusions:** What does his reaction to her death reveal about their relationship and his state of mind?

3. **Key Ideas and Details (a)** What does Macbeth say about the witches when he learns that Birnam Wood is apparently moving and that Macduff "was from his mother's womb / Untimely ripped"? **(b) Infer:** What growing realization do these statements about the witches seem to reflect? **(c) Draw Conclusions:** What is Macbeth's state of mind in his final battle with Macduff? Explain.

4. **Craft and Structure (a)** What occurs in Act V, Scene viii, lines 35–75? **(b) Evaluate:** Would the play be complete if it ended with Macbeth's death but omitted these lines? Why or why not?

5. **Integration of Knowledge and Ideas** Do you think a tragedy could be written about an ordinary person living today? Why or why not?

6. **Integration of Knowledge and Ideas** How do Shakespeare's use of comic relief and his revealing of Macbeth's inner turmoil add new dimensions to tragedy? In responding, use at least two of these Essential Question words: *noble, downfall, tradition, classics.* *[Connecting to the Essential Question: What is the relationship of the writer to tradition?]*

Cite textual evidence to support your responses.

Macbeth, Act V, Scene viii **415**

Concept Connector

Activating Prior Knowledge
Have students return to their responses to the Activating Prior Knowledge activity in which they predicted how the witches' prophecies would or would not come true, and what would happen to Lady Macbeth. Have students compare their predictions to the actual events of the play. What elements did they find most easily predictable? What were the surprises?

Writing About the Essential Question
Have students recall their responses to the Connecting to the Essential Question writing prompt on page 321. Have them work in small groups to compare Macbeth's story with the story of their chosen celebrity or politician. Encourage students to focus on both similarities and differences. Ask groups to share their ideas with the class.

32 **Critical Viewing**
Possible Answer: Macbeth hears the prophecies of the witches. Lady Macbeth and Macbeth conspire to murder King Duncan. Macbeth kills Banquo. Banquo's ghost appears to Macbeth at a banquet, and Macbeth, appears to go mad. In a sword-fight, Macdufff slays Macbeth.

ASSESS
Answers

Before students respond, you may wish to have them write a brief objective summary of the selection. As they answer the questions below, remind them to support their answers with evidence from the text.

1. **(a)** The doctor sees Lady Macbeth acting like she is washing her hands and muttering about blood. The doctor speculates that she has been involved in "unnatural" deeds. **(b)** At first, Macbeth is aghast at murder, yet by the end he wipes out entire families; Lady Macbeth pushed the idea of killing Duncan, yet cannot live with the guilt.

2. **(a)** Macbeth says, "She should have died hereafter." **(b)** His reaction shows that he knew that, if she was not cured of her madness, death was inevitable.

3. **(a)** He says that their words were ambiguous and misleading. **(b)** He realizes that he is doomed. **(c)** He is angry over having been misled and he knows he will die.

4. **(a)** Malcolm and Siward learn of the deaths of Young Siward and Macbeth. Malcolm becomes king. Malcolm thanks everyone. **(b)** The story ends with Macbeth's death, but one expects a final comment.

5. Because ordinary people possess noble qualities, a tragedy could be written about someone today.

6. **Possible answer:** Shakespeare's use of comic relief helps relieve some of the tension found in <u>classic</u> tragedies and often provides a witty commentary or satire of the tragic events unfolding. His revealing of Macbeth's inner turmoil gives Macbeth's <u>downfall</u> more depth—the viewer or reader is forced to see beyond Macbeth's role as the villain of the play and confront his humanity.

415

Answers

1. Macbeth is a central character of high rank and personal quality, with a tragic flaw (ambition). Events triggered by Macbeth's ambition lead to disaster. The play has lively action (murders, sword fights). The play includes comic scenes (with the Porter).

2. Predictions: Macbeth will be king; Banquo's heirs will be kings; Banquo's response: mistrust, may be a lure to evil; Macbeth's response: total belief, kills everyone.

3. Lady Macbeth is a catalyst. Macbeth has considered murder, but she fuels the fire.

4. (a) He allows his ambition to start him down a road that could only lead to more evil. (b) There might have been a kind of moral turning back in confession and surrender, but there would have been no going back to the past situation.

5. Act 1, he imagines killing Duncan. Act 2, phantom dagger, hands that will never be clean. Act 3, Banquo's ghost. His imagination adds to the tragedy because it drives him to do more evil.

6. (a) He shows pride and courage. He will not bend, even when faced with certain death. (b) His realization that life is short and witches cannot be trusted, combined with his bravery, reminds us that things could have turned out better had he made different choices.

7. Facing his limits—knowing that all is lost, the witches lied, and he will die—Macbeth moves beyond them, falling back on the pride and courage that sustained him in better times.

8. (a) The presence of the witches is an important element of the setting, and it helps create an ominous, otherworldly mood. The characters in the play, especially Macbeth, take the witches' prophecies seriously and allow them to influence later actions. (b) The Elizabethans would have understood that the breakdown of order in the highest ranks of society meant a breakdown of order in the whole. This extends the tragedy beyond the realm of the personal.

9. **Possible responses:** (a) We can infer that they understood the

---

After You Read   *Macbeth,* Act V

Literary Analysis

1. **Craft and Structure** Identify all the elements of **Shakespearean tragedy** in *Macbeth,* citing examples from the play.

2. **Key Ideas and Details** Use a chart like this one to show how Banquo's response to the witches emphasizes Macbeth's **tragic flaw.**

3. **Key Ideas and Details** What role does Lady Macbeth play in Macbeth's choice of evil?

4. **Key Ideas and Details** (a) How does Macbeth's tragic flaw lead him to disaster? (b) Once Macbeth kills Duncan, can he turn back? Why or why not?

5. **Key Ideas and Details** Find three passages that show how Macbeth's imagination adds to the tragedy. Support your choices.

6. **Integration of Knowledge and Ideas** (a) What positive qualities does Macbeth display in Act V? Explain. (b) How do Macbeth's positive qualities contribute to the **tragic impulse** revealed in the play?

7. **Integration of Knowledge and Ideas** In what way does the tragic impulse involve going beyond limitations? Support your answer with references to the play.

Reading Strategy

8. **Relate the play to the major themes and issues of its period** by answering these questions: **(a)** How does the belief in witches influence the setting and the characters? **(b)** How do Elizabethan beliefs in the importance of order add to the tragedy?

9. **(a)** What do the doctor's remarks lead you to infer about Elizabethan concepts of and treatments for mental illness? **(b)** Compare and contrast Elizabethan concepts of mental illness with those of today.

 Common Core State Standards

Language

4.c. Consult general and specialized reference materials, both print and digital, to find the pronunciation of a word or determine or clarify its precise meaning, its part of speech, its etymology, or its standard usage. *(p. 417)*

---

mind/wellness connection. His advice (watch her, remove things she could use to injure herself) sounds fairly modern. (b) We are relearning that the mind affects the body, so many would accept the doctor's diagnosis. Current doctors might offer sedatives and therapy.

PERFORMANCE TASKS
Integrated Language Skills

© Vocabulary Acquisition and Use

Word Analysis: Latin Root -turb-

The root -turb- means "to disturb." To experience *perturbation* is to experience "a great disturbance." Knowing the meaning of the root -turb-, define the italicized words below. Then, verify your definitions with a dictionary.

1. At the beginning of the play, a captain reports on the *turbulence* of the battle that is being fought.
2. As the events in *Macbeth* suggest, the Middle Ages was a *turbulent* period in the history of Scotland.
3. Elizabethans believed that a *perturbation* in the heavens meant disorder in society.
4. Macbeth's reaction shows he is extremely *perturbed* by Fleance's escape.
5. After being stirred, the witches' potion was *turbid*.

Using Resources to Build Vocabulary

Descriptive Adjectives: Words Relating to Tragedy

The genre of tragedy carries its own lexicon, or vocabulary. This lexicon includes words—many of them Greek in origin—that relate to different elements of the form or to aspects of the tragic characters themselves. Here are some of these words:

agon	chorus
apostrophe	hamartia
catastrophe	hubris
catharsis	peripeteia

Use a dictionary or a digital resource to look up the meanings of these words, and record their definitions. Then, write a brief description of *Macbeth* using at least three of the words.

Vocabulary: Sentence Completion

Use a word from the vocabulary list on page 400 to complete the sentence, and explain your choice. Use each word only once.

1. The movement of Birnam Wood began with a _____ rustling of trees.
2. The first trees that approached Dunsinane were _____ of the army that followed.
3. Farmers were shocked to see the untouched, _____ wood suddenly move.
4. The trees' unexpected motion made several of the farmers _____ in amazement.
5. This shocking event also made them feel _____ to other strange happenings.
6. They all confessed to a feeling of _____ in their hearts.
7. It was a feeling for which there was no _____.

©**The New Yorker Collection**, 1994, Bruce Eric Kaplan, from *cartoonbank.com*. All Rights Reserved.

"It is a tale told by an idiot, full of sound and fury, signifying nothing, and No. 1 on the best-seller list."

Integrated Language Skills **417**

Assessment Resources

Unit 2 Resources

L1 L2 EL **Selection Test A**, pp. 179–181. Administer Test A to less advanced readers.

L3 L4 EL **Selection Test B**, pp. 182–184. Administer Test B to on-level and more advanced students.

L3 L4 **Open-Book Test 4**, pp. 176–179 As an alternative, give the Open-Book test.

All **Customizable Test Bank**

All **Self-tests** Students may prepare for the **Selection Test** by taking the **Self-test** online.

PHLit Online! All assessment resources are available at **www.PHLitOnline.com**.

Vocabulary Acquisition and Use

Word Analysis

1. *Turbulence*: "commotion, tumult"
2. *Turbulent*: "stormy, unruly"
3. *Perturbation*: "disturbance"
4. *Perturbed*: "uneasy or troubled"
5. *Turbid*: "muddy or disordered"

Vocabulary

1. clamorous
2. harbingers
3. pristine
4. recoil
5. vulnerable
6. perturbation
7. antidote

Using Resources to Build Vocabulary

1. agon: a conflict between the main characters in a drama
2. apostrophe: a speech addressing an absent or imaginary person
3. catastrophe: the final event of the dramatic action
4. catharsis: an emotional release brought about by fear or pity
5. chorus: a group of actors who speak in unison to narrate or comment
6. hamartia: a tragic flaw
7. hubris: the exaggerated pride that brings about the hero's downfall
8. peripeteia: a sudden change in events

Possible response: *Macbeth* is the story of how one man's <u>hamartia</u> brings about not only his downfall but disruption of the whole social order. The prophetic words of the witches and his wife's goading spark Macbeth's <u>hubris</u>, which leads to murder. Macbeth is named king, but in a surprising <u>peripeteia</u>, he is slain by the one man *not* born of woman—Macduff!

Writing

You may use this Writing Lesson as timed-writing practice, or you may allow students to develop the response as a writing assignment over several days.

1. To give students guidance for writing this argumentative text, give them the Support for Writing page from (*Unit 2 Resources*, p. 174).

2. Read with students the comments by critic Stephen Greenblatt about Macbeth in the writing lesson on this page.

3. Work with students to draw up guidelines, based on the assignment for their essays:

   - **Focus** The writer should clearly state his or her opinion about Greenblatt's comment about Macbeth.

   - **Organization** The writer should begin by restating Greenblatt's opinion, as well as whether or not he or she agrees. Then the writer should support his or her opinion with relevant details, imagery, or language from the play, including quotations where appropriate.

   - **Style** An analytical essay requires an academic tone. Students should be respectful of Goldblatt's opinion whether or not they agree with it.

4. Use the **Rubrics for a Response to Literature**, *Professional Development Guidebook*, pp. 250–251, to evaluate students' work.

Writing

Argumentative Text Shakespeare critic Stephen Greenblatt has this to say about Macbeth's plot to assassinate King Duncan:

> The lure is strong enough . . . to make him ignore the threat of divine judgment in the afterlife, but still for a fateful moment he holds back:
>
> *We still have judgement here, that we but teach*
> *Bloody instructions which, being taught, return*
> *To plague th'inventor.*
>
> . . . [I]t is not in some imagined other world that your actions will be judged; it is here and now. Judgment in effect means punishment: whatever violent or dishonest things you do will inevitably serve as a lesson for others to do to you.

In an **analytical essay**, evaluate Greenblatt's commentary. Do you agree that Macbeth dreads the earthly consequences of his actions more than he dreads the fate of his soul—or do you think the opposite is true?

Prewriting Use these steps as you prepare to draft your essay:

- Skim the text, looking for imagery, language, or other stylistic devices that shed light on the nature of Macbeth's crisis. Make a list of these elements.

- Review your list as a whole, and decide whether it supports Greenblatt's conclusion, supports the opposite conclusion, or strikes you as utterly ambiguous. If you decide in favor of ambiguity, ask yourself what thematic purpose such ambiguity might serve.

- Express your position in a sentence or two.

Drafting Introduce the drama, Greenblatt's opinion, and your own. Then, choose two or three key passages to analyze. As you draft, refer to your strongest evidence by quoting it.

Revising Review your draft to ensure that you have considered not only the literal meanings of Macbeth's words, but also any underlying currents of tone, mood, or irony. Could subtle elements of your key passages lead someone to draw a different conclusion? If so, revise to anticipate and address these potential interpretations. Finally, be sure you include correct references and citations.

Model: Including References and Citations

As he contemplates the murder of Duncan, Macbeth expresses a concern for eternal consequences—namely, damnation. He speculates that Duncan has been "So clear in his great office, that his virtues / Will plead like angels trumpet-tongued against / The deep damnation of his taking-off" (I.vii.18–20). Even as Macbeth worries about damnation, though, he is more worried that "pity... Shall blow the horrid deed in every eye," here on earth.

> A direct reference to Macbeth's first soliloquy strengthens the analysis. Parenthetical citations indicate act, scene, and line numbers.

Common Core State Standards

Writing
1.a. Introduce precise, knowledgeable claim(s), establish the significance of the claim(s), distinguish the claim(s) from alternate or opposing claims, and create an organization that logically sequences claim(s), counterclaims, reasons, and evidence.
5. Develop and strengthen writing as needed by planning, focusing on addressing what is most significant for a specific purpose and audience.
Language
1. Demonstrate command of the conventions of standard English grammar and usage when writing or speaking. *(p. 419)*

Teaching Resources

Unit 2 Resources
- L3 L4 **Vocabulary Builder**, p. 169.
- L3 L4 **Support for Writing Lesson**, p. 171.
- L3 L4 **Grammar and Style**, p. 170.
- L4 **Enrichment**, p. 172

- All **Interactive Grammar Lesson:** available under **After You Read** for this selection

- All **Enriched Online Student Edition** Internet Research Activity: available under **After You Read** for this selection

- All *Professional Development Guidebook* **Rubrics for Self-Assessment: Response to Literature**, pp. 250–251

PHLit Online! All resources are available at www.PHLitOnline.com.

Conventions and Style: Adjective and Adverb Clauses

A subordinate clause that modifies a noun or pronoun is called an **adjective clause.** Adjective clauses tell *what kind* or *which one* about the word they modify. When you see a relative pronoun or a relative adjective at the beginning of a subordinate clause, you may be looking at an adjective clause.

Using Adjective and Adverb Clauses

Example: Macbeth kills Duncan, *who is the king of Scotland.*

The adjective clause, introduced by the relative pronoun *who,* modifies the proper noun *Duncan.*

An **adverb clause** is a subordinate clause that modifies a verb, adjective, adverb, or verbal by telling *where, when, in what way, to what extent, under what condition,* or *why.* Adverb clauses start with subordinating conjunctions such as *although, as if, before, unless, wherever,* and *while.*

Example: *Until he heard the witches' prophecy,* Macbeth harbored no thoughts of murder.

Here, the adverb clause modifies the verb *harbored.* The subordinating conjunction is *until.*

Punctuation Tip: When an adverb clause starts a sentence, it is followed by a comma. If an adverb clause ends a sentence, it is usually not preceded by a comma.

© Writing and Speaking Conventions

A. Writing Use each subordinate clause below in a sentence. Then tell which word the clause modifies and what type of clause it is.

1. after he wins a military battle
2. who ruled Scotland
3. because his wife persuaded him

   Example: after he wins a military battle
   Sentence: After he wins a military battle, Macbeth is made Thane of Cawdor.
   Word Modified; Type of Clause: is made; adverb clause

B. Speaking Describe a set design for your favorite scene from *Macbeth.* Include at least one adjective clause and one adverb clause.

Practice Identify each adjective clause and each adverb clause, and tell what word or words it modifies.

1. They encounter the three witches as they are crossing a moor.
2. He remembers everything that the witches have said.
3. Lady Macbeth's ambition is even greater than her husband's.
4. The bloody dagger seems to lead him to the room where the king sleeps.
5. Macbeth becomes king after he kills Duncan.
6. Lady Macbeth, who is plagued by guilt, starts walking in her sleep.
7. She cannot clean the imaginary bloodstains that she sees on her hands.
8. When Macbeth hears of his wife's death, he falls into a state of despair.
9. He hires murderers because he sees Banquo as a threat.
10. Macduff joins Prince Malcolm, who has raised an army to challenge the tyrannical new king.

PH WRITING COACH

Further instruction and practice are available in *Prentice Hall Writing Coach.*

Integrated Language Skills **419**

Conventions and Style
Practice

1. The adverb clause *as they are crossing a moor* modifies *encounter.*
2. The adjective clause *that the witches have said* modifies *everything.*
3. The adjective clause *than her husband's* modifies *greater.*
4. The adjective clause *where the king sleeps* modifies *room.*
5. The adverb clause *after he kills Duncan* modifies *becomes.*
6. The adjective clause *who is plagued by guilt* modifies *Lady Macbeth.*
7. The adjective clause *that she sees on her hands* modifies *bloodstains.*
8. The adverb clause *When Macbeth hears of his wife's death* modifies *falls.*
9. The adverb clause *because he sees Banquo as a threat* modifies *hires.*
10. The adjective clause *who has raised an army to challenge the tyrannical new king* modifies *Prince Malcolm.*

Writing and Speaking Conventions

A. Sample responses:

1. Macbeth becomes king after he wins a military battle. The adverb clause modifies *becomes.*
2. King Duncan, who ruled Scotland, was killed by Macbeth. The adjective clause modifies *King Duncan.*
3. Macbeth kills Duncan because his wife persuaded him. The adverb clause modifies *kills.*

B. Sample Response:

My favorite scene from Macbeth is the one in which the porter imagines himself as hell's porter. When the porter enters, the lights would come up, revealing the dimly lit interior of the castle. The door, on which Macduff knocks, would be visible at one side of the stage.

PH WRITING COACH Grade 12

Students will find instruction on and practice with adjective and adverb clauses in Chapter 13, section 3.

Extend the Lesson

Sentence Modeling

Display for students the following sentences from *Macbeth:*

"So were their daggers, which unwiped we found / Upon their pillows." (Act 2, Scene 3, lines 104–105)

"Macbeth shall never vanquished be until / Great Birnam Wood to high Dunsinane Hill / Shall come against him." (Act 4, Scene 1, lines 92–94)

Tell students that one of these sentences uses an adjective clause and one uses an adverb clause. Ask students to identify the type of clause in each sentence, as well as the word each modifies. (In the first sentence, the adjective clause beginning with *which* modifies *daggers.* In the second sentence, the adverb clause beginning with *until* modifies *vanquished be.*) Have students imitate both sentences on a topic of their own choosing, matching the grammatical and stylistic features as much as possible. Have students share their sentences with the class.

419

The Changing Tragic Hero

1. Tell students that the hero actually appears in many forms, one of which is the tragic hero. Characteristics of this hero include noble birth, a character flaw or error that causes his own downfall, and a fate that is greater than deserved.

2. Direct students attention to the picture of Shakespeare's Macbeth. **Ask:** What situation or events make Macbeth a tragic hero?
   Possible response: his own greed and ambition, how he allowed Lady Macbeth to influence his judgment, and his decision to murder Duncan

3. Direct students attention to the picture of Oedipus. Tell them that this play is the classic story of a tragic hero whose life falls apart when he learns his life story.

4. Direct students to the picture of Faust. **Ask** a volunteer who knows the story to explain the tragedy of Faust.
   Answer: Faust is a doctor who sells his soul to the devil in return for knowledge and learning.

5. **Ask** a volunteer to identify each of the remaining tragic heroes.
   Possible responses: Willy Loman in Miller's *Death of a Salesman* is an ordinary man, and Nora Heimer in Ibsen's *A Doll's House* is an ordinary woman who breaks free of traditional roles.

6. **Ask** students to compare the first two and the last two tragic heroes.
   Possible response: Macbeth and Oedipus are royalty; Nora and Willy Loman are average people.

7. **Ask** students what this comparison indicates about the modern world.
   Possible response: Modern culture is democratic, finding universal value in the plight of ordinary people.

THE CHANGING TRAGIC HERO

RENAISSANCE ENGLAND
The Tragedy of Macbeth
—William Shakespeare (1564 – 1616)

ANCIENT GREECE
Oedipus the King
—Sophocles (496–406 B.C.)

EARLY 19TH-CENTURY GERMANY
Faust
—Johann Wolfgang von Goethe (1749–1832)

LATE 19TH-CENTURY NORWAY
A Doll's House
—Henrik Ibsen (1828–1906)

20TH-CENTURY AMERICA
Death of a Salesman
—Arthur Miller (1915–2005)

420 Celebrating Humanity (1485–1625)

Enrichment: Analyzing a Themes and Symbols

Tragic Heroes

Aristotle first defined the tragic hero as a literary character who brings about his own downfall through a tragic flaw. Other characteristics are that the hero must be noble by birth or through wisdom. His fortune must be reversed through his own actions, he must discover his own mistake too late, and the audience must feel empathy or dramatic irony for the hero's fate. Often the tragic hero starts out no better or worse than the average person.

Activity: Analyze and Compare Two Tragic Heroes Have interested students learn more about one of the tragic heroes illustrated in the spread or another similar character of their choice. Ask them to explain why the character fits the archetype, and compare the character they choose to Shakespeare's Macbeth. Suggest that they record their analysis in the **Enrichment: Analyzing Themes and Symbols** worksheet, *Professional Development Guidebook*, page 243.

Comparing Literary Works

from *Macbeth* by William Shakespeare
• from *Oedipus the King* by Sophocles •
from *Faust* by Wolfgang Von Goethe

Comparing Tragedy Past and Present

Tragedy Tragedy had its origins in ancient Greece, where Aeschylus, Sophocles, and Euripides created immortal verse dramas. Greek tragedy typically featured a high-born figure (called the **tragic hero**) whose **tragic flaw**—a mistake or unwise decision—leads to ruin. The audience felt sorrow and pity for the hero's plight. A chorus commented on the action, and fate or supernatural elements also played a role.

Rediscovered in the Renaissance, ancient tragedies served as models for a golden age of European drama, including the masterpieces of Shakespeare. In the nineteenth century, Romantic verse tragedies, like Goethe's *Faust*, focused on the protagonist's urge to go beyond all limits. Later in the century, this type of drama gave way to modern realistic tragedies like those of Ibsen and Chekhov. Such tragedies featured ordinary heroes whose downfall stemmed from social ills. More recent playwrights, like Arthur Miller, continued in this realistic vein.

As you read the selections from *Oedipus the King* and *Faust*, use a chart like the one shown to compare them to Shakespeare's *Macbeth*.

	Macbeth	Oedipus	Faust
tragic hero	Scottish nobleman		
tragic flaw	murders king and others due to excessive ambition		
fate/supernatural elements	witches and apparitions predict the future		
style elements	verse for high-born characters; soliloquies; asides; no chorus		

© Gather Vocabulary Knowledge

The words *account, reckoning, infinite,* and *constitutionally* appear in these excerpts. Use a **dictionary** to find each word's definition. Then, use other references to explore these words:

- **Specialized Dictionaries:** Use specialized dictionaries, such as those that focus on politics, to discover whether the words have technical meanings. When you encounter the word, decide whether the author intended the technical meaning or not.

- **Book of Quotations:** Use an online or print collection of quotations to find a quotation that contains each of the words. In a sentence or two, analyze the word's connotations in the context of the quotation.

www.PHLitOnline.com

© **Common Core State Standards**

Reading Literature
10. By the end of grade 12, read and comprehend literature, including dramas, at the high end of the grades 11–CCR text complexity band independently and proficiently.

Language
6. Demonstrate independence in gathering vocabulary knowledge when considering a word or phrase important to comprehension or expression.

© **Common Core State Standards**

- **Reading Literature 10**
- **Writing 2, 10**
- **Language 6**

Comparing Tragedy Past and Present

1. Have students read the discussion of tragedies on page 421.

2. Ask students if they can think of other examples of tragedies.

3. Point out that modern tragedies are often found in headlines. For example, accounts of famous movie stars or politicians who fall from grace illustrate classic Greek tragic structure. A tragic hero has a tragic flaw that leads to this downfall. As students mention other tragedies, list them on the board.

4. Have students examine the comparison chart on page 421. Tell students that they can concentrate on a central tragic hero and define his role in these selections. Remind students to use the definitions to the left of each row to guide their understanding of forces in play. They should also go back over what they have read and isolate the style of writing associated with the hero, as compared to other characters.

Gather Vocabulary Knowledge

If specialized reference texts are not available, instruct students to examine all definitions in a standard dictionary. They will discover specialized meanings identified. Guide students to compare and contrast meanings they find for the following words used in multiple areas:

- *account:* business and law
- *reckoning:* business and religion
- *infinite:* math and religion
- *constitutionally:* medicine and politics

Teaching Resources

The following resources can be used to enrich, extend, or differentiate the instruction.

All *Unit 2 Resources,* pp. 185–189.

All Enriched Online Student Edition

All *Common Core Companion,* pp. 82–88; 196–207, 269–276, 336–337.

All resources are available at **www.PHLitOnline.com.**

Background

More About the Author

Sophocles was an unlikely innovator in Greek drama, having been a stable, successful, happy, and influential politician and artist, far less tragic than his most famous character, Oedipus. Family wealth and his remarkable youthful beauty helped Sophocles to study the arts and to serve at times as an ordained priest, a director of an interstate treasury, and a civilian general. This conservative background seems at odds with his innovative bent. His plays altered the previously accepted structure of tragedy, which told three tragic stories at a time. He concentrated on one story alone. He also was one of the first to use scenery painting and rotating prisms that allowed for rapid scene changes, a device still used in modern theater in *A Chorus Line*. He was said to have performed a juggling act so impressive it became legend. He seemed to have lived up to one of his own famous quotations, when he said he wrote men as they ought to be, not as they really were.

Humanities

Bust of Sophocles, copy of Greek 4th c. B.C. original

This marble portrait bust dates back to the Classical Roman Period. With the rise of the Roman Empire, many Roman sculptors produced copies of ancient Greek sculpture. Because many Greek originals were ruined, our knowledge of Greek sculpture is indebted to Roman copies. Many Roman busts of Sophocles have survived to this day. Such artifacts are evidence of his influence and honor.

SOPHOCLES

(496 B.C.–406 B.C.)

Sophocles' (säf´ ə klēz´) life corresponded with the splendid rise and tragic fall of fifth-century Athens. At 16, he was one of the young men chosen by the city to perform a choral ode, dancing and singing in a public celebration of the Athenian naval victory over the Persians at Salamis. In 442 B.C., he was one of the treasurers of the imperial league, which was organized to resist Persia. With Pericles, Sophocles served as one of the generals in the war against the island of Samos, which later tried to secede from the Athenian league. In 413 B.C., he was also appointed to a special government committee when the Athenian expedition to Sicily failed. He died in 406 B.C., two years before Athens surrendered to Sparta in the Peloponnesian War.

Winning Playwright Sophocles' life also coincided with the rise and fall of the Golden Age of Greek tragedy. His career as a dramatist began in 468 B.C. when he entered the Dionysia (dī´ ə nē´ sē ə), the annual theatrical competition dedicated to the god Dionysus (dī´ ə nī´ səs). Competing against the established and brilliant playwright Aeschylus (es´ ki ləs), Sophocles won first prize. Over the next 62 years, he wrote more than 120 plays, 24 of which won first prize; those that did not come in first placed second. Yet only seven of Sophocles' plays have survived intact.

Enriching the Drama Greek plays had their origins in religious festivals honoring the god Dionysus. At first, a chorus narrated stories of the god's life in song. The choral leader would occasionally step forward to recite part of the story alone. Eventually, the recitation grew longer and involved a second speaker. Sophocles increased the number of singers in the chorus and introduced a third speaking part. The addition of a third actor allowed for more dramatically complex dialogue than that of the earlier plays. Sophocles also introduced technical innovations to Greek tragedy, which was presented in an open-air theater with few props. For instance, he was the first to use a crane that lowered actors "miraculously" onto the stage.

Faithfulness to Human Experience In addition to his technical innovations, Sophocles is known for his fidelity to universal human experience. In his plays, the world order consists of human beings, nature, and the inscrutable forces of the gods and fate. Sophocles suggests that while gods can predetermine or influence human action, they do not necessarily define one's character. People are responsible for finding out who they are and where they belong; they must then take moral responsibility for their lives.

422 Celebrating Humanity (1485–1625)

"Numberless are the world's wonders, but none / More wonderful than man." —Sophocles

from Oedipus the King

Translated by David Grene

— BACKGROUND According to the myth on which Sophocles' play is based, King Laius and Queen Jocasta of Thebes learn from an oracle that their son will kill his father and marry his mother. Horrified, they pin together their baby son's feet and give him to a servant to leave on Mount Cithaeron to die. The servant instead gives the baby to a shepherd, who gives him to King Polybus and Queen Merope of Corinth. They name him Oedipus, meaning "swollen feet," and raise him as their own. When Oedipus learns from the oracle that he will kill his father and marry his mother, he thinks this fate refers to Polybus and Merope and so flees Corinth. Enraged by a chariot driver who tries to run him off the road, he kills the driver and his passenger. He then comes to Thebes, which is being terrorized by a monster called the Sphinx, which will let no one enter Thebes until the riddle it poses is solved. Oedipus solves the riddle and, as a reward, marries the recently widowed Jocasta, becoming king of Thebes. He has two sons and two daughters and rules successfully for twenty years. Then a plague breaks out, and the oracle says that it will not end until Laius' murderer is exiled from Thebes.

The following selection, which concludes the play, occurs soon after Oedipus learns that Jocasta is his biological mother and that the man he killed on the road was Laius, his biological father. Horrified by their sins, Jocasta has taken her own life, and Oedipus has blinded himself.

OEDIPUS: . . . come—it's unfit to say what is unfit
to do.—I beg of you in God's name hide me
1520   somewhere outside your country, yes, or kill me,
or throw me into the sea, to be forever
out of your sight. Approach and deign to touch me

❸ **Reading Check**
What does Oedipus learn from the oracle?

from Oedipus the King **423**

423

④ Comparing Tragedies

1. Direct students' attention to the chorus's response beginning in line 1525. Point out that the chorus is speaking both to Oedipus as well as the audience.

2. **Ask** students why these lines are delivered before Creon enters the stage?
   Answer: They prepare the audience for his arrival and explain it.

3. **Ask** students the Comparing Tragedies question: What important information does the chorus supply to the audience in these lines?
   Answer: They say Creon has to come to give Oedipus advice and to respond to what he has asked of them.

4. **Ask** students how Creon fullfills the chorus's explanation.
   Possible response: Creon instructs a servant to bring Oedipus inside so that only his family, and not the general public, witnesses his misery.

⑤ Literature in Context

The Greek Chorus and Players

Sophocles is widely credited for reducing the importance of the role of the chorus through his addition of a third player and skilled use of dialogue.

Connect to the Literature

1. Direct students' attention to the chorus's first lines, beginning on line 1525, and their last lines from 1648 on. Point out that the chorus is assisting the audience's understanding.

2. **Ask** students the first Connect to Literature question: What roles does the chorus perform at the beginning and end of this excerpt?
   Possible response: The chorus helps to explain Creon's roles in the play and reiterates morals and lessons the play has taught.

3. **Ask** students the second question: In what ways does the picture on page 427 help you visualize how the chorus performs?
   Possible response: It shows the chorus as a group wearing their masks, appearing on stage behind the first player. They appear to be moving in unison.

424

---

for all my wretchedness, and do not fear.
No man but I can bear my evil doom.

1525 **CHORUS:** Here Creon comes in fit time to perform
④ or give advice in what you ask of us.
Creon is left sole ruler in your stead.

OEDIPUS: Creon! Creon! What shall I say to him?
How can I justly hope that he will trust me?
In what is past I have been proved towards him
1530 an utter liar.

[*Enter* CREON.]

CREON: Oedipus, I've come
not so that I might laugh at you nor taunt you
with evil of the past. But if you still
are without shame before the face of men
1535 reverence at least the flame that gives all life,
our Lord the Sun, and do not show unveiled
to him pollution such that neither land
nor holy rain nor light of day can welcome.

[*To a* SERVANT.]

Be quick and take him in. It is most decent
that only kin should see and hear the troubles
1540 of kin.

OEDIPUS: I beg you, since you've torn me from
my dreadful expectations and have come
in a most noble spirit to a man

Comparing Tragedies
What important information does the chorus supply to the audience in these lines?

Vocabulary
reverence (rev´ rəns) *v.* show great respect

---

⑤ LITERATURE IN CONTEXT

The Greek Chorus and Players

In Greek tragedies, the role of the chorus was central to the production and to the meaning of the play. The chorus consisted of 12 or 15 dancers called *choreuts,* who were young men about to enter the military. The chorus danced as it sang, moving from right to left during the strophe (strō´ fē), then left to right during the antistrophe (an tis´ trə fē).

Originally, plays included only one actor in addition to the chorus. Thespis, from whom we derive the English word *thespian,* or actor, is said to have been the first actor. The dramatist Aeschylus (es´ kə ləs) is said to have introduced the second actor, and Sophocles the third.

In most dramas, actors played several different parts each. Their costumes were long, flowing garments and expressive masks, which they changed as they changed characters. The actors' shoes also featured a high wooden sole called a *cothurnus* (kō thər´ nəs) to make the individual look taller and more impressive and to heighten visibility in the vast theater.

Connect to the Literature

What roles does the chorus perform at the beginning and end of this excerpt? Also, in what ways does the picture on page 427 help you visualize how the chorus performs?

424 Celebrating Humanity (1485–1625)

Differentiated Instruction   for Universal Access

Enrichment for Gifted/Talented Students
Allow students to stage small sections of the play with an emphasis on the chorus. Students could research how the chorus in Greek drama normally performed. Other students should rehearse delivering the poetic exhortations of Oedipus and Creon, which differ greatly from natural speech. Students could also research how Greek dramas were staged, as well as the origins of Greek drama influenced by ancient Indian theater forms brought back by Alexander the Great in his early conquests.

EL Strategy for English Learners
The term *oracle* may be better understood as a prediction or prophecy, with which students from other cultural backgrounds may be more familiar. Have students discuss people they may know who serve as fortune-tellers or soothsayers and predict the future. Point out that early on in the play, both Oedipus and his wife/mother, Jocasta, keep assuring themselves that different oracles have not predicted events, when they suspect that they are actually true.

that has used you vilely[1]—do a thing for me.

1545 I shall speak for your own good, not for my own.

CREON: What do you need that you would ask of me?

OEDIPUS: Drive me from here with all the speed you can
to where I may not hear a human voice.

CREON: Be sure, I would have done this had not I
1550 wished first of all to learn from the God the course
of action I should follow.

OEDIPUS: But his word
has been quite clear to let the parricide,[2]
the sinner, die.

CREON: Yes, that indeed was said.
But in the present need we had best discover
1555 what we should do.

OEDIPUS: And will you ask about
a man so wretched?

CREON: Now even you will trust
the God.

OEDIPUS: So. I command you—and will beseech you—
to her that lies inside that house give burial
1560 as you would have it; she is yours and rightly
you will perform the rites for her. For me—
never let this my father's city have me
living a dweller in it. Leave me live
in the mountains where Cithaeron is, that's called
1565 my mountain, which my mother and my father
while they were living would have made my tomb.
So I may die by their decree who sought
indeed to kill me. Yet I know this much:
no sickness and no other thing will kill me.
1570 I would not have been saved from death if not
for some strange evil fate. Well, let my fate
go where it will.
Creon, you need not care
about my sons; they're men and so wherever
they are, they will not lack a livelihood.
1575 But my two girls—so sad and pitiful—
whose table never stood apart from mine,
and everything I touched they always shared—
O Creon, have a thought for them! And most
I wish that you might suffer me to touch them
1580 and sorrow with them.

---

1. **vilely** (vīl′ ly) *adv.* wickedly
2. **parricide** (par′ ə sīd) *n.* someone who murders his or her father.

from Oedipus the King **425**

Sidebar

Comparing Tragedies
What does Oedipus' request to Creon show about his attitude toward Thebes? As a **tragic hero,** what noble qualities does he reveal?

Vocabulary
rites (rīts) *n.* ceremonies; rituals

Comparing Tragedies
What role does Oedipus believe fate has played in his life?

Reading Check
What information does Creon want to learn from the God?

Margin Notes

6 Comparing Tragedies

1. Direct students' attention to line 1547 that begins, "Drive me from here..." Point out that "here" refers to Thebes, where he has returned to become king.

2. **Ask** students what Oedipus is asking Creon to do. **Answer:** He is asking Creon to force him to leave Thebes.

3. **Ask** students the first part of the Comparing Tragedies question: What does Oedipus' request to Creon show about his attitude toward Thebes?
   Possible response: He feels he has betrayed Thebes by his actions and deserves to be apart from other human beings.

4. **Ask** students the second part of the Comparing Tragedies question: As a tragic hero, what noble qualities does Oedipus reveal?
   Possible response: He reveals disgust for his horrible actions and a faith in God to punish him for them.

7 Comparing Tragedies

1. Direct students' attention to line 1570 that begins, "I would not have been..." Note that he refers to fate as "evil."
   Ask students to explain what would have happened to Oedipus if fate had not come into play.
   Possible response: He would have died as a child on the mountainside.

2. **Ask** the Comparing Tragedies question.
   Answer: He believes that an evil fate has determined he will not die, despite his suffering.

8 Reading Check

Answer: Creon wishes to learn what course of action he should follow.

Enrichment: Building Context

The Fates
The idea of fate that Oedipus cites in line 1571 is a reference to goddesses in Greek mythology who controlled the destiny of every human. They were also called the Moirae, and they alone determined what would happen from birth to death. One spun the thread of a person's life; another determined how much time was spent on Earth. Another cut the thread when it was time to die. The ministers of the Fates were soothsayers and their oracles.

Activity: Investigating the Fates
Have each student pick one of the Fates to research or investigate how the idea of fate became a part of Western Civilization. Suggest that they record information in the **Enrichment: Building Context** worksheet, *Professional Development Guidebook,* page 222. Direct students to use the results of their research to develop oral presentations. Then have students make their oral presentations to the class.

Evaluate

1. Direct students attention to line 1593, beginning, "O Children..." Have a volunteer read down to line 1601.

2. **Ask** students: For what reasons would Oedipus have blinded himself? How does this punishment fit his "crime"?

   Possible response: Students may offer that Oedipus feels such severe shame and remorse for his actions that he has inflicted upon himself the most severe punishment possible.

❾ Background

Marriage in Ancient Greece

Marriages in Greece were arranged by the bride's father, so it is particularly moving to hear Oedipus anguish over what will become of his daughters without him to protect them. Young women were married not long after they passed through puberty, and men became husbands when they were thirty and had completed military service.

Women rarely owned property in Greece, so the dowry a woman took to marriage usually was all she inherited. A father negotiated a payment of cattle to the son-in-law and had the right to reclaim the dowry if he was not satisfied with how his daughter was treated.

Women lived in separate quarters and rarely left the house. They were expected to educate the children, care for the household, and weave all the cloth.

Men were allowed to have a concubine, but women were expected to remain faithful to their husbands. Marriage between immediate family members was forbidden, as in *Oedipus*, but uncles would marry nieces and half-sisters to keep family property in the family.

Vocabulary
infamy (in´ fə mē) *n.* very bad reputation; disgrace

[*Enter* ANTIGONE *and* ISMENE, OEDIPUS' *two daughters.*]
O my lord! O true noble Creon! Can I
really be touching them, as when I saw?
What shall I say?
Yes, I can hear them sobbing—my two darlings!
and Creon has had pity and has sent me
1585   what I loved most?
Am I right?

CREON: You're right: it was I gave you this
because I knew from old days how you loved them
as I see now.

1590   **OEDIPUS:**   God bless you for it, Creon,
and may God guard you better on your road
than he did me!
                    O children,
where are you? Come here, come to my hands,
a brother's hands which turned your father's eyes,
1595   those bright eyes you knew once, to what you see,
a father seeing nothing, knowing nothing,
begetting you from his own source of life.
I weep for you—I cannot see your faces—
I weep when I think of the bitterness
1600   there will be in your lives, how you must live
before the world. At what assemblages
of citizens will you make one? to what
gay company will you go and not come home
in tears instead of sharing in the holiday?
1605   And when you're ripe for marriage, who will he be,
the man who'll risk to take such infamy
as shall cling to my children, to bring hurt
on them and those that marry with them? What
curse is not there? "Your father killed his father
1610   and sowed the seed where he had sprung himself
and begot you out of the womb that held him."
These insults you will hear. Then who will marry you?
No one, my children; clearly you are doomed
to waste away in barrenness unmarried.
1615   Son of Menoeceus[3], since you are all the father
left these two girls, and we, their parents, both
are dead to them—do not allow them wander
like beggars, poor and husbandless.
They are of your own blood.
1620   And do not make them equal with myself
in wretchedness; for you can see them now
so young, so utterly alone, save for you only.

---

3. **Son of Menoeceus** (mə nē´ sē əs) Creon.

Enrichment: Investigating Culture

The City-States of Greece

Ancient Greece was never a single unified state like present-day Greece. The Greeks organized themselves into loosely aligned city-states, such as Thebes, Athens, and Corinth. Most of these were incorporated by the boundaries of the cities themselves, or by natural formations like mountain ranges. Some, like Athens, included the plains that surrounded the city. Even the Greek colonies were formed as independent city-states.

Activity: Investigating the Greek City-States

Have each student pick a Greek city-state or the concept of Greek city-states to research. Suggest that they record information in the **Enrichment: Building Context** worksheet, *Professional Development Guidebook,* page 222. Direct students to use the results of their research to develop oral presentations. Then have students make their oral presentations to the class.

Touch my hand, noble Creon, and say yes.
If you were older, children, and were wiser,
there's much advice I'd give you. But as it is,
let this be what you pray: give me a life
wherever there is opportunity
to live, and better life than was my father's.

CREON: Your tears have had enough of scope; now go within the
house.

OEDIPUS: I must obey, though bitter of heart.

CREON: In season, all is good.

OEDIPUS: Do you know on what conditions I obey?

CREON: You tell me them,
and I shall know them when I hear.

OEDIPUS: That you shall send me out
to live away from Thebes.

CREON: That gift you must ask of the God.

10 ▼ Critical Viewing
What does this image of
Oedipus and the Chorus
suggest about their
relationship? Explain.
[Interpret]

11 ☑ Reading
Check
Why does Oedipus weep for
his daughters?

from Oedipus the King **427**

Critical Viewing

10 Critical Viewing
Possible response: The chorus is
not acting out a part in the play, like
the actor playing Oedipus is doing,
but it is moving and chanting in unison. The chorus stands behind him in
support of him.

11 Reading Check
Answer: Oedipus weeps because
he knows his daughters will have a
hard life, as they will be linked to his
crimes.

12 Background
Art of the Chorus
The chief role of the chorus was
to provide emotional reaction and
commentary to key moments in the
play. Between episodes, the group
of chorus members sang and danced
while wearing masks that expressed
the current emotion. Masks used in
ancient Greek theater were, like the
rest of Greek theater, larger than life.
Their bold and massive size allowed
for an adequate impression on the
audience within the vast space of the
Greek amphitheater.

Differentiated Instruction for Universal Access

Strategy for Less Proficient Readers
Students may need assistance
in following the narrative
presented in the dialogue or
longer monologues. Stage
a choral reading of key segments where Oedipus or
Creon explains what is happening, such as lines 1558–
1568 or 1605–1619.

Enrichment for Advanced Readers
Have students check out from
the library copies of other
plays by Sophocles, particularly *Antigone* and *Oedipus at
Colonus.* Have them select a
scene or scenes to stage as an
oral reading. Students should
discuss how these scenes
relate to *Oedipus.*

Enrichment for Gifted/Talented Students
Have students write a modern
version of the Oedipus story.
Some critics have suggested
that everything he did, from
killing a man who almost
killed him to unknowingly
marrying his own mother, was
perfectly justified behavior.

427

⓭ Comparing Tragedies

1. Direct students' attention to the chorus's final speech, beginning at line 1648. Point out that the chorus is speaking directly to the audience.

2. **Ask** students why the chorus repeats Oedipus' successes and how he was envied.
   Answer: They remind the audience that Oedipus was once successful and compare what he once was to what he is now.

3. **Ask** students what the chorus means by "breakers of misfortune."
   Answer: They are referring to waves of bad things that have happened to Oedipus.

4. **Ask** students the Comparing Tragedies question.
   Possible response: The chorus is warning the audience that even though someone can be successful and happy, they can lose everything like Oedipus has.

ASSESS

Answers

Before students respond, you may wish to have them write a brief objective summary of the selection. As they answer the questions below, remind them to support their answers with evidence from the text.

1. (a) He earlier ordered that Laius' murderer be exiled. (b) It is ironic that Oedipus finds out he is that murderer, and he must exile himself.

2. (a) He asks Creon to bury Jocasta with all the proper rites and to take care of his daughters.
   (b) This shows that, even in his misery, Oedipus has the strength of character to make sure others are cared for properly.

3. (a) Creon tells Oedipus to stop trying to be the master of his fate and his country. (b) **Possible response:** You are at the mercy of your fate no matter what you do.

4. (a) **Possible response:** Yes, the courageous clarity with which he sees himself is noble—he does not deny responsibility. (b) He begs Creon to carry out his punishment. He has blinded himself, arranged for his daughters' care, and has accepted his fate.

OEDIPUS: But I'm now hated by the Gods.

1640 **CREON:**   So quickly you'll obtain your prayer.

OEDIPUS: You consent then?

CREON: What I do not mean, I do not use to say.

OEDIPUS: Now lead me away from here.

CREON: Let go the children, then, and come.

1645 **OEDIPUS:** Do not take them from me.

CREON: Do not seek to be master in everything,
   for the things you mastered did not follow you throughout your life.

[As CREON and OEDIPUS go out.]

CHORUS: You that live in my ancestral Thebes, behold this Oedipus,—
   him who knew the famous riddles and was a man most masterful;
1650   not a citizen who did not look with envy on his lot—see him now and see the breakers of misfortune swallow him!
   Look upon that last day always. Count no mortal happy till he has passed the final limit of his life secure from pain.

Comparing Tragedies
What does the final speech of the chorus stress about the events depicted in the play?

⓬
⓭

Critical Reading

ⓒ 1. Key Ideas and Details (a) In order to end the plague in Thebes, what command did Oedipus apparently make about the person who murdered Laius? **(b) Analyze:** What about this command is ironic, or surpising and unexpected?

ⓒ 2. Key Ideas and Details (a) What does Oedipus ask Creon to do regarding Jocasta's body and his daughters' future? **(b) Analyze:** What do these requests show about Oedipus' character?

ⓒ 3. Craft and Structure (a) In his final remark, what does Creon tell Oedipus not to seek? **(b) Interpret:** Based on this final scene, what do you think is the theme or central message of the play?

ⓒ 4. Integration of Knowledge and Ideas (a) Make a Judgment: At the play's end, do you think Oedipus is ennobled by suffering? **(b) Support:** Provide reasons and cite detailed and accurate references from the play to support your opinion.

Cite textual evidence to support your responses.

Think Aloud

Reading Strategy: Cause-Effect Relationships
To model the skill of rereading for comparison and contrast, use this "think aloud." Say to students:

I am trying to understand why Oedipus thinks he is hated by the Gods, which he mentions in line 1639. In the previous line, Creon says to him that he must ask a gift of the Gods. This seems to indicate that the Gods have power over the events in Oedipus' life (line 1550). Oedipus blames himself for what has occurred, even though he did not know he was killing his father and marrying the woman who was his biological mother. Therefore, he must believe the Gods made him do these things, which he regrets. I think Oedipus believes that the Gods hate him and have punished him for something he has done (line 1592). The only gift he can ask of them is to be punished with banishment (line 1636), not forgiveness or relief from his woes.

JOHANN WOLFGANG VON GOETHE

(1749–1832)

Because of the tremendous diversity of his talents and interests, Johann (yō hän´) Wolfgang von Goethe (gö´ tə) is best described as a true Renaissance man. He was not only a gifted writer but also a scientist, a painter, a statesman, a philosopher, and an educator.

The son of a wealthy lawyer, Goethe was born in the German town of Frankfurt am Main. After receiving a thorough education from private tutors, he was sent to the University of Leipzig to study law. More interested in the arts than in law, Goethe spent most of his free time writing poetry, studying art, and attending concerts. Nonetheless, he finished his legal studies in 1771.

A Developing Novelist Goethe practiced law for a brief period, during which he wrote *The Sorrows of Young Werther* (1774), an autobiographical novel inspired by an unhappy love affair and the suicide of one of his friends. One of the most important novels of the eighteenth century, *The Sorrows of Young Werther* earned Goethe international fame.

A year after the novel's publication, Goethe accepted an invitation to the court of the reigning duke of Weimar, Charles Augustus. Goethe lived in Weimar for the rest of his life, and for ten years he served as the duke's chief minister. In 1780, he traveled to Italy in an effort to dedicate time and energy to his writing.

Shortly after returning to Weimar, Goethe fell in love with Christiane Vulpius, whom he later married. Through a close friendship with the noted German writer Friedrich von Schiller (1759–1805), Goethe gained valuable guidance and assistance in revising a number of his important works.

A Legendary Figure Probably the most notable of these works was *Faust*. With Schiller's advice and direction, Goethe revised an early draft of the play, adding a prologue. Unfortunately, Schiller died three years before *Faust, Part I* (1808) was published.

The final and greatest achievement of Goethe's literary career was the completion of *Faust, Part II.* The poet's vision of the legendary Faust transformed the traditional character into a newer, more sympathetic one that has fascinated readers and scholars for centuries. Goethe had begun his work on *Part II* while still a young man; because he contributed to the piece throughout his life, *Faust, Part II* ultimately reflects the deep philosophy of life and wry wisdom of the poet's mature years. Goethe never knew of the success of *Faust, Part II,* as it was published in 1832, a few months after his death.

"As soon as you trust yourself, you will know how to live."

— Goethe

Macbeth • Oedipus the King • Faust **429**

Background

More About the Author

Goethe holds a lofty status in German literature, nearly as revered as Shakespeare in English literature. His belief in world literature mirrored his influence on European art during the Romantic Period, which he helped define. He spoke multiple languages and translated many authors. He was at times a minister of state; an expert in taxation, farming, and mining; a musical composer; an opera director; and a scientist, who considered his work in optics and light his greatest achievement. His beliefs in nature were both mystic and poetic. He applied both to his studies of science, as well as to his belief in the perfect man, Faust, who was tempted by ultimate evil. Goethe renewed interest in German folk tales and the country's medieval past. His novel *The Sorrows of Werther* remains in print today, and its love-sick hero has become an archetype. At Weimar, the greatest artists of his time came to share in his universally recognized genius.

From FAUST

Johann Wolfgang von Goethe
translated by Louis MacNeice

BACKGROUND Georg Faust, or Faustus, was a German scholar and traveling magician who lived from about 1480 to 1540. According to legend, Faust sold his soul to the devil in exchange for youth, knowledge, and magical powers. In Goethe's version of the legend, Faust's interests reflect ideas of Romanticism, the literary and artistic movement.

This scene comes from Faust, Part I. *Mephistopheles, or the devil, is urging Faust to formalize their contract by signing it "with one little drop of blood."*

FAUST: Only do not fear that I shall break this contract.
What I promise is nothing more
Than what all my powers are striving for.
250   I have puffed myself up too much, it is only
Your sort that really fits my case.
The great Earth Spirit has despised me
And Nature shuts the door in my face.
The thread of thought is snapped asunder,
255   I have long loathed knowledge in all its fashions.
In the depths of sensuality
Let us now quench our glowing passions!
And at once make ready every wonder
Of unpenetrated sorcery!
260   Let us cast ourselves into the torrent of time,
Into the whirl of eventfulness,
Where disappointment and success,
Pleasure and pain may chop and change
As chop and change they will and can;
265   It is restless action makes the man.

MEPHISTOPHELES: No limit is fixed for you, no bound;
If you'd like to nibble at everything
Or to seize upon something flying round—
Well, may you have a run for your money!
270   But seize your chance and don't be funny!

FAUST: I've told you, it is no question of happiness.

Comparing Tragedies
In what ways are Faust's motivations (lines 260–265) similar to and different from those of Macbeth and Oedipus?

Enrichment: Building Context

The Faust Legend
A real Dr. Johannes Faust or Faustus existed in Germany in the late 1400s or early 1500s. He was a magician, charlatan, and physician who traveled from town to town. His claims of the power of alchemy, astrology, and soothsaying were said to be the result of a pact with supernatural forces. An anonymous *Faust* book was published in 1587 popularizing this legend. Since then, the Faust saga has formed the basis of many works of art.

Activity: Investigating the Faust Story as Art
Have each student pick a book, play, song, opera, or video game that uses the Faust name or theme. Suggest that they record information in the **Enrichment: Building Context** worksheet, *Professional Development Guidebook*, page 222. Direct students to use the results of their research to develop oral presentations. Then have students make their oral presentations to the class.

The most painful joy, enamored hate, enlivening
Disgust—I devote myself to all excess.
My breast, now cured of its appetite for knowledge,
275 From now is open to all and every smart,
And what is allotted to the whole of mankind
That will I sample in my inmost heart,
Grasping the highest and lowest with my spirit,
Piling men's weal and woe upon my neck,
280 To extend myself to embrace all human selves
And to founder in the end, like them, a wreck.

MEPHISTOPHELES: O believe *me*, who have been chewing
These iron rations many a thousand year,
No human being can digest
285 This stuff, from the cradle to the bier[1]
This universe—believe a devil—
Was made for no one but a god!
He exists in eternal light
But us he has brought into the darkness
290 While *your* sole portion is day and night.

FAUST: I will all the same!

MEPHISTOPHELES: That's very nice.
There's only one thing I find wrong;
Time is short, art is long.
You could do with a little artistic advice.
295 Confederate with one of the poets
And let him flog his imagination
To heap all virtues on your head,
A head with such a reputation:
Lion's bravery,
300 Stag's velocity,
Fire of Italy,
Northern tenacity.
Let *him* find out the secret art
Of combining craft with a noble heart
305 And of being in love like a young man,
Hotly, but working to a plan.
Such a person—*I'd* like to meet him;
"Mr. Microcosm"[2] is how I'd greet him.

FAUST: What am I then if fate must bar
310 My efforts to reach that crown of humanity
After which all my senses strive?

---

1. **bier** (bir) *n.* coffin and its supporting platform.
2. **Mr. Microcosm** man regarded as the epitome of the world.

Comparing Tragedies
How is Goethe's verse, as translated by Louis MacNeice, different from the verse used by Shakespeare?

Vocabulary
tenacity (tə nas´ ə tē) *n.* persistence; stubbornness

 **Reading Check**
To what does Faust devote himself?

from Faust **431**

❹ Comparing Tragedies

1. Direct students' attention to lines 271–282 that begin "I've told you…" Point out the last words of lines that rhyme. Do the same for lines 236–240 of *Macbeth*, Act 4.

2. **Ask** students to identify the difference in the rhyme schemes of these passages.
   Answer: Goethe's verse, in translation, rhymes ABADEFEGHIHI, or alternating rhymes. Shakespeare has only the rhyming couplet at the end of the act.

3. **Ask** students the Comparing Tragedies question.
   Possible response: Goethe uses more rhyme in his writing than Shakespeare did.

4. **Ask** students if there are any other differences they can notice between the two authors' styles.
   Possible response: Goethe refers to concepts and abstract terms far more than Shakespeare does in his more natural dialogue.

❺ Reading Check
Answer: Faust says in line 273 that he will devote himself to all excess; in other words, he will overdo the pleasures of life and no longer lust for knowledge.

Differentiated Instruction for Universal Access

Vocabulary for Special-Needs Students
Help students who may be struggling with Goethe's lofty monologues understand that the ideas each character expresses can be stated more simply. Point out that drama of the time was intended more as a poetic reading of ideas and weighty concepts. Break down sets of lines and have students restate the ideas in their own words. Show how Mephistopheles' lines starting at line 282 could be restated as "*I have been eating iron in Hell forever, so I know that no human can understand the sufferings and joys of life.*"

Vocabulary for Advanced Readers
Direct students' attention to the word pairs *painful joy, enamored hate,* and *enlivening disgust* in lines 272 and 273. Explain that these words have contradictory meanings, and that the author combines them for effect. Have students discuss how these opposites can produce a single meaning. A similar pairing of opposites occurs in lines 278–279, 286–287, and 290, with *highest and lowest, weal and woe, devil/God,* and *day and night.* Allow students to offer reasons why Goethe and his translator chose these terms to produce contradiction.

❻ Background

Sturm und Drang

Goethe was part of a movement that swept through German literature and music at the end of the fourteenth century. The title of the movement, *Sturm und Drang,* can be translated as *Storm and Stress* and refers to the difficulties humans have in society, and how nature offers an example of balance in chaos and calm. The artists of *Sturm und Drang,* reacting to the ordered, rational, and optimistic thought of the Enlightenment that came before it, sought to provoke extreme emotions in their audience.

❼ Visual Connections

Whole-Class Activity

Ask students to describe what they see in the picture.
Possible response: At first glance, the mood of the painting is dark, even wild. However, the break in the clouds hints at the calm that will follow the storm's passing, lightening the piece's overall effect.

Small-Group Activity

1. Divide the class into small groups. Tell half of the groups to imagine themselves high on the cliff. Ask the others to imagine they are on a boat on the sea. Have students describe, in their groups and from the assigned perspectives, what might be happening in the painting.

2. Ask one person from each group to summarize the group's ideas. Be sure students compare how the change in perspective affected their descriptions.

Individual Activity

Ask students to write a short story based on the picture. Allow students to choose the perspective, the cliff or the sea, from which they write.

6
7

432 Celebrating Humanity (1485–1625)

Enrichment: Investigating Artistic Schools and Movements

The Age of Enlightenment to the Romantic Era

Artistic schools and movements often emerge as a reaction to or a transformation from the movements that precede them. *The Sturm und Drang* movement arose from the restraint and optimism of the Age of Enlightenment. In turn, it paved the way for the Romanticists who followed. Classicism was another reaction to this approach that sprung up in a variety of art forms of this general time period.

Activity: Investigating Artistic Movements
Have each student pick any of these schools or movements and explore their connections to the movements that came before or after. Suggest that they record information in the **Enrichment: Investigating Artistic Schools and Movements** worksheet, *Professional Development Guidebook,* page 220. Direct students to use the results of their research to develop oral presentations. Then have students make their oral presentations to the class.

MEPHISTOPHELES:
    You are in the end . . . what you are.
    You can put on full-bottomed wigs with a million locks,
    You can put on stilts instead of your stocks,
315   You remain for ever what you are.

FAUST: I feel my endeavors have not been worth a pin
    When I raked together the treasures of the human mind,
    If at the end I but sit down to find
    No new force welling up within.
320   I have not a hair's breadth more of height,
❾ | I am no nearer the Infinite.

MEPHISTOPHELES: My very good sir, you look at things
    Just in the way that people do;
    We must be cleverer than that
325   Or the joys of life will escape from you.
    Hell! You have surely hands and feet,
    Also a head and you-know-what;
    The pleasures I gather on the wing,
    Are they less mine? Of course they're not!
330   Suppose I can afford six stallions,
    I can add that horse-power to my score
    And dash along and be a proper man
    As if my legs were twenty-four.
    So good-bye to thinking! On your toes!
335   The world's before us. Quick! Here goes!
    I tell you, a chap who's intellectual
    Is like a beast on a blasted heath
    Driven in circles by a demon
    While a fine green meadow lies round beneath.

340 **FAUST:** How do we start?

MEPHISTOPHELES: We just say go—and skip.
    But please get ready for this pleasure trip.

[*Exit* FAUST.]

    Only look down on knowledge and reason,
    The highest gifts that men can prize,
345   Only allow the spirit of lies
    To confirm you in magic and illusion,
    And then I have you body and soul.
    Fate has given this man a spirit
    Which is always pressing onward, beyond control,
350   And whose mad striving overleaps

---

❽ ◄ Critical Viewing
How does this painting convey the powers of nature that Faust has experienced?

Comparing Tragedies
Do either *Macbeth* or *Oedipus* long, like Faust, for "the Infinite"? Explain.

❿ **Reading Check**
What does Mephistopheles urge Faust to do?

from Faust **433**

---

❽ Critical Viewing
Possible Response: The painting demonstrates the fury of the ocean in a storm, high winds of a gale, lightning crashing down from the skies, and the strength and resistance of the rocky cliffs. All of these demonstrate the power and strength of nature.

❾ Comparing Tragedies
1. Direct students' attention to line 321, "I am no nearer the Infinite." Have students look to the lines that precede this as well.
2. **Ask** students what it might mean to seek "the Infinite."
   Answer: It could mean everlasting life, the never-ending pleasure, but he mentions force and treasures, so it is more likely he is referring to limitless power.
3. **Ask** students if Oedipus and Macbeth sought limitless power of everlasting life.
   Possible response: Macbeth sought power and Oedipus tried to overcome his fate, but he was also a king who wielded extreme power.
4. **Ask** the Comparing Tragedies question.
   Possible responses: Yes, Macbeth took actions, at first from ambition and then from desperation, that he hoped would secure his destiny—he longs to be the master of his own fate. No, Oedipus at the end of the play clearly understands his limitations and ultimate powerlessness.
5. **Ask** students if Oedipus, Macbeth, and Faust succeeded in achieving the Infinite.
   Possible response: For moments in their lives they had this power, yet for all of them, they paid a heavy price for possessing the gifts only gods enjoy forever.

❿ Reading Check
Answer: Mephistopheles urges Faust in line 334 to stop thinking things through and to follow his urges instead. In line 336, he urges him to stop being an intellectual and to give in to life's base desires.

433

Before students respond, you may wish to have them write a brief objective summary of the selection. As they answer the questions below, remind them to support their answers with evidence from the text.

1. (a) He devotes himself to all excess and rejects his pursuit of the treasures of the human mind, or knowledge. (b) Faust believes that even if he were to gain complete knowledge, he would be no closer to the Infinite, or perfection. He rejects knowledge in exchange for excess, in hopes that pleasure will bring him the Infinite. (c) The Romantics believed intuition and feelings would lift them out of ordinary life. Faust believes knowledge and sensual excess will lift him instead.

2. (a) He suggests an intellectual's pursuit of knowledge is as meaningless as being driven around and around on the same barren ground while missing the fresh grass that is everywhere else— in other words, an impossible task. (b) Mephistopheles is the opposite of reason. He stands for impulse and sensual excess, not reasoned learning.

3. (a) He is counting on Faust's spirit. He will use this against Faust. (b) **Possible response:** He suggests that Faust will never be happy and would have failed even if he had not given into the Devil. (c) **Possible response:** Any attempt to use knowledge or pleasure to make you perfect is impossible, because perfection is unattainable. Faust would need to humble himself to be happy.

4. (a) **Possible response:** Any relentless pursuit of something that may cost you your soul is similar to Faust's bargain with the Devil. Critics are suggesting that society will have to pay someday for its desire for the power given by technology. (b) **Possible response:** I believe that global warming and pollution are the prices we pay for having technology. If we are not careful to control these results, we will, like Faust, have sacrificed the Earth to enjoy the benefits of machines doing our work.

434

Vocabulary
insatiableness (in sā′ shə bəl nes) *n.* the quality of being impossible to fill

355

All joys of the earth between pole and pole.
Him shall I drag through the wilds of life
And through the flats of meaninglessness,
I shall make him flounder and gape and stick
And to tease his insatiableness
Hang meat and drink in the air before his watering lips;
In vain he will pray to slake his inner thirst,
And even had he not sold himself to the devil
He would be equally accursed.

Critical Reading

Cite textual evidence to support your responses.

1. **Key Ideas and Details (a)** To what does Faust say he devotes himself and what does he reject? **(b) Analyze:** How do what he pursues and what he rejects explain what he means by "the Infinite"? **(c) Interpret:** In what ways do Faust's pursuits reflect the Romantics' desire to go beyond ordinary life?

2. **Key Ideas and Details (a) Interpret:** What does Mephistopheles' simile comparing an intellectual to a beast (lines 336–339) suggest about his attitude toward intellectuals? **(b) Infer:** Why does Mephistopheles want Faust and others to "look down on knowledge and reason"?

3. **Key Ideas and Details (a) Analyze:** What quality in Faust does Mephistopheles count on to gain control of him? **(b)** In the final lines, what does Mephistopheles predict will happen to Faust? **(c) Speculate:** Do you agree with this prediction? Why or why not?

4. **Integration of Knowledge and Ideas (a) Connect:** Some critics have called contemporary society, with its devotion to constantly developing technology, Faustian. What do you think they mean? **(b) Make a Judgment:** Do you believe our society is Faustian? Why or why not?

434 Celebrating Humanity (1485–1625)

Assessment Resources

Unit 2 Resources
L3 L4 *Selection Test,* pp. 188–189.

PHLit Online! All resources are available at www.PHLitOnline.com.

After You Read

Macbeth • Oedipus the King • Faust

Comparing Tragedies

 1. Integration of Knowledge and Ideas (a) What is similar about the social status of Macbeth and Oedipus? **(b)** How might the social status of these **tragic heroes** contribute to the awe—a mixed feeling of respect and dread—that the audience feels in watching the **tragedy? (c)** What other elements in each of the three selections help create awe? Explain.

2. Key Ideas and Details How would you define the **tragic flaw** of each hero?

3. Integration of Knowledge and Ideas *Faust* has a chorus of sorts, though it does not appear in this selection; *Macbeth*, however, has no chorus in the usual sense. **(a)** In your opinion, do the Witches in *Macbeth* perform some of the roles that a chorus does? Why or why not? **(b)** Would adding a chorus like that in a Greek drama strengthen or weaken *Macbeth*? Explain.

⏱ Timed Writing

Explanatory Text: Essay

Macbeth and the excerpts you have read reveal how the structure and elements in the work of dramatists changed over time.

Assignment: Write an **explanatory essay** in which you compare and contrast two plays from different periods. Evaluate how the dramatic structure and elements changed from one play to the other. **[40 minutes]**

Use questions like these to focus your analysis.
- Is the play structured to teach a moral, show the downfall of a noble character, or allow for the happy resolution of a misunderstanding?
- Are the characters personifications, social types, or complex individuals?

As you write, follow the conventions of a strong analytical essay:
- Begin your essay with a clear thesis statement.
- Use a clear organizational schema for conveying ideas.
- Support your thesis with relevant and substantial evidence, including well-chosen details from the texts.

As you draft, write legibly. Use appropriate capitalization and punctuation.

5-Minute Planner

Complete these steps before you begin to write:
1. Read the assignment carefully. Take note of key words and phrases.
2. Jot down some initial thoughts. Then, scan the plays for evidence that supports your ideas. **TIP** Create a chart in which to record quotations or details related to each play.
3. Create an outline for your essay that identifies the central idea of each paragraph.
4. Reread the prompt, and draft your essay.

Macbeth • Oedipus the King • Faust **435**

ⓒ Common Core State Standards

Writing

2. Write informative/explanatory texts to examine and convey complex ideas, concepts, and information clearly and accurately through the effective selection, organization, and analysis of content.

10. Write routinely over extended time frames and shorter time frames for a range of tasks, purposes, and audiences.

USE ACADEMIC VOCABULARY

As you write, use academic language, including the following words or their related forms:

   comparison
   contrast
   distinguish
   resolution

For more about academic language, see the vocabulary charts in the introduction to this book.

Answers

Comparing Tragedies

1. (a) They are both kings. (b) Both men are living a life of privilege and power; as they self-destruct, the loss and waste of that status heightens the awe. (c) **Possible response:** The highly dramatic plot twists and characters make these stories more awe-inspiring. Dueling with the Devil instead of a next-door neighbor is an example. Killing your father and marrying your mother are extreme trials to endure.

2. **Possible response:** Macbeth's tragic flaw was his weakness of being persuaded by others. Oedipus' flaw was in not avoiding the very things the oracle had predicted. If he had not married or killed anyone, he would never have fulfilled the prediction. Faust wanted the ultimate and could not settle for less, so he received the ultimate punishment.

3. **Possible response:** The witches in *Macbeth* act in unison and often make the audience aware of larger issues, just like the Greek chorus. They are, however, characters in the drama, not outside commentators like the Greek chorus. (b) **Possible response:** Adding a Greek chorus to *Macbeth* would weaken it because the members of a chorus are not real characters interacting with other characters on stage. Some of the smaller, quieter scenes in *Macbeth* would be ruined by having a chanting chorus on stage.

⏱ Timed Writing

1. Teach the Academic Vocabulary. Discuss the words with students, and their related forms including *comparatively, resolute,* and *resolve.* Review with students the vocabulary they learned before reading the selection, including the the different meanings found. Encourage students to use *account* and *reckoning* as they compare and contrast works from two different time periods.

---

2. Use the prompt to help students identify elements and qualities their analytical essays should have:
   - A thesis statement about the overall similarities and differences between two works from different time periods.
   - A clear organizational structure that categorizes the similarities and differences.
   - Details from the text that support the thesis statement.

Encourage students to focus on these points when they are planning and revising their essays.

Tell students they will have 40 minutes to plan and write the essay. Call students' attention to the 5-Minute Planner. Encourage students to budget their time to allow 5 minutes for outlining, 5 minutes for identifying some initial supporting text references in the works, and 10 minutes for revision and proofreading.

435

Common Core State Standards

- **Reading Informational Text 6**
- **Language 4.d**

About the Texts

1. Introduce the forms, using the instruction on the student page.

2. Tell students that they will identify the elements of newspaper articles as they read.

Reading Strategy

1. Introduce the skill, using the instruction and chart on the student page.

2. Tell students that they will evaluate the author's purpose and perspective as they read.

Think Aloud: Model the Skill

Say to students:

When I am reading a newspaper feature article, I know it will deliver information quickly and in an interesting way. First, I look at the title. Then, I look for the tone of the first paragraph. Finally, I look for the author's use of facts and interesting details. These clues help me to determine the author's purpose and perspective.

Content-Area Vocabulary

1. Have students say each word aloud.

2. Then, use each word in a sentence that makes its meaning clear. Repeat your sentence with the vocabulary word missing and have students fill in the blank.

For more guidance, consult the *Classroom Strategies and Teaching Routines* card on introducing vocabulary.

Reading for Information

Analyzing Functional and Expository Texts

Feature Article • Theater Review

About the Texts

A **feature article** is an informative or entertaining piece of nonfiction writing, found in a print or online periodical, that focuses on a topic of general interest such as a trend, local performance, or significant person. Features include an enticing *lead,* or opening, and a body that provides in-depth analysis.

A **theater review** is a feature article in which the writer gives facts and details about a theatrical production, as well as his or her opinion of it. Some of its features include an overview of the work; a "quick review" device, such as a star ranking indicating quality; and details of where and when the production can be viewed.

Reading Strategy

An **author's purpose** is his or her reason for writing—to inform, to persuade, or to entertain. An **author's perspective,** or **point of view,** on a topic consists of his or her beliefs, judgments, and attitudes about that topic. As you read, **evaluate the author's purpose and perspective** as it is reflected in the following elements:

- The title

- The author's *style,* or overall manner of expression, and *tone,* or the attitude he or she conveys through word choice (formal or informal, serious or light, sarcastic or straightforward); typically established by the lead

- The points made with anecdotes and direct quotes, as well as the facts and interesting details the author chooses to include

Use a chart like the one shown to evaluate the author's purpose.

Text Structures	Example	Effect on Meaning
Title		
Lead		
Positive/Negative Adjectives		
Direct Quotes		
Facts and Details		

Common Core State Standards

Reading Informational Text
6. Determine an author's point of view or purpose in a text in which the rhetoric is particularly effective, analyzing how style and content contribute to the power, persuasiveness, or beauty of the text.

Content-Area Vocabulary

These words appear in the selections that follow. They may also appear in other content-area texts:

pneumatic (noo mat´ ik) *adj.* run or powered by compressed air

excavation (eks´ kə vā´ shən) *n.* the process of making a hole or a cavity by digging and removing

contemporaneous (kən tem´ pə rā´ nē əs) *adj.* originating, existing, or happening during the same period of time

regime (rə zhēm´) *n.* a system of management or government that is in power

---

Teaching Resources

Reading Support

- **L2 L3** *Reader's Notebook*
- **L1** *Reader's Notebook: Adapted Version*
- **EL** *Reader's Notebook: English Learner's Version*

> The title indicates the topic of the article—efforts to design a modern equivalent of the Globe, Shakespeare's original theater.

Smithsonian
MAGAZINE

DESIGNING A GLOBE THEATRE FOR THE 21ST CENTURY

By Eric Jaffe

> Feature articles frequently use vivid descriptions and informal language.

The tractor-trailer planted firmly in the Wal-Mart parking lot did not seem out of place, but the actors who performed *Merchant of Venice* right beside it sure did. When the vehicle arrived it deployed into a full-size stage. Behind the set, pneumatic pods inflated to become ticket-windows and dressing rooms. Sunlight powered the spotlights and speakers. And when the playhouse folded up and drove off, a screen mounted on the side of the trailer replayed the show for all to see.

This is the Globe Theatre—not the one that housed Shakespeare's best dramas, but one conceived by Jennifer Siegal for a modern audience. Siegal's Globe is part homage to the Elizabethan era's itinerant theatre troupe, part shout-out to today's compact, on-the-go gizmos. The Los Angeles-based architect was one of five designers asked to create a 21st-century Shakespearean theatre for "Reinventing the Globe," a new exhibit at the National Building Museum in Washington, D.C., that opens January 13 and runs through August 2007.

Illustration of Jennifer Siegal's "Globetrotter"—a portable Shakespeare theater

Given only brief guidance and a few months to finish, these architects created modern Globes that challenge conventional thoughts about dramatic performances and the spaces that accommodate them, says Martin Moeller, the exhibition's curator. "When the words stay the same but all else changes, you realize how much power the words have," he says.

Theatre designer John Coyne delivered a truly virtual Globe. To reflect today's cross-cultural world, Coyne's performances would occur simultaneously in several locations. Gigantic screens with live streaming would hang above the stages, and characters would interact in real time. So, speaking in Russian from Moscow, Polonius offers advice to Laertes in New York; standing oceans away, Hamlet pierces Claudius with a venom-tipped sword.

Michele (pronounced *Mi-keleh*) Saee, who did not have theatre design experience, modeled a Globe that would capture an actor's fluidity in the structure itself. He proposed tracing the movements of an actor throughout a performance

About Feature Articles

1. Point out to students that the selection is a newspaper feature article.

2. Refer students to the elements of a newspaper feature article on the Preteach page.

3. **Ask** students to predict what information the article will cover, based on its title and first paragraph. **Possible response:** The article is about modern designs for the Globe Theatre.

Evaluate the Author's Purpose and Perspective

1. Refer students to the bulleted elements of the author's purpose and perspective on the Preteach page.

2. Point out that they will evaluate the author's purpose and perspective as they read the article.

3. Suggest that students use a chart like the one shown on the Preteach page to organize their notes.

Differentiated Instruction   for Universal Access

Support for Less Proficient Readers

To make sure students can identify the speakers in a feature article, have them practice identifying quotations. Ask students to make a list of the quotations in the feature article and note the name of each speaker. Have students note when speakers change and how the speakers are identified on the second reference.

EL Strategy for English Learners

English learners may need help with slang and idiomatic expressions such as *shout-out*, *gizmos*, and *hipsters*. Work with English learners to restate unfamiliar phrases using more familiar vocabulary. In addition, explain any unfamiliar references such as the names of characters from Shakespeare's plays.

Evaluate the Author's Purpose and Perspective

1. Remind students that the use of direct quotations can help reveal an author's purpose and perspective.

2. Have students read Siegel's comments in the second and third full paragraphs on this page. **Ask** whether these comments support a positive or negative view on the subject of modernizing the Globe Theatre. **Answer:** The quotes support a positive view.

using electronic monitors then, with the help of a computer, turning these motions into a three-dimensional image that would become the building. "It's like those photos at night where you see red and white lights streaking down the road," Moeller says. "It's almost like you have a history built into one image."

David Rockwell's transparent Globe is intended to erase the barrier between outdoor and indoor settings. H3, the architectural firm guided by Hugh Hardy, created a floating Globe that could bounce around to various New York City boroughs, like so many bar-hopping hipsters, as a way to increase public access.

Siegel, who is the founder of the Office of Mobile Design, says her portable Globe, dubbed the "Globetrotter," is ready to go into production with the right client.

"We're a mobile society that deals with communication devices in a compact way, and theatre can be represented in a similar take," she says. "It doesn't have to be going to this old, stodgy building. It could be much more accessible, transient and lighter."

In some ways, conceptualizing a Globe Theatre for the future requires as much imagination as re-creating the one that stood in Shakespeare's day. Despite the playhouse's prominence, historians still argue over many aspects of the theatre, says Franklin J. Hildy of the University of Maryland, an advisor to the London Globe reconstruction that opened in 1997.

Notable uncertainties include the shape of the stage (some say it was rectangular, others square); how many sides the structure had (with ranges from 16 to 24); even the size of the building itself (some call the diameter 100 feet across, others 90).

Globe reconstructions work off evidence from seven maps of London in that day, texts from Shakespeare's

plays and a site excavation (the original theatre, built in 1599, burned down in 1613 and was restored in the same place). Perhaps the most crucial historical document is a contract to build the Fortune theatre, a contemporaneous playhouse, which instructs builders to copy many of the Globe's dimensions.

Of the Globe's certainties, the stage that jutted out into the crowd was one of its most impressive attributes, says Hildy. "Everywhere you looked there was life, audience, energy." Standing patrons, known as groundlings, surrounded the stage, often shouting at the actors, cracking hazelnut shells—even sitting on stage.

Though Shakespeare's work also appeared at the Rose and Curtain theatres, the Globe hosted most of his famous dramas—including *Hamlet, King Lear* and *Macbeth*—which explains part of its lasting allure, Hildy says.

"The sense has always been that you could feel a closer connection to Shakespeare if you could understand how he saw theatre, how he saw his plays staged," he says. "Shakespeare was working during one of the most successful periods that theatre has ever had. There seems to be a relationship between buildings and that success."

> The writer gives the reader historical background to put the current project in context.

The restored Globe Theatre in London

Vocabulary Development

Content-Area Vocabulary

Review the definitions of the cross-curricular vocabulary with students: *pneumatic, excavation,* and *contemporaneous.* Then, examine each word in its context in the article.

When you have finished with the three listed words, ask students to identify other words in the article that relate to the cross-curricular vocabulary. Have students look up their definitions in a dictionary and then use them in sentences about the topic of the feature article.

The New York Times

April 26, 2007

Theater Review / 'Macbeth'

The Scottish Play, Told With Sound and Fury and Puppets

By LAWRENCE VAN GELDER

The "lead" in this review makes the reader wonder what this theatrical production is all about.

A puppet regime has seized control of the stage of the New Victory Theater. Plotting bloody murder, it slaughters men, women and children in pursuit of power until condign vengeance wreaks its ruin.

"Macbeth" is back in a captivating production that allies the actorly talents of the Chicago Shakespeare Theater with the remarkable talents of the Colla Marionette Company (Compagnia Marionettistica Carlo Colla e Figli) of Italy, which traces its origins to 1835.

In this swift-moving presentation (95 minutes including intermission), playing through Sunday, thirteen puppeteers out of sight above the stage combine with seven actors seated in semidarkness facing the action to render a forceful, visually captivating and clearly articulated version of Shakespeare's tragedy.

Here legions of troops march, caparisoned horses carry caped and tartan-bedecked Scottish noblemen, evil unfolds in the depths of great castles, a flock of birds flutters overhead, and the weird sisters and their fiery cauldron disgorge the prophecies that will lead Macbeth and his lady to deadly doings.

Differentiated Instruction for Universal Access

EL Strategies for English Learners

Lead students on a "selection tour." Direct students to identify elements common to newspapers: the date, text columns, photos, banner, and byline. Additionally, point out words and names that students might struggle with and have students practice saying and using them before reading the selection.

Support for Less Proficient Readers

Inform students that this review is written for an opera based on Shakespeare's *Macbeth*, a play they just completed reading. Remind them to keep the play's plot and characters in mind while reading the review and looking at the accompanying pictures.

About Theater Reviews

1. Tell students that they will now be reading a newspaper theater review.

2. Preview with the students the list of features common to theater reviews that appear on the Preteach page. **Ask:** What other review devices, aside from the star, might writers use to rate a production?
   Possible responses: Students may suggest the use of thumbs, "smiley faces," or letter grades to indicate their assessment.

3. **Ask** students to read the title and the first two paragraphs of the review and make a prediction about the writer's opinion of the performance.
   Possible response: The title and the first paragraph explain that the reviewer had a strong impression of the production, but it is not until the second paragraph that the reviewer indicates that it is a strongly positive impression.

Evaluate the Author's Purpose and Perspective

1. Tell students that they will evaluate the author's perspective as they read the theater review.

2. While they read the review, direct students to find examples of positive or negative adjectives, direct quotes, and facts and details that have an effect on meaning.

3. Remind students to use a chart like the one on the Preteach page to take notes as they read.

1. Remind students to identify the text structures that help them understand the author's perspective.

2. **Ask** students to describe the tone of the review and to support their descriptions with examples from the review.
   Possible response: The use of words such as *captivating*, *remarkable*, and *swift-moving* convey a positive and admiring tone.

Theater Review

The New York Times

Humans, animals, witches—all 130 of them are puppets, most of them three feet tall. Their deeds and misdeeds are carried out in eye-catching sylvan settings and in the corridors and on the parapets of castles whose perspectives make them seem to have been built of genuine stone. In the blackouts between scenes, music composed by Fabio Vacchi intensifies the atmosphere of tension and foreboding.

At least since 1846-7, when Giuseppe Verdi and his librettist Francesco Maria Piave applied themselves to transforming "Macbeth" to opera, Italy has been no stranger to abridging this tragedy; this production retains the play's highlights, including Lady Macbeth's sleepwalking scene, Banquo's ghost, the witches' recipe and the coming of Birnam Wood to Dunsinane.

With puppetry directed by Eugenio Monti Colla and spoken word directed by Kate Buckley, the two companies engineer a shining collaboration.

This "Macbeth" is recommended for audiences 12 and older. For all and in all respects, it is an uncommon treat.

"Macbeth" runs through Sunday at the New Victory Theater.

> The reviewer offers information on where and when performances take place.

> The reviewer supports his point of view or purpose with specific details.

440 Celebrating Humanity (1485–1625)

Vocabulary Development

Content-Area Vocabulary

Review the definitions of the cross-curricular vocabulary with students: *engineer* and *regime*. Then, examine each word in its context in the article.

When you have finished with the two listed words, ask students to identify other words in the article that relate to the cross-curricular vocabulary. Have students look up their definitions in a dictionary and then use them in sentences about the topic of the review.

Critical Reading

 **1. Key Ideas and Details (a)** In the feature article, what does the author say is the reason different versions of the Globe Theater were created? **(b)** Why does the author consider it important to conceptualize a Globe Theater for the future?

2. Key Ideas and Details (a) What is the author's purpose and perspective in the feature article? **(b)** Explain two ways in which he uses direct quotes to support his perspective.

3. Craft and Structure (a) What facts and details in the theater review support the author's opinion of the performance? **(b)** Describe the style and the tone of the review. **(c)** What perspective do this style and tone help to express?

4. Content-Area Vocabulary The Latin prefix *trans-* means "across" or "through." The Latin verb *parēre* means "to be visible." Together, they contribute to the meaning of *transparent*, which means "clear" or "through which things are visible." Using your knowledge of the prefix *trans-*, give the meaning of each of these words: *transmit, transcribe,* and *transpose.* Then, verify your preliminary determination of the meaning of each word by looking it up in a dictionary.

⏱ Timed Writing

Informative Text [40 minutes]

> **Format**
> In a **compare-and-contrast** essay, you analyze the similarities and differences between two or more things. One way to organize your essay is to discuss similarities first and differences second.

Write a **compare-and-contrast** essay in which you analyze and compare the **aesthetic and cultural considerations** that influence modern producers and theater designers when they stage Shakespeare. Integrate ideas and examples from both the feature article and the theater review, providing context as required by your audience's background knowledge. Evaluate the importance and ultimate consequence for theater of each factor you discuss.

> **Academic Vocabulary**
> **Aesthetic and cultural considerations** are ideas concerning style, beauty, and the power of a work to express the experiences of its audience.

5-Minute Planner

Complete these steps before you begin to write.

1. Read the prompt carefully. Underline key words.
2. Scan the texts for details about the reasons people have for adapting Shakespeare. **TIP** Pay special attention to quotations from participants and to descriptions of the impact of their work, as well as to signal words indicating purpose, such as "as a way to."
3. Decide which points you will discuss.
4. Reread the prompt, and begin drafting.

Reading for Information: Feature Article • Theater Review **441**

 Common Core State Standards

Reading Informational Text
7. Integrate and evaluate multiple sources of information presented in different media or formats as well as in words in order to address a question or solve a problem.

Writing
2.b. Develop the topic thoroughly by selecting the most significant and relevant facts, extended definitions, concrete details, quotations, or other information and examples appropriate to the audience's knowledge of the topic.

Language
4.d. Verify the preliminary determination of the meaning of a word or phrase.

Critical Reading

1. (a) The different versions were created for an exhibit at the National Building Museum. (b) The author thinks it is important to challenge traditional ideas about performance spaces.

2. (a) **Possible response:** The author's purpose is to inform. His perspective is that there is no one right way to stage a theater production. (b) He uses quotes to describe the theater designers' work and to explain the controversy surrounding the details of the original Globe Theatre.

3. (a) The author describes the puppets, the staging, the set, and the music. (b) **Possible response:** The style is playful and lively, and the tone is full of praise for the performance. (c) **Possible response:** The style and tone help express the author's perspective, or view, that the play is very good.

4. **Possible response:** To *transmit* is to send. To *transcribe* is to write something out. To *transpose* is to change position.

⏱ Timed Writing

1. Before students begin the assignment, guide them in analyzing key words and phrases in the prompt, using the highlighted notes.

2. Work with students to draw up guidelines for their compare-and-contrast essays based on the key words they identified.

3. Have students use the 5-Minute Planner to structure their time.

4. Allow students 40 minutes to complete the assignment. Evaluate their work using the guidelines they have developed.

Extend the Lesson

Connecting to the Students' World

To give students further practice with persuasive writing and to help them apply the material to their own world, divide the class into small groups. Provide each group with a review of a play being performed in a local theater or of a movie showing in local cinemas. Students should work together to identify the persuasive techniques used by the writer. Ask them to identify the author's opinion and then the word choices, details, and examples that best support that opinion.

441

Write a Persuasive Essay

Common Core
State Standards

Writing
1. Write arguments to support claims in an analysis of substantive topics or texts, using valid reasoning and relevant and sufficient evidence.
5. Develop and strengthen writing as needed by planning, revising, editing, rewriting, or trying a new approach, focusing on addressing what is most significant for a specific purpose and audience.

**Common Core
State Standards**

- **Writing 1.a, b, c, e; 4, 5**
- **Language 1.b, 2.b, 3.a**

Introducing the Writing Assignment

Review the assignment and criteria using the instruction on the student page.

What Do You Notice?

1. Read the excerpt from "Speech Before Her Troops." Discuss with students how the Queen appeals to logic and emotion.

2. Have a student read the highlighted sentence aloud. **Ask** students what makes it special. (**Possible responses:** its strong rhythms; its self-assured tone.)

3. Point out the semicolon that joins the two clauses, and then **ask** how the clauses differ. (**Answer:** The first is very short; the second is very long.)

4. **Ask** students what each clause is about. (**Answer:** the first is about tyrants' fear; the second is about the queen's trust in her people.) **Ask** what the length of each clause suggests about the speaker's attitude toward each subject. (**Possible response:** She is dismissive of tyrants, but has great confidence in herself and in her people.)

5. Suggest that students try joining a short clause with a long one to express competing attitudes.

Frank Kermode on Persuasive Essays

Show students Segment 3 on Frank Kermode on the *See It!* DVD or via the link in the **Enriched Online Student Edition** at www.PHLitOnline.com. Discuss Kermode's opinions on the impact of literary criticism on society.

Persuasive, or Argumentative, Essay English Renaissance writers such as Sir Thomas More argued vigorously for their humanistic ideals in **persuasive essays,** also called *argumentative essays*. A persuasive essay is a prose work that presents a case for or against a position using supporting evidence and convincing language. Follow the steps outlined in this workshop to write your own persuasive essay.

Assignment Write a persuasive essay on an issue of importance to you.

What to Include To succeed, your persuasive essay must feature the following elements:

- a thesis statement that clearly states your position and the action you want readers to take
- well-organized evidence that supports your argument, such as facts, examples, statistics, and personal experience
- responses to alternate or opposing claims
- information that will appeal to your audience's logic and emotions, and that will inspire trust in your credibility and character
- compelling persuasive language that maintains a formal tone
- transitions and varied syntax used to link ideas
- an effective conclusion that sums up the argument

To preview the criteria on which your persuasive essay may be judged, see the rubric on page 449.

To get a feel for persuasive writing, read this excerpt. Notice how Queen Elizabeth I appeals to both her audience's logic and emotions.

from: Speech Before Her Troops

My loving people, we have been persuaded by some, that are careful of our safety, to take heed how we commit ourselves to armed multitudes, for fear of treachery; but I assure you, I do not desire to live to distrust my faithful and loving people. Let tyrants fear; I have always so behaved myself that, under God, I have placed my chiefest strength and safeguard in the loyal hearts and good will of my subjects. And therefore I am come amongst you at this time, not as for my recreation or sport, but being resolved, in the midst and heat of the battle, to live or die amongst you all; to lay down, for my God, and for my kingdom, and for my people, my honor and my blood, even the dust.

WRITE GUY
Jeff Anderson, M.Ed.

What Do You Notice?

Read the highlighted sentence several times. Then, with a partner, discuss the qualities that make it special. You might consider the following elements:

- word choice
- sentence length
- use of punctuation
- vivid details

Share your group's observations with the class.

Teaching Resources

Unit 2 Resources
All **Writing Workshop,** pp. 190–191

All *Common Core Companion,*
pp. 16–31; 40–49

All *Professional Development Guidebook*
**Rubrics for Self-Assessment:
Persuasive Essays,** pp. 256–257.

All *Graphic Organizer Transparencies*
Rubrics for Self-Assessment, p. 174
Plot Diagram, p. 297
Three-Column Chart, p. 299

All *See It!* DVD
Frank Kermode, Segments 3 and 4

PHLit Online! All resources are available at **www.PHLitOnline.com.**

Prewriting and Planning

Choosing Your Topic

Use one of the following strategies to find a topic that provokes in you a strong reaction:

- **Conduct a news scan.** Read newspapers or listen to news programs to learn about current, controversial issues. Avoid issues on which your only opinion is "I like _____" or "I dislike _____." Pick a topic on which you take a clearly articulated stand.

  Weak: I don't like the proposed changes to update the mall.

  Strong: Rather than piecemeal projects, our community needs a coherent revitalization plan.

- **Monitor online discussions.** Internet message boards often contain heated disagreements. Look for boards sponsored by local schools, government agencies, or media sources. Scan message boards for topics that receive many responses—a high number of posts about a topic may indicate controversy.

Narrowing Your Topic

Once you have identified a general interest, focus on a specific aspect that you can fully and completely support. Consider the needs of your intended audience as you make notes about your topic.

> My Interest: Health Care   Narrower Topic: Preventive Care

Gathering Details

Gather facts and arguments to support your position. Use libraries, the Internet, personal interviews, or other resources. Make note also of any facts that contradict your opinion, so you can prepare counterarguments. You might begin by filling out a chart like the one shown.

Purpose	Audience	My Arguments	Counterarguments to Address
To persuade seniors to apply early to college	Seniors at my school	• Choosing early admissions may improve your chances of acceptance. • Applications will just hang over your head if you delay.	• Some schools do not offer early admissions. • Getting in early may limit your financial aid package.

Prewriting and Planning

1. Introduce the prewriting strategies using the instruction on the student page.
2. Have students apply the strategies to choose and narrow a topic and gather details.

Teaching the Strategies

1. Have volunteers share topic ideas from their news scan. Write the ideas on the board. Then, select one topic and ask students what they already know about it. This will help students gauge how much research they need to conduct.
2. Remind students that all Internet sites are not equally reliable. Encourage students to use online discussions as a springboard for new ideas, but to verify information with authoritative resources.

Think Aloud: Model Gathering Details

To model the strategy of gathering details, use the following "think aloud." Say to students:

> Before I write a persuasive essay, I write each fact on an index card. As I prepare to write, I think about my thesis statement. Then, I go through my note cards. I separate them into two piles: facts that support my thesis and facts that are not related. As I write, I use the facts that support my thesis.

Six Traits Focus

✓	Ideas		Word Choice
✓	Organization		Sentence Fluency
	Voice		Conventions

PH WRITING COACH Grade 12

Students will find additional information on persuasive essays in Chapter 9.

Prentice Hall EssayScorer

A writing prompt for this mode of writing can be found on the *Prentice Hall Essay Scorer* at **www.PHLitOnline.com.**

Applying Understanding by Design Principles

Clarifying Expected Outcomes: Using Rubrics

- Before students begin work on this assignment, have them preview the **Rubric for Self-Assessment**, page 449, to learn what qualities their persuasive essays must have. A copy of this Rubric appears in the *Graphic Organizer Transparencies* page 74.
- Review the criteria in the Rubric with the class. Before students use the Rubric to assess their own writing, work with them to rate the Student Model (page 448) using the Rubric.
- If you wish to assess students' persuasive essays with either a 4-point or 6-point scoring rubric, see the *Professional Development Guidebook*, pages 256–257, **Persuasion: Persuasive Essay.**

Drafting

1. Introduce the drafting strategies using the instruction on the student page.
2. Have students apply the strategies as they draft their essays.

Teaching the Strategies

1. Explain to students that a strong opening paragraph provides an important "boost" to their position. Encourage them to craft opening paragraphs that lead to direct statements of their viewpoints. Tell students that using clear, concise sentences will help solidify their position and prepare readers for their argument.

2. Ask students to give definitions and examples of repetition, parallelism, and analogies. Explain that these devices create strong visual images and sound effects that appeal to readers. Advise students not to overly use these devices in their essays; otherwise they will weaken their arguments instead of strengthening them.

3. Guide a discussion of logical, ethical, and emotional appeals. Invite students to talk about which they may want to use and why it would be effective for their essays.

4. Refer students to the graphic organizer chart at the bottom of the page. Have them prepare a chart to develop a list of appeals before deciding which approach to take in their essay.

Six Traits Focus

✔	Ideas	✔	Word Choice
✔	Organization		Sentence Fluency
	Voice		Conventions

Drafting

Shaping Your Writing

Showcase your thesis statement. Introduce a knowledgeable claim on the issue in your first paragraph. To establish the significance of your thesis, begin with examples, facts, or a brief anecdote that will grab readers' attention. Then state your viewpoint in the final sentence of the first paragraph. The chart shown explains some patterns you can use in your introduction.

Develop ideas. Use the body of your writing to defend your ideas. As you develop your argument, help readers understand what is at stake by clearly distinguishing your thesis from opposing claims and then refuting them. Present claims and counterclaims in logical sequence. Make sure you present the strongest evidence on both sides, addressing your audience's concerns and questions. Then, conclude your essay with a memorable restatement of your thesis idea and a clear call for action—a statement of what you want done.

Providing Elaboration

Use rhetorical devices to present appeals. You can use rhetorical devices to grab your audience's interest and persuade them that you are right.

- **Repetition:** Repeat key words to focus your argument.

  Example: The plan is convenient, but is convenience more important than safety?

- **Parallelism:** Repeated grammatical structures can create a memorable rhythm.

  Example: The safety of every student, every teacher, and every visitor is at stake.

- **Analogies:** Use comparisons to help readers grasp ideas.

  Example: Allowing parking along the field is as dangerous as allowing motorcycles to enter a bicycle race.

You can use rhetorical devices to make the following kinds of appeals:

- **Logical appeals** present ideas based on reasoning.
- **Ethical appeals** establish the credibility of information.
- **Emotional appeals** tap into an audience's feelings.

Use a chart like the one shown to develop a list of appeals.

The Importance of Preventative Health Care	
Logical Appeal	If you take good care of yourself, then you reduce your chances of being inconvenienced by a cold or flu.
Ethical Appeal	Doctors say that, whenever possible, prevent yourself and others from catching a cold.
Emotional Appeal	Just a little care can help you avoid the drippy nose, scratchy throat, and aching muscles of a cold or flu.

Common Core State Standards

Writing

1.a. Introduce precise, knowledgeable claim(s), establish the significance of the claim(s), distinguish the claim(s) from alternate or opposing claims, and create an organization that logically sequences claim(s), counterclaims, reasons, and evidence.

1.b. Develop claim(s) and counterclaims fairly and thoroughly, supplying the most relevant evidence for each while pointing out the strengths and limitations of both in a manner that anticipates the audience's knowledge level, concerns, values, and possible biases.

1.e. Provide a concluding statement or section that follows from and supports the argument presented.

Developing Opening Paragraphs

Pattern 1
- Example → Thesis
- Example → statement

Pattern 2
- Fact → Thesis
- Fact → statement

Pattern 3
- Brief anecdote → Thesis statement

Strategies for Using Technology in Writing

If students are using computers, encourage them to consider creating separate files of details for each audience they hope to persuade. Students can list the types of persuasion they feel would be effective for each audience. Key points directed at each audience can also be put into the files. This will make information for specific audiences easily accessible.

444

Writers on Writing

Frank Kermode On Persuasion

Frank Kermode is the author of *"Life in Elizabethan and Jacobean England"* (p. 248).

This passage is excerpted from my essay in *Daedalus, The Journal of the American Academy of Arts and Sciences.* It briefly considers the notion of the common reader from the eighteenth century up to the present day. To Dr. Samuel Johnson, the common reader of the eighteenth century was identified as a member of the leisured class. Now, it is argued, the term applies to people who have benefited by a college education.

"A society containing subtle readers is at least a more interesting, perhaps a richer, society."

—Sir Frank Kermode

from The Common Reader

I have assumed that the modern Common Reader passes through a college or university. The number of people now teaching literature in such institutions is probably greater than the total of critics who formerly existed throughout history, and they must have some effect on the millions of readers who frequent their classes. Does good come of this? The eminent American critic Richard Poirier says he sees "no reason in the world" why common readers should care to read the classics or serious contemporary fiction and poetry; "I don't think it makes them better people, better citizens, better anything." By some criteria he must be right. Indeed, it is immodest to propose that by making people read these things we are improving them, ethically or civically. All we dare claim is that we are making them better readers. We might or might not go on to claim that bad reading has often had disastrous consequences; or that a society containing subtle readers is at least a more interesting, perhaps a richer, society than one that does not; or that good readers are likely to be more resistant to the exploitative forces of "the ruling system." But we should not say we are improving them, except as readers.

> The arts of reading are now entrusted to college and university teachers. Should we assume that this is a wholly good thing?

> Richard Poirier, an eminent critic, denies that enhanced reading skills confer ethical benefits on the student.

> Even if his argument is persuasive, it could be maintained that skillful reading has other socially beneficial effects.

Writing Workshop **445**

Frank Kermode on Persuasion

Review the passage on the student page with the class, using Frank Kermode's comments to deepen students' understanding of the process of writing a persuasive essay.

Teaching From the Professional Model

1. Show students Segment 4 on Frank Kermode on *See It! DVD* or from this page in the **Enriched Online Student Edition.** Discuss Kermode's opinions on the impact of literary criticism on society.

2. **Ask** students why Kermode asks, "Does good come of this?" **Answer:** The question engages readers with the text by challenging them to agree or disagree.

3. Point out that Kermode is using an "expert witness" when he quotes Richard Poirier. Readers might regard this technique as an authoritative reinforcement of their own point of view or as a further challenge to them to argue their own opinions.

4. Explain that in refuting Poirier, Kermode is using a logical appeal. He treats Poirier's opinion respectfully and acknowledges that he may be right. Kermode then builds his own claim logically by pointing out other benefits of reading.

PHLit Online!

Enriched Online Student Edition
Show or assign the video online at www.PHLitOnline.com.

Revising

1. Introduce the revising strategies, using the instruction on the student page.

2. Have students apply the strategies as they revise their persuasive essays.

Teaching the Strategies

1. Have students exchange drafts with a partner. Readers should then mark sentences or paragraphs to make the relationships among ideas clearer.

2. Make sure students understand that good organization can make an argument easier to follow. The careful placement of ideas positions key points where they will have greatest impact.

3. Ask a student to read the example of vague language aloud to the class. Then ask another student to read the vivid image. **Ask** students what makes the second sentence so powerful and vivid. **Answer:** It expresses the idea as a simile, allowing the reader to visualize the idea.

Six Traits Focus

	Ideas	✔	Word Choice
✔	Organization	✔	Sentence Fluency
✔	Voice	✔	Conventions

Revising

Revising Your Overall Structure

Arrange arguments in a logical order. Review your writing to make sure that your evidence is arranged logically and effectively. Follow these steps.

1. Clearly show the connections between ideas, such as the connections between your thesis and supporting reasons, using transition words and phrases, such as *because, therefore, due to,* and *consequently.*

2. In addition, use varied syntax to show the connections between ideas. For example, a complex sentence, combining a dependent and an independent clause, can clearly show the relation between claims and reasons: e.g., *Because the numbers are increasing, immediate action is required.* A compound sentence, joining two or more independent clauses, can be used to link two equally important reasons or to contrast claims and counterclaims: e.g., *Opponents say the plan is the only one that will work, but my alternative has proven effective.*

3. Experiment with arranging your arguments in order of importance, either from least important to most important, or vice versa.

> **Model: Using Transition Words**
>
> In order to play a sport,
> ʌYou are required to pass your classes, which of course motivates athletes to make good grades.
>
> The transition words *in order to* indicate cause and effect.

Revising Your Word Choice

Replace weak language with powerful words or images. To strengthen your arguments, circle passages that are vague or lack force. For each one, brainstorm for charged words, vivid images, and dramatic analogies to help you make your points.

Peer Review: Share your draft with a partner. Discuss your ideas for replacing dull language. Together, choose the most vivid words or phrases.

Vague	Getting into a good college can be tough.	Suddenly, you get nervous about choosing a college.
Vivid	Like a thousand cattle trying to pass through the same gate, vast numbers of students across the nation apply each year for a limited number of places at colleges.	Suddenly, a feeling bubbles up from the pit of your stomach, an achy, acidic feeling of panic.

Common Core State Standards

Writing
1.c. Use words, phrases, and clauses as well as varied syntax to link the major sections of the text, create cohesion, and clarify the relationships between claim(s) and reasons, between reasons and evidence, and between claim(s) and counterclaims.

4. Produce clear and coherent writing in which the development, organization, and style are appropriate to task, purpose, and audience.

Language
3.a. Vary syntax for effect, consulting references for guidance as needed; apply an understanding of syntax to the study of complex texts when reading.

Strategies for Using Transitions

Remind students that transitions show the relationships among ideas. Moreover, different relationships are shown with different types of transitions. Write these examples on the board, and challenge students to suggest additional transitions for each category.

Cause-and-Effect Transitions

because	although	therefore
as a result	so that	consequently

Chronological Transitions

after	before	since
first	next	then

Comparison-and-Contrast Transitions

like	but	neither...nor
instead	however	compared to

Encourage students to keep a list of these transitions to use when revising their essays.

Developing Your Style

Making Sure Your Ideas Are Well Organized

Your persuasive essay probably contains both facts and opinions. Facts can include statistics, examples, and anecdotes. When your facts are well organized, they support your opinions, as in this example:

Opinion: I think we should carpet the school hallway.

Supporting Facts: The carpeting will reduce noise. Mr. Porter, of the maintenance staff, says it will be easier to clean than the existing floors.

As you review the way your facts and opinions are organized, look for logical fallacies, or false connections between ideas:

A **hasty generalization** is based on only a few facts or samples.

Example: I tasted one apple and it was sweet. Therefore, all of the apples in the basket must be sweet.

A **non sequitur** (Latin for "it does not follow") draws a conclusion that does not follow from the evidence given.

Example: Members of Congress are elected by the people and make the laws. Members of Congress know what is best for the people.

A **false analogy** ignores key differences between compared items.

Example: Children are like little adults. Like adults, children can be trusted to make their own financial decisions.

Find It in Your Reading

Read or review "Speech Before Her Troops" by Elizabeth I, page 285.

1. Find two facts and two opinions that she includes in her speech.
2. Find an argument she makes and explain whether it is logical or not.

Apply It to Your Writing

Review your draft. For each paragraph in your draft, follow these steps:

1. Underline the facts or statistics you have used to support your position. Check to see that your facts come from current, reliable sources and that you have cited them accurately.
2. Circle the opinions you have used to support your arguments. Verify that the opinions can be validated by facts, expert opinions, or logical arguments.
3. Evaluate the appeals you have made and revise any faulty logic.

> **PH WRITING COACH**
> Further instruction and practice are available in *Prentice Hall Writing Coach*.

Developing Your Style

1. Introduce persuasive evidence to students using the instruction on the student page.
2. Have the students complete the Find It In Your Reading and Apply It to Your Writing activities.

Teaching the Strategies

1. Have students identify the following statements as facts or opinions.
  a. *People do not trust the information they get from newspapers as they once did.*
  b. *Readership of our newspaper has decreased by 12 percent in ten years.*
  c. *We don't need any more schools!*

Answers: a. opinion; b. fact; c. opinion

2. Provide these examples of logical fallacies and have students identify their type.
  a. *Our neighbor's dog barks all the time. Dogs are nuisances and shouldn't be allowed in apartments.*
  b. *School is just like a job. Students should be paid for attending.*

Answers: a. non sequitur; b. false analogy

3. Discuss student's responses to the Find It in Your Reading questions.

Possible answers:

1. Two facts are that Elizabeth sends a lieutenant general in her stead during the battle and that her advisors told her not to walk among the people. Two opinions are her feebleness as a woman and her heart of a king.

2. She says they will have a victory because of the obedience and courage of the soldiers. This is not logical because it is a hasty generalization. The English will not be victorious just because they are loyal and brave.

Six Traits Focus

	Ideas	✓	Word Choice
	Organization		Sentence Fluency
✓	Voice		Conventions

Differentiated Instruction   for Universal Access

Background for Special-Needs Students

Emphasize to students that information from a book or from any other source is not automatically factual or reliable. Students should answer these questions before taking the information as authoritative:

- Is the source an expert on the topic?
- Is it possible that the speaker or writer is biased?
- Is the information a fact or an opinion?
- If it is an opinion, are there any facts to support it?

Support for Less Proficient Readers

Give students copies of an editorial from a newspaper and then read the editorial aloud. Pause whenever a fact or opinion is expressed. Have students analyze it and decide whether it is a fact or an opinion. If it is an opinion, have them search the editorial for facts that support it. Discuss the opinions and why they do or do not strengthen the thesis of the editorial.

Review the Student Model with the class, using the annotations to analyze the writer's incorporation of the elements of a persuasive essay.

Teaching the Strategies

1. Explain that the student model is a sample and that essays may be longer.

2. Discuss the opening paragraph, pointing out that Jenny raises an interesting issue in the first line. Then she builds on the idea with supporting details and finishes the paragraph with a strong thesis statement.

3. Point out that each paragraph in the body of the essay begins with a clearly stated main idea. The sentences that follow give reasons and facts to support that main idea. **Ask** students to identify the main idea of the second paragraph.
   Answer: The main idea is that the learning process continues after high school.

4. Emphasize that Jenny does not include extraneous information in the essay.

5. Point out that Jenny uses logical appeals to build her arguments. For example, in paragraph three she first describes how jobs require workers to learn new things. She then states a general truth by telling how those who rely solely on old skills will be less effective than their coworkers.

6. Direct students' attention to the final paragraph and point out that Jenny finishes her essay by emphasizing her main points.

Connecting to Real-Life Writing

Tell students that persuasive writing is useful in many jobs. Professional writers are hired to write speeches for politicians, copy for advertisers, and editorials for newspapers. In addition, many jobs require that people who are not professional writers write persuasively to get people to take action. Discuss work situations in which persuasive writing would be appropriate, such as a manager writing a memo to employees explaining a new policy, or an employee writing a memo asking for changes in benefits.

Student Model:

Kristen Metcalf, Black Mountain, NC

Why It Is Important To Be a Student Athlete

You may believe that being a student athlete is a big waste of time. If so, you probably think about having to spend most of your free time at practice or competitions, or about having to stay up late at night doing homework that most students do right after school. You might fear not being able to go to that big party this weekend because of the example you are supposed to be. While it's true that being a student athlete is a huge commitment that calls for a lot of sacrifices and takes a lot of time, it is more than worth it. Every teenager with the opportunity to play a sport should take advantage of it.

One of the main priorities for teenagers is preparing for the "real world." When teenagers go off on their own, there are many things they need to be able to do to make it in the world. They need to be able to take on responsibilities, make smart decisions, set and work for goals, and manage their time well. All of these things are also required by student athletes in order to be successful. So, athletes actually have practice in these important skills outside of the sport itself that lead them to find success as adults.

Most teenagers today want to go to college, and—let's face it—unless you have good grades, you're probably not going to be able to get in. For student athletes, making good grades is a pressing need all the way through school. In order to play a sport, you are required to pass your classes, which of course motivates athletes to make good grades. Along with making good grades come more scholarship opportunities for student athletes.

Maintaining good health is important to everyone. Research shows that healthy habits begun young dramatically improve good health throughout life. When you are a student athlete, you are physically fit from running, lifting weights, or whatever it is your sport requires of you to be prepared. Healthy eating is another component to good health, and the diets that your coaches put you on take care of that. Student athletes learn how to take care of their bodies, making them healthier than most other people.

Take advantage of the opportunities and great outcomes that being a student athlete can bring. If you decide to participate in school athletics, you will find that your life will improve all around.

> Kristen ends her introduction with a clear thesis statement that she defends in the body of the essay.

> Kristen lists examples and facts—she identifies the many benefits of school athletics. See Developing Your Style, p. 447.

> With this paragraph, Kristen addresses the needs of the audience beyond school.

Editing and Proofreading

Focus on commonly confused words. Look for words that are commonly mistaken for one another: for example, *adapt* and *adopt*, *accept* and *except*, or *affect* and *effect*. If necessary, consult a dictionary or handbook to make sure you are using the correct word.

Focus on spelling. The "er" sound can be spelled with different letter combinations. Review your spelling of each word with this sound.

Spiral Review: Conventions Earlier in this unit, you learned about subordinating conjunctions (p. 263) and adjective and adverb clauses (p. 419). Check your persuasive essay to be sure you have used those conventions correctly.

Publishing, Presenting, and Reflecting

Consider one of the following ways to share your writing.

Deliver a speech. Use your persuasive essay as the basis for a speech. See the Communications Workshop on page 450 for presentation strategies.

Submit a letter to the editor. Condense your persuasive essay and re-format it as a letter to the editor for publication in your school or community newspaper.

Create an advertising campaign. Present the key ideas from your essay in a public service print campaign that includes posters and a brochure. Or create a public service announcement for radio broadcast.

Reflect on your writing. Jot down your thoughts on the experience of writing a persuasive essay. Begin by answering this question: How did rhetorical devices help you make your points?

Rubric for Self-Assessment

Evaluate your persuasive essay using the following criteria and rating scale.

Criteria	Rating Scale
	not very very
Focus: How clear is your thesis statement?	1 2 3 4 5
Organization: How effectively do you organize your arguments?	1 2 3 4 5
Support/Elaboration: How well do you use evidence and a variety of appeals to support your position?	1 2 3 4 5
Style: How well do you use rhetorical devices, such as parallelism, repetition, and analogies?	1 2 3 4 5
Conventions: How correct is your grammar, especially your use of commonly confused words?	1 2 3 4 5

Common Core State Standards

Writing

5. Develop and strengthen writing as needed by planning, revising, editing, rewriting, or trying a new approach, focusing on addressing what is most significant for a specific purpose and audience.

Language

1.b. Resolve issues of complex or contested usage, consulting references as needed.

2.b. Spell correctly.

Editing and Proofreading

1. Introduce the editing and proof-reading focuses using the instruction on the student page.

2. Have students read their persuasive essays carefully, marking them for line edits. Make sure they check for errors of the type noted on in the lesson focus and the Spiral Review.

Teaching the Strategies

1. Tell students that it is impossible to proofread thoroughly by reading the draft once. Advise students to concentrate on one type of error each time.

2. You may wish to review a list of commonly confused words with students. Encourage them to make their own personal list.

Six Traits Focus

Ideas		✔ Word Choice
Organization	✔	Sentence Fluency
Voice	✔	Conventions

ASSESS

Publishing, Presenting, and Reflecting

1. Encourage students to practice their oral presentations. Encourage them to record their practice session and use the recording to critique themselves.

2. Before students reformat their essays as letters to the editor, advise them to check the newspaper's guidelines for letters.

3. Encourage students to talk about these additional questions: What part of the writing process remains the most challenging? What parts of the process are getting easier for you?

Strategies for Test Taking

When taking a test that includes a persuasive writing prompt, students should be careful to allow enough time for each step of the process. Though it is likely that a topic will be given, prewriting is still important because this is the stage at which students gather support and determine a position on the topic. Suggest that students use a chart like the one on page 443 to jot down what they know about their audience. If students are asked to choose between two topics, this exercise may also be used to help them identify the topic with which they are more comfortable.

Choose Your Topic and Thesis

Help students choose topics and purposes for their persuasive speeches using the instruction on the student page.

Once they choose topics about which they are passionate, students should make lists of issues that are interesting or disturbing to them.

Direct students to use their lists to help them create theses. Explain that their theses must clearly present the positions they will try to persuade their audiences to accept.

Develop Your Argument and Reasoning

1. Before presenting the three types of persuasive appeals, using the instruction on the student page, explain to students that understanding their audience and the values or concerns they share will help students develop appeals that will be more likely to persuade the audience.
   Present the four forms of argument, using the instruction on the student page. If time allows, have students come up with additional examples.

Deliver a Persuasive Speech

Persuasive speech is language that is used to influence people's thoughts or actions. Most people use persuasion spontaneously as they negotiate their daily lives. In formal speaking situations, however, you must plan persuasive arguments and strategies.

Topic and Thesis

The first step to developing a persuasive speech is to choose a topic about which you are passionate. Jot down a list of issues that interest you. Then, create an arguable **thesis**—your position, or perspective, on the topic. A strong thesis statement is direct and clear, and the goal of your speech should be to persuade your audience to accept the position you set forth in your thesis statement.

Argument and Reasoning

Know your audience. Think carefully about your **audience:** who they are and the values or concerns they share. Understanding your audience will help you develop persuasive appeals that will reach them. There are three main types of persuasive appeals:

- **Ethical Appeal:** Establish your authority as a speaker, by acknowledging both sides of the topic and referring to credible sources.
- **Emotional Appeal:** Present information and evidence in a way that evokes listeners' emotions.
- **Logical Appeal:** Support your thesis with sound *facts* and *reasons.*

You can use different forms of argument to structure your line of reasoning. Use *inductive reasoning* to draw a conclusion after examining specific cases. *Deductive reasoning* involves applying an established principle or conclusion to a specific case. A *syllogism* is a series of three statements or ideas: a general statement, a specific statement, and a conclusion, such as "Reading will improve a student's vocabulary. I need to improve my vocabulary. Therefore, I should read more." An *analogy* is a comparison of one thing to something seemingly unrelated.

Address alternative perspectives. Identify alternative or opposing viewpoints to your position, and answer them in your speech by including logical counterarguments.

Select effective language techniques. As you write your speech, vary your *diction*, or word choice. The use of *Standard American English*—the formal English taught in school—ensures your ideas are clear. Limited use of *informal expressions* or slang can build a bridge to your audience. Keep your audience's knowledge level in mind if you use *technical language* to discuss scientific or technical topics. You may need to define technical terms to ensure that your audience follows your argument.

Also focus on your *syntax*, or sentence structure. The language devices shown in the chart below can make your speech precise and powerful.

Rhetorical Questions	Parallel Structure	Concrete Images	Figurative Language
questions asked for effect that do not require an answer	repetition of grammatical patterns	vivid descriptions of events, places, or people	symbolic or nonliteral language, like similes and metaphors

Activities: Deliver and Discuss a Persuasive Speech

Comprehension and Collaboration For both activities, use an evaluation form like the one shown below.

A. *Rehearse* your speech for friends. Then, deliver it to your class. Afterward, discuss your speech with the class. Respond thoughtfully to classmates' comments and questions. Then, have your audience fill out an evaluation form like the one shown below.

B. Review classmates' comments, synthesizing them by noting where they overlap. Conduct any research needed to answer the concerns raised, and then develop and present an **impromptu speech** offering a *rebuttal,* or answer to your audience's critique of your arguments.

Evaluation Form for Delivery of a Speech

Name of Speech _____

Thesis _____

Types of Persuasive Appeals:

  Ethical: ☐ Example: _____

  Emotional: ☐ Example: _____

  Logical: ☐ Example: _____

Diction:

  Standard English ☐   Informal Language ☐   Technical Language ☐

  Examples: _____

Syntax and Language Devices:

  Rhetorical Questions ☐   Parallel Structure ☐

  Concrete Images ☐   Figurative Language ☐

  Examples: _____

What would the speaker's opponents say in response to this argument?

_____

What did the speaker do well? What could be improved? _____

Develop Your Argument and Reasoning (cont.)

2. Discuss the importance of word choice in formulating an effective argument. Point out that students should look for words that appeal to the readers' emotions when writing an emotional appeal.

3. Remind students to pay attention to sentence structure as they develop their arguments. Give an example of a weak sentence, and then revise the sentence structure to strengthen the argument. For example: Original: *We should all go out and vote today to make a difference.* Revised: *Make a difference—vote today.*

4. Review the chart on the student page to help students focus their attention on persuasive techniques. Have students practice using the four language devices.

Activity: Deliver and Discuss a Persuasive Speech

1. Present the two activities. Explain to students that the degree to which a speech is persuasive will depend a great deal on its delivery. Even the most persuasive words can fall flat if they are not delivered effectively. Have students work in pairs or small groups to rehearse their speeches. After students have delivered their speeches, give them time to examine the evaluation forms filled out by other students. Suggest that students consider the comments on the evaluation forms to help them formulate a rebuttal. Explain that *impromptu* means "spontaneous." The rebuttal will be a less formal argument than the speech.

2. Remind students to be considerate and fair toward their classmates as they fill out the evaluation form.

3. After students complete the activity on the student page, have them discuss which of the students' speeches were most persuasive, as well as which rebuttals were most effective, and why.

4. To evaluate students' delivery, use the **Analyzing Persuasive Techniques** rubric, page 295, in the *Professional Development Guidebook*.

Differentiated Instruction   for Universal Access

Strategy for Special-Needs Students
Many special-needs students can articulate their ideas clearly but may have trouble organizing them and putting them on paper. Suggest that these students work in pairs. Have each student, using a tape recorder, rehearse the speech for a partner. The listener should question the speaker about unclear issues or raise additional points. The taped conversation can form a starting point for revising the speech before presenting it to the class.

EL Strategy for English Learners
These students may have difficulty developing a rebuttal in three minutes. It may also be difficult for them to present an impromptu speech. Have English learners work in pairs for at least 15 minutes to review and discuss the audience's critique of the content of each partner's speech. Then instruct them to work together to write a rebuttal for both speeches. Have two pairs of English learners present their rebuttals to one another.

 **Common Core State Standards**

• Language 4.a, 5, 6

Words from Mythology

1. Teach word origins, using the instruction and samples on the student page.

2. If possible, give additional examples of words of mythological origin. (For example: *mnemonic, chronology*)

Think Aloud: Model the Skills

Say to students:

Sometimes when I look up words, I find that they have interesting stories connected with their origins, especially words that come from mythological references. For example, I learn that the term *Achilles' heel* refers to a person's vulnerable point because Achilles, the hero of Homer's *Iliad,* was invulnerable except for the heel. If I hear or read that a person has an Achilles' heel, I will make the connection that this is a vulnerable and sensitive spot for the person. For example, if Anna's Achilles' heel is her younger sister, I know circumstances related to Anna's sister will cause Anna great pain.

Vocabulary Workshop

Words from Mythology

During the Renaissance, many words with origins in Greek and Roman mythology entered the English language. The renewed interest in the cultures of ancient Greece and Rome inspired English translations of classical writers. As these bodies of literature became familiar, English writers made allusions to their settings, characters, and events. From there, it was a short step to inventing related words that conveyed similar meanings. The chart explains the mythological origin of some common words:

Words	Origin
furious	In Greek mythology, the three **Furies** were the spirits of punishment.
martial	In Roman mythology, **Mars** was the god of war, second in importance only to Jupiter.
mercurial	In Roman mythology, **Mercury** was the winged messenger, fleet of foot.
narcissistic	In Greek mythology, the beautiful youth **Narcissus** fell in love with his own reflection in a pool. He pined away as a result of his unrequited love for himself.
titanic	In Greek mythology, the **Titans** were the race of giants who came before the gods of Olympus.

These words can be found in the literature we read today. For example, in the tragedy *Othello*, Shakespeare writes, "I know not where is that Promethean heat, / That can thy light relume." The allusion is to Prometheus, a figure from Greek mythology who stole fire from heaven. Today, *Promethean* is defined as "creative" or "courageously original." Knowing the classical or Biblical origins of words can help you understand their meanings when you encounter them in your reading.

Practice

Directions: Complete the analogies below, using the chart above to help you. Then, explain the relationship between each pair of words.

1. mercurial : permanent :: _____ : titanic

  a. quick   **b.** small   **c.** sinking   **d.** huge

2. gentle : mild :: martial : _____

  a. military   **b.** enemy   **c.** warlike   **d.** soft

Directions: Use each of these words in sentences that show your understanding of their meaning as inferred from their origins.

3. a. furious   **b.** narcissistic   **c.** mercurial

 **Common Core State Standards**

Language
4.a. Use context as a clue to the meaning of a word or phrase.
5. Demonstrate understanding of word relationships.
6. Acquire and use accurately general academic and domain-specific words and phrases, sufficient for reading, writing, speaking, and listening at the college and career readiness level.

Practice

Answers

1. b. small
   The word pairs are antonyms. *Mercurial* means "quick and changeable," as a reference to the Roman god Mercury's hurried flights. *Titan* means "huge," as a reference to the Titans, a race of giant gods.

2. c. warlike
   The word pairs are synonyms. *Martial* is of mythological origin and refers to Mars, the Roman god of war.

3. a. The furies of ancient Greece often irritated people to a point of their being <u>furious</u>.

   b. The <u>narcissistic</u> actor had life-sized photos of himself all around his dressing room.

   c. The <u>mercurial</u> weather made it difficult to plan a trip to the beach.

Vocabulary Acquisition and Use

Context clues are words or phrases that help readers clarify the meanings of unfamiliar words in a text. By using context clues, you can determine the word or words that complete a sentence. Sentence Completion questions appear in most standardized tests. In these types of questions, you are given sentences with one or more missing words. Your task is to use the context to choose the correct word or words to complete each sentence logically. Try this strategy: (1) Read the entire sentence and anticipate a word that would logically complete it. (2) Scan the answer choices for that word. (3) If the word you anticipated is not there, look for a synonym.

Practice

This exercise is modeled after the Sentence Completion exercises that appear in the Critical Reading section of the SAT.

Directions: Each of the following sentences is missing one or two words. Choose the word or set of words that best completes each sentence.

> **Test-Taking Tip**
> Immediately rule out any answer choices you *know* are wrong.

1. Elizabeth, daughter of Henry VIII, was only 25 years old when she became England's ___?___ queen.
   A. melodious
   B. prodigal
   C. sovereign
   D. pernicious
   E. sanguine

2. Elizabeth proved ___?___, assuming the throne with rigor and wit.
   A. dauntless
   B. sullen
   C. multitudinous
   D. wan
   E. skeptical

3. She tolerated neither ___?___ nor insults, though she herself could be both ___?___ and inconstant.
   A. valor . . . predominant
   B. treasons . . . predominant
   C. valor . . . sullen
   D. treasons . . . sullen
   E. challenge . . . agreeable

4. Unwilling to compromise her power, the "Virgin Queen" would never ___?___ to take a husband.
   A. move
   B. scope
   C. deign
   D. raze
   E. vote

Strategies for
Test Taking

Remind students that when they are answering multiple-choice questions, the correct answer is always given. Sometimes identifying incorrect answers is easier than finding the correct answer. Recommend that students eliminate incorrect choices to improve their chances of choosing the correct answer.

453

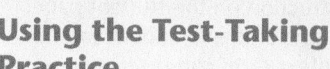

Test-Taking Practice

Critical Reading Test: Paired Passages

Paired reading passages are one type of critical reading passage. Paired passages may be fiction or nonfiction, prose or poetry, and vary in length. Questions that follow will refer to each passage individually and to both passages as a unit. As you read, note similarities and differences between the passages, especially the authors' attitudes, word choices, and styles.

Practice

The following exercise is modeled after the SAT Paired Passages Critical Reading section. This section usually includes 48 questions.

Directions: Read both passages. Then, answer the questions. Passage 1 is by Christopher Marlowe. Passage 2 is by Sir Walter Raleigh.

Common Core State Standards

RL.11-12.1, RL.11-12.2, RL.11-12.4; L.11-12.3, L.11-12.4, L.11-12.6
[For the full wording of the standards, see the standards chart in the front of your textbook.]

Strategy

- **Read Passage 1**, and answer the questions that refer only to the first passage.
- **Read Passage 2**, and answer the questions that refer only to the second passage.
- Finally, answer the **compare-and-contrast** questions.

PASSAGE 1

The Passionate Shepherd to His Love

Come live with me, and be my love,
And we will all the pleasures prove
That valleys, groves, hills, and fields,
Woods, or steepy mountain yields.

5 And we will sit upon the rocks,
Seeing the shepherds feed their flocks,
By shallow rivers to whose falls
Melodious birds sing madrigals.

And I will make thee beds of roses,
10 And a thousand fragrant posies,
A cap of flowers, and a kirtle
Embroidered all with leaves of myrtle;

A gown made of the finest wool,
Which from our pretty lambs we pull;
15 Fair lined slippers for the cold,
With buckles of the purest gold;

A belt of straw and ivy buds,
With coral clasps and amber studs;
And if these pleasures may thee move,
20 Come live with me, and be my love.

The shepherds' swains shall dance and sing
For thy delight each May morning;
If these delights thy mind may move,
Then live with me and be my love.

PASSAGE 2

The Nymph's Reply to the Shepherd

If all the world and love were young
And truth in every shepherd's tongue
These pretty pleasures might me move
To live with thee, and be thy love.

5 Time drives the flocks from field to fold,
When rivers rage and rocks grow cold,
And Philomel becometh dumb,
The rest complains of cares to come.

The flowers do fade, and wanton fields
10 To wayward winter reckoning yields:
A honey tongue, a heart of gall,
Is fancy's spring, but sorrow's fall.

Thy gowns, thy shoes, thy beds of roses,
Thy cap, thy kirtle, and thy posies
15 Soon break, soon wither, soon forgotten,
In folly ripe, in season rotten.

Thy belt of straw and ivy buds,
Thy coral clasps and amber studs,
All these in me no means can move
20 To come to thee and be thy love.

But could youth last and love still breed,
Has joy no date nor age no need,
Then these delights my mind might move,
To live with thee and be thy love.

454 Celebrating Humanity (1485–1625)

1. Which of the following best states the theme of Passage 1?
   A. Love can be felt only in natural surroundings.
   B. Nature provides the raw materials for all human needs.
   C. The pleasures of love are akin to the pleasures of nature.
   D. Love should be both mentally and emotionally stimulating.
   E. The delights of nature far outweigh those of romance.

2. It can most reasonably be inferred from Passage 1 that the speaker
   A. feels a deep connection to nature
   B. has impure motives
   C. is disenchanted with his daily life
   D. has long suffered from unrequited love
   E. is unschooled in the art of love

3. In line 19 of Passage 1, *move* most nearly means
   A. relocate
   B. stir
   C. offend
   D. find
   E. perplex

4. Which of the following best summarizes Passage 2?
   A. Nature may endure, but love is quick to die.
   B. Love does not require gifts or complicated arguments.

   C. Though nature is temporary, our love is permanent.
   D. To love is to ignore the cares and trials of mortality.
   E. Like nature and youth, love is fleeting.

5. It can be inferred that the speaker of Passage 2 finds "truth in every shepherd's tongue" (line 2)
   A. rarely
   B. only when convenient
   C. frequently
   D. only in nature
   E. occasionally

6. It would be most accurate to say that
   A. Passage 1 is a parody of Passage 2
   B. Passage 1 is an excerpt of Passage 2
   C. Passage 2 is a response to Passage 1
   D. Passage 2 is a poor imitation of Passage 1
   E. Passage 2 allegorizes Passage 1

7. The speaker of Passage 2 would most likely describe the speaker of Passage 1 as
   A. deceptive
   B. unintelligent
   C. romantic
   D. naive
   E. remote

Differentiated Instruction   for Universal Access

Support for Less Proficient Students
Read the first passage with students and help them to paraphrase it. Then, go over the first test item as a class, guiding students to eliminate incorrect answer choices.

EL Support for English Learners
Read both passages with the class and help students to summarize each passage. Review the ten questions, making sure that students understand *inferred* in Question 2; *summarizes* in Question 4; and *accurate* in Question 6. Allow students to ask clarifying questions about any of the question choices, being careful not to reveal correct answers. Once students understand the questions, have them complete the test on their own. Allow 5 minutes for reading the passage and 12 minutes for the questions.

Critical Reading:
Paired Passages

1. Introduce the passages using the instruction on page 454.

2. Have students read the first passage silently; then, as a class, analyze each choice in the first test item.
   A—The poem only describes the beloved residing in nature, but never limits love to natural surroundings. (Eliminate)
   B—Provision of human needs is not the main focus or argument. (Eliminate)
   C—Correct answer. The speaker expresses his love through pleasurable gifts from the natural surroundings.
   D—Mental stimulation is never addressed. (Eliminate)
   E—The speaker equally values romance and nature. (Eliminate)

3. Assign the Practice exercise. Have students read the passages and answer the questions on their own. Allow 15 minutes for this process, and announce to students when they have 5 minutes and 1 minute remaining.

Answers

1. C
2. A
3. B
4. E
5. A
6. C
7. D

Question	Pages to Reteach
1	264
2	296
3	306
4	282
5	296
6	296
7	264

455

Editing in Context: Grammar and Writing

1. Introduce the skill using the instruction on the student page. Be sure students understand the strategy set off in the boxed section.

2. You may wish to go over the first test item with students, modeling the "'listen' for errors" strategy. Read the sentence aloud to the class. As you repeat the passage more slowly, ask students to raise their hands when they hear a portion they think sounds incorrect.

3. Point out that the pronoun *his* refers to the noun *writers*, which is plural. The singular pronoun does not agree with the plural noun. Changing the pronoun *his* is required. The correct answer is D.

4. Have students complete questions 2–7 on their own. Allow students 8 minutes to complete the questions.

Editing in Context: Grammar and Writing

Editing-in-context segments often appear in the writing sections of standardized tests. They are made up of a reading passage with numbered sentences. The passages are usually drafts of student essays that contain errors in grammar, style, and usage. For each question, you must decide which of four possible answers will best correct a given sentence.

Practice

This exercise is modeled after the Identifying Sentence Errors portion of the SAT Writing test. The test usually includes 18 such questions.

Directions: Each of the following sentences contains either a single error or no error at all. The error, if there is one, is underlined and lettered. If a sentence contains an error, select the letter of that underlined part. If the sentence is correct, select choice E.

Strategy

"Listen" for Errors
Read the sentence straight through. If you mentally "trip" over one of the underlined portions, it's probably wrong.

1. During the <u>sixteenth century</u>—the first century of the <u>printed book</u>—writers from all <u>levels of society</u> sought to have <u>his</u> works published. <u>No error</u>
   A.
   B.
   C.
   D.
   E.

2. However, it was <u>one</u> of the <u>more dangerous</u> eras in history <u>for</u> those <u>whose names</u> appeared in print. <u>No error</u>
   A.
   B.
   C.
   D.
   E.

3. All books were <u>censored</u> by various <u>government and</u> church authorities, <u>whom</u> in turn were <u>accountable to</u> the monarch. <u>No error</u>
   A.
   B.
   C.
   D.
   E.

4. <u>Even</u> the most innocent <u>complement</u> could be construed as slander; even the <u>most straightforward</u> observation could be <u>mistaken</u> for deceit. <u>No error</u>
   A.
   B.
   C.
   D.
   E.

Strategies for Test Taking

Point out to students that in Editing in Context Tests such as the one on this page, it may be helpful to read the sentences aloud in their heads to hear how the existing sentence sounds. Hearing a sentence can help in identifying awkward or incorrect wording. If reading a portion causes a mental "trip," the sentence probably needs editing.

5. Punishments <u>came</u> in <u>a range of forms</u> and
degrees; <u>it</u> was sometimes a mere reprimand,
<u>sometimes</u> a decade in prison. <u>No error</u>

A.
B.
C.
D.
E.

6. For this reason, the medieval <u>practice</u>
of circulating <u>unpublished</u> manuscripts
continued <u>to thrive</u> <u>well</u> into the 1700s.
<u>No error</u>

A.
B.
C.
D.
E.

7. For courtiers and <u>others of</u> high rank, writing
and circulating anonymous texts <u>were</u> a
<u>relatively safest</u> way of expressing dissent or
<u>affection</u>. <u>No error</u>

A.
B.
C.
D.
E.

 Timed Writing: Position Statement [25 minutes]

In *Utopia*, Sir Thomas More writes: "When a ruler enjoys wealth and pleasure while all about him are grieving and groaning, he acts as a jailor rather than as a king."

Write an essay in which you agree or disagree with More's statement. Do you consider it an overstatement, or a painful truth? What value, if any, might it hold for leaders of our own time? Use reasons and examples from your own knowledge and experience to support your ideas.

> **Academic Vocabulary**
>
> Read the prompt and the assignment twice carefully. Note key words, such as *agree* or *disagree*, that clarify the assignment.

Test-Taking Practice **457**

ASSESS/RETEACH

Answers

1. D
2. E
3. C
4. B
5. C
6. E
7. C

Timed Writing

Position Statement

1. Go over the two paragraphs of the timed writing assignment on the student page.

2. Tell students that they can quickly formulate a thesis statement for their position statements by first making a list of their ideas and experiences. Then, students should organize their thoughts and decide if they agree or disagree with More's statement. Their thesis should be clear and concise.

3. Encourage students to budget adequate time for prewriting and revising/editing. Students should spend about 8 minutes in the prewriting stage, 12 minutes drafting, and 5 minutes revising and editing. Reinforce this strategy by announcing elapsed time at the 8 and 20 minute marks as students respond to the assignment.

4. Use the **Rubrics for Writing for Assessment,** *Professional Development Guidebook,* pages 67–68, to evaluate students' work.

Benchmark

Reteach skills as indicated by students' performance, following the Reteach chart on p. 455. Then, administer the end-of-unit **Benchmark Test** (*Unit 2 Resources,* pp. 195–200). Follow the **Interpretation Guide** for the test (*Unit 2 Resources,* pp. 204–205) to assign reteaching pages as necessary in the *Reading Kit.* Use **Success Tracker** online to automatically assign these pages.

The **Benchmark Tests** and **Success Tracker** are available online at **www.PHLitOnline.com**.

457

Performance Tasks

Assigning Tasks/Reteaching Skills

Use the chart below to choose appropriate Performance Tasks by identifying which tasks assess lessons in the textbook that you have taught. Use the same lessons for reteaching when students' performance indicates a failure to fully master a standard. For additional instruction and practice, assign the *Common Core Companion* pages indicated for each task.

Task	Where Taught/Pages to Reteach	Common Core Companion Pages
1	238, 246, 248–249, 308–311, 321, 360, 406	28–40, 196–207
2	241, 247, 308, 314–315, 321, 342, 349, 377	41–53, 196–207
3	252, 282, 291, 296, 342, 378, 386	103–115, 185–195
4	250, 258, 296, 342, 378, 386	54–60, 297–303
5	250, 258, 296, 386	2–14, 278–285, 304–305
6	268, 271, 290, 316–319, 356–357, 436–440	143–155, 297–303

Assessment Pacing

In assigning the Writing Tasks on this student page, allow a class period for the completion of a task. As an alternative, assign tasks as homework. In assigning the Speaking and Listening Tasks on the facing page, consider having students do any required preparation as a homework assignment. Then, allow a class period for the presentations themselves.

Evaluating Performance Tasks

Use the rubric at the bottom of this Teacher Edition page to evaluate students' mastery of the standards as demonstrated in their Performance Task responses. Review the rubric with students before they begin work so they know the criteria by which their work will be evaluated.

Performance Tasks

Follow the instructions to complete the tasks below as required by your teacher. As you work on each task, incorporate both general academic vocabulary and literary terms you learned in this unit.

 Common Core State Standards

RL.11-12.1, RL.11-12.3, RL.11-12.4, RL.11-12.5; RI.11-12.2, RI.11-12.6; W.11-12.1, W.11-12.2; SL.11-12.4, SL.11-12.5
[For the full wording of the standards, see the standards chart in the front of your textbook.]

Writing

Task 1: Literature [RL.11-12.3; W.11-12.1]
Analyze the Development of a Drama

*Write an **essay** in which you analyze how the author of one of the dramatic works in this unit develops and relates the key elements of the play.*

- Explain which play you chose and briefly summarize the plot.
- Identify key choices the author made in writing the drama. For example, consider where the play is set, how the action is ordered, and how the characters are introduced and developed. Consider also the way in which these elements relate to each other.
- Analyze the impact of the author's choices, discussing how these decisions affect both the play's meaning and the reader's experience.
- Organize ideas so that each idea builds on the one it follows to create a unified whole.
- Provide a concluding section that follows from the explanation presented. In your conclusion, sum up your analysis of the author's key choices and their impact. Include a memorable statement of your opinion of the work.

Task 2: Literature [RL.11-12.4; W.11-12.1]
Analyze Shakespearean Language

*Write an **essay** in which you analyze Shakespeare's word choice in one of the acts of* Macbeth, *which appears in this unit.*

- Identify specific examples of language that you find especially effective in one of the acts of *Macbeth*. Consider the following elements: figures of speech, such as similes or metaphors; specific words that are particularly interesting

or beautiful; and connotative meanings that are especially rich or striking. Explain your choices and the reasons for them.
- Identify any words in the act that readers may not understand. Explain the meanings of these words. If any have multiple meanings, explain which ones are most important.
- Consider how the combined word choices in the act you are analyzing develop the author's tone.
- Cite specific examples from the play to support your ideas. Quote precisely and accurately. Introduce each example with a sentence or phrase that shows its connection to the idea you intend it to illustrate.

Task 3: Informational Text [RI.11-12.2; W.11-12.2]
Analyze the Development of Central Ideas

*Write an **essay** in which you analyze the development of two or more central ideas in a work of literary nonfiction from this unit.*

- Choose a work of nonfiction from this unit, and clearly identify and explain at least two central ideas expressed in the work.
- Discuss how the author introduces and develops each idea.
- Support your claim, identifying specific details that shape and refine each central idea.
- Explain how the central ideas interact and build on one another—reinforcing, adding to, or refining each other—to create a complex analysis of the topic of the work.
- To ensure that readers understand your analysis, include an objective summary of the work.

Performance Task Rubric: Standards Mastery	Rating Scale				
	not very				very
Critical Thinking: How clearly and consistently does the student pursue the specific mode of reasoning or discourse required by the standard, as specified in the prompt (e.g., comparing and contrasting, analyzing, explaining)?	1	2	3	4	5
Focus: How well does the student understand and apply the focus concepts of the standard, as specified in the prompt (e.g., development of theme or of complex characters, effects of structure, and so on)?	1	2	3	4	5
Support/Elaboration: How well does the student support points with textual or other evidence? How relevant, sufficient, and varied is the evidence provided?	1	2	3	4	5
Insight: How original, sophisticated, or compelling are the insights the student achieves by applying the standard to the text(s)?	1	2	3	4	5
Expression of Ideas: How well does the student organize and support ideas? How well does the student use language, including word choice and conventions, in the expression of ideas?	1	2	3	4	5

Speaking and Listening

 Task 4: Literature [RL.11-12.5; SL.11-12.4]

Analyze Text Structure

*Prepare and deliver an **oral presentation** in which you analyze the structure of a poem in this unit.*

- Identify the poem you will analyze, and explain why you chose it.

- Begin your presentation by discussing the overall structure of your chosen poem. For example, does it follow simple chronological order, or does it move about in time? Who is the speaker, and who is being addressed? Do the divisions between stanzas or other sections reflect and reinforce shifts in ideas?

- Identify a specific section of the poem that you will analyze in your presentation. For example, you may discuss how the poem begins, how events are ordered, or how it ends (happily, tragically, or inconclusively). Discuss how the specific section or aspect of the poem contributes to the overall structure.

- Discuss the aesthetic, or artistic, impact of the author's structural choices.

- Explain how the structure affects the poem's overall meaning. Support your ideas with evidence from the text.

 Task 5: Literature [RL.11-12.1; SL.11-12.5]

Draw Inferences

*Prepare and deliver an **oral presentation** in which you cite textual evidence to support inferences drawn from a poem in this unit.*

- Identify the poem you chose. Explain the poem's explicit meaning or key idea. Quote from the text to support your point.

- Identify any ideas or emotions that the speaker suggests but does not explicitly state. Cite details from the poem that help you draw these inferences. Explain how you tied these details together to see connections that suggest implicit meanings.

- Discuss ideas or emotions the poem leaves uncertain or open to interpretation. Consider the reasons for and effects of this ambiguity.

- Incorporate digital media that enhances your presentation. For example, consider images, audio, graphics, or textual elements that help illustrate and clarify your ideas or those expressed in the poem.

Task 6: Informational Text [RI.11-12.6; SL.11-12.4]

Determine Author's Point of View

*Prepare and deliver an **oral presentation** in which you determine the author's point of view and analyze his or her style in a nonfiction work from this unit.*

- Introduce the work you chose. Explain the author's purpose, topic, and central ideas.

- Describe the author's point of view. Explain how the author's stance affects his or her discussion of the topic and helps to shape the central idea.

- Discuss specific aspects of the author's rhetoric and style. Cite details and examples from the text to support your position.

- Define technical language or uncommon words to address your audience's knowledge level of your subject.

? What is the relationship of the writer to tradition?

Something Old, Something New The old rhyme about weddings says that a bride should wear "something old" together with "something new." In that spirit, many writers in this unit combined old and new.

Assignment Choose three authors from this unit who drew from tradition to create something new. Write a **literary analysis** showing how each author used a traditional theme, genre, or stylistic device but refreshed it with a new or inventive approach.

Performance Tasks **459**

Supporting Speaking and Listening

1. Consider having students work with partners or in groups to complete Performance Tasks involving listening and speaking. For tasks that you assign for individual work, you may still wish to have students rehearse with partners, who can provide constructive feedback.

2. As students rehearse, have them keep in mind these tips:

   - Present findings and evidence clearly and concisely.

   - Observe conventions of standard English grammar and usage.

   - Be relaxed and friendly but maintain a formal tone.

   - Make eye contact with the audience, pronounce words clearly, and vary your pace.

   - When working with a group, respond thoughtfully to others' positions, modifying your own in response to new evidence.

Linking Performance Tasks to Independent Reading

If you wish to cover the standards with students' independent reading, adapt Performance Tasks of your choice to the works they have selected. (Independent reading suggestions appear on the next page.)

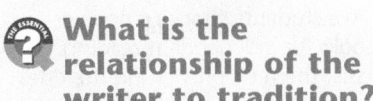

? What is the relationship of the writer to tradition?

1. Remind students of the Essential Question, "What is the relationship of the writer to tradition?"

2. Have students complete their responses to the prompt on the student page. Point out that in this unit, they have read a variety of literature of the British Renaissance and that they should draw on these selections in their responses. Remind them that they can also draw on their own experiences and what they have learned in other subject areas in formulating their answers.

Differentiated Instruction   for Universal Access

Strategy for Less Proficient Readers

Assign a Performance Task, and then have students meet in groups to review the standard assessed in that task. Remind students of the selections or independent readings to which they have previously applied the standard. Have groups summarize what they learned in applying the standard and then present their summaries. Discuss, clarifying any points of confusion. After students have completed their tasks, have groups meet again to evaluate members' work. Encourage members to revise their work based on the feedback they receive.

EL Strategy for English Learners

For each assigned Performance Task, review the instructions with students. Clarify the meaning of any unfamiliar vocabulary, emphasizing routine classroom words such as *connotative*, *interact*, and *implicit* and academic vocabulary such as *evidence*.

Next, have students note ideas for their responses. Pair students, and have them review each other's notes, asking questions to clarify meaning and suggesting improvements. Encourage students to ask for your assistance in supplying English words or expressions they may require.

Independent Reading

Titles featured on the Independent Reading pages at the end of each unit represent a range of reading, including stories, dramas, and poetry, as well as literary nonfiction and other types of informational text. Throughout, labels indicate the works that are CCSS Exemplar Texts. Choosing from among these featured titles will help students read works at increasing levels of text complexity in the grades 11–12 text complexity band.

Using Literature Circles

A literature circle is a temporary group in which students independently discuss a book.

Use the guidance in the *Professional Development Guidebook*, pp. 47–49, as well as the teaching notes on the facing page, for additional suggestions for literature circles.

Meeting Unit 2 CCS Standards

Students can use books listed on this page to apply and reinforce their mastery of the CCS Standards covered in this unit.

Introducing Featured Titles

Have students choose a book or books for independent reading. Assist them by previewing the titles, noting their subject matter and level of difficulty. **Note:** Before recommending a work to students, preview it, taking into account the values of your community as well as the maturity of your students.

Featured Titles

In this unit, you have read a variety of literature of the English Renaissance. Continue to read works related to this era on your own. Select books that you enjoy, but challenge yourself to explore new topics, new authors, and works offering varied perspectives or approaches. The titles suggested below will help you get started.

LITERATURE

The Tragedy of Hamlet
William Shakespeare   EXEMPLAR TEXT

 **Drama** In this classic tale of murder and revenge, Hamlet learns that his uncle has murdered his father in order to seize the crown. Urged on by the ghost of his father, Hamlet swears he will kill his uncle. However, Hamlet is paralyzed by indecision, delaying his revenge until events themselves speed the story to a bloody conclusion.

[Shakespeare's play The Tragedy of Macbeth begins on page 322 of this book. Build knowledge by reading another tragedy by this author.]

The Tempest
William Shakespeare

 **Drama** After his evil brother steals his kingdom, the magician Prospero and his daughter are stranded on a remote island. Years later, when a tempest shipwrecks his brother on the same island, Prospero has the opportunity for revenge, reconciliation, or both—if only his magic powers do not fail him.

The Sonnets
William Shakespeare

 **Poetry** This collection contains all 154 of Shakespeare's sonnets, along with commentary and illustrations. This version includes an introduction by the poet W. H. Auden.

[Four of Shakespeare's sonnets appear on pages 275–278 of this book. Build knowledge by reading all of his sonnets.]

Don Quixote
Miguel de Cervantes   EXEMPLAR TEXT

 **Novel** Don Quixote, an aging man from La Mancha, Spain, sets out with his companion Sancho Panza on a quest filled with misadventures. He is determined to save maidens, right wrongs, and revive the code of chivalry. The fact that these adventures take place largely in Quixote's head only adds to the satiric hilarity.

INFORMATIONAL TEXTS

Historical Texts

Utopia
Sir Thomas More
NuVision Publications, 2007

 **Philosophy** More describes an idealized city-state governed by reason. In a wide-ranging work that anticipates the hot-button issues of the next several centuries, he addresses such topics as women's rights, education, religion, and war.

Contemporary Scholarship

Galileo's Daughter
Dava Sobel

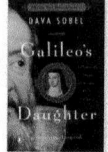 **Science** This scientific biography tells of Galileo's relationship with Virginia, his eldest daughter and confidante. Her letters, translated and masterfully woven into the narrative, illuminate and humanize the life of this towering figure in the fields of astronomy and physics.

The Children of Henry VIII
Alison Weir
Ballantine Books, 1997

 **Historical Narrative** Six times married, King Henry VIII of England left four prospective heirs to the throne after his death. This narrative describes the tumultuous period when three of Henry's children reigned in succession—Edward VI, Mary I, and, finally, Queen Elizabeth I.

A Year in the Life of William Shakespeare: 1599
James Shapiro

 **Biography** Thirty-five-year-old William Shakespeare wrote four plays in 1599. In this biography, James Shapiro discusses how the turbulent events of the time influenced *Henry V, Julius Caesar, As You Like It,* and *Hamlet.*

460 Celebrating Humanity (1485–1625)

Text Complexity: Aligning Texts With Readers and Tasks

TEXTS	READERS AND TASKS
• *The Sonnets* • *The Children of Henry VIII*	**Below-Level Readers** Allow students to focus on reading for content, and challenge them to interpret multiple perspectives.
• *The Tragedy of Hamlet* • *The Tempest* • *A Year in the Life of William Shakespeare: 1599*	**Below-Level Readers** Challenge students as they read for content. **On-Level Readers** Allow students to focus on reading for content, and challenge them to interpret multiple perspectives. **Advanced Readers** Allow students to focus on interpreting multiple perspectives.
• *Don Quixote* (Lexile: 1410L) • *Utopia* (Lexile: 1420L) • *Galileo's Daughter* (Lexile: 1530L)	**On-Level Readers** Challenge students as they read for content. **Advanced Readers** Allow students to focus on reading for content, and challenge them to interpret multiple perspectives.

Preparing to Read Complex Texts

Reading for College and Career In both college and the workplace, readers must analyze texts independently, draw connections among works that offer varied perspectives, and develop their own ideas and informed opinions. The questions shown below, and others that you generate on your own, will help you more effectively read and analyze complex college-level texts.

 **Common Core State Standards**

Reading Literature/Informational Text
10. By the end of grade 12, read and comprehend literature, including stories, dramas, and poems, and literary nonfiction at the high end of the grades 11-CCR text complexity band independently and proficiently.

When reading complex texts, ask yourself...

- What idea, experience, or story seems to have compelled the author to write? Has the author presented that idea, experience, or story in a way that I, too, find compelling?
- How might the author's era, social status, belief system, or personal experiences have affected the point of view he or she expresses in the text?
- How do my circumstances affect what I understand and feel about this text?
- What key idea does the author state explicitly? What key idea does he or she suggest or imply? Which details in the text help me to perceive implied ideas?
- Do I find multiple layers of meaning in the text? If so, what relationships do I see among these layers of meaning?
- How do details in the text connect or relate to one another? Do I find any details unconvincing, unrelated, or out of place?
- Do I find the text believable and convincing?

Key Ideas and Details

- What patterns of organization or sequences do I find in the text? Do these patterns help me understand the ideas better?
- What do I notice about the author's style, including his or her diction, uses of imagery and figurative language, and syntax?
- Do I like the author's style? Is the author's style memorable?
- What emotional attitude does the author express toward the topic, the story, or the characters? Does this attitude seem appropriate?
- What emotional attitude does the author express toward me, the reader? Does this attitude seem appropriate?
- What do I notice about the author's voice—his or her personality on the page? Do I like this voice? Does it make me want to read on?

Craft and Structure

- Is the work fresh and original?
- Do I agree with the author's ideas entirely, or are there elements I find unconvincing?
- Do I disagree with the author's ideas entirely, or are there elements I can accept as true?
- Based on my knowledge of British literature, history, and culture, does this work reflect the British tradition? Why or why not?

Integration of Ideas

Independent Reading **461**

 **Text Complexity: Reader and Task Support Suggestions**

INDEPENDENT READING

Increased Support Suggest that students choose a book that they feel comfortable reading and one that is a bit more challenging.

Pair a more proficient reader with a less proficient reader and have them work together on the more challenging text. Partners can prepare to read the book by reviewing questions on this student page. They can also read difficult passages together, sharing questions and insights. They can use the questions on the student page to guide after-reading discussion.

Increased Challenge Encourage students to integrate knowledge and ideas by combining the Essential Questions and the unit concepts in their approach to two or more featured titles.

For example, students might consider the contrast between More's ideal world in *Utopia* to the realities of life in Renaissance England as revealed in *The Children of Henry VIII*.

Preparing to Read Complex Texts

1. Tell students they can be attentive readers by bringing their experience and imagination to the texts they read and by actively questioning those texts. Explain that the questions they see on the student page are examples of types of questions to ask about works of fiction and nonfiction.

2. Point out that, like writing, reading is a "multidraft" process, involving several readings of complete works or passages, revising and refining one's understanding each time.

Key Ideas and Details

3. Review and amplify the second bulleted point in the Key Ideas and Details box. **Ask:** What key ideas and details in the text illustrate this point of view? **Possible response:** Students may cite ideas and details that are directly related to the author's background or details that convey a contrast with the author's background.

Craft and Structure

4. Review and amplify the fourth bulleted point in the Craft and Structure box. **Ask:** How might the text be different if the author's emotional attitude toward the topic were the opposite?

   Possible response: A different emotional attitude would affect the writing style, the events of the plot, and the way the themes are treated.

Integration of Ideas

5. Review and amplify the second and third bulleted points in the Integration of Ideas box. **Ask:** Why might it be useful to keep track of the ideas that you agree or disagree with in a text?

   Possible response: This will help you separate your feelings about the author's style and technique from the ideas presented.

6. Finally, explain to students that they should cite key ideas and details, examples of craft and structure, or instances of the integration of ideas as evidence to support their points during a discussion of drama, fiction, or nonfiction. After hearing the evidence, the group might reach a consensus or might agree to disagree.

461

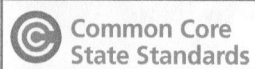

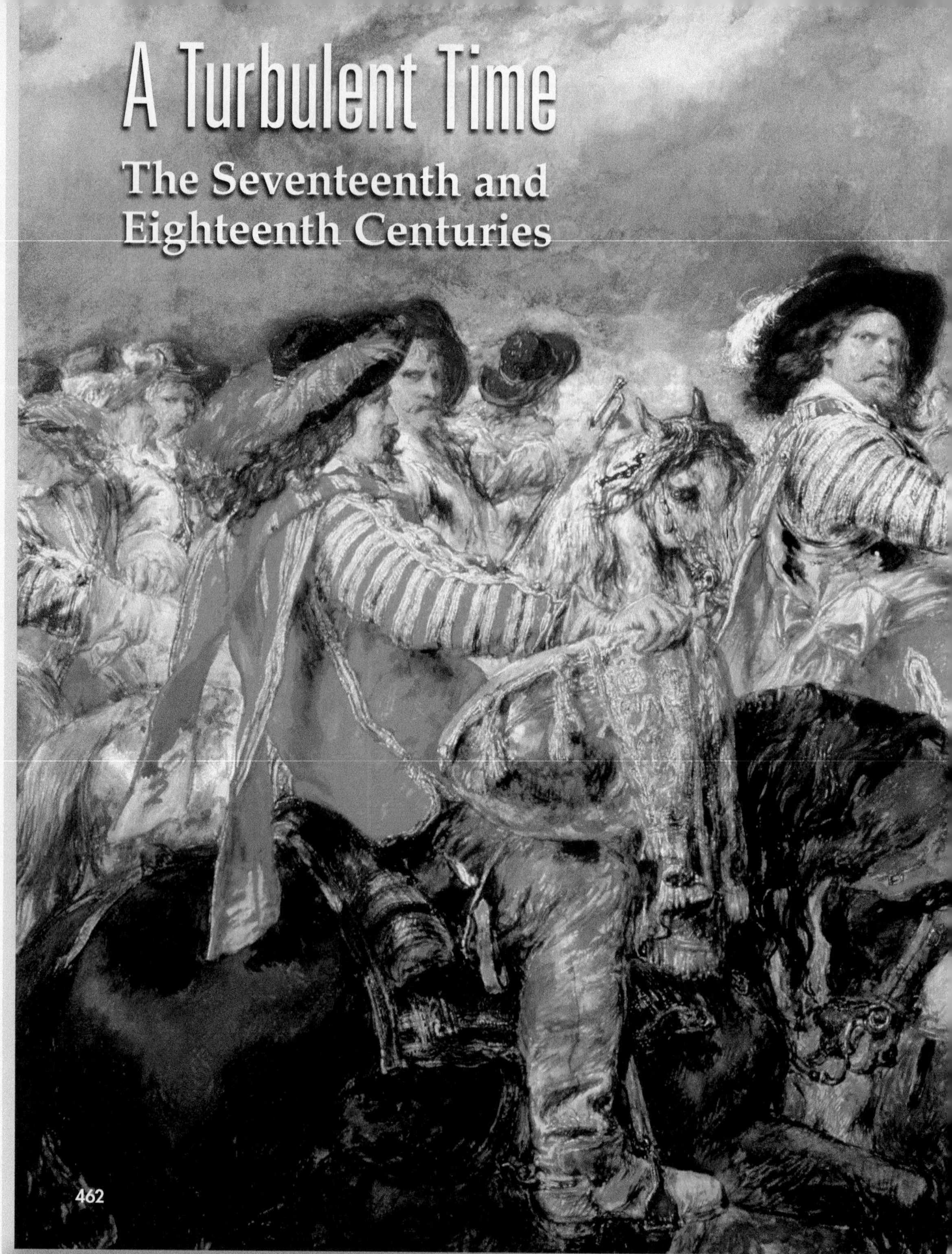
A Turbulent Time
The Seventeenth and Eighteenth Centuries
462

Common Core State Standards

- **Reading Literature 1, 2, 3, 4, 5, 6, 7, 9**
- **Reading Informational Texts 1, 3, 4, 5, 7, 9**
- **Writing 1, 2, 3, 4, 5, 6, 7, 8, 10**
- **Speaking and Listening 1, 6**
- **Language 1, 4, 5, 6**

PHLit Online!
www.PHLitOnline.com

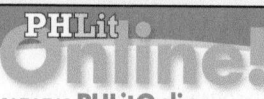

Teaching From Technology

Enriched Online Student Edition
- full narration of selections
- interactive graphic organizers
- linked **Get Connected** and **Background** videos
- all work sheets and other student resources

Professional Development
- the ***Professional Development Guidebook*** online
- additional professional-development essays by program authors

Planning, Assigning, and Monitoring
- software for online assignment of work to students, individually or to the whole class
- a system for tracking and grading student work

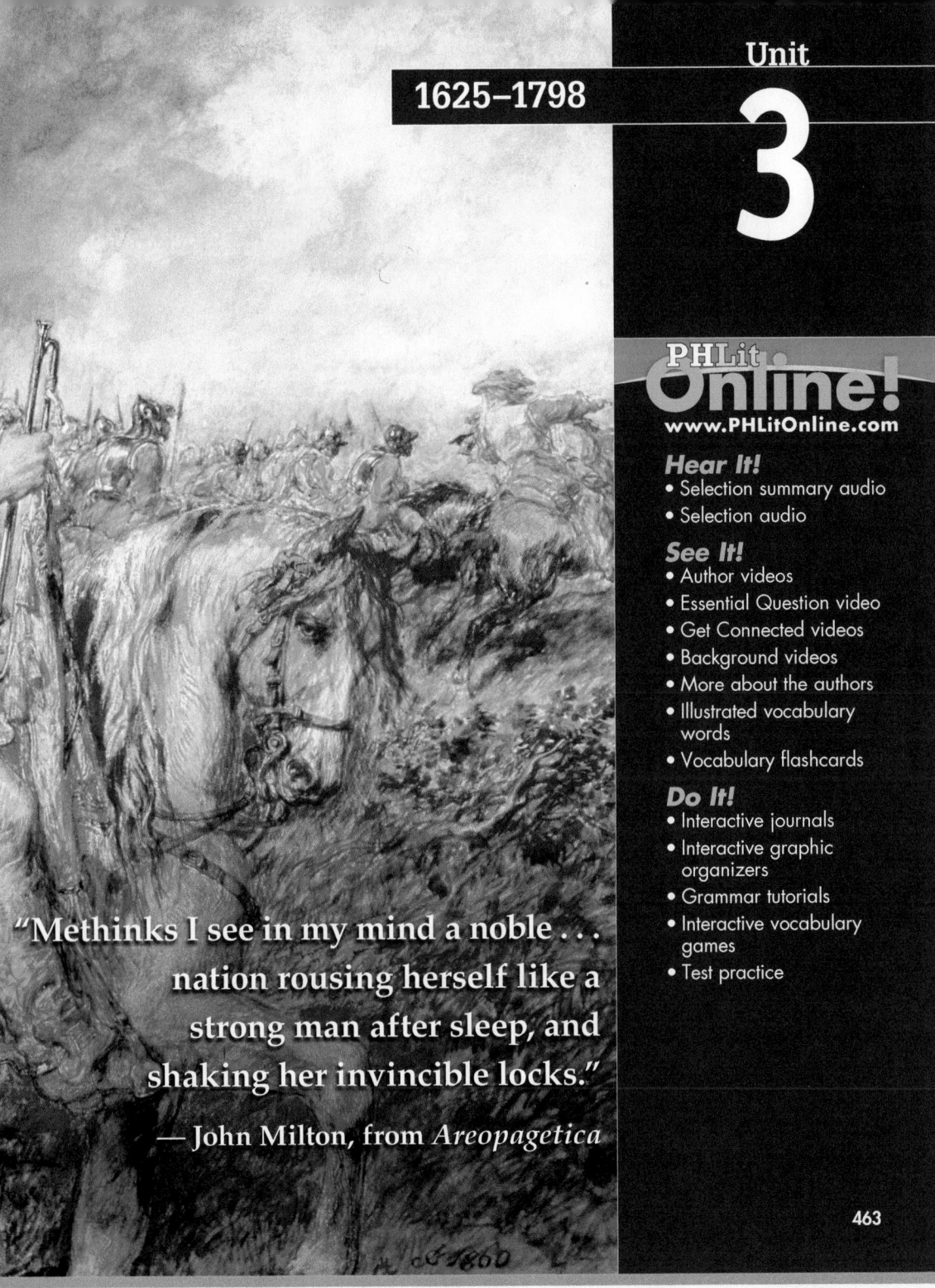

"Methinks I see in my mind a noble . . .
nation rousing herself like a
strong man after sleep, and
shaking her invincible locks."

— John Milton, from *Areopagetica*

PHLit Online!
www.PHLitOnline.com

Hear It!
• Selection summary audio
• Selection audio

See It!
• Author videos
• Essential Question video
• Get Connected videos
• Background videos
• More about the authors
• Illustrated vocabulary words
• Vocabulary flashcards

Do It!
• Interactive journals
• Interactive graphic organizers
• Grammar tutorials
• Interactive vocabulary games
• Test practice

463

Introduce Unit 3

1. Direct students' attention to the title of the Unit, including the time period covered. Have a volunteer read the quotation. **Ask:** What does the quotation suggest about events of the period?
   Possible response: The quotation speaks to upheaval and turmoil, and of the new direction for Britain as it begins a new period in its history.

2. Discuss the artwork, *After the Battle of Naseby in 1645,* painted by Sir John Gilbert in 1860.
   Ask: This painting depicts one of the closing events in the turbulent reign of King Charles I. Do these soldiers look defeated or victorious?
   Possible response: Students might suggest they look victorious, even defiant.

3. Have students speculate about the literature of the period, given the quotation and the art.
   Possible response: Students might offer that the turbulence of the English Civil War led to turbulence in art and literature as well.

Unit Resources

Unit 3 Resources includes these pages:

▶ **Benchmark Tests** assess and monitor student progress.

▶ **Vocabulary and Reading Warm-ups** provide additional vocabulary support, based on Lexile rankings, for each selection. "A" **Warm-ups** are for students reading two grades below level. "B" **Warm-ups** are for students reading one grade below level.

▶ **Selection Support**
   • Reading Strategy
   • Literary Analysis
   • Vocabulary Builder
   • Support for Writing
   • Enrichment

PHLit Online!
All worksheets and other student resources are also available online at www.PHLitOnline.com.

Unit Features

Unit Author
Richard Rodriguez helps introduce the period in the Unit Introduction, provides Recent Scholarship on literature in the Unit, and offers insight in the Writing Workshop.

Extended Study
Students explore in depth the works of John Milton, presented with links to contemporary culture, a Critical Commentary, and a Comparing Literary Works feature.

Comparing Literary Works
Students compare master works in the British tradition with works of world literature.

Primary Sources
Students engage the documents that recorded history as it was made.

Informational Texts
Students learn to use and evaluate various types of informational text.

Themes Across Centuries
Students discover links between canonical literature and the contemporary world.

CLASSROOM STRATEGIES

Differentiated Instruction through Paired Reading **Sharon Vaughn**

"Differentiating instruction promotes learning for ALL students."

W hat is no secret to any practicing teacher is that not every child is reading at grade level. What is more challenging is to provide instruction that includes and supports the learning of these students while continuing to stretch and expand the learning of better readers. Twenty-six percent of 12th graders read below basic levels. You may be thinking, yes, I know exactly who those students are, but what am I supposed to do? Fortunately, teachers can make a difference in promoting the reading and understanding of students in their classes by making adjustments to their typical classroom instructional routines. Differentiating instruction promotes learning for ALL students, not just students with reading difficulties.

Paired Reading for Meaning

Students enjoy working in pairs and can accomplish a great deal when reading and working with a partner using the following structured activity.

1. Pair students to work together. If all of your students read within two grade levels of the text they are reading, then pair students based on their likelihood of successfully working together – or let them pick their own partners. If students are struggling with reading the text, then pair better readers with poorer readers to assure that modeling and support for passage reading are available.

2. Identify students in the pair as Reader #1 and Reader #2. When better readers and poorer readers are paired, allow the better reader to be Reader #1 so that the modeling of good reading occurs first. Of course, students are unaware of the motivation for identifying reader order.

3. Assure that both partners have copies of the same passage to read. It is useful to do this activity with all of the students using the same passage from the Literature Program. In that way, when you "wrap up" with all of the students at the end of the activity, students will be able to learn from each other.

4. Provide students with a learning log to record their responses. The learning log can be a sheet of paper that contains the following information:
   • *Words misread*
   • *Words you need to know more about*
   • *Summary of the most important ideas*

   Adjust learning logs to reflect your goals for the passage. For example, rather than asking students to summarize the most important ideas, you might ask them to identify the author's purpose or to identify the theme and reflect on.

5. Tell Reader #1 to read the passage aloud with expression as though reading professionally. Reader #2 follows along.

6. After Reader #1 has completed the reading, partners then switch roles. Reader #2 reads the same passage aloud with expression and Reader #1 follows along.

7. After reading, students complete the learning log. Initially, it is a good idea to have students work together on one log, and after they are more proficient, they work together but each records his or her own log.

8. Wrap up with the class as a whole. Have students do the following:

- Identify words they misread and demonstrate how to read these words and related words.
- Identify words they need to know more about. Allow other students to build meaning with you as you expand knowledge of these words.
- Ask students about their summaries, author's purpose, or another goal you identified for reading.
- Allow students time to discuss and expand their comments and to make changes to their learning logs based on the group interaction.

Management Tips

- Tell students that it is a good idea to help each other read words they don't know. This way the passage is read aloud twice (once by each student in the pair).
- During reading, students can either keep notes or remember words that they misread and words they need to know more about. Record these words on the learning log. Tell students to go back and reread the sentence before, the sentence the word is in, and the sentence after the word to see if they can figure out the word's meaning.

What the Research Says

There is considerable research supporting the use of well-organized and guided student pairing and small group work as a means of promoting reading fluency and comprehension (e.g., Fuchs, Fuchs, Thompson, Svenson, Yen, Al Otaiba, et al, 2001; Fuchs, Fuchs, Mathes & Simmons, 1997). Research also suggests that students improve their comprehension when they identify key words and access their meaning as well as monitoring words they know and don't know. Finally, students who are able to identify main ideas and summarize are more likely to comprehend what they read (Bryant, Vaughn, Linan-Thompson, Ugel, Hamff, & Hougen, 1999; Edmonds, Vaughn, Wexler, et al., in press; Vaughn, Klingner, & Bryant, 2001).

Teacher Resources

- *Professional Development Guideboook*
- *Classroom Strategies and Teaching Routines cards*

PHLit Online!

Log on as a teacher at **www.PHLitOnline.com** to access a library of all Professional Development articles by the Contributing Authors of Pearson Prentice Hall *Literature*.

Sharon Vaughn, Ph.D.

Sharon Vaughn, Ph.D., is the H.E. Hartfelder/Southland Corporation Regents Chair of Human Development and Professor, University of Texas at Austin. She is the author of numerous books and articles on enhancing reading outcomes for students with reading difficulties.

Supporting Research

Bryant, D.P., Vaughn, S., Linan-Thompson, S., Ugel, N., Hamff, A., & Hougen, M. (1999). Reading outcomes for students with and without reading disabilities in general education middle-school content area classes. *Learning Disability Quarterly, 23:* 238–252.

Edmonds, M.S., Vaughn, S., Wexler, J. et al., (in press). Effective interventions for adolescents with reading difficulties. *Review of Educational Research.*

Fuchs, D., Fuchs, L.S., Thompson, A., Svenson, E., Yen, L., Al Otaiba, S., et al. (2001). Peer-assisted learning strategies in reading: Extensions for kindergarten, first grade, and high school. *Remedial and Special Education, 22:*15–21.

Fuchs, D., Fuchs, L.S., Mathes, P.G., & Simmons, D.C. (1997). Peer-assisted strategies: Making classrooms more responsive to diversity. *American Educational Research Journal, 34:*174–206.

Vaughn, S., Klingner, J. K., & Bryant, D. P. (2001). Collaborative strategic reading as a means to enhance peer-mediated instruction for reading comprehension and content area learning. *Remedial and Special Education, 22*(2), 66–74.

INTRODUCE

Reading the Unit Introduction

A Turbulent Time

Explain to students that this unit covers literature in Great Britain during the seventeenth and eighteenth centuries. The Unit Introduction includes these components:

—a **Snapshot** offering a quick glimpse at the period

—a **Historical Background** section discussing major events

—a **Timeline** that covers the period from 1625–1798, over a span of ten pages

—a **Unit Essay** examining the literature of the period through the lens of three Essential Questions

—**Following-Through** activities

—a recent Scholarship essay.

Introducing the Essential Questions

1. Introduce each of the Essential Questions on the student page.

2. Show the Essential Question video on the *See It!* DVD. Help students relate the Essential Questions to the unit and their own experiences by asking the following:

   Literature and Place Think of locations that have influenced you in meaningful ways. In what ways do these locations influence your perspective on life?

   Literature and Society Consider the writing of one of your favorite writers. In what ways does his or her writing help to shape people's understanding of society?

   Writer and Tradition If you had to write a persuasive piece about a controversial topic, how would your writing benefit from using arguments that are based on traditions of the past?

3. Explain to students that the ideas they have considered in answering these questions also apply to the history of Great Britain. Have them begin reading the Unit Introduction, telling them to look for ideas related to their answers as they read.

Snapshot of the Period

Social turmoil and new growth define this period and its literature. The guns of the English Civil War, which pitted the king against Parliament, echo through the work of poets Andrew Marvell, Richard Lovelace, and John Milton. The Industrial and Agricultural revolutions, sparked by the use of new machines in production and in farming, led to the growth of cities, an increase in urban poverty, and the rise of the middle class. These developments influenced the work of Samuel Pepys, Daniel Defoe, Samuel Johnson, and Joseph Addison, each of whom chronicled the life of the middle class or catered to its leisure needs. At the end of the period, political revolutions in America and in France prepared the way for the revolution in literature known as Romanticism.

The surrender of British General Cornwallis to George Washington at Yorktown, Virginia (1781), led to America's victory in the Revolution.

James Watt's steam engine, shown here, helped bring about the Industrial Revolution.

As you read the selections in this unit, you will be asked to think about them in view of three key questions:

What is the **relationship** between literature and *place?*

How does literature **shape or reflect** *society?*

What is the relationship of the **writer** to *tradition?*

464 A Turbulent Time (1625–1798)

Teaching Resources

The following resources can be used to support, enrich, or extend the instruction for the Unit 3 Introduction.

Unit 3 Resources

Names and Terms to Know Worksheet, p. 2
Essential Questions, pp. 3–5
Follow-Through Activities, p. 6
Listening and Viewing, p. 226

All *Common Core Companion,* pp. 9–14; 33–38

All *Professional Development Guidebook* **Cross-Curricular Enrichment, pp. 224, 231, 233, 235, 242**

See It! DVD **Essential Question Video: Unit 3 Richard Rodriquez,** Segment 1

All resources are available at www.PHLitOnline.com.

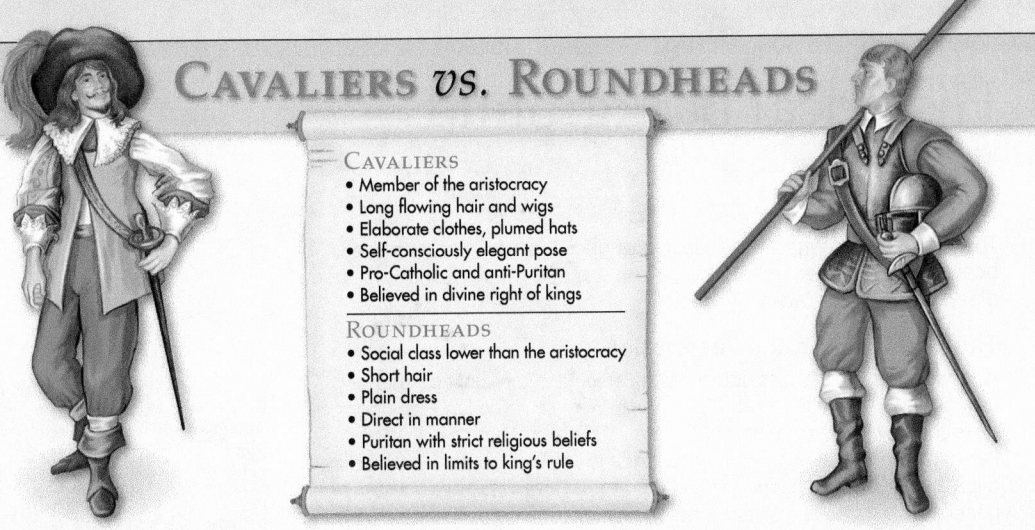

CAVALIERS *vs.* ROUNDHEADS

CAVALIERS
- Member of the aristocracy
- Long flowing hair and wigs
- Elaborate clothes, plumed hats
- Self-consciously elegant pose
- Pro-Catholic and anti-Puritan
- Believed in divine right of kings

ROUNDHEADS
- Social class lower than the aristocracy
- Short hair
- Plain dress
- Direct in manner
- Puritan with strict religious beliefs
- Believed in limits to king's rule

THE INTRODUCTION OF COFFEE TO ENGLAND is a story in which exploration, trade, slavery, the growth of cities, and the rise of the middle class all play a role.

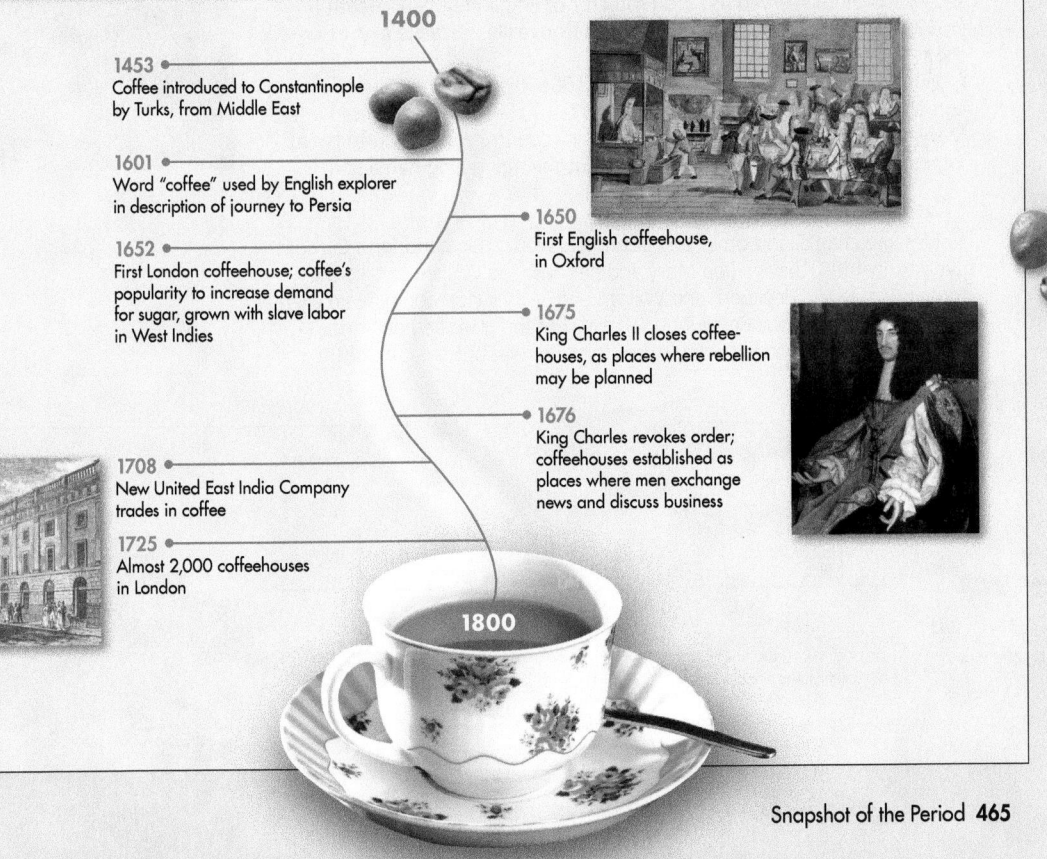

1400

1453
Coffee introduced to Constantinople by Turks, from Middle East

1601
Word "coffee" used by English explorer in description of journey to Persia

1652
First London coffeehouse; coffee's popularity to increase demand for sugar, grown with slave labor in West Indies

1650
First English coffeehouse, in Oxford

1675
King Charles II closes coffee-houses, as places where rebellion may be planned

1676
King Charles revokes order; coffeehouses established as places where men exchange news and discuss business

1708
New United East India Company trades in coffee

1725
Almost 2,000 coffeehouses in London

1800

Snapshot of the Period **465**

Background

History

Tell students that the Industrial and Agricultural revolutions were times during which basic and ground-breaking changes developed in agricultural practice, manufacturing, transportation, and other areas affecting people's lives. These developments were not independent of each other, but were closely related to each other's growth. For example, new practices in agriculture led to an increase in raw materials, which in turn helped to supply other industries, such as the textile industry. Although the Industrial Revolution was not social or political in nature, there were many social and political implications that influenced some of the works presented in this unit.

Differentiated
Instruction   for Universal Access

Culture Connection Point out to students how the introduction of a simple product like coffee impacted exploration, trade, and other aspects of society.

Ask students to compare the impact of the introduction of coffee with the impact of the introduction of personal computers and the Internet. Have students consider how personal computers and the Internet has impacted their world.

Show or assign the **Essential Question** video for this Unit online at **wwwPHLitOnline.com**.

Teaching the Historical Background

The Historical Background section discusses the most significant events of this period: the English Civil War and Restoration, the Glorious Revolution, European Enlightenment, the Industrial and Agricultural Revolutions, American independence, and the French Revolution.

1. Point out that this was a very turbulent period marked by a civil war in England, five other revolutions, the Great Fire of London, as well as an outbreak of bubonic plague in the city.

2. Have students read the Background. Ask students to identify the key political events. Then, have them look for parallel cultural events associated with these political developments. **Answer:** the English Civil War and the monarchy restored, the Glorious Revolution; the development of political parties, Puritans close theaters, John Locke publishes *Two Treatises of Government,* English Bill of Rights, daily newspapers begin publication

Teaching the Timeline

1. Tell students that the Timeline for the period 1625–1798 appears on pages 466–475 of this Unit Introduction. Each portion of the Timeline identifies and illustrates some of the major events in England and the world during that period.

2. Have students survey the entire Timeline before they read the rest of the Unit Introduction.

3. Encourage students to identify additional events from the period and share them with the class.

Historical Background
The Seventeenth and Eighteenth Centuries (1625–1798)

The period begins with the beheading of one king and ends with the beheading of another. In between, a civil war and five revolutions created a new and different world.

The Civil War and the Restoration

A proud king, Charles I, struggled with Parliament over political and religious authority until, in 1642, civil war broke out. The king's supporters were the Cavaliers, with long hair, plumed hats, and high boots. The Parliamentary forces were the "Roundheads," with cropped hair, black hats, and sturdy shoes. Their leaders included Oliver Cromwell, a stern general who thought his new model army could bring divine justice to England. After six brutal years, Charles was defeated, captured, and tried by his "subjects." Condemned to death, he was beheaded in January 1649.

A dead king does not, however, guarantee a democratic or effective government. Impatient with quarreling Parliamentary factions, Cromwell seized power and served as Lord Protector of England until his death (1653–1658). In 1660, Charles II returned from exile in France and assumed the throne in a restored monarchy.

When Charles died without an heir in 1685, his brother, a Catholic convert, became James II. James also had no male heirs, and his daughter, Mary, was a staunch Protestant. The uneasy country was willing to have James as king while it waited for Mary, but the aging king had a son.

"The Glorious Revolution"

Nobles, merchants, and other power brokers would not stand for a Catholic dynasty. In 1688, they invited Mary and her husband William to take the throne. James was deposed, and William and Mary succeeded him, an event hailed as "The Glorious Revolution." The will of the governed had once again determined who would rule, but this time without great bloodshed.

Charles I

TIMELINE

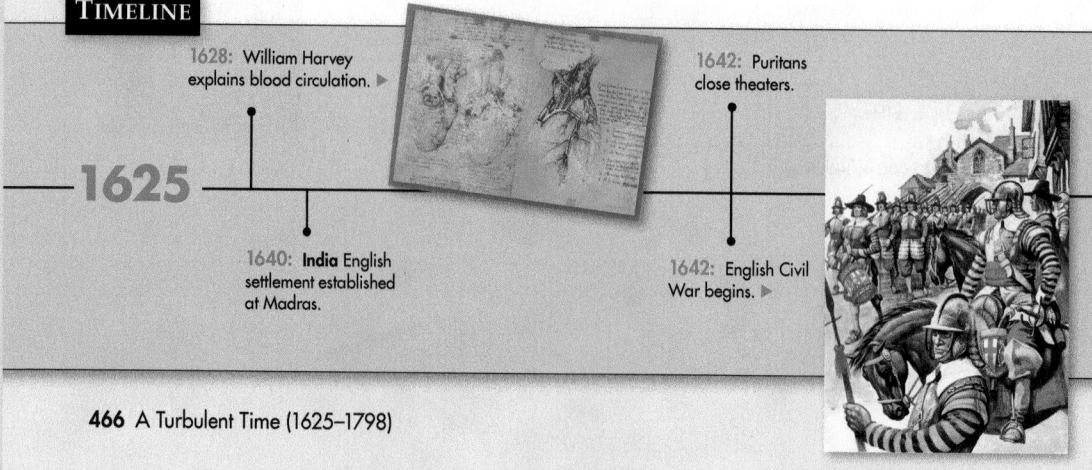

1628: William Harvey explains blood circulation. ▶

1642: Puritans close theaters.

1625

1640: India English settlement established at Madras.

1642: English Civil War begins. ▶

466 A Turbulent Time (1625–1798)

Enrichment: Investigating a Key Person in History

Oliver Cromwell

Cromwell was born into a wealthy family in 1599. Best known for changing England into a republic, he ruled from 1653 to 1658. A strict Puritan, many of his policies sprang from his strong religious faith. After Charles I's execution, Cromwell's government undertook a brutal military conquest of Scotland and Ireland and succeeded in uniting them under one government. Cromwell remained Lord Protector until his death. The Protectorate's collapse led to the restoration of the Stuart monarchy.

Activity: Investigate a Leader of the English Civil War Encourage students to learn more about this Puritan leader. Have them create a timeline and interpret the events in the context of the English Civil War. Suggest that they record their analysis in the **Enrichment: Investigating a Key Person in History** worksheet, *Professional Development Guidebook,* page 233.

Parliament stepped in again in 1701, passing the Act of Settlement to keep the crown in Protestant hands. In 1714, George, the Elector of Hanover in Germany, became king. George I did not speak English and cared little for the country, and Parliament assumed almost complete control.

Other Revolutions

The Industrial Revolution, an explosion of manufacturing involving new technology and new energy sources such as steam, began in the 1700s. Powerful new machinery linked with crop rotation, larger farms, and improved transportation led to an Agricultural Revolution, creating a new abundance with which fewer farmers could feed the swelling population of the cities.

The fourth revolution began in 1775 and ended in 1781. England, a mighty military power, was defeated by American troops fighting on their own soil. America became independent but maintained connections of language, politics, culture, and literature that enriched both countries.

The fifth revolution of the period began on July 14, 1789, when the people of Paris stormed the Bastille, a hated symbol of royal oppression. Shortly after this, King Louis XVI was beheaded and the old order was shattered. Government without kings, already established in America, had now displaced a monarchy in Europe.

At the end of the American Revolution, when Lord Cornwallis led his defeated troops out of Yorktown, the band played a popular tune: "The World Turned Upside Down." It is a good theme song for the whole era.

Key Historical Theme: Civil War and Revolutions

- Struggles between king and Parliament led to a bloody civil war, culminating in the execution of Charles I, and subsequently, to a bloodless revolution deposing Charles II's successor, James II.
- Industrial and Agricultural revolutions boosted manufacturing and farming production.
- Revolutions in America and France showed that people could change their form of government.

1643: **France** Louis XIV becomes king.

1649: **Charles I** beheaded.

◀ 1660: Monarchy restored.

1660

1644: **China** Ming Dynasty ends.

1653: **Oliver Cromwell** becomes Lord Protector. ▶

1658: **Oliver Cromwell** dies. Puritan government collapses.

Historical Background **467**

Connecting to the Literature

1. Point out that the English Civil War was as much a response to the Reformation as it was a quarrel between parliament and king. Students will encounter John Milton's *Paradise Lost*, pages 524–534, in which the civil war between Lucifer and God mirrors the civil war on Earth, and Bunyan's *Pilgrim's Progress*, pages 554–556, an allegory of a Christian on a journey through life.

2. Explain that revolutions in industry and agriculture as well as natural disasters produced social dislocations. Social commentators such as Samuel Pepys, pages 571–577, and Daniel Defoe, pages 590–595, reported on the disasters, and Jonathan Swift, pages 604–627, responded by writing satires of English society and religious disputes.

Key Historical Theme

1. Explain to students that this section of the Historical Background calls out three major political upheavals from the period.

2. The Background suggests that the popular tune "The World Turned Upside Down" was a good theme song for the entire period. **Ask** students to suggest songs to help them remember the individual political upheavals.
   Possible response: "English Civil War" by The Clash, based on "Johnny Comes Marching Home"; Grey Holiday's "Glorious Revolution"; for the Industrial Revolution: "Hard Times at the Mill," by Pete Seeger; and for the French Revolution: "La Marseillaise."

Critical Viewing

Interpret

1. Call students' attention to the illustration of the English Civil War on the Timeline.

2. **Ask:** How does this picture suggest that the action took place during an especially chaotic time period?
   Possible response: The men in the painting are wearing armor and carrying weapons; the horse looks agitated. The soldiers appear to be marching near the outskirts of a fairly large city.

467

As students read "A Turbulent Time," they will examine its information through the lens of three Essential Questions. Each Essential Question is broken down into "stepping-stone," or intermediate, questions. Work through each stepping-stone question with the class. Then, have students pose answers to the Essential Question as it applies to the period.

What is the relationship between literature and place?

1. Before they read this section of the essay, tell students that understanding the division between city and country was critical to this period in history.

2. Have students read this section of the essay. Then, pose the stepping-stone question. **Ask:** How was London the capital of literature, too?
Possible response: Early poets such as Donne, Jonson, and Milton knew only the London of narrow streets and wooden houses. The Puritans blamed the great fire and plague on the behavior of the court; later writers, such as Samuel Pepys and Daniel Defoe, used those disasters as the basis of their literary creations.

3. **Ask** students the second stepping-stone question: How did roads lead to novels?
Possible response: The construction of new turnpikes and canals improved transportation. As people took advantage of this new mobility, a literature of the road developed featuring characters, such as those in Fielding's *Tom Jones,* and their wanderings around the countryside.

4. Then, **ask** the third stepping-stone question: How did a new gathering place capture a lively new readership?
Possible response: Coffee shops sprang up on London street corners. It became fashionable for middle-class Londoners to gather there to read essays in popular magazines of the day such as *The Tatler* and *The Spectator.*

Essential Questions Across Time

The Seventeenth and Eighteenth Centuries (1625–1798)

 What is the **relationship** between literature and *place?*

Bustling city versus quiet country: that age-old division is central to the period. For most of the time, it is the city of London that matters, but gradually, it is the rural landscape that comes to dominate.

How was London the capital of literature, too?

Old London The London of the seventeenth-century poets John Donne, Ben Jonson, and the young John Milton was still the old city of narrow, unpaved streets and timber houses. The river Thames was the main thoroughfare. It was easier to sail to a distant destination than walk or ride, and with only one bridge, ferries were needed to connect the two banks of the river.

During the civil war and the Protectorate of Cromwell, all eyes focused on the Houses of Parliament. These were not the imposing buildings in which Parliament sits today, made famous by postcards. (Those buildings were erected in the 1840s!) Although much smaller, they were still the stages on which the political dramas of the day were enacted.

In 1660, a new king returned from exile, and London threw off its Puritan black, reopened the theaters the triumphant Puritans had closed in 1642, welcomed actresses on the stage for the first time, and celebrated.

London Disasters Become London Literature The party did not last long, however. The Puritans said it was divine retribution on a scandalous court; historians say it was flea-bearing rats from the busy wharves on the Thames. In 1664, the plague struck and

1664: North America
Britain seizes New Netherlands.

1666: Great Fire of London. ▶

◀ **1682: North America**
La Salle claims Louisiana for France.

1660

468 A Turbulent Time (1625–1798)

Enrichment: Analyzing Historical Patterns, Trends, and Periods

The Bill of Rights and John Locke

The 1689 Bill of Rights restated the traditional rights of English citizens to trial by jury and the principle of *habeas corpus*—that no one could be jailed without being charged with a crime. William and Mary accepted the English Bill of Rights in order to ascend the throne. This historic bargain between ruler and subject inspired the political thought of Locke, who felt legitimate government depends on people's consent.

Activity: Analyze Enlightenment Thought

Have students investigate Locke's views on government and its relationship to the English Civil War. Ask them to summarize his philosophy, the events that shaped it, and how it influenced the world. Suggest that they record their analyses in the **Enrichment: Analyzing Historical Patterns, Trends, and Periods** worksheet, *Professional Development Guidebook,* page 231.

the streets of London were filled with carts carrying dead bodies to lime pits. Then, in 1666, a great fire broke out and large areas of London were incinerated. Samuel Pepys captured these twin disasters in his *Diary*, displaying a reporter's cool eye and a citizen's warm concern.

Pepys was writing only for himself, or so he thought (the *Diary*, written in code, was "translated" and published in the 19th century). At least two generations later, however, Daniel Defoe interviewed survivors of the plague and studied records to re-create that perilous time for a broad public, writing the fictional *A Journal of the Plague Year*.

How did roads lead to novels?

Just as London was rebuilt after the fire, the countryside was also being transformed by a series of turnpikes for stagecoaches and canals for barges. The primary purpose was business, but as people took advantage of the new mobility the coach roads offered, a new literary form took inspiration from the road: the novel.

The novel pictured all kinds of characters in their wanderings. Henry Fielding's humorous and good-humored *Tom Jones* was a prime example of a novel on the road. (One later writer, the French novelist Stendhal, would even define a novel as a mirror traveling down a road, reflecting the life around it.)

How did a new gathering place capture a new readership?

All roads still led to London, especially for the bright and ambitious. In London, they would encounter a new kind of gathering place. Suddenly,

---

The BRITISH TRADITION

THE CHANGING ENGLISH LANGUAGE, BY RICHARD LEDERER

No Harmless Drudge, He

On April 15, 1755, Dr. Samuel Johnson—blind in one eye, impoverished, and incompletely educated—produced the first modern *Dictionary of the English Language*.

Johnson set himself the task of making a different kind of dictionary, one of the first that would include all the words in the English language, not just the difficult ones. In addition, he would show how to divide words into syllables and where words came from. He would establish a consistent system of defining words and draw from his own gigantic learning to provide, for the first time in any dictionary, illustrative quotations from famous writers.

Underfunded and working almost alone in a Fleet Street garret room, Johnson defined some 43,000 words and illuminated their meanings with more than 114,000 supporting quotations.

Johnson defined a lexicographer as "a writer of dictionaries, a harmless drudge . . ." However, he was obviously far more than a harmless drudge, and his two-volume dictionary was by far the most comprehensive and readable that had appeared.

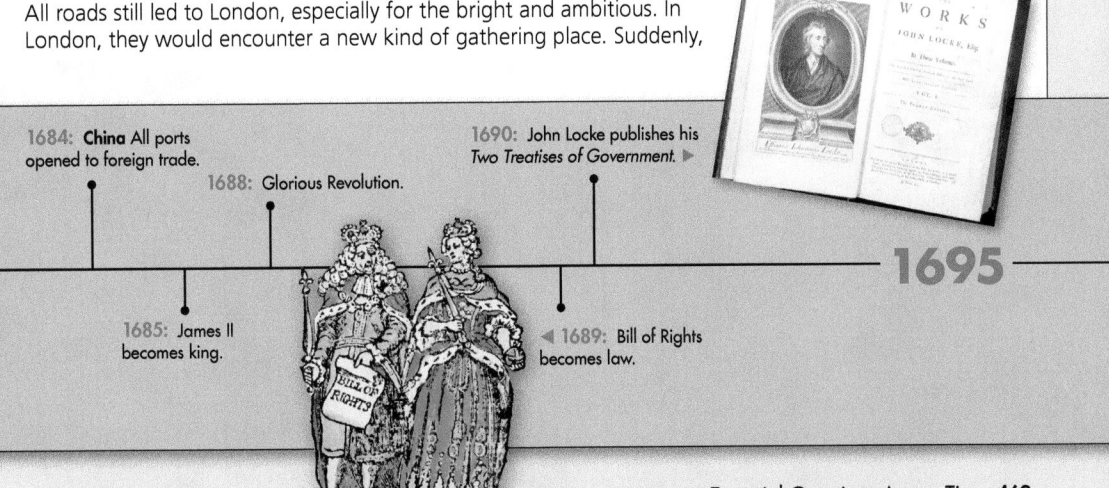

1684: **China** All ports opened to foreign trade.

1685: James II becomes king.

1688: Glorious Revolution.

1689: Bill of Rights becomes law.

1690: John Locke publishes his *Two Treatises of Government.* ▶

WORKS JOHN LOCKE, Esq

1695

Essential Questions Across Time **469**

469

Teaching the Essential Question (cont.)

5. **Ask** the fourth and final stepping-stone question: How did the countryside begin to influence literature?
Possible response: In the latter half of the eighteenth century, poets and other writers began to focus more on nature and draw upon the rural landscape for their inspiration, moral examples, and comfort. For example, Gray's "Elegy Written in a Country Churchyard" had a far more meditative tone than the satire that flourished in the urban world.

Applying the Essential Question

1. Summarize the class discussion of the four stepping-stone questions.

2. Then **ask** students this question: Do contemporary writers tend to focus more on the urban environment or on the countryside for their inspiration?
Possible response: Answers will vary. Ensure that students explain and support their responses with examples from contemporary literature.

---

like mushrooms sprung up overnight, these places were all over the city. There seemed to be one on every corner. Who could account for the unstoppable spread of the coffee house? Will's and White's were among the most fashionable, but they all had many regulars.

They were popular because they offered not only coffee, the beverage that was all the rage at the time, but a place to hang out, to meet friends, to smoke a pipe, and to read the essays in those new-fangled magazines people were talking about. The titles of two famous magazines of the time, *The Tatler* and *The Spectator*, suggest that periodicals were an extension of the observation and gossip that took place around the city and especially in coffee houses. Such gossip, however, was still respectable for a self-conscious and social-climbing middle class—a coffee house was more proper than a tavern.

Samuel Johnson, who had ridden from Litchfield to London to seek literary fame and fortune—sharing a horse with future actor David Garrick, according to legend—embodied the London man of letters at this time. He famously remarked that if a man were tired of London, he was tired of life. In his greatest literary achievement, the *Dictionary of the English Language*, Johnson defined in a single book all the words worth knowing, just as London itself defined all the life worth living.

How did the countryside begin to influence literature?

Even as Johnson was speaking, however, the times were changing. One of the most popular and influential poems of the second half of the eighteenth century is not set in London, but in a country churchyard. Thomas Gray's "Elegy Written in a Country Churchyard" is a sober and thoughtful poem, and its meditative tone is completely different from the biting satire that flourished in an urban world. A mood of nocturnal reverie became the dominant mood of poetry.

Removed from the din and dirt of the city, poets looked to country landscapes for inspiration, moral examples, and consolation. The country replaced the city as the setting and subject for literature.

> **ESSENTIAL QUESTION VOCABULARY**
>
> These Essential Question words will help you think and write about literature and place:
>
> **mobility** (mō bil′ ə tē) *n.* ability to move freely from place to place
>
> **meditative** (med′ ə tāt′ iv) *adj.* deeply thoughtful
>
> **urban** (ur′ bən) *adj.* characteristic of the city, as opposed to the country

TIMELINE

The Daily Courant.

1695

◀ **1702:** First daily newspaper begins publication.

1703: Russia Peter the Great begins building St. Petersburg. ▶

1707: Great Britain created by Act of Union. ▲

470 A Turbulent Time (1625–1798)

Vocabulary Development

Essential Question Vocabulary
Students will use Essential Question Vocabulary (introduced on pp. 470, 471, and 473) when they discuss and write about the literature in the Unit. Have students practice by completing sentence starters such as these:

Fielding's "novel on the road" revealed increased **mobility** in the countryside contributed more to life than just _____.

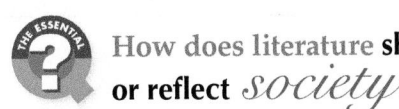

How does literature **shape** or reflect *society?*

The turmoil of the period raised profound questions about order. Civil war toppled a king and so posed the question, What holds the social order together? Fueled by religious differences, the war dramatized still other fundamental questions: If human beliefs differ irreconcilably, what can one know about the order of the world or about the right way to behave? Even economic growth opened questions. Members of the new middle class, their place in the world secured by prosperity, not birth, were haunted by the question, What is my place in the social order? The literature of the time was dedicated to answering such questions.

How did Milton's Grace become Newton's Gravity?

For John Milton, who lived through the Civil War, serving as Cromwell's secretary, literature, religion, and civic duty were all related. His epic *Paradise Lost* takes disobedience as its theme: the rebellious pride of Satan leading to the willful disobedience of Eve. Writing in the dark days when the Puritan religious government had failed, he intended his epic poem "to justify the ways of God to men."

At almost the same time that Milton published *Paradise Lost*, one of England's towering geniuses provided a different vision of God's ways in the world. In 1687, Isaac Newton published his *Mathematical Principles of Natural Philosophy* and everything changed. Newton demonstrated that the universe was governed by natural physical principles. Newton himself was a deeply religious man, but others read his work as proof that the world operated without the constant attention of a divine being. Gravity replaced grace. Some believed in a divine watchmaker who created and wound up the universe and then let it tick on its own.

Belief in a benevolent but detached God was called Deism. Pope's *Essay on Man* tells us: "Know then thyself, presume not God to scan." More and more, emphasis would be placed on understanding humans in their own world and according to the natural laws of that world.

> **ESSENTIAL QUESTION VOCABULARY**
>
> These Essential Question words will help you think and write about literature and society:
>
> **civic** (siv´ik) *adj.* relating to citizenship and affairs of government
>
> **rational** (rash´ ən əl) *adj.* of or based on reason
>
> **proportion** (prō pôr´ shən) *n.* balance; desirable relationship among parts

1715: **France** Louis XV succeeds to throne.

1727: **Brazil** First coffee planted. ▼

1730

1714: **George I** becomes King.

◀ 1719: First organized cricket match takes place.

Essential Questions Across Time **471**

Teaching the Essential Question

How does literature shape or reflect society?

1. Before they read this section of the essay, tell students that a reaction to the religious conflicts of the Reformation led to separation of church and state, and a shift toward a more secular worldview.

2. Have students read this section of the essay. Then, pose the first stepping-stone question. **Ask:** How did Milton's Grace become Newton's Gravity?
Possible response: For John Milton, politics and faith were inseparable. Though Newton was a religious man, his work suggested that the universe was governed by natural laws that human beings could understand. People came to see God as a divine watchmaker who did not intervene directly in human affairs.

Critical Viewing

Analyze

1. Call students' attention to the illustrations of the *Daily Courant* newspaper and the coffee beans.

2. **Ask:** How are these two images related?
Answer: Coffeehouses in London became popular gathering places where people read new publications, like this newspaper, and discussed the news of the day.

Differentiated Instruction for Universal Access

Strategy for Less Proficient Readers
To help students sift through this information-packed text, encourage them to break the text into manageable chunks and read them one at a time. Have them stop and ask themselves questions such as: What does this tell me about the history or literature of this time?

EL Vocabulary for English Learners
Have students skim this selection together and compile a list of unfamiliar vocabulary words. Give a brief overview of what is being described in each section. Then help students define unfamiliar words and ideas as they read.

Enrichment for Gifted/Talented Students
Ask each student to select a writer mentioned in these pages. Have students research the writers and create attractive posters displaying their information. Give students guidelines as to the minimum number of facts to include on their posters.

Teaching the Essential Question

(cont.)

3. **Ask** the second and final stepping-stone question: How did literature focus on conduct?
Possible response: Newton's clockwork universe demanded conduct based upon rational principles rather than fear of an avenging God. Satire pointed out the absurdities of irrational conduct, and the essay supplied the new gentry class with guidance for correct behavior. Novels of the period reflected this focus on reason and logic.

Applying the Essential Question

1. Summarize the class discussion of the two stepping-stone questions on pages 471–472.

2. Then, **ask** students these questions: How do contemporary views about God help shape human behavior? Is this reflected in our literature?
Possible response: Many people believe we can discover God by looking for the divine in nature or in ordinary life activities; right conduct involves striving to improve the lives of other human beings and protecting the environment. Students should supply examples from modern literature, such as *Silent Spring*, that reflect the view of God they identified.

Why did literature focus on conduct?

Satire and Proportion In this new world, writers examined conduct through the lens of reason, not revelation. As a result, satire flourished. Satire ridicules conduct that is not rational, that is out of proportion. Pope's *Rape of the Lock* is a mock epic in which a trivial incident is treated as something earth-shaking. Swift's *Gulliver's Travels* is, with its tiny Lilliputians and giant Brobdingnagians, a study in proportion and the disproportionate things that humans do.

The "How-to" Genres The literary essay began as a "how-to" genre, teaching rational conduct to the new middle classes and helping them find their own identity. As Addison says in his essay "The Aims of *The Spectator*," he hopes the "morning lectures" in his new periodical will provide "instruction agreeable, and ... diversion useful."

The novel also had its start in the "how-to" fashion. Samuel Richardson, a publisher, wrote a book of advice on conduct for apprentices. He then began a series of model letters on problems of conduct in daily life. In 1740, these turned into *Pamela*. Often cited as the first English novel, *Pamela* is epistolary in form; it is a series of letters by a young servant whose virtue is, unsuccessfully, assailed by her master.

Religious belief was also caught up in this question of appropriate conduct. John Wesley founded Methodism, which grew from his early commitment to self-examination and self-discipline, the "method" of belief and worship. His preaching was very influential because it met the need for a renewed sense of personal religious experience.

The BRITISH TRADITION

CLOSE-UP ON DAILY LIFE

Proper Behavior for Children

The eighteenth-century focus on proper conduct applied to children as well. One book on this subject was entitled *Rules for Children's Behavior: At Church, at Home, at Table, in Company, in Discourse, at School, abroad, and among Boys* . . . (1701). Following are some of the "Rules for Behavior in Company":

Sit not down in the presence of Superiors without bidding.

Sing not nor hum in thy mouth while thou art in company.

Play not wantonly like a Mimic with thy Fingers or Feet.

Stand not wriggling with thy body hither and thither, but steady and upright.

In coughing or sneezing make as little noise as possible.

If thou cannot avoid yawning, shut thy Mouth with thine Hand or Handkerchief before it, turning thy Face aside.

Laugh not aloud, but silently Smile upon occasion.

TIMELINE

1730

1740: Prussia Frederick the Great succeeds to the throne. ▼

1749: Henry Fielding publishes *Tom Jones*.

1745: Last Jacobite rebellion in Scotland.

1752: North America Benjamin Franklin invents lightning rod. ▲

472

Enrichment: Daily Life

Agricultural Revolution

Emphasize that agricultural efficiency had social consequences. In the 1700s, rich landowners pushed ahead with enclosure, taking over and fencing in the common lands once shared by villagers. This action consolidated strips of farmland into larger fields. As millions of acres were enclosed, small farmers were forced off their land because they could not compete. Landless farm workers migrated to cities and formed a growing labor pool needed for new industries.

Activity: Analyze an Agricultural Revolution

Ask students to investigate the causes and effects of the Agricultural Revolution that began with the invention of new farm machinery. Have them compare it with the Green Revolution of the twentieth century. Suggest that they record their analyses in the **Enrichment: Daily Life** worksheet, *Professional Development Guidebook*, page 224.

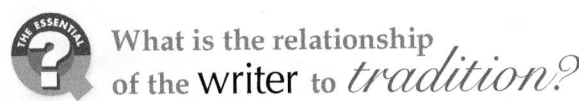

What is the relationship of the writer to *tradition?*

In this period, some literary traditions reach a magnificent conclusion, and some wholly new forms emerge from the chaos of civil war and revolution to meet the needs of a growing, literate, middle-class audience.

What effects did the Renaissance and Reformation have?

From Love to Religion John Donne is a child of the Renaissance—the rebirth of classical learning and themes that began in the fifteenth century—and Reformation—the efforts to reform Christianity that led to the birth of Protestantism. He begins as a witty love poet and ends as the Dean of the old St. Paul's Cathedral, which burned in 1666. His early lyrics continue the Elizabethan tradition, but his Holy Sonnets change the sonnet from a love poem into a religious meditation.

Work Based on the Classics Ben Jonson's poetry is restrained and graceful, like the classical poetry he admired. Poets who succeeded him, "The Tribe of Ben," produced brilliant poems on the *carpe diem* theme. *Carpe diem* is Latin for "seize the day," and the speakers in the poems, male, urge their audience, female, to forget inhibitions and take advantage of the fleeting hours of life. Andrew Marvell's "To His Coy Mistress" adds a serious undertone suggesting the real ravages of time.

Renaissance and Reformation John Milton's work embodies almost all the traditions of both the Renaissance and Reformation. Able to read Greek, Latin, Hebrew, French, and Italian, he wanted to give English an epic poem to match those of Homer and Virgil. He first considered an epic based on the legends of King Arthur because Homer and Virgil had based their epics on mythic histories of their countries.

A devout son of the Reformation, however, he decided that the fit subject for an English epic was the Bible's story of creation and fall. When the hated monarchy had been restored, the poet, blind and disillusioned with politics, dictated his poem about the fall from Eden and the promise of a redeemer who will restore the human race to its rightful heritage.

ESSENTIAL QUESTION VOCABULARY

These Essential Question words will help you think and write about the writer and tradition:

literate (lit´ər it) *adj.* able to read and write

heritage (her´ i tij) *n.* something handed down from the past, such as a culture or tradition

prophet (präf´ ət) *n.* person regarded as divinely inspired

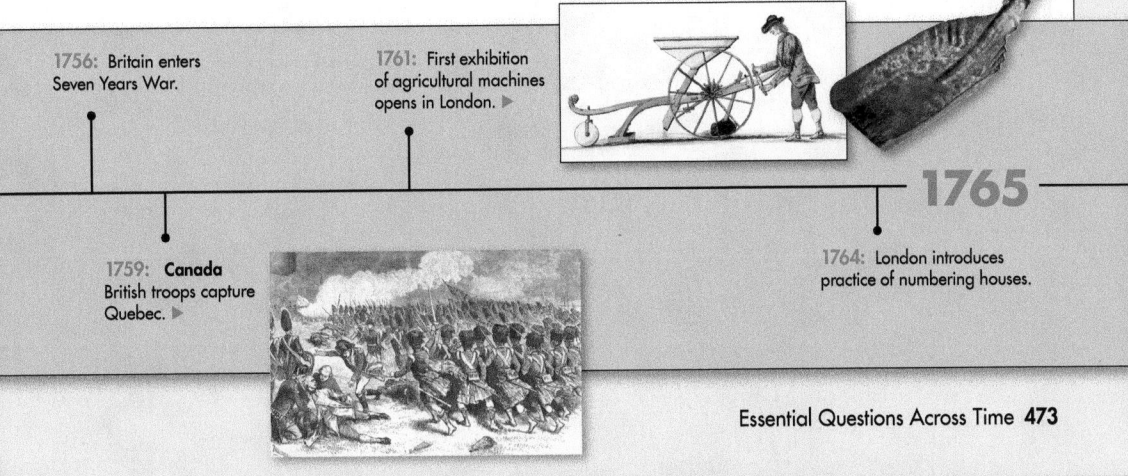

1756: Britain enters Seven Years War.

1761: First exhibition of agricultural machines opens in London. ▶

1765

1759: Canada British troops capture Quebec. ▶

1764: London introduces practice of numbering houses.

Essential Questions Across Time **473**

Enrichment: Technology

The Early Industrial Revolution

Emphasize for students that the Industrial Revolution began with agriculture, with Jethro Tull's seed drill increasing food production. The next advance was the discovery of steam power, which was much more efficient than previous power sources. In a steam engine, improved by James Watt, water is heated by burning fuel such as coal. The resulting steam enters an enclosed cylinder, where it pushes against a piston.

Activity: Analyze the Impact of the Industrial Revolution Ask students to investigate an aspect of the early Industrial Revolution from this period, such as the seed drill, steam engine, iron foundries, or textile manufacture. Have them create a chronology of developments and consider how it impacted society.

Suggest that they record their analyses in the **Enrichment: Investigating Technology** worksheet, *Professional Development Guidebook,* page 242.

The British Tradition
Close-Up on Daily Life

1. Have students read the sidebar feature about proper behavior of children in the eighteenth century.

2. Explain to students that these rules helped mold and shape the character of children in this period.

3. **Ask:** What do these rules suggest about how people in this time period viewed young people?
   Possible response: They were viewed as small adults. They were expected to respect and not interrupt their elders.

Teaching the Essential Question

What is the relationship of the writer to tradition?

1. Before they read this section of the essay, tell students that the turmoil of the Civil War and the revolutions in English society that followed it produced new literary traditions.

2. Have students read this section of the essay. Then, pose the first stepping-stone question. **Ask:** What effects did the Renaissance and Reformation have?
   Possible response: The Renaissance brought about a revival of interest in classical styles and subjects for poetry, as shown in the work of Ben Jonson and his Tribe, while the Reformation spurred poems of faith, like Donne's Holy Sonnets. John Milton's poetry brought together the strands from both these traditions.

Critical Viewing

Analyze

1. Call students' attention to the illustration of Benjamin Franklin's famous experiment with lightning.

2. **Ask:** What do Franklin's scientific studies of lightning have to do with the changes in literature in this period?
   Possible response: They relate to Newton's discovery of the physical laws that govern the universe and the application of reason to understanding the world.

Teaching the Essential Question

(cont. from p. 473)

3. **Ask** the second stepping-stone question: How did Milton create a new role for the poet?
Possible response: Milton's poetry created a new role for the poet as a prophet reminding the nation when it strays from its proper path.

4. Then, **ask** the third and final stepping-stone question: What new forms arose for new audiences?
Possible response: The heroic couplet (iambic pentameter linked in rhyming pairs) reached its peak with the poetry of Alexander Pope. The essay and the novel arose to meet the needs of the new middle-class audience.

Applying the Essential Question

1. Summarize the class discussion of the three stepping-stone questions on pages 473–474.

2. Then, **ask** students this question: Do these literary traditions still influence contemporary literature and film?
Possible response: Many modern writers, such as C. S. Lewis, Madeleine L'Engle, J.R.R. Tolkien, and Tim LaHayne (*Left Behind* series), still write about biblical themes and act like prophets trying to keep people from straying from values. The epic form is very much alive in stories like the *Star War's* saga about heroes like those in classical myths and legends.

How did Milton create a new role for the poet?

Poet as Prophet In his writing, Milton addressed the English as if he were an Old Testament prophet, thundering at a people that had broken its covenant with God. Milton created the role of poet as prophet, a poet reminding a nation of the path from which it had strayed. This idea of the poet had a strong influence on subsequent literature. In the Romantic period, the poets William Blake and Percy Bysshe Shelley assume the role. Another Romantic, Wordsworth, despairing of the state of England in 1802, writes: "Milton! thou shouldst be living at this hour / England hath need of thee."

What new forms arose for new audiences?

The Heroic Couplet Milton's influence was not felt immediately. With the end of the civil war and Puritan rule, poets sought a new mode of expression for a new social order. That mode was the heroic couplet, iambic pentameter lines linked in rhyming pairs. This form perfectly suited an urban aristocratic society that valued clever talk. With the genius of Alexander Pope, the form reaches its peak. The variations he creates within the rigid form give his poetry vitality.

The Essay and the Novel Two new forms came into being in this period to meet the demands of a new middle-class audience: the essay and the novel. Both require a literate audience with money to spend on periodicals and books and leisure time to fill—an audience who want to read about people like themselves and people they would like to be.

The essay is a secular sermon, teaching lessons about life. Where sermons are delivered in houses of worship, essays depended on publication in periodicals to reach their audience. At the same time, periodicals relied on essays to attract readers. That marriage produced an enduring form whose offspring includes today's newspaper columns and television news commentary shows.

The novel had its roots in quasi-religious narratives: the life story of a man or woman struggling to survive and be virtuous in a world that is hostile, evil, or simply indifferent. Coming into flower in the middle of the eighteenth century, the novel is the beginning of a style of literature—self-conscious, self-analytical, socially concerned—that will dominate coming centuries.

John Milton

TIMELINE

1765

1773: North America Boston Tea Party. ▶

1776: North America American Revolution begins. ▼

474 A Turbulent Time (1625–1798)

Enrichment: Investigating a Literary Figure

John Milton

Milton, one of the greatest poets of the English language, is best known for his epic poem *Paradise Lost* (1667). Educated at Christ's College, Milton gave up his plans to become a priest after being expelled. He traveled to France and Italy, where he met Galileo Galilei, whose telescope figures prominently in *Paradise Lost*. In this epic poem, he created a sympathetic portrait of Lucifer. Milton also wrote pamphlets defending religious civil liberties.

Activity: Investigate Milton's Contributions to the British Literary Tradition Ask interested students to learn more about Milton. Encourage them to create a chronology, identify representative works, and analyze influences on his writings and his contributions. Suggest that they record their analyses in the **Enrichment: Investigating a Literary Figure** worksheet, *Professional Development Guidebook*, page 235.

The BRITISH TRADITION

CONTEMPORARY CONNECTION

John Milton: Epic Poet or Computer Visionary?

John Milton wrote his great epic *Paradise Lost* in the mid-1600s. So, what could Milton's poetic description of hell possibly have in common with artificial intelligence, the technology of thinking machines? Pandemonium, that's what!

Paradise Lost describes how Satan was ousted from heaven and set up his own domain. Milton actually created the word *Pandemonium* to name Satan's capital city. It is based on the Greek word *pan*, meaning "all," and the Latin word *daemonium*, meaning "demons." Pandemonium is the place where all the demons gather to argue about which diabolical scheme they will pursue next. Satan, of course, makes the final decision.

In 1958, Oliver Selfridge, a computer pioneer, thought Milton's word for the capital of the nether world was perfect to describe a system of processing information. In pandemonium as it refers to computers, there are four levels of demons. Demons are the working parts of a computer program. The lowest demons receive data. Higher-level demons accumulate and "shout" out their data. Like Satan, the top demon makes the decision about which shout is the loudest and should be followed up.

Certainly, Milton could not have anticipated this use for his word. Being an inventive thinker himself, though, he would probably have applauded it!

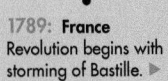

1784: France
First school for the blind established.

1789: France
Revolution begins with storming of Bastille. ▶

1798: William Wordsworth and Samuel Taylor Coleridge publish *Lyrical Ballads*.

1798

Essential Questions Across Time **475**

The British Tradition

Contemporary Connection

1. Have students read the sidebar feature connecting John Milton's demons to computer modeling.

2. Explain that Oliver Selfridge's model for machine learning relies on parallel processing of data. It has proved such an effective learning model that psychologists have used it to model human visual pattern recognition.

3. **Ask:** What are the implications of this computer model for artificial intelligence research?
   Possible responses: Even if the mental processing of computers is not exactly the same as ours, in the future we may be able to make their processing more like our own and give them the ability to understand human language, creativity, and something similar to free will. This may eventually make it possible to design intelligent robots that can learn and develop independently, as well as help us learn more about the functioning of the human brain.

Critical Viewing

Analyze

1. Call student attention to the paintings from the American Revolutionary period.

2. **Ask:** How do these images relate to the literary history of this turbulent time?
   Possible response: The leaders of the American Revolution who took part in the Boston Tea Party and the American independence movement saw themselves as the heirs of the English Bill of Rights and John Locke's theories on government, which in turn grew out of the English Civil War.

Differentiated Instruction for Universal Access

Strategy for Special-Needs Students

Students may benefit from creating a graphic organizer to help them master the unit's Essential Questions. The organizer might consist of three boxes with the Essential Question written at the top of each, with each stepping-stone question listed under the Essential Question with space to write. Have students work in groups of three, with each student creating a box for one of the three Essential Questions.

EL Vocabulary for English Learners

Before students read this Contemporary Connection, discuss the common meaning and word origin of the word *pandemonium,* coined by Milton to describe the supreme council of hell in *Paradise Lost.* Then have them read the feature. Tell them the word was chosen to describe this computer model because the parts of the computer program are organized under a master demon like the top demon (Satan) in Milton's vision of hell.

475

Recent Scholarship

Richard Rodriguez

1. Richard Rodriguez introduces the unit and provides insights into the role of a spectator in London. A selection from his work *Days of Obligation:* "In Athens Once" and his commentary about it appear later in the unit on pages 686–693.

2. Have students read the introductory paragraph about Richard Rodriguez. Tell them that he is an editor at Pacific News Service and a contributing editor and writer for many highly respected publications. His *NewsHour Essays on American Life* won him the 1997 George Foster Peabody Award. His work contains his observations on life.

3. Use the *See It!* DVD to introduce Richard Rodriguez. Show Segment 1 to provide insight into his writing career. You can also view the video from this page in the Enriched Online Student Edition at **www. PHLitOnline.com.** After students have watched the segment, **discuss** what observations on life Rodriguez chooses as subjects for his writing.
   Answer: He chooses to comment on society and cultural differences.

4. **Ask** students what issues they would write about.
   Possible response: Students may suggest issues that relate to their school.

Recent Scholarship

Richard Rodriguez

Talks About the Time Period

From Small Towns to Big Cities

In high school, whenever teachers assigned texts of British literature, I responded most to the idea of London. I lived in Sacramento, at that time, more a town than a city. By senior year, because my body and mind were growing, I began to feel the need of a city—a place of contest and ambition. I left home, as so many seekers of fortune in English novels leave home, for the city.

London, Market for Commodities and Ideas

London at the beginning of the eighteenth century was becoming the center of the world. Most of the world's commodities and many of the world's ideas passed through London. A city of so much invested interest was interested. People required news: of ships, of trade, of exploration. To get the news, people required newspapers. Londoners also wanted to read about themselves, about plays and books, about fashions and personalities.

About the Author

Richard Rodriguez (b. 1944) is a distinguished nonfiction author and journalist who often presents his views on public television. His books include *Hunger of Memory: The Education of Richard Rodriguez* (1982), *Days of Obligation: An Argument with My Mexican Father* (1992), and *Brown: The Last Discovery of America* (2001; 2003).

476 A Turbulent Time (1625–1798)

Birth of *The Spectator*

In 1711, an ex-soldier and ex-scholar named Richard Steele published a journal called *The Spectator*. *The Spectator*'s innovation was to notice and to comment upon the social and moral life of London. Steele enlisted a young writer named Joseph Addison to contribute to the paper. Addison developed the persona of *The Spectator*:

"I am frequently seen in most public places. . . . [But] I live in the world rather as a spectator of mankind than as one of the species. . . ."

Addison's essays are fictional observations of real places and real habits. They remain among the best records we have of how several classes of men and women behaved and thought and spoke in London in the eighteenth century.

Joining "the conversation of cities"

It was my ambition, when I left my schoolbooks behind, to join the conversation of cities. I became a journalist. My fate, as Addison might have foretold: In order to write, one must seek solitude. To create a public voice, one must choose loneliness.

Addison benefited from his solitude as a spectator; he was thrilled to have found readers in the male clubs and coffee houses of London. And he also wanted women readers.

When I was in high school and teachers instructed me to compose an essay, I never wondered about my reader. My reader was the teacher—her ear a pair of spectacles, her voice a fluent red ink.

What one never learns in high school about writing is just how large the world is and how a writer in the world must find an audience—must seduce, amuse, or infuriate a stranger's attention.

The Beginning and End of Print

The reading audience of eighteenth-century London was avid, middle class, growing as the city was growing—whereas we live near the end of a long age of print. Now, fewer people read for their news; fewer still for their pleasure. Today's blogger, tossing words into the void of the Web, must sense this. I sense it, writing for newspapers. Yet one is confident that one is, somehow, recorded. One lives in the age of mass media, after all.

But writing, although lonely, cannot be completed alone. In order to write, in order to continue writing, the writer needs to find, as Addison found, a reader—"you"—someone willing to complete the meaning of this sentence by the act of reading.

© Speaking and Listening: Collaboration

Rodriguez compares his career to that of British author Joseph Addison (1672–1719), who, says Rodriguez, "was thrilled to have found readers in the male clubs and coffee houses of London." These coffee houses were places where people exchanged news and ideas, as well as conducted business.

With a partner, study the picture of an eighteenth-century coffee house shown here. Then, formulate a **media evaluation** that answers the following questions:

- What techniques did the artist use to convey a favorable or unfavorable impression of such a place?
- What social and personal values was the artist promoting?

LONDON COFFEE-HOUSES, PAST AND PRESENT.

477

Speaking and Listening: Collaboration

Media Evaluation

1. Review the assignment with students.
2. Have students examine the picture. They should formulate media evaluations that take into account the questions provided. They may discuss forums for discussion and exchange analogous to eighteenth-century coffee-houses that exist in today's society.
3. After students complete their media evaluations of the picture, have them present their analyses to the class.
4. To help conduct the discussion, use the **Discussion Guide** in the *Professional Development Guidebook*, page 65.

ASSESS

 Common Core
State Standards

• Reading Informational Text 7
• Speaking and Listening 1, 1.a

Integrate and Evaluate Information

1. Review the chart assignment with the class. Then, ask students to use the Activity A chart in the **Follow-Through** worksheet (p. 6 in **Unit 3 Resources**) to complete this activity.
   Possible responses: Literature and Society: Key Concept—Rational conduct; Author—Swift. Writer and Tradition: Key Concept—Renaissance and Reformation; Author—Milton.

2. **Possible responses:** Monarchs and military leaders figured prominently, based on the portrait of Cromwell on p. 467 and the illustration of monarchs on p. 469. These were also times of tragedy, war, and upheaval, based on the images of the Yorktown surrender on p. 464, the Great Fire of London on p. 468, and the storming of the Bastille on p. 475.

3. **Possible responses:** English Civil War—Pro-Catholic supporters of Charles I (the Cavaliers) fought against Puritan Parliamentary forces (Roundheads); the former believed in the divine right of kings while the latter sought to limit the king's power. Glorious Revolution—Catholic James II was deposed and forced into exile; Protestant Mary succeeded him. These events helped amplify the voices of the governed.

4. Responses should reflect local issues and should identify strategies for participating, such as blogging, speaking at local meetings, or writing letters to the editor.

Integrate and Evaluate Information

1. Use a chart like the one shown to determine the key ideas expressed in the Essential Question essays on pages 468–474. Fill in two ideas related to each Essential Question and note the authors most closely associated with each concept. One item has been provided for you.

Essential Question	Key Concept	Key Author
Literature and Place	Threats to London	Samuel Pepys
Literature and Society		
Writer and Tradition		

2. Review the visual sources that appear on the timeline on pages 466–475. Make two generalizations about life during the seventeenth and eighteenth centuries based on the images. Cite specific examples from the essays on these pages to support your generalizations.

3. The seventeenth and eighteenth centuries were marked by civil war and revolution. Choose either the English civil war or the Glorious Revolution and describe the perspectives of those involved in the conflict. What did each side seek? To what was it opposed? What long-term changes in English society did the event help to create? Cite evidence from the multiple sources presented on pages 464–475, as well as from other sources you consult, such as encyclopedias, in your response.

 4. **Address a Question:** In his essay on pages 476–477, Richard Rodriguez recalls that "It was my ambition, when I left my schoolbooks behind, to join the conversation of cities." What "conversations" define your town or city? What forums give citizens a "public voice"? How could you use these forums to "join the conversation"? Integrate information from this textbook and other sources, such as blogs, to support your ideas.

Speaking and Listening: Debate

With other students, form two small groups, the Roundheads and the Cavaliers, and **debate** the following resolution: *A king rules by divine right and cannot be deposed.* Argue for and against the resolution before an audience of your classmates.

 Solve a Research Problem: To participate effectively in the debate, you and your teammates will need to research the following topics:
  • the divine right of kings
  • Parliament's rights to limit the king's power
  • Anglican and Roman Catholic beliefs versus Puritan beliefs
Before you begin, formulate a research plan that includes a variety of print and online sources. Assign a different task to each team member. Before the debate, share information and rehearse arguments. As you present your evidence in the debate, cite the texts you consulted.

 Common Core
State Standards

Reading Informational Text
7. Integrate and evaluate multiple sources of information presented in different media or formats as well as in words in order to address a question or solve a problem.

Speaking and Listening
1. Initiate and participate effectively in a range of collaborative discussions with diverse partners on *grades 11–12 topics, texts, and issues,* building on others' ideas and expressing their own ideas clearly and persuasively.

1.a. Come to discussions prepared, having read and researched material under study; explicitly draw on that preparation by referring to evidence from texts and other research on the topic or issue to stimulate a thoughtful, well-reasoned exchange of ideas.

ESSENTIAL QUESTION VOCABULARY

Use these words in your responses:

Literature and Place
mobility
meditative
urban

Literature and Society
civic
rational
proportion

Writer and Tradition
literate
heritage
prophet

478 A Turbulent Time (1625–1798)

Speaking and Listening

1. Review the assignment with the class, pointing out that students are to stage a debate on the divine right of kings.

2. Analyze the activity and identify its key terms: *resolution; divine right of kings; deposed; resources; Parliament's rights.*

3. Then, have students complete Activity B in the **Follow-Through** worksheet (p. 6 of **Unit 3 Resources**). Remind students to plan arguments and counterarguments.

4. After students have completed the debate, have them discuss which arguments and strategies they found most effective.

The War Against Time

479

Selection Planning Guide

The selections in this section present the great writers of seventeenth-century England. The section opens with four works by John Donne: "Song," "A Valediction: Forbidding Mourning," "Holy Sonnet 10," and "Meditation 17," works that capture the essence of the metaphysical writings that characterized his era and that captivated the twentieth century. Three pieces by Ben Jonson make up the next grouping: "On My First Son," "Still to Be Neat," and "Song: To Celia." Three love poems with the theme of *carpe diem* follow in the next grouping: "To His Coy Mistress" by Andrew Marvell; "To the Virgins, to Make Much of Time" by Robert Herrick; and "Song" by Sir John Suckling.

Humanities

Louise de Keroualle, 1684 by Sir Godfrey Kneller

Kneller was the leading portrait painter in England during the late seventeenth and early eighteenth centuries. Born in Lubeck, Germany, Kneller was a student of Ferdinand Bol and Rembrandt. He came to England in 1674. Kneller was introduced to the king and became court painter to several British monarchs. His work focused almost exclusively on portraits. The subject of this portrait was the mistress of Charles II.

Use these questions for discussion:

1. Describe the dress and manner of the woman in this portrait.
   Answer: She wears a full-length red gown and an elegant pearl necklace. Her posture is somewhat stiff and her hands are posed gracefully.

2. Why do you think Charles II had Kneller paint a portrait of his mistress?
   Possible response: She was very beautiful and was probably a member of his royal court.

Monitoring Progress

Before students read the selections in Part 1, refer to the results for the Vocabulary in Context items on **Benchmark Test 4 (Unit 2 Resources p. 201).** Use this diagnostic portion of the test to guide your choice of selections to teach, as well as the depth of preparation you will provide, based on students' readiness for reading and vocabulary skills.

© Text Complexity: At a Glance

This chart gives a general text complexity rating for the selections in this part of the unit to help guide instruction. For additional text complexity support, see the Test Complexity Rubric at point of use.

Song (Donne)	**More Complex**	Still to Be Neat	**More Accessible**
Valediction Forbidding Mourning	**More Complex**	Song: to Celia	**More Accessible**
Holy Sonnet 10	**More Complex**	To His Coy Mistress	**More Complex**
Meditation 17	**More Accessible**	To the Virgins, to Make Much of Time	**More Complex**
On My First Son (Johnson)	**More Complex**	Song	**More Accessible**

COMMON CORE
Time and Resource Manager

• Works of John Donne
Lesson Pacing Guide

DAY 1   Preteach

- ⓒ Administer the Reading and Vocabulary Warm-ups (*Unit 3 Resources*, pp. 7–10) as necessary.
- ⓒ Introduce the Literary Analysis concept: Metaphysical Poetry.
- • Introduce the Reading Strategy: Analyze Perspective.
- ⓒ Build background with the author and Background features.
- • Develop thematic thinking with Connecting to the Essential Question.
- ⓒ Teach the selection vocabulary.

DAYS 2–3   Preteach/Teach/Assess

- • Distribute copies of the appropriate graphic organizer for the Reading Strategy (*Graphic Organizer Transparencies*, pp. 75–76).
- • Distribute copies of the appropriate graphic organizer for Literary Analysis (*Graphic Organizer Transparencies*, pp. 77–78).
- • Prepare students to read with the Activating Prior Knowledge activities (TE).
- • Informally monitor comprehension while students read.
- • Use the Reading Check questions to confirm comprehension.
- ⓒ Develop students' understanding of metaphysical poetry using the Literary Analysis prompts.
- • Develop students' ability to analyze perspective using the Reading Strategy prompts.
- ⓒ Reinforce vocabulary with the Vocabulary notes.
- • Assess students' comprehension and mastery of the skills by having them answer the Critical Reading, Literary Analysis, and Reading Strategy questions.
- • Have students complete the Vocabulary Lesson.

DAY 4   Extend/Assess

- • Have students complete the Conventions and Style Lesson.
- ⓒ Have students complete the Writing Lesson and write a biographical narrative. (You may assign as homework.)
- • Administer Selection Test A or B (*Unit 3 Resources,* pp. 20–22 or 23–25).

ⓒ Common Core
State Standards

Reading Literature 4. Analyze the impact of specific word choices on meaning and tone, including words with multiple meanings or language that is particularly fresh, engaging, or beautiful.

Writing 3.a. Create a smooth progression of experiences or events.
5. Develop and strengthen writing as needed by planning, revising, editing, rewriting, or trying a new approach, focusing on addressing what is most significant for a specific purpose and audience.

Language 1. Demonstrate command of the conventions of standard English grammar and usage when writing or speaking.
1.b. Resolve issues of complex or contested usage, consulting references as needed.
5. Demonstrate understanding of word relationships in word meanings.

Additional Standards Practice
Common Core Companion, pp. 41–48; 208–218, 226–227; 314–317, 332–335

Daily Block Scheduling
Each day in this Lesson Pacing Guide represents a 40–50 minute period. Teachers using block scheduling may combine days to revise pacing. In addition, teachers may differentiate and support core instruction by integrating components for extended and intensive support as students require. See the Guide to Selected Leveled Resources (facing page).

Guide to Selected Leveled Resources

R T I Tier 1 (students performing on level)

Works of John Donne

Warm Up	Practice, model, and monitor fluency, working with the whole class or in groups.	**Vocabulary and Reading Warm-ups B,** *Unit 3 Resources,* pp. 7–8, 10
Comprehension/Skills	Support and monitor comprehension and skills development, having students complete the activities, graphic organizers, and interactive prompts independently or as a class.	• *Reader's Notebook,* adapted instruction and full selection EL *Reader's Notebook: English Learner's Version,* adapted instruction and adapted selection • **Reading Skill Graphic Organizer B,** *Graphic Organizer Transparencies,* p. 80 • **Literary Analysis Graphic Organizer B,** *Graphic Organizer Transparencies,* p. 82
Monitor Progress	Monitor student progress with the differentiated curriculum-based assessment in the *Unit Resources.*	• **Selection Test B,** *Unit 3 Resources,* pp. 23–25 • **Open-Book Test,** *Unit 3 Resources,* pp. 17–19

R T I Tier 2 (students requiring intervention)

Works of John Donne

Warm Up	Practice, model, and monitor fluency in groups or with individuals.	• **Vocabulary and Reading Warm-ups A,** *Unit 3 Resources,* pp. 7–9 • *Hear It!* Audio CD (adapted text)
Comprehension/Skills	• Support and monitor comprehension and skills development, working in small groups or with individuals. • As students complete the selection in the appropriate version of the *Reader's Notebook,* monitor comprehension frequently with group questions and individual instruction. • Model strategies while guiding students in completing the activities and prompts in the *Reader's Notebook,* as well as the graphic organizers. • Practice skills and monitor mastery with the *Reading Kit* worksheets.	• *Reader's Notebook: Adapted Version,* adapted instruction and adapted selection EL *Reader's Notebook: English Learner's Version,* adapted instruction and adapted selection • **Reading Skill Graphic Organizer A,** *Graphic Organizer Transparencies,* p. 79 • **Literary Analysis Graphic Organizer A,** *Graphic Organizer Transparencies,* p. 81 • *Reading Kit,* Practice worksheets
Monitor Progress	Monitor student progress with the differentiated curriculum-based assessment in the *Unit Resources* and in the *Reading Kit.*	• **Selection Test A,** *Unit 3 Resources,* pp. 20–22 • *Reading Kit,* Assess worksheets

TIER 3 Tier 3 intervention may require consultation with the student's special-education or dyslexia specialist. For additional support, see the Tier 2 activities and resources listed above.

One-on-one teaching   Group work   Whole class instruction   Independent work   A Assessment

For a complete guide to selection support, including support for Advanced students, see the Overview of Resources in the frontmatter.

• Works of John Donne

RESOURCES FOR:
- **L1** Special-Needs Students
- **L2** Below-Level Students (Tier 2)
- **L3** On-Level Students (Tier 1)
- **L4** Advanced Students (Tier 1)
- **EL** English Learners
- **All** All Students

Vocabulary/Fluency/Prior Knowledge

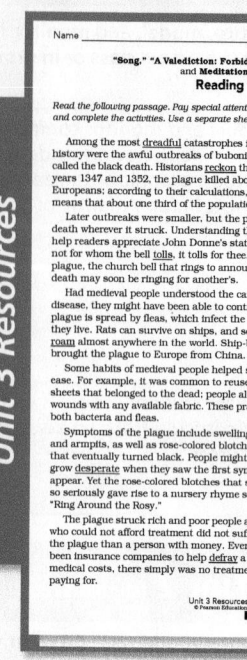

EL L1 L2 Reading Warm-ups A and B,
pp. 9–10

Also available for these selections:

EL L1 L2 Vocabulary Warm-ups A and B,
pp. 7–8

All Vocabulary Builder, p. 13

Reader's Notebooks

Pre- and postreading pages for these selections, as well as Meditation 17, appear in an interactive format in the *Reader's Notebooks*. Each *Notebook* is differentiated for a different group of learners.

The selections in the Adapted and English Learner's versions are abridged.

- **L2 L3** *Reader's Notebook*
- **L1** *Reader's Notebook: Adapted Version*
- **EL** *Reader's Notebook: English Learner's Version*
- **EL** *Reader's Notebook: Spanish Version*

© *Common Core Companion*

Additional instruction and practice for each Common Core State Standard

Selection Support

Skills Development/Extension

Assessment

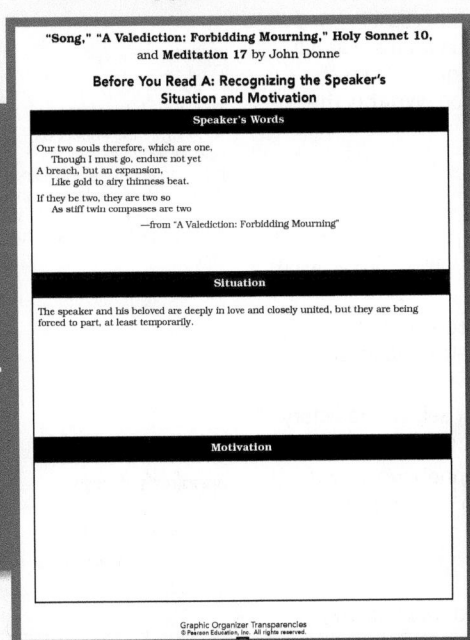

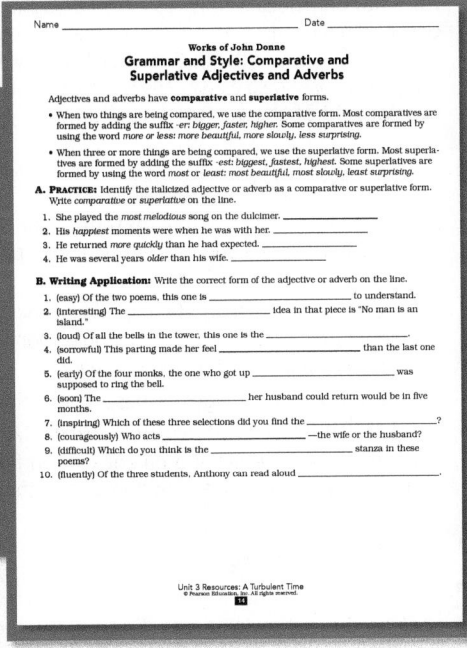

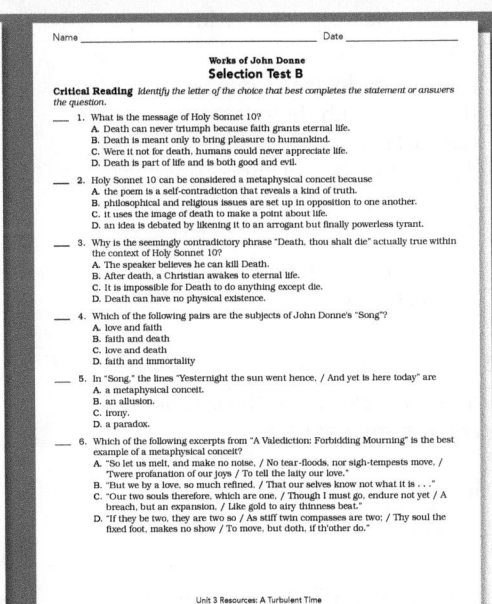

Graphic Organizer Transparencies

Unit 3 Resources

EL L1 L2 Reading: Graphic Organizer A (partially filled in), p. 75

Also available for these selections:

EL L3 Reading: Graphic Organizer B, p. 76

EL L1 L2 Literary Analysis: Graphic Organizer A (partially filled in), p. 77

EL L3 Literary Analysis: Graphic Organizer B, p. 78

EL L3 L4 Grammar and Style, p. 14

Also available for these selections:

All Literary Analysis, p. 11

All Reading, p. 12

EL L3 L4 Support for Writing, p. 15

L4 Enrichment, p. 16

EL L3 L4 Selection Test B, pp. 23–25

Also available for these selections:

L3 L4 Open-Book Test, pp. 17–19

EL L1 L2 Selection Test A, pp. 20–22

PHLit Online!
www.PHLitOnline.com

Online Resources: All print materials are also available online.

- complete narrated selection text
- a thematically related video with writing prompt
- an interactive graphic organizer
- highlighting feature
- access to all student print resources, adapted to individual student needs
- Spanish and English summaries
- adapted selection translations in Spanish

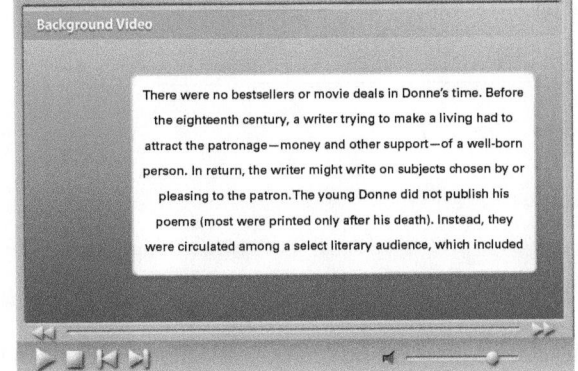

Background Video

Also available:

Get Connected! (thematic video with writing prompt)
All videos are available in Spanish.

Vocabulary Central (tools and activities for studying vocabulary)

Also available:

Writer's Journal (with graphics feature)

❶ 🔍 Connecting to the Essential Question

1. Review the assignment with the class.

2. Prepare students to write by discussing with them famous unusual comparisons, such as "life is like a box of chocolates." **Ask** students to share surprising comparisons they have heard.

3. As students read, have them note unusual comparisons Donne uses.

❷ Literary Analysis

Introduce the skill using the instruction on the student page.

Think Aloud: Model the Skill

Say to students:

When I read these selections from John Donne, I will be looking for three things. First, I will look for philosophical topics or ideas. I will also look for unusual comparisons. For example, I know that one poem used a flea to symbolize a love relationship. The third thing I will look for are paradoxes or seeming contradictions.

❸ Reading Strategy

1. Introduce the strategy, using the instruction on the student page.

2. Give students a copy of **Reading Strategy Graphic Organizer B,** p. 76 in *Graphic Organizer Transparencies,* to fill out as they read.

Think Aloud: Model the Skill

Say to students:

Motivation means "what a person wants." If I know what the speaker in a poem or selection wants and what situation the speaker is in, that knowledge can help me understand what the speaker says.

❹ Vocabulary

1. Pronounce each word, giving its definition, and have students say it aloud.

2. For more guidance, see the *Classroom Strategies and Teaching Routines* card for introducing vocabulary.

Before You Read | *Works of John Donne*

❶ **Connecting to the Essential Question** John Donne was called *witty* not only because his work was amusing, but also because it used clever comparisons. A poetic device that Donne invented was the odd but clever comparison of things that at first seem very different. Noting such comparisons will help as you answer the Essential Question: **What is the relationship of the writer to tradition?**

❷ **Literary Analysis**

Donne and his followers wrote **metaphysical poetry**—poetry characterized by intellectual displays and concern with metaphysical, or philosophical, issues. It uses the following poetic devices:

- **Conceits** are extended comparisons that link objects or ideas not commonly associated. For example, Donne compares two lovers to the two legs of a drawing compass.

- **Paradoxes** are images or descriptions that appear self-contradictory but that reveal a deeper truth: "Death, thou shalt die."

Interpret the conceits and paradoxes you find in Donne's work, and analyze how word choices result in poetry that is fresh and engaging.

❸ **Reading Strategy**

© **Preparing to Read Complex Texts** To understand these poems, **analyze the author's perspective,** or view the author is taking, and **how word choice affects meaning and tone.** Remember that Donne's work is divided into a youthful period, during which he wrote love poems, and a later phase, during which he wrote religious works. Donne's poems are arranged in rough chronological order, so you can see evidence of his change of heart. Also, even though the speaker in each poem is not necessarily Donne himself, the poet is closely identified with the speaker. Use a chart like the one shown to infer the speaker's situation and motivation—these, in turn, will give you clues to the author's perspective.

❹ **Vocabulary**

profanation (präf′ ə nā′ shən) *n.* action showing disrespect for something sacred (p. 484)

laity (lā′ i tē) *n.* those not initiated into a priesthood (p. 484)

trepidation (trep′ ə dā′ shən) *n.* trembling (p. 484)

contention (kən ten′ shən) *n.* dispute; argument (p. 489)

piety (pī′ ə tē) *n.* devotion to sacred duties (p. 489)

covetousness (kuv′ ət əs nis) *n.* greediness (p. 490)

© **Common Core State Standards**

Reading Literature
4. Analyze the impact of specific word choices on meaning and tone, including words with multiple meanings or language that is particularly fresh, engaging, or beautiful.

Speaker's Words

"Sweetest love, I do not go, For weariness of thee, … "

Situation

He has to leave his beloved.

Motivation

He is reassuring her that he is not leaving because he lis tired of her.

PHLit
Online!
www.PHLitOnline.com

Vocabulary Development

Vocabulary Knowledge Rating

Create a **Vocabulary Knowledge Rating Chart** (*Professional Development Guidebook,* p. 33) for the vocabulary words on the student page. Give each student a copy of the chart with the words on it. Read the words aloud, and have students mark their rating of each in the Before Reading column. When students have completed reading and discussing these selections, have them take out their **Vocabulary Knowledge Rating Charts** for the story. Read the words aloud and have students rate their knowledge again in the After Reading column. Clarify any words that are still problematic. Then, have students complete the Vocabulary practice at the end of the selections.

Vocabulary Central, featuring tools and activities for studying vocabulary, is available online at www.PHLitOnline.com.

John Donne (1572?–1631)

Works of John Donne

Donne's life and poetry seem to fall neatly into two contradictory parts. Wild, young Jack Donne wrote clever love poems read by sophisticated aristocrats. In later life, sober Dr. John Donne, Dean of St. Paul's and the most popular preacher in England, published widely read meditations and sermons. Contradiction and conflict were the stuff of Donne's life; they are also at the heart of his poetic style. As Jack or as John, Donne the writer excelled at dramatizing—and wittily resolving—the contradictions of life.

Religious Conflict A distant relative of Sir Thomas More, Donne was raised a Catholic. In the England of Queen Elizabeth I, Catholics faced prejudice and restrictive laws. Although Donne studied at Oxford and Cambridge, he never obtained his degree, probably because of his refusal to compromise his Catholicism by swearing an oath acknowledging the supremacy of the king over the church. Later, he abandoned Catholicism and joined the official Church of England. To this day, scholars debate whether Donne experienced a genuine conversion.

A Secret Marriage After taking part in two naval expeditions against the Spanish, Donne served as private secretary to one of the queen's highest-ranking officials, Sir Thomas Egerton. Bright, clever, and charming, Donne secretly wed Anne More, his employer's niece, in 1601. Again, scholars throw doubt on Donne's motives. Some hold that he married for love; others maintain that he hoped his marriage to the daughter of an influential family would promote his career. If Donne counted on this possibility, though, he was sadly mistaken. Anne's father disapproved of the union, and so Donne's marriage temporarily ruined his chances for social advancement.

For many years, the devoted couple lived plagued by poverty and illness, in the midst of which Donne still managed to write influential poetry. He eked out a living writing religious tracts and serving as temporary secretary to several aristocrats. Donne finally attained a secure position in 1615 when, at the insistence of King James, he entered the clergy.

Success After serving as a royal chaplain, Donne became dean of St. Paul's Cathedral in London in 1621, a post he held until his death. He became one of the most popular preachers of his day. No longer the writer of sly or witty passionate verses, he published widely read sermons and religious meditations. Jack Donne's days were over, and John Donne's fame was spreading.

Works of John Donne **481**

Daily Bellringer

For each class during which you will teach these selections, have students complete one of the five activities for the appropriate week in the *Daily Bellringer Activities* booklet.

Multidraft Reading

To assist struggling readers and to enhance reading for all, assign the text in chunks, as warranted by length, and apply multidraft reading protocols. For each reading, have students set the purpose indicated:

- **First reading**—identifying key ideas and details and answering any Reading Checks.
- **Second reading**—analyzing craft and structure and responding to the side-column prompts.
- **Third reading**—integrating knowledge and ideas, connecting to other texts and the world, and answering the end-of-selection questions.

For more guidance, refer to the *Classroom Strategies and Teaching Routines* card on Multidraft Reading.

❺ Background
More About the Author

Fired and briefly imprisoned for eloping with the seventeen-year-old Anne, Donne reportedly wrote his briefest and, some would say, most accessible poem: "John Donne, Anne Donne, Undone." From this simple beginning, Donne's marriage would inspire some of the most profound love poems in the English language.

The marriage also produced many children. The Donnes had twelve, of whom seven were still living when Anne died in childbirth in 1617.

www.PHLitOnline.com

Teaching From Technology

Preparing to Read
Go to **www.PHLitOnline.com** display the *Get Connected!* slide show for these selections. Have the class brainstorm responses to the slide show writing prompt, entering ideas in the interactive journal. Then, have students complete their written responses as homework.

To build background, display the Background and More About the Author feature.

Using the Interactive Text
Go to **www.PHLitOnline.com** and display the Enriched Online Student Edition. As the class reads the selection or listens to the narration, record answers to side-column prompts using the graphic organizers accessible on the interactive page. Alternatively, have students use the online edition individually, answering the prompts as they read.

❶ About the Selection

This poem expresses what it feels like to be separated from the person one loves. Donne's argument is artfully presented through a conceit that compares a temporary absence to the permanent absence of death.

❷ Activating Prior Knowledge

Ask students to think of people they know who have a dramatic flair. Without giving the person's name, have students write a paragraph, describing the person. Tell students that John Donne was such a person, but that he also had a quiet, meditative aspect to his personality.

❸ Humanities

Fair Is My Love, by Edwin A. Abbey

Although Abbey (1852–1911) was an American painter, muralist, and illustrator, he lived in England.

Use the following question to stimulate discussion:

Do you think this piece of art is a good or poor choice for an illustration of this poem? Why?

Answer: Some students may find it too romantic and not cerebral enough; others may think it is a good choice because it shows such strong emotions.

❹ Critical Viewing

Answer: Students might comment that the man in the painting seems deeply moved by the woman's song, whereas the speaker in the poem hopes his "song" will change how the woman feels.

Fair Is My Love, Edwin A. Abbey. The Harris Museum and Art Gallery, Preston

Song
John Donne

❹ ▲ Critical Viewing
How does the relationship of the man and woman in this painting compare with the relationship described in the poem? **[Compare and Contrast]**

Sweetest love, I do not go,
    For weariness of thee,
Nor in hope the world can show
    A fitter love for me;
5   But since that I
Must die at last, 'tis best
To use¹ myself in jest,
    Thus by feigned² deaths to die.

Yesternight the sun went hence,
10   And yet is here today;
He hath no desire nor sense,
    Nor half so short a way;

1. **use** condition.
2. **feigned** (fānd) *adj.* imagined.

Ⓒ Text Complexity Rubric: Leveled Texts

	Song	Valediction	Holy Sonnet 10	Meditation 17
Qualitative Measures				
Context / Knowledge Demands	Metaphysical verse 1 2 ③ 4 5	Metaphysical verse 1 2 ③ 4 5	Metaphysical sonnet 1 2 ③ 4 5	Religious meditation 1 ② 3 4 5
Structure/Language Conventionality and Clarity	Archaic diction and syntax 1 2 ③ 4 5	Archaic diction and syntax 1 2 ③ 4 5	Archaic diction and syntax 1 2 ③ 4 5	Archaic diction and syntax 1 ② 3 4 5
Levels of Meaning/ Purpose/Concepts	Moderate (love, death) 1 2 3 ④ 5	Moderate (love, parting) 1 2 ③ 4 5	Challenging (immortality) 1 2 3 ④ 5	Moderate (human connection) 1 2 ③ 4 5
Quantitative Measures				
Lexile/Text Length	NP / 213 words	NP / 233 words	NP / 124 words	1140L / 717 words
Overall Complexity	**More complex**	**More complex**	**More complex**	**More accessible**

Then fear not me,
　　But believe that I shall make
15　Speedier journeys, since I take
　　　More wings and spurs than he.

　　O how feeble is man's power,
　　　That if good fortune fall,
　　Cannot add another hour,
20　　　Nor a lost hour recall!
　　　But come bad chance,
　　And we join to it our strength,
　　And we teach it art and length,
　　　Itself o'er us to advance.

25　When thou sigh'st, thou sigh'st not wind,
　　　But sigh'st my soul away;
　　When thou weep'st, unkindly kind,
　　　My life's blood doth decay.
　　　It cannot be
30　That thou lovest me as thou say'st,
　　If in thine my life thou waste,
　　　That art the best of me.

　　Let not thy divining heart
　　　Forethink me any ill,
35　Destiny may take thy part,
　　　And may thy fears fulfill;
　　　But think that we
　　Are but turned aside to sleep.
　　They who one another keep
40　　　Alive, ne'r parted be.

The BRITISH TRADITION

Mind and Feeling

The twentieth-century poet T. S. Eliot celebrated Donne as one of the best—and last—poets to integrate mind and heart: "A thought to Donne was an experience; it modified his sensibility [feeling and perception]." Eliot praised Donne's "direct sensuous apprehension of thought" and his "recreation of thought into feeling."

Eliot claimed that later poets did not "feel their thought as immediately as the odor of a rose" and that "[in] the seventeenth century a dissociation of sensibility set in, from which we have never recovered."

Connect to the Literature

In what ways are lines 27–28 an integration of mind and heart?

Critical Reading

Cite textual evidence to support your responses.

1. **Key Ideas and Details** **(a)** What does the speaker say his reason is for leaving? **(b) Infer:** To what remark of his beloved might he be responding in this poem?

2. **Key Ideas and Details** **(a) Analyze:** How would you outline the speaker's argument? **(b) Speculate:** What might the argument's effect on the beloved be?

3. **Integration of Knowledge and Ideas** Imagine that the speaker's beloved is in tears as he is leaving. Why might the speaker have chosen to present his feelings in the form of witty arguments?

4. **Integration of Knowledge and Ideas** The speaker uses exaggeration to persuade his beloved. Do you think exaggeration is a useful or a valid persuasive tool? Explain.

Song **483**

⑤ The British Tradition
Mind and Feeling

Poet, playwright, and literary critic T. S. Eliot was among the first modern writers to rediscover Donne. His literary analyses of the metaphysical poets played an important role in rescuing their work from centuries of neglect.

Connect to the Literature Have students read "The British Tradition." Present the background information above, then **ask** the Connect to the Literature question. Encourage students to support their answers with evidence from the poem.

Possible response: The thought of leaving his beloved evokes images of weeping and bleeding.

ASSESS

Answers

Remind students to support their answers with evidence from the text.

1. (a) He says that his departure is a preparation for their ultimate separation in death. (b) Students may infer that his beloved had asked if he was leaving because he no longer cared for her.

2. (a) Answers will vary. (b) Students may speculate that the speaker's argument will convince her of his love.

3. **Possible response:** He needs to soothe her fears about separation and to distract her attention with cleverness.

4. **Possible response:** Students may respond that although exaggeration can undermine credibility, it can also make arguments more vivid, persuasive, and powerful.

Text Complexity: Reader and Task Suggestions

Preparing to Read the Texts	Song, Valediction Leveled Tasks	Holy Sonnet 10 Leveled Tasks	Meditation 17 Leveled Tasks
• Using the Background on TE p. 481, explain that Donne wrote the Valediction before a long parting from his wife. • Discuss how a near-death illness might affect one's views of life and death. • Guide students to use Multidraft Reading strategies (TE p. 481).	*Levels of Meanings* If students will have difficulty with the poems' ideas, have them first identify each topic or situation and key conceit used to describe it. Then, have them reread to comprehend the main ideas about parting and love. *Analyzing* If students will not have difficulty with the poems' ideas, have them explain how the conceits help convey key ideas and feelings.	*Levels of Meanings* If students will have difficulty with the poem's ideas, have them focus first on the qualities of death conveyed through personification. Then, have them reread to identify Donne's main point about death. *Analyzing* If students will not have difficulty with the poem's ideas, have them analyze the final paradox and the details Donne provides to support it.	*Levels of Meaning* If students will have difficulty with the meaning, have them first identify the reason the bell tolls. Next, have them explain the conceit comparing a person to part of a continent. *Evaluating* If students will not have difficulty with the meaning, have them evaluate the effectiveness of Donne's argument, considering its logic, supporting details, and use of figurative language.

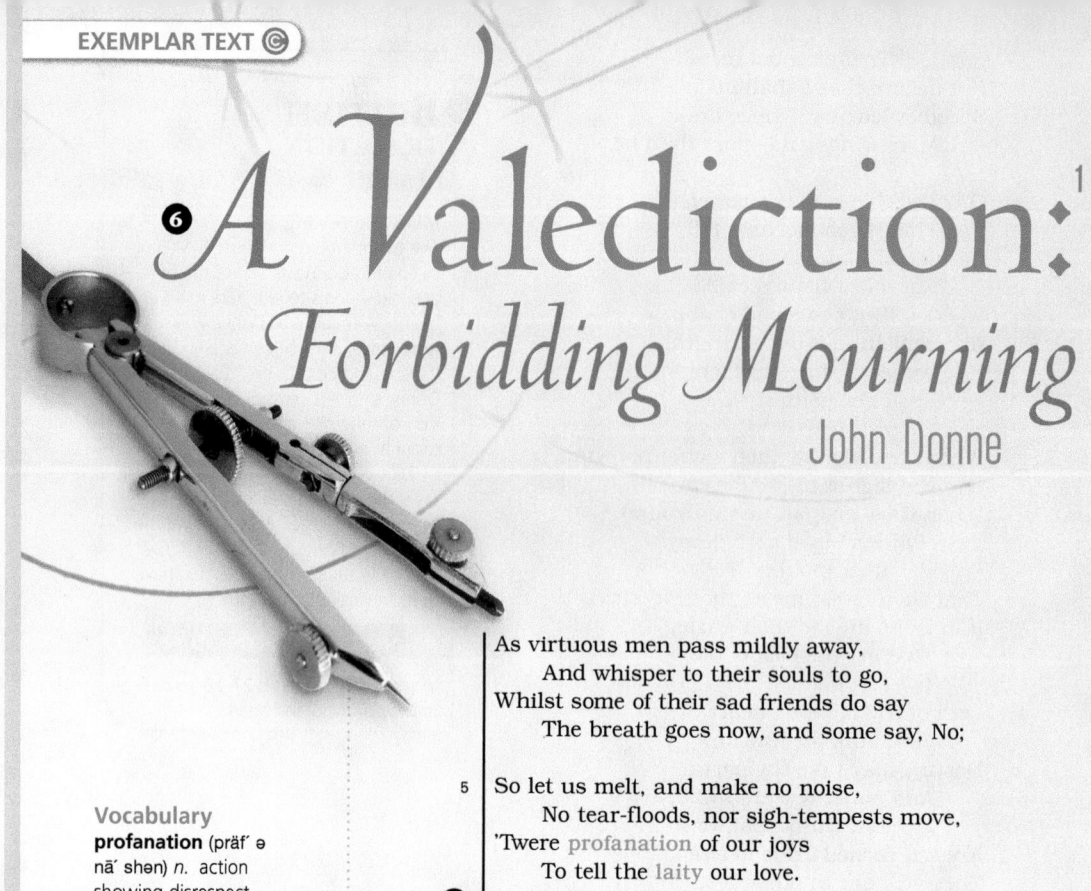

A Valediction:[1]
Forbidding Mourning
John Donne

❻ About the Selection

This is considered to be one of Donne's best love poems. Its numerous references to the science of the day, its intellectual tone, its paradoxes, and its conceit at the end—the comparison involving the compass—make it a showcase for the elements that define metaphysical poetry.

❼ Reading Strategy:

Analyzing Perspective

1. Have volunteers read aloud the first five stanzas (lines 1–20).

2. Discuss with students the meaning and interrelationships of these stanzas. (The first describes tranquil deaths; the second suggests the lovers also behave calmly; the third and fourth suggest that love is inferior when partners cannot stand to be parted for a time; the fifth suggests the speaker's love is superior because knowing each other's minds means the partners do not need to be together in person.)

3. Based on the discussion, have students describe the speaker's situation and motivation throughout the first five stanzas, using a graphic organizer like the one on page 480. (See *Graphic Organizer Transparencies*, p. 76.) **Possible response:** Situation: He is parting from his beloved. Motivation: He wants them to part quietly, with no tears.

4. **Ask** students the Reading Strategy question: Why does the speaker turn parting into a proof of the strength of his love? **Possible response:** He suggests that a dignified parting will demonstrate that their ideal love transcends the limitations of a merely sensual attraction which wanes in the absence of the beloved.

Vocabulary

profanation (präf′ ə nā′ shən) *n.* action showing disrespect for something sacred

laity (lā′ i tē) *n.* those not initiated into a priesthood

trepidation (trep′ ə dā′ shən) *n.* trembling

❼ Reading Strategy
Analyzing Perspective
Why does the speaker turn parting into a proof of the strength of his love?

As virtuous men pass mildly away,
    And whisper to their souls to go,
Whilst some of their sad friends do say
    The breath goes now, and some say, No;

5 So let us melt, and make no noise,
    No tear-floods, nor sigh-tempests move,
'Twere profanation of our joys
    To tell the laity our love.

  Moving of th'earth brings harms and fears,
10   Men reckon what it did and meant;
But trepidation of the spheres,[2]
    Though greater far, is innocent.

  Dull sublunary[3] lovers' love
    (Whose soul is sense) cannot admit
15 Absence, because it doth remove
    Those things which elemented it.[4]

  But we by a love, so much refined,
    That our selves know not what it is,

---

1. **valediction** farewell speech.
2. **trepidation of the spheres** movements of the stars and planets that are inconsistent with a perfect circular orbit.
3. **sublunary** (sub′ loo nər′ ē) referring to the region below the moon, considered in early astronomy to be the domain of changeable and perishable things.
4. **Those things . . . elemented it** the basic materials or parts of their love.

484 A Turbulent Time (1625–1798)

Enrichment: Analyzing a Literary Figure

"A Valediction"

According to Donne biographer Sir Izaak Walton, "A Valediction: Forbidding Mourning" has a specific and tragic biographical context. Anne Donne was in the late stages of a problematic pregnancy when Donne was assigned to a diplomatic mission in France. Filled with foreboding, Anne urged Donne not to go. Donne responded by writing "A Valediction" to ease the pain of their parting.

Shortly after arriving in Paris, Donne had a vision of Anne walking across his room carrying a dead child in her arms. He later learned that on that very day, after an agonizing labor, Anne "had been delivered of a dead child."

Activity: Research on John Donne Have pairs or groups of students conduct research on John Donne's life and work. Have students record information in the **Enrichment: Analyzing a Literary Figure** worksheet, *Professional Development Guidebook*, page 235. Invite them to share and discuss their findings.

7 ▲ Inter-assurèd of the mind,[5]
20   Care less, eyes, lips, and hands to miss.

Our two souls therefore, which are one,
     Though I must go, endure not yet
A breach, but an expansion,
     Like gold to airy thinness beat.

25 If they be two, they are two so
     As stiff twin compasses[6] are two;
Thy soul the fixed foot, makes no show
     To move, but doth, if th'other do.

8
30 And though it in the center sit,
     Yet when the other far doth roam,
It leans, and hearkens after it,
     And grows erect, as that comes home.

Such wilt thou be to me, who must
     Like th'other foot, obliquely[7] run;
35 Thy firmness makes my circle just,[8]
     And makes me end where I begun.

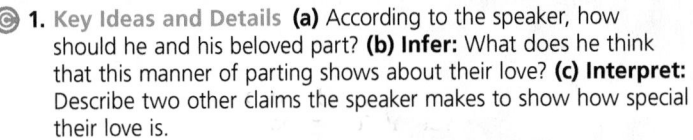

If they be two,
they are two so
As stiff twin
compasses are two...

---

5. **Inter-assurèd of the mind** mutually confident of each other's thoughts.
6. **twin compasses** the two legs of a drawing compass.
7. **obliquely** at an angle; not straight.
8. **just** true; perfect.

Critical Reading

Ⓒ **1. Key Ideas and Details (a)** According to the speaker, how should he and his beloved part? **(b) Infer:** What does he think that this manner of parting shows about their love? **(c) Interpret:** Describe two other claims the speaker makes to show how special their love is.

Ⓒ **2. Key Ideas and Details** The poem compares the lovers to the legs of a compass—she is fixed in place while he moves. What does the comparison indicate about their relationship?

Ⓒ **3. Integration of Knowledge and Ideas** The speaker links love with the order and stability of the world. Support this insight with details from the poem.

Ⓒ **4. Integration of Knowledge and Ideas** Do you, like the speaker, see love as a union of two souls, or do you think that lovers should be independent? Explain.

Cite textual evidence to support your responses.

A Valediction: Forbidding Mourning **485**

Differentiated Instruction   for Universal Access

Support for Special-Needs Students and Less Proficient Readers
Use a large compass (or simulate one with two long rods or pointers) to demonstrate the motions described in Donne's poem. As the class reads lines 25–32 aloud, show how the "fixed foot" leans and rises in response to the "roaming" of the other foot.

Enrichment for Gifted/Talented Students
After discussing Donne's compass conceit, challenge students to develop their own conceits, using other instruments or objects to express a truth about human relationships. They can develop their conceits into poems or provide detailed prose explanations of the conceits.

8 ❓ **Engaging the Essential Question**

1. Review with students the biographical information about John Donne on page 481. **Ask:** Did John Donne seem more to accept or reject traditions in his life? **Answer:** He seemed ready to reject tradition, perhaps in hopes of gain.

2. **Ask:** What is the unusual comparison in this poem? Why is it unexpected? **Answers:** The speaker compares the union of his soul and his beloved's to a compass. The comparison of a mechanical device to human love seems unlikely.

3. **Ask:** Did Donne accept or reject tradition when he chose a compass for the conceit in this poem? **Answer:** He rejected tradition.

4. Remind students to look for other unusual comparisons as they read these selections.

ASSESS

Answers

Before students respond, you may wish to have them write a brief objective summary of the selection. As they answer the questions below, remind them to support their answers with evidence from the text.

1. **(a)** He suggests they part "mildly," "melting" apart and making "no noise." **(b)** It shows unity and their confidence in their love. **(c) Possible responses:** Their love is "refined" and needs no physical reassurance. Their souls will not be separated but will expand like beaten gold to cover the distance between them.

2. **Possible response:** The comparison shows that he relies on the beloved's stable center; his life revolves around her.

3. **Possible response:** The image asserts an unbreakable bond—the lovers are a single entity like the feet of a compass.

4. **Possible responses:** Some students may reply that they agree with this statement, while others may feel that lovers should be independent. Students should offer evidence to support either position.

485

This is one of the best-known poems about death and how it was viewed by Donne and his contemporaries. Donne addresses death directly, as if death were a personal adversary whom the speaker no longer fears. Donne explains why he does not fear death, and his argument is relatively easy to follow.

❿ **Humanities**

***Sir Thomas Aston at the Deathbed of His Wife,* by John Souch**

John Souch was a British portrait painter who did most of his work between 1617 and 1636. This, one of his few surviving portraits, was probably commissioned by Thomas Aston, high sheriff of Cheshire, as a memorial to his first wife, Magdalene.

Use these questions to stimulate discussion:

1. In what ways does this painting reflect the ideas of the sonnet?
   Possible response: It shows that death is not final; memory can overcome it; it reflects the idea that death lives with sickness.

2. Why is the wife, Magdalene, shown twice, do you think?
   Possible response: It shows her in her life as well as in her death. Perhaps it indicates the continuum between life and death or indicates that she has wakened to eternal life, such as Donne mentions in Holy Sonnet 10.

3. What can you infer about the man from this picture?
   Possible responses: Students may respond that his clothes show he is wealthy and in mourning. His hand on the skull may indicate that he has accepted death.

⓫ **Critical Viewing**

Possible response: Both the painting and the poem show a form of everlasting life and a refusal to shrink from death.

❾ HOLY SONNET 10
John Donne

Sir Thomas Aston at the Deathbed of His Wife, John Souch, Manchester City Art Galleries

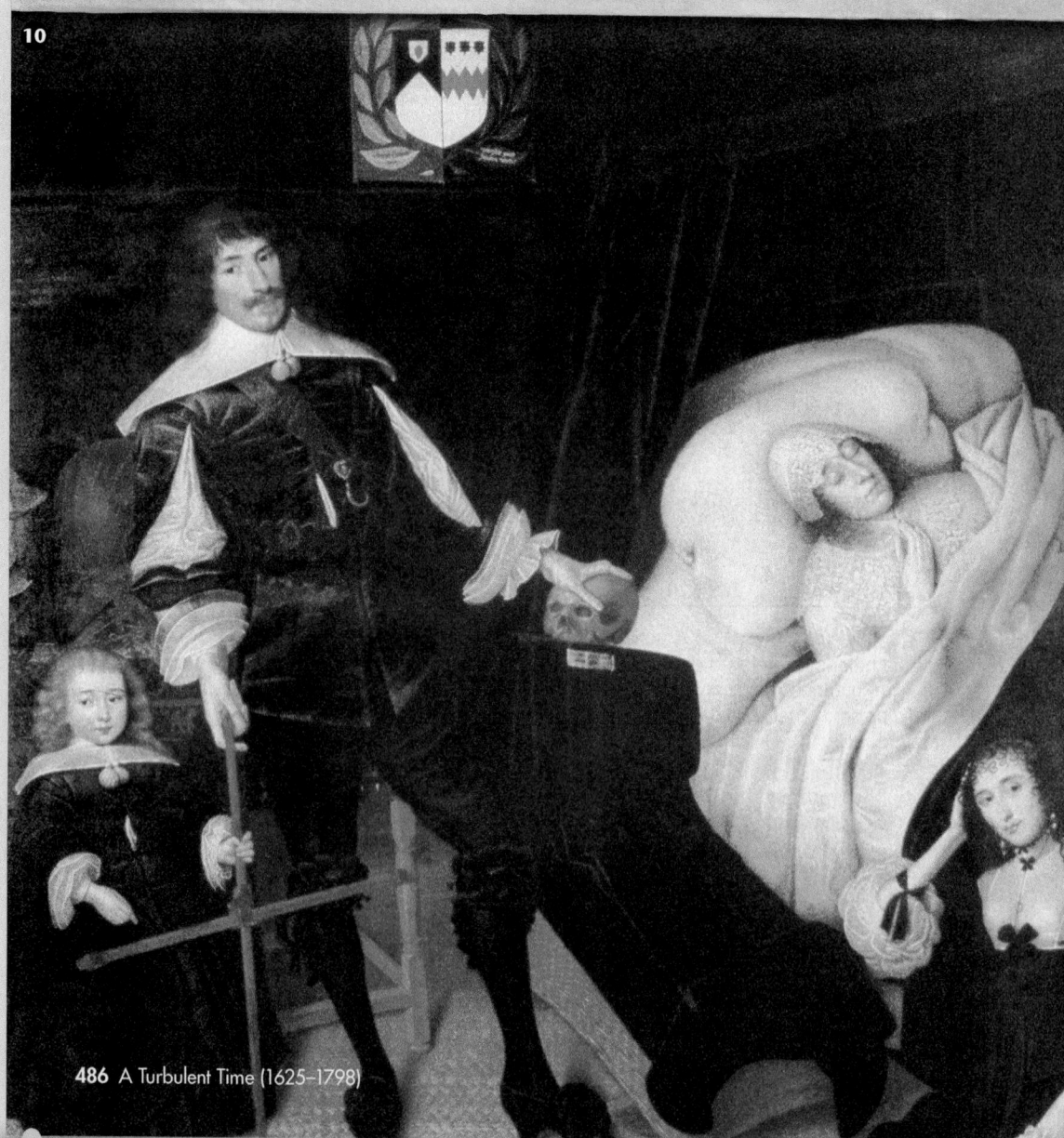

486 A Turbulent Time (1625–1798)

Differentiated Instruction for Universal Access

Culturally Responsive Instruction

Culture Connection Some students may find this painting and poem morbid. Before studying them, discuss cultural attitudes toward death. Point out that, although many modern-day Americans would rather deny death, cultures in other times and places show more acceptance.

The work on these pages shows a very typical seventeenth-century attitude of candid recognition of the reality of death. People were aware (as T. S. Eliot wrote) of the "skull beneath the skin"; they did not flinch from or evade mortality. Near the end of his life, Donne was not afraid to pose in his own death shroud. A statue of the result stands in St. Paul's Cathedral in London, an enduring monument to his era's attitude toward death.

Lead a discussion sharing your own and students' knowledge of current cultural beliefs and practices for dealing with death.

BACKGROUND WRITERS IN DONNE'S DAY OFTEN DEPENDED ON THE SUPPORT OF PATRONS, WEALTHY SUPPORTERS OF THE ARTS. THE YOUNG DONNE DID NOT PUBLISH HIS POEMS (MOST WERE PRINTED ONLY AFTER HIS DEATH). INSTEAD, THEY WERE CIRCULATED AMONG A SELECT LITERARY AUDIENCE THAT INCLUDED PATRONS SUCH AS THE COUNTESS OF BEDFORD. AFTER DONNE WAS DISMISSED FROM HIS POSITION WITH SIR THOMAS EGERTON, HE AND HIS FAMILY DEPENDED IN PART ON PATRONS FOR FINANCIAL SUPPORT. WHEN HE BECAME A CLERGYMAN, DONNE NO LONGER NEEDED TO CAPTURE THE INTEREST OF PATRONS. HE CONTINUED, THOUGH, TO WRITE IMPASSIONED, WITTY VERSE SUCH AS THE HOLY SONNETS.

Death be not proud, though some have called thee
Mighty and dreadful, for thou art not so;
For those whom thou think'st thou dost overthrow,
Die not, poor death, nor yet canst thou kill me.
5 From rest and sleep, which but thy pictures[1] be,
Much pleasure; then from thee much more must flow,
And soonest our best men with thee do go,
Rest of their bones, and soul's delivery.[2]
Thou art slave to fate, chance, kings, and desperate men,
10 And dost with poison, war, and sickness dwell,
And poppy,[3] or charms can make us sleep as well
And better than thy stroke; why swell'st[4] thou then?
One short sleep past, we wake eternally,
⑫ | And death shall be no more; Death, thou shalt die.

1. **pictures** images.
2. **And . . . delivery** Our best men go with you to rest their bones and find freedom for their souls.
3. **poppy** opium.
4. **swell'st** swell with pride.

Critical Reading

⑪ ◄ Critical Viewing The painting shows Lady Aston both when she is alive and when she is dead. Compare the relationship between death and life implied by the painting with that developed in Holy Sonnet 10. **[Compare and Contrast]**

Literary Analysis
Metaphysical Poetry
What paradox does the speaker use to end his argument with Death?

Cite textual evidence to support your responses.

© 1. Key Ideas and Details (a) What "pictures" of death does the speaker mention? **(b) Infer:** What positive lesson about death does the speaker draw from this resemblance?

© 2. Key Ideas and Details (a) Interpret: In what sense is death a slave (line 9)? **(b) Connect:** How does this point justify the opening line?

© 3. Key Ideas and Details (a) Interpret: What does the statement "Death, thou shalt die" mean? **(b) Draw Conclusions:** Why might the speaker react to death by challenging its "strength" and "pride"?

© 4. Integration of Knowledge and Ideas Does the speaker sound like a man talking himself out of fear or like one who has triumphed over fear? Explain.

Holy Sonnet 10 **487**

Differentiated Instruction   for Universal Access

EL   **Pronunciation for English Learners**

1. Some students may have difficulty pronouncing the *-th* consonant blend at the end of *death,* which appears repeatedly in Sonnet 10. They may pronounce only the first consonant, *t* (making the word sound like *debt*), or add extra vowel sounds or syllables.

2. Model and have students practice placing the tongue against the upper front teeth to pronounce *-th.* Provide additional practice with words that end with this blend, such as *with, myth, faith, bath, mouth, teeth,* and *cloth.*

3. Pair English learners with fluent students to practice pronouncing and using the words in sentences. Have fluent English speakers correct English learners as needed.

4. Finally, play a game in which students compete to create and pronounce sentences with the most words ending in *-th.* For example: *I have traveled the length and width of the country from north to south.*

⑫ Literary Analysis:
Metaphysical Poetry

1. Have a volunteer read aloud line 14, the final line of the sonnet.

2. Remind students that paradoxes are images or descriptions that appear to contradict themselves but reveal a truth. Have them look for a seeming contradiction in this line.

3. **Ask** students the Literary Analysis question: What paradox does the speaker use to end his argument with Death?
Answer: He introduces the paradoxical notion that Death itself—in the personified form in which it figures throughout the poem—will die.

ASSESS

Answers

Before students respond, you may wish to have them write a brief objective summary of the selection. As they answer the questions below, remind them to support their answers with evidence from the text.

1. **(a)** The speaker mentions rest and sleep as images of death. **(b) Possible response:** There is much pleasure from rest and sleep, and the speaker believes there must also be pleasure from death. He reflects that the best people rest their bones in death, and in so doing find freedom for their souls.

2. **Possible responses: (a)** The speaker makes the case that death is a slave in the sense that it "obeys," or happens because of, fate, chance, kings, and desperate men. **(b)** If death is a slave, there is no reason to be proud.

3. **Possible responses: (a)** The speaker's belief in eternal life removes death's power or meaning. **(b)** By asserting that death will "die," the speaker makes death seem less powerful and frightening.

4. **Possible response:** The poet sounds like a man who has triumphed over fear by reasoning that death is a preamble to immortality.

487

⓭ ⓮ Meditation 17

John Donne

Nunc lento sonitu dicunt, Morieris.
(NOW, THIS BELL TOLLING SOFTLY FOR ANOTHER, SAYS TO ME, THOU MUST DIE.)

Perchance he for whom this bell tolls may be so ill as that he knows not it tolls for him; and perchance I may think myself so much better than I am as that they who are about me and see my state may have caused it to toll for me, and I know not that. The church is catholic,[1] universal, so are all her actions; all that she does belongs to all. When she baptizes a child, that action concerns me; for that child is thereby connected to that head which is my head too, and ingrafted into that body[2] whereof I am a member. And when she buries a man, that action concerns me: all mankind is of one author and is one volume; when one man dies, one chapter is not torn out of the

1. **catholic** applying to humanity generally.
2. **head . . . body** In the Bible, St. Paul calls Jesus the head (spiritual leader) of all men (1 Corinthians 11:3) and a body in which the faithful are unified (1 Corinthians 12:12).

488 A Turbulent Time (1625–1798)

Think Aloud

book, but translated into a better language; and every chapter must be so translated. God employs several translators; some pieces are translated by age, some by sickness, some by war, some by justice; but God's hand is in every translation, and his hand shall bind up all our scattered leaves again for that library where every book shall lie open to one another. As therefore the bell that rings to a sermon calls not upon the preacher only, but upon the congregation to come, so this bell calls us all; but how much more me, who am brought so near the door by this sickness. There was a contention as far as a suit[3] (in which both piety and dignity, religion and estimation,[4] were mingled) which of the religious orders should ring to prayers first in the morning; and it was determined that they should ring first that rose earliest. If we understand aright the dignity of this bell that tolls for our evening prayer, we would be glad to make it ours by rising early, in that application, that it might be ours as well as his whose indeed it is. The bell doth toll for him that thinks it doth; and though it intermit again, yet from that minute that that occasion wrought upon him, he is united to God. Who casts not up his eye to the sun when it rises? but who takes off his eye from a comet when that breaks out? Who bends not his ear to any bell which upon any occasion rings? but who can remove it from that bell which is passing a piece of himself out of this world? No man is an island, entire of itself; every man is a piece of the continent, a part of the main.[5] If a clod be washed away by the sea, Europe is the less, as well as if a promontory were, as well as if a manor of thy friend's or of thine own were. Any man's death diminishes me because I am involved in mankind, and therefore never send to know for whom the bell

16

---

3. **suit** lawsuit.
4. **estimation** self-esteem.
5. **main** mainland.

Vocabulary
contention (kən ten´ shən) *n.* dispute; argument

piety (pī´ ə tē) *n.* devotion to sacred duties

Literary Analysis
Metaphysical Poetry In the sentence beginning, "No man is an island," what extended metaphor does Donne use to show one person's relationship to all humankind?

17 ☑ Reading Check

According to Donne, for whom does the bell toll?

...Therefore never send to know for whom the bell tolls; it tolls for thee.

Meditation 17 489

---

16 Literary Analysis:
Metaphysical Poetry

1. **Read** aloud or have a volunteer read the sentence in lines 22–23 that begins "No man is an island."

2. **Remind** students that metaphors are comparisons that do not use the words *like* or *as*. Review information on metaphysical conceits, extended comparisons that link objects or ideas not commonly associated.

3. **Ask** students the Literary Analysis question: What extended metaphor does Donne use here to show a single individual's relationship to all mankind?
   Answer: He asserts that man is not set apart from mankind as an island is from the mainland, but is rather a part of a continent, and thereby joined together with the rest of mankind.

▶ **Monitor Progress** To check understanding of the concept, **ask** students to identify the conceit in the lines that span pages 488–489, "all mankind is of one author and is one volume; when one man dies, one chapter is not torn out of the book, but translated into a better language."
   Answer: The conceit compares individual human beings with chapters in a book.

▶ **Reteach** If students have difficulty identifying the conceit, guide them to identify key nouns in the lines: *mankind, author, volume, man, chapter, book.* Help them to group these nouns into two categories to identify the two things Donne compares: mankind and a book.

17 Reading Check

Answer: It tolls for every individual member of the human race; "It tolls for thee."

Differentiated Instruction for Universal Access

Strategy for Advanced Readers
Have students compare Donne's handling of the topic of death in Meditation 17 and in Holy Sonnet 10. Then, have them write a compare-and-contrast essay including citations and specific analyses of Donne's use of conceits and paradoxes in his approach to the topic.

Enrichment for Gifted/Talented Students
Have students prepare a soundtrack to accompany a reading of Meditation 17. Suggest that they choose background music for the reading, as well as appropriate sound effects, including the obligatory tolling of a bell. Have them create audio recordings of the resulting oral presentation or give a live presentation to the class.

489

Before students respond, you may wish to have them write a brief objective summary of the selection. As they answer the questions below, remind them to support their answers with evidence from the text.

1. (a) The bell tolls for a person's death. (b) People share a common humanity; the death of one person affects another.

2. **Possible responses:** (a) Donne says, "Any man's death diminishes me" because he is "involved in mankind." (b) Individuals are connected—no one is isolated or so alone that he or she does not need other human beings, or is not affected by them. (c) The continent comparison emphasizes that humanity is a single entity, and, as a continent would be smaller if part of it washed away. All of humankind is also diminished by the loss of one part.

3. **Possible responses:** (a) The "treasure of affliction" turns into "current money" when people wisely use hardships to grow and transcend them, moving closer to heaven by doing so. (b) Donne finds affliction valuable because people are "matured and ripened by it, and made fit for God" by it. (c) The "tolling bell" tells us of others' afflictions and warns us to be aware of our own vulnerabilities.

4. **Possible response:** Donne may be implying that attachment to worldly things is a distraction from spiritual priorities.

5. **Possible responses:**
Students may respond "no man is an island" could be the <u>theme</u> of our times; the phrase applies even more in today's world than it did in Donne's time. The fates of <u>individuals</u> are more connected to one another than ever, as the world has gotten smaller through developments in communication, transportation, and political alliances.

Vocabulary
covetousness (kuv´ ət əs nis) *n.* greediness

tolls; it tolls for thee. Neither can we call this a begging of misery or a borrowing of misery, as though we were not miserable enough of ourselves but must fetch in more from the next house, in taking upon us the misery of our neighbors. Truly it were an excusable covetousness if we did; for affliction is a treasure, and scarce any man hath enough of it. No man hath affliction enough that is not matured and ripened by it, and made fit for God by that affliction. If a man carry treasure in bullion, or in a wedge of gold, and have none coined into current money,[6] his treasure will not defray him as he travels. Tribulation is treasure in the nature of it, but it is not current money in the use of it, except we get nearer and nearer our home, heaven, by it. Another man may be sick too, and sick to death, and this affliction may lie in his bowels as gold in a mine and be of no use to him; but this bell that tells me of his affliction digs out and applies that gold to me, if by this consideration of another's danger, I take mine own into contemplation and so secure myself by making my recourse to my God, who is our only security.

---

6. **current money** currency; wealth in spendable form.

Critical Reading

Cite textual evidence to support your responses.

1. **Key Ideas and Details (a)** What event does the tolling bell announce? **(b) Analyze:** Why does Donne say the tolling bell applies to him as well as to others?

2. **Key Ideas and Details (a)** What reason does Donne give for saying, "Any man's death diminishes me"? **(b) Interpret:** What does Donne mean by "No man is an island, entire of itself; every man is a piece of the continent"? **(c) Analyze:** How does the comparison of humanity to a continent support the idea that one death affects all people?

3. **Key Ideas and Details (a) Analyze:** In Donne's metaphor, when does the "treasure" of affliction turn into "current [spendable] money"? **(b) Interpret:** Why does Donne find affliction valuable? **(c) Connect:** In what sense does the tolling bell "apply" one person's affliction to another?

4. **Integration of Knowledge and Ideas** Donne says that, once one takes the bell as tolling for oneself, one is "united to God." In urging people to think about their own deaths, what might he be implying about people's attachment to worldly things such as money, success, and popularity?

5. **Integration of Knowledge and Ideas** Does the statement "No man is an island" still apply today? Why or why not? In your response, use at least two of these Essential Question words: *theme, unity, individual.* [*Connecting to the Essential Question: What is the relationship of the writer to tradition?*]

490 A Turbulent Time (1625–1798)

Concept Connector

Reading Strategy Graphic Organizer
Ask students to review the graphic organizers in which they analyzed the speaker's situation and motivation to help them understand key lines of the selections. Then, have students share their organizers and compare their analyses.

Activating Prior Knowledge
Have students return to their responses to the Activating Prior Knowledge activity. Ask them to explain whether their thoughts have changed and, if so, how.

Writing About the Essential Question
Have students compare their responses to the prompt completed before reading the sonnets with their thoughts afterward. Have them work individually or in groups, writing or discussing their thoughts, to formulate their new responses. Then, lead a class discussion, probing for what students have learned that confirms or invalidates their initial thoughts. Encourage students to cite specific textual details to support their responses.

Works of John Donne

Literary Analysis

1. Craft and Structure Identify and interpret a **conceit** that the speaker in "Song" uses to reassure his beloved. Explain what things are being compared.

2. Craft and Structure (a) What **paradox** does the speaker use in the fourth stanza of "Song"? **(b)** Explain the truth underlying this contradiction.

3. Craft and Structure (a) Identify a conceit in Holy Sonnet 10. **(b)** Explain the speaker's point in making the comparison.

4. Integration of Knowledge and Ideas In Meditation 17, Donne uses a conceit comparing suffering and treasure. **(a)** Use a chart like the one shown to analyze the forms of treasure he discusses. **(b)** Explain how each relates to suffering.

> **Main Idea: There are two forms of suffering, just as there are two forms of treasure.**
>
> | First Form of Treasure: _____ | Second Form of Treasure: _____ | Relationship Between Forms of Treasure: _____ |
> | --- | --- | --- |

5. Integration of Knowledge and Ideas (a) What important differences distinguish "Song" and "Valediction" from Holy Sonnet 10? **(b)** Identify an element of metaphysical poetry that all three share, giving examples from each.

6. Craft and Structure In the poems, the speaker uses conceits and paradoxes to move from uncertainty (his own or his listener's) to certainty. In Meditation 17, he uses these devices to inspire uncertainty in his listener. Explain, using examples from each work.

Reading Strategy

7. Analyze how the author's perspective affects meaning by tracing a shift of attitude and perspective in Donne's work. **(a)** How does the perspective in "Song" and "A Valediction: Forbidding Mourning" differ from that in Holy Sonnet 10? **(b)** In what ways does this change affect the meaning, or essential message, Donne communicates in each poem?

8. (a) In each of Donne's works, who is the speaker and what is the speaker's situation? **(b)** What is each speaker's motivation? **(c)** How do the speaker's situation and motivation provide a clue to Donne's perspective in each poem?

9. Choose a line from each work, and describe how knowledge of the speaker's situation and motivation helps you understand the text.

10. During World War II, the British used the phrase "No man is an island" to justify joining the fight against Nazi Germany. Do you think this use of Donne's words accurately reflected his perspective and meaning? Explain.

Common Core State Standards

Writing
3.a. Create a smooth progression of experiences or events. *(p. 492)*
5. Develop and strengthen writing as needed by planning, revising, editing, rewriting, or trying a new approach, focusing on addressing what is most significant for a specific purpose and audience. *(p. 492)*

Language
1. Demonstrate command of the conventions of standard English grammar and usage when writing or speaking. *(p. 493)*
1.b. Resolve issues of complex or contested usage, consulting references as needed. *(p. 493)*
5. Demonstrate understanding of word relationships in word meanings. *(p. 492)*

Answers

1. The speaker compares himself to the sun, which departs and returns every day, with far less motivation than he, as her lover, has to return to her.

2. (a) The paradox is "unkindly kind." (b) Grief can undermine the confidence of the beloved.

3. (a) The conceit is death as a proud person. (b) His intent is to make death seem less powerful.

4. (a) First Form: affliction; Second Form: current money; (b) Relationship: Affliction becomes "current money" when used to make oneself more fit for God.

5. (a) In "Song" and "Valediction," the speaker addresses his true love. In Holy Sonnet 10, the speaker addresses death. (b) All three works have paradoxes. In "Song" the paradox is "unkindly kind"; in "Valediction" it is "Two souls are one"; and in Holy Sonnet 10, it is "Death, thou shalt die."

6. **Sample response:** "Valediction": The speaker answers his beloved's uncertainties with the conceit of the compass; he argues that their souls are as firmly bound together as the two feet of a compass and that even as he travels, his life revolves around her; if she accepts the conceit, she will be certain that their love cannot be harmed. Holy Sonnet 10: The speaker confronts human uncertainty in the face of death with the paradox that death will die; this paradoxical belief moves those who accept it to certainty about their triumph over death. Meditation 17: The conceit of the tolling bell is intended to shake loose readers' certainties about life.

7. (a) The perspective in "Song" and "Valediction" is that of a man speaking to his beloved, whereas the perspective of Holy Sonnet 10 is that of a man examining his faith. (b) The essential message of the first two poems comforts the speaker's beloved about their parting, whereas in the final poem it offers comfort about death.

8. **Sample response for "Song":** Speaker: devout lover; Situation: impending separation;

Motivation: to reassure beloved. These provide a clue to the perspective by showing the speaker's feelings and thoughts.

9. **Sample responses for "Valediction":** Motive: to reassure his beloved; Situation: The speaker is departing; lines 21 to 24: He says their separation will not part their souls but will expand them, reassuring her of his love. **Sample responses for Holy Sonnet 10:** Motive: to reassure himself; Situation: He confronts fears of death; line 9: He says that death is a "slave to fate"; by insulting death, he keeps up his own courage.

10. Students may say that the words do reflect his perspective and meaning, and that Donne would agree that our common fate requires us to help others.

Answers

Vocabulary Acquisition and Use

1. Introduce the skill using the instruction on the student page.
2. Have students complete the Word Analysis activity and the vocabulary practice.

Word Analysis

Answers will vary.

Vocabulary

1. profanation
2. laity
3. trepidation
4. contention
5. piety
6. covetousness

Writing

1. To guide students in writing their narrative text, give them the **Support for Writing** page (*Unit 3 Resources,* p. 15).
2. Have students follow the steps of prewriting, drafting, and revising to complete their biographical narratives.
3. Use the **Rubrics for Biography,** *Professional Development Guidebook,* pages 278–279, to evaluate students' work.

Vocabulary Acquisition and Use

Word Analysis: Latin Prefix con-

The word *contention* begins with the Latin prefix *con-*, which means "together" or "with." *Contention* comes from a Latin word meaning "to strive or struggle with."

Use at least four of the *con-* words listed here to write a paragraph about the works by Donne you have read. If any of the words are unfamiliar, use a dictionary to clarify their meanings.

concentrate	conflict
confront	connect
consequence	console
construct	contact

Then, choose two of the words you used and write a sentence identifying how the prefix *con-* helps create their meaning.

Vocabulary: Analogies

Analogies show the relationships between pairs of words. Complete each analogy using a word from the vocabulary list on page 480. In each, your choice should create a word pair that matches the relationship between the first two words given. Then, explain your answers.

1. *Crime* is to *law* as _____ is to *faith.*
2. The _____ is to the *clergy* as *civilians* are to *military personnel.*
3. *Nervousness* is to _____ as *happiness* is to *smiling.*
4. *Jealousy* is to *envy* as _____ is to *quarrel.*
5. _____ is to *religion* as *patriotism* is to *the nation.*
6. *Hunger* is to *food* as _____ is to *money.*

Writing

Narrative Text Imagine that a publisher has asked you to prepare a *biographical narrative* about John Donne. The essay will introduce a collection of Donne's work by highlighting the most important events of his life. Your assignment is to write a **plan** for your narrative.

Prewriting Review the biographical and background information on Donne in the text. Select the key events in his life, both personal and professional. You can also consult literary encyclopedias in print or online to gather more information.

Drafting Following your prewriting notes, write an outline for your narrative with the correct *sequence of events* that helps your reader to smoothly follow the progress of Donne's life.

Revising Read through your outline and revise points to make sure you can use them to communicate clearly the *significance of key events* to your audience.

> **Model: Revising to Clarify Significance**
> **Weak explanation:** 1615—Donne *became* a clergyman
> **Strong explanation:** 1615—Donne *gained security by entering* the clergy
>
> Specific language best communicates the significance of events.

492 A Turbulent Time (1625–1798)

Assessment Resources

Unit 3 Resources

L1 L2 EL **Selection Test A,** pp. 20–22.
Administer Test A to less advanced readers.

L3 L4 EL **Selection Test B,** pp. 23–25.
Administer Test B to on-level and more advanced students.

L3 L4 **Open-Book Test,** pp. 17–19.
As an alternative, administer the Open-Book Test.

All **Customizable Test Bank**

All **Self-tests**
Students may prepare for the **Selection Test** by taking the **Self-test** online.

PHLit Online! All assessment resources are available at www.PHLitOnline.com.

Conventions and Style: Comparative and Superlative Adjectives and Adverbs

Adjectives and adverbs can take three different forms, as shown in the chart below.

Forms of Adjectives and Adverbs

Positive	Comparative	Superlative
sweet	sweeter	sweetest
witty	wittier	wittiest
mildly	more mildly	most mildly
willingly	more willingly	most willingly
much	more	most
good	better	best

The comparative degree is for comparing *two* persons, places, or things. The superlative is for comparing *three or more*. Some comparatives and superlatives are formed by adding a suffix to the modifier (*-er* or *-est,* respectively). Others are formed by using (respectively) *more* or *most.* Consult a dictionary of English usage as needed to determine correct usage.

Using the Comparative	Using the Superlative
The days of his youth were *wilder* than those of his later life.	At one time, Donne was the most *popular* preacher in England.
During his lifetime, Donne's sermons were read *more widely* than his love poems.	Some people thought John Donne was the *best* poet at that time.

Practice Supply the correct form of the adjective or adverb shown in parentheses.

1. The mature John Donne was _____ than his younger counterpart, Jack. (*religious*)
2. She thought he was the _____ man she had ever met. (*charming*)
3. T. S. Eliot praised Donne's works _____ than many earlier critics had. (*highly*)
4. He says she is the _____ woman for him. (*good*)
5. The speaker says that he will travel _____ than the sun. (*fast*)
6. Death takes the _____ men when they are young. (*fine*)
7. It was determined that whoever rose _____ should be called to prayer first. (*early*)
8. Donne says a person who suffers becomes _____ than one who does not. (*mature*)
9. "Song" is _____ than "Valediction." (*long*)
10. Which of the three poems did you enjoy _____? (*much*)

© Writing and Speaking Conventions

A. Writing For each adjective or adverb below, write one sentence using the comparative form and one using the superlative form.

   1. carefully   **2.** proud   **3.** mighty   **4.** great   **5.** deeply

   Then, consult a dictionary of English usage to ensure that you have correctly formed comparatives and superlatives.

B. Speaking As Death, write and present a response to Donne's argument in Holy Sonnet 10. Correctly use at least one comparative form and one superlative form. Consult a dictionary of English usage to check your formation of comparatives and superlatives.

PH WRITING COACH

Further instruction and practice are available in *Prentice Hall Writing Coach.*

Integrated Language Skills **493**

Conventions and Style

Introduce and discuss the skill using the instruction on the student page.

Think Aloud: Model the Skill

Say to students:

If I want to compare the mildness of two things using the adverb *mildly,* first I will try adding *–er:* "The breeze blew mildlier on our second day at the beach." This doesn't sound right. Next I will try adding the word *more* in front of *mildly:* "The breeze blew more mildly on our second day at the beach." This sounds right. The comparative form of *mildly* is formed by adding the word *more.*

PH WRITING COACH Grade 12

Students will find instruction on and practice with adjectives and adverbs in Chapter 13, section 3.

Practice

1. more religious
2. most charming
3. more highly
4. best
5. faster
6. finest
7. earliest
8. more mature
9. longer
10. most

Writing and Speaking Conventions

Sample responses:

A. Answers will vary. Student's sentences should include the correct comparative and superlative forms of the words given.

B. Answers will vary. Student's responses should include correct uses of at least one comparative and one superlative form.

Extend the Lesson

Sentence Modeling

1. Have students view the following sentences from the text: "But believe that I shall make/ Speedier journeys, since I take/More wings and spurs than he." ("Song," lines 14–16) and "From rest and sleep, which but thy pictures be,/Much pleasure; then from thee much more must flow,/And soonest our best men with thee do go." (Holy Sonnet 10, lines 5–7).

2. **Ask** students to note the use of the Grammar skill and the use of style in the sentences.

3. Have students write their own sentences modeled on the sentences shown. Students should use the Grammar skill and imitate the style of the sentences.

4. Encourage students to share their sentences with the class.

493

On My First Son • Still to Be Neat • Song: To Celia

Lesson Pacing Guide

DAY 1   Preteach

- © Administer the Reading and Vocabulary Warm-ups (*Unit 3 Resources*, pp. 26–29) as necessary.
- © Introduce the Literary Analysis concept: Epigrams.
- • Introduce the Reading Strategy: Comparing and Contrasting.
- © Build Background with the author and Background features.
- • Develop thematic thinking with Connecting to the Essential Question.
- © Teach the selection vocabulary.

DAYS 2–3   Preteach/Teach/Assess

- • Distribute copies of the appropriate graphic organizer for the Reading Strategy (*Graphic Organizer Transparencies*, pp. 79–80).
- • Distribute copies of the appropriate graphic organizer for Literary Analysis (*Graphic Organizer Transparencies*, pp. 81–82).
- • Prepare students to read with the Activating Prior Knowledge activities (TE).
- • Informally monitor comprehension while students read.
- © Develop students' understanding of epigrams using the Literary Analysis prompt.
- • Develop students' ability to compare and contrast using the Reading Strategy prompt.
- © Reinforce vocabulary with the Vocabulary notes.
- • Assess students' comprehension and mastery of the skills by having them answer the Critical Reading, Literary Analysis, and Reading Strategy questions.
- • Have students complete the Vocabulary Lesson.

DAY 4   Extend/Assess

- • Have students complete the Conventions and Style Lesson.
- © Have students complete the Writing Lesson and write a response to literature. (You may assign as homework.)
- • Administer Selection Test A or B (*Unit 3 Resources*, pp. 39–41 or 42–44).

Common Core State Standards

Reading Literature 4. Analyze the impact of specific word choices on meaning and tone, including words with multiple meanings or language that is particularly fresh, engaging, or beautiful.

Writing 1.a. Introduce precise, knowledgeable claim(s), establish the significance of the claim(s), distinguish the claim(s) from alternate or opposing claims, and create an organization that logically sequences claim(s), counterclaims, reasons, and evidence.

Language 1. Demonstrate command of the conventions of standard English grammar and usage when writing or speaking.
4. Determine or clarify the meaning of unknown and multiple-meaning words and phrases based on grades 11–12 reading and content, choosing flexibly from a range of strategies.

Additional Standards Practice
Common Core Companion, *pp. 41–48; 185–195; 314–317, 324–331*

Daily Block Scheduling
Each day in this Lesson Pacing Guide represents a 40–50 minute period. Teachers using block scheduling may combine days to revise pacing. In addition, teachers may differentiate and support core instruction by integrating components for extended and intensive support as students require. See the Guide to Selected Leveled Resources (facing page).

Guide to Selected Leveled Resources

R T I Tier 1 (students performing on level)

On My First Son • Still to Be Neat • Song: To Celia

Warm Up	Practice, **model**, and **monitor** fluency, working **with the whole class** or **in groups**.	**Vocabulary and Reading Warm-ups B**, *Unit 3 Resources*, pp. 26–27, 29
Comprehension/Skills	**Support** and **monitor** comprehension and skills development, having students complete the activities, graphic organizers, and interactive prompts **independently** or **as a class**.	• *Reader's Notebook,* adapted instruction and full selection **EL** *Reader's Notebook: English Learner's Version,* adapted instruction and adapted selection • **Reading Skill Graphic Organizer B**, *Graphic Organizer Transparencies,* p. 84 • **Literary Analysis Graphic Organizer B**, *Graphic Organizer Transparencies,* p. 86
Monitor Progress **A**	**Monitor** student progress with the differentiated curriculum-based assessment in the *Unit Resources.*	• **Selection Test B**, *Unit 3 Resources,* pp. 42–44 • **Open-Book Test**, *Unit 3 Resources,* pp. 36–38

R T I Tier 2 (students requiring intervention)

On My First Son • Still to Be Neat • Song: To Celia

Warm Up	Practice, **model**, and **monitor** fluency **in groups** or **with individuals**.	• **Vocabulary and Reading Warm-ups A**, *Unit 3 Resources,* pp. 26–28 • *Hear It!* **Audio CD (adapted text)**
Comprehension/Skills	• **Support** and **monitor** comprehension and skills development, working **in small groups** or **with individuals**. • As students complete the selection in the appropriate version of the *Reader's Notebook,* **monitor** comprehension frequently with group questions and individual instruction. • **Model** strategies while guiding students in completing the activities and prompts in the *Reader's Notebook,* as well as the graphic organizers. • **Practice** skills and **monitor** mastery with the *Reading Kit* worksheets.	• *Reader's Notebook: Adapted Version,* adapted instruction and adapted selection **EL** *Reader's Notebook: English Learner's Version,* adapted instruction and adapted selection • **Reading Skill Graphic Organizer A**, *Graphic Organizer Transparencies,* p. 83 • **Literary Analysis Graphic Organizer A**, *Graphic Organizer Transparencies,* p. 85 • *Reading Kit,* Practice worksheets
Monitor Progress **A**	**Monitor** student progress with the differentiated curriculum-based assessment in the *Unit Resources* and in the *Reading Kit.*	• **Selection Test A**, *Unit 3 Resources,* pp. 39–41 • *Reading Kit,* Assess worksheets

TIER 3 Tier 3 intervention may require consultation with the student's special-education or dyslexia specialist. For additional support, see the Tier 2 activities and resources listed above.

One-on-one teaching   Group work   Whole class instruction   Independent work   **A** Assessment

For a complete guide to selection support, including support for Advanced students, see the Overview of Resources in the frontmatter.

On My First Son • Still to Be Neat • Song: To Celia

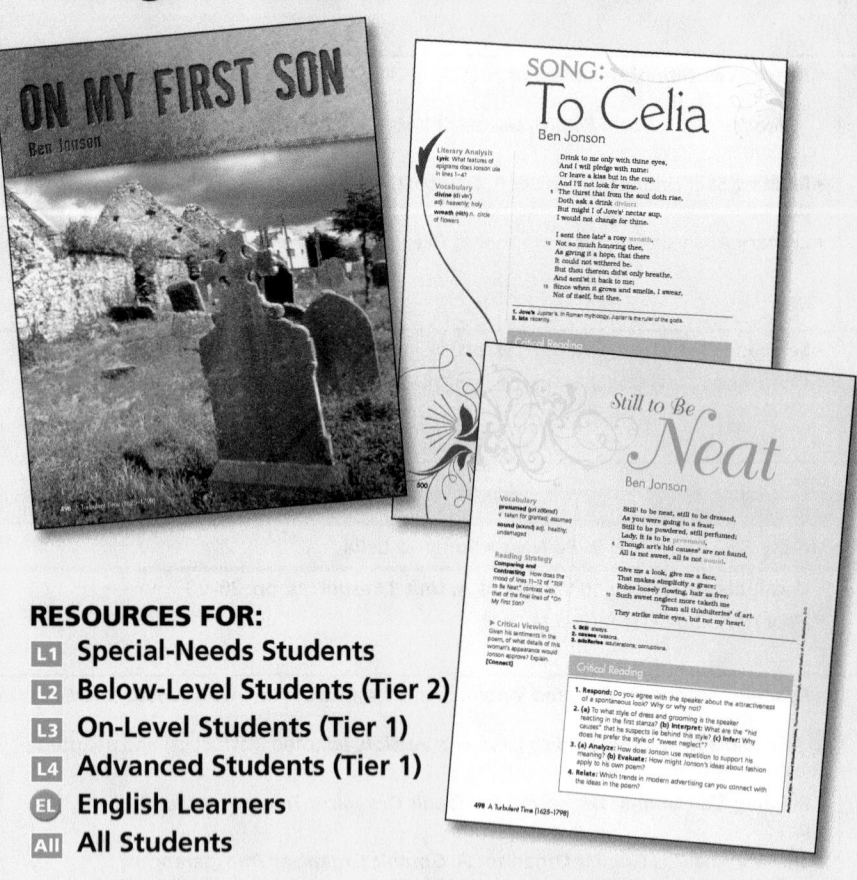

RESOURCES FOR:

- **L1** Special-Needs Students
- **L2** Below-Level Students (Tier 2)
- **L3** On-Level Students (Tier 1)
- **L4** Advanced Students (Tier 1)
- **EL** English Learners
- **All** All Students

Vocabulary/Fluency/Prior Knowledge

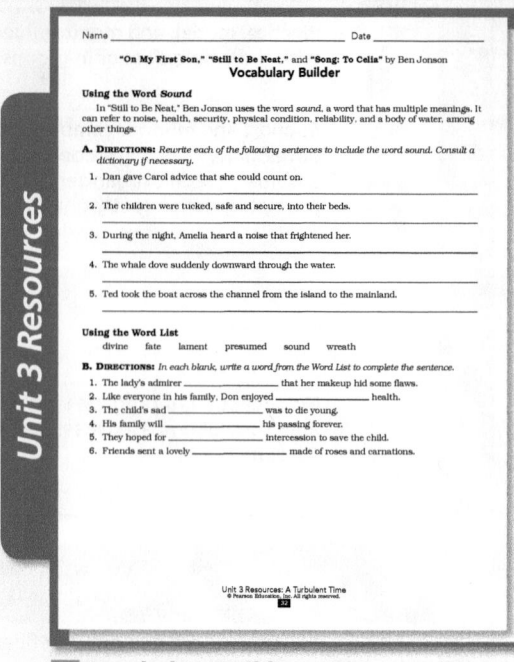

All **Vocabulary Builder,** p. 32

Also available for these selections:

EL L1 L2 Vocabulary Warm-ups A and B, pp. 26–27

EL L1 L2 Reading Warm-ups A and B, pp. 28–29

Reader's Notebooks

Pre- and postreading pages for these selections appear in an interactive format in the *Reader's Notebooks*. Each *Notebook* is differentiated for a different group of learners. The selections in the Adapted and English Learner's versions are abridged.

L2 L3 *Reader's Notebook*

L1 *Reader's Notebook: Adapted Version*

EL *Reader's Notebook: English Learner's Version*

EL *Reader's Notebook: Spanish Version*

© *Common Core Companion*

Additional instruction and practice for each Common Core State Standard

Selection Support

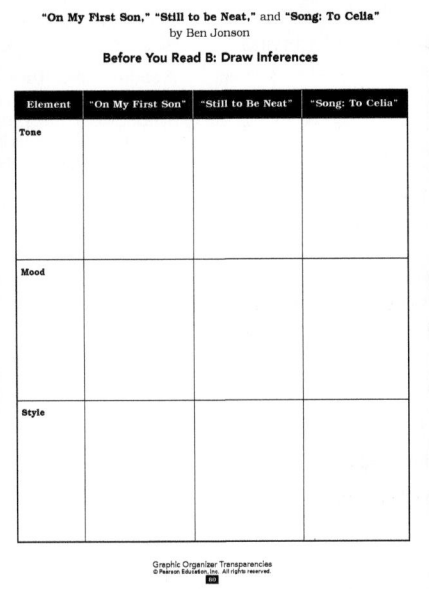

Graphic Organizer Transparencies

"On My First Son," "Still to be Neat," and "Song: To Celia"
by Ben Jonson

Before You Read B: Draw Inferences

Element	"On My First Son"	"Still to Be Neat"	"Song: To Celia"
Tone			
Mood			
Style			

Graphic Organizer Transparencies
© Pearson Education, Inc. All rights reserved.

EL L3 Reading: Graphic Organizer B, p. 80

Also available for these selections:

EL L1 L2 Reading: Graphic Organizer A (partially filled in), p. 79

EL L1 L2 Literary Analysis: Graphic Organizer A (partially filled in), p. 81

EL L3 Literary Analysis: Graphic Organizer B, p. 82

Skills Development/Extension

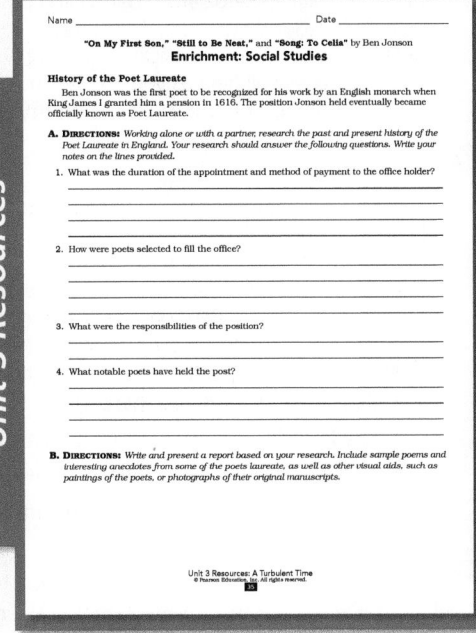

Unit 3 Resources

Name _____ Date _____

"On My First Son," "Still to Be Neat," and "Song: To Celia" by Ben Jonson
Enrichment: Social Studies

History of the Poet Laureate

Ben Jonson was the first poet to be recognized for his work by an English monarch when King James I granted him a pension in 1616. The position Jonson held eventually became officially known as Poet Laureate.

A. DIRECTIONS: *Working alone or with a partner, research the past and present history of the Poet Laureate in England. Your research should answer the following questions. Write your notes on the lines provided.*

1. What was the duration of the appointment and method of payment to the office holder?

2. How were poets selected to fill the office?

3. What were the responsibilities of the position?

4. What notable poets have held the post?

B. DIRECTIONS: *Write and present a report based on your research. Include sample poems and interesting anecdotes from some of the poets laureate, as well as other visual aids, such as paintings of the poets, or photographs of their original manuscripts.*

Unit 3 Resources: A Turbulent Time
© Pearson Education, Inc. All rights reserved.

L4 Enrichment, p. 35

Also available for these selections:

All Literary Analysis, p. 30

All Reading, p. 31

EL L3 L4 Grammar and Style, p. 33

EL L3 L4 Support for Writing, p. 34

Assessment

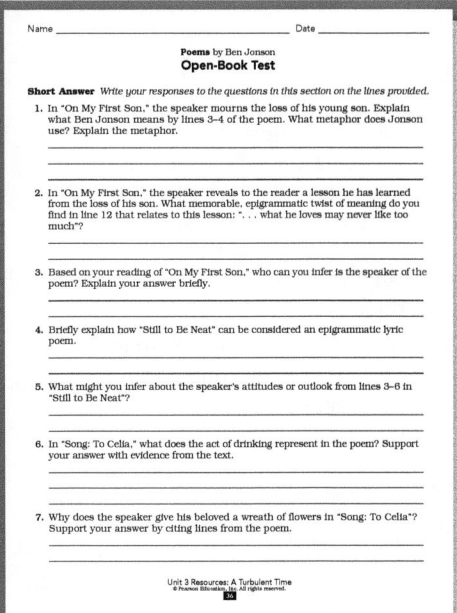

Name _____ Date _____

Poems by Ben Jonson
Open-Book Test

Short Answer *Write your responses to the questions in this section on the lines provided.*

1. In "On My First Son," the speaker mourns the loss of his young son. Explain what Ben Jonson means by lines 3–4 of the poem. What metaphor does Jonson use? Explain the metaphor.

2. In "On My First Son," the speaker reveals to the reader a lesson he has learned from the loss of his son. What memorable, epigrammatic twist of meaning do you find in line 12 that relates to this lesson: ". . . what he loves may never like too much"?

3. Based on your reading of "On My First Son," who can you infer is the speaker of the poem? Explain your answer briefly.

4. Briefly explain how "Still to Be Neat" can be considered an epigrammatic lyric poem.

5. What might you infer about the speaker's attitudes or outlook from lines 3–6 in "Still to Be Neat"?

6. In "Song: To Celia," what does the act of drinking represent in the poem? Support your answer with evidence from the text.

7. Why does the speaker give his beloved a wreath of flowers in "Song: To Celia"? Support your answer by citing lines from the poem.

Unit 3 Resources: A Turbulent Time
© Pearson Education, Inc. All rights reserved.

L3 L4 Open-Book Test, pp. 36–38

Also available for these selections:

EL L1 L2 Selection Test A, pp. 39–41

EL L3 L4 Selection Test B, pp. 42–44

PHLit Online!
www.PHLitOnline.com

Online Resources: All print materials are also available online.

- complete narrated selection text
- a thematically related video with writing prompt
- an interactive graphic organizer
- highlighting feature
- access to all student print resources, adapted to individual student needs
- Spanish and English summaries
- adapted selection translations in Spanish

Get Connected! (thematic video with writing prompt)

Also available:

Background Video
All videos are available in Spanish.

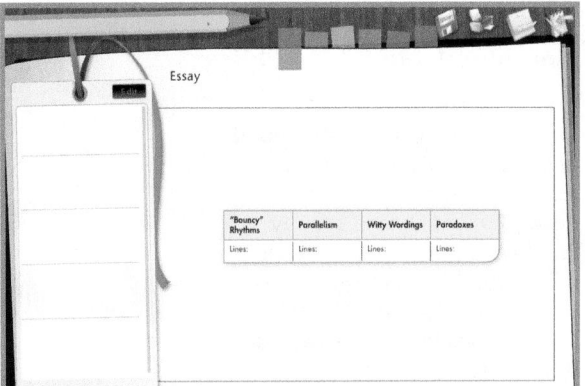

Writer's Journal (with graphics feature)

Also available:

Vocabulary Central (tools and activities for studying vocabulary)

❶ Connecting to the Essential Question

1. Review the assignment with the class.

2. Have students discuss areas of their lives that benefit from balance, for example, eating and exercise habits, relationships, or time spent at work and play. Have them think of people in their lives who value balance. Then, have students complete the assignment.

3. As students read, have them look for passages in Jonson's poems that reflect the classic virtues of balance and clarity.

❷ Literary Analysis

Introduce the skill, using the instruction on the student page.

Think Aloud: Model the Skill

Say to students:

When I read the lines "Drink to me only with thine eyes, / And I will pledge with mine," I can hear that the way the stress falls on nearly every other syllable creates a bouncy rhythm.

❸ Reading Strategy

1. Introduce the strategy using the instruction on the student page.

2. Give students a copy of **Reading Strategy Graphic Organizer A**, page 79 in *Graphic Organizer Transparencies*, to fill out.

Think Aloud: Model the Skill

Say to students:

I compare and contrast the mood of stories, television shows, or movies all the time. If I am feeling down, I might choose a funny or lighthearted book to lift my spirits. If I am choosing a movie for my whole family to watch, I might stay away from films that are depressing or intense.

❹ Vocabulary

1. Pronounce each word, giving its definition, and have students say it aloud.

2. For more guidance, see the *Classroom Strategies and Teaching Routines* card for introducing vocabulary.

494

Before You Read

On My First Son
• *Still to Be Neat*
• *Song: To Celia*

❶ Connecting to the Essential Question In his poetry, Ben Jonson favored qualities like balance, clarity, and proportion, virtues he associated with classical literature. As you read, notice passages in Jonson's poems that reflect the classical virtues of balance and clarity. Identifying these passages will help as you answer the Essential Question: **What is the relationship of the writer to tradition?**

❷ Literary Analysis

A **lyric** is a brief, melodic poem expressing personal thoughts or feelings. In ancient Greece, lyrics were recited or sung to the accompaniment of a lyre (hence the name lyr-ic).

Styles of lyric poetry are often influenced by the *historic period*. Renaissance England, Ben Jonson's era, admired classical Greece. It is natural, therefore, that Jonson used an ancient Greek form called an **epigram** (from the Greek for "inscription"). Epigrams include these features:

• Short lines with bouncy rhythms
• Paradoxical twists, as in "Drink to me only with thine eyes . . ."
• Parallel structures, as in "Still to be neat, still to be dressed, . . ."

As you read, analyze the elements that make Jonson's lines memorable.

❸ Reading Strategy

Preparing to Read Complex Texts By **comparing and contrasting elements** in several poems, you can better understand how Jonson expresses a range of feelings. Remember that these elements are the cumulative result of particular word choices:

• *tone*, or writer's attitude toward the subject
• *mood*, the emotions called up by the poem
• *style*, the author's general approach, varying from highly personal to impersonal and distant

Use the chart shown to compare these elements, including word choices that contribute to them, and to note how Jonson uses them to achieve his *aesthetic purposes*, or goals.

❹ Vocabulary

fate (fāt) *n.* destiny; fortune (p. 497)

lament (lə ment´) *v.* express grief over; mourn (p. 497)

presumed (pri zoomd´) *v.* taken for granted; assumed (p. 498)

sound (sound) *adj.* healthy; undamaged (p. 498)

divine (di vīn´) *adj.* heavenly; holy (p. 500)

wreath (rēth) *n.* circle of flowers (p. 500)

494 A Turbulent Time (1625–1798)

Common Core
State Standards

Reading Literature
4. Analyze the impact of specific word choices on meaning and tone, including words with multiple meanings or language that is particularly fresh, engaging, or beautiful.

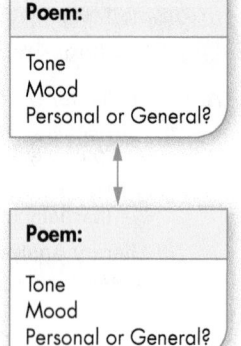

Poem:

Tone
Mood
Personal or General?

Poem:

Tone
Mood
Personal or General?

PHLit
Online!
www.PHLitOnline.com

Vocabulary Development

Vocabulary Knowledge Rating
Create a **Vocabulary Knowledge Rating Chart** (*Professional Development Guidebook,* pp. 32–33) for the vocabulary words on the student page. Give each student a copy of the chart with the words on it. Read the words aloud, and have students mark their ratings in the Before Reading column. Urge students to attend to these words as they read and discuss the selections.

In order to gauge how much instruction you need to provide, tally how many students are confident in their knowledge of each word. As students read, point out the words and their context.

PHLit Online! **Vocabulary Central**, featuring tools and activities for studying vocabulary, is available online at www.PHLitOnline.com.

⑤Ben Jonson (1572–1637)

Author of "On My First Son" • "Still to Be Neat" • "Song: To Celia"

Ben Jonson lived a nearly mythic life. Even in his physical stature, he seemed a little larger than life—he was a big man with boundless energy and enormous courage. Brilliant in his poetry and dangerous in a duel, a classical scholar and a veteran soldier, an astute critic and a brassy talker, Jonson had a colorful, sometimes violent career that culminated in his reputation as an esteemed judge of literature. The friend as well as the chief rival of Shakespeare and Donne, he set literary tastes for a generation of poets.

A Poet at War Adopted in infancy, Jonson worked for his stepfather, a bricklayer, while attending the equivalent of high school under a private tutor. Too poor to study at a university, Jonson joined the army and fought in the wars for Dutch independence from Spain. The brawny Jonson at one point met an enemy champion in single combat before the massed armies of Holland and Spain. Jonson won.

Scandal and Success After returning to England, Jonson became an actor. Despite his turbulent life—jailed for his part in a "slanderous" play, almost hanged for killing a fellow actor in a duel, and even suspected of plotting against the king—Jonson became a major dramatist.

The Importance of a Poet Jonson's own opinion of his work and status may be judged by the fact that when he published his collected works in 1616, he entitled the volume *The Works of Benjamin Jonson*—a style of title used largely with celebrated ancient authors. With this gesture, Jonson may have become the first English-language poet to claim true professional dignity for himself.

Varied Styles Jonson's experiences ranged from tavern brawls to elegant entertainments, and his poetic styles are equally varied. He favored satire in his dramas, poking fun at contemporary character types in plays such as *Volpone* and *The Alchemist.*

Jonson wrote many of his poems in an impersonal style, one suited to inscriptions on monuments. Others are filled with nasty wit. As diverse as his styles are, though, one of his consistent strengths is the clear, direct expression of ideas.

A Lasting Influence In his varied experiences and diverse literary output, Jonson might seem to sum up the age in which he lived. Yet his importance does not end with the seventeenth century. Jonson's influence on writers is still felt today, and his plays continue to be produced.

On My First Son • Still to Be Neat • Song: To Celia **495**

 Daily Bellringer

For each class during which you will teach these selections, have students complete one of the five activities for the appropriate week in the *Daily Bellringer Activities* booklet.

Multidraft Reading

To assist struggling readers and to enhance reading for all, assign the text in chunks, as warranted by length, and apply multidraft reading protocols. For each reading, have students set the purpose indicated:

- **First reading**—identifying key ideas and details and answering any Reading Checks.
- **Second reading**—analyzing craft and structure and responding to the side-column prompts.
- **Third reading**—integrating knowledge and ideas, connecting to other texts and the world, and answering the end-of-selection questions.

For more guidance, refer to the *Classroom Strategies and Teaching Routines* card on Multidraft Reading.

⑤ Background
More About the Author

Historic accounts help us picture Jonson at the Mermaid Tavern, surrounded by admirers and engaged in duels of wit with Shakespeare. Jonson's emphasis on graceful, balanced expression in verse shaped a generation of young poets, offering an alternative to Donne's "rough" lines. Critic Douglas Bush writes, "Jonson demanded, and unceasingly strove for, the ageless classical virtues of clarity, unity, symmetry, and proportion." Jonson was the first English poet with a "school"; he was also the first to insist that poetry was in itself an important vocation. Shakespeare, who did not publish his plays, regarded himself as a working dramatist, a tradesman in words. Jonson, however, risked controversy by publishing his verse in the form of a "Collected Works"—a format previously reserved for theological or historical works.

1 About the Selections

The emotions expressed in Ben Jonson's poems cover a wide range, from heartbreak to love to amusement. Whereas Donne's work argues that death does not matter because it leads to eternal life, Jonson's poem "On My First Son" shows that death sorely wounds those grieving people left behind. In contrast, the poem "Still to Be Neat," which comes from the first act of *Epicoene; or the Silent Woman*, a comedy written in 1609, has a lighthearted tone. In the poem, the speaker expresses his admiration for the natural style of beauty, feeling that powders and perfumes cover up a lack of sweetness and soundness. Jonson developed "Song: To Celia" from some prose pieces written by a third-century Greek writer, Philostratus. Like other Greek and Roman lyrics, it exhibits a sense of balance, proportion, simplicity, and conciseness.

2 Activating Prior Knowledge

Have students suggest reasons they remember a line of poetry or a quotation from a speech. Ask them to cite a few memorable quotations and explain why they are memorable. Then, tell them that Ben Jonson's writing was designed to produce quotable lines and phrases.

Concept Connector ➝

Tell students they will return to their responses after reading the selections.

ON MY FIRST SON

Ben Jonson

496 A Turbulent Time (1625–1798)

Ⓒ Text Complexity Rubric: Leveled Texts

	On My First Son	Still to Be Neat	Song: To Celia
Qualitative Measures			
Context/ Knowledge Demands	Lyric poem; literary knowledge demands 1 2 ③ 4 5	Lyric poem; cultural knowledge demands 1 ② 3 4 5	Lyric poem; literary knowledge demands 1 ② 3 4 5
Structure/Language Conventionality and Clarity	Archaic diction and syntax 1 2 ③ 4 5	Archaic diction 1 ② 3 4 5	Archaic diction and syntax 1 ② 3 4 5
Levels of Meaning/ Purpose/Concept Level	Moderate (love for child) 1 2 ③ 4 5	Accessible (natural vs. artificial beauty) 1 ② 3 4 5	Accessible (love) 1 2 ③ 4 5
Quantitative Measures			
Lexile/Text Length	NP / 108 words	NP / 82 words	NP / 102 words
Overall Complexity	**More complex**	**More accessible**	**More accessible**

Ben Jonson was indebted to ancient Greek and Roman poets, whose work shaped his taste for clear, brief expression. Like ancient poets, Jonson composed poetry with a definite social function. Jonson's poems praising other writers appeared at the beginning of their books. Poems such as "On My First Son" marked the occasion of a death. Songs such as "Still to Be Neat" were written by Jonson for his masques (royal entertainments).

Farewell, thou child of my right hand,[1] and joy;
    My sin was too much hope of thee, loved boy,
Seven years thou wert lent to me, and I thee pay,
    Exacted by thy fate, on the just[2] day.
5 O, could I lose all father,[3] now. For why
    Will man lament the state he should envy?
To have so soon scaped world's, and flesh's rage,
    And, if no other misery, yet age?
Rest in soft peace, and, asked, say here doth lie
10   Ben Jonson his best piece of poetry.
For whose sake, henceforth, all his vows be such,
    As what he loves may never like[4] too much.

---

1. **child . . . hand** literal translation of the Hebrew name Benjamin, the name of Jonson's son. Jonson's son was born in 1596 and died in 1603.
2. **just** exact.
3. **lose . . . father** shed an identity as a father.
4. **like** possibly meant in the old sense of "please."

Vocabulary
fate (fāt) *n.* destiny

lament (lə ment') *v.* express grief over; mourn

Literary Analysis
Lyric Do you think this poem was written to create a sense of permanence? Explain.

Critical Reading

© 1. **Key Ideas and Details (a)** What is the sin the speaker refers to in line 2? **(b) Interpret:** Why does the speaker call this feeling a sin?

© 2. **Key Ideas and Details (a) Interpret:** Why does the speaker wish to "lose all father, now"? **(b) Interpret:** What does he vow in lines 11–12? **(c) Draw Conclusions:** Why would grief lead to these reactions?

© 3. **Key Ideas and Details (a) Interpret:** Does the speaker ever present his feelings of grief directly? Explain. **(b) Evaluate:** Why might this manner of presenting grief strengthen the impression made on the reader?

© 4. **Integration of Knowledge and Ideas (a) Apply:** Contrast the ideas in lines 5–8 with contemporary attitudes. **(b) Evaluate:** Which makes more sense to you?

Cite textual evidence to support your responses.

On My First Son **497**

---

❸ Literary Analysis
Lyric
1. Read aloud the last line. **Ask** students what makes the last two lines so memorable.
   Answer: It seems paradoxical; it is snappy and alliterative.
2. **Ask** students the Literary Analysis question: Do you think this poem was written to create a sense of permanence? Explain.
   Possible response: The poet wanted to create an expression that was more lasting than the life of his dead son.

ASSESS
Answers

Before students respond, you may wish to have them write a brief objective summary of the selection. As they answer the questions below, remind them to support their answers with evidence from the text.

1. (a) The sin is loving his son too much. (b) He would have had his son remain in this inferior world.
2. (a) The speaker is haunted by memories of being a father. (b) The speaker vows that he will never again love anyone so strongly. (c) Grief leaves lasting wounds.
3. (a) No; he does not directly describe how he is feeling. (b) By withholding extravagant expressions of grief, the speaker multiplies the poignancy of such lines as "here doth lie / Ben Jonson his best piece of poetry."
4. (a) Rather than envying the child for having escaped old age, most people today would consider his death a tragedy. (b) Students may respond that they place a higher value on this present life.

© Text Complexity: Reader and Task Suggestions

	On My First Son	Still to Be Neat	Song: To Celia
Preparing to Read the Texts • Using the Background on TE p. 495, discuss with students how poetry might display "clarity, unity, symmetry, and proportion." • Discuss with students the most common topics of lyric poetry. • Guide students to use Multidraft Reading strategies (TE p. 495).	**Leveled Tasks** *Levels of Meaning* If students will have difficulty with the poem's ideas, have them read the poem with a focus on the speaker's chief emotion and the reason for it. Then, as they reread, have them try to comprehend the more difficult ideas. *Analyzing* If students will not have difficulty with the poem's ideas, have them analyze the speaker's question in lines 5–6.	**Leveled Tasks** *Knowledge Demands* If students will have difficulty with the cultural context, have them focus first on details that still apply, then on details specific to Jonson's day. Then, as they reread, have them consider the details that are specific to Jonson's day. *Analyzing* If students will not have difficulty with the cultural context, have them analyze the speaker's attitude toward art.	**Leveled Tasks** *Levels of Meaning* If students will have difficulty with the poem's imagery, have them focus on its central meaning and tone. Then, as they reread, have them consider how specific images help convey that meaning and tone. *Evaluating* If students will not have difficulty with the poem's imagery, have them discuss which images work best to convey the speaker's feelings.

498

Comparing and Contrasting

1. Have students reread the final lines of "On My First Son," and suggest adjectives they might use to characterize its mood. Then have them do the same for lines 11–12 of "Still to Be Neat."

2. **Ask** students the Reading Strategy question: How does the mood of lines 11–12 of "Still to Be Neat" contrast with that of the final lines of "On My First Son"? Encourage them to use the *Reading Strategy Graphic Organizer* to help them construct their responses.
   Answer: The mood of "Still to Be Neat " is lighthearted, as the speaker admits that his heart remains untouched. The final lines of "On My First Son" are restrained and quiet in their grief, but the effect is quite poignant.

❺ **Critical Viewing**

Possible response: Jonson would approve of the woman's free-flowing hair, clear complexion, and relaxed, easy posture. Her dress is casual and unornamented.

ASSESS

Answers

Before students respond, you may wish to have them write a brief objective summary of the selection. As they answer the questions below, remind them to support their answers with evidence from the text.

1. (a) The speaker is reacting to an overdone appearance. (b) The speaker suspects that flaws are masked by perfume and powder. (c) He prefers the style of sweet neglect because it touches his heart as well as his eyes.

2. (a) The repetition of "still to be" indicates the speaker's displeasure regarding the lady's appearance. The repetition of "give me" is softer and reflects the simplicity he prefers. (b) He writes clean, simple verse.

3. Cosmetic advertisements spotlight natural beauty—even though cosmetics are perfect examples of artifice.

Still to Be Neat

Ben Jonson

Vocabulary

presumed (pri zoōmd´) *v.* taken for granted; assumed

sound (sound) *adj.* healthy; undamaged

Reading Strategy

Comparing and Contrasting How does the mood of lines 11–12 of "Still to Be Neat" contrast with that of the final lines of "On My First Son"?

❺ ▶ **Critical Viewing**
Given his sentiments in the poem, of what details of this woman's appearance would Jonson approve? Explain. **[Connect]**

Cite textual evidence to support your responses.

Still[1] to be neat, still to be dressed,
As you were going to a feast;
Still to be powdered, still perfumed;
Lady, it is to be presumed,
5 Though art's hid causes[2] are not found,
All is not sweet, all is not sound.

❼ Give me a look, give me a face,
   That makes simplicity a grace;
   Robes loosely flowing, hair as free;
10 Such sweet neglect more taketh me
❹   Than all th'adulteries[3] of art.
   They strike mine eyes, but not my heart.

1. **Still** always.
2. **causes** reasons.
3. **adulteries** adulterations; corruptions.

Portrait of Mrs. Richard Brinsley Sheridan, Thomas Gainsborough, National Gallery of Art, Washington, D.C.

Critical Reading

1. **Key Ideas and Details** **(a)** To what style of dress and grooming is the speaker reacting in the first stanza? **(b) Interpret:** What are the "hid causes" that he suspects lie behind this style? **(c) Infer:** Why does he prefer the style of "sweet neglect"?

2. **Key Ideas and Details** **(a) Analyze:** How does Jonson use repetition to support his meaning? **(b) Evaluate:** How might Jonson's ideas about fashion apply to his own poem?

3. **Integration of Knowledge and Ideas** Which trends in modern advertising can you connect with the ideas in the poem?

Vocabulary Development

Vocabulary Knowledge Rating
When students have completed reading and discussing the poems, have them take out their **Vocabulary Knowledge Rating Charts** for the poems. Read the words aloud and have students rate their knowledge of words again in the After Reading column. Clarify any words that are still problematic. Have students write their own definitions and example or sentence in the appropriate column. Then, have students complete the Vocabulary Lesson at the end of the selections. Encourage students to use the words in further discussion and written work about the selections. Remind them that they will be accountable for these words on the **Selection Test**, *Unit 3 Resources,* pages 39–41 or 42–44.

499 Still to Be Neat

Still to Be Neat **499**

6 Humanities

Portrait of Mrs. Richard Brinsley Sheridan, by Thomas Gainsborough

Gainsborough was one of the most popular and prolific English painters of the eighteenth century. Famous for his portraiture, Gainsborough retained a passion for landscapes; in his portrait of Mrs. Sheridan, he is able to indulge in both genres with his characteristic lightness of brush stroke and delicacy of color. His subject is the wife of Richard Sheridan, the English playwright best known for *The Rivals* and *The School for Scandal.*

Use the following question for discussion:

How has the artist expressed a sense of naturalness and ease in this portrait?

Possible response: The artist has placed his subject within nature and uses the flowing shapes of branches to echo the woman's casual posture and the flowing lines of her garments.

7 Engaging the Essential Question

1. Draw students' attention to lines 7–9 of "Still to Be Neat."

2. After reading the lines aloud, **ask** students what the speaker's attitude is toward "simplicity." Have students explain their reasoning.
   Possible response: Because the speaker says "give me" in line 7, we can assume he desires simplicity. In addition, he calls simplicity a "grace," which indicates that he feels it is a virtue.

Differentiated Instruction for Universal Access

Strategy for Special-Needs Students
Invite students to find advertisements or pictures of women who fit both types described in this poem. Have them mount these images on posters labeled "Neat" and "Sweet Neglect." Then, ask students to write a paragraph describing their reactions to these images.

Enrichment for Gifted/Talented Students
Tell students that "Song: To Celia" (p. 500) has been set to music. Have students locate the tune or compose their own melody and prepare a performance of the song for the class.

Monitor Progress

1. **Ask** students to identify the three features of epigrams.
   Answer: short lines with bouncy rhythms, paradoxical twists, and parallel phrases or clauses

2. **Ask** students the Literary Analysis question: What features of epigrams does Jonson use in lines 1–4?
   Answer: He uses bouncy rhythms and paradoxical twists.

Reteach

If students have trouble responding, review the definition and features of epigrams found on page 494.

ASSESS

Answers

Before students respond, you may wish to have them write a brief objective summary of the selection. As they answer the questions below, remind them to support their answers with evidence from the text.

1. (a) The soul has a thirst for love. (b) The speaker has asked Celia to "drink" to him with her eyes, to look at him lovingly.

2. (a) We know only that the speaker is in the beginning stages of love for Celia. (b) Students may agree or disagree that more information about the speaker of the poem would add to its effect.

3. Students may feel that the poem captures the true sentiment of the early stages of infatuation.

4. **Possible response:** Jonson's use of <u>precise</u> language and strict form does, at times, seem <u>artificial</u> and unemotional. His adherence to <u>classic</u> Greek and Roman sensibilities does not always allow much raw emotion to come through in his words.

SONG: To Celia
Ben Jonson

Literary Analysis
Lyric What features of epigrams does Jonson use in lines 1–4?

Vocabulary
divine (di vīn´) *adj.* heavenly; holy
wreath (rēth) *n.* circle of flowers

8
Drink to me only with thine eyes,
And I will pledge with mine;
Or leave a kiss but in the cup,
And I'll not look for wine.
5 The thirst that from the soul doth rise,
Doth ask a drink divine;
But might I of Jove's[1] nectar sup,
I would not change for thine.

I sent thee late[2] a rosy wreath,
10 Not so much honoring thee,
As giving it a hope, that there
It could not withered be.
But thou thereon did'st only breathe,
And sent'st it back to me;
15 Since when it grows and smells, I swear,
Not of itself, but thee.

1. **Jove's** Jupiter's. In Roman mythology, Jupiter is the ruler of the gods.
2. **late** recently.

500

Critical Reading

1. **Key Ideas and Details (a)** For what does the soul thirst in lines 5–6 of "Song: To Celia"? **(b) Interpret:** Explain how this idea of the soul's thirst extends the image in lines 1–2.

2. **Key Ideas and Details (a) Assess:** How much do you know about the speaker of "Song: To Celia" or his beloved? **(b) Make a Judgment:** How would more information affect your appreciation of the poem?

3. **Integration of Knowledge and Ideas** Does Jonson's poem seem artificial or false by today's standards, or does it capture true sentiment? Explain.

4. **Integration of Knowledge and Ideas** Does Jonson's emphasis on clarity lessen the emotional impact of his work? In your response, use at least two of these Essential Question words: *classic, precise, artificial*. *[Connecting to the Essential Question: What is the relationship of the writer to tradition?]*

Concept Connector

Reading Skill Graphic Organizer
Ask students to review the graphic organizers in which they have compared and contrasted elements of Jonson's poetry. Then, have students summarize the ways that these three poems are similar and different. Ask volunteers to share their comparisons with the class.

Activating Prior Knowledge
Have students return to their responses to the Activating Prior Knowledge activity. Ask them which lines from Ben Jonson's poems they will most likely be able to remember a year from now.

Writing About the Essential Question
Have students work in groups to discuss how Ben Jonson's poetry reflects his appreciation for balance, clarity, and proportion. Have them write or discuss how this compares to the person they wrote about in Connecting to the Essential Question. Ask students to evaluate whether their understanding of these three "virtues" has changed as a result of their reading. Encourage students to cite specific textual details to support their responses.

Literary Analysis

© **1. Craft and Structure** Jonson favored a form of **lyric** called an *epigram*, a term that comes from a Greek word meaning "inscription." Would "On My First Son" be suitable as an inscription on the subject's tombstone? Explain.

© **2. Craft and Structure** Identify three pairs of parallel phrases or clauses in "Still to Be Neat."

© **3. Craft and Structure** **(a)** Explain how the phrase "sweet neglect" in "Still to Be Neat" appears paradoxical, or self-contradictory, but makes memorable sense. **(b)** How does the *irony*—a surprising difference from the expected—of the phrase add to its effect?

© **4. Craft and Structure** Use a chart like the one shown to identify and characterize lines that give "Song: To Celia" the style of an epigram.

"Bouncy" Rhythms	Parallelism	Witty Wordings	Paradoxes
Lines:	Lines:	Lines:	Lines:

Reading Strategy

5. Comparing Literary Works (a) Compare and contrast elements in Jonson's work by contrasting the tone of lines 9–12 of "On My First Son" with that of lines 1–6 of "Still to Be Neat." **(b)** How do these different tones allow Jonson to achieve different *aesthetic purposes* in these lyrics?

6. Comparing Literary Works (a) For each lyric, identify one or two words or images that help create the *mood*. **(b)** Compare and contrast the moods called up by each of these poems.

7. Comparing Literary Works (a) Identify two details of Jonson's *style* in "On My First Son" that make it a sincere personal statement of grief. Explain. **(b)** Identify two details of Jonson's *style* in "Song: To Celia" that give it a formal, impersonal quality. Explain your choices. **(c)** Are both *aesthetic purposes*—sincerity and formality—equally valuable? Why or why not?

8. Comparing Literary Works (a) Which details in "Still to Be Neat" give it a generalized quality? **(b)** Which details make it seem heartfelt? **(c)** Compare the sentiment in this poem with the sentiment of the other two lyrics.

9. In what occupations today might the elements of Jonson's brief, witty writing style be effective? Explain.

Common Core State Standards

Writing

1.a. Introduce precise, knowledgeable claim(s), establish the significance of the claim(s), distinguish the claim(s) from alternate or opposing claims, and create an organization that logically sequences claim(s), counterclaims, reasons, and evidence. *(p. 502)*

Language

1. Demonstrate command of the conventions of standard English grammar and usage when writing or speaking. *(p. 503)*

4. Determine or clarify the meaning of unknown and multiple-meaning words and phrases based on *grades 11–12 reading and content*, choosing flexibly from a range of strategies. *(p. 502)*

On My First Son • Still to Be Neat • Song: To Celia **501**

Assessment Practice

Writer's Purpose (For more practice, see *All-in-One Workbook*.)

Many tests require students to identify an author's purpose for writing. Use the following passage from "Still to Be Neat" to teach students how to identify a writer's main purpose.

. . . Give me a look, give me a face,/That makes simplicity a grace;/Robes loosely flowing, hair as free;/Such sweet neglect more taketh me/Than all th'adulteries of art,/They strike mine eyes, but not my heart.

Jonson wrote this passage primarily to

A ridicule the lady

B inform the lady that he finds natural beauty more attractive than artificial beauty

C tell the lady that he knows she uses "art" to appear more beautiful

D express his love for the lady

Based on the last three lines, students should determine that the correct answer is **B**.

Answers

1. Students may cite lines 9–10: "here doth lie/Ben Jonson his best piece of poetry." The first phrase suggests a tombstone.

2. Parallel phrases include "Still to be neat, still to be dressed"; "Still to be powdered, still perfumed"; "All is not sweet, all is not sound."

3. (a) Neglect of one's grooming is normally unpleasant, but "sweet" changes it to a carefree naturalness. (b) Jonson is noting something special that others might not appreciate.

4. "Bouncy" Rhythms: 1–4, 9–12; Parallelism: 2 and 4; Witty Wordings: 1 and 3; Paradoxes: 15–16.

5. (a) The bouncy, abrupt lines of "Still to Be Neat" create a mocking tone, while the longer lines and serious language of "On My First Son" give it a more somber and sincere tone. (b) "Still to Be Neat" points out something that Jonson sees as a societal flaw, while "On My First Son" attempts to articulate Jonson's formless grief.

6. (a) "Still to Be Neat": "All is not sweet, all is not sound"; "On My First Son": ". . . flesh's rage," (b) "Still to Be Neat" creates a mood of wistfulness. "On My First Son" evokes a hopeless mood.

7. (a) Jonson speaks directly to his dead son, making the poem intensely heartfelt. Jonson calls his son his "best piece of poetry." (b) "Song: To Celia" provides no personal information about either the speaker or Celia. (c) "On My First Son" is an expression of personal grief. The abstract qualities of "Song: To Celia" express universal feelings of infatuation.

8. (a) Students may cite the formal style and withholding the lady's name. (b) The speaker's yearning for "sweet neglect" is heartfelt. (c) The speaker gives a sophisticated judgment on a woman's appeal. By contrast, "On My First Son" is a sincere expression of grief, and "Song: To Celia" is a true expression of infatuation.

9. Jonson might use his epigrammatic style in speech writing, advertising, or song writing.

501

Vocabulary Acquisition and Use

Multiple-Meaning Words

1. priest
2. perceive, discover
3. reward

Students should create two sentences accurately using a multiple-meaning word. They can then exchange sentences with a partner and use context to determine the meaning of each word in their partner's sentences.

Vocabulary: Synonyms

1. lament
2. divine
3. wreath
4. sound
5. fate
6. presume

Writing

You may use this Writing Lesson as timed-writing practice, or you may allow students to develop the essay as a writing assignment over several days.

1. To guide students in writing this argumentative text, give them the Support for Writing Lesson page (*Unit 3 Resources,* p. 34).

2. Tell students a critical response is a piece of nonfiction writing that presents a reaction to, or an analysis of, a literary work.

3. You may wish to use the Response to Literature rubrics in the *Professional Development Guidebook,* pages 250–251, to evaluate students' critical responses.

Vocabulary Acquisition and Use

Multiple-Meaning Words

Many English words have more than one meaning, such as *sound*, which Jonson uses in "Still to Be Neat." From the context of the lines, you know that the word means "healthy" rather than "noise." Use context clues to determine the meanings of the italicized words in these sentences.

1. After the choir sang, the *divine* delivered his sermon.
2. The agent struggled to *divine* the secret of the coded message.
3. Winning the *prize* thrilled the contestant.

Next, think of another word with multiple meanings and write two sentences in which you use it in different ways. Exchange your sentences with a partner, and use context clues to determine the meanings of each other's word. If context is not sufficient to determine the meaning, use a print or an online dictionary.

Writing

Argumentative Text Some critics complain that Jonson's poetic style is dull. Critic Douglas Bush defends the poet from these criticisms: " … Jonson demanded … the ageless classical virtues of clarity, unity, symmetry, and proportion. … His poems are wholes, not erratic displays of verbal fireworks." Drawing on details from the selections, write a **response** to this idea.

Prewriting Note uses of *imagery, language,* or *stylistic devices* that illustrate or contradict each "classical virtue" that Bush cites. Determine whether your examples support or refute Bush's claim and decide whether you agree or disagree with his view.

Drafting Write a draft of your response that begins by summarizing Bush's point and stating your position. As you write, support your generalizations with *accurate and detailed references* to Jonson's writing.

Revising Review your draft, highlighting generalizations and looking for supporting details for each. Make sure that all quotations are accurate and properly referenced.

Vocabulary: Synonyms

A **synonym** is a word that has the same meaning as another word. Replace each italicized word below with a synonym from the vocabulary list on page 494. Use each vocabulary word only once.

1. "I always *regret* my mistakes of the past," said the sad man.
2. The sunlight streaming into the cathedral produced a feeling of the *sacred*.
3. The *garland* of leaves, colored red and green, brightened the door.
4. The carpenter thought the wood was *strong* and good for building.
5. He felt that an evil *doom* awaited him.
6. The judge told the jury to *suppose* that the accused was innocent.

For instance, the lines "But might I of Jove's nectar sup / I would not change for thine" unify the images of drinking. The reference to Jove, though, is artificial.

Model: Adding Support
Jonson may achieve unity, but in some cases it is at the expense of spontaneous feeling. What is the virtue of formal unity if the poem seems lifeless?

Added details from the poem strengthen support for the generalization.

502 A Turbulent Time (1625–1798)

Assessment Resources

Unit 3 Resources

L1 L2 EL **Selection Test A,** pp. 39–41. Administer Test A to less advanced readers.

L3 L4 EL **Selection Test B,** pp. 42–44. Administer Test B to on-level and more advanced students.

L3 L4 **Open-Book Test,** pp. 36–38. As an alternative, administer the Open-Book Test.

All **Customizable Test Bank**

All **Self-tests** Students may prepare for the **Selection Test** by taking the **Self-test** online.

All assessment resources are available at **www.PHLitOnline.com.**

Conventions and Style: Participles, Gerunds, and Infinitives

One way to make your writing smoother is to combine short sentences using participles, gerunds, and infinitives. A **participle** is a verb form, usually ending in *-ing* or *-ed*, that can be used as an adjective. A **gerund** is a verb form ending in *-ing* that acts as a noun. An **infinitive** is a verb form that appears with the word *to* and acts as a noun, an adjective, or an adverb. You can add modifiers and complements to these verb forms to make **phrases,** or groups of words without a subject or a verb.

Combining with Participial, Gerund, and Infinitive Phrases

Choppy	Better
Ben Jonson was adopted in infancy. Ben Jonson grew up poor.	*Adopted in infancy*, Ben Jonson grew up poor. (participial phrase modifying *Ben Jonson*)
He joined the army. He chose a course.	*Joining the army* was the course he chose. (gerund phrase as the subject)
Jonson could not attend a university. Jonson was not wealthy enough.	Jonson was not wealthy enough *to attend a university*. (infinitive phrase acting as an adverb modifying the adverb *enough*)

Practice In items 1–5, identify the italicized phrase as a participial, gerund, or infinitive phrase. In items 6–10, use the type of phrase indicated in parentheses to combine the two sentences into one, more involved sentence.

1. Her hair, *flowing freely*, was beautiful.
2. *Using a lot of makeup* can hide facial flaws.
3. His goal was *to give clear, brief expression to his ideas*.
4. Jonson, *regarded as a great judge of literature*, guided the trends of his time.
5. The speaker says he hopes *to avoid ever loving anyone so deeply again*.
6. He lost his son. It was a painful experience. (gerund)
7. Jonson returned to England. Jonson became an actor. (participial)
8. The speaker longs for one thing. The speaker would like to forget his identity as a father. (infinitive)
9. Jonson was influenced by the poetry of the ancient Greeks. Jonson liked to write poems with a social function. (participial)
10. Jonson employed satire, a type of humor. Jonson poked fun at contemporary character types. (infinitive)

Writing and Speaking Conventions

A. Writing Use each phrase in a sentence and tell what type of phrase it is.
1. writing with a direct style
2. to dress simply
3. saying goodbye to a child

   Example: writing with a direct style
   Sentence: Writing with a direct style, Jonson became popular.
   Type of Phrase: participial phrase

B. Speaking Respond to the ideas in "Still to Be Neat" as though you are a woman living in Ben Jonson's time. Use at least one participial phrase, one gerund phrase, and one infinitive phrase.

PH WRITING COACH
Further instruction and practice are available in *Prentice Hall Writing Coach*.

Conventions and Style

Introduce and discuss the skill using the instruction on the student page.

Think Aloud: Model the Skill

Say to students:

I know that one way to make my writing smoother is to combine sentences. I can do this by changing the verb form in one of the sentences to make it a gerund, participle, or infinitive.

PH WRITING COACH Grade 12

Students will find instruction on and practice with participles, gerunds, and infinitives in Chapter 13, section 2.

Practice
1. participle
2. gerund
3. infinitive
4. participle
5. infinitive

Sample responses for items 6–10:
6. Losing his son was a painful experience.
7. Jonson returned to England, becoming an actor.
8. The speaker longs for one thing, to forget his identity as a father.
9. Jonson, influenced by the poetry of the ancient Greeks, liked to write poems with a social function.
10. To poke fun at contemporary character types, Jonson employed satire, a type of humor.

Writing and Speaking Conventions

Sample responses:
1. Writing with a direct style, the author was able to expand her audience. (participial phrase)
2. His choice was to dress simply. (infinitive phrase)
3. Saying goodbye to a child is a painful process. (gerund)
B. Answers will vary. Be sure that students use all three forms.

Extend the Lesson

Sentence Modeling
Choose the line given from the selections that students have read:

"Robes loosely flowing…" ("Still to Be Neat")

"…a rosy wreath not so much honoring thee…" ("Song: To Celia")

Ask students what they notice about the first line. Elicit from them that "loosely flowing" modifies "robes." So, "loosely flowing" is a participial phrase. Ask students what they notice about the second line. They should respond that "…not…honoring thee…" is a participial phrase modifying "wreath."

Have students imitate the sentence in a sentence on a topic of their own choosing, matching each grammatical and stylistic feature discussed. Collect the sentences and share them with the class.

To His Coy Mistress • To the Virgins, to Make Much of Time • Song
Lesson Pacing Guide

DAY 1 Preteach

- ⓒ Administer the Reading and Vocabulary Warm-ups (*Unit 3 Resources*, pp. 45–48) as necessary.
- ⓒ Introduce the Literary Analysis concept: *Carpe Diem* Theme.
- • Introduce the Reading Strategy: Analyze Similar Themes.
- ⓒ Build background with the author and Background features.
- • Develop thematic thinking with Connecting to the Essential Question.
- ⓒ Teach the selection vocabulary.

DAY 2 Preteach/Teach/Extend

- • Distribute copies of the appropriate graphic organizer for the Reading Strategy (*Graphic Organizer Transparencies*, pp. 83–84).
- • Distribute copies of the appropriate graphic organizer for Literary Analysis (*Graphic Organizer Transparencies*, pp. 85–86).
- • Prepare students to read with the Activating Prior Knowledge activities (TE).
- • Informally monitor comprehension while students read.
- • Use the Reading Check question to confirm comprehension.
- ⓒ Develop students' understanding of the *carpe diem* theme using the Literary Analysis prompts.
- • Develop students' ability to analyze similar themes by using the Reading Strategy prompts.
- ⓒ Reinforce vocabulary with the Vocabulary notes.
- • Assess students' comprehension and mastery of the skills by having them answer the Critical Reading, Literary Analysis, and Reading Strategy questions.

DAY 3 Assess

- • Have students complete the Vocabulary Lesson.
- ⓒ Have students complete the Writing activity and write a public service announcement. (You may assign as homework.)
- • Administer Selection Test A or B (*Unit 3 Resources*, pp. 57–59 or 60–62).

ⓒ Common Core State Standards

Reading Literature 2. Determine two or more themes or central ideas of a text and analyze their development over the course of the text, including how they interact and build on one another to produce a complex account.

Writing 1. Write arguments to support claims in an analysis of substantive topics or texts, using valid reasoning and relevant and sufficient evidence.

Additional Standards Practice
***Common Core Companion,** pp. 15–22; 185–195*

Daily Block Scheduling
Each day in this Lesson Pacing Guide represents a 40–50 minute period. Teachers using block scheduling may combine days to revise pacing. In addition, teachers may differentiate and support core instruction by integrating components for extended and intensive support as students require. See the Guide to Selected Leveled Resources (facing page).

Guide to Selected Leveled Resources

R T I Tier 1 (students performing on level)

To His Coy Mistress • To the Virgins, to Make Much of Time • Song

Warm Up	**Practice, model,** and **monitor** fluency, working **with the whole class** or **in groups**.	Vocabulary and Reading Warm-ups B, *Unit 3 Resources,* pp. 45–46, 48
Comprehension/Skills	**Support** and **monitor** comprehension and skills development, having students complete the activities, graphic organizers, and interactive prompts **independently** or **as a class**.	• *Reader's Notebook,* adapted instruction and full selection • **EL** *Reader's Notebook: English Learner's Version,* adapted instruction and adapted selection • **Reading Skill Graphic Organizer B,** *Graphic Organizer Transparencies,* p. 88 • **Literary Analysis Graphic Organizer B,** *Graphic Organizer Transparencies,* p. 90
Monitor Progress A	**Monitor** student progress with the differentiated curriculum-based assessment in the *Unit Resources.*	• **Selection Test B,** *Unit 3 Resources,* pp. 60–62 • **Open-Book Test,** *Unit 3 Resources,* pp. 54–56

R T I Tier 2 (students requiring intervention)

To His Coy Mistress • To the Virgins, to Make Much of Time • Song

Warm Up	**Practice, model,** and **monitor** fluency **in groups** or **with individuals**.	• Vocabulary and Reading Warm-ups A, *Unit 3 Resources,* pp. 45–47 • *Hear It!* Audio CD (adapted text)
Comprehension/Skills	• **Support** and **monitor** comprehension and skills development, working **in small groups** or **with individuals**. • As students complete the selection in the appropriate version of the *Reader's Notebook,* **monitor** comprehension frequently with group questions and individual instruction. • **Model** strategies while guiding students in completing the activities and prompts in the *Reader's Notebook,* as well as the graphic organizers. • **Practice** skills and **monitor** mastery with the *Reading Kit* worksheets.	• *Reader's Notebook: Adapted Version,* adapted instruction and adapted selection • **EL** *Reader's Notebook: English Learner's Version,* adapted instruction and adapted selection • **Reading Skill Graphic Organizer A,** *Graphic Organizer Transparencies,* p. 87 • **Literary Analysis Graphic Organizer A,** *Graphic Organizer Transparencies,* p. 89 • *Reading Kit,* Practice worksheets
Monitor Progress A	**Monitor** student progress with the differentiated curriculum-based assessment in the *Unit Resources* and in the *Reading Kit.*	• **Selection Test A,** *Unit 3 Resources,* pp. 57–59 • *Reading Kit,* Assess worksheets

TIER 3 Tier 3 intervention may require consultation with the student's special-education or dyslexia specialist. For additional support, see the Tier 2 activities and resources listed above.

One-on-one teaching   Group work   Whole class instruction   Independent work   A Assessment

For a complete guide to selection support, including support for Advanced students, see the Overview of Resources in the frontmatter.

To His Coy Mistress • To the Virgins, to Make Much of Time • Song

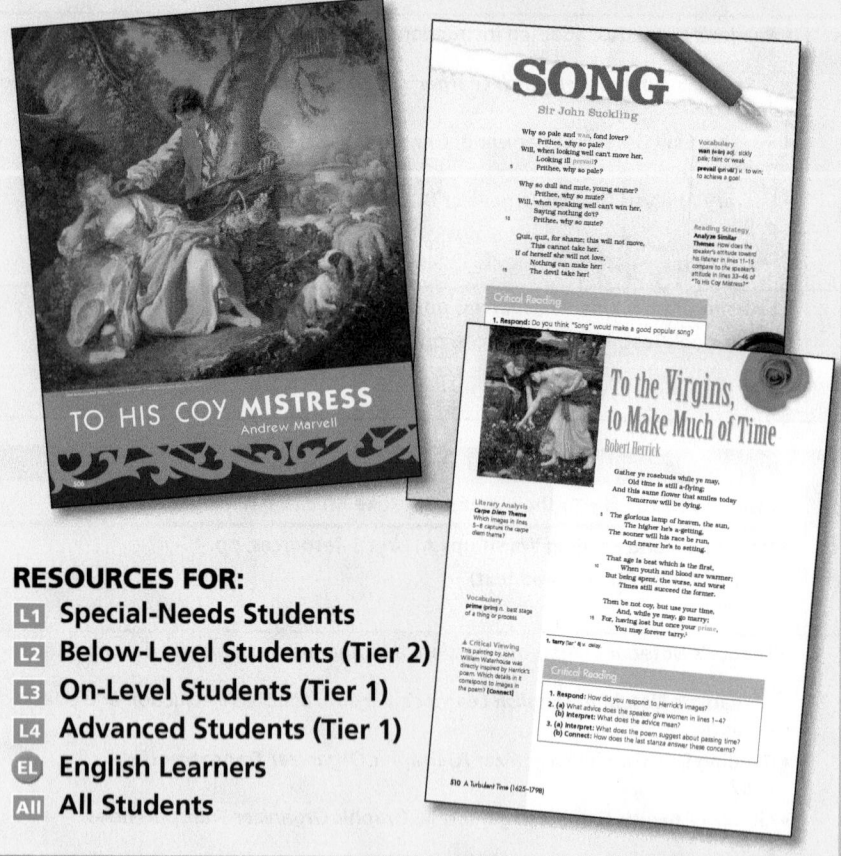

RESOURCES FOR:

- **L1** Special-Needs Students
- **L2** Below-Level Students (Tier 2)
- **L3** On-Level Students (Tier 1)
- **L4** Advanced Students (Tier 1)
- **EL** English Learners
- **All** All Students

Vocabulary/Fluency/Prior Knowledge

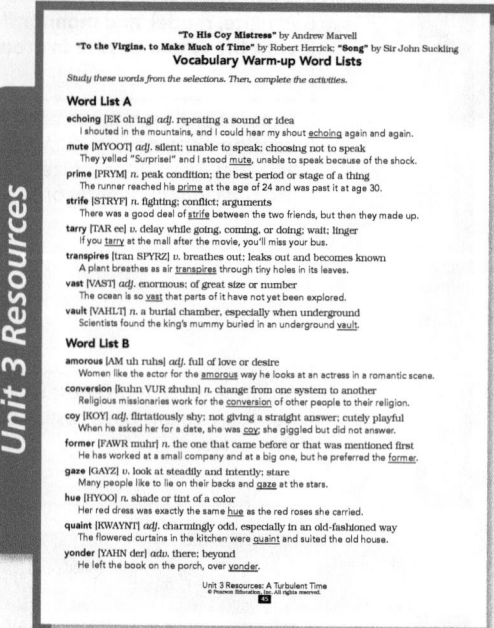

EL L1 L2 Vocabulary Warm-ups A and B, pp. 45–46

Also available for these selections:

EL L1 L2 Reading Warm-ups A and B, pp. 47–48

All Vocabulary Builder, p. 51

Reader's Notebooks

Pre- and postreading pages for these selections appear in an interactive format in the *Reader's Notebooks*. Each *Notebook* is differentiated for a different group of learners. The selections in the Adapted and English Learner's versions are abridged.

- **L2 L3** *Reader's Notebook*
- **L1** *Reader's Notebook: Adapted Version*
- **EL** *Reader's Notebook: English Learner's Version*
- **EL** *Reader's Notebook: Spanish Version*

© Common Core Companion

Additional instruction and practice for each Common Core State Standard

Selection Support

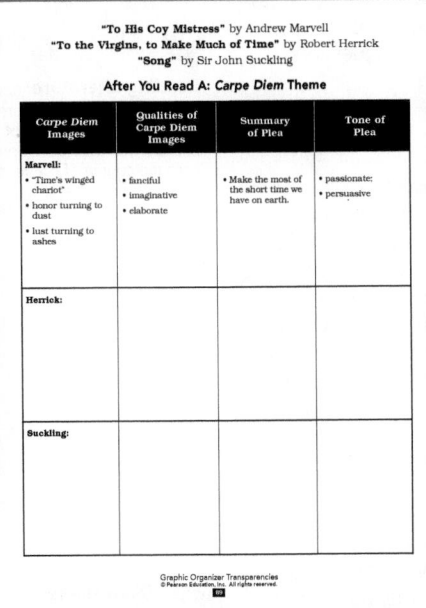

"To His Coy Mistress" by Andrew Marvell
"To the Virgins, to Make Much of Time" by Robert Herrick
"Song" by Sir John Suckling

After You Read A: *Carpe Diem* Theme

Carpe Diem Images	Qualities of Carpe Diem Images	Summary of Plea	Tone of Plea
Marvell: • "Time's winged chariot" • honor turning to dust • lust turning to ashes	• fanciful • imaginative • elaborate	• Make the most of the short time we have on earth.	• passionate; • persuasive
Herrick:			
Suckling:			

EL L1 L2 Literary Analysis: Graphic Organizer A (partially filled in), p. 85

Also available for these selections:

EL L1 L2 Reading: Graphic Organizer A (partially filled in), p. 83

EL L3 Reading: Graphic Organizer B, p. 84

EL L3 Literary Analysis: Graphic Organizer B, p. 86

Skills Development/Extension

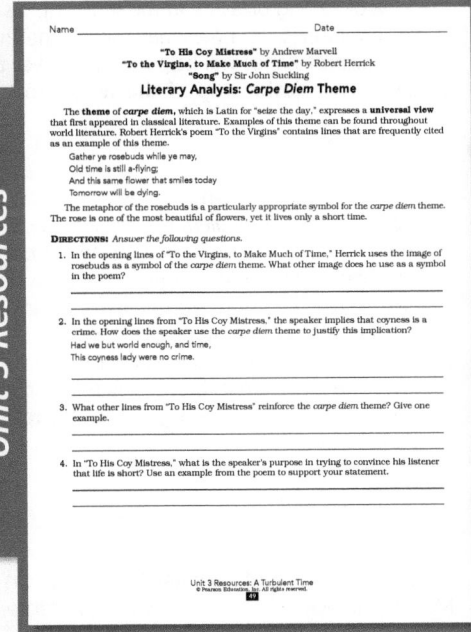

Name _____ Date _____

"To His Coy Mistress" by Andrew Marvell
"To the Virgins, to Make Much of Time" by Robert Herrick
"Song" by Sir John Suckling

Literary Analysis: *Carpe Diem* Theme

The **theme** of *carpe diem*, which is Latin for "seize the day," expresses a **universal view** that first appeared in classical literature. Examples of this theme can be found throughout world literature. Robert Herrick's poem "To the Virgins" contains lines that are frequently cited as an example of this theme.

Gather ye rosebuds while ye may,
Old time is still a-flying;
And this same flower that smiles today
Tomorrow will be dying.

The metaphor of the rosebuds is a particularly appropriate symbol for the *carpe diem* theme. The rose is one of the most beautiful of flowers, yet it lives only a short time.

DIRECTIONS: *Answer the following questions.*

1. In the opening lines of "To the Virgins, to Make Much of Time," Herrick uses the image of rosebuds as a symbol of the *carpe diem* theme. What other image does he use as a symbol in the poem?

2. In the opening lines from "To His Coy Mistress," the speaker implies that coyness is a crime. How does the speaker use the *carpe diem* theme to justify this implication?

Had we but world enough, and time,
This coyness lady were no crime.

3. What other lines from "To His Coy Mistress" reinforce the *carpe diem* theme? Give one example.

4. In "To His Coy Mistress," what is the speaker's purpose in trying to convince his listener that life is short? Use an example from the poem to support your statement.

All Literary Analysis, p. 49

Also available for these selections:

All Reading, p. 50

EL L3 L4 Support for Writing, p. 52

L4 Enrichment, p. 53

Assessment

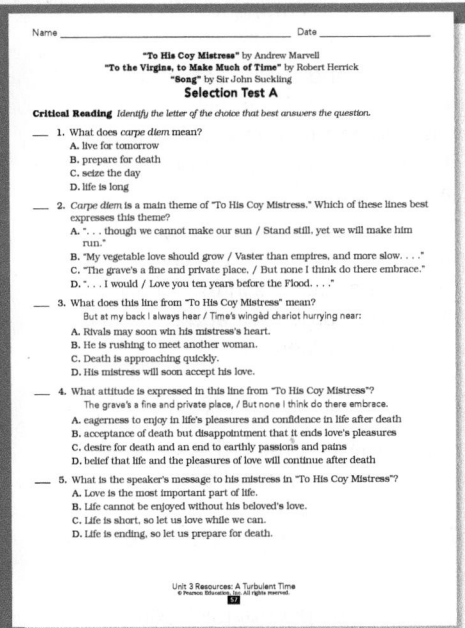

Name _____ Date _____

"To His Coy Mistress" by Andrew Marvell
"To the Virgins, to Make Much of Time" by Robert Herrick
"Song" by Sir John Suckling

Selection Test A

Critical Reading *Identify the letter of the choice that best answers the question.*

___ 1. What does *carpe diem* mean?
A. live for tomorrow
B. prepare for death
C. seize the day
D. life is long

___ 2. *Carpe diem* is a main theme of "To His Coy Mistress." Which of these lines best expresses this theme?
A. ". . . though we cannot make our sun / Stand still, yet we will make him run."
B. "My vegetable love should grow / Vaster than empires, and more slow. . . ."
C. "The grave's a fine and private place. / But none I think do there embrace."
D. ". . . I would / Love you ten years before the Flood. . . ."

___ 3. What does this line from "To His Coy Mistress" mean?
But at my back I always hear / Time's wingèd chariot hurrying near:
A. Rivals may soon win his mistress's heart.
B. He is rushing to meet another woman.
C. Death is approaching quickly.
D. His mistress will soon accept his love.

___ 4. What attitude is expressed in this line from "To His Coy Mistress"?
The grave's a fine and private place, / But none I think do there embrace.
A. eagerness to enjoy in life's pleasures and confidence in life after death
B. acceptance of death but disappointment that it ends love's pleasures
C. desire for death and an end to earthly passions and pains
D. belief that life and the pleasures of love will continue after death

___ 5. What is the speaker's message to his mistress in "To His Coy Mistress"?
A. Love is the most important part of life.
B. Life cannot be enjoyed without his beloved's love.
C. Life is short, so let us love while we can.
D. Life is ending, so let us prepare for death.

EL L1 L2 Selection Test A, pp. 57–59

Also available for these selections:

L3 L4 Open-Book Test, pp. 54–56

EL L3 L4 Selection Test B, pp. 60–62

PHLit Online!
www.PHLitOnline.com

Online Resources: All print materials are also available online.

- complete narrated selection text
- a thematically related video with writing prompt
- an interactive graphic organizer
- highlighting feature
- access to all student print resources, adapted to individual student needs
- Spanish and English summaries
- adapted selection translations in Spanish

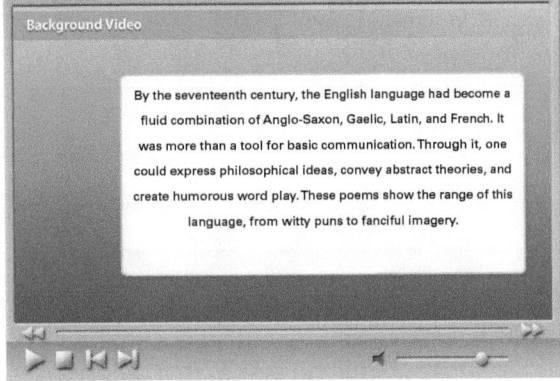

Background Video

By the seventeenth century, the English language had become a fluid combination of Anglo-Saxon, Gaelic, Latin, and French. It was more than a tool for basic communication. Through it, one could express philosophical ideas, convey abstract theories, and create humorous word play. These poems show the range of this language, from witty puns to fanciful imagery.

Background Video

Also available:

Get Connected! (thematic video with writing prompt)
All videos are available in Spanish.

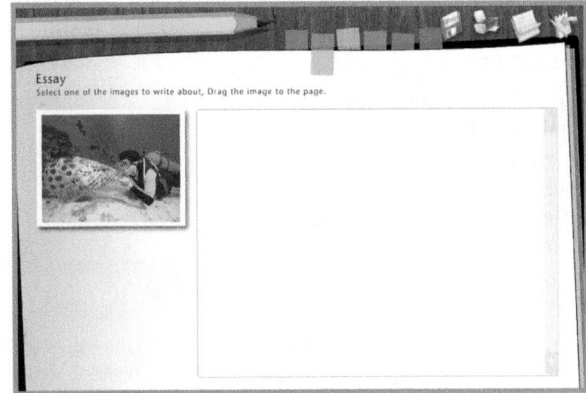

Essay
Select one of the images to write about. Drag the image to the page.

Writer's Journal (with graphics feature)

Also available:

Vocabulary Central (tools and activities for studying vocabulary)

Graphic Organizer Transparencies *(side tab)*

Unit 3 Resources *(side tab)*

❶ ❓ **Connecting to the Essential Question**

1. Review the assignment with the class.

2. Have students brainstorm about occasions when one might take pleasure in the moment. Then have students complete the assignment.

3. As students read, have them look for specific examples of ways in which the speakers in the following poems urge their audience to seize the moment.

❷ Literary Analysis

Introduce the skill, using the instruction on the student page.

Think Aloud: Model the Skill

Say to students:

As I read these poems, I will notice a theme that connects all three: *carpe diem.* I remember that *carpe diem* means "seize the day." It expresses the idea that because time is fleeting, one should act decisively to make the most of life.

❸ Reading Strategy

1. Introduce the skill using the instruction on the student page.

2. Give students a copy of **Reading Strategy Graphic Organizer B,** page 84 in *Graphic Organizer Transparencies,* to fill out as they read.

Think Aloud: Model the Skill

Say to students:

The poems all express the *carpe diem* theme. I should note that each writer deals with the theme in different ways, though. I will look for these differences as I read the upcoming selections.

❹ Vocabulary

1. Pronounce each word, giving its definition, and have students say it aloud.

2. For more guidance, see the *Classroom Strategies and Teaching Routines* card for introducing vocabulary.

Before You Read

To His Coy Mistress •
*To the Virgins, to Make
Much of Time* • *Song*

❶ **Connecting to the Essential Question** These poets all promote the idea of seizing pleasure in the moment. As you read, notice passages in which a poet gives a personal twist to the theme *Seize pleasure now.* Finding such passages will help as you answer the Essential Question: **What is the relationship of the writer to tradition?**

**© Common Core
State Standards**

Reading Literature
2. Determine two or more themes or central ideas of a text and analyze their development over the course of the text, including how they interact and build on one another to produce a complex account.

❷ Literary Analysis

Each poem in this grouping expresses a version of the ***carpe diem* theme** (kär′ pē dē′ em). *Carpe diem* is Latin for "seize the day." The theme might be summed up as: "Time is fleeting, so act decisively to enjoy yourself."

This theme has a classical origin, with the Roman poet Horace being the first to use the phrase *carpe diem.* It was also popular in love poems of the 16th and 17th century, like the ones in this grouping. In such lyrics, a male speaker usually tries to convince a female to grasp the opportunity for love. The *carpe diem* theme may build upon other themes in a poem, such as the fleeting nature of youth or the relationship between human-kind and nature.

❸ Reading Strategy

© Preparing to Read Complex Texts In reading, it is helpful to **analyze and evaluate similar themes** across a variety of selections. Marvell, Herrick, and Suckling all use the *carpe diem* theme, but they do so in different ways:

- Marvell approaches the theme with a mix of whimsical fancy and passionate urgency.

- Herrick delivers a more traditional version of the theme, using familiar imagery to depict the passing seasons.

- Suckling gives the theme a new twist. The speaker in his poem advises a friend to abandon, rather than pursue, a problematic lover.

As you read, use a chart like the one shown to continue analyzing and evaluating how each of these poets expresses this classic theme.

Carpe Diem Theme

Marvell

Herrick

Suckling

❹ Vocabulary

coyness (koi′ nis) *n.* shyness; aloofness, often as part of a flirtation (p. 507)

amorous (am′ ə res) *adj.* full of love or desire (p. 508)

languish (laŋ′ gwish) *v.* become weak; droop (p. 508)

prime (prīm) *n.* best stage of a thing or process (p. 510)

wan (wän) *adj.* sickly pale; faint or weak (p. 513)

prevail (pri vāl′) *v.* win; achieve a goal (p. 513)

**PHLit
Online!**
www.PHLitOnline.com

504 A Turbulent Time (1625–1798)

Vocabulary Development

Vocabulary Knowledge Rating
Create a **Vocabulary Knowledge Rating Chart** (*Professional Development Guidebook,* p. 33) for the vocabulary words on the student page. Give each student a copy of the chart with the words on it. Read the words aloud, and have students mark their rating of each in the Before Reading column. When students have completed reading and discussing the selections, have them take out their **Vocabulary Knowledge Rating Charts** for the story. Read the words aloud and have students rate their knowledge again in the After Reading column. Clarify any words that are still problematic. Then, have students complete the Vocabulary practice at the end of the selections.

**PHLit
Online!** **Vocabulary Central,** featuring tools and activities for studying vocabulary, is available online at **www.PHLitOnline.com.**

ANDREW MARVELL

MARVELL
(1621–1678)

Author of "To His Coy Mistress"

Marvell showed an extraordinary adaptability in a turbulent time. Although he was the son of a Puritan minister and frowned on the abuses of the monarchy, he enjoyed close friendships with supporters of Charles I in the king's dispute with Parliament. He also opposed the government of Oliver Cromwell, leader of the Puritan rebellion and then ruler of England.

Beginning in 1651, however, Marvell worked for Lord Fairfax, the commanding general of the Parliamentary army. Still later, he tutored Cromwell's ward. Marvell gained the sponsorship of the Puritan and great English poet John Milton, whose assistant he became.

Marvell wrote masterful poetry in various veins—some works share the metaphysical qualities of Donne's verse, while others have the classical qualities recommended by Jonson. Although he was thought of chiefly as a satirist until the nineteenth century, much of his work has become classic.

> "We would sit down, and think which way
> To walk, and pass **our long love's day.**"

To His Coy Mistress **505**

 Daily Bellringer

For each class during which you will teach these selections, have students complete one of the five activities for the appropriate week in the *Daily Bellringer Activities* booklet.

Multidraft Reading

To assist struggling readers and to enhance reading for all, apply multidraft reading protocols. For each reading, have students set the purpose indicated:

- **First reading**—identifying key ideas and details and answering any Reading Checks.
- **Second reading**—analyzing craft and structure and responding to the side-column prompts.
- **Third reading**—integrating knowledge and ideas, connecting to other texts and the world, and answering the end-of-selection questions.

For more guidance, refer to the *Classroom Strategies and Teaching Routines* card on Multidraft Reading.

---

⑤ Background
More About the Author

As well as being a gifted satirist and poet, Marvell was also a skilled politician. He and his contemporaries lived during turbulent political times. Marvell was able to keep his balance as England whipsawed from monarchy to commonwealth and back to monarchy. He was elected to Parliament in 1659, a position he held until his death. When the monarchy was restored in 1660, Marvell was able to intercede on behalf of John Milton, saving his former mentor from imprisonment—or worse.

PHLit Online!
www.PHLitOnline.com

Teaching From Technology

Preparing to Read
Go to **www.PHLitOnline.com** and display the **Get Connected!** slide show for these selections. Have the class brainstorm responses to the writing prompt, entering ideas in the interactive journal. Then, have students complete their written responses individually, in a lab or as homework.
To build background, display the **Background** and **More About the Author** features.

Using the Interactive Text
Go to **www.PHLitOnline.com** and display the **Enriched Online Student Edition.** As the class reads the selection or listens to the narration, record answers to side-column prompts using the graphic organizers accessible on the interactive page. Alternatively, have students use the online edition individually, answering the prompts as they read.

❶ About the Selection

Marvell's work has been called "the most major minor verse in English," and this poem shows why so many readers enjoy Marvell. Rich in sensory images and flattery, "To His Coy Mistress" is designed to appeal to feelings as well as to the intellect. Its exaggerated emotion and persuasive tone are humorous to readers who recognize the speaker's goal.

❷ Activating Prior Knowledge

Ask students which statement below best reflects modern attitudes:

Life is short. Do it now.

Look before you leap.

Briefly discuss factors that might be behind the two pieces of advice.

Concept Connector ➡

Tell students they will return to their responses after reading the selections.

❸ Humanities

The Interrupted Sleep, by François Boucher

The legacy of François Boucher (1703–1770) includes some of the finest examples of rococo art. Boucher's style includes excellent brushwork and an eye for drama and decoration. Use this question for discussion:

Is the girl in the painting asleep, or is she being "coy"?

Possible response: Though her eyes are closed, the girl does not look relaxed enough to be asleep. She seems to be aware of what the youth is doing.

The Interrupted Sleep, François Boucher, The Metropolitan Museum of Art

❶ ❷ TO HIS COY MISTRESS

Andrew Marvell

506

Ⓒ Text Complexity Rubric: Leveled Texts

	To His Coy Mistress	To the Virgins, to Make Much of Time	Song
Qualitative Measures			
Context/ Knowledge Demands	Seventeenth-century lyric 1 2 ③ 4 5	Seventeenth-century lyric 1 ② 3 4 5	Seventeenth-century lyric 1 ② 3 4 5
Structure/Language Conventionality and Clarity	Archaic diction and syntax; clear, logical structure 1 2 ③ 4 5	Archaic diction 1 2 ③ 4 5	Archaic diction; informal tone 1 2 ③ 4 5
Levels of Meaning/ Purpose/Concepts	Moderate (*carpe-diem* theme) 1 2 3 ④ 5	Accessible (*carpe-diem* theme) 1 2 ③ 4 5	Accessible (advice to the lovelorn) 1 ② 3 4 5
Quantitative Measures			
Lexile/Text Length	NP / 301 words	NP / 97 words	NP / 78 words
Overall Complexity	**More complex**	**More complex**	**More accessible**

By the seventeenth century, the English language had become a fluid combination of Anglo-Saxon, Gaelic, Latin, and French. It was more than a tool for basic communication. Through it, one could express philosophical ideas, convey abstract theories, and indulge in humorous wordplay. These poems show the range of this language, from witty puns to fanciful imagery.

 Had we but world enough, and time,
This coyness lady were no crime.
We would sit down, and think which way
To walk, and pass our long love's day.
5   Thou by the Indian Ganges' side
Should'st rubies find; I by the tide
Of Humber[1] would complain. I would
Love you ten years before the Flood,
And you should if you please refuse
 10   Till the conversion of the Jews.[2]
My vegetable love should grow
Vaster than empires, and more slow;
An hundred years should go to praise
Thine eyes, and on thy forehead gaze;
15   Two hundred to adore each breast,
But thirty thousand to the rest;
An age at least to every part,
And the last age should show your heart.
For, lady, you deserve this state,[3]
20   Nor would I love at lower rate.
   But at my back I always hear
Time's wingèd chariot hurrying near:
And yonder all before us lie
Deserts of vast eternity.
25   Thy beauty shall no more be found,
Nor, in thy marble vault, shall sound

Vocabulary
coyness (koi′ nis) *n.*
shyness; aloofness, often as part of a flirtation

Spiral Review
Conceits
How does the conceit in lines 1–20 help set a humorous tone?

Reading Check
What is the lady's crime?

---

1. **Humber** river flowing through Hull, Marvell's home town.
2. **conversion of the Jews** according to Christian tradition, the Jews were to be converted immediately before the Last Judgment.
3. **state** dignity.

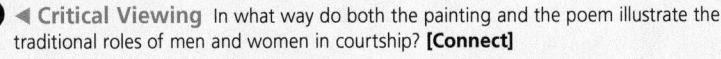 ◄ **Critical Viewing** In what way do both the painting and the poem illustrate the traditional roles of men and women in courtship? **[Connect]**

④ Literary Analysis
Carpe Diem Theme

1. Remind students that *carpe diem*—Latin for "seize the day"—permeates world literature and has come to mean "time is fleeting, so enjoy life."

2. Read aloud the first two lines. Then **ask:** How do these lines express the theme of *carpe diem?* **Answer:** The speaker urges the lady to enjoy love now, while they are still in their youthful prime.

⑤ Reading Strategy
Analyze Similar Themes

1. Have students read the poem.

2. Then, **ask** what the speaker's feelings for the woman are. **Possible response:** Students may say that the fierce images suggest both passion and playfulness.

Spiral Review

Conceits

1. Remind students that they have studied conceits.

2. **Ask** students the Spiral Review question.

   Possible response: The conceit sets a humorous tone because the speaker contends he will spend a preposterous amount of time wooing the lady.

⑥ Reading Check
Answer: From the point of view of the speaker, her crime consists of forestalling his amorous advances.

⑦ Critical Viewing
Answer: Students might comment that both the painting and the poem show men in active pursuit and women being demure in their responses.

Text Complexity: Reader and Task Suggestions

Preparing to Read the Texts	To His Coy Mistress	To the Virgins, to Make Much of Time	Song
	Leveled Tasks	**Leveled Tasks**	**Leveled Tasks**
• Using the information at the bottom of TE p. 508, discuss with students the *carpe-diem* theme. • Discuss with students their own sense of time: Is time "flying" or "crawling"? • Guide students to use Multidraft Reading strategies (TE p. 505).	*Levels of Meaning* If students will have difficulty with the levels of meaning, have them focus first on the argument to the coy mistress. As they reread, have them consider what the argument says about life in general. *Analyzing* If students will not have difficulty with the levels of meaning, have them discuss the poem's attitude toward time.	*Levels of Meaning* If students will have difficulty with meaning, have them focus on words that give advice. Then have them reread the poem for overall meaning. *Evaluating* If students will not have difficulty with meaning, have them compare the poem to Marvell's. Which poem is more persuasive?	*Language/Structure* If students will have difficulty with the poem's language, have them restate it in contemporary English. Then, have them consider the speaker's attitude toward love. *Analyzing* If students will not have difficulty with the poem's language, have them discuss how this poem expresses the *carpe-diem* theme.

Carpe Diem Theme

1. Call students' attention to the last six lines of the poem. Ask them to rephrase them in their own words.

2. Then, **ask** them the Literary Analysis question: What new twist does the speaker apply in order to "solve" the problem of fleeting time? **Answer:** Since the sun (time) cannot be stopped, the speaker proposes to tear through life at such a pace as to force the sun to keep up.

ASSESS

Answers

Before students respond, you may wish to have them write a brief objective summary of the selection. As they answer the questions below, remind them to support their answers with evidence from the text.

1. (a) **Possible response:** The speaker would love his mistress ten years before the flood; his mistress should, if she pleased, refuse until the conversion of the Jews; the speaker would praise his mistress's eyes and gaze at her forehead for a hundred years. (b) These things go very slowly, an appropriate pace if only there were "world enough, and time."

2. (a) Students may infer that the speaker feels his mistress is worth the wait. (b) This willingness shows the sincerity of his feelings for his mistress.

3. (a) The speaker foresees death and an end to loving. (b) The images in the first part of the poem disintegrate.

4. **Possible response:** The speaker saves his proposition for last, after his other arguments have had a chance to persuade his mistress to take his proposal seriously.

5. (a) In the beginning, the lovers have an eternity. In the middle, time is presented as being limited. In the end, the speaker proposes to outrace time itself. (b) Students may respond that Marvell's awareness of fleeting time and human mortality is realistic; his hope that love might make the sun "run" may seem idealistic.

508

My echoing songs; then worms shall try
That long-preserved virginity,
And your quaint honor turn to dust,
30 And into ashes all my lust:
The grave's a fine and private place,
But none I think do there embrace.
  Now therefore, while the youthful hue
Sits on thy skin like morning dew,
35 And while thy willing soul transpires[4]
At every pore with instant fires,
Now let us sport us while we may,
And now, like amorous birds of prey,
Rather at once our time devour
40 Than languish in his slow-chapped[5] power.
Let us roll all our strength, and all
Our sweetness, up into one ball,
❽ And tear our pleasures with rough strife
Thorough[6] the iron gates of life:
45 Thus, though we cannot make our sun
Stand still, yet we will make him run.

Vocabulary
amorous (amʹ ə res) *adj.* full of love or desire

languish (lanʹ gwish) *v.* become weak; droop

Literary Analysis
***Carpe Diem* Theme**
What new twist does the speaker apply in order to "solve" the problem of fleeting time?

---

4. **transpires** breathes out.
5. **slow-chapped** slow-jawed.
6. **Thorough** through.

Critical Reading

Cite textual evidence to support your responses.

1. Key Ideas and Details (a) Name three things the speaker and his mistress would do and the time each would take if time were not an issue. **(b) Connect:** How do these images relate to the charge the speaker makes against his lady in lines 1–2?

2. Key Ideas and Details (a) Infer: Why would the speaker be willing to spend so much time waiting for his mistress? **(b) Interpret:** How does this willingness take the sting out of his complaint?

3. Craft and Structure (a) Analyze: What future does the speaker foresee for himself and his love in lines 25–30? **(b) Connect:** How do the images in lines 21–30 answer the images in the first part of the poem?

4. Craft and Structure Why does the speaker save the urgent requests in lines 33–46 for the end?

5. Integration of Knowledge and Ideas (a) Compare and Contrast: Compare the attitudes toward time at the beginning, middle, and end. **(b) Evaluate:** Is Marvell's idea of love realistic or idealistic? Explain.

508 A Turbulent Time (1625–1798)

Enrichment: Analyzing Theme

The *Carpe Diem* Theme

The *carpe diem* theme is not confined to seventeenth-century England. It can be found among the writings of different cultures and different times. For example, in 2400 B.C., the Egyptian Ptahhotep wrote, "The wasting of time is an abomination to the spirit."

  Activity: The *Carpe Diem* Theme Have students complete the **Enrichment: Analyzing**

Themes and Symbols worksheet, *Professional Development Guidebook*, page 243. First, direct students to fill out the first half of the worksheet as it pertains to "To His Coy Mistress." As the class works through the next two poems, have students complete the chart. Review the completed worksheets as a class, comparing and contrasting students' findings.

Robert Herrick

(1591–1674)

Author of "To the Virgins, to Make Much of Time"

Born into a family of London goldsmiths, Herrick went to Cambridge when he was twenty-two and graduated at the age of twenty-nine. After graduation, he served as a military chaplain. As a reward for his services, he was assigned to a parish in rural England. Here, he performed his churchly duties and wrote religious verse and musical love poems.

Although not politically active, Herrick was evicted from his parish by the Puritans and allowed back only with the Restoration of Charles II. While barred from his church, Herrick returned to his native and beloved London, where he published his poetry in *Noble Numbers* and *Hesperides* (the title comes from an ancient Greek name for a mythical garden at the edge of the world).

Published during a turbulent time and largely ignored by his contemporaries, these verses were rediscovered in the nineteenth century. Today, Herrick is included among the English poets of the seventeenth century who are still worth remembering.

Reading poems like "To the Virgins, to Make Much of Time," modern readers might suppose that Herrick was a bit of a rake or playboy. That impression seems to be further confirmed by a poem like "Upon the Loss of His Mistresses": "I have lost, and lately, these / Many dainty mistresses . . .," whom he goes on to name: Julia, Sappho, Anthea, Electra, Corinna, and Perilla.

The perhaps disappointing biographical truth is that this poet, so rakish in his verse, lived for many years rather soberly as a bachelor church official in the west of England. As one critic points out, the name of Herrick's maid was Prudence.

❾ Background
More About the Author
Robert Herrick is considered by scholars to be one of the greatest of the Cavalier poets—a group of poets who associated with Charles I and his exiled son. Herrick and the Cavalier poets produced most of their work from the late 1630s to 1660. The Cavalier poets were also called the "Sons of Ben" because they admired Ben Jonson so much. Herrick's lyrics show Jonson's influence. While largely unrecognized during his own life, Herrick's work was rediscovered in the nineteenth century.

Differentiated Instruction for Universal Access

Enrichment for Gifted/Talented Students
Have students analyze the poem "To His Coy Mistress," noting the rhythm and rhyme that is used. Then have students write a short poem that deals with the theme of *carpe diem*. As an added challenge, have them write with a set rhyme scheme of their own choosing.

Strategy for Advanced Readers
Ask students to compare and contrast "To His Coy Mistress" with "To the Virgins, to Make Much of Time." Have them cite specific examples from the poems, discussing theme, rhythm, imagery, and speakers' attitudes in a compare-and-contrast essay.

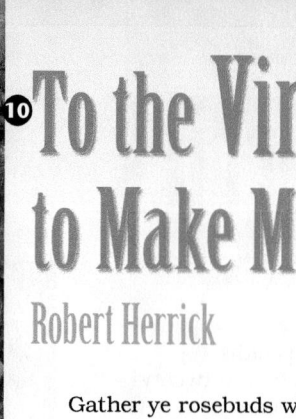

⓾ To the Virgins, to Make Much of Time

Robert Herrick

Gather ye rosebuds while ye may,
    Old time is still a-flying;
And this same flower that smiles today
    Tomorrow will be dying.

5 The glorious lamp of heaven, the sun,
    The higher he's a-getting,
The sooner will his race be run,
    And nearer he's to setting.

That age is best which is the first,
10   When youth and blood are warmer;
But being spent, the worse, and worst
    Times still succeed the former.

Then be not coy, but use your time,
    And, while ye may, go marry;
15 For, having lost but once your prime,
    You may forever tarry.[1]

---

1. **tarry** (tar´ē) *v.* delay.

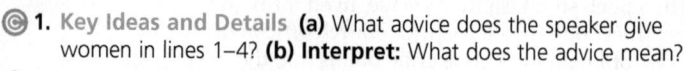
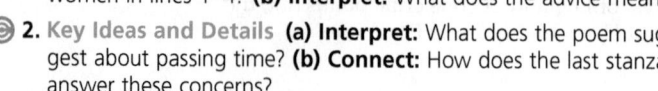
Critical Reading

©

© 1. **Key Ideas and Details** **(a)** What advice does the speaker give women in lines 1–4? **(b) Interpret:** What does the advice mean?

© 2. **Key Ideas and Details** **(a) Interpret:** What does the poem suggest about passing time? **(b) Connect:** How does the last stanza answer these concerns?

Think Aloud

Literary Analysis: *Carpe Diem* Theme

To model the process of working out the answer to the Literary Analysis question, use the following "think aloud":

In order to determine which images in lines 5–8 capture the *carpe diem* theme, I need to first identify key words in the poem. When I read the words *lamp of heaven* and *sun,* I see in my mind the sun, which determines the passing of the days. When I read *race* and *run,* I think of someone going very fast. I can put these thoughts together, and imagine that the sun rising and the sun setting is like a race being run. I can even imagine the rising sun being chased by the setting sun. This helps me understand the author's point about "seizing the day" because the sun rises and sets every day, and sometimes it seems days pass very quickly.

Sir John Suckling (1609–1642)

Author of "Song"

In some ways, Sir John Suckling lived a life more romantic than Marvell's or Herrick's. A privileged young courtier, Suckling inherited his vast estates when he was only eighteen. He later served as a gentleman in the privy chamber of Charles I. Praised as the cleverest of conversationalists, Suckling was said to be able to compose a poem at a moment's notice. He incorporated some of his best lyrics, including the poem "Song," into plays that he lavishly produced at his own expense.

Suckling's military exploits proved less successful than his poems, however. The cavalry troop he raised and lavishly uniformed for the king was defeated in Scotland, and Suckling was mocked for caring more about his men's uniforms than about their military abilities. After joining a failed Royalist plot to rescue a royal minister from prison, he fled to France, where he died in despair at the age of thirty-three. His poems, though, preserve the dash and spirit of his younger days.

Song **511**

Background

More About the Author

Sir John Suckling was another of the Cavalier poets. He also wrote four plays. However, he regarded his military and ambassadorial service as his career. Writing was a casual pastime. Suckling's other hobbies included playing games such as bowling and cards. He is acknowledged as the inventor of the game cribbage. Most of his work appeared after his death in 1642.

Differentiated Instruction for Universal Access

EL Strategy for English Learners

Students may be confused by Suckling's use of the word *Will* in lines 3 and 8 of "Song." Write the following words on three strips of poster board: *Will, /when looking well can't move her, /Looking ill prevail?* Do the same with the following lines: *Will, /when speaking well can't win her,/ Saying nothing do't?* Display each sentence. Then take out the strip that contains the middle clause. Move that strip to the beginning of the sentence to produce a standard English sentence.

Support for Less Proficient Readers

Students may have difficulty visualizing Suckling's "pale and wan" lover. Ask students how they think a young man might look if the woman he desires seems uninterested in him. Then have students draw portraits of the poem's intended audience.

511

Young Man Writing, by Joos van Craesbeeck

Flemish artist Joos van Craesbeeck probably met his future teacher—painter Adriaen Brouwer—in an Antwerp prison. Brouwer was imprisoned for tax debts around 1633, at which time Craesbeeck was working as a prison baker. Craesbeeck often painted peasants and tavern scenes but later moved on to depict the middle classes. Use the following question for discussion:

How does the young man's expression compare or contrast with the speaker's attitude in the poem?

Possible response: The young man in the painting seems serious and thoughtful, like the speaker in the beginning of the poem. The speaker later becomes sharp and impatient, which does not seem to be reflected in the young man's expression.

15 Critical Viewing

Answer: The speaker tells of a young lover who tries to move his lost love by speaking well of her and making her love him. This young lover may be writing poems to her or sketching her image.

14

15 ▼ **Critical Viewing** Consider the speaker's words in "Song." What might the young lover pictured here be writing? Explain. **[Speculate]**

512 A Turbulent Time (1625–1798)

Concept Connector

Reading Skill Graphic Organizer
Ask students to review the graphic organizers in which they have noted details that help them analyze and evaluate similar themes. Then, have students share their organizers and compare details they noted.

Activating Prior Knowledge
Have students return to their responses to the Activating Prior Knowledge activity. Ask them to explain whether their thoughts have changed and, if so, how.

Writing About the Essential Question
Have students compare their responses to the prompt, given before reading the selected poems, with their thoughts afterward. Have them work individually or in groups, writing or discussing their thoughts, in order to formulate their new responses. Then, lead a class discussion, probing for what students have learned that confirms or invalidates their initial thoughts. Encourage students to cite specific textual details to support their responses.

SONG

Sir John Suckling

Why so pale and wan, fond lover?
  Prithee, why so pale?
Will, when looking well can't move her,
  Looking ill prevail?
5 Prithee, why so pale?

Why so dull and mute, young sinner?
  Prithee, why so mute?
Will, when speaking well can't win her,
  Saying nothing do't?
10 Prithee, why so mute?

Quit, quit, for shame; this will not move,
  This cannot take her.
If of herself she will not love,
  Nothing can make her:
15 The devil take her!

Critical Reading

Cite textual evidence to support your responses.

1. **Key Ideas and Details (a)** How does the young lover look and act according to the first ten lines of "Song"? **(b) Analyze:** Explain why the speaker treats the friend's behavior as if it were an attempt to achieve a goal.

2. **Key Ideas and Details (a) Interpret:** In the final stanza, what helpful shift in perspective does the speaker encourage? **(b) Draw Conclusions:** What attitude toward love does the last stanza reflect?

3. **Key Ideas and Details (a) Analyze:** What features of the poem make it suitable as song lyrics? **(b) Hypothesize:** Which would be a good audience for such a song: uneducated farmers, young aristocrats, or both? Explain, using details from the poem.

4. **Integration of Knowledge and Ideas** Do these poets merely repeat the *carpe diem* theme, or do they give it new life? Explain. Use two of these Essential Question words in your response: *universal, contemporary, derivative. [Connecting to the Essential Question: What is the relationship of the writer to tradition?]*

Song **513**

Assessment Practice

Writer's Point of View (For more practice, see *All-in-One Workbook*.)

Many tests require students to identify the writer's point of view. Use the following sample item to show students that a writer's opinion is often revealed through diction.

  Had we but world enough, and time,
  This coyness lady were no crime…
  The grave's a fine and private place,
  But none I think do there embrace.
The speaker views his lady's hesitation as—

A ignorant but harmless
B inappropriate but excusable
C foolish but charming
D spiteful but virtuous

Marvell exaggerates when he uses the word *crime* to describe his lady's coyness, and he ironically calls the grave a "fine and private place." By keeping in mind Marvell's playful diction, students should determine that C is the best answer.

513

Answers

1. "To His Coy Mistress": *Carpe Diem* Image: Time's winged chariot; Qualities: Fanciful; Statement of Plea: Let us sport us while we may; Passionate; "To the Virgins": *Carpe Diem* Image: Old time is flying; Qualities: Simple; Statement of Plea: Gather rosebuds; Reasonable; "Song": *Carpe Diem* Image: Pale, mute lover; Qualities: Simple; Statement of Plea: Quit; Reasonable.

2. Sample answer: People have always had to accept that they will die, and this theme is one way of dealing with the universal subject of death.

3. Students may say that "To the Virgins, to Make Much of Time" is more persuasive because it is simpler and more direct in its argument.

Vocabulary Acquisition and Use

1. T; *Wan* means "pale and unhealthy-looking," which is how someone who has not eaten for days might look.

2. F; A person's *prime* is the best part of his or her life—probably not near the person's death.

3. T; To *languish* is to decline, so a plant that is not watered would probably languish.

4. T; *Prevail* means "win," and a team that scores the most goals would win.

5. F; *Coyness* is reluctance to make a commitment.

6. T; *Amorous* means "showing love and affection."

Writing

1. Go over the assignment with students. Discuss different ways in which students might apply the *carpe diem* theme to a public service announcement.

2. Have students complete the assignment. Suggest that they allot 5 minutes for prewriting, 10 minutes for drafting, and 10 minutes for revising and editing.

After You Read	To His Coy Mistress • To the Virgins, to Make Much of Time • Song

Literary Analysis

1. Craft and Structure Contrast the treatment of the ***carpe diem*** theme in the three poems using a chart like the one shown.

Carpe Diem Images	Qualities: Fanciful? Simple?	Statement of Plea	Humorous? Passionate? Reasonable?

2. Integration of Knowledge and Ideas This theme has appeared in literature over a long period of time. What do you think accounts for its popularity?

Reading Strategy

3. Analyze and evaluate similar themes by noting which of these authors presents the *carpe diem* theme most effectively. Consider such factors as word choice, imagery, interaction with other themes, and sense of drama.

PERFORMANCE TASKS
Integrated Language Skills

Vocabulary Acquisition and Use

Compare the meaning of each underlined vocabulary word with its **context,** or surrounding words, to determine whether the statement is true or false. Write T or F, and explain your answer.

1. He had not eaten for days, and his cheeks were <u>wan</u>.
2. The <u>Prime</u> of Miss Jean Brodie is probably about a woman near death.
3. If a plant is not regularly watered, it will <u>languish</u>.
4. The soccer team that scores the most goals will <u>prevail</u>.
5. <u>Coyness</u> shows commitment to a relationship.
6. An <u>amorous</u> couple is affectionate.

Writing

Argumentative Text Public-service announcements (PSAs) urge people to act wisely. Use the *carpe diem* theme in a **PSA** that calls on people to do something beneficial, such as exercise to maintain health.

- Decide whether you will write a radio or television ad.
- Write the script and revise it to make sure you use effective evidence, logical evidence, and emotional appeals to persuade your audience.

514 A Turbulent Time (1625–1798)

Common Core State Standards

Writing
1. Write arguments to support claims in an analysis of substantive topics or texts, using valid reasoning and relevant and sufficient evidence.

Assessment Resources

Unit 3 Resources

L1 L2 EL **Selection Test A,** pp. 57–59. Administer Test A to less advanced readers.

L3 L4 EL **Selection Test B,** pp. 60–62. Administer Test B to on-level and more advanced students.

L3 L4 **Open-Book Test,** pp. 54–56. As an alternative, administer the Open-Book Test.

All **Customizable Test Bank**

All **Self-tests** Students may prepare for the **Selection Test** by taking the **Self-test** online.

PHLit **Online!** All assessment resources are available at **www.PHLitOnline.com.**

A Nation Divided

515

This chart gives a general text complexity rating for the selections in this part of the unit to help guide instruction. For additional text complexity support, see the Test Complexity Rubric at point of use.			
Sonnet VII (Milton)	**More Complex**	*from* Eve's Apology in Defense of Women	**More Accessible**
Sonnet XIX	**More Complex**	To Lucasta, on Going to the Wars	**More Accessible**
from Paradise Lost	**More Complex**	To Althea, from Prison	**More Complex**
from The Pilgrim's Progress	**More Complex**		

Selection Planning Guide

The selections in this section highlight conflicts that existed in seventeenth-century England. Sonnet VII and Sonnet XIX deal with problems of a personal nature. The excerpts from Milton's *Paradise Lost* deal with the epic conflict between God and Satan. The excerpt from "Eve's Apology in Defense of Women" addresses the long-standing conflict between men and women. "To Lucasta, on Going to the Wars" touches on both the battle for control of England and the conflict between a soldier and a woman who doesn't want him to leave. "To Althea, from Prison" reflects the conflict between Cavaliers and Puritans.

Humanities

King Charles I (1649) Led to His Execution, 1905, by A. S. Forest

This illustration is from *Our Island Story* by Henrietta Elizabeth Marshall (1867–1941). For fifty years it was the standard history of England for children. Charles I's reign was marked by struggles with Parliament and ended with the English Civil War. The picture shows the king being led through the streets of London shortly before his execution for treason.

Use these questions for discussion:

1. How would you characterize King Charles I from this portrait?
   Possible response: The King appears to be walking to his death very bravely. He seems defiant and likely considers himself a martyr.

2. Why do you think the illustrator chose to portray the king in this way?
   Possible response: The artist wanted to dramatize the story of the monarch and the significance of the events to the nation.

Monitoring Progress

Before students read the selections in Part 2, refer to the results for the Vocabulary in Context items on **Benchmark Test 4 (Unit 2 Resources p. 201).** Use this diagnostic portion of the test to guide your choice of selections to teach, as well as the depth of preparation you will provide, based on students' readiness for reading and vocabulary skills.

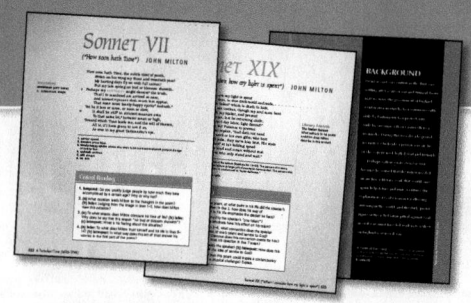

COMMON CORE
Time and Resource Manager

• Poetry of John Milton
Lesson Pacing Guide

DAY 1 Preteach

Ⓒ Administer the Reading and Vocabulary Warm-ups (*Unit 3 Resources*, pp. 63–66) as necessary.

Ⓒ Introduce the Literary Analysis concepts: Epic Poetry and the Italian Sonnet.

• Introduce the Reading Strategy: Using Graphic Organizers.

Ⓒ Build background with the Author in Depth and Background features.

• Develop thematic thinking with Connecting to the Essential Question.

Ⓒ Teach the selection vocabulary.

DAYS 2–3 Preteach/Teach

• Distribute copies of the appropriate graphic organizer for the Reading Strategy (*Graphic Organizer Transparencies*, pp. 87–88).

• Distribute copies of the appropriate graphic organizer for Literary Analysis (*Graphic Organizer Transparencies*, pp. 89–90).

• Prepare students to read with the Activating Prior Knowledge activities (TE).

• Informally monitor comprehension while students read.

• Use the Reading Check questions to confirm comprehension.

Ⓒ Develop students' understanding of epic poetry and the Italian sonnet using the Literary Analysis prompts.

• Develop students' ability to understand graphic organizers by using the Reading Strategy prompts.

Ⓒ Reinforce vocabulary with the Vocabulary notes.

DAY 4 Assess

• Assess students' comprehension and mastery of the skills by having them answer the Critical Reading, Literary Analysis, and Reading Strategy questions.

• Have students complete the Vocabulary Lesson.

DAY 5 Extend/Assess

• Have students complete the Conventions and Style Lesson.

Ⓒ Have students complete the Writing Lesson and write a Response to Literature. (You may assign as homework.)

• Administer Selection Test A or B (*Unit 3 Resources,* pp. 78–80 or 81–83).

Ⓒ Common Core State Standards

Reading Literature 5. Analyze how an author's choices concerning how to structure specific parts of a text contribute to its overall structure and meaning as well as its aesthetic impact.

Writing 1.a. Introduce precise, knowledgeable claim(s), and create an organization that logically sequences claim(s), reasons, and evidence.
1.b. Develop claim(s) fairly and thoroughly, supplying the most relevant evidence for each.
1.e. Provide a concluding statement or section that follows from and supports the argument presented.

Language 4.c. Consult general and specialized reference materials, both print and digital, to find the pronunciation of a word or determine or clarify its precise meaning, its part of speech, its etymology, or its standard usage.
6. Acquire and use accurately general academic and domain-specific words and phrases, sufficient for reading, writing, speaking, and listening at the college and career readiness level.

Additional Standards Practice
Common Core Companion, pp. 54–55; 185–195; 324–331, 336–337

Daily Block Scheduling
Each day in this Lesson Pacing Guide represents a 40–50 minute period. Teachers using block scheduling may combine days to revise pacing. In addition, teachers may differentiate and support core instruction by integrating components for extended and intensive support as students require. See the Guide to Selected Leveled Resources (facing page).

Guide to Selected Leveled Resources

R T I Tier 1 (students performing on level)

Poetry of John Milton

Warm Up	**Practice, model,** and **monitor** fluency, working **with the whole class** or **in groups.**	**Vocabulary and Reading Warm-ups B,** *Unit 3 Resources,* pp. 63–64, 66
Comprehension/Skills	**Support** and **monitor** comprehension and skills development, having students complete the activities, graphic organizers, and interactive prompts **independently** or **as a class.**	• *Reader's Notebook,* adapted instruction and full selection **EL** *Reader's Notebook: English Learner's Version,* adapted instruction and adapted selection • **Reading Skill Graphic Organizer B,** *Graphic Organizer Transparencies,* p. 92 • **Literary Analysis Graphic Organizer B,** *Graphic Organizer Transparencies,* p. 94
Monitor Progress [A]	**Monitor** student progress with the differentiated curriculum-based assessment in the *Unit Resources.*	• **Selection Test B,** *Unit 3 Resources,* pp. 81–83 • **Open-Book Test,** *Unit 3 Resources,* pp. 75–77

R T I Tier 2 (students requiring intervention)

Poetry of John Milton

Warm Up	**Practice, model,** and **monitor** fluency **in groups** or **with individuals.**	• **Vocabulary and Reading Warm-ups A,** *Unit 3 Resources,* pp. 63–65 • *Hear It!* Audio CD (adapted text)
Comprehension/Skills	• **Support** and **monitor** comprehension and skills development, working **in small groups** or **with individuals.** • As students complete the selection in the appropriate version of the *Reader's Notebook,* **monitor** comprehension frequently with group questions and individual instruction. • **Model** strategies while guiding students in completing the activities and prompts in the *Reader's Notebook,* as well as the graphic organizers. • **Practice** skills and **monitor** mastery with the *Reading Kit* worksheets.	• *Reader's Notebook: Adapted Version,* adapted instruction and adapted selection **EL** *Reader's Notebook: English Learner's Version,* adapted instruction and adapted selection • **Reading Skill Graphic Organizer A,** *Graphic Organizer Transparencies,* p. 91 • **Literary Analysis Graphic Organizer A,** *Graphic Organizer Transparencies,* p. 93 • *Reading Kit,* Practice worksheets
Monitor Progress [A]	**Monitor** student progress with the differentiated curriculum-based assessment in the *Unit Resources* and in the *Reading Kit.*	• **Selection Test A,** *Unit 3 Resources,* pp. 78–80 • *Reading Kit,* Assess worksheets

TIER 3 Tier 3 intervention may require consultation with the student's special-education or dyslexia specialist. For additional support, see the Tier 2 activities and resources listed above.

One-on-one teaching · Group work · Whole class instruction · Independent work · [A] Assessment

For a complete guide to selection support, including support for Advanced students, see the Overview of Resources in the frontmatter.

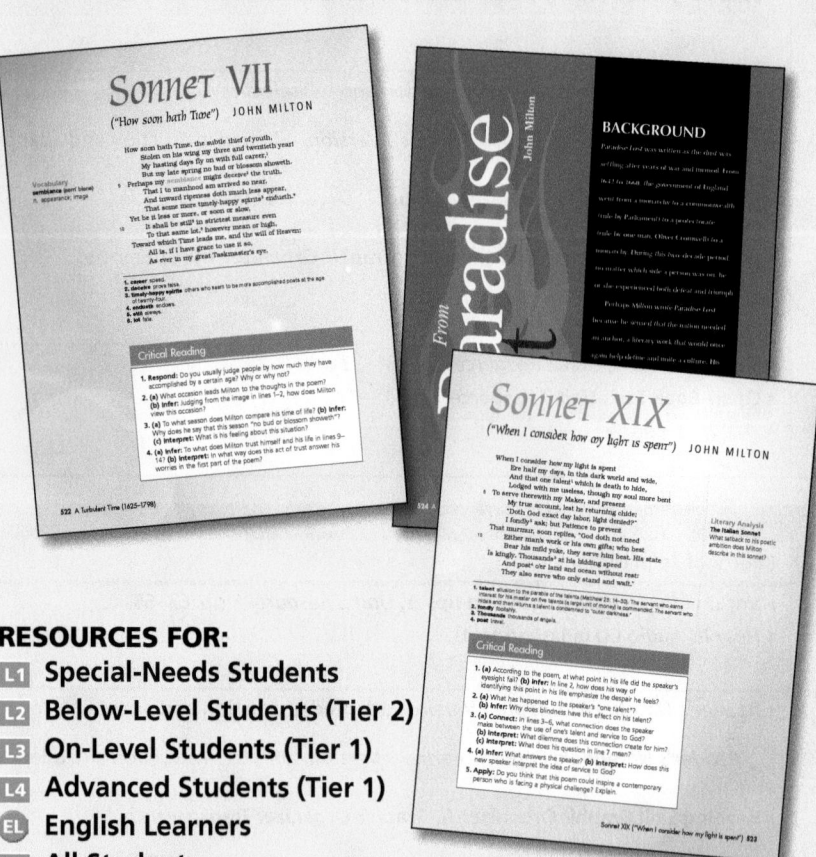

• Poetry of John Milton

Vocabulary/Fluency/Prior Knowledge

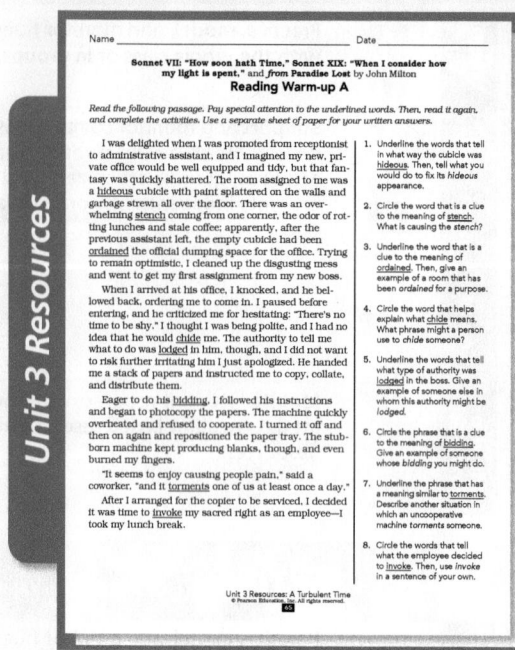

RESOURCES FOR:

- **L1** Special-Needs Students
- **L2** Below-Level Students (Tier 2)
- **L3** On-Level Students (Tier 1)
- **L4** Advanced Students (Tier 1)
- **EL** English Learners
- **All** All Students

EL L1 L2 Reading Warm-ups A and B,
pp. 65–66

Also available for these selections:

EL L1 L2 Vocabulary Warm-ups A and B,
pp. 63–64

All Vocabulary Builder, p. 71

Reader's Notebooks

Pre- and postreading pages for these selections, as well as the excerpt from *Paradise Lost,* appear in an interactive format in the *Reader's Notebooks*. Each *Notebook* is differentiated for a different group of learners.

The selections in the Adapted and English Learner's versions are abridged.

- **L2 L3** Reader's Notebook
- **L1** Reader's Notebook: Adapted Version
- **EL** Reader's Notebook: English Learner's Version
- **EL** Reader's Notebook: Spanish Version

© Common Core Companion

Additional instruction and practice for each Common Core State Standard

Selection Support

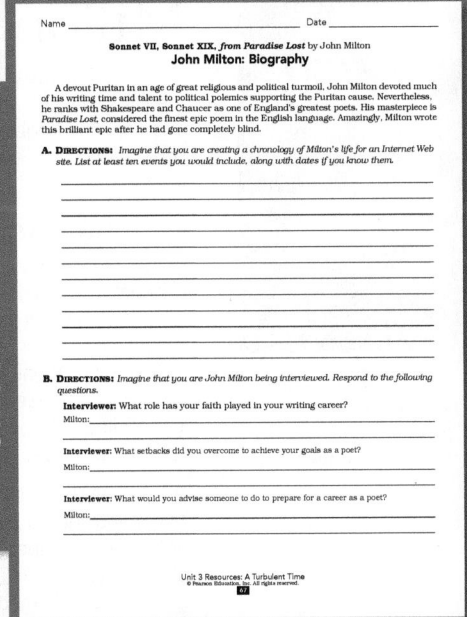
Graphic Organizer Transparencies

EL L3 Literary Analysis: Graphic Organizer B, p. 90

Also available for these selections:

EL L1 L2 Reading: Graphic Organizer A, (partially filled in), p. 87

EL L3 Reading: Graphic Organizer B, p. 88

EL L1 L2 Literary Analysis: Graphic Organizer A (partially filled in), p. 89

Skills Development/Extension

Unit 3 Resources

Name _____ Date _____

Sonnet VII, Sonnet XIX, *from Paradise Lost* by John Milton
John Milton: Biography

A devout Puritan in an age of great religious and political turmoil, John Milton devoted much of his writing time and talent to political polemics supporting the Puritan cause. Nevertheless, he ranks with Shakespeare and Chaucer as one of England's greatest poets. His masterpiece is *Paradise Lost*, considered the finest epic poem in the English language. Amazingly, Milton wrote this brilliant epic after he had gone completely blind.

A. DIRECTIONS: *Imagine that you are creating a chronology of Milton's life for an Internet Web site. List at least ten events you would include, along with dates if you know them.*

_____
_____
_____
_____
_____
_____
_____
_____
_____
_____
_____

B. DIRECTIONS: *Imagine that you are John Milton being interviewed. Respond to the following questions.*

Interviewer: What role has your faith played in your writing career?
Milton: _____

Interviewer: What setbacks did you overcome to achieve your goals as a poet?
Milton: _____

Interviewer: What would you advise someone to do to prepare for a career as a poet?
Milton: _____

Unit 3 Resources: A Turbulent Time
© Pearson Education, Inc. All rights reserved.

All Biography, p. 67

Also available for these selections:

All Literary Analysis, p. 68

All Literary Analysis, p. 69

All Reading, p. 70

EL L3 L4 Grammar and Style, p. 72

EL L3 L4 Support for Writing, p. 73

L4 Enrichment, p. 74

Assessment

Name _____ Date _____

Poetry of John Milton
Selection Test B

Critical Reading *Identify the letter of the choice that best completes the statement or answers the question.*

___ 1. What is the theme of this excerpt from *Paradise Lost*?
  A. service to God
  B. good and evil
  C. consequences of rebellion
  D. historical relationships

___ 2. Milton's epic poem *Paradise Lost* expresses values of seventeenth-century Christian England in that it reflects a prevalent belief in
  A. Greek and Roman classical gods.
  B. earthly angels.
  C. serpents and sea monsters.
  D. Heaven and Hell.

___ 3. Which of the following describes the style in which *Paradise Lost* is written?
  A. unrhymed iambic pentameter
  B. rhymed couplets
  C. quatrains of varying rhyme schemes
  D. run-on lines

___ 4. What is the main clause in the following lines from *Paradise Lost*?
  And chiefly O Spirit, that dost prefer / Before all temples the upright heart and pure, / instruct me, for thou know'st . . .
  A. that dost prefer
  B. for thou know'st
  C. And chiefly thou O Spirit
  D. Instruct me

___ 5. The lines "With loss of Eden, till one greater Man / Restore us, and regain the blissful seat" allude to the
  A. power of God.
  B. punishment of Satan.
  C. coming of Christ.
  D. joy of the angels.

___ 6. Which of the following lines referring to Satan best expresses the conflict between Satan and God?
  A. ". . . the thought / Both of lost happiness and lasting pain / Torments him . . ."
  B. "He trusted to have equaled the Most High . . ."
  C. ". . . he views / The dismal situation waste and wild . . ."
  D. "He soon discerns . . . / One next himself in power, and next in crime . . ."

Unit 3 Resources: A Turbulent Time
© Pearson Education, Inc. All rights reserved.

EL L3 L4 Selection Test B, pp. 81–83

Also available for these selections:

L3 L4 Open-Book Test, pp. 75–77

EL L1 L2 Selection Test A, pp. 78–80

PHLit Online!
www.PHLitOnline.com

Online Resources: All print materials are also available online.

- complete narrated selection text
- a thematically related video with writing prompt
- an interactive graphic organizer
- highlighting feature
- access to all student print resources, adapted to individual student needs
- Spanish and English summaries
- adapted selection translations in Spanish

Get Connected! (thematic video with writing prompt)

Also available:

Background Video
All videos are available in Spanish.

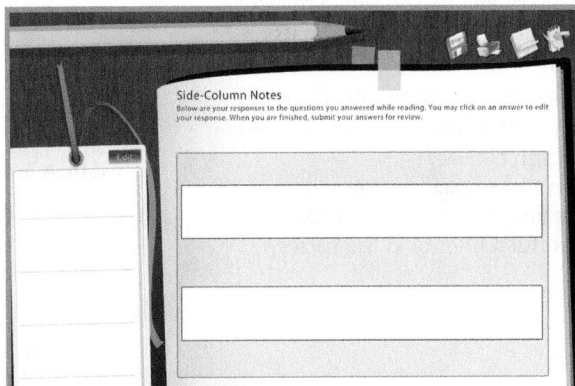

Writer's Journal (with graphics feature)

Also available:

Vocabulary Central (tools and activities for studying vocabulary)

Critical Viewing
Possible response: Adam appears distraught; Eve's clenched hands suggest worry.

Literary History: Milton's World
1. Explain to students that John Milton wrote at a time when speaking out on politics and religion was a potentially dangerous thing to do. Milton believed in the freedom of the individual, however, and he believed that power corrupted leaders. His work reflects these attitudes.
2. Ask students to consider why Milton would risk sharing his attitudes. Then, have them read the article.

Background
The English Civil War
1. Explain to students that Milton's poetic concerns were shaped in part by the English Civil War (1642–1649). The king of England at the time, Charles I, relied on royal privilege rather than diplomacy, ruling for eleven years without calling Parliament into session once. His wars with Spain and France, however, had drained his resources. Charles called a Parliament to ask for funds, but the body refused to grant his request unless he gave over some of his power. Charles refused, and in 1642 the English Parliament declared war on its own king.
2. **Ask:** Why might the Civil War have left a symbolic void in English culture?
Possible response: A reigning king or queen embodies the rightful authority in the society.

▲ **Critical Viewing**
What feeling does this portrayal of Adam and Eve convey? **[Interpret]**

Literary History: Milton's World

In the 1650s, the aged John Milton decided to retell the Biblical story of the creation, fall, and redemption of humanity in two epics, Paradise Lost *and* Paradise Regained. *With these works, Milton reaffirmed Britain's core values after a decade of war.*

Making "Darkness Visible": Milton's Epic Ambition

Milton had compelling reasons for telling this story. By 1652, he was completely blind. Unable to write, he dictated the poem to his daughters, who copied down each word. As he worked, the world crumbled around him. The monarchy he had opposed was restored to England, and he went to jail for a time. Blind, disgraced, and disillusioned, Milton nevertheless persevered. Over perhaps ten years, he dictated nearly 11,000 lines of poetry. The result, critics agree, is the greatest epic in the English language, *Paradise Lost.*

An Overview Like many epic poems, *Paradise Lost* begins in the middle. Milton introduces Satan, who, along with his angel allies, has done the unthinkable—rebelled against God. Expelled from Heaven, they have plummeted into Hell, a place devoid of light, life, and even form: "one great furnace flamed, yet from those flames / No light, but rather darkness visible / Served only to discern sights of woe."

Satan's war with Heaven is Milton's invention. The remainder of the story is the familiar one of Christian tradition. God has forbidden Adam and Eve to eat fruit from the Tree of the Knowledge of Good and Evil. Bent on revenge, Satan tempts Eve into eating the apple. She then persuades Adam to partake. This event, the Fall of Adam and Eve, leads to their (and so humanity's) expulsion from the Garden of Eden. They leave Paradise with a sense of hope: "The World was all before them, where to choose / Their place of rest, and Providence their guide. . . ."

A Cosmic Commentary Apart from telling this grand story, large portions of *Paradise Lost* are dedicated to another grand project— "to justify the ways of God to men." In the story, God sends the angel Raphael to Paradise to warn Adam of the necessity of obedience. In their conversation, Milton is able to speak on a few issues that were controversial in his day.

- **Reason and Free Will** Humanity can see the difference between right and wrong. With that ability comes the freedom to choose between the two.
- **Free Will and Predestination** God knows everything that is, was, and will be. Yet God's foreknowledge does not mean that people's choices are determined in advance by God. People have free will.

The Reformation
In the 1500s, the traditional authority of the Catholic Church in Europe was extensively challenged. Martin Luther (1483–1546) interpreted scripture to show that the faith of the individual was the source of salvation. John Calvin (1509–1564) argued that salvation was predestined by God for his elect. In 1534, Henry VIII of England founded his own church. The Puritans of Milton's day, influenced by Calvin and others, challenged corruption in Henry's church and sought to restore authority to the individual's conscience.

Activity: Analyzing the Reformation Ask students to complete the **Enrichment: Analyzing a Historical Event** worksheet, *Professional Development Guidebook,* page 230, by including the above information and by doing additional research. Students may discuss the ways in which the Reformation compares to other historical events.

By affirming free will, Milton broke with some of the sternest Puritans of his day, who held that men and women were predestined to salvation or damnation. Milton's epic story finds individuals responsible for their own actions and fate and so grants them dignity.

Words in the Void In a sense, *Paradise Lost* is Milton's answer to the great historical crisis through which Britain had just passed. Puritans, including Milton, had challenged the official Church of England. They demanded a return to what they saw as the original principles of the Christian religion. At the same time, religious controversy led to the Civil War (1642–1649) in which Parliament eventually put its own king, Charles I, to death.

These upheavals shattered the symbolic centers of English life and culture, Church and King. With *Paradise Lost*, Milton helped the nation find its bearings again by retelling the central story of its culture. In the figure of Satan, he commemorated the destructive forces that had recently torn through the nation. At the same time, the fall of Satan symbolically puts rebellious urges into their proper place—the netherworld of Hell. It was these tasks, perhaps, that drove the blind Milton to rise above adversity and deliver this epic to his country.

Milton's Legacy Over the centuries, Milton's story of the Fall has become as well known as the biblical version. It has influenced writers as diverse as the poets William Blake, the visionary; and John Keats, the introspective dreamer; as well as the novelist George Eliot, a formidable social critic. By the nineteenth century, study of Milton's epic was considered an essential part of a respectable education, and even relatively uneducated people could be expected to have two books in their homes—the King James Bible and *Paradise Lost*. In telling a story to heal his own time, Milton fed the imaginations of generations to come.

Speaking and Listening: Discussion

Ⓒ Comprehension and Collaboration Since the time of Milton, many writers have attempted to heal the wounds of collective trauma through works of literature.

With a group, discuss your thoughts about the ways in which literature can bring understanding or closure to people after a period of historical crisis. Use these questions to guide your discussion:

• What examples can you cite in which literature, including drama, deals with a real historical crisis?

• Do you think such literature can have meaning for people who have not lived through the crisis in question? If so, how?

Organize your conclusions into a **report** to share your ideas with the class.

Literary History **517**

Background
Milton's Syntax

Milton wrote much of his poetry in Latin. Even in English, his syntax (sentence structure) borrows something from Latin. Because the person, case, and number of words are clearly marked in the language, word order is much freer than in English. The reader will know which adjective belongs with which noun because of their endings. Milton's syntax is Latinate, in that he allows himself greater freedom in word placement than is usual in English.

Critical Thinking

1. What parallels exist between Satan's fall and the Civil War?
   Possible responses: Like Satan, the English had rebelled against their traditional ruler; like Satan, the English king had demonstrated excessive pride.

2. In what way does the idea in *Paradise Lost* of humanity's fate differ from Puritanism?
   Possible response: Milton emphasizes the dignity and loneliness of human freedom, rejecting Puritan ideas of predestination.

3. In what sense does *Paradise Lost* symbolically restore unity to English culture?
   Possible response: The epic retells a story central to English culture, and so affirms the nation's common values.

Speaking and Listening: Discussion
The Healing Power of Literature

1. Read "The Healing Power of Literature" with the class. Allow students time to write their individual responses to the discussion questions. Suggest that they consider books, movies, plays, and songs related to various national or global crises, such as the Vietnam War, the September 11 attacks, or the war in Iraq.

2. Organize small groups for discussion. Ask students to share their written responses with one another.

3. Have groups present their conclusions to the class. As a class, list the works students feel have had the most healing power. Ask students to defend their evaluations.

517

❶ Background

Overview: The Author's Work

Today, John Milton is famous for *Paradise Lost*, but his work did not achieve instant popularity. Although the epic poem was published in 1667, it was not well-known as a unique and remarkable work of literature until the 1700s. At first, its audience was limited to those who knew Milton personally. Toward the middle of the century, the poem was translated into Italian, German, and French, and its audience grew. The writers and critics of the eighteenth century were mainly interested in Milton's imagery—especially his vivid portrayals of the Garden of Eden. Milton's reputation as a writer changed over time, however. In the 1800s, Romantic writers such as Percy Shelley and Lord Byron began to focus on Milton's characterization of Satan as a "dark hero."

The Writer in His Time

John Milton's life spanned a time of upheaval and change in England. His work on *Paradise Lost* was undertaken at the very beginning of the Restoration era—the period of time beginning with the restoration of Charles II to the throne in 1660. Neoclassical writers such as John Dryden and Alexander Pope were coming to the forefront of English literature. These writers valued order, reason, and cleverness over emotional expression and vividly described settings, and they preferred the tight rhyme scheme of the heroic couplet. To them, Milton's unrhymed, dark, and dramatic epic poem may have seemed like a voice from an earlier age.

John Milton
(1608–1674)

John Milton is regarded as one of the greatest poets of the English language, yet he owes this regard to comparatively few poems. Much of his work is in Latin, not English, and during the fifteen years he spent writing political pamphlets and other prose works, he wrote little poetry. Although other poets have surpassed him in quantity, Milton's masterpiece, the epic *Paradise Lost,* is enough to establish him as the equal of Chaucer and Shakespeare. Milton himself never lacked self-confidence, setting his sights on poetic greatness at the start of his career.

A Privileged Childhood

Milton was born in London to a middle-class family and grew up in a highly cultured environment. His father, a professional scribe who drew up contracts and lent money, was also a composer and musician of considerable ability. Deeply religious, Milton's father was devoted to the Protestant cause. At the age of thirteen, Milton started his formal education, the equivalent of high school. He was also tutored at home. He mastered Greek, Latin, and Hebrew, as well as several modern European languages. After this thorough education, Milton went on to college.

518 A Turbulent Time (1625–1798)

©️ Text Complexity Rubric: Leveled Texts

	Sonnet VII	Sonnet XIX	*from* Paradise Lost
Qualitative Measures			
Context/ Knowledge Demands	Italian sonnet 1 ② 3 4 5	Italian sonnet; literary knowledge demands 1 2 ③ 4 5	Literary epic; literary knowledge demands 1 2 3 ④ 5
Structure/Language Conventionality and Clarity	Archaic diction and syntax 1 2 ③ 4 5	Archaic diction and syntax; long sentences 1 2 ③ 4 5	Archaic diction and syntax; long sentences 1 2 3 ④ 5
Levels of Meaning/ Purpose/Concept Level	Moderate (aging and faith) 1 2 ③ 4 5	Challenging (blindness and faith) 1 2 3 ④ 5	Challenging (the fall of man) 1 2 3 ④ 5
Quantitative Measures			
Lexile/Text Length	NP / 127 words	NP / 114 words	NP / 2,062 words
Overall Complexity	**More complex**	**More complex**	**More complex**

God's Poet

When Milton entered Christ's College at Cambridge University, he had already decided to prepare himself for a career as a great poet ("God's poet" was how he described himself). It appears that for a time he also considered entering the ministry. The religious and political situation at the time, though, was quite uncertain, so Milton devoted himself to a life of study. After earning his degrees from Cambridge, he withdrew to his father's house, first at Hammersmith, then at Horton in Buckinghamshire, for nearly six years, where, it is said, he read everything that was written in the ancient and modern languages at his command. It was during this long period of study that he wrote one of his best-known poems, "Lycidas." That work, together with the poems "L'Allegro" and "Il Penseroso," written during his student days, marked the young Milton as a gifted poet destined for fame.

A Man of Ideals

Following his studies, Milton went to continental Europe for a planned two-year Grand Tour, during which he called on the astronomer Galileo (1564–1642). While he was away, Parliament rebelled against King Charles I, eventually replacing the monarchy with a government led by Oliver Cromwell. Learning of the revolt, Milton cut short his trip and returned to England. He began writing pamphlets for the Puritan cause, criticizing the control of the bishops over the English church.

Public Service, Private Loss

In 1649, when the Puritans decided to execute Charles I, Milton wrote a treatise defending this act. Impressed by Milton's brilliantly presented opinions, Cromwell made him Secretary of State for Foreign Tongues. This position required Milton to translate official documents into Latin and to write in defense of the new government against Royalist attacks. It was while serving in this position that he lost his eyesight.

In 1660, Milton's fortunes took a turn for the worse. The monarchy was restored, and Milton was imprisoned for a time. (His friend, the poet Andrew Marvell, may have been instrumental in gaining his release.) Blind and stripped of most of his property, Milton withdrew once again into words—he wrote *Paradise Lost* (1667), the greatest epic of the English language.

Milton as a youth (top) and as a mature man (bottom)

John Milton **519**

© Text Complexity: Reader and Task Suggestions

Preparing to Read the Texts	Sonnet VII	Sonnet XIX	*from* Paradise Lost
• Using the Background on TE p. 516, discuss the possibility that civil unrest in seventeenth-century England helped inspire Milton's great epic. • Discuss with students the role faith played in Milton's poetic ambitions. • Guide students to use Multidraft Reading strategies (TE p. 519).	**Leveled Tasks** *Language/Structure* If students will have difficulty with the sonnet's language, have them summarize the octet (lines 1–8) and sestet (lines 9–14). Then, as they reread, have them focus on imagery and diction. *Evaluating* If students will not have difficulty with the language, have them discuss the sonnet's attitude toward human achievement.	**Leveled Tasks** *Levels of Meaning* If students will have difficulty with the levels of meaning, have them focus first on the speaker's view of his blindness. Then, as they reread, they should consider what the poem says about faith and achievement. *Analyzing* If students will not have difficulty with the levels of meaning, have them discuss the ideas about God and faith in the poems final sestet.	**Leveled Tasks** *Knowledge Demands* If students will have difficulty with the allusions, have them first study the footnotes. Then, have them read the selection in sections. Finally, have them read the selection through. *Analyzing* If students will not have difficulty with the allusions, have them analyze the style elements that help Milton convey his themes.

519

❶ Dark Heroes

1. Poll students to see which ones are familiar with Darth Vader, Magneto, and The Phantom. Then ask students to suggest reasons people seem to be fascinated by these characters.

2. Ask students to name examples of villains from other books or movies. As you write these on the board, have students rate their "degree of evil." That is, are they altogether evil, or is there some redeeming quality to them? Have students compare the villains by giving each one a rating from 1 to 10 (10 being the most evil) and explain their ratings.

3. Explain to students that writers often try to give readers an explanation for a character's actions. Readers often want to know why a character is a villain. Ask students familiar with Darth Vader, The Phantom, or Magneto if they can explain the reason for that character's villainy.

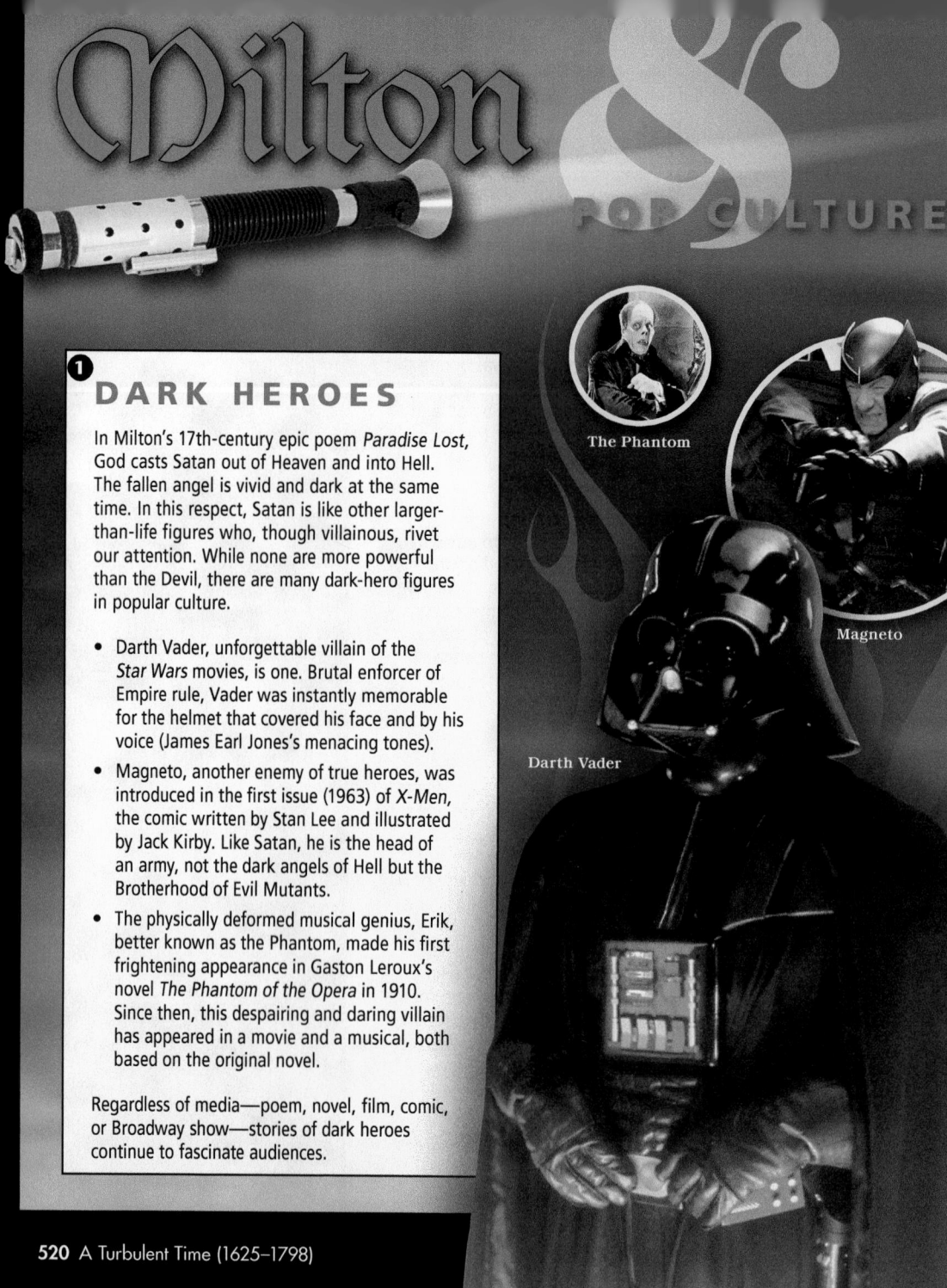

Milton & POP CULTURE

❶ DARK HEROES

In Milton's 17th-century epic poem *Paradise Lost*, God casts Satan out of Heaven and into Hell. The fallen angel is vivid and dark at the same time. In this respect, Satan is like other larger-than-life figures who, though villainous, rivet our attention. While none are more powerful than the Devil, there are many dark-hero figures in popular culture.

- Darth Vader, unforgettable villain of the *Star Wars* movies, is one. Brutal enforcer of Empire rule, Vader was instantly memorable for the helmet that covered his face and by his voice (James Earl Jones's menacing tones).

- Magneto, another enemy of true heroes, was introduced in the first issue (1963) of *X-Men*, the comic written by Stan Lee and illustrated by Jack Kirby. Like Satan, he is the head of an army, not the dark angels of Hell but the Brotherhood of Evil Mutants.

- The physically deformed musical genius, Erik, better known as the Phantom, made his first frightening appearance in Gaston Leroux's novel *The Phantom of the Opera* in 1910. Since then, this despairing and daring villain has appeared in a movie and a musical, both based on the original novel.

Regardless of media—poem, novel, film, comic, or Broadway show—stories of dark heroes continue to fascinate audiences.

The Phantom

Magneto

Darth Vader

520 A Turbulent Time (1625–1798)

Vocabulary Development

Vocabulary Knowledge Rating

Create a **Vocabulary Knowledge Rating Chart** (*Professional Development Guidebook,* p. 33) for this selection, using the selection vocabulary from the next page. Give students a copy of the chart. Read the words aloud, and have students mark their rating in the Before Reading column. Urge them to be alert to these words as they read and discuss the selection.

Tally how many students think they know each word to gauge how much instruction to provide. As students read and discuss the selection, point out the words and their context.

PHLit Online! **Vocabulary Central,** featuring student tools for recording and studying vocabulary, is available online at **www.PHLitOnline.com.**

Before You Read | *Poetry of John Milton*

❷ Connecting to the Essential Question John Milton brings to life a well-known story of the time, about angels who rebelled against God. As you read, notice vivid passages in Milton's description of the underworld in *Paradise Lost*. Seeing such descriptions in your mind's eye will help you answer the Essential Question: **What is the relationship of the writer to tradition?**

❸ Literary Analysis

An **Italian,** or **Petrarchan, sonnet** is a fourteen-line lyric poem with a distinctive structure. The first eight lines, called the octave, rhyme *abbaabba* and present a problem. A six-line sestet with a variable rhyme scheme responds to the octave. In Milton's Italian sonnets, the structure of the octave and the sestet contributes to the structure, meaning, and aesthetic pleasure of the entire sonnet.

An **epic** is a long narrative poem about a hero. For seventeenth-century English writers, ancient epic poets such as Homer—the blind, half-mythical author of the *Iliad* and the *Odyssey*—set the standard for literary greatness. Milton uses the following features of Homeric epics in *Paradise Lost:*

- A story that begins in the middle of the action (*in medias res*)
- An opening invocation in which the poet calls for divine aid in telling his story
- Extended similes, comparisons using *like* or *as*

Look for these epic elements as you read *Paradise Lost,* and analyze how in the sonnets, the structure of the parts contributes to the structure and meaning of the poem.

❹ Reading Strategy

Ⓒ Preparing to Read Complex Texts If you do not understand a passage, repair your comprehension by **using a graphic organizer** like the one shown. This organizer can help you break down long, confusing sentences into smaller parts: main clauses, which can stand by themselves, and supporting clauses, which cannot.

❺ Vocabulary

semblance (sem´ bləns) *n.* appearance; image (p. 522)

illumine (i l⎯oo´ mən) *v.* light up (p. 526)

transgress (trans gres´) *v.* violate a law or command (p. 526)

guile (gīl) *n.* artful trickery (p. 527)

obdurate (äb´ d⎯oor it) *adj.* stubborn (p. 527)

tempestuous (tem pes´ ch⎯oo əs) *adj.* turbulent; stormy (p. 528)

transcendent (tran sen´ dənt) *adj.* exceeding beyond all limits (p. 529)

ignominy (ig´ nə min´ ē) *n.* humiliation; dishonor (p. 529)

Ⓒ Common Core State Standards

Reading Literature
5. Analyze how an author's choices concerning how to structure specific parts of a text contribute to its overall structure and meaning as well as its aesthetic impact.

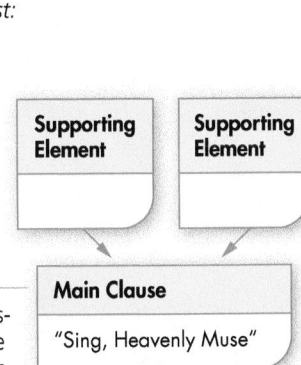

Supporting Element

Supporting Element

Main Clause

"Sing, Heavenly Muse"

Supporting Element

Supporting Element

www.PHLitOnline.com

Poetry of John Milton **521**

Teaching From Technology

Preparing to Read
Go to **www.PHLitOnline.com** in class or in a lab, and display the **Get Connected!** slide show. Have the class brainstorm responses to the slide show writing prompt, entering ideas in the interactive journal. To build background, display the **Background** video and **More About the Author** slideshow.

Using the Interactive Student Edition
Go to **www.PHLitOnline.com** and display the **Enriched Online Student Edition** to the class. As the class reads the selection or listens to the narration, record answers to side-column prompts using the graphic organizers accessible on the interactive page. Alternatively, have students use the online edition individually, answering the prompts as they read.

---

❷ ❓ Connecting to the Essential Question

1. Review the assignment with the class.

2. Have students discuss what makes a "good" story. What makes a story interesting to hear or read? In contrast, why are some stories less interesting? After the discussion, have students complete the writing assignment.

3. As students read, have them look for vivid descriptions, especially in *Paradise Lost.*

❸ Literary Analysis

Introduce the skill using the instruction on the student page.

Think Aloud: Model the Skill

Say to students:

> If Milton's *Paradise Lost* follows the conventions of epic poetry, it should be obvious immediately. After all, the first two characteristics of an epic poem listed here have to do with how the story begins.

❹ Reading Strategy

1. Introduce the strategy using the instruction on the student page.

2. Give students a copy of **Reading Strategy Graphic Organizer B,** page 88 in *Graphic Organizer Transparencies,* to fill out as they read.

Think Aloud: Model the Skill

Say to students:

> Sentences are made up of main and supporting clauses. If I think of a sentence like *During the storm, many people lost their electricity,* the main clause would be *many people lost their electricity* because it could stand on its own as a sentence.

❺ Vocabulary

1. Pronounce each word, giving its definition, and have students say it aloud.

2. For more guidance, see the *Classroom Strategies and Teaching Routines* card for introducing vocabulary.

Readers who know Milton as a literary giant may be surprised to discover that he was not always sure of himself, his abilities, or his future. While Milton expresses his faith in Sonnet VII, he also voices his dissatisfaction.

❷ Activating Prior Knowledge

Ask students to consider this question: In a hundred years, what would you like to be remembered for? Have students write a brief answer to this question.

Concept Connector ➡️

Tell students they will return to their responses after reading.

ASSESS

Answers

Before students respond, you may wish to have them write a brief objective summary of the selection. As they answer the questions below, remind them to support their answers with evidence from the text.

1. (a) He is reflecting upon his twenty-third birthday. (b) He is surprised by how quickly time has passed; he feels cheated by time.

2. (a) He compares it to late spring. (b) He is referring to the fact that he has not yet created a great body of work. (c) Milton is concerned.

3. (a) He puts his trust in God. (b) His trust in God allays his worries about his progress because he sees that he will arrive in life where he is meant to, when he is meant to.

---

❶❷ Sonnet VII

("How soon hath Time") JOHN MILTON

How soon hath Time, the subtle thief of youth,
    Stolen on his wing my three and twentieth year!
    My hasting days fly on with full career,[1]
    But my late spring no bud or blossom showeth.
5 Perhaps my semblance might deceive[2] the truth,
    That I to manhood am arrived so near,
    And inward ripeness doth much less appear,
    That some more timely-happy spirits[3] endueth.[4]
Yet be it less or more, or soon or slow,
10   It shall be still[5] in strictest measure even
    To that same lot,[6] however mean or high,
Toward which Time leads me, and the will of Heaven;
    All is, if I have grace to use it so,
    As ever in my great Taskmaster's eye.

Vocabulary
semblance (sem' bləns)
n. appearance; image

---

1. **career** speed.
2. **deceive** prove false.
3. **timely-happy spirits** others who seem to be more accomplished poets at the age of twenty-four.
4. **endueth** endows.
5. **still** always.
6. **lot** fate.

Critical Reading

Cite textual evidence to support your responses.

© 1. **Key Ideas and Details** **(a)** What occasion leads Milton to the thoughts in the poem? **(b) Infer:** Judging from the image in lines 1–2, how does Milton view this occasion?

© 2. **Key Ideas and Details** **(a)** To what season does Milton compare his time of life? **(b) Infer:** Why does he say that this season "no bud or blossom showeth"? **(c) Interpret:** What is his feeling about this situation?

© 3. **Key Ideas and Details** **(a) Infer:** To what does Milton trust himself and his life in lines 9–14? **(b) Interpret:** In what way does this act of trust answer his worries in the first part of the poem?

Sonnet XIX

("When I consider how my light is spent") JOHN MILTON

When I consider how my light is spent
    Ere half my days, in this dark world and wide,
    And that one talent[1] which is death to hide,
    Lodged with me useless, though my soul more bent
5 To serve therewith my Maker, and present
    My true account, lest he returning chide;
    "Doth God exact day labor, light denied?"
    I fondly[2] ask; but Patience to prevent
That murmur, soon replies, "God doth not need
10   Either man's work or his own gifts; who best
    Bear his mild yoke, they serve him best. His state
Is kingly. Thousands[3] at his bidding speed
    And post[4] o'er land and ocean without rest:
    They also serve who only stand and wait."

4 Literary Analysis
The Italian Sonnet
What setback to his poetic
ambition does Milton
describe in this sonnet?

---

1. **talent** allusion to the parable of the talents (Matthew 25: 14–30). The servant who earns interest for his master on five talents (a large unit of money) is commended. The servant who hides and then returns a talent is condemned to "outer darkness."
2. **fondly** foolishly.
3. **Thousands** thousands of angels.
4. **post** travel.

Critical Reading

1. **Key Ideas and Details (a)** According to the poem, at what point in his life did the speaker's eyesight fail? **(b) Infer:** In line 2, how does his way of identifying this point in his life emphasize the despair he feels?

2. **Key Ideas and Details (a)** What has happened to the speaker's "one talent"? **(b) Infer:** Why does blindness have this effect on his talent?

3. **Key Ideas and Details (a) Connect:** In lines 3–6, what connection does the speaker make between the use of one's talent and service to God? **(b) Interpret:** What dilemma does this connection create for him? **(c) Interpret:** What does his question in line 7 mean?

4. **Key Ideas and Details (a) Infer:** What answers the speaker? **(b) Interpret:** How does this new speaker interpret the idea of service to God?

5. **Integration of Knowledge and Ideas** Do you think that this poem could inspire a contemporary person who is facing a physical challenge? Explain.

Cite textual evidence to support your responses.

Sonnet XIX ("When I consider how my light is spent") **523**

TEACH

3 About the Selection
In Sonnet XIX, Milton muses on his blindness, which he thought he had caused by his voracious reading.

4 Literary Analysis

The Italian Sonnet

Ask students the Literary Analysis question: What setback to his poetic ambition does Milton describe in this sonnet?
Answer: He describes how he fears that his blindness may prevent him from serving God through poetic writing.

ASSESS

Answers

1. (a) He became blind at midlife. (b) The speaker's life is halfway over. He fears the remaining portion of his life will be useless.

2. (a) He has been rendered useless. (b) He will not be able to write, study his work, or read other material without sight.

3. (a) The speaker feels that the purpose of his talent is to enable him to serve God. (b) The speaker's dilemma is that his poetry was his only talent, and he feels he will be unable to serve God. (c) How does God expect him to work when he is blind?

4. (a) Patience answers the speaker. (b) God does not demand work, only faith, devotion, or acceptance.

5. Yes, this poem might inspire someone to accept a physical challenge. It sends the message "make the most of what you have."

Differentiated Instruction   for Universal Access

Support for Special-Needs Students
Have students complete the **Before You Read** and the **Making Connections** pages for these selections in the *Reader's Notebook: Adapted Version*. These pages provide an abbreviated skills instruction, a selection summary, the Before You Read graphic organizer, and a **Note-taking Guide**.

Support for Less Proficient Readers
Have students complete the **Before You Read** and the **Making Connections** pages for these selections in the *Reader's Notebook*. These pages provide an abbreviated skills instruction, a selection summary, the Before You Read graphic organizer, and a **Note-taking Guide**.

EL Support for English Learners
Have students complete the **Before You Read** and the **Making Connections** pages for these selections in the *Reader's Notebook: English Learner's Version*. These pages provide additional vocabulary, vocabulary skills, and vocabulary practice, along with a **Getting Ready to Read** activity.

❺ About the Selection

In the opening lines of *Paradise Lost,* Milton tells of Satan's rebellion against God, and describes how the fallen archangel and his followers, defeated, are cast into a fiery pit. In creating a Satan who is unrepentant, proud, and in his own way heroic, Milton makes a powerful statement about the alluring nature of evil. It would be easy to avoid evil if it were completely repugnant; evil that has admirable qualities is far more insidious and dangerous.

❻ Critical Viewing

Answer: The engraving reflects the years of warfare and turmoil that occurred in England at this time. It depicts a leader and his army.

From **Paradise Lost**

John Milton

524 A Turbulent Time (1625–1798)

❺ BACKGROUND

Paradise Lost was written as the dust was settling after years of war and turmoil. From 1642 to 1660, the government of England went from a monarchy to a commonwealth (rule by Parliament) to a protectorate (rule by one man, Oliver Cromwell) to a monarchy. During this two-decade period, no matter which side a person was on, he or she experienced both defeat and triumph.

Perhaps Milton wrote *Paradise Lost* because he sensed that the nation needed an anchor, a literary work that would once again help define and unite a culture. His explanation of God's reason for allowing suffering in the world, and the dark, proud figure of the rebel Satan pitted against God in civil war, must have led readers to reflect on England's own civil war.

❻ ▶ **Critical Viewing** How is Milton's time period—an era in which England was torn apart by civil war and religious conflict—reflected in this painting? **[Connect]**

Paradise Lost, 1668, From the British Library

Enrichment: Analyzing an Image

Angels

Milton's poem had a profound influence on the way Christians viewed angels. The term *angel* comes from the Greek word *angelos,* which means "messenger." However, angels are not unique to the related religions of Judaism, Christianity, and Islam. Many cultures have benevolent or mischievous spirits that act as messengers between humans and a deity.

The Christian view of angels has changed over time. Angels were not always thought of as looking like humans with a single pair of bird wings, and the notion of the souls of the dead becoming angels appears to have arisen during Victorian times.

Activity: Analyzing an Image Have interested students research artistic depictions of angels, using the **Enrichment: Analyzing an Image** worksheet on page 232 of the *Professional Development Guidebook* to gather and organize their information.

➐ Humanities

Gustave Doré

This engraving was done in the style of Gustave Doré, a French artist who was born in 1832 and who specialized in book illustrations. He created beautiful illustrations for Dante's *Divine Comedy*, Cervantes's *Don Quixote*, and the Bible.

Use the following question for discussion:

Is the style of this engraving in keeping with Milton's literary style?
Possible response: Yes, because it includes vivid details.

Differentiated Instruction for Universal Access

Strategy for Less Proficient Readers

Have students preview the selection by reading the Background and looking at the illustrations. Have them discuss with a partner what they expect to happen in the poem, and write three predictions based on their discussion. As students read the poem, they can compare their predictions to the actual events.

EL Strategy for English Learners

Because Milton's language can be difficult to understand, have students listen to the selection on the *Hear It!* **Audio CDs** before reading it themselves. Students may also work in pairs to read the text in chunks of 10–20 lines, stopping after each chunk to summarize what they have read.

Epic Poetry

1. Remind students of the definition of epic poetry. The epic is a long narrative poem that tells the story of a hero and reflects the values of a culture. For seventeenth-century English writers, the ancient Greek and Roman epic poets, such as Homer, set the standard for literary greatness.

2. **Ask** students the Literary Analysis question: What epic convention does Milton follow in his opening sentence?
Answer: He begins with an invocation to the Muse.

❾ Critical Thinking

Analyze

1. **Ask** students to identify the speaker's purpose in lines 1–26.
Answer: In line 26, the speaker says that he will "justify the ways of God to men."

2. Tell students that *Paradise Lost* was written in the aftermath of the English Civil War. Then **ask** students why this purpose is particularly significant, given the work's historical context.
Answer: *Paradise Lost* can be seen as both an explanation for the suffering that occurs in the world and as a way of giving that suffering meaning.

Literary Analysis
Epic Poetry What epic convention does Milton follow in his opening sentence?

Vocabulary
illumine (i lōō′ mən) *v.*
light up

transgress (trans gres′) *v.*
violate a law or command

Of man's first disobedience, and the fruit
Of that forbidden tree, whose mortal[1] taste
Brought death into the world, and all our woe,
With loss of Eden, till one greater Man[2]
5 Restore us, and regain the blissful seat,
Sing Heavenly Muse,[3] that on the secret top
Of Oreb, or of Sinai,[4] didst inspire
❽ That shepherd, who first taught the chosen seed,
In the beginning how the Heavens and Earth
10 Rose out of Chaos: or if Sion hill[5]
Delight thee more, and Siloa's brook[6] that flowed
Fast[7] by the oracle of God, I thence
Invoke thy aid to my adventurous song,
That with no middle flight intends to soar
15 Above the Aonian mount,[8] while it pursues
Things unattempted yet in prose or rhyme.
And chiefly thou O Spirit,[9] that dost prefer
Before all temples the upright heart and pure,
Instruct me, for thou know'st; thou from the first
20 ❾ Wast present, and with mighty wings outspread
Dovelike sat'st brooding on the vast abyss
And mad'st it pregnant: what in me is dark
Illumine, what is low raise and support;
That to the height of this great argument[10]
25 I may assert Eternal Providence,
And justify the ways of God to men.
    Say first, for Heaven hides nothing from thy view
Nor the deep tract of Hell, say first what cause
Moved our grand[11] parents in that happy state,
30 Favored of Heaven so highly, to fall off
From their Creator, and transgress his will

1. **mortal** deadly.
2. **one . . . Man** Christ.
3. **Heavenly Muse** Urania, the muse of astronomy and sacred poetry in Greek mythology. Here, Milton associates Urania with the holy spirit that inspired Moses ("That shepherd") to receive and interpret the word of God for the Jews ("the chosen seed"). To convey the message of God to his people, Moses wrote the first five books of the Bible, including Genesis, the book on which *Paradise Lost* is based.
4. **Oreb** (ōr′ eb) **. . . Sinai** (sī′ nī′) alternate names for the mountain where God communicated the laws to Moses.
5. **Sion** (sī′ ən) **hill** hill near Jerusalem on which the temple ("the oracle of God") stood.
6. **Siloa's** (sī lō′ əz) **brook** stream near Sion hill.
7. **Fast** close.
8. **Aonian** (ā ō′ nē ən) **mount** Mount Helicon in Greek mythology, home of the Muses. Milton is drawing a comparison between the epic he is now presenting and the epics written by the classical poets, Homer and Virgil.
9. **Spirit** the Holy Spirit, the voice that provided inspiration for the Hebrew prophets.
10. **argument** theme.
11. **grand** first in importance and in time.

Enrichment: Investigating Religion and Myth

Views of Paradise

The description of Paradise differs little among various cultures. An early account of Paradise appears on tablets produced by the Sumer tribe around 5000 B.C. The plain of Babylon, called "Edinn," is described as an innocent, clear, and sun-filled land, where gods are forever young, healthy, and amiable.

In Greek mythology, the inhabitants of Paradise guard the tree that gives the golden apples.

In African tales, Paradise is a beautiful garden with ample food and leisure. There is no death or disease. Humans live in harmony with animals.

Activity: Investigating Religion and Myth Have students conduct further investigation into views of Paradise in religion and myth. Suggest that students use the **Enrichment: Investigating Religion and Myth** worksheet on page 240 of the *Professional Development Guidebook* to collect information.

For[12] one restraint,[13] lords of the world besides?[14]
Who first seduced them to that foul revolt?
The infernal Serpent; he it was, whose guile

35 Stirred up with envy and revenge, deceived
The mother of mankind, what time his pride
Had cast him out from Heaven, with all his host
Of rebel angels, by whose aid aspiring
To set himself in glory above his peers,

40 He trusted to have equaled the Most High,
If he opposed; and with ambitious aim
Against the throne and monarchy of God
Raised impious war in Heaven and battle proud,
With vain attempt. Him the Almighty Power

45 Hurled headlong flaming from the ethereal sky
With hideous ruin and combustion down
To bottomless perdition, there to dwell
In adamantine[15] chains and penal fire,
Who durst defy the Omnipotent to arms.

50 Nine times the space that measures day and night
To mortal men, he with his horrid crew
Lay vanquished, rolling in the fiery gulf,
Confounded though immortal. But his doom
Reserved him to more wrath; for now the thought

55 Both of lost happiness and lasting pain
Torments him; round he throws his baleful eyes
That witnessed[16] huge affliction and dismay,
Mixed with obdurate pride and steadfast hate.
At once as far as angels' ken,[17] he views

60 The dismal situation waste and wild:
A dungeon horrible, on all sides round,
As one great furnace flamed, yet from those flames
No light, but rather darkness visible
Served only to discover sights of woe,

65 Regions of sorrow, doleful shades, where peace
And rest can never dwell, hope never comes
That comes to all; but torture without end
Still urges,[18] and a fiery deluge, fed
With ever-burning sulfur unconsumed:

70 Such place eternal justice had prepared
For these rebellious, here their prison ordained

---

12. **For** because of.
13. **one restraint** commandment that Adam and Eve should not eat of the fruit of the tree of knowledge.
14. **besides** in every other respect.
15. **adamantine** (ad´ ə man´ tēn´) *adj.* unbreakable.
16. **witnessed** gave evidence of.
17. **ken** view; scope of knowledge.
18. **urges** afflicts.

Vocabulary
guile (gīl) *n.* artful trickery

🔟 **Literary Analysis**
Epic Poetry What does the story Milton has chosen to retell reveal about his poetic ambition?

Vocabulary
obdurate (äb´ door it) *adj.* stubborn

12 Reading Check
Whom does Milton call to help him tell his story?

🔟 **Literary Analysis**
Epic Poetry
1. Students will find Milton's syntax complex. Point out that he was deliberately writing in what was known as the "high style" that used sentence forms modeled on Latin grammar.
2. **Ask** students why this syntax is appropriate for an epic poem. **Answer:** An epic is supposed to be lofty.
3. **Ask** students the Literary Analysis question: What does the story Milton has chosen to retell reveal about his poetic ambition? **Answer:** Milton's choice of the grand biblical theme recounting the Fall from the Garden of Eden is extremely ambitious.

11 **Engaging the Essential Question**
1. Read aloud lines 61–69 as students listen with eyes closed. Have them visualize the images in these lines.
2. Have student volunteers describe the mental pictures they formed while listening. Then **ask** students to name details they found particularly vivid. **Possible responses:** Students may say that the image of a great furnace, the flames that do not give off light, and the fiery deluge with its ever-burning sulfur are particularly vivid details.
3. Tell students to look for equally vivid descriptions of Satan as they continue to read the poem.

12 Reading Check
Answer: He calls upon the Muse.

Differentiated Instruction for Universal Access

Strategy for Less Proficient Readers
Milton's words are far easier to understand when they are read aloud, since his long sentences, with clause added to clause, have somewhat the rhythm of speech. Encourage students to say the words to themselves while they read, instead of just moving their eyes along the lines.

Enrichment for Advanced Students
Milton's blindness did not deter him from creating his masterpiece, *Paradise Lost*. Have students research a well-known, creative person who was or is blind, like Ray Charles or Stevie Wonder, and prepare a report on his or her life. Have students present their reports to the class.

13 Critical Viewing

Answer: The artist is depicting the traditional views about the penalties of sin by showing the fallen angel as isolated, with downcast eyes and a posture that suggests he is troubled.

13 ▶ Critical Viewing
What traditional associations with sin explain this artist's rendering of one of Milton's fallen angels? **[Hypothesize]**

In utter darkness, and their portion set
As far removed from God and light of Heaven
As from the center thrice to the utmost pole.[19]
75   O how unlike the place from whence they fell!
There the companions of his fall, o'erwhelmed
With floods and whirlwinds of *tempestuous* fire,
He soon discerns, and weltering by his side
One next himself in power, and next in crime,
80   Long after known in Palestine, and named
Beelzebub.[20] To whom the archenemy,
And thence in Heaven called Satan, with bold words
Breaking the horrid silence thus began:

14 ↓   "If thou beest he; but O how fallen! how changed
85   From him, who in the happy realms of light

Vocabulary
tempestuous
(tem pes′ chōō əs) *adj.*
turbulent; stormy

---

19. **center . . . . pole** three times the distance from the center of the universe (Earth) to the outermost sphere of the universe.
20. **Beelzebub** (bē el′ zə bub′) traditionally, the chief devil, or Satan. In this poem, Satan's chief lieutenant among the fallen angels.

Think Aloud

Vocabulary: Using Context
Direct students' attention to the word *suppliant* in line 112. Use the following "think aloud" to model the skill of using context to infer the meaning of the word. Say to students:

I may not know the meaning of the word *suppliant.* When I read the sentence, however, I can see that the word is an adjective used to describe the noun knee. I also realize that Satan is saying he will never bow or submit to his adversary, God. In saying he will never bow, or kneel, "with suppliant knee," Satan is saying he will never submit. So, *suppliant* is used to describe an attitude of subservience or humility. I think that *sue for grace with suppliant knee* might mean something like "asking for mercy with a humble or subservient attitude."

Clothed with transcendent brightness didst outshine
Myriads though bright: if he whom mutual league,
United thoughts and counsels, equal hope
And hazard in the glorious enterprise,
90 Joined with me once, now misery hath joined
In equal ruin: into what pit thou seest
From what height fallen, so much the stronger proved
He with his thunder:[21] and till then who knew
The force of those dire arms? Yet not for those,
95 Nor what the potent Victor in his rage
Can else inflict, do I repent or change,
Though changed in outward luster, that fixed mind
And high disdain, from sense of injured merit,
That with the Mightiest raised me to contend,
100 And to the fierce contention brought along
Innumerable force of spirits armed
That durst dislike his reign, and me preferring,
His utmost power with adverse power opposed
In dubious battle on the plains of Heaven,
105 And shook his throne. What though the field be lost?
All is not lost; the unconquerable will,
And study[22] of revenge, immortal hate,
And courage never to submit or yield:
And what is else not to be overcome?
110 That glory never shall his wrath or might
Extort from me. To bow and sue for grace
With suppliant knee, and deify his power
Who from the terror of this arm so late
Doubted[23] his empire, that were low indeed,
115 That were an ignominy and shame beneath
This downfall; since by fate the strength of gods
And this empyreal substance[24] cannot fail,
Since through experience of this great event,
In arms not worse, in foresight much advanced,
120 We may with more successful hope resolve
To wage by force or guile eternal war
Irreconcilable, to our grand Foe,
Who now triumphs, and in the excess of joy
Sole reigning holds the tyranny of Heaven."
125   So spake the apostate angel, though in pain,
Vaunting aloud, but racked with deep despair;
And him thus answered soon his bold compeer.[25]

---

21. **He . . . thunder** God.
22. **study** pursuit.
23. **Doubted** feared for.
24. **empyreal** (em pir´ ē əl) **substance** the indestructible substance of which Heaven, or the empyrean, is composed.
25. **compeer** comrade; equal.

Vocabulary
transcendent
(tran sen´ dənt) *adj.*
exceeding beyond all limits

Literary Analysis
Epic Poetry What details in these lines might suggest to some readers that Satan is the hero of Milton's epic?

Literary Analysis
Epic Poetry In what way does Milton's vision of the opposition between Satan and God fit the expectation that epics tell of famous battles?

Vocabulary
ignominy (ig´ nə min´ ē)
n. humiliation; dishonor

 **Reading Check**
Whom does Satan discover lying next to him?

⑭ Literary Analysis
Epic Poetry

1. Remind students of the characteristics of epic poetry; in particular, point out that an epic tells the story of a hero.

2. Explain to students that although Milton's piety was profound, his poem was often lauded for its fascinating depiction of Satan. Romantic poets William Blake and Percy Bysshe Shelley thought Milton's Satan was the real hero of the poem and even applauded his rebellion against the tyranny of Heaven.

3. Instruct students to pay special attention to the characterization of Satan as they read the poem. Then **ask** the Literary Analysis question: What details in these lines might suggest to some readers that Satan is the hero of Milton's epic?
Answer: Students may note that Satan dared to set himself above his peers and set himself on par with God; that Satan dared to raise war against God; or that he suffers a great affliction in Hell.

⑮ Literary Analysis
Epic Poetry

1. Have students read lines 100–124 and have them describe the opposition between God and Satan.

2. **Ask** students the Literary Analysis question: In what way does Milton's vision of the opposition between Satan and God fit the expectation that epics tell of famous battles?
Answer: Milton envisions this opposition as a grand battle, not unlike the battles fought by epic heroes.

⑯ Reading Check
Answer: Satan discovers Beelzebub lying next to him.

Differentiated Instruction for Universal Access

EL Strategy for English Learners
Have students read lines 81–87 and note the use of the word *whom*. Use this example as an opportunity to explain the correct use of *who* and *whom*. *Whom* is the object of the preposition *to*; *who* is the subject of the clause "who in the happy realms of light . . . ."

Vocabulary for Advanced Readers
Have interested students use a dictionary or other resource to look up the meanings of the names Satan and Beelzebub. *Satan* comes from a Hebrew word meaning "adversary," which is appropriate for a former angel who rebelled against God. *Beelzebub* also comes from Hebrew and means "god of flies"—a distasteful name suitable for a fallen angel.

Using Graphic Organizers

1. Remind students about the difference between main and supporting clauses. Main clauses are those that stand by themselves. Supporting clauses cannot stand by themselves.

2. Have students read lines 134–142 and ask them to use the **Reading Strategy Graphic Organizer** to help them distinguish between main and supporting clauses. **Possible responses:** Main clauses:

"I see and rue the dire event," "the mind and spirit remains / invincible," and "vigor soon returns."

18 Literary Analysis

Epic Poetry

1. Have students read lines 159–168 and consider how Milton shows the power and stubbornness of evil.

2. **Ask** students the Literary Analysis question: What assumptions about the epic struggle between good and evil does Milton make in lines 159–168? **Possible response:** Milton's depiction of Satan's stance suggests an assumption on his part that evil is a constant force in life, and that battling evil will be a constant struggle.

---

17 Reading Strategy
Using Graphic Organizers Complete a chart to break the sentence into main and supporting clauses.

18 Literary Analysis
Epic Poetry What assumptions about the epic struggle between good and evil does Milton make in lines 159–168?

"O prince, O chief of many thronèd Powers,
That led the embattled Seraphim[26] to war
130 Under thy conduct, and in dreadful deeds
Fearless, endangered Heaven's perpetual King,
And put to proof his high supremacy,
Whether upheld by strength, or chance, or fate!
Too well I see and rue the dire event[27]
135 That with sad overthrow and foul defeat
Hath lost us Heaven, and all this mighty host
In horrible destruction laid thus low,
As far as gods and heavenly essences
Can perish: for the mind and spirit remains
140 Invincible, and vigor soon returns,
Though all our glory extinct, and happy state
Here swallowed up in endless misery.
But what if he our conqueror (whom I now
Of force[28] believe almighty, since no less
145 Than such could have o'erpowered such force as ours)
Have left us this our spirit and strength entire
Strongly to suffer and support our pains,
That we may so suffice[29] his vengeful ire,
Or do him mightier service as his thralls
150 By right of war, whate'er his business be
Here in the heart of Hell to work in fire,
Or do his errands in the gloomy deep?
What can it then avail though yet we feel
Strength undiminished, or eternal being
155 To undergo eternal punishment?"
Whereto with speedy words the Archfiend replied:
"Fallen cherub, to be weak is miserable,
Doing or suffering:[30] but of this be sure,
To do aught[31] good never will be our task,
160 But ever to do ill our sole delight,
As being the contrary to his high will
Whom we resist. If then his providence
Out of our evil seek to bring forth good,
Our labor must be to pervert that end,
165 And out of good still[32] to find means of evil;
Which oft times may succeed, so as perhaps
Shall grieve him, if I fail not,[33] and disturb

---

26. **Seraphim** (ser´ ə fim´) the highest order of angels.
27. **event** outcome.
28. **Of force** necessarily.
29. **suffice** satisfy.
30. **doing or suffering** whether one is active or passive.
31. **aught** anything.
32. **still** always.
33. **if . . . not** unless I am mistaken.

Enrichment: Understanding Authors

Milton's Gaffe

You may wish to point out to students that even a great poet like Milton could make mistakes. His reference to Briareos and Typhon in line 199 shows that he believed that both of these mythological figures were sent to the underworld by Zeus. The original source for this myth goes back to the ancient Greek poet Hesiod. In his epic poem the *Theogony*, Briareos was not an enemy of Zeus but was instead his ally in the war against the Titans. Moreover, although Zeus did send the Titans to the underworld once the battle had been won, his ally Briareos was not among them.

Activity: Analyzing a Literary Figure
Have interested students investigate the life and works of the Greek poet Hesiod. Invite them to use the **Enrichment: Analyzing a Literary Figure** worksheet on page 235 of the *Professional Development Guidebook* to gather information about where and when Hesiod lived, and about his contribution to literary history.

18 ▲ His inmost counsels from their destined aim.
But see the angry Victor[34] hath recalled
170 His ministers of vengeance and pursuit
Back to the gates of Heaven: the sulfurous hail
Shot after us in storm, o'erblown hath laid
The fiery surge, that from the precipice
Of Heaven received us falling, and the thunder,
175 Winged with red lightning and impetuous rage,
Perhaps hath spent his shafts, and ceases now
To bellow through the vast and boundless deep.
Let us not slip[35] the occasion, whether scorn,
Or satiate[36] fury yield it from our Foe.
180 Seest thou yon dreary plain, forlorn and wild,
The seat of desolation, void of light,
Save what the glimmering of these livid flames
Casts pale and dreadful? Thither let us tend
From off the tossing of these fiery waves,
185 There rest, if any rest can harbor there,
And reassembling our afflicted powers,[37]
Consult how we may henceforth most offend
Our Enemy, our own loss how repair,
How overcome this dire calamity,
190 What reinforcement we may gain from hope,
If not what resolution from despair."
     Thus Satan talking to his nearest mate,
With head uplift above the wave, and eyes
That sparkling blazed; his other parts besides
195 Prone on the flood, extended long and large,
Lay floating many a rood,[38] in bulk as huge
As whom the fables name of monstrous size,
Titanian, or Earthborn, that warred on Jove,
Briareos or Typhon,[39] whom the den
200 By ancient Tarsus[40] held, or that sea beast
Leviathan,[41] which God of all his works
Created hugest that swim the ocean stream:
Him haply slumbering on the Norway foam

---

34. **angry Victor** God.
35. **slip** fail to take advantage of.
36. **satiate** (sā′ shē āt′) satisfied.
37. **afflicted powers** overthrown armies.
38. **rood** old unit of measure equal to seven or eight yards.
39. **Titanian** (tī tā′ nē ən) . . . **Earthborn** . . . **Briareos** (brī ar′ ē əs) . . . **Typhon** (tī′ fən) In classical mythology, both the Titans, led by Briareos, who had a hundred hands, and the Giants (Earthborn), led by Typhon, a hundred-headed serpent monster, fought with Jove. As punishment for their rebellion, both Briareos and Typhon were thrown into the underworld.
40. **Tarsus** (tär′ səs) capital of Cilicia (sə lish′ ə). Typhon is said to have lived in Cilicia near Tarsus.
41. **Leviathan** (lə vī′ ə thən) in the Bible, a great sea monster.

---

19 World
**LITERATURE
CONNECTION**

Reinventing the Epic
When writing *Paradise Lost*, Milton was deeply influenced by classical epics: Homer's the *Iliad* and the *Odyssey*, Virgil's *Aeneid*, and Ovid's *Metamorphoses*. He had read them in the original Greek and Latin and had immersed himself in the ideas and traditions of the ancient world.

Just as the classical poets based their epics on stories that were central to their cultures, Milton based *Paradise Lost* on Genesis, a Biblical account of the world's beginning that was central to his culture. He followed the classical structure, opening *Paradise Lost* with an invocation, or address, to the muse and beginning in the middle of the action. By adapting the ancient epic form to his religious poem, Milton succeeded in combining classical and Christian traditions. Perhaps he also hoped to create a heroic Christian literature that would help pull his divided society together.

Connect to the Literature
What do you think Milton meant when he said that his poem would pursue "Things unattempted yet in prose or rhyme"?

20  Reading Check
What does Satan tell Beelzebub their sole purpose will be?

from Paradise Lost **531**

㉑ Critical Thinking

Analyze

1. Have students compare lines 160–163 with lines 215–220.

2. **Ask** students what, according to these two passages, is one of Satan's main problems?
   Answer: God can turn evil deeds to his own good ends.

3. **Ask:** How does this problem motivate and define Satan?
   Answer: Satan determines to try to bring evil out of good whenever he can, and this becomes his defining purpose.

Spiral Review

Imagery

1. Remind students that they have studied the concept of imagery in an earlier lesson.

2. **Ask** students the Spiral Review question.

   Possible response: The violent imagery suggests a metaphor for the nature and effect of the civil war.

Spiral Review
Imagery
How might the violent imagery in lines 209–241 and elsewhere in the poem relate to the English civil wars?

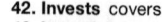

The pilot of some small night-foundered skiff,
205 Deeming some island, oft, as seamen tell,
     With fixed anchor in his scaly rind
     Moors by his side under the lee, while night
     Invests[42] the sea, and wished morn delays:
     So stretched out huge in length the Archfiend lay
210 Chained on the burning lake, nor ever thence
     Had risen or heaved his head, but that the will
     And high permission of all-ruling Heaven
     Left him at large to his own dark designs,
     That with reiterated crimes he might
215 Heap on himself damnation, while he sought
     Evil to others, and enraged might see
 ㉑ How all his malice served but to bring forth
     Infinite goodness, grace and mercy shown
     On man by him seduced, but on himself
220 Treble confusion, wrath and vengeance poured.
     Forthwith upright he rears from off the pool
     His mighty stature; on each hand the flames
     Driven backward, slope their pointing spires, and rolled
     In billows leave in the midst a horrid vale.
225 Then with expanded wings he steers his flight
     Aloft, incumbent[43] on the dusky air
     That felt unusual weight, till on dry land
     He lights, if it were land that ever burned
     With solid, as the lake with liquid fire;
230 And such appeared in hue, as when the force
     Of subterranean wind transports a hill
     Torn from Pelorus, or the shattered side
     Of thundering Etna,[44] whose combustible
     And fueled entrails thence conceiving fire,
235 Sublimed[45] with mineral fury, aid the winds,
     And leave a singèd bottom all involved[46]
     With stench and smoke: such resting found the sole
     Of unblessed feet. Him followed his next mate,
     Both glorying to have scaped the Stygian[47] flood
240 As gods, and by their own recovered strength,
     Not by the sufferance[48] of supernal[49] power.
        "Is this the region, this the soil, the clime,"
     Said then the lost Archangel, "this the seat

---

42. **Invests** covers.
43. **incumbent** lying.
44. **Pelorus** (pə lôr′ əs) . . . **Etna** volcanic mountains in Sicily.
45. **Sublimed** vaporized.
46. **involved** enveloped.
47. **Stygian** (stij′ ē ən) of the river Styx, which, in Greek mythology, encircled Hades (hā′ dēz′), the home of the dead.
48. **sufferance** permission.
49. **supernal** (sə purn′ əl) heavenly.

Vocabulary Development

Vocabulary Knowledge Rating

When students have completed reading and discussing the selections, have them take out the **Vocabulary Knowledge Rating Charts** they worked on earlier. Read the words aloud and have students rate their knowledge of the words again in the After Reading column. Clarify any words that are still problematic. Have students write their own definitions and example or sentence in the appropriate column. Then, have students complete the Vocabulary lesson at the end of this selection. Encourage students to use the words in further discussion and written work about the selections. Remind them that they will be accountable for these words on the **Selection Test**, *Unit 3 Resources*, pages 78–80 or 81–83.

245   That we must change⁵⁰ for Heaven, this mournful gloom
    For that celestial light? Be it so, since he
    Who now is sovereign can dispose and bid
    What shall be right: farthest from him is best,
    Whom reason hath equaled, force hath made supreme
250   Above his equals. Farewell happy fields,
    Where joy forever dwells. Hail horrors! Hail
    Infernal world! and thou, profoundest Hell
    Receive thy new possessor, one who brings
    A mind not to be changed by place or time.

22   The mind is its own place, and in itself
255   Can make a Heaven of Hell, a Hell of Heaven.
    What matter where, if I be still the same,
    And what I should be, all but less than he
    Whom thunder hath made greater? Here at least
    We shall be free; the Almighty hath not built
260   Here for his envy, will not drive us hence:
    Here we may reign secure, and in my choice
    To reign is worth ambition though in Hell:

50. **change** exchange.

22 Literary Analysis
Epic Poetry and Poetic Ambition In what way is the attitude expressed in lines 250–258 fitting both for a hero and a poet?

23 Reading Check
What does Satan say about the mind?

24 ◄ Critical Viewing
Why might the English Civil War have made Milton think of a battle between angels like the one depicted in this picture? **[Connect]**

from Paradise Lost **533**

22 Literary Analysis
Epic Poetry and Poetic Ambition
Monitor Progress

1. **Ask** students to explain what an epic is.
Answer: An epic is a long narrative poem about a hero.

2. Point out that if *Paradise Lost* is an epic, there must be a hero. Ask students to identify who the hero of the poem is.
Possible response: Students may feel that Satan is the hero of the poem because he seems to be the main character.

3. Have students read lines 250–258. Have students identify the attitude expressed in these lines.
Answer: The attitude expressed is one of extreme self-confidence and defiance.

4. Then, **ask** students the Literary Analysis question: In what way is the attitude expressed in lines 250–258 fitting both for a hero and a poet?
Answer: It is fitting for a hero who, despite being subjected to such terrible circumstances, nonetheless stands up against his punishment and asserts himself defiantly. Similarly, it is fitting for a poet because it describes his efforts to overcome the limitations of his mortal existence through his poetic craft.

Reteach

If students are having difficulty, review with them the explanation of an epic on page 521, and have them find details that make Satan seem heroic.

23 Reading Check

Answer: The mind is a powerful tool that can affect one's whole perspective on life.

24 Critical Viewing

Possible response: Students may respond that the war may have inspired Milton to describe fierce and warlike angels, like the ones in this illustration.

Before students respond, you may wish to have them write a brief objective summary of the selection. As they answer the questions below, remind them to support their answers with evidence from the text.

1. (a) Milton writes that Satan deceived Eve out of revenge on God for casting him out of Heaven. (b) Adam and Eve, like Satan, fall because they question God's sovereignty.

2. (a) Milton's Hell is dark, eternally burning, and filled with tortured souls who have no hope of relief. (b) Satan reacts with a sense of personal injury.

3. (a) He threatens an eternal war, fought by force or by guile. (b) Satan's motive is revenge. (c) Failing to regain Heaven for himself, Satan brings about the downfall of Adam and Eve.

4. (a) Satan's attitude, that the mind can make a Heaven of Hell, proves that adversity will not change his mind. (b) Attitude and outlook help to determine an individual's experience of one's situation and place.

5. (a) Satan is rebellious and stubborn, but he is also courageous. Example: "Better to reign in Hell than serve in Heaven" (line 263). (b) Students may say that Satan's determination to make the best of what he has and his desire for freedom at all costs are heroic and admirable. A focus on his fall from grace, however, makes him seem despairing.

6. (a) Milton means that he intends to make God's decisions understandable to people. (b) Students may mention lines 209–220 as a reasonable explanation for why God allows evil in the world.

7. **Possible response:** Lines 60–124 give a traditional description of Hell but invent new details about Lucifer, or Satan, creating a detailed and innovative characterization.

265

Better to reign in Hell than serve in Heaven.
But wherefore[51] let we then our faithful friends,
The associates and copartners of our loss
Lie thus astonished[52] on the oblivious[53] pool,
And call them not to share with us their part
In this unhappy mansion, or once more
With rallied arms to try what may be yet
Regained in Heaven, or what more lost in Hell?"

51. **wherefore** why.
52. **astonished** stunned.
53. **oblivious** causing forgetfulness.

Critical Reading

Cite textual evidence to support your responses.

1. **Key Ideas and Details (a)** Summarize the story of Adam and Eve as Milton tells it in lines 28–36. **(b) Connect:** How is the fall of Adam and Eve connected to the fall of Satan and his cohorts?

2. **Key Ideas and Details (a)** Lines 59–74 describe Hell. What does Milton indicate are its main features? **(b) Interpret:** Explain Satan's reaction in lines 94–99 to his fall into Hell.

3. **Key Ideas and Details (a) Infer:** In lines 116–124, what kind of war does Satan propose to wage against Heaven? **(b) Interpret:** Judging from lines 105–116, what is his motive for such a war? **(c) Hypothesize:** How will this war lead to the fall of Adam and Eve?

4. **Integration of Knowledge and Ideas (a) Interpret:** Explain how Satan's attitude toward Hell in lines 250–252 proves that he is "one who brings / A mind not to be changed by place or time" (lines 252–253). **(b) Draw Conclusions:** Explain how the mind "Can make a Heaven of Hell, a Hell of Heaven" (line 255).

5. **Integration of Knowledge and Ideas (a) Summarize:** Characterize Satan, supporting your description with quotations from the text. **(b) Evaluate:** To what extent does Satan seem admirable? To what extent despairing? Explain.

6. **Integration of Knowledge and Ideas (a) Interpret:** What does Milton mean when he says he wants to "justify the ways of God to men" (line 26)? **(b) Assess:** How good a start has Milton made toward this goal? Explain.

7. **Integration of Knowledge and Ideas** Focus on an especially strong passage in *Paradise Lost*. What devices—word choice, rhythm, characterization, description—help Milton reinvent the story of the fallen angels? In your response, use at least two of these Essential Question words: *invent, innovation, tradition.* *[Connecting to the Essential Question: What is the relationship of the writer to tradition?]*

Concept Connector

Reading Skill Graphic Organizer
Ask students to review the graphic organizers in which they identified the main and supporting clauses of complex sentences. Then, have students share and compare their organizers.

Activating Prior Knowledge
Have students return to their responses to the Activating Prior Knowledge activity, in which they explained what they would want to be remembered for in 100 years. Have students think about how Milton is remembered, and then revise their responses in light of any new knowledge gained from their reading.

Writing About the Essential Question
Have students recall their responses to the Connecting to the Essential Question writing prompt on page 521. Have them work in small groups to identify Milton's relationship to tradition. Ask groups to share their ideas with the class.

Critical Commentary

from "A Defense of Poetry"
Percy Bysshe Shelley

from *Surprised by Sin*
Stanley Fish

Poets and critics have long debated whether Satan in Paradise Lost *is an evil villain or the secret hero of the poem. Romantics like Percy Bysshe Shelley viewed Satan as a heroic Romantic rebel. Writing in 1821, Shelley made the case for that perspective.*

Milton's Devil as a moral being is as far superior to his God, as one who perseveres in some purpose, which he has conceived to be excellent in spite of adversity and torture, is to one who in the cold security of undoubted triumph inflicts the most horrible revenge upon his enemy, not from any mistaken notion of inducing him to repent of a perseverance in enmity, but with the alleged design of exasperating him to deserve new torments. Milton has so far violated the popular creed (if this shall be judged to be a violation) as to have alleged no superiority of moral virtue to his god over his devil. And this bold neglect of a direct moral purpose is the most decisive proof of the supremacy of Milton's genius. . . .

Writing exactly 150 years later, the critic Stanley Fish argued that, far from being an admirable rebel, Milton's Satan has no will or identity of his own.

. . . Satan's independence is an illusion because he is in bondage to the freedom to do as he likes and he becomes the captive of momentary purposes and the plaything of master strategists (God, Milton) who make of him what they will; his will does not exist (he has no "deepest self"), except in a Satanic never-never-Land where evil could be someone's good. This reversal is impossible in a universe where God is God and when Satan admits "myself am Hell" he, in effect, says "myself am not," since hell is the state of disunion from God's sustaining power and hence a state of nonbeing . . . Perhaps the most ironic of his boasts is this one: "What matter where, if I be still the same" (I.256). The sameness of evil is the sameness of chaos, a stability of instability where the identity and form of any atom or cluster of atoms is a matter of chance unless an ordering power is imposed; Satan is condemned to restless wandering until God or some deputy of God finds a use for him and endows him with motives and opinions and powers to fit the role "imposed from without."

© **Key Ideas and Details** What admirable qualities does Shelley attribute to Satan? Why does Fish declare that "Satan's independence is an illusion"?

Critical Commentary

1. Have students read the passage from Shelley's "A Defense of Poetry." Then **ask** students to explain why Shelley says that Milton's Satan is "far superior to his God."
   Answer: Satan is committed to his purpose no matter what kind of adversity he encounters.

2. **Ask** students why Shelley finds Milton to have "violated the popular creed."
   Answer: The "popular creed" would be to portray God as inherently more "moral" than Satan. Shelley thinks that Milton violated this by refusing to make Satan less moral than God.

3. Have students read the comments made by Stanley Fish. **Ask** them to discuss what Fish means by saying that Milton's Satan is "in bondage to the freedom to do as he likes."
   Possible response: Milton's Satan may be limited to actions that are in accord with his narrow purposes. A "master strategist" may have more than one motive for his or her actions, and so, more possible actions from which to choose.

Key Ideas and Details
Answers

1. Milton's Devil persevered in his purpose despite adversity; he stayed true to his chosen course; his revenge is thorough.

2. Fish believes that Satan thinks himself independent, but he is really a shallow character in bondage to one limiting purpose, while the truly powerful "beings" are God and Milton.

Enrichment: Analyzing Themes and Symbols

Lucifer
Students may be interested to learn that *Lucifer*, which means "light-bearer" in Greek, was, according to Christian theology, Satan's name when he was the Angel of Light, before he rebelled against God. You might want to have students evaluate the appropriateness of Satan's punishment given this information. Students will probably find it appropriate that the former angel of light is punished by being cast into darkness.

Activity: Analyzing Themes and Symbols
Encourage interested students to investigate the symbolic use of light and dark in Milton's work. They way wish to compare this with the use of light and dark in other works of literature. Have them use the **Enrichment: Analyzing Themes and Symbols** worksheet on page 243 of the *Professional Development Guidebook.* Ask students to share their conclusions with their classmates.

Answers

1. (a) The sestet in Sonnet XIX has a more regular pattern. (b) Yes; the regularity gives a strong feeling of resolution.

2. (a) Milton changes the pattern by using run-on rhymes. (b) This links the problem and solution even more closely.

3. (a) Satan and the fallen angels have been expelled from Heaven. (b) An epic begins *in media res* (in the middle of things).

4. Milton depicts Satan as being courageous in the face of calamity.

5. **Possible response:** In Sonnet VII, the speaker answers his own concerns about his lack of accomplishment by asserting that whatever he achieves is the will of Heaven. In Sonnet XIX, Milton confronts the obstacle that his blindness poses; he comforts himself with the idea that submission to God's will is all that God requires.

6. (a) Milton reflects Homer by invoking the assistance of the Muse; he connects with the Bible in his retelling of Satan's tale. (b) Rather than standing by, Milton created his great epic.

7. (a) Certainly, Milton made his own "place" in his mind. (b) In *Paradise Lost,* Satan vows to make Heaven out of Hell. Milton also makes a heaven out of hell—by pushing through his blindness to create a sublime epic poem.

8. In the drawing, paradise is lost—it has become a wasteland. The phrase "paradise lost" is a humorous allusion to Milton's work.

9. Students' choices of passages will vary. The graphic organizer should be filled out accurately.

10. (a) The main clause is "I fondly ask." (b) The clause "Doth God exact labor..." is the direct object of the verb *ask.* "When I consider how my light is spent..." expresses Milton's concern with his blindness. "And that one talent..." makes the reader understand that Milton fears nothing more than losing his talent, because it is the only way he knows to serve God.

After You Read | *Poetry of John Milton*

Literary Analysis

1. **Craft and Structure** **(a)** Which **Italian sonnet** has the more regular pattern of rhymes in the sestet? **(b)** Does this regularity strengthen the "solution" the sestet gives to the problem set out in the octave? Explain.

2. **Craft and Structure** **(a)** In Sonnet XIX, how does sentence structure break with the pattern of octave and sestet? **(b)** What effect is achieved?

3. **Key Ideas and Details** **(a)** What major event has occurred before the beginning of Milton's **epic?** **(b)** How does picking up the story after this event follow the conventions of epic form?

4. **Craft and Structure** A traditional epic character has a powerful personality. How does Milton make Satan a suitable epic character?

5. **Integration of Knowledge and Ideas** In Sonnets VII and XIX, Milton reflects on setbacks to his poetic ambition. Use a chart like the one shown to compare the two poems.

Speaker's Situation	Effect on Ambition	Solution	How Solution Helps

6. **Integration of Knowledge and Ideas** **(a)** Explain how, by writing *Paradise Lost,* Milton aspires to the literary greatness of Homer and the Bible. Provide lines from the poem in support. **(b)** Does Milton's ambition contradict the moral of Sonnet XIX: "They also serve who only stand and wait"? Why or why not?

7. **Integration of Knowledge and Ideas** **(a)** What ideas about the power of a poet might lines 254–255 of *Paradise Lost* suggest? **(b)** What parallel, if any, can you draw between the situation of Satan and the ambition of a poet? Explain.

8. **Integration of Knowledge and Ideas** Using your knowledge of *Paradise Lost,* explain the humor of the cartoon shown on this page.

Reading Strategy

9. **(a)** Identify a passage that was hard to understand. **(b)** Explain how to repair comprehension by **using a graphic organizer** to break down sentences into main and supporting clauses.

10. **(a)** Identify the main clause in lines 1–8 of Sonnet XIX. **(b)** Explain what each supporting clause adds to its meaning.

Common Core State Standards

Language
4.c. Consult general and specialized reference materials, both print and digital, to find the pronunciation of a word or determine or clarify its precise meaning, its part of speech, its etymology, or its standard usage. *(p. 537)*
6. Acquire and use accurately general academic and domain-specific words and phrases, sufficient for reading, writing, speaking, and listening at the college and career readiness level. *(p. 537)*

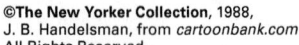

"We're Birds of Paradise all right—paradise lost!"

Assessment Practice

Writer's Purpose

Assessments often ask students to determine an author's purpose. Use the following passage to remind students that writers may directly state their purposes.

> Sing heavenly Muse . . .
> . . . what in me is dark
> Illumine, what is low raise and support;
> That to the height of this great argument
> I may assert Eternal Providence
> And justify the ways of God to men . . .

Milton's main purpose is to—
A convert people to Christianity.
B retell the story of Adam and Eve.
C be compared with Homer, who composed the *Iliad.*
D justify God's actions to humankind.

Students should determine that the correct answer is *D.*

Integrated Language Skills

© Vocabulary Acquisition and Use

Word Analysis: Latin Root -lum-

The Latin root -lum-, found in *illumine*, means "light" or "lamp." It is the basis for many words used in *science* to describe light.

Review the list of words and definitions containing -lum-. Then, use the context of the sentences that follow to determine which words fit best in the sentences that follow. Use each word only once and explain your answers.

illuminant *n.* something giving off light

illuminate *v.* shed light on

lumens *n.* units of light

luminous *adj.* emitting light

1. "This clue may _____ the entire mystery," exclaimed the detective.

2. A more efficient light bulb generates more _____ while using less power.

3. The _____ full moon made the path ahead of them clear.

4. A flickering torch served as their only _____.

Using Resources to Build Vocabulary

Epic Style: Words for the Nether World

In *Paradise Lost*, one of Milton's greatest challenges is to create a vivid picture of Hell. He meets this challenge by using words like the ones below to describe the underworld:

desolation	dreary
forlorn	glimmering
gloom	horrid
mournful	wild

Note how the *connotations*, or associations, of these words serve Milton's purpose. Then, use a print or an electronic *dictionary* or *thesaurus* to find **antonyms**—words with the opposite meaning—of these words. Identify which of those antonyms you think Milton might use to describe Heaven and explain why.

Vocabulary: Synonyms

A **synonym** is a word that has a similar meaning as another word. Write a complete sentence to answer each question that follows. In your answer, replace the underlined word or words with a synonym taken from the vocabulary list on page 521.

1. Does a good portrait give more than a <u>likeness</u> of its subject?

2. What did they use to <u>shine on</u> the dark pool?

3. What do shoplifters want when they <u>commit a wrong</u>?

4. How does <u>sneakiness</u> benefit a spy?

5. How would an <u>inflexible</u> child act?

6. What effect did the <u>violent</u> events have on the crowd?

7. How did the audience feel about the <u>unmatchable</u> musical performance?

8. Did the corrupt senator's <u>shame</u> affect anyone else?

Extended Study: Integrated Language Skills **537**

Vocabulary Acquisition and Use

Word Analysis

1. illuminate—the answer will be revealed

2. lumens—more units of light

3. luminous—brightened the path

4. illuminant—source of light

Vocabulary

Possible responses:

1. Yes, a good portrait gives more than a semblance of the subject.

2. They used a flashlight to illumine the dark pool.

3. Shoplifters want free goods when they transgress.

4. Guile benefits a spy because he needs to avoid detection.

5. An obdurate child might throw a tantrum.

6. The crowd was traumatized by the tempestuous events.

7. The audience was impressed with the transcendant performance.

8. The corrupt senator's ignominy tainted everyone's view of him.

Using Resources to Build Vocabulary

Possible responses:

desolation—splendor

forlorn—hopeful

gloom—cheer

mournful—happy

dreary—sunny

glimmering—shining

horrid—wonderful

wild—calm

Any of the antonyms could be used to describe Heaven, because they are positive terms.

Assessment Resources

Unit 3 Resources

L1 L2 EL **Selection Test A,** pp. 78–80. Administer Test A to less advanced readers.

L3 L4 EL **Selection Test B,** pp. 81–83.

L3 L4 **Open-Book Test,** pp. 75–77. As an alternative, administer the Open-Book Test

All **Customizable Test Bank**

All **Self-tests**
Students may prepare for the **Selection Test** by taking the **Self-test** online.

PHLit Online! All assessment resources are available at **www.PHLitOnline.com**.

Writing

1. To guide students in writing this informative text, give them the Support for Writing page (*Unit 3 Resources,* p. 73).

2. Remind students that their essays should clearly express their thesis and all ideas should be supported with evidence from the text.

3. You might want to have students brainstorm together about other dynamic villains before they begin writing.

4. Use the **Rubrics for Writing Self-Assessment,** *Professional Development Guidebook,* pp. 195–196, to evaluate students' work.

Writing

ⓒ **Argumentative Text** Twentieth-century literary critic Douglas Bush said this of *Paradise Lost*: "Its characterization of Satan is one of the supreme achievements of world literature." Clearly Satan is the villain of the poem. Is he more than that? Do you feel any admiration or sympathy for him as you read?

Write an **essay** in which you present and defend your analysis of the character of Satan in *Paradise Lost.* Consider both positive and negative aspects of his character. In your essay, explain how your view of Satan influences your interpretation of *Paradise Lost* itself.

Prewriting Study the *imagery, language, events, universal themes, speeches,* and *stylistic devices* that Milton uses to characterize Satan. Refer to the Critical Commentary on page 535 to spark your own ideas.

- Use a chart like the one shown to take your notes.
- Consider how Milton balances these positive and negative elements.
- Think about other villains from literature or movies. How does Milton's treatment of Satan compare to the way these villains are presented?
- Write a sentence or two to serve as the thesis of your essay, and develop an outline that shows how you will support the thesis.

Negative Aspects	Positive Aspects
introduction to Satan: (lines 34–40) he is arrogant and destructive	strong will: "All is not lost" (line 106)
"durst defy the Omnipotent" (line 49)	resourceful: "We may with more successful hope resolve / To wage by force or guile eternal war" (lines 120–121)
"obdurate pride and steadfast hate" (line 58)	

Drafting Write a draft of your essay that follows your outline and incorporates evidence from the text of *Paradise Lost* to support your points. State your thesis in the opening paragraph, support it in the body of the essay, and conclude the essay by summarizing what you have proved.

Revising Revise your essay to make it clear and effective.

- Review your draft, making sure you have included *accurate and detailed references to the text* to support your points.
- If your opening paragraph is not lively, consider quoting from the poem or contrasting Satan with another villain to catch readers' attention.
- Check quotations to be sure they are accurate and properly referenced.
- Read the essay carefully to make sure it is grammatically correct and that all words are spelled correctly.

538 A Turbulent Time (1625–1798)

ⓒ **Common Core State Standards**

Writing
1.a. Introduce precise, knowledgeable claim(s), and create an organization that logically sequences claim(s), reasons, and evidence.
1.b. Develop claim(s) fairly and thoroughly, supplying the most relevant evidence for each.
1.e. Provide a concluding statement or section that follows from and supports the argument presented.

Teaching Resources

Unit 3 Resources
- L3 L4 **Vocabulary Builder,** p. 71
- L3 L4 **Support for Writing Lesson,** p. 73
- L3 L4 **Grammar and Style,** p. 72
- L4 **Enrichment,** p. 74

All **Enriched Online Student Edition**
Interactive Grammar Lesson: available under After You Read for this selection
Internet Research Activity: available under After You Read for this selection

Professional Development Guidebook
Rubrics for Writing Self-Assessment: pp. 195–196

 All resources are available at www.PHLitOnline.com.

Conventions and Style: Misplaced and Dangling Modifiers

One way to make your writing clearer is to avoid misplaced and dangling modifiers. A **misplaced modifier** seems to modify the wrong word in a sentence because it is too far away from the word it really modifies. A **dangling modifier** does not sensibly modify any word because the word it should modify does not appear in the sentence. Always check your writing for any words, phrases, or clauses that are misplaced or dangling modifiers.

Fix Misplaced and Dangling Modifiers

Misplaced	Better
Milton hoped to one day achieve poetic greatness *early in his career.* (phrase)	Early in his career, Milton hoped to one day achieve poetic greatness.

Dangling	Better
Seeking revenge against God, Eve is tempted into eating the forbidden fruit. (phrase)	Seeking revenge against God, Satan tempts Eve into eating the forbidden fruit.
While he was working as a translator for the government, his eyesight was lost. (clause)	While he was working as a translator for the government, Milton lost his eyesight.

Practice Fix each misplaced or dangling modifier to make the sentence clear and sensible. You may have to change the wording slightly. In items 1–5, the misplaced or dangling modifier is in italics.

1. Milton dictated the poem to his daughters, *blind and unable to write.*
2. *Gifted*, Milton's destiny was to become a famous poet.
3. *At the age of fourteen*, Milton's formal education was begun.
4. *Learning about the revolt against the king*, Milton's tour of Europe was cut short.
5. His blindness is the burden he bears, *which he calls a "mild yoke."*
6. Losing the battle, Hell becomes the rebellious angels' place of banishment.
7. Satan initiates a battle with God motivated by pride and willfulness.
8. The speaker reflects that time has stolen his youth on his birthday.
9. Concerned about his career progress, comfort is found in the speaker's faith.
10. Satan decides he will make humans commit acts of evil during his conversation with Beelzebub.

© Writing and Speaking Conventions

A. Writing Write a sentence using each phrase or clause as a modifier. Then, tell what word or words the phrase or clause modifies.

    1. getting older   **2.** during middle age   **3.** who serves God

    Example: getting older
    Sentence: The poet, getting older, wrote about time.
    Word Modified: poet

B. Speaking Write and perform a dialogue in which Satan tries to rally his fellow devils. Correctly use one word, one phrase, and one clause as modifiers.

PH WRITING COACH

Further instruction and practice are available in *Prentice Hall Writing Coach.*

Extended Study: Integrated Language Skills **539**

Answers
Conventions and Style

Introduce and discuss the skill, using the instruction on the student page.

Think Aloud: Model the Skill

Say to students:

    One of the most important things to remember as a writer is that you want your readers to understand what you mean. One way to prevent any misunderstanding is to check your writing for misplaced or dangling modifiers.

PH WRITING COACH Grade 12

Further instruction on and practice with modifiers can be found in Chapter 16, section 5.

Practice
Sample answers:

1. Milton, who was blind and unable to write, dictated the poem to his daughters.
2. The gifted Milton was destined to become a famous poet.
3. Milton began his formal education at the age of fourteen.
4. Upon learning about the revolt against the king, Milton cut short his tour of Europe.
5. His blindness, which he calls a mild "yoke," is the burden he bears.
6. Hell becomes the rebellious angels' place of banishment after they lose the battle.
7. Satan, motivated by pride and willfulness, initiates a battle with God.
8. The speaker reflects on his birthday that time has stolen his youth.
9. Concerned about his career progress, the speaker finds comfort in his faith.
10. During his conversation with Beelzebub, Satan decides he will make humans commit acts of evil.

Writing and Speaking Conventions

A. Sample answers:

1. The <u>woman,</u> getting older, began to fear death.
2. During middle age, <u>she</u> hadn't had such concerns.
3. The <u>poet</u> who serves God writes divinely.

B. Student dialogues will vary. Check for proper usage of modifiers.

539

Epics in World Literature

1. Tell students that an epic is a long narrative poem. An epic typically recounts the deeds and adventures of heroic or legendary figures or the history of a nation.

2. Tell students that two of the most famous epic poems are the *Iliad* and the *Odyssey* by Homer, which tell about the Trojan War and the adventures of Odysseus on his voyage home after the war. Have a volunteer who knows any of the conflicts in the poems share them with the class.

3. Explain that an epic typically focuses on the great deeds of a hero. **Ask** students to suggest other genres that focus on a central hero. **Possible answers:** mystery, historical fiction, science fiction, fairy tale.

4. Direct students' attention to the illustrations of some of the world epics. Note that each of these epics originated in a different part of the world. **Ask** students why they believe the epic is a cross-cultural genre. **Possible response:** All cultures dream about an "ideal"; in epics, the protagonist possesses superhuman strength, wisdom, and insight.

5. Inquire if students have read any of the pictured epics. If so, have volunteers tell what they know about the epics they have read.

EPICS
in World Literature

Match numbers on the left with pictures on the right to see illustrations of some of these world epics.

1 *Iliad and Odyssey* (c. 800–700 B.C.)
ancient Greek epics attributed to Homer

Mahabharata (200 B.C.–A.D. 400)
Indian epic attributed to Vyasa

Song of Roland (c. A.D. 1100)
French epic

2 *Song of My Cid* (c. 1140)
Spanish epic

3 *Divine Comedy* (1308–1321)
Italian epic by Dante Alighieri

4 *Paradise Lost* (1667) and
Paradise Regained (1671)
English epics by John Milton

5 *The Song of Hiawatha* (1855)
American epic by Henry Wadsworth Longfellow

Sundiata (1960)
West African epic, created as a novel by D. T. Niane

6 *Omeros* (1990)
Caribbean epic by Derek Walcott

540 A Turbulent Time (1625–1798)

Enrichment: Analyzing Forms and Genres

Epics

The term *epic* or *heroic poem* is applied to a work that meets at least the following criteria: it is a long narrative poem on a serious subject, it is told in an elevated style, and it is centered on a heroic or superhuman figure on whose actions depends the fate of a tribe, a nation, or the human race. The "traditional epics" were shaped by a literary artist from historical and legendary materials that developed in the oral traditions of his or her nation during a period of expansion and warfare.

Activity: Analyze and Compare Two Epics
Have interested students learn more about two of the epics illustrated in the spread. Ask them to discuss how the works fit the criteria above. Suggest that students record their analyses on the **Enrichment: Analyzing Forms and Genres** worksheet, *Professional Development Guidebook,* page 227.

COMMON CORE ▪ EXTENDED STUDY: JOHN MILTON

Comparing Literary Works

from *Paradise Lost* • from the
Divine Comedy: Inferno

Comparing Epics Around the World

The Epic Tradition Epics are long narrative poems describing the adventures of noble characters. Among the earliest epics are *Gilgamesh*, from the Middle East, and the ancient Greek epics attributed to Homer, the *Iliad* and the *Odyssey*. One of the first epics with a known author is the Roman poet Virgil's *Aeneid*. Christian authors Dante Alighieri (the *Divine Comedy*) and John Milton (*Paradise Lost*) imitated classical models and developed their great works using these traditional elements of epics:

- amazing events, such as great battles, and vast settings
- larger-than-life main characters and supernatural creatures who take an interest in human affairs
- themes expressing important cultural values and beliefs
- an elevated style using a serious tone and lofty poetic language

As you read, use a chart like the one shown to help you compare the elements of the excerpt from Dante's epic with those from Milton's *Paradise Lost*. Consider the impact of the choices that each author made.

	Divine Comedy: Inferno	Paradise Lost
subject		the Fall of Humanity
main character(s)		Satan; larger-than-life supernatural character
setting(s)		vivid depictions of Heaven and Hell
theme(s)		original sin; pride and disobedience
style		serious tone; lofty poetic language; blank verse

© **Gather Vocabulary Knowledge**

Dante used related forms of the words *cowered, awe,* and *writhes*. Use a **dictionary** to find each word's part of speech and definition. Then, employ the following references to further explore these words:

- **History of Language:** Use a history of English to research each word's origins. Write a paragraph about the word's emergence in English.
- **Book of Quotations:** Use an online or print collection of quotations to find a quotation containing one of the words. In a paragraph, explain nuances in meaning that are evident from the context of the quotation.

Comparing References Compare and contrast what you learn about the words from these and other related references, printed or electronic.

© **Common Core State Standards**

Reading Literature
3. Analyze the impact of the author's choices regarding how to develop and relate elements of a story or drama.

Language
6. Demonstrate independence in gathering vocabulary knowledge when considering a word or phrase important to comprehension or expression.

PHLit
Online!
www.PHLitOnline.com

from Paradise Lost • *from the* Divine Comedy: Inferno **541**

PRETEACH

© **Common Core State Standards**

- **Reading Literature 3**
- **Writing 2, 10**
- **Language 6**

Comparing Epics Around the World

1. Review the characteristics of epics with students. Remind them that while the original epics were products of the oral tradition in warrior societies, the form has been adapted by later, literate cultures. In adapting the form, writers still maintain one of it's key functions in celebrating their cultures core values and posing it's key dilemmas.

2. Tell students that in the selection they are about to read, Dante, like Milton, adapts epic conventions to a 'Christian' worldview.

Gather Vocabulary Knowledge

Have print and online quotation resources available for students.

Begin by displaying the following quotation from Milton.

"Gratitude bestows reverence, allowing us to encounter everyday epiphanies, those transcendent moments of awe that change forever how we experience life and the world."

Discuss with students how the context helps them understand the meaning of *awe*.

Teaching Resources

The following resources can be used to enrich, extend, or differentiate the instruction.

All *Unit 3 Resources,* pp. 84–85.

All Enriched Online Student Edition

All *Common Core Companion*
pp. 28–40; 196–207, 269–276; 336–337

PHLit
Online!

All resources are available online at
www.PHLitOnline.com.

541

Background

More About the Author

Although known mostly for his poetic works, Dante's influence extends into moral philosophy, rhetoric, and political thought. His writing influences included many of the key figures in classical literature, such as Virgil, Cicero, and Boethius. Although born into a relatively poor family, Dante's knowledge and understanding of contemporary scholastic philosophy and theology were remarkable. His knowledge of political theories and government thrust him into the major political controversies of his day. Around 1313, Dante finished *De monarchia* (*On Monarchy*), which is one of the major works of medieval political philosophy.

Dante
Alighieri
(1265–1321)

Author of the *Divine Comedy: Inferno*

Dante Alighieri (dän′ tā al əg yer′ ē), whose visions of Hell have haunted readers for centuries, is widely considered one of the greatest poets of western civilization. T. S. Eliot wrote, "Dante and Shakespeare divide the modern world between them; there is no third."

Political Chaos Dante was born into a poor but noble family in the Italian city of Florence. At the time, Italy was not a unified nation but a collection of independent city-states where internal political struggles and interstate rivalries often led to warfare. Elected to help run Florence's government, Dante and his party were overthrown in civil warfare that led to exile from his beloved city in 1302. His experience of exile would play an important role in his writing.

Pioneering Italian In Dante's time, most European writers wrote in Latin, the language of scholarship and the Church. Dante believed that poets should write in the vernacular, or language of the people—in his case, Italian. In 1304, he published *De Vulgari Eloquentia*, which argued for the use of the vernacular. He wrote many lyric poems in Italian, and his crowning achievement, the *Divine Comedy*, was also an Italian work.

The Love of His Life Appearing in the *Divine Comedy* is a woman named Beatrice, to whom Dante also dedicated his early love poems. Scholars believe she is based on a real-life person, Beatrice Portinari. Yet evidence suggests that Dante saw the real Beatrice only twice in his life—first when he was nine and then nine years later. Nevertheless, for Dante, Beatrice came to represent an ideal love figure, the guiding force that led him from despair.

> "Midway in our life's journey, I went astray / from the straight road and woke to find myself / **alone in a dark wood. . . .**"

542 A Turbulent Time (1625–1798)

③

FROM THE DIVINE COMEDY:
❶ Inferno   Dante Alighieri
translated by John Ciardi

❷ **BACKGROUND** In his *Divine Comedy*, Dante uses an organizing principle based on the number three, drawn from the Christian concept of the Holy Trinity. Documenting his imagined visit to Hell, Purgatory, and Heaven, he divides the epic into three parts—*Inferno, Purgatorio,* and *Paradiso.*

In Paradise, Dante will be guided by his beloved Beatrice. For his trip through Hell to Purgatory, however, Dante's guide is the poet Virgil, to whom Dante pays homage by calling him "my Master." Virgil takes Dante through the nine circles of Hell, organized by gravity of the sin involved. In this final canto of *Inferno*, the two reach the ninth circle, by the frozen waters of Cocytus[1], where those guilty of the worst sin, treachery, are found. They include Judas Iscariot, who betrayed Jesus, and Brutus and Cassius, two Roman senators who plotted to assassinate the Roman leader Julius Caesar. They also include the angel-turned-devil Satan, here called Lucifer, the ultimate traitor who rebelled against God.

---

1. **Cocytus** (kō sīt′ əs) Greek: "river of wailing."

❹ ▲ **Critical Viewing**
How does the artist's depiction of Lucifer in this engraving compare and contrast with Dante's portrayal of him?
[Compare and Contrast]

from the Divine Comedy: Inferno **543**

Enrichment: Building Context

Dante's World
During Dante's life, Italy was not yet a nation-state. Instead, it was composed of several small city-states: Sicily, Naples, Rome (where the Catholic Church was a political as well as religious authority), Milan, Venice, and Florence (Dante's native city). People were loyal to their city-state, not to Italy as a whole. Dante lived during a period of great political turmoil. Civil warfare led to Dante's exile from Florence, which influenced his writing in the *Divine Comedy*.

Activity: Investigating the City-State Have each student pick a medieval Italian city-state to research. Suggest that they record information in the **Enrichment: Building Context** worksheet, *Professional Development Guidebook*, page 222. Direct students to use the results of their research to develop oral presentations. Then have students make oral presentations to the class.

❺ **Comparing Epics**

1. Direct students to lines 4–5 of the poem.
2. Then, **ask** the Comparing Epics question: What aspect of Dante's style is illustrated in lines 4–5?
   Answer: These lines showcase Dante's skillful use of simile, comparing the moment to a whirling windmill or mist rising from the ground.

Canto XXXIV

Ninth Circle: Cocytus	Compound Fraud
Round Four: Judecca	The Treacherous to Their Masters
The Center	Satan

"On march the banners of the King,"[2] Virgil begins as the Poets face the last depth. He is quoting a medieval hymn, and to it he adds the distortion and perversion of all that lies about him. "On march the banners of the King—of Hell." And there before them, in an infernal parody of Godhead, they see Satan in the distance, his great wings beating like a windmill. It is their beating that is the source of the icy wind of Cocytus, the exhalation of all evil.

All about him in the ice are strewn the sinners of the last round, *Judecca,* named for Judas Iscariot.[3] These are the *Treacherous to Their Masters*. They lie completely sealed in the ice, twisted and distorted into every conceivable posture. It is impossible to speak to them, and the Poets move on to observe Satan.

He is fixed into the ice at the center to which flow all the rivers of guilt; and as he beats his great wings as if to escape, their icy wind only freezes him more surely into the polluted ice. In a grotesque parody of the Trinity, he has three faces, each a different color, and in each mouth he clamps a sinner whom he rips eternally with his teeth. *Judas Iscariot* is in the central mouth: *Brutus* and *Cassius*[4] in the mouths on either side.

Having seen all, the Poets now climb through the center, grappling hand over hand down the hairy flank of Satan himself—a last supremely symbolic action—and at last, when they have passed the center of all gravity, they emerge from Hell. A long climb from the earth's center to the Mount of Purgatory awaits them, and they push on without rest, ascending along the sides of the river Lethe, till they emerge once more to see the stars of Heaven, just before dawn on Easter Sunday.

❺ **Comparing Epics**
What aspect of Dante's style is illustrated in lines 4–5?

"On march the banners of the King of Hell,"
    my Master said. "Toward us. Look straight ahead:
    can you make him out at the core of the frozen shell?"
Like a whirling windmill seen afar at twilight,

---

2. **On ... King** This hymn was written in the sixth century by Venantius Fortunatus, Bishop of Poitiers. The original celebrates the Holy Cross and is part of the service for Good Friday, to be sung at the moment of uncovering the cross.
3. **Judas Iscariot** (is ker´ ē ət) disciple who betrayed Jesus; see the Bible, Matthew 26:14, 48.
4. **Brutus and Cassius** They took part in a plot to assassinate Julius Caesar.

Think Aloud

Vocabulary: Using Context
Direct students' attention to the word *exhalation* in the last line of the first paragraph. Use the following "think aloud" to model the skill of using context to infer the meaning of the word. Say to students:

I may not know the meaning of the word *exhalation*. However, reading the preceding sentences and the sentence in which this word appears, I know the writer is describing the movement of air. He describes the beating of Satan's wings and the blowing of the icy wind of Cocytus. Also, I am familiar with the word *exhale*: to breath out. *Exhalation* must mean the act of blowing out—in this case, evil.

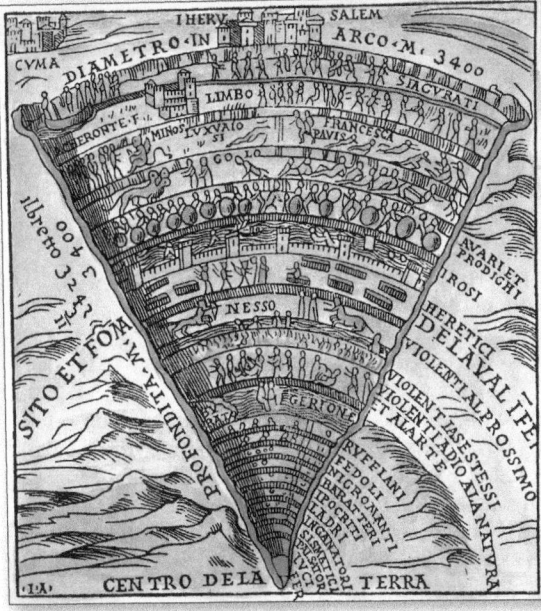

Speculate

1. Have students read lines 21–26 to themselves. Encourage them to focus on the description of the speaker's reaction to seeing Lucifer.

2. Then, **ask** students to speculate on why the speaker says, "I lost life's breath."
Possible response: He feels that he has lost life's breath because the awful sight of evil incarnate literally took his breath away.

7 **Critical Viewing**

Possible response: Dante and Virgil are now in the ninth circle, or in the depths of Hell near the center of the Earth--near the red "centro della terra" on the map of the *Inferno.*

7 ◄ **Critical Viewing** Where on this map of the *Inferno* do Dante and Virgil now find themselves? Use information from the background on the facing page of hints. **[Analyze]**

Vocabulary
cowered (kou´ erd) *v.* crouched, as from fear or cold

5   or when a mist has risen from the ground—
        just such an engine rose upon my sight
    stirring up such a wild and bitter wind
        I cowered for shelter at my Master's back,
        there being no other windbreak I could find.
    I stood now where the souls of the last class
10   (with fear my verses tell it) were covered wholly;
        they shone below the ice like straws in glass.
    Some lie stretched out; others are fixed in place
        upright, some on their heads, some on their soles;
        another, like a bow, bends foot to face.
15 When we had gone so far across the ice
        that it pleased my Guide to show me the foul creature⁵
        which once had worn the grace of Paradise,
    he made me stop, and, stepping aside, he said:
        "Now see the face of Dis!⁶ This is the place
20   where you must arm your soul against all dread."
    Do not ask, Reader, how my blood ran cold
        and my voice choked up with fear. I cannot write it:
        this is a terror that cannot be told.
6   I did not die, and yet I lost life's breath:
25   imagine for yourself what I became,
        deprived at once of both my life and death.

---

5. **the foul creature** Lucifer.
6. **Dis** (dis) in Greek mythology, the god of the lower world or the lower world itself. Here, it stands for Lucifer.

from the Divine Comedy: Inferno **545**

Culturally Responsive Instruction

Culture Focus Point out to students that epics—long narrative poems—appear in the literature and oral traditions of many different cultures. Epic poetry has been used by many cultures all over the world to pass along traditions from one generation to another, often without the use of writing. Epics usually involve subjects such as myths, heroic legends, religious tales, animal stories, or philosophical or moral theories. The earliest-known epic poetry was created by the ancient Sumerians, no later than 3000 BC. Two of the best examples of the oral epic are Homer's *Iliad* and *Odyssey.* Virgil's *Aeneid* is an example of the Latin epic. Other epics include the Old English *Beowulf,* the Arthurian Romance poems describing King Arthur, and the Japanese *Kojiki* and *Nihon shoki.* Ask students to share epic poems or stories from their own cultures, including derivations, such as movies, songs, or television programs.

8 Comparing Epics

1. Direct students' attention to lines 33–35. Point out that Dante here provides a bit of background information about Satan.

2. **Ask** students who Satan once was and what he was like before he was banished to Hell. **Answer:** Satan was once a beautiful angel.

3. Have students recall Milton's description of Satan in the excerpt from *Paradise Lost.*

4. **Ask** students the Comparing Epics question: What background information about Lucifer, or Satan, do lines 33–35 share with Milton's epic? **Answer:** Like Dante, Milton describes Satan as once being good and once "Favored of Heaven." Milton further describes him in the poem as being "in the realms of light, clothed with transcendent brightness."

9 Critical Viewing

Possible response: Virgil looks as though he has positioned himself between the attacking creatures and Dante. It looks as though he is using his robe as a shield to protect Dante.

Comparing Epics
What background information about Lucifer, or Satan, do lines 33–35 share with Milton's epic?

Vocabulary
awe (ô) *n.* feelings of reverence, fear, and wonder

9 ▼ Critical Viewing
Which elements in this engraving emphasize Virgil's role as guide and protector of Dante? **[Analyze]**

The Emperor of the Universe of Pain
 jutted his upper chest above the ice;
 and I am closer in size to the great mountain
30 the Titans[7] make around the central pit,
 than they to his arms. Now, starting from this part,
 imagine the whole that corresponds to it!

8 If he was once as beautiful as now
 he is hideous, and still turned on his Maker,
35 well may he be the source of every woe!
With what a sense of awe I saw his head
 towering above me! for it had three faces:[8]
 one was in front, and it was fiery red;
 the other two, as weirdly wonderful,
40 merged with it from the middle of each shoulder
 to the point where all converged at the top of the skull;
 the right was something between white and bile;
 the left was about the color one observes
 on those who live along the banks of the Nile.
45 Under each head two wings rose terribly,
 their span proportioned to so gross a bird:

---

7. Titans giant deities who were overthrown by Zeus and the Olympian gods of Greece.
8. three faces There are many interpretations of these three faces. The common theme in all of them is that the faces are a perversion of the qualities of the Trinity.

546 A Turbulent Time (1625–1798)

> If he was once as beautiful as now
> he is hideous, and still turned on his Maker,
> well may he be the **source of every woe!**

I never saw such sails upon the sea.
They were not feathers—their texture and their form
    were like a bat's wings—and he beat them so
50   that three winds blew from him in one great storm:
it is these winds that freeze all Cocytus.
    He wept from his six eyes, and down three chins
    the tears ran mixed with bloody froth and pus.[9]
In every mouth he worked a broken sinner
55   between his rake-like teeth. Thus he kept three
    in eternal pain at his eternal dinner.
For the one in front the biting seemed to play
    no part at all compared to the ripping: at times
    the whole skin of his back was flayed away.
60 "That soul that suffers most," explained my Guide,
    "is Judas Iscariot, he who kicks his legs
    on the fiery chin and has his head inside.
Of the other two, who have their heads thrust forward,
    the one who dangles down from the black face
65   is Brutus: note how he writhes without a word.
And there, with the huge and sinewy arms, is the soul,
    of Cassius,—But the night is coming on[10]
    and we must go, for we have seen the whole."
Then, as he bade, I clasped his neck, and he,
70   watching for a moment when the wings
    were opened wide, reached over dexterously[11]
and seized the shaggy coat of the king demon;
    then grappling matted hair and frozen crusts
    from one tuft to another, clambered down.
75 When we had reached the joint where the great thigh
    merges into the swelling of the haunch,
    my Guide and Master, straining terribly,
turned his head to where his feet had been
    and began to grip the hair as if he were climbing;[12]
80   so that I thought we moved toward Hell again.

---

9. **bloody froth and pus** the gore of the sinners he chews, which is mixed with his saliva.
10. **the night is coming on** It is now Saturday evening.
11. **dexterously** *adv.* skillfully.
12. **as if he were climbing** They have passed the center of gravity and so must turn around
    and start climbing.

⑩ Comparing Epics
What is unusual about the climate in this final circle of Dante's Hell?

Vocabulary
writhes (*rīthz*) *v.* twists and turns the body, as in agony

⑪ Reading Check
What torture do Judas Iscariot, Brutus, and Cassius suffer?

from the Divine Comedy: Inferno **547**

⑩ Comparing Epics

1. **Direct** students' attention to Dante's description of the climate of the final circle of Hell. Have students reread the first 80 lines of the poem.

2. **Ask** students what the most common description of Hell is like.
   Answer: Hell is usually described as being a furnace-like underground area, rolling with fire and lava.

3. **Ask** students the Comparing Epics question: What is unusual about the climate in this final circle of Dante's Hell?
   Answer: Dante describes the final circle of Hell as being cold and covered in ice.

4. **Ask** students how Dante's descriptions of Hell differ from Milton's.
   Answer: Milton's descriptions of Hell follow the traditional beliefs: that of a fire-scorched underworld.

⑪ Reading Check

Answer: Judas Iscariot, Brutus, and Cassius are trapped in eternal punishment, each in one of the three mouths of Satan. They are kept in pain as Satan's eternal dinner.

Differentiated Instruction   for Universal Access

Strategy for Special-Needs Students
Students may need assistance with the flow of events. List the main characters on the board. Then, discuss who each character is. Then list the events of the selection so far. Ask students what has happened and what the main characters have seen. Have students continue listing events as they read the selection.

Enrichment for Advanced Readers
Have students check out copies of Dante's *Inferno* from the library. Then, have students each choose one or two other sections to read and analyze. Suggest students offer at least one note of historical context with each section they analyze. Have students present the sections they have read and analyzed to the class.

Enrichment for Gifted/Talented Students
Have students create a miniplay based on the selection. Students can set a modern scene, write new dialogue, and consider alternative endings to the story. Though their version will be different than Dante's, insist that students work with the same narrative device of the epic poem.

One of the oldest techniques used to make prints from relief surfaces, woodcuts have been used since the fifth century. Chinese artists at first used woodcuts to decorate textiles. At the end of the fourteenth century, European artisans further developed the technique when the manufacturing of paper became common. The engravings that accompany Dante's *Inferno* are a variation of a woodcut. Gustave Doré used wood engraving techniques to create the illustrations you see here. In wood engraving, the wood is cut across the grain of the wood. This allows the artist to create much finer and more intricate work. White lines on an engraving appear as the positive image against a black background when printed on a press.

"Hold fast!"

my Guide said, and his breath came shrill/with labor and exhaustion.

"There is no way/but by such stairs to rise above such evil."

Vocabulary
shrill (shril) *adj.* high and sharp in tone; high-pitched

Vocabulary
nimble (nim´ bəl) *adj.* able to move quickly and lightly

"Hold fast!" my Guide said, and his breath came shrill
 with labor and exhaustion. "There is no way
 but by such stairs to rise above such evil."
At last he climbed out through an opening
85 in the central rock, and he seated me on the rim;
 then joined me with a nimble backward spring.
I looked up, thinking to see Lucifer
 as I had left him, and I saw instead
 his legs projecting high into the air.
90 Now let all those whose dull minds are still vexed
 by failure to understand what point it was
 I had passed through, judge if I was perplexed.
"Get up. Up on your feet," my Master said.
 "The sun already mounts to middle tierce,[13]
95 and a long road and hard climbing lie ahead."
It was no hall of state we had found there,

---

13. middle tierce According to the church's division of the day for prayer, tierce is the period from about six to nine A.M. Middle tierce, therefore, is seven-thirty. In going through the center point, Dante and Virgil have gone from night to day. They have moved ahead twelve hours.

548 A Turbulent Time (1625–1798)

Think Aloud

Vocabulary: Using Context
Direct students' attention to the word *vexed* in line 90. Use the following "think aloud" to model the skill of using context to infer the meaning of the word. Say to students:
I am unfamiliar with the word *vexed*. But even if I do not know this word, I may be able to guess what it means. For example, if I read the entire sentence in which it appears, I see that Dante uses the phrase *dull minds* before *vexed* and then clarifies by writing *failure to understand*. Using these clues, I can infer that *vexed* must mean to be puzzled by something.

but a natural animal pit hollowed from rock
with a broken floor and a close and sunless air.
"Before I tear myself from the Abyss,"
100   I said when I had risen, "O my Master,
explain to me my error in all this:
where is the ice? and Lucifer—how has he
been turned from top to bottom: and how can the sun
have gone from night to day so suddenly?"
105   And he to me: "You imagine you are still
on the other side of the center where I grasped
the shaggy flank of the Great Worm of Evil
which bores through the world—you were while I climbed down,
but when I turned myself about, you passed
110   the point to which all gravities are drawn.
You are under the other hemisphere where you stand;
the sky above us is the half opposed
to that which canopies the great dry land.
Under the midpoint of that other sky
115   the Man[14] who was born sinless and who lived
beyond all blemish, came to suffer and die.
You have your feet upon a little sphere
which forms the other face of the Judecca.
There it is evening when it is morning here.
120   And this gross Fiend and Image of all Evil
who made a stairway for us with his hide
is pinched and prisoned in the ice-pack still.
On this side he plunged down from heaven's height,
and the land that spread here once hid in the sea
125   and fled North to our hemisphere for fright:[15]
And it may be that moved by that same fear,
the one peak[16] that still rises on this side
fled upward leaving this great cavern[17] here."
Down there, beginning at the further bound

____

14. **the Man** Jesus, who suffered and died in Jerusalem, which was thought to be the middle of the Earth.
15. **fled North . . . for fright** Dante believed that the Northern Hemisphere was mostly land and the Southern Hemisphere, mostly water. Here, he explains the reason for this state of affairs.
16. **the one peak** the Mount of Purgatory.
17. **this great cavern** the natural animal pit of line 97. It is also "Beelzebub's dim tomb," line 130.

◄ **Critical Viewing** What evidence is there from this image that Dante and Virgil have made it out of hell? **[Analyze]**

Comparing Epics
Would the description of Lucifer in line 107 apply to the Satan of Milton's epic? Why or why not?

Reading Check
What "stairway" did Virgil take to climb out of Hell?

> And this gross Fiend and Image of all Evil
> who made a stairway for us with his hide
> is pinched and prisoned in the ice-pack still.

from the Divine Comedy: Inferno **549**

⑬ Critical Viewing
Possible response: The setting of Hell has been described as a light-less place, and yet Dante and Virgil appear to be conversing upon a mountain at dawn.

⑭ Comparing Epics
1. Direct students to lines 105–107 and ask a volunteer to read the lines.
2. **Ask** students the Comparing Epics question: Would the description of Lucifer in line 107 apply to the Satan of Milton's epic? Why or why not?
   Possible response: It is similar in that both Milton and Dante describe Satan as being the force from which all evil originates.

⑮ Reading Check
Answer: Virgil used the body of Satan, or Lucifer, as steps to climb out of Hell.

Differentiated Instruction for Universal Access

Strategy for Special-Needs Students
Students may need assistance with understanding what happens to Virgil and Dante after their meeting with Satan. Students will benefit from rereading all or parts of the selection on this page. In reviewing the text, prompt students to focus on Virgil's explanation of what happened. Encourage volunteers to explain, in their own words, how Virgil and Dante climbed out of Hell.

Enrichment for Gifted/Talented Students
Have students research the general views, understandings, and knowledge of Dante's contemporaries of the geography of Earth. Have interested students write brief essays describing what was known about the hemispheres and the composition of land and water in Dante's age. Encourage volunteers to share their essays with their classmates.

where a round opening brought in sight the blest
and beauteous shining of the Heavenly cars.
And we walked out once more **beneath the Stars.**

1. (a) Dante cannot write about the
    terror he felt at seeing Lucifer. (b)
    Dante states that he was deprived
    at once of both his life and death,
    almost as if suspended some-
    where between, with the strength
    to describe what he saw.

2. (a) Judas Iscariot, Brutus, and
    Cassius are all sinners, as is
    Lucifer. (b) **Possible response:**
    The frozen water emphasizes the
    inability to change their situa-
    tions; they are stuck in their pre-
    dicaments for eternity.
    (c) **Possible response:** These
    three sinners, in Dante's opinion,
    committed the worst sins.

3. (a) Dante emphasizes Brutus's
    silence as he writhes.
    (b) **Possible response:** The
    inability to express one's self
    could be viewed as an extreme
    form of torture or punishment.

130   of Beelzebub's[18] dim tomb, there is a space
        not known by sight, but only by the sound
      of a little stream[19] descending through the hollow
        it has eroded from the massive stone
        in its endlessly entwining lazy flow."
135   My Guide and I crossed over and began
        to mount that little known and lightless road
        to ascend into the shining world again.
      He first, I second, without thought of rest
        we climbed the dark until we reached the point
140   where a round opening brought in sight the blest
      and beauteous shining of the Heavenly cars.
      And we walked out once more beneath the Stars.[20]

---

18. **Beelzebub's** (bē el′ zə bubz′) Beelzebub, which in Hebrew means "god of flies," was
    another name for Lucifer or Satan.
19. **a little stream** Lethe (lē′ thē); in classical mythology, the river of forgetfulness, from which
    souls drank before being born. In Dante's symbolism, it flows down from Purgatory, where
    it has washed away the memory of sin from the souls who are undergoing purification. That
    memory it delivers to Hell, which draws all sin to itself.
20. **Stars** As part of his total symbolism, Dante ends each of the three divisions of the *Divine
    Comedy* with this word. Every conclusion of the upward soul is toward the stars, symbols of
    hope and virtue. It is just before dawn of Easter Sunday that the Poets emerge—
    a further symbolism.

Critical Reading

Cite textual
evidence to
support your
responses.

1. **Key Ideas and Details (a)** In lines 22–23, what does Dante
    say he cannot describe? **(b) Analyze:** How does he nevertheless
    communicate his experience?

2. **Key Ideas and Details (a)** What do the three figures in Lucifer's
    mouth all have in common, and what do they have in common
    with Lucifer? **(b) Interpret:** Why do you think Dante situates these
    sinners in frozen waters? **(c) Infer:** Why do you think he feels no
    sympathy for these sinners, as he did for many sinners in earlier
    circles of Hell?

3. **Key Ideas and Details (a)** Which aspect of Brutus's torture does
    Virgil emphasize in line 65? **(b) Interpret:** Why might language
    be denied to the inhabitants of the ninth circle of Hell?

After You Read

from *Paradise Lost* •
from the *Divine Comedy: Inferno*

Comparing Epics

1. Integration of Knowledge and Ideas Compare and contrast the ways in which Dante and Milton portray Satan (or Lucifer) in their **epics.** **(a)** What is similar about these epic villains? **(b)** How do they differ physically and in terms of personality?

2. Integration of Knowledge and Ideas **(a)** What is similar and different about the sinful behavior being criticized in each epic? **(b)** Based on the two excerpts, do you think these epics are teaching the same values? Why or why not?

3. Craft and Structure How effective is each selection in achieving the elevated style appropriate to an epic? Cite specific passages to support your opinions.

4. Integration of Knowledge and Ideas Is there evidence in the texts themselves that Dante's epic was written in the Middle Ages and Milton's in the seventeenth century? Explain.

⏱ Timed Writing

Informative Text: Essay

Epics traditionally show their heroes braving the underworld or other dangerous, often supernatural settings to perform great deeds.

Assignment: Write an essay in which you compare and contrast the impact of the authors' choices as to how to portray setting. **[40 minutes]**
Address questions such as these to focus your analysis:

- What do the imagery and descriptive language these authors use to portray Hell have in common? How do they differ?
- What is the effect of Dante's firsthand impression of Hell compared to the effect of Milton's all-knowing narrator?
- Which setting do you find more unusual? Why?
- Which universal themes do these settings suggest? Explain.

As you draft your essay, remember to do the following:

- Write an essay of sufficient length to address the questions you decide to consider.
- Include relevant and substantial evidence and well-chosen details.
- Write legibly and use appropriate capitalization and punctuation conventions.

5-Minute Planner

Complete these steps before you begin to write:

1. Read the assignment carefully. Identify key words and phrases.
2. Weigh the similarities and differences between the two selections.
   TIP As you scan the texts, jot down details that you might use.
3. Create a rough outline for your essay.
4. Reread the prompts, and draft your essay.

Ⓒ Common Core State Standards

Writing

2. Write informative/ explanatory texts to examine and convey complex ideas, concepts, and information clearly and accurately through the effective selection, organization, and analysis of content.

10. Write routinely over extended time frames and shorter time frames for a range of tasks, purposes, and audiences.

USE ACADEMIC VOCABULARY

As you write, use academic language, including the following words or their related forms:

  categorize
  classify
  determine
  indicate

For more information about academic language, see the vocabulary charts in the introduction to this book.

Assessment Resources

Unit 3 Resources
L1 **L2** **EL** **Selection Test,** pp. 87–88.

PHLit Online! Students may use the Self-test, online at **www.PHLitOnline.com,** to prepare for the Selection Test.

Encourage students to focus on these points when they are planning and revising their essays.

Tell students they will have 40 minutes to plan and write the essay. Call students' attention to the 5-minute planner. Encourage students to budget their time to allow 5 minutes for outlining, 5 minutes for identifying some initial supporting text references in the works, and 10 minutes to revise and proofread.

Answers

Comparing Epics

1. (a) **Possible response:** Both Milton and Dante portray Satan as being serpent-like, with wings, forever trapped in Hell. (b) **Possible response:** Milton's Satan speaks, unlike Dante's Satan. Dante's Satan is described as having three heads. Milton's Satan has accepted his banishment to Hell and seems willing to recruit more sinners in his war against God.

2. (a) **Possible response:** Dante's Satan is more intent upon inflicting pain on sinners. The Satan in *Paradise Lost* seems almost proud of his sins. (b) **Possible response:** No, I think that in Dante's *Inferno*, Dante depicts Satan as the ultimate evil; whereas, in Milton's *Paradise Lost*, Milton allows Satan to speak, therefore making his situation seem more human.

3. **Possible response:** Both use lofty language and powerful imagery to treat serious subjects and themes. Students may also mention Milton's elegant long sentences in blank verse.

4. **Possible response:** No, the references in these excerpts are not of the writers' times.

⏱ Timed Writing

1. Teach the Academic Vocabulary. Discuss the words with students, as well as their related forms, including *category, classification, indication,* and *indicative.* Review with students the vocabulary they learned before reading the selection, including the quotation they found. Encourage students to use one of the quotations to illustrate a point they make about the settings in the epics.

2. Use the prompt to help students identify elements and qualities their essays should have.

   - A thesis statement about the authors' choices in portraying settings.
   - Details about the imagery and descriptive language in the works.
   - A discussion of the effect of point of view in the works.
   - Details from the text that support the thesis statement.

551

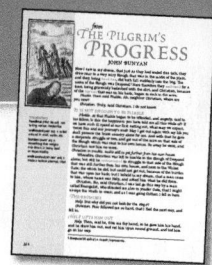

• *from The Pilgrim's Progress*
Lesson Pacing Guide

DAY 1 Preteach

- Administer the Reading and Vocabulary Warm-ups (*Unit 3 Resources*, pp. 89–92) as necessary.
- Introduce the Literary Analysis concept: Allegory.
- Introduce the Reading Strategy: Analyzing Allegory.
- Build background with the author feature.
- Develop thematic thinking with Connecting to the Essential Question.
- Teach the selection vocabulary.

DAY 2 Preteach/Teach/Extend

- Distribute copies of the appropriate graphic organizer for the Reading Strategy (*Graphic Organizer Transparencies*, pp. 93–94).
- Distribute copies of the appropriate graphic organizer for Literary Analysis (*Graphic Organizer Transparencies*, pp. 95–96).
- Prepare students to read with the Activating Prior Knowledge activities (TE).
- Informally monitor comprehension while students read.
- Develop students' understanding of allegory using the Literary Analysis prompts.
- Develop students' ability to analyze allegory using the Reading Strategy prompts.
- Reinforce vocabulary with the Vocabulary notes.
- Assess students' comprehension and mastery of the skills by having them answer the Critical Reading, Literary Analysis, and Reading Strategy questions.

DAY 3 Assess

- Have students complete the Vocabulary activities.
- Have students complete the Writing activity and write a casting memo. (You may assign as homework.)
- Administer Selection Test A or B (*Unit 3 Resources,* pp. 101–103 or 104–106).

Common Core State Standards

Reading Literature 2. Determine two or more themes or central ideas of a text and analyze their development over the course of the text, including how they interact and build on one another to produce a complex account.

Writing 2.b. Develop the topic thoroughly by selecting the most significant and relevant facts, extended definitions, concrete details, quotations, or other information and examples appropriate to the audience's knowledge of the topic.

Additional Standards Practice
Common Core Companion, pp. 15–22; 196–207

Daily Block Scheduling
Each day in this Lesson Pacing Guide represents a 40–50 minute period. Teachers using block scheduling may combine days to revise pacing. In addition, teachers may differentiate and support core instruction by integrating components for extended and intensive support as students require. See the Guide to Selected Leveled Resources (facing page).

Guide to Selected Leveled Resources

R T I Tier 1 (students performing on level)
from The Pilgrim's Progress

Warm Up	Practice, **model**, and **monitor** fluency, working **with the whole class** or **in groups**.	**Vocabulary and Reading Warm-ups B**, *Unit 3 Resources*, pp. 89–90, 92
Comprehension/Skills	**Support** and **monitor** comprehension and skills development, having students complete the activities, graphic organizers, and interactive prompts **independently** or **as a class**.	• *Reader's Notebook*, adapted instruction and full selection **EL** *Reader's Notebook: English Learner's Version*, adapted instruction and adapted selection • **Reading Skill Graphic Organizer B**, *Graphic Organizer Transparencies*, p. 98 • **Literary Analysis Graphic Organizer B**, *Graphic Organizer Transparencies*, p. 100
Monitor Progress	**A** Monitor student progress with the differentiated curriculum-based assessment in the *Unit Resources*.	• **Selection Test B**, *Unit 3 Resources*, pp. 104–106 • **Open-Book Test**, *Unit 3 Resources*, pp. 98–100

R T I Tier 2 (students requiring intervention)
from The Pilgrim's Progress

Warm Up	Practice, **model**, and **monitor** fluency **in groups** or **with individuals**.	• **Vocabulary and Reading Warm-ups A**, *Unit 3 Resources*, pp. 89–91 • *Hear It!* Audio CD (adapted text)
Comprehension/Skills	• **Support** and **monitor** comprehension and skills development, working **in small groups** or **with individuals**. • As students complete the selection in the appropriate version of the *Reader's Notebook*, **monitor** comprehension frequently with group questions and individual instruction. • **Model** strategies while guiding students in completing the activities and prompts in the *Reader's Notebook*, as well as the graphic organizers. • **Practice** skills and **monitor** mastery with the *Reading Kit* worksheets.	• *Reader's Notebook: Adapted Version*, adapted instruction and adapted selection **EL** *Reader's Notebook: English Learner's Version*, adapted instruction and adapted selection • **Reading Skill Graphic Organizer A**, *Graphic Organizer Transparencies*, p. 97 • **Literary Analysis Graphic Organizer A**, *Graphic Organizer Transparencies*, p. 99 • *Reading Kit*, Practice worksheets
Monitor Progress	**A** Monitor student progress with the differentiated curriculum-based assessment in the *Unit Resources* and in the *Reading Kit*.	• **Selection Test A**, *Unit 3 Resources*, pp. 101–103 • *Reading Kit*, Assess worksheets

TIER 3 Tier 3 intervention may require consultation with the student's special-education or dyslexia specialist. For additional support, see the Tier 2 activities and resources listed above.

One-on-one teaching   Group work   Whole class instruction   Independent work   **A** Assessment

For a complete guide to selection support, including support for Advanced students, see the Overview of Resources in the frontmatter.

• from *The Pilgrim's Progress*

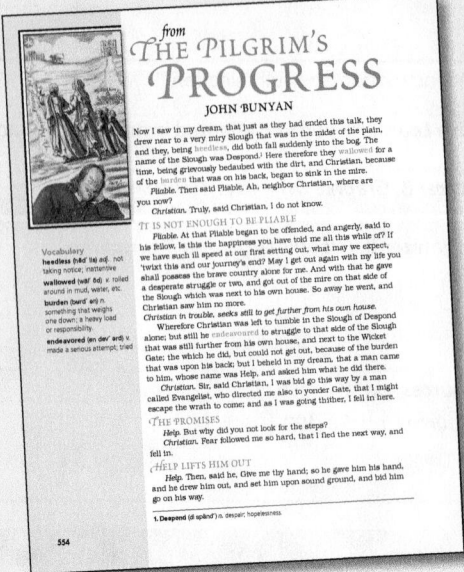

RESOURCES FOR:

L1 Special-Needs Students

L2 Below-Level Students (Tier 2)

L3 On-Level Students (Tier 1)

L4 Advanced Students (Tier 1)

EL English Learners

All All Students

Vocabulary/Fluency/Prior Knowledge

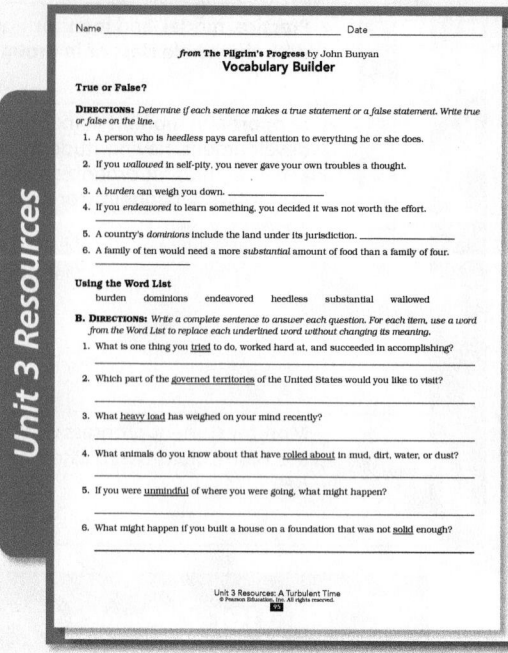

All Vocabulary Builder, p. 95

Also available for these selections:

EL L1 L2 Vocabulary Warm-ups A and B, pp. 89–90

EL L1 L2 Reading Warm-ups A and B, pp. 91–92

Reader's Notebooks

Pre- and postreading pages for this selection appear in an interactive format in the *Reader's Notebooks*. Each *Notebook* is differentiated for a different group of learners.

The selections in the Adapted and English Learner's versions are abridged.

L2 L3 *Reader's Notebook*

L1 *Reader's Notebook: Adapted Version*

EL *Reader's Notebook: English Learner's Version*

EL *Reader's Notebook: Spanish Version*

© *Common Core Companion*

Additional instruction and practice for each Common Core State Standard

Selection Support

from *The Pilgrim's Progress* by John Bunyan

Before You Read A: Interpret an Allegory

Elements of an Allegory	Allegorical Elements in *The Pilgrim's Progress*
Overall symbolism	• Christian's journey = a Christian's journey through life to salvation
Symbols whose names state their meanings	• Christian = a Christian Help = help
Other symbols and their meanings	• Celestial City = Heaven
Main message or lesson	

Graphic Organizer Transparencies
© Pearson Education, Inc. All rights reserved.

Graphic Organizer Transparencies

EL L1 L2 **Reading: Graphic Organizer A** (partially filled in) p. 93

Also available for these selections:

EL L3 **Reading: Graphic Organizer B,** p. 94

EL L1 L2 **Literary Analysis: Graphic Organizer A** (partially filled in), p. 95

EL L3 **Literary Analysis: Graphic Organizer B,** p. 96

Skills Development/Extension

Name _____ Date _____

from *The Pilgrim's Progress* by John Bunyan
Support for Writing: Casting Memo

Your job is to cast the parts for a film based on *The Pilgrim's Progress*. Use the following chart to organize your ideas about suitable actors for the roles. In column 2, describe the qualities each performer will need. In column 3, write the reasons you think a particular actor would be good in the role.

Character	Qualities Needed	Suggested Actor / Reasons
Christian		
Pliable		
Help		
Evangelist		
The King		

Unit 3 Resources: A Turbulent Time
© Pearson Education, Inc. All rights reserved.

Unit 3 Resources

EL L3 L4 **Support for Writing,** p. 96

Also available for these selections:

All **Literary Analysis,** p. 93

All **Reading,** p. 94

L4 **Enrichment,** p. 97

Assessment

Name _____ Date _____

from *The Pilgrim's Progress* by John Bunyan
Open-Book Test

Short Answer *Write your responses to the questions in this section on the lines provided.*

1. From the first sentence of *The Pilgrim's Progress*, what can you infer about the narrator? What state is he in?

2. An allegory is a narrative with both literal and symbolic meanings. Who or what might Christian, the main character in *The Pilgrim's Progress*, symbolically represent?

3. Christian bears a "burden" on his back that causes him to sink deeper into the mudhole. What role does this burden play in *The Pilgrim's Progress*? What might the burden represent?

4. How does the character Help contrast with the character Pliable in *The Pilgrim's Progress*?

5. In *The Pilgrim's Progress*, consider the explanation that Help gives to Christian about the Slough of Despond. What might be the allegorical meaning of the Slough of Despond?

6. Use the chart shown below to identify the allegorical meaning of the following characters and details from *The Pilgrim's Progress*.

Character	Details
the King	
1,600 years	
the steps	
the slough	

Unit 3 Resources: A Turbulent Time
© Pearson Education, Inc. All rights reserved.

L3 L4 **Open-Book Test,** pp. 98–100

Also available for these selections:

EL L1 L2 **Selection Test A,** pp. 101–103

EL L3 L4 **Selection Test B,** pp. 104–106

PHLit Online!
www.PHLitOnline.com

Online Resources: All print materials are also available online.

- complete narrated selection text
- a thematically related video with writing prompt
- an interactive graphic organizer
- highlighting feature
- access to all student print resources, adapted to individual student needs
- Spanish and English summaries
- adapted selection translations in Spanish

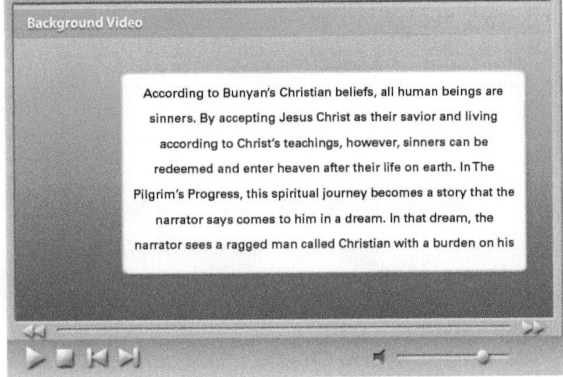

According to Bunyan's Christian beliefs, all human beings are sinners. By accepting Jesus Christ as their savior and living according to Christ's teachings, however, sinners can be redeemed and enter heaven after their life on earth. In The Pilgrim's Progress, this spiritual journey becomes a story that the narrator says comes to him in a dream. In that dream, the narrator sees a ragged man called Christian with a burden on his

Background Video

Also available:

Get Connected! (thematic video with writing prompt)
All videos are available in Spanish.

Vocabulary Central (tools and activities for studying vocabulary)

Also available:

Writer's Journal (with graphics feature)

1 ❓ **Connecting to the Essential Question**

1. Review the assignment with the class.

2. Prepare students to write by asking them to review different authors' purposes.

3. As students read, have them look for examples of Bunyan's principles.

2 **Literary Analysis**

Introduce the skill using the instruction on the student page.

Think Aloud: Model the Skill

Say to students:

As I read, I will look for examples of how Bunyan writes a story on two levels. As I read, I will pay attention to how Bunyan uses people and places as symbols.

3 **Reading Strategy**

1. Introduce the strategy using the instruction on the student page.

2. Give students a copy of **Reading Strategy Graphic Organizer B,** page 94 in *Graphic Organizer Transparencies,* to fill out as they read.

Think Aloud: Model the Skill

Say to students:

To interpret an allegory, I can use the details in the text and my knowledge to determine how something is being used as a symbol. For example, I can look to see if a name of a person or place gives me clues about its symbolism.

4 **Vocabulary**

1. Pronounce each word, giving its definition, and have students say it aloud.

2. For more guidance, see the *Classroom Strategies and Teaching Routines* card for introducing vocabulary.

552

Before You Read | from *The Pilgrim's Progress*

1 **Connecting to the Essential Question** If you talk about your trip down "the road of life," you are using the same symbolism as Bunyan does in his book. As you read, note religious ideas that influence Bunyan's hero, Christian, in this episode of his life's trip. Identifying these ideas will help as you answer the Essential Question: **How does literature shape or reflect society?**

2 **Literary Analysis**

Used in different types of narratives, **allegory** is a literary form in which all the parts of a story have a symbolic meaning. Many works of fiction use *symbols*—objects, people, or places that stand for something beyond themselves. In an allegory, however, every element of the story is symbolic. The allegory in *The Pilgrim's Progress* can therefore be read in two ways:

- On the *literal* level, it tells the story of an adventure-packed journey.
- On the *symbolic* level, it tells the complex account of a Christian soul's journey through life to salvation.

The purpose of an allegory is to teach a moral lesson. To make his lesson clear, Bunyan uses names that reveal the symbolic meanings of characters. A character who assists the hero, for example, is named Help. As you read the excerpt from this allegory, analyze the author's choices of names for the characters. Then, consider the lessons that the allegory teaches as well as the multiple themes that it expresses.

3 **Reading Strategy**

ⓒ **Preparing to Read Complex Texts** By **analyzing the text structure** of an allegory—its literal and symbolic levels—you can better appreciate its *meaning*. Remember, too, that you will be reading just one episode of a longer journey that stands for a Christian soul's search for salvation.

- Review the map on page 556 to see the whole journey.
- Use a chart like the one shown to interpret the meaning of specific characters and places in this part of the journey.

4 **Vocabulary**

heedless (hēd´ lis) *adj.* not taking notice; inattentive (p. 554)

wallowed (wäl´ ōd) *v.* rolled around in mud, water, etc. (p. 554)

burden (bʉrd´ ən) *n.* something that weighs one down; a heavy load or responsibility (p. 554)

endeavored (en dev´ ərd) *v.* made a serious attempt; tried (p. 554)

dominions (də min´ yənz) *n.* governed territories (p. 555)

substantial (səb stan´ shəl) *adj.* large in size or strength (p. 555)

ⓒ **Common Core State Standards**

Reading Literature
2. Determine two or more themes or central ideas of a text and analyze their development over the course of the text, including how they interact and build on one another to produce a complex account.

Interpreting an Allegory

Overall symbolism	Christian's journey = a Christian's journey through life to salvation
Specific symbols with names that signal their meaning	Christian = a Christian Celestial City = heaven
Specific symbols not signaled by their names	
Main message or lesson	

552 A Turbulent Time (1625–1798)

Vocabulary Development

Vocabulary Knowledge Rating
Create a **Vocabulary Knowledge Rating Chart** (*Professional Development Guidebook,* p. 33) for the vocabulary words on the student page. Give each student a copy of the chart with the words on it. Read the words aloud, and have students mark their rating of each in the Before Reading column. When students have completed reading and discussing the selec-tion, have them take out their **Vocabulary Knowledge Rating** charts for the story. Read the words aloud and have students rate their knowledge again in the After Reading column. Clarify any words that are still problematic. Then, have students complete the Vocabulary practice at the end of the selection.

 **Vocabulary Central,** featuring tools and activities for studying vocabulary, is available online at **www.PHLitOnline.com**.

⑤ JOHN BUNYAN *(1628–1688)*

Author of *The Pilgrim's Progress*

The son of a tinker, or traveling mender of pots and pans, John Bunyan had little formal education. Yet he went on to produce *The Pilgrim's Progress*, one of the most widely read books in the English language.

Finding Faith Born near Bedford in central England, Bunyan learned only the basics of reading and instead worked as his father's apprentice, a path on which he would have continued had warfare not intervened. Drafted into the army, he fought on the Parliamentary side in the English Civil Wars. In about 1648, he married a member of a Puritan sect to which he converted. The two religious tracts his wife brought into their home also helped him improve his reading.

Testaments of Faith By 1655, Bunyan had become a popular preacher at his Bedford church. Five years later, however, when Charles II was restored to the throne, it became illegal to preach outside the Church of England. Arrested and jailed for twelve years, Bunyan spent the time profitably, studying the Bible and using it as a guide in writing several books, including a religious autobiography, *Grace Abounding*. He began *The Pilgrim's Progress* during a second, shorter prison term, publishing the first part in 1678 and a second part six years later.

Combining simple yet vivid language and characters with humor and suspense, *The Pilgrim's Progress* proved enormously popular. It went through ten printings in the author's lifetime, was translated into over a hundred languages, and has outsold every other religious work in English except the King James Bible.

> "I BETOOK ME TO MY BIBLE AND BEGAN TO TAKE
> GREAT PLEASURE IN READING; BUT ESPECIALLY
> WITH THE HISTORICAL PART THEREOF....
> I BEGAN TO LOOK INTO IT WITH NEW EYES AND
> READ AS I NEVER DID BEFORE."

from The Pilgrim's Progress **553**

🔔 Daily Bellringer

For each class during which you will teach this selection, have students complete one of the five activities for the appropriate week in the *Daily Bellringer Activities* booklet.

Multidraft Reading

To assist struggling readers and to enhance reading for all, assign the text in chunks, as warranted by length, and apply multidraft reading protocols. For each reading, have students set the purpose indicated:

- **First reading**—identifying key ideas and details and answering any Reading Checks.
- **Second reading**—analyzing craft and structure and responding to the side-column prompts.
- **Third reading**—integrating knowledge and ideas, connecting to other texts and the world, and answering the end-of-selection questions.

For more guidance, refer to the *Classroom Strategies and Teaching Routines* card on Multidraft Reading.

⑤ Background
More About the Author

John Bunyan was a passionately religious man. Obsessed with his own sins, however small, he sought a religion that assured him of salvation. After a pilgrimage and baptism in 1653, he found that assurance in the Baptist religion. Like other famous religious people (Saint Joan of Arc and Saint Theresa), Bunyan heard voices and saw visions.

Despite Bunyan's strict religious beliefs, some consider him a Christian humanist. He believed in people's ability to make their own choices and influence the world.

www.PHLitOnline.com

Teaching From Technology

Preparing to Read
Go to **www.PHLitOnline.com** in class or in a lab and display the **Get Connected!** slide show for this selection. Have the class brainstorm responses to the slide show writing prompt, entering ideas in the interactive journal. Then, have students complete their written responses individually, in a lab or as homework.

To build background, display the More About the Author feature.

Using the Interactive Text
Go to **www.PHLitOnline.com** and display the Enriched Online Student Edition. As the class reads the selection or listens to the narration, record answers to side-column prompts using the graphic organizers accessible on the interactive page. Alternatively, have students use the online edition individually, answering the prompts as they read.

553

❶ About the Selection

The Pilgrim's Progress is told as a dream that the narrator has about Christian on his journey to the Celestial City. Bunyan begins by expressing his hopes that the reader will learn from the text and not be offended that it is fictional. Many strictly religious people of his day believed only nonfiction was appropriate reading material.

Christian begins his journey to Wicket Gate. As he begins his journey, he falls into a swamp called the Slough of Despond. It is here that the excerpt begins.

❷ Activating Prior Knowledge

Ask students to consider how they would tell the journey of an adolescent from age 13 through 18. What name would they choose and how would they describe the dangers, valleys, and joys of this journey?

Concept Connector ➡

Tell students they will return to their responses after reading the selection.

❸ Literary Analysis

Allegory

Remind students that an allegory is a story told on two levels. Then, **ask** students to consider what the Slough of Despond might mean on an allegorical level.

Possible response: The Slough of Despond may refer to despair over the seeming meaninglessness of life or anxiety about the future—problems to which religion proposes answers.

Vocabulary

heedless (hēd′ lis) *adj.* not taking notice; inattentive

wallowed (wäl′ ōd) *v.* rolled around in mud, water, etc.

burden (bʉrd′ ən) *n.* something that weighs one down; a heavy load or responsibility.

endeavored (en dev′ ərd) *v.* made a serious attempt; tried

❸

554

from THE PILGRIM'S ❶ ❷ PROGRESS

JOHN BUNYAN

Now I saw in my dream, that just as they had ended this talk, they drew near to a very miry Slough that was in the midst of the plain, and they, being heedless, did both fall suddenly into the bog. The name of the Slough was Despond.[1] Here therefore they wallowed for a time, being grievously bedaubed with the dirt, and Christian, because of the burden that was on his back, began to sink in the mire.

Pliable. Then said Pliable, Ah, neighbor Christian, where are you now?

Christian. Truly, said Christian, I do not know.

IT IS NOT ENOUGH TO BE PLIABLE

Pliable. At that Pliable began to be offended, and angerly, said to his fellow, Is this the happiness you have told me all this while of? If we have such ill speed at our first setting out, what may we expect, 'twixt this and our journey's end? May I get out again with my life you shall possess the brave country alone for me. And with that he gave a desperate struggle or two, and got out of the mire on that side of the Slough which was next to his own house. So away he went, and Christian saw him no more.

Christian in trouble, seeks still to get further from his own house.

Wherefore Christian was left to tumble in the Slough of Despond alone; but still he endeavoured to struggle to that side of the Slough that was still further from his own house, and next to the Wicket Gate; the which he did, but could not get out, because of the burden that was upon his back; but I beheld in my dream, that a man came to him, whose name was Help, and asked him what he did there.

Christian. Sir, said Christian, I was bid go this way by a man called Evangelist, who directed me also to yonder Gate, that I might escape the wrath to come; and as I was going thither, I fell in here.

THE PROMISES

Help. But why did you not look for the steps?

Christian. Fear followed me so hard, that I fled the next way, and fell in.

HELP LIFTS HIM OUT

Help. Then, said he, Give me thy hand; so he gave him his hand, and he drew him out, and set him upon sound ground, and bid him go on his way.

---

1. **Despond** (di spänd′) *n.* despair; hopelessness.

ⓒ Text Complexity Rubric

from The Pilgrim's Progress

Qualitative Measures	
Context/Knowledge Demands	Religious allegory 1 2 ③ 4 5
Structure/ Language Clarity	Archaic language; long sentences 1 2 ③ 4 5
Levels of Meaning	Challenging (religious symbolism) 1 2 3 ④ 5

Quantitative Measures			
Lexile	1190L	Text Length	766 words
Overall Complexity	**More complex**		

Reader and Task Suggestions

Preparing to Read the Text

- Using the Background on TE p. 553, discuss the importance Bunyan placed on individual choices.
- Discuss with students the technique of creating an allegory in which each character represents an abstract idea.
- Guide students to use Multidraft Reading strategies (TE p. 553).

Leveled Tasks

Levels of Meaning If students will have difficulty with the symbolism, have them work in pairs to create a chart and "map" like those on p. 556, using them to guide a second reading.

Analyzing If students will not have difficulty with the symbolism, have them analyze Bunyan's views on fears and doubt.

What Makes the Slough of Despond

Then I stepped to him that plucked him out, and said, "Sir, wherefore, since over this place is the way from the City of Destruction, to yonder Gate, is it, that this plat[2] is not mended, that poor travellers might go thither with more security?" And he said unto me, "This miry Slough is such a place as cannot be mended; it is the descent whither the scum and filth that attends conviction for sin doth continually run, and therefore is it called the Slough of Despond: for still as the sinner is awakened about his lost condition, there ariseth in his soul many fears, and doubts, and discouraging apprehensions, which all of them get together, and settle in this place; and this is the reason of the badness of this ground.

"It is not the pleasure of the King that this place should remain so bad; his labourers also, have, by the direction of His Majesty's surveyors, been for above this sixteen hundred years, employed about this patch of ground, if perhaps it might have been mended; yea, and to my knowledge," saith he, "here hath been swallowed up at least twenty thousand cart loads; yea, millions of wholesome instructions, that have at all seasons been brought from all places of the King's dominions (and they that can tell, say they are the best materials to make good ground of the place); if so be it might have been mended, but it is the Slough of Despond still, and so will be when they have done what they can.

The Promises of Forgiveness and Acceptance to Life by Faith in Christ

"True, there are by the direction of the law-giver, certain good and substantial steps, placed even through the very midst of this Slough; but at such time as this place doth much spew out its filth, as it doth against change of weather, these steps are hardly seen; or if they be, men through the dizziness of their heads step besides; and then they are bemired to purpose, notwithstanding the steps be there; but the ground is good when they are once got in at the Gate."

---

2. **plat** a flat, low-lying piece of ground.

Critical Reading

1. **Key Ideas and Details** **(a) Summarize:** Sum up what happens to Christian at the Slough of Despond. **(b) Interpret:** What human mood or attitude might the Slough of Despond represent?

2. **Integration of Knowledge and Ideas** What does the selection show about the role of faith in Bunyan's society? In your response, use at least two of these Essential Question words: *devout, piety, redeem.* [*Connecting to the Essential Question: How does literature shape or reflect society?*]

---

④ Literary Analysis
Allegory
On the symbolic level of this allegory, to what might the steps refer?

Reading Strategy
Analyzing Allegory
What does the King symbolize?

Vocabulary
dominions (də min′ yənz) *n.* governed territories or lands

substantial (səb stan′ shəl) *adj.* having substance; large in size or strength

> "It is not the pleasure of the King that this place should remain so bad ... But the ground is good when they are once got in at the Gate."

from The Pilgrim's Progress **555**

---

④ Literary Analysis
Allegory

1. Have students reread page 555.
2. Point out Help's description of the Slough and the steps.
3. Then **ask** the Literary Analysis question: On the symbolic level of this allegory, to what might the steps refer?
   Possible response: The steps refer to the help Christians receive.

⑤ Reading Strategy
Analyzing Allegory

1. Reread the second paragraph.
2. **Ask** students to identify details about the King.
   Answer: He is unhappy that the Slough of Despond exists. He has servants who have been working for 1,600 years.
3. **Ask** students to connect these details with what they know about Christianity and when *The Pilgrim's Progress* was published.
   Answer: Christianity began 1,600 years before *The Pilgrim's Progress* was written.
4. **Ask** the Reading Strategy question: What does the King symbolize?
   Answer: The King symbolizes Jesus Christ.

ASSESS
Answers

Before students respond, you may wish to have them write a brief objective summary of the selection. As they answer the questions below, remind them to support their answers with evidence from the text.

1. (a) Christian and Pliable fall in. Pliable gets out on one side, and Christian journeys to the other side. He cannot get out. Help explains why there is a Slough and shows him the steps out. (b) It might represent sadness, guilt, or despair.

2. **Possible response:** The selection shows that faith was important. The character Help shows that <u>devout</u> believers can help <u>redeem</u> struggling Christians.

Sample response: If John Bunyan were alive today, he might use computer graphics to create a film about Christian's journey. He could tell the story of *The Pilgrim's Progress* through film, using computer graphics to create realistic settings like a swamp in the Slough of Despond. Computer graphics would allow Bunyan to control the swamp environment to portray what he envisioned. Also, he could add fantastical elements like the steps.

MAPPING ALLEGORY

An allegory is like an extended metaphor in which every detail has a literal and a symbolic meaning:

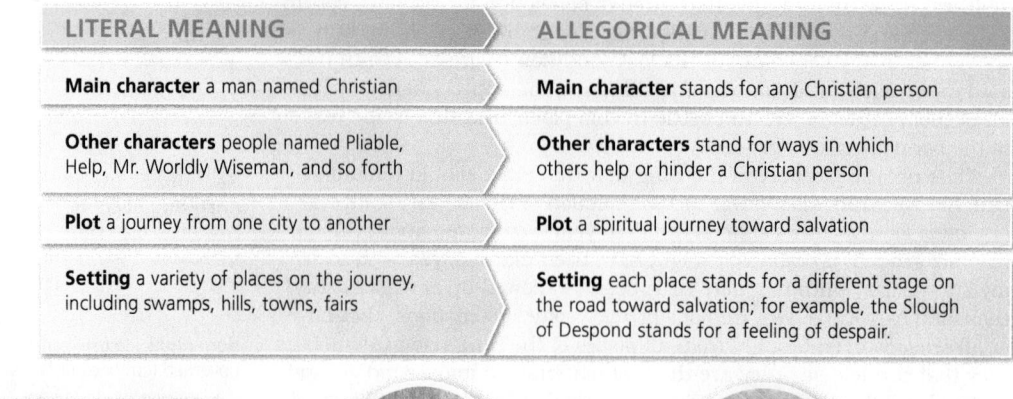

LITERAL MEANING	ALLEGORICAL MEANING
Main character a man named Christian	**Main character** stands for any Christian person
Other characters people named Pliable, Help, Mr. Worldly Wiseman, and so forth	**Other characters** stand for ways in which others help or hinder a Christian person
Plot a journey from one city to another	**Plot** a spiritual journey toward salvation
Setting a variety of places on the journey, including swamps, hills, towns, fairs	**Setting** each place stands for a different stage on the road toward salvation; for example, the Slough of Despond stands for a feeling of despair.

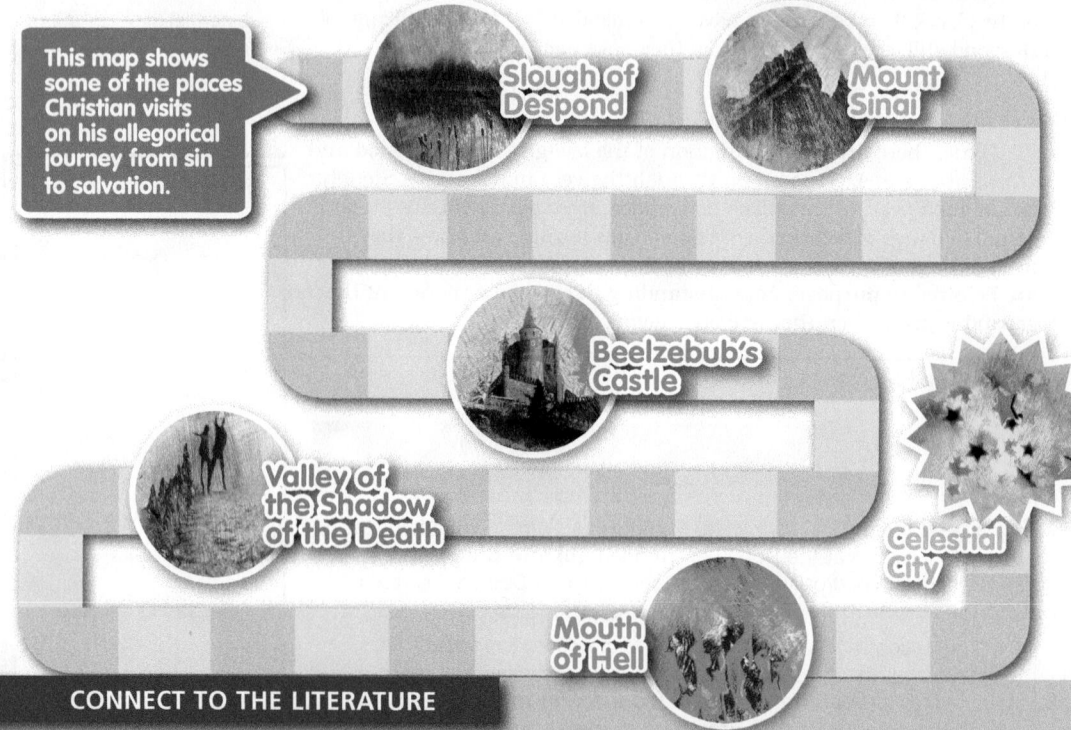

This map shows some of the places Christian visits on his allegorical journey from sin to salvation.

Slough of Despond

Mount Sinai

Beelzebub's Castle

Celestial City

Valley of the Shadow of the Death

Mouth of Hell

CONNECT TO THE LITERATURE

If John Bunyan were alive today, how might he use advanced technology to create his religious allegory?

Concept Connector

Reading Strategy Graphic Organizer
Ask students to review the charts of the allegory. Then, have students share their charts and compare the details they identified and analyzed.

Activating Prior Knowledge
Have students return to their responses to the Activating Prior Knowledge activity about how they would write an allegory about adolescence. Ask them to explain whether their thoughts have changed about events or place names.

Connecting to the Essential Question
Have students compare their responses to the prompt, completed before reading the selection, with their thoughts afterward. Have them work individually or in groups, writing or discussing their thoughts, to define their new responses. Then, lead a class discussion, probing for what students have learned that confirms or invalidates their initial thoughts. Encourage students to cite specific textual details to support their responses.

Literary Analysis

1. Craft and Structure Using details from the selection, explain why *The Pilgrim's Progress* is an **allegory.** Use a chart like the one shown to record elements of the allegory's symbolism.

Character/Place	Symbolic Role in a Christian's Life Journey

2. Integration of Knowledge and Ideas **(a)** What moral lesson or lessons do you think Bunyan was trying to teach in this episode? **(b)** Judging by this episode, how would you explain the popular appeal of *The Pilgrim's Progress*?

Reading Strategy

3. Analyzing text structures will help you appreciate the two levels of an allegory. **(a)** Briefly summarize the literal level of meaning in this episode of the allegory—what happens in the story? **(b)** Then, summarize the symbolic meaning of the events instead of just retelling them.

4. How does the title, *The Pilgrim's Progress,* help clarify the basic overall symbolism of the plot?

PERFORMANCE TASKS
Integrated Language Skills

Vocabulary Acquisition and Use

Use your knowledge of the underlined vocabulary words to determine whether each statement is true or false. Then, explain your answers.

1. A million dollars is a <u>substantial</u> amount of money.
2. A dog that just <u>wallowed</u> in something is likely to be dry.
3. A monarch rules over his or her <u>dominions</u>.
4. By misbehaving, Jill <u>endeavored</u> to please her teacher.
5. A <u>heedless</u> student listens carefully to what the teacher says.
6. A heavy suitcase can be a <u>burden</u> for a traveler.

Writing

Informative Text Imagine that a film is being made of *The Pilgrim's Progress* and your job is to cast the parts. Write a **casting memo** suggesting actors who might play the roles in this selection. Describe the qualities each performer will need or the reasons you think a particular star will suit a particular role. Cite details from the selection to justify your ideas. Use a standard memo format, including headings indicating From, To, Subject, and Date.

from The Pilgrim's Progress **557**

Common Core State Standards

Writing
2.b. Develop the topic thoroughly by selecting the most significant and relevant facts, extended definitions, concrete details, quotations, or other information and examples appropriate to the audience's knowledge of the topic.

Answers

1. **Possible response:** It is an allegory because Bunyan describes a journey on two levels. Pliable: a person who is easily swayed. Slough of Despond: despair one might feel. Help: a guide for a new Christian. Steps: the ways a new Christian can get out of despair. The King: Jesus Christ.

2. **Possible response:** (a) Bunyan's message was that sin keeps people in despair. A new Christian might become discouraged and doubtful, but the Bible, church, or prayer can help. (b) Readers could identify with the experience of fear and doubt.

3. **Possible response:** (a) Christian is a man on a journey. On his way, he falls into a swamp. A man comes to help him out. (b) A person on his Christian journey toward heaven may fall into despair at the beginning. He would need help to rise above it.

4. The word *pilgrim* shows the story is about a person on a religious journey. The word *progress* shows the journey is positive.

Vocabulary Acquisition and Use

1. True. A million dollars is a large amount.
2. False. If a dog rolls in mud or water, it will be wet.
3. True. Dominions are lands a monarch rules.
4. False. If she endeavored, she would behave well.
5. False. A heedless student would be inattentive.
6. True. A heavy suitcase would weigh a traveler down.

Writing

1. Read and go over the assignment with students.
2. Show a sample casting memo. Ask volunteers to identify the information in each line.
3. Have students complete the assignment. Suggest that they allot 5 minutes for prewriting, 10 minutes for drafting, and 10 minutes for revising and editing.
4. Evaluate students' informative texts using the **Rubrics for Business Letters,** *Professional Development Guidebook,* pages 291–292.

557

from *Eve's Apology in Defense of Women*
• To Lucasta, on Going to the Wars
• To Althea, from Prison
Lesson Pacing Guide

DAY 1 Preteach

- Ⓒ Administer the Reading and Vocabulary Warm-ups (*Unit 3 Resources*, pp. 107–110) as necessary.
- Ⓒ Introduce the Literary Analysis concept: Tradition and Reform.
- • Introduce the Reading Strategy: Relating a Work to Its Historical Period.
- Ⓒ Build background with the author and Background features.
- • Develop thematic thinking with Connecting to the Essential Question.
- Ⓒ Teach the selection vocabulary.

DAY 2 Preteach/Teach/Extend

- • Distribute copies of the appropriate graphic organizer for the Reading Strategy (*Graphic Organizer Transparencies*, pp. 97–98).
- • Distribute copies of the appropriate graphic organizer for Literary Analysis (*Graphic Organizer Transparencies*, pp. 99–100).
- • Prepare students to read with the Activating Prior Knowledge activities (TE).
- • Informally monitor comprehension while students read.
- • Use the Reading Check questions to confirm comprehension.
- Ⓒ Develop students' understanding of tradition and reform using the Literary Analysis prompts.
- • Develop students' ability to relate a work to its historical period using the Reading Strategy prompts.
- Ⓒ Reinforce vocabulary with the Vocabulary notes.
- • Assess students' comprehension and mastery of the skills by having them answer the Critical Reading, Literary Analysis, and Reading Strategy questions.

DAY 3 Assess

- • Have students complete the Vocabulary Lesson.
- Ⓒ Have students complete the Writing activity and write a dramatic scene. (You may assign as homework.)
- • Administer Selection Test A or B (*Unit 3 Resources,* pp. 119–121 or 122–124).

Ⓒ **Common Core
State Standards**

Reading Literature 4. Analyze the impact of specific word choices on meaning and tone, including words with multiple meanings or language that is particularly fresh, engaging, or beautiful.

Writing 3.b. Use narrative techniques, such as dialogue, pacing, description, reflection, and multiple plot lines, to develop experiences, events, and/or characters.

Additional Standards Practice
Common Core Companion, pp. 41–48; 208–218

Daily Block Scheduling
Each day in this Lesson Pacing Guide represents a 40–50 minute period. Teachers using block scheduling may combine days to revise pacing. In addition, teachers may differentiate and support core instruction by integrating components for extended and intensive support as students require. See the Guide to Selected Leveled Resources (facing page).

Guide to Selected Leveled Resources

R T I **Tier 1** (students performing on level)			*from* Eve's Apology in Defense of Women • To Lucasta, on Going to the Wars • To Althea, from Prison
Warm Up		**Practice, model,** and **monitor** fluency, working **with the whole class** or **in groups**.	**Vocabulary and Reading Warm-ups B,** *Unit 3 Resources,* pp. 126–127, 129
Comprehension/Skills		**Support** and **monitor** comprehension and skills development, having students complete the activities, graphic organizers, and interactive prompts **independently** or **as a class**.	• *Reader's Notebook,* adapted instruction and full selection **EL** *Reader's Notebook: English Learner's Version,* adapted instruction and adapted selection • **Reading Strategy Graphic Organizer B,** *Graphic Organizer Transparencies,* p. 108 • **Literary Analysis Graphic Organizer B,** *Graphic Organizer Transparencies,* p. 110
Monitor Progress	**A**	**Monitor** student progress with the differentiated curriculum-based assessment in the *Unit Resources.*	• **Selection Test B,** *Unit 3 Resources,* pp. 141–143 • **Open-Book Test,** *Unit 3 Resources,* pp. 135–137

R T I **Tier 2** (students requiring intervention)			*from* Eve's Apology in Defense of Women • To Lucasta, on Going to the Wars • To Althea, from Prison
Warm Up		**Practice, model,** and **monitor** fluency **in groups** or **with individuals**.	• **Vocabulary and Reading Warm-ups A,** *Unit 3 Resources,* pp. 126–128 • *Hear It!* Audio CD (adapted text)
Comprehension/Skills		• **Support** and **monitor** comprehension and skills development, working **in small groups** or **with individuals**. • As students complete the selection in the appropriate version of the *Reader's Notebook,* **monitor** comprehension frequently with group questions and individual instruction. • **Model** strategies while guiding students in completing the activities and prompts in the *Reader's Notebook,* as well as the graphic organizers. • **Practice** skills and **monitor** mastery with the *Reading Kit* worksheets.	• *Reader's Notebook: Adapted Version,* adapted instruction and adapted selection **EL** *Reader's Notebook: English Learner's Version,* adapted instruction and adapted selection • **Reading Strategy Graphic Organizer A,** *Graphic Organizer Transparencies,* p. 107 • **Literary Analysis Graphic Organizer A,** *Graphic Organizer Transparencies,* p. 109 • *Reading Kit,* Practice worksheets
Monitor Progress	**A**	**Monitor** student progress with the differentiated curriculum-based assessment in the *Unit Resources* and in the *Reading Kit.*	• **Selection Test A,** *Unit 3 Resources,* pp. 138–140 • *Reading Kit,* Assess worksheets

TIER 3 Tier 3 intervention may require consultation with the student's special-education or dyslexia specialist. For additional support, see the Tier 2 activities and resources listed above.

One-on-one teaching   Group work   Whole class instruction   Independent work   **A** Assessment

For a complete guide to selection support, including support for Advanced students, see the Overview of Resources in the frontmatter.

from *Eve's Apology in Defense of Women* • To Lucasta, on Going to the Wars • To Althea, from Prison

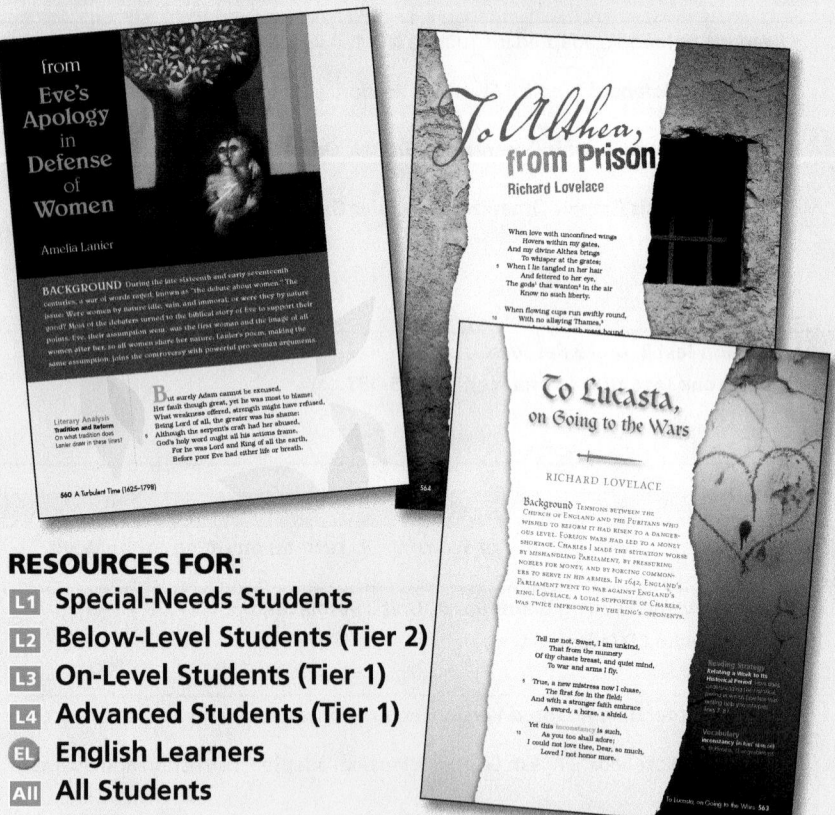

RESOURCES FOR:

- **L1** Special-Needs Students
- **L2** Below-Level Students (Tier 2)
- **L3** On-Level Students (Tier 1)
- **L4** Advanced Students (Tier 1)
- **EL** English Learners
- **All** All Students

Vocabulary/Fluency/Prior Knowledge

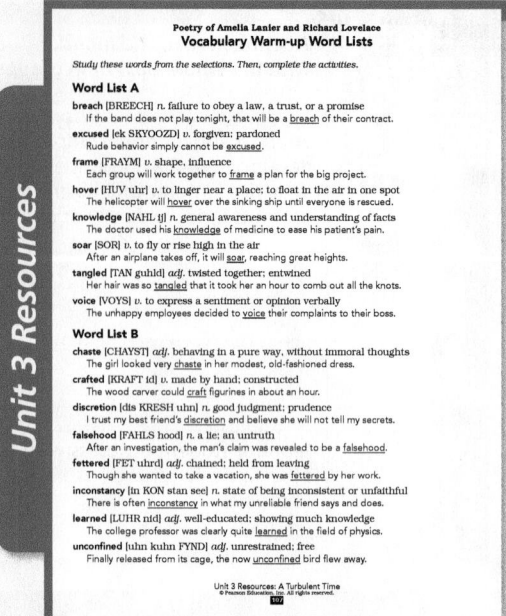

EL L1 L2 Vocabulary Warm-ups A and B,
pp. 107–108

Also available for these selections:

EL L1 L2 Reading Warm-ups A and B,
pp. 109–110

All Vocabulary Builder, p. 113

Reader's Notebooks

Pre- and postreading pages for these selections appear in an interactive format in the *Reader's Notebooks*. Each *Notebook* is differentiated for a different group of learners. The selections in the Adapted and English Learner's versions are abridged.

- **L2 L3** *Reader's Notebook*
- **L1** *Reader's Notebook: Adapted Version*
- **EL** *Reader's Notebook: English Learner's Version*
- **EL** *Reader's Notebook: Spanish Version*

© *Common Core Companion*

Additional instruction and practice for each Common Core State Standard

Selection Support

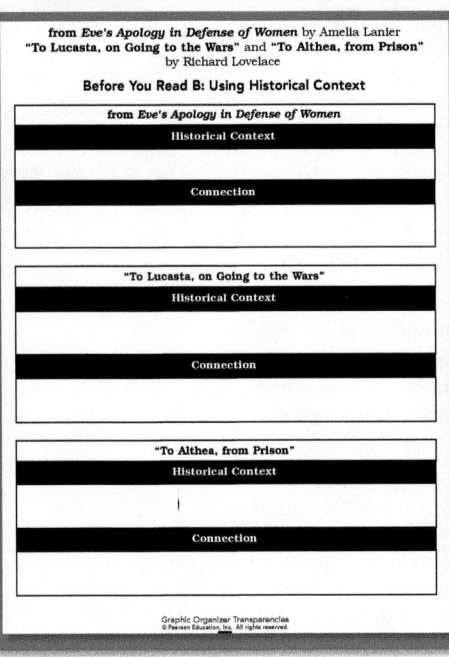

from *Eve's Apology in Defense of Women* by Amelia Lanier
"To Lucasta, on Going to the Wars" and "To Althea, from Prison"
by Richard Lovelace

Before You Read B: Using Historical Context

from *Eve's Apology in Defense of Women*

Historical Context

Connection

"To Lucasta, on Going to the Wars"

Historical Context

Connection

"To Althea, from Prison"

Historical Context

Connection

Graphic Organizer Transparencies
© Pearson Education, Inc. All rights reserved.

Graphic Organizer Transparencies *(sidebar)*

EL L3 **Reading: Graphic Organizer B,** p. 98

Also available for these selections:

EL L1 L2 **Reading: Graphic Organizer A** (partially filled in), p. 97

EL L1 L2 **Literary Analysis: Graphic Organizer A** (partially filled in), p. 99

EL L3 **Literary Analysis: Graphic Organizer B,** p. 100

Skills Development/Extension

Unit 3 Resources *(sidebar)*

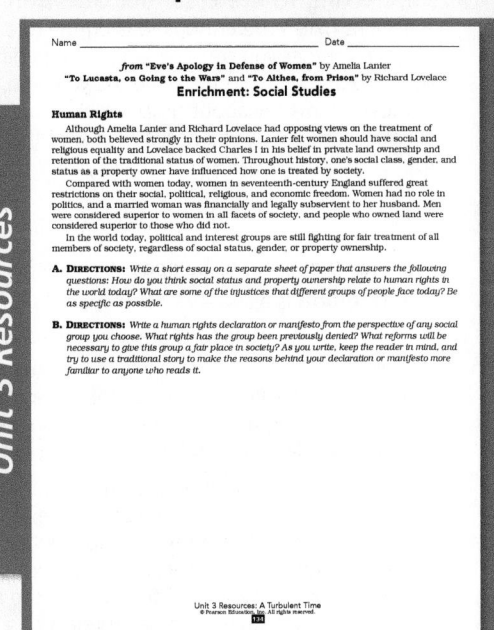

Name _____ Date _____

from "Eve's Apology in Defense of Women" by Amelia Lanier
"To Lucasta, on Going to the Wars" and "To Althea, from Prison" by Richard Lovelace

Enrichment: Social Studies

Human Rights

Although Amelia Lanier and Richard Lovelace had opposing views on the treatment of women, both believed strongly in their opinions. Lanier felt women should have social and religious equality and Lovelace backed Charles I in his belief in private land ownership and retention of the traditional status of women. Throughout history, one's social class, gender, and status as a property owner have influenced how one is treated by society.

Compared with women today, women in seventeenth-century England suffered great restrictions on their social, political, religious, and economic freedom. Women had no role in politics, and a married woman was financially and legally subservient to her husband. Men were considered superior to women in all facets of society, and people who owned land were considered superior to those who did not.

In the world today, political and interest groups are still fighting for fair treatment of all members of society, regardless of social status, gender, or property ownership.

A. DIRECTIONS: *Write a short essay on a separate sheet of paper that answers the following questions: How do you think social status and property ownership relate to human rights in the world today? What are some of the injustices that different groups of people face today? Be as specific as possible.*

B. DIRECTIONS: *Write a human rights declaration or manifesto from the perspective of any social group you choose. What rights has the group been previously denied? What reforms will be necessary to give this group a fair place in society? As you write, keep the reader in mind, and try to use a traditional story to make the reasons behind your declaration or manifesto more familiar to anyone who reads it.*

Unit 3 Resources: A Turbulent Time
© Pearson Education, Inc. All rights reserved.

L4 **Enrichment,** p. 115

Also available for these selections:

All **Literary Analysis,** p. 111

All **Reading,** p. 112

EL L3 L4 **Support for Writing,** p. 114

Assessment

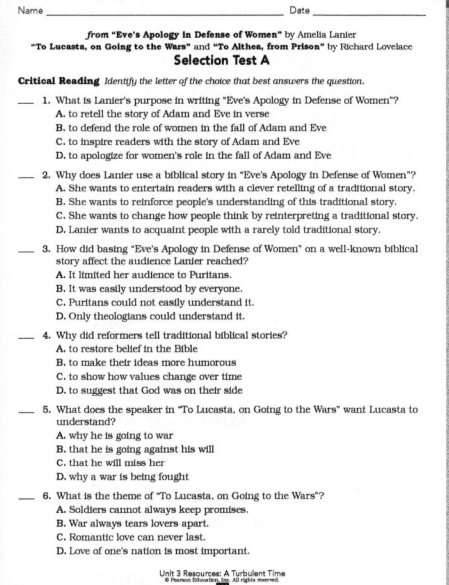

Name _____ Date _____

from "Eve's Apology in Defense of Women" by Amelia Lanier
"To Lucasta, on Going to the Wars" and "To Althea, from Prison" by Richard Lovelace

Selection Test A

Critical Reading *Identify the letter of the choice that best answers the question.*

___ 1. What is Lanier's purpose in writing "Eve's Apology in Defense of Women"?
A. to retell the story of Adam and Eve in verse
B. to defend the role of women in the fall of Adam and Eve
C. to inspire readers with the story of Adam and Eve
D. to apologize for women's role in the fall of Adam and Eve

___ 2. Why does Lanier use a biblical story in "Eve's Apology in Defense of Women"?
A. She wants to entertain readers with a clever retelling of a traditional story.
B. She wants to reinforce people's understanding of this traditional story.
C. She wants to change how people think by reinterpreting a traditional story.
D. Lanier wants to acquaint people with a rarely told traditional story.

___ 3. How did basing "Eve's Apology in Defense of Women" on a well-known biblical story affect the audience Lanier reached?
A. It limited her audience to Puritans.
B. It was easily understood by everyone.
C. Puritans could not easily understand it.
D. Only theologians could understand it.

___ 4. Why did reformers tell traditional biblical stories?
A. to restore belief in the Bible
B. to make their ideas more humorous
C. to show how values change over time
D. to suggest that God was on their side

___ 5. What does the speaker in "To Lucasta, on Going to the Wars" want Lucasta to understand?
A. why he is going to war
B. that he is going against his will
C. that he will miss her
D. why a war is being fought

___ 6. What is the theme of "To Lucasta, on Going to the Wars"?
A. Soldiers cannot always keep promises.
B. War always tears lovers apart.
C. Romantic love can never last.
D. Love of one's nation is most important.

Unit 3 Resources: A Turbulent Time
© Pearson Education, Inc. All rights reserved.

EL L1 L2 **Selection Test A,** pp. 119–121

Also available for these selections:

L3 L4 **Open-Book Test,** pp. 116–118

EL L3 L4 **Selection Test B,** pp. 122–124

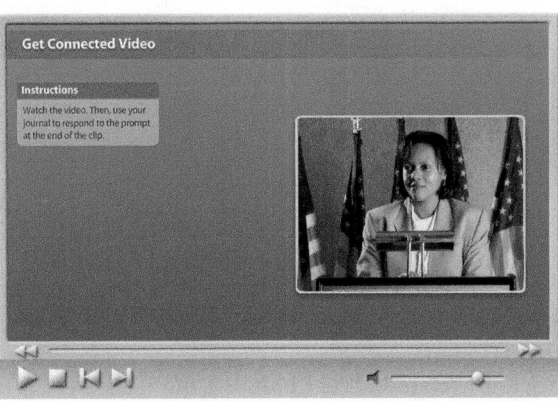

PHLit Online!
www.PHLitOnline.com

Online Resources: All print materials are also available online.

- complete narrated selection text
- a thematically related video with writing prompt
- an interactive graphic organizer
- highlighting feature
- access to all student print resources, adapted to individual student needs
- Spanish and English summaries
- adapted selection translations in Spanish

Get Connected! (thematic video with writing prompt)

Also available:

Background Video
All videos are available in Spanish.

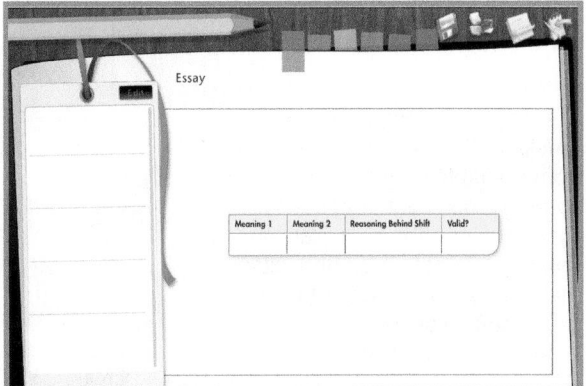

Writer's Journal (with graphics feature)

Also available:

Vocabulary Central (tools and activities for studying vocabulary)

Before You Read

from *Eve's Apology in Defense of Women* • *To Lucasta, on Going to the Wars* • *To Althea, from Prison*

❶ Connecting to the Essential Question

1. Review the assignment with the class.

2. Have students discuss the many roles that women have in society today. Then, have them complete the assignment.

3. As students read, have them note what the speakers say about or to women.

❷ Literary Analysis

Introduce the skill, using the instruction on the student page.

Think Aloud: Model the Skill

Say to students:

I know a writer is supporting tradition when he or she writes, "That's the way we've always done it." I know that the writer is trying to reform tradition when he or she says, "There's a better way." As I read these selections, I will look for clues that the writer provides about societal values, beliefs, roles, and practices, which the writer is supporting or trying to change.

❸ Reading Strategy

1. Introduce the strategy, using the instruction on the student page.

2. Give students **Reading Strategy Graphic Organizer B**, page 98 in *Graphic Organizer Transparencies,* to fill out as they read.

Think Aloud: Model the Skill

Say to students:

As I read this poem, I see that Amelia Lanier uses the story of Eve from the Bible to make a point about women deserving equality. By considering the historical context of this argument, I understand that the Bible was thought to be an expert source on whether women should enjoy basic rights.

❹ Vocabulary

1. Pronounce each word, giving its definition, and have students say it aloud.

2. For more guidance, see the *Classroom Strategies and Teaching Routines* card for introducing vocabulary.

558

---

❶ Connecting to the Essential Question The two authors of these selections have different opinions on the role of women in society. Briefly explain whether you consider yourself a traditionalist, a reformer, or neither with regard to this issue. As you read, notice what the speakers in these poems say about or to female characters. Understanding this contrast will help as you answer the Essential Question: **How does literature shape or reflect society?**

❷ Literary Analysis

Although they seem to be opposite, tradition and reform go together.

- **Tradition** is a society's approved values, beliefs, roles, and practices.
- **Reform** attempts to change traditional practices and ideas.

Amelia Lanier is a clear reformer, fighting against stereotypes of women, whereas Richard Lovelace fights for tradition, going to war and prison for his king and his honor. As you read, note the appearance of themes of tradition and reform in their works.

Comparing Literary Works Even when reformers' proposals are radical, they are often based on traditional beliefs. Lanier, for example, turns to the Bible, a traditional text, to support her new ideas about the equality of men and women. Lovelace, a supporter of the traditional power of his king, finds a new kind of freedom in love and integrity.

Both use a key strategy for interpreters of a tradition: They explore the multiple meanings of value terms such as *strength, honor,* and *freedom.* By redefining such terms, they find new ways to apply traditional ideas. As you read, analyze the impact of the authors' use of these words and the *political, religious, and philosophical assumptions* that their use suggests.

❸ Reading Strategy

Preparing to Read Complex Texts As you read a work, **relate it to the major themes and issues of its historical period** by identifying ideas, assumptions, and references that are typical of its era. Consider also which ideas may be responses to events of the period. To understand how Lanier's and Lovelace's poems reflect their era, complete a chart like the one shown for each work.

❹ Vocabulary

breach (brēch) *n.* breaking or being broken; failure to observe the terms of an agreement (p. 561)

discretion (di skresh′ ən) *n.* care in what one does and says (p. 561)

reprove (ri pro͞ov′) *v.* rebuke or find fault for an action (p. 561)

inconstancy (in kän′ stən sē) *n.* fickleness; changeableness (p. 563)

558 A Turbulent Time (1625–1798)

Common Core State Standards

Reading Literature
4. Analyze the impact of specific word choices on meaning and tone, including words with multiple meanings or language that is particularly fresh, engaging, or beautiful.

Poem

"Eve's Apology"

↓

Historical Context

Seventeenth-century women's rights were restricted; story of Eve was used to justify these restrictions

www.PHLitOnline.com

Vocabulary Development

Vocabulary Knowledge Rating

Create a **Vocabulary Knowledge Rating Chart** (*Professional Development Guidebook,* p. 33) for the vocabulary words on the student page. Give each student a copy of the chart with the words on it. Read the words aloud, and have students mark their rating of each in the Before Reading column. When students have completed reading and discussing the selec-tions, have them take out their **Vocabulary Knowledge Rating Charts** for the story. Read the words aloud and have students rate their knowledge again in the After Reading column. Clarify any words that are still problematic. Then, have students complete the Vocabulary practice at the end of the selections.

Vocabulary Central, featuring tools and activities for studying vocabulary, is available online at www.PHLitOnline.com.

❺ Amelia Lanier (1569–1645)

Author of "Eve's Apology in Defense of Women"

Amelia Lanier (also spelled "Lanyer") saw the need for women's rights three hundred years before the women's movement for equality. Daring to question her society's vision of women and the limited roles it allowed them, she anticipated future ideas of justice for women.

From Court Life to Working Woman Lanier had ties to the royal court, where her father, Baptista Bassano, was a musician to Queen Elizabeth I. Lanier's husband, Alphonso, and her son, Henry, were also court musicians. Despite her court connections, however, Lanier and her husband were not wealthy. When her husband died in 1613, Lanier sought to make a living by opening a school outside London.

A Radical Work In 1611, Lanier published a volume of poetry called *Salve Deus Rex Judaeorum (Hail, God, King of the Jews)*. In this groundbreaking work, of which "Eve's Apology in Defense of Women" is a section, Lanier questioned the privileges of the upper class and called for women's social and religious equality with men.

Although a woman sat on the throne of England during much of Lanier's lifetime, few women in her day published poetry. The poems in *Salve Deus Rex Judaeoroum* reflect her sense that women were underrepresented in the culture of the time. Sections of the work praise her female patrons, while others re-evaluate the role of women in stories from the Bible.

"Dark Lady" or Visionary? In later times, Lanier was perhaps more famous as a possibility for Shakespeare's "dark lady" (the mysterious woman to whom he addresses some of his sonnets) than for her poetry. As scholars have explored the political undercurrents of past literature, though, interest in Lanier has revived. Today, Lanier is considered a visionary feminist who spoke out against injustice.

from Eve's Apology in Defense of Women **559**

🔊 Daily Bellringer

For each class during which you will teach these selections, have students complete one of the five activities for the appropriate week in the *Daily Bellringer Activities* booklet.

Multidraft Reading

To assist struggling readers and to enhance reading for all, assign the text in chunks, as warranted by length, and apply multidraft reading protocols. For each reading, have students set the purpose indicated:

- **First reading**—identifying key ideas and details and answering any Reading Checks.
- **Second reading**—analyzing craft and structure and responding to the side-column prompts.
- **Third reading**—integrating knowledge and ideas, connecting to other texts and the world, and answering the end-of-selection questions.

For more guidance, refer to the *Classroom Strategies and Teaching Routines* card on Multidraft Reading.

❺ Background

More About the Author

Amelia Lanier was unusual for a woman of her time. Her contention in "Eve's Apology in Defense of Women"—that Eve was less responsible than Adam for the fall of humanity—was considered radical in the male-dominated era in which men held hierarchical positions in both the church and at home. Lanier's use of the church as the focus of her feminist writing was significant for two reasons. The church was an integral part of Renaissance life for both nobility and peasantry, and women were already reevaluating their roles in religion.

---

www.PHLitOnline.com

Teaching From Technology

Preparing to Read
Go to **www.PHLitOnline.com** in class or in a lab and display the **Get Connected!** slide show for this grouping. Have the class brainstorm responses to the slide show writing prompt, entering ideas in the interactive journal. Then, have students complete their written responses individually, in a lab or as homework.

To build background, display the Background and More About the Author features for both.

Using the Interactive Text
Go to **www.PHLitOnline.com** and display the Enriched Online Student Edition. As the class reads the selection or listens to the narration, record answers to side-column prompts using the graphic organizers accessible on the interactive page. Alternatively, have students use the online edition individually, answering the prompts as they read.

❶ About the Selection

Lanier would have made a wonderful lawyer. The book from which this passage is taken argues that women should have full equality with men, both socially and in religion. Such ideas were considered quite radical in Lanier's day, and some people might still find them so today.

❷ Activating Prior Knowledge

Ask students if they believe that writers should be outspoken about their beliefs and attempt to change the beliefs of others. For example, should artists promote unpopular ideas?

Concept Connector ➤

Tell students they will return to their responses after reading the selection.

❸ Literary Analysis

Tradition and Reform

1. Have a volunteer read the first stanza of the poem (lines 1–8).
2. **Ask** students: How would you summarize the speaker's arguments?
   Possible response: Adam was created first and had more authority than Eve, so he was more to blame than she was.
3. **Ask** students the Literary Analysis question: On what tradition does Lanier draw in these lines?
   Answer: Lanier draws on the biblical tradition of Genesis.

❶
❷ **from**

Eve's Apology in Defense of Women

Amelia Lanier

BACKGROUND During the late sixteenth and early seventeenth centuries, a war of words raged, known as "the debate about women." The issue: Were women by nature idle, vain, and immoral, or were they by nature good? Most of the debaters turned to the biblical story of Eve to support their points. Eve, their assumption went, was the first woman and the image of all women after her, so all women share her nature. Lanier's poem, making the same assumption, joins the controversy with powerful pro-woman arguments.

Literary Analysis
Tradition and Reform ❸
On what tradition does
Lanier draw in these lines?

But surely Adam cannot be excused,
Her fault though great, yet he was most to blame;
What weakness offered, strength might have refused,
Being Lord of all, the greater was his shame:
5 Although the serpent's craft had her abused,
God's holy word ought all his actions frame,
    For he was Lord and King of all the earth,
    Before poor Eve had either life or breath.

560 A Turbulent Time (1625–1798)

ⓒ Text Complexity Rubric: Leveled Texts

	from Eve's Apology in Defense of Women	To Lucasta, on Going to the Wars	To Althea, from Prison
Qualitative Measures			
Context/ Knowledge Demands	Poetic argument 1 ② 3 4 5	Seventeenth-century lyric 1 ② 3 4 5	Seventeenth-century lyric 1 ② 3 4 5
Structure/Language Conventionality and Clarity	Archaic diction and syntax; long sentences 1 2 ③ 4 5	Archaic diction and syntax 1 ② 3 4 5	Archaic diction and syntax; long sentences 1 2 ③ 4 5
Levels of Meaning/ Purpose/Concepts	Accessible (gender equality) 1 2 ③ 4 5	Accessible (love and honor) 1 2 ③ 4 5	Accessible (love, honor, and freedom) 1 2 ③ 4 5
Quantitative Measures			
Lexile/Text Length	NP / 264 words	NP / 72 words	NP / 169 words
Overall Complexity	**More accessible**	**More accessible**	**More complex**

Who being framed by God's eternal hand,
10 The perfectest man that ever breathed on earth;
And from God's mouth received that strait command,
The breach whereof he knew was present death:
Yea, having power to rule both sea and land,
Yet with one apple won to lose that breath
15   Which God had breathéd in his beauteous face,
Bringing us all in danger and disgrace.

And then to lay the fault on patience's back,
That we poor women must endure it all;
We know right well he did discretion lack,
20 Being not persuaded thereunto at all;
If Eve did err, it was for knowledge sake,
The fruit being fair persuaded him to fall:
No subtle serpent's falsehood did betray him,
If he would eat it, who had power to stay him?

❹
25 Not Eve, whose fault was only too much love,
Which made her give this present to her dear,
That what she tasted, he likewise might prove,
Whereby his knowledge might become more clear;
He never sought her weakness to reprove,
30 With those sharp words, which he of God did hear:
Yet men will boast of knowledge, which he took
From Eve's fair hand, as from a learned book.

Vocabulary

breach (brēch) *n.* breaking or being broken; failure to observe the terms of an agreement

discretion (di skresh′ ən) *n.* care in what one does and says

Vocabulary

reprove (rĭ prōōv′) *v.* rebuke or find fault for an action

Critical Reading ©

© 1. **Key Ideas and Details** **(a)** According to Lanier, what motive did Eve have for tasting of the Tree of Knowledge? **(b)** According to Lanier, why did Eve offer Adam a taste of the apple? **(c) Summarize:** Describe Eve's character according to Lanier.

© 2. **Key Ideas and Details** **(a)** According to the last stanza, what should Adam have done? **(b) Infer:** What view of Adam is suggested by Lanier's description of him?

© 3. **Key Ideas and Details** According to the poem, in what way do men apply a double standard to the story of the Fall?

© 4. **Integration of Knowledge and Ideas** Explain why the interpretation of this story was so important in seventeenth-century arguments about the nature of women.

Cite textual evidence to support your responses.

from Eve's Apology in Defense of Women **561**

---

❹ Critical Thinking
Infer

1. Have a volunteer read the last two stanzas, concentrating on lines 17–18, 21, 25, and 31–32.

2. **Ask** students: What would you say the common attitude was at the time toward the actions of Adam and Eve?
   Answer: Eve was blamed for the Fall, and Adam was seen as the victim.

3. **Ask** students: What can you infer about people's attitudes toward women in general?
   Possible response: People may have perceived women as weak and the source of humanity's troubles.

ASSESS

Answers

Before students respond, you may wish to have them write a brief objective summary of the selection. As they answer the questions below, remind them to support their answers with evidence from the text.

1. (a) Eve's motive was to gain knowledge. (b) Eve wanted to give Adam the apple so that he would have clear knowledge. (c) Eve is loving and thoughtful.

2. (a) He should have reproved her by quoting what God had told him directly. (b) Adam lacks discretion; he took the fruit for no other reason than it was "fair."

3. Men blame Eve for being banished from the Garden of Eden, but they boast about the knowledge gained from Eve's hand.

4. The story of Adam and Eve was used to validate seventeenth-century stereotypes of women.

© Text Complexity: Reader and Task Suggestions

Preparing to Read the Texts	*from* Eve's Apology in Defense of Women	To Lucasta, on Going to the Wars	To Althea, from Prison
• Using the Background on pp. 559 and 562, discuss the two poets' relationships to their era. • Discuss with students what sacrifices might be required to maintain honor and duty. • Guide students to use Multidraft Reading strategies (TE p. 559).	**Leveled Tasks** *Levels of Meaning* If students will have difficulty understanding Lanier's argument, have them first identify her main point. Then, have them consider the reasons she gives to support her main point. *Evaluating* If students will not have difficulty understanding the argument, have them evaluate its validity.	**Leveled Tasks** *Levels of Meaning* If students will have difficulty with the levels of meaning, have them focus first on the basic situation the poem details. Then, have them consider the imagery that helps capture that situation. *Evaluating* If students will not have difficulty with meaning, have them offer their own views about love and honor.	**Leveled Tasks** *Language/Structure* If students will have difficulty with the long sentences, have them sum up the first three stanzas using the structure *When* A, *then* B. Then, have them consider how these points lead to the last stanza. *Analyzing* If students will not have difficulty with structure, have them tell how the imagery expresses the idea of freedom.

⑤ Background
More About the Author

Richard Lovelace embodied the definition of the Cavalier poets, an informal group of soldier poets, named for being a combination of knights and gentlemen. Lovelace was typical of this group, which was also known as the Tribe of Ben because they were admirers and followers of the Elizabethan poet Ben Jonson. They prided themselves on their wit and gallant pursuits of literature, war, and the dashing, exciting life that often included beautiful women and a live-for-the-moment attitude. Lovelace's witty, graceful lyrics snub their nose at the horrors of war, prison, and political upheaval he endured.

PHLit Online!
For more about the author, go online at www.PHLitOnline.com.

⑤ RICHARD LOVELACE (1618–1657)

Author of "To Lucasta, on Going to the Wars" • "To Althea, from Prison"

Richard Lovelace, son of a wealthy family and firm supporter of his king, had the misfortune to live at a time when the English monarchy was under violent assault. The Civil War that culminated in the execution of the king plunged the privileged Lovelace into prison and poverty.

Looks and Talent Before England's Civil War, Lovelace profited by his association with royalty. It is said that, charmed by this winning young man, the king and queen ordered Oxford to grant him a degree before he had completed his studies! Lovelace did not, however, lack talent. While at Oxford, he wrote a play, painted, and played music.

The Price of Loyalty Lovelace was about twenty-six when Parliament challenged the king's authority and civil war broke out. Perhaps because of his personal charm, Lovelace was chosen to demand that Parliament restore the king's authority. Parliament was not impressed, though, and Lovelace was immediately arrested.

A Daring Life While imprisoned, Lovelace wrote "To Althea, From Prison," a moving affirmation of the value of personal integrity, even if it meant imprisonment. When released, he rejoined Charles's forces and spent his fortune equipping the king's army. Upon Charles's defeat in 1645, Lovelace joined the wars against Spain.

An Untimely End Returning to England years later, Lovelace was again imprisoned by the Puritans. During this time, he prepared for publication the volume that included "To Lucasta, on Going to the Wars." No one knows for certain how Lovelace's life ended, but it is believed that the charming young man who had won the heart of his king and queen died in discouragement and poverty at the age of thirty-nine.

Enrichment: Analyzing Music

Popular Music

Help students grasp the ideas of tradition and reform by showing how these apply to popular music. For instance, groups such as the Rolling Stones in the 1960s and Led Zeppelin in the 1970s "reformed" rock music—changed the basic tastes—by returning to much earlier versions of traditional blues songs. In turn, these bands were much imitated, establishing a new tradition.

Activity: Analyzing Music. Have each student pick a style of music to research. Suggest that they record information in the **Enrichment: Analyzing Music** worksheet, *Professional Development Guidebook*, page 236. Direct students to use the results of their research to develop oral presentations and present them to the class.

To Lucasta,
on Going to the Wars

RICHARD LOVELACE

⑦ Background TENSIONS BETWEEN THE
CHURCH OF ENGLAND AND THE PURITANS WHO
WISHED TO REFORM IT HAD RISEN TO A DANGER-
OUS LEVEL. FOREIGN WARS HAD LED TO A MONEY
SHORTAGE. CHARLES I MADE THE SITUATION WORSE
BY MISHANDLING PARLIAMENT, BY PRESSURING
NOBLES FOR MONEY, AND BY FORCING COMMON-
ERS TO SERVE IN HIS ARMIES. IN 1642, ENGLAND'S
PARLIAMENT WENT TO WAR AGAINST ENGLAND'S
KING. LOVELACE, A LOYAL SUPPORTER OF CHARLES,
WAS TWICE IMPRISONED BY THE KING'S OPPONENTS.

Tell me not, Sweet, I am unkind,
    That from the nunnery
Of thy chaste breast, and quiet mind,
    To war and arms I fly.

5   True, a new mistress now I chase,
    The first foe in the field;
⑧ And with a stronger faith embrace
    A sword, a horse, a shield.

Yet this inconstancy is such,
10   As you too shall adore;
I could not love thee, Dear, so much,
    Loved I not honor more.

Reading Strategy
**Relating a Work to Its
Historical Period** How does
understanding the historical
period in which Lovelace was
writing help you interpret
lines 7–8?

Vocabulary
inconstancy (in kän' stən sē)
n. fickleness; changeableness

To Lucasta, on Going to the Wars **563**

---

⑥ About the Selection
Like that of other Cavalier poets,
Richard Lovelace's work reflects an
upper-class attitude that focuses on
such courtly themes as love, honor,
and loyalty. In "To Lucasta," the
speaker explains to his love that she
should be glad that he is going off to
war; he could not love her so such if
he did not value honor so highly.

"To Althea, from Prison" explores
the nature of freedom—that freedom
of thought is true freedom, not an
absence of walls around the body.
This poem is also a political poem
that states the poet's Royalist sentiments explicitly in the third stanza.

**⑦ Activating Prior
Knowledge**
Ask students if they have ever
encountered an injustice that needed
to be addressed. Ask students how
the world should be made aware of
these injustices. Have students write
a paragraph suggesting ways to
rectify the situations, such as writing
letters or talking to others about the
injustices.

Concept Connector ⟹

Tell students they will return to their
responses after reading the selection.

⑧ Reading Strategy

**Relating a Work to Its
Historical Period**

1. Have a volunteer read lines 7–8.

2. **Ask** students: How does the
mention of "faith" and tools of
war, "sword . . . shield" relate to
the time period?
Answer: Lovelace wrote it during
a period of conflict between the
king of England and Parliament
over religion.

3. **Ask** the Reading Strategy question: How does understanding
the historical period in which
Lovelace was writing help you
interpret lines 7 and 8?
Answer: By knowing that he is
referring to religious warfare, you
can appreciate the poet's
motivations.

563

9 **Critical Thinking**

Critical Thinking

Analyze

1. **Ask** students how the poet's writing moves from specific to general in the poem.
   Possible response: Students may respond that the first stanza is about love of one woman; the second is about love of friends; the third is about love of king and, therefore, country; and finally, the fourth is about freedom in general.

2. **Ask:** Do you think this poem is primarily a love poem or an expression of support for the king? What are some reasons for your answer?
   Possible response: Students may respond that it could be a love poem, since it begins and ends with verses about love; however, it could be political because the writer is content to be in jail and sing the praises of the king.

10 **Engaging the Essential Question**

1. Point out to students that while Lovelace is suggesting that society should change its ways, the manner in which he writes about women hardly suggests a change in relationships between the sexes as Amelia Lanier's poetry did.

2. **Ask** students: What are the actions of Lovelace's female characters?
   Answer: Lucasta complains that he goes off to war. Althea comes to the prison to visit; she once draped her hair over him as they looked lovingly at each other.

3. **Ask** students: How does his portrait of Althea match Lovelace's beliefs in freedom and love?
   Answer: He believes in freedom in love and honor, and portrays Althea and himself as being hopelessly in love. However, his political actions have put him in a prison where he can no longer lie with her in happiness, so he has compromised his love and hers by affirming his loyalty to the king and his political struggle. Althea seems powerless to change the situation, other than to visit him and accept that her lover has chosen this course.

9

To Althea, from Prison

Richard Lovelace

When love with unconfined wings
　　Hovers within my gates,
And my divine Althea brings
　　To whisper at the grates;
5　When I lie tangled in her hair
　　And fettered to her eye,
The gods[1] that wanton[2] in the air
　　Know no such liberty.

10

When flowing cups run swiftly round,
10　　With no allaying Thames,[3]
Our careless heads with roses bound,
　　Our hearts with loyal flames;
When thirsty grief in wine we steep,
　　When healths[4] and drafts[5] go free,
15　Fishes that tipple in the deep,
　　Know no such liberty.

1. **gods**

   The word *gods* is replaced by *birds* in some versions of this poem.
2. **wanton**

   play.
3. **cups . . . Thames** (temz) wine that has not been diluted by water (from the river Thames).
4. **healths** toasts.
5. **drafts** drinks.

564

Concept Connector

Reading Strategy Graphic Organizer
Ask students to review the graphic organizers in which they have noted the historical context of each poem. Then, have students share their organizers and compare these historical contexts.

Activating Prior Knowledge
Have students return to their responses to the Activating Prior Knowledge activity. Ask them to explain whether their thoughts have changed and, if so, how.

Writing About the Essential Question
Have students compare their responses to the prompt, completed before reading the poems, with their thoughts afterward. Have them work individually or in groups, writing or discussing their thoughts, to formulate their new responses. Then, lead a class discussion, probing for what students have learned that confirms or invalidates their initial thoughts. Encourage students to cite specific textual details to support their responses.

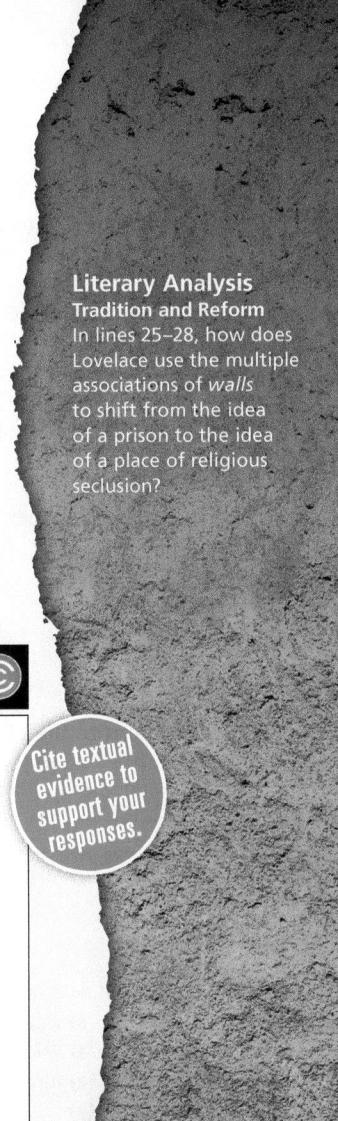

                When, like committed linnets,[6] I
                    With shriller throat shall sing
                The sweetness, mercy, majesty,
20   And glories of my King;
                When I shall voice aloud how good
                    He is, how great should be,
                        Enlarged[7] winds that curl the flood,
                        Know no such liberty.

25   Stone walls do not a prison make,
                    Nor iron bars a cage;
            Minds innocent and quiet take
                    That for an hermitage;[8]
                If I have freedom in my love,
30   And in my soul am free,
                Angels alone that soar above,
                    Enjoy such liberty.

---

6. **committed linnets** caged finches.
7. **Enlarged** released.
8. **hermitage** (hur′ mi tij) a place of religious seclusion.

Critical Reading

1. Key Ideas and Details (a) What does the speaker "now . . . chase" in line 5 of "To Lucasta"? **(b) Interpret:** In what sense does the speaker admit to having two loves? **(c) Draw Conclusions:** In the final two lines, why does the strength of the speaker's love for Lucasta depend on the strength of his other love?

2. Key Ideas and Details (a) In "To Althea," what are three things the poet does in prison? **(b) Interpret:** Explain the kind of "liberty" these activities possess.

3. Key Ideas and Details (a) In the fourth stanza of "To Althea," which two freedoms does the poet say are most important? **(b) Interpret:** What is the meaning of lines 25–26? **(c) Evaluate:** Do you agree with Lovelace's views on freedom? Explain.

4. Integration of Knowledge and Ideas Which of these authors do you think was reflecting dominant social attitudes about women? Which was trying to influence or change those attitudes? Explain. In your response, use at least two of these Essential Question words: *values, independence, reform.* *[Connecting to the Essential Question: How does literature shape or reflect society?]*

Literary Analysis
Tradition and Reform
In lines 25–28, how does Lovelace use the multiple associations of *walls* to shift from the idea of a prison to the idea of a place of religious seclusion?

Cite textual evidence to support your responses.

To Althea, from Prison **565**

---

(11) Literary Analysis
Tradition and Reform

1. Have a volunteer read lines 25–28, as well as the rest of the last stanza.

2. **Ask** students the Literary Analysis question: How does Lovelace use the multiple associations of *walls* to shift from the idea of a prison to the idea of a place of religious seclusion?
   Answer: Through an act of spiritual transcendence, Lovelace turns the prison walls into a sanctuary that protects the speaker from the distractions of daily life.

ASSESS

Answers

Before students respond, you may wish to have them write a brief objective summary of the selection. As they answer the questions below, remind them to support their answers with evidence from the text.

1. (a) He chases a new mistress, "the first foe in the field"—war. (b) His mistresses are Lucasta and honor. (c) Students may say that the speaker cannot love himself if he is not honorable; then he cannot, in turn, love Lucasta.

2. (a) He dreams about Althea, toasts his friendships, and sings the praises of his king. (b) When he has freedom in his love and loyalties, his soul is free and cannot be caged by iron bars.

3. (a) The poet says freedom in love and freedom in one's soul are important. (b) Stone walls and iron bars cannot imprison the soul. (c) Have the class discuss Lovelace's views on freedom and explain whether they agree with him or not.

4. **Possible response:** Lovelace reflects traditional <u>values</u> and attitudes toward women, while Lanier argues for <u>reform</u> of those values and champions more <u>independence</u> for women.

Assessment Resources

Unit 3 Resources

L1 L2 EL Selection Test A, pp. 119–121.
Administer Test A to less advanced readers.

L3 L4 EL Selection Test B, pp. 122–124.
Administer Test B to on-level and more advanced students.

L3 L4 Open-Book Test, pp. 116–118.
As an alternative, administer the Open-Book Test.

All Customizable Test Bank

All Self-tests
Students may prepare for the **Selection Test** by taking the **Self-test** online.

PHLit Online! All assessment resources are available at **www.PHLitOnline.com.**

565

Answers

1. (a) Lanier is trying to reform the belief that women are not equal to men. (b) She uses the biblical story of Adam and Eve to illustrate her argument. (c) She reinterprets the story to give realistic insight into Eve's character and gives Adam blame in proportion to his greater responsibilities.

2. (a) Lovelace is defending the traditions of love, honor, and loyalty. (b) Like King and Gandhi, Lovelace views his imprisonment as an opportunity for contemplation and meditation. He sees prison as a place of seclusion, a sanctuary that protects him from the distractions of daily life.

3. (a) Lanier concludes that Adam was more to blame than Eve, because he was created first and was supposedly more powerful than Eve. (b) Lanier points out that Adam was more powerful because he had God's word, and was "Lord and King of all the earth." (c) Meaning 1: free to love more than one woman; Meaning 2: spiritual freedom; Reasoning Behind Shift: the speaker experienced a spiritual transcendence; Valid?: yes.

4. (a) In Lanier's time, the Bible was considered the ultimate authority. Lanier exploits this faith by reinterpreting the story of Adam and Eve to give realistic insight into Eve's character and accord blame to Adam in proportion to his greater responsibilities. (b) Honor was a quality highly prized in Lovelace's time. In these lines, he explains to his lover that he could not love her as much as he does if he did not value honor so highly. (c) The speaker fiercely and outspokenly supports his king, and he equates this passion with his feelings for Althea.

Vocabulary Acquisition and Use

1. Choice C is correct, because *compliance* means keeping or preserving something, which is the opposite of *breach*.

2. Choice C is correct because *outspokenness* refers to expressing something forcefully or offensively, which is the opposite of *discretion*.

3. Choice A is correct because "to *forgive*" is the opposite of "to find fault," which is the meaning of *reprove*.

566

After You Read	from *Eve's Apology in Defense of Women* • *To Lucasta, on Going to the Wars* • *To Althea, from Prison*

Literary Analysis

 1. Key Ideas and Details (a) In "Eve's Apology," what traditional assumptions is Lanier trying to **reform? (b)** What **tradition** does she use to aid her, and why? **(c)** How does she reinterpret this tradition to make her point?

 2. Integration of Knowledge and Ideas (a) In "To Althea, from Prison," what tradition does Lovelace defend? **(b)** Compare the spirit of lines 29–32 with the principles of a reformer such as Gandhi or Martin Luther King, Jr.

3. Comparing Literary Works (a) In "Eve's Apology," lines 1–8, what conclusion about the Fall does Lanier draw from Adam's strength? **(b)** How does she shift between *weakness* as "moral weakness" and as "powerlessness" to make her point? **(c)** Use a chart like the one shown to note a similar shift in the meaning of *freedom* in "To Althea."

Meaning 1	Meaning 2	Reasoning Behind Shift	Valid?

Reading Strategy

4. Relate poems to their historical period by showing how issues, events, or political assumptions of the period help you interpret these passages: **(a)** "Eve's Apology," lines 25–32 **(b)** "To Lucasta," lines 11–12 **(c)** "To Althea," lines 17–24.

PERFORMANCE TASKS
Integrated Language Skills

Vocabulary Acquisition and Use

Choose the letter of each word's antonym (opposite). Explain each choice.

1. **breach:** **(a)** violation **(b)** cooperation **(c)** compliance
2. **discretion:** **(a)** valor **(b)** loudness **(c)** outspokenness
3. **reprove:** **(a)** forgive **(b)** support **(c)** balance
4. **inconstancy:** **(a)** flirtatiousness **(b)** faithfulness **(c)** certainty

Writing

Narrative Text Today, as in Lovelace's time, soldiers bid farewell to spouses, parents, or other loved ones when going off to war. Write a brief **dramatic scene** portraying such an event.
- Decide what relationship the characters will have.
- Use *dialogue* to reveal the characters' *emotions*.
- Revise your script to include stage directions where necessary.

 Common Core State Standards

Writing
3.b. Use narrative techniques, such as dialogue, pacing, description, reflection, and multiple plot lines, to develop experiences, events, and/or characters.

566 A Turbulent Time (1625–1798)

---

4. Choice *B* is correct because being *faithful* means being loyal and trustworthy, which is the opposite of *inconstancy*.

Writing

Evaluate students' narrative texts using the **General (Holistic) Writing Rubrics**, *Professional Development Guidebook*, pages 282–283.

The Ties That Bind

PART 3

567

Selection Planning Guide

The selections in this section all reveal or comment on the ties that bind together a family, community, or nation. Samuel Pepys's *Diary* provides a firsthand glimpse of how citizens of London pulled together as they dealt with two terrible disasters that struck in the mid-1600s: the bubonic plague and the Great Fire. Although Defoe's *A Journal of the Plague Year* is a work of fiction, it contains profound and heartbreaking insights into the effects the plague had on families and communities. Jonathan Swift also, through his satiric *Gulliver's Travels,* reveals how, for better or worse, religious and national identities inform the actions and thoughts of congregations and citizenry.

Humanities

Outskirts of London (detail) by Jan Griffier

Jan Griffier the Elder (1645/46–1718) was a Dutch landscape painter and graphic artist active in the Netherlands and England. Griffier was a versatile artist who used a variety of genres and media. This landscape portrays daily life in an English market on the outskirts of seventeenth-century London.

Use these questions for discussion:

1. What do the details in the painting reveal about life in London? **Possible response:** Life was still semirural and revolved around church and commerce. There are crowds of people in the market outside London.

2. How might this type of community respond to disasters such as an epidemic and widespread fire? **Possible response:** Many houses, shops, and workplaces of the time were made from wood and would go up in flames. These dual tragedies would have struck this community very hard and resulted in many deaths.

Monitoring Progress

Before students read the selections in Part 3, refer to the results for the **Vocabulary in Context** items on Benchmark Test 4 (*Unit 2 Resources,* p. 201). Use this diagnostic portion of the test to guide your choice of selections to teach, as well as the depth of preparation you will provide, based on students' readiness for reading and vocabulary skills.

© Text Complexity: At a Glance

This chart gives a general text complexity rating for the selections in this part of the unit to help guide instruction. For additional text complexity support, see the Test Complexity Rubric at point of use.

from A Journal of the Plague Year	**More Complex**	*from* A Dictionary of the English Language	**More Accessible**
from Gulliver's Travels	**More Accessible**	*from* The Life of Samuel Johnson	**More Complex**
A Modest Proposal	**More Complex**	Elegy Written in a Country Churchyard	**More Complex**
from An Essay on Man	**More Accessible**	A Nocturnal Reverie	**More Accessible**
from The Rape of the Lock	**More Complex**		

Common Core State Standards

- **Reading Informational Text 1, 3**
- **Writing 7, 8**
- **Language 6**

❶ About the Text Forms

1. Introduce the forms, using the instruction on the student page.
2. Tell students they will identify the characteristics of each form as they read the selections.

❷ Reading Strategy

Introduce the strategy, using the instruction on the student page.

Think Aloud: Model the Skill

Model the strategy of verifying and clarifying facts. Say to students:

To evaluate the reliability of a text as I read, I identify facts that I can check in another source. Most statements that include a name, date, or place can be verified or clarified in some way.

❸  What is the relationship between literature and place?

1. Ask for a volunteer to read the Essential Question aloud.
2. Then, discuss how students should approach the selections with the Essential Question in mind, using the instruction on the student page.

© COMMON CORE ▪ RESEARCH PROJECT

Primary Sources

Diary
The Diary of Samuel Pepys

Policy Statement
Charles II's Declaration to London, 1666

About the Text Forms

❶ A **diary** is an account of a person's experiences and reactions kept daily or at frequent intervals. Some people keep diaries just for themselves. Others hope one day to publish their diaries and so may be more careful in what they say or how they say it. As primary sources, diaries can offer a personal perspective on historical figures and events or provide valuable information about everyday life in the writer's times.

A **policy statement** is an official statement in which a government, a business, or another organization states principles or guidelines to follow. It often addresses a particular situation and aims to achieve a particular result. As primary sources, policy statements can show the political, social, or economic concerns at a particular time.

Reading Strategy

To get the most out of a primary source, follow these steps. As you complete your reading of the text or of a section of the text

- *summarize* what the writer has said, restating the most important ideas
❷
- *draw conclusions* about what the writer says implicitly, identifying his or her assumptions, or unstated beliefs, and implied, or suggested, meanings
- *analyze* the relations among ideas, events, and people in the text, considering how they interact and develop
- **verify and clarify facts.** First, identify factual claims—claims that you can confirm or disprove. Check each claim in another source, noting whether the second source confirms or disconfirms it. In addition, identify unclear passages and determine whether other sources help clarify them.

Support your summary and analysis with strong textual evidence—relevant
❸ quotations from the text. Note any points at which the text leaves matters uncertain, and determine the possible reasons for the uncertainty.

What is the relationship between **literature** and *place?*

As you read, consider the glimpses of seventeenth-century London that each document provides and the way it reflects the city's concerns.

Common Core State Standards

Reading Informational Text
1. Cite strong and thorough textual evidence to support analysis of what the text says explicitly as well as inferences drawn from the text, including determining where the text leaves matters uncertain.

3. Analyze a complex set of ideas or sequence of events and explain how specific individuals, ideas, or events interact and develop over the course of the text.

PHLit Online!
www.PHLitOnline.com

Teaching Resources

Unit 3 Resources
All **Diary and Policy Statements,** p.125
All **Vocabulary Builder,** p.126

Professional Development Guidebook
Enrichment, pp. 222, 229, 230, 236

PHLit Online! All resources are available at **www.PHLitOnline.com**

❹ **Note-Taking Guide**

1. Point out the sample note-taking guide on the student page.
2. Encourage students to use it to help them analyze the two selections in this lesson.

❺ **Vocabulary**

1. Have students preview the selection vocabulary, pronouncing the words and reading their definitions. Have students identify any words with which they are already familiar.
2. Use each word in a sentence with sufficient context to define the word. Then, offer another definitional sentence with the vocabulary word missing, requiring the class to fill in the blank orally. Here is an example:
A <u>malicious</u> act is one that is deliberately harmful. When someone intentionally harms another person, he or she is being [students say "malicious."]

❹ ## Note-Taking Guide

Primary-source documents are a rich source of information for researchers. As you read these documents, use a note-taking guide like the one shown to organize relevant and accurate information.

1 Type of Document (check one)
☐ Newspaper ☐ Letter ☐ Diary ☐ Speech ☐ Advertisement
☐ Government Document ☐ Eyewitness Account ☐ Memorandum ☐ Other

2 Date of Document _____

3 Author _____
Author's Position _____

4 Original Audience _____

5 Purpose and Importance
a What was the original purpose?_____
Write down two details that support your answer. _____
_____
_____

b List two important ideas, statements, or observations from this document.
_____
_____

c What does this document show about the time and place in which it was composed?_____
_____
_____

Reading Strategy
Verifying and Clarifying Facts
Identify facts and statements you may want to verify and clarify using other sources.

This guide was adapted from the **U.S. National Archives** document analysis worksheet.

❺ ## Vocabulary

apprehensions (ap rē hen´ shənz) *n.* fears; concerns (p. 572)

abated (ə bāt´ id) *v.* lessened (p. 572)

lamentable (lam´ ən tə bəl) *adj.* causing grief; distressing (p. 573)

combustible (kəm bus´ tə bəl) *adj.* capable of being ignited and burned; flammable (p. 574)

malicious (mə lish´ əs) *adj.* deliberately harmful; destructive (p. 576)

accounts (ə kountz´) *n.* records of money received and paid out; financial records (p. 577)

pernicious (pər nish´ is) *adj.* causing great injury, destruction, or ruin; deadly (p. 579)

magistrate (maj´ is trāt) *n.* a local official who administers the law or serves as a judge (p. 579)

eminent (em´ ə nənt) *adj.* noteworthy; of high rank; distinguished (p. 579)

notorious (nō tôr´ ē əs) *adj.* widely but unfavorably known; having a bad reputation (p. 579)

deliberation (di lib´ ər ā´ shən) *n.* careful consideration and discussion before reaching a decision (p. 579)

6 Background

The Story Behind the Documents

Samuel Pepys

Samuel Pepys did nothing by halves. His capacity for learning and his devotion to duty were astonishing. He remained at his post with the Royal Navy throughout the plague and saved the navy office during the Great Fire. As was true with almost anyone with government connections in those days, he spent time in prison. However, King Charles rescued him and sent him on several diplomatic missions. Pepys rose to become one of the most important men of his day. The friends of his old age included Sir Christopher Wren, Sir Isaac Newton, John Dryden, and almost every great scholar of the time.

Charles II

Charles II was entitled to become king of England in January 1649, when his father was executed. However, the same group that had killed his father was in control of the country at the time, so Charles II did not become king until the English Civil War ended. He was, however, named King of Scots in February 1649. He returned to England in 1660 and was crowned king of England and Ireland in April 1661—more than twelve years after his father's death.

© COMMON CORE ■ RESEARCH PROJECT

6 THE STORY BEHIND THE DOCUMENTS

Samuel Pepys

Samuel Pepys (pēps) (1633–1703), author of perhaps the most famous diary in English, was in a good position to report on his era. The son of a London tailor, Pepys became a clerk in the navy in 1660 and continued on a rapid rise to fame and fortune, eventually serving as a member of Parliament and secretary of the navy. Pepys began his diary in 1660 and continued it for nine years, when failing eyesight forced him to abandon the project. Writing for himself alone, he used a little-known shorthand that was not deciphered until the nineteenth century, when the diary was published. Today the diary offers a detailed and intimate account of events great and small in Restoration London.

Charles II (1630–1685) was restored to the throne in 1660, the same year Pepys began his diary. Charles's coronation —vividly described in the diary—came after years of exile during the period of England's civil war and subsequent Puritan rule. Excessive in his personal life, he tried to govern with moderation, punishing a few people directly responsible for the execution of his father, Charles I, but otherwise allowing different factions to share in governing. He also supported the arts and, to further scientific advancement, sponsored establishment of the Royal Society—an organization that numbered Samuel Pepys among its early presidents.

The return of the monarchy was greeted with much jubilation in a nation tired of Puritan austerity. Then twin disasters struck: a Great Plague broke out in 1664 and swept through London the following year, and the Great Fire of London devastated the city just one year after that. Samuel Pepys gives vivid and detailed accounts of both events in his diary. In his policy statement of 1666, Charles II responds to the Great Fire by ordering London's citizens to institute practices that would help prevent such calamities in the future.

Charles II

570 A Turbulent Time (1625–1798)

Enrichment: Analyzing a Historical Event

The Great Fire of London

Ask students to name disaster movies they have seen. Point out that most disaster movies are based on events that could or did happen, such as a deadly fire. Both selections in this lesson address the disastrous fire that raged through London in 1666. They provide unforgettable images of real horror.

Activity: Analyzing a Historical Event Have students research the Great Fire of London. Suggest that they record information in the **Enrichment: Analyzing a Historical Event** worksheet, *Professional Development Guidebook*, page 230. This research will improve their understanding of the selections that follow.

from THE DIARY

Samuel Pepys

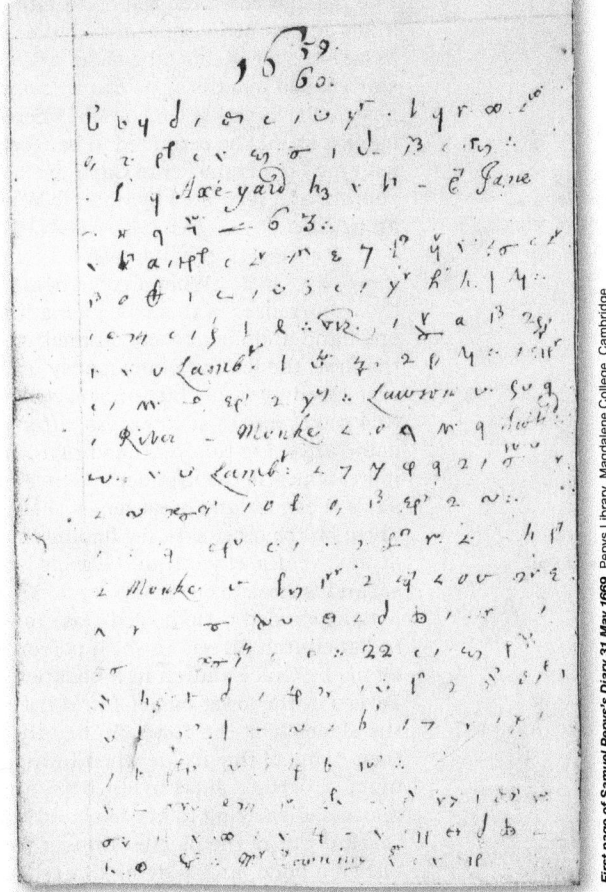

First page of Samuel Pepys's Diary 31 May 1669, Pepys Library, Magdalene College, Cambridge

The Plague

Sept. 3, 1665. (Lord's Day.) Church being done, my Lord Bruncker, Sir J. Minnes, and I up to the vestry[1] at the desire of the Justices of the Peace, Sir Theo. Biddulph and Sir W. Boreman and Alderman Hooker, in order to the doing something for the keeping of the plague from growing; but Lord! to consider the madness of the people of the town, who will (because they are forbid) come in crowds along with the dead corps[2] to see them buried; but we agreed on some orders for

---

1. **vestry** (ves' trē) *n.* church meeting-room.
2. **corps** corpses.

▲ **Critical Viewing**
What evidence on this page of the diary suggests that Pepys never meant to share his writing with the world? **[Infer]**

TEACH

❶ **Background**

History

Samuel Pepys wrote his diary in code, believing that it would not be read by anyone else. The diary has remained popular because it shows an extraordinarily honest and detailed picture of one person's real life, as well as the historical events that he witnessed or took part in. Today, readers who want to learn about seventeenth-century London still turn to Pepys's diary.

❷ **Humanities**

First page of Samuel Pepys's *Diary*, 1 January 1660

Pepys wrote this diary using a particular system of shorthand devised by Thomas Shelton. However, because some passages contained sensitive information, Pepys added further safeguards, using a cipher that he had created, as well as foreign words. The contents remained secret until 1825, when the diary was finally decoded.

❸ **Critical Viewing**

Possible response: We can infer from his use of a code, instead of a recognizable alphabet, that Pepys was not writing for others.

PHLit Online!

These selections are available in interactive format in the **Enriched Online Student Edition**, at **www.PHLitOnline.com**, which includes a thematically related video with writing prompt and an interactive graphic organizer.

571

Diary

1. Have a volunteer read the first diary entry aloud.

2. **Ask** students what they can learn about Pepys from the entry for September 3, 1665.
   Possible responses: Pepys is a Christian who attends church; he is an important member of society who makes decisions and rules; he is compassionate; he is concerned for his own health.

3. Have another volunteer read the second diary entry aloud.

4. Then, **ask** the Primary Sources question in the margin: What do the incomplete sentences and names in the entry for September 14, 1665, suggest about the audience for whom Pepys was writing?
   Possible response: His use of incomplete sentences throughout this passage indicates that Pepys was writing for himself and did not expect anyone else to read the diary. Also, the code in which the diary was written may have contributed to the choppiness of the writing.

the prevention thereof.[3] Among other stories, one was very passionate, methought of a complaint brought against a man in the town for taking a child from London from an infected house. Alderman Hooker told us it was the child of a very able citizen in Gracious Street, a saddler,[4] who had buried all the rest of his children of the plague, and himself and wife now being shut up and in despair of escaping, did desire only to save the life of this little child; and so prevailed to have it received stark-naked into the arms of a friend, who brought it (having put it into new fresh clothes) to Greenwich; where upon hearing the story, we did agree it should be permitted to be received and kept in the town. Thence with my Lord Bruncker to Captain Cocke's, where we mighty merry and supped, and very late I by water to Woolwich, in great apprehensions of an ague. . . .

Sept. 14, 1665. When I come home I spent some thoughts upon the occurrences of this day, giving matter for as much content on one hand and melancholy on another, as any day in all my life. For the first; the finding of my money and plate,[5] and all safe at London, and speeding in my business of money this day. The hearing of this good news to such excess, after so great a despair of my Lord's doing anything this year; adding to that, the decrease of 500 and more, which is the first decrease we have yet had in the sickness since it begun: and great hopes that the next week it will be greater. Then, on the other side, my finding that though the bill[6] in general is abated, yet the city within the walls is increased, and likely to continue so, and is close to our house there. My meeting dead corpses of the plague, carried to be buried close to me at noonday through the city in Fanchurch Street. To see a person sick of the sores, carried close by me by Grace church in a hackney coach.[7] My finding the Angell Tavern at the lower end of Tower Hill, shut up, and more than that, the alehouse at the Tower Stairs, and more than that, the person was then dying of the plague when I was last there, a little while ago, at night, to write a short letter there, and I overheard the mistress of the house sadly saying to her husband somebody was very ill, but did not think it was of the plague. To hear that poor Payne, my waiter, hath buried a child, and is dying himself. To hear that a laborer I sent but the other day to Dagenhams, to know how they did there, is dead of the plague; and that one of my own watermen, that carried me daily, fell sick as soon as he had landed me on Friday morning last, when I had been all night upon the water (and I believe he did get his infection that day at Brainford), and is now dead of the plague. To hear

Vocabulary
apprehensions (ap′ rē hen′ shənz) *n.* fears; concerns

Vocabulary
abated (ə bāt′ id) *v.* lessened

4 Primary Sources

Diary
What do the incomplete sentences and names in the entry for September 14, 1665, suggest about the audience for whom Pepys was writing?

---

3. **but we . . . thereof** Funeral processions were forbidden in London during the plague. However, the law was often ignored.
4. **saddler** *n.* person who makes, sells, and repairs saddles.
5. **plate** valuable serving dishes and flatware.
6. **bill** weekly list of burials.
7. **hackney coach** carriage for hire.

Enrichment: Investigating Health and Medicine

Medical History

In the diary, a child is taken from a plague-ridden household in hopes of saving its life. The child was stripped naked, because people feared that clothes might spread the plague. This belief was not as odd as it may seem. Smallpox, another major killer at the time, was spread by contact with anything that had come into contact with an infected person—even two years later.

Bubonic plague was spread by fleas and by coughing or sneezing. In Pepys's day, though, little was known about the disease. Removing clothes that had been in contact with infected people was an effort to stop the spread of the disease.

Activity: Investigating Health and Medicine
Have students research the bubonic plague. Suggest that they record information in the **Enrichment: Investigating Health and Medicine** worksheet, *Professional Development Guidebook*, page 229.

that Captain Lambert and Cuttle are killed in the taking these ships; and that Mr. Sidney Montague is sick of a desperate fever at my Lady Carteret's, at Scott's Hall. To hear that Mr. Lewes hath another daughter sick. And, lastly, that both my servants, W. Hewer and Tom Edwards, have lost their fathers, both in St. Sepulcher's parish, of the plague this week, do put me into great apprehensions of melancholy, and with good reason. But I put off the thoughts of sadness as much as I can, and the rather to keep my wife in good heart and family also. After supper (having eat nothing all this day) upon a fine tench[8] of Mr. Shelden's taking, we to bed.

The Fire of London

Sept. 2, 1666. (Lord's day.) Some of our maids sitting up late last night to get things ready against our feast today, Jane called us up about three in the morning, to tell us of a great fire they saw in the city. So I rose and slipped on my night-gown, and went to her window, and thought it to be on the back side of Mark Lane at the farthest; but, being unused to such fires as followed, I thought it far enough off; and so went to bed again and to sleep. About seven rose again to dress myself, and there looked out at the window, and saw the fire not so much as it was and farther off. So to my closet to set things to rights after yesterday's cleaning. By and by Jane comes and tells me that she hears that above 300 houses have been burned down tonight by the fire we saw, and that it is now burning down all Fish Street, by London Bridge. So I made myself ready presently, and walked to the Tower,[9] and there got up upon one of the high places, Sir J. Robinson's little son going up with me; and there I did see the houses at that end of the bridge all on fire, and an infinite great fire on this and the other side the end of the bridge; which, among other people, did trouble me for poor little Michell and our Sarah on the bridge. So down, with my heart full of trouble, to the Lieutenant of the Tower, who tells me that it begun this morning in the King's baker's house in Pudding Lane, and that it hath burned St. Magnus's Church and most part of Fish Street already. So I down to the waterside, and there got a boat and through bridge, and there saw a lamentable fire. Poor Michell's house, as far as the Old Swan, already burned that way, and the fire running farther, that in a very little time it got as far as the steel yard, while I was there. Everybody endeavoring to remove their goods, and flinging into the river or bringing them into lighters that lay off; poor people staying in their houses as long as till the very fire touched them, and then running into boats, or clambering from one

---

8. **tench** *n.* type of fish.
9. **Tower** Tower of London.

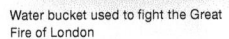

Water bucket used to fight the Great Fire of London

Vocabulary

lamentable (lam´ ən tə bəl) *adj.* causing grief; distressing

6

Reading Check

How did Pepys hear about the fire in the city?

from The Diary **573**

5 Background

Language

Point out to students that when Pepys writes that "Jane called us up," he is not referring to a phone call. This is a British expression for "woke us up by calling to us."

6 Reading Check

Answer: Pepys heard about the great fire from one of his maids named Jane. Later he went and checked it out by walking to the Tower and climbing to one of the high places to observe events on London Bridge.

Differentiated Instruction for Universal Access

Strategy for Less Proficient Readers
Suggest that students list details as they read. Then, after they have finished reading a diary entry, have them go back over the list to identify items that might help them draw conclusions. Working with partners might help them identify facts and details that are related.

EL Strategy for English Learners
This selection may be difficult for students because of both the language and the unfamiliar cultural context. Pick one day from Pepys's diary and work through unfamiliar words and ideas as a class, drawing conclusions when appropriate. Additional images of London or these disasters might aid understanding.

❼ Reading Strategy

Verifying and Clarifying

Ask students the Reading Strategy question: Which facts in this paragraph could you verify in another source?

Possible answers: September 2 as the day the London fire began; more than 300 houses burned that night; the street names detailing where the fire was burning; how the fire started; Pepys's actions, as verified by witnesses

❽ Primary Source: Art

Possible response: Pepys's line "and there I did see an infinite great fire on this and the other side of the bridge . . ." would be an appropriate caption.

❾ Humanities

The Great Fire of London, 1666

At the time of the fire, photography did not exist, so artists were relied upon to create visual records of events of the time. These artists often worked outdoors in the midst of the events they recorded. We do not know who created this painting, which hangs in the Museum of London, England. However, he or she left a vivid record of the disaster. The accuracy of the image is confirmed by the ease with which one can identify important landmarks, such as the Tower of London, on the right, and London Bridge, to the left.

Use these questions for discussion:

1. How might such an event be recorded or shared today?
   Possible response: Photographs and videos are likely ways that it would be recorded, and the information might be shared in newspapers, magazines, the internet, or on television.

2. Why do people keep visual records of such events?
   Possible response: Most people like to have some way of remembering major events, or even of proving that a disaster was as bad as they remember when they relate the stories years later.

❼ Reading Strategy

Verifying and Clarifying

Which facts in this paragraph could you verify in another source?

Vocabulary

combustible (kəm busʹtə bəl) *adj.* capable of being ignited and burned; flammable

❽ ▼ Primary Source: Art

What line from Pepys's account of the fire would be an appropriate caption for this painting? Why? **[Connect]**

pair of stairs by the waterside to another. And among other things, the poor pigeons, I perceive, were loth to leave their houses, but hovered about the windows and balconies till they were, some of them burned, their wings, and fell down. Having stayed, and in an hour's time seen the fire rage every way, and nobody, to my sight, endeavoring to quench it, but to remove their goods, and leave all to the fire, and having seen it get as far as the steel yard, and the wind mighty high and driving it into the city; and everything, after so long a drought, proving combustible, even the very stones of churches, and among other things the poor steeple by which pretty Mrs.— lives, and whereof my old schoolfellow Elborough is parson, taken fire in the very top, and there burned till it fell down. I to Whitehall (with a gentleman with me who desired to go off from the Tower, to see the fire, in my boat), and there up to the King's closet in the chapel, where people come about me, and I did give them an account dismayed them all, and word was carried in to the King. So I was called for, and did tell the King and Duke of York what I saw, and that unless his Majesty did command houses to be pulled down nothing could stop the fire. They seemed much troubled, and the King commanded me to go to my Lord Mayor from him, and command him to spare no houses, but to pull down before the fire every way. The Duke of York bid me tell him that if he would have any more soldiers he shall; and so did my Lord Arlington afterwards, as a great secret. Here meeting with Captain Cocke, I in his coach, which he lent me, and Creed with

❾ *The Great Fire of London,* 1666

574 A Turbulent Time (1625–1798)

me to Paul's,[10] and there walked along Watling Street, as well as I could, every creature coming away loaden with goods to save, and here and there sick people carried away in beds. Extraordinary good goods carried in carts and on backs. At last met my Lord Mayor in Canning Street, like a man spent, with a handkerchief about his neck. To the King's message he cried, like a fainting woman, "Lord! what can I do? I am spent: people will not obey me. I have been pulling down houses; but the fire overtakes us faster than we can do it." That he needed no more soldiers; and that, for himself, he must go and refresh himself, having been up all night. So he left me, and I him, and walked home, seeing people all almost distracted, and no manner of means used to quench the fire. The houses, too, so very thick thereabouts, and full of matter for burning, as pitch and tar, in Thames Street; and warehouses of oil, and wines, and brandy, and other things. Here I saw Mr. Isaake Houblon, the handsome man, prettily dressed and dirty, at his door at Dowgate, receiving some of his brothers' things, whose houses were on fire; and, as he says, have been removed twice already; and he doubts (as it soon proved) that they must be in a little time removed from his house also, which was a sad consideration. And to see the churches all filling with goods by people who themselves should have been quietly there at this time. By this time it was about twelve o'clock; and so home. Soon as dined, and walked through the city, the streets full of nothing but people and horses and carts loaden with goods, ready to run over one another, and removing goods from one burned house to another. They now removing out of Canning Street (which received goods in the morning) into Lumbard Street, and farther; and among others I now saw my little goldsmith, Stokes, receiving some friend's goods, whose house itself was burned the day after. I to Paul's Wharf, where I had appointed a boat to attend me, and took in Mr. Carcasse and his brother, whom I met in the street, and carried them below and above bridge to and again to see the fire, which was now got farther, both below and above, and no likelihood of stopping it. Met with the King and Duke of York in their barge, and with them to Queenhithe, and there called Sir Richard Browne to them. Their order was only to pull down houses apace, and so below bridge at the waterside; but little was or could be done, the fire coming upon them so fast. Good hopes there was of stopping it at the Three Cranes above, and at Buttolph's Wharf below bridge, if care be used; but the wind carries it into the city, so as we know not by the waterside what it do there. River full of lighters and boats taking in goods, and good goods swimming in the water, and only I observed that hardly one lighter or boat in three that had the goods of a house in, but there was a pair of virginals[11] in it. Having seen as much as I could now, I away to Whitehall by

10. **Paul's** St. Paul's Cathedral.
11. **virginals** *n.* small, legless harpsichords.

🔟 **Reading Strategy**
Verifying and Clarifying
From the details in the text, what can you clarify about the role of the River Thames in the Great Fire of London?

⓫ World
LITERATURE
CONNECTION

Famous Diaries in World Literature
Samuel Pepys was not the first to keep a diary. As early as the tenth century, women in the Japanese Imperial Court wrote journals they called "pillow books," because they hid them under their pillows. Sei Shōnagon began hers with a description of dawn, written in graceful Japanese brush strokes. Soon, she was confiding, "I just love it when bad things happen to people I can't stand," believing nobody would ever read her words.

In the eighteenth and nineteenth centuries, diary writing became a popular pastime in Europe and the Americas, as Western culture placed greater emphasis on the individual personality. During World War II, a teenager named Anne Frank kept a diary while hiding from the Nazis in an attic in Amsterdam. She never guessed it would be read around the world someday.

Connect to the Literature
Do you think Pepys would have written a different sort of diary if he had known it would be published? Explain.

⓬ Reading Check

What does Pepys learn about the fire from his visit to the Tower?

from The Diary **575**

Differentiated Instruction   for Universal Access

Support for Special-Needs Students
Create an outline of the September 2, 1666, diary entry. Initially, just write Date, How Pepys Heard News, Where He Went, Where Fire Started, Why It Spread, How People Acted, and so forth, to the end of Pepys's day. Then, as students read, have them pull details from the text to fill in the outline. When students finish, you can use the outline to review the eventful day.

Support for Less Proficient Readers
Suggest that each student pick an incident from his or her life, from the news, or from history and create a diary entry similar to this one. Tell them to be specific and to use facts, but also to include personal observations and comments. Tell them to pick an incident with which they are familiar or which they can easily research, so that they can find enough information.

🔟 **Reading Strategy**
Verifying and Clarifying
Ask students the Reading Strategy question: From the details in the text, what can you clarify about the role of the River Thames in the Great Fire of London? **Possible response:** The River Thames provided a safe zone the fire could not breach. It also prevented the fire from spreading in that direction.

⓫ **World Literature Connection**
Famous Diaries in World Literature
A diary is at once able to reveal the character of its writer and provide insight into the historical period in which it is written. This unique quality makes a diary an invaluable tool for historians. Historians have used diaries kept by Presidents of the United States to learn about these men and periods of U.S history.

One rather unique diary was kept by President Harry S. Truman. Truman wrote notes about each appointment he had during the day. After one visit with a public figure, he jotted down, "This man not only wants to run the country, but the universe and the entire Milky Way." After having dinner at the Mayflower Hotel for Jackson Day Dinner, he wrote, "An enthusiastic meeting. My first political speech as President. Rang the bell, I believe." Truman's diary, like those of Pepys, Frank, and Nin, reveals his character and provides insight into the historical period.

Connect to the Literature
After they have read Famous Diaries in World Literature note, share the additional background information above with students. Then, **ask:** Do you think Pepys would have written a different sort of diary if he had known it would be published?

Possible response: If Pepys had known his diary would be published, he might not have been as honest or detailed in his writing.

⓬ **Reading Check**

Answer: Pepys learns that the fire started at the king's baker's house, burned down St. Magnus's Church, and spread to most of Fish Street.

13 Humanities

The Great Fire
by Marcus Willemsz Doornik, 1666

This map is a good example of the cartographer's (mapmaker's) art, which saw many changes during the seventeenth century. New developments in science and mathematics helped determine longitude, and an interest in exploration helped to create more-accurate maps. Maps of this era were usually engraved, with each color requiring a different engraved plate. Maps such as this one are considered by many to be works of art, as well as utilitarian objects.

Use these questions for discussion:

1. This map shows the area devastated by the Great Fire. What other information can you get from this map?
Answer: London's general layout, major streets, and location of the River Thames.

2. Is this map more effective in practical terms or as a work of art? Explain.
Possible response: It shows clearly the aftermath of the fire, but would not help someone navigate the city. It is primarily a work of art.

14 Primary Source: Art

Possible response: It enhances Pepys's description because it shows the extent of the damage.

15 Primary Sources

Diary

1. Have students reread the text on page 576 silently.

2. Then, **ask** the Primary Sources question from the margin: What emotional reaction does Pepys have toward the fire that is sweeping through London? Cite words and phrases that reveal his feelings.
Possible response: Pepys is clearly distressed by the scene. He says, "It made me weep to see it." He also repeats the word *horrid*.

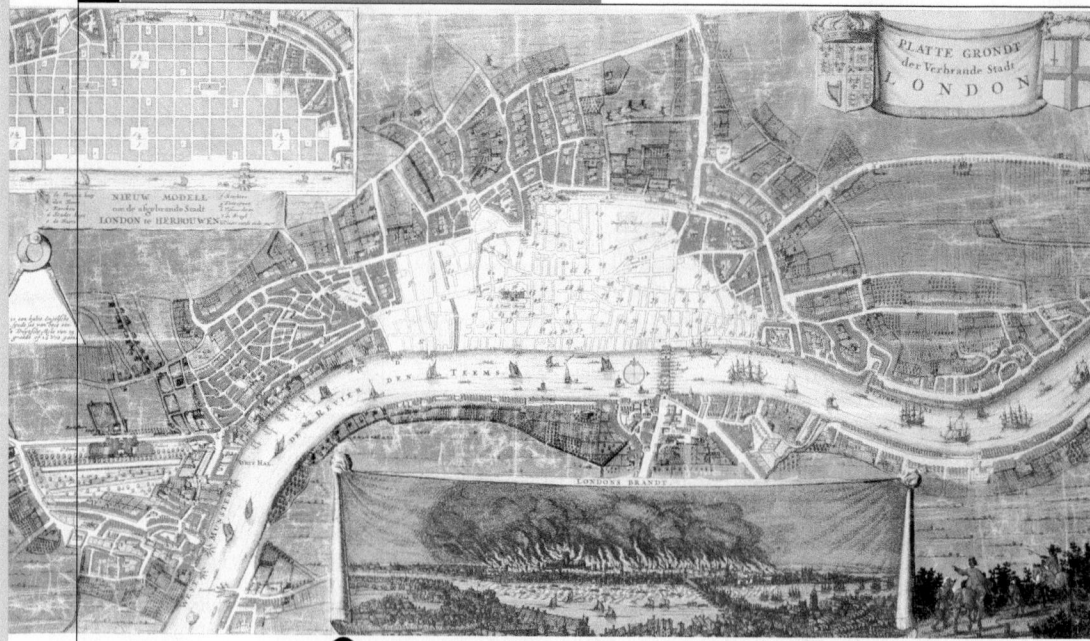

13 *The Great Fire*, 1666, Marcus Willemsz Doornik, Guildhall Library, Corporation of London

14 ▲ Primary Source: Art
This map of London includes an inset depicting the area destroyed by the Great Fire. Does this image enhance Pepys's eyewitness description? Explain.
[Make a Judgment]

Vocabulary
malicious (mə lish′ əs) *adj.* deliberately harmful; destructive

15 Primary Sources
Diary What emotional reaction does Pepys have toward the fire that is sweeping through London? Cite words and phrases that reveal his feelings.

appointment, and there walked to St. James's Park, and there met my wife and Creed and Wood and his wife, and walked to my boat; and there upon the water again, and to the fire up and down, it still increasing, and the wind great. So near the fire as we could for smoke; and all over the Thames, with one's face in the wind, you were almost burned with a shower of firedrops. This is very true; so as houses were burned by these drops and flakes of fire, three or four, nay, five or six houses, one from another. When we could endure no more upon the water, we to a little alehouse on the Bankside, over against the Three Cranes, and there stayed till it was dark almost, and saw the fire grow; and, as it grew darker, appeared more and more, and in corners and upon steeples, and between churches and houses, as far as we could see up the hill of the city, in a most horrid malicious bloody flame, not like the fine flame of an ordinary fire. Barbary and her husband away before us. We stayed till, it being darkish, we saw the fire as only one entire arch of fire from this to the other side the bridge, and in a bow up the hill for an arch of above a mile long: it made me weep to see it. The churches, houses, and all on fire and flaming at once; and a horrid noise the flames made, and the cracking of houses at their ruin. So home with a sad heart, and there find everybody discoursing and lamenting the fire; and poor Tom Hater come with some of his few goods saved out of his house, which is burned upon Fish Street Hill. I invited him to lie at

---

Enrichment: Building Context

Firefighting

Pulling down buildings to stop a fire was the only real fire fighting strategy that had been devised by the time of London's Great Fire in 1666. After the Great Fire, the first fire brigades were created by London's insurance companies (the government did not get involved until 1865). The first fire hose was invented in the Netherlands in 1672. Benjamin Franklin helped create the first fire department in the 1700s,

but it was not until 1830 that the first modern standards for a fire department were introduced, in Edinburgh, Scotland.

Activity: Building Context Have students work in pairs to research early firefighting techniques. Ask students to record what they learn, using the **Enrichment: Building Context** worksheet, *Professional Development Guidebook,* page 222.

my house, and did receive his goods, but was deceived in his lying there, the news coming every moment of the growth of the fire; so as we were forced to begin to pack up our own goods, and prepare for their removal; and did by moonshine (it being brave dry, and moonshine, and warm weather) carry much of my goods into the garden, and Mr. Hater and I did remove my money and iron chests into my cellar, as thinking that the safest place. And got my bags of gold into my office, ready to carry away, and my chief papers of accounts also there, and my tallies into a box by themselves. So great was our fear, as Sir W. Batten hath carts come out of the country to fetch away his goods this night. We did put Mr. Haters, poor man, to bed a little; but he got but very little rest, so much noise being in my house, taking down of goods.

3rd. About four o'clock in the morning, my Lady Batten sent me a cart to carry away all my money, and plate, and best things, to Sir W. Rider's at Bednall Green. Which I did, riding myself in my night-gown in the cart; and, Lord! to see how the streets and the highways are crowded with people running and riding, and getting of carts at any rate to fetch away things. I find Sir W. Rider tired with being called up all night, and receiving things from several friends. His house full of goods, and much of Sir W. Batten's and Sir W. Pen's. I am eased at my heart to have my treasure so well secured. Then home, with much ado to find a way, nor any sleep all this night to me nor my poor wife.

Vocabulary

accounts (ə kountz´) *n.* records of money received and paid out; financial records

Critical Reading

Cite textual evidence to support your responses.

1. **Key Ideas and Details (a)** According to the entry for September 3, 1665, what happened to the saddler's family during the plague? **(b) Infer:** What does Pepys's reaction to this situation show you about his personality?

2. **Key Ideas and Details (a)** What does Pepys recommend to the King and Duke of York during the fire? **(b) Evaluate:** Was the recommendation a good one? Why or why not?

3. **Integration of Knowledge and Ideas (a) Compare and Contrast:** What are some modern disasters that compare with the Great Plague and Great Fire of London? **(b) Evaluate:** Do you think Pepys and others in authority handled disaster as well as their modern counterparts would have? Why or why not?

4. **Craft and Structure (a)** List three details about seventeenth-century London that Pepys includes in his diary. **(b) Evaluate:** How has living in London during the plague and the fire affected what Pepys has to say and the effectiveness with which he says it?

from The Diary **577**

Background

16 **Background**

Prior to the Great Fire, efforts had been made to prevent people from building with wood and using thatch roofs, both of which were known to be tremendous fire hazards. Combined with the city's narrow, winding streets, these building materials made it too easy for fires to spread. It took a disaster, however, for people to take the warnings and restrictions seriously.

16 Charles II's

DECLARATION TO LONDON,
1666

BACKGROUND Following the Great Fire of London, Charles II took personal charge of seeing that the city got back on its feet. On the day the fire effectively ended, the king visited a field where a hundred thousand homeless Londoners were camping out and tried to reassure them about the future. Charles would have liked to rebuild his capital on a grand scale but had neither the money nor the time to do so. Instead, he had to move as quickly as possible to address the widespread homelessness and the disruption of London's trade, so vital to the English economy. Charles was nevertheless determined to create a more modern city that would never again face the kind of devastation the fire had caused. Taking advice from architects like Christopher Wren, scientists like Robert Hooke, and officials like Samuel Pepys who had fought the fire, Charles issued the following policy statement giving guidelines to Londoners about rebuilding their streets, shops, and homes.

578 A Turbulent Time (1625–1798)

In the first place the woeful experience in this late heavy visitation hath sufficiently convinced all men of the pernicious consequences which have attended the building with Timber, and even with Stone itself, and the notable benefit of Brick, which in so many places hath resisted and even extinguished the Fire; And we do therefore declare Our express Will and Pleasure, That no man whatsoever shall presume to erect any House or Building, great or small, but of Brick or Stone, and if any man shall do the contrary, the next Magistrate shall forthwith cause it to be pulled down.

. . . all other eminent and notorious Streets, shall be of such a breadth, as may with God's blessing prevent the mischief that one side may suffer if the other be on fire.

. . . nor will we suffer any Lanes or Alleys to be erected, but where upon mature deliberation the same shall be found absolutely necessary.

. . . no house shall be erected within so many foot of the River.

. . . any houses to be inhabited by Brewers, or Dyers, or Sugar-Bakers, which Trades by their continual Smokes contribute very much to the unhealthiness of the adjacent places, but We require the Lord Mayor and Aldermen of London upon a full consideration, and weighing all conveniences and inconveniences that can be foreseen, to propose such a place as may be fit for all those Trades which are carried on by smokes to inhabit together.

Vocabulary

pernicious (pər nish´ is) *adj.* causing great injury, destruction, or ruin; deadly

magistrate (maj´ is trāt) *n.* a local official who administers the law or serves as a judge

eminent (em´ ə nənt) *adj.* noteworthy; of high rank; distinguished

notorious (nō tôr´ ē əs) *adj.* widely but unfavorably known; having a bad reputation

deliberation (di lib´ ər ā´ shən) *n.* careful consideration and discussion before reaching a decision

Primary Sources
Policy Statement
What are the four main guidelines set forth in this policy statement?

Critical Reading

@ **1. Key Ideas and Details (a)** What does Charles say the recent fire has shown about building construction? **(b) Infer:** What situation does he want to prevent by getting rid of very narrow streets and keeping lanes and alleys to a minimum? **(c) Speculate:** Why do you think he orders that no house be erected too close to the river?

@ **2. Integration of Knowledge and Ideas (a) Infer:** Why does Charles want all London businesses requiring continuous fires to be housed in the same place? **(b) Evaluate:** Do you think this idea is practical? Why or why not?

@ **3. Key Ideas and Details (a) Analyze Cause and Effect:** What main concern of Charles II's London has led him to issue this policy statement? **(b) Draw Conclusions:** What does the statement reveal about London buildings before the fire?

Cite textual evidence to support your responses.

Charles II's Declaration to London, 1666 **579**

Primary Sources
Policy Statement

1. Have a volunteer read the policy statement aloud.
2. Then, **ask** students the Primary Source question in the margin: What are the four main guidelines set forth in this policy statement? **Answer:** 1) Streets are to be widened for fire prevention. 2) No unnecessary lanes or alleys are to be created. 3) No houses are to be built close to the river. 4) Trade shops that create a lot of smoke will be together in one area.

ASSESS

Answers

Before students respond, you may wish to have them write a brief objective summary of the selection. As they answer the questions below, remind them to support their answers with evidence from the text.

1. (a) The fires have shown that it is better to build with brick than timber. (b) Fire can jump from one building to another. If the streets are wider, it is harder for the fire to spread. (c) **Possible response:** Perhaps he wants firefighters to always be able to reach the water source.

2. (a) If all the businesses that maintain fires are together in one area, it will be easier to monitor and control the fire hazard. (b) **Possible response:** Yes, it seems practical to keep similar types of buildings together and away from residential buildings.

3. (a) **Possible response:** The Great Fire caused many people to be homeless and severely disrupted the economy. (b) Many houses were built of timber or stone, but some were made of brick, which is fire-resistant.

Differentiated Instruction for Universal Access

Support for Less Proficient Readers
To aid in understanding, have pairs of students paraphrase the declaration, breaking it down into shorter, more manageable sentences. Encourage students to use a dictionary to look up the meanings of any words they do not understand.

EL Support for English Learners
So that students do not get distracted, point out that many words are capitalized in old documents that would not be capitalized in standard use today. For example, *Timber, Stone,* and *Brick* would not require capitalization in modern writings. However, city names, such as *London*, should always be capitalized.

Answers

Comparing Primary Sources

1. A diary presents personal reflection and might lack specific details. A policy statement's purpose is to inform, so it will be very specific on the points it covers.

2. Great Plague: People are dying everywhere, corpses are carried through the streets, it lasts week after week, there is a sense of desperation. Great Fire: Many houses burned down, people are panicking, people are trying to help one another to save what they can of their belongings. (a) What they have in common is that each event was distressing and disruptive for the city of London; differences are the length of time of the disaster, greater loss of life in the plague, and the loss of buildings in the fire. (b) The plague seems worse, because it lasted longer and because more lives, not buildings, were lost.

3. Pepys's account would be useful because he names many landmarks and streets to explain the location of the fire and how it progresses through the city. He also explains some of the measures taken to stop the fire. Charles II's declaration is useful because it is a city-planning document that provides a sort of "before and after" for the fire.

Vocabulary Acquisition and Use

1. (a) pernicious; (b) Both *malicious* and *pernicious* mean "destructive."

2. (a) Both mean that someone or something is well-known; (b) *Notorious* has a negative connotation, whereas *eminent* does not.

3. (a) A lamentable situation would prompt concerns about how long it might continue. (b) If the concerns lessoned, the person would be less fearful.

4. False. Deliberation requires time, not haste.

5. False. Paper burns more easily than rocks.

6. True. Accounts are financial records.

7. True. A magistrate is a local judge.

580

 COMMON CORE ▪ RESEARCH PROJECT

Diary • Policy Statement

Comparing Primary Sources

Refer to your note-taking guide to answer these questions.

1. **(a)** Summarize each source, supporting your summary with quotations. **(b)** In the entry for September 3, 1665, what does Pepys imply are the reasons he and others agreed to allow the child "to be received and kept" in Greenwich? Cite textual details in support of your response.

2. **(a)** Outline the sequence of events and interaction of people in Pepys's diary entry for September 2, 1666. **(b)** Identify one point that he leaves unclear, and explain why he probably did not clarify it.

3. Compare and contrast the information Pepys provides about the Great Plague with the information about the Great Fire of London in both sources. **(a)** What do the two disasters have in common, and how do they differ? **(b)** Which seems worse, and why? To help you answer the question, gather details on a Venn diagram like the one shown.

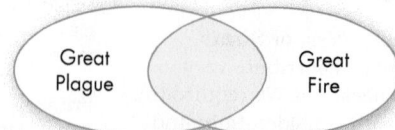

Vocabulary Acquisition and Use

New Vocabulary Answer the questions about the italicized vocabulary words.

1. **(a)** Which word is closest in meaning to *malicious*: *lamentable*, *pernicious*, or *notorious*? **(b)** What do the two words mean?

2. **(a)** What is similar about the meanings of *eminent* and *notorious*? **(b)** What is different about them?

3. **(a)** Why might a *lamentable* situation prompt *apprehensions*? **(b)** If those *apprehensions* then *abated*, would the person be more or less fearful? Explain your answer.

Content-Area Vocabulary Determine whether each statement is true or false. Explain your answers.

4. Someone who moves with *deliberation* is hasty.

5. Rocks are more *combustible* than paper.

6. A company's bookkeeper is often responsible for keeping *accounts*.

7. A *magistrate* might serve as a judge in a local legal matter.

Etymology Study *Magistrate* comes from the Latin *magnus*, meaning "great." A *magistrate* is a person who exercises great authority in certain legal matters. Use a dictionary to show how these *magnus* terms from political science reflect the idea of greatness: *magisterial*, *Magna Carta*, *magnate*, *magniloquent*.

Ⓒ Common Core State Standards

Writing

7. Conduct short as well as more sustained research projects to answer a question or solve a problem; narrow or broaden the inquiry when appropriate; synthesize multiple sources on the subject, demonstrating understanding of the subject under investigation.

8. Gather relevant information from multiple authoritative print and digital sources, using advanced searches effectively; assess the strengths and limitations of each source in terms of the task, purpose, and audience; integrate information into the text selectively to maintain the flow of ideas, avoiding plagiarism and overreliance on any one source and following a standard format for citation.

Language

6. Acquire and use accurately general academic and domain-specific words and phrases, sufficient for reading, writing, speaking, and listening at the college and career readiness level; demonstrate independence in gathering vocabulary knowledge when considering a word or phrase important to comprehension or expression.

580 A Turbulent Time (1625–1798)

Etymology Study:

magisterial: appearing to have great authority; *Magna Carta*: great charter; *magnate*: person of great influence; *magniloquent*: speaking in a style of greatness

Research Task

Topic: The Great Fire of London

Samuel Pepys's account of the Great Fire takes us right to the scene of the ongoing disaster. You cannot duplicate his eyewitness vantage point. However, you can gain a clear perspective on the causes, sequence of events, or results of the fire.

Assignment: Write a research report on one of the following aspects of the Great Fire:

- causes—geographical, architectural, cultural
- sequence of events from beginning to end
- short-term and long-term effects

Formulate a research plan. Begin with a question open-ended enough to support an in-depth, multi-faceted report, such as, "How did the way of life of seventeenth-century Londoners contribute to the Great Fire?" Then, develop stepping-stone questions the answers to which will help you answer your major question. Finally, devise a research plan by listing the types of sources you will consult. Do not rely entirely on texts written for students. In addition to such texts, consult both primary sources and texts written by experts for informed audiences.

Model: Using Stepping-Stone Questions

How did the way of life of Londoners contribute to the Great Fire?

How did people communicate?
How were neighborhoods arranged?
How were streets designed?
What were buildings made of?

Gather sources. Follow your plan. Assemble and organize your evidence, showing how facts support central ideas. Do not rely entirely on any one source.

Synthesize information. Evaluate your information and determine what to use and what to discard. First, distinguish between reliable and unreliable sources, excluding information you find only in unreliable sources. Then, look for and focus on patterns of ideas, excluding irrelevant details. Be flexible: If your question and research plan result in too little or too much information, revise them.

Organize and present ideas. Write your research paper based on a clear organization or outline. The topic of the Great Fire lends itself to visual aids, so consider including paintings, drawings, blueprints, diagrams, and maps. Avoid plagiarism, citing sources for words, ideas, and visuals not your own, using a standard format.

▲ One effect of the Great Fire was the use of fire marks like this one to identify insured property. Firemen, paid by insurance companies, would try to save marked properties.

RESEARCH TIP

The Great Fire has been treated in books for scholars, for general adult readers, for young adults, and for children. Do not waste time on books that are too specialized or too simplified.

Use a checklist like the one shown to review, and possibly revise, your report.

> **Research Checklist**
> ☐ Have I answered the major research question?
> ☐ Have I gathered information from both primary and secondary sources?
> ☐ Have I organized the information in a logical way?
> ☐ Have I incorporated visuals appropriately?

Research Task **581**

TEACH

Contemporary Connection

Neil Gaiman is an award-winning author known for his dark humor and creative talents. In addition to his numerous books of fantasy, he has collaborated on comics and written for film. He has won three Hugos and two Nebulas—top awards in science fiction.

London Past and Present

1. Both English writers and outsiders have been fascinated by London for hundreds of years, making it the setting of many stories. Students have been reading literature from the 1600s and 1700s. Now they will read an excerpt from a modern novel set in a very different London from the city Pepys knew.

2. Knightsbridge of London becomes Night's Bridge in the dark underworld of Gaiman's novel. **Ask** students what may be gained or lost when an actual place name is recast in a fantasy story.
   Possible response: Having something to connect to in the real world can often enhance one's reading of a fantasy story. It might help you to visualize the setting. However, if a reader is overly familiar with the actual place, it may also make it more difficult to picture the fantasy version of it.

London Past

"Don't ever take a city for granted,"

Neil Gaiman wrote in an online essay. "After all, it is bigger than you are; it is older; and it has learned how to wait…." In his novel *Neverwhere,* Gaiman certainly did not take London for granted. Describing a fantastical underground London unknown to the usual inhabitants of "London Above," he pays tribute to the city's long history and to its darker side.

Gaiman's dangerous underground city has a kinship with the London that Pepys describes in his accounts of the Great Plague and the Fire. Both are scary places, filled with turmoil and threat. Pepys may have been unaware that rats were playing a a major role in the plague; however, Gaiman gives great power to rodent-like characters called rat-speakers.

A female rat-speaker named Anaesthesia accompanies Gaiman's hero, Richard Mayhew, in this episode from the beginning of the tale. Mayhew has recently arrived in the underground city "from the London Above." Now, he and Anaesthesia, led by a mysterious woman, must cross the fear-inspiring Night's Bridge. It is the first major test of Mayhew's courage.

582 A Turbulent Time (1625–1798)

Enrichment: Analyzing Forms and Genres

Fantasy

Fantasy novels were once thought of as pure entertainment and not valued as being literature worthy of study. However, many classic works, from medieval romances to *A Midsummer Night's Dream,* contain elements of fantasy. In recent years, fantasy novels have been made into popular films, such as *The Lord of the Rings* trilogy, the Narnia series, and the Harry Potter series. This has increased interest in the genre.

Activity: Review a Fantasy Novel Have individuals or pairs of students find and read a fantasy novel. Then, have students present synopses and reviews of the novels to the class. Suggest that students record information on the **Enrichment: Analyzing Forms and Genres** worksheet, *Professional Development Guidebook,* page 227. After hearing all the book reports, discuss with students which fantasy novelists Gaiman seems most similar to in terms of style and subject.

and Present

Neil Gaiman
Novelist/Graphic Novelist/Poet/Songwriter/Screenwriter

Neverwhere started life in 1996 as a BBC television series in England. Gaiman (b. 1960) later adapted it into a novel in order to develop the characters. The novel became a major success, while the original TV series has faded.

Gaiman is versatile, writing songs and poems as well as screenplays. Even his screenwriting experience is diverse—it includes writing the English-language script for the Japanese anime movie *Princess Mononoke* (1999). Overall, however, Gaiman is best known as the author of the graphic novel series *Sandman*.

Describing his fertile creative process, he wrote, "You get ideas from daydreaming." Clarifying, he continued, "You get ideas from being bored. You get ideas all the time. The only difference between writers and other people is we notice when [it happens]."

from Neverwhere **583**

Neil Gaiman

1. Review the information on Neil Gaiman with students.
2. **Ask:** Do you agree with Gaiman's statement that you can get ideas when you are bored?
   Possible response: Yes, boredom often leads to daydreaming about more interesting things.

from Neverwhere
Neil Gaiman

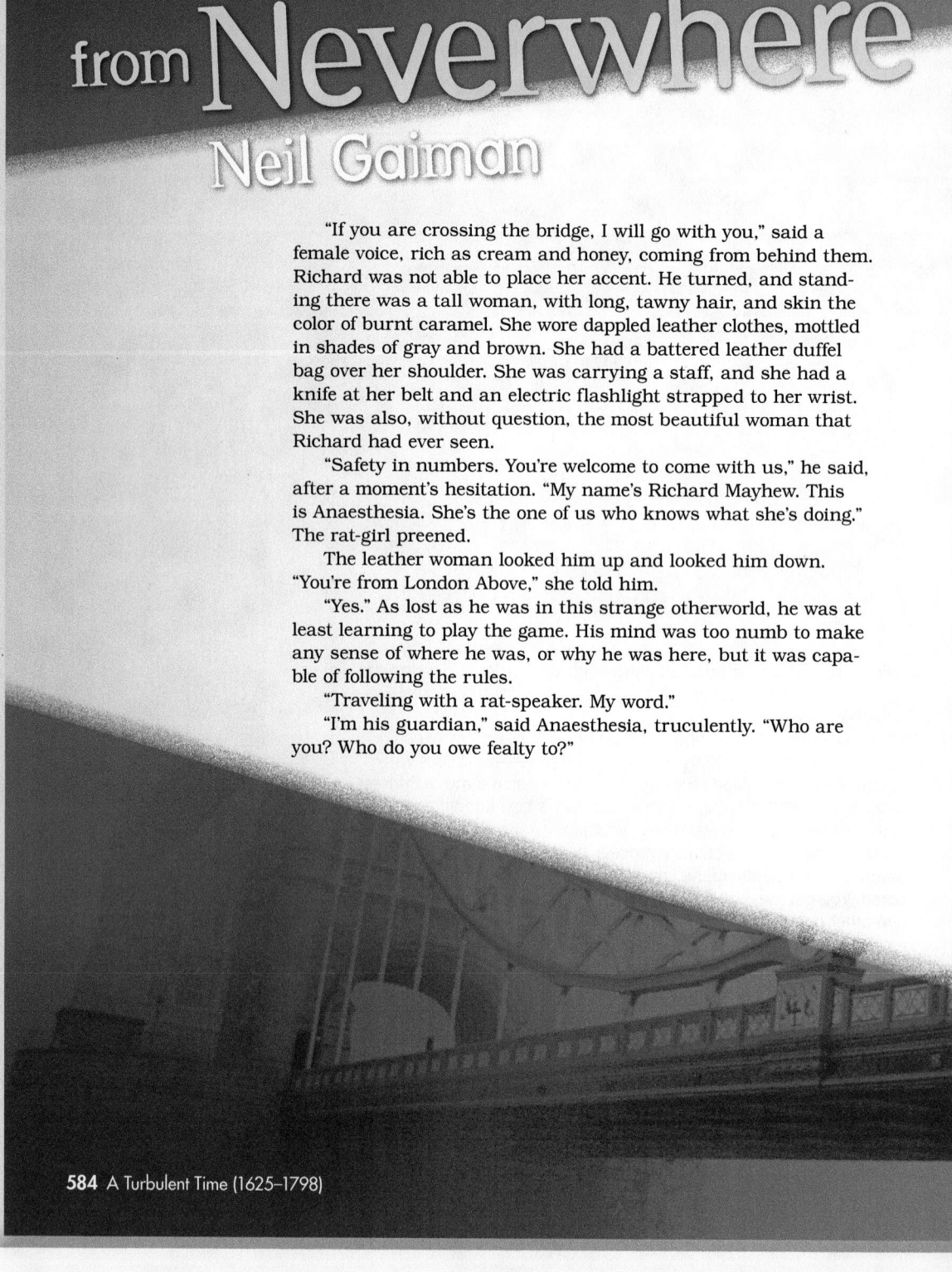

"If you are crossing the bridge, I will go with you," said a female voice, rich as cream and honey, coming from behind them. Richard was not able to place her accent. He turned, and standing there was a tall woman, with long, tawny hair, and skin the color of burnt caramel. She wore dappled leather clothes, mottled in shades of gray and brown. She had a battered leather duffel bag over her shoulder. She was carrying a staff, and she had a knife at her belt and an electric flashlight strapped to her wrist. She was also, without question, the most beautiful woman that Richard had ever seen.

"Safety in numbers. You're welcome to come with us," he said, after a moment's hesitation. "My name's Richard Mayhew. This is Anaesthesia. She's the one of us who knows what she's doing." The rat-girl preened.

The leather woman looked him up and looked him down. "You're from London Above," she told him.

"Yes." As lost as he was in this strange otherworld, he was at least learning to play the game. His mind was too numb to make any sense of where he was, or why he was here, but it was capable of following the rules.

"Traveling with a rat-speaker. My word."

"I'm his guardian," said Anaesthesia, truculently. "Who are you? Who do you owe fealty to?"

The woman smiled. "I owe no man fealty, rat-girl. Have either of you crossed Night's Bridge before?" Anaesthesia shook her head. "Well. Isn't this going to be fun?"

They walked toward the bridge. Anaesthesia handed Richard her candle-lamp. "Here," she said.

"Thanks." Richard looked at the woman in leather. "Is there anything, really, to be scared of?"

"Only the night on the bridge," she said.

"The kind in armor?"

"The kind that comes when day is over."

Anaesthesia's hand sought Richard's. He held it tightly, her tiny hand in his. She smiled at him, squeezed his hand. And then they set foot on Night's Bridge and Richard began to understand darkness: darkness as something solid and real, so much more than a simple absence of light. He felt it touch his skin, questing, moving, exploring: gliding through his mind. It slipped into his lungs, behind his eyes, into his mouth. . .

With each step they took the light of the candle became dimmer. He realized the same thing was happening to the leather woman's flashlight. It felt not so much as if the lights were being turned down but as if the darkness were being turned up. Richard blinked, and opened his eyes on noth-ing—nothing but darkness, complete and utter. *Sounds.* A rustling, a squirming. Richard blinked, blinded by the night. The sounds were nastier, hungrier. Richard imagined he could hear voices: a horde of huge, misshapen trolls, beneath the bridge. . . .

Something slithered past them in the dark. "What's that?" squeaked Anaesthesia. Her hand was shaking in his.

"Hush," whispered the woman. "Don't attract its attention."

"What's happening?" whispered Richard.

"Darkness is happening," said the leather woman, very quietly. "Night is happening. All the nightmares that have come out when the sun goes down, since the cave times, when we huddled together in fear for safety and for warmth, are happening. Now," she told them, "now is the time to be afraid of the dark." Richard knew that something was about to creep over his face. He closed his eyes: it made no differ-ence to what he saw or felt. The night was complete. It was then that the hallucinations started.

Richard began to understand dark-ness: darkness as something solid and real, so much more than a simple absence of light.

from Neverwhere **585**

from *Neverwhere*

1. **Ask** students whether the leather woman is being sarcastic when she says, "Well. Isn't this going to be fun?" and explain how they know.
   Possible response: Yes, she is being sarcastic. We know because she didn't want to cross the bridge alone.

2. **Ask** students what techniques Gaiman uses to help readers feel what Richard is feeling.
   Possible response: Gaiman uses numerous sensory details in his writing to help readers see, hear, and touch everything Richard does. He also uses vivid verbs such as *gliding, rustling, squirming, slithered,* and *creep* to explain what is happening.

from *Neverwhere*

1. **Ask** students why some of the text is italicized on this page. **Answer:** The italic text indicates what is a hallucination.

2. **Ask:** What does Richard realize after his eyes adjust to the light and he tries to calm himself about what they have just been through? **Answer:** Anaesthesia is no longer with them.

He saw a figure falling toward him through the night, burning, its wings and hair on fire.

He threw up his hands: there was nothing there.

Jessica looked at him, with contempt in her eyes. He wanted to shout to her, tell her he was sorry.

Place one foot after another.

He was a small child, walking home from school, at night, down the one road with no streetlights. No matter how many times he did it, it never got any easier, never got any better.

He was deep in the sewers, lost in a labyrinth. The Beast was waiting for him. He could hear a slow drip of water. He knew the Beast was waiting. He gripped his spear. . . . Then a rumbling bellow, deep in its throat, from behind him. He turned. Slowly, agonizingly slowly, it charged at him, through the dark.

And it charged.

He died.

And kept walking.

Slowly, agonizingly slowly, it charged at him, over and over, through the dark.

There was a sputter, and a flare so bright it hurt, making Richard squint and stagger. It was the candle flame, in its lemonade-bottle holder. He had never known how brightly a single candle could burn. He held it up, gasping and gulping and shaking with relief. His heart was pounding and shuddering in his chest.

"We would appear to have crossed successfully," said the leather woman.

He had never known how brightly a single candle could burn.

Richard's heart was pounding in his chest so hard that, for a few moments, he was unable to talk. He forced himself to breathe slowly, to calm down. They were in a large anteroom, exactly like the one on the other side. In fact, Richard had the strange feeling that it was the same room they had just left. Yet the shadows were deeper, and there were afterimages floating before Richard's eyes, like those one saw after a camera flash. "I suppose," Richard said, haltingly, "we weren't in any real danger. . . . It was like a haunted house. A few noises in the dark . . . and your imagination does the rest. There wasn't really anything to be scared of, was there?"

The woman looked at him, almost pityingly; and Richard realized that there was nobody holding his hand. "Anaesthesia?"

From the darkness at the crown of the bridge came a gentle noise, like a rustle or a sigh. A handful of irregular quartz beads pattered down the curve of the bridge toward them. Richard picked one up. It was from the rat-girl's necklace. His mouth opened, but no sound came out. Then he found his voice. "We'd better. We have to go back. She's . . ."

The woman raised her flashlight, shone it across the bridge. Richard could see all the way across the bridge. It was deserted. "Where is she?" he asked.

"Gone," said the woman, flatly. "The darkness took her."

Critical Reading

1. **(a)** What does the leather woman say when she learns that Richard and Anaesthesia have never before crossed Night's Bridge? **(b) Infer:** Do you think that the leather woman has crossed the bridge before? Why or why not?

2. **(a) Summarize:** Briefly summarize what Richard feels and sees in the darkness on Night's Bridge. **(b) Interpret:** What do "night" and "darkness" come to mean to Richard while he is on the bridge?

3. **(a)** Describe the place the leather woman and Richard reach after they cross Night's Bridge. **(b) Speculate:** Are they in the same room they started from? Explain.

Use these questions to focus a class discussion of Neverwhere:

4. Do you think that nighttime in Pepys's London would have been a little bit like the night on Gaiman's bridge? Why or why not?

5. Why are writers like Gaiman and Pepys so interested in depicting a city like London?

Before students respond, you may wish to have them write a brief objective summary of the selection. As they answer the questions below, remind them to support their answers with evidence from the text.

1. (a) "Well. Isn't this going to be fun?" (b) **Possible response:** Yes, she seems to know how difficult it is going to be, and she does not want to cross the bridge alone.

2. (a) Nightmares and hallucinations flash through his mind as he feels a menacing presence all around him. (b) **Possible response:** Night and darkness are real forces that seek to harm him.

3. (a) They are in a "large anteroom, exactly like the one on the other side." (b) **Possible response:** Richard thinks it might be the same room. I don't think it is, though, because the leather woman would not bother to cross through again if she knew that doing so did not take you to a different place.

4. **Possible response:** Yes; Pepys's London had been ravaged by plague and fire. There was probably a pervasive feeling of misery there, too, which would be enhanced by darkness.

5. **Possible response:** Pepys lives just outside of London and views the city as a cultural center. Neil Gaiman was born and raised in England, so London is likely to be a quintessential city in his mind, as well.

• *from A Journal of the Plague Year*
Lesson Pacing Guide

DAY 1 Preteach

- © Administer the Reading and Vocabulary Warm-ups (*Unit 3 Resources*, pp. 129–132) as necessary.
- © Introduce the Literary Analysis concept: Point of View.
- • Introduce the Reading Strategy: Questioning.
- © Build background with the author feature.
- • Develop thematic thinking with Connecting to the Essential Question.
- © Teach the selection vocabulary.

DAYS 2–3 Preteach/Teach/Assess

- • Distribute copies of the appropriate graphic organizer for the Reading Strategy (*Graphic Organizer Transparencies*, pp. 103–104).
- • Distribute copies of the appropriate graphic organizer for Literary Analysis (*Graphic Organizer Transparencies*, pp. 105–106).
- • Prepare students to read with the Activating Prior Knowledge activities (TE).
- • Informally monitor comprehension while students read.
- • Use the Reading Check question to confirm comprehension.
- © Develop students' understanding of point of view using the Literary Analysis prompts.
- • Develop students' ability to question using the Reading Strategy prompts.
- © Reinforce vocabulary with the Vocabulary notes.
- • Assess students' comprehension and mastery of the skills by having them answer the Critical Reading, Literary Analysis, and Reading Strategy questions.
- • Have students complete the Vocabulary Lesson.

DAY 4 Extend/Assess

- © Have students complete the Writing Lesson and write a reflective essay. (You may assign as homework.)
- • Administer Selection Test A or B (*Unit 3 Resources*, pp. 141–143 or 144–146).

© Common Core State Standards

Reading Literature 3. Analyze the impact of the author's choices regarding how to develop and relate elements of a story or drama.

Writing 3. Write narratives to develop real or imagined experiences or events, using effective technique, well-chosen details, and well-structured event sequences.

Language 4.a. Use context as a clue to the meaning of a word or phrase.

Additional Standards Practice
Common Core Companion, *pp. 28–35; 208–218; 324–331*

Daily Block Scheduling
Each day in this Lesson Pacing Guide represents a 40–50 minute period. Teachers using block scheduling may combine days to revise pacing. In addition, teachers may differentiate and support core instruction by integrating components for extended and intensive support as students require. See the Guide to Selected Leveled Resources (facing page).

Guide to Selected Leveled Resources

R T I Tier 1 (students performing on level)

from A Journal of the Plague Year

Warm Up	Practice, **model,** and **monitor** fluency, working **with the whole class** or **in groups.**	Vocabulary and Reading Warm-ups B, *Unit 3 Resources,* pp. 89–90, 92
Comprehension/Skills	**Support** and **monitor** comprehension and skills development, having students complete the activities, graphic organizers, and interactive prompts **independently** or **as a class.**	• *Reader's Notebook,* adapted instruction and full selection **EL** *Reader's Notebook: English Learner's Version,* adapted instruction and adapted selection • **Reading Skill Graphic Organizer B,** *Graphic Organizer Transparencies,* p. 98 • **Literary Analysis Graphic Organizer B,** *Graphic Organizer Transparencies,* p. 100
Monitor Progress **A**	**Monitor** student progress with the differentiated curriculum-based assessment in the *Unit Resources.*	• **Selection Test B,** *Unit 3 Resources,* pp. 104–106 • **Open-Book Test,** *Unit 3 Resources,* pp. 98–100

R T I Tier 2 (students requiring intervention)

from A Journal of the Plague Year

Warm Up	Practice, **model,** and **monitor** fluency **in groups** or **with individuals.**	• Vocabulary and Reading Warm-ups A, *Unit 3 Resources,* pp. 89–91 • *Hear It!* Audio CD (adapted text)
Comprehension/Skills	• **Support** and **monitor** comprehension and skills development, working **in small groups** or **with individuals.** • As students complete the selection in the appropriate version of the *Reader's Notebook,* **monitor** comprehension frequently with group questions and individual instruction. • **Model** strategies while guiding students in completing the activities and prompts in the *Reader's Notebook,* as well as the graphic organizers. • **Practice** skills and **monitor** mastery with the *Reading Kit* worksheets.	• *Reader's Notebook: Adapted Version,* adapted instruction and adapted selection **EL** *Reader's Notebook: English Learner's Version,* adapted instruction and adapted selection • **Reading Skill Graphic Organizer A,** *Graphic Organizer Transparencies,* p. 97 • **Literary Analysis Graphic Organizer A,** *Graphic Organizer Transparencies,* p. 99 • *Reading Kit,* Practice worksheets
Monitor Progress **A**	**Monitor** student progress with the differentiated curriculum-based assessment in the *Unit Resources* and in the *Reading Kit.*	• **Selection Test A,** *Unit 3 Resources,* pp. 101–103 • *Reading Kit,* Assess worksheets

TIER 3 Tier 3 intervention may require consultation with the student's special-education or dyslexia specialist. For additional support, see the Tier 2 activities and resources listed above.

One-on-one teaching   Group work   Whole class instruction   Independent work   **A** Assessment
For a complete guide to selection support, including support for Advanced students, see the Overview of Resources in the frontmatter.

• from *A Journal of the Plague Year*

RESOURCES FOR:

- **L1** Special-Needs Students
- **L2** Below-Level Students (Tier 2)
- **L3** On-Level Students (Tier 1)
- **L4** Advanced Students (Tier 1)
- **EL** English Learners
- **All** All Students

Vocabulary/Fluency/Prior Knowledge

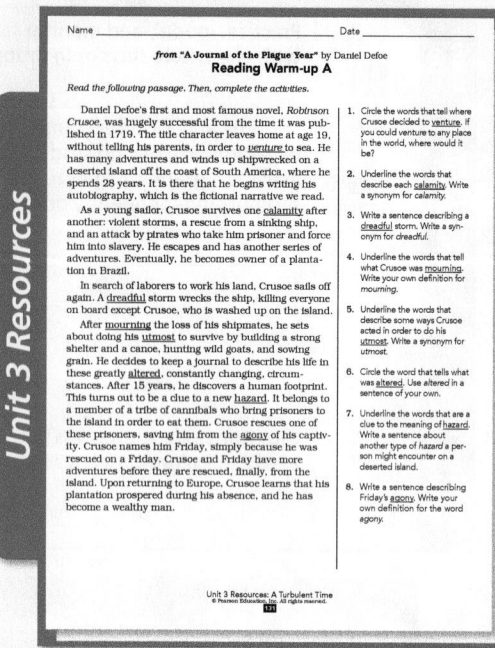

Unit 3 Resources

EL L1 L2 Reading Warm-ups A and B, pp. 131–132

Also available for these selections:

EL L1 L2 Vocabulary Warm-ups A and B, pp. 129–130

All Vocabulary Builder, p. 135

Reader's Notebooks

Pre- and postreading pages for this selection appear in an interactive format in the *Reader's Notebooks*. Each *Notebook* is differentiated for a different group of learners.

The selections in the Adapted and English Learner's versions are abridged.

- **L2 L3 Reader's Notebook**
- **L1 Reader's Notebook: Adapted Version**
- **EL Reader's Notebook: English Learner's Version**
- **EL Reader's Notebook: Spanish Version**

© *Common Core Companion*

Additional instruction and practice for each Common Core State Standard

Selection Support

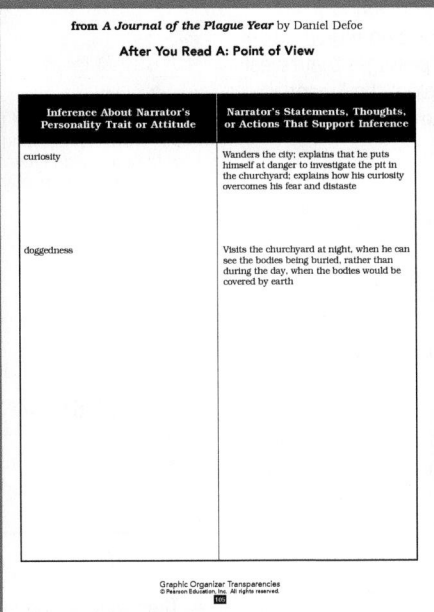

Literary Analysis: Graphic Organizer A (partially filled in), p. 105

Also available for these selections:

EL L1 L2 **Reading: Graphic Organizer A** (partially filled in), p. 103

EL L3 **Reading: Graphic Organizer B,** p. 104

EL L3 **Literary Analysis: Graphic Organizer B,** p. 106

Skills Development/Extension

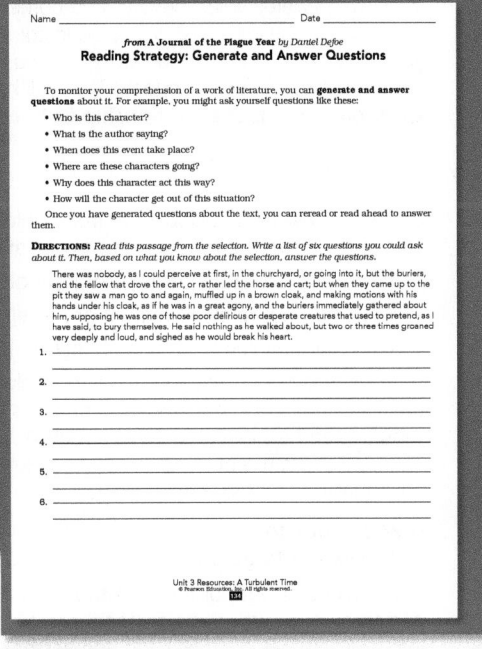

All **Reading,** p. 134

Also available for these selections:

All **Literary Analysis,** p. 133

EL L3 L4 **Support for Writing,** p. 136

L3 L4 **Enrichment,** p. 137

Assessment

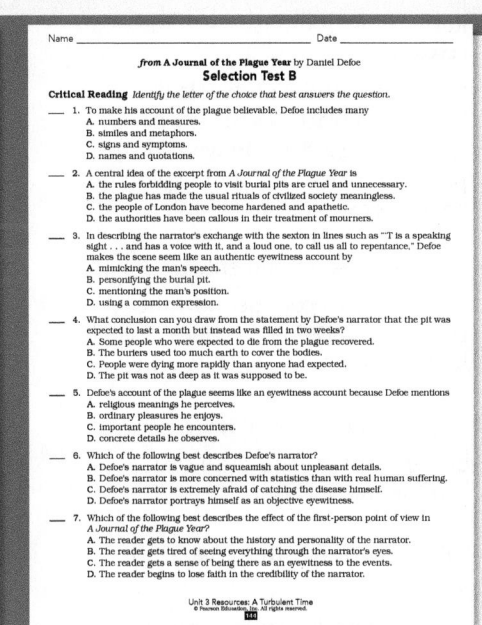

EL L3 L4 **Selection Test B,** pp. 144–146

Also available for these selections:

L3 L4 **Open-Book Test,** pp. 138–140

EL L1 L2 **Selection Test A,** pp. 141–143

PHLit Online!
www.PHLitOnline.com

Online Resources: All print materials are also available online.

- complete narrated selection text
- a thematically related video with writing prompt
- an interactive graphic organizer
- highlighting feature
- access to all student print resources, adapted to individual student needs
- Spanish and English summaries
- adapted selection translations in Spanish

Get Connected! (thematic video with writing prompt)

Also available:

All videos are available in Spanish

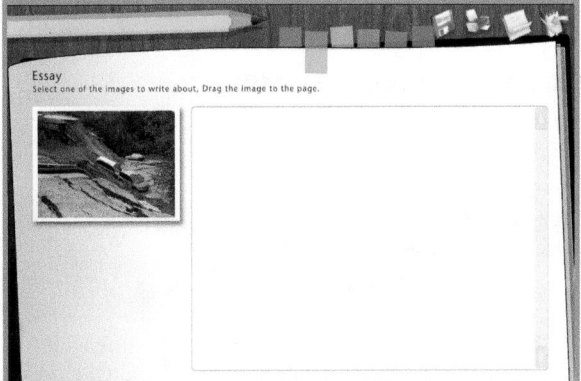

Writer's Journal (with graphics feature)

Also available:

Vocabulary Central (tools and activities for studying vocabulary)

❶ Connecting to the Essential Question

1. Review the assignment with the class.

2. Brainstorm landmark events that have taken place in your city or region. Ask students to work in pairs to discuss what they experienced or witnessed during one such event. Then, have them complete the assignment.

3. Have students consider how the London that Defoe describes takes on a personality of its own.

❷ Literary Analysis

Introduce the skill using the instruction on the student page.

Think Aloud: Model the Skill

Say to students:

A Journal of the Plague Year is written in the form of a journal, so I expect it to be in the first person. Reading the first line, I see that the author uses *I*. Later in that paragraph, he writes about hearing "shrieks ... as *we* passed the streets." Defoe tells his story by reporting direct experiences.

❸ Reading Strategy

1. Introduce the strategy using the instruction on the student page.

2. Give students the **Reading Strategy Graphic Organizer B**, page 104 in *Graphic Organizer Transparencies,* to use as they read.

Think Aloud: Model the Skill

Say to students:

When I read a newspaper, I generate questions based on what I already know. As I read, I find answers to the questions. As I learn more, I generate more questions.

❹ Vocabulary

1. Pronounce each word, giving its definition.

2. See the *Classroom Strategies and Teaching Routines* card for vocabulary instruction.

Before You Read

from *A Journal of the Plague Year*

❶ **Connecting to the Essential Question** In *A Journal of the Plague Year,* Daniel Defoe vividly describes his hometown, London, during a terrible catastrophe in its past. What landmark event in your own region do you think would make a good story? As you read, note passages that reveal how the plague affected London. They will help you explore the Essential Question: **What is the relationship between literature and place?**

❷ ## Literary Analysis

Point of view is the perspective from which a narrator tells a story. Stories told from the **first-person point of view** have these qualities:

• The narrator either participates in or observes the events.

• The narrator refers to himself or herself as "I."

• The narrator can tell you his or her thoughts but not those of others.

Nonfiction diaries and journals almost always use the first-person point of view, since they present a person's daily account of his or her thoughts and experiences. Even though *A Journal of the Plague Year* is fiction, Defoe's use of the first-person point of view makes it seem as if he actually witnessed the events he writes about, as in this passage:

It was about the 10th of September that my curiosity led, or rather drove, me to go and see this pit again, . . .

Reporting only his or her own thoughts and experiences, the first-person narrator provides a personal perspective that helps brings readers into a private world of meaning and aesthetic pleasure.

❸ ## Reading Strategy

© **Preparing to Read Complex Texts** When you realize that you do not understand a passage you are reading, repair your comprehension by **asking questions.** Focus on the basics of the puzzling situation: who is doing what to whom and why? Also, when and where is the action taking place? Use a chart like the one shown to help you ask and answer questions about a passage.

❹ ## Vocabulary

lamentations (lam′ ən tā′ shənz) *n.* expressions of grief (p. 591)

distemper (dis tem′ pər) *n.* infectious disease, such as the plague (p. 592)

delirious (di lir′ ē əs) *adj.* having hallucinations; ranting (p. 592)

resolution (rez′ ə loo′ shən) *n.* determined state of mind (p. 593)

importuning (im′ pôr toon′ iŋ) *v.* pleading with (p. 594)

prodigious (prō′ dij′ əs) *adj.* enormous; huge (p. 595)

© **Common Core State Standards**

Reading Literature
3. Analyze the impact of the author's choices regarding how to develop and relate elements of a story or drama.

Text: Description of Pit

Q. Who was thrown in? **A.** Londoners who died of plague
Q. What happened to them? **A.** They were buried in a mass grave.
Q. Where was the pit? **A.** in Aldgate parish in London
Q. When were they brought there? **A.** at night
Q. Why were they put there? **A.** to prevent the spread of disease

PHLit Online!
www.PHLitOnline.com

Vocabulary Development

Vocabulary Knowledge Rating

Create a **Vocabulary Knowledge Rating Chart** (*Professional Development Guidebook,* p. 33) for the vocabulary words on the student page. Give each student a copy of the chart with the words on it. Read the words aloud, and have students mark their ratings in the Before Reading column. Urge students to attend to these words as they read and discuss the selection.

In order to gauge how much instruction you need to provide, tally how many students are confident in their knowledge of each word. As students read, point out the words and their context.

PHLit Online!

Vocabulary Central, featuring tools and activities for studying vocabulary, is available online at **www.PHLitOnline.com.**

⑤ DANIEL DEFOE

(1660–1731)

Author of *A Journal of the Plague Year*

"A false, shuffling, prevaricating rascal"—that was how fellow author Joseph Addison described Daniel Defoe. In many ways, Addison was not far from wrong. Constantly in debt, Defoe often engaged in shady business deals and declared bankruptcy in 1692, owing a small fortune to his creditors. He was also a sometime government spy and propagandist who even upgraded his own name, originally *Foe*, by adding an aristocratic *De*.

An Innovative Novelist Despite all his flaws, we remember Defoe for an important literary achievement. He practically invented the modern realistic novel. He did so with two books that were written as the memoirs of fictional characters. *Robinson Crusoe* (1719) presents an almost documentary narrative of a man marooned on a desert island. *Moll Flanders* (1722) tells a satirical tale of a poor woman seeking respectability. During his lifetime, Defoe's books were considered so realistic that they were sold as nonfiction. In fact, the first-person narrators were so convincing that Defoe was even accused of "forging a story, and imposing it on the world for truth."

Factual Fiction Defoe brought an even greater factual background to *A Journal of the Plague Year* (1722), his fictional account of the great plague that devastated England from 1664 to 1665. To construct this vivid narrative, Defoe studied official documents, interviewed survivors of the plague, and may have drawn on his own memories as a young child.

The vivid historical re-creation of the plague is a triumph of Defoe's energetic, detailed style in a genre that set English fiction on a new path.

from A Journal of the Plague Year **589**

Multidraft Reading

To assist struggling readers and to enhance reading for all, assign the text in chunks, as warranted by length and apply multidraft reading protocols. For each reading, have students set the purpose indicated:

- **First reading**—identifying key ideas and details and answering any Reading Checks.
- **Second reading**—analyzing craft and structure and responding to the side-column prompts.
- **Third reading**—integrating knowledge and ideas, connecting to other texts and the world, and answering the end-of-selection questions.

For more guidance, refer to the *Classroom Strategies and Teaching Routines* card on Multidraft Reading.

⑤ Background

More About the Author

Daniel Defoe was educated for the Presbyterian ministry but became a merchant instead. He loved politics as much as business and wrote numerous political pamphlets, which earned him faithful friends and dangerous enemies. Between his love of risky business dealings and his strongly held religious and political beliefs, he frequently found himself in trouble with the law. When he turned to journalism, he did it with such skill that he influenced the development of the newspaper. Defoe was married for 47 years, and six of his children survived childhood.

PHLit Online!
www.PHLitOnline.com

Teaching From Technology

Preparing to Read
Go to **www.PHLitOnline.com** in class or in a lab and display the *Get Connected!* slideshow for this selection. Have the class brainstorm for responses to the slideshow writing prompt, entering ideas in the interactive journal. Then, have students complete their written responses individually, in a lab or as homework.

To build background, display the Background and More About the Author features.

Using the Interactive Text
Go to **www.PHLitOnline.com** and display the Enriched Online Student Edition. As the class reads the selection or listens to the narration, record answers to side-column prompts using the graphic organizers accessible on the interactive page. Alternatively, have students use the online edition individually, answering the prompts as they read.

❶ About the Selection

Daniel Defoe combined his journalistic and creative skills to develop an unusual hybrid: a fictional narrative in the form of a journal. Although this "true history" was narrated by a fictional Londoner identified only as H.F., Defoe's research provided the book with a great deal of historical accuracy.

❷ Activating Prior Knowledge

Ask students to name disaster movies they have seen. In telling about the deadly plague of 1664, Defoe provides unforgettable images of real horror. Ask students to predict the sorts of images they expect the book to contain.

Concept Connector ➡

Tell students that they will return to their responses after reading the selection.

❸ Humanities

The Dead Cart

This wood engraving by an unknown artist was created for an early edition of Defoe's *A Journal of the Plague Year,* first published in 1722.

Use these questions for discussion:

1. What was the purpose of the dead cart?
   Answer: The dead cart was used to carry away the bodies of those killed by the plague.

2. What is the artist's attitude toward the subject?
   Answer: The attitude is matter-of-fact; the cart is shown in the context of everyday life.

FROM A JOURNAL OF THE PLAGUE YEAR

DANIEL DEFOE

The Dead Cart, The British Library

590 A Turbulent Time (1625–1798)

ⓒ Text Complexity Rubric

Reader and Task Suggestions

from A Journal of the Plague Year	
Qualitative Measures	
Context/Knowledge Demands	Fictional journal; historical knowledge demands 1 2 3 ④ 5
Structure / Language Clarity	Long sentences; above-level vocabulary 1 2 ③ 4 5
Levels of Meaning	Accessible (epidemic/disaster) 1 ② 3 4 5
Quantitative Measures	
Lexile	1450L	**Text Length**	1,999 words
Overall Complexity	**More complex**

Preparing to Read the Text
- Using the Background on TE p. 589, discuss how Defoe's experience in journalism likely helped him create a realistic journal.
- Discuss the reasons infectious disease spread easily in seventeenth-century London—overcrowding, bad sanitation, and so on.
- Guide students to use Multidraft Reading strategies (TE p. 589).

Leveled Tasks

Knowledge Demands If students will have difficulty with the context, have them skim for unfamiliar place names or terms. Then, have each student research one to submit to a class glossary to use in a final reading.

Evaluating If students will not have difficulty with the context, have them research the plague and evaluate Defoe's accuracy in portraying it.

4

5

The face of London was now indeed strangely altered, I mean the whole mass of buildings, city, liberties, suburbs, Westminster, Southwark, and altogether; for as to the particular part called the city, or within the walls, that was not yet much infected. But in the whole the face of things, I say, was much altered; sorrow and sadness sat upon every face; and though some parts were not yet overwhelmed, yet all looked deeply concerned; and as we saw it apparently coming on, so everyone looked on himself and his family as in the utmost danger. Were it possible to represent those times exactly to those that did not see them, and give the reader due ideas of the horror that everywhere presented itself, it must make just impressions upon their minds and fill them with surprise. London might well be said to be all in tears; the mourners did not go about the streets indeed, for nobody put on black or made a formal dress of mourning for their nearest friends; but the voice of mourning was truly heard in the streets. The shrieks of women and children at the windows and doors of their houses, where their dearest relations were perhaps dying, or just dead, were so frequent to be heard as we passed the streets, that it was enough to pierce the stoutest heart in the world to hear them. Tears and lamentations were seen almost in every house, especially in the first part of the visitation; for toward the latter end men's hearts were hardened, and death was so always before their eyes, that they did not so much concern themselves for the loss of their friends, expecting that themselves should be summoned the next hour. . . .

I went all the first part of the time freely about the streets, though not so freely as to run myself into apparent danger, except when they dug the great pit in the churchyard of our parish of Aldgate. A terrible pit it was, and I could not resist my curiosity to go and see it. As near as I may judge, it was about forty feet in length, and about fifteen or sixteen feet broad, and, at the time I first looked at it, about nine feet deep; but it was said they dug it near twenty feet deep afterwards in one part of it, till they could go no deeper for the water; for they had, it seems, dug several large pits before this. For though the plague was long a-coming to our parish, yet, when it did come, there was no parish in or about London where it raged with such violence as in the two parishes of Aldgate and Whitechapel.

5 **Literary Analysis**
Point of View
Where in the first paragraph does the narrator indicate that he is providing a personal account intended to be read by others? Explain.

Vocabulary
lamentations (lam'ən tā'shənz) *n.* expressions of grief or mourning

6 **Reading Check**
In what ways was the "face of London . . . strangely altered"?

from A Journal of the Plague Year **591**

Questioning

1. Direct students' attention to the bracketed passage on page 592.

2. **Ask:** What reason does the narrator give for wanting to visit the pit at night rather than during the day?

   Answer: He wanted to see the bodies thrown into the pit, which was only done at night.

❽ Critical Thinking

Interpret

1. Point out the bracketed paragraph beginning "There was … " Tell students that in this passage Defoe explains why there was a ban on visiting the pit.

2. **Ask:** What emotions, thoughts, and motivations are revealed by what was happening to these people at the pits?

   Possible response: People must have felt totally hopeless or desperate. They may have felt that they were keeping the disease from their families by throwing themselves into the pit; they may have been delirious as a result of their illness; or they may have been in so much pain that they wished they were dead.

Vocabulary
distemper (dis tem′ pər) *n.* infectious disease such as the plague

INTO THESE PITS THEY HAD PUT PERHAPS FIFTY OR SIXTY BODIES EACH

❼ **Reading Strategy**
Questioning From the information in the paragraph beginning, "It was . . .," what reason does the narrator give for wanting to visit the pit at night rather than during the day?

Vocabulary
delirious (di lir′ ē əs) *adj.* having hallucinations; ranting

I saw they had dug several pits in another ground, when the distemper began to spread in our parish, and especially when the dead carts began to go about, which was not, in our parish, till the beginning of August. Into these pits they had put perhaps fifty or sixty bodies each; then they made larger holes, wherein they buried all that the cart brought in a week, which, by the middle to the end of August, came to from 200 to 400 a week; and they could not well dig them larger, because of the order of the magistrates confining them to leave no bodies within six feet of the surface; and the water coming on at about seventeen or eighteen feet, they could not well, I say, put more in one pit. But now, at the beginning of September, the plague raging in a dreadful manner, and the number of burials in our parish increasing to more than was ever buried in any parish about London of no larger extent, they ordered this dreadful gulf to be dug, for such it was rather than a pit.

They had supposed this pit would have supplied them for a month or more when they dug it, and some blamed the churchwardens for suffering[1] such a frightful thing, telling them they were making preparations to bury the whole parish, and the like; but time made it appear the churchwardens knew the condition of the parish better than they did, for the pit being finished the 4th of September, I think, they began to bury in it the 6th, and by the 20th, which was just two weeks, they had thrown into it 1114 bodies, when they were obliged to fill it up, the bodies being then come to lie within six feet of the surface. I doubt not but there may be some ancient persons alive in the parish who can justify the fact of this, and are able to show even in what place of the churchyard the pit lay better than I can. The mark of it also was many years to be seen in the churchyard on the surface, lying in length parallel with the passage which goes by the west wall of the churchyard out of Houndsditch, and turns east again into Whitechapel, coming out near the Three Nuns' Inn.

It was about the 10th of September that my curiosity led, or rather drove, me to go and see this pit again, when there had been near 400 people buried in it; and I was not content to see it in the daytime, as I had done before, for then there would have been nothing to have been seen but the loose earth; for all the bodies that were thrown in were immediately covered with earth by those they called the buriers, which at other times were called bearers; but I resolved to go in the night and see some of them thrown in.

There was a strict order to prevent people coming to those pits, and that was only to prevent infection. But after some time that order was more necessary, for people that were infected and near their end, and delirious also, would run to those pits, wrapped in blankets or rugs, and throw themselves in, and, as they said, bury themselves. I cannot

---

1. **suffering** allowing.

Enrichment: Analyzing Themes and Symbols

Graveyard Scenes

The famous scene in Daniel Defoe's *A Journal of the Plague Year* in which a father visits the churchyard where his wife and family are to be buried is memorable and evokes sympathy from readers. Many of Defoe's readers would have been familiar with other iconic graveyard scenes from such works as Shakespeare's *Hamlet,* in which Hamlet discovers the skull of "poor Yorick" in a tomb. Another memorable graveyard scene is in *The Tragedy of Romeo and Juliet* in which the star-crossed lovers die.

Charles Dickens used a graveyard as the backdrop for scenes of intrigue and danger in *Great Expectations.*

Activity: Comparing Graveyard Scenes
Encourage students to read one of these other scenes and compare the graveyard's description and significance with those in Defoe's novel. Suggest that they record their analysis in the **Enrichment: Analyzing Themes and Symbols** worksheet, *Professional Development Guidebook* p. 243.

say that the officers suffered any willingly to lie there; but I have heard that in a great pit in Finsbury, in the parish of Cripplegate, it lying open then to the fields, for it was not then walled about, [some] came and threw themselves in, and expired there, before they threw any earth upon them; and that when they came to bury others, and found them there, they were quite dead, though not cold.

This may serve a little to describe the dreadful condition of that day, though it is impossible to say anything that is able to give a true idea of it to those who did not see it, other than this, that it was indeed very, very, very dreadful, and such as no tongue can express.

I got admittance into the churchyard by being acquainted with the sexton who attended, who, though he did not refuse me at all, yet earnestly persuaded me not to go, telling me very seriously, for he was a good, religious, and sensible man, that it was indeed their business and duty to venture, and to run all hazards, and that in it they might hope to be preserved; but that I had no apparent call to it but my own curiosity, which, he said, he believed I would not pretend was sufficient to justify my running that hazard. I told him I had been pressed in my mind to go, and that perhaps it might be an instructing sight, that might not be without its uses. "Nay," says the good man, "if you will venture upon that score, name of God go in; for, depend upon it, 't will be a sermon to you, it may be, the best that ever you heard in your life. 'T is a speaking sight," says he, "and has a voice with it, and a loud one, to call us all to repentance"; and with that he opened the door and said, "Go, if you will."

His discourse had shocked my resolution a little, and I stood wavering for a good while, but just at that interval I saw two links[2] come over from the end of the Minories, and heard the bellman, and then appeared a dead cart, as they called it, coming over the streets; so I could no longer resist my desire of seeing it, and went in. There was nobody, as I could perceive at first, in the churchyard, or going into it, but the buriers and the fellow that drove the cart, or rather led the horse and cart; but when they came up to the pit they saw a man go to and again,[3] muffled up in a brown cloak, and making motions with his hands under his cloak, as if he was in a great agony, and the buriers immediately gathered about him, supposing he was one of those poor delirious or desperate creatures that used to pretend, as I have said, to bury themselves. He said nothing as he walked about, but two or three times groaned very deeply and loud, and sighed as he would break his heart.

When the buriers came up to him they soon found he was neither a person infected and desperate, as I have observed above, or a person distempered in mind, but one oppressed with a dreadful weight

2. **links** torches.
3. **to and again** to and fro.

---

❾ Background

A *sexton* is a person who is charged with keeping the church and parish building prepared for meetings. (A *parish* is a district that has its own church and clergy.) The sexton's duties included caring for church equipment and, often, ringing the church bell and arranging for burials.

❿ Literary Analysis
Point of View

In the paragraph beginning, "His discourse . . . ," which details make Defoe's fictional narrator seem like a real person? Why?

Vocabulary
resolution (rez´ə loo´shən) *n.* fixed or determined state of mind

Reading Check

What provisions does the parish make for disposing of the bodies of plague victims?

❿ Literary Analysis
Point of View

1. **Ask:** What effect might the sexton's arguments against visiting the pit have on students if they were in the narrator's position? **Possible responses:** Some students will say that the sexton's arguments would give them the creeps and they would leave. Some may say that his comments would not bother them.

2. Remind students that, by this time, there were more than 1,000 bodies in the pit, though most of them would have been covered with a thin layer of dirt.

3. Direct students to the bracketed passage beginning "His discourse…" **Ask** students the Literary Analysis question. **Possible responses:** He is torn between leaving the pit and going in. He is horrified by what he hears and he wavers, but the approach of the dead cart renews his curiosity. He feels sympathy for both the "desperate creatures" and the mourner by the grave's edge.

4. Remind students that, although the narrator is fictional, the events in the story are real.

5. **Ask** students how they think a person's life and focus might change in such a situation. **Possible response:** People would give up ordinary pursuits and try to do things that meant the most to them.

⓫ Reading Check

Answer: The parish digs an enormous pit for the corpses, about 40 feet in length, 15 or 16 feet wide, and 9 to 25 feet deep.

Differentiated Instruction for Universal Access

Vocabulary for Less Proficient Readers
Help students to notice differences in words and to determine word meanings in context. For example, in the paragraph that begins "It was about . . . ," have them differentiate between *led* and *drove* and decide which adds more emotion. Also, have them determine in context what *buriers* and *bearers* are.

EL Strategy for English Learners
To help students stay on track, point out such British names as *Houndsditch* and *Whitechapel,* and explain that these are places—not words that need to be understood literally. Give a brief overview of what is being described. Then, help students define unfamiliar words and ideas as they read.

Enrichment for Advanced Readers
Encourage students to find out more about London and its history. They may wish to focus on disasters, such as the plague and the Great Fire, or on the growth and development of the modern city. Knowing more about London will help them better understand both English literature and issues of urban development.

593

⑫ Humanities

Lord, Have Mercy on London, Contemporary English woodcut on the Great Plague of 1665.

This illustration is a woodcut. Its rough style shows that it was intended for distribution, rather than as fine art. The advantage of a woodcut over a painting was that, once the image was carved into a wood block, it could be used to print as many images as needed.

Although the words used are modern English, they reflect the influences of languages that contributed to English.

Use the following questions for discussion:

1. What might be the reason for the confrontation shown at the far right?
Possible response: People who did not know what caused the plague would be reluctant to allow anyone from an infected area to come into their towns, because they would fear getting the disease themselves.

2. How does the overall emotional impact of the image compare with that of the *Journal*?
Possible response: The figure of death, obviously on the attack, is frightening; the people trying to flee seem hopeless; the plea of "Lord, have mercy" is desperate. All these emotions are reflected in the *Journal*.

⑬ Critical Viewing

Possible responses: The *Journal* relates that there are so many people dying that there is no time to build coffins. This is reflected in the image. The people fleeing seem in keeping with the panic revealed in the account.

of grief indeed, having his wife and several of his children all in the cart that was just come in with him, and he followed in an agony and excess of sorrow. He mourned heartily, as it was easy to see, but with a kind of masculine grief that could not give itself vent by tears; and calmly defying the buriers to let him alone, said he would only see the bodies thrown in and go away, so they left importuning him. But no sooner was the cart turned round and the bodies shot into the pit promiscuously,[4] which was a surprise to him, for he at least expected they would have been decently laid in, though indeed he was afterwards convinced that was impracticable; I say, no sooner did he see the sight but he cried out aloud, unable to contain himself. I could not hear what he said, but he went backward two or three steps and fell down in a swoon. The buriers ran to him and took him up, and in a little while he came to himself, and they led him away to the Pie Tavern over against the end of Houndsditch, where, it seems, the

Vocabulary
importuning (im′ pôr tōōn′ iŋ) *v.* pleading with

---

4. **promiscuously** mixed together without care or thought.

⑬ ▼ **Critical Viewing** Explain how the *Journal* helps you make sense of details in this picture. **[Connect]**

594 A Turbulent Time (1625–1798)

man was known, and where they took care of him. He looked into the pit again as he went away, but the buriers had covered the bodies so immediately with throwing in earth, that though there was light enough, for there were lanterns, and candles in them, placed all night round the sides of the pit, upon heaps of earth, seven or eight, or perhaps more, yet nothing could be seen.

This was a mournful scene indeed, and affected me almost as much as the rest; but the other was awful and full of terror. The cart had in it sixteen or seventeen bodies: some were wrapped up in linen sheets, some in rags, some little other than naked, or so loose that what covering they had fell from them in the shooting out of the cart, and they fell quite naked among the rest; but the matter was not much to them, or the indecency much to anyone else, seeing they were all dead, and were to be huddled together into the common grave of mankind, as we may call it, for here was no difference made, but poor and rich went together; there was no other way of burials, neither was it possible there should, for coffins were not to be had for the prodigious numbers that fell in such a calamity as this.

Vocabulary
prodigious (prō´ dij´ əs)
adj. enormous; huge

Critical Reading

© **1. Key Ideas and Details (a)** What was the purpose of the great pit dug in Aldgate? **(b) Infer:** Why do you think the narrator describes the pit in detail?

© **2. Key Ideas and Details (a)** What prompts the narrator to visit the pit? **(b) Interpret:** What does the Sexton mean when he says that visiting the pit will "be a sermon" to the narrator?

© **3. Key Ideas and Details (a) Summarize:** Retell the incident concerning the man in the brown cloak. **(b) Draw Conclusions:** In what way does this incident add a new dimension of meaning to the previous general descriptions of the plague? Explain.

© **4. Craft and Structure** Does Defoe use informative language, emotional language, or both to describe London during this crisis? In your response, use at least two of these Essential Question words: *city, destruction, struggle. [Connecting to the Essential Question: What is the relationship between literature and place?]*

FOR HERE WAS NO DIFFERENCE MADE, BUT POOR AND RICH WENT TOGETHER

Cite textual evidence to support your responses.

from A Journal of the Plague Year **595**

ASSESS

Answers

Before students respond, you may wish to have them write a brief objective summary of the selection. As they answer the questions below, remind them to support their answers with evidence from the text.

1. (a) The pit served as a communal grave for plague victims. (b) The narrator is trying to convey the horrible realities of the plague.

2. (a) The narrator is curious. (b) The Sexton warns the narrator that he will be reminded of his own mortality and will be moved to repent his sins.

3. (a) The man in the brown cloak was mourning the deaths of his wife and his children. When he saw their bodies dumped into the pit with hundreds of others, he cried out in anguish and fainted. (b) After paragraphs of statistics about massive numbers of deaths and bodies dumped by the cart-load, this incident confronts the reader with the grief and loss of the individual.

4. **Possible response:** In describing London during the plague, Defoe uses both informative and emotional language. For example, at the beginning of this passage, his language is informative as he lists the physical parts of the *city* ("the whole mass of buildings…"), but in the next sentence it becomes emotional as he describe the *destruction* the population faced ("sorrow and sadness sat upon every face …"). Students may point out that Defoe's writing both depicts and interprets the *city*.

Concept Connector

Reading Strategy Graphic Organizer
Ask students to review the graphic organizers in which they have listed their questions and answers. Then, have students share their organizers and compare what they have asked and learned.

Activating Prior Knowledge
Have students return to their responses to the Activating Prior Knowledge activity. Ask them to explain whether their thoughts have changed and, if so, how.

Connecting to the Essential Question
Have students compare their responses to the prompt completed before reading the *Journal* with their thoughts afterward. Have them work individually or in groups, writing or discussing their thoughts, to formulate their new responses. Then, lead a class discussion, probing for what students have learned that confirms or invalidates their initial thoughts. Encourage students to cite specific textual details to support their responses.

Answers

1. Students should refer to specific passages and note the use of the personal pronouns *I* or *we*.

2. Defoe wants to give the account a human face.

3. **Possible responses:** The narrator is curious and he is not a coward. He decides to visit the pit at night to observe conditions for himself. He also displays sensitivity in describing the impact of the plague.

4. **Possible response:** The narrator appears to be a fairly accurate reporter of events.

5. **Possible response:** Reading a first-person account of the Great Plague seems more real and personal than a dry but factually accurate, account in a history text.

6. Answers will vary. Students should supply reasons and use examples from the selection in their answers.

7. Students should defend their views with examples and supply reasons why mixing fiction with nonfiction is a good literary technique.

8. (a) **Possible questions:** What aspects of daily life is the narrator referring to when he says that the city was altered? When the disaster occurs, what parts of the city were affected? (b) Students should cite specific details.

9. (a) **Possible responses:** The man is a mourner. He is dressed in a brown cloak. He has lost his wife and children. He is in the graveyard. When their bodies go into the pit he falls down in a swoon. (b) The narrator says he was deeply affected, but he carefully reports the details of what he saw.

10. **Possible response:** You can ask yourself who, when, where, why, and how questions about the passage.

596

After You Read | from *A Journal of the Plague Year*

Literary Analysis

1. Craft and Structure Referring to specific passages, demonstrate that *A Journal of the Plague Year* is written from the **first-person point of view.**

2. Craft and Structure Why do you think Defoe chose a first-person narrator, an "eyewitness," to present this account of the plague year?

3. Key Ideas and Details What is the first-person narrator like? Use a chart like the one shown to make inferences about his personality traits and attitudes based on what he says, thinks, and does in the selection.

Narrator's Personality Trait or Attitude	Narrator's Statements, Thoughts, or Actions That Support Your Inference

4. Key Ideas and Details Does the narrator seem like an accurate reporter of events, or does he seem unreliable? Cite specific details to support your opinion.

5. Integration of Knowledge and Ideas How does reading an account of the Great Plague from the first-person point of view compare to reading about such events in history textbooks? Explain.

6. Integration of Knowledge and Ideas Which would you prefer to read—Defoe's fictionalized first-person account or an actual journal kept by someone during the Great Plague? Why?

7. Integration of Knowledge and Ideas Defoe's account mixes fiction and nonfiction, combining Defoe's research into the events surrounding the actual plague with a fictional narrator and made-up situations. Do you think literary works should avoid mixing fiction and nonfiction? Why or why not?

Reading Strategy

8. Asking questions is a good way to understand difficult passages. **(a)** If you did not understand the changes described in the first paragraph, what are two questions you might ask to *repair your comprehension?* **(b)** How might you answer those questions?

9. (a) Answer these questions about the man in the next-to-last paragraph: Who is he? What does he look like? Where is he? Why is he accompanying the cart? How does he behave? **(b)** Then, explain what the narrator's reporting of this incident reveals about himself.

10. You can ask yourself questions to figure out what a puzzling passage means. How could you also use a questioning strategy to monitor your understanding and decide whether a passage has puzzled you?

Common Core State Standards

Writing
3. Write narratives to develop real or imagined experiences or events using effective technique, well-chosen details, and well-structured event sequences. *(p. 597)*

Language
4.a. Use context as a clue to the meaning of a word or phrase. *(p. 597)*

Assessment Practice

Writer's Point of View (For more practice, see *All-in-One Workbook*.)

Many tests require students to identify a writer's point of view. Use this sample test item.

> The cart had in it sixteen or seventeen bodies: some were wrapped up in linen sheets, some in rags, some little other than naked … they were all dead, and were to be huddled together into the common grave of mankind … for here was no difference made; but poor and rich went together …

Defoe would probably agree that _____.

A people should be buried according to their status

B it is unimportant what happens with our bodies after we die

C death reveals the common humanity of all people

D death can bring shame, even on the rich and powerful

The fact that Defoe comments on this and his use of the words *common grave of mankind* indicate that the correct answer is **C**.

Integrated Language Skills

ⓒ **Vocabulary Acquisition and Use**

Word Analysis: Latin Prefix *dis-*

The word *distemper* includes the Latin prefix *dis-*, which means "the opposite of" or "not." *Distemper* is "the opposite of temper, or balance"—in other words, the state of imbalance when one has a serious disease.

With a small group, write sentences about the selection using at least five of the *dis-* words listed below. Explain the meaning of each *dis-* word you use. Try to figure out the meanings of the following words based on your understanding of the prefix. However, if the meaning of a word is unclear, refer to a dictionary.

disappeared	disinfectant
disbelief	disobey
discomfort	disquiet
disconcert	dispense

Vocabulary: Context Clues

Context clues are words and phrases in a text that help you figure out the meaning of an unfamiliar word. Using context clues in the numbered sentences, choose the word from the vocabulary list on page 588 that best completes the meaning. Then, explain how you arrived at your answers.

1. The death toll from the Great Plague was _____.
2. Many who had the plague became _____ as the disease worsened.
3. Those afflicted with the _____ usually perished in the end.
4. Some mourners made their _____ loudly; others walked in silence.
5. It seemed like the whole city was _____ God to spare their loved ones.
6. It took great _____ for the narrator to walk the streets every night to report on events.

Writing

ⓒ **Narrative Text** The selection by Defoe begins with an account of great change in London. Try writing your own **essay** about a time of change. It need not be as dramatic as the one in Defoe's account, but it should be a significant change that has affected your life.

Prewriting Jot down notes on the situation before and after the change. Also, briefly explain what caused the change and how it affected you.

Drafting In describing the change and its effect, use types of writing as they are appropriate: *persuasive, narrative, descriptive,* and *expository.* Combine concrete *incidents* with *broader themes* that illustrate your ideas about life.

Revision Exchange drafts with a partner. Accept suggestions for making information, thoughts, and feelings more concrete.

Model: Revising to Make Information More Concrete

When I saw what happened to the block where I lived,
I was amazed at the change.
       gasped in amazement

Adding more detail makes a vague and abstract statement more concrete and vivid.

Integrated Language Skills **597**

Vocabulary Acquisition and Use

1. Introduce the skill using the instruction on the student page.
2. Have students complete the Word Analysis activity and the Vocabulary practice.

Word Analysis

1. The Great Plague caused much *discomfort* and *disquiet* among the population of London.
2. Some mourners *disobeyed* the order to prevent people from visiting the pits.
3. The narrator expressed *disbelief* at how changed the city had become.
4. There were no *disinfectants* that could stop the spread of the disease.
5. It took a long time before the effects of the plague had fully *disappeared* from British society.

Vocabulary

1. *prodigious;* the death toll was enormous, which is a synonym
2. *delirious;* the adjective describes an effect of the disease
3. *distemper;* refers to an infectious disease like the plague
4. *lamentations;* mourners express grief
5. *importuning;* synonym for pleading
6. *resolution;* refers to the narrator's state of mind

Writing

1. To guide students in writing about a time of great change, give them the Support for Writing Page (*Unit 3 Resources,* p. 136).
2. Remind students that their essays should involve an incident that had an impact.
3. Use the **Rubric for Reflective Essay** in the *Professional Development Guidebook,* pages 293–294, to evaluate students' narrative texts.

Assessment Resources

Unit 3 Resources

L1 L2 EL Selection Test A, pp. 141–143. Administer Test A to less advanced readers.

L3 L4 EL Selection Test B, pp. 144–146. Administer Test B to on-level and more advanced students.

L3 L4 Open-Book Test, pp. 138–140. As an alternative, administer the Open-Book Test.

All Customizable Test Bank

All Self-tests
Students may prepare for the **Selection Test** by taking the **Self-test** online.

PHLit Online! All assessment resources are available at **www.PHLitOnline.com**.

- **Reading Informational Text 5**
- **Writing 1**
- **Language 4.b**

About the Texts

1. Introduce the forms using the instruction on the student page.

2. Tell students they will use text features to help them understand organization and content as they read.

Reading Strategy

1. Introduce the skill using the instruction and chart on the student page.

2. Tell students they will use text features to help them understand organization and content as they read.

Think Aloud: Model the Skill

Say to students:

When I am reading a transit brochure, I skim the title, headings, and bulleted text to identify the type of information the brochure contains.

Content-Area Vocabulary

1. Have students say each word aloud. Then, use each word in a sentence that makes its meaning clear.

2. Repeat your sentence with the vocabulary word missing and have students fill in the blank.

For more guidance, consult the *Classroom Strategies and Teaching Routines* card on introducing vocabulary.

Reading for Information

Analyzing Functional and Expository Texts

Annual Report • Transit Map and Schedule

About the Texts

An **annual report** is a record providing information to the public on the status of an organization's initiatives and finances. Basic features of annual reports include chapter or section headings; bulleted and bold-faced information; and photos, charts, or graphs.

Transit maps and schedules are posters or brochures designed to transmit travel information graphically. They include simplified geographic representations of an area, a key or legend to explain symbols, and charts showing arrivals, departures, and stops.

Reading Strategy

Text features are elements of a text, such as heads, that signal its organization or clarify the information it presents. Follow these steps to **evaluate information from text features** and to evaluate the effectiveness of the structure they create:

- Identify text features, such as heads, legends, or tables, and their function.

- Based on text features, draw conclusions about the topics and subtopics covered in the text, as well as its organization.

- Use the text features to locate information or to guide you as you read.

- Evaluate whether each text feature contributes to the clarity of the text.

As you read, use a chart like the one shown to evaluate text features.

Text Feature Graphic	How It Clarifies/Organizes
Table of Contents/Index	
Head/Subhead	
Bulleted List	
Table/Chart/Graph	
Map	
Legend/Key	

Reading Informational Text
5. Analyze and evaluate the effectiveness of the structure an author uses in his or her exposition or argument, including whether the structure makes points clear, convincing, and engaging.

Language
4.b. Identify and correctly use patterns of word changes that indicate different meanings or parts of speech.

Content-Area Vocabulary

These words may also appear in other subject-area texts:

congestion (kən jesʹ chen) *n.* excessive crowding or accumulation

sustainable (sə stānʹ ə bəl) *adj.* capable of being maintained or prolonged

consumption (kən sumpʹ shen) *n.* the using of goods or services

economic (ekʹ ə nämʹ ik) *adj.* having to do with the production, distribution, and use of goods and services

---

Teaching Resources

Reading Support
L2 L3 *Reader's Notebook*
L1 *Reader's Notebook: Adapted Version*
EL *Reader's Notebook: English Learner's Version*

The Mayor's Annual Report 2004

To reduce congestion in London

Congestion—whether on the roads, on the Underground, on the buses or on the trains—is the scourge of London's current transport system. The result of many years of under-investment combined with significant rates of increase in London's population, it will not be cured overnight. Nevertheless, the Mayor is committed to ensuring that anti-congestion measures are combined with the necessary improvement in the capacity and quality of service of London's transport system to alleviate congestion in a systematic manner.

> The heading clearly states the goal that is the topic of this section of the report.

Congestion Charging

The congestion charging scheme commenced in central London in February 2003. The scheme directly tackles four key transport priorities for London:

- reducing congestion
- improving bus services
- improving journey time reliability for car users
- making the distribution of goods and services more reliable, sustainable and efficient.

> The bulleted list makes the transport priorities easy to read and remember.

TfL are monitoring the impacts and operation of the scheme as set out in the first Annual Monitoring Report in June 2003. They have since produced two reports setting out their findings: Congestion Charging:

Six Months On was published in October 2003; Congestion Charging: February 2004 Update was published after one year's operation. A Second Annual Monitoring Report is currently being prepared for publication in the Spring.

Reduced traffic levels and congestion

TfL estimate that 65,000 fewer cars per day are being driven into or through the charging zone, with the majority of occupants switching to public transport or diverting around the zone. As a result only 4,000 fewer people are coming to the charging zone each day because of the scheme.

Congestion in the zone has dropped by around 30 percent and is at the lowest level seen since the mid-1980s. The number of vehicles with four or more wheels entering the zone during charging hours has dropped by18 per cent—making journeys to and from the charging zone quicker and more reliable. Journey times to and from the zone have decreased by an average 14 percent and journey time reliability has improved by an average of 30 percent.

About Annual Reports

1. Point out to students that the first selection is an annual report.
2. Ask students to predict what information the report will cover, based on its title and section headings.
   Possible response: The report is about efforts to minimize traffic problems in London.

Evaluate Information from Text Features

1. Refer students to the bulleted information about the features of an annual report on the Preteach page.
2. Point out that they will be looking for these features and analyzing how they are used as they read the selection.

Differentiated Instruction   for Universal Access

Strategy for Less Proficient Readers
Ask students to reread the first paragraph. This introduction gives an overview of the report. It is important that students understand its main points. Ask them to work in pairs to look up any words they don't understand. Have them summarize the paragraph before reading further.

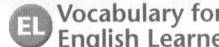 Vocabulary for English Learners
To increase students' comprehension of the report, begin by teaching them the word *congestion*. Remind students that the prefix con- means "together." Explain that the Latin root of *congestion* is *congere*, which means "to heap up." So, by looking at the meanings of the word parts, students can see that *congestion* means "heaped together," or "blocked up."

Evaluate information from Text Features

1. Remind students that a common feature of a report is that details are organized under headings.

2. **Ask** students to identify the two headings on this page.
   Answer: The two headings are "Congestion levels in the charging zone during charging hours" and "Economic Impact."

3. **Ask** students to explain the purpose of the bar graph.
   Answer: The bar graph supports the text above it by showing data for the "total traffic entering the charging zone during charging hours."

Congestion levels in the charging zone during charging hours

Reduced congestion has also assisted the wider improvements in bus service reliability and journey times; the additional waiting time due to unreliability within the charging zone has reduced by around one third since the beginning of the scheme. Routes serving the congestion zone also experience 60 percent less congestion due to traffic disruption than before the charge was introduced.

Economic Impact

Reduced traffic delays, improved journey time reliability, reduced waiting time at bus stops and lower fuel consumption resulting from congestion charging all have economic benefits which are increasingly being recognised. TfL's cost benefit analysis of the overall impact of congestion charging is that it generates £50 million per annum of net benefits to London, principally through reduced congestion.

> The chart shows the progress and effect of the congestion charging program.

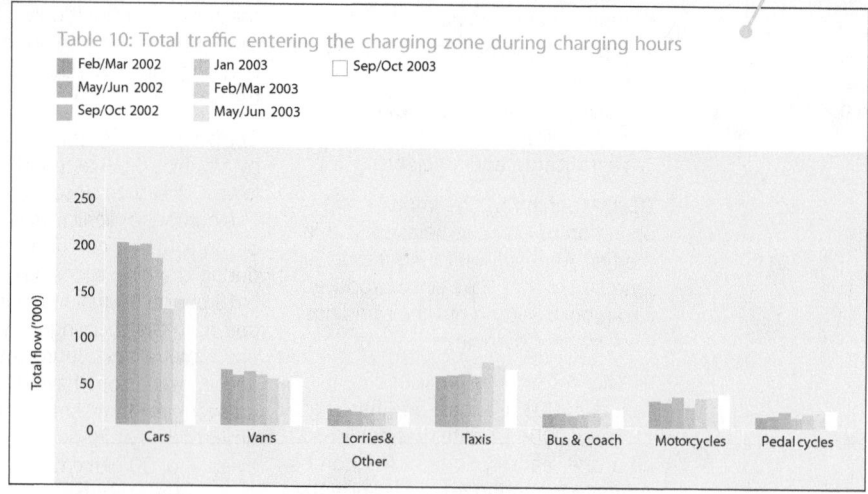

Table 10: Total traffic entering the charging zone during charging hours

- Feb/Mar 2002
- May/Jun 2002
- Sep/Oct 2002
- Jan 2003
- Feb/Mar 2003
- May/Jun 2003
- Sep/Oct 2003

600 A Turbulent Time (1625–1798)

Vocabulary Development

Content-Area Vocabulary: Economics

Review the definitions of the cross-curricular vocabulary with students: *congestion, sustainable, economic,* and *consumption.* Then, examine each word in its context in the annual report.

When you have finished with the four listed words, ask students to identify other words in the report that relate to economics, such as *alleviate, systematic, efficient,* and *reliability.* Have students look up their definitions in a dictionary and then use them in sentences about transportation.

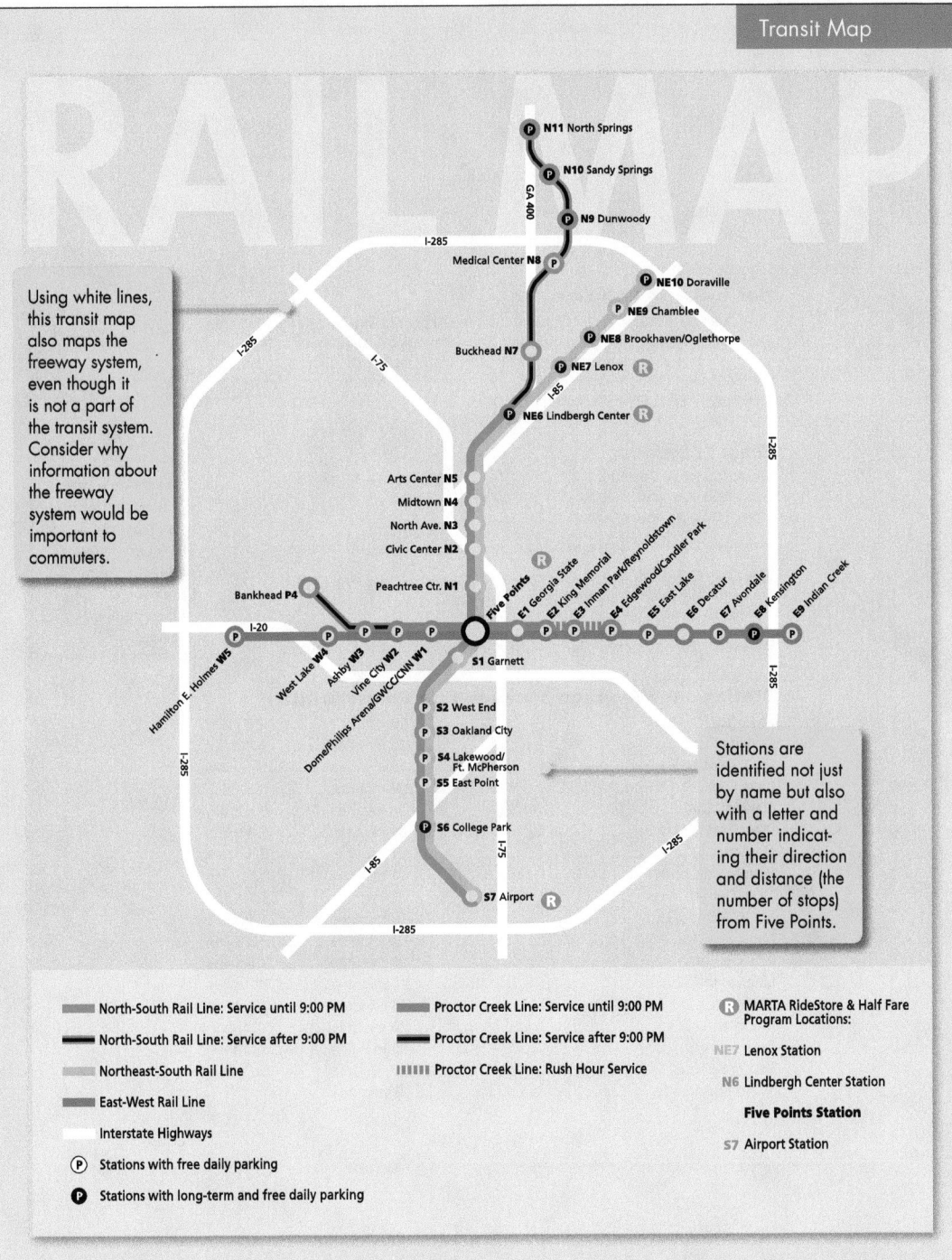

RAIL MAP

N11 North Springs

N10 Sandy Springs

GA 400

N9 Dunwoody

I-285

Medical Center N8

NE10 Doraville

NE9 Chamblee

NE8 Brookhaven/Oglethorpe

Buckhead N7

NE7 Lenox ®

I-75

I-85

NE6 Lindbergh Center ®

I-285

Arts Center N5

Midtown N4

North Ave. N3

Civic Center N2

Peachtree Ctr. N1

Bankhead P4

I-20

Hamilton E. Holmes W5

West Lake W4

Ashby W3

Vine City W2

Dome/Phillips Arena/GWCC/CNN W1

Five Points ®

E1 Georgia State

E2 King Memorial

E3 Inman Park/Reynoldstown

E4 Edgewood/Candler Park

E5 East Lake

E6 Decatur

E7 Avondale

E8 Kensington

E9 Indian Creek

S1 Garnett

S2 West End

S3 Oakland City

S4 Lakewood/Ft. McPherson

S5 East Point

S6 College Park

I-85

I-75

I-285

S7 Airport ®

I-285

I-285

> Using white lines, this transit map also maps the freeway system, even though it is not a part of the transit system. Consider why information about the freeway system would be important to commuters.

> Stations are identified not just by name but also with a letter and number indicating their direction and distance (the number of stops) from Five Points.

Legend	
North-South Rail Line: Service until 9:00 PM	Proctor Creek Line: Service until 9:00 PM
North-South Rail Line: Service after 9:00 PM	Proctor Creek Line: Service after 9:00 PM
Northeast-South Rail Line	Proctor Creek Line: Rush Hour Service
East-West Rail Line	
Interstate Highways	
℗ Stations with free daily parking	
🅿 Stations with long-term and free daily parking	

® MARTA RideStore & Half Fare Program Locations:

NE7 Lenox Station

N6 Lindbergh Center Station

Five Points Station

S7 Airport Station

About Transit Maps

1. Introduce the form of a transit map, using the description on the Preteach page.

2. **Ask** students to locate the names of the rail lines shown on this transit map.
   Answer: The rail lines are the North-South Rail Line, the Northeast-South Rail Line, and the East-West Rail Line.

Evaluate Text Features

1. Tell students to analyze the map's features.

2. Remind students to use a chart like the one on the Preteach page as they read.

3. **Ask** students to explain how someone who lives near Decatur Station could get to Doraville Station.
   Answer: The person would board a westbound train at Decatur Station and disembark at Five Points Station. He or she would then board a northbound train on the Northeast-South Rail line and take it to Doraville Station.

Differentiated Instruction   for Universal Access

Culturally Responsive Instruction
Culture Connection Transportation systems, or transit systems, vary from city to city—and a smaller town might not have one at all. Ask students to share whether they have ridden public transportation.

Have them explain where they got on the train or bus, where they got off, and how many stops they passed along the way. Ask them to tell whether it was a positive or negative experience overall. If a student has not ridden any form of public transportation, ask him or her to describe how it is depicted in television and/or movies.

About Transit Schedules

1. **Introduce** the form of a transit schedule, using the description on the Preteach page.

2. **Tell** students that the schedule shows when a train will arrive at major stations along its route.

3. **Ask** students to locate a station on the line and determine how long it would take to get to the downtown Five Points Station.
Answer: Students' responses will vary. Examples: The average time it takes to get from Airport Station to Five Points Station is 16 minutes. The average time it takes to get from Dunwoody Station to Five Points Station is 22 minutes.

Evaluate Information from Text Features

1. **Tell** students to analyze the schedule's text features.

2. **Remind** students to use a chart like the one on the Preteach page as they read.

3. **Ask** to compare the frequency of trains on weekdays during peak service to the frequency of trains on weekends.
Answer: Trains come every 10 minutes on weekdays during peak service but only every 20 minutes on weekends.

MARTA

North-South Rail Line

Note: If you are traveling Northbound from the Airport to the Buckhead, Medical Center, Dunwoody, Sandy Springs and North Springs rail stations after 9:00 pm, you need to board the northbound train with "Doraville" destination sign, exit at the Lindbergh Center rail station (N6), and transfer to the North Line train with a destination sign of "North Springs."

Train Frequency

Weekday Peak Service: From 6:00 a.m. until 9:00 a.m. From 3:00 p.m. until 7:00 p.m.	Every 10 minutes
Weekday Off-Peak Service:	Every 15 minutes
Weekday Off-Peak Service after 9:00 p.m. Trains run between Lindbergh Center Station and North Springs Station after 8:00 p.m.	Every 20 minutes
Weekend (Saturday and Sunday) Service:	Every 20 minutes

> This schedule does not provide departure times, but it helps commuters understand that trains come along at the specified intervals.

Stations and Average Times to Five Points Station

Airport:	16 minutes	9.0 miles
College Park:	15 minutes	8.2 miles
East Point:	12 minutes	6.4 miles
Lakewood/Ft. McPherson:	08 minutes	4.5 miles
Oakland City:	06 minutes	3.4 miles
West End:	04 minutes	1.9 miles
Garnett:	01 minutes	0.4 miles
Peachtree Center:	01 minutes	0.5 miles
Civic Center:	02 minutes	1.0 miles
North Avenue:	03 minutes	1.4 miles
Midtown:	04 minutes	2.0 miles
Arts Center:	06 minutes	2.5 miles
Lindbergh Center:	10 minutes	5.2 miles
Buckhead:	16 minutes	7.4 miles
Med Center:	20 minutes	12.1 miles
Dunwoody:	22 minutes	13.1 miles
Sandy Springs:	25 minutes	
North Springs:	27 minutes	

602 A Turbulent Time (1625–1798)

Think Aloud Reading Strategy: Analyze Text Features

To model the process of analyzing text features, use the following "think aloud." Say to students:

To interpret transit schedules, it is helpful to compare them with transit maps. If I use both documents together, I can figure out approximate traveling times between stations. For example, I can see on the map that Five Points Station is between West End Station and Arts Center Station. It takes about four minutes to get from West End Station to Five Points Station, and it takes about six minutes to get from Arts Center Station to Five Points Station. If I add these times together, I can guess that it would take me about twenty minutes to travel from West End Station to Arts Center Station.

After You Read

Annual Report •
Transit Map and Schedule

Critical Reading

1. Key Ideas and Details **(a)** According to the annual report, where was the "congestion charging" plan implemented? **(b)** How often did officials monitor the impact of the plan?

2. Key Ideas and Details **(a)** Based on the transit map, how many stops after Georgia State is East Lake? **(b)** Based on the transit schedule, how long does it take to go from Oakland City to Five Points?

3. Craft and Structure **(a)** Identify two text features or graphics used in the annual report, and two in the transit map and schedule. **(b)** Explain how effective each is in presenting information or in helping you navigate the text.

4. Content-Area Vocabulary *Economic* is an adjective meaning "having to do with the production, distribution, and use of goods or services." Using this definition, along with your knowledge of word forms, give the meaning and part of speech of each of these words: *economize, economist, economical.* Check your answers in a dictionary.

Common Core State Standards

Writing

1. Write arguments to support claims in an analysis of substantive topics or texts, using valid reasoning and relevant and sufficient evidence.

Timed Writing

Argument [40 minutes]

Format

In a **position paper,** you present your viewpoint on a specific topic. An effective position paper contains a clear thesis logically supported with well-organized evidence and reasons.

Write a **position paper** in which you argue for or against congestion pricing in large cities. Develop a thesis and the support you will use by **synthesizing ideas and making logical connections** between the annual report and the transit map and schedule. Support your claim with textual evidence.

Academic Vocabulary

When you **synthesize ideas and make logical connections,** you combine related ideas from various texts, noting where they reinforce or build on one another, to support a conclusion.

5-Minute Planner

Complete these steps before you begin to write.

1. Read the prompt carefully and underline key words.

2. Scan the text for details that relate to the prompt. TIP Consider what the transit map and schedule show about the advantages or disadvantages of public transit.

3. Before writing, create an outline to guide you.

4. Reread the prompt, and begin drafting your essay.

Critical Reading

1. (a) It was implemented in central London. **(b)** Officials monitored the plan's impact every six months.

2. (a) East Lake is four stops after Georgia State. **(b)** It takes 6 minutes.

3. (a) **Possible response:** The annual report uses heads and bulleted lists. The map uses a key. The schedule uses a table. **(b)** All of these features help organize the information so readers can find the information they need quickly and efficiently.

4. To *economize* (a verb) is to avoid using goods wastefully. An *economist* (a noun) is someone who studies economics. *Economical* is an adjective that describes something or someone that avoids waste.

Timed Writing

1. Before students begin writing their position papers, guide them in analyzing key words and phrases in the prompt, using the highlighted notes.

2. Work with students to draw up guidelines for their position papers based on the key words they identified.

3. Have students use the 5-Minute Planner to structure their time.

4. Allow students 40 minutes to complete the assignment. Evaluate their work using the guidelines they have developed.

Extend the Lesson

Connecting to the Students' World

To give students further practice with government and public documents and to help them apply the material to their own world, divide the class into small groups. Provide each group with a transit map or schedule for a local route. Students should work together to analyze the text features of the document and provide multiple examples of how to use it.

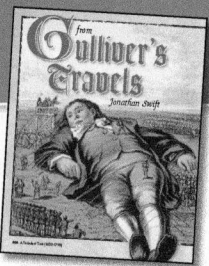

from *Gulliver's Travels*
• A Modest Proposal
Lesson Pacing Guide

DAY 1 Preteach

- ⓒ Administer the Reading and Vocabulary Warm-ups (*Unit 3 Resources*, pp. 153–156) as necessary.
- ⓒ Introduce the Literary Analysis concept: Satire.
- • Introduce the Reading Strategy: Analyzing Text Features.
- ⓒ Build background with the author and Background features.
- • Develop thematic thinking with Connecting to the Essential Question.
- ⓒ Teach the selection vocabulary.

DAYS 2–3 Preteach/Teach/Assess

- • Distribute copies of the appropriate graphic organizer for the Reading Strategy (*Graphic Organizer Transparencies*, pp. 107–108).
- • Distribute copies of the appropriate graphic organizer for Literary Analysis (*Graphic Organizer Transparencies*, pp. 109–110).
- • Prepare students to read with the Activating Prior Knowledge activities (TE).
- • Informally monitor comprehension while students read.
- • Use the Reading Check question to confirm comprehension.
- ⓒ Develop students' understanding of satire using the Literary Analysis prompts.
- • Develop students' ability to analyze text features using the Reading Strategy prompts.
- ⓒ Reinforce vocabulary with the Vocabulary notes.
- • Assess students' comprehension and mastery of the skills by having them answer the Critical Reading, Literary Analysis, and Reading Strategy questions.
- • Have students complete the Vocabulary Lesson.

DAY 4 Assess

- ⓒ Have students complete the Writing Lesson and write a plan for a multimedia presentation. (You may assign as homework.)
- • Administer Selection Test A or B (*Unit 3 Resources*, pp. 165–167 or 168–170).

ⓒ Common Core State Standards

Reading Literature 6. Analyze a case in which grasping point of view requires distinguishing what is directly stated in a text from what is really meant.

Writing 2.a. Introduce a topic; organize complex ideas, concepts, and information so that each new element builds on that which precedes it to create a unified whole; include formatting, graphics, and multimedia when useful to aiding comprehension.

Language 5. Demonstrate understanding of word relationships in work meanings.

Additional Standards Practice
Common Core Companion, pp. 61–62; 196–207, 226–227

Daily Block Scheduling
Each day in this Lesson Pacing Guide represents a 40–50 minute period. Teachers using block scheduling may combine days to revise pacing. In addition, teachers may differentiate and support core instruction by integrating components for extended and intensive support as students require. See the Guide to Selected Leveled Resources (facing page).

Guide to Selected Leveled Resources

R T I Tier 1 (students performing on level)			*from* Gulliver's Travels • A Modest Proposal

Warm Up		Practice, **model,** and **monitor** fluency, working **with the whole class** or **in groups.**	**Vocabulary and Reading Warm-ups B,** *Unit 3 Resources,* pp. 151–152, 153
Comprehension/Skills		**Support** and **monitor** comprehension and skills development, having students complete the activities, graphic organizers, and interactive prompts **independently** or **as a class.**	• *Reader's Notebook,* adapted instruction and full selection **EL** *Reader's Notebook: English Learner's Version,* adapted instruction and adapted selection • **Reading Strategy Graphic Organizer B,** *Graphic Organizer Transparencies,* p. 112 • **Literary Analysis Graphic Organizer B,** *Graphic Organizer Transparencies,* p. 114
Monitor Progress	**A**	**Monitor** student progress with the differentiated curriculum-based assessment in the *Unit Resources.*	• **Selection Test B,** *Unit 3 Resources,* pp. 165–167 • **Open-Book Test,** *Unit 3 Resources,* pp. 159–161

R T I Tier 2 (students requiring intervention)			*from* Gulliver's Travels • A Modest Proposal

Warm Up		Practice, **model,** and **monitor** fluency **in groups** or **with individuals.**	• **Vocabulary and Reading Warm-ups A,** *Unit 3 Resources,* pp. 151–153 • *Hear It!* **Audio CD (adapted text)**
Comprehension/Skills		• **Support** and **monitor** comprehension and skills development, working **in small groups** or **with individuals.** • As students complete the selection in the appropriate version of the *Reader's Notebook,* **monitor** comprehension frequently with group questions and individual instruction. • **Model** strategies while guiding students in completing the activities and prompts in the *Reader's Notebook,* as well as the graphic organizers. • **Practice** skills and **monitor** mastery with the *Reading Kit* worksheets.	• *Reader's Notebook: Adapted Version,* adapted instruction and adapted selection **EL** *Reader's Notebook: English Learner's Version,* adapted instruction and adapted selection • **Reading Strategy Graphic Organizer A,** *Graphic Organizer Transparencies,* p. 111 • **Literary Analysis Graphic Organizer A,** *Graphic Organizer Transparencies,* p. 113 • *Reading Kit,* Practice worksheets
Monitor Progress	**A**	**Monitor** student progress with the differentiated curriculum-based assessment in the *Unit Resources* and in the *Reading Kit.*	• **Selection Test A,** *Unit 3 Resources,* pp. 162–164 • *Reading Kit,* Assess worksheets

TIER 3 Tier 3 intervention may require consultation with the student's special-education or dyslexia specialist. For additional support, see the Tier 2 activities and resources listed above.

One-on-one teaching   Group work   Whole class instruction   Independent work   **A** Assessment

For a complete guide to selection support, including support for Advanced students, see the Overview of Resources in the frontmatter.

from *Gulliver's Travels*
• A Modest Proposal

RESOURCES FOR:

L1 Special-Needs Students

L2 Below-Level Students (Tier 2)

L3 On-Level Students (Tier 1)

L4 Advanced Students (Tier 1)

EL English Learners

All All Students

Vocabulary/Fluency/Prior Knowledge

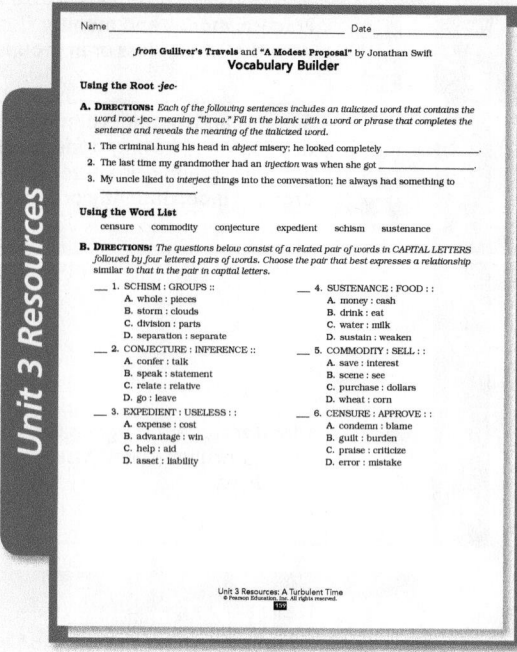

All Vocabulary Builder, p. 159

Also available for these selections:

EL L1 L2 Vocabulary Warm-ups A and B, pp. 153–154

EL L1 L2 Reading Warm-ups A and B, pp. 155–156

Reader's Notebooks

Pre- and postreading pages for these selections, as well as the excerpt from *Gulliver's Travels,* appear in an interactive format in the *Reader's Notebooks.* Each *Notebook* is differentiated for a different group of learners.

The selections in the Adapted and English Learner's versions are abridged.

L2 L3 *Reader's Notebook*

L1 *Reader's Notebook: Adapted Version*

EL *Reader's Notebook: English Learner's Version*

EL *Reader's Notebook: Spanish Version*

© *Common Core Companion*

Additional instruction and practice for each Common Core State Standard

Selection Support

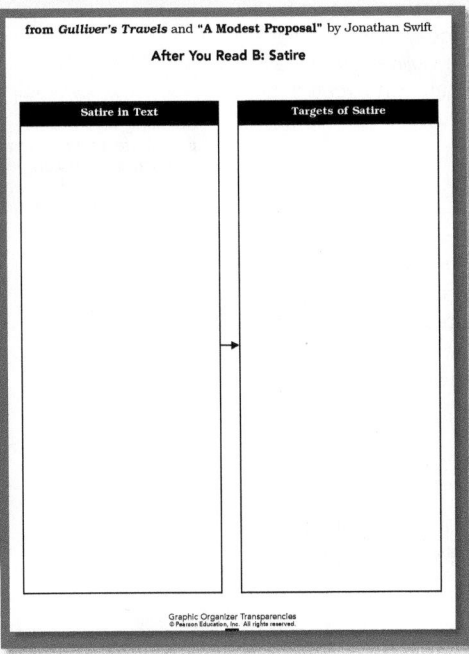

EL L3 **Literary Analysis: Graphic Organizer B,** p. 110

Also available for these selections:

EL L1 L2 **Reading: Graphic Organizer A** (partially filled in), p. 107

EL L3 **Reading: Graphic Organizer B,** p. 108

EL L1 L2 **Literary Analysis: Graphic Organizer A** (partially filled in), p. 109

Skills Development/Extension

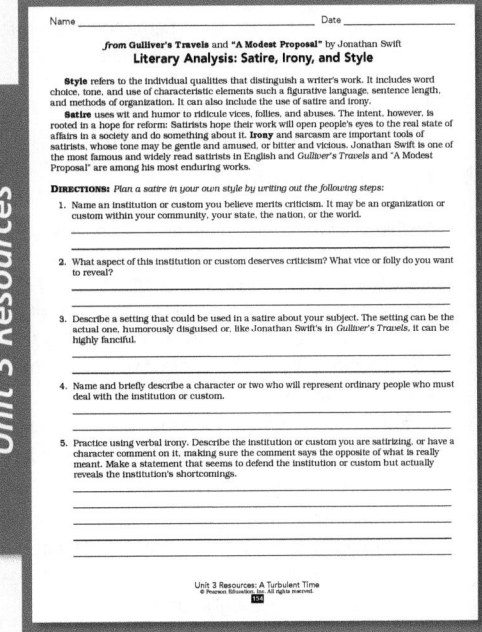

All **Literary Analysis,** p. 157

Also available for these selections:

All **Reading,** p. 158

EL L3 L4 **Support for Writing,** p. 160

L4 **Enrichment,** p. 161

Assessment

L3 L4 **Open-Book Test,** pp. 162–163

Also available for these selections:

EL L1 L2 **Selection Test A,** pp. 165–167

EL L3 L4 **Selection Test B,** pp. 168–170

PHLit Online!
www.PHLitOnline.com

Online Resources: All print materials are also available online.

- complete narrated selection text
- a thematically related video with writing prompt
- an interactive graphic organizer
- highlighting feature
- access to all student print resources, adapted to individual student needs
- Spanish and English summaries
- adapted selection translations in Spanish

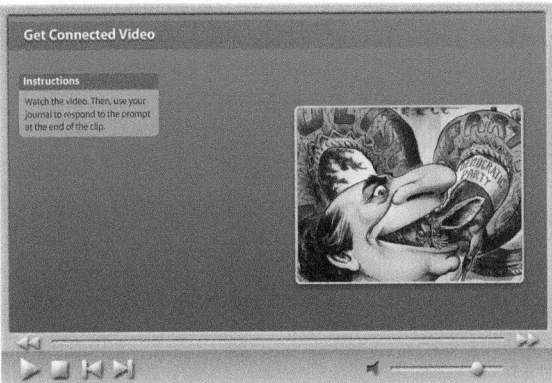

Get Connected! (thematic video with writing prompt)

Also available:

Background Video
All videos are available in Spanish.

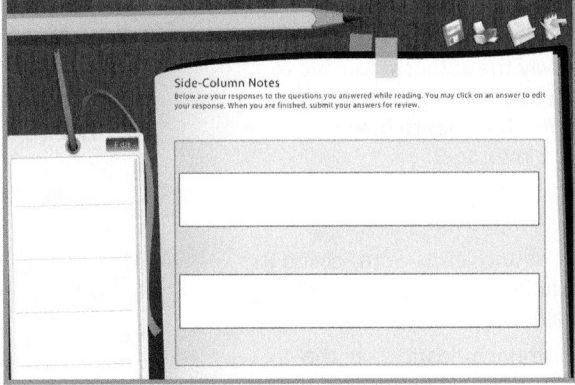

Writer's Journal (with graphics feature)

Also available:

Vocabulary Central (tools and activities for studying vocabulary)

❶ Connecting to the Essential Question

1. Review the assignment with the class.

2. Prepare students to write by suggesting that they make notes about current practices or attitudes that they think should be changed.

3. As students read, have them look for similarities between their lists and Swift's targets.

❷ Literary Analysis

Introduce the skill using the instruction on the student page.

Think Aloud: Model the Skill

Say to students:

I know that satire uses humor to expose and mock human foibles. As I read, I will look for passages that appear exaggerated or amusing. Then I will stop and try to figure out what Swift really means.

❸ Reading Strategy

1. Introduce the skill using the instruction on the student page.

2. Give students a copy of **Reading Strategy Graphic Organizer B, page 108** in *Graphic Organizer Transparencies,* to fill out as they read.

Think Aloud: Model the Skill

Say to students:

The text structure often reveals the way the author wants me to think about ideas. I can look at text features for clues to help me clarify Swift's message.

❹ Vocabulary

1. Pronounce each word, giving its definition, and have students say it aloud.

2. For more guidance, see the *Classroom Strategies and Teaching Routines* card for introducing vocabulary.

Before You Read | from *Gulliver's Travels* • *A Modest Proposal*

❶ Connecting to the Essential Question Like Jonathan Swift in his time, you might want to criticize social practices of today that you find annoying or disturbing. As you read the excerpts from *Gulliver's Travels* and the essay "A Modest Proposal," identify the subjects that Swift targets in his satire. Doing so will help as you answer the Essential Question: **How does literature shape or reflect society?**

Common Core State Standards

Reading Literature
6. Analyze a case in which grasping point of view requires distinguishing what is directly stated in a text from what is really meant.

❷ Literary Analysis

Satire is writing that uses humor to expose and ridicule vice and folly. Satirical writing can appear in many genres—for example, Swift's *Gulliver's Travels* is a *satirical novel* and "A Modest Proposal" is a *satirical essay.* Although satirists unmask evils, they sometimes conceal their point of view by masking their targets in order to avoid the dangers involved in naming real people, places, or beliefs. Swift uses masks such as the following in *Gulliver's Travels*:

- imaginary lands and people, such as Lilliput and the Lilliputians
- fictional conflicts, like the conflict between Big- and Little-Endians

In his essay, Swift uses these devices:

- *understatement*, in which the literal meaning falls short of the topic; saying you cannot think of one objection to a terrifying proposal is an example.
- *hyperbole*, or exaggeration
- *sarcasm*, or a bitter way of saying the opposite of what you mean

Comparing Literary Works In both his novel and his essay, Swift uses the satirical weapon of **irony,** a surprising contradiction between reality and appearance or between the actual and intended meaning of words.

❸ Reading Strategy

Preparing to Read Complex Texts By **analyzing and evaluating information from text features** such as background and footnotes, you can better understand Swift's irony and his point of view. Use a chart like the one shown to analyze text features and show how they clarify Swift's meaning.

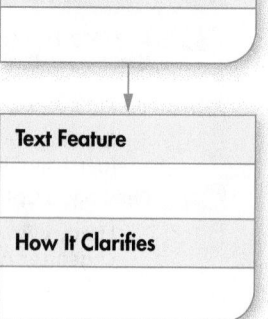

Passage

↓

Text Feature

How It Clarifies

❹ Vocabulary

conjecture (kən jek´ chər) *v.* guess (p. 607)

schism (siz´ əm) *n.* division of a group into factions (p. 608)

expedient (ek spē´ dē ənt) *n.* device used in an emergency (p. 609)

sustenance (sus´ tə nəns) *n.* food or money to support life (p. 618)

commodity (kə mäd´ ə tē) *n.* product that is bought or sold (p. 619)

censure (sen´ shər) *v.* strongly disapprove; condemn (p. 621)

PHLit Online!
www.PHLitOnline.com

Vocabulary Development

Vocabulary Knowledge Rating

Create a **Vocabulary Knowledge Rating Chart** (*Professional Development Guidebook,* p. 33) for the vocabulary words on the student page. Give each student a copy of the chart with the words on it. Read the words aloud, and have students mark their rating in the Before Reading column. Urge students to attend to these words as they read and discuss the selections.

In order to gauge how much instruction you need to provide, tally how many students are confident in their knowledge of each word. As students read, point out the words and their context.

 **Vocabulary Central,** featuring tools and activities for studying vocabulary, is available online at **www.PHLitOnline.com.**

⑤ Jonathan Swift (1667–1745)

Author of *Gulliver's Travels* •
"A Modest Proposal"

Swift was born in Dublin, Ireland, to English parents, although his father died before he was born. With the assistance of relatives, he received a good education and then obtained an appointment in the household of Sir William Temple, a wealthy diplomat who lived on an estate in Surrey, England. Swift hoped for a career in politics, but receiving no support from Sir William, he decided on a career in the church. After Temple's death in 1699, he was given a small parish near London.

Satirist The satirical writing Swift had done while in the Temple household was out of character for a clergyman, but its brilliance was widely acknowledged in 1704 when he published his satires as two separate books: *A Tale of a Tub*, which satirizes excesses in religion and learning, and *The Battle of the Books*, which describes a comic encounter between ancient and modern literature.

Ambition and Achievement When the authorship of Swift's religious satires became known, Swift lost favor in the eyes of many church officials and also lost opportunities for advancement. Although he failed to achieve his goal of becoming a bishop in the Church of England, Swift remained a staunch defender of the Anglican faith. His political allegiance, however, shifted completely in 1710 when he left the Whig party to join the Tory party favored by Queen Anne. He benefited immediately from this move. As the leading party writer for the government, he wrote many pamphlets and wielded considerable political influence.

The Story Behind *Gulliver's Travels* Swift's most famous book, the novel *Gulliver's Travels*, began as a humorous assignment from the Scriblerus Club, a group of Swift's sharp-witted literary friends. These writers, who delighted in making fun of literary pretensions, gave Swift the project of writing a series of amusing, imaginary journeys because they knew he enjoyed reading travel books.

Later Years Although embittered by his failure to be named a bishop, Swift served for more than thirty years as dean of St. Patrick's Cathedral in Dublin. His caustic wit did not flag, as shown in the savage satire "A Modest Proposal" (1729), on starvation in Ireland. His death in 1745 deprived the world of a generous and learned man who despised fanaticism, selfishness, and pride.

from Gulliver's Travels • A Modest Proposal **605**

Daily Bellringer

For each class during which you will teach these selections, have students complete one of the five activities for the appropriate week in the *Daily Bellringer Activities* booklet.

Multidraft Reading

To assist struggling readers and to enhance reading for all, assign the text in chunks, as warranted by length, and apply multidraft reading protocols. For each reading, have students set the purpose indicated:

- **First reading**—identifying key ideas and details and answering any Reading Checks.
- **Second reading**—analyzing craft and structure and responding to the side-column prompts.
- **Third reading**—integrating knowledge and ideas, connecting to other texts and the world, and answering the end-of-selection questions.

For more guidance, refer to the *Classroom Strategies and Teaching Routines* card on multidraft reading.

⑤ Background
More About the Author

Swift suffered from a disease called Ménière's disease. This illness of the inner ear causes nausea and vertigo. Unfortunately, not much was known about the disease in Swift's lifetime. The disease became more acute as Swift aged.

After the death of Queen Anne (1714), Swift's career in England was over. He returned to Ireland, where he began to pour out satires and poetry. Dating to this "exile" are his most famous works, *Gulliver's Travels* and "A Modest Proposal." The biting satire of the latter still has the power to shake up readers. Swift is considered the greatest prose satirist in the English language.

PHLit Online!
www.PHLitOnline.com

Teaching From Technology

Preparing to Read
Go to **www.PHLitOnline.com** in class or in a lab and display the *Get Connected!* slideshow these selections. Have the class brainstorm for responses to the slideshow writing prompt, entering ideas in the interactive journal. Then, have students complete their written responses individually, in a lab or as homework.

To build background, display the Background and More About the Author feature.

Using the Interactive Text
Go to **www.PHLitOnline.com** and display the Enriched Online Student Edition. As the class reads the selection or listens to the narration, record answers to side-column prompts using the graphic organizers accessible on the interactive page. Alternatively, have students use the online edition individually, answering the prompts as they read.

❶ About the Selection

Swift sends Gulliver to Lilliput to do a job he probably never could have done so well at home: make fun of the religious conflicts of his day. By exposing the conflict between the Big-Endians and the Little-Endians over which end of the egg to break, Swift, through Gulliver, comments with wry wit on the religious and political absurdities over which people do serious battle.

In "A Voyage to Brobdingnag," Swift satirizes English attitudes and modern warfare. To do so, he sends Gulliver to Brobdingnag, a place in which the people are twelve times as tall as Gulliver.

❷ Activating Prior Knowledge

List the following on the chalkboard and ask students to make connections among the entries. (Students should recognize that all of these mock or satirize something.)

• *Doonesbury*

• *Saturday Night Live* skits

• Weird Al Yankovic songs

Guide students to explain on their own the humor and significance of the satire. Have students select one of these satirical vehicles in which they are familiar. Have them write a paragraph explaining how it uses humor, exaggeration, or laughter to poke fun at a serious subject. Ask students to explain why the use of humor has more impact on listeners than a serious tone would have.

Concept Connector ➡

Tell students they will return to their responses after reading the selection.

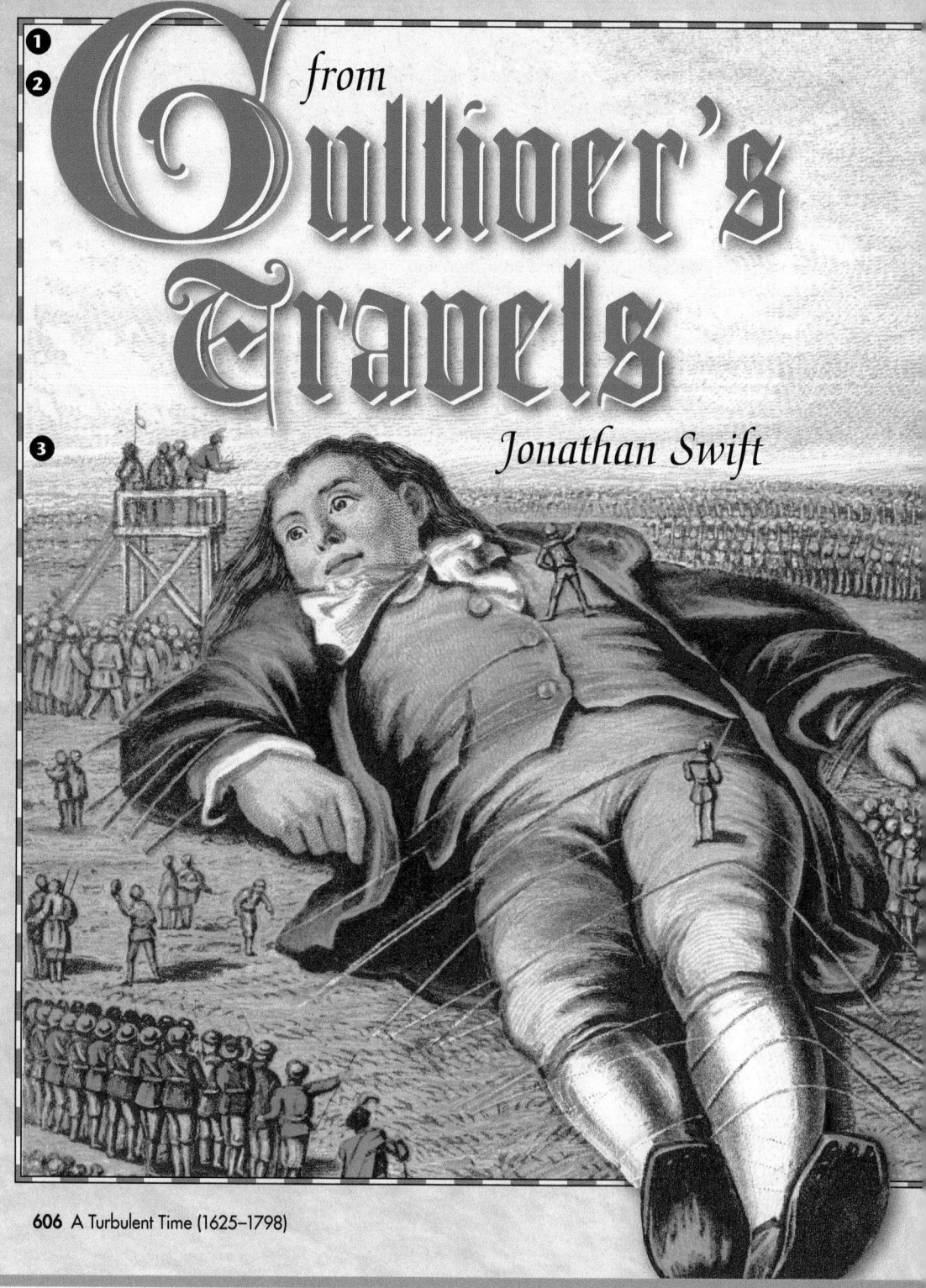

from

Gulliver's Travels

Jonathan Swift

606 A Turbulent Time (1625–1798)

© Text Complexity Rubric: Leveled Texts

	from Gulliver's Travels	A Modest Proposal
Qualitative Measures		
Context/ Knowledge Demands	Satirical fantasy; historical knowledge demands 1 2 3 ④ 5	Satirical essay; historical and literary demands 1 2 ③ 4 5
Structure/Language Conventionality and Clarity	Long sentences 1 2 ③ 4 5	Complex syntax; formal diction; long sentences 1 2 ③ 4 5
Levels of Meaning/ Purpose/Concept Level	Moderate (politics, royalty, and religious disputes) 1 2 ③ 4 5	Challenging (deeply ironic social commentary) 1 2 3 ④ 5
Quantitative Measures		
Lexile/Text Length	1480L / 3,604 words	1810L / 3,401 words
Overall Complexity	**More accessible**	**More complex**

Background

Swift's era was marked by religious and political strife. Reacting against the intolerance displayed in these conflicts, he ridiculed those whose pride overcame their reason. His novel *Gulliver's Travels* satirizes such intolerance by means of four imaginary voyages of Lemuel Gulliver, the narrator, a well-educated but unimaginative ship's surgeon. In "A Voyage to Lilliput," for example, Swift focuses on disputes between the established Church of England and Roman Catholicism, calling the followers of each Little-Endians and Big-Endians, respectively. He also satirizes the religious wars between Protestant England and Catholic France, disguising them as a conflict between Lilliput and Blefuscu. In "A Voyage to Brobdingnag," he suggests that the politicians leading England are guilty of "ignorance, idleness, and vice."

from A Voyage to Lilliput

After being shipwrecked, Gulliver swims to shore and drifts off to sleep. When he awakens, he finds that he has been tied down by the Lilliputians (lil´ ə pyoo͞´ shənz), a race of people who are only six inches tall. Though he is held captive and his sword and pistols are taken from him, Gulliver gradually begins to win the Lilliputians' favor because of his mild disposition, and he is eventually granted his freedom. Through Gulliver's exposure to Lilliputian politics and court life, the reader becomes increasingly aware of the remarkable similarities between the English and Lilliputian affairs of state. The following excerpt begins during a discussion between the Lilliputian Principal Secretary of Private Affairs and Gulliver concerning the affairs of the Lilliputian empire.

We are threatened with an invasion from the island of Blefuscu,[1] which is the other great empire of the universe, almost as large and powerful as this of his Majesty. For as to what we have heard you affirm, that there are other kingdoms and states in the world, inhabited by human creatures as large as yourself, our philosophers are in much doubt, and would rather conjecture that you dropped from the moon, or one of the stars; because it is certain, that an hundred mortals of your bulk would, in a short time, destroy all the fruits

---

1. **Blefuscu** represents France.

4 ◄ Critical Viewing What passages in the text reveal that Lilliputians now trust Gulliver more than they did in the episode depicted here? **[Infer]**

Vocabulary
conjecture (kən jek´ chər)
v. guess

5 ☑ Reading Check
From where do the Lilliputians think Gulliver came?

from Gulliver's Travels **607**

3 Humanities

Illustration from a nineteenth-century edition of *Gulliver's Travels*

The picture shows a large, wide-eyed, and somewhat cherubic-looking Gulliver in the typical English dress of his day. Gulliver seems undisturbed by the extraordinary situation in which he finds himself—tied down to a vast plain and surrounded by endless regiments of Lilliputians.

Use these questions for discussion:

1. Why do you think the artist shows Gulliver looking so relaxed?
Possible responses: Gulliver is not worried about these little people. He may realize that the cords cannot hold him. Gulliver may be amused by what he sees or shocked at the situation.

2. Why are there so many Lilliputians in this picture? Why are they arranged in regiments, or military groupings?
Answer: The number of Lilliputians makes it clear that Gulliver has found himself among an entire race of people who are six inches tall. They may be shown in "formations" to make it clear that the Lilliputians are an organized, legitimate society, capable of doing all the things that full-sized people do.

4 Critical Viewing

Possible responses: The entire conversation with the secretary shows that they trust Gulliver, as well as the fact that Gulliver is allowed to make suggestions.

5 Reading Check

Answer: They think he dropped from the moon or a star.

© Text Complexity: Reader and Task Suggestions

from **Gulliver's Travels**		**A Modest Proposal**	
Preparing to Read the Text	**Leveled Tasks**	**Preparing to Read the Text**	**Leveled Tasks**
• Using the Background on TE p. 605, discuss how the loss of a career may have led Swift to write satire. • Review strategies for using text features such as introductory background notes and footnotes to help clarify Swift's satire. • Guide students to use Multidraft Reading strategies (TE p. 605).	*Knowledge Demands* If students will have difficulty with the historical targets of Swift's satire, have them focus on plot events and settings in their first reading. Then, as they reread, have them concentrate on the general satire of human foibles. *Synthesizing* If students will not have difficulty with the targets of Swift's satire, have them discuss the general impression that his satirical details convey about England in his day.	• Using the Background on p. 605, explain social conditions in Ireland in Swift's day. • Remind students that irony says the opposite of what is meant in order to make a point and is a common tool of satire. • Guide students to use Multidraft Reading strategies (TE p. 605).	*Levels of Meaning* If students will have difficulty with Swift's irony, have them read the selection in sections, pausing periodically to ask themselves, "Does he really mean that? If not, what does he mean?" As they reread, have students focus on main points. *Evaluating* If students will not have difficulty with irony, have them consider whether satire is effective in exposing a social problem to readers who are part of the problem.

Spiral Review

Denotation and Word Choice

1. Remind students that they studied the concepts of denotation and word choice in an earlier lesson.

2. **Ask** the Spiral Review question.

   Possible response: In the context of the selection, *schism* carries a negative meaning. It implies a radical break from an established norm.

⑥ Literary Analysis

Satire

1. Review with students their understanding of satire as writing that uses humor to expose and ridicule human vice and folly. **Ask** students to name "masks" Swift uses to conceal real people, places, or beliefs.
   Answer: Swift uses imaginary lands, made-up characters, and fictional conflicts of belief to conceal the real people and issues.

2. Point out the amusing and satirical nature of the secretary's comments that Gulliver's land and people cannot exist. Tell them that Swift is satirizing those who, even faced with evidence, will not be convinced.

3. Have students read the description of the two empires. **Ask:** What two world powers are ridiculed in this passage?
   Answer: The two nation-states in the satire represent England and France and their inability to see each other's point of view.

4. Remind students that religious conflict between Protestants and Catholics was Swift's chief target here. **Ask:** Is the decision over which end of an egg to break an important issue?
   Answer: No, It is a very trivial one.

5. **Ask** the Literary Analysis question.
   Possible responses: Students might say that Swift is suggesting that all wars are, at root, absurd. Swift picks a trivial issue to show how foolish it is to allow narrow-minded opinions and uncompromising positions to determine public policy.

Literary Analysis
Satire Why do you think Swift chooses the correct way to break eggs as the cause of conflict between Lilliput and Blefuscu?

Vocabulary
schism (siz´ əm) *n.* division of a group into factions

Spiral Review
Denotation and Word Choice Read the vocabulary word *schism* in context. What conclusions can you draw about the positive or negative nuances of *schism*?

and cattle of his Majesty's dominions. Besides, our histories of six thousand moons make no mention of any other regions, than the two great empires of Lilliput and Blefuscu. Which two mighty powers have, as I was going to tell you, been engaged in a most obstinate war for six and thirty moons past. It began upon the following occasion. It is allowed on all hands, that the primitive way of breaking eggs before we eat them, was upon the larger end; but his present Majesty's grandfather, while he was a boy, going to eat an egg, and breaking it according to the ancient practice, happened to cut one of his fingers. Whereupon the Emperor, his father, published an edict, commanding all his subjects, upon great penalties, to break the smaller end of their eggs. The people so highly resented this law that our histories tell us there have been six rebellions raised on that account; wherein one emperor lost his life, and another his crown.[2] These civil commotions were constantly fomented by the monarchs of Blefuscu; and when they were quelled, the exiles always fled for refuge to that empire. It is computed that eleven thousand persons have, at several times, suffered death rather than submit to break their eggs at the smaller end. Many hundred large volumes have been published upon this controversy; but the books of the Big-Endians have been long forbidden, and the whole party rendered incapable by law of holding employments.[3] During the course of these troubles, the emperors of Blefuscu did frequently expostulate[4] by their ambassadors, accusing us of making a <u>schism</u> in religion, by offending against a fundamental doctrine of our great prophet Lustrog, in the fifty-fourth chapter of the *Brundecral* (which is their Alcoran).[5] This, however, is thought to be a mere strain upon the text, for the words are these: That all true believers shall break their eggs at the convenient end; and which is the convenient end, seems, in my humble opinion, to be left to every man's conscience, or at least in the power of the chief magistrate[6] to determine. Now the Big-Endian exiles have found so much credit in the Emperor of Blefuscu's court, and so much private assistance and encouragement from their party here at home, that a bloody war hath been carried on between the two empires for six and thirty moons with various success; during which time we have lost forty capital ships, and a much greater number of smaller vessels, together with thirty thousand of our best seamen and soldiers; and the damage received by the enemy is reckoned to be somewhat greater than ours. However, they have now equipped a numerous fleet,

⑥

---

2. **It is allowed . . . crown** Here, Swift satirizes the dispute in England between the Catholics (Big-Endians) and Protestants (Little-Endians). King Henry VIII who "broke" with the Catholic church, King Charles I, who "lost his life," and King James, who lost his "crown," are each referred to in the passage.
3. **the whole party . . . employments** The Test Act (1673) prevented Catholics from holding office.
4. **expostulate** (eks päs´ chə lāt´) *v.* reason earnestly with.
5. **Alcoran** Koran, the sacred book of Muslims.
6. **chief magistrate** ruler.

Enrichment: Investigating Religion

Swift's Religious Beliefs
Though Swift mocks belief in his tales, it was his own deeply held beliefs that directed his writing career. For Swift, religion meant rational Anglicanism, so both Catholics and Nonconformists were seen as a threat. Swift's reason for leaving the Whigs, with whom he agreed on most points of politics, was that they were too tolerant of Nonconformists. He remained passionately devoted to the Anglican church, even as he wrote pamphlets in Ireland deriding the English government.

Activity: Analyze a Religious Controversy
Ask interested students to learn more about the schism between the Catholic and Anglican Churches and the Nonconformists. Tell them to use print and online sources to research its origin and its impact on events during Swift's day. Suggest that they record their analysis in the **Enrichment: Investigating Religion and Myth** worksheet, *Professional Development Guidebook,* page 240.

and are just preparing to make a descent upon us; and his Imperial Majesty, placing great confidence in your valor and strength, hath commanded me to lay this account of his affairs before you.

I desired the Secretary to present my humble duty to the Emperor, and to let him know, that I thought it would not become me, who was a foreigner, to interfere with parties; but I was ready, with the hazard of my life, to defend his person and state against all invaders.

The empire of Blefuscu is an island situated to the north-northeast side of Lilliput, from whence it is parted only by a channel of eight hundred yards wide. I had not yet seen it, and upon this notice of an intended invasion, I avoided appearing on that side of the coast, for fear of being discovered by some of the enemy's ships, who had received no intelligence of me, all intercourse between the two empires having been strictly forbidden during the war, upon pain of death, and an embargo laid by our Emperor upon all vessels whatsoever. I communicated to his Majesty a project I had formed of seizing the enemy's whole fleet; which, as our scouts assured us, lay at anchor in the harbor ready to sail with the first fair wind. I consulted the most experienced seamen upon the depth of the channel, which they had often plumbed, who told me, that in the middle at high water it was seventy *glumgluffs* deep (which is about six feet of European measure), and the rest of it fifty *glumgluffs* at most. I walked to the northeast coast over against Blefuscu, where, lying down behind a hillock, I took out my small pocket perspective-glass, and viewed the enemy's fleet at anchor, consisting of about fifty men of war, and a great number of transports. I then came back to my house and gave order (for which I had a warrant) for a great quantity of the strongest cable and bars of iron. The cable was about as thick as pack-thread, and the bars of the length and size of a knitting-needle. I trebled the cable to make it stronger, and for the same reason I twisted three of the iron bars together, bending the extremities into a hook. Having thus fixed fifty hooks to as many cables, I went back to the northeast coast and, putting off my coat, shoes, and stockings, walked into the sea in my leathern jerkin, about half an hour before high water. I waded with what haste I could, and swam in the middle about thirty yards until I felt ground; I arrived at the fleet in less than half an hour. The enemy was so frightened when they saw me, that they leaped out of their ships, and swam to shore, where there could not be fewer than thirty thousand souls. I then took my tackling, and, fastening a hook to the hole at the prow of each, I tied all the cords together at the end. While I was thus employed, the enemy discharged several thousand arrows, many of which struck in my hands and face and, besides the excessive smart, gave me much disturbance in my work. My greatest apprehension was for my eyes, which I should have infallibly lost, if I had not suddenly thought of an expedient. I kept

from Gulliver's Travels **609**

LITERATURE IN CONTEXT

❼ The Vocabulary of Religious Conflict

The word *schism*, which Swift uses in describing the conflict between Big-Endians and Little-Endians, is an important term in the history of religious conflict. This term comes from the Greek word *schizein*, meaning "divide," and it can mean simply "to cleave or cut." Traditionally, it has been applied to a split in an organized group (especially a church), the act of trying to cause such a split, or a sect formed by the split. By using this word in describing the controversy between Big-Endians and Little-Endians, Swift signals readers that his fiction refers to a significant religious conflict.

Connect to the Literature

What further divisions have come as a result of Lilliput's schism in religion?

Vocabulary
expedient (ek spē′ dē ənt) *n.* device used in an emergency

❽
Reading Check

How does Gulliver plan to defend the Lilliputians against invasion?

---

❼ Literature in Context
The Vocabulary of Religious Conflict

The word *schism* was originally used to describe groups that broke away from the church because of disagreements over something other than church doctrine. The word did not at first imply heresy, but that changed over time. Hence, *schism* once meant being different but not necessarily wrong. Eventually, it meant both.

When Swift wrote, the world was still reeling from the Reformation, when Protestants split from the Roman Catholic Church. Not long after the initial split, England's King Henry VIII declared that he, instead of the Pope, was the head of the English Church. At the time of the Restoration of the English monarchy, the Act of Uniformity was passed (1662). A period of persecution followed. As a result, almost 2,000 Nonconformist ministers were ejected from their positions. The Conventicle Act of 1664 punished people over age 16 for attending religious meetings that did not conform to the Anglican *Book of Common Prayer*.

In 1685, Charles II's Roman Catholic brother, James II, became king. During the "Glorious Revolution" (1688), James was deposed and William and Mary became joint rulers of England.

Connect to the Literature

Explain to students that the English turmoil of schism after schism created Jonathan Swift's horror of religious disagreement.
Ask: What further divisions have come as a result of Lilliput's schism in religion?
Answer: The religious difference led to war, rebellion, exile, and discrimination in employment.

❽ Reading Check

Answer: Gulliver plans to seize the enemy's whole fleet.

Differentiated Instruction for Universal Access

Support for Special-Needs Students
Pronounce the place names, or use the *Hear It!* Audio CD to help students become more familiar with Gulliver's world. Remind students that the places and people are make-believe, but that the issues they represent are real.

Support for Less Proficient Readers
Have students read from "A Voyage to Lilliput" silently as they listen to the *Hear It!* Audio CD. Then guide students in a discussion about the conflict between the Big-Endians and the Little-Endians and what it suggests about Lilliputian society.

Enrichment for Gifted/Talented Students
Have students work in pairs to illustrate a scene described in "A Voyage to Lilliput." Encourage students to incorporate as many details from *Gulliver's Travels* as possible in their illustrations. You may want to refer students to the examples of fine art throughout this lesson.

Satire and Irony

1. Point out to students that Swift goes back and forth between obvious parallels and hidden or ironic parallels. The narrow channel between the two countries clearly represents the English Channel. Water depth is measured in units that are approximately six feet, as they are in English (the fathom). As was true for both countries, it was sea power that determined one's strength.

2. **Ask** students to explain why Gulliver decides to put on glasses (spectacles).
   Answer: to protect himself from arrows
   Reteach: Remind students that the irony that Swift uses creates a contradiction between reality and appearances.

3. **Ask** students the Literary Analysis question: What is ironic about Gulliver using spectacles as a shield in a military operation?
   Possible responses: Being made of glass, the spectacles seem to be a fragile shield, yet they successfully protect Gulliver's eyes, as the arrows bounce off them. Spectacles are generally used for such quiet, civilian pursuits as reading and writing, and one removes them before fights, rather than putting them on.

4. You may wish to discuss, in light of Swift's belief in rationalism, the way in which Gulliver, with his reading glasses protecting him from arrows, might represent the man of reason and learning triumphing over brute force.

Literary Analysis
Satire and Irony What is ironic about Gulliver using spectacles as a shield in a military operation?

❾

among other little necessaries a pair of spectacles in a private pocket, which, as I observed before, had escaped the Emperor's searchers. These I took out and fastened as strongly as I could upon my nose and thus armed went on boldly with my work in spite of the enemy's arrows, many of which struck against the glasses of my spectacles, but without any other effect further than a little to discompose them. I had now fastened all the hooks and, taking the knot in my hand, began to pull, but not a ship would stir, for they were all too fast held by their anchors, so that the boldest part of my enterprise remained. I therefore let go the cord, and, leaving the hooks fixed to the ships, I resolutely cut with my knife the cables that fastened the anchors, receiving above two hundred shots in my face and hands; then I took up the knotted end of the cables to which my hooks were tied and, with great ease, drew fifty of the enemy's largest men-of-war after me.

The Blefuscudians, who had not the least imagination of what I intended, were at first confounded with astonishment. They had seen me cut the cables and thought my design was only to let the ships run adrift or fall foul on each other; but when they perceived the whole fleet, moving in order, and saw me pulling at the end, they set up such a scream of grief and despair that it is almost impossible to describe or conceive. When I had got out of danger, I stopped a while to pick out the arrows that stuck in my hands and face, and rubbed on some of the same ointment that was given me at my first arrival, as I have formerly mentioned. I then took off my spectacles, and, waiting about an hour until the tide was a little fallen, I waded through the middle with my cargo and arrived safe at the royal port of Lilliput.

The Emperor and his whole court stood on the shore expecting the issue of this great adventure. They saw the ships move forward in a large half-moon but could not discern me, who was up to my breast in water. When I advanced to the middle of the channel, they were yet more in pain, because I was under water to my neck. The Emperor concluded me to be drowned, and that the enemy's fleet was approaching in a hostile manner; but he was soon eased of his fears; for, the channel growing shallower every step I made, I came in a short time within hearing, and holding up the end of the cable by which the fleet was fastened, I cried in a loud voice, Long live the most puissant[7] Emperor of Lilliput! This great prince received me at my landing with all possible encomiums and created me a *Nardac* upon the spot, which is the highest title of honor among them.

His Majesty desired I would take some other opportunity of bringing all the rest of his enemy's ships into his ports. And so unmeasurable is the ambition of princes, that he seemed to think of nothing less than reducing the whole empire of Blefuscu into a province and governing it by a viceroy; of destroying the Big-Endian exiles and compelling that people to break the smaller end of their eggs,

---

7. **puissant** (pyo͞o′ i sənt) *adj.* powerful.

Enrichment: Investigating a Key Person in History

The Stuarts

The "Glorious Revolution" replaced the unpopular James II with his Protestant daughter Mary and her husband William. Mary died in 1694. At William's death in 1702, Mary's younger sister, Anne, became queen. While Anne was the first monarch to rule over Great Britain (England and Scotland were united in 1707), she was the last sovereign to veto an act of Parliament. She was also the last Stuart monarch.

Activity: Investigate Political Figures Ask interested students to learn more about William and Mary or Queen Anne. Have them identify their accomplishments, create a timeline of important events, and describe how the person influenced history. Suggest that they record their analysis in the **Enrichment: Investigating a Key Person in History** worksheet, *Professional Development Guidebook*, page 233.

◄ **❶ Critical Viewing**
What specific details from the text does this picture illustrate?
[Connect]

A Voyage to Lilliput, Illustration from a nineteenth-century edition of *Gulliver's Travels*

by which he would remain sole monarch of the whole world. But I endeavored to divert him from this design by many arguments drawn from the topics of policy as well as justice, and I plainly protested that I would never be an instrument of bringing a free and brave people into slavery. And when the matter was debated in council, the wisest part of the ministry were of my opinion.

This open bold declaration of mine was so opposite to the schemes and politics of his Imperial Majesty that he could never

✓ Reading Check **❷**
Summarize the action Gulliver takes against the fleet of Blefuscu.

from Gulliver's Travels **611**

A Voyage to Lilliput: **Illustration from a nineteenth-century edition of** *Gulliver's Travels*

Here Gulliver indulgently helps the Lilliputians and averts violence by stealing the fleet of their enemies, the Blefuscudians. In the illustration, Gulliver seems intent only on his task, while the Lilliputians cheer their new hero and celebrate such an easy victory.

Use these questions for discussion:

1. Why are the Lilliputians pictured in full military dress?
   Possible response: The Lilliputians could not be sure how Gulliver's efforts would turn out. They are ready for an attack by the Blefuscudians.

2. Why doesn't Gulliver smile and wave in light of the fact that the crowd is delighted by his efforts on their behalf?
   Possible response: Gulliver has done what he felt needed to be done. He has no personal stake in the outcome or any reason to feel proud: He was simply bigger than his opponents.

⓫ Critical Viewing

Answer: The illustration shows Gulliver returning with the Blefuscudian fleet, while the emperor and his court stand on the shore. Gulliver is holding the cable towing the fleet. It also shows that Gulliver is wearing glasses to protect his eyes.

⓬ Reading Check

Answer: He goes to Blefescu armed with cables and bars. He frightens the defenders away from their ships, ties a hook and a length of cable to each ship's prow, puts on spectacles to protect his eyes, cuts loose the anchors, and drags the fleet into Lilliput's harbor.

Differentiated Instruction for Universal Access

 **Support for English Learners**
To help students recognize words and know how they sound, play the *Hear It!* **CD** of this selection, and have students follow along in their textbooks. Identify unfamiliar words, and help students define and pronounce them. For items such as Gulliver's coat, shoes, stockings, spectacles, and jerkin, you may want to find an illustration and point to each of these things. Terms related to the sea and ships (*channel, port, anchor, man-of-war*) may also need identification or describing.

Enrichment for Gifted/Talented Students
Gulliver's Travels is a delightful tale that can be appreciated on the level of pure fantasy. Students may be interested in imagining other adventures Gulliver could have had in Lilliput, and what other advantages and difficulties he might have encountered. Encourage them to use what they know of Gulliver's personality and character to write a scene in which he has further discussions or adventure in the world of Lilliput or, perhaps, in Blefuscu.

Satire

1. Direct student attention to the bracketed passage and point out that it continues onto the next page.

2. **Ask** the Literary Analysis question: Which satirical details in the first paragraph of "A Voyage to Brobdingnag" relate to England and which relate to humanity in general? Explain.
Answer: References to the king and queen, Whig or Tory, and "the scourge of France" point directly to England. Details that refer to humanity in general include references to trade, wars by sea and land, religious schisms, and political parties, and the entire sentence about "those creatures" and their houses, cities as nests and burrows, vanity ("make a figure in dress"), emotions, and faults ("fight," "cheat," "betray").

❶❹ **Reading Strategy**

Analyzing Text Features

1. Direct students' attention to the footnote at the bottom of the page. Point out the line in which Gulliver speaks of England as "my own beloved country."

2. **Ask** students the Reading Strategy question: Based on what you have learned from text features about this historical period, what is satirical about the king laughingly asking whether Gulliver is "a Whig or a Tory?"
Answer: Swift started out as Whig and changed his allegiance to the Tory party. By this time, Swift's career in England was over, he was living in Ireland, and he was writing pamphlets and stories (including this very story) criticizing the English government.

---

forgive me; he mentioned it in a very artful manner at council, where I was told that some of the wisest appeared, at least, by their silence, to be of my opinion; but others, who were my secret enemies, could not forbear some expressions, which by a sidewind reflected on me. And from this time began an intrigue between his Majesty and a junta of ministers maliciously bent against me, which broke out in less than two months and had like to have ended in my utter destruction. Of so little weight are the greatest services to princes when put into the balance with a refusal to gratify their passions.

from A Voyage to Brobdingnag

Gulliver's second voyage leads him to Brobdingnag (bräb´ diŋ nag´), *an island located near Alaska that is inhabited by giants twelve times as tall as Gulliver. After being sold to the Queen of Brobdingnag, Gulliver describes the English social and political institutions to the King, who reacts to his description with contempt and disgust.*

Literary Analysis
Satire Which satirical details in the first paragraph of "A Voyage to Brobdingnag" relate to England and which relate to humanity in general? Explain.

Reading Strategy
Analyzing Text Features Based on what you have learned from text features about this historical period, what is satirical about the King laughingly asking whether Gulliver is "a Whig or a Tory"?

It is the custom that every Wednesday (which, as I have before observed, was their Sabbath) the King and Queen, with the royal issue of both sexes, dine together in the apartment of his Majesty, to whom I was now become a favorite; and at these times my little chair and table were placed at his left hand before one of the saltcellars. This prince took a pleasure in conversing with me, inquiring into the manners, religion, laws, government, and learning of Europe, wherein I gave him the best account I was able. His apprehension was so clear, and his judgment so exact, that he made very wise reflections and observations upon all I said. But I confess, that after I had been a little too copious in talking of my own beloved country, of our trade, and wars by sea and land, of our schisms in religion, and parties in the state, the prejudices of his education prevailed so far, that he could not forbear taking me up in his right hand, and stroking me gently with the other, after an hearty fit of laughing, asked me whether I were a Whig or a Tory.[8] Then turning to his first minister, who waited behind him with a white staff, near as tall as the mainmast of the *Royal Sovereign*,[9] he observed how contemptible a thing was human grandeur, which could be mimicked by such diminutive insects as I. And yet, said he, I dare engage, those creatures have their titles and distinctions of honor, they contrive little nests and burrows, that they call houses and cities; they make a figure in dress and equipage;[10] they love, they fight, they dispute, they cheat, they betray. And thus he continued on, while my color came and went several times, with indignation to hear our noble country, the mistress

---

 8. **Whig . . . Tory** British political parties.
9. *Royal Sovereign* one of the largest ships in the British Navy.
10. **equipage** (ek´ wi pij´) horses and carriages.

Enrichment: Understanding Political Science

Whigs and Tories

Having the Whigs and the Tories facing off was more than politics as usual. This was, in fact, the first time in political history that there were two clearly defined, opposing parties. The Tory party wanted to maintain the prerogatives of the crown and the authority of the Church of England. It was they who were responsible for the passing of laws against the Dissenters. The Whigs, on the other hand, favored reform, the rights of the people, Parliamentary power, and tolerance of Dissenters.

Activity: Understanding the Political Party System Encourage interested students to learn more about the development of the English two-party system and compare it with similar political developments in the United States. Suggest that they record their analysis in the **Enrichment: Understanding Political Science** worksheet, *Professional Development Guidebook*, page 237.

of arts and arms, the scourge of France, the arbitress of Europe, the seat of virtue, piety, honor and truth, the pride and envy of the world, so contemptuously treated. . . .

He laughed at my odd kind of arithmetic (as he was pleased to call it) in reckoning the numbers of our people by a computation drawn from the several sects among us in religion and politics. He said he knew no reason why those who entertain opinions prejudicial to the public should be obliged to change or should not be obliged to conceal them. And, as it was tyranny in any government to require the first, so it was weakness not to enforce the second; for, a man may be allowed to keep poisons in his closets, but not to vend them about as cordials.

He observed, that among the diversions of our nobility and gentry[11] I had mentioned gaming.[12] He desired to know at what age this entertainment was usually taken up, and when it was laid down. How much of their time it employed; whether it ever went so high as to affect their fortunes. Whether mean vicious people by their dexterity in that art might not arrive at great riches, and sometimes keep our very nobles in dependence, as well as habituate them to vile[13] companions, wholly take them from the improvement of their minds, and force them, by the losses they received, to learn and practice that infamous dexterity upon others.

He was perfectly astonished with the historical account I gave him of our affairs during the last century, protesting it was only an heap of conspiracies, rebellions, murders, massacres, revolutions, banishments, the very worst effects that avarice, faction, hypocrisy, perfidiousness, cruelty, rage, madness, hatred, envy, lust, malice, and ambition could produce.

His Majesty in another audience was at the pains to recapitulate the sum of all I had spoken; compared the questions he made with the answers I had given; then taking me into his hands, and stroking me gently, delivered himself in these words, which I shall never forget, nor the manner he spoke them in. "My little friend Grildrig, you have made a most admirable panegyric upon your country. You have clearly proved that ignorance, idleness, and vice are the proper ingredients for qualifying a legislator. That laws are best explained, interpreted, and applied by those whose interest and abilities lie in perverting, confounding, and eluding them. I observe among you some lines of an institution, which in its original might have been tolerable, but these half erased, and the rest wholly blurred and blotted by corruptions. It doth not appear from all you have said how any one perfection is required toward the procurement of any one station among you, much less that men are ennobled on account of their virtue, that priests are advanced for their piety or learning, soldiers for their con-

---

11. gentry the class of landowning people ranking just below the nobility.
12. gaming gambling.
13. habituate (hə bich′ o͞o āt′) **them** to make them used to.

...after *an hearty fit of laughing, (he) asked me whether I were a Whig or a Tory.*

16 ☑ Reading Check

What does the King of Brobdingnag say in response to Gulliver's account of European customs and history?

---

15 **Critical Thinking**
Evaluate

1. **Ask** students to identify the device Swift uses in his conversation with the king to counter Gulliver's enthusiasm and provide the satire.
   Answer: Swift uses the king's questions and comments to ridicule weaknesses and evils in Gulliver's world.

2. **Ask** students to explain how Swift satirizes gambling (gaming).
   Answer: The king's questions suggest that the unscrupulous could use the sport of gambling to take advantage of others; that the foolish (including the nobility) might get hooked on gambling, which keeps them in bad company and diverts them from useful occupations; and that, to cover their losses, those who lose at gambling draw others into this habit.

3. **Ask** students whether they agree with Swift's appraisal of gambling and to explain their positions. How might Swift's evaluation apply to today's culture in which government-sponsored lotteries support social programs?
   Possible responses: Some students may agree with Swift's assessment of this habit, which leads to the poorest element of society wasting valuable resources. Others may feel it is an expedient way to tax human vice and get funds to support necessary social programs. Students should justify their answers.

16 **Reading Check**
Answer: He calls it a heap of conspiracies, rebellions, murders, massacres, and revolutions, and the worst effects faction, hypocrisy, cruelty, rage, hatred, envy, lust, malice, and ambition can produce.

Differentiated Instruction for Universal Access

Strategy for Less Proficient Readers
To help students get the most out of these tales, discuss in class the differences between Gulliver's encounters in Lilliput and in Brobdingnag. Lead students to notice that while Gulliver seems more noble than the Lilliputians, he seems more petty than the King of Brobdingnag. Ask students to identify the aspects of British society that appear in each tale. You may want to list this information on the chalkboard and discuss how, together, the tales offer a more complete picture of Swift's ideas.

Enrichment for Advanced Readers
Gulliver's Travels suggests a wealth of study topics. Students might learn more about the English "Glorious Revolution" and how it affected British political institutions; the impact of the development of gunpowder; Swift's fantasy geography (where on the globe he placed these countries and what is really located there); or even the physics of these stories (could people really be so small or so large and how would it affect their biological structures and abilities?). Have students select and research topics that interest them and share their findings with the class.

613

 Literary Analysis

Satire and Irony

1. Point out Gulliver's claim that an "extreme love of truth" is why he relates all the nasty things the King of Brobdingnag has said.

2. **Ask** students why this claim is doubly ironic.
   Answer: Rather than being reluctant to say nasty things, Swift has it as his main purpose. Later, Gulliver speaks of his cleverness in bending the truth—so much for his love of truth!

3. **Ask** the Literary Analysis question: In Gulliver's remark that he "artfully eluded" the king's questions, what is the difference between the intended meaning and the actual meaning?
   Answer: The intended meaning of Gulliver's remark is that he cleverly avoided the more difficult questions, but the actual meaning is that he lied when he thought the answer would show England in a bad light.

18 Humanities

A Voyage to Brobdingnag

In this illustration, the King of Brobdingnag carefully listens as Gulliver talks. Like a European king, he wears a golden and jeweled crown.

Use these questions for discussion:

1. What does the look on the king's face convey?
   Possible responses: The king seems sadly amused by what he hears. He may feel compassion for Gulliver, or possibly the look is one of reluctance to believe what he is hearing.

2. Gulliver's pose is relaxed. Why do you think the artist chose to represent him in such a relaxed manner?
   Possible responses: The king listens quietly, creating an atmosphere in which Gulliver says whatever comes to mind. Gulliver is unaware of the impact of his stories; what seems normal and civilized to him seems barbaric to the king.

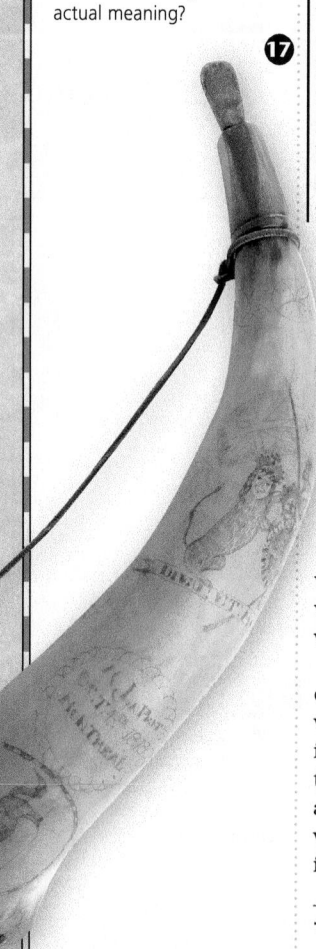

Literary Analysis
Satire and Irony In Gulliver's remark that he "artfully eluded" the King's questions, what is the difference between the intended meaning and the actual meaning?

duct or valor, judges for their integrity, senators for the love of their country, or counselors for their wisdom. As for yourself," continued the King, "who have spent the greatest part of your life in traveling, I am well disposed to hope you may hitherto have escaped many vices of your country. But, by what I have gathered from your own relation, and the answers I have with much pains wringed and extorted from you, I cannot but conclude the bulk of your natives to be the most pernicious race of little odious vermin that nature ever suffered to crawl upon the surface of the earth."

Nothing but an extreme love of truth could have hindered me from concealing this part of my story. It was in vain to discover my resentments, which were always turned into ridicule; and I was forced to rest with patience while my noble and most beloved country was so injuriously treated. I am heartily sorry as any of my readers can possibly be that such an occasion was given, but this prince happened to be so curious and inquisitive upon every particular that it could not consist either with gratitude or good manners to refuse giving him what satisfaction I was able. Yet thus much I may be allowed to say in my own vindication that I artfully eluded many of his questions and gave to every point a more favorable turn by many degrees than the strictness of truth would allow. For I have always borne that laudable partiality to my own country, which Dionysius Halicarnassensis[14] with so much justice recommends to an historian. I would hide the frailties and deformities of my political mother and place her virtues and beauties in the most advantageous light. This was my sincere endeavor in those many discourses I had with that mighty monarch, although it unfortunately failed of success.

But great allowances should be given to a king who lives wholly secluded from the rest of the world, and must therefore be altogether unacquainted with the manners and customs that most prevail in other nations: the want of which knowledge will ever produce many prejudices, and a certain narrowness of thinking, from which we and the politer countries of Europe are wholly exempted. And it would be hard indeed, if so remote a prince's notions of virtue and vice were to be offered as a standard for all mankind.

To confirm what I have now said, and further to show the miserable effects of a confined education, I shall here insert a passage which will hardly obtain belief. In hopes to ingratiate myself farther into his Majesty's favor, I told him of an invention discovered between three and four hundred years ago, to make a certain powder, into an heap of which the smallest spark of fire falling, would kindle the whole in a moment, although it were as big as a mountain, and make it all fly up in the air together, with a noise and agitation greater

---

14. **Dionysius** (dī′ ə nĭsh′ əs) **Halicarnassensis** (hal′ ə kär na sen′ sis) Greek writer who lived in Rome and attempted to persuade the Greeks to submit to their Roman conquerors.

Enrichment: Investigating Technology

Gunpowder

Point out the description on the next page of the "certain powder" that Gulliver describes. What he is describing, of course, is gunpowder. The Chinese invented an early form of gunpowder in the tenth century. The Arabs may have produced the first gun in the early 1300s, using black powder and a bamboo tube reinforced with iron. Black powder was adopted for use in firearms in Europe by the fourteenth century and was being used for peaceful purposes (mining and road building) by the seventeenth century.

Activity: Investigate Weapons Technology
Students might be interested in further researching the use of gunpowder for peaceful purposes or some of the weapons-technology Gulliver describes. Ask them to create a timeline of the technology, identifying its advantages and disadvantages and possible future developments. Suggest that they record their analysis in the **Enrichment: Investigating Technology** worksheet, *Professional Development Guidebook*, page 242.

▲ Critical Viewing **19**
Compare the relationship between Gulliver and the King of Brobdingnag as portrayed by the artist with that portrayed in the text. **[Compare and Contrast]**

A Voyage to Brobdingnag, Illustration from a nineteenth-century edition of Gulliver's Travels

than thunder. That a proper quantity of this powder rammed into an hollow tube of brass or iron, according to its bigness, would drive a ball of iron or lead with such violence and speed as nothing was able to sustain its force. That the largest balls, thus discharged, would not only destroy whole ranks of an army at once, but batter the strongest walls to the ground, sink down ships, with a thousand men in each, to the bottom of the sea; and when linked together by a chain, would cut through masts and rigging, divide hundreds of bodies in the middle, and lay all waste before them. That we often put this powder into large hollow balls of iron, and discharged them by an engine into some city we were besieging, which would rip up the pavement, tear the houses to pieces, burst and throw splinters on

20  Reading Check

What is the King's opinion of most of Gulliver's countrymen?

from Gulliver's Travels **615**

19 Critical Viewing
Answer: In the text, Gulliver sits at a small table at the king's left hand, in front of one of the saltcellars. In this illustration, he sits, with no table or saltcellar in sight, at the king's right hand. In the text, the king is described as making wise reflections on what Gulliver has to say. The artist has captured the look of wise conjecture in this illustration, which shows the king in an attitude of concentrated attention and thoughtfulness.

20 Reading Check
Answer: The king thinks that most of Gulliver's countrymen are ignorant and barbaric. He calls them "odious vermin."

Differentiated
Instruction   for Universal Access

Enrichment for Advanced Readers
Suggest that students read additional works by Jonathan Swift. Provide students with Swift's *A Tale of a Tub*, "The Battle of the Books," or have them read excerpts from Books III ("A Voyage to Laputa") and IV ("The Country of the Houyhnhnms") of *Gulliver's Travels.*

After students have read additional works by Swift, have them form discussion groups in which they compare and contrast the selections they have read. Suggest criteria for comparison, such as metaphors, imaginative details, theme, sentiment, satirical impact, style, or ideas. To extend the activity, have students present brief oral reports on their favorite Swift selections.

Before students respond, you may wish to have them write a brief objective summary of the selection. As they answer the questions below, remind them to support their answers with evidence from the text.

1. (a) When the emperor of the Lilliputians ordered his subjects to break the small end of their eggs, the Blefuscudians supported the Lilliputian rebels who wanted to continue breaking their eggs at the large end. (b) They take their dispute very seriously. It is rooted in their system of beliefs. (c) The fact that he picked something as silly as breaking eggs shows that Swift does not expect the reader to take the dispute seriously.

2. (a) The King of Brobdingnag pets Gulliver like a small pet. He speaks disparagingly of English history and culture. (b) **Possible response:** Gulliver recognizes the utility of gunpowder, but the king views gunpowder as destructive and inhuman.

3. (a) The Lilliputians are tiny and the Brobdingnagians are enormous. (b) Gulliver sees the Lilliputians as smaller in character and the Brobdingnagians as greater. (c) **Possible response:** Gulliver sees himself as superior to Lilliputians, and distances himself from their human follies. In Brobdingnag, he identifies with and defends that folly.

4. Swift uses the king's horror to express his hope that people will eventually turn away from war.

every side, dashing out the brains of all who came near. That I knew the ingredients very well, which were cheap, and common; I understood the manner of compounding them, and could direct his workmen how to make those tubes of a size proportionable to all other things in his Majesty's kingdom, and the largest need not be above two hundred foot long; twenty or thirty of which tubes, charged with the proper quantity of powder and balls, would batter down the walls of the strongest town in his dominions in a few hours, or destroy the whole metropolis, if ever it should pretend to dispute his absolute commands. This I humbly offered to his Majesty as a small tribute of acknowledgment in return of so many marks that I had received of his royal favor and protection.

The King was struck with horror at the description I had given of those terrible engines and the proposal I had made. He was amazed how so impotent and groveling an insect as I (these were his expressions) could entertain such inhuman ideas, and in so familiar a manner as to appear wholly unmoved at all the scenes of blood and desolation which I had painted as the common effects of those destructive machines; whereof he said some evil genius, enemy to mankind, must have been the first contriver. As for himself, he protested that although few things delighted him so much as new discoveries in art or in nature, yet he would rather lose half his kingdom than be privy to such a secret, which he commanded me, as I valued my life, never to mention any more.

> The King was struck with horror at the description I had given . . . and the proposal I had made.

Critical Reading

Cite textual evidence to support your responses.

© 1. **Key Ideas and Details** (a) Describe the conflict between Big-Endians and Little-Endians. (b) **Infer:** Do these two groups take their dispute seriously? Why or why not? (c) **Analyze:** What evidence is there that Swift does not want you to take the dispute seriously? Explain.

© 2. **Key Ideas and Details** (a) Citing the text, give one example of how the King of Brobdingnag shows affection toward Gulliver and one example of how he shows distaste for Gulliver's ideas. (b) **Interpret:** Show how the final disagreement between Gulliver and the King reflects a difference between ingenuity and wisdom.

© 3. **Key Ideas and Details** (a) What is the most important physical difference between Lilliputians and Brobdingnagians? (b) **Interpret:** How does this physical difference suggest other important ways in which they differ? Explain. (c) **Synthesize:** How do Lilliputians and Brobdingnagians each represent a different way of viewing humanity?

© 4. **Integration of Knowledge and Ideas** In the final paragraph, how does Swift use the King's reactions to express his own hopes for humankind?

Think Aloud

Vocabulary: Using Context
Direct students' attention to the word *desolation* in the second paragraph. Use the following "think aloud" to model the skill of using context to infer the meaning of the word.

Say to students:

A good way to figure out the meaning of an unknown word is to look carefully at the sentence in which it appears and also to look at sentences before and after it. I may not know the meaning of the word *desolation*. When I read the sentence, however, I realize that Swift is using the word to describe the effects of the terrible machines and weapons used for laying siege to human cities that he has just described for the king. I know those machines have such massive destructive power that they can batter down the walls of towns and cause the population to scatter. As a result, the area would be left empty of people and create great destruction, so I think *desolation* must mean that the town and its surroundings would be left barren and in ruins.

A Modest Proposal

Jonathan Swift

21 About the Selection

In this satire, Swift mocks the upper class and their insatiable appetites by posing an extreme solution to the problem of Ireland's increasing poverty.

22 Humanities

The Midday Meal, (oil on canvas) by Jakob Emmanuel Gaisser (1825–1899)

The intricate details in the painting serve as a perfect representation of the wealthy class Swift chooses to mock. The painting depicts a family shortly after finishing what was likely a fairly heavy meal. Details such as lavish clothing and jewelry, the food and fine china on the table, well-fed children, and the servant in the background support Swift's view of the appetites of the rich for a luxurious life.

Use these questions for discussion:

1. What details in the picture support the idea that this family's comforts contrast most sharply with the poverty of the Irish population?
   Answer: The gloves tossed on the stool suggest the leisurely and worry-free attitude of the family. The expressions and body language of the figures on the right-hand side of the table suggest they are stuffed.

2. How can illustrations such as this help enhance an essay writer's purpose or arguments?
   Possible response: Students may suggest that illustrations strengthen the writer's purpose by providing visual support for his or her ideas.

23 Critical Viewing

Possible response: The family's extravagant clothing, the ornate room, and their after-dinner torpor show the pursuit of luxury that Swift addresses.

Background

Swift recognized that the best audience for "A Modest Proposal" was the upper class—a group of people who had the ability to make changes for the better in Ireland. On a satirical level, however, Swift's essay mocks this very group of people. He suggests that their relentless pursuit of luxury has developed in them a taste for almost unimaginable delicacies. In this way, they become the perfect target for his modest proposal.

23 ▲ Critical Viewing
In what way does this painting embody the "relentless pursuit of luxury" that Swift addresses through his essay? **[Interpret]**

A Modest Proposal **617**

Differentiated Instruction for Universal Access

Culturally Responsive Instruction

Culture Connection Students may lack the background knowledge and context-building experiences necessary to comprehend the selection. Before students read, locate Ireland on a map or globe and show pictures of the countryside and its people. Explain that Swift was born in Dublin (a major Irish city) to English parents. He cared deeply about the Irish people. During this time period, the Irish people were subject to discriminatory laws because of their religion and made landless in their own country. Instead, wealth and power was transferred to landlords, and the natives were thrust into crushing poverty. The English government refused to pass needed reform laws that might have made their lives better. Swift's essay was responding to this inequality.

Interpret

1. Direct students' attention to the first bracketed passage on this page.

2. **Ask** students to identify what Swift states is the essay's purpose in this paragraph.
   Answer: Swift explains that his purpose is to propose a "fair, cheap and easy method" of solving the growing population problem and making the children of the poor useful to society.

25 **Reading Strategy**

Analyzing Text Features

1. **Ask** students to describe the speaker's attitude toward the poor. Remind them that the narrator of an essay should not to be confused with the author.
   Possible response: He refers to the poor as professed beggars and persons who demand charity, and suggests that the children of the poor are a burden to their parents and the nation.

2. Direct students to the second bracketed passage and the related footnote giving the definition of the word *dam,* as used in the passage.

3. **Ask** students the Reading Strategy question: How does Swift's use of the word *dam*—explained in the footnotes—indicate the irony behind his proposal? In other words how does what he actually says differ from what he really means?
   Possible response: The word *dam,* which normally refers to a female animal, dehumanizes the poor and compares them with animals.

FOR PREVENTING THE CHILDREN OF POOR PEOPLE FROM BEING A BURDEN TO THEIR PARENTS OR COUNTRY, AND FOR MAKING THEM BENEFICIAL TO THE PUBLIC.

It is a melancholy object to those, who walk through this great town,[1] or travel in the country, when they see the streets, the roads, and cabin-doors, crowded with beggars of the female sex, followed by three, four, or six children, all in rags, and importuning every passenger for an alms.[2] These mothers instead of being able to work for their honest livelihood, are forced to employ all their time in strolling, to beg sustenance for their helpless infants, who, as they grow up, either turn thieves for want of work, or leave their dear native country to fight for the Pretender in Spain,[3] or sell themselves to the Barbadoes.[4]

I think it is agreed by all parties, that this prodigious number of children, in the arms, or on the backs, or at the heels of their mothers, and frequently of their fathers, is in the present deplorable state of the kingdom, a very great additional grievance; and therefore whoever could find out a fair, cheap and easy method of making these children sound useful members of the commonwealth would deserve so well of the public, as to have his statue set up for a preserver of the nation.

But my intention is very far from being confined to provide only for the children of professed beggars, it is of a much greater extent, and shall take in the whole number of infants at a certain age, who are born of parents in effect as little able to support them, as those who demand our charity in the streets.

As to my own part, having turned my thoughts, for many years, upon this important subject, and maturely weighed the several schemes of other projectors, I have always found them grossly mistaken in their computation. It is true a child, just dropped from its dam[5] may be supported by her milk for a solar year with little other nourishment, at most not above the value of two shillings, which the mother may certainly get, or the value in scraps, by her lawful occupation of begging, and it is exactly at one year old that I propose to provide for them, in such a manner, as, instead of being a charge upon their parents, or the parish, or wanting food and raiment[6] for the rest of their lives, they shall, on the contrary, contribute to the feeding and partly to the clothing of many thousands.

There is likewise another great advantage in my scheme, that it will prevent those voluntary abortions, and that horrid practice of

Vocabulary

sustenance (sus′ tə nəns) *n.* food or money to support life

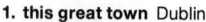

Reading Strategy

Analyzing Text Features How does Swift's use of the word *dam*—explained in the footnotes—indicate the irony behind his proposal? In other words how does what he actually says differ from what he really means?

---

1. **this great town** Dublin.
2. **importuning. . . alms** begging passersby for charity.
3. **Pretender in Spain** James Edward Stewart (1688–1766), a Catholic, was a claimant (or "Pretender") to the English throne despite being barred against succession.
4. **sell. . . Barbadoes** commit themselves as indentured servants on Barbadian plantations.
5. **dam** female parent, usually an animal.
6. **raiment** clothing.

Enrichment: Building Context

Irish Poverty

Ireland in the seventeenth century was primarily a rural agricultural nation populated by people who were among the poorest in the Western World. An English or Anglo-Irish absentee ruling class owned most of the countryside. These landowners lived far from their properties, demanded exorbitant rents, and siphoned off most of Ireland's resources. Swift felt the English upper class was the only group possessing enough wealth and influence to correct these wrongs. Yet, the aristocracy was among the chief offenders. Swift decided to focus attention on the Irish plight. The result was Swift's memorable essay "A Modest Proposal."

Activity: Building Context Encourage interested students to learn more about the conditions that led Swift to write this essay by examining some of the events that led up to it. Suggest that they record their analysis in the **Enrichment: Building Context** worksheet, *Professional Development Guidebook,* page 222.

women murdering their bastard children, alas, too frequent among us, sacrificing the poor innocent babes, I doubt, more to avoid the expense, than the shame, which would move tears and pity in the most savage and inhuman breast.

The number of souls in this kingdom being usually reckoned one million and a half,[7] of these I calculate there may be about two hundred thousand couple whose wives are breeders, from which number I subtract thirty thousand couples, who are able to maintain their own children, although I apprehend there cannot be so many under the present distresses of the kingdom, but this being granted, there will remain an hundred and seventy thousand breeders. I again subtract fifty thousand for those women who miscarry, or whose children die by accident, or disease within the year. There only remain an hundred and twenty thousand children of poor parents annually born: The question therefore is, how this number shall be reared, and provided for, which, as I have already said, under the present situation of affairs, is utterly impossible by all the methods hitherto proposed, for we can neither employ them in handicraft, or agriculture; we neither build houses, (I mean in the country) nor cultivate land: they can very seldom pick up a livelihood by stealing till they arrive at six years old, except where they are of towardly parts,[8] although, I confess they learn the rudiments much earlier, during which time, they can however be properly looked upon only as probationers, as I have been informed by a principal gentleman in the County of Cavan, who protested to me, that he never knew above one or two instances under the age of six, even in a part of the kingdom so renowned for the quickest proficiency in that art.

I am assured by our merchants, that a boy or a girl, before twelve years old, is no saleable commodity, and even when they come to this age, they will not yield above three pounds, or three pounds and half-a-crown at most on the Exchange, which cannot turn to account[9] either to the parents or the kingdom, the charge of nutriment and rags having been at least four times that value.

I shall now therefore humbly propose my own thoughts, which I hope will not be liable to the least objection.

I have been assured by a very knowing American of my acquaintance in London, that a young healthy child well nursed is at a year old a most delicious, nourishing, and wholesome food, whether stewed, roasted, baked, or boiled, and I make no doubt that it will equally serve in a fricassee, or a ragout.[10]

26

---

7. **souls . . . half** censuses from the year 1699 put Ireland's population at approximately 1.2 million.
8. **of towardly parts** highly talented or able.
9. **turn to account** bring a profit.
10. **fricassee** (frik ə sē′) . . . **ragout** (ra go̅o̅′) meat stews.

27 ▲ **Critical Viewing**
Do you think the technique used in this etching best conveys the hardship of poverty? Explain. **[Assess]**

Vocabulary
commodity (kə mäd′ ə tē) *n.* product that is bought or sold

28 **Reading Check**
Who first told Swift about the use of children as a source of food?

A Modest Proposal 619

26 **Humanities**

A famished boy and girl turning up the ground to seek for a potato to appease their hunger, from *The Illustrated London News*

The Illustrated London News was founded by Herbert Ingram in 1842. The publication recorded important historical events. Ingram believed he could aid social reform through his publication. He published his liberal views on child labor, factory conditions, and the poor to educate the public. In fact, he was so popular that he was elected a member of Parliament for Boston, Lincolnshire. Use these questions for discussion:

1. **Ask** students to identify the details in this engraving that suggest poverty.
   Answer: the children's ragged clothes and appearance; the fact that they appear to be digging through the soil to obtain food

2. **Ask** students to explain whether they think Ingram would have published Swift's essay in his paper.
   Possible response: Some students may think that because Ingram had the courage to start his own publication and air his views, he would probably have published "A Modest Proposal." Others may think that Ingram might not have published so provocative a piece which might have alienated his readers.

27 **Critical Viewing**

Possible response: Students may suggest that the detailed depictions and rigid lines convey the hardship of poverty.

28 **Reading Check**

Answer: Swift credits "a very knowing American" of his aquaintance with suggesting the use of children as a source of food.

Differentiated Instruction   for Universal Access

Background for Less Proficient Readers
Remind students that Swift uses irony in "A Modest Proposal." Explain that verbal irony is a discrepancy between what is said and what is meant. As students read the selection, help them understand that Swift writes one thing but means something else entirely.

EL Vocabulary for English Learners
Students may be familiar with the word *modest* as meaning "humble." Explain that *modest* may also mean "free from extravagance," "decent," or "moderate." In this satire, however, Swift uses *modest* ironically to mean the opposite: extravagant, indecent, and extreme.

Enrichment for Advanced Readers
Ask students to use the Internet or other resources to find out how satire differs from parody. Encourage students to find examples of each type of work and share their findings with the class.

29 Literary Analysis

Satire

1. Ask a student to read the bracketed passage aloud to the class. Draw students' attention to the words *breed* and *savages*.

2. Then, **ask** the first Literary Analysis question: What effect do words like *breed* and *savages* have on the tone in this paragraph?
Answer: The words create a harsh, unsympathetic tone.

30 Literary Analysis

Satire

1. Remind students that satire pokes fun at the flaws and shortcomings of human beings.

2. Read aloud the bracketed passage. Then, **ask** students the second Literary Analysis question: In what way does Swift's sarcasm sharpen his satirical attack on landlords?
Answer: Swift's sarcasm suggests that because landlords figuratively "devour" their tenants, it would not be difficult for them to devour their children literally.

Literary Analysis
Satire What effect do words like *breed* and *savages* have on the tone in this paragraph? **29**

Literary Analysis
Satire In what way does Swift's sarcasm sharpen his satirical attack on landlords? **30**

I do therefore humbly offer it to public consideration, that of the hundred and twenty thousand children, already computed, twenty thousand may be reserved for breed, whereof only one fourth part to be males, which is more than we allow to sheep, black-cattle, or swine, and my reason is that these children are seldom the fruits of marriage, a circumstance not much regarded by our savages, therefore one male will be sufficient to serve four females. That the remaining hundred thousand may at a year old be offered in sale to the persons of quality, and fortune, through the kingdom, always advising the mother to let them suck plentifully in the last month, so as to render them plump, and fat for a good table. A child will make two dishes at an entertainment for friends, and when the family dines alone, the fore or hind quarter will make a reasonable dish, and seasoned with a little pepper or salt will be very good boiled on the fourth day, especially in winter.

I have reckoned upon a medium,[11] that a child just born will weigh 12 pounds, and in a solar year if tolerably nursed increases to 28 pounds.

I grant this food will be somewhat dear,[12] and therefore very proper for landlords, who, as they have already devoured[13] most of the parents, seem to have the best title to the children.

Infants' flesh will be in season throughout the year, but more plentiful in March, and a little before and after, for we are told by a grave author an eminent French physician,[14] that fish being a prolific diet, there are more children born in Roman Catholic countries about nine months after Lent, than at any other season; therefore reckoning a year after Lent, the markets will be more glutted than usual, because the number of popish[15] infants, is at least three to one in this kingdom, and therefore it will have one other collateral[16] advantage by lessening the number of Papists[17] among us.

I have already computed the charge of nursing a beggar's child (in which list I reckon all cottagers, laborers, and four-fifths of the farmers) to be about two shillings per annum, rags included, and I believe no gentleman would repine[18] to give ten shillings for the carcass of a good fat child, which, as I have said will make four dishes of excellent nutritive meat, when he has only some particular friend, or his own family to dine with him. Thus the Squire will learn to be a good landlord, and grow popular among his tenants, the mother will have eight shillings net profit, and be fit for work till she produces another child.

---

11. **reckoned upon a medium** estimated as an average.
12. **dear** costly.
13. **devoured** financially destroyed.
14. **grave . . . physician** François Rabelais, a renown humorist and satirist.
15. **popish** Catholic (derogatory).
16. **collateral** parallel; related.
17. **Papists** Roman Catholics (derogatory).
18. **repine** (ri pīn´) *v.* complain.

Enrichment: Investigating a Literary Figure

Isaac Bickerstaff

"A Modest Proposal" is not Swift's only satirical writing. In 1708, a cobbler-turned-astrologer named John Partridge published an almanac of predictions. Jonathan Swift wrote a scathing parody of the almanac using the pseudonym Isaac Bickerstaff. The parody—titled *Prediction For the Ensuing Year By Isaac Bickerstaff*—included a prediction of Partridge's death to take place in March 1708. On the date of the predicted death, Swift insisted that Partridge had died, even though Partridge himself protested.

Activity: Investigating Jonathan Swift's Contributions Have interested students learn more by researching Swift's place in the British literary tradition. Have them use online and print sources to identify key events in his life, his literary works, and his contributions. Suggest that they record their analysis using the **Enrichment: Investigating a Literary Figure** worksheet, *Professional Development Guidebook*, page 235.

Those who are more thrifty (as I must confess the times require) may flay the carcass; the skin of which, artificially dressed, will make admirable gloves for ladies, and summer boots for fine gentlemen.

As to our city of Dublin, shambles[19] may be appointed for this purpose, in the most convenient parts of it, and butchers we may be assured will not be wanting, although I rather recommend buying the children alive, and dressing them hot from the knife, as we do roasting pigs.

A very worthy person, a true lover of his country, and whose virtues I highly esteem, was lately pleased, in discoursing on this matter, to offer a refinement upon my scheme. He said, that many gentlemen of this kingdom, having of late destroyed their deer, he conceived that the want of venison might be well supplied by the bodies of young lads and maidens, not exceeding fourteen years of age, nor under twelve, so great a number of both sexes in every country being now ready to starve, for want of work and service: and these to be disposed of by their parents if alive, or otherwise by their nearest relations. But with due deference to so excellent a friend, and so deserving a patriot, I cannot be altogether in his sentiments; for as to the males, my American acquaintance assured me from frequent experience, that their flesh was generally tough and lean, like that of our schoolboys, by continual exercise, and their taste disagreeable, and to fatten them would not answer the charge. Then as to the females, it would, I think with humble submission, be a loss to the public, because they soon would become breeders themselves: And besides, it is not improbable that some scrupulous people might be apt to censure such a practice, (although indeed very unjustly) as a little bordering upon cruelty, which, I confess, has always been with me the strongest objection against any project, however so well intended.

But in order to justify my friend, he confessed that this expedient was put into his head by the famous Psalmanazar,[20] a native of the island Formosa, who came from thence to London, above twenty years ago, and in conversation told my friend, that in his country when any young person happened to be put to death, the executioner sold the carcass to persons of quality, as a prime dainty, and that, in his time, the body of a plump girl of fifteen, who was crucified for an attempt to poison the emperor, was sold to his Imperial Majesty's Prime Minister of State, and other great Mandarins of the Court, in joints from the gibbet, at four hundred crowns. Neither indeed can I deny, that if the same use were made of several plump young girls in this town, who, without one single groat[21] to their fortunes, cannot stir abroad without a chair, and appear at

---

19. **shambles** slaughterhouses.
20. **Psalmanazar** Here, Swift refers to a fictitious account of cannibalism in Formosa as made by impostor George Psalmanazar.
21. **groat** coin, of trivial amount.

31  **LITERATURE IN CONTEXT**

The Irish Troubles
In the later seventeenth century, just as Swift was growing up, England encouraged Scottish Protestants to emigrate to Northern Ireland and confiscate land owned by Catholics. Political power in Ireland became concentrated exclusively in the hands of the Protestant upper class, which comprised only about ten percent of the population. Catholics were the targets of relentless discrimination. For example, they were not allowed to reside in towns, but had to content themselves with living in rural settings. England's exploitative economic policies combined with crop failures in the 1720s to trigger a crisis; many farmers found it impossible to pay rent to their English landlords, and the streets teemed with beggars. This desolate situation was the background for "A Modest Proposal."

Connect to the Literature

In his essay, Swift appears to condemn the Irish Catholics in the same way as the social class he mocks. What possible motives might Swift have for using such a strategy?

Vocabulary
censure (sen' shər) v. strongly disapprove; condemn

Reading Check
32 What contribution to society will infants make if Swift's proposal is accepted?

A Modest Proposal **621**

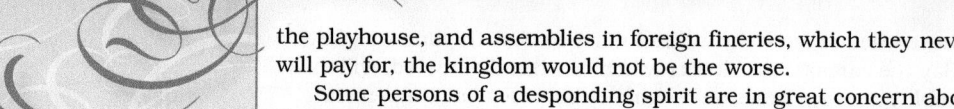

33 Literary Analysis

Satire

1. Direct students' attention to the second of the arguments that appear on the page.
2. **Ask** the Literary Analysis question: What realistic solution to Ireland's problems is suggested in Swift's second argument?
   Possible response: The landlords should not deprive their tenants of all they possess in order to pay rent.

34 Literary Analysis

Satire

1. Remind students that satire pokes fun at the flaws and shortcomings of human beings and institutions.
2. **Ask** students to explain in what way Swift's fifth argument mocks the upper classes of English society.
   Answer: It mocks the desire of the upper classes for expensive things.

the playhouse, and assemblies in foreign fineries, which they never will pay for, the kingdom would not be the worse.

Some persons of a desponding spirit are in great concern about that vast number of poor people, who are aged, diseased, or maimed, and I have been desired to employ my thoughts what course may be taken to ease the nation of so grievous an encumbrance.[22] But I am not in the least pain upon that matter, because it is very well known, that they are every day dying, and rotting, by cold, and famine, and filth, and vermin, as fast as can be reasonably expected. And as to the younger laborers they are now in almost as hopeful a condition. They cannot get work, and consequently pine away for want of nourishment, to a degree, that if at any time they are accidentally hired to common labor, they have not strength to perform it; and thus the country and themselves are happily delivered from the evils to come.

I have too long digressed, and therefore shall return to my subject. I think the advantages by the proposal which I have made are obvious and many, as well as of the highest importance.

For first, as I have already observed, it would greatly lessen the number of Papists, with whom we are yearly over-run, being the principal breeders of the nation, as well as our most dangerous enemies, and who stay at home on purpose with a design to deliver the kingdom to the Pretender, hoping to take their advantage by the absence of so many good Protestants, who have chosen rather to leave their country, than stay at home, and pay tithes against their conscience, to an Episcopal curate.[23]

33 Literary Analysis
Satire What realistic solution to Ireland's problems is suggested in Swift's second argument?

Secondly, the poorer tenants will have something valuable of their own, which by law may be made liable to distress,[24] and help to pay their landlord's rent, their corn and cattle being already seized, and money a thing unknown.

Thirdly, whereas the maintenance of an hundred thousand children, from two years old, and upwards, cannot be computed at less than ten shillings a piece per annum, the nation's stock will be thereby increased fifty thousand pounds per annum, besides the profit of a new dish, introduced to the tables of all gentlemen of fortune in the kingdom, who have any refinement in taste, and the money will circulate among ourselves, the goods being entirely of our own growth and manufacture.

Fourthly, the constant breeders, besides the gain of eight shillings sterling per annum, by the sale of their children, will be rid of the charge of maintaining them after the first year.

34 Fifthly, this food would likewise bring great custom to taverns, where the vintners will certainly be so prudent as to procure the best

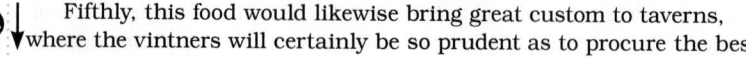

22. **encumbrance** burden.
23. **tithes . . . curate** taxes, paid to the Catholic Church, which Protestants paid against their conscience.
24. **liable to distress** available for seizure by landlords as payment for debts.

Enrichment: Analyzing Forms and Genres

Swift's Epitaph

Swift composed an epitaph for himself before his death on October 19, 1745. The epitaph was written in Latin and came with instructions that it should be deeply cut with large letters and strongly gilded. William Butler Yeats, another Irish poet, is quoted as saying, "Swift sleeps under the greatest epitaph in history." Yeats wrote a loose translation of the epitaph in the following poem:

Swift has sailed into his rest;
Savage indignation there
Cannot lacerate his breast.
Imitate him if you dare,
World-besotted traveler; he
Served human liberty.

Activity: Investigating Epitaphs Have interested students find out more about other epitaphs that have been written about historical figures. Suggest that they record their analysis of historic epitaphs using the **Enrichment: Analyzing Forms and Genres** worksheet, ***Professional Development Guidebook,*** page 227.

receipts for dressing it to perfection, and consequently have their houses frequented by all the fine gentlemen, who justly value themselves upon their knowledge in good eating; and a skillful cook, who understands how to oblige his guests will contrive to make it as expensive as they please.

Sixthly, this would be a great inducement to marriage, which all wise nations have either encouraged by rewards, or enforced by laws and penalties. It would increase the care and tenderness of mothers toward their children, when they were sure of a settlement for life, to the poor babes, provided in some sort by the public to their annual profit instead of expense. We should see an honest emulation[25] among the married women, which of them could bring the fattest child to the market, men would become as fond of their wives, during the time of their pregnancy, as they are now of their mares in foal, their cows in calf, or sows when they are ready to farrow, nor offer to beat or kick them (as it is too frequent a practice) for fear of a miscarriage.

Many other advantages might be enumerated: For instance, the addition of some thousand carcasses in our exportation of barreled beef; the propagation of swine's flesh, and improvement in the art of making good bacon, so much wanted among us by the great destruction of pigs, too frequent at our tables, which are no way comparable in taste, or magnificence to a well-grown, fat yearling child, which roasted whole will make a considerable figure at a Lord Mayor's feast, or any other public entertainment. But this, and many others I omit being studious of brevity.

Supposing that one thousand families in this city, would be constant customers for infants' flesh, besides others who might have it at merry-meetings, particularly weddings and christenings, I compute that Dublin would take off annually about twenty thousand carcasses, and the rest of the kingdom (where probably they will be sold somewhat cheaper) the remaining eighty thousand.

I can think of no one objection, that will possibly be raised against this proposal, unless it should be urged that the number of people will be thereby much lessened in the kingdom. This I freely own, and was indeed one principal design in offering it to the world. I desire the reader will observe, that I calculate my remedy *for this one individual Kingdom of Ireland, and for no other that ever was, is, or, I think, ever can be upon earth. Therefore let no man talk to me of other expedients:*[26] *Of taxing our absentees at five shillings a pound: Of using neither clothes, nor household furniture, except what is of our own growth and*

---

25. **emulation** competition.
26. **expedients** Prior to publication, Swift proposed each of the following reasonable means by which Ireland might find relief, but the government ignored his suggestions. Swift used italics in editions printed during his lifetime to indicate that these proposals were, in fact, serious ones.

Literary Analysis
Satire Explain Swift's use of exaggeration in this passage.

Reading Strategy
Analyzing Text Features
In what ways do the proposals in italics contrast with Swift's "modest proposal" in the body of the essay?

✓ Reading Check

According to Swift's third argument, what benefit will his plan bring to Ireland?

A Modest Proposal **623**

---

35 Literary Analysis
Satire

1. Review with students the Literary Analysis instruction on page 604. Make sure they understand that hyperbole, or exaggeration, is a satirical tool.

2. Have students read the bracketed passage of Swift's sixth argument independently. Then, **ask** students to respond to the Literary Analysis item: Explain Swift's use of exaggeration in this passage. **Possible response:** He uses exaggeration to say that the poor Irish women are breeders whose husbands care little for them. By raising children for market, wives could earn money, and husbands would appreciate them in pregnancy and care for them (as they do their pregnant animals) rather than mistreat them.

36 Reading Strategy
Analyzing Text Features

1. Ask a volunteer to read aloud the italicized text. Point out to students that this text appears in italics to set it apart from the rest of the essay.

2. **Ask** students the Reading Strategy question: In what ways do the proposals in italics contrast with Swift's "modest proposal" in the body of the essay? **Answer:** The proposals in italics are realistic solutions.

37 Reading Check

Possible response: Swift suggests that the nation's stock will increase. People will be proud that they produced the new delicacy themselves, in their own country.

Differentiated Instruction for Universal Access

Strategy for Less Proficient Readers
The long sentences in this essay may cause difficulty for less proficient readers. Work with these students as they read the list of benefits that Swift offers. The first benefit is seven lines long. Model breaking down one extended sentence into several sentences. One way to divide this sentence is to begin with the first word and go through *Papists*. Model changing the verb and syntax in the next clause, "with whom we are overrun," so that it becomes a complete sentence. Have students work with partners and continue the process on their own until they finish the sixth reason. Help partners paraphrase, as necessary. As students offer their summaries, record them on the chalkboard. Address any questions that students may have.

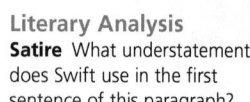

Literary Analysis
Satire What understatement does Swift use in the first sentence of this paragraph?
38

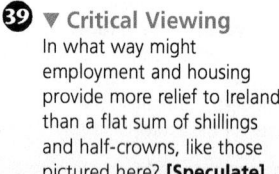

39 ▼ Critical Viewing
In what way might employment and housing provide more relief to Ireland than a flat sum of shillings and half-crowns, like those pictured here? **[Speculate]**

manufacture: Of utterly rejecting the materials and instruments that promote foreign luxury: Of curing the expensiveness of pride, vanity, idleness, and gaming in our women: Of introducing a vein of parsimony, prudence and temperance: Of learning to love our Country, wherein we differ even from Laplanders, and the inhabitants of Topinamboo:[27] Of quitting our animosities and factions, nor act any longer like the Jews, who were murdering one another at the very moment their city was taken:[28] Of being a little cautious not to sell our country and consciences for nothing: Of teaching landlords to have at least one degree of mercy toward their tenants. Lastly of putting a spirit of honesty, industry and skill into our shopkeepers, who, if a resolution could now be taken to buy only our native goods, would immediately unite to cheat and exact upon us in the price, the measure, and the goodness, nor could ever yet be brought to make one fair proposal of just dealing, though often and earnestly invited to it.

Therefore I repeat, let no man talk to me of these and the like expedients, till he hath at least some glimpse of hope, that there will ever be some hearty and sincere attempt to put them in practice.

But as to myself, having been wearied out for many years with offering vain, idle, visionary thoughts, and at length utterly despairing of success, I fortunately fell upon this proposal, which as it is wholly new, so it hath something solid and real, of no expense and little trouble, full in our own power, and whereby we can incur no danger in disobliging[29] England. For this kind of commodity will not bear exportation, the flesh being of too tender a consistence, to admit a long continuance in salt, although perhaps I could name a country,[30] which would be glad to eat up our whole nation without it.

After all I am not so violently bent upon my own opinion, as to reject any offer, proposed by wise men, which shall be found equally innocent, cheap, easy and effectual. But before something of that kind shall be advanced in contradiction to my scheme, and offering a better, I desire the author, or authors will be pleased maturely to con-

---

27. **Laplanders and . . . Topinamboo** Swift refers to natives of inhospitable lands as examples for the Irish.
28. **city . . . taken** Jerusalem, which was taken by Rome in AD 70 while its Jewish inhabitants were occupied with infighting.
29. **disobliging** offending.
30. **country** England.

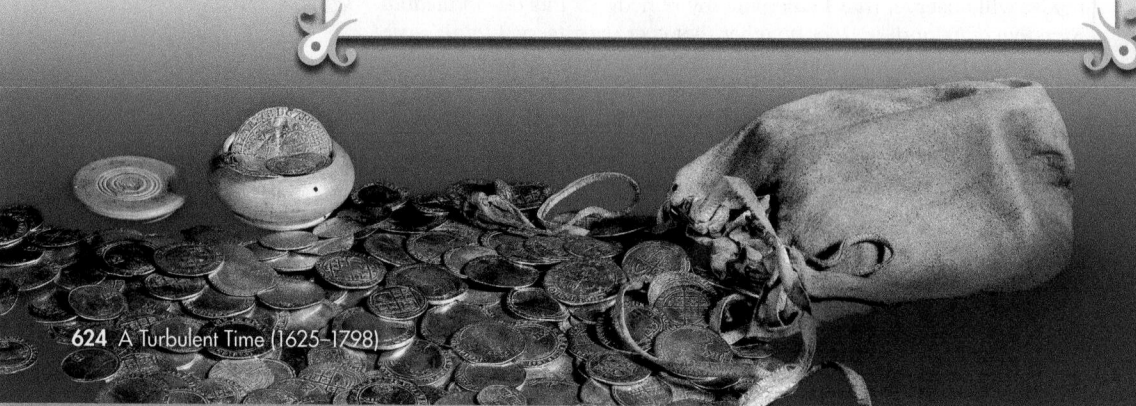

624 A Turbulent Time (1625–1798)

sider two points. First, as things now stand, how they will be able to find food and raiment for an hundred thousand useless mouths and backs. And secondly, there being a round million of creatures in human figure, throughout this kingdom, whose whole subsistence put into a common stock, would leave them in debt two millions of pounds sterling adding those, who are beggars by profession, to the bulk of farmers, cottagers and laborers with their wives and children, who are beggars in effect. I desire those politicians, who dislike my overture, and may perhaps be so bold to attempt an answer, that they will first ask the parents of these mortals, whether they would not at this day think it a great happiness to have been sold for food at a year old, in the manner I prescribe, and thereby have avoided such a perpetual scene of misfortunes, as they have since gone through, by the oppression of landlords, the impossibility of paying rent without money or trade, the want of common sustenance, with neither house nor clothes to cover them from the inclemencies of the weather, and the most inevitable prospect of entailing[31] the like, or greater miseries upon their breed for ever.

I profess in the sincerity of my heart that I have not the least personal interest in endeavouring to promote this necessary work, having no other motive than the public good of my country, by advancing our trade, providing for infants, relieving the poor, and giving some pleasure to the rich. I have no children, by which I can propose to get a single penny; the youngest being nine years old, and my wife past child-bearing.

40 Literary Analysis
Satire Why do you think Swift uses the phrases "sincerity of my heart" and "not the least personal interest" in the final paragraph?

---

31. **entailing** passing to a later generation.

Critical Reading

1. Key Ideas and Details **(a)** What agreement "by all parties" does Swift seek to establish in the second paragraph of the essay? **(b) Analyze:** Why is this agreement necessary for setting the groundwork for the satire?

2. Key Ideas and Details According to Swift's American acquaintance in London, what purpose can be served by well-nursed children who are a year old?

3. Key Ideas and Details **(a)** According to Swift, why will children be a very proper food for landlords? **(b) Draw Conclusions:** What satirical point is Swift making in his reference to landlords?

4. Integration of Knowledge and Ideas What do these selections suggest that Swift wanted to change about society? In your response, use at least two of these Essential Question words: *values, dissatisfaction, ideal. [Connecting to the Essential Question: How does literature shape or reflect society?]*

Cite textual evidence to support your responses.

A Modest Proposal **625**

Answers

1. **Possible responses:** Items in the text: Gulliver's description of gunpowder; Lilliput and Blefuscu; treating infants as a commodity; Targets of Swift's satire: people's enthusiasm for conflict; England and France; the class system.

2. (a) Gulliver's perceptions of the Lilliputians as silly and barbaric is mirrored in the king's view of Europeans. (b) It adds to the satire by showing that people think their own views are correct.

3. **Possible response:** People are often petty, combative, and self-important.

4. (a) The wealthy are Swift's target. (b) Swift reveals his proposal gradually in order to establish its "logic" and to avoid shocking readers. (c) Swift's proposal is outrageous.

5. **Possible responses:** (a) After listing other solutions, Swift writes: "I am not so violently bent upon my own opinion as to reject an offer [that is as] cheap, easy, and as effectual [as my own]." (b) Swift suggests that "men will be as fond of their wives in pregnancy as they are of their mares in foal, . . . and will not beat them for fear of miscarriage." (c) Swift suggests sarcastically that landowners should benefit from this new food source, as they had already devoured the parents.

6. **Possible response:** (a) Students might choose the passage about Gulliver's conversation with the secretary about people who refuse to believe the evidence of their own senses and his recommendation that year-old infants be fattened as food. (b) Students may find the irony more effective in *Gulliver's Travels* because Swift's "A Modest Proposal" is so outrageous. They should justify their responses.

7. **Possible response:** Students might cite *Saturday Night Live* comedy sketches and should provide specific examples of how satire is used.

8. **Possible response:** The cartoon shows a patient in a psychiatrist's office tied up by tiny people, just as the Lilliputians tied up Gulliver. The doctor asks him about his feelings of persecution by little people.

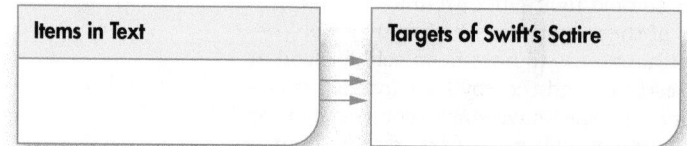

Literary Analysis

1. Craft and Structure Use a chart like the one shown to indicate three targets of Swift's **satire** in *Gulliver's Travels*.

Items in Text		Targets of Swift's Satire
	→	
	→	
	→	

2. Key Ideas and Details **(a)** Compare and contrast Gulliver's impression of the Lilliputians with the King of Brobdingnag's impression of Europeans. **(b)** How does the comparison add to the satire?

3. Key Ideas and Details Summarize the universal and timeless points Swift wants to make in his satirical novel.

4. Key Ideas and Details **(a)** What is Swift's chief satirical target in "A Modest Proposal"? **(b)** Why do you think he only gradually reveals the real nature of the "proposal"? **(c)** What is misleading about the word *modest* in the title?

5. Craft and Structure Demonstrate how Swift uses each of these elements in his essay: **(a)** *understatement* **(b)** *hyperbole* **(c)** *sarcasm*.

6. Comparing Literary Works **(a)** Focusing on a passage in each work, compare and contrast Swift's use of **irony** in his novel and his essay. **(b)** In which passage is the irony more effective? Why?

7. Integration of Knowledge and Ideas Are there any contemporary satires—whether in literature, on television, or in the movies—that resemble Swift's? Explain, citing examples.

8. Analyze Visual Information Use your knowledge of *Gulliver's Travels* to explain the humor in the cartoon on this page.

Reading Strategy

9. (a) Identify a passage in Swift's work that might require you to **analyze text features** in order to discover what is being satirized. **(b)** Demonstrate step by step how such analysis would work.

10. (a) Which text features were most helpful to you in figuring out the targets of Swift's satire in his novel and his essay? Why? **(b)** Which text features helped you better understand Swift's irony? Explain.

▼ *"Tell me more about these little people that are out to get you."*

---

9. **Possible response:** (a) The passage in which the King of Brobdingnag asks Gulliver whether he is a Whig or a Tory. (b) This would require someone who does not know anything about English political parties to examine the footnote and Swift's biography to understand the satire.

10. **Possible response:** (a) The background notes were most helpful because they filled in gaps in knowledge about political and social institutions. (b) The footnotes were more helpful in figuring out irony because they were located near different passages.

Vocabulary Acquisition and Use

Word Analysis: Latin Root -jec-

The word *conjecture* includes the Latin root -*jec*-, which means "throw." *Conjecture* means "to guess by 'throwing' facts or inferences together." Write sentences using at least four of the following words in a paragraph describing what you might think or feel when traveling to another planet, just as Gulliver traveled to new worlds. If any of the words are unfamiliar, use a dictionary to clarify their meanings.

dejection	eject
object	project
reject	trajectory

Then, choose one of the words you used and write a sentence identifying how the "throw" root helps create its meaning.

Vocabulary: Analogies

Analogies show the relationships between pairs of words. Complete each analogy using a word from the vocabulary list on page 604. In each, your choice should create a word pair that matches the relationship between the first two words given. Then, explain your answers.

1. *Vegetables* : _____ :: *homes* : *shelter*.
2. *A* _____ : *merchandise* :: *help* : *assistance*.
3. *Emergency* : *an* _____ :: *moving* : *truck*.
4. *A transmission* : *a message* :: *a* _____ : *a rupture*.
5. _____ : *criticize* :: *praise* : *approve*.
6. *Night* : *day* :: _____ : *certainty*.

Writing

Informative Text Like a modern-day Swift, make a plan for a satiric **multimedia** using *text, images, and sound*. You might include taped scenes or archival footage; photos, video, or cartoons; and sound effects or music.

Prewriting Start by choosing a target. What foolish behavior, trend, or attitude in today's world merits mockery?

Drafting Outline the sequence of your presentation. Then, decide on the *appropriate medium* to present each idea. Select the words, images, or sounds that will best convey your satire at each stage. Decide whether it is better to create those elements or to identify copyrighted sources that might provide the needed material—for example, television, videos, or films; newspapers, magazines, or books; clip-art collections or original drawings. Use a chart like the one shown to record your ideas.

Point	Media	Possible Sources
Reality shows are not "real."	Video clip from a reality show that reveals a convoluted situation.	Download copyrighted content from Internet
	News headlines showing problems people really face.	Scan from local papers

Revising Read through your plan and make any changes needed to clarify your message and to blend different types of media effectively.

Integrated Language Skills **627**

Vocabulary Acquisition and Use

1. Introduce the skill using the instruction on the student page.
2. Have students complete the Word Analysis Activity and the Vocabulary Practice.

Word Analysis

Possible response:
I embarked on the new *project* to travel to the planet Mars with great enthusiasm. The *object* of our mission was to reach the red planet before our rivals could reach the same goal. Our *trajectory* was flawless, so our plan was successful. We explored our neighbor world without a mishap and came back home. Our rivals were *dejected*.

A *project* is a task or undertaking, and the root-part –*ject*, meaning "to throw," suggests that I move the task forward to completion.

Vocabulary

1. sustenance
2. commodity
3. expedient
4. schism
5. censure
6. conjecture

Writing

1. To give students guidance for planning this informative text, give them the Support for Writing page from *Unit 3 Resources*, page 160.

2. Read with students the note for the writing lesson on this page, and then tell students that they should select the text, images, and sounds that will most effectively convey the foolishness of their target.

3. If students have difficulty selecting a target or images and sounds, tell them to review television or film satires for ideas. Remind them that they can create their own taped scenes, cartoons, or images for the presentations.

4. Use the Rubrics for Multimedia Presentation, *Professional Development Guidebook*, pages 266–267, to evaluate students' work.

627

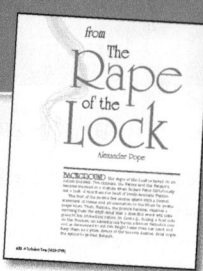

from *An Essay on Man* • from *The Rape of the Lock*

Lesson Pacing Guide

DAY 1 Preteach

- Administer the Reading and Vocabulary Warm-ups (*Unit 3 Resources*, pp. 171–174) as necessary.
- Introduce the Literary Analysis concept: Parody
- Introduce the Reading Strategy: Analyzing Author's Purpose.
- Build background with the author and Background features.
- Develop thematic thinking with Connecting to the Essential Question.
- Teach the selection vocabulary.

DAYS 2–3 Preteach/Teach/Assess

- Distribute copies of the appropriate graphic organizer for the Reading Strategy (*Graphic Organizer Transparencies*, pp. 111–112).
- Distribute copies of the appropriate graphic organizer for Literary Analysis (*Graphic Organizer Transparencies*, pp. 113–114).
- Prepare students to read with the Activating Prior Knowledge activities (TE).
- Informally monitor comprehension while students read.
- Use the Reading Check questions to confirm comprehension.
- Develop students' understanding of parody using the Literary Analysis prompts.
- Develop students' ability to analyze the author's purpose using the Reading Strategy prompts.
- Reinforce vocabulary with the Vocabulary notes.
- Assess students' comprehension and mastery of the skills by having them answer the Critical Reading, Literary Analysis, and Reading Strategy questions.
- Have students complete the Vocabulary Lesson.

DAY 4 Extend/Assess

- Have students complete the Writing Lesson and write a mock-heroic poem. (You may assign as homework.)
- Administer Selection Test A or B (*Unit 3 Resources*, pp. 183–185 or 186–188).

Common Core State Standards

Reading Literature 6. Analyze a case in which grasping point of view requires distinguishing what is directly stated in a text from what is really meant.
9. Demonstrate knowledge of eighteenth-, nineteenth-, and early-twentieth-century foundational works of American literature, including how two or more texts from the same period treat similar themes or topics.

Reading Informational Text 9. Analyze seventeenth-, eighteenth-, and nineteenth-century foundational U.S. documents of historical and literary significance for their themes, purposes, and rhetorical features.

Writing 4. Produce clear and coherent writing in which the development, organization, and style are appropriate to task, purpose, and audience.

Language 4.a. Use context as a clue to the meaning of a word or phrase.

Additional Standards Practice
***Common Core Companion**, pp. 61–62, 75–76; 170–171; 324–331*

Daily Block Scheduling
Each day in this Lesson Pacing Guide represents a 40–50 minute period. Teachers using block scheduling may combine days to revise pacing. In addition, teachers may differentiate and support core instruction by integrating components for extended and intensive support as students require. See the Guide to Selected Leveled Resources (facing page).

Guide to Selected Leveled Resources

R T I Tier 1 (students performing on level)

from An Essay on Man • from The Rape of the Lock

Warm Up	Practice, model, and monitor fluency, working with the whole class or in groups.	Vocabulary and Reading Warm-ups B, *Unit 3 Resources,* pp. 168–169, 171
Comprehension/Skills	Support and monitor comprehension and skills development, having students complete the activities, graphic organizers, and interactive prompts independently or as a class.	• *Reader's Notebook,* adapted instruction and full selection **EL** *Reader's Notebook: English Learner's Version,* adapted instruction and adapted selection • Reading Skill Graphic Organizer B, *Graphic Organizer Transparencies,* p. 116 • Literary Analysis Graphic Organizer B, *Graphic Organizer Transparencies,* p. 118
Monitor Progress	Monitor student progress with the differentiated curriculum-based assessment in the *Unit Resources.*	• Selection Test B, *Unit 3 Resources,* pp. 183–185 • Open-Book Test, *Unit 3 Resources,* pp. 177–179

R T I Tier 2 (students requiring intervention)

from An Essay on Man • from The Rape of the Lock

Warm Up	Practice, model, and monitor fluency in groups or with individuals.	• Vocabulary and Reading Warm-ups A, *Unit 3 Resources,* pp. 168–170 • *Hear It!* Audio CD (adapted text)
Comprehension/Skills	• Support and monitor comprehension and skills development, working in small groups or with individuals. • As students complete the selection in the appropriate version of the *Reader's Notebook,* monitor comprehension frequently with group questions and individual instruction. • Model strategies while guiding students in completing the activities and prompts in the *Reader's Notebook,* as well as the graphic organizers. • Practice skills and monitor mastery with the *Reading Kit* worksheets.	• *Reader's Notebook: Adapted Version,* adapted instruction and adapted selection **EL** *Reader's Notebook: English Learner's Version,* adapted instruction and adapted selection • Reading Skill Graphic Organizer A, *Graphic Organizer Transparencies,* p. 115 • Literary Analysis Graphic Organizer A, *Graphic Organizer Transparencies,* p. 117 • *Reading Kit,* Practice worksheets
Monitor Progress	Monitor student progress with the differentiated curriculum-based assessment in the *Unit Resources* and in the *Reading Kit.*	• Selection Test A, *Unit 3 Resources,* pp. 180–182 • *Reading Kit,* Assess worksheets

TIER 3 Tier 3 intervention may require consultation with the student's special-education or dyslexia specialist. For additional support, see the Tier 2 activities and resources listed above.

One-on-one teaching   Group work   Whole class instruction   Independent work   A Assessment

For a complete guide to selection support, including support for Advanced students, see the Overview of Resources in the frontmatter.

from *An Essay on Man*
• from *The Rape of the Lock*

RESOURCES FOR:

- **L1** Special-Needs Students
- **L2** Below-Level Students (Tier 2)
- **L3** On-Level Students (Tier 1)
- **L4** Advanced Students (Tier 1)
- **EL** English Learners
- **All** All Students

Vocabulary/Fluency/Prior Knowledge

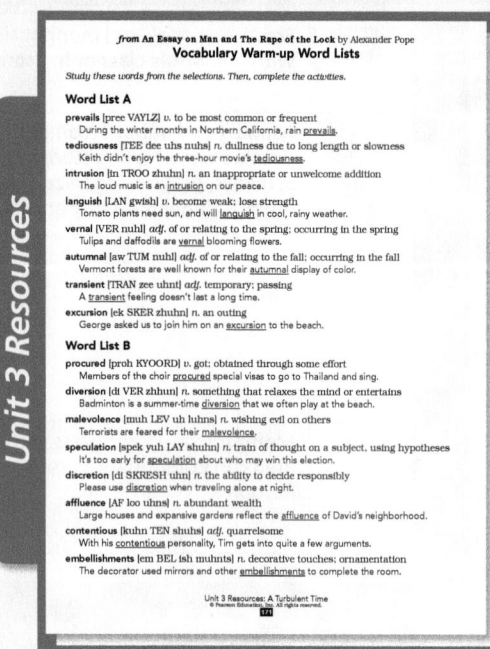

EL L1 L2 Vocabulary Warm-ups A and B, pp. 171–172

Also available for these selections:

EL L1 L2 Reading Warm-ups A and B, pp. 173–174

All Vocabulary Builder, p. 177

Reader's Notebooks

Pre- and postreading pages for these selections appear in an interactive format in the *Reader's Notebooks*. Each *Notebook* is differentiated for a different group of learners. The selections in the Adapted and English Learner's versions are abridged.

- **L2 L3** *Reader's Notebook*
- **L1** *Reader's Notebook: Adapted Version*
- **EL** *Reader's Notebook: English Learner's Version*
- **EL** *Reader's Notebook: Spanish Version*

© *Common Core Companion*

Additional instruction and practice for each Common Core State Standard

Selection Support

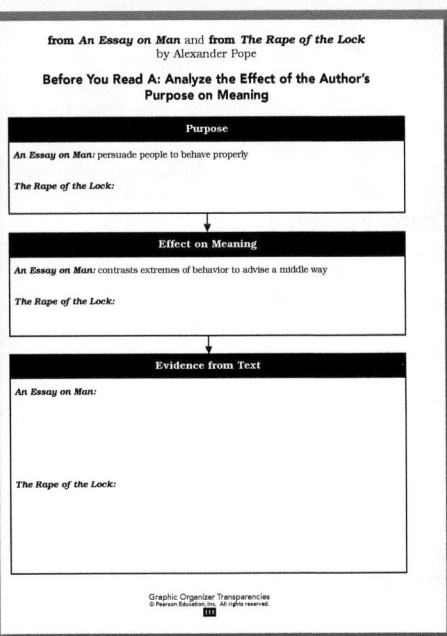

Graphic Organizer Transparencies

EL L1 L2 **Reading: Graphic Organizer A**
(partially filled in), p. 111

Also available for these selections:
EL L3 **Reading: Graphic Organizer B**, p. 112
EL L1 L2 **Literary Analysis: Graphic Organizer A** (partially filled in), p. 113
EL L3 **Literary Analysis: Graphic Organizer B**, p. 114

Skills Development/Extension

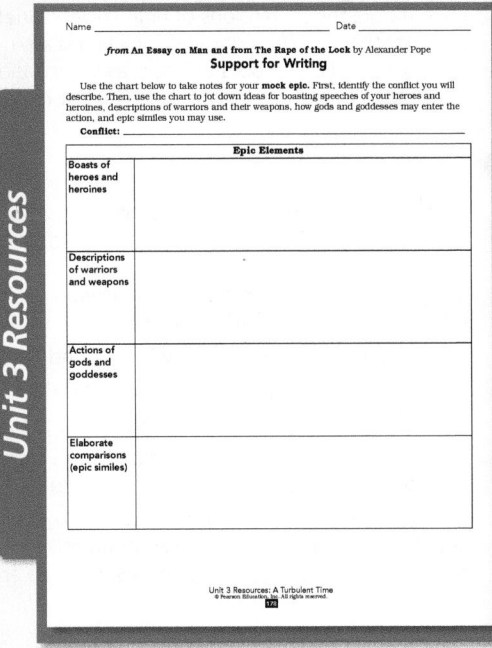

Unit 3 Resources

EL L3 L4 **Support for Writing**, p. 178

Also available for these selections:
All **Literary Analysis**, p. 175
All **Reading**, p. 176
All **Enrichment**, p. 179

Assessment

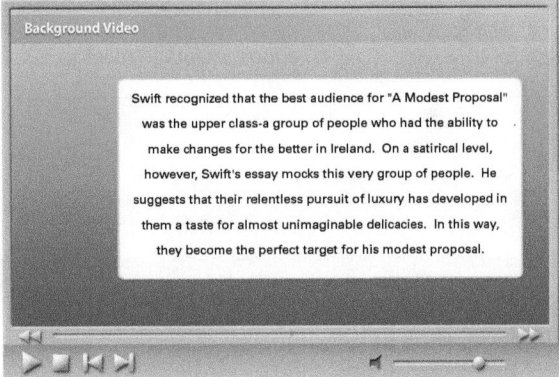

EL L1 L2 **Selection Test A**, pp. 183–185

Also available for these selections:
L3 L4 **Open-Book Test**, pp. 180–182
EL L3 L4 **Selection Test B**, pp. 186–188

PHLit Online!
www.PHLitOnline.com

Online Resources: All print materials are also available online.

- complete narrated selection text
- a thematically related video with writing prompt
- an interactive graphic organizer
- highlighting feature
- access to all student print resources, adapted to individual student needs
- Spanish and English summaries
- adapted selection translations in Spanish

Background Video

Swift recognized that the best audience for "A Modest Proposal" was the upper class-a group of people who had the ability to make changes for the better in Ireland. On a satirical level, however, Swift's essay mocks this very group of people. He suggests that their relentless pursuit of luxury has developed in them a taste for almost unimaginable delicacies. In this way, they become the perfect target for his modest proposal.

Background Video

Also available:

Get Connected! (thematic video with writing prompt)
All videos are available in Spanish.

Vocabulary Central

Vocabulary Central (tools and activities for studying vocabulary)

Also available:

Writer's Journal (with graphics feature)

❶ 🔍 Connecting to the Essential Question

1. Review the assignment with the class.

2. Prepare students to write by prompting them to consider who today might be analogous to the high-society types of Pope's day. Then, have them complete the assignment.

3. As students read, have them look for attitudes that Pope associates with high-society types.

❷ Literary Analysis

Introduce the skill using the instruction on the student page.

Think Aloud: Model the Skill

Say to students:

When I read a mock epic, I need to distinguish between the trivial events taking place and the grandiose way they are described. For example, in *The Rape of the Lock* at the beginning of a card game, the kings, queens, and knaves (or jacks) "Draw forth to combat on the velvet plain" (line 44). To get the joke, I need to picture in what is really going on—people are sitting around a table and taking turns playing their cards.

❸ Reading Strategy

1. Introduce the strategy using the instruction on the student page.

2. Give students **Reading Strategy Graphic Organizer B**, page 112 in *Graphic Organizer Transparencies*, to fill out as they read.

Think Aloud: Model the Skill

Say to students:

If I were telling a story in order to ridicule something I found silly, I would exaggerate the ridiculous aspects of my subject. I might also include overly dramatic language. Because I know Pope's purpose is also to ridicule these techniques are things I can expect, in Pope's poetry.

❹ Vocabulary

Pronounce each word, giving its definition, and have students say it aloud.

Before You Read

from *An Essay on Man* •
from *The Rape of the Lock*

❶ Connecting to the Essential Question In *The Rape of the Lock*, Pope mocks the pretensions of high society. Briefly describe pretentious behavior that you have observed. As you read, noticing the upper-class behavior that Pope mocks will help as you consider the Essential Question: **How does literature shape or reflect society?**

❷ Literary Analysis

Used in poetry, prose, drama, and other basic genres, **parody** is writing that makes fun of another, more serious work or of its author's style. *The Rape of the Lock* is a *mock epic*, or poetic parody of a traditional epic about heroes. Pope applies these conventions of classical epics to his trivial subject, the theft of a lady's lock of hair:

- boasting speeches made by heroes and heroines
- elaborate descriptions of warriors and their weapons
- involvement of gods and goddesses in the action
- **epic similes,** or intricate comparisons in the style of Homer that sometimes use the words *like, as,* or *so*

Note Pope's mocking of epic elements in *The Rape of the Lock*. Also note how, in both poems, he uses antithesis, a rhetorical device in which contrasting words, clauses, sentences, or ideas are placed side by side in parallel grammatical structures:

Whether he thinks <u>too little</u>, *or* <u>too much</u>. *(Essay, line 12)*

❸ Reading Strategy

© **Preparing to Read Complex Texts** To **analyze how an author's purpose affects the meaning of a work,** ask yourself why the author is writing. For example, knowing that Pope's purpose is to poke fun at grand literature and high society, you will understand why he chooses certain words to suggest contrasts between heroic deeds and trivial upper-class pursuits to in turn create a humorous **tone.** As you read, notice how his purpose leads him to make such contrasts throughout the poem.

❹ Vocabulary

stoic (stō′ ik) *n.* person indifferent to joy, grief, or pain (p. 631)

disabused (dis′ ə byo͞ozd′) *adj.* freed from false ideas (p. 631)

obliquely (ə blēk′ lē) *adv.* at a slant; indirectly (p. 634)

plebeian (plē bē′ ən) *adj.* common; not aristocratic (p. 635)

destitute (des′ tə to͞ot′) *adj.* lacking (p. 635)

assignations (as′ ig nā′ shənz) *n.* appointments to meet (p. 639)

© Common Core State Standards

Reading Literature
6. Analyze a case in which grasping point of view requires distinguishing what is directly stated in a text from what is really meant.

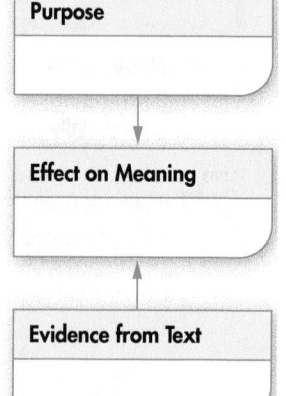

Purpose

↓

Effect on Meaning

↑

Evidence from Text

www.PHLitOnline.com

628 A Turbulent Time (1625–1798)

Vocabulary Development

Vocabulary Knowledge Rating
Create a **Vocabulary Knowledge Rating Chart** (*Professional Development Guidebook*, p. 33) for the vocabulary words on the student page. Give each student a copy of the chart with the words on it. Read the words aloud, and have students mark their rating of each in the Before Reading column.

Urge students to attend to these words as they read and discuss the selections.

In order to gauge how much instruction you need to provide, tally how many students are confident in their knowledge of each word. As students read, point out the words and their context.

PHLit Online! **Vocabulary Central,** featuring tools, activities, and songs for studying vocabulary, is available online at **www.PHLitOnline.com.**

⑤ Alexander Pope
(1688–1744)

Author of *An Essay on Man* •
The Rape of the Lock

Despite a crippling childhood disease and persistent ill
health, Alexander Pope was determined at a young age
to become a great poet. He triumphantly achieved his
boyhood ambition by the time he was in his twenties,
capturing the attention of the leading literary figures of
England. A brilliant satirist in verse, Pope gave his name to
the literary era in which he wrote, which is now called the
Age of Pope and Swift.

A Struggle Against Prejudice Born into the Roman
Catholic family of a London linen merchant, Pope was
a member of a persecuted religious minority. After the
expulsion of King James II in 1688, English Catholics could
not legally vote, hold office, attend a university, or live
within ten miles of London. Probably to comply with the
rule of residency, his family moved first to the village of
Hammersmith and then to Binfield, near Windsor Forest.
In this rural setting, Pope spent his formative years writing
poetry, studying the classics, and educating himself.

"[T]his long Disease, my Life" In addition to facing
religious prejudice, Pope had severe physical problems.
Deformed by tuberculosis of the bone, or Pott's disease,
Pope stood only about four and a half feet tall—"that little
Alexander the women laugh at," he said about himself. Pope
also suffered from nervousness and excruciating headaches
throughout his life. In a line from his poem *Epistle to Dr.
Arbuthnot* (1735), he refers jokingly but also with sadness to
"this long Disease, my Life."

A Turn to Philosophy In the 1730s, Pope's writing moved
out of the satirical mode to become increasingly philosophical. Leaving humor behind, he embarked on a massive work
concerning morality and government but completed only
An Essay on Man and *Moral Essays*. Nevertheless, the entire
body of his work is so noteworthy that critics and fellow
writers alike frequently accord him exceptionally high
praise. The twentieth-century poet Edith Sitwell, for example, called Pope "perhaps the most flawless artist our race
has yet produced."

from An Essay on Man • *from The Rape of the Lock* **629**

⌨ Daily Bellringer

For each class during which you will
teach these selections, have students
complete one of the five activities
for the appropriate week in the *Daily
Bellringer Activities* booklet.

▸ Multidraft Reading

To assist struggling readers and to
enhance reading for all, assign the
text in chunks, as warranted by
length, and apply multidraft reading
protocols. For each reading, have
students set the purpose indicated:

- **First reading**—identifying key
  ideas and details and answering
  any Reading Checks.
- **Second reading**—analyzing craft
  and structure and responding to
  the side-column prompts.
- **Third reading**—integrating knowledge and ideas, connecting to
  other texts and the world, and
  answering the end-of-selection
  questions.

For more guidance, refer to the
*Classroom Strategies and Teaching
Routines* card on multidraft reading.

⑤ Background
More About the Author
Alexander Pope

Alexander Pope, largely self-
educated, was a precocious boy,
eagerly reading Latin, Greek, French,
and Italian, which he taught himself. Despite his curved spine, he
could ride a horse and delighted in
travel. However, reading and writing
remained his main pursuits. Pope's
successful translation of Homer's *Iliad*
was admired by his peers and later
poets. Samuel Taylor Coleridge called
it "an astonishing product of match-
less talent and ingenuity."

Pope is among the most quotable
writers in the English language. Some
of the epigrams from his *Essay on
Criticism* are better known than the
author. Examples include "To err
is human, to forgive, divine," and
"Fools rush in where angels fear to
tread."

PHLit Online!
www.PHLitOnline.com

Teaching From Technology

Preparing to Read
Go to **www.PHLitOnline.com** in class or in a
lab and display the **Get Connected!** slideshow
for this grouping. Have the class brainstorm
responses to the slideshow writing prompt,
entering ideas in the interactive journal. Then,
have students complete their written responses
individually, in a lab or as homework.
To build background, display the Background
and More About the Author features.

Using the Interactive Text
Go to **www.PHLitOnline.com** and display the
Enriched Online Student Edition. As the class
reads the selection or listens to the narration,
record answers to side-column prompts using
the graphic organizers accessible on the interactive page. Alternatively, have students use
the online edition individually, answering the
prompts as they read.

❶ About the Selection

Pope's heroic couplets are the perfect vehicle to balance the contrary attributes of humankind. The passage asks, "What is man?" Its answer is that man is a creature in the middle. Both the glory and the jest of the world, man is above all a riddle.

❷ Activating Prior Knowledge

Have them discuss ways in which cliques and other social groups have been or might be satirized.

Concept Connector ➡

Tell students they will return to their responses after reading the selections.

❸ Humanities

The Thinker by Auguste René Rodin, 1880

Refused admittance to the art school of his choice, Rodin became the foremost sculptor of the nineteenth and early twentieth centuries. Rodin's best-known sculpture style is characterized by a deliberate roughness of form. Use these questions for discussion:

1. **Possible response:** Thinking is hard work. This sculpture may be a metaphor.

❹ Critical Viewing

Possible response: Rodin's image is a contemplative one. Pope's descriptions of doubt, thought, and reason compare well with this image. However, the sculpture reflects calmness, which contrasts with the "chaos of thought" in Pope's work.

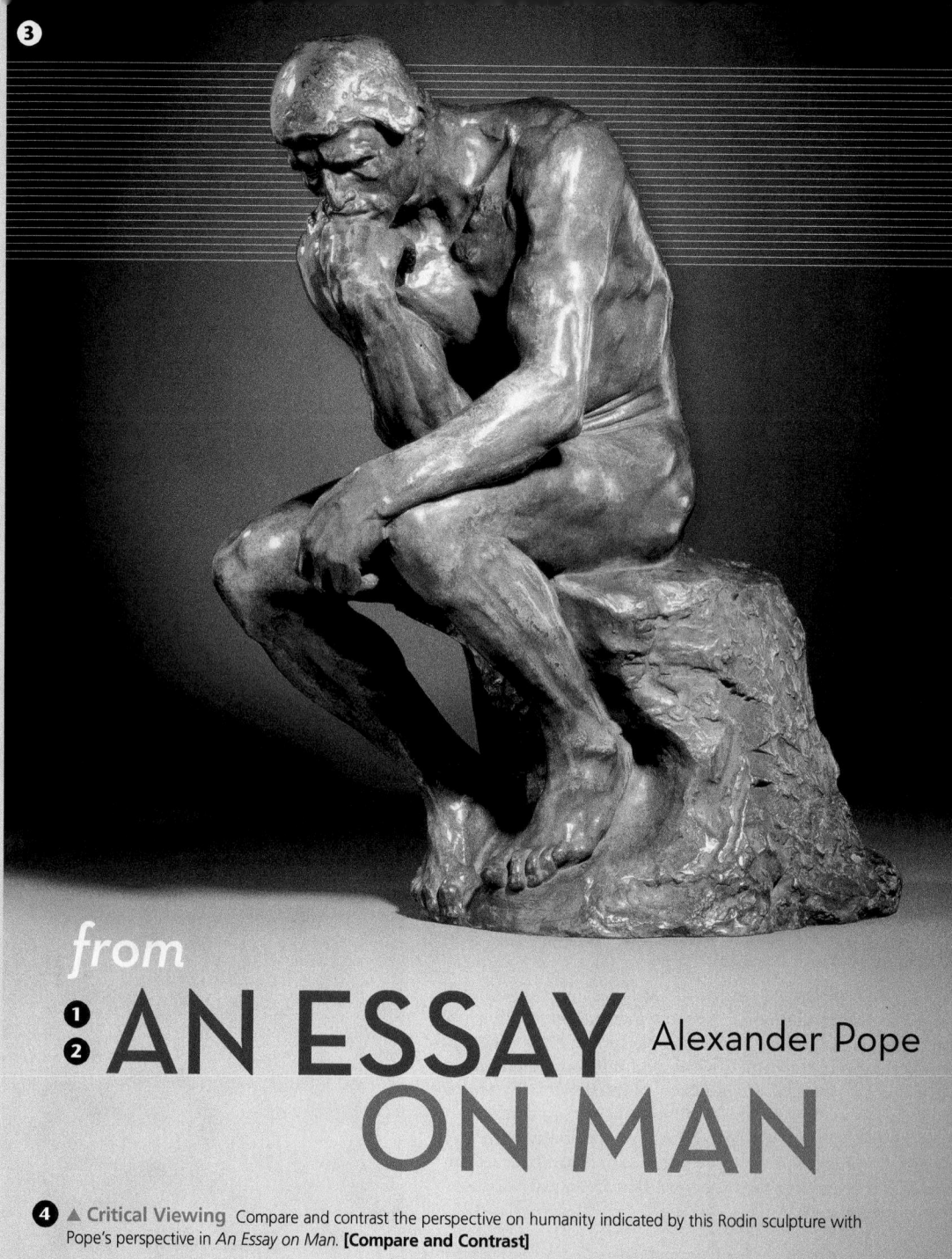

from

❶ ❷ AN ESSAY ON MAN

Alexander Pope

❹ ▲ **Critical Viewing** Compare and contrast the perspective on humanity indicated by this Rodin sculpture with Pope's perspective in *An Essay on Man*. **[Compare and Contrast]**

630 A Turbulent Time (1625–1798)

© Text Complexity Rubric: Leveled Texts

	from **An Essay on Man**	*from* **The Rape of the Lock**
Qualitative Measures		
Context/ Knowledge Demands	Philosophical poem; cultural knowledge demands 1 2 ③ 4 5	Mock epic; literary and cultural knowledge demands 1 2 3 ④ 5
Structure/Language Conventionality and Clarity	Archaic diction; long sentences 1 2 ③ 4 5	Archaic diction and syntax; long sentences 1 2 ③ 4 5
Levels of Meaning/ Purpose/Concept Level	Moderate (human nature) 1 2 ③ 4 5	Challenging (social manners) 1 2 3 ④ 5
Quantitative Measures		
Lexile/Text Length	NP / 142 words	NP / 2,187 words
Overall Complexity	**More accessible**	**More complex**

BACKGROUND *An Essay on Man* is an examination of human nature, society, and morals. In the following passage, Pope cautions against intellectual pride by describing the uncertain "middle state" in which humans have been placed.

Know then thyself, presume not God to scan;
⑤ The proper study of mankind is man.
Placed on this isthmus of a middle state,
A being darkly wise, and rudely great:
5 With too much knowledge for the skeptic side,
With too much weakness for the stoic's pride,
He hangs between; in doubt to act, or rest;
In doubt to deem himself a god, or beast;
In doubt his mind or body to prefer;
10 Born but to die, and reasoning but to err;
Alike in ignorance, his reason such,
Whether he thinks too little, or too much:
Chaos of thought and passion, all confused;
Still by himself abused, or disabused;
15 Created half to rise, and half to fall;
Great lord of all things, yet a prey to all;
Sole judge of truth, in endless error hurled:
The glory, jest, and riddle of the world!

Vocabulary
stoic (stō′ ik) *n.* person indifferent to joy, grief, pleasure, or pain

disabused (dis′ ə byo͞ozd′) *adj.* freed from false ideas

Critical Reading

© **1. Key Ideas and Details** **(a)** What does Pope say should be the object of man's study? **(b) Speculate:** Why do you think Pope says, "presume not God to scan"?

© **2. Key Ideas and Details** **(a)** According to Pope, what prevents man from being a skeptic or a stoic? **(b) Analyze Cause and Effect:** What is the result of man's being neither skeptic nor stoic? Explain.

© **3. Key Ideas and Details** **(a)** What does each "half" of man do? **(b) Interpret:** In your own words, express how man can be both a "lord of all things" and "a prey to all."

© **4. Integration of Knowledge and Ideas** What twentieth-century events suggest that humans are any or all of the following: "The glory, jest, and riddle of the world!" Explain.

Cite textual evidence to support your responses.

from An Essay on Man **631**

⑤ Critical Thinking
Analyze

1. Make sure students understand that *man* in line 2 refers to all humankind.

2. Explain that Pope uses antithesis extensively in this poem. **Ask** students to identify the opposites in the passage and to explain how each half of the pairs of ideas contributes to Popes work. **Possible responses:** The juxtaposition of *reasoning* and *err* (line 10) shows that despite humans' ability to use logic, they make mistake.

ASSESS

Answers

Before students respond, you may wish to have them write a brief objective summary of the selection. As they answer the questions below, remind them to support their answers with evidence from the text.

1. (a) The proper study of man is humankind. (b) Pope thinks humans should understand themselves, not question God.

2. (a) Too much knowledge keeps a person from becoming a skeptic, and too much weakness keeps a person from becoming a stoic. (b) Man lives in doubt, never certain what to do or think.

3. (a) Half of man rises and half falls. (b) **Possible response:** Man's intelligence makes him "lord of all things," but his frailty makes him "a prey to all."

4. **Possible response:** Glorious things range from landing on the moon to the kindness of Mother Teresa. However, the horrible things—war, terrorism—show that humans are still a "riddle."

© Text Complexity: Reader and Task Suggestions

from **An Essay on Man**		*from* **The Rape of the Lock**	
Preparing to Read the Text	**Leveled Tasks**	**Preparing to Read the Text**	**Leveled Tasks**
• Using the Background on TE p. 629, have students consider what makes a line from a poem stand alone as a famous quotation. • Explain that Pope, like many others of his day, viewed all of creation as a Great Chain of Being. • Guide students to use Multidraft Reading strategies (TE p. 629).	*Levels of Meaning* If students will have difficulty understanding Pope's view of the Great Chain of Being, have them focus on each couplet of the poem and the point it makes. Then, have students state the general impression of humanity the passage conveys. *Synthesizing* If students will not have difficulty understanding Pope's view of the Great Chain of Being, have them synthesize each point he makes into a single statement about humanity.	• Using the Background on TE p. 632, help students understand the dispute that inspired the poem. • Explain that this mock-epic pokes fun at upper-class people in Pope's day. • Guide students to use Multidraft Reading strategies (TE p. 629).	*Knowledge Demands* If students will have difficulty understanding court life, have them focus on the poem's basic story. Then, as they reread, have them consider how the lofty tone jarringly contrasts with the poem's actual events. *Synthesizing* If students will not have difficulty understanding the lifestyle, have them focus on details that mock aristocratic life.

6 About the Selection

At Hampton Court, amid the "heroes and nymphs," life is pure and petty amusement. There are games of cards; there are tea and coffee; there are gossip and fashion; and there is even—at least in the scene described here—the game of cutting a lock of hair as a kind of prize from the head of a beautiful woman. Pope treats this situation as if it were a scene from an epic battle.

7 Background

The Petre and the Fermor families were part of a prominent group of intermarrying Roman Catholic families, a group to which Pope's own family also belonged. After Robert Petre cut a lock from Arabella Fermor's hair, the ensuing dispute between the Petres and Fermors likely had a disruptive effect on their entire social circle. John Caryll, an acquaintance of Pope's as well as a member of one of the Roman Catholic families, encouraged Pope to write *The Rape of the Lock* in the hope that seeing the situation in a humorous light would help the Petre and Fermor families to be reconciled. By the time the poem was published and revised, however, the dispute between the families had calmed down, and Robert Petre and Arabella Fermor were both married to other people.

from

The Rape of the Lock

Alexander Pope

BACKGROUND *The Rape of the Lock* is based on an actual incident. Two families, the Petres and the Fermors, became involved in a dispute when Robert Petre flirtatiously cut a lock of hair from the head of lovely Arabella Fermor.

The first of the poem's five cantos opens with a formal statement of theme and an invocation to the Muse for poetic inspiration. Then, Belinda, the poem's heroine, receives a warning from the sylph Ariel that a dreadful event will take place in her immediate future. In Canto II, during a boat ride on the Thames, an adventurous baron admires Belinda's hair and is determined to cut two bright locks from her head and keep them as a prize. Aware of the baron's desires, Ariel urges the spirits to protect Belinda.

632 A Turbulent Time (1625–1798)

Enrichment: Investigating Daily Life

Hairstyles

Hairdressing, has been employed by very nearly every society. During the Copper Age (3200–2300 B.C.) and Bronze Age (2300–700 B.C.), hairstyles were often sophisticated, with braids, and ornaments.

The women of ancient Rome used crude curling irons to create their elaborate hairstyles. By 400 B.C., the women of Greece were beginning to dye their hair, while wealthy Greek men powdered their hair with gold dust. Asia, too, developed complex coiffures, and Japanese women used lacquer to secure their styles.

Activity: Hairstyles in History Have groups of students conduct research on popular hairstyles from a chosen historical period. Suggest that they record information in the **Enrichment: Investigating Daily Life** worksheet, *Professional Development Guidebook*, page 224. Have students share pictures of hairstyles from their research, and lead a discussion of the ways in which hairstyles have been used to make statements.

The Barge, 1895–96 Aubrey Beardsley

⑨ Critical Viewing Does the artist's portrayal of Belinda, who is shown here, correspond to Pope's portrayal of her in Canto III? Explain. **[Connect]**

from The Rape of the Lock **633**

The Barge by Aubrey Beardsley, 1895

The British illustrator Aubrey Beardsley (1872–1898) achieved in his six productive years a strange and wonderful style. His only formal art training was one year at the Westminster School of Art in London. His lifelong illness, tuberculosis, did not leave him the strength to explore any form of expression other than pen-and-ink drawings. He received his first illustration commission by chance through a bookseller he frequented. This commission led to many others and to fame as an illustrator. His career ended abruptly with his death at the age of twenty-six.

In executing this drawing, Beardsley introduced a technique of using dots to give texture and variety to his usually severe lines.

Use these questions for discussion:

1. What deductions can you make about the people with whom Belinda, the woman in the center, interacts?
   Answer: She moves among the rich and privileged. These people may be quite stiff and formal. On the other hand, they may be so bored as to take risks when speaking or acting. They may also be as silly and as vain as Belinda seems to be.

2. How would you describe the detail in this illustration?
   Answer: There is a huge amount of detail which, to the modern eye, seems overdone. Nevertheless this elaborate detailing reproduces the style of rich people of the time.

⑨ Critical Viewing

Possible response: Yes; she is beautifully coifed and dressed, and she holds a fan in an elaborate setting, suggesting a restful afternoon with high-society friends.

Differentiated Instruction   for Universal Access

Strategy for Less Proficient Readers

Less proficient readers will likely struggle with the complex sentences and vocabulary in *The Rape of the Lock*. To help students build a conceptual framework for the poem before they begin to read it, display a timeline of events in the poem. For example, the timeline might begin with "A group of high society men and women gather to socialize at the end of a day." Discuss the entire timeline with students. This will help place events in context, as well as help identify the main ideas and themes.

EL Strategy for English Learners

The complex grammar in *The Rape of the Lock* presents difficulties for English learners. To model the process of constructing meaning from complex sentence structures, write the first four lines of the poem on the board. Then "translate" each phrase into simpler language and discuss the function of each phrase. Point out that the subject of the sentence, a structure (or building), does not appear until line 3. Encourage students to determine what the subject of each sentence is, and to determine what roles the other phrases play.

⑩ Critical Thinking

Interpret

1. Remind students that Pope often used antithesis—placing side by side strongly contrasting words or ideas—to make his point.

2. Then, **ask** students to interpret lines 21–22.
   Answer: Judges, who decide the fate of someone convicted of a crime, quickly deliver a verdict of guilty so that their deliberation will not postpone their dinners.

3. **Ask** students how the use of antithesis strengthens Pope's point.
   Possible response: The two lines help readers see two sides of the same situation, presenting a stark contrast between the selfishness of the judges and the pitiful condition of the wretches who hang as a result.

⑪ Literary Analysis

Parody

1. Have students follow along as you read aloud lines 33–36.

2. To aid understanding and help contextualize this passage, **ask** students to explain what is happening in their own words. Encourage them to look back at previous lines, especially lines 31 and 32.
   Answer: Belinda is playing cards, calling on mythical sylphs such as Ariel to point out important cards.

3. Then, **ask** students the Literary Analysis question: To what trivial subject and epic convention does Pope refer in lines 33–36?
   Answer: Pope refers to the trivial event of a card game, while incorporating the epic element of references to mythology.

Canto III

> Meanwhile, declining
> from the noon of day,
> The sun obliquely
> shoots his burning ray.

Vocabulary
obliquely (ə blēk´ lē) *adv.* at a slant; indirectly

⑪ **Literary Analysis**
Parody To what trivial subject and epic convention does Pope refer in lines 33–36?

Close by those meads, forever crowned with flowers,
Where Thames with pride surveys his rising towers,
There stands a structure of majestic frame,[1]
Which from the neighboring Hampton takes its name.
5   Here Britain's statesmen oft the fall foredoom
Of foreign tyrants, and of nymphs at home;
Here thou, great Anna![2] whom three realms obey,
Dost sometimes counsel take—and sometimes tea.
        Hither the heroes and the nymphs resort,
10 To taste awhile the pleasures of a court;
In various talk th' instructive hours they passed,
Who gave the ball, or paid the visit last;
One speaks the glory of the British Queen,
And one describes a charming Indian screen;
15 A third interprets motions, looks, and eyes;
At every word a reputation dies.
Snuff, or the fan,[3] supply each pause of chat,
With singing, laughing, ogling, and all that.
        Meanwhile, declining from the noon of day,
20 The sun obliquely shoots his burning ray;
⑩ The hungry judges soon the sentence sign,
And wretches hang that jurymen may dine;
The merchant from th' Exchange[4] returns in peace,
And the long labors of the toilet[5] cease.
25 Belinda now, whom thirst of fame invites,
Burns to encounter two adventurous knights,
At omber[6] singly to decide their doom;
And swells her breast with conquests yet to come.
Straight the three bands prepare in arms to join,
30 Each band the number of the sacred nine.[7]
Soon as she spreads her hand, th' aerial guard
Descend, and sit on each important card:
First Ariel perched upon a Matadore,[8]
Then each, according to the rank they bore;
35 For sylphs, yet mindful of their ancient race,
Are, as when women, wondrous fond of place.
        Behold, four kings in majesty revered,
With hoary whiskers and a forky beard;

---

1. **structure . . . frame** Hampton Court, a royal palace near London.
2. **Anna** Queen Anne, who ruled England, Ireland, and Scotland from 1702 through 1714.
3. **snuff . . . fan** At the time, gentlemen commonly took snuff and ladies usually carried a fan.
4. **Exchange** London financial center where merchants, bankers, and brokers conducted business.
5. **toilet** dressing tables.
6. **omber** popular card game.
7. **sacred nine** reference to the nine Muses of Greek mythology.
8. **Matadore** powerful card that could take a trick.

Enrichment: Building Context

Card Games and Leisure

In eighteenth-century England, the gentry were so wealthy that they did not need to work for a living; their days were instead filled with leisure activities, including many different card games. Popular card games of the period included casino, commerce, loo, piquet, quadrille, speculation, and whist.

Then as today, card games offered a backdrop against which people could socialize.

Activity: Research Historical Card Games
Have pairs of students conduct research on the rules and relative popularity of various card games of eighteenth-century England. You may also have some students research other leisure activities of the period. Suggest that they record information in the **Enrichment: Building Context** worksheet, *Professional Development Guidebook,* page 222. Encourage students to discuss how their findings affect their understanding of the characters in *The Rape of the Lock.*

And four fair queens whose hands sustain a flower,
40 Th' expressive emblem of their softer power;
Four knaves in garbs succinct,[9] a trusty band,
Caps on their heads, and halberts[10] in their hand;
And particolored troops, a shining train,
12 Draw forth to combat on the velvet plain.
45   The skillful nymph reviews her force with care:
Let spades be trumps! she said, and trumps they were.
     Now move to war her sable Matadores,
In show like leaders of the swarthy Moors.
Spadillio[11] first, unconquerable Lord!
50 Led off two captive trumps, and swept the board.
As many more Manillio[12] forced to yield,
And marched a victor from the verdant field.[13]
Him Basto[14] followed, but his fate more hard
Gained but one trump and one plebeian card.
55 With his broad saber next, a chief in years,
The hoary majesty of spades appears,
Puts forth one manly leg, to sight revealed,
The rest, his many-colored robe concealed.
The rebel knave, who dares his prince engage,
60 Proves the just victim of his royal rage.
Even mighty Pam,[15] that kings and queens o'erthrew
And mowed down armies in the fights of loo,
Sad chance of war! now destitute of aid,
Falls undistinguished by the victor spade!
65   Thus far both armies to Belinda yield;
Now to the baron fate inclines the field.
His warlike Amazon her host invades,
Th' imperial consort of the crown of spades.
The club's black tyrant first her victim died,
70 Spite of his haughty mien, and barbarous pride.
What boots[16] the regal circle on his head,
His giant limbs, in state unwieldy spread;
That long behind he trails his pompous robe,
And, of all monarchs, only grasps the globe?
75   The baron now his diamonds pours apace;
Th' embroidered king who shows but half his face,
And his refulgent queen, with powers combined
Of broken troops an easy conquest find.

---

9. **succinct** (sək siŋkt´) belted.
10. **halberts** long-handled weapons.
11. **Spadillio** ace of spades.
12. **Manillio** two of spades.
13. **verdant field** the card table, covered with a green cloth.
14. **Basto** ace of clubs.
15. **Pam** knave of clubs, the highest card in the game called "loo."
16. **What boots** of what benefit is.

---

13 Vocabulary
plebeian (plē bē´ ən) adj.
common; not aristocratic

Vocabulary
destitute (des´ tə tōōt)
adj. lacking

14 Reading Check
In what way do Belinda and
her friends pass the time?

from The Rape of the Lock **635**

12 **Background**
The Card Game
Pope describes the card game as if
the kings and queens on the cards
were actually doing battle. Point out
the mock epic elements of this game,
but assure students that they need
not follow every play to know what
is happening. The detail adds to the
mock-heroic tone but does not affect
the outcome of the story.

You may wish to explain, however, that Belinda is being aided by
the sylphs and so wins the first four
"tricks." Then, in lines 66–74, the
baron trumps Belinda's king of clubs
("the club's black tyrant") with his
queen of spades ("warlike Amazon,"
"imperial consort of the crown of
spades"). By line 85, he has taken
Belinda's queen of hearts with his
jack of diamonds. She grows pale
at the thought of defeat. However,
in lines 95–98, we learn that she triumphs, as her king of hearts "springs
to vengeance" in fond memory of his
captured queen.

13 **Vocabulary Builder**
Words From Political Science

1. Call students' attention to the
word *plebian* and its definition.
Explain that it is the adjectival
form of *plebs*, a word not simply
derived from Latin, but actually
used in ancient Rome, where it
referred to lower-class citizens.

2. Explain that *plebian* is usually
used to describe things that are
a bit too common or somewhat
vulgar. **Ask** students what they
think the phrase "plebeian card"
in line 54 means.
Answer: The card is a regular
numbered card—not an ace,
king, queen, or knave.

14 **Reading Check**
Answer: They play omber, a popular
card game of the time.

635

15 Humanities

The Toilette by Aubrey Beardsley, 1895–1896

This drawing was produced by Beardsley for an 1896 edition of *The Rape of the Lock*. Beardsley's signature black-and-white ink drawings are thought to reflect a desire on his part to minimize visual clutter in his work. This drawing may seem like a departure from this ideal because of the extreme detail.

Use this question for discussion:
Who might these two women be, and what clues support this?
Possible response: The seated woman might be Belinda; the other might be a servant or waiting-girl. Clues include the fact that Belinda is seated having her hair done, and the waiting-girl's hair is covered by a cap.

16 Critical Viewing

Possible response: Pope might ridicule the elaborate hairstyle worn by the woman.

17 Reading Strategy

Analyzing the Author's Purpose

1. Have a student volunteer read aloud lines 83–86.

2. **Ask** students what double meanings Pope creates with the words *nations* and *dye*.
   Answer: *Nations* could refer to either political nations or the different suits in the card game; likewise, *dye* could refer to either the different skin tones of various regions or the dyes used to create playing cards.

▶ **Monitor Progress Ask** the Reading Strategy question.
Possible response: These four lines might seem to be a commentary on the tragedy of war; however, within the context of the poem, these lines take on a more ironic tone.

18 Literary Analysis

Mock Epic and Antithesis

1. Have students read line 92 to themselves.

2. Then, **ask** students the Literary Analysis question.
   Possible response: It sets up a contrast between the dramatic phrase "the jaws of ruin" and the *codille,* a much less dramatic defeat.

636

16 ▶ Critical Viewing
Which elements of the situation portrayed in this drawing do you think Pope would choose to ridicule? Why? **[Speculate]**

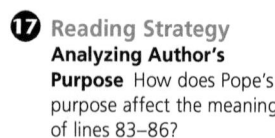

17 Reading Strategy
Analyzing Author's Purpose How does Pope's purpose affect the meaning of lines 83–86?

18 Literary Analysis
Mock Epic and Antithesis Why is line 92 an example of antithesis?

Clubs, diamonds, hearts, in wild disorder seen,
80   With throngs promiscuous strew the level green.
      Thus when dispersed a routed army runs,
      Of Asia's troops, and Afric's sable sons,
            With like confusion different nations fly,
      Of various habit, and of various dye,
85   The pierced battalions disunited fall,
      In heaps on heaps; one fate o'erwhelms them all.
            The knave of diamonds tries his wily arts,
      And wins (oh shameful chance!) the queen of hearts.
      At this, the blood the virgin's cheek forsook,
90   A livid paleness spreads o'er all her look;
      She sees, and trembles at th' approaching ill,
      Just in the jaws of ruin, and codille.[17]
      And now (as oft in some distempered state)
      On one nice trick depends the general fate.

---

17. **codille** term meaning the defeat of a hand of cards.

636 A Turbulent Time (1625–1798)

Enrichment: Analyzing Historical Patterns, Trends, and Periods

Orientalism

In eighteenth-century Europe, decorative items from the Orient, such as porcelain and lacquerware, were very popular. In lines 107–110 of the poem, we read of Japanese lacquer tables and Chinese cups, though the setting is British.

The rise of interest in all things Asian was known as Orientalism. Public interest in the Orient was stimulated by the translation into English in 1705–1708 of the *Arabian Nights.*
Activity: Investigate Orientalism Have pairs or groups of students conduct research on the roots and effects of Orientalism, as well as other arenas in which the trend manifested itself, such as theater and fashion. Suggest that they record information in the **Enrichment: Analyzing Historical Patterns, Trends, and Periods** worksheet, *Professional Development Guidebook,* page 231. Have students share their results, and ask them how the characters in *The Rape of the Lock* likely feel about the Orient.

95 An ace of hearts steps forth; the king unseen
     Lurked in her hand, and mourned his captive queen.
     He springs to vengeance with an eager pace,
     And falls like thunder on the prostrate ace.
     The nymph exulting fills with shouts the sky;
100 The walls, the woods, and long canals reply.
         Oh thoughtless mortals! ever blind to fate,
     Too soon dejected, and too soon elate.
     Sudden, these honors shall be snatched away,
     And cursed forever this victorious day.
105   For lo! the board with cups and spoons is crowned,
     The berries crackle, and the mill turns round;[18]
     On shining altars of Japan[19] they raise
     The silver lamp; the fiery spirits blaze;
     From silver spouts the grateful liquors glide,
110 While China's earth[20] receives the smoking tide.
     At once they gratify their scent and taste,
     And frequent cups prolong the rich repast.
     Straight hover round the fair her airy band;
     some, as she sipped, the fuming liquor fanned,
115 Some o'er her lap their careful plumes displayed,
     Trembling, and conscious of the rich brocade.
     Coffee (which makes the politician wise,
     And see through all things with his half-shut eyes)
     Sent up in vapors to the baron's brain
120 New stratagems, the radiant lock to gain.
     Ah cease, rash youth! desist ere 'tis too late,
     Fear the just gods, and think of Scylla's fate![21]
     Changed to a bird, and sent to flit in air,
     She dearly pays for Nisus' injured hair!
125   But when to mischief mortals bend their will,
     How soon they find fit instruments of ill!
     Just then, Clarissa drew with tempting grace
     A two-edged weapon from her shining case:
     So ladies in romance assist their knight,
130 Present the spear, and arm him for the fight.
     He takes the gift with reverence, and extends
     The little engine[22] on his fingers' ends;
     This just behind Belinda's neck he spread,
     As o'er the fragrant steams she bends her head.
135 Swift to the lock a thousand sprites repair,
     A thousand wings, by turns, blow back the hair;

---

18. **The berries . . . round** Coffee beans are ground in a hand mill at the table.
19. **altars of Japan** small imported lacquer tables.
20. **China's earth** earthenware cups imported from China.
21. **Scylla's** (sil′ ez) **fate** Scylla, the daughter of King Nisus, was turned into a sea bird because she cut off the lock of her father's hair on which his safety depended and sent it to his enemy.
22. **engine** instrument.

⑲ *The*
BRITISH
TRADITION

**Neoclassical Style and
The Heroic Couplet**
Lines 105–106 or any of the rhyming lines in the poem demonstrate Pope's use of the closed heroic couplet, a rhyming pair of iambic pentameter lines that are "closed" because they express a complete thought. This type of couplet is typical of the Neoclassical style of the eighteenth century, which had these characteristics: a reliance on Greek and Roman models, a stress on human limitations, and a concept of the poet as a kind of public speaker addressing society as a whole.
    In keeping with the Neoclassical outlook, the closed heroic couplet allows Pope to indicate human follies and frailties with devices from public speaking, such as antithesis.

Connect to the Literature

In what ways do lines 125 and 126 fit the Neoclassical style and outlook?

⑳ ✓ Reading Check

What is the baron plotting to do?

from The Rape of the Lock **637**

---

⑲ The British Tradition
Neoclassical Style and the Heroic Couplet
While the literature of many European countries used rhyming couplets in some form, the heroic couplet belonged only to England. Its first use in English poetry is not known, but Chaucer was the first to use it extensively, in *The Canterbury Tales*. By the mid-seventeenth century, heroic couplets became the principal meter used in drama.

Connect to the Literature
Remind students of the elements of Neoclassical style. Then, **ask** the Connect to the Literature question: In what ways do lines 125 and 126 fit the Neoclassical style and outlook? **Answer:** The lines refer to the mischief of mortals, a common theme in classical literature; making mischief is a human failing; and the poet addresses the audience, society at large, with this warning.

⑳ Reading Check
Answer: The baron is plotting to cut a lock of Belinda's hair.

Differentiated
Instruction   for Universal Access

Strategy for Special-Needs Students
If students are struggling to recognize how Pope satirizes the elaborate elements of the coffee service in Canto III, have them focus on elements of the scene that suggest the sumptuous environment. You may wish to have students list on the board phrases that point to the lavish environment, such as "silver spouts," "rich repast," and "rich brocade." Have students view the accompanying art throughout this selection as a visual aid.

Enrichment for Advanced Readers
Students may be interested in learning more about Alexander Pope's life and work. Suggest that they try to find two or three facts about him that are not mentioned in the biographical material at the beginning of the selection. You may wish to have them share some of what they learn with the class. Another possibility would be to have students look for information about how Pope's work was received by his contemporaries—what literary figures did Pope associate with, and what was their opinion of his work?

❷❶ Humanities

The Rape of the Lock by Aubrey Beardsley, 1895–1896

This drawing is one of the nine produced by Aubrey Beardsley for an 1896 edition of this poem. The satiric nature of the poem appealed to Beardsley's sense of the burlesque. He depicts the incident of the cutting of the hair with a mocking humor comparable to Pope's. The artist's appreciation of the poet's wit and humor adds an extra element to these drawings.

Use these questions for discussion:

1. Who might the central figure in the foreground be?
   Possible response: It is possible that this is Ariel, a male spirit who intercedes on behalf of Belinda. Although he is dressed like others in the drawing room, he is half their size, and he has an entirely different kind of expression on his face.

2. Why do you think the illustrator does not show Belinda's face?
   Possible response: Belinda does not know what is happening. What is important in this illustration is both the act of cutting and the milieu in which the cutting takes place, both of which the artist captures.

❷❷ Critical Viewing

Possible response: Pope makes trivial events such as a game of cards or an afternoon tea sound important with his flowery language and exalted imagery. In much the same way, the artist captures trivial goings-on with the detail and care that one would normally expect to be given to more important events.

The Rape of the Lock, 1895–96, Aubrey Beardsley

❷❷ **Critical Viewing**
Where in the poem does Pope make a trivial occasion seem important, as the artist does here? Explain. **[Connect]**

Enrichment: Analyzing an Image

Fashion of the Times

The obsession with fashion satirized by Alexander Pope was a phenomenon of the upper classes in the 1700s. Fashions of the European upper class were just as elaborate as hairstyles of the time. Women's dresses were made of luxurious fabrics and decorated lavishly. High fashion also dictated that women wear boned corsets that cinched their waists.

The Industrial Revolution brought dramatic cultural change for both England and the United States. Mass production of goods made stylish clothes available to the middle class.

Activity: Fashion in Art Have pairs of students analyze the image on page 638 with an eye toward the way fashion is portrayed. Is the focus more on the characters or on their clothing? Suggest that students record information in the **Enrichment: Analyzing an Image from Fine Art** worksheet, *Professional Development Guidebook,* page 232. Ask students how the art contributes to their understanding of the poem.

And thrice they twitched the diamond in her ear;
Thrice she looked back, and thrice the foe drew near.
Just in that instant, anxious Ariel sought
140   The close recesses of the virgin's thought;
As on the nosegay in her breast reclined,
He watched th' ideas rising in her mind,
Sudden he viewed, in spite of all her art,
An earthly lover lurking at her heart.[23]
145   Amazed, confused, he found his power expired,
Resigned to fate, and with a sigh retired.
        The peer now spreads the glittering forfex[24] wide,
T' enclose the lock; now joins it, to divide.
Even then, before the fatal engine closed,
150   A wretched sylph too fondly interposed;
Fate urged the shears, and cut the sylph in twain,
(But airy substance soon unites again).
The meeting points the sacred hair dissever
From the fair head, forever, and forever!
155   Then flashed the living lightning from her eyes,
And screams of horror rend th' affrighted skies.
Not louder shrieks to pitying heaven are cast,
When husbands, or when lap dogs breathe their last;
Or when rich China vessels fallen from high,
160   In glittering dust, and painted fragments lie!
        "Let wreaths of triumph now my temples twine,"
The victor cried, "the glorious prize is mine!"
While fish in streams, or birds delight in air,
Or in a coach and six the British Fair,
165   As long as Atalantis[25] shall be read
Or the small pillow grace a lady's bed,
While visits shall be paid on solemn days,
When numerous wax lights in bright order blaze,
While nymphs take treats, or assignations give,
170   So long my honor, name, and praise shall live!
What time would spare, from steel receives its date,[26]
And monuments, like men, submit to fate!
Steel could the labor of the gods destroy,
And strike to dust th' imperial towers of Troy;
175   Steel could the works of mortal pride confound,
And hew triumphal arches to the ground.
What wonder then, fair nymph! thy hairs should feel,
The conquering force of unresisted steel?

---

23. **earthly lover . . . heart** If in her heart Belinda wants the baron to succeed, they cannot
    protect her.
24. **forfex** scissors.
25. *Atalantis* popular book of scandalous gossip.
26. **receives its date** is destroyed.

from The Rape of the Lock **639**

23 Reading Strategy
Analyzing Author's Purpose Why does the author describe the scene in lines 145–160 in such an elevated manner?

24 Literary Analysis
Parody How is Belinda's reaction to the loss of her hair appropriate for a mock epic?

Vocabulary
assignations
(as´ ig nā´ shənz) *n.* appointments to meet

25 Reading Check
What happens to the sylph that flies between the blades of the shears?

23 Reading Strategy
Analyzing Author's Purpose

1. Have several student volunteers read aloud lines 145–160. Encourage the students reading aloud to be dramatic, even overly so.

2. **Ask** students which phrases are elevated or exaggerated.
   Possible responses: Phrases such as "the fatal engine," "the sacred hair," and "forever, and forever" are elevated; phrases such as "screams of horror" are exaggerated. The references to mythical sylphs also add to the elevated tone of the passage.

3. Then, **ask** students the Reading Strategy question.
   Answer: The author describes the scene this way because the elevated language humorously emphasizes how truly trivial the events are, which is the point he is trying to make.

24 Literary Analysis
Parody

1. Have students reread lines 155–160 to themselves.

2. Then, **ask** students the Literary Analysis question: How is Belinda's reaction to the loss of her hair appropriate for a mock epic?
   Possible responses: Her reaction of overly dramatized horror, even the same horror and despair that would accompany a husband's death, plays up the importance of a trivial event. Pope's use of the imagery of the skies and heaven adds to the epic feeling of the language.

25 Reading Check
Answer: The sylph who flies between the shear blades is cut in two; however, because he is "airy substance," his two halves are able to rejoin.

Differentiated Instruction   for Universal Access

Support for Less Proficient Readers
Use the **Literary Analysis Graphic Organizer B**, page 114 in the *Graphic Organizer Transparencies,* to help students understand what to look for in reading a mock epic. Then, in a group, work through a passage of approximately fifteen lines, and have students identify the mock epic elements.

Support for Special-Needs Students
The most important thing to get across to students is that this poem is meant to be funny. Explain that everything is exaggerated. Review what the battle is about, and remind students that the author's purpose is to entertain and ridicule.

EL Support for English Learners
Review with students what is happening in the story, then have students follow along in their texts while listening to the *Hear It!* Audio CDs. Periodically pause the recording to discuss any passages that give them trouble, and help them define unfamiliar words.

Fashions of the Times

During the reign of Louis XIV (1643–1715), France became not only a superpower, but the unchallenged leader of European fashion. All fashion—hair, clothes, makeup, manners—was established in Paris. The latest crazes were advertised by means of elaborately dressed dolls (called *mannequins*) or prints created by well-known artists of the day.

Men's styles were just as elaborate as women's. In fact, the importance of fashion for men is reflected in some of the humorous names in this passage—Dapperwit and Fopling. To be dapper is to be neat and well dressed, while a fop is a vain man who is very fond of fine clothes.

Connect to the Literature

Discuss hairstyling trends in history and in modern times. You may wish to have students bring in pictures of historical hairstyles. Then, **ask** the Connect to the Literature question. **Possible response:** An upper-class woman might have an elaborate hairstyle or wig to prove that she has leisure time to spend on fashion.

27 ## Critical Thinking

Analyze

1. Have several students read aloud lines 1–20. Point out that there has been a break in the action. The text skips from Canto III to Canto V.

2. Point out that in line 9, Pope mentions Homer, author of the *Iliad* and the *Odyssey*. Pope satirically compares the battle over the stolen lock of hair to the Trojan War—fought over the abduction of Greece's Queen Helen—as chronicled by Homer in the *Iliad*.

---

26 **LITERATURE IN CONTEXT**

Fashions of the Times
Pope's focus on Belinda's hair indicates the importance that women's hairstyles played in the upper-class obsession with fashion at this time. During the eighteenth century, the world's first fashion magazine was launched by the French, suggesting that nation's leadership in setting styles. Leonard, hairdresser to the French queen Marie Antoinette (1755–1793), whose picture appears below, established a fashion in which women's hairdos rose as high as four feet. These "hair statues" were augmented with horsehair pads and decorated with gauze and feathers. English hairdressers quickly took up the challenge, decorating women's heads with horse-drawn carriages, zoos of miniature lions and tigers, and, if accounts can be believed, a lit stove complete with pots and pans!

Connect to the Literature

Explain how Belinda and other women of her class might reflect their status in their hairstyles.

640

---

from Canto V

In Canto IV, after Umbriel, "a dusky, melancholy sprite," empties a bag filled with "the force of female lungs, sighs, sobs, and passions, and the war of tongues" onto Belinda's head, the lady erupts over the loss of her lock. Then she "bids her beau," Sir Plume, to "demand the precious hairs," but Plume is unable to persuade the baron to return the hair.

In the beginning of Canto V, Clarissa, a level-headed nymph, tries to bring an end to the commotion, but rather than being greeted with applause, her speech is followed by a battle cry.

"To arms, to arms!" the fierce virago[27] cries,
And swift as lightning to the combat flies.
All side in parties, and begin th' attack;
Fans clap, silks rustle, and tough whalebones crack;
5 Heroes' and heroines' shouts confusedly rise,
And bass and treble voices strike the skies.
No common weapons in their hands are found,
Like gods they fight, nor dread a mortal wound.
       So when bold Homer makes the gods engage,
10 And heavenly breasts with human passions rage;
'Gainst Pallas, Mars, Latona, Hermes[28] arms;
And all Olympus[29] rings with loud alarms:
Jove's[30] thunder roars, heaven trembles all around,
Blue Neptune[31] storms, the bellowing deeps resound;
15 Earth shakes her nodding towers, the ground gives way,
And the pale ghosts start at the flash of day!
       Triumphant Umbriel on a sconce's height[32]
Clapped his glad wings, and sat to view the fight;
Propped on their bodkin spears,[33] the sprites survey
20 The growing combat, or assist the fray.
       While through the press enraged Thalestris[34] flies,
And scatters death around from both her eyes,
A beau and witling[35] perished in the throng,
One died in metaphor, and one in song.
25 "O cruel nymph! a living death I bear,"
Cried Dapperwit, and sunk beside his chair.

---

27. virago (vi rā′ gō) scolding woman.
28. Pallas . . . Hermes gods who directed the Trojan War. Pallas and Hermes supported the Greeks, while Mars and Latona sided with the Trojans.
29. Olympus mountain which was supposed to be the home of the Greek gods.
30. Jove's referring to Jupiter, the ruler of the Gods in Roman mythology: identified with Zeus in Greek mythology.
31. Neptune Roman god of the sea; identified with Poseidon in Greek mythology.
32. sconce's height candleholder attached to the wall.
33. bodkin spears large needles.
34. Thalestris (the lēs′ tris) an Amazon (a race of female warriors supposed to have lived in Scythia) who played a role in the medieval tales of Alexander the Great.
35. witling person who fancies himself or herself a wit.

Think Aloud

Vocabulary: Using Context

Direct students' attention to the word *margin* in line 29. Use the following "think aloud" to model the skill of using context to infer the meaning of the word. Say to students:

I have seen the word *margin* before, but in this line it does not seem to mean what I think it means. Usually when I hear the word, it refers to the blank side columns of a piece of paper. But here, the text says that an "expiring swan" is lying on the margin. So the margin must be some type of solid surface. Also, the margin is called "Maeander's flowery margin." The footnote tells me that the Maeander is a river. If the margin is flowery and can also be lain upon, it must be land. I guess that *margin* refers to the banks of the Maeander River. This makes sense, because just as a paper's margin is the part around the edges, the margin of a river might be the land along the river's edge.

The Battle of the Beaux and Belles Aubrey Beardsley

▲ **Critical Viewing** In what ways is the elaborate decorative style of the drawing similar to the language of the poem? **[Connect]**

A mournful glance Sir Fopling[36] upwards cast,
"Those eyes are made so killing"—was his last.
Thus on Maeander's[37] flowery margin lies
30 Th' expiring swan, and as he sings he dies.
      When bold Sir Plume had drawn Clarissa down,
Chloe[38] stepped in, and killed him with a frown;
She smiled to see the doughty hero slain,
But, at her smile, the beau revived again.

---

36. **Dapperwit . . . Sir Fopling** names of amusing characters in comedies of the time.
37. **Maeander's** referring to a river in Asia.
38. **Chloe** (klō′ ē) heroine of the ancient Greek pastoral romance, *Daphnis and Chloe.*

Reading Check
What "weapons" do the combatants use?

from The Rape of the Lock **641**

Humanities

The Battle of the Beaux and the Belles by Aubrey Beardsley, 1895–1896

This is another of the nine pen-and-ink drawings created by Beardsley for *The Rape of the Lock*. This rococo scene is executed with the skill and mocking wit for which Beardsley is noted. The abundance of ruffles and flounces and the extravagance of embroidery emphasize the silliness of the situation depicted.

Use the following questions for discussion:

1. In what ways are the characters sympathetically portrayed?
Possible response: The characters are attractive and seem quite human despite the exaggeration. Though the continued mourning is silly, the initial reaction seems more reasonable when one sees how carefully done Belinda's hair is.

2. Which character seems to communicate the mocking tone of the picture?
Possible response: The turbaned figure in the middle seems to be the only one not focused on Belinda and appears to have a posture and facial expression that indicate mockery.

Critical Viewing

Possible response: The elaborate drawing parallels the elaborate description in the poem. For example, having a cup of coffee lasts for sixteen lines, and the drink itself is "grateful liquor," "smoking tide," and "fuming liquor." Everything gets decorated and embroidered in the poem, just as it does in the drawing.

Reading Check

Answer: The combatants use "weapons" such as metaphor, song, and facial expressions.

Differentiated Instruction for Universal Access

Culturally Responsive Instruction

Culture Connection The characters in *The Rape of the Lock* are part of the land-owning gentry—meaning that they do not need to work to support themselves. Explain to students that the men of this class often spent their days engaged in sport, such as hunting, fishing, and horseback-riding, while women entertained themselves with needlework and musical pursuits. At night, everyone gathered for a meal and a night of leisure, which might include card games, gambling, and gossip.

Ask students to share activities that their families pursue on vacation, or have students discuss how they would spend their days if they had no need to work. Prompt students to compare and contrast their chosen activities with those of eighteenth-century England. Then ask students whether they think the life they describe would become boring after a while. Suggest to students that perhaps the reason the characters in *The Rape of the Lock* create so much drama out of a small incident is that it adds excitement to an otherwise dull existence.

Spiral Review

Couplet

1. Remind students that they have studied couplets in an earlier lesson.

2. **Ask** students the Spiral Review question.

   Possible response: There are not many differences. They both use iambic pentamter; they both use no-repeating rhymes. Although they both use closed couplets in their poems, Pope uses them more consistently and regularly.

31 **Literary Analysis**

Parody

1. Read aloud lines 51 and 52.

2. Then, **ask** students the Literary Analysis question: How are Belinda's words and action in lines 51–52 appropriate for a mock epic?

   Possible response: Her cry, "Now meet thy fate," is elevated to mimic epic language, and her action of drawing the "deadly bodkin" mirrors the action of epic heroes drawing their weapons. The humor arises from the fact that her weapon is a bodkin—a small decorative pin—wielded as if it were a deadly weapon.

32 **Engaging the Essential Question**

1. Point out that Pope in this poem engages society from the view-point of two very different roles. Because the poem was inspired by real people in Pope's social circle, the poem is tied to the local society of a specific place and is in a sense Pope's personal contribution to the effects of this dilemma on his local society. In another sense, though, Pope's role as poet puts him in a position of speaking to and about society as a whole, rather than just that of his local community.

2. **Ask** students: What high-society attitudes does Pope identify as being extreme or ridiculous?
   Possible response: Pope finds the seriousness with which the incident was treated ridiculous (e.g., lines 35–38 and 65–70).

Spiral Review
Couplet
Does Pope's use of the couplet differ from Chaucer's use? Explain.

31 **Literary Analysis**
Parody
How are Belinda's words and actions in lines 51–52 appropriate for a mock epic?

3. Then, **ask** students: How does Pope view his role or responsibility as a member of his society?
   Possible response: Pope takes on the role of friendly critic.

35 Now Jove suspends his golden scales in air,
     Weighs the men's wits against the lady's hair;
     The doubtful beam long nods from side to side;
     At length the wits mount up, the hairs subside.
         See, fierce Belinda on the baron flies,
40   With more than usual lightning in her eyes;
     Nor feared the chief th' unequal fight to try,
     Who sought no more than on his foe to die.
     But this bold lord with manly strength endued,
     She with one finger and a thumb subdued:
45   Just where the breath of life his nostrils drew,
     A charge of snuff the wily virgin threw;
     The gnomes direct, to every atom just,
     The pungent grains of titillating dust.
     Sudden with starting tears each eye o'erflows,
50   And the high dome re-echoes to his nose.
         "Now meet thy fate," incensed Belinda cried,
     And drew a deadly bodkin[39] from her side . . .
         "Boast not my fall," he cried, "insulting foe!
     Thou by some other shalt be laid as low.
55   Nor think, to die dejects my lofty mind;
     All that I dread is leaving you behind!
     Rather than so, ah let me still survive,
     And burn in Cupid's flames—but burn alive."
         "Restore the lock!" she cries; and all around
60   "Restore the lock!" the vaulted roofs rebound.
     Not fierce Othello in so loud a strain
     Roared for the handkerchief that caused his pain.[40]
     But see how oft ambitious aims are crossed,
     And chiefs contend till all the prize is lost!
65   The lock, obtained with guilt, and kept with pain,
     In every place is sought, but sought in vain.
     With such a prize no mortal must be blessed,
     So Heaven decrees! with Heaven who can contest?
         Some thought it mounted to the lunar sphere,
70   Since all things lost on earth are treasured there.
     There heroes' wits are kept in ponderous vases,
     And beaux' in snuffboxes and tweezer cases.
     There broken vows and deathbed alms are found,
32 And lovers' hearts with ends of riband bound . . .
75   But trust the Muse—she saw it upward rise,
     Though marked by none but quick, poetic eyes . . .

---

39. **bodkin** ornamental pin shaped like a dagger.
40. **Not . . . pain** In Shakespeare's *Othello*, the hero is convinced that his wife is being unfaithful to him when she cannot find the handkerchief that he had given her. Actually, the handkerchief had been taken by the villain, Iago, who uses it as part of his evil plot.

642 A Turbulent Time (1625–1798)

A sudden star, it shot through liquid[41] air
And drew behind a radiant trail of hair . . .[42]
     Then cease, bright Nymph! to mourn thy ravished hair,
80 Which adds new glory to the shining sphere!
Not all the tresses that fair head can boast,
Shall draw such envy as the lock you lost.
For, after all the murders of your eye,[43]
When, after millions slain, yourself shall die;
85 When those fair suns shall set, as set they must,
And all those tresses shall be laid in dust,
This lock, the Muse shall consecrate to fame,
And midst the stars inscribe Belinda's name.

*Not all the tresses that
fair head can boast,
Shall draw such envy
as the lock you lost.*

---

41. liquid clear.
42. trail of hair The word *comet* comes from a Greek word meaning "long-haired."
43. murders . . . eye lovers struck down by her glances.

Critical Reading

1. **Key Ideas and Details (a)** What happens during the game of cards? **(b) Infer:** What does the way they play reveal about Belinda and the baron?

2. **Key Ideas and Details (a)** What does Clarissa help the baron do to Belinda, and what struggle results from it? **(b) Compare and Contrast:** Compare and contrast the card game with the final conflict in the poem. **(c) Synthesize:** What is really at stake in all of the poem's conflicts?

3. **Key Ideas and Details (a)** What happens to the lock of hair in lines 79–88 of Canto V? **(b) Analyze:** In what way is the claim that Pope makes in these lines ridiculous? In what way is it true? Explain.

4. **Integration of Knowledge and Ideas (a) Interpret:** What do you think is Pope's basic criticism of the rituals he describes in the poem? Explain. **(b) Support:** Which passage or passages indicate that Pope has some positive feelings about the rituals he criticizes? Explain.

5. **Integration of Knowledge and Ideas** Pope based this poem on an actual incident. What contemporary incident might inspire a mock epic? Explain.

6. **Integration of Knowledge and Ideas** Are elaborate social rituals, like the ones Pope mocks, always ridiculous? Why or why not?

7. **Integration of Knowledge and Ideas** Was Pope's main goal to change the behavior he mocked or to entertain readers? In your response, use at least two of the following Essential Question words: *exaggerate, reform, charm, preserve.* [Connecting to the Essential Question: How does literature shape or reflect society?]

Cite textual evidence to support your responses.

from The Rape of the Lock **643**

Answers

1. **Possible response:** Lines in Poem: Canto V, 9–16; Activity: fight to retrieve lock of hair; Lines in Poem: Canto V, 21–34; Activity: "battle," women against men; Lines in Poem: Canto V, 53–56; Activity: the baron's defiance of Belinda.

2. (a) These lines offer an elaborate comparison in the style of an epic. (b) By comparing the lovers' quarrel to an epic battle, Pope makes the absurdity of the dispute glaringly obvious.

3. **Possible response:** Comparing a card game to an epic battle shows that the courtship rituals are taken too seriously.

4. **Possible response:** During the "battle" in Canto V, lines 21–58, Pope shows that the love behind the rituals is real.

5. The sprites are small and weak, more like fairies than gods.

6. Both passages place contrasting elements side by side, with similar grammatical structure—the line in *Essay* contrasts thinking too little and too much; those in *Rape* contrast the significant with the insignificant.

7. In *An Essay on Man,* antithesis enables Pope to show that the human condition is full of contradictions. In *Rape* it helps Pope mock the folly of taking oneself too seriously.

8. **Possible response:** Antithesis reflects the theme of *An Essay on Man,* which observes that man is caught between two extremes. *The Rape of the Lock* uses antithesis to achieve humorous effects.

9. Pope pokes fun by describing the consumption of coffee as a profound ritual. He entertains by describing the effects coffee has on the baron's brain.

10. **Possible response:** (a) Knowing that Pope seeks to amuse helps readers to recognize the exaggeration in his description. (b) It might seem to be an intense contest.

644

After You Read — from *An Essay on Man* • from *The Rape of the Lock*

Literary Analysis

© **1. Craft and Structure** Use a chart like the one shown to identify epic elements and the trivial activities to which they apply in *The Rape of the Lock*, Pope's **mock epic.**

Epic Element	Lines in Poem	Activity
Hero's boasts		
Gods and goddesses		
Description of warriors		

© **2. Craft and Structure** **(a)** Why are lines 8–16 in Canto V an **epic simile? (b)** How does this simile add to the absurdity of the action Pope is describing?

© **3. Craft and Structure** Which of the epic elements Pope uses adds most to his criticism of upper-class courtship rituals? Explain.

© **4. Key Ideas and Details** Referring to a specific passage, show that Pope's criticism of upper-class rituals is affectionate rather than stern.

© **5. Integration of Knowledge and Ideas** Classical epics frequently feature gods and goddesses who intervene in human affairs. What qualities of Pope's sprites distinguish them from the gods and goddesses of a classical epic?

© **6. Craft and Structure** Explain how line 12 of *An Essay on Man* and Canto III, lines 13–14, of *The Rape of the Lock* are examples of **antithesis.**

© **7. Craft and Structure** In what way does antithesis help Pope describe the human condition in *An Essay on Man* and mock upper-class pretensions in *The Rape of the Lock*?

© **8. Integration of Knowledge and Ideas** Is antithesis a device that is equally essential in both poems? Why or why not?

Reading Strategy

9. **Analyze Pope's purpose** to show how, in Canto III, lines 105–120, Pope's intention is both to make fun of a social ritual and to entertain readers.

10. **(a)** How does knowing Pope's purpose help you determine the meaning of his comparison of a card game with a serious battle (Canto III, lines 75–86)? **(b)** How might your interpretation of the meaning change if you did not realize Pope's purpose? Explain.

644 A Turbulent Time (1625–1798)

© **Common Core State Standards**

Reading Literature
9. Demonstrate knowledge of eighteenth-, nineteenth- and early-twentieth-century foundational works of American literature, including how two or more texts from the same period treat similar themes or topics. *(p. 645)*

Reading Informational Text
9. Analyze seventeenth-, eighteenth-, and nineteenth-century foundational U.S. documents of historical and literary significance for their themes, purposes, and rhetorical features. *(p. 645)*

Writing
4. Produce clear and coherent writing in which the development, organization, and style are appropriate to task, purpose, and audience. *(p. 645)*

Language
4.a. Use context as a clue to the meaning of a word or phrase. *(p. 645)*

Assessment Practice

Writer's Point of View (For more practice, see *All-in-One Workbook*)

Many tests require students to identify a writer's point of view. Use this sample test item.

. . . A being [man] darkly wise, and rudely great: With too much knowledge for the skeptic side, With too much weakness for the stoic's pride, He hangs between; in doubt to act, or rest; In doubt to deem himself a god, or beast; In doubt his mind or body to prefer; Born but to die, and reasoning but to err. . . .

With which statement would Pope **not** agree?

A Humans are a plague on the face of the earth.

B To err is human.

C Humans are full of contradictions.

D People should recognize their limitations.

Choices *B* and *D* are almost restatements of lines of the poem. The passage points out contradictions in human nature, eliminating *C*. The correct answer is *A*.

Integrated Language Skills

Vocabulary Acquisition and Use

Words from Political Science

Many English words concerning social or political matters have Latin origins. *Plebeian*, meaning "ordinary or common," comes from the Latin word *plebs* meaning, "the common people." Use your background knowledge and context clues to determine the meanings of the italicized words below, and explain those meanings. Consult a dictionary to confirm the definitions and trace the words' Latin origins.

1. In some cultures, property is inherited along *maternal* lines.
2. The United States is not a direct democracy but a *republic*.
3. People need the *society* of others.
4. *Officials* should act in the public interest.
5. A principle of the American legal system is "equal *justice* under the law."

Vocabulary: Synonyms

A **synonym** is a word that has the same meaning as another word. Replace each italicized word in the following sentences with its synonym from the vocabulary list on page 628.

1. "Your underhanded actions *rid* me of any illusions about you," she said.
2. She delivered the message *slyly* so that anyone overhearing their conversation would not understand it.
3. The shabby clothes showed how *poor* the once-rich prince had become.
4. The secretive pair often had *trysts*.
5. The manager's *unemotional* manner never changed whether the team won or lost.
6. She pretended to be sophisticated, but she spoke in a *common* manner.

Writing

Explanatory Text The Enlightenment was an eighteenth-century cultural movement favoring reason and balance. To appreciate the wide influence of the Enlightenment, find and read two American works from the period: the Declaration of Independence and Phillis Wheatley's "To His Excellency, General Washington." Compare them to Pope's "Essay on Man."

Prewriting Note details in the Declaration and in Pope's poem that reflect ideas about human nature. Note details about the language, imagery, tone, and rhyme scheme in Pope's and Wheatley's poems.

Model: Revising for Parallelism
Pope's rhyming couplets emphasize his witty contrasts; Wheately's [are different because they] reinforce her stately voice.

By phrasing contrasting thoughts in grammatically parallel clauses, the writer adds force and clarity.

Drafting In your introduction, briefly summarize Pope's ideas about humanity and describe his poetic style. Then, compare his ideas of human nature to those in the Declaration. Next, compare his style to Wheatley's. Finally, draw a conclusion about Enlightenment values based on your comparisons. (You can learn more about the Enlightenment on page 646.)

Revising Make your comparisons clear by using parallelism, stating similar ideas in similar grammatical form.

Integrated Language Skills **645**

Vocabulary Acquisition and Use

Words from Political Science

1. *Maternal* means "relating to the mother." It is different from the usual male inheritance customs.
2. A *republic* is a group of people, with indirect power, ruled by a president.
3. *Society* is being with others–people need others.
4. *Officials* are those with public duties and so act for the public.
5. *Justice* is being fair to all, or treating all equally.

Vocabulary

1. disabused
2. obliquely
3. destitute
4. assignations
5. stoic
6. plebian

Writing

You may use this Writing Lesson as timed-writing practice, or you may allow students to develop the essay as a writing assignment over several days.

1. To guide students in writing this poem, give them the **Support for Writing Lesson** page (*Unit 3 Resources*, p. 178).
2. Review the elements Pope uses—elaborate descriptions, heroic elements, alliteration, antithesis, and similes.
3. Encourage students to use as many of the elements from Pope's work as they can, and to be as humorous as possible. Remind them that Pope's satire is affectionate, not bitter or hurtful.
4. Use the Writing Lesson to guide students in developing their mock-epic scenes.

Assessment Resources

Unit 3 Resources

L1 L2 EL **Selection Test A**, pp. 183–185. Administer Test A to less advanced readers.

L3 L4 EL **Selection Test B**, pp. 186–188. Administer Test B to on-level and more advanced students.

L3 L4 **Open-Book Test**, pp. 180–182. As an alternative, give the Open-Book Test.

All **Customizable Test Bank**

All **Self-tests**
Students may prepare for the **Selection Test** by taking the **Self-test** online.

PHLit Online! All assessment resources are available at **www.PHLitOnline.com**.

645

from *A Dictionary of the English Language*
• from *The Life of Samuel Johnson*
Lesson Pacing Guide

DAY 1 Preteach

- ⓒ Administer the Reading and Vocabulary Warm-ups (*Unit 3 Resources*, pp. 189–192) as necessary.
- ⓒ Introduce the Literary Analysis concept: Dictionary and Biography.
- • Introduce the Reading Strategy: Analyzing the Author's Purpose.
- ⓒ Build background with the author and Background features.
- • Develop thematic thinking with Connecting to the Essential Question.
- ⓒ Teach the selection vocabulary.

DAYS 2–3 Preteach/Teach/Assess

- • Distribute copies of the appropriate graphic organizer for the Reading Strategy (*Graphic Organizer Transparencies*, pp. 115–116).
- • Distribute copies of the appropriate graphic organizer for Literary Analysis (*Graphic Organizer Transparencies*, pp. 117–118).
- • Prepare students to read with the Activating Prior Knowledge activities (TE).
- • Informally monitor comprehension while students read.
- • Use the Reading Check questions to confirm comprehension.
- ⓒ Develop students' understanding of dictionary and biography using the Literary Analysis prompts.
- • Develop students' ability to analyze the author's purpose by using the Reading Strategy prompts.
- ⓒ Reinforce vocabulary with the Vocabulary notes.
- • Assess students' comprehension and mastery of the skills by having them answer the Critical Reading, Literary Analysis, and Reading Strategy questions.
- • Have students complete the Vocabulary Lesson.

DAY 4 Extend/Assess

- ⓒ Have students complete the Writing Lesson and write an editorial on dictionaries. (You may assign as homework.)
- • Administer Selection Test A or B (*Unit 3 Resources*, pp. 201–203 or 204–206).

ⓒ Common Core State Standards

Reading Informational Text
3. Analyze a complex set of ideas or sequence of events and explain how specific individuals, ideas, or events interact and develop over the course of a text.
4. Determine the meaning of words and phrases as they are used in a text, including figurative, connotative, and technical meanings.
9. Analyze seventeenth-, eighteenth-, and nineteenth century foundational U.S. documents of historical and literary significance for their themes, purposes, and rhetorical features.

Writing 9.b. Apply *grades 11–12 Reading standards* to literary nonfiction.

Language 4.c. Consult general and specialized reference materials, both print and digital, to find the pronunciation of a word or determine or clarify its precise meaning, its part of speech, its etymology, or its standard usage.

Additional Standards Practice
Common Core Companion, pp. 28–48, 75–76; 324–331

Daily Block Scheduling
Each day in this Lesson Pacing Guide represents a 40–50 minute period. Teachers using block scheduling may combine days to revise pacing. In addition, teachers may differentiate and support core instruction by integrating components for extended and intensive support as students require. See the Guide to Selected Leveled Resources (facing page).

Guide to Selected Leveled Resources

R T I Tier 1 (students performing on level)

from A Dictionary of the English Language • *from* The Life of Samuel Johnson

Warm Up

Practice, model, and monitor fluency, working with the whole class or in groups.

Vocabulary and Reading Warm-ups B, *Unit 3 Resources,* pp. 186–187, 189

Comprehension/Skills

Support and monitor comprehension and skills development, having students complete the activities, graphic organizers, and interactive prompts independently or as a class.

• *Reader's Notebook,* adapted instruction and full selection

EL *Reader's Notebook: English Learner's Version,* adapted instruction and adapted selection

• Reading Strategy Graphic Organizer B, *Graphic Organizer Transparencies,* p. 120

• Literary Analysis Graphic Organizer B, *Graphic Organizer Transparencies,* p. 122

Monitor Progress

A

Monitor student progress with the differentiated curriculum-based assessment in the *Unit Resources.*

• Selection Test B, *Unit 3 Resources,* pp. 201–203

• Open-Book Test, *Unit 3 Resources,* pp. 195–197

R T I Tier 2 (students requiring intervention)

from A Dictionary of the English Language • *from* The Life of Samuel Johnson

Warm Up

Practice, model, and monitor fluency in groups or with individuals.

• Vocabulary and Reading Warm-ups A, *Unit 3 Resources,* pp. 186–188

• *Hear It!* Audio CD (adapted text)

Comprehension/Skills

• Support and monitor comprehension and skills development, working in small groups or with individuals.

• As students complete the selection in the appropriate version of the *Reader's Notebook,* monitor comprehension frequently with group questions and individual instruction.

• Model strategies while guiding students in completing the activities and prompts in the *Reader's Notebook,* as well as the graphic organizers.

• Practice skills and monitor mastery with the *Reading Kit* worksheets.

• *Reader's Notebook: Adapted Version,* adapted instruction and adapted selection

EL *Reader's Notebook: English Learner's Version,* adapted instruction and adapted selection

• Reading Strategy Graphic Organizer A, *Graphic Organizer Transparencies,* p. 119

• Literary Analysis Graphic Organizer A, *Graphic Organizer Transparencies,* p. 121

• *Reading Kit,* Practice worksheets

Monitor Progress

A

Monitor student progress with the differentiated curriculum-based assessment in the *Unit Resources* and in the *Reading Kit.*

• Selection Test A, *Unit 3 Resources,* pp. 198–200

• *Reading Kit,* Assess worksheets

TIER 3 Tier 3 intervention may require consultation with the student's special-education or dyslexia specialist. For additional support, see the Tier 2 activities and resources listed above.

One-on-one teaching   Group work   Whole class instruction   Independent work   **A** Assessment

For a complete guide to selection support, including support for Advanced students, see the Overview of Resources in the frontmatter.

from *A Dictionary of the English Language*
• from *The Life of Samuel Johnson*

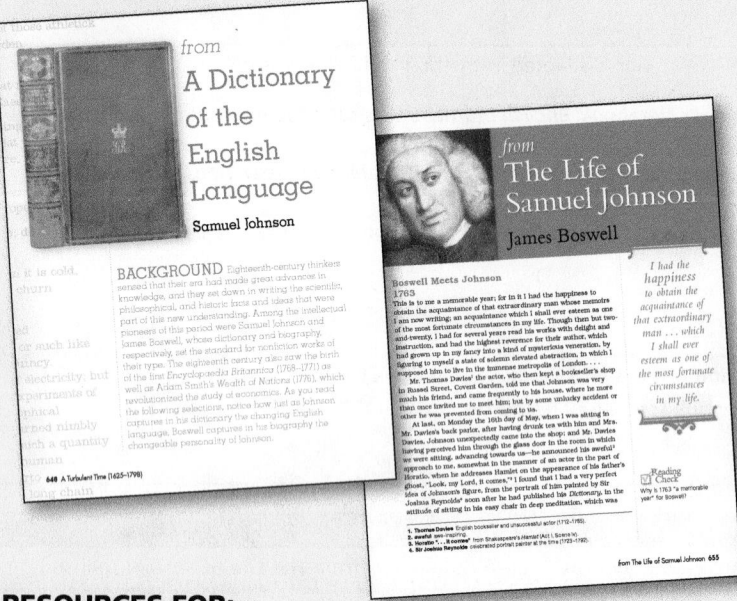

RESOURCES FOR:

L1 Special-Needs Students

L2 Below-Level Students (Tier 2)

L3 On-Level Students (Tier 1)

L4 Advanced Students (Tier 1)

EL English Learners

All All Students

Vocabulary/Fluency/Prior Knowledge

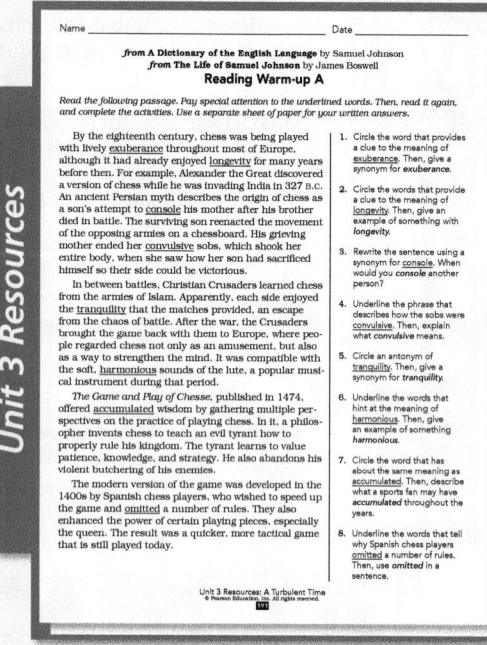

EL L1 L2 Reading Warm-ups A and B,
pp. 191–192

Also available for these selections:

EL L1 L2 Vocabulary Warm-ups A and B,
pp. 189–190

All Vocabulary Builder, p. 195

Reader's Notebooks

Pre- and postreading pages for both selections appear in an interactive format in the *Reader's Notebooks*. Each *Notebook* is differentiated for a different group of learners. The selections in the Adapted and English Learner's versions are abridged.

L2 L3 *Reader's Notebook*

L1 *Reader's Notebook: Adapted Version*

EL *Reader's Notebook: English Learner's Version*

EL *Reader's Notebook: Spanish Version*

© *Common Core Companion*

Additional instruction and practice for each Common Core State Standard

Selection Support

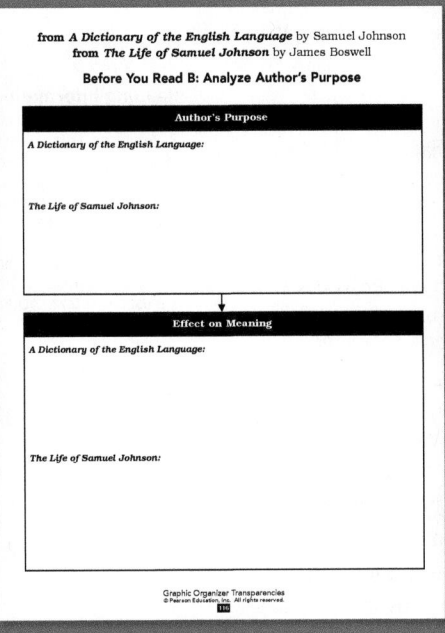

EL L3 Reading: Graphic Organizer B, p. 116

Also available for these selections:

EL L1 L2 Reading: Graphic Organizer A (partially filled in) p. 115

EL L1 L2 Literary Analysis: Graphic Organizer A (partially filled in) p. 117

EL L3 Literary Analysis: Graphic Organizer B, p. 118

Skills Development/Extension

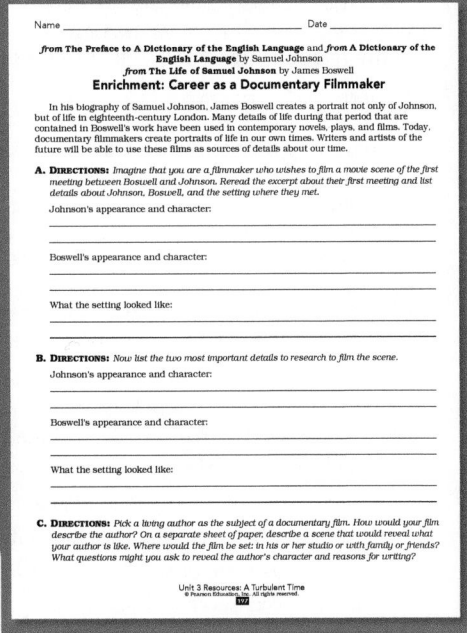

L4 Enrichment, p. 197

Also available for these selections:

All Literary Analysis: p. 193

All Reading, p. 194

EL L3 L4 Support for Writing, p. 196

Assessment

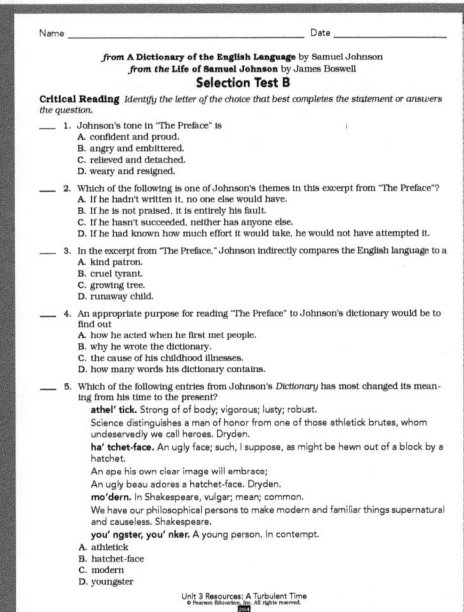

EL L3 L4 Selection Test B, pp. 204–206,

Also available for these selections:

L3 L4 Open-Book Test, pp. 198–200

EL L3 L4 Selection Test A, pp. 201–203

PHLit Online!
www.PHLitOnline.com

Online Resources: All print materials are also available online.

- complete narrated selection text
- a thematically related video with writing prompt
- an interactive graphic organizer
- highlighting feature
- access to all student print resources, adapted to individual student needs
- Spanish and English summaries
- adapted selection translations in Spanish

Get Connected!

Also available:

Background Video (thematic video with writing prompt)
All videos are available in Spanish.

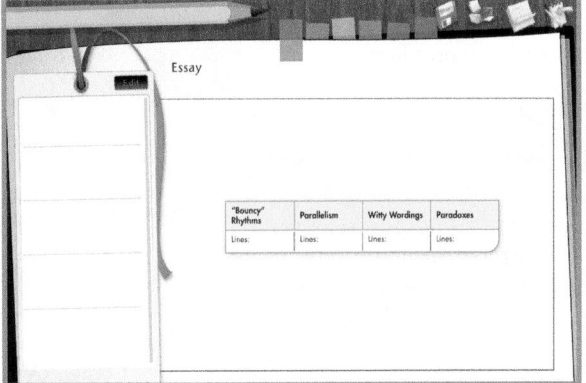

Writer's Journal (with graphics feature)

Also available:

Vocabulary Central (tools and activities for studying vocabulary)

❶ Connecting to the Essential Question

1. Review the assignment with the class.

2. Prepare students to write by asking them to recall when a wrong word led to a misunderstanding.

❷ Literary Analysis

Introduce the skill using the instruction on the student page.

Think Aloud: Model the Skill

Say to students:

> When I listen to someone speak, I can tell some things from his or her diction. I get a sense of whether he is comfortable using language. In the same way, I can be aware of diction in what I read and make guesses about the author's understanding of the topic.

❸ Reading Strategy

1. Introduce the skill using the instruction on the student page.

2. Give students the **Reading Strategy Graphic Organizer B,** page 116 in *Graphic Organizer Transparencies,* to fill out as they read.

Think Aloud: Model the Skill

Say to students:

> I can read to find out what compelled Johnson to write a dictionary and what compelled Boswell to record Johnson's life. Maybe they enjoyed these tasks, because they spent a lot of time and energy on them.

❹ Vocabulary

1. Pronounce each word, giving its definition.

2. For more guidance, see the *Classroom Strategies and Teaching Routines* card for introducing vocabulary.

646

Before You Read

from *A Dictionary of the English Language* • from *The Life of Samuel Johnson*

❶ **Connecting to the Essential Question** Samuel Johnson wrote the first true English dictionary. As you read, note passages in which each author sees himself as an innovator to answer the Essential Question: **What is the relationship of the writer to tradition?**

❷ **Literary Analysis**

A **dictionary** defines words and may provide information about their pronunciation, history, and usage. Samuel Johnson compiled the first standard dictionary of the English language. As you read the excerpt from it, look for features he initiated that are still in use today.

A **biography** is an account of someone's life written by another person. Just as Johnson's *Dictionary* was a landmark, so was Boswell's *Life of Samuel Johnson.* In reading it, note how Boswell uses many details from his own personal knowledge to portray Johnson's character.

Comparing Literary Works Both these selections reveal the *philosophical assumptions and beliefs* of the Enlightenment. This eighteenth-century intellectual movement stressed the following values:

- the importance of regularizing and preserving knowledge
- a perception of reason and judgment as the highest human abilities
- the belief that great authors were authorities on language and life
- elevated **diction,** or word choice, revealing a respect for learning

To comprehend elevated diction, look up unfamiliar words, checking connotations, or emotional associations, as well as literal meanings. As you read, also draw inferences about how Enlightenment beliefs influenced each author.

❸ **Reading Strategy**

© **Preparing to Read Complex Texts** By **analyzing the author's purpose,** or goal, you will better understand a work's *meaning*. For example, knowing that Boswell's purpose was to record the life of an exemplary man, you will realize why he includes detailed stories about Johnson. Over the course of the text, the complex set of ideas develops into a complete picture of the man. Use a graphic organizer to record the author's purpose and how it affects meaning.

❹ **Vocabulary**

caprices (kə prēs′ iz) *n.* whims (p. 649)

adulterations (ə dul′ tər ā′ shənz) *n.* impurities; added ingredients that are improper or inferior (p. 649)

risible (riz′ ə bəl) *adj.* prompting laughter (p. 650)

abasement (ə bās′ mənt) *n.* condition of being humbled (p. 656)

credulity (krə dōō′ lə tē) *n.* tendency to believe too readily (p. 659)

malignity (mə lig′ nə tē) *n.* strong desire to harm others (p. 659)

646 A Turbulent Time (1625–1798)

Common Core State Standards

Reading Informational Text

3. Analyze a complex set of ideas or sequence of events and explain how specific individuals, ideas, or events interact and develop over the course of a text.

4. Determine the meaning of words and phrases as they are used in a text, including figurative, connotative, and technical meanings.

Author's Purpose or Perspective

↓

Effect on Meaning

Vocabulary Development

Vocabulary Knowledge Rating

Create a **Vocabulary Knowledge Rating Chart** (*Professional Development Guidebook,* p. 33) for the vocabulary words on the student page. Give each student a copy of the chart with the words on it. Read the words aloud, and have students mark their ratings in the Before Reading column. When students have completed reading and discussing the selec-

tions, have them take out their **Vocabulary Knowledge Rating Charts** for the story. Read the words aloud and have students rate their knowledge again in the After Reading column. Clarify any words that are still problematic. Then have students complete the Vocabulary practice at the end of the selections.

 **Vocabulary Central,** featuring tools, activities, and songs for studying vocabulary, is available online at **www.PHLitOnline.com.**

Samuel Johnson

(1709–1784)

Author of *A Dictionary of the English Language*

With his fine mind and dazzling conversation, Samuel Johnson was at the center of a circle that included most of Britain's leading artists and intellectuals. So great was his influence on English literature that the second half of the eighteenth century is often called the Age of Johnson.

A Life of Hardship Samuel Johnson overcame severe physical and economic hardships. The son of a bookseller in Lichfield, England, he suffered a series of childhood illnesses that left him weak and disfigured. Bright enough to read Shakespeare as a young boy, he was too poor to attend the schools of the aristocracy and pursued his education largely by reading books in his father's shop. Although he was able to enter Oxford in 1728, lack of funds forced him to leave early.

A Great Work In 1737, Johnson moved to London to try to earn his living as a writer; in 1746, he began work on his *Dictionary of the English Language*. This landmark effort took nine years to complete—difficult years during which his wife died and he continued to be dogged by poverty. When at last the *Dictionary* was published, however, it ensured Johnson's place in literary history. Still, it was not until 1762, when he received a pension from the king, that he did not have to rely on writing for a living. In 1775, he received an honorary degree from Oxford, the school he had been forced to leave.

"When a man is tired of London, he is tired of life; for there is in London all that life can afford."

from A Dictionary of the English Language **647**

Daily Bellringer

For each class during which you will teach these selections, have students complete one of the five activities for the appropriate week in the *Daily Bellringer Activities* booklet.

Multidraft Reading

To assist struggling readers and to enhance reading for all, assign the text in chunks, as warranted by length and apply multidraft reading protocols. For each reading, have students set the purpose indicated:

- **First reading**—identifying key ideas and details and answering any Reading Checks.
- **Second reading**—analyzing craft and structure and responding to the side-column prompts.
- **Third reading**—integrating knowledge and ideas, connecting to other texts and the world, and answering the end-of-selection questions.

For more guidance, refer to the *Classroom Strategies and Teaching Routines* card on Multidraft Reading.

❺ Background
More About the Author

Samuel Johnson and James Boswell will forever be linked by virtue of Boswell's authoritative biography of Johnson. Johnson's marvelous wit—captured by Boswell so admirably in *The Life of Samuel Johnson*—was sufficiently revered during his lifetime and by later generations that the Enlightenment period in which he lived is known today as the Age of Johnson.

Teaching From Technology

Preparing to Read
Go to **www.PHLitOnline.com** in class or in a lab and display the **Get Connected!** slideshow for these selections. Have the class brainstorm responses to the slideshow writing prompt, entering ideas in the interactive journal. Then, have students complete their written responses individually, in a lab or as homework.
    To build background, display the More About the Authors feature.

Using the Interactive Text
Go to **www.PHLitOnline.com** and display the Enriched Online Student Edition. As the class reads the selection or listens to the narration, record answers to side-column prompts using the graphic organizers accessible on the interactive page. Alternatively, have students use the online edition individually, answering the prompts as they read.

❶ About the Selection

Writing a dictionary is a huge and nearly impossible undertaking. In this Preface, Johnson reviews the challenges he faced, acknowledges the flaws in his work, and proudly asserts the value of his accomplishments.

❷ Activating Prior Knowledge

Have students discuss the advantages and disadvantages of having dictionaries to clarify meanings and correct spellings of words. Ask them to consider whether dictionaries preserve a language's form or hinder its development.

Concept Connector ➡

Tell students they will return to their responses after reading the selection.

from

A Dictionary of the English Language ❶ ❷

Samuel Johnson

BACKGROUND Eighteenth-century thinkers sensed that their era had made great advances in knowledge, and they set down in writing the scientific, philosophical, and historic facts and ideas that were part of this new understanding. Among the intellectual pioneers of this period were Samuel Johnson and James Boswell, whose dictionary and biography, respectively, set the standard for nonfiction works of their type. The eighteenth century also saw the birth of the first *Encyclopaedia Britannica* (1768–1771) as well as Adam Smith's *Wealth of Nations* (1776), which revolutionized the study of economics. As you read the following selections, notice how just as Johnson captures in his dictionary the changing English language, Boswell captures in his biography the changeable personality of Johnson.

648 A Turbulent Time (1625–1798)

Ⓒ Text Complexity Rubric: Leveled Texts

	from **A Dictionary of the English Language**	*from* **The Life of Samuel Johnson**
Qualitative Measures		
Context/ Knowledge Demands	Dictionary preface and entries 1 ② 3 4 5	Biography; literary and cultural knowledge demands 1 ② 3 4 5
Structure/Language Conventionality and Clarity	Long sentences; vocabulary 1 ② 3 4 5	Conversational language; vocabulary 1 2 ③ 4 5
Levels of Meaning/ Purpose/Concept Level	Accessible (dictionaries and satirical definitions) 1 ② 3 4 5	Average 1 2 ③ 4 5
Quantitative Measures		
Lexile/Text Length	1290L / 1,083 words	1250L / 2,567 words
Overall Complexity	**More accessible**	**More complex**

from The Preface

It is the fate of those who toil at the lower employments of life, to be rather driven by the fear of evil, than attracted by the prospect of good; to be exposed to censure, without hope of praise; to be disgraced by miscarriage, or punished for neglect, where success would have been without applause, and diligence without reward.

Among these unhappy mortals is the writer of dictionaries; whom mankind have considered, not as the pupil, but the slave of science, the pioneer of literature, doomed only to remove rubbish and clear obstructions from the paths through which learning and genius press forward to conquest and glory, without bestowing a smile on the humble drudge that facilitates their progress. Every other author may aspire to praise; the lexicographer can only hope to escape reproach, and even this negative recompense has been yet granted to very few.

I have, notwithstanding this discouragement, attempted a dictionary of the English language, which, while it was employed in the cultivation of every species of literature, has itself been hitherto neglected; suffered to spread under the direction of chance, into wild exuberance; resigned to the tyranny of time and fashion: and exposed to the corruptions of ignorance and caprices of innovation.

When I took the first survey of my undertaking, I found our speech copious without order and energetic without rule: wherever I turned my view, there was perplexity to be disentangled and confusion to be regulated; choice was to be made out of boundless variety, without any established principle of selection; adulterations were to be detected, without a settled test of purity; and modes of expression to be rejected or received, without the suffrages of any writers of classical reputation or acknowledged authority.

Having therefore no assistance but from general grammar, I applied myself to the perusal of our writers; and noting whatever might be of use to ascertain or illustrate any word or phrase, accumulated in time the materials of a dictionary, which, by degrees, I reduced to method, establishing to myself, in the progress of the work, such rules as experience and analogy suggested to me; experience, which practice and observation were continually increasing; and analogy, which, though in some other words obscure, was evident in others. . . .

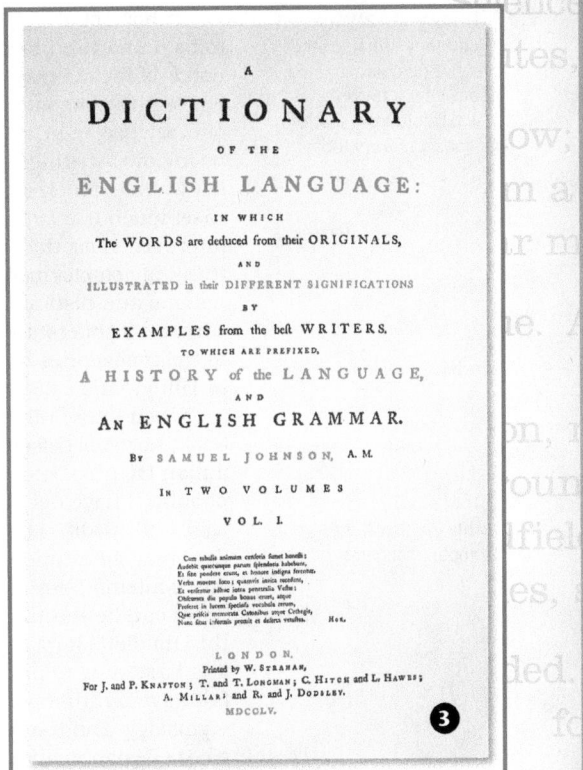

A
DICTIONARY
OF THE
ENGLISH LANGUAGE:
IN WHICH
The WORDS are deduced from their ORIGINALS,
AND
ILLUSTRATED in their DIFFERENT SIGNIFICATIONS
BY
EXAMPLES from the beſt WRITERS.
TO WHICH ARE PREFIXED,
A HISTORY of the LANGUAGE,
AND
An ENGLISH GRAMMAR.
By SAMUEL JOHNSON, A.M.
IN TWO VOLUMES
VOL. I.

LONDON,
Printed by W. STRAHAN,
For J. and P. KNAPTON; T. and T. LONGMAN; C. HITCH and L. HAWES;
A. MILLAR; and R. and J. DODSLEY.
MDCCLV.

❸

❹ ▲ **Critical Viewing**
What does this title page of Johnson's *Dictionary* tell you about the contents? **[Infer]**

Vocabulary
caprices (kə prēs′ iz) *n.* whims

adulterations (ə dul′ tər ā′ shənz) *n.* impurities; added ingredients that are improper or inferior

❺ ☑ Reading Check
In what condition did Johnson find the English language when he began work?

from A Dictionary of the English Language **649**

❸ **Humanities**
This title page of Johnson's *Dictionary* suggests some facts about the history of printing conventions. Students may notice that almost the entire page is set in capital letters, as if the title page were of great importance. Use these questions for discussion:

1. Do you think Johnson would have been proud of this title page?
Possible response: Johnson would likely have been proud of this title page. Not only does it describe his achievement—the dictionary, history of the language, and grammar—but it also credits the work to Johnson.

2. Why do you think Johnson's name appears in relatively small letters?
Answer: Johnson gained fame through his dictionary, but he was not famous before its publication. Also, printing conventions of the day may have called more attention to the title of a work than to its author.

❹ **Critical Viewing**
Possible response: The title page gives a great deal of information about the contents. It explains that the definitions include examples of the use of words from "the best writers" and that the dictionary includes information on the history and grammar of the language. It says that the work consists of two volumes, so readers can infer that the dictionary is extensive. These claims, followed by the quotation by Horace, allow readers to infer that the dictionary is a scholarly work based on research.

❺ **Reading Check**
Answer: When Johnson began work, he found the English language "copious without order and energetic without rule."

© Text Complexity: Reader and Task Suggestions

from **A Dictionary of the English Language**		*from* **The Life of Samuel Johnson**	
Preparing to Read the Text	**Leveled Tasks**	**Preparing to Read the Text**	**Leveled Tasks**
• Using the Background on SE p. 648, have students consider the difficulties of creating a dictionary from scratch. • Explain that Johnson decided to define words and also include quotations illustrating their usage. • Guide students to use Multidraft Reading strategies (TE p. 647).	*Language/Structure* If students will have difficulty with Johnson's language, have them use context clues to help with the meanings of unfamiliar words. Then, have students consult a contemporary dictionary to learn the meanings of others. *Evaluating* If students will not have difficulty understanding Johnson's language, have them evaluate the effectiveness of his definitions and the appropriateness of his humor.	• Using the information at the bottom of TE p. 654, discuss the genre of biography. Note that Boswell's *Johnson* is the first great English biography. • Point out that Boswell admired Johnson but nevertheless included his flaws. • Guide students to use Multidraft Reading strategies (TE p. 647).	*Levels of Meaning* If students will have difficulty recognizing Boswell's main points, have them focus on the direct statements he makes about Johnson, both good and bad. Then, have them look for details that support those statements. *Synthesizing* If students will not have difficulty with Boswell's main points, have them determine the positive and negative qualities he conveys about Johnson and then sum up his portrait.

649

Dictionary

1. Review with students Johnson's description of his task. **Ask** students to name the difficulties he encountered.
Answer: Johnson found the language disordered and confused; he had to identify adulterations in the language; he had to accept or reject "modes of expression," using only grammar and the works of other writers as his guide.

2. Then, **ask** the Literary Analysis question: What do the first five paragraphs reveal about how Johnson's task differed from that of dictionary makers today?
Answer: Because Johnson was creating the first dictionary of English, he could not build on others' work, as dictionary makers do today. He had no experts with whom to confer and no computerized databases of word citations; his word-processing equipment consisted of pen and ink.

▶ **Reteach** If students have difficulty grasping the enormity of Johnson's task, ask them to think about taking notes for a research paper. Have them review the process of finding information, noting sources, writing note cards, and then organizing the cards. Then, invite them to compare this brief process with Johnson's work of collecting definitions, examples of uses, sources, and spellings for two volumes' worth of words.

Dictionary What do the first five paragraphs reveal about how Johnson's task differed from that of dictionary makers today?

Vocabulary
risible (riz´ ə bəl) *adj.* prompting laughter

In hope of giving longevity to that which its own nature forbids to be immortal, I have devoted this book, the labor of years, to the honor of my country, that we may no longer yield the palm of philology, without a contest to the nations of the continent. The chief glory of every people arises from its authors. Whether I shall add anything by my own writings to the reputation of English literature, must be left to time. Much of my life has been lost under the pressures of disease; much has been trifled away; and much has always been spent in provision for the day that was passing over me; but I shall not think my employment useless or ignoble, if by my assistance foreign nations and distant ages gain access to the propagators[1] of knowledge, and understand the teachers of truth; if my labors afford light to the repositories of science, and add celebrity to Bacon, to Hooker, to Milton, and to Boyle.[2]

When I am animated by this wish, I look with pleasure on my book, however defective, and deliver it to the world with the spirit of a man that has endeavored well. That it will immediately become popular, I have not promised to myself. A few wild blunders, and risible absurdities, from which no work of such multiplicity was ever free, may for a time furnish folly with laughter, and harden ignorance into contempt; but useful diligence will at last prevail, and there never can be wanting some who distinguish desert; who will consider that no dictionary of a living tongue ever can be perfect, since, while it is hastening to publication, some words are budding, and some falling away; that a whole life cannot be spent upon syntax and etymology, and that even a whole life would not be sufficient; that he, whose design includes whatever language can express, must often speak of what he does not understand; that a writer will sometimes be hurried by eagerness to the end, and sometimes faint with weariness under a task which Scaliger[3] compares to the labors of the anvil and the mine; that what is obvious is not always known, and what is known is not always present; that sudden fits of inadvertency will surprise vigilance, slight avocations[4] will seduce attention, and casual eclipses of the mind will darken learning; and that the writer shall often in vain trace his memory at the moment of need, for that which yesterday he knew with intuitive readiness, and which will come uncalled into his thoughts tomorrow.

In this work, when it shall be found that much is omitted, let it not be forgotten that much likewise is performed; and though no book was ever spared out of tenderness to the author, and the world is little solicitous to know whence proceed the faults of that which it condemns; yet it may gratify curiosity to inform it, that the *English Dictionary* was written with little assistance of the learned, and

---

1. **propagators** (präp´ ə gāt´ ərz) *n.* those who cause something to happen or to spread.
2. **Bacon . . . Boyle** writers quoted by Johnson in the *Dictionary*.
3. **Scaliger** Joseph Justus Scaliger (1540–1609), a scholar who suggested that criminals should be condemned to writing dictionaries.
4. **avocations** things that call one away or distract one from something.

Enrichment: Investigating Dictionaries and Language Usage

Dictionaries and Their Makers

Johnson's dictionary influenced the language we use today. Other dictionary makers established rules for usage. American Noah Webster (1758–1843) attempted to standardize spelling. Some countries have established academies to preserve language. These academies, however, have not been able to prevent language change, and the task of most modern dictionaries is to record current usage.

Activity: Investigating Technology Have students research the latest form of the dictionary: the e-dictionary. Suggest that they examine online dictionaries and record their findings in the **Enrichment: Investigating Technology** worksheet, *Professional Development Guidebook,* page 242.

without any patronage of the great; not in the soft obscurities of retirement, or under the shelter of academic bowers, but amidst inconvenience and distraction, in sickness and in sorrow. It may repress the triumph of malignant criticism to observe that if our language is not here fully displayed, I have only failed in an attempt which no human powers have hitherto completed. If the lexicons of ancient tongues, now immutably fixed and comprised in a few volumes, be yet, after the toil of successive ages, inadequate and delusive; if the aggregated knowledge and cooperating diligence of the Italian academicians did not secure them from the censure of Beni;[5] if the embodied critics of France, when fifty years had been spent upon their work, were obliged to change its economy[6] and give their second edition another form, I may surely be contented without the praise of perfection, which, if I could obtain, in this gloom of solitude, what would it avail me? I have protracted my work till most of those whom I wished to please have sunk into the grave,[7] and success and miscarriage are empty sounds: I therefore dismiss it with frigid tranquility, having little to fear or hope from censure or from praise.

Selected Entries from A Dictionary

athle´ tick. Strong of body; vigorous; lusty; robust.
    Science distinguishes a man of honor from one of those *athletick* brutes, whom undeservedly we call heroes. Dryden.

bang. A blow; a thump; a stroke: a low word.
    I am a bachelor. That's to say, they are fools that marry; you'll bear me a *bang* for that. Shakespeare, *Julius Caesar.*

to ba´rbecue. A term used in the West Indies for dressing a hog whole; which, being split to the backbone, is laid flat upon a large gridiron, raised about two foot above a charcoal fire, with which it is surrounded.
    Oldfield, with more than harpy throat endu'd,
    Cries, send me, gods, a whole hog *barbecu´d*. Pope.

bu´ffleheaded. A man with a large head, like a buffalo; dull; stupid; foolish.

cream. The unctuous or oily part of milk, which, when it is cold, floats on the top, and is changed by the agitation of the churn into butter; the flower of milk.

electri´city. A property in some bodies, whereby, when rubbed so as to grow warm, they draw little bits of paper, or such like substances, to them. Quincy.

---

5. **Beni** Paolo Beni severely criticized the first Italian dictionary.
6. **economy** organization.
7. **sunk . . . grave** Johnson's wife had died three years earlier.

from A Dictionary of the English Language **651**

---

❼ Reading Strategy
Analyzing the Author's Purpose What information in the last two paragraphs helps you determine Samuel Johnson's purpose for writing his *Dictionary*?

❽ Reading Check
Why, according to Johnson, can "no dictionary of a living tongue ever . . . be perfect"?

---

❼ Reading Strategy
Analyzing the Author's Purpose

1. Remind students that by establishing a purpose before reading—in this case, to find out why Johnson undertook the task of writing a dictionary—they can better answer questions about the material. Tell them to reread the last two paragraphs with the purpose of identifying Johnson's feelings about writing the *Dictionary*.

2. **Ask** students to identify and list Johnson's feelings.
   Answer: Johnson is proud of his accomplishment, on which he has "endeavored well," of presenting even an imperfect work to the world. Even though he apologizes for "much" that may have been omitted, he asserts that "much likewise [was] performed." Johnson is also proud that he did this job on his own, without a rich patron or the security of a university job.

3. Then, **ask** students the Reading Strategy question: What information in the last two paragraphs helps you determine Samuel Johnson's purpose for writing his *Dictionary*?
   Answer: From his feelings about the task and the result, readers can infer that Johnson wrote the dictionary not to gain fame; in fact, he fears that he will receive criticism for the imperfections of the work. He argues that he has achieved something useful and important in reporting on the changing English language.

❽ Reading Check
Answer: According to Johnson, no dictionary can be perfect because, while it is on its way to publication, new words are "budding, and some falling away."

Differentiated Instruction for Universal Access

Strategy for Special-Needs Students
Students may have difficulty evaluating how Johnson's dictionary differed from contemporary ones. Show students a modern dictionary and explain each element of an entry, including pronunciation, etymology, and definition. Then, refer students to an example from Johnson's *Dictionary*. Use the **Literary Analysis Graphic Organizer B** transparency on page 116 of *Graphic Organizer Transparencies* to guide your instruction.

Strategy for Advanced Readers
Have students read Johnson's preface independently. Then, have them consider some of Johnson's dictionary entries. Have partners use modern dictionaries to look up five of the words in Johnson's *Dictionary*. Finally, have students give oral presentations of their research—including any differences in pronunciation, etymology, and definition they have uncovered.

Dictionary and Style

1. Review with students their understanding of diction, or word choice, and how it may reflect an author's or speaker's attitude.

2. Tell students that at one point, Lord Chesterfield had expressed interest in supporting Johnson's dictionary project. The promised help never came close to meeting Johnson's needs, yet when the work was completed, Chesterfield wanted to be regarded as Johnson's patron. Johnson wrote a scathing letter to Chesterfield, saying that during his work he had been "without one act of assistance, one word or encouragement, or one smile of favor."

3. Then, **ask** the Literary Analysis question: What effect does Johnson's word choice have on his definition of *patron*?
Answer: Johnson's diction suggests his contempt for patrons and for those who receive patronage.

▶ **Reteach** If students have difficulty understanding Johnson's attitude toward patronage, conveyed by such word choices as *wretch* and *insolence,* remind them that in The Preface Johnson states with pride that he completed the dictionary "without any patronage of the great."

A Page from Johnson's Dictionary

Literary Analysis
Dictionary and Style ⑨
What effect does Johnson's word choice have on his definition of *patron*?

Such was the account given a few years ago of electricity; but the industry of the present age, first excited by the experiments of Gray, has discovered in electricity a multitude of philosophical wonders. Bodies electrified by a sphere of glass, turned nimbly round, not only emit flame, but may be fitted with such a quantity of the electrical vapor as, if discharged at once upon a human body, would endanger life. The force of this vapor has hitherto appeared instantaneous, persons at both ends of a long chain seeming to be struck at once. The philosophers are now endeavoring to intercept the strokes of lightning.

to fu´rnace. To throw out as sparks from a furnace. A bad word.
> He *furnaces*
> The thick sighs from him. Shakespeare's *Cymbeline.*

gang. A number herding together; a troop; a company;
> a tribe; a herd. It is seldom used but in contempt or abhorrence.

ha´tchet-face. An ugly face; such, I suppose, as might be hewn out of a block by a hatchet.
> An ape his own dear image will embrace;
> An ugly beau adores a *hatchet-face.* Dryden.

lifegua´rd. The guard of a king's person.

mo´dern. In Shakespeare, vulgar; mean; common.
> We have our philosophical persons to make *modern* and familiar things supernatural and causeless. Shakespeare.

pa´tron. One who countenances, supports or protects. Commonly a wretch who supports with insolence, and is paid with flattery.

pi´ckle. Condition; state. A word of contempt and ridicule.
> How cam'st though in this *pickle*? Shakespeare.

plu´mper. Something worn in the mouth to swell out the cheeks.
> She dex'trously her *plumpers* draws, That serve to fill her hollow jaws. Swift's *Miscellanies.*

shill-I-shall-I. A corrupt reduplication of *shall I?* The question of a man hesitating. To stand *shill-I-shall-I,* is to continue hesitating and procrastinating.

Think Aloud

Literary Analysis: Understanding Diction
To model the process of working out the answer to the Literary Analysis question on the student page, use the following "think aloud." Say to students:
I know that words often carry associations called connotations. These connotations hint at a writer's or speaker's attitude toward a topic. I should look to see if the words and phrases Johnson uses carry connotations that suggest his attitude.

I am somewhat dainty in making a resolution, because when I make it, I keep it; I don't stand shill-I-shall-I then; if I say't, I'll do't. Congreve's *Way of the World.*

to sneeze. To emit wind audibly by the nose.

wi´llow. A tree worn by forlorn lovers.

to wipe. To cheat; to defraud.
> The next bordering lords commonly encroach one upon another, as one is stronger, or lie still in wait to wipe them out of their lands. Spenser, *On Ireland.*

you´ngster, you´nker. A young person.
> In contempt.

youth. The part of life succeeding to childhood and adolescence; the time from fourteen to twenty-eight.

Critical Reading

Cite textual evidence to support your responses.

1. **Key Ideas and Details (a)** Among what class of workers does Johnson place writers of dictionaries? **(b) Infer:** What does this ranking suggest about his experience in compiling his *Dictionary?*

2. **Key Ideas and Details (a)** What did the English language lack when Johnson undertook his work? **(b) Infer:** What do you think Johnson hoped his *Dictionary* would make available to English speakers and writers?

3. **Key Ideas and Details (a)** What is Johnson's definition of *modern?* **(b) Compare and Contrast:** Compare and contrast Johnson's definition of this word with our definition of it today. Explain what different values each represents. **(c) Draw Conclusions:** What does your comparison indicate about the nature of language?

4. **Integration of Knowledge and Ideas (a) Analyze:** Which definitions are most revealing of Johnson's character and situation? **(b) Draw Conclusions:** What do these definitions reveal about Johnson?

5. **Integration of Knowledge and Ideas (a) Speculate:** Why do you think *electricity* receives such a long definition? **(b) Connect:** In what ways is Johnson similar to the scientists whose work he eagerly discusses in this entry?

6. **Integration of Knowledge and Ideas** What does Johnson's use of quotations suggest about the role of authors in shaping meanings?

7. **Integration of Knowledge and Ideas** Do you find Johnson's definitions more or less useful than those in modern dictionaries? Explain.

from A Dictionary of the English Language **653**

653

James Boswell ⑪

(1740–1795)

Author of *The Life of Samuel Johnson* ⑩

James Boswell is perhaps the greatest biographer in English letters. In his *Life of Samuel Johnson*, he writes with vigor about his fascinating subject, training his eye on the picturesque and the grotesque.

Celebrity Chaser Born into an aristocratic family in Edinburgh, Scotland, Boswell was educated at several universities. Although he received his degree in law and was admitted to the bar in both Scotland and England, his true passion was literature. His father, a prominent judge, was angered by what he saw as his son's "shallow" values. The extremely sensitive Boswell interpreted this dissatisfaction as rejection. In an effort to overcome his low self-esteem and also find a suitable father figure, he became a celebrity chaser.

In Samuel Johnson, he found not only a friendly celebrity but also the father figure he apparently sought. Deciding to become Johnson's biographer, he devoted many years to compiling detailed records of Johnson's life.

Twentieth-Century Author Boswell's *Life of Samuel Johnson* (1791) was an acclaimed book from its first appearance. Then, in the 1920s, scholars discovered Boswell's private papers, long thought to have been destroyed. In 1950, they began publishing the journals they found among these papers—the first volume was *Boswell's London Journal* (1762–1763)—and the great biographer was reborn as a twentieth-century author!

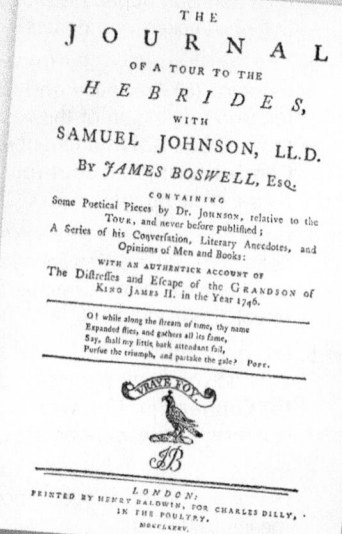

654 A Turbulent Time (1625–1798)

Enrichment: Investigating Genres

Biographies

The first biographies were probably elaborate, though likely inaccurate, inscriptions on the tombs of ancient rulers. Plutarch's *Parallel Lives* contains the first biographies that sought objectivity. The insights and intimacy of Boswell's biography of Johnson influenced many writers. Only since the nineteenth century have biographers in general striven to give a complete picture of their subjects, showing both favorable and unfavorable aspects of their character.

Activity: Investigating Genres Have students read and report on a recently written biography of their choice. Have them use the **Enrichment: Analyzing Forms and Genres** worksheet, *Professional Development Guidebook,* page 227, to track the characteristics of the genre in their selection. Ask students to tell whether or not they recommend the biography and why or why not.

from
The Life of Samuel Johnson

James Boswell

Boswell Meets Johnson
1763

12 This is to me a memorable year; for in it I had the happiness to obtain the acquaintance of that extraordinary man whose memoirs I am now writing; an acquaintance which I shall ever esteem as one of the most fortunate circumstances in my life. Though then but two-and-twenty, I had for several years read his works with delight and instruction, and had the highest reverence for their author, which had grown up in my fancy into a kind of mysterious veneration, by figuring to myself a state of solemn elevated abstraction, in which I supposed him to live in the immense metropolis of London. . . .

Mr. Thomas Davies[1] the actor, who then kept a bookseller's shop in Russel Street, Covent Garden, told me that Johnson was very much his friend, and came frequently to his house, where he more than once invited me to meet him; but by some unlucky accident or other he was prevented from coming to us.

At last, on Monday the 16th day of May, when I was sitting in Mr. Davies's back parlor, after having drunk tea with him and Mrs. Davies, Johnson unexpectedly came into the shop; and Mr. Davies having perceived him through the glass door in the room in which we were sitting, advancing towards us—he announced his aweful[2] approach to me, somewhat in the manner of an actor in the part of Horatio, when he addresses Hamlet on the appearance of his father's ghost, "Look, my Lord, it comes,"[3] I found that I had a very perfect idea of Johnson's figure, from the portrait of him painted by Sir Joshua Reynolds[4] soon after he had published his *Dictionary*, in the attitude of sitting in his easy chair in deep meditation, which was

I had the happiness to obtain the acquaintance of that extraordinary man . . . which I shall ever esteem as one of the most fortunate circumstances in my life.

13 ☑ Reading Check

Why is 1763 "a memorable year" for Boswell?

---

1. **Thomas Davies** English bookseller and unsuccessful actor (1712–1785).
2. **aweful** awe-inspiring.
3. **Horatio "... it comes"** from Shakespeare's *Hamlet* (Act I, Scene iv).
4. **Sir Joshua Reynolds** celebrated portrait painter at the time (1723–1792).

---

14 Reading Strategy

Analyzing the Author's Purpose

1. Remind students of the opening paragraph about Boswell's admiration of Johnson.

2. **Ask** students how they might feel if they found themselves meeting and conversing with someone they admired greatly.
   Possible response: They might feel shy and fearful that they would say something silly or wrong. They might be excited or nervous and thus prone to blurt out words they would later recall with embarrassment.

3. Then, **ask** students the Reading Strategy question: What details in the third paragraph make Boswell's purpose for sharing the story of his first meeting with Johnson clearer?
   Answer: Details about Boswell's rather desperate attempts to make a good first impression and to begin a friendship—such as his concern about being from Scotland—suggest that Boswell is telling this story in order to establish the relationship he will have with Johnson: as a subordinate to this great and "aweful" man.

15 Critical Thinking

Draw Conclusions

1. Explain to students that on the basis of what Boswell reveals about Johnson, they should be able to make assessments about the famous man's personality.

2. Then, **ask** if thus far Boswell's picture of Johnson is a flattering one.
   Answer: No, for the most part, it is not flattering. Johnson is prejudiced against Scots, and while he is quick-witted, he is also quick to criticize someone who offers an opinion contrary to his own.

14 Reading Strategy
Analyzing the Author's Purpose What details in the third paragraph make Boswell's purpose for sharing the story of his first meeting with Johnson clearer?

Vocabulary
abasement (ə bās′ mənt) *n.* condition of being put down or humbled

15

the first picture his friend did for him, which Sir Joshua very kindly presented to me, and from which an engraving has been made for this work. Mr. Davies mentioned my name, and respectfully introduced me to him. I was much agitated; and recollecting his prejudice against the Scotch, of which I had heard much, I said to Davies, "Don't tell where I come from." "From Scotland," cried Davies roguishly. "Mr. Johnson," said I, "I do indeed come from Scotland, but I cannot help it." I am willing to flatter myself that I meant this as light pleasantry to soothe and conciliate him, and not as an humiliating abasement at the expense of my country. But however that might be, this speech was somewhat unlucky; for with that quickness of wit for which he was so remarkable, he seized the expression "come from Scotland," which I used in the sense of being of that country; and, as if I had said that I had come away from it, or left, retorted, "That, Sir, I find, is what a very great many of your countrymen cannot help." This stroke stunned me a good deal; and when we had sat down, I felt myself not a little embarrassed, and apprehensive of what might come next. He then addressed himself to Davies: "What do you think of Garrick?[5] He has refused me an order for the play for Miss Williams, because he knows the house will be full, and that an order would be worth three shillings." Eager to take any opening to get into conversation with him, I ventured to say, "O, Sir, I cannot think Mr. Garrick would grudge such a trifle to you." "Sir," said he, with a stern look, "I have known David Garrick longer than you have done: and I know no right you have to talk to me on the subject." Perhaps I deserved this check; for it was rather presumptuous in me, an entire stranger, to express any doubt of the justice of his animadversion upon his old acquaintance and pupil. I now felt myself much mortified, and began to think that the hope which I had long indulged of obtaining his acquaintance was blasted. And, in truth, had not my ardor been uncommonly strong, and my resolution uncommonly persevering, so rough a reception might have deterred me forever from making any further attempts. Fortunately, however, I remained upon the field not wholly discomfited; and was soon rewarded by hearing some of his conversation, of which I preserved the following short minute,[6] without marking the questions and observations by which it was produced.

"People," he remarked, "may be taken in once, who imagine that an author is greater in private life than other men. Uncommon parts require uncommon opportunities for their exertion."

"In barbarous society, superiority of parts is of real consequence. Great strength or great wisdom is of much value to an individual. But in more polished times there are people to do everything for money; and then there are a number of other superiorities, such as those of

---

5. **Garrick** David Garrick (1717–1779), a famous actor who had been educated by Johnson. Garrick was also one of the managing partners of the Drury Lane Theatre in London.
6. **minute** note.

Think Aloud

Reading Strategy: Analyzing the Author's Purpose
To model the process of working out the answer to the Reading Strategy question on the student page, use the following "think aloud." Say to students:

I know the way a character speaks, moves, and gestures helps me understand what he or she is like. I can draw conclusions about characters in literature much the same way I

draw conclusions about my friends through their posture, tone of voice, physical movements, and eye contact. These small details tell me a lot about their moods, energy levels, interests and motivations. When I pay close attention to details in the texts I am reading, I can better understand a character's motivation and purpose.

birth and fortune, and rank, that dissipate men's attention, and leave no extraordinary share of respect for personal and intellectual superiority. This is wisely ordered by Providence, to preserve some equality among mankind."

"Sir, this book (*The Elements of Criticism,*[7] which he had taken up) is a pretty essay, and deserves to be held in some estimation, though much of it is chimerical."

Speaking of one[8] who with more than ordinary boldness attacked public measures and the royal family, he said, "I think he is safe from the law, but he is an abusive scoundrel; and instead of applying to my Lord Chief Justice to punish him, I would send half a dozen footmen and have him well ducked."[9]

"The notion of liberty amuses the people of England, and helps to keep off the *taedium vitae*.[10] When a butcher tells you that his heart bleeds for his country, he has, in fact, no uneasy feeling."

"Sheridan[11] will not succeed at Bath with his oratory. Ridicule has gone down before him, and, I doubt,[12] Derrick[13] is his enemy."

"Derrick may do very well, as long as he can outrun his character; but the moment his character gets up with him, it is all over."

It is, however, but just to record, that some years afterwards, when I reminded him of this sarcasm, he said, "Well, but Derrick has now got a character that he need not run away from."

I was highly pleased with the extraordinary vigor of his conversation, and regretted that I was drawn away from it by an engagement at another place. I had, for a part of the evening, been left alone with him, and had ventured to make an observation now and then, which he received very civilly; so that I was satisfied that though there was a roughness in his manner, there was no ill nature in his disposition. Davies followed me to the door, and when I complained to him a little of the hard blows which the great man had given me he kindly took upon him to console me by saying, "Don't be uneasy. I can see he likes you very well."

---

7. **The Elements of Criticism** one of the works of Scottish philosophical writer Henry Home (1696–1782).
8. **one** John Wilkes (1727–1797), an English political agitator.
9. **ducked** tied to a chair at the end of a plank and plunged into water.
10. **taedium vitae** (tē′ dē əm vī′ tē) boredom.
11. **Sheridan** Thomas Sheridan (1719–1788), an Irish actor and author. At the time, Sheridan was reading lectures at the Oratory at Bath.
12. **doubt** fear.
13. **Derrick** the Master of Ceremonies of the Oratory at Bath.

I was highly pleased with the extraordinary vigor of his conversation...

17 Reading Check

What quality of Johnson's conversation pleased Boswell?

from The Life of Samuel Johnson **657**

16 Literary Analysis
Biography

1. Review with students that a biography is a story of someone's life written by another person.
2. Have students indicate who is the biographer and who is the subject of the biography in this selection.
   Answer: James Boswell is the biographer; Samuel Johnson's life is the subject of his biography.
3. Have students read the bracketed passage [from "Speaking of one" to "need not run away from"], noting any details that Boswell uses in describing Johnson's "extraordinary vigor."

▶ **Monitor Progress:** Then, **ask:** Has Boswell sufficiently supported his statement about the "extraordinary vigor" of Johnson's conversation? Why or why not?
Answer: Boswell has supported his statement. Johnson seems very quick-witted and articulate. He shows that he is informed about the manners of his day. He uses a Latin term in conversation; he is witty about both the matter of ducking and the butcher; and he produces a pun on the spot about "outrunning character" and the character catching up.

17 **Reading Check**

Answer: The extraordinary vigor—that is, the energy and intelligence—of Johnson's conversation pleased Boswell.

Differentiated Instruction   for Universal Access

Strategy for Less Proficient Readers
Have students read along with you the passages in *The Life of Samuel Johnson* in which Boswell reveals contradictory aspects of Johnson's character. Ask students to make a list of good and bad qualities that Boswell describes.

Enrichment for Gifted/Talented Students
Have students draw front-and-back illustrations showing the facets of Samuel Johnson according to Boswell. Students should incorporate as many of Johnson's contrary characteristics as possible, drawing opposite characteristics on the front and back of each illustration.

Enrichment for Advanced Readers
Tell students that Johnson once said, "Nobody can write the life of a man, but those who have eat and drunk and lived . . . with him." Have students debate this remark and defend their opinions using Boswell's biography and other biographies as examples.

Johnson and Boswell, The Trustees of the British Museum

19 ▲ **Critical Viewing** This engraving shows the ghost of Samuel Johnson haunting Boswell. In what ways does the relationship between the men that it portrays reflect the relationship suggested by Boswell's *Life*? **[Interpret]**

Johnson's Character

The character of Samuel Johnson has, I trust, been so developed in the course of this work, that they who have honored it with a perusal, may be considered as well acquainted with him. As, however, it may be expected that I should collect into one view the capital and distinguishing features of this extraordinary man, I shall endeavor to acquit myself of that part of my biographical undertaking, however difficult it may be to do that which many of my readers will do better for themselves.

His figure was large and well formed, and his countenance of the cast of an ancient statue; yet his appearance was rendered strange and somewhat uncouth by convulsive cramps, by the scars of that 20 distemper[14] which it was once imagined the royal touch could cure,[15] and by a slovenly mode of dress. He had the use only of one eye; yet

---

14. **distemper** scrofula, a type of tuberculosis that causes swelling and scarring of the neck.
15. **royal touch . . . cure** it was at one time believed that the touch of an English monarch had the power to heal. As a child Johnson was taken to Queen Anne to receive her touch in the hope that it would cure him.

20 so much does mind govern and even supply the deficiency of organs, that his visual perceptions, as far as they extended, were uncommonly quick and accurate. So morbid was his temperament, that he never knew the natural joy of a free and vigorous use of his limbs: when he walked, it was like the struggling gait of one in fetters; when he rode, he had no command or direction of his horse, but was carried as if in a balloon. That with his constitution and habits of life he should have lived seventy-five years, is a proof that an inherent *vivida vis*[16] is a powerful preservative of the human frame.

Man is, in general, made up of contradictory qualities; and these will ever show themselves in strange succession, where a consistency in appearance at least, if not in reality, has not been attained by long habits of philosophical discipline. In proportion to the native vigor of the mind, the contradictory qualities will be the more prominent, and more difficult to be adjusted; and, therefore, we are not to wonder that Johnson exhibited an eminent example of this remark which I have made upon human nature. At different times, he seemed a different man, in some respects; not, however, in any great or essential article, upon which he had fully employed his mind, and settled certain principles of duty, but only in his manners and in the display of argument and fancy in his talk. He was prone to superstition, but not to credulity. Though his imagination might incline him to a belief of the marvelous and the mysterious, his vigorous reason examined the evidence with jealousy.[17] He was a sincere and zealous Christian, of high Church of England and monarchical principles, which he would not tamely suffer to be questioned; and had, perhaps, at an early period, narrowed his mind somewhat too much, both as to religion and politics. His being impressed with the danger of extreme latitude in either, though he was of a very independent spirit, occasioned his appearing somewhat unfavorable to the prevalence of that noble freedom of sentiment which is the best possession of man. Nor can it be denied, that he had many prejudices; which, however, frequently suggested many of his pointed sayings that rather show a playfulness of fancy than any settled malignity. He was steady and inflex-
21 ible in maintaining the obligations of religion and morality; both from a regard for the order of society, and from a veneration for the Great Source of all order; correct, nay, stern in his taste; hard to please, and easily offended; impetuous and irritable in his temper, but of a most humane and benevolent heart, which showed itself not only in a most liberal charity, as far as his circumstances would allow, but in a thousand instances of active benevolence. He was afflicted with a bodily disease, which made him often restless and fretful; and with a constitutional melancholy, the clouds of which darkened the brightness of his fancy, and gave a gloomy cast to his whole course of thinking: we, therefore, ought not to wonder at his sallies

Vocabulary

credulity (krə do͞o′ lə tē) *n.* tendency to believe too readily

malignity (mə lig′ nə tē) *n.* strong desire to harm others

22 Reading Check

What are some of Johnson's "contradictory qualities"?

---

16. *vivida vis* lively force.
17. **jealousy** suspicion.

from The Life of Samuel Johnson **659**

20 Critical Thinking
Make Judgments

1. Have students read the bracketed passage. Ask them to focus on Boswell's physical description of Johnson.

2. Then, **ask** if they think this physical description of Johnson is objective.
   Answer: It appears to be objective. Johnson was not, evidently, pleasing to look at, and Boswell does not hesitate to tell readers so. In addition, he says that Johnson walked strangely and cut a rather ludicrous figure on his horse when he rode. Because it is clear that Boswell keenly admired Johnson, readers can infer that these details are included simply because they are part of the overall portrait of the man.

21 Critical Thinking
Analyze

1. Have volunteers take turns reading aloud the bracketed passage.

2. Then, **ask** students what negative aspects of Johnson's character are contained in this description.
   Answer: Johnson's prejudices, his sternness, his tendency to be easily offended, his irritability, his moodiness, and his ability to say nasty things are described.

22 Reading Check

Possible responses: Students may mention Johnson's benevolence and wit, his prejudices, his sternness, and his tendency to be easily offended.

Differentiated Instruction for Universal Access

Culturally Response Instruction

Culture Connection Point out to students that Johnson was a role model and mentor to Boswell. Boswell did not expect his role model to be perfect, yet he admired and tried to emulate him or her. In the culture of the United States, the tendency to make role models from celebrities is common, and famous people can feel the burden of being expected to act and speak in ways that set examples of behavior. Ask students to consider whether a person can or should be a role model simply because that person is famous, and whether young people can admire and emulate celebrities and still be honest about those celebrities' shortcomings, as Boswell was about Johnson's.

㉓ Literary Analysis

Biography

1. Remind students that a good biography presents an accurate and complete picture of the subject against the backdrop of the time in which he or she lived.

2. **Ask** students what it means to present a complete picture of a person's life.
   Possible response: It means to tell both the good and the bad, the exciting and the mundane, about that person's life.

3. Then, **ask** the Literary Analysis question: In what part of the biography—the beginning, middle, or end—would it be appropriate for Boswell to present this analysis of Johnson's character? Why?
   Possible responses: Some students may feel that this summation of Johnson's character is appropriate for the end of Boswell's biography; others may feel that it would be better treated in the middle of the biography, since it contains many contrasting opinions and views that can be teased out and reconciled as the work progresses.

Literary Analysis
Biography
In what part of his biography—the beginning, middle, or end—would it be appropriate for Boswell to present this analysis of Johnson's character? Why?

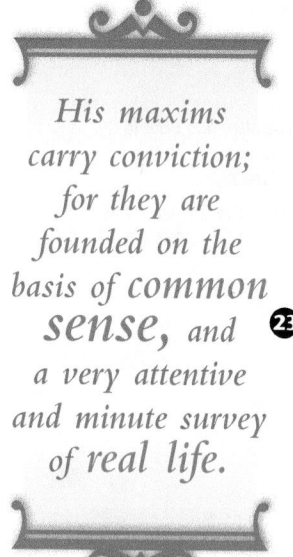

*His maxims carry conviction; for they are founded on the basis of **common sense,** and a very attentive and minute survey of real life.*

of impatience and passion at any time; especially when provoked by obtrusive ignorance, or presuming petulance; and allowance must be made for his uttering hasty and satirical sallies even against his best friends. And, surely, when it is considered, that, "amidst sickness and sorrow," he exerted his faculties in so many works for the benefit of mankind, and particularly that he achieved the great and admirable Dictionary of our language, we must be astonished at his resolution. The solemn text, "of him to whom much is given, much will be required," seems to have been ever present to his mind, in a rigorous sense, and to have made him dissatisfied with his labors and acts of goodness, however comparatively great; so that the unavoidable consciousness of his superiority was, in that respect, a cause of disquiet. He suffered so much from this, and from the gloom which perpetually haunted him and made solitude frightful, that it may be said of him, "If in this life only he had hope, he was of all men most miserable."[18] He loved praise, when it was brought to him; but was too proud to seek for it. He was somewhat susceptible of flattery. As he was general and unconfined in his studies, he cannot be considered as master of any one particular science; but he had accumulated a vast and various collection of learning and knowledge, which was so arranged in his mind, as to be ever in readiness to be brought forth. But his superiority over other learned men consisted chiefly in what may be called the art of thinking, the art of using his mind; a certain continual power of seizing the useful substance of all that he knew and exhibiting it in a clear and forcible manner; so that knowledge, which we often see to be no better than lumber[19] in men of dull understanding, was, in him, true, evident, and actual wisdom. His moral precepts are practical; for they are drawn from an intimate ㉓ acquaintance with human nature. His maxims carry conviction; for they are founded on the basis of common sense, and a very attentive and minute survey of real life. His mind was so full of imagery, that he might have been perpetually a poet; yet it is remarkable, that, however rich his prose is in this respect, his poetical pieces, in general, have not much of that splendor, but are rather distinguished by strong sentiment and acute observation, conveyed in harmonious and energetic verse, particularly in heroic couplets. Though usually grave, and even aweful, in his deportment, he possessed uncommon and peculiar powers of wit and humor; he frequently indulged himself in colloquial pleasantry; and the heartiest merriment was often enjoyed in his company; with this great advantage, that as it was entirely free from any poisonous tincture of vice or impiety, it was salutary to those who shared in it. He had accustomed himself to such accuracy in his common conversation, that he at all times expressed his thoughts with great force, and an elegant choice of language,

---

18. **"If . . . miserable"** from I Corinthians 15:19.
19. **lumber** rubbish.

660 A Turbulent Time (1625–1798)

Think Aloud

Literary Analysis: Biography
To model the process of working out the answer to the Literary Analysis question on the student page, use the following "think aloud." Say to students:

I know that reading a biography is a bit like

getting to know a person. When you first meet someone, you know just a little about him or her. Like Boswell, over time, you gradually discover a person's strengths and weaknesses.

the effect of which was aided by his having a loud voice, and a slow deliberate utterance. In him were united a most logical head with a most fertile imagination, which gave him an extraordinary advantage in arguing: for he could reason close or wide, as he saw best for the moment. Exulting in his intellectual strength and dexterity, he could, when he pleased, be the greatest sophist[20] that ever contended in the lists of declamation; and, from a spirit of contradiction and a delight in showing his powers, he would often maintain the wrong side with equal warmth and ingenuity; so that, when there was an audience, his real opinions could seldom be gathered from his talk; though when he was in company with a single friend, he would discuss a subject with genuine fairness: but he was too conscientious to make error permanent and pernicious[21], by deliberately writing it; and, in all his numerous works, he earnestly inculcated[22] what appeared to him to be the truth; his piety being constant, and the ruling principle of all his conduct.

Such was Samuel Johnson, a man whose talents, acquirements, and virtues, were so extraordinary, that the more his character is considered the more he will be regarded by the present age, and by posterity, with admiration and reverence.

---

20. **sophist** (säf′ ist) *n.* one who makes clever, apparently plausible arguments.
21. **pernicious** (pər nish′ əs) *adj.* wicked; evil.
22. **inculcated** (in kul′ kāt′ əd) *v.* to teach by repetition and urging.

Critical Reading

Cite textual evidence to support your responses.

1. **Key Ideas and Details (a)** How did Boswell meet Johnson? **(b) Infer:** What does their conversation at that meeting tell you about each of them?

2. **Key Ideas and Details (a)** What are some of the topics Johnson discusses that Boswell records "without marking the questions and observations" that produced them? **(b) Infer:** What do Johnson's opinions on these topics suggest about his interests and knowledge?

3. **Key Ideas and Details (a)** Briefly summarize Boswell's remarks on Johnson's character. **(b) Evaluate:** Would Johnson have been less interesting if he had been less "contradictory"? Explain.

4. **Integration of Knowledge and Ideas** Which label, if any, suits each author better, inventor or conservator? Explain. In your response, use at least two of these Essential Question words: *commentary, conventional, authentic. [Connecting to the Essential Question: What is the relationship of the writer to tradition?]*

from The Life of Samuel Johnson **661**

Concept Connector

Reading Strategy Graphic Organizer
Ask students to review the graphic organizers in which they have analyzed the author's purpose. Then, have students share their organizers and compare their interpretations of the author's perspective and its effect on meaning.

Activating Prior Knowledge
Have students return to their responses to the Activating Prior Knowledge activity. Ask them to explain whether their thoughts have changed and if so, how.

 Writing About the Essential Question
Have students compare their responses to the prompt, completed before reading the selections, with their thoughts afterwards. Have them work individually or in groups, writing or discussing their thoughts, to formulate new responses. During a class discussion, encourage students to cite specific textual details to support their responses.

Answers

1. Johnson's definitions are accurate but not the most common meanings. Another sample answer can be found on **Literary Analysis Graphic Organizer A**, page 117 in *Graphic Organizer Transparencies*.

2. (a) Facts include: Johnson rebuked Boswell for foolishness; Johnson had scars; Johnson attempted to supply a friend with theater tickets. Opinions include: Boswell deserved the rebuke; Johnson looked "strange"; Johnson was generous. (b) While the facts are revealing, Boswell's haste in apologizing for Johnson speaks much of Johnson's effect on others.

3. Students should support their responses with quotes.

4. **Possible response:** Johnson says that in his dictionary "much is omitted, . . . much likewise is performed." Boswell refers to Johnson's insult toward his country as "that quickness of wit for which he was so remarkable."

5. Both *Dictionary* and *Life* try to bring order to reality. In Johnson's case, the English language is codified; in Boswell's case, a full life is compressed into a biography.

6. The cartoon suggests that Boswell is wordy.

7. (a) The passage that might best express Johnson's purpose is the one that begins "Having therefore no assistance but from general grammar...."(b) Students may agree that Johnson achieved his purpose, as his work is still of great repute. (c) Johnson wished to convey that authors are important in shaping the meanings of words.

8. (a)The passage "The character of Samuel Johnson has, I trust, been so developed in the course of this work...may be considered as well acquainted with him" best reveals Boswell's purpose. (b) Boswell wants to make clear that Johnson was likable once you got to know him.

After You Read

from *A Dictionary of the English Language* • from *The Life of Samuel Johnson*

Literary Analysis

1. **Integration of Knowledge and Ideas** Use a chart like the one shown to compare the definition of a word in Johnson's *Dictionary* with its definition in a modern **dictionary**.

Johnson's *Dictionary*	Modern Dictionary	Similarities/ Differences

2. **Key Ideas and Details** **(a)** Find three examples of facts and three examples of opinions in the **biography** written by Boswell. **(b)** Which is more revealing of Johnson's character, the facts or the opinions? Why?

3. **Craft and Structure** Find passages from the Preface to the *Dictionary* and from *The Life of Samuel Johnson* that show the formality of the **diction** of the eighteenth-century Enlightenment.

4. **Integration of Knowledge and Ideas** Citing specific passages, contrast Johnson's mixed *tone* of discouragement and pride in the Preface with Boswell's unmixed tone of admiration in *Life*.

5. **Integration of Knowledge and Ideas** Referring to specific passages, demonstrate how both works strive to accomplish an Enlightenment goal of bringing order to messy reality.

6. **Analyzing Visual Information** Using what you know about Johnson and Boswell, explain the humor of the cartoon shown on this page.

Reading Strategy

7. **Analyze Johnson's purpose** for writing his *Dictionary* by reviewing the Preface. **(a)** Which passage best expresses his purpose? Why? **(b)** Do you think Johnson achieved this purpose? Why or why not? **(c)** Explain how knowing Johnson's purpose helps you understand why he included quotations from famous authors in many definitions.

8. **(a)** Identify a passage revealing Boswell's purpose for writing. **(b)** How does his purpose explain the space he devotes to his meeting with Johnson?

©The New Yorker Collection, 1995, Ed Fisher, from *cartoonbank.com.* All Rights Reserved.

"More port for Dr. Johnson. And more ink for Mr. Boswell." ▶

Common Core State Standards

Reading Informational Text
9. Analyze seventeenth-, eighteenth-, and nineteenth-century foundational U.S. documents of historical and literary significance for their themes, purposes, and rhetorical features. *(p. 663)*

Writing
9.b. Apply *grades 11–12 Reading standards* to literary nonfiction. *(p. 663)*

Language
4.c. Consult general and specialized reference materials, both print and digital, to find the pronunciation of a word or determine or clarify its precise meaning, its part of speech, its etymology, or its standard usage. *(p. 663)*

Assessment Practice

Writer's Point of View (For more practice, see *All-in-One Workbook.*)

Many tests require students to identify a writer's point of view or opinion. Use this sample test item.

  Pa´ tron. One who countenances, supports, or protects. Commonly a wretch who supports with insolence, and is paid with flattery.

Based on this definition, Johnson's opinion of a patron

A is unbiased
B is favorable
C is extremely low
D cannot be determined

Lead students to recognize that Johnson's use of the word *wretch* to describe a patron and the phrase "paid with flattery" both reveal a very negative opinion of a patron. **C** is the correct answer.

Integrated Language Skills

Vocabulary Acquisition and Use

Word Analysis: Latin Root -dict-

The Latin root -dict- conveys the idea of something said. In dictionary, it refers to the words "said" in a language. The root also appears in the word dictator, which means "a ruler whose pronouncements are the final word." Knowing the meaning of the root -dict-, use context clues to infer the meaning of each italicized word listed here. Then, use a dictionary to verify your inferences.

1. During the Napoleonic Wars, Britain sought to interdict the flow of goods to France.
2. In the British legal system, a person must be indicted before being tried.
3. A Supreme Court judge releases a dictum of his or her position after many cases.
4. Dictators issue edicts, but in Britain, Parliament makes the laws.
5. In the past, secretaries used shorthand to record messages dictated by their bosses.
6. Skilled playwrights control the diction of each character to reflect his or her background.

Vocabulary: Cognates

Cognates are words that share a common origin but may have different meanings. For instance, patron, one of Johnson's dictionary entries, shares its origin with paternal ("fatherly"). Both come from the Latin pater, which means "father." Cognates can also occur across languages, like the English word night and the German word nacht. Study the pairs of words from Johnson's Preface and Boswell's Life that follow. Determine whether each pair is a cognate, explaining your reasoning. Then, check the words in a dictionary to see if you were correct.

1. caprices ("whims") and capacity ("volume")
2. adulterations ("impurities") and adult ("individual who has reached maturity")
3. risible ("laughable") and ridiculous ("deserving ridicule")
4. abasement ("being put down") and debase ("to corrupt")
5. malignity ("desire to harm others") and aligned ("in line with")

Writing

Informative Text James Boswell's The Life of Samuel Johnson and Benjamin Franklin's The Autobiography are two eighteenth-century classics. Find a copy of Franklin's autobiography (or download it from a Web site, such as the Gutenberg Project, that provides classic works free of charge), and read his account of his first entry into Philadelphia. Then, write an **essay** comparing two "firsts": Boswell's introduction to Dr. Johnson and Franklin's arrival in Philadelphia. Discuss whether Johnson, an Englishman, and Franklin, a colonial American, possess similar traits or share certain values.

Prewriting As you read both texts, take notes about the ways in which each man presents his younger self. Consider the personality traits each displays and the qualities each seems to value, both in himself and others. Review your findings to arrive at a thesis.

Drafting Organize your ideas logically, so that your discussion explores the two texts clearly. Support your ideas with quotations from each work.

Revising Review your draft, highlighting any awkward or wordy phrasing. Revise with more concise and precise word choices.

> **Model: Revising for Impact**
> At his first meeting with Dr. Johnson, young Boswell felt ~~overwhelmed with a sense of awe and a little fearful.~~
> awestruck and intimidated.

Specific language makes an essay stronger.

Vocabulary Acquisition and Use

Word Analysis

1. Interdict means "to prohibit by act or decree of a court."
2. Indicted means "charged with a crime."
3. A dictum is a judge's opinion.
4. Edicts are decrees issued by sovereigns or authorities.
5. Words that are dictated are meant to be set down in writing.
6. Diction is word choice.

Vocabulary

1. Not cognates, caprices and capacity do not share a common origin.
2. Not cognates, words do not share a common origin.
3. Cognates, words share origin.
4. Cognates, words share origin.
5. Cognates, words share origin.

Writing

You may use this writing lesson as timed-writing practice, or allow students to develop the essay as a writing assignment over several days.

1. To guide students in writing this editorial, give them the **Support for Writing Lesson** page (Unit 3 Resources, p. 196).
2. Tell students that they should consider both positions regarding the issue of objectivity before favoring one approach.
3. Use the Writing Lesson to guide students in developing their thesis statements.
4. Use the rubrics for Persuasive Essays in the **Professional Development Guidebook,** pages 256–257, to evaluate students' essays.

Assessment Resources

Unit 3 Resources

L1 L2 EL **Selection Test A,** pp. 201–203. Administer Test A to less advanced readers.

L3 L4 EL **Selection Test B,** pp. 204–206. Administer Test B to on-level students and more advanced students.

L3 L4 **Open-Book Test,** pp. 198–200. As an alternative, give the Open-Book test.

All **Customizable Test Bank**

All **Self-tests**
Students may prepare for the **Selection Test** by taking the **Self-test** online.

PHLit Online! All assessment resources are available at www.PHLitOnline.com.

Elegy Written in a Country Churchyard
• A Nocturnal Reverie
Lesson Pacing Guide

DAY 1 Preteach

- Administer the Reading and Vocabulary Warm-ups (*Unit 3 Resources*, pp. 207–210) as necessary.
- Introduce the Literary Analysis concept: Pre-Romantic Poetry.
- Introduce the Reading Strategy: Paraphrasing.
- Build background with the author and Background features.
- Develop thematic thinking with Connecting to the Essential Question.
- Teach the selection vocabulary.

DAY 2 Preteach/Teach/Extend

- Distribute copies of the appropriate graphic organizer for the Reading Strategy (*Graphic Organizer Transparencies*, pp. 119–120).
- Distribute copies of the appropriate graphic organizer for Literary Analysis (*Graphic Organizer Transparencies*, pp. 121–122).
- Prepare students to read with the Activating Prior Knowledge activities (TE).
- Informally monitor comprehension while students read.
- Use the Reading Check questions to confirm comprehension.
- Develop students' understanding of Pre-Romantic poetry using the Literary Analysis prompts.
- Develop students' ability to paraphrase using the Reading Strategy prompts.
- Reinforce vocabulary with the Vocabulary notes.
- Assess students' comprehension and mastery of the skills by having them answer the Critical Reading, Literary Analysis, and Reading Strategy questions.

DAY 3 Assess

- Have students complete the Vocabulary activities.
- Have students complete the Writing activity and write directions for reciting a poem. (You may assign as homework.)
- Administer Selection Test A or B (*Unit 3 Resources,* pp. 219–221 or 222–224).

© Common Core State Standards

Reading Literature 2. Determine two or more themes or central ideas of a text and analyze their development over the course of the text, including how they interact and build on one another to produce a complex account.

Writing 2. Write informative/explanatory texts to examine and convey complex ideas, concepts, and information clearly and accurately through the effective selection, organization, and analysis of content.

Additional Standards Practice
Common Core Companion, pp. 15–22; 196–207

Daily Block Scheduling
Each day in this Lesson Pacing Guide represents a 40–50 minute period. Teachers using block scheduling may combine days to revise pacing. In addition, teachers may differentiate and support core instruction by integrating components for extended and intensive support as students require. See the Guide to Selected Leveled Resources (facing page).

Guide to Selected Leveled Resources

R T I Tier 1 (students performing on level)
Elegy Written in a Country Churchyard • A Nocturnal Reverie

Warm Up	Practice, model, and monitor fluency, working with the whole class or in groups.	Vocabulary and Reading Warm-ups B, *Unit 3 Resources,* pp. 204–205, 207
Comprehension/Skills	Support and monitor comprehension and skills development, having students complete the activities, graphic organizers, and interactive prompts independently or as a class.	• *Reader's Notebook,* adapted instruction and full selection EL *Reader's Notebook: English Learner's Version,* adapted instruction and adapted selection • Reading Strategy Graphic Organizer B, *Graphic Organizer Transparencies,* p. 124 • Literary Analysis Graphic Organizer B, *Graphic Organizer Transparencies,* p. 126
Monitor Progress A	Monitor student progress with the differentiated curriculum-based assessment in the *Unit Resources.*	• Selection Test B, *Unit 3 Resources,* pp. 219–221 • Open-Book Test, *Unit 3 Resources,* pp. 213–215

R T I Tier 2 (students requiring intervention)
Elegy Written in a Country Churchyard • A Nocturnal Reverie

Warm Up	Practice, model, and monitor fluency in groups or with individuals.	• Vocabulary and Reading Warm-ups A, *Unit 3 Resources,* pp. 204–206 • *Hear It!* Audio CD (adapted text)
Comprehension/Skills	• Support and monitor comprehension and skills development, working in small groups or with individuals. • As students complete the selection in the appropriate version of the *Reader's Notebook,* monitor comprehension frequently with group questions and individual instruction. • Model strategies while guiding students in completing the activities and prompts in the *Reader's Notebook,* as well as the graphic organizers. • Practice skills and monitor mastery with the *Reading Kit* worksheets.	• *Reader's Notebook: Adapted Version,* adapted instruction and adapted selection EL *Reader's Notebook: English Learner's Version,* adapted instruction and adapted selection • Reading Strategy Graphic Organizer A, *Graphic Organizer Transparencies,* p. 123 • Literary Analysis Graphic Organizer A, *Graphic Organizer Transparencies,* p. 125 • *Reading Kit,* Practice worksheets
Monitor Progress A	Monitor student progress with the differentiated curriculum-based assessment in the *Unit Resources* and in the *Reading Kit.*	• Selection Test A, *Unit 3 Resources,* pp. 216–218 • *Reading Kit,* Assess worksheets

TIER 3 Tier 3 intervention may require consultation with the student's special-education or dyslexia specialist. For additional support, see the Tier 2 activities and resources listed above.

One-on-one teaching   Group work   Whole class instruction   Independent work   A Assessment

For a complete guide to selection support, including support for Advanced students, see the Overview of Resources in the frontmatter.

Elegy Written in a Country Churchyard
• A Nocturnal Reverie

Vocabulary/Fluency/Prior Knowledge

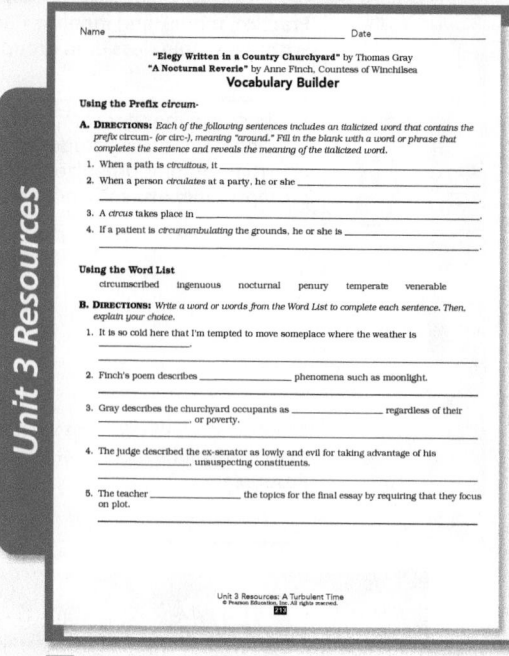

All **Vocabulary Builder,** p. 213

Also available for these selections:

EL **L1** **L2** **Vocabulary Warm-ups A and B,** pp. 207–208

EL **L1** **L2** **Reading Warm-ups A and B,** pp. 209–210

RESOURCES FOR:
- **L1** Special-Needs Students
- **L2** Below-Level Students (Tier 2)
- **L3** On-Level Students (Tier 1)
- **L4** Advanced Students (Tier 1)
- **EL** English Learners
- **All** All Students

Reader's Notebooks
Pre- and postreading pages for both selections appear in an interactive format in the *Reader's Notebooks*. Each *Notebook* is differentiated for a different group of learners. The selections in the Adapted and English Learner's versions are abridged.

L2 **L3** *Reader's Notebook*

L1 *Reader's Notebook: Adapted Version*

EL *Reader's Notebook: English Learner's Version*

EL *Reader's Notebook: Spanish Version*

© Common Core Companion
Additional instruction and practice for each Common Core State Standard

Selection Support

Graphic Organizer Transparencies

EL L1 L2 Literary Analysis: Graphic Organizer A (partially filled in), p. 121

Also available for these selections:

EL L1 L2 Reading: Graphic Organizer A (partially filled in), p. 119

EL L3 Reading: Graphic Organizer B, p. 120

EL L3 Literary Analysis: Graphic Organizer B, p. 122

Skills Development/Extension

Unit 3 Resources

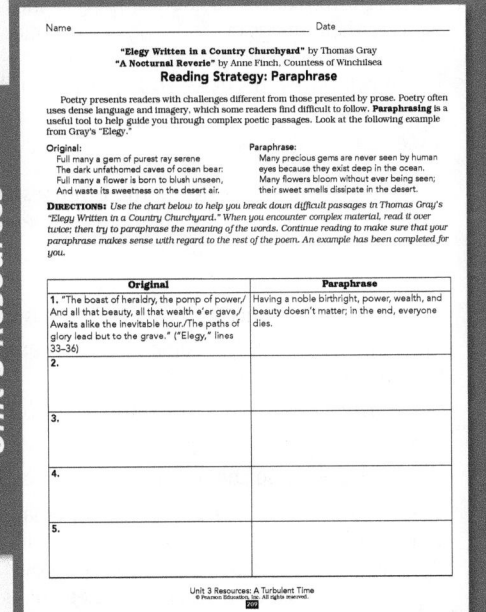

All Reading, p. 212

Also available for these selections:

All Literary Analysis, p. 211

EL L3 L4 Support for Writing, p. 214

L4 Enrichment, p. 215

Assessment

L3 L4 Open-Book Test, pp. 216–218

Also available for these selections:

EL L1 L2 Selection Test A, pp. 219–221

EL L3 L4 Selection Test B, pp. 222–224

PHLit Online!
www.PHLitOnline.com

Online Resources: All print materials are also available online.

- complete narrated selection text
- a thematically related video with writing prompt
- an interactive graphic organizer
- highlighting feature
- access to all student print resources, adapted to individual student needs
- Spanish and English summaries
- adapted selection translations in Spanish

Background Video

Also available:

Get Connected! (thematic video with writing prompt)
All videos are available in Spanish.

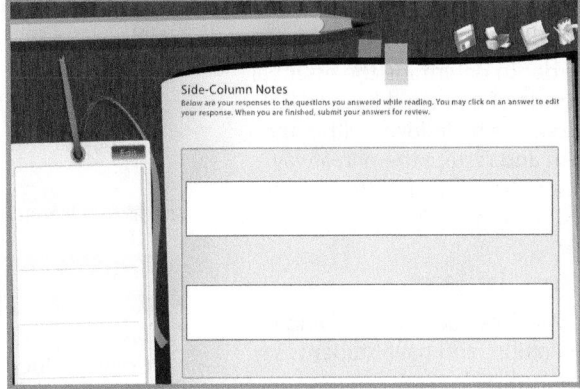

Writer's Journal (with graphics feature)

Also available:

Vocabulary Central (tools and activities for studying vocabulary)

❶ Connecting to the Essential Question

1. Review the assignment with the class.

2. Prepare students to write by discussing places students have found conducive to deep thought and reflection, and the characteristics of those places. Then have students complete the assignment.

3. As students read, have them look for lines in which the poets describe how specific features of their environment affect the way they feel.

❷ Literary Analysis

Introduce the skill using the instruction on the student page.

Think Aloud: Model the Skill

Say to students:

To notice the features that give Pre-Romantic poetry a polished feel, I need to focus on line-level details such as word choice and rhythm.

❸ Reading Strategy

1. Introduce the strategy using the instruction on the student page.

2. Give students a copy of **Reading Strategy Graphic Organizer B**, page 120 in *Graphic Organizer Transparencies*, to fill out as they read.

Think Aloud: Model the Skill

Say to students:

In order to determine the essential message of a poem, I have to figure out the main ideas within the poem and restate them in a way that's clear to me. In other words, I must paraphrase it.

❹ Vocabulary

1. Pronounce each word, giving its definition, and have students say it aloud.

2. For more guidance, see the *Classroom Strategies and Teaching Routines* card for introducing vocabulary.

---

❶ Connecting to the Essential Question Like each of these authors, you might sometimes seek out a special landscape or place when you want to think things over. Noting the qualities of each author's special place as you read will help as you consider the Essential Question: **What is the relationship between literature and place?**

❷ Literary Analysis

Eighteenth-century **Pre-Romantic poetry** shares characteristics of two different styles. Like earlier, Neoclassical poetry, Pre-Romantic poetry is characterized by these features:

• the polished expression of ideas
• the use of balanced phrases and sophisticated vocabulary

At the same time, Pre-Romantic poetry anticipates Romantic literature by introducing these elements:

• a new focus on nature and the life of common folk
• the expression of heightened, sometimes nameless feelings

Look for all these characteristics as you read the following poems.

Comparing Literary Works Like the Romantics who come after them, Gray and Finch express heightened feelings in their poetry. Gray's stroll through a country churchyard lets him discover life's true value. Finch's nighttime walk allows her to feel a deep connection with nature. As you read, compare the emotions these poets experience and analyze two or more themes or central ideas in the poems. Consider how these themes develop and build on one another to produce a deeper meaning.

❸ Reading Strategy

© **Preparing to Read Complex Texts** **Determine the essential message,** or main idea, of a passage in a poem by *paraphrasing* it—identifying its key ideas and restating them in your own words. Use a chart like the one shown to paraphrase passages from these poems as you read.

❹ Vocabulary

penury (pen´ yoo rē) *n.* poverty (p. 669)

circumscribed (sur´ kəm skrībd´) *v.* limited; confined (p. 669)

ingenuous (in jen´ yoo əs) *adj.* candid and frank; naive; simple (p. 669)

nocturnal (näk tur´ nəl) *adj.* occurring at night (p. 673)

temperate (tem´ pər it) *adj.* mild (p. 674)

venerable (ven´ ər ə bəl) *adj.* commanding respect because of age, character, or rank (p. 674)

© **Common Core State Standards**

Reading Literature

2. Determine two or more themes or central ideas of a text and analyze their development over the course of the text, including how they interact and build on one another to produce a complex account.

Original

"Now fades the glimmering landscape on the sight,…"

↓

Paraphrase

Nightfall is making it difficult to see the landscape.

Vocabulary Development

Vocabulary Knowledge Rating

Create a **Vocabulary Knowledge Rating Chart** (*Professional Development Guidebook*, p. 33) for the vocabulary words on the student page. Give each student a copy of the chart with the words on it. Read the words aloud, and have students mark their rating of each in the Before Reading column. When students have completed reading and discussing the group of selections, have them take out their **Vocabulary Knowledge Rating Charts** for the selections. Read the words aloud and have students rate their knowledge again in the After Reading column. Clarify any words that are still problematic. Then, have students complete the Vocabulary practice at the end of the selections.

⑤ Thomas Gray

(1716–1771)

Elegy **665**

Author of "Elegy Written in a Country Churchyard"

The uncertainty of life was something that Thomas Gray understood all too well. The only one of twelve Gray children to survive infancy, he suffered from convulsions as a child. On at least one occasion, his mother was forced to open a vein to relieve the pressure on his brain.

Lavishing affection on her sickly son, Gray's mother saved money from the shop she kept in London and sent him to Eton and Cambridge.

A Quiet Life After making the Grand Tour of Europe with his friend the author Horace Walpole, Gray lived with his mother and aunts in the sleepy village of Stoke Poges. There, in the summer of 1742, he wrote his first important poems. The church and graveyard at Stoke Poges probably inspired his best-known poem, "Elegy Written in a Country Churchyard."

A Near Mishap This beloved poem nearly went astray. Gray sent a copy to Walpole, and it fell into the hands of a dishonest editor. It was retrieved only after a struggle. In the end, the poem came to belong to its readers: It contains some of the best-remembered lines in English poetry.

A Lonely Romantic After age thirty, Gray returned to Cambridge, where he studied classical literature and Celtic and Norse mythology. He died after an attack of gout. His literary output was small—he wrote slowly, striving for perfection—but his poems are counted among the finest in the English language. In them, he expresses new, Romantic yearnings in the formal style of his times. The poet Matthew Arnold suggested that if Gray had lived in another era, his accomplishments might have been even greater.

❶ **About the Selection**

This famous poem uses the melancholy setting of a graveyard at twilight to meditate on the lives of the ordinary people interred there. In soulful song, Gray laments not one particular death, but the obscurity into which death may plunge us all.

❷ **Activating Prior Knowledge**

Tell students that for these two poets, nighttime wanderings lead to profound contemplations about life. Ask students whether they have ever experienced this phenomenon. Have them write a paragraph describing their experiences and/or explaining why they think nighttime might have this effect on people.

Concept Connector ➡

Tell students they will return to their responses after reading the selection.

❸ **Humanities**

British Isles, Church with Tombstones

by Leonore Weber

This photograph evokes a strong sense of the passage of time. Use these questions for discussion:

What deductions might you make about the churchyard's occupants? **Possible response:** Those buried in the churchyard were probably poor and obscure in life.

❹ **Critical Viewing**

Answer: Students may say that the photograph reflects the unpretentious, quiet nature of death among poor and simple people.

❸ ❶ ❷ # Elegy Written in a Country Churchyard

THOMAS GRAY

❹ ▲ **Critical Viewing** The churchyard in this photograph looks untended and forgotten. How does the photograph reflect the meaning of Gray's poem? [Deduce]

666 A Turbulent Time (1625–1798)

© **Text Complexity Rubric: Leveled Texts**

	Elegy Written in a Country Churchyard	A Nocturnal Reverie
Qualitative Measures		
Context/ Knowledge Demands	Pre-Romantic elegy; literary and cultural knowledge demands 1 2 ③ 4 5	Pre-Romantic meditative poem; literary knowledge demands 1 2 ③ 4 5
Structure/Language Conventionality and Clarity	Long sentences; poetic syntax; vocabulary 1 2 ③ 4 5	Long sentences; poetic syntax 1 2 ③ 4 5
Levels of Meaning/ Purpose/Concept Level	Challenging (death, immortality) 1 2 3 ④ 5	Challenging (nature, emotion) 1 2 ③ 4 5
Quantitative Measures		
Lexile/Text Length	NP / 992 words	NP / 367 words
Overall Complexity	**More complex**	**More accessible**

In the eighteenth century, many writers championed reason, clarity, and logic. These values led to the articulate, eloquent couplets of Alexander Pope. They also led to the major scientific discoveries of Sir Isaac Newton, of whom Pope wrote: "God said, Let Newton be! And there was light!" These values might be thought of as belonging to daylight. In contrast, the poems in this grouping are set at twilight or at night. They stress emotion—the not-always-reasonable reaction to circumstances—and mystery—those longings and intuitions of human experience that are not clearly communicable or analyzable. By stressing these "night-time" qualities, these poets anticipate the artistic movement called Romanticism.

---

⑥
> The curfew tolls the knell of parting day,
>   The lowing herd winds slowly o'er the lea,[1]
> The plowman homeward plods his weary way,
>   And leaves the world to darkness and to me.
>
> 5   Now fades the glimmering landscape on the sight,
>   And all the air a solemn stillness holds,
> Save where the beetle wheels his droning flight,
>   And drowsy tinklings lull the distant folds;
>
> Save that from yonder ivy-mantled tower,
> 10   The moping owl does to the moon complain
> Of such as, wandering near her secret bower,
>   Molest her ancient solitary reign.
>
> Beneath those rugged elms, that yew tree's shade,
>   Where heaves the turf in many a moldering heap,
> 15   Each in his narrow cell forever laid,
>   The rude[2] forefathers of the hamlet sleep.

---

1. **lea** meadow.
2. **rude** uneducated.

⑦ ✓ Reading Check

At what time of day is the poem set?

Elegy **667**

⑤ Background
The Enlightenment was an intellectual movement that gained popularity in Europe in the seventeenth and eighteenth centuries. Its emphasis on rational thought pervaded aspects of society from politics to the arts. In many ways, the development of Romanticism was an artistic counter-argument to Enlightenment thinking. Pre-Romantic poets led the way with their emphasis on feelings that transcend the material and rational.

⑥ Reading Strategy

Paraphrasing

1. Call on a volunteer to read aloud lines 1–4.

2. Then, explain that putting a passage into one's own words can be helpful when determining the main idea. Have students suggest various ways to paraphrase each line.
   Possible responses: A bell rings to signal the end of the day; cows head home through the fields; a field worker slowly walks home; the world becomes dark before the poet's eyes.

3. **Ask** students whether they see a pattern among the images in these lines that could be generalized into a broader, all-encompassing statement.
   Possible response: Students may say that many of the images show life winding down at the end of a day.

4. Then, **ask** students to express the main idea of the first stanza.
   Possible response: As the day ends, the poet observes life winding down and darkness setting in.

⑦ Reading Check

Answer: The poem is set at dusk.

ⓒ Text Complexity: Reader and Task Suggestions

Elegy Written in a Country Churchyard		A Nocturnal Reverie	
Preparing to Read the Text	**Leveled Tasks**	**Preparing to Read the Text**	**Leveled Tasks**
• Using the Background on TE p. 667, point to Pope's writings as typical of the Enlightenment. • Discuss the poem's setting of a country graveyard at twilight, and ask what thoughts might occur in such a setting. • Guide students to use Multidraft Reading strategies (TE p. 665).	*Levels of Meaning* If students will have difficulty with Gray's ideas, have them focus on the overall mood and on the message in the final epitaph. Then, as they reread, have them consider how each quatrain relates to that mood and message. *Analyzing* If students will not have difficulty understanding Gray's ideas, have them analyze how imagery and sound effects in individual quatrains contribute to the mood.	• Using the information on TE p. 673, explain that a benign view of nature is central to Romantic thinking. • Remind students to use context and text features to understand unfamiliar terms. • Guide students to use Multidraft Reading strategies (TE p. 665).	*Language/Structure* If students will have difficulty with the poem's language, have them focus on the essential message and overall mood. Then, as they reread, encourage them to use context clues and footnotes to clarify specific lines and statements. *Analyzing* If students will not have difficulty with the poem's language, have them explain how the images and other details work together to convey a particular mood.

❽ Reading Strategy

Paraphrasing

1. Remind students of the paraphrasing technique that can be used to help determine the main idea or ideas in a passage. Encourage students to use this technique as they read lines 17–20 silently.

2. Then, **ask** students the Reading Strategy prompt: Restate the main ideas in lines 17–20 in your own words.
   Possible response: No sounds, whether natural or man-made, will cause the dead to awaken.

❾ Critical Thinking

Distinguish

1. Have a volunteer read aloud lines 25–28 while the other students follow along.

2. **Ask** students which aspects of these lines are rooted in the place and period the poem was written, and which aspects would apply to life in any period.
   Possible response: The details about farming, such as the sickle and team, are rooted in the period, while the theme that humans must work hard on a daily basis and can find satisfaction in their work can be applied to any period or profession.

❿ Literary Analysis

Pre-Romantic Poetry

1. Review with students the characteristics of Pre-Romantic poetry, including the polished expression of ideas, balanced phrases, and sophisticated vocabulary.

2. Tell students to look and listen for these features as you read lines 33–36 aloud.

3. Then, **ask** students the Literary Analysis question: What images and phrasings in lines 33–36 show formal polish?
   Possible responses: Students may cite the parallel structure of lines 33–34; the alliteration in "pomp of power" and assonance in "awaits alike"; the elaborate, periodic sentence structure that withholds meaning until line 35; and the use of abstract nouns such as *power, beauty, wealth,* and *glory.*

❽ Reading Strategy
Paraphrasing Restate the main ideas in lines 17–20 in your own words.

❿ Literary Analysis
Pre-Romantic Poetry
What images and phrasings in lines 33–36 show formal polish?

The breezy call of incense-breathing morn,
    The swallow twittering from the straw-built shed,
The cock's shrill clarion, or the echoing horn,[3]
20   No more shall rouse them from their lowly bed.

For them no more the blazing hearth shall burn,
    Or busy housewife ply her evening care;
No children run to lisp their sire's return,
    Or climb his knees the envied kiss to share.

25 Oft did the harvest to their sickle yield,
    Their furrow oft the stubborn glebe[4] has broke;
How jocund[5] did they drive their team afield!
    How bowed the woods beneath their sturdy stroke!

Let not Ambition mock their useful toil,
30   Their homely joys, and destiny obscure;
Nor Grandeur hear with a disdainful smile
    The short and simple annals of the poor.

The boast of heraldry,[6] the pomp of power,
    And all that beauty, all that wealth e'er gave,
35 Awaits alike the inevitable hour.
    The paths of glory lead but to the grave.

Nor you, ye proud, impute to these the fault,
    If memory o'er their tomb no trophies[7] raise,
Where through the long-drawn aisle and fretted vault[8]
40   The pealing anthem swells the note of praise.

Can storied urn,[9] or animated[10] bust,
    Back to its mansion call the fleeting breath?
Can honor's voice provoke[11] the silent dust,
    Or Flattery soothe the dull cold ear of Death?

45 Perhaps in this neglected spot is laid
    Some heart once pregnant with celestial fire;
Hands, that the rod of empire might have swayed,
    Or waked to ecstasy the living lyre.

---

3. **clarion . . . horn** A clarion is a trumpet. The horn is a hunter's horn.
4. **glebe** soil.
5. **jocund** cheerful.
6. **heraldry** noble descent.
7. **trophies** symbolic figures or pictures depicting the achievements of the dead man.
8. **fretted vault** church ceiling decorated with intersecting lines.
9. **storied urn** funeral urn with an epitaph inscribed on it.
10. **animated** lifelike.
11. **provoke** call forth.

Enrichment: Analyzing Themes and Symbols

Gravestones

Students might be interested to know that gravestones are among the earliest examples of sculpture in the United States, dating back to colonial times. New England gravestones are decorated with elaborate symbolic figures and objects. For example, a skeleton represents death and is often shown snuffing out the candle of life; grapes represent eternal life. Epitaphs written on gravestones are often equally memorable, and even humorous, such as this one: "Here lies as silent as clay Miss Arabella Young / Who on the 21st of May began to hold her tongue."

Activity: Symbol Analysis Have pairs or groups of students conduct research on a common symbol used on colonial gravestones. They may also research other uses and meanings of the same symbol. Suggest that they record information in the **Enrichment: Analyzing Themes and Symbols** worksheet, *Professional Development Guidebook,* page 243.

But Knowledge to their eyes her ample page
    50   Rich with the spoils of time did ne'er unroll;
Chill Penury repressed their noble rage,
      And froze the genial current of the soul.

Full many a gem of purest ray serene
      The dark unfathomed caves of ocean bear:
55 Full many a flower is born to blush unseen,
      And waste its sweetness on the desert air.

Some village Hampden,[12] that, with dauntless breast,
      The little tyrant of his fields withstood,
Some mute inglorious Milton[13] here may rest,
    60   Some Cromwell[14] guiltless of his country's blood.

The applause of listening senates to command,
      The threats of pain and ruin to despise,
To scatter plenty o'er a smiling land,
      And read their history in a nation's eyes,

65 Their lot forbade: nor circumscribed alone
      Their growing virtues, but their crimes confined
Forbade to wade through slaughter to a throne,
      And shut the gates of mercy on mankind,

The struggling pangs of conscious truth to hide,
    70   To quench the blushes of ingenuous shame,
Or heap the shrine of Luxury and Pride
      With incense kindled at the Muse's flame.

Far from the madding[15] crowd's ignoble[16] strife,
      Their sober wishes never learned to stray;
75 Along the cool sequestered vale of life
      They kept the noiseless tenor[17] of their way.

Yet even these bones from insult to protect
      Some frail memorial still erected nigh,
With uncouth rhymes and shapeless sculpture decked,[18]
    80   Implores the passing tribute of a sigh.

---

12. **Hampden** John Hampden (1594–1643), an English statesman who defied King Charles I, resisting the king's efforts to circumvent Parliament.
13. **Milton** English poet, John Milton (1608–1674).
14. **Cromwell** Oliver Cromwell (1599–1658), English revolutionary leader who
defeated King Charles I and ruled England as Lord Protector of the Common-wealth from 1653 to 1658.
15. **madding** frenzied.
16. **ignoble** (ig nō´ bəl) *adj.* not noble; common.
17. **tenor** general tendency or course.
18. **Some . . . decked** contrasts with "the storied urn[s] or animated bust[s]" (line 41) inside the church.

Vocabulary
penury (pen´ yoo rē)
n. poverty

11 Literary Analysis
Pre-Romantic Poetry
How do the images in lines 53–56 give the reader a powerful sense of what is unknown or lost?

Vocabulary
12 circumscribed (sur´ kəm skrībd) *v.* limited; confined
ingenuous (in jen´ yoo əs) *adj.* naive; simple

13 ☑ Reading Check
About whom is the speaker speculating?

Elegy **669**

⓮ Reading Strategy

Paraphrasing

1. Have students follow along as you read aloud lines 85–88.

2. **Ask** students to explain what the phrases "this pleasing anxious being" and "the warm precincts of the cheerful day" mean. Remind them that putting phrases into their own words is helpful when identifying main ideas.
   Possible responses: "This pleasing anxious being" refers to our human form, which is beautiful yet frail and worry-prone. "The warm precincts of the cheerful day" refers to life on Earth's surface, where the sun spreads its cheerful and life-giving warmth.

3. Then, **ask** students the Reading Strategy prompt: Express the key idea of lines 85–88 in your own words.
   Possible response: No one passes away without regretting leaving the world behind.

⓯ Literary Analysis

Pre-Romantic Poetry

1. Have a volunteer read aloud lines 89–92 while the other students follow along.

2. **Ask** students what marks this passage as Pre-Romantic.
   Possible responses: These lines include formal structure and language, an attention to nature, and nameless feelings given new expression.

3. Then, **ask** students the Literary Analysis question: What intense, perhaps irrational feelings are expressed in lines 89–92?
   Answer: Humans long to be cared about and remembered; this yearning survives the tomb and burns "even in our ashes."

670 A Turbulent Time

⓮ Reading Strategy
Paraphrasing Express the key idea of lines 85–88 in your own words.

⓯ Literary Analysis
Pre-Romantic Poetry
What intense, perhaps irrational feelings are expressed in lines 89–92?

Their name, their years, spelt by the unlettered Muse,[19]
    The place of fame and elegy supply:
And many a holy text around she strews,
    That teach the rustic moralist to die.

85 For who, to dumb Forgetfulness a prey,
    This pleasing anxious being e'er resigned,
Left the warm precincts of the cheerful day,
    Nor cast one longing lingering look behind?

On some fond breast the parting soul relies,
90   Some pious drops[20] the closing eye requires;
Even from the tomb the voice of Nature cries,
    Even in our ashes live their wonted fires.

For thee,[21] who, mindful of the unhonored dead,
    Dost in these lines their artless tale relate;
95 If chance, by lonely contemplation led,
    Some kindred spirit shall enquire thy fate,

Haply[22] some hoary-headed swain[23] may say,
    "Oft have we seen him at the peep of dawn
Brushing with hasty steps the dews away,
100   To meet the sun upon the upland lawn.

"There at the foot of yonder nodding beech,
    That wreathes its old fantastic roots so high,
His listless length at noontide would he stretch,
    And pore upon the brook that babbles by.

105 "Hard by yon wood, now smiling as in scorn,
    Muttering his wayward fancies he would rove;
Now drooping, woeful wan, like one forlorn,
    Or crazed with care, or crossed in hopeless love.

"One morn I missed him on the customed hill,
110   Along the heath, and near his favorite tree;
Another came; nor yet beside the rill,[24]
    Nor up the lawn, nor at the wood was he;

---

19. the unlettered Muse In Greek mythology, the Muses were goddesses who inspired artists and writers. *Unlettered* means "uneducated."
20. drops tears.
21. thee Gray himself.
22. Haply perhaps.
23. hoary-headed swain white-haired country laborer.
24. rill brook.

Think Aloud

Literary Analysis: Pre-Romantic Poetry
Direct students' attention to lines 89–92 of "Elegy Written in a Country Churchyard." Use the following "think aloud" to model the skill of analyzing formal poetic language to find meaning. Say to students:

Sometimes the language of Pre-Romantic poetry is so complex that I have to dissect it carefully to figure out what the poet is saying. One thing I can do is look for patterns in sentence structure. For example, lines 89 and 90 have a similar structure. They both end with phrases that refer to someone dying. They both also begin with phrases that indicate emotion. The words *relies* in line 89 and *requires* in line 90 show the connection between the dying person and the emotions described. In each line, the person who is dying hopes others will remember him fondly and feel sadness at his death. This helps me understand lines 91 and 92 better as well. These lines claim that even after we die, the Nature within us still desires to be remembered.

"The next, with dirges due in sad array
    Slow through the churchway path we saw him borne.
115 Approach and read (for thou canst read) the lay
    Graved on the stone beneath yon aged thorn."[25]

The Epitaph

Here rests his head upon the lap of Earth
    A youth, to Fortune and to Fame unknown.
Fair Science[26] frowned not on his humble birth,
120   And melancholy marked him for her own.

Large was his bounty, and his soul sincere,
    Heaven did a recompense as largely send:
He gave to misery (all he had) a tear,
    He gained from Heaven ('twas all he wished) a friend.

125 No farther seek his merits to disclose,
    Or draw his frailties from their dread abode
(There they alike in trembling hope repose),
    The bosom of his Father and his God.

---

25. **thorn** hawthorn tree.
26. **Science** learning.

Critical Reading ©

© **1. Key Ideas and Details** Who are the forefathers to whom the speaker refers in line 16? **(b) Interpret:** In line 35, what is the "inevitable hour" that the rich and ambitious share with their forefathers?

© **2. Key Ideas and Details** According to lines 45–48, what types of people might lie among the forefathers? **(b) Infer:** Why did the forefathers not fulfill their potential? **(c) Interpret:** In what way do the images of the gem and the flower in lines 53–56 express the idea of unfulfilled potential?

© **3. Key Ideas and Details (a) Summarize:** What mark have the forefathers left on history? **(b) Connect:** According to lines 77–84, how is their memory preserved? **(c) Interpret:** What do lines 85–92 suggest about the need to be remembered after death?

© **4. Key Ideas and Details (a) Summarize:** By what standards is the life of the speaker measured in "The Epitaph"? **(b) Draw Conclusions:** What insight into life does the speaker reach?

© **5. Integration of Knowledge and Ideas** Do you find the feelings in the poem artificial or moving? Explain.

Cite textual evidence to support your responses.

Elegy **671**

672

16 ANNE FINCH
Countess of Winchilsea (1661–1720)

Author of "A Nocturnal Reverie"

Anne Kingsmill Finch, Countess of Winchilsea, lived in an era that rejected women intellectuals. Even her friend Alexander Pope poked fun at her, satirizing her as the character Phoebe Clinket in the play _Three Hours After Marriage._ Despite this mockery, Finch pursued her interest in poetry, publishing a volume of verse in 1713, during an era when publication by women was rare.

An Uncertain Childhood Anne Kingsmill's father died when she was only five months old, and three years later her mother died as well. For eight years, she and her sister, Bridget, lived with their grandmother, while their brother, William, lived with an uncle. The children were reunited under their uncle's care in 1672. By the standards of the day, the girls' education was quite progressive. Anne studied classical Greek and Roman literature, the Bible, French, Italian, history, poetry, and drama.

A Poet and Countess In 1682, Anne Kingsmill left home to become a maid of honor to the wife of the duke of York, later James II. In the duke's household, she met her husband, Heneage Finch.

When James II was driven from power in 1688, the Finches endured a period of poverty until Heneage Finch inherited the title Earl of Winchilsea and an estate at Eastwell in Kent. Many of Anne Finch's poems celebrate the rural pleasures of Eastwell.

Though she was not the most famous of poets, her work had an impact on later writers. In 1800, Romantic poet William Wordsworth praised her in the Preface to his groundbreaking book, _Lyrical Ballads._

672 A Turbulent Time (1625–1798)

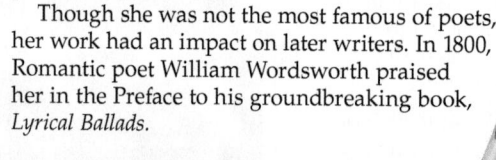

Think Aloud

Vocabulary: Using Context
Direct students' attention to the words _woodbind_ (line 13), _cowslip_ (line 14), and _foxglove_ (line 15) on page 674. Use the following "think aloud" to model the skill of using context to infer meaning. Say to students:

I may not know the meanings of these three words. However, I see in line 13 that the woodbind is something that "springs," and in line 14 that the cowslip "grows." This tells me that these words refer to plants that are growing. This makes sense because

I know the poet has already made other references to nature, such as _grass_ in line 11. When I read lines 15–16, I see that the foxglove checkers the "dusty brakes" with red. The footnote tells me that _brakes_ refers to overgrown areas, so the foxglove must be a growing thing that adds spots of red throughout a thicket. I think that _woodbind, cowslip,_ and _foxglove_ are probably all types of flowers.

A NOCTURNAL REVERIE

Anne Finch, Countess of Winchilsea

In such a night, when every louder wind
Is to its distant cavern safe confined;
And only gentle Zephyr[1] fans his wings,
And lonely Philomel,[2] still waking, sings;
5   Or from some tree, famed for the owl's delight,

---

1. **Zephyr** (zef´ ər) in Greek myth, the west wind; a breeze.
2. **Philomel** (fil´ ō mel´) in Greek myth, nightingale.

Cottage and Pond, Moonlight, Thomas Gainsborough, Victoria and Albert Museum, London

17

18 ▲ **Critical Viewing** What visual elements in this picture help create a mood like that of the poem? **[Analyze]**

A Nocturnal Reverie 673

19 **About the Selection**
In this meditative poem, Anne Finch reflects how in the softness of twilight, the sounds and sights of nature reveal their beauty. The poem celebrates the restorative power of this twilight world, where the mind may roam freely, unfettered by the confusion of the day.

20 **Engaging the Essential Question**

1. Remind students that "Elegy" and "A Nocturnal Reverie" are inspired by places that transport the poets out of everyday life, causing them to ponder life's mysteries. In the poems, these places and thoughts are described in a way that may allow us to take a mental journey similar to the poets'.

2. Tell students to look for phrases that help them connect with the setting of the poems as they continue to read.

Differentiated Instruction   for Universal Access

Enrichment for Gifted/Talented Students
Have students work in small groups to write a song or create musical accompaniment as background music to a reading of an excerpt from "A Nocturnal Reverie." Students should listen to the music several times and find places where rhythm and melody might enhance and emphasize the words and mood of the poem. Remind students that their goal is to blend music with language.

Strategy for Advanced Readers
Have students write essays in which they compare and contrast "Elegy Written in a Country Churchyard" with "A Nocturnal Reverie," using the characteristics of Pre-Romantic poetry as a basis. For example, students might compare and contrast the ways in which the two poems exhibit polished language and balanced phrases, or the degrees to which the poems exhibit a heightened sense of emotion.

㉑ Reading Strategy

Determining the Main Idea

1. Have students read lines 29–38 to themselves.

2. **Ask** students to paraphrase line 38.
   Possible response: This goes on while humans are sleeping.

▶ **Monitor Progress** Then, **ask** students to identify the main idea or ideas in the passage. Students may need time to reread the passage before answering.
Possible response: Animals live and eat freely while men are asleep.

▶ **Reteach** If students include too much detail in their responses (for example, by mentioning specific animals and their activities), remind them that the main idea is the big picture idea and should not include specific details. You may also walk them through the paraphrasing technique, helping them see how putting smaller individual sections into their own words can help them identify the big idea linking them all together.

㉒ Critical Thinking

Infer

1. Have students read lines 43–50 to themselves.

2. Direct students' attention to line 46, and **ask** students what Finch refers to when she says "the inferior world."
   Answer: Finch refers to the simpler way of life among animals in nature.

3. Then, **ask** students: From lines 48–50, what can we infer about why the poet likes to think the natural world "like her own" (line 46)?
   Possible response: The poet grows weary of the confusion and toil of daily life and wishes life were simpler, as it is in nature.

Vocabulary
nocturnal (näk tur´ nəl) *adj.* occurring at night

Vocabulary
temperate (tem´ pər it) *adj.* mild

venerable (ven´ ər ə bəl) *adj.* commanding respect because of age, character, or social rank

She, hollowing clear, directs the wanderer right:
In such a night, when passing clouds give place,
Or thinly veil the heavens' mysterious face;
When in some river, overhung with green,
10 The waving moon and trembling leaves are seen;
When freshened grass now bears itself upright,
And makes cool banks to pleasing rest invite,
Whence springs the woodbind, and the bramble-rose,
And where the sleepy cowslip sheltered grows;
15 Whilst now a paler hue the foxglove takes,
Yet checkers still with red the dusky brakes:[3]
When scattered glow-worms, but in twilight fine,
Show trivial beauties watch their hour to shine;
Whilst Salisbury[4] stands the test of every light,
20 In perfect charms, and perfect virtue bright:
When odors, which declined repelling day,
Through temperate air uninterrupted stray;
When darkened groves their softest shadows wear,
And falling waters we distinctly hear;
25 When through the gloom more venerable shows
Some ancient fabric,[5] awful in repose,
While sunburnt hills their swarthy looks conceal,
And swelling haycocks thicken up the vale:
When the loosed horse now, as his pasture leads,
30 Comes slowly grazing through the adjoining meads,[6]
Whose stealing pace, and lengthened shade we fear,
Till torn-up forage[7] in his teeth we hear:
When nibbling sheep at large pursue their food,
And unmolested kine[8] rechew the cud;

---

3. **brakes** overgrown areas; thickets.
4. **Salisbury** This may refer to a Lady Salisbury, daughter of a friend, not to the town of Salisbury.
5. **ancient fabric** edifice or large, imposing building.
6. **meads** archaic term for meadows.
7. **forage** (fôr ij) *n.* food grazed for by animals.
8. **kine** archaic plural of cow; cattle.

A Turbulent Time (1625–1798)

Concept Connector

Reading Strategy Graphic Organizer
Ask students to review the graphic organizers in which they have paraphrased passages from the selections to help determine the main idea. Then, have students share their organizers and compare the main ideas they identified.

Activating Prior Knowledge
Have students return to the paragraphs they wrote during the Activating Prior Knowledge activity. Ask them if there is anything they would add or modify after studying the two poems.

Writing About the Essential Question
Have students compare their responses to the prompt completed before they completed reading the poems with their thoughts afterwards. Have them work in pairs, discussing their thoughts and formulating a new response that takes both students' ideas into account. Encourage students to look back at the poems and cite specific textual details to give examples or lend support to their responses. Then lead a discussion about which textual details helped students most to imagine the settings of the poems, and why.

35   When curlews cry beneath the village walls,
21   And to her straggling brood the partridge calls;
  Their shortlived jubilee the creatures keep,
  Which but endures, whilst tyrant man does sleep;
  When a sedate content the spirit feels,
40   And no fierce light disturbs, whilst it reveals;
  But silent musings urge the mind to seek
  Something, too high for syllables to speak;
  Till the free soul to a composedness charmed,
  Finding the elements of rage disarmed,
45   O'er all below a solemn quiet grown,
22   Joys in the inferior world, and thinks it like her own:
  In such a night let me abroad remain,
  Till morning breaks, and all's confused again;
  Our cares, our toils, our clamors are renewed,
50   Or pleasures, seldom reached, again pursued.

Critical Reading

1. **Key Ideas and Details** **(a)** Describe the setting of the poem, listing specific images from lines 1–24. **(b) Analyze:** What mood do these images create?

2. **Key Ideas and Details** **(a) Analyze:** Outline the steps that lead from the speaker's "sedate content" to her joy (lines 39–46). **(b) Interpret:** How does the natural world charm the speaker to "composedness"?

3. **Key Ideas and Details** **(a) Infer:** What is the relation between people and their "pleasures" in line 50? **(b) Compare and Contrast:** What is the main difference between the pursuit of pleasures and the "composedness" caused by nature?

4. **Integration of Knowledge and Ideas** If the speaker were taking a nocturnal walk in modern times, do you think her reactions to nature would be the same? Explain.

5. **Integration of Knowledge and Ideas** What qualities of a special place help each author to draw conclusions about life? In your response, use at least two of these Essential Question words: *nature, country, isolation.* *[Connecting to the Essential Question: What is the relationship between literature and place?]*

Cite textual evidence to support your responses.

A Nocturnal Reverie **675**

Assessment Practice

Writer's Point of View (**For more practice, see** *All-in-One Workbook.*)

Use the following sample test item to give students practice in identifying a writer's opinion.

. . . The boast of heraldry, the pomp of power, / And all that beauty, all that wealth e'er gave, / Awaits alike the inevitable hour. / The paths of glory lead but to the grave. . . .

. . . Far from the madding crowd's ignoble strife, / Their sober wishes never learned to stray . . .

Based on this passage, the poet believes that ____.

  A a person's worth can be measured by his or her contributions to literature

  B people who live in the country are more religious than those who live in the city

  C one should seize the day

  D people should live their lives simply because we are all equal in death

D is the correct answer.

Answers

1. Both poets imply that value and dignity lie in the simple beauties of life, not in ambitious pursuits. These themes anticipate Romanticism because they deal with common people and things and the mysteries of life; they emphasize emotion rather than reason.

2. (a) **Possible response:** Lines 89–92 suggest that everyone yearns to be remembered after death. (b) Lines 89–92 "Elegy": Stated Ideas: Humans need to be remembered; nature is part of mankind; Feelings Expressed: wistfulness. Message About Life: Nature is essential to humans in life and death. Lines 39–46 "Nocturnal Reverie": Stated Ideas: Nature makes the human spirit content and inspires human beings by its beauty; Feelings Expressed: ecstasy in sublime; Message About Life: Nature gives human beings solace.

3. Lines 29–32 "Elegy": We should not belittle people who lived simple, obscure lives. Lines 47–50 "Nocturnal Reverie": When it is so peaceful, the speaker wishes to remain outside all night.

Vocabulary Acquisition and Use

The <u>venerable</u> old woman wanted to overcome the <u>penury</u> in the village. She told young people that <u>nocturnal</u> reading could help them escape a <u>circumscribed</u> life. She risked the danger that her <u>temperate</u> manner would make her seem <u>ingenuous</u>.

Writing

Evaluate students' explanatory text using the **Rubrics for Response to Literature**, *Professional Development Guidebook*, pages 250–251.

Literary Analysis

C 1. Integration of Knowledge and Ideas Explain what is **Pre-Romantic** about Gray's concern for the unknown dead of a country graveyard and Finch's loving attention to humble "creatures." How do these *themes* anticipate Romanticism?

C 2. Key Ideas and Details (a) What feelings do lines 89–92 of Gray's "Elegy" convey? **(b)** Compare these feelings to the feelings in lines 39–46 of "A Nocturnal Reverie," using a chart like the one shown.

Lines	Stated Ideas	Feelings Expressed	Themes, or Messages, About Life

C Common Core
State Standards

Writing
2. Write informative/explanatory texts to examine and convey complex ideas, concepts, and information clearly and accurately through the effective selection, organization, and analysis of content.

Reading Strategy

3. *Paraphrase* to **determine the essential message** in lines 29–32 of Gray's "Elegy" and lines 47–50 of "A Nocturnal Reverie."

PERFORMANCE TASKS
Integrated Language Skills

C Vocabulary Acquisition and Use

Use a different vocabulary word from page 664 in place of each familiar underlined word. Explain your choices.

The <u>respected</u> old woman wanted to overcome the <u>poverty</u> in the village. She told young people that <u>nighttime</u> reading could help them escape a <u>limited</u> life. She risked the danger that her <u>mild</u> manner would make her seem <u>naive</u>.

Writing

C Explanatory Text The *recitation* of poetry requires attention to *performance details* to convey the *meaning* of a poem in a way that is *forceful and clear*. Choose a brief passage from one of these poems and write **directions** for reciting it:

- Identify which words to emphasize and where to pause.
- Explain when to change volume or pitch.
- Tell how eye contact and appropriate gestures will engage an audience.

Then, follow the directions and have a partner rate your performance.

Assessment Resources

Unit 3 Resources

L1 L2 EL **Selection Test A,** pp. 219–221. Administer Test A to less advanced readers.

L3 L4 EL **Selection Test B,** pp. 222–224. Administer Test B to on-level and more advanced students.

L3 L4 **Open-Book Test,** pp. 216–218. As an alternative, administer the Open-Book Test.

All Customizable Test Bank

All Self-tests
Students may prepare for the **Selection Test** by taking the **Self-test** online.

PHLit Online! All assessment resources are available at **www.PHLitOnline.com**.

Focus on Literary Forms: The Essay

Selection Planning Guide

The selections in this section focus on the informal essay, a form that came into being in periodicals of the eighteenth century. The excerpt from Joseph Addison's "The Aims of *The Spectator*" provides not only a mission statement for the publication, but also a satirical look at English society. In "Days of Obligation," journalist Richard Rodriguez describes a visit to Tijuana, Mexico.

Humanities

Girl Writing by Lamplight, ca. 1850, by William Henry Hunt

William Henry Hunt (1790–1864) ensured his later reputation with his experiments with watercolor. To better depict interior scenes and to concentrate on effects of light, Hunt combined watercolors with "body"—a mixture of watercolor with an opaque white paint. Other watercolorists followed in Hunt's experimental path.

Use the following questions for discussion:

1. How does the painter dramatize the interior life of his subject?
   Answer: The portrait and other objects on the desk suggest the girl's interests. The fact that viewers cannot read what the girl is absorbed in writing and the fact that her face is in shadow suggest interior thoughts.

2. How does the position of the lamp give the painting depth?
   Answer: The lamp stands between the objects at the edge of the table and the girl behind, creating a transition into the painting's depth.

Monitoring Progress

Before students read the excerpt from "The Aims of *The Spectator*," refer to the results for the Vocabulary in Context items on **Benchmark Test 6 (Unit 3 Resources p. 250).** Use this diagnostic portion of the test to guide your choice of selections to teach, as well as the depth of preparation you will provide, based on students' readiness for reading and vocabulary skills.

© Text Complexity: At a Glance

This chart gives a general text complexity rating for the selection in this part of the unit to help guide instruction. For additional text complexity support, see the Test Complexity Rubric at point of use.

The Aims of *The Spectator*	More Accessible

❶ Defining the Essay

Discuss that essays convey the author's own ideas and opinions. Then, point out that in addition to the formal and informal categories, essays may also be classified by topic. For example, an autobiographical essay presents the writer's perspective on his or her own life, while a reflective essay expresses a writer's thoughts and feelings on a topic of personal significance. **Ask:** Where do you most often see and read essays today?

Possible response: Essays are often found in newspapers (particularly op-ed pages) and magazines. Many Internet bloggers use the essay form.

❷ Modes of Writing

Review the four modes of essay writing listed on this page. Explain that a good essayist often combines different modes to accomplish a broader purpose. Thus, a narrative essay might include descriptive passages, and a persuasive essay might contain expository passages or narrative anecdotes. **Ask:** How might a writer arguing for prison reform strengthen his or her essay by including descriptive, expository, or narrative passages?

Possible response: Descriptive: The author might vividly describe substandard conditions in a local prison. Expository: He or she would present information about how prisons are currently run. Narrative: The author might tell about a visit to a prison.

❸ Close Read: Elements of an Essay

Review the chart with students. Point out the highlighted text in the model on page 679. Explain that in each case, the color of the highlighting matches the color of the category in the chart. Details that illustrate a given category are highlighted in the color of that category.

"A GOOD ESSAY . . . MUST DRAW ITS CURTAIN ROUND US, BUT IT MUST BE A CURTAIN THAT SHUTS US IN, NOT OUT."

— VIRGINIA WOOLF

❶ Defining the Essay

An **essay** is a short work of nonfiction that explores a specific topic and conveys an author's ideas and opinions. In 1580, the French philosopher Michel de Montaigne published a new form of short prose discussions called *Essais.* Over four hundred years later, Montaigne is still credited with creating the modern essay.

Types of Essays Most essays fall into one of two categories:

- **Formal essays** use a serious tone and dignified language, and often analyze public issues or important events.
- **Informal essays,** also called personal essays, use a more casual tone and explore everyday topics in a relaxed, conversational style.

❷ Modes of Writing

Within the two broad categories, essays can be further classified according to the mode of writing used.

- A **narrative essay** tells a true story about real people or events.
- A **persuasive essay,** also called an **argumentative essay,** tries to persuade the reader to accept the writer's opinion or to take a course of action.
- A **descriptive essay,** sometimes called an **observational essay,** uses sensory details to create a portrait of a person, a place, or an object.
- An **expository essay** presents information or discusses an idea.

An essayist often combines different modes of writing. Thus, a persuasive essay might contain narrative examples.

❸ Close Read: Elements of an Essay

These literary elements are called out in the Model text at right.

Author's Purpose: the author's particular reason for writing Example: *Jonathan Swift wrote "A Modest Proposal" to attack British economic and social policies in Ireland.*	**Style:** the author's distinctive way of writing; the overall "sound" of a work Example: *In "The Aims of the Spectator," Joseph Addison uses an elegant style as in the statement "But there will be none to whom this paper will be more useful than to the female world."*
Theme: the main insight into life conveyed by a work Example: *In "Days of Obligation," Richard Rodriguez reflects on what is incomplete or relative in the identity of places and people, using the example of Tijuana.*	**Tone:** the author's attitude toward his or her subject or audience, as expressed in word choice, sentence structure, and so on Example: *In "Shooting an Elephant," George Orwell takes an ironic tone in the sentence "In Moulmein, . . . I was hated by large numbers of people."*

678 A Turbulent Time (1625–1798)

In This Section

- Defining the Essay (p. 678)
- Model: from "The Fallacy of Success" by G. K. Chesterton (p. 679)
- Study: "The Aims of *The Spectator*" by Joseph Addison (p. 682)
- Richard Rodriguez Introduces from "Days of Obligation" (p. 686)
- Study: from *Days of Obligation* by Richard Rodriguez (p. 689)

For more practice analyzing essays, see pages 617, 760, and 1318.

Differentiated Instruction   for Universal Access

Strategy for Special-Needs Students

Students may benefit from turning the information on the student page into a chart for future reference. Suggest that students create a four-column chart with the headings *Narrative, Persuasive, Descriptive,* and *Expository.* Under each heading, students should jot down the characteristics of each type of essay. Then, they may add the titles mentioned on the student page. Later, as they read the essays in this unit, invite students to write the titles of the essays in the appropriate columns.

Strategy for Advanced Readers

Ask students to think of essays they have read for school or on their own. Challenge them to label the essays according to their category (formal or informal), purpose, and type. Ask each student to name an essay; identify its category, purpose, and type; and support these judgments with details from the essay. Remind students that an essay may demonstrate more than one purpose or have characteristics of more than one type.

Model

About the Text Besides his novels, short stories (including the Father Brown detective series), literary studies, poems, and works on religion, the British writer G. K. Chesterton (1874–1936) wrote highly regarded essays. This essay is one of his most admired.

from "The Fallacy of Success," in *Selected Essays*
G. K. Chesterton

4 There has appeared in our time a particular class of books and articles which I sincerely and solemnly think may be called the silliest ever known among men. They are much more wild than the wildest romances of chivalry and much more dull than the dullest religious tract. Moreover, the romances of chivalry were at least about chivalry; the religious tracts are about religion. But these things are about nothing; they are about what is called Success. On every bookstall, in every magazine, you may find works telling people how to succeed. They are books showing men how to succeed in everything; they are written by men who cannot even succeed in writing books. To begin with, of course, there is no such thing as Success. Or, if you like to put it so, there is nothing that is not successful. That a thing is successful merely means that it is; a millionaire is successful in being a millionaire and a donkey in being a donkey. Any live man has succeeded in living; any dead man may have succeeded in committing suicide. But, passing over the bad logic and bad philosophy in the phrase, we may take it, as these writers do, in the ordinary sense of success in obtaining money or worldly position. These writers profess to tell the ordinary man how he may succeed in his trade or speculation—how, if he is a builder, he may succeed as a builder; how, if he is a stockbroker, he may succeed as a stockbroker. They profess to show him how, if he is a grocer, he may become a sporting yachtsman; how, if he is a tenth-rate journalist, he may become a peer; and how, if he is a German Jew, he may become an Anglo-Saxon. This is a definite and business-like proposal, and **5** I really think that the people who buy these books (if any people do buy them) have a moral, if not a legal, right to ask for their money back. Nobody would dare **6** to publish a book about electricity which literally told one nothing about electricity; no one would dare to publish an article on botany which showed that the writer did not know which end of a plant grew in the earth. Yet our modern world is full of books about Success and successful people which literally contain no kind of idea, and scarcely any kind of verbal sense.

It is perfectly obvious that in any decent occupation (such as bricklaying or writing books) there are only two ways (in any special sense) of succeeding. One **7** is by doing very good work, the other is by cheating. Both are much too simple to require any literary explanation. If you are in for the high jump, either jump higher than any one else, or manage somehow to pretend that you have done so.

---

4 Theme Chesterton points to his theme at the outset of the essay: The concept of Success is empty—or even evil—and so should not serve as the "value" that some modern people take it to be.

5 Tone Here, Chesterton delivers a joke, implying that the books are frauds, with breezy efficiency. This passage reflects the overall tone of light satire.

6 Author's Purpose Chesterton's purpose, or reason for writing, is to mock "how-to" books of his day as well as to entertain his readers. He accomplishes both purposes in passages such as this one.

7 Style Chesterton's style combines plain, direct diction ("cheating") with a brisk, punchy balance of phrases and clauses. ("One is . . . , the other is. . . .")

Extended Study: The Essay **679**

---

4 Theme

Draw students' attention to Chesterton's theme as stated in the callout. Point out that because authors do not always state their themes as concisely as this, a reader must often infer the theme from the content. Explain that a theme can generally be summarized in a declarative sentence. **Ask:** What is the theme of *Cinderella* or some other familiar story?

Possible response: *Cinderella:* True worth resides within a person, not on the surface.

5 Tone

Read aloud the bracketed passage. **Ask:** How does the author indicate his disrespect for books about success?

Possible response: He suggests that people who buy such books should ask for their money back.

6 Author's Purpose

Point out that Chesterton strongly suggests his purpose in the essay's title and illustrates it more directly in the highlighted passage. **Ask:** What does "fallacy" mean?

Answer: falsehood

7 Style

Review with students the information in the callout box. Then, invite a volunteer to read aloud the bracketed passage. **Ask:** What effect do you think this style will have on most readers?

Possible response: It will support Chesterton's purpose of criticizing and mocking books about success.

Extend the Lesson

Evaluating Essays

Ask students to read an essay of their own choosing. They might select the essay from a literary magazine, a newspaper, an online site, or a collection of essays. Have students determine why the essay is or is not effective. Tell students to determine the type of essay, the author's purpose in writing the essay, and the historical and cultural context of the essay.

After students read and evaluate their essays, have them work in groups to compare their choices. Some students might read their essays aloud in class, particularly if the essays are timely or humorous.

COMMON CORE
Time and Resource Manager

• The Aims of *The Spectator*
Lesson Pacing Guide

DAY 1 Preteach

- Administer the Reading and Vocabulary Warm-ups (*Unit 3 Resources*, pp. 227–230) as necessary.
- Introduce the Literary Analysis concept: Essay.
- Introduce the Reading Strategy: Analyze Author's Assumptions.
- Build background with the author feature.
- Develop thematic thinking with Connecting to the Essential Question.
- Teach the selection vocabulary.

DAY 2 Preteach/Teach/Extend

- Distribute copies of the appropriate graphic organizer for the Reading Strategy (*Graphic Organizer Transparencies*, pp. 123–124).
- Distribute copies of the appropriate graphic organizer for Literary Analysis (*Graphic Organizer Transparencies*, pp. 125–126).
- Prepare students to read with the Activating Prior Knowledge activities (TE).
- Informally monitor comprehension while students read.
- Use the Reading Check question to confirm comprehension.
- Develop students' understanding of the essay using the Literary Analysis prompts.
- Reinforce vocabulary with the Vocabulary notes.
- Assess students' comprehension and mastery of the skills by having them answer the Critical Reading, Literary Analysis, and Reading Strategy questions.

DAY 3 Assess

- Have students complete the Vocabulary Lesson.
- Have students complete the Writing activity and write a letter to the editor. (You may assign as homework.)
- Administer Selection Test A or B (*Unit 3 Resources*, pp. 239–241 or 242–244).

Common Core State Standards

Reading Informational Text
1. Cite strong and thorough textual evidence to support analysis of what the text says explicitly as well as inferences drawn from the text, including determining where the text leaves matters uncertain.

Writing 1.a. Introduce precise, knowledgeable claim(s), establish the significance of the claim(s), distinguish the claim(s) from alternate or opposing claims, and create an organization that logically sequences claim(s), counterclaims, reasons, and evidence.

Additional Standards Practice
Common Core Companion, pp. 90–97; 185–195

Daily Block Scheduling
Each day in this Lesson Pacing Guide represents a 40–50 minute period. Teachers using block scheduling may combine days to revise pacing. In addition, teachers may differentiate and support core instruction by integrating components for extended and intensive support as students require. See the Guide to Selected Leveled Resources (facing page).

• The Aims of *The Spectator*

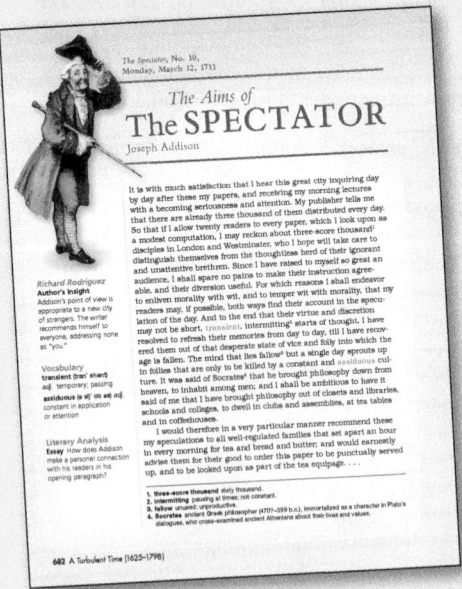

RESOURCES FOR:

- **L1** Special-Needs Students
- **L2** Below-Level Students (Tier 2)
- **L3** On-Level Students (Tier 1)
- **L4** Advanced Students (Tier 1)
- **EL** English Learners
- **All** All Students

Vocabulary/Fluency/Prior Knowledge

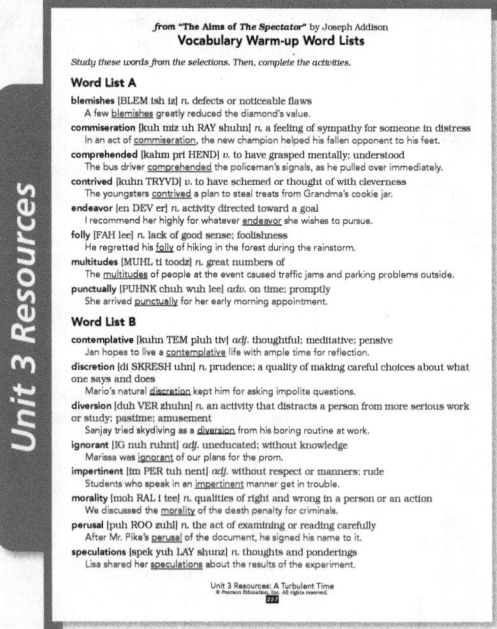

EL L1 L2 Vocabulary Warm-ups A and B, pp. 227–228

Also available for these selections:

EL L1 L2 Reading Warm-ups A and B, pp. 229–230

All Vocabulary Builder, p. 233

Reader's Notebooks

Pre- and postreading pages for this selection appear in an interactive format in the *Reader's Notebooks*. Each *Notebook* is differentiated for a different group of learners.
The selections in the Adapted and English Learner's versions are abridged.

L2 L3 *Reader's Notebook*
L1 *Reader's Notebook: Adapted Version*
EL *Reader's Notebook: English Learner's Version*
EL *Reader's Notebook: Spanish Version*

© *Common Core Companion*

Additional instruction and practice for each Common Core State Standard

Selection Support

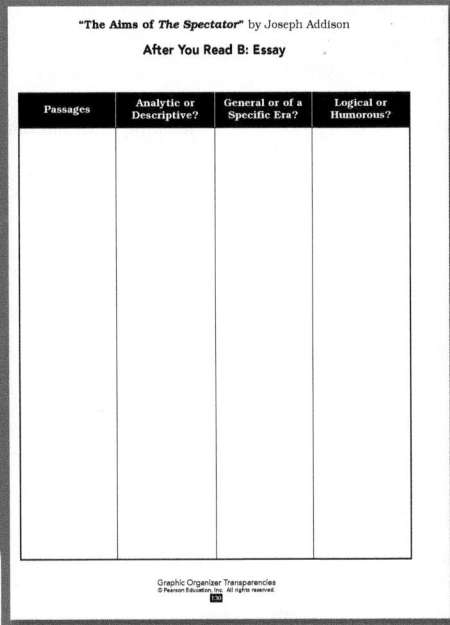

"The Aims of *The Spectator*" by Joseph Addison

After You Read B: Essay

Passages	Analytic or Descriptive?	General or of a Specific Era?	Logical or Humorous?

EL L3 Literary Analysis: Graphic Organizer B, p. 126

Also available for these selections:

EL L1 L2 Reading: Graphic Organizer A (partially filled in), p. 123

EL L3 Reading: Graphic Organizer B, p. 124

EL L1 L2 Literary Analysis: Graphic Organizer A (partially filled in), p. 125

Skills Development/Extension

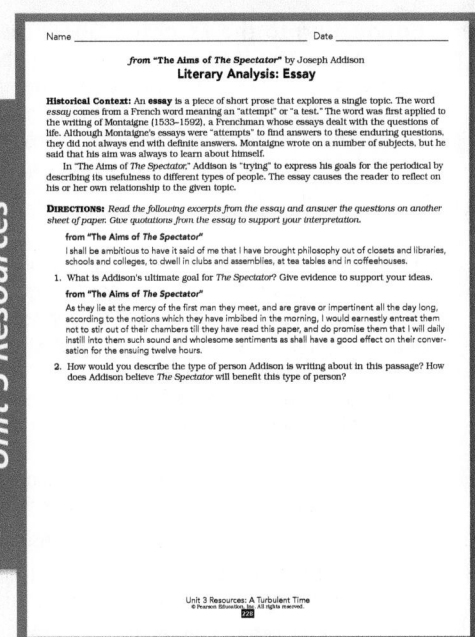

Name _____ Date _____

from "The Aims of *The Spectator*" by Joseph Addison
Literary Analysis: Essay

Historical Context: An **essay** is a piece of short prose that explores a single topic. The word *essay* comes from a French word meaning an "attempt" or "a test." The word was first applied to the writing of Montaigne (1533–1592), a Frenchman whose essays dealt with the questions of life. Although Montaigne's essays were "attempts" to find answers to these enduring questions, they did not always end with definite answers. Montaigne wrote on a number of subjects, but he said that his aim was always to learn about himself.

In "The Aims of *The Spectator*," Addison is "trying" to express his goals for the periodical by describing its usefulness to different types of people. The essay causes the reader to reflect on his or her own relationship to the given topic.

DIRECTIONS: *Read the following excerpts from the essay and answer the questions on another sheet of paper. Give quotations from the essay to support your interpretation.*

from "The Aims of *The Spectator*"

I shall be ambitious to have it said of me that I have brought philosophy out of closets and libraries, schools and colleges, to dwell in clubs and assemblies, at tea tables and in coffeehouses.

1. What is Addison's ultimate goal for *The Spectator*? Give evidence to support your ideas.

from "The Aims of *The Spectator*"

As they lie at the mercy of the first man they meet, and are grave or impertinent all the day long, according to the notions which they have imbibed in the morning, I would earnestly entreat them not to stir out of their chambers till they have read this paper, and do promise them that I will daily instill into them such sound and wholesome sentiments as shall have a good effect on their conversation for the ensuing twelve hours.

2. How would you describe the type of person Addison is writing about in this passage? How does Addison believe *The Spectator* will benefit this type of person?

All Literary Analysis, p. 231

Also available for these selections:
All Reading, p. 232
EL L3 L4 Support for Writing, p. 234
L4 Enrichment, p. 235

Assessment

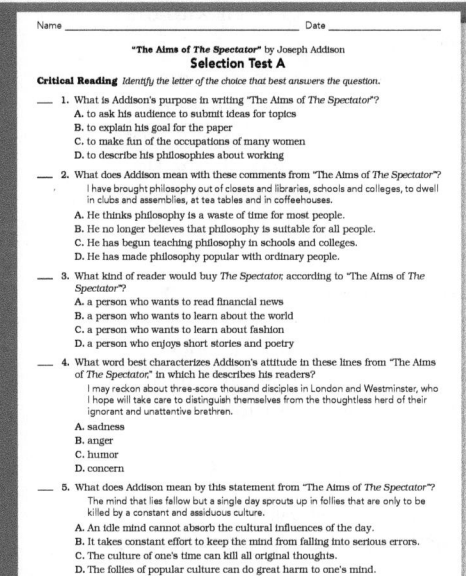

Name _____ Date _____

"The Aims of *The Spectator*" by Joseph Addison
Selection Test A

Critical Reading *Identify the letter of the choice that best answers the question.*

___ 1. What is Addison's purpose in writing "The Aims of *The Spectator*"?
   A. to ask his audience to submit ideas for topics
   B. to explain his goal for the paper
   C. to make fun of the occupations of many women
   D. to describe his philosophies about working

___ 2. What does Addison mean with these comments from "The Aims of *The Spectator*"?
   I have brought philosophy out of closets and libraries, schools and colleges, to dwell in clubs and assemblies, at tea tables and in coffeehouses.
   A. He thinks philosophy is a waste of time for most people.
   B. He no longer believes that philosophy is suitable for all people.
   C. He has begun teaching philosophy in schools and colleges.
   D. He has made philosophy popular with ordinary people.

___ 3. What kind of reader would buy *The Spectator*, according to "The Aims of *The Spectator*"?
   A. a person who wants to read financial news
   B. a person who wants to learn about the world
   C. a person who wants to learn about fashion
   D. a person who enjoys short stories and poetry

___ 4. What word best characterizes Addison's attitude in these lines from "The Aims of *The Spectator*," in which he describes his readers?
   I may reckon about three-score thousand disciples in London and Westminster, who I hope will take care to distinguish themselves from the thoughtless herd of their ignorant and unattentive brethren.
   A. sadness
   B. anger
   C. humor
   D. concern

___ 5. What does Addison mean by this statement from "The Aims of *The Spectator*"?
   The mind that lies fallow but a single day sprouts up in follies that are only to be killed by a constant and assiduous culture.
   A. An idle mind cannot absorb the cultural influences of the day.
   B. It takes constant effort to keep the mind from falling into serious errors.
   C. The culture of one's time can kill all original thoughts.
   D. The follies of popular culture can do great harm to one's mind.

EL L1 L2 Selection Test A, pp. 239–241

Also available for these selections:
L3 L4 Open-Book Test, pp. 236–238
EL L3 L4 Selection Test B, pp. 242–244

PHLit Online!
www.PHLitOnline.com

Online Resources: All print materials are also available online.

- complete narrated selection text
- a thematically related video with writing prompt
- an interactive graphic organizer
- highlighting feature
- access to all student print resources, adapted to individual student needs
- Spanish and English summaries
- adapted selection translations in Spanish

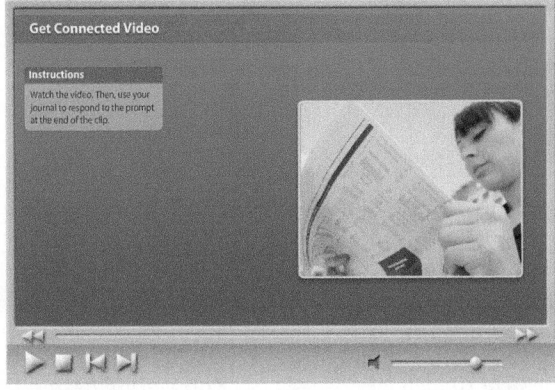

Get Connected! (thematic video with writing prompt)

Also available:

All videos are available in Spanish.

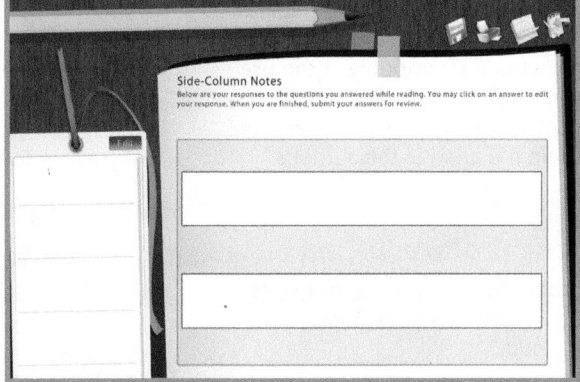

Writer's Journal (with graphics feature)

Also available:

Vocabulary Central (tools and activities for studying vocabulary)

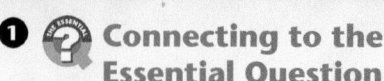
PRETEACH

❶ Connecting to the Essential Question

1. Review the assignment with the class.

2. As homework, have students bring in magazines or newspapers from home, or provide materials from the school library. Have students determine the intended audience for each magazine or newspaper.

3. As students read, have them find passages in which Addison expresses what his audience needs from his magazine and how he will meet those needs.

❷ Literary Analysis

Introduce the skill using the instruction on the student page.

Think Aloud: Model the Skill

Say to students:

As I read an essay, I remember that an essay is a "test" or "experiment" that uncovers connections between experiences. If an essay, like a science experiment, helps me learn something new about the subject of the essay, I know it has been successful.

❸ Reading Strategy

Introduce the skill using the instruction on the student page.

Think Aloud: Model the Skill

Say to students:

I know that in order to understand an author's attitude, I must analyze the author's assumptions. I can use the background information or knowledge I have about the author to help me analyze the author's assumptions.

❹ Vocabulary

1. Pronounce each word, giving its definition, and have students say it aloud.

2. For more guidance, see the *Classroom Strategies and Teaching Routines* card for introducing vocabulary.

Before You Read — *The Aims of* The Spectator

❶ **Connecting to the Essential Question** Just as today's bloggers enjoy the Internet, Addison was excited by the new medium of *his* day, the magazine. As you read, notice passages in which Addison expresses what his audience needs from his magazine and how he will meet those needs. These passages will help as you answer the Essential Question: **How does literature shape or reflect society?**

❷ **Literary Analysis**

An **essay** is a short prose piece that explores a topic as if the author were letting you overhear his or her thoughts. Meaning an "attempt" or a "test," the word *essay* was first applied to writing by the French essayist Michel de Montaigne (1533–1592).

Addison's essay can be seen as a "test," or experiment, to discover connections between experiences and to learn about the self. As you read, notice how the writer links observations and anecdotes to form ideas.

It is no accident that the essay flourished during the eighteenth century. Here are some links between this form and the **historical period:**

- This era saw the development of a rising and well-off middle class.
- Middle-class people wanted to learn more about the world and about themselves. This new class needed a self-definition.
- The essay, often featured in magazines, provided such information, as well as entertainment and moral instruction.

As you read, note how Addison helps readers ask and answer questions such as, *Who am I? What do I need to know and believe?*

❸ **Reading Strategy**

ⓒ **Preparing to Read Complex Texts** To fully appreciate an *author's perspective*, you need to **analyze the author's implicit philosophical assumptions**—unstated beliefs—and **explicit assumptions**—stated beliefs—about a subject. To analyze unstated beliefs, draw inferences and support them with textual evidence. Use a chart like the one shown to find evidence of the *author's perspective*.

❹ **Vocabulary**

transient (tran´ shənt) *adj.* temporary; passing (p. 682)

assiduous (ə sij´ ळ əs) *adj.* constant in application or attention (p. 682)

affluence (af´ lळ əns) *n.* abundant wealth (p. 683)

contentious (kən ten´ shəs) *adj.* quarrelsome (p. 683)

trifles (trī´ fəlz) *n.* things of little value or importance (p. 684)

embellishments (em bel´ ish məntz) *n.* decorative touches; ornamentation (p. 684)

680 A Turbulent Time (1625–1798)

ⓒ **Common Core State Standards**

Reading Informational Text

1. Cite strong and thorough textual evidence to support analysis of what the text says explicitly as well as inferences drawn from the text, including determining where the text leaves matters uncertain.

Explicit Assumption

Author's Perspective

Implicit Assumption

Author's Perspective

PHLit
Online!
www.PHLitOnline.com

Vocabulary Development

Vocabulary Knowledge Rating

Create a **Vocabulary Knowledge Rating Chart** (*Professional Development Guidebook,* p. 33) for the vocabulary words on the student page. Give each student a copy of the chart with the words on it. Read the words aloud, and have students mark their rating of each in the Before Reading column. When students have completed reading and discussing the selection, have them take out their **Vocabulary Knowledge Rating Charts** for the story. Read the words aloud and have students rate their knowledge again in the After Reading column. Clarify any words that are still problematic. Then, have students complete the Vocabulary practice at the end of the selection.

PHLit
Online!   **Vocabulary Central,** featuring tools, activities, and songs for studying vocabulary, is available online at **www.PHLitOnline.com.**

⑤ JOSEPH ADDISON
(1672–1719)

Author of "The Aims of *The SPECTATOR*"

Born in a village in Wiltshire, England, Joseph Addison was educated at the Charterhouse School in London, where he became a friend of classmate Richard Steele. Both young men went on to Oxford, but, after their school days, their paths diverged. The impetuous Steele immersed himself in London life, editing an early newspaper and managing the Drury Lane Theatre, while the more cautious Addison pursued prestigious political positions. Their paths, though, were to cross again.

Scholar, Poet, and Bureaucrat A Fellow of Magdalen College, Oxford, Addison was invited by John Dryden to do translations of Virgil. After four years of European study and travel, he produced an epic, *The Campaign,* celebrating a notable English victory. In 1706, Addison was named undersecretary of state and later went on to other important posts.

A Reunion In 1709, the story is told, Addison happened to read an article in *The Tatler,* a new literary magazine that had become all the rage in London coffeehouses. The article was signed "Isaac Bickerstaff," but Addison immediately recognized the style of his old school friend Richard Steele. Addison soon became a contributor to *The Tatler.* When publication of *The Tatler* ended, the two founded another journal, *The Spectator.*

A Lifetime Partnership As a team, Addison and Steele became the most celebrated journalists in England. Their essays in *The Tatler* and *The Spectator* earned them a permanent place in English literature. Almost every magazine you can buy today uses an informal, popular style derived from the one they originated.

> **❝** *But there are none to whom this paper will be more useful than to the female world.* **❞**

The Aims of *The Spectator* **681**

❶ About the Selection

Thrilled with the success of his paper, Addison sets out to tell his readers what his "aims" are. In an agreeable, witty voice, Addison promises to uplift his faithful readers by treating them to useful ideas and instilling in them sound and useful sentiments.

❷ Activating Prior Knowledge

Have students write a paragraph describing the kinds of publications they read, and when they read them.

Concept Connector ➡

Tell students that they will return to their responses after reading the selection.

❸ Author's Insight

1. Point out that while Addison uses *I* he does not use the familiar *you* with his readers.

2. **Ask** students to list the terms he uses in the first ten lines to describe his readers.
   Answer: Addison uses *great city, readers, disciples,* and *audience* to refer to his readers.

❹ Literary Analysis

1. Have students read the first paragraph of the essay.

The Spectator, No. 10,
Monday, March 12, 1711

The Aims of ❶ ❷
The SPECTATOR

Joseph Addison

❸ *Richard Rodriguez*
Author's Insight
Addison's point of view is appropriate to a new city of strangers. The writer recommends himself to everyone, addressing none as "you."

Vocabulary
transient (tran´ shənt) *adj.* temporary; passing

assiduous (ə sij´ ᵒᵒ əs) *adj.* constant in application or attention

❹ **Literary Analysis**
Essay How does Addison make a personal connection with his readers in his opening paragraph?

It is with much satisfaction that I hear this great city inquiring day by day after these my papers, and receiving my morning lectures with a becoming seriousness and attention. My publisher tells me that there are already three thousand of them distributed every day. So that if I allow twenty readers to every paper, which I look upon as a modest computation, I may reckon about three-score thousand[1] disciples in London and Westminster, who I hope will take care to distinguish themselves from the thoughtless herd of their ignorant and unattentive brethren. Since I have raised to myself so great an audience, I shall spare no pains to make their instruction agreeable, and their diversion useful. For which reasons I shall endeavor to enliven morality with wit, and to temper wit with morality, that my readers may, if possible, both ways find their account in the speculation of the day. And to the end that their virtue and discretion may not be short, transient, intermitting[2] starts of thought, I have resolved to refresh their memories from day to day, till I have recovered them out of that desperate state of vice and folly into which the age is fallen. The mind that lies fallow[3] but a single day sprouts up in follies that are only to be killed by a constant and assiduous culture. It was said of Socrates[4] that he brought philosophy down from heaven, to inhabit among men; and I shall be ambitious to have it said of me that I have brought philosophy out of closets and libraries, schools and colleges, to dwell in clubs and assemblies, at tea tables and in coffeehouses.

I would therefore in a very particular manner recommend these my speculations to all well-regulated families that set apart an hour in every morning for tea and bread and butter; and would earnestly advise them for their good to order this paper to be punctually served up, and to be looked upon as part of the tea equipage. . . .

---

1. **three-score thousand** sixty thousand.
2. **intermitting** pausing at times; not constant.
3. **fallow** unused; unproductive.
4. **Socrates** ancient Greek philosopher (470?–399 b.c.), immortalized as a character in Plato's dialogues, who cross-examined ancient Athenians about their lives and values.

682 A Turbulent Time (1625–1798)

Ⓒ Text Complexity Rubric

The Aims of *The Spectator*			
Qualitative Measures			
Context/ Knowledge Demands	Enlightenment essay; historical and cultural context		
	1 2 ③ 4 5		
Structure/ Language Clarity	Long sentences; above-level vocabulary		
	1 2 ③ 4 5		
Levels of Meaning	Accessible (news)		
	1 ② 3 4 5		
Quantitative Measures			
Lexile	1470L	**Text Length**	968 words
Overall Complexity	**More accessible**		

Reader and Task Suggestions

Preparing to Read the Text
- Using the Background on TE p. 681, stress the novelty of periodicals in Addison's day.
- Discuss the importance of audience in nonfiction, clarifying that Addison's main audience for *The Spectator* was England's growing middle class.
- Guide students to use Multidraft Reading strategies (TE p. 681).

Leveled Tasks
Knowledge Demands If students will have difficulty with the context, have them focus on Addison's purpose of explaining the aims of *The Spectator*. Then, as they reread, have them consider details that aid his purpose.

Synthesizing If students will not have difficulty with the context, have them draw conclusions about London in Addison's day.

> *I have resolved to refresh their memories from day to day, till I have recovered them out of that desperate state of vice and folly into which the age is fallen.*

In the next place, I would recommend this paper to the daily perusal of those gentlemen whom I cannot but consider as my good brothers and allies, I mean the fraternity of spectators, who live in the world without having anything to do in it; and either by the **affluence** of their fortunes or laziness of their dispositions have no other business with the rest of mankind but to look upon them. Under this class of men are comprehended all contemplative tradesmen, titular physicians, fellows of the Royal Society, Templars[5] that are not given to be **contentious**, and statesmen that are out of business; in short, everyone that considers the world as a theater, and desires to form a right judgment of those who are the actors on it.

There is another set of men that I must likewise lay a claim to, whom I have lately called the blanks of society, as being altogether unfurnished with ideas, till the business and conversation of the day has supplied them. I have often considered these poor souls with an eye of great commiseration, when I have heard them asking the first man they have met with, whether there was any news stirring? and by that means gathering together materials for thinking. These needy persons do not know what to talk of till about twelve o'clock in the morning; for by that time they are pretty good judges of the weather, know which way the wind sits, and whether the Dutch mail[6] be come in. As they lie at the mercy of the first man they meet, and are grave or impertinent all the day long, according to the notions which they have imbibed in the morning, I would earnestly entreat them not to stir out of their chambers till they have read this paper, and do promise them that I will daily instil into them such sound and wholesome sentiments as shall have a good effect on their conversation for the ensuing twelve hours.

But there are none to whom this paper will be more useful than to the female world. I have often thought there has not been sufficient pains taken in finding out proper employments and diversions for the fair ones. Their amusements seem contrived for them, rather as they are women, than as they are

---

5. **titular physicians, fellows of the Royal Society, Templars** physicians in title only; members of a group dedicated to scientific research; lawyers or law students with offices in the Inner or Middle Temple.
6. **Dutch mail** mail from Europe bearing news of the war.

The Aims of *The Spectator* 683

LITERATURE IN CONTEXT

World Events

Rise of the Middle Class

In this essay, Addison addresses members of a new and rising social group, the British middle classes. By the mid-1700s, England enjoyed growing prosperity and a high rate of literacy. The careers available in law, medicine, teaching, banking, and government service expanded. As a result, more and more English citizens had the leisure, education, and money needed to enjoy such cultural pursuits as music, art, and reading.

Addison knows his audience, quickly tapping their interests in this essay. He refers, for instance, to the coffeehouses that provided their middle-class patrons with newspapers, gossip, and political debate as well as refreshments. He has great fun with the new custom of the shopping trip. Tongue half in cheek, Addison informs his audience of his intentions: to improve and amuse them.

Connect to the Literature

What benefit does *The Spectator* provide for the men Addison calls "the blanks of society"?

Vocabulary

affluence (af´ loo əns) *n.* abundant wealth

contentious (kən ten´ shəs) *adj.* quarrelsome

Reading Check
To what four groups does Addison recommend his paper?

Concept Connector

Reading Strategy Graphic Organizer
Ask students to review the graphic organizers in which they have listed the author's assumptions and perspective. Then, have students share their organizers and compare inferences.

Activating Prior Knowledge
Have students return to their responses to the Activating Prior Knowledge activity. Ask them to explain whether their thoughts have changed and, if so, how.

Writing About the Essential Question
Have students compare their responses to the prompt, completed before reading the selection, with their thoughts afterward. Have them work individually or in groups, writing or discussing their thoughts, to formulate their new responses. Then, lead a class discussion, probing for what students have learned that confirms or invalidates their initial thoughts. Encourage students to cite specific textual details to support their responses.

683

1. After students have finished reading this paragraph, have them reread its first three sentences. **Ask** students to summarize Addison's description of women. **Answer:** Ordinary women only shop and fix their hair, while "better" women are a mix of beauty and brains.

2. **Ask** students what outcome Addison hopes for by describing two such types of women. **Possible response:** Addison creates competition in which women want to be superior. He hopes to persuade women that by reading his paper, they can develop "all the beauties of the mind" as well as the "ornaments of dress."

ASSESS

Answers

Before students respond, you may wish to have them write a brief objective summary of the selection. As they answer the questions below, remind them to support their answers with evidence from the text.

1. (a) **Possible response:** Addison hopes to maintain a large readership (b) **Possible response:** Addison hopes his readers will "take care to distinguish themselves from the thoughtless herd," and that he will increase the number of women "that move in an exalted sphere of knowledge."

2. (a) Spectators live in the world without doing anything in it. (b) Addison sympathizes with those who want to live a life of the mind. He mocks those who have no ideas of their own and women who only care about hair and clothing.

3. **Possible response:** Modern media observe humanity for the purpose of sympathy and mockery. Human interest stories invite us to sympathize in some cases and mock in others.

4. **❓ Possible response:** Addison would like to present an ideal to be emulated, and values by which one could live. He hopes to inspire people to become more educated, thoughtful, and reflective.

---

❽ *Richard Rodriguez*
Author's Insight
Do not read this paragraph with modern eyes. Women readers are acknowledged as a possible audience; the writer's world suddenly doubles.

Vocabulary
trifles (trī′ fəlz) *n.* things of little value or importance

embellishments (em bel′ ish mənts) *n.* decorative touches; ornamentation

reasonable creatures; and are more adapted to the sex than to the species. The toilet[7] is their great sense of business, and the right adjusting of their hair the principal employment of their lives. The sorting of a suit of ribbons is reckoned a very good morning's work; and if they make an excursion to a mercer's or a toyshop,[8] so great a fatigue makes them unfit for anything else all the day after. Their more serious occupations are sewing and embroidery, and their greatest drudgery the preparation of jellies and sweetmeats. This, I say, is the state of ordinary women; though I know there are multitudes of those of a more elevated life and conversation, that move in an exalted sphere of knowledge and virtue, that join all the beauties of the mind to the ornaments of dress, and inspire a kind of awe and respect, as well as love, into their male beholders. I hope to increase the number of these by publishing this daily paper, which I shall always endeavor to make an innocent if not an improving entertainment, and by that means at least divert the minds of my female readers from greater trifles. At the same time, as I would fain give some finishing touches to those which are already the most beautiful pieces in human nature, I shall endeavor to point all those imperfections that are the blemishes, as well as those virtues which are the embellishments, of the sex.

---

7. **toilet** act of dressing and grooming oneself.
8. **suit of ribbons . . . mercer's or a toyshop** A suit of ribbons was a set of matching ribbons; a mercer's store sold fabrics, ribbons, and so on; a toyshop sold small items of little value.

Critical Reading

Cite textual evidence to support your responses.

1. **Key Ideas and Details (a)** What reason does Addison give for making his instruction "agreeable"? **(b) Support:** Addison felt *The Spectator* would set high standards for readers. Identify two expressions of this attitude.

2. **Key Ideas and Details (a)** How does Addison define the "spectators" of society? **(b) Infer:** What is Addison's attitude toward the "blanks of society" and toward women? Is he sympathetic, mocking, or both? Explain.

3. **Integration of Knowledge and Ideas Apply:** Do modern media encourage "spectatorship" as Addison defines it? Explain.

4. **Integration of Knowledge and Ideas** What kinds of things would Addison like to change about society? In your response, use at least two of these Essential Question words: *values, dissatisfaction, ideal. [Connecting to the Essential Question: How does literature shape or reflect society?]*

Assessment Practice

Writer's Purpose
Many tests require students to identify the writer's purpose. Use the following sample test item.

There is another set of men . . . whom I have lately called the blanks of society, as being altogether unfurnished with ideas, till the business and conversation of the day has supplied them . . . they lie at the mercy of the first man they meet, and are grave or impertinent all the day long, according to the notions which they have imbibed.

Addison uses the phrase "they lie at the mercy of the first man they meet"

A to show that the "blanks" are powerless

B to ironically deflect blame for the "blanks'" opinions onto others

C to praise the men who give the "blanks" direction

D to show the predatory nature of humans

The phrase is ironic; the correct answer is B.

After You Read | *The Aims of* The Spectator

Literary Analysis

1. **Key Ideas and Details** In his **essay** for *The Spectator,* Addison describes audiences for his paper. How does he "test" the usefulness of his paper?

2. **Integration of Knowledge and Ideas** Using a chart like this one, analyze Addison's portrait of his four readers.

Passage	Analytic/ Descriptive	General/Of a Specific Era?	Logical/ Humorous?

Reading Strategy

3. **Analyze the author's philosophical assumptions** in the first paragraph. **(a)** What *explicit assumptions* does he make about the best way to present moral instruction? Cite specific evidence. **(b)** What *implicit assumptions* does he make about using media to promote ideas? Explain.

PERFORMANCE TASKS
Integrated Language Skills

Vocabulary Acquisition and Use

For each word, choose the letter of its synonym, a word that means the same thing. Explain each choice.

1. **affluence:**   **(a)** speed   **(b)** poverty   **(c)** wealth
2. **assiduous:**   **(a)** diligent   **(b)** aggressive   **(c)** helpful
3. **contentious:**   **(a)** mild   **(b)** argumentative   **(c)** proud
4. **embellishments:** **(a)** food   **(b)** remarks   **(c)** decorations
5. **transient:**   **(a)** powerful   **(b)** passing   **(c)** near
6. **trifles:**   **(a)** trivia   **(b)** wonders   **(c)** dangers

Writing

Argumentative Text Like Addison, you observe people in action every day. Write a **letter to the editor** of a local paper describing a kind of behavior you find interesting, amusing, or annoying. Persuade readers to regard the behavior as you do.

- State your position, presenting vivid *examples* of the behavior.
- Support your views with *reasoning* and *emotional appeals*.
- Anticipate and *refute opposing arguments*.

The Aims of *The Spectator* 685

Common Core State Standards

Writing

1.a. Introduce precise, knowledgeable claim(s), establish the significance of the claim(s), distinguish the claim(s) from alternate or opposing claims, and create an organization that logically sequences claim(s), counterclaims, reasons, and evidence.

Answers

1. Addison "tests" the usefulness of his paper by naming all the respective readers to whom it might be useful or interesting.

2. **Sample responses:** Passage: fourth paragraph; Analytic/ Descriptive: blanks form ideas and opinions from others' conversations; General/Of a Specific Era?: general; Logical/Humorous: amusing term for people with limited opinions.

3. (a) He explicitly assumes that the best way to teach morality is by combining the instruction with wit to make for a more agreeable experience. (b) He implicitly assumes that a newspaper with such a large circulation is sure to reach many people, thereby spreading his word successfully.

Vocabulary Acquisition and Use

1. (c) Wealth means having a large amount of money or possessions, which is something that *affluent* persons possess.

2. (a) A diligent person works persistently, or *assiduously*, to achieve his or her goals.

3. (b) A quarrelsome person is *contentious*, or argumentative.

4. (c) A wedding cake usually has many *embellishments*, or decorations.

5. (b) A fad is often *transient*, or passing.

6. (a) *Trifles*, like trivia, are little things that don't matter.

Writing

Evaluate students' argumentative text using the **Rubrics for a Persuasive Essay**, *Professional Development Guidebook*, pages 256–257.

Assessment Resources

Assessment Resources

Unit 3 Resources

All Customizable Test Bank

All Self-Tests

Students may prepare for the **Selection Test** by taking the **Self-Test** online.

All resources are available at
www.PHLitOnline.com

Themes Across Centuries

Richard Rodriguez

1. Call students' attention to the Meet the Author feature on this page. Point out that Rodriguez is a well-known author, journalist, and commentator. You may also wish to have students reread Rodriguez's introduction to Unit 3.

2. Show students Segment 2 on Richard Rodriguez on the *See It!* **DVD** to provide insight into Rodriguez's understanding of Jonathan Swift. After students have watched the segment, **ask** them why Swift is so important to Rodriguez.
   Possible response: Rodriguez admires Swift's talent as a political and social satirist, and Rodriguez finds satire a key element of the social and cultural commentary he writes.

Journalist as Spectator, Then and Now

1. After students read the first section of Rodriguez's comments, remind them that Joseph Addison was the author of "The Aims of *The Spectator.*"

2. **Ask** students to explain the distinction Rodriguez draws between Addison and his persona, the Spectator.
   Possible response: Although it reflected the author's moral sensibility, Addison's persona was separate from the world he observed in a way that the real Addison could not actually be.

3. Explain to students that Rodriguez begins his comments with Addison because he feels a personal connection to the author's persona as the Spectator. This persona is a useful one for writers like Rodriguez because it allows them to observe actual events without involvement or a biased point of view.

Richard Rodriguez Introduces
from Days of Obligation:
from "In Athens Once"

Journalist as Spectator, Then and Now The best journalists achieve a sort of disappearing act, a recitation of facts so transparent it is as though the eye were speaking. Joseph Addison, writing three hundred years ago, styled himself a "spectator" of the great city of London. *Spectator* is a noun I would willingly take for myself, preferring to present myself to the reader as a spectator, at some cool distance from the world I describe.

Joseph Addison, Spectator and Man Joseph Addison was a periodical columnist, writing for magazines. He invented a fictionalized persona who roamed the city of London and reported what he found there. The persona of the Spectator was not Joseph Addison, but resembled him. There is, for instance, a discernible moral sensibility in all Addison's writing that reveals the man. If he writes about that fellow in the corner, with the parrot on his shoulder, it is because he has something in mind to say. It is not simply that he wishes to place a colorful character before us.

Richard Rodriguez, Journalist and Man The journalist in me wants to be informative, to say what is true or factual, and to report exactly what I have seen, without reference to my own sensibility. As a journalist, for example, I visit the teeming, optimistic city of Tijuana, Mexico, situated across the border from San Diego, California.

Tijuana is a city of uncountable millions, and as many aspirations, and as many preoccupations, and as many points of

About the Author

Journalist, essayist, and author Richard Rodriguez won the George Foster Peabody Award in 1997 for his work on PBS's *MacNeil-Lehrer NewsHour.* His writing has appeared in a number of publications, including *The Washington Post,* the *Wall Street Journal,* and *Harper's.*

Teaching Resources

The following resources can be used to enrich or extend the instruction for Contemporary Commentary

Unit 3 Resources
> From the Author's Desk, p. 225
> Listening and Viewing, p. 226

See It! DVD
> Richard Rodriguez, Segment 2

"The best journalists achieve a sort of disappearing act."

view. Most Americans have no sense of Tijuana beyond its old-fashioned notoriety as a honky-tonk draw for sailors during the war.

To me, Tijuana appears as raw and exciting, sometimes as appalling, as I imagine eighteenth-century London must have appeared to Joseph Addison. Large, beautiful houses overlook a city of factories, heavy metal rock bands, gypsies, taxis, street cries, stinking canals. It is a city of contradictions.

My journalistic obligation to the reader is to present numbers and dates as correctly as I can. My journalistic impulse always intends to complicate rather than to simplify issues, to suggest two or several points of view rather than to argue a single position. My journalistic obligation, therefore, is to see this border town from both sides—to describe how Mexico, particularly Mexico City, views Tijuana, as well as how people north of the border regard this city.

But I have also come to Tijuana as a Mexican American, as someone born in the United States to Mexican parents. My status here is in question. Indeed, Tijuana, this city that lies on the border between cultures, must finally remind me of myself—the struggle of cultures in my own soul. Tijuana implicates me and fascinates me for being (as I am) confused by its identity.

The Spectator Becomes a Comic Character Thus, you will see how in this piece, Richard Rodriguez becomes a comic character within the city he has been at such pains to describe from a distance. *They* surround the *I*. The diffidence of Richard Rodriguez is exposed as completely at odds with the messy ease of Tijuana—at odds, too, with the airs he gives himself as a traveler-observer.

▲ **Critical Viewing**
In what way is the man pictured here a "colorful character" and, like Rodriguez, "at odds" with his surroundings? **[Analyze]**

Themes Across Centuries: Author's Insights **687**

687

1. (a) Journalists should be completely transparent in their writing so readers can see straight through to reality. (b) **Possible response:** Many print journalists strive for this transparency. Many television journalists, however, blur the line between journalistic transparency and subjective opinions.

2. (a) Rodriguez sees parallels in the two cities' contradictions. (b) As a journalist, Rodriguez must accurately present the city in all of its complexities. (c) **Possible response:** Students may say that Rodriguez is not likely to remain objective, because he cannot keep himself removed from and uninvolved with the city.

3. (a) Rodriguez sees himself as both Mexican and American, and he sees Tijuana as a city torn between American and Mexican cultures.(b) **Possible response:** Rodriguez wants to convey the facts about his subject as a journalist would, but he also wants to describe his own subjective experience, as a literary artist might.

4. (a) This device makes the point that Rodriguez has become a character in his essay. (b) Students may suggest that the "I" is Rodriguez the man and "Richard Rodriguez" is Rodriguez the journalist and writer.

5. **Possible response:** Students may list such specific words and lines as "la capital" and "in the nineteenth century" as examples of journalistic style; "with bad skin or bad teeth" and "paperweights upon a map" are examples of literary language. Students may say that the more journalistic passages give facts and history, while the literary sections paint a picture that brings the city to life.

6. **Possible response:** Students will likely describe the section toward the end of the essay during which Rodriguez is in the museum in Tijuana as the moment when the author becomes a participant in the world he is observing.

When the journalist becomes a character within his own report, he enters the realm of bias and prejudice, or he enters the realm of literature—depending.

The pieces I write for newspapers are usually published on an opinion page; they intend to persuade. My television essays are reserved for the last part of a news program; they are clearly identified as "commentary." They circle a point of view, but cannot express a point of view. The only journalistic pride I own is the fact that I have been called by some readers "left" and by other readers "right." The journalist in me does not want to be slotted among one band of partisans in an argument.

But the writing I prefer attempts a marriage: journalism wedded to literature.

The journalist Richard Rodriguez writes as fairly as possible of the world around him. The writer Richard Rodriguez finds himself caught up in the world he is watching. He may be morally outraged. Or he may simply be made petulant by the heat. He shows his hand, at any rate.

Critical Reading

1. **Key Ideas and Details (a)** According to Rodriguez, in what way do good journalists perform a "disappearing act"? **(b) Make a Judgment:** Do you think his ideas apply to today's television and print journalists? Explain.

2. **Key Ideas and Details (a)** What connections does Rodriguez draw between Addison's London and modern-day Tijuana? **(b)** As a journalist, in what way must Rodriguez present the border town of Tijuana? **(c) Speculate:** Because of the parallels Rodriguez notes between himself and Tijuana, do you think he can be objective in his presentation of the city? Why or why not?

3. **Key Ideas and Details (a) Infer:** In what ways might the connection Rodriguez feels to Tijuana make him the perfect person to write about the city? **(b) Interpret:** In your own words, explain what Rodriguez means by "journalism wedded to literature."

4. **Craft and Structure (a)** In this commentary, what is the effect of Richard Rodriguez referring to himself in the third person? **(b)** What, if any, is the difference between the "I" in this essay and "Richard Rodriguez"?

5. **Craft and Structure** Note words and phrases that make this a piece of journalism and words and phrases that make it literature. Explain the differences you note, using what you read in Rodriguez's essay.

6. **Integration of Knowledge and Ideas** Consider whether Rodriguez remains a spectator throughout his essay. Identify any moments when you think he becomes a participant rather than an observer.

Cite textual evidence to support your responses.

Think Aloud

Writing a Monologue
To model the skill of narrative writing, use the following "think aloud." Say to students:

When I plan to write my own essays, I first need to consider how I will share my ideas. One approach is as Rodriguez says: "The best journalists achieve a sort of disappearing act, a recitation of facts so transparent it is as though the eye were speaking." I can infer that he means the writer "steps out" of the story in a way that allows the tale to be told while allowing the speaker to integrate his or her ideas without overpowering the reader. Rodriguez also notes that "when the journalist becomes a character within his own report, he enters the realm of bias and prejudice, or he enters the realm of literature—depending." I think he is reminding me to be careful not to overshadow my story or my characters.

from

Days of Obligation:

from "In Athens Once"

Richard Rodriguez

❶ **About the Selection**

In *Days of Obligation,* Richard Rodriguez writes of Tijuana, Mexico, a city of contradictions. Rodriguez writes that the city reminds him of his own contradictions—torn between the cultures of Mexico and the United States. His comments are acerbic yet humorous, mocking yet introspective.

❷ **Activating Prior Knowledge**

Ask students to think about the town or suburb closest to where they live. How similar are the two areas? Then remind students that people are usually most like those who live closest to them, rather than those who live far away. Thus, Tijuana is very different from Mexico City and in many ways like cities of the United States.

Consider Tijuana from Mexico's point of view. Tijuana is
❸ farther away from Mexico City than any other city in Mexico. Tijuana is where Mexico comes to an end.

In Mexico City you will waste an afternoon if you go to bookstores looking for books about Tijuana. The clerk will scarcely conceal his amusement. (And what would be in a book about Tijuana?) People in Mexico City will tell you, if they have anything at all to say about Tijuana, that Tijuana is a city without history, a city without architecture, an American city. San Diego may worry about Mexican hordes crawling over the border. Mexico City worries about a cultural spill from the United States.

❹ ▲ **Critical Viewing**
What does this image suggest about the contents and tone of the essay to come? **[Predict]**

from Days of Obligation **689**

❸ **Critical Thinking**

Analyze

1. Have students locate Tijuana and Mexico City on a map of Mexico. Then, **ask** students to explain the two meanings of the sentence, "Tijuana is farther away from Mexico City than any other city in Mexico."
Answer: Tijuana may indeed be the farthest city in miles from Mexico City. Figuratively, Tijuana is miles away from the culture of Mexico City.

2. **Ask** students what effect this wordplay has on the tone of the essay.
Answer: Students may describe the effect as humorous or lighthearted.

3. **Ask** students what Rodriguez means when he says that Tijuana is "where Mexico comes to an end."
Answer: Tijuana is a border town and, like many border towns, is a mix of cultures.

❹ **Critical Viewing**

Possible response: It may suggest an essay addressing stereotypical Spanish or Mexican culture, celebratory in nature, colorful and light.

Differentiated Instruction   for Universal Access

Support for Special-Needs Students
Lead a quick tour of the essay before the students read Rodriguez's essay. Have students focus on the title, questions in the side margin, photographs, footnotes, and reading check question. Ask students to predict what the essay will be about and its tone. Talk about the location of Tijuana and its proximity to the United States. Ask students whether they have heard anything about Tijuana or other border towns. Explain that border towns usually have a mix of two cultures.

Enrichment for Gifted/Talented Students
Rodriguez provides commentary on both Tijuana and San Diego. Ask students to develop a much more objective view of either city by designing and writing a travel brochure or a multimedia virtual tour. Ask students to research the museums, parks, local customs and celebrations, and other attractions of the city using the Internet or other references. Ask them to share their brochures or multimedia tours with the rest of the class.

⑤ Critical Thinking

Interpret

1. Have students review the bracketed paragraph. **Ask** them to explain what Rodriguez means when he says that Tijuana and San Diego are not in the same historical time zone.
Answer: Although the two cities are in the same geographic time zone, they are out of sync in terms of progress and culture.

2. **Ask** students why Rodriguez describes Tijuana as "Dickensian."
Answer: Like the London of Charles Dickens, scoundrels and eccentrics inhabit the streets of Tijuana.

3. Have students compare the descriptions of Tijuana and San Diego. **Ask** them which city Rodriguez favors.
Answer: He has biting comments on both. Though he points out that San Diego represents progress, he mocks its high-impact plastic and the eating habits of its people. He points out the backwardness of Tijuana, but speaks of the emergence of new ideas there.

⑥ Critical Viewing

Possible response: The picture contains two kinds of landscapes—one mountainous, the other crowded and urban.

From prehistory, the North has been the problem. Mexico City (la capital) has been the platform from which all provincialism[1] is gauged. From the North came marauding[2] tribes, iconoclasts,[3] destroyers of high Indian civilization. During the Spanish colonial era, the North was settled, even garrisoned, but scarcely civilized. In the nineteenth century, Mexico's northernmost territories were too far from the center to be defended against America's westward expansion. In after-decades, the North spawned revolutionaries and bandits, or these fled into the North and the North hid them well.

Beyond all the ribbon-cutting palaver[4] about good neighbors, there remains an awesome distance of time. Tijuana and San Diego are not in the same historical time zone. Tijuana is poised at the beginning of an industrial age, a Dickensian[5] city with palm trees. ⑤ San Diego is a postindustrial city of high-impact plastic and despair diets. And palm trees. San Diego faces west, looks resolutely out to sea. Tijuana stares north, as toward the future. San Diego is the future—secular, soulless. San Diego is the past, guarding its quality of life. Tijuana is the future.

On the Mexican side there is flux, a vast migration, a camp of siege. On the Mexican side is youth, with bad skin or bad teeth, but with a naïve optimism appropriate to youth.

On the American side are petitions to declare English the official language of the United States; the Ku Klux Klan; nativists posing as environmentalists, blaming illegal immigration for freeway congestion.

⑥ ▼ **Critical Viewing**
In what ways does this photograph depict the contradictory worlds Rodriguez describes?
[Connect]

1. **provincialism** narrowness of outlook.
2. **marauding** plundering, raiding.
3. **iconoclasts** those who seek to destroy widely accepted beliefs or ideas.
4. **palaver** conference or discussion.
5. **Dickensian** having the characteristics of a nineteenth century English novel written by Charles Dickens (1812–1870). Dickensian characteristics would include obscure London streets inhabited by scoundrels and villains, wide-eyed innocents, and eccentric characters.

Tijuana
and San Diego are not in the same historical time zone.

690 A Turbulent Time (1625–1798)

Enrichment: Historical Timeline

A Brief History of Mexico

Indians from the north were the first people who lived in what is now Mexico. They settled there about 8000 B.C. By 2000 B.C., classes had developed among the people, including priests, pottery makers, and weavers. By 1000 B.C., the villages had grown into religious centers.

Great Indian civilizations thrived between 259 and 900 A.D. The Indians built great pyramids to the sun and the moon. The climate became drier after 900 A.D., and the people began warring with neighboring tribes for more land.

The last great Indian empire was the Aztec during the mid-1400s. The Spanish conquered the Aztecs in the early 1500s.

Acivity: Historical Timeline Have students research and construct their own timelines of Mexican history from 8000 B.C. to the present. Students might use the Timeline on *Professional Development Guidebook* p.100.

And late at night, on the radio call-in shows, hysterical, reasonable American voices say they have had enough. Of this or that. Of trampled flower beds. Of waiting in line or crowded buses, of real or imagined rudeness, of welfare.

In San Diego people speak of "the border" as meaning a clean break, the end of *us*, the beginning of *them*. In Mexican Spanish, the legality takes on distance, even pathos, as *la frontera*, meaning something less fixed, something more akin to the American "frontier." Whereas San Diego remains provincial and retiring, the intrusion of the United States has galvanized Tijuana to cosmopolitanism.[6] There are seven newspapers in Tijuana; there is American television—everything we see they see. Central American refugees and southern California *turistas* cross paths in Tijuana. There are new ideas. Most worrisome to Mexico City has been the emergence of a right-wing idea, a pro-American politics to challenge the one-party system that has governed Mexico for most of this century.

Because the United States is the richer country, the more powerful broadcaster, Mexicans know more about us than we care to know about them. Mexicans speak of America as "the other side," saying they are going to *el otro lado* when they cross for work, legal or illegal. The border is real enough; it is guarded by men with guns. But Mexicans incline to view the border without reverence, referring to the American side as *el otro cachete*, the other buttock.

Traditionally, Mexican cities are centered by a town square or *zócalo*, on either side of which stand city hall and cathedral, counterweights to balance the secular[7] with the eternal. Tijuana never had a *zócalo*. And, like other California cities, Tijuana is receding from its old downtown.

---

6. **cosmopolitanism** worldly sophistication.
7. **secular** related to worldly, rather than religious, things.

❽ Reading Check

Which city is called "la capital"?

from Days of Obligation 691

The new commercial district of Tijuana, three miles east of downtown, is called the Zona del Río. For several blocks within the Zona del Río, on grass islands in the middle of the Paseo de los Héroes, stand monuments to various of Mexico's heroes. There is one American (Abraham Lincoln) in a line that otherwise connects the good Aztec, Cuauhtémoc,[8] to the victorious Mexican general, Zaragoza.[9] With Kremlin-like dullness, these monuments were set down upon the city, paperweights upon a map. They are gifts from the capital, meant as reminders.

Prominent along the Paseo de los Héroes is Tijuana's Cultural Center, Mexico City's most insistent token of troth.[10] Tijuana might better have done with sewers or streetlights, but in 1982 the Mexican government built Tijuana a cultural center, an orange concrete bomba[11] in the brutal architectural idioms[12] of the 1970s. The main building is a museum, very clean and empty during my visit, except for a janitor who trails me with a vacuum cleaner. Together we tread a ramp past fairly uninteresting displays of Mayan pottery, past folk crafts, past reproductions of political documents and portraits of Mexico's military heroes. The lesson to Tijuana is clear: she belongs to Mexico.

As the exhibits travel in time, south to north, the umbilical approach narrows to gossamer. We reach a display devoted to Tijuana's own history. We find a collection of picture postcards from the

---

8. **Cuauhtémoc** the 11th and last Aztec emperor. When captured in battle, Cuauhtémoc refused to reveal the location of Aztec riches, earning him legendary status among Mexico's leaders.

9. **Zaragoza** General Zaragoza and his militia defeated an invading French army on May 5, 1862. Cinco de Mayo is celebrated each year to commemorate the victory.

10. **troth** loyalty.

11. **bomba** bomb.

12. **idioms** style of expression.

The lesson to Tijuana is clear:

She belongs to Mexico.

692 A Turbulent Time (1625–1798)

twenties, emblazoned in English with "Greetings from Old Mexico."

One sympathizes with the curator's dilemma. How does one depict the history of so unmonumental a city, a city occasioned by defeat and submission to the enemy's will?

The treaty ending the Mexican-American War ruled a longitudinal line between the Gulf of Mexico and the Pacific Ocean. For decades thereafter, Tijuana remained vacant land at the edge of the sea, an arid little clause dangling from Mexico's disgraced nineteenth century.

No one in Tijuana is able to fix for me the derivation of the name of the place. Some say it is an Indian name. Some think the town was named for a woman who lived in a shack at the turn of the century, a Mexican Ma Kettle known in the region as Tía Juana.

Mexico City tried to dispose of the name in 1925. By an act of Mexico's congress, Tijuana was proclaimed to be Ciudad Zaragoza. A good name. A patriot's name. The resolution languished in a statute book on a shelf in Mexico City, two thousand miles away.

⑩ ▲ Critical Viewing
Which details in this postcard support the author's message that Tijuana lacks a clear identity as a city?
[Connect]

Critical Reading

Cite textual evidence to support your responses.

⑩ 1. Key Ideas and Details (a) According to the residents of Mexico City, what two things does Tijuana lack? **(b) Interpret:** In what way does geography play a part in this reputation? **(c) Speculate:** What effects might a city that lacks a specific urban plan or a sense of identity have on the community and people who live there?

⑩ 2. Key Ideas and Details (a) According to the essay, which city is actively moving toward its own future? **(b) Hypothesize:** What challenges might arise when a city progresses and grows very quickly? Cite examples from the essay to support your response.

⑩ 3. Integration of Knowledge and Ideas (a) Instead of a cultural center, which other improvement might have benefited Tijuana? **(b) Compare and Contrast:** In what ways is Tijuana more American than Mexican in its culture? **(c) Analyze Cause and Effect:** What effect might Rodriguez's American background have on his perception of Tijuana's cultural identity?

⑩ 4. Integration of Knowledge and Ideas (a) Infer: Which characteristics of Tijuana are likely to appear in a positive light in a tourism advertisement? **(b) Evaluate:** Are these characteristics truly assets to the city? Explain.

from Days of Obligation **693**

- **Writing 3.a, c, d; 4, 5, 6**
- **Language 2.b**

Write a Reflective Essay

Writing
3.a. Engage and orient the reader by setting out a problem, situation, or observation and its significance.

Reflective Essay In this unit, thought-provoking essays by Joseph Addison and Richard Rodriguez offer revealing glimpses of each writer's personality. These **reflective essays** also encourage readers to consider their own personal experiences more deeply. Follow the steps outlined in this workshop to write a reflective essay.

Assignment Write a reflective essay in which you describe an event from your personal experience and then share insights about its significance.

What to Include The assignment summarizes your *purpose*, and your *audience* will be your classmates. To achieve your purpose and engage the audience, include these elements in your essay:

- an explanation of a personal experience that shaped your beliefs
- an organization that clarifies the significance of the events you describe, and a balance between specific events and beliefs
- clear connections between beliefs and events
- a consistent, personal tone

To preview the criteria on which your reflective essay may be assessed, see the rubric on page 701.

Introducing the Assignment

Review the assignment and criteria using the instruction on the student page.

What Do You Notice?

1. Read the excerpt from *Days of Obligation*. Discuss with students the elements that make it a reflective essay.

2. Have a student read the highlighted sentence aloud. **Ask** what makes it special. (**Possible response:** its unusual words)

3. Point out the coordinating conjunction *but,* then **ask** how this word helps create suspense in the sentence. (**Answer:** It signals that Tijuana did not get sewers or streetlights, and so creates curiosity about what Tijuana *did* get.)

4. Point out that the last phrase of the sentence is an appositive that renames *cultural center*. **Ask** which phrase better satisfies the reader's suspense—*cultural center,* or *orange concrete bomba*—and why. (**Possible response:** the latter, because it brings the physical reality of the cultural center to life)

5. Suggest that students use a descriptive appositive in their essays.

Richard Rodriguez on Reflective Essays

Show students Segment 3 on Richard Rodriguez on the *See It!* DVD or via the link in the **Enriched Online Student Edition** at www.PHLitOnline.com. Discuss Rodriguez's approach to reflective writing.

To get a feel for the reflective essay, read this excerpt from *Days of Obligation* by Richard Rodriguez on page 692.

from: Days of Obligation

Prominent along the Paseo de los Héroes is Tijuana's Cultural Center, Mexico City's most insistent token of troth. *Tijuana might better have done with sewers or streetlights, but in 1982 the Mexican government built Tijuana a cultural center, an orange concrete bomba in the brutal architectural idioms of the 1970s.* The main building is a museum, very clean and empty during my visit, except for a janitor who trails me with a vacuum cleaner. Together we tread a ramp past fairly uninteresting displays of Mayan pottery, past folk crafts, past reproductions of political documents and portraits of Mexico's military heroes. The lesson to Tijuana is clear: she belongs to Mexico.

WRITE GUY
Jeff Anderson, M.Ed.

What Do You Notice?

Read the highlighted sentence several times. Then, with a partner, discuss the qualities that make it special. You might consider the following elements:

- word choice
- sentence length
- use of punctuation
- vivid details

Share your group's observations with the class.

694 A Turbulent Time (1625–1798)

Teaching Resources

Unit 3 Resources
Writing Workshop, pp. 245–246

Common Core Companion, pp. 208–234; 318–321

Professional Development Guidebook
Rubrics for Self-Assessment: Reflective Essays, pp. 293–294.

Graphic Organizer Transparencies
Rubric for Self-Assessment, p. 127
Plot Diagram, p. 297
Three-Column Chart, p. 299

See It! DVD
Richard Rodriguez, Segments 3 and 4

All resources are available at **www.PHLitOnline.com**

Prewriting and Planning

Choosing Your Topic

To choose an event to focus on, use one of these strategies:

• **Freewriting** Write for five minutes about key experiences in your life and beliefs you hold strongly. Jot down as many ideas as you can. Then, look for connections between general beliefs and specific events.

• **Top-Five List** Make a list of five times in your life when you discovered something wonderful. Scan *journals*, if necessary, to help generate this list. For each key event, note what you learned and think about why this discovery has remained important to you.

Narrowing Your Topic

Focus on an insight. Once you have selected an event, focus your essay by stating your key insight in one sentence. Then, develop ideas and examples that explain and support that insight.

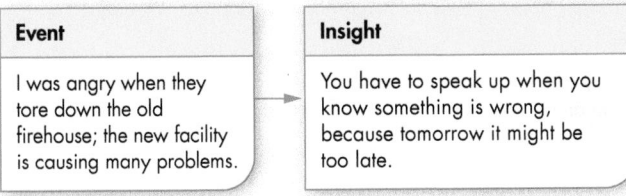

Gathering Details

Make connections. Consider how your experiences relate to themes in the world at large. Organize your thoughts in a diagram like the one shown. Then, conduct research to deepen your knowledge about your subject. Talk with friends and family, or use the library or the Internet to gather details about past events or issues that relate to your personal experience.

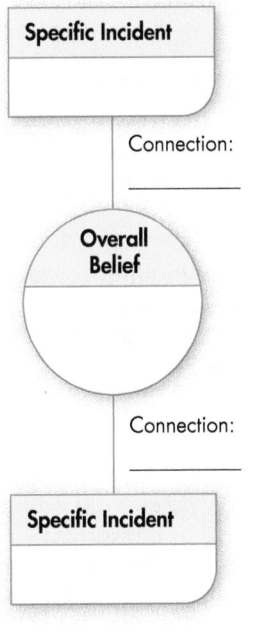

Preparing Rhetorical Strategies

While preparing to write about an event, remember that you can use a variety of different rhetorical strategies in addition to narration, or story telling. These strategies include *description* (when you describe people, things, and places), *exposition* (when you set forth general ideas), and *persuasion* (when you try to convince the reader that your beliefs are true).

Applying Understanding by Design Principles

Clarifying Expected Outcomes: Using Rubrics

• Before students begin work on this assignment, have them preview the **Rubric for Self-Assessment**, page 701, to learn what qualities their reflective essays must have. A copy of this Rubric appears in the *Professional Development Guidebook,* page 293.

• Review the criteria in the Rubric with the class. Before students use the Rubric to assess their own writing, work with them to rate the Student Model (p. 700) using the Rubric.

• If you wish to assess students' reflective essays with either a 4-point or 6-point scoring rubric, see the *Professional Development Guidebook,* pages 293–294.

Prewriting and Planning

1. Introduce the prewriting and planning strategies using the instruction on the student page.

2. Have students apply the strategies to choose and narrow a topic and gather details.

Teaching the Strategies

1. Have students choose topics. Remind students that their potential topics should cover experiences that students would wish to share with others.

2. Have students work in small groups. Students should share their ideas and ask for feedback. Group members should ask clarifying questions such as "Why was this event important?"

3. Tell students to use the graphic organizer to make connections between freewriting ideas and the beliefs they support.

4. Encourage students to create summary sentences.

Think Aloud: Model Choosing Your Topic

To model the strategy of narrowing a topic, use the following "think aloud." Say to students:

Before I write, I think about an experience and what I learned from it. For example, I I learned that persistence pays.

Six Traits Focus

✔	Ideas		Word Choice
✔	Organization		Sentence Fluency
	Voice		Conventions

PH WRITING COACH | Grade 12

Students will find additional information on reflective essays in Chapter 5.

Prentice Hall EssayScorer

A writing prompt for this mode of writing can be found on the *Prentice Hall Essay Scorer* at **www.PHLitOnline.com**.

695

Drafting

1. Introduce the drafting strategies using the instruction on the student page.

2. Have students apply the strategies as they draft their essays.

Teaching the Strategies

1. Remind students that their opening paragraph should include mention of the specific incident that spurred a more general insight.

2. Explain that it is essential that students write with a consistent tone in their essays and resist deviating from that tone.

3. It may help students to think of the body of their essay as the story of the incident that led them to a moment of insight. Suggest that students use a timeline or storyboard to plot out the incident.

4. Encourage students to elaborate on the important details in their essays. The details they mention can be descriptions that help the readers imagine the scene, dialogue that makes an incident come to life, or even an internal monologue revealing the writer's thoughts. Challenge students to elaborate on or explore at least three details in their writing.

Six Traits Focus

✔	Ideas	✔	Word Choice
✔	Organization		Sentence Fluency
✔	Voice		Conventions

Drafting

Shaping Your Writing

Decide where to start. A well-organized reflective essay alternates between *broader themes* or generalizations and *specific incidents*. Your introduction should include both. Consider these organizations for your opening:

- State your overall belief and then give one or two tantalizing details about the incidents that led you to it.
- Describe an event and then tell the surprising insight you drew from it. Your essay will make the full connection clear.

Establish a tone. Introduce an appropriate tone for your essay from the beginning, and stay with it throughout. A serious, straightforward tone is appropriate, but you might also consider using one of these:

- **Ironic tone:** a good tone to use when your details show that things do not always work out as expected or intended
- **Humorous tone:** a logical choice when your examples are amusing

Model: Experimenting With Specific Tones

Ironic Tone
I welcomed my coach's criticism as warmly as any self-centered ten-year-old might. I was quite comfortable postponing any action until the following year, by which time I expected the matter would be forgotten.

Humorous Tone
Having a little brother is not as big a pain as people say. It's worse. Yet, after years of his tattling and tagging along, one incident brought home to me how important family is—even little brothers. I no longer want to sell him to the circus. Not unless they've raised their prices.

Providing Elaboration

Explode a moment. Expand key descriptions by telling more about what happened, what something looked like, or how the people involved—including you—reacted. Mark moments you can "explode," and use the margin to write the details you want to add.

Model: Revising to Explode a Moment

Julie was cute and dated the most popular boys in our school.
 a cheerleader and
She was ∧ a Student Council member. She was also the most
 , and she welcomed an understudy
confident person I knew∧.

These additional details provide more description.

696 A Turbulent Time (1625–1798)

Common Core
State Standards

Writing
3.c. Use a variety of techniques to sequence events so that they build on one another to create a coherent whole and build toward a particular tone and outcome.
3.d. Use precise words and phrases, telling details, and sensory language to convey a vivid picture of the experiences, events, setting, and/or characters.

Strategies for
Using a Graphic Organizer

If students have trouble adopting a tone in their essay, suggest that they try writing a few sentences of the essay in two different ways, using two different tones. Challenge students to model their writing on the excerpts that appear in the graphic organizer on this page.

Students should write a few sentences of their essay in a straightforward tone, and a few sentences using a humorous or ironic tone. Tell students to show their sentences to a partner and ask for feedback about which tone is more effective.

Writers on Writing

Richard Rodriguez On Reflective Writing

Richard Rodriguez is the author of *Days of Obligation* (p. 689).

These paragraphs appear in *Days of Obligation*, a philosophical travel book of mine that ranges over several centuries and back and forth across the U.S.-Mexico border. Each chapter, like the fragment below, is autobiographical. But that is only to say, memory is my guide throughout; memory forces me to reflect on the lessons within my life.

"In my reflective essays, the 'I' moves freely."

—Richard Rodriguez

from *Days of Obligation*

Our last house on "Eye" Street was across from an old cemetery. No memory attached to it. The grass was watered and cut once a month by the city. There were no scrolls or wrought-iron fences; no places to put flowers. There were granite plaques level with the ground. Early dates. Solitary names. Men. Men who had come early to California and died young.

No grandsons or granddaughters came forward in the 1950s when Sacramento needed the land to build a school, a new Sutter Junior High School. A plywood fence was hammered up around the cemetery and, within that discretionary veil, bulldozers chugged and grunted, pulling up moist hairy mounds of what had once been the light of day; trucks came to carry it all away.

In early November, white tulle fog rises from the valley floor. My father is easy with this ancient weather reminiscent of the sea. My father is whistling this morning as he scrambles two eggs. My mother turns away from the window, pulling her blue bathrobe closer around her throat. I am sitting at the kitchen table. I am sixteen years old. I am pouring milk onto Sugar Frosted Flakes, watching milk rise in the bowl. My parents will die. I will die. Everyone I know will someday be dead. The blue parakeet my mother has taught to say "pretty boy" swings upon his little trapeze, while my mother pours coffee.

> Each paragraph is about remembrance or the refusal to remember: civic amnesia; the forgetfulness of ancestors; the middle-aged writer's teenage discovery of death; the adult's inability to remember winter.

> Images of nature are everywhere in this meditation on death—the parakeet, winter fog, clumps of grass upturned by bulldozers. As the contending images suggest: Death is the end of life yet also a part of nature.

> Notice here how the most astonishing ideas of life can come not with a drumbeat or violin, but in an instant of a Saturday morning, between spoonfuls of cereal.

Writing Workshop **697**

Differentiated Instruction for Universal Access

Strategies for Reflective Writing

Give students these suggestions for revising their reflective writing:

- Look for places in your draft where you can include a detail that makes a scene complete. For example, in the excerpt from *Days of Obligation,* Rodriguez includes the detail of his mother pulling her robe tighter around her throat. The detail is a small one, but it gives the reader a vivid picture.
- Include details that appeal to all of the senses, as Rodriguez does. He appeals to a sense of

taste and smell (father cooking eggs), sound (parakeet saying "Pretty boy"), touch (mother and her robe), and sight (milk rising in a cereal bowl). Sensory details help writing come alive.

- Remember that the event or moment at the center of your reflective essay does not have to be an important one. Notice how Rodriguez manages to capture his teenage self's realization that life is short as he was eating cereal on an ordinary morning.

Richard Rodriguez on Reflective Writing

Review the passage on the student page with the class, using Richard Rodriguez's comments to deepen students' understanding of the process of writing a reflective essay.

Teaching the Strategies

1. Show students Segment 4 on Richard Rodriguez on *See it!* DVD or from this page in the **Enriched Online Student Edition**. Discuss Rodriguez's idea that literature shows readers that they are connected to people who are not like them. Ask students how writing about their own lives may connect them to others.

2. Point out that Rodriguez was inspired by many writers but does not believe that writers should be role models. He suggests instead that readers should learn from a writer's words, not from a writer's life. Ask students to think about what their own writing, particularly their reflective essays, might teach readers.

3. Discuss Rodriguez's comments on the excerpt from *Days of Obligation.* Talk about how he acknowledges how memory is faulty and how, as a mature writer, he realizes how different he is from his younger self. Ask students to consider how distance from an event in their life affects how they remember it. Challenge students, as they write their reflective essays, to be aware of how they have changed since the time they are writing about.

4. Have a volunteer read aloud the annotation next to the third paragraph of the model on page 697. Point out how Rodriguez manages to find a meaningful idea about life during an ordinary moment. Challenge students to do the same in their reflective essays.

Enriched Online Student Edition
Show or assign the video online at
www.PHLitOnline.com.

697

Revising

1. Introduce the revising strategies using the instruction on the student page.
2. Have students apply the strategies as they revise their essays.

Teaching the Strategies

1. Encourage students to review their drafts for any places that are "narrative heavy" or "narrative light" and to incorporate additional information to balance their reflective essays.

2. Remind students of the strategy of "exploding a moment" as they revise. If a section of the essay needs more details, they can consider how to explode a moment and add more description or dialogue.

3. Remind students that they can brainstorm and use other idea-generating strategies when revising, especially when they are adding new details.

4. It may help students to think of the connection between incident and insight as a cause-and-effect relationship. Students can use transitional words and phrases that convey cause and effect, such as *therefore, because,* or *as a result,* to help the reader see the connections.

5. Suggest that student partners share their drafts and consider any suggestions the other makes. Remind students to look for tone, clarity of ideas, and connections at this stage, rather than proofreading issues.

Six Traits Focus

✔	Ideas	✔	Word Choice
✔	Organization		Sentence Fluency
✔	Voice		Conventions

Revising

Revising Your Overall Structure

Balance narration with reflection. Review your writing to make sure that you *maintained a balance between specific incidents and general ideas.*

1. Bracket any segments of the essay that describe specific events.
2. Mark in red any passages where you have included a detail that does not set a scene or advance ideas.
3. Use a different color to mark the points where you provide your interpretation of events.

> **Model: Editing to Omit Unnecessary Details**
>
> [I giggled and flirted my way through the next two years.]
> ✔ [During that time, my Dad got a new job and we moved to a different neighborhood.] Through it all, I felt as if I were putting on an act. [In the middle of my junior year, I received my first ACT results.] I was not happy with my scores.

The writer deleted this incident because it did not contribute toward her insight or provide necessary background.

4. Looking at your essay as a whole, determine whether you have maintained a balance between specific events and the interpretation of those events.

Revising Your Sentences

Strengthen your connections. Examine the passages where you shift between events and the generalizations to which they have led you. Consider using transitional words or phrases to clarify the connections for your readers.

Examples:

And that is how . . .
Suddenly I understood that . . .
After this happened, . . .
As a result, . . .
For the very first time, . . .
I gradually became aware that . . .

Peer Review: Ask a partner to identify passages in your essay where your connections could be stronger. Discuss ways to strengthen and clarify the connections.

Evaluate your partner's suggestions. Then, make your revisions and share your work with your partner.

Common Core State Standards

Writing
4. Produce clear and coherent writing in which the development, organization, and style are appropriate to task, purpose, and audience.
5. Develop and strengthen writing as needed by revising, focusing on addressing what is most significant for a specific purpose and audience.

698 A Turbulent Time (1625–1798)

Strategies for
Improving Word Choice

Give students the following suggestions for revising word choice:

- Look for places in your draft where an added detail can expand a moment or bring an idea to life.
- Circle "to be" verbs—such as *am, is, are, was, were, be, being, been.* Challenge yourself to change some of them to more vivid action

verbs. You may need to rewrite the sentences when you change the verb.

- Replace clichéd expressions with more precise and original phrases. For example, replace the trite phrase "my feet were as cold as ice" with "my feet were so cold I thought they would crack into tiny pieces when I walked."

Developing Your Style

Moving From Personal to Universal

A reflective essay moves from personal experiences to universal truths. Be careful to maintain your **personal voice** even when generalizing.

- Maintain your personal tone, even when stating general truths. Look for ways to inject your personality into each section of your essay.
- Be sure that you really agree with the statements you make. Your essay may feel insincere if you say something just because you think it sounds good or because you think your audience will agree.

Here is how one writer revised a universal statement that felt stiff and artificial. The revised version feels more personal and sincere.

Stiff Voice	Personal Voice
Families help us learn and grow. We achieve our best when we have their love and support. Your family's encouragement can help you accomplish anything.	For better or worse, your family knows you better than anyone else. As a result, they won't let you get away with doing anything less than your best. That can be a pain, but it also helps you succeed.

Find It in Your Reading

Read or review Richard Rodriguez's introductory essay on page 686.

1. Find two personal experiences that Rodriguez discusses in the essay.
2. Evaluate the lessons that Rodriguez draws from these experiences.
3. Look for the language that lets you "hear" Rodriguez's unique voice.

Apply It to Your Writing

Review your draft. For each paragraph, follow these steps:

1. Underline the specific events and details that you have included.
2. Circle the broader, more general lessons, observations, or beliefs about life to which these events and details have led you. Then, answer these questions:
   - Do you genuinely believe the statement?
   - Do you state your belief in a personal way?
3. Revise your essay, as necessary, to maintain your personal voice.

Developing Your Style

1. Introduce the concepts of life lessons and the sense of an ending to students using the instruction on the page.
2. Have the students complete the Find It in Your Reading and Apply It to Your Writing activities.

Teaching the Strategies

1. Make sure that students understand that one of the purposes of writing a reflective essay is to discuss an idea that they believe or value. Students' essays will have more value if they articulate why their ideas or beliefs are important.
2. Review with students the options for effective endings that appear in the chart on this page. Discuss how a lackluster conclusion to an otherwise interesting essay can leave readers disappointed.

Find It in Your Reading

1. **Possible response:** He recalls a visit to Tijuana and the pieces he writes for newspapers.
2. **Possible response:** He realizes that becoming a character in his own report could make his writing biased or prejudiced, but it could also make his writing become literature.
3. **Possible response:** Students may cite details about Tijuana in the fifth paragraph, among other things.

Six Traits Focus

	Ideas	✔	Word Choice
	Organization	✔	Sentence Fluency
✔	Voice		Conventions

Differentiated Instruction   for Universal Access

Strategy for Special-Needs Students
During the revision stage, it may help students to articulate the message they hope their essay imparts. Allow student partners to talk about the lessons at the center of their essays. The partners should take turns making notes, as precisely as possible, of what their partners say. Then students should review their essays to see whether the message comes through clearly in the essay.

Strategy for Advanced Writers
Tell students that the connections they draw between an incident and a general insight should challenge the readers. While they should provide plenty of details and information for their readers, they should not feel as though they have to "connect all the dots" for them. Readers will appreciate having to make inferences. It will make reading the essay a more interesting experience.

Student Model

Review the Student Model with the class, using the annotations to analyze the writer's incorporation of the elements of a reflective essay.

Teaching the Strategies

1. Explain that the Student Model is a sample, and that essays may be longer.

2. **Ask** students to identify the specific incident or topic of Ashley's essay and how she connects it to something more general. **Answer:** The incident Ashley chooses is learning that a writer set stories in a place he'd never visited; her general insight is that she had been attempting something foreign in her own life, and it was better to be true to herself.

3. Discuss with students what details make Ashley's account seem balanced between individual and general ideas.

4. Point out how Ashley keeps her prose energetic with a consistent tone and vivid details and imagery.

5. Discuss with students how Ashley reports incidents that lead to her realization and how she states her central insight in her conclusion.

Connecting to Real-Life Writing

Explain that good reflective writing offers readers or listeners an insight into the writer's mind and life. Tell students that reflective writing is often used in speeches, introductions, or toasts to honor friends, family, or co-workers. Managers use it in memos and meetings; religious leaders use it in sermons and lectures; and teachers and coaches use it to communicate what they have learned to their students and protégés.

Student Model: Ashley Philips, Ruston, LA

Coming Home

North Carolina novelist T. R. Pearson told me recently that when he was a teenager, he had set his stories in New York City, though he had never been there. "I thought New York was where it was," he laughed, adding that the fiction he had produced during this period was uniformly bad. Almost accidentally, he had begun to write about the life he really knew—life in little towns like Reidsville, North Carolina. It was only then that he succeeded at what he was attempting. Pearson's remarks set me thinking about my own life. Like Tom Pearson, I had spent a part of my life attempting something foreign and feeling unhappy with the result.

When I was in grade school, I read through every book in our classroom and did special reports. Research thrilled me. Books were the most important part of my life. I knew who I was. And I was happy.

In my freshman year, though, I decided that my own life paled compared with that of my older friend Julie. Julie was popular and dated the most popular boys in our school. She was a cheerleader and a Student Council member. She was also the most confident person I knew, and she welcomed an understudy. I borrowed Julie's clothes and copied her hairstyles, right down to the huge hair bows that were her signature. By the end of the year, I had decided to run for cheerleader.

I giggled and flirted my way through the next two years. Through it all, I felt as if I was putting on an act. In the middle of my junior year, I received my first ACT results. I was not happy with my scores. I began to reevaluate my life. I decided not to run for cheerleader. I paid less attention to who was popular and concentrated on friendships that were comfortable and fun. I threw myself into my science project and was exhilarated when I took top honors at the state science fair. By the end of the year, a teacher had invited me to serve as editor of a literary magazine. I felt that I was home again.

This December, as I sat listening to T. R. Pearson discuss the path that had led him to his true subject, I felt I knew exactly what he was talking about. It was a warm December day. A late fall sun filtered through the pine trees onto my English teacher's deck. Four other students and I sat in deck chairs and listened to Pearson speak about writing. It all felt so natural. This, I thought, is the kind of world I want to live in. I realized then that you can never get anywhere if you leave your true self behind. At that moment, I could not, for all the world, remember why cheerleading or Julie's boys or big hair bows had ever mattered.

Ashley sets up a clear connection between the narrative that follows and her general point: Success depends on being true to oneself.

By carefully selecting details, Ashley includes just enough incidents to support and balance her general insight.

Ashley's short, decisive self-descriptions establish a consistent tone.

Ashley reports incidents that clearly lead to her realization.

In her conclusion, Ashley clearly states her general insight. (See Developing Your Style on p. 699.)

Editing and Proofreading

Focus on commas. Focus on commas between items in a series, commas in compound sentences, and commas that set off appositives.

Focus on spelling. When adding -ly to form an adverb from an adjective ending in -le, drop the -le. *Reasonable* becomes *reasonably*.

Spiral Review Conventions Earlier in this unit, you learned about comparative and superlative adjectives and adverbs (p. 493); participles, gerunds, and infinitives (p. 503); and fixing misplaced and dangling modifiers (p. 539). Check your persuasive essay to be sure you have used those conventions correctly.

Publishing, Presenting, and Reflecting

Consider one of the following ways to share your writing:

Create a radio broadcast. Use your essay as the basis for a radio opinion piece. Rehearse your presentation, looking for ways to match the tone of your voice to the tone of your essay. Try to "tell" incidents or events rather than read them verbatim. If possible, record your presentation so that you can critique it later.

Publish on the Internet. Post your reflective essay on a Web site for student writing. Invite feedback from other writers.

Reflect on your writing. Jot down your thoughts on the experience of writing a reflective essay. Begin by answering these questions:

- What have I learned about moving from the particular to the general, and back again, in my writing?
- What new aspects of the topic did I discover as I developed plans for my essay?

Rubric for Self-Assessment

Evaluate your reflective essay using the following criteria and rating scale, or, with your classmates, determine your own reasonable evaluation criteria.

Criteria	Rating Scale				
	not very				very
Focus: How clearly do you show how a personal experience led you to an insight?	1	2	3	4	5
Organization: How logical is your organization?	1	2	3	4	5
Support/Elaboration: How fully do you describe the events that influenced your beliefs?	1	2	3	4	5
Style: How well do you establish a personal tone?	1	2	3	4	5
Conventions: How correct is your grammar, especially your use of commas?	1	2	3	4	5

Common Core State Standards

Writing
5. Develop and strengthen writing as needed by editing, focusing on addressing what is most significant for a specific purpose and audience.
6. Use technology, including the Internet, to produce, publish, and update individual or shared writing products in response to ongoing feedback, including new arguments or information.

Language
2.b. Spell correctly.

Editing and Proofreading

1. Introduce the editing and proofreading focuses using the instruction on the student page.
2. Have students read their reflective essays carefully, marking them for line edits.

Teaching the Strategies

1. Have students go through their essays and identify any errors in comma usage. As a class, review some comma use errors.
2. Have students read their essays aloud in a soft voice to find run-on sentences or incorrectly punctuated sentences.

Six Traits Focus

Ideas		Word Choice	
Organization		Sentence Fluency	✔
Voice		Conventions	✔

ASSESS

Publishing, Presenting, and Reflecting

1. Ask students to reread their essays, considering which elements might appeal to an audience. Writing containing vivid descriptions and snappy dialogue might work well on the radio.
2. Encourage students to practice delivering their radio presentations to a friend. Students should ask for feedback, paying particular attention to the tone of voice.
3. Ask volunteers to share what they learned from the experience of presenting or publishing.

Strategies for Test Taking

When taking a test that includes a reflective writing prompt, students should be careful not to write an essay about an experience without making a connection to a larger theme, issue, or insight. Most reflective essay prompts encourage students to tell about an experience from their lives that has taught them an important lesson. Encourage students to estimate how much of the essay they should spend retelling the event and how much they should spend explaining its significance. Remind students to balance the two elements as much as possible.

Analyze a Literary Work

1. Read the instructions for Analyze a Literary Work with the students. Provide class time for them to review and reflect on each of the selections in the unit.

2. List each of the literary elements and stylistic devices described on the student page. Be sure students are clear on the differences between each of the elements. Ask students to name any other literary elements or stylistic devices to consider during their analyses. Help students identify one or two selections that exemplify use of the literary devices.

3. After students have selected a work to analyze, allow class time for them to record their observations. Circle the classroom and provide clarification and guidance as needed. Check that students correctly identify literary elements and stylistic devices. Allow students who are working on different selections but who have identified common literary elements to discuss and compare the authors' uses of the elements.

4. To assist students as they begin to write their analytical essays, point out the importance of a strong thesis statement. Ask for volunteers willing to share their thesis statements. Provide suggestions for students whose statements need work.

Oral Interpretation of a Literary Work

An **oral interpretation** is an oral reading of a literary work that conveys the presenter's understanding of the nuances of a text. Long before the invention of the printing press, poets and storytellers performed for their communities, relying on voice and gesture to convey meaning. People still present literary works in this manner today.

Analyze a Literary Work

Review the text. Make a copy of a speech, poem, or soliloquy from this unit. Choose one that you truly enjoy. Then, analyze the work to identify the use of literary elements and stylistic devices, such as the following:

- **Tone:** the author's attitude. Determine if it is formal, earnest, satirical, approving, or critical.
- **Author's Style:** the way a writer uses language to express ideas. Analyze the elements that help reveal a writer's voice. For example, notice sentence lengths, word choice, images, and characters' personalities, as well as uses of symbols, figurative language, and description.
- **Imagery:** descriptions that appeal to the senses. Study the author's images of places, objects, and experiences.
- **Theme:** the overall message of the selection. Consider the writer's purpose and note ideas or images that are repeated.
- **Nuance and Ambiguity:** Literature can be interpreted in many ways. Look for actions or symbols whose meanings are not directly stated, and decide how you understand the author's meaning in these items.

A review of these elements will help you understand the selection's *significant ideas*. Read the work several times to help you understand its layers of meanings or to find areas where you may have questions. Pay attention to denotative, or surface-level meanings. Eventually, connotative meanings—those that are deeper or more subtle—will become apparent. Look to other texts as well to support your ideas. Record your observations by *highlighting, circling words, and making marginal notes*.

Write your analysis. Use your notes to write a brief analytical essay that details your understanding of the text. Focus on your interpretation of any *complexities of the text*. Make specific references to the literary elements noted above and the ways in which they affect your understanding. Also, consider including *rhetorical strategies* in your analysis, such as describing other interpretations or narrating your first impressions of the work. Use this essay to introduce your oral presentation.

Common Core
State Standards

Reading Literature
7. Analyze multiple interpretations of a story, drama, or poem, evaluating how each version interprets the source text.

Speaking and Listening
6. Adapt speech to a variety of contexts and tasks, demonstrating a command of formal English when indicated or appropriate.

Rehearse Speaking Strategies

To perform your oral interpretation effectively, use these techniques:

Technique	Application	Explore It
Eye Contact	Look at everyone in your audience.	Observe how your teachers look at the whole class while teaching.
Gesture/Movement	Use hand gestures and staging to convey action and emotion.	View a recording of a famous actor or poet performing a literary work and note his or her movements.
Vocalization	Reflect characters' accents and dialects, and enunciate and project your voice.	Research the areas in which your characters are said to live and how they might sound.
Voice Register	Use your voice's highs and lows to create emphasis or differentiate characters.	Practice saying the same sentence with different emphasis and pitch.

Enhance your performance. To further develop your interpretation, consider using simple costumes and props, music, pictures, or sound effects. You can ask a friend to assist with such effects during your performance.

Practice. *Rehearse* in front of a mirror and then in front of family or friends. Be sure to practice your *staging* and the use of any props.

Activities: Deliver and Analyze Oral Interpretations

Ⓒ Comprehension and Collaboration For both activities, use an evaluation form like the one below.

A. Present your interpretation, starting off with an introduction based on your essay. Afterward, apply listeners' feedback to revise your delivery.

B. With a small group, listen to a variety of interpretations of the same work. You may use audio or video recordings, your own interpretations, or a combination of the two. Analyze how each version interprets the source text.

Evaluation Form for Oral Interpretation

Title and Author of Literary Selection: _____

Which aspects of the work does the interpreter emphasize? _____

Does the interpreter use gestures? How do they help the performance? _____

How does he or she use voice techniques? _____

How well does the interpreter maintain eye contact? _____

Name one thing the interpreter could do better next time. _____

Rehearse Speaking Strategies

1. Model an oral interpretation performance focusing on the techniques listed on the student page. Ask students to identify and provide feedback for the techniques used throughout the model.

2. Provide opportunities for students to follow the suggestions in the Explore It section of the performance technique table. In particular, ask for student volunteers to share their applications of the Voice Register suggestion.

Activities: Deliver and Analyze Oral Interpretations

1. Divide the class into pairs of students and allow partners to deliver their oral interpretations to each other. As each student shares his or her performance, have the partner fill out an evaluation form like the one shown on the student page. Remind students to provide constructive feedback when filling out the evaluation forms.

2. Before students present their interpretations to the whole class, provide additional time for them to revise their performances based on feedback from the evaluation forms.

3. To evaluate students' analyses, use the **Presenting an Oral Response to Literature** rubric, page 302 in the *Professional Development Guidebook*.

Differentiated Instruction *for Universal Access*

Support for Special-Needs Students
Allow students to work in small groups to analyze a literary work. Together, students should identify the author's use of literary elements, share their observations and understandings of the selection with one another, and divide the delivery of the oral interpretation into sections.

Support for Less Proficient Readers
Assist students with the analysis portion of the assignment by providing copies of selections in which the literary elements or stylistic devices used by an author have already been highlighted or underlined. Ask students to label each passage with the name of the appropriate element. Help students identify the ways in which the highlighted passages affect the meaning of the entire selection.

 Common Core
State Standards

• Language 4, 4.a, c

Etymology: Political Science/History Terms

1. Teach the skills, using the instruction and charts on the student page.

2. Point out that some dictionary entries provide the etymology of the words. Many dictionaries also provide a list of Greek and Latin roots and their meanings.

Think Aloud: Model the Skills

Say to students:

I know that the etymology of a word not only provides the meaning of its components, but also may contextualize the word in a historical sense. After the Normans conquered England in 1066, the new legal system was framed in their French- and Latin-derived language. Therefore, when I come across a word concerning administration, government, or law, I know that it is likely to have a French or Latin origin. For example, if I see a word containing the word root *-jud-*, I know that it likely entered the English lexicon around 1066 and that the word has something to do with law or judging.

Vocabulary Workshop

Etymology: Political Science/History Terms

If you were given the original manuscript of *Beowulf*, you would need an Anglo-Saxon scholar to read it for you, so different is Old English from the language we speak today. In contrast, you could read much of *The Canterbury Tales* on your own. By Chaucer's day, Anglo-Saxon had been transformed into Middle English, a language that shares much of the grammar and vocabulary of our modern tongue. The Norman invasion of England in 1066 brought thousands of French and Latin words into the vocabulary. Since French and Latin were the languages of the ruling class, many of the new words referred to administration, government, and law. The chart below introduces you to key affixes and roots stemming from these words. An understanding of these word parts can help you define unfamiliar terms you encounter in political science and history.

 Common Core
State Standards

Language
4. Determine or clarify the meaning of unknown and multiple-meaning words and phrases based on *grades 11–12 reading and content*, choosing flexibly from a range of strategies.
4.a. Use context as a clue to the meaning of a word or phrase.
4.c. Consult general and specialized reference materials, both print and digital, to find the pronunciation of a word or determine or clarify its precise meaning, its part of speech, its etymology, or its standard usage.

Prefixes	Roots	Suffixes
ab- (Latin): away from *ad-* (Latin): to; toward *an-* (Greek): not; without *ex-, e-* (Latin): outside; out of; away *pro-* (Latin): forward *syn-* (Greek): together; with	*-arch-* (Greek): chief; first; highest; ruler *-dict-* (Latin): say or tell *-doc-* (Latin): teach *-jud-, -jur-* (Latin): to judge; law, swear *-urbs-* (Latin): city *-ven-, -vent-* (Latin): come	*-an* (Latin): belonging to *-ate* (Latin): characterized by *-ation* (Latin): action or process; result *-dom* (Anglo-Saxon): state; condition; domain; rank *-ity-, ty* (Latin): state or quality *-y* (Latin): condition or state

Practice

Practice A: Choose the word from the list that fits each numbered definition. Explain your choices with reference to each word's root and affixes.

anarchy   edict   judiciary
adjudicate   urban   syndicate

1. a decree issued by an authority
2. absence of political authority
3. relating to a city
4. government branch that administers justice
5. an association of individuals formed to carry out a project
6. to judge a case

Practice B: Using a dictionary, trace the etymologies of the following political science and history terms: *prerogative, doom, allegiance, property, deed.* Identify the language of origin and the point at which the word entered the English language.

Practice

Answers
Practice A

1. edict: *e-:* out of; *dict:* tell
2. anarchy: *an-:* without; *arch:* ruler; *-y:* state
3. urban: *-urbs-:* city; *-an:* belonging to
4. judiciary: *-jud-:* to judge; *-y:* state
5. syndicate: *syn-:* together; *dict:* tell; *-ate:* characterized by
6. adjudicate: *ad-:* toward; *jud:* to judge; *-ate:* characterized by

Practice B
Possible responses

prerogative: Latin; 1293

doom: from Old English for judgment or law; circa 1600

allegiance: Anglo-French; 1732

property: Anglo-French; 1760

deed: Old English; circa 1300

Vocabulary Acquisition and Use: Context Clues

Context clues are words or phrases that help readers clarify the meanings of unfamiliar words in a text. By using context clues, you can determine the word or words that complete a sentence. Sentence Completion questions appear in most standardized tests. In these types of questions, you are given sentences with one or more missing words. Your task is to use the context to choose the correct word or words to complete each sentence logically. Try this strategy: (1) Identify the meaning of each answer option. (2) If you are unsure of the meaning of a word, use roots, prefixes, and suffixes, or similar words to help you understand the meaning. (3) Test those potential meanings in the sentence.

Practice

This exercise is modeled after the Sentence Completion exercises that appear in the Critical Reading section of the SAT.

Directions: Each of the following sentences is missing one or two words. Choose the word or set of words that best completes each sentence.

Test-Taking Tip
Pace yourself: Questions are easier early in the test and more challenging later in the test.

1. The critic praised the actress, calling her performance ___?___.
   A. devout
   B. eminent
   C. lamentable
   D. transcendent
   E. transient

2. Due to the manager's ___?___, the staff was whimsically assigned to different projects.
   A. caprices
   B. credulity
   C. discretion
   D. guile
   E. resolution

3. Her earlier ___?___ forgotten, she enjoyed a life of ___?___.
   A. abasement . . . expedients
   B. dominions . . . covetousness
   C. penury . . . affluence
   D. piety . . . distemper
   E. schism . . . resolution

4. The pleas of the ___?___ peasant did not affect the ___?___ noble.
   A. delirious . . . inconstant
   B. importuning . . . obdurate
   C. ingenuous . . . temperate
   D. prodigious . . . dubious
   E. risible . . . substantial

5. The owl set out each evening on its ___?___ search for food.
   A. amorous
   B. heedless
   C. nocturnal
   D. notorious
   E. venerable

6. The speaker's arguments did nothing to ___?___ the situation.
   A. breach
   B. illumine
   C. presume
   D. reconfigure
   E. transgress

Practice

1. Introduce the skill, using the instruction on the student page. Be sure students understand how context clues can reveal the meaning of an unknown word.

2. You may wish to go over the first item with students, applying the "define unfamiliar words" strategy. Read the first item to the class, including all of the answer choices. As you read the list of choices a second time, ask students to raise their hands when they think a word fits the sentence meaning. Point out that *devout* is similar to the word *devoted* and relates to religious commitment. Point out that *eminent* is similar to the word *prominent* and means "outstanding, distinguished, or renowned." *Lamentable* contains the suffix *-able*, meaning "subject to." A performance subject to *lament* would be unsatisfactory and unworthy of praise. *Transcendent* contains the prefix *trans-*, which means "across or beyond" and refers to a quality that surpasses ordinary or merely physical experience. *Transient* also contains the prefix *trans-* and describes a quality of impermanence. After trying these words in the sentence, students may agree that *eminent* works best, selecting *B* as their answer.

3. Assign the remaining items in the Practice Test. Point out that some questions require pairs of words, rather than a single word, for completion. Allow students six minutes to complete the questions.

Answers:
1. B
2. A
3. C
4. B
5. C
6. B

Strategies for
Test Taking

Remind students of the importance of reading Sentence Completion test items thoroughly. Tell students that crossing out incorrect answers can help eliminate confusion and ensure that they do not mark incorrect answers.

Using the Test-Taking Practice

In this Test-Taking Practice (pp. 706–709), students apply the skills in Unit 3. The Practice is divided into three sections.

1. Before assigning each section, review the relevant Unit skills with students. Discuss the characteristics of each type of test and specific strategies for test questions, using the instruction that precedes each Practice.

2. Set a time limit for the multiple-choice items in each Practice, allowing a little more than one minute per question. Use the designated time allowance set for the Timed Writing section.

3. Administer each section. Have students write the starting time at the top of their papers. When half of the time for the multiple-choice items has run out, ask students to write the time next to the answer on which they are working. Have them make similar notes when the time is three-quarters through and again when time is up. Follow a similar procedure for the Timed Writing assignment.

4. Review with students the pacing reflected in their notes.

Reteaching

Have students complete each Practice. Then, use the Reteach charts to determine which skills require reteaching, based on the items students answer incorrectly. Reteach these skills prior to assigning the **Benchmark Test 5 Unit 3 Resources,** pages 147–152.

Test-Taking Practice

 **Common Core State Standards**

RL.11-12.1, RL.11-12.3, RL.11-12.4; L.11-12.1, L.11-12.3, L.11-12.4.a
[For the full wording of the standards, see the standards chart in the front of your textbook.]

Reading Test: Humanities Passage

Humanities passages are one of the four types of reading selections found on standardized tests. These passages come from memoirs or essays and cover subjects in the arts and literature, philosophy, and entertainment media. Questions can focus on main ideas and supporting details, on the author's tone and style, and on the meaning of particular words or sentences. They may require you to make generalizations or analyze causes and effects.

Practice

The following exercise is modeled after the ACT Reading Test, Humanities section.

Directions: Read the following passage, taken from John Donne's "Meditation 17." Then, choose the *best* answer to each question.

> No man is an island, entire of itself: every man is a piece of the continent, a part of the main. If a clod be washed away by the sea, Europe is the less, as well as if a promontory were, as well as if a manor of thy friend's or of thine own were. Any man's death diminishes
> 5   me because I am involved in mankind, and therefore never send to know for whom the bell tolls; it tolls for thee. Neither can we call this a begging of misery or a borrowing of misery, as though we were not miserable enough of ourselves but must fetch in more from the next house, in taking upon us the misery of our neighbors. Truly it were an
> 10   excusable covetousness if we did; for affliction is a treasure, and scarce any man hath enough of it. No man hath affliction enough that is not matured and ripened by it, and made fit for God by that affliction. If a man carry treasure in bullion, or in a wedge of gold, and have none coined into current money, his treasure will not defray him as he travels.
> 15   Tribulation is treasure in the nature of it, but it is not current money in the use of it, except we get nearer and nearer our home, heaven, by it.

Strategy

Scan, then read.

- **First, underline words that indicate the author's attitude.** Look for formal language, diction, and rhetorical devices used to make an argument more persuasive.

- **Second, consider how this language contributes to the writer's message.** Ask yourself what effect the writer's feelings have on the ideas he or she presents.

- Finally, answer the questions using this information to guide you.

Strategies for Test Taking

Tell students that they should read the passage carefully to find text that relates to each question. They should avoid the distraction of an answer choice that has information that does not relate directly to the question.

Have students make sure that there are specific details in the passage that match what the question is asking for and that support their chosen answers. Explain that these specific details are proof that the answer is correct.

1. Which of these best paraphrases lines 1–2?
   A. All men are connected to one another, but that is not true of women.
   B. People who live on islands are not isolated from one another.
   C. All people, by natural right, partly own the land where they live.
   D. No person exists in isolation; we are all connected.

2. Which best explains why Donne refers to the *clod* and the *promontory* in lines 2–3?
   F. Referring to both small and large pieces of land strengthens his argument.
   G. He emphasizes that Europe has both lowland and highland areas.
   H. Citing the landholdings of both the poor and the rich reinforces his point.
   J. Mentioning landforms of all shapes and sizes underlines his point that the world is constantly changing.

3. In the context of lines 1–5, it can reasonably be inferred that *diminishes* means:
   A. reduces the amount of light available.
   B. lessens something in quantity or size.
   C. saddens someone; causes grief.
   D. holds dominion over; controls.

4. Which of these best paraphrases lines 5–6?
   F. When church bells signal that someone has died, we should all attend the services.
   G. When church bells signal that someone has died, a part of each of us dies.
   H. One day, the church bell will toll for each of us, signaling our death.
   J. We should not ask why the church bell tolls but consider how morally we have lived our lives.

5. Why does Donne say in lines 6–7 that feeling the death of another person is not "a begging of misery or a borrowing of misery"?
   A. He believes we will be repaid for it in the end.
   B. He thinks that feeling is false rather than heartfelt.
   C. He argues that we are truly affected by that person's death.
   D. He says that we must pay for these feelings with our treasure.

6. From the context of lines 1–10, it can reasonably be inferred that *affliction* means:
   F. fond feelings for another person.
   G. difficult circumstances that cause suffering.
   H. pretending to have a better social status than one does.
   J. sympathy for people who are suffering.

7. Why is it surprising that Donne uses the phrase "excusable covetousness" in line 10 to refer to afflictions?
   A. It is surprising to say people desire afflictions.
   B. It is surprising to call covetousness excusable, because it is a sin.
   C. It is unusual to say people covet what neighbors own.
   D. Earlier in the piece, Donne condemned covetousness.

8. From the context of lines 12–14, it can reasonably be inferred that *bullion* means:
   F. sores upon the feet.
   G. something of value.
   H. money and jewels.
   J. land and property.

Test-Taking Practice **707**

ASSESS/RETEACH

Reading Test
Humanities Passage

1. Introduce the skill using the instruction on page 706. Be sure students understand the strategy set off in the boxed section.

2. You may wish to go over the first test item with students before they take the test. As a class, analyze each choice in the first test item.

   A—Donne uses the word *man* to refer to all humankind, not to exclude women. (Eliminate)

   B—Donne's use of *island* is figurative language. He does not address habitation on islands. (Eliminate)

   C—Donne does not speak of land ownership. (Eliminate)

   D—Donne suggests that every person is a part of the whole of humankind. Correct answer.

3. Assign the Practice exercise. Have students read the passage and answer the questions on their own. Allow 15 minutes for this process, and announce to students when they have five minutes and 1 minute remaining.

Answers

1. D
2. F
3. C
4. G
5. C
6. G
7. A
8. G

Question	Pages to Reteach
1	664
2	480
3	502
4	664
5	480
6	672
7	480
8	502

Differentiated Instruction   for Universal Access

Support for Less Proficient Students
Read the passage with students and help them to summarize it. Then, go over the first test item as a class, guiding students to eliminate incorrect answer choices.

EL Support for English Learners
Read the entire passage with the class and help students to paraphrase it. Review the ten questions, making sure that students understand *paraphrases* in questions 1 and 4 and *inferred* in questions 3, 6, and 8. Allow students to ask clarifying questions about any of the question choices, being careful not to reveal correct answers. Once students understand the questions, have them complete the test on their own. Allow 5 minutes for reading the passage and 12 minutes for the questions.

707

Grammar and Writing
Editing in Context

1. Introduce the skill using the instruction on the student page. Be sure students understand the strategy set off in the boxed section.

2. Read the first two sentences of the Practice passage; then, go over the second test item with students, modeling the "narrow the answer options" strategy.

3. Point out that the original sentence contains a misplaced modifier and is weakened by passive voice. The antecedent pronoun needs proximity to "the anonymous writer" instead of "the reader's confidence." Change is required, so Choice F is eliminated. Choice G incorrectly inserts an unnecessary article and does not fix the misplaced modifier or passive voice; G is eliminated. Choice H merely rearranges the possessive and maintains passive voice and the misplaced modifier; H is eliminated. Choice J correctly restructures the clause so that the correct noun has closest proximity to the antecedent. The verb usage is strengthened with present tense in active voice. J is therefore the best alternative.

4. Have students complete questions 1 and 3–8 on their own. Allow students 9 minutes to complete the questions.

Grammar and Writing: Editing in Context

Editing-in-context segments often appear in the writing sections of standardized tests. They are made up of a reading passage with numbered sentences, some of which contain errors in grammar, style, and usage. For each question, you must choose the best way to correct a given sentence.

Practice

This exercise is modeled after the ACT English Test.

Directions: For each underlined sentence or portion of a sentence, choose the best alternative. If an item asks a question about the underlined portion, choose the best answer to the question.

> ### Strategy
>
> **Narrow the Answer Options.**
> Make your task simpler by eliminating any answers that you know to be incorrect.

In "A Modest Proposal," Jonathan Swift <u>presents an outrageous and disgusting idea calmly and rationally</u>. Beginning by establishing his credibility, <u>the reader's confidence is gained by the anonymous writer</u>. First, he paints a dismal picture of the difficult lives of the country's poor. Next, the writer promises great advantages from his solution, declaring it will apply <u>not only to beggars but also</u> to other families. Then, the author states that he <u>has spent much time thinking about the problem and weighed different options carefully</u>. <u>He details his calculations about births. He uses mathematics to present an image of rationality.</u> <u>Relying on expert testimony</u>, the writer dismisses another possible solution. Just before finally dropping his bombshell, the writer states that he offers this idea <u>"humbly" or hopes</u> there can be no objection. <u>Only after laying this careful groundwork</u> does Swift allow his anonymous writer to present his insane idea.

Strategies for Test Taking

Point out to students that in Editing in Context Tests, such as the one on this page, some test items simply list choices; students, following the general directions, are expected to choose the best alternative. Items 1, 2, 4, 5, and 7 are examples of this type.

Other test items are preceded by questions. Often, these involve descriptions of the parts of speech and mechanics of words and phrases. Items 3, 6, and 8 are examples of this type.

Since choosing the correct editing alternatives may take more time, students might work through the "short" test items first and then go back to the more detailed test items. Also, if students complete the test with time remaining, they should review their answers to the detailed test items.

1. **A.** NO CHANGE
   B. presents an outrageous and a disgusting idea calmly and rationally.
   C. presents calmly an outrageous, rational, and disgusting idea.
   D. calmly and rationally presents an outrageous and disgusting idea.

2. **F.** NO CHANGE
   G. the reader's confidence is gained by Swift.
   H. the confidence of the reader is gained by the anonymous writer.
   J. the anonymous writer gains the reader's confidence.

3. What is the function of *not only* and *but also*?
   A. They are adjectives.
   B. They are coordinating conjunctions.
   C. They are correlative conjunctions.
   D. They are subordinating conjunctions.

4. **F.** NO CHANGE
   G. has spent careful time thinking about the problem and weighed different options.
   H. has spent much time thinking about the problem and carefully weighing different options.
   J. has carefully spent time thinking about the problem and weighed different options.

5. **A.** NO CHANGE
   B. Because he details his calculations about births, he presents an image of rationality.
   C. He details his calculations about births, but uses mathematics to present an image of rationality.
   D. He details his calculations about births; however, he uses mathematics to present an image of rationality.

6. What word or words are modified by this clause?
   F. the writer
   G. dismisses
   H. another possible
   J. solution

7. **A.** NO CHANGE
   B. "humbly" and hopes
   C. "humbly" but hopes
   D. either "humbly" or hopes

8. What is the function of the underlined words?
   F. prepositional phrase
   G. adverb clause
   H. independent clause
   J. no purpose; the words should be eliminated

Timed Writing: Persuasive Essay [30 minutes]

An old saying goes, "If at first you don't succeed, try, try again." History is full of examples of people who reached their goals by sheer determination. However, persistence alone is not always sufficient to guarantee success.

In an essay, take a position on the above claim. You may argue any point of view. Be sure to back up your statements with sound reasoning and specific examples.

> **Academic Vocabulary**
> Carefully read the prompt and the assignment twice. Note key words and phrases, such as "take a position" or "examples," that clarify the assignment.

ASSESS/RETEACH

Answers

1. A
2. J
3. C
4. H
5. B
6. F
7. C
8. F

Timed Writing
Persuasive Essay

1. Go over the two paragraphs of the timed writing assignment on the student page.

2. Tell students to quickly decide which position to take on the claim. Then they should consider how to persuade someone to agree with them.

3. Encourage students to budget adequate time for prewriting and revising/editing. Students should spend about 8 minutes in the prewriting stage, 17 minutes drafting, and 5 minutes revising and editing. Reinforce this by announcing elapsed time at the 8 and 25 minute marks as students respond to the assignment.

4. Use the **Rubrics for Writing for Assessment,** *Professional Development Guidebook,* pages 258–259, to evaluate students' work.

Benchmark

Reteach skills as indicated by students' performance, following the Reteach charts on pages 707 and 709. Then, administer the end-of-unit **Benchmark Test** *(Unit 3 Resources,* pp. 146–151). The Benchmark Test concludes instruction in the Unit skills. Follow the **Interpretation Guide** for the test *(Unit 3 Resources,* page 259–264) to assign reteaching pages as necessary in the *Reading Kit.* Use **Success Tracker** online to automatically assign these pages.

Reteach

Question	Pages to Reteach
1	539
2	539
3	—
4	503
5	263
6	539
7	—
8	503

PHLit Online!

The **Benchmark Tests** and **Success Tracker** are available online at **www.PHLitOnline.com.**

Performance Tasks

Assigning Tasks/Reteaching Skills

Use the chart below to choose appropriate Performance Tasks by identifying which tasks assess lessons in the textbook that you have taught. Use the same lessons for reteaching when students' performance indicates a failure to fully master a standard. For additional instruction and practice, assign the *Common Core Companion* pages indicated for each task.

Task	Where Taught/ Pages to Reteach	*Common Core Companion* Pages
1	467, 504, 510, 678–679, 552, 556, 702	15–27, 196–207, 261–268
2	469, 474, 492, 516, 541, 556, 558, 597	28–40, 196–207, 261–268
3	502, 521, 538, 552, 598, 604	136–142, 261–268
4	469, 480, 568, 628, 678–679	123–135, 306–312
5	521, 535, 581, 646, 664	103–115, 306–312
6	480, 494, 628, 645, 678–679, 696, 702	41–53, 306–312

Assessment Pacing

In assigning the Writing Tasks on this student page, allow a class period for the completion of a task. As an alternative, assign tasks as homework. In assigning the Speaking and Listening Tasks on the facing page, consider having students do any required preparation as a homework assignment. Then, allow a class period for the presentations themselves.

Evaluating Performance Tasks

Use the rubric at the bottom of this Teacher Edition page to evaluate students' mastery of the standards as demonstrated in their Performance Task responses. Review the rubric with students before they begin work.

Performance Tasks

Follow the instructions to complete the tasks below as required by your teacher. As you work on each task, incorporate both general academic vocabulary and literary terms you learned in this unit.

 Common Core State Standards

RL.11-12.2, RL.11-12.3, RL.11-12.4; RI.11-12.2, RI.11-12.4, RI.11-12.5; W.11-12.2, W.11-12.9.a, W.11-12.9.b; SL.11-12.6
[For the full wording of the standards, see the standards chart in the front of your textbook.]

Writing

Task 1: Literature [RL.11-12.2; W.11-12.2, W.11-12.9.a]

Analyze the Development of Themes

*Write an **essay** in which you analyze the development of two or more themes in a literary work from this unit.*

- Identify a literary work from this unit that presents two or more significant themes. State which work you chose and explain your reasons for this choice.

- Explain the themes the work expresses and identify specific ways in which each theme is introduced and developed. Include an analysis of how the themes interact and build on one another.

- Cite specific details from the literary work under discussion to support your analysis.

- Use appropriate and varied transitions to clarify the relationships among your ideas.

Task 2: Literature [RL.11-12.3; W.11-12.2, W.11-12.9.a]

Analyze the Development of a Narrative

*Write an **essay** in which you analyze and evaluate the development of a narrative work from this unit.*

- Explain which work you chose and briefly summarize the essential elements, such as setting, situation, characters, conflict, and plot.

- Discuss how the author orders events and how he or she introduces and develops characters or new situations.

- Explain how the author's choices about the development of the narrative affect the reading experience and contribute to the narrative's larger meaning or themes.

- Organize your ideas so that each new idea builds on the one it follows to create a unified whole.

- Provide a concluding section that follows from the explanation presented.

Task 3: Informational Text [RI.11-12.5; W.11-12.9.b]

Analyze and Evaluate Text Structure

*Write an **essay** in which you analyze and evaluate the structure of a work of nonfiction from this unit.*

- Identify a work of nonfiction from this unit and provide a brief summary of its central ideas and key supporting details.

- Explain the structure the author chose. To clarify the work's structure for the reader, provide a list, an outline, or a clear description of its structural elements.

- Evaluate the effectiveness of the author's choice of structure. Identify specific ways in which the structure either contributes to or detracts from the meaning, and consider whether the structure itself helps to add interest to the work.

- Organize your essay logically and use thoughtful transitional words and phrases to clarify the flow of your ideas. Provide a concluding section that follows from and supports the evaluation you presented.

710 A Turbulent Time (1625–1798)

Performance Task Rubric: Standards Mastery	Rating Scale				
	not very				*very*
Critical Thinking: How clearly and consistently does the student pursue the specific mode of reasoning or discourse required by the standard, as specified in the prompt (e.g., comparing and contrasting, analyzing, explaining)?	1	2	3	4	5
Focus: How well does the student understand and apply the focus concepts of the standard, as specified in the prompt (e.g., development of theme or of complex characters, effects of structure, and so on)?	1	2	3	4	5
Support/Elaboration: How well does the student support points with textual or other evidence? How relevant, sufficient, and varied is the evidence provided?	1	2	3	4	5
Insight: How original, sophisticated, or compelling are insights the student achieves by applying the standard to the text(s)?	1	2	3	4	5
Expression of Ideas: How well does the student organize and support ideas? How well does the student use language, including word choice and conventions, in the expression of ideas?	1	2	3	4	5

Speaking and Listening

 Task 4: Informational Text [RI.11-12.4; SL.11-12.6]

Analyze Word Choice and Meaning

*Deliver an **oral presentation** in which you analyze the use of language in a nonfiction work from this unit.*

- Introduce the work you chose. Provide information about the author, explain the work's historical context, and briefly summarize its central ideas.

- Provide a broad overview of the type of diction the author employs. Then, identify specific word choices that are critical to the writer's overall purpose and expression of ideas. State why you chose these words and phrases, and explain their figurative, technical, or connotative meanings.

- Consider any key words or phrases the author uses repeatedly and discuss how the meaning of those terms is modified or refined over the course of the work.

- Include examples from the text that illustrate and support your analysis.

- Speak clearly and precisely so that listeners can follow your line of reasoning.

 Task 5: Informational Text [RI.11-12.2; SL.11-12.6]

Analyze Central Ideas

*Deliver an **oral presentation** in which you analyze and evaluate the central ideas in a work of nonfiction from this unit.*

- Explain which work you chose and provide information about the historical context, occasion and purpose for the writing, and the author.

- Identify two or more central ideas expressed in the work. Cite specific details to show how the author introduces, develops, and refines each idea.

- Discuss your assessment of the central ideas. Include an evaluation of how well the two central ideas build on and reinforce one another.

- Provide hand-outs or other materials to help your listeners understand your ideas.

- Organize and develop your presentation logically and clearly, avoiding abrupt shifts in focus and using language that provides clear transitions among ideas.

 Task 6: Literature [RL.11-12.4; SL.11-12.6]

Analyze Word Choice and Tone

*Deliver a **visual presentation** in which you analyze the impact of word choice on tone in a literary work from this unit.*

- State which work you chose and summarize its key elements—setting, characters, events, and themes.

- Describe the tone of the work. Cite at least three specific word choices—especially those with rich connotations or multiple meanings—that contribute to this tone.

- Incorporate visuals, such as drawings, photographs, or word maps, that illustrate the words and phrases you chose and capture the overall tone of the work. Discuss these choices.

- Present your ideas clearly and logically, using formal English and academic vocabulary.

What is the relationship between literature and place?

London as a Character The literature of the period addressed in this unit is filled with vivid personalities, authors, and fictional characters alike. Perhaps the greatest literary star of the period, however, is the city of London.

Assignment Write a **literary analysis** of the work of three authors from this unit. Analyze the role that London played—a "character" in its own drama, a vivid backdrop for action, or an area for a certain social class—in each work.

Supporting Speaking and Listening

1. Consider having students work with partners or in groups to complete Performance Tasks involving listening and speaking. For tasks that you assign for individual work, you may still wish to have students rehearse with partners, who can provide constructive feedback.

2. As students rehearse, have them keep in mind these tips:
   - Present findings and evidence clearly and concisely.
   - Observe conventions of standard English grammar and usage.
   - Be relaxed and friendly but maintain a formal tone.
   - Make eye contact with the audience, pronounce words clearly, and vary your pace.
   - When working with a group, respond thoughtfully to others' positions, modifying your own in response to new evidence.

Linking Performance Tasks to Independent Reading

If you wish to cover the standards with students' independent reading, adapt Performance Tasks of your choice to the works they have selected. (Independent reading suggestions appear on the next page.)

What is the relationship between literature and place?

1. Remind students of the Essential Question, "What is the relationship between literature and place?"

2. Have students complete their responses to the prompt on the student page. Point out that in this unit, they have read a variety of British literature from the seventeenth and eighteenth centuries and that they should draw on these selections in their responses. Remind them that they can also draw on their own experiences and what they have learned in other subject areas in formulating their answers.

Differentiated Instruction   for Universal Access

Strategy for Less Proficient Readers

Assign a Performance Task, and then have students meet in groups to review the standard assessed in that task.

Remind students of the selections or independent readings to which they have previously applied the standard. Have groups summarize what they learned in applying the standard and then present their summaries. Discuss, clarifying any points of confusion. After students have completed their tasks, have groups meet again to evaluate members' work. Encourage members to revise their work based on the feedback they receive.

EL Strategy for English Learners

For each assigned Performance Task, review the instructions with students. Clarify the meaning of any unfamiliar vocabulary, emphasizing routine classroom words such as *evaluate, purpose,* and *analysis* and academic vocabulary such as *conflict.*

Next, have students note ideas for their responses. Pair students, and have them review each other's notes, asking questions to clarify meaning and suggesting improvements. Encourage students to ask for your assistance in supplying English words or expressions they may require.

Independent Reading

Titles featured on the Independent Reading pages at the end of each unit represent a range of reading, including stories, dramas, and poetry, as well as literary nonfiction and other types of informational text. Throughout, labels indicate the works that are CCSS Exemplar Texts. Choosing from among these featured titles will help students read works at increasing levels of text complexity in the grades 11–12 text complexity band.

Using Literature Circles

A literature circle is a temporary group in which students independently discuss a book.

Use the guidance in the *Professional Development Guidebook*, pp. 47–49, as well as the teaching notes on the facing page, for additional suggestions for literature circles.

Ⓒ Meeting Unit 3 CCS Standards

Students can use books listed on this page to apply and reinforce their mastery of the CCS Standards covered in this unit.

Introducing Featured Titles

Have students choose a book or books for independent reading. Assist them by previewing the titles, noting their subject matter and level of difficulty. **Note:** Before recommending a work to students, preview it, taking into account the values of your community as well as the maturity of your students.

Featured Titles

In this unit, you have read a variety of British literature from the seventeenth and eighteenth centuries. Continue to read works related to this era on your own. Select books that you enjoy, but challenge yourself to explore new topics, new authors, and works offering varied perspectives or approaches. The titles suggested below will help you get started.

LITERATURE

Moll Flanders
Daniel Defoe

 **Fiction** Moll Flanders starts out life as "a poor desolate girl" in seventeenth-century England. Gradually, she claws her way up to a life of wealth and security, making mistakes along the way. The novel presents an interesting portrait of a woman who is more a victim of society's evils than an evildoer herself.

[An excerpt from Defoe's A Journal of the Plague Year *begins on page 590. Build knowledge by reading another novel by this author.]*

Gulliver's Travels
Jonathan Swift

 **Satire** Shipwrecked and cast adrift, Lemuel Gulliver awakes to find himself in Lilliput, an island inhabited by people whose six-inch height makes their quarrels over fashion and fame seem ridiculous. His subsequent encounters with equally strange individuals give Gulliver new, bitter insights into human behavior. With its wild distortions and undertones of the grotesque, *Gulliver's Travels* defies the reader's expectations of a conventional traveler's tale.

[An excerpt from Gulliver's Travels *begins on page 606 of this book. Build knowledge by reading the full text.]*

Donne: Selected Poetry
John Donne   EXEMPLAR TEXT

 **Poetry** Enjoy the poetry of Donne's romantic youth and the more spiritual poetry of his later life. This collection contains Donne's famous poem "A Valediction: Forbidding Mourning."

[Donne's poems appear on pages 482–490 of this book. Build knowledge by reading other poems by this author.]

INFORMATIONAL TEXTS

Historical Texts

The Diary of Samuel Pepys
Samuel Pepys
Modern Library, 2001

 **Diary** In his diary, Pepys recorded his observations and impressions of some of the great events of his time, including the Great Plague of 1665 and the Great Fire of London in 1666. Equally engaging are his accounts of everyday life in the seventeenth century.

[An excerpt of the diary begins on page 571 in this book. Build knowledge by reading the full text.]

Selected Letters
Lady Mary Wortley Montagu

 **Letters** Writer and essayist Montagu wrote about her experiences with great humor and a unique perspective. Read her selected letters to learn about the life of this extraordinary woman.

Contemporary Scholarship

A Preface to Paradise Lost
C. S. Lewis
Oxford University Press, 1961

 **Literary Criticism** In this critically acclaimed book, C. S. Lewis, a literary scholar and famed children's author, discusses the importance of the epic as a literary form and provides insight into Milton's *Paradise Lost*.

Samuel Johnson
W. Jackson Bate
Counterpoint, 1998

 **Biography** This biography of Samuel Johnson, author of *A Dictionary of the English Language*, describes both the private and the public life of this extraordinary man of letters. Winner of both the National Book Award and the Pulitzer Prize, the book presents an engaging, modern look at this larger-than-life figure.

712 A Turbulent Time (1625–1798)

Ⓒ Text Complexity: Aligning Texts With Readers and Tasks

TEXTS	READERS AND TASKS
• *A Preface to Paradise Lost*	**Below-Level Readers** Allow students to focus on reading for content, and challenge them to interpret multiple perspectives.
• *Gulliver's Travels* (Lexile: 1210L) • *The Diary of Samuel Pepys* • *Selected Letters*	**Below-Level Readers** Challenge students as they read for content. **On-Level Readers** Allow students to focus on reading for content, and challenge them to interpret multiple perspectives. **Advanced Readers** Allow students to focus on interpreting multiple perspectives.
• *Moll Flanders* (Lexile: 1390L) • *Donne: Selected Poetry* • *Samuel Johnson*	**On-Level Readers** Challenge students as they read for content. **Advanced Readers** Allow students to focus on reading for content, and challenge them to interpret multiple perspectives.

Preparing to Read Complex Texts

Reading for College and Career In both college and the workplace, readers must analyze texts independently, draw connections among works that offer varied perspectives, and develop their own ideas and informed opinions. The questions shown below, and others that you generate on your own, will help you more effectively read and analyze complex college-level texts.

 **Common Core State Standards**

Reading Literature/Informational Text
10. By the end of grade 12, read and comprehend literature, including stories, dramas, and poems, and literary nonfiction at the high end of the grades 11-CCR text complexity band independently and proficiently.

When reading complex texts, ask yourself...

- What idea, experience, or story seems to have compelled the author to write? Has the author presented that idea, experience, or story in a way that I, too, find compelling?

- How might the author's era, social status, belief system, or personal experiences have affected the point of view he or she expresses in the text?

- How do my circumstances affect what I understand and feel about this text?

- What key idea does the author state explicitly? What key idea does he or she suggest or imply? Which details in the text help me to perceive implied ideas?

- Do I find multiple layers of meaning in the text? If so, what relationships do I see among these layers of meaning?

- How do details in the text connect or relate to one another? Do I find any details unconvincing, unrelated, or out of place?

- Do I find the text believable and convincing?

Key Ideas and Details

- What patterns of organization or sequences do I find in the text? Do these patterns help me understand the ideas better?

- What do I notice about the author's style, including his or her diction, uses of imagery and figurative language, and syntax?

- Do I like the author's style? Is the author's style memorable?

- What emotional attitude does the author express toward the topic, the story, or the characters? Does this attitude seem appropriate?

- What emotional attitude does the author express toward me, the reader? Does this attitude seem appropriate?

- What do I notice about the author's voice—his or her personality on the page? Do I like this voice? Does it make me want to read on?

Craft and Structure

- Is the work fresh and original?

- Do I agree with the author's ideas entirely, or are there elements I find unconvincing?

- Do I disagree with the author's ideas entirely, or are there elements I can accept as true?

- Based on my knowledge of British literature, history, and culture, does this work reflect the British tradition? Why or why not?

Integration of Ideas

Independent Reading **713**

Text Complexity: Reader and Task Support Suggestions

INDEPENDENT READING

Increased Support Suggest that students choose a book that they feel comfortable reading and one that is a bit more challenging.

Pair a more proficient reader with a less proficient reader and have them work together on the more challenging text. Partners can prepare to read the book by reviewing questions on this student page. They can also read difficult passages together, sharing questions and insights. They can use the questions on the student page to guide after-reading discussion.

Increased Challenge Encourage students to integrate knowledge and ideas by combining the Essential Questions and unit concepts in their approach to two or more featured titles.

For example, students might compare and contrast the fictional life of Moll Flanders with the real life of Lady Mary Wortley Montagu. Students can focus on how women's roles in the seventeenth and eighteenth centuries are reflected in the literature of the time.

Preparing to Read Complex Texts

1. Tell students they can be attentive readers by bringing their experience and imagination to the texts they read and by actively questioning those texts. Explain that the questions they see on the student page are examples of types of questions to ask about works of fiction and nonfiction.

2. Point out that, like writing, reading is a "multidraft" process, involving several readings of complete works or passages, revising and refining one's understanding each time.

Key Ideas and Details

3. Focus on the fifth bulleted point in the Key Ideas and Details box. **Ask:** What details in the text reveal the relationship between these layers of meaning?

   Possible response: Students may point out that certain themes are connected to the storylines of different characters or that a theme is set up by one character's storyline and resolved by another's.

Craft and Structure

4. Review and amplify the fourth bulleted point in the Craft and Structure box. **Ask:** Do the literal meanings of the author's words always accurately reflect his or her attitude toward the subject of the text?

   Possible response: No. Often, an author will use satire, exaggeration, or irony to express an attitude that is the opposite of the literal meaning of his or her words.

Integration of Ideas

5. **Ask:** Why is it helpful to pay attention to arguments that are unconvincing?

   Possible response: Determining why these ideas are not persuasive can lead to a greater understanding of the entire text.

6. Finally, explain to students that they should cite key ideas and details, examples of craft and structure, or instances of the integration of ideas as evidence to support their points during a discussion of fiction, poetry, or primary sources such as diaries or letters. After hearing the evidence, the group might reach a consensus or might agree to disagree.

713

Index of Authors and Titles

Note: Page numbers in *italics* refer to biographical information for authors, or commentary on titles or literary and historical issues. Nonfiction and informational text appears in red.

R68 Index of Authors and Titles

Index of Skills

Boldface numbers indicate pages where terms are defined.

Reading for Information

Analyzing Functional and Expository Texts

Primary Sources

Reading Strategies

Index of Skills **R73**

Writing Strategies

Prewriting

Drafting

Revising

Critical Viewing

Research and Technology

Speaking, Listening, and Viewing

Test-Taking Practice

Grammar

Reading

Timed writing:

Vocabulary in context

Acknowledgments

Grateful acknowledgment is made to the following for copyrighted material:

Aitken Alexander Associates Ltd "B. Wordsworth" from *Miguel Street* by V. S. Naipaul. Copyright © 1959 by V. S. Naipaul. Used with permission of Aitken Alexander Associates Limited.

Anvil Press Poetry Ltd. "Prayer" from *Mean Time* by Carol Ann Duffy. Published by Anvil Press Poetry in 1993. Copyright © Carol Ann Duffy, 1985, 1987, 1990, 1993, 1994. Used by permission of Anvil Press Poetry.

Georges Borchardt, Inc. From "Disappearing Act" by John Lahr from *The New Yorker,* February 12, 2007. Used by permission of Georges Borchardt, Inc.

Professor Geoffrey Bownas "When I went to visit" by Ki Tsurayuki, "Was it that I went to sleep" by Ono Kamachi, "Once cannot ask loneliness" by Priest Jakuren. Copyright © 1964 by Penguin Books, revised edition 1998. Translation copyright © Geoffrey Bownas and Anthony Thwaite, 1964, 1998. Used by permission of Geoffrey Bownas.

Broadway Video "Where's Frankenstein" from a *Saturday Night Live* episode that originally aired on October 28, 2006, hosted by Hugh Laurie. Copyright © 2006 NBC Studios, Inc. Distributed by Broadway Video Enterprises. Courtesy of Broadway Video Enterprises and NBC Studios, Inc.

Curtis Brown London "Be Ye Men of Valor" (retitled "Wartime Speech"), BBC London, May 19, 1940, from *Blood, Toil, Tears and Sweat: The Speeches of Winston Churchill* edited and with an introduction by David Cannadine. Speeches Copyright © 1989 by Winston Churchill. Used courtesy of Curtis Brown Ltd. on behalf of The Estate of Winston Churchill.

California State Parks Jack London State Historic Park brochure, copyright © 2001 California State Parks. Used by permission of California State Parks.

Cambridge University Press, NY Excerpt from "Letter to Thomas Flower Ellis from Thomas Babington Macaulay on the Passing of the Reform Bill" written in 1831, from *The Selected Letters of Thomas Babington Macaulay,* ed. Thomas Pinney, 5 vols. Used with the permission of Cambridge University Press.

Citysearch.com "A Thoughtful, Poignant, and Chilling Macbeth" October 7, 1999 from *www.shakespearefest.org/macbeth_99.htm#Reviews.* Copyright © Citysearch.com. Citysearch is a registered trademark of Bluefoot Ventures, Inc. and is used under license. Used by permission of Citysearch.com.

Arthur C. Clarke "Extra-Terrestrial Relays" by Arthur C. Clarke from *Wireless World,* October 1945, pp 305-308 © 1945. Used by permission of the author and the author's agents, Scovil Chichak Galen Literary Agency, Inc.

Jonathan Clowes Ltd. "No Witchcraft for Sale," from *African Short Stories* by Doris Lessing. Copyright © 1981 Doris Lessing. Used by kind permission of Jonathan Clowes, Ltd., London, on behalf of Doris Lessing.

Copyright Clearance Center, Inc. for Hearst Communications, Inc. 'Kingdom of Desire' a sensual 'Macbeth' remake Peking opera style" by Robert Hurwitt from San Francisco Chronicle, May 23, 2005, *www.sfgate.com/cgi-bin/article.cgi?f=/c/a/2005/05/23/DDG9LCSI0H1.DTL&hw=kingdom+of+desire&sn=002&sc=981.* Copyright © 2005 by San Francisco Chronicle. Reproduced with permission of San Francisco Chronicle via Copyright Clearance Center.

Cumbria County Council Table of Traffic Flow at Waterhead, Ambleside. A591 from *Transport and Policies 1999/2000, and Local Transport Plan 2001/2–2005/6.* Copyright © Cumbria County Council. Used by permission of Cumbria County Council.

The Charles Dickens Museum Charles Dickens Museum in London Homepage & Online Tour retrieved from *http://www.dickensmuseum.com.* Copyright © 2005 Charles Dickens Museum. Reproduced courtesy of The Charles Dickens Museum, London.

Dorling Kindersley Ltd. "Lancashire and the Lakes" from *DK Eyewitness Travel Guides: Great Britain* by Michael Leapman. Copyright © 1995, 2001 Dorling Kindersley Limited, London. Reproduced by permission of Dorling Kindersley Ltd.

Dutton Signet From *Beowulf* by Burton Raffel, translator. Translation copyright © 1963, renewed © 1991 by Burton Raffel. Used by permission of Dutton Signet, a division of Penguin Group (USA) Inc.

Encyclopædia Britannica Search results: Anglo-Saxon Poetry from *http://search.eb.com/search?query=anglo+saxon+poetry&x=0&y=0.* "English Literature: The Old English Period: Poetry: The major manuscripts" from *http://search.eb.com/eb/article-12747.* Copyright © 2007 by Encyclopædia Britannica. Used with permission from Encyclopædia Britannica, Inc.

Faber and Faber Limited "Journey of the Magi" from *Collected Poems 1909–1962* by T. S. Eliot, copyright 1936, copyright © 1964, 1963 by T. S. Eliot. "The Horses" from *New Selected Poems* by Ted Hughes. Copyright © 1957, 1960 by Ted Hughes. Published in the UK in The Hawk in the Rain by Ted Hughes. "Follower" from *Poems 1965–1975* by Seamus Heaney. Copyright © 1980 by Seamus Heaney. "The Hollow Men" from *Collected Poems 1909–1962* by T. S. Eliot, copyright 1936 and renewed 1964, 1963 by T. S. Eliot. "Two Lorries" from *The Spirit Level* by Seamus Heaney. Copyright © 1996 by Seamus Heaney. "The Explosion" from *Collected Poems* by Philip Larkin. Copyright © 1988, 1989 by the Estate of Philip Larkin. "An Arundel Tomb" from *Collected Poems* by Philip Larkin. Copyright © 1988, 1989 by the Estate of Philip Larkin. "That's All" from *Complete Works: Three* by Harold Pinter. Copyright © 1966 by H. Pinter Ltd. "Not Palaces" by Stephen Spender. From *Collected Poems 1928–1985.* Copyright © 1986 by Stephen Spender. Copyright © 1934 by The Modern Library, Inc. and renewed 1962, 1964, 1986 by Stephen Spender. Used by permission of Faber and Faber.

Farrar, Straus & Giroux, LLC "Follower" from *Poems 1965–1975* by Seamus Heaney. Copyright © 1980 by Seamus Heaney. "The Horses" from *Collected Poems* by Ted Hughes. Copyright © 2003 by The Estate of Ted Hughes. "Two Lorries" from *The Spirit Level* by Seamus Heaney. Copyright © 1996 by Seamus Heaney. "The Explosion" from *Collected Poems* by Philip Larkin. Copyright © 1988, 1989 by the Estate of Philip Larkin. "An Arundel Tomb" from *Collected Poems* by Philip Larkin. Copyright © 1988, 1989 by the Estate of Philip Larkin. "Chapter XXVIII, Part I" from *Omeros* by Derek Walcott. Copyright © 1990 by Derek Walcott. "Midsummer XXIII" from *Collected Poems 1948–1984* by Derek Walcott. Copyright © 1986 by Derek Walcott. Used by permission of Farrar, Straus and Giroux, LLC.

Florida Department of Environmental Protection Marjorie Kinnan Rawlings Historic State Park Brochure from *http://www.floridastateparks.org/marjoriekinnanrawlings/docs/brochure.pdf.* Printed 02/07. Used by permission of Florida Department of Environmental Protection.

Fondo de Cultura Economica From *The Nine Guardians* by Rosario Castellanos, translated by Irene Nicholson. Balún Canán de Rosario Castellanos. D.R. © 1957 Fondo de Cultura Economica. Carretera Picacho-Ajusco 227, C.P. 14200, Mexico, D.F. Used by permission of Fondo de Cultura Económica.

Professor Norman Gash "The case for parliamentary reform: 1831: Lord John Russell: 1 March 1831" by Lord John Russell from *The Age of Peel* by Norman Gash (London, Edward Arnold, 1973) *www.dialspace.dial.pipex.com/town/terrace/adw03/peel/refact/refbill.htm.* Copyright © Norman Gash. "A conservative criticism of parliamentary reform: 1831" by Sir Robert Peel, 2nd Baronet from *The Age of Peel* by Norman Gash (London, Edward Arnold, 1973) *www.dialspace.dial.pipex.com/town/terrace/adw03/peel/refact/refpeel.htm.* Copyright © Norman Gash. Used by permission of Norman Gash.

Greater London Authority From *The Mayor's Annual Report 2004* from *http://www.london.gov.uk/mayor/annual_report/docs/ann_rpt_2004.pdf.* Copyright April 2004, Greater London Authority. Used by permission.

Grove/Atlantic, Inc. "That's All" from *Complete Works: Three* by Harold Pinter. Copyright © 1966 by H. Pinter Ltd. "Come and Go" from Collected Shorter Plays by Samuel Beckett. Copyright © 1968, 1984 by Samuel Beckett. "Next Term We'll Mash You" from *Pack of Cards* by Penelope Lively. Copyright © 1978, 1980 1981, 1982, 1984, 1985, 1986 by Penelope Lively. Used by permission of Grove/Atlantic, Inc.

Jen O'Leary "Weather in the Palm of Your Hand" by Jennifer O'Leary, University of Wisconsin-Madison Space Science and Engineering Center from *www.ssec. wisc.edu/media/features/jan10_06.htm*. Used by permission of the author.

Oxford University Press, Inc. "The Wanderer," from *An Anthology of Old English Poetry*, edited and translated by Charles W. Kennedy. Copyright © 1960 by Oxford University Press, Inc. Used by permission of Oxford University Press, Inc.

Oxford University Press, UK "The Naming of Parts," from *A Map of Verona* by Henry Reed, 1946, copyright © by Henry Reed. Used by permission of Oxford University Press, UK.

Oxford University Press, UK "To Lucasta, Going To the Wars" from *The Poems Of Richard Lovelace*, edited by C.H. Wilkinson, copyright © 1953. "To the Virgins, to Make Much of Time" from The Poems of Robert Herrick, edited by L.C. Martin.

Penguin Books Ltd., London "The Wife of Bath's Tale" from *The Canterbury Tales* by Geoffrey Chaucer, translated by Nevill Coghill (Penguin Classics 1951, Fourth revised edition 1977). Copyright 1951 by Nevill Coghill. Copyright © the Estate of Nevill Coghill, 1958, 1960, 1975, 1977. From *A History of The English Church and People* by Bede (pp 37-40), translated by Leo Sherley-Price, revised by R.E. Latham (Penguin Classics 1955, Revised edition 1968). Copyright © Leo Sherley-Price, 1955, 1968. "Prologue" from *The Canterbury Tales* by Geoffrey Chaucer, translated by Nevill Coghill (Penguin Classics 1951, Fourth revised edition 1977). Copyright 1951 by Nevill Coghill. Copyright © the Estate of Nevill Coghill, 1958, 1960, 1975, 1977. "Pardoner's Tale" from *The Canterbury Tales* by Geoffrey Chaucer, translated by Nevill Coghill (Penguin Classics 1951, Fourth revised edition 1977). Copyright 1951 by Nevill Coghill. Copyright © the Estate of Nevill Coghill, 1958, 1960, 1975, 1977. From *The Decameron* by Giovanni Boccaccio, translated with an introduction and notes by G. H. McWilliam (Penguin Classics 1972, Second Edition 1995). Copyright © G. H. McWilliam, 1972, 1995. "Next Term We'll Mash You" from Pack of Cards by Penelope Lively. Copyright © 1978, 1980 1981, 1982, 1984, 1985, 1986 by Penelope Lively. Used by permission of Penguin Group Ltd., UK.

Random House, Inc. "In Memory of W. B. Yeats", copyright 1940 & renewed 1968 by W.H. Auden from *Collected Poems* by W.H. Auden. "Musee des Beaux Arts", copyright 1940 & renewed 1968 by W.H. Auden from *Collected Poems* by W.H. Auden. Used by permission of Random House, Inc. "Home" by Anton Chekhov from *Modern Library*, copyright © 1999 by Random House, Inc.

Riverbend From "Baghdad Burning" by Riverbend (baghdad.burning@gmail. com)from *The Great Wall of Segregation...*, *http://riverbendblog.blogspot.com*, April 26, 2007.

Riverhead Books, an imprint of Penguin Group (USA) Inc. "I'm Like a Bird" from *Songbook* by Nick Hornby, copyright © 2002 by Nick Hornby. Used by permission of Riverhead Books, an imprint of Penguin Group (USA) Inc.

Rogers, Coleridge & White Ltd. "A Devoted Son" from *Games at Twilight and Other Stories* by Anita Desai. Copyright © 1978 Anita Desai. Reproduced by permission of the author c/o Rogers, Coleridge & White Ltd., 20 Powis Mews, London W11 1JN.

Russell & Volkening, Inc. "The Train from Rhodesia" from *Selected Stories* by Nadine Gordimer. Copyright © 1950 by Nadine Gordimer, renewed in 1978 by Nadine Gordimer. Used by the permission of Russell & Volkening as agents for the author.

Scovil Chichak Galen Literary Agency, Inc. "We'll Never Conquer Space" by Arthur C. Clarke, from *Science Digest*, June 1960. Copyright © 1960 by Popular Mechanics Company. Used by permission of the author and the author's agents, Scovil Chichak Galen Literary Agency, Inc.

Scribner, an imprint of Simon & Schuster "The Second Coming" from *The Collected Works of W.B. Yeats, Volume 1: The Poems* edited by Richard J. Finneran. Copyright © 1924 by The Macmillan Company; copyright renewed © 1952 by Bertha Georgie Yeats. Used with the permission of Scribner, an imprint of Simon & Schuster Adult Publishing Group, All rights reserved.

Smithsonian Institution "Recasting Shakespeare's Stage" by Eric Jaffe from *www.smithsonianmag.com/arts-culture/globe.html*. Copyright 2008 Smithsonian Institution. Used with permission from Smithsonian Business Ventures. All rights reserved. Reproduction in any medium is strictly prohibited without permission from Smithsonian Institution. Such permission may be requested from Smithsonian Business Ventures.

Stage Three Music (US) Inc. "Eli, the Barrow Boy" written by Colin Meloy from *Picaresque*. Copyright © 2005 music of Stage Three/Osterozhna! Music (BMI). Used by permission of Stage Three Music (US), Inc.

The Estate of Ann Stanford "The Wife's Lament" by Ann Stanford from *The Women Poets In English: An Anthology*. Copyright © 1972 by Ann Stanford. Used with permission of the Estate of Ann Stanford.

Taylor & Francis From "The Rape Of The Lock", reprinted from *The Poems of Alexander Pope*, edited by John Butt. Reproduced by permission of Taylor & Francis Books UK.

University of California Press & Carmen Balcells Agencia Literaria *Selected Odes of Pablo Neruda*, by Pablo Neruda, translated by Margaret Sayers Peden, copyright © 1990 by the Fundacion Pablo Neruda, published by the University of California Press. All rights reserved.

The University of Chicago Press Excerpt from "Oedipus The King" by Sophocles, D. Grene, trans., from *The Complete Greek Tragedies*, R. Lattimore and D. Grene, eds. Used with permission of The University of Chicago Press.

Ed Victor, Ltd. "Not Palaces" from *Collected Poems 1928–1985* by Stephen Spender, copyright © 2004 by Stephen Spender. Used by permission of Ed Victor Ltd.

Viking Penguin, Inc. "Araby", from *Dubliners* by James Joyce, copyright 1916 by B. W. Heubsch. Definitive text Copyright © 1967 by The Estate of James Joyce. "Wirers" from *Collected Poems Of Siegfried Sassoon* by Siegfried Sassoon, copyright 1918, 1920 by E. P. Dutton. Copyright 1936, 1946, 1947, 1948 by Siegfried Sassoon. "The Rocking-Horse Winner" from *Complete Short Stories Of D.H. Lawrence* by D.H. Lawrence. Copyright © 1933 by the Estate of D. H. Lawrence, renewed © 1961 by Angelo Ravagli and C. M. Weekley, Executors of the Estate of Frieda Lawrence. "The Book of Sand", from *Collected Fictions*, by Jorge Luis Borges, translated by Andrew Hurley, copyright © 1998 by Maria Kodama; translation copyright © 1998 by Penguin Putnam, Inc. From "In Athens Once", from *Days Of Obligation* by Richard Rodriguez, copyright © 1992 by Richard Rodriguez. Used by permission of Viking Penguin, a division of Penguin Group (USA) Inc. All rights reserved.

Wake Forest University Press "Carrick Revisited" from *Selected Poems of Louis MacNeice*, edited by Michael Longley. Copyright © Wake Forest University Press, 1990. Used by permission of Wake Forest University Press.

The Arthur Waley Estate Excerpts from *The Analects of Confucius*, translated and annotated by Arthur Waley. Copyright © 1938 by George Allen and Unwin Ltd, London. From "The Book of Songs, Song 34 (Thick Grow the Rush Leaves)" translated by Arthur Waley from *The Book Of Songs*. Copyright © 1919, 1941 by Alfred A. Knopf, Inc. Used by permission of The Arthur Waley Estate.

Wikipedia.org "Zorro" retrieved from http://en.wikipedia.org accessed on 6/6/07. "Space Mirror Memorial" retrieved from http://en.wikipedia.org accessed on 6/15/07. "Davy Crockett" retrieved from http://en.wikipedia.org accessed on 6/18/07.

Yale University Press "The Seafarer" from *Poems from the Old English*, translated by Burton Raffel. Copyright © 1960, 1964; renewed 1988, 1922 by The University of Nebraska Press. Copyright © 1994 by Burton Raffel. Used by permission of Yale University Press.

Note: Every effort has been made to locate the copyright owner of material reproduced on this component. Omissions brought to our attention will be corrected in subsequent editions.

Credits

Photo Credits

xlvi: Amra Pasic/Shutterstock; 1: Bridgeman Art Library, London/ SuperStock; 2: r. 2: m. © The Board of Trinity College, Dublin, Ireland/ The Bridgeman Art Library; 2: l. Stapleton Collection/CORBIS; 3: rt. Erich Lessing/Art Resource, NY; 3: rm. British Museum/Art Resource, NY; 3: rb. Andy Crawford/© Dorling Kindersley; 3: bl. Historical Picture Archive/CORBIS; 3: tl. Werner Forman/CORBIS; 4: br. Archivo Iconografico, S.A./CORBIS; 4: bl. The Art Archive / British Museum / Eileen Tweedy; 5: br. Rough Guides Dorling Kindersley; 5: bl. Abbie Enock; Travel Ink/CORBIS; 6: bm. The Granger Collection, New York; 6: br. The Art Archive / British Library; 7: bl. Christophe Boisvieux/CORBIS; 7: br. Frans Lanting/ CORBIS; 8: br. The Granger Collection, New York; 9: br. The Granger Collection, New York; 9: bl. Werner Forman/CORBIS; 10: bl. The Gallery Collection/CORBIS; 10: br. The Granger Collection, New York; 11: bl. The Granger Collection, New York; 11: br. Bettmann/CORBIS; 12: bl. Archivo Iconografico, SA/CORBIS; 12: br. Danny Lehman/CORBIS; 13: br. Stephano Bianchetti/CORBIS; 13: bl. HIP/Art Resource, NY; 15: bl. Prentice Hall; 17: Bridgeman Art Library, London/SuperStock; 19: ©Eyre / Alamy; 20–21: Barry Lewis/CORBIS; 24: t. St. Cuthbert's Holy Island, 1797 (w/c over pencil on textured paper) by Thomas Girtin (1775–1802); Yale Center for British Art, Paul Mellon Collection, USA/ / The Bridgeman Art Library; 26: Matthias Kulka/CORBIS; 31: r. Clive Druett;Papilio/CORBIS; 33: The Grandsons of Gostosmysl: Rurik, Truvori and Sineus, 1986 (oil on canvas), Glazunov, Ilya (b. 1930) / Private Collection, / The Bridgeman Art Library; 34: The Granger Collection, New York; 37: Boris Vallejo, Inc.; 42: b. Kerstin Hamburg/CORBIS; 46: l. istockphoto.com; 47: b. ©The Trustees of the British Museum; 47: TR ©The Trustees of the British Museum; 49: r. HIP/Art Resource, NY; 55: tr. British Museum/Art Resource, NY; 59: BEOWULF: A TALE OF BLOOD, HEAT, AND ASHES. Text copyright ©27 by Nicky Raven. Illustrations copyright ©27 by John Howe. Reproduced by permission of the publisher Candlewick Press, Inc., Cambridge, MA; 61: t. 62: bl. The Granger Collection, New York; 63: t. BEOWULF: A TALE OF BLOOD, HEAT, AND ASHES. Text copyright ©27 by Nicky Raven. Illustrations copyright ©27 by John Howe. Reproduced by permission of the publisher Candlewick Press, Inc., Cambridge, MA; 68: t. ©Smith Richard Frank/CORBIS Sygma; 68: m. Concept and design by Cynthia Krupt; b. The Art Archive/British Library; 69: tr. Richard Cummings/CORBIS; 76: b. 77: 78: 80: t. David Reed/CORBIS; 84: 87: tr. M-Sat Ltd / Photo Researchers, Inc.; 90: l. The Granger Collection, New York; 92–93: The Granger Collection, New York; 93: t. Stapleton Collection/CORBIS; 96–97: Reproduced with the cooperation of Alexandra Szyk Bracie and Historicana www.szyk.com; 100: l. The Yeoman, Arthur Szyk for The CANTERBURY TALES, Reproduced with permission of Alexadra Szyk Bracie and Irvin Ungar; 102: l. The Monk, Arthur Szyk for The CANTERBURY TALES, Reproduced with permission of Alexadra Szyk Bracie and Irvin Ungar; 104: l. The Student, Arthur Szyk for The CANTERBURY TALES, Reproduced with permission of Alexadra Szyk Bracie and Irvin Ungar; 109: The Wife of Bath, Arthur Szyk for The CANTERBURY TALES, Reproduced with permission of Alexadra Szyk Bracie and Irvin Ungar; 111: r. Matt Stroshane/Getty Images, Inc.; 111: no credit necessry; 111: The Miller, Arthur Szyk for The CANTERBURY TALES, Reproduced with permission of Alexadra Szyk Bracie and Irvin Ungar; 112: Richard Ross/CORBIS; 113: The Summoner Arthur Szyk for The CANTERBURY TALES, Reproduced with permission of Alexadra Szyk Bracie and Irvin Ungar; 114: l. The Pardoner, Arthur Szyk for The Canterbury Tales, Reproduced with permission of Alexadra Szyk Bracie and Irvin Ungar; 118: b. Three Monks, Arthur Szyk for The CANTERBURY TALES, Reproduced with permission of Alexadra Szyk Bracie and Irvin Ungar; 131: s. Lambeth Palace Library, London, UK/ Bridgeman Art Library, London/New York; 144: Bridgeman Art Library; 151: br. www.cartoonstock.com; 155: bl. Old golden frame on white background; 155: bl. ©Viktor/Fotolia; 155: tl. ©suzannmeer; 157: r. Summerfield Press/CORBIS; 158: The Decameron, 1916 (oil on canvas), Waterhouse, John William (1849–1917) / © Lady Lever Art Gallery, National Museums Liverpool, / The Bridgeman Art Library; 160: b. Scala/Art Resource; 162: l. The Granger Collection, New York; 167: St. George and the Dragon, c.1606 (oil on canvas), Rubens, Peter Paul (1577–1640) / Prado, Madrid, Spain, Giraudon / The Bridgeman Art Library; 185: Michel Setboun/ CORBIS; 188–189: Photo by Mansell/Time & Life Pictures/Getty Images; 190–191: Fine Art Photographic Library, London/Art Resource, NY; 193

Giraudon/Art Resource, NY; 193: Giraudon/Art Resource, NY; 196: b. www.cartoonStock.com; 201: Photographersdirect.com; 207: tr. The Granger Collection, New York; 211: t. The Gallery Collection/CORBIS; 211: bl. Geoff Dann/© Dorling Kindersley, Courtesy of the Anthony Barton Collection; 211: bmr. Geoff Dann/© Dorling Kindersley, Courtesy of the Anthony Barton Collection; 211: bml. Geoff Dann/© Dorling Kindersley, Courtesy of the Anthony Barton Collection; 211: br. Geoff Dann/© Dorling Kindersley, Courtesy of the Anthony Barton Collection; 214: b. CORBIS; 234–235: Scala/Art Resource, NY; 236: br. Private Collection/ The Stapleton Collection/ The Bridgeman Art Library; 236: t. 237: br. Scala/Art Resource, NY; 237: bl. The Granger Collection, New York; 237: bmr. The Granger Collection, New York; 237: bml. Science Museum/Science & Society Picture Library; 238: br. Gianni Dagli Orti/CORBIS; 238: bl. Bettmann/ CORBIS; 239: King Richard I and his Barons, Anonymous / British Library, London, UK, © British Library Board. All Rights Reserved / The Bridgeman Art Library; 239: bl. Jim Zuckerman/CORBIS; 239: br. ©Prisma Bildagentur AG / Alamy; 240: bl. Paule Seux/Hemis/CORBIS; 241: bl. The Granger Collection, New York; 242: b. The Granger Collection, New York; 243: tr. National Trust/Art Resource, NY; 243: br. Gregg Newton/Gregg Newton/CORBIS; 243: bl. Andy Willimams/Loop Images/CORBIS; 243: rm. Victoria & Albert Museum, London / Art Resource, NY; 244: bl. Blue Lantern Studio/CORBIS; 244: Bettmann/CORBIS; 245: br. Bettmann/CORBIS; 247: br. Bettmann/CORBIS; 249: b. Prentice Hall; 249: t. ©Edinburgh University Library, Scotland/ The Bridgeman Art Library; 250: t. ©Hatfield House, Hertfordshire, UK/ The Bridgeman Art Library; 251: Burstein Collection/CORBIS; 251: 253: r. 255: Burstein Collection/CORBIS; 257: r. 258: Victoria & Albert Museum, London/Art Resource, NY; 265 rt. www.cartoonStock.com; 267–268: Museum of Fine Arts, Houston, Texas, USA/ Agnes Cullen Arnold Endowment Fund/ The Bridgeman Art Library; 273: r. 274: Private Collection/ The Stapleton Collection/ The Bridgeman Art Library; 277: tr. The Granger Collection, New York; 277: ml. Private Collection/ © Philip Mould Ltd, London/ The Bridgeman Art Library; 277: rm. 277: rb. No. 3856 Henry Wriothesley, 3rd Earl of Southampton (1573–1624), c.1594 (gouache on vellum) by Nicholas Hilliard (1547–1619) Fitzwilliam Museum, University of Cambridge, UK/ The Bridgeman Art Library; 277: bml. 277: bl. North Wind Picture Archives; 277: tl. The Art Archive/Victoria and Albert Museum London/Sally Chappell; 277: tm. The Art Archive/Victoria and Albert Museum London/Sally Chappell; 277: r. Judith Miller/© Dorling Kindersley/Joseph H. Bonner; 277: ml. istockphoto.com; 281: Hans the Younger Holbein (1497/8–1543), Dutch, "Portrait of Henry VIII", 16th century. Oil on canvas. Belvoir Castle, Leicestershire. The Bridgeman Art Library Ltd.; 285: tr. "Dangers Averted" medal, celebrating the defeat of the Spanish Armada, c. 1589, gold cast and chased by Nicholas Hilliard (1537–1619) Fitzwilliam Museum, University of Cambridge/Bridgeman Art Library , London/New York; 286: Elizabeth I, Armada Portrait, c. 1588 (oil on panel) by George Gower (1540–1596) (attr. to). Woburn Abbey, Bedfordshire, UK/ The Bridgeman Art Library, London/New York; 288: bl. Picture Desk, Inc./Kobal Collection; 290: t. istockphoto.com; 292: m. Getty Images; 292: bl. Getty Images; 293: t. 294: l. Polygram/The Kobal Collection, Bailey, Alex; 295: t. Studio Canal/Working Title/The Koball Collection/Sparham; 297: Private Collection/The Bridgeman Art Library; 298: RÈunion des MusÈes Nationaux / Art Resource, NY; 303: The Return of the Prodigal Son, Lionello Spada/Erich Lessing/Art Resource, NY; 307: Ellen Terry (as Lady Macbeth), 1889, oil on canvas 87"x 45", Tate Gallery on loan to National Portrait Gallery London, Art Resource, NY; 312: © AF archive / Alamy/TOSHIRO MIFUNE; THRONE OF BLOOD; KUMONOSU JO; DIRECTED BY AKIRA KUROSAWA FILM COMPANY CRITERION 15 January 1957; 313: b. Photofest; 313: tr. MIRISCH-7 ARTS/ UNITED ARTISTS / THE KOBAL COLLECTION; 313: tl. MGM / THE KOBAL COLLECTION; 316: b. National Portrait Gallery, London/Superstock.; 318: ml. Mary Evans Picture Library; 318–319: b. 324: t. Erich Lessing / Art Resource, NY; 328: t. New Walk Museum, Leicester City Museum Service, UK/ The Bridgeman Art Library; 330: b. Darren Robb/Getty Images; 332: b. t. City of Westminster Archive Centre, London, UK/ The Bridgeman Art Library; 343: t. Steve Gorton/© Dorling Kindersley; 347: Photofest; 350: b. The Pierpont Morgan Library, Art Resource, NY; 352: t. The Granger Collection, New York; 366: t. The Art Archive / Garrick Club; 371: t. Scene from Macbeth, Cattermole, By Permission of the Folger Shakespeare Library, Washington, D.C.; 379: t. Earl & Nazima Kowall/CORBIS; 380: Victoria & Albert Museum, London / Art Resource, NY; 387: b. The

R86 Credits

1133: b. Paula Bronstein/Getty Images; 1135: tr. Colin McPherson/CORBIS; 1135: tl. Pete Turner/Getty Images; 1135: b. The Granger Collection, New York; 1136: Topham/The Image Works; 1136: Art Resource, NY; 1139: Hulton-Deutsch Collection/CORBIS; 1141: Christie's Images/CORBIS; 1142: John Conrad/CORBIS; 1143: Photodisc/Getty Images; 1144: Underwood & Underwood/CORBIS; 1144: age fotostock / SuperStock; 1145: The Image Bank/Getty Images; 1147: Gilles Mermet / Art Resource, NY; 1147: Gilles Mermet / Art Resource, NY; 1148: Gilles Mermet / Art Resource, NY; 1155: Hulton-Deutsch Collection/CORBIS; 1156: E.O. HoppÈ/CORBIS; 1158: Jean Kugler/Getty Images; 1163: PhotothÈque R. Magritte-ADAGP / Art Resource, NY, ©1998 C. Herscovici, Brussels/Artists Rights Society (ARS), New York.; 1171: Bettmann/CORBIS; 1172: The Granger Collection, New York; 1172: Bkgrnd Freyda Miller/CORBIS; 1174: Michael Goldman/Getty Images; 1176: Art Projects International; 1177: 1179: Getty Images; 1180: Michael St. Maur Sheil/CORBIS; 1182: Sophie Bassouls/Sygma/CORBIS; 1182: 1183: Paul Hardy/CORBIS; 1184: Paul Hardy/CORBIS; 1187: © Gilles Mermet / Art Resource; 1188: Getty Images; 1189: t. Private Collection, © The Bloomsbury Workshop, London / The Bridgeman Art Library International; 1189: b. Private Collection, The Stapleton Collection/ The Bridgeman Art Library International; 1189: 1190: t. Marilyn Monroe, Andy Warhol, © Andy Warhol Foundation/CORBIS. TM 2006 Marilyn Monroe, LLC by CMG Worldwide, Inc / www.MarilynMonroe.com © Andy Warhol Foundation for the Visual Arts / ARS, New York; 1190: br. Getty Images; 1190: bl. 1192: RÈunion des MusÈes Nationaux / Art Resource, NY; 1193: 1195: The Garden of Love, Walter Richard Sickert, Fitzwilliam Museum, Cambridge; 1196: RÈunion des MusÈes Nationaux / Art Resource, NY; 1197: age fotostock / SuperStock; 1198: Private Collection, / The Bridgeman Art Library International; 1200: Julian Barrow/Getty Images; 1200: 1201: Andreas Altwein/dpa/CORBIS; 1210: b. Library of Congress, Prints & Photographs Division, NYWT&S Collection; 1217: Getty Images 1219: Hulton-Deutsch Collection/CORBIS; 1220–1221: Ron Dahlquist / Super; 1223: Image1 / SuperStock; 1224–1225: border Gala / SuperStock; 1226: Michael Halminski / SuperStock; 1228–1229: Steve Vidler / SuperStock; 1230–1231: age fotostock / SuperStock; 1231: Ben Mangor / SuperStock; 1232: Digital Vision Ltd. / SuperStock; 1233: The Granger Collection, New York; 1234: St. Patrick's Close, Walter Osborne, National Gallery of Ireland; 1235: Robbie Pleck / SuperStock; 1238: © The Metropolitan Museum of Art / Art Resource, NY; 1239: British Museum / Art Resource, NY; 1243: Bettmann/CORBIS; 1244: Stockbyte /Getty Images; 1245: Stockbyte /Getty Images; 1247: Izzy Schwartz/Getty Images; 1249: Marvin E. Newman/Getty Images; 1250: Jonathan Kitchen/Getty Images; 1251: C Squared Studios/Getty Images; 1255: Stockbyte / Getty Images; 1256: Marvin E. Newman/Getty Images; 1258: Bettmann/CORBIS; 1259: Kevin Summers/Getty Images; 1260: Kevin Summers/Getty Images; 1262: Kevin Summers/Getty Images; 1264: Beth Dixson/Getty Images; 1267: Bildarchiv Preussischer Kulturbesitz / Art Resource, NY; 1269: t. Michael Nicholson/CORBIS; 1269: m. Hulton-Deutsch Collection/CORBIS; 1269: b. The Granger Collection, New York; 1270: Bettmann/CORBIS; 1271: t. Nathan Benn/CORBIS; 1272: Bettmann/CORBIS; 1274–1275: © pzAxe/Fotolia; 1276: Getty Images; 1278–1279: AFP/Getty Images; 1282: Bettmann / CORBIS; 1283: Snark/Art Resource, NY; 1293: Hulton-Deutsch Collection/CORBIS; 1296: Portrait of N. Pietrunkevic, Nikolai Ge, Scala/Art Resource, NY; 1297: Sleepless Night, Nikolai Romadin, Scala/Art Resource, NY; 1302–1303: Hulton-Deutsch Collection/CORBIS; 1305: b. courtesy of Royal Literary Fund and Special Collections, U of Birmingham; 1306: Hulton-Deutsch Collection/CORBIS; 1308: The Art Archive / Imperial War Museum; 1308: The Art Archive / Imperial War Museum; 1313: The Granger Collection, New York; 1314: Paul Souders/CORBIS; 1319: Steve McDonough/CORBIS; 1320: ©Orwell Archive; 1323: Colin McPherson/CORBIS; 1324: HIP / Art Resource, NY; 1327: HIP / Art Resource, NY; 1330: Private Collection/ The Stapleton Collection/ The Bridgeman Art Library; 1337: Micheline Pelletier/CORBIS; 1338: Ron Stroud/Masterfile; 1340: Jean Miele/CORBIS; 1343: Peter Turnley/CORBIS; 1344: David Bergman/CORBIS; 1355: BASSOULS SOPHIE/CORBIS SYGMA; 1356: ©Bettmann/CORBIS; 1358: "Boy on a Wall: Rat Island, 1989" from TIEPOLO'S HOUND by Derek Walcott. Copyright © 20 by Derek Walcott. Reprinted ty Permission of Farrar, Straus and Giroux, LLC. From the collection of Michael and Judy Chastanet.; 1358: Ryan McVay/Getty Images; 1363: ©Smith Richard Frank/CORBIS Sygma; 1366: Hulton-Deutsch Collection/CORBIS; 1369: The Irish Times; 1370: Starry Night, Vincent van Gogh, Digital Image © The Museum of Modern Art/Licensed by SCALA / Art Resource, NY; 1373: JLImages / Alamy; 1375: Thierry Orban/CORBIS SYGMA; 1376: Ulrik Tofte/Getty Images; 1376: Ulrik Tofte/Getty Images; 1379: Getty Images; 1380: Getty Images; 1385: Getty Images; 1386: Arthur S. AubryGetty Images; 1388: Daniel Nevins / SuperStock; 1391: AP/Wide World Photos; 1392: Scott Stulberg/CORBIS; 1394: Scott Stulberg/CORBIS; 1397: Getty Images; 1398: image reproduced with the kind permission of the Dean and Chapter of Chichester Cathedral; 1402: t. Nicolas Elder/Globe Photos; 1402: b. Hulton-Deutsch Collection/CORBIS; 1403: GK Hart/Vicky Hart/Getty Images; 1404: PIER/Getty Images; 1406: Getty Images; 1407: t. Colin McPherson/CORBIS; 1407: b. Getty Images; 1408: Artkey/CORBIS; 1408: Artkey/CORBIS; 1410: Getty Images; 1410: Getty Images; 1412: l. Fridmar Damm/zefa/Corbis; 1412: r. Colin McPherson/CORBIS; 1413: istockphoto.com; 1415: Colin McPherson/CORBIS; 1416: Franck Guiziou/Hemis/CORBIS; 1417: Martin Harvey/CORBIS; 1422: Grace Davies/Omni-Photo Communications, Inc.; 1423: Blaine Harrington III/CORBIS; 1431: Getty Images; 1432: © David Noton Photography / Alamy; 1434: © Orit Allush / Alamy; 1434: © Orit Allush / Alamy; 1436: Christopher Pillitz/Getty Images; 1438: Tim Graham/Getty Images; 1441: William Coupon/CORBIS; 1442: Steve Nagy/Design Pics/CORBIS; 1443: NASA/JPL; 1444: US Geological Service; 1444: Hiroyuki Matsumoto /Getty Images; 1448: AITCH/Getty Images; 1449: t. CORBIS; 1449: b. istockphoto.com; 1449: mb. ESA/K. Horgan/Getty Images; 1449: mt. DRA/Getty Images; 1459: mc. PHERSON COLIN/CORBIS SYGMA; 1460: Luke MacGregor/Reuters/CORBIS; 1462: Tim Mosenfelder/CORBIS; 1462: Tim Mosenfelder/CORBIS; 1486: bcl. ©Bettmann/Corbis

Staff Credits

The people who made up the Pearson Prentice Hall Literature team—representing design, editorial, editorial services, education technology, manufacturing and inventory planning, market research, marketing services, planning and budgeting, product planning, production services, project office, publishing processes, and rights and permissions—are listed below. Boldface type denotes the core team members.

Tobey Antao, Margaret Antonini, Rosalyn Arcilla, Penny Baker, James Ryan Bannon, Stephan Barth, **Tricia Battipede,** Krista Baudo, Rachel Beckman, Julie Berger, Lawrence Berkowitz, Melissa Biezin, **Suzanne Biron,** Rick Blount, **Marcela Boos, Betsy Bostwick,** Kay Bosworth, Jeff Bradley, Andrea Brescia, Susan Brorein, Lois Brown, **Pam Carey,** Lisa Carrillo, **Geoffrey Cassar,** Patty Cavuoto, Doria Ceraso, Jennifer Ciccone, Jaime Cohen, Rebecca Cottingham, Joe Cucchiara, Jason Cuoco, **Alan Dalgleish, Karen Edmonds, Irene Ehrmann,** Stephen Eldridge, Amy Fleming, Dorothea Fox, Steve Frankel, Cindy Frederick, Philip Fried, Diane Fristachi, Phillip Gagler, **Pamela Gallo,** Husain Gatlin, **Elaine Goldman,** Elizabeth Good, John Guild, Phil Hadad, Patricia Hade, Monduane Harris, Brian Hawkes, Jennifer B. Heart, Martha Heller, John Hill, Beth Hyslip, Mary Jean Jones, Grace Kang, Nathan Kinney, Roxanne Knoll, **Kate Krimsky,** Monisha Kumar, Jill Kushner, Sue Langan, Melisa Leong, Susan Levine, Dave Liston, **Mary Luthi, George Lychock, Gregory Lynch, Joan Mazzeo, Sandra McGloster,** Salita Mehta, Eve Melnechuk, Kathleen Mercandetti, Artur Mkrtchyan, Karyn Mueller, Alison Muff, Christine Mulcahy, Kenneth Myett, Elizabeth Nemeth, Stefano Nese, Carrie O'Connor, April Okano, Kim Ortell, Sonia Pap, Raymond Parenteau, Dominique Pickens, Linda Punskovsky, **Sheila Ramsay,** Maureen Raymond, Mairead Reddin, **Erin Rehill-Seker, Renee Roberts, Laura Ross,** Bryan Salacki, Sharon Schultz, Jennifer Serra, **Melissa Shustyk,** Rose Sievers, Christy Singer, Yvonne Stecky, **Cynthia Summers,** Steve Thomas, Merle Uuesoo, Roberta Warshaw, Patricia Williams, Daniela Velez

Additional Credits

Lydie Bemba, Victoria Blades, Denise Data, Rachel Drice, Eleanor Kostyk, Jill Little, Loraine Machlin, Evan Marx, Marilyn McCarthy, Patrick O'Keefe, Shelia M. Smith, Lucia Tirondola, Laura Vivenzio, Linda Waldman, Angel Weyant

R88 Credits

Student Edition Pages